Current Biography Yearbook 2008

EDITOR
Clifford Thompson

SENIOR EDITORS
Miriam Helbok
Mari Rich

PRODUCTION EDITORS
Forrest Cole
Richard Joseph Stein

ASSISTANT EDITOR
Bertha Muteba

CONTRIBUTING EDITOR
Kieran Dugan

COPY ASSISTANT
Jessica McHugh

STAFF WRITERS
Christopher Cullen
William Dvorak
Dmitry Kiper
Majid Mozaffari
Jamie E. Peck
Margaret E. Roush
Maria A. Suarez

CONTRIBUTING WRITERS AND EDITORS
Matt Broadus
Sara J. Donnelly
David J. Kim
Nicholas W. Malinowski
Christopher Mari
Tracy O'Neill
Kenneth J. Partridge
Claire Stanford
Hope Tarullo
Julia Weist

EDITORIAL ASSISTANT
Carolyn Ellis

THE H. W. WILSON COMPANY
NEW YORK   DUBLIN

SIXTY-NINTH ANNUAL CUMULATION—2008

PRINTED IN THE UNITED STATES OF AMERICA

International Standard Serial No. (0084-9499)

International Standard Book No. – 978-0-8242-1095-3

Library of Congress Catalog Card No. (40-27432)

Table of Contents

Preface v

List of Biographical Sketches vii

Biographical Sketches 1

Obituaries 627

Classification by Profession—2008 707

2001–2008 Index 711

PREFACE

The aim of *Current Biography Yearbook 2008*, like that of the preceding volumes in this series of annual dictionaries of contemporary biography, now in its seventh decade of publication, is to provide reference librarians, students, and researchers with objective, accurate, and well-documented biographical articles about living leaders in all fields of human accomplishment. Whenever feasible, obituary notices appear for persons whose biographies have been published in *Current Biography*.

Current Biography Yearbook 2008 carries on the policy of including new and updated biographical profiles that supersede earlier articles. Profiles have been made as accurate and objective as possible through careful researching of newspapers, magazines, the World Wide Web, authoritative reference books, and news releases of both government and private agencies. Immediately after they are published in the 11 monthly issues, articles are submitted to biographees to give them an opportunity to suggest additions and corrections in time for publication of the *Current Biography Yearbook*. To take account of major changes in the careers of biographees, articles are revised before they are included in the yearbook.

Classification by Profession–2008 and *2001–2008 Index* are at the end of this volume. *Current Biography Cumulated Index 1940–2005* cumulates and supersedes all previous indexes.

For their assistance in preparing *Current Biography Yearbook 2008*, I thank the staff of *Current Biography* and also the staffs of the company's Computer and Manufacturing departments.

Current Biography welcomes comments and suggestions. Please send your comments to: The Editor, *Current Biography*, The H. W. Wilson Company, 950 University Ave., Bronx, NY 10452; fax: 718-590-4566; E-mail: cthompson@hwwilson.com.

Clifford Thompson

List of Biographical Sketches

Akon, *Musician* 1

Laylah Ali, *Artist* 3

Edgar Arceneaux, *Artist* 6

Dick Bavetta, *National Basketball Association referee* 10

Diana Beresford-Kroeger, *Botanist, biochemist, gardener, and writer* 13

Robert Bigelow, *Aerospace entrepreneur and real-estate magnate* 17

Roy Blunt, *U.S. representative from Missouri and House minority whip* 20

Andrew Bogut, *Basketball player with the Milwaukee Bucks* 24

Lee C. Bollinger, *President of Columbia University and First Amendment scholar* 28

Dee Dee Bridgewater, *Singer* 33

Josh Brolin, *Actor, writer, and director* 36

Campbell Brown, *Television journalist* 40

Sam Brownback, *U.S. senator from Kansas* 44

Elisabeth Bumiller, *Journalist and writer* 48

Ed Burns, *Television writer, former teacher, and former police detective* 52

Jack Cafferty, *Television journalist* 55

Lois Capps, *U.S. representative from California* 58

Wendy Carlos, *Composer* 62

E. Jean Carroll, *Journalist and advice columnist* 66

David Carson, *Graphic designer* 68

Safra A. Catz, *Co-president of Oracle Corp.* 72

George Clooney, *Actor, director, producer, and social activist* 74

Roger Cohen, *Journalist and columnist* 80

Jerome R. Corsi, *Political pundit, businessman, and writer* 83

Miguel Cotto, *Boxer* 86

Tom Coughlin, *Coach of the New York Giants football team* 90

Katie Couric, *Television journalist and anchor of* CBS Evening News 95

Roy DeCarava, *Photographer* 99

Caleb Deschanel, *Cinematographer and film director* 103

Philip-Lorca diCorcia, *Photographer* 106

James Downey, *Writer for, producer of, and actor on the television show Saturday Night Live* 109

Ann E. Dunwoody, *U.S. Army four-star general* 111

Monta Ellis, *Basketball player with the Golden State Warriors* 114

Neil Estern, *Sculptor* 117

Warren Faidley, *Photojournalist and professional storm chaser* 119

Feist, *Singer and songwriter* 123

Douglas J. Feith, *Former U.S. government official* 125

Prince Fielder, *Baseball player with the Milwaukee Brewers* 128

Bobby Flay, *Chef, television host, and writer* 131

Flight of the Conchords, *Musical-comedy duo and actors* 133

Harrison Ford, *Actor* 139

Terry Francona, *Manager of the Boston Red Sox baseball team* 144

Tom Friedman, *Artist* 148

John Gagliardi, *Coach of the St. John's University football team* 151

Jennifer Garner, *Actress* 154

Keith Gessen, *Magazine editor, literary critic, and writer* 157

Ghostface Killah, *Rapper* 160

Lois Gibson, *Forensic artist* 165

Yousaf Raza Gilani, *Prime minister of Pakistan* 168

Marcello Giordani, *Opera singer* 171

Joe Girardi, *Manager of the New York Yankees baseball team* 176

Rudolph Giuliani, *Businessman and former mayor of New York City* 181

Bruce Golding, *Prime minister of Jamaica* 187

Suhas Gopinath, *Internet entrepreneur* 191

Carol W. Greider, *Molecular biologist and educator* 194

Kathy Griffin, *Comedian, television personality, and actress* 197

David Harvey, *Geographer* 201

PJ Harvey, *Singer and songwriter* 204

Ricky Hatton, *Boxer* 208

Tyrone B. Hayes, *Biologist, endocrinologist, and educator* 212

Dana Hee, *Stuntwoman, tae-kwon-do champion, and motivational speaker* 215

Robert Hellenga, *Writer* 218

Agnes Heller, *Philosopher, writer, educator, and social activist* 222

Susan Hockfield, *President of the Massachusetts Institute of Technology and neurobiologist* 227

David Horsey, *Political cartoonist and columnist for the* Seattle Post-Intelligencer 231

Trevor Immelman, *Golfer* 234

Sheila Jackson Lee, *U.S. representative from Texas* 237

Al Jaffee, *Cartoonist and illustrator* 240

Joe Jamail, *Trial lawyer* 243

Bobby Jindal, *Governor of Louisiana* 247

Boris Johnson, *Mayor of London* 250

Zach Johnson, *Golfer* 254

Cullen Jones, *Swimmer* 256

Kaká, *Soccer player* 259

John Kao, *Businessman, writer, and political consultant* 262

Millard Kaufman, *Screenwriter and novelist* 265

Raymond Kelly, *New York City police commissioner* 269

Michael Kitchen, *British actor* 273

Herb Kohl, *U.S. senator from Wisconsin and owner of the Milwaukee Bucks
     basketball team* 276

Charles Krauthammer, *Columnist and essayist* 280

Dennis J. Kucinich, *U.S. representative from Ohio* 284

Raymond Kurzweil, *Inventor, computer scientist, futurist, entrepreneur, and
     writer* 289

Svetlana Kuznetsova, *Russian tennis player* 294

David LaChapelle, *Photographer and film and video director* 298

Bernard Lagat, *Track and field athlete* 302

Anthony Lane, *Film critic* 305

Tracy Letts, *Playwright and actor* 308

Janna Levin, *Astrophysicist, cosmologist, writer, and educator* 312

Monique Lhuillier, *Fashion designer* 316

Keith Lockhart, *Conductor of the Boston Pops Orchestra* 318

John Mackey, *Co-founder and chief executive officer of Whole Foods Market* 322

Tony Malaby, *Jazz saxophonist* 326

Leonard Maltin, *Film historian and critic* 329

Eli Manning, *Football player with the New York Giants* 333

Marta, *Soccer player* 336

Brian May, *Musician and astrophysicist* 339

Jane Mayer, *Political writer* 343

Mitch McConnell, *U.S. senator from Kentucky* 346

Montgomery McFate, *Anthropologist* 352

James McNerney, *Chairman, president, and chief executive officer of Boeing* 355

Dmitry Medvedev, *President of Russia* 358

Douglas A. Melton, *Molecular embryologist and cell biologist* 361

Stephenie Meyer, *Writer* 365

Sue Mingus, *Band organizer and memoirist* 368

Elvis Mitchell, *Film critic, television and radio host, and filmmaker* 371

Mohammed bin Rashid Al Maktoum, *Ruler of Dubai* 374

ix

Jane Monheit, *Jazz singer* 379

Michael B. Mukasey, *U.S. attorney general* 382

Mike Mullen, *Chairman of the Joint Chiefs of Staff* 387

My Morning Jacket, *Music group* 390

Ingrid Newkirk, *President and co-founder of People for the Ethical Treatment of Animals* 394

Kori Newkirk, *Artist* 398

Michele Norris, *Radio journalist and co-host of* All Things Considered 402

Jean Nouvel, *French architect* 405

Michelle Obama, *Lawyer, hospital administrator, and wife of President-elect Barack Obama* 408

Kelli O'Hara, *Actress and singer* 412

Garrett Oliver, *Beer expert, brewmaster, and writer* 415

Omarion, *Singer* 418

Kenny Ortega, *Choreographer and director* 421

Alexander Ovechkin, *Hockey player with the Washington Capitals* 425

Ellen Page, *Actress* 429

Vikram Pandit, *Chief executive officer of Citigroup* 432

Jon Pareles, *Music critic* 438

Tony Parker, *Basketball player with the San Antonio Spurs* 440

David Paterson, *Governor of New York* 443

Ron Paul, *U.S. representative from Texas* 446

Kimberly Peirce, *Filmmaker* 451

Nelson Peltz, *Chief executive officer of Triarc Companies and Trian Fund Management* 454

Irene Pepperberg, *Animal behaviorist* 459

Dana Perino, *White House press secretary* 461

Amy Poehler, *Comic actress* 464

Susan Polgar, *Chess grandmaster* 467

Samantha Power, *Writer, activist, and educator* 470

Rakim, *Rapper* 473

Ignacio Ramonet, *Journalist, activist, and educator* 476

Ian Rankin, *Writer of crime fiction* 479

Raven-Symone, *Actress and singer* 483

Luke Ravenstahl, *Mayor of Pittsburgh* 486

José Reyes, *Baseball player with the New York Mets* 490

Doc Rivers, *Coach of the Boston Celtics basketball team* 494

Robin Roberts, *Television journalist, sportscaster, and writer* 497

Rudy Rucker, *Science-fiction writer, mathematician, and computer programmer* 500

Patricia Russo, *Former chief executive officer of Alcatel-Lucent Technologies* ... 504

C. C. Sabathia, *Baseball player with the Milwaukee Brewers* 508

Sheryl Sandberg, *Chief operating officer of Facebook* 511

Eric Schmidt, *Chief executive officer and chairman of Google Inc.* 514

Pepper Schwartz, *Sociologist, educator, and writer* 519

Christian Scott, *Jazz trumpeter* 523

Robert Siegel, *Radio journalist and co-host of* All Things Considered 526

David Simon, *Journalist and television writer and producer* 530

Gail Simone, *Comic-book writer* 534

Cameron Sinclair, *Co-founder and executive director of Architecture for
    Humanity* 537

David A. Sinclair, *Molecular biologist and longevity researcher* 541

Curtis Sittenfeld, *Writer* 544

Slash, *Rock musician* 547

Stacey Snider, *Co-chair and chief executive officer of DreamWorks SKG* 552

Jerry Speyer, *Real-estate developer* 555

Susan Stamberg, *Radio journalist* 558

Cass R. Sunstein, *Legal scholar, writer, and educator* 561

Johnny Temple, *Publisher and musician* 564

Lhadon Tethong, *Human-rights activist* 567

Michael Thomas, *Writer* 571

Luca Turin, *Biophysicist and scent creator and critic* 573

Lydia Villa-Komaroff, *Molecular biologist, educator, and businesswoman* 576

Cecily von Ziegesar, *Writer* 579

John P. Walters, *U.S. drug czar* 582

Jeff "Tain" Watts, *Jazz drummer* 586

Jennifer Weiner, *Writer* 588

Spencer Wells, *Population geneticist and head of the Genographic Project* 592

Juan Williams, *Print and broadcast journalist and writer* 595

Lauryn Williams, *Track and field athlete* 599

Jules Witcover, *Writer and political journalist* 602

Yehudi Wyner, *Composer, pianist, and educator* 607

Yuen Wo Ping, *Filmmaker and choreographer of martial-arts movies* 610

Tim and Nina Zagat, *Survey and guidebook publishers* 614

Robert B. Zoellick, *President of the World Bank* 617

Mark Zuckerberg, *Founder and chief executive officer of Facebook* 622

Current Biography Yearbook 2008

Scott Gries/Getty Images

Akon

Apr. 16, 1973– Musician

Address: c/o Melvin Brown, Konvict Music Group, P.O. Box 831, Waynesboro, VA 22980

While the Senegalese-American musician Akon has produced tracks or been a guest vocalist for such diverse recording stars as Sir Elton John, Gwen Stefani, Monica, R. Kelly, and Ladysmith Black Mambazo, his popularity among teens and young adults stems mainly from his own albums and radio hits, including *Trouble* (2004) and *Konvicted* (2006), which blend contemporary R&B with hip-hop. He told Tamara Warren for *Remix* (December 1, 2006), "R&B songs are more complicated than hip-hop because there are more melodies involved. . . . The drums were always the main drive on [my] tracks, and that's how it is for hip-hop, too. I can understand why people call me a hip-hop artist, because I sing stuff that hip-hop artists rap about." That "stuff" often includes references to his African heritage as well as the years he spent in prison for auto theft. His lyrics regarding women have provoked outrage in some circles, with critics accusing him of sexism or misogyny. His fans, however, respond to his unique singing style. Jody Rosen wrote for *Slate* (April 10, 2007, on-line), "There's at least one good reason for Akon's success: the tone of his voice. He sings in a high, lilting, slightly nasal tenor, which frequently slides into mournful little trills. It's an exotic sound, carrying hints of Akon's West African roots: Senegalese mbalax music and the Muslim muezzin's call to prayer. . . . No recent African-American star has sounded quite so African."

Akon has given conflicting answers to questions about aspects of his private life, beginning with the date and place of his birth. He told Laura Checkoway for *Vibe* (April 2007), "The only thing I hide is my age. Once the entertainment industry got age on you, the countdown begins. Before I lie to you, I'd rather say nothing." Akon, whose real name is Aliaune Thiam, was born on April 16, 1973. Various news sources list his place of birth as St. Louis, Missouri; New Jersey; or Senegal. Checkoway reported that Akon was born in St. Louis; his father, Mor Thiam, was a Senegalese jazz percussionist, and his mother, Kine Thiam, was a dancer. Mor Thiam, a musical star in his own country, had immigrated to the United States at the invitation of the legendary modern-dance choreographer Katherine Dunham, who wished to collaborate with him in live performances. Akon's childhood was "filled with art and privilege, trips to Senegal for summer vacation, and karate lessons after school," Checkoway wrote. She also noted that the family moved often, living in Miami, Florida, and Jersey City, New Jersey, and that in each place Akon would "[run] with tough crews" before "returning to a comfortable middle-class home." Sometimes he led his classmates to believe that he had grown up in Africa and did not understand English. "I never revealed the fact that I spoke English fluently," he said to Checkoway. "While they're talking about me, I'm listening, with them thinking I don't know what they're talking about."

By all accounts Akon attended high school in northern New Jersey, where he began selling drugs, carrying an unlicensed gun, and stealing cars. (However, he has been known to greatly exaggerate his criminal record.) In about 1993 he met the Haitian-American musician Wyclef Jean and began recording tracks in Jean's studio in East Orange, New Jersey. Jean was a member of the hip-hop group the Fugees, who exploded onto the national music scene in 1996 with their multiplatinum album *The Score*, on which Akon appeared as a guest vocalist.

In the early 1990s Akon moved to Atlanta, Georgia, to attend Clark Atlanta University on a basketball scholarship; he left the school without completing a degree. He recorded a demo called "Operations of Nature" and signed with the major label Elektra/East West Records, but the company soon dropped him from its roster of artists. By his own account, later in the 1990s he started a car-theft ring with hubs in Chicago, Illinois; New Jersey; and Atlanta. He used some of the money to fuel his musical pursuits, buying expensive studio equipment and recording more tracks. "While the performer's rap sheet does include a half-dozen arrests, Akon has only been convicted of one felony, for gun possession," according to the investigative Web site smokinggun.com (April 16, 2008). "That 1998 New Jersey case ended with a guilty plea, for which the singer was sentenced to three years probation. Another 1998 bust, this one in suburban Atlanta, has been seized upon by Akon and transformed into the big case that purportedly sent him to prison (thanks to his snitching cohorts) for three fight-filled years. In reality, Akon was arrested for possession of a single stolen BMW and held in the DeKalb County jail for several months before prosecutors dropped all charges against him. So there was no conviction. There was no prison term between 1999 and 2002. And he was never 'facing 75 years,' as the singer claimed in one videotaped interview."

In Atlanta Akon began to build a reputation as a professional songwriter and guest vocalist on other artists' albums. He told Tom Sinclair for *Entertainment Weekly* (August 13, 2004), "Being a convicted felon, I couldn't really get a job, so making music was the best [option]." Akon's songwriting process remained consistent with each new project. He told Warren, "I think about the concept first, then I come up with the chorus. Once I got the chorus, then I create the beat around the chorus."

Akon enlisted his longtime friend Devyn Stephens as his agent. Stephens shopped Akon's newest demo around and received offers from several major labels. Ultimately Akon signed with Street Records Corp. (SRC), an imprint of Universal Records. In 2004 SRC released Akon's debut album, *Trouble*, an account of Akon's path to redemption. The album was an enormous hit; it went multiplatinum and spawned a hugely popular single, "Locked Up," a collaboration with the rapper Styles P. SRC also released a remix of "Locked Up," featuring several European rappers, which was particularly successful in France, which has a large Senegalese population. Another single, the mournful "Lonely," also became a hit . That track included a speeded-up sample of the 1964 pop hit "Mr. Lonely," by Bobby Vinton. The success of Akon's "Lonely" put Vinton in the *Billboard* Top 10 for the first time in 34 years.

As Akon's popularity grew, so did the number of myths surrounding him. Akon has claimed that he purchased a diamond mine in South Africa in 2005 with revenue from sales of *Trouble*. Whether or not that is a true story, media outlets reported it as one, as they did with a variety of conflicting accounts of Akon's marriage, children, and criminal record. He alternately denied and confirmed being married and refused to answer definitively questions about his rumored polygamy.

In 2006 Akon provided guest vocals for the Detroit, Michigan–based rapper Obie Trice's song "Snitch." Through Obie Trice he met the rapper Eminem, who performed on Akon's 2006 album, *Konvicted*. Akon produced, wrote, and recorded at his home studio all but one of its songs. "Smack That," a collaboration with Eminem, immediately became a hit single and went on to receive a Grammy Award nomination. Akon said, as quoted by many sources, "I knew I wanted Eminem to be on the track, but he is very careful about appearing on too many other people's songs. When he called and said he was ready to go into the studio, I knew it was a blessing. I was on the first flight to Detroit." On the Web site of his Konfidence Foundation, which is "devoted to the welfare and education of the kids of Senegal," Akon stated, "Eminem was the only white boy to come into the rap game and take it over, and I'm the first one from Africa to come in and take it over. . . . And now I'd like to inspire other kids to do the same."

Gail Mitchell wrote about *Konvicted* for *Billboard* (November 18, 2006, on-line), "Club banger 'Smack That' gives way to the live piano and violins lacing the ballad 'Never Took the Time.' Then there's funky jazz via the love song 'I Can't Wait' before Akon's past rears up on the anti-gangsta 'Tired of Runnin'.' Tying it all together are Akon's soothing vocals." Not all critics were impressed by *Konvicted*. Chris Ryan wrote for *Vibe* (January 2007), "For all the production flourishes here . . . Akon is almost comically one-dimensional in tone, regardless of subject matter. Whether inviting a girl back to his place . . . or noting 'even a child can pull a trigger,' he stays forlorn, soft-focus, and whiny." Jody Rosen wrote for the *Slate* article, "The essence of Akon's gangsta R&B isn't gangsterism at all. It's misogyny. If your idea of romance involves greased stripper poles and women waiting on all fours to receive a hard smack, Akon is the Don Juan for you."

In April 2007 Akon sparked controversy by dancing provocatively with a fan onstage during a performance in Trinidad; the two mimed sexual intercourse in front of a packed house. The girl was later revealed to be a minor, with most sources reporting her age as 14 or 15. Akon responded to that news with a public apology in which he said that he had not known the girl's age when he invited her on stage to dance. He also complained that the club was supposed to be an 18-and-over venue and that the club's security guards had not enforced the rule. After the conservative talk-show host Laura ("Dr. Laura") Ingraham exhorted her listeners to protest Verizon's sponsorship of Gwen Stefani's tour with Akon, Verizon was inundated with phone calls and e-mail messages from irate customers. (Akon produced the title track of Stefani's album *The Sweet Escape*.) The grassroots campaign led Verizon to cancel its sponsorship of Stefani's tour. Akon told Nui Te Koha for the Australia *Sunday Herald Sun* (July 22, 2007), "It was blown way out of proportion. People don't understand the culture of Caribbean dancing. That's how they dance." He later released a track, "Sorry, Blame It All on Me," that alluded to the episode.

In June 2007 another controversy erupted after an Akon performance in Fishkill, New York. Akon stopped his set, claiming that an audience member had thrown something at him; at his request, the crowd pointed out the offender, and a guard sent a youth to the stage. Akon threw the boy into the audience, where he slammed into a woman who later claimed to have suffered a concussion as a result. A video of the event circulated on the Internet. In December Akon pleaded not guilty to charges of harassment and endangering the welfare of a minor.

Those incidents do not appear to have damaged Akon's reputation among his fans. In addition to the U.S., he has a large following in Western Europe, Israel, and West Africa, particularly in Senegal, where he is treated as a hero. He told Margeaux Watson for *Entertainment Weekly* (February 2, 2007), "Yo, it's crazy. It seems like that kind of ma-

nia don't even exist no more. It was definitely an honor to go back and receive that kind of welcome. It encourages me to work harder. They look at me like, 'He's one of us. If he made it, I can probably make it too.'" Akon's album *In My Ghetto* was released in July 2007. *In My Ghetto 2* came out the following year. Akon's latest album, *Freedom*, was scheduled to go on sale on November 25, 2008.

Akon owns Konvict Muzik, a subsidiary of Interscope Records. In early 2007 he launched Konvict Clothing, a line of streetwear, and Aliaune, a higher-priced collection. Akon lives in Atlanta. He reportedly has four sons.

—S.J.D.

Suggested Reading: *Remix* p26 Dec. 1, 2006; *Slate* (on-line) Apr. 10, 2007; *Scottish Daily Record* p17 July 24, 2007; *Vibe* Apr. 2007;

Selected Recordings: *Trouble*, 2004; *Konvicted*, 2006; *In My Ghetto*, 2007; *In My Ghetto 2*, 2008

Ali, Laylah

1968– Artist

Address: c/o 303 Gallery, 525 W. 22d St., New York, NY 10011

"I often describe my work as psycho-political, meaning it is where the loose ends of my psyche meet the world," the artist Laylah Ali told the curator Cylena Simonds, for the Web site of the London, England-based Institute of International Visual Arts (inIVA). Ali, described by Ana Otero for the Art:21 Web site (November 13, 2007) as one of America's "most celebrated and enigmatic contemporary artists," came to prominence in the late 1990s, with a much-discussed series of untitled, cartoon-like watercolor paintings referred to as Greenheads. She went on to develop her style further in intricate ink drawings and portraits. By creating in her work a juxtaposition of the endearing and the haunting, and by offering fresh takes on such traditional artistic forms as the illustration and the portrait, Ali has developed a style that, according to the Web site of the Institute of Contemporary Art, in Boston, Massachusetts, "initially charms and disarms viewers, drawing them into a world fraught with tension and mystery." A main focus of her work has been to investigate what she sees as oppressive social dynamics and the stereotyping of people. Ali's "intention is always to poke and prod the preconceived notions humans have about one another," S. L. Berry wrote for the *Indianapolis Star* (November 22, 2002). Heather Felty, a curatorial assistant at the Museum of Contemporary Art in Chicago, Illinois, described Ali's work to Ann Wilson Lloyd for the *New York Times* (Au-

Courtesy of 303 Gallery

gust 8, 1999) as questioning "social structures, racial perceptions and complicated power struggles behind basic interactions." At the same time, Ali has been linked with the group of African-American artists identified as "post-black," a term indicating their declared freedom to ignore or embrace themes of race.

Another distinguishing characteristic of Ali's work is that, as Berry wrote, it takes the "Socratic approach to art-making," compelling viewers to bring their own interpretations to the work, answer for themselves the questions it raises, and perhaps, in the process, draw conclusions related to larger issues of perception, identity, and power. "Ali's Greenheads has sparked a good deal of debate, from discussions of race, class, and political content in visual art to conversations about the richness (or legitimacy) of genre-crossing between fine art and illustration. Always, though, people ask: how are we supposed to know what these paintings are really about? . . .," Tisa Bryant wrote for the *Believer* (December 2006). "Her paintings are free of . . . slogans, captions, and loaded titles. . . . Viewers and curators alike are left to mine their own perspectives and imaginations for answers." Critics have noted the deceptive simplicity of Ali's images, and as Deanna Truman-Cook wrote for the *Iowa City Press–Citizen* (September 22, 2007), "The images of her works have been referred to as everything from creatures to cartoons to monsters and aliens. The only thing people don't refer to them as are people." What Catherine Fox, writing for the *Atlanta Journal–Constitution* (October 25, 2002), called the "intentional ambiguity" in her pieces compels viewers to provide their "own narrative or explanation, and the pared-down style makes every detail seem like an important clue. But, whatever one makes up, it's hard to avoid themes of pain, confrontation, inhumanity, violence and power struggle." Ali's art refrains from references to specific political or social events or struggles; rather, as Holland Cotter put it in the *New York Times* (June 30, 2000), her work suggests conflicts that are "generic, of a kind always happening somewhere some time." Nor is her work explicitly autobiographical. Ali told Bryant, "I really wanted to resist any easy connection to the artist—people always want to go there, to the pathology of the artist, rather than examining themselves. I think I need to disappear a bit in order for the viewer to engage more fully."

The daughter of an African-American father and a white mother, Laylah Ali was born in Buffalo, New York, in 1968. She grew up in a predominantly white neighborhood in Buffalo, where she gained an awareness of issues that she would later explore in her art. "I was the only black kid in my school," she told Cate McQuaid for the *Boston Globe* (August 29, 2008). "I've been able to negotiate different social places because of that. . . . More people are seeing this now because of Barack Obama, but there have always been biracial people in the U.S., with the ability to move between these worlds and notice what's different and what's not different. I developed heightened powers of observation not just from curiosity but for survival." Ali, who has described her family as "very American," was also shaped by her consciousness of the existence of different social classes. "My mom's family had come from some money," she told McQuaid. "It was gone, but they still had the idea of what it's like to have nice silver, a nice oriental rug. They had an aspiration from what they had lost. Dad's family was from the farming Mississippi South. He

grew up working the land. I keep asking him questions and finding out more things. He walked five miles to school and had no electricity at home."

Many observers have found significance in the artist's having come into the world in 1968, a tumultuous year that saw the bloodiest period of the Vietnam War, widespread antiwar protests, civil rights and black power struggles, the sexual revolution, the assassinations of Martin Luther King Jr. and Senator Robert F. Kennedy, and other historic movements and events. "Watching footage and hearing speeches from the civil rights era were extremely influential on my politics and aspirations while growing up," Ali told Lloyd. "But it also created a model for social revolution that has been impossible to recreate in the 1980s and 1990s. The impulses for social change are still there, but less connected and thus less politically influential. Sometimes I think my work is about the desire to take radical action. Or to create heroes who come to save the day." Perhaps because she grew up in the aftermath of 1968, in an era of "mixed messages," as one observer put it, rather than of the clashing certainties that defined that year, her art—while known for its passion—also contains subtlety and ambivalence not generally associated with the era in which she was born.

Ali earned a B.A. degree in studio art and English from Williams College, in Williamstown, Massachusetts, in 1991. She went on to attend the Whitney Museum Independent Study Program in New York and the Skowhegan School of Painting and Sculpture, in Maine, before receiving an M.F.A. degree in painting from Washington University, in St. Louis, Missouri, in 1994. Her first solo show was at the Hallwalls Contemporary Art Center, in her native Buffalo. It was when she began exhibiting her now-famous, signature Greenheads, in 1998, that Ali became known in the art world. She began painting the Greenheads, according to McQuaid, while she was teaching creative writing and art history part-time at the Commonwealth School in Boston. "It started with figures I made in '96," Ali told an interviewer for the PBS television series *Art:21*, on which she was a featured artist in 2005. "I put this big green head on this brown superhero body, but not really a superhero—because it was an emaciated, silly, almost child's body that didn't look like our conception of a superhero. It had on Underoos [a brand of children's underwear], or something between a 1940s' bathing suit and super-hero gear. I looked at it and thought, 'What am I looking at? What have I done? What does this mean?' The figure was like a question mark. I would look at it, and I had no idea what it was. That prompted further examination. As I worked further I wanted to see more. Eventually they were put in blue backgrounds with a white floor, very simple settings, but it set them apart. From there, things have remained relatively simple and focused, but a bit more complicated than the earlier ones."

Ali's Greenheads were a series of stick-legged, cartoon-like figures with bulbous green heads and brown-skinned, androgynous bodies set against pleasant backgrounds. Because they are innocuous, cute, innocent, and simple on the surface, it may take the viewer a moment to notice what Frances Richard, writing for *Artforum International* (April 1, 2005), called the "brutal group antics" in which they are engaged—including amputation, lynching, and punishments of various sorts. Their lively outfits contain "culturally loaded signs," as noted on the Art:21 Web site, consisting of either pointy hats reminiscent of Ku Klux Klan garb, running shoes, religious or military uniforms, or masks, along with such props as dodgeballs or nooses, which "[tweak] our impulse to use such visual cues to figure out who these people are and what is going on," Sarah Valdez wrote for *Art in America* (May 1, 2005). "The quietude of these scenes makes them all the more unsettling," Richard Huntington observed for the *Buffalo News* (January 17, 2003). "Beneath Ali's clear, flawless blue skies horrible things happen." The disturbing juxtaposition of appealing visuals and hideous content forces the viewer to supply a narrative. The gouache (opaque watercolor) paintings are precise and carefully planned out, each painting taking months to complete. "They are planned in groups," Ali told Simonds, "so their relationships with each other are more strategic." Observers have pointed out that the cartoon has always been an effective medium for the discussion of complicated issues and that Ali's work is reminiscent of comic serials in the Japanese "superflat" tradition. Untitled and wordless, the paintings have been compared even more often to hieroglyphs. "Sometimes I feel like I'm making an extended alphabet, or that images encapsulate parts of an idea," she told the PBS interviewer. "By using parts of that alphabet or hieroglyphic system, I can recombine them and come up with new meanings. Because they're so crisp and have definite shape, sometimes I think it feels like they're letters." Ali has also named television as another stimulus. "TV had a huge influence," she told McQuaid. "My generation was completely saturated with TV. It was my best friend, my pet, my brother, my sister. I grew up looking at a two-dimensional screen all the time: *Scooby Doo*, *Love Boat*, Vietnam imagery. *Roots* was very disturbing."

Ali's collection was seen as a darkly humorous, absurdist, metaphorical take on society, with observers calling the Greenheads "Everymen." "I think of them as being very cerebral, smart and doing problematic things, like in real life. We pretend it's people who don't think about things who are causing trouble. Real trouble is often meticulously planned . . . ," she told Lloyd. "I'm not creating a little fantasy world. They are very much related to the world in which I live—and to the weird, unpredictable complexity of human encounters and responses to other people's race, gender and sexuality." Christine Temin wrote for the *Boston Globe*

(April 20, 2001), "The Greenheads are stand-ins for people, of course. Their remove from human reality allows us to approach them with a certain neutrality. . . . Sometimes, it's hard to tell the oppressor from the oppressed in Ali's works, which suggest that there's a bit of both in all of us." The material signifiers—such as belts—in the paintings provide some suggestions for supplying possible meanings. "If we're going to use that word, power, belts connote some kind of power," she told the PBS interviewer. "Imagine policemen without belts. You couldn't take them seriously." Elsewhere in her work, dodgeballs point to violent and oppressive social dynamics. ("Being the only black child in a white elementary school," she added, "dodgeball was not enjoyable.") Ali told Simonds that in the Greenheads series, she was focusing on "moments around physical violence, whether political violence or inter-personal violence, or somewhere in between. . . . The earlier work concentrated on the details of the physical interactions. Those figures tended to be less individualistic and more a part of teams—and their dress reflected that by being more like uniforms or athletic wear." As Ali's exploration of her themes has evolved over the years, her gouaches have developed into portraits of more pink-skinned, alienated individuals, perhaps captured before or after the act of violence instead of during it. In 2005 Ali collaborated with the choreographer and director Dean Moss on *Figures on a Field*, a stage interpretation of her work, mounted at the Massachusetts Museum of Contemporary Art (MASS MoCA) and The Kitchen in New York.

Ali's most recent work, exhibited in 2007 and 2008, is collectively titled Drawings from the Typology Series. Although aesthetically a departure from her signature gouache style, the Typology drawings can be read as a logical extension of her earlier work, as they explore the various ways in which identity is created, interpreted, and classified. Ali "takes symbolic imagery," Megan Blackhouse wrote for the Melbourne, Australia, *Age* (November 5, 2005), "and twists things around, adding unexpected markers of racial identity, class or social mobility. The result is small black and white ink drawings that play with the way we invest value and meaning into what are essentially inanimate objects." The intricately patterned ink-and-pencil drawings depict hybrid character types, singly or in pairs, that are—according to the University of Arizona Museum of Art's Web site—"culled from an imaginary anthropology." The drawings, Otero wrote, "recall the 19th-century racist pseudo-science of 'typology,' with which scientists attributed physiological characteristics and personality traits to the global races." In contrast to the painstakingly planned-out gouaches, Ali has referred to her Typology drawings as "automatic" and spontaneous. The pieces in Typology also differ from her earlier work in that the representations of action are mostly replaced by a study of types. The viewer, however, still plays a crucial role in assigning meaning to the work. "I have become interested in exploring 'types' and blurring the distinctions between the obvious and absurd ways that people are visually categorized," she told Simonds. "Yet types are also useful in that they contain within them instant narrative. So we all understand the immediately revealed, usually derogatory, narrative contained within a stereotype. And we are sympathetic to other kinds of typology: she is a working class mother; he is a Democrat. We use this kind of shorthand all the time. In my new drawings, I aim to fuse recognisable types with question marks, fuse known narratives with things that are not as easily articulated. The inbuilt narratives within what is recognisable give the viewer a place to start. So, we might start with what looks like a kiss, but what kind of kiss is this? Who are these people?"

Ali has had solo exhibitions at venues including 303 Gallery, in New York; the Museum of Modern Art in New York; the Institute of Contemporary Art in Boston; the Museum of Contemporary Art in Chicago; the Contemporary Art Museum in St. Louis; the Gertrude Contemporary Art Space, in Melbourne; the Albright-Knox Art Gallery, in Buffalo; the MASS MoCA, in North Adams; and the Yerba Buena Center for the Arts, in San Francisco, California. She exhibited her work at the Venice Biennale in 2003 and the Whitney Biennial in 2004. Books and catalogues featuring her work include *Laylah Ali: Types*; *Laylah Ali: Typology*, and *Notes with Little Illustration*. In 2006, as part of a program that is sponsored by a number of foundations and provides artists with grants and other support, Ali was selected as one of the first United States Artist Fellows. When Simonds asked her in 2007 about her future plans, Ali said that "fledgling painting ideas are knocking around my head, readying themselves for the next series of paintings, which always takes me a fair amount of time to complete."

Ali, who teaches courses in drawing and painting at Williams College, works and lives in Williamstown. She is married to Michael Nixon, an elementary-school teacher.

—M.M.

Suggested Reading: *Artforum International* p189 Apr. 1, 2005; *Atlanta Journal-Constitution* Preview Q p6 Oct. 25, 2002; *Believer* (on-line) Dec. 2005; *Boston Globe* (on-line) Aug 29, 2008; *Buffalo News* Gusto G p22 Jan. 17, 2003; *Indianapolis Star* Weekend G p32 Nov. 22, 2002; *Massachusetts Review* p153+ Spring/Summer 2008; *New York Times* II p33 Aug. 8, 1999

Selected Books: *Laylah Ali*, 2002; *Types*, 2005; *Notes with Little Illustration*, 2007; *Typology* (with Alex Baker and Kara Walker), 2007

Arceneaux, Edgar

(AR-sen-oh)

July 7, 1972– Artist

Address: c/o Susanne Vielmetter Los Angeles Projects, 5795 W. Washington Blvd., Culver City, CA 90232

The African-American artist Edgar Arceneaux "is interested in the relationship between artistic processes, most often drawing, and psychology, physics, and philosophy," Aimee Chang wrote for the Web site of the Hammer Museum at the University of California at Los Angeles (UCLA). "His explorations . . . favor a nonlinear and nonobjective logic, paying attention instead to unintended connections, interstitial spaces, and, in his words, 'a different way to construct relationships between things.'" Arceneaux has become known internationally for creating room-sized multimedia installations—often consisting of drawings, sculpture, found objects, and film projections—that encourage viewers to question their assumptions about such concepts as language, culture, race, class, and memory and to view the world according to new systems of meaning. Arceneaux's fondness for incorporating highly specific references to history,

Susanne Vielmetter Los Angeles Projects

mythology, science, pop culture, literature, and language into his work has earned him a reputation for both intellectualism and playfulness. After presenting solo exhibitions at galleries and museums all over the world, Arceneaux was the 2006 recipient of the William H. Johnson Foundation Prize, a $25,000 award that is named for an African-American painter who came to prominence during the Harlem Renaissance and that supports the work of minority artists early in their careers. In the spring of 2008, The Alchemy of Comedy . . . Stupid, an installation Arceneaux created in conjunction with the comedian David Alan Grier, was included in the Whitney Biennial in New York City, the top national showcase for contemporary art. Arceneaux's most recent solo exhibition, Correlations and Isomorphisms, was presented at the Susanne Vielmetter Los Angeles Projects, in California, from September through October 2008.

Edgar Arceneaux was born on July 7, 1972 in Los Angeles, California. Very little has been published about the artist's early life. He earned his B.F.A. degree from the Art Center College of Design, in Pasadena, California, in 1996. From 1998 to 2001 he attended art institutions including the Banff Centre for the Arts, in Banff, Alberta, Canada; Project Row Houses in Houston, Texas; the Skowhegan School of Painting, in Skowhegan, Maine; and Fachhochschule Aachen in Aachen, Germany. In 2001 he received his M.F.A. degree from the California Institute of the Arts, in Valencia, California, where he worked closely with Charles Gaines, a professor at the school and a fellow African-American artist who creates conceptual pieces that focus on "the postmodern sublime and metonymy," according to his biography on the United States Artists Web site. During his schooling Arceneaux developed the ability to "draw like a dream" and a "vibrant, restless intellect," as Jeffrey Kastner put it in an article for Artforum International (February 1, 2006). Arceneaux's early works were pencil renderings; he enjoys pencil work because of its "immediacy," as he told Vincent Johnson, who interviewed him for the Pomona College Museum of Art Web site (Fall 2001). "It's a little more direct, a little more tactile . . . ," he told Johnson. "Also, the ability to simultaneously erase and leave a trace of an action is something that likens itself to the act of remembering."

One of Arceneaux's early works, a pencil drawing of the heads of three pop-culture icons with similar-sounding names, entitled Spock, Tuvac, Tupac, demonstrates the artist's fondness for finding surprising connections between apparently dissimilar ideas. Spock, who is white, and Tuvac, who is black, are fictional extraterrestrial characters who appeared on different "generations" of Gene Roddenberry's science-fiction television series Star Trek. "Tupac" refers to Tupac Shakur, the popular black hip-hop artist, known for his introspective lyrics, who was shot to death in September 1996. Completed in 1997, the drawing "is like a page from some Dadaist illustrated encyclopedia of popculture," Kastner wrote, referring to Dadaism, the early-20th-century artistic and literary movement that rebelled against society by rejecting its conventional logic in favor of chaos and irrationality. Kastner described the drawing, which is in the collection of the Museum of Contemporary Art in San Diego, as depicting "three brothers from another mother joined by linguistic adjacency and the artist's deadpan, pitch perfect rendering, into an uncanny triumvirate." In 2000 some of Arceneaux's other pencil drawings appeared as part of Sitegeist, an exhibit focusing on "lived space," according to the show's statement, as quoted by Robert L. Pincus in the San Diego Union-Tribune (October 5, 2000). Arceneaux curated Sitegeist with his fellow artist Dwayne Moser at the Porter Troupe Gallery, in San Diego, California. Arceneaux's light graphite renderings depicted what he called "idealized memories that are left over from childhood," as quoted by Pincus. Pincus wrote that Arceneaux's pieces, which included drawings of a Los Angeles pharmacy and a water-damaged mural, "vibrate with intimacy. In his exacting delicate drawings, places materialize as if they had a life separate from sky and everyday landscape."

Over the next several years, Arceneaux incorporated his drawings and sculptures into larger, multimedia installations. He was inspired to create the piece The Trivium when he purchased albums by Pharoah Sanders, a jazz saxophonist popular in the 1970s, and Pharoah Monch, a contemporary rap artist, and noted the shared name of the artists, who were separated by generations. "The play on language was to evidence further the intertwining narratives and texts," Arceneaux told Johnson. As with Spock, Tuvac, Tupac, Arceneaux created pencil drawings on vellum (paper made from processed animal skin) that explored the relationships not only between those two artists but among the jazz musician Thelonious Monk, the 14th-century Italian poet Dante Alighieri, and the Greek philosopher Socrates. For the finished installation, which was first exhibited at Pomona College in 2001, Arceneaux fixed the drawings to the gallery walls loosely and coupled them with other, found images of his subjects. As many art critics noted, by juxtaposing images of Socrates and Dante, major figures, respectively, of Western philosophy and literature, who are typically associated with European "high" culture, with images of American hip-hop and jazz artists, Arceneaux's work explored issues of class and social structure. Arceneaux compared his installation's free-associative, even unfinished, quality to bebop, a form of jazz characterized by fast tempos and improvisation, which became popular in the mid–20th century. "[With jazz] there was a certain breaking away of forms and a constant process of reinventing; it was not necessarily being tied to any certain conclusion or direction," Arceneaux told Johnson.

Many have identified Rootlessness–Sugar Hill, A Heuristic Model (2002) as the exhibit that marked Arceneaux's entrance into the mainstream art world. First shown at the Susanne Vielmetter Los Angeles Projects in 2002, the large multimedia installation juxtaposes two journeys: the forced journey of Africans from their homelands to America, where they became slaves, as described in Alex Haley's book and the subsequent, same-titled, made-for-television movie *Roots*, and the journey of the characters in the *Star Trek* series from Earth to outer space. The exhibit, which includes a painting, news clippings, books, videos, and artifacts from both series, creates "a genealogy of memorabilia . . . [which] gleans memories gathered in our collective tele-visual pop cultural history," as Reina Alejandra Prado Saldivar wrote in an essay for the Web site of the Smithsonian Center for Latino Initiative. According to Arceneaux's statement for the exhibit, as quoted by Prado, the artist set out to explore "the social memory of place" and "the unbridgeable gap between loss and desire."

Arceneaux began one of his best-known installations, the ongoing Drawings of Removal, in 1999. It has been installed just twice, in 2002 in a huge room in the Studio Museum in Harlem, in New York City, and in 2003 at the Hammer Museum. Described by Chang as "a meditation on the fleeting nature of the present and the function of memory," the project is based on a road trip that Arceneaux took with his parents to his father's hometown of Beaumont, Texas, in 1998. The town had changed so much in the 40 years that had elapsed since his father's last visit that it was almost unrecognizable. "The house [my father] grew up in is completely gone, [the site] is just a grassy field with a tree stump," Arceneaux told Chang. "The geography itself had changed. They'd put in new streets—literally reconfiguring the landscape." For the installation, which incorporates performance, Arceneaux uses the exhibition space as his studio. Inspired by his memories of the trip, as well as his father's descriptions of what the town was once like, he creates pencil and pen sketches on large sheets of paper, pastes them in layers on the bare walls of the exhibition space, cuts some of the paper to reveal the layers beneath, transplants fragments of some sheets to others, and erases and redraws whole sections of the work, all during visiting hours, so members of the public can watch him at work. As the creative process becomes a part of the ever-changing installation, the piece also includes materials suggestive of his labor, such as empty coffee cups and Mountain Dew cans, art-history books, a garbage can, a CD player, and scattered CDs. Arceneaux told Chang, "The work not only represents the idea of loss or of the gap between memory and desire, but is literally active. Something is being built and something is breaking down."

Arceneaux's Borrowed Sun, which opened in 2004 at the Susanne Vielmetter Los Angeles Projects, is perhaps his most critically acclaimed installation. Described by Holland Cotter for the *New York Times* (November 18, 2005) as "an open-ended essay in cultural memory spun around a single image, the sun, which radiates endless associations," the multimedia installation draws connections between the sun and three historical individuals: Galileo, the revolutionary astronomer who advanced the then-heretical idea that the sun was at the center of the solar system; Sun Ra, a musician, poet, and philosopher, who created an influential musical genre called Space Age jazz; and the contemporary minimalist artist Sol Lewitt, whose first name means "sun" in Latin. One of the installation's most notable pieces is *Blocking Out the Sun*, a series of slides projected on the gallery wall, showing Arceneaux holding up his thumb to the setting sun at various points along the Pacific coast. (The gesture is a reference to astronomers' practice of masking the sun to determine the clarity of the surrounding atmosphere.) Another projection, *Permutation Without Permission*, is a homemade film of Arceneaux and a friend on a freestanding brick wall tracing a reproduction of a 1976 Lewitt drawing of concentric circles. The "screen" on which that piece is projected is actually the brick-wall sculpture itself, entitled *Broken Sol*. Some critics found the collection of pieces oblique; Glen Helfand wrote for *Artforum International* (January 1, 2006): "[Arceneaux] manages to combine pseudoscientific chartmaking and figurative drawing with admirable consistency, yet this installation ultimately felt like hermetic noodling rather than a heartfelt attempt to represent the sense of awe engendered by its subject." Many others, though, found delightful meaning in Arceneaux's unusual juxtapositions. Kastner wrote, "The exhibition is a kind of room-size philosophical machine in which the physical and the metaphysical are repeatedly woven together and teased apart to produce new and unexpected connections."

In January 2005 Arceneaux, along with the University of Chicago, received an award from the Joyce Foundation, which supports Midwest cultural organizations in commissioning works by artists of color. The University of Chicago commissioned Arceneaux to create a short, 35-millimeter film installation, in collaboration with students from the University of Illinois–Chicago and two Chicago-area high schools, about the stand-up comedy of David Alan Grier, a performer best known for his roles on the sketch-comedy show *In Living Color*. For that project Arceneaux followed Grier through four stand-up performances in three Chicago locations and documented the development of his material from rehearsal to performance. "Like an alchemist, [Grier] is striving toward perfection . . . ," Arceneaux told Dan R. Goddard for the *San Antonio Express-News* (April 16, 2006). "At first, the routine is rather crude, but by the fourth performance, he's surrounded by people laughing. I recorded him going through the process of deciding which jokes are funny and which are not."

The completed video installation, The Alchemy of Comedy . . . Stupid, was first exhibited at the University of Illinois in 2006. The installation included numerous wall projections and television monitors showing different segments from Grier's performances of the same routine. In many of the segments, Grier is introspective about events in his own life, such as his tumultuous relationship with his father; in others, he appears awkward—for instance, when his jokes are not met with laughs. One projection is silent and shows only a close-up of Grier's facial expressions during his routine. Audio taken from the different performances is played overhead but scattered around the room, making it possible to pick up only fragments of jokes. Holly Myers wrote for the *Los Angeles Times* (November 10, 2006): "Arceneaux's interest lies primarily, it seems, in what the pleasure of the punch lines tends to obscure: the fumbled words, the awkward gestures, the anxious glances. Fracturing the jokes just enough to disable the humor, he illuminates the cracks between them, exposing an economy of expression considerably more nuanced—and fraught—than the sort of comedic persona one typically encounters on television." The installation, exhibited most recently at the Spring 2008 Whitney Biennial, in New York City, also includes sculptures and drawings. The latter include a large drawing of a giant wheelchair containing the embers of a fire, a reference to Grier's wheelchair-bound father, to whom he makes reference throughout his act, and a print of 12 images of a burning match, a tribute to Richard Pryor, one of Grier's comedic influences, who accidentally set himself on fire in 1980. Many critics admired "the elaborate dissection of something magical—a good joke—into its composite parts," as Myers put it in her description of Arceneaux's show. Others, such as Alan G. Artner, writing for the *Chicago Tribune* (April 13, 2006), were less taken with the installation, which "touches upon every medium for which [Arceneaux] has been acclaimed, though that does not turn out to be an advantage," in Artner's view. "The related works fail to extend the video, which is in itself one of those empty-vessel pieces that rely on the most cerebral responses to fill it because its actual achievements in idea and technique are small."

In Arceneaux's most recent solo exhibition, entitled Correlations and Isomorphisms and mounted by the Susanne Vielmetter Los Angeles Projects in the fall of 2008, he showed new works in mediums including drawing, painting, sculpture, and film, all of which, according to the exhibition's press release, explored "the origins and laws of our physical reality." By incorporating ideas from science, mythology, philosophy, and religion in his works, Arceneaux also examined the shared perspectives in seemingly contrasting views on the origins of the universe. Some of the major pieces in the exhibition were abstract images of constellations made with graphite, dirt, gesso, and enamel on canvas and paper; another, called *Circle Disk Rotation*, was a video of a mysterious cosmic disk that revolved between circles and spheres. Describing a painting called *Eyes Floating in the Abyss*, which showed three pairs of eyes hovering on a green and black wash, Courtney J. Martin wrote for artforum.com: "If the eyes refer to the trinity (the dealer, the collector, and the artist!), they also allude to the ways in which figuration in painting has always played with the tension between spirituality and corporeality."

In addition to his many solo exhibitions, Arceneaux regularly creates shows in collaboration with fellow African-American artists working in Los Angeles. In 2004 he and Rodney McMillian, for example, explored the life and magnetic appeal of the pop-music megastar Michael Jackson. The Michael Jackson Project (2003–04), installed at the Susanne Vielmetter–Culver City gallery in Los Angeles, featured many pieces that conveyed "intense, dislocated moments," Julien Myers wrote for *Frieze* magazine (May 2004), related to elements from Jackson's childhood and his hometown—Gary, Indiana. "What these pieces have to tell us about Jackson is unresolved—it's not clear, after all, that he is much more than a cipher for either artist—but they suggest that the singer's radical experiments in self-construction and historical revision may have ghastly consequences." Arceneaux collaborated with his former mentor, Charles Gaines, on a piece called *Snake River*, which was supported and exhibited by the city's REDCAT Gallery and Austria's Lentos Kunstmuseum Linz in 2006. *Snake River* consisted of a split-screen video simultaneously showing footage of the Snake River and a chamber group rehearsing in an elegant concert hall. "During the two-hour span of the video, a nonverbal narration unfurls," Leah Ollman wrote for the *Los Angeles Times* (October 4, 2006), "a loose progression from the intimate to the more detached, from sensual toward mechanical, organic to constructed, and in terms of aesthetic sensibility, from romantic to modern." Arceneaux worked with McMillian as well as the Los Angeles–based artists Vincent Galen Johnson and Olga Koumoundouros and the Canadian artist Matthew Sloly on the installation The Philosophy of Time Travel, which opened at the Studio Museum in Harlem in the summer of 2007. The pieces in that show were concerned with the fictional theory of time travel developed in Richard Kelly's 2001 science-fiction movie *Donnie Darko* and Sun Ra's "Afrofuturist ideas about blacks in outer space propelled by music," as Ann Compton reported for *Art in America* (October 2007). Compton noted that the installation asked a question: "What if time were not fixed, but rather allowed past and present to meet in new and unexpected ways?"

Arceneaux's pieces are part of numerous public collections at institutions including the Carnegie Museum of Art, in Pittsburgh, Pennsylvania; the Walker Art Center, in Minneapolis, Minnesota; the Los Angeles County Museum of Art; the San Francisco Museum of Modern Art; and the New York Public Library. Arceneaux is the recipient of a 2005 Creative Capital Grant and a 2006 ArtPace Residency in Antonio, Texas. In 2003 he published two books in conjunction with installations titled, respectively, Lost Library and 107th Street, Watts.

Kastner described Arceneaux as "an affable, intensely focused Angeleno." Arceneaux has been identified, along with many of his fellow African-American collaborators, as a member of a new generation of black artists whose work, dubbed "post-black," forgoes explicit discussions of race and instead deals with race, as well as other subjects, in more conceptual ways. Known for his collaborations, Arceneaux, who continues to live and work in the Los Angeles area, has become a pillar in the city's artistic community. He told Jori Finkel for the *New York Times* (June 10, 2007): "This community—my inner circle of artists—is interested in having a dialogue that is politically and socially engaged. . . . The art world is so social, and sometimes I'm the only black face in the crowd. That's part of the reason I work so hard to maintain this community."

—M.E.R.

Suggested Reading: *Artform International* p228 Jan. 1, 2006, p192+ Feb. 1, 2006; *Los Angeles Times* E p6 Oct. 4, 2006; *New York Times* E p43 Nov. 18, 2005, II p29 June 10, 2007; Pomona College Museum of Art Web Site; *San Antonio Express-News* Life J p10 Apr. 16, 2006; *San Diego Union-Tribune* Entertainment p37 Oct. 5, 2000; Susanne Vielmetter Los Angeles Projects Web Site; UCLA Hammer Museum Web Site

Selected Exhibitions: The Remnants Project, 1998; The Project, 1999; The Trivium, 2001; Rootlessness, 2002; Drawings of Removal, 2002; Library as Cosmos, 2003; Library as Chaos, 2003; 107th Street, Watts, 2003; Borrowed Sun, 2004; The Michael Jackson Project, 2004; An Arrangement with the Tormentors, 2004; Alchemy of Comedy . . . Stupid, 2006; The Philosophy of Time Travel, 2007; The Agitation of Expansion, 2008; Correlations and Isomorphisms, 2008

Ronald Martinez/Getty Images

Bavetta, Dick

Dec. 10, 1939– National Basketball Association referee

Address: National Basketball Referees Association, c/o Perennial Strategy Group, 1455 Pennsylvania Ave., N.W., Suite 225, Washington, DC 20004

Dick Bavetta, a 34-year veteran of the National Basketball Association (NBA), has been called "the Cal

Ripken Jr. of referees"—a reference to the durable Baltimore Orioles shortstop and third baseman—for his longevity in the field of officiating. Bavetta is one of the most recognizable and well-liked figures in a profession usually characterized by anonymity. "I understand my role. I'm a grade-B actor. The players are the stars, and the game is the production. I'm like the guy you see on the street. You know the face but not the name. I've always accepted that," he noted to David DuPree for *USA Today* (February 20, 2004). Since he began his tenure in the NBA, during the 1975–76 season, he has never missed an assigned game, and he currently holds the record for most officiated games in the league's history, with more than 2,200. Throughout his 34 seasons, he has consistently been among the NBA's highest-rated officials and has refereed more than 220 play-off games and more than 20 NBA Finals games. Bavetta's journey to the top of the NBA's officiating ranks was not an easy one. While refereeing games in the semiprofessional Eastern League (the forerunner of the Continental Basketball Association), he was accepted by the NBA only after having tried out unsuccessfully in the previous nine seasons. It took him another 11 years to be assigned to his first play-off game. Now a postseason fixture, Bavetta has since gained a reputation for being one of the most efficient and knowledgeable officials in the league, in addition to being "a favorite among coaches for his willingness to admit, after a game, that he might have blown a call or two," as noted by David Firestone for the *New York Times* (December 4, 1998). Garry St. Jean, a former coach and former general manager of the Golden State Warriors, explained to Firestone, "He's not just one of the top referees in the game. He's also the guy who will dance with the mascots, and give the ball to a 5-year-old at his first game during a time out, and say hello by name to the ball boys and equipment managers. He just makes you light up when you see him on the floor."

The younger of two sons, Richard T. Bavetta was born on December 10, 1939 in the Park Slope section of Brooklyn, New York. His father was a lieutenant in the New York Police Department; his mother was a homemaker. His older brother, Joe, became a police detective. Bavetta attended Power Memorial High School, where he played basketball. (Power Memorial became a basketball juggernaut in the 1960s, when Lew Alcindor—later known as Kareem Abdul-Jabbar—led the school's team to three straight New York City Catholic championships and a 72-game winning streak.) Bavetta continued to play basketball at St. Francis College in Brooklyn, where he graduated with a degree in economics in 1962. Commenting on his playing skills, Bavetta noted to DuPree, "I was mediocre, at best. I didn't even make the travel team. I just played in the home games." After receiving his M.B.A. degree from the New York Institute of Finance, he started working as a stockbroker for the Wall Street brokerage firm Salomon Brothers. At night he played basketball in a Wall Street league at New York's Downtown Athletic Club. After Joe Bavetta, who doubled as a part-time basketball official, refereed one of his younger brother's games, Dick Bavetta was coaxed into officiating at a game along with him. He was instantly hooked.

In 1966 Bavetta signed up for a 10-week officiating class in order to get certified for youth-league games. He began refereeing games in public and parochial high-school leagues at night and later worked games in the semiprofessional Eastern League on the weekends. The Eastern League paid him only $45 per game and did not compensate him for expenses. "People were looking for me, wondering why I wasn't at work on Tuesdays and Fridays. That's because they played Catholic and public high school games at 3:30 in the afternoon on those days . . . ," he recalled to DuPree. "I'd leave Brooklyn on a Saturday afternoon, drive to Pennsylvania and work one night in Scranton and the next night in Wilkes-Barre, finishing the last game at 10 o'clock Sunday night, knowing I had to be back on Wall Street at 7 the next morning." Longing for a chance to officiate in the NBA, he started attending regional tryouts at camps for NBA officials. Though he wrote numerous letters to league officials in the hope that they would consider him for a referee job, Bavetta was rejected for nine straight years. Then, in 1975, the NBA hired him following the retirement of the legendary Mendy Rudolph (the first league referee to officiate at 2,000 games). Bavetta, who is five feet 11 inches tall and a lean 156 pounds, has cited his unimposing size as one of the main factors that had kept the NBA from taking him on. He explained to Terry Pluto for the Akron, Ohio, *Beacon Journal* (February 9, 1997), "They used to like their officials to be big guys. Guys whom you'd see for the first time and you'd have instant respect. Look at me? Tell me what you see?"

Although his dream had been realized, Bavetta's new career resulted in a 50 percent pay cut, an extensive travel schedule, and less time spent with his family, which included two daughters. His wife, Francis, was opposed to his career change, and the two divorced just before he joined the NBA. (They remained friends.) "I don't blame her," Bavetta said to Pluto. "She is a great girl. When we married, she thought I was going to be a stockbroker, working 9 to 5." Bavetta made his NBA debut on December 2, 1975 at New York's Madison Square Garden, in a regular-season game between the New York Knicks and the Boston Celtics. His first 10 years in the league proved to be the toughest of his career. Calling his officiating skills during that period "marginal, at best," Bavetta consistently ranked in the bottom third among officials in performance evaluations and led NBA referees in technical fouls called and ejections of players. (Officials prone to calling frequent technical fouls and making ejections are often disregarded by players and coaches, which, in turn, often leads them to amass even higher totals in those categories.) As a result, he was not assigned to play-off games. He recalled to Pluto, "Every year, I sweated it out, wondering if they'd rehire me. . . . I was fighting for respect out there." While impressing NBA executives was difficult for him, he discovered that it was even harder to win respect from his peers. During a late-1970s game between the Philadelphia 76ers and the New Jersey Nets, when Bavetta overruled a last-minute call made by his colleague Earl Strom, reversing the outcome of the game, Strom physically assaulted him. Pluto noted that during that time, a *Boston Globe* journalist—referring to the rail-thin, incompetent deputy played by Don Knotts on the *Andy Griffith Show* and to a famous prison uprising—wrote that "sending Dick Bavetta to ref a big game is like sending Barney Fife to quell the Attica riots." Nonetheless determined to succeed, Bavetta dedicated himself to becoming a better official. In the off-season he refereed games on the Jersey Shore for the New Jersey summer pro league and games in the famed Rucker League in New York's Harlem neighborhood, in which he recalls being the only white official. "The guys in Harlem probably thought I was either the best official in the world or completely crazy to keep going back, year-after-year," he quipped to Pluto. In addition to officiating games seven days a week, he acquired an encyclopedic knowledge of the NBA rulebook.

Bavetta's two daughters, Christine and Michelle, willing to share what he has called his "vagabond lifestyle," came to live with him in 1980, while they were in their teens. Getting a second chance at fatherhood proved to be a pivotal development in Bavetta's life. "Reflecting back, I was just ordinary, a mediocre official at best," he explained to DuPree. "But when Christine and Michelle came to live with me, they provided a purpose for me, and things just started taking off. . . . It was almost that they provided stability. I thought at the time that I'd teach them about life, but they taught me." In 1983 he became the first official to undergo a training regimen in the off-season. (Normally, officials, who on average run five to eight miles in a game, would wait until mid-summer to get into shape.) He began running six to eight miles every morning (even on game days) and taking three-hour "power" naps in the afternoons. He also started wearing up to five pairs of socks at a time during games, because, as he later recalled to Sarah Lorge Butler for *Runner's World* (June 2007, online), "My feet were getting sore from the running. . . . So during the summer, I said, let me just experiment, add a couple of pairs of socks. I always used to wear two or three anyway. So I just added two more pairs of socks. Felt comfortable with five. Wasn't too restrictive to my feet. Went to a half size bigger [shoe]. I said, as long as I'm not missing games. Might be missing calls, but I'm not missing games, I'm going to stick with this. So it's been a comfortable existence for me and a healthy existence for me."

During the 1980s Bavetta became an officiating crew chief and quickly developed a reputation as one of the best-conditioned referees in the league. (Determined by seniority, crew chiefs are in charge of basketball games; calls by other officials are either approved or overruled by them.) He was assigned to his first play-off game in 1986. (NBA officials are now required to have a minimum of seven years' experience before they can referee games in the postseason. In addition, prior to 1988 each NBA game was officiated by a two-person crew with a staff of 35, an arrangement that made it difficult for referees to cover every area of the basketball court in time, which often diminished crews' play-calling efficiency—given the high speed of the game and the athleticism of the players; that year the National Basketball Referees Association, or NBRA, instituted three-person crews and expanded each staff to 60, in an effort to recruit younger prospects.) One of Bavetta's most memorable experiences as a referee occurred on November 9, 1984, in a nationally televised game between the Celtics and their rivals the 76ers. Beginning early in the third quarter, Bavetta was forced to officiate by himself, after his crewmate Jack Madden broke his leg in a collision with the Celtics guard Dennis Johnson. Then, midway through the fourth quarter, the Celtics forward Larry Bird and 76ers forward Julius "Dr. J." Erving—considered two of the greatest players of all time—were ejected for punching one another during a bench-clearing brawl. Bavetta recalled to Liz Robbins for the *New York Times* (February 5, 2006), "I guess the N.B.A. figured, 'If this guy could handle this, he could handle anything.'" Later in the decade Bavetta had a second altercation with Earl Strom: the veteran official choked him in the dressing room during halftime of a 1989 game for allegedly being a "homer," a derogatory term for officials who side with home crowds. (Early in Bavetta's career, his officiating often seemed to favor the winning team or to be in-

fluenced by the crowd.) Strom reportedly apologized to Bavetta two weeks after the incident.

In the 1990s and 2000s, Bavetta went from being a "homer" to being seen as the league's best "road ref." A fixture in the postseason, he consistently ranked among the highest-rated officials in terms of performance evaluation. In addition to being an authoritative call-maker and rulebook expert, he became especially known for his willingness to admit mistakes. In the early 1990s Bavetta and his officiating crews started a post-game routine of meeting in his hotel room each night to evaluate their performance on videotape, offering one another criticism. "My thing is communication," he explained to Pluto, who described him as "the perfect official." Bavetta added, "I believe in talking to people, letting them know why we called something. Early in my career, that was considered a sign of weakness. Most of the older officials said, 'Just make the call. You don't have to explain anything. If they don't like it, T-them up [call a technical foul].' But that has never been my personality." Discussing Bavetta's skills as a communicator—which include the ability to defuse tension—his fellow official Bennett Salvatore explained to DuPree, "That's his greatest strength. He's very approachable, and his body language says, 'You can come talk to me,' and after that, he listens. . . . He evaluates the situation and then responds in one of three ways. He either does it with a very stern answer, with humor or he'll give you an answer from left field. . . . You can be yelling at him and your emotions are running high and he'll listen to you and then say, 'By the way, did you see that sumo wrestling show the other day?' and then he'll walk away. The player or coach is left standing there thinking, 'This guy is nuts.'" During one game, when the player Charles Barkley tried to contest one of his calls, Bavetta, who happened to know that Barkley was a soap-opera fan, managed to avoid a confrontation with him by shifting the conversation to the character Erica Kane (played by Susan Lucci) on the daytime drama *All My Children.*

By the early 2000s, Bavetta had become not only one of the most respected but also one of the highest-paid referees in the league, earning upwards of $200,000 per year. In 2003 Bavetta's consecutive-game streak, which was nearing 2,000, was put in jeopardy when the Indiana Pacers forward Jalen Rose accidentally punched him in the nose during a game against the New York Knicks. (The punch was intended for the Knicks' center Patrick Ewing.) Instead of leaving the game, Bavetta opted to have his nose surgically repaired after the contest, then returned the next day to referee a New Jersey Nets game. In February 2004, in a game between the Knicks and the Utah Jazz, he became only the fourth NBA referee in the league's history to officiate 2,000 games—and the first to do so in consecutive contests. (Prior to achieving the milestone, Bavetta noted that he had never particularly paid attention to such records.) When he refereed his

2,135th game, on February 8, 2006, he broke Jake O'Donnell's record for the most games officiated in the history of the NBA, making him the official "gold standard for basketball referees," as noted by a writer for PR Newswire (February 7, 2006). The same writer added, "What makes Bavetta's record even more intriguing is that his 2,135 games will have been consecutive."

The following season, on December 16, 2006, Bavetta made headlines after ejecting a record 10 players in response to a brawl that took place during a game between the Knicks and the Denver Nuggets. To date Bavetta has officiated at more than 2,200 regular-season games, 228 play-off games, and 24 NBA Finals games. Garry St. Jean said to DuPree about Bavetta, "He epitomizes everything we want our game to be. He just has a way about him. He loves his job, and it exudes from him. He makes you feel confident. When he's the ref, you can concentrate on the game and not have to worry about the officiating."

In June 2008 the *New York Times* reported that Bavetta's name had come up in an FBI probe into allegations that Game Six of the 2002 Western Conference finals between the Lakers and the Sacramento, California, Kings—which the Lakers won, 106–102—had been rigged. The allegations came from the disgraced NBA official Tim Donaghy, who had referred the game with Bavetta and Bob Delaney. Donaghy, who had been forced to resign from the league in July 2007 after betting on and manipulating more than 100 games in which he had officiated, described Bavetta and Delaney as "company men" and claimed that the two had favored the Lakers so as to extend the finals to a seventh game. Those allegations notwithstanding, the NBA commissioner, David Stern, defended Bavetta and showed his support by assigning him to referee at the 2008 NBA Finals, in which the Celtics faced the Lakers. According to a recently released league-commissioned report, Donaghy, who is currently serving a 15-month federal prison sentence, was the only guilty party in the 2002 game-fixing scandal.

Dick Bavetta is a "people person" with a "marvelous sense of humor," according to DuPree. He lives in Ocala, Florida, with his wife, and has an additional home in Lake George, New York, where he frequently works out in the off-season. In addition to his NBA duties, Bavetta has done extensive charitable work. During the 2007 NBA All-Star Weekend, he took part in a short-distance charity race against the former player and current Turner Network Television (TNT) studio analyst Charles Barkley; the event helped to raise $75,000 for the Las Vegas, Nevada, chapter of the Boys and Girls Club of America. Since 1986 he has financed the Bavetta Scholarships, which offer parochial high-school scholarships to minority girls and underprivileged children. He is a member of the board of directors of the Double H-Hole in the Woods Ranch, located in upstate New York, where he has worked since 1992 with critically ill children with

cancer or HIV. He is also the upstate New York regional director for the Juvenile Diabetes Foundation. At 68, he shows no signs of slowing down, explaining to Robbins, "I still feel like I'm celebrating my 16th birthday. I'm blessed with good health—why not keep doing it?"

—C.C.

Suggested Reading: *ABC News Transcripts* (online) Feb. 10, 2006; (Akron, Ohio) *Beacon Journal* H p2+ Feb. 9, 1997; *New York Times* B p2 Dec. 4, 1998, p2 Feb. 5, 2006; PR Newswire *US* Feb. 7, 2006; *Runner's World* p132 June 2007; *USA Today* C p1+ Feb. 20, 2004

Courtesy of the University of Michigan Press

Beresford-Kroeger, Diana

July 25, 1944– Botanist; biochemist; writer; gardener

Address: P.O. Box 253, Merrickville, Ontario K0G 1N0, Canada

"Through our gardens all of us can, together, heal our planet . . . our home," the botanist, biochemist, and writer Diana Beresford-Kroeger has said, as quoted on the Web site of the Canadian television program *Recreating Eden*, which aired a documentary about her life and work in 2008. Beresford-Kroeger "has a lot of revolutionary things to say about the ways we plan, construct, and maintain the natural world around us, particularly in the garden," a writer noted for the Web site of the University of Michigan Press, which has published two of her books. "Her laboratory—spiritually, emotionally, and physically—is the garden, from which spring her ideas about saving the world through rethinking how we put our gardens together." Beresford-Kroeger earned four university degrees and spent 10 years in biomedical laboratories, researching aspects of heart function and manmade blood, before devoting herself to gardening—in particular, to planting and maintaining her own gardens, in which she grows rare and endangered species of trees and other plants. In the conviction that reforestaton must start with individuals rather than governments, she has sent millions of seeds from her gardens to scientists and others who have pledged to start what she has called epicenter forests: "You plant a tree—one tree, two, three, four trees—you protect them from all kinds of predation, and the trees within ten years will start producing seedlings, and the seedlings will make the forest," she explained to Bruce Gellerman for the National Public Radio show *Living on Earth* (April 25, 2008, on-line). "When you replant the forest, you mend the planet," she has said, as quoted on the *Recreating Eden* Web site.

The diversity of plant species in Ontario and other parts of the Great Lakes region of Canada, where Beresford-Kroeger lives, has diminished greatly since whites settled in North America, creating what Beresford-Kroeger has described as a highly unbalanced condition in the natural world that is unhealthy for humans and other living organisms. Moreover, that unnatural lack of diversity, she has said, has deprived researchers of the chance to discover many aspects of the complex ways in which living organisms have interacted for millennia—in particular, ways that involve chemicals. A species of tree known as the wafer ash, for instance, "is a chemical factory . . . , and its products are part of a sophisticated survival strategy," Jim Robbins wrote after interviewing Beresford-Kroeger for the *New York Times* (August 11, 2008). "The flowers contain terpene oils, which repel mammals that might feed on them. But the ash needs to attract pollinators, and so it has a powerful lactone fragrance that appeals to large butterflies and honeybees. The chemicals in the wafer ash, in turn . . . , provide chemical protection for the butterflies from birds, making them taste bitter." Beresford-Kroeger has often advised contemporary scientists and others to consider not only recent discoveries but also indigenous herbalism—knowledge gained over generations among native peoples about particular plants and ways in which humans can make use of them. She has devoted much time and energy to gathering such information, which, she has warned, is fast disappearing in the modern world, because most people no longer value it.

In lectures, magazine articles, and, until recently, guided tours of her gardens as well as in her books, Beresford-Kroeger has promoted the concept of "bioplanning": planting trees, in cities especially, for specific purposes (to combat the effects of air pollution and global warming, for instance), based on each species' "ecofunctions"—"medicinal, environmental, nutritional, pesticidal and herbicidal properties," in the words of Jim Robbins. Thus, for example, Beresford-Kroeger has advocated planting black walnut trees and honey locust trees along roads, because those species, according to Alison Kroulek, writing for celsias.com (September 9, 2008), a Web site devoted to finding practical ways to combat climate change, "are especially good at filtering pollutants from the air." Beresford-Kroeger has also made claims for some trees' salutary effects on humans' well-being. For example, she believes that chemicals from the hawthorn tree help to prevent blood clots in humans, that birch trees release compounds that can aid patients recovering from prostate cancer and kidney problems, and that substances emitted by cedars may strengthen the immune system, act as a heart stimulant, and aid breathing. While some scientists have agreed that such benefits may be real, they have also said that they are reserving judgment about such theories until controlled scientific studies are carried out to test them.

In the University of Michigan Press interview, Beresford-Kroeger said, "If you garden do not forget nature. This is what the Bioplan is all about. The Bioplan tells you how to bring nature back into any garden. And by this I mean, you will bring back birds, butterflies, dragonflies, all the native pollinators, frogs and their cousins the snakes, mammals, and the kingdom of beneficial insects. All of these creatures need water, food, and a safe place if they are to stay in your garden. The ideas of the Bioplan are simple, but they are not being used. A garden is not just for flowers, in my opinion. It should have more than that to satisfy the soul. It should have diversity. A Bioplan brings diversity into any garden."

Beresford-Kroeger's books include *Bioplanning a North Temperate Garden* (1999), which was published in the U.S. in 2004 as *A Garden for Life: The Natural Approach to Designing, Planting, and Maintaining a North Temperate Garden*. In the foreword to that book, the celebrated British naturalist Miriam Rothschild praised it as "one answer to *Silent Spring*"—a reference to the book by the biologist Rachel Carson that, when it appeared in 1962, awakened people to the dangers of pesticides and their role in environmental and ecological degradation. The internationally renowned biologist Edward O. Wilson, who wrote the foreword to Beresford-Kroeger's book *Arboretum America: A Philosophy of the Forest* (2003), told Jim Robbins, "Her ideas are a rare, if not entirely new approach to natural history. The science of selecting trees for different uses around the world has not been well studied." Beresford-Kroeger's most recent work of nonfiction, *Arboretum Borealis*, about the boreal forests in Canada, is due to be published in the near future. Also accepted for publication is a book of her essays, *The Global Forests*. In addition, Beresford-Kroeger is the author of a collection of short stories, *Time Will Tell* (2004), and has written a second book of short stories, about gardening, to be titled "Sun Dogs."

Beresford-Kroeger was born Diana Beresford to John Leslie Beresford and Eileen A. Beresford on July 25, 1944 in England. When she was 11, in circumstances not revealed in easily available sources, both of her parents died. Afterward, for about two years, she lived in southern Ireland with her uncle Denny in a Gaelic-speaking community. "There's a wardship system in the ancient Gaelic world in Ireland, where a child who is an orphan becomes the child of everybody. I was the child of everybody," she told Bruce Ward for the *Ottawa (Ontario, Canada) Citizen* (November 23, 2003). Beresford-Kroeger, who is fluent in Gaelic, recalled to Ward, "I was brought to all the different farms up in the mountains and was told in Gaelic about the pisreogs—the Gaelic word for ancient cures, the knowledge of plants, the traditional systems. [Members of the community] never looked at the world in the terms you and I do. Poverty was their baseline for living. But their richness was in their spirit and in their mind and their knowledge about the natural world was phenomenal."

When Beresford-Kroeger was 13, a judge gave her the option of living with members of her wealthy extended family in England or with another uncle, Patrick O'Donoghue, in the Irish city of Cork. She chose the latter. O'Donoghue was a chemist, and as Beresford-Kroeger wrote in her book *Arboretum America*, as quoted by Ward, he "insisted that knowledge was no burden and that erudition in a woman was more important than in a man." Her uncle owned thousands of books, and Beresford-Kroeger began to read voraciously after she moved into his house. She told Ward, "That was my companionship, books. . . . [G. K.] Chesterton, Hilaire Belloc, Shakespeare and all the Gaelic works. You name it and I ate my way through it." O'Donoghue encouraged Beresford-Kroeger to analyze and discuss what she had been reading. "I had an extraordinary childhood," she told Ward. "On one side of the fire my uncle would sit and we'd have physics. He'd read physics to me—electromagnetic force or something like that—and I'd be on the other side and I'd talk about hydrodynamics, spin theory or whatever. This was my life. . . . Then I started studying and I kind of mopped up everything. I was a walking mop."

Beresford-Kroeger attended the University College of Cork, earning a B.S. degree in classical botany and medical biochemistry. She also earned an M.S. degree while in Ireland. She next pursued a Ph.D. degree in organic chemistry and radionuclear chemistry at the University of Connecticut, in Storrs. "I would say in my academic life I have met the top brains in the world . . . ," she told Ward. "They would look at not what you had in your pocket, but what you had in your heart. That was the most important thing: who are you, who are you in your soul? And they took me and they taught me all these things. And I was a very avid listener." After she earned her doctoral degree,

Beresford-Kroeger worked for 10 years as a researcher in molecular biology and hemodilution at the University of Ottawa School of Medicine. While there she co-wrote several papers on the chemistry of artificial blood and the heart in professional periodicals including *Progress in Clinical and Biological Research* (1978), *Cardiovascular Research* (1979), the *American Heart Journal* (1980 and 1982), and the *Canadian Journal of Physiology and Pharmacology* (1984). According to Cameron Smith, writing for the *Toronto (Ontario, Canada) Star* (May 18, 1996), Beresford-Kroeger has also earned a diploma in veterinary surgery.

Some years earlier Beresford-Kroeger had gotten married to the photographer Christian H. Kroeger. In the late 1970s she and her husband began to create a 160-acre garden on their property with the goals of both preserving Canada's rarest trees and conducting botanical research. They set aside eight acres of their property for Beresford-Kroeger's outdoor research laboratory. Within a dozen years or so, their gardens contained hundreds of representatives of endangered species, among them black hellebore flowers from Bosnia, English morello cherry trees, and black potatoes from the Magdalen Islands, in the Gulf of St. Lawrence, which were first seen by Europeans in the 16th century. With time the gardens grew to encompass several habitats: a water garden—that is, one with plants that live in water; a vineyard; a potager, or ornamental garden; a mixed orchard (containing shrubs and trees that produce edible fruits, such as blueberries and apples); and a large garden of perennials—flowers that live for more than two years. Beresford-Kroeger has handled more than 6,000 plant species and has successfully grown specimens from places as far removed from Canada as Japan, Siberia, and the Balkans. Her gardens contain rare Chinese peonies, more than 100 varieties of hellebores (a popular genus of garden plants, some of which contain alkaloids and other chemicals that have been used for medicinal purposes for centuries and can be poisonous in large quantities); and more than 100 tree species, including rare fir trees, Siberian cherry trees, and disease-resistant chestnuts, butternuts, and elms. (In North America in the 20th century, Dutch elm disease killed tens of millions of elm trees; chestnut blight, a fungal disease, dessimated most populations of chestnut trees; and another fungus killed most of the butternut trees—also called white walnut trees—in some parts of the continent.)

In 1997 Beresford-Kroeger began to focus on collecting specimens of the tree species that had once been plentiful along the St. Lawrence River Basin in Ontario: shag bark hickory, butternut, sweet black walnut, burr oak, hackberry, Canadian red oak, and wafer ash, among others. The basin had once been "one of the richest species areas in the world for trees," she told Julia Elliott for the *Vancouver (British Columbia, Canada) Sun* (July 17, 1999). "It was a warm pocket because of [the Great Lakes]. All of the tropical trees were left there because the glaciers didn't reach that far [during the last Ice Age]. And what has happened over the years, in the last hundred years, is they've all been cut down." After she planted seedlings of the various species, Beresford-Kroeger identified individuals that proved strong enough to survive the cold Canadian winters. Those seedlings became her breeding material. Her work—and that of botanists and gardeners throughout eastern Canada— suffered a tremendous but not irrevocable setback when a severe ice storm in January 1998 damaged or killed countless trees. In 1999 she gave away seeds from some of the trees to people in Canada and the U.S. who had pledged to plant them. Many of those people, Heller told Elliott, "are all really worried about global warming and they're all really worried about the environment."

Beresford-Kroeger's book *Bioplanning a North Temperate Garden* was published in Canada in 1999. Its technical-sounding title notwithstanding, it is aimed at lay gardeners. The book offers drawings of a basic bioplanned garden and suggestions for adapting the plan for less-than-ideal plots, such as small urban sites. Information about 1,200 specific species and varieties includes facts about each plant's ecofunctions: whether it attracts insects or birds and can provide food, medicinal substances, or dyes. Beresford-Kroeger also shared with readers accounts of her experiences with her own gardens. The book includes photographs by Beresford-Kroeger's husband. In a review of *Bioplanning a North Temperate Garden* for the Canadian magazine *Gardening Life* (June 22, 1999, online), Karen York described the book as "inspiring" and as "truly a must-read for anyone concerned with exploring and preserving nature's fragile web." Beresford-Kroeger's book *A Garden for Life: The Natural Approach to Designing, Planting, and Maintaining a North Temperate Garden*, which was published in the U.S. in 2004, "appears to be the same" as *Bioplanning a North Temperate Garden*, Nina Palmin of the Library of Congress told *Current Biography*; Beth Crim, however, in a review for *Library Journal* (2004), as quoted on Barnes & Noble's Web site, called *A Garden for Life* a "revision" of the earlier book.

Bruce Ward, commenting on Beresford-Kroeger's book *Arboretum America* (2003), wrote, "You know how we're all supposed to be thinking outside the box? Diana goes way past that. She grabs the box in both hands and smashes it to splinters. Her thinking stretches from the stars to the microscopic hairs on the underside of certain leaves. The book is a guide to the native trees of the North American continent, but that's like saying *War and Peace* is about Russia. Because when Diana walks around a tree, it becomes a voyage of discovery. So the book amounts to a distillation of her thinking and her detailed plan for reconstructing the biosphere." A reviewer for Nielsen Bookdata wrote, in an article posted on the Norwegian Web site studia.no (2004), "*Arboretum America* is, at the very least, the Bible of Trees. But its ambitions are

grander than that. Author Diana Beresford-Kroeger, a self-described 'renegade scientist,' aims for no less than the salvation of the planet— through the miracle of trees. There are many books on both subjects. Some warn, some inform, while others meditate on the disappearance of the forests or the meaning of trees. Few books, though, touch on all of these subjects as *Arboretum America* does."

Beresford-Kroeger has hosted several Canadian television and radio shows. She has contributed articles to Canadian magazines including *Nature Canada*, the *Canadian Organic Grower*, and the *Merrickville Phoenix*, her local newspaper; her articles have also appeared in periodicals published by such organizations as the Irish Garden Plant Society, the Wiltshire Gardens Trust, and the American Horticultural Society. For some years Beresford-Kroeger led tours of her gardens as a means of raising money for charities. In 1994, for example, tours of her daffodil garden—with more than three dozen varieties, it is one of the largest in North America—generated funds for surgical teams helping victims of the war in Bosnia, in the former Yugoslavia. In 1995 she auctioned off rare plants and seeds as a benefit for the organization Doctors without Borders.

Beresford-Kroeger lives on the outskirts of Merrickville, near Ottawa, with her husband. The couple's daughter, Erika Beresford-Kroeger, is a sales representative for an Ontario real-estate company. Diana Beresford-Kroeger told the University of Michigan Press interviewer that her "dream" was to one day see "corridors of life, of Bioplanned gardens working in concert together. I want to see these in every part of the North American continent. Then the migrations of songbirds with all their majesty can move from nesting to maturation on this continent. When a man in Florida says goodbye to the hummingbird, a man in Toronto can say hello. You see we all live together in a fragile web of connectivity with nature on this planet. Simply, it is our home."

—W.D.

Suggested Reading: *Living on Earth* Web site Jan. 23, 1998; *New York Times* F p2 Aug. 12, 2008; *Ottawa (Ontario, Canada) Citizen* C p6 Nov. 23, 2003; *Recreating Eden* Web site; *Toronto (Ontario, Canada) Star* July 17, 1999; University of Michigan Press Web site; *Vancouver (British Columbia, Canada) Sun* G p2 July 17, 1999; *Contemporary Authors* (on-line)

Selected Books: *Bioplanning a North Temperate Garden*, 1999 (republished as *A Garden for Life: The Natural Approach to Designing, Planting, and Maintaining a North Temperate Garden*, 2004); *Arboretum America: A Philosophy of the Forest*, 2003; *North American Trees: An Ecological Green Guide*, 2003; *Time Will Tell*, 2004

Courtesy of Bigelow Aerospace

Bigelow, Robert

May 12, 1944– Real-estate magnate; aerospace entrepreneur

Address: Bigelow Aerospace, 4640 S. Eastern Ave., Las Vegas, NV 89119

In July 2006 Bigelow Aerospace, a company founded by the Las Vegas, Nevada, real-estate tycoon Robert T. Bigelow, launched *Genesis I*, a one-third–size prototype for an inflatable commercial space station. A year later the firm successfully sent a second, similarly miniaturized module, *Genesis II*, into orbit, bringing closer to fruition Bigelow's longstanding dream of helping mankind establish a presence in outer space. Both *Genesis* crafts, which continue to function and transmit pictures back to Earth, were built using materials that originated with Bigelow Aerospace and technology licensed from the National Aeronautics and Space Administration (NASA). Bigelow, who made a fortune as the founder of the Budget Suites of America hotel chain and other business ventures, has spent $100 million of his own money and has expressed his willingness to devote $400 million more toward the creation of a commercial space station. In February 2008 Bigelow Aerospace announced that it was close to striking a deal with United Launch Alliance, a company with the rockets and other materials necessary to launch a full-size space station into orbit. Bigelow hopes to conduct the initial launch in late 2011 and carry crew members to the space station, dubbed *Sundancer*, by 2012. While initial media reports suggested that he was seeking to build a "space hotel" for wealthy tourists, Bigelow has since clarified his intentions, explaining that the station will cater to scientists, corporations, and countries that are interested in developing their own space programs. "I recognize that everything I have spent so far and what I might spend in the future could all be for nothing," Bigelow told David Shiga for *New Scientist* (January 12, 2008). He added, "If you are not willing to take on that kind of risk, then don't be in the game." "Where's the inspiration in America?" he asked rhetorically during an interview with Michael Belfiore and Bill Sweetman for *Popular Science* (March 2005). "If you asked 50 people or 500 people, 'What is America's inspiration today?' what would they say? To win the war in Iraq? That doesn't create a dream in some kid's mind. An inspiration has to be something you carry with you 24/7."

Robert Thomas Bigelow was born on May 12, 1944 in Las Vegas, where he has lived ever since. His mother, Jewel Thebo Bigelow, was a homemaker; his father worked in the real-estate business. While growing up, during the Cold War and the dawn of the space age, Bigelow was fascinated by science, space travel, and paranormal activity. He and his friends would sometimes see mushroom clouds rise into the atmosphere as military researchers tested atomic weapons in the desert 75 miles away. Bigelow also read science-fiction novels and was captivated by stories of UFOs (unidentified flying objects). When he was 10 he heard that two years earlier, his grandparents had reported having their car run off the road by a mysterious aircraft whose powers of navigation greatly surpassed those of known air vehicles; later, some of his friends and their parents told similar stories. "I got the message from all this that there was a lot out there that we knew nothing about, and the UFO reports made me think that our rocket age must be very immature compared to these other things that were flying around," he told Shiga. "So I embarked on a lifetime quest to get into space if I possibly could." At age 15 he vowed to help humans live in space someday.

Realizing that he would need a great deal of money to fulfill his dreams, Bigelow decided to pursue a career in business rather than science. After his graduation from Arizona State University, in Tempe, in 1967, with a B.S. degree in business administration, he joined his father in the real-estate field. He started out as a broker and soon, as the owner of Bigelow Development, took charge of construction projects; throughout the 1970s and 1980s, he focused on building hotels, warehouses, apartment buildings, and private homes. For five years he sat on the board of directors of a savings-and-loan association, of which he was the second-biggest shareholder, and for a similar period, he directed a commercial bank of which he was the largest shareholder; he also ran his own mortgage company. In 1988 he founded Budget Suites of America, a hotel chain that has capitalized on the Southwest's growing economy. With locations in Texas, Arizona, and Nevada, the chain offers customers facilities where they can live for weeks or months. The thousands of one- and two-bedroom suites, which are usually 90 percent occupied, contain fully equipped kitchens; the rent, from $199 to $299 per week, includes utilities, unlimited local telephone calls, and cable television. Extra fees are charged for linens, dishes, pots and pans, and maid service. Transient families, construction workers, and, in Nevada, casino workers comprise a large part of the clientele. The market for extended-stay hotels grew by 3.3 percent per year from 1992 to 1995, and by 1999 the chain was worth an estimated $600 million. When his additional Las Vegas real-estate holdings and other businesses are also taken into account, Bigelow is believed to be worth more than $1 billion (not enough for him to be included in the 2008 *Forbes* list of the 400 richest Americans or the 1,125 richest people worldwide).

In 1995 Bigelow formed the National Institute for Discovery Science, which was devoted to the study of reported paranormal activity, such as appearances of UFOs, seemingly inexplicable mutilations of cattle, and out-of-body experiences. Bigelow has interviewed more than 200 people who alleged that they were abducted by aliens. "Because of the diversity of the folks involved and the credibility of their backgrounds, as well as the fact that this is a global phenomenon, I think they should be taken seriously," he told John Johnson Jr. for the *Los Angeles Times* (August 30, 2006). The now-defunct institute operated out of Bigelow's Nevada ranch, called Skinwalker. (The name refers to beings that supposedly can change their shapes at will.) "One of the main reasons [Bigelow is] so eager to get his [space] stations launched is that he thinks they might provide a step toward making contact" with extraterrestrials, as Vince Beiser wrote for *Wired* (October 23, 2007, on-line).

In March 1999 Bigelow founded Bigelow Aerospace, and he soon began talking about designing a luxury space cruise ship capable of taking passengers on trips to the moon. While some questioned whether a private citizen could accomplish what NASA had not, Bigelow insisted that entrepreneurship was the key to colonizing space. "It's up to private enterprise to get the general public into space in our lifetimes," Bigelow told Joel Glenn Brenner for the *Washington Post* (July 25, 1999). "It is imperative that we create user-friendly, market-driven projects like this one or it will never happen." Responding to the suggestion that he lacked scientific knowhow, Bigelow said, "I know a lot more about aerospace than NASA knows about business."

By early 2000 Bigelow Aerospace had 17 employees (currently, there are 120), among them Gregory Bennett, an engineer who had spent 15 years working on the International Space Station and whom Bigelow hired as vice president of development. The firm later announced plans to build a 60,000-square-foot Nevada compound, complete with a rocket-shaped building, which, because of its surrounding moat, would look as if

it were positioned on a launch pad. Bigelow's ambition was still to build a cruise liner, and several high-profile figures publicly supported his idea. "This is completely within the realm of possibility," the former astronaut Buzz Aldrin (who set up the ShareSpace Foundation, in 1998, to promote affordable space tourism for laypeople) told Brenner. "For 30 years we've been waiting for a chance to go back to the moon. But it's never been a matter of technology, only desire."

Bigelow abandoned the cruise-ship idea after he read about TransHab, an inflatable space station that NASA began designing in 1997 and abandoned three years later. In 2002 he licensed the technology from NASA, and as part of the agreement, he was permitted to work with the engineers who had created the design. William Schneider, the NASA scientist responsible for TransHab's basic structure, became a frequent visitor to Bigelow's compound, and he was impressed by what he saw. "It was mind-boggling, because this is the vision that I really wanted," Schneider told Michael Belfiore and Bill Sweetman. "Here's these things, all sitting there, and of course some of them are mock-ups, but the rest were inflatable, and I said, 'Man, he's serious. He's not playing around.'" Bigelow's prototype station comprised a center cabin and three inflatable units, "each slightly larger than a shipping container [about 8.5 x 8.5 x 40 feet] and shaped like a giant watermelon," as Vince Beiser wrote. Each of the inflatable sections was wrapped in 16 inches of synthetic skin, which included five sheets of a protective material similar to Vectran or Kevlar. (Bigelow has not disclosed its composition.) Tanks in the station's core kept the units inflated, and an air bladder protected the ship's internal atmosphere. Inside, the station "feels like an empty submarine," Beiser wrote. The individual modules were designed so that occupants could divide the space as needed, using fabric bands to create distinct spaces for living and scientific experimentation. "You'll be able to float around in your shirtsleeves," Beiser reported. "Or put on a spacesuit and step out into the void for a change of scenery."

As work on the station progressed, Bigelow earned a reputation for being secretive and eccentric. Afraid of information leaks, he forbade his workers from using e-mail or voicemail, and he hired armed guards to patrol the grounds, which were enclosed with barbed-wire fences. (The guards wore shirts with pictures of space aliens on the shoulders.) In the summer of 2004, when he and several of his engineers were discussing whether a certain laboratory was the right venue for vibration tests, Bigelow suddenly decided to end the meeting and fly his team to Pasadena, California, for a firsthand inspection. The scientists toured the facility and ate lunch before flying back to Las Vegas the same afternoon.

In 2001 Bigelow asked the Federal Aviation Administration (FAA) for permission to launch his inflatable modules into orbit. He had chosen a design whereby three of the capsules, which he told the Associated Press (May 4, 2001) resembled "fat hot dogs," would link to form a single station. FAA officials asked Bigelow "for patience and for a lot of details," Bigelow said, explaining that the FAA had never received such a request. "The papers and forms don't exist for an application like this." Though Bigelow was working with technology he had purchased from NASA, he still accused that agency of making it difficult for private citizens to make headway into space. As an example, he cited the agency's efforts to prevent Dennis Tito, a multimillionaire businessman, from visiting the space station. "NASA views space as its own monopoly," he said, adding, "It will be very difficult to break that monopoly." Three years later, realizing that even if he could launch his station, he would still need a way to transport customers and crew back and forth, he created America's Space Prize, a $50 million award to be given to the first company to develop a reliable shuttle service. The deadline for the contest is January 2010.

In November 2004 the FAA gave Bigelow the go-ahead to launch a prototype of his space station. "This will go a long way to establishing a good precedent for the inflatables," Mike Gold, a lawyer for Bigelow Aerospace, told Leonard David for CNN.com. Less than two years later, in July 2006, Bigelow sent *Genesis I* into orbit. "I wouldn't be the least bit surprised if we have a number of different systems fail," Bigelow told the Associated Press (July 12, 2006) shortly before the launch, which took place in Russia's Ural Mountains. Despite Bigelow's reservations *Genesis* performed as intended, and the 2,800-pound, 14-foot-long, four-foot-wide craft inflated to twice its width after reaching orbit. *Genesis* carried insects and photographs of Bigelow Aerospace employees, and its dozen cameras relayed images back to Earth. "We're ecstatic," Bigelow told the Associated Press. "We're just elated. We have a sense of being on a great adventure." In an interview with the *Christian Science Monitor* (July 17, 2006), George Whitesides, director of the National Space Society, a space-advocacy group, called Bigelow's launch "incredibly significant." Comparing *Genesis* with other millionaires' pet space projects, Whitesides added, "This is the only real, funded project that's trying to create a destination in space privately, as opposed to the other folks, who are creating private launch vehicles." In August 2006 data showed that *Genesis* was holding its air at least as well as the International Space Station, and scientists predicted it would take 150 to 200 years for all of the air to leak out.

Speaking at the National Space Symposium in April 2007, Bigelow unveiled a list of potential space-station customers, laying to rest the idea that he was merely courting wealthy tourists. "The suborbital business is going to be a resounding success," he said, according to *Satellite News* (April 16, 2007), and he cited corporations, high-tech research firms, and countries that were eager to de-

velop their own space programs as possible clients. "We're in the business to make an economic benefit and hopefully help mankind along the way," he added. Bigelow set a price of $12 million per ticket and encouraged customers to put down 10 percent deposits. While some wealthy adventurers, such as the Microsoft executive Charles Simonyi, had already paid for weeklong trips to the International Space Station, Bigelow's fees were far lower than those charged for weeklong trips to that facility, and his firm promised to allow clients to stay in space four times as long.

In July 2007 Bigelow Aerospace launched *Genesis II*, and as with its predecessor, the module inflated according to design. While *Genesis II* was launched without incident, the module encountered problems after going into orbit. "One of the subsystems went off-line, and we had to reboot the spacecraft's onboard computers," Bigelow told Geoffrey Little for *Air & Space* (January 1, 2008, online). The reboot was necessary to keep the station from losing altitude. *Genesis I* had faced similar problems, and it, too, had to be rebooted, after a computer subsystem failed. There were also problems related to *Genesis II*'s cargo. The ship's storage in Russia for six weeks prior to its launch led to the deaths of all the insects before they reached space. In addition, communication problems kept Bigelow's team from activating an onboard bingo game, as had been planned. "We're gaining experience and learning how to operate missions on orbit," Bigelow told Little. "We want to test to fault. That's our goal." In addition to ants, cockroaches, and scorpions, *Genesis II* carried a variety of small cameras and other items that people had paid $295 to have placed on board.

In August 2007 Bigelow revealed that rising costs had forced him to scrap a third test launch and instead build his new *Galaxy* module on the ground. He also expedited the launch of *Sundancer*, which is slated to become the first privately funded manned and operational space station. In February 2008 Bigelow Aerospace announced plans to launch *Sundancer*, as well as crew members and cargo, via Atlas rockets provided by United Launch Associated, a partnership between Boeing and Lockheed Martin. If a deal is reached, the first launch—which will likely take place in Cape Canaveral, Florida—could come as early as 2011. Six missions are set to follow in 2012: the first two would be for the purpose of transporting building materials, while the next four would ferry supplies and work crews. "After that, we're expecting our launch rate to double," Gold told Todd Halvorson for *Florida Today* (February 6, 2008).

According to the California Space Authority (2006, on-line), Bigelow "has completed many years of post-graduate business courses." He holds many aerospace-related patents. Bigelow has rarely granted interviews and until recently refused to be photographed by the press. He lives in Nevada with his wife, Diane, to whom he has been married for more than four decades. For years he never revealed to her his interest in space travel, because, as he told Belfiore and Sweetman, "it's possible that that kind of dream would never happen." The Bigelows' son Rod Lee Bigelow died in 1992 of a self-inflicted gunshot wound in what his father has maintained was an accident. The couple's other child has a daughter, Blair, who was 15 in early 2008. Blair's name was embroidered on the outer fabric of *Genesis II*, as can be seen in a photograph that appeared in *Air & Space Magazine* (January 1, 2008, on-line). The Bigelows have contributed $7 million to the University of Nevada, $3.7 million of it for a professorship of consciousness studies, which was to include consciousness "especially as it exists after bodily death," as Lisa Ferguson wrote for the *Las Vegas Sun* (March 3,

1998, on-line). The university's Rod Lee Bigelow College of Health Sciences and the Bigelow Physics Building benefited from the remainder of the Bigelows' donation. The couple have also made substantial contributions toward cancer research. Robert Bigelow won the 2006 Arthur C. Clarke Innovator's Award, from the Arthur C. Clarke Foundation, and the 2007 Space Foundation Award for Space Achievement.

—K.J.P.

Suggested Reading: *Christian Science Monitor* p3 July 17, 2006; *Florida Today* A p1 Feb. 6, 2008; *Los Angeles Times* A p1 Aug. 30, 2006; *New Scientist* p42 Jan. 12, 2008; *Wired* (on-line) Oct. 23, 2007

Alex Wong/Getty Images

Blunt, Roy

Jan. 10, 1950– U.S. representative from Missouri (Republican); House minority whip

Address: 217 Cannon House Office Bldg., Washington, D.C. 20515

In November 2002, when Roy Blunt of Missouri was unanimously elected majority whip of the U.S. House of Representatives by his fellow Republican members of that body, his predecessor, the newly elected House majority leader, Tom DeLay, presented him with a velvet-covered hammer. The gift was meant to signify the difference between the two politicians: DeLay, nicknamed "The Hammer," had a reputation for strong-arming col-

leagues into voting along party lines, while Blunt, who had served as DeLay's chief deputy, was seen as softer and more compassionate. "The velvet hammer hurts just as much," Blunt told Deirdre Shesgreen for the *St. Louis Post-Dispatch* (November 17, 2002), hinting that he had no intention of coddling House legislators. "It's just not as loud." Blunt has said that his easygoing approach is effective in carrying out his main responsibility, which is to drum up (or "whip up") votes for pending legislation and occasionally to ask lawmakers to support bills to which they have expressed opposition. "You do this job with patience [and] with understanding members' districts as well as they do," he told Shesgreen. "You have to be willing to say, 'I've been to your district. You can take this vote'"—that is, voting "yes" at the request of Blunt and other Republican Party leaders will not get them in trouble in their home states. In November 2008 Blunt was reelected to the House for the sixth time.

Blunt's rise to majority whip—the third-highest position in what was then a Republican-dominated House—was viewed as remarkably swift: the Missouri representative attained the position after only six years in Washington, D.C. Prior to becoming whip, Blunt had forged close ties with the White House and had served since the start of his second two-year term in office as DeLay's chief deputy. As whip Blunt has distinguished himself by successfully guiding lobbyists to influence House members and win tight votes. "Here in Washington, Blunt has converted what had been an informal and ad hoc relationship between congressional leaders and the Washington corporate and trade community into a formal, institutionalized alliance," Thomas B. Edsall wrote for the *Washington Post* (May 17, 2005). "Lobbyists are now an integral part of the Republican whip operation on par with the network of lawmakers who serve as assistant whips."

After DeLay stepped down as House majority leader, in January 2006, in the face of felony charges related to alleged campaign-finance violations, Blunt announced his desire to succeed him. (Blunt had served as acting majority leader in the four months following DeLay's indictment.) Hedging his bets, Blunt refused to resign from his whip position while he campaigned for the post of majority leader. In an article for *National Review* (January 20, 2006, on-line), Rich Lowry wrote that Blunt "will be in a position to show his favor or disfavor toward members, win or lose. That gives him a huge amount of leverage." Blunt was favored to win, but in the election, held in February 2006, he lost to Congressman John Boehner of Ohio. Following the congressional elections of 2006, in which Democrats took control of both the House and Senate, Blunt won election as House minority whip.

Roy D. Blunt was born on January 10, 1950 in Niangua, Missouri, to Leroy Blunt, a state legislator at one time, and the former Neva Letterman. He grew up on a dairy farm. In 1970 he graduated from Southwest Baptist University, in Bolivar, Missouri, with a B.A. degree in history. He then worked for a while as a high-school teacher. In 1972 he earned an M.A. degree in history and government from Southwest Missouri State University, in Springfield. That year he made his first foray into politics, as a volunteer for the congressional campaign of the Republican John Ashcroft. Ashcroft, who lost that election, would later prove to be an important political connection, as he went on to serve as a Missouri governor, a U.S. senator, and the U.S. attorney general. In 1973 Missouri's Republican governor, Christopher "Kit" Bond, appointed Blunt to the position of Greene County clerk, a post he held until 1984. From 1976 to 1982 Blunt was an adjunct instructor at Drury College (since renamed Drury University), in Springfield. In 1980, at the request of U.S. senator John Danforth, he ran for lieutenant governor of Missouri. He lost that election, but four years later he was elected Missouri's secretary of state. Blunt retained that office until 1993, when he began a three-year stint as president of Southwest Baptist University. Earlier, in 1992, Blunt had made a bid for governor, even though fellow Republicans Bill Webster, the Missouri attorney general, and Wendall Bailey, the state treasurer, were also seeking the office. Blunt lost in the hard-fought three-man primary, and some claimed that his attacks on Webster, the eventual Republican candidate, helped a Democrat, Mel Carnahan, win the governorship.

In 1996, following the announcement by U.S. congressman Mel Hancock of Missouri that he would retire at the end of his term, Blunt decided to run for his seat, representing the state's Seventh Congressional District. In the Republican primary, in which he faced a former regional administrator for the Small Business Administration, he won 56 percent of the vote; on Election Day in 1996, Blunt won handily, capturing 65 percent of the vote. "He wanted to climb the ladder in Missouri. And when that didn't work out, just four years later, he turns around and runs for Congress and has had perhaps more success in Washington easily than he's had back here in Missouri," Steve Kraske, a political reporter for the *Kansas City (Missouri) Star*, told Alex Chadwick on the National Public Radio program *Day to Day* (September 29, 2005). Before the election Blunt had visited Hancock, who told him to aim for the freshman spot on the influential House Republican Steering Committee, the panel in charge of placing representatives on committees. "That puts you in the room with everybody here," Blunt remembered Hancock saying, according to Thomas B. Edsall and Shailagh Murray in the *Washington Post* (October 1, 2005). (Other sources say it was DeLay who first told Blunt to seek that committee seat.) After meeting with Hancock, Blunt called DeLay, and before long, according to Edsall and Murray, Blunt had become "the protégé of one of the most powerful men in town." "I left that meeting thinking, this is a great guy to work with," Blunt said of his talk with DeLay.

As a member of the House Republican Steering Committee, Blunt worked to secure committee assignments for other freshman Republicans. In 1999, after Blunt's reelection, DeLay chose him, from a pool of 48 deputy whips, as his chief deputy. "I had a lot of great talent to pick from but the thing that stood out most about Roy was, the minute he came into the House he wanted to be part of the whip team," DeLay told Shesgreen. "He almost made a nuisance of himself, coming into the office [saying], 'What can I do? You got a job for me?'" Again showing what many have described as an ability to align himself with influential people, Blunt served on George W. Bush's presidential exploratory committee and became one of the first congressmen to endorse Bush in the 2000 presidential campaign. He later became the chief liaison between House Republicans and the campaign. After Bush took office Blunt began having breakfasts regularly with Bush's chief strategist, Karl Rove, at the White House.

In 2001, while trying to help the Republican leadership pass a bill giving President Bush more power in negotiating trade agreements, Blunt proved he could use lobbyists to influence House members and win close votes. After meeting with various coalitions, including pro-trade and energy groups, Blunt dispatched lobbyists to secure votes from Republicans and Democrats alike. "Democrats also consult regularly with lobbyists and rely on them for key political and legislative advice," Shesgreen wrote for the *St. Louis Post-Dispatch* (September 11, 2001). "But Blunt's efforts seem to be more sophisticated, with meetings about once a week." "The reason we're going to be successful is because of the effort Roy Blunt has laid out here," Dan Mattoon, a lobbyist and Republican political adviser, told Shesgreen. "What's being done right now is finding ways in which we can achieve 218 votes in the House, not only working with Republicans but also finding like-minded Democrats." The trade bill passed by a vote of 215–214.

By the spring of 2002, as it became clear that De-Lay was on his way to becoming House majority leader, many political observers pegged Blunt as his likely successor. "He'd be a great whip because he understands what it takes to get our entire group to go along with the leadership," Republican congressman Rob Portman of Ohio told Susan Ferrechio and Derek Willis for the *Congressional Quarterly Daily Monitor* (April 8, 2002). "You need a special sense of the conference to do this job and do it well," Portman added, referring to the Republican Conference, the organizational body for Republican House members. "And he has it." Even some of his political opponents welcomed the idea of Blunt's promotion. An official with the AFL-CIO, a labor union typically aligned with Democrats, told Ferrechio and Willis, "I think the change will be that he is less confrontational and easier to get along with than Mr. DeLay. It may lead to more cordial relations with the Democrats." In addition to his success in helping the Republicans to secure votes needed for legislation whose passage was uncertain, Blunt showed himself to be an aggressive fund-raiser, collecting more than $550,000 in the 13 months ending in April 2002. Responding to charges of being "too aggressive," Blunt said he was an equally "aggressive giver" and felt obligated to help the party expand its majority in Congress.

In July 2002 Blunt underwent surgery for removal of his left kidney, after doctors found a softball-sized tumor on it. There were no signs of tumor cells elsewhere, and he received no follow-up treatment. In November 2002, after he won his fourth term in Congress, House Republicans unanimously elected him House majority whip. Colleagues praised the Missouri representative, citing his affability and effectiveness in both getting legislation passed and raising money for the GOP. (In advance of the 2002 congressional elections, Blunt helped funnel $24 million to Republican congressmen engaged in contentious races.) "You want to say yes to Roy Blunt," Republican congressman Christopher Shays of Connecticut told Shesgreen. "He treats you with respect, he's got good reasons, and you like him. The bottom line is, he's awesome at it." Almost immediately after Blunt took over as majority whip, pundits began mentioning him as a possible future Speaker of the House, since, because of term limits, then-Speaker Dennis Hastert was required to give up his seat in 2006, and some speculated that he would do so two years earlier. "[Blunt is] smooth on TV and good at his job, which is counting votes," a Republican aide told Jim VandeHei for the *Washington Post* (November 18, 2002).

In April 2003 Blunt married his second wife, Abigail Perlman, a prominent lobbyist for Altria, the parent company of the tobacco giant Philip Morris. Philip Morris has contributed large amounts of money to Blunt's political campaigns, and a son from his first marriage, Andrew Blunt, is a lobbyist for that firm. In June 2003 the *Washing-*

ton Post reported that in the previous year, within hours of becoming the majority whip, Blunt had tried to sneak a provision benefiting Philip Morris into the legislation that created the Department of Homeland Security. "It is highly unusual for a House Republican to insert a last-minute contentious provision that has never gone through a committee, never faced a House vote and never been approved by the speaker or majority leader," Jim VandeHei noted in the *Washington Post* (June 11, 2003). Blunt's addition to the bill would have made it more difficult for companies to sell counterfeit cigarettes over the Internet. While Blunt claimed that he was not the author of the legislation, he maintained that it was designed to stop terrorist groups from making profits on sales of tobacco. "National news accounts have documented this disturbing source of funds for some of the most dangerous terrorist organizations," Blunt said, according to CBSnews.com (June 11, 2003). "It's a serious homeland security issue, and this proposal would help the United States thwart terrorists who engage in cigarette trafficking and sales to finance their operations." Many saw the incident as evidence that the Missouri legislator was beholden to lobbyists, including his wife. "Now everything he does is suspect," an unnamed Republican aide told Eleanor Clift for *Newsweek* (June 23, 2003). Some speculated that DeLay—rumored to be feuding with Blunt—had leaked the Philip Morris story to the *Washington Post*, though the majority leader insisted that he had not. "There's a rift being concocted by the press," DeLay told Gebe Martinez for *Congressional Quarterly Weekly* (July 11, 2003). "Roy Blunt's doing a great job; [he is] a very close friend of mine."

In July 2003 Blunt was diagnosed with early-stage prostate cancer. The disease was said to be unrelated to his kidney tumor, and within a month of having his prostate removed, he toured his congressional district and declared himself cured.

In April 2005 Blunt began using what became known as his "lobbyist-whip" operation to mobilize support for the Central American Free Trade Agreement, a bill that was in danger of stalling on the House floor. He courted enough Democratic votes to offset those of Republicans who opposed the legislation, and the measure passed. "We are following all the rules," Blunt told Alan K. Ota for *Congressional Quarterly Weekly* (April 29, 2005), defending his lobbyist-whip system. "There's no reason why we should not work together. Lobbyists have a healthy understanding of where interests intersect." Gary Ruskin, the director of the Congressional Accountability Project (a nongovernmental group set up by the consumer activist Ralph Nader), disagreed, telling Ota, "What we are seeing is the corporate control of Congress. This lobbyist-whip system opens the door to abuse." By May 2005 Blunt and his operatives had won more than 50 straight victories for the Republican leadership. "Working outside the glare of public attention, Blunt has maximized the organization's influence by delegating authority to Washington business and trade association lobbyists to help negotiate deals with individual House members to produce majorities on important issues," Edsall wrote (May 17, 2005).

In September 2005 DeLay was indicted by a Texas grand jury on charges that he had violated campaign-finance laws. Under Republican Conference rules he was forced to give up his post as majority leader until further notice. Blunt then persuaded Hastert to name him interim majority leader. Blunt said he hoped DeLay would eventually reclaim his position. "I'm confident that's going to happen," he told Ota for Congressional Quarterly Today (September 30, 2005).

On January 7, 2006 DeLay announced that he would not resume his position as majority leader, thus setting the stage for an election to fill the position. Blunt's main challenger, Ohio congressman John A. Boehner, emphasized his outsider status, in light of the DeLay indictment and a scandal involving the prominent lobbyist Jack Abramoff, which had caused some to question the Republican Party's ethics. Blunt had ties to both DeLay and Abramoff; in addition to working under DeLay in his early years in Congress, he had helped Abramoff by writing letters opposing the construction of a Louisiana casino that might have drawn business away from a pair of competing establishments run by two of Abramoff's clients. Worried about losing their majority to the Democrats in the upcoming 2006 elections, some Republican members of the House accused both Boehner and Blunt of having too many ties to lobbyists. When a third candidate, Arizona congressman John Shadegg, entered the race for majority leader, he promised "a clean break from the scandals of the recent past," as David Nather wrote for Congressional Quarterly Weekly (January 13, 2006).

As the election for majority leader approached, Blunt sparked criticism by refusing to relinquish his post as majority whip. "Not only does he theoretically keep the whip spot as a soft landing if he doesn't win the majority-leader race, he is able to lobby members for their support with the knowledge right there in the foreground that even if he's not majority leader in a couple of weeks, he will still be whip," Rich Lowry wrote. "He is losing the outside game, in the editorials and in the blogosphere. What hurts him is the perception that he is an old-style, horse-trading, risk-averse politician. Holding the whip spot plays into that perception." While Blunt claimed early in the race that he had secured the 117 votes needed to win, he lost the election, winning a plurality in the first round of voting but losing to Boehner in the runoff, after Shadegg dropped out. "We are trying to send a message that we want change," Kentucky congressman Edward Whitfield told Ota for Congressional Quarterly Today (February 2, 2006). Blunt said that his campaign had been sabotaged by a handful of House members who had "planted" stories in the press about a need for change, according to John H.

Fund in the American Spectator (March 2006). "The five or six people that will talk to the media about what bad shape we're in are not reflective of 225 of their colleagues," Blunt told Fund.

In November 2006, after the Democrats regained control of the House of Representatives as well as the Senate, Blunt found himself running for the position of minority whip. Shadegg again emerged as a challenger, touting his affiliation with the Republican Study Committee (RSC), a conservative group that, for the first time ever, claimed more than half of all House Republicans as members. Blunt supporters maintained that many of the Missouri congressman's high-ranking aides were RSC members, and they pointed out that he had amassed a solid conservative voting record over the years. Amid continued calls for an all-new leadership team—DeLay had already stepped down, and Hastert had announced that he would not seek a top leadership spot in the Democrat-led House—Blunt downplayed his association with the so-called old guard and emphasized his experience. He won the minority-whip post by a vote of 137–57. The new leadership team, he said, would "get rid of the bad habits we may have developed in our 12 years in the majority," according to Kate Zernike in the New York Times (November 18, 2006). Arizona congressman Jeff Flake, who had supported Shadegg, expressed disappointment over Blunt's victory, however, telling Zernike, "It's just easier to follow a reform agenda with new leaders. It's not impossible to do with the old. It's just harder. So we have a harder road now."

Since the 2006 elections, Blunt has been critical of the Democrats' spending bills and efforts to impose timelines for troop withdrawal from Iraq. In May 2007, after House Democrats failed to come up with enough votes to override the president's veto of a bill that would have established a deadline for troop withdrawal, Blunt released a statement calling for a "long-term strategy for success," according to PR Newswire US (May 2, 2007). He has also reasserted his conservative positions, courting right-wing blogs and creating his own video channel on the popular Web site YouTube. "Congressman Blunt has always been a conservative . . . ," his spokesperson Burson Snyder told Susan Davis for Roll Call (March 27, 2007). "All of his efforts are a direct offshoot of the desire to get back a majority." While some House members have continued to question Blunt's convictions, others have praised him for being the type of politician who would be unhappy with anything but a leadership role. On November 4, 2008 Blunt defeated his Democratic opponent, Richard Monroe, and two other candidates and won a seventh term as congressman.

Six months before his second marriage, Blunt divorced his first wife, Roseann, ending their 35-year union. Like their son Andrew, their daughter, Amy, is a lobbyist. Their other son, Matthew, was elected governor of Missouri in 2004. In 2006 Blunt and his second wife adopted an 18-month-old boy, Alexander Charles Blunt, from Russia.

—K.J.P.

BOGUT

Suggested Reading: *Congressional Quarterly Today* Nov. 15, 2006; *Congressional Quarterly Weekly* July 11, 2003, Sep. 30, 2005, Jan. 13, 2006; National Public Radio *Day to Day* Sep. 29, 2005; *National Review* (on-line) Jan. 20, 2006; *Roll Call* Mar. 27, 2007; *St. Louis (Missouri) Post-Dispatch* B p1 Nov. 17, 2002; *Time* p22 Jan. 23, 2006; *Washington Post* A p19 Nov. 18, 2002, A p19 May 17, 2005; *Weekly Standard* Oct. 10, 2005; *Who's Who in America, 2007*

Bogut, Andrew

(BOH-gut)

Nov. 28, 1984– Basketball player

Address: Milwaukee Bucks, 1001 N. Fourth St., Milwaukee, WI 53203

In his first season with the Milwaukee Bucks, the forward and center Andrew Bogut led his team to a spot in the National Basketball Association (NBA) play-offs. In doing so, Bogut, an Australian native and the first player chosen in the league's 2005 lottery draft, became only the fourth number-one draft pick in NBA history to make the postseason as a rookie. (David Robinson, Chris Weber, and Tim Duncan were the first three.) Bogut missed 15 games in an injury-plagued second season, and months before he began his third year with the Bucks, the seven-footer drew criticism for remarks he made about some of his fellow players. "The public's image of NBA players is true," Bogut told David Sygall for the Sydney, Australia, *Sun-Herald* (June 17, 2007). "A lot of them get caught up in the hype and do video clips with rappers and all that crap. They want bling bling all over themselves and drive fast cars. But that's just the way the culture is in America—if you've got it flaunt it and if you don't, you can't." Bogut later apologized, telling Bob Wolfley for the *Milwaukee (Wisconsin) Journal-Sentinel* (October 10, 2007), "The point I was trying to get across was coming from Australia where we have 80 million people, a very laid back country, to America . . . all that bling bling—all that stuff—it's something I didn't grow up with. It definitely was a shock to me [at first] but being around it for three years, it's fine to me now."

While Bogut has earned something of a reputation for speaking his mind, his candor has not overshadowed his accomplishments on the basketball court. After leading the Australian national team to a junior world championship in July 2003, Bogut left for Salt Lake City, Utah, where Rick Majerus, then the coach of the University of Utah men's basketball team, the Utes, offered him an athletic scholarship. In two seasons with the Utes, Bogut established himself as one of the top college players in the country, and in his sophomore year, he helped his team make the "Sweet 16" round of the National Collegiate Athletic Association (NCAA) tournament. After that season he earned many honors, including being named Consensus National Player of the Year, and declared himself eligible for the NBA draft. In his rookie season he averaged 9.4 points and 7.0 rebounds per game and finished third in voting for the league's All-Rookie team. As he prepared for his third season, Bogut told reporters that he was looking forward to strengthening his game. While observers have noted his solid play, many believe that he has not yet posted the kinds of spectacular numbers of which he is capable. "I've got a long way to go to get to the player I want to be in my career . . . ," Bogut told Lee Crossley for *MX* (August 29, 2007), an Australian newspaper. "I've shown glimpses but I definitely have to improve."

The younger of two children, Andrew Michael Bogut was born on November 28, 1984 in Melbourne, Australia. His parents, Michael and Anne Bogut, had immigrated to Australia as teenagers in the 1970s to escape the civil war in their native Croatia. Bogut has credited his father, a mechanic who arrived in Australia unable to speak English, with inspiring his tireless work ethic. "No-one said he'd make it, and yet he is one of the best in Australia at what he does," Bogut told Paul Kent for the Sydney *Sunday Telegraph* (November 27, 2005). He also said that his father "didn't always do it for the money. He's a real stickler for making it perfect. Even when the job isn't his." It was in his father's garage that Bogut discovered his love of basketball, as he would often toss a ball into a metal ring bolted to the wall. When he turned 11 he joined his first club (or youth) team and began taping Australia's weekly NBA highlights show and watching each episode repeatedly. He had growth spurts at 12 and 16; in between he played on the perimeter of the court, away from the area under the basket, where tall centers are usually positioned. Consequently, he honed his ball-handling and shooting skills—attributes that would later serve him well.

Meanwhile, Bogut was having difficulty making friends, and his parents were having trouble fitting in with the other club parents. Part of the problem stemmed from their ethnic background. "I got a lot of crap for having a European surname when I was in high school," Bogut told Adam Harvey for the Perth, Australia, *Sunday Times* (November 13, 2005). He said to Kelli Anderson for *Sports Illustrated* (February 21, 2005), "As a young teenager I probably wasn't as talented as some other kids, but I knew I had the potential. Yet coaches told me I'd never make it. I'd go home and cry about how much I wanted to make it. I would practice for hours and hours, and I knew other kids weren't doing that."

If Bogut was already more motivated than his peers, he reached a new level of dedication at the age of 15 (some sources say 14), when he was cut from Victoria, Australia's under-18 team. "After that he vowed he would never be last again," his mother told Anderson. Bogut's parents hired a personal trainer, and in addition to morning work-outs, the boy spent two and a half hours practicing each day after school. As part of his sessions, Bogut was required to wear ankle weights and plastic blinders that made it impossible for him to look at the ball while dribbling. "After half a practice I could barely walk," Bogut told Anderson. "It was crazy, but that's where I got my game." Seven months later Bogut began working out with the Victoria Titans, a team in Australia's National Basketball League. Ken Shields, the former coach of Canada's national basketball team, attended one of the team's practices and mentioned Bogot to Rick Majerus, then the coach of the University of Utah squad.

Bogut later signed on to play for the Australian Institute of Sport, a government agency that grooms talented teenage athletes for Olympic competition. Thanks to his success with the institute team, European professional teams began to offer him seven-figure contracts, but he decided to postpone turning professional and to accept Majerus's offer of a scholarship. "In Europe the money's always going to be there," he told Chris Wilson for the *Canberra (Australia) Times* (May 15, 2004). "So I thought I'd experience college—it's a once in a lifetime thing—and if I didn't like it I'd leave the next day." Bogut signed his letter of intent in April 2002, but due to difficulties connected with his high-school transcript, he was unable to begin playing for Utah in December 2002 as planned. Instead, he remained in Australia and played for the junior national team. In July 2003, in Greece, Bogut led that squad to a world title, averaging 26.3 points and 17 rebounds per game. He was named most valuable player of the tournament. At that point, as a year had passed since Bogut had signed the agreement with the University of Utah, he could have turned professional or chosen to attend a different college. "I stuck with Utah, because they stuck with me," he told Mike Sorensen for the Salt Lake City *Deseret Morning News* (January 17, 2006).

As a freshman Bogut had to adjust to Majerus's hard-edged coaching style. "Everyone who goes through the program gets to a point where he really thinks about whether he loves the game enough to stay and play under Majerus, because he is so competitive and so demanding," Bogut told Anderson. "People say there was a lot of turmoil between us, but it was nothing like that. I learned more that year than I had in my whole life. Not so much fundamentals as strategy." In other interviews Bogut has spoken less favorably of Majerus, who left Utah in January 2004, midway through Bogut's freshman season, due to health problems. (He currently coaches at St. Louis University, in Missouri.) When Joe Beatty, a reporter for the *Daily Utah Chronicle*, asked Bogut what advice he would give colleges considering hiring Majerus, he said, according to University Wire (February 21, 2006), "I'd leave it up to them, but I wouldn't go there if Majerus were there." He added that while Majerus

had helped him become a better player, "he took confidence away from me, the way he coaches and the type of guy he is." Despite that problem, Bogut performed satisfactorily, averaging 12.5 points and 9.9 rebounds per game. At the end of the season, he was named freshman of the year in the Mountain West Conference.

After Majerus's departure Bogut again received offers from European teams. In an effort to re-recruit his team's star player (Bogut had not quit school but was thinking of leaving), Utah's new head coach, Ray Giacoletti, flew to Australia after the spring semester and met with Bogut and his family. During the fewer than 24 hours that Giacoletti remained in Australia, he persuaded Bogut to return to Utah and take advantage of a strategy that promised to be better suited to his skills. "He didn't have to say much when he came over because his actions speak louder than words," Bogut told Mike Harrington for the *Buffalo (New York) News* (March 19, 2005).

Before he returned to Utah, Bogut played for the Australian national team, the Boomers, at the 2004 Summer Olympics, in Athens, Greece. In five games he averaged 14.8 points and 8.8 rebounds, and he scored 11 points and grabbed eight rebounds in a contest with the United States team, whose center, Tim Duncan, Bogut had long admired. "He did a great job on the offensive glass," Duncan told Grantley Bernard for the Melbourne *Herald Sun* (December 22, 2005). "He made some big baskets for them and showed some great touch right around the basket." Australia lost to the U.S. by 10 points and failed to win a medal.

After his Olympic experience Bogut appeared to play with new confidence, and in his sophomore year at Utah, he ranked 19th in the NCAA in scoring and second in rebounding, averaging 20.4 points and 12.2 rebounds per game. He also led the nation in double-doubles (games in which he achieved double digits in two categories, such as points and rebounds), with 26. On the strength of his 715 total points that year, Bogut became the third Utah player to break 1,000 points in only two seasons. He started in all 35 games and played eight all the way through, without leaving the floor. In the NCAA tournament Bogut led the Utes past the University of Texas–El Paso in the first round and Oklahoma, which had been favored to win, in the second. In the latter contest Bogut nearly posted a triple-double, scoring 10 points, grabbing 11 rebounds, and making seven assists. Utah lost in the tournament's "Sweet 16" round, as the University of Kentucky used double- and triple-team defensive schemes against Bogut. Despite the heavy coverage he scored 20 points, more than any other player during that game. After the Utes were eliminated, Bogut was named Consensus National Player of the Year. He also received the prestigious Naismith College Player of the Year and John R. Wooden Awards, and the Associated Press, ESPN, and *Sports Illustrated* named Bogut NCAA Player of the Year. Soon afterward he announced that he was leaving Utah to join the NBA.

Doug Benc/Getty Images

Desmond Mason (left) and Andrew Bogut (right) of the Milwaukee Bucks battle for position with the Orlando Magic's Adonal Foyle (center).

In the lead-up to the 2005 NBA draft, observers predicted that Bogut would be among the first three players chosen, though some basketball experts wondered whether his outstanding college record should be attributed to Utah's playing in the Mountain West Conference, a relatively weak division. Bogut also faced rumors (which some said could be traced to Majerus) that he suffered from a degenerative eye disease. In his pre-draft workout with the Milwaukee Bucks, the team that had earned the number-one pick through the league's lottery system, Bogut showed up wearing a suit and carrying a copy of his résumé. "Best interview of anybody I've ever had with the Bucks," the team's owner, U.S. senator Herb Kohl of Wisconsin, told Marty Burns for *Sports Illustrated* (October 24, 2005). "Great questions. Great answers. Very impressive. When he left, I said, 'That guy's a winner.'"

On June 28, 2005 Bogut became the first Australian player to be picked first in the NBA draft. He signed a five-year contract worth roughly $26 million. Under league rules the first two years of a rookie player's contract are guaranteed, and the team later has the option of renewing for the third and fourth seasons. In June 2007, having already renewed the contract for a third year, the Bucks took advantage of their final option and signed Bogut through the 2008–09 season. After signing his initial deal, Bogut established the Andrew Bogut 4 Foundation, which helps underprivileged children in Croatia, Australia, Utah, and Milwaukee. (In college he wore a jersey with the number four.) "I think it's good to give back," he told Charles F. Gardner for the *Milwaukee Journal Sen-*

tinel (July 2, 2005). "Quite honestly, it's a lot of money for anybody, and I don't think one person deserves that much money in their life. If I can give back to people who have nothing, especially youths who might be stuck in crime or drugs, maybe putting a basketball in their hands will get them out of that." In August 2005 Bogut became "The Bogey Man," accepting the nickname as part of a $5 million endorsement agreement with the athletic-apparel manufacturer Nike. "I'll probably get a lot of crap for it, but it will be well worth it," he told a Fox News sports Web site in Australia, according to Linda Hamilton in the *Deseret Morning News* (August 19, 2005).

In his first season with the Bucks, Bogut, playing both the forward and center positions, participated in all 82 games, starting 77 of them. He averaged 9.4 points, 7.0 rebounds (more than any other rookie that year), and 2.3 assists per game, helping the Bucks post a 40-42 record and earn a spot in the Eastern Conference play-offs. The NBA commissioner, David Stern, was among those who praised him, and as Milwaukee surged toward the postseason, he told the *Geelong (Victoria) Advertiser* (April 15, 2006), "I think he's living up to those expectations and doing better than a lot of people thought he would, the so-called basketball experts." After the Detroit Pistons eliminated the Bucks in five games, Bogut said publicly that his squad needed players besides Michael Redd, who averaged 27.2 points in the play-off series, to step up and contribute. "We won some games this year with Michael, but you can't win consistently," Bogut told Colin Fly for the Associated Press (May 5, 2006). "[The Pistons] have a lot of guys that can take over a game, and we need to get that way." Bogut also admitted that he, too, needed to improve. In addition, he told Fly that he hoped to acquire a leadership role. "I really want to try and take over the reins a little bit more," he said. "I think I can be that guy, but I have to earn the respect of my teammates and my coaches and better respect in the league before I can start doing those things."

The day after the Bucks' season ended, Bogut was named to the NBA's All-Rookie team, having received the third-highest number of votes. Despite that honor he was upset about the way the season had ended. "It's disappointing, but I think there have to be some dramatic changes made next season," he told Tim Buckley for the *Deseret Morning News* (May 5, 2006).

During the 2006 off-season, Bogut returned to Australia, where he rejoined the national basketball team. Paid $120 per day, or $250 on game days—a tiny fraction of his NBA salary—Bogut relished the opportunity to play in front of home crowds who otherwise would not see him in the flesh. "I think it is something special, especially for the young kids," he told Peter Kogoy for the *Australian* (July 6, 2006). "Being out with the guys is also good fun at these camps." In August the team traveled to Saitama, Japan, where Bogut performed well, scoring 20 points and grabbing six rebounds in a game that Australia lost to the U.S., 113–73.

Bogut improved in his second season with the Bucks, though he missed the final 15 games after spraining his left foot, and the team failed to make the play-offs. He averaged 12.3 points and 8.8 rebounds per game, and his 55.3 shooting percentage was the seventh-best in the league. In February 2007, midway through the season, Bogut told Ron Reed for the *Herald Sun* (February 15, 2007) that the team's poor performance was taking the fun out of playing. "We're obviously struggling, losing games, and it's become a bit of a grind," he said. "It's not as enjoyable as it should be." On March 15, 2007, with the Bucks at the bottom of the Eastern Conference standings with a record of 23–41, their coach, Terry Stotts, was fired. That news came the same day that Bogut learned he had been fined $25,000 for making a rude gesture toward a spectator in Toronto, Canada, the day before. One week later, as a result of an injury he had suffered during a game against the Los Angeles Lakers weeks earlier, Bogut was officially sidelined for the rest of the season.

Bogut spent the next four months in Australia, visiting with his parents and girlfriend, Jess; training in a gym; and visiting the site of his own training facility, which is being built in Melbourne. Back in Milwaukee Bogut bought a Siberian husky and traded his high-rise apartment for a house on the outskirts of the city. Looking ahead to the 2007–08 season, Bogut said he hoped to help a new Bucks recruit, Yi Jianlian, a native of China, adjust to life in the NBA. "I think international players take it a bit harder when they get to the league," he said. "I think [Yi] has a chance to be very, very good. I think he will be all right once he meets some people." Bogut has said that he sometimes feels lonely in the U.S., telling Kent that there is a lack of camaraderie in the NBA. "Basically, after a game guys go their own way," he said. "It's as much a business as it is anything else."

In June 2007 Bogut made headlines with his comments about the NBA, telling Sygall that many young players are overly obsessed with jewelry and fast cars. "About 80 per cent of them go broke by the time they retire or come close to it," Bogut said. "But it's just the culture over there," he added. "I would never want my child to be brought up in an environment like that, where if you have money you're supposed to flaunt it and make everyone jealous." His remarks raised many hackles in the U.S., just as remarks he had made before being drafted had irritated many Australians: in that instance, in response to a question as to how he would compare himself with Luc Longley, another native Australian now in the NBA, Bogut said there was no comparison between him and Longley or other Australians who preceded him in the NBA (Andrew Gaze, Chris Anstey, and Shane Heal). "I'm not as slow as Luc Longley, I'm more athletic, I can shoot better, I'm more competitive," he said, according to Dave Hughes, writing for the *West Australian* (June 29, 2005). Bogut later maintained that his remarks had been taken out of context, telling Bruce Arthur for the Regina, Saskatchewan, *Leader-Post* (July 19, 2005), "Australian media's some of the worst media in the world, I think. Obviously, we're part of the Commonwealth, and British tabloids—I think the Aussies learned really well from them."

From the start of his NBA career, Bogut told reporters that he would rather be blunt than dishonest. "If I don't look good with the things I say, that's something I'm going to live with," he told Arthur. Bogut told Sygall that he wants "people to think of me as someone who works very hard, who has gone through a lot of crossroads along the way." "I don't want to be seen as arrogant but I know that sometimes that's how it will come across," he added. "I have a lot of respect for the game and I hope it respects me back."

Milwaukee's new head coach, Larry Krystkowiak, told Loren Jorgensen for the *Deseret Morning News* (October 11, 2007) that, despite Bogut's less-than-stellar first two seasons, "I'm anticipating some positive things happening for him." "It's a situation where I'm constantly reminding people that this would be his rookie year if he would have stayed in school," he said to Jorgensen. "He's put on some weight and he's getting more and more comfortable with his game." Bogut and the Bucks began the 2007–08 season on October 31. During that season he averaged 14.3 points and 9.8 rebounds per game. On January 13, 2008, in a game against the Phoenix Suns, Bogut scored 29 points—a career high.

—K.J.P.

Suggested Reading: *Australian* p38 July 6, 2006; *Buffalo (New York) News* B p5 Mar. 19, 2005; (Melbourne, Australia) *Herald Sun* p94 Feb. 15, 2007; *Milwaukee (Wisconsin) Journal Sentinel* C p2 Oct. 10, 2007; (Salt Lake City, Utah) *Deseret Morning News* D p6 Oct. 11, 2007; *Sports Illustrated* p56 Feb. 21, 2005; (Sydney, Australia) *Sun-Herald* p92 June 17, 2007; (Sydney, Australia) *Sunday Telegraph* p60 Nov. 27, 2005

Stephen Chernin-Pool/Getty Images

Bollinger, Lee C.

Apr. 30, 1946– President of Columbia University; First Amendment scholar

Address: Columbia University, 535 W. 116th St., 202 Low Memorial Library, Mail Code 4309, New York, NY 10027

"If you were called upon to invent a perfect university president, you couldn't do better than Lee Bollinger," Nicholas Lemann wrote for the *New Yorker* (December 18, 2000). A First Amendment scholar and now the head of Columbia University, in New York City, Bollinger is widely thought to represent a new breed of visionary college presidents, who not only act as chief administrators but speak out on controversial social and political issues. Throughout his academic career Bollinger has been vocal about such issues as the importance of diversity in educational settings and the necessity of preserving freedom of speech. In 1987, for example, Bollinger, then a professor of law, appeared before the Senate Judiciary Committee to testify against the Supreme Court nominee Robert Bork,

whose views on the U.S. Constitution he saw as a threat to First Amendment rights. Later, as president of the University of Michigan, Bollinger energetically defended the school's use of race as a factor in its admissions process in two lawsuits, which eventually reached the U.S. Supreme Court. In September 2007 (a time of great political tension between the U.S. and Iran), Bollinger, as president of Columbia, made international headlines after the university invited Mahmoud Ahmadinejad, Iran's controversial leader, to speak before an audience at the university; he introduced the Iranian president on stage with a series of pointed accusations.

While Bollinger sometimes attracts heated criticism, those who have worked with him typically describe him as approachable, patient, and intellectually serious. "[He is] never content with the easy answer," Jeff Lehman, a longtime colleague, told Maryanne George for the *Detroit Free Press* (March 2, 2001). "Lee is happiest when he is struggling with a genuinely complex issue."

Lee Carroll Bollinger was born on April 30, 1946 in Santa Rosa, California, and grew up in Baker City, Oregon. His father was a journalist and later in life became the publisher of a Baker City newspaper called the *Democrat-Herald*. Bollinger attended the University of Oregon and majored in social history. As a freshman he met Jean Magnano, who was majoring in education and psychology. Jean was attracted to Lee's intelligence and love of the outdoors, and in 1968, soon after they graduated, the couple married and moved to New York City. They both attended Columbia University: Lee pursued a law degree and was a *Law Review* editor, and Jean studied for a master's degree. That period was a tumultuous one for the country as a whole and for the university. The Vietnam War was raging, and Columbia was an epicenter of student protest—in April 1968, the semester before the Bollingers arrived, antiwar protesters had famously taken over the university president's office. Bollinger recalled to Barbara Kantrowitz for *Newsweek* (March 11, 2002), "We came here very naive and with very little money and lived under terrible conditions." Still, Bollinger thrived in the challenging intellectual climate of the school.

After graduating from law school, Bollinger served as a clerk for Warren Burger, then the chief justice of the Supreme Court. In 1973 he was offered an assistant professorship at the University of Michigan Law School, and the Bollingers moved to Ann Arbor. Jean cared for the couple's two young children, Lee and Carey. Bollinger became a much-loved professor, and in 1987 he was appointed dean of the law school. That same year, as a well-known scholar of the First Amendment, which guarantees the right to free speech, Bollinger appeared before the U.S. Senate during the confirmation hearings for Robert Bork, a conservative whom President Ronald Reagan had nominated to fill a vacancy on the Supreme Court. Bork was a proponent of originalism, a theory of constitutional interpretation that holds that the intentions of the document's original drafters—rather than any more recent or contemporary considerations—should be of primary importance. Bollinger argued that Bork's confirmation could lead to limits on free speech, and his testimony was regarded as a major factor in the rejection of Bork's nomination.

In 1989 Bollinger again made headlines when he defended the University of Michigan's decision to ban recruiters for the Federal Bureau of Investigation (FBI) from visiting the campus because of the organization's discriminatory practices. (The agency had been found guilty of denying promotions and desirable job assignments to Hispanics.) Bollinger's staunch belief in equality came under scrutiny later that year, however, when a graduate student charged that the university's new anti-bias code was so generalized that it violated the First Amendment. Bollinger's critics faulted him for not speaking out against the code, which defined discriminatory behavior as any act "that stigmatizes or victimizes an individual on the basis of race, ethnicity, religion, sex, sexual orientation, creed, national origin, ancestry, age, marital status, handicap or Vietnam-era veteran status," according to Lee Mitgang, writing for the Associated Press (June 11, 1989). Bollinger told Mitgang that the issue was one of priorities: "Should the university be the place in society where there is ultimate protection of free speech, or is it a place where you want to preserve civility and discourse? Those are two very different models, both with strong appeals." The code was ultimately deemed unconstitutional by a federal court.

Bollinger left Michigan in 1994 to take a job as a professor of government and provost (a senior administrator) at Dartmouth College, a small Ivy League school in New Hampshire. He remained there for only two years: in November 1996 he was unanimously chosen (following a lengthy debate among regents about his liberal political views) as the 12th president of the University of Michigan. Many at Dartmouth were reportedly sorry to see him go. According to the University of Michigan *University Record* (November 14, 1996), Lawrence D. Kritzman, a Dartmouth professor, called Bollinger "a man of vision . . . [and] deep intellectual passion and commitment," noting, "From the day of his arrival on the Dartmouth campus Lee Bollinger has had an enormous impact." James O. Freedman, Dartmouth's president, said, "The University of Michigan is to be congratulated on an absolutely wonderful appointment," and he predicted that Bollinger would be "one of the most distinguished university presidents in the country."

Bollinger assumed his presidential duties on February 1, 1997, and his formal inauguration took place the following September. He explained in his inaugural address, as posted on the school's Web site, that the delay had been meant to "maximize both the chances of good weather and the distance from examinations (when everyone gets a little grouchy)." In the address he emphasized the importance of resisting political influence in academia, maintaining diversity among students, and preserving both an autonomous faculty and transparent administration. Between February and September the university community had gotten to know Bollinger, and most observers felt he was performing well. "He has taken [the school] in a new direction," Louis D'Alecy, a physiology professor and chairman of the university's Senate Advisory Committee on University Affairs, told Maryanne George for the *Detroit Free Press* (September 18, 1997). "We had 15 years of the corporate model—the top-down, build, build, build, CEO management style. . . . His style is relaxed, accessible and confidence-generating." Bollinger's approachability soon became a trademark of his presidency at the university. He moved his office from an inaccessible location to a spot that allowed students to drop by easily. One evening in November 1997, following a Michigan football victory against Penn State, a large group of students stormed the lawn of Bollinger's home, shouting his name. Rather than ordering the boisterous crowd to leave, Bollinger and his wife invited them into the house, where they settled into his study, dining room, and even his bedroom to relax and celebrate. Bollinger, in a move unusual for university presidents, also found time to teach an undergraduate class, in an effort to stay connected to the students. (The topic was freedom of speech and the media.)

The semester after Bollinger's inauguration was challenging. In October 1997, for example, following reports that the school's basketball team had violated National Collegiate Athletic Association rules, Bollinger launched an expensive and lengthy investigation, which revealed, among other things, that an athletic booster named Ed Martin had inappropriately given money and gifts to players. Besides appointing a new athletic director in the wake of the incident, Bollinger made several other appointments during his first months in Michigan, including Nancy Cantor as the university's first female provost and Chacona Johnson, a black woman, as his chief of staff.

In April 2000, following a series of student protests regarding the sweatshop conditions in Third World factories producing University of Michigan apparel, the sportswear company Nike terminated a lucrative licensing agreement with the school. Bollinger accused the company of punishing Michigan for its involvement with the Worker Rights Consortium, a student-driven labor-rights coalition, and reiterated the university's commitment to human rights. Despite that loss of potential income, throughout his presidency Bollinger was widely considered a responsible steward of the university's finances and a master fund-raiser. Under his watch private donations to the school increased from $180 million in 1997 to $220 million in 2007. State appropriations increased by more than 20 percent, and federal grants to the university almost doubled, to $600 million.

One of Bollinger's major accomplishments as president of the university was the establishment, in 1999, of the Life Sciences Initiative, which included the building of a massive new biotechnology facility, the Life Sciences Institute. Much of the funding for the project came from a multibillion-dollar settlement the state had received from the tobacco industry. Undoubtedly, however, it was Bollinger's defense of the university's affirmative-action program that earned him the most national attention. Like many other schools, the University of Michigan awarded points to applicants for factors other than grade-point average and standardized test scores; admissions officers considered the quality of applicants' high-school curriculums, the geographic areas they came from, their leadership skills, and their racial backgrounds. Debates about political correctness and affirmative action were becoming common in the 1990s, and college-admission processes across the country were coming under increased scrutiny. In 1997, just months after he assumed the presidency, the Center for Individual Rights, a conservative Washington, D.C.–based organization, filed two lawsuits on behalf of students who claimed to have been denied admission to the University of Michigan because they were white: Jennifer Gratz and Patrick Hamacher were the plaintiffs in one case, involving the undergraduate program, and Barbara Grutter was the plaintiff in a suit against the law school.

Bollinger, along with other university officials, defended the consideration of race in admissions procedures. In the *National Review* (October 14, 2002), he was quoted as saying, "This principle of [affirmative action] is a deep part of the educational philosophy of American higher education. Without the diversity it provides, the character and the quality of our great public universities would decline." He frequently pointed out that for students from homogeneous communities, freshman year might offer the first opportunity to interact with those of other backgrounds and points of view. Lemann, explaining that minorities typically earned lower scores on standardized tests, wrote, "A race-blind, by-the-numbers admissions operation at an elite university will produce an almost all white and Asian class."

There were many who disagreed. Carl Cohen, a philosophy professor and one of the university's most outspoken opponents of affirmative action, told Ed Bradley for the TV program *60 Minutes* (October 29, 2000), "[Considering race] is evil. It's not meant to be evil, but it's fundamentally wrong in a good society. . . . Treat the races without discriminating on the basis of skin color. I've devoted my life to much of that. And I'm not going to stop now when people are doing it for what they think are good reasons." According to Lemann, Cohen had been "the person primarily responsible for the lawsuits." In the mid-1990s, after obtaining university documents through the Freedom of Information Act, Cohen had discovered that the school set a distinctly lower set of admission standards for minority students. In the pre-medical program, for instance, a score of 1,320 on the SAT was the minimum required for most students, while 1,170 was the minimum for minority students. After those standards became public, the university changed its policy to one that awarded points for certain criteria: a perfect grade-point average was worth 80 points, for example, while student athletes were awarded 20 points, offspring of alumni were awarded four points, and minority students were awarded 20 points.

In December 2000 a district judge ruled that while the school's former policy had been illegal, its current policy was permissible. As expected, however, the decision was appealed, and in January 2001 Bollinger testified in federal court. He claimed that the policies complied with the Supreme Court's 1978 ruling in *Regents of the University of California vs. Bakke*, which had found that race could be considered as a factor in university admissions, but that quota systems were not to be used. In March 2001 the federal court ruled that the University of Michigan's consideration of race in admissions decisions (for both the law school and the undergraduate school) was illegal. The university announced its determination to appeal, and it was widely expected that the cases would eventually reach the Supreme Court.

The ensuing controversy greatly increased Bollinger's public profile. In early 2001 he was short-listed to replace Harvard University's outgoing president, Neil Rudenstine. When the job went to another candidate, Michigan students, faculty, and Bollinger himself reported being pleased with the decision. Although Bollinger repeatedly pledged his commitment to Michigan during the following months—and despite the fact that private donors and regents had collaborated on a compensation package worth a reported million dollars annually to keep him at Michigan—in October of that year Bollinger accepted a position as the 19th president of Columbia University, located in the racially and socially diverse New York City neighborhood of Morningside Heights. He told reporters, "I didn't seek this out. Columbia brought this to me and after giving it very serious and hard consideration, it seemed to make the most sense," as quoted by Rachel Green and Elizabeth Kassab for the *Michigan Daily* (October 4, 2001). In June 2003, over a year after Bollinger left Michigan, the Supreme Court upheld the constitutionality of using race as a factor for admissions policies; the ruling was the first the court had made on affirmative action in a quarter-century. The court, however, also ruled, in a 6–3 decision, that the University of Michigan's undergraduate admission policies, which set distinctly different criteria for minorities, were unconstitutional. (The law school's policies were approved.)

As at Michigan, Bollinger's tenure at Columbia has thus far been marked by periods of controversy. Felicity Barringer wrote for the *New York Times* (February 22, 2003, on-line), "As one of his first acts as president of Columbia University, [Bollinger] declared the [one-year] curriculum at the heart of the Graduate School of Journalism 'insufficient.' At the same time, he refused to select either of two finalists for the school's vacant deanship. Like a smartly delivered cue ball, Mr. Bollinger's message . . . sent a collection of faculty members and alumni ricocheting off one another in anger and confusion. Within weeks, journalists from Canada to South Africa, some proud that they had never taken a journalism course, were arguing about what academic training reporters need, if any." Bollinger initially wanted to expand the program to two years, in order to provide more comprehensive training; his proposal triggered an outcry over the tuition costs that would entail. Instead, the revamped program offered two one-year tracks—the original master of science degree, with its practical, generalized courses, is still offered, as is a new master of arts degree that requires highly specialized courses in such areas as science journalism or business reporting. Bollinger appointed the respected journalist Nicholas Lemann, known for his work at the *Washington Post* and the *New Yorker*, among other publications, as dean.

In 2005 Bollinger faced intense media scrutiny when a group of students alleged that certain professors in Columbia's Middle Eastern studies program were guilty of anti-Israel bias; the accusations were highlighted in a short film called "Columbia Unbecoming," by the pro-Israel student group the David Project. While the accused professors denied charges of anti-Semitism, Bollinger formed a committee of professors and administrators to review the allegations and examine the department. Bollinger was largely criticized, however, for the strong opinions of his selected committee members, as well as for his own comments regarding the Middle East, which many interpreted as entirely pro-Palestinian. Others were frustrated by what they saw as Bollinger's vague stance on the issues raised: Bollinger—who has been called "Clintonian" (after President Bill Clinton) in his efforts to find consensus—was quoted at times affirming his commitment to the professors' freedom of academic expression and at other times insisting that certain academic freedoms were not unlimited.

In September 2007 Bollinger endured perhaps the greatest media firestorm of his career, when Columbia University's School of International and Public Affairs invited the president of Iran, Mahmoud Ahmadinejad, to speak at the university. Ahmadinejad has earned international attention for, among other things, his outspoken criticism of American foreign policy and Western culture generally, his aggressive anti-Israel position, his persistent efforts to build a nuclear program, and his alignment with Holocaust deniers. The invitation ignited a fury of debate, with politicians, scholars, students, and members of the media speculating about the implications of allowing Ahmadinejad to express his views on a respected academic stage to a global audience. Various Jewish organizations

were outraged and held protests; a spokesman for Yad Vashem, Israel's official memorial to the victims of the Holocaust, told the *Mideast Mirror* (September 24, 2007), "It is unfortunate that Columbia University, an institution ostensibly dedicated to the pursuit of truth and knowledge, should choose to provide a man so divorced from reality and historical truths with a platform to spout his venomous ideology." On the floor of the U.S. Senate, Joseph Lieberman, a U.S. senator from Connecticut, said, as quoted by Anderson Cooper on CNN (September 24, 2007), "Personally, I feel it was a terrible mistake for Columbia University to invite him to speak, because he comes, literally, with blood on his hands." When asked by Cooper whether he regretted having Ahmadinejad speak, Bollinger replied, "There are different approaches . . . to this. Some people think it is better never . . . to listen to or confront people who hold such terrible beliefs, have done terrible things. And others, and I happen to be one of them, . . . believe deeply in confronting people and confronting ideas, and really trying to understand what the world is like through that."

Ahmadinejad gave his speech on September 24, 2007. In introducing the Iranian leader, Bollinger said, according to transcripts posted on the Web site of the Centre for Research on Globalisation, that the president exhibited the signs of "a petty and cruel dictator," and appeared, because of his views, "either brazenly provocative or astonishingly uneducated." Bollinger asked Ahmadinejad to address such issues as Iran's nuclear program, his attitudes towards Israel, and his brutal crackdown on dissidents, but concluded, "In all candor, Mr. President, I doubt that you will have the intellectual courage to answer these questions, but your avoiding them will in itself be meaningful to us. I do expect you to exhibit the fanatical mind-set that characterizes so much of what you say and do." Ahmadinejad responded by saying, through a translator, "In Iran, we don't think it's necessary before the speech is even given to come in with a series of claims and to attempt in a so-called manner to provide vaccination of some sort to our students and our faculty. I think the text read by the gentleman here, more than addressing me, was an insult to information and the knowledge of the audience here. In a university environment, we must allow people to speak their mind, to allow everyone to talk so that the truth is eventually revealed by all. Most certainly he took more than all the time I was allocated to speak. And that's fine with me. We'll just leave that to add up with the claims of respect for freedom and the freedom of speech that is given to us in this country." His speech, which blended quotes from the Koran with anti-Western rhetoric, touched on few of the issues Bollinger had raised. At one point, asked by an audience member about the well-documented persecution of homosexuals in Iran, Ahmadinejad responded, "In Iran, we don't have homosexuals, like in your country," a comment that sparked laughter from the audience.

Bollinger's introduction was the focus of much debate, which continued for months after the visit. Many saw his comments as rude and antithetical to his professed ideal of free speech. One observer wrote to the *Chronicle of Higher Education* (October 19, 2007), "The president of Iran and I do not agree on much, but I do agree with him that the lack of courtesy shown to him at Columbia was shocking. There is no excuse for the lack of decorum that Lee C. Bollinger, Columbia's president, demonstrated." Others saw the introduction as a way to ease the criticism Bollinger had attracted simply by allowing the invitation or as a way to appease Columbia's many Jewish alumni. Bollinger told Rich Sanchez for the TV news program *Out in the Open* (September 24, 2007) that he wrote the confrontational introduction as a way of insuring a robust and sincere dialogue: "There's always risks that, when you have something like this, it will degenerate into a bland conversation and . . . that really major things, major beliefs, very serious matters are minimized and not truly confronted." Moreover, Bollinger continued, "As part of the arrangement with the president, it was very clear that the only way this would happen would be for me to be able to introduce this with very sharp questions and very sharp statements." While much of the talk regarding Bollinger's handling of Ahmadinejad's visit was critical, there were several supportive voices. An editorial in the *Pittsburgh Tribune-Review* (September 25, 2007) read: "Every American should thank him for speaking truth to the insanity that is Mahmoud Ahmadinejad." In November 2007 100 discontented members of Columbia's faculty signed a document criticizing Bollinger's leadership in a variety of areas, including his governance of the university and his stances on Middle Eastern issues, including his remarks about Ahmadinejad. The professors presented the criticisms to Bollinger at a staff meeting but did not call for his resignation. Bollinger defended his record as well as his introduction to the Iranian president, and afterward he likened his experience at the meeting to "watching open-heart surgery" on himself, as Tamar Lewin and Amanda Millner-Fairbanks wrote for the *New York Times* (November 14, 2007).

September 2007 was also notable for Bollinger as the month in which he reached an agreement with Manhattan borough president Scott M. Stringer regarding Columbia's plans to significantly expand its facilities into the surrounding community. As part of the agreement, Bollinger promised to help fund affordable housing, use environmentally sustainable materials in the construction of school buildings, create a number of public parks and playgrounds, and found a community center. The agreement is a significant step in a 30-year plan first announced in 2004, which has been a source of dissension in the neighborhood, particularly among those business owners whose property the university proposes to purchase. In July 2008, in light of the refusal of two commercial-property owners to sell their businesses, Bollinger released a statement that expressly indicated the university's intent to invoke eminent-domain laws to seize the commercial properties. The Empire State Development Corp., the agency that will decide whether eminent-domain laws apply in that case, concluded, based on two separate studies, that the part of Harlem set to undergo construction was "mainly characterized by aging, poorly maintained and functionally obsolete industrial buildings, with little indication of recent reinvestment to revive their generally deteriorated conditions," as quoted by Timothy Williams in the *New York Times* (July 18, 2008). In September 2008 the agency's board held a public hearing that elicited emotional reactions from community members who opposed the university's plan to remove the two resistent businesses from the area. As of October 2008 the board had not yet voted on whether to approve Columbia's request. In addition to Stringer, the plan, which is expected to cost some $7 billion in total, has gained the support of New York State's governor, David A. Paterson, U.S. congressman Charles B. Rangel, and the New York City Council.

Bollinger has written or edited of a number of books, including *The Tolerant Society* (1986), *Images of a Free Press* (1991), and *Eternally Vigilant: Free Speech in the Modern Era* (2002). He lives in New York City with his wife, Jean, who is now an artist, known for her evocative graphite drawings. Their children both hold law degrees—Lee's from the University of Michigan and Carey's from Columbia.

—M.E.R.

Suggested Reading: *Chronicle of Higher Education* p54 Oct. 19, 2007; *Columbia News* (on-line) Sep. 24, 2007; *Detroit Free Press* A p1 Jan. 18, 1997, J p1 Jan. 10, 1999, B p1 Mar. 26, 2003; *Michigan Daily* (on-line) Nov. 10, 1997; *New York Jewish Week* p1 Mar. 4, 2005; *New York Times* (on-line) Nov. 14, 2007, Sep. 5, 2008; *New Yorker* p46 Dec. 18, 2000; *Newsweek* p54 Mar. 11, 2002; *Washington Post* A p6 Sep. 30, 2007

Selected Books: as author—*The Tolerant Society*, 1986; *Images of a Free Press*, 1991; as editor—*Eternally Vigilant: Free Speech in the Modern Era* (with Geoffrey R. Stone), 2002

ing and her performances in stage productions including *Sophisticated Ladies* and *Lady Day*. Since the early 1990s her jazz albums—among them *Keeping Tradition* (1992), *Dear Ella* (1997), *This Is New* (2002), and *Red Earth* (2007)—have enjoyed wide acclaim, as have her live performances. Andrew Gilbert wrote for the *Boston Globe* (October 14, 2005), "Bridgewater is an artist whose musical virtuosity is inseparable from her instincts as an entertainer. On the bandstand she'll flirt outrageously with men in the front row and act out a song's lyric. . . . Her patter between tunes often turns into stream-of-consciousness riffs on love and sex. An unabashed ham, she'll launch into an impromptu version of a pop song from her adolescence, then trail off into silence with a ditzy look straight out of Lucille Ball's repertoire."

Dee Dee Bridgewater was born Denise Eileen Garrett on May 27, 1950 in Memphis, Tennessee, to Matthew Garrett and Marion Hudspeth. Her father was a teacher and jazz trumpeter who played with the famed singer Dinah Washington; according to family lore, Washington once stood over Dee Dee's cradle and said, "She's gonna be a singer just like me." When Bridgewater was three years old, the family moved to Flint, Michigan. Raised as a Catholic, she attended a convent school and has said that for a while as a child she wished to become a nun. As a girl she sang in her church choir. She was exposed early on to jazz, because of her father's career and her mother's fondness for the jazz great Ella Fitzgerald's records, and she listened to a variety of other music as well. "I was in love with Elvis Presley and James Brown and Ricky Nelson," she told S. R. B. Iyer for the *Columbus (Ohio) Dispatch* (April 29, 1996). "I wanted to grow up and marry Johnny Mathis. I listened to everything, except classical. I loved country-and-western music." During high school Bridgewater formed a short-lived vocal trio called the Iridescents.

After graduating, in 1968, Bridgewater enrolled at Michigan State University and joined a jazz quintet led by the saxophonist Andy Goodrich. When the quintet played at a festival at the University of Illinois, in 1969, the director of that school's jazz band, John Garvey, recruited Bridgewater to sing in a six-week tour of the Soviet Union. While on tour she met Cecil Bridgewater, a jazz trumpeter; the two married in 1970. The Bridgewaters moved to New York City that year to pursue their musical careers, and in 1972 Dee Dee Bridgewater joined the Thad Jones–Mel Lewis big band, which performed at the famous Village Vanguard jazz club. Bridgewater has credited her time in that group with educating her as a singer, telling Jacqueline Trescott for the *Washington Post* (April 15, 1978), "Just about all the musical knowledge I have came from the band period. Thad is an incredible arranger, and to be in front of all that music, 17 pieces, I learned you have to be another instrument. I was anxious to be known as a musician. I didn't want to be just the band singer." She later told Geoff Chapman for the *Toronto Star* (February

Bridgewater, Dee Dee

May 27, 1950– Singer

Address: c/o EmArcy Records, Universal Classics & Jazz, Stralauer Allee 1, D10245 Berlin, Germany

In describing the veteran jazz singer Dee Dee Bridgewater, critics have tended to reach for superlatives. Writing for the *Orange County (California) Register* (March 1, 1999), Steve Eddy called her "probably the greatest living scat singer." In a piece included in his book *Weather Bird*, Gary Giddins, one of the country's most respected jazz writers, pronounced Bridgewater to be "the most capable jazz singer of her generation." And David W. Bothner declared for the *Pittsburgh Post-Gazette* (June 14, 1996), "The quirky Bridgewater is perhaps the most talented jazz singer of her generation, a vocalist who draws the harmonic smarts and girlish embellishments of Sarah Vaughan and the scatrhythms of Carmen McRae together with an eclectic, highly visual stage persona. She is an unpredictable stylist who is always expanding traditional boundaries and shifting gears within a performance. It's nothing to see her drop out of a steamrolling scat into an extended a cappella suite and end with an imitation of Tina Turner dancing." Bridgewater first gained attention in the early 1970s, as a member of the Thad Jones–Mel Lewis jazz band, before landing her Tony Award–winning role as Glinda in the Broadway production of *The Wiz*. After trying her hand at film acting and releasing several albums in which she flirted with R&B and pop, she moved in the 1980s to Paris, France, where she became celebrated for her sing-

18, 1999) that her experience with the band "taught me how important it is to sing the melody. Without that you can never be a good improviser. I also learned how to breathe and project my voice over 15 horns and a rhythm section, and Thad also taught me the importance of arrangements." In 1974 Bridgewater released the jazz album *Afro Blue* and auditioned for a part in the Broadway musical *The Wiz*, an African-American retelling of *The Wizard of Oz*. Chosen to play the part of Glinda, she won a Tony Award in 1975 for best supporting actress in a musical. The award did not please her at first. As she recalled to Trescott several years later, "When I first got the nomination letter, I fainted: I didn't deserve it. Then when I won, it sent me into a depression for a year. I just didn't think I deserved it, and there were some people who agreed with me out loud. But now I feel I must have been good." Also in 1975 she divorced Cecil Bridgewater; in 1977 she married Gilbert Moses, the director of *The Wiz*. Meanwhile, in 1976, Bridgewater had left that show and moved to Los Angeles, California, to pursue a career in acting and also pop music, after dealings with one record company failed to work out to her satisfaction. "People promised me things that didn't happen," she told Trescott. "But it was a learning experience. Now I know I have to keep control of my career in my own hands." Bridgewater's acting credits include roles in the films *The Wiz* (1978), *The Fish That Saved Pittsburgh* (1979), and *The Brother from Another Planet* (1984) and the sitcom *Benson*.

In the late 1970s and early 1980s, Bridgewater made forays into R&B, funk, and disco, with the albums *Dee Dee Bridgewater* (1976), *Just Family* (1977), *Bad for Me* (1979), and a second eponymous record, in 1980. Later in the 1980s she traveled to Paris to perform in a production of *Sophisticated Ladies* and discovered that she loved the city. That discovery, together with the turmoil stemming from her divorce in 1985 from Moses, prompted her to stay in France. "I loved the country and the people and stayed longer than I thought I would," Bridgewater told Matt Byrne for the Australian *Sunday Mail* (August 19, 2007). In Paris she was the first black performer to play the role of Sally Bowles in *Cabaret*, and she also appeared in the one-woman show *Lady Day*, about the singer Billie Holiday. (Her later performance in London as Holiday earned her an Olivier Award.) "[The French] started to call me their modern Josephine Baker, which was a huge compliment when you knew how much they adored her," she told Byrne. "But the most important thing I found in France was acceptance. In France, people judge you on your talent and your character and for fourteen years I never went back to America." She has also said that she preferred France to the United States because of how she was categorized in the U.S. "In the United States, I was a black artist," she said to Don Heckman for the *Los Angeles Times* (November 14, 1995). "In Europe, I'm an artist."

During those years Bridgewater recorded the albums *Live in Paris* (1986) and *Victim of Love* (1990) before releasing the live album *In Montreux* (1990), her first recording for the prestigious Verve label. (The title refers to the famous annual jazz festival in Montreux, Switzerland, where the album's tracks were recorded.) Her following album, *Keeping Tradition*, was nominated for a Grammy Award in 1993. Then, in 1995, Bridgewater began what would be a series of tribute albums, the first called *Love & Peace: A Tribute to Horace Silver*. Dee Dee and Cecil Bridgewater had toured with Silver, a famous jazz pianist, in 1970. Bridgewater had often asked him if she could sing with him, but he had invariably turned her down. Bridgewater recalled to Bob Young for the *Boston Herald* (June 28, 1995) sneaking on stage with Silver once, so much did she wish to collaborate: "I had been asking Horace all along this tour if I could sit in. He always said no. Now when Horace plays, his head is in the keyboard and his hair is in his face and he doesn't see a lot of the time. So I figured I would slide on stage and start singing, and he wouldn't do anything. He started the tune and I sang the first words, and he stopped the band. 'What are you doing on stage?' he demanded, and before I could answer, he said 'Get off right now!' It was one of the most embarrassing moments of my life. . . . [With the tribute album] he's accepted that I've kind of forced myself into his life." *Love & Peace* sold 41,000 copies in France in only four months—a substantial number for a jazz album—rising to number 16 on the pop charts.

In 1997 Bridgewater released *Dear Ella*, which included 12 songs made famous by Ella Fitzgerald, including "Mack the Knife" and "A-Tisket, A-Tasket." When asked why she had recorded that album, Bridgewater told Charles J. Gans for the *Oregonian* (December 13, 1997), "The idea was born out of the extreme sense of loss that I felt after Ella passed away [in 1996]. I thought that there were going to be at least three or four big recording tributes to Ella, but there was nothing. When I called the record company [Polygram], they jumped on the idea. Two days later—after I thought about the ramifications—I called back and said, 'I don't think it's such a good idea, let's cancel it.' But they wanted me to do it. I was petrified by the whole idea of comparison, criticism. . . . I decided that I wanted it to be something that would be a reflection of how important her career was." The consensus among critics who compared the two singers was that while Fitzgerald's voice possessed a bounce and lightness, Bridgewater's treatment of her predecessor's songs was frequently darker; some found fault with Bridgewater's interpretations, while others found them refreshing. A reviewer for the *San Diego Union-Tribune* (October 16, 1997), T. Michael Crowell, wrote, "Unlike current favorite Cassandra Wilson, whose smoky way with a song is all her own, Bridgewater is something of a throwback, a singer who steers a traditional course, more often than not with jazz standards. This is not a criticism. Few singers possess the vocal prowess—a crystalline voice and broad range—of Bridgewater. She is right at home with Ella Fitzgerald. . . . She takes a straight-ahead line on each of the 13 tunes, but remains herself with her own sassy, smart readings. Bridgewater and Ella are kindred spirits. But Bridgewater has a more sultry approach. If Ella could dazzle with her flexible vocal beauty, Bridgewater adds heat and a come-hither pace." Less positively, Lloyd Sachs wrote for the *Chicago Sun-Times* (November 9, 1997), "There is no doubting the influence of Ella Fitzgerald on Dee Dee Bridgewater. What singer hasn't been touched by Ella's magic? Still, the spirit of the departed legend isn't easy to find on Bridgewater's *Dear Ella*. . . . Whereas Ella had a lighter-than-air essence, Bridgewater makes large, soulfully intense statements (a notable exception is her affecting reading of 'Midnight Sun,' one of Ella's best ballads). Whereas Ella made the big band a seamless extension of her style, Bridgewater uses one to pump herself up. And whereas Ella asserted a pure, joyful spirit scatting through tunes such as 'How High the Moon,' Bridgewater is a cutely self-conscious fun-seeker. Beyond all that, *Dear Ella* is so polished and reeking of class in alternating among toney new big band and string charts and smaller settings, it's impossible to relax with it."

Dear Ella earned two Grammy Awards, for best jazz vocals and best jazz arranging (by Kenny Burrell). Of winning the Grammy for best jazz vocals, Bridgewater said to Dan Ouellette for the *San Francisco Chronicle* (April 19, 1998), "This award confirms what people have been saying, that I'm one of jazz's important singers." The singer, who had also produced the album, explained to Dean Smith for the *Charlotte (North Carolina) Observer* (April 10, 1998), "As a producer, winning the Grammy is a confirmation that I'm going in the right direction. For the record company, it's a big indication for them that I'm a bona fide producer. I like producing; I like putting the creative forces together. After having been a victim of different producers and different record companies, at least in jazz, I know what I want to do and how I want to do it. I have to be able to have control."

Bridgewater's next album, *This Is New*, a tribute to the German-born songwriter Kurt Weill, was released in 2002. Weill, who was Jewish, fled to the United States during the rise of the Nazi Party; he was perhaps best known for the music he composed for *The Threepenny Opera* in 1928, including the song "Mack the Knife." After being invited to sing in a Kurt Weill festival in Poland, Bridgewater decided to create and produce an album that would integrate the exuberance of Weill's songs with her own innovative vocal stylings. The album represented a departure from Bridgewater's more recent work in that it did not focus on jazz standards, of which she had grown weary. She said in an interview with Owen McNally for the *Hartford (Connecticut) Courant* (October 10, 2002), "Weill gave me a whole new lease on life. . . . I love

Weill's music because of its dramatic quality. The songs come from musicals and operettas. They are narratives. This music appeals to my theatrical side because it lends itself to dramatization in performance." *This Is New* was well-received, with Howard Reich writing for the *Los Angeles Times* (August 4, 2002) in a representative review, "A musical free spirit if ever there was one, Bridgewater always has defied categorization, and her anything-goes brand of vocalizing reinvigorates the music of Kurt Weill. One would be hard-pressed to name another female singer working today who can finesse the theatrical elements of Weill's songs while also infusing them with comparably brilliant scat singing, propulsive swing rhythm, and gorgeously lush tone colors. Like a great cabaret artist, Bridgewater knows how to tell a story in classics such as 'The Saga of Jenny' and 'Alabama Song,' but she also can spin a soaring, practically operatic vocal line in 'Lost in the Stars.' Where lesser singers approach these masterworks with too much reverence, Bridgewater radically reimagines them with sometimes purring, sometimes growling vocal effects." Her unusual approach to production also earned praise. "Bridgewater produced the album and has introduced a few unexpected instrumentations and rhythms throughout," S. Y. Wang noted for the Singapore *Straits Times* (June 28, 2002). "'Bilbao' is enlivened by a torrid flamenco introduction, while J. J. Mosalini's bandoleon lends an ambience to 'Youkali.' The strident rhythm of 'Alabama Song' is interspersed with a habanera interlude and a witty quotation from Benny Golson's 'Blues March.' . . . Such exotic touches and occasionally unsettling effects are wholly appropriate for Weill, whose cross-continental career often dealt with the theme of alienation and sardonic humor. . . . As a producer, [Bridgewater] has sequenced the songs brilliantly, the album concluding with two outstanding numbers."

Three years later Bridgewater released *J'ai Deux Amours*, whose title translates from French as "I Have Two Loves." The *Boston Globe* (October 14, 2005) reviewer called the album Bridgewater's "lush valentine to France," and Bridgewater explained to the writer, "This album was really my way to say thank you to France for having opened its arms and adopted me, calling me one of their own." She felt that France had allowed her to reimmerse herself in jazz; years earlier she had said to David W. Bothner, "I'm grateful to France for saving me. I rediscovered my jazz roots and developed again as a jazz singer in that supportive environment. France has a special fascination with jazz music and black-American musicians. I had the luxury there to rehone my jazz and scatting chops and develop as an artist again on my own terms." Indeed, the country had shown its support for Bridgewater, awarding her its highest musical honor, the Victoire de la Musique (for best jazz vocal album), in 1998 for *Dear Ella*. A review of *J'ai Deux Amours* in the *Straits Times* (April 29, 2005) read,

"In her latest album, she expresses through songs her love for her adopted country. . . . The selection of the title track is laden with significance. Its opening line, 'J'ai deux amours / mon pays et Paris' ('I have two loves / my country and Paris'), sums up the sentiment of every Francophile expatriate. Then there is the song's association with Josephine Baker, the cabaret artiste who performed and won acclaim in Paris in the 1920s, thus paving the way for other black Americans in later generations."

The idea for Bridgewater's most recent album, *Red Earth: A Malian Journey* (2007), took hold several years before the recording was released. Undertaking an investigation of her ancestry, Bridgewater traced her forebears back 150 years to slaves in Mississippi. Since no earlier records existed, she began listening to various types of West African music, knowing that most African slaves brought to the Americas had come from western African countries. In 2004 she visited Mali with her third husband, Jean-Marie Durand, and Chieck Tidiane Seck, a Malian composer who introduced her to other Malian singers and musicians. "I'm a very intuitive person," Bridgewater told Joe Klopus for the *Kansas City Star* (October 11, 2007). "I decided to just listen to music. I thought when I heard the music of the country my ancestors are from, I would recognize it. When I heard the music of Mali, it struck a very deep chord, and I just knew. They have a lifestyle that is very nomadic. So many things about their culture are similar to the way I was raised. Everywhere I was going I was seeing people who looked like people I knew. . . . After that first trip I decided my next album would be a project about Malian music and the meeting between Malian music and jazz." Because *Red Earth* differed so greatly from her previous work, some Bridgewater fans failed to appreciate the album. The singer viewed that response philosophically, telling Siddhartha Mitter for the *Boston Globe* (October 14, 2007), "I have my traditional fans who don't like it. I say I'm sorry, but I've moved into another area. I feel that with this album I have truly found my own voice."

Bridgewater is an ambassador for the United Nations Food and Agricultural Organization and hosts a program, *JazzSets with Dee Dee Bridgewater*, on National Public Radio. She has homes in Nevada and France. Bridgewater married Jean-Marie Durand in 1991. She has three children: Tulami Bridgewater, China Moses, and Gabriel Durand.

—T.O.

Suggested Reading: *Boston Globe* D p18 Oct. 14, 2005, N p5 Oct. 14, 2007; *Boston Herald* p42 June 28, 1995; *Charlotte (North Carolina) Observer* E p3 Apr. 10, 1998; *Hartford (Connecticut) Courant* p10 Oct. 10, 2002; *Kansas City Star* G p9 Oct. 11, 2007; *Los Angeles Times* F p1 Nov. 14, 1995, p68 Aug. 4, 2002; *Pittsburgh Post-Gazette* p17 June 14, 1996; *San Diego Union-Tribune* p26 Oct. 16, 1997; *San Francisco Chronicle* p41 Apr. 19, 1998; (Singapore) *Straits Times* (on-line) June 28, 2002, Apr. 29, 2005; *Toronto Star* (on-line) Feb. 18, 1999

Selected Recordings: *In Montreux*, 1990; *Keeping Tradition*, 1992; *Love & Peace: A Tribute to Horace Silver*, 1995; *Dear Ella*, 1997; *This Is New*, 2002; *Red Earth: A Malian Journey*, 2007

Valerie Macon/AFP/Getty Images

Brolin, Josh

Feb. 12, 1968– Actor; writer; director

Address: c/o I\D Public Relations, 8409 Santa Monica Blvd., W. Hollywood, CA 90069

For most of the 22 years since he launched his career as an actor, Josh Brolin was known less for his on-screen performances than for his family ties: his father is the actor James Brolin, who gained celebrity as a character on the popular 1970s television series *Marcus Welby, M.D.*; his stepmother, since 1998, is the legendary singer and actress Barbra Streisand. Josh Brolin's credits—mostly television roles and small parts in forgettable films—were further obscured by his high-profile romances with the actresses Minnie Driver and Diane Lane, the latter of whom he married in 2004. Then, in 2007, he won enthusiastic critical praise for his supporting performance in *American Gangster*, directed by Ridley Scott and starring Denzel Washington, and for his lead turn in *No Country for Old Men*, written and directed by Joel and Ethan Coen. Hollywood observers hazarded the guess that Brolin might earn an Academy Award nomination for his work in each film. While that honor did not materialize, the mere speculation represented a major achievement for an actor who had spent two decades in relative obscurity. "The fact that my name and [the word] Oscar is even coming out of people's mouths, well, I can't even tell you how that sounds to me," Brolin told Cindy Pearlman for the *Chicago Sun-Times* (November 4, 2007). "Let's just say that in life you should just respect the moment. I'm very respectful."

Josh J. Brolin was born on February 12, 1968 in Los Angeles, California. His father is best known for his portrayal of Dr. Steven Kiley, a colleague of the title character (played by Robert Young) in *Marcus Welby, M.D.* (1969–76); he later appeared on TV as Peter McDermott in the series *Hotel* (1983–88), Lieutenant Colonel Bill "Raven" Kelly in *Pensacola: Wings of Gold* (1997), and the governor and presidential candidate Robert Ritchie in *The West Wing* (2002). Josh Brolin's mother, Jane Agee, was an aspiring actress who later worked for the California Department of Fish and Game. Despite his father's fame Brolin was raised out of the public eye. Starting in the mid-1970s, his family, which included his younger brother, Jess, lived on a ranch in Paso Robles, California, 200 miles from Los Angeles. "Where I grew up was very isolated," Brolin told Bob Ivry for the Bergen County, New Jersey, *Record* (August 13, 1997). "In Hollywood or New York, acting is usually the talk of the town, or who you've seen on the street that day. For us, it was farming. It was getting up at 5:30 in the morning and feeding 48 horses. It was that simple."

Brolin had no thoughts of becoming an actor until the early 1980s, when he saw a production of the play *Tamara*, by John Krizanc and Richard Rose. Set in fascist Italy in the 1920s, *Tamara* consists of a series of scenes that take place simultaneously. (The play can be staged only in a building with many rooms and hallways.) The playgoers choose which characters they want to watch; they can switch to different characters whenever they wish, so that "there are, in principle, several hundred thousand possible plays to see," as Eileen Blumenthal wrote for the *New York Times* (November 29, 1987). "It was awesome," Brolin told Jamie Portman for the *Calgary (Alberta, Canada) Herald* (September 8, 1997). "I was knocked out by the way you could follow one actor into a scene and then change halfway through and follow another one." Soon afterward Brolin enrolled in acting classes.

After he completed middle school, in Paso Robles, Brolin attended a high school in Santa Barbara, California. While there he appeared in a student production of Tennessee Williams's *A Streetcar Named Desire*. His extracurricular interests included competing in sports and playing the drums in a punk-rock band. He worked in restaurants at night when he was 15 and 16 and reportedly considered becoming a professional chef. Brolin's parents divorced in about 1984; afterward, the teenager engaged in "rageful kinds of things," as he put

it in an interview with Nancy Mills for *Cosmopolitan* (August 1996). He told Mills that he spent some time in jail, but he would not reveal to her what crimes he had committed. Brolin acquired his first stepmother in 1986, when his father married the actress Jan Smithers. He has a stepsister, Molly, from that union, which ended in divorce in 1995.

When he was 16 Brolin won the part of Brand Walsh in the film *The Goonies* (1985), about a group of children searching for lost pirate treasure. He read for the role four times before the director of the movie, Dick Donner, and the producer, Steven Spielberg (whom he did not recognize at his auditions), added him to the cast. The film was a hit, and Brolin received more than 2,500 fan letters. His father, who tried to discourage him from pursuing a career in acting and urged him to study law, was quick to deflate his expanding ego. "My father slammed me up against the wall and told me he would tear my head off if I ever showed that attitude again," he told Vernon Scott for United Press International (August 13, 1986). "Believe me, that made an impression."

In his next film, *Thrashin'* (1986)—a "mindless skateboard movie aimed at kids," according to Scott—Brolin had a starring role. When he saw the completed picture, his performance horrified him. "I don't belong in lead roles because I'm not good enough," he told Scott. "So I'm looking for smaller roles, supporting roles, to build up my knowledge of acting while I take classes on my own time." In 1987 he appeared in the TV movie *Prison of Children*. "The role was small but I liked what I did," he told Scott. "It restored my confidence." Brolin was also cast in a half-dozen episodes of the short-lived 1987 TV series *Private Eye*. On the set of that show he met Alice Adair (identified as Deborah Adair in some sources), whom he married in 1988. At around that time Brolin studied with the famed acting coach Stella Adler in New York City.

In 1989 Brolin acted alongside his father in *Finish Line*, a TV movie about a competitive runner who, feeling pressure from his father, turns to using steroids. To prepare for the role, he gave up smoking and temporarily took up running. Later that year he joined the cast of *The Young Riders*, a television series set in the Old West. He appeared in 67 episodes of the show, which was co-directed by James Brolin and aired until 1992. Meanwhile, in around 1990 Josh Brolin had co-founded a repertory company called the Reflections Festival. The group mounted a rotating series of three American plays each season at the GeVa Theatre (now the Geva Theatre Center), in Rochester, New York. From time to time during the next five years, Brolin acted in and directed Reflections Festival productions and wrote plays for the troupe. In 1992 Brolin and Adair divorced, but they continued to live together with their son, Trevor, and daughter, Eden.

Brolin's next project was the 1994 television series *Winnetka Road*, which was pulled off the air after a month. "I decided that not working at all was preferable to doing a series like that," he told

Jamie Portman. "What I really want to do is work with the best people I can." Also in 1994 Brolin played a small role in the film *The Road Killers*. In 1995 he appeared on an episode of the TV show *The Outer Limits*. That same year his mother was killed in a car accident, and Brolin inherited the 97-acre Paso Robles ranch. He moved there with his family, and several years passed before he changed any of his mother's décor. "Along with inheriting the ranch, I inherited a pretty hefty mortgage, so any money I make goes into it," he told Nancy Mills.

In 1996 Brolin acted in the films *Gang in Blue*, *Bed of Roses*, and *Flirting with Disaster*, the last with an ensemble cast, directed by David O. Russell, that included Ben Stiller, Patricia Arquette, Tea Leoni, Alan Alda, Lily Tomlin, George Segal, and Mary Tyler Moore. Brolin played a bisexual federal agent with a fetish for armpits; in one often-referenced scene, he licked Arquette's underarm. "I love those characters," he told Michele Norris for the National Public Radio program *All Things Considered* (November 9, 2007). "They're fun, you know? There's billions of characters to play. . . . There's always something different to put into a character." Brolin received high marks for his performance, and better roles began coming his way. "There's more confidence in my ability to do something that's put in front of me after *Flirting with Disaster*," he told Ivry. "I've been getting leading-man offers and funky, wild roles. And I get recognized on the street. I'm usually the guy that people go, Did we go to high school together? But I had one woman come up to me and lift her arm."

In 1997 Brolin appeared in the films *My Brother's War*, *Nightwatch*, and *Mimic*. The latter two, like *Flirting with Disaster*, were produced by Miramax, co-founded by Harvey and Bob Weinstein. "I like working for [the Weinsteins] a lot, because they're very innovative," Brolin told Rene Rodriguez for the *Dallas Morning News* (April 24, 1998). "I get along with them really well, and I like their mentality. They're like the Malcolm X of Hollywood: by any means necessary." In *Nightwatch*, a thriller starring Nick Nolte and Ewan McGregor, Brolin played a law student who cuts off his own thumb. "I passed out," he told Janet Weeks for *USA Today* (April 30, 1998). "I guess I was hyperventilating. . . . The crew thought I was doing some brilliant acting maneuver." In *Mimic*, a horror film directed by Guillermo Del Toro, Brolin played an agent of the federal Centers for Disease Control who battles enormous cockroaches in New York City.

In 1998 Brolin met the British actress Minnie Driver. The two co-starred in the poorly received film *Slow Burn* (2000). The next year, six months after announcing their engagement, they split up. Between 1999 and 2003 Brolin appeared in a string of critically derided films, among them *The Mod Squad*, *Best Laid Plans*, *Hollow Man*, *Slow Burn*, *D. C. Smalls*, *Coastlines*, and *Milwaukee, Minnesota*. He returned to the stage in 2000, when he and the

actor Elias Koteas replaced Philip Seymour Hoffman and John C. Reilly, respectively, in a New York City production of Sam Shepard's *True West*. In a review for the *New York Times* (July 18, 2000), the theater critic Ben Brantley panned both actors' performances: "Mr. Brolin and Mr. Koteas convey the comic sense of Mr. Shepard's play but none of its troubling emotional sensibility. And without the fear beneath the laughter, *True West* just isn't very funny." In 2003 he depicted the title chracter in the NBC series *Mr. Sterling*. The show, which lasted only nine episodes, told the story of a young, independent U.S. senator who fights for change on Capitol Hill. "I liked [Sterling's] dichotomous nature—very smart, but very kind of angry," Brolin told Bridget Byrne for the Associated Press (March 9, 2003). "I think there's an arrogance to him that I'm just starting to understand, that I didn't see before, that I'm not sure if I like. His intention is in the right place, but I think he has this thing that 'If everybody would do things more my way, it would be better.'"

In 2004 Brolin played a dentist in Woody Allen's *Melinda and Melinda*. The following year he portrayed the American explorer, trapper, trader, and Indian fighter Jebediah Smith (1798–1831) in the six-part, award-winning TV miniseries *Into the West*. That same year he married Diane Lane. In December 2004 police were called to the couple's Los Angeles home, and Brolin was arrested on suspicion of domestic abuse. Lane never pressed charges, and later, in interviews, Brolin insisted that the incident was a misunderstanding. "It was the most misconstrued, awful thing that was the best lesson we ever had, because we both went, 'Oh, people are actually [watching],'" he told Gregory Kirschling for *Entertainment Weekly* (October 19, 2007). "If you call the cops, somebody has to go to jail. But what happened to being able to have a fight and screaming and doing your thing, especially since the kids weren't there."

In 2005 Brolin played a villainous treasure hunter in *Into the Blue*, about a group of young divers who discover the underwater wreckage of a plane loaded with cocaine. In a write-up for the *Chicago Tribune* (August 24, 2007), the critic Allison Benedikt called Brolin's performance "awesomely bad-to-the-bone." In 2006 Brolin appeared in *The Dead Girl*, a thriller whose ensemble cast included Brittany Murphy, Toni Collette, and Marcia Gay Harden. Most reviewers praised the film but few mentioned Brolin, who had a small role as the boyfriend of Murphy's character.

Brolin next appeared as an evil doctor in Robert Rodriguez's *Planet Terror*, the first part of *Grindhouse* (2007), a "double feature" inspired by the low-budget zombie and car-chase films of the 1960s and 1970s. (Quentin Tarantino wrote and directed *Death Proof*, the second part of the movie.) Despite its critical acclaim, *Grindhouse* was a box-office disappointment. While on the set of *Planet Terror*, Brolin learned that Joel and Ethan Coen, the makers of such films as *Fargo*, *Raising Arizona*, and *The Big Lebowski*, were engaged in casting for their next project, *No Country for Old Men*. Brolin had read the Cormac McCarthy novel on which the film was to be based, and he asked Rodriguez to help him shoot an audition video. Despite the high quality of the tape, which Rodriguez shot with a $950,000 camera, it did not convince the Coens that Brolin was right for the role he was seeking—that of Llewelyn Moss, a Texas welder and Vietnam War veteran who happens upon the scene of a botched drug deal and attempts to keep the money he finds. After the Coens met with Brolin, however, they gave him the part. When the filming of *No Country for Old Men* was complete, Brolin flew to New York City to play a corrupt police officer named Trupo in Ridley Scott's *American Gangster*, which starred Denzel Washington as the infamous 1970s Harlem drug lord Frank Lucas and Russell Crowe as his nemesis, the honest police officer Richie Roberts.

American Gangster was released in early November 2007, a week before *No Country for Old Men* came to theaters. In a review of *American Gangster* for *Rolling Stone* (October 18, 2007), Peter Travers called Brolin's acting "chillingly good," while Manohla Dargis, a *New York Times* (November 2, 2007) critic, described his depiction as a "knockout performance." "In the film, the only truly loathsome villain" is Trupo, Richard Schickel wrote for *Time* (November 2, 2007), "played with wonderful brutality by Josh Brolin, who encourages us to think that the only real crime is to interrupt the smooth flow of criminal entrepreneurship."

Brolin played a more sympathetic character in *No Country for Old Men*. For much of the film, Llewelyn Moss is on the run from drug dealers bent on reclaiming their money. The script contained little dialogue; Brolin portrayed his character largely through facial expressions and body movements. "The questions I had were about the book and that sort of thing, but what I didn't think about was guys I knew who were extremely quiet," Brolin told John Anderson for *Newsday* (November 4, 2007). "Because the big challenge of this part was to convey ideas without dialogue, really, and that was scary. I just didn't want to overcompensate for that by scratching where I didn't have an itch, or grunting where there was nothing to grunt about. Just be in the moment. So I was very adamant about telling the Coens, 'If you see me having a false moment, or a moment where a moment doesn't belong, tell me.' But they never told me." Two weeks before he started to work on the film, Brolin was in a motorcycle accident and suffered a broken collarbone. The injury helped him get into character, as Moss is shot in the same arm Brolin was forced to keep in a sling.

No Country for Old Men was met with rave reviews, and critics—just as they had after the opening of *American Gangster*—speculated that Brolin might earn an Academy Award nomination. "Holding his own in distinguished company after long dwelling in TV and schlock, Brolin gives off young Nick Nolte vibes as an ordinary man who tries to outsmart some big boys in order to get away with the score of his life," Todd McCarthy wrote for *Variety* (May 18, 2007). "Despite some heady competition, the supple and ever-surprising Brolin gives what will surely be a career-making charismatic performance," Kenneth Turan wrote for the *Los Angeles Times* (November 9, 2007). In an assessment for *Time* (November 9, 2007), Richard Schickel described Brolin as "terrific as a totally twisted cop in *American Gangster*, but he's equally good as a totally innocent good ole boy here." Brolin "is quietly terrific as neo-cowboy Moss, resourceful and tough," Gary Thompson wrote for the *Philadelphia Daily News* (November 9, 2007).

Brolin's last film role in 2007 was that of a chauvinistic police officer in *In the Valley of Elah*, co-starring Tommy Lee Jones and Charlize Theron. Also in 2007, for the first time Brolin wrote and directed a film—a short called *X*, which stars his teenage daughter, Eden. Diane Lane's daughter, Eleanor Lampert, was also in the cast. In December *X* was accepted by the Santa Barbara International Film Festival.

Brolin planned to use his newfound fame to land better roles. "Look, I'm going to take full advantage of this situation just because I love working with great filmmakers," he told Susan Wloszczyna for *USA Today* (November 19, 2007). "But I've been around for a while, and I'm not going to play into the hype that I'm some great, you know, discovery." In 1999 Brolin co-founded the Tramp Art Theatre Club, which has chapters in San Francisco and Los Angeles; his play *Dirty Deeds Done Dirt Cheap*, which he co-wrote (with the Brothers Tramp) and directed, premiered in Los Angeles in the summer of 2007.

In 2008 Brolin played the lead role in the Oliver Stone–directed film *W*, about the life of President George W. Bush. The film, most critics noted, was not a typical Stone biopic: rather, it was straightforward, fact-based, and not hyperbolic. Brolin spent months researching the president's Texas accent and his mannerisms, gait, and facial expressions. In the film, Roger Ebert wrote for the *Chicago Sun-Times* (October 15, 2008), "the focus is always on Bush (Josh Brolin): His personality, his addiction, his insecurities, his unwavering faith in a mission from God, his yearning to prove himself, his inability to deal with those who advised him." Some reviewers noted that Brolin may have even received inspiration from his own life story: "Brolin, who himself knows what it's like to have a celebrated father, tears into the Oedipal aspect of the role," Mick LaSalle wrote for the *San Francisco Chronicle* (October 17, 2008). "W.'s pain, shame, embarrassment and resentment are all made real." Brolin was slated to appear in the director Gus van Sant's film about Harvey Milk, one of the first openly gay elected officials in the U.S., who was assassinated in 1978. In that motion picture, which was due to arrive in theaters before the end of 2008, Brolin was cast as Dan White, Milk's killer.

Brolin's hobbies include day trading and auto racing. In 2000 he won first place in the celebrity/pro race at the Toyota Grand Prix, held in Long Beach, California.

—K.J.P.

Suggested Reading: *Calgary (Alberta, Canada) Herald* B p11 Sep. 8, 1997; *Entertainment Weekly* p21 Oct. 19, 2007; imdb.com; *Los Angeles Times* E p4 Oct. 28, 2007; *San Luis Obispo (California) Tribune* Nov. 30, 2007; United Press International Aug. 13, 1986; *USA Today* B p11 Nov. 19, 2007

Selected Films: as actor—*The Goonies*, 1985; *Thrashin'*, 1986; *The Road Killers*, 1994; *Gang in Blue*, 1996; *Bed of Roses*, 1996; *Flirting with Disaster*, 1996; *My Brother's War*, 1997; *Nightwatch*, 1997; *Mimic*, 1997; *The Mod Squad*, 1999; *Best Laid Plans*, 1999; *Hollow Man*, 2000; *Slow Burn*, 2000; *Milwaukee, Minnesota*, 2003; *Melinda and Melinda*, 2004; *Into the Blue*, 2005; *The Dead Girl*, 2006; *Grindhouse*, 2007; *No Country for Old Men*, 2007; *In the Valley of Elah*, 2007; *American Gangster*, 2007; *W*, 2008; *Milk*, 2008; as writer and director—*X*, 2007

Selected Television Shows: *Highway to Heaven*, 1986; *Prison for Children*, 1987; *21 Jump Street*, 1987; *Private Eye*, 1987–88; *Finish Line*, 1989; *The Young Riders*, 1989–92; *Winnetka Road*, 1994; *The Outer Limits*, 1995; *All the Rage*, 1999; *Mister Sterling*, 2003; *Murder Book*, 2005; *Into the West*, 2005

Selected Theatrical Productions: as writer and director—*Dirty Deeds Done Dirt Cheap*, 2007

Courtesy of CNN

Brown, Campbell

June 14, 1968– Television journalist

Address: CNN, 820 First St., N.E., Washington, DC 20002

"My passion has always been hard news," the broadcast journalist Campbell Brown, who made her debut as a CNN (Cable News Network) anchor in early 2008, told Diane Clehane for *mediabistro.com* (February 26, 2007). "That's how I cut my teeth in this business. Those are the stories I get most excited covering. All the highs in my career have been when I've been out there covering major news events, be it Hurricane Katrina or the first Iraqi election—to be there experiencing it on the ground: There's nothing like it." Brown, who worked for NBC News from 1996 through mid-2007 and as a co-anchor of NBC's *Weekend Today* for four years beginning in 2003, has developed a reputation as versatile, credible, evenhanded, and comfortable in her job. As a Washington, D.C.–based White House and Pentagon reporter for NBC, she covered major domestic and international events, among them the impeachment of President Bill Clinton; the bombing of Kosovo, in the former Yugoslavia, by NATO in 1999 during the war in the Balkans; the 2000 American presidential campaign and controversial election of George W. Bush; the September 11, 2001 terrorist attacks on the U.S.; the war in Iraq that the U.S. launched in 2003; and the Abu Ghraib prisoner-abuse scandal, also in Iraq. She won an Emmy Award for her emotionally charged reporting on location in the aftermath of Hurricane Katrina, in the late summer of 2005, during which she criticized on the air the belated and inadequate response of the Bush administration to the catastrophe. Howard Kurtz, a longtime media reporter for the *Washington Post* and host of the CNN media-analysis program *Reliable Sources*, interviewed Brown immediately after she quit NBC and three months before she began anchoring *CNN Election Center*; he wrote for the *Post* (July 30, 2007), "For the first time in her career, Brown will have to carry a show built around her personality, in an environment where outrage gets the highest ratings." Earlier, during a conversation with Terry Judd for the *Muskegon (Michigan) Chronicle* (December 1, 2005), Brown had commented, "As a journalist, if you are doing your job well, no one likes you. And if you are hosting the *Today Show*, everyone needs to like you." She also told Judd, "I look at my job as to challenge on all fronts and not champion one position. If you try to ask questions, not to accept answers at face value but to try to dig a bit and paint a picture, that gives viewers the whole story."

One of three sisters, the journalist was born Alma Dale Campbell Brown on June 14, 1968 in Ferriday, a small, racially mixed town in eastern Louisiana, near Natchez and the Mississippi River. Her father, James H. "Jim" Brown Jr., was a Democratic state senator before he became the Louisiana secretary of state and, later, the state insurance commissioner; he lost the last job, and then served a six-month prison sentence, after lying to the FBI about an insurance company, in a case tied to a corruption scandal involving Louisiana's four-term governor Edwin Edwards. Jim Brown is currently a political consultant. Brown's mother, the former Dale Campbell, was a homemaker; she is now an artist known as Dale Fairbanks. (Brown's parents divorced, and both remarried.) "When we were kids it was clear to us that our stay-at-home Mom had greater ambitions, but ambitions that she was quieting for a time," Brown wrote for the Web site allday.msnbc.msn.com (May 11, 2007). "She instilled in us the belief that we must follow our passions."

Brown grew up in Ferriday in what Lois Smith Brady, writing for the New York Times (April 9, 2006), described as "a big Catholic family . . . full of hunters, politicians and good cooks." "It was all about Cajun food and tight-knit families and big parties," Brown said to Brady about her early years. As a teenager she attended a private boarding and day school—the Madeira School—in McLean, Virginia, until the age of 16, when she was expelled for "sneaking off campus to go to a party," in Kurtz's words. Brown earned a B.A. degree in political science in 1991 from Regis University, a Roman Catholic college in Denver, Colorado. "When I graduated . . . . I had no idea what I wanted to do but I knew I wanted to travel," she told Diane Clehane. Excited by the advent of democracy in formerly Communist countries in Eastern Europe, she moved to Prague, in what was then Czechoslovakia, where she taught English for a year. After she returned to the U.S., she became a "self-described Colorado ski bum," according to Kurtz. Next, Brown moved to the nation's capital, where she secured a series of internships with NBC-affiliated television stations. Then, on the strength of her résumé and a videotape that she mailed to 200 stations nationwide, she was hired as a reporter of local news for the NBC-affiliated television station KSNT-TV, in Topeka, Kansas. She next worked successively at WWBT-TV, in Richmond, Virginia, and WBAL-TV, in Baltimore, Maryland. "I could not for the life of me get a job in D.C.," she told Kurtz. A freelance reporting assignment for WRC-TV, the local NBC station in Washington, D.C., led to her getting a full-time job with NBC in 1996. For the next two years, she worked as a correspondent for NBC News. Her beat included domestic events, including the crash of a Swissair plane

off the coast of Canada on September 2, 1998, and international happenings, such as the visit of Pope John Paul II to Cuba in 1998. The Pope's visit coincided with the first public revelations about President Bill Clinton's affair with Monica Lewinsky when she was a White House intern. In an interview with Tim Russert on CNBC (July 19, 2003), Brown recalled the reactions of some of her colleagues when they first heard about the Clinton-Lewinsky scandal: "I remember somebody screaming, like, 'Oh my God! Come see this. Come see this.' And we all gathered around the one computer that was working and read it and just were shocked. And people started leaving immediately. I mean, all the big anchors and everyone left." Then she added, in reference to her low position on the newsroom totem pole, "And I got left in Cuba." Brown also gained experience as an occasional substitute anchor for NBC's late-night broadcast Nightside.

A turning point for Brown came later in 1998, when she was assigned to cover politics for The News with Brian Williams, on MSNBC. She reported on Clinton's impeachment trial on charges of perjury in 1999 and NATO's bombing of Kosovo, in the same year, during the war in the Balkans that erupted after the breakup of Yugoslavia. In 2000 she spent several months reporting on the campaign of the Republican nominee for the presidency, George W. Bush, during which she was on the road continually. "I came home once, to change my clothes from fall to winter," she recalled to Lois Smith Brady. Because of widespread problems with voting machines in Florida on Election Day, neither Bush nor his Democratic opponent, Vice President Al Gore, could be declared immediately as the winner, and for the next 35 days, Brown reported on the vote recounts and other events in Florida that culminated in the 5–4 decision by the U.S. Supreme Court that in effect gave the presidency to Bush. "The most fun I ever had was on the campaign trail and covering the White House," she told a Grand Rapids (Michigan) Press (April 3, 2008) interviewer. Brown reported on the response of the Bush administration to the September 11, 2001 terrorist attacks and, later, on the invasions and occupations of Afghanistan and Iraq, beginning in 2001 and 2003, respectively. She reported on the first election in Iraq following the downfall of the longtime Iraqi dictator, Saddam Hussein; the prisoner-abuse scandal involving U.S. troops at Abu Ghraib, which became front-page news in early 2004; and Hussein's incarceration, in 2004, and trial, in 2006.

Meanwhile, in 2003, Brown had moved from Washington to New York, where she became the co-host of NBC's Weekend Today, which was then the country's top-rated weekend news and talk show. She also began appearing increasingly often onscreen as a correspondent and occasionally as a substitute anchor for NBC Nightly News with Brian Williams. Referring to one difference between working as a correspondent and sometime anchor for NBC News and anchoring *Weekend Today*, a soft-news morning show, Brown told Kurtz that she had been "accustomed to grilling then–White House spokesman Ari Fleischer" and that she did not "have to do that to the woman coming in to make pasta."

During and after Hurricane Katrina, which struck the Gulf Coast of the U.S. in late August 2005, Brown provided on-the-scene accounts of the destruction, deaths, and tremendous hardships that affected millions of people in Louisiana (especially in and around New Orleans), Mississippi, and the Florida Panhandle. Brown had arrived in Louisiana before the hurricane made landfall; according to Paul Bedard, writing for *U.S. News & World Report* (September 18, 2005, on-line), she "lived out of a car, and ate PowerBars and SpaghettiOs." On the night of September 2, a nine-year-old orphan named Charles Evans gave her a tour of the Ernest N. Morial Convention Center (now called the New Orleans Morial Convention Center), an unofficial evacuation center to which thousands of New Orleanians (as many as 20,000, as was widely reported) had fled from flooded neighborhoods, only to find that there were no provisions for them there. As Brown told NBC-TV viewers from that site, for several days those sheltered in the center—the vast majority of whom were low-income African-Americans—had no water (and thus no sanitary facilities), food, electricity, or medical supplies or care. Dehydration and/or lack of necessary medications led to the deaths of several people, whose corpses remained among the living. Some evacuees took advantage of the nearly complete absence of order or of law-enforcement figures to prey on others in acts of theft and even rape. Charles Evans, who was at the center with a few cousins and his 76-year-old great-grandmother, made a deep impression on Brown, as she later told David Bauder for the Associated Press (September 18, 2005): "I haven't been able to stop thinking about this child," she said. She also told Bauder, "People have made a lot [out] of the emotion that was in my voice that night. It was totally spontaneous, it was totally unrehearsed. It was simply a human reaction to what I was hearing and what I had seen." In addition, she said to Bauder, "I'm struggling to define my role as a journalist in the midst of all this. I have lost my objectivity. I am emotionally involved. I can't pretend that I'm not." Earlier, in a conversation with Eric Deggans for the *St. Petersburg (Florida) Times* (September 8, 2005), she had said, "Watching the power struggles play out between New Orleans officials and the state and federal government has been beyond frustrating. . . . They let the bureaucracy get in the way of saving lives. A lot of people died, I believe unnecessarily. And there has to be some accountability." Brown's post-Katrina reporting boosted her name recognition significantly, and she shared the 2006 Emmy Award for outstanding coverage of a breaking news story in a regularly scheduled newscast, for the segment of *NBC Nightly News with Brian Williams* called "Hurricane Katrina: Moment of Crisis," which aired on September 1, 2005.

According to Paul Bedard, for a long time NBC executives had urged Brown "to 'girlie up' her image, as her competitors have." But her "gutsy and heartfelt reports" from New Orleans and "her undolled-up looks and go-get-'em attitude" while she reported on the Hurricane Katrina disaster "jazzed NBC insiders" and "cemented her position as NBC's top choice to replace" Katie Couric as the co-host of NBC's *Today* show. Couric was then in her 15th year with *Today*, and it had become public knowledge that both ABC and CBS had been trying to lure her to their nightly news shows. On April 5, 2006 Couric announced her intention to leave the program at the end of the following month, and later that day CBS revealed that she was to be the next host of the *Evening News*; the day after that NBC revealed that Meredith Vieira would fill Couric's shoes on the *Today* show.

In July 2007 Brown announced that she would be leaving NBC News to anchor her own prime-time show on CNN beginning in February 2008. (She was due to give birth to her first child in December 2007 and planned to take some time off.) Some media observers speculated that Brown's decision to sever her ties with NBC stemmed from her disappointment at being passed over as Couric's successor on *Today*. "It's been written to death: 'Oh my God, she's leaving because she didn't get Katie's job,'" Brown told Kurtz. "Of course I wanted that job. Who wouldn't want that job? It's one of the best jobs in television." Brown also said that she felt that her duties with *Weekend Today* had taken her too far from hard political news and that she wanted to return to such assignments full-time. "In cable you can go a little more in depth, be a little more inside baseball," she told Kurtz. "In broadcast, you have to simplify things, and on occasion you're forced to dumb things down." Jonathan Klein, the president of CNN/U.S., described Brown as "a political reporter, and that's one thing there's precious little of in prime-time television," as quoted by the *Grand Rapids Press* (April 3, 2008) interviewer. "There's a lot of talk, but there are very few people who have the insight that she does, and the experience."

In part to ease her introduction to CNN viewers, network executives named Brown the anchor of a new, temporary program called *CNN Election Center*, which airs between 8:00 p.m. and 9:00 p.m. on weeknights, after *Lou Dobbs Tonight* and before *Larry King Live*. "It's the ultimate soft launch," the *Grand Rapids Press* reporter wrote. "The timing also gives Brown the chance to show her talents at a high-water mark for a network where interest ebbs and flows depending on the news." *Election Center*, which premiered on January 14, 2008 and was scheduled to be dropped after the November 2008 elections, was designed to offer discussions of the 2008 presidential campaign and other political news as well as issues of widespread concern. Most of the installments have begun with Brown's description of a given topic, the presentation of relevant news clips, and Brown's conversation with people particularly knowledgeable about the subject, followed by a discussion by a panel of other experts. The installment that aired on August 1, 2008, for example, called "Roads to Ruin: Why America Is Falling Apart," focused on the deterioration of U.S. roads, bridges, and other infrastructure. Brown was joined by Governor Arnold Schwarzenegger of California, a Republican; Governor Ed Rendell of Pennsylvania, a Democrat; and Michael Bloomberg, the mayor of New York City, who is currently a registered Independent. Brown showed footage of the collapse during rush hour on August 1, 2007 of I-35W, a bridge that crossed the Mississippi River in Minneapolis, Minnesota, resulting in the deaths of 13 people and injuries to 145. The Minnesota commissioner of transportation, a Minnesota congressman, and a victim of the collapse spoke via videotape, and then Brown interviewed Stephen Flynn, a senior fellow in national-security studies with the Council on Foreign Relations, who declared that one year after the I-35W disaster, next to nothing had been done to address the nation's infrastructure crisis. On the September 12, 2008 installment of *CNN Election Center*, Brown's topics included the collision of a commuter train with a freight train on September 12 in Los Angeles, California, which resulted in two dozen deaths, and the effects of Hurricane Ike, which had struck Texas a few days earlier; several CNN correspondents, among them Ted Rowlands, Erica Hill, Gary Tuchman, and Ali Velshi, discussed Texans' reactions to orders to evacuate various areas and the destruction caused by the hurricane. Another subject on September 12 was the interview the previous day of the Republican vice-presidential candidate, Governor Sarah Palin of Alaska, by Charles Gibson, the anchor of *ABC World News with Charles Gibson*, which Brown discussed with Gloria Borger and Jeffrey Toobin, both CNN political analysts, and Dana Millbank, a *Washington Post* political correspondent. On September 15, 2008 Brown and several other CNN correspondents talked about the 500-point drop in the Dow Jones Industrial Average that day, following the news that the 158-year-old investment house Lehman Brothers had gone bankrupt and that the financial-services firm Standard & Poor had downgraded to "junk status" the debt of Washington Mutual, the largest savings-and-loan association in the U.S. Brown's next topic was whether ads in support of the 2008 presidential candidates were "crossing the line" in terms of honesty; the panelists were David Brody, a CNN contributor and Christian Broadcasting Network national correspondent; Alex Castellanos, a Republican consultant; and Roland Martin, a CNN political analyst and supporter of U.S. senator Barack Obama, the Democratic presidential nominee.

Election Center replaced Paula Zahn's show, which had fared poorly in the 8:00 p.m. time slot against the opinionated network commentators and interviewers Keith Olbermann and Bill O'Reilly, of MSNBC and Fox News, respectively. According to Jacques Steinberg, writing for the *New York Times* (October 4, 2008), Brown initially had difficulty finding "a voice and identity for her program," but with the motto "No bias, no bull" as the basis of her approach, she has succeeded in attracting an impressive number of viewers: an average of 826,000 nightly from March 10 through September 28, Steinberg reported. (The corresponding figures for Olbermann and O'Reilly were about 1.1 million and 2.7 million, Steinberg wrote.) "As journalists, and certainly for me over the last few years, we've gotten overly obsessed with parity, especially when we're covering politics," Brown told Steinberg. "We kept making sure each candidate got equal time—to the point that it got ridiculous in a way." She also said to Steinberg, "You're not going to see me ever be partisan. I'll never take a position on a candidate or an issue." After Election Day, November 4, 2008, Jonathan Klein of CNN told Steinberg, *Election Center* will be renamed, with Brown remaining as its anchor. Her mission will be to focus on politicians who won election or reelection and who will make up the new administration and Congress.

On a few occasions Brown has drawn critical comments. One stemmed from a CNN special, entitled *Campaign Killers: Why Do Negative Ads Work?*, hosted by Brown, that aired on January 17, 2008. In it she referred to an ad placed in the *New York Times* on September 9, 2007 by the organization MoveOn and headlined "General Petraeus or General Betray Us?" The ad accused General David H. Petraeus, who had been serving as the commanding general of the multinational force in Iraq since January 26, 2007, of being dishonest with the American people about the course of the war in Iraq. In *Campaign Killers* Brown said, "General David Petraeus made his reputation taking on insurgents in Iraq. But when he came to Capitol Hill in September, he was confronted by American insurgents, a liberal anti-war group called MoveOn.org." Brown's description of MoveOn representatives as "insurgents" struck reporters for the liberal watchdog group Media Matters for America as unfair. Others among Brown's critics have contended that because she is married to a former Bush administration official who has repeatedly voiced a hardline view of Iran, she cannot be dispassionate or unbiased in her accounts of news about that nation.

Brown has repeatedly defended the mainstream media against charges that its journalists are too soft in their questioning and portrayal of the federal government, particularly regarding foreign policy. She has argued that only major media corporations can afford to dedicate the resources necessary to cover adequately such events as the war in Iraq and the aftermath of Hurricane Katrina. "That's commitment only mainstream media can make," she told Judd. "I still believe there is one place, the mainstream media, that is the best place for quality journalism. I think you will find people in the mainstream media who are still trying to challenge power, no matter what party they represent." When Russert asked her in 2003 whether, as a White House correspondent, she felt that journalists were seduced by the power and prestige of working there, she responded: "This is, you know, the center of the universe. That you do get caught up in. [But] I think it almost has the opposite effect in terms of the seduction of the president or his aides or whatever, because you go in there and every day, it is a huge fight, and maybe it wasn't the case with previous administrations—I can only speak about this one—but to get anything, any little bit of information. . . . I think the relationship, frankly, [of administration representatives] with reporters in the White House especially now is pretty antagonistic. It would be very difficult for the Bush White House or any of the top aides to seduce the White House press corps at the moment given the sort of acrimony that exists."

Brown lives in New York with her second husband, Dan Senor, whom she married in 2006, after her conversion to Judaism, Senor's religion. Senor is a Fox News analyst; formerly, he was a Republican strategist and the chief spokesperson for the Coalition Provisional Authority in Iraq. Guests at their wedding were asked not to bring gifts but instead to contribute to a fund that pays for medical care at the Cleveland Clinic, in Ohio, mostly for seriously injured Iraqi refugee children. The couple have one son, Eli James, who was born in December 2007.

—M.M.

Suggested Reading: *Cleveland (Ohio) Jewish News* (on-line) Oct. 10, 2007; CNBC News Transcripts: *Tim Russert* (on-line) July 19, 2003; *Grand Rapids (Michigan) Press* B p5 Apr. 3, 2008; *mediabistro.com* Feb. 16, 2007; *Muskegon (Michigan) Chronicle* B p2 Dec. 1, 2005; *New York Times* p13 Apr. 9, 2006, p7 Oct. 4, 2008; *St. Petersburg (Florida) Times* A p6 Sep. 8, 2005; *Washington Post* C p1+ July 30, 2007

Brownback, Sam

Sep. 12, 1956– U.S. senator from Kansas (Republican)

Address: 303 Hart Senate Office Bldg., Washington, DC 20510-1604

On October 17, 2007, two days before he dropped out of the race for the Republican presidential nomination, U.S. senator Sam Brownback of Kansas told Sarah Pulliam for *Christianity Today* (October 18, 2007) that abortion is "the lead moral issue of our day, just like slavery was the lead moral issue 150 years ago." A prominent figure in the Christian right wing on Capitol Hill, Brownback entered the Senate in 1997, after a special election held to choose a successor to the longtime Republican senator Bob Dole. At the time of that election, Brownback was serving his first term in the U.S. House of Representatives, where—emboldened by the return of the House and the Senate to Republican control in 1994, for the first time in four decades—he and many other freshmen Republicans had embarked on a crusade to drastically shrink the federal government and achieve other goals enumerated in a Republican manifesto called the Contract with America. "I had never lived under a GOP Congress," Brownback, who was 38 years old in 1994, told Terry Eastland for the *Weekly Standard* (August 7, 2006). "We were going to change the world and do it in six months."

Since he made that remark, Brownback—who won a full, six-year term in the Senate in 1998 and was reelected in 2004—has pursued, with very few deviations, a strongly conservative Republican

Paul J. Richards/AFP/Getty Images

agenda that calls for "support for God in public life," as David D. Kirkpatrick wrote for the *New York Times* (October 14, 2005). In addition to his staunch opposition to abortion, Brownback has fought for the legalization of school prayer and opposed government-sanctioned fetal-stem-cell research and gay marriage. He has voted for every federal tax cut and against every tax increase and has proposed that each taxpayer be given the choice of paying a flat tax rather than conventional income taxes. He has also consistently backed measures that expand free trade, and has called for reforming the Social Security system by enabling workers to opt out of that plan and maintain their own retirement accounts instead. He has championed the creation of charter schools and school voucher programs; fought legislation that limits political free speech by imposing restrictions on campaign advertising; and supported tort-reform measures that would bar lawsuits against the manufacturers, distributors, importers, and sellers of guns and that set caps on noneconomic and punitive damages in medical malpractice suits. He has voted against any increase in the minimum wage; against the banning of oil and gas drilling in the Arctic National Wildlife Refuge, in Alaska; against measures that would strengthen CAFE (Corporate Average Fuel Economy) standards for cars and trucks; against the Patients' Bill of Rights; and against legislation calling for mandated reductions in the emission of greenhouse gases from energy plants and factories.

At the same time Senator Brownback has expended much effort in areas not commonly associated with conservative Republican lawmakers, working to stamp out sex trafficking, for example, which he has called "the ugly side of globalization"; to stop the ethnic and tribal genocide in the Darfur region of Sudan; and to secure increased funding for the treatment and elimination of AIDS and malaria in Africa. Within the U.S. he has worked to fund literacy and job-training programs and promote Bible study in prisons, with the goal of shrinking recidivism rates; to secure funding for the construction of the National Museum of African American History and Culture as part of the Smithsonian Institution; and, by means of a congressional resolution, to offer an apology from the federal government to Native Americans for centuries of oppression, broken treaties, hostile policies, and dishonest business dealings. In an op-ed column for the *New York Times* (December 22, 2004), Nicholas Kristof described Brownback as "one of the most conservative, religious, fascinating—and, in many ways, admirable—politicians in America today." "Sure, Mr. Brownback is to the right of Attila the Hun, and I disagree with him on just about every major issue," Kristof wrote. "But . . . let me point to reasons for hope. Members of the Christian right, exemplified by Mr. Brownback, are the new internationalists, increasingly engaged in humanitarian causes abroad—thus creating opportunities for common ground between left and right on issues we all care about."

One of the four children of Robert and Nancy Brownback, Samuel Dale Brownback was born on September 12, 1956 in Garnett, Kansas, near the town of Parker, where he grew up on his parents' 800-acre farm. His mother and father still live on their farm, raising cattle, wheat, corn, and other so-called row crops. His siblings are his sister, Mary, and brothers Alan, now a veterinarian, and James, a farmer. Brownback recalled to Terry East-

land that when the local radio farm broadcaster reported market news, "conversation stopped around our table." Such information "stirred my interest in international affairs," he added, "since what was going on in the Soviet Union or Brazil or Australia affected our markets for wheat and soybeans." At Prairie View High School, in the nearby town of LaCygne, Brownback played quarterback for the football team. During his high-school years, he was elected president of the Kansas chapter of Future Farmers of America; in 1976–77 he served as the organization's national vice president and became a skilled speaker.

In 1975 Brownback enrolled at Kansas State University, in Manhattan, where he studied agricultural economics. He joined the Alpha Gamma Rho fraternity, most of whose members pursue careers in the agriculture or food industries. As an undergraduate he was elected student-body president. In 1976 he campaigned for former California governor Ronald Reagan in his failed bid for the Republican presidential nomination. Brownback worked as a farm broadcaster for radio station KKSU in 1978–79. After he earned a B.S. degree, with honors, in 1979, he entered the University of Kansas School of Law, in Lawrence. In 1980 he was a volunteer worker in Reagan's successful run for the presidency, in a race against the incumbent, Jimmy Carter. "I just thought Reagan got it right," Brownback told Eastland. "Here was finally somebody who made a whole lot of sense to me, who understood the difference between right and wrong, and who was willing to stand up for what's right."

Brownback earned a J.D. degree from the University of Kansas School of Law in 1982. Beginning that year until 1986, he worked for a private-practice law firm in Manhattan, Kansas. Concurrently, he taught at the University of Kansas School of Law and, from 1983 until 1986, served as the attorney for the towns of Ogden and Leonardville, near Manhattan. In 1986, when he was 30, the Kansas Board of Agriculture appointed him secretary. He held that position until 1993, when the Kansas Department of Agriculture was created in place of the board. During those years he took a leave of absence, from 1990 to 1991, to work on trade and tariff pacts as a White House fellow in the office of the U.S. special trade representative (Carla Hills at that time).

In 1994, when James "Jim" Slattery announced that he would give up his seat in Congress as the representative of Kansas's Second District to seek the governorship, Brownback announced his desire to succeed him. Brownback defeated the more conservative Bob Bennie, an agricultural-chemicals salesman, in the Republican primary. In the general election he faced John Carlin, a Democrat, who, after serving as governor of Kansas, from 1979 to 1987, had become so unpopular that when he had again sought that position, in 1990, he lost the primary. Although Brownback had never held elective office, he had substantial name recognition, thanks to his contacts with many other members of the Future Farmers of America during his teens and his work as Kansas secretary of agriculture. In addition, he campaigned tirelessly, emphasizing his belief in fiscal conservatism and smaller government rather than his positions on social issues, and he capitalized on his knack for developing instant rapport with a wide array of voters. On Election Day he carried each of the two dozen counties in the Second Congressional District, which stretches from Nebraska, on the north, to Oklahoma, on the south, and encompasses Topeka (the state capital), Manhattan, and huge swathes of prairie and farmland; he defeated Carlin by a margin of nearly two to one.

Brownback's 1994 victory was among those that enabled the Republicans to capture a majority in the House and Senate for the first time in 40 years. Under the leadership of the Speaker of the House, Republican congressman Newt Gingrich of Georgia, the newly elected Republicans vowed to usher in a host of federal reforms, prominently outlined in their Contract with America. Indeed, Brownback and his compatriots pushed for reforms even more radical than those proposed in that document. He and 30 other freshmen congressmen urged the elimination of four Cabinet-level departments—Commerce, Education, Energy, and Housing and Urban Development—which they dismissed as unnecessary, inefficient bureaucracies. Although the freshmen failed to realize that goal and most of the others listed in the Contract with America, they "moved the leadership dramatically," as Grover Norquist, the president of Americans for Tax Reform and a former Gingrich adviser, told Lisa Leiter for *Insight on the News* (March 20, 1995).

In the spring of 1995, Brownback was diagnosed with melanoma, a potentially fatal form of skin cancer. While he underwent two successful operations, the experience led him to think about his priorities. As he explained to John J. Miller for the *National Review* (May 8, 2006), "I had devoted my life to building [my] resume. But what did it really matter? Life is not a resume." By his own account, he emerged from that period of soul-searching with renewed spiritual vigor and a determination to connect his work with his Christian faith. (Raised a Methodist, he had joined an evangelical church after his marriage.) During that time, in a widely publicized gesture, he washed the feet of one of his longtime aides at an event hosted by the Christian men's group Promise Keepers. His action, Brownback told David Kirkpatrick, was a "biblical model of what servant leadership is."

In June 1996, more than two years before the end of his fifth term in the U.S. Senate, the Republican Bob Dole, Kansas's senior senator, announced that he was resigning his seat to devote himself full-time to his quest for the presidency. Kansas's governor, William Graves, and other state Republican officials chose Lieutenant Governor Sheila Frahm to fill Dole's seat until the special election to be held the following November. Graves and his col-

leagues felt confident that voters would choose Frahm, a moderate Republican who supported abortion rights, to complete the remainder of Dole's term. Her powerful backers notwithstanding, Brownback immediately announced that he was challenging Frahm for the Republican nomination in the special primary to be held in August 1996. Supported by conservative Christian groups and promising voters that his top priority would be "a return to basic values," Brownback won the primary with 55 percent of the vote. On Election Day that November, after a hard fight, he defeated the Democratic candidate, Jill Docking, by "campaigning on the 'three R's'—reduce (the size of government), reform (Congress) and return (to traditional values)," as a reporter for the *Economist* (March 11, 2006) summarized his platform. On Election Day in 1998, Brownback received more than twice as many votes as his Democratic opponent to win a full six-year term in the Senate. Six years later he won reelection with two-and-a-half times as many votes as the Democratic nominee.

The site of the geographic center of the lower 48 states, Kansas ranks 15th in area among the 50 states and is home to some 2.76 million people, placing it 33d in population. In 2000, according to the U.S. Census, 91.19 percent of Kansans were white, 6.41 percent black, 2.10 percent Asian, 1.78 percent Native American, and .12 percent native Hawaiian or Pacific islander. Until 1940 the population in rural areas was greater than the urban total; by 2000 nearly 70 percent of Kansans lived in towns or cities, and only about 1 percent identified themselves as farmers. Still, at least 90 percent of the land in Kansas is devoted to agriculture. Among registered voters in Kansas, Republicans outnumber Democrats by three to two.

With few exceptions among the hundreds of bills he has sponsored or voted for during his eight years in the Senate, Brownback has not deviated from the Republican Party line. In 1999, for example, during the 106th Congress, he co-sponsored a bill that proposed a constitutional amendment requiring the federal government to balance its budget within seven years of the amendment's ratification by the states. As recorded in Thomas, a search engine maintained by the U.S. Library of Congress, he also sponsored a resolution "to establish a special committee of the Senate to address the cultural crisis facing America" that would "study the causes and reasons for the substantial social and cultural regression" and "the impact that such negative cultural trends and developments have had on our broader society, particularly in regards [sic] to child well-being," and "explore a means of cultural renewal and make recommendations, including such recommendations for new legislation." During the 107th Congress (2001–02), he sponsored a bill to add to the Constitution an amendment that would give Congress "power to prohibit the physical desecration of the flag of the United States" and a resolution designating November 27, 2000 as "a national day of prayer and fasting," on which to "seek guidance from God to achieve greater understanding of our own failings," "learn how we can do better in our everyday activities," and "gain resolve in how to confront those challenges which we must confront"—in particular, "the threat of terrorism, violent extremist organizations, and states that permit or host organizations that are opposed to democratic ideals." He also co-sponsored a bill "to protect the right to life of each born and preborn human person in existence at fertilization," which stated, in part, "a human father and mother beget a human offspring when the father's sperm fertilizes the mother's ovum, and the life of each preborn human person begins at fertilization. . . . Americans and our society suffer from the evils of killing even one innocent born or preborn human person, and each day suffer the torture and slaughter of more than 3,500 preborn persons." None of those proposed measures became law.

Also during the 107th Congress, Brownback introduced a bill to designate "God Bless America" as the U.S.'s national song and another seeking to prohibit the cloning of human beings. In 2004, during the 108th Congress, he co-sponsored a bill to "terminate" the entire Internal Revenue Code of 1986 and replace it with a new tax system that would "appl[y] a low rate to all Americans," "provid[e] tax relief for working Americans," "protec[t] the rights of taxpayers and reduc[e] tax collection abuses," "eliminat[e] the bias against savings and investment," "promot[e] economic growth and job creation," and "not penalize marriage or families." He also introduced a bill to withdraw the federal Food and Drug Administration's approval of the so-called morning-after drug, RU-486, which prevents pregnancy by disrupting the process in which a fertilized egg gets implanted in the womb.

Also during the 108th Congress, Senator Brownback introduced resolutions to "protect, promote, and celebrate" motherhood and fatherhood and to designate April 2005 as American Religious History Month; another of his bills was aimed at having the words "In God We Trust" appear on the faces of the $1 coins being issued to honor each U.S. president. He also introduced a bill to "clarify" federal law to prohibit "the dispensing, distribution, or administration of a controlled substance for the purpose of causing, or assisting in causing, the suicide, euthanasia, or mercy killing of any individual." He introduced a measure to "ensure that women seeking an abortion are fully informed regarding the pain experienced by their unborn child." As in every congressional session, he proposed adding as an amendment to the Indian Health Care Improvement Act (which requires periodic reauthorization) an acknowledgement of "a long history of official depredations and ill-conceived policies by the Federal Government regarding Indian tribes" and an offer of "an apology to all Native Peoples on behalf of the United States."

Regarding international matters, in 2005 Brownback introduced a bill to fund efforts to combat malaria, tuberculosis, and other infectious diseases worldwide, and he tried to gain support for legislation that would ease the process by which North Koreans could apply for asylum or refugee status in the U.S. He has become a prominent advocate for actions to end the violence in the Darfur region of eastern Sudan, where, since 2002, the Sudanese government and the janjaweed—Arab militiamen armed largely by that government—have engaged in genocide against Darfur's black African tribespeople. After he visited Darfur in early 2004, Brownback spoke on the floor of the Senate (July 22, 2004), saying, as transcribed for votesmart.org, "Are we going to look back on this one and say, 'never again,' or are we going to get in on this one now and say, 'no, let us stop it'? . . . When will the death of innocent men, women and children—who want nothing more in this world than to be left alone to farm their land and provide for their families—be too much for the conscience of the international community to bear?"

Brownback co-sponsored the Darfur Peace and Accountability Act (2006), which imposed sanctions, such as the freezing of assets and denial of visas, against "perpetrators of crimes against humanity" in Darfur and other parts of Sudan and urged that any ships transporting Sudanese oil be denied entry in U.S. ports. He also co-sponsored the Senate's Civilian Protection resolution (2006), which stated the necessity for presidential action in Darfur, including efforts to bring NATO peacekeepers to the region and bolstering any United Nations missions there, and the Sudan Accountability and Divestment Act (2007), which prohibits American firms doing business with the Sudanese government from receiving federal contracts. Financial disclosure forms that he released in May 2007, as the Federal Election Commission requires of presidential candidates, revealed that Brownback and his wife had divested themselves of many thousands of dollars' worth of mutual-fund holdings so as to avoid profiting from the earnings of companies involved in trade with Sudan.

Brownback is a member of the U.S. Commission on Security and Cooperation in Europe, known as the Helsinki Commission; an independent federal agency composed of nine U.S. senators, nine members of the House, and officials from the Departments of State, Defense, and Commerce, the commission is part of the Organization for Security and Cooperation in Europe, formed in 1975. It currently includes 56 nations in North America, Europe, Africa, and Central Asia, which work collectively on issues involving military security, human rights, the environment, and economic matters. For two years (2005–06) Brownback chaired the commission. He also currently serves on the Senate Committee on Appropriations and its Subcommittee on Financial Services and General Government; the Senate Committee on the Judiciary and its Subcommittee on the Constitution; and the Joint Economic Committee, which is composed of Democrats and Republicans from the House and Senate. Most recently, as a member of the last-named committee, as posted on jec.senate.gov (February 28, 2008), Brownback disputed the findings of committee Democrats regarding the costs of the war in Iraq. According to the Democrats' report, the cost of the war will exceed $2.6 trillion; according to Brownback, "The report's methodology and assumptions are, at the very least, very controversial and debatable. Moreover, by making standard economic assumptions, over $1 trillion of war costs estimated in the report vanish." (In testimony before the committee on February 28, 2008, the Nobel Prize–winning economist Joseph I. Stiglitz stated that the overall cost of the war will reach $3 trillion.)

In December 2006 Brownback announced his intention to pursue the 2008 Republican presidential nomination. Despite his appeal to right-wing elements in his party, he failed to attract donors or voters, and he dropped out of the race in October 2007. In response to an invitation from the *New York Times* to submit an op-ed piece headed "What I'd Be Talking About If I Were Still Running," Brownback wrote (March 2, 2008), "This was the central idea I tried to bring to the presidential race: we need to rebuild the family and renew the culture in America. Marriage is in crisis. Divorce and adultery, cohabitation and out-of-wedlock births, and a mentality that views children as a burden are all part of the problem. . . . The best way to reduce poverty, fight crime and improve education is to rebuild the family. Families should be able to keep more of what they earn and have more options in terms of education. We need to enact common sense measures to restrict abortion, encourage adoption and promote abstinence. We need to encourage broadcast decency and to address the effects of violence and pornography on our culture. We need a culture that knows right from wrong, encourages virtue and discourages vice. While I realize these topics can be very personal and difficult to talk about, that does not mean we can ignore them. The future of our land depends in large part upon the strength of our families and our culture."

Brownback has named the British politician and humanitarian William Wilberforce (1759–1833) as one of his role models. A convert to evangelicalism, Wilberforce campaigned for many years to end the slave trade, and he founded a society for the suppression of vice. With James B. Wadley, Brownback wrote *Kansas Agricultural Law* (1989, 1994). He is also the author of *From Power to Purpose: A Remarkable Journey of Faith and Compassion* (2007), which its publisher describes as "a personal narrative of a man with a sense of mission for America and a heart for God."

Brownback is married to the former Mary Stauffer, an attorney, who has been a full-time homemaker since early in her marriage. From Monday through Thursday, the senator lives in an apartment in Washington, D.C.,; the rest of the week, he lives with his family in a Topeka suburb. The Brownbacks have three biological children—Abby, Andrew, and Elizabeth, born in 1986, 1988, and 1990, respectively. When medical problems precluded their having a fourth child, they adopted a boy from Guatemala and a girl from China—Mark and Jenna, born in 1997 and 1998, respectively. In 2002 Brownback converted to Catholicism.

—M.H.

Suggested Reading: *American Spectator* p14+ Aug./Sep. 2003; Club for Growth Web site; *Congressional Quarterly Weekly Report* Supplement p17 Nov. 9, 1996; *CQ Weekly* p18+ Jan. 5, 2002; *Economist* p30 Mar. 11, 2006; *National Review* p38+ May 8, 2006; *New Republic* p15+ Dec. 18, 2006; *Rolling Stone* p50+ Feb. 9, 2006; Sam Brownback's Senate Web site; *Washington Post* C p1+ June 7, 2006; *Weekly Standard* p23+ Aug. 7, 2006

Selected Works: *Kansas Agricultural Law* (with James B. Wadley), 1989, 1994; *From Power to Purpose: A Remarkable Journey of Faith and Compassion*, 2007

Bumiller, Elisabeth

May 15, 1956– Journalist; writer

Address: New York Times, *1627 I St., N.W., Suite 700, Washington, DC 20006*

The journalist and author Elisabeth Bumiller started her stint as a *New York Times* White House correspondent on September 10, 2001, one day before the terrorist attacks that would set the direction and tone of the George W. Bush White House. "I signed up for a different presidency," Bumiller told Rebecca Zeifman for *Northwestern* (Summer 2005), the alumni magazine of her undergraduate alma mater, Northwestern University. "Pre-9/11 [the Bush administration] wasn't thought of as a big presidency," she added. "In fact [the administration] became completely the opposite." Her new assignment, she continued, presented her with "relentless, around-the-clock demands. It hasn't stopped, actually."

In reporting from the Bush White House, Bumiller was accused of being both too hard and too soft on the president. As evidence of Bumiller's willingness to criticize him, some have cited the story she wrote about Bush's May 2003 speech aboard the USS *Abraham Lincoln*, where, wearing a U.S. Navy flight suit, he spoke in front of a banner reading, "Mission Accomplished," which referred to U.S. military operations in Iraq. "George W. Bush's 'Top Gun' landing on the deck of the carrier *Abra-*

Alex Wong/Getty Images for Meet the Press
Elisabeth Bumiller

ham Lincoln will be remembered as one of the most audacious moments of presidential theater in American history," Bumiller wrote for the *New York Times* (May 16, 2003). The remainder of the story focused on ways the Bush administration had used the media—particularly television—to influence public opinion. On the other hand, some media observers complained that she, like many other members of the White House press corps, failed to ask enough pointed questions in the lead-up to the invasion of Iraq, in March 2003.

Negative views of her White House coverage notwithstanding, Bumiller received high marks for her book *Condoleezza Rice: An American Life* (2007), about the second African-American, and second female, U.S. secretary of state. (The first African-American was Rice's immediate predecessor, Colin L. Powell; the first woman was Madeleine Albright, who served under President Bill Clinton.) The book, which Bumiller wrote during a 15-month leave of absence from the *Times*, is "scrupulously fair and most notable for its above-the-battle tone," Robert Dallek, a historian and the author of books about several American presidents, wrote for the *New York Times* (December 27, 2007). As part of her research, Bumiller spoke with 150 of Rice's critics and colleagues, and she conducted eight one-hour interviews with the secretary herself. Bumiller, a former *Washington Post* style correspondent, has said that she has always been fascinated by Rice. "It was a book about race and politics and national security and gender and foreign policy," she told Bob Carlton for the *Birmingham (Alabama) News* (December 16, 2007). "There was just a lot. It was a very rich palate." Bumiller has been married since 1983 to another

New York Times reporter, Steven R. Weisman. She is the author of two books that she wrote while living abroad—in India, from 1985 to 1988, and then Japan, from 1989 to 1992: *May You Be the Mother of a Hundred Sons: A Journey Among the Women of India* (1990) and *The Secrets of Mariko: A Year in the Life of a Japanese Woman and Her Family* (1995). Bumiller also helped Jennifer Berman (a urologist) and Laura Berman (a sex therapist) write their book *For Women Only: A Revolutionary Guide to Overcoming Sexual Dysfunction and Reclaiming Your Sex Life* (2001; revised edition, 2005).

Elisabeth Bumiller was born on May 15, 1956 in Aalborg, Denmark. Her younger sister, Trine Bumiller, is an artist. Her mother, Gunhild, a native of Denmark, was a nurse; her father, Theodore R. "Ted" Bumiller, an American, was an architect turned filmmaker and producer. After graduating from the University of Cincinnati, in Ohio, and working for less than a year as an architect, Ted Bumiller spent $2,000 on camera equipment and set out to see the world. For 11 months in 1955 and 1956, he drove his Jeep 45,000 miles, touring India, among other places, and compiling footage for his first film, *By Jeep Around the World.* "He was larger than life," Bumiller wrote in an obituary of her father for the *Cincinnati Enquirer* (June 29, 2004). When she was three years old, Bumiller moved with her parents from Denmark to Cincinnati. Her parents later divorced; her mother subsequently married a Cincinnati lawyer, John K. Rose.

Bumiller attended Walnut Hills High School, in Cincinnati, a public institution that has been ranked among the top secondary schools in the U.S. There, she became interested in journalism, when she began writing for the school's newspaper, the *Walnut Hills Chatterbox.* She went on to study journalism at Northwestern University, in Chicago, Illinois. In her junior year she began writing about politics for the campus newspaper, the *Daily Northwestern*; her duties included reporting on meetings of the Associated Student Government. "Elisabeth was a star even at the *Daily*," the *Los Angeles Times* columnist Geraldine Baum told Zeifman. "She was always flawless, sentence after sentence of copy." Bumiller earned a reputation for being a hard worker; in 1977, on the eve of graduation, she postponed celebrating in order to finish a story about the school's just-announced tuition hikes. After earning a B.A. degree in journalism, she enrolled at the Columbia University Graduate School of Journalism, in New York City, where she earned an M.A. degree in 1979.

Shortly before Bumiller graduated from Columbia, she learned that one of her professors had recommended her for a job at the Style section of the *Washington Post.* Though the position would require her to cover society functions, not politics—her main interest—in the nation's capital, Bumiller jumped at the opportunity. "The *Post* was the most exciting paper in the country at the time," she told Zeifman. "It was a great experience, and I met everybody in town." Determined to make the most of her beat, Bumiller focused on politics whenever possible, using cocktail parties to gain access to lawmakers. "I wasn't just writing about flowers and dresses," Bumiller said. "I tried to get some news out of it." She also wrote profiles of people including the White House press secretary, James Brady, and traveled with First Lady Nancy Reagan to the wedding of Princess Diana and Prince Charles, in London, England. In many of her stories, Bumiller displayed an eye for detail, writing about what her subjects ate for breakfast, for example, and their activities when not at work. In 1983 Bumiller married Steven R. Weisman, a *New York Times* White House correspondent whom she had met four years earlier at a fund-raising event for Jimmy Carter, during his unsuccessful bid for a second term as president.

In 1985 the *New York Times* offered Weisman a position as head of its New Delhi, India, bureau. The couple moved to India, and Bumiller continued writing for the *Washington Post*'s Style section, first as a full-time employee and later as a contractual contributor. (According to Kim Eisler in the *Washingtonian* [August 2001], Weisman's boss, the *New York Times*'s executive editor, A. M. Rosenthal, told Bumiller to quit the *Washington Post*, since the newspapers were such "fierce" rivals.) Bumiller filed Style stories from India for two years before taking a leave of absence to write her first book, *May You Be the Mother of a Hundred Sons: A Journey Among the Women of India.* A nonfiction work about women at different levels of Indian society, the book includes profiles of people ranging from Bombay actresses to peasants whom she met while living with a farm family. It also focuses on an array of complex issues, including overpopulation; widespread illiteracy; and many parents' decision to abort female fetuses or kill newborn females. (In Indian culture female children are often seen as undesirable, since families must pay expensive dowries when their daughters are married.) Since she lived in India for only three and a half years and knew that she was not an expert on her subject, Bumiller "wrote from the point of view of one American woman," as she told Kathleen Hendrix for the *Los Angeles Times* (June 7, 1990). "I wrote a book I would have wanted to read before I went to India [but that] was not available." In a review for United Press International (June 8, 1990), Kathleen Silvassy described *May You Be the Mother of a Hundred Sons* as "a comprehensive work that successfully embraces the broad mosaic of life for Indian women." She added that Bumiller "strikes the fine balance required of being both sympathetic and critical within her obvious fascination with the subject." By contrast, in a review for *Newsday* (May 27, 1990), the Indian-born novelist Bharati Mukherjee accused Bumiller of "Eurocentrism," according to Hendrix. "A vision of the author emerges: an earnest and intrepid notebook-waving white missionary-chronicler bringing righteous rage to bear on nasty local ways," Mukherjee wrote.

In 1989 the *New York Times* named Weisman its Tokyo bureau chief, and Bumiller moved with her husband from India to Japan, where the couple remained until 1992. In 1990 she gave birth to her first child, Madeleine. Initially, Bumiller felt uninspired by Tokyo, while her continued love for India led her to subscribe to Indian magazines and seek out Indian cuisine. "It's true," she told Hendrix. "Japan pales by comparison. It's pleasant. It's very interesting. It's more important right now to the United States. But India was an adventure. It was many things, but it was never boring."

Before long, however, Bumiller regained the urge to write, and after taking Japanese lessons and reading extensively about the country, she set out to "explore Japanese society through the experience of one family," in her words, as quoted by Michael Harris in the *Los Angeles Times* (November 6, 1995). From February 1991 through April 1992, Bumiller, with the help of an interpreter, observed the Tanaka family (the name is a pseudonym), paying particularly close attention to Mariko Tanaka, a 44-year-old working wife and mother of three whose household included her ailing, elderly parents. The resulting book, *The Secrets of Mariko: A Year in the Life of a Japanese Woman and Her Family*, examines the seemingly ordinary family's complicated dynamics. Mariko, who had two part-time jobs and shouldered all the burdens of homemaking in addition to total care of her parents, maintained her equanimity through activities outside her home, including music lessons and participation in community festivals. "For Americans who have been fed the image of a remote and disciplined Japanese society, this story offers a close-up, sometimes startling, picture of real people," Sherry Jacobson wrote in a review for the *Dallas Morning News* (April 14, 1996). In an assessment for the *Washington Post* (November 19, 1995), Elizabeth Ward wrote, "Bumiller manages to tell us a great deal about Japan by gracefully digressing from her portrait of Mariko at the numerous points where the family's concerns intersect with broader social questions. Education, work habits, alcoholism, the care of the aged, living standards, Japan's wartime responsibilities, marriage, divorce, local politics, the expectations imposed on women and many other issues are treated just as they crop up in the course of the year."

Bumiller and her family moved back to the U.S. in 1992, after the *New York Times* promoted Weisman to deputy foreign editor. The couple settled in New York City, where Bumiller gave birth to her second child, Theodore. In 1995, overcoming her unwillingness to work for the same publication as her husband, she joined the *Times* as a metro reporter. "I liked being a general assignment metro reporter a lot because I loved New York City," Bumiller told Zeifman. "I had more freedom in those days, and I liked just having the whole city to write about." In 1999 she covered the U.S. Senate race between the Democratic first lady Hillary Rodham Clinton and the Republican candidate,

Congressman Rick Lazio, who had won the nomination after the presumptive GOP nominee, Mayor Rudolph Giuliani of New York, dropped out of the race. She was also one of three writers to contribute to the *Times*'s Public Lives column, which focuses on prominent individuals. From 1999 to mid-2001 she held the title of City Hall bureau chief.

In 2001 the *Times* promoted Bumiller to White House correspondent, and she and her family moved again, this time to the Washington, D.C., area. (The following year her husband, who had served as a member of the *Times*'s editorial board beginning in 1995, was named chief diplomatic correspondent, a job connected, like Bumiller's, with the newspaper's Washington bureau.) Bumiller started her new beat on September 10, 2001, the day before Middle Eastern terrorists hijacked four jetliners and flew two of them into the twin towers of the World Trade Center and one into the Pentagon; the fourth crashed in a Pennsylvania field. At the *New York Times* Washington bureau office on the morning of the attacks, Bumiller watched TV reports of the first plane hitting the north tower of the World Trade Center. As rumors spread that the White House was being evacuated, she hurried to the scene to interview fleeing presidential staff members. One employee had a TV monitor, and Bumiller watched as the second plane hit the trade center's south tower. "A Somber Bush Says Terrorism Cannot Prevail" was the headline of the first article she wrote as the *Times*'s White House correspondent; datelined September 12, 2001 and written with input from David E. Sanger, it reported on the speech President Bush gave from the Oval Office "hours after returning from a zigzag course across the country, as his Secret Service and military security teams moved him from Florida . . . to command posts in Louisiana and Nebraska before it was determined the attacks had probably ended . . . ," as Bumiller wrote. "His speech came after a day of trauma that seems destined to define his presidency," she noted.

For the next five years, until mid-2006, Bumiller reported on the administration's policies, many of which were influenced by the events of September 11, 2001. She has said that she often found it difficult to get information from the White House, as Bush and his colleagues had a reputation for secrecy. "It's always hard to cover the White House," she told Zeifman. "Any White House does not want to tell you what's going on. It's just harder to get information out of [this administration] than other recent White Houses—Republican or Democrat." She also told Zeifman, "At every press conference I stand up every time and ask a question. No matter what."

Bumiller, like other White House reporters, faced criticism following the March 6, 2003 press conference in which Bush outlined his plans for invading Iraq. Some felt that Bumiller and her colleagues did not ask the president enough tough questions, ones that might have revealed the weaknesses in his arguments justifying the invasion. "I think we were very deferential because . . . it's live, it's very intense, it's frightening to stand up there," she told a *Baltimore Sun* reporter, according to the *American Prospect* (March 30, 2004, online). "Think about it, you're standing up on prime-time live TV asking the president of the United States a question when the country's about to go to war. There was a very serious, somber tone that evening, and no one wanted to get into an argument with the president at this very serious time."

Others insist that Bumiller always pushed the Bush administration for answers. "Reporting is an oasis, and White House reporting is a pretty dry desert," the *Washington Post* correspondent Dana Milbank told Zeifman. "Bumiller has a nice anti-authority streak, and she doesn't suffer fools." Bumiller's most famous criticism of the administration appeared in an article on Bush's "Mission Accomplished" speech, which he delivered on the deck of the USS *Abraham Lincoln*. The story dealt with ways Bush had tried to manipulate his own image. Bumiller has said that the White House was often upset by her writing. "It's a contentious relationship," she told Zeifman. "Our intentions are not the same here, and this administration is especially hard to crack." "Elisabeth was a tireless hunter of color and detail that we were often reluctant to share," Nicolle Devenish, an assistant to the president for communications, told Zeifman. "But in the end I think we learned to understand each other, and more often than not we were able to come to a middle ground on most stories." When researching stories on Washington, D.C., figures, Bumiller would often employ what she called the "outside-in" method of reporting, whereby she would first interview people outside the White House and then approach people increasingly close to the president. "I think people think I expect handouts, that they think my job is to listen to what Scott McClellan says at the briefing every day and then put it in the paper," she said to Zeifman, referring to the then–White House press secretary. "That's not my job. You talk to these large concentric circles outside of the White House, and you do it every time, no matter what."

Bumiller has traced her idea to write about Condoleezza Rice—who served as George W. Bush's national security adviser before becoming secretary of state—to a conversation in late 2005 with a family friend, who suggested that Rice would make a good subject for a book. In June 2006 Bumiller began a 15-month leave of absence from the *New York Times*, working on the biography as a public-policy scholar with the Woodrow Wilson International Center and a transatlantic fellow with the German Marshall Fund. "For me, it was a way to write about this woman who had always fascinated me and who I had covered as White House correspondent," Bumiller told Bob Carlton. "But also it was 50 astonishing years of American history that she had lived through." Bumiller came to see Rice, who grew up in Birmingham, Alabama, the daughter of a middle-class pastor, as similar to Bush, in that they were "both products of their own elite." "Bush came from the old East Coast establishment, and Condi Rice was of a Southern black professional class—with real distinct manners in each elite," she told Carlton. "They both look very self-confident on the surface, but they also harbor deep resentments underneath. I think Condi Rice has been underestimated, like the president, her entire life—as an African-American, as a woman, and for many years, as the youngest person in the room."

Critics praised Bumiller for producing a balanced portrayal of Rice, who, according to Dallek, is presented as "neither hero nor villain," despite her role in promoting the Iraq War. Dallek went on to call Bumiller's book a "compelling portrait." In a critique for the *New York Times Book Review* (January 20, 2008), Jacob Heilbrunn wrote that Bumiller "brings a keen eye to Rice, probing not only her tenure as a policy maker and her close ties to George W. Bush, but also her personal and professional past." He added, "Several books about Rice have already appeared, but this one is probably the most measured, insightful, and comprehensive." In a review for the *Los Angeles Times* (December 11, 2007, on-line), Stanley Meisler wrote that Bumiller "has labored to present an evenhanded look at Rice. She shows some sympathy for her subject and even more understanding."

In September 2007 Bumiller returned to the *New York Times* as a national-affairs correspondent. Her coverage of the Republican John McCain's presidential campaign attracted a lot of attention when, during an interview with McCain in March 2008, she pressed him to elaborate on his conversa-

tion with John Kerry in 2004 in which the men discussed the possibility of his becoming Kerry's running mate and thereby joining the Democratic ticket. The irritation that McCain expressed regarding her questions, and his refusal to answer them because, in his words, there was "no living American in Washington" who did not know about that meeting, led her to ask, as quoted on ABCNews.com (March 7, 2008) and many other Web sites, "Can I ask you about your . . . why you're so angry?" "Pardon me?" McCain said. "Never mind, never mind," Bumiller responded, stirring McCain to say, "I mean it's well known. Everybody knows. It's been well chronicled a thousand times. John Kerry asked if I would consider being his running mate." "Right," Bumiller said. "And I said categorically no, under no circumstances," McCain continued. "That's all very well known." Bumiller then continued the interview with an unrelated question.

Bumiller lives near Washington, D.C., with her husband and two children.

—K.J.P.

Suggested Reading: *Birmingham (Alabama) News* F p1 Dec. 16, 2007; *Los Angeles Times* E p1 June 7, 1990; *Northwestern* (on-line) Summer 2005; *Washington Post* X p4 Nov. 19, 1995

Selected Books: *May You Be the Mother of a Hundred Sons: A Journey Among the Women of India*, 1990; *The Secrets of Mariko: A Year in the Life of a Japanese Woman and Her Family*, 1995; *Condoleezza Rice: An American Life*, 2007

Burns, Ed

Nov. 28, 1946– Television writer; former teacher; former police detective

Address: c/o HBO, 1100 Ave. of the Americas, New York, NY 10036

Though he is widely hailed as the co-creator of one of the best television programs ever made, Ed Burns never sought a career in the entertainment industry. A native of Baltimore, Maryland, he spent 20 years working in law enforcement and seven serving as a teacher in Baltimore's troubled public schools before beginning his tenure as co-writer and producer of the critically acclaimed dramatic series *The Wire*, which debuted on the cable channel HBO in 2002 and concluded in March 2008. Along with his partner, David Simon, Burns operated outside Hollywood norms to create a program portraying the harsh realities of inner-city life. The program has been hailed for what Neil Drumming, writing for EW.com, called its "complex, novelistic style," "naturalistic" dialogue,

"heroes and villains—played by a brilliant cast of virtual unknowns—[who] were often indistinguishable," and story lines that "were never neatly tied up by episode's end." Recently, Burns helped pilot a program designed to keep Baltimore's most disruptive students from dropping out of school. For his most recent project, he wrote and co-produced a miniseries on the Iraq war, entitled *Generation Kill*, which aired on HBO in July and August 2008. With Simon, Burns co-wrote the 1997 nonfiction book *The Corner*, about a poor Baltimore family struggling with the effects of drug addiction.

Edward Burns was born on November 28, 1946 and grew up in Baltimore. Upon graduating, at age 22, from Loyola College, where he had majored in history and minored in philosophy, he was drafted into the military and served in the Vietnam War. Following his discharge he returned to his native city and began a career in law enforcement that lasted some 20 years, eventually becoming a detective and investigating many drug and homicide cases. "I never felt hopeless," he said about his time on the police force, in a conversation with Terry Gross for the National Public Radio (NPR)

Stephen Shugerman/Getty Images

Ed Burns

program *Fresh Air* (November 22, 2006, on-line). "I really enjoyed what I was doing because I had a chance to find what I thought was the most dangerous group in this city. . . . So I was taking down guys that, you know, were doing all sorts of murders to further their drug activities." Despite that initial enthusiasm, Burns came to feel that his effectiveness at fighting crime was stymied by the police department's shortsightedness. "Where the frustration would come in," he told Gross, "was the fact that there . . . was no follow-up. So you would go into an area, you would take down a guy who controlled, say, the towers in a housing project, and you would basically reduce the murder rate there to zero for maybe a year or so, but then it would pick back up. . . . There was no effort to try to stabilize the area once you'd gotten one of these violent gangs out." Burns also pointed to the department's concern with the number of arrests made rather than the effects on communities of those arrested: "They're into stats. If it took me two years to bring down, say, a [major drug dealer] . . . that's one stat, one guy. . . . I can go up on the corner in one day and pick off five or six guys, no problem. There's no . . . point scale system in the game."

Burns's experiences as a policeman led him to view the U.S. government's "war on drugs" as ultimately counterproductive. "They're not warring on drugs," he told Radley Balko for *Reason Magazine* (March 7, 2008), "they're warring on drug addicts and the users and the small-time dealers. They're warring on neighborhoods. They're warring on people who can't stand up to them. They're not warring on major dealers." That critique would later find voice in the plots and themes of *The Wire.*

After retiring from the police force, in 1992, Burns decided to become a teacher, because of the desperate need for instructors in Baltimore's inner-city schools. Jumping into the job with little training, he was initially shocked at the conditions in which he had to work. "I've been to Vietnam and I was a Baltimore police homicide detective," he said to Mary Carole McCauley for the *Baltimore Sun* (September 21, 2005). "Nothing was as hard as my first year of teaching. . . . It was the most emotionally draining thing I've ever done." As he told Alejandro Danois for the Associated Press (September 6, 2006), "It's stunning how bad the school system is . . . it takes your breath away. The distance from middle school to the courtroom is five years." Though the children he taught at Hamilton Middle School were only 12 or 13 years old, they had seen an untold amount of trauma in their lives. "We had a group of 120 kids in the seventh grade and thirteen had been shot, two of them twice," he told Terry Gross. Many children, to whom he referred as "corner kids," were already embarking on lives of crime; Burns noted that students challenged teachers in ways that foreshadowed their dealings with the police. But as difficult as they were to teach, Burns never blamed his students for what he saw as the fundamental disconnect between the school's policies and the children's experiences. "When you put them in a classroom with a curriculum that doesn't compute with their world, everybody has a way of surviving," he told HBO.com—ways that include defying authority. Realizing that "a bad teacher is what [the students] expect," he made an attempt at "modeling a caring behavior," becoming "the adult who's consistent, who's always there, who always comes through with what he said . . . that's a whole new world for them." He also said, "What you try to do is present an image that the kids—maybe at some time later on in life, even if they're sitting in prison or something—can reflect on."

Burns's experiences as both a policeman and a teacher gave him a deep understanding of people on the bottom rung of the socioeconomic ladder. "You're just there as a visitor . . . ," he told Gross. "You have to start seeing the world through their eyes. . . . You've got to keep yourself open. You've got to just keep breaking down who you are so you can more and more appreciate the world you're looking at." It was that empathy that spurred him to co-write *The Corner* (1997), an account of his firsthand observations of a family ravaged by poverty and addiction. He worked on the book with his longtime friend David Simon, a journalist whom he had met during his days as a detective, when Simon, then a reporter for the *Baltimore Sun,* used him as a source for a story on the arrest of the drug kingpin Melvin Williams. "He's a very opinionated soul," Simon said of Burns to a writer for *Teacher Magazine* (September 1, 2006), "but the opinions—they're grounded." *The Corner* was hailed by Sara Mosle for the *New York Times* (November 23, 1997) for showing its subjects "a respect backed up not by cheap sentiment or easy moralizing but by the dangerous, backbreaking labor of intrepid reporting." The book was made into a television miniseries for HBO in 2000 and won three Emmy Awards for its unflinching portrayal of the pernicious effects of both urban blight and the drug war.

It was partly on the strength of *The Corner*'s success that Simon and Burns were able to get approval from executives for their next project, *The Wire*. Though decisionmakers at HBO were initially reluctant to produce a "cop drama," a type of show that had traditionally been the province of network television, Simon and Burns convinced the station that they could rework the genre in an original and even subversive way. In a memo to HBO executives, as quoted by Margaret Talbot in the *New Yorker* (October 22, 2007), Simon wrote that it would be a "profound victory . . . to take the essence of network fare and smartly turn it on its head, so that no one who sees HBO's take on the culture of crime and crime fighting can watch anything like *C.S.I.* or *N.Y.P.D. Blue* or *Law & Order* again without knowing that every punch was pulled on those shows." After more than a year of negotiations, HBO executives agreed. Only one year after retiring from teaching, Burns began a third career—in television.

HBO's subscriber-based format gave Simon and Burns the freedom to portray, without restraint, the city of Baltimore as they had seen it all their lives. Each season of *The Wire*, which debuted in 2002 and ran for five seasons, portrayed a different milieu of life in the city, drawing parallels over the course of the series among various failed institutions, from the school system to the police department to the gang hierarchy. Season One examined the drug trade from both police and criminal viewpoints; Season Two, the port; Season Three, the city bureaucracy; Season Four, the school system (drawing upon Burns's experiences as a teacher); and Season Five, the press (based in part on Simon's time at the *Baltimore Sun*). Since ratings were not as much of a concern for HBO as for network television, Burns and Simon were permitted to make demands on the show's viewers, requiring that they follow long story lines that did not tie up neatly at the end of each episode. "We can do things no other show can do," Burns told Ben Marshall for the London *Guardian* (February 10, 2007). "It's wonderful, because you can plan something in episode nine that doesn't blossom until 35."

The Wire received low ratings among viewers, due partly to its complexity and partly, according to Simon, to its predominantly African-American cast. "There are people who see that many black faces staring back at them and say, 'This is not my story,'" Simon told Neil Drumming for EW.com. (It is perhaps significant that the second season, which featured the largest number of white actors, was also the highest-rated.) However, all seasons of the show were extremely popular among critics. Jacob Weisberg's piece in *Slate* (September 13, 2006,

on-line) was indicative of the consensus: "*The Wire* is surely the best TV show ever broadcast in America. . . . No other program has ever done anything remotely like what this one does, namely to portray the social, political, and economic life of an American city with the scope, observational precision, and moral vision of great literature." In addition to its innovative structure, critics praised the show for portraying both policemen and outlaws in ways that went beyond the simple good-versus-evil duality presented by most police dramas. "They have created [criminal] characters that are at once loathsome and utterly fascinating," Ben Marshall wrote. "To then get us to empathise with these men is extraordinary. Equally, the cops—caught between the dealers and the vicissitudes of city hall—are, even at their most honest and likable, grippingly dysfunctional."

Simon and Burns went to great lengths to portray the economic underclass in a realistic and unsentimental way, writing dialogue to accurately reflect current street language. Because they wanted to include "faces and voices of the real city," as Margaret Talbot reported, they cast many local unknown and/or first-time actors, whose life experiences mirrored those of their characters. City officials and former *Baltimore Sun* reporters played characters based on themselves, and the former drug dealer Melvin Williams, whom Burns himself had helped put in prison years earlier, played a community deacon. The show's realism also made it popular with the very people it portrayed, namely inner-city minorities; it was widely bootlegged and circulated around poor neighborhoods and was the first HBO series to be syndicated to BET (Black Entertainment Television). "*The Wire* is the truth," Ben Marshall quoted a "junked-up 17-year-old" as saying for the *Guardian* (April 16, 2005). "The only unrealistic thing 'bout *The Wire* is that [nobody] in *The Wire* watch *The Wire*. Cos in Baltimore, man, everyone watch that show."

Though Simon and Burns acknowledge that *The Wire* brought attention to certain sociological issues over the course of its five-season run, they also recognize that no television show can resolve those issues on its own. As a more concrete way of helping to improve society, Burns recently helped found, with a grant from the Abell Foundation, an experimental program at Baltimore's troubled William H. Lemmel Middle School. The program takes "corner kids" out of regular classes and immerses them in practical, hands-on activities, serving the dual purpose of engaging troublemakers in school and removing them from class so that other children can learn. Burns stressed to the writer for *Teacher Magazine* the importance of understanding and making allowances for the students' everyday realities: "They don't get love, they don't get attention, they don't get decent meals. So minus all of that, to start coming right in and expecting the three Rs and all of that—[a troubled student] can't work with that. And it becomes a very cruel process of suspension, running the halls, getting kicked out of the classroom until he decides he's had enough [and drops out]."

Burns currently resides in West Virginia with his wife, Anna. He has a son and daughter from a previous marriage, and his wife brought a daughter to their union. He recently finished working with Simon on *Generation Kill*, a seven-hour miniseries for HBO about the U.S. invasion of Iraq, based on the award-winning book by Evan Wright. Like *The Wire*, the miniseries, which aired in July and August 2008, looked at the human cost of American institutional failures—this time, the mistakes the government made in planning and carrying out the Iraq war.

"Burns is unquestionably cynical, but he may be the most relentlessly optimistic cynic in the country," the *Teacher Magazine* writer noted. "He loves teaching, but he finds most teachers unimpressive. He hates bureaucracy, but he's been an active part of acutely dysfunctional institutions. He thinks American education is hopelessly screwed up, but that it's also the country's only hope." Simon half-jokingly told Margaret Talbot that Burns "is only working in TV till somebody realizes that they ought to give him all the money to fix our social problems."

—J.E.P.

Suggested Reading: *Baltimore Sun* C p1 Sep. 21, 2005; *Fresh Air*, NPR.org, Nov. 22, 2006; HBO Web site; *Instructor* p72 May 1, 2007; (London) *Guardian* p4 Feb. 10, 2007; *New York Times* Arts and Leisure p1 July 6, 2008; *Newsday* B p4 Sep. 7, 2006; *Teacher Magazine* p32 Sep. 1, 2006

Selected Books: *The Corner* (with David Simon), 1997

Selected Television Shows: *The Wire*, 2002–08; *Generation Kill*, 2008

Courtesy of Jack Cafferty

Cafferty, Jack

Dec. 14, 1942– Television journalist

Address: CNN Studios, 10 Columbus Circle, New York, NY 10019

"I'm not some hair-sprayed, programmed anchorette who's wound up for an hour, wheeled into the desk . . . and the computer turns me on and off and the script comes out like it's supposed to," the television news anchor and commentator Jack Cafferty told Lynn Elber for the Associated Press (July 3, 2006). Despite, or more likely because of, that refusal to fit any typical anchor mold, Cafferty has remained a popular fixture on the broadcast news landscape for several decades. As host of "The Cafferty File" on the Cable News Network (CNN), he has been outspoken on a variety of hot-button topics, including illegal immigration, the George W. Bush administration's handling of the effects of Hurricane Katrina, and the Iraq war. As a result he has received negative responses to some of his rants, many of which have angered and offended ethnic groups and politicians. In defense of his behavior, Cafferty told Elber, "I'm 63 years old, put four kids through college, survived two marriages, paid an awful lot of taxes and I figure I'm as qualified as the next person to take a look at the world around me and have some opinions on what I see. They're not always right but they're always heartfelt and they're always real."

Cafferty began his career in broadcast journalism in Reno, Nevada, in the 1960s, going on to become a news anchor for an NBC affiliate in Des Moines, Iowa, in the early 1970s. In 1977 he was hired by NBC to host its New York City news show *The NewsCenter*, and soon afterward he became the co-anchor of the long-running local program *Live at Five*, where he was mostly overshadowed by his popular *Live at Five* co-anchor, Sue Simmons. Cafferty's profile grew substantially when he was later given his own show, *Newsline New York*, on the local Fox television network affiliate. In 1999 Cafferty joined the short-lived CNNfn network before co-hosting the CNN show *American Morning*. Since 2005 he has been a commentator for *The Situation Room*, of which "The Cafferty File" is a segment.

Cafferty was born on December 14, 1942 in Chicago, Illinois, the older of the two children of Tom and Jean Cafferty. He grew up in Reno, where his father was a popular broadcaster nicknamed "Cactus Tom" because he frequently wore a cowboy hat and boots. Tom Cafferty served as a disc jockey for the radio station KKOH and the city's first television station, KOLO-TV. Cafferty and his brother, Terry, were raised in a turbulent household. "My mom, Jean, battled booze and painkillers and, at times, deep depression," Cafferty wrote in his book, *It's Getting Ugly Out There: The Frauds, Bunglers, Liars, and Losers Who Are Hurting America* (2007), in an excerpt posted on the CNN Web site. "My dad, Tom, was a complex, fascinating man: a hard-drinking, sometimes abusive parent when drunk, but a charming, outspoken local radio and television celebrity when sober." Cafferty's father introduced him to drinking at an early age. "[He] used to take me into bars and saloons around Reno when I was a kid, 11, 12, 13 years old," he told Andrea Sachs for *Time* (September 15, 2007). "By the time I was mid-teens, I was having a beer in these joints or I was having a beer at home. It was a very natural outgrowth of the environment I was in." Despite the turmoil that sometimes characterized his upbringing, Cafferty has credited his parents with helping to shape the positive aspects of his character. "Whatever [their] heartaches and weaknesses, they taught me the importance of integrity, of truth telling, and of being able to give a man your word," he wrote in his book. "I also learned from watching my dad at his best—in the studio. His gift for relating to everyday people made him a friend of the common man. People sensed he had character and honor. Maybe some of that rubbed off on me."

After high school, Cafferty, who had aspirations of becoming a doctor, enrolled in the premed program at the University of Nevada at Las Vegas. In 1961, during his sophomore year, he landed a job as a morning disc jockey for the country-music station KBET. Over the next several years, Cafferty also hosted a number of public events, including the 1962 Miss Sparks Pageant, in Sparks, Nevada. He decided during his junior year to follow in his father's footsteps. "By the time I was in about my third year, I was making enough money in broadcasting to support myself," Cafferty told Forrest Hartman for the *Reno Gazette-Journal* (March 3, 2004). "So I thought, 'What the hell? I'll do this.'" After leaving school he became the host of a television show on KOLO-TV. "I was a forest ranger for the kids' program, *Ranger Jack*," he told Hartman. "It was a live program in the afternoon. I think it was at 5 o'clock, and we ran Three Stooges comedies and Popeye cartoons." Following his stint with KOLO-TV, Cafferty served as the director and local news announcer for the NBC network affiliate KCRL-TV (now called KRNV), in Reno. He was forced to step down in 1968, when the Air National Guard called him to active duty, following North Korea's seizure of the *USS Pueblo*. He was assigned to the Missouri National Guard's public-information office, in Kansas City. To supplement his meager service pay, Cafferty took a job as an

evening reporter and weekend news anchor at WDAF-TV. Following his discharge from the National Guard, Cafferty remained briefly at WDAF-TV before moving to Des Moines, Iowa, in 1974 and joining the NBC affiliate WHO-TV, as a news director and anchor for the 6 p.m. and 10 p.m. newscasts. Thanks to the ratings success of both broadcasts, Cafferty was invited to New York City to audition for WNBC, the flagship station of the NBC television network. "New York City's the biggest market in the country, and I'd never been here before," he told Hartman. "So, I'm like some hayseed coming in here. I flew into LaGuardia [airport] on the day of the audition. I was by myself, and the plane kind of circled around the foot of Manhattan where the World Trade Center used to be and the Statue of Liberty. I looked out the window of the plane and I thought, 'Holy God.' I'd never seen anything like that." Despite his awe, Cafferty performed well at the audition, and in 1977 he accepted an offer of a six-month contract from WNBC. In addition to serving as a local weekend news anchor, Cafferty hosted *Strictly Business*, a nationally syndicated business program. His raw style, which would become his trademark, quickly became evident: in July 1977, when he filled in for the news anchor Chuck Scarborough during a local broadcast and was asked to comment on the weather in New York City, Cafferty responded, "It sucks." In 1979 Cafferty was named the co-anchor of NBC's hour-long news show *Live at Five* (later called *News 4 New York*), with Sue Simmons. When it first aired, *Live at Five* drew criticism for mixing celebrity features with hard news stories. According to Marvin Kitman, writing for *Newsday* (November 14, 1989), "It sometimes seemed there were two minutes and 45 seconds of news; the rest was a commercial for the NBC network's shows and stars." The show nonetheless remained on the air for more than 25 years. During his time on the program, Cafferty failed to rival Scarborough or Simmons in popularity. In 1989, after over a decade at WNBC, Cafferty joined WNYW, the flagship station of Fox Broadcasting, as the anchor of *Newsline New York*, a news and interview program that was modeled after ABC's *Nightline*, and of the evening broadcast for *Fox 5 News at 7*. "He was concerned that his image was getting too soft," Sue Simmons told Verne Gay for *Newsday* (February 22, 1990). "I got the feeling—although he never told me this—that he wanted people to know he could do the job as well as Ted Koppel or Bryant Gumbel."

Cafferty's opportunity to demonstrate that ability came on January 25, 1990, while he was reporting on Avianca Airlines flight 52 from Bogota, Colombia, which had crashed on Long Island en route to John F. Kennedy Airport, in the New York City borough of Queens. After learning about the crash at 10 p.m., Cafferty went on the air at 11 p.m. and covered the disaster, carrying the story over to an expanded edition of *Newsline*—a three-hour block of programming that provided viewers with a comprehensive account of the area's worst crash in 15 years. Cafferty's capable reporting of the incident garnered him newfound respect among critics. "Suddenly, Cafferty was a serious newsman. He wasn't interviewing some silly starlet or smirking over a one-liner dropped by a supporting *Live at Five* cast member," Gay wrote. "He was calmly, concisely and, for the most part, unemotionally delivering the news." Cafferty remained at *Newsline New York* and *Fox 5 News* until 1992, when he became the co-anchor, with Kaity Tong, of *News at Ten* on WPIX (since renamed CW 11). Six years later Cafferty was fired by the network and replaced by Jim Watkins. He subsequently joined CNN. "I was kind of getting burned out on local news," he said to Hartman. "It's bleeding, burning things and car crashes and entertainment news, and there's precious little I think that's probably that worthwhile in terms of pure journalism. . . . When I had a chance to go to CNN, it was to do business news originally, and I've always had a kind of an interest in that. It wasn't a tough decision to make, and it actually has turned out to be maybe the best part of my career."

Cafferty began working for CNN's now-defunct financial-news channel CNNfn. "The chance to deal with information that's a little more grown-up is very appealing to me. Local news is what it is. But the kind CNNfn does is different," he told Richard Huff for the New York *Daily News* (December 23, 1998). "I wanted to do something that was more interesting on a personal level. When you raise four kids you develop an interest in the economy whether you want to or not." In 1999 Cafferty anchored the morning program *Before Hours*, and over the next four years he served as the host for such CNN shows as *Money Morning* and *In the Money*. After appearing on CNN's *American Morning* in 2004, Cafferty joined *The Situation Room*, a popular early-evening news program hosted by Wolf Blitzer, in 2005. As the host of "The Cafferty File," a featured segment on the show, Cafferty poses questions to viewers on relevant political topics and reads their responses on the air. He often sounds off on the topics himself, and his provocative on-air commentary—while appealing to many—has made him highly controversial.

Despite initially supporting the Bush administration's decision to invade Iraq in 2003, Cafferty became a vocal opponent of the administration, following the disclosure that the war had been launched despite intelligence reports offering no evidence that Iraq possessed weapons of mass destruction (WMDs). Cafferty garnered criticism in 2006 for calling former U.S. secretary of defense Donald Rumsfeld a "war criminal" on the air. Although he apologized at the urging of CNN officials, he told Sachs, "I will go to my grave as Jack Cafferty, Private Citizen, believing that these people committed war crimes." He also argued that the war in Iraq had been launched for reasons unrelated to that country's alleged ties to terrorists. "In my humble opinion the Bush administration used

9/11 as an excuse to start the war in Iraq," he said, as quoted in the transcript of a live chat posted on the *Huffington Post* (September 12, 2007). "People make a lot of money during wartime . . . $600 billion we've spent there so far . . . and a lot of that money has gone to friends of the administration. And of course there is all that oil. I don't think for a single second there was anything honorable about the decision to invade a sovereign country. [Iraq] had nothing to do with 9/11 and had done nothing to the United States."

Cafferty again made headlines in 2006, after he criticized Vice President Dick Cheney for granting the Fox News network an exclusive interview regarding his accidental shooting of a friend of his during a hunting trip. Cafferty contended that Cheney had taken the easy route by granting an interview to a network sympathetic to the administration. According to a transcript available on CNN.com (February 15, 2006), Cafferty said, "But I would guess it didn't exactly represent a Profile in Courage for the vice president to wander over there to the f-word network for a sit down with [the anchor] Brit Hume. That's a little like [the criminal] Bonnie interviewing [her partner] Clyde, ain't it? Where was the news conference? Where was the access to all of the members of the media?" Cafferty has been equally critical of the Democratic Party for its reluctance to press for an end to the war in Iraq, telling the *Huffington Post*, "The Democrats were handed a golden opportunity to challenge President Bush on the war when they were given control of Congress in the midterm elections last year [2006]. So far they have done absolutely nothing. It seems the Democrats are the greatest thing the Republicans have going for them sometimes." Cafferty sparked controversy with an on-air remark he made about Arab people during a broadcast of *The Situation Room* in November 2004. According to a transcript of the show, Cafferty said, "The Arab World is where innocent people are kidnapped, blindfolded, tied up, tortured and beheaded, and then videotape of all of this is released to the world as though they're somehow proud of their barbarism. Somehow, I wouldn't be too concerned about the sensitivity of the Arab world. They don't seem to have very much." In response, representatives of the American-Arab Anti-Discrimination Committee (ADC) declared on their Web site, "Jack Cafferty continues to express a simplistic view of the Arab and Muslim worlds, oftentimes conflating them. His comments malign the Arab and Muslim peoples and [imply] that they are somehow inherently prone to violence."

Cafferty's statements directed at China have stirred up the most controversy so far in his career. On April 9, 2008, during a discussion of U.S.-China relations, Cafferty referred to the hard-line stance toward China held by successive U.S. administrations after mainland China became Communist, in 1949, and the friendlier approach adopted in recent years, especially after Beijing was chosen as the site of the 2008 Olympics. He said, "So I think our relationship with China has certainly changed. I think they're basically the same bunch of goons and thugs they've been for the last 50 years." That statement angered many Chinese-Americans and prompted the Chinese Foreign Ministry to demand an apology. Cafferty's later explanation that he was referring to the Chinese government and not its people, and an apology issued by Jim Walton, the president of CNN, were deemed insufficient by many Chinese-Americans, and thousands of them descended on the network's Los Angeles and Atlanta studios to demand Cafferty's dismissal. The remark also led to two lawsuits: a $1.3 billion defamation suit filed by a primary-school teacher and a beautician as well as another filed by 14 lawyers.

According to Cafferty, his plainspokenness is a reflection of his frustration with politics. "I think that our government spends a good part of their waking hours figuring out what batch of lies they're going to tell us next," he told Sachs. "I don't believe most of what I'm told by the politicians. I think virtually everything they say for public consumption is said with an agenda. I just don't think that we have a very honest relationship with our government in this country, and it makes me angry." Many of Cafferty's opinions are included in the book It's Getting Ugly Out There: The Frauds,

Bunglers, Liars, and Losers Who Are Hurting America (2007), in which he also discussed his successful struggle to overcome alcoholism and stop smoking with the help of his second wife, Carol.

"I'm not a big city guy," Cafferty told Hartman. "I grew up in Reno and the mountains and Lake Tahoe and Pyramid Lake. I'm kind of a small-town country bumpkin, I guess." Cafferty has portrayed reporters in the films It Could Happen to You (1994), City Hall (1996), Night Falls on Manhattan (1997), and Just the Ticket (1999). He has won an Emmy Award, the New York Associated Press State Broadcasters Award, and the Edward R. Murrow Award. Cafferty lives in Cedar Grove, New Jersey. His second marriage ended with the sudden death of his wife in early September 2008.

—W.D.

Suggested Reading: (New York) Daily News p76 Dec. 23, 1998; Reno (Nevada) Gazette-Journal D p1 Oct. 6, 2001; San Francisco Chronicle (on-line) June 28, 2006; Time (on-line) Sep. 15, 2007

Selected Books: It's Getting Ugly Out There: The Frauds, Bunglers, Liars, and Losers Who Are Hurting America, 2007

Capps, Lois

Jan. 10, 1938– U.S. representative from California (Democrat); nurse; educator

Address: 1110 Longworth House Office Bldg., Washington, DC 20515

Lois Capps, a Democratic U.S. representative from California, joined the 105th Congress on March 17, 1998, a week after a special election was held to fill the seat vacated when her husband, Walter H. Capps, unexpectedly died, in October 1997, less than a year into his first term in the House. Capps is one of three dozen women who have served in Congress as a result of what has been dubbed "widow's succession"; of that group, she is among the small number who have served more than one full term. For about a quarter-century during her 37-year marriage, Capps worked as a nurse or nursing educator, in hospitals and public schools, and for about 10 years, she taught college-level courses in early childhood development. After a car accident kept her husband away from the campaign trail for several months in 1996, she took to the hustings herself to speak in his behalf. After his term began she often traveled with him to speak with his constituents and served as an unofficial adviser to him in the nation's capital. Her taste of a legislator's life and her determination to carry on her husband's work led her to enter the political arena after his

Nancy Ostertag/Getty Images

death. Todd S. Purdom, who followed her during her first bid for public office, wrote for the New York Times (March 7, 1998), "Mrs. Capps, with a nurse's empathetic bedside manner, campaigns with an ease that belies her lack of experience."

Eight months after she won the special election, Capps was elected to her first full term in the House, as the representative from California's 22d Congressional District. She has been reelected five times and has not faced serious opposition since 2000, when she captured 53 percent of the votes cast. Her winning percentages in 2002, 2004, 2006, and 2008 were 59.1, 63.1, 65.2, and 71, respectively. Since 2005, as a result of California's state-mandated redistricting based on data gathered in the 2000 U.S. census, Capps has represented the 23d Congressional District, an extremely narrow, 200-mile-long area that encompasses the Pacific coastal areas of San Luis Obispo, Santa Barbara, and Ventura Counties and has often been cited as a glaring example of gerrymandering.

Capps's specialties in Congress include public-health and nursing issues. "A classic California liberal," as Purdom described her, she has introduced legislation to address the nationwide nursing shortage and to improve services for treating mental-health problems and handling cases of domestic abuse; has championed the expansion of Medicare coverage; has condemned cigarette advertising that is specifically designed to attract girls and women; has voted in favor of embryonic-stem-cell research and against the ban on so-called partial-birth abortion; and co-founded and co-chairs the House Nursing Caucus. She has led efforts to fight oil drilling in California and in the state's coastal waters and has tried to eliminate hunting and the imposition of visitor fees in protected areas of the state. She opposed the legislation that permitted the use of military force in Iraq in 2003, and she supported a 2007 bill (which failed to become law) that would have required President George W. Bush to set deadlines for the withdrawal of American troops from Iraq. Other legislation for which she voted "no" called for a permanent cut in the estate tax and the building of a fence along the U.S.–Mexico border. In addition, she opposed legislation granting to U.S. spy agencies greater power to eavesdrop on foreign suspects without court orders and a bill that proposed a constitutional amendment banning same-sex marriage. In the current, 110th Congress, Capps missed only 1.2 percent of votes, and she voted with the majority of Democratic representatives more than 97 percent of the time. In that Congress she was a member of the House Committee on Energy and Commerce and three of its subcommittees (Telecommunications and the Internet; Health; and Environment and Hazardous Materials) and the Natural Resources Committee and two of its subcommittees (Fisheries, Wildlife and Oceans; and National Parks, Forests and Public Lands).

In remarks made at a meeting of the Santa Barbara Clergy Association, as posted on the group's Web site (April 9, 2007), Capps said, "In all the work I do in Congress, I continue to feel the power of the words my husband, Walter, used when he ran for Congress, words that encapsulate, for me, my faith and my politics: 'We are best as people

when we work for the common good, when we exercise regard for those who are least among us. We are strongest as a people when we are directed by that which unites us rather than giving [in to] the fears, suspicions, innuendoes and paranoias that divide us.'" In the same speech Capps listed her priorities as a citizen, person of faith, and member of Congress: caring for the poor, being a good steward of the environment, halting what she described as the "unjust" war in Iraq, "welcoming the stranger"—that is, immigrants to the United States—and "living humbly in God's grace."

The congresswoman was born Lois Ragnhild Grimsrud on January 10, 1938 in Ladysmith, Wisconsin, to Jurgen Milton Grimsrud and the former Solveig Magdalene Gullixson. She grew up in Wyoming and Montana, in towns in which her father worked as a Lutheran minister. She received a B.S. degree in nursing, with honors, from Pacific Lutheran University, in Tacoma, Washington, in 1959, and then taught at the Legacy Emanuel Hospital School of Nursing, in Portland, Oregon. In 1960 she moved to New Haven, Connecticut, where for the next three years, she held nursing positions, among them head nurse, at the Yale/New Haven Hospital. Shen then served for one year as a visiting nurse in nearby Hamden. Also in 1960 she married Walter Holden Capps, who was then pursuing a master's degree in theology at the Yale Divinity School. In 1964 she herself earned an M.A. degree in religion from Yale. That year her husband joined the faculty of the University of California at Santa Barbara (UC–Santa Barbara) as a professor of religious studies. For about 23 years between 1968 and 1998, while raising a son and two daughters, Lois Capps worked as a school nurse for districts in Santa Barbara and its surrounding communities. In 1985–86 she directed a teenage-pregnancy and -parenting project in Santa Barbara, and she later directed Santa Barbara's Parent and Child Enrichment Center. In 1990 she earned a second master's degree, in education, from UC–Santa Barbara. For about 10 years starting that year, she taught early childhood education at Santa Barbara City College.

Capps was powerfully influenced by the beliefs of her husband, in particular his convictions regarding ethical behavior. In public forums in the 1960s Walter Capps had vigorously opposed the war in Vietnam. A course that he introduced at UC–Santa Barbara in 1978, called "Religion and the Impact of Vietnam," became enormously popular on that campus—it "regularly drew 900 undergraduate students," as reported in a biography of him on the Web site of the Walter H. Capps Center for the Study of Ethics, Religion, and Public Life, which was set up at the university in 2002 "to honor and further [Capps's] legacy." In addition, the course was transmitted to television stations nationwide via satellite. "For many Vietnam veterans this course provided a first opportunity to tell their stories," according to the Capps Center biography. Walter Capps was also active at the Center for the

Study of Democratic Institutions, a Santa Barbara think tank, and worked to establish help centers for Vietnam veterans throughout the U.S. He was well known as a humanist and outspoken liberal when, in 1994, he tried to win the seat for California's 22d Congressional District (which encompassed all of San Luis Obispo County and most of Santa Barbara County) in the U.S. House of Representatives. He lost by a slim margin to Andrea Seastrand, an extremely conservative Republican state assemblywoman, who benefited from the Republicans' huge gains in that year's elections, when the GOP won control of both the House and the Senate for the first time in four decades. Walter Capps ran for the same seat again in 1996, and although he was unable to campaign during the late spring and the entire summer, because of injuries sustained when his car was struck by a vehicle whose driver was drunk, he defeated Seastrand that November, becoming the first Democrat to win that congressional seat since World War II. He served in Congress from January 3 until October 28, 1997, when he suffered a fatal heart attack.

One month later Lois Capps, then 59, announced that she would attempt to serve out the remainder of her husband's term. She already had some experience in politics, having stumped for her husband during his convalescence after his automobile accident and traveled with him after his election "to see first-hand the needs of the people he represented," as she told a reporter for the Alternative Press (November 17, 1997, on-line). To assist her in her campaign, she put together a staff of people who had become fiercely loyal to her husband while working on his 1996 campaign and who wanted his principles, ideas, and goals to survive him. The special primary election held in January 1998 to fill Walter Capps's vacated seat was a so-called open primary, in which all registered voters could cast their ballots for a candidate affiliated with any party. With less than 43 percent of registered voters going to the polls, Lois Capps, the only Democrat among the six hopefuls, won 45 percent of the vote; although she finished in first place, she had not secured a majority of the votes, making a runoff election necessary. Her opponent in the runoff, held on March 10, 1998, was Tom Bordonaro Jr., the top vote-getter among the three Republicans in the primary. The runoff was the only major American election scheduled for that month, and it attracted the energetic participation in the nominees' campaigns of an unusually large number of organizations. Among them were the National Rifle Association (which opposes virtually all efforts to limit gun ownership) and the Campaign for Working Families (whose primary goal is the rescinding of all legislation that permits abortions); both of those groups supported Bordonaro. Those supporting Capps included the National Abortion Rights Action League (now known as NARAL Pro-Choice America) and the AFL-CIO, a major labor union. On the day of the special election, Capps emerged victorious, with 54 percent of the vote.

Capps faced Bordonaro at the polls again eight months later, in the regularly scheduled congressional election. By that time, as a writer for Human Events (October 16, 1998) pointed out, she was "less the widow than the lawmaker with a record"; she had voted on the floor of Congress against a bill requiring that any tax increases win the approval of two-thirds of the House and had also voted for Republican-sponsored legislation that called for $80 billion in tax cuts. Thanks in part to carefully crafted ads that linked Bordonaro with the Speaker of the House, Republican congressman Newt Gingrich of Georgia, whose approval ratings had been plummeting, Capps won the general election, with 55 percent of the vote.

During her first full term in Congress, Capps introduced a bill to make the Carrizo Plain Natural Area, in San Luis Obispo County, a designated national conservation area; passed by the House, the bill has never become law. Along with Representative Carolyn Murphy of New York State, she co-sponsored the reintroduction of the Patient Safety Act, which aims to ensure high-quality nursing care in hospitals and to protect from retaliation registered nurses who bring concerns about patient care to public attention. As the end of a suspension of offshore oil drilling drew near, she joined other legislators in discussing with Interior Secretary Bruce Babbitt the possibility of a federal buy-back of offshore oil-drilling leases. In 2003 the federal government reached an agreement with leaseholders whereby it could someday buy back the leases. Capps also pushed for ending the federal Adventure Pass program, according to which visitors to national forests and other public lands must pay fees. Her efforts in that regard failed, and in 2004 Congress voted to extend the program for 10 years. "We already pay taxes to support these public lands and we shouldn't have to pay another to get access to our own lands," Capps told Zeke Barlow for the Ventura County Star (November 23, 2004, on-line).

In October 2000 the Youth Drug and Mental Health Services Act and the Youth Drinking Elimination Act, which Capps had introduced, were signed into law, as part of the Children's Health Act. The following month, despite her loss of the endorsement of the Teamsters union because she favored the expansion of trade relations with China, she won reelection with 53 percent of the vote, with her Republican opponent, former Santa Barbara County supervisor Mike Stoker, earning only 44 percent. In 2001 she and others introduced the Nurse Reinvestment Act (signed into law in 2002), which authorizes the provision of scholarships and other educational opportunities to nursing students and fosters partnerships between nursing schools and nurse training centers.

In 2001 Capps became the target of criticism from newspaper columnists, government-spending watchdog groups, and the conservative radio-show host Rush Limbaugh when she obtained $50,000 from the federal government for a program that enabled Santa Barbara gang members to have tattoos removed. (Research has shown that the presence of visible tattoos correlates with violent behavior and decreases individuals' chances of getting jobs.) As quoted by Kelly Beaucar Vlahos on foxnews.com (January 11, 2002), David Williams, the vice president of Citizens Against Government Waste, complained, "Why should someone in Arizona or Wisconsin have to pay for this program? That's our biggest beef with this pork. Let the local government or county pay for it." Capps dismissed such criticism, telling Vlahos, "Responding to the needs of my constituents is my top priority and I'm proud to work with law enforcement and health care officials when they request my help."

In 2002 Capps was among 117 House members who voted against the transport of radioactive waste through Santa Barbara and Ventura Counties for burial at a site in Nevada. "There are too many unanswered questions, on security and safety, for my constituents and for people across the country. Pure and simple, it's an accident waiting to happen," she told Jenifer Ragland for the *New York Times* (May 9, 2002). Capps supported measures to increase funding for cancer research and stroke prevention and joined a bipartisan initiative to craft a bill allowing for funds from Medicaid to be used to help victims of domestic violence. She was also successful in pushing for the passage of an amendment that effectively barred new oil drilling in the waters off her district's coast. In an action that surprised some political observers, she joined 27 other House Democrats in voting for President George W. Bush's $1.35 trillion tax cuts.

In 2003 Capps announced that—contrary to earlier statements in which she had promised to limit her congressional service to three terms—she would seek reelection again. "I see things a little differently now," she explained, as quoted by David Hawkings and Brian Nutting in *Congressional Quarterly's Politics in America 2004*. The next year she proposed legislation to ban drilling for oil or gas in the Los Padres National Forest. "[The Bush] administration is preparing to open up miles and miles of the Los Padres to new oil and gas development," she told Julie Cart for the *Los Angeles Times* (February 19, 2004). "I think it's time they hear from us directly that we do not want new oil and gas drilling on the Central Coast: Not off our shores and not in our forests." Nevertheless, the U.S. Forest Service approved the plan in 2005. After one of the oil pipes burst, in 2007, Capps issued a press release in which she noted that the spill "confirms what I have been saying for years: drilling for oil is a dirty business."

In 2006 Capps butted heads with Congressman Duncan Hunter, a California Republican, over his proposal—inserted into a House defense bill—to turn Santa Rosa Island, part of the Channel Islands National Park, into a resort where, for several months annually, members of the military, military veterans, and their guests could hunt deer and elk. "The inclusion of this ridiculous proposal in the Defense bill is a travesty," Capps said to Stacey Weible for the *VC Reporter* (October 5, 2006, online), an alternative Ventura County news source. "Kicking the public off a National Park it paid more than $30 million for to continue indefinitely a lucrative private hunting operation is clear violation of the public trust. I will be introducing legislation to reverse this terrible provision." In 2007 U.S. senator Dianne Feinstein of California inserted into the Fiscal Year 2008 Omnibus Spending Bill the portion of Capps's legislation that was designed to make Hunter's proposal inoperative. That goal was accomplished with the House's passage of the omnibus spending bill.

In August 2007 Capps inserted into the State Children's Health and Medicare Protection Act a measure to expand Medicare coverage for children in Santa Barbara County. Both the House and the Senate passed that legislation, which included a provision to expand the State Children's Health Insurance Program (known informally as S-chip), but they failed to override President Bush's veto of it. Also in 2007 Capps began a crusade against the R. J. Reynolds Tobacco Co., the manufacturer of Camel No. 9 cigarettes, and women's magazines that accepted ads for that product. In an opinion piece for the *Washington Post* (October 12, 2007), she wrote, "There's a disturbing hot item being pushed this fall by a number of leading women's fashion magazines. As a mother, grandmother and former school nurse, I'm sorry to say that this 'must-have' is Camel No. 9 cigarettes, cynically brought to our girls and young women by the folks at R.J. Reynolds, the tobacco company that thought cartoon character Joe Camel was a responsible product spokesman." She continued, "While we have come to expect this kind of sleazy marketing from tobacco companies, a big disappointment is that they've found an ally in women's fashion magazines. That's right, America's most popular magazines for women, which set trends for the country and have historically served as respected sources for articles on women's health and fitness, have sold out the well-being of their readers to help Big Tobacco in its search for new victims." Capps and other members of Congress wrote letters to many women's magazines urging them not to accept such ads. In November R. J. Reynolds announced that the company would cease its print advertising in 2008.

In October 2008 Capps voted in favor of an expanded version of the Emergency Economic Stabilization Act, a "bailout package" aimed at curbing the growing financial crisis in the U.S. The bill, which was passed that month and signed into law by President Bush, generated controversy because it authorized the government to use taxpayer money to purchase bad debts from financial firms. With several other congresswomen, Capps was a co-author of the Breast Cancer and Environmental Research Act, which calls for the allocation of funds for federal research into connections between the environment and breast cancer. That act also became law in October 2008.

On other fronts, Capps has co-sponsored legislation that aims to make renewable resources—among them wind and solar power, wood and waste from products manufactured from wood, ethanol, and biomass energy, which is derived from municipal and industrial waste—the source of 20 percent of the nation's energy. She has also co-sponsored a bill that would require by 2016 that vehicles made in the United States get at least 33 miles per gallon. In the matter of immigration reform, she has advocated legislation that would establish a "humane guest worker program," as she described it in an article for the *Ventura County Star* (May 2, 2006) entitled "Immigration Reform Must Be Comprehensive and Compassionate." Capps summarized her positions on immigration, the environment, and several other pressing issues in her talk to the Santa Barbara Clergy Association in April 2007. She was reelected in November 2008, beating her Republican opponent, Matt Kokkonen, a financial planner, with 71 percent of the vote.

Writing for thehill.com (May 2, 2006), Charles Case described Capps as "a brisk, elegant woman . . . who is naturally polite and inquiring." Her house in Santa Barbara, a remodeled 1906 horse barn, has solar panels and other "green" features. In her community she is active in the organization Veterans for Peace. In 2002 the magazine *Washingtonian* named her the nicest member of Congress.

Capps's daughter Lisa was a psychologist who specialized in autism, taught at the University of California at Berkeley, and co-wrote three books; she died of lung cancer at the age of 35 in 2000. Lois Capps remains close to Lisa's two young sons as well as their father and his second wife. Capps's other daughter, Laura Capps, is the communications director for U.S. senator Edward M. Kennedy of Massachusetts; in 2007 she married Bill Burton, the national press secretary for U.S. senator Barack Obama of Illinois, who remained in that position during Obama's successful run for the presidency in 2008. Lois Capps's son, Todd Holden Capps, is a composer who has written scores for television and film. He is the father of Capps's third grandson.

—W.D.

Suggested Reading: *Congressional Quarterly Weekly Report* p687 Mar. 14 1998; Lois Capps's Web site; *Los Angeles Times* A p1 Jan. 27, 1998, B p1 Feb.19, 2004; *New York Times* A p6 Mar. 7, 1998; nurseweek.com July 17, 2000; Santa Barbara Clergy Association Web site Apr. 9, 2007; thehill.com May 2, 2006; *VCReporter* (online) Oct. 5, 2006; *Biographical Dictionary of Congressional Women*, 1999; *Congressional Quarterly's Politics in America 2004; Who's Who in America 2007*

Carlos, Wendy

Nov. 14, 1939– Composer

Address: c/o East Side Digital, P.O. Box 7367, Minneapolis, MN 55407

The first classical album whose sales topped one million copies was devoted to music by Johann Sebastian Bach, but no traditional orchestral instruments—violins, cellos, violas, clarinets, oboes, bassoons, flutes, trumpets, tubas, horns, drums, pianos—were used to make it. A long-playing vinyl phonograph record called *Switched-On Bach*, it won the Grammy Award for best classical album of 1968. It also earned two Grammy Awards for its engineer and performing artist, Wendy Carlos (then known as Walter Carlos), who, in collaboration with the producer Rachel Elkind, created it entirely with a revolutionary new electronic musical instrument, the Moog synthesizer. "There are two things that were complementary in *Switched-On Bach*," Robert Moog, its inventor, told Pascal Wyse for the London *Guardian* (February 11, 2005). "One is the use of the synthesizer to make all these neat sounds, and the other is the consummate musical skill that Carlos had in using a tape recorder and a mixer to lay down one track at a time and then combine them. We take it for granted, but

Vernon L. Smith, courtesy of Wendy Carlos

back then very few people knew how to do it so it came out sounding right—and it was a big mystery. Conventional wisdom said you couldn't really do it." *Switched-On Bach* "sent the message to everybody that a synthesizer is a musical instrument," Frank J. Oteri, the composer advocate at the American Music Center, noted for *New Music Box* (April 2007, on-line). "And it helped make the synthesizer mainstream, rather than just some thing in a laboratory that professors were doodling around with to make . . . weird, electronic pieces."

Carlos's *Switched-On Brandenburgs*, Volumes 1 and 2, and *The Well-Tempered Synthesizer*, all released in 1969, were also created with the Moog machine. The Canadian piano virtuoso Glenn Gould, whose interpretations of the music of Bach are still ranked among the world's finest, famously said, as quoted on various Web sites, that "Carlos's realization of the Fourth Brandenburg Concerto is, to put it bluntly, the finest performance of any of the Brandenburgs—live, canned, or intuited—I've ever heard." With the score that Carlos wrote for Stanley Kubrick's motion picture *A Clockwork Orange* (1971), synthesized music reached Main Street, U.S.A., and a new era in the production of film music was ushered in. Carlos later wrote some of the music used in Kubrick's film *The Shining* (1980) and the soundtrack for the animated movie *Tron* (1982).

Carlos's innovative compositions for the album *Sonic Seasonings* (1972) introduced the genre known as ambient music—works designed to require of the listener less than full concentration while offering more than amorphous atmospheric sounds. Carlos was also a pioneer in the use of digital synthesis in music composition; her album *Digital Moonscapes* (1984) was written for a "replica" orchestra, after she compiled a "library" of about 500 tones, having programmed "several hundred details . . . for each note of each instrument with various dynamic levels and performing methods," as she wrote for her Web site.

In an interview with James R. Oestreich for the *New York Times* (April 2, 1997), Carlos explained why the first recording she and Elkind made contained not Carlos's own compositions but some of Bach's: "I came to [use the synthesizer] just trying to show people: 'I'm a composer, and I'm going to do things electronically. But you probably won't want to listen to that, so wait. Let me show you first that electronic music can sound like music.'" She added, "And boy, did I ever sign on the dotted line with Mephistopheles"—an acknowledgment that although the popularity of the *Switched-On* recordings brought financial rewards, it proved to be frustrating professionally. "To be candid, it was irritating to me," Carlos told Frank J. Oteri. "It felt like a detour, and it still does. . . . It represented so little of my strengths, and so much what I could only 'sort of do,' and I'm still a bit embarrassed by that, being considered a classical performer first." In an interview with Chris Twomey for *Exclaim* (December 1998/January 1999), Carlos said, "I'm a composer who does some performing."

"Don't be afraid to use things that other people have invented—to stand on the shoulders of giants," Carlos told Amy Duncan for the *Christian Science Monitor* (March 26, 1987). "Steal only the best from the past. The newness is in combining things in a way that they've never been combined before." *Secrets of Synthesis*, released in 1987, is an audio documentary, narrated by Carlos, about her synthesizer-generated music. From 1992 to 1995, working with the synthesizer expert and composer Larry Fast, Carlos invented DigiSurround Stereo Sound, a "digital process of soundtrack restoration," in her words. Using that process, for a dozen years beginning in the mid-1990s, she concentrated on digitally remastering *Switched-On* and others among her albums. Her discography also includes *By Request* (2003), which offers music by Bach, Tchaikovsky, Wagner, Burt Bacharach and Hal David, John Lennon and Paul McCartney, and Carlos herself. *Rediscovering Lost Scores*, Volumes 1 and 2 (2005), contain compositions that she wrote but that were not used in the films *The Shining*, *Tron*, and the widely panned *Woundings* (also called *Brand New World*, 1998).

In a lengthy interview with Arthur Bell for *Playboy* (May 1979)—the only one she has ever granted on the subject—Carlos discussed her decision to undergo gender-reassignment surgery earlier in the 1970s and the years-long, self-imposed isolation that followed, during which she turned down many requests for interviews and public appearances. *Switched-On Brandenburg* (1979) was the first album that she released under the name Wendy Carlos. Carlos's Web site contains accounts of the solar eclipses she has witnessed and photographed in far-flung parts of the world since 1963. Some of her eclipse photos have been published in *Sky and Telescope* and other astronomy publications.

The composer was born Walter Carlos to Clarence Carlos and his wife in Pawtucket, Rhode Island, on November 14, 1939. The family included Carlos's brother. Their father owned and managed a small textile factory started by his own father. As a very young child, Walter felt that he was meant to be a girl. "My awareness of it happens to be one of my first memories," Carlos told Bell. "I remember being *convinced* I was a little girl, much preferring long hair and girls' clothes, and not knowing why my parents didn't see it clearly. I didn't understand why they insisted on treating me like a little boy." Carlos had a difficult time at school, enduring much abuse at the hands of his classmates. Nevertheless, he excelled in every academic subject. He began studying piano at age six, and at 10 he wrote his first full-length composition, a trio for piano, clarinet, and accordion. With a tuning hammer and rubber wedges that his parents bought for him, he taught himself how to tune a piano, first to produce the usual, so-called equal-temperament, 12-tone octave, and later to produce nonstandard tunings. At home at age 14, Carlos built a computer that won a Westinghouse Science Fair prize. As a teenager he read *On the Sensations of Tone as a Physiological Basis for the Theory of Music*, by Hermann Helmholtz, and *Genesis of a Music* (1949), by Harry Partch. Partch, a 20th-century music theorist and composer, wrote dozens of works in an array of tonal systems for instruments of his own construction; Carlos recalled to Oteri having "tried building little instruments, a wannabe Harry Partch." As a teenager Carlos took several months of organ lessons. At 17 he composed an electronic music piece, consisting of manipulated tape-recorded tones.

After graduating from high school, Carlos attended Brown University, in Providence, Rhode Island, where he majored in both music and physics. He earned a B.A. degree in 1962, then moved to New York City to pursue a graduate degree at the Columbia–Princeton Electronic Music Center, at Columbia University (renamed the Columbia University Computer Music Center in 1994), the first facility of its kind in the U.S. "I was entranced by the new tools, and could see that this was a ripe new method of making musical sounds, no more nor less," Carlos recalled for wendycarlos.com. Carlos studied under such electronic-music pioneers as Otto Luening and Vladimir Ussachevsky, who together had founded the center in 1958, but he was unmoved by the type of music being produced at Columbia. "I thought what ought to be done was obvious, to use the new technology for appealing music you could really listen to," Carlos said in an interview with Carol Wright for *New Age Voice* (November 1999, on-line). "Why wasn't it being used for anything but the academy-approved 'ugly' music? You know, the more avant-garde than thou-ers, atonal or formally tedious twelve-tone strait-jacket." Carlos's graduate-school compositions included *Dialogues for Piano and Two Loudspeakers* (1963), *Variations for Flute and Electronic Sounds* (1964), *Episodes for Piano and Tape* (1964), and *Pomposities for Narrator and Tape* (1965). Carlos earned a master's degree in music composition in 1965.

The year before, while still at Columbia, Carlos had met Robert Moog at an Audio Engineering Society convention in New York City. "It didn't take long to establish a budding friendship," Carlos wrote in an appreciation of Moog posted on wendycarlos.com (2005), shortly after Moog's death. "It was a perfect fit: he was a creative engineer who spoke music; I was a musician who spoke science. It felt like a meeting of simpatico minds, like he were my older brother, perhaps." As one of Moog's first customers, Carlos worked with him to improve Moog's newly invented synthesizer, "zeroing in on what would permit genuinely 'musical' electronic music to be made," as she wrote for her Web site. ("Artist feedback drove all my development work . . . ," Moog told Frank Houston for *Salon.com* [April 25, 2000]. "I'm a toolmaker. I design things that other people want to use.") Housed in a beautiful wooden cabinet that greatly pleased Carlos aesthetically, the first Moog synthesizer was very large and cost $11,000 (equivalent to about $70,000 in 2008). "To work it most effectively, one had to be a conductor, performer, composer, acoustician, and instrument builder. Carlos was all of those," Arthur Bell wrote.

Carlos and Moog continued to collaborate while Carlos supported himself as a recording engineer and composer of sound effects and music for commercials. During that period Carlos met Rachel Elkind (now Elkind-Tourre) at a New York recording studio; a singer of jazz and show music, Elkind had earlier worked as a secretary to Goddard Lieberson, then the president of Columbia Records. Elkind became Carlos's best friend and "silent partner," as Carlos has labeled her—she chose to remain in the background, according to Carlos—and Carlos has credited Elkind with much of her success. For a decade, beginning in about 1970, the two lived together (platonically) in the brownstone that Elkind and her mother owned on Manhattan's West Side, and they worked together there as well, in the elaborate recording studio that they assembled on one floor. Elkind "brought an important quality of spontaneity to my music, and helped me to shed some of the stuffier conceits one can acquire from formal music studies," Carlos wrote for her Web site.

Meanwhile, serendipitously, at around the time that Carlos had become skilled at manipulating Moog's synthesizer (thanks to Carlos's input, the device had improved significantly), Columbia Records expressed to Elkind the company's interest in marketing an electronic version of music by Bach. "We wanted to show that the synthesizer was capable of being a real musical instrument," Carlos told Robert Siegel for the National Public Radio program *All Things Considered* (August 22, 2005, on-line). "And what better way than to find a kind of music that was familiar, unthreatening, like Bach's music?" The recording of the 10 selections that constitute *Switched-On Bach* was extraordinarily labor-intensive, because the Moog synthesizer produced only one note at a time; moreover, as Carlos recalled to Carol Wright, it "was very unstable and would go out of tune constantly." "If the tonal quality didn't change much over the phrase, you could get down a measure or two. . . . You would play a phrase, back up, and check. Retune and continue. To create a chord, you'd play the second line, then the third. With counterpoint, you'd play the melodies that wove together. Eventually, we got all the parts to make the piece." "The result was, by any standards, remarkable," according to a writer for the BBC Web site h2g2 (August 21, 2006). "Gone was the weedy voice of the harpsichord shouting to make itself heard over the string section. From the scintillating *Sinfonia to Cantata #29*, through the noble and religious *Jesu, Joy of Man's Desiring*, . . . to the joyfully exuberant third movement of the *Brandenburg #3*, it was plain that Bach's music had found not just a fresh new voice but also a uniquely clear one. Every single note was audible, and Carlos' interpretations captured the spirit of each piece perfectly, alternating between bright and dark but always lyrical." Although many music critics frowned upon that approach to Bach, which they felt trivialized his work, the public responded enthusiastically. Remarkably for an album of classical music, *Switched-On Bach* went platinum and earned three Grammy Awards (and Moog suddenly found himself inundated by orders for synthesizers).

The year 1969 saw the release of three additional *Switched-On* albums, the last of which—*The Well-Tempered Synthesizer* (a play on the title of Bach's *Well-Tempered Clavier*)—included Carlos and Elkind's interpretations of music by Monteverdi, Scarlatti, and Handel as well as Bach.

At the beginning of the 1970s, Carlos and Elkind, experimenting with a vocoder—an electronic device that synthesizes speech—produced a synthesized version of part of the fourth movement of Beethoven's Ninth Symphony, which incorporates voices. When some of their friends reacted negatively to their interpretation, Elkind suggested that Carlos "write a piece of music that introduced the vocoder gently, slowly, until it became really clear that you were hearing that synthesizer singing!," as Carlos recalled to Chris Twomey. "And then you could listen to the Beethoven and not flinch." While composing what was to become *Timesteps*, Carlos received from a friend a copy of Anthony Burgess's novel *A Clockwork Orange*; soon after reading it, Carlos learned that Stanley Kubrick was making a movie of the book. On the strength of *Timesteps* and Carlos's adaptations of Beethoven's Ninth—a work dear to the heart of *Clockwork*'s sociopathic antihero—Kubrick hired Carlos and Elkind to write some of the music for the film. The pair's contributions to the soundtrack, which included excerpts from *Timesteps* and other Carlos pieces as well as orchestral selections chosen by Kubrick, impressed most critics. "As sheer music," Don Heckman wrote for the *New York Times* (August 27, 1972), "it is a giant step past the banalities of most contemporary film tracks." The soundtrack album (1972) reached 34th place on *Billboard*'s pop-albums chart. Carlos's remastered soundtrack CD, released in 1998, contains *Timesteps* in full, along with compositions by Carlos that Kubrick did not use and synthesized versions of the orchestral pieces from the original soundtrack. Carlos's "Clockwork Black," a track on her album *Tales of Heaven and Hell* (1998), "reexamines" what she wrote for Kubrick's film, as she put it. By then Carlos had abandoned the Moog synthesizer in favor of two synthesizers invented by Raymond Kurzweil.

Carlos's passion for eclipses and her desire to photograph them have carried her to exotic locations. In some, such as Tibet and Bali, she was exposed to alternate musical tunings and scales. Their influences, and the availability of the newly invented digital synthesizer, inspired her to compose works that are included on her album *Beauty in the Beast* (1986). "At last it's possible to get all of the range of dissonance or consonance under your finger tips," Carlos told Amy Duncan. "You can use ethnic scales which have no relation to Western music . . . and graft them onto our own current vocabulary. This is unheralded in music history." "In the closing 'A Woman's Song,'" Allan Kozinn wrote in a review of *Beauty in the Beast* for the *New York Times* (May 31, 1987), "Ms. Carlos brings together a Bulgarian folk tune, an Indian tambura drone, and a handful of purely electronic sounds (spacy, tingling and heavily phase-shifted) to create a thoroughly cross-cultural piece." For her next album, *Secrets of Synthesis* (1987), Carlos spoke about her experiences with electronic music and offered audio samples. The making of *Secrets of Synthesis*, she wrote for her Web site, "had evolved into an ideal project to complete my long contract with CBS/Sony, a fitting summary of what had been learned in the process."

Carlos joined with the comic/musician "Weird Al" Yankovic to record parodies of Sergei Prokofiev's *Peter and the Wolf* and Camille Saint-Saens's *Carnival of the Animals—Part Two*. Their album went on sale in 1988. "We all need a vacation now and then . . . ," Carlos wrote for her Web site. "For me the project was a chance for some musical fun and tomfoolery, working with a bright, witty collaborator, before getting back to more adventurous tuning and timbre projects." Drawing on the originals, Carlos composed music to accompany Yankovic's lighthearted poems.

In 2001 Carlos purchased a newer Kurzweil machine, the K2600S, a 76-key so-called sampling workstation. "The first month I couldn't get enough of the convincing 'triple strike' piano sound, and began practicing long hours again, as I used to," Carlos recalled for her Web site. "It was great to get back at making music, the skills of moving fingers precisely and expressively. The chore of remastering all my older albums had dragged me away from that. I'm not a great performer, as I've often said, but I do sight read well, and enjoy improvising new things as well as hacking away at the classical repertoire." The remastered albums bear the label East Side Digital.

In 2005 Carlos earned the SEAMUS (Society of Electro Acoustic Music in the United States) Lifetime Achievement Award. She lives in a loft in New York City with her dog and two cats.

—J.E.P.

Suggested Reading: *Christian Science Monitor* p23 Mar. 26, 1987; (London) *Guardian* p8 Feb. 11, 2005; *New Age Voice* (on-line) Nov. 1999; *New Music Box* (on-line) Apr. 2007; *Perfect Sound Forever* (on-line) May 2007; *Playboy* p75+ May 1979; Wendy Carlos Web site

Selected Recordings: *Switched-On Bach*, 1968; *Switched-On Brandenburgs, Volumes 1 and 2*, 1969; *The Well-Tempered Synthesizer*, 1969; *A*

Clockwork Orange, 1972; *Sonic Seasonings*, 1972; *The Shining*, 1980; *Tron*, 1982; *Digital Moonscapes*, 1984; *Beauty in the Beast*, 1986; *Secrets of Synthesis*, 1987; *Tales of Heaven and Hell*, 1998; *Peter and the Wolf and The Carnival of the Animals—Part Two*, 1988; *By Request*, 2003; *Rediscovering Lost Scores*, Volumes 1 and 2, 2005

Robert Wright, courtesy of HarperCollins

Carroll, E. Jean

Dec. 12, 1943– Journalist; advice columnist

Address: AskEJean.com, P.O. Box 70, Warwick, NY 10990

"The once gentle, helpful American advice column has grown fangs," William Grimes wrote for the *New York Times* (March 30, 1997). "Readers who write in these days are likely to get a faceful of attitude along with their answers, if the answers ever arrive in the course of the winding narratives. In dozens of alternative weeklies and mass-market monthly magazines, the advice column has waved farewell to Dear Abby and Ann Landers, and in the process it has become something else: one of the most vital, unpredictable literary forms going, built around a vivid and decidedly cynical personality." One of the personalities Grimes cited was that of E. Jean Carroll. As the author of the column "Ask E. Jean," published in the popular women's magazine *Elle* since 1994, Carroll offers blunt, no-nonsense advice on a number of topics, many pertaining to love and relationships. A consistent theme in her messages to readers has been the need

for women to take charge of—and enjoy—their lives. "A lot of times, people know the answer" they are seeking, Carroll told Cheryl Lavin for the *Chicago Tribune* (March 14, 1996). "They just need to hear someone else say it. You have to give them permission to do what they want to do." Indeed, the essence of much of her advice, as she explained to Joan Kelly Bernard for *Newsday* (March 22, 1994), is, "Do it! Just do it! No matter what the question is, many times that's all they want to hear." Since 2007 Carroll has written a column for the Web site DearSugar.com. Her books include collections of her columns as well as the biography *Hunter: The Strange and Savage Life of Hunter S. Thompson* (1993).

The writer was born Betty Jean Carroll on December 12, 1943 in Detroit, Michigan, to Tom and Betty (McKinney) Carroll. She grew up with her three younger siblings outside Hunterstown, Indiana, in what she described to *Current Biography* as "an 1855 schoolhouse." Her mother was a politician in Allen County, Indiana; her father, who originally wanted to name his first-born daughter Elizabeth, was an inventor who, Carroll stated in her interview with *Current Biography*, came up with the idea for sugarcoated cereal. She claimed in the same interview that the Kellogg's food company used her father's idea but that, as with his other innovations, he saw no money from it. (The family also owned a furniture store.) Carroll attended Indiana University (IU), where, she recalled, her main interests were becoming a beauty contestant and meeting male swimmers and basketball players; she was crowned Miss Indiana University in 1963 and Miss Cheerleader USA the next year. Because she knew that she would be young only once, her philosophy at the time, as she recalled to *Current Biography*, was, "You don't put your nose in a book at 19—you live!" She received an "F" in the only journalism course she attended, but not due to a lack of interest or effort on her part. As Carroll told *Current Biography*, she thought that writing "was a cool thing to do," but she became frustrated that her professor continued to teach traditional methods of journalism at a time when Tom Wolfe, Hunter S. Thompson, and others were pioneering New Journalism—a style that used such techniques of literary fiction as scenes, dialogue, and first-person points of view. After graduation, Carroll spent a year working as a market researcher for Procter & Gamble, a manufacturer of prescription drugs as well as personal-care and cleaning products. She told *Current Biography* that that experience served as her "school of journalism," because the job required her to go door-to-door and interview housewives and their families about the company's products. "We had great conversations," she told Joan Kelly Bernard. "I'd get into the female psyche. I learned to interview. Their whole lives would start spilling out."

After she had gotten married and moved to Montana, Carroll's journalism career began in 1979, when she successfully submitted to the men's magazine *Esquire* a quiz she had written on the literary giants Ernest Hemingway and F. Scott Fitzgerald. It was at that point that she decided to write as E. Jean Carroll, telling Cheryl Lavin that the "E" stands for "Elizabeth." She added, "When I sold my first piece to *Esquire*, I was so excited. It was the happiest day of my life. I always wanted to write. But I didn't think Jean Carroll was enough. I thought the E. in front of it looked fancy, and now I'm stuck with it." (Elsewhere, she has said that the initial does not stand for anything.) She continued to contribute to *Esquire*, where she later became a contributing editor, and freelanced for other magazines, including *Outside*, *Rolling Stone*, *New York*, and *Playboy*. Her articles have appeared in collections including *Out of the Noosphere: Adventure, Sports, Travel, and the Environment: The Best of Outside Magazine* (1992) and *Sand in My Bra and Other Misadventures: Funny Women Write from the Road* (2003). Carroll wrote for the NBC sketch-comedy show *Saturday Night Live* for a season (1986-87) and was nominated for an Emmy Award.

In 1994 Carroll's "Ask E. Jean" advice column debuted in the September issue of *Elle* magazine. The publication's newly appointed editorial director, Amy Gross, had been impressed with Carroll's articles in *Esquire* and decided to offer her the job. As Bernard wrote, "Gross was struck by Carroll's way of responding to whoever her subject was. It was unprogrammed, warmhearted, funny.'" Gross told Bernard that Carroll was "a wild woman beyond the inhibitions of normal constraints. I wanted to hear wild women. I didn't want to hear polite, middle-of-the-road anything." Carroll's blunt observations and no-nonsense advice reaches 4.5 million readers every month, and the writer, who often addresses her readers by such sobriquets as "honey," "sweetheart," or "silly poopface," has gained a large following. She has answered questions representing many subjects and various levels of seriousness, from dealing with a co-worker's body odor to suspecting one's wife of cheating to coping with AIDS. "I'm very strong in my life. Not to say I'm not riddled with flaws of every kind. But I can take on all these problems," Carroll told Bernard. Joyce Gottlieb, a New York City social worker who ran the West Side Mood Disorders Support Group, told Bernard about Carroll's column, "I like her on serious topics. She's very good, really on target." In the June 2008 issue of *Elle*, one reader asked whether she should be permitted to have an extramarital affair since her depressed and controlling husband had not been sexually intimate with her for five years. Carroll responded, "You are permitted to have an affair. But first you must tell your husband: 'Yo Sweetheart, my perpetual appeals for you to 'touch' me are tuckering me out. Therefore, I'm going to enjoy a little nook-nook with my trainer.' You may then proceed with the fling . . . or your husband might decide to see a physician, find out what is physically/mentally wrong with him, return home with a sack of Viagra, and embark on the exquisite hang-

ing and banging of an intimate marriage. Either way, life's too short to go without bliss!" As published in the May 2005 issue of *Elle*, another reader wrote, "Dear E. Jean: My boyfriend of one year is driving five hours to take his ex-girlfriend to 'their' restaurant for her birthday. It also happens to be our one-year anniversary. Should I be bothered?" Carroll replied, "You Delectable Dupe! Never allow a lad to drive anywhere with an ex-girlfriend. Never. Unless you're three times cuter, eight times smarter and four years younger than she—and then still keep an eye on him." The *Ask E. Jean* television show aired for two seasons on NBC's cable network America's Talking, starting in 1994. The show, based on the *Elle* column, featured Carroll advising callers. *Entertainment Weekly* (December 30, 1994) called Carroll the "most entertaining cable talk-show host on a channel you don't get or never watch." For a special installment in May 1995, Carroll filmed the surgery she underwent after finding a lump on her breast (which was later revealed to be benign). The show was canceled in 1996, when America's Talking became MSNBC. Since then, Carroll has doled out advice on a number of shows, including *Today*, *The O'Reilly Factor*, *American Morning*, and the enormously popular *Oprah*.

Carroll, having been married "the normal amount," in her words, counts her two ex-husbands as good friends. Her first marriage, to the writer and *National Geographic Adventure* deputy editor Stephen Byres, lasted 14 years. "It came to an end. It doesn't mean it failed," she explained to Lavin. "We had 14 great years. Then I wanted to do something else and so did he. I came to New York to do a story and didn't leave." Her second marriage, to John Johnson, a former New York television newscaster, lasted four years. "I'm just not meant to be married," she told *Current Biography*.

Carroll has written four books, including *Female Difficulties: Sorority Sisters, Rodeo Queens, Frigid Women, Smut Stars and Other Modern Girls* (1985); *Hunter: The Strange and Savage Life of Hunter S. Thompson* (1993); *A Dog in Heat Is a Hot Dog and Other Rules to Live By* (1996), a collection of her advice columns; and *Mr. Right, Right Now!: How a Smart Woman Can Land Her Dream Man in 6 Weeks* (2003). *Hunter*, a biography of the hard-living "gonzo" journalist Hunter S. Thompson, received much critical acclaim. Carroll—who herself was called "feminism's answer to Hunter Thompson" by David Quammen in the *New York Times* (November 1, 1981)—based much of the book on a 12-day stay at Thompson's Colorado ranch. Her 2002 article "The Cheerleaders" was featured in *Best American Crime Writing*, an annual collection. Written for *Spin* magazine, the article focused on a small, seemingly perfect upstate New York town dealing with a string of murders, suicides, and other tragic deaths.

In 2002 Carroll and her sister, Cande, a Web designer, founded GreatBoyfriends.com. The idea for the Web site, which allows women to recommend their ex-boyfriends, male friends, or brothers as potential romantic partners for other women, was conceived while Carroll was reading through letters she had received. "I'm reading a stack of 'Ask E. Jean' questions, and there's 'Help me find a man,' 'Help me find a man.' And then there's 'Help me find a man. I just broke up with this great guy because he's moving to California.' And I thought, 'What would happen if she could recommend this great guy to all the girls in California?'" she explained to Heather Salerno for the Westchester County, New York, *Journal News* (July 23, 2005). The site grew quickly, particularly after it was featured on a 2003 installment of *Oprah*. That same year, the duo launched GreatGirlfriends.com; the Knot Inc., which publishes materials dealing with various stages of romance and family life, acquired both sites in 2005. Carroll remains a consultant for GreatGirlfriends.com and is a media spokeswoman for GreatBoyfriends.com. Her sister managed the sites until early 2008. In 2003 Carroll started Catch27.com, which spoofed the popular social-networking site MySpace. Catch27 users were assigned monetary value based on their attractiveness, and members who wanted to be friends with other users would have to beg, trade, or pay (with their credit cards) for the privilege. The site ceased operating after a couple of years. In addition to running her own Web site, AskEJean.com; producing "Ask E. Jean" videos for YouTube.com; and writing her column for *Elle*, in 2007 Carroll signed on to write an advice column for DearSugar.com, a division of Sugar Publishing, which runs the popular celebrity gossip site PopSugar.com. As of October 2008 she was writing a sex manual for college students.

Carroll lives in a cabin in Warwick, New York, with her three dogs—a Great Pyrenees, a poodle, and a pit bull. When asked by Lavin whom she consulted for advice, Carroll responded, "The great philosophers: Plato, [Ralph Waldo] Emerson and, above all, [Henry David] Thoreau. Can't you hear him in my advice? 'Walk to the beat of a different drummer'? 'Simplify, simplify, simplify'? And the great novelists: [Leo] Tolstoy, [Charles] Dickens, Jane Austen. And I learn more from my dogs than anybody. No matter how much you screech at them, they always forgive you."

—M.A.S.

Suggested Reading: askejean.com; *Chicago Tribune* Tempo p1 Mar. 14, 1996; *New York Times* Style p1+ Nov. 24, 2002; *Newsday* B p13 Mar. 22, 1994; (Westchester County, New York) *Journal News* E p1 July 23, 2005

Selected Books: *Female Difficulties: Sorority Sisters, Rodeo Queens, Frigid Women, Smut Stars and Other Modern Girls*, 1985; *Hunter: The Strange and Savage Life of Hunter S. Thompson*, 1993; *A Dog in Heat Is a Hot Dog and Other Rules to Live By*, 1996; *Mr. Right, Right Now*, 2003

David Carson, courtesy of Ginko Press

Carson, David

Sep. 8, 1955– Graphic designer

Address: David Carson Design, 418 E. Ashley Ave., Folly Beach, SC 29439

David Carson, a former professional surfer and schoolteacher turned graphic designer, is considered the principal figure in distressed, layered typography, a movement in the design world responsible for breaking virtually every typesetting rule of thumb. Beginning his design career in obscure, specialist magazines such as *Transworld Skateboarding* and *Beach Culture* in the late 1980s, Carson rose to prominence as art director of the music magazine *Ray Gun* early in the following decade. Instead of adhering to the conventions of traditional magazine design, such as justified text and standardized column sizes, Carson used an intuitive approach that produced a semi-abstract, often unreadable style, which Patricia A. Riedman described for *Advertising Age* (August 1, 1993) as "the typographical equivalent of a flailing mosh pit at a Lollapalooza show." The hallmarks of Carson's style included omitting page numbers, deliberately running photos upside-down, overlapping blocks of copy, using dark texts against dark backgrounds, running text across two pages, mixing upper-case and lower-case letters with seeming randomness, and featuring stories that begin on the inside of a magazine and conclude on the front cover. "I had no idea how to get color to come out of a photograph or how to crop a picture," Carson recalled to Wevonneda Minis for the Charleston, South Carolina, *Post and Courier* (August 28, 2004), discussing the early stages of his career. "One of the reasons I've been so successful is that I've never learned all of the things that you are not supposed to do." Carson's work for *Ray Gun* perfectly captured the zeitgeist of the time (which saw the "grunge" era of rock music) and spawned countless imitators in advertising design, bringing him international fame and, as an independent designer, a client list that included companies ranging from Microsoft to Mercedes-Benz. He has also designed album covers for such musical acts as Nine Inch Nails, U2, and David Byrne.

While Carson's detractors have called his work unabashedly self-indulgent (he was once denounced by the Italian-American designer Massimo Vignelli as the "king of non-communication"), the majority of observers have noted the important impact of his work on the otherwise largely utilitarian and obscure world of graphic design. "I'd call Carson a popularizer," the designer and historian Steven Heller explained to Peter Plagens and Ray Sawhill for *Newsweek* (February 26, 1996). In 1995 Carson co-authored, with Lewis Blackwell, *The End of Print,* which has become the top-selling graphic-design book of all time, with purchases of more than 200,000 copies in five languages worldwide. He is also the author of *2nd Sight: Grafik Design After the End of Print* (1997), *Fotografiks* (1999), and *Trek* (2000). From 1989 to 2004 Carson won—by his count—more than 170 awards for his work in graphic design, including the Designer of the Year award from the International Center for Photography. Since 1995 Carson's main focus has been working as the chief designer of his own company, David Carson Design Inc. In 2004 he was named creative director of the Gibbes Museum of Art, in Charleston, South Carolina. He told Sam Whiting for the *San Francisco Chronicle* (March 5, 1996), "For some reason I have a visual intuition that allows me to design things in an interesting way, and I don't know where that came from. Because I don't have this formal training, I seem to drift in a different direction."

David Allen Carson was born on September 8, 1955 (one source says 1956) in Corpus Christi, Texas, and moved with his family to New York City four years later. His father was a test pilot for the U.S. Air Force, and his mother was a painter. Due to his father's peripatetic profession, Carson spent much of his youth traveling all over North America, Puerto Rico, and the West Indies. He was raised mostly in the affluent community of Palos Verdes, California, an area that featured ideal spots for surfing; he immersed himself in the surfing culture, a pursuit that would influence his free-spirited approach to the design process. In the late 1970s, while he attended San Diego State University, his talent at surfing enabled him to compete professionally, and at one point he ranked as high as eighth in the world. Infinity Surfboard, a popular surfboard manufacturer, sold a David Carson model that he designed. In 1977 Carson graduated from San Diego State with a degree in sociology. The following year he began teaching grades seven through 12 at Real Life Private School, in Grants Pass, Oregon. As a hobby he designed logos for his friends and the school; at the time he considered himself more of an artist than a graphic designer. In fact, Carson had never heard the term "graphic design" when, in 1980, he received a flyer in the mail announcing a two-week graphic-design workshop at the University of Arizona, in Tucson, intended for his high-school students. Intrigued, he decided to sign up for the course himself. Under the teacher and design luminary Jackson Boelts, whom he has called one of the first great influences on his work, Carson developed logos, inspired by signs on old Mexican storefronts and office buildings. Carson said to Tiffany Kjos for the *Arizona Daily Star* (February 23, 2003) about Boelts, "He was instrumental in me making a radical career change. I doubt if I'd have gotten into it had I had a different teacher."

Carson began to pay attention to signs and the ways that they communicated various messages. When he returned to California, he quit his teaching job and re-enrolled at San Diego State University to study commercial art. He left after only a month and then, at the urging of his grandmother, transferred to the Oregon College of Commercial Art, in Ashland. While there he started sending samples of his work to an art director who had been working for one of his friends at a magazine in San Clemente, California. During a phone conversation with Carson, the art director mused aloud about the possibility of replacing someone in the office; despite the fact that there was no opening on the staff, Carson immediately packed his bags, left school (after only a six-month stay), and moved to San Clemente, showing up at the office of the stunned art director, who subsequently hired him. The magazine, *Action Now,* issued by Surfer Publications, covered territory that Carson knew quite well: music, fashion, and board sports, including surfing. For the next six months, he gained experience by working on small accounts as an unpaid intern. After the magazine folded, he taught sociology three days a week at Torrey Pines High School in Del Mar, California; he held the position from 1982 to 1987.

In 1983 Carson attended a three-week graphic-design workshop in Rapperswil, Switzerland. The instructor was the Swiss graphic designer Hans-Rudolph Lutz, who became another mentor for Carson. Lutz inspired his students to use type to which they responded viscerally; Carson honed a style largely shaped by that intuitive approach. Upon returning to the U.S., he continued teaching and began working four days a week as a designer for the underground magazine *Transworld Skateboarding*. At that point he started experimenting with unusual typefaces and unconventional layouts. During his three and a half years at the magazine, he developed a signature style that gave birth to the so-called dirty grunge font. Carson recalled to Peter Plagens and Ray Sawhill that the magazine "had 200 pages every month, in full color, and no budget restrictions. I had an audience that wanted something experimental." He later moved to the East Coast, where he had a short-lived stint as an art director of a Massachusetts-based magazine, *Musician*. (His highly unusual style got him fired after only 17 issues.) Rejecting offers from Condé Nast and the *New Yorker*, Carson then decided to go to Nashville, Tennessee, to do design work for a country-music festival. In 1989 he returned to Los Angeles to become a designer for the surfer magazine *Beach Culture*.

Although that enterprise lasted for only six issues, from 1989 to 1991, it sparked a new generation of would-be designers. Carson became the leader of what critics called the "deconstructivist" trend in graphic design. Using unconventional fonts from the Émigré type foundry, created in the early 1980s by the designers Rudy VanderLans and Zuzana Licko and considered "the Home Depot of the post-modern graphics business," to quote Plagens and Sawhill, Carson purposely ran lines of font that collided on the page, used experimental photography and illustration, and abolished any sense of a standard, orderly page grid of the sort that kept layouts neat and polished, their graphics purposely innocuous, and their designers anonymous. Letters wandered across pages with a seeming randomness that belied Carson's careful planning. Rick Poyner wrote in his book *Typography Now: the Next Wave*, "*Beach Culture* rapidly became both cause celebre and designer's *bete noire* for the deconstructive frenzy with which Carson dismantled the typography of contents pages, headlines, and text," as quoted by Riedman. According to Carson, the six issues garnered 160 awards for type photography, editorial design, and illustration. After the demise of *Beach Culture*, he brought his singular methods to *Surfer* magazine, where he served as a designer and art director from 1991 to 1992. In one instance, while preparing a layout for *Surfer*, Carson accidentally cut his finger with an X-Acto knife and was so taken with the drops of blood that fell on the layout that he left them in the final design. Joni Casimiro, his successor at *Surfer*, told Plagens and Sawhill, "His work reflects his work habits—disarray."

In November 1992 Carson and Marvin Scott Jarrett founded the Santa Monica, California–based alternative-music magazine *Ray Gun*, which deemed itself "the bible of music & style." With a circulation of 150,000, the 80-page monthly introduced Carson's radical methods to an international readership. Serving as the art director for 30 issues from 1992 to 1995, Carson threw out every conventional notion of typesetting. Pushing his previous innovations even further, he distorted text and pictures, designed overlapping blocks of copy, and stretched fonts to the point at which many articles were unreadable. *Ray Gun* was the first magazine to banish page numbers, offer a table of contents with nothing to indicate articles' locations, and run stories from back to front or bottom to top. The magazine also worked with an ever-changing palette of typefaces, introducing new ones with every issue. Carson's declared aim was not to confuse readers but to enhance memory retention. "The intent is never to make something illegible," Carson explained to Patricia Riedman. "The starting point is always to solve a particular problem that an article demands, and in doing that some things become a little more difficult to read, or require the reader to be less passive. Those pages aren't meant to be read literally." In 1993 *I.D.* magazine honored Carson for his pioneering design work, naming him one of the "*I.D.* Forty" in its first annual selection of leading design innovators.

Among many examples of Carson's experimental work with *Ray Gun*, in a story titled "Gutter," about the Australian band Midnight Oil, the word "gutter" is bisected horizontally and spread over two pages, while the letters spelling the band's name appear out of sequence. A piece on the sketch-comedy troupe Kids in the Hall ran without parentheses, dashes, or accents and with a mystifying spacing of letters; a cover ostensibly focusing on the group Beastie Boys was left blank except for two inches at the top; another cover ran upside-down; and a story on the group Pavement began on the inside of the magazine and ended on the front cover. Jim Davies, writing for *Campaign* (December 1, 1995), called *Ray Gun* "a triumph of Carson over content." Carson was criticized for self-indulgence, a quality he has called essential for fostering creativity. He told Terry Jamieson for the Glasgow, Scotland, *Herald* (November 10, 1997), "I don't see it as a negative thing. I always thought it was a curious criticism as if the writer wasn't self-indulgent about their writing. It's the type of field where you can be creative and have some fun and I think you should." In 1995, after a disagreement over a cover featuring David Bowie, Carson parted ways with *Ray Gun* and Jarrett. (While Jarrett insisted on showing the musician's face, Carson wanted the cover to feature only Bowie's neck.)

Later that same year Carson founded his own design firm, David Carson Design Inc., along with Mike Jurkovac and the renowned *Vogue* photographer Albert Watson, setting up offices in San Diego and New York City. During his tenure at *Ray Gun*, Carson had already ventured into the world of advertising as a design consultant for such clients as Levi's, Nike, Pepsi, General Motors, Converse, and Kentucky Fried Chicken. He also directed commercials and titling (involving the design of uppercase text for ads and logos) for American Express, Coca-Cola, Hardees, and Sega. By the mid-1990s Carson's status as a "rock star designer" had reached its height. The most sought-after graphic designer of the decade, he was chosen as designer of the year by the International Center for Photography and won the New York–based Information Management Institute's award for best book design of the year for his work on Watson's volume of photographs, *Cyclops*. That prompted Neville Brody, one of the pioneers in avant-garde graphic design, to hail Carson's work as a contribution to what Brody called "the end of print"—a term referring to the way the ever-changing media landscape challenged traditional notions of form and presentation. In November 1995 Carson responded to Brody's comment by co-authoring *The End of Print*, a book about his work, on which he collaborated with the *Creative Review* editor Lewis Blackwell. *The End of Print* has sold more than 200,000 copies to date.

Taking full advantage of his popularity, which was unprecedented for a graphic designer, Carson signed onto a wide variety of projects. He designed album covers for David Byrne and Nine Inch Nails; made several experimental films, including one narrated by the writer William S. Burroughs; created a video loop for the music group U2's *Zoo TV* tour; and produced a collage for the film *Addicted to Love*, in which Meg Ryan portrayed a biker who is also a collage artist. Under Cyclops Productions with Jurkovac and Watson, Carson directed more commercials, including popular TV ads for Lucent Technologies. He designed worldwide ad campaigns for Microsoft and Giorgio Armani and appeared in advertisements endorsing Apple Computers and Samsung computer monitors. In 1996 he launched a San Francisco–based pop-culture quarterly, *Speak*, with the publisher Dan Rolleri. Having tired of magazines that were about "just music and skateboards," Carson approached *Speak* with an eye toward serious content (in contrast to his work for *Ray Gun*, which had proudly emphasized style over substance.) "After four years, I couldn't look at articles that were just pop band biographies," he explained to Robert Yates in an interview for the London *Guardian* (May 1, 1996). *Speak*'s editorial content reflected social consciousness, which Carson attributes to his years as a teacher, and included an eclectic mix of articles, ranging from pieces on Western artists who went to Southeast Asia to inform locals about land mines to interviews with 21-year-old paraplegics, as well as "anti-fashion" spreads and alternative-music profiles and reviews. Carson was also more restrained on the design front.

Carson published two more graphic-design books in the latter half of the 1990s: *2nd Sight* (1997) and *Fotografiks* (1999). The former, co-authored by Lewis Blackwell and considered a follow-up to *The End of Print*, is an in-depth look at Carson's intuitive creative process. *Fotografiks* features a wide array of images, including street markings and graffiti.

In 1998 Carson's design firm expanded to include both U.S. and international clients, among them AT&T, British Airways, Kodak, Lycra, Packard Bell, Sony, Suzuki, Toyota, Warner Bros., CNN, Cuervo Gold, Johnson AIDS Foundation, MTV Global, Princo, Lotus Software, Fox TV, Nissan, and Mercedes-Benz. That same year he published his fourth book, *Trek*, which features nearly 500 pages of his signature design work. While some critics called it self-congratulatory, most praised the volume. Carson became art director for the popular surfer-clothing brand Quicksilver, a position he held from 2000 to 2003. Afterward he continued working on various projects for the brand, which included designing its annual surfing magazine, *Explorations*. In 2004 he was named creative director of the Gibbes Museum of Art, in Charleston. He won a first-place award from the Advertising Federation of Charleston for a postcard he made for the Gibbes's Andy Warhol exhibit. A T-shirt for the same exhibit garnered Carson a second-place award, and marketing materials he designed for a Red Grooms exhibit won him a third-place award. Although he has receded from the spotlight in recent years, his stylistic innovations continue to influence designers all over the world. In 2007 Carson was featured in Gary Hustwit's acclaimed documentary *Helvetica*, about the sans-serif typeface and its impact on global visual culture. He designed and wrote an afterword for a book about the life and work of a contemporary Ecuadorian artist—*Wolfgang Bloch: The Colors of Coincidence*—which was scheduled for publication in 2008.

In 2000 Carson set up a studio in Charleston to be closer to his children, Luci and Luke. He currently resides in Folly Beach, South Carolina; he also has a studio in New York and in Zurich, Switzerland. During the winter Carson spends his time at his house on Tortola, in the British Virgin Islands, where he pursues his first love: surfing. He noted to Minis, "When I think there's a good storm that's going to send great waves down there, I go." —C.C.

Suggested Reading: *Advertising Age* p16+ Aug. 1, 1993; *Campaign* Dec. 1, 1995; (Charleston, South Carolina) *Post and Courier* F p1+ Aug. 28, 2004; *Creative Review* p46+ Apr. 1, 2004; (Glasgow, Scotland) *Herald* p16+ Nov. 10, 1997; (London) *Guardian* T p10+ May 1, 1996; (London) *Independent* p57+ Dec. 6, 1997; *Los Angeles Times* E p1+ Nov. 30, 2005; *Newsweek* p64+ Feb. 26, 1996; *San Francisco Chronicle* B p1 Mar. 5, 1996; (Toronto, Canada) *Globe and Mail* May 18, 1995; (Tucson) *Arizona Daily Star* D p1 Feb. 23, 2003

Selected Books: *The End of Print* (with Lewis Blackwell), 1995; *2nd Sight*, 1997; *Fotografiks*, 1999; *Trek*, 2000

Courtesy of Oracle

Catz, Safra A.

Dec. 13, 1961– Co-president of Oracle Corp.

Address: Oracle Corp., 500 Oracle Pkwy., Redwood Shores, CA 94065

"If I dropped dead tomorrow, Safra Catz would be the CEO of Oracle," Lawrence ("Larry") J. Ellison, the co-founder and chief executive officer of the Oracle Corp., said in 2005, as Rochelle Garner reported for Bloomberg News (December 19, 2006, on-line). Catz joined Oracle in 1999 as a senior vice president; she served as chief financial officer for about three years and has held the post of co-president since 2005. In 2004 she played a key role in Oracle's bitterly contested takeover of People-Soft, which produces so-called application software for the management of data pertaining to personnel, customers, finance, manufacturing, and other business matters. The acquisition of People-Soft transformed the California-based Oracle into the world's second-largest creator of business-management software (the first being the German company SAP A.G.). That purchase and the buyouts of some three dozen other companies have increased Oracle's market value by more than 50 percent and have made it a one-stop source of software for databases, business management, and middleware (software that connects computers). Catz's financial acuity, discipline, and aggressiveness in buyouts and other Oracle activities have helped her to become one of the highest-ranking women in corporate America, which is still overwhelmingly a male domain in the top echelons. In the business world, women "have to be better" than men, Catz said at a Women's High-Tech Coalition con-

ference held in May 2005, as quoted by Rochelle Garner. "You have got to work harder, work longer, be louder." *Fortune* magazine reported that in 2005, Catz's total compensation from Oracle amounted to $26.1 million, making her the highest-paid female executive in the nation. Her achievements and recognition by the media notwithstanding, Catz is known for maintaining a shroud over her personal life, often declining interviews and, as a result, remaining more or less a mystery to all but her closest associates.

The older of two daughters, Safra Ada Catz was born on December 13, 1961 in Holon, Israel, to Leonard and Judith Catz. Her father was the chairman of the Physics Department at the University of Massachusetts–Boston until his retirement, in 2005; Judith Catz, a Holocaust survivor, died in 2004. Catz's sister, Sarit, is a stand-up comedian and television writer/producer; she has worked on episodes of *Full House* and is currently the head writer of the independently produced TV pilot *What She's Having*. The Catz family immigrated to the United States when Safra was six. Safra Catz received a B.A. degree in business from the Wharton School of the University of Pennsylvania, in Philadelphia, in 1983 and then earned a J.D. degree from Harvard Law School, in Cambridge, Massachusetts, in 1986. That year she joined the investment bank Donaldson, Lufkin & Jenrette (later acquired by Credit Suisse First Boston). She served as a senior vice president for three years beginning in 1994 and was named managing director in 1997.

Ellison told John Markoff for the *New York Times* (July 3, 2000, on-line) that while working on software-industry deals at Donaldson, Lufkin & Jenrette, Catz helped to expand Softbank, a Japanese software giant founded by Masayoshi Son. In 1999, when the extensive travel required by her job became too onerous, she joined Oracle. Catz had become friends with Ellison years earlier, while working at Donaldson, Lufkin & Jenrette, and Ellison—who was "enchanted by her intellect," according to Victoria Murphy Barret, writing for *Forbes* (August 11, 2006, on-line)—appointed her a senior vice president. Later in 1999 Catz was named executive vice president of the company, a title also held by Gary L. Bloom. Her appointment followed the resignation of Oracle's president at that time, Raymond J. Lane, reportedly after Lane clashed with Ellison. According to Andy Serwer, writing for the *Fortune* Web site cnnmoney.com (November 13, 2000), "Some suggest that Ellison pitted Catz against Lane." In 2004 Ellison named Catz co-president with Charles E. Phillips Jr. and Gregory Maffei. Concurrently, in 2005, Catz took on the post of interim chief financial officer when Maffei stepped down. As the director of Oracle's global operations, she became known as "the efficiency queen," as Barret put it, because of her drastic cuts in company spending; according to Barret, she consolidated 70 employee database centers into one and reduced the number of Oracle's call centers from "dozens" to five, located in several time zones.

By the early 2000s most of the companies that relied on the types of database-software provided by Oracle already owned such software, and the pace at which Oracle's revenues were growing began to slow. In an effort to offset the dwindling database sales, Ellison decided to purchase companies that were flourishing in the application-software business. (An application is a program that organizes and tracks information in a database, increasing the value of that database. Applications programs help to automate such corporate tasks as updating employee records and processing orders.) On June 6, 2003, under Catz's direction, Oracle announced a takeover bid to acquire one of the most successful among those companies—PeopleSoft, whose recent acquisition of one of its rivals, the J. D. Edwards Co., had greatly increased its share of the market, placing it second to SAP. Oracle first offered PeopleSoft $16 a share, or $5.1 billion, then raised its bid to $19.50 a week later and to $26 per share the following February; then, in May 2004, Oracle lowered the bid to $21 per share. Meanwhile, PeopleSoft's management had filed a $2 billion civil lawsuit against Oracle to prevent the buyout. In addition, the U.S. Justice Department had filed a federal suit against Oracle, on the grounds that its absorption of PeopleSoft would hurt competition, raise product prices, and limit innovation in the industry. In June 2004 Catz appeared in federal court to testify on behalf of Oracle, stating that a few years earlier, Craig A. Conway, PeopleSoft's CEO and a former Oracle executive, had contacted Ellison to discuss a possible merger of the two companies. (By 2004, however, according to a September 13, 2005 New York Times article by Laurie J. Flynn, the relationship between Ellison and Conway had become marked by "intense animosity.") Catz further asserted that the merger would not raise prices and would foster a more competitive market, and that PeopleSoft's existing costumer base would receive support for their purchases for 10 years. In September 2004 a federal judge, Vaughn R. Walker, ruled in favor of Oracle, stating that the plaintiffs had failed to prove that the merger was "likely to substantially lesson competition in a relevant product and geographic market," as Steve Lohr and Laurie J. Flynn reported for the New York Times (September 10, 2004). In November 2004 a majority of PeopleSoft's shareholders voted to accept Oracle's latest offer, $24 per share, but PeopleSoft's board of directors rejected that amount as insufficient. Then, early the next month, the two companies signed what Oracle, in a press release dated December 13, 2004 (on-line), called "a definitive merger agreement," according to which Oracle was to pay PeopleSoft $26.50 per share, or a total of about $10.3 billion. Oracle thereby moved into the number-two spot in the business-management software market, behind SAP.

In reporting on Judge Walker's decision, Steve Lohr and Laurie J. Flynn noted, "Many industry experts agree that the software industry will likely go through a winnowing in the years ahead," and they quoted Michael Cusumano, a professor of management at the Massachusetts Institute of Technology, as writing that it was "probably true that there are too many software companies in the world by a factor of three or more." In 2005 Oracle's mergers and acquisitions group, headed by Catz, spurred that winnowing process by acquiring majority stakes in 12 additional companies, among them Retek, for $643 million, and I-flex, for about $900 million. "In I-flex, Oracle picks up what's known as the world's best-selling banking software and one that's used by 575 banking customers in 115 countries," Lisa Vaas wrote for eweek.com (August 5, 2005). In January 2006 Oracle paid $5.85 billion to purchase Siebel Systems, thus becoming the world's largest seller of sales-automation software, also known as customer-relationship-management software. Several months earlier Laurie J. Flynn had written for the New York Times (September 13, 2005) that, even with that acquisition, SAP would remain "a far bigger supplier of business applications over all," but that Ellison anticipated that ownership of Siebel would move Oracle "closer to our goal of being No. 1 in applications globally." In 2007, among other purchases, Oracle acquired Stellent, for $440 million; Hyperion Solutions, for $3.3 billion; and Agile Software Corp. and Bharosa, for cash payments to each of $495 million.

Michael Liedtke, writing for the Associated Press (September 21, 2007), reported that by mid-September 2007, Oracle's market value had "climbed by about $40 billion, or more than 50 percent," since it had begun "snapping up the company's smaller rivals" in 2004. "Although Oracle still trails SAP in revenue from business-applications software, the gap separating the two appears to be closing," Liedtke wrote. Buoyed by such encouraging developments, in June 2007, at an Oracle conference held in Israel, as Raphael Fogel wrote for the InfoWorld Web site (June 25, 2007), the "usually soft-spoken" Catz "uncharacteristically savaged rivals"—SAP, Microsoft, and IBM. "SAP failed to meet the goals that it declared in its financial statements," she noted, for example. "We managed to beat expectations for 17 straight quarters while SAP missed forecasts in three out of four quarters." She also said, "SAP has succumbed to the curse of the winners. They lost sight of the competition. We have the competition in view all the time." Catz said in addition that Oracle allocates as much as $2 billion annually to research and development. "No small part of this money goes to helping customers with system integration," according to Fogel, who quoted Catz as saying, "I am visiting our clients and watching many products that we already purchased, such as Hyperion and Siebel, and I am happy to say to my customers that they don't have any integration problem any more." That is because Oracle handles integration problems for them, enabling them, in Fogel's words, "to focus on their business while [Oracle] considers the knotty issues of integrating the systems of the 30 companies it bought with its own."

In an interview with Aaron Lazenby and Margaret Terry Lindquist that was posted on the Oracle Web site (May 2007), Catz said, "When people buy our products, they're not buying something that is disposable. It's really a commitment to the future. . . . Once you purchase a product from us, our responsibility increases dramatically and it is really our job to make you successful, because we can't be successful unless that happens." She also divulged that she was the "executive sponsor" for the government of Great Britain. "We were able to develop for them a very special and revolutionary program that allows different government entities throughout the U.K. to acquire products from us and to benefit from our best practices in streamlining and transforming all these different groups. . . . I personally work with the Department for Work and Pensions and the Foreign Office and a number of other groups that are using our technology. . . . I get personally involved in their implementations and I'm updated on the state of affairs. . . . I watch to make sure that [their developments] are going according to plan." She told the interviewers that above all else, the key to Oracle's ongoing success is its understanding of its customers' goals and problems. "The more we know about what's going on with our customers, the better off we are as partners and vendors. It ultimately translates into having better products, better consulting, and better service. . . . It's a great experience to watch a customer benefit from our products, because we do believe that we can help them. And when they reap the benefits of the relationship, it's very satisfying."

While Catz told Barret in her 2006 interview that she did not want to be CEO of Oracle, Ellison "has called her his heir apparent," according to Rochelle Garner, who also wrote that "analysts see Catz as Ellison's right-hand woman." Jeffrey Henley, the company's chairman, told Barret that Catz and Ellison are "on the same wavelength." Rob Enderle, a technology consultant, told Garner that Catz "conceals all aspects of herself except for what she thinks [Ellison] wants to see, and she does that very successfully. He's the star and makes sure he stays the star. She may have realized there's only downside risk in talking to the press." He added, "If Larry dies, there's every chance we'd find a different Safra Catz."

Catz has served on Oracle's board of directors since 2001; she is also a member of Oracle's Education Foundation. In September 2008 Jeff Epstein, previously the CFO of the on-line video-game publisher Oberon Media, was hired as Oracle's CFO; when he assumed that position, the next month, Catz relinquished that title; she retained the post of co-president.

Catz and her husband, Gal Tirosh, a soccer coach, live in Los Altos, California, with their teenage sons, Daniel and Jonathan.

—W.D.

Suggested Reading: bloomberg.com Dec. 18, 2006; *Forbes* (on-line) Aug. 11, 2006; infoworld.com June 25, 2007; *New York Times* (on-line) July 3, 2000; Oracle Corp. Web site

---

Clooney, George

May 6, 1961– Actor; director; producer; social activist

Address: c/o Stan Rosenfield & Associates, 2029 Century Park E., Suite 1190, Los Angeles, CA 90067

"I'm an actor, but I'm also a businessman and a bit of a hothead," George Clooney told Dana Kennedy during an interview for the *New York Times* (June 25, 2000). Hollywood, Clooney continued, "is run by fear, but I've always had a line that I would not cross. It may have cost me some jobs, but at least I can look myself in the eye in the mirror every morning." The actress and comedian Roseanne, whose immensely popular sitcom Clooney quit in 1989 because he believed his portrayal of his character was inadequate, told Kennedy much the same thing. "Everyone in Hollywood is scared and they'll totally compromise themselves to get ahead," she said. "But George is his own man. He's not for sale." In 1994, after a decade in which he had often served as "a seventh banana in mediocre

TV," as he described himself to Kennedy, Clooney landed a role in the television series *ER*: that of Doug Ross, a physician who worked in a fictional Chicago, Illinois, hospital emergency room. During his five seasons with *ER*, the show ranked either first or second in popularity in the Nielsen ratings, and early on in its run, Clooney was pegged its "resident heartthrob," as many journalists noted. He became a megacelebrity, stalked without letup by paparazzi, and in 1997 *People* magazine named him the "sexiest man alive." (The magazine bestowed the same title on him in 2006.)

Meanwhile, Clooney was on his way to becoming one of the very small number of popular television actors who later built highly successful careers as actors in film. His performances in movies including *One Fine Day; Out of Sight; Three Kings; A Perfect Storm; O Brother, Where Art Thou?; Ocean's Eleven; Good Night, and Good Luck; Syriana; and Michael Clayton* have earned him many plaudits and honors, among them an Academy Award for best supporting actor (for his portrayal of the character Bob Barnes in *Syriana*) and an Oscar nomination for best actor in a leading role (the title character in *Michael Clayton*). "Film fans used

George Clooney

Frazer Harrison/Getty Images

to speculate about whether Clooney could become the Cary Grant of our time, and now we know he's our Clark Gable and William Holden and Dean Martin, too," the movie critic Jim Emerson wrote for rogerebert.com (April 4, 2008), referring to three A-list actors of years gone by. Acknowledging Clooney's ability to maintain a mystique and glamorous aura reminiscent of Hollywood's golden age, *Time* (March 3, 2008) ran a cover story on the actor titled "The Last Movie Star."

In 2005 Clooney was also nominated for Academy Awards, and won a bevy of other prizes, as the co-writer (with Grant Heslov) and director of *Good Night, and Good Luck*. That film is about the pioneering television journalist Edward R. Murrow and Murrow's role in exposing the unsavory tactics of the Republican U.S. senator Joseph R. McCarthy and members of the House Committee on Un-American Activities, who led attempts to root out alleged Communists in government and the entertainment industry in the late 1940s and 1950s. Clooney knew that the subject was unlikely to lead to huge box-office receipts. "No one is encouraging me or anyone else to do things that aren't going to make any money," Clooney told David Carr for the *New York Times* (September 18, 2005). "On the other hand, 20 years from now, you want to be able to say to people that you stood for something besides your own career." The actor David Strathairn, who portrayed Murrow in the film, said to Carr, "[Clooney] paid a lot of dues to get where he is, and now there are a lot of doors open to him. . . . He has the good luck, the charm and the guts to do what he wants, and this film is what he chose to do." When Ian Parker asked him, during an interview for the *New Yorker* (April 14, 2008),

what sort of director he is, Clooney answered, "I'm fun. I do know that. I keep the set fun." He added, "I'm as prepared as anybody you'll meet, or anybody I've worked with. Doesn't mean I'm as good, I'm just prepared. I can show you storyboards this thick, with every single shot and every single scene. Every frame. Literally every shot."

The production companies associated with *Good Night, and Good Luck*, *Syriana*, and *Michael Clayton* included Section Eight, which Clooney and the director Steven Soderbergh founded in 1999. In addition to those films, Section Eight, which closed its doors in 2006, helped to produce two dozen other pictures, among them *Ocean's Eleven* and its two sequels, *Far from Heaven*, *Confessions of a Dangerous Mind*, *K Street*, *Rumor Has It*, and *The Good German*. Section Eight's successor is the Smoke House Production Co., headed by Clooney and Grant Heslov. Another of Clooney's companies, Maysville Pictures, produced the TV movie *Fail Safe* and the film *Rock Star*.

In addition to his work for the small and big screens, Clooney has devoted his time to humanitarian activities. Since 2006 he has strived to push the United Nations, as he put it in a speech to the U.N. Security Council on September 14, 2006, to "take real and effective measures to put an end" to the violence in the Darfur region of Sudan. (Since 2002 the Sudanese government and the janjaweed—Arab militiamen armed largely by that government—have engaged in genocide against Darfur's black African tribespeople.) In January 2008 the United Nations secretary-general, Ban Ki-moon, named Clooney a messenger of peace, a title given to celebrities who are known for their ability to raise public awareness of urgent problems and are recruited to promote the United Nations' efforts to maintain peace. Clooney is a co-founder of the organization Not on Our Watch, whose mission, according to its Web site, is "to focus global attention and resources towards putting an end to mass atrocities around the world" and to give "a voice to the victims" of such atrocities. "Early in his stardom, George Clooney figured out how to convey both a grateful amusement at his own good luck and good looks, and a serious awareness of the power he's got while the going is good," Lisa Schwarzbaum wrote for EW.com (April 1, 2008). "That's also how he became a walking American character ideal, with a responsible carbon footprint and a villa in Italy. Clooney appears to be a guy who knows how not to sweat the small stuff, while making his commitment to big stuff look really exciting."

The second of the two children of Nicholas "Nick" Clooney and Nina (Warren) Clooney, George Timothy Clooney was born on May 6, 1961 in Lexington, Kentucky. His father's sister Rosemary Clooney was a very popular singer and actress in the 1940s and 1950s; her first husband, José Ferrer, was an Academy Award–winning actor. For five years in the 1960s, Nick Clooney anchored a television news program in Lexington; next, in

Columbus and then Cincinnati, Ohio, through the early 1970s, he hosted his own morning variety and talk program, *The Nick Clooney Show*, and later returned to news anchoring. For years he wrote a column for the *Cincinnati Post*, and in 2004 he ran without success, as a Democrat, for a seat in Congress. The Clooneys' income rose and fell along with the ratings of Nick Clooney's shows. At the age of five, George began to make guest appearances on *The Nick Clooney Show*, performing as a leprechaun on St. Patrick's Day and a bunny at Easter and occasionally singing. By his early teens he had begun helping out on the sets of that and other local programs his father hosted, among them *Bowling for Dollars* and *The 3:30 Morning Movie*.

Clooney attended a series of four elementary and middle schools in Kentucky and Ohio. Eventually his parents, seeking to make the lives of their son and daughter, Ada, more stable and enable them to experience a small-town environment, settled in Augusta, Kentucky, near Cincinnati. At Augusta High School George Clooney played on the school basketball and baseball teams, outstandingly on the latter. At 16 he tried out without success for the Cincinnati Reds, a Major League Baseball club. In 1980, after his high-school graduation, he entered Northern Kentucky University, in Highland Heights, near Cincinnati, where he intended to major in broadcasting and, by his own admission, spent an excessive amount of time partying. One day in the spring of his freshman year, José Ferrer and two of his sons invited Clooney to the set of a movie that was being filmed in Lexington. Seeing the shoot and earning a bit part in the film (the never-released *And They Are Off*) so excited him that he quit college and resolved to pursue a career in acting—despite his father's warnings about the odds against becoming a success in that field. With such jobs as cutting tobacco and sketching caricatures of people at a summer festival, he saved enough money to buy an old car, and in the fall of 1981, he drove to Los Angeles. There, he lived for a year in the home of his aunt Rosemary, whose career had languished and who was grappling with addictions to drugs and alcohol. His aunt, who was twice divorced, "taught me a lot by example about what mistakes not to make because she made them all," George Clooney told Louis B. Hobson for the *Toronto (Ontario, Canada) Sun* (November 24, 2002).

According to an article his mother wrote for the *Cincinnati Post* (August 21, 2006), for nearly two years George Clooney did not land a single acting job; his earnings from other work, mostly in construction, supported him and paid for acting classes with the famous Hollywood teacher Milton Katselas. (According to other sources, he had earlier found a few, brief acting jobs.) Clooney's performance in a class production, according to Dominic Wills, writing for the British Web site Tiscali.co.uk, led to a deal with an agent. His first paying role came in a commercial for the Japanese company Panasonic, the next in an episode of the short-lived TV detective show *Riptide*, in 1984. Then he won a minor part in a new sitcom, called *E/R* (not related to the later *ER*), which aired 22 times, between September 1984 and July 1985, before its cancellation. Clooney also won small roles in episodes of sitcoms including *Crazy Like a Fox* (1985), *Throb* (1986), and *The Facts of Life* (1985–86). In 1988 and 1989 he appeared in 11 episodes of the extremely popular sitcom *Roseanne*, as a womanizing factory manager. Other TV shows in which he was cast included the drama *Sunset Beat* (1990, one episode); the sitcom *Baby Talk* (1991, four episodes); and the police drama *Bodies of Evidence* (1992 and 1993, 16 episodes). Clooney left the cast of *Baby Talk* after heated arguments with its producer, Ed. Weinberger (who had also produced *The Mary Tyler Moore Show* and *Taxi*), and told his father that he feared (unnecessarily, as it turned out) that Weinberger would blacklist him. "It was very dangerous for George to quit *Baby Talk*, but I told him it was the right thing to do," Nick Clooney told Dana Kennedy. "No matter how frightening it feels to jump into the void, you keep your integrity and eventually something even better comes along." During one season (1993–94) of the five-year run of the critically admired *Sisters*, whose cast was headed by Swoosie Kurtz, George Clooney played the husband of one of the sisters, earning $40,000 per week for his work. The husband was killed off at the end of that season.

Clooney has described himself during that period as "the best-paid unknown actor in Hollywood." His relative anonymity ended on September 19, 1994, when the series *ER* premiered on NBC. Developed from a two-decade-old script by the novelist Michael Crichton, *ER*—which recently completed its 14th season—is set in the emergency room (ER) of a fictitious Chicago hospital. Clooney was cast as Doug Ross, a pediatric resident. A womanizer who drank too much, Ross had excellent professional skills and treated his patients with great sensitivity; in one episode he was shown delivering a vital medical device, purchased with his own money, to a boy living in a city housing project. According to Bernard Weinraub, writing for the *New York Times* (June 15, 1997, on-line), Clooney gave up the chance to star in a new series, to be called *Golden Gate*, after he read an *ER* script, because he "knew at once that playing the role of the lecherous, good-natured pediatrician would define his career," as Weinraub reported. Clooney, who appeared in just over 100 episodes in his five seasons with *ER*, earned critical notice for his portrayal of Ross, picking up nominations for an Emmy Award in 1995 and 1996 and for a Golden Globe Award in three straight years (1996–98). With his fellow cast members, he earned the Screen Actors Guild Award for outstanding performance by an ensemble in a drama series in 1997, 1998, and 1999.

Meanwhile, in 1987, Clooney had made his debut on the silver screen, in the forgettable movie *Grizzly II: The Predator*. His next films, among them *Return to Horror High* (1987) and *Return of the Killer Tomatoes* (1988), were equally undistinguished. Clooney told George Hadley-Garcia for the *Japan Times* (April 10, 2008, on-line) that he had long known that "the transition from TV actor to movie actor" would be "very rocky." "Most people do not make that transition," he continued. "A lot of guys try, a very few make it." In 1996 he starred in the vampire horror thriller *From Dusk Till Dawn*, written by Quentin Tarantino and directed by Robert Rodriguez. While the blood-and-gore–drenched film received scant praise from critics, Clooney impressed many of them: he struck Janet Maslin, the reviewer for the *New York Times* (January 19, 1996), as "truly dashing," and Mick LaSalle, writing for the *San Francisco Chronicle* (January 19, 1996), as having a "magnetic presence." For his work in *From Dusk Till Dawn*, he won a Saturn Award, as best actor, from the Academy of Science Fiction, Fantasy, and Horror Films.

Clooney next starred in the Michael Hoffman–directed comedy *One Fine Day* (1996), portraying a journalist and divorced father who falls in love with a divorced mother who is a high-powered architect (played by Michelle Pfeiffer). The movie was a modest box-office success, and many critics made note of Clooney's big-screen charisma. Lisa Schwarzbaum wrote for *Entertainment Weekly* (December 20, 1996), "Clooney proves himself to be a true movie star and romantic leading man. His charm, his energy, even his ease with children . . . carry *One Fine Day* into irresistibility."

As his name and face recognition grew, freelance commercial photographers began hounding Clooney, following his every move. In 1996 he organized an actors' boycott of the Paramount Television–owned celebrity-gossip show *Entertainment Tonight*, after another Paramount show, *Hard Copy*, bought videos of Clooney, taken by paparazzi (dubbed, more recently, "stalkerazzi"). The boycott was successful: Paramount issued a statement, according to Bill Carter, writing for the *New York Times* (November 13, 1999), in which the firm "promised that *Hard Copy* would now reject tape in which the subject had been harassed to provoke a reaction or that showed stars' children without authorization."

In 1997 Clooney was cast as Batman in the action film *Batman and Robin*, which also starred Arnold Schwarzenegger and Uma Thurman. Both the film and his performance failed to impress critics. Also in 1997 Clooney appeared opposite Nicole Kidman in the action film *The Peacemaker*, directed by Mimi Leder. His performance, and the film—the first to emanate from the DreamWorks studio—got mixed reviews. Next, Clooney starred in the Stephen Soderbergh–directed thriller *Out of Sight* (1998), as Jack Foley, an escaped convict who romances a federal marshal (Jennifer Lopez). In his review of *Out of Sight*, Stephen Hunter wrote for the *Washington Post* (June 26, 1998), "Clooney is the most impressive he's been on film. Jack Foley feels real, not like some Hollywood improvisation.

Foley is charming, handsome, graceful, cultured, energetic, and disciplined." Clooney had a minor role as a platoon leader in the director Terrence Malick's war film, *The Thin Red Line* (1998), and then co-starred in the director David O. Russell's satirical movie about the 1991 Gulf War, *Three Kings* (1999). His turn as Captain Archie Gates in *Three Kings* spurred Owen Gleiberman to write for *Entertainment Weekly* (October 8, 1999), "Clooney, more than ever, displays his extraordinarily facile gift for acting cool and unflappable in the midst of utter chaos. Everything he says spins by with mocking egotistical zip. His action-figure urgency holds *Three Kings* together." During the filming of *Three Kings*, Clooney accused Russell of mistreating the cast and crew, and during one argument the men attacked each other physically. "It was a really bad experience," Clooney told Kennedy. Meanwhile, Clooney was also appearing regularly on *ER*; his contract with NBC called for him to remain with the series through the 1998–99 season, and, as he told Weinraub, he intended to fulfill its terms, despite his burgeoning film career. "I get too much credit" for honoring the contract, he said to Weinraub. "But the truth is I'm doing what I'm supposed to do and not something extraordinary." Indeed, he attributed the surge in the number of parts coming his way to his work on *ER*.

In 1999, with funding from Warner Bros. and individual investors, Clooney and Soderbergh formed the production company Section Eight. (The number refers to a military discharge given for reasons of mental illness.) As Laura M. Holson wrote for the *New York Times* (January 17, 2005), Clooney and Soderbergh's aim was "to give emerging directors a voice in an increasingly hostile studio system in which executives are afraid to offend worldwide audiences and independent filmmaking has largely disappeared." Section Eight produced two dozen films, among them some commercial flops—*Insomnia, Welcome to Collinwood, Full Frontal*, and *Confessions of a Dangerous Mind* (all in 2002), the last of which marked Clooney's debut as a director; *Criminal* and *Keane* (2004); *The Jacket, Bubble*, and *The Big Empty* (all 2005); *A Scanner Darkly, The Half Life of Timofey Berezin*, and *The Good German* (all 2006); and *Wind Chill* (2007). Section Eight's critical successes included *Ocean's Eleven* (2001) and its second sequel, *Ocean's Thirteen* (2007); *Good Night, and Good Luck* and *Syriana* (both 2005); and *Michael Clayton* (2007). For HBO, Section Eight produced two short-lived series: *K Street* (2003), a sober view of Washington, D.C., lobbyists and politicians, and *Unscripted* (2004), about the enormous difficulties faced by the vast majority of people who aspire to careers in show business. Both series presented a mixture of reality and fiction and dialogue that was mostly improvised.

In 2000, soon after Clooney left *ER*, he produced for television the live, two-hour, black-and-white drama *Fail Safe*, an adaptation for TV by Walter Bernstein of the screenplay Bernstein had written for the highly acclaimed, same-titled 1964 film. The original film, directed by Sidney Lumet, was based on a 1962 novel by Eugene Burdick and Harvey Wheeler about the possibility of a nuclear war's being triggered by a mechanical accident. With *Fail Safe*, the first television drama to be broadcast live in 39 years, Clooney aimed to pay homage to the so-called golden age of television of the 1950s, when live dramas were commonplace, and also to present "a cautionary tale about how fear can metastasize into destruction," as David Carr wrote. The prime-time drama, which made use of 18 cameras and two sound stages on the Warner Bros. lot, was performed twice, without mishap, by Richard Dreyfuss, Harvey Keitel, Noah Wyle, Brian Dennehy, Hank Azaria, and Clooney himself, first for East Coast audiences and then for those on the West Coast. Comparisons with the Hollywood film, whose stars included Henry Fonda and Walter Matthau, and complaints about the inevitable commercial interruptions muted the universal critical praise Clooney's version of *Fail Safe* received.

Clooney next appeared on the big screen in *A Perfect Storm* (2000), an adaptation of Sebastian Junger's 1997 nonfiction chronicle of the last, fatal voyage of a Gloucester, Massachusetts, fishing boat that disappeared during a monstrous storm off the coast of Nova Scotia in 1991. Also in 2000 Clooney co-starred, with John Turturro and Tim Blake Nelson, in Joel and Ethan Coen's much-praised comedy *O Brother, Where Art Thou?* Clooney played Ulysses Everett McGill, who, having escaped from a prison chain gang while shackled to the dimwitted Turturro and Nelson characters, undertakes an *Odyssey*-like journey through rural Mississippi during the Great Depression of the 1930s in search of money, his wife, and his favorite hair pomade. Clooney "has never seemed more alive on screen," Robert Wilonsky wrote for the *Dallas Observer* (January 11, 2001), while A. O. Scott, the *New York Times* (December 22, 2000) reviewer, wrote that Clooney's "elusive, highly mannered performance . . . appears to belong, as much as the vintage roadsters and ice-cream suits, to a vanished era."

In 2001 Clooney produced the comedy *Rock Star*, featuring Mark Wahlberg as a singer in a cover band. Clooney also appeared that year in the hit *Ocean's Eleven*, a remake, directed by Steven Soderbergh, of a 1960 crime caper starring Frank Sinatra, Sammy Davis Jr., and other members of the group of entertainers dubbed the Rat Pack. Clooney played Danny Ocean, an ex-convict, who leads an attempt to rob a string of Las Vegas casinos. By all accounts, Clooney fit the role of Danny to a T. Clooney also starred in the film's sequels, *Ocean's Twelve* (2004) and *Ocean's Thirteen* (2007), both directed by Soderbergh. The three *Ocean's* films took in more than $1 billion at the box office.

Earlier, Clooney had made his directorial debut, with *Confessions of a Dangerous Mind*, based on the life and writings of Chuck Barris, who hosted or produced such popular 1960s and 1970s TV game shows as *The Dating Game*, *The Newlywed Game*, and *The Gong Show* and has claimed to have worked secretly as an assassin for the Central Intelligence Agency (CIA). The film, with a screenplay by Charlie Kaufman, starred Sam Rockwell as Barris; Clooney played the CIA agent who recruits him. Critics disagreed about Clooney's direction of the film. Robert Koehler wrote for *Variety* (December 9, 2002), "Clooney has absorbed his time with the Coen brothers, David O. Russell and partner Steven Soderbergh to create an enveloping cinematic world that only rarely teeters into excess or self-seriousness," while Kenneth Turan, in an assessment for the *Los Angeles Times* (December 31, 2002), complained, "With its multiplicity of overstylized looks and slick gimmicks, *Dangerous Mind* was doubtless more stimulating to direct than it will be for audiences to experience." Also in 2002 Clooney starred in Soderbergh's *Solaris*, a poignant science-fiction tale, which is a remake of the same-titled 1972 film by Andrei Tarkovsky. He played a divorce attorney in the poorly received Coen brothers comedy *Intolerable Cruelty* (2003).

In an interview with Virginia Rohan for the Bergen County, New Jersey, *Record* (October 2, 2005), Clooney explained why he chose to write and direct his next project, *Good Night, and Good Luck* (2005): "I grew up on a newsroom floor, watching my father work with . . . these really wonderful reporters, watching them piece a news show together, and [Edward R.] Murrow was always the highwater mark that everyone aimed for. So, it was my love of that, and it was certainly a tip of my hat to my dad." The film was shot in black and white, as TV viewers had always seen Murrow, and incorporated footage of Senator Joseph R. McCarthy and hearings of the House Committee on Un-American Activities for added realism. Clooney portrayed Fred W. Friendly, who collaborated with Murray in the production of the latter's scathing 1954 documentary about McCarthy's witch hunts of alleged Communists. "The picture is partly an ode to the early days of broadcast journalism and partly a call to arms, a reminder of the standards that contemporary media (of all sorts) ought to be upholding," Stephanie Zacharek wrote for Salon.com (September 23, 2005). "But what's remarkable about *Good Night, and Good Luck* is the way Clooney, Heslov and the actors make those ideas work so well dramatically." The movie received six Academy Award nominations, including those for best picture, director, and actor.

In 2005 Clooney starred in and co–executive produced *Syriana*, about the oil industry's influence on events occurring in the oil-rich Middle East. To prepare for his role as a betrayed CIA operative, Clooney gained weight and grew a beard, making himself look considerably older; he also found himself feeling unusually sad, as he told Ian Parker. His portrayal earned him both a Golden Globe Award and an Academy Award in the supporting-actor category. According to Claudia Puig for *USA Today* (November 22, 2005), Clooney's "world-weary but heroic agency veteran is the emotional center of the film. Clooney does a masterful job portraying a smart guy who knows he should probably take a desk job in D.C., but is hooked on the adrenaline rush of top-secret overseas assignments." During the shooting of *Syriana*, Clooney severely injured his back; he later had several operations to repair the damage, but he still feels considerable pain.

In 2007 Clooney starred in *Michael Clayton* as the title character, an in-house "fixer" at a large New York law firm, who tampers with evidence and information for the benefit of his employers; the film examines Clayton's inner struggle with his reprehensible job. *Michael Clayton* was nominated for several Academy Awards, including best actor for Clooney.

Clooney's third directorial effort was the comedy *Leatherheads* (2008), a fictional 1920s period piece about the players on one of America's earliest professional football teams. The film followed the character Dodge Connolly (Clooney), a team captain determined to put professional football on the map, despite his fledgling league's financial struggles and the immense popularity of college football. The film received mixed reviews, with many critics praising its re-creation of the era; Shawn Levy wrote for the *Oregonian* (April 4, 2008, online), for example, "Clooney directs with golden love: Muddy football fields, creaky train carriages, smoky speakeasies and plush hotel lobbies all are caressed in romantic light and crisp period detail. . . . Clooney proves the best sort of sentimentalist: keen on rescuing whatever's most delicious from the past, whether it's captured in a song, an article of clothing, a catchphrase or an attitude." In his assessment for the *New York Times* (April 4, 2008), A. O. Scott described *Leatherheads* as "by a wide margin the weakest movie" directed by Clooney. It is "interesting to note that all three of the movies he has directed . . . share a passing concern with the ethical problems of journalism and the conundrums of celebrity culture at various points in 20th-century history. What is harder to comprehend is how Mr. Clooney turned out such a sloppy, haphazard and tonally incoherent piece of work [as *Leatherheads*]. *Leatherheads* lurches hectically between Coen brothers–style pastiche and John Saylesian didacticism, while Mr. Clooney works his brow and his jaw and waits in vain for his charm to kick in and save the day. Unless he's just vamping until the director shows up and gives him some clear instructions." Also in 2008 Clooney apeared in *Burn After Reading*, a comedic crime film written and directed by Joel and Ethan Coen.

In addition to his work in entertainment, Clooney has made headlines for his charitable activities and social activism. After the terrorist attacks of September 11, 2001, he helped to organize a celebrity telethon, *America: A Tribute to Heroes*, that raised over $30 million for the victims' families. For several years he has devoted energy to urging the United Nations and others to stop the genocide in the Darfur region of Sudan, which has claimed the lives of hundreds of thousands of people and displaced hundreds of thousands of others. Using his name and face recognition to draw attention to the tragedy and to the urgent need to help its victims, he has visited Darfur and refugee camps in Chad several times. "The key to being an advocate is that you are really informed on the subject matter so you don't do it damage," Clooney told Andrew Gumbel for the *Hamilton (Ontario, Canada) Spectator* (September 30, 2006). "Now, there are people out there who want to question anything that any celebrity does. They'll say that what I do is self-serving. What do they think, that I need to be more famous? I'm just trying to participate in the human condition."

Joel Stein wrote in the 2008 *Time* cover story on Clooney, "Somehow this guy . . . really is a movie star. Maybe the only one we have now. There are plenty of huge box-office draws (Will Smith, Tom Hanks, Julia Roberts, Ben Stiller, Adam Sandler, Johnny Depp) and even more famous celebrities (Brad Pitt, Tom Cruise, Angelina Jolie, Jennifer Lopez, Lindsay Lohan), but no one besides Clooney is so gracefully both." In 2000 Dana Kennedy wrote that Clooney "in person is as charming as advertised and entirely without airs, though his easy manner seems to mask a very guarded nature." Clooney was married to the actress Talia Balsam from 1989 to 1993. He has told reporters that he intends to remain single. In addition to his villa on the banks of Lake Como, in Italy, Clooney owns an estate in the Studio City section of Los Angeles and is having a house built in Mexico.

—W.D.

Suggested Reading: clooneystudio.com; *GQ* p67+ Jan. 2003; *Hamilton (Ontario, Canada) Spectator* D p18 Sep. 30, 2006; imdb.com; *New York Times* II p19 June 15, 1997, II p11 June 25, 2000, C p1+ Jan. 17, 2005; *New Yorker* p40+ Apr. 14, 2008; *Time* p46+ Mar. 3, 2008; *Vanity Fair* p270+ Oct. 2003, p108+ July 2006, p340+ Nov. 2006

Selected Films: as actor—*Return to Horror High*, 1987; *Return of the Killer Tomatoes!*, 1988; *From Dusk Till Dawn*, 1996; *One Fine Day*, 1996; *Batman and Robin*, 1997; *The Peacemaker*, 1997; *Out of Sight*, 1998; *Three Kings*, 1998; *The Thin Red Line*, 1998; *Fail Safe*, 2000; *A Perfect Storm*, 2000; *O Brother, Where Art Thou?*, 2000; *Ocean's Eleven*, 2001; *Intolerable Cruelty*, 2003; *Ocean's Twelve*, 2004; *The Good German*, 2006; *Ocean's Thirteen*, 2007; *Burn After Reading*, 2008; as actor and director—*Confessions of a Dangerous Mind*, 2002; as co-writer (with Grant Heslov), actor, and director—*Good Night, and Good Luck*, 2005; as actor and producer—*Syriana*, 2005; *Michael Clayton*, 2007; as actor, director, and producer—*Leatherheads*, 2008

Selected Television Shows: *Riptide*, 1984; *E/R*, 1984–85; *Crazy Like a Fox*, 1985; *Throb*, 1986; *The Facts of Life*, 1986; *Roseanne*, 1988; *Sunset Beat*, 1990; *Bodies of Evidence*, 1992–93; *Sister*, 1992–93; *ER*, 1994–2000

Courtesy of the *New York Times*

Cohen, Roger

Aug. 2, 1955– Journalist; columnist; nonfiction writer

Address: New York Times, *620 Eighth Ave., New York, NY 10018*

In May 2007 it was announced that Roger Cohen's column "Globalist," which had appeared twice weekly in the *International Herald Tribune* since 2004, would become a medium for Cohen's views and commentary as well as his reporting of world events. The *Tribune's* executive editor, Michael Oreskes, said to *Business Wire* (May 2, 2007) on that occasion, "Roger's 'Globalist' has been a triumph! He has combined tireless reporting and sharp analysis to shed real light on world issues. He has richly earned this opportunity to add his own opinions to the wealth of material he offers our readers." In the same month, Cohen became an op-ed columnist for the *Tribune's* parent publication, the *New York Times*. Cohen, who joined the staff of the *Times* in 1990, has held various positions at other news organizations, including the *Wall Street Journal* and Reuters, contributing articles and commentary focusing primarily on international relations. He is also the author of three books: *In the Eye of the Storm: The Life of General*

H. Norman Schwarzkopf, written with the Italian journalist Claudio Gatti; *Hearts Grown Brutal: Sagas of Sarajevo*, the culmination of Cohen's years as a correspondent for the *New York Times* in the former Yugoslavia in the 1990s; and *Soldiers and Slaves: American POWs Trapped by the Nazis' Final Gamble*. When asked in an interview with *Independent Media Weekly* (February 12, 2007) about his favorite aspect of his work, Cohen answered, "The freedom to take on any subject I like for the column and the latitude to express my feelings and thoughts about an immense range of subjects, from politics to culture and football. I like the interaction with my readers that comes from having a column. The exchanges are often stimulating."

Roger Cohen was born on August 2, 1955 in London, England. His family subscribed to two London-based newspapers, the *Daily Telegraph* and the *Times*, and Cohen, a fan of the football team of the city's Chelsea area, was a devoted reader of the sports pages. The desire to write for a living ran deep in him; he told the *Independent Media Weekly*, "I always loved writing and was always very curious about the world. I figured that if I could find a way to get someone to pay me to travel around the world and try to evoke it in words, that would suit me." After earning his master's degree in French and history at Oxford University, in 1977, he moved to Paris, France, where he served as a reporter for *Paris Metro*, taught English, and did freelance writing. Cohen co-founded *Speakeasy*, a newspaper for French students learning English, with the publisher Fernand Nathan. In 1979 he began working for the news agency Reuters as a foreign correspondent; in the following year he was sent on assignment to Brussels, Belgium, after which he returned to London. In 1983 he took the position of chief foreign correspondent at the *Wall Street Journal*, working at the newspaper's European office, in Rome, Italy. There, he began writing about the Italian economy but was soon sent instead to Beirut, in Lebanon, the scene of a civil war. After reporting from Lebanon, Cyprus, Greece, and Turkey, he moved to the *Wall Street Journal's* South American office, in Rio de Janeiro, Brazil. He covered stories in that country and in Argentina, Paraguay, Chile, Peru, and Venezuela.

It was at the *New York Times*, beginning in January 1990, that Cohen truly made a name for himself as a journalist. Initially he worked as a media reporter. After only one year, he was offered the prestigious position of Jerusalem bureau chief. The offer came at about the time that Cohen asked to take four weeks off to complete the book *In the Eye of the Storm: The Life of General H. Norman Schwarzkopf*, a biography of the commander of multinational forces in the 1991 Gulf war, co-written with Claudio Gatti. The publishing company Farrar, Straus, & Giroux, according to Howard Kurtz in the *Washington Post* (March 15, 1991), had offered him "a handsome sum for a few weeks of collaboration with a friend [Gatti]." The *Times's* managing editor, Joseph Lelyveld, discouraged the project, as did its executive editor, Max Frankel, who told Kurtz that Cohen "had to choose" between the book and the promotion. "I guess he thought he could do both. I told him, 'You've got to meet your priorities, we've got to meet our priorities.'" Choosing to work on the book, Cohen lost the bureau-chief position to Clyde Haberman. His and Gatti's hastily written book received lukewarm reviews. John Eisenhower wrote for the *Chicago Tribune* (August 25, 1991) about *In the Eye of the Storm*, "Its construction is loose and disjointed. Repetition is sometimes exasperating, and material of secondary importance is often given too much space. . . . Nevertheless, *In the Eye of the Storm* is a useful contribution to our knowledge of an important figure, and it is well to have it now. Old Soldier Schwarzkopf is obviously a man who has no intention of conforming to Army mythology and simply fading away. We need more understanding of this complex man, and this may be the best source we will have until the general himself publishes his memoirs."

In 1992 Cohen rebounded, becoming the *Times*'s European economic correspondent and moving to Paris. Next, in 1994, he was made the paper's Balkan bureau chief, based in Zagreb, Croatia, in the former Yugoslavia, another region in the throes of civil war. There, the former Yugoslav republic of Serbia aided the Serbs in neighboring Bosnia in their campaign of "ethnic cleansing" against Muslims, who ran Bosnia's government. Some of Cohen's most celebrated work was completed during his tenure in that position. Evoking the tragedy of a land contaminated by ethnic conflict, Cohen wrote for the *Times* (August 14, 1994), "Bosnia today overflows with hatred. It is in every village, every war-lacerated community. Lost kin and lost homes have fueled an avenging fury. . . . The Bosnian Serbs cling to the fantasy that the Muslims they have butchered are the victims of an aberration that led them to convert to Islam during the centuries of Ottoman rule in Bosnia, and that one day they will revert to being Christian Slavs. The Muslim-led Bosnian Government refers to its enemy as the 'Belgrade regime [Serbia],' as if the Serbs of Bosnia did not exist. War, not diplomacy, is seen by the Government as the only way to 'liberate' Bosnia. But what is Bosnia? A millennial state fighting against a large-scale Serbian invasion, the government says. In truth, an expanse of breathtakingly beautiful land ruled, since the collapse of the medieval kingdom, by various outside authorities—Ottoman, Austro-Hungarian, Communist—and subject to outbreaks of hostility between its Muslim, Serb, and Croatian inhabitants."

In 1995 Cohen received the Overseas Press Club of America Burger Human Rights Award for his investigative journalism concerning a Serb-run concentration camp, Susica, in Bosnia. He was able to garner much information about the camp through extensive interviews, particularly those conducted with one of the guards, Pero Popovic, a Serb. At the time, most Serbs claimed that the camps were detention centers for prisoners of war, but Cohen's series of articles helped to reveal the truth. Following the publication of those articles, several Serbs were indicted as war criminals for the murder, rape, torture, and dispossession of Bosnian Muslims in the first international war-crimes tribunal held since the end of World War II. In 1995, following Cohen's reports on Serb-initiated attacks on Muslims, the Central Intelligence Agency found that 90 percent of the war crimes in Bosnia had been committed by Serbs. Cohen, however, aware of the mutual initiation of aggression, wrote for the *Times* (September 24, 1995) that the Bosnian war had "been fought through attempts to reinvent, change and obscure history in order to justify killing and destruction. Each side, in varying degrees, has scoured and twisted the past in order to grab what it could." Encouraging American intervention, he argued, "These people are condemned to try to overcome the specters that now savagely divide them, in order to live together. They cannot be permanently divided because their history—beyond all its violence—ties them together. Indeed, the attempt to destroy history is an attempt to hide that basic fact. . . . The flailing of Europe in the last four years has made it clear that American leadership in the Balkans is irreplaceable. So America is being called on to secure a peace, guarantee it with troops and cast enough light on the past in order to build the future. It worked in Germany and Japan [after World War II]. It might work in Bosnia."

In the book *Hearts Grown Brutal: Sagas of Sarajevo* (1998), Cohen told the stories of four Bosnian families in arguing that the United States' intervention in the Balkan conflict had been inadequate. "Bosnia did not satisfy the Pentagon's criteria for the use of American power," Cohen wrote, as quoted in the *Boston Globe* (September 15, 1998). "The administration was presented with an intractable mess, but it could find neither the determination nor the moral conviction to rectify it. Bosnia's dismemberment was consummated through this failure." While Cohen drew some criticism for what was seen as an overly subjective view of the conflict, the book was lauded by many critics. E. William Smethurst Jr. declared for the *Chicago Tribune* (October 4, 1998), "*Hearts Grown Brutal* is a powerful and passionate evocation of the unspeakable horrors of the Bosnian genocide. In the course of his narrative, Roger Cohen . . . delivers a history lesson, a series of brutal indictments and an anguished cri de coeur over senseless and irreparable loss. Cohen's command of language is brilliant and seamless. His elegiac and lapidary prose intensifies the emotional impact of the unfolding tragedy." *Hearts Grown Brutal* received an Overseas Press Club Citation for Excellence in 1999.

Cohen persisted in advocating for greater Western military intervention in the Balkans war, disparaging government and military officials who considered efforts toward a resolution of the conflict to be futile. In one of his most vehement criticisms of Western military inaction, he wrote (October 4, 1998), "Perhaps lazy thinking about the consistency of [Serbian president Slobodan] Milosevic's destructive policies, twisted memories, contorted history and Western cynicism have contributed more decisively to the bloodshed than any fabled Balkan predisposition to kill and to mutilate. One of the more unforgettable gestures of the latest Balkan conflicts was the nonchalant wave of the hand of Gen. Sir Michael Rose, the commander of United Nations forces in Bosnia in 1994, that always accompanied his dismissive mantra: 'This is the Balkans, you know.' The phrase . . . amounted to a form of renunciation. In it was captured a widespread, often subliminal, view that if the people in the Balkans are really intent on killing each other, there is not much to be done about it." Cohen ended the article by writing, "The fact remains that, through a decade of Balkan violence, the one Western act that demonstrably contributed to peace—albeit the deeply flawed peace in Bosnia—was the concerted NATO bombing of Serb positions in Bosnia in August and September 1995."

After his tenure as Balkan bureau chief, Cohen worked as a correspondent for the *New York Times* in Paris, then became bureau chief in Berlin, Germany, in 1998. While in Berlin, he wrote a series of articles concerning immigration to Europe, particularly Turkish immigrants in Germany. Deftly putting into context the issues surrounding immigration, Cohen wrote, "As the advance of the European Union encroaches on national sovereignty and the wealth of Europe draws the world's dispossessed migrants, a nationalist reaction has set in, marked by jingoistic hymns to national cultures, anti-immigrant tirades and the scapegoating of foreigners for everything from rising crime to rotten schools. It is no longer Communism that haunts Europe: it is the outsider." Because of the comparative cheapness of relocating to Europe, immigrants were more likely to settle there than in the United States. While in 1999 only 30,000 people applied for asylum in the U.S., 365,000 applied for asylum in the European Union. Cohen's series included articles about the cultural gap between first- and second-generation immigrants; the influx of Eastern European sex workers in Western Europe; exploitation of immigrants in transit; and the rise of neo-Nazi ideology in central European political groups. Those articles earned him the Peter Weitz Prize from the German Marshall Fund, an Overseas Press Club citation, and the Arthur F. Burns Prize from the Foreign Office of the Federal Republic of Germany in 2001.

A month after assuming the position of deputy foreign editor at the *Times*, in August 2001, Cohen became acting foreign editor. The following spring he was named foreign editor and the *New York Times*'s international writer-at-large. The *Times* took on full ownership of the *International Herald Tribune* in 2003, and in 2004 Cohen began writing the "Globalist" column for the *Tribune*.

Cohen published his third book, *Soldiers and Slaves: American POWs Trapped by the Nazis' Final Gamble*, in 2005. Focusing on 350 U.S. soldiers taken prisoner by the Nazis and assigned, because they were Jewish or thought to be so, to the brutal Berga slave-labor camp, *Soldiers and Slaves* is based largely on interviews conducted with former Berga prisoners of war. Reviewers of the book unanimously praised Cohen's illumination of the plight of American soldiers at Berga but differed in their opinions of his writing. Tom Brokaw's review of the book, featured in the *International Herald Tribune* (May 16, 2005), read, "While all of the big pieces have been assembled on history's table for some time now, it is the discovery of the little-known episodes that constantly expands our appreciation, fascination and revulsion for the brutal clash of civilizations in the heart of the 20th century. Roger Cohen's meticulously reported and passionately felt book *Soldiers and Slaves* is just such a discovery." While Michael Kiene, assessing *Soldiers and Slaves* for *Parameters* (Winter 2005/2006), found that "Roger Cohen does a great service by shedding light on a little-known episode of the Holocaust, one in which the victims were Americans" and that "Cohen's flowing prose makes *Soldiers and Slaves* eminently readable," a critic wrote for *Publishers Weekly* (February 7, 2005), "The book is well organized, but the writing style is not always smooth; it's Cohen's level of detail that makes this journalistic history come alive."

In 2006 Cohen became the *International Herald Tribune*'s first editor-at-large. In the following year he was named an op-ed columnist for the *New York Times*. Though the breadth of his column is great, covering topics as varied as neoconservatism, the U.S. senator and presidential candidate Barack Obama's family as a symbol of globalization, and the Arab-Israeli conflict, Cohen's most consistent theme has been the way in which current events jeopardize or strengthen international political stability. His first op-ed column, entitled "Sarkozy's New Order" (August 23, 2007), discussed French-American diplomatic relations following a meeting between U.S. president George W. Bush and French president Nicolas Sarkozy in Maine. "French-American relations are always complex," he wrote in the column, which, like much of Cohen's writing for the *Times*, also appeared in the *International Herald Tribune*. "Seldom have two countries been more reluctant, or stubborn, allies. The universalizing ambitions of both nations, their thirst to embody and spread the ennobling values of mankind, lead to tensions at the best of times. When things go south, as they did with Iraq, you get freedom fries and other less trivial forms of vilification. So a warming of relations is good news if you believe, as I do, that when the trans-Atlantic bond is broken, the world grows more unstable. Still, the ironies of the amiable Maine picnic were hard to swallow. On one end of the corn on the cob you had a French president who seems determined to make his office more accountable, more accessible, more open, and invoking American-style checks and balances to achieve that. On the other, you had an American president who, in the name of the war on terror, has, with Dick Cheney, been bent on placing the authority of the White House as far as possible beyond the offsetting power of the legislative and judicial branches." In another article (December 17, 2007), Cohen again raised the question of nationhood in an increasingly globalized world, one in which the Euro has become a transnational currency and Belgian reactionary factions propose moving toward federalism. Comparing Belgium's nationhood to a famed Belgian artwork, he wrote, "Belgium's favorite Surrealist son, René Magritte, is famous for his painting of an apple on which he wrote: 'This is not an apple.' He did the same for a pipe. Today he might aptly produce a rendering of his native land and inscribe on it: 'This is not a country.' It looks like a prosperous one, with its lace and chocolate stores, and beautiful Bruges, and its glassy sprawl of European Union institutions, and its very own tennis champion, Justine Henin. But for more than a half-year Belgium has been unable to form a government because its 10.4 million citizens can't decide what the state is for. . . . The map of Europe is not fixed. But I suspect its overall stability is. I am attached to Belgium—two of my children were born here—and I'd favor its preservation, but I can't say it's necessary within an overarching E.U. As for a Belgian government, it would be nice to have one, but not essential. There's no Belgian franc to go wobbly. There's no monetary policy to

set. There's scarcely a country to govern, given how far European integration on the one hand and national devolution on the other have gone. This is the 21st-century world the United States will face: a mysterious Europe with a more identifiable phone number living its postmodern version of paradise as its nation states get less meaningful or dissolve; and a rising Russia and China hurtling the other way, toward 19th-century-style nationalism, militarism and assertiveness. Such dissonance will require American flexibility and imagination, enough to understand that the essence of the Belgian crisis is: this is not a crisis."

Cohen lives in Brooklyn, New York, with his wife, the sculptor Frida Baranek, and their four children. He has said that he considers his greatest achievement to be the publication of *Hearts Grown Brutal* and that he hopes someday to publish a novel.

—T.O.

Suggested Reading: *Boston Globe* E p2 Sep. 15, 1998; *Independent Media Weekly* p16 Feb. 12, 2007; *International Herald Tribune* (on-line) May 16, 2005; *New York Times* (on-line) Aug. 14, 1994, IV p1 Oct. 4, 1998; *Washington Post* C p1 Mar. 15, 1991

Selected Books: *In the Eye of the Storm: The Life of General H. Norman Schwarzkopf* (with Claudio Gatti), 1991; *Hearts Grown Brutal: Sagas of Sarajevo*, 1998; *Soldiers and Slaves: American POWs Trapped by the Nazis' Final Gamble*, 2005

Corsi, Jerome R.

Aug. 31, 1946– Political pundit; writer; businessman

Address: WorldNetDaily, P.O. Box 368, Catharpin, VA 20143

Jerome Corsi is known chiefly as the author of two best-selling books, each aimed at damaging the reputation of a Democratic candidate for president. The first, *Unfit for Command: Swift Boat Veterans Speak Out Against John Kerry* (2004), written with John O'Neill, focuses on the U.S. senator from Massachusetts and 2004 Democratic nominee. Published three months before that year's election, the book alleges that Kerry—a decorated Vietnam War veteran—misrepresented his actions as a swiftboat commander in Vietnam and accuses him of abetting Communists through his subsequent antiwar activities. The second, similarly timed book, *The Obama Nation: Leftist Politics and the Cult of Personality* (2008), levels attacks against Barack Obama, a U.S. senator from Illinois and the coun-

try's first African-American major-party nominee for president. That book hints strongly at continuing drug use on Obama's part and portrays him as concealing a militant black nationalism and dangerous links to radical Islam. Many felt that Kerry lost the 2004 election to the incumbent, George W. Bush, in large part because of Corsi's book—as well as the actions of a group, organized by O'Neill, called Swift Boat Veterans for Truth—and since then, as Toby Harnden wrote for the Canadian *National Post* (August 16, 2008), "the term 'to be swiftboated'—meaning to be smeared by rightwingers—has entered the political lexicon." Both books have been widely and strongly condemned as hatchet jobs filled with unsubstantiated claims, inaccuracies, and thinly veiled lies.

Corsi, previously an academic and a financial-services and insurance executive, was a marginal figure on the right fringe of the conservative movement before 2004, when, as Max Blumenthal wrote for the *Nation* (August 20, 2008, on-line), he emerged overnight as "a conservative folk hero," assuming the role of "court bard of the conservative movement." With *Unfit for Command* and *The Obama Nation*, Corsi unapologetically stated that

Andrew C. Stettner, courtesy of Pocket Books

Jerome R. Corsi

his mission was to prevent the election of the Democratic nominees; his strategy was to turn their respective strengths—Kerry's war heroism and Obama's "compelling life story," as Eugene Robinson put it in the *Washington Post* (August 15, 2008, online)—against them. Corsi has publicly broken with Republicans to endorse the far-right Constitution Party. Among his other books are those advancing the theories that oil is not, as is generally believed, a finite commodity; that officials in the U.S. government, among others, are helping to arm Iran with nuclear weapons; and that there is a covert plan to integrate Canada, the U.S., and Mexico into one nation. Corsi is a regular contributor to the Web sites WorldNetDaily and Human Events.

Jerome Robert Corsi was born on August 31, 1946 in East Cleveland, Ohio, one of the two sons of Alice and Louis Corsi. His father, a committed Democrat, worked for the Brotherhood of Railroad Trainmen, an important labor group and a forerunner of the United Transportation Union. As Steve Giegerich wrote for *Leader's Edge Magazine* (June 2005), published by a subsidiary of the Council of Insurance Agents & Brokers, "There is nothing about Jerry Corsi's childhood that would even remotely suggest he would one day become a conservative lightning rod. In fact, quite the opposite is true." Corsi told Giegerich, referring to the Democratic president Franklin Delano Roosevelt, that he was "raised in a family that adored FDR. They thought he was one of the best presidents America ever had. Some of my earliest political memories had to do with FDR." Corsi's first job was as a public-relations worker for his father's labor union; his first book, *Collective Bargaining and Compulsive Arbitration*, written when he was only 17, was strongly pro-labor.

Corsi enrolled at what is now Case Western Reserve University, in Cleveland, earning a bachelor's degree in economics and political science in 1968. During his undergraduate years, which coincided with the Vietnam War, widespread antiwar protests, and the introduction of federally funded social programs launched to build the so-called Great Society championed by Democratic president Lyndon Baines Johnson, Corsi—unlike many in his generation—felt drawn to the political right. (According to Ben McGrath, writing for the *New Yorker* [August 25, 2008], Corsi had been attracted to Republican positions at a much earlier age and "said that he was six years old when he began to question his father's admiration for [the 1952 Democratic presidential nominee] Adlai Stevenson.") President Johnson's "war on poverty did not appeal to me," Corsi told Giegerich. "They were embarking on social engineering without being certain it would work." In 1968, according to Giegerich, Corsi turned down a paid position in the Republican Richard M. Nixon's ultimately successful campaign for the presidency. Instead, he attended graduate school at Harvard University, in Cambridge, Massachusetts, earning a Ph.D. degree in political science in 1972. (According to Giegerich, Corsi, a strong supporter of the Vietnam War, had avoided military service because of a diagnosis of hereditary eczema.) His dissertation, entitled *Prior Restraint, Prior Punishment, and Political Dissent: A Moral and Legal Evaluation*, examined the historic 1964 U.S. Supreme Court ruling in *New York Times v. Sullivan*, which defined modern American defamation law, ensuring freedom of political speech and protecting freedom of the press. The civil rights movement had led to numerous libel suits brought against news organizations that had reported on racial injustice in the southern states; the *New York Times* argued that the suits were filed in order to discourage the media from reporting on segregation. The Supreme Court ruled that for a public official to sue successfully for defamation, he or she must prove "actual malice," an extremely difficult standard to meet, because one had to prove that the defendant had known that a published statement was false or had acted with reckless disregard for the truth. Those criteria made it almost impossible for public figures to win cases against publishers. "In the name of free speech, courts protect false speech," the former Nixon administration official John Dean wrote for findlaw.com (August 22, 2008). Dean added that Corsi is immune from lawsuits when writing about figures such as Kerry and Obama "because he can hide behind a body of law that protects lies and insults on the assumption that they will be corrected in the marketplace of public debate." In fact, Dean argued, some voters who were unaware of the law were surprised when Kerry and Obama did not sue Corsi, assuming that therefore "there must be some truth to Corsi's claims" in his books.

After earning his doctorate Corsi spent most of the 1970s as a professor and researcher at the University of New Mexico and the University of Denver. According to Giegerich, he "devoted years to development of technology that allowed New Mexico Department of Labor officials to obtain sworn testimony on unemployment claims over the telephone." After the Republican Ronald Reagan entered the White House, in 1981, Corsi left academia to work under the president, whose anti-Communist stance he admired. At the U.S. Agency for International Development, Corsi spent a year training embassy employees survival techniques used by hostages.

In 1982 Corsi moved to the financial sector, specializing in the relatively new financial instruments known as annuities, which were lucrative in American banking at the time. In 1986 he established Marketing One Securities, a third-party business that offered such investment options as annuities and mutual funds to savings-and-loan institutions and other firms, as ways for those firms to provide new investment strategies to customers. Beginning in 1998 Corsi established three different third-party firms—Independent Financial Marketing Group, Bankmark, and U.S. Financial Marketing Group; he had sold all of them by 2005. According to an oft-cited article in the *Boston Globe* (August 20, 2008), in 1995 Corsi became involved in a failed mutual-fund investment scheme in Poland, in which he and two partners were accused of cheating a group of Minnesota investors, who lost a total of $1.2 million. While an FBI investigation into the affair was inconclusive, several investors sued Corsi successfully but received no compensation, as Corsi had placed all of his assets in his wife's name.

Corsi's career move from business to political writing began in earnest in 2004, when John Kerry, a decorated Vietnam War veteran turned antiwar activist and later a Democratic U.S. senator from Massachusetts, ran for president against the incumbent, George W. Bush. According to several sources, Corsi had harbored a strong animosity toward Kerry for his involvement in the antiwar movement and believed that he was a Communist at heart. "I always said if he ran for president I'd come out against him," Corsi told Giegerich. Corsi teamed up with a college acquaintance, a Texas lawyer named John O'Neill, who, like Kerry, had served on a swift boat (though not Kerry's) during the Vietnam War and who had opposed Kerry's antiwar stance. O'Neill established an anti-Kerry organization called Swift Boat Veterans for Truth (SBVT). In the summer of 2004, a few months before the presidential election, Corsi and O'Neill published *Unfit for Command: Swift Boat Veterans Speak Out Against John Kerry*, attacking Kerry—who was emerging as the Democratic presidential nominee—as unpatriotic, claiming that he had lied about his military actions and his injuries in order to receive medals, and alleging that Kerry's antiwar activities amounted to treason and to collusion with Communists. While the book contained testimony from soldiers who had never served with Kerry, many who had served with him rallied to his side, calling the accusations unfounded. Nonetheless, *Unfit for Command* and its word-of-mouth publicity resonated with the public to such an extent that many saw the book as helping to determine the outcome of the election, which Bush won.

Meanwhile, the group Media Matters for America had attacked the book, with its president and CEO, David Brock, writing a letter to the heads of major book-store chains, urging them to consider "the responsibility of books sellers when it becomes established that prominent non-fiction books are based on false information." As quoted by US Newswire (August 20, 2004), Brock wrote, "There is something fundamentally wrong when a book that is rampant with falsehoods and misinformation is published and sold as non-fiction. . . . Customers should be made aware that *Unfit for Command* is a paid political hatchet job, full of false allegations and lies." Media Matters for America also exposed numerous inflammatory comments made by Corsi between 2001 and 2004 on a right-wing Web site, FreeRepublic.com. Corsi, who later acknowledged that he had made the comments and apologized for them, claiming that they were satirical, was quoted by US Newswire (August 6, 2004) as writing on the Free Republic site, "Let's see exactly why it isn't the case that Islam is a worthless, dangerous Satanic religion? Where's the proof to the contrary?" He also wrote that Islam "is like a virus—it affects the mind—maybe even better as an analogy—it is a cancer that destroys the body it infects. . . . No doctor would hesitate to eliminate cancer cells from the body." In addition to several other, even more incendiary comments about Islam and Muslims, Corsi crudely attacked Catholicism, Judaism, and homosexuals as well as the Democrats Al Gore and Hillary and Bill Clinton. After his comments were exposed, Corsi was quickly dropped from the book-promotion campaign. That episode notwithstanding, with Bush's reelection, Corsi became a star among right-wing Republicans.

Corsi's other volumes include a children's book, *The King, the Dragon, and the Witch*, and several books on marketing, insurance, and banking. In 2005 he and Craig R. Smith published *Black Gold Stranglehold: The Myth of Scarcity and the Politics of Oil*, a book claiming that the public has been duped into believing that oil is a finite fossil fuel when, according to Corsi and Smith, it is a constantly regenerating product of the earth. The same year he also wrote *Atomic Iran: How the Terrorist Regime Bought the Bomb and American Politicians*, in which he accused U.S. Democrats, among others, of abetting the Iranian government's plans to acquire a nuclear bomb. The following year he co-authored, with Michael D. Evans, *Showdown with Nuclear Iran: Radical Islam's Messianic Mission to Destroy Israel and Cripple the United States* and also published *Minutemen: The Battle to Se-cure America's Borders*, co-written with Jim Gil-christ, a founder of the Minutemen, a group of self-appointed, armed patrollers of U.S. borders. In that and his subsequent book, *The Late Great U.S.A.: The Coming Merger with Mexico and Canada*, pub-lished in 2007, Corsi advanced the theory that President Bush is pursuing a secret "globalist agen-da" of unifying and integrating Mexico, Canada, and the U.S. into one nation with a common cur-rency, the "amero," modeled on the European Union and its currency, the euro.

Corsi declared in January 2005 that he was mov-ing from New Jersey to Massachussetts to try to win John Kerry's Senate seat in 2008. He later said that his wife had "vetoed" the plan. Corsi has said that he is not a member of the GOP; in a September 25, 2007 article for WorldNet Daily entitled "Why I Am Not Republican," he expressed his view that the party had abandoned its conservative princi-ples and betrayed the "moral Christians brought into the GOP by Ronald Reagan," asking, "Why is it that once Republicans like George W. Bush win office, they ignore the agenda of the conservatives and moral Christians who elected them, to the point of ridiculing our goals and objectives?" Also in 2007 Corsi announced his backing of the Consti-tution Party, which calls for dramatic reductions in the size of government, an end to immigration, a ban on abortion even in cases of rape and incest, and, according to Blumenthal, a platform founded on the belief that the "US Constitution established a Republic under God, rather than a democracy." After he announced that he would run for presi-dent in 2008, Corsi instead backed Chuck Baldwin as the Constitution Party's nominee.

In August 2008, three months before the sched-uled presidential election, Corsi published *The Obama Nation: Leftist Politics and the Cult of Per-sonality* (whose title is a play on the word "abomi-nation"). As Corsi told Jim Rutenberg and Julie Bosman for the *New York Times* (August 13, 2008), his goal in writing the book was "to defeat Obama. I don't want Obama to be in office." Corsi sought to portray Obama (who is a Christian) as a danger-ous Muslim extremist who subscribes to radical ra-cial politics, hides his "black rage," and has not stated clearly that he ever stopped taking illegal drugs. (Obama has said that he has not used illegal drugs since the age of 20.) Corsi claimed that Oba-ma was "the most un-vetted candidate we have had in recent history," as quoted by Rob Jennings in the Morristown, New Jersey, *Daily Record* (August 24, 2008), and that his (Corsi's) investigative work was simply a way of informing voters. *The Obama Na-tion* was published by a division of Simon & Schuster run by Mary Matalin, a longtime Republi-can strategist. Thanks in part to conservative orga-nizations' strategy of buying copies in bulk and to a publicity campaign that included more than 100 radio interviews with Corsi across the country, the book debuted at number one on the *New York Times* best-seller list. (Corsi's radio interviews in-cluded one on *The Political Cesspool*, a white-supremacist program hosted by James Edwards.) Newspaper editorials condemned *The Obama Na-tion* in the strongest terms, with the one in the *Washington Post* (August 15, 2008) titled "Par for Mr. Corsi: An expert at misrepresentation takes on Barack Obama." In the *New Yorker* (September 1, 2008), Hendrik Hertzberg wrote, "On a foundation of small, medium-sized, and extra-large false-hoods, *The Obama Nation* erects a superstructure of innuendo, guilt by (often nonexistent) associa-tion, baseless speculation, and sinister-sounding but irrelevant digression. The result is an example of what used to be known, in the glory days of ideologically driven totalitarianism, as the Big Lie." The Obama campaign released a 40-page re-port, "Unfit for Publication," debunking the claims in Corsi's book, and also put on its Web site a point-by-point refutation of Corsi's allegations.

Corsi lives in New Jersey with his second wife, Monica, and their daughter.

—M.M.

Suggested Reading: *ABCNews.com* Sep. 5, 2008; *FindLaw.com* Aug. 22, 2008; *Leader's Edge Magazine* (on-line) June 2005; *Morning Edition*, National Public Radio (on-line) Aug. 15, 2008; *Nation* (on-line) Aug. 20, 2008; *New Yorker* Aug. 25, 2008; *WorldNetDaily.com* Sep. 25, 2007

Selected Books: *Unfit for Command: Swift Boat Veterans Speak Out Against John Kerry* (with John O'Neill), 2004; *Black Gold Stranglehold: The Myth of Scarcity and the Politics of Oil* (with Craig R. Smith), 2005; *Atomic Iran: How the Terrorist Regime Bought the Bomb and American Politicians*, 2005; *Minutemen: The Battle to Secure America's Borders*, 2006; *Showdown with Nuclear Iran: Radical Islam's Messianic Mission to Destroy Israel and Cripple the United States* (with Michael D. Evans), 2006; *The Late Great U.S.A.: The Coming Merger with Mexico and Canada*, 2007; *The Obama Nation: Leftist Politics and the Cult of Personality*, 2008; for children—*The King, the Dragon, and the Witch*, 1972

Cotto, Miguel

Oct. 29, 1980– Boxer

Address: Top Rank Inc., 3980 Howard Hughes Pkwy., Suite 580, Las Vegas, NV 89109

On November 10, 2007 Miguel Cotto successfully defended his World Boxing Association (WBA) welterweight title when he defeated "Sugar" Shane Mosley, a former world champion in three weight classes, by unanimous decision. Kevin Iole, writ-ing for Yahoo! Sports (November 10, 2007, on-

Miguel Cotto

Nick Laham/Getty Images

line), proclaimed, "Whatever superlatives you apply, it is clear that Miguel Cotto has arrived at the top of the boxing heap," and Keith Idec added for the Passaic County, New Jersey, *Herald News* (November 12, 2007), "[Cotto] is undoubtedly an elite-level boxer, one who could creep into the top five of pound-for-pound lists after a masterful performance against one of the best boxers of this era." After enjoying one of the greatest amateur boxing careers in the history of his native Puerto Rico and competing in the Olympic Games in 2000, Cotto turned pro the following year, achieving a 30–0 record with 25 knockouts prior to his fight with Mosley. He nonetheless remained a relative unknown, owing to his lack of high-profile contenders until that time. In addition, he found himself in the shadow of his idol Felix Trinidad, a former multi-division world champion and perhaps the most beloved Puerto Rican fighter of all time. Cotto's victory over Mosley changed matters, inspiring Bernard Fernandez to write for the Philadelphia *Daily News* (November 12, 2007), "Cotto's emergence is the latest sign that boxing, which has been in a deep slumber, might finally be awakening."

In April 2008 Cotto successfully defended his title against Alfonso Gomez, defeating him in the fifth round by a technical knockout. That July he suffered his first career loss, in an unsuccessful title defense against Antonio Margarito at the MGM Grand in Las Vegas, Nevada. While Cotto's high-profile fights have helped to bring him into boxing's spotlight, some sportswriters have predicted that, because boxing tends to thrive on controversy and the outrageous behavior of its practitioners, his reserved demeanor may prevent him from achieving the levels of celebrity and wealth enjoyed by past champions. Cotto, for his part, has let his fighting speak for itself: his percentage of knockouts—79—remains one of the highest in the sport. He was named Puerto Rico's Fighter of the Year in 2004 and 2005 and Boxer of the Year in 2008 by the World Boxing Association. He is currently the ninth-ranked fighter, pound-for-pound, in the world. "I'm available for all the big names in the business," Cotto declared to Keith Idec. "And I'm ready for them."

The youngest of three sons, Miguel Angel Cotto was born on October 29, 1980 in Caguas, Puerto Rico. His father, Miguel Angel, was an officer in the National Guard, and his mother was a homemaker. Cotto grew up in a family of former boxers that included his father, his uncle Evangelista, his older brother Juan, and his cousin Abner. Initially, Cotto pursued boxing for reasons other than family tradition or love of the sport. As posted on the HBO Web site, he recalled, "When I was 11 years old, my weight was 156 pounds, and I tried to lose weight with boxing. . . . I lost weight, but I started to feel something for boxing." Under the guidance of his father and uncle, Cotto began training at Caguas's Bairoa Gym, famous as the training site of the former Puerto Rican world champions Hector "Macho" Camacho, Orlando "Cholo" Fernandez, and Jose "Curry" Carrazo; his uncle would later become his official trainer. When Cotto reached his teens, he started fighting on the amateur circuit, winning four Puerto Rican championships in two weight classes: the 132-pound division in 1997, 1998, and 1999 and the 140-pound division in 2000. After participating in several international tournaments, including the Pan American Games, he was asked to represent Puerto Rico as a light welterweight (140 pounds) in the 2000 Olympic Games, held in Sydney, Australia. He was eliminated in the first round, after losing a 17–7 decision against the Uzbekistan fighter Muhammad Abdullaev, who went on to win the gold medal. As quoted on the HBO Web site, Cotto disagreed with the judges' ruling, explaining, "I felt that I did the best I could at the Olympics. Unfortunately, some judges don't see it that way. But I was very happy with my performance, and I felt that I won that fight." Following his defeat in the Olympics, Cotto decided to turn pro, leaving behind an impressive amateur record of 125–23. One writer deemed him "the greatest amateur boxer" to ever hail from Puerto Rico.

On February 23, 2001, at the age of 20, Cotto made his professional debut in Austin, Texas, against the Louisiana native Jason Doucet. He took control of the fight early on, scoring two knockdowns in the first two minutes, before the referee ruled the fight a first-round technical knockout, or TKO. (A TKO occurs when a boxer is judged to be unable to continue fighting.) Cotto said about the fight, as posted on the Top Rank Web site, "I was just happy to get the first win under my belt. [Doucet] had a lot of courage and was very strong." He won his next five fights in similar fashion before a serious car accident jeopardized his boxing career. Driving to the gym for a 5:30 a.m. workout in August 2001, he fell asleep at the wheel and crashed into a concrete wall, breaking his right arm and shoulder in four places. Despite being told by doctors that he would need to recover for 18 months before he could train again, Cotto—who had a six-inch titanium rod inserted into his right shoulder—returned to the gym just three months later. In January 2002, when he made his comeback in the ring, he showed no signs of being at a disadvantage, knocking out Joshua Smith in the second round. He won his next four fights, all by knockout or technical knockout, before meeting an opponent who lasted the distance. Even that fighter—John Brown, a four-time world-title challenger—was knocked down in the second round and staggered in the eighth before losing in a unanimous decision. Cotto later said to Sean Stowell for the Max Boxing Web site, speaking through an interpreter, "Without a doubt the accident changed me. It made me think about a lot of things, especially my career. I could have never had a career, so now I have to take full advantage of that."

On February 1, 2003 Cotto competed in his first title bout, against Cesar Bazan, a former holder of the World Boxing Council (WBC) lightweight belt. Bazan proved to be a tough opponent, despite suffering a bloody nose in the second round, but Cotto gradually wore him down with his trademark left hooks and thunderous body shots. When the referee stopped the fight, with 16 seconds left in the 11th round, Cotto was crowned the WBC international super-lightweight (also called junior-welterweight) champion, solidifying his reputation as a talented all-around fighter. Despite being mislabeled as a "wade-in, body-banging brawler," as noted by Bernard Fernandez, Cotto had demonstrated his skill as both an infighter and boxer-puncher, combining power with fast footwork and endurance. (Infighters maintain close proximity to their opponents, unleashing a wide variety of punching combinations; boxer-punchers mete out the same barrage of hooks and uppercuts as infighters while also using hit-and-move tactics, wearing opponents down before scoring knockouts, usually in the later rounds.)

Cotto went on to defend his title against five challengers in less than a year. He knocked out Rocky Martinez in the second round on June 28, 2003 in Bayamon, Puerto Rico; landed a series of jabs that forced Demetrio Ceballos to submit in the seventh round on September 13, 2003, in Las Vegas, Nevada; ended Carlos Maussa's unbeaten streak on December 6, 2003 in Bayamon; scored three knockdowns against Victoriano Sosa (a cousin of the baseball player Sammy Sosa) for a third-round victory on February 28, 2004 in Las Vegas; and won a unanimous decision over Lovemore N'dou in Las Vegas on May 8, 2004. After a four-month respite, Cotto claimed his second professional title with a win against the Brazilian power puncher Kelson Pinto, who had defeated Cotto

twice as an amateur and posted a perfect record of 20–0. The left-handed Cotto, who in previous fights had adopted a stance normally used by right-handed fighters, this time kept his hands high in front of him to ward off Pinto's attacks. In the sixth round, after Cotto had scored his third knockdown, the referee declared him the winner by technical knockout. Cotto obtained the World Boxing Organization (WBO) junior-welterweight championship and brought his pro record to 21–0, with 17 knockouts. Following the fight, during which he wore trunks that had the names of all past Puerto Rican world boxing champions sewn on, Cotto said, according to his Web site, "Today, there's one more. I've got to be honest, I was very nervous. But you know, when you look at my record and you look at his, and the progress that I've made, I knew I would win."

Cotto continued his dominance in the WBO junior-welterweight division, defending his title six times. Following impressive TKO victories over Randall Bailey and DeMarcus Corley, he faced Muhammad Abdullaev, the last man to defeat him as an amateur, for his third title defense, in June 2005. At New York's Madison Square Garden on the eve of the city's annual Puerto Rican Day Parade, with more than 10,000 people in attendance, Cotto did not disappoint: he controlled the fight from the opening round until the ninth, when Abdullaev, his right eye closed by Cotto's left hooks, signaled to the referee to stop the fight. As posted on the Top Rank Web site, Cotto explained, "[Abdullaev] still had the same style from when I fought him in the Olympics. He was strong and came forward through the fight, just as he did in the Olympics, but tonight I worked him well. He's a great athlete, but he was hurt and he knew his body couldn't go on any longer." The following day Cotto was grand marshall of the parade.

Cotto's next fight proved to be one of the most challenging of his professional career. On September 24, 2005 in Atlantic City, New Jersey, the previously undefeated contender Ricardo Torres (21–0) became the first fighter to knock Cotto down since the latter's turning pro, even breaking one of his eardrums. Cotto rallied to send Torres to the canvas in the sixth round and knock him out with a left hook, with one minute and 24 seconds remaining in the seventh. After the fight Cotto said, as posted on the Top Rank Web site, "I didn't expect it to be so tough and to go back and forth like it did. I'm glad people saw that I can take a punch and fight back. All the time I was thinking I had to win the fight, no matter how. I didn't care how I won, I had to win. It showed the public that I can hit, and I can take a punch." Six months later, in front of 15,000 fans at the Coliseo de Ruben Rodriguez in Bayamon, Cotto battled Gianluca Branco to score a seventh-round technical knockout in his fifth title defense. He returned to Madison Square Garden for his sixth and final title defense, going the distance—12 rounds—against Paulie Malignaggi, who was previously undefeated. By the end of the fight,

Cotto had broken Malignaggi's right cheekbone and severely bloodied his nose. The three judges scored the fight 116–111, 116–111, and 115–112, all in favor of Cotto, to give him the win by unanimous decision.

In late 2006 Cotto announced that he would relinquish his WBC and WBO titles to move up in class to the more competitive welterweight division, which featured four of the top fighters in the sport: Floyd Mayweather, Ricky Hatton, Jose Luis Castillo, and Shane Mosley. Cotto's promoter—Bob Arum, founder of the Las Vegas–based company Top Rank—was initially hesitant to let Cotto move up, since Mayweather, whom Arum also represented, had just moved to the welterweight division himself; for Top Rank, having top contenders in different weight classes seemed the more lucrative arrangement. Cotto, however, wanted the opportunity to take on better-known fighters for larger purses. In December 2006, in his first fight as a welterweight, he battled his fellow Puerto Rican Carlos Quintana for the vacant World Boxing Association (WBA) welterweight championship. After withstanding a number of body shots, Quintana surrendered the fight to Cotto prior to the sixth round, giving him his third professional title. Frank Gonzales Jr. wrote for the East Side Boxing Web site, "Cotto seems to move in slow motion at times, while imposing the tempo of a fight and striking when the moment is right. Against the mobile Quintana, Cotto pressed the action and was able to cut off the ring and land those body shots that do so much damage. He looks real comfortable at 147 [pounds]." Three months later Cotto retained his belt with a TKO of Oktay Urkal in the 11th round.

Cotto's next fight, against Zab Judah, the former International Boxing Federation (IBF) and WBO junior-welterweight title holder and the undisputed welterweight champion of the world, was his most controversial. Judah, a southpaw, came after Cotto early in the first round with a left uppercut and two straight jabs to the face, then lost his momentum after Cotto delivered an accidental low blow that sent him face-first to the mat. Another accidental low blow from Cotto downed Judah again in the third. In the subsequent rounds, both fighters suffered cuts over their right eyes after butting heads repeatedly. After staggering Cotto in the seventh with punches including a left uppercut, Judah seemed to have regained his momentum, but Cotto quickly countered with his own flurry of punches, dropping Judah to one knee in the ninth before scoring a knockdown and TKO in the 11th. Judah has since demanded a rematch, citing what he saw as the bias of the referee and the low blows—which he called intentional—as the main causes of his loss.

On November 10, 2007 Cotto took on Shane Mosley at Madison Square Garden. Mosley, a three-division, four-time former world champion, once regarded as the best "pound-for-pound" boxer in the world, was Cotto's toughest and most high-profile opponent to date. Before a crowd of 17,135, Cotto won a unanimous decision over Mosley in a close, 12-round fight in which the advantage shifted back and forth; in the end, Cotto's relentless jabs wore Mosley down. "I showed everything about Miguel Cotto . . . ," Cotto said to Franklin McNeil for the Newark, New Jersey, *Star-Ledger* (November 12, 2007). "I said before that I wasn't worried about [Mosley's] speed. I was never hurt; I felt good throughout the fight."

For his next title defense, many sportswriters believed Cotto would fight Floyd Mayweather, Ricky Hatton, or Oscar De La Hoya during the 2008 Cinco de Mayo weekend. As it turned out Mayweather retired following his victory over Hatton in December 2007, and De La Hoya decided against meeting Cotto in the ring, instead fighting Steve Forbes in a tune-up bout later that May. In the end Cotto defended his championship against the Mexican boxer Alfonso Gomez on April 12, 2008 in Atlantic City, New Jersey. Gomez proved to be no match for Cotto, who knocked him to the floor three times before the referee ended the fight after five rounds, granting Cotto the win by TKO. The following July Cotto suffered his first loss as a professional boxer, in a match against Antonio Margarito. In that fight, which took place at the MGM Grand in Las Vegas, Cotto landed a flurry of punches and used clever footwork to avoid blows by his opponent during the early rounds. Then, in the later rounds, Margarito wore Cotto down by trapping him against the ropes. In the 11th round Margarito knocked Cotto to the floor twice, and Cotto's trainer threw in the towel.

Robert Morales wrote for the Los Angeles *Daily News* (November 8, 2007), "Cotto is likeable. One would be hard pressed to find a nicer guy in the sport. But whereas Trinidad has an unconstrained personality, Cotto's could be considered withdrawn." Cotto's promoter, Arum, however, said to Morales, "Miguel is Miguel. He's a great, great fighter. He's a great young man. We who are close to him know that he has a great personality. I don't want him to be a phony. I don't want him to be what he isn't."

Miguel Cotto and his wife, Melissa, live in Caguas, Puerto Rico. They have three children: Miguel Angel, Alondra, and Miguel. "I am very comfortable in Puerto Rico," he explained to Sean Stowell. "It's my home. I don't feel I'm missing out on anything here."

—C.C.

Suggested Reading: Canadastar Boxing Web site; HBO Official Web site; (Los Angeles) *Daily News* C p5+ Nov. 8, 2007; Max Boxing Web site; Miguel Cotto Official Web site; *New York Times* D p4 Nov. 12, 2007; (Passaic County, New Jersey) *Herald News* C p1 Nov. 12, 2007; Philadelphia *Daily News* D p100 Nov. 12, 2007; Top Rank Official Web site

Harry How/Getty Images

Coughlin, Tom

(CAWF-lin)

Aug. 31, 1946– Football coach

Address: Giants Stadium, 50 State Route 120, East Rutherford, NJ 07073

Tom Coughlin, the head coach of the New York Giants since 2004, has guided college and professional football teams for nearly four decades. Coughlin is famous—or notorious, as some would say—for his steely glare, for putting immense pressure on his players to work hard and win, and for insisting that the men abide by his strict, "old-school" rules. He always starts team meetings five minutes ahead of schedule, for example, and he has imposed fines for lateness even on players who arrived two minutes *before* the appointed time. While members of his teams have sometimes objected to rules that they consider arbitrary, most have acknowledged his ability to motivate athletes to win. "I've never seen somebody who wants to win so badly as Coach Coughlin, but it carries over to us, and that's what you need to get to the ultimate plateau," Jimmy Smith, who played with the Jacksonville Jaguars under Coughlin from 1994 to 2002, told Michael Silver for *Sports Illustrated* (September 20, 1999). The other teams Coughlin has coached since 1969 include three college squads, at the Rochester Institute of Technology, Syracuse University, and Boston College, and two in the National Football League (NFL)—the Philadelphia Eagles and the Green Bay Packers. After the 2006 season, in which the Giants won eight games and lost the same number, Coughlin told Tom Canavan for the Associated

Press (August 22, 2006), "I do want our players to know that what I do has their best interest at heart and the best interest of the New York Giants. There is no agenda. There is no nothing. I don't have a chip on my shoulder or a big ego. I don't have any of that stuff, but I do have knowledge of the game and I do have a deep belief in what it takes to win." That belief bore fruit on February 3, 2008 at Super Bowl XLII, when—after virtually unanimous media predictions of victory by the New England Patriots—the Giants triumphed, 17–14, in what has been described as one of the most spectacular upsets in Super Bowl history.

The eldest of the seven children of Louis and Betty Coughlin, who were of Irish descent, Thomas Richard Coughlin was born on August 31, 1946 in the town of Waterloo, in the Finger Lakes region of New York State, about halfway between Syracuse and Rochester. Coughlin attended Waterloo Central High School, where he stood out in class, as an honors student, and on the sports field, as the captain of the baseball, basketball, and football teams, all of which he led to league titles. As a young man he had a strong work ethic and self-discipline. Friends also remember him as being highly competitive. Andrew Osborne, a former classmate of Coughlin's, told Scott Pitoniak for the *Rochester Democrat and Chronicle* (February 3, 2008), "It didn't matter if he was delivering groceries on his bike or walking home, he'd treat it like it was a race. He was always pushing himself to do more and be better." During his senior year Coughlin scored 19 touchdowns, setting a school record that still stands. Waterloo Central High School's football stadium now bears his name.

After his high-school graduation, in 1964, Coughlin attended Syracuse University on a full football scholarship; he played wingback with the All-American backs Larry Csonka and Floyd Little and the future Hall of Fame coach Ben Schwartzwalder. Little told Aditi Kinkhabwala for the Bergen County, New Jersey, *Record* (January 28, 2008, online) that Coughlin never complained that he did not get to run the ball as often as his All-American teammates. "It was all about teamwork and winning—always," Little remarked. In 1967, during his senior year, Coughlin broke Syracuse's single-season passing record and won the Orange Key Award as the school's outstanding scholar-athlete. That same year Coughlin married his high-school sweetheart. He graduated from Syracuse in 1968 with a B.A. degree in education; in 1969 he earned an M.A. degree in the same field, also from Syracuse. That year he held his first coaching job, with Syracuse's freshman football team.

In 1970 Coughlin became the head coach of the Rochester Institute of Technology (RIT) football team, the Tigers, with whom he began to earn his reputation as a strict disciplinarian. "It was brutal, no place for wimps . . . ," Mark MacCabe, a former Tiger, told Pitoniak, recalling Coughlin's summer workouts. "There were times when you wanted to strangle the guy, but you were too pooped to try." The practices were so difficult that nearly half of the players left the team before the season started. During his three years at RIT, Coughlin led the team to a cumulative 16–15–2 record—an impressive feat, considering that most of the Tigers' opponents were teams from Division III schools that were generally thought to have stronger players. "We often didn't match up talent-wise with our opponents, but thanks to Coach Coughlin we were usually tougher, mentally and physically, and we were always better prepared," Ken Wegner, a former Tiger, recalled to Pitoniak. "He was tough, but he was fair. The thing we respected about him was that he never asked you to do anything he wouldn't do. As long as you worked hard, mentally and physically, you'd be fine."

In 1974 Coughlin accepted an assistant's post, that of offensive-backfield and quarterback coach, for the Syracuse University football team. In 1978 he was promoted to offensive coordinator. In 1979, under his direction, the Syracuse Orangemen won the Independence Bowl, their first bowl trophy in 13 years. His success led to his being hired as quarterback coach for Boston College, in Massachusetts, in 1981. There he coached a future Heisman Trophy winner—the quarterback Doug Flutie, who went on to have a long career as a professional. In 1982 Coughlin helped lead the Boston College Eagles to the Tangerine Bowl (now known as the Capital One Bowl), which the Auburn University team won that year. In 1983 the Eagles defeated Notre Dame to win the Lambert-Meadowlands Trophy at the Liberty Bowl, becoming the Eastern Division champions for the first time in 42 years.

Coughlin left Boston College in 1983 to take on what turned out to be a series of assistant-coach positions with professional teams. He was the wide-receivers coach for the Philadelphia Eagles (1984–85) and the receivers coach for the Green Bay Packers (1986–87) and the Giants (1988–90). With the Giants, Coughlin served under the head coach, Bill Parcells, who became both a mentor and a friend; from Parcells, he learned such strategies as maintaining a "power defense" and lengthy offensive drives. Coughlin also worked with the defensive coordinator Bill Belichick. During the 1990 season Coughlin helped fine-tune the skills of receivers including Mark Ingram, Lionel Manuel, Odessa Turner, and Stephen Baker. That year the Giants achieved a regular-season record of 13–3, going on to compete in Super Bowl XXV. There, they defeated the Buffalo Bills, 20–19.

In 1991 Coughlin returned to Boston College as the head coach, replacing Jack Bicknell, his former boss, who had been known as a friendly and thoughtful coach. The college's Athletics Department decision makers expected Coughlin to bring a tougher edge to the football program. "I hope to build a team here that will play like the Giants did this past year. With a lot of power," Coughlin told Will McDonough for the Boston Globe (March 2, 1991). As he had at RIT, he toughened the practice schedule and drills, emphasizing work ethic and

accountability. Dwight Shirley, a former Boston fullback, recalled the Eagles' first meeting with the new coach to William C. Rhoden for the New York Times (October 22, 1992): "He came in and told everyone to sit up straight, put all eyes on him. Then he said, 'We will have no fat people on this team.' Some of the linemen just kind of looked at each other. But it was true, we were kind of a flabby team." The team, numbering some 120 players, became both leaner and smaller—many players quit. "I think that's what the coach wanted, to get down to the people who could last. That's us," a star player, the quarterback Glenn Foley, told Leigh Montville for Sports Illustrated (October 5, 1992). The team ended the 1991 season with four wins and seven losses.

The Eagles won their first five 1992-season games and tied in the sixth. The team advanced to the Hall of Fame Bowl, where they played the Tennessee Volunteers in January 1993. Boston performed poorly; they were outrushed by Tennessee by nearly 100 yards, and many of their yards were gained only in the fourth quarter, when Boston was down 38–7. Coughlin remarked to William N. Wallace for the New York Times (January 2, 1993) that his team had displayed "probably the poorest tackling performance . . . I've ever seen in my life." Still, fans were pleased with Coughlin's leadership. The team finished the season with a record of 8–3–1, their first winning record in five years. Although Coughlin was reportedly offered the position of head coach of the New York Giants at the end of the season, he confirmed at a press conference in January 1993 that he would remain in Boston, indicating that the loss to Tennessee had left him feeling that he had not lived up to his own standards as a coach. "There was one thought I could not shake," Coughlin told Frank Litsky for the New York Times (January 6, 1993). "Had I achieved my commitment to Boston College and accomplished what I wanted to accomplish? We stand for winning, doing things right, the amateur game of collegiate football in its finest hour."

The 1993 season was the Eagles' best under Coughlin. After starting the season 0–2, he led the team to a 9–3 record, winning eight consecutive late-season games, including a November contest against Notre Dame's Fighting Irish that was widely dubbed the "Holy War" (because Boston College and Notre Dame were the only two Catholic universities that compete in the NCAA's Division I-A tournament). Ranked number one after their upset defeat of the formerly number-one–ranked Florida State Seminoles the week before, Notre Dame had been heavily favored in the contest. But Boston's David Gordon scored a last-second 41-yard field goal to give the win to the Eagles, 41–39, and keep Notre Dame from the national championship. Coughlin then led the 1993 team to defeat the University of Virginia (31–13) in the Carquest Bowl (now known as the Champs Sports Bowl).

On February 21, 1994 Coughlin surprised his Boston colleagues by announcing that he had accepted the positions of head coach and director of football operations for the Jacksonville, Florida, Jaguars, one of two NFL expansion teams slated to begin play in 1995; his contract was reportedly worth $4 million over five years, making him the highest-paid rookie coach in NFL history. At a news conference Coughlin called the offer "a once-in-a-lifetime opportunity," as quoted by the Associated Press (February 22, 1994). In an unusual circumstance for the coach of an expansion team, Coughlin was given the ultimate say in all coaching and recruiting decisions. He hired five of his Boston College assistants and spent the 1994 season building his 53-man roster, scouting and recruiting players from the February allocation draft and the expansion draft in April 1995. Two of the players he acquired turned out to be especially valuable: Mark Brunell, a backup quarterback from the Green Bay Packers, and Tony Boselli, a left tackle from the University of Southern California. In the summer before the 1995 season, the Jaguars underwent rigorous training in what became known as "Camp Coughlin." The world of professional football thus became familiar with Coughlin's lengthy list of rules, among them: coaches may not wear sunglasses on the practice field; players may not wear hats or slouch at team meetings, wear ankle socks at practice, wear white socks while on the road, have beards or wear jewelry, or watch television within 90 minutes of a game. The players were required to wear helmets during warm-ups and were forbidden to kneel or sit at practice. Explaining one of the reasons for his rules, Coughlin said, as quoted by Peter King in *Sports Illustrated* (August 7, 1995), "You only get one time to make a first impression. You can't start easy and then get strict on players." Coughlin's approach seemed to work: the Jacksonville Jaguars became the most successful expansion team in NFL history. While a slew of injuries forced them to play with a different offensive starting lineup in each of their 16 games, the Jaguars won four of their 16 games during their inaugural season, which, at that time, was more than any previous expansion team had in its first year.

Coughlin became known for motivating his players the night before games by yelling out what he predicted would be the next day's important matchups. Jaguar linebacker Kevin Hardy recalled to King for *Sports Illustrated* (July 16, 1997) that when, on the eve of a game, Coughlin matched him with the Denver Broncos' tight end Shannon Sharpe, "you hear that and you think, Wow, I've got a pretty important role here. I went into the Denver game honestly thinking that how I did against Shannon Sharpe would be the big factor in the game." The Jaguars' eight wins and eight losses in the regular season earned them a spot in the play-offs as a wild-card team. After winning their first three play-off games, the Jaguars advanced to the National Football Conference (NFC) championship game. Their opponents were the New England Patriots, coached by Bill Parcells. Before the game Parcells was widely quoted singing Coughlin's praises. As reported by Dave Anderson for the *New York Times* (January 7, 2004), Parcells said, "Tom is one of the best two or three coaches I've ever been around. Because he's fearless—fearless. He's not afraid of anything." Although the Jaguars lost the game, 20–6, Coughlin was honored as NFL Coach of the Year by United Press International.

In the next three seasons, Coughlin led the Jaguars to solid winning records and play-off spots, which generated tremendous support for the team from the Jacksonville, Florida, community. In each season from 1997 through 1999, the Jaguars' regular-season records of 11–5, 11–5, and 14–2, respectively, enabled them to reach the play-offs. In 1997 the Jaguars overcame the season-ending injury of their starting quarterback, Mark Brunell, and started with Rob Johnson, their underused backup quarterback, who had not appeared on the field even once during the previous season. That year the Jaguars scored 394 points in the regular season, the third-highest number in the league. In 1999 the Jaguars finished the season with the league's best record, 14–2, and advanced to the second round of the play-offs, where they met the Tennessee Titans—the team responsible for their two regular-season losses. At half-time the Jaguars were leading, 14–10, then failed to gain any additional points or to prevent the Titans from amassing 23 more during the second half. After the 1999 season Coughlin and his staff were selected to coach the NFL's Pro Bowl, which is analogous to baseball's All-Star Game. Rather than treating it as a casual exhibition game, Coughlin played to win. The Jaguars' Pro-Bowl offensive tackle, Leon Searcy, recalled to John Oehser for *Football Digest* (October 1, 2000) that the Pro Bowl players were not accustomed to Coughlin's intensity. "A lot of guys were like, 'Relax, TC,'" Searcy said. "A lot of guys who don't know him think of it as stern, but it's the way he is. You've got to respect a man like that, who doesn't wade in and out. . . . You need a little discipline in your life. You need someone who's going to be a little stern."

The Jaguars finished the 2000 season with a 7–9 record, leaving them in last place in their division and without the chance to appear in the play-offs. In 2001 Coughlin was forced to renegotiate several players' contracts to take into account the NFL's salary-cap rules. The team lost some key players and replaced many of them with rookies. The Jaguars' regular-season record, 6–10, again removed them from contention for the play-offs. Attendance at games dwindled, and fans expressed increasing frustration with the team's poor performance. Nevertheless, in May 2002 the Jaguars' major owner, Wayne Weaver, described Coughlin as "still in the top five or six coaches in the NFL" in an interview with Devan Stuart for the *Business Journal* (May 17, 2002) and announced that Coughlin's contract was being extended to the end of the 2004 season.

In the 2002 off-season, 10 players left because of the salary cap, and Jacksonville acquired several veteran second-string players to replace them. In 2002 the Jaguars again lost more games (10) than they won (six). On January 3, 2003 Coughlin was fired. "We are at a point in this business where we see we need innovative ideas and approaches," Weaver explained to Devan Stuart, as quoted by the *Business Journal* (January 3, 2003). "Tom was disappointed. He's a very proud man who knows he's done his job. . . . Whatever Tom Coughlin does in the future, he will be successful."

Parcells, then the head coach of the Dallas Cowboys, reportedly invited Coughlin to work as his offensive coordinator, but Coughlin turned down that offer in the hope that a head-coach position would come his way. Late in 2003 Jim Fassel, the New York Giants' head coach, announced that he was leaving the team, following a dismal season plagued by fumbles, drops, and missed scoring opportunities. After a brief interviewing process, throughout which Coughlin always appeared to be the top choice, in January 2004 the Giants named him as the team's new head coach. "Tom Coughlin is the man we wanted 11 years ago and he is the man we wanted now," the Giants' general manager, Ernie Accorsi, told Lynn Zinser for the *New York Times* (January 7, 2004). "Aside from his family, Tom has one interest: winning." The following April Coughlin made a draft-day trade for the University of Mississippi quarterback Eli Manning and picked up the Boston College guard Chris Snee (who had recently fathered a child with Coughlin's daughter Katie) in the second round. As Coughlin commenced his tough routine of preseason practice and instituted his lengthy list of rules, fans and sports media speculated about the effect that his coaching style would have on the struggling Giants. Players soon registered complaints with the NFL players' union regarding Coughlin's rules and his tendency to fine people for breaking them.

Despite some resistance from his team—the linebacker Antonio Pierce recalled to a reporter for the *Pittsburgh Post-Gazette* (February 3, 2008), "Everybody pretty much hated his guts"—Coughlin's tactics had immediate positive results. The Giants won four out of their first five games, among them a 20–14 upset against the Washington Redskins. After a series of midseason losses, Coughlin benched his starting quarterback Kurt Warner and started Eli Manning, who led the Giants to a last-minute victory against the Cowboys in the season's last game, ending an eight-game losing streak. The Giants finished the season with a 6–10 record. The team enjoyed more success the next year; with 11 wins and five losses in the regular season, they earned a spot in the play-offs. In their postseason game against the Carolina Panthers, the Giants lost, 23–0. The running back Tiki Barber (one of five Pro Bowl Giants that year) publicly criticized what he considered Coughlin's failure to prepare the team for the play-offs, specifically for "not setting . . . goals high enough," as Barber said, according to Michael Silver in *Sports Illustrated* (September 4, 2006). "The talk all season was 'Restore Giant pride' and 'Get to the playoffs,' and we did that. But anyone who thought we had a successful season is misguided."

When the players arrived at training camp in 2006, they were greeted by a poster, hung by Coughlin, bearing words by Winston Churchill: "Victory is never final. Defeat is never fatal. It's courage that counts." After posting a 4–0 record in their preseason games and winning six out of their first seven, the Giants suffered such midseason problems as injuries, intra-team disagreements, and poor execution. After a September loss to the Seattle Seahawks (42–30), the tight end Jeremy Shockey told reporters that the team had been "outplayed and out-coached," as quoted by Nunyo Demasio in *Sports Illustrated* (December 11, 2006); the comment struck Coughlin as "extremely disappointing." In October the *New York Times* reported that Barber was retiring at the end of the season to pursue a broadcasting career—news that sparked significant public and fan resentment. Key players were injured, and the performances of Manning and the defense suffered. The Giants lost six out of their last eight games, ending the season with an 8–8 record. Coughlin described the team's frustration with their offense to Tom Canavan for the Associated Press (November 21, 2006): "You're out of sync, you're out of whack. There is no momentum, there isn't any flow to your game because your offense isn't playing very well." The very next Sunday the Giants gave up a 21-point lead over the Titans in the fourth quarter to lose the game, 24–21, and fans and members of the sports media called for Coughlin's ouster. At a December 24, 2006 home game against the New Orleans Saints, which the Giants lost, 30–7, some fans left the stadium early in the fourth quarter while chanting "Fire Coughlin." The Giants made it to the postseason as a wild-card pick, losing in the first round to the Philadelphia Eagles, 23–20. There were rumors that Coughlin would be replaced by the Notre Dame coach Charlie Weis. In January 2007, after meeting with Coughlin several times, two of the Giants' owners, Jonathan Tisch and John Mara, announced that they had extended Coughlin's contract for another year. According to the Associated Press (January 10, 2007), Tisch declared, "He has a vision and he understands how that vision can move forward."

Coughlin made a few notable changes in preparation for the 2007 season. He hired Steve Spagnuolo as the new defensive coordinator and Chris Palmer as the new quarterback coach. He also made a conscious effort to establish warmer connections with his players. He created a team leadership council, with whom he discussed important matters. "My whole philosophy has been to communicate with the players better," he told Damon Hack for *Sports Illustrated* (January 21, 2008). "I share my thoughts with [the leadership council], they share their thoughts with me, and they take the message to the team." Players also remarked that Coughlin had lightened up a bit, joking and chatting. He even took his team bowling and arranged a team-only casino night during training camp. "The changes he's made have exceeded anything I ever expected," the defensive end Michael Strahan told Jim Trotter for *Sports Illustrated* (October 29, 2007). "The guy actually is a personality now. He's funny, he gets the room laughing. He makes you feel like you can enjoy being at work. That's important."

The Giants started the season with two losses, and fans prepared themselves for another frustrating year. But the team surprised all their critics by winning the next six games, and they earned a spot in the play-offs after their 15th, penultimate regular-season game. In their final match of the season, on December 29, 2007, the Giants faced the undefeated New England Patriots; the undisputed stars of the NFL and the focus of the media, the Patriots had broken many offensive and defensive records as they aimed to complete a "perfect," undefeated season (a feat last achieved in 1972, when the Miami Dolphins went 15–0). After leading at halftime, 21–16 (marking the first time all season that the Patriots trailed at the midpoint), the Giants gave up 22 points in the last 19 minutes to lose, 38–35. Despite that defeat, fans and the media acknowledged that the Giants had made an excellent showing.

The Giants entered the play-offs as a wild-card team, with a record of 10–6. Although the sports media repeatedly expressed negative expectations about their prospects, in their first game, on January 6, 2008, the team defeated the Tampa Bay Buccaneers, 24–14. A week later the Giants faced the Dallas Cowboys, who had beaten them twice in the regular season and were heavily favored. Nevertheless, the Giants won, 21–17. After the game Coughlin appeared exhilarated, telling Hack, "What I think you are seeing is the team concept to the nth degree." The NFC championship game pitted the Giants against the Green Bay Packers in Green Bay, Wisconsin, where winds made the air temperature bitterly cold. The game went into overtime when the Giants' place kicker Lawrence Tynes missed two potentially game-winning field goals in the fourth quarter, then sank a 47-yard field goal that led to the Giants' victory—their 10th road-game win in a row.

Super Bowl XLII, held on February 3, 2008, was among the most exciting games and biggest upsets in Super Bowl history. The Giants' four-man defensive line pressured the Patriots' Tom Brady throughout the game, sacking him five times—more than he had ever been sacked in a single game. As a result the Patriots' outstanding offense had difficulty gaining any momentum. The Patriots led 7–3 in the second quarter, a score that remained until the fourth quarter, when Manning hit David Tyree in the end zone to take the lead. The Patriots answered with an efficient 80-yard drive to bring the score to 14–10. With just two minutes and 42 sec-

onds left in the game, Manning led the team to the Patriots' 44-yard line, where, on third down, he appeared to have been sacked—then threw a surprise, 32-yard bomb to Tyree, who leapt into the air and, in another amazing play, caught the pass on his helmet. The Giants scored a few plays later, when Manning threw to Plaxico Burress (who was playing with an injured knee ligament) in the end zone's back corner, to take the lead, 17–14, the game's final score. Coughlin and the team were ecstatic about their improbable victory. "Every team is beatable, you never know," Coughlin told Judy Battista for the *New York Times* (February 4, 2008). "The right moment, the right time, every team is beatable." The Giants' owner John Mara called the win "the greatest victory in the history of this franchise, without question," as quoted by David K. Li in the *New York Post* (February 4, 2008, on-line). The team continued to celebrate the following Tuesday, February 5, in a tickertape parade through downtown Manhattan and a party at Giants Stadium, in New Jersey. Manning was honored as the Super Bowl's most valuable player. In March 2008 Coughlin signed a four-year contract with the Giants worth about $21 million. The following September Coughlin published *A Team to Believe In: Our Journey to the Superbowl*; written with the sportswriter Brian Curtis, it chronicles the Giants' improbably successful 2007–08 season. The book also describes Coughlin's struggles as a coach and why he changed his approach to the game and his players.

In the summer of 2008, the Giants' roster underwent some notable changes. The star defensive end Michael Strahan announced his retirement, and Coughlin traded to the New Orleans Saints the team's starting tight end Jeremy Shockey, who had been known both for his talent and his edgy persona and prominent ego. The trade was widely thought to reflect the philosophy that Coughlin had outlined during training camp, as quoted by Paul Shwartz in the *New York Post* (July 24, 2008): "Team over self is why we win." Seven weeks into the 2008–09 season, the Giants had won five games and lost one, putting them in first place in their division. The team's only loss came on October 13, 2008 against the Cleveland Browns (35–14), a game in which a number of Giants were unable to play due to injuries.

Coughlin and his wife, Judy, have four children—Tim, Brian, Keli, and Katie—all of whom are married; the couple have five grandchildren. His family, who know him as a loving taskmaster, often chide him about his obsessive organization and his refusal to relax. In 1999 his son Brian told Silver, "He talks a big game, but my mom's the boss at home, no question about it." In 1996 Coughlin founded the Jay Fund Foundation, named in honor of Jay McGillis, who played football for Coughlin at Boston College, then died of leukemia at the age of 21. Now run by Coughlin's daughter Keli, the foundation raises money to assist juvenile victims of leukemia and their families and to support research in leukemia and other childhood cancers. Coughlin regularly hosts events and parties for pediatric oncology patients for the Make a Wish Foundation and often arranges for the children to attend Giants' practice sessions.

—M.E.R.

Suggested Reading: *Boston Globe* E p12 Feb. 4, 2008; *Football Digest* p30 Oct. 1, 2000; *New York Times* D p1+ Jan. 7, 2004, (on-line) Feb. 4, 2008, July 27, 2008; *North Jersey Record* (on-line) Jan. 28, 2008; *Rochester Democrat and Chronicle* (on-line) Feb. 3, 2008; *Sports Illustrated* p52+ Sep. 20, 1999, p33 Sep. 27, 2004, p144 Oct. 29, 2007

Selected Books: *A Team to Believe In: Our Journey to the Superbowl* (with Brian Curtis), 2008

Peter Kramer/Getty Images

Couric, Katie

NOTE: An earlier article about Katie Couric appeared in *Current Biography* in 1993.

Jan. 7, 1957– Television journalist; anchor

Address: CBS Evening News, 524 W. 57th St., New York, NY 10019

On September 5, 2006, when she made her debut as anchor of the *CBS Evening News*, Katie Couric became the first solo female host of a nightly network-television news program. After 15 years as the co-host of NBC's *Today*, a morning news and entertainment show increasingly known for its soft-news features and light mood, Couric regarded the CBS job as a welcome challenge and an opportunity to reconnect with her hard-news roots. CBS executives, for their part, hoped to breathe new life into *Evening News*, which was trailing its competitors, NBC's *Nightly News* and ABC's *World News*, in the Nielsen ratings. In courting Couric CBS executives had told her that they envisioned the *Evening News* as becoming "more personal, more accessible, a little less formal, a little more approachable," as she told Joe Hagan for *New York* (July 16, 2007). In her September 5 broadcast, Couric demonstrated both her strength as a one-on-one interviewer on weighty subjects and her facility in presenting "fluff" (news about a celebrity couple's baby); she also introduced "freeSpeech," a *CBS Evening News* segment in which laypersons and famous figures speak their minds on various topics. As that night's program ended, the camera pulled away, giving viewers a glimpse of Couric's widely admired legs. Joe Hagan called the telecast "unmistakably Katie," adding, "A slightly more serious, more polished version of her morning-show persona, but Katie nonetheless."

Couric came to the *CBS Evening News* during a transitional time in the network's history. In March 2005 Bob Schieffer had become the temporary replacement for the longtime anchor Dan Rather, who had left the network following a scandal in which reporters for *60 Minutes Wednesday* were accused of citing false documents in a story critical of President George W. Bush's National Guard service. Couric's CBS debut was a ratings success, with an estimated 13.5 million viewers tuned in. Before long, however, those numbers began dropping, and by May 2007 only 5.5 million people were watching—fewer than before Couric's arrival. CBS responded by firing the *Evening News*'s producer and adopting a more conventional approach to presentation of the news. Some speculated that audiences' unwillingness to accept a female network weekday-evening-news anchor, combined with Couric's sometimes disparaged perkiness, led to the show's poor ratings. Couric thought, as she told Hagan, that "maybe a new anchor from another network was jarring enough. So perhaps we should have done a more traditional newscast and as time went on sort of wiggled out of that slowly." In the months preceding her first anniversary as *Evening News* anchor, several articles highly critical of her performance appeared in major periodicals, among them one by Jaime J. Weinman for *Maclean's* (May 28, 2007) entitled "It's the Katie Couric Death Watch." "If it turns out it wasn't a perfect fit, then, you know, I'll do something else that's really exciting and fulfilling for me," Couric told Hagan. Rick Kaplan, who took over as the executive producer of *Evening News* in March 2007, told Gail Shister for the *Philadelphia Inquirer* (April 22, 2007), "Katie is the anchor until she decides to ride off into the sunset and do something else. There is no one, no one, wringing their hands around here."

Over the course of her career, Couric, who worked as a general-assignment reporter and NBC Pentagon correspondent before joining *Today*, has covered a wide range of stories, including the shootings at Colorado's Columbine High School and the terrorist attcks of September 11, 2001. In 2000, two years after her husband died of colon cancer, she taped one of her more memorable segments, undergoing an on-air colonoscopy. Couric earned a Peabody Award for that colon-cancer report. Her other honors include the 2001 Radio-Television News Directors Association Edward R. Murrow Award for Overall Excellence; six Emmy Awards; a National Headliner Award; an Associated Press Award; the Society of Professional Journalists' Sigma Delta Chi Award; two American Women and Radio and Television Gracie Awards; the Harvard University School of Public Health's Julius B. Richmond Award; and the Danny Kaye Humanitarian Award, given by UNICEF.

Katherine Anne Couric was born on January 7, 1957 in Arlington, Virginia, to John M. Couric, a journalist and public-relations executive, and Elinor Couric, who worked part-time for the Lord & Taylor department-store chain after raising Katie and her sisters, Emily and Clara, and brother, John Jr. (Emily Couric was a Virginia state senator when she died, in 2001, of pancreatic cancer.) Elinor Couric also volunteered at the local branch of Planned Parenthood. As the youngest sibling, Katie was often the center of attention. A competent, confident, and outgoing student at Yorktown High School in Arlington, she earned membership in the National Honor Society and engaged in extracurricular activities including track and field, gymnastics, cheerleading, and writing for the student newspaper. In an interview with Bruce Weber for the *New York Times* (April 9, 1992), she described herself as "the kid whose essay the teacher would read in front of the class." After her high-school graduation, in 1975, Couric enrolled at the University of Virginia at Charlottesville. There, she joined the sorority Delta Delta Delta and served on the campus newspaper, the *Cavalier Daily*, as an associate editor. She also interned at local radio stations. After she earned a B.A. degree in American studies, with honors, in 1979, she set about getting work as a television reporter, which her father had advised her paid more than reportorial jobs with newspapers.

Couric landed her first job—desk assistant, an entry-level position—by talking her way past a secretary and into the office of ABC News's assistant bureau chief in Washington, D.C. Less than a year later, she accepted an invitation from the bureau's chief, George Watson, to move with him to the Washington bureau of the Cable News Network (CNN). At CNN she held the post of assignment editor, which entailed intermittent on-air reporting. At that time Couric's voice was high-pitched and squeaky; to Reese Schonfeld, CNN's president then, she sounded like a 16-year-old, and after he heard one of her broadcasts, he ruled out any future on-air appearances for her. "I'll never forget how depressed she was that day," Chris Curle, a CNN co-anchor then, told Barbara Matusow for the *Chicago Tribune* (May 5, 1991).

Undaunted, Couric worked with a voice coach in Atlanta, Georgia, where she had moved in 1982 to take the job of CNN associate producer. She was later named the producer of *Take Two*, a daily two-hour CNN news-and-information show; after awhile she became a full-time correspondent for the program. In 1984, as a temporary CNN on-air political correspondent, she reported on that year's presidential campaign and several U.S. Senate races. After Election Day CNN "advised her to leave," as Don Farmer, one of *Take Two*'s anchors, told Barbara Matusow.

Before the year was out, Couric had found work as a general-assignment reporter for WTVJ, in southern Florida. She covered news connected with immigration, crime, and drug-related issues for two televised newscasts a day. She produced a WTVJ special about homeless people in downtown Miami, Florida, and wrote and produced an award-winning series on child pornography. Despite her growing proficiency behind the camera, she was still "terrible" in live broadcasts, as her producer, Tammi Leader, recalled in an interview with Joanne Kaufman for *TV Guide* (February 6, 1993). "She didn't know how the earpiece worked, she didn't know how to address the camera. She screwed up all the time. She was smart and knew how to put stories together, but her presentation was terrible." Couric has claimed that at that time she was not interested in anchoring anyway. "I'm not glamorous," she told Barbara Matusow. "I always thought of myself as the workhorse, street-reporter type. And besides, my bosses never encouraged me."

In 1986 Couric returned to Washington, D.C., where she became a general-assignment reporter for the 11:00 p.m. newscast of the NBC affiliate WRC; most often she reported on fires, murders, and government corruption. In 1989, her final year there, she won a local Emmy Award and an Associated Press Award for an exposé of an unscrupulous dating service for disabled people. "You can throw anything at her and she can handle it," Bret Marcus, then the WRC news director, told Roxanne Roberts for the *Washington Post* (May 21, 1991). "Anything" did not include anchoring, however. Nervous and nearly overwhelmed by the demands of her job, Couric assessed her on-air performances as "terrible," as she recalled to Roberts, adding, "and I was a wreck." When her contract came up for renewal, Marcus advised her to seek work as a full-time anchor with a smaller station, where the professional risks would be minimal. Alternatively, he suggested that she try out for the position of NBC's deputy Pentagon reporter, a low-profile post that might prepare her for a higher-level network job.

With the help of NBC's Washington bureau chief, Tim Russert, and NBC's chief Pentagon correspondent, Fred Francis, Couric joined the network's Pentagon staff as a deputy correspondent. "I was looking for a general-assignment reporter," Russert told Matusow, "and I had viewed roughly sixty tapes from all over the country, but I kept glancing up at the monitors and noticing Katie Couric. She was always so competent and unflustered, whether she was covering hard news, soft news, the homeless, or [Washington, D.C.'s mayor, Marion] Barry." Couric had impressed Francis with her live reporting from Dover, Delaware, in April 1989, after an accidental explosion killed 47 servicemen aboard the battleship USS *Iowa*. "It was network-quality stuff," he told Matusow.

In December 1989, for reasons that remain in dispute, U.S. military forces invaded Panama. While Francis reported from Panama City, Couric covered the Pentagon. One week after the invasion, NBC news executives, grappling with the urgent situation, asked Couric to anchor the *Saturday Nightly News*. She became so popular with her sources, Francis recalled to Joanne Kaufman, that "one day one of [them] sent her flowers." Earlier in 1989 Couric had married John Paul "Jay" Monahan, a lawyer who later became a legal analyst for NBC.

In June 1990 Couric was named the *Today* show's national correspondent, based in Washington, D.C. In an interview with Verne Gay for *New York Newsday* (June 11, 1990), she reiterated that reporting was her "first love" and that she was not interested in becoming an anchor. "I'd be happy doing this for the rest of my life," she said. In August 1990 U.S. troops were deployed to the Persian Gulf region in response to Iraq's invasion of its neighbor Kuwait. Couric's reporting on what is now called the first Persian Gulf War boosted her name recognition and enhanced her reputation for trustworthiness among viewers.

In February 1991 Couric became the substitute co-anchor for the *Today* show, working alongside Bryant Gumbel and replacing Deborah Norville during the latter's six-week maternity leave. During Norville's final week, *Today*'s Nielsen ratings had been 3.8 (meaning that, on average, 3.8 percent of American households had tuned in to it each night). By the end of Couric's first week, the ratings had risen to 4.3, only a 10th of a point behind *Good Morning America*'s. The ratings remained high throughout Norville's absence, during which Couric conducted the first postwar television interview with General H. Norman Schwarzkopf, who had achieved celebrity status as the leader of the allied military effort to expel Iraqi forces from Kuwait. Others whom she interviewed included King Hussein of Jordan.

Maintaining a bright, cheerful demeanor even during her most serious interviews, Couric seemed to be the solution to *Today*'s ratings problem. "Everybody knew we had seen the future and it was

Katie," one NBC official quipped to the *New York Times* (April 8, 1991) reporter Lena Williams. When Norville's leave ended, she announced that she had decided to care for her newborn son full-time, and in April 1991 NBC executives officially handed the co-anchor baton to Couric. She also became a contributing anchor for the news-magazine program *Dateline NBC*. In July 1991 Couric gave birth to her first child, Elinor Tully "Ellie" Monahan.

Among other notable events in her career during that time, on October 13, 1992 Couric conducted a 20-minute impromptu interview with President George H. W. Bush after he wandered into the room in which she was interviewing the First Lady, Barbara Bush. According to the Poynter Institute (August 31, 2006, on-line), she "surprise[d]" the president "with tough questions." She later interviewed former presidents Jimmy Carter and Bill Clinton; President George W. Bush; Vice President Dick Cheney; Secretary of State Colin Powell; Prime Minister Tony Blair of Great Britain; Prime Minister Ariel Sharon of Israel; and Crown Prince Abdullah of Saudi Arabia, who had never before consented to an interview for U.S. television.

In her 1992 interview with Bruce Weber, Couric offered an explanation for her popularity with viewers: "People get a sense that I really enjoy talking to who I'm talking to, that I don't see it as a duty, that I see it as a pleasure. I think I have the ability to laugh at myself, which perhaps people find appealing. And I don't think I'm better than other people. I don't have an air of superiority. If anything, I think I'm a bit of a reverse snob. I don't like snobby people myself." Perhaps most important to the success of *Today* was Couric's restoration of the family atmosphere that had been missing since the departure, in 1990, of Jane Pauley, a 13-year veteran of the show. In addition, Couric immediately established rapport with the sometimes difficult-to-please Bryant Gumbel. "I think we complement each other," she said to Joanne Kaufman. "I'm not at my best when Bryant isn't next to me, and I don't think he's at his best when I'm not there to give him a hard time or make fun of him or make sure he doesn't take himself oh-too-seriously." "She's been terrific," Gumbel told Roxanne Roberts. "Katie's easygoing, she's bright, she's curious, she's fun to be with. I've yet to hear someone say a bad thing about her." (Ironically, early-morning viewers' easy acceptance of Couric was often attributed in part to the very same "too-cute" appearance that had plagued her earlier in her career.) In August 1993, in addition to her *Today* duties, Couric began co-anchoring the weekly newsmagazine *Now, with Tom Brokaw and Katie Couric*; the show ended its run in September 1994.

In January 1996 Couric gave birth to a second daughter, Caroline Couric Monahan. Early the following year her husband was diagnosed with colon cancer; he succumbed to the disease in January 1998. Couric absented herself from *Today* for only one month after his death. "I have two small children who depend on me for a lot more than food, clothing and shelter—they depend on me as an example of how to go on," she later told Claudia Glenn Dowling for *Life* (January 1999). Also in 1998 Couric reportedly signed a $28 million contract to co-host the *Today* show through 2002. (Matt Lauer had replaced Gumbel as her co-host in January 1997.)

In the wake of her husband's death, Couric committed herself to raising awareness of colon cancer and of the relatively simple test that can detect its presence in its early stages. In March 2000 she launched the National Colorectal Cancer Research Alliance (NCCRA) and underwent a colonoscopy live on *Today*, as part of her series on colon cancer. For about a year after the much-talked-about segment, experts noted a 20 percent increase nationally in colon-cancer screenings—the "Couric effect," as some dubbed it. The series earned Couric a 2001 George Foster Peabody Award. Also in 2000 Couric began gaining notice for her lighter hair color and stylish clothing. Her new look was seen as part of a wider industry trend, as many female journalists were moving away from the drab attire they had adopted in an effort to gain equal footing with their male counterparts. Around that time Couric began to field offers of jobs from other networks, including CBS. "The prospect of leaving NBC made me a little sick to my stomach," she admitted to interviewers for *People* (January 14, 2002). In 2002 Couric signed a contract with NBC that totaled at least $60 million for four years. By that time *Today* had become NBC's highest-earning program, garnering revenues in excess of $350 million per year.

On April 5, 2006, the start of her 16th year as the host of *Today*, Couric announced her intention to leave the program at the end of the next month. She did not mention NBC's efforts to keep her, which included offers of generous extra benefits, such as Fridays off. Later that day CBS, which had wooed her for months, revealed that she was to be the next host of the *Evening News* and a contributor to *60 Minutes*. "Will viewers accept their evening news from someone wearing mascara?" Marc Peyser and Johnnie L. Roberts asked in *Newsweek* (April 17, 2006), echoing a question that other media specialists had raised. "The fact is, Couric is cut from entirely different cloth than any of her predecessors, including the handful of women coanchors. She's the most up-close-and-personal news broadcaster ever on television." *CBS Evening News* had been languishing in third place in the Nielsen ratings, behind NBC's *Nightly News* and ABC's *World News*, and Leslie Moonves, CBS's CEO and chairman, hoped Couric would bring new energy to it.

An estimated 13.5 million people viewed Couric on September 5, 2006, her first day as anchor of the *Evening News*. By May 2007 only about 5.5 million were watching the show each night—the lowest number the show had seen in two decades. As the program's ratings fell, Couric faced criticism from some of her CBS colleagues. Some complained about what they considered the un-

necessarily large, five-person staff she had brought with her from NBC—evidence, they said, of her tendency to behave like a diva; others were outraged that her high salary made it necessary for network executives to fire talented veteran producers. Money also became an issue at *60 Minutes*: in order to accommodate Couric, veteran reporters including Morley Safer and Lesley Stahl were asked to accept pay cuts. Meanwhile, media observers continued to question Couric's abilities as a journalist. "I think I underestimated the feeling that some might have that I was a morning-show personality and not a credible news person," Couric told Hagan. "Which I, quite frankly, think is patently unfair." Her merits as a journalist were further called into question in April 2007, when one of her "Katie Couric's Notebook" pieces—articles posted on her CBS News blog—was revealed to have been plagiarized from a *Wall Street Journal* article. The public later learned that Couric did not write the blog entry and that other staffers often handled the column.

In March 2007 CBS fired *Evening News*'s executive producer, Rome Hartman, replacing him with Rick Kaplan, the former president of MSNBC. Known as a harsh taskmaster, Kaplan worked to implement a more traditional format and eliminated many of the segments he believed were hampering the program, including Couric's sit-down interviews. "A lot of things that made Katie successful in the morning probably don't work in the evening news broadcast," Sean McManus, the president of CBS News, told Hagan. The new approach meant that Couric enjoyed less screen time; those loyal to her said that CBS executives had gone back on their promises to let Couric—who is also the managing editor of *Evening News*—run the newsroom.

A year later it appeared that that strategy was not working. In late February 2008 Couric met with both the president and the chairman of CBS about the possibility of her having to leave the anchor position after the 2008 presidential election. Although no decision was made at that meeting, rumors about her potential departure became national news. During one week the following April, *Evening News* had a nightly average of 5.4 million viewers—fewer than for any other five weeknights in the history of the program. Some speculated that Couric had become a "lame-duck" anchor. To some extent that changed after September 24, 2008, when Couric interviewed that year's Republican vice-presidential candidate, Governor Sarah Palin of Alaska—one of the very few interviews Palin had given up until then (and even afterward). The interview received a huge amount of publicity, leading thousands of viewers to watch clips from it on YouTube and inspiring takeoffs on the weekly comedy show *Saturday Night Live*. Although the attention did not significantly boost Couric's ratings, it did help her "reassert her role as an anchor," Jacques Steinberg wrote for the *New York Times* (October 10, 2008).

Couric remains active with the NCCRA, which supports research by nine scientists. The organization has raised more than $27 million since its inception. Couric was also instrumental in establishing the Jay Monahan Center for Gastrointestinal Health at New York–Presbyterian Hospital/Weill Cornell, in New York City, which opened in March 2004. She has written two books for children: *The Brand New Kid* (2000) and *The Blue Ribbon Day* (2004). Couric lives in New York City with her two daughters.

—K.J.P.

Suggested Reading: CBS News (on-line); (Cleveland, Ohio) *Plain Dealer* E p1 May 30, 2006; *Entertainment Weekly* p24 Oct. 20, 2000; (Merrillville, Indiana) *Post-Tribune* A p2 Sep. 6, 2006; *New York* p18+ July 16, 2007; *Newsweek* p 36+ Apr. 17, 2006; *Philadelphia Inquirer* H p1+ Apr. 22, 2007; Poynter Institute Web site

Selected Books: *The Brand New Kid*, 2000; *The Blue Ribbon Day*, 2004

DeCarava, Roy

(dee-cuh-RAH-vah)

Dec. 9, 1919– Photographer

Address: The Witkin Gallery, 415 W. Broadway, New York, NY 10012

"I want to photograph Harlem through the Negro people," the acclaimed photographer and teacher Roy DeCarava wrote in an application for a John Simon Guggenheim grant in the 1950s, as quoted by Glenn McNatt in the *Baltimore Sun* (November 13, 1998). "Not the famous and the well known, but the unknown and the unnamed, thus revealing the roots from which spring the greatness of all human beings." DeCarava has made a career of pursuing that goal, photographing the residents of his native New York City neighborhood of Harlem with a documentary-like style that has been described as the "snapshot aesthetic," through which he creates works of art by using natural light to capture people in real-life scenes.

DeCarava, who grew up amid the culturally and artistically rich Harlem Renaissance and began his career in the 1940s, is today recognized as one of the most important and influential African-American photographers. David Usborne, writing for the London *Independent on Sunday* (August 26, 2001), quoted the photographer and filmmaker James Hinton as saying that DeCarava was "the first black man who chose . . . to document the black and human experience in America" and "the first to devote serious attention to the black aesthetic as it relates to photography and the black experience in America." As McNatt put it, DeCarava's pictures

have become "some of the most beloved images" of 1950s America. "He photographed ordinary people in ordinary situations, employing what soon became recognized as a signature style of great empathy and tenderness." DeCarava's best-known book, *The Sweet Flypaper of Life* (1955), which contains of numerous shots of the people and places of Harlem, has been praised by critics for its emotional honesty, and his photographs of legendary jazz musicians in New York's nightclubs have added to his reputation. His photographic style has been noted for its minimal use of light; his pictures are generally in black and white and often dark. Richard Lacayo, writing for *Time* (February 12, 1996), noted that "his most enduring pictures dare you to see in the dark. They're so heavily shadowed that your eyes have to adjust to the carbon-tone depths." DeCarava told C. Gerald Fraser for the *New York Times* (June 6, 1982), "To me, the only thing that's black in a photograph is a black subject. I'm not talking about people. But, say, a black wall. Darkness is not black; in a practical sense it's never really quite black. You get a very dark gray, which allows you to penetrate it so that you can see into your darks. They are beautiful; you can see into them."

The only child of Andrew and Elfreda DeCarava, Roy Rudolph DeCarava was born on December 9, 1919 in Harlem. He never knew his father; Andrew and Elfreda divorced when their son was very young, and Elfreda raised the boy on her own. Hoping to foster musical ability in him, she bought DeCarava a violin when he was five years old and sent him, in a suit, to take lessons. He told Michael Kernan for the *Washington Post* (March 30, 1986) that the suit alone "cost her four paychecks," and consisted of "black velvet short pants and a vest and a white silk shirt with a wide collar, and man, when I had to go down the street to my lessons with that violin case, I ran as fast as I knew how." DeCarava also showed a penchant for drawing. At eight he was producing chalk art on the streets and sidewalks of his neighborhood, and he gained some attention from his neighbors when he drew the figure of a cowboy that stretched from one side of 105th Street to the other. "I was the best cowboy artist on the block," he recalled to Kernan. "I made a lot of them. Sometimes we had chalk, sometimes just plaster of Paris we found in the street."

As a teenager DeCarava attended the Harlem branch of the New York City Textile High School. When he realized that the branch was not on a par academically with the main branch, in Manhattan's Chelsea neighborhood, he and a friend transferred there, finding themselves the only African-Americans in the student body. At the Chelsea branch DeCarava studied art history and was exposed to the work of great painters, including Vincent Van Gogh, Michelangelo, and Leonardo da Vinci. After graduating, in 1938, he found work painting signs for the Work Projects Administration, a federally funded program created by President Franklin D. Roosevelt's New Deal legislation

Carroll Blue, courtesy of Icarus Films
An image from the film Conversations with Roy DeCarava

to curb unemployment during the Great Depression. DeCarava later won a graphic-design scholarship, which allowed him to attend the art and engineering college Cooper Union, in downtown Manhattan, while continuing to pursue work as a painter and designer. Facing an unwelcoming environment as a minority student, he stayed at the school for only two years before attending the now-renowned Harlem Community Art Center, where he came into contact with a number of African-American cultural innovators, including the poet and writer Langston Hughes and the artists Romare Bearden and Jacob Lawrence. He also took classes at the privately funded George Washington Carver School.

In 1943, during World War II, DeCarava served as a topographical draftsman in the U.S. Army. When he returned to New York City, he began to work as a commercial painter and silkscreen artist. He had his first solo show in 1947, at Serigraph Galleries. When he purchased a handheld 35-millimeter camera for $19.95 to document images he wanted to paint, he soon discovered that his preferred medium was, in fact, the photograph. "I originally planned to be an artist, studying painting and printmaking," he told McNatt. "I only started taking photographs as reference material for that, and it sort of took over." He told Kernan that photography quickly became his means of expressing his artistic voice, saying, "I didn't know what I wanted to paint, but photography told me right away." DeCarava also decided not to use color in most of his work. "It's bright," he told Fern Robinson for *American Visions* (December 1, 1999). "It's documentary. An orange is orange. You can't get away from that."

By 1947 DeCarava had made the decision to concentrate solely on photography, and he began to document the people and places of his urban neighborhood. He told Kernan that being behind the lens gave him the confidence to approach potential subjects. "I was very shy, scared to death of people, and somehow the camera gave me a license, a way of relating to people. They weren't suspicious or paranoid in those days, they didn't ask what I was taking [the photographs] for, was I going to make money off them or what. They were flattered." In 1950 DeCarava had his first solo photography show, at the Forty-Fourth Street Gallery, and Edward Steichen, then the curator of photography at the Museum of Modern Art (MoMA) in New York City, was invited to attend. Steichen was impressed with what he saw and bought prints for the museum. He also advised DeCarava to apply for a prestigious John Simon Guggenheim fellowship. DeCarava followed his advice and, in 1952, became the first black photographer to win the fellowship, using the grant money to continue his work in Harlem.

DeCarava has said that he set out not to document his community but to express himself by using a visual medium to portray his environment. According to Vicki Goldberg, writing for the *New York Times* (February 11, 1996), DeCarava wrote in his Guggenheim application, "I do not want a documentary or sociological statement, I want a creative expression, the kind of penetrating insight and understanding of Negroes which I believe only a Negro photographer can interpret." Despite the grant, DeCarava had trouble getting his pictures published. That changed when Langston Hughes offered to write a fictional narrative to accompany the photographs and said that he would also work to have the resulting book published. In addition, Hughes chose the pictures that would go into the book. DeCarava told Steve Appleford for the *Los Angeles Times* (November 10, 1996), "I respected him so much that I did something that I had never done before and I will never do again: I gave him carte blanche. I gave him 500 pictures and said, 'Go ahead.'"

The result of that collaboration was the 1955 book *The Sweet Flypaper of Life*, which was well received by critics, sold out its first printing, and garnered two awards. The photographs were intimate, revealing snapshots of families at home and of life on the streets of Harlem; critics noted the candid nature of the subjects and the near-documentary feel of the "snapshot aesthetic." According to Robinson, *The Sweet Flypaper of Life* is "an achingly beautiful book of dramatic black-and-white photographs that showed the dignity and determination of a people through the faces of the residents of Harlem." Lacayo wrote, "If the book is sometimes guilty of the blandness of concerned photography, it also contains pictures that mark the beginning of DeCarava's best work. . . . His street pictures speak in the international language of the snapshot aesthetic. Figures are cut by the edges of the frame. Serendipitous little details, like the windblown edge of a scarf, take on large but ambiguous meaning." The photographs showcased what would become DeCarava's signature image: that of humans in tender and honest moments. According to Robinson, one picture of a father surrounded by his four children "speaks about adoration—the father's for his children and his children's for him. His arms may not be long enough to enfold all of his children, but certainly his heart is big enough."

The underlying theme of the African-American struggle against poverty and oppression was also perceptible in the photographs of *Flypaper*; Lacayo pointed to one photograph in particular, *Graduation*, in which a young girl in a graduation gown, bathed in sunlight, faces a litter-strewn tenement courtyard cloaked in darkness. Lacayo wrote, "Because of the way it seems to guide her into a more confined future, the light feels ominous. Because the girl is black, the hint of dwindling expectations has an additional gravity for her situation and for DeCarava's account of it." DeCarava has said that the overall theme of the photographs was one of human survival and tenacity; he told Robinson, "In spite of the poverty, you see people with dignity and a certain quality that contrasts with where they live and what they're doing."

In 1955 DeCarava's work was displayed in the Museum of Modern Art's historic Family of Man exhibition, which toured a number of museums throughout the world. (The exhibit catalog has sold millions of copies and is still in print.) That year he also opened the Photographer's Gallery, on the Upper West Side of Manhattan. Open by appointment only, it sold and exhibited the work of photographers including Harry Callahan, Minor White, and Berenice Abbott. The gallery did not succeed financially, however, and DeCarava closed it in 1957. He then supported himself as a commercial photographer, picking up freelance photojournalism assignments from such magazines as *Fortune, Newsweek, Time,* and *Life*.

During the late 1950s and early 1960s, DeCarava also photographed legendary jazz musicians, among them Louis Armstrong, John Coltrane, Billie Holiday, Miles Davis, Duke Ellington, Count Basie, Roy Haynes, and Elvin Jones, in nightclubs around the city. DeCarava's pictures of those performers have been noted for their dark hues; using only the light available in the clubs, DeCarava created a distinctive look that reflected the emotional intensity of the music. "I'm always working in inadequate light," DeCarava told Kernan. "I'm fascinated by jazz and jazz musicians, and that always means a dark room somewhere. I try to capture the performer's intensity, the concentration. It's so beautiful to see. It's like watching anyone do something, a baby trying to stand up: that intense dedication, oblivious. It's an expression of love. I try to suggest it in the pictures."

Kernan described the process of interpreting the images in DeCarava's photos, writing, "A saxophonist's forehead gleams with sweat. A man's face emerges from deep darkness as you stare, then another, then another. You have to look harder at Roy DeCarava's pictures." Sarah Boxer, writing for the *New York Times* (March 27, 1996), described a photograph of Elvin Jones: "One can clearly see the sweat running down his forehead, but the cymbal seems to have been blotted out. The sound is all in the face."

In the early 1960s, during the height of the civil rights movement, DeCarava also began to photograph many of the era's marches and protests, such as the 1963 March on Washington, at which the civil rights leader Martin Luther King Jr. gave his now-famous "I Have a Dream" speech. DeCarava said he did not attend the marches with the intention of taking photographs. "I went, I guess, out of a sense of responsibility," he said to Appleford. "I took a lot of pictures. It was funny the way it turned out. I really didn't go there to take pictures, I just wanted to be there." He has also said that the most enduring pictures he took at the marches were not of historic occurrences but of ordinary people exhibiting pride and emotion. "By that time I had realized that it wasn't about the particulars, it wasn't about the subject matter, except the general subject matter of the human condition," he told Appleford. "The advantage of going to a place like the March on Washington is the freedom to shoot. Nobody was going to ask why you were photographing. The pictures that I took and valued could have been taken anywhere." Also in 1963 DeCarava founded the Kamoinge Workshop, which fostered a supportive environment for young African-American photographers. The name was taken from a Bantu word that means "group effort," and the photographers, who included Adger Cowans and Louis Draper, were successful in hosting numerous exhibitions before DeCarava left the workshop in 1966.

In 1968 DeCarava picked up a job as a contract photographer for *Sports Illustrated* magazine that would last for 10 years. He has since said that that period, in which he focused on commercial photography, was irrelevant to his overall career; indeed, journalists have noted that DeCarava was not very prolific from about 1965 to 1975. After he was hired as an associate professor of photography by Hunter College, in New York City, in 1975, and appointed professor in 1978, he began to have a greater creative output. Andy Grundberg wrote for the *New York Times* (May 16, 1982) that while "his style [had] not shifted radically from that of the 50's and early 60's," his use of selective focus and attention to detail and contrast had become stronger. In 1979 DeCarava's work was featured in the Mirrors and Windows exhibition, curated by MoMA's director of photography, John Szarkowski. The organization Friends of Photography published a monograph in 1981 titled *Roy De-Carava: Photographs*, which featured 82 plates of

DeCarava's work. In 1982 a 129-print exhibition of his work took place at the Witkin Gallery, in New York City, and an exhibition of his work with jazz musicians, dubbed The Sound I Saw, was held at the Studio Museum in Harlem in 1983. In 1984 *The Sweet Flypaper of Life* was reissued in a larger, updated edition. DeCarava received an honorary Ph.D. from the Rhode Island School of Design in 1985 and another from the Maryland Institute College of Art in 1986. He was appointed distinguished professor of art at Hunter in 1988.

The 1980s and early 1990s saw DeCarava grow in popularity, as he continued to photograph, lecture, and teach. In 1996 he was honored by MoMA with a major, 200-print retrospective of his work. The show traveled the Unites States until 1999, earning the attention of photography and art critics alike. Maren Stange noted for *Art in America* (March 1996) that while some of his photographs "lay claim to irony," they were mainly "rooted in an older, more central modernist esthetic. In this representational mode, it is primarily form, rather than subject, that conveys emotional and psychological meaning." Stange described DeCarava's *Hallway* (1953) as portraying "at once a dismally claustrophobic tenement hallway . . . and, in the structurally central void with its impossibly narrow opening, a rich symbol of unknowable interiority." Abigail Foerstner, writing for the *Chicago Tribune* (June 23, 1996), commented on DeCarava's intimate pictures of family and friends in their environment: "Throughout, his work exudes the sense of sanctuary found at the front stoops and kitchen tables of the places people call home." Kenneth Baker noted the use of natural light in DeCarava's photographs, writing for the *San Francisco Chronicle* (February 3, 1998) that "the content of DeCarava's work is frequently deepened by its formal beauty. He likes to use available light and always shoots in black and white, so many of his pictures reveal their details slowly. The process of discovering them is unforgettably moving and gratifying."

A book of DeCarava's Jazz Age photographs, *The Sound I Saw: Improvisation on a Jazz Theme*, was published in 2001. DeCarava had had the idea for the book since the 1960s but had shelved the project in the same decade, after becoming dissatisfied with the photograph-reproduction quality and frustrated with publishers who expressed confusion over the book's seemingly disorganized nature. Almost 40 years later his wife, Sherry, persuaded him to try again, and the book became only the second he had published since *The Sweet Flypaper of Life* in 1955. He told David Usborne that the book was "almost 99 per cent the same as the original [prototype]. It took a tremendous amount of intense labour to do it and the fact that it came out so well is—well, I feel very lucky." *The Sound I Saw* combined DeCarava's celebrated portraits of jazz legends with his poetry about the music. Bill Harris, writing for the Detroit, Michigan, *Metro Times* (January 16, 2002), took note of the book's

lack of organization; in his view, the seemingly "arbitrary arrangement" of pictures was like the "best improvisation, offering the chance to create one's own analogies, metaphors and plots." Regina Woods, writing for *Black Issues Book Review* (September 2001), observed, "DeCarava's images take us behind his eyes to reveal the emotional intensity, the beauty and the reverence with which he experiences the world of jazz. We discover the rich tonal nuances of shadows, the quiet stillness in chaos and the eternity in well-chosen moments." DeCarava told Usborne, "The whole point about musicians is that I felt they were neglected because they were musicians. They had no value beyond their playing—when they got off the stage they disappeared and I said, 'My God, but this is a human being.' Do you have to be playing to have value? I want you as the viewer to experience that person not as an individual necessarily, or, rather not as a name. You can look at this book, and you can look at it a thousand times, and each time you look at it differently."

In 2006 DeCarava was the recipient of a National Medal of Arts from the National Endowment for the Arts. Over the course of his career, he has also been involved with a number of arts-related organizations; in the late 1940s he was on the Committee for the Negro in the Arts, and in the early 1960s he founded and chaired the American Society of Magazine Photographers' Committee to End Discrimination Against Black Photographers. He also protested, with the Ad Hoc Emergency Cultural Coalition, a MoMA exhibit in 1969 called Harlem on My Mind. The exhibit was criticized for failing to enlist organizational input from Harlem-based artists. DeCarava withdrew his photographs from the show as a result.

DeCarava continues to teach at Hunter College and lives in the Bedford-Stuyvesant neighborhood of Brooklyn, New York, with his wife. The couple have three children: Susan, Wendy, and Laura. Commenting on his career, DeCarava told Usborne, "I was famous, then I got buried, then I was famous again, then I got buried again and then I was famous again. I don't think they even know who I am on [my] street. I am just the old man who lives next door."

—W.D.

Suggested Reading: *American Visions* p20 Dec. 1, 1999; *Art in America* p35 Mar. 1996; (London) *Independent on Sunday* p19 Aug. 26, 2001; *Time* p73 Feb. 12, 1996; *Washington Post* H p1 Mar. 30, 1986

Selected Books: *The Sweet Flypaper of Life*, 1955; *The Sound I Saw: Improvisation on a Jazz Theme*, 2001

Evan Agostini/Getty Images

Deschanel, Caleb

(deh-shah-NEL)

Sep. 21, 1944– Cinematographer; film director

Address: c/o Dark Light Pictures, 812 N. Highland Ave., Hollywood, CA 90038

"Most people think cinematographers are drawn to movies because they give us a vast canvas on which we can create big epics, but I've always been drawn to movies by actors and the chance to be there at the moment of a great performance." So said Caleb Deschanel, a practitioner of the art and craft of cinematography for the past four decades, during a talk with John Bailey of the American Society of Cinematographers (ASC), as posted on the Web site thewords.com. He added, "I'm drawn to the human face because it's so powerful." Trained in filmmaking at two colleges and the American Film Institute, Deschanel directed the photography for such varied motion pictures as *The Right Stuff, The Natural, Fly Away Home, The Patriot,* and *The Passion of the Christ,* all of which earned Academy Award nominations for achievement in cinematography. "Deschanel takes his cue from the drama in a given moment," Anthony D'Alessandro wrote for *Daily Variety* (January 7, 2005). "It's what sets each of his films apart visually, whether he's reflecting the simplicity of Chauncey Gardiner in *Being There* with overcast grays or the athletic talents of Roy Hobbs in *The Natural* with sunrise hues." Deschanel has often found inspiration for his cinematography in works of art, especially 19th-century Romantic paintings. "They absolutely use light to express emotional elements. That's

what [cinematographers] do," he explained to Lynn Elber for the Associated Press (March 5, 1997, on-line). He has also compared cinematography to jazz. "In jazz, you're not just playing a strict form of music; you're dancing around the music, playing around it," he told Elber. "Film is probably more like that than like a string quartet, where you have everything precisely laid out, where you're following an exact script." He added, "For me, my work doesn't exist as a still frame. It doesn't exist as a composition. It really exists within an entire film, where it's a mosaic." Deschanel has directed two feature films, *The Escape Artist* and *Crusoe,* but prefers cinematography to direction. As he told Vanessa Franko for the *Capital* (April 15, 2004), "The problem with me directing is that as a cinematographer I get offered a lot of great movies to do and as a director it's more of a struggle to get things off the ground. You have to be totally dedicated."

Caleb Deschanel was born on September 21, 1944 in Philadelphia, Pennsylvania. Raised as a Quaker, he grew up on the outskirts of Philadelphia until his family moved to Gambrills, Maryland, before he started high school. He received his first camera, a Brownie Hawkeye, as an 11th-birthday gift. Deschanel attended a private college-preparatory academy, the Severn School, in Severna Park, Maryland. In his teens he enjoyed sailing on the Severn River. After he graduated from high school, in 1962, his family moved to Denver, Colorado. That summer Deschanel returned to the East Coast to attend Johns Hopkins University, in Baltimore, Maryland. He initially pursued a degree in pre-medical studies, his mother having urged him to follow in the footsteps of his grandfather, a physician. After taking several elective courses in art history, he changed his major to that field and then to film. With others in a class taught by the humanities professor Richard Macksey, he made a 16mm film. Deschanel has cited as influential in his development as a cinematographer works by Ingmar Bergman, Federico Fellini, and such French New Wave directors as Jean-Luc Godard and François Truffaut, which were shown on campus as part of an extracurricular film series. His friends at Johns Hopkins included Walter Murch, who later gained fame as a Hollywood sound editor and mixer. As a senior Deschanel served as editor of the university's campus newsletter; he also took pictures for that publication and for the student yearbook. During one summer he provided photos on assignment for a New York City–based still photographer. At Murch's suggestion, after Deschanel earned a B.A. degree from Johns Hopkins, in 1966, he enrolled at the film school of the University of Southern California (USC), in Los Angeles. At USC he became acquainted with several renowned figures in film, among them the cinematographer Haskell Wexler, whom he has described as one of his mentors, and the director Francis Ford Coppola. With another student, the future director George Lucas, he produced several short films. He and his fellow students "loved" the film program "so much and worked so hard, we used to sneak in at night to do films," as Deschanel told Kerry Serini for the Annapolis, Maryland, *Capital* (May 9, 2005). He left USC in 1968 and the next year enrolled at the newly opened American Film Institute Conservatory, in Los Angeles. There, he interned with the cinematographer Gordon Willis, who later became famous for his work on Coppola's *The Godfather*. "I literally wrote down everything I could about everything [Willis] was doing," Deschanel told Vanessa Franko. He earned a certificate (some sources say master's degree) from the conservatory in 1969.

In an interview with Jeanne Johnson for *Johns Hopkins Magazine* (April 2002, on-line), Deschanel described the job of a cinematographer as "infinitely malleable," because it requires adapting to changes in such factors as the weather, casting, performances, and studio pressures and politics; such adjustments necessitate modifications in production design, lighting, camera movement, lens type, and many other aspects of photography. Benefiting in part from his connections in the film industry, Deschanel gradually built his résumé. In 1974 he landed his first major screen credit, as a photographer in the camera-and-electrical department on the film *A Woman Under the Influence*, written and directed by John Cassavetes. Two years later Deschanel wrote, directed, and photographed the documentary *Trains*, which won a Silver Bear for best short film at the Berlin International Film Festival. In 1978 Deschanel served as second-unit photographer on Coppola's *Apocalypse Now*. The following year he took charge of the cinematography on *The Black Stallion*, produced by Coppola and directed by Carroll Ballard. Adapted from a novel by Walter Farley, *The Black Stallion* is about a boy who, after a shipwreck, is stranded on an island with an Arabian stallion; after the two are rescued, the boy helps train his equine friend to race. By most accounts, the movie was visually stunning; some critics complained, though, that, the gorgeousness of the scenes overpowered the story and diluted the adventurous elements. The film earned a best-cinematography prize from the Los Angeles Film Critics Association. In 1979 Deschanel also directed photography for the dark comedy *Being There*; adapted by Jerzy Kosinski from one of his own novels and directed by Hal Ashby, the film starred Peter Sellers as a reclusive, illiterate, boundlessly naïve and childlike gardener who, after years of isolated television viewing, is forced to venture into the outside world, where he is hailed by the rich and powerful for his apparent wisdom and prescience. The National Society of Film Critics honored *Being There* with its award for best cinematography in 1980.

The Escape Artist (1982), the first of the two feature films that Deschanel has directed, is a fantasy about a precocious orphan named Danny who aspires to be a famous illusionist. Rita Kempley, writing for the *Washington Post* (November 19, 1982), called the film "brilliant and eccentric," while other critics found the film's intentional weirdness—in its setting and characters—vexing. "Don't ask in what town, or even when, the movie is set, for both period and locale are left deliberately vague," David Ansen wrote for *Newsweek* (June 14, 1982). "Hoping to make the movie seem 'timeless,' designer Dean Tavoularis has jumbled together every decade from the '20s to the present. It's all tantalizingly atmospheric, and mostly inscrutable. But any movie in which major characters inexplicably vanish and the sequence of events is so arbitrarily scrambled is a movie too out of control to be held accountable for meaning." "Though Danny has within him the stuff of a nearly perfect kid-hero, the movie that surrounds him is a tentative mess, not quite fantasy, not quite an adventure, not quite a comedy, not quite coherent on any level," Vincent Canby declared in the *New York Times* (May 28, 1982).

Deschanel's second attempt at feature-film direction, a retelling of the classic Daniel Defoe story *Robinson Crusoe*, about a man shipwrecked on a desert island, fared little better with critics. *Crusoe* (1989) was shot mainly on a small island in the Seychelles (an archipelago nation in the Indian Ocean, near Madagascar), with interiors filmed in Yugoslavia. Reviewers praised the film's lush look but faulted the motion picture's simplistic anti-slavery message. Dave Kehr, for example, wrote for the *Chicago Tribune* (April 21, 1989), "Given the apparently infinite richness of the story, Deschanel . . . has coaxed only two ideas from it which turn out to be fairly contradictory. *Crusoe* pits an empty pictorialism against a strident social consciousness." Jay Carr, meanwhile, wrote for the *Boston Globe* (April 28, 1989), "The gorgeous imagery can go only so far to paper over the holes in the weak script."

Earlier, in 1983, Deschanel had earned his first Oscar nomination, for his cinematography on the director Philip Kaufman's *The Right Stuff*, based on the same-titled book by Tom Wolfe, about the test pilot Chuck Yeager and the first seven astronauts in the U.S. space program. The cast included Mary Jo Deschanel, whom the cinematographer had married in 1972, in the role of Annie Glenn, the wife of the astronaut John Glenn. Gary Arnold, in a review for the *Washington Post* (October 16, 1983), wrote admiringly of "the illusion of claustrophobia and tingling, stomach-churning sensory apprehension" that Kaufman and Deschanel conveyed in "the subjective moments of confinement inside cockpits and space capsules," while Peter Nichols wrote for the *New York Times* (June 13, 2003), in an assessment of the newly released DVD of *The Right Stuff*, that "much of its richness depends on light and color" and that "Deschanel's cinematography textures desert grit and big-city hoopla."

In 1985 Deschanel received his second Academy Award nomination, for his work on Barry Levinson's *The Natural* (1984), a loose adaptation of a Bernard Malamud story, in which Robert Redford portrayed a 1930s baseball player. For some scenes Deschanel borrowed ideas from the American painter Edward Hopper, much of whose work was created in the same decade. "Deschanel does beautiful, sun-drenched, slow-motion work here, and even if he and Levinson come closer to elevating baseball to mythic levels than Malamud might have liked, it's hard to argue with the way it works," Dave Roth wrote for a Barnes and Noble review (on-line). Hal Erickson, in a critique for the All Movie Guide (on-line), wrote, "*The Natural* elevates the art of slow-motion photography to new heights; while this technique would become precious and boring in later baseball films, it works beautifully here, as does the decision" by Levinson and Deschanel "to convey the symbolism inherent in the story in purely visual rather than blatantly verbal terms." Deschanel also directed the cinematography for *The Black Stallion Returns* (1983) and *The Slugger's Wife* (1985).

Determined to spend more time with his wife and two daughters, in the latter part of the 1980s and the early 1990s, Deschanel took a six-year sabbatical from the silver screen. During that period he directed commercials and episodes of television shows, among the latter, in 1990, three segments of the acclaimed series *Twin Peaks*. In 1994, with the producer Vincent Arcaro, Deschanel formed the production company Dark Light Pictures. Headquartered in Hollywood, the firm specializes in the production of movie trailers and television commercials for companies including Coca-Cola, AT&T, Budweiser, Perrier, Reebok, Tylenol, UPS, Nestlé, Carnation, Sprint, Bacardi International, and Microsoft.

Deschanel returned to cinematography, and earned another Oscar nomination, for *Fly Away Home* (1996). In that film, which incorporated elements of a true story, a 13-year-old girl (played by Anna Paquin) raises a nest of orphaned goslings in Canada and trains them to fly south for the winter with the help of her father, an inventor (Jeff Daniels). The movie was well received, and Deschanel's cinematography, consisting of many aerial shots, earned enthusiastic praise. "The 15 Canada geese were filmed from hatchlings to glorious flying creatures, creating unusually intimate portraits," Peter Stack wrote for the *San Francisco Chronicle* (September 13, 1996). "The filmmakers shot the birds seamlessly, with astonishing skill normally found only in *National Geographic* specials." In a review for the *Cincinnati Enquirer* (September 13, 1996), Margaret A. McGurk wrote that the aerial scenes in *Fly Away Home* are "wondrous, beautiful as symphonies, and worth the price of admission alone."

In 1997 Deschanel directed the photography for the contemporary scenes—shot in Halifax, Nova Scotia, Canada—in James Cameron's film *Titanic*. He served as cinematographer for *Hope Floats* (1998), *Message in a Bottle* (1999), *Anna and the King* (1999), and *The Patriot* (2000), in the last of which the actor Mel Gibson played a farmer turned

fighter in the American Revolution. Its director, Roland Emmerich, and Deschanel gave *The Patriot* "a lyrical style, full of sylvan imagery, heroic postures and eye-popping violence," Michael Wilmington wrote for the *Chicago Tribune* (June 28, 2000). *The Patriot* brought Deschanel his fourth Academy Award nomination and won the prize for outstanding achievement in cinematography from the American Society of Cinematographers in 2001.

Mel Gibson chose Deschanel as cinematographer on *The Passion of the Christ* (2004), which depicts in explicit detail Jesus's final 12 hours. Before that assignment Deschanel had never learned about or had interest in the biblical accounts of Christ's life. "It's embarrassing to say," he told Mark Olsen for the *Los Angeles Times* (February 27, 2005), "but honestly, I didn't know the story. And I found it really moving and thought it was really powerful emotionally. To me it was this wonderful pacifist message . . . the idea of resisting revenge and forgiving the people who are attacking you." He told Franko that he felt drawn to a story like Christ's, in which—in events highly unorthodox for a Hollywood product—the hero never escapes his oppressors. "It's fascinating to think you can create a dramatic structure like that. It doesn't have the satisfaction of revenge that you get in an average Hollywood film," he explained. Gibson's decision to have the characters speak Aramaic and Latin also appealed to him. "It was just so far-out an idea, I thought, 'Wow, this is great, I just have to do this, this is really going to be something,'" he told Olsen.

To prepare for shooting, Gibson and Deschanel viewed previous cinematic depictions of the events leading up to Christ's crucifixion. Gibson, as Deschanel told D'Alessandro, "didn't feel they were right, probably stemming from his idea of an unrelenting brutality in his movie." The two agreed that the film should reflect the influence that paintings, especially the works of such Italian masters as Caravaggio and Raphael, have had on people's conceptions of Christ's appearance and life. Deschanel's extensive research gave him "a catalog of ideas" from which to draw, as he recalled to Olsen. "There isn't any specific shot in the movie that references any specific painting," he explained. "They were more inspirational." The film was shot in Matera, Italy, and Rome's Cinecitta film studios. Like many others, Gibson was impressed not only with Deschanel's skill but also his modesty. "He gave me exactly what we agreed it would be," Gibson told Olsen. "I said to him one day, in an astounded manner, 'It's like a moving Caravaggio,' and he said, 'That's what you wanted, isn't it?'" For his work on the film, Deschanel earned his fifth Oscar nomination. Despite, or because of, the heated controversy surrounding the film (stemming from such issues as the way Jews were portrayed in it and the belief of Gibson's father that the Holocaust is largely a myth), and notwithstanding its mixed critical reception, *The Pas-*

sion of the Christ became one of the top-grossing films in history and remains the highest-grossing R-rated film ever made.

Deschanel handled the cinematography for *National Treasure* (2004), *Ask the Dust* (2006), *Killshot*, and *The Spiderwick Chronicles*, the last two of which were scheduled for release in 2008. He recently finished work on *My Sister's Keeper*, which is due to arrive in theaters in 2009.

An interview with Deschanel appears in the documentary *Visions of Light: The Art of Cinematography* (1993). In 2004 he was named the cinematographer of the year at the Hollywood Film Festival; received a Distinguished Alumni Award from Johns Hopkins University; and earned a career achievement award from the National Board of Review, which has no commercial ties to the film industry. He and his wife, the former Mary Jo Weir, live in Los Angeles. They are the parents of the ac-

tresses Emily Deschanel and Zooey Deschanel.

—M.B.

Suggested Reading: (Annapolis, Maryland) *Capital* A p1+ Apr. 15, 2004, C p2 May 9, 2005; Associated Press Entertainment News Mar. 7, 1997; *Daily Variety* Jan. 7, 2005; imdb.com; *Johns Hopkins Magazine* (on-line) Apr. 2002; *Los Angeles Times* Feb. 27, 2005

Selected Films: *The Black Stallion*, 1979; *Being There*, 1979; *The Right Stuff*, 1983; *The Black Stallion Returns*, 1983; *The Natural*, 1984; *The Slugger's Wife*, 1985; *Fly Away Home*, 1996; *Hope Floats*, 1998; *Message in a Bottle*, 1999; *Anna and the King*, 1999; *The Patriot*, 2000; *The Passion of The Christ*, 2004; *National Treasure*, 2004; *Ask the Dust*, 2006; *Killshot*, 2008; *The Spiderwick Chronicles*, 2008; as director—*The Escape Artist*, 1982; *Crusoe*, 1989

Andrew H. Walker/Getty Images

diCorcia, Philip-Lorca

1953– Photographer

Address: c/o Gagosian Gallery, 522 W. 21st St., New York, NY 10011

In 1981 the French philosopher and critic Roland Barthes wrote in his treatise *Camera Lucida*, "It seems that in Latin 'photograph' would be said '*imago lucis opera expressa*'; which is to say: image revealed, 'extracted,' 'mounted,' 'expressed' (like the juice of a lemon) by the action of light."

Perhaps no contemporary photographer so exemplifies Barthes's understanding of photography as does Philip-Lorca diCorcia. DiCorcia, who was described by a writer for the London *Guardian* (June 12, 2003) as being "known for his tricks with light," has achieved art-world celebrity for his sophisticated lighting techniques, through which he seemingly arrests his subjects in time and in the space between the hyper-realistic and the surreal. A given photograph of diCorcia's might be touted by one critic for its value as documentation and praised by another for its baroque fabrication. "The more specific the interpretation suggested by a picture, the less happy I am with it," he told Peter Galassi, a curator at the Museum of Modern Art, in New York City, for a book on diCorcia published by the museum. It is that purposeful confusion between the fictive and the historical, rendered by dramatic lighting, that marks diCorcia's work. His photographs have been exhibited around the world, from the Nikon Salon in Tokyo, Japan, to the Institute of Contemporary Art in Boston, Massachusetts.

Philip-Lorca diCorcia was born in Hartford, Connecticut, in 1953 to Italian-American parents. Little is known publicly about his early life, beyond the fact that his mother—who named him Philip-Lorca after the Spanish poet Federico García Lorca and named his sister, Auden, after the poet W. H. Auden—abandoned the family when the diCorcia children were very young. While studying at the University of Hartford, diCorcia developed an interest in photography; soon afterward he transferred to the School of the Museum of Fine Arts in Boston's Fenway Cultural District, where he received his diploma in 1975 and his postgraduate, fifth-year certification in 1976. One of his earliest exhibitions took place at the Fogg Art Museum at Harvard University, in Cambridge, Massachusetts, in 1977. Following his years in Boston, di-Corcia attended Yale University, in New Haven, Connecticut, where he earned his master's degree in fine arts in 1979. He then moved to Los Angeles, California, where, with little success, he sought a job in the film industry. Next, he moved to New York and became an assistant to the British rock-and-roll photographer Red Saunders.

In 1980 diCorcia received a grant from the National Endowment for the Arts (NEA) to pursue photography, and by 1984 he had begun freelancing regularly for various publications, including *Condé Nast Traveller*, *Fortune*, *Harper's Bazaar*, *Details*, and *Esquire*. He received a second NEA grant in 1986 and, in 1987, won a prestigious fellowship from the John Simon Guggenheim Memorial Foundation. A work by diCorcia was included in a 1989 show at the Artists Space, in New York City, titled Witnesses: Against Our Vanishing, which centered on AIDS and its effects on Americans. DiCorcia's contribution to the exhibit, a color photograph titled *Vittorio*, depicted an AIDS patient in a hospital, surrounded by balloons and other symbols of cheer. "Focus is everywhere soft and sweet," John Russell wrote about the photograph for the *New York Times* (November 16, 1989, online). "For the time it takes to activate the camera, pain and despair and indignity are defeated." The exhibition temporarily lost $10,000 in funding after the NEA's chairman, John Frohnmayer, withdrew the agency's support from the show, declaring in a statement quoted by the *New York Times* (November 9, 1989) that some of the images were in "questionable taste" and that "between the time the [NEA] panel approved the grant and the way the show developed, it turned into a political statement." (Frohnmayer's decision came soon after the U.S. Congress passed legislation forbidding funding for projects that in the judgment of the NEA or the National Endowment for the Humanities could be considered obscene.) Following an outcry from the arts community, Frohnmayer restored the grant money for Witnesses, but the NEA continued to receive political pressure to avoid controversial subjects, so much so that when diCorcia received his third NEA grant, in 1989, he was made to sign a contract promising not to produce work that could be considered obscene.

In light of that development, the photographer's next move was subversive: he used the NEA funding to pay male prostitutes and hustlers on Santa Monica Boulevard, in Hollywood, California, to pose for his series of color photographs called Strangers. DiCorcia meticulously choreographed each photograph, using his assistant to help him test the composition and lighting for each scene before approaching the young men. There was no direct indication, in terms of visual content, that the men were prostitutes or hustlers; most of the pictures show the men in everyday scenes, sitting outside a drive-through fast-food restaurant, for example, or looking out the window. Each photograph's title was simply the subject's name, age, place of

birth, and amount of money he accepted from di-Corcia. One photograph, *Eddie Anderson; 21; Houston, Texas; $20*, taken from within a shop, shows a shirtless young man gazing inside the front window, which is emblazoned with the words "Peace on Earth"; a hamburger, a miniature jukebox, and a paper cup rest on the sill. Photographs from the series were exhibited at New York City's Museum of Modern Art in 1993.

Joanne Silver wrote in a review of the exhibit for the *Boston Herald* (December 12, 1993), "By blurring the line between fact and fiction, normalcy and society's fringes, diCorcia constructs a chilling mirror of our world, in which the familiar can appear more alien than the unknown, and strangers can reflect features in ourselves that make us squirm." An earlier review by Charles Hagen, published in the *New York Times* (April 30, 1993), more closely analyzed the series: "Many of [diCorcia's] subjects present themselves as figures of fantasy, a fact that further heightens the confusion in these pictures between theatricality and authenticity. . . . Mr. diCorcia's images are more often ambiguous in their meanings, and as a result they remain unsettling and powerful. The pictures are so obviously posed and the scenes so clearly based on stereotypes that it becomes difficult to distinguish the realities of the men's lives from Mr. DiCorcia's theatrical rendering of them. The men are like actors, and as such they become as much representatives of fictional types as individuals. Mr. DiCorcia makes no attempt to look behind the masks that these men offer to the world; if anything, he plays up their public images, helping them act out the characters they have constructed for themselves. In the end, it is this split between self and persona that provides the real drama of Mr. DiCorcia's moving, challenging pictures." Susan Kandel's review in the *Los Angeles Times* (October 3, 1997), published after the exhibit's debut on the West Coast, expressed a similar view: "What we see are not individuals but types, emptied of their particularity and pictured as tawdry icons. What diCorcia offers each [male subject], then, is an arena in which to act out what is already an act."

DiCorcia's next series, entitled Streetworks, secured his position as one of America's great street photographers. For that series, rather than carefully composing his frames, diCorcia installed cameras and strobe lights at designated locations in cities around the world, randomly capturing images of people as they went about their daily routines. An exhibit of the photographs took place at the Whitney Museum of American Art Biennial, in New York, in 1997. The show generated further interest in diCorcia's work as a study of reality and theatricality, for while in Streetworks he took unstaged photographs of people in their regular lives, the lighting he used bathed the subjects in what seemed to be an almost supernatural glow. Ken Johnson, writing for the *New York Times* (December 25, 1998), referred to the lighting in one of the photographs as "Caravaggiesque light" (a reference to the 16th-century Italian painter Caravaggio), while Louis Templado wrote for *Asahi Shimbum* (October 7, 1999) that the light was "always strong and autumnal, falling from the side and casting random passersby in a statuary stillness." Discussing his work with Templado, diCorcia lamented, "Many people point out that my work seems cinematic. . . . It's the most tiring trend in the art world today. What I want to do now is make something that people won't consider filmic." He also rejected the categorization of his work as documentary, saying, "I don't want a journalistic bent to my work." In 1997 diCorcia began a relationship with *W* magazine, handling approximately one fashion shoot per year.

From 1999 to 2001 diCorcia shot photographs for his exhibition Heads, which would later appear in book form. The exhibition traveled to many museums worldwide, including the Pace Wildenstein Gallery, in New York. As in Streetworks, diCorcia used a strobe-light-and-camera process. This time his equipment was attached to scaffolding in New York's Times Square, his camera farther from his subjects and his lens longer. The photographs showed only the subjects' faces, leaving their heads surrounded by darkness. While his previous series had been classifiable as street photography, with the city figuring as a central character in his work, the photographs in Heads were portraits. Although the intensity of lighting and many of the facial expressions lent the images a sense of drama, the photographs were anything but theatrical or forced; the subjects were all caught in the candor of everyday life. "Unaware of the camera," Michael Kimmelman wrote for the *New York Times* (September 14, 2001), "they are absorbed in thought or gaze absently; they are how we act most of the time, walking down the street, in a crowd, focused on something or nothing. But enlarged and isolated, their expressions become riddles, intensely melodramatic and strangely touching. Mr. DiCorcia's pictures remind us, among other things, that we are each our own little universe of secrets and vulnerable. Good art makes you see the world differently, at least for a while, and after seeing Mr. DiCorcia's new 'Heads,' for the next few hours you won't pass another person on the street in the same absent way."

Heads and its associated book figured in a court case brought against diCorcia in 2005 by a retired diamond merchant named Ermo Nussenzweig, who learned that a photo of him, taken in Times Square in 2000, appears in the book and that DiCorcio had made a limited edition of 10 prints of that photo and sold them for between $20,000 and $20,000 apiece. Nussenzweig, an Orthodox Jew, charged that diCorcia had unlawfully violated his privacy by taking the picture of him without his consent; moreover, he maintained, his religious forbade the reproduction of his image by any means, because of the prohibition against graven images in the Ten Commandments. Nussenzweig also charged that diCorcia had violated New York

State laws that ban the use of a person's likeness without consent for commercial purposes. In 2006 Justice Judith J. Gische of the New York Supreme Court (not the state's highest court) dismissed the suit, on the grounds that the photograph was a work of art, not a commercial product. "New York has been fairly liberal in its protection of what constitutes art," Justice Gische wrote in her decision, as quoted by Mark Fass in the *New York Law Journal* (February 13, 2006) and posted on law.com; its courts, the judge continued, have "recognized that art can be sold, at least in limited editions, and still retain its artistic character." She continued, "This analysis recognizes that First Amendment protection of art is not limited to only starving artists. . . . A profit motive in itself does not necessarily compel a conclusion that art has been used for trade purposes." Moreover, she ruled, Nussenzweig had filed his complaint after the expiration of the one-year statute of limitations that apply in such cases. Nussenzweig lost both his first appeal and a second one.

In 2003 DiCorcia's exhibition A Storybook Life was shown at the Whitechapel Gallery, one of the most prestigious exhibition spaces in London, England. The series, comprising 76 small photographs taken from the 1970s through the 1990s, was originally meant to be presented as a book. A Storybook Life showed "regular" life: people watching television, taking baths, or napping. Writing for the London *Guardian* (June 12, 2003), Elisabeth Mahoney enthusiastically commended diCorcia's work: "These are thrilling photographs of some deadly dull moments of being. . . . What transforms them from being snapshots is the lush, cinematic lighting, imbuing each scene with a drama and poetry it would lack in everyday life." In 2006 some of the images from A Storybook Life were published in a photography anthology titled *So the Story Goes*, which also included photographs taken by Nan Goldin, Tina Barney, Sally Mann, and Larry Sultan.

DiCorcia's next exhibition was not met with similar praise. Lucky Thirteen, which featured photographs of 13 pole dancers shot in almost complete darkness, their bodies dramatically lit, received mixed reviews, many of which construed the images of dancers connected to poles as interpretations of Crucifixion iconography. In the *New York Sun* (September 15, 2005), Daniel Kunitz praised the show for the "tension between movement and stasis, light and dark, as in Baroque paintings," and proclaimed, "Mr. DiCorcia is not making a moral judgment here. Religion provides the look, modern irony the ethos: These women are both fallen and uplifted, desirable and imperfect, straining and still, sad or perhaps taken up by the ecstasy of exertion. That lack of judgment, along with the way that so much about these clear, simple pictures remains uncertain—in tension, rather than intentional—is what makes them so unsettlingly powerful. It is we who are lucky." In contrast, Francis Hodgson, writing for the London *Fi-*

nancial Times (March 4, 2005), derided the photographs in Lucky Thirteen, in part for what she perceived as their violence against women: "One recurring element is . . . disturbing, and jars with the mildness all around. The 12 poses that diCorcia has shown are distressingly violent: all are predictably intertwined with the pole. The references are fairly obvious: we are in the visual realm of Marsyas or St. Sebastian. It is close to the Crucifixion, but the torture is unaccompanied by any idea of redemption." In 2007, when Lucky Thirteen moved to the Institute of Contemporary Art in Boston, the Boston Globe (May 20, 2007) writer Ken Johnson reviewed it favorably: "[The women in the photographs] look as much like gymnasts as erotic entertainers, and, like diCorcia's street scenes, with their Caravaggio-esque lighting, these images have a historical resonance that calls to mind figures of goddesses, angels, and other mythic beings from Baroque paintings. . . . They are anything but pornographic, and yet they are viscerally sexy. Visitors will find it hard to tear their eyes away."

DiCorcia has one son and lives in New York City.

—T.O.

Suggested Reading: Design Week p36 June 5, 2003; New York Times C p1 Sep. 12, 1991; New York Sun p13 Sep. 15, 2005

Selected Art Exhibits: Heads, 2001; A Storybook Life, 2003; Lucky Thirteen, 2005

Brian Ach/WireImage.com

Downey, James

1952(?)– Television writer; producer; actor

Address: Saturday Night Live, NBC Studios, 30 Rockefeller Plaza, New York, NY 10112

On February 23, 2008 the NBC comedy show *Saturday Night Live*, informally known as *SNL*, ran a sketch about the media's coverage of the 2008 presidential campaign. During the skit reporters hurled tough questions at Senator Hillary Clinton, played by Amy Poehler, while giving Senator Barack Obama, her challenger for the Democratic Party nomination, portrayed by Fred Armisen, a far easier time. Days later, during a debate with Obama, Clinton herself referred to the piece, whose script was penned by the longtime *SNL* writer and producer James Downey, leading political pundits to consider the influence *Saturday Night Live* has on national politics. Such a development "tells you that you might have articulated something that was vaguely out there, but had yet to be stated in a comedy form," Downey told Dave Itzkoff for the *New York Times* (March 3, 2008). "Some things make you laugh because they're funny, and other things, the effect is: 'Hey, that's right. That makes sense.'"

The brother of the filmmaker Robert Downey and an uncle of the actor Robert Downey Jr., James Downey was born in about 1952. He attended Harvard University, in Cambridge, Massachusetts, graduating in 1974. He told Lloyd Kramer in an interview for the ABC program *Day One* (October 11, 1993) that he majored in Russian studies; according to some sources, he studied mythology and folklore. As a student Downey wrote for the *Harvard Lampoon*, a famed campus humor magazine. He was so devoted to the publication that he often slept in the magazine office. He later earned a fellowship that enabled him to travel throughout Eastern Europe.

In 1976 Downey took a writing job at *Saturday Night Live*, a late-night comedy/variety show that had premiered on NBC the previous year. Doug Kenney, a friend of his and a fellow Harvard graduate, who had founded the humor magazine *National Lampoon*, had recommended him for the position. Known for its topical, cutting-edge comedy, *Saturday Night Live* was an instant success, launching the careers of such comic actors as Chevy Chase, Dan Aykroyd, and John Belushi. "In the beginning no one had any idea of the significance of the show in terms of career or economics," Downey told Doug Hill for the *Bend (Indiana) Tribune* (October 2, 1994). "It was like a children's crusade; people would camp out here and not think about anything but the show." Downey began recommending that NBC hire other former *Harvard Lampoon* scribes, and thanks to him, several other Harvard alumni who went on to build successful TV-writing careers got their first show-business breaks at the network. "Jim Downey is Patient Zero on this whole thing," Mike Reiss, a former lead writer for the TV series *The Simpsons* and the co-creator of another, *The Critic*, told Paul Cullum for *Daily Variety* (February 8, 2005). "He was the first guy to really make the jump from *Harvard Lampoon* into television."

By the start of the fifth season, many of *Saturday Night Live*'s high-profile stars had moved on, leaving its producer, Lorne Michaels, unsure of how to continue. He asked NBC for a six-month break, but network executives refused, forcing him to make the most of his depleted cast. During that year—the 1979–80 season—Downey stepped from behind the scenes and joined the "Not Ready for Prime-time Players," as the *Saturday Night Live* regulars were known. Following that season, which is generally considered one of the worst in the show's history, Michaels left. He tapped Downey to become one of the new producers, but the network opted instead to promote associate producer Jean Doumanian, who later became known as a friend of and producer for the filmmaker Woody Allen. In response, Downey quit the show.

In 1982 Downey became the head writer for the NBC talk show *Late Night with David Letterman*, and he was again responsible for bringing *Harvard Lampoon* veterans onto the writing staff. He returned to *Saturday Night Live* in 1984, a year in which he wrote one of his more prescient political sketches. The skit was set in the war room of the Democratic presidential nominee, former vice president Walter Mondale, who was plotting to win his home state, Minnesota—which later turned out to be the only state in which Mondale gained more votes than the Republican incumbent, Ronald Reagan, on Election Day.

In the mid-1980s Downey became an *SNL* producer, a capacity in which he helped writers refine their material for the air. "There's no question Downey is a central and in many ways revered figure at *Saturday Night Live*," Hill wrote. "He's considered a master comedy writer, and he still writes some of the show's most brilliant sketches, but his principal contribution is shepherding the other writers' scripts from conception through rewrites." "Calling Jim 'a writer' doesn't do him justice," Dave Mandel, another of the show's writers, told Hill. "Piece after piece, show after show, he makes things better."

During his tenure as producer, Downey struggled to maintain the show's quality, as many cast members left to pursue careers in Hollywood. "Nowadays, anyone coming here knows what the formula is: a couple of hit characters, then you get a movie," he told Hill. "They want to keep their options open with the industry on the West Coast, so you get a more measured kind of involvement. It makes the show harder to do. That's not just sentimentality; it's simply true."

By the end of the 1994–95 season, NBC executives, led by Don Ohlmeyer, had grown unhappy with the show's direction and began pushing Michaels, who had returned to the staff, to make changes. "[Ohlmeyer had] been relentlessly trying to get me fired for like nine months before he ever laid eyes on me," Downey told Tom Shales and James Edward Miller for the book *Live from New York: An Uncensored History of Saturday Night Live* (2003). In 1995—the same year many of the show's veteran cast members were replaced by young comedians—Downey was fired from his post as producer and head writer. Michaels was able to keep him on the payroll by giving him the task of writing and producing "Weekend Update," a weekly faux-newscast sketch. "Me and Jim were kind of like alone at *SNL*, you know, especially when the new bunch came in," Norm MacDonald, who hosted "Weekend Update" during that period, told Shales and Miller. "In many ways they resented Jim, because he was much smarter and funnier than them."

In 1998 Downey and MacDonald were fired. Many observers attributed their termination to the frequent "Weekend Update" jokes concerning the former football player, actor, sports commentator, and accused murderer O.J. Simpson, a longtime friend of Ohlmeyer's. Ohlmeyer has claimed that he was not offended by the Simpson material in particular but simply did not find "Weekend Update" funny. In 2000 Ohlmeyer left NBC, and Downey returned to the *Saturday Night Live* writing staff. That year he wrote one of his most famous sketches, a send-up of a presidential debate between Al Gore and George W. Bush. Will Ferrell, playing Bush, poked fun at that candidate's tendency to mispronounce words, saying his campaign could best be summed up with the word "strategery." Darrel Hammond, who played Gore, pedantically repeated the term "lockbox," which the former vice president, then widely viewed as uncharismatic and robotic, had used repeatedly in one of his real debates with Bush. After the sketch aired, Gore's aides reportedly used the tape to coach him on how to better present himself. Lawrence O'Donnell, a political commentator, told the anchor of NBC's *News with Brian Williams* (October 13, 2000) that the sketch was "the most important political writing of this election year." "Nowadays, since I came back again after being fired as 'Update' guy, I sort of have a mandate to write topical political stuff, although I do other kinds of things, too," Downey told Shales and Miller.

While the Democratic Party held primaries to determine its 2008 presidential nominee, Downey wrote a number of sketches about the contest. On February 23, 2008 the show ran a skit that suggested that the press had been harder on Clinton than Obama. Days later Clinton complained during a debate about her treatment by the moderators, Brian Williams and Tim Russert. She said, according to David Bauder in the blog *Huffington Post* (February 27, 2008), "In the last several debates I seem to get the first question all the time. I don't mind. I'll be happy to field it. I just find it curious if anybody saw *Saturday Night Live*, you know, maybe we should ask Barack if he's comfortable and needs another pillow." The February 23 episode also featured a pro-Clinton monologue from the host and former cast member Tina Fey, leading some to claim that the show was trying to influence the election. "I'm just trying to make the sketches funny," Downey told Bill Carter for the *New York Times* (March 13, 2008), adding that of the two candidates, he favored Obama. (While Downey told Carter that he is a registered Democrat, other sources have reported that he is a Republican, and that his Clinton-Obama sketches are designed to undermine both candidates.) On March 1, 2008 Clinton herself appeared on the show and performed in a sketch with Poehler. Producers invited Obama to appear on a later episode, but the candidate, who had made an appearance on a November 2007 episode, declined. "I hope it was scheduling and not because he hates us," Downey told Carter.

Beginning in September 2008 *SNL* returned to the national spotlight, when Tina Fey returned to the show to portray Governor Sarah Palin of Alaska, the Republican Party's vice-presidential nominee. Fey appeared in skits with Poehler, who played Hillary Clinton or Katie Couric. The satirical pieces drew a great deal of attention, not only because of Fey's spot-on impressions of Palin but because much of what she said was almost identical to what Palin had said in her real interviews with Couric and the news anchor Charles Gibson as well as in the vice-presidential debate, televised on October 2, 2008. On October 18, 2008 Palin herself made a brief appearance on the show.

Downey, who writes his material by hand on legal pads, has appeared on some 60 installments of *Saturday Night Live*, playing bit parts even when not an official member of the cast. He has had small roles on the TV show *Kate & Allie* (1989) as well as in the films *Billy Madison* (1995), *Dirty Work* (1998), and the director Paul Thomas Anderson's acclaimed *There Will Be Blood* (2007).

As part of the *SNL* writing team, Downey has won three Emmy Awards for outstanding writing (in 1977, 1989, and 2002). In total, he has written for almost 500 *SNL* episodes. In 1993, while he was producer, *Saturday Night Live* won an Emmy in the category of outstanding variety, music, or comedy series.

—K.J.P.

Suggested Reading: *Daily Variety* A p1 Feb. 8, 2005; *New York Times* E p1 Mar. 3, 2008, E p1 Mar. 13, 2008; *South Bend (Indiana) Tribune* E p7 Oct. 2, 1994; *Washington Post* C p1 Jan. 14, 1998; Shales, Tom and James Edward Miller. *Live from New York: An Uncensored History of Saturday Night Live, as Told by Its Stars, Writers and Guests,* 2003

Selected Television Shows: as writer—*Saturday Night Live*, 1976–; *Late Night with David Letterman*, 1982–84; as producer—*Saturday Night Live*, 1985–1995; as actor—*Kate & Allie*, 1989

Selected Films: as actor—*Billy Madison*, 1995; *Dirty Work*, 1998; *There Will Be Blood*, 2007

Courtesy of the United States Army

Dunwoody, Ann E.

1953– U.S. Army four-star general

Address: U.S. Army Materiel Command, 9301 Chapek Rd., Fort Belvoir, VA 22060

On July 23, 2008 the U.S. Senate confirmed President George W. Bush's nomination of Lieutenant General Ann E. Dunwoody of the U.S. Army to be the first female four-star general in the United States. Dunwoody was scheduled to assume the leadership of the U.S. Army Materiel Command (AMC), in Fort Belvoir, Virginia, in the fall of 2008. In that position she will be in charge of the soldiers, civilians, and contractors responsible for providing troops with everything they might need on and off the battlefield: food, clothing, toiletries, vehicles, tents, and equipment ranging from canteens and rucksacks to programmable radios, guns, and ammunition. "I grew up in a family that didn't know what glass ceilings were," Dunwoody said in an army press release, issued on June 23, 2008, that was widely quoted in the print media and on the Internet. "This nomination only reaffirms what I have known to be true about the military throughout my career: that the doors continue to open for men and women in uniform." When President Bush nominated Dunwoody for four-star rank, in June 2008, she was one of only two women ever to have acquired three stars in the U.S. Army (the first being Claudia Kennedy, who retired in 2000). As of the end of June 2008, there were also three female two-star generals and 15 female one-star generals. Although the total number of women in the army with one-star rank or higher is more than at any time in the past, it represents only about 5 percent of army generals currently in active service. In an article for the *New York Times* (June 30, 2008), Rachel L. Swarns noted that Dunwoody's "quiet, determined climb into the Army's upper echelon highlights both the widening role that women are playing in the armed forces and the difficulties they encounter in reaching the top."

While most four-star generals earn that prestigious rank after serving in combat, Dunwoody has worked primarily in planning and logistics—the latter being the acquisition, maintenance, distribution, and transport of equipment and supplies. (Recent events in Afghanistan and Iraq notwithstanding, federal law bars females from engaging in full-scale combat.) Dunwoody is also a skilled parachutist, and in 1990 and 1991, during Operation Desert Shield and then Operation Desert Storm, she served as division parachute officer in the 82nd Airborne Division, accompanying that unit and managing logistics during its deployment in Saudi Arabia. During her more than three decades in the army, the general has also served as deputy commander of the Army Materiel Command, commanding general of the United States Army Combined Arms Support Command, and commanding general of the First Corps Support Command.

Ann E. Dunwoody was born in 1953 in New York State to Harold H. Dunwoody and Elizabeth H. Dunwoody. She comes from a long line of soldiers: her paternal great-grandfather and grandfather and her father all graduated from the U.S. Military Academy at West Point, in New York, and served in wars overseas. Dunwoody's father attained the rank of one-star general. Her brother, Harold H. Dunwoody Jr., also attended West Point, and her sister, Susan Dunwoody Schoeck, was the third woman in the army to become a helicopter pilot. The family moved frequently during Ann's childhood. She lived for a time in Germany and later attended the SHAPE (Supreme Headquarters Allied Powers Europe) high school in Belgium, graduating in 1969. She then entered the State University of New York at Cortland, where she was a competitive gymnast and tennis player. She earned a B.S. degree in physical education in 1975. Soon afterward she joined the army, in part because it was then the only branch of the U.S. military that allowed women to become paratroopers. (Paratroopers are trained to parachute from planes and are most commonly assigned to airborne units.) She received a direct commission as a second lieutenant. "I planned to only stay in the Army to complete my two-year commitment, but it wasn't too long before I realized that there are no other shoes I would rather fill than the ones I'm wearing right now," she told Dawn S. Onley in an interview for *Military Logistics Forum* (October 5, 2007). In 1976 Dunwoody graduated from both the Quartermaster Officers' Basic Course, which prepares soldiers to lead logistics platoons, and the Basic Airborne School and was assigned to Fort Sill, Oklahoma. While there she joined the 100th Supply and Transport Battalion, serving as a platoon leader, company executive officer, and battalion adjutant. She went on to command the 226th Light Maintenance Company.

Dunwoody's next assignment, after she had completed the Quartermaster Advanced Course, called for her to serve as community adjutant for the Eighth Infantry Division. She then traveled to Germany to command the 29th Area Support Group of the Fifth Quartermaster Detachment. In 1984 she became quartermaster captains assignment officer at the Military Personnel Center, in Alexandria, Virginia. Four years later she earned an M.S. in logistics management from the Florida Institute of Technology, in Melbourne. In 1990 she joined the 82nd Airborne Division, based in Fort Bragg, North Carolina. While there she began to experience discrimination that she attributed to her being female. "It was like coming into the dark ages," she told Eric Schmitt in an interview for the *New York Times* (August 2, 1992, on-line). "Some senior officers perceived that their bosses would think less favorably of them if they allowed me to be assigned to the division in a critical position." While she held the rank of major, her superiors ordered her to keep track of equipment—a task generally given to lower-ranking personnel. In time she proved herself and—thanks in part to her athletic prowess—received more challenging assignments. "She impressed a lot of people in that environment, a high-density male environment, a high-testosterone environment," Lieutenant General David W. Barno told Rachel L. Swarns. Dunwoody served as division property book officer and executive officer of the 407th Supply and Transportation Battalion, the largest battalion in the 82nd Airborne Division, before she was deployed to Saudi Arabia, where the division was stationed during Operations Desert Shield and Desert Storm—two phases of the conflict that followed Iraq's invasion of its neighbor Kuwait in 1990. While overseas she served as division parachute officer. When she returned to the U.S., she was named deputy chief of staff, G4 branch, a logistics position.

In 1992 Dunwoody became the first woman to lead a battalion of the 82nd Airborne Division, taking over as commander of the 407th Supply and Transportation Battalion, which provides logistical support. In October 1993 she became commander of the 782nd Main Support Battalion of the 92nd Airborne Division. Three years later she graduated from the Industrial College of the Armed Forces, in Washington, D.C., with an M.S. degree in national resources strategy. In June 1996 she was assigned to Fort Drum, New York, where she commanded the 10th Mountain Division (Light Infantry) Support Command. She next served as executive officer to the director at the Defense Logistics Agency (DLA), at Fort Belvoir. The DLA "provides supply support and technical and logistics services to the Army, Air Force, Navy and Marine Corps and several federal agencies," according to the agency's Web site. In July 2000 Dunwoody became commanding general of the First Corps Support Command (Airborne), which is based at Fort Bragg. Until August 2002, when she moved on, she helped to deploy a Logistics Task Force in conjunction with Operation Enduring Freedom, the name given to the U.S. war in Afghanistan, and a Joint Logistics Command in Uzbekistan. The Joint Logistics Command was in support of Combined Joint Task Force 180, which was created to combat terrorist groups in Afghanistan and promote the establishment of a democratic government there.

From 2002 to 2004 Dunwoody served at Scott Air Force Base, in Illinois, where she led the Surface Deployment and Distribution Command. That period, during which the U.S. military continued its global "war on terror" and launched an invasion of Iraq, marked the "largest deployment and redeployment of troops since World War II," according to Elizabeth M. Lorge, writing for *Defense Department Documents and Publications* (June 23, 2008). In September 2004 Dunwoody became the commanding general of the U.S. Army Combined Support Command, at Fort Lee, Virginia. That promotion marked the first time a female had earned the rank of commanding general at Fort Lee. "In the midst of a global war on terrorism, I know we must be able to transform on the run," Dunwoody said during her swearing-in ceremony, as quoted by Jeffrey Kelly in the *Richmond (Virginia) Times Dispatch* (September 3, 2004). In November 2005 Dunwoody was nominated to become a lieutenant general and assigned to the Pentagon, where she became the first woman to serve as deputy chief of staff for logistics. That promotion made her the highest-ranking woman on active duty in the army. While serving at the Pentagon, Dunwoody oversaw a reorganization of her department and established a so-called Reserve Mobilization Directorate, which communicates daily with the Army National Guard Bureau and Army Reserve. "We wanted to evolve into an organization that was a catalyst for change," she told Dawn S. Onley. "The result is a more readily recognizable organization that ensures the goals, objectives, and priorities are in place to best support the Army." By 2007 the U.S. had been at war for six years—the longest it had ever fought with an army composed solely of volunteers. Using techniques drawn from Lean Six Sigma, a business-management strategy originally designed by the Motorola corporation, army logisticians sought to modernize their practices and determine the best ways to deploy and redeploy soldiers and equipment. "To maintain and sustain a ready Army, we had to rid ourselves of the legacy systems, processes and policies and deliver agile, modern, integrated and synchronized systems to support our new expeditionary and campaign quality Army," Dunwoody told Onley.

In September 2006 Dunwoody was named chairman of the board of directors of the Defense Commissary Agency (DCA). The DCA's commissaries, or military supermarkets, which it maintains across the globe, offer for little more than cost food and other products for active military personnel and retirees and their families. In June 2008 Dunwoody was sworn in as the first female deputy commanding general of the U.S. Army Materiel Command. According to the AMC Web site, "If a Soldier shoots it, drives it, flies it, wears it, communicates with it, or eats it—AMC provides it." "AMC has established an incredible reputation throughout the Army," Dunwoody said, according to Melissa Bohan, writing for *Defense Department Documents and Publications* (June 18, 2008). "When folks see the AMC patch, they know they will get the help they need. Warfighters truly know and appreciate the capability AMC brings to the table. They will never go to war without us."

On June 23, 2008 President Bush nominated Dunwoody to become the first female four-star general in U.S. military history. (By law, the army's roster can include no more than 11 active-duty four-star generals at any given time.) "Lt. Gen. Dunwoody's leadership, character and career have best prepared her to lead the Army Materiel Command," Secretary of the Army Preston M. "Pete" Geren said, according to the States News Service (June 23, 2008). "She will bring 33 years of experience to over 56 thousand Soldiers, DA [Department of the Army] Civilians, and their Families in 40 states and 50 countries as she serves as the next commanding general of Army Materiel Command." "This is an important day for the Dunwoody family, the military and the Nation," Gen. George W. Casey said, according to Lorge. "Lt. Gen. Dunwoody's nomination not only underscores her significant contributions and success throughout 33 years of service, but also shows the level of possible opportunity in our Army's diverse, quality all-volunteer force." U.S. senator Hillary Clinton of New York said that the nomination of Dunwoody "not only reflects her own remarkable achievements as an officer, but also serves as a symbol of the tremendous strides by women who serve this country in uniform," according to the Associated Press (July 2, 2008).

Dunwoody has been described as an exceptional leader and creative thinker who would prefer that people not mention her gender when discussing her achievements. "Her issue is, when are people going to stop being surprised?" Jeanette Edmunds, a retired major general, said to Swarns.

Dunwoody's honors include the Distinguished Service Medal, the Legion of Merit with one Oak Leaf Cluster, the Defense Meritorious Service Medal, the Defense Superior Service Medal, the Army

Commendation Medal, the Army Achievement Medal, the National Defense Service Medal with Bronze Star, the South West Asia Service Medal, and the Kuwait Liberation Medal. In her leisure time she enjoys running, sailing, and playing tennis. Dunwoody has been married to Craig F. Brotchie, a retired air-force colonel, since about 1990. She and her husband have a puppy named Barney.

—K.J.P.

Suggested Reading: *Defense Department Documents and Publications* June 23, 2008; globalsecurity.org July 23, 2008; *Military Logistics Forum* (on-line) Oct. 5, 2007; *New York Times* A p17 June 30, 2008; (Petersburg, Virginia) *Progress-Index* A p1 June 25, 2008; *Richmond (Virginia) Times Dispatch* B p1 Sep. 3, 2004; *Washington Post* A p2 June 24, 2008; *Who's Who in America 2008*

Brian Bahr/Getty Images

Ellis, Monta

(MON-tay)

Oct. 26, 1985– Basketball player

Address: Golden State Warriors, 1011 Broadway, Oakland, CA 94607

Monta Ellis's career with the National Basketball Association (NBA) had a somewhat inauspicious start. During the 2005 NBA draft he was not picked until well into the second round; he was eventually chosen—a disappointing 40th overall—by the California-based Golden State Warriors. He sat out much of the 2005–06 season, given little chance to prove his capabilities. That was a less-than-stellar season for the team as a whole, and the Warriors, who had not made a play-off appearence in over a decade, once again failed to do so. During the next season, however, Ellis, who had averaged 6.8 points per game during his rookie season, was given more time on the court and averaged 16.5 points, 4.1 assists, and 3.2 rebounds per game, capturing the NBA's Most Improved Player Award. Thanks in large part to his performance, the Warriors made their first play-off appearance since 1994. Ellis has signed an endorsement contract with And1, a sports-apparel company, which has capitalized on his burgeoning name recognition with the slogan "Who is Monta Ellis?" His teammates, who gave him a standing ovation when he was deemed most-improved player, have noted that despite the increased attention, he has remained levelheaded. "To be so young and to have all the exposure and success he's been getting, it's great," the veteran Golden State forward Stephen Jackson told Marcus Thompson II for *Inside Bay Area* (November 20, 2007). "A lot of kids can't mature as fast as he has. Just to see how he's handled it—not letting it get to his head, continuing to be humble about what he has—that shows a lot about his growth." In August 2008 Ellis injured an ankle while riding his moped—an activity forbidden by his contract. To punish him for that infraction, the following October the Warriors suspended him for 30 games without pay.

Monta Ellis, who was born in Jackson, Mississippi, on October 26, 1985, has long shown clear signs of maturity and determination. Growing up in a dangerous area of Jackson, he stayed out of trouble by concentrating on basketball. "I've been around drugs, killing, violence and fights all my life," he told Jeremy Hudson for the Jackson *Clarion-Ledger* (February 20, 2005). "Instead of picking up drugs and guns, I decided to pick up a basketball and use what God gave me to go where I need to go and do what I need to do." When Ellis was two, his father left the family and moved to Texas; he did not stay in touch. As a result, Ellis and his mother, Rosa, developed a strong bond. She told Hudson, "I've had to be his momma and daddy. He's been up under my wing all his life." Rosa was a prison guard at the Hinds County Detention Center, in Raymond, Mississippi, until Ellis's NBA salary allowed her to quit her job. Rosa did what she could to keep Ellis and his older brother, Antwain, safe, including instituting strict curfews. "[Monta] stayed out of all of the trouble that was around," she told Hudson. "Kids would come over and try to get him to go out and play, but he wanted to stay to himself. He would wait for dark to come, then he would go out and shoot ball by the light of a street pole." Wanting to avoid the crime-ridden local park, Ellis frequently played just outside his home, using a milk crate nailed to a pole or an empty trash can as a basket. In a 2007 interview posted on the NBA Web site, Ellis was asked when he got his first basketball. He replied, "We played with tin [foil] balls or we would find a kick ball to play with. I never had my own basketball."

Antwain Ellis, also a highly proficient basketball player, led Lanier High School to a state championship in 1999; Monta Ellis sometimes served as his brother's ballboy. When Antwain's best friend and Lanier teammate, Ronnie "P.J." Gaylor, was murdered in a dispute over $30 in drug money, however, Antwain lost interest in the game and began to behave erratically. Ellis told Michael Lee for the *Washington Post* (January 28, 2006, on-line) that his brother "lost it. One day, he scared me so bad, I didn't know he was my brother." Watching his brother's talent and NBA potential dissipate, Ellis resolved to pursue basketball seriously. "That's where he got his drive from," Rosa told Lee. "He watched his brother go from a star to nothing now. . . . He always said, 'I'm not going to let it happen to me, like it happened to 'Twain.' He set a goal for himself."

After he entered Lanier High, Ellis became a guard on the school's basketball team, the Bulldogs. He quickly became a valued player and was named the national sophomore of the year by the editors of *Student Sports*. As word of Ellis's skills spread, high-school gymnasiums across the state began to sell out whenever Lanier played, and Ellis was featured on billboards erected in Jackson that read, "The Greatest Show on Hardwood." He helped lead the Bulldogs to state titles in 2002 and 2005, under Coach Thomas Billups, and by the end of his high-school career, he had scored 4,617 points—breaking a city scoring record once held by Othella Harrington, now with the Charlotte Bobcats of the NBA, by about 1,000 points.

As Ellis's high-school graduation approached, in 2005, excitement about his prospects mounted. He was named the *Parade* Co-Player of the Year, an honor he shared with Greg Oden, a student from Indiana; called Mississippi's Mr. Basketball by the *Clarion-Ledger*; and ranked 24th nationally by *USA Today*. That year Ellis also achieved one of his most-cherished personal goals when he was accepted into the McDonald's All-American Game, featuring the country's top high-school basketball players. Ellis had envisioned himself at the event ever since a hero of his, the Cleveland Cavaliers player LeBron James, participated in 2003. "Watching LeBron and guys like that, it was just sitting in the back of my head that if I went in the gym and worked hard, I'd make that game, and God made my wish come true," Ellis told Bill Spencer for the *Clarion-Ledger* (February 24, 2005).

Speculation began to build over whether Ellis would declare for the NBA draft immediately or enter Mississippi State University on a basketball scholarship. He decided to vie for a spot in the NBA, signing with an agent in April 2005 and thus renouncing his college eligibility. He had been contemplating the draft since his freshman year of high school, he told reporters, citing as role models such players as Travis Outlaw of Starkville, Missis-

sippi, who went straight to the Portland Trail Blazers after high school as a first-round pick. "All that just pushed me to go for it," Ellis told Todd Kelly for the *Clarion-Ledger* (April 26, 2006). "It's really stuck in my head since I was a ninth grader. A lot of players might do it for the money. Of course the money is there, but I look at it as a chance for a job at the highest level. I'll be doing it because I love the game of basketball."

In June 2005 Ellis and his family, along with several friends and supporters, gathered in Jackson to watch the draft on television. After several hours of anticipation, the first round was over, many of the guests had left the party, and Ellis had not yet been picked. The Warriors finally selected him as the 10th pick in the second round—the 40th overall. Second-round picks are not guaranteed contracts, and a disappointed Ellis told Kelly for a later *Clarion-Ledger* article (June 29, 2005), "There was a lot going through my mind [during the draft]. I know half the guys who were drafted—and I know I'm way better than them. But it's a blessing to get drafted by the Warriors. Now I'm just going to go in and work hard and prove everybody wrong." Billups was surprised at the outcome of the draft, telling Kelly, "I'm disappointed because I thought Monta was a first-rounder. A lot of things can happen. People can change their minds. Sometimes people will tell you they're going to pick you, but then they pick someone else." (There has been some speculation that a knee injury and subsequent surgery had made Ellis seem less appealing to teams during the draft.)

Despite his initial concerns about the draft results, Ellis did receive a contract, signing for two years with the Warriors for $450,000 per season, well below the figures offered to first-round picks but above the $398,762 minimum guaranteed to rookies. After signing he moved into a relatively modest, four-bedroom house in Alameda, California, in the San Francisco Bay Area. He invited two of his cousins to live with him during his rookie year.

Ellis sat out all but three of the team's first 31 games during the 2005–06 season. Then, in February 2006, with a number of the Warriors injured, he was given extra time on the court. He quickly began outperforming all eight of the other players selected during high school in the previous draft. (Five had been picked before him, in the first round.) "I'm a better player and everybody knew that," Ellis told Marcus Thompson II for the *Monterey County (California) Herald* (February 15, 2006). "So, I just had to come out and prove it. And so far, I am." Although the Warriors did not make it to the play-offs during the 2005–06 season, Ellis was happy simply to be in California. He told Greg Beacham for the Associated Press (April 6, 2006), "I like it a whole lot better than living in Mississippi. The weather's not too hot or too cold, and I don't have to worry about watching my back every five seconds. . . . When I got off that plane [for the first time], I was just thinking, 'Wow, I really made it out of Mississippi.'" Like other sportswriters, Beacham was impressed not only by Ellis's warm personality but by his progress as a professional player; he wrote, "[Ellis's] bursts of exceptional talent, explosive drives, acrobatic layups, and improving defense have marked him throughout the league as a player to watch."

During the 2006–07 season, under the former Dallas Mavericks coach Don Nelson, who had replaced Montgomery, Ellis was paired with Baron Davis for the starting backcourt. The pair proved to have an exciting chemistry. Janny Hu wrote for the *San Francisco Chronicle* (November 14, 2006), "Nelson says he has never had a point guard as big and skilled as Baron Davis, and that he has never had a point guard as young and able as Monta Ellis. . . . At a lithe 6-foot-3, Ellis is one of the quickest ballhandlers in the league. At a bruising 6-3, Davis is one of the most intimidating. When Ellis pushes the pace, Davis is free to roam around the free-throw line, set picks, and put himself in post-up and catch-and-shoot positions. Both are perimeter threats. Both can penetrate. So it's little wonder that after seven games—the last two with Davis and Ellis starting together—the Warriors have one of the top-ranked offenses."

In a game against the Seattle Supersonics on November 19, 2006, Ellis achieved a career-high 31 points, leading the Warriors to victory. By late December the Warriors had reached eighth place in the Western Conference, although the team returned from the road with a number of hurt players, including Ellis, who had sustained a shoulder injury during a game with the Miami Heat. On January 24, 2007 Ellis made a jump shot that fell through the hoop as the buzzer sounded, giving his team the win in a game against the New Jersey Nets. "I looked up and I saw zero-zero on the clock, and it doesn't get any better than that," Nelson told Hu for the *San Francisco Chronicle* (January 25, 2007). In April the Warriors clinched their first play-off spot since 1994, with a victory against the Portland Trail Blazers, and in May they defeated the Dallas Mavericks to become the first number-eight seed to beat a number-one seed in a best-of-seven series. That feat also marked the Warriors' first win in a play-off series since 1991. (The Warriors, closed out by the Utah Jazz later in the month, did not make it to the 2007 Western Conference Finals.)

During his rookie year Ellis had averaged 6.8 points, 1.6 assists, and 3.1 rebounds per game; his sophomore season saw him improve those averages to 16.5 points, 4.1 assists, and 3.2 rebounds per game. In April 2007 Ellis received the NBA's Most Improved Player Award, beating out the Sacramento Kings player Kevin Martin in one of the closest finishes in recent NBA history. Ellis told a reporter for the Associated Press (April 26, 2007), "I worked so hard this summer to put myself in this position to win this award, and I just want to thank everybody around me for giving me the opportunity and keeping me on my toes." He frequently credited Nelson, in particular, for his progress.

In October 2007 Ellis hit his head on a teammate's hip while training at a camp in Kailua, Hawaii, and injured his neck. Despite initial fears about the severity of the damage, he recovered within three weeks. The 2007–08 season thus started slowly for him, but he went on to score 31 points against both the Philadelphia 76ers and Phoenix Suns in one three-night span in November. That feat made him the team's third-leading scorer, and his popularity with the public and the media continued to increase. In December 2007 Ellis scored a then-career-high 35 points during the Warriors' victory over the Minnesota Timberwolves. The next month Ellis achieved a new career high—39 points—in a game against the New Jersey Nets. In February 2008 he became the ninth guard ever to shoot successfully at least 60 percent of the time over the course of one month: he made 60.2 percent of his shots, averaging 26 points per game. "Monta's on fire. He's one of the hardest players in the league to guard," his teammate Matt Barnes told an espn.com interviewer, a comment quoted widely on the Internet. "If you come up on him, he'll go by you. If you back off, he can hit his shot. Monta's becoming a superstar and is really tough to stop."

In July 2008 Ellis signed a six-year, $66 million contract with the Warriors. The next month he severely sprained his ankle; afterward, he reported that the accident had occurred during a pickup-basketball game. A few days later he confessed that the injury had happened when he fell off his moped. Ellis's contract stipulates that riding a motorcycle or moped is forbidden; consequently, in October 2008 the Warriors suspended Ellis for 30 games without pay.

Away from the court, Ellis prefers to stay at home to play video games, including NBA Live 2006, on which he is featured. He is engaged to his high-school sweetheart, Tandra Johnson, a former player on the Lanier girls' basketball team; no wedding date has been set. He remains close to his mother, who travels between Mississippi and California. She helps advise him on his finances, chiding him if he buys too many CDs or video games. (His one major extravagance thus far has been a 2005 Cadillac Escalade with a television and top-of-the-line stereo system.) He plans to one day build a community center in Jackson. He told Michael Lee, "I want to make it better for the kids and my nephews that are there now, so they won't have to struggle like I did to find a place to play basketball."

—W.D.

Suggested Reading: Associated Press Apr. 6, 2006, Nov. 27, 2007; *Inside Bay Area* Nov. 20, 2007; (Jackson, Mississippi) *Clarion-Ledger* D p1 Mar. 26, 2004, A p1 Feb. 20, 2005, D p1 Mar. 13, 2005, A p1 Apr. 26, 2005, D p1 June 29, 2005, D p1 Apr. 9, 2006; *Monterey County (California) Herald* Feb. 15, 2006; *San Francisco Chronicle* E p2 Nov. 14, 2006, D p1 Jan. 25, 2007, D p1 Nov. 28, 2007; *Washington Post* (on-line) Jan. 28, 2006

Courtesy of the National Sculpture Society

Estern, Neil

Apr. 18, 1926– Sculptor

Address: 432 Cream Hill Rd., West Cornwall, CT 06796

"I like sculpting nudes . . . , and I have done many, both male and female," the sculptor Neil Estern told Dena Merriam for *Sculpture Review* (Spring 1994). "But nudes tend to be anonymous, and I am naturally drawn to people who have had an impact on our lives and changed the course of history to some degree. I think of it as three-dimensional biography. I want to make my subjects vivid and alive so that the viewer can immediately relate to their special qualities. For me, doing a public figure represents an exciting challenge, although it can be very daunting also." Estern has fashioned statues and busts of such towering figures in American history as President Franklin Delano Roosevelt and First Lady Eleanor Roosevelt, President John F. Kennedy, and New York City mayor Fiorello H. La Guardia. Others of his subjects, individuals who have also made major contributions to or had indelible influences on society, include U.S. senator and representative Claude Pepper of Florida; President Jimmy Carter; J. Edgar Hoover, the longtime head of the FBI; U.S. senator Robert A. Taft of Ohio; Frederick Law Olmsted and Calvert Vaux, the architects of Central Park, in New York City; and, in the United Kingdom, Prince Charles and Princess Diana. Estern's bronze relief of the songwriter Irving Berlin is in the collection of the National Portrait Gallery, a division of the Smithsonian Institution, in Washington, D.C., and his bust of the actor Danny Kaye is in the collection of the Brooklyn Museum, in the New York City borough of Brooklyn.

According to a writer for the National Park Service, in a description for nps.gov of the Franklin Delano Roosevelt Memorial in Washington, D.C., "The portrait and figurative sculptures of Neil Estern attempt to go beyond a mere recording of physical characteristics. His work captures the energy or the repose, the tidiness or the rumple, the wrinkles, the tilts, the gestures and body language—those details that animate a specific personality with a presence as unique as a fingerprint." "[Estern's] goal is that the viewer sense the personality of the subject, not simply recognize the historical personage," Benjamin Forgey wrote for the *Washington Post* (April 27, 1997). Trained in the fine arts, Estern worked for two decades in the toy industry before devoting himself full-time to portrait sculpture. In the 1950s he created the clay model for Patti Playpal, the first successful life-size doll to be marketed in the U.S.; it is the subject of the book *The Art of Patti Playpal* (2004), by Jennifer A. H. Kohn and her co-authors, who characterized it as "the most spectacular doll of the twentieth century." Estern has participated in group and solo shows at locations including the National Academy of Design, in New York City, and the Brooklyn Museum. At present, he told *Current Biography*, his projects include a statue of Lady Bird Johnson, the wife of President Lyndon B. Johnson.

An only child, Neil Carl Estern was born on April 18, 1926 in New York City to Marc and Molly (Sylbert) Estern. His father was a negotiator for a toy-industry trade group. Estern grew up in Brooklyn. Starting early in life, he enjoyed making things out of clay from the children's sets that his father would buy for him. At the age of 12, Estern started attending a Saturday-morning class in drawing and painting at the Pratt Institute, a leading American art school, which has a branch in Brooklyn. Sometimes, he has recalled, he would stop working on the day's project and, instead, mold his extremely pliable kneaded erasers into various shapes. After he completed grammar school, Estern attended the School of Industrial Arts (later renamed the High School of Art and Design), in Manhattan, where at that time each student took four art classes daily. Estern found helpful and fun the classes in which live models posed and students sketched them. Instruction in sculpting, though, was minimal. Estern told *Current Biography* that the school's objective was to prepare students for commercial jobs, as illustrators or designers of window displays, for example. He learned that two of his teachers were sculptors; like many others who aspired to make a career in the fine arts, their main incomes came from their work as educators. At his high-school graduation ceremony, in about 1943, New York City's mayor, Fiorello H. La Guardia, handed out the diplomas.

Having decided that he was far more interested in fine art than commercial art, Estern enrolled at the Tyler School of Fine Arts, a division of Temple

University that is located near Philadelphia, Pennsylvania. He also took classes at the Barnes Foundation, in nearby Merion, which is both a museum and an educational facility. In 1947 Estern earned both a B.F.A. (bachelor of fine arts) degree and a B.S. degree in education from the Tyler School—the latter for practical reasons, in case he was unable to support himself as an artist. Within days of his college graduation, he married a fellow student, the former Anne Graham.

Estern soon discovered that he had little chance of earning a living as a fine artist, not least because his specialty—realist, or classical, art—was no longer in vogue among the buyers and sellers of art; rather, the demand was for abstract, or nonrepresentational, art. "The art establishment is all concerned with novelty, with something different, something shocking," Estern noted years later to David Karp, a reporter for the *St. Petersburg (Florida) Times* (April 16, 2002). With the help of his father, he got a job as a wax modeler with the Ideal Toy Co., molding heads, limbs, and torsos for dolls. In the late 1950s Abe Katz, who was then the president of the company, assigned him the task of creating a life-size doll. Within two weeks Estern had sculpted a clay model of a 35-inch doll. Named Patti Playpal, the doll was introduced in March 1959 at the American International Toy Fair. With some of her outfits designed by Estern's wife, Patti Playpal became an instant success. It was the "first big doll to really catch on," according to a *Time* (December 14, 1959) reporter; indeed, her popularity was so great that, in November of that year, a giant Patti Playpal balloon debuted at the annual Macy's Thanksgiving Day Parade, in New York City. Estern later sculpted other life-size dolls for Ideal: Patti's siblings or friends, Peter Playpal, Saucy Walker, Bye Bye Baby, Penny Playpal, Suzy Playpal, Bonnie and Johnny, Shirley Temple, and Patti Pattite. He also completed freelance projects for other toy manufacturers, among them Hasbro, Kenner Products, and Goldberger Dolls. According to Kohn and her co-authors, he refused to work with Mattel, because he believed that that company's Barbie doll (which had been introduced in 1959 at the same toy fair) failed to teach wholesome values to young girls.

A big break for Estern came in the early 1960s, when New York City officials recruited the American Institute of Architects to sponsor a competition for a monument to honor the recently assassinated president John F. Kennedy. The winning design for the monument, which was to be erected at a newly constructed fountain at Grand Army Plaza, in Brooklyn, called for a bust of the slain president, and Estern was commissioned to sculpt it. Set upon a pedestal covered in Vermont marble, the bust was unveiled in May 1965. (In 2002 it was removed because of damage attributed to weather, and Estern was asked to make changes to the design. As of mid-2008 it had not been reinstalled.) The materials that Estern uses for his models are clay or plaster. His completed sculptures are then cast in bronze at any of several foundries.

In 1964 the Port Authority of New York and New Jersey commissioned Estern to design for La Guardia Airport a statue of Fiorello H. La Guardia, who served as mayor of New York City from 1934 to 1945 and was known as an unusually honest, passionate reformer. Lack of funds forced the authority to abandon the project. Estern kept the plaster model, and in 1986 a picture of it came to the attention of Al McGrath, a founder of the group Friends of La Guardia Place, which is dedicated to the beautification of an area south of Washington Square Park in Manhattan. McGrath submitted the design to the Manhattan community board whose approval was required for such public works. Estern's statue portrays the former mayor in vigorous mid-stride, talking animatedly, his hands about to clap—the way he often looked and moved, as the hundreds of photographs and newsreels that Estern used for research showed. The sculptor also relied on his own memories of the fiery, feisty La Guardia in creating the sculpture. "He was always railing against something, some injustice or corruption," Estern told Marvine Howe for the *New York Times* (September 25, 1994). The "dynamic posture" of the statue, as McGrath put it, according to Howe, displeased some New York City residents, who, at several public hearings, contended that it made La Guardia look foolish. Among them was John Bennett, who offered as an alternative his own, sedate model, which depicted the mayor "in an almost Napoleonic pose," Douglas C. McGill wrote for the *New York Times* (October 9, 1987). In 1988, after almost a year of debate, the community board, with the backing of New York City's Art Commission and a number of people who had known La Guardia personally, endorsed Estern's design. Almost six years passed before enough money was raised to pay for the bronze cast of Estern's model. Erected in La Guardia Place, the statue was dedicated on October 19, 1994. Two years later Estern won an award from the Greenwich Village Society for Historic Preservation for his work.

In the 1970s Estern and four others—the sculptors Tom Hardy, George Segal, and Robert Graham and the landscape architect Lawrence Halprin—were commissioned to design different parts of the proposed Franklin Delano Roosevelt Memorial in Washington, D.C. Halprin designed four outdoor "rooms," placed in a 7.5-acre space, that offer a chronological look at Roosevelt's 12 years as president. Estern portrayed the 32d president, whose previous jobs included assistant secretary of the U.S. Navy, as he appeared at a wartime conference held in Yalta, in what was then the Soviet Union, in February 1945, two months before his death. The statue, which is nine feet tall, shows Roosevelt seated, with a thoughtful expression and with his large U.S. Navy cape draped over much of his body, its hem resting on the ground; in addition to his head and part of his neck, only his hands and one leg are visible. Sitting near him is his famous dog, Fala. Many handicapped people and advocates criticized the design, arguing that Roosevelt's inability to walk unaided—polio had caused the paralysis of his legs before he became president—was one of his defining characteristics and should not be hidden. But Estern disagreed, telling Sam Libby for the *New York Times* (February 11, 1996), "Roosevelt would never have allowed a sculpture of him in a wheelchair." Yielding to the demands of some organizations for the disabled, he added wheels to the chair on which the president sits. (Robert Graham's sculpture of the president in a wheelchair was added to the memorial in 2000.) Estern also designed a statue of Eleanor Roosevelt for the memorial. The First Lady is seen standing serenely, wearing a simple cloth coat, with her hands clasped at her waist. Behind her is a reproduction of the symbol of the United Nations, a reference to her service as the first chairperson of the United Nations Human Rights Commission. After years of delays stemming from lack of funds, construction of the Roosevelt memorial began in 1994. The children's book *Shaping a President: Sculpting for the Roosevelt Memorial* (1997), by Kelli Peduzzi, describes the process through which Estern came up with and executed his design.

Claude Pepper, who served as a U.S. senator from 1936 to 1951 and in the U.S. House of Representatives from 1963 until his death, in 1989, was instrumental in pushing Congress to appropriate money for the Roosevelt memorial. He was also an outspoken liberal, a tireless fighter for the disadvantaged among his constituents, and a champion of a fair deal for the elderly. Estern's statue of Pepper, erected on the Florida State University campus in Tallahassee, was unveiled in late 2003. It shows the bespectacled politician dressed in a three-piece suit and standing with his left hand outstretched and his right hand clenched at the level of his shoulder. In a press release posted on the Web site of the Claude Pepper Foundation, Estern was quoted as saying, "In my sculpture of Claude Pepper I want those who knew him personally as well as those who knew him only by reputation to immediately recognize the man for who he was and what he stood for."

Estern served as president of the National Society of Sculptors (NSS) from 1994 to 1996 and again from 2007 to 2008; currently he sits on the society's past-presidents advisory board. In 2008 the NSS bestowed its Medal of Honor on Estern. He has also won the NSS's Lindsey Morris Prize (1984) and Mildred Vincent Prize (in 1988 and 1992). His other honors include the 1990 Dessie Greer Prize, the 1997 Daniel Chester French Medal, and the 1999 Isaac N. Maynard Award, the last-named from the National Academy of Design. Estern and his wife, Anne Graham Estern, have three grown children: Peter, a lawyer; Evan, a cinematographer; and Victoria, a onetime owner of a company that specialized in lighting equipment for filmmakers. The Esterns lived in Brooklyn until 2006, when they moved to West Cornwall, Connecticut. Anne Graham Estern has published three books for children.

—M.A.S.

Suggested Reading: *New York Times* B p1+ Oct. 9, 1987; *Sculpture Review* p21+ Spring 1994; Kohn, Jennifer A. H., and others. *The Art of Patti Playpal*, 2004; *Who's Who in America*

Selected Works: doll—Patti Playpal, 1959; sculptures—*President John F. Kennedy*, Brooklyn, New York City, 1965; *Mayor Fiorello H. La Guardia*, Manhattan, New York City, 1994; *President Franklin Delano Roosevelt*, Washington, D.C., 1997; *First Lady Eleanor Roosevelt*, Washington, D.C., 1997; *Congressman Claude Pepper*, Florida State University, 2003

Faidley, Warren

May 11, 1957– Photojournalist; professional storm chaser

Address: P.O. Box 31808, Tucson, AZ 85751

Warren Faidley, a journalist and photographer, travels around the United States in pursuit of tornadoes, hurricanes, lightning storms, blizzards, and earthquakes. Since 1989, when *Life* magazine published his dramatic shot of lightning striking a utility pole, Faidley has earned his living capturing images and video footage of dangerous weather. His work has appeared in *National Geographic*, *Scientific American*, and *Newsweek*, among other publications, and has been featured on such outlets as the Discovery Channel and the Weather Channel. Although he is not a trained meteorologist, he has become a respected authority on severe storms; he appears regularly on television, has written several books on the subject, and worked as a technical adviser on the 1996 film *Twister*. Faidley wrote on his Web site (cyclonecowboy.com), "Accomplishing a rare shot is like playing chess on an earth-sized board. It's complex and a constant mental game—requiring an unlimited amount of patience. In fact, if I was not a storm photographer I might be a treasure hunter—the attractions are similar. Big investment in time, life, research and money—but big payoff if you strike it rich. It might not fetch me a million in gold doubloons, but the mental rewards are similar."

Warren E. Faidley was born on May 11, 1957 in Topeka, Kansas, the heart of what is known informally as "tornado alley." (The term refers to the states in which strong tornadoes occur most frequently—Texas, Oklahoma, Nebraska, and South Dakota in addition to Kansas.) Less than a year after Faidley was born, his father, a civil-service computer programmer, was relocated to Mobile, Alabama, an area known for its hurricanes. "I remember huddling with my mother, sister, and baby brother in the hallway of our home after a storm warning," Faidley wrote in his book *Storm Chaser: In Pursuit of Untamed Skies* (1996), as

Courtesy of Warren Faidley

Warren Faidley

quoted on the Rain Farm Press Web site. "On at least one occasion, I tried to sneak out to take a look, only to be grabbed by my mom." (The book, which became a best-seller, includes not only autobiographical anecdotes but tips on photography, simple explanations of weather, and many color pictures.) Faidley's teachers often moved his seat as far as possible from the windows, because he continually gazed out. He eagerly awaited the yearly TV broadcast of the film *The Wizard of Oz* and was mesmerized by the tornado scene; he imagined that a heroic photographer had captured the images and was disappointed to learn later that the sequence was the work of special-effects experts. Once, a neighbor's house was hit by lightning. Faidley recalled the incident in *Storm Chaser*: "I ran down the street following the fire engine, and when I reached the front yard, I saw a huge, shirtless man standing at the door, rubbing his beet-red potbelly. Sipping from a beer can, he told the people gathered around the house that he was watching the *I Love Lucy* show when a lightning bolt hit the roof antenna. The charge went into the house and blew up his television set. Lightning leaped from the television and hit him in the stomach, he said, singeing his skin. He quickly became the celebrity of our neighborhood. For days, kids knocked on his door and asked to see his belly and the charred television set in the back yard. He enjoyed the attention and conducted detailed tours, holding another beer can." When he was nine years old, while boating with his father in Mobile Bay, Faidley himself had a narrow escape from dangerous weather: as a squall in the distance began heading toward their tiny craft, Faidley's father gunned the boat's engine and reached shore barely ahead of the storm.

In late 1966 Faidley's family moved to Tucson, Arizona. There, young Warren led goggle-wearing groups of friends on bike-riding expeditions to view heavy rainstorms and dust devils—vortices of hot air that resemble small tornadoes. Faidley once succeeded in penetrating a dust devil on his bike. He wrote in *Storm Chaser*, "The interior of the devil was still and virtually dust-free, illuminated by a weird orange hue, caused, I suppose, by sun filtering through the spinning wall of fine desert grit. . . . But the show abruptly ended when one of the walls crashed into me. I was thrown clear of the funnel, which disintegrated into wispy strands of slowly falling dust. I was greeted by fellow chasers who, having lost sight of me, feared that I had been lifted away. I was elated. My chase had been a success." He had less luck on another occasion: while he walked along the bank of a flooded lake after a storm, the bank collapsed, pitching him into the roiling, muddy water. Just when he thought he could hold his breath no longer, the current carried him to a shallow patch from which he scrambled to safety. Such adventures did little to endear him to neighborhood parents, who warned their children to avoid "that Faidley kid," as he has recalled to several journalists.

Faidley earned an A.A. degree in art from Pima Community College, in Tucson, in 1980, and then went on to attend the University of Arizona. He had hoped to become a navy pilot, but his eyesight was too poor. Instead, he studied photojournalism, and as an undergraduate he freelanced for local newspapers and wire services. In 1983 he photographed a major Arizona flood. "It was the first weather stuff I'd shot, and that's when I learned nobody was shooting weather," Faidley told Leo W.

Banks for the *Los Angeles Times* (July 8, 1992). "I had houses collapsing into rivers and I thought, 'This is fun.'" He graduated that year with a B.A. degree and took a job as a staff photographer at the *Tucson Citizen*. Before long he grew bored with the routine assignments and disillusioned by office politics. In about 1987 he quit the daily paper to become a freelance weather photographer. During one thunderstorm in Tucson, Faidley made his way through thick cobwebs—and the resident spiders—to set up his camera beneath an overpass and aim it at a fuel depot several yards away. Suddenly, a lightning bolt hit a nearby pole. "It was like a bomb exploding next to me," Faidley told Banks. "The light blinded me. I smelled the ozone and felt the shock wave from the electricity." Knocked off his feet when the lightning struck, he nevertheless succeeded in getting a photo. That picture is still widely acknowledged to be one of the closest and most revealing images ever taken of a lightning strike. Phil Krider, the director of the University of Arizona's Institute of Atmospheric Physics, told Banks that the photo "showed the discharge at the point where the lightning was striking. . . . I've seen maybe a half-dozen such photos in 20 years. This was the most unusual. We don't really understand the physics of how lightning strikes the ground. The photo provided some new information." Faidley sold the photo to *Life*. Days after it appeared in the magazine, in Feburary 1989, hundreds of editors asked Faidley for similar photos. "Until the *Life* photo, I was an ex-newspaper photographer, eating Rice-a-Roni and bread for dinner," he told Banks. "It really gave me a boost." In 1989 Faidley opened Weatherstock, an agency specializing in storm- and weather-related photography. That year he filmed *Thunderstorm*, the first storm-chase video ever released commercially.

During the early days of his career, as Faidley explained to Daryn Kagan for the show *CNN Live* (April 26, 2005, on-line), "there were really no guidelines. There was no Internet, there were no [storm] chase manuals. I had to do it all from the seat of my pants. And, of course, a few times I ended up driving right under forming tornadoes or getting way too close to a storm, being hit by baseball-size hail, which is not a lot of fun." Faidley's black sports utility vehicle, which he calls "the Archangel," is now loaded with sophisticated computers, cellular phones, and communications equipment. (Built to his own specifications, the Archangel is the "world's first Fortified Storm Intercept Vehicle," according to Faidley.) While chasing severe weather has become increasingly popular with hobbyists and thrill seekers in the years since he took his first photos, Faidley has often emphasized the dangers involved. He told Stacy Jurado for the *Springfield (Missouri) News-Leader* (October 30, 2003), "I know what I am doing and I take the right precautions. What I do is not for untrained amateurs—that's why newspapers and magazines pay me to take the pictures."

Faidley's first close-up encounter with a tornado took place on April 26, 1990 in Red Rock, Oklahoma. The tornado, with wind gusts of more than 300 miles an hour, hit a house directly in front of his vehicle. "There was pink insulation falling on the windshield. I half expected body parts to fall," he wrote on his Web site. "My foot was shaking on the accelerator and I felt like throwing up. You can hear the mix of excitement and terror in my voice as I shot the video footage." (The tornado registered as an F5, the most violent and destructive kind on the Fujita Scale, which is used to rate the intensity of such storms.) Faidley's experiences with tornadoes attracted the attention of Hollywood filmmakers, and he was asked to work as a technical consultant for *Twister* (1996). Although his name does not appear in the film's credits, he provided guidance on several aspects of professional storm chasing (such as how the chase vehicle should be equipped), and a photo taken by him (of a 1994 tornado in Texas) was featured on the promotional poster for the movie. When asked if any of the movie's characters are based on him, Faidley has pointed out that the film depicts a group of scientists, not photojournalists. He has said that while the filmmakers took certain artistic liberties for the sake of drama—it is rare for dozens of tornado sightings to occur on a single day, as they do in the film, for example—many of his own real-life experiences are even stranger. He told Walt Belcher for the *Tampa Tribune* (September 10, 2004) that he once saw a man in a yellow raincoat calmly sitting on a park swing during Hurricane Frances. "Tiles were peeling off of rooftops, and the rain was beating down, and he seemed oblivious. If I had been working for a newspaper, it would have been a great front-page shot," Faidley said. Once, while chasing a tornado, he came upon a young child standing in the middle of a deserted highway. "When I think back—it's like I've journeyed though a modern day fairy tale. Weirdoes, strange women, beautiful women, mentors, jealous and vengeful competitors, oddballs, crazies, heros, crooks, evil scientists, pranksters, demonic authors, and fellow chasers who have come and gone," Faidley wrote on his Web site. "You think *Twister* was interesting? Ha—that was nothing!"

In early May 1999 Faidley documented an extremely rare event, when more than 60 tornadoes struck on three successive days in Oklahoma, Kansas, Arkansas, and Tennessee. Soon after he began his pursuit of the twisters, his car got stuck in a ditch. While trying to extricate himself, he glanced up to see a large tornado approaching right in front of him. Knowing that the funnels were moving 50 to 60 miles per hour and that he would not have time to set up his usual camera, Faidley pulled out a hand-held digital model and shot 15 minutes of footage. He told Michael Goldman for the photography magazine *Millimeter* (October 1999) that most of the danger he encountered during the trip stemmed not from the tornadoes but from the surprisingly high number of amateur storm chasers in the area. "It would have been comical if it wasn't so dangerous," he said. "There were mom-and-pop types out in pickup trucks, college kids in vans, and they were all racing down the road. What can be really dangerous is trying to watch the storm while also keeping an eye on the crazy traffic." (He has blamed the film *Twister* for exciting much of the general public's interest.) While he shares amateurs' delight in dramatic weather, he believes that people should keep in mind the toll that severe storms can take. He explained to Kagan, "It's one thing to shoot a tornado that's out over the open fields, beautiful setting, picturesque sky. And then it's a whole different feeling when you see that tornado go into a populated area. And that's something, you know, I'm always thinking about in the back of my mind when I'm out there chasing."

Faidley has had extensive experience shooting hurricanes as well. In August 1992 he flew into Miami, Florida, while many others were leaving that city: Hurricane Andrew, one of the deadliest storms in U.S. history, was approaching the coast. All night Faidley awaited the arrival of the storm in a concrete parking garage, which shook when the storm hit. Venturing outside, he was knocked to the ground by 160-mile-per-hour winds. The hurricane caused the deaths of dozens of people and inflicted an estimated $10 billion in property damage. Faidley became one of the only photojournalists ever to cover a Level 5 hurricane, the most dangerous kind. He was also on the scene in 2005 to photograph the devastation wrought by Hurricane Katrina, another among the nation's most costly and deadly storms. Faidley told Paul L. Allen for the *Tucson Citizen* (September 2, 2005), "Gas lines were broken open, areas blocked off. . . . Cars that were damaged looked like they had been in a 70-mph collision. The damage surprised even me."

Faidley's experiences during Katrina and other storms inspired his latest book, *The Ultimate Storm Survival Handbook* (2006), which offers ways to prepare for and remain safe during snowstorms, tornadoes, ice storms, and hurricanes. Faidley has also contributed to books for children. He provided the pictures for *Lightning* (1992), an elementary-level science book written by Steven Kramer. "Exceptionally fine, full-color photographs—each a work of art—perfectly illustrate the text, powerfully and spectacularly showing the majesty and might of this phenomenon," Meryl Silverstein wrote for the *School Library Journal* (July 1992). "Written material and pictures can stand independently, but together they create a masterpiece." Faidley collaborated again with Kramer for *Eye of the Storm: Chasing Storms with Warren Faidley* (1997). In a review for *Booklist* (March 15, 1997), Stephanie Zvirin described as "spectacular" Faidley's images of "lightning, tornadoes, and hurricane winds ripping the landscape and candid shots of himself on the road in his specially outfitted car. Kramer's text is just as noteworthy. With entries from Faidley's diary and

personal comments, it reveals the drama and danger inherent in Faidley's unusual profession." Faidley's latest children's book is *Wild Weather* (2005), a collaboration with Caroline Harris.

In March 2007 tornado alley was hit by some 65 storms in a single day. Faidley appeared on CBS's *Early Show* on March 30 to comment on the unusually high number and deadly nature of the tornadoes, which killed almost 50 people. Faidley explained to the show's anchor, Harry Smith, that the storms were connected to global warming. "You know, the earth is getting warmer," he said. "There's no doubt about that. The statistics show that no matter who you listen to. And, of course, storms love heat. Heat is energy to storms." Faidley has often spoken publicly on issues of environmental concern. He has also donated his services to various educational and philanthropic groups, including the American Red Cross. The Storm Angels Foundation, a group he founded with the aim of assisting storm victims, recently ceased operations due to lack of sponsorship.

In 2008 Faidley documented in his on-line blog, stormchaserblog.com, his experiences chasing that year's most severe hurricanes; some of his dramatic photographs were available for purchase. In August 2008 he captured images of the waves, winds, and destruction caused in Gulfport, Mississippi, by Hurricane Gustav, which affected parts of Texas, Louisiana, Alabama, and Florida as well as Mississippi. A few weeks later, in September, Faidley recorded damage in Galveston, Texas, caused by Hurricane Ike, the third-most-destructive hurricane ever to hit the United States and the largest Atlantic hurricane ever recorded. In addition to areas of the South, Ike's residual winds caused destruction and death in such inland states as Ohio, Indiana, and Pennsylvania.

Faidley, who is single, lives in Tucson. He is a member of the National Weather Association, the National Press Photographers Association, the Society of Professional Journalists, the National Association of Storm Chasers and Spotters, the American Meteorological Society, and the Picture Agency Council of America. His recreational interests include World War II–era aviation, pre-1900 nautical history, skiing, auto racing, and competitive cycling.

—M.E.R.

Suggested Reading: CNN (on-line) May 31, 1997, Apr. 26, 2005; cyclonecowboy.com; *Los Angeles Times* E p1 July 8, 1992; *Millimeter* Oct. 1999; *Springfield (Missouri) News-Leader* E p9 Oct. 30, 2003; stormchaser.com; stormchaserblog.com; *Tuscon (Arizona) Citizen* A p4 Sep. 2, 2005; *Tampa (Florida) Tribune* p4 Sep. 10, 2004; *Virginian-Pilot* J p3 June 23, 1996

Selected Books: *Lightning* (with Steven Kramer), 1992; *Storm Chaser: In Pursuit of Untamed Skies*, 1996; *Eye of the Storm: Chasing Storms with Warren Faidley* (with Steven Kramer), 1997;

Wild Weather (with Caroline Harris), 2005; *The Ultimate Storm Survival Handbook*, 2006

Karl Walter/Getty Images

Feist

(fyste)

Feb. 13, 1976– Singer; songwriter

Address: Cherry Tree, 2220 Colorado St., Santa Monica, CA 90404

The chameleonic singer-songwriter Feist has run the gamut from punk music to quiet, folksy indie rock with the abandon of a woman who once donned a sock puppet and lamé leotard to perform with the electroclash musical act Peaches. That very flexibility and willingness to draw upon varied genres have helped to make her solo albums, *Monarch (Lay Your Jeweled Hand Down)*, *Let It Die*, and *The Reminder*, so esteemed by music journalists, with a critic for *People* (June 4, 2007) writing about *The Reminder*: "This Canadian singer-songwriter has a little bit of everything on her third solo album. There's lilting bossa nova ('So Sorry'), sultry jazz-pop ('My Moon My Man'), atmospheric folk ('The Park'), even some old-time gospel ('Sealion'). And Feist handles it all with a deft touch that seamlessly connects the dots." Her fusion of various musical styles, sensitive lyrics, and soft voice, which has inspired comparisons to honey, have made Feist the darling of indie rock. Among her honors are four Grammy Award nominations in 2008 and seven Juno Awards, for New Artist of the Year and Alternative Album of the Year, in

2005, and five Junos, including Artist of the Year, in 2008.

Leslie Feist was born on February 13, 1976 in Nova Scotia, Canada. Both of her parents pursued artistic endeavors; her mother, Lyn, met her father, Harold Feist, a noted abstract-expressionist painter, while studying ceramics under him at the Alberta College of Art and Design, in Canada. Shortly after Leslie Feist's birth, her parents divorced; she moved with her mother and older brother, Ben, to Regina, Saskatchewan, also in Canada, to live with her maternal grandparents. Later, the family moved to Calgary, Alberta. There, she enjoyed writing short stories and singing in choirs. She has called the latter an excellent learning experience, telling *USA Today* (October 22, 2007), "That's a really good way to begin, because you're nestled inside harmony in a physical way." She began experimenting more with her voice after her father gave her a microphone and effects rack for Christmas one year; her surprise at the way she could manipulate her voice with that equipment increased her fascination with music. "I discovered that setting No. 29 made you sound like you were in an enormous cavern. I would do little self-choirs and make long, experimental pieces of singing, wailing into the cavern with multiple harmonies," she explained to the writer for *USA Today*. One challenge for the young Feist was having very few local female singers for role models. "Having had no girls or women in my town singing," she told *Time-Out London* (April 5, 2007), "I modeled myself after the community I was in, which was dudes. So I was kind of singing with this deep voice."

At age 15 Feist founded an all-girl punk band called Placebo, for which she was lead singer. "I didn't have an incredible voice," she told Olivia Stren for *Toronto Life* (July 2007, on-line), "so I yarled." Placebo won a high-school battle-of-the-bands contest, whose prize was to open at Infest, a musical festival headlined that year by the Ramones, the Violent Femmes, and Bad Brains. The following year, at 17, Feist moved out of her mother's home and began working as a cook to support herself. Although she had previously considered attending university, Placebo had come to dominate her time, energy, and focus. As she and her bandmates performed at venues on the punk-music circuit, Feist began to feel the strain of her lifestyle; in 1995 she was forced to take a break from touring because of damage to her vocal cords.

To recover, Feist found a doctor in Toronto, where her father lived, who specialized in music-related maladies. She moved into the basement of her father's house and used a holistic approach to heal her throat, including exercise and Tai Chi; meanwhile, she rested her voice. While doing so, she learned to play the guitar. After six months her voice had healed, but Feist, tired of punk, did not return to Placebo. Instead, she began bartending and booking acts for a restaurant/pool hall/night club, Rivoli, and waitressing at Lava Lounge, a restaurant-lounge owned by the Rivoli proprietors. In that way she met the manager of the indie band Rheostatics, who promptly hired her as his assistant. She continued booking events, including cabaret nights at a club called Weave. Feist then began singing and playing guitar for an indie band called By Divine Right, which was formed in 1989 by José Miguel Contreras and Mark Goldstein; she performed on their record *Bless this Mess*.

In 1999 Feist moved into an apartment with a friend of a friend, Merrill Nisker, who would soon gain attention as an electroclash musician with the stage name Peaches; her lyrics focused primarily on issues of gender and sexuality. Often, while Peaches created beats in her room, Feist wrote lyrics in hers. Feist contributed vocals to Peaches's first album, *The Teaches of Peaches*, and collaborated with Nisker on a song called "Give 'Er," which appeared on the album *Impeach My Bush*. Additionally, Feist performed onstage with Peaches at her early shows, calling herself Bitch Lap Lap, wearing a pink lamé leotard, rapping with a sock puppet, and—after a fashion—tap dancing. Feist explained to Stren, "It was what we did in our living room—playing dress-up, jumping on the couch rapping to other records—but we were onstage." Peaches introduced Feist to Chilly Gonzalez, who would go on to produce her records. The three soon moved to Europe for Peaches's tour. During that time Feist made her own debut, with an unpolished album titled *Monarch (Lay Your Jeweled Hand Down)*, produced by Dan Kurtz.

In 2001 Feist contributed vocals and guitar work to recordings by the Canadian indie collective Broken Social Scene; she received a Juno Award in 2003 for her work on their album *You Forgot It in People*, which sold 90,000 copies worldwide. Meanwhile, after Peaches decided to work as a solo act, Feist and Gonzalez continued touring together throughout Europe in support of Gonzalez's record *Presidential Suite*. While on tour Gonzalez helped Feist to record some of her songs at the Paris, France, studio of the music producer Renaud Letang; the songs would be included on *Let It Die*, released in 2003 by the indie-music label Arts & Crafts (distributed by Interscope/EMI). Defying the expectations of all involved, since the songs were not mainstream, the album—consisting of six original tracks and five covers—was a success. Kelefa Sanneh wrote for the *New York Times* (April 21, 2005), "On the album, Ms. Feist tosses off one enthralling song after another, casually revealing her little surprises as if each one were no big deal. 'Mushaboom' starts with some strummed guitar and a couplet that undoes itself: 'Helping the kids out of their coats / But wait, the babies haven't been born.' Almost before you notice them, horns and keyboards creep into the mix, and so, slyly, does the title—the nonsense word becomes a sotto voce rhythm instrument." The album sold approximately 500,000 copies worldwide, a huge success for an indie record. While indie credibility might be compromised by such popularity (as Olivia Stren put it, "You can't be indie and sing for soccer moms on 97.3 EZ Rock"), Feist maintained her indie status with the "grace of her unusual voice, both sultry and soaring, and her scrappy guitar-playing style," in Stren's opinion. The album earned Feist two Juno Awards in 2005, for alternative album of the year and new artist of the year. Feist soon embarked on an extensive tour of North America and Europe.

While on the *Let It Die* tour, Feist wrote the songs for her next album, *The Reminder*, which she recorded within two weeks in Paris following the tour. For that purpose she rented a house near the Seine River with her band, including Gonzalez, Mocky, Jamie Lidell, Jesse Baird, Bryden Baird, Afie Jurvanen, and Dafyd Hughes. In a May 30, 2007 interview with Heiko Hoffman for the Pitchfork Media Web site, Feist explained the choice to record in the house: "I wanted to live where I made the record. I didn't want to take any vehicle in the morning to go to work. We slept upstairs and it was like summer camp. Everyone had their own room and we'd go down in the morning—still in your bathrobe—eat something, make a tea, hang out, and then decide what to work on that day." Forgoing the traditional style of recording, which involves many overdubs, Feist and the band recorded in a manner they called "town hall," in which everyone played and sang around one microphone simultaneously. *The Reminder* was met with critical acclaim. Christopher Gray wrote for the Boston *Phoenix* (June 4, 2007, on-line), "Feist's third solo album is a soundtrack for watching your lover walk out the door. From misty-eyed paralysis to teenage triumph, *The Reminder* . . . bespeaks the adrenaline-soaked moments of clarity that strike when your flame leaves you for the first or last time. . . . *The Reminder* reprises *Let It Die* in pace and formula but is more emotive and comfortable." In a review for the *New York Times* (April 15, 2007), Jon Pareles called the album "a modestly scaled but quietly profound pop gem: sometimes intimate, sometimes exuberant, filled with love songs and hints of mystery." One of the songs, "1, 2, 3, 4," appeared in a commercial for the third-generation iPod nano. The commercial gave an enormous boost to sales of Feist's music; during the week of September 9, 2007, when the commercial first aired, *The Reminder* was selling about 6,000 copies per week, a number that was more than tripled during the month after the initial airing. The single made it to number 10 on *Billboard*'s Pop 100 Chart. Feist was nominated for four Grammy Awards for *The Reminder*, including best female pop vocal, best new artist, best pop vocal album, and best short form music video. *The Reminder* was chosen as *Time*'s number-three album of 2007, one of *Spin*'s Top 40 Albums of 2007, and one of *Rolling Stone*'s Top 50 Albums of 2007.

Feist is romantically involved with Kevin Drew of Broken Social Scene. The two share a home in Toronto. She also keeps a home in Paris. In 2008 Feist toured the U.S., Canada, Europe, and Australia.

—T.O.

Suggested Reading: *New York Times* (on-line) Apr. 21, 2005; (Ontario, Canada) *Spectator* G p15 Dec. 4, 2007; *TimeOut London* (on-line) Apr. 5, 2007; *Toronto Life* (on-line) July 2007; *USA Today* B p10 Oct. 22, 2007

Selected Recordings: *Monarch (Lay Your Jeweled Hand Down)*, 1999; *Let It Die*, 2003; *The Reminder*, 2007

Jewel Samad/AFP/Getty Images

Feith, Douglas J.

(fythe)

July 16, 1953– Former U.S. government official; attorney

Address: Georgetown University, 301 InterCultural Center, 37th & O Sts., N.W., Washington, DC 20057

Douglas J. Feith is one of the more controversial figures in modern-era U.S. politics, a neoconservative whose intelligence and deeply held beliefs made him an effective agent of the agenda advanced by the administration of President George W. Bush. After obtaining his law degree from Georgetown University, in 1978, he held a succession of national-security posts during Ronald Reagan's presidency. It was as undersecretary of defense in the Bush administration, however, that he undertook the actions for which he will likely be remembered: heading the group that presented the administration, prior to the 2003 invasion of Iraq, with intelligence—much of it discredited—linking

Iraq with the terrorist network Al Qaeda; and questioning the application of the Geneva Conventions' rules for treatment of military detainees as they pertained to those in U.S. custody during the so-called war on terror—questioning that resulted in the detainees' being denied protection by those rules. Feith resigned from his position in 2005 and then taught for two years at the Georgetown School of Foreign Service. In 2008 he published the memoir *War and Decision*, in which he set out to justify the Iraq war and his role in it.

One of the three children of Dalck and Rose Feith, Douglas Jay Feith was born on July 16, 1953 in Philadelphia, Pennsylvania, and grew up in the Philadelphia suburbs. His father was a Polish-born Holocaust survivor who lost most of his family in concentration camps; he went on to found Dalco Manufacturing, which supplied metal parts to businesses in the electronics industry. Politics was a frequent topic of conversation in the Feith household. "[Neville] Chamberlain wasn't popular in my house," Feith told Jeffrey Goldberg for the *New Yorker* (May 9, 2005), referring to the British prime minister famous for his policy of appeasing the Nazi leader Adolf Hitler in the period preceding World War II. Feith explained to Goldberg that in his teen years, which coincided with the Cold War between the U.S. and the Soviet Union, the Vietnam War, and widespread antiwar protests, he did "a lot of reading, relative for a kid," about World War II. "What I was hearing from the antiwar movement, with which I had a fair amount of sympathy . . . were thoughts about how the world works, how war is not the answer. I mean, the idea that we could have peace no matter what anybody else in the world does didn't make sense to me. . . . The kind of people who put bumper stickers on their car that declare that 'war is not the answer,' are they making a serious comment? What's the answer to Pearl Harbor? What's the answer to the Holocaust? . . . The surprising thing is not that there are so many Jews who are neocons but that there are so many who are not."

Following his graduation from Philadelphia's Central High School, in 1971, Feith attended Harvard University, in Cambridge, Massachusetts, graduating magna cum laude in 1975. While at Harvard he attended lectures by, and came to admire the work of, Professor Richard Pipes, the head of the university's Russian Research Center. "We were part of a rather small minority in Cambridge who thought that working to bring about the collapse of the Soviet Union was not only a noble pursuit, but a realistic project," he said of Pipes in a speech he made in 2004 at Harvard's Kennedy School of Government. Feith was also inspired by the writings of the British political philosopher Edmund Burke, whose works form part of the basis of modern conservatism.

After he graduated from Harvard, Feith served as an intern for a U.S. Senate subcommittee headed by Senator Henry M. "Scoop" Jackson, a Democrat from Washington State who believed strongly in military intervention in the cause of freedom. Feith attended the Georgetown University Law Center, in Washington, D.C., graduating magna cum laude in 1978. He worked for three years as a lawyer with the private firm Fried, Frank, Harris, Shriver & Kampelman before obtaining his first job in government: in 1981, during the administration of President Ronald Reagan, he obtained a position as a Middle East specialist on the National Security Council. He was later transferred to the Pentagon, where he worked, from 1982 to 1984, as special counsel to Richard Perle, assistant secretary of defense for international security, who became a mentor for Feith.

In 1984 Feith was promoted by Secretary of Defense Caspar Weinberger to deputy assistant secretary of defense for negotiations policy. His most notable action in that post was to argue successfully against the ratification of changes to the Geneva Conventions that would have made the minimum standards for treatment of detainees apply more broadly to military prisoners, even those who had violated the rules of war. In 1986 he returned to private life, and upon his departure from the government, he received the highest Defense Department civilian award, the Distinguished Public Service Medal. He co-founded the law firm Feith & Zell, based in Washington, D.C. The firm's clients included the aerospace manufacturer Lockheed Martin and the defense contractor Northrop Grumman. In 1989 Feith founded International Advisors Inc., an organization devoted to securing U.S. military and economic assistance for Turkey.

In 1996, along with Perle and David Wurmser, Feith was part of discussions that formed the basis for the influential report "A Clean Break: A New Strategy for Securing the Realm," meant to advise Israeli prime minister Benjamin Netanyahu on policy. The paper has been criticized for its extreme right-wing position, with Sidney Blumenthal, writing for Salon.com (August 3, 2006), calling it a "neocon manifesto against the Middle East peace process." For his part, Feith, who is often identified as one of the authors of the paper, has denied that role, writing for his Web site, "I neither wrote it, nor signed it. I do not believe I even saw it before it was published. . . . The paper's principal author was David Wurmser. . . . As he researched the paper, he shared some of his thoughts with a half dozen people, including me, and asked us for our reactions and our own ideas." Feith's "main contribution" to the paper, he wrote, "was the suggestion that Israel could help both itself and the United States by 'graduating' from the U.S. economic aid program."

In 2001 Feith returned to government service as undersecretary of defense for policy in the George W. Bush administration. In charge of roughly 1,500 employees, he was the third-ranking civilian in the Pentagon, working under Secretary of Defense Donald Rumsfeld and Deputy Secretary Paul Wolfowitz. In the wake of the September 11, 2001 terrorist attacks on the U.S. by members of the group Al Qaeda, Feith helped to build a case for the invasion of Iraq, which was thought to have weapons of mass destruction (WMD) that posed a threat to the U.S. Feith had a history of advocating for regime change in Iraq; he was one of a group who had consulted in the late 1990s with the Iraqi opposition leader Ahmad Chalabi (who was later found to have given false information about Iraq's stockpile of weapons in the hope of encouraging the U.S. invasion), and he successfully pushed for the enactment of the Iraq Liberation Act, signed into law by President Bill Clinton in 1998. Without specifically advocating a U.S. invasion, the act had stated a desire to undermine the rule of Saddam Hussein: "It should be the policy of the United States to support efforts to remove the regime headed by Saddam Hussein from power in Iraq and to promote the emergence of a democratic government to replace that regime." Feith cited the 1998 act when making a case for war.

Feith's role in the Bush administration's rollback of the Geneva Conventions, an international treaty governing treatment of prisoners of war, was a source of controversy. In 2002 the Bush administration sought to examine the constraints of the Geneva Conventions when it came to interrogating suspected terrorists, including members of Afghanistan's Taliban faction and other detainees at the U.S. facility at Guantánamo Bay, Cuba. In his communications with the president, Feith reasoned that Al Qaeda fighters were not entitled to prisoner-of-war status, or its resulting protections, because they did not meet the Geneva Conventions' four criteria for granting such status: wearing a uniform with an insignia; carrying arms openly; having an official chain of command; and obeying the conventions' rules of war. Taliban fighters, according to the argument, should also be denied such status. President Bush signed a memorandum authorizing that interpretation, making Guantánamo Bay a place of unrestricted interrogation tactics until 2006, when the U.S. Supreme Court's decision in *Hamdan vs. Rumsfeld* asserted that the Bush administration's reinterpretation of the Geneva Conventions was illegal. When asked by Philippe Sands, writing for *Vanity Fair* (May 2008), whether "moral authority [meant] anything" when it came to the issue of denying detainees the protection of the Geneva Conventions, Feith told Sands, "The problem with moral authority [is] people who should know better, like yourself, siding with the a**holes, to put it crudely." With regard to that quote, Feith wrote in a letter to *Current Biography*, "I was referring to the fact that the administration acted in line with the letter and spirit of Geneva when it denied POW status to detainees who had not satisfied Geneva's conditions for such status. U.S. moral authority should not be considered damaged by such a position. I told Mr. Sands that it would be wrong for knowledgeable lawyers such as himself to side with non-knowledgeable critics of the Administration's policies on this matter. It does not promote respect for the law when critics falsely accuse U.S. officials of ignoring the law."

Feith created two new divisions at the Department of Defense, the Office of Special Plans and the Policy Counterterrorism Evaluation Group. The former was charged with planning an invasion and eventual reconstruction of Iraq, while the latter combed CIA data in search of previously unexamined links between terrorist organizations such as Al Qaeda and potential state sponsors of terrorism. In 2003 Feith responded in writing to questions from the Senate Select Committee on Intelligence; in his written communication, he stressed a link between Saddam Hussein and Al Qaeda. His argument drew on reports, which the CIA itself viewed as lacking in credibility, linking the two. Though the intelligence community apparently saw little of value in the memo, its content was leaked to the public via the *Weekly Standard*, a conservative journal, and ideas from it were subsequently incorporated into speeches delivered by administration officials.

Feith has stated that his communication with the Senate committee did not present new intelligence and that it was merely a critique of the CIA's position that there was no credible link between Al Qaeda and Hussein. He has also maintained that the memo was based in part on intelligence that he had obtained through the CIA director, George Tenet. While conceding that the intelligence was later discredited, he said on the TV program *Fox News Sunday with Chris Wallace* (February 11, 2007, on-line) that "that was the best information that the government had" at that time.

Feith drew fire for his role in delivering faulty information about Saddam Hussein's alleged stockpiles of weapons of mass destruction—the elimination of which was the original stated purpose of the 2003 U.S. invasion of Iraq. (No such weapons were found.) Despite the criticism, he has continued to express the view that Iraq had a WMD program of some sort, even if he was mistaken about details at the time he built a case for the war. "We did not find WMD stockpiles . . . ," he admitted when questioned by Wolf Blitzer for CNN (February 11, 2007, on-line). "Although we did not find the stockpiles, we found that [Hussein] had the facilities, he had the personnel, he had the intention. It wasn't the way the C.I.A. described." Despite those admitted mistakes, and despite many Congress members' assertions that they were misled into supporting the war, Feith has downplayed the role of specific intelligence in justifying the Iraq conflict: "The main rationale was not based on intelligence," he told Jeffrey Goldberg. "It was known to anyone who read newspapers and knew history. Saddam had used nerve gas, he had invaded his neighbors more than once, he had attacked other neighbors, he was hostile to us, he supported numerous terrorist groups. It's true that he didn't have a link that we know of to 9/11. . . . But he did give safe haven to terrorists."

Feith's department was involved in an intelligence scandal in 2004, when his subordinate Lawrence Franklin came under FBI investigation for allegedly leaking classified information to the Israeli government. In October 2005 Franklin pleaded guilty to three counts of mishandling or passing on classified information. Feith refused to comment publicly on the proceedings, in part because he was also under investigation, though there was not sufficient evidence to bring him to trial. In January 2005, citing personal reasons, he announced that he would resign in the summer.

After leaving his post at the Pentagon, Feith was appointed to a teaching position at Georgetown University's School of Foreign Service. He received a chilly reception there from both students and faculty, with 72 professors, administrators, and graduate students signing a letter of protest to his appointment. When asked by Jason DeParle for the *New York Times* (May 24, 2006) how he felt about such expressions of disapproval of his actions, Feith said that he welcomed debate "in a proper, civil and rigorous way." He also denied some faculty members' accusations that he had advocated torture and that he had lied in order to lead the country into war. Despite generally positive feedback from his students, Georgetown declined to renew his teaching contract after two years. When Julia Cai, a reporter for the *Hoya* (April 25, 2008), asked him whether he believed his political views and actions accounted for the college's decision, he said, "I think it is the only reason."

In 2007 a report on Feith's prewar intelligence operations by the Pentagon's acting inspector general, Thomas Gimble, concluded that while he had acted inappropriately by disseminating intelligence at odds with "the consensus of the Intelligence Community," he had not broken any laws. Though Feith expressed relief that he was not going to be charged with a crime, he said that Gimble's reprimand was "wrong" and "bizarre" and reflected "confusion about the way policy and intelligence officials relate to one another in the real world," as quoted by David S. Cloud and Mark Mazzetti for the *New York Times* (February 9, 2007). In another report, made public in June 2008, the Senate Intelligence Committee arrived at similar conclusions about Feith's distortions and politicization of prewar intelligence.

In 2008 Feith published the memoir *War and Decision*. In the book he detailed his actions as a member of the Bush administration and defended himself against accusations that he had knowingly relied on flawed intelligence from the demonstrably unreliable Ahmad Chalabi. He blamed faulty intelligence on the CIA and criticized the agency for what he saw as a bias toward intelligence they themselves have gathered. "When the C.I.A. produced or obtained reports that supported its analysts' thinking, the agency often described the reports as 'credible,' without necessarily explaining why," he wrote, as quoted by Eli Lake for the *New York Sun* (April 15, 2008). "When reports contradicted its analysts' theories, however, the CIA commonly described them as 'unconfirmed'—though they were no more lacking in corroboration than the reports described simply as 'credible.'" He also reprinted various declassified documents detailing his department's predictions of what could potentially go wrong in Iraq, in an attempt to refute those who have accused the administration of shortsightedness with regard to the difficulties they would encounter.

In interviews given since the publication of his memoir, Feith has expressed his view of the Iraq war as flawed in execution but justified. In an interview for the CBS program *60 Minutes* in April 2008, he told the correspondent Steve Kroft, "We developed plans to try to give meaning to the concept of liberation rather than occupation. And one of . . . my great regrets is that the United States wound up setting up an occupation government in Iraq for 14 months. Which I think was a . . . serious mistake." He held firm, however, on what he saw as the preemptive war's essential rightness: "In an era where WMDs can put countries in a position to do an enormous amount of harm, the old idea of having to wait until you actually see the country mobilizing for war doesn't make a lot of sense." When asked if he still thought the invasion was justified, given what the government now knows about Saddam Hussein's regime, Feith responded, "I think the president made the right decision given what he knew. And given what we all knew. And to tell you the truth, even given what we've learned since."

Despite the wealth of criticism he has faced, Feith believes he will be vindicated in the end. "When history looks back," he told Jeffrey Goldberg, "I want to be in the class of people who did the right thing, the sensible thing, and not necessarily the fashionable thing, the thing that met the aesthetic of the moment." According to CBS News, Feith is donating all of the profits from his memoir to a fund he created to help Iraq war veterans and their families. He has written numerous op-ed articles over the years, for the *Wall Street Journal*, *Commentary*, the *New Republic*, and other publications. He has four children; according to Marquis Who's Who, he and his wife, Tatiana, are separated.

—J.E.P.

Suggested Reading: *New York Sun* Arts and Letters p9 Apr. 15, 2008; *New Yorker* p36 May 9, 2005; *Vanity Fair* p82 Jan. 2007; Feith, Douglas J. *War and Decision: Inside the Pentagon at the Dawn of the War on Terrorism*, 2008

Selected Books: *War and Decision*, 2008

Fielder, Prince

May 9, 1984– Baseball player

Address: Milwaukee Brewers, Miller Park, One Brewers Way, Milwaukee, WI 53214

After three full seasons in baseball's major leagues, the first-baseman Prince Fielder of the Milwaukee Brewers has established himself as one of the sport's most fearsome left-handed hitters. In 2007 he supplanted Willie Mays as the youngest player in the history of the game to rack up 50 home runs in one season. He also joined his father, Cecil Fielder, an All-Star power-hitting first baseman who played for 13 seasons—most notably in Toronto, Detroit, and New York—as the only father and son to each hit 50 home runs in a single season. Fielder's 2007 home-run total also led the National League and was instrumental in the postseason push by the Brewers, their first since 1982. Despite his team's second-place finish in the National League Central Division, Fielder, who ended the season ranked second in the league in slugging percentage and third in runs batted in (RBIs), was voted third in the contest for the league's most valuable player. Although his home-run hitting power has earned him the inevitable comparisons to his father, Fielder has defined himself as more of an all-around hitter. "I don't even consider myself a power hitter," he told Wayne Coffey for the New York *Daily News* (July 28, 2002). "I just try to get

Chris Graythen/Getty Images

hits. When I'm hitting doubles, that's when I know I've got my stroke."

The older of two children, Prince Semien Grant Fielder was born on May 9, 1984 in Ontario, California, to Cecil and Stacey (Granger) Fielder. At that time he and his family lived in a trailer while his father played for the Kinston Blue Jays, a minor-league affiliate of the Toronto Blue Jays of Major League Baseball (MLB). Fielder was around four or five when he first tried hitting a baseball, and his father soon advised him on his batting stance. "I came home from a road trip and saw him batting righthanded, and I said, 'Hey man, turn around,'" Cecil Fielder told Coffey. "You go back in history, from Babe Ruth to Barry Bonds, and most of the great hitters were lefthanded." Young Prince had a prodigious appetite, and, like his father, he was unusually large from his earliest years, according to Albert Chen, writing for *Sports Illustrated* (May 28, 2007). In 1990, after his father had played for five years with the Toronto Blue Jays and one season for the Hanshin Tigers of the Japanese Central League, Fielder and his family settled in Detroit, Michigan, where Cecil Fielder had signed a five-year deal with the Tigers, the city's major-league ball club. During those years Fielder's mother entered beauty contests, winning the Mrs. Michigan title and becoming first runner-up in the Mrs. America pageant. By age 11, meanwhile, Prince Fielder had become a fixture in the Tigers' clubhouse, and he accompanied his father to every road game during summers. He first showed a hint of his power-hitting potential at age 12, when he launched a ball into the upper deck during a batting practice at Tiger Stadium. He left Detroit the next year, when his father was traded by the Tigers to the New York Yankees, in exchange for Ruben Sierra and Matt Drews.

During the 1996 season Fielder attended batting practices and regular-season games at Yankee Stadium and witnessed firsthand the Yankees' championship run, which made a huge impression on him. "I remember how much fun they were having, grown men playing baseball, laughing, really enjoying it," he told Peter Kerasotis for *Florida Today* (November 7, 2002). "How many other jobs do grown men have where they can have that much fun?" Fielder's father ended his major-league career in 1998, after a season in which he divided his playing time between the Anaheim Angels and the Cleveland Indians. Prince Fielder and his family eventually settled in Melbourne, Florida, where he attended the Florida Air Academy, a military and college-preparatory school, for three years before enrolling at Eau Gallie High School, playing for both schools' baseball teams. By his sophomore year Fielder had fully demonstrated his raw power, once hitting a ball that soared beyond the playing field and shattered the window of a gas station across the street. He also drew attention for his weight—more than 300 pounds. "I realized I had to lose some weight to be a serious baseball player," he told Albert Chen. He lost 50 pounds between his sophomore and senior years; in the latter, while playing first base, he hit .524 with 10 home runs and 41 RBIs in 82 at-bats. *Baseball America* ranked him as the 24th-best overall baseball prospect in the nation and as the top prospect among first basemen for the 2002 MLB draft; he

was voted All–Space Coast Baseball Player of the Year (2002) by *Florida Today*. Fielder's weight, however, was a serious concern for major-league scouts, who viewed him as a designated hitter, not a position player. Determined to participate in the 2002 draft, he began working with a personal trainer hired by his father. After losing another 60 pounds, Fielder, who had accepted a scholarship to attend Arizona State University, became the seventh-overall pick in the draft when he was signed by the Milwaukee Brewers. With his father serving as his agent, Fielder signed a contract for an undisclosed amount that included a $2.4 million signing bonus.

At age 18 Fielder made his professional debut with a Brewers' minor-league affiliate, the Ogden Raptors of Utah, in the Pioneer League. He made an immediate impression by hitting a game-tying, ninth-inning grand-slam home run against the Idaho Falls team, whom the Raptors defeated. In his first season with the Raptors, Fielder hit .390 with 10 home runs, 12 doubles, and 40 RBIs in only 41 games. He was promoted in 2003 to the Brewers' Class A affiliate, the Beloit Snappers, in the Midwest League, where he played alongside two of the team's other heralded minor-league prospects—Rickie Weeks and Tony Gwynn Jr., the son of the Hall of Fame player. After hitting .341 in April, Fielder struggled in May, with a .242 batting average, then regained his momentum and batted .330 over the next two months. He finished the season with impressive totals and was among the league leaders in the major offensive categories, including batting average (.313), slugging percentage (.526), home runs (27), runs batted in (112), and intentional walks (16). The Pioneer League named Fielder among its top prospects and voted him to its all-star team. *Baseball America* named him one of the Midwest League's highly ranked prospects, and he was honored as the Midwest Player of the Year, the Milwaukee Brewers Minor League Player of the Year, and the *USA Today* Minor League Player of the Year.

In 2004 Fielder, along with Weeks and Tony Gwynn Jr., received a promotion to the Huntsville Stars, the Brewers' Class AA affiliate. After the first half of the season, which saw him record a .256 average, 14 home runs, and 46 RBIs, he was selected as the cleanup hitter for the All-Star Futures Game. During that period his relationship with his father became strained, for several reasons. Fielder claimed that his father had taken $200,000 of his $2.4 million signing bonus without his permission. After one game he was served—in front of his coaches and fellow players—with legal papers naming him as a defendant in a lawsuit against his father, who owed almost $400,000 to banks and casinos. (The process server had been unable to find his father.) It was later revealed that Cecil Fielder had squandered his entire fortune, more than $40 million, on gambling and bad business ventures. Fielder also alleged that his father publicly slapped his sister when she asked him to increase her mother's financial support. (Cecil and Stacey Fielder divored in 2004.) Currently, Fielder and his father are estranged.

Fielder finished the 2004 season with a .272 batting average and 78 runs batted in and tied for third place in the Class AA league home-run tally, with 23. The next year he played for the Nashville Sounds of the Pacific Coast League (PCL), the Brewers' Class AAA minor-league team. Fielder was called up in August to join the team's major-league ball club, as interleague play between the National and American Leagues was about to begin. Serving as the designated hitter, he recorded his first major-league hit against the pitcher Hideo Nomo of the Tampa Bay Devil Rays and his first major-league home run against the Minnesota Twins pitcher Matt Cain. In 39 games with the major-league team, he hit .288 with two home runs and 10 RBIs. Fielder spent the remainder of the 2005 season with the triple-A team in Nashville, Tennessee, ending the year with a .291 average and 28 home runs, to be ranked as the number-three prospect in the PCL. He was voted to the All-Star second team by *Baseball America* and named the Triple-A All-Star DH (designated hitter) and the Milwaukee Player of the Year for the second year in a row.

During the off-season Lyle Overbay, a Brewers first baseman, was traded, paving the way for Fielder to become the major-league team's starting first baseman. After a slow beginning—he was hitless in his first 11 at-bats and struck out seven times—Fielder set the team record for most home runs by a rookie (previously held by the outfielder Greg Vaughn in 1990), when he hit his 18th home run of the season, against the Pittsburgh Pirates in July 2006. At the end of that season, he had 28 home runs and 81 runs in 157 games, with a .271 average. He finished seventh in the voting for the National League Rookie of the Year; he was named to the Topps Major League Rookie All-Star team and won distinction as the Brewers' best newcomer.

In March 2007, during spring training, Fielder negotiated a new contract with his team. After straining his right quadriceps muscle in the preseason, he tied a team record when he reached base seven times (with three singles, a double, and three walks) in the Brewers' regular-season opening game, against the Florida Marlins. From April 30 to May 6 he hit .440 with four home runs, 12 RBIs, and eight runs scored and was named the National League Player of the Week. He set another franchise record in May, when he hit his 12th home run of the month—and his 18th of the season. Also in May he set a new team record for the most home runs in a month by hitting his 13th home run—his 19th of the season—to tie for the major-league lead with Alex Rodriguez of the New York Yankees. Fielder earned National League Player of the Month honors in May, during which he hit .321 with 13 home runs and 28 RBIs. In June he led the National League with 27 home runs and was the

second-leading vote-getter for the All-Star Game, held at AT&T Park in San Francisco, California; he also took part in the home-run-hitting contest but failed to advance past the first round.

In August, as the Brewers were battling the Chicago Cubs for the lead in the National League division race, Fielder received a three-game suspension, after a heated exchange with the umpire Wally Bell over Bell's ejection of Fielder's teammate Geoff Jenkins, who had argued a call by the umpire; after an appeal Fielder's suspension was reduced to two games. On September 18 he became the fifth player in the history of the franchise to record 100 RBIs and score 100 runs in the same season. On September 26 he hit two home runs, to become the youngest player ever to hit 50 home runs—as well as the National League home-run leader. (His offensive production was not enough to propel the Brewers past the Cubs, who finished two games ahead of Milwaukee to win the National League Central Division title.)

Fielder received a slew of accolades for his record-setting 2007 season. He won the Golden Sledgehammer Award, given to the player who hits home runs the greatest distance during the course of the season. He was also voted his team's most valuable player by the Baseball Writers Association of America and received the National League Outstanding Player of the Year Award from the Major League Players Association; the Hank Aaron Award for the National League's best offensive player; and the National League Silver Slugger Award. (His defensive play has not received equal praise.)

In the 2008 season Fielder did not match his 2007 home-run record; nonetheless, he had a fairly good year, with 34 home runs, 102 RBIs, 86 runs, and 84 walks. For the week of September 15–22, Fielder was named National League Player of the Week.

The five-foot 11-inch, 260-pound Fielder watches his food intake carefully, as he is highly prone to weight gain. "The first thing you notice when sizing up Prince Fielder is his enormous tattoos," Dennis Semrau wrote for the Madison, Wisconsin, *Capital Times* (March 31, 2006). "Somehow, though, they are appropriate given the size of the expectations that follow . . . Fielder wherever he goes." Fielder and his wife, Chanel Fielder, have two sons, Jadyn and Haven.

—B.M.

Suggested Reading: (Brevard County) *Florida Today* D p1 June 5, 2006; (Madison, Wisconsin) *Capital Times* D p1 Mar. 31, 2006, C p3 June 18, 2002; MLB.com; *Sporting News* p41 June 17, 2002; *Sports Illustrated* p34+ May 28, 2007

Bryan Bedder/Getty Images

Flay, Bobby

Dec. 10, 1964– Chef; television host; writer

Address: Mesa Grill, 102 Fifth Ave., New York, NY 10011

"My food is bold, gutsy, to the point," the chef Bobby Flay told Jerry Shriver for *USA Today* (May 28, 1999). "It's all about flavor. I don't think you can serve bland food anymore to anyone." Flay, one of the most popular chefs featured on the Food Network cable-television channel, is known for his powerfully flavored southwestern cuisine, vividly colored with various corns, chilis, beans, cilantro, and tomatoes. He has hosted several television shows, including *Grillin' & Chillin'*, *The Main Ingredient*, *Hot Off the Grill*, *Food Nation with Bobby Flay*, *BBQ with Bobby Flay*, *Boy Meets Grill*, and *Throwdown with Bobby Flay*, and has appeared on *Iron Chef America* and the *CBS Morning Show*. Additionally, he has written several cookbooks, among them *Bold American Food*, *From My Kitchen to Your Table*, *Boy Meets Grill*, *Bobby Flay Cooks American*, *Boy Gets Grill*, *Bobby Flay's Grilling for Life: 75 Healthier Ideas for Big Flavor from the Fire*, *Bobby Flay's Grill It!*, and *Bobby Flay's Mesa Cookbook*. The famously energetic Flay owns and serves as executive chef at the restaurants Mesa Grill and Bar Americain, in New York; Bobby Flay's Steak, in Atlantic City, New Jersey; and Mesa Grill in Las Vegas, Nevada.

Robert William Flay was born on December 10, 1964 to Bill and Dorothy Flay and raised in the Yorkville neighborhood of Manhattan, in New York City. His father, a lawyer and restaurant manager, and mother, a paralegal who worked for the cosmetics company Estée Lauder, divorced when Flay, was a child. Samantha Miller and Lisa Kay Greissinger reported for *People* (July 13, 1998) that by age seven, Flay "was exhibiting some unusual tastes. At the supermarket he pestered his mother for cake mixes. At home he clamored to assemble deviled eggs. He even asked for an Easy Bake toy oven." In Yorkville Flay fell in with what he described to the *People* reporters as "a pretty tough group." After being expelled from several schools, he graduated from the La Salle Academy, a Catholic school, in 1982. Meanwhile, hoping to prevent Flay from entering a life of delinquency, his father arranged for him to work as a busboy at the New York theater-district restaurant Joe Allen, of which Bill Flay was a partner. Sometimes his father would even come to the restaurant unexpectedly, to make sure his son had gone to work. Flay progressed from busboy to kitchen helper; when the proprietor, Joe Allen, realized that Flay had potential as a chef, he sponsored his education at the French Culinary Institute, in Manhattan. Flay graduated from the school in 1984.

Flay was soon hired as an assistant chef at the Brighton Grill. A week later the chef was fired, but Flay, at only 20, knew he was too inexperienced to act as head chef of a busy restaurant. "It was a case of too much too soon," he explained to Bea Lewis for *Newsday* (September 17, 1989). He went to work instead under Jonathan Waxman at Bud and Jams, where he developed an interest in southwestern fare, which he found appealing because, as he told Lewis, "the colors are vibrant, the flavors are explosive, and the cuisine can be light and contemporary." Hoping to develop his understanding of southwestern food, he toured the U.S., studying varieties of corn and rare chilis and learning to create spices. When he returned to New York, in 1988, he became, at only 24, the executive chef of Miracle Grill in Manhattan's East Village. A review of the restaurant in *New York* magazine "set us on the map," Flay told Bea Lewis. In 1990, while cooking for a Meals-on-Wheels benefit, he met Debra Ponzek, the chef at Montrachet, a French restaurant. The two married the following year.

It was also in 1991 that Flay and Jerome Kretchmer opened the restaurant Mesa Grill, on Fifth Avenue in New York. The southwestern-themed restaurant featured appetizers including grilled tuna tostada with jicama and mango and such entrees as blue-corn–encrusted salmon cakes. About two weeks after the restaurant's opening, Bryan Miller wrote for the *New York Times* (February 1, 1991) about the chef, "His cooking is as colorful as a desert sunset, and well focused." Miller wrote another review of the restaurant two months later, again for the *New York Times* (March 29, 1991), which read, "The sassy Tex-Mex fare at Mesa Grill surpasses anything of its kind elsewhere in New York City. And the sizzling social scene, characterized by loose-fitting Italian suits, ubiquitous ponytails and more exposed legs than at Churchill Downs, further stokes the campfires. . . . The food, by

Bobby Flay, formerly of Miracle Grill, is intelligently balanced and colorful." Quickly garnering praise, Mesa Grill was named the best restaurant of 1992 by Gael Greene in *New York* magazine. Interviewed by William Rice for the *Chicago Tribune* (March 11, 1993), Flay said about his area of culinary specialty, "Southwest is more of a made-up cuisine. The dishes have a strong fresh flavor profile and vivid colors. It strikes the eye and then hits the palate. Very few dishes are slow-cooked. I use ingredients indigenous to the Southwest, but I don't restrict myself to them. But there's a limit. I don't let my cooks mix in Asian ingredients, even though everyone in New York is doing that. I tell them to stay with the focus. What comes out is very American."

In 1993 Flay opened his second restaurant, the Spanish- and Mediterranean-themed Bolo, in Manhattan's Chelsea area. Reviewing the restaurant for the *New York Times* (January 7, 1994), Ruth Reichl wrote, "From the bold graphic collages on the wall to the Gaudí-style tiles around the oven, Bolo vibrates with the humorous edginess of Spain's most interesting city [Barcelona]. The food has the same exuberance. It is a high-wire act that sometimes slips, but even when it does, you find yourself admiring the bravery of the attempt. This food has guts and energy; when it doesn't work, it is rarely because it is too timid." That year Flay was also given the James Beard "Rising Chef" Award, a prestigious culinary honor. He followed the success of Mesa and Bolo with the publication of a cookbook, *Bobby Flay's Bold American Food*, for which he went on a nine-city tour. The chef saw a "direct relationship" between his "bold" recipes and his early life, as he told Kirsten A. Conover for the *Christian Science Monitor* (July 7, 1994): "I was a very rebellious kind of kid. I hung around with tough kids. It made me streetwise. I'm glad I went through it, but I wouldn't go back. That's the way I cook, brash and bold, it's not about subtleties." The book greatly increased Flay's prominence.

In 1995 Flay—who had divorced Ponzek the year before—married Kate Connelly, who was a host of the Food Network's show *Robin Leach Talking Food*. The couple had a daughter, Sophie, in 1996. Also in 1996 Flay began co-hosting the Food Network show *Grillin' and Chillin'* with Jack McDavid, a Philadelphia, Pennsylvania, restaurateur. Chris Sherman reported for the *St. Petersburg Times* (May 16, 1996) that on the program, which showed the two men using different ingredients to cook similar meals, Flay "play[ed] city-slick straight man to the country-cousin persona of McDavid." *Grillin' and Chillin'* marked the beginning of Flay's status as a celebrity chef. He followed up with the books *From My Kitchen to Your Table* (1998) and *Boy Meets Grill* (1999). Flay became so closely associated with grilling that he was asked to host two other grilling shows, *Hot Off the Grill with Bobby Flay* and *Boy Meets Grill*. The latter won Flay a daytime Emmy Award.

Flay may not have known, when he agreed to participate in an "Iron Chef" challenge against the famous chef Masaharu Morimoto in 2000, how famous the event would become. *Iron Chef*, a television show on which two chefs compete to create—in one hour—the best four or five dishes based on one special ingredient (chosen by the producers), was a hit in Japan. In the Iron Chef challenge between Flay and Morimoto, the ingredient was crab. During the filming of the show, in Manhattan, Flay not only cut his finger badly while racing to complete his dishes, but also received electric shocks, due to a water leak in the temporary kitchen set up for the show. Morimoto won, but Flay, thinking that he was the victor, jumped atop the counter and pumped his fists enthusiastically. An angry Morimoto said of Flay, as quoted by Rick Marin in the *New York Times* (June 6, 2001), "He is not a chef." Noting that Flay had stood on his cutting board, Morimoto added that in Japan, "cutting boards and knives are sacred to us." Viewers were hungry for more, and in 2001 the Food Network staged a grudge match between the two, this time with $10,000 worth of Japanese lobsters as the common ingredient. Flay won the rematch. (Morimoto disagreed with the decision, saying, as Marin reported, "With all those spices, he's killing the subtle flavor of the Japanese lobster.") The Iron Chef competitions were so popular that in 2005, the Food Network began airing a new show, *Iron Chef America: The Series*, with Alton Brown as host.

Turning his attention to what he called his "bread and butter"—that is, his restaurants—Flay added a tapas menu at Bolo in 2003. "The new tapas menu shows Mr. Flay at his best," William Grimes wrote for the *New York Times* (June 4, 2003). "Mr. Flay has built a career on big bold flavors and lots of spice. But he is judicious and, in his own way, restrained. A light rice-flour batter makes a crisp but nearly transparent wrapping for tender rings of squid, whose natural sweetness shines through. A few dots of anchovy vinaigrette and a drizzle or two of bright-green parsley pesto do the rest. Crunchy, sharp-tasting green-onion croutons, likewise, add an ingenious finishing touch to a potent brew of steamed baby clams and saffron-tomato broth. Again and again, Mr. Flay orchestrates his flavors masterfully. . . . Many chefs have come to grief speeding merrily down the unmarked roads of fusion cuisine. Mr. Flay has managed to develop distinctive dishes that draw on Spanish flavors and spices in a disciplined way." The Mesa Grill in Las Vegas opened in 2004.

In 2005 Flay, having divorced Connelly, married the actress Stephanie March. In the same year he opened another restaurant in New York, Bar Americain, which featured brasserie-style dishes, such as pulled pork and ricotta on crispy squash in black vinegar sauce and roasted duck with duck confit and duck liver rice. While the *Newsday* (June 17, 2005) writer Joan Reminick celebrated the brasserie, writing that Flay "has good reason to be happy. Bar Americain does a nation proud,"

Frank Bruni of the *New York Times* (June 22, 2005) was less impressed by the food, lamenting, "That broiler needs better tending. Two of the four steaks I sampled weren't cooked to the requested doneness. . . . Mr. Flay is not averse to repeating himself and to taking easy paths—to pandering, in a sense. Time and again he tethers a peppery jolt to a honeyed calmative or vice versa." The next year Flay opened Bobby Flay Steak in Atlantic City, while Wolfgang Puck, his cooking idol, launched a restaurant there called American Grille. Craig La-Ban, writing for the *Philadelphia Inquirer* (October 15, 2006), preferred Flay's restaurant, writing, "If genuine personality is what you seek, Bobby Flay Steak is a better bet. . . . Much of the menu here is borrowed from Flay's Bar Americain in New York, from the spice-rubbed steaks to the raw bar. But I also sense some original effort here from Flay in his quest to redefine the classic steakhouse to the vivid hues of his Southwestern frame of mind. The results are fun and flavorful, if not necessarily subtle."

In 2006 the Food Network also began airing *Throwdown with Bobby Flay*, a program in which Flay travels across the country challenging Americans to compete with him at making their specialty dishes, usually such "down-home" items as chicken and waffles or chicken-fried steak. Although the show has enjoyed a widespread viewership, it has been criticized for lacking instructional content. Frank Bruni has been one of its harshest critics, writing for the *New York Times* (October 3, 2007), "Bobby Flay still dispenses advice on *Boy Meets Grill*, but spends much of his television energies on flashier, less pedagogic projects. Take *Throwdown*. Mr. Flay cooks on this show, but not principally to educate viewers who might aspire to cook as well as he does. *Throwdown* pits him against a nonprofessional chili or burger maker whose yard or home Mr. Flay visits and whose work he is trying at once to replicate and to trump. He's a slumming celebrity cooking in the service of bragging rights or humiliation."

In the summer of 2008, Flay opened Bobby's Burger Palace, or BBP, a restaurant in Lake Grove, on Long Island, New York. As she revealed in her critique for the *New York Times* (October 5, 2008), Joanne Starkey was not favorably impressed: "Every burger sampled was overcooked and dry. . . . A few of the specialty burgers were nearly salvaged by their moist toppings." Other reviewers echoed Starkey's remarks, judging the food as good but not great and as overpriced. Also in 2008 Flay launched a line of kitchenware, which is available at Kohl's department stores.

In 1993 the French Culinary Institute, where Flay studied, presented him with the Outstanding Graduate Award and named him a Master Instructor.

—T.O.

Suggested Reading: *Newsday* p31 Sep. 17, 1989, B p10 Jan. 12, 2005; *New York Times* (on-line) Feb. 1, 1991, F p5 June 2, 1999, B p2 June 1, 2001, F p1 Oct. 3, 2007; *New York Post* p58 Apr. 2, 2000; *Philadelphia Inquirer* M p1 Oct. 15, 2006; *Washington Post* B p1 May 2, 1994

Selected Books: *Bold American Food*, 1994; *From My Kitchen to Your Table*, 1998; *Boy Meets Grill*, 1999; *Bobby Flay Cooks American*, 2001; *Boy Gets Grill*, 2004; *Bobby Flay's Grilling for Life*, 2005

Selected Television Shows: *Boy Meets Grill*, 2003–; *Throwdown with Bobby Flay*, 2006–

Flight of the Conchords

Musical-comedy duo

Clement, Jemaine
Jan. 10, 1974– Musician; actor; comedian; filmmaker

McKenzie, Bret
June 29, 1976– Musician; actor; comedian; theater director

Address: c/o HBO, 1100 Ave. of the Americas, New York, NY 10036

Since they teamed up in 1998, while they were university students in their native New Zealand, Jemaine Clement and Bret McKenzie—known together as Flight of the Conchords—have gained a significant cult following for their dry, understated comedic style and their acoustic parodies of a wide spectrum of musical genres, from folk to funk, "gangsta" rap to rock love ballads. They first won attention with performances at dozens of notable comedy festivals around the globe, where they earned several awards, the respect of fellow comedians, and the allegiance of a core following. They received rave reviews and played sold-out shows at the prestigious Fringe Festival in Edinburgh, Scotland, in 2002, 2003, and 2004. Then, in 2006, their smash-hit performance on the HBO comedy special *One Night Stand* launched Flight of the Conchords into semi-stardom, leading to their eponymous HBO sitcom, which premiered in June 2007. The show follows Clement and McKenzie as they play exaggerated fictional versions of themselves, awkward members of a two-person band from New Zealand trying to make it in New York City; it also features original Flight of the Conchords songs, woven into each episode. Receiving mostly positive reviews, the show was recently renewed for a second season, slated to debut in the fall of 2008. Clement and McKenzie have been surprised by the scale of their success but not by the

Jemaine Clement (left) and Bret McKenzie

appeal of their low-key New Zealand brand of comedy in other cultures. Clement told Christine Fenno for *Entertainment Weekly* (June 2007, on-line) that there is "something gained" in the translation of their humor to an American setting. "Because, you know, we're quite low energy. And that's unusual here . . . usually people are running on stage with their hands up in the air. And we just . . . sit there. I think people find that funny, that we're not shouting. There's something funny about being on a big stage and not making a big effort to fill it up."

Jemaine Clement—the member of the duo with glasses, a cleft chin, and sideburns, who resembles "a hybrid of [the comedian] David Cross and someone very handsome," as Troy Patterson wrote for *Slate Magazine* (June 15, 2007)—was born in New Zealand on January 10, 1974, the eldest of three sons. He grew up in Masterton, a town near Wellington, the country's capital. Little is known about his immediate family. His father was originally from Australia. His mother, a fan of the singing group the Jackson Five, named Clement after one of the Jackson brothers, Jermaine. (Available sources do not explain the absence of an "r" from Clement's given name.) Although he was shy and quiet as a child (traits that he has retained in adulthood), he had an early interest in comedy. From about age nine to 17, he practiced his vocal impressions by imitating the voices he heard on television. Clement recalled in an interview for the fan Web site whatthefolk.com that at age 11 or so he watched the television comedy series *Blackadder*, starring Rowan Atkinson, and thought, "I want to do something like that." Of on-stage comedy, Clement told Sarah Kuhn for *Back Stage East* (June 14, 2007), "I loved watching it, and I remember go-

ing to live comedy shows a couple of times and seeing how the audience reacts and just thinking it was quite exciting; it was like a rock concert, really." Clement got his own start in comedy during high school, when he had to repeat his senior year after failing an exam. Writing for *USAweekend.com* (June 17, 2007), Lorrie Lynch quoted Clement as saying, "I was older than the other kids. . . . I'd always wanted to do something creative, so I developed a new persona and entertained the class." He attended Victoria University of Wellington, where he studied drama and film and began writing and performing his own comedic material. At an audition Clement met a fellow writer/performer, Taika Waititi; together they formed a comedy duo called Humourbeasts and began performing throughout New Zealand and Australia. Referring to the lack of competition in New Zealand's less-than-thriving comedy scene, Clement told Kuhn, "It's very easy to break in. I would say anyone could get a gig. There's one dedicated comedy club in the whole country." During the 1990s Clement worked with Waititi in writing and performing for the New Zealand TV sketch-comedy shows *Skitz* and *Tellylaughs*.

Bret Peter Tarrant McKenzie, who, Patterson wrote, "has a face like a knife and eyes to make all the girls swoon," was born on June 29, 1976 in Wellington, the second of three sons. His mother, Deirdre Tarrant, was a dance teacher, choreographer, and founder/director of New Zealand's Footnote Dance Company. McKenzie and his brothers regularly accompanied their mother overseas, where she worked stints as a choreographer, dance teacher, and dance examiner. McKenzie's father, Peter McKenzie, was a lawyer, actor, and singer. Sarah

Boyd reported for the Wellington *Dominion Post* (August 12, 2006) that the boys' grandfather was "an important figure in their lives," often engaging in activities with them after school, when their parents were working. McKenzie's parents encouraged him and his brothers to become involved in sports, dance, and music as children. As a result McKenzie learned to play instruments including guitar, ukulele, keyboard, and drums. Both of his brothers still live in Wellington; his older brother, Justin, works at a liquor company, and his brother Jonathan has a job in telecommunications. McKenzie told an interviewer for HBO (on-line) that he held his worst job when he was 11 years old, explaining, "We had a bowling alley in my town, but it didn't have the machines that picked up the pins. So I was one of the boys who picked up the pins." Like Clement, McKenzie studied drama and film at Victoria University of Wellington. He played instruments in several bands, including keyboard in the seven-person soul, funk, and reggae band the Black Seeds.

Clement and McKenzie crossed paths in 1998, while working on a project with the filmmaker Duncan Sarkies. As Clement explained during an interview for HBO, the two met under fortuitous circumstances: "Bret had a guitar but didn't know how to play guitar. And I knew how to play guitar, but I didn't have a guitar. So . . . Bret came over to my place with his guitar and I told him how to play it." The two aspiring performers became roommates. With three others, including Waititi, they formed a comedy act and toured New Zealand and Australia, performing under the names So You're a Man and Generation Y Literati. Soon Clement and McKenzie, growing tired of auditioning for TV shows and commercials, decided to form a band. Both men have said that the decision to write their own songs, rather than play covers of others' material, was based on their relative lack of musical experience. "It takes ages to learn somebody else's song because you have to remember it all," Clement told Brian Logan for the London *Guardian* (August 12, 2003). "But if you make up your own, who's gonna pull you up for being wrong?" McKenzie recalled to Bess Manson for the *Dominion Post* (October 1, 2003) the simplicity of their first songs' chord progression: "It was like A A A A, D A A A." (In more recent interviews, the pair have boasted of having learned up to 11 chords. "You can always tell when we've learned a new chord," Clement told Logan, "because we'll use it in our next three songs.") Clement and McKenzie did not initially intend to perform musical comedy, as McKenzie told a journalist for the New Zealand *Nelson Mail* (July 17, 2003); rather, they just wrote funny songs. Their becoming a musical-comedy act was an incidental outcome of their first gig at a small New Zealand club. "We were supposed to be supplying the music for a comedy night," McKenzie said to Logan, "but—and I can't remember how it happened—we ended up being one of the acts." The pair's name, Flight

of the Conchords, came from a dream that McKenzie had about a "V formation of flying V guitars that kind of looked like Concordes," as he told HBO. The spelling of "Conchord" was inspired by musical chords. (Clement and McKenzie also considered the name "Tanfastic," after a New Zealand brand of suntan lotion.)

The successful first night of their act led to subsequent gigs throughout New Zealand and Australia. "It was always going to be a strange band," McKenzie admitted to Dave Itzkoff for the *New York Times* (June 10, 2007). "It might have been a very different story if we ended up playing rock venues. We just ended up playing comedy clubs." They received a positive response and slowly began to cultivate a following. Although they billed themselves as a folk duo, they satirized folk musicians as well as some of their favorite artists and groups from other musical genres, including James Brown, Parliament, Prince, Bob Dylan, and Leonard Cohen. Other musical influences include Stevie Wonder, Wings, Cat Stevens, Beck, Crowded House, Hall and Oates, and the New Zealand artists Neil and Tim Finn. Much of the Conchords' deadpan, understated humor came through during their awkward dialogue with each other between songs, when they discussed such purposely mundane subjects as a trip to the post office. "If we can act as though we're the genuine article," McKenzie told Logan, referring to folk musicians, "people will find it funnier. We've been trying to come up with banter that's as boring as possible." The pair soon began traveling the globe—spending more money than they earned—to perform on stages at comedy festivals. They took their first full-length show in 2000 to a small pub at the 2000 Calgary Fringe Festival, in Calgary, Canada.

In 2001 Flight of the Conchords performed their show entitled "Folk the World" to sold-out audiences at Bat's Theatre in New Zealand. The show featured songs on subjects including angels making love in the clouds, the desire to touch the "fishy bit" of a mermaid, and the story of a person being eaten by his starving friends while on a lifeboat. Tim Cardy wrote for the New Zealand *Evening Post* (May 5, 2001), "Decked out in super flares and an overdose of polyester, the two plucked guitars and banged bongos, while helped along by several surprise guest musos, including ukulele and cello players. The songs ranged in style from corny early 70s folk rock to overdone Latin American, pseudo-Hawaiian, bluegrass, pomp rock and a good dose of funk . . . But what took Folk The World to another level was the wit and musicianship Clement and McKenzie also brought to the stage. Not only was each song very funny, but each could be enjoyed even if you didn't take in the lyrics."

In 2002 Clement and McKenzie took their "Folk the World" show to the Edinburgh Fringe Festival, the largest arts festival in the world. During that event the relatively unknown act slowly began to garner an audience, especially among fellow performers. McKenzie told Logan, "We became a kind of show for other comedians to see after their shows. . . . They liked it because it was quite different to what they do." A journalist for the *New Zealand Herald* (May 13, 2002) wrote, "An extremely dry, deadpan wit is on display here as Clement and McKenzie chat in a series of verbal riffs that celebrate the unlikely and the preposterous to equally rollicking effect. . . . What really sets them apart is the fact that the music itself is first-rate—some of their songs deserve radio play—and it runs the gamut from hip hop to bebop, with a fusion jazz underpinning." Flight of the Conchords earned a 2002 Spirit of the Fringe Award, honoring both their talent and their creative spirit. Following the 2002 festival Clement and McKenzie met with casting directors and media executives in Los Angeles, California, to discuss a possible project, but they were not sure what they wanted the project to be. McKenzie told Logan, "They'd ask us, 'So, what do you guys wanna do?' It was a dream opportunity to say, 'We want to make a film.' And they would have gone, 'Well, here's 20 million.' . . . It was really exciting, but you needed to have a clear idea of what you wanted to do. And we didn't really have any idea at all." They did, however, record and release an album, *Folk the World Tour*, in 2002, featuring live performances of several songs.

The following year, at the 2003 Edinburgh Fringe Festival, Flight of the Conchords took the stage late at night, in a secluded venue underneath a bridge. That uninviting site notwithstanding, their show, "High on Folk," gained widespread popularity as the year's "buzz comedy act," as it was dubbed by Brian Logan. Of the 2003 performance, Logan wrote, "The musicianship is impressive: Clement and McKenzie's folk-rap crossover, 'The Hiphopopotamus Meets Rhymenoceros,' sounds like a beatbox Bohemian Rhapsody. And there's more, from Ennio Morricone to acoustic electronica and beyond. There are also blissfully funny lyrics." The show was nominated for a Perrier Award, the United Kingdom's most prestigious comedy award, honoring the most outstanding up-and-coming stand-up comedy/comedy cabaret act. The duo stayed in the U.K. and Ireland for three weeks, performing more than 40 shows; one took place at Her Majesty's Theatre in London's West End, with other comedians on the Perrier Award shortlist, before an audience of 1,400. Flight of the Conchords also participated in a six-part pilot series for BBC Radio about the band's bumbling, misguided attempts to make it big in London; narrated by the Welsh actor and comedian Rob Bryan and featuring several other Fringe comedians, the series, almost completely improvised, was recorded on a portable mini-disc machine in various London locations. It was eventually picked up by BBC's Radio 2 and aired in September 2005, earning a bronze Comedy Award at the Sony Radio Academy Awards in the following year. Meanwhile, in 2004 the pair made their third appearance at the Edinburgh Fringe Festival, where, as a well-known act this time, they had their choice of stages. They performed their show "Lonely Knights" before sold-out audiences and stayed in London to perform a 10-night gig at the Soho Theater.

As Flight of the Conchords gained increasing popularity, each member continued to pursue his own creative projects, which were many and varied. McKenzie directed and performed in a number of successful New Zealand theater productions, including *Dirt* (1998), which was named best original production at the Chapman Tripp Theatre Awards; *AAARGH!!!* (2000); and *Live Tansmissionz* (2002). He gained cult recognition as an extra in the film *Lord of the Rings: the Fellowship of the Ring* (2001). Among fans of that film, whose main character is Frodo Baggins, McKenzie's role as a silent but distractingly attractive elf earned him the nickname "figwit," an acronym for "Frodo is great . . . who is that?!" (The line is meant to represent the excited reactions of viewers who find McKenzie so attractive onscreen that he steals their attention away from the film's main character.) At least one Internet site is devoted chiefly to McKenzie's turn as an elf, and many others mention it. Shot in his home town of Wellington, the film and its sequels employed quite a few residents as extras, including McKenzie's brother and father. McKenzie also toured with his band, the Black Seeds, and recorded three albums (*Keep on Pushing*, 2001; *On the Sun*, 2003; and *Pushed*, 2003). In 2003 McKenzie released a four-track record with a group of musicians called the Dub Connection. He also played gigs around New Zealand with the Wellington International Ukelele Orchestra.

During his time away from the Conchords, Clement performed with Taika Waititi as the Humourbeasts. They took their award-winning show, "The Untold Tales of Maui," to stages all over the world in 2004. Clement also earned awards as a writer and voice actor for a number of New Zealand radio shows, including *Trashed* and *The Sunglasses Store*. He wrote and appeared in the action comedy *Tongan Ninja* (2002) and, along with a fellow comedian, Guy Capper, wrote a clay-animation film called *The Pen*, about two sheep chatting in a bar. *The Pen* appeared at film festivals in 2007. Those numerous and varied projects notwithstanding, Clement told Margaret Agnew for the Christchurch, New Zealand, *Press* (October 20, 2004), "There's other things I'd like to be doing as well. I always feel like I'm missing out on something."

At the 2004 Melbourne Comedy Festival, where the duo took home the award for best newcomer, Flight of the Conchords caught the attention of the U.S. networks Fox and NBC; they accepted an offer from NBC to develop a TV series, but the deal later fell through. In the spring of 2005, Clement and McKenzie attracted the interest of another big name, the cable network HBO. After they performed at the U.S. Comedy Arts Festival in Aspen, Colorado, where they received the award for best alternative comedy act, HBO executives invited them to perform in Los Angeles for their stand-up comedy special *One Night Stand*. Following the success of that special—and in light of its popularity in later months on the video-sharing Web site YouTube—HBO signed Clement and McKenzie to create a 12-episode sitcom series, scheduled to air beginning in June 2007; in the series they would star as fictional versions of themselves. Clement told Tom Howard for *Time Out* (September 12, 2007) that their dealings with HBO executives progressed quickly. "In England a meeting is: 'Well we hope you can work with us if you're at all interested,'" he said. "In America it's more like: 'We want you to start on Monday.' I'm sure that's part of how we got swept over here. You have to be stronger willed than we are to say no to the Americans."

On several previous occasions Clement and McKenzie had pitched the show to media executives in New Zealand without success. Once Clement proposed the show to a co-worker at a TV production company where he was employed around the time that he and McKenzie formed the Conchords. "I said, I'm doing this band thing, and I think that may be a good show, with two guys trying to get gigs and stuff—basically the same idea [as the HBO series]. And he just screwed up his face really," Clement recalled to Thomas Rogers for salon.com. Clement and McKenzie have frequently remarked—likely somewhat in jest—on the humorlessness of New Zealanders and the frustrating lack of recognition they have received in their native country. "New Zealand is where comedy goes to die," McKenzie quipped to Charlie Amter for the *Los Angeles Times* (July 5, 2007). "It's so hard to get anything in New Zealand," Clement told Cardy. "You feel a little bit under-appreciated and you go: 'I'm sure if we did this thing in America people would like it or if we did it in England.' It's good to find out that you are right."

As co-writers, executive producers, and stars of the new series, Clement and McKenzie faced many challenges in adapting their on-stage performance to a half-hour TV series. For example, they needed to give their characters, also named Jemaine and Bret, greater dimension. Clement told Kuhn for *VNU Entertainment News Wire* (June 27, 2007, online) that on stage, he and McKenzie "had vague . . . personas, but we had to [create] characters that you could tell stories about." The Jemaine character, he said, is "an exaggeration of what I'm like on a bad day. When I get grumpy and I'm sick of doing something, I'm slightly like that character." For the television show to work, the pair also had to create some kind of conflict between the Jemaine and Bret characters. Unlike many comedy duos, however, whose acts are based on the illusion of conflict and competition, Clement and McKenzie always agreed with and helped each other while on stage. "We tried to make [the original relationship] into a sitcom, and you couldn't—that structure didn't really help in creating stories, so we had to add a

little more antagonism between the characters," McKenzie told Rogers.

Shot on location at bars and on streets and apartment stoops in the Lower East Side neighborhood of New York City's borough of Manhattan, the show follows the roommates and bandmates Bret and Jemaine as they fumble through their attempts to secure gigs, get the hang of living in New York, and find true love. They are helped (or hindered) by their manager, Murray (played by Rhys Darby), who also happens to be the New Zealand consul, and constantly followed by Mel (Kristen Schaal), the sole member of their fan club. The story lines tend to be absurd, the conflicts humorous and inconsequential. In one episode Jemaine discovers that he has been dating Bret's ex-girlfriend; in another Jemaine decides that an audiotape would be an adequate substitute for Bret in live performances; and in another, Bret becomes obsessed with constructing a helmet that resembles his own hair. In meetings with the duo, Murray insists on parliamentary-style roll call, and every few episodes Bret quits the act, only to return shortly thereafter. The group's songs—about two per episode—are incorporated into the story lines as music-video–like segments, often resembling iconic videos from the past. "One of the challenges of the show was to incorporate songs we'd already written so they felt like they organically fitted in," McKenzie recalled to Howard. As in their live performances, the humor of the show—which has no laugh track—is not punchline–based; rather, it comes from the quiet, deadpan delivery of lines (many of them improvised) and from long, awkward silences. McKenzie told Rogers, "James [Bobin, the series' director], Jemaine and I, we're all big fans of understated comedy shows. That's a style we enjoy. I guess we made the show to amuse ourselves rather than being conscious of a particular audience." The show's aesthetic has been compared to that of the filmmaker Wes Anderson's work.

The series *Flight of the Conchords* premiered in the United States in June 2007 and received mainly positive reviews. Rogers wrote, "Unlike most musical comedy groups, Flight of the Conchords are legitimately funny. Their lyrics are neither sophomoric nor overly precious, and their deadpan delivery is frequently hilarious." Reviewers also complimented the quality of Clement and McKenzie's songwriting and singing. Howard wrote, "The sections that give *Conchords* a real edge are the self-penned songs that the duo burst into at key moments. They add a fantasy element, but are included in such a way so as not to hold up the narrative or the laughs." In one episode McKenzie, having taken a job as a sign holder to supplement the band's meager income, falls for a co-worker and sings, as quoted by Rob Owen for Scripps Howard News Service (June 13, 2007), "I want to tell her how hot she is, but she'll think I'm sexist / Oh, my god, she's so hot, she's making me sexist." In another episode, when Clement's girlfriend breaks up with him, he croons, "I'm not weeping 'cos you won't be there to hold my hand / For your information there's an inflammation in my tear gland / I'm not upset 'cos you left me this way / My eyes are just a little sweaty today." A number of critics found the show too awkward to be funny. In a review representative of that reaction, Ray Richmond wrote for Reuters (June 14, 2007) that *Flight of the Conchords* "has its moments of wiggy charm but lacks an essential ingredient: star charisma. Its two leads . . . are deadpan and clever but so cloyingly doofy that they're not only tough to root for but difficult to watch for extended periods as well." In September the show premiered in the United Kingdom and New Zealand, where it was also met with mostly good reviews.

Flight of the Conchords' second album is an EP that contains six songs from the first season of their TV series. Released on August 7, 2007 on the indie-rock label Sub Pop records, the album is titled *The Distant Future*, after a line in a celebratory song written for robots to listen to in the future, after humans have become extinct. In April 2008 Flight of the Conchords released their first full-length studio-recorded album. The eponymously named record, which contains 15 original songs, sold 52,000 copies in its first week and debuted at number three on the *Billboard* music chart. At the 2008 Vodafone New Zealand Music Awards—or the Tuis—Flight of the Conchords won four awards, in the categories of album of the year, best group, breakthrough artist of the year, and international achievement.

On August 17, 2007 HBO announced the renewal of *Flight of the Conchords* for a second season, originally set to premiere in the spring of 2008. In October 2007 Clement and McKenzie returned to Wellington to write the material for the second season, because, as McKenzie told Howard, the pair had "used up most of [their] stockpile of songs up to now." DVDs of the first season of *Flight of the Conchords* were released in November 2007. In September 2008 *Flight of the Conchords* was nominated for four Emmy Awards, in the categories of outstanding writing for a comedy series, outstanding original music and lyrics (one each for the songs "Inner City Pressure" and "The Most Beautiful Girl [In the Room]"), and outstanding directing of a comedy series. Filming for the second season, which was to include 10 episodes, began in September 2008; the season premiere was expected to air later in the fall. Despite the duo's growing success, Clement and McKenzie recently told a reporter for the British music magazine *Q* that the second season of *Flight of the Conchords* would likely be its last. "The second series seems to me like it would be a good end to the show," Clement said, as quoted by Kelly Andrew in the *Dominion Post* (September 1, 2008, on-line). According to McKenzie's mother, Deirdre Tarrant, who also spoke to *Q* magazine, Clement and McKenzie's decision to end the television series is related to their desires to "break into a few other things," such as scriptwriting and acting.

Thus far in their career, virtually all of Clement and McKenzie's side projects have flourished. In 2004 McKenzie launched a solo music project in which he performed as a character called the Video Kid, with a debut album, *Prototype*, and in 2006 McKenzie's band, the Black Seeds, released a new album, *Into the Dojo*. Clement appeared in a series of commercials for Outback Steakhouse, thanks to his exposure on the 2006 HBO special. He told Kuhn (June 14, 2007), "The people making [the ads] saw the special. I guess out of me and Bret, I'm the bigger one; I look like I eat more steak than him." Clement has written and directed several films, including the mock documentary *What We Do in the Shadows* (2006), exploring the lifestyles of three vampires, which were shown at New Zealand film festivals in early 2007. He also starred in *Eagle vs. Shark* (2007), a quirky comedy about two misfits who fall in love, directed by his fellow Humourbeast Taika Waititi. That film won the award for best screenplay at the 2007 U.S. Comedy Arts Festival and was nominated for the Grand Jury Prize at the 2007 Sundance Film Festival. It appeared in select theaters in the United States in 2007.

Flight of the Conchords has continued to perform at increasingly bigger venues throughout the world to critical acclaim. The act was scheduled to appear in January 2009 at the new O2 arena in London, which seats 20,000 people. Clement has a leading role in the film *Gentleman Broncos*, a comedy directed by Jared Hess that was set to premiere in 2009.

The laid-back Clement and McKenzie seem largely unchanged by their success, remaining self-deprecatory and seemingly puzzled by the idea of their celebrity. They stress to interviewers that they are neither wealthy nor famous, especially not in New Zealand, where comedians are not seen as "cool" the way they are in the United States. For the past year or so, they have divided their time among New York, Los Angeles, and Wellington, the last-named city being the base of their other artistic groups and projects and a location that Clement has described as "a good place to be creative." Both Clement and McKenzie have girlfriends from New Zealand, whom they "imported" to New York City while filming the HBO series. Clement told Itzkoff, "People are always surprised to hear that I'm a comedian. Like, people will say: 'But you're not funny. You don't even talk.'" McKenzie agreed, adding, "Jemaine and I are both particularly understated. When we're hanging out with other New Zealanders, we're still two of the quieter ones."

—M.E.R.

Suggested Reading: *Fresh Air* (on-line) Nov. 9, 2007; (London) *Guardian* Features p14 Aug. 12, 2003; *New York Times* (on-line) June 10, 2007; *New Zealand Herald* Entertainment May 13, 2002; Salon.com Features June 15, 2007; *VNU Entertainment News Wire* (on-line) June 27, 2007

Selected Recordings: *Folk the World Tour*, 2002; *The Distant Future*, 2007; *Flight of the Conchords*, 2008

Selected Television Shows: *Flight of the Conchords*, 2007–

Ford, Harrison

NOTE: An earlier article about Harrison Ford appeared in *Current Biography* in 1984.

July 13, 1942– Actor

Address: c/o McQueeney Management, 10279 Century Woods Dr., Los Angeles, CA 90067

Having spent a career dodging giant boulders, saving the galaxy, chasing the One-Armed Man, and fighting Nazis, Imperial Storm Troopers, evil cult members, and terrorists from the all over the world, Harrison Ford has been arguably the world's most popular screen action hero for the better part of the last three decades. With his films grossing just over $3 billion, Ford was the highest-earning actor of all time as recently as 2002, much of that profit springing from the immense popularity of the *Star Wars* and Indiana Jones films released over the 12-year span from 1977 to 1989. His memorable characters in those series—the wise-cracking mercenary Han Solo in the former and the whip-wielding archaeologist Indiana Jones in the latter—also propelled him to the status of pop-culture icon and led to a series of films that featured Ford in the role of the manly, flawed hero, including *Blade Runner* (1982), *The Fugitive* (1993), *Patriot Games* (1992), *Clear and Present Danger* (1994), *Air Force One* (1997), *K-19: The Widowmaker* (2002—Ford's debut as executive producer), and *Firewall* (2006). Ford was nominated for Golden Globe Awards for his roles in the 1985 film *Witness* (which also brought him an Academy Award nomination), *The Mosquito Coast* (1985), *The Fugitive* (1993), and *Sabrina* (1996). At 65 Ford reprised his role as Indiana Jones in the series' much-anticipated fourth installment, *Indiana Jones and the Kingdom of the Crystal Skull*, which arrived in theaters in May 2008.

Over the course of his career, Ford has approached his characters by attempting to capture their "emotional reality," as he told Michael Fleming for *Playboy* (August 1, 2002). Most critics have agreed that his acting is both subtle and natural to the point of seeming effortless; still, given the preponderance of tough, sarcastic, and ultimately heroic men on Ford's résumé, he has never been known for his dramatic range. "I don't think that there's a lot that is dissimilar between the character and the person," Ford's *Star Wars* co-star Carrie Fisher told Gerard Clark for *Time* (February 25,

1985). "It's no accident that [Ford] plays a lot of heroes. . . . He has that quality." Ford is "Everyman. He's us . . . ," the filmmaker and producer George Lucas noted to Jim Windolf for *Vanity Fair* (February 2008). "In the end, Harrison is a movie star because he's a character actor. He is like Clark Gable, who was also a character actor, and Humphrey Bogart, who was a character actor. Those people were not Adonis, superhero guys. But that's why they're so endearing. That's why everybody loves them. That's why they're so much fun to watch on-screen, because they're vulnerable."

Of mixed Irish-Catholic and Russian-Jewish descent, Harrison Ford was born in Chicago, Illinois, on July 13, 1942 to Dorothy and Christopher Ford. With his younger brother, Terrance, Ford grew up in the suburbs of Park Ridge and Morton Grove, Illinois. Ford's father worked as a producer of television commercials and did acting and voiceovers for radio. A shy child, with little interest in either sports or academics, Ford aspired to be the man who delivered coal to his family's home every day, because, as Ford noted to Brian D. Johnson for *Maclean's* (July 15, 1991), "he could see the result of his labor." In junior high school, in contrast to the heroes he would later portray, Ford was bullied regularly. "The favorite recess activity was to take me to the edge of a sharply sloping parking lot, throw me off, wait for me to struggle back to the top, then throw me off again," as he told Richard Corliss for *Time* (May 29, 1989). "The entire school would gather to watch this display."

After an undistinguished high-school career, Ford attended Ripon College, in Ripon, Wisconsin, where he majored in philosophy. An indifferent student at first, Ford found his niche when he took a drama class in his junior year to fulfill an elective requirement. "I was terrified to get up in front of people, but I really enjoyed the storytelling part," he told Karen S. Schneider for *People* (August 4, 1997). "It was the first time I felt comfortable with what I was doing." He threw himself wholeheartedly into drama, acting in student productions and doing a season of summer stock in Williams Bay, Wisconsin. Ford left Ripon two credits short of earning a degree. He married his college sweetheart, Mary Marquardt, in 1964 and drove their Volkswagen to Hollywood, California, to pursue his dream of acting.

Before long, Ford signed a $150-a-week contract with Columbia Pictures' New Talent program, an attempt to revive the star-building system of an earlier era, under which young men and women took acting classes and bit parts while being groomed for stardom. The process went against Ford's grain. "Styling your hair, dressing you—it was all so deadly wrong, calculated to remove all those particularities which made you interesting in the first place," he told Edwin Miller for *Seventeen* (July 1983). Ford quickly gained a reputation for being difficult. Following his motion-picture debut, with a one-line appearance as a bellboy in *Dead Heat on a Merry-Go-Round* (1966), the head of the new-

Harrison Ford

Frederick M. Brown/Getty Images

talent program called Ford into his office and told the young actor that he was "never going to make it" in the business; he then told what Ford called "the Tony Curtis story," in an effort to persuade him to quit the profession. "He said the first time Tony Curtis was ever in a film he delivered a bag of groceries. The talent guy took one look at Curtis and knew he was a movie star," Ford recalled to Lawrence Grobel for *Playboy* (September 1993). "And I leaned across the desk and said, 'I thought that you were supposed to think that he was a grocery delivery boy.' He said, 'Get out of here.'"

After his bit parts in *Luv* (1967) and *A Time for Killing* (1967), Columbia dropped Ford, finding him, in his words, "too difficult." Three days later Ford signed with Universal Pictures, which cast him in small roles in television movies and shows. Universal also lent Ford to the Italian filmmaker Michelangelo Antonioni for *Zabriskie Point* (1970) and to Columbia for *Getting Straight* (1970). Disillusioned with the studio bureaucracy, weary of bit parts, and needing money, Ford decided to take up an occupation that would help him support his growing family and give him the financial stability to reject roles that would not advance his career. Ford learned carpentry from library books and from his experience of remodeling his own home in Hollywood Hills. Referred by a friend, he was hired by the famous Brazilian musician Sergio Mendez to remodel his garage. Impressed with Ford's work, Mendez recommended him to his friends, and Ford began working steadily as a carpenter, a job that he thoroughly enjoyed, earning enough money to be able to pass up small television roles in favor of more substantial film projects. (During those years Ford had appeared in small

parts in such TV series as *The Virginian, Ironside, The Mod Squad, The F.B.I., Gunsmoke*, and *Love, American Style*.)

Through an old friend from the Columbia program, Fred Roos, Ford secured an audition for the George Lucas film *American Graffiti* (1973). That low-budget coming-of-age story followed a group of teenagers during one night in Modesto, California, in 1962. When Ford was offered $485 per week to play the supporting part of Bob Falfa—the out-of-town hot-rodder who challenges the local auto-cruising champion, Big John Milner (Paul Le Mat), to a drag race—he felt insulted. "I said, 'You're out of your f—king mind,'" Ford recalled to Schneider. "'I make twice that much as a carpenter.'" With the offer increased to $500 per week, and an assurance from Roos that the film had the potential to be a hit, Ford agreed to take the role. Indeed, *American Graffiti* was a huge commercial and critical success, grossing $117 million (50 times the amount invested in it). While Ford was not singled out in the reviews for *American Graffiti*, its producer, Francis Ford Coppola, tapped him for a role in *The Conversation* (1974). That film, written and directed by Coppola, won the grand prize at the Cannes Film Festival and was nominated for an Academy Award for best picture. Ford next took roles in a number of television movies, including *The Trial of Lieutenant Calley* (1974) and *Dynasty* (1976), but critical appreciation continued to elude him.

Continuing his carpentry work, Ford was hired to build a portico entrance to Coppola's Los Angeles office, where Lucas was auditioning actors for his next film, *Star Wars* (1977). Lucas asked Ford to help with auditions by reading the lines of the character Han Solo, a cocky, intergalactic soldier of fortune. According to Hollywood legend, Ford, annoyed at not being asked to audition for the part, impressed Lucas by lending just the right touch of cynicism to his voicing of Solo's lines, though Ford contends that he was just "grumpy by nature in those days," as he told Schneider. Set "long, long ago in a galaxy far, far away," the now-classic science-fiction film concerns Princess Leia Organa (Carrie Fisher) of the planet Alderaan, the leader of the Alliance to Restore the Republic, and her effort to mount a rebellion against the evil Galactic Empire. Led by the power-mad emperor Grand Moff Tarkin (Peter Cushing) and the once-noble Darth Vader (played by David Prowse under a heavy mask with the voice of James Earl Jones), the Galactic Empire, which has already destroyed Leia's planet, has plans to take over all planets in the Republic. Leia's allies are the young Luke Skywalker (Mark Hamill), the wise Jedi warrior Obi-Wan Kenobi (Alec Guinness), and Solo. Ford's seemingly effortless performance as Solo won him the admiration of actors and critics. The film itself earned critical and audience approval for its visual splendor, epic story, and well-crafted characters and was the first film ever to gross more than $10 million in one weekend and $300 million in its first year of distribution, by far the largest box-office take in motion-picture history up to that time.

Star Wars' sequel, *The Empire Strikes Back* (1980), was the first film Ford was "happy with" when seeing himself on screen. Produced by Lucas and directed by Irvin Kershner, the sequel is widely considered the best of the three *Star Wars* films by fans and critics, both for its imaginative visual effects and for the complexity of the characters. *Empire* features the first inkling of romance between Han Solo and Princess Leia and ends with a cliffhanger, as Darth Vader places Solo in a carbon freezing chamber. It was Ford who suggested the dialogue spoken as Solo is about to become a human ice cube: grief-stricken, Princess Leia confesses, "I love you," to which Solo—instead of saying "I love you, too," as in the script—responds, "I know."

The third film in the original *Star Wars* trilogy, *The Return of the Jedi* (1983), produced by Lucas and directed by Richard Marquand, dramatically concludes the many strands of the Rebels' journey: Princess Leia frees Solo from the frozen chamber, Skywalker overcomes the temptation to join the "dark side," and Darth Vader, who turns out to be Luke's father, reconnects with the good side of his nature, hurling the evil emperor to his death before dying himself. While most critics found the film a mesmerizing visual adventure, many thought that the human and dramatic elements were overwhelmed by special effects and parodic allusions to other works of fantasy. Nevertheless, audiences made the film the third-ranking box-office grosser up to that time.

Meanwhile, Ford had deliberately widened his range with a number of small but significant roles, such as those of a psychically shattered Vietnam veteran in Jeremy Paul Kaga's *Heroes* (1977), a commando officer in *Force Ten from Navarone* (1978), and an inscrutable army colonel in Francis Ford Coppola's Vietnam epic *Apocalypse Now* (1979). He also had a starring role as Rick Deckard, the glumly reticent 21st-century cop tracking and gunning down rebellious replicates (genetically engineered humanoid robot slaves) in the "cyberpunk" film *Blade Runner* (1982), adapted from Phillip K. Dick's novel *Do Androids Dream of Electric Sheep?* (1968). Commercially unsuccessful upon its release, the film has since become a cult classic. Ridley Scott, the director of *Blade Runner*, credited Ford with "an immense understanding of the entire movie-making process" and with having "tremendous" input into "the story level as well as . . . his own character."

As Scott pointed out, Ford had become a star not with *Star Wars* but with *Raiders of the Lost Ark* (1981): "Before that, Ford was not a well-known actor, but the man who played Han Solo." Conceived by Lucas and directed by Steven Spielberg, *Raiders* has as its protagonist Professor Indiana Jones, a tough, globe-trotting, treasure-hunting archaeologist reminiscent of the pulp heroes of 1930s and 1940s film serials. Jones competes with the Nazis to unearth the Ark of the Covenant, the golden casket that was said to be used by the ancient Hebrews to hold the tablets on which the Ten Commandments were inscribed—and that now holds untold mystical powers. Ford was behind the improvising of one of the film's most memorable and humorous scenes, in which a swordsman challenges the whip-wielding "Indy" to a fight, demonstrating his prowess with a series of impressive maneuvers. Though the script called for an elaborate fight scene that would have taken three days to shoot, Ford—suffering from dysentery in the brutal heat of Tunisia, where *Raiders* was filmed—suggested to Spielberg that Indy simply shoot the swordsman, and Spielberg, also fed up with the working conditions, quickly agreed. The resulting sequence perfectly captured the film's wry spirit. Widely regarded as a masterpiece of pop cinema, *Raiders* was both a critical success and one of the biggest box-office draws in history, grossing more than $231 million. "The spirit of the piece is beautifully captured in Harrison Ford's performance," David Ansen wrote for *Newsweek* (June 15, 1981). "He's a wry hero, but he's a real one—exuding just that quiet, sardonic masculinity that made stars like Bogart and Gable at once larger than life and down to earth."

The sequel to *Raiders*, *Indiana Jones and the Temple of Doom* (1984), is widely considered the weak link in the original trilogy, due to its graphic scenes involving the occult and to the weakness of its secondary characters. (One scene, involving a mystical tribe's tradition of heart removal, led executives to create the PG-13 film rating.) The film finds Indiana Jones surviving a plane crash in the Himalayas and stumbling upon an Indian village whose magic jewel has been stolen, along with the village's children, by a cult that inhabits an underground fortress. Indiana's quest to retrieve the stone results in bizarre and heart-racing scenes involving a voodoo doll, an elaborate mine-car race, a pit of flames, and Indy's becoming brainwashed after being forced to drink blood. Vincent Canby, writing for the *New York Times* (May 23, 1984), called Ford's "an exceptionally skillful comic performance, demonstrating easy charm and timing." Despite mixed critical assessments, *Temple of Doom* was considered the summer's must-see movie, grossing $333 million worldwide.

The campy third film in the series, *Indiana Jones and the Last Crusade* (1989), follows Indy and his cantankerous, scholarly father, Henry Jones (Sean Connery), on their search for the Holy Grail, the cup used—according to biblical lore—by Christ during the Last Supper. The Nazis are also seeking the Grail, which, according to legend, gives eternal youth to any person who drinks from it. Critics, while finding little that was new in the action-packed finale, generally approved of the "archaeological dig through Hollywood cliches, ending with a classic ride into the sunset," as Brian D. Johnson put it in *Maclean's* (June 5, 1989). Of Ford's performance, Roger Ebert wrote for the *Chi-*

cago Sun-Times (May 24, 1989): "What he does seems so easy, so deadpan, that few other actors could maintain such a straight and credible presence in the midst of such chaos." A hit with fans, The Last Crusade grossed almost $500 million worldwide.

During the 1980s and 1990s, Ford appeared in other critically acclaimed films, such as the romantic comedy Working Girl (1988); the dark 1986 tale The Mosquito Coast (for which he received a Golden Globe nomination); Frantic (1988), Roman Polanski's mystery set in Paris, France; the psychological thriller Presumed Innocent (1990); and Regarding Henry (1991), about a ruthless lawyer who loses his memory when he is shot in the head during a robbery. Perhaps Ford's most notable role during that era was that of John Book, a Philadelphia detective investigating the murder of a police officer, in Witness (1985). When a young Amish boy, Samuel Lapp (Lukas Haas), the sole witness to the brutal murder, implicates another Philadelphia cop (played by Danny Glover), Book finds that corruption extends to the police department's upper levels. Hunted himself for what he has discovered, Book goes into hiding as a member of the Amish community, where he falls in love with Samuel's mother, Rachel Lapp (Kelly McGillis). Nominated for an Oscar for his portrayal of the jaded police officer, Ford's performance impressed critics, who credited him with having expanded his range.

In the Academy Award–nominated suspense film The Fugitive (1993), loosely based on the 1960s television series of the same title, Ford played Richard Kimble, a physician who is unjustly accused, tried, and convicted of murdering his wife. After escaping during a prison bus crash, he seeks to discover his wife's true murderer, while being pursued by U.S. Marshal Samuel Gerard (Tommy Lee Jones, who won an Academy Award for his role). Writing for Maclean's (August 9, 1993), Johnson called The Fugitive "a simple but riveting exercise in suspense, kept taut by superb performances from Ford and Tommy Lee Jones." He noted that Ford was "ideally cast" as Kimble and that his performance contained "an intensity that quivers between fear and rage." In Patriot Games (1992) and Clear and Present Danger (1994), based on novels by Tom Clancy, Ford played the heroic Jack Ryan, a CIA analyst who is dispatched around the world to take on national and international conflicts. While earning mixed reviews, the films were financial successes. Ford's ability to generate box-office profits was recognized in 1994 by the National Association of Theater Owners, which named the actor Star of the Century.

After appearing in Sabrina (1995) and The Devil's Own (1997), Ford starred in Air Force One (1997) as the fictional U.S. president James Marshall, whose flight home is hijacked by Kazakhstan terrorists who have taken his daughter and wife hostage. Receiving mixed reviews, Air Force One grossed some $300 million at box offices world-wide. At his insistence Ford, who prefers to do most of his own stunts, received real punches to the face during filming; he also injured his rotator cuff. (On-set injuries were not new to Ford, who tore a knee ligament and ruptured a disc in his spine while making the Indiana Jones films.) "Harrison doesn't care if he has all sorts of black marks on his body," Wolfgang Petersen, the director of Air Force One, told Schneider. "When his face was really red and swollen, I'd just push back close-ups a few days."

In the late 1990s and early 2000s, Ford appeared in films that drew only lukewarm critical reception. In 1998, the same year he was named People magazine's Sexiest Man Alive, Ford starred opposite Anne Heche in the desert-island romantic comedy Six Days and Seven Nights. In 1999 he appeared opposite Kristen Scott Thomas in Random Hearts, about a widow and widower who discover that their spouses, who have perished in the same plane crash, had been having an affair with each other. In What Lies Beneath (2000), about a seemingly normal couple with a terrible secret, Ford played his first "bad guy" role. As he explained to Fleming, he had never avoided playing villains; rather, casting directors had simply not envisioned him in such roles.

Though Ford regularly has a hand in shaping his films' stories and scripts, K-19: The Widowmaker (2002) was the first film for which he was credited as executive producer. Loosely based on events that took place in 1961, at the height of the Cold War, the film, starring Ford and Liam Neeson, tells the story of the Soviet Union's first nuclear ballistic submarine, which suffered a malfunction on its maiden voyage and nearly triggered a nuclear world war. Directed by Kathryn Bigelow, the suspenseful film earned positive reviews for its complexity and its bravery in telling a Cold War story from the Russian perspective. Other, more critical reviewers pointed out the actors' poor Russian accents and the limited appeal of such a story to contemporary American audiences. Indeed, the film had a dismal box-office showing, a rarity for a Ford action picture. Ford next made two films that also failed to attract a significant audience: the police action comedy Hollywood Homicide (2003) and the computer-security thriller Firewall (2006).

After a significant slowdown in Ford's career, the release on May 22, 2008 of the highly anticipated Indiana Jones and the Kingdom of the Crystal Skull brought fresh attention to his iconic role and to Raiders of the Lost Ark, which had inspired a generation of action filmmakers. In addition to Ford, the film stars Karen Allen, reprising her Raiders role as Marion Ravenwood; Shia LaBeouf as Mutt Williams, Jones's adventurous young sidekick and (it is revealed) the son of Indy and Marion; and Cate Blanchett as Irina Spalko, the stern Soviet colonel and the film's main villain. Set in 1957, the story follows Indy and Mutt as they set out to locate Indy's former colleague Harold Oxley (John Hurt), who disappeared in the Nazca Mountains in Peru after discovering a mysterious crystal skull, the focus of many legends of the local Ugha tribe. During his quest Indy battles Spalko and her convoy of Soviets, who also seek the skull, for what they believe is its great psychic power. The media made much of the fact that Ford was 65 when the film was released—older than Connery was when he played Indiana Jones's father. Still doing most of his own physically demanding scenes, Ford told Windolf that he found it easy to relate to Indiana Jones. "There's something about the character that I guess is a good fit for me," he said, "because the minute I put the costume on, I recognize the tone that we need, and I feel confident and clear about the character." The film, and Ford's work in it, got mixed reviews. Those who greeted both enthusiastically included Pete Hammond, who described the movie for Hollywood.com as "a rousing, exciting, even nostalgic adventure that makes for a great time at the movies" and wrote of Ford, "There is no question that Harrison Ford and Indiana Jones were made for each other and even after nearly two decades apart, the marriage between actor and his most iconic role is still a perfect fit. Smartly, Ford lets Indy age, so even though he's probably Hollywood's only gray-haired action hero this summer—and there are more lines in his face—he's still got it. You believe he can still pull off all this derring-do which is pretty remarkable for an actor now eligible for Social Security checks." By contrast, David Denby, a *New Yorker* (June 2, 2008) critic, wrote, "It was a mistake for Spielberg and George Lucas . . . to revive *Indiana Jones* after so many years. *Crystal Skull* isn't bad—there are a few dazzling sequences, and a couple of good performances—but the unprecedented blend of comedy and action that made the movies so much more fun than any other adventure series is mostly gone." Ford, according to Denby, "can't be described as a man relaxing into middle age. He's in great shape physically, but he doesn't seem happy. He's tense and glaring, and he speaks his lines with more emphasis than is necessary, like a drunk who wants to appear sober. In the earlier movies, Indy was often surly, but his scowl turned into a rakish smile—he dared you to think he was afraid to do something, and then, before you had quite registered the dare, he raced away and did it. Ford combined swagger with charm, and he was quick; he moved as if he had steel springs in his legs. He rolls and jumps well enough in *Crystal Skull*, but his hostile unease in some of the dialogue passages is a real killjoy." As of October 17, 2008 the film has grossed over $317 million in the U.S.

Ford will star in Wayne Kramer's *Crossing Over*, about immigrants seeking legal status in the U.S., which was scheduled for release in December 2008.

Ford prefers to keep a low profile and is often portrayed in the media as being reticent or even grumpy. He is notoriously difficult to interview because he resists revealing details about his life. "What I do for a living is the most interesting thing about me," he told Grobel. "I don't have a mystique, and because there is no mystique, there is no mystery." While he feels "most comfortable, most at peace around a movie set," as quoted by *People* (March 15, 1999), Ford dislikes the celebrity lifestyle; he has never had a publicist and has kept the same manager, Patricia McQueeney, since he began acting. Ford told Fleming, "Nothing is good about being famous. You always think, If I'm successful, then I'll have opportunities. You never figure the cost being a total loss of privacy. That's incalculable." Ford's hobbies include doing carpentry work, riding one of his many motorcycles, and piloting one of his private planes across the country, activities that allow him to escape the pressures of celebrity. Those who have worked with Ford speak fondly of him, noting his politeness and his mischievous sense of humor.

From his marriage to Marquette, Ford has two sons, Benjamin and Willard. He married the screenwriter Melissa Mathison, whom he met on the set of *Apocalypse Now*, in 1983. Their union produced two children, Malcolm and Georgia; Ford and Mathison separated in 2000 and divorced in 2004. Ford currently lives with his fiancée, the actress Calista Flockhart, and her adopted son, Liam, in Hollywood Hills. The actor earned a Lifetime Achievement Award from the American Film Institute in 2000. Discussing the durable popularity of his screen persona, he told Fleming, "I was never the hippest thing around, which means that I wasn't in the position to be replaced by the next hippest thing. I'm more like old shoes."

—M.E.R.

Suggested Reading: *Maclean's* p56 June 5, 1989, p44 July 15, 1991, p52 Aug. 9, 1993; *New York Times* E p1+ May 22, 2008; *People* p90 Aug. 4, 1997; *Playboy* p20 Sep. 1993, p59 Aug. 1, 2002; *Time* p82 May 29, 1989; *Vanity Fair* p116 Feb. 2008

Selected Films: *Dead Heat on a Merry-Go-Round*, 1966; *Luv*, 1967; *A Time for Killing*, 1967; *Getting Straight*, 1970; *Zabriskie Point*, 1970; *American Graffiti*, 1973; *The Conversation*, 1974; *Star Wars*, 1977; *Heroes*, 1977; *Force Ten from Navarone*, 1978; *Apocalypse Now*, 1979; *Hanover Street*, 1979; *The Frisco Kid*, 1979; *The Empire Strikes Back*, 1980; *Raiders of the Lost Ark*, 1981; *Blade Runner*, 1982; *Return of the Jedi*, 1983; *Indiana Jones and the Temple of Doom*, 1984; *Witness*, 1985; *The Mosquito Coast*, 1986; *Frantic*, 1988; *Working Girl*, 1988; *Indiana Jones and the Last Crusade*, 1989; *Presumed Innocent*, 1990; *Regarding Henry*, 1991; *Patriot Games*, 1992; *The Fugitive*, 1993; *Clear and Present Danger*, 1994; *Sabrina*, 1995; *The Devil's Own*, 1997; *Air Force One*, 1997; *Six Days Seven Nights*, 1998; *Random Hearts*, 1999; *What Lies Beneath*, 2000; *K-10: The Widowmaker*, 2002; *Hollywood Homicide*, 2003; *Water to Wine*, 2004; *Firewall*, 2006; *Crossing Over*, 2008; *Indiana Jones and the Kingdom of the Crystal Skull*, 2008

Jim McIsaac/Getty Images

Francona, Terry

Apr. 22, 1959– Baseball manager

*Address: Boston Red Sox, 4 Yawkey Way,
Boston, MA 02215-3296*

When the officials of the Boston Red Sox were considering Terry Francona as the next manager of their Major League Baseball team, in the fall of 2003, the club's general manager, Theo Epstein, expressed one concern about him, as Peter King reported for *Sports Illustrated* (April 5, 2004): "Is he too nice?" At that time the highly disparate Red Sox players had gained notoriety as rowdy, undisciplined, and urgently in need of an assertive manager. Francona, who is famously patient, candid, and friendly, had rarely yelled in public and had never criticized his players when speaking to reporters. Indeed, while managing the Philadelphia Phillies, from 1996 through 2000, he had become known as a "players' manager." Despite the Phillies' persistent losses and Philadelphia fans' frustrations, he had remained an enduring source of what many have labeled positive energy. Speaking of the Phillies, Francona told Doug Lesmerises for the Wilmington, Delaware, *News Journal* (February 7, 1999), "I don't ever try to hide the fact that I like them. The more they're around ya, they grow on ya. I mean, if they didn't, something's wrong."

Francona turned out to be a perfect fit for the Red Sox. Since he took the helm, he has notched 470 wins and 340 losses in five regular seasons (2004–08). In his first year as manager, he led the team to its first World Series championship since 1918. He thereby ended the legendary "curse of the Bambino," the superstition that the Red Sox had

been cursed ever since the team traded their star player, Babe Ruth, to the New York Yankees, in 1919. The team won its 2004 World Series trophy, and its next one, three years later, in four straight games, making Francona the first manager in baseball history to win all of his first eight World Series games.

Francona's well-known ability to relate to each of his players, ranging from the stars to the bullpen pitchers to the bench players, and from those with easygoing personalities to those seen as prickly, stems in part from his experiences during his nine years as a player. He started his professional career in 1980 as the Montreal Expos' "golden boy," a first-round draft pick and outstanding hitter. Later, he spent several seasons trying to overcome injuries; he ended his playing days in the minor leagues. "He is unbelievable," the Red Sox relief pitcher Javier Lopez told John Lowe for the *Detroit Free Press* (October 30, 2007). "One thing is he always has the players' backs"—that is, he always supports them. "He is always going to accept responsibility. That's why we are a family. He trusts everybody to get the job done."

The son of John Patsy "Tito" Francona and his wife, Birdie, Terry Jon Francona was born on April 22, 1959 in Aberdeen, South Dakota. His father played first base and outfield for nine major-league teams in succession during the 1950s and 1960s, among them the Cleveland Indians, the St. Louis Cardinals, the Philadelphia Phillies, the Atlanta Braves, the Oakland Athletics, and the Milwaukee Brewers. When the elder Francona retired from baseball, in 1970, the family moved to a suburb of Pittsburgh, Pennsylvania. During his childhood Terry Francona was a "baseball brat," traveling with his father to road games; he often sat behind home plate and followed every play closely. "Most kids are running around the ballpark," Tito Francona told John F. Bonfatti for the Associated Press (March 30, 1997). "Every time I looked up, [Terry] was watching the game." As a student at New Brighton High School, near Pittsburgh, Francona excelled in both basketball and baseball. In the latter sport he played first base and outfield. He finished his junior season with an astonishing batting average: .769.

During his senior year Francona was wooed by baseball recruiters. He was drafted in the second round by the Chicago Cubs, but he decided instead to accept a full baseball scholarship to attend the University of Arizona. In 1980, as a senior, he helped the school's baseball team, the Wildcats, to win the College World Series. He was named college player of the year by *Sporting College News* and amateur player of the year by USA Baseball, the governing body for amateur baseball. (The Wildcats have since honored Francona by retiring his jersey number.) His accomplishments on the field attracted the attention of major-league recruiters, and the Montreal Expos' scouting director, Jim Fanning, made him the team's first-round pick in the June 1980 amateur draft. Francona spent his first season with the Expos' double-A team, the Memphis, Tennessee, Chicks. During the 1981 season he divided most of his time between Memphis and the Expos' triple-A team in Denver, Colorado, where he played outfield, collected 181 hits, and earned a .352 batting average. He also played 34 games with the Expos, his major-league debut coming on August 18, 1981. Francona stepped into the Expos' lineup full-time the following September 13 and hit his first major-league home run three days later. In 1982 he finished the season with a .321 batting average, the second-best in the National League, and earned a reputation as a consistent contact hitter. In a June 1983 game against the St. Louis Cardinals, Francona experienced a season-ending injury to his right knee that required surgery. "I thought it was just a temporary setback, and actually it was," Francona told Bonfatti. "In fact, I thought I was a better player after that. I got stronger. I got to watch the game a little bit and I thought I learned a lot."

In 1984, his knee having healed, Francona returned to active play. After 58 games he led the National League with a .346 batting average. Then, on June 14, in a game against the Pittsburgh Pirates, after making a bunt that enabled a runner to reach second base, he damaged his left knee while trying to evade the pitcher as he headed to first base. The injury, in addition to preventing him from returning to the field that season, irreparably damaged his career as a player. "Not having one knee is one thing," Francona told Lesmerises. "But [if] you don't have either knee? I was never the same hitter again. I didn't have anything to push off of." In his 1985 season with the Expos, Francona's batting average was only .267, and he played only occasionally in the field. The Expos tried unsuccessfully to trade Francona, at his request, and he ended up signing a one-year contract with them. He left the team in 1986 and then played single seasons with the Chicago Cubs, the Cincinnati Reds, the Cleveland Indians, and the Milwaukee Brewers; with each, his physical limitations led to his being let go. Francona concluded his professional baseball career with the triple-A Louisville Cardinals at the end of the 1991 season.

The experience of being a bench player on so many teams gave Francona a big-picture perspective on the game. "You get all wrapped up in yourself [as a starter], especially when you're younger, and I got away from that," Francona told Bonfatti. "I never wanted to be caught off-guard pinch-hitting. I knew always when there was a chance I was going to hit. I think, without really knowing it, that prepares you to manage." Francona's first offer of a managing job, that of hitting instructor for the Chicago White Sox's rookie-level Gulf Coast League club in Sarasota, Florida, came in 1991, from his friend and former Cincinnati Reds teammate Buddy Bell. In 1992 Francona managed the single-A South Bend White Sox, a midwestern team. From 1993 to 1995 he managed the double-A Birmingham Barons. After the Barons won the

Southern League title in 1993, *Baseball America* named Francona the minor-league manager of the year. In 1992 and 1994 Francona also managed in the Arizona Fall League. He became known for his unshakable positivity and his ability to communicate with his players on a personal level.

Francona received greater than normal media attention in 1994, when Michael Jordan, the star Chicago Bulls player, announced that he was leaving the National Basketball Association to try his hand at professional baseball and joined Francona's Birmingham Barons. The sold-out stadiums, influx of press and autograph-seekers, and questions about whether Jordan should even have been allowed to play the game greatly complicated Francona's job. Observers credited Francona with handling the situation with great poise and refusing to allow Jordan's aura to interfere with the team's performance. Francona developed an excellent relationship with Jordan and admired his work ethic and his genuine respect for the game during his one season with the Barons. Although 1994 was a losing season for Francona—the only one he experienced in the minor leagues—several baseball magazines identified him that year and the next as a top prospect for a manager's position in the major leagues.

In 1996 Buddy Bell, then the general manager of the Detroit Tigers, hired Francona as the team's third-base coach. During a frustrating season in which the Tigers lost 109 out of 164 games, Francona gained a greater appreciation of the importance of composure by observing Bell "just about lose his mind a couple times," as he recalled to Lesmerises. "I remember seeing the players look at him—so I tried to learn from that." In October 1996 Francona was placed on the short list of possible successors to Jim Fregosi, who had recently been dismissed as manager of the Phillies after six seasons. Among those who vouched for Francona's suitability for the job were Michael Jordan, who placed a call to Philadelphia's general manager, Lee Thomas, during the interview process. In October 1996 Francona accepted the job as the 48th manager of the Phillies. At age 37 he was the youngest manager in professional baseball at that time.

Like many other teams, the Phillies had been struggling to recapture fans' affections since the 1994 baseball strike, which arose because of a salary-cap dispute and led to the cancellation of all games after August 12, including the entire postseason. As the team's new manager, Francona sometimes found himself the object of fans' bitterness over the strike and their frustration with the Phillies' losing records. "It was tough. This really shocked me," Francona told Gordon Edes for the *Boston Globe* (April 14, 2004). "I was on the highway, everybody's going 70, and people still recognized me so much they could do this"—gesture rudely to him with their middle fingers. Meanwhile, Francona's humility; self-effacing demeanor; "players-first" coaching philosophy, which emphasized helpful, understanding communication; and stress on the fundamentals of "playing the game right" earned him many friends in both the Phillies organization and the league.

Still, during Francona's four seasons with the team, the Phillies never won more games than they lost. Although the team's record in the second half of the 1997 season, 44–33, was the league's third-best, they finished that season with 68 wins and 94 losses. In December of that year, Francona was given a one-year contract extension and was recognized by the Phillies' general manager, Ed Wade, for his "relentless enthusiasm," as Paul Hagan wrote for the *Philadelphia Daily News* (December 12, 1997). In 1998 Francona guided the team to better totals—75 wins and 87 losses, which placed them third in their division and enabled them to remain in the race for the wild-card spot to enter the play-offs as late as mid-August. In 1999 the Phillies' win–loss record was 77–85, again leaving them in third place in their division.

With 65 wins and 97 losses, the Phillies' 2000 season was their worst during Francona's time as manager, and they were widely described as the worst team in baseball. Sports analysts, noting Francona's failure to improve the Phillies' performance significantly, predicted correctly that he would soon lose his job. At an August 2000 press conference, Francona displayed a sense of humor regarding all the criticism he was receiving from the media and fans, saying, as quoted by *Baseball Digest* (June 1, 2005), "I'm bald. I have a big nose. I've been released five times. I have thick skin. I'll make it." Francona spent the 2001 season with the Cleveland Indians, as a special assistant for baseball operations. That year he was also the coach of Team USA in baseball, guiding the national squad to a 7–3 record and a silver medal in the Baseball World Cup, held in Taipei, Taiwan. In 2002 and 2003 he served as the bench coach for the Texas Rangers and the Oakland Athletics, respectively.

Francona faced a lot of pressure when, on December 4, 2003, he was hired as the manager of the Boston Red Sox, one of the most scrutinized positions in all of sports. The previous manager, Grady Little, had been let go after failing to remove from the mound the weary-armed starting pitcher, Pedro Martinez, in the eighth inning of the seventh and final game of the 2003 American League Championship Series (ALCS)—a decision widely seen as having paved the way for the Yankees' comeback from a three-run deficit in that game and their victory in the series. Francona's reputation as a "nice" manager notwithstanding, Red Sox executives were attracted to his assertiveness and his use of statistics rather than gut instinct in making on-the-field decisions.

From early in the 2004 season, it was clear that Francona worked well with the Red Sox, seeming to manage the team with a combination of resolute decision-making and respectful distance—for instance, he resisted micromanaging his players' decisions on the field and always waited for a private moment with a player before offering a critique.

Midway through July 2004, after 81 games, the Red Sox posted the league's third-highest average figures in both batting average (.280) and pitching (with a 4.12 earned-run average, or ERA), but their weaknesses in the field had produced an unimpressive, 41–40 record. Francona and the Red Sox management made the controversial decision to trade the team's most prominent shortstop, Nomar Garciaparra, who had suffered injuries and a strained relationship with the team's administrators; Garciaparra went to the Chicago Cubs in a complicated four-team deal that gave the Red Sox the shortstop Orlando Cabrera, the first baseman Doug Mientkiewicz, and the outfielder Dave Roberts. Their arrivals enabled Francona to make roster adjustments that led to a stronger defense. After losing only one of a succession of 17 games in August and September, the Red Sox finished with a 98–64 season record, securing the wild-card spot in the postseason.

The Red Sox swept the Los Angeles Angels, 3–0, in the best-of-five-game Division Series and moved on to the American League Championship Series, in which they faced their bitterest rivals, the Yankees. The Red Sox's starting pitcher, Curt Schilling, aggravated an ankle injury during the first game of the seven-game series, on October 12, 2004, and the Red Sox lost that contest and the next two. Then Francona led the Red Sox to win four in a row (including a game in which Schilling pitched with a barely healed ankle), thereby capturing the American League pennant and becoming the first team ever to overcome a three-game deficit in postseason play. The Red Sox went on to handily defeat the National League champions, the St. Louis Cardinals, in four consecutive games. While Francona, in his usual modest manner, complimented the hard work of his players at press conferences and in interviews, many observers attributed the victory to his deft substitutions and expert handling of a shrunken roster.

The 2005 season was one in which several important players, including Schilling and Keith Foulke, spent a significant amount of time on the disabled list, and other veteran players failed to perform as well as they had in the previous season. Nonetheless, the Red Sox entered the play-offs as a wild-card team, with a 95–67 record, and Francona became the first manager ever to guide the club to the postseason in his first two seasons. In the Division Series the Red Sox lost to the Chicago White Sox, the eventual World Champions. In the off-season Francona made a number of useful trades and acquired the pitchers Josh Beckett and Jonathan Papelbon, both of whom proved to be key players in 2006. In March of that year, Francona accepted a two-year contract extension, covering the 2007 and 2008 seasons. Later in 2006 he notched his 200th win with Boston, in less time than all but one of the team's previous managers. That year the team posted the fewest errors in the American League. Still, the season was marred by player injuries, and the Red Sox finished with a record of 86–

76, leaving them in third place in their division, behind the Yankees and the Toronto Blue Jays, and ineligible for the play-offs.

During the following off-season the Red Sox acquired the Japanese Olympic pitcher Daisuke Matsuzaka and the shortstop Julio Lugo. Early in the 2007 season, the team ranked first in their division. By mid-season Beckett had emerged as the team's most consistent starting pitcher and Papelbon as the star closer, and the club boasted the best record in the American League. On September 22, 2007, by winning the American League East title (for the first time since 1995), the Red Sox secured their play-off spot, becoming the first team in their league to do so. In the play-offs the team swept the Los Angeles Angels in three games. On October 12 the Red Sox won the first game of the American League Championship Series, against the Cleveland Indians, then lost the next three games. Francona went on to lead the Red Sox to three decisive wins against the Indians, winning the American League pennant. In the World Series, which started on October 24, the Red Sox faced the Colorado Rockies in that franchise's first series appearance. With expert pitching by Beckett, who struck out nine batters in Game One, and Mike Lowell's game-winning home run in Game Four, the Red Sox swept the Rockies in four straight contests. Francona became the first manager in baseball history to win all of his first eight World Series games. He was credited as the architect of a new, budding powerhouse baseball dynasty in Boston and was honored with an invitation to a White House dinner in January 2008.

In February 2008 Francona signed a three-year contract extension that was worth a total of $12 million and included the option for the Red Sox to renew his contract, for two years and a lucrative sum, at the end of that period. The Red Sox's general manager, Theo Epstein, told Anthony McCarron for the New York *Daily News* (February 25, 2008) that Francona was now beginning to get the credit he deserved. "He flew under the radar screen until this second World Series and he started to get it after that," Epstein said. "Hopefully, this contract reflects the status he has not only in our organization, but in the game."

The Red Sox opened the 2008 season on March 25, in a game held in Tokyo, Japan, against the Oakland Athletics as a part of the MLB Japan Series; that series also included exhibition games against Japanese teams. Despite injuries to some of the team's best players, among them the pitchers Curt Schilling and Josh Beckett, and the trade of the star slugger Manny Ramirez to the Los Angeles Dodgers in late July, Francona guided his team to an impressive season record of 95–67 and a wildcard berth in the play-offs. In October 2008 the Red Sox defeated the Los Angeles Angels in four games in the American League Division Series and advanced to the ALCS, where they faced the Tampa Bay Rays. Down 3–1 after the fourth game in the seven-game series, the Red Sox defeated the Rays

in Games Five and Six. In Game Five the Sox overcame a seven-run deficit in the seventh inning to secure an 8–7 win, marking the best comeback victory in any postseason game since 1929. The Red Sox lost, 4–2, in Game Seven, however, thus failing to advance to the World Series. In light of the injuries and other difficulties that had beset the team—Francona himself had been stricken with the flu during the last ALCS game—Francona considered the season to be a success. "This game is kind of crazy," he told Ian Browne for MLB.com (October 21, 2008). "I laugh when people say it winds down. No, it comes to a crashing halt. You're going 100 miles an hour and then it's over."

Francona is a two-time survivor of pulmonary embolisms—a complication of what is known as deep-vein thrombosis (DVT), in which blood clots travel from veins deep within the legs to the lungs, where, if not dissolved with drugs, they can be fatal. The first attack, which involved clots in both lungs, occurred in 2002, 10 days after he had had knee surgery. The second, while not diagnosed with certainty as an embolism, was treated by increasing the amount of blood thinner Francona was taking—the standard treatment for DVT. He wrote briefly about his experiences for the Web site of the Coalition to Prevent Deep-Vein Thrombosis. Francona has also experienced back problems that have required multiple surgeries. He expected to undergo a surgical procedure in the 2008 offseason for abnormalities that have caused numbness in both arms for several months. His health problems are described in the book *Red Sox Rule: Terry Francona and Boston's Rise to Dominance* (2008), by Michael Holley.

Francona and Jacque, his wife since 1982, live in Boston. Their four children—Nicholas, Alyssa, Leah, and Jamie—have all been active in sports. Nick was drafted by the Red Sox when he completed high school, in 2004, but decided instead to attend the University of Pennsylvania, where he pitches, left-handed, for the school team. At a December 4, 2003 press conference, according to Michael O'Connor, writing for the *Boston Herald* (December 5, 2003), Francona admitted that he had missed Game Seven of the 2003 ALCS between Boston and New York because he attended a basketball game in which his daughter Leah played. "My dad always taught me to enjoy the game of baseball and treat it with respect," he told O'Connor. "But more important, my parents taught me to respect people."

—M.E.R.

Suggested Reading: *Baseball Diges*t p58+ June 1, 2004; *Boston Globe* F p1 Apr. 14, 2004; Boston Red Sox Web site; *Detroit Free Press* Sports p4 Oct. 30, 2007; (New York) *Daily News* Sports p58 Feb. 25, 2008; *Philadelphia Daily News* Sports p124; *Sports Illustrated* p114 Apr. 5, 2004; (Wilmington, Delaware) *News Journal* D p1 Feb. 7, 1999

Courtesy of Friedman Studio

Friedman, Tom

Apr. 29, 1965– Artist

Address: c/o Gagosian Gallery, 522 W. 21st St., New York, NY 10011

"I love experimental philosophy, work that breaks down and creates systems for understanding humanity, life and consciousness," the multimedia sculptor Tom Friedman told Ariella Budick for *Newsday* (October 12, 2001). Since his student days in the 1980s, Friedman has sought to deepen such understanding through his sculpture. He attracted attention early on with his laboriously, meticulously executed transformations of common materials—toothpicks, styrofoam balls and cups, cereal boxes, sugar cubes, spaghetti—into objects many have found to be unusually thought-provoking. Examples include a smooth, shiny, perfect pink sphere made out of 1,500 pieces of chewed bubble gum; a wispy, full-sized male figure fashioned from clear plastic drinking straws, who urinates a perfect arc of straws joined end to end; a black garbage bag sitting atop a white pedestal and bulging with its contents—approximately 3,000 other garbage bags, placed one inside the next. "I call what I do 'making objects to think about,'" Friedman told Rosie Millard for the *New Statesman* (June 21, 2004). Jeffrey Kastner wrote for the *New York Times* (December 17, 2000) about the artist, "His practice has often been likened to a magic act: a highly evolved routine that conjures astonishing things from mundane materials, that transforms the everyday into the extraordinary with humor, intelligence and perceptual misdirection." Friedman's work was exhibited publicly for

the first time at a group show held at the University of Illinois Gallery 400, in Chicago, in 1990, shortly after he graduated from the master's program in fine art at that school. Since then his artwork—which also includes two-dimensional drawings, paintings, and manipulated photographs and scrupulously realistic life-size replicas of insects—has appeared in dozens of group and solo shows, at such prestigious locations as the Museum of Modern Art, the New Museum of Contemporary Art, and the Guggenheim Museum, in New York City; the International Biennial of São Paolo, Brazil; the South London Gallery, in England; and the Art Institute of Chicago.

In a review of a large solo show that visited six museums in 2000 and 2001, Anita Budick wrote for *Newsday* (October 12, 2001), "As in so much of his oeuvre, a constant tension simmers between obsession and explosion, between the urge to control and the powerful counter-force of entropy. A parallel tension roils between the base materials Friedman uses—the plastic cups, the sugar cubes, the toilet paper—and the ideal forms he constructs. Friedman works a kind of magic upon his materials, a mysterious yet playful spinning of chaff into gold. But Friedman is not after alchemy: He doesn't fundamentally change the nature of anything. He just shows it to us in new, exciting ways." After seeing the same show, the senior art critic for the *Village Voice* (April 11, 2000), Jerry Saltz, wrote, "Going beyond obsession, quirkiness, mind-boggling cleverness, and extreme labor intensiveness, his art has acquired a richer, more serendipitous, multidimensional quality." Friedman told Budick that his ideal viewer is "someone who doesn't respond immediately, but who is willing to take [a piece] with them, to let it plant a seed and think about how it relates to their world and their ideas." "I don't feel like I own the meaning of work," Friedman also said. "I'm more interested in how the meaning branches out and develops a life of its own." Friedman and his work are the subjects of five books. They include the two-volume set *Tom Friedman* (2003), published in Italy by Fondazione Prada (April 2, 2003), a project of the entrepreneur and fashion designer Miuccia Prada, who edited those books.

Thomas H. Friedman was born on April 29, 1965 in St. Louis, Missouri. He has one brother. From a young age he took an interest in how things were constructed and experimented with making objects himself. The 1970s TV series *The Six Million Dollar Man* inspired him to make a bionic arm, as he recalled to Jeffrey Kastner. Friedman attended Washington University in St. Louis, earning a B.F.A. degree in graphic illustration in 1988. Then, having concluded that his ideas would be better expressed by fine art than by commercial art, he enrolled in a master's program in art at the University of Illinois at Chicago. During his first year of graduate school, he had difficulty in finding his creative direction and felt that he had "hit a brick wall," as he recalled to Kastner. At the beginning of his second year, spurred in part by his readings in Zen Buddhism, he resolved to start afresh: as he explained to Kastner, "I decided I would just take everything out of my studio and work on creating this absolutely pristine space. I cleared everything out. I taped and spackled everything, cleaned the floor and the fixtures, built a wall in front of the windows, painted everything absolutely white. The room conveyed this sense of possibility. There was something about the focus and clarity and simplicity that made sense to me. It was like [the 20th-century composer] John Cage said: in order to understand music, you have to understand silence." Through the introduction of a series of ordinary objects into the space and experimentation with their placement and uses, Friedman began to see art differently, appreciating its ability to "focus your attention in a way that was different from your everyday, more peripheral experience of things," in his words. He told Kastner that he decided to base his work on four elements: "the material I would choose; my process for altering that material; the form that process would create, and how I presented it."

The works in Thesis, Friedman's first group exhibition, at the University of Illinois Gallery 400 in 1990, consisted of pieces he had made to fulfill the requirements of his master's degree in sculpture. The interest generated by that show landed him two group exhibitions at Feature Inc., a New York City gallery, and at two Chicago galleries later that year. The objects he exhibited at Feature Inc., as listed by Kastner, included "a piece of paper poked by a pin as many times as possible without tearing, affixed to the wall with the pin used to perforate it; 3,000 black garbage bags stuffed inside one another until no more could be added; . . . a perfect little sphere, a half millimeter in diameter, of the artist's own feces, centered atop a white pedestal." The last-named sculpture disappeared more than once when patrons oblivious to the presence of the tiny sphere sat down on the pedestal; since Friedman, as he assured the gallery, had large reserves of the material used to produce it, he repeatedly recreated it.

Friedman's work was represented in four group and three solo shows in 1991 and in one solo and six group shows in 1992, among them one at the Galerie Monika Spruth, in Cologne, Germany. Among his eight group exhibitions in 1993 was the invitational exhibition of painting and sculpture sponsored by the American Academy of Arts and Letters, in New York City. The next year Friedman participated in shows at the Galarie Analix, in Geneva, Switzerland, and the Galerie Jennifer Flay, in Paris, France, among other venues. In 1995 he was honored with a small solo show, called Project 50: Tom Friedman, in the lobby gallery of the Museum of Modern Art (MoMA) in New York City. The pieces in that exhibition, he told Kastner, were meant to "lead away from the object and draw in other references on the journey" and then lead the viewer back to the starting point. The MoMA

sculptures included Friedman's bubble-gum ball, adhering at eye level to the corner formed by two walls; an aspirin into which the artist had carved his own likeness; a smooth, well-used bar of white soap into which was shallowly embedded a perfect black spiral (or concentric circles, according to some reviewers) constructed out of bits of Friedman's public hair; a small, round, gray-brown clump of dust (not titled) resting directly on the gallery floor; Loop, which consisted of the contents of a box of spaghetti, with each cooked strand glued end to end with two others to create a single, unbroken, three-dimensional tangle. On a 36-inch-square piece of paper labeled Everything 1992–1995, Friedman had copied, in blue ink in nearly microscopic writing, every entry in the American Heritage Dictionary of the English Language. Of the latter piece, Bruce Hainley wrote for ArtForum (November 1995), "It contains [the words] 'everything' and 'nothing,' but are you looking at the words or the nothing between all the words? [Friedman] will show you everything being made up of nothing at all. Things, thoughts, beauty exist because the possibility of their annihilation rubs all around them." Regarding Everything and others among Friedman's "feats of miniaturism," as he dubbed them, Holland Cotter wrote for the New York Times (April 7, 1995), "Work like this seems to exist in the realm of ritual (think of such examples of devotional virtuosity as . . . miniature Korans carved in nutshells), partly in folk art (ships in bottles) and partly in sheer personal obsessiveness. . . . Mr. Friedman is less interested in creating shattering effects than in introducing a perceptual blip or two into the everyday data flow. . . . [His] skewed vision of the world . . . tends to be open-ended and slightly pixilated; it accommodates both jokes (there are many) and cosmological musings, the latter prompted by the little orbits on the bar of soap, the floating planet made of gum, and the little ball of gray dust sitting in a kind of corona of its own disintegration over there in the corner. Disintegration—of the body, of the universe—is certainly a cause for anxiety, and there are all kinds of ways to cope with it. . . . Mr. Friedman's conceptually nimble shaping and ordering" is one.

In 1996 the Art Institute of Chicago mounted a two-man show called Affinities: Chuck Close and Tom Friedman. Although Close's large-scale portraits bear no similarity in appearance to Friedman's conceptual sculptures, the exhibition's curator, Madeleine Grynsztejn, hoped "to point to a continued thread in American art making that specifically focuses on issues of process and which revolves around a kind of laboriousness," she told Garrett Holg for the Chicago Sun-Times (June 2, 1996). Reviews of Affinities ranged from fair to good; even critics who believed the link between the two artists tenuous appreciated Grynsztejn's effort. "This is a show, then, that, in its apparent conceptual and visual fuzziness offers something to both poles on a fairly wide continuum," Alan G.

Artner wrote for the *Chicago Tribune* (May 3, 1996). "It offends no one and perhaps cannily makes a few friends of viewers who thanks to Close have become a little more tolerant, even understanding, of Friedman's challenging and, ultimately, engaging art."

Friedman's fourth exhibition at the Feature gallery in New York City, in 1997, "represents several years of his eccentrically herculean labors, often expended on the most ephemeral of materials . . . ," Roberta Smith wrote for the *New York Times* (October 24, 1997). "At once whimsical and uncannily devotional, Mr. Friedman's work continually circles art's first principles, poking at them, exalting them, isolating them, drawing them out in the open for better viewing. The main principle, of course, is that art usually involves the transformation of inert, everyday materials into something that can feed the spirit, if you pay enough attention to it. To insure our attention, Mr. Friedman flirts with different kinds of invisibility, executing enticing disappearing acts that pull us into his game." The transformed objects in this exhibition included a long piece of nylon monofilament hung from the ceiling and knotted thousands of times, which, according to Smith, resembled "a string of tiny glass beads." Smith also reported, "Working in Play-Doh, [Friedman] recreates every pill in *The Physician's Desk Reference*, scattering them about in a kind of medicinal color spectrum. Similarly encyclopedic, and also in Play-Doh, is a work subtitled *Small World*. In the somewhat naive manner of a small child, it recreates 500 things, among them a ladder, a clipboard, a space missile and a 12-inch stick. But as each item is about a half-inch high, the piece is a tour de force display of patience, focus and skill, like everything else in this terrific show."

In 2000–01 the retrospective Tom Friedman: The Epic in the Everyday appeared at the Museum of Contemporary Art in Chicago; the Yerba Buena Centre for the Arts, in San Francisco; the Southeastern Centre in Winston-Salem, North Carolina; the Aspen Art Museum, in Colorado; the New Museum of Contemporary Art in New York City; and the Feature Inc. Gallery. The show earned Friedman a nomination for the prestigious Hugo Boss Prize, with which the Guggenheim Foundation recognizes achievement in contemporary art. Resting in what looked like a huge pool of blood on the floor was a piece that "transfixed" Jerry Saltz: a life-size rendering of Friedman's mangled body, complete with shattered bones and exposed entrails and brain matter—a self-portrait that the artist described as "in a state of fragmentation produced by a motorcycle accident," according to DesignBoom.com. The blood and dismembered corpse—constructed entirely of colored construction paper—struck Jeffrey Kastner as "visually stunning, technically dumbfounding, at once deeply disturbing and laugh-out-loud funny." "Echoing Vesalius's extraordinary 16th-century anatomical drawings, arts-and-crafts paper proj-

ects, World War II and police evidence photographs, the Scarecrow in *The Wizard of Oz*, a piñata, a medical model, and Duane Hanson's 1967 motorcycle crash, this sensational sculpture is a tour de force," Saltz wrote. "Moving away from lightness or one-liners," he continued, "[Friedman is] taking his art to a more human place. For longtime observers, this is akin to watching a prodigy grow up without losing his particular precocious genius." Also in that show was a blank sheet of paper $32^1/_2$ inches on each side, called *1000 Hours of Staring* (1992–97), which Friedman claimed that he had literally stared at for a total of 1,000 hours during one five-year period. "This can seem, at first, like a Conceptual Art hoax, but it could be said to honor, in glorious isolation, the intense visual scrutiny that all successful artists expend on their work, the long hours of looking, looking, looking in order to figure out how to make it better," Roberta Smith wrote.

Subsequently, Friedman's work appeared in solo and group shows at venues including the Stephen Friedman Gallery in London, England (2002); the Prada Foundation in Milan, Italy (2002); the Mildred Lane Kemper Art Museum in St. Louis, Missouri (2006); the Gagosian Gallery in Los Angeles, California (2006); the Guggenheim Museum in New York (2007); the Museum of Contemporary Art in Shanghai, China (2007); and the Gagosian Gallery in Moscow, Russia (2007). In a reference to *Untitled* [Foil Guitarist] (2004), which made its debut at the Kemper Art Museum, a critic for the *US States News* (September 21, 2006) described it as "a rare figurative sculpture as well as a witty visual pun on 'heavy metal.'" "When I think about comedy," Friedman told Kastner, "I think about seeing something differently: I don't want to say 'truth,' but more like an overview. Which is interesting, because one of the Buddhist definitions of humor is 'overview'—when you can separate yourself from the situation and see both the importance and absurdity of it at the same time."

Monsters and Stuff, a solo Friedman show, opened at the Gagosian Gallery in London, in 2008. Explaining in a statement for gagosian.com (May 2008) why he chose that title for the exhibit, Friedman wrote that he wanted "both to create a conceptual backdrop, and to keep it open-ended. From a figurative standpoint, 'monsters' represents the abnormal, which is open-ended, whereas 'and stuff' states an unresolved conclusion. We desire resolve." In a preview of the show for the London *Guardian* (May 31, 2008), Jessica Lack wrote, "The easy way of describing Tom Friedman's art would be to say that he makes miniature versions of everyday objects from Cheerio packets to bars of soap. Except that it is not entirely accurate. Certainly he manipulates the everyday, offering us sculptures from detritus—a spider's web made from a strand of hair, or a skeleton of a bird made from toenail clippings—but he has also magnified objects, giving weight to the most innocuous of artefacts. He brings out the child in everyone, and it takes an iron will not to steal one of his works. Monsters And Stuff is . . . a sci-fi nut's paradise. With green mutants built from lollipops and golf balls, zombies, giants, and a man being chased by a fly twice his size, its comic genius outshines Iron Man."

"Despite the show-stopping flair of Mr. Friedman's aesthetic sleight-of-hand, the artist himself is surprisingly low-key, intensely serious about his concept and craft," Kastner wrote in 2000. Friedman works in a studio in Northampton, Massachusetts, and lives nearby with his second wife, Mary Ryan. From his first marriage, to Julie Lichtenberg, an artist, he has a son, Oliver.

—J.E.P.

Suggested Reading: *Art Journal* p68+ Spring 2008; *ArtForum* (on-line) Mar. 2002; *ArtsEditor* (on-line) Feb. 1, 2004; Gagosian Gallery (on-line); *Parkett* No. 64 p50+ Jan. 2002; Tomio Koyama Gallery (on-line); Hainley, Bruce. *Tom Friedman*, 2001; McDonald, Alison and Domenica Stagno, editors. *Tom Friedman 1989–2008: Essays*, 2008

Courtesy of St. John's University

Gagliardi, John

(guh-LAHR-dee)

Nov. 1, 1926– College football coach

Address: Athletic Dept., St. John's University, P.O. Box 7277, Collegeville, MN 56321

John Gagliardi, the winningest coach in the history of college football, may also be the most unusual.

Since he took over the coaching duties of his Colorado high-school team in 1943, at the tender age of 16 (the squad's previous coach having been called to war), Gagliardi has gone against the grain of conventional coaching methods through an approach that has been summed up as "Winning with No's." Among the "No's" (which currently number 108) are no calisthenics, no tackling during practice, no playbooks, no cutting players, no whistles, no compulsory weightlifting program, no captains (all seniors are captains), and, significantly, no calling him "coach"; he tells players to call him "John." Taking the place of those forbidden elements are the coach's instinct, discipline, and belief in placing players' needs over standard procedure. Gagliardi explained to a writer for the *Houston Chronicle* (October 15, 2006), "I never played college football, so I don't know what they're supposed to be doing." Naming three legendary coaches, he added, "I never had a [Bill] Parcells or [Ara] Parseghian or anybody like that, a [Vince] Lombardi. So I didn't know what the heck they were doing. I had to figure it out myself." While the majority of his peers would probably regard adopting his style as career suicide, the 82-year-old Gagliardi—the coach of the St. John's University Johnnies of Collegeville, Minnesota, for the last 56 seasons—has racked up four Division III national championships, 27 conference titles, and—as of mid-October 2008—458 wins, perhaps demonstrating the wisdom of the first "No" on his list: "No single way to coach football." In 1993 the National Collegiate Athletic Association (NCAA) named an award in his honor, and more recently, in August 2006, Gagliardi became the first active head coach to be enshrined in the College Football Hall of Fame. In 2008 he surpassed Eddie Robinson for most games as a college head coach. Gagliardi shows no signs of slowing down, telling the *Houston Chronicle* writer, "I know I can't coach forever. So it's probably a good time to announce that I'm going to coach probably for another one or possibly two more . . . decades."

The fifth of the nine children of Ventura and Antoinetta Gagliardi, John Gagliardi was born on November 1, 1926 in Trinidad, Colorado. Gagliardi's father had emigrated from southern Italy in 1910, working in the Colorado coalmines for several years before opening his own blacksmith shop in Trinidad; when the need for his blacksmith services waned, he started an auto-body shop. John Gagliardi was one of only seven boys in his class at Trinidad's Holy Trinity Catholic High School (now known as Trinidad Catholic High School), most of whom were sons of Italian immigrants. The boys became very close, often gathering behind the school to play games of shinny hockey, which John Henderson, writing for the *Denver Post* (November 7, 2003), called "a brutal game using milk cans, sticks and a lot of teeth." Gagliardi distinguished himself as the school's best athlete and particularly stood out as a member of the football team, for which he played quarterback and served as captain. In 1943, prior to his senior year, the school's football coach left to serve in World War II. When the school's principal, Father Sebastiani, considered eliminating the football program indefinitely, Gagliardi—then 16 years old—persuaded Sebastiani to allow him to take over coaching responsibilities for the team as a player-coach. In his new role Gagliardi quickly made changes, deeming many of the rules the team had followed in the past to have been unnecessary if not detrimental. To the delight of his teammates, he abandoned all forms of calisthenics and running drills. He also let the players drink water between plays, which the previous coach had forbidden in order to toughen the athletes. "I grew up in a coal-mining region in Colorado, and I remember the mules sweating like crazy when they came out of the mines," Gagliardi explained to Ira Berkow for the *New York Times* (November 6, 2003). "They were given water and it surely didn't hurt them. When the miners came out, they got water. It only helped. So I figured, how couldn't it be good for my football players, too?" Acting largely on instinct, Gagliardi focused on repetition, having team members run plays until they had perfected them. Mounting a triple-threat offense (running, passing, and kicking) and continuing to play quarterback, Gagliardi led the Tigers to their first-ever league championship.

While studying at Trinidad Junior College, Gagliardi remained coach of the Tigers, leading them to a total of four conference titles in six seasons. He enrolled at Colorado College, in Colorado Springs, where he earned a bachelor's degree in education in 1949; during his stay there he also coached the nearby St. Mary's High School football team. After graduating he was hired to run the football, basketball, and baseball programs at Carroll College, in Helena, Montana. Prior to his arrival, the college had considered dropping the football program, due to its lack of success and a resulting lack of interest in the team. Over the next four years, Gagliardi led the Fighting Saints football squad to three Frontier Conference championships and compiled an impressive 24–6–1 record. Additionally, he led the basketball and baseball teams to championships.

In 1953 Gagliardi's success caught the attention of officials at St. John's University, in Collegeville, Minnesota, who needed to fill the coaching spot being vacated by the football player-turned-coach Johnny "Blood" McNally, a charter member of the Professional Football Hall of Fame. As the football coach at St. John's, Gagliardi faced the task of turning around a team that had not won a conference title in 15 years. The outgoing coach, McNally, left Gagliardi with the ominous declaration, "Nobody could win at St. John's." That fall, however, Gagliardi led the Johnnies to a conference title. Jim Lehman, a quarterback-turned-running back during Gagliardi's debut season, recalled to Dean Spiros for the Minneapolis *Star Tribune* (November 7, 2003), "We had kids on the ballclub who were Korean [War] vets, and they were the same age as John. He immediately captured everybody's

respect. There was no doubt: This was the coach. He was very firm, and he was a perfectionist. He just took charge. When he presented his theories, the light would go on and you'd say, 'This is good.' It was a matter of just being so well prepared. You believed in him. John brought the best out of you."

Gagliardi was also commissioned to coach the university's hockey and track teams. Using the same principles he had brought to his work at Carroll College, he helped the track team capture championships and secured a 42–25–1 record with the hockey team over five seasons. (He still owns the best career-win percentage of any hockey coach in the school's history.) On the gridiron, Gagliardi had only one losing season (1956, 3–4–1) in the 1950s and amassed a 38–18–1 overall record that decade. One of the keys to his immediate and consistent success was his ability to relate to his players; he was able to instill discipline while giving team members a strong sense of autonomy and seeing to their needs. In 1957, after Gagliardi's star player Dick Miller, the best player in the conference at the time, was injured in practice during a tackling drill known as "bull in the ring," Gagliardi immediately eliminated tackling in practices. Instead, the sessions came to focus on noncontact techniques aimed at perfecting plays. Gagliardi also abolished long practices (none exceeds an hour and a half); playbooks ("players never read them," according to the coach, who instead makes them memorize all of the plays); practices in the rain or in extreme temperatures (he claims to be the first coach ever to hold football practice inside a gymnasium); and player cuts (on average, more than 150 students turn out to be part of the team each season). In addition, "I've never thought about goals, or how many games my teams can win," he explained to Ira Berkow. "Really, it's the old cliché—I play them one game at a time."

In the 1960s Gagliardi enjoyed three perfect seasons (1962, 9–0; 1963, 10–0; 1965, 11–0), two National Association of Intercollegiate Athletics (NAIA) championships (1963, 1965), three Minnesota Intercollegiate Athletic Conference (MIAC) titles (1962, 1963, 1965), and a victory in the Mineral Bowl game (1969). The Johnnies' one losing season that decade, in 1967 (3–5), would be the last of Gagliardi's career to date. The team popularized the use of the "triple option" in its offensive game. That strategy involved three different ways to move the ball up the field: the quarterback could either hand the ball off to the fullback, throw it to the halfback, or run it himself. One of Gagliardi's standout players during that era was Bernie Beckham, who, despite a modest five-foot seven-inch, 170-pound frame, won the Most Valuable Player award in the 1963 NAIA championship game after rushing for 51 yards, running for one touchdown, throwing for another, and making 12 tackles. Gagliardi has attributed his success to the sorts of players epitomized by Beckham—"ordinary people doing ordinary things extraordinarily well." Gagliardi received job offers from a number of high-profile teams, including the Miami Dolphins and Minnesota Vikings of the National Football League (NFL), but he declined them all. "If Notre Dame had offered me a job, I would have gone, but they never did," he told Liz Clarke for the *Washington Post* (November 1, 2003). "I've been satisfied with every job I've ever had—even being an auto-body man. Heck, I was content."

The Johnnies enjoyed a golden era of success in the 1970s, winning six conference titles and finishing the decade without a losing season. In the mid-1970s Gagliardi set about adding a fourth dimension to his already-successful triple option. Using his four children as guinea pigs, he began experimenting in the family's backyard with the quadruple option, which added to the triple-option formation a slot receiver, who was put in position to receive a possible pass from the quarterback. Implemented in 1976, the quadruple option proved so baffling to opponents that it became virtually unstoppable. The Johnnies were undefeated that season, which saw Gagliardi capture his third national championship. The team led the NCAA Division III in three categories: total offense, with an average of 451.8 yards per game; rushing offense, with 348.9 yards per game (a record that still stands); and scoring offense, with 42.5 points per game. They outscored their opponents 480–141 in 11 games, with an average score of 43.6 points per game, compared with 12.8 for their opponents. Jeff Norman, the quarterback for the 1976 Johnnies squad, explained to Dean Spiros that "one of the main reasons we won the national championship" was that "John designed the offense to fit the personnel. He has no ego when it comes to winning games. He doesn't care what offense he uses or who is running it. The focus is on winning football games; no show, no pretense." Gagliardi has also displayed an uncanny ability to detect opposing teams' tendencies and weaknesses without passing sleepless nights or spending an inordinate number of hours in his office. (He reportedly always makes it home for dinner.) Unlike other college organizations that boasted future NFL prospects, Gagliardi created dominating teams from local talent, without recruiting. One writer compared the St. John's program's expenditure on recruiting to what Florida State University spends on postage. Gagliardi has refused to let individuals' egos get in the way of the camaraderie of the team; for instance, he forbids player celebrations—such as dancing in the end zone—after the scoring of touchdowns, prohibits so-called trash-talking, and never posts statistics or newspaper clippings in the locker room. "I just try to go by the Golden Rule," Gagliardi explained to Harvey Meyer for *Italian America* (July 31, 2004). "Treat everyone the way you'd want to be treated."

Gagliardi came closest to leaving St. John's in the early 1980s, when the University of California (UC) at San Diego sought to hire him. Discussing the offer, whose attractions included warm weather and a house with an ocean view, Gagliardi called his flirtation with UC–San Diego "the closest thing I've ever had to having an affair," as noted by Chris Dufresne for the *Los Angeles Times* (November 4, 1998). He concluded, though, that Minnesota was going to be his permanent home; his children often rode horses in the backyard during the summer and skated on the adjoining lake in the winter. "It was paradise," Gagliardi said to Dufresne. The Johnnies were dominant in the MIAC in much of the decade, winning three conference titles (1982, 1985, 1989) and reaching the postseason on four occasions, including the NCAA national semifinals in 1989. After finishing 8–2 in 1985, with an NCAA first-round play-off berth, the Johnnies returned the following season anticipating the same level of success. Then, the night before the Johnnies' second game of the season, against St. Thomas, two St. John's students were fatally struck by a train in nearby St. Joseph. Visibly affected by the tragedy, the team lost their home game the next day, 56–21. The loss set the tone for the rest of the season, and the Johnnies finished with a 4–4–1 record, the last nonwinning season of Gagliardi's career to date. Dan Grant, a receiver on the 1986 team, explained to Spiros, "You don't see the tenacity John has until you see his reaction to losing." The Johnnies bounced back the next season with an 8–3 record and reached the NCAA quarterfinals.

By the time Gagliardi ended his fourth decade of coaching, in the 1990s, his impressive win total had begun to bring him and his relatively unknown Johnnies organization some national attention. On October 16, 1993 St. John's defeated Bethel University, 77–12, giving Gagliardi his 300th college victory and making him the fifth member of the exclusive "300 club" of football coaches, alongside Pop Warner (313), Amos Alonzo Stagg (314), Bear Bryant (323), and Eddie Robinson (408). That season the Johnnies averaged an astonishing 61.5 points per game, setting a daunting college-football record. That same year the NCAA's Division III named its player-of-the-year award in Gagliardi's honor. The namesake of such an award "should have the decency to be dead," Gagliardi quipped to Dufresne. The attraction of Gagliardi's no-cut philosophy for prospective players also generated millions of dollars in revenue for the university. Some star high-school players chose St. John's over other schools, where they might have been starters, for the experience of playing under the celebrated coach. The Johnnies amassed a stunning 96–17–2 record during the 1990s.

Coming into the 2000 season, Gagliardi stood just 44 victories shy of Eddie Robinson's record for wins. His team reached the NCAA national semifinals in three straight years (2000–02) and was the NCAA national runner-up in 2000, leaving him with 400 victories at the start of the 2003 season. On November 8 of that year, St. John's won a come-from-behind 29–26 victory over its rival, the previously unbeaten Bethel, to earn the MIAC championship and make Gagliardi the winningest coach in the history of college football. Reaching the

NCAA play-offs undefeated, the Johnnies won their first three home-field games before squaring off against Mount Union in the Stagg Bowl for the NCAA Division III championship. Mount Union was heavily favored to win, having defeated opponents in 109 of its previous 110 games and won seven of the last 10 Division III titles. St. John's, however, capped their remarkable season with a 24–6 victory over the Goliath-like team. Gagliardi went on to win the Division III Coach of the Year honor and was named the Minneapolis *Star Tribune*'s Sportsperson of the Year. When rumors started surfacing that Gagliardi would end his career on that high note, the coach asked Michael Rand of the *Star Tribune* (December 22, 2003), "What am I going to do, go sit on a park bench and play checkers with some guy who can't hear me?" In the four seasons since he set a new mark for career wins, the Johnnies have compiled a 39–8 record and have reached the postseason in each of the last two years. Prior to the 2006 season, on August 11, 2006, Gagliardi became the first active head coach to be enshrined in the College Football Hall of Fame. In 2007 the Johnnies compiled a record of 10–2 and advanced to the second round of the Division III play-offs, where they lost to Central (Iowa) College, 37–7.

In 2008 Gagliardi reached yet another milestone: coaching his 589th game, a 9–6 loss to the Concordia-Moorhead Cobbers, he broke Eddie Robinson's record for most games as a college head coach. He also won the Amos Alonzo Stagg Award, presented annually by the American Football Coaches Association (AFCA) to recognize a person who has demonstrated outstanding commitment to football. Gagliardi recently finished his 60th season as a college head coach and his 56th season at St. John's. As of October 2008 his career record stood at 458–124–11, with a .772 winning percentage—the highest percentage among the top-10 all-time win leaders. (Of the more than 25,000 head coaches in the history of college football, only 10 have presided over at least 300 victories.)

Gagliardi and his wife have lived for a half-century in an on-campus house adjacent to a lake in Collegeville, Minnesota. They have four grown children and 18 grandchildren. Gagliardi's approach to football has been the subject of four books, including *NO-How Coaching: Strategies for Winning in Sports and Business from the Coach Who Says 'NO!'* (2001), by Jim Collison, and Austin Murphy's *The Sweet Season* (2002). Off the field Gagliardi is known for his modesty, quick wit, and self-deprecating humor. Good health permitting, he plans to coach as long as his teams continue to win. His daughter Nancy told Austin Murphy for *Sports Illustrated* (November 17, 2003), "His biggest fear in life was that he would get old and start losing. In the last couple years he's realized that's not gonna happen. I think after all these years he's finally having fun." Gagliardi said to Harvey Meyer, "Somebody once asked me what I wanted on my tombstone. I said it should read, 'I'd rather be coaching.'"

—C.C.

Suggested Reading: (Albany, New York) *Times Union* C p1+ Dec. 13, 2003; *Denver Post* D p1+ Nov. 7, 2003; *Houston Chronicle* p2+ Oct. 15, 2006; *Italian America* p14 July 31, 2004; *Los Angeles Times* D p1+ Nov. 4, 1998; (Minneapolis, Minnesota) *Star Tribune* S p2+ Nov. 7, 2003; *New York Times* D p1 Nov. 6, 2003; *Sports Illustrated* p54+ Aug. 31, 1992, p44 Nov. 17, 2003; St. John's University Official Web site; *Washington Post* A p1+ Nov. 1, 2003; Collison, Jim. *NO-How Coaching*, 2001; Murphy, Austin. *The Sweet Season*, 2002

Chris Jackson/Getty Images

Garner, Jennifer

Apr. 17, 1972– Actress

Address: c/o Endeavor Agency, 9601 Wilshire Blvd., Third Fl., Beverly Hills, CA 90210

Jennifer Garner has been acting since she was a young girl growing up in West Virginia. Soon after she moved to New York to become a stage actress, she landed the role of Sydney Bristow, a college student leading a dangerous double life as a CIA agent, on the television series *Alias*. The show made Garner a star, and she saw her film career blossom, winning lead roles in major films including *Daredevil*, *Elektra*, and *13 Going on 30*. Though well-known in Hollywood for her willingness to do her own fight scenes and stunt work, Garner has resisted being typecast, taking film roles in everything from romantic comedies to dramatic thrillers to the quirky independent film *Juno*. And while she has had to deal with the pressures of instant fame and a devastating divorce from her first husband (the actor Scott Foley), Garner has handled life's ups and downs with rare grace and dignity; she has since married the actor Ben Affleck and become a mother. Garner, whom Chris Connelly, writing for *Marie Claire* (October 2007), called "Hollywood's most down-to-earth star," often spends her free time at home with her family and rarely discusses details of her personal life. Confessing to Garth Pearce for *Times Online* (August 8, 2004) that she was "clumsy and uncomfortable" as a teenager, Garner said, "My teenage awkwardness has not really left me, in one way. You don't see me at Hollywood parties if I have no reason to be there. I would feel fake and would not know how to act or what to say."

Jennifer Garner was born in Houston, Texas, on April 17, 1972. Four years later her family moved to Charleston, West Virginia, where Garner grew up in the South Hills area. Her father, Bill, was a chemical engineer; her mother, Pat, was a part-time English teacher who devoted most of her time to homemaking. Garner was the second of three daughters. Raised in a conservative household, she and her sisters, Melissa and Susannah, attended the local Methodist church every Sunday and were not allowed to wear makeup or pierce their ears until they were 16 years old. Her parents were always supportive of her creative endeavors, however, and from a young age, Garner was active in community dance and theater groups. She studied ballet and was a member of the Charleston Light Opera Guild's dance company, playing roles in *Annie Get Your Gun* and *The Music Man*. Later, while attending George Washington High School, she starred in the Appalachian Youth Jazz-Ballet Company's presentation of *Cinderella* and played the lead roles in the guild's productions of *Gypsy* and *A Chorus Line*. Her childhood friend Elizabeth Cary Brown told Rusty Marks for the *Charleston Gazette* (December 30, 2007) about Garner, "She was never afraid to be crazy. She was never afraid to express her personality and get out in front of the crowd. She thrived on it." Though Garner loved being on stage, she never imagined at the time that she would become a professional actress. "Growing up where I did, the thought of working on a television show or in a movie . . . that existed on a parallel plane, you know?" Garner told Chris Connelly. Referring to characters on the sitcom *Gilligan's Island*, she added, "When I was a kid, the Professor was the Professor and Mary Ann was Mary Ann—[the actors] did not have personal lives. . . . I never watched that stuff ever, ever, ever and thought, *I want to be that.*"

After graduating from high school, in 1990, Garner attended Denison University, in Granville, Ohio, with intentions of studying chemistry. She soon became involved with the school's theater program, however, and realized that acting was her true passion. She graduated in 1994 with a B.F.A. degree in theater. At her mother's urging she moved to New York and began auditioning for stage roles. A month later she was chosen as an understudy for the Broadway production of Ivan Turgenev's *A Month in the Country*. Struggling to make ends meet, she auditioned successfully for small TV roles, even though, as she has since admitted, she was ashamed at the time to be doing television work. Soon after earning roles in two made-for-TV movies, she appeared on episodes of *Law & Order* and *Spin City* and also landed small parts in movies, including the 1997 releases *Deconstructing Harry* and *Mr. Magoo*. After moving to Los Angeles, California, she was cast in 1998 as a lead in the TV series *Significant Others*. The show, a drama about three friends struggling to adjust to adulthood, was canceled after three episodes due to poor ratings. Garner continued to work as a guest star on the popular TV series *Felicity*. That drama followed Felicity Porter (played by Keri Russell), a recent high-school graduate who decides to attend a university 3,000 miles away from home in order to follow the object of her high-school crush. Garner's role on *Felicity* introduced her to the show's producer, J. J. Abrams, who would play a vital role in her career years later, and also to her fellow actor Scott Foley. Foley and Garner began dating that year and were married on October 19, 2000. The previous year Garner had earned a supporting role in the *Party of Five* spin-off *Time of Your Life*, starring Jennifer Love Hewitt; the show was canceled during its first season, but thanks to the exposure it brought Garner, she received roles in major motion pictures, including *Dude, Where's My Car?* (2000) and *Pearl Harbor* (2001).

In 2000 Abrams started work on a new TV series for ABC. *Alias* revolved around a female college student who spent her nights working as a CIA double agent. (Abrams had come up with the idea for the show while working on *Felicity* and imagining how that drama would have differed had the title character been hired by the CIA for dangerous covert missions.) Needing an actress to fill the lead role, that of Sydney Bristow, Abrams thought immediately of Garner. "There was something about her that I just thought was really special," he explained to Robert Bianco for *USA Today* (January 31, 2002). "I always thought she had something in her personality that was funnier and sexier and smarter and more mischievous than anything I'd seen her do. And when I wrote Sydney, I wanted to show that." Garner, who despite Abrams's enthusiasm faced a series of auditions, was determined to win the part. After learning that later stages of the audition process would require her to demonstrate some fighting moves, she found a tae kwon do instructor through the phone book and attended lessons every day for a month. The practice paid off, and Garner earned the role. With her 10 years of ballet study and her resulting athletic prowess, Garner had the essential components of an action-movie star. She insisted on doing her own stunts and often went to great lengths to make fight scenes spectacular. Premiering in 2001, the action-packed drama did not become an instant ratings success; devoted fans and rave reviews, though, not only saved *Alias* from cancellation but soon made Garner a star. She realized how successful *Alias* had become when she went shopping for Christmas presents that year. "It was freaky and terrifying," she told *MoviesOnline* (January 19, 2007). "I mean in July I could have gone shopping and nobody would have seen me or said anything, and it wouldn't have been a big deal at all, but in December, in that short amount of time, I couldn't even take a step without somebody stopping me." Still, Garner was pleased to play a character who could serve as a strong role model for young women. "I run into women on the street who tell me, 'I took a self-defense class because of you' or 'I got stronger and broke up with my boyfriend because your character had the strength to be on her own,'" she told Nancy Mills for the London *Mail on Sunday* (March 11, 2007). "That's very gratifying."

During the show's run Garner was nominated for several awards, winning the 2002 Golden Globe for best performance by an actress in a drama television series. She also won the 2005 Screen Actors Guild Award for outstanding performance by a female actor in a drama series and took home two People's Choice Awards in 2006, for favorite female action star and favorite female television star. Due to her success on television, she began to receive more film roles. She made a brief appearance in Steven Spielberg's *Catch Me If You Can* (2002) before appearing opposite Ben Affleck in *Daredevil* (2003), a movie adaptation of the Marvel Comics series. Garner played Daredevil's love interest, Elektra Natchio, a character known in the comic-book universe for her incredible—and ruthlessly wielded—fighting abilities. The action role was a perfect fit for the *Alias* star, and despite being panned by critics, the film did well at the box office. The following year the romantic comedy *13 Going on 30* allowed Garner to demonstrate her comedic talents. She played Jenna Rink, a 13-year-old girl who becomes a 30-year-old woman overnight, only to discover that the life she had dreamed of has come at a price. Though the movie was widely seen as a less successful version of the 1988 film *Big*, Garner received accolades from many critics, who found her performance convincing and charming.

While shooting that film Garner had struggled with the demise of her marriage to Foley. She explained to Garth Pearce, "I was brokenhearted to end the marriage. I wanted to be married for as long as my parents. This sounds a cliché, but we really were victims of Hollywood. Everything is speeded up here—it is a fast-lane life, and if something is not working, it is considered best to end it without much thought. If we lived where I was brought up, we would probably still be together." In late 2004 she began dating her *Daredevil* co-star, Ben Affleck. Garner revisited her *Daredevil* role in the

spin-off *Elektra* in 2005, and later that year, Garner and Affleck were married. Garner told Cindy Pearlman for the *Chicago Sun-Times* (January 21, 2007), "I can say that I took getting married again incredibly seriously and still do. If you ask [Affleck], I don't think he would say it was easy getting me to this point. We worked pretty hard to get to this point."

By November 2005 *Alias*'s ratings had dropped, and ABC announced that the series would be canceled after its fifth season. When asked about the timing of the show's end, Garner told Dan Snierson for *Entertainment Weekly* (November 30, 2005), "It feels like the right thing; it feels like we've told the story. But I can't really talk about it without getting sad. Obviously it's been such a huge force in my life. . . . It feels like a graduation. Graduation is hard."

Garner starred in three major films released in 2007: *Catch and Release*, *The Kingdom*, and *Juno*. *Catch and Release*, about a woman who must cope with her fiancé's death and the secrets she discovers about his life, allowed Garner to communicate the perspective on relationships she had formed after her divorce. "I don't have this fantasy about marriage anymore," she said, as quoted by *MSN Entertainment* (August 15, 2005, on-line). "Everyone says it takes hard work. Well, it kind of does—and I'm much more pragmatic about romance than I used to be. I wanted to see [Foley] as a white knight and was crushed whenever anything normal happened. I wanted to be the princess. Now I'm much more willing to see myself as human and flawed, and accept someone—the whole picture." *The Kingdom*, which co-starred Jamie Foxx, Chris Cooper, and Jason Bateman, found Garner playing Janet Mayes, an FBI agent investigating the terrorist bombing of a U.S. compound in Saudi Arabia. In *Juno*, she portrayed a woman who is unable to have children and arranges to adopt the baby of the pregnant teenage title character. Even though Garner's performance was shot in only two weeks, the film, which received rave reviews, an Academy Award nomination for best picture, and the Oscar for best original screenplay, was heavily dependent on her character, in the view of its director, Jason Reitman. "If Jennifer wasn't Jennifer, the film wouldn't work," Reitman told Johanna Schneller for the Toronto, Canada, *Globe and Mail* (September 29, 2007).

In late 2007 Garner returned to the stage, starring in *Cyrano de Bergerac* with Kevin Kline on Broadway. The *New York Times* (November 2, 2007) critic Ben Brantley praised Garner's return to her theater roots, calling her "captivating" and adding, "The latest in a series of boldface film and television actresses to test their stage legs . . . Ms. Garner seems by far the most comfortable." (A taping of the play was scheduled to air on PBS in January 2009 as part of its *Great Performances* series.) Also in 2007 Garner was named one of *Glamour* magazine's women of the year, not only for being a successful working mother but also for her humble demeanor and charity work, which included visiting and aiding New Orleans children affected by Hurricane Katrina, helping to fund cancer research, and supporting the Children's Defense Fund and the American Lung Association.

Garner and Affleck's daughter, Violet Anne Affleck, was born in Los Angeles on December 1, 2005. "Having a baby fills your life," Garner told Cindy Pearlman. "No matter what you've done, there's something bigger, which is your child. I know it sounds trite, but I've been in heaven with her." Affleck and Garner have raised Violet without the help of a live-in nanny and schedule their work so that one of them can be with their daughter at all times. In August 2008 Garner announced that the couple were expecting their second child. Although Garner lives in Los Angeles for her work, her attachment to her home state, West Virginia, is apparent. She and her husband and daughter make frequent trips there to visit her family, and Violet was baptized at the Charleston Methodist church Garner attended throughout her childhood. Garner has said that she would like to be able to work in West Virginia but that films and television shows are rarely, if ever, shot in the state due to a lack of tax incentives for production companies. In 2007, upon hearing that comment, Corey Palumbo, a West Virginia state lawmaker and former high-school classmate of Garner's, sponsored a bill to offer a 22 percent tax credit for any film, TV, or commercial project shot within the state. The West Virginia Film Industry Investment Act was approved and enacted on January 1, 2008. The previous month Garner's hometown newspaper, the *Sunday Gazette-Mail*, named her West Virginian of the year, citing her work ethic and dedication to the state.

Garner is working on three movies slated for release in 2009: *The Ghosts of Girlfriends Past*, with Matthew McConaughey and Michael Douglas; *This Side of the Truth*, starring the British actor Ricky Gervais; and *Be With You*, which Garner will star in and produce through Vandalia Films, the company she formed with her personal assistant, Juliana Janes, in 2005. "Every job has a flip side," she said to Garth Pearce. "You cannot have the greatness of this job [that is, acting in film], which is challenging and ridiculously well rewarded, without other things. I have perks beyond my dreams. I can make a sick child smile, help raise money for charities and make things happen that I would never have believed. That is all good. The bad is that you lose the illusion of having a personal life that is truly private. But the good by far outstrips the bad."

—M.A.S.

Suggested Reading: *Charleston Gazette* A p1 Dec. 30, 2007, A p1 Oct. 3, 2007; *Chicago Sun-Times* D p5 Jan. 2, 2007; *In Style* p110 May 2007; *Marie Claire* (on-line) Oct. 2007; *USA Today* D p3 Jan. 25, 2007

Selected Television Shows: *Significant Others*, 1998; *Time of Your Life*, 1999–2001; *Alias*, 2001–2006

Selected Films: *Catch Me If You Can*, 2002; *Daredevil*, 2003; *13 Going on 30*, 2004; *Elektra*, 2005; *Catch and Release*, 2007; *The Kingdom*, 2007; *Juno*, 2007

Selected Theater Performances: *Cyrano de Bergerac*, 2007–08

Courtesy of Viking/Penguin

Gessen, Keith

Jan. 9, 1975– Magazine editor; literary critic; writer

Address: n+1, 68 Jay St. #405, Brooklyn, NY 11201

The writer and editor Keith Gessen has made a name for himself as a practitioner of critical theory. In *n+1*, the literary journal he co-founded with Benjamin Kunkel, Mark Greif, and Marco Roth in 2004, he and others have analyzed and criticized literature, pop culture, and modern society through book reviews, fiction, and essays. "There are these problems in the contemporary world," he said in an interview with the *New York Inquirer* (November 9, 2006, on-line). "What can we say about them, what can we know, what do they mean? Sometimes the book review is a pretty good way of getting at these questions; sometimes it's a short story. Long essays, if they are direct and have a clear argument, can also do it." Controversial in some literary circles for its critiques of other magazines, the Brooklyn, New York–based, left-leaning *n+1* seeks to challenge what its editors view as misguided social, political, and cultural movements and institutions. Now published twice yearly in a print run of 7,500 copies, it has become much-talked-about in the literary world. David Itzkoff wrote for the *New York Times* (April 27, 2008), "With its well-timed attacks on old-guard stodginess as well as young-Turk mawkishness, *n+1* quickly made itself heard."

Gessen has also gained attention as a translator of Russian literature, notably Svetlana Alexievich's acclaimed 1997 work *Voices from Chernobyl: The Oral History of a Nuclear Disaster*, published in English in 2005, and as a writer of ambitious book reviews and essays published in *New York*, the *Washington Post,* the *New Yorker*, and elsewhere. In April 2008 he published his first novel, *All the Sad Young Literary Men*, whose title alludes to that of F. Scott Fitzgerald's story collection *All the Sad Young Men*. The book follows the intellectual pursuits and personal failings of a group of Ivy league–educated writers as they drift through their post-college days—a story not unlike that of Gessen's own life.

The writer and editor was born Kostya Gessen on January 9, 1975 in Moscow, Russia. His mother, Elena, called Yolka, was a literary critic and translator; his father, Alexander, was a computer scientist. His older sister, Masha, is a writer. Gessen's parents "were from a particular milieu in Russia, a particular intellectual, social milieu," he said in an interview with bigthink.com (May 13, 2008). When Gessen was six years old, his family immigrated to the United States, settling in Newton, Massachusetts, a suburb of Boston. "I'm partly from Moscow and I'm partly from Newton, and those things have shaped me in complex and confusing ways," Gessen told bigthink.com. In Newton his parents "sort of managed to reconstruct" with other Russian immigrants the life they had known in their home country, Gessen said. "But . . . they were cut off from the American world that surrounded them." For Gessen, "it was confusing because I very much wanted to be an American. I wanted to fit in with the rest of the kids and I wanted to engage with American life. . . . I didn't wanna sit at home with my parents and the Russian books and drinking tea all the time." (Those desires led him to change his given name to Keith.) Still, he added, "I sensed, even though I didn't acknowledge [it] until a bit later, that my parents' world was a very rich world."

Gessen enrolled at Harvard University, in Cambridge, Massachusetts, where he played on the football team and wrote his honors thesis on *Criterion*, the journal edited by the American-born British poet, playwright, and essayist T. S. Eliot. While in college Gessen also spent time in Moscow, translating wire-service stories into English for the Russian news agency Interfax. He then returned to Cambridge, where he earned a bachelor's

degree in 1997. Next, he began contributing book reviews to newspapers and literary magazines and working as a contributing editor and writer for *Feed*, one of the many Web "zines" that emerged during the mid-1990s. Since 2000 Gessen has had book reviews and essays published in *American Scholar*, the *Washington Post*, the *American Prospect*, *Forward*, the *New Yorker*, the *New York Review of Books*, *New York*, and slate.com. He has also written original analytical pieces on literature, pop culture, and society for the publications *Hermenaut* and *Dissent*.

Gessen's critical writing frequently concerns the state of humanity as it relates to literature, entertainment, and art. In a piece called "Simpsons at the Gates," available on the *Hermenaut* Web site (April 26, 2000), Gessen cited the popular animated cartoon *The Simpsons* as an example of a show that frequently and haphazardly makes unexplained references to earlier television shows and other artifacts of pop culture. Such shows, Gessen argued, create a language of allusion special to Gessen's generation—one in which works alluded to in the shows mean little or nothing to the average viewer, who is not familiar with the source, so that for most viewers the allusion *becomes* the source. Gessen wrote, "If we imagine the function of an allusion to be like notes played on a piano— . . . hitting some chord in the memory, and resonating beyond it—then allusions to television shows are like a piano played without pedals. We hear the notes but they do not resonate so deeply. But what happens if one show subsumes all these notes, if an allusion to a television show on *The Simpsons* actually replaces that show entirely, so that we do not hear the note at all?"

Like his essays, Gessen's book reviews find the writer exploring ideas that relate to the works under examination while extending beyond them, with significance for modern culture. In a review of *The Corrections* (2001)—Jonathan Franzen's postmodern novel about a family—published in the *American Prospect* (November 5, 2001), Gessen took into account the previous decade of postmodern writing in order to illustrate the irony that Franzen's popular novel, intended as a critique of consumer culture, was straightforward enough in style and plot to become popular in the mainstream.

In the early 2000s Gessen attended the graduate creative-writing program at Syracuse University, in Syracuse, New York. In the summer of 2004, operating out of his New York City apartment, he, Kunkel, Greif, and Roth founded *n+1*, with the idea of publishing work that was politically and socially significant—yet free of the pretense they felt was too common in the literary world. They took inspiration in part from the popular American political and literary quarterly *Partisan Review*, which during its heyday, in the mid-20th century, had included groundbreaking cultural critiques from a group of writers known as the "New York Intellectuals," who included Philip Rahv, Mary McCarthy, and Dwight Macdonald. The *n+1* editors were also looking to create their own version of the journals and Web zines from the mid-to-late 1990s that had impressed them as being the "intellectual hope of a generation," as Greif put it to A. O. Scott for the *New York Times Magazine* (September 11, 2005).

In addition to publishing the writing of outside authors, the magazine would serve as a home for the unpublished work of its editors. Gessen told Scott, "Here I am with all this fiction no one would want to publish, and here's Mark [Greif] with these essays no one's going to publish, and after a while we felt like we had this critical mass of stuff that nobody would want to publish." With each editor investing $2,000 of his own money, Gessen and his colleagues published the first issue of *n+1* in the fall of 2004. The issue opened with what would become a regular column of criticism, "Intellectual Situation," followed by a politics section; short stories; and critiques of books, intellectual figures, and pop culture. An important aspect of the magazine, the editors decided, would be its relevance to contemporary times. Gessen told Itzkoff, "A lot of the best intellectual magazines are oriented toward the past, and we wanted to be oriented more toward the present." To emphasize that aim, the first issue contained a statement of the editors' commitment to achieving social and intellectual progress through writing. It read in part, "The idea of progress is not uncomfortable to us. Who will drive progress? To every tradition, and every art, and aspect of culture, and line of thought, a step is added. This dream of advance in every human endeavor, in line with what we need, not just what we're capable of, is futurism humanized. It is wanted in a time of repetition. It is needed whenever authorities declare an end to history. It is desperate when the future we are offered is the outcome of technology."

The first issue also included articles that sought to show readers how *n+1* differed from literary magazines that had paved the way for it. According to Itzkoff, "Beyond the simple red cover of its first issue, *n+1* defined itself by the magazines it denounced, and all but challenged them to a duel." The writers took shots at the *New Republic* and the *Weekly Standard* and reserved the "Intellectual Situation" for Dave Eggers's popular and quirky literary journal, *McSweeney's*. Written anonymously, the column argued that *McSweeney's* represented little progress either intellectually or stylistically. "As far as content goes . . . the innovation of the Eggersards [Eggers and those associated with him] was their creation of a regressive avant-garde," the critique read. "The first regression was ethical. Eggersards returned to the claims of childhood. Transcendence would not figure in their thought. Intellect did not interest them, but kids did. Childhood is still their leitmotif. The second regression was technical and stylistic. In typography and tone the Eggersards adopted old innovations, consciously obsolete maneuvers from earlier moments of creative ferment." Within a short time

n+1 gained attention. James Wood, a *New Yorker* literary critic, told Itzkoff that the publication's indictment of other, similar magazines "seemed like a necessary, Oedipal clearing of the undergrowth," and added, "We all have to make ourselves orphans at some point." Kunkel's first novel, *Indecision* (2005), was well received, which generated further publicity for *n+1*. With the magazine's circulation increasing, the editors were able to move into an office in the Dumbo (Down Under Manhattan Bridge Overpass) section of Brooklyn, New York.

Despite the attempt of the editors to set *n+1* apart from other contemporary literary efforts, Scott wrote that it and another magazine published by McSweeney's Books, the *Believer*, were essentially part of the same idealistic mindset. He wrote, "Modest though the magazines are in scale and appearance, there is nonetheless something stirringly immodest—something 'authentic and delirious,' as e.e. cummings once wrote—about what they are trying to do, which is to organize a generational struggle against laziness and cynicism, to raise once again the banners of creative enthusiasm and intellectual engagement." *n+1* is not without its detractors. Stefan Beck wrote for the *New Criterion* (January 1, 2006) that the journal "strives for seriousness (or thinks it does) to compensate for the many little magazines that don't. Unfortunately, that means it can poison the well in a way that a quirky amusement like *McSweeney's* could never dream of. . . . An *n + I* reader . . . may believe that the magazine's strain of pseudo-thoughtful logorrhea is the same thing as real argument—the kind that takes a side and proposes what to do."

Over the next several years, Gessen continued to write and edit for *n+1* and publish literary criticism and essays in other newspapers and magazines. He also served as the English-language translator of Svetlana Alexievich's *Voices from Chernobyl: The Oral History of a Nuclear Disaster*, published in the U.S. in 2005. The book contains interviews with victims of the 1986 explosion at the Chernobyl nuclear power plant in Pripyat, Ukraine, which forced many residents to evacuate and others to suffer and die from exposure to radiation. The book, which received the 2005 National Book Critics Circle Award for general nonfiction, was praised for its poignant accounts of the lives disrupted by the tragedy.

In April 2008 *All the Sad Young Literary Men* was published. Critics, aware of Gessen's status in the literary world, drew parallels between the novel and the author's life; Itzkoff noted that "the idea of literary fame is central" to the book. In it, three college graduates pursue writing careers and romantic relationships, while struggling with their flaws and uncertainty about the future. The character Mark, who has spent time in Russia and married and divorced a Russian woman, attempts to complete his doctoral dissertation but finds himself constantly distracted by the temptations of online dating Web sites and Internet pornography;

Sam is working on the "great Zionist novel," more to escape an empty relationship than to write about Israel; and Keith, a magazine writer, is the character perhaps most closely modeled on Gessen. Gessen also incorporated allusions to Russian history and culture into the book. In one passage quoted by Jonathan Yardley for the *Washington Post* (April 20, 2008, on-line), Gessen compared Russia's post-communist struggles to Mark's squandered intellect, writing, "Mark was like those stunned post-Soviet Russians during the draconian free market reforms, watching their ten-thousand-ruble lifetime savings, still active in their memories, turn overnight into fifty dollars. The Devaluation, it was called. And it hurt." In writing about Russia, Gessen had been aided by his discovery of writers of a previous generation—including Saul Bellow—who had been born of Russian parents and come as children to the U.S. Gessen told bigthink.com, "Discovering those people and feeling like, in fact, I had a very similar experience to those people . . . allowed me to, I think, develop a way of writing about Russia and thinking about Russia."

The novel received mixed reviews. Judith Shulevitz wrote for *Slate* (April 21, 2008, on-line), "One of the pleasures of Gessen's novel is how well he reproduces the speech patterns of brainy, left-wing Ivy leaguers. . . . Marginally less pleasurable, but not unenjoyable, is the work the novel forces us to do of separating Keith the character, with his self-congratulatory self-deprecation, from Gessen the author. The difficulty of this exercise explains, in part, both the novel's comic bite and its faintly bitter aftertaste. Keith charms us with his candor but puts us off with his disturbingly authentic sense of superiority. We chuckle with Keith, but we wonder about Gessen: Are we supposed to laugh with him or gloat with him?" The review in *New York* (April 28, 2008), which has published Gessen's work in the past, was perhaps the most negative of all assessments of the book—but offered qualified praise: "For about 40 thrilling pages, Gessen delivers one of the purest joys in all of literature: the ecstasy of watching a much-hyped young littérateur fall flat on his face. The book's opening is self-satisfied, boringly solipsistic, and full of embarrassing pomo moves that Gessen doesn't have nearly the pizzazz to pull off: gratuitous photos in the middle of the text . . . uninventive charts about character behavior, a screen shot of an e-mail in-box. . . . And yet, as the characters maunder on, Gessen's charm somehow takes over. His sly, tumbling prose is consistently funny, and in the end he's scraped up an impressive little heap of truth from severely unpromising ground.'"

Gessen's short story "Like Vaclav" was published in *Best New American Voices 2005*. In June 2008 he started a blog—keithgessen.tumblr.com. The blog is devoted to whatever interests him, ranging from the state of the economy to his dreams. His translation into English of *Scary Fairy Tales*, by Lyudmila Petrushevskaya, will be pub-

lished in 2009. Gessen, who is divorced, lives in Brooklyn, near the Brooklyn Museum. As of mid-October 2008, he was taking care of his grandmother in Russia and intended to remain there for some months. His sister, Masha Gessen, lives in Moscow; she is the author of *Ester and Ruzya: How My Grandmothers Survived Hitler's War and Stalin's Peace* (2004) and *Blood Matters: From Inherited Illness to Designer Babies: How the World and I Found Ourselves in the Future of the Gene* (2008), originally published as a series of articles in *Slate*. Masha Gessen has also contributed articles to *n+1*.

—W.D.

Suggested Reading: *n+1* Web site; *New York Times* Style p1 Apr. 27, 2008; *New York Times Magazine* p38 Sep. 11, 2005; *Slate* (on-line) Apr. 21, 2008

Selected Books: *Voices from Chernobyl: The Oral History of a Nuclear Disaster* (as translator), 2006; *All the Sad Young Literary Men*, 2008

Ethan Miller/Getty Images

Ghostface Killah

May 9, 1970– Rapper

Address: c/o Def Jam Recordings, 825 Eighth Ave., New York, NY 10019

When the Wu-Tang Clan, a hip-hop group many have called the most influential of all time, recorded its debut album, *Enter the Wu-Tang (36 Chambers)*, the rapper Ghostface Killah—often called simply Ghostface—performed the first verse of the leadoff track, "Bring da Ruckus." Despite a lack of radio airplay, *Enter the Wu-Tang* (1993) became a sensation, catapulting the nine-member group from the New York City borough of Richmond (better known as Staten Island) into the international limelight. Emerging when hip-hop artists such as MC Hammer were crossing over onto the pop charts, the Wu-Tang Clan created a harsh new sound, mixing gritty street lyrics and references to 1970s kung-fu movies with foreboding musical accompaniments. "The group brought the street-brotherhood mentality back to rap," James Mayo wrote for the *Denver Westword* (July 26, 2001). "With ruminations on topics like numerology, Five Percenter Islamic philosophies and Kung Fu, the group elevated the lyrical game and set it amidst sinister, sparse backdrops. The Wu-Tang Clan has established a legacy that undeniably will live on in the annals of hip-hop."

The Wu-Tang Clan was also unique in that its record contract, with a subsidiary of RCA, allowed each group member to sign with other labels and produce solo albums. While all nine members—as well as many of the supporting players who have shown up on Wu-Tang Clan releases—have recorded their own albums, Ghostface has established himself as arguably the most artistically consistent and critically heralded. His first solo album, *Ironman* (1996), is regarded by many as a hip-hop classic, as is its follow-up, *Supreme Clientele* (2000). While *Bulletproof Wallet* (2001) was not as well received, his subsequent efforts—*The Pretty Toney Album* (2004), *Fishscale* (2006), *More Fish* (2006), and *The Big Doe Rehab* (2007)—have won widespread acclaim, and many critics have lauded his colorful, often abstract wordplay and talent for telling heavily detailed stories of inner-city life. "Ghostface's reckless, passionate rhymes make an impact because they don't always make sense," the critic Kelefa Sanneh wrote, reviewing one of the rapper's performances for the *New York Times* (April 29, 2004). "He gives himself over to the seduction of slang, often content to let his pungent phrases create their own dreamlike logic."

Ghostface, whose real name is Dennis Coles, was born on May 9, 1970 on Staten Island, New York. He grew up in the Stapleton Houses, a public-housing development located near the Verrazano Bridge, which connects Staten Island to the borough of Brooklyn. When Ghostface was six his father abandoned the family, and afterward his mother struggled to provide for her children. (It is not clear how many siblings Ghostface has.) Ghostface's mother would often sing around the house, and her collection of classic soul and R&B records would prove to be a big influence on her son's music. Ghostface also loved hip-hop, and by the time he was 15, he was writing his own rhymes. Though Ghostface has said that he had a difficult childhood and has frequently made references to the drugs and violence that were prevalent in his neighborhood, he has credited his early surroundings, as well as his later experiences in the music industry, for giving him a clear perspective on the world. "Me being in the streets made me the person who I am right now," he told Lee Henderson for the music Web site PopMatters (April 10, 2006). "In a way, I'm kinda glad I went through what I went through. 'Cause I see things from a 360-degree angle, not just one angle. I had a chance to be around thugs and street people, *and* the corporate side of things. And other countries and other cities. I look at everything as it really is, not just what it appears to be."

By the late 1980s Ghostface had befriended many of the rappers who would become members of the Wu-Tang Clan. The group of friends, many of whom hailed from the nearby Park Hill housing projects, enjoyed smoking marijuana and watching old martial-arts movies together—diversions from their surroundings. The group was the brainchild of Robert Diggs, a rapper and producer who, in 1991, had cultivated a suave, lady-killer persona to record an album under the name Prince Rakeem. (Diggs and two other future Wu-Tang members had previously been part of the rap trio Force of the Imperial Master.) In 1992 Diggs faced trial for attempted murder, and after being cleared of the charges (he claimed it was a case of self-defense), he decided to create a new kind of hip-hop group. Named for the 1981 Hong Kong film *Shaolin and Wu Tang*, the group comprised nine rappers: RZA, as Diggs rechristened himself; GZA, his cousin; Ol' Dirty Bastard; Ghostface Killah; Method Man; U-God; Inspectah Deck; Raekwon; and Masta Killa. Ghostface took his name from Ghostface Killer, a character in the 1979 film *The Mystery of Chess Boxing*, also known as *Ninja Checkmate*.

In 1992 the members of the Wu-Tang Clan combined their money and recorded a single, "Protect Ya Neck." As would become typical of their work, the song lacked a repeated chorus and featured verses from eight of the nine rappers. It was also built around a stark beat and minimal musical backing, leading many radio deejays to declare the song "too raw" to be played on the air, according to A. James, writing for the *Independent Weekly* (October 19, 2005). Raw or not, the song sold more than 10,000 copies and landed the group a deal with Loud Records, a subsidiary of the major label RCA. Loud's founder, Steve Rifkind, paid the group $60,000—to be split among all nine members—and put $30,000 of his own money toward the recording of a full-length album. "He told me he didn't have enough money and he didn't understand hip-hop much, but when I told him my vision, he believed in it," RZA told Mariel Concepcion for *Billboard* (December 1, 2007).

Released in November 1993, *Enter the Wu-Tang (36 Chambers)* climbed to number 41 on the *Billboard* 200 album chart, a remarkable feat considering that the disc's most successful single, "C.R.E.A.M.," reached only number 60 on the *Billboard* Hot 100 singles chart. The album opens with the song "Bring da Ruckus," on which Ghostface handles the leadoff verse, rapping, "Ghostface, catch the blast of a hype verse / My Glock bursts, leave in a hearse, I did worse / I come rough, tough, like an elephant tusk / Your head rush, fly like Egyptian musk." "Every track on *Enter the Wu-Tang* is packed with fresh, inventive rhymes, which are filled with martial arts metaphors, pop culture references (everything from Voltron to Lucky Charms cereal commercials to Barbra Streisand's 'The Way We Were'), bizarre threats of violence, and a truly twisted sense of humor," Steve Huey wrote for the All Music Guide Web site. "Their off-kilter menace is really brought to life, however, by the eerie, lo-fi production, which helped bring the raw sound of the underground into mainstream hip-hop." Many critics have since called the album one of the most influential releases in hip-hop history, and in 2003, when *Rolling Stone* compiled its list of the "500 Greatest Albums of All Time," it ranked the album at number 386. "Hip-hop had been harder, but it had rarely been this dirty," a writer stated for that magazine (November 1, 2003, on-line). In early public appearances Ghostface often wore a white mask. (Some said that the disguise was intended to hide his face from the police). He stopped wearing the mask when he realized that audiences were having difficulty understanding his verses.

The contract that the Wu-Tang Clan signed with Loud Records stipulated that all members would be able to record solo albums for labels of their choosing. In 1995 Ghostface contributed verses to three solo projects by Wu-Tang members: Ol' Dirty Bastard's *Return to the 36 Chambers: The Dirty Version*, GZA's *Liquid Swords*, and Raekwon's *Only Built 4 Cuban Linx*. With respect to the last-named record, Ghostface is often described as a co-star, since he performs on many of the tracks. The album is generally regarded by fans and critics as one of the finest Wu-Tang–related releases. "The fellow Clan members who show up as guests are re-cast under gangster aliases, and Ghostface Killah makes himself an indispensable foil, appearing on the vast majority of the tracks and enjoying his first truly extensive exposure on record," Huey wrote for All Music Guide. The following year Ghostface released his own solo album, *Ironman*, named after a Marvel Comics superhero. Since then Ghostface has often gone by the name Ironman, as well as Tony Starks—a play on "Tony Stark," the name of Iron Man's alter ego. Like the Wu-Tang solo albums that preceded it, *Ironman* was produced by RZA, who bolstered his usual beats with "moody traces of lush strings, baroque riffs and samples from '60s soul records . . . ," according to S. H. Fernando Jr., writing for *Rolling Stone* (November 20, 1996, on-line). "In short, *Ironman* is yet another solid Wu-Tang production for hip-hop fiends to sink their fangs into."

Ghostface did not release another solo album until 2000. In the previous four years, he collaborated on albums by other hip-hop artists, including Mobb Deep, RZA, Cappadonna (often referred to as an unofficial member of Wu-Tang), and Method Man & Redman. In December 1997 he was arrested in the New York City neighborhood of Harlem and charged with carrying a loaded .357 Magnum firearm, which police claimed to have found in the glove compartment of his car. Ghostface was also charged with illegally wearing a bulletproof vest. Adding to his legal troubles was the fact that, at the time of the arrest, Ghostface was assumed to be recuperating from malaria, a disease he claimed to have contracted while touring overseas; a week earlier he had cited malaria as an excuse for not appearing in court to face an unrelated 1995 robbery charge. Ghostface pleaded guilty to that charge and served four months of a six-month sentence.

The Wu-Tang Clan's second album, the two-disc *Wu-Tang Forever* (1997), debuted at number one on the *Billboard* 200 and was met with mostly positive reviews. "For good reason, RZA hasn't fiddled with his basic production formula on his new effort. *Wu-Tang Forever* is cleaner and more stripped down than the dense, raw *Enter the Wu-Tang*, but the familiar pieces of B-movie dialogue and loops of strings and piano are still present. And though some of the first album's madcap energy is gone, the music's effect is still mesmerizing," Nathan Brackett wrote for *Rolling Stone* (June 26, 1997, on-line). In a review for *Entertainment Weekly* (June 6, 1997, on-line), Matt Diehl gave the album an "A," writing that it "continues the group's artistic grand slam. Like their forebears in Public Enemy, Wu-Tang are musical revolutionaries, unafraid to bring the noise along with their trunk of funk."

In 2000 Ghostface released his sophomore album, *Supreme Clientele*. He was again credited with recording one of the better Wu-Tang solo albums. In a review for PopMatters, Mike Pace wrote, "Aside from the occasional aggravating skit that drones on for too long, the album is chockfull of spit-polished Wu-isms and catchy-as-hell beats, as well as knob-turning from none other than the RZA, Inspectah Deck, and the Mathematics, making it the closest thing to a true Wu record that we've seen in awhile." Anthony DeCurtis wrote for *Rolling Stone* (March 16, 2000, on-line), "The Wu-Tang Clan is filled with rappers whose rhymes are so claustrophobic as to be almost impossible to decipher, let alone comprehend, but Ghostface Killah's lines may be the toughest to crack. While RZA and GZA, for example, draw on obviously esoteric sources (mystical Islam, kung-fu films, science fiction), Ghost's references—the streets, food, soul music—are the stuff of everyday life. But his urgent, overpowering flow is designed to maintain the unrehearsed immediacy of freestyle rapping, in which cadence, sound and unconscious association triumph over logic." *Supreme Clientele* later made *Vibe* magazine's list of the top 10 greatest rap albums of all time.

Also in 2000 the Wu-Tang Clan released its third album, *The W*. The collection received mixed reviews, with some critics dismissing the work as unorganized and chaotic. "With nine voices, nine styles competing for your ear, even the most carefully crafted Wu-Tang album flirts with chaos, and the listener is left to separate milestones from mistakes," Kelefa Sanneh wrote for the *Village Voice* (December 20, 2000). "*The W* bursts with inspiration, but what does it all mean? You can't help wishing there was someone in charge." The critic Kris Ex expressed a more favorable view in his assessment for *Rolling Stone* (November 21, 2000, on-line), writing that the album "simply reaffirms this Wu-world order." The following year Ghostface released his third album, *Bulletproof Wallets*, which received less acclaim than his other work. Ghostface failed to gain permission to use several key samples from other songs, and some tracks had to be pulled from the finished album. As a result, "people didn't really get to hear the full potential," Ghostface told Ben Johnson for the *Staten Island Advance* (December 13, 2007). Some of the critics who did not like the album cited its reliance on R&B samples and its unusually clean production style. "Sprucing up the scratchy soul samples of his sophomore *Supreme Clientele* into a relatively pristine mainstream gloss, Ghostface Killah also, unfortunately, removed much of the flair from the most distinctive sound in the Wu-Tang camp," John Bush wrote for All Music Guide.

The Wu-Tang Clan's fourth album, *Iron Flag* (2001), garnered positive reviews, with some hailing it as the best Wu-Tang record in years. "Leave it to the Wu-Tang Clan to defy hip-hop's first law of career dynamics: When a rapper announces he's back, he's over," Jon Pareles wrote for *Rolling Stone* (January 31, 2001). "Clan members repeatedly announce, 'The Wu is back' on *Iron Flag,* the collective's fourth album amid countless solo albums and spinoffs. In truth, on *Iron Flag,* the Wu are not just back—they're overhauled and determined to compete." In 2002, after disputes with the record label Epic, Ghostface signed with the legendary hip-hop imprint Def Jam and started his own subsidiary, Starks Enterprises. Under the advice of Def Jam executives, he officially dropped the "Killah" portion of his name (he would later restore it), and in 2004 he released *The Pretty Toney Album*. The disc, like Ghostface's three previous efforts, received mostly high marks. In a review for the music Web site *Pitchfork Media* (May 5, 2004), Rollie Pemperton wrote that the album "far surpasses 2001's *Bulletproof Wallets*, finally finding the missing link between street cred and commercial respect." The critic David Jeffries also thought it better than Ghostface's previous album, declaring in his review for All Music Guide, "It's partly a party album like 2001's *Bulletproof Wallets*, but freer, more inspired, and tempered with pure street tracks that were missing last time round." Some critics again lamented the move away from the traditional Wu-Tang sound and toward more soul-inspired accompaniment. "Don't get us wrong; as a rapper, he still connects with his offkilter flow and streetwise vulgarity," Darryl Sterdan wrote for the Ontario, Canada, *London Free Press* (May 8, 2004). "But like a lot of Wu stars, his kung fu hits

hardest when backed by the ominous tracks of Clan kingpin RZA, who only drops two cuts here, leaving Ghost to make do with clubby grooves and Motown melodies ill-suited to his gritty persona. All of which make *Pretty Toney* pretty dull."

In a 2004 interview with AllHipHop.com, reprinted on the Wu-Tang Clan Web site, Ghostface revealed that he had stopped smoking marijuana, in part because he suffered from diabetes. Ghostface also spoke about his religious affiliation, denying his involvement with the Five Percent Nation, an Islamic group, but confirming that he practices Islam. Responding to a question about whether his music videos, which sometimes feature scantily clad women, violate Muslim tenets, Ghostface responded, "Well, Islam for me means Peace and Submission, so I submit to the will of Allah. At the same time, I know we are in a time where things have changed."

In March 2006 Ghostface released *Fishscale*, one of his most critically applauded albums. Before it went on sale, he had voiced frustration with Def Jam, claiming that the label had not done enough to promote *The Pretty Toney Album*. Ghostface had been selling progressively fewer albums with each solo release, despite the respect he was earning from peers and critics. In an interview for *XXL* (March 24, 2006, on-line), Ghostface told Noah Callahan-Bever that he had had "a lot of bad luck with record companies," adding, "I gave [Sony] like three bombs [good albums]. They couldn't do nothing with it. Those three bombs worked out my credibility, where people respect me. I came to Def Jam, gave them a nice album. It made a lot of headlines, but there was nothing behind it."

Ghostface has claimed that he wrote much of *Fishscale*—named for an uncut and expensive form of cocaine—while in bed for three months, nursing an injured leg. "It would have taken me forever to write this record if I hadn't broken my ankle," he told a crowd in Austin, Texas, according to Sean Moeller's piece for the Web site *Daytrotter*. As with his previous albums, *Fishscale* featured a great deal of seemingly nonsensical wordplay, though many of the songs detailed the inner-city cocaine trade—a topic that had become popular with rap audiences. "You know, the game is funny, because you never know which way to go with these people [fans] nowadays," he told Callahan-Bever. "So one minute they like this, next minute, they like that." The album earned mostly raves. For the *New York Times* (March 27, 2006), Sanneh wrote, "Through it all, Ghostface remains perhaps the most lovable rapper in the world: a wounded warrior with raps to match his speeding heartbeat." In a piece for the *Village Voice* (April 22, 2006), Robert Christgau, often called the "dean of American rock critics," wrote that Ghostface's stories "are as vivid, brutal, and thought-out as any noir," adding, "His high wail renders extreme anxiety beautiful." Writing for *Rolling Stone* (March 20, 2006), Jonathan Ringen called the album an "ambitious disc with almost no filler." *Rolling*

Stone, *Spin*, *Blender*, and other publications placed the album on their lists of the best albums of 2006. In the *Village Voice* "Pazz and Jop" poll, which surveys hundreds of critics, the album ranked number three.

Ghostface ended 2006 with *More Fish*, a sequel to *Fishscale*. The collection featured members of the Theodore Unit, Ghostface's hip-hop crew, and Sun God, his 17-year-old son. While the critical response was not as overwhelmingly positive as that for *Fishscale*, *More Fish* earned mostly favorable reviews. "Six discs into his solo career, Ghostface Killah handily delivers everything that his fans expect: nostalgic soul samples, richly detailed scenes of street life, and an abundance of inventive wordplay ('A shark's teeth ain't sharp enough / I'm like Mount St. Helen when the god erupt')," Simon Vozick-Levinson wrote for *Entertainment Weekly* (December 8, 2006, on-line), while Nathan Rabin wrote for the *Onion* on-line-newspaper's A.V. Club site (January 2, 2007), "*Fishscale* was named after a particularly expensive and pure form of cocaine. *More Fish*'s sonic fix is of a lesser quality, but it still packs a potent punch."

In late 2007 Ghostface found himself weighing solo interests against those of the Wu-Tang Clan, as both he and the group were scheduled to release new albums on December 4. Ghostface lashed out against his group mates in the press, claiming that they were infringing on a release date he had already claimed. He also said that he had not been paid for recent Wu-Tang Clan tours and alleged that Rifkind had tried to stop his solo album from coming out. RZA asked Ghostface to push back his release date, and when he refused, Wu-Tang moved its album back a week, to December 11. The controversy did not end there, though, as Ghostface told the press that he was unhappy with the Wu-Tang album, *8 Diagrams*. In particular, he criticized RZA's production style, which had evolved to include live instruments. "RZA is fumbling the ball . . . ," Ghostface told Rob Harvilla for the *Village Voice* (December 4, 2007). "His music wasn't sounding like how it was when we first came in. And it's hurting us."

As planned, Ghostface unveiled his seventh album, *The Big Doe Rehab*, on December 4. Vozick-Levinson, who gave the record a "B+," wrote for *Entertainment Weekly* (November 30, 2007), "By the end of the Rehab stint, you'll find that this Ghost is very much alive." "*The Big Doe Rehab* isn't as distinct as last year's *Fishscale*, but it's close," Christian Hoard wrote for *Rolling Stone* (December 13, 2007). "Ghost's bouncy, more direct approach on cuts like 'Walk Around' shows off his ability to turn crack-slinging narratives into big, hooky pleasures." While many critics also liked *8 Diagrams*, some felt that it was not as good as past Wu-Tang releases. Writing for the *New York Times* (December 10, 2007), Sanneh called it a "quirky, uneven" effort, and a critic for the *Los Angeles Times* (December 18, 2007) complained that the album comprised "largely tepid arrangements that

fail to generate much excitement." Critiquing the album for *Pitchfork Media* (December 11, 2007, on-line), Nate Patrin admitted that the "bleak moments outweigh the triumphant ones," though he added, "Of course, in due time—maybe it'll take years—*8 Diagrams* will sink in as a compelling, well-regarded album." Ghostface eventually downplayed his conflict with the Wu-Tang Clan, telling Johnson, "It's all good. It is what it is. I love my Wu-Tang brothers, every last single one of them. We just got misunderstandings."

Ghostface has expressed interest in making movies, and in 2004 he launched his own production company, Starks Films. He had a cameo in the 2007 comedy *Walk Hard: The Dewey Cox Story*, starring John C. Reilly, and appears in a small role in the 2008 superhero film *Iron Man*. In November 2007 MTV Press published *The World According to Pretty Toney*, a collection of many of the musings that Ghostface contributed to the cable channel MTV2. In the same month a limited-edition Ghostface doll, which comes with real gold chains and can utter six catchphrases, went on sale.

Ghostface sends money to countries and organizations in Africa each month in order to help feed children there. "That's just me doing my time," he told Henderson. "I'm a servant for God. That's my duty." Now that he has young daughters (sources do not say how many), Ghostface has also been making an effort to clean up the language in his songs. "Music right now is not good music," he told Maxine Shen for the *New York Post* (December 4, 2007). "It's degrading, there are certain things that your daughters shouldn't hear." In an interview for the Web site Askmen.com, Ghostface said that hip-hop music is "just a stepping stone" for him and added, "This is what I do but I think my purpose in life is even . . . bigger than this. And I'm waiting for God to deliver the revelations to me so I can carry out his mission."

—K.J.P.

Suggested Reading: *Billboard* Dec. 1, 2007; (North Carolina) *Independent Weekly* p51 Oct. 19, 2005; PopMatters Web site Apr. 10, 2006; *Staten Island (New York) Advance* W p24 Dec. 13, 2007

Selected Recordings: With the Wu-Tang Clan—*Enter the Wu-Tang (36 Chambers)*, 1993; *Wu-Tang Forever*, 1997; *The W*, 2000; *Iron Flag*, 2001; *8 Diagrams*, 2007; solo—*Ironman*, 1996; *Supreme Clientele*, 2000; *Bulletproof Wallets*, 2001; *The Pretty Toney Album*, 2004; *Fishscale*, 2006; *More Fish*, 2006; *The Big Doe Rehab*, 2007

Courtesy of Lois Gibson

Gibson, Lois

Feb. 25, 1950– Forensic artist

*Address: Houston Police Dept., 1200 Travis St.,
Houston, TX 77002*

Lois Gibson earned her place in the *Guinness Book
of World Records* not by giving the longest piano
performance ever recorded or sewing the smallest
football jersey in existence, but by creating sketches that have helped law-enforcement agents to
identify and capture more than 1,000 criminal suspects—a figure that makes her the world's most
successful forensic artist. Gibson, who has worked
full-time for the Houston, Texas, police department since 1989 and has taught forensic-art
courses at Northwestern University since 1999, is
notable not only for her sheer volume of work but
also for her unusually high success rate—30 percent—for producing sketches that can be used to
correctly identify perpetrators. (By contrast, use of
fingerprints has only a 10 percent success rate.)
She has worked with several law-enforcement
agencies, including the Federal Bureau of Investigation (FBI), the Drug Enforcement Administration
(DEA), and the U.S. Bureau of Alcohol, Tobacco,
Firearms, and Explosives. Once assaulted as a
young woman, Gibson is able to relate to crime victims unusually well in order to obtain details about
the culprits' physical appearances for her sketches;
she feels highly motivated to help other victims.
"There was like an energy force inside of me and
you could let it be a loose cannon of hurt," she told
Pam Easton for the Associated Press (October 16,
2004). "But I took the feelings I had [about being at-
tacked] and I hitched it up to my efforts and I have

all this energy to help anybody now. And all I have
to do is draw faces."

The second child of Don Herbert, a carpenter,
and Eva Herbert, a homemaker, Lois Gibson was
born on February 25, 1950 in Humansville, Missouri, the only baby in the small hospital at the
time, as she told *Current Biography*. She has two
sisters, Adonna and Laura, and two brothers, Brent
and Mark. During her childhood in Kansas City,
Missouri, she drew pictures on paper bags, since
her working-class family did not have the money
to spend on drawing paper. She was a good student
who spent a lot of time painting. Gibson went on
to study psychology at Wichita State University
and Kansas Wesleyan University, in Salina, without earning a degree. As a young woman she
moved to Los Angeles, California, to work as a photographic model. She got a job on television as a
dancer on *The Real Don Steele Show*, a Saturday-
night dance-party variety program, and began dating the actor James Caan.

In 1971 Gibson opened the door of her West-
wood apartment for a man posing as a neighbor;
she would later discover that he was a serial rapist.
The man attacked and raped Gibson, then left her,
bleeding and unconscious, for dead. Gibson, like
two-thirds of rape victims, did not report the attack, feeling too much shame to talk about it; she
feared that the police might consider the rape her
own fault. In a strange coincidence, four weeks later, while driving in Los Angeles, she saw her attacker being arrested on drug charges. Talking with
Jane Clinton for the *Sunday Express* (September 9,
2007), a British publication, she described seeing
her attacker in custody as a "relief" and as being
"like a miracle." Soon afterward, she left California, choosing her next destination—Texas—by
closing her eyes and placing her finger on a map.

In Texas Gibson returned to school, attending
the University of Texas at Arlington before enrolling at the university's Austin campus, where she
received her bachelor's degree in fine arts in 1976.
While attending college, she painted more than
700 watercolor portraits at a Six Flags amusement
park and drew about 3,000 pastel portraits at River
Walk in San Antonio, Texas. She then studied at
the University of Texas Health Science Center at
the San Antonio Dental School from 1977 to 1978.
Next, she moved to Houston, Texas.

In 1981, while watching television with a friend,
Gibson saw a news report that changed her life.
The report involved the rape of a dance teacher in
front of a class of several young girls; the only information given about the attacker was that he was
five feet 10 inches tall with brown hair and brown
eyes. "I was absolutely enraged, as was my girlfriend," Gibson told Clinton about the news report,
"and it was at that moment that I decided I could
do something to help. The descriptions given out
in the news were so vague I thought if I could just
sketch something I might be able to help catch the
attacker." In order to confirm that belief, she asked
her friend to go to a gas station, then call her to de-

scribe an attendant. Gibson made a sketch based on her friend's description of the attendant's features, then showed it to her friend, who was shocked at the resemblance between the sketch and the attendant—whom Gibson had never seen. In 1982 Gibson approached the Houston Police Department, seeking employment as a sketch artist; because there were (as there are now) so few forensic artists in the country, the Houston police were skeptical about Gibson's usefulness. But thanks to her persistence (she called the police department 20 times over the course of two weeks), they took her on as a part-time forensic artist. Her job was to interview crime victims to obtain physical descriptions of perpetrators, sketch the suspects from the descriptions, and then distribute the sketches so that they could be used as identification tools. At first she often received only $25 per sketch, paid out of the police department's coffee fund. After seven and a half years, during which her sketches helped solve roughly one in every three cases in which she was involved, the department made her a full-time employee in October 1989.

To hone her skills Gibson attended the FBI National Academy, in Quantico, Virginia, in 1986. One important tool she gained from the academy was the FBI Facial Identification Catalog, comprising pictures of various types of facial features to aid victims in describing their assailants. The catalog includes 146 pictures of noses, 208 eye variations, 130 types of lips, and 146 chin types as well as 48 pictures each of cheekbones, ears, hair styles, and foreheads and a handful of images of facial hair and skin irregularities. Gibson also learned how to recreate the faces of disfigured, decomposed, or burned bodies and to establish the race and gender of deceased individuals from otherwise unrecognizable corpses. Marla Lawson, a forensic artist who helped to apprehend Eric Robert Rudolph, known variously as the Centennial Park Bomber and the Olympic Park Bomber, explained to Christy Oglesby for CNN (November 27, 2007) how forensic sketch artists may elicit information from only a skull: "If you turn the skull of a white male sideways, it's almost like a truck hit it. It's just straight up and down flat. The forehead protrudes very little and the chin sinks in. But for African-Americans, they slightly slope at the forehead and they protrude slightly at the mandible and they have these great cheekbones. Their skulls weigh more than white people's skulls, and their teeth will be whiter and brighter usually."

One of Gibson's early cases involved the 1988 rape of a five-year-old girl, which was witnessed by two of the girl's friends. When Gibson questioned the three girls separately about the physical appearance of the assaulter, each selected the same eyes, mouth, chin, hair, and skin problem from the FBI catalog. They said, however, that his nose most resembled Gibson's own. Using a mirror, she sketched her own nose into her picture of the facial features she had drawn. Within a month the rapist was arrested for public intoxication, and police

thought he so resembled Gibson's sketch that they immediately called the young girls in to view suspects in a lineup. Each little girl pointed to the arrested man as the rapist. When police searched his apartment, they found his journal, which detailed the attack. In 1991 another of Gibson's sketches bore such an uncanny resemblance to a perpetrator that he was caught only days after shooting a police officer, Paul Deason, and running over him with his car, dragging him 60 feet. Deason, who had pulled his attacker over for a traffic violation, was in such grave condition at the time of Gibson's interview with him that he does not remember speaking to her about the suspect. Still, she was able to glean enough information that a few days later, when an off-duty DEA officer caught a man stealing a chainsaw in a Sears store, he immediately recognized him as Deason's shooter and arrested him on the spot. Police later found patches of Deason's skin and shreds of his uniform stuck to the underside of the man's car.

Another early success for Gibson was her work in uncovering the killer of Alfonso Orosco, who was murdered on July 19, 1964, while working at his Houston beer store. The night of the murder, Orosco was in the store with his brother, his 11-year-old son, Al, and an employee. According to the police report, the killer entered the store and ordered a soft drink after setting a false fire alarm near the store. As a fire truck sped past the store, the employee went outside, curious to see the cause of the commotion, while the killer held Orosco at gunpoint, demanded money, and, upon being given Orosco's wallet, shot him in the chest. Police investigators identified and charged Ora David Lott within a week of the homicide, but by then Lott had fled Houston. In 1993 Al Orosco called the Houston Police Department to inquire about any developments in the almost 30-year-old case. The investigation had been dropped by the police department years earlier, but when Orosco called, Investigator C. P. Abbondondalo became interested in the case and had Gibson sketch Lott. In order to make the sketch helpful, Gibson "aged" Lott by 30 years, drawing what she believed he would look like in 1993, based on a photograph taken of him in 1964. When investigators from the Gulf Coast Violent Offenders Task Force tracked Lott from Houston to New Orleans, Louisiana, and then to Los Angeles, he answered the door at his home but denied that he was the man they sought. After being shown the sketch drawn by Gibson, however, he admitted that "he knew he'd done something wrong thirty years ago," as Abbondondalo told the *Houston Chronicle* (October 26, 1994). That same year, Gibson completed sketches of a man who entered Rhonda Krehbiel's home in Newton, Kansas, forced Krehbiel's young daughter and the daughter's friend into a closet, then beat Krehbiel to death. The two girls, who were six and five years old, were the only witnesses. Several months later, when Chester Higgenbotham, accompanied by his wife and son, was brought in for questioning about another violent crime, his son—seeing Gibson's sketch of Krehbiel's killer on the wall—turned to his mother and said, as quoted by Roy Wenzl for the *Wichita Eagle* (May 18, 2005), "Mom, look. It's a picture of dad". Higgenbotham was convicted of both murders and is currently serving two 40-year sentences at Lansing Correctional Facility.

Gibson has said that to her knowledge, she is the only forensic artist to use pastels rather than pencils. Other characteristics that make her exceptional in her field—the ones cited by her colleagues—are Gibson's compassion and disarming manner, which help put victims at ease so that they are able to describe those who have attacked them. More than sketching well, Gibson deftly gains access to others' guarded memories. "You have to be patient, you have to comfort," she told Pam Easton. "They are overwhelmed with the fear. . . . If I can relax you enough, I can have you to remember your fifth-grade teacher." "To have someone with Lois Gibson's talents and also her compassion for the victim and ability to work with the victim to get the best possible description is so important to law enforcement," Lieutenant Dan Norris of the Montgomery County Sheriff's Department told Charlie Bier for the *Houston Chronicle* (April 14, 2004). Gibson has also been particularly effective in working with children, first welcoming them and giving them toys and candy. "I have seen her take children into her office. Those kids sometimes have just seen their mother stabbed to death, or they've been raped . . . ," Lieutenant Mike Little of the Houston Police Department told Roy Wenzl. "Those kids come out of her office smiling. And inside her office is a sketch that Lois got out of a six-year-old kid's memory. And you know, when we catch the guy, it's sometimes because of that sketch." So profound is her rapport with child victims that while her general success rate for identification is 30 percent, it is 60 percent with children, according to Gibson. When asked how she makes victims feel so comfortable, Gibson told Sandra Hughes during a CBS News interview (January 21, 2004), "All you got to do is care, and that's easy for me."

One of Gibson's recent cases involved the sketching of the decaying body of a two-year-old girl found in a plastic box in Galveston Bay, Texas. The box had been washed ashore, then found by a fisherman, and because it had been months since the girl's death, identification was extremely difficult. Gibson sketched what she believed the girl would look like if still alive. Five days after Gibson's sketch was released to news sources, Sheryl Sawyers identified the girl in the picture—whom the press had dubbed Baby Grace—as her grandchild, Riley Ann Sawyers. Although DNA testing has not yet confirmed that conclusion, soon after Sawyers identified the corpse, Riley's mother, Kimberly Trenor, submitted an affidavit admitting that on July 24, 2007 she and her husband, Royce Clyde Ziegle, beat and tortured her daughter to death, enraged by the child's misbehavior. The couple then purchased gloves, bleach, and a plastic container. After treating the body with bleach, they left it in their barn for two months in the container, later throwing the corpse into the water by the Galveston Causeway. When interviewed along with Sheryl Sawyers and the baby's father, Robert Sawyers, on *CNN's Larry King Live* (November 29, 2007), Gibson proclaimed, "I did this for Sheryl. Sheryl, I want you to know I did it for you. When I was driving to Galveston to look at the little girl that was murdered—I didn't know her name and I didn't know who you were. And I said a grandmamma is going to have to see this picture to solve this. And I went to see her in person and I could see that she was so beautiful. And you know how I made the sketch look so beautiful. And I wanted to reach out with that image. I didn't know where you were or who you were, but I needed it to get solved so we could find out who did this to her and so I could be at peace. . . . And, Sheryl, I just want you to know I did it for you, and I'm so glad you saw that image."

A less macabre job completed by Gibson involved one of the most famous American photographs ever taken, Alfred Eisenstaedt's August 14, 1945 shot of a sailor kissing a nurse on V.J. Day (marking the U.S.'s victory in the war with Japan) in New York's Times Square, which was published in *Life* magazine. Eisenstaedt died in 1995 without having revealed the identities of the sailor and nurse captured in his photograph. More than 10 men have claimed to be the sailor, including a retired New York police detective and a Rhode Island fisherman. One of them, George Mendoza, paid a computer lab to "un-age" his face by 60 years in his attempt to prove himself the sailor. In August 2007, however, Gibson confirmed that Glenn McDuffie, age 80, was the sailor kissing the nurse in Eisenstaedt's photograph. To do so, Gibson asked McDuffie to pose, holding a pillow in the same fashion in which the sailor held the nurse, and took more than one hundred photographs of him. She then measured his wrists and hat size to compare them to those in the photograph, because such measurements do not change much over time. When asked by Diane Sawyer in an August 7, 2007 interview for ABC News about her certainty that McDuffie was the sailor in the photo, Gibson replied, "Well, first of all, I'm 100%. First of all, I took over 100 pictures. And I got a pose that's almost identical. . . . The ear is exact. But your ears grow all your life, so it's bigger. And the distance from the bottom of the eye to the top of the nose, . . . that's the same shape. It's the same distance." Gibson also cited the similarities in hairline, nostrils, and facial bone structure.

Gibson has long been an advocate for those in her field. Although, as she told Pam Easton, "one hundred percent of the time, when a reasonably trained artist, reasonably talented, does a sketch, it is going to at least look similar" to the person he or she is sketching, there are many who remain skeptical about the usefulness of sketch artists or consider computer-generated images from facial-composite software programs to be adequate substitutes for artists' work. Gibson told Alex Branch for a February 23, 2004 article in the *Fort Worth Star Telegram* that the law-enforcement community "has yet to embrace" forensic art. "I think it's [a] real problem because there are already qualified people who can't get full-time work." As of 2004 there were only 30 certified forensic artists in the country. Gibson, for her part, feels that "computers can't capture the emotion, shadowing or intricate details [artists] can put on a page," as Easton wrote. Gibson went on to explain that although facial-composite software has improved, it cannot replace the rapport between artists and victims that is often necessary to piece together details of suspects' appearances. When interviewed for a feature in the *Police Federation of England & Wales Magazine* (August 2006), a frustrated Gibson said, "I am the only voice promoting forensic art. . . . I am actually trying to make something happen before I die. I may not see it happen, but other artists need to pick up and do what I do. There are tens of thousands of artists with enough talent to draw faces well enough to do the work. I'm just trying to help others identify murderers and stop people who rape."

Since 1980 the forensic artist has been married to Sid Gibson, with whom she has two children, Brent and Tiffany; an earlier marriage, to John Law-son, ended in divorce. As part of her attempt to develop the field of forensic art further, Gibson has taught at Northwestern University since 1999 and has published two books, *Faces of Evil* (with Deanie Mills, 2005) and *Forensic Art Essentials* (2007). She was featured, at her urging, in the 2005 *Guinness Book of World Records* as the most successful forensic sketch artist; by the estimate of Houston Police Chief Harold Hurtt, at the time she had completed 1,074 successful sketches. In a February 15, 2004 interview with Paula Zahn of CNN, Gibson attributed her dedication to forensic art to the attack on her in the 1970s: "I realize I wanted to catch people because I wanted to get back at the guy that hurt me and tried to kill me. . . . And that's why I go through this work, because I want the people that I'm with to feel what it feels like to get justice, because I know what it feels like to want it so bad."

—T.O.

Suggested Reading:Associated Press Oct. 16, 2004; *Augusta (Georgia) Chronicle* A p10 May 12, 2005; *Houston Chronicle* p13 May 26, 2005; (London) *Daily Telegraph* Features p15 Jan. 21, 2004; *Wichita (Kansas) Eagle* A p1 May 18, 2005; *USA Today* (on-line) Aug. 3, 2007

Selected Books: *Faces of Evil* (with Deanie Mills), 2005; *Forensic Art Essentials*, 2007

Gilani, Yousaf Raza

June 9, 1952– Prime minister of Pakistan

Address: Prime Minister Secretariat, Islamabad, Pakistan

The National Assembly of Pakistan elected Yousaf Raza Gilani prime minister in March 2008, at a crucial, uncertain, and defining moment for his country. Pakistan faces several interrelated crises, including a standoff among military rule, civilian constitutional democracy, and theocracy; an economic crisis; and the need to define its role in the U.S.'s regional policy, including the "war on terror." Known as a loyal member of the Pakistan People's Party (PPP), which is chiefly associated with its assassinated leaders, Zulfikar Ali Bhutto and his daughter, Benazir Bhutto, Gilani is the first prime minister from the PPP who is neither a member of the Bhutto family nor a native of their home province, Sindh. Elected as part of a broad but far-from-cohesive coalition that was opposed to the autocratic rule of then-president Pervez Musharraf, Gilani is seen as a low-key but principled consensus-builder who is capable of reaching across party lines. After beginning his career in the cabinet of the military dictator Zia ul-Haq (who was responsible for having Zulfikar Ali Bhutto dismissed

Courtesy of the Government of Pakistan

and executed), Gilani pledged allegiance to the populist Benazir Bhutto, General Zia's rival, shortly before Zia was killed in a mysterious plane crash in 1988. Gilani served as speaker of the National Assembly under Bhutto's tumultuous—and heavily corrupt—premierships in the late 1980s and 1990s. When Musharraf took control of the country at the end of the decade, he is said to have coerced all rivals to join his party, and when Gilani refused, he was sentenced to prison on corruption charges. As Saeed Shah noted for the Toronto *Globe and Mail* (March 24, 2008), Gilani's loyalty to the PPP won him "enormous kudos in the People's Party, which is built on the iconography of suffering for the cause." Opposing the military's repeated intrusion in politics and calling for the strengthening of the state's judicial and parliamentary institutions, Gilani became prime minister in one of the most chaotic eras in the short history of Pakistan.

Syed Makhdoom Yousaf Raza Gilani was born on June 9, 1952 in Karachi, Pakistan. ("Syed" is a title denoting direct lineage from the prophet Muhammad.) He comes from a well-connected, powerful, and influential family of politicians and landowners from the ancient city of Multan, in Punjab, the most populous and prosperous province in Pakistan. The Gilanis, who claim that their ancestors came from the Iranian province of Gilan, trace their origins to Abdul Qadir Gilani, a well-known 12th-century religious figure associated with Sufism, a branch of Islam. Gilani's paternal grandfather and granduncles joined the All India Muslim League in the 1940s and signed the resolution that led to the creation of Pakistan as a state separate from India in 1947—the year India gained its independence from Britain. Several of Gilani's uncles were politicians; one of them, Hamid Raza Gilani, was a long-serving member of Pakistan's National Assembly and Senate as well as a federal minister. Gilani's father, Alamdar Hussain Gilani, who was also active in the creation of Pakistan, was a health minister of Punjab. Yousaf Gilani is also related, through his mother, to Pir Pagara, the leader of a faction of the Pakistan Muslim League (PML). Gilani attended St. Mary's Convent School and then La Salle High School, in Multan, before enrolling at Forman Christian College and then the Government College in Lahore. He then received a master's degree in journalism from the University of Punjab, in Lahore, in 1976. After the death of his father, in 1978, he entered politics, joining the centrist/conservative PML.

Early leaders of Pakistan, which is predominantly Muslim, tried to combine the ideals of democracy and theocracy, making for contradictions that underlie many of the nation's continuing difficulties. In 1954, in the face of poor economic conditions and growing unrest, Pakistan's leaders dismissed the democratic government and declared a state of emergency, creating a precedent for the undermining of civilian governments, ostensibly for the sake of national security. Religious, ethnic, and regional tensions have also become political tools in the struggles among various factions, further undermining national stability and unity. In the nation's first 10 years, Pakistan's civilian governments repeatedly fell apart, with no fewer than seven prime ministers leaving office; that period of instability paved the way for the military coup of 1958, when General Ayub Khan declared martial law and imposed over a decade of military rule. After a war with India, several devastating natural disasters, and a civil war that led to the secession of Bangladesh (formerly East Pakistan) in 1971, civilian rule returned later that year, when Ayub Khan's successor, General Yahya Khan, was replaced by the autocratic leader of the center-leftist Pakistan People's Party, Zulfikar Ali Bhutto. General Zia ul-Haq deposed Bhutto in 1977, declaring martial law; Bhutto was hanged in 1979. Zia moved the country away from secular politics and toward an increased role of religion in the law, the military, and civil service, while significantly strengthening the role of the president. In 1988 Zia died in a mysterious plane crash; Ghulam Ishaq Khan succeeded him as president, and Zulfikar Ali Bhutto's daughter Benazir was elected prime minister. In the 1990s power alternated between Bhutto and the PPP on one side and Zia's protégé, Nawaz Sharif, on the other; Bhutto and Sharif were each elected prime minister twice and voted out of office following allegations of corruption. In 1999, amid Pakistan's ongoing conflict with India over the disputed territory of Kashmir, Sharif and the military leader Pervez Musharraf disagreed over policy and the role of the military in government. Sharif sacked Musharraf, who then staged a bloodless coup. With Bhutto and Sharif in exile, Musharraf gradually undermined the power of the prime minister—who under the constitution is designated as the nation's chief executive—and assumed the dual role of army chief and president. Promising to settle the increasing tensions between Islamists and secularists and to strengthen the economy, Musharraf received substantial financial and political backing from the U.S., particularly after the 2001 terrorist attacks in New York City and Washington, D.C., positioning himself as a U.S. ally in the so-called war on terror. Though Musharraf was credited by many with managing Pakistan's economy well, he received criticism for his increasingly autocratic rule. In the fall of 2007, amid rising ethnic and religious violence and widespread discontent with the Musharraf regime, as well as the return of Bhutto and Sharif to contest upcoming parliamentary elections, Pakistan's Supreme Court threatened to invalidate Musharraf's latest, less-than-democratic presidential electoral victory—prompting the general to dismiss the judges who opposed him. In the run-up to the parliamentary elections, Bhutto was assassinated, with her supporters pointing the finger at Musharraf as having orchestrated her murder.

Earlier, during the period of martial law declared by General Zia, Gilani had joined the Pakistan Muslim League's Central Working Committee. He was elected as district council chairman for Multan in 1983 and as a member of the National Assembly in 1985. When Zia appointed Muhammad Khan Junejo prime minister that year, Gilani served in Junejo's cabinet, first as minister of housing and works and then as railways minister. Gilani had disagreements with Junejo and was marginalized in the PML, leading him to approach Benazir Bhutto about joining her party. At the time the move was seen as a risk, as the PPP had itself been marginalized since the killing of Bhutto's father. After Zia dismissed the Junejo government in May 1988, months before Zia's death, Gilani formally joined the PPP, winning a seat in the National Assembly by defeating the PML's Nawaz Sharif. In the Bhutto government of 1988–90, Gilani served as minister of tourism and then as minister of housing and works. While Bhutto was voted out of office in 1990, Gilani retained his seat in that year's elections, beating one of his uncles for the position. When Bhutto returned to the premiership, in 1993, after Sharif lost his post, Gilani was elected speaker of Parliament—serving until Bhutto was again dismissed for corruption, in 1996. In 1997 Gilani suffered the first electoral defeat of his career, losing his parliamentary post in a pro-Sharif environment in which the PPP did not win a single seat in Punjab. "That period was a low point in Pakistan's failed experiments with democracy, with Sharif and Bhutto persecuting each other when in power and seeking to paralyze parliament when in opposition," Stephen Graham wrote for the Associated Press (March 25, 2008). Reuters reported, as printed in the *International Herald Tribune* (May 14, 2008), "Bhutto and Sharif fought mercilessly for power during the 1990s, a decade associated with rampant corruption and government incompetence that paved the way for Musharraf's 1999 military coup."

When Musharraf took over he promised to rid the country of corruption, going so far as to form an anti-corruption agency, the National Accountability Bureau (NAB). "The process degenerated, however, into a witch-hunt for political opponents," the Pakistan Newswire (November 22, 2004) reported. "It is now crystal clear that NAB operates selectively and has become an apparatus to institutionalize state-sponsored terror for opponents. It has now become customary to join the ruling PML to evade the establishment's wrath." It was alleged that Musharraf coerced opposition members to switch parties and charged them with corruption if they did not do so. Gilani was arrested by the NAB in February 2001, convicted of misusing public funds and making illegal appointments, and sentenced to 10 years in prison. During his sentencing Benazir Bhutto's husband, Asif Ali Zardari, reportedly told the court, "Gentleman! Today you have convicted the person who will be the chief executive of Pakistan in [the] future." While in prison Gilani wrote a book, whose title in English, according to infopak.gov, is "Cry from Yusuf's Well," in which he advocated the democratization of Pakistan and the curbing of the military's role in politics. On October 7, 2006 the Musharraf government, perhaps for the sake of appearances,

released Gilani from prison. (An amnesty agreement in October 2007 allowed Bhutto to return from exile).

Earlier, in August 2007, Gilani had stated that his leader-in-exile, Bhutto, would never accept Musharraf as both head of the army and head of a civilian government; that the prime minister's role (filled at that time by Shaukat Aziz) had been reduced to that of rubber-stamping the president's policies; and that it was time to hand power back to an elected government. In October 2007 the government dropped all corruption charges against Bhutto but not Sharif, prompting speculation that Musharraf was preparing for a power-sharing agreement with the PPP. The next day Musharraf won a controversial election for yet another term as president, but opposition parties declared the election unconstitutional, and the Supreme Court had to rule on its legitimacy. Less than two weeks later, Bhutto returned to Pakistan, with her celebratory homecoming procession disrupted by bombings. In early November, amid violence, Musharraf declared a state of emergency, suspended the constitution, and dismissed the senior judges of the Supreme Court. Later that month Musharraf allowed Sharif to return to Pakistan. At the end of November, in the hopes of remaining a civilian president, Musharraf handed over control of the military and was sworn in for his second five-year term, which was confirmed by the new Supreme Court he had installed earlier in the month. Although some felt that Bhutto might consider entering into an alliance with Musharraf, others—opposed to his rule—were preparing for elections for the National Assembly, hoping to weaken the president by removing his parliamentary rubber stamp. On December 27 Bhutto was assassinated; three days later her husband, Zardari, who had served in her second administration, assumed leadership of the PPP. The party continued to push Bhutto's populist campaign platform, based on the "Five E's"—employment, education, energy, environment, equality—and won the majority of the votes in the general elections held in February 2008. Sharif's faction in the PML also scored major victories, while Musharraf's faction suffered many defeats, resulting in a coalition, anti-Musharraf government headed by the PPP. Gilani had beaten Sikandar Hayat Bosan (to whom he had lost in 1997) to win back his seat. While Zardari was clearly running the PPP, he was ineligible to stand for prime minister because he was not a member of the National Assembly.

At first Gilani seemed to dismiss the notion that he might become prime minister, joking that the post would be an express route back to prison. In fact, Gilani's years in prison had brought him, in the eyes of many, an air of integrity; he appeared incorruptible in his quest for a democratic solution to Pakistan's troubles. He also had an inoffensive, low-key style that many felt would hold together a fragile coalition government as it worked to carry out necessary reforms. Both Sharif and the formerly pro-Musharraf faction withdrew their parties' candidates and backed Gilani. (In a March 24, 2008 broadcast on National Public Radio, the India-based correspondent Philip Reeves told listeners, "The real power within the coalition will lie with Asif Ali Zardari—Bhutto's widower—and with former Prime Minister Nawaz Sharif. They weren't eligible for the prime minister['s job] themselves since they don't hold seats in parliament. But they are the leaders of the coalition's two core parties, so they will call the shots. The fate of Gilani's government will, in fact, depend on whether these two men can continue to cooperate.")

On March 24, 2008 the National Assembly elected Gilani prime minister, with 264 votes to only 42 for Musharraf's nominee, Chaudhry Pervaiz Elahi. Gilani made his acceptance speech to chants of "Long live Bhutto" and "Go Musharraf go," ordering the immediate release of the judges under house arrest, a move seen as a rebuke to Musharraf. He also called for a U.N. investigation into the murder of Bhutto, rejecting the earlier government's verdict that she was killed by Islamic terrorists. "We didn't get this moment for free," he said, as quoted by Graham. Referring to the deaths of his party's leaders, he added, "This moment came due to continued struggle and martyrdom." Gilani said that he would strengthen democracy and ensure the independence of the judiciary as well as freedom of the press in Pakistan.

Gilani's challenges were many, including a fractured coalition; the judicial crisis; an insurgency on the part of the Muslim fundamentalist group the Taliban; the National Assembly's seeming inability to control the country's military and intelligence services; and, perhaps most urgently, a failing economy. The first crack in the coalition appeared in the parties' divergent strategies for reinstating the sacked judges. A reinstatement would have led to a probable overturning of Musharraf's electoral victory, and the PPP had reportedly come under intense pressure from the U.S. to support Musharraf. In an apparent reversal of campaign promises, Gilani and the PPP refused to order the judges' reinstatement, prompting nine of the ministers supported by Sharif to pull out of the coalition government in May. Gilani refused to accept their resignations. In August 2008 Zardari and Sharif announced that impeachment proceedings would begin against President Musharraf, on the grounds of the firing of judges, the illegal imposition of emergency rule, and gross mismanagement of the economy. The move was also seen as a way to curb the powers of the presidency, including the ability to dissolve Parliament and thus escape impeachment. Musharraf soon resigned. Running as a PPP candidate in the National Assembly, Zardari won election as president on September 6, 2008. Two weeks later, in an example of the challenges Gilani and Zardari face, a bomb exploded at the entrance to the Marriott Hotel in Islamabad, Pakistan, near the prime minister's house, where government leaders were dining after the president's speech to the National Assembly. The attack, which killed dozens of people, bore "all the hallmarks of a terrorist operation carried out by Al Qaeda or its associates," a U.S. intelligence official told Carlotta Gall, writing for the *New York Times* (September 21, 2008, on-line). Gilani and Zardari, in response, vowed to root out terrorism in Pakistan.

On his first trip to the United States as prime minister, Gilani urged President George W. Bush and others to support democracy in Pakistan and the larger region, alluding to the U.S.'s past support of dictatorships in nations including Pakistan. He told the audience at a meeting of the Council on Foreign Relations on July 29, 2008, as transcribed for the council's Web site, "One of the greatest tragedies of the modern era is that after achieving the liberation of Afghanistan [in its war with the Soviet Union in the 1980s], the world failed to reconstruct a postwar Afghanistan built on the democratic principles of coalition, consensus and compromise. We failed to rebuild civil society and promote democratic institution(s). The fundamental mistake was that we were not consistently committed to the values of freedom, democracy and self-determination that undermined the basic tenets of terrorism. With all due respect, the United States thought short term, but not long term. The world must not repeat the mistake again in Pakistan. . . . Democracy and human rights should be the centerpiece of your policy at home and abroad. Selective and expedient [application] of the values of democracy is not only immoral, but in the long run counterfunctional. Dancing with the dictators has always come back to haunt the world."

Gilani is married and has five children.

—M.M.

Suggested Reading: Associated Press Mar. 25, 2008; *BBC News* (on-line) Mar. 24, 2008; National Public Radio (on-line) Mar. 24, 2008; (Toronto) *Globe and Mail* A p12 Mar. 24, 2008

Selected Books: *Chah-e-Yusuf ki Sada* ("Cry from Yusuf's Well"), 2006

Giordani, Marcello

Jan. 25, 1963– Opera singer

Address: c/o Mindi Rayner Public Relations, 1655 Flatbush Ave., Suite B409, Brooklyn, NY 11210

Thanks to radio, television, and the World Wide Web, the general public is familiar with the names of many dozens of pop, rock, and soul singers. Among opera singers, by contrast, only a few superstars have achieved widespread recognition. Those include Enrico Caruso, in the early part of the 20th century, and, in the latter half, Plácido Do-

Opernhaus Zurich, courtesy of Marcello Giordani

Marcello Giordani

mingo, José Carreras, and Luciano Pavarotti, whose performances as the Three Tenors reached millions of people via television. Other immensely talented and accomplished singers are virtually unknown outside the world of opera but are, within that domain, revered by critics and opera devotees alike. Prominent among them is Marcello Giordani, a native of Sicily, in Italy, whom Scott Barnes, writing for *Opera News* (March 2008), described as "arguably, the greatest leading tenor of his generation, possessed of a masculine, sexy Mediterranean sound that releases into a thrilling high C and beyond." Unlike most of his peers, Giordani ended his formal education with high school and never attended a music conservatory or college; he studied voice with individual teachers and developed his acting techniques on his own, largely by observing others. Now 45, he launched his career in Italy at the age of 23, when he sang the role of the Duke in a production of Verdi's *Rigoletto*; he made his international debut two years later, in Switzerland, in the same role. In 1994 serious problems with his voice and loss of confidence led him to study intensively with the voice coach Bill Schuman, and he learned more efficient, less stressful ways to achieve breath control, a beautiful tone, vocal agility, resonance, and other requirements of superlative singing. He has since appeared in many of the world's major opera houses in roles from more than 40 operas, all but two of them (Richard Strauss's *Der Rosenkavalier* and Tchaikovsky's *Eugene Onegin*) by Italian or French composers. Among those roles are the title characters in Berlioz's *La Damnation de Faust*, Verdi's *Don Carlo* and *Ernani*, Massenet's *Werther*, Offenbach's *The Tales of Hoffmann*, and Gounod's

Faust; Don José in Bizet's *Carmen*; Edgardo in Donizetti's *Lucia di Lammermoor*; the male lead in Gounod's *Roméo et Juliette*; the Chevalier Des Grieux in Puccini's *Manon Lescaut* and Massenet's *Manon*; and Pinkerton in Puccini's *Madama Butterfly*. Giordani's repertoire also includes the Verdi Requiem. In 2007 he was cast as Don Alvaro in a production of Verdi's *La Forza del destino* at the Maggio Musicale Fiorentino, in Florence, Italy; that performance was carried by satellite to movie theaters throughout the United States and Europe. Also during the 2007–08 season, Giordani appeared in five productions at the Metropolitan Opera House (known informally as the Met) in New York City, including two—*Madama Butterfly* and *Roméo et Juliette*—in which he replaced other singers on extremely short notice, in demonstrations of his flexibility and outstanding memory as well as his vocal gifts. "I'm very fortunate in that many opera houses, like the Met, ask me what I'd like to do and try to accommodate me," he told Dominic McHugh for MusicalCriticism.com (August 6, 2007). In an event televised in all parts of the world, Giordani sang on April 20, 2008 at Yankee Stadium, in New York City, during the Mass conducted there by Pope Benedict XVI.

In a review of the Met's production of Puccini's *Manon Lescaut* in January 2008, Harry Rolnick wrote for ConcertoNet.com (January 30, 2008) that "the real reason why this *Manon Lescaut* was a triumph" was Giordani's performance: "Giordani as Des Grieux has a voice which brings back memories of the greatest tenors of the so-called Golden Age. His voice has the richness, the intonation, and above all the *sweep* of a [Richard] Tucker, a [Jussi] Björling, almost a Pavarotti. True, the latter made it look easy, and Giordani impresses you with just what magic he has. But the audience was incredibly impressed, as they should have been. It would be useless to choose which parts he made his own. Every note he [sang] resounded through the Met, . . . and every act was a triumph for this incredible tenor." When Dominic McHugh asked Giordani to describe himself as a singer, he responded, "If I may say so, I'm not just a singer but an artist. I try to be versatile, eclectic, a complete artist. I'm not just a specialist in Italian music. People say, 'Oh well, if you're an Italian singer you must always sing Italian opera,' but I think that would be rather limiting and a little boring! I want to be a complete performer, singing different kinds of music equally well."

The youngest of four brothers, Giordani was born Marcello Guagliardo to Michele Guagliardo and his wife, Santa, on January 25, 1963 in Catania, on Sicily's east coast. According to Brian Kellow in *Opera News* (February 2002), the difficulty that non-Italians had in pronouncing his surname led him to change it at the start of his career. Giordani was raised in a working-class environment in the port town of Augusta, near Catania. His was "a very Sicilian family," he told T. L. Ponick for the *Washington Times* (November 9, 1997).

"Very normal, no singers, no musicians." Giordani's father worked as a prison guard before becoming the owner of a prosperous gas station. His father loved opera; impressed by his son's vocal talents, he arranged for Marcello to take voice lessons from Maria Gentile in Catania. Giordani told Kellow that hearing recordings by Giuseppe di Stefano, a tenor who enjoyed great popularity for a brief period in the mid-20th century, reinforced his love of operatic singing when he was entering his teens. "I went crazy for [di Stefano's] beautiful sound, legato, phrasing," he recalled.

After Giordani graduated from high school, at age 18, he took a job at a local bank. The work bored him, and after a year he quit to take lessons with a local voice coach. His decision frightened his mother and brothers. "They were against it, leaving a secure job with a good salary, pension, health insurance, to do this," he recalled to Ponick. "They thought it was madness." "I was the only one in the family with rebellion and ambition," he added. Giordani's father, however, supported his decision; indeed, Giordani has said that his father had long encouraged him to pursue a career in music.

By the age of 20, Giordani was studying with the singer and coach Nino Carta in Milan, Italy, and had begun to give recitals there. "God smiled on me in every sense," he remarked to Matthew Gurewitsch for the New York Times (January 21, 2007). "I was born a tenor, and you know what that means. Tenors are a rare commodity. You can work immediately. And step by step, I found people who believed in me." In 1983 he met Luciano Pavarotti in Catania, when that city bestowed its Bellini d'Oro Prize on both Pavarotti and Maria Gentile. "I sang for him the second part of 'A te o cara!' from I Puritani, with a C-sharp which made a big impression on him," Giordani recalled in his on-line newsletter (December 2007). "I saw his broad smile and heard him wish me a brilliant future."

In 1986, at 23, Giordani won a prize in a competition for singers at the Festival dei Due Mondi, in Italy, better known as the Spoleto Festival, for the city in which it is held. Thanks in part to the good impression he made there, later that same year he made his professional debut, in the role of the Duke of Mantua in Verdi's Rigoletto, at the Teatro Sperimentale in Spoleto. Soon afterward he appeared in another major role, that of Cavaradossi, the lover of the title character, in Puccini's Tosca. Those performances disappointed him. "I had no technique, just high notes," he told Kellow. "My voice was three different registers." Nevertheless, the Italian man who managed his career from 1986 to 1988 secured other roles for him for which he was not properly prepared vocally.

An audition with Marcello Viotti, the artistic director of the Lucerne, Switzerland, opera house, brought Giordani a contract to sing in Rigoletto there in February and October 1988. Those Lucerne concerts marked the start of his international career. While in Lucerne he courted Wilma Ahrens, a member of the opera-house staff; a Swiss native, Ahrens soon became his constant companion. Fluent in five languages, she helped him to become fluent in English and aided him with other languages associated with the operatic repertory. The two married in 1990, and in interviews Giordani has often spoken about his wife as an invaluable anchor for him. "When you finish in the evening and if you have a success or no success, it doesn't matter," he told Ivana Segvic for the Daily Cougar (February 1, 1994, on-line), a University of Houston, Texas, student publication. "You go back to your room and if you have nobody you can speak your experience or your feeling to, you become depressed. It's important because I leave all my stress." He also said to Segvic that his wife "sings with me even if she is in the audience. She breathes with me and suffers with me. I need people like her."

In June 1988, in the role of Rodolfo in Puccini's La Bohème, Giordani made his debut in the Teatro alla La Scala, familiarly known as La Scala, in Milan, one of the world's most famous opera houses. Also that year he performed in the same role in Rio de Janeiro, Brazil; in Verdi's Don Carlo at the Festival di Szeged Ungheria, in Hungary; and in Madama Butterfly in Tokyo, Japan.

In 1988 Matthew Laifer, an American, became Giordani's agent and brought him to Portland, Oregon. There, Robert Bailey, then the general director of the Portland Opera, cast him in Bizet's opera The Pearl Fishers; Giordani sang the role of Nadir, one of the two male leads. "At that time, Marcello had a kind of naïve stage presence," Bailey, who worked with Giordani in Portland for a total of seven seasons, told Kellow. "Very sincere and earnest, but [he was] not terribly comfortable onstage with his body—but incredibly appealing, because he was without any pretense. And the voice was so beautiful. It had a gorgeous, velvety quality and seemingly endless range. When he was onstage taking direction, he would have one eye on the stage director and one eye on Nino [Carta]. He needed that kind of assurance as he was finding his way. He would say, 'Did that work? Is this the way to do it?' But he was a born performer." In a review of The Pearl Fishers for the Sunday Oregonian (November 13, 1988), David Stabler wrote that Giordani, singing in French, "used his voice intelligently, once he settled down, and portrayed Nadir equally as having brains as well as brawn. While he made some most un-French vocalisms that betrayed his Italian background, the quality of his voice was beautiful and intriguing—flexible, ringing, colorful."

Speight Jenkins, the general director of the Seattle Opera, attended Giordani's performance in The Pearl Fishers, and soon afterward he cast him in Lucia di Lammermoor and Madama Butterfly. Jenkins told Gurewitsch that Giordani's singing in Lucia di Lammermoor was unlike anything he had heard before. "I had never heard the duet in Act I in that opera with a final high E flat for the tenor," he said, referring to other singers' substitution of a lower note that they know will not present a problem for them. "Marcello was spectacular throughout, lyric yet very strong, clearly a tenor on the way to big lyric parts." Martin Bernheimer, reviewing for the *Los Angeles Times* (May 5, 1989) one of Giordani's *Madama Butterfly* performances, observed that Giordani "introduced the contradiction of an amiable, robust persona and a slender, delicate tenor. His warm, brightly focused, lyric resources might be better suited to bel-canto than verismo"—that is, purer, more beautiful tones rather than earthy realism—"but his is obviously a major talent. Remember the name."

Also in 1989 Giordani appeared in Bellini's *La Straniera*, at the Spoleto Festival USA in Charleston, South Carolina; in productions of Gounod's *Faust* in Portland and Baltimore, Maryland; and in *Madama Butterfly* and Verdi's *La Traviata* in Bilbao, Spain. Between 1990 and the beginning of 1994, he added to his repertoire the roles of Fernand in *La Favorita* and Tonio in *La Fille du Regiment*, both by Donizetti; the Italian Singer in *Der Rosenkavalier*; and Gualtiero in *Il Pirata* and Arturo in *I Puritani*, both by Bellini. During that period he sang with opera companies in cities including Trieste, Italy; Chicago, Illinois; Houston, Texas; Toronto, Canada; Philadelphia, Pennsylvania; and Vienna, Austria. He made his New York City debut in 1993, in a Met performance held in Central Park, in the role of Nemorino in Donizetti's *L'Elisir de'Amore*. During that period he also appeared on television, in a Public Broadcasting Service (PBS) program called *Pavarotti Plus! Live from Lincoln Center*.

The death of his father, in 1993, was a tremendous blow for Giordani. He was still grappling with that loss when, in 1994, Riccardo Muti, the artistic director of La Scala, dropped him from the cast of *Rigoletto* two days before he was to have appeared onstage. "He told me I wasn't ready, because I didn't have one note—the low E-flat in 'Questa o quella,'" Giordani recalled to Brian Kellow. "He said, 'It's better if you don't sing. [The audience] will kill you.' I accepted that." Giordani also told Kellow that during that time he awakened one morning with a severe pain in his chest and thought that he might be having a heart attack. "It was just because I was really tight," he said. According to Kellow, Giordani's "vocal problems had increased to the point where he was terrified to sing a B-flat." "This career takes great stamina, great mental attitude," Giordani told Barnes. "Plus you have to be prepared musically and vocally. . . .When I had my vocal crisis, I lost my confidence. I needed to close the gates on some old information and open them to . . . new information." "Old information" referred to some of what he had learned from earlier teachers, which he believes was counterproductive. "In Italy, we have lost the teaching tradition," he told Octavio Roca for the *San Francisco Chronicle* (September 21, 1999). "Teachers often try to force an artificial way to manipulate the voice: It is not natural." "Some-

times voice teachers teach not technique but imitation," he said to Anne Midgette for the *New York Times* (November 23, 2003). "You need somebody to explain the mechanism of your body. Once you understand singing, it is easy. But it becomes very difficult when you are trying to manipulate it to do different things."

Determined to overcome his vocal problems, Giordani came to New York City to work with the coach Bill Schuman, a former tenor. (Contrary to various accounts, he did not cancel several months' worth of engagements; he bowed out of one or two.) "The first thing [Schuman] did was open my body and let me trust my voice again," he told Midgette. Schuman told Scott Barnes, "When Marcello came in to this studio, he really had to re-educate himself, and he did it so humbly and thoroughly. He wasn't on the core of his voice, his vocal cords weren't closing completely, his high notes were gone. It was a joke—this man who had made his name from his high notes couldn't hit a B-flat!" "After three months, I learned new things, got my confidence back," Giordani recalled to Ponick. "[Schuman] showed me how to open up my body so things are easier. My whole voice came back, like I was 22 again."

Giordani resumed his career in October 1994, in a performance of *Rigoletto* in Hamburg, Germany. Later that year he sang in *Lucia di Lammermoor* in Portland and San Francisco. In 1995 he appeared as Alfredo in a production of *La Traviata* by the Royal Opera House in London. In an example of the sorts of mixed reviews he has sometimes earned, Andrew Porter, writing for the London *Observer* (July 9, 1995), reported that Giordani "sang a clean, true, 'standard' Alfredo," while Hugh Canning, the reviewer for the London *Sunday Times* (July 9, 1995), found his singing "rough, ill-tuned and graceless." In December of that year—in what he described to Pearl Amanfu for naxos.com (November 2003) as "without a doubt" the defining moment of his career up to that date—Giordani made his debut at the Metropolitan Opera House, in the role of Rodolfo in *La Bohème*. "Although it sounds contradictory, he probably needs to try less hard," Mary Campbell wrote in an assessment of his performance for the Associated Press (December 12, 1995). "When he pushes his voice for maximum volume, his tone thins out and begins to sound strident." The *New York Times* (December 13, 1995) critic, Kenneth Furie, warned, "This can be only a preliminary report" on Giordani as Rodolfo: "Flashes of color in Act I suggested that the voice had yet to warm up, and sure enough, it suddenly came together for 'Questa e Mimi' in Act II, which was fluid and pointed. The rest of the way he sounded generally confident, if somewhat hard on top. But Rodolfo's most important singing comes in Act I." Giordani's portrayal of Rodolfo at the Met the next year pleased Anthony Tommasini, another *New York Times* (November 4, 1996) reviewer. After noting that Giordani had "done variable work since his Met debut," Tommasini declared, "At his best, however, as he mostly was on this occasion, he has a radiant voice and a true sense of Italianate style."

Earlier in 1996 Giordani and others had joined Pavarotti at the opening celebration of the newly restored Detroit Opera House, in Michigan. In 1997 Giordani made his debuts as Des Grieux in Massenet's *Manon* at the Met and as the Duke in Verdi's *Simon Boccanegra* at Covent Garden, in London. He sang in five performances of the latter, which proved to be the last complete operas conducted by the world-renowned George Solti before his death a few months later. By the end of the Covent Garden engagement, to Giordani's delight, Solti was addressing him as "Marcello" rather than "Mr. Giordani"—a sure sign of the maestro's esteem for him. "In many ways, he was like a father-figure to me . . . ," he told Pearl Amanfu. "When I am depressed or feeling down, thinking of him brings me back up." In November 1997 Giordani appeared as Romeo in seven performances of Gounod's *Roméo et Juliette* at the Washington Opera House. After attending one of them, Ponick wrote that Giordani's "authoritative yet lyrical voice is an instrument of vast resources fully capable of gut-wrenching emotion. He is controlled and contemplative in tender moments and approaches in the more powerful passages a brilliant, orchestra-overwhelming resonance that eerily recalls Plácido Domingo. Mr. Giordani's Romeo rides a roller coaster of youthful passion, and the journey is thrilling, terrifying and breathtaking. He is truly one of the new young superstars." Giordani added to his repertoire the role of Gennaro in Donizetti's *Lucrezia Borgia* in 1998, the title character in Berlioz's *La Damnation de Faust* and Raoul in Meyerbeer's *Les Huguenots*, both in 1999, and Rodolfo in Verdi's *Luisa Miller* in 2000. In 2001 Giordani became the first Italian in the history of the Metropolitan Opera to sing in Russian, in the role of Lensky in *Eugene Onegin*. Also that year he participated in a performance of Verdi's Requiem at Carnegie Hall, in New York City; the next year, at the same venue, he sang the role of Maurizio in a concert version of Francesco Cilea's opera *Adriana Lecouvreur*.

Between March 2003 and October 2004, in a prodigious feat of memorization, Giordani learned eight new roles, among them some of the most difficult in the operatic repertoire: the title character in Rossini's *William Tell*—"the opera that unleashed the first full-voice high C on an unsuspecting world," as Anne Midgette noted; Henri in the French version of Verdi's *Vêpres Siciliennes*; Calaf in Puccini's *Turandot*; Don José in Bizet's *Carmen*; Enzo Grimaldi in Ponchielli's *La Gioconda*; Arrigo in Verdi's *I Vespri Siciliani*; des Grieux in Puccini's *Manon Lescaut*; and Cellini in Berlioz's *Benevenuto Cellini*. "It is always a goal of mine to try new ideas," he told Pearl Amanfu. "Singers are like painters. We are always looking for new colours and attempting to paint new rainbows." In December 2003 Giordani appeared as Cellini in the director Andre Serban's production of *Benevenuto Cel-*

lini—the first-ever mounting of that opera at the Met. In a critique of one of his performances, Frederick M. Winship wrote for United Press International (December 29, 2003), "He has a voice of necessary Wagnerian weight"—a reference to the power demanded of singers in operas by the German composer Richard Wagner—"with a bright upper register and gives an entirely creditable, often ardent performance in one of opera's most challenging roles, flawed only by a few lapses in the pitch of his top notes." David Patrick Stearns, in a critique for andante.com (December 4, 2003), wrote, "Even though Marcello Giordani . . . was given to tonal dryness by the cruel tessitura"—vocal range—"his burnished tenor put him miles ahead of any Cellini I've ever heard. . . . With his dashing stage presence, Giordani was within striking distance of being ideal in the part."

In 2004 Giordani sang in nine venues (twice in one of them, the Zurich Opera House, in Switzerland), in operas including *I Vespri Siciliani*, *La Gioconda*, *Carmen*, *Madama Butterfly*, *Manon Lescaut*, *Tosca*, and *Turandot*. He fulfilled 14 engagements the following year, including his debut in the title role—that of a real-life poet who was executed during the French Revolution—in *Andrea Chénier*, the best-known work of Umberto Giordano. In a review of a later performance of that role, at the Zurich Opera House, an *Opera Now* (March/April 2007) critic wrote, "Giordani thrilled in the punishing title role, singing with a passion, confidence and triumphant ringing top that never let him down—an ideal Chénier, full of sincerity and commitment." His portrayal of Chénier at the Teatro Massimo Bellini in Catania stirred Sergio Sciacca to write for *La Sicilia* (April 2007, as translated from the Italian), "Giordani . . . possesses a robust vocal power: he climbs with ease to the peaks of the musical scale giving powerful color to even the highest notes. At the same time, he traces with a fine brush the romantic nuances of the Poet. . . . His intimate singing is extremely beautiful, with an inner lyricism which was as compelling as the acclaimed summits of his high notes." Giordani's 2006 performances included his turn as Pinkerton in a production at the Met of *Madama Butterfly* guided by the film director Anthony Minghella. Peter G. Davis, in a critique for *New York* (September 26, 2006), lambasted Minghella's rendition, which originated at the English National Opera in London, but had high praise for Giordani, writing, "It's a rare pleasure to hear an ardent-voiced Italian tenor of this quality sing his own language with such authority and musical taste." Anthony Tommasini, writing for the *New York Times* (September 26, 2006), praised both the production and Giordani's performance, reporting that though he thought the singer "looked a little beefy to play the dashing American naval officer . . . he sang with full-bodied Italianate passion, warm, rich tone and clarion top notes. And I have never seen him act with more involvement and subtlety."

Giordani opened the Met's 2007–08 season in the role of Edgardo in *Lucia di Lammermoor*, directed by the Tony Award winner Mary Zimmerman. Noting the lyric as well as dramatic qualities of Giordani's voice, F. Paul Driscoll, in an assessment of that *Lucia*, wrote for *Opera News* (December 2007), "Giordani, a full-toned, more spinto Edgardo than the norm, was admirably ardent in Act I, properly impassioned in Act II and positively riveting in the tomb scene of Act III." Giordani sang the title role in the Met's production of *Ernani* in March and April 2008 and that same month participated in two concert performances—the first, of Puccini's *Edgar* with the Opera Orchestra of New York at Carnegie Hall, in New York City, and the second, of Berlioz's *Les Troyens*, at Symphony Hall in Boston, with the Boston Symphony Orchestra, in the role of Aeneas. In August 2008 Giordani performed in the "Meet in Beijing 2008—Cultural Events," a series of concerts held in Beijing during the Olympic Games. That month he also sang at the Centro de Bellas Artes in San Juan, Puerto Rico. In September 2008 he sang at the Met in a tribute to Pavarotti, who had died a year earlier. Giordani was among the singers who appeared in the Met's "Live in HD" 2008–09 series, in which performances were shown in movie theaters.

Giordani still works with Bill Schuman when he is in New York; he also relies on other coaches to gain a fuller understanding of the music, lyrics, and backgrounds of particular operas. When he was preparing for the role of Cellini, a 16th-century Italian painter, sculptor, goldsmith, soldier, and musician, for example, as he told Anne Midgette, he wanted answers to such questions as, "Why do the instruments play this way at this moment? Why is this passage written in four-four time and this one in three-four time? Why is it written allegretto, fast? [The coaches and I] spend hours doing this." For the Cellini role he also "did an in-depth study" of Cellini's life, as he told Pearl Amanfu: he read Cellini's famous autobiography, visited places in Florence and Paris where Cellini had worked, and read political and social histories of the period in which he lived. "When I sing a role like Cellini I feel as though I am not Giordani anymore, but that I am the man himself—I *am* Cellini," he told Amanfu.

Giordani has recorded two albums as a soloist: *Marcello Giordani: Tenor Arias* (2003) and *Marcello Giordani: Sicilia Bella* (2004), and he can be heard on recordings of Verdi's *Jérusalem* and a collection of songs composed by Steven Mercurio called *Many Voices* (2006). He appears on DVDs of productions of *La Gioconda*, *La Bohème*, *Madama Butterfly*, and *Manon Lescaut*, and he lent his voice to the soundtrack of the director Michael Hoffman's version of Shakespeare's *A Midsummer Night's Dream* (1999).

Giordani and his wife have two sons, Michele Francesco and Gerard-André, who were 10 and nine years old in early 2008. The family has a home in Augusta, in Sicily, and an apartment in New York City. Giordani's sons attend school in New York when he is there for performances.

—W.D.

Suggested Reading: Marcello Giordani's Web site; MusicalCriticism.com Aug. 6, 2007; naxos.com Nov. 2003; *New York Times* Arts & Leisure p39+ Nov. 23, 2003, p29 Jan. 21, 2007; *Opera News* p22+ Dec. 2002, p12+ Aug. 2005, p12+ Mar. 2008; *Washington Times* D p1 Nov. 9, 1997

Selected Recordings: *Verdi—Jérusalem*, 2001; *Tenor Arias*, 2003; *Sicilia Bella*, 2004

Selected DVDs: *Madama Butterfly*, 2006; *La Bohème*, 2007; *La Gioconda*, 2007; *Manon Lescaut*, 2008

Ezra Shaw/Getty Images

Girardi, Joe

(jeh-RAR-dee)

Oct. 14, 1964– Baseball manager

Address: New York Yankees, 161st St. and River Ave., Bronx, NY 10451

On October 30, 2007 the New York Yankees named the former catcher Joe Girardi, who had played in baseball's major leagues for 15 years, as the team's new manager. Girardi succeeded Joe Torre, with whom he won three World Series titles as a player and under whom he served as a bench coach in 2005. The announcement came as a surprise to many baseball insiders, who viewed the legendary Yankees' first baseman Don Mattingly, a member of the team's coaching staff from 2004 until 2007, as the leading candidate to replace Torre; but in contrast to Mattingly, who had no managerial experience, Girardi had managed a rookie-filled Florida Marlins team, keeping them in play-off contention throughout the 2006 season. While his fiery demeanor and tumultuous relationship with the Marlins' owner and management led to his dismissal after only one season, Girardi's toughness is regarded as an asset in the high-pressure environment of New York. "He's been a world champion player, played in this environment; he's been a coach; he's been a major league manager; he's meticulous in his approach," the Yankees' general manager, Brian Cashman, told Ronald Blum for the Associated Press (October 30, 2007) about Girardi—who, in addition, has served as an on-air baseball commentator. "Three characteristics that probably describe his beliefs are hard work, accountability and discipline." Girardi is also well known for his aggressive coaching style, which represents a clear departure from Torre's laid-back approach. "From one Joe to another, Girardi brings with him a fire and determination not seen in the Yankees universe in years," Frank Russo wrote for the Yankees blog NYYFans.com (March 31, 2008, on-line). "The exact opposite of Torre, he will set the tone for his team. Intense is a word that best describes the Peoria, Illinois native. . . . [Torre] was never a believer in throwing inside to opposing batters, no matter the circumstances. Thankfully, Girardi will not be as passive as his predecessor. . . . Under his leadership, this Yankees team is going to show an attitude that has been sorely lacking for years."

The fourth of five children, Joseph Elliott Girardi was born on October 14, 1964 to Jerry and Angela Girardi in Peoria, Illinois, an industrial town located nearly 200 miles southwest of Chicago. His mother, a child psychologist, was diagnosed with ovarian cancer when Girardi was 13; she succumbed to the illness six years later. His father held several jobs, as a salesperson, a bricklayer on the weekends, and the manager of Girardi's, a family-run restaurant. His older brothers, John and George, are medical doctors; his younger brother, Jerry, is an accountant; and his sister, Maria, is a mathematics professor at the University of South Carolina. In Girardi's family, "there were a lot of mouths to feed, college educations," as he told Nancy Armour for the Associated Press Online (March 4, 2001). "My parents did everything they could to give us a better life." Girardi got a taste of hard work beginning at the age of six, while helping his father at his weekend bricklaying job. "I was the grunt. I used to carry the bricks and blocks and cement for him," he told Joe Capozzi for the Palm Beach (Florida) Post (October 30, 2005). He also worked as a busboy and waiter at the family restaurant. Meanwhile, when he was five, his brother John taught him to play chess, which he

still enjoys; he has likened the game, in terms of the strategy required, to baseball. In addition, Girardi—raised as a Catholic—was an altar boy.

Beginning early on, sports played a significant role in Girardi's life. His father took him to Chicago Cubs games at Wrigley Field. "From the time I was 6 or 7, I can remember coming to this park," he told Michael Romano for the Denver, Colorado, Rocky Mountain News (June 26, 1994). "In the third grade, the teachers asked us to write an essay about what we wanted to do in life. Of course, I wrote that I wanted to play for the Chicago Cubs." Girardi played the sport in pickup games, as part of the Oakwood Oaks, a neighborhood team. Beginning at age 10 he was the third baseman and pitcher for the Sea Merchants, a traveling all-star baseball team in East Peoria, on which he was the youngest player. When the team's catcher suffered a thumb injury, Girardi filled in, so impressing his coach, Dave Rodgers, that he continued in the position after the original catcher's thumb had healed. Rodgers recalled to Kevin Kernan for the New York Post (November 4, 2007) that Girardi was a particularly obedient player who closely followed the coach's advice—which included avoiding air conditioning, as the coach believed that it made players stiff and sore. "The whole Girardi family had to go without air conditioning," Rodgers told Kernan. "I don't know if anybody else on the team listened to me but Joe. I always had to be careful of what I said because Joe would follow it to the letter."

After attending the Father Sweeney School, a parochial school for academically gifted children, Girardi enrolled at the Spalding Institute, a Catholic high school, where he was a member of the baseball team. While he also played on the football team during his junior and senior years, Girardi was determined to become a major-league baseball player. His performance during a baseball tournament in Springfield, Illinois, resulted in offers of athletic scholarships from several colleges. After graduating from the Spalding Institute, in 1982, Girardi chose to study at Northwestern University, a Big Ten Conference school in Evanston, Illinois, where he was an industrial-engineering major and a member of the Alpha Tau Omega fraternity. In a conversation with Bruce Lowitt for the Tampa (Florida) Tribune (March 13, 2004), Girardi referred to industrial engineers as "people who try to make systems run more efficiently. It's problem-solving. Kind of like being a catcher." Girardi was voted an All–Big Ten catcher and an academic All-American three times while playing on the college's baseball team. He fulfilled his dream of a professional career when the Chicago Cubs selected him as their fifth overall pick in the Major League Baseball (MLB) draft on June 3, 1986, the day before he received his B.S. degree.

Girardi was assigned to the Chiefs, the club's affiliate in Peoria. During that time "his doting father always had a home-cooked meal waiting" for him, as Michael Romano noted. ("He took a lot of ribbing from his teammates," his father told Romano.)

Girardi said to the reporter, "A lot of people don't realize how big of a struggle the minor leagues can be. I was making $700 a month. I was only able to survive and eat well—because I was living at home. I always had that support system." In his first professional season, he appeared in only 68 games due to a fractured ankle and had a .309 batting average. The following year he hit .290 for the Spirits, the Chicago Cubs' Class A affiliate in Winston-Salem, North Carolina, and was voted to the All-Star team in the Class-A Carolina League. He was then promoted to the Cubs' Double A team in Pittsfield, Massachusetts. During an impressive season in 1987, he led the Eastern League in several categories, including fielding percentage, putouts, assists, total chances, and percentage of runners caught attempting to steal bases. He was also selected to play in the Eastern League's All-Star Game.

On the subject of Girardi's mother's death, which had occurred when the athlete was in college, Michael Romano reported that Girardi "was behind the plate" the day after the funeral, "doing whatever he could to block out the pain of his loss." During his time in the minor leagues, however, he began to feel the full effects of his mother's passing. "I always thought I was playing to keep my mother alive," Girardi told Romano. "Then she was gone. And I never really dealt with it. But in 1987, just about the time of year my mom died, it hit me: There's no reason at all to keep playing this game. I can't keep my mom alive anymore, so why don't I go home and get a job. At that moment in life, I was gone—I was done with baseball." He added that his college girlfriend and future wife, Kim, "brought me to the Lord and made me realize that I was playing baseball because God gave me gifts and talents."

Girardi made his major-league debut in April 1989, when the highly touted catcher Damon Berryhill was placed on the disabled list, and became the first rookie to catch an opening game for the Cubs since 1966. After making five errors in one month, he was sent down to the Cubs' triple-A team in Iowa, following Berryhill's return. Girardi was called back six weeks later, after Berryhill underwent season-ending shoulder surgery for a torn rotator cuff. Over the remainder of the regular season, Girardi shared catching duties with Rick Wrona; he hit .248 with one home run and 14 runs batted in (RBIs) while helping the Cubs capture their second National League East division title in a decade. The Cubs lost the best-of-five National League Championship Series (NLCS) 3–2 to the San Francisco Giants, who were eventually defeated in four games by the Oakland Athletics in the World Series.

In 1990, Girardi's first full season in the major leagues, he was designated the Cubs' starting catcher, as Berryhill was still recovering from surgery. (Berryhill returned to the Cubs that September.) Girardi appeared in 133 games and had a .270 batting average with 24 doubles, 36 runs, 38 RBIs,

and eight stolen bases for a Cubs team that finished in fifth place in their division. Defensively, he had 61 assists, which was second-best among all catchers in the National League; his eight stolen bases were the most by a Cubs catcher since 1924. The next year Girardi competed against Berryhill for the starting-catcher position during spring training; Berryhill won the job after hitting .340, considerably better than the .150 average of Girardi, who spent most of the 1991 season on the disabled list with a lower-back injury. Upon his return, in August, he also suffered a broken nose, in a collision at home plate with John Kruk of the Philadelphia Phillies. In 1991 Girardi was limited to only 21 games, in which he hit .191. The next year he batted .270 and collected 73 hits, 19 runs and 12 RBIs in 91 games before an injured left hand ended his season in late September. Girardi's tenure with the Cubs ended two months later, when he was made available for the 1992 major-league expansion draft and selected 19th overall by the Colorado Rockies, a new franchise.

Girardi served as the Rockies' starting catcher during their inaugural season, in 1993. Still bothered by his hand injury, he spent two months on the disabled list; he nonetheless managed to hit .290 with 35 runs and a team-leading 12 sacrifice hits in 86 games, while also posting a career-best .397 slugging percentage. Girardi missed 60 games of the strike-shortened 1994 season, after undergoing surgery to remove the damaged bone in his left hand; he also spent two weeks on the disabled list with inflammation in his left patellar tendon. He finished the season with a .276 batting average, four home runs, and 34 RBIs in 93 games. Girardi established career highs in home runs (eight), runs batted in (55), and runs scored (63) and also had a 14-game hitting streak in May, to help the Rockies win the National League Wild Card spot in 1995; they went on to lose in four games to the Atlanta Braves in the best-of-seven National League Division series in October, during which Girardi managed only two hits. A month later he was traded to the New York Yankees for the relief pitcher Mike DeJean.

Yankees fans did not initially embrace Girardi, who had supplanted the highly popular Mike Stanley as the team's starting catcher. "When they announced my name [during the team's annual welcome-home dinner], I got booed bad, and these were supposed to be a thousand of the Yankees' most loyal fans," Girardi told Michael Sokolove for the *New York Times* (June 4, 2006). He said to Matt Michael for the Syracuse, New York, *Post-Standard* (November 4, 1996), "My wife, Kim, kept telling me, 'You're here for a reason. Stop fighting it.' She was always there for me. A lot of times the wives go unnoticed, but most of us couldn't survive without our wives." Apparently undaunted, he hit .294 with two home runs, 45 RBIs, and 13 stolen bases in 124 regular-season games and recorded a .996 fielding percentage to help the Yankees to a 92–70 record and a first-place finish in the

American League Eastern Division. Another regular-season highlight for Girardi was Dwight Gooden's no-hit game—the eighth regular-season no-hitter in franchise history—for which he was the catcher. Afterward, Gooden attributed his feat to Girardi's selection of pitches and said that he had never worked with a better catcher. "It changed the fans' reaction toward me a lot," Girardi told Matt Michael. The Yankees defeated the Texas Rangers, the league's Western Division champions, in the American League Division Series (ALDS) and beat the American League Wild Card–winning Baltimore Orioles in the best-of-seven American League Championship Series (ALCS). They advanced to the World Series, another best-of-seven contest, against the Atlanta Braves, whom they defeated, four games to two. Girardi contributed to the victory by hitting a triple in Game Six. In his first season in New York, Girardi had earned a World Series ring. After that season Girardi became a free agent and accepted a two-year, $5.5 million contract (with a $3.4 million option in 1999) to remain with the Yankees.

In 1997 Girardi handled most of the catching duties for a Yankees team that relied more on pitching and defense than power hitting. He also served as a mentor to backup catcher Jorge Posada during Posada's first full season in the majors. That year Girardi hit .264 with 105 hits, 38 runs, 50 RBIs, and 23 doubles in 112 games, while also throwing out more than 22 percent of players attempting to steal bases. The Yankees ended the regular season with a 96–66 record and won the American League Wild Card berth; they failed to advance past the Cleveland Indians in the 1997 ALDS, losing the best-of-five-game series, 3–2. Posada began to assume more of a starting role over the next two years, although Girardi still saw considerable playing time. "Joe was very selfless in helping Jorge," Joe Torre said to Bruce Lowitt. "Knowing that someone is the heir-apparent for your job and that you can just about reach out and touch the day it's going to happen, it takes a very special guy to do what Joe did." Girardi said to Lowitt, "I've always felt there's always going to be someone you meet in your life who's either stronger, smarter, faster, more talented. The only thing I concern myself with is not ever letting anyone take my job because he outworked me. Talent levels you can't control, so I never really worried about it." In 1998 he appeared in 78 games (74 were starts) and posted a .276 batting average, with 70 hits, 31 runs, 31 RBIs, and three home runs; in 1999 he played in 65 regular-season games and collected 50 hits, 23 runs, 27 RBIs and two home runs to go along with his .239 batting average. He was also the catcher during the Yankees' pitcher David Cone's perfect game in July 1999, against the Montreal Expos. The Yankees won the World Series in both seasons.

In December 1999, after three years with the Yankees, the 35-year-old Girardi turned down a one-year deal with the team and instead signed a three-year, $5.5 million contract to return to the Chicago Cubs, his first major-league team. As the team's starting catcher, he hit a respectable .278 with 15 doubles, six home runs, and 40 RBIs in 106 games during the 2000 season. He also had solid defensive numbers, posting a .993 fielding percentage while committing only five errors in 754 total chances and throwing out 25 of 88 would-be base stealers. Girardi also made his first—and only—major-league All-Star game appearance, as a substitute for the injured Mike Piazza of the New York Mets. Over the next two years he shared catching duties with Todd Hundley, who had signed a four-year, $23.5 million contract with the Cubs in December 2000, and saw his playing time and his offensive numbers gradually diminish. In 2001 he started 61 games to Hundley's 67 while hitting .253 with three home runs and 25 RBIs. He also collected his 1,000th major-league hit in May, during the Cubs' 4–1 victory over the Milwaukee Brewers. In 2002 he made 67 starts behind the plate (Hundley made 71) and batted .226 with one home run and 13 RBIs. Regarded as a natural leader, Girardi was designated the team's co-captain and the player representative. On June 22, 2002 he addressed the fans outside the third-base dugout at Wrigley Field, announcing that the game between the Cubs and the St. Louis Cardinals was being canceled; it was later discovered that the cancellation was due to the death of the 33-year-old Cardinals pitcher Darryl Kile, from an apparent heart attack.

When the Cubs decided not to offer him a contract following the 2002 season, Girardi signed a one-year deal to serve as the backup catcher for Mike Matheny of the Cardinals in 2003. He began the season on the disabled list, as the result of a herniated disc in his back and neck that he had suffered during a spring-training game in March. Although the injury was initially thought to be career-ending, he made his debut with the Cardinals on June 11, after missing 61 games. An unrelated lower-back injury in late June caused him to miss another 56 games. Girardi started five games behind the plate and hit .130 in 16 games in his only season with the Cardinals. After that year he announced his retirement as a major-league player.

Girardi's broadcasting career began in September 2003, when he was offered a job as a color commentator for ESPN Radio. Following an appearance as a player in a March 2004 spring-training exhibition game in Japan with the Yankees, he assumed sports-broadcasting duties with the Yankees' regional YES television network and also served as the host of one of the network's programs, the youth-oriented sports show Kids on Deck. In the 2006 postseason he provided pregame analysis for the Fox network. Meanwhile, he had returned to baseball competition in 2005, after accepting a position as a bench coach with the Yankees under Joe Torre. (A bench coach offers advice to the head coach and takes over if the latter is ejected from a game.) Girardi had already turned down a coaching position with the Florida Marlins, which would have included a guarantee to succeed Jack McKeon as the team's manager in 2006. Then, following the 2005 season and McKeon's resignation, Girardi signed a three-year deal with the Florida Marlins, making him the youngest manager in franchise history. Although many were predicting a 100-loss season for the team, which had not only the lowest payroll in MLB but a roster made up mostly of rookies, the first-time manager defied expectations, leading the Marlins to a respectable 78–84 record while also keeping the team competitive in the National League Wild Card race (which was won by the Los Angeles Dodgers). Girardi's "no-nonsense managing style," as Bart Hubbuck called it in the *New York Post* (October 31, 2007), included "instituting a . . . ban on facial hair and keeping the youngest team in baseball on a short leash." Girardi earned National League Manager of the Year honors from Major League Baseball and the *Sporting News*.

Girardi's rookie year as a big-league manager, while successful, was not without controversy. During a televised Marlins game, he was captured on camera while grabbing the pitcher Scott Olsen by the collar and pulling him into the dugout tunnel after Olsen had complained about not being given sufficient time to warm up. Girardi also continually clashed with officials in the team's front office, including the Marlins' owner, Jeffrey Loria. In August 2006, during a home game against the Dodgers, Loria—who was seated behind the Marlins' dugout—became incensed when Girardi failed to argue a strike-call by the home-plate umpire. Loria yelled at the umpire and then at Girardi, who in response uttered profanity in telling Loria, in effect, to remain quiet. Following the game they spoke with each other during a 90-minute closed-door meeting, after which they claimed to have resolved their differences. Reporters, however, speculated that Loria had nearly fired Girardi. In any case, the episode added new strain to an already contentious relationship, and at the end of the 2006 season, Girardi was relieved of his duties as the Marlins' manager.

Girardi became a leading candidate for several other managerial openings. A week after leaving the Marlins, he interviewed for the vacant Cubs' managing job previously held by Dusty Baker. He also withdrew his name from consideration for the Washington Nationals' manager position, recently vacated by Frank Robinson, who had retired at the end of the 2006 season. In the end Girardi decided not to manage in 2007, citing a desire to spend more time with his family. In November 2006 he accepted an offer to return to the YES network as a game analyst and as the co-host of *Behind the Plate*, with the former Yankees' catcher John Flaherty. Meanwhile, major-league teams were still hotly pursuing Girardi; in June 2007 he turned down the chance to manage the Baltimore Orioles.

After Torre led the Yankees in 2007 to their 12th consecutive play-off appearance, the team finished second in the American League East for the first time in 10 seasons and also failed to advance past the first round of the play-offs for the third straight year. The team's owner, George Steinbrenner, regarded those developments as unacceptable for the team with the highest payroll in baseball. After Torre rejected the terms of his contract extension at the end of the 2007 season, Girardi was seen as a potential successor, along with Tony Peña, Torre's first-base coach, and Don Mattingly, the legendary former Yankees first baseman and Torre's bench coach in 2006, whom many saw as the leading candidate. At the time the media also reported that Girardi and the Los Angeles Dodgers were discussing a managing position. During a six-hour interview held at the Yankees' complex in Tampa, Florida, in October 2007, Girardi impressed the team's executives with his preparation and analytical skills. "The spring-training component; the regular season; pregame preparation; advance scouting; how you select coaches and why; your evaluations of players; your media-relations abilities. Ultimately a lot of things came up right and helped me gravitate to Joe Girardi," Brian Cashman told Peter Abraham for the Westchester County, New York, *Journal News* (October 31, 2007). The Yankees signed Girardi to a three-year contract worth $7.8 million.

Girardi said that he would come to the Yankees' post having "gained wisdom," in Peter Abraham's words, during his experience as the Marlins' manager. "What I've learned . . . is the importance of relationships; the importance of everyone being on the same page and the importance of sticking together," Girardi said, according to Abraham. "If you don't have a situation like that, it is not a great workplace." At a press conference held in November at Yankee Stadium, Girardi announced his coaching staff for 2008, which included three members of the 2007 staff: Peña; hitting coach Kevin Long; and Rob Thomson, who was promoted from field coordinator to bench coach. Newcomers include the bullpen coach Mike Harkey and two former Yankees' players: David Eiland, the team's new pitching coach, and Bobby Meacham, the third-base coach. Girardi also decided to wear the number 27 on his jersey, to indicate the team's quest for their 27th world championship. Girardi, who enjoys a close relationship with his father, an Alzheimer's patient, shared with Ronald Blum for the Associated Press (November 2, 2007, on-line) his father's reaction to his new coaching position. "I try not to get emotional, but my father hasn't spoke in a month. And when the lady who takes care of my father . . . showed him the picture of me as the new Yankee manager, my father said, 'Oh yeah.'"

On September 21, 2008 Girárdi, along with nearly 60,000 people in the stands, witnessed the last game to be played at the original Yankee Stadium, which opened in 1923. The Yankees beat the Orioles in that game, 7–3; two days later the Bronx Bombers were eliminated from the play-offs. (The new Yankee Stadium, which is across the street from the old one, is set to open for the 2009 season.)

Girardi lives in Coral Springs, Florida, with his wife, Kim, also a graduate of Northwestern University, and their three children, Serena, Dante, and Lena. During his playing days many noted that Girardi, unlike many other professional athletes, was happy to sign autographs for free. He told Matt Michael, "I used to be one of the kids that used to hang out over the wall in Wrigley Field, so I know the excitement of seeing ballplayers and what it meant to me to get an autograph."

—B.M.

Suggested Reading: *Chicago Sun-Times* p80 Mar. 30, 1992, p12+ Oct. 20, 1996; *ChicagoTribune* C p8+ June 22, 1988, N p5 May 28, 2001, N p8 Dec. 20, 2002, C p3 Aug. 9, 2006; (Fort Lauderdale, Florida) *Sun-Sentinel* C p1 Aug. 8, 2006; *New York Times* B p25+ Mar. 27, 1997, p81+ June 4, 2006, D p1 Nov. 2, 2007; (Newark, New Jersey) *Star-Ledger* p63 Oct. 29, 1999; *Palm Beach (Florida) Post* C p1 Oct. 20, 2005; *St. Louis Post-Dispatch* F p9 Sep. 28, 2003; *USA Today* C p13 Feb. 17, 2000; (Westchester County, New York) *Journal News* C p1+ Oct. 31, 2007; yesnetwork.com

Joe Raedle/Getty Images

Giuliani, Rudolph

NOTE: An earlier article about Rudolph Giuliani appeared in *Current Biography* in 1988.

May 28, 1944– Businessman; former mayor of New York (Republican)

Address: *Giuliani Partners, 5 Times Sq., New York, NY 10036*

"Him?" So read the cover text of *New York* magazine's March 5, 2007 issue, which featured a photograph of Rudolph Giuliani. The cover expressed surprise that Giuliani—the notoriously combative former New York mayor who succeeded in "cleaning up" the city but was accused by some of trampling civil liberties in doing so, the Republican known to have supported gay rights, abortion rights, and gun control—had emerged as the front-runner for the 2008 GOP presidential nomination. In the fall of 2007, Giuliani appeared to be a very serious contender, with poll numbers that placed him either at the top or in the top three. But by the end of January 2008, after receiving no significant support in state primaries, he withdrew from the race and endorsed U.S. senator John McCain of Arizona. Giuliani first gained fame as a U.S. attorney for the Southern District of New York, a post in which he secured indictments and convictions of prominent figures from both the Mafia and Wall Street. After failing in his first bid for the mayoralty, in 1989, he served in that office for two four-year terms beginning in 1994. He occupied the international spotlight on September 11, 2001, the day of the terrorist attacks on New York and Washington, D.C.; the efficiency and compassion he demonstrated in the wake of the tragedy brought him a reputation for competence in the face of crisis, a quality apparently attractive to many in an age defined by fears of terrorism. In 2006 he launched his campaign for the presidency, running on a platform that emphasizes national security.

An only child, Rudolph William Louis Giuliani was born in the New York City borough of Brooklyn on May 28, 1944 and grew up in Brooklyn and Long Island, New York. His parents, Harold Giuliani and Helen (D'Avanzo) Giuliani, were both children of Italian immigrants. His father, a former amateur boxer and onetime felon, was working as a plumber's assistant in the Brooklyn Navy Yard at the time of his son's birth; his mother, a former spelling champion, was a bookkeeper. Helen Giuliani impressed upon her son the importance of education, reading biographies and history books to him when he was very young. In 1948, with jobs scarce, Harold Giuliani went to work for his wife's younger brother, who owned a bar—the site of a number of illegal operations, such as gambling and loan-sharking. In addition to working behind the bar, Harold acted as a collector and enforcer. He kept that aspect of his life a secret from his son, instead inspiring him with tales of the courage and goodness of Helen's other brothers, some of them firefighters and policemen. Politics was also a frequent topic of conversation in the Giuliani household. (Harold Giuliani was a Democrat, Helen a Republican.)

In 1951 Harold Giuliani moved the family to Garden City South, Long Island, in part to keep his young son away from the occasional violence that his work at the bar entailed. (Later they moved again, to the small Long Island town of Bellmore.) Harold, who had dropped out of school at 15, wanted Rudy to keep up his studies so that he could succeed in an honest profession. Giuliani attended Bishop Loughlin Memorial High School in Brooklyn. The student body, Catholic and all male, was largely working-class, but most of its members went on to college. After graduating from high school, in 1961, Giuliani considered attending a seminary but enrolled instead at Manhattan College, in the New York City borough of the Bronx, a Catholic school that was then for men only. Though Giuliani majored in political science (with a minor in philosophy), at the time he did not foresee a career in politics, giving more thought to pursuing journalism, medicine, or the priesthood. He did, however, gain experience in politics while serving as class president during his sophomore year and as president of his fraternity, Phi Rho Pi, which became his main extracurricular interest. A registered Democrat at the time, Giuliani worked on Long Island on Robert F. Kennedy's senatorial campaign. He earned an A.B. degree in 1965.

Ultimately choosing to pursue a law degree, Giuliani entered New York University, where he found his coursework highly stimulating; he graduated magna cum laude with a J.D. degree in 1968. He had been mentored in law school by Irving Younger, a former U.S. attorney, who persuaded him to become a prosecutor. Instead, Giuliani took a clerkship with a federal judge, Lloyd MacMahon, of the Southern District of New York. Also in 1968 Giuliani wedded Regina Peruggi, his second cousin; the two had dated sporadically since high school. During that time Giuliani was able to avoid military service in the Vietnam War through student deferments in 1963, 1967, and 1968 as well as through a rare occupational deferment that he received with the help of MacMahon.

In 1970, at the urging of MacMahon, Giuliani became an assistant U.S. attorney for the Southern District of New York. The ambitious young man lobbied strenuously to work on the most prestigious cases. He earned a reputation as a brilliant, and sometimes shockingly ferocious, prosecutor with a particular hatred for municipal corruption. A defining moment in his career as a prosecutor came in 1974, during a bribery trial in which he cross-examined Bertram Podell, a Democratic congressman from Brooklyn. Giuliani's questioning was so intense that Podell asked for a courtroom recess before submitting a guilty plea. Giuliani's personal life, meanwhile, suffered from his ambition, and by the mid-1970s his marriage was deteriorating.

In 1975, during the administration of President Gerald R. Ford, Giuliani took a position in the Department of Justice as an assistant to Judge Harold Tyler, the deputy attorney general. When Jimmy Carter became president, in 1977, Giuliani followed Tyler to New York to work for the law firm of Patterson, Belknap, Webb & Tyler, eventually becoming a partner.

In 1980 Giuliani changed his political affiliation to Republican and returned to Washington to assume the position of associate attorney general—the number-three position in the Department of Justice—under Attorney General William French Smith in the administration of President Ronald Reagan, who entered the White House in 1981. In his two years in that post, in addition to supervising all 94 U.S. district attorneys, Giuliani helped steer the focus of the Department of Justice from white-collar crime to illegal sales and use of narcotics, immigration, organized crime, and prison reform. While working for the Department of Justice, Giuliani began dating Donna Hanover, a Miami, Florida–based newscaster. In 1982, having had his first marriage annulled, he married Hanover in a Roman Catholic ceremony.

In 1983, at Giuliani's request, Reagan appointed him to the top spot in the U.S. Attorney's Office in the Southern District of New York for a four-year term. Giuliani brought to the position key political contacts in the Department of Justice, which enabled him to win assignments on high-profile cases. As a U.S. attorney Giuliani was determined to overhaul a legal system that, to his mind, had come to value the rights of the accused over those of the victim. "During the '50s and '60s," he said to Richard Stengel for *Time* (February 10, 1986, online), "we socialized the responsibility for crime. We broke down the line between explanation and excuses, and explanations became excuses. . . . For purposes of ethics and law, we elevate human beings by holding them responsible. Ultimately, you diminish human individuality and importance when you say, 'Oh, well, you're not really responsible for what you did. Your parents are responsible for it, or your neighborhood is responsible for it, or society is responsible for it.' In fact, if you harm another human being, you're responsible for that." His goal, he continued, was "to make the justice system a reality for the criminal."

Giuliani quickly earned a reputation as a zealous and innovative prosecutor. While continuing to target organized crime and narcotics, he oversaw a stream of white-collar arrests. According to *Biography Magazine* (January 2002), Giuliani was extremely effective, recording 4,152 convictions with only 25 reversals. One of his earliest successes involved a crackdown on drug-dealing in Manhattan's Lower East Side. Although the ultimate effect of those arrests, in many cases, was simply the relocation of drug peddlers to other boroughs of New York City, Giuliani's actions showed his commitment to focus on street-level crime and gained him the appreciation of government officials and the public.

Giuliani's relentless pursuit of organized crime led to his highest-profile cases. Using the Racketeering Influenced and Corrupt Organizations (RICO) Act to attack Mafia leadership, Giuliani presided over three sensational organized-crime cases that had national implications: the "Colombo Case," the "Pizza Connection Trial," and "The Commission of La Cosa Nostra." In the Colombo case, whose outcome Giuliani has referred to as one of his 10-best indictments, Giuliani's office secured convictions of Carmine Persico and eight other members of the Colombo crime family on charges of racketeering in the restaurant and construction industries. In the "Pizza Connection Trial," Giuliani's office charged New York's Bonanno crime family with conspiring with the Sicilian Mafia to distribute billions of dollars' worth of heroin and cocaine through pizzerias in the U.S., from the East Coast to the Midwest; 17 of 21 defendants were convicted. "The Commission of La Cosa Nostra" became Giuliani's signature Mafia case. (Time magazine dubbed it the "Case of Cases.") Although the names of many of the defendants were already in the FBI's files, legal scholars noted the unusual focus of Giuliani's organization of the case, as it challenged the Mafia at the highest, or "commission," level. Giuliani's office took advantage of over a decade's worth of FBI surveillance to build the preliminary case, which was so promising that Attorney General Smith and the FBI director, William H. Webster, both longtime Giuliani allies, allowed him to expand his investigation and employ agents in 14 U.S. cities to help map the nationwide pattern of Mafia activity. The final indictment that Giuliani's office handed down alleged that the "Commission" directed Mafia activity throughout the United States and backed crimes ranging from extortion to murder. The men accused of being part of the Commission were Persico; Anthony Salerno, the alleged head of the Genovese crime family; Antonio Corallo, said to be the head of the Luchese family; Gennaro Langella, another Colombo family leader; and Phillip Rastelli, a Bonanno family boss. Paul Castellano, the Gambino family head, was indicted along with the five other men but was murdered in 1985, before the trial.

Giuliani was also successful in the area of white-collar crime. He steered to completion a tax-fraud case that had been in progress when he was appointed U.S. attorney—that against the commodities trader Marc Rich. Giuliani obtained a guilty plea and a fine of $200 million from companies owned by Rich, who fled to Switzerland to avoid prosecution before receiving a presidential pardon from Bill Clinton in 2001. In 1985 Giuliani's office secured a guilty plea from Edward A. Markowitz in one of the largest tax-fraud cases in U.S. history; Markowitz had been behind an income-tax deduction scheme for celebrities that created nearly $450 million in false deductions. Also during that period Giuliani's office handed down indictments of several Wall Street executives accused of insider trading—using privileged information about the mergers and acquisitions of companies before that information is available to the public in order to guarantee the profitability of their stock-market transactions. Those prosecuted included such well-known figures as Ivan Boesky and Michael Milken.

Although Giuliani compiled an extensive record of convictions, many criticized his techniques and accused him of overzealousness and of grandstanding to promote his career. (While many of Giuliani's predecessors had avoided the limelight, Giuliani enjoyed engaging with the media and was often seen on television.) Giuliani's wide-ranging investigations into organized crime included an increased use of wiretaps and surveillance, which some lawmakers saw as setting dangerous precedents that threatened civil rights. Giuliani, in response, accused his detractors of being jealous of his success or of being overly liberal and ready to fault any aggressive prosecutor, particularly a Reagan appointee. "If I don't tip in favor of law enforcement, who will?" Giuliani asked rhetorically in a conversation with Michael Winerip for the New York Times (June 9, 1985). "The civil libertarians won't. The defense lawyers won't. The liberal editorial writers won't." Giuliani's detractors took particular issue with his eagerness in using the media to drum up publicity by calling news conferences to announce indictments and making the so-called "perp walk"—or public arrest in which the suspect is escorted in handcuffs past a pre-assembled cadre of press reporters—a standard procedure. In fact, in some instances, Giuliani's zest for publicity had decidedly negative consequences, as was the case with the Wall Street executives Richard Wigton, Robert Freeman, and Timothy Tabor, who were arrested at work and paraded through a throng of press that had been alerted by Giuliani's office. The charges against all three men were later dropped, but their professional reputations had been ruined, and many blamed Giuliani's tactics. "Rudy was a person for whom the world was only black-and-white," another lawyer who worked in the U.S. Attorney's Office told Peter J. Boyer for the New Yorker (August 20, 2007). "There were no gray shadings." For his part, Giuliani—according to Winerip—said, "My view is: The way you end corruption, you scare the daylights out of people." Giuliani left the U.S. Attorney's Office at the end of his term, in 1989, and went to work in private practice for White & Case in New York City. In 1990 he joined the law firm Anderson, Kill, Olick & Oshinsky, also in New York.

Meanwhile, Giuliani had set his sights on becoming New York's mayor. After winning the 1989 Republican nomination in the mostly Democratic city but losing to David Dinkins, an African-American, in that year's general election, Giuliani returned to challenge Dinkins in 1993. Although Dinkins trumpeted a two-year decline in crime rates, improvements in city services, and a balanced budget, voters remained concerned about crime as well as the issues of jobs, affordable housing, and the quality of public schools. Many thought he had done a poor job of responding to the 1991 riots in the Crown Heights section of Brooklyn, and Giuliani's advertisements sought to take advantage of that perception, portraying Dinkins as weak and ineffective. Giuliani, having lost in 1989, "did not stop running until the next election was over," as Michael Powell wrote for the *New York Times* (July 22, 2007). "His political task seemed clear. He could not count on peeling black votes away from a black mayor. So he cultivated Jews, ethnic whites and the Hispanic middle class." Giuliani promised to crack down on crime, privatize government services, and lower taxes as well as promote "quality of life." Dinkins criticized Giuliani's plan to limit stays in homeless shelters to 90 days, calling it an example of his lack of compassion, and otherwise characterized Giuliani as mean-spirited. One of Giuliani's greatest political mishaps, highlighting what many saw as his racial insensitivity, occurred in September 1992. Speaking outside City Hall at a rally of thousands of police officers who were protesting Dinkins's proposal for a civilian board to review police misconduct, Giuliani offered a speech disparaging the mayor's proposals to increase police accountability. Many of the off-duty officers in attendance were drinking alcohol, and some held racist signs directed at Dinkins and shouted racial epithets at elected officials entering City Hall. Giuliani's involvement in the event, which culminated in a near-riot as the protesters blocked the entrance to the Brooklyn Bridge, likely gained him few votes and sparked animosity and division among the city's residents. Giuliani offended African-Americans throughout his campaign as he spoke bluntly about what he perceived to be the failure of the city's black leadership in recent years. On Election Day Giuliani swept white ethnic neighborhoods in Brooklyn, Queens, and Staten Island; kept his hold on the Republican vote; drew small support from crossover Democrats; and won over only 10 percent of African-American voters. The result was a 2 percent margin of victory over Dinkins. Giuliani became the 107th mayor of New York City and the first Republican to hold the office since John V. Lindsay, in 1965.

When Giuliani took office, in early 1994, New York City had 2,000 murders a year, a shrinking tax base, and a dearth of private-sector jobs; in addition, one in six citizens received public assistance. Giuliani introduced innovative strategies for reducing crime, limiting public assistance, encouraging economic growth, and generally improving "quality of life." He boosted tourism by eliminating the commercial-rent tax in most areas of the city and reducing the hotel-occupancy tax. He also eliminated the unincorporated-business tax, helped to create private-sector jobs, reduced the number of city employees, and ushered in a population boom in the city. Early on Giuliani displayed the political heterodoxy that would define him lat-

er in his career. In his first year in office, for example, he broke with the Republican Party to endorse the incumbent Democrat Mario Cuomo for governor rather than his ultimately successful Republican challenger, George Pataki. Giuliani leaned to the political left on some issues, such as gay rights, gun control, and abortion, but drew sharp criticism from liberals over his welfare policies, inattention to education and social services, and aggressive police force.

Giuliani made crime reduction the signature feature of his tenure as mayor. He hired more officers, increased their prominence on the streets, and held New York Police Department (NYPD) commanders accountable for their actions. In alliance with the NYPD commissioner William Bratton, Giuliani embraced George Kelling and James Q. Wilson's now-famous "broken windows" theory, according to which the discouragement of minor offenses sends the message that more serious crimes will not be tolerated. Accordingly, the police under Giuliani targeted such low-level crimes as creating graffiti and jumping turnstiles in the subway as well as "lifestyle" offenses such as public drunkenness. Giuliani's policies had an immediate effect: in his first term crime rates, particularly rates of violent crime, plummeted—murders and robberies fell to their lowest points in 25 years. Giuliani also used city ordinances to replace shady businesses in Manhattan's Times Square with more reputable commercial centers, such as Music Television and the Virgin Megastore. It should be noted, however, that after the early 1990s, crime rates began to drop significantly nationwide in many other urban areas as well as New York City. Furthermore, a considerable number of economists, sociologists, and crime experts questioned the degree to which the implementation of the "broken-window" theory contributed to New York City's declining crime rate; more effective, experts said, was the increase in the number of police officers on the street. (The crime rate in New York undoubtedly dropped under Giuliani, but why that happened again became an issue in the months preceding the 2008 presidential primary election.)

As the crime rate dropped, however, charges of police misconduct rose. Between 1993 and 1997 payments by the city to victims of police brutality rose 38 percent, to $27.5 million. Giuliani's "quality of life" campaigns against street vendors, the homeless, jaywalkers, squeegeemen (people who, ininvited, cleaned the windshields of cars stopped at red lights, in hopes of earning tips), and publicly funded art projects were seen by some as infringing on citizens' civil rights. Andrew Kirtzman, a New York journalist and the author *of Rudy Giuliani: Emperor of New York*, told reporters for an undated article on the Web site of CNN, "To combat the sense of lawlessness on the street, Giuliani used his police force as an army. And in a very short time, New York started to look a lot better. On the other hand, the tactics they were using started to antagonize people, especially minority communities." Giuliani's desire to decrease public-assistance benefits and privatize social services were met with similar resistance from New Yorkers who saw his policies as going against a long tradition in New York of helping the needy. Jack Newfield, writing for the Nation (June 17, 2002) in the wake of Giuliani's tenure as mayor, remarked: "Giuliani was a mayor of excess, with some big accomplishments and some spectacular lapses into cruelty and fanaticism." Giuliani suggested that negative reactions to his policies stemmed from his commitment to disrupting the status quo. "People didn't elect me to be a conciliator. If they wanted a nice guy, they would have stayed with Dinkins," he told Eric Pooley for Time (December 31, 2001–January 7, 2002, on-line). "They wanted someone who was going to change this place. How do you expect me to change it if I don't fight with somebody? You don't change ingrained human behavior without confrontation, turmoil, anger." Members of his inner circle described some of Giuliani's actions as being driven by stubbornness rather than racism or lack of compassion. "I never thought Rudy Giuliani was a racist," Fran Reiter, one of Giuliani's deputy mayors, said to Michael Powell. "But he was obsessed with the notion there were certain groups he couldn't win over. And he wasn't even going to try." Near the end of Giuliani's first term, former New York mayor Edward I. Koch told Barry Bearak and Ian Fisher for the New York Times (October 19, 1997): "He is a good mayor, but he'll never be a great one. . . . He can't accept disagreement. When it occurs, he wants to destroy you." Despite his controversial style, in 1997 Giuliani won reelection in a landslide victory over Manhattan borough president Ruth Messinger.

Giuliani's second term as mayor is largely associated with three highly publicized incidents involving violence on the part of the police. In July 1997 officers arrested Abner Louima, a Haitian-born security guard, in the Flatbush section of Brooklyn, and sexually assaulted him at a precinct house. Louima was hospitalized for two months following the assault and was later awarded $8.75 million in the largest police-brutality settlement in the city's history. (Louima initially testified that two of policemen involved, Justin Volpe and Charles Schwartz, had yelled "It's Giuliani time" during the attacks. Although Louima later recanted that part of his testimony, the phrase echoed in public discussions and the media.) In February 1999 Amadou Diallo, an unarmed West African immigrant, was shot and killed by policemen outside his home, which led to citywide demonstrations; some protesters carried placards on which were written such phrases as "Stop Giuliani's Reign of Terror." The four officers involved in the shooting—Edward McMellon, Sean Carrol, Kenneth Boss, and Richard Murphy—were acquitted of misconduct, which infuriated many. A year later Patrick Dorismond, an off-duty security guard, was approached by an undercover policeman who asked Dorismond if he knew where he could buy drugs. Dorismond took offense at the request, and a physical altercation ensued; a second undercover officer fatally shot Dorismond during the fight. At that time, in the aftermath of the Diallo murder and subsequent police acquittals, racial tensions were already running high. Giuliani asked New Yorkers to withhold judgment about the Dorismond incident until the facts were in, but the following day he publicly came to the defense of the NYPD, authorized the release of Dorismond's juvenile-arrest record, and characterized the victim as being "no altar boy," which some interpreted as a rationalization, or even justification, for the shooting. Giuliani immediately came under siege for his comments and actions with regard to the incident; his unconditional support of the police department led many New Yorkers to feel that the cost of Giuliani's crime-reduction strategies was too great.

In 2000 Giuliani briefly considered a run for the U.S. Senate seat being vacated by Daniel Patrick Moynihan. He withdrew from the race, however, in the face of health problems and public-relations troubles having to do with his personal life. He was diagnosed with prostate cancer that year, and his affair with Judith Nathan, which had become tabloid fodder, accelerated the proceedings of a bitter public divorce from his second wife, Donna Hanover. Barred by law from seeking a third term as mayor and mired in low approval ratings, Giuliani seemed to have passed the peak of his political career.

That perception changed dramatically on September 11, 2001, when terrorists flew two passenger jets into the twin towers of the World Trade Center, causing New York's two tallest buildings to collapse and killing nearly 3,000 people. Within two hours of the tragedy, Giuliani was on the phone with the news channel CNN, providing updates to newscasters around the world. "You have to remember that for most of the day, [President] George W. Bush was in flight," Kirtzman told CNN (on-line). "It was really Rudy Giuliani who was on the air most of the day, being very decisive and being very reassuring, telling people that we had weathered this extraordinary catastrophe, but that New York was going to be here today, and it was going to be here tomorrow." Giuliani was frequently on television and the radio throughout the day of the attacks, informing the public about safety steps the city was taking and reassuring viewers and listeners that no chemical or biological weapons had been used against New York. Giuliani's longtime executive assistant Beth Petrone-Hatton was inspired by Giuliani to continue working that day despite the death of her husband in the disaster. "He was probably the most 'on' I have ever seen him," she told Pooley. "On the one hand, he was devastated, destroyed. He knew he'd lost a lot of friends [in the attacks]. But he also knew he had to calm the city down. . . . [His performance] was so well orchestrated that you would have thought he had prepared for it forever."

In the weeks following the disaster, Giuliani kept New Yorkers abreast of the city's goings-on; overruled advisers who wanted, for security purposes, to severely limit commercial and tourist activity in the city; and pushed the New York Stock Exchange and the city's Major League Baseball teams to continue operating and serve as symbols of endurance following the attacks. Six weeks after the tragedy, Giuliani's approval rating, which had bottomed out at 36 percent in February 2001, reached 70 percent. On September 23, 2001, at the first major public event in the city after the attacks, Giuliani addressed a crowd of 20,000 gathered at a prayer service at Yankee Stadium. After being introduced by the famed TV personality Oprah Winfrey as "America's mayor," Giuliani offered an inspirational message, telling the crowd, as reported by *Biography Magazine* (January 2002), "To those who say our city will never be the same, I say, you are right. It will be better." Many of Giuliani's strongest critics offered their praise of his calm leadership in the weeks following the attacks. "Since the catastrophe, [Giuliani] has exerted the leadership which he's always had. What was different was that he was sensitive and warm and compassionate and showed nuances with respect to emotion that he never showed before," Edward Koch told CNN. Giuliani received expressions of support from international leaders including Jacques Chirac, Nelson Mandela, Tony Blair, and Vladimir Putin and was granted an honorary knighthood by Queen Elizabeth II of Great Britain. In addition, he was named *Time* magazine's "Person of the Year" for 2001.

Following the attacks Giuliani sought to amend New York's constitution in order to serve an unprecedented three-month extension of his mayoral term, until April 2002, or even a third term as mayor. While some applauded the idea, others saw it as an act of egotism, one that could dampen the goodwill he had recently built up. Giuliani insisted that he merely wished to provide the city with continuity in a difficult time. (Giuliani's proposal was turned down by the state assembly.) In recent years Giuliani has begun to receive criticism for his handling of several aspects of the recovery period following the attacks. He has been blamed by some for insisting, before the attacks, against the advice of many experts, that the city's emergency command center be placed at the World Trade Center; for the city's lack of preparedness on September 11; for the haste of the recovery effort; and for inattention to various safety concerns: for example, though Giuliani declared that the air quality around Ground Zero was safe, it was later discovered that dangerous airborne chemicals including benzene, asbestos, and dioxin surrounded the site, where clean-up crews developed a host of health problems.

Shortly after leaving office Giuliani established a consulting firm, Giuliani Partners, in New York City. According to the company's Web site, its mission is to help "leaders solve critical strategic issues, accelerate growth, and enhance the reputation and brand of their organizations in the context of strongly held values." A subsidiary of the partnership, Giuliani Security & Safety LLC (formerly Giuliani-Kerik), focuses on security consulting; other branches include Giuliani Safety & Security Asia and Giuliani Compliance Japan. In March 2005 Giuliani joined the Houston, Texas–based law firm of Bracewell & Giuliani (formerly Bracewell & Patterson), which opened a Manhattan office; he helped develop an informal alliance between Bracewell and Giuliani Partners, which could not merge due to ethical considerations. Meanwhile, he conducted a highly lucrative lecture tour, speaking on topics relating to leadership and the 2001 terrorist attacks. In 2004 Giuliani addressed the Republican National Convention, held that year in New York.

On November 10, 2006 Giuliani filed papers to form a presidential exploratory committee. Three days earlier the Republican Party had lost both houses of Congress to the Democrats, largely, it was thought, because of voter dissatisfaction with the war in Iraq. "The general mood of the country," Giuliani told Boyer, "in some ways, is very similar to the general mood that New York City was in in 1993"—the year he was elected mayor. "It's a country in which people believe we're going in the wrong direction. It's kind of eerie. It's about the same percentage, it's about sixty-five, seventy per cent who think we're going in the wrong direction. People in New York felt the same thing." Giuliani is an unorthodox Republican candidate, given his past support for abortion rights, gay rights, gun control, and immigration, stances that put him at odds with much of the Republican base. His campaign began inauspiciously, when a confidential 126-page memo in which his office outlined his political vulnerabilities was leaked to the New York *Daily News*. Even more damaging than the information itself was that Giuliani had allowed it to become public, which was seen as a display of amateurism that did not bode well for a candidate running on a platform of national security. Giuliani stumbled in early Republican debates as well—giving equivocal answers to questions about his views on abortion, for example—leading some to question the seriousness of his intentions. Peggy Noonan, a columnist and former speechwriter for Ronald Reagan, wrote for t*he Wall Street Journal* about Giuliani's performance in one debate, as reported by Boyer, "There is an embarrassing ad-hocness, a bush-leagueness to this. It's as if he hasn't thought it through, as if he's just deciding everything each day. But by the time you're running for president you should have decided."

The campaign focused largely on Giuliani's performance on September 11, 2001; it also emphasized law and order, leadership, national security, and the candidate's support for the war in Iraq. Giuliani emerged as the front-runner for the 2008 Republican presidential nomination, besting his main rivals—U.S. senator John McCain of Arizona, former Massachusetts governor Mitt Romney, and former Arkansas governor Mike Huckabee—in many polls. The former mayor benefited chiefly from reports about the effectiveness of his response to the terrorist attacks on New York, which suggested to many that he could manage national crises in a capable manner. In a development that was surprising to many and seemed potentially very valuable for the Giuliani campaign, in November 2007 the influential Christian televangelist Pat Robertson endorsed Giuliani's candidacy, despite the former mayor's views on abortion and gay rights. As quoted by CNN (November 7, 2007, online), Robertson called Giuliani "a proven leader who is not afraid of what lies ahead and who will cast a hopeful vision for all Americans." He added, "In all of the crises which confront our nation and the world, we need a leader with a bold vision who is not afraid to tackle the challenges ahead."

Giuliani's strength, however—his actions in the wake of the terrorist attacks—began to wear thin in some quarters. (As quoted by many sources, the Democratic presidential contender Joseph Biden, a U.S. senator from Delaware, quipped, "There's only three things [Giuliani] mentions in a sentence: a noun and a verb and 9/11.") A Democratic presidential consultant, Bob Shrum, told Stephen Rodrick for *New York* (March 5, 2007), "There's a reason Giuliani's using 9/11 as an asset. It's his *only* asset. He's not even running on his mayoral record. He's running on a few weeks. September 11 doesn't change the fact that Rudy has no foreign-policy experience, and his foreign-policy record is limited to having the same position on Iraq as George Bush." On January 8, 2008, in the New Hampshire primary, Giuliani finished fourth, receiving 9 percent of the vote. He then settled on an unusual approach: concentrating on Florida and ignoring the rest of the primaries. Despite the money and effort devoted to Florida, Giuliani finished third in that state's primary, capturing only 15 percent of the vote. The next day, January 30, 2008, he announced that he was withdrawing from the race, and he endorsed John McCain, who seven months later became the Republican Party's presidential nominee. On September 3, 2008 Giuliani spoke at the Republican National Convention, praising McCain and his running mate, Governor Sarah Palin of Alaska, and dismissing Senator Barack Obama of Illinois, the Democratic Party's presidential nominee, as inexperienced.

Giuliani is the co-author, with Ken Kurson, of the book *Leadership* (2002), detailing his turbulent tenure as New York City's mayor. In September 2007 he received the Margaret Thatcher Medal of Freedom, named for and presented by the former British prime minister. Giuliani married Judith Nathan in 2003; from his marriage to Donna Hanover, he has two children, Andrew and Caroline. He lives in New York.

—N.W.M.

Suggested Reading:*New Yorker* (on-line) Aug. 20, 2007; *New York* (on-line) Sep. 11, 2002, Mar. 5, 2007; *New York Times* A p1 July 22, 2007; *Time* p40 Dec. 31, 2001–Jan. 7, 2002, (on-line) June 24, 2001

Selected Books: *Leadership* (with Ken Kurson), 2002

Tony Karumba/AFP/Getty Images

Golding, Bruce

Dec. 5, 1947– Prime minister of Jamaica

Address: Office of the Prime Minister, 1 Devon Rd., Kingston 10, Jamaica

Days after the People's National Party (PNP) lost to the rival Jamaican Labour Party (JLP) in Jamaica's closely contested September 2007 general elections, the outgoing prime minister, Portia Simpson-Miller, warned her successor, Bruce Golding, that his administration was in for "sleepless nights and nightmares," according to Edmond Campbell, writing for the *Jamaica Gleaner* (September 18, 2007, on-line). Speaking at a swearing-in ceremony for his ministers of state and parliamentary secretaries, Golding used his predecessor's words to criticize the PNP government that had just been voted out. "We have been told that we are going to be visited by a nightmare, [but] we already are wrestling with that nightmare," Golding said, according to Campbell. "We come to government inheriting a debt of almost $1 trillion, that is an enormous nightmare." He also said, "We have a crime rate in which the murder total this year, if it continues on the same trajectory, is likely to be in excess of 1,300," and added, "We have a nightmare in crime."

Golding's rise to the office of prime minister came five years after he rejoined the JLP. He left the party in 1995, after its leadership failed to embrace a number of his proposed reform initiatives. Golding had also felt that Jamaica's two-party system was helping to foster the nation's "garrison politics"—a system in which certain portions of the country functioned as armed fiefdoms, with gunmen using violence to ensure support for particular parties or candidates. After leaving the JLP, Golding formed the National Democratic Movement (NDM), a party that, despite early support in public-opinion polls, failed to win any seats in Parliament in the 1997 or 2001 elections.

Golding resigned as NDM president in 2001 and spent part of 2002 hosting a radio program. In September of the same year he returned to the JLP, signing a "memorandum of understanding" that highlighted the party's commitment to several key reforms, including the elimination of garrison politics. Possibly spurred by Golding's return, the JLP fared better than had been expected in the 2002 elections, and Golding was later elected party chairman. Three years later he was named JLP leader, and on September 3, 2007, after the party captured 50.1 percent of the popular vote and won 33 of the nation's 60 parliamentary seats, Golding became prime minister. (In Jamaica the party that wins the majority of parliamentary seats appoints the members of the new government, including the prime minister.)

The JLP's victory marked the first time in 18 years that the party had been in control of the government. At his inauguration ceremony Golding told Simpson-Miller that he looked forward to working with her on solving Jamaica's problems. "In our two pairs of hands rest so much of the hopes of the people of Jamaica," he said, according to *El Caribe de Hoy* (October 2007). "We have a choice. Those hands can engage in hand-to-hand combat or we can join those hands together to build a nation that is strong, just, peaceful and prosperous."

The third of the four children of Tacius and Enid Golding, both teachers, Orette Bruce Golding was born on December 5, 1947 in Clarendon, the third-largest of the 14 parishes (administrative subdivisions that are analogous to counties) in Jamaica. The couple's second child, their only daughter, died soon after birth. Golding was born in his godmother's house, where his mother, who wanted to be close to her doctor, was staying temporarily. His birth was officially registered at Ginger Ridge, in St. Catherine Parish, where his family lived. Tacius Golding was the head of the Ginger Ridge School then, but after he had a dispute with Edward Thompson, a prominent man in Ginger Ridge, Thompson persuaded the townspeople not to rent housing to him. Tacius Golding later succeeded in renting a place to live near the school.

When Bruce Golding was two years old, the family moved to the St. Faiths district of St. Catherine. That year his father was elected to Jamaica's House of Representatives. For the next 22 years, Tacius Golding represented West St. Catherine in the country's legislature. By the time Bruce was five, two years shy of the usual enrollment age, he was attending classes at Watermount Elementary School. For six months in 1954 he lived with an aunt in Skibo, Portland Parish, and attended Skibo Elementary School, where his aunt was a teacher and his uncle headmaster. He then moved back to St. Faiths and entered Macca Tree Elementary School, where his father had once been headmaster. A half-year later his mother took a teaching position at Alpha Academy, in Kingston, Jamaica's capital city, and Golding became a student at the Alpha Primary School. In his third year there he earned qualifying marks for secondary school in the Common Entrance examination, a standardized test. Since he was not yet 10 years old, however, he was denied free tuition in secondary school. Golding took issue with the government's rules, and with his test scores in hand, he went to St. George's College, hoping to plead his case to the headmaster. (In England and former British colonies such as Jamaica, high schools or preparatory schools are often called colleges.) After hearing the boy argue with his secretary, the headmaster accepted Golding as a student, though he insisted that his parents pay tuition fees.

Golding studied at St. George's for five years, taking his Senior Cambridge examinations—secondary-level standardized tests—in 1962. He earned a Grade II certificate with distinction in English and mathematics. Meanwhile, in 1961, at the age of 12, Golding had developed an interest in politics, traveling with his father as he campaigned in advance of a countrywide plebiscite on whether Jamaica should remain part of the West Indies Federation. (The majority voted to withdraw.) Beginning in 1962, a general-election year, Golding set up the sound systems at public meetings, and he would often spend his after-school hours in Parliament, listening to political debates. After the decision of Jamaicans to withdraw from the West Indies Federation, Great Britain agreed to discuss with island officials the possibility of independence as a member of the British Commonwealth of Nations. With a constitution in place, Jamaica officially declared its independence on August 6, 1962. In elections held several months earlier, the JLP had captured 26 parliamentary seats, while the PNP earned 19. Founded in 1938 by Norman Manley, the PNP is seen as the more left-leaning of Jamaica's two major parties. The JLP was formed in 1943 by Sir Alexander Bustamante, who became the first prime minister of an independent Jamaica.

In 1963 Golding transferred to Jamaica College, where he took classes to prepare for his A-level, or advanced-level, examinations. Three years later he earned passing marks in economics, religious studies, and history. Earlier, midway through his second year at Jamaica College, Golding was appointed a school prefect, a position also held by his classmate Peter Phillips, who would go on to become vice president of the PNP. The following year Golding became head boy. In 1966 he enrolled at the University of the West Indies at Mona, Jamaica. In 1967, following the redrawing of parliamentary districts, rumors spread that Tacius Golding would lose his long-held seat. Determined to help his father remain in office, Golding put his studies on hold and took charge of the campaign. Thanks to his son's help, Tacius Golding won the election, by 878 votes. In 1968, a year before he graduated from the University of the West Indies with a bachelor's degree in economics, Bruce Golding was elected vice chairman of the JLP Constituency Executive for West St. Catherine. As a student he was appointed to the board of directors of the National Lotteries by then–Prime Minister Edward Seaga.

In 1969, less than three weeks after Golding finished taking his university examinations, the JLP held a special conference and selected the 21-year-old as its candidate for the West St. Catherine seat in the Jamaican Parliament. That same year he became central executive of the party, and in 1970 he helped found the JLP's youth affiliate, Young Jamaica. General elections were held in 1972, and Golding won a seat in Parliament by 893 votes. Thus, the 24-year-old Golding became the youngest Jamaican parliamentarian ever, a record he still holds. Later in 1972 he became a member of the board of governors of the Institute of Jamaica, the government's cultural agency. After Seaga gained control of the JLP, in 1974, Golding was elected general secretary of the party.

Golding lost his parliamentary seat in 1976, as political violence stemming from a variety of problems (prominent among them widespread poverty) swept Jamaica and elections were conducted during a declared state of emergency. The following year he decided to forgo another run for the House and instead focus on his duties as JLP general secretary. He was appointed to the Senate, the upper house of Jamaica's Parliament, and helped the JLP prepare for the 1980 elections. In that plebiscite the party regained control of the government and won 51 of 60 parliamentary seats. (In Jamaican politics, the governor-general, the ceremonial head of state, appoints the 21 members of the Senate. The prime minister recommends 13 members, while the leader of the opposition party chooses the other eight.)

After the JLP's 1980 victory, Golding was reappointed to the Senate, and he became minister of construction for the new government. According to Golding's official 2007 campaign biography, his nine-year stint as construction minister brought many successes: construction grew by 43 percent, after having declined throughout the PNP-controlled 1970s; 25,000 new units of housing were built; rent laws were established to protect tenants and encourage new construction; a major road-improvement program was launched; and a registration system was created for engineers and architects.

Golding returned to the House of Representatives in 1983, after winning a seat from the South Central St. Catherine District. (The district was later renamed Central St. Catherine.) Golding was reelected by increasingly larger margins in the 1989 and 1993 general elections. He served as acting prime minister on the frequent occasions when the prime minister and deputy prime minister were out of the country. The PNP regained control of the government in the 1989 general election, and Golding became shadow minister of finance ("shadow" refers to his membership in the opposition party) and chairman of the Public Accounts Committee. He played a role in several notable government investigations, including the so-called furniture scandal, in which PNP leaders were accused of spending $1.5 million of government money to outfit their homes and offices with luxury fixtures and appliances.

In the early 1990s Golding began pushing for government reforms. First on his list was the elimination of "garrison politics," which allowed gunmen to control portions of the country, using intimidation to ensure support for particular candidates. "It was a personal evaluation," Golding told Linda Diebel for the *Toronto Star* (May 9, 1996), explaining his decision to take on a system of which he had long been a part. "I asked myself, 'What difference did I make to the scheme of things in the 20-odd years I was there?' And I was quite shocked by the answer. . . . I had to admit that things were getting worse, not better, and that I had been at the centre during this prolonged period of degeneration"—"degeneration" referring to the political situation and violence. In 1995 Golding, frustrated that JLP leaders were reluctant to support his proposed reforms, resigned from the party and formed the National Democratic Movement. Breaking from the JLP required him to withdraw his support from Seaga, his political mentor. "I was pretty close to him," Golding told Diebel. "I was closer than anybody has been, and the nature of Jamaican party politics is that a loyalty line is drawn. But I'd been through that too often. And, I felt that my country was running out of time"—that is, traveling further down the path of social and political chaos.

Golding later told P. Damian for *El Caribe de Hoy* (September 2005) that, contrary to what many believed, his decision to defect from the JLP and form his own party was not the result of a falling-out with Seaga. "Part of the difficulty is that things are said anecdotally and then they become fact," Golding explained. "I challenge you to find any statement I made, any speech I gave where I was critical of Mr. Seaga or even the Labour Party. I criticized a system . . . that I thought was wrong. I thought politics in Jamaica had become so tribalized, that the country's interest had become the victim and the casualty."

The NDM failed to win a single parliamentary seat in the 1997 general election, and the party was again shut out in the 2001 by-elections, held to fill vacancies. "People who are willing to support a third party idea are not willing to support a third party idea until they see a third party idea gathering strength," Golding told Damian. "So what happens is that they are willing to join, but they are not joining until you join. But you are also not joining until I join. So everybody is standing back to see. So that's where you need a core of activists and the core of activists in Jamaican politics are in the PNP and the JLP. They are not sitting in the wings." In 2001 Golding resigned as president of the NDM, a position he had held since the party's formation. Temporarily stepping out of the political arena, in April 2002 he began hosting a radio show, *Disclosure*, which climbed to the second spot in radio ratings. Golding rejoined the JLP in September 2002, after the PNP announced an upcoming general election. Golding's reconciliation with JLP leaders followed a long negotiation process, and JLP party officials signed a "memorandum of understanding," committing themselves to fighting tribalism and revisiting the ideas of setting a fixed election date and creating a separation of powers—which would allow Jamaican voters to elect parliamentarians and the prime minister in separate elections—among other reforms. "It was an enormous decision to make because a lot was at risk," Golding told Damian, describing his return to the JLP. "A lot was at stake—my own credibility, my own commitment to the things in which I believed and my anxiety to ensure that in returning it was not purely to see what impact that may have on the election, but also that there would be a genuine undertaking and commitment given to areas of reform."

Elections were held three weeks after Golding's return, and the JLP, which had lagged in opinion polls, drew a surprising 48 percent of the vote to capture 26 parliamentary seats. Golding was named to the Senate and became shadow minister of foreign affairs and foreign trade. In November 2003 he was elected party chairman, and in February 2005, a month after Seaga stepped down, he ran unopposed for the office of party leader (a position separate from that of chairman). In April 2005 he was again elected to the House, representing West Kingston, and named leader of the opposition. Some members of the media criticized Golding for running to represent West Kingston, a garrison Seaga had formerly controlled. "Whatever one may say about the positives of West Kingston, it still is a garrison seat that hosts a number of politically affiliated dons and thugs," Loui Mcneil wrote for the Web site Jamaicans.com (June 1, 2005). "Golding's choice was to prove his manhood by staying outside and destroying the garrison mentality, or staying within the garrison and beating his chest as the new don. He chose the latter." Not long after Golding was elected to the West Kingston seat, three policemen were murdered in the city's Tivoli Gardens district. Police officers retaliated by killing two of the alleged gunmen. Golding found himself in a difficult position. "He can condemn the killers and urge the police to bring them to justice in a rush. But he cannot invite the police into Tivoli 'cause that will be his political doom there. Might even cost him his life," Mcneil wrote. "And he can't too strongly defend Tivoli, because that will be his political doom elsewhere."

By November 2006, however, Golding was making modest political gains. Polls showed that his approval rating had climbed from 31 percent to 35 percent between July and October 2006, while Prime Minister Portia Simpson-Miller—the first woman to hold that office in Jamaica's history—had seen her approval numbers drop from 60 to 54 percent. Some attributed the change in public attitude to ad campaigns designed to change the widely held image of Golding as cold and aloof. "The JLP started electronic ads featuring Mr. Golding and his family members," the pollster Bill Johnson told the *Weekly Gleaner* (November 9, 2006). "They are trying to soften him up and I think it has had an effect." As Golding campaigned for the upcoming election, which had not yet been scheduled but was supposed to take place before October 2007, he promised that the JLP would establish a fixed election date within its first 100 days of regaining power. Golding claimed that that could be accomplished by means of a majority vote in Parliament, but others argued that altering the relevant clause in the constitution would affect other clauses and necessitate referenda.

In July 2007 the PNP dissolved Parliament and announced that elections would be held the following month. In the weeks before the election, both parties made "change" a major part of their campaign rhetoric, even though the PNP had been in power for 18 years. The JLP, which had been seen as leaning to the right in the political spectrum, championed a host of social programs, such as free health care and government-paid secondary-school tuition. The JLP also pushed for more investment from foreign companies. "The government . . . reported 2.5 percent [economic] growth last year—the highest growth rate they have recorded in 15 years," Golding told Jacqueline Charles for the *Miami (Florida) Herald* (August 30, 2007). "And they regard that as something to celebrate? This government has so lowered our standards that mediocrity now becomes a goal." Golding also promised to hire more police officers in an attempt to lower Jamaica's high murder rate.

On August 19, 2007 a highly destructive hurricane, Dean, hit Jamaica, forcing the postponement of the elections, which had been scheduled for the following week. Despite dire predictions, another storm, tropical depression Felix, did not strike Jamaica on September 3, the day of the rescheduled elections, so weather was not a factor as voters went to the polls. That night the JLP was declared the winner, with 50.1 percent of the vote and 33 seats captured in Parliament. Given the narrow margin, Simpson-Miller refused to concede defeat, charging the JLP with election violations, such as putting on the ballot candidates who held dual citizenships. Addressing supporters just before midnight, Golding said, "The majority of the people have placed their trust in us," according to *El Caribe de Hoy*. "We must honor that. We must not betray that trust." Simpson-Miller conceded the next day, though she said that the PNP might still challenge "a number" of the seats it lost.

Golding was sworn in on September 11, 2007. Seaga, who had been largely absent during the campaign, further fueling rumors of animosity between him and Golding, was in attendance at the swearing-in ceremony, as was Simpson-Miller. In his inaugural speech Golding called himself the "chief servant of the people," according to Charles, and he invited his predecessor to play a role in reforming the country. "I want to sit down with you, Portia," he said, according to *El Caribe de Hoy* (October 2007). "Let's talk about Jamaica. Let's talk about the dream that I believe we share for a Jamaica whose people are at peace with each other, where equality and justice reign supreme, where every child can go to a good school and every adult to a decent job, where everyone might not be rich, but no one has to be poor." He also pledged to clean up the government and make it harder for politicians to abuse the system. "Corruption in Jamaica is much too easy," he said, according to Horace Helps, reporting for Reuters (September 11, 2007). "It is too risk-free. . . . Public officials will be impeached and removed from office if they are found guilty of corruption." He added, as Jacqueline Charles reported for the *Miami Herald* (September 12, 2007), that free tuition for secondary school would begin immediately, with hospital fees disappearing by April 2008. "There is much that can be done to improve the quality of governance and the quality of people's lives that do not require large spending," he said, according to Charles. "It requires political will."

On September 17, 2007 Golding held a swearing-in ceremony for his ministers of state and parliamentary secretaries. Referring to the "sleepless nights and nightmares" Simpson-Miller had predicted for the new government, Golding told his team, "We expect to have sleepless nights, because I expect that you are going to be working night and day to deal with the problems that confront this country and, therefore, it is going to rob you of some of the sleep that you would normally get at nights," according to the *Jamaica Gleaner* (September 18, 2007, on-line). Days earlier Golding had said that his father "always supported my being in politics, he was my mentor," according to Howard Campbell in the *Weekly Gleaner* (September 13, 2007). "I suspect that if he was alive today that this was what he expected"—Golding's becoming prime minister —"from those early days." Assessing his career, Golding added, "I think what I'll perhaps regard as one of my lasting contributions to this country is that I challenged the system in the mid-1990s and put my political future at risk. I think that helped change the agenda of public discussion."

Golding has been married to his wife, Lorna, since 1972. The couple have three children. Their son, Steven, is a graduate of Johns Hopkins University, in Baltimore, Maryland. Their daughter Sherene attended Howard University and Georgetown University Law School, both in Washington, D.C., as well as Rutgers University, in New Jersey. Their daughter Ann-Merita graduated from Howard University.

—K.J.P.

Suggested Reading: *El Caribe de Hoy* p16 Sep. 2005, p18 Oct. 2007; Government of Jamaica Web site; *Jamaica Observer* (on-line) Sep. 12, 2007; (Jamaica) *Weekly Gleaner* p17 Sep. 13, 2007; jamaicans.com June 1, 2005

Courtesy of Globals Inc.

Gopinath, Suhas

Nov. 4, 1985– Internet entrepreneur

Address: Globals Inc., 485 E. Middlefield Rd., Mountain View, CA 94043

"I want to be like Bill Gates," Suhas Gopinath proclaimed to Indrajit Basu for United Press International (November 28, 2003). When he was 16 years old, Gopinath was officially declared the youngest CEO in the world: he is the founder, CEO, and president of Globals Inc., an information-technology (IT) firm that specializes in cost-effective Web and software technology for small corporations and educational institutions. Gopinath had already made a name for himself earlier, at 14: a product of the worldwide "dot-com" movement, which gave rise to the so-called "teentrepreneur"—allowing almost anyone with computer savvy to start up an Internet-based company—he established the horizontal portal CoolHindustan.com, which provided up-to-date information on events in India, an innovation that brought him recognition as the youngest Web developer in history. Despite having run into a series of legal obstacles as a result of his youth, Gopinath has expanded Globals Inc. into a multinational corporation with offices in more than 11 countries, including the United States, England, Germany, Russia, Italy, Spain, Australia, India, and Bangladesh. In 2008, the year he turned 23, Gopinath became the youngest person to be appointed as a Young Global Leader by the World Economic Forum. Recalling his ambitious plans for Globals, the Indian prodigy explained to Jay Shankar for Agence France Presse (November 6, 2003), "I wanted to develop a platform for youngsters to develop their talents and to help them understand and get exposed to technology." He added, "When I look around I see [a] lot of guys of my age hanging out with their girlfriends. I do not feel bad as I have a mission to make my company another Microsoft."

The younger of two children, Suhas Gopinath was born on November 4, 1985 in Bangalore, India, the capital of the southern Indian state of Karnataka. He grew up in a middle-class family that emphasized the importance of education. His father, M. R. Gopinath Rao, is an electronics engineer who worked for India's Ministry of Defense; his mother, Kala, is a homemaker. Commenting on his upbringing, Gopinath noted to Current Biography, "My parents always advised me from a very young age to lead a simple life, with humbleness and modesty irrespective of one's success, money or fame." When he was very young, he aspired to become a veterinarian; at age eight he started an animal-protection service with his friends called the Global Awareness Club. Each day Gopinath and the other members went around their neighborhood with sticks to protect stray dogs from harm by abusive children.

Gopinath's ambition to work with animals gave way to his fascination with the World Wide Web, after he began accompanying his older brother, Shreyas, to a local Internet café. Shreyas, who later earned an M.B.A. degree from the Indian Institute of Management, Lucknow (IIM Lucknow), was pursuing an undergraduate engineering degree at the time and was using the café to complete his school projects. A turning point in Gopinath's life came when his brother gave him a Hotmail.com e-mail account for his 13th birthday. He recalled to Current Biography, "I was overjoyed as my first Internet identity was created, and went to my school and distributed my e-mail address with its username and password to all my friends, because I had a misconception that my friends also [needed] to know my password when they [needed] to send me e-mail." His monthly allowance of just 25 rupees (approximately 50 cents in U.S. currency) was not enough for him to go to the Internet café every day, as the café charged 125 rupees per hour of Internet usage; but Gopinath eventually persuaded the café's owner, Shubha Dev, to let him open and manage the shop during lunch hours (1 p.m. to 4 p.m.) in return for free Internet use. It was during that three-hour span that Gopinath began reading books on the Internet moguls Bill Gates, Michael Dell, and Sir Richard Branson, which helped fuel his entrepreneurial spirit. He was also greatly influenced by the Indian businessman R. Chenraj Jain, the founder and chairman of a premier group of schools and colleges across India, whom he has cited as his mentor. (Jain is currently a Globals Inc. board member.)

Gopinath quickly learned the fundamentals of Internet use, then moved on to more complicated areas, such as figuring out source codes to Web sites. He also read numerous e-books and gained further knowledge through discussions in Web-developer forums. His preoccupation with the Web caused his grades to suffer; he even failed a mathematics exam. He noted to Current Biography that that "was the first time" he had ever failed in school and that his mother asked him "to swear on her" that he would stop visiting the Internet café and concentrate on his studies. (His parents were not swayed by his argument that Bill Gates had dropped out of Harvard University before founding Microsoft.) Gopinath eventually managed to balance his school requirements with his Web pursuits, continuing to teach himself at the Internet café.

In 2000, when he was 14 years old, Gopinath launched the Web site CoolHindustan.com, an Internet portal that offered free e-mail and voicemail services. The site quickly became popular among nonresident Indians in the United States and England, allowing them to send audio greetings to their families in India. Gopinath recalled to Hasnain Kazim for Spiegel (May 16, 2007, on-line), "I wanted to provide Indians all over the world with a forum to post public events, tips for eating out and everything else they're interested in." Just a week after he launched the portal, he was contacted by Network Solutions, a New York–based technology company owned by Verisign Inc., which expressed interest in hiring him. (He did not go to work there.) Not long afterward the company awarded him a certificate as a professional Web developer. With that designation, Gopinath, at 14, was officially recognized as the youngest Web developer in the world, as well as the youngest in history. A Fortune 1000 company (which he has not identified by name) then offered him a $2,000-a-week salary, chauffeur service, and an executive apartment to work as a full-time freelancer, but he declined. He explained to Pratiksha Thanki for the Times of India (January 12, 2007), "It was a tempting offer for a middle class boy like me. But I never wanted to settle down in the US and become an NRI [non-resident Indian]." (He has also said that he did not want to move away from his family.) In

2004, after a controversial news article on India-Pakistan relations appeared on the site (as a result of a PHP script that Gopinath had developed that provided automated updates from popular Indian news feeds), CoolHindustan.com fell prey to a group of anti-Indian hackers who changed the logo on the Web site to "Cool Pakistan." Responding to mounting family pressure, he shut down the portal.

Concurrently with his work on CoolHindustan.com, Gopinath launched the firm Globals Inc., to offer Web-based services for small and mid-sized companies. CoolHindustan.com operated as a means of drawing prospective customers to Globals Inc. Wanting to become a model for Indian youth, Gopinath attempted to register the company in India but was refused permission by the government because he was a minor. Still only 14, he decided to register the company in the United States, in San Jose, California, after proposing the idea to Clifford Leslie, a part-time student at a technical university. During that time Gopinath made a short visit to the U.S. to officially launch his company; Gopinath, Leslie, and Gopinath's friend Vinay M. Nellogi (also known as Vinay M.N.) are credited as the co-founders of Globals Inc. Not long after its launch, Gopinath's company was denied an outsourcing contract—worth half a million dollars—with the Singapore-based company Smith and Gale, also because of his age. "Many people didn't take me seriously," he recalled to Kazim. When he began to develop facial hair, he grew a moustache in order to appear older. He even met with India's then-president, Abdul Kalam, to try to have certain age-limit regulations for businesses lowered from 18 years to 16 years, but he was unsuccessful.

In 2003, at Asia's largest IT event and trade fair, BangaloreIT.com, held in Bangalore, Gopinath announced his intentions for Globals Inc. Calling the presentation a "memorable experience," Gopinath noted to Current Biography, "We were able to exhibit our competence and projects which we had already done. That impressed many visitors and media persons who visited our booth. Post event, we were able to market our services more easily because we had already proven our competence." That exposure helped to give Globals Inc. credibility in the eyes of many. In addition to its work with small companies, Globals began winning commissions to create Web sites for large corporations, advertisers, and educational institutions. "Most of the projects we undertake are small ones which do not require a memorandum of understanding or any legal pacts," he noted to Jay Shankar. While carving a profitable niche for the company, Gopinath assembled a team of employees who were 20 to 22 years old. One of the company's most widely used products, a software program that allows schoolteachers to record grades and attendance more accurately, has been distributed to 1,000 schools across India. Commenting on his plans for the company, Gopinath noted to Current Biography, "Our goals for the future [are] to develop a world-class product in the field of education and to develop on-demand Web-based applications for various domains, by which we can create more employment to the eligible unemployed youth."

In 2005 Gopinath was officially recognized by the Rotary Club as the youngest CEO in the world. Around that time CNBC and the organization e-Business Canada named him the youngest entrepreneur in the world; he was also recognized as the world's youngest CEO by many other media outlets, including the BBC, CBS News, the Washington Times, Indian Express, and the Times of India. Since 2005, when Gopinath moved the company back to India, Globals Inc. has amassed more than 200 customers around the world and has set up offices in 11 countries. Roughly 65 percent of the company's revenues come from Europe. In 2006 Gopinath became the youngest person in the history of Karnataka to win the prestigious Rajyotsava Award, presented by the Indian government to individuals in a wide variety of fields in recognition of their accomplishments. Gopinath's proudest achievement came later that year, when India's Limca Book of Records listed him as the world's youngest executive. He noted to Nandini Vaish for India Today (October 22, 3007), "It made my family proud."

In March 2008 Gopinath was among 17 Indians and 245 people in total from around the world—all under 40—to be chosen as Young Global Leaders by the Geneva, Switzerland–based World Economic Forum; his inclusion made him the youngest-ever Young Global Leader. He told Current Biography that the honor includes participation in a leadership program at Harvard University. Gopinath's obligations as a Young Global Leader include attending meetings with prominent business leaders, politicians, and intellectuals from around the world to discuss global problems. Upon finishing his leadership program at Harvard, he will participate in the World Economic Forum's annual meeting in Davos, Switzerland, in 2009. Bruce Nussbaum wrote in his Business Week blog, Nussbaum on Design, as noted by Ashfaque Swapan for India West (March 21, 2008), "In a growing universe of private social networks, the YGL network has got to be one of—if not THE—most exclusive SN around. The YGL grouping is perhaps the paramount network in the globe."

Gopinath lives with his parents and brother in Bangalore. He pursued a bachelor's degree in information science for two years at the M. S. Ramaiah Institute of Technology in Bangalore but discontinued his studies due to his new obligations with the World Economic Forum and increased responsibilities with his company. He has been designated as the Indian representative for the United Nations Youth Federation and Action Program and serves as a coordinator for Indo-Pak Youth programs. He is also actively involved with the animal-rights organization PETA. In his free time he enjoys hiking

and going to wildlife resorts with his friends and cousins. Often working as many as 16 hours a day, Gopinath travels abroad extensively for his firm and frequently lectures on entrepreneurship to students at various institutions around the world. Gopinath concluded to Pratiksha Thanki, "Whatever little time I get, I spend it with my family. I can't afford to watch movies or go for holidays."
—C.C.

Suggested Reading: Globals Inc. Web site; *India Express* Nov. 6, 2003, Sep. 17, 2005; *India Today* p60 Oct. 22, 2007; *Spiegel* (on-line) May 16, 2007; *Times of India* Jan. 12, 2007; United Press International Nov. 28, 2003

Courtesy of Johns Hopkins University

Greider, Carol W.

(GRY-der)

Apr. 15, 1961– Molecular biologist; educator

Address: Dept. of Molecular Biology and Genetics, Johns Hopkins University School of Medicine, 725 N. Wolfe St., Baltimore, MD 21205

"What intrigues basic scientists like me is that any time we do a series of experiments, there are going to be three or four new questions that come up when you think you've answered one," the molecular biologist Carol W. Greider said after she learned that she had won the 2006 Lasker Award for Basic Biomedical Research, sometimes referred to as the American Nobel Prize. "Our approach shows that while you can do research that tries to

answer specific questions about a disease, you can also just follow your nose," Greider added, as quoted by Audrey Huang in a press release issued by Johns Hopkins Medical Institutions (September 17, 2006, on-line). Greider shared the Lasker Award with her graduate-school mentor, Elizabeth H. Blackburn of the University of California, and John W. "Jack" Szostak of Harvard Medical School, for their prediction and subsequent confirmation that successful cell division depends upon a particular enzyme in the nucleus that operates at both ends of each chromosome, at sites called telomeres. Greider identified that enzyme—now called telomerase—in 1984, at the age of 23, while engaged in Blackburn's laboratory in research that fulfilled the requirements for her doctoral degree. The work of Greider and her collaborators, whose investigations focused on a one-celled animal that lives in ponds and (in the case of Szostak) yeast cells, also paved the way for many studies that have connected telomeres and telomerase to cancer and the aging of cells in humans. In announcing the Lasker Award winners, the selection committee hailed the scientists for "pursuing curious observations, devising bold experiments, rigorously testing ideas, throwing aside conventional thought and working with great persistence," as quoted by Juhi Yajnik in the-scientist.com (September 18, 2006).

In an account of their work for the journal *Cell* (January 23, 2004) called "Tracking Telomerase," Greider and Blackburn wrote, "Time will tell which connections between telomerase and health will endure; further, new, unforeseen connections may yet emerge. We did not set out to find a new approach to cancer therapy or study specific disease mechanisms. We were simply interested in how chromosomes are maintained. It may seem highly improbable: a new medical approach from studying the chromosome fragments of a pond creature? Yet the history of medicine is filled with examples of advances from improbable places. Fundamental mechanisms are conserved across species, although one particular species may accentuate a particular mechanism. Given the diversity of life, no doubt many new fundamental mechanisms remain to be found."

Since 1997 Greider has taught and conducted research at the Johns Hopkins University School of Medicine, in Baltimore, Maryland, where she has held the title Daniel Nathans professor of molecular biology and genetics and has headed the department in that branch of science since 2003. Previously, from 1988 to 1997, she worked at the Cold Spring Harbor Laboratory, on Long Island, New York. In addition to the Lasker prize, her many honors include the Gertrude Elion Cancer Research Award, from the American Association for Cancer Research (1994); the Gairdner Foundation Award (1998); the Rosenstiel Award in Basic Medical Research (1999); the Richard Lounsbery Award, from the National Academy of Sciences (2003); the Wiley Prize in Biomedical Sciences

(2006); and the Paul Ehrlich–Ludwig Darmstaedter Prize (2008).

Carol Widney Greider was born in San Diego, California, on April 15, 1961 and was raised in Davis, near the Davis campus of the University of California (U.C.). Her father, Kenneth R. Greider, was a physics professor at that school; he is the author of *Invitation to Physics* (1973). Greider's mother, a biologist, died when Carol was six and her brother, Mark, was seven. Her father's approach to life and work influenced her indelibly. "My father would talk about academic freedom and the importance of liking what you do," she said during an interview with the American Society for Cell Biology (1999, on-line). "He would say, 'You can do whatever you want, but you have to like whatever you do.'" As a teenager Greider was known as "the Flier" among her friends because of her skill in equestrian vaulting, a sport in which handstands and other gymnastic movements, dancing, and balancing tricks are performed solo or in teams on the back of a walking or cantering horse.

In high school Greider enjoyed her science courses and developed a particular interest in marine biology. Unlike many of her classmates, who chose to attend the University of California at Davis or Berkeley, she enrolled at the Santa Barbara branch of the school. "I didn't want to do what everyone else was doing," she told Regina Nuzzo for the National Academy of Sciences Web site (June 7, 2005). Beatrice M. Sweeney, a professor of biology at U.C.-Santa Barbara's College of Creative Studies, took Greider under her wing. Sweeney, who had supervised Greider's mother when she was a postdoctoral fellow, encouraged Carol to try her hand at laboratory research. During her freshman year Greider assisted in Sweeney's lab, where research focused on connections between cell biology and circadian rhythms (daily cycles in organisms' physiological processes). By her sophomore year Greider had become fascinated with biochemistry, and she started working in the laboratory of Leslie Wilson, a professor of biochemistry in the university's Department of Molecular, Cellular, and Developmental Biology. "You can't really know without being in a lab the style of science that it does," she told Nuzzo. "But once you get into an environment that fits your own scientific way of thinking about problems, it just clicks." In her junior year Greider studied at George-August Universität in Göttingen, Germany, a major European molecular-biology research center, where she gained additional laboratory experience. Greider earned a B.A. degree in biology from U.C.-Santa Barbara in 1983.

As a college senior Greider had applied to an array of graduate schools, but she received offers of interviews from only two. "I had great research experience, great letters of recommendation, and outstanding grades, but I had poor GREs," she explained to Regina Nuzzo, referring to her scores on the Graduate Record Examination, which, like the SAT for undergraduates, students seeking graduate-school admission must take. Greider's unimpressive scores on the GRE and other standardized tests stemmed from her dyslexia, a condition from which she had suffered unknowingly during her earlier years, according to Nuzzo. Greider gained admission to the University of California at Berkeley after an interview with the molecular biologist Elizabeth H. Blackburn. "I really liked my conversation with Liz, and there were a number of other people in the department that would be potentially fun to work with, so I went there," she told Nuzzo.

In her research, Blackburn studied a single-celled pond organism called Tetrahymena, which is unusual in that it has two nuclei, the larger of which contains more than 40,000 chromosomes—nearly a thousand times the number in humans. (Normally, with the exceptions of red blood cells and reproductive cells—sperm in males, eggs in females—every human cell has 46 chromosomes.) Working with Joseph Gall at Yale University, Blackburn had determined the molecular structure of telomeres—the "caps" at both ends of chromosomes that maintain the chromosomes' integrity, or completeness, and that in normal cells prevent one chromosome from fusing with another. Like all the parts of chromosomes, telomeres contain genetic information in the molecules from which they are constructed—molecules of DNA (deoxyribonucleic acid), called nucleotides. (DNA contains all the information necessary for the myriad activities of cells and is the mechanism by which traits pass from one generation to the next. In part, it is made of sequences of four chemical bases: adenine, thymine, guanine, and cytosine.) Telomeres consist of hundreds or thousands of repeating blocks of a short DNA sequence; the sequences are specific to each species of animal. In an analogy that Blackburn and Greider have often used in interviews, telomeres can be compared to aglets, the little plastic or metal sleeves on the ends of shoelaces that prevent the lace from fraying or unraveling. During mitosis—the process of division by which nearly all cells reproduce—chromosomes and the genetic information they contain are copied, thus producing two nuclei and, at the culmination of the process, two cells. For the most part, chromosome duplication is carried out with the help of an enzyme known as DNA polymerase. But DNA polymerase cannot duplicate telomeres; indeed, during cell division, nucleotides from the telomeres get lost during the duplication process. To prevent the progressive loss of a chromosome's genetic information every time it is reproduced—that is, over several or many generations—another mechanism must be at work. Among the different theories that scientists proposed concerning that mechanism, Blackburn and her colleague Jack Szostak hypothesized that there must be an enzyme devoted specifically to rebuilding telomeres.

By means of the technique known as autoradiography, Greider found the enzyme in 1984, after working in Blackburn's lab for nine months, often for 12 hours a day. The discovery came on Christmas Day, when, alone in the lab, she developed an X-ray that showed the pattern that had been predicted for the enzyme (christened "telomere terminal transferase" and later renamed "telomerase"). (She and Blackburn described the methods they used to identify the enzyme in their article "Tracking Telomerase.") Blackburn has attributed the discovery to Greider's curiosity and willingness to take on any challenge. "For a student to want to get involved in this project was almost unheard of," she told Rebecca Skloot for the Johns Hopkins Medicine Web site (2001). "Students want to do safe things, and this was not safe. It could have completely crashed and burned. But Carol had a sense of adventure, she said, 'Hah, this is interesting, I want to do it.' And she did." Repeated experiments confirmed Greider's discovery, which she and Blackburn announced publicly in a paper published in *Cell* (December 1985) entitled "Identification of a Specific Telomere Terminal Transferase Activity in Tetrahymena Extracts." "It was a fundamental discovery, right up there with figuring out how DNA is replicated and how cells divide," Lea Harrington, now a professor of medical biophysics at the University of Toronto, told Skloot. "People had been asking how organisms maintain the genetic material at the ends of their chromosomes since the '70s. Telomerase was the answer." Telomerase, as Greider and others later established, is only one of several agents involved in the regulation of telomere length. Others include telomere binding proteins, telomere capping proteins, and DNA replication enzymes.

Greider's doctoral dissertation was entitled "Identification and Characterization of Telomere Terminal Transferase." After she earned her Ph.D., in 1987, Greider spent two years (1988–90) as an independent fellow at Cold Spring Harbor Laboratory, which was then directed by James D. Watson, one of the co-discoverers of the structure of DNA. While at Cold Spring Harbor, Greider worked without a supervising researcher, in her own laboratory. She continued to study telomerase and discovered that it is copied from RNA (ribonucleic acid); specifically, it is a ribonucleoprotein polymerase. In 1990, after she obtained funding that enabled her to hire a graduate student to work with her, Cold Spring Harbor appointed her to the position of assistant investigator. She was promoted to associate investigator in 1992 and investigator in 1994. She later told the American Society for Cell Biology interviewer that the environment at Cold Spring Harbor Laboratory was "very nice" for a young scientist like herself. "Senior faculty . . . are very committed to making sure junior faculty do well, partly because it is such a small place," she said.

During that period Greider teamed up with Calvin Harley, a professor of biochemistry at McMaster University, in Hamilton, Ontario, Canada, to study telomere length. In 1990 she and Harley discovered that telomere length is related to cellular aging. With every division of a cell as it ages, they determined, its telomeres shorten; pieces of the telomere's repeating sequences of DNA are not replaced. In human cells (with exceptions), the telomeres on the chromosomes of a child are longer than those of a young adult, whose telomeres, in turn, are longer than those of an elderly person. (The exceptions are the stem cells that are required for tissue renewal and the cells that produce sperm; in females, all eggs are present, in an immature state, at birth.) Indeed, in organisms that reproduce sexually, the regeneration of the lost pieces of the telomeres, by means of telomerase, occurs only prenatally. After birth, in all normal cells except for stem cells that are required for tissue renewal and the reproductive cells, telomerase is absent or virtually absent (or "unexpressed," as some sources put it—that is, inactive). With each cell division, the telomeres get shorter, making the chromosomes increasingly unstable; eventually, after an average of between 50 and 100 divisions, the cell ceases to divide, entering a nondividing state known as senescence, or it is programmed to die.

Those facts led Greider and Harley to investigate the connection between telomerase and cancer, since a distinguishing characteristic of cancerous cells, or tumor cells, is that they keep dividing unceasingly: in other words, they become immortal, remaining alive until the host organism dies. Other scientists had found telomerase activity in about 90 percent of cancerous cells. Greider, Harley, and five of their co-workers discovered, as they announced in the *EMBO Journal* (Volume 11, 1992), a publication of the European Molecular Biology Organization, that "in immortal cells which express telomerase activity," as the title of their paper put it, "telomere shortening associated with chromosome instability is arrested." Among the implications of that finding are, first, that if telomerase were added to cells or made active in them, the lives of the cells might be extended, and second, that if the activity of telomerase could be blocked in cancerous cells, the cells might once again become mortal. Unlike many other chemical agents used in the treatment of cancer, a substance that would interfere with the action of telomerase would not damage normal cells.

In 1993 Harley left McMaster University to join the fledgling biotechnology firm Geron Corp., in Menlo Park, California. Greider turned down an offer to work for Geron but became a founding member of the company's scientific advisory board. She remained independent and continued to work at Cold Spring Harbor, but according to Lewis D. Solomon, in his book *The Quest for Human Longevity: Science, Business, and Public Policy* (2005), she "became enmeshed with Geron's research agenda because she had embarked on a project with Harley." In 1995 Greider, Kathleen Collins, and R. Kobayashi succeeded in cloning the genes for two protein components of telomerase in Tetrahymena and, using cancer cells grown outside the human body, found that the enzyme could be inhibited, leading to shortening of the telomeres and the subsequent deaths of the cells. Then, in 1997, Greider parted ways with Geron, on the grounds that the company's frequent public announcements about its scientists' research clashed "with what I saw as a very straightforward, honest science principle: Don't overstate things," as she told Nuzzo. "The rhetoric in an academic area and in a business are very different." In addition, in a paper entitled "Telomere Length Regulation," published in the *Annual Review of Biochemistry* (July 1996), she expressed her doubts about the prediction, made by Harley and other Geron scientists, that telomerase might hold the secret to prolonging the human life span. "Although the role of telomere length in signaling cellular senescence is not fully understood, telomere length is clearly not directly correlated with organismal aging," she declared.

In 1996 President Bill Clinton appointed Greider to the National Bioethics Advisory Commission, which offered guidance to federal agencies on ethical issues connected with bioscientific projects. She participated in many public-policy debates and contributed to reports devoted to protocols for research involving human subjects and such controversial issues as human stem-cell research and cloning. She served on the commission until 2001, when it disbanded. (It was succeeded by the President's Council on Bioethics.)

Meanwhile, in the early 1990s, Greider had married Nathaniel Comfort, at that time a science writer for the Cold Spring Harbor public-affairs office. In 1997, when Comfort joined the History Department at George Washington University, in Washington, D.C., Greider landed an associate professorship at Johns Hopkins University School of Medicine. She was promoted to professor two years later and named the Daniel Nathans professor and director of the Department of Molecular Biology and Genetics in 2003. Concurrently, since 1999, she has been a professor in the Department of Oncology. In her conversation with Nuzzo, she talked about the enjoyment she gets as a mentor to aspiring scientists. "Graduate students are a little more open to trying different things . . . ," she said. "I select for people that like to be very independent. It's more like having a day to day collaboration with smart people, and I find that fun."

In 2003 Greider was elected to the National Academy of Sciences. In her inaugural article for the academy, entitled "Functional Analysis of the Pseudoknot Structure in Human Telomerase RNA," published in the *Proceedings of the National Academy of Sciences* in 2005, Greider and one of her postdoctoral fellows, Jiunn-Liang Chen, argued that the looplike part of RNA is static and, contrary to a widely held belief among biochemists, does not switch back and forth between two different conformations. That study of RNA structure turned out to be relevant to emerging research that linked dyskeratosis congenita (a rare, progressive, inherited disease arising from abnormalities in bone marrow, where stem cells produce red blood corpuscles) to RNA mutations. "Suddenly,

the studies that we had done, very careful studies on the structural function of RNA, were pertinent to this disease," she told Nuzzo. "It's another example of curiosity-driven research ending up having a direct medical implication." Greider and her co-workers have since conducted research on stem cells and their possible relation to telomerase mutations. Currently, they are studying mice genetically engineered to inherit dyskeratosis congenita.

In 2008 Greider and Blackburn shared the Paul Ehrlich–Ludwig Darmstaedter Prize, awarded by the Paul Ehrlich Foundation, for their work with telomerase.

Greider lives in Baltimore with Nathaniel Comfort and their two young children, Charles and Gwendolyn. Occasionally, in her lab, she has had her graduate students and postgraduate fellows form pyramids with herself at the top, as a reminder to them that their work is supporting hers. In her scant leisure time, she has competed in triathlons, in which she runs, swims, and bikes. Her husband is a specialist in the history of biology. Formerly the deputy director of the Center for History of Recent Science at George Washington University, Comfort is an associate professor at the Institute of the History of Medicine at Johns Hopkins University. He is the author of the book *The Tangled Field: Barbara McClintock's Search for the Patterns of Genetic Control* (2001). His name has appeared in the acknowledgments sections of some of Greider's journal articles.

—W.D.

Suggested Reading: American Society for Cell Biology Web site; hopkinsmedicine.org; National Academy of Sciences Web site; *New York Times* (on-line) June 9, 1992; *Smart Woman* (on-line) May 5, 2007

Griffin, Kathy

Nov. 4, 1960– Comedian; actress

Address: c/o United Talent Agency, 9560 Wilshire Blvd., Suite 500, Beverly Hills, CA 90212

The comedian Kathy Griffin "occupies one of the most precarious places in the Hollywood firmament: She's an insider who bites back like the ultimate outsider," Nicholas Fonseca wrote for *Entertainment Weekly* (June 13, 2008). "She's happy to attend any star-studded party that will have her, but as soon as she leaves, Griffin is even happier to share the absurd, hypocritical, and often hilarious tales of the rarefied world behind the velvet rope." Griffin's sarcastic and bawdy humor has attracted admirers as well as controversy. Her stand-up acts are often aimed at celebrities' outrageous behavior and have targeted a wide range of public

Kathy Griffin

Scott Wintrow/Getty Images

personalities, from the singer Whitney Houston to the television and radio host Ryan Seacrest. "I've found that life is just high school," Griffin told Adam Sternbergh for New York magazine (August 1–8, 2005). "And I read this criticism of me somewhere that went 'When Kathy Griffin rants, she sounds like the kid who was picked on in high school and now she's mad at the cheerleaders.' Of course! I am! Most of us were! Because there weren't that many cheerleaders." Her unrestrained style of comedy has gotten her banned from several talk shows, including The Tonight Show with Jay Leno and The View, fired from her assignment as a red-carpet commentator for E! Channel in 2005 (after she had joked that an 11-year-old actress, Dakota Fanning, was in drug rehab), and condemned by the Catholic League, the largest Catholic civil rights organization in the U.S., for her acceptance speech at the 2007 Creative Arts Emmy Awards ceremony.

Griffin spent seven years with the Los Angeles, California, comedy troupe the Groundlings before embarking on her stand-up career in the 1990s. The redheaded performer received small roles in films and on television before being cast as Vicki Groener, opposite Brooke Shields, on the NBC sitcom Suddenly Susan (1996–2000). After the conclusion of that series, Griffin developed a fan base in the Los Angeles area with a stand-up act that centered on famous people and her personal experiences with them. "I am fascinated by how celebrities, by and large, don't have a good sense of humor about themselves, and yet they're so ridiculous," she told Julie Hinds for the Detroit Free Press (June 22, 2006, on-line). Griffin has proclaimed herself "Queen of the D-list" (a reference to the film indus-

try's Ulmer Scale, which places the most popular and top-grossing actors and directors on the "A" list and the lesser lights on the "C" list) and has openly admitted to her craving for publicity. Her Emmy Award–winning "reality" series, Kathy Griffin: My Life on the D-List, debuted in 2005 on the Bravo cable channel. The show follows Griffin through her daily life and professional appearances, which range from a sold-out show at New York's Madison Square Garden to a trip to entertain troops in Iraq to her hosting of the 2007 GAY-VN awards, considered the Oscars of the gay adult-entertainment industry. Although Griffin has amassed a large fan base through her reality series and successful comedy tours, she has insisted that she will remain on the "D" list. "I embrace it. I'm a D-lister for life," she told Shelley Fralic for the Vancouver (British Columbia) Sun (July 14, 2006). "I try to have some shame and dignity. But I don't have any."

Kathleen Mary Griffin was born on November 4, 1960 (some sources say 1961) in Oak Park, Illinois, to John and Margaret Griffin. She is the youngest of five children (she has three brothers and one sister) in an Irish-Catholic family. Her father was an electronics-store manager, and her mother worked as a hospital administrator. Griffin has said that she knew as early as age five—when she would gather her family in their kitchen and sing and dance for them—that she wanted to be a performer. Watching 1960s and 1970s television sitcoms, most notably The Mary Tyler Moore Show, helped Griffin discover her ambition. "I wanted to be Rhoda," she told Allan Johnson for the Chicago Tribune (October 10, 1997), referring to Valerie Harper's role as the Moore character's wise-cracking best friend. "I wanted to be like all the sidekicks on TV shows." Griffin attended Catholic school until eighth grade, when she persuaded her parents to allow her to attend public high school. She told Patricia Harty for Irish America (April/May 2007), "My only reason was the high school was so big I knew that there would be a better drama department." (Griffin has said that she strayed from religion as a teenager and told Blase DiStefano for the September 2005 issue of OutSmart magazine that she is now a "complete militant atheist.")

During her years at Oak Park and River Forest High School, Griffin developed her comedic talents as a way to fend off bullies. "Fair-skinned with freckles and wiry, red hair, I was picked on," she recalled to Luaine Lee for the Houston Chronicle (June 5, 2007). "The boys used to bark out the window when I'd pass with my schoolbooks and call me 'dog' and every name in the book. It was my survival mechanism. I thought, 'If I can be funnier or quicker than they are, then I have something on them and they might back off.' And they did." Though Griffin belonged to what she called a "drama clique" in high school, she told Erin Carlson for the Associated Press (August 22, 2006), "I've always kind of identified with the outsider looking in."

Griffin's first acting job was in a commercial for the Chicago White Sox baseball team. After graduating from high school, in 1978, she moved to Los Angeles with her newly retired parents. She studied drama at the Lee Strasberg Institute and, in the mid-1980s, joined the local improvisational comedy troupe the Groundlings. Her fellow members included Lisa Kudrow, who later starred in the sitcom *Friends*, and the future *Saturday Night Live* cast members Phil Hartman and Jon Lovitz. Griffin soon found that she had a knack for comedy. At the urging of the Groundling member Judy Toll (who later wrote and worked on the television series *Sex and the City*), she opened Friday-night performances with a five-minute monologue about things that had happened to her over the course of the week. "Kathy would go out and just talk to the audience, and it was so easy and funny," Kudrow told Kevin West for *W* (February 1, 2006). "We would talk about how she should do stand-up. Oh my God, it was invented for her." Griffin heeded her colleagues' advice and started her stand-up career in the early 1990s, becoming part of the new "alternative stand-up" scene emerging in California, which found comedians mining their own lives extensively for their performances. Griffin's material often revolved around her love life and her day jobs as a waitress and temp.

Griffin began to land small roles on various television shows, among them *The Fresh Prince of Bel-Air*, *Mad About You*, *Caroline in the City*, and *ER*. She also had roles in several films, including *The Unborn* (1991), *Shakes the Clown* (1991), *It's Pat* (1994), and *Pulp Fiction* (1994). In 1996 she became a contributing writer and ensemble member for the Fox network's comedy sketch/variety show *Saturday Night Special*, produced by the comedian and actress Roseanne; the show was canceled after six episodes. That same year Griffin made an appearance on the hit NBC sitcom *Seinfeld*. She played Sally Weaver, whose onetime college roommate is the fiancée of the character George Costanza (Jason Alexander). Griffin's off-camera interaction with the show's star, the comic Jerry Seinfeld, inspired material for her *HBO Comedy Half Hour* special later that year. "I just thought that he kind of acted like a big star," she explained to Alan Pergament for the *Buffalo* (*New York*) *News* (January 29, 1998). "I asked for an autograph and he turned to me and said, 'Oh, yeah, that's about the last thing I have time for right now.'" As a result, she said, "I did a whole story [in my act] where I just slammed him. And for some reason he liked it. He wrote me a very funny letter . . . and then they wrote that my character would come back to the show." In 1998 Griffin returned for a second appearance on *Seinfeld*. In that episode her character has a one-woman show titled "Jerry Seinfeld Is the Devil."

Meanwhile, in 1996, Griffin was cast on the NBC sitcom *Suddenly Susan*. The show, which followed the staff of a fictional San Francisco magazine, starred Brooke Shields as the columnist Susan Keane and Judd Nelson as her boss, Jack Rich-

mond. Griffin played Vicki Groener, Susan's quick-witted, sarcastic co-worker. *Suddenly Susan*'s debut season earned impressive ratings and saw the show ranked fourth among the year's most-watched television programs. "It's really what I've always wanted," Griffin told Bob Thomas for the Associated Press (June 1997). "I love the best-friend parts, the character parts. I like to go in, get the laugh and then leave. My dream is to be one of those actors that somebody looks at and says, 'Oh, I know her, but I don't know her name.'" On the strength of that show's success, Griffin landed her own hourlong HBO comedy special, *Hot Cup of Talk*, in 1998. After *Suddenly Susan* was canceled, in 2000, Griffin kept busy with voiceover and television work, including roles on *The X-Files* and *The Simpsons*, as well as an appearance in the rapper Eminem's music video for "The Real Slim Shady." In February 2001 Griffin married Matthew Moline, a computer technician.

Griffin returned to stand-up in 2002, with a weekly show at the Los Angeles comedy club Laugh Factory. Instead of anecdotes about her love life, her new act focused on Hollywood and the antics of famous people. Much of the material was inspired by the years of relative fame she enjoyed during the run of *Suddenly Susan*. "All of a sudden, I'm working with Brooke Shields every day, and I'm going to [the tennis champion] Andre Agassi's house, and I'm presenting on an awards show, and then I'm hosting an awards show," she told Julie Hinds. "And you get to see all that backstage stuff. I was sort of immersed in the world of celebrity and never knew that celebrities were so ridiculous until I saw for myself." In her act she has accused the talk-show host Oprah Winfrey of having a Jesus complex, pronounced the actress Nicole Kidman's Botox injections to be "out of control," and referred to the singer Clay Aiken as "Clay Gayken." Kristi Turnquist wrote for the Portland *Oregonian* (January 12, 2007), "Griffin's approach mirrors the public appetite both for celebrity news and for knowing how the star-making machinery works. . . . But Griffin also reflects the other side of our celeb fascination: the urge to poke holes in the carefully constructed facades of the famous. Like a one-woman celeb-bashing blog, Griffin has a keen eye for who deserves to be taken down a peg." Despite the number of enemies she has made in Hollywood, Griffin—who has claimed to admire most of the people she skewers—has found that some celebrities respond positively to her humor. "I've said some pretty heinous things, and it's odd, but I've found the bigger the star, the better they are about it," she told Nick A. Zaino III for the *Boston Globe* (May 25, 2007).

Even though her stand-up act was proving successful, Griffin found that it did not bring her the level of celebrity she wanted. In an attempt to become more famous, she signed on to participate in the ABC reality-television game show *Celebrity Mole: Hawaii* in 2003. The game followed seven celebrity contestants as they solved puzzles and completed tasks to earn cash prizes, while also trying to figure out who among them was purposely sabotaging the game. Griffin won the competition, earned the grand prize of $233,000, and counts her appearance on the show as the moment she became a D-list celebrity. (In Griffin's estimation, the "A" list is made up of movie stars, the "B" list of TV stars, and the "C" list of supporting players in either medium. The "D" list, in her view, comprises people well-known for appearing on reality shows.) "I have gone from 'B-list' to 'D-list'. I skipped 'C' altogether," she said, as quoted by the *Edmonton Sun* (January 10, 2003). Also in the reality-television vein, she hosted the first season of NBC's show *Average Joe*, on which a beautiful woman must seek her soul mate among a group of average-looking men.

After attending one of Griffin's stand-up shows in 2003, the NBC Entertainment president Jeff Zucker introduced Griffin to executives at the NBC-owned Bravo network in hopes of developing a sitcom for her. Deciding that her real life was much more interesting than a scripted show would be, the network launched *Kathy Griffin: My Life on the D-List* in August 2005. For that program camera crews follow the performer through her daily life and professional gigs. Her parents, husband, assistants, and friends have also been featured in the show. Griffin's professional engagements broadcast on the show have included a performance at an Arizona state penitentiary; her participation in the Gay and Lesbian Mardi Gras celebration in Sydney, Australia; her hosting of a corporate sales convention for Redken, a hair-care products manufacturer; and a show at Carnegie Hall, in New York City. *My Life on the D-List* has also chronicled some of the woes that have befallen Griffin in recent years, including her separation and divorce from her husband in 2006 (she later claimed that he had been stealing her money) and the death of her father from heart failure on February 17, 2007. Griffin has recorded stand-up specials for the network, with four to date: *Kathy Griffin . . . Is Not Nicole Kidman* (2005), *Kathy Griffin: Strong Black Woman* (2006), *Kathy Griffin: Everybody Can Suck It* (2007), and *Kathy Griffin: Straight to Hell* (2007).

My Life on the D-List earned the Bravo network its highest ratings ever in 2007 and won that year's Creative Arts Emmy Award for Outstanding Reality Program. In perhaps her most controversial act to date, Griffin, accepting the award at the September 8, 2007 ceremony, said, "A lot of people come up here and they thank Jesus for this award. I want you to know that no one had less to do with this award than Jesus. He didn't help me a bit." She went on to use a vulgar expression in connection with Jesus and concluded, "This award is my god now!" Explaining her speech, she told Larry King on CNN's *Larry King Live* (September 17, 2007), "I always think it's funny when the rappers and the starlets and the athletes . . . get an award and they thank Jesus, as if Jesus doesn't have anything better to do than make sure that someone got their Peo-

ple's Choice Award or whatever. . . . Jesus is not busy in Darfur. He's very busy helping Hollywood celebrities win awards." Her speech made national news and infuriated Christian groups. The Catholic League successfully demanded that Griffin's speech be censored during the show's television broadcast, and the Miracle Theater, a religious-themed entertainment group based in Pigeon Forge, Tennessee, placed a full-page ad in *USA Today* denouncing the comedian's remarks. "Isn't it funny that everyone has gotten so high and mighty that they're worried about my little Jesus joke?" Griffin asked Fred Shuster for the *Chattanooga (Tennessee) Times Free Press* (February 27, 2008). "But it paid off big time. I was in every magazine and all over the news. You have to wonder whatever happened to humor in this country. A lot of it is probably just garden-variety sexism. They're not used to hearing stuff like that from a woman. But I'm cracking up because, at the age of 47, I'm 'the envelope-pushing comedian Kathy Griffin.'" *My Life on the D-List* won a second Creative Arts Emmy in 2008 as well as the GLAAD Media Award for Outstanding Reality Program, from the Gay and Lesbian Alliance Against Discrimination. Nevertheless, as of October 24, 2008 the future of the series was uncertain: Griffin and Bravo had failed to agree on Griffin's salary for the next season. Griffin claimed that Bravo had ignored her requests for more money and that she had been talking to another network about the possibility of moving the series. "You'd think that having won a second freakin' Emmy would entitle me to a few more bucks," she told Bill Zwecker for the *Chicago Sun Times* (October 10, 2008).

The comedian has been open about the cosmetic surgery and other procedures she has undergone, including a nose operation, Botox injections, and liposuction; she claims to have had no such work done in recent years. In 1999 a liposuction procedure landed Griffin, who already wore size-four clothes, in a hospital emergency room—the result of a bad reaction to the anesthetic, which caused her bladder to shut down. "I was thin, but I was the fattest person in L.A.," she told Luaine Lee. "I almost died from that . . . liposuction. I had it done all over and it didn't work at all. . . . I'm not against plastic surgery, but I will tell that when stuff goes wrong, it's permanent." Four years later, a botched LASIK eye operation to correct her nearsightedness left her with permanently blurry vision in her right eye. Subsequent procedures have failed to correct the problem, and Griffin is outspoken about the risks of LASIK.

Griffin hosted Bravo's first *A-list Awards* show on June 12, 2008 and released her first comedy album, *For Your Consideration*, five days later. Her latest nationwide tour with her stand-up act was scheduled to continue until February 2009. She recently recorded voice work for the animated film *Around the World in 50 Years 3D*, set for release in 2009. Griffin lives in a mansion in the Hollywood Hills area of Los Angeles with her two dogs,

Chance and Pom Pom. She is known as a "gay icon," a phrase reserved for celebrities who have a large following among gay people, and she has performed at numerous events for the homosexual community and often participated in AIDS benefits. "The truth is, I really like being on the D list," Griffin told Sean Smith for *Newsweek* (June 12, 2006, on-line). "I feel it's the best of both worlds. I get to have a fancy house, but I don't have people going through my garbage."

—M.A.S.

Suggested Reading: *Chicago Sun-Times* p3 Oct. 20, 1996; *Entertainment Weekly* p34 June 13, 2008; KathyGriffin.net; *New York* p71+ Aug. 1–8, 2005; *New York Times* Arts & Leisure p18 June 15, 2008; *W* p170+ Feb. 1, 2006

Selected Television Shows: *Saturday Night Special*, 1996; *Suddenly Susan*, 1996–2000; *Celebrity Mole: Hawaii*, 2003; *Kathy Griffin: My Life on the D-List*, 2005–

Selected Films: *The Unborn*, 1991; *Shakes the Clown*, 1991; *Pulp Fiction*, 1994; *It's Pat*, 1994; *The Cable Guy*, 1996; *Muppets from Space*, 1999; *The Intern*, 2000; *On Edge*, 2001; *Dirty Love*, 2005; *Her Minor Thing*, 2005

Courtesy of John Wiley & Sons, Inc.

Harvey, David

Oct. 31, 1935– Geographer

Address: The Graduate Center of the City University of New York, 365 Fifth Ave., New York, NY 10016-4309

David Harvey is widely considered one of the most important geographers of the contemporary era. His provocative, innovative thinking on such topics as urbanization, economic and social justice, imperialism, globalization, and neoliberalism has greatly influenced his own field and many related social sciences. Nicholas Lemann wrote for the *New Yorker* (April 9, 2001), "After the Second World War, most of the Ivy League universities abolished their departments of geography, and the subject inexorably began to slip, at least in the mind of the general public, into the realm of junior-high-school memorization of place-names and climatic zones. But geography is back. In the past couple of decades, a group of mostly British, mostly left-wing scholars [including] David Harvey . . . have created a field known, variously, as 'critical geography' and 'the new geography.'" Lemann explained that the new geographers have been "promoting a new, more cunning way of looking at maps. When you think about it, geography is a rich subject. Much of the politics and economics of the world revolves around the question of who controls what space, and to what end."

Harvey, who has long taught a popular course on the 19th-century German philosopher Karl Marx, is currently a professor at the City University of New York (CUNY) Graduate Center. His course on Karl Marx's *Capital, Volume 1: A Critique of Political Economy* is currently available free of charge on-line at davidharvey.org. Harvey has written many books, including *Explanation in Geography* (1969), *Social Justice and the City* (1973), *The Condition of Postmodernity: An Enquiry into the Origins of Cultural Change* (1989), *Spaces of Hope* (2000), *The New Imperialism* (2003), *A Brief History of Neoliberalism* (2005), and *Spaces of Global Capitalism: Towards a Theory of Uneven Geographical Development* (2006). *The Limits to Capital* (1982), a study of Marx's political and economic ideology, is considered by many to be Harvey's magnum opus. Praising Harvey's interdisciplinary approach to his work, in 2005 Doug Henwood wrote for the *Left Business Observer*, a left-leaning newsletter, "Maybe it has something to do with his coming from geography, which occupies an anomalous position in the disciplinary universe, but I'm in awe of the way [Harvey] can write about philosophy and capital flows, gentrification and imperialism, all in the pages of a single book." In a review for *Canadian Geographer* (March 1999), Bruce Braun wrote that Harvey's works have "challenged geographers to develop analytical approaches and theoretical concepts adequate for the political project of imagining better possible worlds."

David William Harvey was born on October 31, 1935 in Gillingham, Kent, England. During World War II his father worked in a dockyard repairing ships. "I got a very close-up view of the military activities that were going on during World War II as a kid. [I learned] a lot about relations to the world and the British presence in the world, and what that was all about, from a very early age," Harvey told Harry Kreisler for an interview series known as "Conversations with History," held at the Institute of International Studies of the University of California, Berkeley, and posted on the school's Web site (March 2, 2004). "Since my father was close to the navy and the naval tradition, I always thought from an early age that knowing the world and sailing the world was very important. I was always drawn to the idea of knowledge of the world." As a boy Harvey "[ran] away in my imagination," as he told Jeff Byles for the *Village Voice* (August 7, 2001), and he often daydreamed about the countries represented in his stamp collection. As a teen he roamed the Kent countryside on his bicycle and made a hobby of perusing maps.

Harvey won a scholarship to attend St. John's, a constituent college of the University of Cambridge, in England. He remained there throughout his undergraduate and graduate years and was awarded his Ph.D. in geography in 1962. His doctoral thesis concerned the production of hops (used primarily in the manufacture of beer) in 19th-century Kent.

"Most of the people who taught me at Cambridge came out of either a military background or the colonial experience, so geographical knowledge had been very important to those two spheres of action," Harvey told Kreisler. "After World War II there was a withdrawal of geography very much into an association with regional planning, development, and so on, and so it became very much more a local discipline about what was going on in localities and the like. But . . . there was very little theoretical apparatus for this; it was more of an ad hoc empirical discipline. One of the ambitions I [had] was to give a theoretical basis to it, a theoretical center to what seemed to me to be a fascinating empirical set of issues."

Harvey lectured in geography at the University of Bristol, in England, from 1961 until 1969, the year he published the landmark book *Explanation in Geography*, which called for theory and scientific methodology to be applied to the field. James D. Sidaway wrote for the *Annals of the Association of American Geographers* (March 2007), "*Explanation in Geography* became a philosophical statement for human geography organized around a scientific framework. Almost anywhere in the world of Anglophone geography, someone in a geography department will have a copy on their bookshelves."

For much of the 1960s, Harvey leaned somewhat to the left politically, but he was by no means a radical. Writing *Explanation in Geography* so engrossed him that he was largely oblivious to the social revolution and youth protests occurring throughout the world in 1968. In 1969 Harvey took a teaching job at Johns Hopkins University, in Baltimore, Maryland; there, he underwent what some scholars have characterized as an intellectual about-face, one that saw him go from being a positivist, quantitative scientist to a dialectical Marxist. He explained to Kreisler, "I went to Baltimore in the wake of the '68 uprising, riots, whatever you want to call them, around the death of Martin Luther King, and I was shocked at the conditions I found there. I was really, really shocked that in the wealthiest country in the world, people live in chronic impoverishment. I was really upset. So I started to participate much more in the political activism around that. Of course, the anti-war movement was in full swing, so I participated in that." He continued, "At that time, I felt that the theoretical framework I had been using for my own work wasn't adequate for that political situation. I thought, 'Well, we should read Marx, just for interest.' . . . I found it a very compelling framework within which I could formulate problems, think through things in terms of my intellectual work."

Harvey began to work with the Black Panthers, a revolutionary organization dedicated to social change and defense of African-Americans. In December 1969 he slept on the pavement outside the group's Baltimore headquarters as a human shield, to protect those inside from police brutality. (One of their leaders, Fred Hampton, had just been killed in a police raid.)

Harvey became involved in issues of housing and rent control in Baltimore, and he was commissioned to write a series of reports on urban renewal for city officials. In doing so he was strongly influenced by the writings of the 19th-century German social scientist and philosopher Friedrich Engels (a colleague and benefactor of Marx), who wrote extensively about housing problems in Germany and England. Harvey explained to Kreisler that Engels believed "the bourgeoisie had only one way to solve its housing problem: it moved it around. When I started to look at what some of the [Baltimore government] proposals were, they were about gentrification, which, in effect, would displace [homeless and poor] people and just simply move the problem around. So I made a big pitch in these reports, saying, 'If you're going to address this question, you can't address it in a way that simply moves it around. In order not to move it around, we have to deal with basic questions about income distribution, wealth and the like, and, also, of course, racism, and housing markets and so on.' This was a very important principle that came out of reading Engels." He continued, "When you actually laid it out . . . using these kinds of concepts, people understood what you meant. The only time they turn around and walk the other way is when you tell them where it came from."

In 1973 Harvey published *Social Justice and the City*, a widely cited classic of urban theory. In it Harvey argued that geographers could not stay detached or objective in the face of mounting societal ills. He wrote, according to *David Harvey: A Critical Reader* (2006): "There is a clear disparity between the sophisticated theoretical and methodological framework which we are using and our ability to say anything really meaningful about events as they unfold around us. . . . In short, our paradigm is not coping well." Bruce Braun wrote that Harvey has characterized the body of his work since *Social Justice and the City* "as an attempt to advance Marxian theory in order to make it 'robust enough' to handle the complex urbanization processes and experiences of urban life found in capitalist modernity."

Beginning in 1987 Harvey served as the Halford Mackinder professor of geography at the University of Oxford, in England. He returned to Johns Hopkins in 1993 and also began to travel frequently as a guest lecturer. In the late 1990s he served as a Miliband fellow at the London School of Economics, and in 2001 he became a distinguished professor in the Department of Anthropology at the CUNY Graduate Center, where he remains. Some observers have pointed out that CUNY provides a natural home for Harvey, as it is widely considered a model public institution, in an era when privatization has left few options for those who believe in higher education as a right. Additionally, the interdisciplinary nature of anthropology suits Harvey's own eclectic interests and studies.

Harvey has been most recently recognized for his books *The New Imperialism* (2003) and *A Brief History of Neoliberalism* (2005). According to Harvey, the global capitalist system rests on the accumulation of wealth through uneven geographical development—for instance, the formation of slums concurrent with building booms—as well as the exploitation of labor; that theory informs his analysis of what he views as the class warfare that has been waged from above since the economic crises of the 1970s. The crisis of capitalism, as Harvey sees it, is the inability to absorb capital surpluses, which pose the danger of inflation, and therefore the system must always find new places to colonize and expand in order to continue functioning.

Neoliberalism—what might be called a free-market fundamentalism that advocates deregulation, privatization, free trade, and state withdrawal from the economy—emerged in the 1970s, according to Harvey, as a response to the dual crisis then facing the ruling elite: after the post–World War II boom, the economy had stagnated, and the protest movements of the late 1960s presented a challenge to the power structure. Harvey has pointed out what he sees as the gaps between neoliberal theory and practice. In theory, the state would back away from economic policy in favor of individual liberty and freedom—but in actual practice the plutocratic state works to redistribute wealth and power upward. In theory, there would be a trickle-down effect, in which capitalism enriches all, while in practice, power and advantage rest with a tiny portion of the population.

The concept of "accumulation by dispossession" is central to Harvey's argument. Wealth is redistributed, he explains, either by privatizing health care, public housing, education, and even water (things that Harvey terms public goods) or by taking advantage of debt, forcing people to sell their assets and rights cheaply. Harvey sees the banking community's response to the fiscal crisis of the mid-1970s in New York City as an important laboratory for neoliberalism—a dress rehearsal of sorts—after which members of the elite class realized that they could seize opportunities presented by crises to push through their policies. "The city ran up a lot of debts," Harvey told Joseph Choonara for the *Socialist Review* (February 2006). "One reason was as a response to the urban crisis of the 1960s in the U.S. Money was poured into inner cities by the federal government to deal with race problems, unemployment and so on. Out of that came strengthened unions and increased employment in the public sector." With the economic downturn of the early 1970s, the federal government was no longer prepared to fund those projects, however, and the city began to borrow from banks. When the real-estate market that was fueling much of that borrowing crashed, in 1973, "the city found itself vulnerable to the bankers. The bankers saw this as a possibility for them to launch a coup against the city—reshaping it according to a very different model." He continued, "The bankers had wanted to discipline New York City in the 1960s and early 1970s. The crisis of 1973-75 gave them their chance. They implemented a pioneering 'structural adjustment programme,' shearing off a lot of public services and renegotiating contracts. It was a full frontal attack on the population of the city. Then of course they had to reconstruct it, because they had tremendous interests in real estate values, especially in Manhattan. This is when they started using public largesse to rebuild the city around their project." Thus, in Harvey's reading, the postwar liberal ideal of a welfare state was giving way to the neoliberal ideal, in which the unrestrained market is paramount. That mechanism was then used on a global scale to redistribute wealth from the Third World (via entrenched local elites) back to the advanced industrialized countries. Harvey told Sasha Lilley for the *Monthly Review* (June 19, 2006), "Of course this then became the [direction] that [U.S. president Ronald] Reagan went and then it became . . . the standard way the International Monetary Fund [IMF] starts to discipline countries that run into debt around the world."

Another key testing ground for neoliberalism, according to Harvey, was the U.S.-backed 1973 overthrow of Salvador Allende's democratically elected socialist government in Chile. Under the new dictatorship of General Augusto Pinochet, U.S. bankers and economists again had a laboratory in which to experiment with neoliberal policies. On a broader scale, in order to deal with the problem of excess capital that had created the economic crisis of 1973, the U.S. Department of the Treasury and the IMF began to lend large sums (in significant part, Saudi Arabian profits from oil) to Third World countries (notably in Latin America) in need of development aid. When those countries were unable to pay back their debts, neoliberal policies were prescribed by the U.S. and the international financial institutions it controlled.

Neoliberalism, Harvey has said, became the order of day under the conservative governments of Reagan and British prime minister Margaret Thatcher, during which privatization took place on an unprecedented scale; the U.K. and, especially, the U.S. were no longer manufacturing centers but financial centers. Such financial domination, according to Harvey, has led to a crisis of over-accumulation similar to that which occurred in the 1970s, and neoconservatives have responded by waging war and seeking imperial control over the world's resources.

Because of the timely subject matter of Harvey's books, they received notice in the mainstream press. John H. Summers wrote for the Providence, Rhode Island, *Phoenix* (January 30–February 5, 2004, on-line), for example, "The conquest of Iraq is the central political fact of our time. . . . Yet the big questions go begging for answers: Why did the American government invade Iraq? And why has the government announced its intention to dominate the world by force? The absence of credible explanations cries out for answers. . . . *The New Imperialism*, then, merits the widest possible public."

Perhaps not surprisingly, Harvey's positions have sparked loud disagreement. Jeff Byles quoted Ross Clark, a regular contributor to the London *Spectator*, who complained about Harvey's work "that whereas history was supposed to be about chaps and geography about maps, now geography was about chaps, too: 'It is about homeless chaps, hard-up chaps, and downtrodden chaps of all kinds.'" Clark felt that the field of geography had devolved into "a general depository for Marxist academics who don't quite fit in any other university department." In a review of *David Harvey: A Critical Reader* for *Capital and Class* (Spring 2007), Greig Charnock, a professor of international politics at the University of Manchester, wrote, "For all the rhetoric of theoretical open-mindedness, Harvey remains a resolutely 'unreconstructed' Marxist. And if one central conclusion is to be drawn from this reader, it is surely that Harvey's greatest strength, as well as his most serious weakness, is his commitment to classical Marxism."

James D. Sidaway assessed Harvey's impact on the study of geography: "Whereas the discipline's institutional position, role, focus, and viability continue to be subjects of concern and lively debate, there is no doubt that human geography's intellectual status and contribution to the wider social sciences have been greatly enhanced by David Harvey's work and by those who have pursued the lines and directions opened by it."

"Geography was [once] a service discipline," Harvey told Byles. "It served the military and it served the state. But in the '60s and '70s some of us started to take a line that was anti-capitalist, anti-state, and anti-military. We opened up a space for what you might call a critical intellectual geography." Neil Smith, a former student of Harvey's and now a highly respected professor and author in his own right, told Byles, "If you think of the world as a giant jigsaw puzzle, the puzzle was thrown into the air in the '60s, and now the pieces are starting to come down. Only the pieces that are coming down are no longer the pieces that went up."

Harvey, who lives in New York City, was elected a member of the American Academy of Arts and Sciences in 2007. He has won numerous awards, including the Anders Retzius Gold Medal from the Swedish Anthropological and Geographical Societies, the Patron's Medal from the Royal Geographical Society, and the Lauréat Prix International de Géographie Vautrin Lud.

—M.M.

Suggested Reading: *Annals of the Association of American Geographers* p212+ Mar. 2007; *Canadian Geographer* p105+ Spring 1999, p335+ Summer 2001; *Capital and Class* p149 Spring 2007; *Left Business Observer* (on-line) 2005; *New Yorker* p131 Apr. 9, 2001; University of California, Berkeley Web site Mar. 2, 2004; *Village Voice* p72 Aug. 7, 2001

Selected Books: *Explanation in Geography*, 1969; *Social Justice and the City*, 1973; *The Limits to Capital*, 1982; *The Condition of Postmodernity: An Enquiry into the Origins of Cultural Change*, 1989; *Spaces of Hope*, 2000; *The New Imperialism*, 2003; *A Brief History of Neoliberalism*, 2005; *Spaces of Global Capitalism: Towards a Theory of Uneven Geographical Development*, 2006

Harvey, PJ

Oct. 9, 1969– Singer; songwriter

Address: c/o Island Records, 825 Eighth Ave., New York, NY 10019

"People have this image of me as melancholy, depressed, dark, sad, constantly serious," the singer/songwriter PJ Harvey told Dan Cairns for the London *Sunday Times* (May 16, 2004). "And it's the same with my live shows. When people write about them, it's always 'dark queen of rock,' 'angst-ridden,' 'caterwauling.'" Since her recording debut, in the early 1990s, Harvey has been given many other, similar labels by the press, ranging from "melancholic feminist" to "hunking, hairy,

Kevin Winter/Getty Images

PJ Harvey

end. If it rains, it's flooded and your animals can be wiped out. It just keeps things in perspective. It reminds you of how vulnerable you are." Perhaps because there were few other girls her age in the village, Harvey became a tomboy, insisting at one point that the boys call her Paul. (As she entered adolescence she began calling herself Polly again.) Despite describing herself as shy, Harvey has felt the desire to perform since an early age. "It's a very great need," she told Dan DeLuca for the *Philadelphia Inquirer* (May 31, 1995). "Long before I started writing songs, when I was 4 or 5 years old, I would read poems or perform with marionette puppets in front of whoever came over to the house. It's just a desire to show people what I can do." (DeLuca also reported that Harvey is "uncomfortable with . . . public self-examination." She told him, "I don't talk to people about the way I'm feeling. I wouldn't be writing music if I could.") Harvey entertained her parents' friends with her own plays and was involved in the theater and music programs at school. The greatest influence on her creative pursuits was her parents' record collection, which included albums by Captain Beefheart, Bob Dylan, the Rolling Stones, Jimi Hendrix, Johnny Cash, Elvis Presley, John Lee Hooker, and Howlin' Wolf. "I was exposed to all these very compassionate musicians at a very young age," Harvey said in a 1996 *Rolling Stone* interview, as quoted by Hilton Als in the *New Yorker* (August 20, 2001). "And that's always remained in me and seems to surface more as I get older and have more experience myself. I think the way we are as we get older is a result of what we knew when we were children." Because of her mother's work, "we'd often end up with bands staying with us at weekends. Most of them were blues bands or boogie-woogie bands. There would be sax players, and I used to get free lessons." Her mother bought her a saxophone, and at 14 Harvey joined her first band.

At 18 Harvey took up the guitar, an interest encouraged by her mother, who "bought me loads of [Bob Dylan's] songbooks so I could learn the chord structures," as Harvey recalled to Robert Hilburn. "What I learned from Dylan is to go straight for the heart in your music. I think people often get caught up too much in the specifics of a song and try to intellectualize it, when the important thing is just to strike an emotion. Sometimes just a breath in a song can make you weep." After high school Harvey studied sculpture. (Sources conflict as to where she studied, with some indicating a school in London, others the Yeovil Art School.) During those years she also wrote stories, as she told Hilton Als: "Words would be the spark of the idea that would make pieces of work, always words and never anything else." When she was 19, "the music and words came together," as Als put it. Harvey told the journalist, "I suddenly was able to make a thing out of them, something that could be tangible almost—a song instead of just writing on a page. Something that I could stand up and perform." From that point on, "[my] sculpture stood over

leather-clad monster." While she does not deny that her lyrics—coupled with her stripped-down blues style—can make her sound by turns angry, depressed, remorseful, vulnerable, and sexually charged, Harvey believes she has been unfairly pigeonholed as a singer of songs with dark themes. "I think the most ridiculous misconception about me has to be this kind of angry-woman, man-hating feminist angle, which really isn't an issue with me," Harvey said to Michael Dwyer for the Sydney, Australia, *Sun Herald* (November 19, 2000). "Really! I'm not exaggerating. Interviewers are scared of me. Men are scared of me. Once you're saddled with something it's very hard to shift it. So I'm securely fastened within my dark woman of rock syndrome." The aforementioned descriptions have not prevented critics from lauding each of Harvey's recordings. With her debut, *Dry*, she won a reputation as a welcome and refreshing new voice in music, and she has sustained her following with her subsequent albums: her sophomore release, *Rid of Me*; *To Bring You My Love*, which earned two Grammy Award nominations; *Is This Desire?*; *Stories from the City, Stories from the Sea*; *Uh Huh Her*; and *White Chalk*.

One of two children (she has an older brother), Polly Jean Harvey was born on October 9, 1969 and grew up in the village of Yeovil, in Dorset, England. She was raised on a small farm by her father, a stone quarryman, and her mother, a sculptor and part-time concert promoter. "You most certainly develop a healthy respect for the elements when you live in the country," Harvey explained to Robert Hilburn for the *Los Angeles Times* (May 7, 1995). "If it snows where we live, you are cut off. Sometimes you can't get into town for weeks on there, away from my body. It felt antiseptic and distant from me, like it wasn't connected, because it wasn't. Performing made me feel connected to the thing I was doing."

Harvey toured Europe with the experimental band Automatic Dlamini. In 1991 she formed a trio, PJ Harvey, with the bassist Stephen Vaughan and the drummer Robert Ellis. Speaking with Als, Ellis recalled the band's first performance, at a toga party held in a skittle hall (similar to a bowling alley): "As soon as we struck up, everybody, absolutely everybody, walked out of the building. There was a barman at one end and we were down at the other end, just looking at each other while playing. And then the next thing I knew there was this woman coming down the alleyway, like a bowling ball, straight at me. She just shouted, as I was playing, 'Don't you realize nobody likes you? Why don't you stop?'" Undaunted, the band soon signed with the Too Pure record label, which released their first single, "Dress," in the fall of 1991, followed in February 1992 by "Sheela-Na-Gig." The next month Too Pure released *Dry*, PJ Harvey's first, self-produced album.

Dry received unusual acclaim for a debut, and PJ Harvey was soon attracting attention in Europe and the United States. Marty Hughley, writing for the *Oregonian* (November 20, 1992), speculated that "Harvey's songs are gaining attention primarily because she deals with sexual politics in a fashion that's both intimate and incisive, twisting with contradictory passions: pride, lust, remorse, anger, frustration." The "intimacy" Hughley mentioned has often been referred to by critics as "vulnerability," and Harvey's approach to "passions" is frequently described as dark and brooding—qualities that apparently resonate with Harvey's fans. In discussing the success of *Dry*, Als wrote, "Harvey married the humor and the hardness of the blues form to what she knew about her own culture that was hard and—to her mind—filled with humor. Her intellectual concerns were expressed in semi-abstract, often controversial lyrics, sung in whoops, shrieks, and whispers over the rough sheen of constantly soaring and collapsing guitar work." The *Village Voice*, the *New York Times*, and *Rolling Stone* chose *Dry* as album of the year, with *Rolling Stone* singling out Harvey as the best songwriter and best new female singer of the year. As Thom Duffy noted for *Billboard* (March 6, 1993), John Peel, an important figure in the British independent-music scene, said: "I do think [Harvey's] was the most distinctive voice we heard last year by some distance. You're initially so taken aback by what you're hearing. But you go back again and again and it implants itself on your consciousness."

PJ Harvey signed with Island Records in 1993, and their sophomore album, *Rid of Me*, was released the same year. In comparison with the spare quality of their debut album, *Rid of Me* offered songs of greater density and complexity. At the end of 1993, Island Records issued *4-track Demos*, a collection of unreleased material and the band's alternate versions of earlier songs. Meanwhile, following the release of the successful *Rid of Me*, Harvey decided to record and perform on her own. To compose the songs for her first solo release, she isolated herself in her seaside home, near Yeovil. Upon her return to the studio, the producers Mark Ellis (better known as Flood) and John Parish worked on the album, titled *To Bring You My Love*, which many predicted—correctly—would be Harvey's commercial breakthrough. DeLuca wrote about the album, "*To Bring You My Love*'s tightly coiled songs play out parables of feminine rage, rapture, hunger and deliverance on a mythical landscape, strewn with biblical imagery. . . . This work is free of the stop-start auditory assault tactics that made . . . *Rid of Me* such a difficult listen. The album's accessibility speaks to Harvey's desire to reach a sizable audience. And a listen to [the] title cut, aimed at her fans ('I've traveled over dried earth and floods / Hell and high water / To bring you my love') is convincing evidence of the sacrifices she's made to get the job done." During that period Harvey signed with the management team—led by Paul McGuiness—that represented the wildly popular group U2.

At the time of the world tour in support of *To Bring You My Love*, Harvey added a theatrical touch to her onstage and video performances, dressing in elaborate costumes that were a mixture of the elegant and the macabre. She told Hilburn in 1995 that the idea behind the costumes was to "deal in extremes. You can see right away that there is something wrong with this person [in the video and onstage]. It's not just someone trying to look beautiful. It's someone who has gone a bit over the top. It makes you think, 'There's something strange going on, something very strange in fact.'" Several years later she told Jane Stevenson for the *Toronto Sun* (October 29, 1998) about the costumes, "I look back on it now—I cringe and think, 'Oh, my God, how could I have done that?' But I do think it was something I'd have to have tried at some point." *To Bring You My Love* received a Mercury Prize nomination and two Grammy Award nominations. The album sold more than one million copies and was listed as the number-one album of the year by *USA Today*, the *New York Times*, and the *Los Angeles Times* critics' poll, which, according to the PR Newswire (June 30, 1998), cited the win as "the biggest landslide in 15 years." Harvey was named artist of the year by *Rolling Stone* and *Spin* magazines.

Harvey's *Is This Desire?* was released in late 1998, and despite not reaching the level of popular success achieved by her previous album, it was lauded by critics. Gina Arnold wrote for the *Village Voice* (October 6, 1998): "The album is Harvey's fourth . . . and like [her previous recordings] it's unswervingly truthful emotionally. But she's made the music become less provocative, replacing forceful hard rock with spare and muted tracts awash with bleak, mood-inducing sound effects and foreboding industrial tones. Harvey's musical metier is textures, and she's still growing more adept at varying them, but for all that her songs often sound as if the brain behind the music is burdened by relentless sonic pessimism. . . . To listen to her sing is again to become engulfed by the sulky, sultry, atmosphere of obsession. . . . It is one perfectly hewn chunk of truth, and truth, as we know, is beauty. . . . Though set within a quiet framework—hushed and somber beats, a lush grand piano, and only the occasional soaring melody, usually sung at a snail's pace—*Is This Desire?* seethes with lovesickness; there is nothing worth seeking but love, love, love. But the knowledge Harvey's harrowed voice invariably conveys is that no perfect love exists."

While composing the songs for her next album, Harvey divided her time between her seaside home in England and New York City, where she took on her first acting role, in Hal Hartley's short film *The Book of Life*; she played a modern version of the biblical figure Mary Magdalene. Her living arrangements during that period were reflected in her album's title, *Stories from the City, Stories from the Sea*. Released in 2000, the album included guest performances by Thom Yorke, from the group Radiohead, among others, and saw the return of Rob Ellis and Mick Harvey (a multi-instrumentalist, not related to PJ Harvey, who had performed on *Is This Desire?*). While Harvey's music was becoming less raw—and bore more signs of a producer's touch—with each new release, critics continued to applaud her efforts. In a representative review, Mary-Rose MacColl opined for the Queensland, Australia, *Courier Mail* (November 25, 2000) that *Stories* is "more accessible than her earlier work, without losing one iota of the presence and power she developed with *Rid of Me* or the passion she imparts on *To Bring You My Love*. Songs like 'Big Exit' and 'The Whore's Hustle and the Hustler's Whore' make sure you're paying attention, but there's poetry and yearning here, too. For me, the album confirms Harvey's place among the world's best musicians." In 2001 Harvey toured as the opening act for U2.

Harvey's *Uh Huh Her* was released in the autumn of 2003. Again, she had retreated to her seaside home to write the songs. According to Cairns, the album "may prove a rude awakening" for fans "whose first exposure to her work was 2001's Mercury Prize–winning *Stories from the City, Stories from the Sea*." He continued to describe the album: "Its 13 tracks remove the relatively lush sonic upholstery that cushioned *Stories* in favour of a thrilling, bone-rattling barrage, interleaved with moments of hushed, accordion-flecked intimacy whose closeness and apparent candour make you want to shield yourself from their passion. Amid all the speculation, misattribution and lyric-unpicking, there is an inescapable essence in Harvey's work—whether she cares to admit it or not—which is that, diary or drama (or a combination of both), her songs express things. Rapture, sadness,

rage, love, lust, confusion, alienation, despair. And so forcefully and powerfully do they do this that, even as we dimly recognise that the impact they have on us is primarily due to the responses they trigger in our own psyches, we cannot help but be curious about the person who created them. A person who, according to those who know her, spends most of her time as a nomad, touring, recording, collaborating . . . who cannot settle in one place, or with one person, for long; who eats little . . . who stands on stage, transformed in diaphanous cocktail dresses and stiletto heels, exercising total control over her adoring audiences; who fashions time bombs disguised as albums and moves on to her next project the minute they've been delivered."

Harvey's most recent release, *White Chalk* (2007), represents a departure from her previous work. The 11 tracks of the album, primarily ballads on which she plays piano, have a haunting quality. Harvey spoke about the mood of the record with Simon Cosyns for the England *Sun* (September 21, 2007): "Darkness is just one aspect. As an artist, I feel I try to reflect the world around me . . . and that has many different qualities. Some of them dark. Some of them light and beautiful." She continued: "I love this record very much. I even play it for myself at home, which is very unusual for me." Most critics praised Harvey's newest recording. Jim DeRogatis wrote for the *Chicago Sun Times* (September 30, 2007): "[Harvey] radically redefines her sound by eliminating the guitar, building a stark, minimalist set of 11 songs around quietly lilting piano, and trading her full-throated roar for a little-girl sing-song that brings to mind Bjork or Tori Amos at their mellowest. The difference is that, like a great Gothic novelist, Harvey contrasts this evocation of innocence with a terror lurking in the hazy shadows. 'Dear darkness, I've been your friend for many years,' she sings at one point, while at another, she adds, 'All of my being is now in pining.' The question remains: Where does this pain come from? Harvey's eighth disc is named for the white chalk hills of her native Dorset, England, but if it's really such an awful place and the source of so many bad memories, why does she stay? Is the misery all just an act? When the artist's passion is so compelling, it doesn't really matter. Absent such a powerful delivery, songs such as 'Devil,' 'Dear Darkness' and 'When Under Ether' could fall on the wrong side of Goth parody. But as surprising a departure as this disc is musically, and as chilling and downbeat an experience as it is lyrically, it is ultimately irresistible and absolutely entrancing."

Harvey has collaborated with numerous artists, including Nick Cave, Mark Lanegan, Gordon Gano of the Violent Femmes, and Josh Homme of Queens of the Stone Age, and she is scheduled to release an album in 2008 with John Parish. She also helped produce the debut album of Tiffany Anders, and she helped write, record, and produce Marianne Faithfull's most recent release, *Before the Poison.* In addition, Harvey has dabbled in other arts, exhibiting her sculptures in galleries in the United Kingdom and publishing her poetry.

—F.C.

Suggested Reading:*Billboard* p1 Mar. 6, 1993; *Boston Globe* p31 Dec. 7, 1992; *Chicago Sun Times* D p12 Sep. 30, 2007; (London) *Sun* Sep. 21, 2007; (London) *Sunday Times* p18 May 16, 2004; *Los Angeles Times* p8 May 7, 1995; *New Yorker* p99 Aug. 20, 2001; *Oregonian* p34 Nov. 20, 1992; *Philadelphia Inquirer* E p1 May 31, 1995; PR Newswire June 30, 1998; (Queensland, Australia) *Courier Mail* M p3 Nov. 25, 2000; *San Francisco Chronicle* D p1 July 14, 1993; (Sydney, Australia) *Sun Herald* p12 Nov. 19, 2000; *Toronto Sun* p68 Oct. 29, 1998; *Village Voice* p63 Oct. 6, 1998; *Washington Post* G p10 Mar. 5, 1995

Selected Recordings: *Dry*, 1992; *Rid of Me*, 1993; *To Bring You My Love*, 1995; *Is This Desire?*, 1998; *Stories from the City, Stories from the Sea*, 2000; *Uh Huh Her*, 2003; *White Chalk*, 2007

Hatton, Ricky

Oct. 6, 1978– Boxer

Address: c/o Punch Promotions, 25 Queens Dr., Hyde, Cheshire SK14 5LQ, England

The British boxer Ricky Hatton is one of the most popular figures in the sport in his country. Until his defeat in a highly publicized bout against the acclaimed American boxer Floyd Mayweather Jr., in December 2007, Hatton—nicknamed "the Hitman"—had an unbeaten record of 43 fights, 21 of which were world-championship title bouts. (Hatton gained another win when he defeated the American boxer Juan Lazcano in June 2008.) His fighting style has been likened to that of an older generation of boxers. Writing for the London *Daily Mail* (April 13, 1999), Ian Gibb described Hatton as "something of a throwback with his short-punching style to head and body."

Hatton won his first professional title in February 1999, defeating Tommy Peacock to become the British Central Area light-welterweight champion. He went on to win the World Boxing Organization (WBO) Intercontinental light-welterweight title in late 1999 and made five successful title defenses. In 2001 Hatton added the World Boxing Union (WBU) Intercontinental light-welterweight title to his collection, with his fourth-round knockout of Tony Pep. In the early and mid-2000s, he successfully defended his WBU title 15 times. Hatton's surprise victory against then-reigning International Boxing Federation (IBF) light-welterweight champion Kostya Tszyu elevated his status in in-

ternational boxing circles as well as in his native England. Hatton developed a reputation as a hard puncher with his ninth-round knockout of World Boxing Association (WBA) light-welterweight champion Carlos Maussa, in 2005, and his first-round knockdown of WBA welterweight titleholder Luis Collazo, in 2006. The following year, after earning a unanimous decision to win the IBF and International Boxing Organization (IBO) light-featherweight titles, Hatton scored a fourth-round knockout of Jose Luis Castillo to retain the IBO title while also capturing the World Boxing Council (WBC) light-welterweight title. In July 2007 Hatton surrendered the latter title to challenge Floyd Mayweather Jr. for the WBC welterweight title. Hatton suffered a 10th-round technical-knockout loss to Mayweather. Following his defeat of Lazcano, Hatton put his plans for retirement on hold, hoping for a second fight against the then-retired Mayweather.

Richard Hatton was born on October 6, 1978 to Carol and Ray Hatton in Stockport, a town in Greater Manchester, England. Both of his parents worked for Ferodo Limited, a brake-parts-manufacturing company. When Hatton was 18 months old, his family moved to the village of Hyde, where his parents opened their first pub, the Oddfellows Arms. They later managed pubs in Marple and Hattersley, where the family lived on a council estate, a form of public housing. While growing up, Hatton played several sports, including cricket and soccer. At age 10 Hatton, who was a fan of the martial-arts film star Bruce Lee, took kickboxing lessons for a short time. "I wasn't bad, but these short legs of mine just weren't built for kicking, and that's when I switched to boxing," he told Brian Doogan in an interview posted on the ESPN Web site (December 4, 2007). Hatton followed in the footsteps of his great-grandfather Daniel Slattery, a well-known bare-knuckle fighter in Ireland, and his uncle, a 1930s boxer who was known as Spider Hatton. Hatton's father had played professional soccer with the Manchester City Football Club, from 1966 to 1971, before suffering a career-ending injury to his Achilles tendon. "I always thought that football ran in the family through my dad and my grandfather, until I was told about my great grandfather," Hatton told Gibb. "So maybe boxing is in the blood."

Hatton's father brought him to a boxing gym in Hyde that was owned by Bill Crawley, the first person in the sport to take note of Hatton's talent. "I remember when he walked into the club and we took him to be assessed. He was just [10], and we had a little joke telling him we only trained champions," Crawley told Richard Pendlebury for the London *Daily Mail* (December 8, 2007). "Even then Ricky said he wanted to be world champion so we just said 'Well, we'll see what we can do for you.' When we took him to the pads to see how he punched he was hitting with the power of a 16-year-old." Hatton fought at the amateur level beginning at the age of 11, winning his first match on

Dave Hogan/Getty Images

Ricky Hatton

points. During his early teens, at Manchester City's School of Excellence, he also played soccer. Hatton soon gave up the sport, however, when it began interfering with his boxing. "It was probably for the best, for while I enjoyed both sports it was getting to the stage where I knew I had to choose between them. That made up my mind for me," he told Alan Hubbard for the London *Independent* (May 14, 2000). When he was 16 years old, Hatton left school and worked for his father's newly launched carpet business, R Carpets. At that time he also began to give serious consideration to pursuing a career in professional boxing. "When I used to train with the professionals in the evening, I'd see all these guys who . . . get paid for doing something they loved," he told Ed Caesar for the London *Sunday Times* (November 18, 2007, on-line). "I thought, 'I'm on my hands and knees all day!' That's when I knew, definitely, I wanted to be a professional."

At the age of 17, Hatton began to train with the former professional boxer Billy "the Preacher" Graham, who was impressed with Hatton when he first walked into Graham's gym, Phoenix Camp, in Salford, Manchester. "I'd heard all these things about Richard Hatton, and lots of people had told me that he was the best thing since sliced bread," Graham said to Caesar. "Others had told me he was just a strong kid, and when everyone his age caught up with him he'd be nothing special. . . . The first round I saw him spar, the hair physically stood up on the back of my neck. He was the best 17-year-old I'd ever seen, and I told him right then that if he tried and he wanted it bad enough, he could do anything he wanted." As an amateur fighter, Hatton compiled a record of 73 victories and only sev-

en losses, capturing seven junior national titles and an Amateur Boxing Association (ABA) championship. (The ABA governs amateur boxing in the United Kingdom.) In 1996 Hatton advanced to the semifinals of the World Junior Championships, in Havana, Cuba, where he lost to Timur Nergadze of Russia. Disgusted at not reaching the finals, Hatton tossed his bronze medal into a drawer and announced the following year that he was turning professional.

Hatton made his professional debut on September 11, 1997, at the Kingsway Leisure Centre in the town of Widnes, England, scoring a first-round technical knockout in a four-round match against a fellow Brit, Colin McAuley. (A technical knockout, or TKO, is declared when a referee judges one boxer to be unable to continue fighting.) His U.S. boxing debut came the following December, when he earned a four-round unanimous decision against Robert Alvarez, at New York City's Madison Square Garden. Hatton remained unbeaten in 1998, competing in eight professional matches and scoring first-round knockouts in four. During his final match of the year, against the Birmingham, England, boxer Paul Denton, in December, Hatton suffered a cut above his eye that nearly cost him the match—and his undefeated record. In February 1999 he captured his first title, in Lancashire, England, after scoring a second-round TKO of Tommy Peacock, to win the vacant British Boxing Board of Control's Central Area light-welterweight title. (The British Boxing Board of Control is the governing body of professional boxing in the United Kingdom.) Two months later he added another title to his collection, capturing the vacant WBO Intercontinental light-welterweight crown, with his fifth-round technical knockout of the Guyanan fighter Dillon Carew. In his final two bouts of the year, Hatton successfully defended his WBO title against Bernard Paul and Mark Winters while also earning Young Boxer of the Year honors from the British Boxing Writers Association (BBWA).

In 2000, following a third-round TKO of Leoncio Garces, Hatton retained his WBO Intercontinental light-welterweight belt by knocking out Pedro Alonso Teran in the fourth round at the Liverpool Olympia, in Liverpool, England; Ambioris Figuero in the fourth round at the Spectrum Arena, in Cheshire, England; and Gilbert Quiros in the second round at the Fox Theatre, in Detroit, Michigan. In September he successfully fought off a challenge from then-reigning WBA Intercontinental light-welterweight title-holder Giuseppe Lauri, whose belt he also captured. With that victory, Hatton was unbeaten in 20 matches, with 16 knockouts. The next year he beat the British boxer Jonathan Thaxton, known as a formidable puncher, to win the British Boxing Board of Control's light-welterweight title. The match was reportedly one of the bloodiest of Hatton's career. About 15 seconds into the first round, Thaxton opened up a cut on Hatton's left eyebrow. By the fifth round Hatton had landed several potshots of his own, opening up cuts on Thaxton's face. Although Hatton failed to deliver a knockout against Thaxton, he won the classic 12-round match, on points. Soon after the bout, Hatton underwent plastic surgery to make him less vulnerable to facial cuts. His fourth-round victory, in March 2001, against the Canadian boxer Tony Pep earned him the vacant light-welterweight title from the WBU, a lightly regarded boxing sanctioning body.

Four months later Hatton retained that title with his defeat of the British boxer Jason Rowland, his 24th straight win and 19th "inside the distance," a boxing-industry term for winning before a fight's allotted time. During the remainder of the year, he also successfully defended his title, with a fifth-round TKO against John Bailey; a second-round knockout against Freddie Pendleton; and a second-round TKO against Justin Rowsell. Hatton's next title defense came in February 2002, when he faced Mikhail Krivolapov, against whom he recorded a ninth-round TKO. Upon realizing how resilient the Russian fighter was, Hatton took a more patient approach, thereby tiring him out. "I could see he was using up a lot of energy moving around the ring and eventually I gave him enough rope to hang himself with," Hatton told Frank Wiechula for the *People* (February 10, 2002), a London periodical.

Hatton found himself on the canvas for the first time in his professional career during the first round of a June 2002 title-defense bout against the Irish fighter Eamonn Magee. Hatton rebounded from the knockdown to earn a 12-round unanimous decision. The bout, which was held at the Manchester Evening News Arena (also known as the MEN Arena), garnered attention from reporters, who regarded the match as one of the most interesting in years and also noted the crowd's enthusiasm for Hatton. According to Pearson Guy, writing for the Stoke-on-Trent, England, *Sentinel* (June 2, 2002), "The Manchester 23-year old was cheered on by the majority of the 15,000 crowd in scenes not witnessed domestically since the halcyon days of [the popular boxers] Nigel Benn and Chris Eubank. And the manner of his victory and the acclaim which went with it have marked Hatton out as an undisputed British boxing great." Three months later Hatton scored a controversial points decision against Stephen Smith, after John Smith, Smith's father and trainer—angered by the reluctance of the referee, Mickey Vann, to take action when Hatton elbowed his son during the fight—entered the ring and shoved Vann. As a result of his father's actions, Vann disqualified Smith, giving Hatton the victory. The resulting media fracas and Smith's embarrassment over the incident led Smith to retire from boxing.

In December 2002 Hatton successfully defended his WBU light-welterweight title, with a fourth-round knockout against Joe Hutchinson. The following year, in April, he retained his belt by earning a 12-round unanimous decision against the American fighter Vince Phillips, also a former world champion. After the match Hatton under-

went plastic surgery to repair a gash above his eye, which he had suffered during his match against Phillips. "I don't worry about it any more," he was quoted as saying by the *Birmingham Post* (April 7, 2003). "If you feel sorry for yourself, it's going to affect your performance and you're more likely to get cut again. It's a shame, but I've come back from cuts before. This time, I won't come back before it's healed properly, because the fights are getting bigger now and you can't take any chances."

During the rest of the year, Hatton notched title-retaining victories against Aldo Nazareno Rios, who stopped fighting in the 10th round, and the Ghanaian fighter Ben Tackie. Despite Tackie's reputation as a formidable puncher, Hatton recorded a 12-round unanimous decision, in what he has described as his best career win. In an assessment of the bout, Ron Lewis wrote for the London *Times* (December 15, 2003), "What was so impressive was the way Hatton constantly varied his attack. As well as his movement, he used his jab to good effect and often led with a short straight right—a difficult punch to disguise. He constantly confused the experienced Ghanaian." In 2004 Hatton defended his title four times, recording a sixth-round TKO of Dennis Holbaek Pedersen; a 12-round unanimous decision against Carlos Wilfredo Vilches; a fifth-round TKO of Michael Stewart; and a 10th-round knockout of the American fighter Ray Oliveira.

Hatton's breakout year was 2005, when he faced off against the then-reigning International Boxing Federation world light-welterweight champion Kostya Tszyu, then considered one of the best welterweights of all time and one of the top "pound-for-pound" boxers in the world. Tszyu was the overwhelming favorite, with many speculating that Hatton's substantial weight gain between fights would hurt his chances against Tszyu. In response to such predictions, Hatton told Niall Hickman for the London *Express* (April 14, 2005), "There's no use denying it, I do put on weight when I'm not in full training . . . but any idea that I won't be anything other than 100 per cent ready to face Tszyu is quite incredible. It's the biggest fight of my life and I've already been in training for four weeks just slowly taking off the pounds." The much-awaited bout took place on June 5, in front of 22,000 fans at the MEN Arena. During the first two rounds Hatton caught Tszyu with two left hooks and backed him against the ropes with a series of punishing uppercuts. Tszyu recovered somewhat over the next three rounds, landing right hooks against Hatton. In the seventh round Tszyu delivered a low blow that sent Hatton down on one knee. Hatton regained some momentum in the eighth round, with a series of solid right hooks. At the end of the ninth round, Hatton responded to a series of low blows from Tszyu with a below-the-belt shot that forced Tszyu to the mat, resulting in a standing ovation. Hatton continued his aggressive assault over the next two rounds, dominating Tszyu with a combination of hooks, uppercuts, straight rights, and jabs. With Tszyu quitting at the end of the 11th round, Hatton was declared the winner and awarded the IBF light-welterweight title. The victory extended Hatton's undefeated record to 38.

In November 2005 Hatton added the World Boxing Association light-welterweight title to his collection when he scored a ninth-round knockout of the Colombian boxer Carlos Maussa. With his victory, Hatton succeeded in unifying the WBA and IBF titles. Immediately after the match, Hatton underwent surgery to treat the cuts that he had sustained and was sidelined for six months. The following year Hatton's desire to compete against better-known boxers led him to fight in a higher weight class. Hatton was forced to relinquish his IBF light-welterweight title in March 2006, after refusing to participate in a mandatory title defense against the Australian fighter Naoufel Ben Rabah. He also surrendered his WBA title, before moving up to compete in the welterweight division. In May 2006 Hatton captured the WBA welterweight belt with a 12-round decision against the reigning title-holder, Luis Collazo. Three months later Hatton relinquished the title and returned to the light-welterweight class.

In January 2007 Hatton reclaimed his IBF light-welterweight title while also capturing the vacant IBO light-welterweight title, with his 12-round unanimous decision against the Colombian boxer Juan Urango. In late June Hatton recorded a fourth-round knockout of Jose Luis Castillo to defend his IBO light-welterweight title and win the vacant WBC International light-welterweight belt. Oliver Holt, writing for the London *Mirror* (January 25, 2007), described Hatton's bout-ending shot to the ribs as "one of the most vicious body punches of the decade." After the match Hatton expressed interest in facing the six-time world champion Floyd Mayweather Jr., who had announced his retirement in early June, following his 12-round split-decision victory against the then-reigning WBC junior-middleweight title-holder Oscar de la Hoya. Mayweather had surrendered the WBC junior-middleweight belt and retained his WBC welterweight belt. In July Mayweather came out of retirement to defend his welterweight title against Hatton, who returned to the welterweight division. Hatton regarded the bout as the biggest fight of his career; the media concurred, referring to the contest as the biggest match-up of undefeated welterweights since Oscar de la Hoya and Felix Trinidad battled in 1999. During the pre-match press conference, Hatton and Mayweather exchanged insults, with Hatton ridiculing Mayweather's decision to appear as a contestant on the ABC television series *Dancing with the Stars*. Mayweather taunted Hatton, calling him "Vicky Fatton."

On December 9, 2007 Hatton and Mayweather, each unbeaten in their previous matches, met for the first time at the MGM Grand in Las Vegas, Nevada. Hatton fared well early in the fight, surprising Mayweather with a hard left hook in the first round. Mayweather gained momentum over the third and fourth rounds, opening a cut above Hatton's right eye and delivering a flurry of powerful combinations. Hatton was docked a point for hitting Mayweather in the back of the head during the sixth round. Over the next two rounds Mayweather responded with a flurry of sharp punches. In the 10th round Mayweather sent Hatton to the canvas twice to retain his welterweight title and hand Hatton his first defeat. In an interview for Reuters, Mayweather praised Hatton's effort. "He was definitely the toughest competitor I ever faced. I threw a lot of body punches and he kept coming. No wonder they call him the 'Hitman.'" In June 2008 Hatton retained his IBO light-welterweight title, with his 12-round unanimous decision against the American fighter Juan Lazcano. Hatton, who left his longtime trainer, Billy Graham, in July, was scheduled to return to Las Vegas in November 2008, for a title bout against the reigning IBF light-welterweight champ, the American boxer Paulie Malignaggi. To prepare for that match, Hatton trained in Las Vegas with Floyd Mayweather Sr.

After he announced that he would quit boxing at the end of 2008, Hatton reconsidered his plan, having decided that he wanted to fight Mayweather again, if the latter could be enticed out of retirement. He told Mark Irwin for the London *Sun* (October 18, 2008), "I know if he does step back into the ring, I've got half a chance of getting my revenge."

Away from the boxing ring, Hatton is the owner of Punch Promotions, which is run by his father. In addition, he has his own line of sports apparel. On January 1, 2007 Hatton became a Member of the British Empire (MBE) at a ceremony at Buckingham Palace, for his accomplishments in sports and his work with local charities. Hatton has written an autobiography, *The Hitman: My Story* (2006). He is a devout fan of the Manchester City Football Club, whose anthem, "Blue Moon," serves as the entrance music at his bouts. Hatton lives in Hyde, Manchester, with his son and his girlfriend, Jennifer Dooley, in a home that is named the "Heartbreak Hotel," after a song by Elvis Presley, one of his favorite musicians. During his free time he can often be found playing darts and drinking beer with his friends at his family's pub, the New Inn, in Hattersley.

—W.D.

Suggested Reading: ESPN (on-line) Dec. 5, 2007; (London) *Independent* p16 Jan. 11, 1999, (on-line) May 14, 2000; (London) *Sunday Times* (on-line) Nov. 18, 2007

Courtesy of the University of California at Berkeley

Hayes, Tyrone B.

July 29, 1967– Biologist; endocrinologist; educator

Address: Dept. of Integrative Biology, 3060 Valley Life Sciences Bldg. #3140, University of California, Berkeley, CA 94720-3140

"Everybody has this fundamental interest in little crawly things and animals, and some of us grow out of it, and some of us don't," Tyrone Hayes said, with laughter, to Alison Pierce for the San Francisco, California, publication *SF Weekly* (June 2, 2004). Rather than growing out of his interest in such creatures, Hayes has developed it into a celebrated career as a biologist and one of the country's foremost authorities on amphibian endocrinology. The author of dozens of papers published in scientific journals, Hayes gained the attention of the mainstream press after linking pesticides to alarming anatomical and physiological changes among amphibians native to North America—in particular, malformations in reproductive organs; he has also sounded the alarm over the implications of his findings for human health. "I've been looking at frogs my whole life and, up until I was 21, I'd seen only one frog with a limb deformity. . . . I thought it was so unusual," he told Ayala Ochert in an interview posted on *California* (December 2002, on-line), an alumni publication of the University of California (UC) at Berkeley. "Now, I can drive across the country and see ponds where 20 percent of the frogs have limb deformities, in completely different places geographically. On any given day I can go out and find you a deformed frog." Hayes discovered a link between exposure to the widely used pesticide atrazine and developmental problems in amphibians, including both male and female sexual functions. Hayes's work prompted a letter from the National Resources Defense Council to the Environmental Protection Agency (EPA) that pointed to links between the pesticide and prostate cancer as well as negative effects on amphibians. Syngenta, atrazine's primary manufacturer, challenged Hayes's findings; in a May 5, 2003 document posted on the Syngenta Crop Web site, the company maintained that "scientists have seen no association between atrazine and frog population declines." Hayes's work nonetheless contributed to a ban on atrazine by the European Union in 2003.

Hayes has been tireless in his efforts to alert the general public, as well as the scientific community, about the negative effects of atrazine. "Look, the people who we're poisoning are our country; they're our economy. They're paying my salary. But they're not at that EPA hearing. They're not invited to any scientific conferences," he told Kerry Tremain in an interview for *Sierra* (July/August 2004, on-line). In addition, Hayes is a dedicated and award-winning teacher whose students at UC Berkeley "seem to froth with the infectious enthusiasm that he projects," Pierce wrote. Jean Lee, writing for the *Journal of Young Investigators* (January 2004, on-line), reported that Hayes's teaching philosophy is that his students "should know all that I know." Lee wrote that Hayes "is quite happy to say to his lecture students, 'I don't know the answer to your question. But you know what? No one knows right now! I can even go next door to my fellow professors who are working on this stuff right now and find out, but they still might not know! That's what makes it so exciting!'"

The oldest of three sons, Tyrone B. Hayes was born on July 29, 1967 in Columbia, South Carolina, to Romeo and Susie Hayes. He became interested in amphibians at a young age and studied the development of various creatures that inhabited the Congaree Swamp, nine miles from his home. One of his favorite childhood pastimes involved catching tadpoles, which he then kept on the front porch of his family's house. Jean Lee quoted him as saying to a group of his endocrinology students at UC Berkeley, "I was fascinated by how one cell could turn into a tadpole, and further [become] a frog . . . a completely different organism! One is aquatic and is able to swim and has gills, while the other has four legs, hops around, and breathes with lungs on land." As a child he received a book about frogs as a present from his mother, a homemaker. (Some sources indicate that the gift came from his grandmother.) His father provided him with several issues of *National Geographic* that he had collected from houses in which he installed carpet. "Those magazines were the beginning of it," Romeo Hayes told Elizabeth Royte for *Discover* (February 1, 2003). "Even then he knew he wanted to be a scientist." While his parents supported his passion for frogs, they also stressed the importance of his broader education. "In my home, the kids had no chores. Your 'chore' was to do well in school; that was your job," Hayes told Ochert. Royte reported that when Hayes began dating, he took his prospective girlfriends to the Congaree Swamp—so they could help him catch frogs.

During high school Hayes entered and won several state and national science competitions. As a freshman he observed the effects of temperature on the skin color of a group of lizards by housing the reptiles in a doghouse, where they were shielded from sunlight, and then exposing their extremely thin, sensitive skin to varying temperatures at different hours of the day. During his senior year he studied a group of turtles that he kept in a man-made concrete pond he had built in his backyard with the help of his father. After he scored well on his Preliminary Scholastic Aptitude Test (PSAT), Hayes was contacted by recruiters from top colleges, including Harvard, in Cambridge, Massachusetts, the oldest institution of higher learning in the United States. He applied only to Harvard, mentioning in his personal statement his interest in armadillo biology. His lack of interest in other schools and decision to focus only on prestigious Harvard did not reflect cockiness on his part: Hayes has claimed that he found out about the school only after he "heard of it on [the sitcom] *Green Acres* and figured it must be good," a recollection he shared "without a trace of irony," as Royte noted.

Hayes was awarded a full undergraduate scholarship to attend Harvard, where he planned to study medicine. He found the transition to college life difficult. Unlike him, "most of the blacks at Harvard were from private schools," as he told Royte. "They knew what was going on. Their parents had gone to school there. They flew to Bermuda at spring break." Feeling out of place, he spent most of his time in the lab, which was "the only place I felt at home," as he said to Royte. The summer after his freshman year, Hayes began to reconsider his plan to become a physician after he started working in the research lab of Bruce Waldman, an associate professor in the Department of Organismic and Evolutionary Biology at Harvard, who had been studying frogs and toads for more than 25 years. Hayes became a fixture in Waldman's lab, helping him to conduct studies involving kin recognition in toads and the effects of the environment on tadpole metamorphosis. "I realized what a person who enjoyed what I did might do for a living," Hayes told Royte. "I saw the whole picture coming together." He subsequently changed his major to organismic and evolutionary biology. At one point during his college career, Hayes struggled to budget his time, which caused his grades to suffer, and he was placed on academic probation; he has recalled being unable to approach his parents for advice, since neither had attended college. Support from Waldman and from Hayes's girlfriend (and future wife) kept him from dropping out. His undergraduate research consisted of un-derstanding the development of frogs, particularly the effect that hormones have on them. For his senior thesis Hayes observed the effects of water temperature on the growth, metamorphosis, sex determination, and sex differentiation of wood frogs (*Rana sylvatica*), work that earned him summa cum laude honors when he graduated from Harvard with a bachelor's degree in biology, in 1989.

Hayes next traveled to the West Coast, where he had been accepted into the doctoral program in integrative biology at UC Berkeley. Over the next three and a half years, he continued the endocrine research on frogs that he had begun as an undergraduate. For his dissertation he investigated the role of hormones on the growth, development, and metamorphosis of amphibians. Upon completing his doctorate, in 1993, he embarked on his first field trip to East Africa, a journey he funded himself after failing to obtain a grant from the National Geographic Society due to his lack of experience. There, Hayes studied the skin colors of the African reed frog. (The male and female frogs of most species have the same skin color until they reach sexual maturity, at which point the coloring of the male reed frog is usually green while that of the female is reddish with white spots. The male also has a large vocal pouch—not present in the female—that he inflates to produce a mating call.)

Following his observation that several of the male reed frogs had developed the white spots that are characteristic of the female, Hayes theorized that as tadpoles mature into frogs, they become vulnerable to environmental changes, such as contaminants in their water or food supply, that can trigger color changes in their extremely thin, permeable skin. During his trip he tested the effects of hormones and other chemical compounds on sexual differentiation in frogs. He exposed the male reed frogs to natural and synthetic estrogens, which also produced white spots. He also found that increased exposure to testosterone produced voice pouches in the female reed frogs while the metamorphosis from tadpole to frog was accelerated by an increase in thyroid hormones.

In 1994, after his return from Africa, Hayes served briefly as a postdoctoral fellow at the National Institutes of Health (NIH) before accepting a position the same year as an assistant professor at UC Berkeley. He was promoted to associate professor in 2000 and full professor in 2003, winning tenure at the age of 30. During that time Hayes obtained a patent for the process he had developed for screening reed-frog larvae for reactions to compounds such as chemical pollutants; he called the process the Hyperolius Argus Endocrine Screen (HAES) test. In 1997 Ecorisk Inc., a Washington State–based environmental research and consulting firm, commissioned him to participate in a project sponsored by Syngenta, a global agricultural business, to test the safety of one of its products: atrazine, the second-leading weed killer, used most often in corn production and forest clear-cutting (the cutting down of all the trees in particular areas). The results were to be reported to the EPA. Atrazine contaminates surface water and groundwater, and people with private drinking wells are especially at risk of exposure; atrazine was one of nearly 900 pesticides that the EPA had identified for re-registration and measurement against current safety guidelines. Hayes was asked to evaluate the scientific literature regarding atrazine's effects on frogs, to determine if the pesticide was harmful to them. When his evaluation yielded inconclusive findings, he undertook a nearly three-year study to test the effect of the herbicide on reed frogs, working with the help of his students at UC Berkeley's Department of Integrative Biology. Hayes had initial reservations about performing the study, for which Syngenta paid his lab $250,000. "I honestly thought that the compound wouldn't do anything," he told William Souder for *Harper's* (August 1, 2006). "There was no basis that I knew of for a hypothesis that it would. My concern was how it would look to my colleagues. Would it look like I had prostituted myself to a company to do studies that weren't going to produce anything?"

In 1999 Hayes and his students collected 900 African clawed frog tadpoles (*Xenopus laevis*, a species regarded as "the lab rat of amphibians"); they divided the frogs among 30 coded and water-filled aquarium tanks, half of which contained atrazine and half of which did not. After 40 days, during which the tanks were cleaned and the solutions replaced every three days, Hayes examined the tadpoles, which had matured into frogs, and discovered that in 80 percent of cases in which male frogs were exposed to doses of atrazine as low as one part per billion parts of water (a relative amount equivalent to a grain of salt dissolved in a one-gallon aquarium), their larynxes were constricted. The smaller larynxes might affect the ability of the male frogs to attract mates. At the time the EPA guidelines stated that the safe level of atrazine in drinking water was three parts per billion. Nearly a third of the male frogs that were exposed to atrazine were unable to reproduce. There were incidents of deformities such as multiple sets of testes in several of the frogs, while others developed both testes and ovaries.

In early 2000, upon the recommendation of the other Ecorisk panel members, Hayes conducted additional testing—financed partly with money from departmental grants and from awards he had won, after Ecorisk was slow to approve additional funding. With the help of his students, he observed that atrazine levels as low as 0.1 parts per billion, or one-10th the amount in the previous study, triggered the appearance of multiple nonfunctioning ovaries and testes in the sex organs of the male frogs; the testes produced eggs rather than sperm. Even after he informed Ecorisk of his findings, the research firm did not report them to the EPA and continued to delay funding for the follow-up studies. Hayes responded by resigning from the panel in November 2000.

In January 2001 Hayes met with officials from Ecorisk and refused their invitation to rejoin the panel. He later recalled that he and the panel's leader, Ronald Kendall, discussed an arrangement whereby Hayes would continue his research studies with private funding, from Syngenta—an offer that Hayes viewed with suspicion. "Right after I left [the panel], I told them I had repeated the work and intended to go ahead with publication. What is it that they were trying to purchase? . . . They were trying to buy the data," he told Goldie Blumenstyk for the *Chronicle of Higher Education* (October 31, 2003, on-line). Using grants obtained from UC Berkeley and the National Science Foundation (NSF), Hayes performed the test on African clawed frog tadpoles two more times, then published the results in April 2002 in the renowned journal *Proceedings of the National Academy of Sciences*. The day after Hayes's findings were published, Syngenta issued a statement in the *Wall Street Journal* calling his research inconclusive. In June the Ecorisk panel members pointed to Syngenta-funded studies conducted by three independent teams of university researchers who repeated Hayes's experiments but did not obtain the same results. As part of the pesticide-reapproval process, the EPA prepared to evaluate scientific data from Hayes and the panel members to ensure that atrazine complied with current health and environmental safety standards. The Natural Resources Defense Council, a conservation group, and the U.S. Fish and Wildlife Service's Division of Environmental Quality—citing two studies, including Hayes's—lobbied the EPA to ban atrazine in the United States, citing the pesticide's possible effects on the environment and on human health. In November 2002 the Kansas Corn Growers Association and the Triazine Network, a group of about 1,000 growers and herbicide manufacturers, questioned the accuracy of Hayes's studies and petitioned the EPA to ignore his findings. Both organizations were found to have received funding from Syngenta. (Royte reported that the week before Hayes was to turn in his data to the EPA, his computer was struck by 500 viruses.) Hayes proposed replicating the experiments on the African clawed frogs in three separate research facilities simultaneously: the lab at UC Berkeley and two others selected by Syngenta and the EPA; he was turned down.

In October 2002 Hayes had published in *Environmental Health Perspectives*, an on-line biomedical publication, and *Nature* (October 31, 2002) similar results of experiments involving the indigenous northern leopard frog (*Rana pipiens*). In the study, conducted during the summer of 2001, he examined specimens of native leopard-frog tadpoles and groundwater samples he had collected (to measure atrazine levels) near farmland and from ponds, rivers, and streams in eight locations in the midwestern and western United States, including Indiana, Wyoming, Nebraska, and Utah. Hayes focused on sites where atrazine was used regularly and where it was not used at all. He discovered that nearly a third of the males were exposed to atrazine, and that even with levels as low as 0.1 parts per billion, the atrazine triggered the production of estrogen, causing the testes to develop ovaries and eggs. After examining the gonads of the male frogs, he observed that 10 to 92 percent of the frogs from seven of the eight locations had hermaphroditic traits. He detected the highest incidences of gonadal abnormalities among the male frogs that were collected near eastern Wyoming's North Platte River, a location that is far from farmland and in which use of atrazine is not typical.

In October 2003 the EPA announced that exposure to atrazine did not pose a potential cancer risk and approved the reregistration of the pesticide. (The agency, whose lengthy licensing process has become less stringent in recent years, has come under criticism for promoting the interests of big business.) Upon the recommendation of the Scientific Advisory Panel (SAP), the EPA also mandated that scientists at Syngenta oversee additional experiments monitoring the effects of atrazine on African clawed frogs, which they conducted in 2005 and 2006. The EPA finished its detailed review of atrazine in mid-2006 and again approved the reregistration of atrazine. The European Union, meanwhile, had imposed a ban on atrazine in 2005, after the pesticide was found in drinking-water supplies. Studies on animals have linked atrazine to human infertility, muscular degeneration, heart disease, and cancer.

Hayes revealed to Kerry Tremain that in 2002, on the day after he called his mother to tell her that he had published his findings on frogs in *Nature*, she called him back to say, "Honey, I don't want to hurt your feelings, but I went down to the Barnes & Noble and they've never heard of that magazine." Hayes told Tremain, "She made me realize that the things that counted the most for me—getting tenured and published—are the least relevant. Here you have this important information, but so very few people have access to it." As a result of that epiphany, Hayes began speaking before a wide variety of groups in the U.S. and abroad about the effects of pesticides on humans and animals; he has addressed gatherings ranging from the Used Oil and Household Hazardous Waste Conference to meetings of breast-cancer organizations and the National Water Security Board of Nepal. "I don't know why we're continually surprised that pesticides, which are designed to take away life, create these kinds of effects," he told Tremain. "It's not just that environmental health is related to public health. They are one and the same." Hayes has continued to conduct research on the pesticide. In January 2006 he published findings from two studies in *Environmental Health Perspectives*. He concluded in one study that frogs that are exposed to a combination of atrazine and other pesticides suffer more severe damage than those that are exposed only to atrazine. In the other study he discovered that male tadpoles develop similar gonadal abnormalities when exposed to the female hormone estradiol or a compound that suppresses testosterone. (Components of medications taken by people, those substances are present in human waste and have been found in streams and groundwater.) His current research studies the effects of mixtures of pesticides on early development of amphibians and the potential role of pesticides in the decline of amphibian populations.

For his efforts Hayes has received several awards in the field of endocrinology, including the Bartholomew Award (1998) from the Society of Integrative and Comparative Biology's Division of Comparative Physiology and Biochemistry; the International Outstanding Young Investigator Award (1999); the College of Letters and Science Award for Distinguished Research Mentoring of Undergraduates (2001) and the Distinguished Teaching Award (2002) from UC Berkeley; the National Geographic Emerging Explorer Award (2004); and the Jennifer Altman Award (2005). He continues to teach integrative biology at UC Berkeley and heads the Hayes Lab, where he helps student research assistants hone their laboratory, grant-writing, and presentation skills. Hayes's lab, as Royte reported, is the most ethnically diverse in the department; the scientist told Royte that he makes an effort to work with gifted students who, as he once did, require nurturing. He is also part of UC Berkeley's Health Sciences Initiative, aimed at incorporating the physical and biological sciences in treatment of health problems of the 21st century. He and his wife, Katherine Kim, have two children, Tyler and Kassina, both of whom visit Hayes's lab frequently and have accompanied him on trips to collect specimens for study. The five-foot three-inch Hayes often wears his shoulder-length hair in braids or in a ponytail. He prefers to wear shorts and T-shirts in the lab; for public-speaking engagements he usually dons a black suit, an iridescent necktie, and long, dangling earrings.

—B.M.

Suggested Reading: *California* (on-line) Dec. 2002; *Chronicle of Higher Education* (on-line) Oct. 31, 2003; *Discover* (on-line) Feb. 1, 2003; *Harper's Magazine* p59 Aug. 1, 2006; *Sierra* p20 July/Aug. 2004; *SF Weekly* News/Featured Stories June 2, 2004

Hee, Dana

Nov. 9, 1961– Stuntwoman; tae-kwon-do champion; motivational speaker

Address: A & M Agency, 130 Siringo Rd., Suite 202, Santa Fe, NM 87505

After finding herself at the brink of suicide in her early 20s, Dana Hee began to develop her self-esteem by studying two of the martial arts—karate

Dana Hee

Courtesy of Dana Hee

and tae kwon do. Thanks to her natural abilities, hard work, and determination, within a half-dozen years she had earned many prizes in tae-kwon-do competitions, notably a gold medal at the 1988 Summer Olympics, in Seoul, Korea. That success launched her careers as a model, actress, and Hollywood stuntwoman; she has served as a double for Uma Thurman in *Batman and Robin* (1997); Gwyneth Paltrow in *A Perfect Murder* (1998); Nicole Kidman in *The Peacemaker* (1997), *Practical Magic* (1998), and *Moulin Rouge!* (2001); and Kristanna Loken in *Terminator 3: Rise of the Machines* (2003). She has also performed stunts for a bevy of other movies, among them *My Favorite Martian* (1999) and *Charlie's Angels* (2000) and for such TV series as *Star Trek*, *Baywatch*, *Melrose Place*, *Dharma & Greg*, *The X-Files*, *CSI: Miami*, *Alias*, and *D.R.E.A.M. Team*. Her specialties are kickboxing, precision driving, rock climbing, and horseback riding. On her Web site Hee acknowledged that she is "one of the biggest chickens out there. But what makes me appear courageous is that I no longer let my fears stop me from doing what I want to do." In recent years Hee has devoted herself mainly to giving inspirational and motivational lectures to corporate and government workers and members of community groups. "Through my ongoing quest to face my fears and push beyond my perceived limitations, I have discovered specific tools to achieve success," Hee declared on her Web site. "It is my belief that these tools are available to each and every one of us. All we need is a set of guidelines, a positive, inspired mind set, and a big kick in the pants from an expert Martial Artist! . . . The code words are, 'I CAN!'"

Dana Hee was born Dana Lynn Davidson on November 9, 1961 in Baton Rouge, Louisiana. When she was three years old, her parents, who had divorced earlier, abandoned Hee and her two brothers, and the children were placed in the care of the Masonic Home, an orphanage in Alexandria, Louisiana. Eight years later the children's father returned and took them to California, where she apparently lived alternately with him and her mother, an alcoholic, and her stepfather, whose behavior she has described as abusive. One day when she was 14, her mother nearly strangled her, and Hee ran away from home. For the next two years, she drifted in and out of government shelters, halfway houses, detention centers, and a commune for runaways, all in the San Francisco Bay Area. At 16 Hee became the foster child of the parents of a school friend of hers. As a student at Lynbrook High School in San Jose, California, she joined the track and field team, performing particularly well in the high jump. Her accomplishments in those activities led her to dream about competing in the Olympics. She told *Current Biography*, "I felt that if I could win an Olympic gold medal . . . then my life would be turned around." Hee graduated from high school in 1980.

After the Stanford University track coach Denny Spangler agreed to train her while she attended a community college, Hee turned down a full track scholarship to Linfield College, in McMinnville, Oregon. Her goal was to win a scholarship to Stanford after she completed her core undergraduate requirements at the community college. She worked with Spangler for three months, and then, after what she described to *Current Biography* as "a particularly discouraging practice," she stopped. "I just turned and walked away," she recalled. "I never even said goodbye, or thank you to my coach. I was too afraid to face his reaction." Hee told *Current Biography* that the following years were "fraught with continued turmoil" because of her "ongoing habit of running from any chance, challenge, or dream," which stemmed from her lack of confidence and what she has termed an "I can't" mentality. One day when she was 23, she attempted suicide. By her own account, that act of desperation proved to be a turning point in her life, leading her to resolve that from then on she would strive to conquer her fears.

During that period Hee matriculated at De Anza College, a community college in Cupertino, California, where she enrolled in a course in karate and joined the karate club. Guided by the instructor Irv Ploke, she earned an advanced brown belt in Shotokan karate. She then studied moo-duk-kwan tae kwon do with Debbi Pedersen, Chris Jensen, and Marty Mackowski at Mackowski's gym, in San Mateo, California, where her future husband, Brian Hee, also trained. The couple married in 1984. Dana Hee began to compete in local tae-kwon-do contests in the early 1980s. By 1986 she had dropped out of college and quit her job in order to develop her skills in the sport full-time; she practiced six hours a day, six or seven days a week. During the next three years, she won silver medals at the 1986, 1987, and 1988 U.S.A. Taekwondo National Championships. She won a bronze medal at the World University Games, in Berkeley, California, in 1986, and placed fifth at the World Championships, in Barcelona, Spain, in 1987.

Also in 1987, with the Summer Olympics scheduled to take place the next year in Seoul, South Korea, the Olympic Committee added tae kwon do, Korea's national sport, to the roster of events as a so-called demonstration sport; tae-kwon-do winners would receive medals that were smaller than those distributed to winners of official Olympic sports, and their medals would not be included in each nation's official count. Practiced in Korea, in various forms and under different names, for some 2,000 years, tae kwon do evolved out of many martial arts from Korea and surrounding areas and is marked by influences from karate and kung fu. After the 20th-century Japanese occupation of Korea ended, in 1945, the first tae-kwon-do school was established. Since then tae kwon do has become one of the world's most popular martial arts. In an attempt to standardize the rules, the World Taekwondo Federation (WTF) was founded in the early 1970s. (Another organization, the International Taekwon-Do Federation, was formed a decade earlier and still claims many followers, but the WTF's rules have become the standard.)

In Olympic tae-kwon-do contests, competitors are judged according to their sparring techniques and accuracy. Each competitor receives one point for a strike to his or her opponent's trunk with either a punch or a kick and two points for a kick to the head (punches to the head are not allowed). If a competitor is knocked down and the referee begins but does not complete the knockout count, a point is awarded to his or her opponent. Each match consists of three rounds of two minutes each; the winner is determined by knockout or when a competitor accumulates 12 points, gains a seven-point lead, or has the most points at the end of the three rounds. In cases of ties, the referee determines which opponent showed the most initiative, and the winner is given the match on superiority instead of points.

Hee won a place on the 1988 U.S. Olympic tae-kwon-do team by earning gold medals at each of three trials. During the last of the trials, she suffered a deep-tissue bruise in her back; in order to heal, she was forced to halt her training two weeks before the start of the Games in Seoul. Then, at the Games, as she told Current Biography, she had to contend with "racing-heart syndrome and exercise-induced asthma." Hee competed in the lightweight division (55–60 kilograms, or 121–132 pounds). She won the quarterfinal match, on points, against Ong Bee Eng of Malaysia. She won both the semifinal and final contests by superiority, defeating Chen Jiun-Feng of Taiwan in the former and Karin Schwartz of Denmark in the latter, thereby earning a gold medal. The United States

Olympic Committee elected her along with three other Olympic athlete delegates to represent the U.S. in the 1989 International Olympic Academy in Athens, Greece.

After Hee returned to the U.S., United Airlines, for which she then worked, recruited her to serve as a speaker for its United Way fund-raising campaign. Her success in that role led United Way of the San Francisco Bay Area to tap her for a similar assignment. In 1990 she learned from an editor for the magazine Inside Kung Fu that James Lew, a top Hollywood stunt coordinator and martial-arts actor and choreographer, was seeking a stuntwoman skilled in martial arts for work on a film. Hee's meeting with Lew led to her first job in Hollywood, as a stuntwoman on Undercover Blues (1993), a motion picture directed by Herbert Ross and starring Kathleen Turner and Dennis Quaid. Hee soon secured similar work on films including Demolition Man (1993), The Shadow (1994), Terminal Velocity (1994), Stranger by Night (1994), The Brady Bunch Movie (1995), Independence Day (1996), The Long Kiss Goodnight (1996), Soldier (1998), Lethal Weapon IV (1998), Charlie's Angels (2000), Swordfish (2001), and Gangs of New York (2002), as well as Batman and Robin, A Perfect Murder, The Peacemaker, Practical Magic, Moulin Rouge!, My Favorite Martian, and Terminator 3: Rise of the Machines. In addition to Nicole Kidman, Gwyneth Paltrow, Uma Thurman, and Kristanna Loken, she has served as a double for actresses including Cameron Diaz, Sandra Bullock, Rene Russo, Jamie Lee Curtis, Geena Davis, Jennifer Garner, Nastassja Kinski, Daryl Hannah, Penelope Ann Miller, and Shelley Long. Hee also performed stunts for many television shows. In 1995 she worked on the movie Mortal Kombat as a trainer and stunt double for Talisa Soto, who played the character Princess Kitana; in its sequel, Mortal Kombat: Annihilation (1997), Hee performed stunts for four actresses and portrayed the character Mileena. On a television spin-off, Mortal Kombat: Conquest, she served as the stunt double for the lead actress, Kristanna Loken, and played the character Siann on six episodes during the show's first season, in 1998. By then she had become expert in such skills as boxing and kickboxing, falling from heights, precision driving, skiing (in snow or water), escaping fires or explosions, equestrian arts, archery, wire work, ice skating, and rappelling.

Physical problems stemming from her work as a stuntwoman led Hee to abandon that career, for the most part, and launch one as an inspirational speaker. Her clients have included IBM, Hewlett Packard, the New Mexico Natural Resources Conservation Service, and Future Farmers of America. She has also served as a commentator for local, national, and international tae-kwon-do events.

Hee has twice received a Taurus World Stunt Award (whose winners are selected by the members of the Taurus World Stunt Academy)—the first in 2000, for her aerial work in the movie Charlie's Angels, and the second in 2001, for best fight choreography, for her work in the TV movie *Alias*. In 2004 she was nominated for the same award, for her work in *Terminator 3*, in the category of best action sequence with a vehicle. At the United States Taekwondo Grandmasters Society Second Annual Awards Ceremony, held in April 2007, Hee was honored with the Female Competitor of the Year Award.

Hee maintains a home on a 15-acre organic-fruit orchard in New Mexico. Her companions there include three horses, three dogs, chickens, and rabbits. Her marriage to Brian Hee ended in divorce.

—F.C.

Suggested Reading: *Albuquerque (New Mexico) Journal* p1+ Apr. 22, 2007; Dana Hee Web site; Internet Movie Database Web site

Selected Films: *Demolition Man*, 1993; *The Shadow*, 1994; *Terminal Velocity*, 1994; *Stranger by Night*, 1994; *The Brady Bunch Movie*, 1995; *Mortal Kombat*, 1995; *Batman Forever*, 1995; *Independence Day*, 1996; *The Long Kiss Goodnight*, 1996; *Barb Wire*, 1996; *Mortal Kombat Annihilation*, 1997; *The Peacemaker*, 1997; *Batman & Robin*, 1997; *Soldier*, 1998; *Lethal Weapon IV*, 1998; *Practical Magic*, 1998; *A Perfect Murder*, 1998; *Charlie's Angels*, 2000; *Swordfish*, 2001; *Ghosts of Mars*, 2001; *Gangs of New York*, 2002; *Terminator 3: Rise of the Machines*, 2003

Selected Television Shows: *Baywatch*, 1989; *Melrose Place*, 1992; *Red Shoe Diaries*, 1996; *Team Knight Rider*, 1997; *Dharma & Greg*, 1997; *Mortal Kombat: Conquest*, 1998–99; *D.R.E.A.M. Team*, 1999; *Three Wise Guys*, 2005

Courtesy of Little, Brown and Co.

Hellenga, Robert

Aug. 5, 1941– Writer; educator

Address: 343 N. Prairie St., Galesburg, IL 61401

"I used to have this feeling that at some point everything would become clear, and if I really put my mind to it, I could understand everything," the writer Robert Hellenga told Wendy Smith during an interview for *Newsday* (August 2, 1998). "But now I guess I've given up, and that leaves story as the basis. When you've reached a point where your understanding goes as far as it can, you tell a story:

'I can't explain it; let me tell you what happened.' And at the heart of every good story is a mystery, because if you could explain it in other terms, you wouldn't need the story." Hellenga is the author of short stories, scholarly essays, and five novels: *The Sixteen Pleasures*; *The Fall of a Sparrow*; *Blues Lessons*; *Philosophy Made Simple*; and *The Italian Lover*. All of those books except the third are connected, and all are grounded in Hellenga's experiences as the father of three beloved daughters; as a devotee of Italy, blues guitar, and gourmet cuisine; and as a popular, enthusiastic member of the English Department at Knox College, in Galesburg, Illinois, for 40 years. In his first and fifth novels, set largely in Italy, the main character is Margot Harrington, a specialist in the preservation and restoration of old or damaged books. The protagonist of the fourth is Rudy Harrington, the father of Margot and her two sisters, who, as the story opens, is ending a long career in academia. The second novel is centered on Alan "Woody" Woodhull, a professor of classics at a midwestern college, whose marriage has disintegrated following the murder of the eldest of his three daughters in a terrorist bombing in Italy. In *The Italian Lover*, Hellenga again focused on Margot, many years after the events of *The Sixteen Pleasures*, and paired her up with Woody. "I'm a great believer in discovering things as you write and not planning too much," he told Wendy Smith. "I try to sit down, not with the attitude 'I've got to grind this stuff out' but 'What will I learn about this character today as I'm fooling around?' I do a lot of planning too, but I want to be open to the story's possibilities."

"One of the most widely praised novelists in America, Robert Hellenga is also, paradoxically, one of the least well-known," Alan Cheuse wrote for the *Chicago Tribune* (March 12, 2006). "Despite scores of positive reviews for his first three novels, for one reason or another you just don't find his name on most lists of America's most admired fiction writers. Let's say his name. Let's add him to the lists. Because with the publication of *Philosophy Made Simple*, his fourth book, Hellenga once again has produced a novel that adds immeasurably to the pleasures of reading contemporary fiction. His ability to ground his intelligence in the everyday and produce novels that are smart and intellectually engaging while at the same time emotionally compelling is a rare thing. Many's the writer who tries it, but the results are almost always off to one side or the other. Not so for Hellenga . . . as this new book makes plain."

Robert Riner Hellenga was born in Milwaukee, Wisconsin, on August 5, 1941 to Theodore Edward ("Ted") Hellenga and the former Marjorie Johnson. His surname is of Dutch origin. He grew up in Three Oaks, a village in southern Michigan, where he and his parents regularly attended a Methodist church. Ted Hellenga's job involved sales of produce, and in the summer it took him to Milwaukee (about 180 miles northwest of Three Oaks). Hellenga and his mother spent summers in Milwaukee with him, and there, young Robert became acquainted with his father's helpers, most of whom were Italian. "In retrospect I see that this is how I got my first sense of Italy as something opposed to small-town Midwestern Protestant culture—a theme that has shaped a lot of my writing," Hellenga noted on his personal Web site. In an interview for bookbrowse.com (2005), he recalled that when he was young, one of his grandmothers read stories about King Arthur to him, and his mother would read to him novels by Charles Dickens. "Literature has always played a very important role in my life," he said.

Hellenga attended Three Oaks High School (1955–59) and then the University of Michigan, graduating in 1963 with a B.A. in English with high honors; he was elected to Phi Beta Kappa, the national honor society. In August of that year he married. With his wife, he spent the next academic year in Northern Ireland, where, supported by an International Exchange Fellowship, he studied Greek and English at Queen's University–Belfast. The next academic year he studied comparative literature at the University of North Carolina, under a Woodrow Wilson Fellowship. In 1965, with a National Defense Education Act (NDEA) fellowship, he enrolled in the doctoral program in English at Princeton University, in Princeton, New Jersey. His dissertation examined Thomas Underdowne's 1587 translation into Renaissance English of a Latin version of the third-century romance *Aethiopica* ("Ethiopian History"), written in Greek by Heliodorus. Hellenga's first two daughters were born while he was at Princeton. Immediately after he earned a Ph.D., in 1968, he joined the English Department at Knox College, in Galesburg, Illinois.

Founded by opponents of slavery in 1837, Knox has been named in the influential (and controversial) rankings of best American colleges produced annually by *U.S. News & World Report*. Hellenga

taught introductory courses in composition, fiction, poetry, philosophy and literature, and classical mythology; for higher-level students, he taught classes in subjects including the English Renaissance; the British writers Thomas Malory, William Shakespeare, and John Milton; Greek drama; and literary criticism. In 1973–74 he co-directed the Newberry Library Seminar in the Humanities, in Chicago, Illinois, a graduate-level program offered to undergraduates enrolled at Knox or any of the other 13 member institutions of the Associated Colleges of the Midwest (ACM). That year seminar students carried out research on topics related to the theme "The Search for Community." In 1982–83 Hellenga directed the ACM's program in Florence, Italy, where he taught courses entitled "Virgil and Dante" and "The Concept of the Renaissance." His wife and children (his third daughter had been born by then) also spent the year in Florence. Since 2002 Hellenga has held the titles George Appleton Lawrence distinguished service professor emeritus of English and distinguished writer-in-residence at Knox. He has continued to teach courses in fiction writing and classical mythology.

"I did not set out to be a writer," Hellenga recalled in an essay for the *Gettysburg Review* (Autumn 2001) called "A Writer's Christmas." "I set out . . . to be a teacher. It seemed presumptuous to write new stuff when there was so much great old stuff. What was the point?" With time, though, Hellenga became increasingly interested in Knox College's creative-writing program. "I didn't pay too much attention to it when I first came," he wrote in his *Gettysburg Review* essay, "but everyone made such a fuss over the student stories that I thought, I can write stuff like this, and then maybe people will make a fuss over me." He added, "It worked, but it took a long time."

The year 1973 marked Hellenga's debut as a published author, with the appearance in print of a short story ("Russian Dreams," in the *Iowa Review*) and a scholarly article ("Hamlet in the Classroom," in *College English*). During the next two decades, 10 other stories by him were published, in the *Chicago Review, Columbia, Ascent, Farmer's Market*, the *Chicago Tribune Magazine, TriQuarterly, Crazyhorse*, the *Mississippi Valley Review*, and the *California Quarterly*. "The Mountain of Lights," published in the *California Quarterly* in 1982, was listed in *Best American Short Stories 1983* and reprinted in *Best Short Stories from the California Quarterly, 1971–1985*. Hellenga also wrote additional articles for professional journals, among them "Shakespeare: Our Contemporary?," for the journal *Teaching Shakespeare*; "Elizabethan Dramatic Conventions and Elizabethan Reality," for *Renaissance Drama*; and "What Is a Literary Experience Like?," for *New Literary History*. Meanwhile, Hellenga had also written two novels. The first was never published. The second, *The Sixteen Pleasures*, received 39 rejections before Soho Press, a small, independent New York City firm, bought the rights to publish it, for $5,000. By that time some three years had passed since Hellenga had finished writing *The Sixteen Pleasures*; indeed, he had almost completed his next book, *The Fall of a Sparrow*.

The title of *The Sixteen Pleasures* (1994) refers to *I Modi* ("The Ways"), a 1520s volume of sexually explicit engravings by Marcantonio Raimondi (based on erotic paintings by Giulio Romano) that accompanied 16 sonnets by the Italian poet Pietro Aretino. The most important work of Renaissance erotica, it was condemned by Pope Clement VII, who ordered that all copies be destroyed. As far as is known, only a few fragments of *I Modi* still exist. *The Sixteen Pleasures* is set in 1966, in the aftermath of the flood that inundated much of Florence on November 4 of that year. The protagonist, Margot Harrington, is an American book conservator who works at the Newberry Library; she has come to Florence to help salvage some of the millions of volumes damaged by the floodwaters, or, in her words, "to save whatever could be saved, including myself. . . . I wanted to break the mold in which my life was hardening, and I thought this might be a way to do it." While ministering to books in a convent library, she discovers that a copy of *I Modi* has survived there, hidden between the pages of a prayer book. The convent's head is eager to raise money for the convent and keep *I Modi* from falling into the hands of her nemesis, the local bishop, and at her request, Margot sells the book. "Everything about the narrator and heroine of this novel is appealing right from the first paragraph, in which she sets out the basic facts . . . ," a reviewer for the *New Yorker* wrote in 1994, as quoted on Hellenga's Web site. "What is amazing here is how intensely you care about everything that happens to this woman, and not just in the obvious matters of love and money: the suspense is so sharp that you find yourself checking ahead to make sure she doesn't miss a train. Like her, the book is modest, resourceful, and without malice–it is high-minded and fine. So after skipping ahead to slow your heart you go back to read each elegantly moving word." Mark Mitchell, in a critique for the *New York Times Book Review* (May 8, 1994), reacted differently; after he described *The Sixteen Pleasures* as "well told," he complained, "There are aggravations as well as pleasures here, however. Margot is, in truth, less interesting than the book in her care (except for her relationship to that book): she is a serviceable protagonist, not a memorable one. And the author's habit of using Italian words and phrases when English ones would do seems self-conscious. Nonetheless, Mr. Hellenga has written a lively first novel that communicates the heady peril, as well as the adventure, of Florence after the flood."

Portions of Hellenga's second novel, *The Fall of a Sparrow* (1998), are also set in Italy. One inspiration for its plot was the bombing by neofascists on August 2, 1980 of the waiting room of Bologna, Italy's, main train station. The explosion killed 85 people, many of them tourists, and injured more than 200 others. The apprehension of the perpetrators was hampered by members of the Italian military-intelligence agency, who tried to pin responsibility for the bombing on a group that had no part in it. Also figuring in Hellenga's story is the association that relatives of the victims formed, with the goal of ensuring that the investigation would be carried out honestly and transparently and the bombers brought to justice. The protagonist in *The Fall of a Sparrow* is Alan "Woody" Woodhull, a middle-aged classics professor at the fictional St. Clair College, in rural Illinois. (There is a real four-year college and a real community college with that name, in Canada and Michigan, respectively.) The story opens half a dozen years after the murder of the first of Woody's three daughters, Carolyn (nicknamed Cookie), in the Bologna bombing. In the wake of the tragedy, Woody and his wife have grown distant; his wife's increasing immersion in Catholicism leads her to renounce her worldly life and join a convent. Meanwhile, Woody, though still powerfully gripped by grief, has attempted to return to a semblance of normalcy. For the first time since Cookie's death, he throws a party at his house, and before the night is over, one of his students, the daughter of a major St. Clair College benefactor, has seduced him. The ensuing affair, which imperils his job, and his deepening involvement with the Italy-based association of Bologna bombing-victims' relatives, spurs him to travel to Bologna, where he attends the trial of several of the terrorists; he also meets the father of a female terrorist and later visits the woman in prison. In addition, he becomes romantically involved with his Italian landlady. "Hellenga's masterful and compassionate novel . . . [is] suffused in the humanist tradition, erudite and wise . . . ," a reviewer for the *Economist* (April 10, 1999) wrote. "For all its musings and gloomy theme, [it] is a novel steeped in pleasure and the love of life." In a critique of *The Fall of a Sparrow* for *Multicultural Education* (Spring 1999), Ted D. Ayres wrote, "Hellenga writes with a dry and subtle humor and he writes well, putting his words to good use. He clearly speaks with knowledge and experience as he writes about campus politics and as he touches upon the sometime arrogance and narrow-mindedness of academe. Likewise, he appears to know about Italy. . . . In this book, he also writes with seeming authority on a number of diverse topics, e.g., bats, the blues, guitars, cooking, classical literature, teaching, and the timely topic of terrorism. The depth of his actual knowledge may be subject to debate, but he writes convincingly and with confidence. While *The Fall of a Sparrow* is not a great book, it is a good book, and a very entertaining read." In an article called "The Best Novels You've Never Read," in *New York* (June 4, 2007), the political columnist and feminist Katha Pollitt wrote, "*The Fall of a Sparrow* didn't get the love lavished on Hellenga's first novel, *The Sixteen Pleasures,* but to my mind it's an even richer, profounder book. *The Fall of a Sparrow* raises all the old deep questions about cosmic justice and the lack thereof, but also has much to say about Oriental carpets, Delta blues, Parmesan cheese, Latin poetry, and finding a new life when your old one has exploded." The *Los Angeles Times* and *Publishers Weekly* included *The Fall of a Sparrow* in their lists of the best books of 1998.

"A Writer's Christmas" was published while Hellenga was working on *Blues Lessons*. "My first two novels," he wrote in that essay, "begin with a father and three daughters, just like the old fairy tales. Just like our family (except that in the novels the family is destabilized by the death or disappearance of the mother). Then the main character, who is stuck in his or her life, goes to Italy and has some adventures and discovers some good things. The advantage of writing about Italy is that it gives me a good reason to go to Italy, but I think I'd better not do that again, so my third novel will be set in Chicago. No one will go to Italy unless I get really really stuck, nor will the main character have three daughters. I want to get away from that too. But I can't get away from it entirely. Without a daughter I don't know what to do, so I have given my protagonist an illegitimate daughter, fathered when he was a senior in high school, and this daughter is becoming increasingly important. I can't help myself. I can't displace my own daughters from the center of my imagination. They are the mainspring. Three wonderful sister-daughters who—unlike the three sister-daughters in the fairy tales—all get along with each other, who have all found love and meaningful work in the world, and who are all glad to be home for Christmas."

Blues Lessons (2002) "expands on themes touched upon in his earlier work: parenthood, loss and the place of art in one's life," as Valerie Ryan wrote in a review of the book for the *Seattle Times* (February 10, 2002). The story begins in the mid-1950s in the town of Appleton, Wisconsin. While still in high school, Martin Dijksterhuis impregnates his girlfriend, Corinna "Cory" Williams, the daughter of the foreman on his family's apple orchard. Neither his parents nor Cory's, who are black, accede to Martin's request to marry Cory, and to ensure that he will attend college, Martin's mother and father pay Cory's family to leave town permanently. Infuriated, Martin joins the navy, turning his back on school, his family, and the family business. After he completes his stint in the military, he works as a clerk in a railroad post office until he finds his true vocation—playing the blues. He enters his daughter's life when the child is eight years old. Martin's story unfolds as the civil rights movement gains strength and increasing emphasis is placed on awareness of black culture and traditions. In a representative review, John Green wrote for *Booklist*, as quoted on Amazon.com, "What seems at first to be a trite love story becomes something much better, a large-hearted novel that is finally about vocation: What are we to do, how are we to do it, and with whom? Hellen-

ga's lush sense of place and powerful prose prove sturdy enough to handle these themes." "Hellenga imparts his personal passion for music, explores issues of place, race, class and destiny with a sure hand and doesn't preach," Valerie Ryan wrote. "All in all, a treat to read."

The title of Hellenga's fourth novel, *Philosophy Made Simple* (2006), is also the title of a book that Rudy Harrington, the main character, reads throughout the course of the story. It is 1966; the Arno has overflowed its banks in Florence, and Rudy's daughter Margot has gone there to rescue sodden books. Unhappy in his empty nest—his wife died years earlier, and his other two daughters live elsewhere—Rudy retires from his job, sells his house, and moves to Texas, where he has bought an avocado orchard sight unseen. In his new environment he forges new friendships, takes on new responsibilities—including the care of a former circus elephant—and gains insights about life through his readings in philosophy. The philosophical discussions struck some critics as heavy-handed or "too simple," "dangerously close to patronizing its characters and readers," as Polly Shulman wrote for *Newsday* (March 12, 2006), but the book as a whole earned much praise. "Hellenga is up to something serious beneath the charmingly picaresque tale of Rudy Harrington. . . . [whose] unlikely adventures are accompanied by his earnest reflections on the meaning of it all, understood in the largest terms possible . . . ," Rebecca Newberger Goldstein wrote for the *New York Times Book Review* (April 23, 2006). "Harrington's determination to filter what he is experiencing through the ideas of Plato et al. are touchingly sincere and sometimes comically naive. Harrington may fall short in grasping Kant's notion of the *Ding an sich*, the thing in itself. . . . But Hellenga does not intend us to think any less of him."

In *The Italian Lover* (2007), Margot Harrington is living in Florence, where, over the course of three decades, she has established herself as a skilled book conservator. She has also had a long series of amorous relationships, none of which brought her as much happiness as she is currently enjoying with her new lover, Woody Woodhull. Woody is helping Margot to write a screenplay about the events surrounding her discovery and sale of *I Modi*. Meanwhile, the recently divorced filmmaker who has come to Florence to work on that project intends to use a very different screenplay. The actor and actress who will star in the film add to the volatility of the situation. "Part of what makes this book so enjoyable is Hellenga's simple treatment of complex emotions and situations," Stephanie Rebein wrote for the *Tampa (Florida) Tribune* (November 4, 2007). "His direct, plain-spoken prose is a pleasure to read and helps keep the complex plot on course. His fans will surely be thrilled with this latest installation of a story arc spanning 25 years. And for those new to his work, although it isn't necessary to read his novels in order, the rich history of Margot to be found in *The*

Sixteen Pleasures and later in *Philosophy Made Simple*, along with Woody's story from *The Fall of a Sparrow*, makes this work, where both are main characters, even more of a treasure." The Cleveland, Ohio, *Plain Dealer* (September 30, 2007) critic, Kevin R. Long, wrote, "Hellenga uses a deceptively light touch to restart Margot's story, dividing *The Italian Lover* into preproduction, production and postproduction sections that mirror the film. His segments can be choppy, and a few moments strain, but most of this story about art, literature, love and handling happiness is a joy." "I've been waiting a long time for *The Italian Lover*, and, believe me, it's about time Robert Hellenga got around to writing it," Andrea Hoag wrote for the *Denver (Colorado) Post* (November 24, 2007). "It has been 12 years since . . . *The Sixteen Pleasures* kept me up on a two-day reading binge. . . . Can *The Italian Lover* live up to my lofty expectations? Mercifully, *Grazie Dio*, the answer is a resounding yes! . . . Among the many escapist pleasures in *The Italian Lover*, the most fulfilling is the fact that a 50-something woman from the Midwest can lead a life full of glamour—and *amore*—in Italy." In an assessment for *Booklist* (September 15, 2007), Bill Ott wrote, "There's almost too much plot here, as we watch each of the main characters negotiate the turbulent waters of a love affair, but Hellenga masterfully keeps all the stories afloat, with one feeding the other like themes in a fugue. In the end, the novel is a life-affirming ode to what Hellenga calls the spirit of the Renaissance, 'the discovery of this world, the wind in your hair, the rough pavement beneath your feet, a man's hand on your breast."

Hellenga's honors include fellowships from the National Endowment for the Humanities (1975–76), the Illinois Arts Council (1981–82), and the National Endowment for the Arts (1989) and a PEN Syndicated Fiction Award (1988). He lives in Galesburg with his wife, Virginia Hellenga, who teaches Latin at Monmouth College, in Illinois. The couple's daughters are Rachel, an exhibit developer at the Museum of Science and Industry, in Chicago; Heather, a fifth-grade teacher in Galesburg; and Caitrine, a veterinarian in Glen Carbon, Illinois. The Hellengas have three grandchildren. In "A Writer's Christmas," Hellenga wrote, "I no longer ask, 'What is the meaning of life?' Or at least I put the question differently now than I did when I was younger. My question now is simpler: 'What experiences make life meaningful?' I have settled for an adjective rather than a noun. High on my list: sexual intercourse, walking in the woods, selling a novel, teaching a good class, getting married, having children, cooking dinner, playing the guitar. The usual."

—F.C.

Suggested Reading: bookbrowse.com 2005; *Gettysburg Review* p501+ Autumn 2001; *Newsday* B p11 Aug. 2, 1998, C p30 Mar. 12, 2006; Robert Hellenga Web site

Selected Books: *The Sixteen Pleasures*, 1994, *The Fall of a Sparrow*, 1998; *Blues Lessons*, 2002; *Philosophy Made Simple*, 2006; *The Italian Lover*, 2007

Heller, Agnes

May 12, 1929– Philosopher; writer; educator; social activist

Address: New School, Rm. 1019, 6 E. 16th St., New York, NY 10003

The 2008–09 edition of *The Occupational Outlook Handbook*, an annual guide published by the United States Department of Labor, offers information about more than 250 jobs—about 90 percent of the vocations through which Americans earn their livelihoods. Among the uncommon jobs not mentioned is one that Agnes Heller has held for her entire working life, which now spans more than half a century: philosopher. Virtually unknown by the general public, Heller is a giant among her peers in academia. Born in Budapest, Hungary, 79 years ago, she entered her teens during World War II. The horrors of the war, and in particular the murder by German Nazis of Heller's father and millions of other civilians, ranging from newborns to the very elderly, at Auschwitz and other concentration camps designed expressly for the extermination of

huge numbers of humans, "exercised an immense influence on my whole life, particularly on my work," Heller told Csaba Polony during an interview in March 1997 for leftcurve.com. "I was always interested in the question: How could this possibly happen, how can I understand this? . . . How could people do things like this? So I had to find out what morality is all about, what is the nature of good and evil, what can I do about crime, what can I figure out about the sources of morality and evil? That was the first inquiry. The other inquiry was a social question: What kind of world can produce this, what kind of world allows such things to happen? What is modernity all about? Can we expect redemption? So it was ideas like these that interested me, and very passionately from the beginning onwards. And I felt that I had a debt to pay as a survivor [of the war]. Writing moral philosophy and philosophy of history for me then became a way to pay my debt as a survivor to the people who could not survive."

As an undergraduate in Budapest, Heller embraced the tenets of Marxism. The many abuses by the Hungarian government and other Communist regimes whose leaders claimed to have adopted

Agnes Heller

Karl Marx's doctrines led her to examine the enormous disparity between Marx's ideas about the creation of just societies and the nature of the societies set up in his name—and the reasons for those failures of Eastern Europe's Communist states. As part of a circle of like-minded political theorists (among them her second husband, Ferenc Fehér), known collectively as the Budapest school of socialist philosophy, Heller was subjected to persecution by government agents. In the late 1970s, under governmental pressure, she and her family immigrated to Australia, where she taught at La Trobe University, in a Melbourne suburb, for nearly a decade. In 1986 she and her family moved to New York City, where she joined the faculty of the New School, a university that is devoted to the liberal arts, fine arts, and performing arts. All the while her "single greatest political desire," as she wrote for *Dissent* (Fall 1999), an intellectual quarterly about politics and culture, was "that Hungary and its neighbors finally become 'normal' modern states"—that is, "democratic, with political systems that rest on the rule of law, equality before the law, free parliamentary elections with multiparty competition, and the protection of human rights and the rights of citizens." Her wish came true in 1990, when the Communist Party lost its grip on Hungary and the nation became a democratic republic. "As long as I lived in communist Hungary I could not voice my political ideas," she wrote for *Dissent*; "while living in Australia and in the United States I could speak out but I couldn't be a political participant. Now I finally have the opportunity both to speak and to act as a citizen of my country. Of course, my voice is just one among many. Often it is a voice of dissent. But this is just what I

dreamed about for almost sixty years—to be able to voice dissent or consent in the media of my own country, as an independent intellectual."

During an interview with Katie Terezakis for *Radical Society* (October 2002, on-line) about her book *The Time Is Out of Joint: Shakespeare as Philosopher of History* (2002), Heller said, "My philosophical work . . . concentrates, if you picture it geometrically, on history, society, and politics, on the one side, and ethics on the other, with a theory of justice in the middle." She said that she wrote other books (among them *The Time Is Out of Joint*), which do not fit into her "main philosophical corpus," for her own enjoyment. "I was always emphatically interested in art, music, tragedy, beauty," she explained. "My main body of work being complete, I'm free to indulge in writing about these interests." Heller is the author, co-author, or editor of upwards of 40 books, the earliest published in Hungary. Among those published before she turned 30 is a compilation whose title in English is "Selected Studies in Aesthetics" (1953); another, "The Disintegration of the Ethical Norms: Ethical Questions in the Works of Dezső Kosztolányi" (1957), focuses on a 20th-century Hungarian poet and writer. The titles of those and others among Heller's books reveal the wide-ranging aspects of philosophy, sociology, history, literature, and other human endeavors that have gripped her attention. Those available in English that she wrote as sole author include *The Theory of Need in Marx* (1976); *A Theory of Feelings* (1979); *On Instincts* (1979); *A Theory of History* (1982); *Everyday Life* (1984); *Beyond Justice* (1987); *General Ethics* (1988); *A Philosophy of History in Fragments* (1993); *An Ethics of Personality* (1996); *A Theory of Modernity* (1999); *The Concept of the Beautiful* (1999); and *The Immortal Comedy: The Comic Phenomenon in Art, Literature, and Life* (2005). Books that Heller wrote with Ferenc Fehér (who died in 1994) include *Hungary 1956 Revisited: The Message of a Revolution a Quarter-Century After* (1983); *Doomsday or Deterrence? On the Antinuclear Issue* (1986); *Eastern Left, Western Left: Totalitarianism, Freedom, and Democracy* (1987); *The Postmodern Political Condition* (1989); *From Yalta to Glasnost: The Dismantling of Stalin's Empire* (1991); *The Grandeur and Twilight of Radical Universalism* (1991); and *Biopolitics: Public Policy and Social Welfare* (1994).

Works by Heller that have not appeared in English include books with such titles (translated into English) as "The Aristotelian Ethics and the Antique Ethos" (1966); "Social Role and Prejudice: Two Studies Concerning Everyday Life" (1966); "Instincts, Aggression, Character: Introduction to Marxist Social Anthropology" (1977); "Lectures on the Rise of the Middle Class" (1992); "Nietzsche and the Parsifal: Prolegomena to a Personality Ethics" (1994); "The Existentialist Metaphysics of Leibniz" (1995); "Poetry and Thinking" (1998); "Resurrection of the Jewish Christ" (2000); "Philosophical Ballgames: Studies in the History of Philosophy" (2002); "Picaresque in the Shadow of Auschwitz: Four Studies" (2003); "On the Unresolvability of the Jewish Question" (2004); "Incarnation: Philosophical Studies" (2005); and "Here I Am: Philosophical Explanations of the Book of Genesis" (2006).

Heller's life and work are the subjects of eight books, six of which are by Italian, French, German, or Portuguese writers. The two that are available in English are Simon Tormey's *Agnes Heller: Socialism, Autonomy and the Postmodern* (2001) and John Grumley's *Agnes Heller: A Moralist in the Vortex of History* (2005). "Of Radical Democrats and Great Republics: Agnes Heller's Political Thought," presented by the political scientist Anthony Kammas at the 2006 Annual Conference of the Midwestern Political Science Association, offers a detailed analysis of her writings on democratic citizenship and politics. In "The Social Ethics of Agnes Heller," in *Qualitative Inquiry* (August 2002), the ethicist Clifford G. Christians discussed another principal facet of her philosophy: the possibility of the existence of good people, their activities as citizens, their capacity for maintaining close personal relationships, and the implications of those phenomena for the institution of social justice. On her curriculum vitae (on-line), Heller characterized the work whose title in English is "Ape on a Bike" (1998) as her "autobiography"; an "interview novel" representing a collaboration with János Köbányai, it was originally published in Hungarian and has been translated into German, Persian, and Dutch.

Heller's most recent honor was the 2006 Sonning Prize, awarded every other year by the University of Copenhagen, in Denmark. That country's most prestigious cultural award, it recognizes people who have made significant contributions to the understanding and promotion of European culture. The Sonning Prize selection committee noted that Heller had described Europe's culture for a half-century with "a creative talent, a political cleverness, moral energy and intellectual integrity," according to the *International Herald Tribune* (February 21, 2006), and that she had skillfully and compellingly illuminated important facets of human existence, in part through analyses of the ideas of European philosophers and writers including Aristotle, Shakespeare, Immanuel Kant, Friedrich Nietzsche, Søren Kierkegaard, Martin Heidegger, and György Lukács, the last of whom was a mentor, colleague, and friend of Heller's.

"All my friends remark that I haven't really changed a lot since my teenage years," Heller told Katie Terezakis in 2002. "My interests, values, my commitments may have changed, but my character has changed very little. . . . I'm not an ironic person who can keep inventing herself. I simply love life, my life. That is why I sympathize with the Shakespearean heroines who absolutely feel gratitude to life, yet must deal with its situations as they are. I think this gratitude permeates all my work."

Agnes Heller was born on May 12, 1929 in Budapest to intellectual Jewish parents. Her father, Pal Heller, was a prominent member of a Hungarian political party. "I learned a great deal from him and he ensured that we knew what was going on," she told Simon Tormey for the Web site *Radical Philosophy* (March/April 1999). During World War II the German Nazi regime took control of Hungary, and some 440,000 Hungarian Jews were sent to Auschwitz, a Nazi-run concentration camp in Poland; there, most of them perished, either in the gas chambers or from starvation or disease. Heller's father was among those who died at Auschwitz; the lives of many members of Heller's extended family as well as many of her friends and her second husband's father—and of millions of other Jews, Romani people (Gypsies), homosexuals, and others deemed undesirable by the Nazis—also ended at Auschwitz or at other concentration camps.

Heller and her mother evaded capture by the Nazis during the war and remained in Budapest after it ended. Meanwhile, during her mid-teens, Heller had "embraced Zionism," as she recalled to Polony: "I believed that redemption comes from Zion and I planned to go to Palestine." By 1947 she had given up that conviction and plan. Instead, she enrolled at Eötvös Loránd University (formerly, and still often called, the University of Budapest), with the intention of majoring in physics and chemistry. She wanted "to show that women are as good as men" in science, as she told Simon Tormey for *Radical Philosophy*, citing as inspirational to her the achievements of the Polish-born French scientist Marie Curie, who won Nobel Prizes in physics and chemistry in 1903 and 1911, respectively.

A turning point in Heller's life came during her first year in college, when her then-boyfriend took her to a lecture delivered by the literary critic and Marxist thinker György (or Georg) Lukács for his course on the philosophy of culture (culture in its broadest sense). As she listened to Lukács speak, she told Csaba Polony, "I began to realize that I hadn't understood a thing about what he was talking. But there was one thing that I did understand: what he talked about was the thing that is the most important of all the things in the world and that I must understand it. So this and my experience of the holocaust combined for me, because basically it was something which was concerned with the sense of life. It became far more important for me than the hard sciences to understand the world in which I am living. I realized that I didn't want to be a chemist or physicist, I wanted to understand the world. The consciousness of the debt that I had to pay because of the holocaust then came together with the understanding that I do not understand one thing about the world."

Heller switched her course of study to philosophy and social theory and took classes in Hungarian literature as well. Following Lukács's example, she joined the Hungarian Communist Party. She was drawn to the political and socioeconomic ideas of communist philosophy, which promoted common ownership of the means of production in society and the creation of a virtually classless social structure in which everyone would be equal. "It offered what I was searching for," Heller told Polony. "It offered an explanation of why there is suffering in the world and it offered an earthly redemption, a second coming of something." Within two years Heller had become disillusioned with the Hungarian Communist Party, which, after it had come to power in 1945, had adopted the totalitarian tactics practiced by Joseph Stalin, the longtime dictator of the Soviet Union. For example, Hungary's Communist leaders had begun to stage many show trials, in which people who had been tortured by government agents after their imprisonment were forced to confess to crimes of which they were innocent and for which they were later executed. The party's methods, Heller told Polony, "turned out very soon" to be "phony." "You need redemption and the freedom to think with your own mind," she said. "You need both, but there was a clash between the two. The Party offered a scheme for redemption but it never allowed you to use your own mind." Noting the disparity between Marxian theory and practice, she quoted a friend of hers as having said, "The essence is good but all the appearances are evil." Heller's public criticism of the Hungarian brand of communism resulted in her expulsion from the party in 1949; after some time, however, her membership was reinstated. Also in 1949 she married István Hermann, who later became a member of the Hungarian Academy of Sciences and has written many books, among them one about the work of Lukács.

In 1952 Heller completed her undergraduate work and gave birth to a daughter, Zsuzsanna. She then entered a Ph.D. program at the Hungarian Academy of Sciences, with Lukács as her adviser. For her doctoral thesis she analyzed the writings of the 19th-century Russian socialist and philosopher Nikolay Gavrilovich Chernyshevsky (or Tchernyshevsky), who argued that self-sacrifice was necessary for those who serve a revolutionary cause. Heller disagreed, claiming that that idea was inconsistent with Marxian theory; rather, she contended, radical social change required the "rational egoism" of those seeking it. In her thesis, according to Simon Tormey in his book *Agnes Heller*, she argued that "no social program can be realized without the participants' interest and that only consensus among individuals can lead to collective action." Heller completed her dissertation, titled *Tchernyshevsky and the Problem of Rational Egoism*, in 1955. That year she joined the faculty of the University of Budapest as an assistant professor of philosophy.

On October 23, 1956 Hungarian students and others took to the streets to protest against their nation's government. In less than two weeks, the revolt had been crushed by Soviet forces; a Soviet-backed regime, led by János Kádár, was installed. The actions of the Soviet government in suppress-

ing a popular people's revolution further dimmed Heller's views about Marxism. In 1957 the new Hungarian regime began to round up dissidents and revolutionaries, and Heller was again expelled from the Communist Party. She was also barred from holding any positions in institutions of higher learning, which effectively ended her ability to publish. She was, however, permitted to work as a research assistant to Lukács, and that job enabled her to give a series of lectures about ethics at the University of Budapest. Her talks included thinly veiled critiques of communist ideology; she argued, for instance, that the concept of class "interest" denied autonomy to the individual, thus subsuming each person's will within a greater, collective will. She told Polony, "It was obvious that if you accepted the Party line and followed it step by step, you could not pursue philosophy because you had to accept certain things you didn't believe to be true." Heller was punished for her subversive rhetoric: she was forced to stop working with Lukács and ordered to teach at schools below the college level. In an e-mail message to *Current Biography*, Agota Szilagyi, the director of the Information Resource Center at the American Embassy in Budapest, who was a student of Heller's in a Hungarian high school, compared Heller's demotion to Leonardo da Vinci's being forced to work as a wallpaperer.

In 1962, her marriage to Hermann having ended, Heller married Ferenc Fehér, a member of the Institute of Sociology of the Hungarian Academy of Sciences and a brilliant philosopher whose interests ranged from political theory to the theory of aesthetics. The next year Heller was permitted to join the institute, as a senior research fellow, and while she was not allowed to teach, she was free to conduct research and write. In 1964 she gave birth to a son, Yuri Fehér. At around that time Lukács, Heller, Fehér, and other prominent philosophers joined to form what was later referred to as the Budapest school (not to be confused with the Budapest school of documentary filmmaking), a forum for the discussion of Marxism. The group advocated reform of Marxist theory as well as practice; as Tormey wrote in *Agnes Heller*, "They were inspired by the idea of a 'renaissance of Marxism,' a flowering of the critical, oppositional potential they believed lay within Marxism." For a while the group's activities were tolerated by the Hungarian government, which was beginning to adopt some small reforms in the economic sphere and other areas.

In 1968 democratization measures in Czechoslovakia and the fear among the other Communist governments of Eastern Europe of their consequences led to the invasion of Czechoslovakia by five of its fellow members of the Warsaw Pact (the Soviet bloc's equivalent of NATO, the North Atlantic Treaty Organization). In a daring act of defiance, Heller and a number of her colleagues condemned the invasion in a publicly disseminated letter. Nevertheless, the letter's signatories remained on their jobs until 1973, when, in what became known in Hungary as the Philosopher's Trial (though it did not occur in a courtroom), the Hungarian Communist Party issued a resolution aimed at Heller and her colleagues. The essence of the resolution, Heller told Polony, was that "since in Hungarian scientific institutions Marxism-Leninism should be practiced, those people who are alien and hostile to Marxism-Leninism have no place in Hungarian scientific institutions. Consequently such people have to be removed from their jobs." Heller, Lukács, Fehér, and others working at the Institute of Sociology were dismissed. For several years they lived as "pariahs," as Heller put it in her interview with Polony, subsisting on what they could earn "by teaching language day and night" and working as translators. During that time they were "constantly subjected to police harassment, we were followed in the streets, they sent informers and spies to our apartments, and my husband, Feri, also spent a few days in prison. . . . It was a very unpleasant kind of life," she told Polony.

Earlier, in 1970, Heller's book *Everyday Life* had been published in Hungary; it was soon translated into Italian and Spanish and in the late 1970s appeared in German. When she learned that an English translation was planned, she told the publisher that she would translate it herself from the original Hungarian version and shorten it as well. In the preface to the English edition, which appeared in 1984, Heller wrote that she had not given in to the temptation to revise the book to reflect the evolution of her thinking and acquisition of additional knowledge since she had first written it, in 1967–68. She then explained, "*Everyday Life* was written in the midst of a period when the slogan of the 'renaissance of Marxism' was coined. The first objective of the book was exactly what the title suggested: outlining a theory of everyday life. However, the enterprise was even more ambitious. I decided to embark on new paths by working out a philosophical method, on the one hand, and the outlines of a new philosophical framework, on the other hand, while remaining faithful to the spirit of Marx and, at the same time, breaking with certain dominant traditions of 'historical materialism.' It is in this book that I established the very framework of my philosophy which I have never changed since, short of elaboration or occasional modification." She also wrote, "How everyday life can be changed in a humanistic, democratic, socialist direction is the practical issue the book addresses." According to Tormey, "What [*Everyday Life*] demonstrates is a desire to engage with an intellectual debate of broader significance and scope."

In her book *The Theory of Need in Marx* (1976), Heller painted a humanist picture of Marxism and argued that the humanization of the communist political and social system would help the citizens overcome feelings of alienation. By that time, however, most members of the Budapest school had lost any interest in reform, having decided that a reformed version of Marxism could not become reality. In 1977 Heller, Fehér, and several other dissidents associated with the Budapest school left Hungary. In an article for the *Washington Post* (March 7, 1978), Michael Getler wrote that they had been "quietly pressured" into emigrating. In the fall of that year, Heller and Fehér settled in Australia, where Heller had gotten a position in the Sociology Department at La Trobe University, outside Melbourne. "Though I was teaching philosophy, it was philosophy with an eye to the subject matter of the department," she noted to Tormey.

In her book *Renaissance Man* (1978), Heller discussed the essence of what it means to be human from the perspective of philosophical anthropology, which draws upon the humanities, the social sciences, and, to a limited extent, the natural sciences to gain an understanding of humans as cultural and social beings. Her book *A Theory of History* was published in 1982. In it, in a departure from Marxian analysis, Heller criticized approaches to a philosophy of history that failed to include the concept of human freedom and individuality. Heller and Fehér's book *Hungary 1956 Revisited* appeared in 1983. John C. Campbell wrote for *Foreign Affairs* (Winter 1983/1984), "Not a retelling but a reinterpretation of the events of 1956 and their meaning for Hungary and for the world. The authors . . . have a definite point of view, which is radical and socialist but not communist. They see the revolution as defying simple explanation: it was both nationalist and socialist, and was directed not only against Moscow but also the Western powers which were jointly responsible for the infamous Yalta-Potsdam system and which failed both Hungary and the cause of freedom in 1956. A book which invites debate and merits a careful reading." In the next few years, Heller published several additional books as author or co-author.

In 1986 Heller and Fehér moved to New York City to join the graduate faculty of the New School for Social Research (now known as the New School). "It was a new environment and had one great attraction, which was the chance to teach in a philosophy department," she told Tormey. Since 1988 Heller has taught at the New School as the Hannah Arendt professor of philosophy. After the demise of communism in Hungary, Heller was elected to the Hungarian Academy of Sciences. For the last 18 years she has divided her time between New York and Budapest, where she is a member of the Faculty of Arts at the Institute for Art Theory and Media Studies at Eötvös Loránd University. During that time she has written two dozen books and many articles for professional journals. The latter include "The Absolute Stranger: Shakespeare and the Drama of Failed Assimilation," in *Critical Horizons* (February 2000); "A Tentative Answer to the Question: Has Civil Society Cultural Memory?," in *Social Research* (Winter 2001); "9/11, or Modernity and Terror," in *Constellations: An International Journal of Critical & Democratic Theory* (March 2002); "The Unmasking of the

Metaphysicians or the Deconstructing of Metaphysics?," in *Critical Horizons* (Vol. 5, 2004); "The Three Logics of Modernity and the Double Bind of the Modern Imagination," in *Thesis Eleven* (May 2005); and "The Gods of Greece: Germans and the Greeks," in *Thesis Eleven* (May 2008).

In May 2008 Ben-Gurion University, in Israel, awarded Heller an honorary doctoral degree. The award citation, as quoted in a New School press release (June 23, 2008, on-line), described her as "a model of personal and intellectual courage" and stated, in part, that the honor expressed the university's "admiration of a Holocaust survivor who has dedicated her life to examining the moral and ethical issues of our lives, posing fundamental questions about history, culture, democracy and modernity; . . . appreciation of a woman who bravely withstood persecution by a totalitarian regime in her native Hungary, unwilling to compromise her independent thought and integrity; . . . acknowledgement of an award-winning scholar whose prolific body of work and teaching continues to inspire generations of students; . . . [and] profound esteem for a person who did not hesitate to reexamine her ideas, never losing her belief in the spirit of man and the values of mutual responsibility and brotherhood."

—W.D.

Suggested Reading: leftcurve.org Mar. 1997; radicalphilosophy.com Mar./Apr. 1999; Grumley, John. *Agnes Heller: A Moralist in the Vortex of History*, 2005; Tormey, Simon. *Agnes Heller: Socialism, Autonomy and the Postmodern*, 2001

Selected Books: *The Theory of Need in Marx*, 1976; *Renaissance Man*, 1978; *A Theory of Feelings*, 1979; *On Instincts*, 1979; *A Theory of History*, 1982; *Everyday Life*, 1984; *Beyond Justice*, 1987; *General Ethics*, 1988; *A Philosophy of History in Fragments*, 1993; *An Ethics of Personality*, 1996; *A Theory of Modernity*, 1999; *The Immortal Comedy: The Comic Phenomenon in Art, Literature, and Life*, 2005; with Ferenc Fehér—*Hungary 1956 Revisited: The Message of a Revolution a Quarter-Century After*, 1983; *Doomsday or Deterrence? On the Antinuclear Issue*, 1986; *Eastern Left, Western Left: Totalitarianism, Freedom, and Democracy*, 1987; *The Postmodern Political Coalition*, 1989; *From Yalta to Glasnost: The Dismantling of Stalin's Empire*, 1991; *The Grandeur and Twilight of Radical Universalism*, 1991; *Biopolitics: Public Policy and Social Welfare*, 1994

Hockfield, Susan

Mar. 24, 1951– President of MIT; neurobiologist

Address: Office of the President, MIT, 77 Massachusetts Ave., Cambridge, MA 02139-4307

When the neuroscientist Susan Hockfield assumed her duties as the 16th president of the Massachusetts Institute of Technology (MIT), in Cambridge, Massachusetts, in December 2004, she became both the first woman and the first scientist with a biology background to hold that position in the history of the school. Her arrival was seen as a breakthrough: by MIT's own admission, as revealed in a 1999 report by female faculty members, the work environment there was male-dominated. Furthermore, the school had built its reputation in the 19th and 20th centuries through its focus on engineering and technology, not the life sciences. Hockfield's appointment was thus perceived in the media and in academic circles as emblematic of a shift in the school's direction; with an emphasis on gender equality and a move to merge the research of the already convergent fields of engineering, technology, and biomedical science, MIT seemed to be taking cues from its history of breaking new ground.

Hockfield solidified her reputation early in her career, beginning her research in 1980 at the acclaimed Cold Spring Harbor Laboratory, on Long Island, New York, with her study of the nervous

Darren McCollester/Getty Images

system. In 1985 she became an assistant professor of neurobiology at the Yale University School of Medicine, in New Haven, Connecticut, where she was promoted to full professor in 1994. She also continued her work as a neuroscientist, leading a team in its 1997 discovery of a protein linked to a form of human brain cancer known as glioma. She took on her first administrative position in 1998, when Yale appointed her dean of the Graduate School of Arts and Sciences; in that post she became known for working to bring more women into the faculty and increasing the diversity of the student body. She was also a key player in the battle between graduate students and the school's administrators over stipends and quality-of-life issues, working with the students to help meet some of their requests and drawing criticism from them when she refused to meet with the union they had organized, which was not recognized by the school. In 2002 she was made provost of Yale, occupying the post for two years before becoming MIT's president. Since she took on that position, Hockfield has, among other actions, created a program to research the world's growing energy problems; worked on a plan to match federal grant money for low-income students; and initiated a $750 million expansion of the school to include facilities that will bring science and engineering departments under the same roof.

Susan Hockfield was born on March 24, 1951 in Chicago, Illinois, the second of four girls. Her mother, Fayetta, was a homemaker; her father, Robert, was a patent lawyer who later rose to a position of prominence at General Electric. His work with the company required the family to move to a new city every two years, and it was not until Hockfield was 10 that they settled in Chappaqua, New York. As a small child she spent time in such common pursuits as riding her bike and sewing; it was her passion for assembling and disassembling objects that set her apart from others her age. She was also interested at a young age in science and math and has said that her family assumed, for those reasons, that she would become a doctor. She told Liz Karagianis for the MIT publication *Spectrum* (Spring 2005, on-line), "I always imagined that anything I wanted to do would be a real possibility for me."

Hockfield attended Chappaqua High School and then the University of Rochester, in Rochester, New York, where she studied cellular biology with the idea of attending medical school afterward. After one of her advisers persuaded her to take a summer job at a neuroscience laboratory, she discovered that she was more interested in performing research than in becoming a physician. "It was the thing I had been looking for, searching for, all my life," she said to Cornelia Dean for the *New York Times* (May 3, 2005) of her newfound passion for neuroscience. Hockfield graduated from college a semester early, in 1973. After working in the neuroscience lab for several years, she enrolled at the Georgetown University School of Medicine, in Washington, D.C., where she earned her Ph.D. degree in anatomy in 1979, completing a dissertation in the area of neuroscience. She then pursued postdoctoral work as a National Institutes of Health (NIH) fellow at the University of California at San Francisco, joining a research team that was investi-

gating pathways in the nervous system connected with feelings of pain.

In 1980 Hockfield joined Cold Spring Harbor Laboratory as a junior investigator. At the time scientists were beginning to study monoclonal antibodies as a means of exploring the structure of the nervous system. Antibodies are proteins in the human body that battle invading bacteria and viruses; monoclonal antibodies are formed when tumor cells, which replicate continuously, are fused with mammalian cells, which produce antibodies. The result of that cell fusion is the hybridoma, a cell that produces antibodies continuously. Using electron microscopes, scientists are able to observe antibodies as they move toward specific sites. At Cold Spring Harbor, using that approach to study the nervous systems of the leech and the cat, Hockfield discovered a protein that regulates changes in the structure of neurons, cells that transport information. Hockfield was promoted to senior staff investigator at the laboratory in 1982. She has said that she found her time at Cold Spring Harbor to be extremely rewarding. While there she met the professor and doctor Thomas Byrne, whom she married in 1991.

In 1985 Hockfield became an assistant professor of neurobiology at the Yale University School of Medicine. She returned to Cold Spring Harbor every summer until 1997 to work as program director of the Summer Neurobiology Program. She became an associate professor at Yale in 1989 and received tenure in 1991; three years later she was promoted to full professor. Hockfield also continued her work in neuroscience. In 1997 she led a team of researchers in search of proteins involved in the brain's development; one member of the team, Diane Jaworski, who was then a postdoctoral fellow, sought proteins that bind hyaluronan, a sugar component of the molecules that surround cells. In the process Jaworski discovered a protein that was produced solely by gliomas—deadly brain tumors in humans. The new protein was called BEHAB (brain-enriched hyaluronan binding) by Hockfield's team. Prior research had revealed that hyaluronan-binding proteins helped cells move around during tissue development; Jaworski found not only that glioma cells, exclusively, secrete BEHAB in adult human brains but that hyaluronan proteins are also linked to invasive cancers. To test whether BEHAB increased glioma's invasiveness, Hockfield's team introduced BEHAB into normal rat glioma cell lines, then placed the cell lines back into the rats' brains. Hockfield told Marcia Barinaga for *Science* (November 14, 1997) that the BEHAB fragment "increased the invasive potential of these cells." In the April 1, 1998 issue of the *Journal of Neuroscience*, Hockfield and her team published their findings, expressing hope that scientific methods would eventually be able to halt the production of BEHAB and thus slow the spread of glioma cells.

In 1998 Hockfield was appointed dean of the Graduate School of Arts and Sciences at Yale, a post in which she oversaw the academic and administrative policies for the school's roughly 2,300 graduate students. She was the first member of Yale's medical-school faculty to become dean of the graduate school. She took the position amidst ongoing campus-wide protests from graduate students alleging poor treatment by the university's administration. Many of those students were attempting to organize as a union—the Graduate Employees and Students Union (GESO)—in order to obtain better teaching-assistant stipends and other benefits. Protests included mass demonstrations as well as the withholding of grades for undergraduates. (Graduate students taught many undergraduate courses.) In August 1998 Hockfield attempted to reach out to the graduate students by organizing the first matriculation ceremony for them in the school's history; she also worked with administration officials to increase stipends, improve healthcare benefits, and expand training programs for the graduate students. Despite the changes she sought, Hockfield was the target of a protest in 1999 led by GESO-affiliated graduate students who grew frustrated when she refused to meet with them to discuss their goals. Hockfield noted that she could not meet with them because Yale did not recognize GESO as representing graduate students. In September 1999, after speaking with department officials, Hockfield reorganized Yale's graduate administrative structure. She replaced three associate deanships with two associate- and two assistant-dean positions and brought in the former associate provost Ellen Ryerson as a deputy dean to assist her; Hockfield explained that the restructuring was an attempt to better address the concerns brought up by graduate students.

By the end of her tenure as dean, Hockfield had been credited with having greatly influenced the policies of Yale's McDougal Graduate Student Center, where she had expanded training courses, career-services programs, and student-life programs for graduate students. She had worked with the Graduate Student Assembly to facilitate interaction between graduate students and faculty, helped make available free health care to graduate students in Ph.D. programs, increased the standard nine-month stipend for students in the humanities and social sciences from $10,500 to $15,000, and pushed for stipend increases for students in dissertation fellowships and the sciences. She was also acknowledged for her work toward increasing campus diversity; she had created the Office for Diversity and Equal Opportunity with the goal of recruiting more minority students and was instrumental in attracting more women to the faculty. Hockfield had also started the Graduate Mentor Award program, to recognize faculty members who excelled at guiding and teaching graduate students, and expanded training for graduate students learning English as a second language.

Hockfield was appointed William Edward Gilbert Professor of Neurobiology in 2001 and, although appointed to a second term as the graduate-school dean in early 2002, was named by Yale's president, Richard C. Levin, as provost that December. As provost Hockfield was, after Levin, the university's chief academic and administrative officer. She began the new position in January 2003; by February she had found herself caught up again in the struggle of graduate students seeking to unionize. When it was learned that GESO had authorized a graduate-student strike, Hockfield issued a statement, quoted by Kevin Canfield in the *Hartford Courant* (February 20, 2003), in which she said it was "disturbing that any group would attempt to disrupt the education of our students to advance its own ends. The university will make every effort to fulfill its commitments to our educational programs, even while some may seek to disrupt instruction." The graduate students did go on strike. Hockfield's handling of the episode has been both praised and criticized. The neuroscience professor who initially brought her to Yale, Pasko Rakic, told Marcella Bombardieri and Jenna Russell, writing for the *Boston Globe* (August 27, 2004), that Hockfield had emerged from the fray with the students' respect. "If you give them bad news, they hate you," he said. "But she told them, and they didn't hate her." A leader of the graduate-student union, Mary Reynolds, conveyed to Bombardieri and Russell an opposing view, telling them that Hockfield was not open to dialogue. "I found that she shut down discussion and refused to speak to students in the union," Reynolds said. "She was not a consensus builder. The administration was opposed to the union, but that shouldn't stop her from speaking to graduate students."

On August 26, 2004 MIT announced that Hockfield had been appointed its president, ending a six-month campaign by the school's officials to find a successor for Charles M. Vest. Her appointment was noteworthy not only because she was MIT's first female president but because her background was in neuroscience; MIT had earned a reputation primarily for engineering and technology, and Hockfield's arrival signaled a new focus on life sciences as well. That year was the first in the school's history in which research funding from the NIH exceeded or equaled that provided by the Department of Defense, and MIT had recently begun to place more emphasis on cognitive and brain science and biomedical research. Hockfield told Mark Jewell for the Associated Press State & Local Wire (December 6, 2004), "My being a life scientist does not mark a departure from where MIT has been. It's a logical extension of where MIT has been for a long, long time." She added that she intended to work with MIT scientists to merge engineering with the life sciences, fostering collaboration, for example, among experts in such fields as genetics and robotics. She also said, "There has been tremendous progress in the life sciences in terms of computational approaches, bringing mathematical approaches to understanding data in the life sciences, nanotechnology and information systems." In addition, she noted that installing a woman as MIT's head was a sign of progress, telling Jewell, "I feel very strongly that my generation now owes it to subsequent generations to continue this progress so that MIT and universities around the nation became what we truly can call a great meritocracy." Despite the advances suggested by Hockfield's appointment, however, Jewell pointed out that as of 2004, women "still comprise[d] just 42 percent of undergraduates, 29 percent of graduate students and 17 percent of faculty" at the school.

One of Hockfield's first newsworthy actions as president of MIT was to join with two other prominent university presidents, Shirley M. Tilghman of Princeton University and John L. Hennessy of Stanford University, to write a 700-word essay in response to statements made by Lawrence H. Summers, then the president of Harvard University, about women in science. At a conference in January 2005, Summers had said that biological differences between men and women might explain why fewer women were found in science and engineering; his controversial remarks and the public reaction to them became a focus of media attention. The essay by Hockfield, Tilghman, and Hennessy appeared on the op-ed page of the *Boston Globe*'s February 12, 2005 edition; while the piece made only one reference to Summers (who later resigned), it argued that "speculation that 'innate differences' may be a significant cause of underrepresentation by women in science and engineering may rejuvenate old myths and reinforce negative stereotypes and biases."

In June 2005 Hockfield announced her first major initiative, a program aimed at researching solutions to the world's mounting energy problems, which include the increasing consumption of finite resources and the need for sustainable and "clean" energy sources to address the threat of global warming. The following year, after hearing from a research council of faculty and outside experts she had assembled, Hockfield introduced the MIT Energy Initiative (MITEI), which is focused on campus-wide energy research, outreach, and classroom education. The program also includes joint research ventures; in November 2007 MIT and the Chevron Corp. announced an energy-research program to develop technology for obtaining energy from deep-water reserves.

In July 2006 Hockfield created a committee to look into allegations that a Nobel laureate and prominent neuroscience professor at MIT, Susumu Tonegawa, had sent e-mail messages to a young postdoctoral fellow, Alla Karpova, discouraging her from accepting a job offer from the school because doing so would place her in competition with him. That November the committee declared that while Tonegawa had acted inappropriately, he had done so in part because he was unfairly excluded from the hiring process, and he would not be punished. Hockfield and others also determined that the competitive atmosphere among the school's neuroscience centers was the true cause of Tonegawa's actions and needed to be addressed. "We cannot allow internal competitiveness to undercut the integrity, values, and mission of the Institute as a whole," Hockfield said in a statement that accompanied the committee's report, quoted by Bombardieri for the *Boston Globe* (November 3, 2006).

Currently, MIT is in the midst of a $750 million expansion, described by Bombardieri for the *Boston Globe* (September 14, 2006) as Hockfield's "first stamp on the Massachusetts Institute of Technology's physical campus since she took office." The expansion will include both housing and academic facilities totaling about one million square feet and including a cancer-research center as well as management, architecture, and technology centers. MIT hosted the MIT Energy Conference in April 2008, bringing together experts in technology, policy, industry, and finance with the goal of developing solutions to the energy crisis. Hockfield was a featured speaker. The next MIT energy conference, "Accelerating Change in Global Energy," will be held in 2009.

In an op-ed piece published in the *Washington Post* (September 11, 2008), Hockfield argued for an increase in federal funding for energy research. "The potential gains—from the economy to global security to the climate—are boundless," she wrote. "Other nations are also chasing these technologies. We must be first to market . . . the most innovative solutions. We must make sure that in the energy technology markets of the future, we have the power to invent, produce, and sell—not the obligation to buy."

Hockfield holds honorary degrees from Brown University, in Providence, Rhode Island, Tsinghua University, in Beijing, China, and the Watson School of Biological Sciences, at Cold Spring Harbor. She is a member of the American Academy of Arts and Sciences, a trustee of the Carnegie Corp. of New York, a director of the General Electric Co., and a trustee of the Woods Hole Oceanographic Institution. She has served on the National Advisory Neurological Disorders and Stroke Council of the NIH and is also on the board of overseers of the Boston Symphony Orchestra.

In January 2008 Hockfield was elected to join the World Economic Forum, a Geneva, Switzerland–based organization that hosts debates among top world leaders about key social and economic issues. She has written more than 90 scientific papers on the biology of the nervous system. Hockfield lives with her husband and their teenage daughter, Elizabeth Hockfield Byrne, in Cambridge. Thomas Byrne is on the staff of Massachusetts General Hospital, in Boston, and also teaches neuroscience at MIT.

—W.D.

Suggested Reading: Associated Press State & Local Wire Dec. 6, 2004; *Boston Globe* A p1 Aug. 26, 2004; *M2Presswire* Dec. 16, 2002; *New York Times* (on-line) May 3, 2005; *Science* p1226 Nov. 17, 1997; *Spectrum* (on-line) Spring 2005; *Yale Alumni Magazine* (on-line) Summer 1998

Courtesy of the Seattle Post-Intelligencer

Horsey, David

Sep. 13, 1951– Political cartoonist; columnist

Address: Seattle Post-Intelligencer, P.O. Box 19099, 101 Elliott Ave. W., Suite 200, Seattle, WA 98119

"To me, if you're working for a newspaper, you're a journalist," the editorial cartoonist and columnist David Horsey said to David Astor for *Editor & Publisher* (December 4, 1993). "I see myself as a journalist who happens to draw." Horsey, who was not yet 30 when he joined the staff of the *Seattle Post-Intelligencer* (*P-I*), in Washington State, in 1979, has twice won the Pulitzer Prize for his editorial cartoons: in 1999, when he was recognized mainly for his views on the Clinton-Lewinsky scandal, and in 2003, for his takes on subjects including homeland-security measures; the war in Iraq; U.S. oil companies' influence on policymaking during the administration of President George W. Bush; and revelations regarding pedophilia among Roman Catholic priests. His cartoons are syndicated to more than 200 newspapers nationwide, and he has published a half-dozen collections of his work and co-edited and illustrated additional books. "When I first started at the *P-I*, I

worried about being profound every day, but now I realize that few cartoonists can do that, and perhaps no one," he told John Marshall for the *Seattle P-I* (August 29, 1992). "Now, I take whatever comes—and the ones that are award winners or really hit home are very rare. That's probably true of every creative person. I settle for singles most days and, once in a while, hit a home run."

"Cartoons are a collection of symbols," Horsey told a reporter for *A&S Perspectives* (Summer 1999), a newsletter published by the University of Washington School of Arts and Sciences. "Most of the time, I'm looking for a metaphor that will fit the topic—some common symbol or image that can be twisted and turned to say what I want to say. The only problem is, those symbols and images can mean different things to different people. People can read things in a lot of different ways. If they are going to get mad at me, I want them to get mad at what I really meant to say. So I have to choose my metaphors carefully." Three of Horsey's most recent cartoons—about the U.S.'s troubled economy, what is known as the subprime-mortgage crisis, and proposals to send more troops into Afghanistan (published on July 16, 19, and 22, 2008, respectively)—illustrate that point. In the first, which is based on the story of the Dutch boy who saved his country by plugging up a hole in a dike with his finger, water pours through many holes in a huge, cracked wall labeled "U.S. Economy"; a small boy, identified as the Federal Reserve Board, who has stopped three leaks with two fingers and a toe, stares in terror at the many other leaks that he is powerless to stanch. The second cartoon shows Horsey's 2008 version of a scene from Frank Capra's film *It's a Wonderful Life* (1946). Townspeople have come to their banker, George Bailey, the hero, to withdraw their savings. "The money's not here," Horsey's George says, paraphrasing the movie character. "It's in Joe's house and the Kennedy house and a hundred others!" "Uh, not exactly, George," his co-worker says in an aside. "I forgot to tell you I sold their loans to a hedge fund and they got bundled with a bunch of risky mortgages and pawned off on unwitting investors and Asian banks!" In the third cartoon a young couple are looking at a poster for a new movie called *Afghanistan II*. "If you think we won the *first* time, *think again*," the poster reads. The young woman is saying to her friend, "I am so not ready for this sequel." Roger Oglesby, the publisher of the *Seattle P-I*, told Neil Modie for that newspaper (April 8, 2003) that Horsey "has an ability to capture complex ideas in cartoon images like nothing I've ever seen. He's a remarkable journalist. But he is really more than that. He's a remarkable human being, too. He's passionate about what he does, generous, caring. And that's most important of all. He's really a terrific person."

Horsey has also written about many topics for the *P-I*'s opinion section. In one piece (September 18, 1998), he rejected the assertion that year-round schooling is better for American children and emphasized the importance of summer vacations. In another (March 5, 2006), he discussed the correlation between women's liberation in developing nations and global population control. In a third (May 19, 2008), about the current presidential campaigns of Senators John S. McCain and Barack Obama, he questioned the candidates' tendencies to view people who live in small towns as somehow "more American" than city-dwellers. Horsey is also the author of a regular *P-I* column called "Horsey's Burning Questions," in which readers send in their opinions about the topics at hand, ranging from the debate on stem-cell research to the nuisances of airline travel. In January 2008 Horsey launched DavidHorsey.com, a Web site affiliated with the *Seattle P-I*, in which he blogs and posts his cartoons.

David Horsey was born on September 13, 1951 in Evansville, Indiana, to Raymond Wiles Horsey, a musician, and Jeanne Marie (Jaeger) Horsey, a teacher. His father was the son of pioneer settlers in Skagit County, in northwestern Washington State. After a stint in the Army Air Corps as a French-hornist in marching bands and violinist in units that entertained wounded troops, his father played with hotel dance bands. In 1954 the family, which included Horsey's sister, Janice, moved to Seattle. Raymond Horsey took teaching jobs at local schools and eventually became the head of the music department at Ingraham High School, in Seattle. Horsey's mother, who was of Norwegian descent, was born on the Coeur d'Alene Indian Reservation in Idaho, where her father owned a general store. As an adult she campaigned for the purchase of Braille textbooks for blind students in Seattle public schools; she learned Braille and founded the Seattle Area Braillists, a group of volunteers who transcribed textbooks into Braille.

Horsey began to show interest in drawing as a toddler and drew his first editorial cartoon in seventh grade for a class project. His father introduced him to politics when he was a boy. "My dad would bring me along to lots of events," he told the *A&S Perspectives* reporter. "He was a staunch Republican. My earliest political memory is of an Eisenhower election celebration when I was five years old." (The Republican candidate Dwight D. Eisenhower won his second election as president in 1956.) With his father, Horsey attended the 1964 Republican National Convention, where U.S. senator Barry Goldwater of Arizona was nominated to run against the incumbent president, Lyndon B. Johnson, a Democrat. (Johnson won.)

As a youth Horsey played the French horn with the Seattle Youth Symphony. At Ingraham High School, where he was an honor student, he drew cartoons for the student newspaper; most of them reflected the conservative views his father had instilled in him. After his high-school graduation, he enrolled at the University of Washington. The Vietnam War was still raging, and Horsey, exposed to the fierce opposition to the war expressed by many students and professors, found his political views

changing. He also gained a newfound appreciation of his artistic talent: during a weight-training class in his freshman year, he drew a caricature of the instructor, who, to Horsey's surprise, suggested that he consider working for the college newspaper, the *Daily*. He followed the teacher's advice and in time became the paper's editor. Horsey had planned to study graphic design, but his positive experiences in the *Daily*'s offices led him to change his major to communications. In 1974, while still an undergraduate, he borrowed $2,000 from his mother to self-publish a collection of cartoons, *Politics and Other Perversions*.

After Horsey received a B.A. degree, in 1976, the *Daily Journal American*, a newspaper published in Bellevue, near Seattle, hired him as a political reporter to cover the Washington State Legislature, in Olympia. His job also required him to produce a weekly illustrated column and editorial cartoons. In 1979 William Asbury, then the managing editor of the *Seattle Post-Intelligencer* and a former adviser to the University of Washington *Daily*, learned that a rival newspaper, the *Seattle Times*, had hired an editorial cartoonist. In response, he recruited Horsey to produce editorial cartoons and columns for the *Seattle P-I*. Although Horsey loved to draw, he had never planned to earn a living as an artist. "I had not made that my career goal," he told David Astor for *Editor & Publisher* (December 4, 1993). "I was happy to be a reporter, but I realized this was a great opportunity. There are lots of reporters in the world and not many cartoonists." Horsey has said that his reporting background not only gave him the political knowledge that an editorial cartoonist must have but has also helped him maintain his professional integrity.

Horsey's second collection of cartoons, *Horsey's Rude Awakenings*, was published in 1981. In 1986, as a Rotary Foundation scholar, Horsey earned an M.A. degree in international relations from the University of Kent, in Canterbury, England. His next book, *Horsey's Greatest Hits of the '80s*, appeared in 1989. With Maury Forman, an historian of political cartooning, he edited *Cartooning AIDS Around the World* (1992), which includes drawings by Dan Wasserman, Kambiz Derambakhsh, Garry Trudeau, Pat Oliphant, and others. The cartoons address such issues as widespread stereotypes about AIDS and its victims, government policies on health care, and rising death rates from AIDS in the U.S. and abroad. Horsey and Forman organized an exhibit of 43 of the cartoons, which was mounted at 29 American universities and is now in the permanent collection of Ohio State University.

In 1993 Horsey traveled to Brussels, Belgium, as one of only 25 Americans chosen for the European Community Visitorship Program (now the European Union Visitors Program), which, according to the Web site eurunion.org, "invites young, promising leaders from countries outside the European Union to visit Europe to gain a first-hand appreciation of the EU's goals, policies and peoples and to increase mutual understanding between professionals from non-EU countries and their EU counterparts." After his fourth collection, *The Fall of Man* (1994), was published, Horsey spent a year in Washington, D.C, at the offices of the Hearst Corp. (which owns the *Seattle P-I*) to take a closer look at the activities of the three branches of the federal government. During the Lewis and Clark bicentennial, in 2005, Horsey followed the journey of the continental explorers Meriwether Lewis and William Clark from the Continental Divide, at a site between Montana and Idaho, to Cape Disappointment, at the southwestern tip of Washington, on the Pacific Ocean. He described his trip in October of that year, in seven "dispatches" illustrated with dozens of his photographs.

In 1999, while on vacation with his family in Mexico, Horsey received a phone call from *P-I* ordering him to return to the newsroom immediately. Back in Seattle, he learned that he had won that year's Pulitzer Prize for editorial cartooning. The prizes, regarded as the nation's highest honor in print journalism, are awarded by Columbia University, in New York City. Horsey's winning collection of cartoons largely covered the scandal that erupted in early 1998 when the public learned that President Bill Clinton had engaged in sexual activities with Monica Lewinsky when she was a White House intern, in 1995 and 1996—behavior that Clinton at first denied. "It was great fun to be the illustrator of this smarmy tale," Horsey told Joanna Wolper for *Editor & Publisher* (April 17, 1999). "It was like a sleazy soap opera nicely contained in one year." One of Horsey's cartoons, published on January 4, 1998, shows Clinton asleep, dreaming of a classroom in which the teacher is asking a group of youngsters, "Now, class, what is most memorable about America's forty-second president?" The children are gazing at a statue of Clinton striking a heroic pose while his trousers are down around his ankles, revealing boxer shorts decorated with hearts; the caption reads, "Bill Clinton's worst nightmare." In another, published on November 10, 1998, the Republican House Speaker, Newt Gingrich, is depicted as Captain Hook, from the story *Peter Pan*, screaming "Curse you, Peter Pan!" while desperately trying to save himself from the jaws of a crocodile labeled "'98 election"; Monica Lewinsky, drawn as Tinker Bell, follows a soaring Clinton, who has escaped unscathed from the croc. "Golly! Maybe I really *don't* have to ever grow up!" the president crows. That cartoon appeared a week after the 1998 mid-term elections, in which, despite the GOP's attacks on Clinton's morality, the Republican majority in the House shrank.

When Horsey was awarded another Pulitzer Prize, in 2003, he became the first editorial cartoonist in 18 years to win a second Pulitzer award. That year his work included cartoons commenting on the administration of President George W. Bush; the lead-up to the war in Iraq, which was launched in March 2003; and corporate corruption. Horsey has also won other honors for his cartooning. He received a Global Media Award from the Population Institute in 1991 and won first place in the 1994 Best of the West journalism competition. In 1995 he became the first cartoonist to receive an Environmental Media Award, and in 1998 the National Press Foundation honored him with the Barryman Award, for cartoonist of the year. Horsey has also won 14 regional awards from the Society of Professional Journalists, including, in 1999, the Susan Hutchison Bosch Award, which recognizes uncommon courage in journalism, for his work with the *P-I* as well as his government reporting for the *Daily Journal American*. Jim Borgman, a *Cincinnati Enquirer* editorial cartoonist and the judge of the 1994 Best of the West contest, told the *P-I* (May 16, 1995), "When you climb out over the mountains of pedestrian cartoons seen on American editorial pages, and then walk about another thousand miles, that's where you find David Horsey working, way out there on his own. Horsey draws as if he's never read the formulas for cobbling together a typical cartoon." In 2004 Seattle University awarded Horsey an honorary doctorate for his achievements, and the University of Washington Department of Communication inducted him into its Alumni Hall of Fame.

Horsey told Meghan Peters for a profile posted on the University of Washington Department of Communications Web site (2008, on-line) that he considers among his most successful works a map called "The World According to Ronald Reagan," which he made in the mid-1980s. Sales of the map totaled "tens of thousands of copies," according to Peters. Horsey has shown his work in several local exhibits, among them The Expanding Universe of David Horsey, a retrospective mounted at the Frye Art Museum in 2004, and Left, Right & Wrong: Celebrating the Art of Editorial Cartooning, shown at the Art Institute of Seattle in early 2008. Horsey published his fifth collection of cartoons, *One Man Show*, in 1999; it was followed by *From Hanging Chad to Baghdad* (2003) and *Draw Quick, Shoot Straight* (2007).

Although he has admitted to having a liberal bent, Horsey has made a point of drawing cartoons that address issues from opposite parts of the political spectrum. "I don't want to be predictable and because I think there are lunatics and fools on all sides, I try to step away from it once in a while when it's justified and take a shot at my own side," he told Terry Gross for the National Public Radio program *Fresh Air* (April 11, 2003). Horsey is usually not fazed by complaints about cartoons on such controversial issues as abortion, race, and religion, but sometimes he has felt compelled to respond to his critics. In early 2008, for example, some readers berated him regarding a cartoon addressing the federal government's steps to help financially troubled investment firms while ignoring mortgage borrowers facing foreclosure because of those firms' careless activities. The cartoon, published on March 27, was based on the biblical story of the Prodigal Son, in which a father forgives the son who, after demanding his inheritance, acts recklessly and loses all of it. The yarmulke Horsey drew on the head of the father in his cartoon led to charges of anti-Semitism from some readers, who felt that the drawing played into stereotypes by, in a sense, blaming Jewish bankers and investors for the nation's current economic downturn. In an entry on his Web site, DavidHorsey.com, the cartoonist apologized, writing, "I did not intend to disparage Jews. . . . The choice of setting for the cartoon was simply literal—the Prodigal Son story came out of ancient Judea, so I decided to take that as my visual metaphor." Horsey immediately made available another copy of the cartoon without the yarmulke, even though many national newspapers had already printed the original.

Despite such incidents, no *P-I* editor has ever asked Horsey to alter a cartoon. "There is a certain amount of independence about being a cartoonist, a job with a great cachet from being able to spout off every day in the newspaper in a space of your own," he told Marshall. "And it is a generally enjoyable job, pretty rewarding—one of the few jobs in journalism where you control your own product."

Horsey lives in Seattle with his wife, the former Nole Ann Ulery, whom he met while in high school. The couple have one daughter, Darielle, and one son, Daniel.

—M.A.S.

Suggested Reading: *A&S Perspectives* (on-line) Summer 1999; DavidHorsey.com; *Editor & Publisher* p34 Dec. 4, 1993; *Seattle Post-Intelligencer* C p1 Aug. 29, 1992, A p1 Apr. 13, 1999

Selected Books: *Horsey's Rude Awakenings*, 1981; *Horsey's Greatest Hits of the '80s*, 1989; *The Fall of Man*, 1994; *One Man Show*, 1999; *From Hanging Chad to Baghdad*, 2003; *Draw Quick, Shoot Straight*, 2007

David Cannon/Getty Images

Immelman, Trevor

Dec. 16, 1979– Golfer

Address: c/o PGA Tournament Players Club Network Office, 110 TPC Blvd., Ponte Vedra Beach, FL 32082

On April 13, 2008, on the 16th hole of the fourth and final round of the Masters Golf Tournament, in Augusta, Georgia, Trevor Immelman made a double bogey—that is, he shot two strokes over (worse than) par, "par" being the score standard for each hole; he thus found himself a mere three strokes ahead of golf's living legend Tiger Woods, who had just finished the day with an 18th-hole birdie. (A birdie is one stroke under par on a hole.) Immelman ran into trouble on the 17th hole, where his second shot landed in a sand trap. The South African was able to hit out of it and save par, bringing him within one hole of winning his first major title. On the 18th hole Immelman's drive landed in a deep divot, and once again it looked as if he might collapse under pressure and squander his lead. Instead, he placed his eight-iron shot on the green and again managed par, thereby winning the tournament. "I knew I had to go out there and just stick to my game, and stick to my game plan and play one shot at a time and just be tough," he said, according to Larry Dorman, writing for the *New York Times* (April 14, 2008, on-line). Immelman had led or co-led the Masters field after each round of the tournament, marking the first time since 1980 that a player had topped the leader board from start to finish.

Immelman's victory came after a year of health-related setbacks. While competing at the 2007 Masters, he contracted a stomach parasite, and the ensuing illness caused him to lose more than 20 pounds. Then, in December 2007, shortly after winning the Nedbank Challenge, a prestigious tournament in his home country, he underwent surgery to remove a golf-ball-size tumor from his diaphragm. While the growth turned out to be benign, Immelman missed two months of play. When he returned to the Professional Golf Association (PGA) Tour, he struggled to regain his form, failing to place higher than 40th in any of the five tournaments leading up to the 2008 Masters. He hit his stride, however, in Augusta, where, heading into the final round, he stood at 11 strokes under par—two ahead of his closest competitor. In that round he shot a three-over-par 75, and while it was by far his worst score of the tournament—his previous scores had been 68, 68, and 69—he held off Woods and the rest of the pack. A day earlier, according to Martin Blake, writing for the Melbourne, Australia, *Age* (April 15, 2008), the South African golf legend Gary Player had predicted Immelman's victory, saying on Immelman's voicemail, "There will be bad breaks, but I know you're going to win."

The younger of two boys, Trevor Immelman was born on December 16, 1979 in Somerset-West, a suburb of Cape Town, South Africa. His father, Johan, served as commissioner of the professional South African Tour, also known as the Sunshine Tour. Trevor and his brother, Mark, who is nine years older, grew up with an interest in the sport, watching tapes of major tournaments, such as the Masters, from an early age. Mark went on to become a standout golfer at Columbus State University, in Columbus, Georgia, and later accepted a coaching position at the school. Trevor took up the sport at the age of five, the same year he met Gary Player, the first South African golfer to win a Masters title. Player has kept in touch with Immelman throughout his career, acting as a mentor. "He's been kind of like another type of a father to me," Immelman told Blake.

Due to his prodigious golf skills, Immelman soon became something of a celebrity. "All of South Africa knew him from when he was, like, 6 or 7, almost like a Tiger Woods," the South African golf superstar Ernie Els told Jeff Brooke for the Toronto *Globe and Mail* (March 28, 2007). Before long Immelman was telling his parents that he wanted to become a professional. Once, when he was seven, Immelman "grabbed my ears and said, 'I'm going to be the greatest golfer in the world,'" Dudley Wolhuter, a member of Cape Town's Nomads Golf Club, told Jeremy Fowler for the *Orlando (Florida) Sentinel* (April 14, 2008). "I told him to get out of here." By the time he was 12, Immelman had become a scratch golfer—the term given to players capable of shooting par or better—and from 13 to 17, he devoted his summers to the sport. In 1996 he made South Africa's amateur squad and competed in the Eisenhower Trophy, an event held in Chile. In 1997, after playing in Japan and the U.S., he placed second at Royal St. George's, a British amateur tournament. He also made it to the final round of the New Zealand Amateur and the U.S. Junior Amateur events. The following year he won the U.S. Public Links title, and in 1999 he qualified for the Masters, making the cut—or advancing past the second round—and finishing 56th. Throughout his amateur career Immelman received support from his parents, who took out extra mortgages on their home to help finance his travels.

Immelman turned professional in 1999 but failed to qualify that year for the European Tour. Instead, he spent much of 2000 on the second-tier Challenge Tour, on which he won the Kenya Open.

That same year, playing on the Sunshine Tour, he won the Vodacom Players Championship. In 2001 he became a full-time member of the PGA European Tour, after which he struggled to justify the hype that had surrounded him during his amateur years. While other young players, including Sergio Garcia, Adam Scott, and Justin Rose, were winning tournaments and establishing themselves as breakout stars, Immelman eked out an 88th-place finish on the tour's Order of Merit, a list that ranks golfers according to their earnings. "I want to be the best in the world, I want to win majors and compete," he told Phil Casey for the *Irish News* (May 4, 2002). "That is the main goal but you have to take it one shot at a time. I think I am getting there."

Immelman's first European Tour victory came in January 2003, when he won the South African Airways Open. The tournament was played at Erinvale Golf Club, the Somerset-West course where Immelman had played throughout his youth. He won the event in dramatic fashion, forcing a sudden-death play-off with a birdie putt on the 18th hole. He made birdie once more on the play-off hole, defeating his countryman Tim Clark. "I can't tell you how many times I've walked down these fairways dreaming about a chance to do this," Immelman said, according to the UK Newsquest Regional Press (January 16, 2003). "There are no words to describe this." Later that month he won the Dimension Data Pro-Am, a Sunshine Tour event. In November 2003 Immelman and Rory Sabbatini, representing South Africa, won the World Golf Championships World Cup, held on Kiawah Island, South Carolina.

In January 2004 Immelman successfully defended his South African Airways Open title, once again triumphing at Erinvale. He made seven birdies in his final round and became the first golfer since Player to win the event in back-to-back years. (Player's successive wins were in 1976 and 1977.) Four months later Immelman traveled to Germany and picked up his third European Tour victory, winning the Deutsche Bank–SAP Open TPC of Europe. During the last eight holes of his final round, he shot four under par, and on the 17th he made a crucial, par-saving 18-foot putt. He made birdie on the final hole, where Padraig Harrington, who finished second, later missed a birdie putt that would have forced a play-off. Commenting on Immelman's play, John Hopkins wrote for the London *Times* (May 24, 2004), "There is an impressive air about him, a steeliness that hints at greater things to come."

In April 2005 Immelman appeared in his second Masters, shooting 65 in the third round and finishing in a tie for fifth place. That same year Player selected him to be a member of South Africa's President's Cup Team, an honor that qualified him for two years on the U.S. PGA Tour. (The President's Cup is an international contest that pits U.S. players against competitors from other nations in a series of matches.) "That was fantastic for me," Immelman told Tom Yantz for the *Hartford (Connect-*

icut) *Courant* (June 28, 2006). "You know to get selected into that team, it was probably the highlight of my career so far." While Immelman's play was not memorable—he went 1–3 as a member of the President's Cup Team—the experience of spending a week with superstars of golf, including Vijay Singh, Michael Campbell, and Mike Weir, proved to be educational. "I learned so much from them and got to spend valuable time with them in a team room situation or practice rounds when they were sharing information freely," he told Yantz.

In 2006 Immelman won his first PGA Tour event, the Cialis Western Open, held in Lemont, Illinois. He ended his final round by sinking a 32-foot birdie putt, putting himself at 12 under par—two strokes ahead of Tiger Woods, who had already finished playing, and Matthew Goggin and Singh, who were still on the course and in contention. Immelman had intended to play it safe and two-putt for par, which would have kept him one stroke ahead of Woods, but he unintentionally made the first putt. "It's one of those putts that you're actually not even looking at the hole because there was probably three yards of break on that," he told *Africa News* (July 10, 2006). "I was really just trying to throw it up there to the right side and hope that I got the right pace on it." The victory came two months after Immelman nearly won a pair of other tournaments: the Wachovia Championship, which he lost in a play-off against Jim Furyk, and the EDS Byron Nelson, which he lost by one stroke to Brett Wetterich. At the end of 2006, Immelman won the PGA's Rookie of the Year award.

While playing at the 2007 Masters, where he finished in 55th place, Immelman began to feel ill, and he was later diagnosed with having a stomach parasite. The illness caused him to miss a month of golf, and he lost more than 20 pounds. In December he withstood a late-round challenge from Justin Rose to win the Nedbank Golf Challenge, held in Sun City, South Africa. En route to winning the tournament, which some call "Africa's major," according to Lorne Rubenstein, writing for the *Globe and Mail* (April 14, 2008), he chipped in twice on the first nine holes, making up for the bogeys he would post on each of the final three. Shortly after the Nedbank victory, Immelman began feeling pain in his ribcage and having difficulty breathing. A visit to the doctor revealed a golf-ball-size tumor on his diaphragm, which he promptly had removed. The surgery to remove the growth—which was non-cancerous—left a seven-inch scar and kept him off the golf course for two months. "It's the usual cliché but it put a lot of perspective on things, especially as 10 days prior I was winning such a big tournament down in South Africa," he told James Corrigan for the London *Independent* (April 12, 2008). "You kind of go from feeling bullet-proof to lying in a hospital bed wondering if things are going to go your way."

After returning to the PGA Tour, Immelman had trouble equaling his success at the Nedbank event. He failed to make the cut in four of the eight tournaments leading up to the 2008 Masters, held in April, and he finished no better than 40th in the five events directly preceding play in Augusta. Despite those setbacks Immelman played well throughout the Masters, leading or co-leading the field throughout the tournament, which ranks among golf's most prestigious. After posting scores of 68, 68, and 69 in his first three rounds, he entered the final day with a two-stroke lead over Brandt Snedeker, his playing partner. Tiger Woods, the top-ranked player in the world, was six shots back. Immelman bogeyed on the first, eighth, and 12th holes, and after a double bogey on the 16th, he found himself three strokes ahead of Woods, who, thanks to a birdie on the 18th, had moved into second place. Immelman caught bad breaks on the 17th and 18th holes, landing in a sand trap and deep divot, respectively, but he made par both times, holding on to win his first major tournament. His three-over-par 75 was the highest final-round score by a Masters champion since Arnold Palmer's 1962 victory. "It's been the ultimate roller coaster, and I hate roller coasters," Immelman told Fowler. "I missed the cut last week and now I'm the Masters champion. That's the craziest thing I've ever heard of." The win ended Woods's chances of winning all four of golf's major tournaments in the same year, a feat he had previously described on his Web site as "easily within reason."

Following his Masters win Immelman enjoyed newfound fame. On April 14 he appeared on the *Late Show with David Letterman*, where he read a top-10 list titled, "Ways Trevor Immelman's Life Has Changed Since Winning the Masters." The number-one entry read, "Get to put my arm around Tiger Woods and say, 'Maybe next year.'" Following his win at the Masters, Immelman lost the Stanford St. Jude Championship in June, coming in close behind the winner, Justin Leonard, and tied for 19th place at the British Open, in July, and for 50th place at the Deutsche Bank Championship, in early September. Along with 144 other professional golfers, Immelman participated in the FedEx Cup Tour Championship in the fall of 2008. He placed 16th—better than he had in the 2007 FedEx tournament, in which he was 40th. In 2008 Immelman played a total of 22 events; his scoring average was 71.85. As of October 2008, he was ranked number 22 in the world.

Immelman lives and trains in Lake Nona, a wealthy community in Orlando, Florida. He and his wife, Carmenita, have a son, Jacob, who was born in 2006. In addition to golfing, Immelman, like his father, brother, and two of his uncles, plays the drums. He became a close friend of Tico Torres, the drummer for the rock band Bon Jovi, after the two met at a Scottish pro-am tournament (one in which both professionals and amateurs compete).

—K.J.P.

Suggested Reading: (London) *Sunday Times* May 5, 2002; *Los Angeles Times* D p1 Apr. 14, 2008; *Milwaukee (Wisconsin) Journal Sentinel* July 10, 2006; *Newsday* A p45 Apr. 14, 2008; *Orlando (Florida) Sentinel* D p1 Apr. 14, 2008; *USA Today* C p8 July 10, 2006

Brendan Hoffman/Getty Images

Jackson Lee, Sheila

Jan. 12, 1950– U.S. representative from Texas (Democrat)

Address: 2435 Rayburn House Office Bldg., Washington, DC 20515

The one response rarely triggered by the words and deeds of Sheila Jackson Lee is neutrality. A member of the U.S. House of Representatives from Texas's 18th Congressional District, which encompasses much of Houston and its surrounding areas, Jackson Lee has been praised by many as a champion of causes including affirmative action, programs for disadvantaged youth, women's rights, education, immigration reform, and human rights overseas. Her detractors have called her a publicity hound and cited reports of her personal conduct, which has led her staff members to resign at a rate perhaps unparalleled on Capitol Hill. Elected to her first term in 1994, in a year when Democrats across the nation fared poorly at the polls, Jackson Lee defeated her Republican opponent by a large margin and went on to win reelection with ease in subsequent contests. She currently serves as whip of the Congressional Black Caucus. Jackson Lee was a municipal judge and then a Houston City Council member before beginning her tenure in the U.S. Congress. "I want to be a change-maker . . . ," she told *Ebony* (March 1999), "to make a difference, open doors that have been slammed shut, tread upon ground that has not been trod upon and reach beyond myself and help someone else."

The congresswoman was born Sheila Jackson on January 12, 1950 in the New York City borough of Queens. She grew up in a working-class family and was among the first wave of New York public-school students who were bused to schools outside their neighborhoods for the sake of integration. She felt inspired by the work of Martin Luther King Jr. and others in the civil rights movement to push the boundaries of what a young African-American woman could achieve. "The atmosphere in which I grew up was filled with a never-say-never attitude," Jackson Lee told *Ebony*. "So there wasn't anything, despite growing up in the '50s and '60s and seeing discrimination, that I thought I could not do. Because the question was always asked, why not? Why couldn't you do it? So the obvious answer would be yes you can. You just need to try."

Following her graduation from Jamaica High School, in Queens, Jackson Lee attended Yale University, in New Haven, Connecticut, as part of the first class in which female students were admitted. She received a B.A. degree in political science with honors in 1972, then enrolled at the University of Virginia School of Law, receiving her J.D. degree in 1975. Meanwhile, in 1973, she had married Elwyn C. Lee; the couple later moved to Houston, where Elwyn Lee had been offered a job at the University of Houston. He currently serves as the school's vice chancellor for student affairs for the University of Houston system and vice president for student affairs at the University of Houston.

In Houston Jackson Lee went to work in 1980 as a corporate lawyer for United Energy Resources. She remained there until 1987, also serving as chairperson of the Black Women Lawyers Association from 1980 to 1981 as well as president of the Houston Lawyers Association from 1983 to 1984. Earlier, she had obtained her first government experience, serving for a year beginning in 1977 as staff counsel to the U.S. House Select Committee on Assassinations.

After two unsuccessful attempts to attain local judgeships, Jackson Lee won the post of Houston municipal judge in 1987. She served in that position for three years, leaving when she was elected to the Houston City Council in 1990. While on the city council, Jackson Lee grew popular with Houston residents for her efforts at curbing gun violence and initiating after-school and summer programs for disadvantaged youth. She was forced from office in 1994, due to the implementation of term limits for city-council members.

That year Jackson Lee announced her bid for a seat in the U.S. House of Representatives. The Democratic incumbent in the 18th Congressional District, Craig Washington, was vulnerable because of his opposition to the North Atlantic Free Trade Agreement (NAFTA) and two federally funded projects in Houston, the construction of a space station and of a superconducting super collider; all were seen as important in bringing jobs to Houston. Jackson Lee defeated Washington in the Democratic primary with 63 percent of the vote; in the general election in the mostly Democratic district, she won an easy victory over the Republican candidate, Jerry Burley. (Her victory came at a time when Republicans took control of both houses of Congress for the first time in four decades.) Jackson Lee was sworn in as a member of the House of Representatives in January 1995.

As a Democrat representing a largely liberal, urban community, Jackson Lee vowed to fight for such progressive causes as women's rights, civil rights, immigration reform, and social programs to help the underprivileged and improve their socioeconomic status. For a role model she looked to the black legislator Barbara Jordan, who had represented the 18th Congressional District from 1973 to 1979 and had made a name for herself as a member of the Judiciary Committee during the Watergate hearings. "The lessons that have to be learned by Democrats [are] that we have to stand for something," Jackson Lee told Lloyd Gite for *Black Enterprise* (June 1995) months after being elected. "I'm more than happy to listen and to learn from those who have been there. But I'm also willing to stand for what I believe in."

In 1991 Texas's 18th Congressional District had been redrawn so that African-American voters would be better represented. In 1996 a federal panel of judges ruled that that instance of gerrymandering was unconstitutional, and the district's boundaries were redrawn once more. Jackson Lee nonetheless won the subsequent election handily. Meanwhile, she had been active in Congress. She strongly urged the House to allocate funds for summer-job programs for urban youth, without which, she argued, young people would be more likely to turn to crime and gang activity. She also played a key role in amending the Foreign Operations Appropriations Bill to provide funding for the African Development Foundation. While some of her female and minority colleagues in Congress tried to downplay the importance of race and gender in their legislative activities, she turned a spotlight on it. "As women, African-American women, we are free to be emotional, soft nurturers, and we do bring that to the United States Congress," she told Lisa Jones Townsel for *Ebony* (March 1997). When speaking on the floor of the House, though, "I put 'femaleness' behind me; I don't even think about it," she told Townsel. "With respect to my colleagues, whether they are Democratic or Republican, I feel very comfortable in approaching them on issues and convincing them that they should be a sponsor on some legislation or that they should vote on an issue or that we should work together." As whip of the Congressional Black Caucus, she is responsible for getting its members to support certain causes and show up for key votes.

Jackson Lee has often stood her ground in support of unpopular causes or against causes that have much support elsewhere. In 1996 she was the only member of the Texas delegation who did not vote for the legislation resulting in the Defense of Marriage Act, which restricted recognition of homosexual unions. With regard to other hot-button issues, Jackson Lee has voted over the years against bans on so-called partial-birth abortion, against an amendment to the Constitution outlawing desecration of the U.S. flag, and in favor of a ban on oil drilling in the Arctic National Wildlife Refuge. Though she has generally voted along party lines, she has differed with other Democrats on some issues—favoring, for example, the permanent normalizing of U.S. trade relations with China, which she sees as beneficial to Houston's economy and to human rights. With regard to human-rights abuses in other overseas nations, she has advocated sanctions against the government of Sudan, where militias have carried out a campaign of violence against non-Arab groups. On the domestic front, in 1998 she addressed the problem of infant abduction and "baby-switching" in hospitals, crafting a bill that would strengthen hospital-security measures and increase penalties for those involved in such activities. "It's devastating and a nightmare for a parent to know they've taken home the wrong baby," Jackson Lee's spokesman told the *Washington Post* (October 1, 1998). "Who knows how many of these go unreported?"

In 1998 Jackson Lee came to the defense of affirmative action, working to defeat a proposition that would have ended its inclusion in Houston city agencies' hiring practices. A similar measure had recently passed in California, and Jackson Lee wished to prevent the same result in Houston, one of several cities where propositions with exactly the same wording had been put on ballots. She worked to educate voters on what she believed to be the beneficial aspects of affirmative action and helped draft the wording of the proposition. In California the wording had reflected a bias against affirmative action; voters were asked whether they wanted to ban "preferential treatment." In Houston, however, voters were asked simply whether they wished to ban affirmative action in city contracting and hiring. "We worked very hard on the wording to minimize confusion," Jackson Lee told Eric L. Smith for *Black Enterprise* (January 1998). "It was clear that this measure would end affirmative action, and we were not going to stand for that in Houston." Voters ultimately voted in favor of affirmative action, thanks in no small part to Jackson Lee's efforts.

The 105th Congress also saw Jackson Lee, as a member of the Judiciary Committee's Subcommittee on Commercial and Administrative Law, take the initiative on legislation to ensure child-support and alimony payments by parents in the event of bankruptcy proceedings involving those parents. In 1999, in the 106th Congress, Jackson Lee focused on the issue of sexual violence and so-called hate crimes, initiating two bills targeting date rape and bias-related violence, respectively. The Hate Crimes Prevention Act imposed stricter jail terms on those convicted of serious crimes motivated by victims' race, religion, gender, or sexual orientation. The Hillory J. Farias and Samantha Reid Date Rape Prevention Drug Act raised penalties for possessing and/or distributing GHB (gamma hydroxy-butyric acid) and ketamine, common "date-rape drugs," or drugs used to incapacitate potential victims or affect their ability to remember events. The legislation was named for two women who died after ingesting GHB.

Also in 1999 Jackson Lee proposed an amendment to a House appropriations bill to guarantee funding to the National Aeronautics and Space Administration (NASA); in addition, she worked to see that part of NASA's funding is used to recruit graduates of historically black colleges and universities. In efforts on behalf of technology education, she has helped to pass legislation requiring the National Science Foundation to give some of its surplus computers to elementary and secondary schools. With Senator Edward M. Kennedy of Massachusetts, in the 106th Congress Jackson Lee cosponsored a bill to honor all members of minorities who served the U.S. in World War II.

Much of the negative publicity Jackson Lee has received has centered on personal conduct rather than policy positions. She came under fire in 2002 for potential ethics violations after the discovery that she used a chauffeured government vehicle each morning to get from her residence to her office, little more than one block away. (No official reprimand has been issued.) In 1999 Continental Airlines demanded that Jackson Lee improve her behavior toward the airline and its personnel, after one incident in which she complained loudly during a flight that she had not received the seafood meal she had requested, and many instances in which she made several reservations in the same week for flights from Washington, D.C., to Houston, taking the flight that turned out to be most convenient for her—and leaving the airline unable to fill the other seats. Her treatment of her aides has given the congresswoman possibly the highest staff-turnover rate on Capitol Hill. One former legislative counsel recalled that Jackson Lee threatened twice to fire her during the subordinate's first week on the job, and another aide claimed that he quit after Jackson Lee threw a cell phone at him. Jackson Lee has declined to speak to the press on any of those subjects. A more serious controversy involved her ties to Kenneth J. Lay, the chairman of the energy company Enron from 1986 to 2000, who was a major fund-raiser for Jackson Lee in 1994; following the collapse of Enron due to financial mismanagement and dishonest bookkeeping, a development that adversely affected many in the congresswoman's district, Jackson Lee was uncharacteristically silent on the issue of corporate malfeasance. On a different front, Jackson Lee once drew derision by complaining that the names given—hurricanes—such as Andrew and Katrina—are "lily-white," suggesting that some hurricanes be given names of African-American and other racial and ethnic origin. That and other comments over the years have led some to accuse the congress-woman of raising the issue of race in situations that do not warrant it.

In 2002 Jackson Lee was among the minority of representatives who voted against authorizing the invasion of Iraq. After President George W. Bush succeeded in obtaining the authorization, she convened an emergency meeting of Democrats to try to come up with alternatives to military action. Meanwhile, she drafted a competing resolution that would bring home all but 50,000 U.S. troops from the Middle East; increase humanitarian aid to Iraq; restart the Middle East peace process, which has sought to resolve the Israeli-Palestinian conflict; and reaffirm U.S. support for the U.N. Security Council. Though the resolution and the meeting of Democrats failed to prevent the U.S. invasion, they established Jackson Lee as an important voice of opposition to the war, a stance that much of the public has since come to embrace. (Dissatisfaction with the course of the war was seen as a major factor in the return of Congress to Democratic control in the 2006 elections.)

In 2003 Jackson Lee introduced a sweeping proposal to overhaul the current immigration system. As quoted by David Bacon in *Colorlines Magazine* (December 22, 2004), she called the guest-worker program advocated by President Bush "a flat Earth program," one that would create a group of second-class citizens. Under it, Mexicans and others living in the U.S. without visas would obtain legal status as temporary contract laborers for U.S. businesses; while they would be "protected by labor laws" and "enjoy the same working conditions that the law requires for American workers," they would be encouraged to return home when their approved periods of work expired. By contrast, the proposal for the Comprehensive Immigration Fairness Reform Act, written and introduced by Jackson Lee, would offer the foreign workers a chance for permanent legal residency. Jackson Lee stressed that her bill was aimed not at granting amnesty but at creating a path to citizenship in exchange for certain actions on the part of immigrants. She explained her concept to David C. Ruffin for the *Crisis* (July/August 2006) as "earned access to legalization": "It means get in line, learn the language, do community service, pay fines and wait for five or six years. Ultimately, you may not make it. If you meet the criteria, we will consider giving you legal permanent resident status, which then allows you to get on the pathway to citizenship." The bill did not pass, but Jackson Lee has remained a firm advocate for immigrants' rights, especially with regard to refugees from Liberia and Haiti. "Families are torn apart" through the denial of citizenship to immigrants, she lamented to Bacon, "and we're not adding to our security, but only to the misery of human beings who want to give their best to this country. We have a system that's not helping anyone."

In 2007 Jackson Lee was a co-sponsor of proposed legislation for the Assault Weapons Ban and Law Enforcement Protection Act, which failed in committee but will likely be reintroduced in a different form. She campaigned for U.S. senator Hillary Clinton of New York during the 2008 Democratic presidential primary race; after Senator Barack Obama of Illinois won the nomination, she threw her support behind him. On that year's Election Day, she beat her opponent, the conservative Republican John Faulk, with nearly 80 percent of the vote.

Jackson Lee has received many honors for her efforts as a lawmaker, including the 2006 Award for Policy at the 16th Annual Phillip Burton Immigration & Civil Rights Awards, the Revelation Urban Development Institute's Drum Major Award for Public Service, and the National Technical Associ-

ation of Scientists and Engineers' Top Women in the Sciences Award. In 1999 *Ebony* named the congresswoman one of the "100 Most Fascinating Black Women of the Century." In addition to serving as whip of the Congressional Black Caucus, Jackson Lee chairs the Congressional Children's Caucus, is senior whip of the Democratic Caucus, and co-chairs the Pakistan Caucus. She is a member of the Judiciary Committee, the Homeland Security Committee, and the Foreign Affairs Committee and sits on various subcommittees of those bodies. Jackson Lee and her husband have two grown children, Jason and Erica.

—J.E.P.

Suggested Reading: *Black Enterprise* p32 June 1995; *Colorlines Magazine* p11 Dec. 22, 2004; *Ebony* p100 Mar. 1999; jacksonlee.house.gov; *Politics in America 2008*

Courtesy of Abrams Books

Jaffee, Al

Mar. 13, 1921– Cartoonist; illustrator

Address: MAD *Magazine, Dept. 354, 1700 Broadway, New York, NY 10019*

For more than four decades, the comic-strip artist and illustrator Al Jaffee has satirized popular culture, politics, and society from the inside back cover of the long-running humor magazine *MAD*. Known as the "fold-in," Jaffee's popular contribution to the magazine has parodied American cur-

rent events since it first appeared, in 1964; according to Neil Genzlinger, writing for the *New York Times* (March 30, 2008), "Today you could teach a pretty good course in modern American history just using Mr. Jaffee's fold-ins." The feature comprises a large drawing with a question in a panel above it and a panel with text below. When the drawing is physically folded into uneven thirds, so that the inner sides of the left and right columns touch, a new image and bottom text are formed, displaying a humorous answer to the question. Found in the magazine under the heading "Here We Go With Another Ridiculous *MAD* Fold-In" and originally intended to parody the "fold-outs" of popular mainstream magazines, the fold-in has become a core feature of *MAD*'s satirical and sarcastic content. *MAD*, founded by William Gaines and Harvey Kurtzman in 1952, offers comic-strip parodies of movies and TV shows as well as original illustrated content, including the well-known "Spy vs. Spy" panel and cover art that always features the iconic, gap-toothed character Alfred E. Neuman. Today the fold-in, too, has achieved an iconic status; it has been referred to on television, in music, and in other print publications, becoming part of the same pop-culture milieu its originator mocks. Jaffee has also been recognized, although to a lesser extent, for his panel "Snappy Answers to Stupid Questions," another long-running *MAD* feature.

Jaffee started his career drawing children's material for Timely Comics, the forerunner of Marvel Comics, but it was not until he met Kurtzman and joined *MAD* in the 1950s that he began to receive recognition for his work. In the same decade he left *MAD* to follow Kurtzman into two failed humor-magazine ventures, then returned in 1958 to work as a writer and occasional artist. He suggested the fold-in to the editors in 1964 and, after it proved popular, became the feature's sole artist and primary creative force—a position he has held ever since. Jaffee told Genzlinger that as of March 2008—at the age of 87—he had done at least 400 fold-ins; Genzlinger noted, "No current [MAD] contributor . . . goes back further than Mr. Jaffee. And while other *MAD* features, like Spy vs. Spy, have changed artists over the years, only Mr. Jaffee has drawn the fold-in." On his ability to stay abreast of youth culture for material, Jaffee told Genzlinger, "I work for a magazine that's essentially for young people, and to have them keep me going, I feel very lucky. . . . I'm like an old racehorse. When the other horses are running, I want to run too."

Allan Jaffee was born on March 13, 1921 in Savannah, Georgia. His parents were originally from Lithuania; in an interview with John Koch for the *Boston Globe Magazine* (August 27, 2000, on-line), he described his upbringing as "dysfunctional." When he was six years old, his mother took him and his brothers to live in Lithuania in a small Jewish community known as a shtetl, where they stayed from 1927 until 1933. Jaffee told Koch that he credits the subversive humor of that community with helping to shape his own comedic tendencies. At the time Lithuanian society was marked by anti-Semitism. According to Jaffee, "It was an oppressive society. . . . [Jews] couldn't work in government offices, and there were many places you couldn't go. . . . And so, a kind of sardonic sense of humor develops. I listened to the comments these old Jews would make about the government and its leaders, and it would be sort of satirical. There was . . . a tremendous, subversive undercurrent." When the Nazi leader Adolf Hitler rose to power in Germany, in 1933, Jaffee's father came to Lithuania to bring his family back to the United States, where they settled in New York City.

During his time in Lithuania, Jaffee managed to stay connected to the American comic strips he had grown fond of; before he left Savannah, he had made his father promise to mail them to him. He told Koch, "Every six months or so, a huge roll of newspaper comic strips arrived at the post office. My brother [Harry] and I would be in ecstasy for months. We literally learned to read and write English from reading the comic strips." At the time Jaffee was a fan of the rebellious antics of the characters Hanz and Fritz in *Katzenjammer Kids*, a comic created by Rudolph Dirks in 1897. He also enjoyed the daily strip *Mutt & Jeff* and read *Little Orphan Annie*, a strip that displayed social awareness and focused on an orphan girl. He told Koch that those comics nurtured his and his brother's creativity. "We copied them—we would sit down and draw those characters," he said. "And we would invent our own little comic strips. We got into it very early, and my brother became a fine artist, but I went the other way."

In New York Jaffee attended the High School of Music and Art, where other students included his future *MAD* colleagues John Severin, Al Feldstein, and Kurtzman. (Jaffee would not meet Feldstein

and Kurtzman until later.) In school he learned basic art techniques and created his first comic-strip character, Inferior Man, a parody of Superman. Jaffee told Koch that Inferior Man was "a little accountant by daytime, and by nighttime, he ran out in his underwear and jumped from roof to roof, usually missing." Jaffee showed the cartoon to the successful writer and illustrator Will Eisner, who purchased it and placed it on filler pages of published comic books. That success led Jaffee to begin selling work to comic-strip publishers including Timely, which would later become the pioneering superhero empire Marvel Comics. Timely published a number of Jaffee's animal-themed children's comics, including *Ziggy Pig and Silly Seal* and *Super Rabbit*.

In 1942 Jaffee served in World War II, using his artistic abilities to draw informational booklets and training aids for the U.S. Army's rehabilitation programs. When he returned to civilian life, he continued to draw for Timely, working on the teen romance series *Patsy Walker*. Working on that series afforded Jaffee the opportunity to meet Kurtzman, who drew the comic's filler pages. Kurtzman started *MAD*, published by William Gaines, in 1952 and later invited Jaffee to come aboard as an illustrator. Then, in 1956, Kurtzman had a falling out with Gaines over ownership rights and left to start a new comic magazine, *Trump*. Jaffee decided to follow him into the new venture, which would later be financed by *Playboy*'s publisher, Hugh Hefner. The magazine—which Jaffee described to Gavin McInnes for Viceland.com as "a very slick version of what Harvey's idea of *MAD* had been"—lasted for only three issues, the third of which was never published. Undeterred, Kurtzman, Jaffee, and their colleagues put up money to start another magazine, *Humbug*, which ran for a total of 11 issues, until they ran out of money, in 1958. When *Humbug* folded, Jaffee decided to return to *MAD*. "I didn't know if MAD considered me the enemy for leaving, but I took a chance and called Feldstein," he told Mark Evanier for the book *MAD Art: A Visual Celebration of the Art of MAD Magazine and the Idiots Who Create It* (2002). Feldstein harbored no resentment toward Jaffee and hired him to work as a story writer and occasional artist.

In 1964 Jaffee conceived the idea to parody the "fold-outs" of popular magazines such as *Life* and *Playboy*, which featured full-color two-page spreads that readers could unfold. At first Jaffee did not think Feldstein or Gaines would approve of the idea, "because it mutilates the magazine," as he told Genzlinger. To his surprise they approved, and the first fold-in appeared in the April 1964 issue. Explaining the logic behind the fold-ins, Jaffee told Evanier, "The inside back cover of *MAD* was the perfect place for them, and it was black-and-white then. So instead of a magnificently printed fold-out, we had a cheaply printed Fold-In. It was right in keeping with the sensibility of the magazine." He told Koch, "It's unique in *MAD* in that it is an editorial cartoon. *MAD* doesn't carry editorial cartoons: It carries jokes. And also, it's interactive: The reader gets to do something." Indeed, Jaffee's penchant for editorializing was evident in his earliest fold-ins. In the second one, from the June 1964 issue, a drawing of that year's Republican presidential candidates alongside the question "Who wants to be president more than anything?" could be folded to reveal a drawing of future president Richard Nixon, under the answer, "Who wants anything?" An interactive feature on the fold-ins assembled by Genzlinger, Tom Jackson, and Sylvia Rupani-Smith for the *New York Times* Web site noted that "the fold-in has often been uncannily prescient, as with this one . . . published . . . a full four years before Richard M. Nixon did indeed become president." The writers also observed, "Sometimes the fold-in has been more of an editorial statement than a joke." In July 1968 Jaffee provided commentary on the drafting of school dropouts during the Vietnam War; a drawing of students outside a job center with the question, "What is the one thing most school dropouts are sure to become?" folds in to reveal a student in a cannon above the text, "cannon fodder."

Jaffee has also used the fold-in to comment unfavorably on drugs and other addictive substances. A fold-in from July 1971 offered his take on the drug abuse by U.S. soldiers serving in Vietnam; the question "What deadly missions are more and more servicemen voluntarily going on?" yielded the answer, "drug trips." Pop culture has also been a target; a September 1978 fold-in depicts a colorful butterfly under the text, "What colorful fantastic creature is still being exploited even after it has wiggled and died?" The fold-in transformed the butterfly into an image of the deceased rock pioneer Elvis Presley, who—then a year after his death—was still a major source of revenue for the music industry. Criticism of U.S. political leaders has also frequently surfaced in the fold-ins; when President Bill Clinton and his wife, Hillary Rodham Clinton, were accused of fraudulent real-estate activity during the Whitewater scandal of the early and mid-1990s (they were never formally charged), the September 1994 question "What part of the Clinton crime plan seems destined to fail?" yielded the answer, "Covering up Whitewater."

In 1968 *MAD* began printing the inside covers in color, prompting some—including Jaffee—to worry that he would have trouble incorporating color into the complexities of the fold-in. He adapted successfully, although, as he has noted, color has made the process more time-consuming. "I didn't believe I could do it," he told Evanier. "What prompted me to try was that Bill [Gaines] said he'd pay three times the black-and-white rate for an inside cover in color. I thought I was upping my income, but the color ones take three times as long, sometimes more." While he now uses a computer program to handle typographic tricks, Jaffee has always drawn the fold-in by hand. He never folds it during the drawing process. "I'm working on a hard, flat board," he told Genzlinger. "I cannot fold it. That's why my planning has to be so correct."

Jaffee's other successful creation for *MAD* is the "Snappy Answers to Stupid Questions" feature, an illustrated panel that offers three lively and sarcastic responses to what Jaffee perceives to be thoughtless questions; the feature was described by Genzlinger as "basically a running clinic on how to insult someone." One panel from the October 1965 issue, for example, depicts a man stuck in a tree as the result of a car accident. A bystander is seen asking him, "Have an accident?" On a side bar Jaffee has printed three possible "snappy" responses: "No, thanks. I already have one"; "No, I'm a modern sculptor"; and "No, I'm starting a junk yard." The regular panel became Jaffee's second most popular *MAD* feature, spawning eight books of collected material over the years, including *MAD's Snappy Answers to Stupid Questions* (1968) and *MAD's Al Jaffee Spews Out More Snappy Answers to Stupid Questions* (1988).

Jaffee has also drawn and created other features and panels for *MAD*. For the June 1963 issue he illustrated and wrote a feature called "If Kids Designed Their Own Xmas Toys," which consisted of crude drawings of dolls and rocket ships— supposedly done by children—that Jaffee made into physical replications that were faithful to the misshapen figures and skewed proportions of the drawings. His humorous panels devoted to inventions, such as a "spray shield" attached to a soda can (October 1979), have become popular over time and were collected in the 1978 book *Al Jaffee's Mad Inventions*. Jaffee has also contributed puzzle features, illustrations for parodic pieces, and magazine covers. The *MAD* tie-in books for which Jaffee has provided art and text include *MAD Morality* (1972), *MAD's Vastly Overrated Al Jaffee* (1983), and *Al Jaffee's Mad Book of Magic and Other Dirty Tricks* (1988). He has also published non–*MAD*-related work, such as *Al Jaffee Gets His Just Desserts* (1980) and numerous illustrated books featuring Willie Weirdie, an original character. A published collection of fold-ins, *MAD: Fold This Book! A Ridiculous Collection of Fold-Ins*, was published in 1997.

In 2005 the alternative-pop musician Beck paid tribute to Jaffee with the video for his single "Girl." The video, directed by the Motion Theory production team, featured signs and city blocks folding in on themselves to reveal hidden messages. On Jaffee's 85th birthday, in 2006, the comedian Stephen Colbert invited Jaffee on his satirical news show, *The Colbert Report*, and presented him with a birthday cake that, when folded, read, "Al, you are old." In 2008 Abrams Image published the best of *Tall Tales*, a vertical comic strip Jaffee drew for the *Herald Tribune* between 1957 and 1963. Fantagraphics published a two-volume set of *Humbug* later in 2008.

Jaffee, who lives in New York with his wife, Joyce, continues to draw the fold-in from his studio on the East Side of Manhattan. Although a tremor in his drawing hand that has developed in recent years initially presented him with a challenge, he told McInnes that he uses his other hand to steady it: "It's been working for a couple of years now, and when that stops working I'll find some other solution." Despite his age, Jaffee possesses a seemingly irrepressible creative zeal. "If I were fired tomorrow from *MAD*, I think the old creative juices, the old invention, would surge," he told Koch. "And either I would be storming the galleries and creating tons of stuff for them or trying to invent a line that fits me that's half crazy humor and half fine art."

—W.D.

Suggested Reading: *New York Times* Arts and Leisure p1 Mar. 30, 2008; Viceland.com; Evanier, Mark. *MAD Art: A Visual Celebration of the Art of MAD Magazine and the Idiots Who Create It*, 2002

Selected Books: *MAD's Snappy Answers to Stupid Questions*, 1968; *MAD Morality*, 1972; *Al Jaffee's Mad Inventions*, 1978; *Al Jaffee Gets His Just Desserts*, 1980; *MAD's Vastly Overrated Al Jaffee*, 1983; *MAD's Al Jaffee Spews Out More Snappy Answers to Stupid Questions*, 1988; *Al Jaffee's Mad Book of Magic and Other Dirty Tricks*, 1988; *MAD: Fold This Book! A Ridiculous Collection of Fold-Ins*, 1997; *Tall Tales*, 2008; *Humbug*, 2008

Courtesy of Joseph Jamail

Jamail, Joe

Oct. 19, 1925– Trial lawyer

Address: Jamail & Kolius, One Allen Ctr., 500 Dallas St., Suite 3434, Houston, TX 77002-4793

For most of the 55 years that he has practiced law, the Texas trial lawyer Joe Jamail has been known ubiquitously as the "King of Torts," for his record of winning spectacular settlements for plaintiffs in malpractice, negligence, and product-liability cases. While claiming more trial victories than anyone else, he has also become one of the most financially successful lawyers in the history of U.S. civil and corporate law: in the late 1970s he was included in the *Guinness Book of World Records* for

winning the largest-ever individual personal-injury suit, in *Coates v. Remington Arms*, with a $6.8 million settlement; in 1985 he won the biggest lawsuit in history, in *Pennzoil v. Texaco*, with a nearly $11 billion verdict; and in 1999 he represented investors defrauded by the computer disk-drive maker MiniScribe and their accounting firm, Coopers & Lybrand, in *United States National Bank of Galveston, et al. v. Coopers & Lybrand, et al.*, for which he won a $568 million jury verdict. To date he has amassed more than $12 billion in jury awards and more than $13 billion in other verdicts and settlements and has served as lead counsel in more than 200 personal-injury cases in which settlements were in excess of $1 million. Jamail has also been responsible for the national recall of three hazardous products: the Remington 600 rifle, the Honda All-Terrain 3-Wheel Vehicle, and the prescription drug Parlodel. Known for his uncanny ability in selecting juries, extensive preparation, and zealous advocacy on behalf of his clients, Jamail has frequently drawn criticism for his scathing ad hominem attacks on opposing attorneys. In 2003 Jamail published an autobiography, *Lawyer: My Trials and Jubilations*, co-written with Mickey Herskowitz. Jamail said to Steve Quinn for the *Dallas Morning News* (November 30, 2003), "I'll tell you this. I'm proud to be a lawyer. It's the last place to fight for people legitimately without swords, knives, and machine guns and tell the corporate world they are not going to get away with this."

The second of the five children of Joseph and Marie (Anton) Jamail, Joseph Dahr Jamail Jr. was born on October 19, 1925 in Houston, Texas. His grandparents and other relatives immigrated to Houston from Lebanon at the turn of the 20th century. (The family name was originally Gemayel; immigration officials recorded it incorrectly, resulting in its current spelling.) In Texas Jamail's great-uncles started what would become a successful produce business; during the 1920s and 1930s, his father and uncle followed their lead, running a prosperous chain of produce markets in the Houston area. Jamail has recalled that in those years, which brought the Great Depression, his parents gave food to unemployed strangers. The compassion his family showed toward those less fortunate would influence his work in the courtroom. The family business also catered to a wide mix of people, including blue-collar workers and farmers, which contributed to Jamail's ability to deal with people from all backgrounds. A "neighborhood runt," as Steve Quinn put it, Jamail was often picked on by bullies, until he became determined to fight back.

After graduating from St. Thomas High School in 1942, at the age of 16, Jamail enrolled at Texas A&M University, then transferred after a short time to the University of Texas (UT) at Austin. Less than a semester passed before Jamail, flunking all of his premed courses, forged his parents' signatures to join the Marine Corps. After serving in the Pacific theater during World War II, he returned home, only to spend much of his time for several months drinking in bars. Eventually his father gave him a car and $300 to start a new life somewhere else. Jamail relocated to Lafayette, Louisiana, where he attended Southwest Louisiana Institute for a year. During that time, an encounter at a Lafayette bar with a family friend, a Louisiana lawyer named Kaliste Saloom, got him interested in the legal field. After visiting Saloom and watching him work with clients, Jamail thought, as he recalled to Quinn, "I can get paid for this?" Jamail then returned to the University of Texas, managing to have removed from the university's records his failing grades from his first stint at the school.

Upon receiving a B.A. degree in history, in 1949, Jamail enrolled at UT's law program. As has been widely reported, he was unaware of the exam required to enter law school; he simply arrived and began taking classes. Jamail failed a course in tort law during his freshman year and was advised by his professor to seek another line of work. Jamail nonetheless persevered, even persuading the law school's dean to sign his diploma after it was discovered, shortly before graduation, that he had never taken the entrance exam. He told Claudia Feldman for the *Houston Chronicle* (October 21, 2003), "I believe in second chances. If it weren't for the many people who have helped me over the years, I'd be selling bananas. People need help. People need breaks." Prior to graduating, Jamail had tried and won his first case, after suing a brewing company on behalf of a barmaid who had cut her hand while opening a beer bottle.

Once out of law school, Jamail started defending insurance companies for Fulbright, Crooker, Freeman, and Bates (later Fulbright and Jaworski), a white-shoe law firm in Houston. He quickly grew dissatisfied there, later recalling to Anthony Head for *Texas Super Lawyers* (October 2004), an annual publication of *Texas Monthly*, "I lasted about 20 minutes in that kind of corporate law-by-committee environment." He next went to work for the district attorney's office in Harris County, Texas, where he handled a wide variety of cases. Wanting to have autonomy in his cases, he formed his own practice in 1954, to work as a "sore-back lawyer" (legal slang for a lawyer who specializes in personal-injury cases). He first made headlines in 1959, after winning an $85,000 award for the widow of a man who had killed himself by driving—drunkenly, it was alleged—into a tree that was obscured from view. In the case, *Glover v. the City of Houston* (also known as "the Case of the Killer Tree"), Jamail was able to invalidate the coroner's toxicology report by explaining that he had used an unreliable gauge of drunkenness, drawing blood from the dead man's stomach cavity.

In the early 1960s Jamail tried a case that helped bring about the later passage of a products-liability law in Texas. He represented a man named Olin Robertson, who had lost both of his hands and a foot in an accident that involved a faulty electrical box. The accident occurred on the premises of the company Texaco, where Robertson had been sent by his employer, McCullough Tool. McCullough agreed to keep him on the payroll; Texaco viewed the accident as a simple workman's-compensation case and gave him a check for only $12,000. After Robertson was refused an additional $2,500 for a leg prosthesis, he decided to sue Texaco. At the time Texas courts did not review cases of product liability, seeing negligence as the only basis for a suit in such cases. While holding to the general charge of negligence, Jamail modified the suit to include the electrical-box manufacturer, Rig-A-Lite, which he held responsible for making a box with a defective seal that had allowed water to leak in over a period of several years, resulting in the short-circuit responsible for Robertson's accident. The jury awarded Robertson a settlement of $580,000, marking the first case in U.S. tort law in which an individual was awarded $500,000 or more. Not long afterward, Texas passed a products-liability law, and *Newsweek* hailed Jamail as the new "King of Torts." (Tort law provides remedies in civil cases for individuals who have been wronged in circumstances not involving contracts.)

In the late 1960s and 1970s Jamail won a series of ever-escalating jury awards in personal-injury cases. One of them involved an African-American woman, Elnora Spriggs Williams, who had become paralyzed in a 1969 car wreck caused by a faulty steering wheel. When Jamail presented her case to an all-white, all-male jury, in 1972, he drew the ire of some in the courtroom by saying, as noted in his autobiography, "She didn't crawl in here and she isn't crawling out. *She is no Aunt Jemima.* She is a human being. Either you are big enough to look at it that way or you're not." Jamail was able to show that the wheel of Williams's 1963 Chevrolet Impala was defective by demonstrating that a model of the car's chassis, which the defense had used as an exhibit during the trial, was also severely flawed. The jurors found General Motors liable for over $1.5 million (the judge reduced the amount to $1 million), and Williams became the first black woman in American history to receive a million-dollar verdict. Another case involved four members of the Godfrey family, who had been killed en route to a ski vacation in Aspen, Colorado, after the plane in which they were traveling crashed into a mountainside as a result of a blizzard. The plane was the property of Capitol National Bank, of which William G. Godfrey was a co-founder; the pilot was employed by the bank's holding company. The two family members who survived, eight-year-old Andy and 11-year-old Mark, suffered emotional trauma while waiting for two days to be rescued; Mark later lost his left foot and part of his right leg, Andy all the toes of his left foot. In 1977 Jamail helped the two brothers and their younger sister (who had not been on the flight) win a $14 million out-of-court settlement from Capitol National Bank, at the time the highest personal-injury settlement ever awarded. Jamail wrote in his autobiography, "This was not a suit that the bank or its holding company wanted to defend. Nor did I relish the idea of putting Mark and Andy on the witness stand to relive their escape from a bottom-less white pit."

In 1978 Jamail represented a former courtroom opponent, an Austin insurance attorney named John Coates, in a case that involved the Remington Mohawk 600 rifle. Following an afternoon of hunting with his teenage son, Will, Coates was in the family car, where Will was unloading the rifle. The weapon's faulty safety switch caused it to discharge, and Coates was shot in the back; he was paralyzed and lost a kidney. After consulting with an arms expert, Jamail discovered that the design of the rifle had made it impossible for Will and other users to unload it in the "safe" position. He went on to interview a Remington dealer in Texas, who had years earlier warned a Remington representative of the gun's defects. Instead of taking quality-control measures, the representative instructed him to replace any defective weapons with new ones, in order to avoid a recall. During the court proceedings, after Remington experts contended that the gun was free of defects, Jamail's partner, Gus Kolius, used a blank cartridge to demonstrate the gun's flaw to the jury. Jamail, after pressing the company several times to raise their settlement offer, won a $6.8 million award for Coates. That landed Jamail in the *Guinness Book of World Records* for the largest individual settlement ever awarded in a personal-injury suit. A day after the press conference to announce the settlement, Remington recalled all of its model 600 and 660 rifles.

Known for a blunt style that emphasizes basic legal principles and concepts of right and wrong over technicalities, Jamail has had a profound effect on the way tort law is practiced. Commenting on his style, Bill Powers of the University of Texas School of Law explained to Steve Quinn, "He almost always uses very traditional theories of liability. His forte has always been his technique. He

takes the core legal principles and tells a great story to the jury under those traditional principles: If they are violated, then someone ought to pay." One of Jamail's main strengths is his skill at selecting juries. His former colleague Warren Burnett noted to Toni Mack for *Forbes* (May 4, 1987), "After the voir dire examination [of potential jurors], Joe has a good idea of where the passion is in each juror. He might ask Mr. Jones, 'Where do you come from?' If Mr. Jones smiles and says, 'Arkansas,' later on there'll be some allusion in the trial to Arkansas. Joe is one of the few lawyers who remember who's on the jury all the way through."

Jamail's legendary courtroom skills were put to the test when he represented Pennzoil in a case against a larger oil company, Texaco, in 1985. While he had expanded his practice years earlier to include corporate law, and had been earning a reported $10 million to $25 million annually in legal fees, the David-versus-Goliath oil case would prove to be the crowning achievement of his already successful career. *Pennzoil v. Texaco* was emblematic of the corporate greed often associated with the 1980s. The management of Getty Oil had made an informal agreement to sell the company to Pennzoil. Just days after Pennzoil thought it had secured an agreement to purchase Getty, Texaco bought the company instead, in a backdoor deal with Getty Oil's management. As Anthony Head observed, "Getting a jury to care about two big oil companies fighting over more money seemed a daunting task." After spending weeks contemplating the best way to argue the case, Jamail decided to represent it as a matter of honor. "[Pennzoil] didn't have a signed contract, but we had a word. We had a handshake. So I was looking for people [for the jury] with long marriages, long church affiliations . . . people whose word meant something," he noted to Head. "I had to try to make them understand that they didn't give up their common sense when they got to court. And it worked for me." Jamail presented an overwhelming amount of evidence to support Pennzoil's claims that Getty Oil had accepted its $5.4 billion merger proposal, only to scrap the deal when Texaco made a $10.2 billion offer. Jamail effectively won the case when he cross-examined one of Getty's lawyers in the takeover deal, Martin Lipton. As noted in his autobiography, Jamail asked Lipton, "Are you saying that you have some distinction between just us ordinary people making contracts with each other and whether or not it's a $10 billion deal? It's a different standard in your mind?" Lipton replied, "Yes, indeed." On November 20, 1985 the jury awarded Pennzoil a staggering $10.53 billion, the biggest such figure in history. Texaco, one of the biggest corporations in the world at the time, went into bankruptcy two years later. Jamail's own earnings from the case were in the hundreds of millions of dollars. Commenting on the long-term impact of the monumental verdict, Jamail explained to Claudia Feldman, "It changed the way big corporations manage their takeover practices. Before, they were like a group of sharks going after each other, and the little sharks always got gobbled up. We tried to stop that with the Pennzoil case. Also, we proved the importance of the oral contract."

In 1981 Jamail was a visiting professor at the University of Texas, where he taught tort law, thus beginning a series of guest professorships at law schools around the country. During the late 1980s and early 1990s, Jamail was responsible for the national recall of two products: the Honda All-Terrain 3-Wheel Vehicle and the prescription drug Parlodel. A 16-year-old girl, Sonya Renee Webster, had suffered a broken neck and became a quadriplegic after being thrown from an unstable Honda vehicle. Although Honda had previously won more than 100 cases involving accidents with that product, Jamail won a $16.5 million settlement for Webster from the Tokyo-based company. In response to the jury verdict, Honda recalled the vehicle. Parlodel, a delactation prescription drug manufactured and sold by Sandoz Pharmaceutical Co., caused a severe stroke in a woman, Clarissa Diane Trawick, who had recently given birth. While efforts had been made to remove Parlodel from the market, stemming from similar incidents involving the drug, Sandoz actively promoted it all over the country without warning of its dangers. Once Jamail filed Trawick's lawsuit, the drug was discontinued and removed from the market; he later won a multimillion-dollar judgment in the case.

In 1993 Jamail suffered his first loss in nearly a quarter-century when he represented Northwest and Continental airlines in a $3 billion antitrust case against American Airlines. Northwest and Continental contended that American Airlines had engaged in predatory pricing practices, introducing a "value-pricing" plan that resulted in millions of dollars in losses for the other two companies. Seeing the inherent value in low fares, the jurors were unconvinced by the plaintiffs' argument that American was guilty of antitrust violations. In 1994 the Delaware Supreme Court threatened to bar Jamail from practicing again in the state because of behavior the justices deemed "extraordinarily rude, uncivil, and vulgar," as noted by Benjamin Weiser for the *Washington Post* (March 10, 1994). Jamail had been representing his longtime friend J. Hugh Liedtke, the Pennzoil chairman, in a dispute between Paramount Communications Inc.—of which Liedtke was an outside director—and QVC Network Inc. The case involved Viacom Inc.'s offer to acquire Paramount. At one point during the QVC lawyer William Johnston's cross-examination of Liedtke, Jamail told Johnston, "I'm tired of you. You could gag a maggot off a meat wagon." Discussing the Delaware court's rebuke, Jamail told Weiser, "The judges are confused by real-life advocacy. They want to make lawyers dance to their tune of mediocrity. . . . I can only assume that they are frustrated in their jobs." Instead of hurting his reputation, Jamail's abrasive behavior seemed only to add to his stature, and in 1995 his peers named him the number-one trial

lawyer in the U.S. In 1999 Jamail was named "Trial Lawyer of the Century" by the California Trial Lawyers Association, *Texas Monthly*, and other publications.

Joe Jamail lives in Houston. He has a vacation home in Galveston. He was married to his college sweetheart, Lillie "Lee" Mae Hage, a prominent Houston philanthropist, from August 28, 1949 until her death, on January 15, 2007. Jamail has three sons: Joseph Dahr III, a lawyer with his father's firm; Randall Hage, a music producer; and Robert Lee, a business manager. Jamail has given $100 million in endowments to the University of Texas and has donated 10s of millions more to various educational and health institutions in Houston and Austin. Sites at UT named after him include the football field, a swimming pool, a law-school pavilion, and the legal-research center; the school has erected two statues on campus in his honor. A skatepark (for skateboarders, motocross bikers, and Rollerbladers) bearing the names of Lee and Joe Jamail opened in Houston on June 1, 2008.

Jamail is frequently cited by *Forbes* magazine as one of the wealthiest lawyers in the world, with an estimated net worth of $1.5 billion. Now in his 80s, he has continued to garner frequent media attention for his involvement in high-profile cases. In 2007 he successfully represented several thousand former clients of the controversial Texas trial lawyer John O'Quinn, in a complex multimillion-dollar arbitration dispute. In 2008 he was appointed lead counsel for the media giant Clear Channel Communications Inc. in a case (subsequently dropped) brought against several banks that allegedly reneged on their promise to fund a $19.5 billion leveraged buyout of the radio broadcaster and billboard advertiser. Jamail's colleague and friend Ronald Krist noted to Mary Flood for the *Houston Chronicle* (September 9, 2007), "Joe is at his happiest when he has a case going."

—C.C.

Suggested Reading: (Austin, Texas) *American-Statesman* K p5 Dec. 7, 2003; *Chicago Tribune* C p1+ July 25, 1989; (Cleveland, Ohio) *Plain Dealer* E p7 July 25, 1993; *Dallas Morning News* E p3+ Nov. 30, 2003; *Forbes* p33 May 4, 1987; *Houston Chronicle* p1+ Oct. 21, 2003, A p1+ Sep. 9, 2007; Joe Jamail Official Web site; *New York Times* A p28 Nov. 26, 2004; *People* p45 Jan. 6, 1986; *Texas Super Lawyers* (on-line) Oct. 2004; Jamail, Joe, with Mickey Herskowitz. *Lawyer: My Trials and Jubilations*, 2003

Matthew Hinton/AFP/Getty Images

Jindal, Bobby

*June 10, 1971– Governor of Louisiana
(Republican)*

*Address: Office of the Governor, P.O. Box 94004,
Baton Rouge, LA 70804*

"I look at my success this year as the ultimate embodiment of the American Dream," Piyush ("Bobby") Jindal, a Republican from Louisiana, said to Lavina Melwani for *Little India* (December 2004) about his election in 2004 to the U.S. House of Representatives. At the time Jindal had just become the first Indian-American in nearly 50 years to achieve that feat—one that he eclipsed when he became, in October 2007, the first nonwhite person to be elected governor of Louisiana since the Reconstruction era and the first Indian-American governor-elect in U.S. history. He was sworn into office as governor in January 2008.

Jindal has been described in the media as a "policy whiz kid" and a "wunderkind," terms that reflect the speed with which the former Rhodes Scholar went on to positions of prominence. He became head of the Louisiana state Department of Health and Hospitals at the age of 24, director of a federal Medicare commission at 27, president of the University of Louisiana system at 28, and a U.S. representative at 33; when he took the oath of office, on January 14, 2008, he became, at 36, the nation's youngest governor. Jindal's ethnicity has been a major point of interest in political circles and of contention among Indian-Americans. His conservative stances—which include support for a ban on abortion and for the teaching of the "intelligent design" theory—have polarized the opinions

of Americans of Indian descent, as have his Anglo-derived nickname and conversion to Catholicism; his views have likewise surprised political analysts who expect minorities to follow a liberal ideology. As Adam Nossiter put it for the *New York Times* (October 22, 2007), Jindal is "a highly unusual politician, having become the nation's first Indian-American governor in a Southern state where race is inseparable from politics." Nevertheless, Jindal has become a popular Republican figure and governor since he took office. He was praised for his response to the destruction brought upon Louisiana by Hurricane Gustav in August 2008. Until August 29, 2008, when U.S. senator John McCain of Arizona, the 2008 Republican presidential nominee, announced that Governor Sarah Palin of Alaska would be his running mate, many speculated that, despite Jindal's slim résumé, Jindal would be McCain's choice for the second spot on the GOP ticket.

The politician was born Piyush Jindal on June 10, 1971 in Baton Rouge, Louisiana, the state capital. His parents had immigrated to the U.S. that year from New Delhi, in the Republic of India, so that Jindal's mother, Raj Jindal, could pursue a graduate degree in nuclear physics at Louisiana State University (LSU). (She was pregnant with Bobby at the time.) Bobby Jindal told Suz Redfearn for *Little India* (June 1996) that his father, Amar, had come from "an extremely poor, agrarian family" in the Punjab region of India. When they arrived in Baton Rouge, Jindal's parents rented an apartment on the LSU campus, supported by Raj's teaching stipend while Amar looked for work. After Raj found a job with the state Department of Labor and Amar became a civil engineer, the family moved into a home in a middle-class section of Baton Rouge, around the time that Jindal's brother, Nikesh, was born.

At the age of five, Jindal decided to call himself "Bobby," a name he has used ever since. (He told Redfearn that the character Bobby Brady from the popular 1970s sitcom *The Brady Bunch* influenced his choice.) "It was probably one of those things where no one at school could say my name," Jindal said. It was at Baton Rouge Magnet High School that Jindal's ambition began to take hold; he served as president or vice president of numerous school groups and was voted "most likely to succeed" by his class. During that time Jindal was also a computer-programming intern at LSU and, with a friend, started a newsletter for users of Apple computers, distributing copies at local computer stores. Jindal told Melwani that growing up in Baton Rouge was a positive experience for him, despite his minority status: "I found it to be a very welcoming environment. I certainly never felt anything other than welcomed at school and on the playground and among friends. Baton Rouge is a university town. . . . There are people from all over the country, all over the world." It was also during high school that Jindal converted from Hinduism to Catholicism. "I was a teenager and my grandfather had passed away," he told Melwani. "It was really the first time I had thought about life and what happens after death and the importance of religious beliefs. I had always been raised to believe in God and to pray to God, but I felt like this was how God was calling me to worship Him."

Jindal attended Brown University, in Providence, Rhode Island, where he found himself one of very few students with conservative views. He told John J. Miller for the *National Review* (May 14, 2007, on-line), "I was just about the only person who was pro-life, the only person who thought Ronald Reagan was a good president. Believe me, anybody who leaves Brown as a conservative has had his beliefs tested." At Brown Jindal started a chapter of the College Republicans and became its president; the chapter still exists on the campus. "Being at Brown forced me to think much harder about the positions I held and why," Jindal said to Alissa Cerny for the *Brown Daily Herald* (October 19, 2006, on-line). "At Brown, you are constantly challenged to re-examine your views. You can't be complacent because there will always be someone who will disagree and can put together a persuasive argument."

During the summers Jindal conducted research in medical laboratories and served as an intern for Republican U.S. representatives from Louisiana. At one point Jindal asked for more responsibility. "I thought, 'Oh boy, an eager-beaver college student,'" Representative Jim McCrery said of his first impressions of Jindal. "I told him to write a paper on how to improve Medicare. I figured that would keep him busy and I wouldn't see him again." But before the internship concluded, Jindal finished the paper. "It was an excellent piece of work," McCrery said. "It identified problems, discussed budgetary implications, and suggested reforms." In 1991 Jindal graduated early from Brown, magna cum laude, with degrees in biology and public policy; he had written two theses on the state of health care that were later published in medical journals. "I originally thought I was going into medicine," Jindal told Melwani, "but then I realized that if I went into health policy I could help make the system better for . . . doctors and therefore help . . . more patients than I could have if I just went into medicine itself."

After his graduation Jindal took a job with the Exxon Corp., working in the area of public policy. Nine months later he became a Rhodes Scholar at Oxford University, in England, where he received a master's degree in political science. After he returned to the U.S., Jindal went to work for Mckinsey and Co., a highly regarded international consulting firm based in Washington, D.C.; he was appointed as a senior consultant. He told Redfearn that the experience was invaluable, as he spent time assisting the senior management of numerous health-care companies in "out-of-the-box thinking."

Jindal's prior work with Representative McCrery helped him to secure his first position in government. In 1995, with a gubernatorial election approaching in Louisiana, Jindal asked McCrery to assist him in his bid to become the next state health secretary. McCrery introduced his former intern to the Republican candidate, Murphy James ("Mike") Foster, who was so impressed by Jindal that upon winning the governorship he hired the young man. At 24 Jindal found himself in charge of Louisiana's Department of Health and Hospitals (DHH). The department, whose budget totaled $5.6 billion, was deeply in debt at the time. Within his first few weeks in the post, Jindal announced his discovery that the federal government owed over $400 million to the state. By the end of his tenure, Jindal had succeeded in eradicating the department's budget deficit and had posted three consecutive budget surpluses, each exceeding $220 million. According to the Web site of the National Bipartisan Commission on the Future of Medicare, during his time at the DHH, "the department's budget was cut by 25 percent and the number of employees reduced by 1,000," and Louisiana "moved from 37th to 3rd best nationally in health screenings for children, increased its childhood immunizations from 50 percent to nearly 90 percent and offered new and expanded services to elderly and disabled persons."

In 1998 Jindal was appointed executive director of the National Bipartisan Commission on the Future of Medicare, in Washington, D.C. The 17-member commission, created by Congress in the Balanced Budget Act of 1997, was charged with examining the Medicare program and making recommendations for ways to improve it; its members, however, were not able to reach a consensus. In Jindal's next job, from 1999 to 2001, he served as president of the University of Louisiana system, one of the largest higher-education systems in the nation, consisting of eight campuses with an enrollment of 80,000 students and 8,000 faculty and staff. In that position he implemented a nine-point strategic plan to improve and promote academic excellence through an emphasis on the university's strengths.

In March 2001 the newly elected Republican president George W. Bush nominated Jindal to be assistant secretary for planning and evaluation at the United States Department of Health and Human Services (HHS). Under Jindal's leadership the Secretary's Regulatory Reform Committee made more than 255 recommendations for streamlining the country's health-care system; of those, 27 were implemented before the release of the committee's final report, according to an HHS news release (February 13, 2003, on-line). Jindal also led the department's Research Coordinating Council, which oversees $30 billion in annual spending at HHS.

In 2003, with Foster nearing the end of his second term as governor, Jindal stepped down from his position at HHS to make a run for the office. Jindal placed ahead of the other candidates in the nonpartisan "jungle primary" before going against then–lieutenant governor Kathleen Babineaux Blanco, a Democrat, in the runoff election, which he lost by four percentage points. Many political analysts attributed the defeat to ads created by Blanco's campaign that were critical of Jindal's management of the state health department—accusing him of being a "cold-blooded numbers cruncher," as Russell McCulley put it in *Time* (October 4, 2007, on-line). Race discrimination was also said to be a factor. An on-line article from Agence France Presse (October 18, 2007) noted, "Subsequent analysis showed that despite Jindal's ardent support for right-wing 'Christian' causes, he fared poorly against the more liberal Blanco in 26 rural voting districts that were carried by Ku Klux Klan leader David Duke's unsuccessful run for governor in 1991."

Not long after his run for governor, Jindal decided to make a bid for the seat representing Louisiana's First Congressional District, a known Republican stronghold. He won in a landslide, capturing 78 percent of the vote; he was reelected with 88 percent of the vote in 2006. As a U.S. congressman, Jindal voted conservatively on many key issues, opposing embryonic stem-cell research while favoring restrictions on interstate transport of minors seeking to get abortions. He also supported the teaching of the "intelligent design" theory, which attributes human evolution to divine intervention. According to Russell McCulley, among Louisiana's voters Jindal's stances "helped him overcome the twin liabilities (in some circles) of intellectualism and ethnicity—traits that arouse suspicion in some of Louisiana's rural stretches, and that many say also helped tip the scales against him in 2003." As McCulley noted, Jindal's support for the Republican agenda extended to his controversial vote against a bill seeking billions of dollars in recovery aid to Louisiana in the wake of Hurricane Katrina; the bill contained a rider from Democrats who sought the phased withdrawal of U.S. troops from Iraq.

As a result of her declining popularity, Blanco decided not to run for a second term as governor. In 2007 Jindal made a second bid for the office, running on a platform of ethical reform in government; he spent time in the rural areas of the state where he was unpopular in 2003. Jindal's opponents in the race were the Democrats Walter Boasso and Foster Campbell and an Independent, John Georges. As in the previous election campaign, Jindal's competitors ran commercials criticizing his tenure at the state health department, but this time Jindal fired back. "I still believe that in an election you can tell people why they should vote for you, not why they shouldn't vote for somebody else," he told Jan Moller for the New Orleans, Louisiana, *Times-Picayune* (August 16, 2007). "But we're not going to let people distort our record." In response to the negative ads, Jindal's campaign sent out news releases with point-by-point rebuttals. By the end of election night, on October 20, 2007, he had received some 625,000 votes, more than 50 percent of the ballots cast. In his first post-election speech, Jindal mentioned the victory of the LSU football team that same day; according to Nossiter, "The message could not have been clearer: I'm one of you, a normal, red-blooded football-loving Louisiana guy." As governor-elect, Jindal stood to inherit the reins of the state that ranks at the bottom of the nation in terms of per capita income, health, and education level—but first in infant mortality. In addition, flooding from Hurricane Katrina had displaced tens of thousands of Louisiana's citizens in 2005, and rebuilding efforts were still ongoing. Nonetheless, Jindal appeared undaunted in interviews, telling Nossiter for the *New York Times* (October 19, 2007, on-line), "The storms didn't cause all of our problems—they revealed a lot of our problems. It's an incredible opportunity to change the state."

In an article for the *Washington Post* (October 28, 2007), N. C. Aizenman reported on the mixed sentiments of Indian-Americans over Jindal's victory. "Many feel downright giddy at the thought that for the first time, an Indian American will hold the top job in a state. . . . But plenty of Indian Americans recoil at Jindal's socially conservative views," Aizenman wrote. Amardeep Singh, an English professor at Lehigh University, in Pennsylvania, told Aizenman, "It's a soul-searching moment because it raises all these questions about identity and the kind of public profile that Indian Americans have to cut in order to succeed in American life." When Melwani told Jindal in 2004 that "the conventional wisdom is that the Republican Party is not hospitable to minorities and immigrants," and asked why he was attracted to the party, Jindal said, "My allegiance to the Republican Party has everything to do with the core values at the center of the party. The Republican Party believes in the value and freedom of all individuals. It believes in less government in our lives, not more. It stands for lower taxes, less spending and less government control of our health care systems. The Republican Party also represents the conservative values that Louisiana residents find most important in their lives. The Republican Party wants every individual to work toward and achieve his own American Dream."

Within the first five months of his term, Jindal signed several noteworthy bills. He approved laws that require employers to allow workers to bring guns onto company parking lots; authorize the chemical castration of certain convicted sex offenders; establish a "Teacher Bill of Rights"; and set up a voucher plan that secured $10 million for tuition for inner-city children at private schools (including parochial schools). He also restructured the state's Labor Department. Those five months were not free of controversy, however. In June 2008 recall petitions were filed against Jindal and other lawmakers after the governor announced that, notwithstanding one of his campaign promises and his opposition to giving state legislators raises, he would not veto a bill that doubled the lawmakers' salaries. Later, he reversed his position and vetoed the bill. "The bottom line is that allowing this excessive legislative pay raise to become law would so significantly undercut our reform agenda and so significantly diminish the people's confidence in their own government that I cannot let it become law," he told Ed Anderson for the *Times-Picayune* (June 30, 2008, on-line).

Jindal was rumored to be one of several potential running mates for Senator John McCain, the Republican presidential nominee in 2008. In July of that year, Jindal announced that he had never discussed with McCain the possibility of his serving as vice president and that he would not be running with the senator. Jindal was praised for his response to Hurricane Gustav, which struck Louisiana in August 2008. During televised news conferences, the governor kept his constituents informed about the storm and its aftermath and about rescue efforts. "Bobby Jindal has been pitch perfect during Gustav," Douglas Brinkley, the author of *The Great*

Deluge, about the aftermath of Hurricane Katrina in 2005, told Pete Whoriskey for the *Washington Post* (September 3, 2008). "He promised to be a hands-on administrator, and I think he delivered. He had such an easy factual grasp of the situation. It's almost the exact opposite of Blanco and [New Orleans Mayor C. Ray] Nagin during Katrina."

Jindal lives in Baton Rouge with his wife, Supriya. The couple have a daughter, Selia, and two sons, Shaan and Slade. In August 2006 Jindal delivered Slade himself, after his wife went into labor in the bedroom of their home.

—W.D.

Suggested Reading: *American Spectator* p16+ July/Aug. 2007; *Brown (University) Daily Herald* (on-line) Oct. 19, 2006; *Esquire* p225+ Oct. 2008; *Little India* (on-line) Dec. 2004; *Nation* p27+ July 21–28, 2008; *New York Times* (on-line) Oct. 22, 2007; *Time* (on-line) Oct. 4, 2007; *Washington Post* (on-line) Oct. 28, 2007

Johnson, Boris

June 19, 1964– Mayor of London; journalist; novelist

Address: Greater London Authority, City Hall, The Queen's Walk, London SE1 2AA, England

Boris Johnson, who was elected mayor of London, England, in May 2008, enjoys a celebrity in his country that transcends politics. He began his career in the mid-1980s as a journalist, becoming editor of the right-wing *Spectator* in 1999 before winning a seat as a member of Parliament (MP), with the Conservative Party, in the following year. His parliamentary work generated far less attention than the various facets of his outsize presence, from his unruly blond mop of hair to his upper-crust pedigree, from his sex-scandal-ridden journalism career to his propensity for outspokenness and costly verbal blunders—the last two of which have brought him such labels as "buffoon." His supporters, on the other hand, see him as an irreverent, blunt, entertaining, and endearing breath of fresh air in the choreographed world of politics. Perhaps acknowledging both points of view, Johnson once famously declared, "My friends, as I have discovered myself, there are no disasters, only opportunities. And, indeed, opportunities for fresh disasters." With the backing of England's Conservatives, Johnson toned down the rowdier aspects of his persona in order to win an upset mayoral victory over the once-popular incumbent, Ken Livingstone. In addition to his political and journalistic pursuits, Johnson is known as the author of fiction and nonfiction books and for his appearances on the popular satirical program *Have I Got News for You.*

Cate Gillon/Getty Images

Alexander Boris de Pfeffel Johnson was born on June 19, 1964 in New York City, the eldest of the four children of Stanley Johnson, a prominent British politician, and the former Charlotte Fawcett, a painter; his father also has two children from a subsequent marriage. Much has been written about the lineage of the mayor, a self-described "one-man melting pot." (He has regularly pointed to that lineage, and to the mixed ancestry of his wife, when defending himself against charges of racism.) On his father's side Johnson is the great-grandson of Ali Kemal, a Turkish journalist and the last interior minister of the crumbling, post–World War I Ottoman empire, who was killed by a mob of Turkish nationalists loyal to Mustafa Kemal Atatürk, the revolutionary who seized power in the 1920s. Kemal's son, Osman Ali, who was British-born, changed his given name and took the surname of his English grandmother, becoming Wilfred Johnson. Boris Johnson's maternal grandfather was a famous lawyer and member of the European Commission on Human Rights; his godmother is the novelist Rachel Billington. Two of Johnson's siblings, Rachel and Jo, are well-known writers, and his father-in-law, Sir Charles Wheeler, was a celebrated broadcaster. As Sholto Byrnes explained in an article for the New Statesman (March 27, 2008), "Broad networks in media and politics are not unusual. The extent of the ties that Boris can draw on, however, harks back to a different time. . . . Its foundation is class and family, not pure politics."

Stanley Johnson was working in New York for the United Nations at the time of Boris's birth. Because of his father's career, Johnson's family moved often during his childhood, living in places that included rural Exmoor, in England, and Brussels, Belgium. Johnson is said to have undergone treatment for hearing problems as a child. By all accounts, the members of the Johnson family were both close and highly competitive with one another. Johnson attended the European School in Brussels, where he became friends with Marina Wheeler, who would later become his second wife. In 1973, as his parents' marriage was failing, he became a boarding student at Ashdown House Preparatory School, in East Sussex. From there, he won a scholarship to Eton, Britain's most exclusive private secondary school. His housemaster, Sir Eric Anderson, told Johnson's friend and biographer, Andrew Gimson, as quoted by Brian Wheeler for BBC News (May 4, 2008), that the young Johnson tended to live by his "wits rather than preparation" and that he was "a satirist and a humorist rather than a rebel." Developing an enduring interest in history and the classics, according to Gimson, Johnson found a hero in the Athenian statesman Pericles (495–429 B.C.), one of the earliest known champions of democracy. In 1983 Johnson enrolled at Balliol College, at Oxford University, where he studied classics and became involved in several influential student societies, including the Bullingdon Club, the university's infamously rowdy student-dining club, as well as Oxford Union, a debating society. According to several of his contemporaries, Johnson, who was already passionate about politics, campaigned hard and successfully to win the presidency of Oxford Union, which is viewed as a springboard to a career in politics.

After graduating, in 1986, Johnson became a management consultant, a job in which he is said to have lasted less than a week, later famously declaring: "Try as I might, I could not look at an overhead projection of a growth profit matrix and stay conscious." He then became a reporter trainee for the London Times, which fired him within a year for having made up a quote and attributed it to his godfather, the historian Colin Lucas—apparently to add spice to an otherwise uninteresting story about an archaeological dig. Johnson next spent some time as a writer for the local Wolverhampton paper, the Express and Star, before joining the conservative London Daily Telegraph in 1987. From 1989 to 1994 he was the paper's European Community correspondent, based in Brussels; he made a name for himself by lambasting the European Union (EU) institutions on which his father had once served but which had since become a favorite target of Conservatives. In 1994 he became the paper's assistant editor and chief political columnist. Also that year he began writing political columns for the Spectator (founded in 1828), described by Byrnes as the "cheerleading magazine of the right," and in 1999 he was made its editor.

"The magazine has become Johnson's own political torpedo, a publication fashioned in his own image following a round of savage sackings after he became editor . . . ," Sonia Purnell wrote for the London Independent on Sunday (July 7, 2002). "True to form, most of the hard graft and day-to-day running of The Spectator is handled by the immensely able journalist Stuart Reid, his lesser-known deputy. But Johnson still manages to pick up the plaudits and the glory." Under Johnson's tenure the magazine's circulation rose from 57,500 to almost 70,000. Apart from weekly articles attacking the ruling Labor Party and lamenting the weakness of the Conservatives at the turn of the century, Johnson's Spectator had the dubious distinction of also being a constant source of sex scandals, with numerous reports of extramarital affairs involving editors, writers, politicians, and Johnson himself, who was dubbed "Boudoir Boris"—and whose magazine came to be called "The Sextator." Johnson also began to gain celebrity status for his repeated TV appearances on such shows as Have I Got News for You, a satirical news quiz show, on which he is said to have attracted a cult following for, among other things, his self-deprecating humor. In 2006 he produced a popular historical documentary and accompanying book, The Dream of Rome, drawing parallels between the Roman Empire and modern Europe. He has written a regular column for GQ magazine as well as a book about fast and expensive cars and has penned several other books, including an account of his 2000 electoral campaign; a book of poetry; three collections of his journalistic writings; and a novel, Seventy-Two Virgins (2004). As a measure of his celebrity, a book of "Johnson-isms," containing his verbal blunders and other quotes, was published in 2007 under the title The Little Book of Boris, compiled by Iain Dale. Gimson's sympathetic biography of Johnson appeared the same year.

Meanwhile, Johnson had entered politics, running unsuccessfully for a parliamentary seat in Clwyd South, a Labor stronghold, in 1997 before being elected MP in the Conservative district of Henley-on-Thames in 2000. On being named editor of the *Spectator*, in 1999, he had promised the newspaper's owner, Conrad Black, that he would not seek office but would focus on the magazine; but as he confessed to his friend Charles Moore, as quoted by Wheeler: "I want to have my cake and eat it." (As Geoffrey Wheatcroft wrote for the July 15, 2000 edition of the *Independent*, Johnson had followed "a riveting tradition. In the past 60 years, no fewer than four editors of *The Spectator* have been, or become, MPs.") When Andrew Gimson, writing for the *Sunday Times* (September 17, 2006), asked Black why he put up with Johnson's scandalous behavior and political activities, he replied, "We kind of endured it because the paper was doing well. Our view is that Boris's performance was outrageous, but the chief criterion is what's good for *The Spectator*, and Boris was a good thing for *The Spectator*."

Still, as many had predicted, Johnson's penchant for speaking his mind and his overambitious schedule led to problems, including a dismal parliamentary attendance record and the publication of articles that embarrassed or annoyed his peers in Parliament, who began to see him as a liability. In 2004 he was appointed as the opposition party's shadow minister for the arts, but he soon came under fire on other fronts. On October 16, 2004 the *Spectator* published an unsigned editorial criticizing citizens of Liverpool, England, for wallowing in their "victim status" after Kenneth Bigley, a hostage in Iraq who was a Liverpool native, was beheaded. The article also alluded to a disaster in Hillsborough—a soccer match at which fans were crushed to death—claiming, contrary to police reports, that drunken fans were to blame for the fatalities. Although he had not written the piece, Johnson, as editor, accepted responsibility for it. The leader of the Conservative Party at the time, Michael Howard, resisted calls for Johnson's sacking, instead sending him on an "apology tour" of Liverpool. Only a few weeks later, Johnson was demoted from his party's front bench as another scandal broke. It emerged that Johnson had had a long-term affair with a journalist at the *Spectator*, Petronella Wyatt; although he vehemently denied his involvement, describing the accusation as "an inverted pyramid of piffle," Wyatt's mother confirmed it, adding that her daughter had had to undergo an abortion as a result of the affair. Johnson, a father of four, was publicly thrown out of his family home (he was later forgiven by his wife, the successful lawyer Marina Wheeler) and fired as shadow arts minister by Howard for lying about the affair. Johnson's political career was revived when his former schoolmate from Eton and Oxford, David Cameron, assumed the leadership of the Conservative Party and appointed him in December 2005 as shadow minister for higher education, on the condition that he resign from his post at the *Spectator*. (He remains a columnist for the *Daily Telegraph*.) Even though he was soon involved in

several other controversies, including another alleged affair, he kept his parliamentary post. He is known for helping to push the Conservative plan for "top-up fees" for universities—in effect, an attempt to partially privatize higher education. (There is only one private university in Great Britain.)

Conservatives viewed the 2008 London mayoral election as an opportunity to make inroads against the Labor government. The post of elected mayor of London was created in 2000 by the Labor government of Prime Minister Tony Blair, and for years afterward one man's name was synonymous with the position: that of "Red" Ken Livingstone. The Socialist mayor had fallen out with the centrist Labor Party and had run in 2000 as an Independent, albeit one who was backed by Blair; hugely popular, known as a maverick, Livingstone achieved celebrity status, becoming one of the only politicians—other than Johnson—to be referred to by his first name only. (He ran for reelection in 2004 as a member of the Labour Party.) The mayor, while limited in power, has direct control over the city's police department and transportation system. Perhaps more importantly, many see the mayor of London as an important figure in the political balance of power in the country. The Conservatives, who had been out of power nationally for over a decade, looked to the mayoralty as having the potential to influence public opinion in an environment that had seen disenchantment with both the Labor government of Gordon Brown and the tenure of Livingstone. A win in London followed by a successful mayoralty, some pundits predicted, would increase the chances of Cameron and the Conservatives in a national election. But to win in London, the Conservatives would have to both reclaim the political center by broadening their appeal and put forward a celebrity with name recognition on a par with Livingstone's. As Tony Travers, an expert on local government elections at the London School of Economics, told Simon Edge for the Scottish edition of the *Daily Express* (April 4, 2008), "In many ways this is a proxy war between David Cameron and Gordon Brown." Apparently the Conservatives had approached several high-profile potential candidates before making the proposal to Johnson—whose liabilities as an office-seeker were clear—but all had declined. A Johnson candidacy would pose problems other than the danger of damaging the Conservatives' image: among others, he might succeed and then move on to challenge Cameron for the leadership of the party. But as Calvin Trillin wrote for the *New Yorker* (April 14, 2008), "According to one theory . . . a Johnson victory would present Cameron with a bonus beyond party momentum—the breaking of the 'posh barrier.' The theory holds that the willingness of London voters to support someone as posh as Boris Johnson would indicate a willingness to turn the national government over to Cameron, who is even posher."

Johnson announced his candidacy in the summer of 2007, resigning as shadow minister for higher education but remaining an MP. As the election approached, Conservatives made preemptive efforts at damage control, surrounding Johnson with handlers—most notably Lynton Crosby, a political consultant who had been behind the Australian prime minister John Howard's victory in 2004—to keep him in line and "on message." Johnson gave up alcohol for the duration of the campaign, got a haircut, stopped telling jokes in public, and promised to stay out of the social spotlight and avoid faux pas. The press quickly dubbed him Robo-Boris, a scripted and boring version of his true self. Londoners, particularly its sizeable minority communities, were strong Livingstone backers, but many residents of the city's peripheral, mostly middle-class areas were open to Johnson. Crosby's strategy of focusing on conservative suburban voters and playing on fears of crime— promising to ban "anti-social behavior" on buses and trains and put more and better-equipped police on the streets—appeared to help Johnson. The Johnson campaign attacked the image of corruption and waste with which both Socialist and multiterm leaders in Great Britain have often been associated, taking advantage of voters' Labor and Livingstone "fatigue" and promising a "value-for-money" relationship with citizens—a timeworn strategy arguably given new luster by Johnson's maverick image. Livingstone, who had presided over the financial resurgence of the city, made a successful bid to have London host the 2012 Olympics, and instituted a popular toll to limit traffic congestion in central London, tried for his part to emphasize fears that Johnson would cut programs for the disadvantaged. (Johnson once said, as quoted by Felicity Arbuthnot in the left-wing British daily the *Morning Star* [August 13, 2007], "We seem to have forgotten that societies need rich people, even sickeningly rich people, and not just to provide jobs for those who clean swimming pools and resurface tennis courts.") Livingstone also suggested that Johnson was a homophobe and a racist. Johnson had been endorsed by the whites-only, far-right British National Party (BNP), support that Johnson rejected immediately.

Johnson has been accused of racism on numerous occasions. Following the July 7, 2005 bombings in London, an act attributed to Islamic terrorists, he had written for the *Spectator* (July 16, 2005) about the dangers of "extremist Islam," stating that Islam, "judged purely on its scripture—to say nothing of what is preached in the mosques . . . is the most viciously sectarian of all religions in its heartlessness [toward unbelievers]." He had also written an article in 1999 criticizing the Macpherson Report, which had been commissioned after the 1993 killing of a black teenager, Stephen Lawrence; Johnson faulted the report, which called the killing a racist act and criticized the subsequent police investigation, with stirring hysteria. In another article, for the *Daily Telegraph* (January 10,

2002), Johnson criticized Prime Minister Tony Blair's visit to the Congo, saying that when Blair arrived, "the tribal warriors will all break out in watermelon smiles to see the big white chief" and that "it is said the Queen has come to love the Commonwealth, partly because it supplies her with regular cheering crowds of flag-waving piccaninnies." He responded to the subsequent accusations of bigotry by stating, as quoted by Afsun Qureshi-Smith in the Canadian *National Post* (May 12, 2008), "I'm down with the ethnics. You can't un-ethnic me. My children are a quarter Indian, so put that in your pipe and smoke it."

"If Boris is the classic upper-class character out of P. G. Wodehouse, then Ken Livingstone is the caricature of an aging Marxist revolutionary," James Kirchick wrote for the *Weekly Standard* (May 19, 2008). "A common observation made by journalists covering the race was that this was the first time in British politics that the candidates were known merely by their first names: 'The Boris and Ken Show.'" Another similarity between Johnson and Livingstone was that they both had uneasy relationships with their respective parties, which viewed them as irreverent fringe figures. Despite—or because of—that image, Johnson defeated Livingstone on May 1, 2008 with 53 percent of the vote. (Across the country the Conservatives, who picked up 256 parliamentary seats, beat the Labor Party, which lost 331 seats in its worst performance in more than four decades.) Travers told Edge that the election had demonstrated two significant things: "The first is the incredible power of celebrity. . . . The second thing is that, after eight years of Ken Livingstone, the electorate believes it's time for a change. . . . That shows that people think that seven or eight years is enough for anyone. Getting fed up with people is one of the traits of British democracy, as Margaret Thatcher and Tony Blair also discovered." A jubilant Johnson announced that he was stepping down as MP for Henley-on-Thames, and as quoted by Susan Easton in *Human Events Online* (May 4, 2008), he pledged to "work flat out from now on to earn [Londoners'] trust and dispel some of the myths that have been created about me."

Johnson told Andrew Porter for the *Daily Telegraph* (June 7, 2008) that his victory demonstrated "not that London has become a Conservative city. But that the Tories can be trusted to run big, multiracial cities with huge problems of poverty and everything else. . . . I'm determined to see if we can make sense of this idea of civic Conservatism," a notion that reminded some of U.S. president George W. Bush's vow to practice "compassionate conservatism." Echoing others, Andrew Gimson was quoted by Brian Lysaght in *Bloomberg News* (May 11, 2008) as saying: "He's always been very, very serious about getting to the top. People laugh at me when I say that [he may be prime minister one day]." In his first weeks in office, Johnson announced a ban on alcohol consumption on public transport as well as some surprisingly progressive initiatives, such as youth-worker programs. Five months after he became mayor, he forced the resignation of Iain Blair, the embattled Metropolitan Police Commissioner. During his campaign Johnson had called for an expansion of the mayor's authority in hiring and firing the police chief, and Blair's resignation was widely seen as a demonstration of Johnson's assumption of new powers as mayor. Blair had been weakened by several scandals, including allegations of corruption, charges of racism and discrimination within Scotland Yard, and the fatal shooting by police of Jean Charles de Menezes, a Brazilian electrician, in a subway station in 2005 during an anti-terrorism raid. After the death of de Menezes, who had been mistaken for a suicide bomber, the police had tried to cover up their actions.

Johnson has resumed writing his column for the *Daily Telegraph*. When Lynn Barbe, writing for the *Observer* (October 19, 2008), asked him whether he had gone back to drinking alcohol, he responded: "Oh God, yes. I did find [giving it up] one of the most tedious things I've ever done. The only thing was it did help me lose weight a bit, but I soon made it up again with eating. I think giving up alcohol is cruel, cruel, one of the cruellest and most deceitful things you can do to your body. I've taken more out of alcohol than alcohol has taken out of me. It's a great gift of the gods, in my view." Known for riding his bicycle to work, Johnson lives in London with his second wife, Marina Wheeler, and their children, Lara Lettice, Milo Arthur, Cassia Peaches, and Theodore Apollo.

—M.M.

Suggested Reading: BBC News (on-line); *Daily Express* (Scottish Edition) News p34 Apr. 4, 2008; (London) *Daily Telegraph* Features p14 June 7, 2008, (on-line) Sep. 3, 2006; *New Statesman* Mar. 27, 2008; *New Yorker* p26+ Apr. 14, 2008; Gimson, Andrew. *Boris: The Rise of Boris Johnson*, 2007

Selected Books: *Friends, Voters, Countrymen*, 2002; *Lend Me Your Ears*, 2004; *Seventy-Two Virgins*, 2004; *The Dream of Rome*, 2006

Johnson, Zach

Feb. 24, 1976– Golfer

Address: c/o PGA Tour, 112 PGA Tour Blvd., Ponte Vedra Beach, FL 32082

"I'm Zach Johnson from Cedar Rapids. That's about it. I'm a normal guy," the golfer Zach Johnson said after he won the 2007 Masters Tournament, as quoted by Chris Dufresne in the *Los Angeles Times* (April 9, 2007). Born and raised in Iowa, Johnson—who was virtually unknown until his unexpected victory—is consistently described as hardworking, unassuming, and unflaggingly optimistic. After turning professional, in 1998, Johnson spent years playing on small circuits before earning a place in the Professional Golf Association (PGA) Tour in 2004. His climb to the top ranks of professional golfers was based not on flashy playing but on consistency and focus. Susan Harman described his no-frills style for the *Iowa City (Iowa) Press-Citizen* (April 10, 2007): "Johnson has done it with a flat swing that is functional but hardly the fluid, free-flowing look that begs 'oohs' and 'ahs' when the ball is struck. He has done it with a deft putting touch and a marvelous short game. He has done it by hitting his drives in the fairway. He has done it with a nearly perfect mindset for golf—never too high or too low, always based in the present, always believing anything is possible." Johnson himself attributes his success to his attitude. "I think the biggest thing, first and foremost, is to have fun," he told Todd Budnick in an interview for the PGA Web site (July 12, 2006) before the John Deere Classic. "This game will kind

Sam Greenwood/Getty Images

of slap you around pretty quick, especially if you're on a high; it'll bring you down low really quick. The more you play, I think you start to understand that, one, it's very humbling; but two, the good nature and fun, that's what keeps you coming back. Alongside of that, when the days go sour or not very good, you've got to find positives in those, whatever they may be . . . It's a mental struggle at times, a mental fight. That's why I love it. You can never perfect it, so have fun and be positive." After his Masters victory, in which he defeated Tiger Woods and other stellar golfers to win a purse of $1,305,000, he told John McGrath for the Tacoma, Washington, *News Tribune* (April 9, 2007), "Winning the Masters won't change Zach Johnson."

The oldest of three children, Zachary Harris Johnson was born on February 24, 1976 in Iowa City to David Johnson, a chiropractor, and Julie Johnson. He has a younger sister, Maria, and a younger brother, Gabriel, who was an all-conference golfer at Clarke College, in Dubuque, Iowa. As a youngster in Cedar Rapids, Johnson was a devoted Little League baseball player; he was the starting wide receiver on his seventh-grade football team and earned all-city honors as left wing on the soccer team as a senior at Regis High School. Johnson began playing golf at Cedar Rapids' Elmcrest Country Club when he was 12, but he was not a prodigy. Neither was he the best player on the Regis golf team, which won an Iowa 4A State Golf Championship in 1992, with Johnson in the number-two spot. Johnson attended Drake University, in Des Moines, Iowa—one of only two schools that had offered him a golf scholarship. With Johnson again in the number-two position, Drake's golf team earned three consecutive National Collegiate Athletic Association (NCAA) Central Region bids, qualifying for the national finals in 1997 and winning two Missouri Valley Conference titles, in 1997 and 1998.

After he graduated from Drake, with a bachelor's degree in business management and marketing, in 1998, Johnson decided to pursue golf professionally, even though his coaches, his parents, and Johnson himself believed that he had little chance of reaching the highest echelons of the sport. To fund his professional activities, the members of the Elmcrest Country Club formed a syndicate, selling shares at $500 each to raise a total of approximately $40,000. None of Johnson's backers—including his father, who bought eight shares—expected to have their money returned. (They later got their investments back with interest.) Johnson joined the Prairie Golf Tour, earning $7,000 in prize money the first year with one win and $14,000 the next year with two wins. Those victories encouraged him to continue golfing. "You know, I really didn't want to go back to school. You know, I really didn't want to get a job," he reflected to Joe Posnanski for the *Kansas City Star* (April 9, 2007). "The one thing that I kind of clung to was the fact that every year I improved." Still, when Johnson entered the Nationwide Tour (second in importance after the PGA Tour), his performance was below average, and he soon found himself back on smaller circuits, including the Dakota and the TearDrop tours. In 2001 he joined the third-tier National Golf Association (NGA) Hooters Tour (named for a restaurant chain), which pays the fifth-highest purses in golf. That year Johnson won the final three events in the regular season, gaining the nickname "Back-to-Back-to-Back-Zach." Winners in the NGA Hooters Tour got all the chicken wings they could

eat. "I thought those were the best days of my life," Johnson told Dufresne. "Chicken wings and everything." The next year Johnson won one event on the NGA Hooters Tour, and in 2003 he returned to the Nationwide Tour, with considerably greater success. In addition to his wins in the Rheem Classic and the Envirocare Utah Classic, Johnson had 11 top-10 finishes; he also led the tour in putting and was fifth in driving. Named the Nationwide Player of the Year, he earned $494,882, more than anyone else on that tour, and secured a spot on the PGA Tour.

During his first year on the PGA Tour, in 2004, Johnson won the BellSouth Classic (now known as the AT&T Classic), whose previous winners included Tiger Woods and Phil Mickelson. Johnson won by one stroke, having overcome four bogeys (a score of one over par) in five holes for a 72-hole total of 275, 13 under par. His victory brought him $810,000. "It feels amazing," Johnson told Rick Brown for the *Des Moines Register* (April 5, 2004) of the victory. "I've said it a hundred times and I'll say it again." He nonetheless failed to meet any of the 17 criteria that would have qualified him for the Masters. "I'm not disappointed," he told Jerry Potter for *USA Today* (April 5, 2004). "Of course, I'd like to play in the Masters, but my time will come." Since he had finished in a tie for 17th place in the BellSouth two years earlier, the 2004 victory signaled a marked improvement. "I'm going to be around for a while," Johnson told Rana Cash for the *Atlanta (Georgia) Journal-Constitution* (April 5, 2004), after coming in one under par—or birdying—the last hole. Johnson made his Masters debut in 2005, but he missed the cut—that is, he failed to score well enough during the first 36 holes of the tournament to continue on to the second 36 holes. At the 2006 Masters Johnson again missed the cut, beginning what would become a several-month-long slump. He told Todd Budnick that year that he was concentrating on changing his technique. "I kind of reevaluated at the end of last year and wanted to simplify things and make things a little easier on myself week to week, both on weeks and off weeks, and I think we've pretty much accomplished that," he said. "I think where things are, things are going in the right direction for sure, it's just a matter of getting more opportunities to win." He remained modest, however. "I seem to be hitting it pretty well," he told Budnick. "I would never say I'm an elite ball striker. I drive it pretty well and I putt it pretty good. That's what I would say most weeks. But I'm starting to hit it pretty good, consistently pretty solid." That year he was the runner-up at the BellSouth Classic and the Memorial Tournament, and he placed third in the WGC (World Golf Championships) Accenture Match Play Championship.

With those outcomes Johnson won a much-coveted spot on the U.S. Ryder Cup team, which engages in a biennial competition with the European PGA team. The U.S. squad is composed of the top-10 players on the U.S. Points List plus two players chosen by the coaches. Johnson finished ninth on the U.S. Points List. "The whole team thing is something that makes me want it really, really bad. It would be an honor and a privilege," he told Rick Brown for the *Des Moines Register* (June 15, 2006) two months before the final rankings. He continued, "Even though this is an individual sport, playing on a team, and having a team mindset with camaraderie and chemistry, is something I think I'd just relish." Although the U.S. team performed disappointingly as a whole and lost by a wide margin, Johnson was a standout during the tournament, making seven birdies; the other 11 Americans made a combined total of eight. "Zach was just all-world," the U.S. team's captain, Tom Lehman, told Rick Brown for the *Des Moines Register* (September 24, 2006). Johnson told Rick Brown the next day that playing in the competition was "an absolute thrill" and that he looked forward to playing again in 2008.

On April 8, 2007 Johnson won the Masters Tournament, in Atlanta, Georgia, in a contest with such golf superstars as Tiger Woods and Phil Mickelson. Over the course of a weekend of uncharacteristically poor playing by his celebrated competitors, Johnson finished with a score of 289, two strokes ahead of Woods, Retief Goosen, and Rory Sabbatini, all of whom tied for second place. At one over par, his score tied Sam Snead's 1954 finish and Jack Burke Jr.'s 1956 finish for the highest winning score ever at the Masters (a dubious honor, since in golf, the higher the score, the worse the play). Throughout the tournament, but especially on the final day, Easter Sunday, Johnson avoided paying attention to the score. "Today was a day of perseverance and patience," he told Leonard Shapiro for the *Washington Post* (April 9, 2007). "I felt like I had a chance to move up on the board. I don't even know what I shot. And being Easter Sunday, I felt there was another power walking with and guiding me." Johnson is the first person not ranked among the top-50 golfers in the Official World Golf Ranking to win a Masters. With his victory he jumped from the 56th spot to the 15th on the ranking charts, and he won $1,305,000. "This is surreal," he told Lynn DeBruin for the *Rocky Mountain News* (April 9, 2007). "Looking back on it, it's amazing where I came from." In the days that followed Johnson's win, commentators speculated about that very subject—where Johnson had come from—and also about where he might be headed. Alan Shipnuck, writing for *Sports Illustrated* (April 10, 2007), described Johnson's victory as "a surprise but not a fluke." "Expect this flinty grinder to be a regular factor at the majors, where tougher setups perfectly suit his controlled game," Shipnuck wrote, adding, "And, by the way, success couldn't happen to a nicer guy." Despite the exponentially increased level of media attention trained on him, Johnson remained modest. "I'm not a rock star. Far from it . . . ," he told an Associated Press (April 12, 2007) reporter. "I won a very prestigious event. But at the same time, you've got to stay in the present."

On May 20, 2007 Johnson won the AT&T Classic, defeating Ryuji Imada with a birdie on the first hole of a play-off. At the Target World Challenge, held on December 16, 2007, he finished in second place, seven strokes behind Tiger Woods. In the 2008 Masters Immelman tied 20th place. Also in 1008 he won the Valero Texas Open and, by mid-October, had tied four times—for ninth place at the World Golf Championships–CA Championship, 10th at the Justin Timberlake Shriners Hospitals for Children Open, 16th at the World Golf Championships–Bridgestone Invitational, and 20th at the Mercedes-Benz Championship

Johnson and his wife, the former Kimala Barclay, married in 2003. They live in Mary Lake, Florida, with their son, David William Johnson, called Will, who was born in early 2007.

—C.S.

Suggested Reading: *Los Angeles Times* D p1+ Apr. 9, 2007; pga.com July 12, 2006; pgatour.com; *Sports Illustrated* p42+ June 15, 2004; (Tacoma, Washington) *News Tribune* C p1+ Apr. 9, 2007; *Washinton Post* E p1+ Apr. 9, 2007

Jones, Cullen

Feb. 29, 1984– Swimmer

Address: USA Swimming, 1 Olympic Plaza, Colorado Springs, CO 80909

The odds were stacked against the men's U.S. Olympic swimming team during the 2008 Summer Games, held in Beijing, China. The team had not won the 4x100-meter relay since 1996; that race had been dominated by the Australian team in 2000, and many predicted that in 2008 the Americans would not stand a chance against France's formidable swimmers. In an unexpected turn of events, however, the U.S. team—Michael Phelps, Jason Lezak, Garret Weber-Gale, and the only African-American squad member, Cullen Jones—smashed the world record on August 11 by four seconds, with a 3:08.24 win in the 4x100 relay. At 24, Jones became only the second African-American swimmer (Anthony Ervin was the first, in 2000) to win a gold medal in swimming in Olympic competition.

Jones, who has trained in swimming since the age of five, is among the world's greatest sprinters, as those who specialize in the 50-meter freestyle are known. He is a standout on the men's U.S. Olympic swimming team, in part because he is the only African-American on the squad and only the third black swimmer to compete for the U.S. since the Games began, in 1896. (The others are Ervin and Maritza Correia, in 2004.) In addition, the Jones has resolved to try to decrease the rate of ac-

Matthew Stockman/Getty Images

Cullen Jones

and lifeguards were on hand to resuscitate him. When Jones came to, he coughed up a pint of water; then, as he told John Henderson for the *Denver Post* (May 4, 2008), he immediately said, "What's the next ride I'm getting on?" Within a week of that incident, Jones's mother had enrolled him in a swimming class. At eight he began swimming competitively. "Cullen was happy anywhere he could find water," his mother, a health-and-safety policy manager for the Public Service Electric and Gas Co., told Meredith Galante for the Newark, New Jersey, *Star Ledger* (August 3, 2006). "He would compete in a meet, and then ask to go back in the water just to play." As a young boy Jones also took gymnastics lessons, which helped him with swimming because, as he told Bob Schaller for the USA Swimming Web site, "When the coaches taught me flip turns at swim practice, they didn't have to tell me twice because I had learned how to flip in gymnastics."

When Jones was young his family relocated to the town of Irvington, New Jersey, immediately outside the city of Newark (some sources list his hometown as New Brunswick, New Jersey). Swimming helped Jones to avoid the drug activity and gang-related violence in his neighborhood. He participated in the Newark Swim Club, which practiced at the pool at the Newark campus of Rutgers University, and competed in the Newark Long Course Swim Championship when he was 13. For high school he enrolled at St. Benedict's Preparatory School, also in Newark, and became active on the school's swim team under his coach and mentor, Edward Nessel, a former state Amateur Athletic Union (AAU) champion. Jones told Schaller that he gave up his other pursuits in favor of swimming. "As a kid I was definitely that pool rat that you couldn't get out of the water," he said. "I stopped playing basketball in high school—I didn't go out for the team—because I wanted to focus on swimming." Jones's father, a former college basketball player, was initially reluctant to embrace his son's chosen athletic activity, preferring that he pursue basketball or football instead. "Ron would come to every practice and exchange banter with me," Nessel told Galante. "Ron felt his son should be shooting hoops, but Cullen didn't really like it. He only played to please his father." When Jones's parents pulled him out of swimming competitions, his grades began to fall, and his parents promptly allowed him to return to the sport. Jones has credited his mother for that decision: "She was just like 'OK, you need the structure of swimming,'" he told Craig Lord for the London *Times* (March 23, 2007). "I was never pulled out again." Nessel convinced Ronald Jones that his son's training would be worthwhile. "I told Ron that I was going to make Cullen the best swimmer in the state and send him to college for free," Nessel told Galante.

Ronald Jones eventually became one of his son's biggest supporters. The swimmer said in his interview with Schaller, "Once he saw swimming was what I wanted to do, he was 100 percent behind

cidental drowning among African-American and Hispanic children—a rate that is three times greater than that among their white counterparts—through his efforts in several programs. One of them, Make a Splash, was started by USA Swimming (the "national governing body of competitive swimming in the United States," according to its Web site); another, Begin to Swim, was organized by the Young Men's Christian Association (YMCA) and is dedicated to teaching children of color how to swim and remain safe in water. Jones has expressed the hope that his Olympic win will help increase the popularity of swimming among blacks, who represent less than 1 percent of the nation's 232,000 competitive swimmers. "I've got big plans," Jones told Scott Fowler for McClatchy Newspapers after he won the gold medal, as quoted by Courtland Milloy in the Bergen County, New Jersey, *Record* (August 14, 2008). "I want more minority kids to go to a swimming pool and try to swim because of me. I want kids to say, 'Look, a black swimmer. And he's got a gold medal!' And I want them to get in the water because of it."

Cullen Jones was born on February 29, 1984 in the New York City borough of the Bronx to Ronald and Debra Jones. He developed a passion for being in the water at a young age, following a near-death experience. When he was five years old, his parents took him to an amusement park, Dorney Park & Wildwater Kingdom, in Allentown, Pennsylvania, where, despite the objections of his mother, he went down a water slide in a flotation device. Although he heeded his father's advice and held on to the device tightly, he landed upside-down in the water at the bottom of the slide and lost consciousness. His mother jumped in and pulled him out, me—even when he and I knew I wasn't any good at it! He would sacrifice all the time—selling something he had or going without [things] to, say, buy me new goggles." Ronald Jones, a nonsmoker, died of lung cancer in 2002, when Jones was 16. "It was so sudden; one day he was healthy and the next day he was sick and dying—it happened fast, even though he did fight it with a lot of determination," Jones told Schaller. His father's death motivated Jones to excel in swimming; he told Lord, "I pretty much dedicated my entire career to him." Not long afterward Nessel quit his job as a pharmacist to become a full-time swimming coach, taking Jones on as his main pupil. Nessel, whose two sons had died, looked upon Jones almost as an adopted son. Jones told Ned Barnett that his father and Nessel are "the reason I continue to swim" and shared a memory of the two men: "I remember there was a horrible rain storm in New Jersey. It was an outdoor pool. I'm swimming and I get to the wall, and I look up and I see my coach. He's got on large glasses and a safari hat—a sun hat—and my dad is standing next to him with his umbrella just trying not to get wet, but they were cheering me on. It's one of those things I'll never forget. I'll die with that memory." Jones learned valuable lessons from his coach; Nessel taught him not to "fight the water" and warned him that starting too quickly during a race often means losing steam toward the end. With Nessel's help Jones began to receive recognition; during his senior year, in 2002, he won both state and regional prep-school championships in the 50-yard freestyle. Jones told Galante that Nessel was so determined to help him reach the top of his sport that he "would always walk me to the blocks before a race. He would tell me to 'breathe.' That was always the most important thing—to calm down and breathe."

Jones's training paid off when he was accepted on a scholarship to North Carolina (NC) State University. There he joined the school's swimming and diving team, also known as the Wolfpack, while majoring in English with a minor in psychology. In 2004, under coach Chad Onken, Jones won the 50- and 100-yard Atlantic Coast Conference (ACC) titles for NC State, becoming one of the fastest sprinters in ACC history. In his interview with Schaller, Jones said that the NC State team was like "family" to him. "We had our Wolfpack Appreciation Day at a meet against Georgia Tech. . . . At the meet [the team] presented me with a ring for winning the ACC . . . 50 and 100, and had my Mom there," he said. "I mean . . . the time, the effort, the gesture—even the thought itself—that means so much." By the end of his college career, Jones had seven ACC championships under his belt, in the 50- and 100-meter freestyle and the 200-meter medley relay.

During his college years Jones made an unsuccessful bid for a spot on the U.S. team at the 2004 Olympic trials, failing to make it past the 50-meter preliminaries. Overcome by the pressure of the event, he "froze a little bit," as he explained to Beth

Harris for the Associated Press (November 29, 2007). He bounced back in 2005, when he made his international debut in the World University Games in China, receiving the gold medal in the 50-meter freestyle. In October of that year, he was named to the National "B" Team, USA Swimming's second-tier squad of swimmers, and in April 2006 he set the championship record for the 50-meter freestyle, at 21.31 seconds, in the semifinals at the FINA World Short Course Championships, also in China. He graduated from NC State in 2006.

That summer Jones had a breakthrough performance at the ConocoPhillips USA Swimming National Championships in Indianapolis, Indiana, when he beat one of his role models, Gary Hall Jr., in the 50-meter freestyle. Also that summer Jones signed a six-year contract, estimated to be worth around $2 million, with Nike Inc. With the backing of the sportswear giant, Jones began to train for the 2008 Olympics and mounted a campaign to tour public schools in the Raleigh, North Carolina, area to educate students about water safety. "Nike has provided me the opportunity to develop as an athlete and a person," Jones said after signing the deal, according to Swimming World Magazine (August 30, 2006, on-line). "When I evaluated who could help me both in chasing my dream of representing the U.S. in the Olympics and being able to speak out to the African-American and Hispanic communities about the importance of water safety, drowning prevention and learning to swim, I felt that Nike had the best access to a platform where I can reach millions of kids and deliver this message. The thought of joining Tiger Woods, Michael Jordan, and Lance Armstrong in the Nike family is awe inspiring."

In November 2006 Jones was named "breakout performer of the year" at a prestigious swimming-awards event—the Golden Goggles Awards—for his double-gold-medal performance that summer at the Mutual of Omaha Pan Pacific Championships, in Victoria, British Columbia, commonly referred to as the "Pan Pacs." There, he won the 50-meter freestyle event in 21.84 seconds, then the sixth-fastest time ever, as a member of the U.S. team that set the new world record in the 400-meter freestyle relay, and he became the first African-American swimmer to break a world record. The following year was a challenging one for Jones; he was disappointed when he took home the silver medal in the 50-meter freestyle, finishing behind his teammate Ben Wildman-Tobriner, at the March FINA World Championships in Melbourne, Australia, and he came in second to Wildman-Tobriner again at the August U.S. nationals, where he lost by two-100ths of a second. Jones told Harris, "I got a taste of what . . . [success] felt like and I got really lackadaisical in my training. I just got really happy with where I was." Sabir Muhammad, a former sprinter for Stanford University and a U.S. national team member, told Harris that in sprinting the margin of victory is often extremely small. "What a lot of people really need to understand about sprinting is that on any given day you're separated by a hundredth of a second," he said. "Just the simple fact [that Jones] . . . is consistent with swimming under 22 seconds, which the percentage of swimmers that can do that is very small, is remarkable."

In 2007 Jones returned to New Jersey to teach swimming and water safety in the YMCA's Begin to Swim program, funded by the Toyota Motor Corp. and held at YMCA sports facilities. According to a study conducted by USA Swimming, while about three Caucasian children out of 10 are unable to swim, about six out of 10 African-American children lack that skill, a number that often reflects their parents' inability to swim. At Begin to Swim classes, Jones talks to participants about safe behavior in the pool and his experiences as a swimmer. He told Aimee Berg for WCSN.com (April 15, 2008), "I believe there's a reason I'm in the position I'm in. If there's just one kid that I haven't talked to yet, then I need to do it for that kid. But also for myself."

In 2008 Jones left his longtime coach Brooks Teal and, acting on advice from Mark Schubert, the head coach of the U.S. national team, hired the coach David Marsh to train him. The two started working together on April 7, only 81 days before the U.S. Olympic trials. "With every sprinter I've ever coached, I've done some stroke changing," Marsh told Aimee Berg. "But in this short of a window, there isn't time." Jones "needs to get substantially faster," he continued, "and there are several ways to do it. First, we have to connect his strength to his swimming strength. There's vertical strength"—Jones can jump 35 inches vertically—"and prone strength and we have to apply the vertical to water. Second—the starts. There's always hundredths of a second to find there. Third—race strategy. And fourth—probably most important, his focus and confidence when he steps on the blocks." Marsh also said, "You don't need to reinvent an athlete like Cullen. He's a world-class sprinter."

Although Jones set an American record of 21.59 seconds in the 50-meter freestyle swim during the preliminary Olympic trials, on July 4, 2008, his third-place finish the next day in the same event eliminated him from the official 50-meter race. With his third-place finish in the 100-meter freestyle final on July 5, which he swam in 48.35 seconds, he qualified for the 4x100-meter relay. On August 11, 2008, at the 2008 Olympic Games, the U.S. men's swimming team made history in the 4x100-meter relay with a world-record time of 3:08.24 and won the gold medal. Jones began the third leg ahead of his rival on the French team, but by the end of his required distance, he was a half-body length behind. The U.S. team anchor, Jason Lezak, then succeeded in beating one of the French swimmers by eight-100ths of a second. After his team's victory, Jones told Elliott Almond for the *San Jose Mercury News*, as quoted by Milloy, "The stigma that black people don't swim ended today."

Jones swims five to six hours a day, six days a week. He will appear in *Parting the Waters*, a documentary film by Do Tell Productions about a swim team comprised of inner-city youths from Boston. Principal photography for the film was completed in August 2008. Jones's girlfriend, Maritza Correia of Puerto Rico—who in 2004 became the first female swimmer of color to compete for the U.S. in the Olympics—will also appear in the documentary. Tattooed on the back of Jones's neck is his father's basketball-jersey number, 41.

—W.D.

Suggested Reading: *Denver Post* C p18 May 4, 2008; (London) *Times* p86 Mar. 23, 2007; (Newark, New Jersey) *Star-Ledger* p15 Aug. 3, 2006; (Raleigh, North Carolina) *News & Observer* A p1 Aug. 17, 2006; USA Swimming Web site

Koji Watanabe/Getty Images

Kaká

Apr. 22, 1982– Soccer player

Address: A.C. Milan, Via Filippo Turati, 3-20121, Milan, Italy

"Kaka is the best player in the world, without a doubt," the retired Brazilian soccer player Pelé told a reporter for the *Western Daily Press* (June 19, 2007)—high praise, indeed, from the man who is universally acknowledged to be among the greatest practitioners of the sport in history. Now 26, Kaká has played for two of the world's most successful soccer clubs: since 2002 for the national team of Brazil, his native land, and since 2003 for the Italy-based, professional team A.C. Milan. Although other players are deemed more skillful at dribbling and shooting, he is recognized as the "ultimate attacking midfielder" who is outstanding at both setting up goals and moving seamlessly into a deadly striking role. "Kaka is the complete player, and is simply a more effective all-round player than anyone else," Barnaby Chesterman wrote for Agence France Presse (December 2, 2007), echoing what many others have said. As the Web site of the International Football Federation, FIFA.com (November 30, 2007), explained, "Positioned behind the main striker, in the role of what the Italians call the *trequartista*—part creator, part scorer—Kaka is often the player who conjures the final pass, but equally often he is on hand to apply the finish." Noted for his distinctively stylish technique, Kaká struck Dennis Greenan, writing for the Italian News Agency ANSA (March 24, 2004), as a "slim, aristocratic-looking figure who glides over the grass, head held high like the true greats, with a swan-like nobility," while Rob Hughes wrote for the *International Herald Tribune* (December 18, 2007) that he "appears at his best to move on his own [plane], in his own time." According to Richard Williams, writing for the London *Guardian* (April 25, 2007), "His devastating sprint [is] a thing of seemingly unhurried beauty, his body swaying as one change of direction blends seamlessly into another." As Gabriele Marcotti wrote for the London *Times* (June 23, 2007), "He combines Brazilian flair with European directness. He is a product of two footballing cultures, a man who has all the virtues and none of the vices of either." (Soccer is known as football outside the U.S.) "Someone with Kaka's talent and qualities comes along only once every 50 years," the former Brazilian national-team coach Carlos Alberto Parreira told Duncan Castles for the London *Daily Mail* (February 21, 2005). "He is the future example for every player in the Brazil team." At the end of the 2006–07 season, Kaká swept soccer's most important player-of-the-year awards. He is also unusual among his peers in that he is an outspoken evangelical Christian.

Kaká was born Ricardo Izecson dos Santos Leite on April 22, 1982 in Brazil's capital, Brasília, to Bosco Izecson Pereira Leite, a civil engineer, and Simone Cristina dos Santos Leite, a math teacher. As with most Brazilian soccer players (and other Brazilians in the public eye), he is known by his nickname. Since "Kaka" has scatological connotations in many languages (though not in Portuguese, the national language of Brazil), he added an accent to the second "a," in an effort to change the way people pronounce it. Many sportscasters, journalists, and fans refer to him as Ricky Kaká. Kaká lived for his first six years in Brasília and then moved with his family, which includes his younger brother, Rodrigo, to São Paolo, Brazil's largest city. At around age 10, he joined the São Paolo Football Club, slowly rising up the ranks of its junior teams and signing a pro contract with the organization at 15. But he was too small and thin and

tired too easily to compete with the other, more physical players his age, so team officials placed him on a special diet and, according to several sources, arranged to have him undergo hormone treatments. By age 18 he had grown sufficiently to be able to "start expressing his talent," as Turibio Leite de Barros Neto, the sports-medicine coordinator at the University of São Paulo, told Rob Hughes for the *International Herald Tribune* (December 1, 2004).

A few months later, in October 2000, Kaká broke the sixth of the seven vertebrae in his neck in a swimming-pool accident. Such mishaps have left many others paralyzed; in Kaká's case, the bone healed within two months, and he recovered completely, resuming practice with his team afterward. "In that period I saw that God was with me," he told Jeremy Wilson for the London *Guardian* (May 19, 2007), and he came to regard playing soccer as his "mission." In his professional debut, in early 2001, while serving as a substitute in a match between São Paulo and Botafogo (a team from Rio de Janeiro, Brazil's former capital), Kaká scored two goals, including the match winner, in under five minutes. In his first season he scored 12 goals in 26 appearances. (In Brazil the soccer season begins in May and ends in December; in Europe it usually extends from the fall of one year to the spring of the next.) In 2001 he joined Brazil's pre-Olympic squad and the under-21 national team. The next year he was voted Brazil's best player of 2001. In January 2002 he made his debut with the under-21 Brazilian national team, in a 6–0 rout of Bolivia. In the summer he traveled with the so-called dream team (whose members were arguably the best in the world) to the World Cup, hosted that year by Japan and Korea; except for 20 minutes in which he participated in a game between Brazil and Costa Rica, he devoted himself to learning through watching. The next year Kaká got substantially more playing time during the CONCACAF Gold Cup, sponsored by the Confederation of North, Central American, and Caribbean Association Football, in which Brazil finished in second place. The association named Kaká one of the top players of the tournament.

According to Duncan Castles, writing for the London *Daily Mail* (February 21, 2005), Kaká's next career move, his "big-money transfer to Europe," was "inevitable." Two Brazilian national-team veterans—Rivaldo, who was then playing with A.C. Milan, and Leonardo, who had played for that team from 1997 to 2001—were instrumental in guiding Kaká to join A.C. Milan; owned by Silvio Berlusconi, Italy's prime minister at that time, A.C. Milan is part of Serie A, an Italian league, and is one of the winningest clubs in soccer history. When Kaká arrived, in 2003, members of the team included several other Brazilians, among them Serginho, Dida, and Cafu. "That Brazilian influence was the main reason I chose Milan," Kaká, who had refused the higher transfer fee and salary offered by the owner of the British club Chelsea, told Kevin Kelly for the *Sun* (November 8, 2003). In a widely quoted remark, Luciano Moggi, the general manager of Milan's rival Juventus, said, "Kaka? We would never sign anyone with a name like that"; Berlusconi responded by describing the $8.5 million transfer as "peanuts." (Four years later he refused a reported $115 million bid for Kaká.)

At a press conference on August 19, 2003, Kaká said, as quoted by Agence France Press (August 19, 2003), "I'm looking to [complement] the speed and technique of Brazilian football with the tactical discipline of Italian football." He accomplished that goal almost immediately, gaining admittance to the club's first team without the two years of development and adjustment that even his coaches had expected would be necessary. "I remember his first training session at Milanello: we all knew that a fabulous player had arrived," Milan's head coach, Carlo Ancelotti, later said, according to Agence France Press (December 2, 2007). Rivaldo and the Portuguese native Rui Costa, two of the world's best attacking midfielders, were supposed to have mentored Kaká for at least his first year, but "within months," as Rob Hughes wrote (December 1, 2004), "Kaka was the fixture, the two veterans were the deputies." Kaká made his debut with the team on September 1, 2003, and in his first 30 league games, he scored 10 goals. At the end of an outstanding year for the team, Milan won the Scudetto (league title), along with the European Super Cup, and Kaká was named Serie A Foreign Footballer of the Year. Milan immediately renegotiated his contract, extending it until at least 2009. ⸱

With both the media and opposing coaches watching him more closely, the 2004–05 season "was more difficult than last year" for him, as Kaká told Rediff.com (2004). Referring to those who guarded him, he said, "I am known in Italy now, the markers know me and they are tough here. . . . The coaches are very attentive to the details. They really study things and that is a big difference here. They look at your movement, your positioning, they study you and work out how to stop you." Milan ended in second place, after Juventus, in Serie A and finished runners-up to Liverpool after a penalty shoot-out in the Champions League final, the winning of which is perhaps the most coveted prize in European club football. Nevertheless, Kaká was voted best midfielder of the latter tournament and also led Brazil to victory in the Confederations Cup tournament, scoring a goal against Argentina in the final match.

The 2005–06 season saw Kaká score 14 goals in 35 league matches for Milan, once again earning him the title of Serie A Foreign Footballer of the Year. He was also one of Brazil's key players in the 2006 World Cup, in Germany, scoring the team's first goal of the tournament. "Kaka no longer looks like the floppy-haired choirboy and is instead one of the most physically imposing members of the squad," Alex Bellos wrote for the London *Guardian* (June 17, 2006). His team did not progress past the quarterfinals, a major disappointment for Bra-zil, the reigning champions, who were huge favorites, expected to walk over the opposition and put on a show. "We had many great players but it seems they were tired and the teamwork was crippled," Kaká said in an interview for a fan site, rick-ykaka.com, later that year. In addition, A.C. Milan was implicated in a Serie A match-fixing scandal; the Italian league penalized the team by deducting 30 points at the beginning of the 2006–07 season, all but ruining their chances for the Scudetto. Milan had also sold their main striker, Andriy Shevchenko, to Chelsea, leaving Kaká without his most formidable offensive partner. Nevertheless, that season proved to be Kaká's best to date, with many observers arguing that Shevchenko's departure and a greater responsibility for attack had led to Kaká's becoming the centerpiece of the team's offense. Most observers cited the Champions League's two semifinal games, in the spring of 2007, which pitted A.C. Milan against Manchester United, as the defining moments of Kaká's award-winning season. Overshadowing United's Cristiano Ronaldo, widely considered his equal, Kaká scored three times in two games, once by literally splitting the defense and slotting the ball past United's goalie as that team's defenders collided behind him. In an interview with Simon Kuper for the *Financial Times* (February 16, 2008), Kaká described that goal as the perfect move. On May 23, 2007, at the Olympic Stadium in Athens, Milan won the Champions League trophy with a 2–1 victory over Liverpool. Scoring 10 goals in the tournament, four more than the next-highest scorer, Kaká was named Champions League Player of the Season. That season Milan won the Champions League, the European Super Cup, and the Club World Cup. Kaká swept the player-of-the-year honors, being named the Union of European Football Associations' Club Footballer of the Year, the FIF-Pro (Federation Internationale de Footballeurs Professionnels) World Player of the Year, World Soccer Magazine Player of the Year, and, most importantly, the FIFA World Player of the Year, and he won the prestigious Ballon d'Or from the French magazine *France Football*. In a vote by national team managers and captains, Kaká received 1,047 points; his nearest rival, the 20-year-old Argentinian Lionel Messi, received 504, and the third-place winner, the 22-year-old Cristiano Ronaldo, 426. Recently, Kaká has been hampered by knee problems, fatigue, and inconsistency, and Cristiano Ronaldo has outshined him.

Milan struggled in the 2007–08 season, slipping to fifth place in Serie A and thus missing out on the next season's Champion's League tournament; some thought that the team's struggles were due to the relatively advanced average age of its players. Much of the time Kaká clearly played while injured. He underwent arthroscopic surgery on a knee in May 2008, after the season ended, and was said to have recovered relatively well. Over the summer Milan signed Ronaldinho to play alongside Kaká and the teenage sensation Pato. The trio has been affectionately dubbed "Ka-Pa-Ro."

In soccer the number 10 is a shorthand way of referring to great archetypal attacking playmakers, and Kaká has often been compared to those ranked as 10s. (He has refused to change the number, 22, on his jersey, however.) Playing right behind the center forward in neither the conventional midfield nor attacking position, he is "a free spirit" who plays "between the lines," in Chesterman's words. He told Jeremy Wilson for the London *Guardian* (May 19, 2007), "My job is to create chances for the attackers, but I can move further forward and be more decisive." Possessing power, fluidity, what soccer aficionados term explosive pace, and seemingly endless imagination, he is "able to shoot from range with either foot, equally adept at scoring or creating, at once elegant and efficient, blessed with a deceivingly quick first step along with a keen sense of positioning and timing," as Mark Zeigler wrote for the *San Diego Union-Tribune* (December 26, 2007). His "acceleration is astonishing and allows him to ghost past players and into space," Chesterman wrote, adding, "He doesn't need to do three step-overs to beat a man, he simply drops his shoulder and bursts clear."

Kaká has signed lucrative endorsement deals with the sportswear company Adidas and the designer couturier Giorgio Armani. His current annual salary—€9,000,000, or more than $14 million—makes him the highest-paid soccer player in the world. He reportedly contributes 10 percent of his income to his church. After scoring a goal he typically points upward, to indicate that God is the source of his success, and occasionally he has lifted his jersey to reveal an undershirt bearing the words "I belong to Jesus" in English. He also has the words "God is faithful" stitched on the tongues of his boots. Since 2004 he has served the United Nations World Food Programme as one of its eight celebrity "ambassadors against hunger."

In December 2005 Kaká married the 18-year-old Caroline Celico, after a three-year engagement. During the soccer season the couple live in Milan. Their first child, a son named Luca, was born in June 2008. In 2007 Kaká was granted Italian citizenship, mostly so that A. C. Milan can count him as a domestic player and therefore sign an additional foreign player. He will continue to play internationally for Brazil. His brother, nicknamed Digao, also plays with Milan, but not with its first team.

—M.M.

Suggested Reading: Agence France Presse Dec. 2, 2007; FIFA.com Nov. 30, 2007; *International Herald Tribune* Sports p19 Dec. 1, 2004, p20 Dec. 19, 2007; (London) *Daily Mail* p75 Feb. 21, 2005; (London) *Guardian* Sports p6 May 19, 2007, p12 June 17, 2006; (London) *Sun* Football Nov. 8, 2003

Kao, John

(KAY-oh)

Dec. 14, 1950– Businessman; writer; political consultant

Address: 39 Mesa St., Suite 200, The Presidio, San Francisco, CA 94129

Before he became a prominent expert on creativity, the author of two best-selling books on innovation, and the founder of a company that advises such businesses as IBM, Nokia, and Intel on how to encourage creativity and innovation in their employees, John Kao had already pursued careers as a professional keyboardist, psychiatrist, college professor, and movie and theater producer. "It is only in the last 10 or 15 years that it's become clear to me that I was filling out a pattern," Kao told Cornelia Dean for the *New York Times* (June 24, 2008, online), referring to the connection between his nonlinear career path and his passion for innovation. Kao has proposed implementing a national program that would efficiently and creatively address problems in such areas as health care, energy, and education. "The problem in America is not that we don't have lots of good ideas," he told Matthew Bandyk for *U.S. News & World Report* (October 29,

Robert Gumpert, courtesy of Business Innovation Factory

2007). "The problem is aligning our innovative capabilities to pay off on big ideas and big challenges of the day so that we can have innovation operate at a national level."

Kao's parents left China shortly before the Communist takeover of the country, in 1949, to attend Northwestern University, in Chicago, Illinois. His father, who trained as a physician, had received a university research fellowship just before the borders closed. An only child, John J. Kao was born on December 14, 1950 in Chicago and raised in Garden City, New York. As a youth, he tried to absorb American culture while maintaining his Chinese heritage. "I was like a little astronaut," Kao told Laura Silverman for *Transpacific* (March 1, 1997). "I'd go out every day into the American world and then come home at night to this very different world, and it was up to me to make the connections between the two." When he was nine years old, Kao started a literary magazine at his school, putting together an editorial board and organizing a school-wide literary contest. "I just kind of figured out that it was more fun being in the principal's office, organizing a contest, than it was learning whatever I was supposed to be learning in fourth grade," Kao told Silverman. "And that's pretty much been par for the course all the way through."

Though his parents encouraged him to become a research scientist, Kao dreamed of becoming a psychoanalyst. He was also a talented student of jazz piano. Kao attended Yale University, in New Haven, Connecticut, and majored in behavioral science and philosophy. At one point during his studies, a professor introduced him to the iconoclastic composer and guitarist Frank Zappa. Kao told Zappa how much he revered his work and ended up playing the keyboards on tour with Zappa's band, the Mothers of Invention, for three months in 1969. At the end of the summer, in a year that saw the height of the Vietnam War, he was motivated to return to school to avoid being drafted; he graduated in 1972. Though he recalled to Dean that his decision to attend the Yale School of Medicine was partially driven by "some family pressure," Kao greatly enjoyed his medical-school experience. His interest in human behavior led him to study Jungian psychoanalysis, but during his psychiatry residency, he realized that he was interested in pursuing neither clinical nor academic medicine. He obtained a fellowship from Harvard University, in Cambridge, Massachusetts, that allowed him to enroll in the business school while finishing his psychiatry residency; he had a vague notion of using his business degree and his training in psychiatry to help CEOs or "people who were developing new things," as Kao told Silverman.

Kao received his M.B.A. degree in 1982, and shortly thereafter he began teaching at the Harvard Business School. In 1983, as a junior faculty member, he proposed teaching a course on creativity and entrepreneurship. It was unprecedented for a professor teaching for less than two years to make such a proposal, and most of his colleagues opposed the idea, on the grounds that creativity could not be taught in a classroom setting. Kao offered to do all the necessary preparatory work himself in addition to the regular work for his classes and was ultimately granted permission. The course—Entrepreneurship, Creativity, and Organizations—proved to be extraordinarily popular, attracting 200 students in its first session. During the course Kao presented corporate case studies and asked his students to resolve the businesses' problems by trial and error, using creative strategies. He emphasized expanding and invigorating the businesses through improvisation and innovation. In 1989 he published many of his case studies in a textbook, also titled *Entrepreneurship, Creativity, and Organizations*. Kao continued to teach popular courses on corporate creativity for 14 years at Harvard, as well as at schools including the Massachusetts Institute of Technology and the University of Copenhagen, in Denmark.

In 1986 Kao heard about the work of Howard Green, a professor at the Harvard Medical School, who was doing research on growing sheets of skin in the lab for use on burn victims. Recognizing a business opportunity, Kao helped launch BioSurface Technologies, a company that commercialized the manufacturing of skin, cartilage, and other human tissue, for medical replacement procedures. "I did everything," Kao told Silverman. "I wrote a business plan, I raised the money, I recruited a CEO, I kind of whipped it all together—and then there was this magical day when we had money in the bank and investors and a management team, and I walked into this lawyer's office and signed my name 400 times, and we had a company." Kao later sold BioSurface Technologies to Genzyme, one of the most successful biotech companies in the country. He subsequently launched several other successful companies, including another biotech company, K.O. Technology (now called Variagenics), which focuses on cancer treatment, and Advanced Video Communications, which provides such services as video conferencing.

While attending business school, Kao had become interested in the film industry, and in the mid-1980s he began to network aggressively in Hollywood. Through various connections, he met the writer and director Steven Soderbergh, then a newcomer. Soderbergh had written a screenplay called *sex, lies, and videotape*, about four young adults and their complicated, intertwined sex lives. Kao helped produce the movie, which Soderbergh directed, for $1.2 million. Released in 1989 to great critical acclaim, it won the Palm d'Or, the highest prize, at that year's Cannes International Film Festival, and James Spader, who played one of the main characters, won best-actor honors. (Soderbergh was later nominated for an Academy Award for best screenplay.)

Kao next had the idea to make a movie about an American baseball player in Japan. As executive producer, he raised money, commissioned a screenplay, and oversaw the production of *Mr. Baseball* (1992), a modest hit starring Tom Selleck.

While busy with other ventures over the next few years, Kao remained interested in the entertainment field, and in 1998 he produced the stage play *Golden Child*, which was written by David Henry Hwang and was nominated for three Tony Awards.

In 1996 Kao published *Jamming: The Art and Discipline of Business Creativity*. In that book he advocated a management system in which employees work within a defined structure but are encouraged to be creative in developing new ideas and products. He likened the creative process needed in business settings to that used by jazz musicians in jam sessions. "[You] must ruthlessly trash outmoded obstructions to creativity: standard operating procedures, protocols, norms of behavior, a confining brand image, rules, the revered memory of old successes, and so on," Kao wrote in *Jamming*, as quoted by Stephen G. Minter for *Occupational Hazards* (August 1996). "This is always difficult because it obliges people continuously to revise their sense of themselves and their place in the organization." He suggested that managers create office environments that encourage playful and productive interaction and that they be careful not to stifle their employees' creative impulses. Published in 12 languages, *Jamming* reached number 14 on the *BusinessWeek* best-seller list and was generally hailed as a useful resource. Some critics, however, found fault with the book. "Kao makes jamming seem too easy," Ronald Henkoff wrote for *Fortune* (September 9, 1996). "He owes it to his readers to consider the sometimes darker complexities of creativity. Innovation can be destabilizing, unpredictable, and threatening."

In 1997 Kao left Harvard and moved to San Francisco, California. That year he co-edited *Innovation: Breakthrough Thinking at 3M, Dupont, GE, Pfizer, and Rubbermaid*. In each of the book's five chapters, a business leader describes the ways in which his or her company has incorporated innovation into its organizational structure. That year Kao also produced a short companion film to *Jamming*, which combined video and audio recordings of jazz musicians with various business case studies. In a critique for *Training Media Review* (November 1997), Jeanne Baer praised the video for its entertaining qualities and concluded, "There are a few cases of circular logic and jargon-laden explanations that may set an analytical viewer's teeth on edge, but on the whole, *Jamming* presents a convincing argument for the need to become more 'improvisational.'"

In 1997 Kao also founded the Idea Factory, a firm that consults with major corporations on fostering business creativity, planning strategically for the future, and using intuition to make better decisions. The Idea Factory helps develop software and other on-line tools to support collaboration, participates in redesigning businesses' physical space to foster creativity, and offers training programs and workshops, among other services. Initially, the Idea Factory's central office was located in San Francisco, in a large, high-ceilinged loft that contained a grand piano. (The firm's headquarters have since been moved to Singapore.) Kao served as the Idea Factory's CEO until 2001, opening several branch offices throughout Europe and Asia; raising millions of dollars to establish Idea Factory Capital Partners, a venture fund; and developing a number of start-up companies.

In 2000 Kao, along with a group of partners, purchased Ealing Studios, in London, England. Since then Kao has worked to convert Ealing, the oldest film studio in the world, into a cutting-edge digital entertainment company. "My job is to put a container around an idea so that it has tangibility, resources are attracted to it and it starts to have a life," Kao told Andrew Davidson for *Management Today* (April 30, 2001).

In the early 2000s Kao found himself in great demand as a lecturer on subjects related to innovation: he spoke, for example, about the ways in which the U.S. health-care system could be improved through creative means and the ways in which the innovations of East Asian corporations are changing the global economy. During that time he founded Kao & Co., whose services include, according to the company Web site, "helping an organization to clarify its desired future state, generating ways of communicating its desired future state to a variety of constituents, designing an innovation strategy, and supporting the efforts of innovation teams and senior leadership to execute in a variety of ways."

In 2007 Kao published *Innovation Nation: How America Is Losing Its Innovation Edge, Why It Matters and What We Can Do to Get It Back*, a book that discusses the global trends behind the shift of economic dominance from the United States and Western Europe to Asia. One reason for the shift in power, according to Kao, is the recent improvement of educational institutions in Asia, coupled with the declining quality of science and math education in the U.S. Furthermore, Kao blames the restrictive immigration policies instituted by the federal government after the terrorist attacks of September 11, 2001 for the inability of American corporations to recruit highly educated Asian scientists and engineers. "The rest of the world is getting smarter about innovation," Kao told Bandyk. "We've gone from an arms race in the Cold War to a brain race in the 21st century."

Kao, who intentionally published the book just before the 2008 U.S. presidential-election cycle, suggested the creation of a Department of Innovation, overseen by the U.S. Congress, which would coordinate 20 regional groups made up of CEOs, scientists, cultural leaders, policy makers, and technologists, focused on finding creative approaches to specific national problems. He envisions research centers at which young people would study in "regionally strategic fields such as agricultural biotech in Iowa, energy in Montana and aerospace in California," as quoted by Heidi Benson in the *San Francisco Chronicle* (November 24, 2007, on-line).

Without action, Kao told Cornelia Dean, "[The U.S.] will have an elite class of educated, cosmopolitan, global citizens who have a ticket of entry to the major leagues and a much larger group of marginally employable people who have been sold a bill of goods by a consumption economy." Dubbed "scary, insightful, and ultimately very useful" by Bruce Nussbaum, writing for *BusinessWeek* (October 22, 2007), *Innovation Nation* was critically acclaimed, and its premises have been endorsed by such organizations as the National Academy of Sciences and the Brookings Institute. It was chosen by the editors of *BusinessWeek* as one of the 10 best books of the year.

Kao had met U.S. senator Hillary Rodham Clinton in 2004, when both were members of a Defense Department advisory group. In 2006 Kao served as an adviser on Clinton's Senate reelection campaign, and the following year he was a consultant on her presidential bid. Clinton became the target of some derision for working with an innovation expert. In the *Huffington Post* (May 16, 2007, online), E. A. Hanks criticized Clinton's decision to hire Kao and noted that it was "alarming" that his "faux-inspirational babble" might influence Clinton's or any other political campaign. "Innovation doesn't come from a pamphlet, even a $70,000 one," Hanks wrote, referring to the amount Clinton paid Kao, "and it can't be squeezed into a stump speech here or there."

Despite skepticism from some quarters regarding his methods, Kao remains optimistic about the country's ability to address its problems creatively. He believes that because Americans do not attach lasting stigma to failure, the U.S. is an excellent place to try new ideas. "The world needs us, even if it does not believe it does," he told Dean.

Kao lives in San Francisco with his wife, Lauren, and their three children.

—M.E.R.

Suggested Reading: *BusinessWeek* p122 Oct. 22, 2007; *Fortune* p183 Sep. 9, 1996; *Management Today* p58 Apr. 30, 2001; *New York Times* (online) June 24, 2008; *San Francisco Chronicle* (online) Nov. 24, 2007; *Transpacific* p60 Mar. 1, 1997; *U.S. News & World Report* p22 Oct. 29, 2007

Selected Books: as writer—*Jamming: The Art and Discipline of Business Creativity*, 1996; *Innovation Nation: How America Is Losing Its Innovation Edge, Why It Matters and What We Can Do to Get It Back*, 2007; as co-editor—*Innovation: Breakthrough Thinking at 3M, Dupont, GE, Pfizer, and Rubbermaid*, 1997

Kaufman, Millard

Mar. 12, 1917– Novelist; screenwriter

Address: c/o McSweeney's, 849 Valencia St., San Francisco, CA 94110

In October 2007, at the age of 90, Millard Kaufman became a first-time novelist, with the publication of *Bowl of Cherries*, a comical tale narrated by a verbose 14-year-old genius who is awaiting execution in Iraq. Set in locations including a prison in the fictional Assama Province, where buildings are made from "evacuative biodegradables," or human waste, the novel was widely praised by critics, who noted Kaufman's biting satire, erudite vocabulary, and mix of coarse and refined humor. "While the book is unique, parts have the feel of some of the great comedic novels of the past 50 years," Jason Kuiper wrote for the *Omaha (Nebraska) World-Herald* (October 7, 2007). "There are touches of Thomas Pynchon's absurdist humor and John Kennedy Toole's *A Confederacy of Dunces* for general zaniness." Other reviewers compared the book to works by Joseph Heller and Kurt Vonnegut.

For Kaufman *Bowl of Cherries* marked a high point in what had already been a long, varied career. He worked briefly as a journalist before serving in World War II, then became a Hollywood screenwriter. In the 1950s he garnered two Academy Award nominations, for his screenplays for

Courtesy of Millard Kaufman

Take the High Ground! and *Bad Day at Black Rock.* Kaufman also co-created the visually impaired cartoon character Mr. Magoo, who constantly stumbles into precarious situations. In his late 1980s, after a project he had been working on fell through,

Kaufman decided to "try writing a novel," as he recalled to Steffie Nelson for the *Los Angeles Times* (October 31, 2007). "It always kind of interested me, but as long as I was busy I never got around to doing it." Many years ago Kaufman heard the writer W. Somerset Maugham lecture at the University of California at Los Angeles. "There are three rules for writing a novel," Maugham said on that occasion. "Unfortunately nobody knows that they are." "I thought, well, under circumstances like that," Kaufman remarked to Nelson, "how can I lose?"

One of two children and an only son, Millard Kaufman was born to Fred Kaufman and his wife on March 12, 1917 in Baltimore, Maryland. His family owned few books, and it was not until he reached junior high school that his love for reading was awakened. Assigned to read one chapter every week of William Makepeace Thackeray's *The History of Henry Esmond*, Kaufman finished the whole book in one sitting, by reading "all through the night . . . ," as he said in a 2007 interview with *Current Biography*. "I was fractured by it." He said in the same interview that he became interested in cinema at the age of 16 or 17, when he was working as a seaman on a freighter. One night, after the ship docked in Portland, Oregon, the captain gave each of the workers $3 for food and lodging. Kaufman spent some of the money to see a movie; the film he chose, *The Informer*, left him in awe. "I saw it over and over again—the whole night I spent watching this picture," he said. (Years later, while working for MGM, he befriended Dudley Nichols, who wrote the script for *The Informer*, after meeting him in the studio's commissary.)

Kaufman earned a bachelor's degree in English literature from Johns Hopkins University, in Baltimore, in 1939. As an undergraduate he met the woman he would marry, Lorraine, when both of them ingested cobra venom as part of a medical experiment being conducted by the father of one of Kaufman's friends. After college Kaufman moved to New York City. There, he got a job as a copyboy with the New York *Daily News*, earning $13.70 per week. He also wrote for the Long Island daily paper *Newsday*. In one assignment for the latter, in 1941, he and a co-worker donned pairs of shorts and visited a Long Island town that had recently passed a law prohibiting the wearing of revealing clothing out of doors. Police officers, tipped off by the men's editor, arrested them as soon as they arrived. "The paper bailed us out," Kaufman recalled to Scott Simon for the National Public Radio program *Weekend Edition Saturday* (October 27, 2007).

After the U.S. entered World War II, in December 1941, Kaufman joined the Marines and spent three years overseas. While serving in the South Pacific, he participated in the Battle of Guadalcanal and took part in operations on Guam and Okinawa. "I weighed a hundred and eighty-two pounds when I went overseas, and when my wife met me afterward she didn't recognize me—I weighed a hundred and twenty-eight," Kaufman told Rebecca Mead for the *New Yorker* (September

17, 2007). Because of the residual effects of two diseases he had contracted during the war—malaria and dengue fever—Kaufman and his wife moved to San Francisco, California. "I didn't really feel like I could spend the heat of the summer or the cold of the winter in New York anymore," he told Mead.

Kaufman intended to seek work in journalism, but on a lark he traveled to Los Angeles to "see what this business of writing pictures is all about," as he told Teddy Wayne for *Radar* (September 2007). Dore Schary, the chief of production at Metro Goldwyn Mayer (MGM) then, was fascinated by the Marines (he himself had been too old to fight in World War II), and partly for that reason he hired Kaufman as a scriptwriter. Kaufman acquired an agent, who suggested that he write something about the war. The result was *Take the High Ground!* (1953); set in a Texas boot camp, the movie was directed by Richard Brooks and starred Richard Widmark and Karl Malden. The film earned Kaufman his first Academy Award nomination, for story and screenplay. "As a recruiting poster or a preface to greetings from Uncle Sam, this is as able an achievement as a practical-minded critic can conceive," Bosley Crowther wrote for the *New York Times* (November 20, 1953). "The script . . . is an assembly of simple episodes that have color, colloquial humor and straight, ready-made character."

During the 13 years that Kaufman worked for MGM, he "did all kinds of work . . . including handling [improving] pictures which were not yet pictures," as he recalled to Simon. "They were screenplays which fell into a deep hole. They were not done well enough to have been shot and made into movies, and they were not done poorly enough to be simply burned." In 1950 Kaufman served as a "front," taking screenwriting credit for the film *Gun Crazy*, also called *Deadly Is the Female*, which had been written by Dalton Trumbo. Trumbo was among the so-called Hollywood 10, a group of writers who were jailed after refusing to testify before the U.S. House of Representatives' Un-American Activities Committee, whose mission was to identify suspected Communists in the public and private sectors. Kaufman had met Trumbo only once, and he did not receive any money for having his name on the script; rather, as he told Wayne, his action "benefited my conscience." "It's a peculiar thing to go off and spend three years [during World War II] in which—I hope this doesn't sound highfalutin—you're getting your ass shot off and you think you're fighting fascism, and then you return to your democratic country and find that a form of fascism has broken out here. Which I did my best to resist, and this was one of the ways." (In 1992 the Writers Guild of America publicly announced that Trumbo had written the script for *Gun Crazy*.)

Kaufman's most celebrated film, *Bad Day at Black Rock* (1955), earned the writer an Oscar nomination for best screenplay. Directed by John

Sturges, the movie is about a World War II veteran, John Macreedy (played by Spencer Tracy), who visits a small Arizona town in search of the father of a fellow soldier—a man of Japanese descent who died while saving Macreedy's life and has been awarded, posthumously, a medal of honor. The film deals with racism in a way that many consider to be ahead of its time. "As an indictment of traditional American 'frontier justice' and a portrait of the individual vs. the mob," Dan Craft wrote for the (Bloomington, Illinois) *Pantagraph* (March 10, 2000), "*Bad Day* is something of a contemporary reworking of 1952's *High Noon*, only on a much more intense and exciting plane. . . . In the guise of a mystery—what happened to the dead soldier's father, a local farmer?—Sturges and . . . Kaufman address some of the weightiest issues facing modern post-war America. And they do it without seeming preachy or determined to hammer home A Message." "Making racism uncomfortable for bigots has been a gradual process," Kaufman told Edvins Beitiks for the *San Francisco (California) Examiner* (December 23, 1999). "It's not that I think *Black Rock* was any great innovator, but I think there's less pressure now when you make a movie about racial difficulties."

While Kaufman was working on *Bad Day at Black Rock*, he himself became a target of Congress's anti-Communist crusade, after he signed a petition urging Fox studio executives to return to another Hollywood 10 member, Albert Maltz, the rights to one of his books. Maltz's status meant that his book would never be made into a film in the U.S.; a British company, however, was willing to finance such a project, provided that the author regained the rights to the story. "The book was never pulled out of Fox, though. They just dumped it. But I was in deep water; they published my name in *Red Channels*," Kaufman told Marc Weingarten for *LA Weekly* (October 18, 2007, on-line), referring to a pamphlet that contained the names of suspected Communist sympathizers.

Kaufman occasionally clashed with MGM executives. In one instance, he was told to make several changes to the script for *Raintree County* (1957), a Civil War drama starring Elizabeth Taylor and Montgomery Clift. In particular, his bosses objected to the suggestion in the script that Taylor's character might have had a black mother, and they did not want Clift's character, an abolitionist, to enlist with the Union Army. "It was the '50s, when they were reliving the Civil War, so it was all this, 'We're going to lose the Southern market, blah, blah,'" Kaufman told Beitiks. "The Taylor story line was central to the picture. I fought for it. I got it. But Montgomery Clift . . . . They had him joining the Union Army because it was the only way he could get into the South to find his wife."

Kaufman's subsequent writing credits include, for the silver screen, *Never So Few* (1959), a World War II drama directed by John Sturges, starring Frank Sinatra and Steve McQueen; *Living Free* (1972), an adaptation of the same-titled nonfiction book by Joy Adamson about the lioness she raised in Africa; and *The Klansman* (1974), based on the novel by William Bradford Huie about racism in a small Alabama town in the 1960s, starring Lee Marvin and Richard Burton. For television, Kaufman wrote the scripts for *The Nativity* (1978) and *Enola Gay: The Men, the Mission, the Atomic Bomb* (1980).

Outside of screenwriting Kaufman is perhaps best known for co-creating, with the animator John Hubley, Mr. Magoo—an iconic cartoon character who, due to extreme nearsightedness and his frequent refusal to acknowledge that his eyesight is poor, often gets himself into amusing predicaments. Mr. Magoo made his debut in 1949, in a Columbia Pictures cartoon called *The Ragtime Bear*. The National Federation for the Blind later labeled the character a cruel joke at the expense of the visually impaired, but Kaufman has insisted that he never intended to hurt anyone's feelings. He and Hubley based the character on a pair of similar uncles, who "insisted on seeing the world through eyes that interpreted it in a highly subjective manner," as Kaufman told the *Los Angeles Times* (October 30, 1995). "They saw only what they stubbornly wanted to see." "We made a big mistake, John and I, in giving Magoo eyeglasses," he told Simon. "His inability to see was entirely symbolic—that is his insistence on his own way. But by giving him glasses, we were accused, between 20 and 40 years later, of being terribly, viciously, politically incorrect, making fun of people who couldn't see. That wasn't the idea at all."

When he was 82 Kaufman told Dale Keiger for *Johns Hopkins Magazine* (February 2000) that no one had offered him "a truly first-class screen job for about 10 years." "Pictures have always been a product aimed at young people, and there follows the corollary that in order to understand the thought processes of kids, you have to have a young person do it. Of course, you can go overboard. *Black Beauty* wasn't written by a horse." Kaufman used some of his time to write a nonfiction book, *Plots and Characters: A Screenwriter on Screenwriting* (1999), which Keiger described as "a candid, irreverent, and entertaining book of advice on writing movie scripts" containing many funny anecdotes drawn from the author's 50 years of experience in Hollywood. In his book Kaufman complained good-humoredly about the relatively low status of screenwriters in the Hollywood hierarchy. During the interview with Keiger, he said, "I have been aggressively fighting the primacy of the director, and before that the producer. I do feel that the relationship among producer, director, and writer is out of whack. I don't claim to be unprejudicial on this subject, but I think the primary contribution to any movie is made by the writer."

In 2003 Kaufman began working on a script for the director Jake Scott, a son of the director Ridley Scott. "We didn't see eye to eye, and it came to nothing," Kaufman told Weingarten, adding that he believes that he is the oldest Writers Guild of

America member to have written a script. "I had had a long run, but I realized that I needed something to do in order to keep me out of trouble," he told Weingarten. "So I thought I'd write a novel." "I don't know what I'm writing until I see it on paper," he told Steffie Nelson, "and that was the case [with the novel]. I wanted to get it down and take a look at it and see what direction it could go. And there were a number of directions I could have gone, and I went in all of them." He recalled to Weingarten that although he had no interest in writing a "war novel," he felt compelled to weave into the plot the war in Iraq launched by the U.S. in 2003. "Since the beginning of recorded time, which is about 6,500 years or so, we've never had peace in the world," he said to Weingarten. "There's always a goddamn flare-up somewhere. I couldn't have ignored that, but I kept it in the background." Another issue he wanted to explore was the age-old problem of how to dispose of human waste. "Well, it seems to me that we as a human race have gone through a qualitative change when we stopped being nomads and moved to cities," he said. "Nomads could crap anywhere and it wasn't a problem. Suddenly, in cities, crap became a big waste issue."

In *Bowl of Cherries* Kaufman touched on both topics, as the book's protagonist, Judd Breslau, finds himself imprisoned and sentenced to death in Assama, Iraq, whose residents have figured out a way to make buildings from human excrement. As Breslau—a 14-year-old genius who has been expelled from Yale University—awaits death by "ganching," or being thrown from a building onto bamboo spikes, he tells his life story through flashbacks. After leaving Yale, Breslau takes a job at a Baltimore think-tank, where an Egyptologist, who is certain that the ancients used sound waves to build the pyramids, has the young scholar attempt to levitate rocks by playing the tuba. After Breslau falls in love with the Egyptologist's daughter, the action moves to a Colorado farm and to an adult-film studio located in the anchorage of the Brooklyn Bridge.

"That weird incongruity between highbrow/lowbrow humor is only part of what makes *Bowl of Cherries* so irresistible," Ron Charles wrote for the *Washington Post* (September 23, 2007). "Kaufman's comic imagination, his ability to mix things scatological and historical, political and philosophical, reminds one of those young'uns Kurt Vonnegut and Joseph Heller. The ridiculous slapstick in Assama is straight from Woody Allen's *Don't Drink the Water*, and a cameo appearance by a goofy President Bush will take you back to *Dr. Strangelove*. But Kaufman seems to have more heart than those '60s satirists; his precious young hero pulls on our sympathies even as he trudges on through absurdity." Writing for the Cleveland, Ohio, *Plain Dealer* (October 28, 2007), Karen R. Long called the novel "sharp and strange, unlike anything else you'll read this year. It dabbles in atmospherics like those in the television series *Lost* and mixes in elements of *Three Kings*, the George Clooney Gulf War movie, to tell of a boy's coming-of-age." In a review for the *San Francisco Chronicle* (October 21, 2007), Jenna Krajeski praised the novel as "deliriously funny," adding, "It's a suspenseful, hyper and strange work, with a flurry of abrupt cautions administered like literary shock therapy."

Describing the process of writing *Bowl of Cherries*, Kaufman told Weingarten, "I found it enjoyable, but, I don't know if it's my age or what, I'd just go over and over sections looking for the apposite word. I guess I had this exalted view of fiction writing, that it was a higher art, but it's really just like anything else—you sit your ass down and you write the goddamn thing." Kaufman dislikes typewriters and has admitted to feeling afraid of computers and the Internet, so he wrote the book in longhand and had his secretary type the manuscript. He relied on the *Encyclopedia Britannica* for nearly all his research, and he said his use of esoteric or multisyllabic words—which pleased many reviewers—was in keeping with the spirit of his protagonist. "A number of friends have told me that they need a dictionary to read the book, but this kid in the novel is a goofball, a precocious kid, and he would do things like that—use big words that no one understands," he told Weingarten.

Bowl of Cherries was published in October 2007 by McSweeney's; founded by the writer Dave Eggers, it is thought to appeal primarily to young, hip, urban readers. Kaufman had never heard of McSweeney's, but after his literary agent died, he gave his manuscript to a friend, who passed it to another friend, who then sent it to the publisher. According to Kaufman, his editor at McSweeny's, Eli Horowitz, rarely suggested changes and always gave him the final say. Kaufman told *Current Biography* that, like virtually everyone at McSweeney's, including Eggers, he was surprised that the novel received such glowing reviews. "I was astounded to find out that I've been enjoying the hell out of this," he said, referring to interviews and other aspects of his literary success.

Kaufman is currently at work on his second novel; he is "not sure what it's gonna be," according to Nelson. He told Mead that he writes diligently every day, in part because he was impressed by something the film legend Charlie Chaplin said to him when they met on a beach in Italy one day long ago. Much of the morning and early afternoon had been overcast, and at 3:00 p.m., just as the sun started to come out, Chaplin went back to the hotel. "Unless I write every day, I don't feel I deserve my dinner," he told Kaufman.

Kaufman lives in Los Angeles with Lorraine, a psychologist who still maintains her practice. (The writer David Chase has said that she was the inspiration for the character Dr. Jennifer Melfi on the HBO series *The Sopranos*.) The Kaufmans have two daughters, Mary and Amy, both psychologists, and a son, Frederick, a writer.

Kaufman has taught at Johns Hopkins University and the Sundance Institute, in Utah. The Writers Guild Foundation has named him a living legend. He remains an avid reader; each year he rereads F. Scott Fitzgerald's *The Great Gatsby* and Dashiell Hammett's *The Maltese Falcon*. His favorite novel is *Bleak House*, by Charles Dickens, whom he considers "the greatest writer of prose in the English language," according to Weingarten.

—K.J.P.

Suggested Reading: (Cleveland, Ohio) *Plain Dealer* Books M p4 Oct. 28, 2007; *LA Weekly* (on-line) Oct. 18, 2007; *Los Angeles Times* E p1 Oct. 31, 2007; *New Yorker* p36+ Sep. 17, 2007; *Omaha (Nebraska) World-Herald* E p8 Oct. 7, 2007; *Radar* (on-line) Sep. 2007; *Washington Post* Book World p6 Sep. 23, 2007

Selected Books: *Plot and Characters*, 1999; *Bowl of Cherries*, 2007

Selected Films: *The Ragtime Bear*, 1949; *Unknown World*, 1951; *Take the High Ground!* 1953; *Bad Day at Black Rock*, 1955; *Raintree County*, 1957; *Never So Few*, 1959; *Living Free*, 1972; *The Klansman*, 1974; *The Nativity*, 1978; *Enola Gay: The Men, the Mission, and the Atomic Bomb*, 1980

Gabriel Bouys/AFP/Getty Images

Kelly, Raymond

Sep. 4, 1941– New York City police commissioner

Address: One Police Plaza, New York, NY 10038-1403

When he was named the commissioner of the New York City Police Department (NYPD) in 2002, Raymond W. Kelly returned to a post he had held for a little more than a year in the 1990s. In 1993, during his first stint as commissioner, under Mayor David N. Dinkins, terrorists detonated a bomb beneath one of the twin towers of the World Trade Center, killing six people and injuring more than a thousand. Kelly began his second tour of duty as the head of the NYPD as an appointee of Mayor Michael R. Bloomberg, less than four months after the far more devastating terrorist attacks of September 11, 2001, which resulted in the destruction of both trade-center towers and the deaths of nearly 3,000 people. With upwards of 37,000 uniformed officers, the NYPD is the largest law-enforcement agency in the nation, and Kelly is "widely seen as the second most powerful person in city government," as William K. Rashbaum wrote for the *New York Times* (November 15, 2005). Under Kelly there has been a sharp reduction in crime and generally improved relations between the police and the city's black and Latino populations, and the counterterrorism program that he has created is one of the most comprehensive of those in operation among the world's cities. When Rashbaum interviewed him nearly three years ago, Kelly insisted that he had no fear that another terrorist attack, a rise in crime related to the worsening economy, or any other event might tarnish his reputation and spur him to give up his job. "It sounds corny, but I never have avoided the challenges—I relish them—I think it's what makes me tick, to a certain extent," he said. "That would be the last reason I would leave, because things would turn bad; that would be the reason I would stay, quite frankly."

Kelly is a 30-year veteran of the U.S. Marine Corps Reserves. He worked in a number of capacities with the NYPD before his first stint as commissioner and in a series of jobs before his most recent NYPD appointment, including positions with the U.S. Treasury Department, Interpol (formally, the International Criminal Police Organization), the U.S. Customs Service, and the investment bank and securities-trading and brokerage firm Bear Stearns. He has earned two graduate degrees in law and a master's degree in public administration. Mayor Bloomberg described Kelly to William K. Rashbaum as a "phenomenally competent guy," adding, "I think he's the best police commissioner we've ever had, and I think Ray could do anything."

Of Irish ancestry, Raymond Walter Kelly was born on September 4, 1941 in New York City to James F. Kelly, a milkman, and Elizabeth Kelly, who worked at a Macy's department store. He was raised first on the Upper West Side of the city's borough of Manhattan and later in the borough of Queens. He played football while at Archbishop Molloy High School, a Catholic institution in Queens, and graduated in 1959. He then attended Manhattan College, in the New York City borough of the Bronx, where he earned a bachelor's degree in business administration (B.B.A.) in 1963. As an undergraduate Kelly envisioned a possible career in the military and enlisted in the Marine Corps Reserves. He also joined the Police Cadet Program, which aimed to prepare—and inspire—college students to join the New York City Police Department. In 1963 Kelly graduated first in his class from the New York Police Academy, for which he received the Bloomingdale Trophy, an engraved .38 caliber pistol. In 1965, as a first lieutenant in the Marine Corps, Kelly served in the Vietnam War, leading his troops in 12 months of combat. "Everything I know about leadership I learned in the Marine Corps," Kelly remarked to a crowd at an annual Fleet Week Gala, where he was honored for his public service with a Freedom Award, according to Paul Kane in *Defense Department Documents and Publications* (June 8, 2006). "I keep a well-worn copy of the *Guidebook for Marines* beside my desk." (Kelly retired from the Marine Reserves as a colonel in 1995.) Returning to the NYPD in 1966, Kelly earned a reputation for his disciplined leadership and competence. Concurrently, while quickly rising through the ranks, he earned a J.D. degree from the St. John's University School of Law, in Queens, in 1971, and a master of laws (L.L.M.) degree from the New York University Law School, in 1974.

By 1980 Kelly had reached the position of captain (the top civil-service position in the NYPD). Four years later, after earning a master's degree in public administration (M.P.A.) from Harvard University's John F. Kennedy School of Government, which he attended on a scholarship, he was promoted to deputy inspector by then–police commissioner Benjamin Ward. He was the commanding officer of the 77th Precinct when, in 1985, he was assigned to take over the troubled 106th Precinct in the Ozone Park section of Queens, shortly after disclosures that several of the precinct's officers had used stun guns to torture suspected drug dealers. (The officers were later convicted on assault charges.) Praised for his handling of the difficult assignment, in 1987 Kelly became a deputy chief, a one-star position. In 1988 he was given a two-star rank, that of assistant police chief, and named head of the Office of Management Analysis and Planning at police headquarters. On February 9, 1990 Commissioner Lee P. Brown appointed Kelly first deputy police commissioner, the department's second-highest post. "Obviously, this is a culmination of a dream," Kelly told Leonard Buder for the *New York Times* (February 10, 1990). During his two years in that position, Kelly pushed for departmental reforms and an increase in the number of officers on city streets. He also championed an approach to law enforcement called "community policing," based on the idea that visible support of and interaction with communities can help control crime.

In the early 1990s members of the NYPD, whose officers were disproportionately white, were involved in incidents with the public that led to allegations of corruption and racism. Crime rates had also increased dramatically; in 1990 an all-time high of 2,245 murders were reported. In September 1992 members of the police union staged a massive, racially charged demonstration in response to a proposal by Mayor Dinkins (the city's first black mayor) for an all-civilian board to review complaints regarding officer conduct. Kelly publicly denounced the police protests, calling them "an embarrassment to the department," as quoted by Craig Wolff in the *New York Times* (September 23, 1992). "I recognize the right of officers to demonstrate," he told Wolff. "But when it gets into unlawful conduct or conduct unbecoming a police officer, that's when it has gone too far." In August 1992 commissioner Lee Brown abruptly resigned (reportedly, to spend more time with his wife, who was suffering from cancer), and Kelly became acting police commissioner.

On October 15, 1992 Dinkins announced his selection of Kelly as police commissioner, calling his choice "not a difficult judgment to make." "He's a cop's cop," Dinkins said, according to Alan Finder in the *New York Times* (October 17, 1992). "He's intelligent, well educated, organized." As police commissioner Kelly aimed to reduce crime, improve New Yorkers' quality of life, and better the NYPD's relationship with minorities. On his first day as commissioner, during a broadcast of the radio show *The Breakfast Club*, with host Art Whaley, on the black-owned radio station WLIB, Kelly described his plans to increase the numbers of African-Americans and Latinos in the NYPD. On many Sundays he visited predominantly African-American churches to ask for support and recruit police candidates. Continuing his "community policing" efforts, he developed a program called Safe Streets, Safe City, resulting in the largest increase in uniformed ranks in the department's history and a boost in the number of officers patrolling city streets. In regard to so-called quality-of-life issues, he took steps to reduce the presence on the streets of prostitutes, panhandlers, and "squeegee men," who would—uninvited—wash the windshields of motorists stopped at traffic lights and then solicit payment.

On February 26, 1993 the World Trade Center was attacked by terrorists, who detonated a car bomb in the garage underneath Tower One (the North Tower), killing six people and injuring more than 1,000. Kelly was the first top city official to respond to the blast (the mayor was overseas), and he took part in the investigation that resulted in the arrests and convictions of four of the accomplices, who were sentenced to life in prison.

In the 1993 race for mayor of New York, Rudolph W. Giuliani defeated David Dinkins. During his campaign Giuliani had criticized the performance of the police department under Dinkins, arguing that the police had failed to ensure "New Yorkers' civil right to safety," as quoted by Alison Mitchell in the *New York Times* (December 3, 1993). After Giuliani was sworn in, on January 1, 1994, William J. Bratton, formerly the police commissioner of Boston, Massachusetts, became New York's new police commissioner. Bratton instituted a series of aggressive anti-crime measures that came to define Giuliani's years as mayor.

During that period Kelly held a series of federal law-enforcement jobs. In 1994 President Bill Clinton appointed him director of International Police Monitors in Haiti during the multinational mission, dubbed Operation Restore Democracy, to facilitate the return of the exiled president, Jean-Bertrand Aristide. (Aristide had been democratically elected in 1990 but was overthrown seven months later in a coup led by Lieutenant General Raoul Cedras, the head of the armed forces.) Kelly established an interim, international police force and trained Haitian police recruits. After he completed the mission, in 1996, President Clinton and the chairman of the Joint Chiefs of Staff awarded Kelly the Exceptional Meritorious Service Commendation and the Commander's Medal for Public Service, respectively. From 1996 to 1998 Kelly served in the U.S. Treasury Department as undersecretary for enforcement, a subcabinet position in which he oversaw 40 percent of federal law-enforcement activities, including those connected with the U.S. Customs Service, the Alcohol, Tobacco, and Firearms Bureau, and the Secret Service. Concurrently, from 1996 to 2000, he was the vice president for the Americas of Interpol.

In 1998 Kelly took on the job of commissioner of the Customs Service, overseeing the agency's 20,000 employees and $20 million budget. The move was technically a demotion, given that he had overseen the agency, along with others, in his previous position. He explained, as quoted by William Roberts in the *Journal of Commerce* (August 20, 1998), that his decision to accept the position stemmed from his knowing that "this is where the action is." The Customs Service had recently faced increasing criticism for failing to accomplish the goal of speeding up the processes of legal trade while also stopping illegal drug trade at U.S. borders. Viewing modernized technology as a means to tackle both problems, Kelly petitioned the Senate to fund, for example, the purchase of gamma-ray machines and other devices for better screening of cargo. He also took steps to curb racial profiling, in response to reports that the Customs Service was unfairly singling out black and Hispanic people for searches at airports and other ports of entry. Kelly developed objective criteria for agents to identify suspicious behavior. For his accomplishments the U.S. Treasury Department awarded Kelly the Alexander Hamilton Medal for Exceptional Service.

In January 2001 Kelly resigned from the Customs Service to serve as the global head of corporate security for the investment bank Bear Stearns in New York City. On September 11, 2001 he witnessed the terrorist attacks on the World Trade Center from the windows of his apartment in Lower Manhattan. "People [were] saying that the building could never come down," Kelly remarked to Kane Farabaugh, a writer for *Voice of America News* (December 19, 2007), "and seeing it crumble, obviously, it was a life altering moment you might say for me." The event triggered Kelly's desire to return to public service.

Shortly after the multibillionaire businessman Michael R. Bloomberg was elected mayor of New York, in November 2001, then–police commissioner Bernard B. Kerik announced his resignation. That same month Bloomberg announced his intention to appoint Kelly to the position, making Kelly the only person ever to serve two nonconsecutive terms as police commissioner. Crime in the city had dropped substantially during the Giuliani administration, but relationships between police officers and the city's minority communities had often been strained. In two notorious incidents, unarmed black men—Amadou Diallo and Patrick Dorismond—were shot and killed by police, in 1999 and 2000, respectively. At his swearing-in ceremony, on January 4, 2002, Kelly identified three main goals: the reduction of violent crime and quality-of-life offenses, improved relationships with black and Latino communities, and heightened vigilance against terrorism. He also announced the creation of a new department to oversee the city's response to threats of terrorism as well as a new program to improve the safety of shelters for the homeless.

In March 2002 Kelly issued an order to his top commanders banning the use of racial profiling as a practice leading to arrests, car stops, and other law-enforcement actions. "There is at least the perception, in some people's minds, that racial profiling goes on," he said, as quoted by Al Baker in the *New York Times* (March 14, 2002), "and we want to have a clear statement of what the policy of this department is as far as racial profiling is concerned." Donna Liberman, the executive director of the New York Civil Liberties Union, described the ban as "an important and long overdue step forward," as Baker reported. The following month Kelly disbanded the controversial Street Crime Unit, a group of plainclothes detectives who had been widely accused of practicing a confrontational policing style that focused unduly on blacks and Hispanics. (In 1999 the New York State attorney's office had found that blacks and Latinos were much more likely than whites to be stopped and frisked by police officers, particularly by members of the Street Crime Unit.) Kelly's efforts to improve race relations were recognized by minority leaders.

Forced to economize because of budget cuts made necessary by falling property-tax receipts, Kelly has introduced carefully targeted initiatives and modern technology to combat crime. In one program, Operation Spotlight, introduced in 2002, sophisticated devices were used after arrests to identify people who repeatedly committed petty crimes or misdemeanors; such people were sent to a special part of the criminal court, where their cases received priority. Within seven months, the number of jail sentences exceeding 30 days had increased by 55 percent. Operation Impact, introduced in early 2003, increased police presence in 61 neighborhoods where the numbers of shootings and other crimes were rising. In the year ending in June 2003, the numbers of homicides in those areas had dropped nearly 47 percent, robberies (theft involving violence or the threat of violence) had fallen 43 percent, and theft had dropped 31 percent.

In response to the September 11, 2001 attacks, Kelly created a counterterrorism program of unprecedented scope and expanded to about 1,000 the staff of the existing counterterrorism unit, which before that date had numbered about two dozen officers. He recruited unusually qualified experts, including Michael Sheehan, a retired Army Special Forces colonel, who was named deputy commissioner for counterterrorism, and David Cohen, a 35-year veteran of the Central Intelligence Agency (CIA), as deputy commissioner for intelligence. Many members of the unit are stationed overseas. With new training programs, Kelly improved the department's ability to gather and analyze information and strengthened communication between the NYPD and the federal government. Specialized patrol officers and helicopters with sophisticated cameras and other equipment have improved the monitoring of the city. In mid-2007 Kelly launched the Lower Manhattan Security Initiative, a plan to install some 3,000 surveillance cameras and more than 100 instruments that record passing license plates. As of March 2008 the information gathered was being monitored around the clock at a central location, dubbed the Real Time Crime Center, with access to global crime databases. Kelly told Kane Farabaugh that he gauges his program's success by the lack of terrorist attacks in New York City. "We never declare victory," Kelly told Farabaugh. "We say that we're doing everything we reasonably can do to protect the city and we're gonna do it tomorrow as well."

On another front, Kelly has also had to deal with the serious repercussions of the fatal shootings of two civilians by police officers. In the first, which occurred in January 2004, Timothy Stansbury Jr., an unarmed black 19-year-old, was shot and killed by a police officer on the roof of a housing project; the following day Kelly announced that there appeared to be no justification for the shooting and pledged to reexamine the department's tactics and training. His statement was criticized by the police union but applauded by community members as a welcome and unusual effort at candor. The next month a grand jury voted not to indict the officer, describing the shooting as an accident. Kelly later suspended him for 30 days without pay, took away his weapon, and reassigned him to an administrative position. In the second incident, outside a strip club in the predawn hours of November 25, 2006, Sean Bell, an unarmed 23-year-old African-American, and two of his friends were shot a total of 50 times by four undercover and plainclothes police officers who believed one of them had a gun. Bell, whose wedding was to have been held that day, died at the scene, and the two others were severely wounded. The incident sparked citywide outrage toward the NYPD and racially charged protests. While Bloomberg quickly labeled the shooting "inexplicable," Kelly refrained from assigning blame until more facts were obtained, a choice that drew some criticism. "There were, and are, still too many unanswered questions," Kelly said, as quoted by Patrick Healy in the New York Times (November 30, 2006). Kelly ordered that the officers' guns be confiscated, explaining to Healy: "It's a privilege to have a gun; you don't have a right to have a gun." He also appointed a special panel to review the NYPD's guidelines for undercover officers. In June 2007 the panel recommended 19 changes to procedures; among those adopted was the requirement that all officers involved in shootings undergo breath-analysis tests. In March 2007 the three officers involved in the Bell shooting were indicted by a grand jury; their trial, in February 2008, ended with the acquittals of all of them. Their acquittals further ignited racial tensions in the city and led to massive public demonstrations that blocked traffic in Brooklyn and Manhattan.

In light of questions that arose regarding the quality and effectiveness of the department's training of officers, in January 2007 Kelly commissioned the Rand Corp., a private nonprofit organization, to conduct a six-month independent review of the NYPD's training and practices. The Rand investigators' report, released in November 2007, concluded that while whites were stopped on the street about as often as members of minority groups, officers were more likely to frisk, search, and arrest the latter and to use force against them, especially in the borough of Richmond (commonly referred to as Staten Island). "The other recommendations," as Al Baker reported for the New York Times (November 21, 2007), "were to review the boroughs with the greatest disparities; to train newly hired officers in stop-and-frisk policies; to modify the internal audits of street stops; and to flag and investigate those officers who make more racially disparate stops."

Also in February 2008 the NYPD released new figures showing that the number of blacks (28) among the roughly 700 officers who make up the department's upper tier had remained unchanged from 2002 to 2007. (Promotions up to the rank of captain are determined by civil-service exams; promotions above captain are discretionary.) Despite Kelly's assertion, as Al Baker reported in the New

York Times (May 11, 2008), that he had promoted blacks in greater numbers and at a faster pace than members of any other racial or ethnic group, the report sparked criticisms from civil rights groups that the NYPD was not doing enough to promote minorities.

In September 2008, in another tragic incident involving the NYPD, Iman Morales, a mentally disturbed man, fell to his death when an officer shot him with a Taser gun. Morales had been standing naked on a narrow perch at a window in his apartment in the Bedford-Stuyvesant neighborhood of Brooklyn and waving a fluorescent light at officers when an order was given to fire the gun. In light of questions regarding why the order was given to shoot at an unarmed man, and police-manual instructions that advise against shooting in cases in which a suspect might fall from a high point, Kelly instituted refresher training for the 400 police officers who work in the Emergency Service Unit. "Last year, we handled 87,000 calls to aggressive emotionally disturbed people," Kelly told Michael Wilson for the *New York Times* (September 29, 2008). "Obviously, the vast majority of them went

well. You didn't hear about them. But we're human beings. Sometimes we make mistakes. Reporters make mistakes. People on Wall Street make mistakes."

In his leisure time Kelly enjoys cooking and playing the drums. He has not taken a vacation since he was hired in 2002. He lives with his wife, Veronica, in Battery Park City in downtown Manhattan, and has two grown sons: Gregory, a former Marine who is now a TV news anchor for Fox News, and James. He has received honorary degrees from Marist College, Manhattan College, the College of St. Rose, St. John's University, and the State University of New York.

—M.E.R.

Suggested Reading: *Governing* p30+ Oct. 2004; *Journal of Commerce* A p1 Aug. 20, 1998; *New York Times* B p4 Sep. 23, 1992, p1+ Oct. 17, 1992, A p1+ Dec. 3, 1993, B p1+ Feb. 5, 2002, B p3 Mar. 14, 2002, A p1+ Nov. 15, 2005, A p1+ Nov. 30, 2006; *Voice of America News* Dec. 19, 2007

Kitchen, Michael

Oct. 31, 1948– British actor

Address: c/o International Creative Management, Oxford House, 76 Oxford St., London W1D 1BS, England

"Whether I'm playing a hero or a villain, I don't regard playing a part as pretending to be somebody else," the 60-year-old British actor Michael Kitchen told John Lisners for the London *Daily Mail* (June 5, 1992). "I know they are inevitably me, or rather a development or extension of very personal facets. I don't act, I maximize my assets." Described by Brian Courtis, writing for the Sydney, Australia, *Herald* (November 3, 2002), as someone "whose very presence tends to serve as a stamp of quality on a television drama," Kitchen is among the most accomplished actors in the United Kingdom. After working backstage in a prestigious British theater and acting in another during his youth, he attended the famed Royal Academy of Dramatic Art (RADA). In the 1970s he commenced a distinguished stage-acting career with the Royal Shakespeare Company and the Royal National Theatre. Kitchen had many roles as a character actor on television and in movies in the 1980s and 1990s. As the incarnation of the devil in the made-for-TV play *Brimstone and Treacle*, a stealer of babies in the British TV series *Chancer*, and an attorney turned date-rapist in the made-for-TV movie *The Guilty*, Kitchen was praised for his depiction of villains. Others among the dozens of films in which he has appeared include *Out of Africa*, *The*

Courtesy of ITV

Russia House, *Enchanted April*, *GoldenEye*, and *Mrs. Dalloway*. In the past half-dozen years, he has become known for his depiction of the reserved detective Christopher Foyle in the World War II–era drama *Foyle's War*, which premiered on the British television network HTV (now called ITV) in 2002. The 19 episodes, the last of which aired in 2008 in the United Kingdom, also captivated audiences in the United States, Canada, Sweden, and Australia.

"Every line is sculpted to perfection, every emotion controlled to resurrect almost forgotten manners and attitudes," Courtis wrote. "Kitchen transmits his impression with such a sensitive touch that you always feel that sense of reality and never simply an interpretation." According to Jonathan Meades, writing for the London *Times* (November 16, 2002), "Kitchen's instrument is his face. He has used it to create a gestural language of the utmost suppleness and complexity. . . . His sheer control is awesome. His repertoire causes us to rethink the possibilities of facial musculature."

Michael Kitchen was born on October 31, 1948 in Leicester, in central England, to Arthur Kitchen, the manager of a local meat factory, and Betty Kitchen, a hairdresser. He has a brother, Jeffrey. As a boy he was a member of the Church of Martyrs cub scouts and attended the City of Leicester Boys Grammar School, where he appeared on stage for the first time, in a production of Shakespeare's *Cymbeline*. (During that performance another pupil accidentally hit him on his head, and he was sent to the Leicester Royal Infirmary, where he received three stitches.) When he was 15 years old, Kitchen was one of 80 young actors chosen from among the 1,300 who auditioned for productions of Shakespeare's *Coriolanus* and *A Midsummer Night's Dream* at London's National Youth Theatre. He also worked for one year (1965) as an assistant stage manager at the Belgrade Theater in Coventry, England. With a grant from the Leicester City Council, he attended the Royal Academy of Dramatic Art, in London, from 1966 to 1969. While there he was awarded the Emile Littler Award for outstanding talent and aptitude.

During the 1970s Kitchen built a reputation as a stage actor, performing in England with the Royal Shakespeare Company (in *Othello*, *Macbeth*, *Romeo and Juliet*, and *Richard II*) and the Royal National Theatre (in Harold Pinter's *The Homecoming*, among other plays). In 1975 his good looks as well as his ability earned him the title role in an adaptation for the stage of Oscar Wilde's only novel, *The Picture of Dorian Gray* (1890), about an uncommonly handsome young man who never ages but whose evil nature and vile actions magically transform an oil portrait of him. Kitchen had made his television debut on May 9, 1970, at age 21, on the BBC's weekly program *Thirty-Minute Theatre*, in a humorous installment about schoolchildren called *Is That Your Body, Boy?* Around that time Kitchen also appeared in other small roles in British television series, movies, and miniseries, among them *Man at the Top* (1971), *Z Cars* (1971), *Unman, Wittering, and Zigo* (1971), *Dracula A.D. 1972* (1972), *The Brontes of Haworth* (1973), *Marked Personal* (1973), *The Early Life of Stephen Hind* (1974), *Savages* (1975), *A Divorce* (1976), and *Enemy* (1976). He played the starring role in the television movie *The Four Beauties* (1973), about a young journalist who stays at a country bed-and-breakfast, where the landlady and her three daughters all fall in love with him. He also appeared in dramatic productions broadcast on the TV series *Play for Today*.

In 1976 Kitchen was cast in the original production of Dennis Potter's drama *Brimstone and Treacle*, which was to appear on *Play for Today*. Kitchen's character, Martin—an extremely mentally and emotionally disturbed man and possibly an incarnation of the devil—is the guest of a middle-aged writer and his wife; while in their home he rapes the couple's handicapped daughter. After the episode was filmed, the BBC's director of television programs, Alasdair Milne, banned it from the airwaves, on the grounds that the rape scene was inappropriate for TV audiences. The play aired 11 years later, with the approval of Milne's successor, Michael Checkland. (In the interim, a different version was made into a movie, in 1982, with the singer Sting in the part of Martin.) A writer for tv-cream.org wrote of Kitchen's portrayal, "As well as his unflinching eye contact and sinister/childlike demeanor, Kitchen's character shows his otherworldliness with brief glances and asides to camera." During that period Kitchen reportedly turned down roles in several other TV movies, one in the lighthearted detective series *Shoestring* and another in the comic series *Shelley*, because he considered them to be insignificant. "The only power I have on my side of the screen is the word No," Kitchen told Lisners.

Kitchen was a cast member of BBC television or radio productions of *King Lear* (1982), *The Comedy of Errors* (1983), *Love Song* (1985), and *The Browning Version* (1985). In his first important film role, he appeared in the critically acclaimed, Academy Award–winning film *Out of Africa* (1985); directed by Sydney Pollack, it was an adaptation of a memoir by the Danish writer Karen von Blixen, whose pen name was Isak Dinesen. Kitchen played Berkeley Cole, the best friend of Denys Finch Hatton (portrayed by Robert Redford), a lover of von Blixen (Meryl Streep). The film, which grossed more than $87 million in the United States, exposed Kitchen's talents to an international audience.

In about 1988 Kitchen and his wife, Rowena Miller, whom he had met when she worked as a dresser at the Royal Shakespeare Company, became parents for the first time. To earn more money, Kitchen began to seek roles on television. "For an actor there is more satisfaction to be had from the stage, from the point of view of power, controlling and manipulating the audience," Kitchen told Lisners. "But however much satisfaction I got out of theatre, the financial reward is sadly lacking and I was frightened at the prospect of supporting a family on theatre wages." Kitchen won roles on British television series or movies including *The Justice Game* (1989), *Crossing to Freedom* (1990), *Fools of Fortune* (1990), *The Russia House* (1990), and *The War That Never Ends* (1991). In 1991 he appeared as the evil Roman in two episodes of the British science-fiction/mystery drama *Chancer*, whose script was written by Simon Burke. Burke reportedly wrote the part of Steven Vey, the main character in his next television project—the two-part thriller *The Guilty* (1992)—with Kitchen in mind. Vey is a brilliant, handsome young attorney who appears to be headed for a judgeship on the British high court. After getting drunk at a party, he accompanies his secretary home and rapes her. Desperate to keep the woman from revealing what happened and thereby ruining his career, Vey conspires to murder her. Kitchen told Lisners that portraying violent acts in *The Guilty* or in any other production had never bothered him. His goal, he said, was to relate to all his characters. "My art is about exploring more deeply situations that we are all familiar with," he told Lisners. "I would guess that few people, men or women, have not had some sort of rape fantasy. That is not to imply enjoyment, but simply extending the possibilities of questions like: 'What if that happened to me?'" Kitchen's performance in *The Guilty* received positive reviews, reinforcing his reputation for his skill at showing even the most unlikable villains as multifaceted rather than one-dimensional.

Also in 1992 Kitchen appeared in the Academy Award– and Golden Globe–winning romantic film *Enchanted April*, which was adapted for the silver screen from a 1922 novel by Elizabeth von Arnim. He was cast as George Briggs, a gentle, visually impaired veteran of World War I, who rents his villa in Italy to four English women seeking to come to grips with their lives; in the course of their stay, he falls in love with the gorgeous Lady Caroline (played by Polly Walker), who has tired of the incessant attentions of the men in her social circle and realizes with delight that Briggs is not even aware of her physical beauty. In 1993 Kitchen was nominated for a British Academy of Film and Television Arts (BAFTA) Award in the best-actor category for his role in the BBC two-part miniseries *To Play the King*. Kitchen portrayed an unnamed, liberal king of England who threatens to expose the secrets of a cunning and corrupt Conservative politician who has become prime minister. In the same year he appeared alongside Anthony Hopkins and Kyle MacLachlan in the director David Hugh Jones's cinematic version of Franz Kafka's nightmarish 1925 novel, *The Trial*. In 1994 Kitchen had the starring role in the miniseries *Dandelion Dead*, a dramatization of the true story of Herbert Rowse Armstrong, a solicitor who in 1921 was arrested and charged with the arsenic-poisoning of his wife and his attempt to poison a rival lawyer. The actor was next cast in the television movies *Doomsday Gun* (1994), *Fatherland* (1994), *Dirty Old Town* (1995), and *Kidnapped* (1995). In 1995 he had a supporting role in the blockbuster James Bond film *GoldenEye*; he portrayed the intelligence officer Bill Tanner, who provides briefings to Bond (played by Pierce Brosnan) and other special agents. He reprised that role in the well-received 1999 Bond offering, *The World Is Not Enough*.

In the film adaptation of Virginia Woolf's classic 1925 novel, *Mrs. Dalloway*, Kitchen had the part of Peter Walsh, an impractical man whom Clarissa Dalloway (played by Vanessa Redgrave) loved before she married the dull but reliable Richard Dalloway (John Standing). Released in theaters in June 1998, the film follows Mrs. Dalloway as she ponders decisions she has made during the past decades; meanwhile, she is preparing an elaborate dinner party. Kitchen's role as Mrs. Dalloway's first love is a pivotal one in the story, as noted by Edward Guthman for the *San Francisco Chronicle* (March 6, 1998): "Planning the party brings its own tensions and memories but it's the arrival of Clarissa's former boyfriend, played beautifully by Michael Kitchen, and a tragic piece of news . . . that throws her off course." In the TV miniseries *Reckless: The Movie* (1998), Kitchen depicted a man attempting to break up the relationship between his former wife and her fiancé. Also on the small screen, he was cast in the hospital drama *Always and Everyone*. In 2000 he had a role in the motion picture *Proof of Life*, starring Meg Ryan and Russell Crowe.

When the popular British television series *Inspector Morse* came to the end of its run, in 2000, the British writer Anthony Horowitz was commissioned to write a series that might appeal to the same viewers. With the idea that Kitchen would play the lead in such a drama, Horowitz recruited the actor to join him in creating the character who became Detective Chief Superintendent Christopher Foyle. A longtime widower with one son, Foyle is a career police officer who lives and works in Hastings, in southern England. World War II is raging, and Foyle tries in vain to get a job with the War Department. After a period during which he regards his work as irrelevant to the war effort, he comes to see it as an important part of the struggle, not least because he is helping to preserve stability in a part of England where many expect the Germans to invade. Foyle works with a police sergeant, Paul (played by Anthony Howell), and he has a young driver, Samantha (Honeysuckle Weeks). Each episode of *Foyle's War* ran for about 100 minutes. In each of them, Foyle attempts to solve a local mystery that is connected with contemporary events, involving, for example, German emigrés, conscientious objectors, fascist sympathizers, and the consequences of Nazi air attacks. "It's a whodunnit, but there's much more to it than normal because of the era," Kitchen told Fraser Middleton for the Glasgow, Scotland, *Evening Times* (October 26, 2002). "The war affected everybody's lives so much that it's impossible to deflect it from the mind in *Foyle's War* and that's the way it should be. It's a very emotive backdrop and one which actually was used to their advantage by unscrupulous people. Looting and housebreaking rates soared during the black-out years and domestic murders also remained very high." *Foyle's War* was an immediate hit with critics and viewers in the United Kingdom. It has also enjoyed critical acclaim in Australia, the United States, Sweden, and Canada. ITV executives have announced that the sixth season of *Foyle's War*, which began in April 2008, will be the show's last. The impending end of the series sparked an uproar from its many fans. In response, the network is reportedly considering extending the series for another season or creating a spin-off show.

In 2003 Kitchen starred as Greg Brentwood in the campy three-part British television drama *Alibi*. Brentwood throws a surprise anniversary party for his wife, Linda (Phyllis Logan), in the hope of reviving their rocky relationship. At the party the caterer, Marcy (Sophie Okenodo), notices Linda flirting with Martin, Greg's business partner; later, she stumbles upon Greg disposing of Martin's corpse. After Greg convinces her that Martin's death was an accident, Marcy agrees to help him cover up the death and evade the police. Kitchen also had the lead role in *Falling*, a 2005 television movie adapted from a novel by Elizabeth Jane Howard; he was cast as Harvey Kent, a gardener with sinister intentions, who inserts himself into the life of Daisy (Penelope Wilton), a vulnerable writer.

Kitchen has narrated two dozen audio-books, and he provided the narration for the popular British reality show *Faking It* in 2006. His voice was also used in the cartoon series *Shakespeare, The Animated Tales* (1992).

Despite his celebrity, especially in England, Kitchen has always shunned the spotlight. "I simply prefer to spend my time doing other things out of the business," he told Marion McMullen for the *Coventry Evening Telegraph* (November 22, 2003). "I always imagined it was possible to achieve a successful career in film and theatre without parties, publicity, etc. So far, so good." He lives in a house that he built himself, in Dorset, England, with his wife and two sons. For recreation, he enjoys playing tennis, sailing, listening to music, and working on do-it-yourself projects. A few years ago he climbed Mount Kilimanjaro to raise money for the Village Education Project, a nonprofit organization that works to eliminate the barriers to education for children in rural villages.

—M.E.R.

Suggested Reading: *Coventry (England) Telegraph* p20 Apr. 14, 2007; (Glasgow, Scotland) *Evening Times* p16 Oct. 26, 2002; (London) *Daily Mail* p33+ June 6, 1992; (London) *Times* Features p28 Nov. 16, 2002; (Sydney, Australia) *Sun Herald* Television p5 Nov. 3, 2002

Selected Films: *Unman, Wittering and Zigo*, 1971; *Dracula A.D. 1972*, 1972; *The Four Beauties*, 1973; *King Thrushbeard and the Proud Princess*, 1974; *The Early Life of Stephen Hind*, 1974; *Savages*, 1975; *A Divorce*, 1976; *Enemy*, 1976; *No Man's Land*, 1978; *Towards the Morning*, 1980; *Bedroom Farce*, 1980; *Breaking Glass*, 1980; *The Bunker*, 1981; *King Lear*, 1982; *The Comedy of Errors*, 1983; *The Browning Version*, 1985; *Love Song*, 1985; *Out of Africa*, 1985; *Dykket*, 1989; *Ball-Trap on the Cote Sauvage*, 1989; *Crossing to Freedom*, 1990; *Fools of Fortune*, 1990; *The Russia House*, 1990; *The War That Never Ends*, 1991; *Enchanted April*, 1992; *Hostage*, 1992; *The Trial*, 1993; *To Play the King*, 1993; *Doomsday Gun*, 1994; *Fatherland*, 1994; *Dirty Old Town*, 1995; *Kidnapped*, 1995; *GoldenEye*, 1995; *Wilderness*, 1996; *A Royal Scandal*, 1996; *Mrs. Dalloway*, 1998; *Reckless: The Movie*, 1998; *The World Is Not Enough*, 1999; *Second Sight: Parasomnia*, 2000; *The Railway Children*, 2000; *Proof of Life*, 2000; *Lorna Doone*, 2000; *New Year's Day*, 2001; *Crisis*, 2003; *Alibi*, 2003; *Falling*, 2005; *Mobile*, 2007

Selected Television Shows: *Man at the Top*, 1971; *Z Cars*, 1971; *ITV Saturday Night Theatre*, 1971; *Country Matters*, 1973; *The Brontes of Haworth*, 1973; *Marked Personal*, 1973; *Thriller*, 1974-1976; *BBC2 Playhouse*, 1979–80; *Maybury*, 1981; *Freud*, 1984; *Play for Today*, 1971–87; *Chancer*, 1991; *Shakespeare: the Animated Tales*, 1992–94; *The Hanging Gale*, 1995; *Pie in the Sky*, 1994–95; *Reckless*, 1997; *Sunnyside Farm*, 1997; *Always and Everyone*, 1999; *Oliver Twist*, 1999; *The Secret World of Michael Fry*, 2000; *Faking It*, 2003, 2006; *Foyle's War*, 2002–2008

Kohl, Herb

Feb. 7, 1935– U.S. senator from Wisconsin (Democrat); owner of the Milwaukee Bucks

Address: 330 Hart Senate Office Bldg.,Washington, DC 20510

Campaigning on the slogan "Nobody's senator but yours," Wisconsin's senior U.S. senator, Herb Kohl, a Democrat, has been elected to four consecutive six-year terms. Known as a moderate who occasionally has supported Republican-sponsored legislation, Kohl has rarely made headlines or vied for the limelight. The issues he has championed, such as fair treatment for midwestern dairy farmers, tend not to be high on his party's list of priorities. Over the years he has established himself as an advocate for children and opponent of several key corporate mergers, and while he voted to give President George W. Bush the authority to launch the invasion of Iraq in 2003, he has since called for the establishment of timelines for troop withdrawal, labeling the situation in Iraq a "civil war."

Kohl's first election victory came in 1988, three years after he purchased the Milwaukee Bucks National Basketball Association (NBA) franchise,

Alex Wong/Newsmakers

Herb Kohl

thus ensuring that the team would remain in Wisconsin. Kohl earned millions of dollars in the late 1970s, when he and his relatives sold the family's retail-store chains, and he financed his campaign with more than $7 million of his own money. In subsequent elections—in 1994, 2000, and 2006—he has beaten his Republican challengers by increasingly greater margins, garnering 58.3, 61.6, and 67.4 percent of the vote, respectively. Kohl is a noted philanthropist, and projects such as the University of Wisconsin's Kohl Center, a sports arena that his $25 million donation helped to finance, have made him a difficult candidate to defeat. David Littig, a political scientist at the University of Wisconsin at Green Bay, told Brian Tumulty for the Gannett News Service (October 27, 2006) that Kohl has "a kind of grandfatherly, kind image. You'd have to have a very strong challenger to go up against him. He kind of walks around with a halo on his head."

One of four children, Herbert H. Kohl was born on February 7, 1935 in Milwaukee, Wisconsin. His parents, Max and Mary Kohl, were poor Jewish immigrants from Poland and Russia, respectively. Max Kohl worked in a bottle-cap factory before starting his own grocery store, Kohl's, in 1920. His first supermarket opened in 1946. As a boy Herb Kohl helped his father in his stores by sweeping the floors and restocking shelves. In his free time he enjoyed playing stickball with friends, including Bud Selig, who would go on to own the Milwaukee Brewers baseball franchise (in which Kohl was one of the original investors) and to become the commissioner of Major League Baseball. As a student at the public Washington High School in Milwaukee, Kohl played guard on the school's bas-

ketball squad. "'I wasn't a standout by any means but I've always enjoyed the game," he told Mike Ivey for the *Capital Times* (January 10, 1998). After his high-school graduation, Kohl attended the University of Wisconsin at Madison, where he roomed with Selig and earned a B.A. degree in 1956.

Kohl continued his education at Harvard University, in Cambridge, Massachusetts, earning an M.B.A. degree in 1958. At Harvard, he told Susan Young for the school's on-line bulletin (December 1999), he "learned how to devise and implement a strategy and, most important, about the importance of working well with people." While in graduate school Kohl became an avid fan of the Boston Celtics basketball team, rarely missing a home game. From 1958 to 1964 he served in the U.S. Army Reserve. Meanwhile, he had been helping to build the family business, and in 1970 he became president of Kohl's. By 1972, with the help of his two brothers, he had turned Kohl's into a multimillion-dollar operation, including grocery stores, department stores, and pharmacies and some 6,000 workers. During his eight years as president, Kohl made a point of interviewing each of the chain's new employees before they were officially hired. In 1978 the family sold the business to British-American Tobacco Industries. (Kohl's is now among the nation's 50 top retail businesses, and currently the senator's fortune is said to total more than $200 million.) From 1975 to 1977, at the request of Wisconsin's governor Patrick Lucey, Kohl also served as the chairman of the state's Democratic Party. For nearly a decade beginning in 1979, Kohl was president of his own firm, Herbert Kohl Investments.

In 1985, when the Bucks were making arrangements to leave Milwaukee, Kohl purchased the team, in part, as he told Eli Shupak for *Canadian Jewish News* (January 3, 2002), because he "wanted to help the community keep" it in the city. The franchise cost between $18 million and $20 million, according to various sources. Kohl has said that his motive in buying the Bucks was not profit-driven. "I've often said it was the worst business investment I ever made, because it's not a money investment," he told the Associated Press (May 16, 1986), "but it's the best thing I ever did." Days after Kohl bought the team, the Milwaukee philanthropists Jane and Lloyd Pettit announced plans to build a new arena for the Bucks and other local sports teams. The Bradley Center, named for Jane Pettit's late father, opened in 1988.

That same year, after Wisconsin's longtime Democratic U.S. senator William Proxmire announced plans to retire, Kohl, who had never held public office, launched a campaign for the seat. "I held back until literally the last moment," he recalled to Susan Young. "'OK, I'll run,' I finally said, and before I had a chance to change my mind, the press knew, and I was committed." With the slogan "Nobody's senator but yours," Kohl defeated former Wisconsin governor Tony Earl in the Democratic primary. He faced the Republican Susan Engeleiter, a longtime member of the state legislature, in the general election. "I'm not a politician, I'm a businessman," Kohl told Alf Siewers for the *Christian Science Monitor* (October 20, 1988), in an attempt to distance himself from his opponent. He said that his ability to finance his own campaign— he ultimately spent $7 million of his funds— would keep him from yielding to special interests. "Initially there was a question about whether that would be a detriment—people might think that I was buying the election," he said to Susan Young. "The local newspaper took a poll and asked, 'Are you offended by Herb Kohl spending his own money to run for office?' Something like 88 percent said, 'Not at all.'" Kohl's platform included raising taxes for the wealthy, creating a national health-insurance plan, and cutting military spending. In a televised debate Engeleiter challenged Kohl's criticism of military contracts, claiming that as the owner of Kohl's, he had sold coffee cakes to the U.S. Defense Department for $7.52 each. A Kohl spokesperson later said that the coffee cakes had been unusually large to meet military standards, and that in any event Kohl no longer owned the bakery. Kohl paid out of pocket for a series of television commercials, which added to the exposure that already came with having his name linked to one of the area's largest retail chains. On Election Day, in one of that year's closest Senate races, he captured 52 percent of the vote to defeat Engeleiter.

During his first term in office, Kohl established himself as an advocate for children. He successfully lobbied to revive the Senate Judiciary Committee's Juvenile Justice Subcommittee, which had been dissolved in the 1980s; in 1991 he became the chairman of the panel, which studies "the need for any changes to the juvenile justice laws," according to a Senate report. "Kids don't get enough attention from people in public life," Kohl told Karen J. Cohen for the *Wisconsin State Journal* (June 27, 1993). "Any statistic will demonstrate what we spend on kids . . . doesn't compare to what we spend on other groups." He sponsored the Gun-Free School Zones Act, a 1990 law that made it illegal to carry firearms in school zones. (The Supreme Court later deemed the law unconstitutional, and in 1995 it was replaced by a similar law whose constitutionality has not been challenged.) Gun-control activists also praised Kohl for helping to draft sections needed to pass the controversial 1993 Brady Handgun Violence Protection Act, also known as the Brady Bill.

As he adjusted to life in Washington, D.C., Kohl stayed true to his anti-politician persona, flying back to Wisconsin most weekends and showing little interest in socializing with Senate colleagues or becoming part of the political scene. "If there is a system here of how people sort of hang out with each other, if I am judged by that system, I won't be judged well because I am not a big hanger-outer," he told Cohen.

In the Capitol, Kohl revealed himself to be a fiscal conservative willing to separate himself from Democratic president Bill Clinton on matters of finance. In 1993, for example, he attempted, unsuccessfully, to eliminate a proposed fuel tax from Clinton's budget bill. He also added an amendment to Clinton's economic-stimulus package—a measure that ultimately failed—that would have required Congress to offset the program's costs by cutting $8 billion elsewhere. "I have only been here for five or six months but I have seen Sen. Kohl involved in a wide variety of important activities," Wisconsin's junior senator, the Democrat Russ Feingold, told Cohen. "He was a pivotal person in both bills . . . in terms of representing the concerns Democrats had." While Kohl's critics maintained that his laid-back demeanor was indicative of ineffective leadership, Feingold insisted to Cohen that his colleague "doesn't speak unless he really wants to say something. He doesn't speak just to hear himself talk. I won't name names but there are some people" who do. Kohl ran for reelection in 1994, capturing 90 percent of the vote in a Democratic primary and 58 percent in the general election.

In April 1995 Kohl announced that he would donate $25 million for the construction of a new sports arena at the University of Wisconsin. The Kohl Center, as it became known, opened in 1998. Kohl disliked watching games from the luxury boxes, and as at Bucks games, he preferred sitting with the fans. "His idea of a good time at a basketball game is not in a suite having a Pepsi and dipping shrimp," Al Fish, the arena's manager, told Andy Baggot for the *Wisconsin State Journal* (January 17, 1998). "It's being behind the bench hearing the interplay between the coaches and the players."

In 1996 Kohl fought to abolish the Northeast Dairy Compact, an agreement that gave New England states the power to set unnaturally high milk prices, which he said was unfair to midwestern dairy farmers. He told Susan Young, "Because of a law from the 1940s, our dairy farmers get paid less for their milk than those in all other states." The Senate voted 50–46 to disband the compact in 1999, by which time the U.S. secretary of agriculture was supposed to have created new rules for milk pricing. In 1999, in an effort to help Vermont's then-Republican senator Jim Jeffords win reelection, a group of New England senators sought to extend the compact another two years. To thwart them, Kohl filibustered for two days in November 1999, effectively bringing Senate business to a halt. He abandoned his filibuster after Democratic leaders and the chairman of the Senate Agriculture Committee, Richard Lugar, promised to take up the matter at a later date. In September 2001 Kohl persuaded 41 of his colleagues to sign a letter calling for the dissolution of the Northeast Dairy Compact. The compact expired soon after, and in 2002 Kohl was instrumental in creating the Milk Income Loss Contract (MILC) program, through which the government supplements the incomes of dairy farmers when milk prices fall. In its first three years, the program paid out $2 billion, of which Wisconsin farmers received $413 million. Kohl later received the Wisconsin Farm Bureau Federation's Distinguished Service to Agriculture Award.

In 2000 Kohl again won 90 percent of the vote in the Democratic primary and cruised to a lopsided reelection victory over his Republican challenger, John Gillespie, the founder of a ranch that helps troubled and potentially delinquent teenage boys. During the campaign Gillespie had charged Kohl with not doing enough on behalf of Wisconsin residents. "I think people are becoming more aware that he runs very, very nice television ads, but there's not a lot of substance behind them," Gillespie told the Associated Press (November 2, 2000). While the *Milwaukee Journal Sentinel* endorsed Kohl for reelection, the paper's editors echoed some of Gillespie's concerns, writing, as quoted by the Associated Press, "Kohl's most conspicuous failing is that he rarely if ever supplies the bold, effective leadership that is occasionally required by members of Congress. As a result of his unwillingness or inability to champion controversial issues, the people of Wisconsin are not getting the representation they deserve." Some political observers accused Kohl of purposely sidestepping controversy. In addition, opponents of abortion blasted him for voting against a 1997 bill aimed at banning so-called partial-birth abortions. Kohl has said that while he favored outlawing the procedure, he opposed the bill because it did not allow for exceptions when a mother's health was at risk. Susan Armacost, the director of Wisconsin's Right to Life, said of Kohl's position, according to J. R. Ross, an Associated Press (November 2, 2000) reporter, "It's a way for people who really don't want to make partial birth abortion illegal to make it sound like they really care about the issue." In response to Kohl's vote, the First Breath Alliance, a Milwaukee-based anti-abortion group, circulated a petition demanding that the senator be recalled. The group collected 50,000 fewer signatures than were needed to force a recall.

In January 2001 Kohl introduced in the Senate the Child Care Infrastructure Act, which aimed to amend the 1986 Internal Revenue Code to provide tax credits to employers who provided child-care facilities for the dependents of their employees. (The bill, which had seven co-sponsors as of mid-2006, all of them Democrats, has never emerged from Senate committees.) Later in 2001, in the wake of the terrorist attacks of September 11, Kohl sought to discourage knee-jerk military action. "We would take a tragic situation and make it infinitely worse if we just lash out," he said, according to the 2006 *Almanac of American Politics.* In October 2002, however, he voted to give President Bush the authority to invade Iraq and oust that country's leader, Saddam Hussein. In March 2007, as sectarian violence worsened in Iraq, leading Kohl and others to label the situation there a civil war, the senator said that he favored implementing a timetable for troop withdrawal. "After four long years [U.S. troops] have been stretched to the breaking point," he said on the floor of the Senate, according to his official Web site. "They now referee a bloody civil war that bears no resemblance to the original conflict we authorized them to engage in. The time for military solutions is over, and the difficult work of political compromise lies before the Iraqis with little our soldiers can do to help." In April 2007 a group of 25 protestors from the University of Wisconsin's Campus Anti-War Network staged a demonstration in the senator's office, urging him to fight for an immediate pullout of U.S. forces from Iraq. At one point during the protest, Kohl offered to hold a conference call with the students, but for unspecified reasons, it never took place.

Kohl is a member of the Senate Judiciary Committee's Subcommittee on Antitrust Competition Policy and Consumer Rights, and he has worked to block several key corporate mergers. In 1997 he successfully urged the Federal Communications Commission chairman Reed Hundt to prohibit a proposed merger between AT&T and the phone company SBC, and in 1998 he held hearings that helped prevent British Airways from joining forces with American Airlines. Alongside Ohio senator Mike DeWine, in 2004 Kohl sponsored a bill that would have made oil cartels illegal. In early 2007, after Democrats took control of Congress, Kohl became the chairman of the Senate's Special Committee on Aging, enabling him to pursue a major medical initiative: instituting mandatory background checks for nursing-home employees. "I think the nursing home industry does a really good job," Kohl told James Berklan for *McKnight's Long-Term Care News* (May 1, 2007). "I'm amazed at the level of care that's improved over the years. Today, it's very good. I don't come at it from any other standpoint." He added, "But at the same time, we can do better."

In September 2008, in the face of the imminent bankruptcies of a number of major American financial institutions, the Bush administration proposed a $700 billion bailout plan to try to prevent a serious recession or even a possible depression. Kohl's reaction was characteristically measured. In a press release issued by his office on September 25, 2008 (on-line), he stated, "We have yet to see the details of the final bailout package. I am reserving judgment. I understand the delicate situation we are in, and the risks we face, but I am wary of being rushed into a decision. I would prefer a solution that does not provide the $700 billion all at once but provides part of it now and more later if necessary. . . . Any bailout plan needs rigorous oversight, and it should also give the taxpayers a chance to share in any profits that result." Though he believed it to be "deeply flawed," Kohl voted to pass the bill in the Senate because, as he told the *Northwestern* (October 2, 2008), "failure to act would be disastrous."

Kohl's low-key style as a politician resembles the way he has handled ownership of the Bucks: he rarely steals the spotlight from his team. "He's the antithesis to Mark Cuban," Kohl's cousin David Hansher, a Wisconsin judge, told Frederic Frommer for the Associated Press (November 23, 2001), referring to the notoriously animated Dallas Mavericks owner. "He will not jump up and scream and yell. He just does not think it's appropriate to be overly demonstrative." As when he was running his family business, Kohl has met with each new Bucks employee—everyone from equipment managers to players. During the 2000 play-offs Kohl attended practices and cheered his players on. "He was telling us to stay focused, play hard, just let it happen out there on the basketball court," the Bucks' forward Tim Thomas told Frommer. "We were a young team, and he was like everybody's father." While the Bucks franchise is now reportedly worth more than $200 million, Kohl admitted in 2008 that the team loses money each year. He said he is open to the idea of bringing in business executives as partial owners of the team. The squad has also struggled on the court, and as of 2006, the Bucks had a record of 812–859 since Kohl became owner. However, the team made the play-offs in the 2002-03, 2003-04, and 2005-06 seasons.

In the lead-up to the 2006 election, finding a candidate to run against Kohl proved to be difficult for Wisconsin Republicans. The state's former governor Tommy Thompson declined, as did Tim Michels, who had previously challenged Russ Feingold, and State Senator Glenn Grothman. Robert Gerald Lorge eventually stepped in, though the little-known Republican received minimal support from his party. As of August 2003 Lorge had raised a mere $102,415 and Kohl $4,875,117, most of which was his own money. Though Kohl, pending what many expected would be a Democratic takeover of Congress, stood a chance of becoming chairman of three panels—the Senate Special Committee on Aging, the Agriculture Appropriations Subcommittee, and the Judiciary's Subcommittee on Antitrust, Business Rights and Competition—he seldom talked about the power he might soon enjoy. "I suspect if he was in a competitive race we'd be hearing about it," David Wegge, a political-science professor at St. Norbert's College, in De Pere, Wisconsin, told Tumulty. "Usually politicians are pretty good at their own personal PR. I think that is part of who he is as a politician." Kohl won handily, garnering 67.4 percent of the vote.

Kohl has often been described as affable, kind, and unassuming as well as quiet. He is known for wearing baseball caps and ordering peanut-butter sandwiches in the Senate dining room. In several years, although he owed no money in federal income tax, in part because of his large charitable donations, he sent payments to the Internal Revenue service. "I believe that people who have money should pay some amount in taxes," he told Susan Young. "We all have an obligation to our generation and the next to give some of our money back

so that we can keep this country going and improving." Never married, Kohl enjoys campaigning in schools and spending time with young people. Kohl "doesn't have any enemies," the Republican lobbyist Toby Roth told Craig Gilbert and Katherine M. Skiba for the Milwaukee Journal Sentinel (October 1, 2000). "He's not a grandstander," former Democratic congressman Bob Kastenmeier told those reporters. "He's a very gentle and essentially private person." In 1990, as a private citizen, Kohl founded the Herb Kohl Educational Foundation, an organization that, as of August 2007, had awarded more than $6 million to Wisconsin students, teachers, and schools and currently disburses hundreds of thousands of dollars yearly in scholarships.

Gilbert and Skiba have labeled Kohl a pessimist, and bad publicity and Bucks losses have been known to distress him. "I know when we lose, I'm very unhappy," he told Don Walker for the Milwaukee Journal Sentinel (January 25, 2006). "When we win, it's true about most of the things I've done in my life, I'm happy. I'm not euphoric. But losing is really bad."

—K.J.P.

Suggested Reading: Canadian Jewish News p34 Jan. 3, 2002; Harvard Business School Bulletin Online Dec. 1999; Herb Kohl's U.S. Senate Web site; McKnight's Long-Term Care News p62 May 1, 2007; Milwaukee (Wisconsin) Journal Sentinel A p1 Oct. 1, 2000; (Wisconsin) Capital Times A p1 Jan. 10, 1998; Wisconsin State Journal A p1 June 27, 1993

Krauthammer, Charles

Mar. 13, 1950– Columinst; essayist

Address: Washington Post Writers Group, 1150 15th St., N.W., Washington, DC 20071

From the start of his career as a columnist and essayist, Charles Krauthammer has always drawn upon his own emotions. "I write about what gets me mad," Krauthammer told Carla Hall for the Washington Post (August 17, 1984). "I find it hard to set out stuff that I have no passion about." After more than 20 years of writing for publications including the New Republic, Time, and the Washington Post, Krauthammer has become one of the most influential and controversial commentators in the United States. His political viewpoint, always difficult to pinpoint, has undergone a shift over time. When he began writing, in the early 1980s, he was a self-described liberal, if more conservative than most who so identify themselves. He remained a liberal throughout that decade, one that saw him win a National Magazine Award in 1984 and a Pulitzer Prize in 1987—and publish his only book, a

Charles Krauthammer

collection of his essays titled *Cutting Edges: Making Sense of the Eighties*, in 1985. During the 1990s his writings began to take on a distinctly more conservative tone, and by the middle of the decade, he was considered a neoconservative, the label with which he is most frequently identified today. The label does not fit all of his views, however. Unlike many conservatives, he favors legalized abortion and is highly critical of the notion of "intelligent design"; at the same time, he has supported the war in Iraq as a necessary step in fostering democracy in the Middle East. In 2004 the American Enterprise Institute (AEI) for Public Policy Research presented him with its Irving Kristol Award, named for the man considered to be the founder of neoconservatism. In his introduction of Krauthammer, a transcript of which is available on the AEI Web site (February 10, 2004), Vice President Richard B. Cheney praised the columnist's dedication and thoughtfulness. "The most impressive aspect of his work is the sustained level of quality over a period of more than 20 years," Cheney said. "This is not a columnist who merely fills space and meets deadlines. Charles Krauthammer always writes with care. In his columns and essays, there is always a powerful line of reasoning, and behind it the workings of a superior intellect. When you read his words, you know you are dealing with a serious person, who assumes the same of you." Krauthammer, who has excelled at explaining shifts in U.S. foreign policy, is credited with naming, delineating, and—to an extent—helping to put into effect such concepts as the Reagan doctrine, unipolarity, and democratic realism. In accepting the Bradley Prize, given by the Lynde and Harry Bradley Foundation for Intellectual and Civil

Achievement, in 2003, Krauthammer reflected on why he had begun writing. "History is shaped by its battle of ideas, and I wanted to be in the arena," he said, as quoted by Judith Person in the *Washington Times* (October 10, 2003), "not because I want to fight, but because some things need to be said. And some things need to be defended."

Charles Krauthammer was born on March 13, 1950 in New York City. His father, Shulim, was an Austro-Hungarian immigrant who had made a fortune as a teenager in France by distributing mushrooms throughout Western Europe. Forced to flee France during World War II, Shulim Krauthammer met his wife, Thea, in Cuba, where she had gone after fleeing Belgium during the war. Shulim, who held a law degree, worked as a real-estate executive in Montreal, Canada, where his son grew up speaking French. Charles Krauthammer attended McGill University, in Canada, graduating first in his class in 1970 with a degree in political science and economics.

From 1970 to 1971 Krauthammer studied political science as a Commonwealth Scholar at Balliol College, at Oxford University, in England. Then, after admiring the orderly nature of the notebooks of a friend who was studying medicine, Krauthammer decided to go into that field himself. "Medicine promised not only moral certainty, but intellectual certainty, a hardness to truth, something not to be found in the universe of politics," Krauthammer explained in the introduction to *Cutting Edges*, as quoted by Richard Eder in the *Los Angeles Times* (November 10, 1985). Upon returning to the United States, in 1971, Krauthammer enrolled at Harvard Medical School, in Boston, Massachusetts, where he was the Dupont-Warren fellow in psychiatry. He had decided to pursue that discipline because he viewed it as the ideal blend of the concreteness of medicine and the abstract quality of philosophy.

The summer after his first year of medical school, Krauthammer suffered an accident at the outdoor swimming pool of the Children's Inn, a motel next to Boston's Children's Hospital: he dove off the springboard into too-shallow water and hit his head on the bottom, breaking his neck and severely injuring his spinal cord. With his legs paralyzed, he was unable to swim to the surface. "I knew exactly what had happened," he recalled to Hall. "And I knew I was going to die, because I couldn't swim. And at a certain point, when that happens, you don't panic anymore. And it was at that point that they pulled me out." Thereafter Krauthammer was paralyzed from the waist down and confined to a wheelchair; he had partial use of his arms and hands, but he had to relearn how to write. He returned to medical school in the fall, taking exams orally when he was unable to write and observing medical operations but not helping to close wounds, which would have required him to handle surgical instruments. "I made a very early decision to stay in medical school, to keep my life on track until I could figure out what had happened . . . ," Krauthammer explained to Hall. "I was very unhappy and set back, but railing just seemed to me to be pointless. After all, I had done it. And there was no one to blame for it. And the 'why me?' question never appealed to me. Everybody has their tragedy. And this happened to be mine. Some have greater ones than others. The question I asked myself is 'How am I going to live?'" Krauthammer rarely mentions his disability in his writing and has come to express a disdain for what he terms "survivor chic"—by which he means a tendency in America to make heroes out of survivors. ("The worst thing," he told Hall, "is when they tell me how courageous I am. That drives me to distraction.") He sued the builders of the swimming pool and settled out of court five years later for approximately $1 million.

After earning his M.D. degree, Krauthammer began his residency at Massachusetts General Hospital. During the final year of his residency, from 1977 to 1978, he served as the chief resident in psychiatry as well as the chair of a research seminar on psychosomatic medicine. He helped to make the discovery that mania, while usually an aspect of manic-depressive disorder, can also be a secondary result of such factors as tumors or drug use; he and Gerald Klerman, his instructor and an expert on manic illness, co-authored a paper on the discovery in 1978. When Klerman moved to Washington, D.C., later that year to work for the U.S. Department of Health and Human Services as director of the Alcohol, Drug Abuse, and Mental Health Administration, he appointed Krauthammer director of the agency's division of science. Krauthammer served in that capacity for the next two years, though he was gradually becoming less and less interested in psychiatry, explaining to Hall, "I don't have the temperament to be a psychiatrist."

While he was still at the U.S. Department of Health and Human Services, Krauthammer—then a Democrat—met Martin Kaplan, a speechwriter for Vice President Walter Mondale, at a dinner party and mentioned that he would be interested in speechwriting. When Kaplan became Mondale's head speechwriter, he hired Krauthammer, despite his lack of experience. In taking the job, Krauthammer left medicine behind for good. At the end of his stint with Mondale, in 1981, Krauthammer joined the staff of the New Republic, serving from 1981 to 1982 as associate editor and from 1982 to 1988 as senior editor. His main contribution to the magazine, however, was as an essayist, and in 1984 his work for the New Republic won the National Magazine Award—the highest award in magazine writing—for essays and criticism. In 1983 Krauthammer had begun writing a monthly essay for Time, and two years later he began writing a column for the Washington Post, which is now syndicated in more than 100 newspapers. In a 1985 Time article titled "The Reagan Doctrine," Krauthammer introduced that term, which described President Ronald Reagan's Cold War strategy of diminishing international Soviet influence by

covertly backing resistance movements in Africa, Asia, and Latin America. That year People for the American Way gave Krauthammer its First Amendment Award, for his 1984 New Republic essay "America's Holy War," an examination of the conflict between secularists and religious conservatives in the U.S.

Krauthammer published a collection of his essays, Cutting Edges: Making Sense of the Eighties, in 1985. Consisting of 40 pieces, most of which had originally appeared in the New Republic, the book explored topics ranging from AIDS to Albanian politics. Some reviewers noted that Krauthammer's essays suffered in book form, sometimes appearing out of date and commenting on issues that had been resolved since the pieces were first published. Most, though, admired his elegant prose, clear thinking, and balanced approach to his subjects. That very balance annoyed a few critics. "He is judiciously equidistant between Left and Right on all sorts of issues; he stands for 'centrism' in politics; his tone is Solomonic . . . ," Joseph Sobran wrote for the National Review (January 31, 1986). "He is a very bright young man, and a lot of his essays make fine points, especially one on nuclear deterrence, which resolves the conundrum better than any other piece I've seen on the subject. But that perpetual priggishness, that bogus objectivity, though not too noticeable in any single essay, gets very wearing after two hundred pages." Still other reviews, however, found Krauthammer's collection to be timely. "For all his vigilance, even Mr. Krauthammer occasionally succumbs to the columnist's occupational disease and simplifies things for the sake of a debating point," John Gross wrote for the New York Times (November 12, 1985). "But in general the standard of these pieces is exceptionally high; they were well worth collecting, and they remain as stimulating as they were when they first appeared."

Over the course of the next decade, Krauthammer's political views gradually shifted. While they have often been difficult to classify, the general consensus finds him to have been a centrist Democrat in the 1980s and a neoconservative by the late 1990s. In 1987, after only one full year as a syndicated columnist for the Washington Post, Krauthammer won the Pulitzer Prize for commentary. In 1990 he scaled back his commitment at the New Republic, becoming a contributing editor; he also took on the title of contributing editor at the Weekly Standard. Additionally, he began appearing as a weekly panelist on the television talk show Inside Washington. That year he put forward one of his most influential ideas, that of the "unipolar world." After introducing the concept in the Henry M. Jackson Memorial Lecture he delivered in Washington, D.C., on September 18, 1990, Krauthammer adapted his lecture for publication in Foreign Affairs. (Jackson was a Democratic U.S. senator who favored military intervention in support of democracy abroad.) "Unipolarity" described the unique position of the United States as the world's only superpower after the demise of the Soviet Union, in 1991. "The most striking feature of the post–Cold War world is its unipolarity," Krauthammer wrote in his article "The Unipolar Moment." "No doubt, multipolarity will come in time. In perhaps another generation or so there will be great powers coequal with the United States, and the world will, in structure, resemble the pre–World War I era. But we are not there yet, nor will we be for decades. Now we are the unipolar moment." He argued against the notion that the absence of a second superpower indicated a reduced threat of war, and he contended that the unipolarity of the U.S. gave the nation the duty to act unilaterally.

In 1996 one of Krauthammer's essays was included in *Backward and Upward: The New Conservative Writing*, edited by Michael Rust. In a review of the book, a writer for *Insight on the News* (April 15, 1996) asserted that Krauthammer's essay on the Cold War stood out from the rest, calling it "concise, angry and quite splendid." In 2002 President George W. Bush appointed Krauthammer to the President's Council on Bioethics. In that capacity Krauthammer has expressed opposition to human cloning and euthanasia while supporting federal funding of embryonic stem-cell research. That year Krauthammer also received the Guardian of Zion Award from Bar-Ilan University, in Israel; the award is given to Jews who have demonstrated support for the state of Israel, as Krauthammer has in his writing. In 2003 Krauthammer was among the first recipients of the Bradley Prize, presented by the Lynde and Harry Bradley Foundation, a conservative grantmaking organization. In accepting the $250,000 award, Krauthammer said, as quoted by Person, that he hoped it "would inspire others who are not in the liberal monopoly to stand up."

In 2004 the American Enterprise Institute for Public Policy Research gave Krauthammer its Irving Kristol Award. At the award dinner, Vice President Cheney introduced Krauthammer as "a man I admire very much, and am proud to call a friend" and added, "The complexities of this era have certainly brought out the finest attributes of this writer—his wisdom, his deep moral sensibility, and his conviction that freedom is the right of all mankind and must be defended." The award's citation that year read, "To Charles Krauthammer: Fearless journalist, wise analyst, and militant democrat, who has shown that America's interests and ideals are indivisible, and that the promotion of freedom is hard-headed realism." In his speech that evening, titled "Democratic Realism: An American Foreign Policy for a Unipolar World," Krauthammer expanded on his earlier topic of unipolarity. Because the U.S. is the world's single superpower, he argued, the nation must pick its battles with care so as not to overextend itself. "Call it democratic realism," he said. "And this is its axiom: *We will support democracy everywhere, but we will commit blood and treasure only in places where there is a strategic necessity—meaning, places central to the larger war against the existen-*

tial enemy, the enemy that poses a global mortal threat to freedom."

As Krauthammer has become more closely identified with the neoconservative movement, his supporters and his critics have grown more polarized. In 2005 the *American Prospect* named him one of the five "top offenders" on its list of pundits responsible for advocating the Iraq war, a matter in which they were "colossally wrong." Writing for the November 21, 2006 on-line edition of that publication, Matthew Yglesias called Krauthammer "very possibly the worst journalist working in America today, a relentlessly pernicious force, never right about anything, who feels his commentary should not be shackled by the small-minded bonds of accuracy or logic." That same year the *Financial Times* named Krauthammer the most influential commentator in the United States, and on April 23, 2006 the Anti-Defamation League (ADL) gave Krauthammer its Hubert H. Humphrey First Amendment Freedoms Prize, honoring the eloquence with which he expresses his views. "In his decades as a public intellectual, Charles Krauthammer has weighed in on almost every important issue at some point, including such hot-button subjects as stem cell research, the debate over creationism and intelligent design and the Iraq war," Abraham H. Foxman, the ADL national director, said in his speech, as quoted by Targeted News Service (May 1, 2006). "In some instances, this extraordinarily shrewd political commentator has argued the [Bush] administration's position better than the administration." Krauthammer's more recent columns include "Limousine Liberal Hypocrisy," published in *Time* (March 16, 2007, on-line), in which he attacked "the eco-pretensions of the rich and the stupefying gullibility with which they are received"; "The Real Hill-Bill Problem" (*Washington Post*, November 23, 2007), in which he pointed to what he saw as the danger of electing as president Hillary Rodham Clinton; and "On Iraq, a State of Denial" (*Washington Post*, November 23, 2007, on-line), in which he called the Iraq conflict "a war seemingly lost, now winnable."

Krauthammer wrote extensively about the 2008 presidential campaign, in which he consistently supported the Republican nominee, U.S. senator John McCain of Arizona. In his column of October 17, 2008, titled "Who's Playing the Race Card?," he declared McCain innocent of inserting the issue of race into the campaign as a way of hurting Senator Barack Obama's chances of being elected and found Obama guilty of employing that tactic to paint the McCain campaign as racist and thereby hurt McCain's chances of becoming president. Krauthammer also criticized Obama for his associations with William Ayers, a co-founder in 1969 of the long-defunct militant left-wing group the Weather Underground, and with the Reverend Jeremiah A. Wright Jr., the pastor of the church to which Obama and his wife had belonged for 20 years. In particular, Krauthammer faulted Obama for not distancing himself from Ayers, who had participated in bombings of several public buildings when Obama was about eight years old. Ayers later became a professor of education at the University of Chicago, and in the latter half of the 1990s, he and Obama served on the board of directors of the Chicago Annenberg Challenge, a project to improve public-school education. (The challenge was named for Walter Annenberg, a friend of the Republican president Ronald Reagan. Other members of the board included the president of the University of Chicago and several people prominent in Republican circles in Chicago.) In addition, Ayers had hosted a gathering in his home to introduce people to Obama when the latter first ran for political office, in 1996. (Krauthammer's charges notwithstanding, Ayers and Obama had never been close, as those who knew both men told reporters for several newspapers.) In the case of Wright, Obama had remained a member of the Trinity United Church of Christ in Chicago long after Reverend Wright had made highly derogatory remarks about the U.S. during a sermon—remarks that became public knowledge after a video of the sermon was mounted on YouTube. After Wright made additional divisive remarks during television interviews that aired after the YouTube video began circulating, Obama left Trinity United; soon afterward he gave a speech, titled "A More Perfect Union," in which he made a clear distinction between his religious ties and his political connections. In a column titled "McCain for President" (October 24, 2008), Krauthammer declared that he rejected the widespread complaints that McCain had been conducting a "dirty campaign." "The double standard here is stunning," he wrote, noting several instances of what he labeled lies about McCain in Obama-for-president TV ads. He continued, "McCain's critics are offended that he raised the issue of William Ayers. What's astonishing is that Obama was himself not offended by William Ayers. . . . Moreover, the most remarkable of all tactical choices of this election season is the attack that never was. Out of extreme (and unnecessary) conscientiousness, McCain refused to raise the legitimate issue of Obama's most egregious association—with the race-baiting Rev. Jeremiah Wright. Dirty campaigning, indeed." Then he asked rhetorically, referring to the phone in the White House reserved for calls to the president about imminent, life-threatening dangers to the U.S. from foreign powers, "Who do you want answering that phone at 3 a.m.? A man [Obama] who's been cramming on these issues for the past year, who's never had to make an executive decision affecting so much as a city, let alone the world? A foreign policy novice . . . ? . . . Or do you want a man [McCain] who is the most prepared, most knowledgeable, most serious foreign policy thinker in the United States Senate? A man who not only has the best instincts but has the honor and the courage to, yes, put country first, as when he carried the lonely fight for the surge that turned Iraq from catastrophic defeat into

achievable strategic victory?" Earlier in the column, he wrote, "I'd rather lose an election than lose my bearings."

Krauthammer lives in Chevy Chase, Maryland, with his wife, Robyn, an artist whom he met while both were students at Oxford. The couple's son, Daniel, is a student at Harvard University.

—C.S.

Suggested Reading:American Enterprise Institute Web site; *New York Times* C p16 Nov. 12, 1985; *Washington Post* B p1 Aug. 17, 1984

Selected Books: *Cutting Edges: Making Sense of the Eighties*, 1985

Alex Wong/Getty Images

Kucinich, Dennis J.

NOTE: An earlier article about Dennis J. Kucinich appeared in *Current Biography* in 1979.

(koo-SIN-itch)

Oct. 8, 1946– U.S. representative from Ohio (Democrat)

Address: 2445 Rayburn House Office Bldg., Washington, DC 20515

The Democratic U.S. congressman Dennis J. Kucinich of Ohio has overcome many hurdles in both his personal life and political career. He has endured a poverty-stricken childhood, physical ailments, a period as the mayor of Cleveland that ended in ignominy, two failed presidential bids, and a press that frequently paints him as eccentric for his veganism and spiritual beliefs. Still, Kucinich has won a small but loyal band of supporters who admire his idealism and tenacity. "A lot of people don't agree with Dennis on specific issues, but nobody ever doubts where he stands," Andy Juniewicz, Kucinich's press secretary and friend, told Amanda Paulson for the *Christian Science Monitor* (December 31, 2007, on-line). "He's probably the most courageous elected official I've ever known. Whatever the odds, if he believes he's right, he'll buck those odds and push for what he believes is right." Kucinich often stands alone in his views. During his bid for the 2008 Democratic presidential nomination, he pointed out that he was the only candidate in favor of universal, single-payer health care and the only one calling for immediate withdrawal of troops from Iraq. He told Paulson, "[Ralph Waldo] Emerson once wrote, 'Trust thyself: every heart vibrates to that iron string. . . .' I've been reading that essay since I was 10 years old."

The eldest of seven children in a Roman Catholic family, Dennis John Kucinich was born on October 8, 1946 in Cleveland, Ohio, to Frank Kucinich, a truck driver and former U.S. Marine of Croatian descent, and Virginia Kucinich, a homemaker of Irish ancestry. Kucinich has four brothers (Frank, Gary, Perry, and Larry) and two sisters (Theresa and Elizabeth Ann). Gary followed his older brother into politics, serving during the early 1980s on the Cleveland City Council and later making unsuccessful mayoral and congressional bids. Perry, an artist diagnosed with paranoid schizophrenia, died in December 2007 of unknown causes.

The Kuciniches were evicted from a series of lodgings when, struggling to survive on Frank's wages, they were unable to pay rent or landlords discovered seven children crammed into apartments meant for far fewer people. By the time Kucinich was 17 years old, his family had lived in more than 20 different apartments and had also spent time living in their car. "The car was parked near a Pepsi-Cola bottling plant. My mother would go down to the store and ask them to heat up a bottle for the baby," Kucinich told Sheryl Gay Stolberg for the *New York Times* (January 2, 2004, on-line). "My dad was trying to keep working. It was total chaos." For a few months, while his mother was suffering from a bout of postpartum depression, Kucinich and some of his siblings lived in an orphanage. "My background gave me a first-hand chance to experience the deprivation which is only parlor conversation for the elite," Kucinich has said, according to Edward P. Whelan, writing for *Cleveland* magazine (December 1977).

In high school Kucinich stood well under five feet tall and weighed under 100 pounds. Despite his slight build, he played football at St. John Cantius High School, a small, parochial school in the white, working-class neighborhood in which he lived. (He also played baseball.) After his freshman

year Kucinich was diagnosed with a heart murmur, which prevented him from playing sports, but he continued to work as a manager for various varsity teams. He remained close with his high-school football coach, Pete Pucher, whom Kucinich credits for teaching him a strong sense of discipline. (Later, when Kucinich became mayor, he hired Pucher as the city's properties director.)

In addition to his sports activities, Kucinich participated in numerous school clubs, worked on the yearbook, was a member of the debate team, and played the lead in his senior-class production of *The Mouse That Roared*. In order to pay his Catholic-school tuition, Kucinich worked during the summers as a golf caddy at a suburban country club. The job required him to wake up at 5:30 a.m. and hitchhike 12 miles from his home to the club.

In 1964 Kucinich graduated in the top 10 percent of his class. He began supporting himself, working as a hospital orderly and a copy boy for the Cleveland *Plain Dealer*, among other positions. In 1967 Kucinich entered Cleveland State University to study speech and communications, and in 1970 he transferred to Case Western Reserve University, also in Cleveland. Kucinich earned both a bachelor's and a master's degree from Case in 1973.

Kucinich has said that when he was a boy, the nuns who taught him instilled in him a desire to dedicate his life to public service. (He particularly remembers a nun who bought him a new pair of pants after hearing him being teased about his shabby clothing.) In high school Kucinich began to consider seeking political office and once told a friend that he intended to be mayor by the time he was 30. Kucinich devoted hours to reading about Cleveland and its history, and he started a file of clippings about local politics and politicians. He attended civic events and spent his spare time at city hall, talking to anyone he could buttonhole.

When Kucinich was growing up, Cleveland was changing rapidly. As businesses moved to the Sun Belt or elsewhere and members of the upper middle class moved to the suburbs—thus shrinking the city's tax base—poor whites from Appalachia, Hispanics, and poor blacks from the South moved into the city, searching for jobs but finding ever-worsening blight. In the summer of 1966, riots broke out in Hough, a black Cleveland ghetto, and other racial confrontations took place early in 1967. Alarmed, the local business and financial community allocated money for civic improvements and supported the black mayoral candidate Carl Stokes, who won the 1967 election with the help of strategic campaign financing. When Kucinich earned his master's degree in mass communications at Case, the subject of his thesis was the media coverage of the tensions between Stokes and James Stanton, the City Council president.

Kucinich entered electoral politics in 1967, running unsuccessfully against the incumbent West Side city councilman John Bilinski, a supporter of Stokes. Two years later, with the help of an enthusiastic group of student volunteers, he edged out the 64-year-old Bilinski by just 16 votes. During the campaign Kucinich had in effect run against Stokes, the first black mayor of a major city, as much as he had against Bilinski, and after his election he remained Stokes's great adversary, thus making himself a hero to the white ethnic groups—largely Hungarian, Slovak, and Polish—who made up the city's majority but who felt ignored and disenfranchised by their mayor. (Stokes, who died in 1996, declared publicly that Kucinich was never a racist, although some attempted to portray him as such.)

In 1971, when Stokes decided not to run for a third two-year term as mayor, Kucinich left Democratic Party ranks to support the Republican Ralph Perk, a candidate of Czech/Slovak heritage. Kucinich formed the organization Democrats for Perk and was a major force in rallying ethnic support for the candidate, who won the election.

In 1972 and 1974 Kucinich made unsuccessful bids to represent Ohio's 23d Congressional District, made up mostly of suburbs in Cuyahoga County. Still a member of the City Council, Kucinich was a vociferous gadfly, exposing city hall shenanigans and railing against the city's financial and political establishment. While he isolated himself from many of the other members of the council in doing so, he became a household name in Cleveland.

During Perk's mayoralty, Cleveland's drift toward bankruptcy accelerated. The population, 914,808 in 1950 and 750,689 in 1970, had dropped to 650,000 by 1975, a decline reflecting the movement of industry out of the city and the abandonment of housing by landlords. During those years the city suffered an annual loss in its tax base of some $30 million. A widely discussed potential solution to the city's short-term debt problem would have been to finance long-term bonds on the strength of increased property taxes—a potentially unpopular move. "In this dilemma," Alexander Cockburn and James Ridgeway wrote for the *Village Voice* (January 22, 1979), "Perk hit upon a simple solution: if you can't pay for the city, sell it off." According to Cockburn and Ridgeway, the city's transit system, with assets of $72 million and net operating revenues of $28 million, was sold to the newly established Regional Transit Authority, dominated by businessmen and lawyers, for $8.9 million in the form of loans to the system and $1.1 million for parking lots that had been thrown into the deal. In addition, Cleveland Stadium was leased to "civic minded businessmen" for $370,000, of which less than $1,000 was ultimately paid.

In 1977 Kucinich decided to challenge Perk. Aiming his campaign at the working-class residents of the city's ethnic neighborhoods, he promised to end political patronage, institute tax reform favorable to working people, cut out tax abatements for the expansion of big business downtown, work for increased consumer protection and low-cost public transportation, and trim govern-

ment, or at least minimize its expansion. Kucinich focused particularly on the issue of the city-owned Municipal Electric Light and Power System. One of the oldest publicly owned utilities in the country, Muny Light, as it is called, had gone deep into debt beginning in the 1960s. By 1970 it owed $20 million to its creditors, chiefly its rival, the privately owned Cleveland Electric Illumination Company (CEI). The city-owned company, which served 20 percent of Cleveland, including working-class neighborhoods on the West Side, buys most of its power from CEI. Perk had agreed to sell Muny Light to CEI for $158 million and cancellation of its debt, but many Clevelanders opposed the sale, fearing that CEI would raise its rates if it became a monopoly. During his campaign Kucinich pledged never to sell Muny Light.

Kucinich won the nonpartisan primary of October 1977, with State Representative Edward F. Feighan placing second and Perk third. In the lively, vituperative runoff campaign against Feighan, who had the backing of the Democratic Party, Kucinich labeled his opponent a tool of party bosses and continued to pound away at populist themes, especially the matter of Muny Light. In the November 8 election Kucinich narrowly defeated Feighan, with less than 52 percent of the vote. At 31, Kucinich was the youngest person ever elected to head a major American city.

Once in office, Kucinich set about fulfilling his campaign promises—or trying to. With the help of his political mentor, Sherwood Weissman (who, at 48, was one of the oldest members of the new city hall team), Kucinich put legal clout into the fight to save Muny Light. Although the City Council ultimately overrode his veto, he tried to hold the line on tax abatement, and he also trimmed the city government payroll by laying off 300 employees. He strengthened the Consumer Affairs Department, put $5 million—most of it from the Community Development budget—into desperately needed new sewers, and personally directed the snow-removal teams—inadequate as they were—during the severe storms of early 1978. Additionally, Kucinich turned down $41 million from the federal government for a downtown monorail, declaring that what the city really needed was public transportation that would carry people between their homes and work. In a symbolic demonstration of the grass-roots nature of his administration, Kucinich met with business leaders for breakfast at Tony's Diner, a small, working-class West Side restaurant, rather than at the exclusive downtown Union Club.

Kucinich faced many problems during his tenure—including the arrest of the school-board president for indecent exposure—but the first that brought his mayoralty to a crisis point was the confrontation between him and Richard D. Hongisto, the police chief he had appointed on the recommendation of his safety director, James Barrett. As a sheriff in San Francisco, California, Hongisto had earned a national reputation for his compassionate liberalism, including the championing of gay rights. Regarded with suspicion when he first arrived in Cleveland, Hongisto soon became a popular figure, both within the police department and with the general population. It soon became apparent, however, that Hongisto was as ambitious a politician and as astute a media manipulator as the mayor. Within months of his appointment the police chief was accusing Kucinich of pressuring him to commit "unethical acts," which he later said included hampering a cleanup of the vice squad and assigning political favorites of Kucinich's to certain jobs within the police department. The mayor angrily fired Hongisto for insubordination during a televised news conference on March 24, 1978.

Hongisto's firing unleashed a storm of previously suppressed animosity toward Kucinich and his administration, and soon petitions were being circulated for the mayor's ouster. Business leaders, disgruntled city employees, angry city councilmen, and other critics of the Kucinich administration regarded the mayor's adviser, Bob Weissman, as a latter-day Rasputin and his youthful high-level appointees, who had been drawn from the ranks of his campaign organization, as arrogant, combative, and inexperienced.

In April 1978 the mayor's director of human resources ordered three men to conduct an after-hours search of the office of one of her subordinates, a Republican holdover who was suspected of graft. When the incident became known, the newspapers touted it as Cleveland's Watergate (a reference to the scandal that ended Richard Nixon's presidency), and the City Council ordered an investigation. That move strained the deteriorating relations between the mayor and the council to the breaking point, with Kucinich, in one speech, describing members of the council as buffoons, fakers, and liars. The council retaliated by refusing to act on any measures or appointments initiated by the mayor.

Dislike of Kucinich ran so deep that the Mafia planned to assassinate him. One scheduled hit, set to take place during the city's Columbus Day parade in 1978, was thwarted when Kucinich was taken to the hospital because of an ulcer. A backup plan was supposedly set for a hit at Tony's Diner, where Kucinich had breakfast every morning, but when it became apparent that Kucinich would not be reelected, Mafia leaders reportedly decided that it was not worth the potential trouble to assassinate him.

By the time of the recall election on August 13, 1978, the mayor's ouster was supported by 24 of the 33 City Council members, leaders of both the Republican and Democratic parties, the Teamsters union, the Cleveland branch of the labor organization AFL-CIO, and all three major Cleveland newspapers, including the *Plain Dealer*, which had supported his mayoral candidacy less than a year before. Nonetheless, Kucinich managed to win the recall by just 236 votes out of some 120,000 cast.

Kucinich's narrow victory hardly spelled a solution to his problems in governing Cleveland. When it became known that the city had accumulated over the years a $52 million deficit in its bond-fund accounts, Moody's Investors Service downgraded the city's bond rating, and Standard and Poor's Corp. suspended its rating altogether. Those actions, in effect, ruled out the private-investment market as a source of funds. On October 26, 1978 a local court ordered the city's bankrupt water department into receivership, and the nearly bankrupt school system was unable to open classes until the end of October because of the teachers' strike.

The city owed notes, which came due in December 1978, for $14 million in short-term loans to six Cleveland banks, and in addition, $1.5 million was owed to its own treasury. In mid-December Kucinich presented the banks with a fiscal rehabilitation plan that included a mechanism for refinancing the loans. The plan called for an increase in the city's income tax, a multimillion-dollar bond issue that would be made possible by the fiscal strength created by the tax revenues, and a fiscal overseer. According to the consensus of news reports, the banks were ready to accept the report until the major bank, the Cleveland Trust Co., balked, refusing to roll over its loan to the city unless Kucinich agreed to sell Muny Light. The other banks followed the lead of Cleveland Trust, as did the City Council under the leadership of George L. Forbes in a special session on the night of December 15, 1979. Accordingly, shortly after midnight, Cleveland officially went into default. (Bankruptcy would not occur unless and until the banks took the final step of calling in the notes. Still, Cleveland was the first major American city since the Great Depression to go into default.) "While many persons can share responsibility for this sad episode," an editorial in the *Plain Dealer* (December 16, 1979) stated, "the major blame for the problem must rest with Mayor Kucinich." Kucinich responded: "At least we didn't sell our soul." On December 18, 1979, in a show of protest, Kucinich withdrew his savings from Cleveland Trust, and that same day, in an ironic development, his brother Perry, then 22 and under psychiatric care, robbed a bank in another part of Cleveland. (He was ultimately deemed incompetent to stand trial.)

Later, Kucinich and the council compromised, agreeing to let the public vote on the issues of raising payroll taxes from 1 to 1.5 percent and selling Muny Light. The banks agreed not to call in their notes until after the referendum, scheduled for February 27, 1979. In the meantime, trying to avoid massive layoffs of city employees, the city deferred payment of many of its bills, including $7.5 million owed to state pension funds, and the funds' administrators were moving to put liens on city revenues.

Kucinich reportedly still had strong support in the ethnic wards that had elected him, but he was, "to put it baldly, generally regarded as a lunatic," according to Cockburn and Ridgeway. The writers added that Kucinich "has in fact acted, as he says, on his belief that public institutions are viable and that government must not be surrendered to the private sector." At the polls on February 27, 1979 the voters approved a 5 percent increase in the city income tax and the retention of Muny Light. Despite that small show of support, nine months later they voted Kucinich out of office.

Kucinich attempted to enter the private sector but met many roadblocks. Because of his tarnished reputation, companies that had at first agreed to hire him rescinded their offers—usually as the result of external pressure from investors. Kucinich decided to leave Cleveland and head West on what he has characterized to journalists as a quest for meaning. He stayed for a time with a friend, the actress Shirley MacLaine, who is known for her belief in various New Age practices. MacLaine introduced him to Christine Griscom, a spiritual teacher and healer. Under Griscom's guidance Kucinich, who has endured much derision from the press because he once claimed to have seen a UFO, began to explore alternative spirituality and healthier living. (Kucinich currently avoids consuming any animal products, maintaining a strict vegan diet that has been credited with alleviating the symptoms of his Crohn's disease.)

In 1982 Kucinich returned to Cleveland to run for secretary of state, but lost. He had funded the campaign with his own money, and as a result, on his tax return that year, he listed his annual income at $38. The bank was threatening foreclosure on the modest house he had purchased in 1971, and Kucinich was forced to borrow money from friends, including $20,000 from MacLaine, to save his home. Kucinich served briefly on the Cleveland City Council, after a spot opened up in 1983 because one member became ill. (His brother Gary was also on the council at that time.) At the end of that term Kucinich entered the Ohio gubernatorial race as an Independent, but he dropped out early in the campaign.

Kucinich spent much of the following years in California and New Mexico, continuing his spiritual explorations and working sporadically as a lecturer and radio host. In 1986 he founded his own moderately successful business-consulting firm, K Communications, which he later renamed Kucinich Communications. Kucinich made failed congressional bids in 1988 and 1992 and wrote an autobiography that was rejected multiple times. (In 2007 Kucinich finally published *The Courage to Survive*, the story of his early years.)

In 1993 Kucinich was sitting on the beach in Malibu, California, when a reporter from the *Plain Dealer* called to tell him that Cleveland had announced a $146 million expansion of Muny Light. The paper ran an article admitting that Kucinich had been right in his refusal to sell the utility and had actually saved the city millions of dollars. Vindicated, Kucinich to returned to Ohio, and using the slogan "Because He Was Right," he cam-

paigned for a seat in the Ohio State Senate. He was elected in 1994, and two years later he defeated the Republican incumbent Martin Hoke for a seat representing Ohio's 10th Congressional District in the U.S. House of Representatives. (During his congressional campaign Kucinich's posters read, "Light Up Congress.") He has retained his seat in every congressional election since.

Kucinich is known as a staunch believer in unionized labor and still holds a card from the International Alliance of Theatrical Stage Employees, Moving Picture Technicians, Artists and Allied Crafts (IATSE), which he joined in his youth. Early in his congressional tenure he helped thwart an effort to weaken the Clean Air Act, and he has since been recognized for his commitment to the environment and his belief in the importance of alternative energy sources.

Kucinich is a member of the House Committee on Education and Labor and the House Committee on Oversight and Government Reforms. He chairs the Subcommittee on Domestic Policy and is a member of the Congressional Progressive Caucus. He has advocated the creation of a cabinet-level U.S. Department of Peace and has attracted some 70 of his fellow representatives to co-sponsor the legislation calling for the department, which would address issues of child abuse, domestic violence, and gang activity in the U.S., in addition to international issues.

When George W. Bush called for the invasion of Iraq and the implementation of the Patriot Act, Kucinich was one of the president's most outspoken opponents and was one of the few who voted against each measure. He has been steadfast in calling for an immediate withdrawal of U.S. troops in the region.

Kucinich, disheartened by the country's direction, entered the 2004 presidential race. Although it is an understatement to say that his candidacy was considered a long shot, he had a small band of faithful supporters. During his campaign Kucinich vowed to curb unemployment, provide single-payer health care, protect Social Security, and return the nation to bilateral trade by dissolving the North American Free Trade Agreement (NAFTA) and withdrawing the U.S. from the World Trade Organization (WTO). Kucinich's stance on abortion was less easily characterized. Throughout his political career he had voted as a pro-life liberal, but during the campaign he appeared to have adopted a pro-choice agenda. During an installment of the CNN program *Crossfire* (February 21, 2003), Kucinich was asked by the moderator Robert Novak, "Do you think to get in the Democratic party now you have to be pro-abortion? . . . You did a switch-over." Kucinich replied, "No, I expanded my view. . . . This is a very divisive debate, and I think it's important to simultaneously affirm that a woman has the right to choose under the constitution, and at the same time work, as I have my whole life, to see that abortions are not necessary by having sex education and birth control and then prenatal care, postnatal care and childcare." Kucinich scored in the single digits in almost every poll conducted during the campaign.

In 2007 Kucinich, who had filed impeachment papers against Vice President Richard B. Cheney for lying to Congress and the American people about the reasons for invading Iraq, again declared his intent to run for president, campaigning under the slogan "Strength Through Peace." As he had during his previous bid, he fared poorly in the polls, and he was often excluded from official debates. At the end of January 2008, Kucinich withdrew his candidacy in order to focus on his reelection to the House of Representatives. (He won a seventh term on November 4, 2008.)

In June 2008 Kucinich once again introduced articles of impeachment in the House, this time directed at President Bush. He read 35 articles, among them the accusation that Bush had adopted "a calculated and wide ranging strategy" to deceive citizens and Congress into believing Iraq posed an immediate danger to the United States; another charged Bush with failing to spur the government to prepare for and effectively handle the devastation caused by Hurricane Katrina. While Kucinich's effort was unsuccessful, it provided a comprehensive record of what many view as grave misdeeds on the part of the Bush administration.

Kucinich has been divorced twice. His first wife, Helen, reportedly divorced him because he was too focused on his career. He married his second wife, Sandra, in 1977. The two have a daughter, Jacqueline, who is now a reporter. That marriage dissolved in the late 1980s. In 2005 Kucinich met his current wife, Elizabeth Harper, a statuesque redhead from England, who is six inches taller and more than 30 years younger than the congressman. Eli Sanders and Dan Savage wrote for the Seattle-based alternative paper the *Stranger* (October 10, 2007, on-line): "Their love story is quintessential Kucinich. He met her when she came to his office on Capitol Hill two years ago to discuss monetary policy as part of her then-new job with the American Monetary Institute—a job she'd taken after a stint at the House of Lords in London, some time working in one of Mother Teresa's homes for poor children in India, and studies in religion and international conflict resolution. . . . Kucinich, who had been single for 20 years, and who, in 2003, had told a political forum in New Hampshire that his perfect soul mate would be 'fearless in her desire for peace in the world and for universal, single-payer health care,' found himself awestruck. After the meeting, he phoned a friend and exclaimed that he'd met his future wife. Elizabeth also had a love-at-first-sight moment. She later told an interviewer for the *Tampa Tribune* that upon meeting Kucinich, 'I felt such hope for America. It made my heart sing.'" Kucinich and Harper married within months of meeting.

Kucinich received the 2003 Mahatma Gandhi Peace Award from the Religious Society of Friends organization Promoting Enduring Peace, and he keeps a bust of the revered Indian peace activist in his Capitol Hill office. He also displays a cloth given to him by the Dalai Lama, a painting given to him by members of the Brahma Kumaris religious tradition, and two large crucifixes. "Obviously, I connect with all religions," Kucinich explained to Amanda Paulson. "All manners of belief and even non-belief come from a common font."

—F.C.

Suggested Reading: *Christian Science Monitor* (on-line) Dec. 31, 2007; CNN.com Feb. 21, 2003; *Esquire* p182 Nov. 1, 2007; *New York Times* (on-line) Jan. 2, 2004; *Village Voice* p68 Jan. 20, 2004

Selected Books: *The Courage to Survive*, 2007

Gabriel Bouys/AFP/Getty Images

Kurzweil, Raymond

(KERZ-wile)

Feb. 12, 1948– Inventor; computer scientist; futurist; entrepreneur; writer

Address: Kurzweil Technologies, 15 Walnut St. #2, Wellesley, MA 02481

When he was five years old, the computer scientist, inventor, and entrepreneur Raymond Kurzweil "had the notion that inventions could change the world," as he recalled in his most recent book, *The Singularity Is Near: When Humans Transcend Biology* (2005). That belief was reinforced when young Kurzweil read about the exploits of the fictional Tom Swift, a brilliant inventor and the teenage hero of an early 20th-century series of juvenile adventure stories. "Tom would get himself into a terrible predicament, in which his fate and that of his friends, and often the rest of the human race, hung in the balance," Kurzweil wrote in *The Singularity Is Near*. "Tom would retreat to his basement lab and think about how to solve the problem. . . . To this day, I remain convinced of this basic philosophy: no matter what quandaries we face—business problems, health issues, relationship difficulties, as well as the great scientific, social, and cultural challenges of our time—there is an idea that can enable us to prevail. Furthermore, we can find that idea. And when we find it, we need to implement it. My life has been shaped by this imperative."

Since his own teenage years, when he became fascinated with artificial intelligence (AI) and a facet of AI called pattern recognition, Kurzweil has come up with ideas for—and built, as products of the 10 companies that he has founded—inventions that have immeasurably improved the lives of countless people. Prominent among them is the Kurzweil Machine Reader, unveiled in 1976, which can interpret text printed in any of hundreds of fonts and convert it to synthesized speech, allowing blind, partially sighted, or neurologically impaired people access to material that would otherwise be unavailable to them. More recently, Kurzweil introduced the Kurzweil 1000 Reading System, a pocket-size device containing a digital camera, which is programmed to convert into lifelike speech not only text on paper but electronic text, words on such places as road signs, and labels on cans or other curved surfaces, which its scanner can decipher even at odd angles; among other functions, the Kurzweil 1000 can transform words into speech as the user types them. Kurzweil is also a pioneer in the science of voice recognition, whereby spoken words are converted into printed text; his large-vocabulary speech-recognition system was the first to be commercially marketed. With the Kurzweil 250, the first electronic machine capable of reproducing with remarkable verisimilitude the sounds of orchestral instruments, Kurzweil revolutionized the music industry. The variety of organizations and other entities that have honored him—among them the American Library Association, the American Composers Orchestra, the Canadian National Institute for the Blind, the White House Conference on Small Business, *Design News Magazine*, the Massachusetts Software Council, Carnegie Mellon University, the Intellectual Property Owners Association, and the Association on Higher Learning and Disability—indicates the breadth of Kurzweil's influence. Among his most prestigious honors are the National Medal of Technology (1999) and the $500,000 Lemelson-MIT (Massachusetts Institute of Technology) Prize (2000). In 2002 he was inducted into the National Inventors Hall of Fame, founded by the U.S. Patent Office.

Kurzweil is also a futurist—a visionary thinker who analyzes events of the past and present to make predictions about the coming decades or centuries. In his books *The Age of Intelligent Machines* (1990) and *The Age of Spiritual Machines: When Computers Exceed Human Intelligence* (1999) as well as *The Singularity Is Near*, he has described anticipated changes; his column "The Futurecast" appeared in *Library Journal* from 1991 to 1993, and he contributed to the book *Are We Spiritual Machines? Ray Kurzweil Vs. the Critics of Strong A.I.* (2002), edited by Jay W. Richards. Kurzweil believes that technology is advancing exponentially, not linearly, finding that to be true particularly in the cases of information technology, genetic engineering and other technological aspects of genetics, and nanotechnology (whereby microscopically small machines are built at the molecular level); for that reason he predicts that by the middle of the 21st century, humans will be able to "transcend" the limitations of their physical selves and "merge" with AI systems by "downloading" their conscious and unconscious minds into computers and maintaining their bodies with internal, microscopic robots. Kurzweil, like many other futurists, refers to the point in human history at which that will happen as the Singularity. At that point, he wrote in *The Singularity Is Near*, "we will gain power over our fates. Our mortality will be in our own hands. We will be able to live as long as we want (a subtly different statement from saying we will live forever). We will fully understand human thinking and will vastly extend and expand its reach. By the end of this century, the nonbiological portion of our intelligence will be trillions of trillions of times more powerful than unaided human intelligence." That nonbiological intelligence, he predicted, "will continue to represent the human civilization, which is already a human-machine civilization. In other words, future machines will be human, even if they are not biological. This will be the next step in evolution. . . . Our civilization will remain human—indeed, in many ways it will be more exemplary of what we regard as human than it is today, although our understanding of the term will move beyond its biological origins." In an admiring review of *The Singularity Is Near* for the *Skeptical Inquirer* (July/August 2006), the likeminded James N. Gardner wrote, "Just how far will our nonbiological progeny move beyond those origins? In Kurzweil's exuberant view, very far indeed. In fact, he predicts that the ultimate destiny of brainy thinking machines will be to saturate the entire universe with intelligence."

Spurred partly by his determination to overcome his Type II diabetes without insulin, lower his cholesterol levels, and live longer than his father—all of which he has accomplished—and partly by his eagerness to experience the arrival of the Singularity, Kurzweil has become an expert on healthful diets and anti-aging therapies. He is the author of *The 10% Solution for a Healthy Life: How to Eliminate Virtually All Risk of Heart Disease and Cancer* (1993) and the co-author, with Terry Grossman, a physician who devises so-called life-extension regimens, of *Fantastic Voyage: Live Long Enough to Live Forever* (2004).

The first of the two children of Fredric and Hannah Kurzweil, Raymond C. Kurzweil was born on February 12, 1948 in the New York City borough of Queens. His sister, Enid Kurzweil Sterling, is an accountant who runs her own business. One of Kurzweil's grandmothers was among the first European women to earn a Ph.D. in chemistry. His father was a conductor, composer, and music teacher; his mother worked as a visual artist. Jewish natives of Vienna, Austria, his parents immigrated to the U.S. in 1938 to escape the Nazis. "Ideas were the religion of our household," Kurzweil told Brian O'Keefe for *Fortune* (May 2, 2007); his parents "saw science and technology as the way of the future and a way to make money and not struggle the way they did." His mother and father encouraged their son's creativity, and when he was five, he began to construct models of cars, boats, and rocket ships and decided that he would become an inventor. At age eight he built a miniature stage with a robotic device that moved both puppets and scenery, and he created what he called "virtual" baseball games. As a member of a youth organization associated with the Unitarian church, Kurzweil participated in civil rights marches. Also as a church member, Kurzweil learned about different religions, but, as he wrote in *The Singularity Is Near*, the religion he was "raised with" was "veneration for human creativity and the power of ideas."

In 1960, when Kurzweil was 12, he began to browse the many electronics stores on Canal Street in Lower Manhattan, New York City, collecting parts to build his own computers. Kurzweil wrote in *The Singularity Is Near* that while he was "absorbed in the contemporary musical, cultural, and political movements" of his peers during the cultural revolution of the 1960s, he also had a passion for computer technology. He gained access to an IBM 1620 computer, which he used to write programs with the help of an uncle who was an engineer at Bell Labs, the research facility of AT&T. In 1963, at age 15, Kurzweil wrote a program to help with his summer job of processing statistical information for Head Start, the federally funded childhood-development program. His software was so effective that IBM acquired it and distributed it to researchers with its mainframes. Kurzweil next created a pattern-recognition computer program that analyzed existing musical compositions—such as those of Mozart or Beethoven—and composed new music in a similar vein. The program landed Kurzweil an appearance in 1965 on the television program *I've Got a Secret*, where he performed a piano piece written by his computer. That software also earned Kurzweil first prize in the category of electronics and communications at the 1965 International Science Fair, and he was among 40 Westinghouse Science Talent Search winners that year.

After he completed high school, in 1966, Kurzweil enrolled at the Massachusetts Institute of Technology, in Cambridge. He took all nine computer-science courses available at that time as well as classes in literature and creative writing; one of his teachers was the playwright Lillian Hellman. He maintained a friendship with Marvin Minsky, the founder and co-director of MIT's artificial-intelligence laboratory, and, according to Elliott Frieder and Kristin Joyce in the MIT publication *Spectrum* (Fall 2001, on-line), he "worked laboriously on the one main computer that was made available for all students and professors" at MIT in those years. He also became friendly with Aaron Kleiner, an MIT management student who later became his business partner. In 1968, as an undergraduate, he created a computer program that matched high-school students with particular colleges by means of information gathered from the students and colleges. That program, which "could do flawlessly in ten seconds what took us ten hours to do manually with far less accuracy," as Kurzweil wrote in *The Singularity Is Near*, became popular immediately, and the New York publishing company then known as Harcourt, Brace & World soon bought it from Kurzweil for $100,000 plus royalties. The money was enough to pay for the rest of his college education and also helped to pay for medical bills incurred by his father, who died of heart disease in 1970, at age 58. A few months earlier, Kurzweil had graduated from MIT with a B.S. degree in both computer science and literature.

Articles about Kurzweil's life skip to 1974, when he and Kleiner co-founded Kurzweil Computer Products Inc., which continued Kurzweil's work on pattern-recognition software. Kurzweil and Klein had decided to tackle the challenge of designing a program whereby a computer could read typed or printed characters in any font and of varying degrees of clarity. (Existing programs could recognize only a few, specific fonts, and only if the characters were clear.) The "omni-font" optical character-recognition (OCR) software that Kurzweil's team came up with accomplished that goal. (It is currently marketed as TextBridge.) Around that time, in 1975, during a chance encounter with a blind man, Kurzweil learned that only a small percentage of books became available in Braille, usually years after their publication. That meeting inspired him to link the omni-font OCR program with an as-yet nonexistent machine that could read text documents aloud. Toward that end Kurzweil and his colleagues, with input from a team of blind scientists and engineers chosen by the National Federation of the Blind (NFB)—representing some of the intended users of the device—developed the first so-called charge coupled device (CCD) flatbed scanner and the first text-to-speech synthesizer. (A CCD is a light-sensitive semiconductor chip that might be thought of as the digital equivalent of film.) The Kurzweil Reading Machine, which could "read" printed material out loud in a synthesized voice, was unveiled at a press conference on January 13, 1976. The news anchor Walter Cronkite used it to deliver his signature sign-off message at the end of that night's airing of the *CBS Evening News*, and schools and libraries began to order it. In 1978 a commercial version of Kurzweil's OCR was introduced. Organizations including Lexis (an on-line legal-research service) and Nexis (a news service) used it to build on-line databases of documents. In 1980 Kurzweil sold Kurzweil Computer Products to the Xerox Corp. He served as a consultant to Xerox until 1995.

Meanwhile, in 1976 the blind singer-songwriter Stevie Wonder had become the first person to own a Kurzweil Reading Machine. Wonder told Elliott Frieder and Kristin Joyce that the device "changed my life": "I could read anything I wanted with complete privacy: music, lyrics, letters from my children, the latest best sellers and magazines, memos from my business associates. It gave blind people the one thing that everyone treasures, which is independence." During a visit Kurzweil made to Wonder's recording studio in 1982, Wonder "lamented the state of the art in music production," according to Jay Leventhal, writing for *AFBAccessWorld* (September 2004, on-line). In his book *The Age of Spiritual Machines*, Kurzweil explained, "On the one hand, there was the world of acoustic instruments, . . . which provided the rich complex sounds of choice for most musicians. While musically satisfying, these instruments suffered from a panoply of limitations. Most musicians could play only one or two different instruments. Even if you could play more than one, you couldn't play more than one at a time. Most instruments only produce one note at a time. There were very limited means available to shape the sounds. On the other hand, there was the world of electronic instruments, in which these control limitations disappeared. . . . There was only one problem. The sounds you had to work with in the electronic world sounded very thin." At the urging of Wonder, Kurzweil set about designing a synthesizer, with a computerized keyboard, that could reproduce the sounds of orchestral instruments. He set up Kurzweil Music Systems in 1982, and two years later, with the help of engineers and scientists who were also musicians, he unveiled the Kurzweil 250; according to Kurzweil Technology (on-line), it "is considered to be the first electronic musical instrument to successfully emulate the complex sound response of a grand piano and virtually all other orchestral instruments." As an article on the NFB Web site pointed out in 2000, "The technology Kurzweil created allowed musicians for the first time to play the sounds of any acoustic instrument, to play them polyphonically (i.e., multiple notes at a time), and to apply the full range of computer control techniques such as sequencing, layering, and sound modification to the rich sounds of acoustic instruments." In a test of the Kurzweil 250, professional pianists were unable to distinguish between the music produced by Kurzweil's

invention and that emanating from a grand piano. Young Chang, a Korea-based piano manufacturer, bought Kurzweil Music Systems in 1990.

In the 1980s, as he wrote in *The Singularity Is Near*, Kurzweil's "interest in technology trends and their implications took on a life of its own . . . , and I began to use my models to project and anticipate future technologies. . . . This enabled me to invent with the capabilities of the future by conceiving and designing inventions using these future capabilities." In 1982 Kurzweil and Kleiner launched another company, Kurzweil Applied Intelligence (KAI), with the aim of developing computer-based speech-recognition technology—that is, a voice-activated word processor. Five years later Kurzweil introduced a commercially marketable system that recognized an unprecedented number of spoken words. KAI's principal product, Kurzweil VoiceMed (now Kurzweil Clinical Reporter), enabled physicians to produce medical reports by talking slowly into their computers, with brief pauses between words. Kurzweil's more recent product Voice Xpress Plus, which takes advantage of personal computers' greatly expanded memories and other improvements, can translate into print words spoken at a speed of approximately 100 words per minute (about half the speed of conversational speech). In 1995, two years after KAI went public, two of its executives were discovered to have been falsifying sales records to make the company more appealing to investors; the two were found guilty of accounting fraud and received jail terms. Kurzweil, who was co–chief executive officer at that time, was not implicated in the scandal. "I was focusing on the technology," he told Brian O'Keefe. "There was this small conspiracy, which was deeply shocking." In 1997 Lernout & Hauspie, a Belgian speech-recognition-technology company, bought KAI. During the previous year Kurzweil had launched Kurzweil Educational Systems, whose mission was to further print-to-speech technology. In 1997 it produced the Kurzweil 1000 Reading System, software that enables a computer to speak printed text aloud in various voices. The Kurzweil 1000 earned for its inventor and his colleagues the 1998 Vision Award, presented jointly by Stevie Wonder and the business-software company SAP America. The Kurzweil 3000, which also debuted in 1997, helps those suffering from dyslexia, attention deficit disorder, and other impediments to reading; it was the first print-to-speech system that reads from electronically displayed images of pages.

Earlier, in 1987, Kurzweil had made a film, *The Age of Intelligent Machines*, which surveyed advances in AI technology and featured Stevie Wonder and such computer-science experts as Marvin Minsky, Roger Schank, and Raj Reddy. The film won a half-dozen prizes, among them the CINE Golden Eagle Award. Kurzweil expanded on the material in the film in his first book, *The Age of Intelligent Machines*, published in 1990 by MIT Press. Named the most outstanding computer-science book of 1990 by the Association of American Publishers, the 565-page, heavily illustrated volume traces the philosophical and mathematical roots of AI, including ideas of Plato, Euclid, Newton, Einstein, and Wittgenstein; describes the state of the art; and makes predictions, some of which—about the emergence of the World Wide Web, the reliance by the U.S. military on "intelligent" weapons, and the superiority of a computer over a human in chess—proved highly accurate. Interspersed throughout the book are two dozen essays by others, among them Douglas R. Hofstadter and Allen Newell. Kurzweil urged that AI be used for benevolent purposes, noting that "computer technology is already a powerful ally of the totalitarian" and that computer identification technology is "capable of helping Big Brother track and control individual transactions and movements." "But none of these issues make Mr. Kurzweil question the unbridled development of this technology," Jay L. Garfield, a professor of philosophy, complained in an assessment for the *New York Times Book Review* (September 9, 1990).

Some critics similarly faulted Kurzweil's book *The Age of Spiritual Machines: When Computers Exceed Human Intelligence* and *The Singularity Is Near*. Among them was Oliver G. Selfridge, who, in a review of the former for *Psychology Today* (September/October 1999), wrote that Kurzweil "offers up his theories with a kind of relaxed abandon that gives the imagination a good whirl. . . . It's true that technology has made astounding leaps since the 1950s, and Ray Kurzweil himself was behind many of them. . . . But for every leap we easily find limitations"—for example, unlike humans, voice-recognition systems cannot yet distinguish a single voice from among many nearby voices, as at a party. Caspar Henderson, the reviewer for the *Ecologist* (July 1999), noted, "Among the arguments that lend his position credibility is the fact that, relentlessly, problems identified as insurmountable barriers to computers acquiring human abilities—or more—are being broken down." "Writing in an often jocular tone," Henderson continued, "Kurzweil does what he can to tackle the heavy moral and philosophical issues surrounding what he seems to see as a steady march forward. . . . But there are many issues he does not address. . . . If Kurzweil is right, the combined effect of the changes he predicts will, at the very least, completely redraw notions of scarcity and the value of human labour in industrialised economies. Who will profit, politically and financially? What will this mean for the protection and conservation of the nonhuman living world? In a world where the distinction between real and the virtual erodes . . . will nature lose out even more?" Henderson concluded, "*Spiritual Machines* should carry a health warning to the effect that it should only be ingested through a filter of knowledge of the ancient Greek tragedies. . . . An observation made over a hundred years ago by Friedrich Nietzsche holds good: 'Technology is the premise whose

thousand-year conclusion mankind has not yet dared to draw.'"

Two reviews of the 672-page *The Singularity Is Near* illustrate divergent views of Kurzweil's ideas. In the Christian-oriented publication *First Things* (June/July 2006), the political scientist Charles T. Rubin wrote, "For Kurzweil, there is no problem for which some idea does not open the door to a solution. The power of human ideas to change the world is undergoing a vast acceleration. . . . The descendants of human intelligence will, in search of the resources necessary to meet the ever increasing computational demands of their ever more complex virtual worlds, move out into a universe that Kurzweil believes is likely devoid of other intelligence. In barely imaginable forms they will everywhere transform into patterns the chaos that chance has created, until the universe becomes mind thinking itself. . . . Kurzweil . . . is well aware that great dangers come along with great power. Because he believes that his 'law of accelerating returns' means that the technological developments creating these dangers are inevitable, however, the only thing to be done is to find technological responses. Fortunately, he argues, nanotechnology can help solve the dangers created by genetic engineering, and artificial intelligence will be necessary to solve the problems created by nanotechnology. So that's taken care of—except that Kurzweil admits that there is no technical solution to the problem that artificial intelligence might take a dislike to its human creators. His almost completely apolitical view of the world produces an absurd response to this dilemma: 'We have no choice but to strengthen our defenses while we apply these quickening technologies to advance our human values, despite an apparent lack of consensus on what those values should be.' . . . Kurzweil is sure a machine-based pattern is 'human,' because for him what is human is the ability to self-transcend. . . . So if self-transcending human beings become something else, that something else remains human. And if extinction of biological man is the price of what we can become, Kurzweil is ready to pay it." By contrast, James N. Gardner, the author of the book *Biocosm: The New Scientific Theory of Evolution: Intelligent Life Is the Architect of the Universe* (2003), described *The Singularity Is Near* as "not primarily a set of predictions about the future of computing or even technology in general. Rather it is a uniquely well-informed, technically literate, and blindingly honest speculation about the very future of evolution itself. *Singularity* is a book that Charles Darwin would have written were he steeped in the ongoing technological revolution that is engulfing our world. As such, it should be required reading for anyone seriously interested in exploring what lies over the horizon in life's journey from primordial bacterium to transcendant mind."

In the last decade Kurzweil has started four companies: FAT KAT (Financial Accelerating Transactions from Kurzweil Adaptive Technologies, 1999), which is using so-called genetic (evolutionary) algorithms and artificial neural networks to make decisions regarding the stock market; Kurzweil Cyber Art Technologies, which, in Kurzweil's words, "creates software that creates art," including such products as Ray Kurzweil's Cybernetic Poet and AARON the Cybernetic Artist; KurzweilAI.net (2001), which offers a daily newsletter and more than 700 articles about the future of technology and features a virtual hostess named Ramona, who, thanks to natural-language-processing technology, can converse with users; and Ray & Terry's Longevity Products (2003), founded and run jointly with Terry Grossman, which sells nutritional "food products" and supplements. Kurzweil himself consumes about 200 vitamin and mineral capsules or pills daily. He told Steve Lohr, writing for the *New York Times* (December 27, 2004), "Genes are sequential programs. We are learning how to manipulate the programs inside us, the software of life. And personally, I really believe that what I'm doing is reprogramming my biochemistry."

The Kurzweil Foundation, set up in 1986, gives scholarships to people with disabilities that affect reading and learning. In 2004 the foundation sent to all Massachusetts elementary schools the book and CD versions of *Forever Poems for Then and Now*, a book of poems by Kurzweil's wife, Sonya R. Kurzweil, and daughter, Amy. Sonya Kurzweil, whom Kurzweil married in the mid-1970s, is a developmental psychologist; currently, she runs her own clinic and teaches at Harvard Medical School. Amy is a senior at Stanford University. Kurzweil's son, Ethan, a Stanford graduate, is enrolled at Harvard Business School. Kurzweil and his wife live in Newton, Massachusetts. His movie *The Singularity Is Near*, which he wrote, co-directed, and produced, is a combination documentary and drama; it was scheduled for release in 2009. Also expected to arrive in theaters in 2009 was a documentary film about Kurzweil, *Transcendent Man*, directed by Robert Barry Ptolemy.

—W.D.

Suggested Reading: American Federation for the Blind Web site; *BusinessWeek* (on-line) Feb. 12, 1998; cnnmoney.com; *Fortune* (on-line) May 2, 2007; kurzweiltech.com; MIT *Spectrum* (on-line) Fall 2001; *New York Times* C p1+ Dec. 27, 2004, (on-line) Oct. 3, 2005; singularity.com; *Wired* (on-line) Apr. 2000, Apr. 2008; *Leaders of the Information Age*, 2003; *Who's Who in America* (on-line) 2008

Selected Books: *The Age of Intelligent Machines*, 1990; *The 10% Solution for a Healthy Life: How to Eliminate Virtually All Risk of Heart Disease and Cancer*, 1993; *The Age of Spiritual Machines: When Computers Exceed Human Intelligence*, 1999; *Fantastic Voyage: Live Long Enough to Live Forever* (with Terry Grossman), 2004; *The Singularity Is Near: When Humans Transcend Biology*, 2005

Selected Films: *The Age of Intelligent Machines*, 1987

Kuznetsova, Svetlana

(kuuz-net-SOH-vuh, svet-LAH-nuh)

June 27, 1985– Russian tennis player

Address: c/o International Tennis Federation, Bank Ln., Roehampton, London SW15 5XZ, England

Since she made her professional debut, in 2000, Svetlana Kuznetsova has emerged as one of a group of highly touted Russian female tennis players—the others are Maria Sharapova, Elena Dementieva, and Anna Chakvetadze—who are currently dominating the women's professional circuit. Formerly the world's number-one-ranked junior player, Kuznetsova has gone on to win nine Women's Tennis Association (WTA) singles titles. The most significant victory of her career to date came in 2004, with her straight-set upset of Dementieva during the finals of the United States Open, in which she became the lowest-ranked player ever to win that event. After claiming her first Grand Slam title that year, Kuznetsova struggled with inconsistent play, and she failed to advance past the quarterfinals of a Grand Slam tournament in 2005. Then, in the following year, she reached the finals of the French Open while also winning a career-best three singles titles. In 2007 Kuznetsova advanced to her second U.S. Open final in three years and achieved a career-high number-two ranking among the world's female tennis players, to overtake Sharapova as the leading Russian woman in the sport. In addition to her accomplishments in singles matches, Kuznetsova is an accomplished doubles player, with 13 WTA titles to her name. "You can't get satisfied playing tennis, I think," Kuznetsova said to an interviewer for futuretennisstars.com. "You just all the time want to do more."

Svetlana Aleksandrovna Kuznetsova was born on June 27, 1985 in St. Petersburg, Russia, to Galina Tsareva and Alexandr Kuznetsova. She hails from a family of talented cyclists. Her father, a cycling coach, has trained six Olympic and world champions, including his wife and his son, and currently trains the members of Lokomotiv, a professional cycling team in St. Petersburg; her mother is a six-time world sprint-cycling champion and

Greg Wood/AFP/Getty Images

Svetlana Kuznetsova

holds 20 world records in the sport. Kuznetsova's brother, Nikolai, won a silver medal in the men's 4,000-meter track-cycling event at the 1996 Summer Olympic Games, in Atlanta, Georgia. By contrast, Kuznetsova, after learning how to ride a bike at age four, tried cycling competitively but quickly lost interest. "I had two cycle races against 15-year-old guys when I was eight," she told John Roberts for the London *Independent* (February 28, 2004). "I did well in the first race and finished last. I got so bored in the second race that I didn't finish it. My father told me to try something else, like swimming. But I liked tennis more." Speaking with the interviewer for futuretennisstars.com, Kuznetsova, who is moderately fluent in English, said, "I think I can express myself in the court. . . . The same as singers sing songs."

By 1999 Kuznetsova was among the top-20-ranked junior players in Russia. "St. Petersburg is not like Moscow and I ran out of people to play against and I had to leave," she told Chris Jones for the London *Evening Standard* (May 10, 2005). "We didn't have any famous men or women tennis players." Her parents took her to Barcelona, Spain, to attend the Sánchez-Casal Academy, an elite tennis facility for promising European players named after its founders, the former professional players and longtime men's-doubles partners Emilio Sánchez Vicario and Sergio Casal. (Kuznetsova's family chose Spain because her father had previously spent time there—specifically, in the city of Tortosa, which had been home to the preseason training camp for his cycling team.) In Barcelona Kuznetsova stayed in an apartment with her mother, going back to St. Petersburg for two weeks a year. Sánchez sent to the Internet tennis publication *On the*

Line a reminiscence about Kuznetsova's arrival at the academy that has been widely distributed—in varying translations—on the Web: "The first time we met Sveta, our staff . . . shared a common reaction: she was so shy she would not look at you, she had no confidence in herself, but every time she hit the ball the noise it made was scary. It was something we had not seen or heard before from a girl, maybe slightly similar to Andy Roddick."

Impressed by how well she hit the ball at such a young age, the instructors at the academy worked on helping her to develop an "all-court" game—that is, to learn to play well against a variety of opponents on different court surfaces (including clay, hard court, grass, or indoor carpet) and in different weather conditions. Kuznetsova played the junior circuit in 1999, appearing in both singles and doubles events at several hard-court and clay-court tournaments. She reached the singles semifinals of two tournaments—the Donetsk Cup in Ukraine and the Samara Cup of Russia—and won the doubles title at the Mera Cup in Poland, with her fellow Russian player Marianna Yuferova. During international competition with other junior players, Kuznetsova was sometimes bemused by the corporate sponsorship that some of her opponents enjoyed; in particular, she has recalled "playing a Swiss junior who was fully decked out in all the latest gear, courtesy of some corporate sugar-daddy," as Joe O'Connor phrased it in the Canadian *National Post* (August 18, 2005). The Swiss player was "getting for free, everything," Kuznetsova told O'Connor. "If you are Russian, you don't understand this. You are spending your last money to get your racquets, to get your strings, to get your shoes."

In 2000, her first year as a professional, Kuznetsova claimed three singles titles at four clay-court tournaments: the Mostostal Trophy, the Mera Cup, the Garrone International Junior, and the Leciva Czech Junior Open, where she also reached the finals of the doubles event before losing to Iveta Gerlova and Zuzana Zemenova of the Czech Republic. The year 2001 saw Kuznetsova's first participation in junior Grand Slam tournaments, in which she enjoyed some success in the singles and doubles events. She reached the third round of singles competition at the Australian Open Junior Championships, the first Grand Slam event of the tennis season, and that tournament's junior women's doubles final (with her fellow Russian player Anna Bastrikova), in which she lost in three sets (7–6, 1–6, 6–4) to Petra Cetkovska and Barbora Strycova of the Czech Republic. Although she and her partner, Claudine Schaul of Luxembourg, failed to make it past the first-round doubles match at the Junior Championships at Wimbledon, Kuznetsova advanced to the singles quarterfinals before falling to Elena Baltacha in a third-set tie-breaker. Her best results came at the U.S. Open Junior Championships, where she was a finalist in the singles and doubles tournaments. Kuznetsova and Galina Fokina recorded a straight-set victory over Jelena

Janković of Yugoslavia and Matea Mezak of Croatia in the doubles final, but Kuznetsova suffered a three-set loss, 4–6, 6–3, 6–4, to the French player Marion Bartoli, who also defeated her at the final of the Australian Hardcourt Junior Championships, 6–0, 6–3. That same year she captured singles titles at the Banana Bowl and the ITF/Cagliari in Italy while also reaching the finals of the 23d Gerdau Tennis Cup, the International Junior Championships of France, and the Burger King Orange Bowl Tennis Championships. In doubles competition she was a finalist at the Gerdau Tennis Cup, the Osaka Mayor's Cup, and the Mobilux Junior Open. At the end of 2001, Kuznetsova was designated the junior player of the year and the top-ranked junior player in the world by the International Tennis Federation (ITF).

In 2002, after reaching the doubles finals of the Australian Open Junior Championships (with Mezak) and the International Junior Championships of France (with Su-Wei Hsieh of Taiwan), Kuznetsova partnered with Arantxa Sánchez Vicario, the former top-ranked female tennis player in the world and the sister of her coach, Emilio Sánchez. The team went on to win doubles titles at the Women's Tennis Association tournament in Sopot, Poland; the Helsinki Open; and the Toyota Princess Cup in Tokyo, Japan. They were finalists at the Wismilak International in Bali and the Japan Open in Tokyo. That year Kuznetsova continued to climb up the singles rankings, defeating Denisa Chladkova of the Czech Republic to claim her first WTA singles title—as a qualifier—at the Helsinki Open. She also triumphed over her doubles partner Sánchez Vicario to reach the finals of the Wismilak International in Bali, where she fought off four match points in the third set against Spain's Conchita Martinez to win her second WTA title. By the end of 2002, she had risen in singles ranking, from 257th in the world in 2001 to 43.

Following Arantxa Sánchez Vicario's retirement, at the end of 2002, Kuznetsova accepted an offer to team up with the Czech-born veteran Martina Navratilova. In 2003 the pair captured doubles titles at the Gold Coast Tournament in Australia; the Dubai Duty Free Women's Open; the Rogers Cup in Toronto, Canada; the Telecom Italia Masters in Rome, Italy; and the Sparkassen Cup in Leipzig, Germany. Their best result in Grand Slam competition was at the U.S. Open, where they reached the finals before losing 6–2, 6–3 to Virginia Ruano Pascal of Spain and Paola Suarez of Argentina. They made it into the quarterfinals of Wimbledon and into the third round of the Australian Open Championships and the French Open. In singles play Kuznetsova was a quarterfinalist at Wimbledon and the JP Morgan Chase Open and a semifinalist at the Acura Classic. She finished the year 2003 ranked number 36th in the world.

In 2004 Navratilova ended her partnership with Kuznetsova and started playing with the American Lisa Raymond, then one of the world's best in doubles competition and her doubles partner in the year's upcoming Olympic Games in Athens, Greece. Kuznetsova began working with a new coach, Angel Gimenez, and a new partner, Elena Likhovtseva. Kuznetsova and Likhovtseva captured the Gold Coast title while advancing to the finals of the Australian Open Championships, the French Open, the U.S. Open, the Dubai Duty Free Women's Open, the Pacific Life Open, the NASDAQ 100 Open, and the Hastings Direct International Championships; they also reached the quarterfinals of Wimbledon and the JP Morgan Chase Open. Kuznetsova was also a doubles finalist, with Arantxa Sánchez Vicario (who had come out of retirement), at the Wismilak International in Bali. Her biggest win as a singles player came with her straight-set defeat (6–3, 7–5) of Elena Dementieva at the finals of the 2004 U.S. Open—the second all-Russian finals match in tennis history. (The first had occurred between Anastasia Myskina and Dementieva at the 2004 French Open, where Dementieva squandered two match points to lose a close fourth-round match, 1–6, 6–4, 8–6, to Myskina.) Kuznetsova also added two singles titles—the Hastings Direct International Championships and the Wismilak International—to her record and reached the finals of the Dubai Duty Free Women's Open, the Qatar Total Open, the J&S Cup, and the China Open. At the 2004 Olympics she competed in both the women's singles and the women's doubles events. In singles play Kuznetsova, the sixth seed, lost in three sets to second-seeded Amélie Mauresmo of France; as the top seeds in the women's doubles tournament, she and Likhovtseva made it to the second round before losing a three-set match to Sandrine Testud and Nathalie Dechy of France. Kuznetsova was also a member of Russia's winning 2004 Fed Cup team.

In 2005 Kuznetsova ended her doubles partnership with Likhovtseva and joined forces with Alicia Molik. The new team defeated the American pair of Lindsey Davenport and Corina Morariu to win the women's doubles title at the Australian Open; they also captured the doubles title at the NASDAQ 100 Open, where they beat Lisa Raymond and Rennae Stubbs of Australia. At the U.S. Open quarterfinals, they lost a three-set match to Navratilova and Anna-Lena Groenefeld. Kuznetsova teamed up with other players in Grand Slam matches, reaching the finals of Wimbledon with Amélie Mauresmo before losing to Anke Huber of Germany and Cara Black of Zimbabwe and advancing to the second round of the French Open with Mary Pierce. She did not fare as well in individual play, failing to win a singles title in 2005. At the U.S. Open her straight-set defeat (6–3, 6–2) by countrywoman Ekaterina Bychkova made her the first female defending champion to lose in the first round. She had better results at the Australian Open and Wimbledon, where she was a quarterfinalist, and the French Open, where she suffered a fourth-round loss to Justine Henin-Hardenne of France, who also defeated her in the finals of the J&S Cup. In non–Grand Slam competition, she reached the semifinals of the Toray Pan Pacific Open and the Hastings Direct International Championships and also advanced to the quarterfinals of the Pacific Life Open, the Ladies German Open, and the Kremlin Cup. She became embroiled in a doping scandal after she tested positive for the banned substance ephedrine during an exhibition match; she suffered no official consequences because the test had been conducted during an informal competition.

After failing to win a singles title in 2005, Kuznetsova recorded her first victory of 2006 in April, against Maria Sharapova at the Sony Ericsson WTA Tour Championships, in Miami, Florida. Her next appearance in a finals match came at the French Open, where she lost 6–4, 6–4 to Henin-Hardenne. She made it as far as the third round of Wimbledon before she was sidelined for a month with an abdominal injury. Following losses to Martina Hingis at the Rogers Cup and Henin-Hardenne at the Pilot Pen Tennis Championships, Kuznetsova improved on her results at the 2006 U.S. Open, reaching the fourth round before losing to Jelena Janković. That defeat was followed by victories at the Wismilak International Tennis tournament and the China Open. Her only doubles title came with Mauresmo at the Hastings Direct International Championships, where they defeated Huber and Navratilova, 6–2, 6–4. She also played mixed doubles with her countryman Yuri Schukin at the 2006 Hopman Cup, losing in the round-robin stage. Kuznetsova finished the year as the fourth-highest-ranked female tennis player in the world. She recorded the most wins on the WTA tour (60) and the most matches played on the tour (80).

In 2007 Kuznetsova followed up a disappointing fourth-round exit against Shahar Peer at the singles event of the Australian Open with final appearances at the Pacific Life Open (against Daniela Hantuchová), the Qatar Telecom German Open (against Ana Ivanović), and the Rome Tennis Masters (against Janković). She reached the quarterfinals of Wimbledon before losing in straight sets (6–3, 6–4) to Venus Williams. Her first singles title of 2007, at the Pilot Pen Tennis tournament, came amid unusual circumstances. After Kuznetsova triumphed in the fourth round, defeating Agnieszka Radwańska of Poland, her next three opponents—Francesca Schiavone (quarterfinal), Elena Dementieva (semifinal), and Ágnes Szávay (final)—pulled out of their respective matches due to injury or illness.

At the 2007 U.S. Open, Kuznetsova was seeded in the weak lower half of the draw along with Sharapova, whom she was expected to meet in the semifinals, but she quickly became a favorite to reach the finals after Sharapova's shocking third-round loss to the 30th-seeded Radwańska. Kuznetsova struggled early in her semifinal match against Anna Chakvetadze, who also underperformed. "I played the worst first set. I couldn't put the ball in, and I was really embarrassed by my game," Kuznetsova told Howard Fendrich for the Associated Press (September 7, 2007). "When the nerves get in the middle, it's tough." She was dominant over the next two sets, winning 22 of 25 points while saving 11 of 16 break points and committing only four errors to set up a final meeting with Justine Henin (who had dropped her married name following a separation from her husband, from whom she was later divorced). Though Kuznetsova's play had improved slightly since her previous semifinal match, she remained inconsistent, committing 29 unforced errors while failing several times to win her service game against Henin, who captured her second U.S. Open title with a straight-set victory (6–1, 6–3). Kuznetsova performed better at the 2007 Fed Cup championship, where her victory against Francesca Schiavone of Italy gave the Russian team a 3–0 victory (in a best-of-five format), bringing them their third title in four years. In October Kuznetsova also had semifinal finishes at the Porsche Tennis Grand Prix in Germany and the Kremlin Cup in Moscow. An injury to her right shoulder forced her to retire in the quarterfinals of the Zurich Open. Her best showing in doubles competition came at the Dubai Tennis Championships, where she and Alicia Molik reached the finals but lost, 7–6, 6–4, to Cara Black and Anke Huber; she and Molik were quarterfinalists at the Qatar Open as well. Kuznetsova also partnered with Russia's Nadia Petrova, with whom she advanced to the quarterfinals of Wimbledon, the Qatar Telecom German Open, and the Canadian Open.

In early 2008 Kuznetsova announced plans to skip the Fed Cup to concentrate on unseating Henin from the top spot. While she failed to overtake Henin in 2008, she defeated Ana Ivanovic for the Australian Open title and made it to the finals in the Dubai Tennis Championships, where she lost to Elena Dementieva. She represented Russia at the 2008 Olympics in Beijing, starting out as the third-seeded player. In the first round she lost to China's top female player, Ni La. Kuznetsova recently began working with a new coach, the legendary Soviet-era tennis player Olga Morozova.

The five-foot nine-inch Kuznetsova lives in St. Petersburg but continues to train at the Sánchez-Casal Academy with her coach, Stefan Ortega. She told an interviewer for rediff.com (January 14, 2005) that "it's hard to have really close friends" on the WTA tour "because we're all rivals and competitors." She added that among the Russian players, her closest friends included Vera Zvonareva and Elena Likhovtseva. Kuznetsova has also criticized Maria Sharapova's focus on physical appearance. "If someone wants to make a fashion statement they should go on stage, not on a tennis court," she told rediff.com. "On court, you don't have time to worry about other things aside from tennis. It's your game which should count the most, not your outfits." Kuznetsova's leisure-time activities include playing soccer, snowboarding, and listening to pop, dance, and rock music. In addition to Russian and English, she speaks Spanish. In an interview for ASAP Sports (September 12,

2004, on-line), Kuznetsova mentioned that she admired the tennis player Lleyton Hewitt. "I just love watching Hewitt . . . fight . . . ," she said. "I mean, I just like the people who is fighting, you know, and who does . . . everything to win."

—B.M.

Suggested Reading: (Canada) *National Post* B p11 Aug. 18, 2005; ITF.com; (London) *Evening Standard* p60 May 10, 2005; *Los Angeles Times* D p1 Sep. 12, 2004; *New York Times* VIII p1 Sep. 12, 2004; *South China Morning Post* p16 Dec. 21, 2004; *Weekend Australian* p54 Jan. 20, 2007

Marsaili McGrath/Getty Images for Sundance

LaChapelle, David

Mar. 11, 1963– Photographer; film and video director

Address: c/o Fred Torres at Fine Art Account Inc., 527 W. 29th St., Third Fl., New York, NY 10001

"Each time you aim a light, you change reality." That oft-quoted statement is attributed to David LaChapelle, one of the most successful photographers of the past two decades. Sparing no expense, LaChapelle has used sophisticated lighting and other effects—and drawn on his considerable imaginative powers—to create the often outlandish, sometimes surreal visual worlds that serve as settings for his photographs of a wide range of celebrities, from the soccer star David Beckham to the singer Missy Elliott. Raised in Connecticut and North Carolina, LaChapelle moved to New York

City at age 18 and befriended the legendary artist Andy Warhol, who helped the budding photographer break into magazine work. He quickly rose to prominence for his vivid, original style and has become known for his colorful, computer-enhanced images, his ironic take on popular culture, and his ability to inhabit the realms of art and commercial photography simultaneously. His work has appeared in many magazines, including *Interview*, *Details*, *Rolling Stone*, the *New York Times Magazine*, and *Vanity Fair*. He has also exhibited at galleries, among them the Helmut Newton Foundation, in Berlin, Germany; the Tony Shafrazi Gallery, in New York City; and Palazzo Reale, in Milan, Italy.

The youngest of three children, David LaChapelle was born on March 11, 1963 in Fairfield, Connecticut. (Sources differ as to when he was born. For the April 30, 2006 edition of the Sydney, Australia, *Herald Sun*, for example, Emma Brockes wrote that LaChapelle was 37, "or thereabouts; he seems to have been 37 since at least 2002.") His father, a technology executive, grew up during the Great Depression. His mother was one of the last people to come into the United States through Ellis Island; she emigrated from Lithuania after World War II. LaChapelle described her to Stephen Saban for the London *Independent on Sunday* (May 19, 2002) as "an artist who never got to be an artist." She would often take elaborate family portraits, directing her husband and children to pose alongside houses, cars, and even dogs that did not belong to them. It was she who set up the first photograph David took, at age six; it showed his mother in a bikini top, holding a martini glass during a family vacation in Puerto Rico.

When LaChapelle was 12 his family relocated to Raleigh, North Carolina. The move "introduced me to the scary and banal landscape that America is," he told Joe Gioia for Salon.com (October 13, 1999). Openly gay beginning in his early teens, he received support from his parents but was ostracized and became a frequent target of bullying at school. "I remember being 14 years old and not wanting to live," he told Emma Brockes, "but I couldn't do it [kill himself] because my parents were so nice. I thought it would ruin their lives. And it would have." He looked to cultures beyond that of Raleigh for hope that a better life awaited him. "I had a poster of Elton John on my wall," he told Brockes, "and I knew there was a place somewhere in the world where people who were different and creative were accepted and were having a good time." (In 1976 John had announced publicly that he was bisexual; years later he declared that he was gay.)

At 15 LaChapelle left home for New York City, where he got a job bussing tables at Studio 54, a glamorous and hedonistic disco club then in its heyday. "I loved seeing people, celebrities, behaving outrageously," he told Gioia. "I liked the colorfulness and strangeness of the '70s." Before long his father arrived and drove him back to North Carolina. With his father's encouragement,

LaChapelle enrolled in the high-school program of the North Carolina School of the Arts, where he studied photography but did not graduate. Being there "saved my life," he told Saban; he received valuable instruction and found kindred spirits in his creative fellow students.

At 18 LaChapelle was back in New York, where he took classes at the School of Visual Arts and worked odd jobs, including a brief stint as a prostitute. "I guess it felt glamorous to be objectified in that way," he told Hilary Rose for the Australian publication *QWeekend* (February 3, 2007). "Because I was with older, nicer men, I rationalised that I was providing some sort of social service. [But] it messes up something that should be kept pure and special and turns it into work."

At a concert by the rock group Psychedelic Furs, in a chance occurrence, LaChapelle met the iconic pop artist Andy Warhol. "[Warhol] said, 'Oh, you should be a model,'" LaChapelle told Alix Sharkey for the London *Observer* (February 5, 2006). "'But drop by the office, show me your pictures.'" LaChapelle showed him the portfolio of nudes he had taken of his male friends at art school, and Warhol pronounced them to be "great." (LaChapelle soon learned that Warhol called many things "great.") LaChapelle began shooting for Warhol's magazine, *Interview*, as well as various other publications. He and his boyfriend, Louis Albert, a dancer, lived simply, in a tiny apartment with no heat or phone.

LaChapelle's life changed in 1986, when Louis died of AIDS, a disease that had only recently been identified. In denial, LaChapelle did not get tested for HIV, the virus that causes AIDS, until 1992. "When Louis died there wasn't even a test," he told Sharkey. "The fact that I wasn't [HIV] positive was a huge shock." In the wake of his loss, he began working for the AIDS advocacy group Act-Up, and he has donated money and photographs to AIDS charities ever since. "Everyone thinks the Eighties were so cool," he told Sharkey, "but there was a big dark cloud"—the AIDS crisis—"hanging over that period. It was really like a war. Watching your friends die one by one." Shortly after Louis's death, in what were perhaps the results of a manic period (LaChapelle suffers from bipolar disorder), he joined the Marines—which he left a few months later—and married a woman. When asked why he had done those things, he told Sharkey, "I don't know! Even today, I have no idea." (LaChapelle told Brockes that his disorder is cyclical, flaring up in the spring, and that he now controls it in part through his diet. Discussing the positive side of his manic periods, the photographer told Brockes, "You're so creative and you get all this stuff done. I live for a whole year off the ideas that come out of it.") He moved to London, England, with his bride, from whom he soon grew estranged, preferring to spend days at a time using hard drugs and partying with trendy "club kids" including the performance artist and clothing designer Leigh Bowery and the singer Boy George. "It was like the epi-

centre of hype, creativity, outrageousness," he told Sharkey of his time in London, "but it really freaked me out. In the end it was like, I can't take any more. And I was from New York, I thought I'd seen it all, but that was a whole other level of artistic wackiness. It was a subculture of insanity." Despite those distractions, LaChapelle greatly expanded his portfolio during that period, shooting for *Interview* and the *Face*. "The one thing I learnt from London that has been so crucial to everything I believe in," he told Saban, "is originality, not appropriating things, not copying other people's art. It's a common thing [in the U.S.], so common that people don't even look down on it, they don't even question it. But in London you can't walk down the street if you do that—they'll throw eggs at you."

LaChapelle took that lesson back to New York, where he continued to shoot for *Interview* and *Details* and spent time with Warhol in the months leading up to the older man's death, in 1987. LaChapelle frequently cites the artist as the biggest influence on his own style: "Working at *Interview* was really my college . . . ," he told Eleftheria Parpis for *Adweek* (September 19, 2005, on-line). "[Warhol] didn't stick to one medium or one look. He did silk screens, drawings, photography. He ran a magazine, had a television show and he did films. He never limited himself to what people said he should do or could do or, you know, what a serious artist does or anything like that. He did commercial art. He didn't really separate commercial work and fine art. It was all the same to him." That view of art is apparent in LaChapelle's work, which translates well from the pages of magazines to the walls of galleries. "The way I look at it is, magazines are the galleries," he told Amy Spindler for the *New York Times* (November 29, 1994), "and the museum is the refrigerator. If someone rips out the photo and puts in on the fridge, that really is something."

LaChapelle also shares Warhol's interest in the concept of celebrity; he is known for photographing celebrities in ironic ways, such that viewers may wonder if the subjects are in on the joke. Some critics view his work as lacking in depth or substance; others contend that a self-conscious materialism was part of the point of, for example, his photographic depiction of the pop star Britney Spears as a hot-dog vendor and his shots of the singer Lil' Kim, shown nude with a pattern by the fashion designer Louis Vuitton painted on her skin. "LaChapelle's portraits do not celebrate celebrity so much as devour it," Joe Gioia wrote. "Of course, celebrity consumed returns as an indelible imago—a god ready to be eaten again and again. LaChapelle is clearly in touch with how this active process of deification works today." Quoting LaChapelle as saying, "Celebrities provide an escape from the mundane. They are photographed so we can worship them—so they are worthy of our worship," Gioia concluded, "No photographer's work has better exposed that orgiastic extremity of fame."

In the same vein as Warhol's famous images of soup cans, popular culture and Americana are frequent subjects for LaChapelle. He has credited a 1994 *Details* assignment, in which he photographed rock musicians with their parents, with helping him to clarify his style. "It was a breakthrough in my work," he told Eleftheria Parpis for *Adweek* (May 18, 1998). "These pictures were the real America gone mad." LaChapelle has developed a reputation for using artifacts of "low" culture in his photographs of pop icons, as when he photographed the actress Tori Spelling in a limousine with discarded MacDonald's wrappers at her feet. "Modern America wasn't in pictures because people look at it as ugly," he told Spindler. "But you have to embrace it, because there's no going back now." He is fond of quoting the writer Truman Capote's famous maxim, "Good taste is the death of art."

LaChapelle published his first book, *LaChapelle Land*, in 1996. A compilation of his work up to that date, it consists of vivid, surreal (or, as he prefers to say, "escapist") portraits of larger-than-life figures, among them Lil' Kim, the pop megastar Madonna, and the actress Pamela Anderson. "With the publication of *LaChapelle Land* . . . he has found his niche in the Pantheon of celebrated celebrity photographers, alongside Annie Leibowitz and Herb Ritts," Jose Villarrubia wrote for the *Lambda Book Report* (December 31, 1996). LaChapelle was both enthusiastic and humble upon the book's publication. For years, "all I wanted was to make enough money shooting pictures to survive in New York," he told Gioia. "I never expected this."

The mid-to-late 1990s brought much success for LaChapelle, both financially and critically. "Social satirists are rarely rewarded as richly as LaChapelle, especially by Madison Avenue," as Joe Gioia observed. By the turn of the millennium, he had shot an extravagant Citibank ad featuring Elton John; the front and back covers of Madonna's video collection; Madonna as a glowing dragon-goddess for the cover of *Rolling Stone*; a campy, Lolita-esque *Rolling Stone* cover featuring a young Britney Spears; and an ad campaign for the children's musical *Seussical*. He won several awards, including the VH-1 Fashion Awards' Photographer of the Year honor (1996), the International Center of Photography's Applied Photography of the Year Award, and best Cutting Edge Essay and Style Photography honors at *Life* magazine's Alfred Eisenstadt Awards for Magazine Photography (the "Eisies").

LaChapelle's second book of photographs, *Hotel LaChapelle*, was published in 1999. At the end of the book, he included an explanation for the title, as quoted on Amazon.com: "When people come for a photo session with me, they are giving themselves over, sort of checking in. When you stay at a hotel you're living for one day in a place where you don't normally live. That feeling can be true with photographs, too." The book featured surreal,

outlandish photographs of both celebrities and fictional characters, sometimes blurring the boundary: the goth-rock singer Marilyn Manson appears as a crossing guard giving out lollipops to children; the actor Leonardo DiCaprio looks like the screen legend Marlon Brando; and a nurse is shown holding a face in a pair of tweezers. The book earned this description from Gioia: "LaChapelle's photography is all flesh and blood; extravagantly immediate. His photos connect more to the visceral pleasures and terrors of the theater, and its origins in ancient religious sacrifice, than to the rather abstracted cerebral feelings usually aroused by film."

It was also in the 1990s that LaChapelle became known for pushing the boundaries of commercial acceptability, by shooting provocative images— such as an ad for Diesel jeans depicting two male sailors kissing on V-J Day (the day of Japan's surrender in World War II), or the black rapper Tupac Shakur depicted as a slave working on a plantation (meant as a reference to the origins of African-American music). He was also fond of photographing his muse and friend, the well-known transsexual Amanda Lepore, persuading her in 1999 to show up at his London gallery opening completely unclothed, her body painted as if suntanned, with an unpainted area in the shape of a bikini. Though such boldness lent his work an aura of edginess that made him greatly sought after, it also occasionally brought scandal down on his head—as in 1997, when the actress Mira Sorvino, after appearing in a photo spread for *Allure* magazine, grew irate over LaChapelle's use of computer effects to make her look like Joan Crawford. (She had refused to pose as the screen idol.) The photographer Richard Avedon came out in support of LaChapelle, telling Amy Spindler for the *New York Times* (June 17, 1997), "There is no such thing as photographic reality," and adding that LaChapelle had the potential to be his genre's René Magritte, a reference to the famous Belgian surrealist painter. (Spindler pointed out what she saw as a touch of hypocrisy in Sorvino's response, writing, "She has . . . not complained about digital retouching on the same photo that perfected her skin, lengthened her legs, and thinned her waist.") PMK, the publicity firm representing Sorvino, never sued LaChapelle as it had threatened to do but banned him from working with their celebrity clients (the ban was lifted five years later). "It was a loss to their clients," LaChapelle told Saban of the incident. "And, you know, at the end of the day I'm better off not working with clients who don't want to work with me or publicists who don't want me to work with their clients. Because I won't get along with them; they won't understand what I want to do. They want the kind of photographs that are safe, and I don't do safe photographs."

LaChapelle's career was apparently not harmed by that episode; some would argue that the publicity only helped him grow more famous. In 2001 he was invited to direct a music video for Elton John's single "This Train Don't Stop There Anymore."

The video featured Justin Timberlake as a young Elton John going through the motions of greeting various people before taking to the stage. John liked the video enough to invite LaChapelle to direct another, for his 2002 song "Original Sin," this time featuring Mandy Moore as a pimply, teenage Elton John fan who dreams of seeing the musician in concert.

In 2005 LaChapelle made a significant departure from his work up to that time when he directed *Rize*, a documentary about the Los Angeles, California, dance style known as "krumping." He was introduced to the dance while working on the music video for Christina Aguilera's single "Dirrty;" choreographers saw some of the dancers performing it and brought it to his attention. "I went to the room, where there was music playing, and saw them and lost my mind," he told Carina Chocano for the *Los Angeles Times* (June 12, 2005). The dancers, Chocano wrote, "were doing what looks like a manic, desexualized, sped-up version of a lap dance, called 'the stripper dance.'" LaChapelle told Chocano, "It was something I'd never seen before, and my first thought was I wanted other people to see it. I think when you see something beautiful, your tendency is to share it. I just thought, I have to film this."

LaChapelle soon went to the impoverished neighborhood of South-Central Los Angeles, to film the story of the unique dance. The phenomenon is credited to a former drug dealer, Tommy Johnson, who upon his release from prison decided to make a career of entertaining children as Tommy the Clown. He taught many children his hip-hop clown dance, which inspired some of his students to start dance groups of their own. Johnson founded Tommy's Hip-Hop Clown Academy as well as an event called "Battle Zone," in which groups could compete; some of the groups developed a wilder, more aggressive version of the dance, called "krumping." The poorly funded public schools of the South-Central area had few after-school activities, and krumping provided an outlet for the boredom and anger that otherwise drove many youngsters to join gangs. LaChapelle was inspired by his subjects' ability to create their own paths in the face of grim circumstances. "They're from the hardest families in the hood," he told Nicholas White for *People* (July 11, 2005). "They have fathers who are founding members of the [gangs] Crips or Bloods, mothers who are drug addicts or in prison. Yet in the face of all this adversity, these kids have developed a new art form." Chocano wrote about *Rize*: "Unlike the recently released, much-discussed L.A. race opera *Crash* [a film drama], *Rize* avoids stereotypes, facile conclusions and dime-store ironies. By following the story without preconceptions, LaChapelle was able to capture an organic phenomenon in constant flux and, through it, gain a deeper understanding of the lives of the people involved."

LaChapelle has continued to take on diverse projects. To each of them he brings his desire to create an alternate reality. As he told Karl Plewka for *Interview* (September 1998), "Escapist defines my pictures because that's how I feel when I am taking them." In the past three years, LaChapelle has directed music videos including those for Gwen Stefani's "Rich Girl" and Amy Winehouse's "Tears Dry on Their Own," bringing the number of videos he has directed to more than 30. He has shot several commercials, such as Burger King's ad for the Bacon Cheddar Ranch chicken sandwich, a spot featuring the singer Darius Rucker, the supermodel Brooke Burke, and the *Playboy* Playmate Colleen Shannon. He has also participated in many group and solo photographic exhibitions, including the Helmut Newton Foundation's high-profile show Men, War and Peace (2007), held in Berlin, and has published two more books: *Artists and Prostitutes* and *Heaven to Hell* (both 2006). The most recent of the 350 photos in LaChapelle's latest retrospective, which ran from September 2007 to January 2008 in the Palazzo Reale, in Milan, explored the idea of the apocalypse; the photographs incorporated influences as varied as the Renaissance artist Michelangelo, the photojournalist Dorothea Lange, the French Romantic painter Theodore Géricault, and Warhol's pop art. His show Auguries of Innocence was on exhibition at the Tony Shafrazi Gallery, in New York, in the fall of 2008.

LaChapelle, who is single, lives in Hollywood Hills, California, and has an apartment in New York City. He has two cars, though he does not know how to drive (his assistant drives them). "I love people and humanity, and I know that . . . we're doing the best we can, and hopefully we can even do better," he told Serena Altschul for CBS News (March 4, 2007, on-line). LaChapelle's resistance to cynicism sets him apart from many of his art-world peers. "People are afraid not to be cynical because otherwise they'd be naïve," he told Alix Sharkey. "But you don't have to be an apolitical airhead, you can still have ideas and values without having to judge everybody and everything you come across."

—J.E.P.

Suggested Reading: *Adweek* Creative May 18, 1998, Creative Sep. 19, 2005; (London) *Independent on Sunday* p10 May 19, 2002; (London) *Observer* p14 Feb. 5, 2006; Salon.com Oct. 13, 1999; (Sydney, Australia) *Sun Herald* News p61 Apr. 30, 2006

Selected Books: *LaChapelle Land*, 1996; *Hotel LaChapelle*, 1999; *Heaven to Hell*, 2006; *Artists and Prostitutes*, 2006

Selected Films: *Rize*, 2005

Jonathan Ferrey/Getty Images

Lagat, Bernard

(lah-GAHT)

Dec. 12, 1974– Track and field athlete

Address: c/o USA Track & Field, 132 E. Washington St., Suite 800, Indianapolis, IN 46204

Bernard Lagat arrived in Beijing, China, for the 2008 Olympic Games as a reigning world champion in the 1,500-meter and 5,000-meter outdoor events, an Olympic bronze medalist (at the 2000 Games, in Sydney, Australia), and an Olympic silver medalist (at the 2004 Games, in Athens, Greece). He also arrived as an American. The Kenyan native, who ran in 2000 and 2004 under the flag of his homeland, had become a naturalized U.S. citizen and was now one of the strongest members of his adopted country's track-and-field team. While his performance in Beijing was ultimately disappointing—he did not make it past the 1,500-meter semifinals and finished ninth in the 5,000-meter finals—he was proud to have been wearing the uniform of Team U.S.A. Before the World Championships, he had told Luke Cyphers for ESPN.com (August 2, 2007), "If I win, it's not going to be a former Kenyan winning. It's going to be Lagat the American."

The fifth of 10 children, Bernard Kipchirchir Lagat, nicknamed Kip, was born on December 12, 1974 in Kapsabet, Kenya. His parents, Richard Kiplagat Leting and Marsalina, of the Nandi tribe, had been runners before becoming full-time farmers. For them, winning community races often meant earning such valuable and practical prizes

as blankets, machetes, tin sheeting, and axes. Richard, now about 75 years old, is the elder of the Rift Valley Province village, home to some 90 families.

Lagat's siblings are also accomplished runners. His oldest sister, Anjalina Chepchumba, was nationally ranked in her youth; the third-born, William Cheseret, is a marathon runner; the sixth-born, Everlyne Jerotich, is a cross-country champion; and the eighth-born, Robert Cheseret, has excelled in 5,000-meter and 10,000-meter events. Two other siblings, Nathan and Tecla, are military runners, and Irine and Violah, the two youngest, are gifted student athletes. It was, however, the family's second-born, Mary Chepkemboi, the 1984 African champion in the 3,000-meter event, who most inspired Lagat. "Every time I looked at her I wanted to be like her," he told David Powell for an interview posted on the International Association of Athletics Federations (IAAF) Web site (August 2, 2008). "She told me I could be somebody out of this when I didn't know what being somebody out of running was. She said I could be a world leader, a gold medallist, an Olympic champion, and those are the things that still resonate in my mind. She said it a long time ago but it is as if she said it yesterday."

Kapsabet is the birthplace of numerous elite Kenyan runners, including Kipchoge Keino, a four-time Olympic medalist and head of the Kenyan National Olympic Committee, for whom the local stadium is named. Like many athletes from the area, Lagat began running simply to get from place to place; he ran about a mile to Kipsirwo Primary School, ran home in the middle of the day to eat lunch, ran back to school for afternoon classes, and then ran home in the evening. In 1992, when he was a sophomore at Kaptel High School, his sister Mary gave him his first pair of running shoes and encouraged him to train seriously.

Lagat entered the Jomo Kenyatta University of Agriculture and Technology, in Kenya, and in 1996 he became the only college runner to make the 1,500-meter finals at the Kenyan Olympic trials. While he did not qualify for the Games, held that year in Atlanta, Georgia, he was recruited soon after the trials to run for Washington State University, in Pullman, which was actively recruiting promising African runners. Lagat's father sold a small piece of land to pay for a plane ticket, and Lagat moved to the United States to accept the scholarship that the university had offered him. He applied himself enthusiastically to his studies, taking classes in management-information systems and econometrics, but his early performances on the field were hampered by a knee injury. Despite his inability to train at full capacity, Lagat placed seventh in the Pacific-10 Conference cross-country championships in his freshman season. (Commonly known as the Pac-10, the college athletic conference, based in the Western U.S., sponsors several sports, including baseball, football, golf, gymnastics, and track and field.)

Over his college career, Lagat won four Pac-10 championships, the mile and 3,000-meter races at the 1999 National Collegiate Athletic Association (NCAA) Indoor Championships, and the 5,000-meter race at the 1999 NCAA Outdoor Championships; he was named the Mountain Pacific Sports Federation's male athlete of the year three times and reached All-American status nine times in track and twice in cross country.

Lagat graduated from Washington State University in 1999, and the following year, racing for Kenya, he won a bronze medal in the 1,500-meter event at the Sydney Olympics, with a time of 3:32.44 minutes. He continued to prove his prowess, earning a silver medal at the 2001 World Outdoor Championships in the 1,500-meter race, with a time of 3:31.10 minutes, and taking home a World Cup in the 1,500-meter event the year after.

In 2003 Lagat was at the center of what might have become a career-ending scandal. That year he was forced to withdraw from the World Championships after testing positive for erythropoietin (known as EPO), a banned substance that increases endurance by stimulating the growth of red blood cells. His parents, who had traveled from Africa for the first time to see him race, were reportedly devastated. Lagat, who had adamantly maintained his innocence, was exonerated after it was discovered that his urine sample had been improperly stored during a heat wave, skewing the results. His second urine sample came back clean. Lagat has described the period between the two tests as among the bleakest of his life, and he later unsuccessfully sought compensation from the IAAF on the grounds that he had been unable to compete in several lucrative meets during his suspension.

Lagat's fears that the EPO incident and ensuing legal battles might damage his reputation with fans proved to be unfounded. In January 2004, at a meet in Boston, Massachusetts, the crowd greeted him warmly. "I was expecting people to boo, to say, 'There's the druggie,'" Lagat told Cyphers. "But they cheered so much. For months I'd been wondering, Why did this happen to me? I was contemplating quitting. But they welcomed me like they would an American. I almost cried."

Lagat became an American citizen on May 7, 2004, after which he faced dire logistical problems. The government of Kenya does not acknowledge dual citizenship and strips its natives of their Kenyan citizenship when they become nationalized in other countries; additionally, the Olympic Charter requires athletes to be citizens of the countries they represent. Lagat had not expected to be awarded American citizenship until well after the 2004 Games, in Athens, but the process went quickly, leaving him technically unable to compete for either country. (A period of three years must pass before an athlete competes for his or her new country, unless a waiver is granted by the country of origin; Kenyan sports officials refused Lagat such a waiver.)

Ultimately, Lagat did not announce his change in citizenship, and he competed in the Games as a Kenyan. He reasoned that that decision did not compromise his interests, since he had not undertaken the change for purely financial reasons, unlike many of his fellow Kenyan runners, who changed their citizenship in order to race under the flags of oil-rich Gulf states. He told Ted Robbins for the National Public Radio show *Morning Edition* (June 23, 2008, on-line), "I just wanted to raise my family here, live here, work here and, you know, just be one of the American people."

The 2004 Olympics provided an abundance of drama for track-and-field fans. During the second heat of the 1,500-meter event, Lagat was clipped by an American competitor, Alan Webb, 300 meters from the finish line. Lagat's shoe was partially dislodged from his foot, and he struggled awkwardly with it for several meters before managing to kick it off entirely. He finished the heat in second place, behind the Spanish racer Reyes Estevez.

Lagat's greatest rival during the Games was arguably Morocco's Hicham el-Guerrouj. In August 2004, shortly before the two met in Athens, they had competed at the Weltklasse Zurich, an annual event held in Switzerland. Lagat, running the fastest 1,500-meter event recorded that year, with a time of 3:27.40, had defeated el-Guerrouj, who had won the Weltklasse Zurich in each of the previous seven years. (Lagat's victory in Zurich was not ratified as an American record because of his citizenship complications.) The Moroccan runner triumphed during the Olympics, however, becoming the first athlete since 1924 to take home gold medals in both the 1,500-meter and 5,000-meter races. In the 1,500-meter race, el-Guerrouj beat Lagat by just .12 seconds; most sports observers called the match one of the most exciting of the Athens Games. Lagat was exceptionally gracious in his defeat, telling reporters that el-Guerrouj was an inspiration to him. Lagat recalled to Cyphers, "I ran the smartest race I've ever run. It was two good athletes at their best, neck to neck, stride for stride. What more could you ask? Can you imagine what it took for him to dig and find an extra gear to pass me? It wasn't just anybody who beat me. It was Hicham, maybe the greatest ever."

Later in 2004 Lagat won the 3,000-meter race at the World Indoor Championships, with a time of 7:56.34. That marked the start of a winning streak that continued at the Powered by Tyson Invitational in Fayetteville, Arkansas, on February 11, 2005, when he charted a record-breaking 3:33.34 for the 1,500 meters, en route to a record-breaking 3:49.89 finish for the indoor mile. In August 2005 he set a new U.S. record in a 1,500-meter race in Rieti, Italy, with a time of 2:29.30. (In determining eligibility for setting a national record, the governing body for U.S. track-and-field events requires only that an athlete be an American citizen competing in a sanctioned race.)

In June 2006, at his U.S. Outdoor Championships debut, Lagat racked up a double victory, winning both the 1,500-meter race (with a time of 3:39.29) and the 5,000-meter race (with a time of 13:14.32). He told a reporter for the Associated Press (June 26, 2006) that he was initially unaware of the historic nature of that accomplishment: "It means a lot. I didn't know that nobody had done it [before at the U.S. nationals]. . . . This is my first nationals, and I'm proud to be here."

Lagat became eligible to compete for the United States in international track events the night before the 2007 IAAF World Track and Field Championships, in Osaka, Japan. There, he had a surprise victory, coming from behind during the last 100 meters of the 1,500-meter event and defeating Alan Webb with a time of 3:34.77. His win marked the first time in almost a century that an American had captured the gold medal in a major, international 1,500-meter race. As he ran a victory lap, Lagat shouted repeatedly, "I did this for America." Lagat also won the 5,000-meter race at the World Championships, making him the first athlete of any nationality ever to win a double victory at the event. Watching back in Kenya, his extended family began screaming so excitedly that neighbors came to see what was happening.

At the Olympic trials held in July 2008 in Eugene, Oregon, Lagat won both the 5,000-meter and 1,500-meter qualifying races. (He was the only runner to win two qualifiers.) The other top-three qualifiers in the 1,500-meter race, Leonel Manzano and Lopez Lomong, were also naturalized American citizens. Lagat told Steve Kelley for the Seattle Times (July 7, 2008), "It shows that America is the place where dreams can happen. I can't find that in Europe, or in my [native] country. The three of us are living the American dream."

Because of Lagat's double victories in Japan and Oregon, speculation reached a fever pitch that he would take home two gold medals from China. No U.S. Olympian had won the 5,000-meter event since 1964, and no U.S. competitor had ever won both the 5,000 and the 1,500 during the Games. (Only Paavo Nurmi of Finland and el-Guerrouj had accomplished the double win, in 1924 and 2004, respectively.) "Bernard proved in Osaka, thanks to determination and passion, that he can do it," the now-retired el-Guerrouj said, according to Runner's World (April 21, 2008, on-line). "Before, his problem was that he didn't believe it, but now he thinks he can." Frank Litsky wrote for the New York Times (June 29, 2008), "Bernard Lagat's quest seems almost too ambitious. . . . It sounds like a pipe dream, but he achieved that double in last year's world championships in Osaka, so why not again?" Lagat's sister Mary told Jere Longman for the New York Times (May 19, 2008), "When he is running, I will feel like I am running. If he gets the gold medal, I'll get the gold medal."

Crushing such hopes, Lagat finished sixth in the second of two heats and missed qualifying for the 1,500-meter event by two-100ths of a second.

"From the first round," David Epstein wrote for Sports Illustrated (August 17, 2008, on-line), "the savvy veteran who appeared to effortlessly vanquish the competition at the U.S. Trials just did not look like his light-footed self. . . . Lagat, who usually floats past the finish line wearing a smile the size of . . . Arizona, was visibly straining as he leaned for the line and practically stumbled across it. After the race, [he] had no excuses, and no explanation. 'My workouts have been fine, the heat was not a problem, the food has been fine,' Lagat said. 'I gave everything I had.'" Lagat made it to the finals of the 5,000-meter race, but, running with a sore Achilles tendon and a throat infection, he finished ninth, with a time of 13:26.89.

On August 31, 2008 Lagat won the 1,000-meter event at the British Grand Prix in Gateshead, England, with a personal-best time of two minutes, 16.18 seconds. "I was injured three weeks before the [Olympic] Games," Lagat told an interviewer for the Seattle Times (September 1, 2008). "I had problems with my Achilles tendon, so this makes up for that. Now I'm looking forward to the rest of the season. I intend to go out there and show everyone I can still run fast over 1,500 meters."

In 2004 Lagat, whose family had struggled to pay for his education when he was a child, started a foundation that provides the school fees each year for 20 Kenyan students, based on their academic merit. He lives in Tucson, Arizona, with his wife, Gladys Tom, a nutritionist. The pair met at Washington State University and moved to Tucson in 2002, when Lagat's longtime coach, James Li, took a job at the University of Arizona. Lagat and Tom, who is a Canadian of Chinese descent, have a young son, Miika. The athlete is, by all accounts, a doting father. When not training, he delights in working on his home and having barbecues. Cyphers wrote, "Except for his lack of a beer belly, Lagat is the picture of the comfortable suburban dad."

—T.O.

Suggested Reading: Arizona Republic p1 July 2, 2008; Houston Chronicle p9 June 26, 2006; Indianapolis Star C p9 June 25, 2006; Los Angeles Times p5 Feb. 23, 2002; New York Times D p1 June 24, 2008; Runner's World (on-line) Apr. 21, 2008; Seattle Times C p1 July 7, 2008; USA Today C p7 Aug. 30, 2007; Washington Post E p1 Aug. 30, 2007

Lane, Anthony

Dec. 5, 1962– Film critic

Address: New Yorker, *4 Times Sq., New York, NY 10036*

Very few film critics have seen their work read for its own sake, regardless of the material they review. Among that select group is the British-born Anthony Lane, one of most respected contemporary movie critics, popular with audiences and filmmakers alike. A reviewer for the *New Yorker* magazine since 1993, Lane is known for his trenchant humor, erudition, and tendency to transcend the borders separating "high" from "low" art. As Nicolas Lezard wrote for the London *Guardian* (November 15, 2003): "If the film is good art, or a delight, Lane will communicate precisely, concisely and illuminatingly the relevant merits; if the film sucks, he has some fun." Observers have noted that Lane's reviews are often more engaging and entertaining than the movies he discusses. Recognized for what many have described as his enthralling lead paragraphs, Lane has developed a recognizable, celebrated style of writing that is also sometimes seen as his principal weakness: he has occasionally been criticized, mostly by those who subscribe to more academic and theoretical discussions of cinema, as self-promoting and lacking in substance. On the other hand, he has been praised for his ability to provide a broader cultural context for film viewing by infusing his work with references to literature, art, history, and politics; maintaining his critical detachment by ignoring the marketing campaigns and other hype surrounding a given release; and consistently delivering intelligent and incisive accounts of the wide variety of films he reviews. Little of a personal nature was known publicly about Lane, who still lives in England, until the publication of *Nobody's Perfect* (2002), the well-received anthology of his writings on both film and literature for the *New Yorker*. While even that book did not offer much biographical information, it included a photograph of the writer and the year of his birth, surprising the many people who had assumed that Lane, then 40, was a much older man. Tom Beer wrote for *Newsday* (September 29, 2002), "Lane's dry wit and classy tastes suggested a septuagenarian who had seen better cinematic days and looked on present-day Hollywood flounderings with bemusement."

Anthony Lane was born on December 5, 1962 in the United Kingdom. As a child he lived in England, Ireland, and Germany when his father, a British army officer, was stationed in those countries. After attending boarding schools, he enrolled at Cambridge University's Trinity College, where he studied English literature. In an interview with Robert Birnbaum for the literary Web site Identity Theory (October 3, 2002), Lane referred to "that thing that one does around college time—when one grows older you don't physically have the time for—which is when you are discovering [an author] and you are just ravenous and you [read all of that author's books]." Discussing the work of novelists he explored, he added, " I did all of [Elmore] Leonard and then I had a [Raymond] Chandler kick and a [Vladimir] Nabokov kick and then other people, some of whom I was told to read at college. The pleasure of being able to feast upon the writers you love, or the directors that you suddenly become obsessed by—that is probably harder in college now. When I was at Cambridge in England in the '80s they still had nice scratchy old prints of these [films] that were going around the college clubs and you would go to the art cinema and you would see triple bills of [Ingmar] Bergman and [Jean] Renoir and [Howard] Hawks and it was sometimes rather grim going—especially if it was Bergman—but you got the homework done, you started to populate the hinterland."

After graduating, in 1984, Lane moved to London, England, where he "failed instantly and almost impressively to get a job," as he told Beer. He then returned to Cambridge for a couple of years to pursue graduate work on the writings of the poet and critic T. S. Eliot. Back in London Lane found work as a freelance writer and book reviewer for the *Independent* newspaper and quickly built a reputation as a rising talent. In 1989—three years after the *Independent* was founded—he became the paper's deputy literary editor, and in 1991 he was appointed film critic for the *Independent on Sunday*. An article in the London *Daily Telegraph* (December 14, 2003) described Lane as "one of the literary-minded graduates who made the *Independent* superior reading in its early days." Lane himself has often been critical of British journalism. "I associate mean-spirited journalism with England.

That's what we do, that's what we're good at," he told Birnbaum. "It almost lives to be vicious, that almost is its point. It's particularly scathing of anyone who has had the temerity to do well in any field. It presumes that the only possible consequence of success is to fail." He concluded, with regard to his move to the *New Yorker*, "The pleasure of getting out of British journalism cannot be overstated." In the introduction to *Nobody's Perfect*, Lane wrote that one of the benefits of getting a job at the *New Yorker* was that he "no longer felt the slightest compunction to bang the drum for British cinema, an activity only slightly more useful than arguing the case for a fleet of Swiss submarines." (He lamented to Birnbaum that the French filmmakers Renoir, François Truffaut, and Jean-Luc Godard "looked at America, loved the films there and ploughed that love and knowledge back into French films. No one did that in England.")

In 1993, looking for a writer to succeed perhaps the most famous and influential American film critic of all time—Pauline Kael, who had retired from the *New Yorker* two years earlier—the magazine's ambitious new editor, Tina Brown, asked Lane to take on that daunting job. In the introduction to his book, Lane recalled the moment Brown contacted him: "I was sitting in London when the call came from Tina's office; I think I actually *stood up* to receive it, much as I would if a letter had come from the Vatican." His assignment at the weekly publication would be to deliver a review every other week (he would alternate with David Denby, the magazine's other in-house movie critic); in off-weeks, he could write about his other interests, ranging from literature to photography and people deemed worthy of in-depth profiles.

Lane's well-received, 752-page book, *Nobody's Perfect* (whose title was taken from the last line of the Billy Wilder film *Some Like It Hot*), is a collection of the first decade of his work for the *New Yorker*. Lane, who writes mostly at night, explained his technique to Birnbaum: "I wait till peace and quiet and write as I go. I don't enjoy writing. I enjoy rewriting. I like editing myself down. It is journalism. I'm not sitting there waiting for the muse to descend. I'm lucky I have subjects." In his interview with the *Telegraph*, he elaborated: "People think that you have these things called ideas and that writing is a matter of imposing them on the subject material, whereas it's only in the writing that I discover what it is that I think. And I can only write to deadline. I can't do the blank sheet. You know, 'Chapter One: he adored New York . . .'" He added, "I'm not a creative writer. I don't write poetry or novels or drama but criticism, which is the eunuch of the family." As many reviewers have noted, writing for the *New Yorker* allows Lane to display his talents fully, as most critics are much more constrained than he is in terms of time and space. "Lane doesn't write from the boilerplate that confines so many of his brethren," Edward Guthmann wrote for the *San Francisco Chronicle* (September 1, 2002). "There's a contract among U.S. journalists and the editors who process their copy, an agreement that one shouldn't wax too fancy or arcane; that one will not presume too high a level of cultural literacy on the reader's part; that 'big' words will be torpedoed in favor of simple, direct language. Lane . . . understands that gorgeous, expressive language isn't necessarily murky or difficult to read."

Lane's writing style has been described as a mixture of sardonic wit and understatement, and while he is known largely for his humorously devastating takes on some films, as Ian Thomson wrote for the London *Spectator* (November 30, 2002), "the ribbing is done in a spirit of knockabout showmanship rather than spite." For example, in his *New Yorker* (June 4, 2001) review of the Michael Bay film *Pearl Harbor*, starring Ben Affleck as Rafe and Kate Beckinsale as Evelyn, Lane wrote that the movie "tells a tale familiar to every child in America: how a great nation was attacked and humbled by the imperious pride of Ben Affleck. . . . As Pearl Harbor lay smoldering, and the triumphant Japanese admiral uttered the words 'I fear all we have done is to awaken a sleeping giant,' I got up to leave. After all, that was pretty much the line that brought [the World War II drama] *Tora! Tora! Tora!* to a close. Then I glanced at my watch, sighed, and sat down again; forty-five minutes still to go, and we're off into an entirely new narrative, with Alec Baldwin recruiting the boys for yet another mission. 'Do you know what top secret is?' he asks—the second-best question of the film, topped only when Evelyn finds Rafe packing a suitcase, and, quick as a flash, says, 'Packing?'" Lane was equally unsparing in his critique of the George Lucas film *Star Wars: Episode III—Revenge of the Sith* (May 23, 2005): "The general opinion of *Revenge of the Sith* seems to be that it marks a distinct improvement on the last two episodes, *The Phantom Menace* and *Attack of the Clones*. True, but only in the same way that dying from natural causes is preferable to crucifixion."

Perhaps surprisingly, given the sophistication of his writing, Lane is as likely to review and praise a "trashy" blockbuster film as an intellectual art-house one, arguing that most movies that are seen as classics today were dismissed as mere popular entertainment when they were first released. As biting as his humor can be, Lane has suggested that he considers pronouncing a verdict on a given film to be his least important function; he sees his job, rather, as describing the experience of watching the film. He has expressed the hope that readers will turn to his book not for his judgments of films but as a way to "summon the era in which these movies were being put out and received and watched." In that spirit he has recommended that critics either review films immediately upon release or wait "fifty years," as he told Birnbaum, to "cast a cold eye." Lane is also known for often going against conventional wisdom about movies, distancing himself in his analyses from the general acclaim or popularity of a given film. His critique of the hugely successful 1994 film *Forrest Gump*, the story of a retarded man set against the backdrop of historic events of the second half of the 20th century, is instructive in that regard; he lambasted the movie, which won six Academy Awards. "It's a film that tells you not to worry about anything . . . ," he told fellow panel members on the television program *Crossfire* (February 14, 1995). "I don't think it's the business of motion pictures to legislate for the morals of the nation, and this picture tells you how to think. It tells you not to think certain things. It tells you to sweep through life, don't notice what is going on around you. . . . It's the first movie that actually encourages the audience to become mentally challenged themselves."

Lane has won praise not only from readers and fellow critics but from movie directors and others in the filmmaking industry. As the show-business publication *Daily Variety* (March 15, 2000) reported, in a poll of film-industry heavyweights who excoriated movie critics in general, Lane was the only reviewer to score highly when judged on "film literacy, reliability, verisimilitude and quality of writing." As Chris Garcia wrote for the *Austin American-Statesman* (November 3, 2002), several top directors count Lane as their favorite critic. Garcia also, however, quoted some of Lane's detractors, writing that he is "something of a lightweight in the eyes of more academic-minded film critics. Venom is frequently flung from pedants such as the *Chicago Reader*'s Jonathan Rosenbaum, who has dismissed Lane as a 'stand-up comedian,' and former *New York Press* critic Godfrey Cheshire, who called Lane's prose 'gaseous and cute' and Lane himself 'the most embarrassing high-profile film writer in the United States.'" One of the strongest rebukes has come from John Powers in *LA Weekly* (September 11, 2002), who wrote, "The aristocratic ease that makes Lane so pleasurable to read is inseparable from his limitations. Caught up in the dazzling virtuosity of his leaps and twirls, he rarely breaks through the ice to see what might be swimming around in the chilly deep below; he never forces us to see a director in a brand-new way. He's the ideal reviewer for today's denatured Hollywood product . . . because very little is at stake in his work beyond the splendors of his own performance." Powers lamented the passing of the torch from such figures as Kael and Andrew Sarris to Lane because, he argued, Lane is less passionate about movies than his predecessors and is "far more deeply engaged by books, but he's canny enough to know there's more glory and dough in writing about movies." Similarly, in an otherwise glowing review of *Nobody's Perfect* for the *New York Times Book Review* (September 1, 2002), in which she referred to Lane's "infernally contagious" writing style, Laura Miller wrote, "It's impossible to imagine anyone sensible . . . banging his head over an Anthony Lane review the way people often did over Kael's; there just isn't that much at stake. This difference is partly the result of Kael writing during a period of great movie-

making (Lane has less to work with), but it's also because she was American and therefore inclined to take both movies and her own opinions in deadly earnest." Miller went on to ask: "Why is this man . . . reviewing movies? Not once did his film reviews have me wondering how late the video store stays open, but I could not read him on the writers he loves without being seized with a desire to read them too." In fact, though he has written in-depth profiles of filmmakers, among them Alfred Hitchcock, Luis Buñuel, and Billy Wilder, some of his strongest pieces, according to reviewers, have been examinations of works by such literary icons as Nabokov, Eliot, Evelyn Waugh, P. G. Wodehouse, Andre Gide, and Shakespeare.

Lane continues to fill his sometimes devastating *New Yorker* film critiques with humor. "Like many people, I was under the impression that the new Meryl Streep film was called *Mamma Mia*. The correct title is, in fact, *Mamma Mia!*, and, in one keystroke, the exclamation mark tells you all you need to know about the movie . . . ," he wrote in his July 28, 2008 review of the film, which co-stars Pierce Brosnan. "From the opening minutes, in which Sophie (Amanda Seyfried), a young pleasure seeker on the eve of her wedding, greets her two bridesmaids as they arrive on a jetty, yelping with delight like unweaned puppies, you can tell that everyone in this story is just going to have the *best* time. *Ever*. Sophie resides on a Greek island— an island like any other, where gnarled old ladies drop whatever they're doing in the olive grove and tunefully join in on nineteen-seventies Swedish pop songs. She lives there with her mother, Donna (Meryl Streep), who has been running a shabby hotel for many years, and who wears dungarees to signal her lack of reliance on a man." Later in the piece Lane described his reaction to some of what he saw as the more forced musical sequences in the film: "The legal definition of torture has been much aired in recent years, and I take *Mamma Mia!* to be a useful contribution to that debate. . . . I thought that Pierce Brosnan had been dragged to the edge of endurance by North Korean sadists in his final [James] Bond film, *Die Another Day*, but that was a quick tickle with a feather duster compared with the agony of singing Abba's 'S.O.S.' to Meryl Streep through a kitchen window. . . . There is no delicate way of putting this, but anyone watching Brosnan in mid-delivery will conclude that he has recently suffered from a series of complex digestive problems, and that the camera has, with unfortunate timing, caught him at the exact moment when he is finally working them out. What has he done to deserve this?"

In 2001 Lane won a Best American Magazine Writing Award, given by the American Society of Magazine Editors, for pieces including "The Maria Problem," about the film *The Sound of Music*; the award was given in the category of reviews and criticism. In the book *The Best American Magazine Writing 2001*, edited by Harold Evans (Tina Brown's husband), which includes "The Maria

Problem," Lane is described as "a rare critic who is unafraid to express, and even instill, delight. His reviews are laugh-out-loud funny, but also insightful and evocative. His stylish prose and pinpoint perceptions make him one of the most elegant writers of our time." In 2008 *Intelligent Life*, the lifestyle magazine of the *Economist*, named Lane one of the top 30 critics in the world. Lane is married to the well-known British journalist and bestselling novelist Allison Pearson. The couple have two children and live in England.

—M.M.

Suggested Reading: *identitytheory.com* Oct. 3, 2002; *LA Weekly* (on-line) Sep. 11, 2002; (London) *Daily Telegraph* p21 Nov. 22, 2002; (Long Island, New York) *Newsday* D p31 Sep. 29, 2002; *New York Times* (on-line) Sep. 1, 2002

Selected Books: *Nobody's Perfect: Writings from The New Yorker*, 2002

Bryan Bedder/Getty Images

Letts, Tracy

July 4, 1965– Playwright; actor

Address: Steppenwolf Theatre Co., 1650 N. Halsted St., Chicago, IL 60614

"Countless American playwrights have mined pain and pathos, but [Tracy] Letts . . . is today's most explosive extractor," Patrick Healy wrote for the *New York Times* (July 20, 2008). "He has written just five plays in 18 years, yet those five contain enough damage for a lifetime oeuvre." An actor as well as a writer, Tracy Letts is the author of the plays *Killer Joe, Bug, Man from Nebraska, August: Osage County*—which won the Pulitzer Prize for drama and the Tony Award for best play in 2008—and *Superior Donuts*. His main characters include a Texas trailer-park drug dealer, a paranoid Gulf War veteran squatting in an Oklahoma motel, a middle-aged family man from Nebraska, and a cancer-ridden mother of three in Oklahoma. "I'm not as good a playwright as Tom Stoppard, I don't know as many words as Richard Greenberg, and I'm not as smart as Tony Kushner," Letts told Mary Houlihan for the *Chicago Sun-Times* (November 21, 2003). "But I write what I like, what I think about. I'm more interested in writing characters who don't have a great facility for language, who are a bit more everyday. I find them ultimately more interesting. How do these people express themselves? That's what intrigues me. And I think there is a place for this sort of dialogue on stage." Letts has been a member of the Steppenwolf Theatre Company, in Chicago, Illinois, since 2002.

The youngest of three brothers, Tracy Letts was born on July 4, 1965 to Dennis and Billie (Gipson) Letts in Tulsa, Oklahoma. His siblings are Shawn, a jazz musician, and Dana, a technical-support specialist at an Oklahoma state-university library. His father, an educator and actor, taught English at the college level, mostly at Southeastern Oklahoma State University, in Durant. His mother taught journalism at the same school. Billie Letts has written four novels; one of them, *Where the Heart Is* (1998), was chosen for Oprah's Book Club and was made into a 2000 film starring Natalie Portman and Ashley Judd. Dennis Letts acted in that and in more than 40 other films for TV and the silver screen as well as in university and community theatrical productions; for almost three months before his death, in February 2008, he also played the part of Beverly Weston, the father, in *August: Osage County* on Broadway.

When Tracy Letts was three, his family lived in Champaign, Illinois, where his father was pursuing a doctorate; his mother worked as a high-school teacher in a nearby town. That year he was the object of what may have been an aborted abduction: as his mother recalled to an interviewer for the Web site *Readers Read* (2004), a woman posing as Billie Letts telephoned the manager of the day-care center Tracy was attending and said that a family emergency made it necessary for him to be picked up outside the school immediately. After he waited on a swing in the center's playground for a half hour, Tracy, feeling cold, returned to the classroom, where his mother came for him at the usual time. The police never determined the identity of the imposter.

In first grade, Letts told Patrick Healy, he wrote a story called "The Psychopath." "The cover showed a man hanging in the closet, and he had also shot himself in the head," Letts recalled. As a youngster he became an avid moviegoer; accompanied by his parents, he watched films usually deemed unsuitable for children, such as *Serpico.* "The only movie we left was *Taxi Driver,*" he said to Healy. "The only reason we left was because we were in the drive-in, and so we were in a car, and [my parents] were feeling very uncomfortable." He later read published versions of *Who's Afraid of Virginia Woolf?* and other plays in his father's collection. As a child his brother Shawn would direct plays in which Tracy participated and always insisted that Tracy say his lines and follow stage directions perfectly.

When Tracy Letts was 10, his maternal grandfather committed suicide, and after his death Letts's grandmother became addicted to drugs. Periodically, she would be found unconscious on the street and then institutionalized, "smuggl[ing] pills into the hospital by hiding them in her vagina," as Healy reported. At his mother's behest, Letts once filmed his grandmother in her hospital room with his Super 8 movie camera. "The film is this . . . old lady in bed talking nonsense," Letts told Healy. "It's got to be the most depressing three minutes ever shot." He also recalled, "One day, when my mother wasn't around, my dad finally said to my grandmother: 'Please, please kill yourself with these pills. You're destroying my wife's life.'"

Letts told Healy that with adolescence he changed from "eager-to-please kid into tortured teenager—girls, drugs, depression, hormones." At age 15 he got his first role at a community theater near Durant: the director wanted Dennis Letts to accept a part and cast Tracy as a way of enticing his father to join the ensemble. Letts later won parts in productions of plays including Israel Horovitz's *The Indian Wants the Bronx* and Thornton Wilder's *The Skin of Our Teeth.* After he graduated from Durant High School, he spent one term at Southeastern Oklahoma State University before quitting. During that semester, he told Healy, he indulged in "a lot of drugs and drinking." Letts has described himself as a recovering alcoholic. At one time he also smoked a pack of cigarettes daily.

Letts next moved to Dallas, Texas, in search of acting jobs. By age 20 he was living in Chicago, where he took a temp job with an ad agency and at times relied on food stamps to get by. He also became heavily involved with some of the storefront theaters that proliferated in Chicago then, writing scenes for actor friends of his. He briefly tried his luck in Hollywood in the late 1990s before moving back to Chicago, having realized that he preferred to work in theater rather than film or television. He has appeared in a half-dozen films, among them *Paramedics* (1987) and *Guinevere* (1999), and on a few TV shows, among them installments of *Home Improvement,* in 1995, *Seinfeld,* in 1997, and *The Drew Carey Show,* in 1998. Letts has attributed much of his success as a playwright to his experiences as an actor, when he must "really crawl inside" a part and "see how it works," as he told *Time* (June 23, 2008).

In about 1990, inspired in part by a newspaper account of a homicidal family in Florida, Letts wrote *Killer Joe.* In Letts's play the family lives in Texas and consists of a highly dysfunctional father and stepmother, Ansel and Sharla, and Ansel's son, Chris, and daughter, Dottie, from a previous marriage. Chris is a drug pusher; other dealers, to whom he owes $6,000, have threatened to kill him. Chris decides that his only alternative is to have his biological mother murdered, so as to obtain the money from her life-insurance policy. Chris and Ansel hire a corrupt Dallas police officer—Killer Joe—to murder her, using Chris's 20-year-old sister, a virgin, as a "retainer." Discussing the play with Kate Kellaway, a writer with the London *Observer* (March 5, 1995), Letts explained, "Violence in *Killer Joe* has become a means of self-expression; the characters are spiritually starved, the world they live in is spiritually desolate. They have never read a book. They have grown up in a culture of poverty, drugs, cheap sex and violence." The British director Wilson Milam staged its premier production, in 1993, at the Next Lab Theatre, in Chicago, and then brought the play to the Traverse Theatre, in Edinburgh, Scotland, where it won the Scotsman Fringe First Award; it has since been presented in more than two dozen countries in nearly as many languages.

In a *New York Times* (October 19, 1998) review of a production of *Killer Joe* directed by Milam at the SoHo Playhouse, in New York City, where it ran for nine months, Ben Brantley described the work as "compellingly watchable, a pungent reminder that characters in the theater don't have to be poetic or even passionate to hold your interest." "Life may be sloppy and squalid in *Killer Joe*, but it is presented with surgical precision," Brantley continued. "The material could easily register as white-trash Gothic with a comic-book spin, a sort of *Tobacco Road* according to Wes Craven. Yet while *Killer Joe* is often deeply funny, it is cheap in neither its humor nor its shock effects, some of which run to the X-rated. This is partly because Mr. Letts's Texas trailer-park dialogue sounds so natural, only occasionally straining for effect. . . . Mr. Letts isn't serving two-ton moral themes. *Killer Joe* is no sign-waving study in the banality of evil or even the evil of banality. But it does present a portrait of a purely American world that is so numbed out that carnage fits comfortably into the everyday domestic landscape. It's a hazy environment in which violence on television and violence in life have bled into a single, continuing drone." In a critique of a more recent production mounted at the Magic Theatre, in San Francisco, California, Michael Wade Simpson wrote for culturevulture.net (June 16, 2006), "Trailers and 'trailer trash' are, in and of themselves, a kind of stale, classist joke, so just the choice of milieu places the play's author . . . in a risky place. However, the narrative journey from the first whiff of black comedy to a jaw-dropping, gut-grabbing hilariously sick climax is handled masterfully." Among those who responded less enthusiastically was Misha Berson, the *Seattle Times* (April 13, 2001) theater critic, who wrote, "In its own shameless, sometimes hilarious and occasionally chilling fashion, this well-traveled Tracy Letts potboiler is another American foray into pulp satire—that is, taking our worst national traits and supersizing them. . . . Letts knows how to structure a thriller, and he also has a smart ear for dialogue. Some of his tastier Harold Pinter-meets-Quentin Tarantino exchanges achieve a hard-boiled American absurdism that's both funny and eerie. But occasionally, *Killer Joe* reaches for psychological resonance, and there it falters. The dialogue gives rather clunky hints of harrowing, Oprah-esque childhood traumas." Berson concluded, "One probably shouldn't read too much into this little thriller, after the laughter fades. . . . It's really part of that hardy American tradition of taking sleaze to the extreme." The text of *Killer Joe* is contained in the book *New Playwrights: The Best Plays of 1998* (2000).

Letts's next play, *Bug*, premiered in 1994 at the Gate Theatre, in London, under the direction of Wilson Milam. The action takes place in a dingy room in a rundown motel on the outskirts of Oklahoma City, where Agnes, a divorced waitress who uses cocaine as well as alcohol to dull her painful memories, has fled from her abusive ex-husband, who is soon to be released from prison. Through a lesbian friend of hers, Agnes meets Peter, a handsome, homeless veteran of the 1991 Gulf War. Peter moves in with Agnes, sleeping at first on the floor and then joining her in bed. He soon expresses his conviction that their room is infested with bugs released in a conspiracy plotted by the ambiguous Them. In Act II Agnes has become as paranoid as he is. "Letts is amusing in showing how paranoia can spread so quickly, particularly among the loveless and the loopy; the scene in which Peter thinks he has discovered the source of his bug is delightfully grotesque," a *Boston Globe* (June 12, 2002) reviewer wrote. "Still, this is a shallow and barely coherent analysis of paranoia. And the laughs are far enough apart that it lacks the visceral punch of *Killer Joe*. Letts feels more at home, or says he does, with poor folk than rich ones, and the lack of sentimentality in his palette is commendable. But because he draws them as so obviously delusional, there's nothing particularly interesting about their plight." By contrast, a production of *Bug* at the Curious Theatre, in Denver, Colorado, struck Katharine Swan, writing for *L.A. Splash* (October 30, 2005, on-line), as "an unforgettable exploration of the madness and fear that plague conspiracy theorists. . . . The degeneration of the characters creates a compelling web that ensnares the audience as dysfunction turns, suddenly and explosively, to insanity." At the beginning of the play's 11-month run at the Barrow Street Theatre, in New York City, Ben Brantley wrote for the *New York Times* (March 1, 2004), "The visceral wallop of *Bug* is likely to come as a shock even to fans of Mr. Letts' *Killer Joe*. . . . While it could hardly be de-

scribed as understated, *Bug* has a subtlety and sureness of composition that testifies to top-flight craftsmanship. Mr. Letts, in other words, is much more than a shock artist, although if you're in a mood for cheap thrills, he provides plenty of those too." Elyse Sommer, who also saw the Barrow Street Theatre production, wrote for *Curtain Up* (2004, on-line), "Letts has been quoted as seeing characters like Peter as the unhealthy manifestation of healthy paranoia about powerful institutions' activities. The young Frankenstein antics in *Bug* could certainly prompt sober reflection on a world in which too many young men are killed and mentally as well as physically maimed—as exemplified by Gulf War veteran Peter's delusions. That said, don't scratch that itch to look for deep meanings but just grab the edge of your seat and indulge the guilty pleasure of following Letts do his takes on *Marathon Man* and *Psycho*, and gleefully pile incredibility upon incredibility for a final crescendo of kitschy theatricality." The director William Friedkin, working from Letts's screenplay, made a film of *Bug* (2006), starring Ashley Judd, Michael Shannon, and Harry Connick Jr. The motion picture won an award from the International Federation of Film Critics (known as FIPRESCI, from the organization's French name) at the 2006 Cannes Film Festival. In the U.S., much to Letts's dismay, it was marketed as a horror film, thus disappointing fans of the horror genre and failing to attract moviegoers interested in well-crafted psychological character studies.

The protagonist of *Man from Nebraska* (2003) is Ken Carpenter, a middle-aged insurance salesman whose marriage has degenerated into a relationship marked mostly by unemotional civility. Greatly distressed by his sudden loss of faith in God, Ken follows the advice of his pastor and travels alone to England, which he remembers fondly from his time in the military. His friendship with Tamyra, a black barmaid who works at his hotel, and her boyfriend, Harry, a sculptor, help Ken emerge from his spiritual crisis and reach out to his wife and daughter with new understanding. *Man from Nebraska* premiered at the Steppenwolf Theatre in late 2003. It was a finalist for the Pulitzer Prize for drama in 2004, and *Time* named it one of the 10 best plays of 2003. Reviews of the play were decidedly mixed, however. Among those who admired *Man from Nebraska* was Hedy Weiss, who described it in a review for the *Chicago Sun-Times* (December 1, 2003) as a "beautifully observed tale of seemingly ordinary souls at bay" and "a tremendously mature and multifaceted portrait of the American psyche at large in the world at the dawn of the 21st century." Other critics complained that *Man from Nebraska* was overly simplistic. Paul Hodgins, for example, the reviewer for the *Orange County (California) Register* (March 20, 2006), who saw the play performed by the South Coast Repertory, in Costa Mesa, California, in 2006, declared, "Letts is no match for the other playwrights who have examined the dark, unknowable depths of human longing. . . . You leave *Man from Nebraska* with the feeling that Letts has manipulated character and plot lines for the sake of an uplifting and conventional ending, ignoring a more emotionally complex and honest story in the process. To some (especially Midwesterners), the result might seem patronizing."

In the prologue to *August: Osage County* (2007), the alcoholic father, Beverly Weston, a would-be poet and retired professor who likes to quote the poet T. S. Eliot, hires a young Native American woman to care for him and his drug-addicted, alcoholic, acid-tongued wife, who has mouth cancer. In Act I, Beverly mysteriously disappears, and Violet has summoned her three adult daughters to come home to help look for him and comfort her—which entails being subjected to her vicious barbs. As described by Peter Marks in a critique of the play for the *Washington Post* (December 13, 2007), Violet is "so scabrous you could imagine her reducing Martha to tears in the first minutes of *Who's Afraid of Virginia Woolf?*" All of the daughters are psychologically damaged and involved with men "who have cheated on them, plan on cheating or are unsuited to them in ways that will be revealed as just plain unappetizing," in Marks's words. In addition to a Pulitzer Prize and a Tony Award, *August: Osage County* won the New York Drama Critics' Circle and Drama Desk Awards for best play. Nevertheless, its critical reception ranged from ecstatic to dismissive. Representative of the latter was that of Peter Marks (who chaired the Pulitzer Prize jury that chose the play as the year's best): "For all its spiritual and literary pretensions . . . ," he wrote in his review, "*August: Osage County* proves to be a disappointingly hollow experience. After three hours and 20 minutes in the company of Letts's spiteful, bilious, warring clan, there is nothing close to the kind of shattering payoff that you anticipate from a work of this scale and ambition. You're worn down by the sheer volume of revelation, and ultimately, by the ordinariness of what's revealed." Hilton Als, the reviewer for the *New Yorker* (December 24, 2007), was similarly unimpressed, writing, "The family's secrets feel as contrived as the play's regionalism—a corny mint julep laced with Valium. Letts, a potentially great writer, is at his most brilliant and intense when he writes small chamber pieces, in which his rough and scary metaphors are in synch with his disillusioned, mad characters. But here, in his Broadway début, he clearly intends to prove himself a 'major' playwright. To do so, he parodies his roots, rather than revealing them. Letts could very well end up winning prizes for *August: Osage County*. But so did the playwright Preston Jones, with his *Texas Trilogy*, in the mid-seventies. Like Letts, Jones was a provincial writer of promise who was pulled onto the Broadway boards too soon for his own good. Now his work is rarely performed at all."

Charles Isherwood, the *New York Times* reviewer, saw the play at its opening, at the Steppenwolf Theatre, in August 2007, and at its Broadway de-

but, the following December, and came away from both stagings highly, if not totally, pleased. "*August: Osage County* is a ripsnorter full of blistering, funny dialogue, acid-etched characterizations and scenes of no-holds-barred emotional combat, but I would not say it possesses the penetrating truth or the revelatory originality of a fully achieved work of art," he wrote in his August 13, 2007 review, concluding, "With this tastily nasty, ferociously enjoyable tale of a family shredded to tatters by inherited legacies of pain and suffering, Mr. Letts appears ready to emerge as a major contender in American playwriting." In his assessment of the Broadway production (December 5, 2007), he raved, "I'd bet the farm that no family has ever been as unhappy in as many ways—and to such sensationally entertaining effect—as the Westons. . . . *August* is probably the most exciting new American play Broadway has seen in years. Oh forget probably: It is, flat-out, no asterisks and without qualifications, the most exciting new American play Broadway has seen in years. Fiercely funny and bitingly sad, this turbo-charged tragi-comedy . . . somehow finds fresh sources of insight, humor, and anguish in seemingly worn-to-the-stump material: the dysfunctional dynamics of the American family. In *August: Osage County* can be heard echoes of other classic dramas about the strangling grip of blood ties—from Eugene O'Neill's *Long Day's Journey into Night* to Sam Shepard's *Buried Child*—but Mr. Letts infuses his dark drama with potent energies derived from two more populist forms of American entertainment. The play has the zip and zingy humor of classic television situation comedy and the absorbing narrative propulsion of a juicy soap opera too."

Superior Donuts (2008) is the first play of Letts's to be set in Chicago. "It began when I realized there were practically no more independently owned doughnut shops on the West Side these days," Letts told Hedy Weiss for *Beacon News Online* (June 29, 2008). The setting of *Superior Donuts* is an old shop in the racially diverse Uptown section of Chicago. It is owned by an elderly Vietnam War draft dodger named Arthur Przybyszewski and is badly in need of refurbishing. Arthur's sole worker, Franco, an energetic black teenager, dreams of modernizing the place. According to *BroadwayWorld.com* (July 25, 2008), the play "explores the challenges of embracing the past and the redemptive power of friendship." *Superior Donuts* premiered on June 19, 2008 at Steppenwolf's Downstairs Theatre, where it ran for two months. The reactions of Chicago critics ranged from lukewarm to highly positive. "I'm expecting *Superior Donuts* to be known as the one after *August*," Letts has said, as the Steppenwolf actress Amy Morton told Patrick Healy.

According to Healy, Letts has "a well-earned dark side that mixes with a surprising sweetness and exuberant humor." Letts's seven-year-long romantic relationship with the actress Holly Wantuch ended with her death, in 1997, from a stroke linked to a congenital heart defect. Letts has made his home in Chicago for nearly two decades. He lives with Nicole Wiesner, an actress. Wiesner appeared in Glen Berger's comic play *Great Men of Science Nos. 21 and 22*, in a production that Letts directed at the Lookingglass Waterworks Theatre, in Chicago, in 2004. She is an artistic associate of the Trap Door Theatre, also in Chicago. Letts's current projects include writing the screenplay for *August: Osage County*; its producers, Jean Doumanian Productions and Steve Traxler, president of Jam Theatricals, are executive producers of the Broadway production.

—T.O.

Suggested Reading: *American Theatre* p42 Sep. 2004; *Chicago Magazine* (on-line) July 2007; *Chicago Sun-Times* p9 Nov. 21, 2003; *Chicago Tribune* C p1 Apr. 8, 2008; *New York Times* E p1 Oct. 19, 1998, (on-line) July 20, 2008; *Readers Read* (on-line) July 2004; *Seattle Times* E p3 Apr. 13, 2001; *Time* p124 June 23, 2008

Selected Plays: *Killer Joe*, 1993; *Bug*, 1994; *Man from Nebraska*, 2003; *August: Osage County*, 2007; *Superior Donuts*, 2008

Selected Films: *Paramedics*, 1987; *Guinevere*, 1999

Courtesy of Janna Levin

Levin, Janna

1968– Astrophysicist; cosmologist; educator; writer

Address: Dept. of Physics and Astronomy, Barnard College of Columbia University, 3009 Broadway, New York, NY 10027

As a specialist in theoretical physics, astronomy, and cosmology, Janna Levin regularly grapples with big questions—so big that they are discussed in terms of light years. Levin, an assistant professor of astronomy and physics at Barnard College, in New York City, uses mathematics to investigate characteristics of the universe, which is believed to stretch nearly 30 billion light years and to contain at least 50,000 billion billion stars—perhaps more than the number of grains of sand on all the beach-

es on Earth. (A light year is the distance that light travels in a single year, nearly six trillion miles.) Inextricably bound to questions about the size, structure, and evolution of the universe is another fundamental question: is the universe finite or infinite? If the universe—or cosmos—is finite, a person in a rocket ship flying from Earth (hypothetically) in only one direction would approach Earth again billions of years later, just as a person walking (hypothetically) in one direction from a starting point in, say, Columbus, Ohio, would eventually arrive back in that city. With few exceptions, physicists and astronomers have long assumed that the universe is infinite, much the way people once believed that the world is flat. One reason for that assumption, at least among 20th- and 21st-century scientists, is connected with the general theory of relativity, which was proposed by Albert Einstein in 1915. According to that extraordinarily revolutionary theory, the gravity of any star, such as the sun, warps space (and time); thus, space (or spacetime, in the lingo of scientists) may be described as curved. That theory was corroborated by an experiment carried out during a solar eclipse in 1919, which showed, precisely as Einstein had predicted, that the gravity of the sun bends, or deflects, light rays from distant stars. The general theory of relativity led, mathematically, to the deduction that the universe is expanding, possibly without limit. Einstein himself, however, did not address the question of whether space is finite or infinite. Levin's research has led her to suggest that a finite universe is not only possible but probable; after all, as she has pointed out, scientists have never found anything in the natural world that appears to be infinite. "A finite universe, and indeed a finite universe with several extra dimensions, may be a prediction of a theory beyond Einstein's—the long coveted Theory of Everything," Levin wrote in a description of her research for her Web site. A physical theory of everything—another of Levin's research interests—is "the greatest ambition consuming theoretical physics," as she wrote. In the 20th century, she continued, the mathematicians and logicians Kurt Gödel and Alan Turing, the latter of whom is considered the father of computer science, and the mathematician and computer scientist Gregory Chaitin "proved that our knowledge of numbers themselves is fundamentally incomplete. . . . There are true relations among the numbers about which we can only prove that we can never prove them. Many times in the history of physics, theories have been shaped by such profound limits"—the limit of the speed of light, for example, and the limits of measurement described by the branch of physics known as quantum mechanics. "Alongside these should be listed the profound incompleteness in our knowledge of numbers—there can never be a mathematical theory of everything." Levin is seeking "to define the limits [that] mathematical incompleteness might set on a physical theory of everything. Just as Relativity emerged from the limit of light's speed and Quantum Theory emerged from the limits of measurement, deep insight into the universe and its origins could emerge by confronting the limit of mathematical incompleteness."

In an interview with David Kestenbaum for the National Public Radio program *Talk of the Nation* (July 12, 2002), Levin said, "Space is the whole story. And that's one of the really tough things to get over when you're first working on general relativity in Einstein's theory, and that is to accept that space is the whole thing. That is the whole universe. It is not expanding into anything. It's the whole story." In addition to her groundbreaking research in cosmology, Levin has written two critically acclaimed books, one a work of nonfiction and the other a novel of ideas. In *How the Universe Got Its Spots: A Diary of a Finite Time in a Finite Space* (2002), presented in the form of unsent letters to her mother, Levin wove descriptions of the cosmos and discussions of her research-related ideas with descriptions of her life in London, England, as a postdoctoral fellow (1999–2003) and her reactions to various personal experiences. For her second book, *A Madman Dreams of Turing Machines: A Story of Coded Secrets and Psychotic Delusions, of Mathematics and War Told by a Physicist Obsessed by the Lives of Turing and Gödel* (2006), she reimagined the lives of Kurt Gödel and Alan Turing. Although the book was heavily based on biographies and other historical accounts, Levin and her publisher chose to classify it as a novel; the book jacket calls it both "completely imagined" and "entirely true." *A Madman Dreams of Turing Machines* brought Levin the 2007 PEN/Robert Bingham fellowship for writers, which honors "an exceptionally talented fiction writer whose debut work represents distinguished literary achievement and suggests great promise," according to the PEN American Center Web site. The novel also won the 2007 Media Ecology Association's Mary Shelley Award for outstanding fictional work and was a runner-up for the PEN/Hemingway Award.

During the 2003–04 academic year, Levin was the first scientist in residence at the Ruskin School of Drawing and Fine Art, as the department of fine art of Oxford University, in England, is known. "There were times when I thought that there's nothing I'd love more than to have become a painter, except I know that if I were a painter I'd be saying to someone, I wish I became a scientist, because I know that when I was exclusively focused on science I've said, I should have been a writer," she acknowledged on her Web site. Levin has maintained that in their quests to uncover truths, the worlds of science and art overlap. "We are in the questions we ask," Levin wrote in an article for *New Scientist* (August 19, 2006). "We are there, implicitly, in the search for meaning. And our stories do matter. Science without storytelling collapses to a set of equations or a ledger full of data. We are after more than that. For all of the respect paid to objectivity, science is ultimately a human endeavor embroiled in our complex themes. Stripping our discoveries of their narrative thread might lubricate scientific progress, but lending our discoveries to fiction gives our suppressed stories a chance to bloom."

The youngest of three sisters, Janna Jhone Levin was born in Texas in 1968 to Richard and Sandy Levin and spent most of her childhood in Chicago, Illinois. She and her sisters were raised to believe that their gender did not limit their opportunities in life. Her father, a surgeon, "was always pointing out women of influence—doctors, politicians, athletes—with admiration. He was entirely disappointed if a girl opted for cheerleading over playing basketball, that sort of thing. My mother was definitely outspoken about women's issues and gender politics," Levin said, as quoted on her Web site. "It was a given that my sisters and I would go to college. It was a given we could do whatever we wanted. No one ever thought, let alone suggested, there was anything we couldn't do on the basis of our gender." (One of Levin's sisters is a veterinarian; the other is a lawyer.) During Levin's junior year of high school, her family moved to Florida, and she began to feel "restless," as she put it on her Web site. On her 17th birthday Levin and a friend of hers were injured when the friend's car tumbled off a footbridge and landed on its roof in a canal. The accident led her to realize that she no longer wanted to remain in her high school. Acting on the advice of one of her teachers, Levin left school before she earned a diploma and enrolled at Barnard College, an all-women's school associated with Columbia University, in New York City. (The two schools are now formally linked.) At Barnard she intended to major in philosophy. An undergraduate course in astronomy led her to change her plans. As she recalled in *How the Universe Got Its Spots*, the professor, Joseph Patterson, "pierced my drowsiness with this one fact: Our bodies are made from elements synthesized in stars. These gloved hands of mine, these gloves, are reshaped atoms made only in the centers of stars. I admit I missed most of what he said before and most of what he said after, but I knew something had shifted for me."

In 1987 Levin won the Henry A. Boorse Prize in Physics, a Barnard award. She graduated from Barnard in 1988 with a B.S. degree in astronomy and physics. She then entered the Massachusetts Institute of Technology (MIT), in Cambridge, Massachusetts, where she earned a Ph.D. in theoretical physics in 1993. Her dissertation was entitled "MAD Gravity and the Early Universe: A Possible New Resolution to the Horizon and Monopole Problems." In the abstract she wrote about the possibility that "the universe grows old while it is still hot. We call this era of prolonged aging the MAD era." As a postdoctoral fellow Levin worked at the Canadian Institute for Theoretical Astrophysics, in Toronto, from 1993 to 1995, and at the Center for Particle Astrophysics at the University of California at Berkeley, from 1995 to 1998. For four years beginning in 1999, she conducted research, wrote papers, and presented talks as an advanced fellow at the Department of Applied Mathematics and Theoretical Physics at Cambridge University, in England. Her boyfriend (and later husband), Warren Malone, a bluegrass musician, handled domestic chores in their warehouse flat in London (a 45-minute train ride from Cambridge), where their neighbors included filmmakers and others active in the arts. Having friends who are artists and musicians "stretches me, so that I don't collapse in on myself," Levin told Jill Neimark for *Science & Spirit* (November/December 2002, on-line). "It's such a relief to be accepted for who I am rather than being seen as my work."

In England Levin worked with the astrophysicist Joseph Silk, her onetime mentor at Berkeley, who had joined the faculty of Oxford University in 1999. She focused on several questions concerning the cosmos that Einstein did not address in his general theory of relativity. In addition to discussing the origin and expansion of the universe, Einstein determined that the gravity of stars and galaxies (aggregations of stars, gases, and dust, such as the Milky Way, that are bound by gravity) could warp space into different geometric configurations. The shapes of the warps—concave, flat, or hyperbolic—affect the paths in which light travels through the universe. But Einstein did not speculate about the overall shape or topology of the cosmos—that is, about whether the universe is infinite (an assumption widely held since 1576, when the English writer Thomas Digges offered that heretical idea) or is shaped in a way that makes it finite. Levin told David Kestenbaum that people preferred to think of the universe as infinite "because it seemed easier than adding new mathematics into [Einstein's] theory, but now that we're moving on—we're making some steps beyond Einstein's theory—we're starting to be able to realistically ask those questions." Levin believes that scientists may discover the shape of the cosmos by measuring the differences in temperatures in space since light began radiating through the universe, about 300,000 years after the Big Bang (the moment when, theoretically, the universe—including time

as well as space and matter—came into existence). While satellites have collected data showing that the temperatures of radiation are virtually identical in every direction, they have also located places where temperatures differ from the average temperatures by plus or minus 1/100,000th of a degree.

Levin and others have imagined a cosmos shaped something like a doughnut. In the 1970s the Russian physicist Dmitry Sokoloff tried to confirm that idea by scrutinizing images of distant galaxies in an attempt to find an image of Earth's galaxy, the Milky Way, at a moment in the past. (The reason an image of the Milky Way might be found in another part of the universe is that the light reaching Earth from the Milky Way originated tens of thousands or hundreds of thousands of light-years in the past; because of the expansion of the universe, in the more-distant past the Milky Way was in a different location with respect to other galaxies.) Sokoloff never found an image of the Milky Way, but his inability to do so does not mean that such an image of it does not exist; rather, the image may be too faint to detect at present. If scientists ever conclude that the universe is finite, they will have to reconsider all the long-held theories that are based on the concept of an infinite universe that is expanding without limit.

Levin has also studied black holes, which she described on her Web site as "the most outrageous inhabitants of our universe, as well as the most elusive." A black hole is what remains when all of a star's fuel burns up; the star collapses into a sphere many magnitudes smaller than it had been. The sphere is extremely dense and exerts an extremely powerful gravitational pull. The force of its gravity is so great that even light becomes trapped inside what is known as the star's escape boundary (also called its event horizon). Although black holes are invisible to observers elsewhere in the universe, sometimes their effects on other stars can be detected. While she was working in England, Levin studied the possible effects of the collision of two black holes or of two black holes in orbit around each other. As she wrote on her Web site, "As black holes orbit each other, space itself ripples in response to the motion creating gravitational waves. If the black holes are rapidly spinning, then the orbit can be extremely irregular, even chaotic. Chaos imposes a fundamentally new perspective on the merger of black holes, gravitational wave detection, and possibly curved spacetime in general." Levin proposed that the calculations that scientists had been using to predict the effects of such cosmic events lacked the complexities that chaos would introduce. (In the case of such cosmic events, and many phenomena on Earth, "chaos" is a mathematical concept.) Levin's suggestion that chaos should be added to the standard calculations of such cosmic events elicited a defensive backlash from some eminent academics. "I got a pretty violent reaction," Levin told Anjana Ahuja for the London *Times* (February 11, 2002). "Some people . . . said it was important. Others flipped out and were just hysterical. They said there was clearly no chaos. I suppose they assumed that I thought they were being simple-minded; they felt I was disparaging their methods, which I certainly was not—they are all amazing people doing great work."

Levin was living and working in England when she wrote her first book, *How the Universe Got Its Spots: A Diary of Finite Time in a Finite Space* (2002). "I had been writing a lot of technical articles, and I was so tired of writing in such a formal way, and it felt like I was reaching such a small audience," she told Kestenbaum, referring to her motivations for committing to paper what might be described as both a memoir and a popular-science book about cosmology. The book contains descriptions of her research and philosophical ruminations about the universe, along with accounts of her sometimes isolating experiences as a scientist and often difficult relationship with her boyfriend. Although a few critics complained that Levin had failed to strike a satisfactory balance between her discussions of cosmic events and her musings on personal concerns, most found it to be both intellectually and emotionally engaging. "This intimate account of the life and thought of a physicist is one of the nicest scientific books I have ever read—personal and honest, clear and informative, entertaining and difficult to put down," Alejandro Gangui wrote for *American Scientist* (September/October 2002). "[Levin's] female perspective is refreshing, and her personal account is firmly aimed at non-experts, . . . yet avoids patronising readers," Valerie Jamieson wrote for the *Times Higher Education Supplement* (October 4, 2002). *Discover* magazine named *How the Universe Got Its Spots* one of the 20 best science books of the year.

After completing her research at Cambridge, Levin spent nearly a year as the first scientist in residence at the Ruskin School of Drawing and Fine Art in Oxford, supported by a Dream Time fellowship from the National Endowment for Science, Technology, and the Arts, a British funding group. In that capacity Levin, who since childhood has loved to draw and paint, wrote pieces for and about London artists and musicians, including catalog essays and book chapters. She also began writing what became her next book, the novel *A Madman Dreams of Turing Machines*, about two of the most brilliant, original, and influential thinkers of the 20th century: Kurt Gödel and Alan Turing, both of whom suffered greatly in their personal lives, Gödel because of severe mental illness and Turing because of Great Britain's intolerance of homosexuality. (British authorities punished what they called his "indecent acts"; they were unaware that Turing, in top-secret work, had cracked the Nazis' Enigma Code for the British in World War II.) Levin's book contains alternating scenes in which each man appears without the other. Gödel and Turing never met, but their professional and private lives had much in common—some of Turing's work grew out of Gödel's theories—and both died

tragically: Gödel starved himself to death in the paranoid fear that he would be poisoned, and Turing committed suicide by eating a cyanide-laced apple. A third character in the novel is the nameless physicist who narrates the story and ponders the ideas and experiences of Gödel and Turing. As a way of organizing her ideas while writing, Levin sketched out scenes and other parts of the book into a kind of storyboard, which she would redraw and reorganize as her thoughts evolved.

"Levin turns dry history into a literate and revealing examination of the power and the peril of creative genius," Laurence Marschall wrote for *Natural History* (July/August 2007), in one of many admiring reviews of *A Madman Dreams of Turing Machines*. In another, John Allemang wrote for the Toronto, Canada, *Globe and Mail* (September 21, 2006), "Though her book comes with endnotes on historical accuracy, this isn't a case of a scientist being nervous around her new genre. Levin makes the transition seem effortless, as if equations and adjectives were instruments in the same pursuit." "The ultimate achievement of this book is not in its creative biographical studies, but in its exploration of the sociology of ideas," Harold Heft wrote for the Montreal, Canada, *Gazette* (December 23, 2006), while Mark Sarvas, in a critique for the *Philadelphia Inquirer* (October 1, 2006), wrote, "Levin's novel is, at its heart, an effective meditation on interconnectedness, language and free will . . . a paean to misunderstood heroes, as well as an elegy to a lost golden area of discovery." Sarvas and Ariel Swartley, writing for the *Los Angeles Times* (August 21, 2006), both found Levin's handling of her narrator less than felicitous, while a reviewer for *Publishers Weekly* (August 25, 2006), in one of the few unenthusiastic assessments of the book, wrote, "Levin is sympathetic to all concerned, but doesn't quite make a larger point, dramatic or otherwise."

In 2004 Levin returned to New York City, to become an assistant professor of astronomy and astrophysics at Barnard College. As a prominent woman in male-dominated fields, Levin has frequently been asked to comment on her experiences in academia. Levin told Ahuja that science departments were "the last bastion of maleness" and that "the whole system is structured under the assumption that you have a housewife and your wife's life doesn't matter." In an essay for *Newsweek* (September 25, 2006) entitled "This Topic Annoys Me," she wrote, "I don't ever want to talk about being a woman scientist again. . . . I was never very good at telling those stories because truthfully I never found them interesting. What I do find interesting is the origin of the universe, the shape of space-time and the nature of black holes. . . . Why should curing sexism be yet another terrible burden on every female scientist? After all, I don't study sociology or political theory. I study the history of the cosmos written in the laws of physics. That's a story I tell pretty well."

In 2003 Levin won a Kilby International Award, "created to honor unsung heroes and heroines who make significant contributions to Society through Science, Technology, Innovation, Invention, and Education," according to the Web site of the Texas-based foundation that supports that prize. She took a leave of absence from Barnard during the spring 2008 semester. In March 2008 Levin launched her podcast, titled *Janna Levin Reports from the Cosmos*. Each installment features discussions of topics in cosmology, among them black holes, the Big Bang, and the nature of the universe. The podcast is available through Levin's Web site.

Levin and her husband live in New York City with their two young children.

—M.E.R.

Suggested Reading: Janna Levin's Web site; *New Scientist* Features p2828 Sep. 19, 1998, Opinion p40 Apr. 6, 2002; *New York Times* F p1 Mar. 11, 2003; *Perspectives* p44+ Aug. 19, 2006; *Seed Magazine* (on-line) Mar. 6, 2007; *Talk of the Nation/Science Friday* (on-line) July 12, 2002

Selected Books: *How the Universe Got Its Spots: Diary of a Finite Time in a Finite Space*, 2002; *A Madman Dreams of Turing Machines: A Story of Coded Secrets and Psychotic Delusions, of Mathematics and War Told by a Physicist Obsessed by the Lives of Turing and Gödel*, 2006

Lhuillier, Monique

(LOO-lee-ay, moh-NEEK)

Sep. 15, 1971– Fashion designer

Address: *Monique Lhuillier, 1201 S. Grand Ave., Los Angeles, CA 90015*

Monique Lhuillier is one of the top designers of bridal gowns and evening wear in the United States. The experience of planning her own wedding cemented her decision to enter the bridal-wear industry, in the mid-1990s. "You know, I feel that for the regular woman her wedding day is her Oscar or her red-carpet moment. . . . She just wants it to be so perfect so I treat that with as much respect as I would if I were dressing a celebrity going down the red carpet," Lhuillier told a reporter for the *Philippine Daily Inquirer* (November 12, 2006, on-line). "People come to me for their special moments because they know I'm there to make them look their best."

Diane Monique Lhuillier was born on September 15, 1971 in Cebu City, the capital of the province of Cebu, in the Philippines. She is the youngest of two daughters and two sons. Her father, Michael, of French heritage, worked at various times as a jeweler, real-estate investor, and diplomat. Lhuillier has told journalists that she never saw her mother, Amparito, a Filipino former model, without earrings, lipstick, or an impeccable coiffure. "My mother was very glamorous. My parents would entertain a lot and my sister and I would sit and watch her dress," she told Rose Apodaca Jones for *Women's Wear Daily* (September 23, 2004). Amparito designed and made most of her children's clothing, working from the garage of their home. After friends became interested in her designs, she purchased more sewing machines and hired local seamstresses to produce the garments. When the enterprise threatened to outgrow the garage, Amparito acquiesced to her husband's plea that she curtail her activities.

At the age of 15, Lhuillier was sent to the now-defunct Chateau Mont-Choisi, a boarding school in Lausanne, Switzerland. Determined to pursue a career in fashion design, she sought her parents' permission to attend school in New York City, but they were reluctant to let her do so. Los Angeles, California, seemed to them to be a safer location. Frequent trips to visit her maternal grandparents had familiarized Lhuillier with that city, and her siblings had recently begun attending school in the Los Angeles area. Lhuillier enrolled at the Fashion Institute of Design and Merchandising, attending classes at the school's Los Angeles campus and moving into a house with her siblings. For her final project Lhuillier made a wedding dress with hundreds of hand-sewn rosettes. Her work earned her a scholarship funded by Jakob Schlaepfer, a Swiss textile company, to attend the school's advanced program. After she completed the advanced program, in 1995, Lhuillier sought work in the luxury-apparel field, but she found that few high-end fashion companies were based in Los Angeles. She took a job at a small French sportswear firm, Melivier. Dissatisfied because of the lack of glamour, she quit.

Now unemployed, Lhuillier had time to focus on her impending marriage to Tom Bugbee, a business student she had met during her college years. While many journalists repeat a probably apocryphal story about the difficulties Lhuillier had in finding a wedding dress, she has said that she purchased the third gown she tried on, a traditional design by Ron LoVece. "I had my parents with me, and they said, 'You look like a princess,'" she told Stacy Thiel for *New York Weddings* (Fall 2005, on-line). "I thought, Okay, let's take it. I was a really easy bride." She did, however, personally create 25 dresses for members of her bridal party and various relatives. "I didn't know [my design focus] would be bridal until I was shopping for my dress. That's what opened my eyes," she told Thiel. "I thought I could infuse something different into the bridal world."

Monique Lhuillier

Lhuillier was married at the Ritz Carlton in Marina del Rey, California, on May 20, 1995. "I had business cards waiting for me [after the event]. They were left by people asking if I could design for their weddings," she told Allison Adato for *People* (June 14, 2004, on-line). "That's when I knew I could make a business out of this."

In 1996 Lhuillier discovered that a bridal trade show (at which designers show their creations to vendors) was to be held in Las Vegas, Nevada, a month hence. She quickly made six wedding gowns and a small collection of bridesmaids' dresses. With the help of friends, she traveled to the site of the show and set up her rented booth. By the end of the show, five bridal stores, including Mon Amie Bridal, a prominent boutique in Costa Mesa, California, had agreed to carry her line. Bugbee quit his job to help run the company. "Without him, I would still be small," Lhuillier told Maria Cokel for the on-line magazine *Beauty Buzz* (Fall 2000). "I don't look at the business side. I stay with the creative part."

Lhuillier's bridal gowns cost an average of $6,000 each. Most of the designs have A-line skirts, which Lhuillier believes flatter all body types. She also feels that exposing a bride's shoulders and arms keeps the dress from being overpowering. "I hardly ever design a dress with sleeves so it doesn't become frumpy," she told Cokel. "The sleeves on my dresses are mesh and very sheer." According to *Women's Wear Daily* (October 27, 2006), Lhuillier has described her aesthetic as "chic, feminine, [and] modern." Her designs are a favorite with fashion editors, and they have been featured in *Vogue, Glamour, InStyle, Vanity Fair, Elle, Brides,* and *Modern Bride,* among other publications.

In 2001 the first Monique Lhuillier boutique opened, in Beverly Hills, California. The designer provided tissues in the dressing rooms for teary-eyed mothers, energy bars for stressed brides, and a VIP room for the celebrity clients she was attracting. For her spring 2001 collection, Lhuillier included an evening-wear line. The luxury retailers Neiman Marcus and Saks Fifth Avenue were among the first buyers, thus cementing the designer's status in the fashion world. She told Lola Ogunnaike for *USA Weekend* (July 22, 2007, on-line), "I look at what void I have in my closet and try and fill that. Usually, if it strikes a chord with me, it strikes a chord with the customer." Lhuillier launched her first ready-to-wear line in 2003. Her daytime clothing have received mixed reviews. The fashion critic Laird Borrelli wrote for Style.com (February 7, 2006), "Daywear isn't what people come to Lhuillier for; it's her special way with a gown that keeps them lining up for more."

The first major celebrity to wear a Lhuillier evening gown was Angelina Jolie, at the 2002 Golden Globe Awards ceremony. Thanks in large part to that exposure, the designer's clothing is now often seen on the red carpet. For various awards shows Lhuillier has dressed such stars as Sharon Stone, Reese Witherspoon, Carrie Underwood, Katie Holmes, Hilary Swank, Sarah Jessica Parker, Jennifer Connelly, Janet Jackson, and Mariah Carey. She has also designed wedding gowns for a number of public figures, including the singer Pink; the star of the TV show *Grey's Anatomy,* Kate Walsh; and former vice president Al Gore's youngest daughter, Sarah. Among her most famous bridal clients is the pop singer Britney Spears, who chose a Lhuillier gown for her wedding to Kevin Federline, in September 2004. Lhuillier was forced to sign a confidentiality agreement before the top-secret nuptials.

Lhuillier, who has been inducted into the exclusive Council of Fashion Designers of America, has won many honors for her work, including being named bridal designer of the year by *Wedding Bells* magazine in 2006. That year her son, Jack Nicholas Lhuillier Bugbee, was born, on January 17. "It's really a great thing. Now I feel complete. I've been married almost 12 years, and the business was always our focus. Now, to have a family life outside of that has really been wonderful for me," Lhuillier told the *Philippine Daily Inquirer.* Additionally, the toy manufacturer Mattel asked her to design an exclusive Barbie doll. The doll's dress features a colorful sash, a detail that has become something of a trademark for the designer, and sold for $140. Late in the year Lhuillier returned to her native country for a benefit fashion show and was awarded a medal of merit by President Gloria Macapagal-Arroyo.

In 2007 Lhuillier appeared as a guest judge on an episode of the hit Bravo series *Project Runway,* and she designed a collection of dinnerware, stemware, and flatware for Royal Doulton. In October 2007 she moved her flagship store from Beverly Hills to a more spacious location, in the Melrose area of Los Angeles. The opening attracted several devoted celebrity clients, including Kristen Bell, Maria Shriver, Rebecca Gayheart, and Dita Von Teese. Lhuillier has a second eponymous flagship store, in Minneapolis, Minnesota.

Monique Lhuillier Inc., which has annual revenues of more than $20 million, has grown to include a line of handbags, and the designer plans to expand into footwear and perfume. Lhuillier particularly enjoys making public appearances at trunk shows across the country. "I get to meet the brides, the mothers and the grandmothers. It's so wonderful! I love to talk and sometimes keep the stores open longer than I should!" she told Cokel. "It also gives me feedback on the dresses, on how they fit, feel, and how I can improve them."

—M.A.S.

Suggested Reading: *Beauty Buzz* (on-line) Fall 2000; *New York Weddings* (on-line) Fall 2005; *People* (on-line) June 14, 2004; *Philippine Daily Inquirer* (on-line) June 25, 2006, Nov. 12, 2006; *USA Weekend* (on-line) July 22, 2007; *W* p310 Sep. 1, 2005; *Women's Wear Daily* p17 Sep. 23, 2004, p16 Oct. 27, 2006

Lockhart, Keith

Nov. 7, 1959– Orchestra conductor

Address: Boston Pops Orchestra, 301 Massachusetts Ave., Boston, MA 02115

"Mozart and Beethoven had no trouble thinking of themselves as entertainers," the orchestra conductor Keith Lockhart told Clarke Bustard for the *Richmond (Virginia) Times Dispatch* (October 19, 1997). "Why should we? I enjoy helping create the effect that music has on people, and I like the chance to entertain." Lockhart has served since 1995 as the musical director—another term for "conductor"—of the Boston Pops Orchestra, which performed its first concert in 1885, four years after its parent organization, the Boston Symphony Orchestra, made its debut, in Massachusetts's capital city. Enormously popular in the Pops's home city, Lockhart is famous for his "charisma and youthful good looks," as Doug Robinson wrote for the Salt Lake City, Utah, *Deseret News* (March 29, 2003), as well as for his dynamic, balletic style of conducting, his showmanship, and his fondness for innovative programming; he himself once cited his "stamina" and "versatility" as his major qualifications for his job, according to Susan Diesenhouse, writing for the *New York Times* (May 14, 1997). Leon Botstein, the music director of the American Symphony Orchestra, described Lockhart to Diesenhouse as "a gifted musician" who was "a brilliant choice to lead the nation's only really successful pops institution."

Now 49, Lockhart has led more than 1,000 concerts with the Pops, with another 65 performed especially for the PBS television series *Evening at Pops* and various TV specials, and he has guided the orchestra on 28 national and a half-dozen international tours. During each concert season the Pops—whose composition is essentially that of the Boston Symphony Orchestra minus the principal instrumentalists—offers a combination of light classical music, big-band favorites, popular songs, traditional American tunes and patriotic favorites, Latin and Celtic songs, film scores, music written for theatrical shows, and "novelty" compositions that defy classification. Lockhart also conducts the Boston Pops Esplanade Orchestra, made up largely of freelance musicians, which concertizes during the summer months out-of-doors, on the banks of the Charles River; its annual Fourth of July concert, which has been broadcast nationally on CBS-TV for many years, typically attracts 300,000 concert-goers and 20 million TV viewers. The 2002 July 4 broadcast earned an Emmy Award nomination for outstanding classical music/dance program; an installment of *Evening at Pops* called "Fiddlers Three"—in which the classical violinist Nadja Salerno-Sonnenberg, the jazz violinist Regina Carter, and the Irish-American fiddler Eileen Ivers performed the world premiere of Christopher Brubeck's *Interplay for Three Violins*—won the 2002 ASCAP Deems Taylor Award in the "television broadcast" category. "With all due respect to all the other conductors who conduct here [in Boston], there is no harder ticket to get . . . than a ticket for a Keith Lockhart concert," Dennis Alves, the Pops's director of artistic planning, told Doug Robinson. "When people come to the Pops, they want to see Keith Lockhart."

Five years passed between Lockhart's completion of his formal, academic music training, in 1983, and his first job with a professional orchestra—that of assistant conductor with the Akron Symphony Orchestra, in Ohio. He later worked with the Cincinnati Symphony, Cincinnati Pops, and Cincinnati Chamber Orchestras, also in Ohio. Concurrently, in 1998 he began conducting the Utah Symphony Orchestra; the 2008–09 season was scheduled to be his last with that group. Lockhart has also served as a guest conductor with many other major orchestras. Since 2007 he has held the post of artistic director of the Brevard Music Center, in North Carolina, a summer institute for music students. "The barrier between symphony concerts and pops is very inconvenient for me, therefore I refuse to acknowledge it," he told Anthony Tommasini during an interview for the *New York Times* (May 14, 1995). "My career has been based, in a sense, on the belief that we live in an age that is increasingly less impressed with arbi-

Ronald Martinez/Getty Images

Keith Lockhart

trary divisions." Lockhart told Robinson, "I love the way my plate is balanced, but there are some gear-grinding transitions."

The first of two children, Keith Alan Lockhart was born on November 7, 1959 in Poughkeepsie, New York. His father, Newton Lockhart, was an electrical engineer with IBM; his mother, Marilyn, a mathematician, left her computer-technician job at IBM to raise Lockhart and his brother, Paul (now a history professor at Wright State University). Lockhart's father played trumpet in high school and bugle while in the U.S. Navy, and he played the harmonica on family camping trips. He also owned a large record collection. Lockhart told Richard Dyer, who interviewed him for the *Boston Globe* (May 7, 1995), that he vividly remembered the first time he heard a recording of the 20th-century Russian composer Igor Stravinsky's *The Rite of Spring*—a work that broke so decisively with earlier genres that a riot broke out among the audience at its premiere, in 1913. "I was overwhelmed, amazed," Lockhart told Dyer. "I had found my kind of music." His parents granted his wish to have piano lessons, and at age seven he began studying with Gwendolyn Stevens; he would remain her pupil for 11 years. Lockhart told Dyer, "She was the major influence and inspiration for my musical life." Stevens recalled to Dyer that Lockhart "was just a tiny little thing the first time he set foot in my house, but already he noticed everything. He was very bright, with a good ear, and very musical, so the whole thing took off right away. He was a very natural, gifted pianist, very facile. I took him through all the main repertory." Stevens also said, "He wasn't the easiest student I ever had. He didn't always follow through—he

would get bored with practicing. He could do a lot of things in school at the last minute because of his natural intelligence, but you can't play Beethoven's Opus 22 that way"—a reference to the composer's 11th piano sonata. "There was a whole succession of competitions and other things he didn't win in those days because he didn't know how to go far enough."

During his years at Roy C. Ketcham High School, in Wappingers Falls, New York, Lockhart became fond of then-current pop and rock music, including that of the rock giants Queen and Led Zeppelin and the singer-songwriter James Taylor, as well as folk-rock music by Simon and Garfunkel. He joined the high-school marching band and the wind ensemble, took clarinet lessons, and, at 16, directed several student musicals, including productions of *Babes in Arms* and *The Pajama Game*. In the summer of 1974, he studied piano at the Brevard Music Center; the next summer, with a teacher's-aide scholarship, he studied bass clarinet there. In his free time he enjoyed playing sports, particularly baseball.

Lockhart won a music and academic scholarship to attend Furman University, in Greenville, South Carolina, where he studied piano performance and German. He spent his junior year in Vienna, Austria, studying piano with Maria-Regina Seidlhofer at the University of Music and Performing Arts. For his senior piano recital at Furman, he played Beethoven's Piano Sonata no. 31 and Maurice Ravel's *Le Tombeau de Couperin*. As a senior he played clarinet with the Greenville Symphony and earned additional money accompanying an Elvis Presley impersonator on the piano. In 1980 Lockhart attended the intermediate conducting class at the Aspen Music Festival and School, in Colorado. There he was taught by the conductors Sergiu Comissiona and Leonard Slatkin. He told Dyer that the Aspen program marked a "turn-around point" in his education and experience as a conductor; it was "useful because it was my first experience on the big pond; I was buying groceries in the same store as professional musicians."

Lockhart graduated from Furman in 1981 with a B.A. degree in German and a second bachelor's degree, in music, both summa cum laude. According to Robinson, he also completed a minor in clarinet and, in his words, "half a degree" in computer science, chemistry, and English. "I was just a learning junkie," Lockhart told Robinson. "But I always came back to music because I loved it." The next month he enrolled at Carnegie Mellon University, in Pittsburgh, Pennsylvania, to pursue an M.F.A. degree in orchestral conducting under Istvan Jaray, Werner Torkanowsky, Otto-Werner Mueller, and Harold Farberman. "Because I was the only conducting student, I got all the conducting opportunities," he told Dyer. He took the podium for productions of two operettas—Gilbert and Sullivan's *The Mikado* and Johann Strauss's *Die Fledermaus*—and for a performance of the contemporary American composer George Crumb's song cycle *Ancient Voices of Children*. He also worked with a contemporary-music ensemble. He completed the requirements for his master's degree in 1983.

From 1983 to 1989 Lockhart taught voice and music as a faculty member of Carnegie Mellon; he also served as an assistant conductor of the All University Orchestra (which welcomed instrumentalists majoring in any discipline at Carnegie Mellon) and conducted the school wind ensemble. In addition, he conducted local productions of such musical shows as *Candide*, *Sweeney Todd*, and *Sunday in the Park with George*. Concurrently, from 1987 to 1990 he was the music director of the Pittsburgh Civic Orchestra, an all-volunteer, amateur ensemble. During that period he tried without success to secure a conducting job with a professional orchestra. "What I have to show for my trouble is a file of 135 rejection letters," he told Dyer. "My resume wasn't flashy, to say the least. . . . So I couldn't get my foot in the front door."

Lockhart's luck changed when Robert Neu, then the executive director of the Akron Symphony Orchestra, in Ohio, saw a videotape of him at work. "The tape was grainy and he was conducting some college ensemble, but there was something about his conducting that was wonderful to see; he knew what he was doing," Neu recalled to Dyer. Lockhart was hired as the Akron Symphony Orchestra's assistant conductor; commuting from Pittsburgh to Akron, he conducted the associated youth orchestra and the main orchestra's holiday and educational concerts. He displayed his penchant for theatricality in a performance of *Peter and the Wolf*, a composition for children with words and music by Sergei Prokofiev, in which melodies played on a flute, a clarinet, an oboe, and three French horns represent, respectively, the bird, the cat, the duck, and the wolf in the story; Lockhart had members of the orchestra dress as the animals their respective instruments represented. In 1989 he was named one of two conducting fellows of the Los Angeles Philharmonic Institute. From 1990 to 1992 Lockhart held the post of assistant conductor with the Cincinnati Symphony Orchestra, and from 1992 to 1995, he held the same post with its offshoot the Cincinnati Pops Orchestra. In 1991, in the absence of the latter orchestra's regular music director, Erich Kunzel, he conducted the televised, Fourth of July pops concert while dressed as Uncle Sam. Lockhart later launched a series of educational concerts for the Cincinnati Pops, called "Casual Classics," with the goal of attracting people who seldom or never listened to classical music. "We tried to find theatrical and visual ways to hook people into the music without resorting to the techniques of Music History 101," he told Dyer for the *Boston Globe* (February 7, 1995). At one Cincinnati Symphony concert, according to musicianguide.com, he "jumped out of a giant birthday cake onstage," and at another, "he made his entrance on inline skates." At a third, which was dedicated to music by largely unheralded female composers, he and an actress portraying the 19th-century musician Clara Schumann (whose husband was the celebrated composer Robert Schumann) engaged in occasional conversation. For three years beginning in 1992, Lockhart served concurrently as the associate conductor of Cincinnati's symphony and pops orchestras, and from 1992 to 1999, he was music director of the Cincinnati Chamber Orchestra.

In 1993 John Williams—a five-time Academy Award–winning composer as well as a conductor—stepped down as the musical director of the Boston Pops, and what would turn into a two-year search for his successor began. Marshall Burlingame, the Boston Symphony Orchestra's librarian, who had previously worked for the Cincinnati Symphony, suggested to the Boston Pops's coordinator, Dennis Alves, that Lockhart be invited to try his hand at conducting the orchestra. Because Alves was impressed by Lockhart's leadership of the Chicago Symphony Orchestra as a guest conductor, Lockhart got that chance; he made his debut with the Pops on June 7, 1993. He led two additional, well-received concerts in 1994. Commenting on his abilities, Ellen Pfeifer wrote for the *Boston Globe* (May 21, 1994) that although Lockhart "look[ed] like just a kid," he had "an authoritative and charming presence on the podium and a music-making style that is both technically solid and interpretively lively." She also noted, "His return this week reinforced the positive impression" he had made the previous June. The impact Lockhart's work had on Seiji Ozawa, who was then the Boston Symphony Orchestra's music director, sealed the management's decision to hire Lockhart as Williams's permanent replacement. "Immediately, I knew he could conduct wonderfully, and that this was a man of character and personality, a musician at home in many different areas of music," Ozawa told Richard Dyer for the *Boston Globe Magazine* (May 7, 1995). "Keith loves the whole idea of communication between the orchestra and the audience." Ozawa told Susan Diesenhouse that Lockhart was well qualified to lead the Pops, which he declared was "the best tool to bridge" the barrier between "classical and all the other music in the world." "Keith is young, very talented," he told Diesenhouse. "He does well with youth audiences and has lots of ideas. Some will succeed; others won't. But it's critical to keep experimenting. If you stagnate, you're dead. Keith is not afraid to try." Lockhart's new position became official on February 6, 1995, when he signed a contract with the Boston Pops; the deal also called for him to direct the Boston Symphony's Young People's Concerts. At a press conference at the orchestra's home venue, Boston's Symphony Hall, John Williams said, as quoted by Dyer in the *Boston Globe* (February 7, 1995), "Keith is a wonderful find; he is the product of the best training, and he brings youth, enthusiasm, energy and commitment to renew our beloved Pops."

When Lockhart conducted his first concert as permanent conductor, on May 10, 1995, the Boston Pops was "the best-known, most recorded and arguably most popular orchestra in the United States," as Anthony Tommasini wrote; an annual total of almost 900,000 people attended its concerts, and the TV program *Evening at Pops* drew about 40 million viewers a year. The May 10 concert, which aired on *Evening at Pops*, showcased Lockhart's "eclectic bent," as Amy Biancolli wrote for the Albany, New York, *Times Union* (July 9, 1995): he led the orchestra in performances of show tunes and works by John Williams, Antonin Dvorak, and Richard Wagner. By the time he conducted the Pops's July 4 concert that year, Lockhart's popularity—thanks in part to an aggressive advertising campaign by orchestra officials—had reached levels usually associated with rock stars and celebrity athletes. In an article for the *New York Times* (July 10,1995), Nadine Brozan reported that "people in the audience wore T-shirts with his picture on them. Women screamed when he ascended to the stage. Men shouted to him." A decade later Geoff Edgers reported for the *Boston Globe* (July 3, 2005) that since Lockhart had joined the Pops, attendance at the orchestra's concerts in Symphony Hall had averaged 92 percent of capacity.

The first album recorded by the Pops under Lockhart's direction was released in 1996. A classical crossover hit called *Runnin' Wild*, it offered a highly varied menu, including the songs "Chattanooga Choo-Choo," by Mack Gordon and Harry Warren; "The Nearness of You," by Hoagy Carmichael; the traditional Russian "Song of the Volga Boatmen"; Joseph Winner's 19th-century folksong "Little Brown Jug," which was popularized by Glenn Miller; Miller's "Moonlight Serenade"; and

"The Anvil Chorus," from Verdi's opera *Il Trovatore*. In the album's jacket photo, Lockhart is shown kicking up his heels, wearing a white T-shirt, black jacket with tails, black shorts, and high-top sneakers, one black and the other red. Writing about a half-year after *Runnin' Wild* went on sale, Susan Diesenhouse reported that Lockhart and the Pops had earned "mostly glowing reviews" for the 156 concerts they had performed together up to that date, and that revenues from Pops concerts had increased far more than could be accounted for by higher ticket prices and an extended performance schedule.

Lockhart and the Pops have since recorded another 10 albums: *American Visions* (1997), with tracks by composers including Ferde Grofé, Jerome Kern, and John Williams; *The Celtic Album* (1998), which was nominated for a Grammy Award in a new category, "classical cross-over"; *Holiday Pops* (1998); *A Splash of Pops* (1999), whose cover showed Lockhart in concert attire, his arms stretched out and his legs spread wide, apparently landing with a splash on his back in a swimming pool; *Stars and Stripes Forever* (2000); *Latin Album* (2000), with music from Argentina, Brazil, Mexico, and Peru, among other places, and pieces with Spanish themes, such as *El Salón México*, by Aaron Copland; *Encore!* (2000), with music by composers including Leroy Anderson, Georges Bizet, Gerard Fahy, and F. W. Meacham, all of which were recorded on Lockhart's previous albums; *My Favorite Things: A Richard Rodgers Celebration* (2002), with selections from musicals including *Oklahoma!*, *The Sound of Music*, *Carousel*, and *The King and I*; *American Anthem* (2001); *Sleigh Ride* (2004); *America* (2004); and, most recently, *Oscar & Tony: Award-Winning Music from the Stage and Screen* (2007).

A typical Pops concert consists of three sections. In the first, the orchestra plays light classical music, examples of which include Mouret's Rondeau, more familiarly known as the theme from the PBS television series *Masterpiece Theater*; the "Wedding March" from Mendelssohn's *Midsummer Night's Dream*; waltzes by Johann Strauss, such as "On the Beautiful, Blue Danube"; dances from Tchaikovsky's ballets *The Nutcracker* or *Swan Lake*; "Polovstian Dances," from Borodin's opera *Prince Igor*; and the hornpipe from Handel's *Water Music*. The second section features a soloist or music group or other types of performers. Adopting the practice of his immediate predecessors, John Williams and, before him, Arthur Fiedler, who led the Boston Pops for a dozen years and 50 years, respectively, Lockhart has shared the stage at Pops concerts with an eclectic mix of guest artists and performers, among them the illusionists Penn and Teller; the Los Angeles Guitar Quartet; the alternative country-rockers My Morning Jacket; the Irish band the Chieftains; the piano rocker Ben Folds; and the cast of the TV series *Sesame Street*. In the third, concluding part of most Pops concerts, the orchestra plays a medley of film music, patriotic songs, show tunes, big-band hits, or other, often familiar music. In 2002 Lockhart conducted the Pops in the pre-game show of Super Bowl XXXVI, at the Louisiana Superdome, in New Orleans. Compositions commissioned and premiered by the Pops under Lockhart include *Spumonte* (1998), by Dan Welcher, *With Voices Raised* (1999), by Stephen Flaherty and Lynn Ahrens, *The Neville Feast* (2003), by Christopher Rouse, and a huge number of arrangements of Broadway, film, and popular music.

In a review for the *New York Times* (July 31, 1997) of Lockhart's debut with the New York Philharmonic, conducting a free concert in New York City's Central Park, Anthony Tommasini wrote, "Mr. Lockhart is a kinetic, confident and musicianly conductor. . . . His leaps from the podium . . . seem the result of irrepressible excitement, not affectation." Lockhart's exuberant conducting technique involves his entire body. "It's gesture to elicit response," Lockhart told Robinson. "You're not just following along up there. You're causing it to happen. If you put three different conductors in front of an orchestra and one was 325 pounds, and the other was thin and jerky, and the other was a grand old maestro who was slow, you would get three different responses from the orchestra. You know what you want from an orchestra and it just comes out. It's part of the communication between conductor and orchestra." In 1998, at Tech Night at the Pops, a special concert for students and alumni of the Massachusetts Institute of Technology (MIT) presented annually since 1898, Lockhart wore a red and silver jumpsuit fitted with sensors that recorded his heart and respiration rates, muscle tension, skin conductivity, movements, and other bodily activity. The suit was designed by an MIT graduate student, Teresa Marrin, with the aim of collecting data "that might explain how Mr. Lockhart's rhythm, timing, natural gestures and even emotion become music . . . ," as Julie Flaherty reported for the *New York Times* (June 11, 1998). "To add to the spectacle" that the peculiarly clad Lockhart presented, Flaherty continued, "a computer program translated his body's signals into a dance of colorful, swirling geometric shapes."

In 1998 Lockhart took on another job, as the music director of the Utah Symphony, based in Salt Lake City. Since that orchestra's regular season extends from late September through the end of winter, his new responsibilities did not interfere with his work with the Pops, which performs from May through July. "The reason I took on this position is that I very deeply believe I can do it, that I can make a go of it," he told Joel Campbell for the Salt Lake City *Deseret News* (January 29, 1998). "For the first time in my life it is not a financial imperative to seek employment." He made his debut with the Utah Symphony in September 1998, in a concert that featured Gustav Holst's *The Planets*. Currently, the orchestra gives upwards of 70 concerts annually in Abravanel Hall, in Salt Lake City; it also performs in other communities in Utah and neighboring states. Every year it accompanies four productions mounted by the Utah Opera, with which it has been formally linked since 2002. *Symphonic Dances*, Lockhart's only recording to date with the Utah Symphony, was released on the Reference Recordings label in 2006. The album includes Rachmaninoff's Symphonic Dances, Leonard Bernstein's Symphonic Dances from *West Side Story*, and Gabriela Lena Frank's *Three Latin American Dances*, a work that the orchestra commissioned and introduced in concert in 2004. John Sunier's enthusiastic review of the album for *Audiophile Audition* (on-line) reported that the recording contained "brilliant music in brilliant sonics, plus a new composition you'll want to . . . hear again." Lockhart began his final season with the Utah Symphony Orchestra in September 2008.

Lockhart was married to Ann Louise Heatherington from 1981 to 1983 and to the Boston Symphony Orchestra first violinist Lucia Lin from 1996 to 2004; both marriages ended in divorce. From his second marriage he has one son, Aaron, who was born in 2003. In 2007 Lockhart married Emiley Zalesky, an assistant district attorney in Boston.
— W.D.

Suggested Reading: *Boston Globe Magazine* p16+ May 7, 1995; Boston Symphony Orchestra Web site; Columbia Artists Management Inc. (CAMI) Web site; Keith Lockhart's Web site; musicianguide.com; *New York Times* II p27 May 14 1995, p11 May 14, 1997; (Salt Lake City, Utah) *Deseret News* A p1+ Mar. 9, 2003; *Sarasota (Florida) Herald-Tribune* G p1+ Jan. 17, 1999

Selected Recordings: with the Boston Pops Orchestra—*Runnin' Wild*, 1996; *American Visions*, 1997; *The Celtic Album*, 1998; *Holiday Pops*, 1998; *A Splash of Pops*, 1999; *Stars and Stripes Forever*, 2000; *Latin Album*, 2000; *Encore!*, 2000; *American Anthem*, 2001; *My Favorite Things: A Richard Rodgers Celebration*, 2002; *Sleigh Ride*, 2004; *America*, 2004; *Oscar & Tony: Award Winning Music from the Stage and Screen*, 2007; with the Utah Symphony Orchestra—*Symphonic Dances*, 2006

Mackey, John

Aug. 15, 1953– Co-founder and CEO of Whole Foods Market Inc.

Address: Whole Foods Market Inc., 550 Bowie St., Austin, TX 78703

"For years, people would say, 'I'd like to eat healthier, but it tastes terrible,'" the entrepreneur John Mackey told Galina Espinoza and Alicia Dennis for *People* (November 4, 2002). "We've proven that

Courtesy of Whole Foods

John Mackey

natural cuisine can be intensely pleasurable." A six-time college dropout, Mackey is the co-founder and chief executive officer (CEO) of Whole Foods Market Inc., the largest chain of natural and organic foods in the world. Whole Foods started in 1978 as one store with 19 employees in Austin, Texas; currently it comprises more than 270 stores with 54,000 employees in the United States, Canada, and Great Britain, and in fiscal 2007 its annual sales totaled $6.6 billion. Mackey's vision succeeded in large part because he correctly foresaw a change in the way the American consumer would think about and buy food. "The old idea was A&P and Shop Rite: the milk always in one place and the meat in another, the Muzak and fluorescent lights and wheels rolling over linoleum producing a supermarket trance that was exactly the same in Connecticut as in California," Jon Gertner wrote for the *New York Times* (June 6, 2004). "The old idea was Mom going to the store once a week and rarely reading labels. The old idea was male grocery executives and store managers and a clientele that was almost exclusively women. In Mackey's view, consumer evolution necessitates a change in the look and feel of grocery stores."

Whole Foods' overall corporate structure is unique in the supermarket world. Instead of answering to company executives, store managers (called "team leaders") and employees ("team members") have final say over what their individual stores stock. Employees vote on company initiatives, such as health-care coverage, and information about the salaries of everyone in the company, including executives, is available to all of them. The company also has a salary cap, according to which an executive can earn no more than 19 times the average pay of a full-time Whole Foods employee. (Thus, in 2006, when the average wage was $31,990, the maximum salary for executives was $607,810.) Whole Foods sells only products that conform to the company's strict guidelines and organic standards, which ban the use by its suppliers of pesticides, artificial additives or sweeteners, and preservatives. In addition, the company has adopted standards to ensure that suppliers of meat or poultry raise their animals humanely. Charles Fishman, writing for *Fast Company* (July 2004), characterized Mackey as "a man who has done more to improve the quality, sustainability, healthfulness, and purity of the food Americans eat—from farm field and barnyard to kitchen table—than anyone else in the past 25 years." Whole Foods donates at least 5 percent of its annual profits to charity.

Mackey himself is something of an enigma. "He is pro-employee but anti-union; pro-consumer but charges eye-watering prices. He is a vegan but pokes fun at 'crunchy granola types,' and celebrates the fact that 'Republicans shop in our stores, upsetting many of our core customers,'" John Arlidge wrote for the London *Observer* (January 29, 2006). Mackey told Dan Rather for the CBS News weekly program *60 Minutes* (June 4, 2006), "The more profit we make, the more stores we can open, the more donations we can make to our community, the more responsible citizens we can be for the environment. It's all interactive. It's all connected together. There's no separation." "And that may be the key to Whole Foods' success," R. Michelle Breyer wrote for the *Austin American-Statesman* (May 10, 1998). "From the beginning, Mackey was a capitalist who wasn't afraid to be a capitalist in an industry where that wasn't necessarily popular." Mackey opposes the formation of unions because, he told Breyer for the same newspaper (June 6, 2003), "they are resistant to change and they create an adversarial relationship to management." Mackey was criticized in 2007 when the public learned that for seven years he had posted on-line messages anonymously on a Yahoo! financial site, touting Whole Foods and bashing his competitors. The Securities and Exchange Commission as well as Whole Foods' board of directors investigated the matter, and Mackey was cleared of wrongdoing.

The first of three children, John P. Mackey was born in Texas on August 15, 1953 to William S. and Margaret Mackey. His father was an accounting professor until he became the chief executive officer of Lifemark, a health-care company. His mother was a schoolteacher and homemaker. Mackey grew up with his brother and sister in Houston, Texas. While he attended the city's Memorial High School, Mackey's ambition was to become a professional basketball player. After he was dropped from his school's varsity basketball team during his junior year, he persuaded his parents to move three miles away so that he could attend Spring Branch High School and join its team. "I said, 'I don't accept this. I'm going to prove that this was a mistake and I have worth,'" he recalled to Wendy Zellner for *BusinessWeek* (December 7, 1998). He won a place on the Spring Branch varsity team and played well with them.

Mackey graduated from high school in 1971. Interested in philosophy and religion, he enrolled at the University of Texas at Austin. Over the course of the next six years, he alternately attended and dropped out of that school and Trinity College in San Antonio, Texas, six times, never earning a degree. In 1975, during his last stint at the University of Texas, Mackey stopped eating meat and moved into a university vegetarian co-operative residence with the goal of getting a girlfriend. "I was in my early 20s and open to alternative lifestyles. I thought, 'I bet you get a lot of attractive, interesting women in a vegetarian co-op,'" he told John Arlidge. The experience of living in the co-op permanently changed his dietary habits. "It was the first time I realized what you ate could affect how you felt," he told Zellner. In addition, Mackey soon began dating another co-op resident, Renee Lawson Hardy.

For a while after he left college permanently, Mackey worked for the Good Food Stores, a now-defunct local grocery chain. By 1978 he had become interested in the retail business, and he and Hardy decided to start their own health-food store. With $10,000 from Mackey's father, $7,000 from money Hardy had inherited, and additional money raised by Mackey, the two budding entrepreneurs bought an old Victorian mansion in downtown Austin and opened Safer Way Natural Foods (a play on the name of the supermarket chain Safeway). On the first floor of the building, they opened a store, and on the second they launched a health-food restaurant. The third floor served as their living quarters—little more than a bed in one room. "We didn't even have a shower," Mackey told Charles Fishman. "Renee and I would take showers in the . . . dishwasher in the restaurant, you know, using the spray hose."

To appeal to customers with a variety of food preferences, Mackey and Hardy stocked Safer Way Natural Foods not only with traditional health foods but also with refined sugar and other items usually shunned in such stores. Nevertheless, business was slow. In its second year Safer Way generated a small profit, and Mackey began to consider expanding the business. He closed the restaurant and persuaded the owners of another health-food store, the nearby Clarksville Natural Grocery, to join forces with him and Hardy. Speaking to Zellner, Mark V. Skiles, one of the Clarksville owners, recalled Mackey's pitch: "If you don't come in with me, I may put you out of business because I can sell cheaper than you can." In 1980, with another loan from Mackey's father and money raised from a Safer Way customer, he and his new partners (among them Craig Weller, another of Clarksville's owners) opened Whole Foods Market, less than a mile from Mackey's first store, which he had closed earlier.

The new, 11,000-square-foot store, stocked with everything from tofu and herbal tea to alcoholic beverages and red meat, became an instant success. After a flood in May 1981 caused $400,000 in damages, placing the survival of Whole Foods in peril, loyal customers showed up the next day to help clean up the store. Investors and the federal Small Business Administration helped Mackey and his partners get back on track financially, and only a month later, the store reopened. Whole Foods' success continued, and by 1985 the chain consisted of four stores—three in Austin and one in Houston. Whole Foods' first acquisition, Bluebonnet Natural Grocery in Dallas, took place in 1986. The company has since acquired several more natural-food chains, among them Bread & Circus and Fresh Fields, both in the northeastern U.S.; Mrs. Gooch's Natural Food Markets in California; and Wellspring in North Carolina. Inspired by Bread & Circus stores' fresh produce, meat, and seafood sections, Mackey added similar departments to Whole Foods locations in the early 1990s. A decade later 65 percent of Whole Foods' sales were generated from those areas. With the rise of health-consciousness among consumers, Whole Foods grew rapidly; by 2004 it owned 157 stores in the U.S., Canada, and Great Britain. While American grocery stores averaged a growth in sales of 2.5 percent per year from 1999 to 2004, Whole Foods averaged growth of 19.2 percent.

Meanwhile, Mackey had become knowledgeable about the cruel and inhumane conditions that most animals endure at factory farms—a form of agribusiness in which large numbers of animals are crowded into huge buildings and confined in extremely small pens. In 2003 he became a vegan: he stopped buying or eating not only meat or poultry but also anything produced by animals (milk, for example) or containing animal products (leather, for instance). The exception is that he eats eggs from the chickens that he and his wife raise on their ranch, because, as he told Charles Fishman, "I know those chickens are happy. They live in chicken heaven." Whole Foods has since adopted "animal compassion standards" aimed at improving the quality of life of the livestock sold to the company, and it imposed a ban on the use of hormones and antibiotics to ensure the safety of its meat and poultry. In November 2003 Mackey was named the Ernst & Young Entrepreneur of the Year.

Mackey's critics have complained about his competitive, sometimes cutthroat tactics. Jon Gertner wrote, "It's not difficult to get numerous former employees and executives to say unflattering things about Mackey, who is widely known to be tough to work for. Yet it is hard to find anyone who has ever been involved with the company who doubts Mackey's commitment, or who questions whether Whole Foods is an innovative enterprise." Mackey has never apologized for his capitalist-driven work ethic. "A lot of people believe making a profit is unethical . . . [and] based on exploitation," he declared to R. Michelle Breyer. "Profit is the lifeblood of every business. It's like air." He also rejects the complaint by some longtime customers that he has "sold out" by building Whole Foods into a multibillion-dollar corporation. "As a company changes and evolves, some people are going to always remember the good old days as being better," Mackey told Dan Rather. "America has a romance with small businesses and it has mistrust with large business. Whole Foods is out to prove that wrong. I don't see any inherent reason why corporations cannot be just as caring and responsible as small business." Still, Mackey is unlike all but a handful of CEOs in the U.S. According to USA Today's review of the top 50 largest companies listed in Standard & Poor's 500 index in April 2008, the average CEO in those firms was paid $15.7 million in 2007. In late 2006 Mackey announced that he was reducing his annual salary to $1. "I continue to work for Whole Foods not because of the money I can make but because of the pleasure I get from leading such a great company, and the ongoing passion I have to help make the world a better place, which Whole Foods is continuing to do," he wrote for the company's Web site. "I am now 53 years old, and I have reached a place in my life where I no longer want to work for money, but simply for the joy of the work itself and to better answer the call to service that I feel so clearly in my own heart."

In June 2007 Whole Foods opened its first European store, in London. That December the federal Environmental Protection Agency named it Green Power Partner of the Year for the fourth time, citing it as having purchased the largest amount of renewable-energy credits from wind farms in American history—enough to offset 100 percent of the electricity used in all of the firm's North American stores. At the end of its 2007 fiscal year, Whole Foods reported that annual sales had totaled $6.6 billion.

Earlier, after Whole Foods had announced on February 21, 2007 its intention to buy the natural-foods chain Wild Oats Market for $565 million, the Federal Trade Commission (FTC) began to investigate the merger. In a June 5, 2007 press release, the FTC announced that it would file a lawsuit to try to stop the merger, on the grounds that the transaction would increase prices and "violate federal antitrust laws by eliminating the substantial competition." In a post on his corporate blog on June 19, 2007, Mackey accused the FTC of "bullying tactics" and maintained that the merger would not eliminate competition, because many other food retailers, among them Trader Joe's, HEB, Safeway, and Wal-Mart, still accounted for a large part of the retail grocery market. In August 2007 a federal-court judge denied the FTC's motion and allowed Whole Foods to complete its merger with Wild Oats. The FTC appealed that ruling, and as of July 2008, the matter had not been resolved.

Concurrently, in July 2007 the FTC revealed that it had compiled messages that Mackey had posted on the on-line forum Yahoo! Finance under the pseudonym "Rahodeb" (an anagram of his wife's first name) from January 1999 through August 2006. In the more than 1,400 postings, Mackey had repeatedly touted the virtues of Whole Foods and bashed Wild Oats. Later in July Mackey wrote on his blog that he had done it for fun, and he issued an apology. Soon afterward the Securities and Exchange Commission (SEC), along with the Whole Foods board of directors, announced that they were beginning their own investigations of Mackey's actions. During the SEC's investigation Mackey was barred from posting anything on his corporate blog. In April 2008 the SEC cleared him of any wrongdoing; the Whole Foods board of directors, which took no action against Mackey, added to the company's code of business conduct a ban on executive postings on Web forums not authroized by the company.

Prices in Whole Foods stores are generally higher than those at other grocery stores; indeed, some have nicknamed the chain "Whole Paycheck." Mackey has often explained that the prices reflect the higher costs of producing food of greater quality. Since the downturn in the U.S. economy that began in 2006, Whole Foods has suffered some losses. The company's third-quarter profit for 2008 was $33.9 million, 30 percent less than the total for the same quarter the year before. Whole Foods announced in August 2008 that it plans to cut expenses in lieu of closing stores or downsizing its payroll. The company has also launched a program designed to inform the public about its less-expensive items, and it will offer some discounts.

Mackey has dismissed the contention that consumers' demand for organic food is merely a passing fancy. "Something that's been going on for 30 years is hardly a fad," he told Steven Gray for the Wall Street Journal (December 4, 2006). "For people who are really interested and committed to an organic-food lifestyle, it's not a fad for them any more than Christianity is a fad for Christians, or Judaism is for Jewish people. It's a value system, a belief system. It's penetrating into the mainstream. I don't see that disappearing anytime soon." Still, regarding the future of Whole Foods in particular, he said during an interview for the PBS program The NewsHour with Jim Lehrer (February 20, 2007), "Someone will come along and do it better than we do. I mean, that's always what happens. No business stays on top in its niche forever. Everything has a life cycle. It has its day in the sun, and then it fades. And that will happen to Whole Foods, as well."

In 1992 Mackey married Deborah Morin, a yoga instructor and one-time software consultant. The couple live on a 720-acre ranch outside Johnson City, Texas. On weekdays Mackey remains in Austin to handle his business. By choice, he and his wife have no children. Mackey has said that he remains close to the three daughters of a previous girlfriend, Mary Kay Hagen. He told John Arlidge, "The youngest was two when I first got together with Mary Kay, so I helped to raise her up. I got some of the fatherhood stuff that way."

—M.A.S.

Suggested Reading: *BusinessWeek* p79 Dec. 7, 1998; *Fast Company* p70 July 2004; *(London) Observer* p50 Jan. 29, 2006; *New York Times Magazine* p44+ June 6, 2004; Whole Foods Market blogs

Valerie Trucchia, courtesy of Tony Malaby

Malaby, Tony

1964– Jazz saxophonist

Address: Clean Feed Records, Rua Do Alecrim 21 A, 1200-014 Lisboa, Portugal

"With grandeur in mind, Malaby takes explicit phrases and knots 'em together until he's fashioned a lariat wide enough to ensnare whatever notions gallop by," the critic Jim Macnie wrote for the *Village Voice* (March 23, 1999), describing the playing of the jazz saxophonist Tony Malaby. Macnie dubbed Malaby a "prudent expressionist," praising, as other critics have, his ability both to adhere to set musical structures and dazzle audiences with free-form avant-garde passages. "Despite a performance style that sometimes seemed to shift musical idioms from one phrase to the next, Malaby's solos unfolded with remarkable clarity and logic," Howard Reich wrote for the *Chicago Tribune* (May 19, 2004), reviewing one of the musician's live performances. "Or, to put it in other terms, any musician who can cover this much terrain without losing focus or his listeners' attention knows precisely what he's doing."

Malaby plays in roughly 20 bands. While he has released several albums as a bandleader—one of which, *Sabino*, was hailed by the *New York Times* and the *Philadelphia City Paper* as one of the best jazz albums of 2000—he has more often played as a sideman for such jazz luminaries as Paul Motian and George Schuller. Though he has lived in the New York City area since the 1990s, Malaby has not always followed the path trod by his predecessors and contemporaries in that city, who have often equated success with leading a band. "I'm not obsessed or driven to be a leader . . . ," he told Alain Drouot for *Down Beat* (May 2007). "I try to do things my own way, not the New York way."

Of Mexican-Irish descent, Antonio Malaby was born in 1964 in Tucson, Arizona, and grew up in a Spanish-speaking household in a neighborhood called Barrio Hollywood. Many of the songs he has recorded, such as "Sabino" and "Adobe Blues," have titles that allude to his southwestern heritage. While Tucson is not known as a center for jazz, Malaby has said that his hometown was a good place to come of age as a musician. In Arizona, "you have to forge your own path . . . ," he told Gene Armstrong for *Tucson Weekly* (April 15, 2004). "A lot of times, people who grew up in cities that had a really developed jazz scene with lots of teachers and lots of traffic, and so many musicians with so much agenda, they give in to the pressures around them [and] are maybe not influenced in the right ways. You know, the idea that you're not hip if you don't [have certain] records."

Malaby began playing music at John Spring Junior High School, where he learned to play alto saxophone—in part because that seat in the school's jazz band happened to be open. Under the tutelage of Jim Nordgren, Malaby gained skill as an improviser. "Nordgren got us into the 'anything goes' mode," Malaby told Armstrong. "He would show us a tune and say, 'Why don't you just blow?' He really helped me learn at a young age how to play through this melody and play with this melody and play completely away from this one." Nordgren expanded Malaby's musical horizons in other ways, taking him to his first rock-and-roll concert, which featured Tower of Power and Average White Band.

One of Nordgren's standout pupils, Malaby amazed his teacher one year by rewriting a trumpet solo for saxophone. "I asked him how he learned to transpose," Nordgren recalled to Armstrong. "His reply was, 'I checked out a book last summer and figured it out.'" After he moved on to Tucson High School, Malaby studied under another influential teacher, Lou Rodriguez, who introduced him to the music of the legendary bebop saxophonist Charlie Parker. During Malaby's senior year Rodriguez brought the acclaimed tenor saxophonist Dexter Gordon to the school to teach a master class. "That was what really made me realize that's what I wanted to do," Malaby said to Armstrong. "It was the first time I saw that close and personal the kind of sound I had only heard before, that kind of power. It was being really touched by [Gordon's] presence that made me want to do this for the rest of my life."

Rodriguez also worked to get Malaby a scholarship through the Tucson Unified School District's Fine Arts Department. As a result Malaby studied classical technique with Elizabeth Ervin, a professor at the University of Arizona. Ervin "worked with me on my phrasing—how to phrase a melody, how to breathe, how to 'sing' the melody, how to find a line," he told Armstrong. "She taught me how to take playing to the next step." Around the same time Malaby began sneaking into jazz concerts on North Fourth Avenue, where he met professional saxophonists including Greg Armstrong and Mike Porter. In 1982, rather than attending the University of Arizona—where "the type of music I really wanted to pursue wasn't really happening," as he told Armstrong—he enrolled at Arizona State University (ASU), in Tempe, largely on the advice of Rodriguez. There, Malaby made the switch from alto to tenor saxophone. The change came about when he happened to pick up his roommate's tenor and found himself enjoying the feel of the instrument as well as its range. During his undergraduate years Malaby taught music in Phoenix, Arizona, high schools, where he met the then-14-year-old Angelica Sanchez, whom he would later marry.

In 1990 Malaby left Arizona to study music at William Paterson University, in New Jersey. He also began playing with the Joey DeFrancesco Quintet, and before long he found steady work as a member of the Mingus Big Band—a group committed to playing the music of the legendary jazz bassist and composer Charles Mingus. While the Mingus Big Band gave Malaby a chance to learn from master players, it also required him to fight some of his more experimental urges. Malaby told Matt Rand for the Web site All About Jazz, referring to the avant-garde players he met and to the musicians in the Mingus Band, that he would "get swayed from this camp or that camp and get the opinions from angles. I just didn't want that. I wanted to have one voice, a creative voice that could deal with both parameters. And so I wanted to get away from all that and start with a clean slate, just kind of come up with something." After two years on the East Coast, he moved back to Arizona and began teaching at ASU. Malaby reconnected with Sanchez, who was studying at the university; the two later moved together to the so-called Jazz Apartment, a building in Tempe, Arizona, near Phoenix, that was home to many aspiring musicians. The apartment building was within bicycling distance of ASU, and Malaby and Sanchez, a pianist, would often rehearse with their neighbors. "We had a great scene . . . ," Malaby told Jeremy Voas for the Phoenix New Times (November 23, 2000). "Being up at 2 or 3 in the morning, listening to music with other musicians, with the door open. It was a great hang. Everybody really watched out for each other." In 1993 Malaby teamed with the

trombonist Joey Sellers for an album called Cosas. In a review for the Web site All Music Guide, David Dupont described the album's tracks as "evocative musical conversation pieces. Each tune summons a mood from the buoyant bop of 'Terrible Twos' to the melancholy of 'Matriarchal Conspirator,' and the two hornmen weave their improvisations from the melodic strands."

Both Malaby and Sanchez began playing shows in Arizona, but even after forming ties to the Los Angeles, California, jazz community, they soon found the local scene artistically limiting. "The older and better I got, the harder it was to be here," Malaby told Voas. "Musically, [Phoenix] is a very conservative city. The people like jazz, but they like it swinging and polite. My wife and I wanted the music to be a lot more aggressive. After a while, we were so frustrated here." In 1995 Malaby and Sanchez decided to move to New York City, after a friend's apartment became available. To pay the bills Sanchez taught music, and both she and Malaby worked at Tower Records. Malaby soon fell in with local musicians and started touring the country. Though he found success in the New York scene, he was reluctant to talk his way into groups. "I'm not a hustler," he told Rand. "I won't go up to someone and say, 'Hey, I really want to play with you—can I be in your band?' I just don't believe in that. I think you need to earn that." The same year that he moved to New York, Malaby released an album, The Dave Scott/Tony Malaby Quartet. Writing about the album for the Web site Saxophone.org, Jason DuMars called Malaby "one of the best tenor players on the scene right now." He added, "Malaby's playing is a coalescence of warm sound, rich melodic vocabulary, and crystal technique. Listening to the material on this disc leaves you feeling that there is nothing outside the reach of Malaby's tenor." DuMars, stating an opinion with which many critics would later agree, noted Malaby's ability to play cutting-edge music without losing himself in "raunchy, squeaking, wretched sounds," as some other players do. "Malaby and Scott speak to each other and the audience with their own voices and never for the sake of trying to be different or avant garde," he wrote.

Malaby married Sanchez in 1998. The couple later moved to Jersey City, New Jersey, just outside New York City. "Me and Angie dig it," Malaby told Ben Waltzer for the Newark, New Jersey, Star-Ledger (April 13, 2003), describing their neighborhood, which has increasingly become a home for professional musicians. "Our neighbors compliment us on the music we play, although sometimes they say things like, 'I keep waiting for you guys to play the tune. It sounds like you're always warming up!'" Malaby continued playing with a number of notable jazz musicians. In 1998 he toured with Marty Ehrlich's Travelers' Tales. Reviewing one of the group's performances for the Boston Globe (November 23, 1998), Bob Blumenthal wrote, "[Malaby's] solos on both tenor and soprano were marked by great logic and patience, often taking ideas from the melodies or the previous soloist and working them into statements that reinforced the unity of the entire performance. The tenor choruses on 'The Black Hat,' Ehrlich's tribute to clarinetist John Carter, were a prime example of Malaby's ability to marshal extensive technical forces without sacrificing overall coherence."

In 2000 Malaby released *Sabino*, his first album as a bandleader. The disc, for which he composed six of the eight tracks, earned praise from the Jazzmatazz.com (November 2000) critic Jules Epstein, who noted Malaby's fascination "with melodic phrases that he then works—stretching, amending, rethinking, pushing jazz to the verge of freedom but always with that melodic phrase retained, at least tentatively." Epstein wrote that the album presents Malaby as a "potent hornman, and at least the opening track has a taut structure that keeps the melody within a framework the listener can attend to." Elsewhere, however, Epstein criticized several tracks for being "over-long and too loosely structured," noting "a need for compositional refinement." Mark Corroto was more positive in his review for All About Jazz, writing that Malaby's music "has a very disciplined outside [or avant-garde] feel." He added, "Connoisseurs of creative voices in jazz will appreciate Malaby's singular voice." The disc earned a place on the *New York Times* jazz critic Ben Ratliff's list of the best albums of 2000. The *Philadelphia City Paper* also named *Sabino* one of the year's top 10 jazz releases. In 2001 the *Village Voice* placed Marty Ehrlich's Travelers' Tales' album *Malinke's Dance* on its best-of list for 2000, and the critic Gary Giddins cited Malaby for "bringing more bite to this session than to his own *Sabino*."

Malaby released his sophomore album, *Apparitions*, made up solely of his compositions, in 2003. The session featured the bassist Drew Gress as well as two drummers, Tom Rainey and Michael Sarin. "Although song titles allude to Malaby's exploration of his Mexican-American heritage, it's an emotional rather than literal influence," Sean Patrick Fitzell wrote for All About Jazz. "Malaby's writing sets the parameters for the music, blurring the line between composition and improvisation." Writing for *Down Beat* (March 2004), Greg Buium compared Malaby to such notable tenor saxophone players as Tim Berne, John Coltrane, and Joe Lovano, citing his "thick swirls, halting phrases, frills and barks that quickly turn into puzzles." The year 2003 also saw the release of Angelica Sanchez's debut album, *Mirror Me*. Sanchez composed all the tracks on the record, on which she is accompanied by Malaby, Rainey, and Michael Formanek on bass.

Reenlisting Gress and bringing in the veteran drummer Paul Motian, Malaby released his next album, *Adobe*, in 2004. Five of the album's nine tracks were Malaby's original compositions. In his review for All About Jazz, Germein Linares wrote, "Ideas of jazz past and present flow throughout the album, with rightful comparisons to Sonny Rollins' piano-less trios of the '60s. Malaby and crew do more than scour through jazz' yesterdays for modern templates, though. There is an interconnected, easily accessible nature to this album that speaks of today." Critiquing the album for *Japan Times* (January 25, 2004), Michael Pronko wrote, "Malaby's momentum charges ahead with fluent, distinctive expressions. Mature and confident enough to play with a natural gruffness, his phrasing is sparse, but brilliant." He also noted, "Cerebral, challenging postbop is not supposed to be this likable." In a piece for *Time Out New York* (November 20, 2003), Steve Smith wrote, "More than any of Malaby's prior recordings, *Adobe* serves notice of a major talent in the ascendant."

In 2004 Malaby, alongside Sanchez and the drummer Tom Rainey, released *Alive in Brooklyn*, a live session recorded at Barbe's, a nightspot in the New York City borough of Brooklyn. (A second *Alive in Brooklyn* record followed in 2006.) The album's three cuts were completely improvised. In a review for the on-line jazz magazine *One Final Note* (September 30, 2004), Dupont called the music "amorphous." "On *Alive in Brooklyn* Malaby and friends seem to be seeking the ghost of Miles Davis in those late 1960s days when he was shifting to electronic music," Dupont wrote, adding, "The trio seems rambling toward definitive statements, but never gets there." Despite his criticisms, Dupont ultimately called the band "an enjoyable act to hear." "Malaby is known as a Mr. Inside-Outside—rarely does a player considered such a superb technician in the traditional sense also display such gifts for freer forms," Phil DiPietro wrote for All About Jazz (March 25, 2004). The trio toured outside New York City, and in a review for the *Chicago Tribune* (March 19, 2004), Howard Reich called its performance at the Chicago Cultural Center a "glorious musical joy ride." He found that the band deserved to be the "talk of the jazz world," adding, "Not that a band as adventurous and stylistically free-ranging as this ever will make much of an impression on the mainstream jazz marketplace. Its music is too difficult to categorize, its performance style too mercurial, its improvisations too densely packed with ideas."

In 2006 Malaby was featured on *Synapse*, a session led by the trombonist Brian Allen. (Rainey, a frequent collaborator of Malaby's, played drums.) In a review for All About Jazz, Glenn Astarita wrote that Malaby "pronounces fire and brimstone during most of this session as the band follows by an evolutionary process drenched with interleaving exchanges." He concluded, "It's a strong date, often empowered by the artists' collective ability to get to the point, make a statement or two, then back off and redirect energies into newer frontiers." Critiquing the album for the Web site Bagatellen (September 29, 2006), Troy Collins wrote, "The spontaneous improvisations that make up *Synapse* are marvels of empathetic rapport." Praising the saxophonist's skill with both "tender euphonious lyricism" and "expressive exclamations," he observed, "Malaby's breathy, dulcet explorations are complemented by Allen's slurred whinnies and fractious phrases. When Allen ratchets up the intensity level with brassy post-bop angularity and turgid, gutbucket bleating, Malaby expels waves of sound, swirling and churning with serpentine energy." That same year Malaby played on critically acclaimed records by the Paul Motian Band and the pianist Kris Davis. Reviewing Davis's album *The Slightest Shift* for the *Chicago Sun Times* (July 30, 2006), Lloyd Sachs wrote, "Malaby, who seems to be everywhere these days, lays down long, sinuous, dark-toned lines—the album is nothing if not gloomy, albeit in a compelling way—into which the Canadian-born Davis injects short, jagged, nervy phrases that can lead even as they follow."

In 2007, having "earned a reputation as one of New York's stalwart improvisers," according to Nate Chinen, writing for the *New York Times* (December 30, 2007), Malaby released another album of his own, *Tamarindo*, featuring the bassist William Parker and the drummer Nasheet Waits. Chinen wrote that Parker and Waits "bring a driving purpose to the task" and that "meanwhile Mr. Malaby, simmering as often as he squalls, coherently pushes the music forward." Writing for JazzReview.com, Astarita called *Tamarindo* "a high-impact free-form progressive jazz extravaganza brought to us by three hard-hitting heavyweights of the genre." Citing the musicians' talent for building on each other's playing, Greg Camphire, in a review for All About Jazz, wrote, "The feeling one gets listening closely to this powerful combo is the sense of the three players orbiting each other in interlocked, overlapping concentric circles, with the framework of each composition serving as a kind of center of gravity for each musician to spin off of and elaborate upon." In his interview with Rand, Malaby explained that his approach to performing is based on the idea of working with, not playing over, the music of his collaborators. "Tom Rainey [the drummer] has been talking to me about it for years, but it just wouldn't sink in," Malaby said. "He was like 'Don't take a solo; play, but don't take a solo.' . . . And it really hit me 10 years later in a real physical way. . . . It feels like I'm not taking a solo, not leading, that the guys are not accompanying me. It feels like we're all intertwined."

With the recently formed Tony Malaby Cello Trio, which includes Fred Lonberg-Hold on cello and John Hollenbeck on drums, Malaby recorded *Warblepeck* (2008). Writing for allaboutjazz.com (October 27, 2008), Roberto Curtis described the album as "as experimental as it is fun." "The group's virtuosity creeps up behind the obvious ingenuity and body slams you with sonic indulgence," Curtis continued. "Though impossible to say who's in the driver's seat, Malaby's command of the tenor saxophone's altissimo register is remarkably tight as he dances through the three-way improvisation. It may just sound like noise to the undiscerning ear, but rest assured there is method and beauty in the mayhem."

Over the course of his career, Malaby has played with a number of big-name jazzmen, including Tim Berne, Mark Helias, George Schuller, and Fred Hersch. Though he and Sanchez have made their home on the East Coast, Malaby told Armstrong that he often draws inspiration from the relative tranquility of his hometown. "I think the intensity of New York—just where I live, it's noisy and dirty and crowded—combined with the type of person that I am—I have really extended antennae, and everything is filtering into me way too much—is just really overwhelming," he said. "One of the ways to shut that down is to visualize and meditate on where I come from, the physical beauty of the things and places out there. It's going back to where you live, where you grew up. And when I am able to get there, that's where I am really able to compose and tap into that really free space where we all want to love, where all of us who are creative people want to live."

Even if he sometimes looks to Arizona for inspiration, Malaby aims to create music that transcends the region. "In trying to create an identity," he told Waltzer, "you rebel against where you came from, your parents' thing, and in some sense against the American thing." He and Sanchez, he said, "became jazz musicians. And if you're a jazz musician, you live outside the changes of being a normal American. You try to create your own identity."

—K.J.P.

Suggested Reading: *Down Beat* p25 May 2007; (Newark, New Jersey) *Star-Ledger* p1 Apr. 13, 2003, p20 Feb. 17, 2006; *Phoenix (Arizona) New Times* Nov. 23, 2000; Tony Malaby's Web site; *Tucson (Arizona) Weekly* (on-line) Apr. 15, 2004

Selected Recordings: *Cosas*, 1993; *The Dave Scott/Tony Malaby Quartet*, 1995; *Sabino*, 2000; *Apparitions*, 2003; *Adobe*, 2004; *Alive in Brooklyn*, 2004; *Alive in Brooklyn, Vol. 2*, 2006; *Tamarindo*, 2007; *Warblepeck*, 2008

Maltin, Leonard

Dec. 18, 1950– Film historian; critic

Address: Entertainment Tonight, *Paramount Television, 5555 Melrose Ave., Los Angeles, CA 90038*

"Everyone likes talking about the movies—wherever I go, people stop me and want to talk about the movies," the film critic and historian Leonard Maltin told Laurie Freeman for *Electronic Media* (January 8, 2001). For more than 25 years, Maltin has offered his opinions of motion pictures and provided historical information about the movie industry as a commentator on the syndicat-

Mark Mainz/Getty Images

Leonard Maltin

ed television program *Entertainment Tonight*, and his annual handbook *Leonard Maltin's Movie Guide* is the best-selling book of its kind. Maltin's first such guide, called *TV Movies*, contained 8,000 entries and was published in 1969, when he was only 18 years old; the 2009 edition, published in mid-2008, includes more than 17,000 entries. The work was described by Dwight Garner, writing for the *New York Times Book Review* (September 3, 2006), as "the go-to choice for both film geeks and casual couch potatoes," and a writer for *Esquire* (October 1999) declared that it "has become the single most important reference book in every American home." The book has spawned such companion volumes as *Leonard Maltin's Family Film Guide* (1999) and *Leonard Maltin's Classic Movie Guide* (2005), the latter of which covers movies released before 1960. According to Marla Matzer, writing for *Forbes* (September 11, 1995), "Maltin learned early on an important publishing lesson: that the key to profitability is recycling the same basic data into different formats, in effect selling the same information again and again." In an anecdote that reveals the extent of his reputation as a human encyclopedia of film and the film industry, Maltin recalled to Rob Salem for the *Toronto (Ontario, Canada) Star* (January 21, 1992), "Getting accurate running times [the lengths of films in minutes] is a constant headache. Even the studios don't know. [My researchers and I] get completely different lengths from different people in the very same department. I once asked a guy fairly high up at one of the studios how they keep track of running times, you know, for official studio records. And he just looked at me. 'We get them from your book,' he said." Maltin "is invaluable be-

cause there is only one Leonard Maltin," the former *Entertainment Tonight* producer Bill Olson told Dennis McLellan for the *Los Angeles Times* (December 6, 1994). "Above all, he's an expert—a world-renowned film buff—but he's a fan underneath all of that. He just loves it and he never tires of it."

Leonard Maltin was born on December 18, 1950 in New York City to Aaron and Jacqueline (Gould) Maltin. His father was a lawyer and immigration judge; his mother was a singer. He grew up in Teaneck, New Jersey, a suburb of New York. At a young age he became passionate about movies— particularly those from the 1920s and 1930s— watching them on television and in theaters in his neighborhood and nearby towns; because crime was less of a concern in those days, his parents permitted him to take public transportation on his own before he reached adolescence. "I never wanted to be a critic per se," he told Laurie Freeman. "What interested me early on was movie history. As a kid, I was watching *Laurel and Hardy*, *The Little Rascals*, *The Three Stooges*, silent comedies. I loved all of this stuff and was curious to learn more about it, the people, the era, how they were made. I went to the library, took out what few books there were (the first book I ever bought was a biography of Charlie Chaplin at a library sale) and did a lot of writing. I loved to write—creative writing was my favorite subject. I started writing about those movies and those people based on my research and my viewings of the movies I managed to see. I never imagined there was a career to be made doing that."

In fifth grade Maltin and a friend wrote their own movie-fan magazine, and by the time Maltin had entered Teaneck High School, as he recalled to Dennis McLellan, "I was pretty well eating, sleeping, breathing movies. That was it. I fell into a crowd in New York of die-hard old movie buffs who had several little private film societies that would gather several times a week and show rare films, double and triple features." At 13 Maltin started contributing articles to the publication *Film Fan Monthly*, based in Vancouver, British Columbia. When Maltin was 15 *Film Fan's* owner (only 19 himself) decided he did not want to keep the magazine. Along with a check that included money mailed in for subscriptions and advertisements, the owner turned over the magazine to Maltin. For nine years beginning in 1966, Maltin edited and published the magazine, producing it amateurishly at first, by his own account—in his bedroom for a while. The 25 back issues currently available include that of July/August 1966, which features a biography and filmography of the actor John Barrymore by Maltin and a comparison of Captain America and Batman; May 1967, with Maltin's cover article about the actress Miriam Hopkins and a piece about the "worst serials of the 1930s"; February 1971, with an article "chronicling Hollywood veterans in current movies," among them Mae West, Don Ameche, Joan Bennett, and Ray Milland; June 1974, with a "lengthy feature" about Popeye the Sailor Man, in which Maltin "review[ed] the cartoon character's long career"; February 1975, with a "candid profile/interview" of Gloria Swanson "with rare photos" and a photographic tribute to the recently deceased Larry Fine, one of the Three Stooges; and June 1974, with Maltin's interview of Jackie Cooper. Although the circulation of *Film Fan Monthly* increased from 400 to 2,000 during Maltin's tenure, he "never made any money out of it," as he told Paul Byrnes for the *Sydney (Australia) Morning Herald* (September 16, 1987). "It was a labour of love."

As a high-school student, Maltin once traveled to Hollywood to interview the silent-film star Buster Keaton. In 1968, during his senior year, Maltin's English teacher introduced him to an editor at Signet Books, an arm of the New American Library (now a division of the Penguin Group). The editor was interested in publishing a movie reference book that would be more useful than an existing one—*Movies on TV*, by Steven H. Scheuer—which had debuted 10 years earlier under the Bantam Books imprint. After the 17-year-old Maltin suggested the additions of directors' names, the running time of each movie, and a rating system with four stars, he was signed on to write the new guide. Written in just five months, with the help of two researchers whom Maltin recruited, the 8,000-entry *TV Movies* went on sale the following year. The title changed to *Leonard Maltin's TV Movies* in 1985 and to *Leonard Maltin's TV Movies and Video Guide* in 1987; it became *Leonard Maltin's Movie and Video Guide* in 1993 and *Leonard Maltin's Movie Guide* in 2004. The guide was updated every other year until 1988, when it became an annual. The guide published in 2004, which was identified on the cover as the 2005 edition, appeared on the *New York Times* best-seller list for nine weeks, in the "advice and how-to" category. The 2008 edition, published in mid-2007, has 1,648 pages and weighs 1.6 pounds; bearing a cover price of $9.99, it contains upwards of 17,000 entries, including 400 that appeared in the guide for the first time, and listings for more than 8,000 DVDs and 13,000 videos. Maltin, who has not watched every movie listed, relies on researchers for assistance in compiling the guide.

One example of a four-star movie in Maltin's 2008 guide is the classic *Casablanca* (1942), whose entry notes that the film runs for 102 minutes and was directed by Michael Curtiz. The entry lists the names of 13 actors and actresses who appeared in the film, among them Humphrey Bogart, Ingrid Bergman, Paul Henreid, Claude Rains, Conrad Veidt, Peter Lorre, Sydney Greenstreet, and Dooley Wilson. Maltin then wrote: "Everything is right in this WW2 classic of war-torn Morocco with elusive nightclub owner Rick (Bogart) finding old flame (Bergman) and her husband, underground leader Henreid, among skeletons in his closet. Rains is marvelous as dapper police chief, and nobody

sings 'As Time Goes By' like Dooley Wilson. Three Oscars include Picture, Director, and Screenplay (Julius & Philip Epstein and Howard Koch). Our candidate for the best Hollywood movie of all time. Spawned short-lived TV series in the 1950s and 1980s. Also shown in computer-colored version." In an example of what Maltin labeled a "bomb," the entry for *Johnny Be Good* (1988), directed by Bud S. Smith and starring Anthony Michael Hall, Robert Downey Jr., Paul Gleason, and Uma Thurman, reads: "Offensive, bottom-of-the-barrel comedy about star high-school jock Hall and how various colleges attempt to illegally recruit him. The seriousness of the issue completely eludes the makers of this turkey. R-rated scenes were added for homevideo version."

Earlier, after his high-school graduation, Maltin had enrolled at New York University, where he majored in journalism and earned a B.A. degree in 1972. In his spare time he contributed freelance articles to film journals and national publications, among them *Variety* and *TV Guide*. He also wrote books: *Movie Comedy Teams* (1970, revised in 1985), *Behind the Camera* (1971, reprinted as *The Art of the Cinematographer*), *The Great Movie Shorts* (1972, reprinted as *Selected Short Subjects*), and *The Disney Films* (1973, revised in 2000). He contributed to *A Concise History of the Cinema* (1971), *The Complete Guide to Film Study* (1972), *The American Film Heritage* (1972), and *Directors in Action* (1973), and he edited *The Real Stars* (1973) and *The Laurel and Hardy Book* (1973). The second edition of *TV Movies* was published in 1974. That same year, at a film-society screening, Maltin met Alice Tlusty, a publishing-company secretary and fellow movie lover. "I got depressed one time," he admitted to McLellan, "because I didn't really have any social life and I didn't know how to pursue one, but I didn't really want to give up what I was doing because I liked it. I'm awfully happy I met Alice when I did." The two married in March 1975. In 1976 Maltin was a guest curator in the Department of Film at the Museum of Modern Art in New York City.

Meanwhile, in 1973, Maltin had joined the faculty of the New School for Social Research (now known as the New School), in New York City; he taught there until 1981. The titles of three of his courses were Sixty Years of Animation; The Many Worlds of Animation; and A Serious Look at Funny Cartoons. In 1982, thanks to an interview with the *Today* show's media and art critic Gene Shalit about Maltin's book *The Great Movie Comedians* (1978), he landed a steady job on *Entertainment Tonight*. "[Shalit and I] had this really loose, lively, funny conversation, and 3,000 miles away, somebody at Paramount Television saw that and called the man who was then running *Entertainment Tonight*, . . . and said, 'You're looking for a film critic, aren't you?'" Maltin told Virginia Rohan for the Bergen County, New Jersey, *Record* (June 17, 2007). "Two days later, my phone rang, and here I am." He was one of very few movie critics on television at the time and the first to work in a Hollywood film studio. "He was an everyperson reviewer," one of the show's former executive producers, James Bellows, told Marla Matzer. "He wasn't a chichi, big-city type." Over the years Maltin has interviewed Robert De Niro, Meryl Streep, and other movie stars for *Entertainment Tonight*. Some celebrities, he has said, will agree to be interviewed only by him. "I'm not the world's greatest interviewer," he told Beth Pinsker for the *Dallas Morning News* (September 23, 1995). "It's not that I'm so good, it's that so many people are so bad. And by bad I mean that they don't know anything about the people they interview. They haven't really seen the movies. I can finish people's sentences. It scores points."

In 1986 the Maltins became the parents of a daughter, Jessica. Around that time Maltin's *ET* segments began to focus on movie history, with interviews of all-but-forgotten silent-movie stars and demonstrations of how movies achieved special effects before the digital age. Maltin was happy to take a break from reviewing. "That was really becoming a chore," he told Rob Salem for the *Toronto Star* (January 21, 1992). "I had never had a daily reviewing job before. And this was the early '80s—not a great spurt of movie making. This was a time when *Friday the 13th* and *Porky's* were both riding high, and the sequels were coming hot and heavy, and there were a lot of movies with cute robots in them."

Maltin co-authored, with Richard W. Bann, *Our Gang: The Life and Times of the Little Rascals* (1977, reprinted as *The Little Rascals: The Life and Times of Our Gang*). Maltin's book *The Great Movie Comedians* was followed in 1980 by *Of Mice and Magic: A History of American Animated Cartoons* (revised in 1987) and *The Great American Broadcast: A Celebration of Radio's Golden Age* (1997), the last of which "took more than 10 years to produce," as Ruth Bayard Smith reported for the *New York Times Book Review* (November 9, 1997). "Maltin brings the same seemingly boundless enthusiasm and encyclopedic recall previously devoted to film to the so-called Golden Age of broadcasting—the period from the early 1920's to the 1950's . . . ," Smith wrote. "He writes with gusto about many of the participating actors, directors, announcers, writers and sound-effects workers. He also discusses the tremendous impact radio and advertising had on American society as well as the tensions between the radio, music and newspaper industries. And, of course, he addresses the celebrated programming of the era, from comedy and drama and soaps to children's shows and live musical performances. The book contains first-person narratives and anecdotes—some timeworn, some new—but is also filled with an impressive array of photographs of memorabilia and radio practitioners. Unfortunately, the citations for the sources of this material is skimpy; thus, the book is great to read, but limited as an historical reference."

From the late 1980s through the early 1990s, Maltin wrote, produced, and hosted such television specials as *Cartoons for Big Kids* (1989), *The Lost Stooges* (1990), *Cartoon Madness: The Fantastic Max Fleischer Cartoons* (1991), *The Making of The Quiet Man* (1992), and *Young Duke: The Making of a Movie Star* (1993), about the early life of John Wayne. Maltin joined the STARZ! television network in 1994; in five-minute segments titled "Leonard Maltin's Movie Break," he comments on films. He has also hosted film festivals on STARZ! From 1996 to 1999 he wrote a column about films for the bimonthly magazine *Modern Maturity* (now known as *AARP The Magazine*) and was the movie critic for the magazine *Playboy* from 1998 to 2004. Articles by him have also appeared in national publications including *American Film*, *Disney Magazine*, *Esquire*, the *Los Angeles Times*, *Smithsonian*, and the *New York Times*. Since 1998 Maltin has served as an adjunct professor at the School of Cinematic Arts at the University of Southern California. From 2001 to 2004 he hosted what he called a half-hour "movie conversation" show, *Hot Ticket*, for Paramount Television (now known as CBS Paramount Television), which produces and distributes *Entertainment Weekly*. Currently, he hosts *Secret's Out*, a weekly series aired on the Reelz channel that showcases largely overlooked films. His quarterly newsletter, *Movie Crazy*, is available by subscription.

Maltin was instrumental in the decision by Richard W. "Dick" Cook, the chairman of Walt Disney Studios, to issue a series of DVDs called *Walt Disney Treasures*, beginning in 2001. Two years earlier, as he recalled to Susan King for the *Los Angeles Times* (December 3, 2002), Maltin had told Cook, "You have all this wonderful material in your vault. Some of it has never been on video and some that has hasn't been presented in the best way. And now with DVD there are so many opportunities created, things that can be done to showcase this wonderful stuff. And [Cook] said, 'Let's do it.'" The series makes available what Dave Kehr, writing for the *New York Times* (December 20, 2005), described as "the less commercial titles in the Disney canon," chosen and introduced on each DVD by "the invaluable" Maltin, as Kehr put it. The titles include *Walt Disney: On the Front Lines* (2004), a collection of short films and one feature film *(Victory Through Air Power)* commissioned by the U.S. government during World War II, and *Disney Rarities: Celebrated Shorts 1920s–1960s* (2005), which offers a half-dozen of Disney's silent, 1920s "Alice's Wonderland" shorts and the Oscar-winning shorts *Ferdinand the Bull* (1938), based on a children's book by Munro Leaf, and *Toot, Whistle, Plunk and Boom* (1953), an introduction to four families of musical instruments. Other DVDs in the *Treasures* series present movies featuring such Disney characters as Oswald the Lucky Rabbit and his successor, Mickey Mouse; Donald Duck; Pluto; and Goofy.

Maltin served as the president of the Society for Cinephiles in 1990–91 and as president of the Los Angeles Film Critics Association in 1995–96. His honors include the 2001 Annie Award from the International Animated Film Society and the 2005 American Society of Cinematographers Award of Distinction. A longtime advocate for film preservation, he won the 1993 Anthology Film Archives of America Preservation Award and in 1997 was named to the National Film Preservation Board, helping to select the 25 films added to the Library of Congress's National Film Registry annually. In 2006 the librarian of Congress named him to the board of directors of the National Film Preservation Foundation.

Maltin lives with his wife and daughter in Toluca Lake, a district of Los Angeles, California. Jessie Maltin helped him in the preparation of *Leonard Maltin's Family Film Guide.*

—M.A.S.

Suggested Reading: *Calgery (Alberta, Canada) Herald* ES p14 June 1, 2002; *Forbes* p305 Sep. 11, 1995; leonardmaltin.com; *Los Angeles Times* F p1 Dec. 6, 1994; *Toronto (Ontario, Canada) Star* B p1 Jan. 21, 1992

Selected Books—as author or co-author: *Movie Comedy Teams*, 1970, 1985; *Behind the Camera*, 1971; *The Great Movie Shorts*, 1972; *The Disney Films*, 1973, 2000; *Our Gang: The Life and Times of the Little Rascals* (with Richard W. Bann), 1977; *The Great Movie Comedians*, 1978; *Of Mice and Magic: A History of American Animated Cartoons*, 1980, 1987; *The Great American Broadcast: A Celebration of Radio's Golden Age*, 1997; *Leonard Maltin's Movie Crazy: For People Who Love Movies*, 2008; as editor—*Leonard Maltin's Movie Guide* (formerly *TV Movies*) 1969, 2008; *The Real Stars*, 1973; *The Laurel and Hardy Book*, 1973; *Leonard Maltin's Movie Encyclopedia*, 1994; *Leonard Maltin's Family Film Guide*, 1999; *Leonard Maltin's Classic Movie Guide*, 2005

Selected Television and Video/DVD Projects (in various capacities): *The Art of Disney Animation*, 1988; *Cartoons for Big Kids*, 1989; *The Lost Stooges*, 1990; *Cartoon Madness: The Fantastic Max Fleisher Cartoons*, 1991; *The Making of The Quite Man*, 1992; *Young Duke: The Making of a Movie Star*, 1993; *Walt Disney Treasures*, 2001–

Manning, Eli

Jan. 3, 1981– Football player

Address: New York Giants, Giants Stadium, East Rutherford, NJ 07073

Following in the footsteps of a successful family member can be difficult. The National Football League (NFL) quarterback Eli Manning of the New York Giants started out with two sets before him: those of his father, Archie Manning, a celebrated college athlete who went on to be a quarterback for the New Orleans Saints, and those of his brother Peyton Manning, currently a quarterback for the Indianapolis Colts and considered one the greatest to have played the game. The number-one NFL draft pick in 2004, Eli Manning was chosen by the San Diego Chargers and traded immediately to the Giants. He became the team's starting quarterback during his first season, which proved to be one of transition and growth, and the Giants finished with a dismal record. The following two seasons saw the Giants reach the play-offs but lose during the first round, and given the fanfare that had surrounded Manning's signing with the team, there was much discussion of his inability to perform to expectation. The young quarterback silenced his critics in dramatic fashion on February 3, 2008, when he led his team to an upset championship victory over the New England Patriots, in one of the most exciting Super Bowl games ever played.

Stephen Lovekin/Getty Images

The youngest of the three boys of Archie and Olivia Manning, Elisha Nelson Manning was born on January 3, 1981 in New Orleans, Louisiana, into a family with deep roots in football. Archie Manning was a star player at the University of Mississippi, in Oxford—or Ole Miss, as it is affectionately known—coming in third in voting for the Heisman

Trophy during his senior year. He played for the Saints for the first 11 of his 14 seasons in the NFL, and although the franchise never enjoyed a winning season during his tenure, he was always highly respected and lauded for his athleticism. Archie Manning was twice selected for the Pro Bowl, in 1978 and 1979, and had 2,011 career completions, ranking 17th in NFL history in that category. For the last three seasons of his career, he played successively for the Houston Oilers and the Minnesota Vikings.

Eli Manning's brother Cooper, the oldest of the sons, was a star wide receiver at Isidore Newman High School, in New Orleans. He was recruited by Ole Miss, but before he could play a single game there, doctors diagnosed him with spinal stenosis, a narrowing of the spinal column, which threatened severe injury if he continued to play football. Peyton, the middle son, was the starting quarterback at Isidore Newman beginning in his sophomore year (when Cooper was a senior) and amassed an impressive record during his three years as that position, including an undefeated senior season. Instead of following his father and older brother to Ole Miss, Peyton accepted an invitation to play for one of the school's rivals, the University of Tennessee, a decision that infuriated many Ole Miss fans and cost the Manning family several friendships. Peyton Manning helped his college team win the national championship twice and was a Heisman Trophy finalist in each season. He was the first overall pick in the 1998 NFL draft, signed by the Indianapolis Colts. In February 2007, in Super Bowl XLI, he steered the team to victory over the Chicago Bears.

Inevitably, endless comparisons have been made between Eli Manning and his father and brother Peyton, with regard to both personality and quarterback skills. Peyton is known for being methodical, obsessing over statistics, and leading his team with "tough love," while Eli has often been called laid-back, quiet, and shy. His demeanor earned him the nickname "Easy" in high school. Eli was also starting quarterback at Isidore Newman, where he amassed more yards than Peyton (7,389 to 7,207) but fewer touchdowns (81 to 92). A 17-year-old Eli Manning said to John McClain for the *Houston Chronicle* (October 4, 1998) about the constant comparisons with other family members: "It's not hard being Archie's son and Cooper and Peyton's little brother. Because I'm a quarterback, I get compared to my dad and Peyton, but I don't consider that tough. I consider it an honor."

For college Eli Manning chose to follow his father to the University of Mississippi, in part because Peyton's former quarterback coach at Tennessee, David Cutcliffe, had moved to Ole Miss. Before Manning's arrival in Oxford, the town was peppered with bumper stickers that read "Eli's Coming," and the Three Dog Night song of the same name played from countless stereos. During his freshman year Manning redshirted (that is, he did not participate in varsity play), which allowed him to practice with the team while maintaining four years of playing eligibility; he was nonetheless one of the most popular players on autograph day. In the following season, as backup quarterback, he spent much of his time watching game film. He had the opportunity to show his skill when he was called to replace the starting quarterback during the 2000 Music City Bowl. Ole Miss was down 49–16 against West Virginia when Manning entered the game during the fourth quarter; he completed 12 of 20 passes for 167 yards and threw three touchdowns. While his stellar play was not enough to secure a win, Manning proved that he was ready to become the starting quarterback.

During his first start, on September 1, 2001, Manning helped the Ole Miss Rebels defeat Murray State, 49–14, in the process setting two school records, with five touchdown passes in one game and 18 consecutive completed passes. He finished his first season as a starter with 2,948 yards and 31 touchdowns. By the midpoint of his second season as a starter, Manning already held 18 school records—many of which had belonged to his father—but despite his exemplary performance, the Rebels suffered a five-game losing streak, which spoiled their chances for postseason play. Manning logged career-high statistics in many categories: he led the Southeastern Conference (SEC) in passing yards per game, with an average of 257, and in total offense, with 249 yards per game; he passed for 3,088 yards, with 20 touchdowns and 15 interceptions. As Peyton had done, Eli Manning returned to school for his senior year instead of entering the NFL draft. Prior to that season talk of Eli's winning the Heisman Trophy was plentiful, as he had increased his number of school records to 45. Manning threw for 3,341 yards with 27 touchdowns and nine interceptions his senior season, leading the Rebels to one of the best seasons in Ole Miss's history. Like his father and brother before him, he was a finalist for the Heisman Trophy, finishing third in the balloting. He was named the SEC Player of the Year and won the Unitas Golden Arm Award and the Maxwell Trophy for College Football Player of the Year. In his college career Manning threw for 10,119 yards and 81 touchdowns, becoming the school's career passing leader.

There was much speculation about Manning's place in the 2004 NFL draft, in which the San Diego Chargers had first pick. While that season saw a number of talented new quarterbacks, such as Philip Rivers and Ben Roethlisberger, most observers believed that Manning would be chosen first. The Manning family believed so as well, and behind closed doors they expressed their dismay at the prospect of Eli Manning's playing for the Chargers, given the team's poor record (4–12) the previous season. Manning suggested that he might sit out the year and wait for the next draft. The San Diego franchise publicly expressed its disgust at what it saw as the arrogance of the Manning family. On draft day, though, the Chargers picked Manning anyway. The team then traded him to the New York Giants for a 2004 third-round draft pick, a 2005 first-round pick, a 2006 fifth-round pick, and Rivers, whom New York had chosen fourth overall.

Manning and the Giants' new coach, Tom Coughlin, had come to a team whose previous year's record was also 4–12. It was expected that Manning would play backup for his first season while he adjusted to professional play. The Giants let go of their popular quarterback Kerry Collins, after he refused to accept a smaller salary, and hired the veteran quarterback and former Super Bowl champion Kurt Warner to help with Manning's transition. In the summer before the 2004 season, Manning inked a contract that included a signing bonus and other incentives worth as much as $54 million in total.

Warner started the first 10 games of Manning's rookie season, but after the Giants lost three straight games, Coughlin decided to start Manning. The young quarterback lost his first game, against the Atlanta Falcons, and had trouble finding his rhythm in the next several contests. After six losses under Manning's leadership, fans and the press voiced their disapproval. The complaints were especially vitriolic because his fellow rookie Roethlisberger—who had started for the Pittsburgh Steelers since the second game of the season—was having an exceptionally good rookie year. (The next year Roethlisberger, at 23, became the youngest quarterback to win the Super Bowl.)

Manning maintained an air of calm during the poor performances of his first season, suggesting repeatedly that he needed to train further, watch more films, and gain greater confidence in his ability to compete at the professional level. Despite the criticism in the press, the Giants expressed a willingness to be patient with Manning. Comparisons with Peyton Manning proved helpful for the rookie quarterback, as Eli's older brother had led the Colts to a dismal 3–13 record in his first season but had later emerged as one of the most successful quarterbacks of all time. During the final game of the season, Eli Manning showed signs of maturity and quick decision making, which allowed the running back Tiki Barber to score a last-second touchdown. Although the Giants' 2004 season was as bad as the one before it, their dramatic win in the final game left the team and their fans with a glimmer of hope. "There couldn't have been a better drive to end the season," Barber said, as quoted by Peter King in *Sports Illustrated* (September 5, 2005). "It sent us into the off-season knowing our quarterback knew exactly what to do in a clutch situation." Manning ended his first season having thrown for six touchdowns, nine interceptions, and more than 1,000 yards; he had a quarterback rating of 55.4. (The quarterback rating, also known as passer rating, is a measure of overall performance, taking into account total touchdowns, yards, completions, and interceptions. The league average was 82.8 that year.)

By midway through Manning's second year, the team had improved tremendously, and the Giants were enjoying a winning season. Manning had begun to show moxie, especially in the fourth quarter. The Giants ended the regular season at the top of the National Football Conference (NFC) East, with an 11–5 record, landing them in the postseason. (They lost their first game, against the Carolina Panthers.) Manning finished the season with 3,762 yards, 24 touchdowns, 15 interceptions, and a quarterback rating of 75.9.

Opening day of the 2006 season found Manning playing against his brother, as the Giants squared off against the Colts. The win went to Peyton, but the contest was hard-fought. Manning followed that first-week loss with an impressive overtime defeat of the Philadelphia Eagles, in which he threw a career-high 371 yards. The Giants performed unevenly for the remainder of the season, managing a five-game winning streak and then struggling due to injury. They ended the regular season with a record of 8–8, qualifying for the playoffs, where they lost to the Eagles thanks to a last-second field goal.

The Giants began the 2007 season with two losses, which soon brought cries for Coughlin's removal and complaints that Manning's salary was inflated. The team then won the next seven games. Many of those were tough battles, and Manning's quarterback rating stayed relatively low due to the frequency of interceptions. The criticism continued, especially in New York, even when it appeared that the Giants had secured a play-off berth. After the Giants' first 11 games, Ralph Vacchiano, writing for the New York *Daily News* (December 2, 2007), summed up the sentiments of the press and many Giants fans: "Fifty starts into an NFL career that began with the promise—and demand—of greatness, it's clear to everyone that Eli Manning is no Roethlisberger or [Tom] Brady, nor is he the second coming of his older brother, Peyton. Yet determining exactly what he is hasn't been easy for a city that has turned the over-analysis of Eli into a brand new sport. He's too laid-back and doesn't show enough fire. . . . Then sometimes, he's calm and cool in tough situations. He's 'skittish', as GM Jerry Reese said last week. . . . Then sometimes, he has his best games under pressure. He has flashes of brilliance that justify every draft pick the Giants traded for him on Draft Day 2004. . . . Then he turns around and has a four-interception stinker like the one he threw at the Minnesota Vikings last week."

The final game of the 2007 regular season, albeit a loss, helped the Giants to enter the play-offs with determination. The New England Patriots, 15–0, were on a path to becoming only the second NFL team—after the 1972 Miami Dolphins—to finish the season undefeated. During the game Manning completed 22 of 32 passes, throwing for 251 yards, four touchdowns, and only one interception. The Patriots won, 38–35, but the Giants left the field knowing that their opponents were not invincible.

The Giants entered the play-offs in the wild-card spot, and as underdogs they had to play each game on the road. That seemed to work to the Giants' advantage, as they had enjoyed a streak of wins away from home. They defeated the Tampa Bay Buccaneers, 24–14, to advance to the NFC Divisional Championship, where they defeated the NFC number-one seed Dallas Cowboys. In the NFC Championship, against the Green Bay Packers, Manning helped the Giants to an overtime win, in a game that saw some of the coldest temperatures in modern NFL history. In the Super Bowl they would face the Patriots.

Many were surprised that Eli was the member of the Manning family to play in Super Bowl XLII; his brother's team had been defeated by the San Diego Chargers during the AFC Divisional Championship. The Giants, for their part, had had a taste of nearly defeating the storied, heavily favored Patriots, and they were determined to walk away from the Super Bowl as champions. On February 3, 2008, during the most-watched Super Bowl in history, the Giants were behind 7–3 at halftime, but their defense had been punishing the Patriot quarterback Tom Brady, thus limiting his effectiveness. The Patriots and Giants traded touchdowns in the second half, making the score 14–10, in favor of New England. With 2:45 left in the game, Manning was left with one drive to score.

On third down at their own 44-yard line, the Giants needed five yards for a first down. In what has since been called the greatest play in Super Bowl history, Manning—who seemed about to be sacked, as three Patriots converged around him—avoided tackle, circled out of the pocket, and lobbed a pass to the wide receiver David Tyree, who leapt into the air above tight coverage and caught the ball. As Tyree fell backward, he pinned the ball between his hand and helmet, maintaining possession as he hit the ground. During the next set of downs, Manning threw a touchdown pass to the wide receiver Plaxico Burress; the Patriots were unable to recover in the final 35 seconds, and the Giants won, 17–14. Manning was named MVP of the Super Bowl. "Not Peyton Manning's little brother, not Eli who slumps, none of that," the veteran Giants player Michael Strahan said, as Arthur Staple reported for Newsday (February 5, 2008). "Eli Manning is the world champion. I hope everybody remembers that, respects that, understands that because this team goes nowhere without him. Eli Manning has taken us to the Super Bowl and Eli Manning has won it for us."

In the opening game of the regular season in 2008, Manning helped the Giants beat the Washington Redskins, 16–7. Ten days later his three touchdown passes contributed to the Giants' win, 41–13, in a game against the St. Louis Rams. The following week he threw the touchdown pass that spelled a come-from-behind victory over the Cincinnati Bengals, and the next week the Giants beat the Seattle Seahawks, 44–6. Their defeat at the hands of the Cleveland Browns was their only loss in their first seven games. The Giants' other two wins through late October came in contests with the San Francisco 49ers and the Pittsburgh Steelers.

In April 2008 Manning married his college girlfriend, Abby McGrew, who works in fashion design. The couple live in Hoboken, New Jersey.

—F.C.

Suggested Reading: *Hartford (Connecticut) Courant* May 7, 2004; *Houston (Texas) Chronicle* p21 Oct. 4, 1998; National Football League Web site; (New York) *Daily News* p52 Dec. 2, 2007; New York Giants Web site; *New York Times* Sports p1 Oct. 19, 2001; *Sports Illustrated* p130 Sep. 5, 2005

Paul Gilham/Getty Images

Marta

Feb. 19, 1986– Soccer player

Address: Östra Idrottsallén 22 903 42, Umea, Sweden

In Brazil until the late 1970s, it was illegal for women to play soccer. Although they have done so lawfully for more than two decades, Marta—the country's greatest female player and one of the best women soccer players in the world—has had to struggle for years against male chauvinism. Historically, Latin American countries have been much slower than European nations to accept all-female professional soccer leagues; because so many Brazilians view women's soccer as a novelty, Marta (who, like most Brazilian athletes, uses only her given name professionally) joined a Swedish women's soccer club, Umea IK. "There is much more interest in women's football [in Sweden]. Here, I get help, in Brazil I didn't get any help," Marta told Sophie Mongalvy for the Agence France Presse (April 20, 2007).

Since its founding, in 1985, Umea IK has established itself as an outstanding women's club. FIFA (the Fédération Internationale de Football Association, or International Federation of Soccer Associations) has ranked it fourth among the world's strongest women's teams, behind the national teams of the United States, China, and Norway. Marta is a striker and midfielder best known for her lightning speed, her agile maneuvering, and the power of her left foot. Speaking of her abilities, Renê Simões, who coached Brazil's women's team during the 2004 Summer Olympics, told Alex Bellos for the London *Observer* (June 3, 2007), "Her ball control at speed is fabulous. She thinks fast. She is always scoring. I think in the history of women's football only [American] Mia Hamm has been a better player. But Marta is much more creative. And she is only 21. In two years' time, she will overtake Mia to be the best." According to Robert Woodard, writing for *Black Sports the Magazine* (November 2007), Marta "plays with a spontaneity and inventiveness that defies description. When she has the ball, there is a buzz of expectation in the crowd. You can see the concern in the body language of defenders as she glides past them. No single defender can contain her. Her moves and total control of the ball make that impossible. What makes her so special is that there are great dribblers, great passers and great shooters. Few players in soccer history can lay claim to being great in all of those skills. Marta can do it all. She has the vision to see the game clearly and the complete package of skill, strength and speed to make it happen." In an article for *FairGame Magazine* (September 26, 2007), Gayle Bryan wrote after watching a game between the Brazil and Norway teams, "The first time Brazil served a long ball toward the end line and Marta took off after it, I was reminded of the often-used . . . expression, 'She looked like she was just shot out of a cannon.' She's that fast." FIFA named Marta the Women's World Player of the Year in both 2006 and 2007, and in the latter year, she made seven goals in the Women's World Cup, helping the Brazilian national women's soccer team to win the silver medal. Thanks to such achievements, she is slowly becoming a national icon in Brazil. In 2007 *Sports Illustrated* (December 31, 2007–January 7, 2008) listed Marta among the best female athletes of the year.

The youngest of four siblings, Marta Vieira da Silva was born on February 19, 1986 in Dois Riachos, in the northeastern state of Alagoas, Brazil. Her father, Aldario, a barber, abandoned the family when Marta was a baby, leaving her mother, Tereza, to provide for her, her sister, Angela, and her two brothers, Jose and Valdir. Without her father's income, the family became extremely poor.

Marta remembers, as she told Bellos, that even the slightest extra expense cut into the food budget. "We didn't have enough money even to buy a football. If my mum had done that we would have gone without food." When a ball was not available, Marta and her playmates would fashion one out of crumpled paper or plastic bags. In the account of her early years offered by Robert Woodard, her father was still living with his wife and children when Marta began playing soccer, when she was seven.

By that time, the Brazilian law that permitted females to play soccer had been in effect for years. (U.S. sources differ as to what year the law went into effect.) Nevertheless, local boys ridiculed Marta for playing what they considered a man's game. "They would insult me, say that I had no shame," she recalled to Bellos. "Sometimes, I'd try to fight them. I might have been small but I was a tough little girl. I would get angry and let fly." Marta's brothers, too, tried to dissuade her from playing. Moreover, at that time, most Brazilians assumed that any female who wanted to play soccer was a lesbian. Added to those difficulties was the embarrassment felt by boys whose skills fell short of hers. In her first experience with league play, on a five-per-side indoor game, Marta outperformed many of her teammates and opponents. After she had competed in a local tournament for two years, she was banned from playing. "Another team said that they would withdraw from the tournament if I continued to play," as she recalled to Bellos. "There was a huge controversy and the championship organizer thought it would be better if I didn't play any more." For a brief period Marta played with a local women's team associated with the club Centro Sportivo Alagoano; not long after she joined that team, it disbanded, due to lack of financial support.

In 2000 a former coach advised the 14-year-old Marta to attend a communal tryout for the professional women's soccer clubs of Rio de Janeiro and São Paulo. After traveling for three days and 1,000 miles on a bus, Marta arrived in Rio, where, on the second day, she was drafted by the club Vasco de Gama. (She has not attended school since that time.) Considered the premier women's club in Brazil, Vasco de Gama often supplied players to the Brazilian women's national team, which had recently placed third in the World Cup—their best finish up to that date. Marta played well for Vasco de Gama. She drew national attention in 2001, when she was the top scorer in a Brazilian youth tournament. The following year she was the standout Brazilian player during the Under-19 World Cup. Marta stayed with Vasco da Gama for two seasons, until 2002, and then transferred to the short-lived club Santa Cruz, with which she remained for one season.

In the summer of 2003, at 17, Marta helped Brazil win a gold medal at the Pan-American Games, held that year in the Dominican Republic. The following month she made her World Cup debut, in the United States. Although Brazil was defeated in the quarterfinals, Marta's performance garnered her the Golden Ball, awarded for the tournament's best individual performance. Immediately afterward Roland Arnqvist, the manager of the Swedish team Umea IK, sought out Marta with the aim of signing her to his club. Finding her was not easy, however, because, as he explained to Bellos, "Brazil is not like Europe, where every house has a telephone." When he reached her Marta enthusiastically signed the contract, thrilled by the prospect of playing for a celebrated women's professional team. Marta became the first Brazilian woman to play in Europe. Some critics believed that she would find it impossible to adjust to the Swedish style of play as well as to the cold weather. But Marta succeeded in marrying her style and creativity with the Swedish sense of team play, and she became fluent in Swedish., which she speaks with a pronounced Portuguese accent. (The national language of Brazil is Portuguese.) The cold weather, however, "was a challenge," as she admitted to Bellos.

Umea IK is one of the 12 teams in Sweden's Damallsvenskan league. In Marta's first season, ending in mid-2004, she helped Umea IK win the UEFA (Union Européenne de Football Association, or Union of European Football Associations) Women's Cup final against the Frankfurt team, 8–0 in total. (In the final stages of cup play, each team plays each of the others twice; the winner is decided by the total number of goals.) Umea IK placed second in the Swedish league, one point behind Djurgarden, who also beat them in the Swedish Cup final.

During Marta's sophomore season, in 2004–05, she scored 21 goals and helped Umea IK to an undefeated regular season and the league title. The team lost to Djurgarden again in the Swedish Cup final. That year Umea IK reached only the quarterfinals of the UEFA Women's Cup. In 2005–06 Marta again scored 21 goals, and Umea IK again went undefeated, capturing the league title. In the Swedish Cup finals, Umea IK lost to Linköpings FC. The team made it to the semifinals in the UEFA Women's Cup. In the UEFA Cup final the following season, Umea IK lost to the most successful British women's soccer team, Arsenal LFC, 1–0 in total. In 2006 the team won the Swedish Cup, with Marta scoring a hat trick (three goals), including the game-winning goal in the final moments. The 2007–08 season is currently underway; as of January 2008, Umea IK had made it to the finals of the UEFA Cup, which were scheduled to conclude in late March.

In the meantime Marta continued to play with the Brazilian national team, which won a silver medal at the 2004 Summer Olympics Games, in Athens, Greece, and a gold medal at the 2007 Pan American Games. The Brazilian men's soccer team has dominated the sport internationally for more than 50 years, and with Marta's help Brazilian women, too, are becoming a dominant force on soc-

cer's world stage. In late 2007 the women's national team displayed their skills at the World Cup. During group play Brazil beat each of their opponents—China, Denmark, and New Zealand—in shutouts (no goals by the opposing teams) and were the only national team to emerge from the first stage undefeated. During that stage Marta scored four of Brazil's eight goals. In the quarterfinal match Brazil defeated Australia, 3–2; Marta made one goal, on a penalty kick, midway through the first half. The semifinal match was discussed excitedly in the press, as Brazil was to face the United States team, who were enjoying a long streak of wins and had routinely beaten Brazil over the years. The former United States midfielder Shannon Boxx commented to Stephen Wade for the Associated Press (September 25, 2007), "Marta has so much confidence when she is on the ball. Their whole team is crafty, but she is the one you cannot lose focus on because then she'll take it to you. She may put you to sleep, then all of a sudden she'll be ready." In that match Marta scored two of Brazil's four goals for a shutout against the U.S. For the first time the Brazilian women advanced to the World Cup final. There, they met the defending champions, Germany, who won, 2–0. Marta's superlative overall performance garnered her the Golden Ball, for overall individual performance, and the Golden Boot, for most goals scored (seven). Robert Woodard described one of Marta's goals as the culmination of "one of the greatest moves I've ever seen in a game" and as "one of those magical sports moments that no one who saw it will ever forget."

In the 2008 Summer Olympics, held in Beijing, Marta and her Brazilian team came in second to the U.S. In September of that year, she was drafted by a newly formed, Los Angeles, California–based league, called Women's Professional Soccer, whose official launching was scheduled to take place in 2009. She was still under contract to her Swedish team, so the league was negotiating for her services, reportedly for a salary of as much as $350,000 per season.

For four years Marta was a finalist for the FIFA Women's World Player of the Year Award. She placed third in 2004 and second in 2005 and won the award in 2006 and 2007. Recently she won a top honor in Brazil, when she was invited to leave her footprints in wet cement on the Walk of Fame, in front of the Estadio Maracana, a huge Brazilian soccer stadium. Her prints, the first from a woman, are next to those of Brazil's (and the world's) greatest soccer players. One of those players, Pelé, bestowed high praise on her by referring to her as "Pelé with skirts," according to Woodard. Marta earns more than any other player in her league, but far less than what professional male players earn; she sends part of her earnings to family members in Brazil. She has a home in Umea.

—F.C.

Suggested Reading: Agence France Presse Apr. 20, 2007; Associated Press Worldsteam Sep. 25, 2007; *Black Sports the Magazine* p28+ Nov. 2007; FIFA Web site; (London) *Observer Sport Monthly* (on-line) June 3, 2007

Gareth Cattermole/Getty Images

May, Brian

July 19, 1947– Guitarist; co-founder of the rock group Queen; astrophysicist

Address: Duck Productions Ltd., P.O. Box 141, Windlesham, Surrey GU20 6YW, England

"I think music is about our internal life," the guitarist, songwriter, singer, and astrophysicist Brian May said to Madeleine Brand, who interviewed him for the National Public Radio program *Day to Day* (May 8, 2008, on-line). "It's part of the way people touch each other. That's very precious to me. And astronomy is, in a sense, the very opposite thing. Instead of looking inwards, you are looking out, to things beyond our grasp." May is a co-founder and the lead guitarist of the immensely successful British rock band Queen, whose record sales have topped 150 million (or 190 million or as many as 300 million, according to some sources) and which has performed to sold-out crowds in stadiums all over the world. "In its mid-1970's heyday," a *New York Times* (November 25, 1991) reporter wrote, "the group created an image of playful decadence while fabricating elaborate studio productions on its albums, overdubbing multiple guitar and vocal lines," and it forged "a hugely popular hybrid of hard-rock, pop, heavy-metal,

cabaret and a hint of opera." Writing for allmusic.com (formerly the All Music Guide Web site), Stephen Thomas Erlewine described Queen's music as "a bizarre yet highly accessible fusion of the macho and the fey." According to the music Web site Shaw Star, 18 of Queen's albums have topped charts in one or more countries, and the band has had 17 first-place singles. The most popular of Queen's songs include "Bohemian Rhapsody," "We Are the Champions," "Under Pressure," "Radio Ga-Ga," "Stone Cold Crazy," "Crazy Little Thing Called Love," "We Will Rock You," "Tie Your Mother Down," "Headlong," "I Want It All," and "Hammer to Fall," the last five of which were written and composed by May.

"Despite its enormous popularity," Stephen Thomas Erlewine wrote, "Queen was never taken seriously by rock critics." Three decades after the band released its first album, at the ceremony in which May was inducted into the Songwriters Hall of Fame (along with Queen members Roger Taylor, John Deacon, and, posthumously, Freddie Mercury), May said, according to BBC News (June 13, 2003, on-line), "I do think that maybe now people are looking [in] more depth to what we did. Yes, we were pretty flashy and we were pretty loud and at moments we seemed very outrageous, but there was a lot of honest craftsmanship that went on behind that." Both Queen, as a group, and May, as an individual, were inducted into the Rock and Roll Hall of Fame, in 2001 and 2004, respectively.

With a one-of-a-kind electric guitar that, as a teenager, he designed and constructed with his father, and with coins rather than plastic picks, May plays in a wide variety of styles, making use of such techniques as multi-track layering, sweep picking, and finger tapping and producing unusual sounds that have reminded listeners of those emanating from orchestras or synthesizers. "He is as singular an artist as we have ever seen and he breathes the rarified air of the One Note Guys: players so exceptional that you can pick them out with just a single sound," Matt Blackett wrote of May for *Guitar Player* (January, 2008), ranking him with such masters of the guitar as Jimi Hendrix, Eddie Van Halen, Carlos Santana, Eric Clapton, and Jeff Beck. According to an article published in *Circus* magazine (March 1975) early on in Queen's history, "It's impossible to have heard Queen without having been riveted and stunned by Brian May's guitar. A screaming flash on the frets, May's notes seem to sonically seek and destroy in the merciless manner of a Hendrix or [a Pete] Townshend." Following the death of Queen's dynamic, over-the-top frontman, Freddie Mercury, in 1991, May formed the Brian May Band, with whom he recorded *Back to the Light* (1993) and *Another World* (1998). Since 2004 he has performed with Roger Taylor, the singer Paul Rodgers, and a variable roster of other musicians in a band called Queen + Rodgers. On June 3, 2002, during the celebrations that marked Elizabeth II's 50th year on the British throne, May opened the outdoor jubilee concert by performing the British national anthem, "God Save the Queen," on the roof of Buckingham Palace. In 2005 the queen named him a Commander of the British Empire.

In 2007 May completed his Ph.D. in astrophysics—an endeavor he had put on hold nearly 30 years earlier. With Sir Patrick Moore, who has hosted the British television series *The Sky at Night* for half a century, and the cosmologist Chris Lintott, he wrote the book *Bang! The Complete History of the Universe* (2006), which is aimed at a lay audience. Commenting on the fields of music and astronomy, May said to Emma Brockes for the London *Guardian* (October 19, 2006), "I think there's a sort of purity about both of them. Because you can immerse yourself in thoughts of the universe, or in music, and you're really abstracted. You're a million miles away from all your worries and personal problems and the dust and smoke of where you are. . . . You're in this world where you're in your head but you're connected to something wonderful around you. They're both indescribable experiences. I remember thinking, when I was quite young, if all there is to life is just staying alive, then why would we bother? Life has to be about more than just being. There has to be something higher. And to me the higher things are exactly these: music and art, beautiful images, and thoughts of the way things work. I love that. Moments of discovery."

The only child of Ruth Fletcher May and Harold May, Brian Harold May was born on July 19, 1947 in Hampton, a section of London, England. His father was a draftsman with the British Ministry of Aviation; his mother was a homemaker. When he was five May's parents arranged for him to have piano lessons every Saturday. Although he would have preferred to spend the hour playing outside, he continued to take piano lessons until he was nine. At six he began experimenting with his father's banjo ukulele (which has a banjo-like body and a ukulele-type neck). On his seventh birthday his parents gave him a Spanish-style acoustic guitar. Around that time he also developed interests in astronomy and photography. As a child he watched the BBC-TV series *The Sky at Night*, which has aired monthly since 1957 with the same host—the amateur astronomer, writer, and xylophonist Patrick Moore, who was knighted in 2001 for his role in popularizing astronomy. May loved the program's theme music, by the 20th-century Finnish composer Jean Sibelius, and persuaded his father to buy him a recording of the Sibelius piece. When he was 14 May built a reflecting telescope with a four-inch mirror. He recalled to a *Circus* magazine (July 6, 1976) writer, "I can remember getting up about 4 a.m. to see Jupiter, running out in the road trying to find a place where I could get a line on it with me telescope, and actually seeing it with its moons and everything." Also as a teenager, dissatisfied with his acoustic guitar, which struck him as too bulky, he worked with his father to construct an electric guitar from scratch—his

now-legendary Red Special; the neck was fashioned out of mahogany from a discarded century-old fireplace mantel, the body from a piece of oak. In the book *Queen: In Their Own Words* (1992), edited by Mick St. Michael, May is quoted as saying that in its construction, he also used part of a knitting needle and valve springs from an old motorcycle. He honed his guitar skills by playing along to records by such artists as Buddy Holly and the Everly Brothers; his interest in song structure and harmonies led to him to analyze the composition of each piece and then improvise solos of his own. May has also cited among his influences Jimi Hendrix and the groups Cream, the Shadows, and the Beatles.

From 1958 to 1965 May attended the Hampton School, an independent day school for boys in London. After his graduation he enrolled at Imperial College in London to pursue a degree in physics and mathematics. As an undergraduate in 1967 and 1968, he played in a band called 1984 (a name inspired by the title of George Orwell's famous 1949 novel about a future dystopian society). In 1968 May received a B.S. degree and enrolled in the graduate program in astrophysics at Liverpool Polytechnic (now Liverpool John Moores University). For his doctoral research he studied cosmic or interplanetary dust, also called zodiacal dust, discovered within the solar system by the German astronomer Walter Grotrian in 1934. He organized astronomy-related trips to Switzerland and Tenerife, in the Canary Islands, mentored in the latter location by the Spanish astronomer Francisco Sanchez. May also co-authored two scientific papers: "MgI Emission in the Night-Sky Spectrum," which appeared in *Nature* in 1972, and "An Investigation of the Motion of Zodiacal Dust Particles: Radial Velocity Measurements on Fraunhofer Line Profiles," published in *Monthly Notices of the Royal Astronomical Society* in 1974.

Meanwhile, 1984 having disbanded in 1968, May had formed a new band, called Smile, with the bassist Tim Staffell and the drummer Roger Taylor. Like 1984, Smile occasionally opened for artists including Jimi Hendrix and Pink Floyd. In 1970 Tim Staffell left the band; a school friend of his, the vocalist Freddie Mercury (born Farrokh Bulsara in Tanzania), a former frontman for the group Wreckage, joined May and Taylor, and at Mercury's suggestion, the men changed the name of their band to Queen. By then May had abandoned his academic pursuits, primarily for lack of time in his busy schedule: in addition to his work toward his doctorate and his musical activities, he had been teaching math at the Stockwell Park Secondary School in southwest London. When his Imperial College adviser told him that the draft of his dissertation required more work, he decided that he "needed to move on," as he explained to Marcus Chown for *New Scientist* (October 14, 2006). "At the time, there was an opportunity with Queen we really couldn't let pass."

In 1971, with the bass guitarist John Deacon on board, Queen began playing occasional gigs and recording their first album. Called *Queen*, it was released in 1973 on the EMI label in Great Britain and the Elektra label in the U.S. and attracted only scattered critical attention. Among those whom it impressed forcefully was Gordon Fletcher, who, in a review for *Rolling Stone* (December 6, 1973), wrote, "Rumor has it that Queen shall soon be crowned 'the new Led Zeppelin,' which is an event that would certainly suit this observer just fine. There's no doubt that this funky, energetic English quartet has all the tools they'll need to lay claim to the Zep's abdicated heavy-metal throne, and beyond that to become a truly influential force in the rock world. Their debut album is superb." Fletcher continued, with a reference to the British rock group Yes, "The Zeppelin analogy is not meant to imply that Queen's music is anywhere near as blues-based as the content of *Led Zep I & II*. No, their songs are more in the Who vein, straight-ahead rock with slashing, hard-driving arrangements that rate with the finest moments of *Who's Next* and *Quadrophenia*. Yet there's a certain level of intelligence with which the show is presented, a structured sanity that coexists alongside the maniacal fury that gives me the impression that the band must have had a lot of Yes songs on their turntables in the three years this album was taking shape. . . . There's a song on the album . . . called 'Modern Times Rock 'N' Roll,' and that's exactly what Queen's music is. They're the first of a whole new wave of English rockers, and you'd best learn to love 'em now 'cause they're here to stay. Regal bearings aside, *Queen* is a monster." Fletcher praised each member of Queen, describing May as "a master of fuzz, wah and sustain" and adding, "His solos are persistent, hard-hitting and to the point."

Like its predecessor, *Queen II* (1974), the band's second release, went gold (selling at least a half-million copies)—as did all of the band's next 16 recordings, several of which went platinum (at least one million copies sold) or multi-platinum. For part of 1974 Mercury, Taylor, and Deacon worked on Queen's third album, *Sheer Heart Attack*, without May, who, during the group's first North American tour, had fallen ill with hepatitis and then developed a stomach ulcer that required surgery. When May returned to the group, as he recalled to the writer for *Circus* magazine (March 1975), "I was able to look at Queen as if I were an outsider— I'd never realized what it sounded like, or how much the group had to offer. They'd got so much done without me—they were really good about it. All I had to do was to go in and put my bits on. The only thing that really suffered from my illness was that I only have about three and a half songs on this album." Among the tracks on *Sheer Heart Attack* (1974) were "Killer Queen," "Lily of the Valley," "Stone Cold Crazy," "Now I'm Here," "Dear Friends," and "Brighton Rock," the last three of which May wrote. *Sheer Heart Attack* became the

group's first album to hit the U.S. Top 20 album charts, peaking at number 12, and it reached the number-two spot on the British charts.

Queen's third offering was *A Night at the Opera* (1975); produced by Roy Thomas Baker, the album was reportedly the most expensive ever made up to that time, largely because of the complexities of recording the nearly six-minute track "Bohemian Rhapsody," which was made in five different studios. "We didn't think it was too much . . . ," May told David Chiu for the *New York Times* (December 27, 2005). "The great thing was to have no limits." A highly eclectic collection, *A Night at the Opera* contains pedal-to-the-metal rockers ("Death on Two Legs," "I'm in Love with My Car,"), examples of progressive rock ("The Prophet's Song") and of pop rock (the music-hall–style "Lazing on a Sunday Afternoon"), a pop ballad ("You're My Best Friend"), folk rock (May's "39"), and "Bohemian Rhapsody," with lyrics and music by Freddie Mercury, which is widely considered Queen's signature song. "Nothing succeeds like excess—at least that's the case with Queen's breakthrough classic, *A Night at the Opera*," Daniel Durchholz, the co-author of *Musichound Rock: The Essential Album Guide*, wrote in an assessment for Amazon.com. "On one level, the title is a reference to the band's operatic pretensions. . . . Of course, *A Night at the Opera* was also the title of a Marx Brothers movie, and the reference isn't lost on Queen, who seldom scaled the heights of pomp-rock without a knowing wink. The album is remembered for its meticulously produced bombast, but the truth is that there's a wide variety of material here. . . . *A Night at the Opera* is viewed by most as the quintessential Queen album, and justifiably so."

None of the members of Queen have ever revealed what "Bohemian Rhapsody" is really about. Ostensibly, the song is the cri de coeur of a young man who has impulsively or accidentally killed someone, has sold his soul to the devil, and now faces execution. It consists of six distinct parts: an a cappella introduction sung in four-part harmony that closes with music performed on a grand piano; a two-minute ballad; a guitar solo; a mock-operatic section containing many overdubbed voices (which made live performances of that section impossible); a muscular hard-rock portion; and a cathartic "outro" that ends with the sound of a gong. "Bohemian Rhapsody" enjoyed extremely heavy rotation on British radio stations, and the single remained at the top spot on British charts for nine weeks in 1975—a record then—and another five in 1991, when it was re-released; in each of those years, sales of the single topped a million copies. Moreover, Queen also made a music video of the song; called a "promotional" video then, it was among the first to accompany the release of a single and helped enormously to lift sales. In 1977 the British Phonographic Industry (BPI), Great Britain's main recording-industry trade association, named "Bohemian Rhapsody" the best single of the previous 25 years. According to Stephen Thomas Erlewine, "With its bombastic, mock-operatic structure punctuated by heavy metal riffing, [the song] encapsulates [Queen's] music." When David Chiu asked May if "Bohemian Rhapsody" was Queen's best recording, May answered, "Who knows? It's certainly had the biggest effect on the greatest number of people around the world."

May wrote four songs for Queen's *A Day at the Races* (1976): "Long Away," "Teo Toriatte," "White Man," and "Tie Your Mother Down," the last of which became one of the band's biggest hits. *A Day at the Races* (which also shares its title with a Marx Brothers movie) reached the number-one and the number-five spots on British and U.S. album charts, respectively. Queen's sixth studio album, *News of the World* (1977), included the hits "We Will Rock You" and "We Are the Champions," which were also sold as a double-A–sided single; both are now among the most widely played sports anthems in music history. Queen released two albums in 1979: *Jazz*, which contained May's international hit "Fat Bottomed Girls," and *Live Killers*. The following year two new Queen albums went on sale: *The Game*, which had two number-one singles—"Crazy Little Thing Called Love" and "Another One Bites the Dust"—and *Flash Gordon Original Soundtrack*, which, according to Erlewine, was "coldly received" but nevertheless went gold.

Queen received a big boost in 1981 with the single "Under Pressure," which was written and performed with the musician David Bowie. "Under Pressure" reached the top spot on British singles charts and has been used in dozens of TV ads, TV programs, and movies. The performer Vanilla Ice included a virtually identical portion of "Under Pressure" in his biggest hit, "Ice Ice Baby" (1981), and the song was included in both the Royal Philharmonic Orchestra's album *The Queen Collection* (1982) and the recording *The London Symphony Orchestra Plays the Music of Queen* (1994). "Under Pressure" is included on Queen's *Greatest Hits* (1981) album, which sold nine million copies, and on the band's record *Hot Space* (1982), which went gold. Sales of each of the group's next four albums—*The Works* (1984), *A Kind of Magic* (1986), *Live Magic* (1986), and *The Miracle* (1989)—surpassed a million copies.

The lack of much critical acclaim notwithstanding, in the 1970s and 1980s Queen consistently broke concert attendance records all over the world, not least because of their onstage pyrotechnics and light shows and the charismatic Mercury's captivating antics. Queen's 20-minute performance in July 1985 at the Live Aid concert at London's Wembley Stadium is widely considered by many of the band's fans to be among its finest. A concert that Queen gave at the same stadium in 1986, like a half-dozen of their other shows, can be seen on DVD.

During the latter part of the 1980s and early 1990s, May became severely depressed, due to the breakup of his first marriage, the death of his father, and Mercury's deteriorating health, resulting from AIDS. Mercury's illness—hidden from the public until the day before his death, in November 1991—forced Queen to stop touring. The band's studio album *Innuendo* (1991), the last to be released before Mercury died, includes the hit single "These Are the Days of Our Lives"; credited to the group as a whole, the song won the 1992 BRIT (British Phonographic Industry) Award for best single. (Mercury can also be heard on Queen's album *Made in Heaven*, which was released in 1995.) In a benefit concert for AIDS charities held in Mercury's honor in April 1992 at Wembley Stadium, the surviving members of Queen performed alongside musicians including Elton John, David Bowie, Led Zeppelin's Robert Plant, Liza Minnelli, Guns N' Roses, and Metallica. The concert, broadcast worldwide, was reportedly viewed by a billion people.

Without Deacon or Taylor, who pursued projects on their own, May formed the Brian May Band, recruiting the drummer Cozy Powell, the guitarist Mike Caswell, the bassist Neil Murray, and three backup vocalists: Maggie Ryder, Miriam Stockley, and Chris Thompson. May's first album with that band, *Back to the Light*, appeared in 1993. A reviewer for *Rolling Stone* (May 27, 1993) wrote, "Probably the most shocking thing Queen fans are going to discover on Brian May's first solo album is just how good a singer he is. . . . The more than competent fashion in which he handles all the lead and background vocals on *Back to the Light* leads one to conclude that a goodly number of those 1001 'Mama mias' on 'Bohemian Rhapsody' were probably his." In an assessment posted on metaluk.com (August 8, 2003), Chris Clayton wrote, "*Back to the Light* is a flawless collection of songs. . . . The fact that the album explores both dark and light (musically and emotionally) over its twelve tracks is just one thing that sets it apart from the rest. As May's very first post-Queen offering . . . , this album stands up to the test of time. Not only does the poodle-haired maestro deliver his heaviest material to date, he laces the album with delicious melodies and mixes it all up. The flavors are intoxicating." The Brian May Band's second, and last, album, *Another World* (1998), was released a few months after Cozy Powell died in a car accident.

Since 2005 May has performed with the band Queen + Paul Rodgers, whose principal members, in addition to May, are Roger Taylor and Rodgers, a singer formerly with the groups Bad Company, the Firm, Free, and the Law. The band's debut concert took place in South Africa in March 2005, as part of an AIDS awareness campaign launched by South Africa's former president Nelson Mandela. Later that year Queen + Paul Rodgers performed in 32 European arenas. The band's first, live album, *Return of the Champions* (2005), offered Queen standards as well as songs associated with Bad Company and Free. Their second, studio album, *The Cosmos Rocks*, a collection of new songs by May, Taylor, and Rodgers, arrived in stores in September 2008 in Europe and the following month in North America. The worldwide Rock the Cosmos Tour was launched in support of the album, with stops scheduled in Asia, Europe, and South America in late 2008 and in North America in early 2009. The band's debut concert in the Ukraine, called "Let the Cosmos Rock," was scheduled to be shown in digital-video theaters in the U.S. in November 2008.

Earlier, May, Taylor, and the British comedian and writer Ben Elton had collaborated to write the so-called jukebox musical *We Will Rock You*. The show opened in London in 2002 and proved to be a commercial, though not critical, success. Productions were later mounted in more than a dozen other cities, in Europe, Asia, Africa, Australia, and the U.S., and as of October 2008, the musical was running in theaters in Great Britain, Germany, and Canada. In his 2006 interview with Marcus Chown, May traced his decision to complete his work toward his doctoral degree to his meeting with Francisco Sanchez in Madrid, Spain, when *We Will Rock You* opened there. May also told Chown, "You get to this age and you think, I'm still alive when some friends aren't, and you ask yourself, 'Why am I here? What should I be doing?'" As extremely little research on zodiacal dust had been conducted since he had set aside his dissertation, May had no trouble reviewing the literature on that subject published in the last three decades. He completed his thesis, titled *A Survey of Radial Velocities in the Zodiacal Dust Cloud*, in 2007. When Matt Blackett asked him, "What's more exciting to you now, playing Wembley or getting your PhD?," May responded, "It's a very different kind of excitement. To me there's great fulfillment in getting the PhD because it was hanging over me as a shadow in the background all those years while I was playing guitar. I kept thinking, 'Wouldn't it be nice if that great pile of papers in my loft actually turned into something useful?' So it's a wonderful feeling of accomplishment. But there is *nothing* like playing guitar on stage. Your whole mind, body, and soul are bound in that moment. . . . If I had to choose it would be those live moments, shared with a great group of people. It really would have to be that."

About three years earlier, at the urging of Patrick Moore, with whom May had become friendly long before, May agreed to co-write a book about the origin and history of the universe. The third collaborator was the cosmologist Chris Lintott, Moore's co-presenter on *The Sky at Night*. The trio aimed to write in laypeople's terms, in contrast to the physicist Stephen Hawking's book *A Brief History of Time* (1988), which has been described as an "unread best-seller": although more than nine million copies of it have been sold, relatively few buyers understood enough to read much of it. Moore

reportedly wrote the book in a matter of weeks, and then May and Lintott reworked it. "I figured that if I understood it, there was a good chance that people would in general, and that if I didn't understand it, then there was work to be done," May told Emma Brockes. Lavishly illustrated, *Bang! The Complete History of the Universe* was published in Great Britain in 2006 and went on sale in the U.S. in the fall of 2008.

According to Matt Blackett, May is "soft-spoken and articulate" and is "the consummate English gentleman." In 2007 he was appointed to the titular position of chancellor of Liverpool John Moores University. He lives in London's West End with his second wife, the actress Anita Dobson, whom he married in 2000. From his first marriage, to Chrissy Mullen, he has three children: James (known as Jimmy), Louisa, and Emily, who were born in 1978, 1981, and 1987, respectively.

—C.C.

Suggested Reading: *Boston Globe* (on-line) Jan. 31, 1993; *Circus* (on-line) July 6, 1976; *Guitarist* (on-line) Nov. 2001; *Guitar Player* (on-line) Jan. 2008; (London) *Daily Mail* (on-line) Nov. 18, 2006; (London) *Guardian* p10+ Oct. 19, 2006; (London) *Times* (on-line) Sep. 29, 1992; *New Zealand Herald* (on-line) May 26, 2007; *Total Guitar* (on-line) Dec. 1, 1998; *Washington Post* T p6+ Mar. 3, 2006

Selected Recordings: with Queen—*Queen*, 1973; *Queen II*, 1974; *Sheer Heart Attack*, 1974; *A Night at the Opera*, 1975; *A Day at the Races*, 1976; *News of the World*, 1977; *Jazz*, 1979; *Live Killers*, 1979; *The Game*, 1980; *Flash Gordon Original Soundtrack*, 1980; *Greatest Hits*, 1981; *Hot Space*, 1982; *The Works*, 1984; *A Kind of Magic*, 1986; *Live Magic*, 1986; *The Miracle*, 1989; *Innuendo*, 1991; *Made in Heaven*, 1995; as solo artist—*Back to the Light*, 1993; *Another World*, 1998; as member of Queen + Paul Rodgers—*Return of the Champions*, 2005; *The Cosmos Rocks*, 2008

Selected Books: *Bang! The Complete History of the Universe* (with Patrick Moore and Chris Lintott), 2006

Mayer, Jane

1955– Political writer

Address: c/o *The* New Yorker, 4 Times Square, New York, NY 10036

Jane Mayer's career as a political journalist has spanned the administrations of four U.S. presidents and over three decades of landmark events, scandal, and controversy. As a staff writer for the

Courtesy of the *New Yorker*

Jane Mayer

New Yorker, she has written about such topics as Linda Tripp, the former Pentagon staffer who leaked the news of President Bill Clinton's relationship with Monica Lewinsky; the search for Osama bin Laden, the head of the terrorist network Al Qaeda; and the political content of the weekly television drama *24*, which follows the adventures of a government agent named Jack Bauer as he fights terrorism.

Mayer co-wrote the books *Landslide: The Unmaking of the President, 1984–1988* (1988, with Doyle McManus), the story of the Ronald Reagan administration's role in the Iran-Contra affair, and *Strange Justice: The Selling of Clarence Thomas* (1994, with Jill Abramson), about the 1991 confirmation of the polarizing U.S. Supreme Court justice. Her most recent book, a solo effort titled *The Dark Side: The Inside Story of How the War on Terror Turned Into a War on American Ideals* (2008), focuses on the questionable tactics used by the George W. Bush administration in its fight against Islamic radicalism. The book quickly made the *New York Times* and *USA Today* best-seller lists and generated widespread media interest in the author, whose research skills and acumen were widely praised by reviewers. In 2008 *The Dark Side* was named a finalist for a National Book Award (the winners were to be announced at the end of November), and Mayer received the John Chancellor Award for Excellence in Journalism from the Columbia University Graduate School of Journalism for the "depth and detail of her reporting on the Bush Administration's war on terror," according to *Columbia News* (September's 18, 2008, on-line).

Jane Meredith Mayer was born in 1955 in New York City. Her father, William Mayer, is a composer, and her mother, Meredith Nevins Mayer, is a painter, printmaker, and former president of the Manhattan Graphics Center, which seeks to teach printmaking to a new generation of artists. Mayer's maternal grandfather, Allan Nevins, was a Pulitzer Prize–winning writer and historian and a co-founder of *American Heritage* magazine. Mayer is also a great-great-granddaughter of Emanuel Lehman, who in 1850 co-founded the financial-services firm Lehman Brothers. She has a sister, Cynthia (called Mindy), also a journalist, and a brother, Steven, a concert pianist.

In 1973 Mayer graduated from the Ethical Culture Fieldston School, a progressive private institution in New York City. She studied abroad during the 1972–73 academic year at the Bedales School, a British institution known for its liberal bent and academic rigor. Mayer then attended Yale University, in New Haven, Connecticut, and while a student there she worked as a stringer for *Time* magazine. After graduating from Yale, in 1977, Mayer went back to England to study briefly at the University of Oxford.

Upon Mayer's return to the U.S., she began her journalism career at the *Rutland Herald*, a Vermont daily. She started out by writing birth and death notices and was then promoted to cover local news. She has recalled her tenure there fondly, telling Felicity Barringer for the *New York Times* (April 16, 2001, on-line), "We worked all afternoon and early evening. Then we broke to go swimming in the [area's] quarries and eat hash browns in the diner until dawn."

Within a few years Mayer had left Vermont and moved to Washington, D.C., to work as a reporter for the *Washington Star*. The *Star*, a rival of the more popular *Washington Post*, was bought by Time Inc. in 1978 and shut down with only two weeks' notice in August 1981. Mayer then moved back to her native New York City, where, in 1982, she joined the staff of the *Wall Street Journal*, reporting on news related to the television industry. She wrote pieces on such topics as federal budget cuts for public television, the controversy over the use of endangered orangutans in television commercials and programs, and the lives and careers of network executives. In November 1983 Mayer moved to the *Journal*'s Washington bureau and began covering the intersection of media and politics, which included analyzing the news coverage of that year's presidential campaigns of the incumbent, Ronald Reagan, and the Democratic contender, Walter Mondale. A year later Mayer became the newspaper's first female White House correspondent.

Mayer has said that she disliked writing news based on formal White House briefings, and she often looked beyond the official press releases to find compelling stories. In October 1984, for example, President Reagan traveled to Grenada in the wake of the U.S. overthrow of that island nation's military government; Mayer arrived in Grenada a week earlier to do research and found that Reagan's jaunt, meant to celebrate the American victory over what he characterized as the Soviet-Cuban militarization of the island, was costing U.S. taxpayers between $3 million and $5 million. As a result of that story, she was blacklisted by the White House and was unable to obtain further information about Reagan's schedule. "You can pay a price for this kind of reporting," Mayer told Bruce Porter for the *Columbia (University) Journalism Review* (January/February 1995).

In the mid-1980s clandestine arrangements were made within the Reagan White House to circumvent congressional oversight and provide funds to the Contra rebels in Nicaragua—using profits made by selling arms to Iran, despite an existing embargo. The Iran-Contra affair, as the tangled chain of events came to be called, was the end result of Reagan's insistence on aiding the guerrilla fighters battling the Communist-backed Sandinista government of Nicaragua, along with his desire to negotiate the release of several American hostages being held by pro-Iranian groups in Lebanon and to encourage a pro-Western Iranian foreign policy. In late 1986 reports of the illegal arms deal broke in the Lebanese press. Eager to write a book on the inner workings of the Reagan White House, in 1987 Mayer signed a $100,000 deal with the publisher Houghton Mifflin and enlisted Doyle McManus, a veteran national-security reporter who had covered the Iran-Contra affair for the *Los Angeles Times*, as her collaborator. Mayer temporarily left her post at the *Wall Street Journal* to concentrate on the book.

Landslide: The Unmaking of the President, 1984-1988 was published in September 1988 with a first printing of 100,000 copies and debuted at number five on the *New York Times* best-seller list. The book focuses largely on the Iran-Contra affair and made national news with its revelations that in 1987 White House aides briefly considered removing Reagan from office because he was reportedly too depressed to perform his duties. (Howard Baker, then the newly appointed White House chief of staff, ultimately judged that Reagan was fulfilling his duties sufficiently and put an end to the idea.)

The book received mostly positive reviews for its presentation of the events surrounding the Iran-Contra affair. "The real interest of *Landslide*," Christopher Lehmann-Haupt wrote for the *New York Times* (September 19, 1988, on-line), "lies in the extraordinary clarity of its complex narrative. As a result, the reader can follow the unfolding of the Iran-contra affair with an understanding of its details that no previous account that I know of has managed to convey." Jeffrey Hart, critiquing the volume for the conservative-leaning *National Review* (February 10, 1989, on-line), however, felt that it was slanted. "The spin that *Landslide* attempts to put on history is that Reagan was the Wizard of Oz, a shallow master of illusion, and that

all his alleged achievements are illusions too," Hart wrote.

On September 26, 1992 Mayer married William Hamilton, the deputy national editor of political coverage for the *Washington Post*. Five months later the couple moved to Santa Monica, California, after Hamilton accepted a position as the *Post*'s West Coast correspondent. On June 8, 1993 their daughter, Kate, was born, and in September 1994 Mayer and her family moved back to Washington, D.C.

In November 1994 Mayer's second book, *Strange Justice: The Selling of Clarence Thomas*, was published. Co-authored with a fellow *Wall Street Journal* reporter, Jill Abramson (now the managing editor of the *New York Times*), the book examines the events that surrounded the appointment of the controversial Supreme Court justice—including the accusations made by Anita Hill, a former colleague of Thomas's, who claimed that he had sexually harassed her while they were both working for the U.S. Equal Employment Opportunity Commission.

In a review for the *New York Times* (September 6, 1999, on-line), Margo Jefferson called *Strange Justice* an "impressively reported and documented book." While Mayer and Abramson never claimed to have solved the mystery of what went on between Thomas and Hill, their research, which included conducting more than 100 interviews and examining thousands of pages of documents over the course of three years, led them to identify a pattern of behavior—an avid interest in pornography and actions that led to complaints from employees, for example—that suggested that Thomas may have indeed harassed Hill as she claimed. "It took forever to get people to open up," Mayer said on CNN's *Larry King Live* (November 3, 1994, on-line). "I trekked to Savannah, Georgia, and spent time with Clarence Thomas' mother. I went out to Oklahoma to see if Anita Hill was in fact a flake, the way she had been portrayed."

Although *Strange Justice* was nominated for both a National Book Critics Circle Award and a National Book Award, some readers were outraged by its portrayal of Thomas. Howard Kurtz wrote for the *Washington Post* (November 11, 1994), "Inevitably, perhaps, conservatives in the press are striking back, dismissing the book as irrelevant or attacking its sources. . . . In short, the carefully researched book, attempting to build a factual case, is being drawn into the same ideological maelstrom that surrounded Thomas vs. Hill from the start." Mayer and Abramson refused invitations to appear on television shows to debate critics of the book. "I am not the kind of journalist who enjoys a shouting match or thinks it's useful," Mayer told Kurtz. "I've spent three years of my life on this book, and I don't want it reduced to a sound bite at top decibels. . . . Since when did writing books become a blood sport?" In 1999 *Strange Justice* was made into a television film starring Regina Taylor as Hill and Delroy Lindo as Thomas.

In 1995 Mayer joined the *New Yorker* as a staff writer. In March 1998 she wrote a long article about Linda Tripp, the middle-aged government employee who had befriended the young White House intern Monica Lewinsky and secretly taped her phone confessions of sexual trysts with President Bill Clinton. Mayer's piece revealed that Tripp had been arrested for grand larceny at age 19 and had lied about it on her security-clearance form. Larry Klayman, a lawyer who had repeatedly filed lawsuits against the Clinton administration in an effort to prove government corruption and who was then the chairman of the conservative group Judicial Watch, felt that the information might discredit Tripp's testimony in the Lewinsky-Clinton case, and in May he subpoenaed Mayer, seeking access to her notebooks and research documents. Although Mayer maintained that she had gotten her information solely through legitimate means, he accused her of being in Clinton's employ and charged that she had illegally searched Tripp's FBI files. Weeks later a federal judge ruled in Mayer's favor, stating that the materials Klayman had requested were protected under journalistic privilege.

In recent years Mayer has written on a wide variety of other topics for the *New Yorker*. Her subjects have included a group of Democratic billionaires intent on defeating George W. Bush in 2004; Vice President Dick Cheney's former physician, who had admitted to abusing narcotics; and the disgraced congressman James Traficant, who had been indicted on 10 felony counts of bribery and tax evasion. She has also written extensively about the war on terror and the Bush administration's involvement in the programs and legal decisions that resulted in the torture of prisoners at Guantánamo Bay, Cuba, and elsewhere. Her research led her to write *The Dark Side: The Inside Story of How the War on Terror Turned Into a War on American Ideals*, which was published in July 2008. She told Amy Goodman for the radio show *Democracy Now!* (July 18, 2008), "What I've tried to do in *The Dark Side* is take all the facts and put them back in order, so people can understand this as a chapter of history, one great big story. And it basically begins right after 9/11 with a handful of lawyers in the Justice Department reinterpreting the laws in order to justify these programs [that resulted in the abuse of the prisoners]." In her review of the book, Jennifer Schuessler wrote for the *New York Times* (July 22, 2008, on-line), "In *The Dark Side*, Ms. Mayer provides . . . the most vivid and comprehensive account we have had so far of how a government founded on checks and balances and respect for individual rights could have been turned against those ideals." Similarly, Andrea Sachs wrote for *Time* (July 28, 2008), "[Mayer's] account of secret prisons, black-hooded renditions in the middle of the night and unexplained detainee deaths is necessary reading for those who would understand how the Bush Administration came to turn away from the light."

Mayer told Tammy Haddad for the *National Journal* (August 8, 2008, on-line) that despite the avalanche of press attention the book had received, Bush administration officials had maintained "just plain radio silence." She continued, "I can say, I've actually heard from some of the sources. This book is not just based on talking to critics of the administration. It's talking to lots of people on the inside: inside the White House, inside the CIA and the FBI and the military. And it's been really gratifying. I've actually gotten some really wonderful phone calls from people who've said, 'You know, you got it. Thank goodness someone told the story.'"

Mayer and her family live in Chevy Chase, Maryland. In an interview for the PBS show *Bill Moyers Journal* (July 25, 2008, on-line), she said that she is most motivated to delve deeply into a story when she is told by officials, "You can't know this." She explained, "For an investigative reporter . . . it's like someone waving a red flag at a bull."

—M.A.S.

Suggested Reading: *Columbia (University) Journalism Review* p60 Jan./Feb. 1995; *Democracy Now!* (on-line) July 18, 2008; *Larry King Live* (on-line) Nov. 3, 1994; *New York Times* (on-line) Sep. 19, 1988, May 27, 1998, Sep. 6, 1999, Apr. 16, 2001, July 22, 2008; *People* p145 Nov. 14, 1994, p54 Sep. 26, 1998; *Washington Post* D p1 Nov. 11, 1994

Selected Books: *Landslide: The Unmaking of the President, 1984-1988* (with Doyle McManus), 1988; *Strange Justice: The Selling of Clarence Thomas* (with Jill Abramson), 1994; *The Dark Side: The Inside Story of How the War on Terror Turned Into a War on American Ideals*, 2008

McConnell, Mitch

Feb. 20, 1942– U.S. senator from Kentucky (Republican)

Address: 361-A Russell Senate Office Bldg., Washington, DC 20510

"How do you define bipartisanship? My view is that bipartisanship is when some Democrats join Republicans to do things that Republicans would like to do," Mitch McConnell, a Republican from Kentucky and the U.S. Senate minority leader, told Albert Eisele and Mary Lynn F. Jones, editors of the *Hill* (January 17, 2001), a political publication. He continued, "I'm sure there are others, particularly the mainstream press, that define bipartisanship as Republicans agreeing to do things Democrats have been trying to do for years." In the course of his political career, McConnell has been called many things, among them "master strategist," "champion of fundraising," and "political genius," but also

Chip Somodevilla/Getty Images

Mitch McConnell

"an obstructionist," the "Darth Vader of campaign-finance reform," a "new type of Public Enemy #1," and even "the worst senator in the U.S. Senate." But McConnell reportedly does not mind such criticism. According to his wife, U.S. secretary of labor Elaine Chao, although her husband has a calm demeanor, he "loves the fight." Chao told Marc Fisher for the *Washington Post* (October 12, 1999), "For Mitch, a life of adoration is not a life worth being proud of. He takes delight in frustrating his enemies. Their damnation becomes the highest praise." Indeed, since 1984, when McConnell became the first Republican since 1968 to win a statewide election in Kentucky, the now four-term senator has been frank about his staunch partisanship and unwavering in his opposition to campaign-finance reform, the issue with which he is most closely associated. By undertaking the publicly unpopular but—at least among Republicans—widely held position in support of unlimited campaign spending, and by raising enough funds to donate substantially to the campaigns of fellow Republicans in competitive races, McConnell has become a popular and valued figure within his own party. Zachary Roth and Cliff Schecter, writing for *Washington Monthly* (October 1, 2006), noted that the politically skilled McConnell lacks the commanding demeanor or communication style of many other senators—and that he has thus taken on strategic work rather than high-profile causes to make his way to the upper echelons of the Republican Party. "Like the short, unathletic kid who wins a place on the high-school basketball team by hustling, playing defense, and washing the uniforms," they wrote, "he has gained the support of his colleagues by shrewdly focusing on the less glamorous, be-

hind-the-scenes grunt work, while acting as the frontman for unpopular causes that bring negative publicity others would rather avoid." Serving on the Ethics and Rules Committees in the 1990s, McConnell was responsible for such tasks as assigning office space and overseeing the Senate restaurant; by becoming chairman of the National Republican Senatorial Committee in 1998, he was able to exert significant influence as a fund-raiser and political strategist for Republican candidates for the U.S. Senate. Having demonstrated his influence and staying power and having helped the Republicans maintain their numbers within the Senate, McConnell was elected unopposed as the majority whip in 2003. In January 2007, as the Republicans had lost their majority in the Senate in the November 2006 elections, McConnell became minority leader, a post in which he continues to serve his party and his state as a leading fund-raiser.

Addison Mitchell McConnell was born on February 20, 1942 to Julia Shockley and Addison Mitchell McConnell Sr. and raised in South Louisville, a section of Louisville, Kentucky. At age two he was diagnosed with polio. Fearing that pressure on the boy's legs would cause them to develop abnormally, doctors advised McConnell's mother to keep her son off his feet. She did so for several years, helping him to exercise his legs three times a day and repeatedly explaining to him, "You can walk, but you can't walk," as McConnell recalled to Marc Fisher. He added, "I had a lesson taught me about how persistence and tenacity can overcome adversity." (As an adult, Fisher noted, the senator has "a slight hitch in his gait.") McConnell's interest in politics began when he was a boy; his fifth-grade class photo shows him wearing a button that reads "I Like Ike" (a slogan of Dwight D. Eisenhower's presidential campaign), and at age 14 he watched TV coverage of both the Democratic and Republican national conventions. McConnell was president of the student body at each school he attended, including duPont Manual High School, where his name is listed in the Alumni Hall of Fame. He was elected student-body president of the University of Louisville College of Arts and Sciences, where he was also a member of the fraternity Phi Kappa Tau; he graduated with honors in 1964. At the University of Kentucky Law School, where he earned a degree in 1967, he was elected president of the student bar. He joined the 100th Training Unit, U.S. Army Reserve, in Kentucky, but was unable to serve in Vietnam because of poor eyesight. Instead, he interned in Washington, D.C., for the Republican U.S. senator John Sherman Cooper of Kentucky, for whom McConnell has continued to express admiration. McConnell claims to have learned from Cooper "the right way to do the job of a senator," as David Mudd phrased it for *Louisville* magazine (April 1995). While Cooper was more liberal than McConnell was to become, McConnell noted that Cooper "subscribed to the Thomas Jefferson axiom that representatives are to be leaders, no mere instruments of their constituents' collective will," as Mudd put it. After working for several other elected officials in Washington, in 1978 McConnell was elected judge-executive for Jefferson County, which includes Louisville.

When McConnell began talking about his plan to run as a Republican for a U.S. Senate seat in the 1984 election, few people took him seriously, as Kentucky had long been a solidly Democratic state. In May 1984 McConnell easily defeated three other Republicans in the Kentucky primary, winning 79.2 percent of the vote. (Each of the others had run unsuccessfully for Senate seats many times in the past, and together they were considered by many to be merely "token opposition.") McConnell's opponent in the general election was the Democratic incumbent Walter "Dee" Huddleston, who had served comfortably since 1973. McConnell campaigned on a socially conservative platform and launched a barrage of TV ads suggesting that Huddleston did not spend enough time at the U.S. Capitol. (One ad featured bloodhounds sniffing around Washington, unable to locate Huddleston's scent.) The advertising helped—as did, probably, the popularity of the incumbent Republican president, Ronald Reagan, who trounced his Democratic challenger, Walter Mondale, that year; McConnell overcame a 35-point deficit in the polls to defeat Huddleston by less than half a percentage point, becoming the first Republican to win a statewide election in Kentucky since 1968. Many point to that first, narrow victory as an experience that confirmed McConnell's adamant support of unrestricted campaign fund-raising as a necessary "equalizer" in difficult elections. Once elected, McConnell worked hard to secure his place in the Senate, aligning himself with party leaders and beginning early to plan his reelection campaign, with a focus on collecting money from political action committees (PACs), or interest groups that donate funds to campaigns of politicians they believe will promote their agendas. In 1985 and 1986, of the total $869,801 he raised, McConnell collected $246,600 from PACs, and in 1989 and the first quarter of 1990, PAC money accounted for nearly $600,000 of the $2.7 million he collected, placing him 12th in the Senate in funds received from PACs in that period.

For decades, campaign finance has been a recurring national issue. As election campaigns have become increasingly pricey, concern has grown over the perceived link between the donations that candidates receive from corporations and special-interest groups and the decisions of those candidates once they are elected and become legislators. In 1971 Congress passed the Federal Election Campaign Act (FECA), which consolidated all campaign-reform efforts and placed limitations and regulations on campaign contributions from various groups. Since then, however, donors have found ways to circumvent the limitations, particularly by donating large amounts of "soft money," campaign contributions to political parties or sin-gle-issue groups, which are not limited under FECA. Such contributions are subsequently spent on advertisements that implicitly favor one candidate. Legislators have looked for ways to reform the system, but the fact that different parties depend on different kinds of donations has made compromise difficult.

McConnell entered the campaign-finance debate in 1990, as he saw Senate Democrats working with outside experts—and some Republicans—to overhaul campaign-finance laws with a bill proposing voluntary spending limits and incentives such as partial public financing of campaigns. While on a party retreat in West Virginia, McConnell garnered Republican support for his own 30-point proposal. On May 11, 1990, along with 34 Republican co-sponsors, McConnell presented the bill, which rejected public funding and campaign spending limits and instead proposed a complete ban on contributions from political action committees, groups that receive and spend a significant amount of soft money. While everyone recognized McConnell's expertise on the subject of campaign finance, many were puzzled by his proposal, as it contrasted sharply with his own fund-raising practices, which involved ample donations from PACs. Others saw the bill, which contained no attempts to compromise with Democrats and stood little chance of getting their support, as a strategic maneuver to block the success of any effort at reform. While denying that he was against nonpartisan compromise on the issue, McConnell admitted to Helen Dewar for the Washington Post (May 21, 1990), "I am the obstacle if the goal is to pass a bill that benefits the Democrats." Dewar pointed out that McConnell's proposal to ban PACs may have reflected his own difficulty in raising PAC money as an underdog candidate in 1984, an experience that fueled his impression that PACs "tilt the scales" to favor incumbents. In Kentucky, where the incumbents were mostly Democrats, banning money from PACs would benefit Republicans. In a column for USA Today (May 21, 1990), McConnell criticized the Democrats' reform bill for its emphasis on public funding, writing, "With our nation facing a serious budget deficit, it is curious that there is this concerted effort to spend hundreds of millions of taxpayer dollars on political campaigns. Where are they going to get the money?" Despite McConnell's efforts, the Senate rejected the Republican bill with a vote that strictly followed party lines, 55-45, and instead passed the Democrat-sponsored bill, 59-40. In late November 1991 the House passed their version of the Senate Democrats' campaign-finance-reform bill. When a version of the bill reached President George H. W. Bush, in 1992, he vetoed it.

In 1990 McConnell was reelected to the Senate, defeating Jefferson County judge-executive Harvey Sloane. Dewar reported for the Washington Post (October 31, 1990) that McConnell had raised nearly $2 million for his election campaign and Sloane only $500,000. McConnell pointed to those figures as evidence that unlimited fundraising allows challenger parties to succeed in states ruled by opposing parties, while Sloane complained that the same figures demonstrated the incumbent-favoring nature of elections. McConnell told Dewar that his interest in campaign finance had sprung from a course on U.S. political parties and elections that he taught in the 1970s at the University of Louisville. "I became convinced—and I'm no less convinced now—that this is one of the most important subjects in any democracy," he said. "It is the rules of the game in our democracy." McConnell has frequently mentioned campaign spending in connection with freedom of speech, referring to a 1976 Supreme Court ruling that found that FECA's limitations on the use of money for campaign purposes violated the First Amendment, since money was required for any large-scale political message. In 1992 McConnell seemed to contradict his own argument in defense of free speech when he proposed a bill that would allow victims of sexual assault to sue publishers, producers, sellers, exhibitors, and distributors of pornography if it could be proven that the pornography was a significant motivating factor in the crime. The bill was supported by many Republicans and antipornography groups such as Feminists Fighting Pornography, who saw it as a way to address what they called a link between pornography and violence; critics, including some women's groups, the American Booksellers Association, the Writers Guild, the Motion Picture Association of America, and other media organizations, saw the bill as a means of achieving "back door" censorship and disagreed with the idea of blaming third parties for such crimes. Available sources suggest that the bill died before leaving the Senate Judiciary Committee.

Following the November 1994 elections—which gave Republicans majorities in both houses of Congress for the first time since the 1950s—McConnell, as the new chairman of the Senate Appropriations Subcommittee on Foreign Operations, emerged as an outspoken voice on foreign policy. "One might get the impression from the election that Republicans as a group are isolationists," McConnell told Lally Weymouth for the *Washington Post* (January 8, 1995), implying that that impression was wrong. Calling himself an "internationalist," McConnell said that foreign aid should be used as a tool to "directly complement our national security and economic interests." McConnell named the Middle East, South Korea, and the former Soviet republics as national-security priorities, stressing the importance of preventing the reemergence of the Russian empire. He also, however, supported cutting foreign aid overall by 20 percent, abolishing the Agency for International Development, and stopping aid to certain countries in Africa and Latin America that were not making what McConnell saw as significant efforts to reform their economies. McConnell also opposed sending U.S. troops or foreign aid to the former Yugoslavia, the scene of civil war and

so-called ethnic cleansing in the 1990s, as he could discern no U.S. national security interests there. McConnell said to Weymouth that, particularly in the post–Cold War era, "you have to put yourself on a diet when it comes to intervention, devise a meticulous approach to the use of the military and target foreign aid to areas where U.S. interests lie."

Throughout the 1990s McConnell continued to be a key player regarding the recurring issue of campaign-finance reform. In 1994 he led an all-night filibuster to stop a campaign-finance-reform bill, sponsored by the Wisconsin Democrat Russ Feingold and the Arizona Republican John McCain (which resembled the 1990 bill in its limitations on campaign spending and options for public financing) from going to committee. In an example of his combativeness on the issue, McConnell said at a press conference, as quoted by David E. Rosenbaum for the *New York Times* (October 1, 1994), "I make no apologies for killing this turkey of a bill." McConnell offered no alternative reform bill and appeared to have abandoned his stance on banning contributions from PACs. Fred Wertheimer, then the head of the citizen-action group Common Cause, told David Mudd, "For years [McConnell] claimed that what he was concerned about was the proposed solution to the corrupt campaign-finance system. . . . But now that the Republicans are in the majority, he flatly declares reform shouldn't be on the agenda at all. He used the public finance angle as a cover." In December 1996, as Senators McCain and Feingold prepared to introduce another bipartisan campaign-finance-reform bill, one that contained a ban on PACs, McConnell promised again to lead the efforts to obstruct its passing. As Amy Keller and Damon Chappie reported for the *Palm Beach (Florida) Post* (December 8, 1996), McConnell—proudly calling himself "the principal obstacle on campaign finance reform"—told a meeting of GOPAC, a Republican PAC, in November 1996, "The Senate has killed an awful lot of things that needed killing. We'll kill it. . . . You watch it." McConnell led a filibuster to prevent passage of the McCain-Feingold reform bill in 1996 and led many other filibuster efforts in subsequent years to "kill" other versions of the reform bill. In March 2002, when efforts to filibuster a reform bill failed, and President George W. Bush signed into law the Bipartisan Campaign Reform Act of 2002, McConnell worked with legal scholars to file suit against the FEC, challenging the constitutionality of the ban on soft money as a violation of free speech. The suit was brought before the Supreme Court, which upheld some but not all of the regulations of the 2002 act.

Since he began fund-raising for his 1984 campaign, McConnell not only helped Republicans maintain a majority in the Senate from 1995 until 2007; he has also helped Kentucky Republicans by funding their campaigns, counseling them on campaign strategies, and even persuading individuals to run for office. Working primarily through the Bluegrass Committee, his own Kentucky-based

PAC, in recent decades McConnell has personally had a hand in most competitive elections at all levels in Kentucky, and he is credited with almost single-handedly revitalizing the Republican Party in Kentucky. (By 2002 the GOP had come to dominate both U.S. Senate seats and all but one congressional district, despite the fact that Kentucky Democrats outnumbered Republicans two to one.) In 1994, during the presidency of the Democrat Bill Clinton, McConnell persuaded a clergyman and Christian-bookstore owner, Ron Lewis, to run in a district that had not elected a Republican in 100 years and to adopt a socially conservative, anti-Clinton message; the same year he helped Ed Whitfield, a Democrat until then, to run as a Republican in a similarly GOP-averse district. Both candidates won. In 1996 McConnell's organizations helped elect the Republicans Anne Northrup and Geoff Davis to the House and Jim Bunning to the Senate. The following year McConnell took over the chairmanship of the National Republican Senatorial Committee (NRSC), the group that provides Republican U.S. Senate candidates with campaign advice and funds raised by the national party. Prior to the 1998 elections, facing angry voters following the lengthy process that led to the impeachment of President Clinton, McConnell counseled Republicans to overwhelm opponents with negative advertising; the strategy worked, and Republicans avoided losses in the Senate. By 1999, in his role as NRSC chairman, McConnell had raised $38 million for his Republican colleagues. Steven Law, executive director of the NRSC and McConnell's former chief of staff, said to Fisher about McConnell's unmatched success at fund-raising, "The senator just says it direct: This is our need and this is the amount. And he gets a yes or a no. He enjoys it. And he's not ashamed of it." In November 2002 McConnell won his fourth term in the Senate by the widest margin of any Republican in a statewide election in Kentucky's history. Following the 2006 elections, when Democrats gained majorities in many state legislatures and won many gubernatorial seats across the country, Kentucky Republicans maintained a majority in the state Senate as well as a Republican governor, Ernie Fletcher, whom McConnell had helped persuade to run in 2003.

When the Tennessee Republican Bill Frist became Senate majority leader, in January 2003, McConnell—having been elected unopposed—became majority whip, a position in which he was responsible for mobilizing party votes on key issues. In February of the same year, McConnell learned that he had arterial blockages. At the advice of Frist, who is also a physician, he underwent triple-bypass heart surgery and soon recovered. After the 2006 congressional elections, as Republicans lost control of both houses of Congress (due largely to voter dissatisfaction with the course of the war in Iraq), McConnell was elected Senate minority leader. Because Frist had declared that he would serve only two terms (of two years each) in the top Senate post, McConnell had been energeti-

cally securing votes for the position himself since he became whip. "He has systematically and methodically gone to every [Republican] member [of the Senate]. The only real purpose of that meeting is for him to make sure he's got that vote," Tripp Baird, a former aide to Senator Mel Martinez, told Zachary Roth and Cliff Schecter.

McConnell has voted in accordance with the Republican Party almost all of the time. He opposes tax increases and abortion, supports oil drilling in the Arctic National Wildlife Refuge, favors the rights of gun owners, supports crop subsidies, and has been an outspoken supporter of the Iraq war, seeing it as a necessary part of the so-called war on terror. In 2002 he worked with Republicans and Democrats to set federal standards for the process of conducting elections. Also that year he offered an amendment to a Medicare prescription-drug bill to limit damages from malpractice lawsuits as well as lawyers' fees. In June 2003 McConnell strongly advocated that the U.S. take action in response to human rights abuses committed against citizens of Myanmar (formerly known as Burma) by the ruling military junta; in April 2006 McConnell, along with the musician Peter Gabriel, urged the United Nations to take stronger action in the area as well, as he judged the junta's activities to be threatening the entire region. McConnell's support of the policies of President Bush—particularly his support of the war in Iraq—and his unclear position on Bush's immigration bill, which sought to provide a path to citizenship for illegal aliens and set up a new guest-worker program, have in recent months led to a splintering of the Republican Party in Kentucky and to decreased support from McConnell's usually loyal Kentucky constituents. On August 21, 2007 a Survey USA poll showed McConnell's approval rating at just 48 percent. Larry Forgy, a Republican from Kentucky and former gubernatorial candidate, was considering challenging McConnell for his party's nomination in the 2008 Senate race. Forgy told Ralph Z. Hallow for the Washington Times (August 21, 2007), "The average Kentuckian feels we are giving away this country with both hands. Jobs are going, essentially the primacy of the people who made this country great is going, and Mitch McConnell is lumped with the Washington types on this." After reportedly attracting many supporters, including the Kentucky politician Ernie Fletcher, Forgy did not file as a candidate for that office.

In late September 2008, in the midst of a major economic crisis that included a collapse of credit and securities markets and several major financial institutions, McConnell was one of the most vocal supporters of the $700 billion bailout plan. According to that plan, designed by Treasury Secretary Henry M. Paulson and Federal Reserve Chairman Ben S. Bernanke, financial institutions would pass their most distressed assets on to the U.S. Treasury. Legislators from both parties were torn on whether to pass the proposal—which all parties agreed had many imperfections, one of them being that taxpayers would be footing the bill for the debts incurred by banking and investment firms— or to postpone action so that the details of the plan could be debated. Many warned that the latter course might result in even greater financial turmoil. McConnell broke with many conservative members of his party and, along with the Speaker of the House, Democratic congresswoman Nancy Pelosi of California, and others, pushed for quick passage of the bill. "When there's a fire in your kitchen threatening to burn down your home, you don't want someone stopping the firefighters on the way and demanding they hand out smoke detectors first or lecturing you about the hazards of keeping paint in the basement," McConnell said, as quoted by David M. Herszenhorn in the *New York Times* (September 23, 2008, on-line). "You want them to put out the fire before it burns down your home and everything you've saved for your whole life." The bailout plan by was rejected by a majority of members of the House on September 29, 2008, and the markets responded with dramatic losses. After much debate and compromise, the Senate approved another version of the bill on October 1, 2008. The House approved the bill the following day, and on October 3, 2008 President Bush signed it into law.

During his campaign for his fifth consecutive term in the Senate, against the Democratic businessman and former gubernatorial candidate Bruce Lunsford, McConnell repeatedly reminded voters about the significant influence and power he had built up during his nearly 25 years in office and the federal aid that he had acquired for the state, for projects benefiting towns, airports, and universities. "The biggest issue in this race is whether or not our small state is going to continue to have a person of significant clout in Washington or whether we are to trade that person in for a rookie," McConnell declared, as quoted by Carl House in the *New York Times* (October 23, 2008). Despite fears of a recession and widespread dissatisfaction with the Bush administration, McConnell was narrowly reelected on November 4, 2008, in a national election that also resulted in significant Democratic gains in the House and Senate and the decisive victory of the Democratic presidential candidate, Senator Barack Obama of Illinois, over Republican senator John McCain of Arizona. As a Senate leader, McConnell will probably be charged with the task of trying to unite the ideologues and moderates among Senate Republicans. Given the lack of formidable challengers to his post as Senate minority leader and in light of the failure of Democrats to earn enough Senate seats to secure a 60-vote majority, which would allow them to cut off filibusters, Dan W. Reilly, writing for politico.com (November 5, 2008), identified McConnell as perhaps "the most powerful Republican." Reilly further observed: "McConnell is positioned to be both the ultimate dealmaker and the Republican firewall against a leftward tilt in American government."

Regardless of his involvement with other matters of importance, McConnell will likely be remembered for his association with issues of campaign finance. On October 16, 2006 the *Lexington Herald Leader* published a breakdown of the $220 million he has raised during his Senate career, through the McConnell Senate Committee, Bluegrass PAC, the National Republican Senatorial Committee, and the McConnell Center for Political Leadership, which he founded in 1991. Fisher wrote for the *Washington Post* that McConnell's office is filled with gifts and awards from many of his largest donors, including "the National Rifle Association's Eagle award, a framed tobacco leaf, a tobacco cutter from Philip Morris USA, presents from the horse racing industry, and the farm Bureau's Golden Plow award." McConnell has called lobbyists "the voice of the people," arguing that their bad reputation is unwarranted. McConnell told Fisher, "Going door to door is applauded in this country as an act of civic responsibility, but writing a check is condemned. Why is that? I don't think that's a tainted exchange." By most accounts, McConnell is sincere in that belief; many have said that he is more honest than many Washington politicians—most of whom rely on PAC money—on the issue of campaign finance. Even Senator Feingold, a sponsor of the campaign-finance bill that McConnell fought for years, has said, as quoted by Peter H. Stone in the *National Journal* (February 15, 1997), that McConnell is "a person who is truly concerned with free speech; he's determined and he's direct."

McConnell is married to his second wife, Secretary of Labor Elaine Chao, whose former positions include Peace Corps director, president of the United Way, and distinguished fellow at the Heritage Foundation. McConnell and Chao met in 1989, when Chao was serving in the first Bush administration. McConnell has three daughters from a previous marriage. He currently serves on the Appropriations Committee; the Rules and Administration Committee; and the Agriculture, Nutrition and Forestry Committee.

—M.E.R.

Suggested Reading: *CQ Weekly* p184+ Jan. 25, 2003, Supplement p24+ Oct. 30, 1999; *Louisville I* p 46 Apr. 1995; *National Journal* Campaign Finance p314 Feb. 15, 1997; *New York Times* B p13 Sep. 7, 1995, A p1+ Sep. 23, 2008; *Washington Monthly* p 27+ Oct. 1, 2006; *Washington Post* A p1 Oct. 12, 1999

Courtesy of the United States Institute of Peace

McFate, Montgomery

Jan. 8, 1966– Anthropologist

Address: P.O. Box 73583, Washington, DC 20056

"The greatest leaders, the greatest tacticians, like Napoleon and [Douglas] MacArthur, are able to figuratively leave their body and look down on the bigger picture," the retired admiral Jay Cohen, an undersecretary of the U.S. Department of Homeland Security, told Louisa Kamps for *Elle* (April 2008). He added that the anthropologist Montgomery McFate is able to "go to that ethereal place where your mind and dreams are stretched. . . . I enjoy her intellect, her enthusiasm—and her naïveté that by our efforts we can make a difference." McFate has taken on an unusual position for someone in her field: a cultural consultant to the United States military in Iraq and Afghanistan. In 2005 she proposed the formation of the Human Terrain System (HTS), a project subsequently implemented by the Foreign Military Studies Office of the U.S. Army, in which social scientists are embedded in combat brigades to share their expertise on the culture of the local population. "The idea," McFate said to Tom Foreman for CNN (October 13, 2007, on-line), is that the social scientists serve, "you might say, as an angel on the shoulder of the brigade commander, to help him develop better courses of action that involve less lethal force." In one such course of action, McFate began a job-training program in a village in Afghanistan in an effort to lessen the financial desperation that leads many young men to join paid insurgent forces. Now a senior adviser to the HTS project, McFate has been the target of much criticism from her peers in academia. Hugh Gusterson, a professor of cultural studies at George Mason University, wrote, as quoted by Matthew B. Stannard in the *San Francisco Chronicle* (April 29, 2007), "The anthropologist turned military consultant Montgomery McFate . . . [and others] are suggesting a form of hit-man anthropology where anthropologists, working on contract to organizations that often care nothing for the welfare of our anthropological subjects, prostitute their craft by deliberately earning the trust of our subjects with the intent of betraying it." Taking a more positive view, Felix Moos, a professor of anthropology at the University of Kansas, supports activities such as McFate's, telling David Glenn for the *Chronicle of Higher Education* (November 30, 2007), "A better-educated military will kill fewer people, not more."

Montgomery McFate was born on January 8, 1966, the only child of Frances Pointer and Martin Carlough, whom she has called "hippie parents." She grew up in Waldo Point, a houseboat community in Sausalito, California, and was raised mostly by her mother, an artist, who won custody of McFate in a 1968 ruling, after Carlough had recommended himself as a parent by claiming to be the living incarnation of Buddha. Carlough, a Korean War veteran, had been discharged from the marines because of his failing mental health. McFate recalled to the *San Francisco Chronicle* (April 29, 2007), "He used to walk around downtown in this pink denim jacket and it said, 'I am God' in giant rhinestone letters. It's my first memory of my father." When his daughter was 10 years old, Carlough committed suicide by jumping off the Golden Gate Bridge. When Kamps asked McFate what had inspired her work with the military, she answered that her father's experience had made her want to explore "the deep personal consequences" for "individuals in extreme situations that involve violence."

McFate attended Tamalpais High School, in Mill Valley, near Sausalito, where—despite her mother's advice to "get ahead on her looks," in Stannard's words—she excelled academically. In 1985 McFate enrolled at the University of California at Berkeley; during her first day there, her mother died of a stroke. After completing her bachelor's degree, in anthropology, she commenced graduate studies at Yale University, in New Haven, Connecticut, where she received a doctorate in anthropology, writing her dissertation on the Irish Republican Army and its supporters in Northern Ireland as well as British counterinsurgents there. "In Northern Ireland," George Packer wrote for the *New Yorker* (December 18, 2006), McFate discovered that "insurgency runs in families and social networks, held together by persistent cultural narratives." Disheartened by what she viewed as the impracticality of academia, McFate shifted focus, earning a degree from Harvard Law School, in Cambridge, Massachusetts, in 1997. There, she met her husband, Sean McFate, a U.S. Army officer.

After obtaining her law degree, McFate was hired as a litigation associate at the firm Baker & McKenzie, in San Francisco, California. She left after only a few months. "I got there, and they took me up to my 24th floor office . . . and shut the door," she recalled to Stannard, "and I'm sitting there with a view of the bay and all of a sudden I just started to cry. . . . 'This is all wrong. This is not what I should be doing. What am I doing here?'" She next joined Sean McFate in Germany, where he was posted. In 2000 the couple returned to the United States. Montgomery McFate received a fellowship at the Office of Naval Research to interview soldiers and Marines returning from war fronts, beginning in 2003. She found that many in the military felt ill-equipped to deal with the insurgencies in Iraq and Afghanistan—the armed resistance on the part of those countries' local populations to the governments set up with the help of the U.S. For example, the U.S.'s Task Force 121 commando team had been using a 19th-century British anthropology manual to prepare for their mission in Afghanistan. According to George Packer, one Marine stationed in Iraq told McFate that his unit had been unable to shape local public opinion favorably because "we were focussed on broadcast media. . . . But this had no impact because Iraqis spread information through rumor. We should have been visiting their coffee shops."

In 2004 McFate received a call from a science adviser to the Joint Chiefs of Staff; he had been contacted by U.S. military officers in Iraq who were seeking help and admitted, as quoted by Packer, that they had "no idea how this society works." The science adviser turned to McFate, "one of the few anthropologists he could find in the Defense Department," in Packer's words. McFate's initial effort was to create a computer database cataloguing anthropological information she and her colleagues deemed necessary for American military personnel overseas. At a conference in 2004, she stressed the importance of being schooled in the culture of the adversary. One example she gave was that because an extended arm with a palm facing out means "stop" in America but "welcome" in Iraq, Iraqis had been killed by American soldiers who were policing traffic and who, lacking knowledge of the local culture, believed that Iraqis who continued driving despite the "stop" gesture were suicide bombers.

In 2005 McFate published several papers advocating the creation of what she called the Human Terrain System and emphasizing that military success in Iraq and Afghanistan depended on cultural education. "Why has cultural knowledge become such an imperative?" she wrote for *Military Review* (March/April 2005). "Primarily because traditional methods of warfighting have proven inadequate in Iraq and Afghanistan. U.S. technology, training, and doctrine designed to counter the Soviet threat are not designed for low-intensity counterinsurgency operations where civilians mingle freely with combatants in complex urban terrain. . . .

Since the end of the 'hot' phase of the war, coalition forces have been fighting a complex war against an enemy they do not understand." She reasoned that the work of anthropologists is not incongruous with policy making and military operations, pointing out, for example, that "anthropology actually evolved as an intellectual tool to consolidate imperial power at the margins of empire. In Britain the development and growth of anthropology was deeply connected to colonial administration." In another article, published in *Joint Forces Quarterly* (July 1, 2005), she wrote, "Cultural knowledge of adversaries should be considered a national security priority. . . . Recognizing and utilizing pre-existing social structures are the key to political stabilization in Iraq." The efforts of McFate and others resulted in the launch of the Human Terrain System, a $40 million project in which "human-terrain" teams made up of five members each—a leader, a cultural analyst, a regional-studies analyst, a research manager, and a human-terrain analyst—are embedded in military brigades as cultural consultants. McFate serves as a senior social-science adviser for HTS. Marcus B. Griffin, a professor of anthropology and member of the Human Terrain System, wrote in an article for the *Chronicle of Higher Education* (November 30, 2007) that HTS "acts as a cultural broker to reduce miscommunication and help Iraqis and Americans work more effectively as partners."

Some anthropologists did not support the creation of the Human Terrain System, seeing it, in Stannard's words, as part of "a diabolical future where science meant to improve humanity becomes a weapon of mass destruction." McFate had sparked the ire of many in the field with comments she made in the *Military Review* article; she wrote, for example, "DOD [Department of Defense] yearns for cultural knowledge, but anthropologists en masse, bound by their own ethical code and sunk in a mire of postmodernism, are unlikely to contribute much of value to reshaping national security policy or practice. . . . Anthropologists, whose assistance is urgently needed in time of war, entirely neglect U.S. forces." She further angered her peers when she told Stannard, "The military is so willing to listen now . . . and for anthropologists to sit back in their ivory tower and spit at these people that are asking for their help—I think there's something unethical about that. If you're not in the room with them, you won't influence their decisions." Despite such reports as that from Colonel Martin Schweitzer, commander of the 82d Airborne Division unit, who claimed that as a result of working with an HTS team his unit's combat operations had been reduced by 60 percent, some, including the Brown University anthropology professor Catherine Lutz, continued to oppose the HTS. "There is no evidence," she told Kamps, that the Human Terrain program "does anything but prolong the war, and to the extent that it prolongs the war even a day, it creates more deaths." Following the publication of a *New York Times* article profiling the Human Terrain System, one anthropologist, Richard A. Shweder of the University of Chicago, contributed an article to the *Times* (October 27, 2007) mocking the HTS: "The anthropologists are not really doing anthropology at all, but are basically hired as military tour guides to help counterinsurgency forces accomplish various nonlethal missions. These anthropological 'angels on the shoulder,' as Ms. McFate put it, offer global positioning advice as soldiers move through poorly understood human terrain—telling them when not to cross their legs at meetings, how to show respect to leaders, how to arrange a party. They use their degrees in cultural anthropology to play the part of Emily Post."

On October 31, 2007 the American Anthropological Association (AAA) released a statement censuring anthropologists' participation in the Human Terrain System. The statement concluded that "the HTS program creates conditions which are likely to place anthropologists in positions in which their work will be in violation of the AAA Code of Ethics" and that "its use of anthropologists poses a danger to both other anthropologists and persons anthropologists study. Thus the Executive Board expresses its disapproval of the HTS program. In the context of a war in Iraq that it widely recognized as a denial of human rights and based on faulty intelligence and undemocratic principles, the Executive Board sees the HTS project as a problematic application of anthropological expertise, most specifically on ethical grounds. We have grave concerns about the involvement of anthropological knowledge and skill in the HTS project. The Executive Board views the HTS project as an unacceptable application of anthropological expertise." The "ethical grounds" referred to are the concerns that information gained by anthropologists from relationships with natives based on trust will be used against the natives. Gusterson said to Stannard, "You pitch a tent . . . among the people you want to understand, you live with them, you catch their diseases, you eat their horrible food, you share their joys and pains. The thought that you would cultivate those relationships of trust and intimacy and then . . . go to the Pentagon and say 'these are the people you should kill, these are the people you shouldn't kill,' that's extremely problematic for people with that methodology."

McFate has rebutted such accusations, telling the *New York Times* (October 5, 2007), "I'm frequently accused of militarizing anthropology. But we're really anthropologizing the military." She told Kamps that the Human Terrain teams now do not advocate violence when faced with conflict but attempt to find peaceful solutions. If, for example, they discover that an Afghan native is an agent of the Taliban, they ask, "Why is this person a member of the Taliban? Are they ideologically committed? Are they doing it because their family is threatened? Do they need the money?" McFate has returned her critics' scorn, saying to Kamps, "If you're sitting in your little office, at your little university, what opportunity do you have to influence how the brigade does business? Absolutely none! . . . Not that I'm advocating taking over countries, but that's the situation we find ourselves in now, and to pretend otherwise is to hide your head under a blanket and say, 'Naanananana.'" In the summer of 2007, with military leaders including General David Petraeus, the commander of multinational forces in Iraq, McFate helped update the army and Marine Corps's *Counterinsurgency Field Manual.*

McFate recently came under scrutiny when *Wired* and several other publications discovered that her mother-in-law, Mary Lou Sapone, had worked for gun and pharmaceutical manufacturers as a spy, infiltrating the gun-control and animal-rights movements for many years, and that McFate and her husband had worked for Sapone during that time. McFate has denied charges of spying, maintaining that she researched only broad policy topics for her mother-in-law, who never disclosed the names of her clients to McFate. However, a résumé of McFate's acquired by the *Mother Jones* reporters James Ridgeway, Daniel Schulman, and David Corn, who wrote about the accusation regarding Sapone in the July 30, 2008 issue of that magazine, cast doubt on her explanation. The résumé read in part, "Collect and analyze intelligence on European activities of major international environmental organization for a company specializing in domestic and international opposition research, special investigations, issues management and threat assessment," and "Assist in confidential litigation support research." McFate declined to comment further on the matter.

George Packer described McFate as having "hair cut stylishly short and an air of humorous cool." McFate is a senior fellow at the United States Institute of Peace. She was presented with a Distinguished Public Service Award by the secretary of the navy for her scholarship at the Office of Naval Research. She told Packer that she is "passionate about one issue: the government's need to actually understand its adversaries."

—T.O.

Suggested Reading: *Joint Forces Quarterly* p42+ July 1, 2005; *New York Times* (on-line) Oct. 5, 2007; *New Yorker* (on-line) Dec. 18, 2006; *San Francisco Chronicle* (on-line) Apr. 29, 2007; *USA Today* (on-line) Nov. 27, 2007; *Wall Street Journal* (on-line) Aug. 17, 2007

Brendan Smialowski/Getty Images

McNerney, James

Aug. 22, 1949– Chairman, president, and CEO of Boeing

Address: Boeing Corporate Offices, 100 North Riverside, Chicago, IL 60606

In March 2005 the Boeing Co., the world's leading aerospace firm and the largest manufacturer of commercial jetliners and military aircraft, sought a new chief executive officer. The nearly century-old company had recently suffered through scandals involving its top officers, one related to conflict of interest in a defense-contracting deal, the other to an illicit romantic affair. Needing a new CEO who not only had excellent business credentials but was known for integrity, Boeing found the person it sought in James ("Jim") McNerney. McNerney, who left his position as the chairman and CEO of 3M (the Minnesota Mining and Manufacturing Co.) to head Boeing, possessed an attractive set of characteristics: aerospace experience from his years of heading the Aircraft Engines division at General Electric, the company where he was employed for 18 years; a record of increasing companies' profitability by introducing greater discipline; and a reputation as a straitlaced family man known to avoid business dinners in favor of coaching his son's ice-hockey team. The wisdom of Boeing's decision was borne out in the years that followed, as Boeing's own reputation—and its profits—rose. Even John Leahy, the chief commercial officer at Boeing's rival company Airbus, was quoted in the London *Financial Times* (July 1, 2005) as saying about McNerney, "He is one of the industry stars."

The oldest of five children, Walter James McNerney Jr. was born on August 22, 1949 in Providence, Rhode Island. His father, Walter James McNerney Sr., was a professor of health policy who also served as president of the Blue Cross Blue Shield Association. As a child Jim McNerney lived in Ann Arbor, Michigan, Pennsylvania, and Chicago, Illinois. After he graduated from the New Trier Township High School, in Chicago, he attended Yale University, where he competed in varsity hockey and baseball, playing the latter alongside future president George W. Bush. After graduating in 1971, with a degree in American Studies, he took jobs teaching sailing on Lake Michigan and working on a Colorado ranch before finding positions in the health-insurance and pharmaceutical fields: he spent a year at the insurance company British United Provident and another year at G.D. Searle & Co., which is now part of the drug company Pfizer. McNerney next attended Harvard University, in Cambridge, Massachusetts, where he earned his master's degree in business administration in 1975.

After graduating McNerney began working as a brand manager at Procter & Gamble, a Fortune 500 company whose products include Tide laundry detergent, Crisco cooking oil, Pampers diapers, and Max Factor cosmetics. Among the brands that he managed were Ivory soap, Bounce fabric-softener sheets, and Downy liquid fabric softener. In 1978 he left that job to begin working as a management consultant at the German office of McKinsey & Co. In 1982 he started his career at General Electric (G.E.). Beginning as the general manager of G.E.'s mobile-communications department, he became president of General Electric Information Services in 1988. In the next year he was named executive vice president of General Electric Capital; he became president and chief executive officer of G.E. Electrical Distribution and Control in 1991 and president of the company's Asia-Pacific division in 1992. In 1995 McNerney assumed the post of president and chief executive officer of G.E. Lighting, followed by an important three-year stint as president and CEO of G.E. Aircraft Engines, from 1997 to 2000. While in that position, McNerney boosted the division to number one in the aerospace industry, besting Pratt & Whitney. By 1999 sales had reached $11 billion yearly, up from $6.3 billion in 1996, and profits had soared from $1.2 billion to $2.1 billion. It was also during his tenure as president and CEO of G.E. Aircraft Engines that McNerney closed a deal with Boeing to provide GE90 engines for the Boeing 777 jet. In 2000, when the legendary chairman of G.E.'s board, John F. ("Jack") Welch, announced his retirement, many considered McNerney to be his logical successor. Instead, Jeffrey R. Immelt was chosen as G.E.'s new chairman and CEO, after which McNerney left the company, having "lost out in the bitter race to succeed Jack Welch for what must count as the most prestigious job in American business," as a writer for the *Economist* (July 29, 2006) put it. McNerney had been courted by several companies, including Microsoft and Lucent; in the end he accepted an offer to serve as chief executive officer and chairman of 3M, becoming the first outsider to helm the company in its nearly 100-year history.

The Minnesota-based 3M, which is described on its Web site as being "fundamentally a science-based company," manufactures office supplies, provides health-care products and services, and operates businesses in several other areas; its many products include Post-It Notes, Thinsulate clothing insulation, and Scotch tape, and it has customers in 200 countries. Because General Electric, too, was a diversified company with operations in many parts of the world, it was anticipated that when McNerney replaced L. D. ("Desi") DeSimone on January 1, 2001, he would be comfortable running a company of such scale and diversity, even though he had not previously worked for 3M. "He understands the diverse business circumstances here," DeSimone told Justin Bachman for the Associated Press and Local Wire (December 6, 2000) about McNerney. "He has worked internationally, and he has a personal style that will fit very, very well with 3M. I don't see the hurdles you might expect [for a newcomer]." At the time of his arrival, the company's sales were sluggish; McNerney hoped to make each 3M product first or second in its market, decrease production costs, increase accountability within the company, and cut products that were not profitable. To tighten 3M's businesses, McNerney introduced the Six Sigma quality program, according to which a company's operational performance is measured statistically, with the aim of having no more than 3.4 defects per million items produced. Further, while McNerney did not cut the research-and-development budget, he did pressure its scientists to focus on products that were financially viable and to do so more efficiently, so that new products could be introduced to the market more rapidly.

While that disciplined approach to business practice was met with support at 3M, other actions brought criticism, such as McNerney's decision to lay off 10 percent of the company's employees. In 2004 a lawsuit was filed against 3M, alleging age discrimination in the Six Sigma program. (A Ramsey County, Minnesota, judge granted the plaintiffs class-action status in April 2008. As of October 2008 the case was still pending.) The program yielded the desired results, however; in 2004 sales had increased by $4 billion since McNerney's arrival at 3M, reaching a record $20 billion. Two departments McNerney focused on have also flourished: the display and graphics division is now 3M's fastest-growing sector, and the health-care division is now the most profitable in the company, grossing $4 billion in sales. During his tenure at 3M, McNerney also acquired the precision-lens company Corning for $680 million. According to the Associated Press (July 1, 2005), Paul Guehler, a former corporate vice president for research and

development at 3M, praised McNerney's practices, saying, "I think Jim did the right things for 3M at the right time." In 2004 *Industry Week* named him CEO of the Year and *Business Week* named him one of its Best Managers of 2003, because 3M had "been flying since McNerney rolled out his . . . productivity overhaul in 2001." The publication predicted, however, that McNerney would not stay at 3M long, noting, "The big question for McNerney now is: What's next? Or make that: Where next? . . . Given his ambition and wanderlust, 3M probably won't be McNerney's last stop."

Business Week was correct in its prediction. In 2005 the Chicago-based Boeing Co. approached McNerney, who had sat on its board of directors since 2001, about taking over the CEO position. The company had done so twice before, but both times McNerney had expressed his satisfaction at 3M. On July 1, 2005, however, McNerney assumed Boeing's top post, as chairman, president, and CEO, explaining to the reporter for the *Economist*, "I came to the conclusion that my task at 3M was largely done after five years—the company was back on track. Most of all, I realised that this [the CEO and chairman post at Boeing] was the job I really wanted to do next." Boeing offered him a pay package worth $53 million in salary, bonuses, and stock options, up from his $34 million pay package at 3M. McNerney was the third chairman and CEO of Boeing in only a year and a half, and although Boeing was on the upswing financially when McNerney assumed his position there, he inherited several problems, having to do primarily with the company's reputation.

In December 2003 the Pentagon had begun an investigation into the bidding war between Boeing and Lockheed Martin Corp. over a government contract to lease and/or sell one hundred KC-767A aircraft tankers to the United States Air Force. Boeing's chief financial officer, Michael M. Sears, and a former air force official, Darleen Druyun, were accused of conflict of interest after it was revealed that Sears had offered Druyun a job paying a minimum of $250,000 per year in exchange for favoring Boeing over Lockheed Martin in the bidding war. Druyun had accepted the job after ensuring Boeing's acquisition of the contract and passing on to Boeing information about Lockheed Martin. Sears was fired immediately (he and Druyun were later sentenced to prison), and Boeing's CEO, Philip Condit, resigned, replaced by Harry Stonecipher. Boeing suffered further humiliation when an employee sent an anonymous letter to senior executives alerting them to an ongoing affair between Stonecipher and a Boeing vice president, Debra Peabody, which violated the company's ethics rules. Stonecipher was dismissed on the grounds that his affair "reflected poorly" on his judgment and could "impair his ability to lead the company going forward," as Boeing's non-executive chairman, Lewis Platt, told *Business Week* (March 8, 2005). Among other allegations against Boeing executives were the theft of 25,000 pages of proprietary documents from Lockheed Martin and abuse of attorney-client privilege to cover up a study showing that Boeing paid female employees less than male employees.

Given such recent history at Boeing, when McNerney succeeded Stonecipher one of his priorities was to improve the ethical standards at Boeing, a company that employs more than 150,000 people. "Some Boeing managers find their new boss rather cold in his manner," the *Economist* reporter noted, "a marked contrast to the robust, outgoing personalities of his accident-prone predecessors. He is, it is true, every inch a GE man—calm, focused and exuding an air of managerial professionalism, as you would expect from a veteran of the world's most respected company." Wall Street placed so much faith in McNerney that upon his appointment, Boeing stock shares climbed $4.33, to $66 per share, their highest point in four years. In an interview with the *Los Angeles Times* (July 1, 2005), Lewis Platt explained the phenomenon, saying, "Jim has a strong reputation for integrity and ethical business standards." *Business Week* reported on July 18, 2005 that "for McNerney, cleaning up Boeing's toxic culture" was "Job One." That "toxic culture" included, along with ethical violations, resistance to change or innovation and a seeming disregard for rules. One move that symbolized a coming change in the culture of Boeing was McNerney's decision to move the annual executive retreat from the Mission Hills Country Club, in Palm Springs, Florida, where Stonecipher and Peabody were reported to have begun their affair, to the Hyatt Regency in Orlando, and to shorten the three-day event to one and a half days; the new CEO thus signaled that he meant business. He hoped to better unify the company, which had seen infighting among executives and had never properly integrated its operations with those of the McDonnell Douglas Corp., which it had acquired in 1997. As incentive to increase collaboration within the company, McNerney made pay and bonuses partially contingent on working with other units. Other kinds of behavior tied to pay and bonuses included following ethics rules and embodying the six leadership principles he laid out in the "Living Boeing Values" guide, which is aimed at fostering integrity and eliminating abusiveness.

McNerney's reforms were efficacious: Boeing's fourth-quarter earnings during his first year as CEO skyrocketed, its net income more than doubling to $460 million from $186 million. Revenue increased 7 percent, to $14.2 billion. On the New York Stock Exchange, Boeing stock gained $3.31, up to $71.62. By the end of the year, Boeing had received 1,029 orders for jets, a record for the company. One year later, in December 2006, Boeing stock had increased by a whopping 44 percent since the beginning of McNerney's tenure. As for McNerney's generous pay package, one Boeing official, John Dern, told Julie Creswell for the *New York Times* (December 29, 2006), "Jim McNerney's compensation. . . . recognizes the value that he

brings to Boeing and the company's performance has borne that out." A Boeing shareholder, Don Delves, said to Creswell, "McNerney is expensive, but we're getting one of the top . . . people in the horse race to replace Jack Welch at G.E."

In 2007 McNerney faced a major challenge, announcing on October 10 that the launch of Boeing's 787 Dreamliner would be delayed at least six months due to mismanagement of small suppliers and parts. Boeing's stock dropped 7 percent, and McNerney replaced the head of the 787 Dreamliner program, Mike Bair, with Pat Shanahan. According to Boeing, the first 787 Dreamliner was to lift off in the spring of 2008 and make its first deliveries by the end of the year. However, there were more delays, and the plane's first flight was tentatively scheduled for late 2008, with the first commercial deliveries pushed to the third quarter of 2009. As of October 2008 Boeing had nearly 900 orders for the aircraft. Despite the troubles with the Dreamliner, as of the third financial quarter of 2007, Boeing reported its net income at $1.11 billion, up from one year before. McNerney told the *Chicago Tribune* (October 25, 2007) that Boeing's "focus on growth and productivity is driving strong financial performance."

In the third quarter of 2008, a machinists' strike, which had begun in September of that year, caused earnings to drop by 38 percent. The strike lasted for over seven weeks, concluding on October 27, when a tentative deal was reached with the help of a federal mediator. As described by Micheline Maynard for the *New York Times* (October 29, 2008, online), the deal included a 15 percent raise for workers over four years and some limits on Boeing's use of outside contractors, and it lengthened the lifetime of workers' contracts from three to fours years and provided each employee with $8,000 in bonuses over a three-year period. Boeing's shares rose 11 percent following the announcement of the agreement.

McNerney "is described as a low-key, personable executive who rarely raises his voice," Peter Pae wrote for the *Los Angeles Times* (July 1, 2005). In addition to his duties at Boeing, McNerney is presiding director of Procter & Gamble and chairman of the United States–China Business Council. He is married to Haity McNerney, whom he met while working at G.E. The couple have one child; McNerney has two children from an earlier marriage.

—T.O.

Suggested Reading: *Aerospace Daily & Defense Report* News p5 July 1, 2005; *Business Week* p44 July 18, 2005; *Chicago Tribune* C p1 Feb. 2, 2006; *Economist* July 29, 2006; *Los Angeles Times* C p1 July 1, 2005; *New York Times* A p1 Dec. 29, 2006

Medvedev, Dmitry

(mehd-VYED-yehf, dee-MEE-tree)

Sep. 14, 1965– President of Russia

Address: Kremlin, Sobornaya Ploshad, Moscow, Russia

When the 42-year-old Dmitry Medvedev took the oath of office as Russia's new president, on May 7, 2008, he became the country's youngest head of state since Nicholas II, who was crowned tsar in 1894. In Russia's March 2, 2008 presidential election, which marked the first time his name was on the ballot for an elective office of any kind, Medvedev captured a little over 70 percent of the approximately 75 million votes cast, with the nearest of his three competitors gaining less than 18 percent. Medvedev's predecessor, Vladimir Putin, who was prevented by the nation's constitution from running for a third term, had hand-picked Medvedev to fill his shoes and arranged for his successor to name him prime minister. Unlike Putin and many others in the powerful *siloviki*—people in government who, when Russia was part of the Soviet Union, were members of the security forces, intelligence agencies, or secret police, known collectively as the KGB, as well as the military— Medvedev is a former law professor and legal scholar with expertise in Russia's civil code; he has written several highly respected legal textbooks. He is also a businessman, serving from 2000 to 2008 as chairman of the board of the state-controlled monopoly Gazprom, Russia's largest company and the world's largest extractor of natural gas. Medvedev has been a protégé of Putin's since the early 1990s, when both men worked in the administration of the mayor of St. Petersburg (then called Leningrad), Anatoly Sobchak; most recently Medvedev served as Putin's first deputy prime minister. Medvedev is considered a liberal in Russia, because he favors a reduced state role in business and has expressed a desire to further human rights, freedom of expression, transparency in foreign policy, and reforms in government. In a speech given after his swearing-in, as quoted by Luke Harding in the London *Guardian* (May 7, 2008, on-line), Medvedev promised to improve the lives of ordinary Russians so that they would feel "comfortable, confident and secure," and he vowed to battle corruption. He also declared, "I'm going to pay special attention to the fundamental role of the law. We must achieve a true respect in law, and overcome . . . legal nihilism, which is hampering modern development." The very popular Putin is widely expected to continue to exert his influence through Medvedev, who has pledged his support for Putin's policies and goals. In August 2008 Medvedev ordered Russian forces to invade the nearby sovereign nation of Georgia, with the expressed purpose of protecting pro-Russian separatists living in South Ossetia and Abkhazia.

The ensuing violence led to strains in Russia's relations with European nations and the U.S. During the conflict, which came to an end later in the month, Medvedev's popularity in Russia grew, and while Putin was still regarded as the country's true leader, Medevedev was often visible in the news media.

The only child of Anatoly and Yulia Medvedev, Dmitry Anatolievich Medvedev was born on September 14, 1965 in St. Petersburg, then called Leningrad, in Russia, in what was then the Soviet Union. (His given names sometimes appear with the spellings "Dmitri," "Dmitrii," "Dmitriy," and "Anatolyevich.") Medvedev was raised in a modest apartment bloc in Kupchino, a suburb of St. Petersburg. His father taught physics at the Leningrad Technological Institute, and his mother taught Russian language and literature at Leningrad Pedagogical Institute. According to Grant Slater, writing for the information service Russia Profile (2008, on-line), his parents were "steeped in the intellectual culture" of Leningrad, "the Soviet Union's most liberal city." Medvedev's parents and some of his teachers encouraged him without success to pursue a career in science. "Already by the age of 14 he firmly said no; he insisted that he would go into the law," one of his math teachers, Irina Grigorovskaya, told Owen Matthews for *Newsweek* (February 16, 2008, on-line). During his youth Medvedev was an ardent collector of British classic-rock and hard-rock records, most of which had been blacklisted by the Soviet government. He acquired taped copies of albums by his favorite bands—among them Black Sabbath, Led Zeppelin, Pink Floyd, and Deep Purple—through the black market, which was ubiquitous in the Soviet Union then.

After he completed high school, Medvedev majored in law at Leningrad State University (now St. Petersburg State University), supporting himself by working in construction and as a street cleaner. He took classes taught by a liberal lawyer, Anatoly Sobchak, who had taught Putin roughly a decade earlier. Medvedev graduated in 1987 and remained at the same school to earn a doctorate in private, corporate, and securities law, in 1990; concurrently, he worked there as an assistant lecturer on civil law from 1987 to 1990, when he became an associate professor, a position he retained until 1999. Earlier, when Medvedev was 23, he chose to be baptized in the Russian Orthodox Church, at a time when the hostility with which the Communist government regarded organized religion was starting to diminish. The next year he married his childhood sweetheart, Svetlana Linnik; in 1996 he and his wife became the parents of a son, Ilya.

In the late 1980s the Communist Party's hold over the Soviet Union was waning, and policies introduced by Mikhail Gorbachev, who was both the general secretary of the party and president of the Soviet Union, began to push the country toward democracy. In 1989, while Medvedev was pursuing his doctoral degree, he aided Sobchak in his

Alexander Nemenov/AFP/Getty Images

Dmitry Medvedev

quest for a position in the Congress of People's Deputies of the Soviet Republic, a semi-democratic parliament created by Gorbachev. Sobchak's advocacy of the introduction of a free market and other major changes provoked the animosity of some Soviet officials, and during Sobchak's election campaign, the KGB confiscated Sobchak's campaign pamphlets. Thereupon Medvedev and other volunteers "stayed up late into the night to print another set by hand," as Grant Slater reported. Sobchak won a seat in the parliament, and Medvedev went to work for him as a legal adviser.

In 1990 Sobchak was elected chairman of the Leningrad City Council. The council set up the machinery for a direct election for the city's mayor. Sobchak won that election in 1991 (the year the Soviet Union disbanded). Medvedev served as his legal adviser and as a consultant to Leningrad's committee for external affairs, then headed by Putin. While Sobchak was occupied with writing the constitution of the Russian Federation and setting up the new government, Medvedev and Putin joined to perform some of the duties of running the city. Putin was involved with property matters and dealings with foreign officials, while Medvedev provided legal advice and other services. The two worked under Sobchak until 1996, when he lost his bid for reelection.

Meanwhile, in 1990 Medvedev had co-founded a state-controlled company called Uran (the nature of which is not disclosed in readily available sources), and the next year saw the publication of the first of his law textbooks—a comprehensive volume on the Russian civil code that won praise from legal experts. According to Derek Brower in the *Petroleum Economist* (April 2008), one of his

legal textbooks is required reading in some courses in Russian universities. In 1993 Medvedev joined Ilim Pulp, a paper-processing company, as legal-affairs director. He also founded a holding company with a major stake in Ilim Pulp, remaining with it until 1999. In 1994 Medvedev co-founded a consulting group, Balfort, with former college classmates of his, and in 1998 he became chairman of the board of directors of Bratsky Forestry Complex. Those positions enabled him to live on a significantly more lavish scale than he had previously.

When Russia's president Boris Yeltsin appointed Putin prime minister, in August 1999, Putin recruited Medvedev to join him in Moscow. In November of that year, Medvedev was appointed deputy head of government administration. When Yeltsin resigned, one month later, Putin became president, and he named Medvedev deputy head of presidential administration. In the weeks preceding the presidential elections scheduled for February 2000, Medvedev served as Putin's campaign manager. Putin won that election, and Medvedev stayed on in the administration (sources differ as to his exact title). In addition to his administrative tasks, he handled special assignments; for example, he headed a commission overseeing reform of the civil service and investigated how best to overhaul the country's judicial system.

In 2000 Medvedev also became chairman of the board of directors at Gazprom, a gas corporation in which the Russian government owns a controlling stake. Gazprom is the world's largest gas company; it also owns media outlets and banks and provides a quarter of the gas used by Europeans. In 2001 Gazprom took control of the independent television network NTV, which specialized in news programs; in response, a number of journalists left NTV to work at TNT, another network. Since 2005 Gazprom has also been involved in ongoing disputes with its neighbor the Ukraine over natural-gas prices and has cut or reduced service to that nation several times. When Medvedev became president, he gave up his seat as Gazprom's chairman. His successor was the former Russian prime minister Viktor Zubkov.

Medvedev became Putin's chief of staff in 2003 and two years later was appointed first deputy prime minister. He was also placed in charge of important social programs and initiatives, called Russia's National Projects. In that capacity he oversaw projects aimed at improving agriculture, health care, education, housing, and an initiative to bolster Russia's low birth rate. Those projects earned Medvedev favorable national media coverage, and his popularity rose. In 2005 many began to speculate that he would succeed Putin. The more politically experienced and conservative defense minister, Sergei B. Ivanov, was also seen as a possible successor. Medvedev was viewed as the leader of the more liberal faction of the government, which supported a market-based economy and expressed a pro-West attitude. As a result, he was more popular than Ivanov with Russian investors. In his various jobs Medvedev had been successful in avoiding any connections to the *siloviki* (Russian for "force"), former KGB security agents and associates, among them Ivanov. Nonetheless, Medvedev was also recognized for his loyal backing of Putin's statist policies, which included the dismantling of the private oil company Yukos, a move unpopular with many investors.

At a news conference held at the Kremlin on December 10, 2007, Putin announced that he supported Medvedev as his successor. The next day Medvedev gave a speech in which, according to a *New York Times* transcript (December 11, 2007, on-line), he referred to "the necessity of continuing the implementation of the course our country has been moving along for eight years, the course chosen by the people during these years, the course which prevented the collapse of our economy and of the social sphere in our country, the course which prevented civil war, the course which is being conducted by President Putin." During the speech, he called on Putin to serve as prime minister at the conclusion of his second term as president. (Under Putin, as many observers have noted, many of the economic and political reforms adopted after the collapse of the Soviet government have been totally or partially reversed.)

Medvedev's opponents in the race for the presidency were Gennady Zyuganov, the leader of the Communist Party; Vladimir Zhirinovsky, a controversial and outspoken nationalist; and Andrei Bogdanov, an obscure liberal. Medvedev never debated the other candidates on television, confining himself to making campaign speeches throughout the country, expressing his support of the Putin administration. Megan K. Stack, writing for the *Los Angeles Times* (March 3, 2008), observed, "In appearances across the country, Medvedev lavished praise on Putin's eight years in office and carefully avoided striking any policy notes that might clash with the president's agenda. He smiled cheerfully at Putin's side even as he was mocked in cartoons and street corner jokes as the puppet of a powerful master." In one such joke, quoted by Derek Brower, Putin and Medvedev are customers in a restaurant. After Putin orders a steak, the waiter asks him, "And the vegetable?" "He'll have the steak, too," Putin responds. But Medvedev's ideas differ from Putin's in some areas. For example, Medvedev has called for an end to the Russian practice of seating government officials on corporate boards, and he has been critical of corporate and government corruption, which is endemic throughout Russia; during his presidential campaign he spoke of the need to reform the Russian judicial branch and further separate the legislative and executive branches.

In the March 2, 2008 election, Medvedev won 70 percent of the vote and was named Russia's president-elect. According to an opinion piece in the *Economist* (March 8, 2008), "The real selection of Dmitry Medvedev took place last December, when Vladimir Putin announced him as his successor, while promising also to become Russia's next prime minister. The balloting on March 2nd, when 70 percent of voters endorsed Mr. Putin's choice, was mere ritual. It was not so much the election that was rigged (though figures were massaged), but the whole political process leading up to it. Had Mr. Putin picked anyone else, the result would have been the same, for this was his election." "Russia's new political system born in 1989 is now in a state of degradation and has been thrown back to Soviet times," Andrei Buzin of the Russian civilian organization GOLOS, which monitors elections, said at a news conference, as reported by Michael Stott for Reuters (March 3, 2008). Bernard Kouchner, the French foreign minister, told Adrian Blomfield for the London *Daily Telegraph* (March 4, 2008), "The election was conducted Russian-style, with a victory known in advance."

Sam Greene, a scholar-in-residence at the Carnegie Moscow Center, a division of the Carnegie Endowment for International Peace, told Luke Harding that when he took office, Medvedev faced "enough problems to make his hair go grey." Those problems include, on the domestic front, a rapidly rising rate of inflation; growing dissatisfaction, especially among Russia's large number of pensioners and others with fixed incomes, with increasing food and utility prices; the deplorable state of the health-care system (the average life expectancy for men is about 61.5 years, and for women, about 74; in the U.S., the corresponding figures are 75.2 and 81); and a declining population: in January 2008, according to the Russia State Statistic Service, approximately 142 million people lived in Russia, more than three million fewer than in 2000, a decrease of about 2 percent. In Russia, women of child-bearing age have an average of 1.4 children, while in the U.S., the figure is about 2.1. In addition, Russia was seriously affected by the global financial crisis that gripped world markets in mid-2008; globally, by the end of October of that year, its economy had become one of the most insecure, and Medvedev had reportedly created, but not publicly announced, a program that would invest money from Russia's oil-reserve fund into preferred shares in some of the country's biggest banks and firms.

Medvedev and Russia's standing with Europe and the U.S. declined in August 2008 when the president ordered Russian forces to enter its neighbor Georgia, purportedly to protect two "breakaway" regions, South Ossetia and Abkhazia, that are loyal to Russia. Each of the regions is home to a distinct ethnic group from the nearby Caucasus Mountains, and when the Soviet Union annexed Georgia after the Russian Revolution, it created autonomous regions for the two groups. Since the breakup of the Soviet Union, in 1991, the two groups have resisted Georgian efforts to annex them and have aligned themselves with Russia. (Many members of the groups hold Russian passports). Medvedev ordered the Russian military to intervene in the ongoing conflict "to protect the life and dignity of Russian citizens wherever they are," as he told the Interfax news agency, as quoted by the BBC News (August 8, 2008, on-line). He added, "We will not allow their deaths to go unpunished. Those responsible will receive a deserved punishment." Medvedev had acted in response to Georgia's invasion of Tskhinvali, the capital of South Ossetia, and rumors of "ethnic cleansing" on the part of the Georgian military. In addition to sending in troops, Russia had directed air strikes on parts of Georgia. Seven of the G8 countries—the U.S., Canada, the United Kingdom, France, Germany, Italy, and Japan (Russia is the eighth member of the G8)—called on Russia to halt the violence. During the conflict Russian forces also crossed from the separatist regions into undisputed Georgian territory, prompting further international criticism. President George W. Bush, as quoted on globalsecurity.com (August 12, 2008), said, "Russia's actions this week have raised serious questions about its intentions in Georgia and the region. These actions have substantially damaged Russia's standing in the world. And these actions jeopardize Russia's relations with the United States and Europe." A cease-fire was agreed upon on August 12, but as of October 9, some Russian troops remained in Georgia, as Ellen Barry reported for the *New York Times* (October 10, 2008).

Earlier, in late August 2008, Medvedev had issued a decree formally recognizing South Ossetia and Abkhazia as independent of Georgia. "It is not up to Russia to recognize unilaterally the independence of Abkhazia and South Ossetia," French president Nicolas Sarkozy said, as quoted by Jamey Keaten for the Associated Press (September 9, 2008). "There are international rules. These should be respected." According to Keaten, Medvedev declared, "Our decision is irrevocable. Two new states have come into existence. This is a reality which all our partners, including our EU partners, will have to reckon with." Despite Medvedev's public statements regarding the conflict, many still considered Putin to be Russia's real leader. Lynn Berry wrote for the Associated Press (August 15, 2008), for example, "The ongoing conflict has confirmed what has become increasingly obvious in recent weeks: Putin is still the one in charge. President Dmitry Medvedev has been the Kremlin's voice in recent days, but Putin set the tone from the beginning. And when Medvedev suddenly made an uncharacteristically blunt statement, he seemed to be imitating the mannerisms and language of his powerful mentor."

The five-foot four-inch Medvedev enjoys swimming, jogging, and yoga. One of his favorite bands, Deep Purple, played at the Kremlin in February 2008 at a concert marking the 15th anniversary of the founding of Gazprom.

—W.D.

Suggested Reading: BBC News (on-line) Mar. 3, 2008; (London) *Daily Telegraph* p16 Mar. 4, 2008; (London) *Financial Times* p2 Dec. 11, 2007; (London) *Guardian* (on-line) May 7, 2008; *Los Angeles Times* A p1 Mar. 3, 2008; *Newsweek* (on-line) Feb.16, 2008; russiaprofile.com

---

Melton, Douglas A.

Sep. 26, 1953– Molecular biologist; embryologist; educator

Address: Dept. of Molecular and Cellular Biology, Harvard University, 7 Divinity Ave., Rm. 465, Cambridge, MA 02138

For a dozen years after he earned his Ph.D. degree, in 1980, Douglas A. Melton built a solid career in molecular and cellular biology at Harvard University, studying African clawed frogs and tadpoles to unravel some of the mysteries of embryonic development, during which a fertilized egg begins to develop into one organism or another. That phase of his professional life ended dramatically one day in 1993, when his critically ill six-month-old son was diagnosed with Type I diabetes. "When something happens to your child, it gets your full attention," Melton told Steve Mirsky for *BioInteractive* (November 2006, on-line), a publication of the Howard Hughes Medical Institute, one of the several institutions with which Melton is affiliated. "And I did what any parent does. I said, 'I'm not going to stand by and do nothing. What can I do?' Some parents raise money to help support research. Other parents lobby for public policy. In my case, I was fortunate to have the scientific training that allowed me to move my research focus to an area that would be immediately relevant to diabetes." For the past 15 years, Melton has strived to find a cure for diabetes, from which both of his children suffer and which in 2007 was the fifth-leading cause of death in the United States. In doing so he has become a leader in the field of embryonic stem-cell research, an avenue of scientific investigation that has sparked enormous controversy. Those who oppose the use of frozen human embryos (produced in test tubes by combining sperm with an unfertilized egg) for research maintain that it is nothing less than murder, because, they believe, human life begins at the moment when a sperm penetrates an egg. Melton and other scientists who work with embryonic stem cells, by contrast, believe, as Gareth Cook wrote for the *Boston Globe* (March 20, 2005), that "the creation of a human being is a process, like the development of an acorn into an acorn tree. It makes no sense, they [say], to think of the cells they work with as babies." "You could almost say that there is a moral obligation to do

Justin Ide/Harvard News Office

Douglas A. Melton

these experiments," Melton said to Cook, referring to the potential of embryonic stem-cell research to lead to cures not only for diabetes but for many other diseases, genetic defects, and instances of paralysis resulting from accidents, among other serious health problems. In 2006, by circumventing federal funding restrictions with private funds, Melton and his colleagues created 17 new embryonic stem-cell lines, which have been made available without charge to other scientists; that number has since increased to more than 50. The following year his name appeared on *Time* magazine's list of the world's 100 most influential people. In 2008 Melton and a colleague transformed a cell from the pancreas of a mouse into one that secretes insulin, a vital hormone whose presence in humans in insufficient quantities is a symptom of diabetes. Melton is currently working toward applying their breakthrough finding for the benefit of humans.

There are two main types of diabetes. Type I, which usually manifests itself suddenly in childhood or the teenage years, is the most severe form and the most difficult to control. It arises when the body's immune system destroys the specialized cells in the pancreas that produce insulin, a hormone that is vital in the transport and storage of glucose (sugar), as well as in the cells' conversion of glucose into energy, the cells' synthesis of proteins, and the storage of fats. Between 5 and 10 percent of diabetics suffer from that form of the disease. In Type II diabetes, which usually strikes adults over the age of 40, the pancreas produces an insufficient quantity of insulin, or the body loses its ability to use the hormone effectively. About 90 percent of diabetics are victims of that form of the disease. When untreated, diabetes causes such symptoms as frequent, copious urination; excessive thirst or hunger; blurry vision; extreme fatigue; sudden, unaccountable weight loss; protracted itchiness or other skin disorders; and prolonged irritability or depression. In severe cases, untreated diabetes can lead to coma and death. By maintaining a proper diet, testing blood-sugar levels at intervals throughout the day, and taking insulin, either by mouth or via injections, diabetics can control the disease, but treatment cannot duplicate a nondiabetic's natural mechanisms for producing and using insulin. The bodily systems and organs of diabetics are repeatedly subjected to unnatural stresses throughout the day, and for that reason the disease often causes serious complications, including cardiovascular (heart and blood vessel) disease, which can lead to heart attacks and strokes; kidney failure; visual impairments and blindness; and nerve damage, which, in thousands of cases every year, results in amputations of toes, feet, and the lower parts of legs. Diabetics are also three times as likely as nondiabetics to die of the flu or pneumonia, and on average, those suffering from diabetes die 15 years earlier than nondiabetics. Specialists believe that because diabetes remains undiagnosed in millions of people, the death toll from the disease is actually far higher than records indicate: when an undiagnosed diabetic dies of a stroke, for example, the cause of death is listed as stroke, but the true, underlying cause is usually diabetes. In testimony on stem-cell research before the U.S. Senate Committee on Appropriations' Subcommittee on Labor, Health and Human Services, Education, and Related Agencies on January 10, 1999 (as transcribed on the Web site of Harvard's Department of Molecular and Cellular Biology), Melton said, "Diabetes is an insidious disease, and remains widely misunderstood by the general public. Insulin is not a cure for diabetes, it is merely life support."

At that same, 1999 subcommittee meeting, before he talked about the possibility that stem-cell research will enable scientists to discover cures for many diseases, Melton described the difficulties of caring for his diabetic son, Samuel: "The daily regimen of Sam's blood checks and insulin injections (up to 5/day) are coupled with our need to [balance] his diet and exercise: a serious challenge in dealing with a 7 year old soccer player. The medical troubles for Sam are compounded by the vigilance and worry that extract a heavy toll on the rest of the family. For example, my wife is regularly up in the late hours of the night doing blood checks while Sam sleeps: we wonder is his blood sugar too low? Will he find the middle ground between a 'low' or coma and being too 'high' in the morning? I can't recall a night since Sam was diagnosed when we slept peacefully, free of the worry that the balance between his food, insulin and exercise was not good enough. I'm unwilling to accept the enormity of this medical and psychological burden and I am personally devoted to bringing it to an end for Sam and all type I diabetics."

Douglas Arlie Melton was born on September 26, 1953 in Chicago, Illinois, and grew up on that city's South Side. His father was a grocery-store manager, and his mother worked as a court reporter. When not at school, he spent much of his teens playing basketball and tennis. In a conversation with David Ewing Duncan for *Discover* (July 5, 2005), he described his high-school years as "rather difficult," in part because of repercussions stemming from the assassination of Martin Luther King Jr., in 1968, and the killing by Chicago police officers of Fred Hampton, a member of the Black Panthers, in 1969. After he completed high school, in 1971, Melton attended the University of Illinois at Urbana-Champaign, where he became passionately interested in biology. "For the first time in my life, I felt myself part of an intellectual world," he told Duncan. He earned a B.S. degree with honors in 1975, and later that year, having won a Marshall scholarship (funded by the British government), he enrolled at the University of Cambridge, in England, where he earned a B.A. degree in history and the philosophy of science in 1977.

Eager to work hands-on in science and not simply spend his life "commenting on what other, very smart people thought about," as he told Steve Mirsky, Melton remained at Cambridge to pursue a Ph.D. in molecular biology. He worked under the eminent developmental biologist John Gurdon, a pioneer in what is known variously as nuclear transplantation, nuclear transfer, and nuclear cloning. In that process, the nucleus of an adult cell from a donor animal is inserted into another animal's oocyte, or egg (also known as the female germ cell or gametocyte), from which the nucleus has previously been removed. Unlike the egg in its original form, in which the nucleus contained half the number of chromosomes necessary to create a whole organism, the nucleus of the adult donor cell contains the full number of chromosomes associated with all individuals of that species of animal. The re-nucleated egg is considered an embryo, because it now has a full complement of chromosomes. (Normally, the other half is supplied during mating, when the male germ cell, or sperm, penetrates the egg. Like eggs, sperm contain half the number of chromosomes necessary to create a whole organism.)

The embryo can now be handled in either of two ways. It can be transferred to the uterus of another female, the recipient animal, where, potentially, it can grow into a clone, or exact copy, of the donor animal; that process is called reproductive cloning. Alternatively, the embryo can be placed in a growing medium, or culture, in a laboratory dish (commonly called a petri dish), where, potentially, it can produce embryonic stem cells. Potentially, such cells can divide repeatedly to become virtually any type of cell that is found in the adult donor animal. Using a forerunner of the method that Ian Wilmut, a later student of Gurdon's, famously used to clone Dolly, a sheep, Gurdon created cloned frogs from tadpoles. Like Gurdon, Melton worked with aquatic, carnivorous, clawed frogs from Africa belonging to the genus Xenopus. With his completed dissertation, entitled "The Expression of Transfer RNA Genes and Other DNAs Microinjected in Xenopus Oocytes," Melton earned a Ph.D. in molecular biology from Cambridge in 1980.

Melton then moved to Cambridge, Massachusetts, where in 1981 he was named an assistant professor in Harvard University's Department of Biochemical and Molecular Biology (later renamed the Department of Molecular and Cellular Biology). He was promoted to associate professor in 1984 and to professor in 1988. Since 1999 he has held the title of Thomas Dudley Cabot professor of natural sciences. At Harvard he continued to study frogs to discover "what happens right after fertilization that is important for telling cells what to become," as he explained to Duncan. His research illuminated how the ectoderm, mesoderm, and endoderm—the three primary layers of the days'-old embryo—are formed. In one experiment, one of Melton's postdoctoral students, Ali Hemmati-Brivanlou (currently the director of molecular embryology at Rockefeller University), removed a compound called activin (one of many naturally occurring proteins known as growth factors) from a fertilized frog egg; as a result, the embryo failed to develop properly. Further investigation revealed that the lack of activin had curbed development of the mesoderm, which differentiates into many parts of the frog embryo: muscle, bone, connective tissue, the heart, blood, and other elements of the circulatory system, the reproductive system, and the middle layer of the skin, among other tissues and organs. Without activin, most of the cells in the frog embryo became brain cells, or neurons, which are a form of nerve cells. "Many people found interesting the hypothesis we put forth, which now seems to have even more experimental support: that the nervous system forms by a kind of default mechanism," Melton told Duncan. "It's the easiest thing for the embryo to form. That was sort of surprising, because neurobiologists wanted to believe that neurons were the highest, most complicated types of cells."

One morning in 1993, Melton's then six-month-old son, Sam, awakened with what appeared to be an ordinary virus. When, later in the day, his symptoms became significantly worse, Melton and his wife, Gail O'Keefe, brought him to the emergency room at Children's Hospital in Boston, Massachusetts (with which Melton has been associated since 1994). The baby was close to death when a perceptive nurse tested his urine for sugar; the glucose level was far above normal, indicating that Sam had diabetes. Melton took a leave of absence until Sam's condition became stabilized, then returned to his laboratory with a renewed sense of purpose. Now, he was resolved to focus on the causes of and possible cures for diabetes, "one of the most common chronic diseases affecting children, a group upon which it has an especially devastating impact," as he said in his 1999 testimony before the Senate subcommittee. (Melton's daughter, Emma, was diagnosed with Type I diabetes in 1998, when she was 14.)

For several years Melton studied pancreatic development in frogs and mice. In the late 1990s he expanded his lab's work to include human embryonic stem cells, which, in normal development, mature into the approximately 210 types of human cells. First, he determined that no adult stem cells would be suitable for use in his research; indeed, although stem cells (in very small numbers) have been found in the brain, bone morrow, blood, blood vessels, skeletal muscle, skin, and liver, none have been located in the pancreas. He next considered using as his experimental material beta cells, the specialized cells, located in the part of the pancreas called the islets of Langerhans, that produce and release insulin. But those cells may not have sufficient capacity to divide to produce a useful number of cells; within the pancreas, beta cells reproduce "by simple division in the mature phase rather than descending from a progenitor, the adult stem cell," as a writer for *Scientific American* (December 2004) pointed out, and no reliable way has yet been found to spur them to reproduce in the laboratory. An attractive experimental material for Melton's research presented itself in the form of embryonic stem cells that can be derived from the human embryos produced in fertility clinics and then frozen in liquid nitrogen for future use by prospective parents. (In 2006 there were an estimated 500,000 in storage in the U.S.) The vast majority of them are never used, however, and often they are discarded. Nevertheless, many people condemn the use of embryonic stem cells in research as immoral, asserting that embryos are humans, and therefore any manmade process that snuffs out their lives is immoral. Melton strongly disagrees with that belief; as he told William J. Cromie for the *Harvard University Gazette* (March 4, 2004), "The material from which these stem cells are derived has the potential to form a life. But this potential is very low. Those who say that frozen embryos are identical to children are making a mistake. . . . We need to draw a strong line between what has the potential for life and what is alive."

On August 9, 2001 President George W. Bush, in the first televised speech to the nation since his inauguration the previous January, announced his decision to allow federal funding for stem-cell research only on existing stem-cell lines. Although in June 2001 the National Institutes of Health had reported that about 30 such cell lines were known to exist worldwide, the president asserted that there were more than 60. According to Katharine Q. Seelye, writing for the *New York Times* (August 10, 2001), many medical researchers and proponents of embryonic stem-cell research rejected Bush's proposal as unacceptable, because, as Seelye put it, "the existing cell lines, or self-sustaining colonies of cells, were not adequate in number or sufficiently robust to serve the needs of American scientists." Melton held the same view; as he told

Cromie in March 2004, "I could not convince myself that any of the cell lines would be available or useful." In that month only about 15 were publicly available, and, as Melton and others wrote for the *New England Journal of Medicine* (March 25, 2004), "they var[ied] considerably in their usefulness for research." Melton resolved to develop his own cell lines through private funding.

Earlier, in 2000, at a backyard barbecue, Melton had met Doug Powers, a scientist working at Boston IVF, in Massachusetts, a clinic that specializes in in-vitro fertilization, the process in which eggs are fertilized in a laboratory and then implanted in the potential mother. In his conversation with Powers, Melton learned that Boston IVF had in storage many human embryos that would never be used. Later, he proposed a collaboration between the clinic and his laboratory, and after consultations with bioethicists, Boston IVF agreed to work with him. In 2003, with private funding from Harvard, the Juvenile Diabetes Research Foundation International, the Howard Hughes Medical Institute, and a Maryland-based research group, Melton and his team worked with a Boston IVF team to develop 17 new stem-cell lines from thawed embryos. (Because of President Bush's ruling, the work could not be accomplished in any laboratory that had equipment bought with any funds from the federal government.) Melton and a dozen of his colleagues described the derivation of the new embryonic stem-cell lines in the March 25, 2004 issue of the *New England Journal of Medicine*. "The material we used was slated for destruction," Melton told Cromie. "From that point of view, one could almost consider our position pro-life. We took something that was going to be destroyed and isolated cells from it that could improve the lives of people suffering from disease and trauma." Samples of the new lines were offered to other researchers at no charge, because, as Melton told Claudia Dreifus for the *New York Times* (January 24, 2006), "there's a long scientific tradition of making the fruits of one's research available to others."

In April 2004 Harvard announced the opening of the Harvard Stem Cell Institute, which Charlie Schmidt, in a press release from the university's Department of Molecular and Cellular Biology (online), described as a "'virtual' center without walls" whose goal was to support not only the work of Melton and his laboratory but the efforts of scientists at other sites. Melton, who has co-directed the institute since its launching, told Dreifus that because of the ban on federal funding, Harvard had to build a new laboratory "that was separate from everything else here at Harvard. And we had to separate the money in a really scrupulous way. We have an accountant who makes sure that not a penny of federal funding goes to embryonic stem cell research. We have separate everything—light bulbs, computers, centrifuges. This can be burdensome. Most of the activities at this university receive federal money in some indirect way. So you have to ask yourself, 'How can you do the research without any imprint of federal funding?' And we're not just talking about equipment and real estate; it's people. Let's suppose there's a graduate student who's receiving a federally funded fellowship, can he or she participate in thinking about this research or even look at the data? The answer is no." In September 2006 President Bush vetoed a bill that would have loosened the restrictions on federal funding for stem-cell research, allowing couples to donate their frozen embryos to scientists. In July 2007 Bush vetoed a similar bill.

To date, Melton and his colleagues have created more than 50 new embryonic stem-cell lines. In an article published on-line in *Nature* on August 27, 2008, Melton, his Harvard colleague Joe Zhou, and three other scientists associated with Harvard described how they transformed one type of cell found in the pancreas of a mouse into a type that is capable of secreting insulin. Melton and Zhou achieved that feat by injecting a combination of three genes into cells in the pancreas of a living mouse, in a process known as direct reprogramming. (Their report also appeared in the October 2, 2008 print issue of *Nature*.) Not yet tested on humans, the technique is regarded as a potential way to treat people suffering from Type 2 diabetes. "It's a really dramatic discovery," Kathy Myburgh, a biologist at Stellenbosch University, in South Africa, told Alana Rank for the South African daily *Business Day* (August 30, 2008). "One of the reasons it's so interesting is that the transformation of the cells was achieved inside the mouse: most researchers remove cells, try and transform them in a tissue culture in the lab, and then re-implant them. This was done inside the live animal." Melton is currently working to perfect the technique and hopes to begin clinical trials on diabetes patients within two to five years. Melton has already identified hundreds of genes that may prove capable of transforming embryonic stem cells into particular specialized cells.

In another noteworthy accomplishment, in August 2008 a team of researchers from the Harvard Stem Cell Institute created disease-specific stem cells—linked to maladies including diabetes and Parkinson's disease. Their work will enable scientists to observe aspects of the development of those diseases in the lab. The cells can be reprogrammed to behave like those of embryos, creating a way for scientists to "watch what goes right or wrong," as Melton told Sharon Kirkey for the Canwest News Service, as posted on *Canada.com* (August 7, 2008). "In these complex genetic diseases, we're so ignorant at the moment we don't even know when a patient gets diabetes if they all get it the same way. There could be 50 different ways to get Type 1 diabetes." Melton noted that those stem-cell lines could help researchers understand what mutations are responsible for a disease and locate "the weak point where you could try to prevent, or treat it"; they may also "make it possible to find new treatments, and eventually drugs, to slow or even stop

the course of a number of diseases." The stem cells have been made available to other researchers.

Melton is the author or co-author of more than 130 peer-reviewed scientific articles. He is a member of the National Academy of Sciences, the National Academy's Institute of Medicine, and the American Academy of Arts and Sciences. His honors include the Richard Lounsbery Medal, from the National Academy of Sciences; the Elliott P. Joslin Medal, from the Joslin Diabetes Center in Boston; and Harvard's George Ledlie Prize.

—W.D.

Suggested Reading: *Canada.com* Aug. 7, 2008; *Discover* p57+ June 2005; Howard Hughes Medical Institute Web site; *New York Times* F p2 Jan. 24, 2006

Courtesy of Little, Brown and Co.

Meyer, Stephenie

Dec. 24, 1973– Writer

Address: c/o Author Mail, Little, Brown and Co., 237 Park Ave., New York, NY 10017

Lev Grossman wrote for *Time* (April 24, 2008, online) that Stephenie Meyer, the author of the vampire-themed Twilight Saga series of novels, "is a huge success at selling books, but she's becoming something more. People dress up like her characters. They write their own stories about them and post their tales on the Internet. When she appears at a bookstore, 3,000 people go to meet her. There are Twilight-themed rock bands. Meyer has, like one of her vampires, turned into something rare and more than merely human: a literary phenomenon." The four books in the saga—*Twilight* (2005), *New Moon* (2006), *Eclipse* (2007), and *Breaking Dawn* (2008)—have collectively sold a reported 10 million copies, and an eagerly awaited film adaptation of the first book was scheduled for release in November 2008.

Meyer's books have been praised particularly for their exclusion of violence, drugs, and explicit sex. The author, a devout Mormon, told Grossman, "I get some pressure to put [in] a big sex scene. But you can go anywhere for graphic sex. It's harder to find a romance where they dwell on the hand-holding." The novelist explained to Damian Whitworth for the London *Times* (May 13, 2008), "I know a lot of kids who relate to my books because they don't drink and they are not sexually active. There are a ton of them but they don't get a lot of representation in literature or television or movies. Kids who are just good kids and follow the rules—they are out there and they don't get any playtime." In *Time* (April 30, 2008, on-line), Meyer was featured on a list of the world's 100 most influential people, and in that issue Orson Scott Card, a writer of fantasy and science fiction whom Meyer has often cited as an inspiration, paid tribute to her work: "In an era when much of the romance genre has been given over to soft porn, and dark fantasy is peopled with one-dimensional characters bent on grim violence, many readers have become hungry for pure romantic fantasy—lots of sexual tension, but as decorous as Jane Austen. Meyer did not calculatedly reach for that audience. Instead, she wrote the story she believed in and cared about. She writes with luminous clarity, never standing between the reader and the dream they share. She's the real thing. Still, who'd have thought it? Today, [Austen's] Mr. Darcy is a vampire."

Meyer was born Stephenie Morgan on December 24, 1973 in Hartford, Connecticut, to Stephen and Candy Morgan. She has five siblings: Emily, Heidi, Paul, Seth, and Jacob. (Meyer is the second-oldest.) The unusual spelling of her first name was the idea of her father, who simply added an "ie" to the end of his own name. When Meyer was four years old, the family moved to Phoenix, Arizona, where her father worked as the chief financial officer of a contracting firm. Meyer was an avid reader from an early age. "I read the fattest books I could get my hands on," she told Jaimee Rose for the Phoenix *Arizona Republic* (November 10, 2007). She has frequently cited Austen and Card as two of her favorite authors.

Meyer attended Chaparral High School, in Scottsdale, Arizona, graduating in 1992. She wrote on her official Web site, "[Scottsdale was] the kind of place where every fall a few girls would come back to school with new noses and there were Porsches in the student lot. (For the record, I have my original nose, and never had a car until after I was in my twenties)." She won a National Merit Scholarship, through which she studied English literature at Brigham Young University (BYU), a Mor-

mon-affiliated school in Provo, Utah. "On the list of the biggest party schools in the country, BYU consistently and proudly finishes dead last," Meyer—who has never smoked, used drugs, or drunk alcohol—wrote for her site.

In 1994, during her summer break from college, Meyer came into contact with Christiaan "Pancho" Meyer, who had just returned from a Mormon mission in Chile. The two had attended the same church growing up; despite seeing each other on a weekly basis, they had never spoken at length. That summer, however, they began dating, and in December they were married. Meyer finished her degree at BYU, moved with her new husband to Glendale, Arizona, and worked for a brief time as a receptionist. After the arrival of her first son, Gabe, in 1997, Meyer became a stay-at-home mother, while her husband worked as an auditor. Two other sons followed: Seth, in 2000, and Eli, in 2002. Her main creative outlets became, as Grossman wrote, "scrapbooking and making elaborate Halloween costumes." That changed on June 2, 2003, when Meyer woke up from a vivid dream. (She remembers the exact date because it coincided with her sons' first swimming lessons.) She wrote on her Web site, "In my dream, two people were having an intense conversation in a meadow in the woods. One of these people was just your average girl. The other person was fantastically beautiful, sparkly, and a vampire. They were discussing the difficulties inherent in the facts that A) they were falling in love with each other while B) the vampire was particularly attracted to the scent of her blood, and was having a difficult time restraining himself from killing her immediately." Meyer did not know why she had dreamt of a vampire; she had never read the Bram Stoker novel *Dracula*, watched the popular television show *Buffy the Vampire Slayer*, or seen any horror movies. Still, as she went about making breakfast for her children and gathering their bathing suits, she found herself unable to stop thinking about the dream and decided to write it down. After that, she wrote more of the story every day, usually when her children were asleep. "[My husband became] kind of mad at me," Meyer told Whitworth. "He said: 'You never sleep, you never talk to me, I never get to use the computer. What are you doing?'"

Meyer admitted to her husband that she was writing, purely for her own enjoyment. She allowed her older sister, Emily, to read her work, which was 130,000 words long by the time it was finished. Emily encouraged her to find a publisher, and Meyer turned to the Internet to learn how to submit her manuscript. "You don't wrap it up in brown paper like they do in the movies," she told Cecelia Goodnow for the *Seattle Post-Intelligencer* (October 8, 2005). Discovering that most publishing companies did not read the work of authors who were not represented by agents, Meyer began contacting literary agencies. She caught the interest of Jodi Reamer at Writers House, who agreed to represent her. On December 1, 2003 the publisher

Little, Brown and Co. offered the writer $300,000. Meyer, who had been hoping for $10,000 to pay off the debt on her minivan, was horrified when her agent rejected the offer and asked for more. The publishing company ultimately settled on a $750,000 three-book contract.

The first book, *Twilight*, introduces Bella Swan, an unremarkable 17-year-old who moves to Forks, Washington, to live with her divorced father. There, she meets the handsome and charming Edward Cullen and his family, a clan of vampires who have vowed to fight their urges for human blood and instead feed on animals. The pair quickly fall in love. The vampires live in rainy Forks because their skin shimmers unnaturally when exposed to sun; Meyer discovered the real-life town during an Internet search for the rainiest place in the U.S. (In 2007 Forks's mayor, Nedra Reed, proclaimed September 13, the fictional Bella's birthday, as Stephenie Meyer Day.)

Within months of *Twilight*'s publication, in August 2005, word-of-mouth reports had helped the book to reach the top of best-seller lists. It was named one of *Publishers Weekly*'s best books of year and one of the American Library Association's 10 best books for young adults, among other honors. While *Twilight* was marketed to young adults and the series has attracted a readership made up largely of teenage girls, Meyer told Gregory Kirschling for *Entertainment Weekly* (August 10, 2007), "I didn't write *Twilight* thinking, 'Oh, I will appeal to 16 year olds with this.' I don't believe that you need to write down to teenagers." Nor did Meyer feel that she needed to hew to the conventions of other vampire literature. "I am not into horror novels and have never been a horror fan. So when I was writing *Twilight* with no view to publication, just to entertain myself, I played with the basic vampire legend," she told Robyn Doreian for the Sydney, Australia, *Sun Herald* (December 23, 2007). "Research might have meant I couldn't have as much fun with it."

New Moon, the sequel, was published in September 2006 and spent more than 30 weeks at the number-one spot on the *New York Times* young-adult best-seller list. The third book, *Eclipse*, published in August 2007, sold 150,000 copies in its first day in stores, knocking J. K. Rowling's *Harry Potter and the Deathly Hallows* to the number-two position in the *New York Times* rankings within weeks. The fourth and reportedly final installment in the *Twilight Saga* series, *Breaking Dawn*, sold 1.3 million copies within 24 hours of its arrival in bookstores on August 2, 2008.

Meyer has often been likened to Rowling: both write fantasy novels, both were the mothers of small children when they wrote their first books, and each has attracted a fanatical following. Meyer told Whitworth, "I'm a big fan [of Rowling]. All of us YA [young adult] writers are, especially those of us who write big books. If it weren't for her, our books wouldn't even have gotten a chance. People wouldn't put an 800-page YA book on the shelf because there was no way kids were going to read it. Now everyone knows that kids love big books, you just have to make them interesting for them." She continued, "[But] everyone is looking for the next J.K. Rowling. It's not going to happen. . . . She was, is, something that will not be repeated."

Meyer's book signings have often been held in large auditoriums to accommodate the throngs of fans, many of whom have dressed in gothic clothing or T-shirts with *Twilight*-inspired artwork and slogans. Some venues have provided red makeup so that readers can adorn their necks with fake vampire bites.

For much of 2008 Internet message boards and fan sites have been flooded with news of the upcoming movie based on *Twilight*, directed by Catherine Hardwicke. "I put in a clause in the contract that the movie had to be PG-13 so I could go see it," Meyer, who has never seen a film with an R rating because of her religious convictions, told Whitworth.

Despite the popularity of Meyer's books, they have been subject to some criticism. "Wading through the books themselves—1,700-plus pages to date—can be a punishing proposition," Scott Renshaw wrote for the *Salt Lake City Weekly* (March 6, 2008). "Meyer serves up dialogue exposition by the bucketful and appears determined to describe the precise facial expression and vocal intonation of every character during every utterance." Lev Grossman held a similar opinion. "Meyer floods the page like a severed artery. She never uses a sentence when she can use a whole paragraph. Her books are big (500-plus pages) but not dense—they have a pillowy quality distinctly reminiscent of Internet fan fiction." Meyer admitted to being hurt by the negative reviews but told Grossman, "I don't think I'm a writer; I think I'm a storyteller. The words aren't always perfect."

Meyer's first adult novel, *The Host*, was published in May 2008. The story concerns a parasitic race of aliens who have taken over Earth, and romance figures largely in the plot. The book was voted the best of the month by Amazon.com, and in the citation the reviewer, Mari Malcolm, wrote, "Likely the first love triangle involving just two bodies, it's unabashedly romantic, and the characters (human and alien) genuinely endearing. Readers intrigued by this familiar-yet-alien world will gleefully note that the story's end leaves the door open for a sequel—or another series."

In August 2008 Meyer took an unplanned, open-ended break from work on her next book, "Midnight Sun"—a retelling of *Twilight* from Edward's perspective—after a copy of the unfinished manuscript was illegally posted on-line. "I did not want my readers to experience *Midnight Sun* before it was completed, edited and published," Meyer wrote for her Web site (August 28, 2008). "I think it is important for everybody to understand that what happened was a huge violation of my rights as an author, not to mention me as a human being." She also explained that she felt "too sad about what has happened to continue working" on the story and would instead focus on other writing projects and on spending more time with her family.

Meyer, whose favorite band is the alternative-rock group Muse, often listens to music when she writes and has provided on her Web site a list of songs that inspired her during the writing of each book.

Meyer lives in Cave Creek, Arizona, with her family. Her husband resigned from his job in 2007 to take care of their sons while Meyer attends promotional events. Some of the events are billed as "proms," and readers show up in long gowns and tiaras to meet Meyer and get their books signed. The author told Jaimee Rose of her fans, "I have all these teenage adopted daughters. . . . They're impossible not to adore."

—M.A.S.

Suggested Reading:*Arizona Republic* Living p1 Nov. 10, 2007; *Entertainment Weekly* p74 Aug. 10, 2007; (London) *Times* p4 May 13, 2008; (Melbourne, Australia) *Age* A p25 May 17, 2008; *Seattle Post-Intelligencer* E p1 Oct. 8, 2005; Stephenie Meyer's Web site; (Sydney, Australia) *Sun Herald* p48 Dec. 23, 2007; *Time* (on-line) Apr. 24, 2008, Apr. 30, 2008

Selected Books: *Twilight*, 2005; *New Moon*, 2006; *Eclipse*, 2007; *The Host*, 2008; *Breaking Dawn*, 2008

Courtesy of Sue Mingus

Mingus, Sue

Apr. 2, 1930– Band organizer; writer

Address: The Jazz Workshop, 484 W. 43d St., Suite 43S, New York, NY 10036

Four months after the death of her second husband, the acclaimed jazz bassist and composer Charles Mingus, in 1979, Sue Mingus was asked to organize a tribute concert at New York City's Carnegie Hall. Despite her lack of experience as a bandleader, she agreed to do so, choosing seven musicians who had played with her husband on *Mingus Ah Um* and *Mingus Dynasty*, two of his noted 1950s recordings. "I had no idea what I was doing," Sue Mingus told Fred Kaplan for the *New York Times* (July 29, 2007), describing the leadup to the first performance of Mingus Dynasty, as the band would be known. The ensemble played to critical acclaim, and under Sue Mingus's direction it soon began touring the country.

The original incarnation of Mingus Dynasty stayed together for about 10 years, and in 1991 Sue Mingus formed a second group devoted to her late husband's work, the 14-piece Mingus Big Band. The group, which features a revolving roster of more than 100 musicians, has held residencies at two New York City clubs and played shows around the world. Sue Mingus later formed the 10-piece Mingus Orchestra, which features instruments not commonly associated with jazz, such as the French horn and the bassoon. Through all her work with the three bands, as well as her 2002 memoir, *Tonight at Noon: A Love Story*, Sue Mingus has sought to keep Charles Mingus's music and legacy alive. During his lifetime the musician had a reputation as a tempestuous, angry man, and perhaps in part for that reason, in the period immediately following his death, he was not held in the same high regard as Duke Ellington, the only jazz composer to have left behind more material. Many have credited Sue Mingus with changing the way that history views Charles Mingus, who is now seen as a major 20th-century composer. "Charles was many things," Sue Mingus told the Merrillville, Indiana, *Post-Tribune* (April 6, 2007). "He was a fighter. He was anti-war, anti-nuclear bombs, anti-racism. He was also peaceful and spiritual. He spent hours composing at a piano. Tenderness doesn't get write-ups. I don't see those things as contradictory. It's all there in the music."

Sue Mingus, whose maiden name is Graham, was born on April 2, 1930. She grew up in Milwaukee, Wisconsin, where she enjoyed a privileged childhood. Her father, an aristocratic Jewish man who had once served in the British royal cavalry, was the inventor of the variable-speed drive, a device that regulated timing in heavy machinery. Her mother, who had been educated at a convent, came from a prominent family that traced its lineage to a signer of the Declaration of Independence. "Our meals were formal occasions," Sue Mingus wrote in *Tonight at Noon*, "at which my brothers wore ties and freshly ironed shirts, a bell summoned the maids, and my father carved at the head of the table." Like her mother, Sue played the piano. While her record collection included works by the jazz singer Billie Holiday, she knew little of the genre, as her family preferred classical music and opera.

Mingus studied at Smith College, in Northampton, Massachusetts, before living in the European capitals Paris and Rome. While abroad she married Alberto Ungaro, an Italian sculptor. By 1964 the two were separated, and Sue Mingus was living in New York City. In July of that year, she met Charles Mingus. At the time she was acting in an underground film (according to some sources, she was also a model), and a friend from the project suggested that she visit the Five Spot nightclub to hear a concert by the jazz saxophonist Ornette Coleman, who had been commissioned to write the film's score. Mingus was performing there the same night, and when Sue first saw the bassist, he was sitting alone at a table, eating a steak. "I'd barely heard of Mingus, though echoes of his reputation had filtered down: the ornery, sometimes violent, often unjust, blustery figure who fired his musicians onstage, hired them back, denounced the audience for inattention, picked fights, mastered his instrument, dominated his music, vented his political beliefs on stage, presented a larger-than-life personality, and created on-the-spot performances for all to see," she wrote in her memoir. "He was the essence of a sixties 'happening.'"

The couple's initial meeting was far from romantic: after dismissing Coleman as a "calypso player," Charles poked fun at Sue's crooked teeth, expressing disbelief that she had won a part in a movie. Despite their radically different backgrounds—Mingus, who had Asian and Native American as well as black ancestors, grew up in the poor Watts section of Los Angeles, California—Sue was drawn to him. The next week she returned to the Five Spot to hear Mingus play, and several weeks later, they happened to meet in Central Park, where both had gone to see a performance of *Othello*. Mingus asked her to dinner but changed his mind on the way, instead taking her to Grand Central Station, where, in a secluded passageway, he told her that he loved her. "I laughed off his words. They were sounds in a station from a man I hardly knew," Sue wrote. "Still, I went on listening." Over the course of the summer, the two met often, even though Mingus was still married to his third wife. That autumn, soon after performing a critically heralded set at the Monterey Jazz Festival, in California, Mingus asked Sue to help him start his own mail-order record label. Within months they had established Charles Mingus Enterprises.

For the first few years of their relationship, Sue and Charles fought often. She sometimes asked him to leave her apartment, after which he would scream to her from the street. After one argument, according to Michael Eck, writing for the Albany, New York, *Times Union* (September 1, 2002), Charles sent her a full-length mirror with a note that read, "Look at yourself for company, you can't get along with anyone else." Sue went to many of his concerts, watching as, on some occasions, he berated the audience and members of his band. "There were times when I wished I could have plunked down my money at the door, heard the extraordinary music, witnessed the prodigious event that was Charles, and drifted onto the street, a free woman," she wrote. "But I was caught in his struggle now, no longer outside, trapped in the middle of his vast appetites and imagination, his sexuality, his angry intelligence, his nonsense and his pain."

While Mingus was busy composing, recording, and touring, Sue edited two underground New York City newspapers, the *New York Free Press* and *Changes*. She also raised two children, a boy and a girl, from her marriage to Ungaro. She and Mingus moved in together in about 1972 and were married in 1975, first in a ceremony performed by the poet Allen Ginsberg and later at City Hall. Two years later Mingus began to lose feeling in his legs and hands, and on the day after Thanksgiving 1977, he was diagnosed with the nerve disorder amyotrophic lateral sclerosis—commonly referred to as Lou Gehrig's disease—and told that he had six months to live. He was soon confined to a wheelchair, and after he and Sue exhausted conventional treatments, they began experimenting with a wide variety of alternative forms of medicine. "Charles was so courageous and so full of grace," Sue told Gene Stout for the *Seattle Post-Intelligencer* (September 20, 2002). "All the sides of Charles the world doesn't know about came to the fore. . . . You have to call for help for everything. But he never cursed the gods, and he had a sense of humor. He kept us all full of vitality."

As a last resort the couple went to Cuernavaca, Mexico. There, Charles Mingus received treatment from a 72-year-old Indian "witch doctor," who, in addition to performing "bloodless surgery," as Aram Saroyan reported for the *Los Angeles Times* (September 15, 2002), administered iguana blood mixed with wine. None of the cures worked, and Mingus died on January 5, 1979. "Mexico offered hope," Sue told Owen McNally for the *Hartford Courant*, as reprinted in the *Korea Herald* (April 26, 2002). "It extended his life." She added, "We thought we could beat the rap. Paralyzed as he was, Charles would take me out and wine and dine me in a disco, of all things. His imagination could always come up with something wonderful and completely unexpected." In accordance with Charles's last wishes, Sue scattered his ashes in the Ganges River, in India, where she performed a Hindu ritual.

Four months after her husband's death, Sue Mingus was asked to put together a two-day tribute at Carnegie Hall, in New York City. "I looked through the albums and chose the players from those two seminal albums he did in the late '50s for Columbia," she told Marcus Crowder for the *Sacramento Bee* (January 29, 2006). "We had seven people in the band—four horns and a rhythm section. . . . Everybody had to have played with Mingus to give it authenticity, except for the bass, of course." The group was dubbed Mingus Dynasty, after the title of one of his albums. The tribute concert was well received, and despite the objections of some hardcore fans, Sue decided to take the band on the road. "The ensemble sounded so authentic and full-spirited that we decided to keep it going as Mingus Dynasty," she told Dan Ouellette for *Down Beat* (April 2002). "We received a lot of flak at first, especially from Europe where Charles was so beloved. To his fans there, having Mingus music without Mingus was unthinkable." Though not a jazz musician or bandleader, Sue took control of the group, instructing the players on such points as how long to play a solo. On an early Mingus Dynasty tour, some of the musicians made fun of her inexperience. "It hurt, but I was an outsider," she told Kaplan. "I'm not a jazz musician, yet here I was telling seasoned jazz musicians things like, 'Please make your solo shorter.' But I soon realized that I did have one power—I paid the checks. And there was the power of Charles's music, which has an openness that forces musicians to free themselves, and they appreciated that."

Mingus Dynasty continued performing throughout the 1980s. In 1989 Sue Mingus hired additional musicians to stage a performance of *Epitaph*, an ambitious symphonic work that Charles Mingus started writing at the age of 17 and worked on thereafter all his life. He tried performing the two-hour piece once, in 1962, but insufficient rehearsal time led to disastrous results, and many have called the failed concert one of the biggest disappointments of his career. Comprising 4,000 measures of music written on 500 sheets of paper, the work was discovered by a musicologist who was archiving Mingus's compositions. The 1989 concert, at Lincoln Center, in New York, was a success, and it "showed me that it was doable and inspired me to double the size of the band and make it 14 pieces," Sue Mingus told the Springfield, Illinois, *State Journal-Register* (April 25, 2002).

In 1991 Sue Mingus formed the 14-piece Mingus Big Band, and that year she landed the group a weekly engagement at the Fez, a venue in the basement of Time Café, in New York City's East Village area. "The press was chortling into their palms. 'Who wants to hear Mingus music four times a month?'" Sue told the *State Journal-Register*. The band soon became a major draw, and its Thursday-night appearances attracted tourists and local jazz aficionados alike. "When someone like Glenn Miller or Artie Shaw dies and a sideman takes over the band, it's called a ghost band because it just isn't the same," the veteran jazz critic Nat Hentoff told Liz Leyden for the Montreal, Quebec, *Gazette* (March 1, 1999). "But with the Mingus Big Band—and I'm not exaggerating—you can feel Mingus. It's

because of Sue. She knows which musicians to choose, she knows who understands the music." Over time Sue built up a roster of more than 100 musicians. Unlike the original Mingus Dynasty, the Mingus Big Band hired people capable of mastering Mingus's notoriously challenging music. Sue supervised the ensemble's tours and recording sessions, choosing musicians for each trip and deciding which songs would be performed. "My interest is simply that the band shows the enormous scope and variety of Charles's composition," she told Bill Beuttler for the *Boston Globe* (February 27, 2004).

In 1993 the Library of Congress bought Mingus's archives, including scores, photos, and personal papers. That purchase marked the first time that the library had acquired a jazz composer's written works (either musical or literary), and it reflected the major shift that had taken place in terms of the way Mingus was viewed. "People did not think of Charles as a composer the way they did Duke Ellington," Sue told Ashante Infantry for the *Toronto Star* (June 24, 2006). "When you have such an original voice and sound, it takes a while for people to grow up to that." In the late 1990s, in response to the high number of unauthorized Mingus bootlegs sold in stores around the world, Sue created Revenge Records. The label issued official editions of live Mingus recordings, which Sue priced lower than the pirated versions.

In 2000 Sue formed a third group, the Mingus Orchestra. The 11-piece ensemble, which focuses on Mingus's symphonic pieces, soon had its own regular New York City engagement, and like the big band, it visits schools and provides workshops for young musicians. It also draws its members from a large pool of players. With all three groups Sue Mingus instructs the musicians to avoid playing pieces exactly as her husband wrote them. "Charles left a lot of freedom and space within the compositions for musicians to bring in their own voices and personalities," she told Infantry.

In 2002 Sue published *Tonight at Noon: A Love Story*, a memoir. She based much of the book (named for one of Charles Mingus's compositions) on journal entries she wrote in Mexico, during the final year of her husband's life. "Sue Mingus survives and perpetuates her husband with a loving, exacting portrait," Saroyan wrote, adding that the book "has the emotional fluency and power of Mingus' own music." *Tonight at Noon* was named a notable book by the *New York Times* and book of the year by the *Los Angeles Times*. An album of the same name, also released in 2002, featured the rock musician Elvis Costello, who wrote lyrics for one track.

In 2005 Sue partnered with Sunnyside Records and Universal Music Jazz France to create Sue Mingus Music, her second record label. That year she released *I Am Three*, a CD featuring songs by all three Mingus groups. (The disc's title comes from the famous first line of Mingus's autobiography, *Beneath the Underdog*.) Over the years Sue has produced a dozen Mingus Big Band recordings and has also published two educational books, *Charles Mingus: More than a Fake Book* and *Charles Mingus: More than a Play Along*. In 2007 Blue Note Records released *Cornell 1964*, a two-CD recording of a concert that Mingus and his sextet gave at Cornell University. Ed Michel, a producer at Fantasy Records, had discovered tapes of the concert nearly two decades earlier, but at the time Sue was too busy organizing the performance of *Epitaph* to consider releasing them. She stored them with a friend, the legendary Atlantic Records executive Nesuhi Ertegun, and after he died, in 1989, the tapes were found in a mislabeled box. They went missing once more before Sue authorized the Blue Note album. Also in 2007 she began to hand over control of the three groups, hiring a booking firm to coordinate tours. "The shame is,

you finally learn everything, then you die," she said to Kaplan. She added, referring to Charles Mingus's legacy, "The important thing is, if I walked away today, all of this would survive."

—K.J.P.

Suggested Reading: *Chicago Tribune* C p13 Oct. 15, 2000; *Down Beat* p20 Apr. 2002; *Los Angeles Times* R p10 Sep. 15, 2002; (Merrillville, Indiana) *Post-Tribune* D p10 Apr. 6, 2007; *New York Times* (on-line) July 29, 2007; *Newsday* D p36 May 19, 2002; *Seattle Post-Intelligencer* p6 Sep. 20, 2002

Selected Books: *Charles Mingus: More than a Fake Book*, 1991; *Charles Mingus: More than a Play Along*, 2000; *Tonight at Noon: A Love Story*, 2002

Michael Buckner/Getty Images

Mitchell, Elvis

1958– Film critic; television and radio host; filmmaker

Address: National Public Radio, 635 Massachusetts Ave., N.W., Washington, DC 20001-3753

In 2005, less than a year after he left the *New York Times*, the film critic Elvis Mitchell accepted a job with Columbia Pictures. Mitchell, a prolific writer whom some have called the nation's leading African-American film critic, was to have overseen new projects for the studio's East Coast branch.

Some saw the move as a natural one, since Mitchell had long cultivated personal relationships with actors and filmmakers. Throughout his four-year stint at the *New York Times*, he had openly pursued outside interests, socializing with stars and lecturing at Harvard University. According to some reports he had also entertained job offers from two other Hollywood studios as well as *Billboard* magazine. "He literally knows everybody," Mark Urman, president of distribution for ThinkFilm, told Phyllis Furman for the New York *Daily News* (February 15, 2005).

As it happened, Mitchell never took the studio job, and within a year he had resumed his duties for the National Public Radio (NPR) program *Weekend Edition*, to which he had contributed film reviews since 1985, with one interruption. Since that time Mitchell has continued to pursue a variety of creative projects: in January 2008 he and the director Timothy Greenfield-Sanders debuted their documentary, *The Black List: Volume One*, at the Sundance Film Festival. That same month they sold the film, which examines the lives of prominent black Americans, to the cable channel Home Box Office (HBO).

Known for his hip, stream-of-consciousness writing style and penchant for using pop-culture references, Mitchell has contributed to such publications as *Rolling Stone*, *Spin*, and the *Village Voice*. "As a critic, he was a lightning rod for his times," Harvey Weinstein, a head of the film studio Miramax, told Carl Swanson for *New York* (May 3, 2004), following Mitchell's departure from the *Times*. "And as a journalist, he was an underappreciated asset." While editors have generally praised Mitchell's work, some have said that he does not respond well to deadlines and is prone to taking on too many projects at once. His wealth of assignments outside the *Times* may have been one reason that, in 2004, the paper's management decided to make his colleague A. O. Scott the *Times*'s chief film critic. Mitchell left soon after Scott's promotion, and while some have speculated that he was fired, he told David Mills for the blog *Undercover Black Man* (March 7, 2007), "I just left because I felt like it was time to go."

Elvis Mitchell was born in Detroit, Michigan, in 1958. One of nine children, he grew up in what he called "a one-street ghetto" in the city's East Side neighborhood, according to Anderson Jones, writing for the *Detroit Free Press* (September 11, 1994). Mitchell's parents had moved north from Mississippi in 1949; his father held two jobs, loading crates for a dairy company by day and working at a laundry at night. "My father bought me freedom; he worked like a convict most of his adult life and never complained about it, barely missing a day," Mitchell wrote for the *New York Times* (September 24, 2000). As a child Mitchell enjoyed reading comic books and watching movies, and he gradually developed an encyclopedic knowledge of popular culture. He was enamored of *Spider-Man* and other Marvel Comics titles, which "were these empowerment fantasies with people who were basically shunned by society," he said to Jones. "What inner-city black child could not relate to those?" He also told Jones, "Undoubtedly the biggest influences on my writing [were the magazine] *Esquire* and Ralph Ellison's novel *Invisible Man*. I learned that being able to mix humor and passion and, hopefully, intelligence are the way to go."

Mitchell attended Wayne State University, in Detroit, on a theater scholarship, but left after two years, finding his classmates "pretentious," as he told Mills. Six months later he returned to the school, where, after briefly studying philosophy, he decided to major in English. During his college years Mitchell got a job as a film critic for a Detroit public-radio station. In 1979 he met the famous *New Yorker* film critic Pauline Kael, and their subsequent friendship, which lasted until her death, in 2001, played a major role in shaping his career. Kael was in Detroit to be interviewed for a radio show, and since Mitchell knew the show's producer, he visited the studio and chatted with Kael before her segment. When the time came for Kael to go on the air, she grabbed his arm, insisting that Mitchell join her in the booth. "She was the first person outside of my family who had any real confidence in me as a writer," he told Mills. After he graduated from Wayne State University, in 1982, Mitchell became the TV critic for the *Oakland Press*, a Pontiac, Michigan, newspaper. Kael advised him to try for a position at the *Detroit Free Press*, recommending him in a letter to that paper's editors. The paper turned Mitchell down. "So I thought: 'If I can't get hired with a letter from the film critic of the *New Yorker*—the most famous film critic in the United States, and arguably in the world—it's time for me to leave,'" he told Mills.

Mitchell moved to Los Angeles, California, and began writing for such publications as the *L.A. Herald*, *Rolling Stone*, and *Spin*. "I was originally writing about television because at that point, when I came out here, everybody was a film critic," he told Mills. "But TV was going through a really exciting period in [the 1980s]." In 1985 Mitchell took a job reviewing films for the newly launched NPR program *Weekend Edition*. Two years later he moved back to his hometown and began a two-year stint as film critic for the *Detroit Free Press*. He later returned to Los Angeles, where he resumed his role as an in-demand freelancer, going years without holding a full-time job. "I want to do what I want to do," he told Jones. "I look at my life as being a series of adventures and as long as I'm in a position where I don't have to support a family I can try stuff out and I'm the only person that gets hurt by it, I might as well give it a shot." "He's definitely got a restless streak to him," the publisher of *Spin*, Bob Guccione Jr., said to Jones. "But then, I think all artists are restless."

In 1988 Lorne Michaels, the producer of the NBC sketch-comedy series *Saturday Night Live*, offered Mitchell a writing position. Mitchell turned him down, citing the show's hierarchical structure and his distaste for office politics. In 1992 the Paramount Pictures executive Brandon Tartikoff hired Mitchell as a production executive. Mitchell was fired six months later, after he refused to stop reviewing films for NPR; according to Jones, he was so upset that after his dismissal he could not "bring himself to watch a movie distributed by the studio." In 1994 Mitchell joined the team of on-air panelists for *Last Call*, a short-lived late-night Detroit TV discussion program. Among his co-hosts, Mitchell was known as smart yet unreliable, even showing up late for the show's pilot installment. "You're hating him when he's not there," Mitchell's co-host Tad Low told Jones. "You're ready to replace him, and then he gets there and there is nobody else." Mitchell was nervous about appearing before a studio audience, but producers were confident that they had hired the right person. "He obviously has a great knowledge of everything involved in the media, he knows a lot of inside stories that nobody else seems to know and he's a great talker and he's a funny guy," the producer Edward Horwitz told Jones. "He's a great conversationalist."

In 1997 Mitchell became the film critic for the *Fort Worth (Texas) Star-Telegram*. In his first year with the paper, he received an award for criticism from the American Association of Sunday and Feature Editors. Two years later, in December 1999, Mitchell was one of three writers tapped to replace the outgoing *New York Times* film critic Janet Maslin. Under the paper's new arrangement, Mitchell shared reviewing duties with Stephen Holden, who had worked under Maslin, and A. O. Scott, who had been a book critic for *Newsday*. As Mitchell began writing for the *New York Times*, some readers complained about his unconventional style and frequent pop-culture references. "Now that Elvis Mitchell is at the *Times*," an unnamed film producer told Jonathan Bing for *Variety* (March 13–19, 2000), "one has to go to the newsstands to get all the hip magazines to know what he's talking about. I'm pretty trendy and I still have to wade through all of his hip club references to find out what he's talking about." Indeed, Mitchell's early *New York Times* pieces featured a wide range of pop-cultural references. In his review of *The Patriot* (June 28, 2000), a film about the American Revolution, for example, he wrote, "We have the willful anachronism of Benjamin and his group hiding out with a group of African-Americans who are so enlightened in dress and lifestyle that the scene might be from an Erykah Badu video."

In his four years with the *New York Times*, Mitchell established himself as "bigger than life," according to Swanson, appearing on TV shows and socializing with movie stars in addition to his reviewing duties. In an unusual move, the paper hired a freelance editor to "focus" Mitchell's copy, as his pieces had a "stream-of-consciousness quality," according to Swanson. Explaining the difficulty he sometimes had with *New York Times* editors, he told Mills, "It was sort of a struggle to try to get stuff in. Not because they didn't like what I was writing, but just because anything that's kind of contemporaneous just got lost, because a lot of editors there just weren't in touch with the ongoing popular culture in the way that I was. Because I feel that movies and television and music all intersect."

Throughout his tenure at the *New York Times*, employment at which marks a career high for many journalists, Mitchell was rumored to be considering other jobs, including the top position at Warner Independent Films. "Elvis has this sort of Candide-like air about him," Jay Stowe, the executive editor of *Outside*, told Swanson. "It's not naïveté, exactly, but an aura of doing what he wants and seeming surprised, in all innocence, when people take offense." In 2004 Mitchell became a visiting lecturer at Harvard University, in Cambridge, Massachusetts, teaching two courses, one of them a seminar called "The African-American Experience in Film: 1930-1970." For the other, a lecture course on film criticism, Mitchell screened such movies as *Kill Bill, Vol. 2* and *The Warriors* and assigned 500-to-800-word reviews.

In April 2004 the *New York Times* named A. O. Scott as its lead film reviewer, effectively ending the collaborative arrangement editors had devised for the two critics. Steven Erlanger, the paper's cultural news editor at the time, was responsible for the decision, and Mitchell responded by resigning from the paper. "I just said I have to leave," Mitchell said in an interview for the on-line column *Richard Prince's Journal-isms* (May 5, 2004). "That wasn't the way I came in." Mitchell added that he would not ask Erlanger to reverse his decision, since "that would have caused as much difficulty." He also said that he was not sure he wanted to continue working in film criticism. "There is a feeling that the Elvis Mitchell thing was mishandled and that the [*Times*'s] Arts and Leisure section is in total disarray," a source told Keith J. Kelly for the

New York Post (May 13, 2004). The celebrated African-American scholar Henry Louis Gates said to Swanson that Mitchell was "certainly the most powerful black film critic in history, full stop. It was a great day for the race when he got that job [at the *Times*], and it would be a shame for him to lose that platform."

In February 2005 reports surfaced that Columbia Pictures had hired Mitchell as an executive production consultant. Deborah Schindler, former president of Red Om Films, the actress Julia Roberts's production company, was given an equal position. Mitchell was to have been charged with mining film festivals for new talent and combing Columbia's extensive library for films that might be remade. It was rumored that Mitchell's ties to Amy Pascal, chairman of the Sony Pictures Entertainment Group, helped him land the job. "Establishing a strong film presence in New York has been a longtime goal of mine, and I can't think of two people who can execute my vision better than Deb and Elvis," Pascal told Liza Foreman for the *Hollywood Reporter* (February 15, 2005, on-line). Foreman reported that in January 2005 Mitchell had already begun his duties at Columbia, attempting to acquire for the studio *Hustle & Flow*, an entry at that year's Sundance Film Festival. (He lost out to Paramount Pictures/MTV Films.) In response to Mitchell's decision to pursue a career in the movie business, NPR opted to part ways with the critic, deeming his continued employment as a conflict of interest.

After a year away from *Weekend Edition*, Mitchell returned in 2006, reviewing *The Pink Panther* on February 4 and discussing in a piece in the next week how films have examined the issue of race over the years. "He never actually took the job with Columbia so there is no conflict of interest," an NPR spokesman, Chad Campbell, told Prince for *Journal-isms* (February 27, 2006). "He never showed up for work," a source told the New York *Daily News* (October 24, 2005), in one of the few press accounts of why the job fell through. "He's told people that he and Columbia never concluded their discussions. But it was a done deal. It was a huge opportunity. No one can figure out why he blew it off." In January 2008, at the Sundance Film Festival, Mitchell and the director Timothy Greenfield-Sanders debuted *The Black List: Volume One*, their film about prominent black Americans, including Kareem Abdul-Jabbar, Sean Combs, Chris Rock, and Colin Powell. That same month they sold the film to HBO. In addition to serving as producer, Mitchell conducted all of the onscreen interviews. In April 2008 the cable channel Turner Classic Movies announced that Mitchell would host his own interview show, *TCM Presents Elvis Mitchell: Under the Influence*, beginning the following July. Mitchell's guests have included such high-profile actors as Laurence Fishburne and Bill Murray. In November 2008 he was slated to interview the show-business figures Edward Norton, Joan Allen, Richard Gere, and John Leguizamo.

In 2007 Mitchell, who is known for his sharp fashion sense and long dreadlocks, played himself on an episode of the HBO series *Entourage*. Since 1996 he has hosted *The Treatment*, a syndicated radio program about popular culture. The show is based in Los Angeles, where Mitchell lives. A member of the National Society of Film Critics, he has also hosted the radio show *Life and Times* and served as a correspondent for the CNN cable TV program *Newsstand: Entertainment Weekly*. In addition, he has appeared on the TV show *Roger Ebert & The Movies*.

—K.J.P.

Suggested Reading: *Daily Variety* p5 Dec. 3, 1999; *Detroit Free Press* G p1 Sep. 11, 1994; *New York* May 3, 2004; *New York Times* VI p62 Sep. 24, 2000; *Variety* p49 Mar. 13, 2000

Selected Radio Programs: *Weekend Edition*, 1985-2005, 2006– ; *The Treatment*, 1996–

Selected Television Shows: *TCM Presents Elvis Mitchell: Under the Influence*, 2008–

Selected Films: *The Black List: Volume One*, 2008

Ramzi Haidar/AFP/Getty Images

Mohammed bin Rashid Al Maktoum

July 22, 1949– Ruler of Dubai

Address: Emirates Towers, P.O. Box 72127, Dubai, UAE

"He looks much as his ancestors might have nearly two centuries ago when they took over this tiny fishing village on the shores of the Persian Gulf. But Sheikh Mohammed bin Rashid Al Maktoum, the ruler of Dubai and the prime minister of the United Arab Emirates [UAE], is a thoroughly modern prince," Afshin Molavi wrote for *Newsweek International* (August 6, 2007). Best known in the West as a major player in the thoroughbred horse-racing world and for his grandiose and perhaps "over-the-top" real-estate mega-developments, the ruler of the emirate of Dubai—"the most famously booming city-state in the Persian Gulf," as Ahmed Kanna put it in *Middle East Report* (Summer 2007)—is one of the region's wealthiest and most influential figures. Sheikh Mohammed, whose persona and family have become synonymous in the minds of many with the thriving city they govern and essentially own, has been described as an enlightened despot, a visionary modernizer, a competitive workaholic, "ultramodern, apolitical and open for business," a "CEO Sheikh," and, according to Scott MacLeod, writing for *Time* (April 30, 2006), "a very ambitious chap." His "bold vision of transforming Dubai . . . ," MacLeod wrote, "and raising [gross domestic product] from $8 billion to $37 billion in 15 years is urban planning on a cosmic scale." While he rose from crown prince to ruler of the emirate only in 2006, after the death of his older brother, Sheikh Maktoum bin Rashid Al Maktoum, Mohammed has been the de facto ruler for more than a decade. Power in Dubai passed to Sheikh Mohammed from his late father, Sheikh Rashid, who, helped by the discovery of oil in the area five decades ago, "transformed Dubai from a collection of rag tag buildings surrounding a port to the economic hub of the Gulf region," as Stuart Millar and Jamie Wilson noted for the London *Guardian* (December 10, 2001).

While money from the sale of oil has played a crucial role in the story of Dubai and has fueled many of Sheikh Mohammed's most ambitious projects, he has successfully diversified his emirate's economy beyond its dwindling oil supplies, courting foreign investors to develop new business sectors that include tourism, trade, construction, information technology, and finance. Under Sheikh Mohammed's guidance, Dubai has been transformed into one of the world's fastest-growing cities, with an economy expanding at a rate of about 16 percent a year. (The sheikh himself is one of the world's richest people.) Sheikh Mohammed has his share of critics, who charge him with, among other things, doing business with anybody—regardless of reputation or intent—who has money; taking advantage of the instability in the region; and exploiting cheap labor. Nevertheless, as Julia Wheeler put it for the BBC (January 5, 2006, on-line), "Internationally, Sheikh Mohammed is perceived as someone with whom the West can do business." For his part, Sheikh Mohammed has said, according to Graeme Wilson, the author of the biography on the Dubai leader's official Web site: "I do not know if I am a good leader, but I am a leader. And I have a vision. I look to the future, 20, 30 years. I learned that from my father, Sheikh Rashid. He was the true father of Dubai. I follow his example. He would rise early and go alone to watch what was happening on each of his projects. I do the same. I watch. I read faces. I take decisions and I move fast. Full throttle."

Mohammed bin Rashid Al Maktoum is the third son of Sheikh Rashid bin Saeed Al Maktoum. (In Arabic, "bin" means "son of.") He was born on July 22, 1949 in what was then the independent Persian Gulf sheikhdom of Dubai and is now one of the seven emirates that make up the United Arab Emirates. In about 1830 the Al Maktoum family took over Dubai, then a small, backwater fishing and pearling settlement located fortuitously on the shipping routes of the Persian Gulf. Before they were known as the United Arab Emirates, the collection of neighboring Gulf provinces were called the Trucial States or Trucial Sheikhdoms, in reference to an 1892 agreement with the British, who wanted to protect their interests in the region and their sea route to India; the sheikhs agreed, in return for British protection, not to enter into relationships with other states or empires without British consent. That arrangement allowed the Al Maktoums to focus on business, establishing Dubai as a tax-free port to attract traders, shippers, and merchants. Oil was discovered in the Gulf provinces in the late 1950s and 1960s, just after the death of Sheikh Mohammed's grandfather. By the end of the latter decade, Britain, its international influence diminished, was forced to end its arrangement with the seven Trucial Sheikhdoms. On February 18, 1968 Mohammed's father, Sheikh Rashid, and Abu Dhabi's ruler, Sheikh Zayed, met to discuss the formation of a federation. The Union Accord, formalized in December 1971, included six emirates: Abu Dhabi, Dubai, Sharjah, Al Fujairah (also spelled Fujayrah), Ajman, and Umm al-Qaywayn; Ras al-Khaymah joined the following year. The agreement created a Supreme Council made up of the rulers of all seven emirates, with the presidency going to the hereditary ruler of the Al Nahyan clan of Abu Dhabi, which possessed by far the largest oil reserves, and the post of vice president and prime minister going to the hereditary ruler of the Al Maktoum family of Dubai. Sheikh Zayed bin Sultan al Nahyan of Abu Dhabi, the new ruler of the UAE, nationalized oil, which, along with a massive influx of foreign investment in the 1970s, led to the exponential growth of Dubai's economy and population as foreign workers, mostly from the Indian subcontinent (India, Pakistan, Bangladesh, Sri Lanka, and Nepal) and the Middle East, flocked to the booming port city. Dubai grew from just under 60,000 people in 1968 to nearly 185,000 in 1975, roughly doubling each decade thereafter; its population today is estimated at 1.5 million.

Sheikh Mohammed's early years were spent in the Al Maktoum home in Shindagha, Dubai, surrounded by his family, which was headed by his grandfather Sheikh Saeed, the ruler of Dubai. An "athletic and energetic child," according to Graeme Wilson, Sheikh Mohammed enjoyed hunting and falconry, a traditional Arabian sport. His father also taught him how to ride horses, and the young prince was reportedly an avid equestrian from an early age. In 1955, after a couple of years of private tutoring in Arabic and Islamic studies, he was sent to the Al Ahmedia Primary School in Dubai. After roughly two years there, he was sent to Al Shaab School, where he spent another two years before moving on to Dubai Secondary School. He received a different sort of education at home, sitting beside his grandfather during the latter's informal daily *majlis*, or public meetings. On September 9, 1958 his grandfather died, and Mohammed's father, Sheikh Rashid, became Dubai's ruler. By all accounts, Sheikh Mohammed was a sharp student with "an almost photographic memory," according to Wilson, and his father began grooming him to take over the armed forces and police someday. In the meantime, he wanted his son to have a British education, and in August 1966 Sheikh Mohammed enrolled at the prestigious Bell School of Languages in Cambridge, England. There, the young man took an interest in poetry, rowing, hunting, and horses. He completed a six-month training course at Mons Officer Cadet School, in Aldershot, England, graduating with the Sword of Honor award for "achieving the highest mark of any Foreign and Commonwealth officer cadet" in his year, as Wilson wrote.

On November 1, 1968, when Sheikh Mohammed was 19 years of age, his father named him head of Dubai Police and Public Security. Three years later Sheikh Rashid and the rulers of the neighboring emirates signed a constitution, creating the UAE. In December 1971 Sheikh Maktoum, Sheikh Rashid's eldest son, who was both crown prince of Dubai and prime minister of the UAE, appointed his younger brother Sheikh Mohammed as minister of defense, with the rank of general, making the 22-year-old the youngest minister of defense in the world at the time. Almost immediately Sheikh Mohammed had to respond to the destabilizing effects of the Arab-Israeli war, an attempted coup in the neighboring emirate of Sharjah, and a hijacking at Dubai International Airport, among others incidents. In the 1970s his father, who was rapidly strengthening the economy of Dubai, began delegating major tasks to his third son, putting him in charge of Dubai's oil—a crucial element of the tiny emirate's fortunes—as well as the Dubai Dry Docks, which would become the largest facility of its kind in the region and a major global shipyard, bridging Europe and the Far East and positioning Dubai as a leading transport hub. On August 25,

1977 Sheikh Mohammed was put in charge of operations at Dubai International Airport.

In May 1981 Sheikh Rashid fell seriously ill. Three of his sons stepped into the huge void created by their father's extended convalescence: Sheikh Maktoum, Sheikh Hamdan, and Sheikh Mohammed. While they worked together successfully, Mohammed was seen as wielding greater power than his older brothers. Sheikh Rashid died on October 7, 1990, with Sheikh Maktoum taking over as ruler of Dubai; on January 4, 1995 he named Sheikh Mohammed crown prince of the emirate. On January 4, 2006, upon Maktoum's death, Sheikh Mohammed became ruler of Dubai. The following day, as a formality, he was elected vice president of the UAE.

Today, Dubai, which in many ways was modeled on the city-states of Singapore and Hong Kong, is often referred to—derisively by some, admiringly by others—as the Las Vegas of the Persian Gulf; Steve Kroft of the CBS television news magazine *60 Minutes* (February 3, 2008, on-line) called it "the setting for a modern day gold rush" and "the playground and business capital of a new Middle East." While the emirate's oil resources made for an unprecedented economic boom under the hands-on guidance of Sheikh Mohammed, it can be argued that his foresight, opportunism, and business-friendly policies have been a continuation of his forefathers' approach.

One of Sheikh Mohammed's most important achievements has been to make Dubai's wealth largely independent of oil, which now accounts for only between 5 and 10 percent of its gross domestic product. He has done so by taking advantage of Dubai's location—it is roughly equidistant from Singapore and London, England—to attract both workers and foreign investors from various nations, including Iran and India. The regional conflicts that have plagued Dubai's neighbors in the last several decades, including the civil war in Lebanon, the Islamic revolution in Iran, the Iran-Iraq and Gulf wars, and the Soviet invasion of Afghanistan, have also played into its rulers' hands, providing them with both highly skilled and unskilled labor fleeing their war-torn and economically ravaged homelands and turning the city-state into one of the region's few stable, modern, and pragmatic business partners of Western countries and companies. But the fact that Dubai is seen as a land of opportunity for citizens of the Middle East and the Indian subcontinental countries, as well as Western expatriates, arguably owes as much to the Al Maktoums' creation of an attractive, capitalism-friendly environment as it does to the lack of opportunities elsewhere. Dubai "provides investors with a comfortable, Western-style, property-rights regime, including freehold ownership, that is unique in the region," Mike Davis, an activist and the author of books including *Planet of Slums*, wrote in his scathing critique of the city-state's modus operandi for the *Socialist Review* (July 14, 2005, on-line). "Included with the package is a broad tolerance of booze, recreational drugs, halter tops, and other foreign vices formally proscribed by Islamic law. (When [expatriates] extol Dubai's unique 'openness,' it is this freedom to carouse—not to organize unions or publish critical opinions—that they are usually praising.)" Famous for its high, tax-free salaries, Dubai is seen as a place to make money quickly. "In a region where everything is political, Dubai's greatest distinction—and the secret of its prosperity—is that it is almost utterly apolitical. Here, globalization's triumph has been almost complete," Afshin Molavi wrote. "Economically, it is inspiring imitators throughout the Arab world. Everyone, it seems, is setting up free-trade zones, cutting taxes, creating industrial 'cluster cities' and undertaking gargantuan feats of real estate and infrastructure in an attempt to lure tourists, trade and investment along the lines of the 'Dubai model.'" What some might call opportunism, others have called a wildly successful, pragmatic survival mechanism for a small state surrounded by bigger, wealthier states. "I am often asked, 'What are Dubai's political ambitions?'" Sheikh Mohammed wrote in an op-ed piece for the *Wall Street Journal* (January 12, 2008). "Well, here's my answer: We don't have political ambitions. We don't want to be a superpower or any other kind of political power. The whole region is over-politicized as it is." Dubai's tiny local population, and the fact that Sheikh Mohammed is not a head of state but rather the ruler of a province, mean that "much of the regional politics is left to the capital, Abu Dhabi—[making] it a more manageable place than more populous and troubled Arab countries. Dubai is not particularly threatened either from without or within," as Roula Khalaf wrote for the *Financial Times* (May 4, 2007). As with many states that derive their income from lucrative nationalized resources, Dubai does not tax its citizens or foreign workers and therefore is not accountable to them as a democratic government would be; there has not been, in fact, any real push for democracy from the international community, businesses, or the local population. "In Dubai, there is no real opposition to the ruling Maktoum family. That's partly because 'locals' make up only one eighth of the population," Molavi wrote, going on to argue that "it would be wrong to call Dubai undemocratic. . . . It is more ademocratic, says the journalist Othman al-Omeir, the well-known publisher of the online liberal Arab newspaper Elaph.com. 'Sheik Mohammed has shown us that efficient management of the state, a lightly regulated private sector and social freedoms might be more important at this moment in Arab history than free elections.'" In response to the global financial crisis of 2008, for instance, Sheikh Mohammed encouraged investor confidence by injecting 10s of billions of dollars into the national banking sector with a speed not possible in a democracy.

Sheikh Mohammed works closely with Mohammed al-Gergawi, Sultan bin Sulayem, and Mohammed Alabbar, who, as Dubai's most important businessmen, run both the private and state-owned companies that the sheikh created in order to "take the lead on development projects," according to Roula Khalaf. The first developments, initiated by his father but then quickly passed on to Mohammed while still in their infancy, were the dredging of the Dubai creek to build the Jebel Ali port and industrial area, which became a tax- and tariff-free zone, and the creation of Dubai International Airport. Sheikh Mohammed is personally credited with the success of the airport and its showcase, the first of many of his pet projects, the state-owned Emirates Airlines. The first commercial Emirates flight took off on October 25, 1985. The airport and airline have cemented Dubai's reputation as one of the world's busiest cargo and tourism hubs. "People think we're just building Dubai," Sheikh Mohammed said, according to Khalaf. "But no, we're accommodating 1.5 billion people in the central world, here, between the east and west."

Since Sheikh Mohammed took the reins of Dubai's business development—and particularly in the last decade and a half—its economy has soared. Dubai presents itself as a "one-stop shop" for business opportunities and financial services, sports and entertainment, shopping, travel and tourism, information technology, construction and real estate. In 1995, shortly after being named crown prince, he announced the inauguration of the Dubai Shopping Festival, a month devoted to a commercial bonanza, which attracts hordes of customers. In addition, since then, he has brought several high-profile annual sporting events to the city, including a Professional Golf Association tournament, the Dubai Desert Classic; an Association of Tennis Professionals tournament; and the Dubai World Cup, the world's most lucrative horse race. Attracted by the shopping, entertainment, beaches, resorts, and, most recently, such landmarks as ostentatious hotels and other structures, tourists are flocking to "Sheikh Mo's" emirate. According to 2004 figures, roughly five million tourists were visiting the city every year, and that number is growing. Although the massive and flamboyant structures that have been constructed recently are seen by some observers as white elephants, many argue that they were not built to make a profit, at least not directly. Referring to the so-called seven-star Burj Al Arab hotel, the construction magnate Khalaf Al Habtoor told Matthew Swibel for *Forbes* (March 15, 2004) that even though it operates at a loss, the hotel functions as an advertisement for Dubai: "People don't visit Paris without seeing the Eiffel Tower, do they?"

The words "endless ambition" often appear in articles about the sheikh, which note that he seemingly wants everything in Dubai to be the largest of its kind in the world; not surprisingly, he is regularly accused of arrogance and of having an obsession with trophy-like status symbols. "There's a little bit of Donald Trump in him, at least when it comes to showmanship," Kroft said. (Sheikh Mohammed asked Kroft rhetorically, "If you can have it in New York, why can't . . . we have it here?") Not content to limit his investments to the Persian Gulf, the sheikh has developed businesses internationally, many under the portfolio of one of his private companies, Dubai International Capital. He owns the Tussauds Group, the Travelodge hotel chain, and the Doncasters Group, an engineering company, and he has a stake in the automobile giant Daimler-Chrysler, among many other investments. (A multibillionaire, the sheikh is one of the richest people in the world, although it is difficult to distinguish between state and family assets, making it also hard to attach an accurate figure to his net worth.)

Some have charged that Dubai's economic boom has been built on what is akin to slave labor. Human-rights organizations have declared that hundreds of thousands of overworked, mostly Asian and subcontinental laborers there are forced to accept extremely low wages (often less than a dollar an hour) and live in subhuman conditions in what amount to secret camps, eyesores well hidden from the public spotlight. According to those reports, as part of their business-friendly approach, the Maktoums have removed state protection of contract workers and allowed companies to exploit them. The UAE's system of "in-sourcing" labor keeps the unemployment rate at zero but calls for sending workers home when their jobs are done or if they "create trouble," which includes organizing unions. The workers often face dangerous conditions or go for months at a time without being paid.

March 2006 saw rioting among the more than 2,000 construction workers who were building what was to become Dubai's showpiece—the Burj Dubai, which, when completed, will be the world's tallest building. Because of media censorship, particularly in the area of labor issues, accurate figures regarding the number of strikes and riots in the past few years are difficult to obtain, but according to some observers, they have become increasingly common. In a November 2006 report for Human Rights Watch entitled "Building Towers, Cheating Workers," Hadi Ghaemi and Sarah Leah Whitson presented detailed evidence of widespread exploitation in Dubai. The same year, Sheikh Mohammed and his subordinates began a program of labor reform. So far, the reforms have not satisfied human- and labor-rights groups or, as several recent investigative reports have revealed, the workers themselves. Sheikh Mohammed and others have argued that the conditions are not unique to Dubai and merely reflect market forces and the workings of capitalism. One justification that has been offered for the labor conditions is that the workers come to the emirate voluntarily and receive far better wages than they would in their home countries; critics counter that in taking that position, the sheikh has abdicated his responsibility to regulate the private sector. Some fear that Dubai, with its many disgruntled workers, and with its liberal Las Vegas–style night life (which includes the availability of alcohol and rampant prostitution), is a breeding ground and potential target for terrorism. Such fears came to light when, in 2005, Sheikh Mohammed's company bought Britain's P&O, a massive ports and ferries group, which once ran six important ports in the U.S.; in response, many American lawmakers vowed to refuse to allow any Arab company to control U.S. ports. Despite Dubai's having endangered itself as a staunch ally of the United States, backing the 1991 U.S.-led war on Iraq (though not the 2003 invasion) and allowing its ports to be used by U.S. Navy warships in the Gulf, Sheikh Mohammed was denounced by many in the media as a terrorist-backing dictator. "Sheik Mo's kingdom has at least 300,000 Iranians, a near equal number of expatriate Palestinian Arab mercenaries and many British expats in decision-making positions," read an op-ed piece that ran in the *Pittsburgh Tribune Review* (April 8, 2007). "Sheik Mo shipped nuclear equipment from Pakistan to Iran, North Korea and Libya; he recognized the Taliban in Afghanistan; and, according to the FBI, he allowed their banking system to be used by Osama bin Laden prior to the 9/11 attacks." The allegations of Sheikh Mohammed's dealings with nuclear arms and terrorists were never confirmed, and there has never been any proof of links between the Dubai ruler and bin Laden's terrorist network, Al Qaeda. Nonetheless, Sheikh Mohammed sold his U.S. assets in order to avoid confrontations that might have hurt his businesses.

In 2004 Sheikh Mohammed and his brother Sheikh Hamdan were alleged to have enslaved young boys from Africa, South Asia, and the Indian subcontinent for use as camel jockeys. A class-action lawsuit, filed in the U.S., claimed that tens of thousands of boys were victims of "one of the greatest humanitarian crimes of the last 50 years." Camel racing, both a traditional sport and (for owners) a status symbol, is very popular in the emirate. According to the suit, as quoted by Andrew Gumbel in the London *Independent* (September 15, 2006), "Because [the sport] is extremely dangerous and arduous, especially for children, the Arab sheikhs would not make their own children jockeys and trainers. The sheikhs instead bought boys who had been abducted and trafficked across international boundaries and enslaved as young as two years old." Investigative reporters and antislavery groups described a situation in which children were abused, undernourished, and given hormones in order to keep them small enough to ride the camels. Although the case was dismissed because of lack of evidence (it was refiled in 2007), in 2005 the UAE banned the use of child jockeys, repatriating thousands of children and making plans to replace them with lightweight robots. But some observers have claimed that the use of child jockeys, acquired through human trafficking rings, persists.

Despite that controversy, Sheikh Mohammed is recognized internationally as a major philanthropist. He gave a reported £1 million pounds to Bob Geldof's Live Aid benefit-concert fund in the 1980s and has donated undisclosed sums to help the people of Bosnia and Afghanistan, among other war-torn regions. In May 2007, at the World Economic Forum in Jordan, he announced plans to set up a $10 billion educational fund in the Middle East, one of the largest charitable donations in history. As quoted by Mark MacKinnon in the Toronto *Globe and Mail* (May 21, 2007), he said, "There is a wide knowledge gap between us and the developed world in the West and in Asia. Our only choice is to bridge this gap as quickly as possible, because our age is defined by knowledge." In his *Wall Street Journal* piece, the Sheikh expanded on that idea, writing, "Education and entrepreneurship are the twin underpinnings for building a safer world. With these two institutions, we'll have fewer angry young people, fewer frustrated youths ready to embrace radicalism because they have nowhere else to turn." Some saw the donation as at least partly a pragmatic business move; Eckart Woertz, the head of the economics program at the Dubai-based Gulf Research Centre, told Mark MacKinnon: "It's philanthropy, yes, but it's also important for Dubai. If Dubai wants to keep its growth rate, it needs an influx of knowledge."

Known as one of the most influential figures—and one of the biggest spenders—in the world of thoroughbred horse racing, Sheikh Mohammed has done much to revolutionize and internationalize the sport. He owns one of the world's top breeding and racing stables, the Godolphin stud farm in Dubai, along with several stud farms in England, Ireland, and the United States, and his annual Dubai World Cup boasts the largest horse-racing purse on the planet. Graeme Wilson quoted him as stating that he has always felt a kinship with horses: "A love for horses runs in my blood. Don't forget that horses have been bred for centuries by Arabic tribes, they were used for hunting and fighting and they symbolise our history. Horse riding is more than merely sitting on a horse's back. It is nobility and chivalry." Sheikh Mohammed is not only a prize-winning horse owner but a champion in endurance races ("the equestrian equivalent of a marathon," according to Wilson). His sons Sheikhs Rashid, Hamdan, Ahmed, and Majid, have carried on the family tradition with the UAE national team, regularly topping world and Asian rankings and winning several championships. In recognition of his charitable contributions to the sport, in October 2008 Sheikh Mohammed was named "racing's single greatest benefactor" during the prestigious Pride of Racing Awards ceremony.

Sheikh Mohammed is also known as a Nabati poet. Nabati verse is a literary form native to the Arabian peninsula and the Gulf and, according to Wilson, "represents a distinct literary voice for the people of that region." Influenced by the classical poets Al Mutanabi, Al Buhtori, and Abu Tammam, he began writing verse in school. Later, he published poems under a pseudonym to be sure that any praise he won would not be due to his status. "Nowadays," Wilson wrote, "he is widely acknowledged as one of the finest exponents of Nabati verse and his work is published under his own name." The symbols that run through his poetry are the desert and the wildlife of the region, including gazelles and lanner falcons.

On February 1, 2008 Sheikh Mohammed named his second son, Sheikh Hamdan bin Mohammed, to succeed him as Dubai's crown prince. The same day, Sheikh Mohammed named his third son, Maktoum, who oversees Dubai's information-technology and media sectors, as deputy ruler of Dubai, ensuring that the system of rule by the Maktoum brothers would continue. Sheikh Moham-

med lives in Dubai, where he maintains his executive office in Emirates Towers. He has 17 children and two wives. He married his senior wife, Sheikha Hind bint Maktoum bin Juma Al Maktoum, in 1979 and his second wife, Princess Haya bint Al-Hussein, who is a daughter of the late King Hussein of Jordan, in 2004. His memoir is scheduled to be published in 2008.

—M.M.

Suggested Reading: *60 Minutes* (on-line) Oct. 14, 2007; *Financial Times* p11 May 4, 2007; *Forbes* p92 Mar. 15, 2007; *Middle East Report* Issue 243, Summer 2007; *Newsweek International* (on-line) Aug. 6, 2007; *New Statesman* p135 Sep. 4, 2006; sheikhmohammed.co.ae; (Toronto) *Globe and Mail* B p4 Apr. 22, 2006

Evan Agostini/Getty Images

Monheit, Jane

Nov. 3, 1977– Jazz singer

Address: c/o William Morris Agency, 1325 Ave. of the Americas, New York, NY 10019

When Jane Monheit released her debut album, *Never Never Land*, in 2000, she became the most talked-about new artist in jazz, inspiring comparisons to her idol, the legendary Ella Fitzgerald, as well as her contemporary Diana Krall. "At age 22, jazz vocalist Jane Monheit is so good at what she does already, she's a little scary . . . ," Misha Berson wrote for the *Seattle Times* (September 28, 2000). "Simply the best young jazz singer to

emerge in a few years, [she] is a talent to watch in the future—and savor in the present." As *Never Never Land* and Monheit's sophomore effort, *Come Dream with Me* (2001), became best-sellers and drew praise from many critics, others complained that her popularity owed as much to her being an attractive young white woman as to her talent, or that the sales of her albums—which featured many jazz standards—merely reflected the public's nostalgia. Most, however, have attributed the singer's success to the quality of her voice. In an assessment of Monheit's 2007 album, *Surrender*, which topped the *Billboard* jazz chart, a reviewer wrote for the All Music Guide Web site, "At once crisply assertive and lovingly sensual, vocalist Jane Monheit is the jazz equivalent of the young and charming grade school teacher you secretly nurtured a crush on." The writer went on to call Monheit "a sophisticated bombshell of a performer with a voice that is, like her appearance, voluptuous and flawlessly pretty."

Jane Monheit was born on November 3, 1977 to David and Marjorie Monheit and grew up in Oakdale, on Long Island, New York. Music played an important role in her family: her aunt and grandmother were both professional singers; her younger brother, David, plays guitar; her father, the owner of a tool-supply business, plays bluegrass banjo music; and her mother performed in musical theater. "There was never a time when I wasn't listening to music constantly, because it is such a big part of my family life," she told Lori Blackman in an interview for CNN (December 29, 2000, online). "I spent so much time at my grandparents' house and there was never a time when there wasn't a jazz album playing there." As it happened, Monheit—who decided at an early age that she wanted to sing jazz—attended school in a district that offered a jazz program from elementary through high school. She studied clarinet and music theory as well as voice. John Leddy, who taught Monheit music during those years, recalled to Robbie Woliver for the *New York Times* (June 18, 2000), "Even at 9 she would talk about Ella Fitzgerald. She's the only kid I know who could carry on a conversation like that." By the time she had enrolled at Connetquot High School, Monheit had become such an accomplished vocalist that Leddy allowed her to lead the jazz choir. As she explained to Robbie Woliver, "There wasn't that much more for me to learn, so they let me teach, they let me write and they let me arrange." Interested in musical theater as well, Monheit played the lead in every one of her high school's theatrical productions. Outside school she performed standards and love songs at clubs and weddings on the South Shore of Long Island.

At the age of 17, Monheit moved to New York City to study at the Manhattan School of Music, where she received vocal training. "When I first got to college," she told Dan Ouellette for *Down Beat* (December 2004), "I was a teenage girl in a boys' club. They thought, she's just a singer, what could she know about music? It was a constant battle where every time I opened my mouth to sing I felt I had to spew out my knowledge all at once. I wasn't into melody but vocal gymnastics. It was like, 'Look at how I know the chord changes. I'm as [good] as you are.'" Peter Eldridge, a teacher at the school and a founding member of the jazz vocal group New York Voices, helped her to progress beyond that stage by encouraging her to focus on songs' lyrics. "My whole world changed," Monheit recalled to Ouellette. "My big breakthrough came with Ivan Lins' 'Love Dance,' which I still sing all the time. Originally, I had so much trouble getting to the root of the song, but then Peter told me to look at the words. He said, 'You've had boyfriends and you know this story. You've been there before. You're not a little kid.' And I thought, I can admit that to myself. I can understand womanly feelings. I'm finally settling into that now—when I improvise during the body of a tune I try to make my melodic choices reflect the lyric." Monheit graduated in 1999. Meanwhile, she had begun singing at piano bars in the Greenwich Village section of Manhattan.

In 1998 Eldridge encouraged Monheit to enter the vocal competition sponsored by the Thelonious Monk Institute, a nonprofit educational organization. After failing to make the initial cut, she received an invitation to try again once more funding became available for the competition. The then–20-year-old placed second, losing only to the 60-year-old jazz veteran Teri Thornton and becoming the youngest runner-up in the competition's history. In the audience on the night of the finals were Mary Ann Topper of the Jazz Tree Artists Agency and Carl Griffin of the record label N-Coded Music. Topper, who had managed the Grammy Award–winning jazz vocalist Diana Krall early in Krall's career, became Monheit's agent, and Griffin signed the singer to her first record deal.

Two years later Monheit released her debut album, *Never Never Land*. Featuring her renditions of such classic ballads as "Please Be Kind," "Never Let Me Go," and "I Got It Bad," the album became the number-two-selling jazz album in the country within four and a half months; it spent 68 weeks on the jazz charts and was voted best recording debut by the Jazz Journalists Association. In a review for *Down Beat* (September 8, 2000), Fred Bouchard wrote, "Monheit offers a nicely understated debut that bodes well for an ingenue. Her voice is airy, sweet and soft, a little nasal at the high end; yet she can set it on edge, and she's learned good diction and phrasing." *Never Never Land* made Monheit the year's most talked-about new jazz vocalist and brought her a number of high-profile engagements, at venues including Carnegie Hall, Lincoln Center, Birdland, and the Village Vanguard (all in New York City) and the Hollywood Bowl, in Los Angeles, California.

Monheit's sophomore effort, *Come Dream with Me* (2001), was comprised mostly of standards, with an emphasis again on ballads. Upon its release the record became the number-one jazz album on the *Billboard* chart and garnered warm reviews. "Monheit's softened soprano sounds so natural, so personable that it's as if she were spilling her secrets over a couple of beers at a neighborhood tavern," Geoffrey Hines opined for the *Washington Post* (May 4, 2001). Ted Panken wrote in a review for *Down Beat* (September 1, 2001), "Clear, precise, agile, polished and tasteful, Monheit's intent, first and foremost, is to express as directly as possible the meaning of the lyric." He went on to explain why he had given the album only three stars out of a possible five. Monheit's earlier epiphany about lyrics notwithstanding, Panken complained about "the disjunction between the torchy material and the resolute optimism of Monheit's persona. After repeated listenings, I still don't believe that spring is hanging her up the most or that she's through with love or that she's longing to find something to live for. . . . Perhaps it's unrealistic to expect a 23-year-old to be capable of imparting more than Monheit does to the arena she works in. Her voice is a beautiful instrument . . . and if she stays with jazz, it will be interesting to hear the paths along which she develops."

Monheit's third album, *In the Sun*, was released in 2002. Rather than performing only standards, the singer expanded her repertoire to include bossa nova–influenced tunes by the Brazilian pianist and composer Ivan Lins. Critics hailed the album as Monheit's best work up to that time. "Jane Monheit lights a fire with her voice," Steven Winn gushed for the *San Francisco Chronicle* (October 6, 2002). "It's not all flaming passion, but a guttering low warmth that works its way deeply inside a song. . . . Monheit brings her distinctive, penetrating style to each cut and almost always makes it feel like a natural fit." The album's song "Since You've Asked" was nominated for a Grammy Award in the category of best instrumental arrangement accompanying vocals.

Some jazz enthusiasts suggested that the singer's success was attributable to her being young, white, and good-looking or to other factors not connected with her music. In an article for the *New York Times Magazine* (December 31, 2000), the respected critic David Hajdu singled out Monheit as being representative of what was wrong with contemporary jazz. "Monheit, who has emerged as a young siren in the tradition of a swing-era chanteuse, seems to embody mainstream jazz's wholesale submission to nostalgia," he wrote. "Absorbed with the glories of its past and tentative about its future, jazz has grown content to revel in the conservative pleasures of ennobling sentiment. The musical environment that has made Jane Monheit a phenomenon is a jazz world George W. Bush would understand." Among those who disagreed with Hajdu's assessment of Monheit's appeal was Stephen Holden, a music and film critic for the *New York Times*, who told Andrew Marton for the *Fort Worth (Texas) Star-Telegram* (February 3, 2002), "That strikingly beautiful voice is really more beautiful than the other good voices around. Not only does Monheit have good taste as a singer, but she doesn't feel the need to do a lot of flamboyant decorating to show off her range."

As for Monheit herself, she tried to ignore the criticism as much as possible and dismissed accusations that she was too inexperienced to understand and sing jazz. She said to Fred Bruning for *Newsday* (August 2, 2001), "You can sing a love song that is full of high drama when you are 15 years old and your junior high boyfriend broke up with you. And you feel those things and you believe those things because that is the oldest you've ever been. And that is your life experience and you do have something to talk about. I believe that. I believe that we all have our story to tell and it's always valid at any age." Later, in an interview for the Rochester, New York, *City Newspaper* (January 26, 2005, on-line), Monheit said, "I think the misconception about jazz is that in order for life experience to have value when applied to your music, it has to be bad life experience. What . . . is up with that? . . . Why can't this music be about joyfulness and happiness and love? Has everybody missed the point about Ella Fitzgerald? This woman sang from the most beautiful, glorious, happy place."

Monheit's first album on the Sony label, *Taking a Chance on Love* (2004), comprised her versions of a dozen songs from the Metro-Goldwyn-Mayer (MGM) songbook, including the title track; "In the Still of the Night"; "Embraceable You"; and "Dancing in the Dark," which was nominated for a Grammy Award in the category of best instrumental arrangement accompanying vocals. In contrast to past criticism that her singing did not match the themes of her material, Dan Ouellette wrote, "Monheit's in-concert delivery has in the past been marred by a lack of emotion, with theatrics trumping soul. But this is changing." On *Taking a Chance on Love*, Ouellette added, "her vocals are impeccable: pitch-perfect, full-ranged with a touch of huskiness, a spice of sass and a savoir faire for singing simultaneously from earth and sky. She covers Cole Porter and Jerome Kern–Oscar Hammerstein with lovely, charming renditions. It's as if, just like the Hollywood films she's mined for material, Monheit sings fantasy—comely, easy on the ears, smartly produced. It doesn't always emerge from a deep well of soul, but when she digs in, the songs feel truly lived in."

In 2005 Monheit released a holiday-themed recording, *The Season*, which marked her first credit as co-producer (with Al Schmitt). Her 2007 album, *Surrender*, like several of her previous albums, combines jazz standards with pop and bossa nova songs. "What is different," according to the reviewer for the All Music Guide Web site, "is the focus and presentation of Monheit. Rather than featuring her here simply as a singer fronting a jazz band, *Surrender* is a cinematic showcase, a Broadway-sized coming-out party that finds Monheit's voice framed against sweeping orchestration and glossy, Technicolor arrangements. This is Monheit the vocal diva, the superstar." Monheit's latest album, *Lovers, Dreamers, and Me*, recorded on the Universal Japan label, arrived in stores in 2008.

Writing for the *Hartford (Connecticut) Courant* (May 2, 2003), Jeff Rivers reported that Monheit "says she was a bit of an 'ugly duckling' through her high school years, which left her unprepared for how critics and fans have responded to her sensuous face, cascading dark hair and zaftig figure stretched out over her 5-foot, 8-inch frame." In 2002 Monheit married Rick Montalbano, whom she met at the Manhattan School of Music. Montalbano is the drummer in his wife's regular touring band, which also includes the guitarist Miles Okazaki, the tenor saxophonist Ari Ambrose, and the bassist Neil Miner. Monheit maintains a very close relationship with her parents. She and Montalbano live in New York City.

—H.T.

Suggested Reading: *Down Beat* p40 Dec. 2004; *Fort Worth (Texas) Star-Telegram* Arts p3+ Feb. 3, 2002; *Hartford (Connecticut) Courant* D p3+ June 2, 2000; *Los Angeles Times* Calender p3+ May 20, 2001; *New York Times* Long Island Weekly p7+ June 18, 2000; *New York Times Magazine* p32+ Dec. 31, 2000; *Newsday* B p7+ Aug. 2, 2001; (Rochester, New York) *City Newspaper* (on-line) Jan. 26, 2005

Selected Recordings: *Never Never Land*, 2000; *Come Dream with Me*, 2001; *In the Sun*, 2002; *Taking a Chance on Love*, 2004; *The Season*, 2005; *Surrender*, 2007; *Lovers, Dreamers, and Me*, 2008

Alex Wong/Getty Images

Mukasey, Michael B.

July 28, 1941– U.S. attorney general

Address: U.S. Dept. of Justice, 950 Pennsylvania Ave., N.W., Washington, DC 20530-0001

In September 2007, when President George W. Bush nominated him for the post of U.S. attorney general, Michael Mukasey was widely described as a highly capable, nonpolarizing figure likely to receive support from Democrats and Republicans alike. With only 16 months remaining for the Bush administration, with Congress in the control of Democrats, and with Americans increasingly expressing disapproval of the administration's handling of the war in Iraq, the president "didn't need another fight," as Tom Raum wrote for the Associated Press (September 18, 2007). "So he picked a consensus candidate for attorney general who had strong credentials in the war on terror and the support of one of the Senate's most liberal members"— Charles E. Schumer of New York, who had recommended Mukasey for a position on the U.S. Supreme Court in 2003. During his Senate confirmation hearings, however, Mukasey angered a number of senators and many other observers by refusing to label as torture the interrogation method known as waterboarding, which simulates drowning. According to the Geneva Conventions and U.S. law, torture is illegal, but Mukasey argued that even though he found waterboarding "repugnant," he could not comment on its legality, since he had not been briefed on what the technique entails. Many Democrats condemned Mukasey's stance, and on November 8, 2007 the Senate approved his appointment by a vote of 53 to 40—the smallest

number of "yes" votes for an attorney general in more than 50 years. Mukasey's appointment came at a difficult time for the U.S. Justice Department. Alberto Gonzales, Mukasey's predecessor, had stepped down in August 2007, after charges from a growing number of Republicans as well as Democrats that he had overseen the politically motivated firing of nine U.S. attorneys and given false testimony regarding the government's warrantless surveillance programs. The scandals surrounding Gonzales demoralized many of the Justice Department's 110,000 employees and "cast doubt on the government's ability to prosecute cases fairly," as Lara Jakes Jordan wrote for the *Times of Trenton* (November 10, 2007). Mukasey's decision in early January 2008 to investigate another potential scandal, which came to the attention of the public after Gonzales's departure—the destruction of CIA videotapes that purportedly showed suspected terrorists being subjected to waterboarding—heartened those who had feared that Mukasey condoned the controversial interrogation technique. However, some of Mukasey's more recent actions, during the last weeks of the Bush administration, such as his approval of revised FBI guidelines that ease the standards required to investigate a person for involvement in terrorist activities, have sparked a new round of criticisms from Democrats, civil-liberties groups, and other observers.

The son of Orthodox Jewish parents, Michael Bernard Mukasey was born on July 28, 1941 in the New York City borough of the Bronx. His only sibling, a sister, was 12 years older. His father ran a coin-laundry business, and the family was poor. As a child Mukasey attended a small Jewish school in the South Bronx before being accepted into the prestigious Ramaz School, on Manhattan's Upper East Side, in second grade. The Ramaz School is connected to Kehilat Jeshurun, a Modern Orthodox synagogue with a "politically conservative congregation," as Amy Goldstein and Dafna Linzer described it for the *Washington Post* (September 18, 2007). Mukasey has remained involved in the Kehilat Jeshurun community; his wife was a teacher at and later the principal of Ramaz's lower school.

After he graduated from the Ramaz School, in 1959, Mukasey enrolled at Columbia College, in New York City, where he considered a career in journalism and spent a summer reporting for United Press International. (During other summers in his college years, he worked for a lumber company and beer distributor.) He earned an A.B. degree in 1963 and then entered the Yale University Law School, in New Haven, Connecticut. His fellow students there included Joseph I. Lieberman and Paul Tsongas, future U.S. senators from Connecticut and Massachusetts, respectively. He received a law degree in 1967.

In the same year Mukasey went to work as an associate for the now-defunct New York City law firm of Webster, Sheffield, Fleischmann, Hitchcock, and Brookfield. He left the practice in August 1972 to become an assistant at the U.S. Attorney's

Office for the Southern District of New York. During his stint as an assistant U.S. attorney, Mukasey befriended Rudolph Giuliani, a fellow lawyer who would later become the mayor of New York City and a 2008 candidate for president. (After Giuliani began to campaign for the presidential nomination, Mukasey signed on as a judicial adviser to him.) Mukasey presided over both of Giuliani's mayoral inauguration ceremonies, the first of which was postponed a day, so as not to conflict with the Jewish Sabbath. "He loved being an assistant U.S. attorney," a colleague said of Mukasey, speaking with Susan Schmidt and Dafna Linzer for the *Washington Post* (October 11, 2007). "I think that's what defined him."

In 1975 Mukasey was named chief of the Corruption Unit at the U.S. Attorney's Office. A year later he moved to the private sector, becoming an associate with the New York City law firm Patterson, Belknap, Webb, and Tyler. He stayed with the practice until 1987, when President Ronald Reagan tapped him to become a federal judge. He officially took the bench at the U.S. District Court for the Southern District of New York in 1988 and remained there until 2006, when he returned to Patterson, Belknap, Webb, and Tyler as a partner. During his 18 years as a federal judge, Mukasey earned a reputation for being tough but fair. "Do not mistake [his] courtesy for weakness," Patrick Burke, a lawyer who often argued cases before Mukasey, told Timothy O'Connor for the Westchester County, New York, *Journal News* (September 18, 2007). "Those who do, do so at their peril." "He's not an ideologue for the sake of being an ideologue," his former clerk Andrew Ruffino told Goldstein and Linzer, saying that Mukasey never let his politics or religion cloud his judgment.

In 1996 Mukasey presided over one of his most high-profile cases: the trial of Omar Abdel-Rahman, widely known as the blind sheikh. Along with 11 conspirators, Abdel-Rahman was charged with plotting a number of terrorist attacks in New York City, including the 1993 World Trade Center bombing. William M. Kunstler, the lawyer representing one of the defendants, argued that Mukasey should recuse himself from the trial, since he was an Orthodox Jew and a Zionist and the accused were Muslim. After consulting with his rabbi, Haskel Lookstein, Mukasey refused to do so. Mukasey went on to earn praise for his efforts to preserve fairness during the proceedings. He allowed Earl Gant, one of the defendants, to leave prison, since the likelihood of his leaving the U.S. was negligible and he was not a danger to the community. Mukasey even let Gant—who eventually pleaded guilty to a lesser charge—make a religious pilgrimage to Mecca. "He overlooked the fear of the moment and did what you would hope someone would do—take an objective view of who this man was," Andrew Patel, Gant's lawyer, told Emma Schwartz for *U.S. News & World Report* (October 1, 2007). The judge received death threats throughout the trial, and he and his wife remained under the protection of U.S. marshals for years afterward. Despite the high-pressure nature of the case, Mukasey kept order. Early in the trial, as he was questioning jurors, a fire alarm sounded in the courthouse, leading some to believe that the building was under attack. "Mukasey never flinched," Gail Appleson wrote for the *Seattle Times* (October 14, 2007). "In an authoritative voice, he told those in the room to be calm and stay in their seats; it probably was a false alarm. No one budged. Mukasey was right: a child had pulled the alarm."

The Abdel-Rahman case presented Mukasey with many challenges, as he had to consider the defendants' rights to free speech and religious expression. He also had to figure out ways to conduct the trial without making confidential information public. "The arguments we've been having the last six years are the arguments we were having then," the prosecutor Andrew C. McCarthy told Schmidt and Linzer, explaining that the case dealt with many of the complicated issues that would become commonplace following the terrorist attacks of September 11, 2001. Years later Mukasey wrote that the trial "unintentionally provided terrorists with a rich source of intelligence," adding that the proceedings were what alerted Osama bin Laden to the fact that U.S. officials knew of his involvement in the terrorist plots.

In October 2005, following a nine-month trial, a federal jury convicted Abdel-Rahman; three months later he was sentenced to life in prison without parole. The Second U.S. Circuit Court of Appeals upheld the verdict and praised Mukasey for his work on the case. "Mukasey presided with extraordinary skill and patience, assuring fairness to the prosecution and to each defendant, and helpfulness to the jury," President Bush said, quoting the appellate court's opinion, when he announced Mukasey's nomination, according to the *Weekly Compilation of Presidential Documents* (September 24, 2007). "His was an outstanding achievement in the face of challenges far beyond those normally endured by a trial judge." Not everyone was as pleased with Mukasey's handling of the case. Ronald Kuby, who represented several of the defendants, accused the judge of stifling his clients' civil liberties. "It was like facing a second prosecutor, one cloaked in a black robe," Kuby told Donna Leinwand and Kevin Johnson for *USA Today* (September 17, 2007). "It seemed that Judge Mukasey woke up every morning trying to figure out ways to use his formidable intelligence to distort the law in favor of the government."

Mukasey again tackled national-security issues in the aftermath of the September 11, 2001 terror attacks. Even though his courthouse was located mere blocks from the World Trade Center—which had been destroyed when terrorists flew hijacked jetliners into the twin towers—the judge worked quickly to reopen it and keep trials in progress. That became especially important in the weeks following the attacks, as the government sought "material witness" warrants, which gave permission to detain anyone suspected of having knowledge of terrorist plots or being possible flight risks. Material-witness hearings, closed to reporters, were conducted on the top floor of the courthouse. (Mukasey met with members of the press in his office and explained that secrecy was vital.) Colleagues have said that Mukasey signed more warrants than anyone else. "He was chief judge at the time, and I think through a sense of duty more than anything else, he signed more warrants than his colleagues because he had done terrorism cases, he lived in Manhattan, and he already had the benefit of a security detail," a former colleague told Schmidt and Linzer. "Nothing scared him."

Some defense lawyers charged Mukasey with skirting the law, since he forbade them from speaking about their cases in public and sealed all court transcripts. "The government was pushing the seals"—that is, producing a large quantity of paperwork—"and he was agreeing with the government's position every time," one lawyer told Schmidt and Linzer. "It's no secret that he is a pro-government judge." Randall B. Hamud, a lawyer representing the California college student Osama Awadallah, claimed that Mukasey had turned a blind eye to police mistreatment of terror suspects. "He wouldn't let me show him my client's injuries, which he got in detention," Hamud said. "Suspects were shoddily treated. They were in chains and quivering because they were so afraid of the guards, and Mukasey said nothing." "If my experience was atypical because he was in a bad mood, then that's one thing," Hamud added. "But if not, then you have to ask serious questions about his ability to be attorney general of the United States." Other lawyers, among them Alexander E. Eisemann, insisted that Mukasey did not tolerate the abuse of detainees. Eisemann's client, Hussein al-Attas—who was eventually convicted of conspiracy—was denied clothing and forced to endure extreme temperatures until Mukasey intervened. "Anytime Mukasey can go the government's way, he'll do it," Eisemann told Schmidt and Linzer. "But he is a very good judge and would make a perfectly good attorney general."

By the spring of 2002, Bush administration lawyers were considering Mukasey for promotion to the U.S. Court of Appeals for the Second Circuit. Then, in June, he drew the case of Jose Padilla, a U.S. citizen accused of plotting to detonate a "dirty bomb." Bush had sought to declare Padilla an "enemy combatant," and the suspect's lawyers had challenged the action. "White House lawyers decided they could not offer Mukasey the appellate post without seeming to undermine his impartiality in a case important to the administration," Schmidt and Linzer wrote. Later that year Mukasey ruled on the Padilla case, upholding the government's power to declare U.S. citizens "enemy combatants" but insisting that the accused must have the right to consult with lawyers and formally challenge the designation. In presiding over the case, Mukasey came to believe that traditional courts are "strained and mismatched" when it comes to dealing with terrorism cases. He subsequently said that he favored the creation of special national-security courts, which would allow judges to hear cases in secret. "If there is anybody who has a handle on the debate on terrorism issues, it's him," David N. Kelley, a U.S. attorney from 2003 to 2005, told Schmidt and Linzer. "He is one of the only people who has sufficient practical experience together with the intellectual ability."

Mukasey retired from the bench in 2006. He then returned to Patterson, Belknap, Webb, and Tyler. In September 2007 President Bush nominated Mukasey for attorney general. The announcement came nearly a month after Alberto Gonzales—facing criticism over the U.S. attorney firings and his congressional testimony regarding government surveillance—stepped down. "Judge Mukasey is clear-eyed about the threat our Nation faces," Bush said as he announced the nomination, according to the *Weekly Compilation of Presidential Documents*. "As a judge and a private lawyer, he's written on matters of constitutional law and national security. He knows what it takes to fight this war effectively, and he knows how to do it in a manner that is consistent with our laws and our Constitution. And when confirmed by the Senate as Attorney General, he will work to ensure that our law enforcement and intelligence officers have the tools they need to protect the United States and our citizens."

Many saw Mukasey as the latest in a line of uncontroversial appointments that Bush, dogged by low approval ratings and growing public opposition to the war in Iraq, was forced to make during his second term in office, "often to replace highly partisan and divisive officeholders," as Raum wrote. "In his first term, there were three criteria. Loyalty, loyalty and loyalty," Stephen Wayne, a political scientist at Georgetown University, told Raum. "The fourth, which occasionally came in, was competence. At this point, I think he wants people who will basically support his administration and have decent credentials." William Kristol, the editor of the conservative newspaper *Weekly Standard*, called Mukasey "one of the country's top trial judges," adding, "He can't be caricatured as a partisan apologist, and the Democrats won't be able to lay a glove on him."

While Mukasey was labeled a conservative, some observers pointed to the Padilla ruling, which partially rejected some of Bush's policies, as proof that the judge was an independent thinker who was not constrained by party politics. "He's much more middle-of-the-road to me," Ambrose Wotorson, a lawyer who tried cases before Mukasey, told O'Connor. "Maybe he's what you might call a New York conservative." Some right-wing politicians criticized Mukasey for being too liberal, citing the Padilla decision and the case of Jia-Ging Dong, who had sought asylum in the U.S. after officials in China, his home country, ordered his wife to have an abortion. Mukasey denied asylum, angering opponents of abortion.

Mukasey sidestepped controversy in his first day of confirmation hearings, held on October 17, 2007, telling the Senate Judiciary Committee that he did not support the torture of suspected terrorists. Specifically, he condemned the so-called Bybee memo, a 2002 Justice Department document that supports the use of torture. Torture, he told the senators, is "antithetical to everything this country stands for." He also said that the country has an obligation to establish legal opinions that prohibit torture, so that Central Intelligence Agency interrogators can be sure their methods are legal. "We can't expect them to put their careers and their freedoms on the line if they don't have confidence that the authorizations given to them are sound," Mukasey said. He was also critical of the Bush administration, telling Senator Schumer that he had recently read and enjoyed *The Terror Presidency*, by Jack L. Goldsmith, which accuses the president of "unilateralism," or pursuing policies without input from Congress. "I would certainly suggest that we go to Congress whenever we can," Mukasey said. "It always strengthens the hand of the president to do that." Distancing himself from the Gonzales scandal, Mukasey said that he would not let party affiliations influence personnel decisions at the Justice Department. "Hiring is going to be based solely on competence, ability, and dedication and not based on whether somebody has an 'R' or a 'D' next to his name," he said. Asked to comment on the government's controversial warrantless eavesdropping program, Mukasey asserted, "I'm not familiar with that program," according to Philip Shenon, writing for the *New York Times* (October 18, 2007). "For me to make a categorical statement with regard to that program one way or the other, I think, would be enormously irresponsible."

The confirmation hearings turned contentious on their second day, when Mukasey refused to take a definitive stand against waterboarding, an interrogation technique in which water is poured onto the cloth-covered face of a prisoner who is strapped to a board higher at the foot than at the head, producing the sensation of drowning. When asked about waterboarding Mukasey said that he could not say whether the practice amounted to torture. He did, however, say that if waterboarding is torture, it is unconstitutional. "That is a massive hedge," Senator Sheldon Whitehouse, a Democrat from Rhode Island, said, according to James Rowley and Robert Schmidt in the *New York Sun* (October 19, 2007). "I am very disappointed in that answer; I think it is purely semantic." Mukasey also drew flak from Democrats for defending the president's spying program, by pointing out that Congress had authorized the president to use force against the Al Qaeda terrorist network after the events of September 11, 2001.

On October 23, 2007 a group of 10 senators, including Schumer and Whitehouse, sent Mukasey a letter asking him to clarify his position on waterboarding. In his response the judge said that even though he believed that waterboarding was "repug-

nant" and "over the line," according to Russell Berman in the *New York Sun* (October 31, 2007), he could not say with certainty whether it constituted torture. Democratic members of the Senate Judiciary Committee announced soon afterward that they would vote against Mukasey's confirmation, and Senators Hillary Clinton and Barack Obama, both Democratic presidential hopefuls, followed suit. In response President Bush took the unusual step of inviting reporters into the Oval Office, where he complained, "Judge Mukasey is not being treated fairly," according to Scott Shane and David Stout in the *New York Times* (November 1, 2007). Referring to waterboarding, Bush said, "It doesn't make any sense to tell the enemy whether we use those techniques or not," adding, "And the techniques we use by highly trained professionals are within the law. That's what's important for America to know."

Observers speculated that Mukasey's reluctance to label waterboarding as torture resulted from his wanting to protect government officials—including Bush—from future repercussions. "Fear of opening the door to criminal or civil liability for torture or abuse, whether in an American court or in courts overseas, appeared to loom large in Mr. Mukasey's calculations as he parried questions from the committee this week," Shane and Stout wrote. "Some legal experts suggested that liability could go all the way to President Bush if he explicitly authorized waterboarding."

On November 6, 2007 the Senate Judiciary Committee approved Mukasey by a vote of 11–8. All nine Republicans on the panel and two Democrats, Dianne Feinstein of California and Schumer, voted to confirm him. "I am voting today to support Michael B. Mukasey for attorney general for one critical reason: the Department of Justice—once the crown jewel among our government institutions—is a shambles and is in desperate need of a strong leader, committed to depoliticizing the agency's operations," Schumer wrote in an op-ed piece for the *New York Times* (November 6, 2007). On November 8, 2007 only 53 members of the full Senate (46 Republicans, six Democrats, and one Independent) voted to approve Mukasey's appointment—a smaller total than that for any attorney general in 50 years, but enough to make him the third attorney general of the Bush presidency.

During Mukasey's first week on the job, the Justice Department reopened its investigation into the involvement of staff attorneys in the endorsement of the president's anti-terror surveillance program, which includes the federal government's tapping, without warrants, of international phone calls between U.S. citizens and foreign terror suspects. The Office of Professional Responsibility had launched the probe in 2006, but Gonzales had blocked the investigation, claiming that the White House had not granted the necessary security clearances. "It seems like an extraordinary beginning," New York congressman Maurice Hinchey told a *Wall Street Journal* (November 14, 2007) reporter. "We may have an attorney general who understands his obligations and responsibilities are to the people of the United States and not the president." Days later, in what many saw as an attempt to start ridding the Justice Department of partisan politics, Mukasey reassigned U.S. Attorney Rachel K. Paulose, a controversial Minnesota lawyer whom colleagues regarded as "ideologically over-the-top and autocratic," according to Richard B. Schmitt, writing for the *Los Angeles Times* (November 20, 2007).

In January 2008 Mukasey launched an investigation into the destruction of CIA videotapes that had allegedly documented the waterboarding of two suspected Al Qaeda members. The tapes were reportedly made in 2002 and destroyed three years later. CIA officials claimed that they lawfully disposed of the tapes in order to protect the identities of the interrogators. Mukasey tapped John Durham, a first assistant U.S. attorney from Connecticut, to lead the probe, which is being conducted by FBI agents. As news of the tapes surfaced, members of the 9/11 Commission—the government panel charged with investigating the events leading up to the September 11, 2001 terrorist attacks—accused the CIA of having obstructed their efforts.

In June 2008, at an annual conference of Washington federal judges, Mukasey declared that the military tribunals established by the Military Commissions Act of 2006 to examine the cases of the so-called enemy combatants held at Guantánamo Bay were "in the best traditions of the American legal system." Later that month the Supreme Court ruled, 5–4, that detainees, such as those being held at Guantánamo Bay, have a constitutional right to challenge their detention in federal court and that the tribunals established by Congress were not reasonable substitutes for such hearings. In July 2008, as the first war-crimes trials began in civilian courts, Mukasey urged Congress to write new rules, in conformance with the Supreme Court's decision, known as *Boumediene v. Bush*, that would guide terrorism suspects who wanted to contest their imprisonment. He also spoke out in opposition to the court's decision. "The United States has every right to capture and detain enemy combatants in this conflict and need not simply release them to return to the battlefield, as indeed some have after their release from Guantánamo," Mukasey said, as quoted by the *International Herald Tribune* (July 22, 2008). In a speech that he made earlier that month to Congress, Mukasey encouraged lawmakers to approve a proposal from the Bush administration that affirmed that the United States was in a continued state of war with Al Qaeda. (Such a designation is significant because it would provide the legal framework for Bush or his successor to claim congressional approval for various tools of warfare.) "As Sept. 11, 2001, recedes into the past, there are some people who have come to think of it as a kind of singular event and of there being nothing else out there," Mukasey said, as quoted by the *New York Times*

(August 30, 2008). "In a way, we are victims of our own success, our own success being that another attack has been prevented."

By July 2008 many who had previously supported the selection of Mukasey had grown critical of what they saw as his reluctance to challenge the policies of the Bush administration or to investigate the wrongdoings committed under Gonzales. "[Mukasey is] certainly head and shoulders above his predecessor," Senator Patrick Leahy, a Democrat from Vermont, told Eric Lichtblau for the *International Herald Tribune* (July 25, 2008). Leahy went on to say that Mukasey was "letting the worst excesses of the Gonzales era stand, and that disappoints me." In August 2008 Mukasey heartened some of his critics when, in remarks delivered before the American Bar Association, he acknowledged the contents of two Justice Department watchdog reports that had been released earlier that summer, which found that under Gonzales high-ranking officials in the Justice Department had failed to stop illegal hiring practices and had favored conservatives over liberals. "There's no denying it: the system failed," Mukasey said in his speech, as quoted by Marisa Taylor in the *Miami (Florida) Herald* (August 13, 2008). While he refused to take drastic measures, such as prosecuting the attorneys named in the reports or firing those who had been hired under the unfair system, Mukasey said that he had put a stop to the unlawful practices and that he intended to contact the applicants who had been rejected for political reasons and encourage them to reapply for jobs within the department.

In October 2008 Mukasey irked a number of Democrats, as well as some Republicans, when he approved a set of new standards established by the Justice Department to govern the conditions under which agents can interview witnesses and use informants, undercover surveillance, and other investigative techniques. The rules generally made it easier for the FBI to investigate activities indicating the possibility of terrorism. Mukasey, along with Robert S. Mueller, the director of the FBI, said that the new standards "provide the FBI with the authority and flexibility it needs to protect the nation from terrorist threats." One of the most controversial aspects of the new guidelines was a section that allows FBI agents to investigate a person based on his or her general patterns of behavior or the agents' mere suspicions of terrorist activity, without any specific evidence of wrongdoing. The new guidelines were opposed by civil-liberties groups concerned with the possibility of abuse and were seen by many as "one of the final steps by the Bush administration to extend its far-reaching counterterrorism policies into the next administration and beyond," as Eric Lichtblau put it in an article for the *New York Times* (October 4, 2008).

Given his longstanding friendship with Rudolph Giuliani, Mukasey has said that he will recuse himself from all judicial matters in which Giuliani may figure, including the ongoing criminal investigation of Bernard Kerik, a friend of Giuliani's who served as New York City's police commissioner. Mukasey's son, Marc, is a lawyer with Bracewell and Giuliani, the former mayor's firm. Marc Mukasey represented Giuliani in 2006, when Bronx prosecutors wanted him to testify in the Kerik investigation.

Michael Mukasey has been married to the former Susan Bernstock since 1974. In addition to their son, the couple have a daughter, Jessica Mukasey Barkoff, and two grandchildren.

—K.J.P.

Suggested Reading: *CQ Weekly* p2763 Sep. 24 2007; *New York Times* A p1+ Sep. 18, 2007; *Seattle Times* A p8 Oct. 14, 2007; *USA Today* (on-line) Sep. 17, 2007; *U.S. News & World Report* p29 Oct. 1, 2007; *Washington Post* A p1 Sep. 18, 2007, A p1 Oct. 11, 2007; (Westchester County, New York) *Journal News* A p1 Sep. 18, 2007

Mark Wilson/Getty Images

Mullen, Mike

Oct. 4, 1946– Chairman of the Joint Chiefs of Staff

Address: U.S. Dept. of Defense, Pentagon, Rm. 2E676, Washington, DC 20318-0400

Shortly before he became chairman of the Joint Chiefs of Staff, the most senior post in the United States military, in October 2007, Mike Mullen, then chief of naval operations, was asked by a Pentagon official what concerned him most about the state of the country's armed services. Mullen, who has been affiliated with the U.S. Navy since 1964, responded, "The Army," according to Pauline Jelinek, in the *Washington Post* (June 13, 2007, online). Many have praised Mullen—who worried that the army's soldiers were shouldering a disproportionate share of the burden in Iraq and Afghanistan—for taking a big-picture view of the military and not simply focusing on his own branch of service. Defense Secretary Robert Gates, who recommended Mullen for the Joint Chiefs chairmanship, praised the naval officer's ability to "look to the future in terms of where we need to be 5 years from now or 10 years from now," according to David S. Cloud in the *New York Times* (June 9, 2007).

Labeled a "pragmatist" by many observers, Mullen replaced Marine Corps general Peter Pace, whom Gates declined to nominate for a second term in office for fear of triggering a contentious confirmation process in the Democratic-controlled Congress. Mullen was seen by many as a "break from the past," as Thomas Donnelly of the American Enterprise Institute told Jelinek, because he had not been directly involved with the decision to go to war with Iraq in 2003. Upon taking office Mullen stressed the need for political and economic progress in Iraq, where U.S. forces were struggling to quell sectarian violence. "Those security forces can only do this for so long without the other two legs of that three-legged stool—security, politics and economics—kicking in," he told Tim Carpenter for the *Topeka (Kansas) Capital-Journal* (October 25, 2007). He also said it was important to look beyond current conflicts and prepare for threats from other adversaries. "We reset, reconstitute and revitalize our armed forces, especially our ground forces, and we properly balance our risks around the globe," he said, according to Nancy A. Youssef, writing for the Knight Ridder Washington Bureau (October 1, 2007). "So fighting in Iraq and Afghanistan will one day end; we must be ready for who and what comes after. That's the promise we've made."

The oldest of five children, four of them boys, Michael Glenn Mullen was born into a Catholic family on October 4, 1946 in Los Angeles, California. (Most sources, including his official Joint Chiefs of Staff biographical profile, identify him with the first name Mike.) Only one of Mullen's relatives, an uncle, spent any time in the military. During World War II his mother, the former Jane Glenn, had moved from Sioux City, Iowa, to Hollywood, where his father, Jack, a Chicago native, had settled. Both were "drawn by the glitz of the burgeoning movie business," as Peter Spiegel wrote for the *Los Angeles Times* (July 30, 2007). Only his father enjoyed any measure of acting success, appearing in a few live theater roles. Mullen's parents met while doing publicity work for Republic Pictures, the company that represented the popular singing cowboys Roy Rogers and Gene Autry.

After World War II Jack Mullen's publicity career blossomed, and he became one of Hollywood's most respected press agents. (His wife was both a homemaker and a secretary for the comedian Jimmy Durante.) Jack's work meant that the family sometimes got a taste of Hollywood glamour; once, Mike and his siblings spent Christmas with the screen siren Ann-Margret. Despite his high-profile job, Jack did his best to maintain a normal home life. The family attended Mass every Sunday and took regular trips to Newport Beach. "Pop was very, very clear about not mixing family with business, and he rarely conducted his business at the house," Mullen's brother Kevin told Spiegel. Mullen attended Notre Dame High School, in Sherman Oaks, where he established himself as a star basketball player. He was named most valuable player in a league that also included Rick Adelman, who went on to become a National Basketball Association player and coach. "The rigorous academics, the sense of teamwork on the basketball court and the support of great friends and skilled teachers all gave me the confidence I needed to succeed in the Navy," Mullen said of his high school, according to Eric Leach, reporting for the *Daily News of Los Angeles* (December 6, 2005).

Mullen's friends and family members thought he would play college basketball in California, and they were surprised when he announced plans to study at the U.S. Naval Academy, in Annapolis, Maryland. Some have speculated that he chose Annapolis because he was infatuated with East Coast basketball and wanted to pay for his own education. No one thought Mullen would remain with the navy beyond his four years of college and required five years of service. Mullen was not an outstanding student in the Naval Academy's class of 1968—a group that included Jim Webb, now a U.S. senator from Virginia; Marine Commandant Michael Hagee; and Oliver North, a controversial player in the Iran-Contra Affair during the administration of President Ronald Reagan. "I bet if you asked Mike did he ever think he'd be chief of naval operations, he'd just start laughing," the retired rear admiral William W. Cobb Jr., a classmate of Mullen's, told Spiegel. "We were taking things one step at a time."

After his graduation Mullen was deployed to Vietnam, where he served as a navigator and antisubmarine warfare officer aboard the USS *Collett* and weapons officer and operations officer aboard the USS *Blandy*. (Both ships were destroyers.) "During that tour, Admiral Mullen was part of operations so intense that the gun barrels on his ship glowed red," President George W. Bush said at a tribute to General Pace, according to the *Weekly Compilation of Presidential Documents* (October 8, 2007). "That was the beginning of a distinguished career."

In 1973 Mullen became commander of his own ship, the *Noxubee*, a gasoline tanker. The promotion was unusual for someone, like Mullen, whose rank was only lieutenant. He nearly squandered the opportunity by piloting the ship into a buoy in the Hampton Roads harbor, in southeastern Virginia. "Scraping a buoy is considered not a good thing," a navy officer told Spiegel. Mullen has said it took "five years of stellar reviews to dig out of the hole," according to the officer. "The lesson that taught him was perseverance." While Mullen was struggling with the *Noxubee* assignment, his father died. Jack had quit smoking and taken up tennis, and friends and family were stunned when he suffered a fatal heart attack. Mullen has credited his father with teaching him to "be responsible and to seek responsibility," according to Spiegel, as well as to "be trustworthy and be someone who can trust others."

In 1975 Mullen returned to Annapolis, where he became company officer and executive assistant to the commandant of midshipmen at the Naval Academy. Three years later he became chief engineer on the USS *Fox*, and he later served as executive officer aboard the USS *Sterett*. (Both the *Fox* and the *Sterett* were guided-missile cruisers.) In 1983 Mullen enrolled at the U.S. Naval Post Graduate School, in Monterey, California, and two years later he earned an M.S. degree in operations research. In the same year he became commander of the USS *Goldsborough*, a guided-missile destroyer. He commanded the ship until 1987. That year he was honored as top commanding officer, the U.S. Navy's most prestigious award. From 1989 to 1991 Mullen served as an assistant to the director of the Operational Test and Evaluation Directorate of the Office of the Secretary of Defense, and in 1991 he completed the advanced management program at Harvard University. From 1992 to 1994 Mullen was commander of the USS *Yorktown*, another guided-missile cruiser, and then he spent two years as a director at the Bureau of Naval Personnel.

From 1996 to 1998 Mullen was the commander of the navy's Cruiser Destroyer Group Two. For the next two years, he served as the director of surface warfare in the Office of the Chief of Naval Operations. In 2000 he became commander of both the U.S. Second Fleet and NATO (North Atlantic Treaty Organization) Striking Fleet Atlantic. The following year Mullen returned to the Office of the Chief of Naval Operations, becoming deputy chief of naval operations for resources, requirements, and assessments. Mullen was working in the Pentagon on September 11, 2001 when American Airlines Flight 77—one of four jetliners hijacked by Islamic extremists that day—crashed into the building. As smoke filled his office, Mullen made his way to the parking lot and walked roughly six miles to the nearby navy yard. He has said that the quiet following the attack reminded him of *On the Beach*, a 1950s movie about nuclear war.

In January 2003 Mullen announced that the navy intended to cut more than 50 programs from its 2004 budget and use the money to modernize its equipment. "We need to take it all," Mullen told Jason Sherman for *Defense News* (January 20, 2003).

"Since we do not expect the top line to rise sufficiently to cover the shortfall in modernization accounts, we must find modernization money from within the Navy." Later that year Mullen became vice chief of naval operations, and in 2004 he took over as commander of U.S. Naval Forces in Europe and the NATO Joint Force Command. During that time he was based in Naples, Italy, and was responsible for missions in the Mediterranean, the Balkans, and Iraq.

Mullen has said that his stint in Naples helped him understand the ways in which the world was changing. "Fledgling new countries in the Balkans [are] taking democracy on the wing," he told Jim Garamone for the American Forces Press Service (April 19, 2005). "West African nations [are] learning new ways to cooperate with each other. Old and new NATO allies [are] helping train Iraqi security forces. The face of the future is being drawn in colors and shapes and sizes we wouldn't have dreamed of just a few short years ago. But the one constant, and what made the biggest impact on me, has been the need to create a safe and secure environment that allows democracy to flourish and in so doing, creates opportunities for millions of families to live better, safer, freer lives." In response to the threat posed by Islamic extremists, Mullen decided that the military needed to break away from outdated Cold War strategies and work more closely with the FBI and the CIA. He also came to view the Pentagon as being too focused on competition among the military's branches and on budget battles. "They forget it's one team and one fight," Mullen once told a Washington official, according to Tom Bowman, reporting for the National Public Radio program All Things Considered (June 14, 2007).

In March 2005 President Bush nominated Mullen to become the chief of naval operations, one of the Joint Chiefs of Staff. (The other positions are the marine corps commandant, air force chief of staff, and army chief of staff.) After he officially became the 28th chief of naval operations, on July 22, 2005, Mullen wasted no time in getting to work. On his second day in office, he sent a memo urging sailors to "renew their vows to defend the country and to do so with all deliberate speed," according to Andrew Scutro for Defense News (August 1, 2005). Mullen then fired Vice Admiral Joe Sestak, who had earned three stars under the outgoing chief, Vern Clark. Some sources described Sestak as arrogant and verbally abusive; the widely quoted official reason for the firing was that he had allowed a "poor command climate" to prevail.

Mullen's key strategy points, he explained, would be maintaining readiness, building the fleet in preparation for future conflicts, and continuing the process of transforming the navy's personnel system. Another of his objectives was to create a "thousand-ship navy," or broad coalition of navies and coast guards from various countries, according to Mike Barber in the Seattle Post-Intelligencer (August 3, 2006). They would cooperate, Barber wrote, "to address everything from humanitarian concerns and piracy to preventing terrorists from getting their hands on mass-killing weapons." Mullen also said it was important to provide high-quality treatment for servicemen returning home with post-traumatic stress disorder. "We didn't do this very well out of Vietnam, and my generation sees the dramatic downside in too many cases, of not getting this right," he told Barber. "We're not going to let it happen again." Mullen said he wanted to see the number of ships in the navy rise from 281 to 313, though he acknowledged that that would be an expensive undertaking.

In 2005 Mullen, concerned that U.S. Army and Marine Corps forces were being overburdened in Iraq and Afghanistan, sent thousands of sailors overseas on relief duty, for jobs normally assigned to soldiers. "Clearly the ground forces . . . have borne the brunt of what has occurred since 9/11," he told Barber. By May 2007 more than 13,000 sailors were part of the "individual augmentee" program, with about 7,000 of those stationed in the Middle East. Speaking to a group of sailors at Pearl Harbor, Hawaii, Mullen underscored the seriousness of the country's so-called war on terror. "I honestly believe this is the most dangerous time in my life," he said, according to Gregg K. Kakesako in the Honolulu Star-Bulletin (May 8, 2007). "The enemy now is basically evil and fundamentally hates everything we are—the democratic principles for which we stand. . . . This war is going to go on for a long time. It's a generational war."

In June 2007 President Bush, acting on the recommendation of Robert Gates, nominated Mullen to become chairman of the Joint Chiefs of Staff, after it was decided that Peter Pace would not be nominated to serve a second term. (The Bush administration reportedly decided to replace Pace amid fears that Democrats, who had taken control of Congress in 2006, would use his confirmation hearings to focus on mistakes made in Iraq.) "He has the vision, strategic insight, experience and integrity to lead America's armed forces," Gates said of Mullen, according to Jelinek. Washington observers noted that Mullen in some ways symbolized a change of course, because he had not been a top Pentagon staff member when the decision was made to invade Iraq. "Mullen is not considered one of the brainy futurists or crusaders who once surrounded Defense Secretary Donald Rumsfeld," Tom Bowman said on All Things Considered. "All the people at the top of the Pentagon today, including Admiral Mullen, are problem solvers," Loren Thompson, an analyst, told Bowman, stressing Mullen's reputation for being a pragmatic leader. "When they look at the war, they don't consider it a crusade for democracy. They think about how to fix a problem that clearly is not going very well."

While some sources reported that Mullen disagreed with Bush's January 2007 "surge" plan, which committed more than 20,000 additional troops to Iraq, Mullen said during his July 2007

Senate Armed Services Committee confirmation hearing that he agreed with the proposal. "We had rigorous and thorough discussions and debates," Mullen said, according to National Public Radio (July 31, 2007, on-line). "The president then made his decision, and I am in support of that decision and working to make it succeed." Mullen added that the troop buildup was having some positive effects, but that more work needed to be done. "I believe the surge is giving our operational commanders the forces they needed to execute more effective tactics and improve security," he said, according to the Public Broadcasting Service television program NewsHour (July 31, 2007, on-line). "That is happening. Security is better, not great, but better." Mullen said that one of the biggest mistakes the U.S. had made in Iraq was disbanding the army that had operated when Saddam Hussein led that nation. Mullen called that army a "potentially valuable asset for security, reconstruction, and provision of services to the Iraqi people," according to National Public Radio. Now that the army was disbanded, Mullen added, it had become "a recruiting pool for extremist groups."

Mullen was sworn in as chairman of the Joint Chiefs of Staff on October 1, 2007. "He will bring judgment and candor to decisions that may mean the difference between life and death for young Americans who are serving our nation," Bush said, according to Ben Feller, writing for the Associated Press (October 1, 2007). The president also poked fun at Mullen's upbringing in Los Angeles, which has long been considered a bastion of liberal politics. "After all, he is humble, well-grounded and filled with common sense. Not exactly what one thinks about when they think of Hollywood values."

In a town hall meeting later in October with 200 U.S. Army and Air Force sergeants, Mullen was asked by one attendee why the U.S. had not reintroduced a draft. He responded, as quoted by Carpenter, "This is the most combat-ready, combat-hardened military we've ever had in our history. I treasure that. I'd worry about moving to a draft and integrating all that into where we are right now, risking the professional level that we have risen to." Addressing the issue of Iran—a country believed to be aiding Iraqi insurgents and developing nuclear weapons—Mullen said, "I'm not one to take military options off the table. However, I'm a firm believer they should be options of last resort. I'd worry a great deal about getting into a conflict with a third country in that part of the world right now."

In contrast to many of the more hawkish members of the Bush administration, Mullen is seen as an advocate of engaging with—rather than invading—Iran, and he has said that while he is satisfied with the current military situation in Iraq, where the U.S. troop "surge" is credited with bringing about relative stability, he is frustrated by the lack of political progress in the country. Mullen has also recently spoken out on the status of the war in Afghanistan, which he said is likely to enter a "downward spiral" phase, as quoted by Eric Schmitt in the New York Times (October 10, 2008). "The trends across the board are not going in the right direction. I would anticipate next year would be a tougher year," he said.

Mullen has been described as an independent thinker and an approachable, supportive leader. He is married to the former Deborah Morgan. He has two sons, John and Michael, both of whom are naval officers and one of whom has served in Iraq.
—K.J.P.

Suggested Reading: All Things Considered (on-line) June 14, 2007; Daily News of Los Angeles N p3 Dec. 6, 2005; Defense News p10 Jan. 20, 2003, p18 July 18, 2005, p4 Aug. 1, 2005; Honolulu Star-Bulletin May 8, 2007; Los Angeles Times A p18 June 10, 2007, A p1 July 30, 2007; Morning Edition (on-line) Oct. 24, 2007; New York Times A p13 June 9, 2007; Seattle Post-Intelligencer B p5 Aug. 3, 2006; Topeka Capital-Journal A p1 Oct. 25, 2007; Washington Post (on-line) June 13, 2007

My Morning Jacket

Music group

James, Jim
Apr. 27, 1978– Vocalist; songwriter; guitarist

Blankenship, "Two-Tone" Tommy
Feb. 7, 1978– Bassist

Hallahan, Patrick
Apr. 27, 1978– Drummer

Koster, Bo
Aug. 22, 1974– Keyboardist

Broemel, Carl
Jan. 30, 1974– Guitarist

Address: ATO Records, 44 Wall St., 22d Fl., New York, NY 10005

"We've never wanted to be a rock band or an R&B band or be one kind of band," Jim James, the lead singer, guitarist, and principal songwriter for the Louisville, Kentucky–based group My Morning Jacket, was quoted as saying in the Vancouver (British Columbia) Province (June 10, 2008). "We just enjoy celebrating music and having fun with it; making it loud, making it sad and funny. We feel lucky that people are excited about hearing the music we make." Once classified as specialists in "southern rock," a tag generally reserved for the music of such 1970s groups as Lynyrd Skynyrd and the Allman Brothers Band, My Morning Jacket

Autumn DeWilde, courtesy of Girlie Action
My Morning Jacket (left to right): Carl Broemel, Two-Tone Tommy, Jim James, Bo Koster, Patrick Hallahan

has over the course of five studio albums forged an increasingly eclectic sound, earning comparisons to acts ranging from Neil Young to the British experimental rock outfit Radiohead. The group's early albums were characterized by an abundance of "reverb," an echo effect used to treat James's vocals as well as many sounds from the instruments. "Reverb is the thing that makes mere mortals into gods," James told Kitty Empire for the London *Observer* (August 31, 2003). "It makes things sound great."

After recording its first two albums for the independent Darla label, My Morning Jacket signed with ATO, a subsidiary of RCA Records, and released the critically acclaimed *It Still Moves* (2003). Following the 2004 departure of the group's founding guitarist, Johnny Quaid—James's cousin—and the keyboardist Danny Cash, My Morning Jacket recruited two new members and released *Z* (2005), its most experimental album to that point. With little radio airplay the band continued to build its fan base through relentless touring, earning a reputation as one of contemporary rock's best live acts. While My Morning Jacket has never had much chart success—as of June 2008 its best-selling album, *Z*, had sold a comparatively modest 212,000 copies—some have speculated that *Evil Urges* (2008), its latest effort, could finally bring the band mainstream recognition. In a review for *Spin* (June 2, 2008, on-line), Shannon Zimmerman called *Evil Urges* My Morning Jacket's "most accomplished and ambitious record, masterfully sifting through genres." "In the digital age, who listens from beginning to end?" Zimmerman asked.

"Hook-happy and deeply felt, *Evil Urges* makes a compelling case that we should."

Formed in 1998, My Morning Jacket is the brainchild of Jim James, who was born James Olliges Jr. on April 27, 1978. Growing up in the Louisville neighborhood of Hikes Point, James loved music from an early age. As a preteen he would leap around his bedroom, pretending to play along with records by Sepultura, one of his favorite heavy-metal bands. He started playing the guitar at the age of 12 and soon afterward decided to pursue a career in music. He began listening to the work of a diverse range of artists, including Roy Orbison, Bob Dylan, Etta James, Sam Cooke, Ray Charles, and Pink Floyd. James has also cited Jim Henson, the creator of the children's puppet characters the Muppets, as a major influence on his music. "I feel weird sometimes talking about the Muppets, because I know people are looking for some sort of musical inspiration," James told Joan Anderman for the *Boston Globe* (July 4, 2003). "But Jim Henson opened my eyes to what can be done to make people laugh and smile and cry, what you can do to people in a wondrous realm. I get tired of hearing about love and whiskey and cigarettes." In junior high school James and the drummer Patrick Hallahan (born on April 27, 1978), a friend since the fourth grade, formed their first band. The group split up soon afterward, since James and Hallahan feared that being in a band together might ruin their friendship. (Hallahan eventually became My Morning Jacket's third drummer.)

James attended the University of Kentucky, in Lexington. He dropped out after a year and a half to focus on music, originally conceiving of My Morning Jacket as a solo project. (While sources differ as to the origin of the name, the most common story is that James, while visiting the ruins of a favorite college bar that had burned down, found a robe emblazoned with the letters "MMJ," which he imagined stood for My Morning Jacket.) His act became a quartet when he joined forces with the bassist "Two Tone" Tommy Blankenship (born on February 7, 1978), the drummer J. Glenn, and Johnny Quaid. (The keyboardist Danny Cash joined later.) Quaid's family owned a large soybean and cattle farm in nearby Shelbyville, Kentucky, where the band built its own recording studio in an apartment over a three-car garage. Called Above the Cadillac, the studio was used to record the first three My Morning Jacket albums. The band famously recorded James's vocals inside an 80-foot grain silo, as well as in a garage and a bathroom—spaces that provided natural reverb. "We just mike them up and turn those spaces into reverb chambers," James told Eric Brace for the *Washington Post*, as reprinted in the *Ottawa (Ontario, Canada) Citizen* (February 21, 2004). "I admit it. I love reverb. I can't sing without it."

In 1998 James mailed the band's demo tape to the independent Southern California label Darla Records. He had read about the label's owners, James Agren and Chandra Tobey, in *Spin* magazine and decided that "they looked like nice people," he told Nancy Einhart for *SF Weekly* (May 28, 2003). "I made, like, a red foil mix-tape cover and wrapped it all up in real romantic packaging and stuff." James's unusual approach paid off, and in 1999 Darla released the band's debut, *The Tennessee Fire*. In a review for the All Music Web site, Terrance Miles wrote that the album's songs "evoke warm (and somewhat lonely) memories of a gothic country night." Commenting on the abundance of reverb on the album, he added, "At first you wonder if the sound will overtake the songs, but after the first chorus you realize that the beauty of these simple and emotive songs is only enhanced by the addition of this effect, and by the end of the first song, you can't even tell that it's there." Critics generally praised the album. Many called My Morning Jacket a "southern rock" group, a label that likely had less to do with the band's songs than with its members' scruffy appearance and penchant for playing barefoot. "We may be long-haired dudes from Kentucky, but if people spent time with the records, they'd discover we're not a jam band or a Southern rock band," James told Mary Huhn for the *New York Post* (May 30, 2004). "I just say it's rock 'n' roll."

While My Morning Jacket was still largely unknown in the U.S., it was becoming famous in Denmark, where Darla had released the group's sophomore album, *At Dawn* (2001), and an influential Danish music journalist had written a favorable article about it. The group also became the subject of a Dutch documentary film and embarked on four headlining tours of Denmark, Belgium, and the Netherlands. "It was amazing," Quaid told John Cook for the *Chicago Tribune* (May 9, 2003). "Some promoter called and said, 'You're blowing up over here,' and in a couple of weeks we hopped a plane." *Oor*, a popular Dutch music publication, ranked the band first on its 1999 critics' poll. Between trips to Europe, the group continued touring the U.S., where, playing to much smaller audiences, it slowly expanded its fan base. Like its predecessor, *At Dawn* earned mostly positive reviews. "On its second album for Darla Records, My Morning Jacket are perfect. That is to say, they haven't changed a bit, and we like them that way," Miles wrote for the All Music site. In a review for the influential on-line music publication *Pitchfork Media*, Christopher Dare called the band's music "the perfect soundtrack to a summer road trip, or just something you wrap around yourself on the way to work each morning."

In 2002 the British music magazine *NME* called My Morning Jacket America's best new band. After performing at that year's South by Southwest Music Conference and Festival, an annual event held in Austin, Texas, the group was featured in many national music publications, including *Blender* magazine. With the increased attention came offers from major labels. The band signed with ATO, an RCA subsidiary founded by the singer Dave Matthews. "I'm really, really grateful in a lot of ways

that it's taken people a while to catch on to us," James told Jeffrey Lee Puckett for the Louisville *Courier-Journal* (September 6, 2003). "Putting out two records that were moderately successful gave us a chance to really solidify as a band and become friends and to know what we want." September 2003 saw the release of the band's major-label debut, *It Still Moves*, the last of their albums to be recorded at the farm studio. The album was met with widespread acclaim, and in a review for *Rolling Stone* (September 9, 2003, on-line), the critic David Fricke compared the band to Radiohead and Fleetwood Mac, among others. Noting the slow pace of many of the songs, he wrote, "My Morning Jacket are going nowhere fast—but in all the right ways." In a review for *Pitchfork Media*, Joe Tangari wrote that the band "have made the move to the bigs in tremendous style, and as far as I can tell they haven't compromised a thing to be there." He gave the album a rating of 8.3 out of a possible 10—high praise from the Web site's notoriously hard-to-please critics.

In June 2004 My Morning Jacket performed a memorable set at Bonnaroo, a music festival held in Manchester, Tennessee. Thunderstorms raged as the band played, and the concert has since been dubbed "Return to Thunderdome." Later that year Quaid and Cash quit the band. While James has been reluctant to discuss that development, he has indicated that the guitarist and the keyboardist were growing uncomfortable with being on the road constantly. "Whenever anyone's in a place they don't want to be, it creates a negative space, and that expands to include everyone," James told Puckett for the *Courier-Journal* (October 8, 2005). "They're much happier people now that they're doing what they want." James, Blankenship, and Hallahan considered disbanding or continuing as a trio, then decided to hold auditions for new members. They hired the first two musicians who tried out, the keyboardist Bo Koster (born on August 22, 1974) and the guitarist Carl Broemel (born on January 30, 1974). Being asked to join was especially meaningful for Koster, an Indiana native who had been struggling to make his name in the Los Angeles, California, music scene. "One day I was driving around feeling really bad and heard the end of [My Morning Jacket's] 'I Will Sing You Songs' on the radio," Koster told Puckett. "I almost started crying. I thought, man, this is what I want to do. How do I do this?" Despite being new to the band, Koster and Broemel made substantial contributions to the next album, *Z* (2005). Quaid's departure meant that the band could no longer record on the farm, and for the first time, My Morning Jacket opted to work with an outside producer, John Leckie, who had collaborated with such luminaries as Radiohead, Pink Floyd, and George Harrison. "We were excited . . . ," James told Joshua Hammann for the *Courier-Journal* (September 28, 2005). "We got tired of reading about the farm all the time and tired of all that stuff. The time was right, and we were excited to go do something new and get out of there. We had sucked all the magic out of that place." For *Z* James cut back on reverb in favor of other effects and created a far more experimental album than any the band had recorded.

Z generated even more buzz than *It Still Moves.* In his review for the Web site the AV Club, Noel Murray wrote, "If it takes some time to adjust to, it's only because it's hard to recognize a classic right away." *Entertainment Weekly* (September 30, 2005, on-line) gave *Z* an "A–," with its critic Tom Sinclair writing that the band's members "evoke the musical essence of various titans while achieving a wholly distinctive sound of their own." In a review for *Rolling Stone* (October 20, 2005, on-line), Fricke wrote, "America is a lot closer to getting its own Radiohead." To the extent that *Z* earned negative press, it was mostly related to a "spyware" program that Sony, owner of ATO Records, had included on the CD. With the spyware—which was also included on albums released by the Foo Fighters and Alicia Keys—anyone who played the album on his or her computer was "vulnerable to hacking, identity theft and monitoring by outside parties," according to August Brown, writing for the *Los Angeles Times* (January 4, 2007). The group's management company later provided spyware-free copies to unhappy fans upon request. In 2005 My Morning Jacket appeared in the Cameron Crowe film *Elizabethtown.* Perhaps poking fun at its "southern rock" label, the group performed the Lynyrd Skynyrd staple "Free Bird."

In June 2006, the same month that the band played two shows accompanied by the Boston Pops orchestra, My Morning Jacket again performed at Bonnaroo, this time closing the festival with a three-and-a-half-hour set. In September of that year, the band released the live album *Okonokos,* which was recorded at the Fillmore, a famous music venue in San Francisco. Thanks to its appearances at festivals such as Bonnaroo and the Coachella Valley Music and Arts Festival, which is held each year in Indio, California, My Morning Jacket became known as one of the country's best live bands. "The greatest thing about live music is that it's something you can't replicate," James said, as quoted in the *Vancouver Province.* "It's something very communal, and I think society is lacking that." Despite its success as a live band, My Morning Jacket has struggled to sell records. Some have suggested that the band has yet to capture on record the power and vitality of its concerts. "Here's a band that thrives on spectacle, that really wants to be the center of the universe and can justify that presence there," Norm Winer, a program director at the Chicago, Illinois, radio station WXRT-FM, told Ben Sisario in an interview for the *New York Times* (June 15, 2008). "And yet in the studio it's so subdued."

In preparing to record its fifth album, My Morning Jacket enlisted the producer Joe Chiccarelli, who has worked with the Shins and the White Stripes. Having listened to demo recordings of some of James's new songs, Chiccarelli persuaded the band to record in New York City. "I said to Jim, 'This is not the record to go and hide away in the woods,'" he told Sisario. "These are much more open and accessible, groove-oriented, rhythmic sounds. This is a city record." Released in June 2008, *Evil Urges* was more experimental than *Z,* prompting Sisario to call it "the band's most ambitious and challenging work, full of left-field electronic experiments and songs that seem to rebel against every expectation." Critical reaction was mixed, though mostly positive. In a review for the All Music site, Andrew Leahey wrote that the album "cements My Morning Jacket's transformation from grizzled, reverb-drenched classic rockers to experimental, genre-bending innovators." Less favorably impressed was Eric Harvey, who, reviewing the album for *Pitchfork Media* (June 9, 2008), wrote, "There are few fiery guitar freakouts, folk-influenced melodies, soaring space-rock bridges, or psychedelic flourishes here; instead, the empty space is mostly filled with serviceable falsetto funk and glassy-eyed soft rock." He rated the album a 4.7 out of 10. *Rolling Stone* (June 12, 2008, on-line), meanwhile, gave the album four out of five stars, and its critic Will Hermes wrote, "James seems well aware that any definition of 'classic rock' that doesn't include Prince, Radiohead and Wilco is pretty bereft. Now, with *Evil Urges,* he can add My Morning Jacket to that list." In May 2008, about a month before the album was released, James fulfilled one of his childhood dreams when he and the band performed on *Saturday Night Live.*

In addition to *Elizabethtown* James appeared in the 2007 film *I'm Not There,* which focuses on a variety of characters to trace, loosely, the life of the rock icon Bob Dylan. Although My Morning Jacket continues to call Kentucky its home base, in the spring of 2008, James moved from Louisville to the New York City neighborhood of Chelsea. His bandmates live in other parts of the country.

—K.J.P.

Suggested Reading: *Boston Globe* E p12 July 4, 2003, D p18 Oct. 14, 2005; *Los Angeles Times* E p18 Oct. 9, 2003; (Louisville, Kentucky) *Courier-Journal* V p8 Sep. 28, 2005, S p4 Oct. 8, 2005; *New York Times* Arts and Leisure p1+ June 15, 2008; *San Diego Union-Tribune* Dec. 28, 2006; (San Francisco, California) *SF Weekly* May 28, 2003

Selected Recordings: *The Tennessee Fire,* 1999; *At Dawn,* 2001; *It Still Moves,* 2003; *Z,* 2005; *Evil Urges,* 2008

Newkirk, Ingrid

*July 11, 1949– President and co-founder of
People for the Ethical Treatment of Animals*

Address: PETA, 501 Front St., Norfolk, VA 23510

Ingrid Newkirk, the controversial co-founder and president of the nonprofit group People for the Ethical Treatment of Animals (PETA), is not deterred by critics' claims that she is a dangerous fanatic. "I am tough," Newkirk told Stephen Romei for the *Australian* (March 26, 2001). "I have been called every name in the book. Personally, it is inconsequential if people hate me." Since Newkirk co-founded PETA, in 1980, the organization has generated headlines, notoriety, and enemies. Newkirk—sometimes dressed in an animal costume—has protested outside the offices of major corporations and government agencies, thrown fake-blood–stained money at fashion-show audiences, and walked nude through European cities to protest the fur trade. Angering many, she has helped mount campaigns comparing the suffering of slaughterhouse animals to that of Jews during the Holocaust and claiming a connection between dairy products and former New York City mayor Rudolph Giuliani's bout with colon cancer. "We're stunt queens. We have to be," Newkirk told Gary Younge for the London *Guardian* (February 24, 2006).

Despite frequent criticism of its tactics in the mainstream press, PETA has attracted several high-profile supporters, including such celebrities as Alec Baldwin, Pamela Anderson, Kim Basinger, and Eva Mendes. Largely as a result of pressure from the organization, some companies, including Avon, Benetton, and Tonka, have halted much of their product testing on animals, and the Pentagon discontinued wound tests that called for pigs, goats, and other animals to be shot. PETA—which has affiliates in the United Kingdom, Germany, India, and the Netherlands, among other countries—now boasts 300 employees, $300 million in annual revenue, and 1.8 million members, making it one of the world's largest animal-rights organizations.

Born Ingrid Ward on July 11, 1949 in Surrey, England, Newkirk, an only child, spent her early years in India, where her father's job as a navigational engineer took the family and where her mother became involved in the charitable organizations of the humanitarian activist Mother Teresa. The Newkirks were fond of pets; they kept many dogs, cats, chipmunks, birds, and even mongooses. (In England Newkirk had been especially close to Sean, a family dog, and she was angered and upset when her parents euthanized him without her knowledge before the move to India.) Newkirk studied at a Catholic convent school in New Delhi, India, for nine years. She told Richard Behar for *Forbes* (March 20, 1989), "The nuns would smash us across the face with the full force of their hands for the most trivial of reasons, like talking during dinner. It was a desolate, very lonely experience. It scars you for life. At first, you're desperate to get in touch with your parents, but by the time you do go home you really hate and resent them."

Newkirk told Howard Rosenberg for the *Los Angeles Times* (March 22, 1992) that in India, she was "surrounded by suffering. There were lepers in the streets, diseased people, dogs with maggots in their backs, bullocks pulling carts overloaded with bricks, and there were beggars everywhere, breathing exhaust fumes." The work of the Indian writer and social reformer Rabindranath Tagore (1861–1941) was one of Newkirk's early influences. "One of his disciples came to our school and spoke to us well-off little girls," she told Rosenberg. "I didn't realize it then, but I think that his words, combined with what I saw every day, had a lasting impact."

Newkirk and her parents moved to Florida when she was 18. They settled at Eglin Air Force Base, where her father had an engineering job. A year later Newkirk met the American racecar driver Steve Newkirk; the two married and settled in Poolesville, Maryland, a Washington, D.C., suburb. At 22 Newkirk resolved never to have children and was voluntarily sterilized. "I really felt that I knew that so long as there were children who needed homes it was only vanity to have your own," she told Younge.

While in Maryland Newkirk studied to become a stockbroker. Her career path changed dramatically in 1972, when she discovered that a neighbor of hers had moved away, abandoning her cats when she left. Newkirk took the cats to a local animal shelter and was so disgusted by the facility's poor maintenance that she persuaded the management to hire her as a kennel cleaner. "It was the biggest dump I'd ever seen," Newkirk told Susan Reed and Sue Carswell for *People* (October 22, 1990). "Dogs cringed as you approached them. Animals sat in their own filth while workers sat on garbage cans smoking and laughing the day away." When a local television news crew prepared a report on the shelter's poor conditions, Newkirk was fired for agreeing to be interviewed by them. She was subsequently rehired, to replace the shelter's ousted director.

Imbued with a new purpose, Newkirk spent 18 months working as a deputy sheriff for the county, helping to prosecute animal-cruelty cases. During that time she visited a farm at which animals had been abandoned and left to starve. When she discovered the only survivor—an emaciated pig—she began to have doubts about her lifestyle and food choices. She told Daniel Redwood for *HealthWorld Online* (2005), "I realized I was prosecuting somebody for being cruel to one pig while I was paying someone I didn't know to be cruel to another pig. There were lots of little incidents like that where I thought, 'Oh dear, I shouldn't do that. I need to find something different to eat or wear.'" She became a vegan, never eating meat or any food containing animal products and eschewing leather goods.

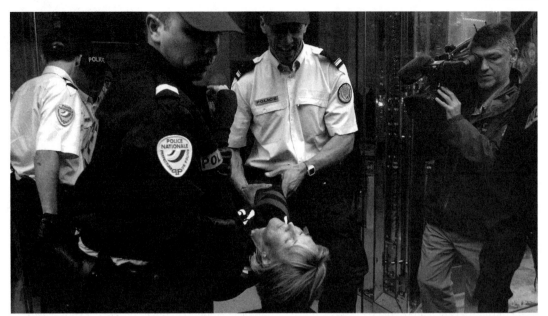

Eric Feferberg/AFP/Getty Images
Policemen remove Ingrid Newkirk from a demonstration held in a Jean Paul Gaultier store.

In 1978 Newkirk became the first female pound master of Washington, D.C. One of her earliest acts was to put an end to the practice of selling shelter animals to research laboratories. She later became director of cruelty investigations for the Washington Humane Society and chief of animal disease control for the District of Columbia Commission on Public Health.

In 1980 Newkirk met a pound volunteer named Alex Pacheco, who introduced her to the influential book *Animal Liberation*, by the Australian philosopher Peter Singer. In the book Singer argued that all species are equal and that, contrary to the Bible's declaration that humans have dominion over other animals, humans do not have a manifest right to control other creatures. Singer's ideas transformed Newkirk into a passionate activist. She told Rosenberg, "All of my life, I'd been thinking that we should treat animals as kindly as we can within the context of using them. It took someone else to say to me, 'Maybe they're not ours to use at all.' It doesn't matter if you love animals or think they're cute. It's about justice."

Soon after they met, Newkirk and Pacheco founded PETA, running the organization, which initially attracted only five volunteers, from Newkirk's home in Takoma Park, Maryland. The fledgling group passed out leaflets, performed guerrilla theater to dramatize issues, and visited schools to spread awareness of animal rights. Newkirk's marriage ended in divorce during PETA's first year; her long hours of work with the group had made it difficult to maintain the relationship.

Before long PETA members began going undercover into research and farming facilities to gather evidence of animal cruelty. In 1981 PETA received national publicity after a successful undercover effort to expose abuse at the federally funded Institute for Behavioral Research, in Silver Spring, Maryland. Pacheco had entered the facility as a volunteer and gathered video footage of surgically mutilated monkeys, leading to a police raid and the subsequent conviction (later overturned on appeal) of the program's director, Edward Taub. PETA fought for custody of the monkeys, and the legal battle eventually reached the Supreme Court. While the court awarded custody to the National Institutes of Health (NIH), a division of the U.S. Department of Health and Human Services (HSS), and the animals were later euthanized, the incident brought PETA into the spotlight as a powerful force in animal rights. PETA caused a media stir again when, in 1984, it publicized videotapes from the Head Injury Clinical Research Center at the University of Pennsylvania, in Philadelphia, that revealed abusive treatment of baboons. The compilation of footage, called *Unnecessary Fuss*, was screened by PETA at a hotel on the school's campus and attended by members of the local media. When the NIH increased funding to the lab the next year, PETA organized a mass demonstration at NIH headquarters; as a result, NIH officials agreed to view the footage, and the lab was shut down. "PETA gave a good kick-start to the [animal-rights] movement in the '80s," Bernard Unti, the executive director of the American Anti-Vivisection Society, told Rosenberg. "The Silver Spring case demonstrated there was cruelty in the laboratory. And the head-injury case demonstrated that the cruelty was not an exception."

In 1986 Newkirk and 11 other protestors were arrested after dressing up in chicken costumes during a demonstration outside HSS offices in Washington, D.C. (The protest was connected to the Silver Spring custody case.) Newkirk told Kate Callen for United Press International (August 6, 1986), "We want the public to know that the National Institutes of Health sees animals as disposable garbage." In 1987 an animal-rights group calling itself the Band of Mercy broke into the Animal Parisitology Institute, in Beltsville, Maryland, removing 25 cats and seven pigs that were being used for experiments involving toxoplasmosis, a parasitic infection that can be particularly dangerous to pregnant women and people with AIDS. While Newkirk publicly denied PETA's involvement in the incident, some believed that the groups were connected in some way, because Newkirk had publicly revealed the Band of Mercy's activities.

By the end of the 1980s, PETA had become the largest and most influential animal-rights group in the U.S., with 325,000 members, a staff of more than 100, and an annual budget of $8 million. In 1989 the group was sued for defamation by the Las Vegas entertainer Bobby Berosini, after Newkirk released a secretly recorded videotape that allegedly showed him mistreating orangutans he used in his show at the Stardust Hotel-Casino. In 1990 Berosini won the suit, and PETA was ordered to pay $4.2 million in damages. The Nevada Supreme Court reversed the decision in 1994, however, and Berosini was ordered to reimburse PETA for legal fees. The court ruled that the tape did, in fact, accurately portray the entertainer's actions and that PETA was within its rights to accuse him of harming the animals.

PETA next made headlines nationally in 1996, after a member entered the restaurant at the Four Seasons Hotel, in New York City, and threw the frozen corpse of a raccoon onto the plate of *Vogue*'s editor, Anna Wintour. Wintour, who has publicly written about her penchant for fur clothing and who has repeatedly refused to remove fur ads from *Vogue*'s pages, has been a frequent PETA target. Newkirk told Mary Braid for the London *Independent* (November 28, 1998), "You would have to bury [Wintour] under a truck load of raccoons to get her attention. She is a hard woman."

By then PETA's efforts to expose animal cruelty had become very worrisome for animal researchers and the corporations and government agencies that employed them. In 1997 the group infiltrated Huntingdon Life Sciences, a product-testing facility in East Millstone, New Jersey. In response, the company's president, Alan Staple, filed a civil lawsuit against PETA under the federal Racketeering Influenced Corrupt Organization (RICO) Act. He argued that PETA had been acting in a criminal manner by harassing the scientists who worked there to such an extent that their careers and reputations had been destroyed. Explaining Staple's reliance on the RICO Act, Gina Kolata wrote for the *New York Times* (March 24, 1998, on-line), "To Mr. Staple,

PETA was a terrifying group that used strategies no different from those used by gangsters." Huntingdon had lost more than half its accounts in the wake of the infiltration, and Staple told Kolata that it was "fear [of] the specter of PETA showing videotapes and demonstrating in front of their headquarters"—not fear of claims of cruelty—that had caused his clients to pull out. In the end, a settlement was reached: PETA destroyed or returned documents it had collected from Huntingdon, and Staple dropped the lawsuit.

In March 2000 PETA introduced the "Milk Sucks . . . Got Beer?" campaign, a parody of the milk industry's "Got Milk?" ads. For the new campaign PETA members visited college campuses with free bottle openers and pamphlets claiming that beer was healthier than milk and that the dairy industry treated cows inhumanely. That provoked an outcry from a number of officials and groups, including Mothers Against Drunk Driving (MADD). "If PETA's misguided purpose is to denounce the dairy industry, they certainly aren't advancing their ball by advocating alcohol consumption by college students," David Botkins, a spokesman for the Virginia attorney general's office, told the Associated Press (March 20, 2000, on-line). PETA halted the campaign in response to the negative publicity, but not before more than 1,500 students had joined the group's College Activist Network.

After ending the "Got Beer?" campaign, PETA organized other campaigns to spread its message about dairy products. One of them, highlighting the link between the dairy industry and the veal industry, satirized the missing-child photographs found on milk cartons, replacing children's pictures with that of the fictional "Charlie," a calf destined to be turned into veal. The new ads were placed on grocery bags and distributed heavily around college campuses. "Many people don't know that there's a slab of veal in every single glass of milk," Newkirk told Andrew Noyes for the American University *Eagle* (March 27, 2000, on-line). "If they did, they would spit it out." Criticism quickly arose that PETA was being insensitive to the plight of parents with missing children. Later in 2000 the organization faced criticism again for parodying the "Got Milk?" ads—this time with billboards that depicted New York City mayor Rudolph Giuliani with a milk moustache, along with the words "Got Prostate Cancer?" The ads angered Giuliani, who threatened PETA with a lawsuit for what he saw as an exploitation of his illness. PETA later apologized and dropped the campaign. In a letter to Giuliani, quoted by the Associated Press (September 1, 2000, on-line), Newkirk wrote, "The dairy parody was meant to expose the ill-health effects of milk. The effort was not intended as an attack on you, and we're sorry it was taken that way." She told Romei, "My father died this year of milk- and meat-related illness. . . . I could put his face on a billboard and no one would give it a second glance. I put Giuliani up there and our website had 60,000 hits in three days."

In 2003 the ad campaign widely considered one of PETA's most inflammatory to date was launched, as members of the group began to tour the world with an exhibit entitled "Holocaust on Your Plate," which placed graphic images of factory farming and slaughterhouses next to images of Jews in Nazi concentration camps during World War II. PETA based the exhibit on the writings of the late Nobel laureate and author Isaac Bashevis Singer, who wrote of the similarity between concentration camps and the slaughterhouse killings he later observed in the U.S. "It's just what . . . Singer saw when he was living above the Chicago stockyards," Newkirk said in the speech quoted by Keane. "He had fled Nazi oppression, and when he saw the lines of cattle and shackles and electric prods—the bewilderment, fear and resistance—he said, 'This is what I have just come from. I cannot impose this on any other living creature.'" The exhibit was funded by an anonymous Jewish philanthropist and supported by Jewish PETA employees and Jewish vegetarian groups, yet it nonetheless drew harsh criticism for its supposed insensitivity to the suffering of millions of people at the hands of the Nazis. Because of the uproar, in May 2005 Newkirk issued a formal apology. She wrote, as quoted by Miriam Porter in the *Canadian Jewish News* (May 26, 2005), "[The exhibit] was designed to sensitize people to different forms of systematic degradation and exploitation, and the logic and methods employed in factory farms and slaughterhouses are analogous to those used in concentration camps. We realize that many people—Jews and non-Jews alike—cannot see through the pain and horror of what was done to human beings to agree, but to our minds, both systems are hideous and devastating."

PETA did not significantly change its ad tactics after the "Holocaust on Your Plate" incident, during which Newkirk spoke the oft-quoted line, "Six million people died in concentration camps, but six billion chickens will die this year in slaughterhouses." In December 2007 the group was threatened with a lawsuit from the California Milk Processor Board, the creator of the "Got Milk?" ads, over its new anti-milk campaign, "Got pus? Milk does," which spread the belief that antibiotics used to treat mastitis in cows contaminates their milk.

In addition to its controversial ad campaigns, PETA's alleged connections to, and verbal support of, various extremist and violent pro-animal organizations, including the Animal Liberation Front (ALF), have drawn ire. Jacquie Calnan, the president of Americans for Medical Progress, a Washington-based interest group, told Bill Sizemore for the *Virginian-Pilot* (December 13, 2000), "Every week I hear of some scientist getting a threatening letter, phone call or e-mail. None of it is under PETA's signature. But PETA is contributing by its notoriety, by its demonization of scientists." She continued, "Very promising students are choosing not to go into the life sciences. . . . Some folks say we have lost a generation because of the animal rights influence, and specifically PETA's influence, in the schools. PETA will say that's a victory. I say that is a blow to medical progress." While Newkirk has said PETA does not engage in violent actions, she has expressed support for the lab breaks-ins and vandalism conducted by ALF and has often acted as the group's unofficial spokesperson. Newkirk defended her organization in 2002 when allegations emerged that PETA had donated money to both ALF and the Earth Liberation Front (ELF), groups linked to bombings and acts of arson. The Center for Consumer Freedom (CCF), a nonprofit organization that claims to represent consumers' rights, had been tracking PETA's monetary contributions, and in February of that year, at a congressional hearing on domestic terrorism, CCF representatives gave evidence that presented PETA in a negative light. Newkirk told Jade Carpenter for the Illinois State University *Daily Vidette* (March 28, 2002), "The CCF is against all kinds of movements, including Greenpeace, MADD, and the Center for Science in the Public Interests. Basically this group does not want regulations on anything. The CCF was founded with an $800,000 grant from . . . Philip Morris," a tobacco company that has had an acrimonious relationship with PETA because of its animal testing. Newkirk continued, "[The CCF has] insinuated we gave money for illegal purposes, and we have never done that." In 2005 reports of PETA's alleged ties to ALF and ELF emerged again, during a Senate hearing. Newkirk declined to appear, but PETA's counsel, Jeffrey Kerr, asserted, as quoted by Terry Frieden on CNN (May 19, 2005, on-line), "PETA has no involvement with alleged ALF or ELF actions. PETA does not support terrorism. PETA does not support violence."

Critics have derided Newkirk's leadership style and PETA's internal workings. John Newton, a fellow activist, told Sizemore, "They're brutal on their people. . . . If you're not radical enough, they drive you out," and Merritt Clifton, a former PETA member who left to start the publication *Animal People*, said, "Ingrid Newkirk rules PETA like a guru cult. Sooner or later, everyone who questions her or upstages her, no matter how unintentionally, ends up getting shafted." In her own defense, Newkirk told Sizemore, "I believe we should be . . . a lean, mean fighting machine. This is not a rest home for people who just have warm feelings about animals."

Newkirk—who is the subject of the 2007 HBO documentary *I Am an Animal: The Story of Ingrid Newkirk and PETA*—has written several books, among them *You Can Save the Animals: 251 Simple Ways to Stop Thoughtless Cruelty* (1999), *Making Kind Choices: Everyday Ways to Enhance Your Life Through Earth- and Animal-Friendly Living* (2004), and *50 Awesome Ways Kids Can Help Animals: Fun and Easy Ways to Be a Kind Kid* (2006). Her most recent book, *One Can Make a Difference* (2008), consists of essays written by medical experts, celebrities and other public figures, and laypeople, in which they described how they have effected positive change through their actions. Newkirk maintains a blog, blog.ingridnewkirk.com.

To protect her safety, she does not reveal where she lives; her offices frequently receive hate mail and even animal corpses from opponents. Newkirk has decreed in her will that her skin be turned into leather products, her feet made into umbrella stands, her liver cooked in the style of the French delicacy foie gras, and her flesh grilled into "Newkirk Nuggets" at a public barbecue.

—W.D.

Suggested Reading: Associated Press (on-line) Mar. 20, 2000, Sep 1, 2000; *Australian* p11 Mar. 26, 2001; *Brandweek* (on-line) Dec. 17, 2007; CNN (on-line) Feb. 28, 2003; *Forbes* p43 Mar. 20, 1989; *HealthWorld Online* 2005; (London)

Guardian p31 Nov. 28, 1998, p12 Feb. 24, 2006; (London) *Independent* p31 Nov. 28, 1998, p18 May 7, 2004; *Los Angeles Times Magazine* p18 Mar. 22, 1992; *New York Times* (on-line) Mar. 24, 1998; *People* p59 Oct. 22, 1990, p34 Jan. 18, 1993; *Virginian-Pilot* Dec. 13, 2000

Selected Books: *Save the Animals!: 101 Easy Things You Can Do*, 1990; *You Can Save the Animals: 251 Simple Ways to Stop Thoughtless Cruelty*, 1999; *Free the Animals: The Story of the Animal Liberation Front*, 2000; *Making Kind Choices: Everyday Ways to Enhance Your Life Through Earth- and Animal-Friendly Living*, 2004; *50 Awesome Ways Kids Can Help Animals: Fun and Easy Ways to Be a Kind Kid*, 2006; *Let's Have a Dog Party!: 20 Tail-wagging Celebrations to Share With Your Best Friend*, 2007; *One Can Make a Difference*, 2008

Newkirk, Kori

1970– Artist

Address: The Project, 37 W. 57th St., Third Fl., New York, NY 10019

The Los Angeles, California–based mixed-media and installation artist Kori Newkirk is associated with a group of other African-Americans— including Edgar Arceneaux, Rodney McMillan, and Mark Bradford—who together form the "post-black" school, a phrase coined by Thelma Golden, curator of the Studio Museum in Harlem. According to Golden, as noted by Regina Hackett for the *Seattle Post-Intelligencer* (August 10, 2007), the term "post-black" applies to the work of those who are "adamant about not being labeled 'black' artists, though their work was steeped, in fact deeply interested, in redefining complex notions of blackness." Newkirk is known chiefly for works incorporating hair beads and murals painted with hair pomade, materials symbolic of African-American experience and, more importantly for the artist, evocative of Newkirk's childhood. In much of his work, he has created representations of recognizable subjects (sharks, suburban landscapes, and helicopters, for example) with nontraditional materials that include hair extensions, glitter, and neon wall texts, as a means of portraying common things in new and revealing ways. Discussing his work and that of other "post-black" artists, Newkirk explained to Jori Finkel for the *New York Times* (June 10, 2007), "We're all making work that can be difficult sometimes, with an incredible investigation into materials and a strong basis in conceptual art. I would say we're all making work that doesn't hit people over the head with the race conversation anymore. It's a juicy conceptualism—a ghetto-fabulous conceptualism—based on reality and the intricacies of daily life."

Over the last decade Newkirk has had solo exhibitions at the Rosamund Felsen Gallery in Santa Monica, California, Johnson County Community College, in Overland Park, Kansas, the Project in New York City and Los Angeles, the Cleveland Museum of Art, and Locust Projects in Miami, Florida, among many other venues. He has also been featured in dozens of prestigious group exhibitions, including Freestyle, at the Studio Museum in Harlem (2001); One Planet Under a Groove: Hip Hop and Contemporary Art, at the Bronx Museum (2001); Gene(sis): Contemporary Art Explores Human Genomics, at the Henry Art Gallery in Seattle, Washington (2002); Beyond Stereotype, at Cortland's Dowd Fine Arts Gallery at the State University of New York (2002); Hair Stories, at the Scottsdale Museum of Contemporary Art (2003); and the Whitney Biennial, in New York (2006). In 2004 Newkirk was the recipient of the $25,000 William H. Johnson Prize, awarded annually since 2002 to an up-and-coming African-American artist. A 10-year survey of Newkirk's work, Kori Newkirk: 1997–2007, was presented at the Studio Museum in Harlem from November 2007 through March 2008. His works are in the permanent collections of several museums as well as in private collections, including that of the actor/comedian David Alan Grier; many of his pieces have asking prices of $20,000 or more. Alice Thorson wrote for the *Kansas City Star* (May 26, 2002), "The wonder of Newkirk is his ability to create objects of great beauty, but it's genius to have managed to turn vehicles of consciousness-raising into highly desirable—and lucrative—commodities."

Kori Newkirk was born in 1970 in the New York City borough of the Bronx. He grew up mainly in the town of Cortland, in central New York State, but often made trips with his parents back to the city of his birth to visit museums and galleries. Newkirk's exposure at a young age to such differ-

Courtesy of Andrew Berardini/Artforum
Newkirk (right) with artist Yoshua Okon

ent locales gave him what he has called "a secondary double-consciousness," that of "the city mouse and the country mouse," as quoted by a writer for *Vibe* (August 9, 2007, on-line). Interested in arts and crafts early on, he had access to "a lot of natural things" to work with in his small town, as he told Jessica Hemmings for *Surface Design Journal* (Fall 2006). Central New York's cold climate led Newkirk to take up skiing and ice skating. While he attended Cortland High School, in the mid-1980s, he began taking an interest in metals, after his art teacher started bringing such magazines as *American Craft* to the classroom. He also started using the family blender to experiment with paper-shredding and dyes. At that point he planned to study fibers in college. He graduated from Cortland High School in 1988, then enrolled at the School of the Art Institute of Chicago. Dissatisfied with the school's fibers program after one class, he decided to study painting.

During those years Newkirk participated in an undergraduate exchange program at the University of Brighton, in England (formerly known as Brighton Polytechnic). While there, he became fascinated with the emerging Young British Artists movement, especially the work of the sculptor Rachel Whiteread. That group of conceptual artists, painters, sculptors, and installation artists—who also included Damien Hirst, Sarah Lucas, Gary Hume, and Fiona Rae—gained attention for their unusual exhibits, which featured innovative use of throw-away materials; for example, Lucas's *Willy* (2000) is a sculpture, reminiscent of garden gnomes, made entirely out of cigarettes. Whiteread, the first woman to win the prestigious Turner Prize, is best known for her casted sculptures. Newkirk received

his B.F.A. degree in 1993; inspired by the Young British Artists to create works that would defy the standard methods and notions of painting by using untraditional materials, he made what he has described as "stripy paintings" before a casual conversation with a friend convinced him that he should pursue projects with more personal themes. Not long afterward, he produced a painting called "I come from a long line of Cadillacs," inspired by his family's fondness for that luxury vehicle. (He explained to Alice Thorson that his father and his father's 13 siblings drove Cadillacs.) The painting shows a family tree with a series of Cadillac images and indicates deceased family members with upside-down cars. For his next piece he used hair of African-Americans, collected from local barbershops, to create an 18-foot-long mural with a Cadillac logo.

In 1997 Newkirk received his M.F.A. degree from the University of California at Irvine. That summer he became an artist in residence at the Skowhegan School of Painting and Sculpture, in Skowhegan, Maine. While reading the *New York Times* one day in August, he came across an article on the African-American tennis player Venus Williams; the article, about Williams's first participation in the U.S. Open, seemed to Newkirk to place as much emphasis on the pony beads in her hair as on her playing ability. (Her opponents had expressed their worry that the beads could fall to the court's surface and cause them to trip.) Newkirk recalled to Hemmings that Williams's beaded hairstyle "had a resonance" with him because it had been "something I always wanted as a child but could not have." "From the initial thought and image—the back of Venus's head, beads swinging—I started thinking about the hairstyle generally, and [the musician] Stevie Wonder [who wore beads in his hair] in the 1970s, and this great episode of [the sitcom] *Facts of Life* where Tootie was a model and got fake braids with beads, and my own history of wanting braids and beads when I was young, and those beaded curtains people used to put up in the 1970s," he explained to Rujeko Hockley during an interview for the Studio Museum in Harlem. Newkirk found his initial experiments with pony beads to be unfulfilling, however, and abandoned the materials for several years. After his stint at Skowhegan, he spent years teaching art classes at a high school in South Central Los Angeles whose student body was heavily Latino and black. That experience helped inspire Newkirk to reflect on the subject of race in his future works. His students "were brilliant," he explained to the writer for *Vibe*, "and they tend to be dismissed."

In 1999 Newkirk's work was displayed publicly in his first solo exhibition, Midnight Son, at the Rosamund Felsen Gallery in Santa Monica. That show saw the appearance of his first beaded-curtain work, *Jubilee*. For the curtain Newkirk placed red, yellow, and orange beads against a blue-beaded background to create an image of a wall of fire; the piece alludes to the fires that raged in Los Angeles in 1992, during the riots that followed the acquittal of the police officers charged with beating an African-American, Rodney King. Commenting on the tedious process of arranging beads, Newkirk explained to Hockley, "The process isn't about mechanical production, it's about labor intensity and the beads going through someone's hands. This goes back to the actual labor of braids and hair. I'm thinking about watching my sister getting her hair done on Saturday mornings growing up, and the time and energy involved in that process. It's all related." Newkirk also displayed one of his early sculptures, *Legacy*, a circular work comprising nine Afro combs, each one six feet two inches tall (Newkirk's height). Thorson wrote, "The formation reads on the one hand as a giant crown, on the other as a circle of abstracted humans. It is up to the viewer to decide whether the enclosure represents a jail of sorts or a ring of protection against outside forces." The following year his work was displayed in another solo show at the Project in New York.

Newkirk first gained critical notice in the 2001 group exhibition Freestyle at the Studio Museum in Harlem. In addition to his pony-bead curtains, he debuted another of his trademark works: *All Over*, a life-size silhouette of a police helicopter, painted on a wall with black hair pomade. Newkirk told David Ramsey for the Syracuse, New York, *Post-Standard* (February 17, 2002) about his use of pomade, which was a common household item during his youth, that "it's a lot about the smell of it and memory." Newkirk has credited a passage from Paul Beatty's 1997 novel *The White Boy Shuffle* as his inspiration for the work; in the novel, the narrator describes a police helicopter searching for a suspect in a black neighborhood. Sarah Valdez wrote for *Art in America* (September 1, 2001) about the painting, "It's mean-looking, gloppy, solid-colored and shiny, rendered a little rough around the edges. The piece requires explanatory text (which appears on a wall panel) to be viewed as more than a gigantic aircraft. Its components assimilated, however, an epiphany might sink in: what to some is an unusually convenient means of transport is, to others, a preying 'ghetto bird.' Or perhaps it's not any realization at all, but acknowledgement of a fact of life." She added, "By monumentalizing this airborne threat to young inner-city dwelling black men (be they criminal or not), Newkirk imbues an infuriating situation with the richness of personal memory. But it's not to evoke pity. The ephemerality of *All Over* . . . bespeaks a recklessness reminiscent of a Freudian acting out—a smearing of [excrement] on a wall, making a sticky mess that someone will have to clean up later. Newkirk makes his point in an unreasonable manner that suits his topic and is appealing." The Freestyle show also featured the work of 27 other African-Americans; through it, Newkirk became affiliated with a new "post-black" movement in art, which differed from previous African-American artistic movements by stressing its prac-

titioners' freedom to create work without an overt thematic or stylistic preoccupation with race. The Studio Museum's curator, Thelma Golden, who coined the phrase "post-black" art, explained in the Freestyle exhibition catalog that its representative works "embrace the dichotomies of high and low, inside and outside, tradition and innovation, with a great ease and facility." In a review of the show, Jerry Saltz wrote for the *Village Voice* (May 22, 2001), "Freestyle is stylistically free, hardcore without being hard-line." Newkirk said to Jori Finkel about himself and a group of other "post-black" artists (Arceneaux, McMillan, and Bradford), "We're all friends, and we all support each other in as many ways as possible. We hang out together. If one of us has an opening, everyone will be there. As artists of color, we all face the same obstacles, so we have been able to band together."

Newkirk's work was included in seven additional group exhibitions as well as two solo shows in 2001. In an exhibition at the Bronx Museum, titled One Planet Under a Groove: Hip Hop and Contemporary Art, he satirized hip-hop culture's fascination with the terms/concepts "ice" and "bling" by using gum wrappers and tinfoil to make representations of diamond-encrusted medallions and tooth coverings. Catherine Fox wrote for the *Atlanta Journal-Constitution* (April 4, 2003), "The piece speaks to hip-hop fashion and materialism and both the pathos and ingenuity of the wannabe, who engineers stuff out of materials at hand." The following year Newkirk's work appeared in 10 group shows, including one in his hometown of Cortland, at the Dowd Fine Arts Gallery at the State University of New York (SUNY). For that exhibit, titled Beyond Stereotype, Newkirk placed in a room four giant snowflakes made from pigmented and solidified hair pomade (one nine feet tall, two six feet tall, and one a foot tall). Commenting on the show, he explained to David Ramsey, "Imagine if snow was this big, imagine a big, massive snowflake. It's larger than life, right? I'm trying to show how snow is such a daily part of our winter existence in Central New York. I'm just trying to amplify the snow." He also said that "the context of this black guy making snowflakes out of pomade" made the work "a little bit" about race, though he added, "I'm not trying to teach a lesson or anything. I'm just trying to look at what it's like to grow up in Central New York." In another show, titled Gene(sis): Contemporary Art Explores Human Genomics, at the Henry Art Gallery in Seattle, he constructed a molecular diagram made up of tiny basketballs to confront the notion that tall black males have genetically based skills that make them good at basketball. (Despite his height, he reportedly hates the sport.) Also in 2002 Newkirk had his work represented in three solo shows, among them an exhibit at the James Van Damme Gallery, in Brussels, Belgium, and another at Johnson County Community College, in Overland Park, Kansas. For the latter he showcased several pony-beaded cityscapes, including one inspired by his former high-school students, titled *Nowhere*, which recreated the smoggy skyline of Los Angeles with shiny brown beads.

Newkirk's work was represented in five solo shows and eight group shows in 2003 and in two solo and six group shows the following year. During that time most of Newkirk's mixed-media work involved an examination of his growing up in Cortland and what he found to be the threatening aspects of "whiteness." For solo exhibitions at the Project in New York and Los Angeles and at the Fabric Workshop and Museum in Philadelphia, Pennsylvania, he created winter landscapes that featured white sharks made of fiberglass (*Win Slow*, 2003), white neon icicles (*Maybury*, 2003), and encaustic white inlays (*Tully*, 2003). One photograph featured at all three shows, titled *Haywood* (2002), depicts Newkirk standing naked in a winter setting, his dark skin juxtaposed against an overwhelmingly white background. Commenting on the piece in a review of his show at the Project in Los Angeles, Christopher Miles wrote for *Artforum International* (January 1, 2004), "Standing naked against a wintry landscape, the figure became a screen for the projection of identities—beast, bigfoot, manimal, specter, even, to use a word Newkirk's work encourages one to use in all its dangerousness, spook. It's this kind of insightfulness and incitefulness to open-ended and uncomfortable readings and associations that reveals Newkirk to be a shrewd negotiator of identity politics—a canny, latter-generation practitioner deeply interested in the problematics of allusion and capable of asking viewers to deal directly with questions of color as well as transparency, opacity, sharpness, crystallization, violence, consumption, internalization, purity, shape, symbol, silhouette, and profile." In a critique of Newkirk's show at the Project in New York, Derek Conrad Murray, writing for *Art in America* (November 1, 2003), observed, "The exhibition read like a personal investigation into the artist's relationship with whiteness. Newkirk's metaphoric use of the shark warns against the peril lurking beneath white's beauty and allure. Clearly, the artist was engaged in a search for compelling forms and symbols that communicate experiences of alterity. In this successful foray into a fresh and experimental visual language, Newkirk tapped into a greater need for a fully articulated voice of postblackness." Discussing the elements uniting his works, Newkirk explained to Hockley, "People don't always remember or think of black people living in the country. So my work, in all its various manifestations, is maybe linked by this desire to talk about the black body in a way that hasn't been addressed, in places that haven't been addressed. It's a direct response to the urbanization of the black body, the reduction of the spaces where black bodies are seen to exist. It's a way to see myself in the art world and the larger world."

In December 2004 Newkirk became the third recipient of the prestigious William H. Johnson Prize, which came with an award of $25,000. (Named for an artist who won widespread acclaim for his depictions of African-American daily life in the early 20th century, the award is given annually to an emerging black artist.) Newkirk took part in three solo shows and four group shows in 2005. In one of the solo shows, at Locust Projects in Miami, he debuted his first video, the five-minute *Bixel*, which "features the tall, thin Mr. Newkirk dancing with wonderful, campily wild grace across a verdant lawn. Wearing a silver foil loin cloth and occasionally consuming silver glitter, he conjures, and sends up, drag, Isadora Duncan, peyote ritual, colonial intrusion and, finally, hunting; the effect is alternately zany, unsettling and scary," as Roberta Smith noted for the *New York Times* (March 17, 2006), calling *Bixel* a "knockout video debut." At another solo show, at the Project in New York, Newkirk included a photograph of himself called *Juke*, which shows him reclining on a grassy area in a suit and tie, leaving the viewer to decide whether he is a relaxing office worker or the prospective victim of an impending assault. Smith explained, "Look up 'Juke' on Wikipedia, and you'll find references to eugenics, football, stabbing and the first harmonica instrumental to become an R&B hit, which all seem vaguely pertinent."

In 2006 Newkirk's work was displayed at two solo and five group shows at sites including galleries in London, England, and Senegal, in West Africa; the Zacheta National Gallery of Art, in Poland; and the Arts Center in Sheboygan, Wisconsin. For that year's Whitney Biennial, in New York, titled Day for Night, he exhibited the four-sided pony-bead painting/sculpture *Glint*, in which nighttime scenes of urban and suburban landscapes were juxtaposed against one another to critique racial stereotypes. Newkirk remained busy in 2007, with one solo show and five group exhibitions. The solo show, Kori Newkirk: 1997–2007, at the Studio Museum in Harlem, is a 10-year survey of Newkirk's work. In addition to his trademark pony-bead curtains and hair-pomade murals, Newkirk debuted another video at the exhibit, *Titan*, which showed him running down a street with intravenous drips laced with neon tubes attached to his body, leading Karen Rosenberg to write for the *New York Times* (November 16, 2007), "'Post-black' seems less relevant as a description than 'extraterrestrial.'" In 2008 the same solo show was mounted at the Pasadena Museum of California Art. Also in 2008 Newkirk's work was included in two group exhibitions: Depletion, at the Tel Aviv Museum of Art, in Israel, and Southern Exposure, at the Museum of Contemporary Art in Sydney, Australia.

Newkirk currently works in a studio in Los Angeles. While working, he enjoys listening to a variety of music, including songs by Mary J. Blige, Sam Cooke, the Notorious B.I.G., Nina Simone, and Fishbone.

—C.C.

Suggested Reading: *Artforum International* p160 Jan. 1, 2004; *Art in America* p134+ Sep. 1, 2001, p160 Nov. 1, 2003; *Kansas City Star* J p1+ May 26, 2002; *New York Times* Mar. 17, 2006, June 10, 2007, Nov. 16, 2007; *Surface Design Journal* Fall 2006; (Syracuse, New York) *Post-Standard* p16+ Feb. 17, 2002; *Village Voice* p51+ May 22, 2001

Selected Works: *Jubilee*, 1999; *Legacy*, 1999; *All Over*, 2001; Beyond Stereotype (exhibit), 2001; *Nowhere*, 2002; *Haywood*, 2002; *Win Slow*, 2003; *Maybury*, 2003; *Tully*, 2003; *Bixel*, 2005; *Juke*, 2005; *Titan*, 2007

Stephen Voss, courtesy of National Public Radio

Norris, Michele

(MEE-shel)

Sep. 7, 1961– Radio journalist; co-host of All Things Considered

Address: National Public Radio, 635 Massachusetts Ave., N.W., Washington, DC 20001

As an engineering student at the University of Wisconsin, Michele Norris spent more time analyzing the wording of the problems she tackled than solving them. "Engineering was interesting, but it was a diversion," Norris, who abandoned science en route to becoming a successful print, television, and radio journalist, said in a 2003 interview with the Web site JournalismJobs.com. "Although it did help me because it teaches you to think logically.

So it wasn't a waste of time. But I've always been interested in writing and storytelling and ultimately found my way to my calling."

In December 2002 Norris became a host of the long-running National Public Radio (NPR) afternoon program *All Things Considered*, which attracts some 12 million listeners each day; her current co-hosts are Melissa Block and Robert Siegel. The first black anchor in the show's history, Norris came to radio after spending several years writing for major newspapers, including the *Los Angeles Times* and the *Washington Post*, and almost a decade as a correspondent for ABC news. As a print and television journalist, Norris often covered education, poverty, and inner-city issues, and while she has said that she enjoys reporting on those topics, one of the things that drew her to NPR was the prospect of exploring a wider variety of subjects. "The show is incredibly elastic, which is part of its success," Norris told Steve Carney for the *Los Angeles Times* (October 11, 2002). "They cover the news and then go beyond that." She explained to Carney that when she listens to the show on her car radio, "they bring all of these interesting people in my life and place them in the passenger seat next to me on the way home."

The daughter of Belvin and Betty Norris, both postal workers, Michele Norris was born on September 7, 1961 in Minneapolis, Minnesota. Her family made a point of keeping up with current events. "I grew up in a household where my parents devoured the papers and the evening news and instructed their children to do the same, up to quizzes at the dinner table," Norris told Raoul V. Mowatt for the *Chicago Tribune* (December 4, 2002). In an interview with the Web site Modern-Mom.com, Norris described her family as "loud and tight-knit." "I never had to guess at my parents' feelings about me," she said. "They placed high expectations on our shoulders but then they surrounded us with love and support and they were generous with the gift of time. They pushed us to aim high and do our best, and they were there when we stumbled or when we didn't know if we had what it takes."

Norris wrote for the student newspaper at Washburn High School, in Minneapolis, but did not initially set out to be a reporter. She enrolled in the Inroads program, a national initiative aimed at preparing minority students for careers in math and science, and after high school she decided to study electrical engineering at the University of Wisconsin. "It seemed like a good career choice at 17," she told Jon Tevlin for the Minneapolis *Star Tribune* (May 7, 2006). Norris stuck with engineering for more than three years before switching to journalism. "I completely freaked my parents out," she told Tevlin. "Engineers made things and changed the world in tangible ways." Despite their surprise, Norris's parents came to support her decision. She transferred to the University of Minnesota and—by working nearly full-time at a local restaurant and writing for the *Minnesota Daily*—managed to pay for another three years of school. She thought she would graduate in 1985 but then found out that she was several language credits short of earning a diploma. Rather than staying in Minnesota to finish her schooling, she accepted an internship at the *Los Angeles Times*. (The University of Minnesota gave her a diploma in 2005.) During her college years Norris had lived with Lizz Winstead, a comedian who went on to create the Comedy Central cable-TV program *The Daily Show*. Winstead, who was looking for her show-business break, recorded jokes on their answering machine, and as Norris began applying for journalism jobs, prospective employers sometimes called and heard comedy routines.

While interning at the San Diego bureau of the *Los Angeles Times*, Norris struggled to please a demanding editor, who often made her redo stories several times. Foreshadowing the kind of reporting that later became her trademark, her first assignment was to examine why essential goods were more expensive in poor neighborhoods than in rich ones. "I left with fewer clips than the other interns, but my editors pushed me to do deeper stories, and I got the job," she told Tevlin, explaining how she came to work at the paper full-time.

Norris moved on to the *Chicago Tribune* before taking a job with the *Washington Post*, where she won high praise for an in-depth series about a six-year-old boy living in a crack house. (The work earned her a Livingston Award, given to the best journalists under the age of 35.) Following the story meant "lots of soul searching conversations with my editors," Norris told Susan Paterno for *American Journalism Review* (March 1998), explaining some of the moral challenges that came with the two-month assignment. "We wanted to maintain journalistic integrity, but we bent the rules in other ways. We kept [the boy] out of harm's way, and we gave him food so he wouldn't get hungry." "No mother ever gave birth to a journalist," Norris added. "You're a human first. You bring your humanity to your story." The series of articles was reprinted in *Ourselves Among Others*, a book that also included essays by the former South African president Nelson Mandela and the writer Gabriel García Márquez.

While living in Washington, D.C., Norris met her future husband, Broderick Johnson, a lawyer in President Bill Clinton's administration. (He would later serve as a senior adviser to the presidential candidate John Kerry.) After interviewing Johnson in the course of preparing a story, she invited him to a party where guests were playing board games; during a round of Scattergories, Norris and Johnson discovered that they were the only two people in the room who had heard of the English rock band Traffic. "I looked at him and said, 'I'm marrying that man,'" she told Tevlin.

Television producers from NBC had approached Norris in 1989, after hearing her speak at the Livingston Award ceremony. Later, ABC officials also contacted her, and in 1993 Norris, finally persuad-

ed, left the *Washington Post* to work for the latter network. "I realized I had done a lot of the work I wanted to do in print and here was an opportunity to build some new skills," she told Journalism-Jobs.com. While the move from print to television was a gamble, Norris had something of a safety net. "The folks at the *Washington Post* were extremely gracious and the publisher, Don Graham, [said] if you want to go and check this out—we'd hate for you to leave—but if you go there and you hate it or they hate you, the first call you make is to me and come back home." Norris was a regular contributor to the "Closer Look" segment on ABC's *World News Tonight*, hosted by Peter Jennings. "Switching to TV I was jumping into the deep end," Norris told Tevlin. "People were saying, 'They are expecting you to fail.' Well, I was thankfully too naïve to know that. I had to put my ego in my purse every day and just be a student. It's a tough, tough business."

In 1999 Norris gave birth to a daughter, Aja, who was named for a song by the rock band Steely Dan. When Aja was 18 weeks old, Norris discovered that she was pregnant for a second time. Learning of her second pregnancy, network executives began talking about relieving her of some of her duties, but Jennings and his editor talked them out of it. "They said, 'Norris has been even more productive through her first pregnancy and since she came back. Let's give her the benefit of the doubt here and expect that she can handle this. She hasn't given us any reason to think otherwise,'" Norris told Mark Lasswell for *Broadcasting & Cable* (August 15, 2005). "Peter could have remained silent or seconded their concern. I [myself] wondered if I would be able to handle it. But to have the man with the name on the broadcast, the franchise, say, 'Let's not worry unless she gives us reason to worry' meant a tremendous amount." She later gave birth to a son, Norris.

In 2002, needing a new host for *All Things Considered*, NPR producers approached Norris, who had won a Peabody Award and an Emmy Award for her role in ABC's coverage of the September 11, 2001 terrorist attacks. "The timing wasn't great," Norris told JournalismJobs.com. "I was under contract and I had a great job that I loved. But it was a special opportunity and they were fairly persistent." Her children were also a factor: working from NPR headquarters in Washington, D.C., would mean fewer trips into the field. "It was one of those rare opportunities, in which you could take a gigantic step forward in your career without taking a concomitant step away from your family."

Norris had long been a fan of *All Things Considered*. "After listening to the show almost all my adult life, realizing I'm going to be part of that daily conversation with 12 million listeners is the most exciting part of my journalism career," she told Mowatt. Norris was intrigued by the possibility of devoting more time and attention to each story. "When I first went into television, I was doing six-minute features," she told Drew Lindsay for the

Washingtonian (March 2007). "Then they were four-minute features, then two minutes. NPR was a place where you had a chance to get to the fourth question. It was a place where people didn't leave the heart of their story in their notebook at the end of the day." She also welcomed the chance to report on a wider array of topics. "You're talking to authors, musicians, and thinkers," she told Clea Simon for the *Boston Globe* (October 24, 2002). "You hear from commentators, and they're not always people who have degrees or pose with the president. They're people who have unique views."

Norris's first pieces for NPR included a story on standardized testing in Massachusetts schools, a profile of the singer Jubilant Sykes, and a look at how comedians help us examine race relations in the U.S. She told JournalismJobs.com that the transition from television to radio was somewhat easier than the one from newspapers to television had been. "It's not to say anything disparaging about ABC because they really had a well thought-out plan for that transition. But I don't think I've ever received the kind of institutional support for anything I've done like I have at NPR. They have really thought this through and anticipated the training I would need to make a quick transition." Norris said that the most difficult thing about the job was adjusting to the show's schedule: *All Things Considered* airs at 4 p.m. "It is an extremely early deadline," she told JournalismJobs.com. "Our morning meeting is at ten. Basically, we have a very compressed day. We produce two hours of live programming between 11 and four o'clock. Do the math. Every day is a miracle on the order of loaves and fishes. And we do it with a teeny staff."

Bruce Drake, NPR's vice president for news and information, said that he did not choose Norris simply for her ability to report on difficult social issues. "Her range is broad," he told Carney. "She's comfortable reporting on everything from Washington politics to popular culture." Drake also said that Norris's race was not a major factor in her hiring. "We're very pleased that Michele will bring diversity to the show, but it's not something that would drive a decision like this," he said. Norris told Carney that she was proud to provide a black voice in the media: "Growing up, I know what it's like to turn on the TV and not always see people who look like you."

In the days after Hurricane Katrina, which devastated much of the Gulf Coast in late August 2005, Norris met Sharon White, a New Orleans woman who had been evacuated to a shelter in Baton Rouge. Norris followed White's story for over a year, filing a series of reports tracing her progress. She also presented stories on New Orleans residents who refused to leave their homes and search-and-rescue missions conducted by the Texas National Guard. In August 2006 the National Association of Black Journalists honored Norris for her reporting on Hurricane Katrina.

Norris has said that radio allows her to use writing and storytelling skills she developed in print journalism and enhance her stories with sound. "There's something incredibly powerful about the intimacy of radio and the way that it plays on the listener's imagination," she told Journalism-Jobs.com. "A soldier knocks on someone's door to deliver bad news. You can describe that in print. You can show that in television. But somehow when you combine the descriptive powers and the ambient sound that they use so well here at NPR to take the listener to that place, it's a powerful medium." Norris has said that she receives regular feedback from NPR listeners, who tend to be passionate about the programming. "I meet someone, and after they figure out what I do, they tell me how much NPR means to them," she told Tim Feran for the *Columbus (Ohio) Dispatch* (June 19, 2006). "I never heard that with ABC. I never heard ABC talked about by viewers in such reverential terms. I think, if we went off the air tomorrow, people would march in the streets."

Gwen Ifill, a Public Broadcasting System correspondent, has described Norris's reporting style as "humane." "She can see beyond the story to the human element almost instantly," Ifill told Tevlin. "As a listener, you feel like you are eavesdropping on a private conversation, even when it's with an important newsmaker." Ifill, also a personal friend of Norris's, continued, "If you are in trouble, she'll talk you down off the ledge. I know she's going to give me the best advice, even if it's something I don't want to hear." In her free time Norris enjoys gardening; listening to a wide variety of music, including jazz and indie rock; and cooking for her husband and children. She admitted to Modern-Mom.com that juggling career and family can be "like juggling chainsaws . . . while riding a skateboard . . . during a tornado." She joked, "That old adage about having your cake and eating it too? It should come with a warning about indigestion."

—K.J.P.

Suggested Reading: *Boston Globe* C p14 Oct. 23, 2002; *Broadcasting & Cable* p12 Aug. 15, 2005; *Chicago Tribune* C p1 Dec. 4, 2002; *Columbus (Ohio) Dispatch* B p1 June 19, 2006; *Los Angeles Times* p33 Oct. 11, 2002; (Minneapolis) *Star Tribune* E p1 May 7, 2006; *Washingtonian* p76 Mar. 2007

Jacques Demarthon/AFP/Getty Images

Nouvel, Jean

(noo-VEL, zhahn)

Aug. 12, 1945– French architect

Address: Ateliers Jean Nouvel, 10 Cité d'Angoulême, 75011 Paris, France

"Every architecture is an opportunity to create what I call the missing pieces of the puzzle," Jean Nouvel said in an interview with Arthur Lubow for the *New York Times Magazine* (April 6, 2008). "To find how you can create more poetry with the place where you are and the program you have. You research what will be the most emotional, the most perfect, the most natural." Nouvel, a French architect, is known not for any single aesthetic sensibility but for his ability to tailor his projects to their surroundings; he begins the process of designing buildings not by drawing but by articulating an idea for relating a structure to its cultural environment. He has identified himself as a hedonist, whose ultimate aim is to create buildings that "give pleasure to other people," as he told Lubow. "What I like is the poétique of the situation." In a career that has spanned three decades, Nouvel has designed more than 200 major structures all over the world, including high-rise residential and office buildings, cultural centers, museums, and theaters. While his work does not reflect a signature style, Nouvel has been recognized for his playful use of transparency, light, and reflection as well as his elegant use of modern technology. In March 2008 Nouvel was honored with the Pritzker Prize, widely considered the field's most prestigious award. The award committee noted, "[Nouvel's]

inquisitive and agile mind propels him to take risks in each of his projects, which, regardless of varying degrees of success, have greatly expanded the vocabulary of contemporary architecture."

The son of high-school teachers, Jean Nouvel was born on August 12, 1945 in the town of Fumel, in southwestern France. As a young man he wanted to be a painter, but his parents urged him to pursue a career that would bring him a stable living, such as mathematics or science. As a compromise, Nouvel decided to study architecture. He enrolled at the renowned French art academy L'école des Beaux Arts, in the city of Bordeaux, in 1964. The next year he failed the entrance examination for architecture school in Bordeaux. When he retook the test in Paris the following year, 1966, his scores put him in first place. That distinction allowed him, while he was still a student at Paris's L'École Nationale Superieure des Beaux Arts, to take a job as an assistant to two renowned thinkers, the architect Claude Parent and the cultural theorist Paul Virilio, who together ran an experimental architecture firm; that experience helped form his artistic perspective. Nouvel's time in school also coincided with the left-wing student strikes and protests that erupted in France in 1968, events that represented a shift in French values from conservatism to progressivism. Perhaps as a result of those influences, Nouvel rebelled against the teachings of the Beaux Arts school, which "valued the drawing of beautiful details over research and critique," as Lubow put it. Once, when asked to design a children's library for his thesis presentation, Nouvel instead wrote an analysis of drawings completed by French children who had been asked what a library looks like. Like many of his attempts at rebellion, that one met with resistance; his thesis was rejected.

Around that time, Parent and Virilio made Nouvel a project manager for an 80-unit apartment complex, despite his lack of experience. "I knew nothing, and the construction manager understood I knew nothing," he told Lubow, but the experience was valuable. In 1970, two years before Nouvel graduated with a degree in architecture, he opened his own architecture office with François Seigneur. Nouvel secured many of his early commissions, mostly for residential units in provincial France, from his former employers. Parent and Virilio also helped him become the architect for the Paris Biennial; he designed the art exhibits for 15 years and gained important contacts throughout the art and theater worlds. From 1972 to 1984 Nouvel partnered at different times with Gilbert Lezenes, Jean-François Guyot, and Pierre Soria. In 1976 he co-founded the French architecture movement known as Mars 1976, and in 1978 he helped establish the French architectural union Syndicat de l'Architecture.

The project that marked Nouvel's international breakthrough is the Institut du Monde Arabe (IMA), or the Arab World Institute. Commissioned by French president François Mitterrand in the

1980s and completed in 1987, the building is a cultural center, museum, and library, built to foster knowledge of Arab culture. It sits along the Seine River, between the Ile Saint-Louis and the campus of Jussieu University. Its two main façades differ greatly from one another. Aligned with the towers of the Notre Dame Cathedral, the northern façade contains an etching of a computer-generated image of the skyline across the river, made of fritted glass—ceramic-based paint screenprinted onto glass. For the building's south façade, its most notable feature, Nouvel designed a wall made up of an intricate network of mechanical aluminum diaphragms, which are controlled by a computer and automatically open and close according to the day's temperature and brightness, to simulate the natural lighting in the Middle East. The network of diaphragms resembles a moucharabieh, or a Middle Eastern latticework screen. "The vocation of the building was to talk about Arab culture," Nouvel explained to Lubow. "If it is a homage, then it has to use the two main aspects of Arab architecture, geometry and light." Passing through the unmarked entrance, a visitor discovers high ceilings, a long stairway, and several glass elevators. The IMA was awarded the Aga Khan Award for Architecture, which honors architectural concepts that address the needs of Islamic communities, as well as a Silver Medal from the French Academy of Architecture.

In 1989 Nouvel brought in a partner, Emmanuel Cattani, and his firm expanded to about 100 people. Over the next several years, Nouvel designed a number of major projects. In the 1980s he had won a commission to remodel the opera house in Lyons, France, originally constructed in 1831, a project that imposed some difficult constraints; the city wanted to expand the theater and improve its acoustics but did not want to do away with the old building, particularly its ornate façade. Nouvel designed an entirely new theater encased within the historic "shell" of the original structure. He increased the space by digging a deep basement and building a steel and glass barrel vault on top of the building, which lights up at night. The completed project, named Opera Nouvel, was controversial, due to both its expense (the equivalent of more than $89 million) and the complications that delayed its opening by four years. Nonetheless, the overall effect of the design—a dramatic juxtaposition of the baroque and the modern—was well received. The design earned Nouvel a Silver Medal and has become a vibrant fixture of the Lyons nightscape since its opening, in 1994.

In a project completed the same year, an art museum called the Fondation Cartier (Foundation Center), in the Montparnasse district of Paris, Nouvel showed his skill at using light, reflection, and transparency to play with people's visual perceptions. The building's exterior is made up of a series of overlapping panes of glass, separating the interior garden from the street, with no visible frame. Writing for the London *Guardian* (May 21, 2001),

Jonathan Glancey described the effect of Nouvel's design: "As discreet as a fine French scent, this filigree museum and gallery performs another of Nouvel's disappearing tricks: in some lights and from some angles, it seems barely there. The building is almost transparent, rising up gently behind a sequence of screens that enjoyably confuse our notion of where the building begins and ends, of what is substantial and what is simply a trick of light." A contrast to the ponderous structures being erected in Paris during that time, the Fondation Cartier is considered a masterpiece of 20th-century architecture.

Nouvel has designed a number of large towers, each with a style that relates to its location. For the Dentsu Tower, completed in 1998 in Tokyo, Japan, Nouvel created a feeling of lightness throughout the building, despite its tremendous size. (The building, one million square feet, stands 60 stories high.) He accomplished that in part by covering the entire façade with thousands of rectangles of reflective fritted glass. "By giving the tower a sweeping crescent shape and a glass skin with a hundred different permutations of grey, the structure completely vanishes," Deyan Sudjic wrote for the London *Observer* (March 10, 2002). "The building appears to float entirely weightless, a limpid beautiful presence on the skyline." On the inside, Nouvel maintained the sense of airiness by stacking atria and using stainless steel surfaces that reflect the sky. Nouvel used a different aesthetic for the Torre Agbar (Agbar Tower), a bullet-shaped, 38-story structure that houses the Agbar water company, completed in 2005 in Barcelona, Spain. The tower's exterior has a layer of aluminum in earth tones and a complex grid of clear or multicolored, translucent panels of blue, yellow, green, orange, fuchsia, and red—colors that are drawn from the nearby Montserrat mountain range. As the panels open and close like blinds, in a pattern controlled by a computer, the reflection of the sun creates the illusion of a trickling fountain. LED (light-emitting diode) lights illuminate the tower at night. The tower also features visual allusions to the work of the city's most famous architect, Antoni Gaudi, who used a similar parabolic shape and "Modernismo" decorations in his designs.

Nouvel's plans for the yet-to-be-built Tour Sans Fins (Tower Without Ends) have come to be seen as representing the peak of the architect's imaginative powers. Commissioned in 1989, the tower was to be located in Paris, and at a quarter-mile in height, it would have been Europe's tallest building. With its base concealed in a crater, the tower was designed to appear "ethereal" as it stretched toward the sky. The lower floors would have been made of granite, which would have transitioned to aluminum, then stainless steel, and then glass, so that the top would have disappeared into the clouds. With a base 138 feet in diameter, the building would have been the world's thinnest skyscraper. Plans for the tower were halted during the real-estate slump of the 1990s, when Nouvel's firm sank into bankruptcy; the Tour Sans Fins nonetheless remains one of Nouvel's most iconic designs.

"That was a very hard period for me," Nouvel told Lubow of the 1990s. "I was not in a very confident position. I had a partner working with me who never told me we were in trouble, and in three months we were done." For a decade beginning in 1994, when he reconstituted his firm with Michel Pelissie, under the name Ateliers Jean Nouvel, the architect was a salaried employee while he repaid his personal debts and back taxes. Nouvel's friends have said that he is generally unconcerned about matters of finance. "I've never met anybody who cares less about money," his friend Gilbert Brownstone told Lubow. "He loves Italian food and great wine. As long as he has that, he can't be bothered."

Since the firm's reemergence, business has been steady, and Nouvel's international reputation has continued to grow. In 2001 Nouvel received his first major commission in the U.S.: the design for the new Guthrie Theater, in Minneapolis, Minnesota. Looking to connect the theater to its geographical context, Nouvel designed the building with an industrial exterior that resembles nearby silos and flour mills. He covered the exterior in dark blue steel, imprinted with images from past Guthrie productions, which appear to hover as the sun goes down, as if they were "ghosts" on the walls, as Nouvel explained to Richard Lacayo for *Time* (June 19, 2006). Nouvel also endeavored to relate the theater to the Mississippi River, which it faces on the west. Though he was provided with a 900-foot-long site on which to build, Nouvel used only the site's western end, stacking the theater's three stages to create an enormous 10-story building. The theater lobbies are elevated, so that people who are mingling before or after a show have picturesque views of the river and the city across the water. Perhaps the building's most magnificent structure is the "lobby bridge," a covered outdoor boardwalk that juts out 178 feet from the theater, 60 feet over the city's West River Parkway, toward the river. "I cannot imagine this building in Paris or in New York City," Nouvel told Mary Abbe for the Minneapolis *Star Tribune* (March 31, 2008). "It would be ridiculous. It is completely linked to the specifics of the program, the situation, the dialogue with the existing buildings and the river."

Like many of Nouvel's buildings, the Guthrie Theater was not universally appreciated; many members of the Minneapolis community found the building's design to be bleak, bulky, and lacking the warmth and beauty found in more traditional theaters. Nouvel took another risk with the Musée du quai Branly (Quai Branly Museum), commissioned by the then–president of France, Jacques Chirac, in 1996 to house works representing cultures worldwide. The project itself was controversial, as it involved dismantling many historical collections of non-European cultural artifacts that had formerly been on display in anthropological museums. With its bold forms, bright colors, and jungle-like textures, the Musée du quai Branly,

completed in 2006, struck a stark contrast to the more neutral environments of most cultural exhibits. The entrance to the exhibition area is a dark, tunnel-like ramp, suggestive of a dim pathway into a forest. In the exhibit area light is restricted with wood-and-glass walls imprinted with images of jungle foliage, with spotlights to illuminate the artifacts, giving the room a mysterious air. Continents are represented with different shades of linoleum—red, terra-cotta, indigo, and ocher—while "islands" float above the main exhibition level. The building's exterior is equally bold; nearly 30 large boxes protrude haphazardly from the northern façade, while another large, elevated, hall-like exhibition space mimics a bend in the Seine River. Nouvel's intention was to remove the artifacts from the typical, "clinical" museum environment and free them from Western interpretations. "It's not an Occidental building," Nouvel told Lubow. "For me it is a world done with colors and shapes linked to an interpretation of Africa and Oceanic and American culture." While much of the public has been delighted by the unusual museum, many anthropologists, museologists, and others have found it to be excessively dramatic and condescending to its content. Michael Kimmelman wrote for the *New York Times* (July 2, 2006), "If the Marx Brothers designed a museum for dark people, they might have come up with the permanent-collection galleries: devised as a spooky jungle, red and black and murky, the objects in it chosen and arranged with hardly any discernible logic, the place is briefly thrilling, as spectacle, but brow-slappingly wrongheaded."

In recent years Nouvel has begun to make his mark with projects in New York City. Completed in 2007 in the SoHo neighborhood of the borough of Manhattan, Nouvel's 15-story luxury apartment building at 40 Mercer Street makes use of glass in innovative ways. The building is curtained in sleek, insulated glass walls, which are either transparent or in shades of red or blue. Some of the walls can slide open. The interior contains details, such as wood-and-stainless-steel kitchens and back-painted glass-tile bathrooms, that make reference to the historic architecture of the surrounding neighborhood. Another project, a 23-story luxury-apartment complex in Manhattan's West Chelsea neighborhood, is expected to be completed in 2008. The complex will feature panels of glass that reach from floor to ceiling on each apartment's west and south sides, which face the Hudson River. "This kind of glass housing tells you about the kind of democracy and transparency that all of our society should have," Rick Bell, the executive director of the New York chapter of the American Institute of Architects, told David Freelander for the *New York Sun* (April 5, 2007). "The building is not walling itself off from the city. . . . [Nouvel's] use of light and glass reflects and refracts the life of the city going on around it." In 2006 Nouvel was selected by the Hines real-estate firm to expand New York's Museum of Modern Art (MoMA). Inspired by the artist Hugh Ferriss's moody late-1920s renderings of the cityscape, which to Nouvel evoked what Lubow called "classic New York," he designed a thin, twisting, 75-story skyscraper, which, when completed, will include not only an expansion of MoMA's galleries but also a luxury hotel and residential condominiums.

Nouvel's firm, which today employs some 140 people in offices in Europe and New York City, is currently working on more than 40 projects in 13 countries. In addition to the Pritzker Prize, Nouvel has received many other honors, among them the Chevalier Ordre de Merit (1987), the Grand Prix National d'Architecture (1987), the Commandeur des Ordre des Artes et des Lettres (1997), the Gold Medal from the French Academy of Architecture (1998), the Golden Lion from the 7th International Architecture Exhibition, Venice Biennale (2000), the Royal Gold Medal from the Royal Institute of British Architects (2001), the Wolf Foundation Prize in the Arts (2005), and the Arnold W. Brunner Memorial Prize in Architecture (2006).

Lubow described Nouvel as "a bulky man with an enormous shaved head, an intense gaze, bushy black eyebrows and an all-black wardrobe." The architect often holds his meetings over long meals and otherwise develops his ideas away from the office, while swimming, vacationing, or lying in his bed—where he often remains until mid-morning. "When you have to think a lot, find a vocabulary, the feeling, the symbols, you can only do that alone . . . ," Nouvel told an interviewer for *Building Design* (May 7, 2004). "Of course, the bed is a very comfortable place, and clearly when I can do that in the morning, it is good, because my brain is clearer." Nouvel has been married and divorced twice. With his first wife, the filmmaker Odile Fillion, he has two grown sons, Bertrand, a computer scientist, and Pierre, a director, producer, and set designer at Factoid, Pierre's own theater. With his second wife, Catherine Richard, he has a teenage daughter, Sarah. He lives in Paris with Mia Hagg, a Swedish architect.

—M.E.R.

Suggested Reading: jeannouvel.fr; (London) *Guardian* Features p14 May 21, 2001; (London) *Observer* p10 Mar. 10, 2002; (Minneapolis, Minnesota) *Star Tribune* News A p1 Mar. 31, 2008; *New York Times* (on-line) May 17, 1993, July 2, 2006, Apr. 6, 2008; *Time* p58+ June 19, 2006

Selected Works: Arab World Institute, Paris, France, 1987; Opera Nouvel, Lyons, France, 1994; Foundation Center, Paris, France, 1994; Dentsu Tower, Tokyo, Japan, 1998; Agbar Tower, Barcelona Spain, 2005; Guthrie Theater, Minneapolis, Minnesota, 2006; Quai Branly Museum, 2006; 40 Mercer Street Residences, New York, New York, 2007

Obama, Michelle

Jan. 17, 1964– Lawyer; hospital administrator; wife of President-elect Barack Obama

Address: University of Chicago Medical Center, 5841 S. Maryland Ave., Chicago, IL 60637

Michelle Obama, a lawyer and hospital administrator, first stepped onto the national political stage in February 2007, when her husband, Barack, entered the race to become the Democratic nominee in the 2008 presidential election. Toby Harnden wrote for the London *Telegraph* (March 2, 2007, on-line) that her admirers believe the aspiring First Lady combines "the poise of Jackie Kennedy with the brain of Hillary Clinton and the uncomplicated charm of Laura Bush." However, Obama has had her share of detractors as well, in large part because of what Michael Powell and Jodi Kantor described in an article for the *New York Times* (June 18, 2008, on-line) as her "complicated public image." On the campaign trail for her husband, she has exhibited, as Michelle Cottle wrote for the *New Republic* (March 26, 2008), a "famously un-Stepford stump style—the sarcasm, the candor, the compulsion to ignore the cardinal rule of political wifedom by portraying her husband as something less than God-made-flesh—that thrills even as it unnerves, prompting eyebrow-arching and hand-wringing over how sassy is too sassy." Months later, Patrick Healy wrote for the *New York Times* (October 27, 2008), "While some of Senator Barack Obama's advisers once viewed Mrs. Obama as an unpredictable force who sometimes spoke her mind a little too much, she is now regarded within the campaign as a disciplined and effective advocate for her husband. She has also, advisers believe, gone a long way toward addressing her greatest unstated challenge: making more voters comfortable with the idea of a black first lady." For his part, Barack Obama has left no doubt as to his feelings about his wife, whom he has often referred to as the family's "rock." "She's strong and smart and grounded," he told Annette Witherage for the London *Sunday Mail* (June 8, 2008). "She's brutally honest, which is good for keeping my head on straight."

Obama was born Michelle LaVaughn Robinson in Illinois on January 17, 1964 to Marian Robinson, a former secretary, and Fraser Robinson, who worked for Chicago's water department and also served as a volunteer for Democrats at the local level. Obama and her older brother, Craig, were raised in a modest home on the South Side of Chicago, a historically black area. Barack Obama paid tribute to his in-laws in a speech posted on his Web

Emmanuel Dunand/AFP/Getty Images

Michelle Obama

site (June 15, 2007): "They faced what other African-American families faced at the time—both hidden and overt forms of racism that limited their opportunities and required more effort to get ahead. And they faced an additional obstacle. At age 30, Fraser was diagnosed with multiple sclerosis. And yet, every day of his life, even when he had to rely on a walker to get him there, he went to work at the local water filtration plant while Marian stayed home with the children. And on that single salary, Fraser Robinson provided for his family." Obama has described her family as traditional and close-knit. They ate dinner together each evening, played board games, and occasionally went on inexpensive family vacations. Marian encouraged Obama and Craig to study hard and excel in school, and they listened to her advice: Obama was admitted to the competitive Whitney M. Young Magnet High School, where she was treasurer of her class, and Craig won a basketball scholarship to Princeton University, in New Jersey. (He is now a highly regarded basketball coach at Oregon State University.) During her junior year of high school, Obama visited her brother and became determined to join him at Princeton, then widely regarded as among the most conservative and least diverse schools in the Ivy League. In 1981 she did so, as part of a class of more than 1,100—fewer than 100 of whom were black.

Obama has recalled feeling stigmatized many times throughout her years at Princeton. When she was a freshman, for example, her roommate's mother became upset that her daughter had been paired with a black student and asked that the room assignments be changed. Although Obama, who majored in sociology and minored in African-American studies, had friends of all races, social life at Princeton was largely segregated, with most minority students spending their free time at the Third World Center, a facility at which they could participate in seminars, cultural events, and recreational activities. Obama, known for her stylish appearance and large collection of Stevie Wonder albums, soon established herself as a leader in on-campus discussions of race and met with school administrators about the direction of the African-American studies program.

In Obama's senior thesis, "Princeton-Educated Blacks and the Black Community," she examined the effects of a Princeton education on black alumni. Surveying some 90 black Princeton graduates, she discovered that while most of them closely identified with the broader black community as students, after leaving the school they largely abandoned their previous social circles and became increasingly involved with whites. After Barack Obama entered the race for the Democratic presidential nomination, the school initially kept the 96-page thesis from public scrutiny. When it was released, in February 2008, it elicited criticism for what some conservative commentators interpreted as Obama's resentment and anger. She wrote, as quoted on www.politico.com (February 26, 2008): "Predominately White universities like Princeton are socially and academically designed to cater to the needs of the White students comprising the bulk of their enrollments." Drawing on her own experiences, she explained, "As I enter my final year at Princeton, I find myself striving for many of the same goals as my White classmates—acceptance to a prestigious graduate school or a high-paying position in a successful corporation." She continued, "I hoped that [my] findings would help me conclude that despite the high degree of identification with Whites as a result of the educational and occupational path that Black Princeton alumni follow, the alumni would still maintain a certain level of identification with the Black community. However, these findings do not support this possibility."

After graduating with a B.A. degree cum laude from Princeton, in 1985, Obama continued her education at Harvard Law School, in Cambridge, Massachusetts, and earned her J.D. degree in 1988. She then took a job as a junior associate at Sidley Austin, a corporate law firm in Chicago, where she specialized in intellectual-property law. In 1989 she was assigned to mentor Barack Obama, who was working as a summer associate at Sidley Austin. She immediately liked the handsome Harvard student but turned down his many invitations to go out with him because she thought it would be inappropriate for them to date, given their respective positions at the firm. She eventually agreed to get together to have ice cream and see a movie—*Do the Right Thing*, a film by Spike Lee about racial tensions in the New York City neighborhood of Bedford-Stuyvesant. When she accompanied Barack to a meeting of one of the community self-help groups with which he worked, she was inspired by his vision of "the world the way it is and the way it could be," as a reporter for the London *Sunday Times* (June 22, 2008, on-line) wrote in a profile of the couple. That day she "fell in love with him," as she recalled in the film that introduced Barack Obama at the 2008 Democratic National Convention.

In 1991, the year her father died, Michelle Obama decided to leave Sidley Austin to pursue a career in public service. "I looked out my window at my neighborhood and sort of had an epiphany that I had to bring my skills to bear in the place that made me," she told Powell and Kantor. "I wanted to have a career motivated by passion and not just money." Obama was hired as an assistant to Richard Daley, then mayor of Chicago, and subsequently became the city's assistant commissioner of planning and development. In 1992 she and Barack were married by the Reverend Jeremiah Wright at Chicago's Trinity United Church of Christ. (Wright, known for his polarizing oratory, later became an embarrassment to the Obama campaign, and in 2008, despite having been members of the congregation for years, the Obamas severed their ties to their controversial pastor.) The young couple, still saddled with student loans, moved into a small condominium in the Hyde Park section of Chicago, and adorned their walls with inexpensive art from Africa and Hawaii, places that figure in Barack Obama's diverse background.

In 1993 Obama became the founding executive director of the Chicago branch of Public Allies, a training program affiliated with AmeriCorps National Service that helps young adults develop the skills necessary for careers in the public sector. She encouraged discussion and debate among her young charges. "I hate diversity workshops," Obama told Powell and Kantor. "Real change comes from having enough comfort to be really honest and say something very uncomfortable."

In 1996 Obama became the associate dean of student services at the University of Chicago, and her husband—who had been teaching constitutional law at the University of Chicago Law School and practicing civil rights law at a small firm—was elected to the Illinois State Senate, representing the state's 13th District. Two years later Michelle Obama gave birth to the couple's first daughter, Malia Ann. Her husband, meanwhile, was becoming an increasingly popular figure in the state Senate. Reelected in 1998 and 2002, he became known for his ability to generate bipartisan support for legislative reform in such areas as ethics and health care. His senatorial duties led him to spend more and more time away from his family, and, as he wrote in his best-selling book *The Audacity of Hope* (2005), by the time the couple's second daughter, Natasha (nicknamed Sasha), was born, in 2001, "my wife's anger toward me seemed barely contained. 'You only think of yourself,' she would tell me. 'I never thought I'd have to raise a family alone.'"

The Obamas were determined to work out their problems. "I came into our marriage with a more traditional notion of what family is. It was what I knew growing up—the mother at home, the father works, you have dinner around the table," Michelle Obama explained to Leslie Bennetts for *Vanity Fair* (December 27, 2007, on-line). "And then I married a man who came from a very different kind of upbringing. He didn't grow up with a father; his mother traveled the world. So we both came to this marriage with very different notions about what children need, and what does a couple need to be happy." She continued, "I had to give up some of my notions, and so did he. That's part of being married; everyone compromises." In 2002 Michelle Obama took on a challenging job as the executive director of community affairs at the University of Chicago Medical Center, which comprises several hospitals, outpatient facilities, and teaching institutions. In that capacity she focused on neighborhood outreach, volunteer recruitment, and staff diversity, among other areas.

Barack Obama had made an unsuccessful bid for a seat in the U.S. House of Representatives in the 2000 primaries; then, in 2004, he defeated four opponents in a landslide Democratic primary victory, winning his party's nomination for a seat in the U.S. Senate. Michelle Obama became known during the campaign as a formidable advocate for her husband. Once, while Barack was making a speech at Chicago's Liberty Baptist Church, a group of raucous protesters, who were questioning his loyalty to the black community, gathered outside the building. "[Michelle Obama] came out the back door, and there were a bunch of hoodlum thugs ready to do a full-blast demonstration," Ron Carter, a witness to the event and a former associate of the Black Panther Party, told Lauren Collins for the *New Yorker* (March 10, 2008, on-line). When Obama loudly confronted the group, Carter reported, "they all froze, guys who would slap the mayor, who would slap Jesse Jackson."

On July 27, 2004, just minutes before Barack Obama delivered the eloquent keynote address at that year's Democratic National Convention, which thrust him into the national spotlight, campaign officials frantically tweaked his speech; Michelle Obama was there to offer her own advice and support, and observers have commented on the couple's seemingly telepathic manner of communicating in the frenzied environment. As Barack walked out of the wings, Obama reportedly pulled him aside and used humor to ease his nervousness, admonishing him, according to Collins: "Just don't screw it up, buddy!"

Barack Obama was elected to the U.S. Senate in November 2004. Michelle Obama decided to remain in Chicago with her daughters while her husband worked in Washington, D.C., several days a week. When he was home, she made sure that he did his share of housework and parenting—taking out the garbage, making the beds, and reading to their daughters.

In 2005 Obama was promoted to vice president of community and external affairs at the University of Chicago Medical Center. (She received a significant raise with the promotion, and the family's financial standing was also improved considerably by the publication that year of *The Audacity of Hope*.) During her tenure at the medical center, with which she is still affiliated, she helped revise the organization's contracting system so that more business goes to firms owned by women and minorities, and she trained counselors, most of them local black residents, to hand out health-clinic referrals to patients waiting in clogged emergency rooms. Weighing in on the center's research agenda, Obama put a stop to a proposal to enlist black teenagers as research subjects to test the human papillomavirus vaccine, which is designed to prevent cervical cancer. "The prospect of white doctors performing a trial with black teenage girls summoned the specter of the Tuskegee syphilis experiment of the mid-20th century, when white doctors let hundreds of black men go untreated to study the disease," Powell and Kantor explained.

Though Barack Obama had gained national attention with his work in the U.S. Senate and with the publication of *The Audacity of Hope*, Michelle Obama was surprised by her husband's decision to run for the U.S. presidency. "He [had only] just won his U.S. Senate seat," she told Bennetts. "We entered [the presidential race] knowing it was going to be really, really hard. For us, the question was: are we ready to do something really hard again, right after doing something that [had been] really hard?" The Obamas discussed the idea at length before agreeing that Barack's candidacy was "something that was bigger than everybody," Craig Robinson told Bennetts.

In February 2007 Barack Obama announced that he was entering the Democratic presidential primary race, and the following month, not wanting to take a full leave of absence from her job, Michelle Obama reduced her work schedule significantly to help him. A talented public speaker, she campaigned up to four days a week, drawing crowds in the thousands. In contrast to her husband, whose speaking style has been described as inspirational but not down-to-earth, Michelle Obama has developed an earthier persona on the campaign trail. Often speaking about growing up in Chicago, the difficulties of being a working mother, and her relationship with Barack, she has been credited with helping to humanize her husband. She has playfully accused him of failing to pick his socks up from the floor and of waking up with bad breath—information that some have seen as endearing and others have regarded as too personal. "Occasionally, it gives campaign people heartburn," David Axelrod, a strategist for the Obama campaign, told Collins. "She's fundamentally honest—goes out there, speaks her mind, jokes. She doesn't parse her words or select them with an antenna for political correctness."

On February 18, 2008 Obama commented during a speech in Wisconsin, "For the first time in my adult life, I am proud of my country." (She repeated the line, in a slightly modified form, later in the day during another speech.) Although she quickly clarified that she had been referring to the fact that so many young or previously discouraged voters were becoming part of the political process, the comment was played repeatedly on news programs, providing fodder for conservative critics who questioned her patriotism. Rumors spread that she had once given a speech in which she used the racial slur "whitey." She told Powell and Kantor, "You are amazed sometimes at how deep the lies can be. I mean, 'whitey'? That's something that [the black sitcom character of the late 1970s and early 1980s] George Jefferson would say. Anyone who says that doesn't know me."

Honest and blunt, Obama has not shied away from discussing the country's problems in her speeches. "Life for regular folks has gotten worse over the course of my lifetime, through Republican and Democratic administrations," she told a crowd in Wisconsin, according to Nancy Gibbs and Jay Stewart-Small, writing for *Time* (June 2, 2008). In light of that and other similarly themed speeches, conservative media outlets have regularly portrayed Obama as angry and militant. The April 2008 cover of the *National Review* featured an unflattering portrait of her labeled "Mrs. Grievance," and the accompanying article, by Mark Steyn, asserted: "Almost every time the candidate's wife speaks extemporaneously she seems to offer some bon mot consistent with [a] bleak assessment [of America]."

Obama's critics "attack her with an exuberance that suggests there are no taboos anymore," Gibbs and Stewart-Small wrote, referring to the element in many of the criticisms of overt or subtle racist elements. On June 3, 2008, when Barack Obama won the requisite number of delegates to give him his party's nomination, he and his wife performed a celebratory gesture that they had picked up from young staffers—bumping their fists together playfully. During the introduction to a segment on nonverbal communication, E. D. Hill, an anchor of the Fox network program *America's Pulse*, referred to the gesture as "a terrorist fist jab." Later that month the bar scrolling beneath footage of Michelle Obama on Fox News referred to her nonsensically as "[Barack] Obama's baby mama," a derogatory term for an unwed mother.

While her views and manner have attracted negative comments, Obama's appearance has seldom been discussed in less than admiring terms, and she is often described as regal or statuesque. Journalists have frequently mentioned her elegant sense of style, and she was included on the *Vanity Fair* list of the best-dressed international figures of 2008, with the magazine's editors dubbing her the "Queen of Sheath."

Obama makes her home in the Hyde Park section of Chicago. She has said that if the family ends up in the White House, her main priority would continue to be raising Malia and Sasha. (Her fierce devotion to her daughters is rarely doubted, even by her most vocal detractors.) Regarding the official agenda that First Ladies are expected to adopt, she has expressed an interest in encouraging public service among young people and in exploring ways to help women better balance work and family. On August 26, 2008 Obama spoke at the 2008 Democratic Convention, in Denver, Colorado. She spent much of her speech describing her own background, as well as her husband's, shedding light on their shared struggles and values. "You see, Barack doesn't care where you're from, or what your background is, or what party, if any, you belong to," Obama told the convention, as quoted by Adam Nagourney in the *New York Times* (August 26, 2008). "You see, that's just not how he sees the world. He knows the thread that conects us—our belief in America's promise, our commitment to our children's future—he knows that that thread is strong enough to hold us together as one nation even when we disagree." Following her speech, Obama was joined on stage by her daughters, and Barack appeared before the convention on a large screen, by video hookup, from a supporter's home in Kansas City, Missouri. Obama's speech was acclaimed by Democrats, and her appearance as a whole was widely thought to be part of a broad effort by the campaign to reintroduce the Obama family to the public and to portray them as "embodiments of the American dream," as Nagourney put it.

Obama told Richard Wolffe for *Newsweek* (February 25, 2008, on-line) that she had been particularly touched by a 10-year-old girl she met while campaigning in South Carolina; the girl had explained that if Barack Obama became president, she knew that she herself could do anything she wanted in life. "She could have been me," Obama said. Referring to her role in a presidential campaign, she continued, "Because the truth is, I'm not supposed to be here, standing here. I'm a statistical oddity. Black girl, brought up on the South Side of Chicago. Was I supposed to go to Princeton? No. . . . They said maybe Harvard Law was too much for me to reach for. But I went, I did fine."

On November 4, 2008, in a contest that drew a record number of voters to the polls, Barack Obama was elected the 44th president of the United States. Michelle Obama and the couple's daughters joined her husband on a stage in Chicago's Grant Park, where the president-elect delivered his historic victory speech to a crowd of 10s of thousands.

—M.E.R.

Suggested Reading: *Boston Globe* A p1 June 15, 2008; *Crain's Chicago Business* p29 May 5, 2008; (London) *Sunday Times* (on-line) June 22, 2008; (London) *Telegraph* (on-line) Mar. 2, 2007; *New Republic* p23 Mar. 26, 2008; *New York Times* A p16 Oct. 28, 2008, (on-line) June 18, 2008; *New Yorker* (on-line) Mar. 10, 2008; *Time* p28 June 2, 2008, p40 June 23, 2008; *Vanity Fair* (on-line) Dec. 27, 2007

O'Hara, Kelli

Apr. 16, 1976– Actress; singer

Address: c/o Gersh Agency, 41 Madison Ave., 33d Fl., New York, NY 10010

"When Kelli O'Hara stands onstage at the Lincoln Center Theater, singing '[I'm in Love with] a Wonderful Guy'—or any of the other Rodgers and Hammerstein standards in *South Pacific*—she'll often think, 'This is me, on Broadway, singing this classic song,'" Marshall Fine wrote for the New York *Daily News* (March 29, 2008, on-line). "Inevitably, it reminds O'Hara of her first trip to New York as a 20-year-old, when she sat next to the Lincoln Center fountain and thought, 'Wouldn't it be the biggest dream to work here someday?'" O'Hara, now a three-time Tony Award nominee, got her big break in 1999, as an understudy for the musical *Jekyll & Hyde*. When the female lead became ill, O'Hara stepped in, and since then her career trajectory has often been described as the stuff of fantasy.

The youngest of three children, the actress was born on April 16, 1976 in Tulsa, Oklahoma, to Laura and Patrick O'Hara. When she was three years old, the family moved to Elk City, Oklahoma, to help her aging grandfather run his farm. O'Hara sang in the local church and entertained her friends and relatives with an occasional country-and-western song. The family ultimately settled in Edmond, Oklahoma, where O'Hara attended high school. In 1994 she entered Oklahoma City University (OCU) to study voice with Florence Birdwell, who had also trained the Oklahoma native and Broadway star Kristen Chenoweth.

In 1998 O'Hara participated in the Metropolitan Opera National Council (MONC) Auditions, a program aimed at discovering promising young opera singers and helping them develop their careers. O'Hara won the statewide MONC competition, but despite her success she was more interested in pursuing a career in musical theater. "Mrs. Birdwell and I had some arguments about that, especially after the Met auditions," O'Hara told James D. Watts Jr. for the *Tulsa (Oklahoma) World* (June 13, 1999). "But I thought that opera would be a great foundation for any singing, because you learn how to care for your voice as well as how to use it."

Scott Wintrow/Getty Images

Kelli O'Hara

After graduating from OCU, in 1998, with a bachelor's degree in vocal performance, O'Hara moved to New York City, where she enrolled in the acclaimed Lee Strasberg Institute and contacted Chenoweth, who had graduated a few years earlier. "I owe a lot to her, because she helped me get an audition with her agency," O'Hara told Watts. "It wasn't very long before the agency said the *Jekyll & Hyde* tour was looking for an [understudy] and ensemble person."

The young singer was hired for the job, and when the lead actress, Andrea Rivette, became sick from a viral infection, O'Hara was tapped to play the role of Emma Carew, Jekyll's fiancée. She did so for several performances, including one in Tulsa that was attended by a large group of family members, friends, and OCU students. Following that exposure O'Hara was cast in 2001 to play Young Phyllis, a showgirl, in a revival of Stephen Sondheim's *Follies*. The musical follows a group of middle-aged performers who gather to reminisce when the theater in which they once worked is slated to be demolished.

While O'Hara was in rehearsals for *Follies*, she auditioned for the musical *Sweet Smell of Success*. "I ended up going [to the audition] on my lunch break," O'Hara told Rick Rogers for the *Daily Oklahoman* (June 9, 2002). "Marvin [Hamlisch, the composer], Craig [Carnelia, the lyricist] and Nick [Hytner, the director] were also taking their lunch break, but I begged to be let in. At the time, I didn't know who any of these people were, which probably helped my nerves. . . . Within a week, I learned that I had been cast." The musical, based on a 1957 film starring Burt Lancaster and Tony Curtis, tells the story of a gossip columnist, J.J.

Hunsecker (played by John Lithgow on Broadway), who holds career-ruining power over the celebrities he covers. O'Hara was cast to play Susan, Hunsecker's rebellious younger sister. Although the show was nominated for seven Tony Awards (Lithgow won as best lead actor in a musical), critical reviews were mixed. O'Hara told Rogers, "Press is press, and we can't change that. We have to do the same show and believe in it as we always have."

O'Hara spent early 2003 appearing Off-Broadway in *My Life with Albertine*, a musical inspired by the work of Marcel Proust, and at California's La Jolla Playhouse, where she starred in *Beauty*, a fairy tale–inspired show by the playwright Tina Landau. She was then cast to play Clara Johnson, a developmentally disabled young woman, in a production of *The Light in the Piazza*, when it opened in Seattle, Washington. The musical was based on the 1960 novella by Elizabeth Spencer, which also inspired a 1962 film. The story follows Clara, who is visiting Florence, Italy, with her mother, Margaret, when she falls in love with Fabrizio, a handsome local. At first Margaret disapproves of the relationship; she has been exceedingly protective since Clara was kicked in the head by a pony at the age of 10, stunting her mental development, but she ultimately relents. O'Hara stayed with the musical as it moved in 2004 to the Goodman Theatre, in Chicago, Illinois, and then in 2005 to New York City's Vivian Beaumont Theater, at Lincoln Center. (Concurrently, from August 2004 to January 2005, she played Lucy, a beautiful young woman bitten by a vampire, in *Dracula, the Musical*. While O'Hara received some positive notices, the show itself was widely panned.) Of portraying Clara, O'Hara told Rob Kendt for the *Los Angeles Times* (January 28, 2007), "It was the most challenging thing I've ever done, because I wanted it so badly to be real. I didn't want somebody coming to the show who was handicapped or had a handicapped person in their life to say, 'She has no idea what it means to be this way.' So I was always in pain in my mind, and it was hard for me to do that every day." The role earned O'Hara her first Tony Award nomination, and she took home an Outer Critics Circle Award as outstanding featured actress in a musical.

In 2006 O'Hara was cast to star in the Broadway revival of *The Pajama Game*, alongside Harry Connick Jr. Scored by Richard Adler and Jerry Ross—the team also responsible for *Damn Yankees*—the musical had been a major hit when it originally opened on Broadway, in 1954. The main characters include Babe Williams (played by O'Hara), the head of the workers' grievance committee in a pajama factory, and Sid Sorokin (played by Connick), the factory superintendent. Complications ensue when the two fall in love. Although Connick was a seasoned performer, with several albums and films to his credit, he had yet to act in a Broadway production, so there was some initial skepticism about his suitability for the role. The doubts proved unfounded: the two leads were so convincing in their roles that gossip spread that the pair had become romantically involved outside the theater. However, O'Hara told Campbell Robertson for the *New York Times* (June 4, 2006), "if there was something going on, we wouldn't have chemistry onstage. There's a sense of attraction, of flirtation, you have with a person, and if you give in to that attraction, it's gone onstage. The talk only fuels our fire."

The show and its cast received excellent reviews, with O'Hara often singled out for her commanding presence and compelling voice. Ben Brantley, for example, wrote for the *New York Times* (February 24, 2006), "As long as these stars are on the stage of the American Airlines Theater, where this frisky tale of a union dispute at a pajama factory opened last night, grown-up audiences have the chance to witness something rarely seen anymore: a bona fide adult love affair, with all its attendant frictions, translated into the populist poetry of hummable songs and sprightly dance. Mr. Connick, best known as a velveteen crooner, and Ms. O'Hara, who here rockets past the promising ingénue status she attained with *Light in the Piazza*, provide the fiery kick in a show that goes down as easily and intoxicatingly as spiked lemonade at a summer picnic." O'Hara received her second Tony Award nomination for her work.

O'Hara was cast in 2007 as the female lead in *Sunday in the Park with George* at the University of California, Los Angeles (UCLA) Freud Playhouse. The acclaimed Broadway actress Bernadette Peters had originated the role, and theater aficionados eagerly waited to see if O'Hara could meet the standard set by her predecessor. While the play itself did not receive universally positive reviews, O'Hara acquitted herself well. Lauren Evans wrote for the UCLA *Daily Bruin* (February 7, 2007, on-line) that "O'Hara's wild gamut of facial expressions and vocal range was the focal point of the show."

In March 2007 O'Hara was cast to sing as the cockney flower girl Eliza Doolittle during a one-night concert staging of *My Fair Lady* at Avery Fisher Hall, in New York City. The performance also featured the television star Kelsey Grammer, as Henry Higgins, and was accompanied by the New York Philharmonic. Charles Isherwood wrote for the *New York Times* (March 9, 2007), "Confirming her status as the most accomplished Broadway ingénue to emerge in years is Kelli O'Hara . . . undertaking the role of Eliza Doolittle for the first time—and, if there is a benevolent spirit presiding anywhere in the vicinity of Broadway, please not the last." He continued, "It would be hard to overestimate the contribution of Ms. O'Hara. The bright purity and richness of her soprano ideally suit Eliza's songs, and her musicianship is superb. Even so, *My Fair Lady* can seem synthetic and bloated if Eliza hits the notes without capturing your heart. Dramatically as well as musically Ms. O'Hara's performance was touched with warmth, humor, spirit and true delicacy of feeling. When she gave voice to a mixture of all of these, in that soaring song about the thrill of discovery, 'I Could Have Danced All Night,' you instantly knew just what this excitable little flower girl was singing about. This was the sound of pure joy. And what a joy it was to hear."

A month later O'Hara had her solo concert debut, at Carnegie Hall, in New York City. She sang songs from her Broadway roles as well as tracks from a forthcoming CD, *Wonder in the World*, which was released in May 2008. *Wonder in the World* includes the original song "Here Now," which is dedicated to her grandfather, along with pop standards and covers of James Taylor and Billy Joel tunes. The album was arranged and orchestrated by Harry Connick Jr., who also sang in an occasional duet with O'Hara and played the piano. Seth Cohen wrote for the All About Jazz Web site (January 23, 2008), "Kelli O'Hara combines her youthful vigor with the presence and professionalism of a seasoned veteran, and she sets the bar high with her spot-on vocals."

In 2008 O'Hara played Nellie Forbush in a revival of the celebrated Broadway musical *South Pacific*, written by Richard Rodgers and Oscar Hammerstein soon after World War II. The original production ran for almost five years, garnered numerous Tony Awards, and inspired a hit 1958 film version. Rumors circulated that the production company had been thinking of casting the Hollywood star Scarlett Johansson in the revival, but the director Bartlett Sher, who had worked on *The Light in the Piazza*, was convinced that O'Hara was the better choice. He told Sean O'Driscoll for the Associated Press (April 1, 2008), "She was perfect for it. We wanted a very natural sound and that suits her voice. She could sing the whole show unmiked if necessary. We could have gone with a big name but it could have drained the show. I wanted the sound to be vital and real."

Based on a book by James Michener, the musical takes place on a South Pacific island during World War II. Nellie Forbush, a U.S. military nurse, falls in love with a French plantation owner (played in the revival by the Brazilian opera singer Paulo Szot), who has sired two mixed-race children. Although Forbush, a naive midwesterner, has deep-seated prejudices, she seems to ultimately overcome them. O'Hara told Jeff Lunden for *All Things Considered* (April 3, 2008, on-line), "I hear people gasping when I use the word 'colored,' which I expected. But [in 1949], they didn't even need to say the word. . . . The audience knew what the problem was." O'Hara was referring to the fact that the line containing the word had been cut from the original production; it was restored in the revival, however. "We actually have to over-explain it," O'Hara continued. "And so when we do . . . you hear people audibly gasping. It makes me feel dirty. . . . I want to apologize, but I don't, because I think that gets us to the end of the play. And that's why it's so rewarding."

The show, which contains such classic tunes as "Some Enchanted Evening" and "I'm Gonna Wash That Man Right Outa My Hair," received stellar reviews, as did its cast. Charles Isherwood wrote for the *New York Times* (May 18, 2008), "Ms. O'Hara's Nellie is wholesome without being corny as those Kansas fields, sweet without causing the mouth to pucker. And she sings with a radiance that is the sound of hope and happiness made manifest, in a voice that could melt the heart of the most unregenerate musical hater." He continued, "Ms. O'Hara's Nellie does not shine so brightly simply because she has dusted off an old archetype otherwise left unexamined. For all the warmth and charm Ms. O'Hara brings to the role, her Nellie Forbush is also richly shaded with glimmers of confusion and anxious self-awareness. The performance is like a sunny sky given definition and interest by a few artfully scattered clouds." O'Hara earned her third Tony Award nomination for her turn in *South Pacific*.

Besides her work on Broadway and in the recording studio, O'Hara has acted in an occasional film and television program. Her screen credits include *The Dying Gaul* (2005), a dark thriller about a love triangle; an episode of *The American Experience* (2007), in which she portrayed Alexander Hamilton's mistress; and three episodes of the soap opera *All My Children* (2007). She also provided the voice of a neurotic radio producer for the PBS cartoon *Click and Clack's As the Wrench Turns*, which aired in the summer of 2008. (The animated show was based on the popular radio program *Car Talk*.)

On July 28, 2007, in a mountaintop ceremony in Vermont, O'Hara married Greg Naughton, an actor and singer/songwriter whom she had known since 2002. Her father-in-law is the two-time Tony Award winner James Naughton.

—F.C.

Suggested Reading: *Daily Oklahoman* Living p1 June 9, 2002; *Los Angeles Times* F p6 Jan. 28, 2007; (New York) *Daily News* (on-line) Mar. 29, 2008; *New York Times* E p1 Feb. 24, 2006, B p12 June 4, 2006, E p3 Mar. 9, 2007, C p1 May 18, 2008; *Tulsa (Oklahoma) World* June 13, 1999

Selected Musical Productions: *Jekyll & Hyde*, 1999; *Follies*, 2001; *Sweet Smell of Success*, 2002; *My Life with Albertine*, 2003; *Beauty*, 2003; *The Light in the Piazza*, 2003; *The Pajama Game*, 2006; *Sunday in the Park with George*, 2007; *South Pacific*, 2008

Oliver, Garrett

July 29, 1962– Beer expert; brewmaster; writer; lecturer

Address: Brooklyn Brewery, 79 N. 11th St., Brooklyn, NY 11211

"When people say they don't like beer they almost certainly have never tried the real thing," the beer expert Garrett Oliver told Damaso Reyes for the New York *Amsterdam News* (July 24, 2003). "Saying 'I don't like beer' is like saying 'I don't really care for food.' Beer has that wide a range." As a world-recognized authority on traditional American-made beers as well as a professional brewer whose original recipes have earned the company for which he works—Brooklyn Brewery—international praise, Oliver has presided at more than 500 beer tastings in the U.S. and overseas. With Timothy Harper he co-wrote *The Good Beer Book* (1997), and as solo author he wrote *The Brewmaster's Table: Discovering the Pleasures of Real Beer with Real Food* (2003), the latter of which won an International Association of Culinary Professionals (IACP) Book Award in 2004 and, also that year, was a finalist for a James Beard Foundation Book Award. The food writer Mark Bittman noted for the *New York Times* (June 16, 2004) that Oliver "has become widely acknowledged as an expert not only in making beer, but in tasting it, pairing it [with foods] and talking about it." Oliver worked

Courtesy of Brooklyn Brewery

for the Manhattan Brewing Co. as an assistant brewmaster for about two years and as brewmaster for about one. In 1994 he was hired by the Brooklyn Brewery, one of the approximately 1,500 craft breweries now operating in the U.S.; unlike the so-called industrial beer makers, each of the craft breweries produces a strictly limited number of barrels of beer and usually tries to make its beers distinctive. As the brewmaster and vice president of production at Brooklyn Brewery, Oliver is responsible for developing recipes and overseeing all aspects of the production of the firm's beers. He told Current Biography, "The brewmaster is essentially the 'chef' of the brewery." The 10 varieties that Brooklyn Brewery currently offers are sold in 21 states and in Canada, the United Kingdom, Ireland, Finland, Denmark, Sweden, Japan, and China. In an article for the New York Times (October 19, 2007), Oliver described as "watery" the beers that have dominated the American market for several decades. Referring to the period (1920–33) known as Prohibition, when the manufacture and sale of all alcoholic beverages were illegal in the U.S., as well as the large number of craft breweries that operated in the U.S. in the 19th and early 20th centuries, he added, "If we truly want to restore the vibrant beer culture that flourished in this country before Prohibition, craft brewers need to retain the values and goals—creating beers that are flavorful, interesting to drink and made from proper beer ingredients—that put us on the map in the first place. Let's not undo American beer again."

Garrett Oliver was born on July 29, 1962 in the New York City borough of Queens. His mother was the membership director for the New York Academy of Sciences; his father helped to develop television commercials for the advertising firm Young & Rubicam. An excellent cook, his father sparked his interest in pairing beer with fine food. "That certainly influenced me," Oliver told Current Biography. "I could write a book on my parents' influence. . . . I can certainly say that they both stressed the importance of education."

Oliver attended Boston University, in Massachusetts, where he majored in broadcasting and film. After he graduated, in 1983, he got a job with the Home Box Office (HBO) TV network. Later that year he moved to London, England, where he became a stage manager for rock groups. At his first visit to a London pub, he ordered a glass of the local English bitter. "I wasn't even sure that I liked it," he told Damaso Reyes, also remarking that until that time, he was not partial to beer and had mostly drunk brands not known for their quality. During his stay in London, he grew fond of traditional English beers, especially the Fuller's line, which includes, most notably, London Pride, ESB, and Chiswick Bitter. After a year Oliver left England to travel on the European continent, tasting many other beers along the way. He "really fell in love" with some of them, as he recalled to Current Biography.

Upon his return to the U.S., Oliver found that the light taste of the American beers he bought at the supermarket no longer satisfied him. At that time (and now) the American beer market was dominated by such mass-market beers as Coors and Anheuser Busch's Budweiser—beverages that Oliver described to Damaso Reyes as "yellow fizz,"

because they tasted so watered down. "That's why I started home-brewing," he told Current Biography. "It wasn't that I was interested in brewing—I started brewing in order to have some real beer." After producing a series of unsatisfactory beers, he consulted other home brewers, and his skills improved. In the mid-1980s he founded the New York Home Brewers' Guild, and at one of the group's meetings, he befriended Mark Whitty, the former head of the Samuel Smith Brewery, in Yorkshire, England, who now had the same position in New York City, with the Manhattan Brewing Co. Oliver called his first successful homemade beer Blast!, the name of a magazine edited by the British writer and painter Wyndham Lewis (1882–1957). Oliver told Current Biography, "Amateur brewers are not allowed to sell their beer. Home-brewing is a great hobby, but it's a hobby. It bears little resemblance to professional brewing, just as being a chef is very different than being a home cook. That said, you can make great beer and great food at home. I made a wide variety of styles, but probably more English-style pale ales than anything else." He also noted that the brewing process "is certainly time-consuming. At its simplest, it can involve using a pre-made syrup; that's what I call the 'Betty Crocker' version. Starting from scratch is much more elaborate, and involves the full brewing process, including sugar conversion and extraction, etc. It can easily take all day."

Upon his return to the U.S., Oliver had been re-hired by HBO and assigned to produce short films. He quit the network in 1987 to take a position at a law firm. In 1989, after the assistant brewmaster of the Manhattan Brewing Co. left, Mark Whitty offered Oliver the position. One of the first working breweries to open in New York City in decades, the Manhattan Brewing Co. had started to produce beer—and opened a pub in which to serve it—in 1984 in Lower Manhattan. Oliver was given the freedom to work on his own recipes, and Whitty imparted to him his wealth of knowledge of brewing.

Produced for at least 8,000 years, beer is an alcoholic beverage made from grain, or cereals: barley (primarily), wheat, corn, rice, or oats. Water, yeast, hops, and occasionally fruits or other ingredients are added; in large quantities, beer is manufactured in breweries. Yeast is a microscopic organism that consumes the sugars in grain and converts them into alcohol and carbon dioxide; hops, the female flowers of the hop vine, add a bitter flavor and act as a preservative. The manufacture of beer involves many steps; differences in ingredients and fermentation and in the time spent in carrying out various steps account for differences in appearance and flavor. The main types of beers are ale (brown ale, porter, stout) and lager (pale lager, pilsner, light lager, and dark lager). Some beers are produced year round, while others are manufactured only during one or another season. Draft (or draught) beer is usually defined as beer that is dispensed from kegs or other large containers, as in a saloon, rather than from cans or bottles.

In 1991, for financial reasons, the Manhattan Brewing Co. closed. To support himself, Oliver wrote articles about beer and conducted beer tastings. Then, in 1993, a group of business partners reopened the brewery and hired Oliver as brewmaster, with control of the firm's products. Within months Oliver had created five new, traditional-style beers with both U.S.- and British-grown ingredients. His beers included a brown ale, a golden ale, a British amber ale, an extra stout, and an Indian pale ale. Reviewing the beers for the London *Guardian* (September 25, 1993), Roger Protz wrote, "The Brown Ale . . . packs a greater punch than the average English mild and has great toasted-malt character from the use of roasted barley." He also noted that Oliver's British amber ale "has a fine bitter-sweet nutty palate and a dry, hoppy finish" and that the extra stout "tastes the way dry Irish stouts did until the mass marketing mentality took over and squeezed the roasty, hoppy character out of them. . . . The aroma and palate are rich with bitter chocolate and coffee and the long finish is bitter-sweet, with developing hop notes." Oliver told Protz that he made beers that appealed to him. "When I agreed to become brewmaster, I told the partners it was important I should like the beer," he said. "If the customers like it, but I don't, the beer gets dumped."

In 1994 Oliver left Manhattan Brewery to become the brewmaster at Brooklyn Brewery, which had been founded 10 years earlier by Steve Hindy, previously an Associated Press correspondent, and Tom Potter, a onetime lending officer at a bank. At first Hindy and Potter had sold their two varieties, a lager and a brown ale, from the back of a truck, going store to store. Their limited resources forced them to have their beers manufactured at the F. X. Matt Brewery in Utica, New York. After Oliver arrived, he reformulated both beers and set up facilities for brewing the beers in a warehouse in an industrial section of the Brooklyn neighborhood called Williamsburg. There, he began to craft new year-round beers for the company. Currently, the company produces Brooklyn Lager, Brooklyn Pilsner, Brooklyn Brown Ale, Brooklyn East India Pale Ale, Brooklyn Pennant Ale '55 (named for the Dodgers baseball team, which played in Brooklyn until 1957 and won the World Series in 1955), Brooklyn Local 1, and Brooklyner Weisse ("weisse" means "white" in German). He also developed seasonal beers, among them Brooklyn Summer Ale, Brooklyn Winter Ale, Brooklyn Oktoberfest, Brooklyn Post Road Pumpkin Ale, Brooklyn Monster Ale, and Brooklyn Black Chocolate Stout. According to Damaso Reyes, "All the beers brewed by Brooklyn are steeped in tradition, so much so that even German natives are impressed by Oliver's weisse, not believing one of the benchmarks of German brewing could be faithfully recreated in New York." Oliver also creates a new beer every two months under the Brooklyn Brewery's Brewmaster Reserve Program; the beers are available for only a few weeks. Oliver told *Current Biog-*

raphy that the program "keeps things fast-paced and creative around [the brewery]." As of 2007, Karl Knoop, Brooklyn Brewery's operations manager, told a Hudson County, New Jersey, *Jersey Journal* (June 7, 2008) reporter, Brooklyn Brewery was in the top 30 domestic breweries, and Brooklyn Lager was the fifth-most-popular draft beer in New York City. Knoop also said, "If you walk into a bar with five tap handles, there is a good chance Brooklyn Lager is one of those taps."

Critics have generally praised Oliver's Brooklyn Brewery creations. The Boston-based beer connoisseurs Jason and Todd Alström, who own the popular rating site beeradvocate.com and publish the magazine *Beer Advocate*, gave Brooklyn Brewery's flagship beer, Brooklyn Lager, a "B" rating. Jason Alström described it as "a good solid brew, the only thing that bothered me about it was the hop flavour seems to be too much and the beer is not as crisp as you would expect a lager to be." They gave Oliver's winter seasonal beer, the Brooklyn Black Chocolate Stout, "A–"; Todd Alström wrote that it was "an incredibly tasty and powerful stout" and represented the "best use of chocolate malt that I've ever seen for the style." The article in the *Jersey Journal* noted that Brooklyn Summer Ale is "a refreshing thirst quencher," adding, "This beer is not too heavy, except in flavor. Excellent with salads, seafood, and quiches, it's good for brunches and light lunches during the summer months."

Oliver is also recognized for his ability to pair particular beers with particular foods to best effect. He told Mark Bittman, "To me, beer and wine are both beverages meant to be served with food. And good beer, real beer, often offers things that most wine does not, like carbonation and caramelized and roasted flavors—aspects that sometimes make beer the preferable choice. And the most wonderful thing about beer is that it has that ability to 're-set' your palate"—that is, remove whatever taste remains in the mouth from whatever was eaten last. He also said that with food, wine "contrasts" better, while beer "harmonizes" better, giving as an example the traditional pairing of chocolate cake with port, a wine produced in Portugal: "You like the idea of the port, but you don't taste anything. But if you eat that cake with the right beer—a framboise, or a chocolate stout—it dovetails beautifully. Unfortunately, people don't necessarily think in that direction." Oliver has demonstrated his pairing abilities and skill as a beer taster at sites in many parts of the world. He has hosted tastings and given talks about beer at such prestigious venues as the James Beard House, Gramercy Tavern, the Waldorf-Astoria Hotel, the Sommelier Society of America, and the American Institute of Wine and Food, all in New York City, and the Culinary Institute of America, in Hyde Park, New York. Overseas, he has presided at events in cities including London and Leeds, in England; Copenhagen, in Denmark; and Rio de Janeiro and São Paulo, in Brazil. He spoke at the 2004 International Association of Culinary Professionals (IACP) conference, in Baltimore, Maryland; the 2006 Cape Wine Conference, in South Africa; and the 2008 Good Experience Live (GEL) conference, in New York City. He has also hosted tastings and lectured at such institutions as the Museum of Natural History and the Jewish Museum, in New York City; the Smithsonian Institution, in Washington, D.C.; and MassMOCA, the Massachusetts Museum of Contemporary Art, in North Adams.

Oliver produced *The Good Beer Book* with the help of Timothy Harper, a freelance writer. In an undated review for *Booklist*, as quoted on Amazon.com, Ray Olson wrote, "Harper and Oliver's beer book is twice good: it is about good—flavorful, zesty, attractive—beer, and it is a good—amusing, informative, lively—book. It covers beer history, how and of what beer is made, the major styles of lagers and ales, the rebirth of American craft brewing, the rise of brewpubs, big brewers' response to craft brewing, and proper beer handling and tasting, and it provides advice on beer and food, annotated lists of outstanding American and European breweries, a little gazetteer of brewpubs and beer bars, some home brew recipes, online and periodical resource lists, and a glossary. Other books are more comprehensive on one or another, even several, of these matters (e.g., there are book-length beer gazetteers), but none treats them all so well at so reasonable a price." Damaso Reyes wrote that Oliver's next book, *The Brewmaster's Table: Discovering the Pleasures of Real Beer with Real Food*, "gives insight to both the history of beer from ancient times . . . to the present day. After reading the lively and well-written book you will not only know just about everything there is to know about beer, but also how to match beer with food, something the Europeans have been doing for centuries but we are still learning about here in America. According to Oliver it is the variety and flexibility of beer that makes it, much more so than wine, the perfect companion to foods from Chinese to Thai to American BBQ."

Oliver has served for 17 years as a judge for the Professional Panel Blind Tasting of the Great American Beer Festival. He has also been a judge at the annual Great British Beer Festival competition and the Brewing Industry International Awards competition. Oliver has been a guest on National Public Radio (NPR) programs and on television news shows on CBS, CNN, ABC, PBS, the History Channel, the Travel Channel, and A&E. He has been commissioned by Oxford University Press to act as editor in chief for *The Oxford Companion to Beer*, scheduled for publication in 2011.

Oliver's honors include the Russell Schehrer Award for Innovation and Excellence in Brewing (1998) from the Institute for Brewing Studies and the 2003 Semper Ardens Award for Beer Culture (2003), a Danish prize. He was named the *Cheers* Beverage Media's "Beverage Innovator of the Year" in 2006. In 2007 *Forbes* named him one of the top-10 tastemakers in the U.S. for wine, beer, and spirits. A few years ago, when Josh Abraham, writing

for gothamist.com (May 31, 2005), asked him to name his favorite beer, Oliver responded, "I'm sure I've had close to 1,000 different beers. So I have too many favorites to list. I have a particular love for the more complex Belgian styles and for British cask-conditioned ales when they're done properly." He told *Current Biography*, "Any time you can take a hobby and make it into your job, it's a wonderful thing. I've had the opportunity to meet people and to brew all over the world. I'm a very lucky man."

—W.D.

Suggested Reading: garrettoliver.com; (Hudson County, New Jersey) *Jersey Journal* June 7, 2008; (London) *Guardian* p45 Sep. 25, 1993; (New York) *Amsterdam News* p23 July 24, 2003

Selected Books: *The Good Beer Book* (with Timothy Harper), 1997; *The Brewmaster's Table: Discovering the Pleasures of Real Beer with Real Food*, 2003

Scott Gries/Getty Images

Omarion

Nov. 12, 1984– Singer

Address: c/o Richard De La Font Agency, 4845 S. Sheridan Rd., Suite 505, Tulsa, OK 74145

"Coming from a boy group and a young genre, it's hard to make the transition into adulthood and still be respected," Omarion, a Grammy Award–nominated R&B musician and former member of the boy band B2K, explained to Cori Bolger for the

Jackson, Mississippi, *Clarion-Ledger* (August 25, 2005). "Now that I'm coming into my manhood, I can have control of my career and destiny. It doesn't rely on other people and I can go where I want to, physically, spiritually and mentally. It's a lot of responsibility, but nothing I can't bear." Like Justin Timberlake, formerly of the group 'N Sync, Omarion has successfully made the often difficult transition from instant boy-band stardom to a career as a solo performer; his extreme versatility as a singer, dancer, songwriter, and, recently, record producer has inspired comparisons to the likes of the pop superstar Michael Jackson. Dancing, in particular, is "very important to my career," as Omarion noted to Richard Harrington for the *Washington Post* (December 29, 2006). "That was something Michael Jackson had: the ability to excite people differently than the next person could. He could just move his arm, and it was 'Wow!' I want to be able to excite people in that way and have them say, 'I wonder what Omarion's going to do next,' because it challenges me. At the same time, it makes my whole entertainment spontaneous."

As the lead singer of the hip-hop/R&B quartet B2K, Omarion anchored the group's eponymous 2001 debut album and their sophomore effort, *Pandemonium* (2003). Omarion's solo albums, *O* (2005) and *21* (2006), each received critical acclaim and reached the top spot on the *Billboard* chart, making the singer one of few to have achieved back-to-back number-one debuts on both the Hot 100 and the R&B charts. The latter album also featured two hit singles, "Entourage" and the Timbaland-produced "Ice Box." *Face Off*, Omarion's collaboration with the rapper Bow Wow, reached stores in December 2007. In addition to his musical endeavors, Omarion has ventured into acting, with roles in the movies *You Got Served* (2004), *Fat Albert* (2004), *Feel the Noise* (2007), and *Somebody Help Me* (2007). In 2005 he had a recurring role in the UPN TV series *Cuts*, about a family-run barbershop. He explained to Bolger in 2005: "I don't want to be 35 and a 100-millionaire like Jay-Z and Puffy. I want to learn the game now and soak it up and by 23 make a lot of money." He added, "I want to be somebody who hangs tough in the industry. I want to own teams and have the Omarion shoe one day. I want to be an entrepreneur."

The oldest of the seven children of Leslie Burrell and Trent Grandberry, the singer was born Omari Ishmael Grandberry on November 12, 1984 in Inglewood, California. "Omari," a name of Swahili origin, means "God the highest"; the suffix "ion" in his stage name was inspired, according to some sources, by "eon"—meaning, as the singer defines it, "forever." Omarion's mother, a hairstylist, raised him and his siblings by herself; she encouraged him when he was very young to pursue a life in the entertainment business. Little is known of his father; it has been reported that he introduced his son early on to the music of Marvin Gaye and

the group Earth, Wind and Fire. Omarion started performing at the age of five, appearing in local theater and in nationally televised commercials for McDonald's and Kellogg's Corn Pops cereal. He said to Margena A. Christian for *Jet* (May 9, 2005), "I was like the only Black kid to have a Pops commercial." He became a music performer at a young age as well. As he recalled to Alicia Quarles for Associated Press Online (March 15, 2007), he was already part of a rap group, the Wild Kingdom, when his mother told him, "'Omari, you might want to sing.' I said, 'Why?' She said, 'Because you know singers get all the women.' I was like, 'Okay.' It stuck with me."

Even as he pursued performing opportunities, Omarion became involved in the gang activity that was ubiquitous in Inglewood, joining a gang called the Under Age Criminals. "A lot of people don't really expect [gang activity] to come from a person like me, because I'm a singer," he explained to Corey Levitan for the *(Torrance, California) Daily Breeze* (March 18, 2005). "But at the same time, Inglewood is Inglewood, just like any 'hood. Gangs are a popular thing here. It's pretty tough and if you don't belong, you pretty much can get hurt in the line of crossfire. . . . When I look back on it now, I think, 'Dang, I was doing a lot of crazy stuff when I was younger. I really could have got hurt.'"

Music helped to steer Omarion away from petty theft and other crime. His older half-brother, Marques Houston, had been performing in the teen group Immature (now known as IMX) for years when he introduced Omarion to the group's manager, Christopher Stokes. In the late 1990s, during the height of the popularity of boy bands, Stokes helped form a new band, consisting of Omarion, his cousin Jarell "J-Boog" Houston, Dreux Pierre "Lil' Fizz" Frederic, and De'Mario Monte "Raz-B" Thornton. The band, initially called Y2K to parallel the worldwide anticipation of the new millennium, instead chose the name B2K, which means "Boys of the New Millennium." In early 2001 the group performed in Los Angeles, California, in front of executives at Epic Records, who instantly felt that B2K had the potential to become as popular as the highly successful act Boyz II Men. Max Gousse, a vice president at Epic, told Nekesa Mumbi Moody for the Dubuque, Iowa, *Telegraph Herald* (February 16, 2003) about the members of B2K, "They're all perfectionists and they each serve a purpose in the group."

Omarion's talents as lead singer and dancer contributed greatly to the foursome's immediate success. B2K's first single, the dance number "Uh Huh," reached the top spot on the singles chart not long after its release, in late 2001. On March 12, 2002 Epic released the group's eponymous debut album to critical acclaim. Jason Birchmeier wrote for the All Music Guide Web site, "Epic Records definitely did its homework before unleashing B2K into the pop market. The boy band of clean-cut and suave young black men is everything a marketing department dreams about: attractive teens-becoming-men who make the girls melt with a little bit of a rugged, tough-guy attitude and flashy clothes." The album, whose highlights included the hit singles "Gots ta Be," "Understanding," and "Why I Love You," went on to achieve gold status in sales. The same month that the album was released, hype surrounding the band resulted in approximately 1,000 fans' storming a record store in a Concord, California, shopping mall during a B2K autograph-signing session, which forced police to close down the mall temporarily. Other, similar incidents included one at a show at the New York venue Planet Hollywood, where unruly fans had to be physically restrained in order for the group to perform. Such fan frenzy attended the group's aptly titled Scream and Scream 2 tours, which saw near-riots among those awaiting the band. In the summer of 2002, B2K toured Europe as an opening act for the group Destiny's Child. On December 10, 2002 B2K released the follow-up to their debut, *Pandemonium*, which included the singles "Bump, Bump, Bump," "Girlfriend," and "What a Girl Wants." Despite mixed reviews, the album achieved platinum status, selling over a million copies. Between the two albums B2K released a remix collection and a Christmas EP, titled *Santa Hooked Me Up*. By year's end, B2K had received a number of awards, including BET's Viewer's Choice Award, a *Billboard* Music Award for the single "Uh Huh," and the Best Group Award from the editors of *Vibe* magazine.

In 2003 B2K embarked on a third successful Scream tour and starred together in the critically panned movie *You Got Served*, about competing crews of hip-hop dancers in Los Angeles. Later that year disagreements among the group's members, among other factors, led to B2K's dissolution. Their final performance together was at a December 2003 concert in Washington, D.C., after which Omarion was briefly hospitalized with head and back pain. The breakup was underscored when Omarion was the only group member to show up for a Philadelphia, Pennsylvania, concert, which unexpectedly became the scene of his solo debut. He explained to Margena A. Christian for *Jet* (January 26, 2004), "It is true that B2K broke up but it's not about me leaving or them leaving. It's about us growing up and wanting to do our own thing. We have been together since we were 14 years old. The guys are like my brothers and I love them and only wish the best for them in everything they do, but the time was coming that we were all more focused on our solo projects than we were in the group." While several of B2K's members accused Stokes (who wrote and directed *You Got Served*) of cheating them of money earned during the Scream 3 tour, Omarion disputed those claims, saying to Christian that he had received "plenty of money."

With Stokes continuing to serve as his manager, Omarion began working on his solo material. On February 22, 2005 he released his debut effort, *O*, which featured his collaborations with the noted producers the Neptunes and Rodney Jenkins. The album entered the *Billboard* album chart at the top spot; it was released concurrently with his same-titled autobiography, published by Pocket Books, in which he gave an intimate account of his growing up in Inglewood and escaping a life of crime through music. Despite entering the charts at number one, the album went on to have comparatively modest sales; that surprised many, as *O* featured a number of singles that scored high on the charts, including "Never Gonna Let You Go (She's a Keepa)," with Big Boi of the group Outkast, which was included on the soundtrack of the romantic film comedy *Hitch*. Reviewers criticized Omarion's ostensible transformation from innocent boy-band member to "bad boy." They were silenced later that year, however, when *O* garnered a Grammy Award nomination for best contemporary R&B album. The singer was also featured on the rapper Bow Wow's hit song "Let Me Hold You," which reached the number-four spot on the *Billboard* 100 chart, making it Omarion's first top-10 single as a solo performer.

A controversy surrounding Omarion arose in the summer of 2005, when the singer was touring in London, England. Following the terrorist bombings that occurred in that city on July 7, a press release purporting to be from Omarion's publicist asked the singer's fans to pray for his safe return to the U.S., while making no mention of the more than 50 people killed or hundreds injured in the attacks. Though a statement on Omarion's Web site denied any connection between the singer and the press release, the episode temporarily marred his reputation. In December 2006, after months of heavy touring, Omarion released his second album, *21*, named to reflect his transition from boyhood to manhood. The record, which entered the *Billboard* chart at number one, drew immediate comparisons to Janet Jackson's album *Control* and Stevie Wonder's *For Once in My Life*, as it was considered to be a breakthrough project for the performer. Omarion had a lot more creative control in the making of the album than he had had with *O*. "It played out wonderfully," he told Richard Harrington. "It was, 'Yes, I want to do this record. . . . No, I don't really like this, let's try something else,' and not having everybody look at you with a raised eyebrow, like, 'He doesn't really know what he's talking about.' But I've been doing this since I was 15, and, for me, it was good to be able to make a suggestion or to have a comment or a question and not be overlooked; when I was a little younger, if I said something, they might not have taken it as seriously or into consideration." He added to Alicia Quarles, "For this album it was definitely a more mature side of me. Not just with the topics or the writing, but just my image as well. If you look at the front cover of the CD . . . there is a real grown-up feel. That is the image I was looking for." Harvey Mason Jr. and Damon Thomas, known collectively as the Underdogs, served as the main producers of the album, which also featured the production work of Pharrell Williams and behind-the-scenes help from Timbaland, who produced the album's biggest hit to date, "Ice Box." *21* received generally favorable reviews for its eclectic mix of dance tracks (including "Entourage") and slow songs (such as "Just Can't Let You Go"). Omarion said to Harrington, "There's still . . . a lot of things business-wise, that I want to do that I haven't been able to do yet. I feel good, and I feel really, really blessed to have had longevity in the industry as long as I have. But I can't ever stop staying hungry because there's always something new, something fresh, always something somebody else is doing, so I'm constantly thinking of creative stuff."

Omarion's long-awaited collaborative album with the rapper Bow Wow, titled *Face Off*, appeared on December 11, 2007. The album did not meet commercial expectations but received generally favorable reviews, with Simon Vozick-Levinson writing for *Entertainment Weekly* (December 7, 2007, on-line), "The formerly pint-size MC (Bow Wow, né Lil') and the ex-boy-band singer (Omarion, late of B2K) made an adorable pair on Bow's 2005 puppy-love ode 'Let Me Hold You.' With *Face Off*, they united again to serenade lady fans—this time with a whole album of raunchier tunes—and their charm proves undeniable. Neither dude will likely be recognized as a world-class vocalist on his own. But together, Bow (he of quicksilver flow) and O (he of slender harmonies) are urban-pop Wonder Twins." Gail Mitchell added for *Billboard* (on-line), "A couple of tracks sound derivative, but for the most part fans of the duo will embrace this album as well as the twosome's maturing sound." In the summer of 2008, Omarion announced that his as-yet untitled third studio album would be released on Timbaland's record label, Mosley Music Group.

The fall of 2007 also brought the releases of two films featuring Omarion: *Feel the Noise*, in which he portrayed a young man from the South Bronx who dreams of success as a rapper, and the horror film *Somebody Help Me*, directed by Christopher Stokes, in which the singer starred alongside his best friend and frequent collaborator, Marques Houston. A sequel to *You Got Served* is planned. With Houston and Stokes, Omarion founded a production company, the Franchise Boys. His hobbies include playing basketball, football, and video games and watching movies. Omari is currently single. Rumors have linked him romantically to the pop star Rihanna.

—C.C.

Suggested Reading: Ask Men Official Web site; Associated Press Online Mar. 15, 2007; (Jackson, Mississippi) *Clarion-Ledger* F p17 Aug. 25, 2005; *Jet* p58+ Oct. 21, 2002, p56+ Jan. 26, 2004, p56 May 9, 2005; *St. Louis Post-Dispatch* p4+ July 24, 2003; (Torrance, California) *Daily Breeze* K p16 Mar. 18, 2005; *Washington Post* T p6+ Dec. 29, 2006

Selected Recordings: with B2K—*B2K*, 2002; *Santa Hooked Me Up*, 2002; *Pandemonium*, 2002; as solo artist—*O*, 2005; *21*, 2006; with Bow Wow—*Face Off*, 2007

Selected Films: *You Got Served*, 2003; *Fat Albert*, 2004; *Feel the Noise*, 2007; *Somebody Help Me*, 2007

Selected Television Shows: *Cuts*, 2005

Mark Mainz/Getty Images for NCLR

Ortega, Kenny

Apr. 18, 1950– Choreographer; director; producer

Address: c/o Schwartzman PR, 10801 National Blvd., Suite 410, Los Angeles, CA 90064-4139

"Musicals are my greatest love, without question," the choreographer and director Kenny Ortega told Tiffany Bakker for the Sydney, Australia, *Sunday Telegraph Magazine* (September 10, 2006). Ortega, whose mediums include the stage, television, the silver screen, and spectacles such as the opening and closing ceremonies of the Olympic Games, has served as a driving force behind the resurrection of the movie musical, which fell into disfavor after its heyday, in the 1930s and 1940s. "For a long while there I thought maybe I'd missed the boat in terms of being born at the wrong time—musicals not being a current sort of way of entertaining," he told an interviewer for ABC News (August 17, 2007). In 1987, 24 years after his first performance in public, at age 13, and a half-dozen years after his first choreography job in Hollywood, Ortega's career got a tremendous boost, thanks to the extraordinary success of the motion picture *Dirty Dancing* (1987), which he choreographed; the film concludes with "the most goosebump-inducing dance scene in movie history," as one writer put it. Ortega's work has been seen on television on episodes of series including *Chicago Hope* and *Ally McBeal* and on special shows starring entertainers including Cher, Michael Jackson, Barbra Streisand, Madonna, Elton John, and Kiss. His direction and choreography of the hugely popular made-for-television movie *High School Musical* (2006) brought his work to the attention of a new generation of teens and "tweens" (children ages eight through 12). *High School Musical* earned him an Emmy Award for outstanding choreography; an ALMA Award, from the Hispanic advocacy group National Council of La Raza, for outstanding director of a television series, mini-series, or television movie; and a Director's Guild of America Award for outstanding directorial achievement in children's programs. *High School Musical: The Ice Tour* (2007), which Ortega directed and produced, led Peter Hartlaub, writing for the *San Francisco Chronicle* (October 22, 2007), to declare, "If this ice show proves nothing else, it's that . . . Kenny Ortega is a genius."

Kenneth John Ortega was born on April 18, 1950 in Palo Alto, California. He grew up with one brother and one sister in nearby Redwood City, not far from San Francisco. According to Douglas Sadownick, writing for the *Los Angeles Times* (May 11, 1988), one of his parents was Cuban, the other Spanish. By his own account, he fell in love with dance at age three or four. "I watched my mother and father dance around the living room," as he recalled to Tiffany Bakker. "They were swing dancing because they were war kids"—a reference to World War II, when the popularity of swing was at its peak. "Seeing their happiness in each other's arms, watching my mother twirl and hearing her laughter—it really affected me." At age 13 Ortega saw *West Side Story* at a local drive-in movie theater. "*West Side Story* changed my life . . . ," he told Bakker. "It was like, 'OK, now I know where I want to be. I know what I want to do.'" Shortly after that epiphany, Ortega began performing in public with two California repertory groups, at the Hyatt Music Theatre, in Burlingame, and the Circle Star Theatre, in San Carlos. He attended Sequoia High School, in Redwood City, where he was powerfully influenced by his exacting drama teacher, Ray Doherty. "He demanded excellence, research, work, homework and if he didn't see it, he called you on it," Ortega told Bakker. In the same interview, he cited the singer and actress Judy Garland as strongly affecting "what turned me on about music and performance." Also crucial in his artistic development were the performances in movies of the dancer, singer, and actor Gene Kelly, who became his idol.

Right after he graduated from high school, in 1968, Ortega formed an opera company with friends. He would put together crews from among "200 kids," as he recalled to Bakker, and recruit enough musicians for a full orchestra. The company staged two or three productions each year. (No readily available sources offer any details about them.) In the 1970s Ortega began a 10-year collaboration as a choreographer and director with the Tubes, known as a theater-rock band; he accompanied them on five world tours. From the latter part of that decade until the mid-1980s, the Tubes attracted much attention for their elaborate live performances, a mixture of rock and what were widely described as "quasi-pornography" and "over-the-top" sociopolitical satires. After seeing a Tubes show, the singer and actress Cher hired Ortega to choreograph one of her television specials in the late 1970s.

On the heels of the publicity that the Cher television special generated, Ortega landed a job as assistant to the choreographer Toni Basil on the feature film *The Rose* (1979), about a Janis Joplin–like rock star (played by Bette Midler). Then he was hired to choreograph the roller-skating routines in the film *Xanadu* (1980), starring Olivia Newton-John. *Xanadu*'s cast also included Gene Kelly, who, as Ortega recalled to Bakker, "took me under his wing." One day Kelly brought Ortega to his home, where he explained, by means of dance sequences from one of Kelly's greatest motion-picture hits, *Singin' in the Rain*, how to choreograph for film. Until then Ortega had known nothing about the art of cinematic choreography, because his experience in dance had been limited to theater. "Basically, you design your choreography with the camera in mind. So once the director takes it into the editing room, he's not putting together his version of your work," Ortega told Lawrence Van Gelder for the *New York Times* (January 29, 1988). Kelly revealed to Ortega that for *Anchors Aweigh* (1945), the first of three movie musicals in which he teamed up with Frank Sinatra, he had taught Sinatra how to dance by using baseball as a reference. "There's a connection" between sports and dance, Kelly told Ortega, as the latter recalled to Lynn Smith in an interview for the *Los Angeles Times* (August 12, 2007). "They belong in the same body."

Soon after shooting *Xanadu*, Ortega was commissioned to direct and choreograph a Broadway show entitled *Marilyn: An American Fable*, which loosely followed the life and career of the Hollywood icon Marilyn Monroe. The show closed after only 17 regular performances in late 1983. In a scathing review of *Marilyn* for the *New York Times* (November 21, 1983), Frank Rich described the play as "incoherent to the point of being loony" and as "so confused that it never gets around to its heroine's death. If nothing else, it must be the first exploitation of the Monroe legend that even denies necrophiliacs a good time." Nevertheless, Alyson Reed, who portrayed Monroe, won the 1984 Drama Desk Award for outstanding actress in a musical. Moreover, thanks in part to his work in *Marilyn*, Ortega won the job of choreographing the singer Madonna's video "Material Girl" (1985), which recreated the scene in the movie *Gentlemen Prefer Blondes* (1953) in which Marilyn Monroe sang "Diamonds Are a Girl's Best Friend."

Ortega's "energetic" choreography for the films *St. Elmo's Fire* (1985), *Ferris Bueller's Day Off* (1986)—for which he also served as second-unit director—and *Pretty in Pink* (1986) "shaped the way teens moved in 1980s films," according to a writer for Hollywood.com. The parade scene in *Ferris Bueller's Day Off*, in which the title character (portrayed by Matthew Broderick) lip-syncs the Beatles' version of the 1961 single "Twist and Shout," is among Ortega's best-known pieces of choreography.

Ortega's greatest cinematic success during the 1980s came with the movie *Dirty Dancing* (1987), a semi-autobiographical story written by Eleanor Bergstein and directed by Emile Ardolino. Set in 1963, in the months before the assassination of President John F. Kennedy, it starred Patrick Swayze as Johnny, a veteran "dirty dancer" and blue-collar dance instructor at a resort hotel reminiscent of those that flourished in the Catskill Mountains of New York in the mid-20th century. Also in a leading role was Jennifer Grey as Baby, the college-bound daughter of the hotel's physician; inexperienced in matters of the heart, Baby becomes a student and dance partner of Johnny's and later his lover. The movie, which cost $5 million to produce, became a runaway hit, earning $170 million at the box office. It was particularly popular among young teenage girls and catapulted Swayze and Grey to celebrity status. Among the many critics who dismissed the plot as hackneyed, a sizable number characterized the dance sequences as unusually entertaining or even spectacular.

Ortega next served as a choreography consultant for Roger Vadim's remake of *And God Created Woman* (1988) and as choreographer for *Salsa* (1988), about a fatherless Puerto Rican family in Los Angeles. The ambition of the son, a young man named Rico, is to win a salsa dancing contest. *Salsa*'s cast included a total of about 260 dancers, many of whom were discovered at salsa clubs in American cities. "I see a lot of myself in these kids," Ortega told Douglas Sadownick. "Like me, these young men and women are using dancing to flee the things in their cultures they don't like. But they also love their families and their culture too. That great contradiction makes me want . . . fire from my dancers." "My emphasis . . . is on a passionate reality, not alignment and technique," he added, referring to his direction of the dancers. Most reviewers agreed that the movie favored dance over narrative and passion over technique. "Nothing happens in the cliché-ridden script that isn't thoroughly predictable," Janice Berman wrote for New York *Newsday* (May 7, 1988). "If we'd known and cared more about the people in them, the dance sequences would have been great fun. Kenny Ortega, as he proved to far better effect in *Dirty Dancing*, knows how to make people move

and to create the sensation of a disco, or even a world in motion, a feeling of pleasure in rhythm, a sense of a community of dancers." Douglas Sadownick rued the decision of the director, Boaz Davidson, to include only the dancers' upper bodies in some sequences: "*Salsa* just might be the hottest, dirtiest dancing of the season, but we'll never know. The ads promise some flashy footwork, but the camera framing stubbornly insists on cutting its subjects off at the knees. . . . Ortega . . . could easily claim self-defense in killing . . . Davidson. Certainly Davidson's penchant for cutting away from the dancers to close-ups of elbows murders whatever artistry Ortega had evolved."

In 1990 Ortega directed and choreographed a television show, *Hull High*, which was almost immediately canceled. For his next big project, he choreographed and directed the film *Newsies* (1992), a musical set in New York City in 1899. Based on fact, *Newsies* starred Christian Bale as the leader of a strike by newsboys (youngsters, also known as newsies, who hawked newspapers on city streets), whose major employers were Joseph Pulitzer and William Randolph Hearst, the publishers of the *New York World* and the *New York Journal*, respectively. For a novice feature-film director, *Newsies* was an ambitious project to tackle, not least because many believed that the live-action motion-picture musical was an obsolete genre. As Barry Koltnow wrote for the *Chicago Tribune* (April 16, 1992), "Kenny Ortega must believe in life after death. Otherwise, he would not have made his debut as a feature film director with an old-fashioned, uplifting, hell-clicking, toe-tapping, finger-snapping, boy-meets-girl, boy-overcomes-impossible odds, dancing-in-the-streets, big-finale movie musical like *Newsies*. Hasn't he heard that the musical is dead?" Ortega hoped that *Newsies* might revive the genre, but it received mostly thumbs-down reviews. Janet Maslin complained in the *New York Times* (April 8, 1992), for example, "Mr. Ortega, whose great strength ought to have been in handling these musical sequences, unaccountably breaks up songs with dialogue and sometimes limits a musical outburst to only a few bars; never does he allow a song-and-dance number to build to a rousing finale. The choreography, by Mr. Ortega and Peggy Holmes, is similarly strange, at one point managing to combine turn-of-the-century Irish jigs with the hip-hop moves of the present. The musical outbursts do not grow organically from the film's other action, nor do they otherwise feel authentic, since the dancing looks forced and the sound is noticeably lip-synched. . . . Few of the cast members have much chance to shine, since the film's idea of charm is seriously misguided." Among the minority of critics who praised *Newsies* was Paul Sherman, who wrote for the *Boston Herald* (April 10, 1992), "Although a tad too long, *Dirty Dancing* choreographer Kenny Ortega's directorial debut is an impressive blend of story, song, dance, acting, and production values. . . . Songs and dances, which go for a *West Side Story* sort of boyish athleticism, may not be impressive when taken out of context, but often the mix of the songs, dancing, sets, and performances make them quite appealing." Its mixed critical reception notwithstanding, *Newsies* reached cult-classic status amongst its fans. Ortega had less success both critically and at the box office with his next cinematic directorial effort, *Hocus Pocus* (1993); he also choreographed that film, which starred Bette Midler, Kathy Najimy, and Sarah Jessica Parker as witches out to steal the souls of children to ensure their own immortality. Later in the 1990s he served as choreographer for the film *To Wong Foo, Thanks for Everything, Julie Newmar* (1995), starring Patrick Swayze, Wesley Snipes, and John Leguizamo as three drag queens.

Ortega directed and choreographed a number of installments of television series, including episodes of *Second Noah, Fame L.A., Wasteland, Chicago Hope, Resurrection Blvd., Grounded for Life*, and *Ally McBeal*. With Judy Chabola, he cochoreographed large-scale ensemble dance routines for the 1996 Summer Olympic Games, in Atlanta, Georgia, guiding the 5,500 dancers who participated in the opening ceremony and the 3,500 who performed in the closing ceremony. He and Chabola won the American Choreography Award for outstanding achievement in a television variety show or special in 1997 for their work on the Olympic ceremonies. The next year Ortega won the American Choreography Award again, this time for his work on an episode of *Chicago Hope*, in which he set the movements for group dance numbers including "Brain Salad Surgery." In 2001 Ortega was nominated for an Emmy Award for outstanding choreography for an episode of *Grounded for Life*. He won further accolades for his work at the 2002 Winter Olympics ceremonies, in Salt Lake City, Utah. Serving as both a director and choreographer for the opening and closing ceremonies, Ortega, with the help of many assistants, designed the movements of dancers and skaters while handling props and pyrotechnics and taking into account the physical demands of the wintry climate. He shared an American Choreography Award and the Emmy Award for outstanding choreography with Sarah Kawahara, a figure-skating choreographer, and Doug Jack, a field choreographer (whose specialties include arranging people on playing fields so that en mass they form recognizable shapes). With the directors Ron de Moraes and Bucky Gunts, he shared the Emmy for outstanding direction of a variety, music, or comedy program. From 2002 to 2006 Ortega directed the television series *Gilmore Girls*, which followed the lives of a 30-something single mother (played by Lauren Graham) raising her teenage daughter (Alexis Bledel). The television show was known for its witty, fast-paced dialogue and sensitive rendering of the mother-daughter relationship. Under Ortega's direction several members of the *Gilmore Girls* cast won television-industry awards.

On January 20, 2006 the made-for-TV film *High School Musical* premiered on the Disney Channel. Ortega had agreed to direct it because he had been "looking for a little film, something under the radar, something to get back behind the camera and into features," as he explained to Richard Huff for the New York *Daily News* (November 28, 2007). *High School Musical*'s main characters—Troy (Zac Efron), a basketball player, and Gabriella (Vanessa Anne Hudgens), an overachieving student—are auditioning for parts in their high-school musical, despite their friends' disparagement of their aspirations. They face fierce competition from two zealous theater geeks—Sharpay (Ashley Tisdale) and Ryan (Lucas Grabeel). The story emphasizes that being true to oneself and being unafraid to dream are of paramount importance for teenagers. Among the first reviews of the film was that of Anita Gates, a *New York Times* (January 20, 2006) critic, who described the movie as "dippy" and wrote that Ortega's "all-student-body dance numbers hint at a combination of influences: a little Bollywood and a little of Patricia Birch's work from *Grease*. His directing influences are unfathomable." Gates and other disparagers viewed *High School Musical* in a different light after it became an entertainment-industry phenomenon: some 200 million people in more than 100 countries reportedly watched the film, and it spawned a quadruple-platinum soundtrack album as well as a national concert tour. In July 2006 Disney reported that, thanks to sales of the *High School Musical* album, its quarterly music revenues totaled $35 million more than in the same period the previous year. Moreover, within about six months the DVD of the movie had sold upwards of 2.7 million copies. "Hating a phenomenon like *High School Musical* no longer makes you appear tasteful," as Virginia Heffernan wrote for the *New York Times* (August 17, 2007), in a review of *High School Musical 2*. "It makes you seem stupid, as if you hated all of market capitalism, or all winners." "Ortega is *Musical*'s secret weapon," Ken Tucker wrote for *Entertainment Weekly* (May 26, 2006): "He keeps the plot moving and the kids jumping, staging a terrific gym set piece in which Troy's team bursts into song while bouncing basketballs in time with the music." Ortega attributed the movie's popularity to its optimism, saying in an interview for ABC News (August 17, 2007), "I think it's been so successful because we've created a world where you can dream, a world where you can hope, a world where you can be courageous, a world where you don't have to stick to the status quo to define who you are as a young person." *High School Musical* greatly increased Ortega's name—and face—recognition; as he told the New York *Daily News* (November 28, 2007), "In the past, it was a certain audience—older, loved dance— that knew me. This is bigger and more awesome than I ever thought for myself. It was quite unintentional. The Disney Channel likes to shoot behind-the-scenes. . . . I came to discover, as I walk through a mall or go to the movies, kids are coming up and saying, 'Are you the dance man?' 'Are you the director of *High School Musical*?' Now, it's, 'Are you Kenny Ortega?'"

Also in 2006 Ortega directed *Cheetah Girls 2*, a sequel to a 2003 Disney Channel movie about a multiethnic quartet of teenage girls striving for success in the music world. The positive portrayals of Hispanics in *Cheetah Girls 2* earned Ortega the Imagen Foundation's Imagen Award for best director. Soon afterward the Ortega-directed *High School Musical 2* (2006) aired on TV. For the scene in that movie in which baseball players sing "I Don't Dance," Ortega re-created the moves Gene Kelly showed Frank Sinatra. The 17.2 million people who watched *High School Musical 2* when it debuted set a record for a cable telecast. "Proving that lightning can and does strike twice, *High School Musical 2* actually surpasses the first movie in sheer energy and verve," Laura Fried wrote for *Variety* (August 13, 2007). "Indeed there's much to admire" in *High School Musical 2*, Virginia Heffernan wrote, such as "some knockout songs." "But, come on, there's also so much to hate. . . . It's badly lip-synched, badly danced and doused in self-tanner. . . . The actors seem at times to be directed for cramped television and at others for giant, overlighted musical theater."

The fall of 2007 saw Disney's launch of the Ortega-directed and -produced *High School Musical: the Ice Tour*, which performed shows nationally. A critic for the *San Francisco Chronicle* (October 22, 2007) wrote, "Skating choreographers were brought in to help, but you could see Ortega's influence everywhere. Who else but the guy who choreographed that wicked awesome *Dirty Dancing* closing sequence could pull off an ice show where half the production takes place in the summer?" Most recently Ortega directed *High School Musical 3*; the first in that series to get a theatrical release, it arrived in theaters in the fall of 2008. The film was praised as highly choreographed escapist fun. The movie "splash[es] brightly across the screen like a spilled bag of Skittles," Ann Hornaday wrote in a representative review for the *Washington Post* (October 24, 2008). "A nonstop barrage of poppy power ballads and ambitious production numbers, this is a movie that unapologetically subscribes to the 'more is more' school of entertainment, with each sequence proving somehow more dazzling than the last. . . . As he's proved before in such classics as *Dirty Dancing* and *Newsies*, Ortega is a master choreographer, especially with big group numbers." As of mid-October 2008, plans were afoot for the production of *High School Musical 4*. Also in 2008 Ortega appeared as himself in the hit concert film *Hannah Montana & Miley Cyrus: Best of Both Worlds Concert*. He is set to direct the film *Footloose*, a remake of a 1984 movie, which is slated to open in 2010.

In 2002 the organization Nosotros honored Ortega for his achievements in improving the images of Hispanics in the entertainment industry. Two years later he won the Career Achievement Award

from the Academy of Dance on Film. Ortega lives in Los Angeles with his Yorkshire terrier, Manly, who appeared in *High School Musical 2* as the pet of the character Sharpay.

—T.O.

Suggested Reading: (Australia) *Sunday Telegraph Magazine* p17 Sep. 10, 2006; *Boston Globe* D p3 Nov. 2, 2007; *Chicago Tribune* F p11 Apr. 16, 1992; *Hispanic Business* p56 Dec. 2006; imdb.com; *New York Times* (on-line) Aug. 17, 1997; Schwartzman PR Web site

Selected Films: *Xanadu*, 1980; *Dirty Dancing*, 1987; *Salsa*, 1988; *Newsies*, 1992; *Hocus Pocus*, 1993; *High School Musical*, 2006; *High School Musical 2*, 2007; *High School Musical 3*, 2008

Selected Television Shows: *Gilmore Girls*, 2002–06

Ovechkin, Alexander

Sep. 17, 1985– Hockey player

Address: Washington Capitals, 627 N. Glebe Rd., Suite 850, Arlington, VA 22203

"You can't watch that kid and not like hockey," Mike Babcock, the coach of the Detroit Red Wings, declared to Michael Farber for *Sports Illustrated* (March 24, 2008), referring to the Washington Capitals' left-wing starter, the Russian-born Alexander Ovechkin. "He's so pumped up." In 2005, when Ovechkin—then 19—joined the National Hockey League (NHL), after three years with Russia's professional Super League, sports journalists predicted that his superlative offensive abilities would win games for the Capitals, who had been struggling near the bottom of their division; those writers also believed that Ovechkin could help revitalize the NHL, which had lost many fans in 2004–05, when every game was cancelled because of a labor-management dispute. After three seasons with the Capitals—whose home arena is the Verizon Center, in Washington, D.C.—Ovechkin's speed, creative stick handling, willingness to barrel through other teams' defense, broad smile, and obvious enthusiasm for the sport have made him one of the best-known and most-talked-about players in the NHL. Drawing comparisons to such NHL greats as Dale Hawerchuk, Steve Yzerman, Rick Nash, and Wayne Gretzky, Ovechkin—or Ovie, as his teammates call him—has already become a superstar, breaking several franchise and league records and consistently making remarkable plays. In January 2008 the six-foot two-inch, 216-pound Ovechkin signed a 13-year, $124 million contract with the Capitals, the largest in NHL history. "If there was ever an athlete who you'd pay to see no matter

Dave Sandford/Getty Images for the NHL
Alexander Ovechkin

what his team did, he'd be the guy," the Columbus Blue Jackets coach Ken Hitchcock told Farber. "I'd watch him in the warmup. He transcends. I think he's the evolution of our game, a young, reckless, skilled player."

The youngest of the three sons of Tatiana Nikolaevna Ovechkina and Mikhail "Misha" Ovechkin, Alexander Ovechkin was born on September 17, 1985 in Moscow, in what was then the Soviet Union. His mother became a basketball star after her recovery from a childhood accident in which her leg was so mangled that doctors wanted to amputate it. As the starting point guard and captain of Russia's national women's basketball team, she helped her squad to win one world championship, six European titles, and Olympic gold medals in 1976 and 1980. Recently voted best female point guard of the 20th century by readers of the Russian newspaper *Sport Express*, she is currently the president of the women's basketball team Dynamo Moscow. Ovechkin's father signed a contract to play professional sports in Russia's Dynamo league when he was a teenager. At 17 he tore a major muscle in his thigh and was forced to give up active play. Instead, he became a taxicab driver and, later, the director of his wife's team. Alexander Ovechkin seemed naturally attracted to hockey starting in early childhood; while other children would use cardboard boxes to make forts, he would tip them sideways to serve as makeshift goals. At age eight he joined a youth hockey league and discovered that many of his peers had begun skating years earlier and could already skate backward figure-eights. Determined to improve, the young Ovechkin demanded that his father wake up early to practice skating with him before his schoolday

started, and he often stayed late after his evening hockey sessions for extra practice. "He would skate there until his legs fell off," Ovechkin's father told April Witt for the *Washington Post* (November 26, 2006). "He'd come home every evening just completely exhausted. He would drop in the hallway, and we'd pick him up and just carry him to his room." While careful not to push his son, Ovechkin's father purchased NHL trading cards and videos of Wayne Gretzky's games, which he and Alexander would dissect together. Thanks to his efforts, Ovechkin's skills soon surpassed those of his teammates.

On September 19, 1995, when Ovechkin was 10, his oldest brother, Sergei, died at age 22 from injuries sustained in a car accident. Heartbroken but not wanting to sit idly at home, Ovechkin played with his team the next day. "His brother wasn't even in the ground yet . . . ," his father recalled to Witt. "He played while tears were flowing down his cheeks. He cried the entire game, but he played. He wanted to play." In remembrance of Sergei, Ovechkin blows a kiss to the sky whenever he makes a goal. (A significant number of sources report erroneously that Sergei died in 2000.)

The NHL took note of Ovechkin's prowess as a member of the Moscow Dynamo junior hockey league. When Ovechkin was 15 Don Meehan, a Canadian sports agent, met with him to discuss his plans, even though Alexander would not be eligible to play in the NHL until he turned 18. Ovechkin began his professional career in Russia at age 16, playing with Dynamo Moscow with men up to two decades older than him. At 17 he became the youngest skater in history to play for the Russian national team, with whom he held his own despite his relative lack of experience. Among those in his age group, he excelled. In the 2002 World Under-18 Junior Championships, for example, Ovechkin's 14 goals in eight games set records, and he helped his team gain a gold medal. In September 2002, as the youngest player in the Four Nations tournament, which featured top junior players from Russia, the Czech Republic, Finland, and Sweden, Ovechkin led all scorers, with six goals in three games—two more than the total for the entire Swedish team. That season Ovechkin scored six goals in six games for Russia's national team, helping them win the gold medal at the 2003 World Junior Championship. Playing with the Dynamo during the 2003–04 season, Ovechkin notched 13 goals and 24 points (the sum of goals and assists), and his team won a silver medal at the World Junior Championships. Meanwhile, Ovechkin was preparing for a career as a border guard at the Military Institute in Moscow. (Military service is compulsory in Russia, but the law is applied differently for particular individuals, and Ovechkin's studies apparently fulfilled the requirements.)

When Ovechkin turned 18 the Washington Capitals, ranked 28th among the 30 NHL teams, won the 2004–05 draft lottery, giving them the first draft pick. George McPhee, the Capitals' general manager, who had met privately with Ovechkin the year before, told Witt, "We were all excited. I called our chief amateur scout. I said, 'If you had to pick today, who would you take?' He said, 'It's got to be Ovechkin.' . . . We just felt like Alex's character and his physical playing really separated him from any other player we could see." The Capitals selected Ovechkin in the first round of the NHL draft on June 26, 2004, but before they agreed on a contract, the start of the season was delayed because of stalled negotiations between the National Hockey League Players Association (NHLPA) and the league over proposed salary caps for players. In February 2005, after five months of negotiations, Commissioner Gary Bettman announced the official cancellation of the 2004–05 NHL season. The NHL "lockout," as it became known, marked the first time in North American professional sports that an entire season was lost due to a labor dispute.

During the lockout Ovechkin played for Dynamo Moscow until the middle of the season, when he walked out because of disagreements about his salary and the size of the apartment the team had provided for him. With the encouragement of his mother, who now handles most of his business affairs, Ovechkin accepted a $2 million offer with Avangard, a team in the Siberian city of Omsk. Before the season began Ovechkin learned that the NHL lockout had ended, on July 22, 2005. He received from McPhee an offer of a base salary of $984,200, with several incentive-based bonuses that gave him the opportunity to earn significantly more than $2 million. Eager to compete with players in the NHL, which is considered the number-one hockey league in the world, Ovechkin recalled to Witt: "I think about the money. You can take the money and not be happy. Or you can take the dream." With his mother's approval, Ovechkin voided his one-year contract with the Omsk team, which contained a clause allowing him to do so, and signed with the Capitals. Ovechkin's former team, the Moscow Dynamo, subseqently sued Ovechkin, arguing that the Dynamo had contractual rights to him during the 2005–06 season, and that he should return to Moscow to play. In January 2006 the matter was dismissed by a U.S. district court.

In his first season as the Capitals' starting left wing, which began on October 5, 2005, Ovechkin—wearing a jersey with an "8," his mother's number when she played basketball—was the team's leading scorer. On January 13, 2006 he recorded his first hat trick, with a game-winning goal in overtime, helping the Capitals beat the Anaheim Mighty Ducks, 3–2. The event that solidified Ovechkin's "rock-star status," as Witt put it, came on January 16, 2006, in the third period of a game against the Phoenix Coyotes. As he was skating toward the goal, preparing to fire the puck backhanded into the net, the defenseman Paul Mara knocked Ovechkin off his feet. Sliding on his back, with the stick over his head, Ovechkin managed to flick the

puck into the net. The shot, replayed over and over on television and the Internet, was so impressive that it became known simply as "the goal"; it earned Ovechkin a new nickname: "Alexander the Great." Other players confirmed that the shot was a result of skill, not luck. "As he fell, he had the presence of mind to change the angle of his hand and his stick so that he could kind of shoot with the stick behind his head . . . ," the Capitals' veteran goalie Ollie Kolzig told Witt. "Once we saw that on replay, we all lost our minds on the bench. . . . A talent like his only comes by once in a lifetime." Though the Capitals failed to make the play-offs, Ovechkin set a team record, with 52 goals, as well as league records, with 435 shots at the goal and 106 regular-season points. He was also the first player in NHL history to rack up more than 50 goals and 100 points in his rookie season. In a landslide vote by the Professional Hockey Writers' Association, Ovechkin was named the franchise's first NHL rookie of the year.

A newcomer to North American culture, Ovechkin worked hard to accustom himself to his surroundings and fit in with his team. He played poker with his teammates, insisted on speaking English to journalists (even before he knew the language well), and asked that he be assigned a roommate from North America rather than a Russian. He ended up rooming with the London, Ontario–born right wing Brian Willsie. "I want to be in the team," Ovechkin told Farber for *Sports Illustrated* (January 9, 2006). "I want to understand coach and teammates. I not want to speak Russian and somebody translate for me." With his broad smile, ebullience, and joyful demonstration on the ice, Ovechkin won over his teammates and fans. Despite his almost immediate status as one of the league's superstars, Ovechkin maintained an attitude of modesty and respect. "It's interesting," McPhee told Barry Svrluga for the *Washington Post* (February 5, 2006), "because he's come here and sort of made our team a team based on all those intangibles that are important—the respect for the coaches and his teammates, the respect for the game, the preparation for the game."

Selected to play for Russia at the 2006 Winter Olympic Games, in Turin, Italy, Ovechkin led the team with five goals, including the winning goal in the match with Canada. He was the only player named to the all-tournament team (an all-star team whose members are selected by the international media) who was not a member of the gold-medal winners, the Swedish team, or the silver-medal winners, the Finnish team. Although Russia won no medals at those Games, the team's obvious improvement since the collapse of the Soviet Union was largely attributed to Ovechkin's leadership. "Ovechkin's love of hockey and homeland has spread among his teammates," Karen Crouse wrote for the *New York Times* (February 23, 2006). "For the first time in years, the Russians are playing as if they are intent on outscoring their opponent and not just outshining one another." In May 2006

OVECHKIN

Ovechkin played for Russia in the International Ice Hockey Federation's Men's Ice Hockey Championship, scoring six goals and three assists in seven games, before the team lost to the Czech Republic in the quarterfinals.

Having proven himself in offense during his rookie year, in the 2006–07 season Ovechkin worked on improving his defense and offense, including skating speed and the ferocity of his hits. "He's all over the place," the Capitals' captain, Chris Clark, told Tarik El-Bashir for the *Washington Post* (December 19, 2006). "He's not just hitting guys, he's running over guys. If he's not shooting the puck on net, he's driving to the net. He's making something happen on every shift." On January 9, 2007 fans voted Ovechkin into the starting lineup for the NHL All-Star Game, held two weeks later. In the first weeks of February, however, as the Capitals struggled to earn a spot in the play-offs, Ovechkin began to experience what appeared to be an offensive slump, scoring only one goal in seven games. Consequently, the team recorded 10 losses and only three wins in February. "When Ovechkin doesn't score, and I'm not saying it's him, but if you look at the last year and a half, he's a big part of our offense," the Capitals' head coach at that time, Glen Hanlon, told El-Bashir (February 19, 2007). The Capitals had only a mediocre season, with just 28 wins out of 68 games, failing yet again to earn a play-off spot. Ovechkin was a member of the Russian team that won a bronze medal in the 2007 World Ice Hockey Championship.

Ovechkin has continued to lead his team offensively, and sports journalists have taken note of the tighter on-the-ice chemistry between Ovechkin and the Capitals' 2006 draft pick Nicklas Backstrom, a center. On March 21, 2008 Ovechkin made two goals in the last eight-and-a-half minutes of a game against the Atlanta Thrashers that the Capitals won, 5–3. With those goals—the 105th and 106th of his career—Ovechkin became the league leader in goals and the first player since 1996 to score 60 goals in a single season. In the Capitals' next three, winning games, Ovechkin scored two more goals, breaking the franchise record of 60, set by Dennis Maruk in 1981–82. Ovechkin finished the regular season with 65 goals, the most ever scored by a left-winger, and 112 points, making him the league leader in both categories.

In their first play-off appearance since 2001, the Capitals faced the Philadelphia Flyers in the Eastern Conference's quarterfinals, a best-of-seven series that began on April 11, 2008. After being held to one goal and four assists in the series' first five games, Ovechkin scored two goals in the sixth game, helping the Capitals secure a 4–2 win. In the seventh game, which took place the following day, Ovechkin scored the team's second goal, which brought the score to 2–2. After 16 unsuccessful shots at the goal in the last 20 minutes, the Capitals met the Flyers in overtime and lost the game. "We're disappointed . . . ," Ovechkin told El-Bashir for the *Washington Post* (April 23, 2008). "

. . . We have lots of chances, but we don't put it in the net. In overtime, it's about luck. Today we don't have luck." Nevertheless, Ovechkin and the Capitals were credited with a triumphant season. Ovechkin played for Russia's national team in the International Ice Hockey Federation World Championships, a 16-team tournament held in Canada in May 2008. Scoring a remarkable 12 points (six goals and six assists) in nine games, he led Russia to its first World Championship gold medal since 1993. He made the second-highest number of goals in the tournament and was named to the all-tournament team. As of October 23, 2008 the Capitals' record stood at 3–3 for the season, with Ovechkin scoring a total of two goals and making two assists.

In both 2006 and 2007, Russian NHL players selected Ovechkin as the winner of the Kharlamov Trophy, which honors the best Russian player in the league. In 2008 the Professional Hockey Writers Association awarded Ovechkin the Hart Memorial Trophy, which recognizes the player who is most valuable to his team, and his peers honored him with the Lester B. Pearson Award for being the most outstanding player. (He was the first Capital to receive either of the latter two awards.) Also in 2008 Ovechkin was named the D.C. Sportsman of the Year by the Greater Washington Sports Alliance. During his three years in the NHL, Ovechkin has been recognized as the league's rookie of the month, offensive player of the month, and number-one star of the month.

Ovechkin lives in a house near downtown Arlington, Virginia. Frequent visitors include his parents and his brother Mikhail, nicknamed Misha, who stays in the United States part of the year to keep him company and study English. Ovechkin enjoys playing cards or watching movies with his family and spending time with his girlfriend, Veronica, a student in St. Petersburg. At night he sometimes dreams of winning the Stanley Cup, professional ice hockey's most coveted prize. "It's to the point where I feel the cup," he told Witt. "I can feel touching it, raising it above my head."

—M.E.R.

Suggested Reading: capitals.nhl.com; *Sports Illustrated* R p8 Nov. 4, 2002, p56 Jan. 9, 2006, p94 Mar. 24, 2008; *Washington Post* E p1 Feb. 5, 2006, W p14 Nov. 26, 2006, E p5 Dec. 19, 2006, E p4 Feb. 19, 2007

Valerie Macon/AFP/Getty Images

Page, Ellen

Feb. 21, 1987– Actress

Address: ID Public Relations, 8409 Santa Monica Blvd., West Hollywood, CA 90069

After describing *Juno* as "just about the best movie" of 2007, the critic Roger Ebert, writing for the *Chicago Sun-Times* (December 14, 2007), lavished praise on Ellen Page, the actress who, at age 19, portrayed the title character. "Has there been a better performance this year than Ellen Page's creation of Juno? I don't think so," Ebert wrote. "If most actors agree that comedy is harder than drama, then harder still is comedy depending on a quick mind, utter self-confidence, and an ability to stop just short of going too far. Page's presence and timing are extraordinary." Many other critics, too, applauded Page's turn as a pregnant teenager who decides to give her baby up for adoption, in a role that required the actress to exhibit both sarcastic wit and childlike fragility. "She has a gift for making her motor-mouth lines sound like they're really coming from her head, and an instinct for mixing almost supernatural self-possession with flashes of vulnerability," the film critic David Edelstein said in his review for the National Public Radio program *Fresh Air* (December 7, 2007). Her work in *Juno*, which was directed by Jason Reitman, brought Page nominations for an Oscar and a Golden Globe Award and a bevy of other awards, as have her performances in some of the two dozen films and television series in which she has appeared since she began her acting career, at age 10. Those honors include the 2003 ACTRA Maritimes Award, from the Alliance of Canadian Cinema,

Television, and Radio Artists, for her work in the film *Marion Bridge*; the 2004 Atlantic Canadian Award, given out at the Atlantic Film Festival, for her performance in the motion picture *Wilby Wonderful*; and two Gemini Awards (which celebrate excellence in English-language Canadian television), in 2004 and 2005, for her performances in *Mrs. Ashboro's Cat* and *ReGenesis*, respectively.

Ellen Philpotts-Page was born on February 21, 1987 in Halifax, the capital of the Canadian province of Nova Scotia. Her mother, Martha Philpotts, is a teacher; her father, Dennis Page, is a graphic designer. According to Dominic Wills, writing for tiscali.co.uk (2008), her father had a son and daughter from a previous marriage, and her parents separated during her childhood; her father later remarried. When Page was 10 years old, talent scouts seeking child actors for a TV movie called *Pit Pony* visited the public Halifax Grammar School, where she was a student, and cast her in a small role. The film was successful, and Page signed on for the spin-off TV series. "My parents never pushed me into this at all, but they've really supported me," she told Jill Rappaport for *Dateline NBC* (January 13, 2008), explaining that she enjoyed a relatively normal childhood. "And their main thing is that I do remain grounded and keep my head on my shoulders." When she was 13 Page was offered a role on a U.S. sitcom, but her parents insisted that she turn it down, since taking the part would have meant moving to Los Angeles, California. "It's a good thing," Page told the WENN Entertainment News Wire Service (January 21, 2008). "I would have had to move to LA and I can't even imagine what I would be like now. They [her parents] said keep up your grades and then you can act." During those years Page played competitively on two soccer teams. She also enjoyed hiking and snowboarding. "I'm pretty adventurous," the self-professed tomboy told Ginny Chien for the *Los Angeles Times* (January 6, 2008).

From 2001 to 2002 Page portrayed Treena Lahey on the Canadian TV comedy *Trailer Park Boys*, a show known for its raunchy humor. "I am not sure she enjoyed her work on *Trailer Park Boys* that much because of the humour on the show—she is so much of a gentle soul, and for her to be able to embrace that I would think would have been beyond her ken," the actor John Dunsworth, who played her drunken father in the series, told Lee-Anne Goodman for the *Peterborough Examiner* (December 15, 2007). Dunsworth told Robyn Young for the *Halifax Daily News* (January 23, 2008), "Who can put a finger on the magic when some people just have it? She's incredible."

In 2002, the same year that she appeared in the film *The Wet Season* and the TV show *Rideau Hall*, Page worked alongside the actress Molly Parker in the independent Canadian film *Marion Bridge* and decided to pursue acting as a career. "For the first time, I felt something different," she told David Ansen and Devin Gordon for *Newsweek* (January 28, 2008). "I felt myself being overcome by something I can't necessarily explain. But I wanted to keep feeling that and finding out what that was and learning more about it."

Over the next couple of years, Page appeared in a string of TV movies, among them *Mrs. Ashboro's Cat*, *Homeless to Harvard: The Liz Murray Story*, *Going for Broke*, and *I Downloaded a Ghost*. She also had a recurring role on *ReGenesis*, a Canadian TV science-fiction series. Her film work included *Touch & Go*, *Love That Boy*, and *Wilby Wonderful*, all Canadian releases. According to Dominic Wills, Page attended the Queen Elizabeth High School before transferring to Shambhala High School, a non-denominational private school that incorporates a brief period of meditation in every student's daily schedule. Page's favorite teacher, Jane Hester, has recalled the young actress as smart, funny, and similar to the character she would later play in *Juno*. In an interview with Young, Hester called Page a "normal Nova Scotian girl," adding, "She's just going to be who she is; she's just going to be honest about herself and that's what she's got going for her." During downtime on film sets, Page taught herself how to juggle, and she would sometimes use the skill to amuse her classmates.

In 2005, the same year she graduated from high school, Page appeared in *Mouth to Mouth* and *Hard Candy*, films that heightened her profile and allowed her to tackle dark, challenging subject matter. In *Mouth to Mouth*, she played a runaway teenager who hitchhikes through Europe and joins a cult-like underground organization called SPARK, or Street People Armed with Radical Knowledge. While the film received mixed reviews, critics praised Page's performance. "An intensely direct performer, Page is also subtly adept at hinting at something held back, in this case through the merest tilt of a jaw that hints at a skeptical strength taking root within a girl who has little reason to trust anyone," Ella Taylor wrote for *LA Weekly* (May 31, 2006). In his review for the *Los Angeles Times* (June 2, 2006), Mark Olsen, having seen some of Page's later movies, was less impressed, writing, "Page's performance here is developmental at best, and though she shows flashes of the strong-willed, seductive decisiveness that has marked her subsequent roles, she mostly looks slightly confused, unsure of herself and under-directed."

In *Hard Candy*, directed by David Slade, Page played Hayley Stark, a 14-year-old who drugs and tortures the pedophile who murdered her best friend. "*Hard Candy*, however it's wrapped, is a tough one to swallow," Rob Nelson wrote for the *Village Voice* (April 11, 2006). "Still, the acute precociousness of our score-settling Lolita strains credibility only if you fail to accept the film's effortless assertion that American pop—e.g., the Internet and, yes, extreme cinema-on-demand—has lowered the minimum-age requirements for just about everything, including principled payback." Nelson went on to write that Page, "a Molly Ringwald type who was only 15 when the movie was made, leaves little doubt as to whether a kid can play a grown-up's icky game and win." Describing Page's performance for *Entertainment Weekly* (April 12, 2006), Owen Gleiberman wrote, "Looking like a baby Sigourney Weaver, she takes off from the script's dexterous sarcasms to play Hayley with an enlightened lack of mercy, an ability to stare down her enemy by thinking just like him. To watch *Hard Candy* is, at moments, to be very afraid, but the scariest thing about it is the fury of Page's talent." In an interview with Gina Piccalo for the *Los Angeles Times* (December 2, 2007), David Slade, who had auditioned more than 300 girls before he cast Page as Hayley, recalled Page's commitment to the part: "She often said, 'I will cry. I will break down. I will look like I'm in a mess. That's part of my process.'" Slade added, "When she's in character, you can't talk to her about anything else. When [in the film] she believes her friend was murdered, she believes it to the exclusion of the world. Yet, she's not this impenetrable dark soul. She's also this breath of fresh air." In 2006 Page appeared as Kitty Pryde in *X-Men 3: The Last Stand* (2006), the final film in a trilogy based on a popular Marvel Comics series. While some of her friends teased her for "selling out" and taking a part in an action blockbuster, Page has said that she had fun portraying a comic-book heroine. "Doing a film like that has helped me do the last five films I've shot," she told Piccalo, referring to the increase in offers that followed the release of that high-profile film.

It was after seeing Page in *Hard Candy* that the director Jason Reitman, the son of the acclaimed comedic filmmaker Ivan Reitman, began considering her for the title role in *Juno*. "You saw a career opening up before your eyes," he told Piccalo, likening her performance to Jodie Foster's star-making turn in the 1976 film *Taxi Driver*. "When I met her, it wasn't even a second thought," Reitman added. "It's a combination of her fearlessness and her intellect. It was literally like meeting Juno. She comes right at you with her intelligence and her sense of humor." "She's way too smart for her age," Reitman told Chien. "It's embarrassing sometimes to have a conversation with her." *Juno* was written by Diablo Cody, a first-time screenwriter who had gained attention with her memoir, *Candy Girl: A Year in The Life of an Unlikely Stripper* (2006), which described her experiences as an exotic dancer. *Juno* is about a snarky teenage outsider who gets pregnant and decides to give the baby to a yuppie couple, played by Jason Bateman and Jennifer Garner. "I just fell in love with [the script]," Page told Jill Rappaport. "It was something that I really, really, really wanted to do. I feel pretty lucky." In particular, Page was struck by Juno's distinctive way of expressing herself, a characteristic many critics have praised. "One of the things that I was blown away by when I first read the script was the dialogue," she told Bob Strauss for the *Daily News of Los Angeles*, as printed in the *Baltimore Sun* (January 11, 2008). "Although it was unique and witty and all of that, to me it felt very fluid, it felt very rhythmic and it felt very organic. And although I didn't speak the exact same way as Juno spoke when I was 16, I definitely had my own unique language with my friends, which was different from how I communicated with my parents and in work environments."

After Page's character learns that she is pregnant, she briefly considers having an abortion; her decision to have the baby adopted has led some to label *Juno* a pro-life film. Page, who has identified herself as pro-choice, told Strauss that to politicize *Juno* is to miss the film's point. "I think people have an idea of a movie they want to make, and it's not about a woman who has an abortion," she said. "For example, our film was about a young girl who decides to have her baby and give it to an uptight yuppie couple. That was Diablo's idea of the film, but it's great that she shows that there's an extremely viable choice that needs to be there for young women. And she deals with it in an incredibly well-done way." She added, "But this is what the film is about. If Juno had an abortion, it would be a short film."

Page has also said that she liked Juno's attitude and regarded the chartacter as refreshing, even unique. "Juno is a teenage female lead we've never seen before," she told Johanna Schneller for the Toronto *Globe and Mail* (January 23, 2008). "She feels genuine, honest. That's what people are responding to." Many critics agreed, and in his review for *Time* (December 7, 2007), the film critic Richard Schickel wrote, "In this effort Cody and Reitman are particularly blessed by Ellen Page's performance. She has a way of making her preternatural articulateness seem real rather than forced, a way of indicating her vulnerability without pressing us for sympathy. Hers is a lived-in character, perking along, tougher than she looks, naturally funnier in speech and outlook than she probably knows. *Juno* is not a great movie; it does not have aspirations in that direction. But it is, in its little way, a truthful, engaging and welcome entertainment." In his review for the *New York Times* (December 5, 2007), the film critic A. O. Scott wrote that *Juno* "outgrows its own mannerisms and defenses, evolving from a coy, knowing farce into a heartfelt, serious comedy." He added, "A good deal of the credit for this goes to Ms. Page, . . . who is able to seem, in the space of a single scene, mature beyond her years and disarmingly childlike. The naïveté that peeks through her flippant, wised-up façade is essential, since part of the movie's point is that Juno is not quite as smart or as capable as she thinks she is." Writing for *Entertainment Weekly* (December 7, 2007), Lisa Schwarzbaum called Page "radiantly no-nonsense," and she went on to grade the film an A–. In Page's interview with Rappaport, she responded to one critic's statement that she embodied Juno the way Audrey Hepburn did Holly Golightly, the iconic lead character of the film *Breakfast at Tiffany's*. "I don't want to sound like, you know, too self-deprecating or what have you,"

Page said, "but, you know, I definitely just—I feel like I have so much to learn and so much I want to do and so on. So it's hard to absorb such kind of insane comments."

In addition to her Academy Award and Golden Globe nominations, Page received leading-actress award nominations from BAFTA (the British Academy of Film and Television Arts), the Broadcast Film Critics Association, the Screen Actors Guild, and the Online Film Critics Society. She earned awards in that category from the film critics' associations of Chicago, Florida, Central Ohio, Las Vegas, and Toronto, and "breakthrough" awards from the Hollywood Film Festival, the National Board of Review, the Phoenix Film Critics Society, the International Press Academy (whose prizes are called the Satellite Awards), and the Independent Film Project (the Gotham Award).

In 2007 Page also appeared in the Canadian films *The Tracey Fragments*—playing "an emotionally unstable teenager looking for her little brother," according to Goodman—and *The Stone Angel*. In *An American Crime* she played a real-life young girl, Sylvia Likens, who in 1965 was raped, tortured, and eventually murdered by the Indiana family whom her parents had hired as caregivers. During filming Page starved herself in an attempt to connect with the horrors Sylvia had faced. "At one point, while we were shooting, she was lying on the cellar floor, which is where a lot of it happened," the film's director, Tommy O'Haver, told Piccalo. "I noticed how skinny she was. I turned to her and I said, 'Ellen, have you been eating?' She said, 'Well, no, because Sylvia wasn't being fed.' She said, 'I'm doing this for you, Tommy.' I just couldn't believe it." The film ran into distribution problems and was not released in theaters; in May 2008 the cable-television company Showtime aired it, and it received several positive reviews. Page appeared in the film *Smart People*, released in April 2008. In that romantic comedy, starring Dennis Quaid and Sarah Jessica Parker, Page portrayed the politically conservative Vanessa Wetherhold, who is "Juno rewritten by Ayn Rand," as A. O. Scott observed in the *New York Times* (April 11, 2008, on-line).

Page is said to have a handful of films in preproduction, including "Light-house"; "Whip It," which will mark the directorial debut of the actress Drew Barrymore; and "Jack and Diane," in which she potrays a teenage lesbian living in New York. In February 2008 it was reported that she had signed on to star in "Drag Me to Hell," a horror film to be directed by Sam Raimi. Page is also set to star in a BBC Films adaptation of Charlotte Brontë's *Jane Eyre*, which is due for release in 2009. Explaining to Chien how she chooses her roles, Page said that it "feeds my soul when I can approach a character who is honest and well-written and whole. I guess I just feel strongly about remaining connected to myself." "When you do this, you do have to understand to a certain extent that it's a business," she told Howard Gensler for the *Phila-*

delphia *Daily News* (December 14, 2007). "But I don't really feel like compromising my happiness or integrity, because life is too short and there are a lot of things that my heart's attached to. So I pick roles that I want to play that I feel branch away from stereotype, and a lot of the actresses I really like have done that."

During many of her interviews surrounding the release of *Juno*, Page wore a badge that read "Nova Scotia: Canada's Ocean Playground." She enjoys traveling, reading, and playing the guitar. In 2007 she spent a month backpacking in Europe. She lives with friends in Halifax.

—K.J.P.

Suggested Reading: *Baltimore Sun* E p14+ Jan. 13, 2008; *Chicago Sun Times* B p1 Dec. 14, 2007; *Dateline NBC* (transcript) Jan. 13, 2008; *Halifax*

(Nova Scotia) Daily News p3 Jan. 23, 2008; *Los Angeles Times Magazine* p28+ Jan. 6, 2008; tiscali.co.uk 2008; *Toronto (Canada) Star* E p1 Jan. 23, 2008; *USA Today* D p1+ Jan. 10, 2008

Selected Films: *Pit Pony*, 1997; *Marion Bridge*, 2002; *The Wet Season*, 2002; *Mrs. Ashboro's Cat*, 2003; *Touch & Go*, 2003; *Homeless to Harvard: The Liz Murray Story*, 2003; *Going for Broke*, 2003; *Love That Boy*, 2003; *I Downloaded a Ghost*, 2004; *Wilby Wonderful*, 2004; *Hard Candy*, 2005; *Mouth to Mouth*, 2005; *X-Men 3: The Last Stand*, 2006; *An American Crime*, 2007; *The Tracey Fragments*, 2007; *Juno*, 2007; *The Stone Angel*, 2007; *Smart People*, 2008

Selected Television Shows: *Trailer Park Boys*, 2001–02; *Rideau Hall*, 2002; *ReGenesis*, 2004–05

Courtesy of Citigroup

Pandit, Vikram

Jan. 14, 1957– CEO of Citigroup

Address: Citigroup, 399 Park Ave., New York, NY 10043

On December 11, 2007 Vikram Pandit was chosen as the new chief executive officer (CEO) of Citigroup, one of the world's largest banks, which had been in turmoil for some time. Analysts and investors immediately wondered whether Pandit would be up to the task of turning the company around, given descriptions of him such as that by the *Financial News* (October 23, 2007, on-line), which

referred to Pandit as "the epitome of a new breed of product specialists with an encyclopaedic knowledge of risk . . . who gained promotion through technical brilliance rather than people skills." In the year preceding the resignation of Pandit's predecessor, Charles Prince, Citigroup's stock prices had fallen an astonishing 40 percent. In the spring of 2007, Prince had laid off some 26,500 employees in an effort to cut costs, and in November 2007 he reported $5.9 billion in company write-downs, or devaluing of assets, due to the debt incurred on investments following the nation's subprime-mortgage crisis. (He resigned the same month.) Pandit's quick rise up the ranks of Citigroup began in April 2007, when the hedge fund that he had founded two years earlier, Old Lane Partners, was purchased by Citigroup for $800 million, and Pandit was named CEO of Citigroup's Citi Alternative Investments (CAI). In October 2007 Pandit was promoted to head the newly created Institutional Clients Group, a division overseeing Citigroup's numerous capital markets and investment-banking businesses; just two months later, after a five-week search, the relative newcomer became the company's chief executive. In 2008, in the face of one of the most tumultuous financial environments in recent history, Pandit resisted calls to break up Citigroup's many financial businesses; instead, he instituted other changes, among them a reduction of jobs, the divestment of many of Citigroup's noncore businesses, and the sale of shares to foreign investors.

Pandit is perhaps not the type of person most would expect to head a Wall Street investment firm. While he is a numbers specialist who has made a career of mastering the minutia of investment banking, he is also known for being quiet and shy and has never sought the limelight. He told Landon Thomas Jr. for *New York* (May 20, 2002) that he had never embraced the "Gordon Gecko idea of Wall Street," a reference to the flamboyant, power-hungry fictional investor in the film *Wall Street* (1987) who gave a speech that included the widely quoted proclamation, "Greed is good." Earlier in Pandit's career, during his tenure as co-president and chief operating officer of the Institutional Securities Group of the financial-services firm Morgan Stanley, Thomas described Pandit as "a slight, bespectacled man who speaks in such a soft, self-effacing voice that he barely registers on a tape recorder. He is an unlikely corporate killer, which, say Morgan Stanley hands who know him well, is the secret of his success."

Vikram Pandit was born on January 14, 1957 to a moderately affluent family in Nagpur, India, an urban center known as "Orange City" for its busy orange trade and located in the state of Maharashtra, on the country's southwestern coast. His mother's name was Shailaja; his father, Shankar, worked as the director of a pharmaceutical company. According to his father, Pandit was such a shy child that he did not talk to anyone outside his immediate family. Because of the relocations required by his father's job, he attended several different schools while growing up. From 1959 to 1964 his family lived in Bombay, India, where Pandit attended Dadar Parsee Youth Assembly High School. When he was 12 his family relocated to Mombassa, Kenya, in Africa. At each school that he attended, Pandit stood out as an academic leader in his class. "Vikram was a studious person," Pandit's father told Vaihayasi P. Daniel for the Web site Rediff.com (December 18, 2007). "I would not say that he was a bookworm. He enjoyed every small aspect of his activities—games or debating. He had learned how to analyze the situation—a sort of lateral thinking—and to come to solutions and make the best of it. He is very successful in that." Pandit's father was transferred to New York City at around the time that Pandit, then 16, enrolled in New York's Columbia University; Pandit, his father, and Pandit's older sister, Alka, lived together in the Rego Park neighborhood in the city's borough of Queens. Pandit graduated from Columbia in 1976 with B.S. degree in electrical engineering; he earned his M.S. degree in the same field from Columbia the following year. When he was 20 years old, his father returned to India, while Pandit moved to the Columbia University campus in the Morningside Heights neighborhood of Manhattan. Having already earned the credentials to be a professional engineer, Pandit nonetheless wanted to earn his Ph.D. from Columbia. At the suggestion of an academic adviser, he decided to study finance. "What attracted me to the industry was that this was a business that could be interesting and a lot of fun," Pandit told Thomas. "But to do well, you have to put a lot of yourself into it. I have to admit there is a sense of accomplishment that comes along with it." While earning his doctorate, Pandit taught economics at Columbia and also served for a time as an assistant professor at the University of Indiana, in Bloomberg. For his dissertation, according to Rajnish Mehra, a professor at the University of California (Santa Barbara), who was on Pandit's dissertation committee, Pandit was assigned one of the toughest asset-pricing problems that his advisers could find—on the subject of "recursive equilibrium in the case of heterogeneous households," as Ben White and David Wighton reported for the London *Financial Times* (December 15, 2007). Mehra told White and Wighton, "We had no idea how to solve it so we gave it to him and he made good progress." Pandit earned his doctorate in 1986.

Meanwhile, in 1983, Pandit had accepted a position as an associate at Morgan Stanley. Just seven years after he was hired, he became a managing director of the firm and head of its equity capital markets, which the Forbes Media Co.'s Web site Investopedia defines as markets that exist "between companies and financial institutions [and are] used to raise the equity capital for the companies"—"equity capital" being money given to companies in exchange for part ownership in those companies. In that position he designed trading systems aimed at reducing transaction costs. In 1991 Pandit and his colleague Ivan Freeman developed a new kind of hybrid security, or financial agreement combining two or more forms of investment, called Preferred Equity Redemption Cumulative Stock (PERCS). Although PERCS was based on previously known financial instruments, Morgan Stanley's competitors had failed to develop similar strategies. "There are no new ideas," Pandit told Tom Pratt for the *Investment Dealer's Digest* (December 2, 1991). "Buy-writes [a kind of security with which PERCS shares similarities] have been around forever; this just brought together three or four things that were already out there. It's like one-stop shopping—a publicly traded, liquid instrument with a built-in buy-write." By 1994 Pandit was running the firm's equity-derivatives business, a position in which he continued to develop proprietary trading and oversee the growth of Morgan Stanley's successful prime-brokerage business. (Equity derivatives are investments whose value depends on the stock price of the company in which one invests. Proprietary trading is a financial firm's investment for itself rather than its clients, and prime brokerage refers to "a special group of services that many brokerages [or financial institutions] give to special clients," according to Investopedia.)

In 1997 Morgan Stanley merged with Dean Witter, a stock-brokerage firm that catered to the middle class. Phillip Purcell of Dean Witter became the CEO of the new firm, which adopted the new name Morgan Stanley Dean Witter. (The name was eventually changed back to Morgan Stanley for the sake of name recognition.) The merger was intended to create a financial powerhouse that could offer a wide spectrum of services to a diverse group of investors. According to many executives, Purcell failed to cultivate a unified culture at the firm following the merger. The Morgan Stanley brokers and Dean Witter brokers remained largely separate in their views on the direction of the company. In 2000 Morgan Stanley suffered significant losses on many of its investments when the so-called "dot-com bubble" of the late 1990s "burst," and several talented brokers left the firm, including Peter Karches, formerly the president and chief operating officer of the company's institutional-securities division. Purcell's popularity sharply declined, especially among those board members who were part of Morgan Stanley prior to the merger and who accused Purcell and former Dean Witter brokers of underperforming. Following Karches's departure, Purcell announced a number of personnel changes, among them the appointment of Pandit and Stephan Newhouse as co-presidents and co–chief operating officers of Morgan Stanley's Institutional Securities Group, the company's most profitable business, encompassing its trading, banking, and research units. Among Pandit's major responsibilities were overseeing the business's trading, sales, and infrastructure, while Newhouse's duties involved investment-banking operations outside the U.S. Commenting on the changes, Purcell told Business Wire (September 25, 2000), "Over the last 20 years, Mr. Newhouse and Mr. Pandit have had extensive experiences across the businesses of the Group and we believe they are the ideal team to lead the business during the ongoing period of rapid change in our industry."

On April 4, 2003 Pandit demonstrated his expertise in the area of emerging markets when he gave a notable speech at the Consulate General of India in New York, an event organized by the Indo-American Chambers of Commerce. He argued that India, because of its high economic growth rate and vast population of English-speaking, educated, skilled workers—especially in sectors such as information and technology—was poised to be the world's fourth-strongest economy by 2020. "According to estimates by Chetan Ahya, chief economist at J.M. Morgan Stanley in India, the country is projected to be the next trillion dollar economy," Pandit said, as quoted by Tanmaya Kumar, writing for India Abroad (April 18, 2003). "For that, a 7.5 percent GDP [gross domestic product] growth will have to be sustained over the next decade and we must remember that even a one percent growth in GDP could translate into $80 billion." Pandit further noted that Morgan Stanley was prepared to take advantage of such a situation. In October 2003 Newhouse was named the new president of Morgan Stanley, replacing Robert G. Scott, and Pandit became the sole president of the Institutional Securities Group.

As Morgan Stanley's stock continue to lag behind that of its competitors, board members heightened their calls for Purcell's resignation. In 2004 Purcell reacted by instituting drastic changes, asking former Dean Witter colleagues to rejoin the board and requesting loyalty from current executives. According to the Daily Deal (April 4, 2005), Purcell offered to make Pandit president of Morgan Stanley under the condition that he would promise to support Purcell in his position as CEO. Pandit reportedly refused to make such a promise (as did John Havens, Pandit's chief deputy head of institutional equities, who was given a similar offer). As a result, the position of president was given to Zoe Cruz, the former head of the fixed-income division, and Stephen Crawford, the chief administrative officer, who became co-presidents of Morgan Stanley. In a slightly different version of the story, a former co-worker of Pandit's told David Wells for the Financial Times (May 6, 2005) that the Morgan Stanley board had disapproved of Pandit's proposed appointment, due to what they considered to be his questionable decision-making capabilities: "He is a visionary but he's risk averse and doesn't make decisions easily or quickly." In March 2005 Pandit left Morgan Stanley, along with his colleagues Havens and Guru Ramakrishnan. Writing for the Financial Times (April 19, 2007), Deborah Brewster and Wighton described Pandit's departure as remarkably quiet, in keeping with his low-key personality: "On March 28, 2005, after a conversation with Philip Purcell . . . Mr. Pandit put on his coat and without saying goodbye to any of his staff, walked out of the bank's headquarters." Many analysts interpreted Pandit's departure as yet another example of Purcell's failure to keep talent at the firm. It was generally agreed that the loss of Pandit was a significant blow to the company; David Bruns, a money manager with Federated Global, was quoted in the Financial Times (March 30, 2005) as saying about Pandit, "He was the one individual who could have replaced Purcell." Purcell's standing with both employees and investors continued to plummet; he resigned in June of that year.

In April 2005 Pandit, along with Havens and Ramakrishnan, founded Old Lane Partners LP, a firm that employed multiple strategies for managing hedge funds and private-equity funds. (A hedge fund is an aggressive set of investments aimed at high returns.) Old Lane was considered one of the most notable hedge-fund launches of that year; the firm was able to raise $2 billion worth of assets in just one day. In December 2005 Old Lane announced a strategic investment in the Toronto, Canada–based hedge fund Diversified Global Asset Management (DGAM), known for its innovative use of cutting-edge risk-management strategies to create "market-neutral, low-volatility portfolios." In August 2006 Old Lane teamed up with JM Financial to create the JM Financial India Fund, which would raise money for domestic and overseas investment in Indian companies, specifically in sectors such as retail, consumer goods, light manufacturing, pharmaceuticals, health care, financial services, and business-process outsourcing. Old Lane was the leading investor in the fund. On February 10, 2007 India Business Insight reported that the JM Financial India Fund had invested in two companies, Sona Group and International Tractors, in addition to its previous investment in the company Genesis Colours. By April

2007 Old Lane was estimated to have acquired $4.5 billion worth of assets.

In April 13, 2007 Citigroup, the largest financial-services company in the world, purchased Old Lane Partners and its interests for an estimated $800 million. Citigroup representatives stated that the purchase was a part of Citigroup's effort to increase its alternative-investment platform, but the move was largely interpreted as a very expensive way to bring Pandit, a star banker, to Citigroup during a time of financial crisis. Since his appointment, in 2004, Citigroup's CEO, Charles Prince, had failed to post significant growth in share prices and had therefore failed to earn the support of investors. Prince had also recently announced plans to lay off 26,500 employees—8 percent of the company's worldwide staff of 327,000—and reduce expenses by $4.6 billion by 2009 in an effort to save costs. Of the acquisition of Old Lane, Prince was quoted in the London *Independent* (April 14, 2007) as saying, "This transaction is an investment as much as it is an acquisition. It is an investment in world-class talent at Old Lane; in a senior leadership team with a track record of building profitable businesses in institutional securities; and an investment in Vikram and John." Pandit was installed as the CEO of CAI, a department composed of Citigroup's Investment Banking Group and the Alternative Investment Division. Pandit told Bill McIntosh for the White Plains, New York, *Daily News* (April 13, 2007): "Citi's network, financial depth, intellectual capital and infrastructure resources should allow us to continue to capture premium returns for our investors across all strategies. As part of CAI, we look forward to leveraging those strengths, together with the tremendous platform we have already established at Old Lane, to deliver world class performance." Soon after his appointment, several publications began to identify Pandit as an eventual contender for the position of CEO, following Prince's expected retirement—though Pandit denied any interest in the job.

Citigroup posted its second consecutive strong quarter in July 2007, with an 18 percent increase in income. Soon afterward, in August, the credit markets collapsed, an event that adversely affected all banks and most aspects of the U.S. and global markets; in particular, high default rates on subprime mortgages, or mortgages approved for high-risk borrowers, also contributed to the crisis. That month Citigroup's stock prices were just 2 percent higher than they had been four years earlier, an insignificant increase when inflation is considered.

On September 5, 2007 Citibank announced that it was liquidating Tribeca Global Investments LLC, its $2.4 billion multistrategy flagship fund, and making Old Lane Partners its new leading fund. According to Havens, the move was intended to "avoid overlap," but many analysts had already cited a number of problems with Tribeca. Writing for the White Plains *Daily News* (September 6, 2007), Emma Trincal predicted upward movement for Pandit, noting, "Tribeca's liquidation could

represent Mr. Pandit's first bold move in his management of a $59 billion alternative platform that comprises private equity, hedge funds, real estate and structured products."

In early October 2007 Citigroup reported that it expected $3.3 billion in losses and write-downs from its securities and banking businesses. Shortly afterward an investment fund run by the government of Abu Dhabi, of the United Arab Emirates, lent Citigroup $7.5 billion in capital. On October 11, 2007 Prince announced that he was combining the businesses Citi Markets and Banking (CMB) and CAI to form a new division, the Institutional Clients Group, and naming Pandit as its head. The reorganization sparked a number of additional shifts; Havens became the new chief executive of CAI, while Tom Maheres, the head of trading, and Randy Barker, the top fixed-income executive, resigned. In his new position Pandit was charged with overseeing Citigroup's numerous capital markets and investment-banking businesses as well as alternative investments, a significant responsibility in light of the mounting pressure from investors on Citigroup to resolve its credit-market problems.

On November 4, 2007 Citigroup reported $5.9 billion in write-downs, and Charles Prince submitted his resignation. The firm announced that Sir Win Bischoff would serve as the acting chief executive officer during the search for a successor, and that Robert E. Rubin, a onetime U.S. treasury secretary and formerly the chairman of the executive committee of Citigroup, as the new chairman of the board. As the search began, analysts named Pandit as a contender for the position of CEO, but they also noted that his lack of experience in dealing with consumer banking and in heading a public company might put him at a disadvantage. Indeed, Pandit was seen as a financial "whiz kid" and technocrat but not as the charismatic leader many felt would be necessary to restore confidence in investors and bring Citigroup back to profitability. Other candidates who were mentioned in the press as possible replacements included Robert B. Willumstad, the chairman of American International Group and a former Citigroup president; Richard Kovacevich, the chairman of Wells Fargo; and Michael Neal, the vice chairman of General Electric's commercial-finance operations. Rubin, who in the past had strongly denied interest in the position of CEO, publicly supported the appointment of Pandit.

On December 11, 2007 Citigroup announced that it had chosen Pandit as the new—and, at 50, youngest ever—CEO of Citigroup. By selecting Bischoff as the new chairman, Citigroup became the first major Wall Street firm to separate the roles of chief executive and chairman. While many marveled at the speed with which Pandit had been promoted through the company (having been hired just eight months earlier), few were truly surprised by his appointment, as he had been viewed as a candidate for the position since he joined the company. Rubin, as well as the founder and former

CEO of Citigroup, Sanford Weill, expressed their approval of the selection, noting Pandit's sharp analytical skills and knowledge of emerging markets. Given Pandit's well-known quietness, as well as his lack of experience running a public company, his selection was largely interpreted as one of substance over style. Most seemed to agree that Pandit had the financial know-how to tackle the current Citigroup crises. Robert Greenhill, a former colleague at Morgan Stanley, and others suggested to Ben White for the *Financial Times* (December 12, 2007) that Pandit was "not likely to lead inspirational cheers at company meetings," in White's words. "[Pandit] may not be a pyrotechnics artist," Greenhill said, "but I don't think what Citi needs right now is pyrotechnics or charisma." Another former Morgan Stanley executive told the same publication (December 15, 2007): "[Pandit] is a great strategist but he is also a nuts and bolts guy who really gets things done." Others, however, wondered whether Pandit might encounter problems in leading and inspiring the company to increased future growth. One investor, speaking with the *Financial Times* (December 15, 2007), expressed the desire of shareholders for an inspirational figure: "We needed someone like Sandy Weill to get the place excited again, and he ain't it."

Many investors, in particular, hoped that Pandit's long-term plans would include breaking up some of the many businesses Citigroup had acquired over the years. Meredith Whitney, a prominent banking analyst, was quoted in the *International Herald Tribune* (December 13, 2007) as calling the dismantling of Citigroup a necessity and the only way to avoid "a highly disruptive year" with "massive layoffs, almost prohibitively expensive technology investments and credit-loss reserves that are at least 50 percent too low." Indeed, other analysts predicted that Pandit would likely need to initiate job cuts of up to 10 percent of the 320,000-strong workforce. Publicly, Pandit's appointment was met with some hesitance. The day it was announced, Citigroup's shares fell $1.54, to $33.23, among a general decline in financial stocks. William Smith, the chief executive of SAM Advisors, which holds stock in Citigroup, was quoted in the London *Independent* (December 12, 2007) as calling the appointments "disappointing." He went on to say, "Pandit is probably a decent manager, but he is a segment manager. He is not a CEO."

Pandit told analysts during a conference in December 2007, as quoted by David Ellis for CNN Money (December 11, 2007, on-line), that he planned to "undertake an objective and dispassionate review of all our businesses." He declined to comment on whether he would dismantle Citigroup, stating, "You have to give me some time to go through our due process." Pandit's tone during that interview, which many found to be icy, sparked further discussion of his leadership abilities. On December 24, 2007 Pandit spoke with Maria Bartiromo for *BusinessWeek* about his general plans for Citibank, which included reviewing productivity levels, evaluating each individual business to ensure that it was "positioned for the future we see in financial services," and reaching out to consumers, "making sure [our people] feel excited about the future." Pandit remarked to Bartiromo, "And really we've got a lot of resources here, and it's not about needing more. It's about making sure we allocate them to the right place to create more profitability and good returns for shareholders." Pandit promoted one of his closest associates, Don Callahan, to the post of chief administrative officer, in which he would oversee operations and technology, marketing and branding, and corporate affairs. Pandit also asked Lewis B. Kaden, the vice chairman, to expand his role, to include more of a focus on corporate government, strategy, senior recruitment, and regulatory and government affairs. Following the retirement of Robert Druskin from the position of chief operating officer, Pandit appointed Chief Financial Officer Gary Crittenden to take his place.

On January 19, 2008 Pandit announced subprime write-downs of $17.4 billion in Citigroup's fourth quarter, a figure that was far worse than most observers had expected. In order to offset the damage, Pandit announced the reduction of quarterly dividends from 54 to 32 cents a share and the infusion of $12.5 billion in investor capital into Citigroup (in addition to the $7.5 billion from Abu Dhabi), from sources that included Prince Alwaleed bin Talal of Saudi Arabia—who owns 3 percent of Citigroup; the Kuwait Investment Authority; the Singapore Investment Corp. (GIC); and Sanford Weill. "The severe markets in which we have been operating these last few months have revealed that we have some areas that require a great deal of work," Pandit told employees, as quoted by Thomas Granahan in *Investment Dealers Digest* (January 21, 2008). "It is clear that we need to put into place superior risk management, more disciplined expense control and balance sheet management, and the right mix of assets to drive our core capabilities in service of our clients. Our unacceptable fourth quarter results highlight the need to be open to change, to be bold in our thinking and to act with thoughtful urgency." While U.S. newspapers referred to the foreign investments in Citigroup and other American financial institutions with derogatory headlines such as "America selling itself to the highest bidder," Granahan noted that Citigroup's fourth-quarter results were not Pandit's fault. They were, however, his immediate responsibility. "Essentially, Pandit never had the luxury of a honeymoon period that many new CEOs are afforded," Granahan wrote. "Citigroup's woes are so deep, and the name so powerful, that there's no time for that."

Over the next few months Pandit announced measures aimed at cutting costs and preserving Citigroup's most important businesses. In March 2008 he announced the sale of shares of numerous businesses, including the Brazilian credit-card servicer Redecard and $45 billion of Citigroup's mortgage assets. The same month Pandit made several personnel changes, as part of the creation of a new command structure, which, in his view, would "get across the value of teamwork and collaboration" and bring Citigroup closer to customers, as he told the Associated Press reporter David Enrich (May 6, 2008). The new structure would also give more autonomy to Citigroup's overseas business, which had been outperforming its United States counterparts. Analyzing Pandit's choices, Marino Marin, the managing director at the boutique investment bank Gruppo, Levey & Co., told Madlen Read for the Associated Press (March 31, 2008), "[Pandit's] not selling Citigroup in pieces, but he's dividing Citigroup into pieces to measure them better and manage them better." Pandit's incremental changes were met with both tentative approval from financial analysts and impatience from investors, who asked Pandit to articulate a clearer vision and enact more drastic changes.

In May 2008, after posting a loss of $5.1 billion in the first quarter of 2008, Pandit introduced a detailed three-year cost-cutting plan. The plan included job reductions, the sales of about $500 billion worth of assets, and the divestment of many of Citigroup's non-core businesses. Pandit planned to focus on improving the company's four main businesses: credit cards, wealth management, corporate banking, and investment banking. In July 2008 Citigroup reported $2.5 billion in quarterly losses on write-downs—less than many investors had feared. Pandit noted that the figure was actually a sign of progress, considering the company's $5.1 billion loss the previous quarter. That same month Citigroup announced several personnel changes, including the resignation of Michael S. Klein, who had been a top executive at the bank for 23 years. In September 2008 Sallie L. Krawcheck, formerly the CEO of Citi Global Wealth Management, dubbed by the *New York Times* (September 23, 2008) "the most prominent woman on Wall Street," was dismissed.

The global financial crisis dramatically worsened in the autumn of 2008. Markets plunged when IndyMac, the largest mortgage lender in the U.S., was seized by federal regulators, and again when, in early September, the major mortgage lenders Fannie Mae and Freddie Mac were placed under conservatorship, thus becoming public entities owned by the federal government. In the same month many of the world's major financial institutions posted record losses. While the global investment firm AIG received a bailout from the Treasury Department and Lehman Brothers declared bankruptcy, many other banks sought partnerships to help them stay afloat. In late September 2008, in a deal orchestrated by the Federal Deposit Insurance Corp., Pandit agreed to purchase for one dollar a share Wachovia's banking business, which includes many branches in New York and New Jersey. Shortly before the deal was closed, the financial services company Wells Fargo, which had lost

the original auction involving Wachovia, offered to buy the firm for $7 per share, a deal that Wachovia accepted. On October 5, 2008 Pandit filed a lawsuit against Wachovia and Wells Fargo, seeking $60 billion in damages for breach of contract. Despite the failed Wachovia deal, Pandit has continued to express optimism about Citigroup's future. In a memorandum sent to Citigroup employees in September, Pandit wrote, as quoted by Andrew Ross Sorkin for the *International Herald Tribune* (October 15, 2008), "It is clear our industry is in a state of change, but I am confident that this should be an opportunity for Citi." Citigroup is one of nine large banks that will receive a total of more than $125 billion from the U.S. government, as part of the $700 billion bailout package passed by Congress in early October 2008.

Pandit's father told White and Wighton that Pandit is "a very simple person at heart. He derives pleasures from simple things in life." Another former colleague told the journalists that Pandit is "saner than almost anyone I know on Wall Street." Pandit lives with his wife, Swati, and their two teenage children in a luxurious 10-room apartment on Manhattan's Upper West Side, once owned by the actor Tony Randall, which he reportedly purchased for $17.8 million in September 2007. Pandit also owns homes in Greenwich, Connecticut, and on Manhattan's East Side. Although he is known to be a workaholic, with few "distracting interests" outside work, he reportedly finds time to spend with his children before they go to bed. (Pandit joined the Westchester Golf Club but, unlike his peers on Wall Street, almost never plays the game—because, as he has admitted, he is simply not very good at it.) According to his father, Pandit travels to India every year or so to visit his large family. He serves on the boards of Columbia University, Columbia Business School, the Indian School of Business, and Trinity School. He is a past member of the boards of NASDAQ, the New York City Investment Fund, and the American India Foundation.

—M.E.R.

Suggested Reading: *BusinessWeek* p23 Dec. 24, 2007; (London) *Financial Times* p9 Dec. 15, 2007; (London) *Independent* p36 Dec. 12, 2007; *New York* (on-line) May 20, 2002; *New York Times* C p1+ Dec. 12, 2007, (on-line) Nov. 3, 2007; Rediff.com Dec. 18, 2007; *United States Banker* p22+ Apr. 2008; *Wall Street Journal* Eastern edition C p1+ Dec. 12, 2007

Courtesy of the *New York Times*

Pareles, Jon

Oct, 25, 1953– Music critic

Address: New York Times, *620 Eighth Ave., New York, NY 10018*

For the Web site RockCritics.com, Steven Ward wrote, "Whenever I interview rock writers for this site, I always ask them to name their favorite music critics—writers that make them want to read about pop music. Many of these writers drop the name of Jon Pareles." The head pop-music critic for the *New York Times* since the late 1980s, Pareles has written about the music of performers as varied as Kurt Cobain, RZA of the Wu-Tang Clan, and Madonna. Pareles served as an editor at *Crawdaddy!* magazine in the late 1970s before working successively at *Rolling Stone* and the *Village Voice*. In 1985 he turned down an editorship at the *Voice* to become a full-time staff writer at the *New York Times*, emerging as the paper's lead pop critic several years later. Pareles co-edited a book, *The Rolling Stone Encyclopedia of Rock & Roll*, in 1983, and has helped to update it twice.

Born in Connecticut on October 25, 1953, Jonathan Pareles took an interest in music from a very young age. He started playing the piano when he was six, soon discovering that he had perfect pitch. For the "Ask a Reporter" section of the *New York Times* Web site (September 2000), he explained that he began writing about music for his high school's newspaper "because I wanted people to know about some music I liked." During high school he played keyboards and flute in rock bands. He attended Yale University, in New Haven, Connecticut, where he studied classical music

and joined the Yale Guild of Carilloneurs, who played the organ-like consoles that brought sounds from the large bells in Yale's bell tower. Having access to an Arp 2600 synthesizer at the school's electronic-music studio, he told Ward, "helped me understand a lot of the electronic music to come." During his college years Pareles played keyboards and flute in various rock and jazz groups and wrote music reviews for the *Yale Daily News*. He also served as music director for WYBC-FM, Yale's radio station. Pareles graduated from Yale in 1974 with a B.A. degree in music.

Following his graduation Pareles moved to Boston, Massachusetts, where he briefly considered becoming a deejay but turned instead to writing. He contributed freelance pieces to the music magazines *Crawdaddy!* and *PopTop* and the *Real Paper*, an alternative weekly. In 1977 he moved to New York City to take a job as a copy editor at *Crawdaddy!*, where he was later promoted to music editor. Pareles has named Timothy White (now the editor of *Billboard*), Mitch Glazer, and Charles M. Young as being among the talented contributors to the magazine at the time. Pareles appreciated the eclectic music scene he found in New York City. "It was a lucky time to come to New York," he told Ward: "The moment when the city was germinating the ideas that would dominate the next generation. Punk, hip-hop, dance music and art-rock were all new and all mixed up with each other; Philip Glass was playing at the Peppermint Lounge, Fab Five Freddy was rapping with Max Roach at the Kitchen in SoHo. There was always something new to discover."

In 1979, Pareles told Ward, he "deserted a sunken ship" and left *Crawdaddy!*—which folded because "its status as a tax write-off had run out"—for a job at *Rolling Stone*. He had been freelancing for that famous magazine, then in its heyday, and his former *Crawdaddy!* colleague Tim White, by then an editor at *Rolling Stone*, had spoken well of his abilities to higher-ups. Pareles served as assistant music editor there for approximately one year. "I learned a lot," he told Ward of his time at the magazine, "watching [the editor] Jann Wenner take up a cover story, devour it, point out precisely what its unanswered questions were and then jet off to other business—but I didn't have a lot of say. Or perhaps I wasn't pushy enough." Pareles played the keyboards in the magazine's in-house band, the Dry Heaves, along with White, Wenner, Kurt Loder, and others. "Playing an instrument and being in a band help you appreciate what musicians have to learn, how groups make decisions and how songs feel from the inside," he told Ward. He added, "I guarantee the world did not lose much of a keyboard player when I became a writer."

Pareles left *Rolling Stone* in 1980 to take a temporary job filling in for Robert Christgau as a senior editor at the *Village Voice*. Pareles admired Christgau, he told Ward, for being "one of the people who were fighting, and winning, the battle to have rock criticism addressed intelligently by writers." He appreciated the *Voice*'s "tradition of treating writers respectfully" and was pleased when his six-month assignment stretched to a year and a half. "It was a wonderful gig," he told Ward.

After leaving the *Village Voice*, Pareles began to write on a freelance basis for the *New York Times* and various other publications. In 1983 he co-edited, with Patricia Romanowski, *The Rolling Stone Encyclopedia of Rock & Roll*, described by its publishers as "the authoritative volume on the world's music makers—from the one-hit wonders to the megastars" and as "the bible of rock and roll." "This book belongs on the shelves and coffee tables of anyone interested in music . . . ," Valerie MacEwan wrote for PopMatters.com (November 2001). "The fact finding sources and the methodology utilized by the contributors add to the credibility of the volume. Many artists responded personally to information requests." Pareles helped update the book in 1995 and 2001.

Pareles's freelance job at the *New York Times* was supposed to end when two of the paper's full-time writers, Stephen Holden and John S. Wilson, returned from extended vacations; after they did, however, the new arts-section editor decided to retain him. In 1985 the *Village Voice* offered Pareles its music-editor position, which Christau had vacated. After "agonizing over the choice," he told Ward, Pareles decided he "preferred writing to editing, and ended up using the offer to persuade the *Times* to put me on staff." He has cited Robert Palmer, a *Times* senior staff writer who helped him obtain the job, as one of the major influences on his work. "Palmer was a seemingly effortless, straightforward writer who was always listening to everything . . . ," he told Ward. "Palmer had a taste for the noisy and un-tempered—from the blues to raga, he loved music that couldn't be reduced to Western notation—that has proved to be extremely durable. And when he brought me to the *Times*, he was a good example to follow because he was one of the few bylines there . . . who wrote conversationally, not sounding stuffy or taking on an English accent."

In the late 1980s Palmer left the *Times*, and Pareles became the newspaper's chief pop-music critic. Despite the *Times*'s somewhat conservative image, Pareles followed Palmer's tradition of being "quick on the uptake for punk, hip-hop, no wave and all kinds of other avant-gardes." He also helped recruit writers, including Ann Powers, Neil Strauss, and Ben Ratliff, whom he viewed as being highly talented and who have gone on to become successful critics. Though he felt stymied at times by the paper's style (having to eschew profanity, both severe and mild, and having to refer to subjects as "Mr." or "Ms."), he also found that the stodginess of the paper's management worked to his advantage. "The editors don't second-guess the pop critics," he told Ward. "When I got there they were all from an older generation that cared more about classical music, and even now, with an early baby-boomer hierarchy, they assume we know

more about the subject than they do. We get treated something like . . . a science correspondent or the head of the New Delhi bureau; we're sending back dispatches from the distant reaches of Musicville." As a result, he said, he and his colleagues are free to find a balance between music they find interesting and music that does not necessarily appeal to them but has achieved mainstream significance.

One of Pareles's stated goals in writing about various types of music is to "fight provincialism." "No one has to like everything—there are huge amounts of mediocrity out there—but no one should be afraid of certain music or deliberately ignorant of it," he told Ward. "Cliquey types who listen to just one kind of music, whether it's classic rock or hip-hop, are only depriving themselves." The critic prefers to write for newspapers rather than magazines, because of how quickly his work appears in newspapers and because newspapers reach a wide audience who might not otherwise read about music. "With a newspaper," he told Ward, "readers might be finishing a feature on Lincoln Center or looking for a book review and suddenly find themselves reading about hip-hop or Brazilian music just because it's on the page, and maybe it will give them a new bit of information or make them curious. You get more serendipity in newspapers." Pareles wrote for the "Ask a Reporter" feature that in addition to introducing music to others, he writes to make himself think critically. "Writing about anything—even if it's what you did last summer—forces you to clarify and focus your thoughts, to decide what's important and what's not," he explained. "When I'm writing, I have to think not just whether I like something but about what I like in it, how it works, and what to tell other people about it."

Pareles contributes frequently to the *New York Times*'s ArtsBeat blog, writing about cultural events that he has attended around the world, including such festivals as South by Southwest, in Austin, Texas; the Pitchfork Music Festival, in Chicago, Illinois; and New Orleans's Mardi Gras celebration. "I'm a geek," he told Dan Ouellette for *Mediaweek* (November 19, 2007). "I love the online world and digital gadgets," which include interactive features. "There's an immediacy to it and an opportunity to play with form." He enjoys the increased breadth of coverage the blog affords him, telling Ouellette that it is "a salve for my conscience because I can't possibly cover in print all the acts that I like when I go to festivals." He compared the "short, quick hits" contained in a one-page blog to "the two and a half minute single in pop music."

Pareles's *New York Times* music critiques have frequently placed new works in a historical context. In his April 27, 2008 review of Madonna's album *Hard Candy*, for example, Pareles wrote, "The sound of *Hard Candy* is partly the sound of an era when New York dance clubs were an experiment in improbable social interactions—gays, socialites, breakdancers, artists—that became a pipeline to pop radio. Pulling such mixed audiences onto the dance floor was a good pretest for wider pop appeal. . . . Yet along with the nostalgia that won't alienate older fans—and who else can afford golden-circle tickets for arena tours?—*Hard Candy* also taps into exactly the sounds that current hip-hop reclaims from the disco era: electro keyboard riffs, filtered voices and bits of Latin percussion." He also commented on Madonna's unabashedly businesslike attitude: "Presenting herself not only as an object of desire but as a material girl with her eye on the profits was one of the many smart moves she made from the beginning. By flaunting her control and her triumphs, Madonna gave fans a stake in her long-term prospects, something that loyalists should be able to appreciate as her sex appeal inevitably fades—although Madonna is still svelte, toned and dressing in lingerie as often as she pleases." While covering many major mainstream releases, Pareles has also devoted space to the work of lesser-known artists or to the more obscure work of well-known performers. In a July 16, 2007 review of the Pitchfork Music Festival (mounted by the same-named popular music-criticism Web site), he wrote about a closing song performed by Yoko Ono and Thurston Moore. "[Ono's] set's best

stretch was its avant-garde extreme: 'Mulberry,' with Thurston Moore of Sonic Youth on guitar. He used his vocabulary of guitar noises—bell tones, motorcycle roars, feedback shrieks, pure sustained notes, crackling distortion—to follow her and goad her, pushing past reflexes toward something searing and untamed. It wasn't music for any pop chart or commercial format, and part of the crowd had already left. But it was the kind of performance that made Pitchfork's picky few wholeheartedly applaud."

Pareles lives with his wife in the Manhattan borough of New York City and works mostly from his home. In addition to his work for the *Times*, he occasionally writes freelance articles for other publications. "Don't tell anybody," he said to Ward, "but the job is really an excuse for my continuing education."

—J.E.P.

Suggested Reading: *Media Week* (on-line) Nov. 19, 2007; rockcriticsarchives.com

Selected Books: as editor—*The Rolling Stone Encyclopedia of Rock & Roll* (with Patricia Romanowski), 1983, 1995, 2001

Parker, Tony

May 17, 1982– Basketball player

Address: *San Antonio Spurs, One AT&T Center, San Antonio, TX 78219*

Tony Parker has helped the San Antonio Spurs win three National Basketball Association (NBA) titles and—born in Belgium to an African-American father and a Dutch mother—has earned the distinction of being the first European-born player to win most-valuable-player (MVP) honors in a league championship series. He is arguably even better known as the husband of Eva Longoria, a star of the ABC television drama *Desperate Housewives*. Parker and Longoria married in July 2007, about a month after the Spurs captured their third NBA championship of the 2000s. When asked which he cherished more, his wedding ring or his championship ring, Parker told Steve Ginsburg for the Perth, Australia, *Sunday Times* (June 17, 2007), "Can't choose," and added, "Both are very good."

Now heralded as the best European point guard ever to play in the NBA, Parker was the 28th and final player selected in the first round of the league's 2001 draft. He came to the U.S. after two seasons in a French professional league, where, while facing a relatively low level of competition, he learned a great deal from his veteran teammates. Described by many as exceptionally mature, Parker took over as the Spurs' starting point guard only five games into his rookie season. That year he

Ronald Martinez/Getty Images

played in 77 games, averaging 9.2 points, 2.6 rebounds, and 4.3 assists per contest. Those statistics won him a spot on the All-Rookie First Team, an honor never before bestowed on a foreign-born player.

In his second NBA season, Parker posted improved numbers and helped lead San Antonio to its first title since 1999. The season culminated with a victory over the New Jersey Nets in the league's best-of-seven finals. The Spurs lost to the Los Angeles Lakers in the following year's play-offs, then defeated the Detroit Pistons in 2004–05; Parker had averaged 16.6 points per game throughout the regular season. The Spurs fell to the Dallas Mavericks in the 2005–06 play-offs, then regrouped the following season, sweeping the Cleveland Cavaliers in the NBA Finals. Parker, who averaged 20.8 points per game during the postseason, was named MVP of the championship series.

The oldest of three brothers, William Anthony Parker Jr. was born on May 17, 1982 in Bruges, Belgium. His father, also called Tony, was a standout basketball player: as a student at Loyola University Chicago, in Illinois, he averaged 17.4 points per game en route to becoming the school's seventh-highest all-time leading scorer. After a failed tryout with the Chicago Bulls of the NBA, he moved to Europe, where he played for professional teams in the Netherlands, Belgium, and France. While overseas Tony Parker Sr. married Pamela Firestone, a model. She gave birth to their first son while the couple were living in Belgium. Parker's brothers, Terence, nicknamed T.J., and Pierre, who are two and four years younger, respectively, were born in France.

Parker showed signs of athleticism early on. As a toddler he started playing with basketballs, and to a lesser degree, he came to enjoy playing soccer. His father enrolled him and his brothers in a basketball camp. In 1995, on one of his yearly trips to visit his paternal grandparents, in Chicago, Parker watched the Bulls play the Dallas Mavericks, and after the game he had his picture taken with Michael Jordan in the locker room.

When he was 14 Parker enrolled at France's National Institute of Sports and Physical Education (known by its acronym, Insep), a high school for promising young athletes. "I never meet a player like him, and I am coaching and teaching since I am 25, 26," Lucien Legrand, a coach at the institute who was then 55, told Harvey Araton for the *New York Times* (June 8, 2003). "He wants to play, play, play." When Parker was in his first year, Legrand selected him for the team that would compete in the European championships. The following year Parker started playing against adults in a third-tier French professional league. Impressed by the youth's abilities, the coach Pierre Vincent tapped him to play on France's 1998 Junior National team. Vincent told Araton, "At the championships, [Parker] was the best player even though he was two years younger than most of the others." Parker rejoined the Junior National Team in 2000 and helped the squad win a European title. He was also named the tournament's MVP.

In 1999, after turning down scholarship offers from U.S. colleges including Georgia Tech and the University of California at Los Angeles, Parker signed with the French professional team Paris Saint Germain Racing (later renamed Paris Basket Racing). In two seasons with that team, he averaged 10.0 points, 1.9 rebounds, and 3.9 assists per game. In 2000 he competed in the Nike Hoop Summit, held in Indianapolis, Indiana, where he and the International Select Team, made up of players from many countries, narrowly lost to Team USA. Parker scored 20 points, made seven assists, and grabbed four rebounds, earning the attention of scouts and the Spurs' general manager, R. C. Buford. "He didn't get excited when he made a basket," Buford told Jonathan Feigen for the *Houston (Texas) Chronicle* (May 9, 2002). "He didn't make faces or chest bumps when guys made dunks. He was poised."

In a pre-draft workout with the Spurs, Parker's play was disappointing, and the Spurs' head coach, Gregg Popovich, sent him home. "And then we set up another interview, another workout, where we stacked it and had some people go after him physically, and he was fantastic," Popovich told Steve Ginsburg. Relatively short at six feet two inches, Parker failed to attract many teams in the draft's first round; the Spurs made him the 28th and final pick. "I think we got a steal," Parker's Spurs teammate Steve Smith told T. A. Badger for the Associated Press Worldstream (November 24, 2001). "He's eager to get out there and play. In time, he'll get smarter and stronger." Before Parker could commit to the NBA, the Spurs had to buy out the remainder of his Paris Basket Racing contract. "I told the owner [of Paris Basket Racing] that my heart is in the States," Parker told Johnny Ludden for the *San Antonio (Texas) Express-News* (June 28, 2001).

While Parker was expected to ride the bench for much of his rookie season, Popovich started him after just four games. "It was a tough decision to start him, because I wanted to make sure it was fair to him," the coach told David DuPree for *USA Today* (November 28, 2007). "He's not only starting at the most difficult position in the league, but he's 19 and he's from a foreign country and didn't know any of these guys." In his first six starts with the Spurs, Parker averaged approximately 14 points, four rebounds, and six assists, helping his team tally six straight wins. Although Parker was suddenly competing against players he had once idolized and had stayed up late to watch on television—his teammates included the NBA superstars David Robinson and Tim Duncan—he had no difficulty focusing on the game. "I can't be a fan," he told Badger, "because I have to defend them."

Parker played in 77 games during his rookie season, averaging 9.2 points, 2.6 rebounds, and 4.3 assists per game—good enough to earn him a place on the NBA All-Rookie First Team. He fared even better during the play-offs, averaging 15.5 points in 10 postseason contests. In the Spurs' first-round match-up against the Seattle Supersonics, Parker went head-to-head with Seattle's star veteran Gary Payton, outplaying him during most of the series.

The Spurs won their series against Seattle in five games. Parker played well; in the third game of the series, he scored 24 points and made five assists. "I think we were all a little apprehensive [about Parker] at first," Duncan told Tim Povtak for the *Orlando (Florida) Sentinel* (May 8, 2002). "You have to be, having someone that young at point guard. But he proved me wrong every night out. He's for real." In the conference semifinals, the Spurs lost to the Lakers.

In his 2002–03 campaign, Parker was viewed as one of Popovich's "four diamonds in the rough," as Greg Boeck wrote for *USA Today* (April 18, 2003). Along with the others—the journeyman Stephen Jackson, the undrafted player Bruce Bowen, and the rookie Manu Ginobili, none of whom were big-name players—Parker propelled the Spurs to a 60–22 record. Parker played in all 82 regular-season games and showed remarkable improvement, averaging 15.5 points, 5.3 assists and 2.6 rebounds per game. He scored 32 points, then a career high, in three games, and in the play-offs, he averaged 14.7 points, 2.8 rebounds, and 3.5 assists in 24 games. He played progressively better throughout the postseason, and in the Western Conference finals, against the Dallas Mavericks, he averaged 16.3 points and four assists per game. Duncan told Al Iannazzone for the Bergen County, New Jersey, *Record* (June 4, 2003), "In just these two years, he's grown threefold from the player he was coming in here."

In 2003 the Spurs defeated the Nets in six games to win their first NBA championship since 1999. Throughout the championship series, Parker played well against Jason Kidd. In Game Three Parker scored 26 points, 11 in the fourth quarter. After missing the first seven games of the 2003–04 season with a sprained ankle, Parker continued to be a standout player, averaging 14.7 points, 3.2 rebounds, and 5.5 assists per game in the remaining 75 matches. Once again Parker excelled in the postseason, averaging 18.4 points per game. His efforts were not enough to keep the Spurs from losing to the Lakers in the conference semifinals, however.

Parker showed even greater improvement during the 2004–05 season, posting what were then career-best averages in points (16.6), rebounds (3.7), and assists (6.1). In February 2005 he scored 20 or more points in five straight games, and he finished the year ranked 13th in the NBA in assists. The Spurs amassed a 59–23 record and cruised through the play-offs to meet the Detroit Pistons in the NBA Finals. Parker averaged 17.2 points per game in the postseason, and in June 2005 the Spurs won their second title in three years, besting the Pistons in seven games.

In September 2005 Parker and the French national basketball team, for which he had served as captain since 2003, won a bronze medal at Euro-Basket '05, Europe's championship tournament. The final victory over Spain earned France its first medal since 1959. During the 2005–06 NBA season, Parker was voted a member of the league's All-Star team for the first time. He again improved on his previous season's scoring numbers, averaging 18.9 points per game and helping to guide the Spurs to a 63–19 record. Parker led the Spurs in scoring and assists, marking the first time in the team's history that a point guard finished first in both of those statistical categories.

As in past years Parker played even better during the play-offs, averaging 21.1 points, 3.6 rebounds, and 3.8 assists in 13 contests. After defeating the Sacramento Kings in the first round, the Spurs again missed a chance to win back-to-back league titles, losing a seven-game series to the Dallas Mavericks in the conference semifinals. That season also saw Parker make his debut as a musician: in March 2006, during the NBA's All-Star Weekend, he performed hip-hop songs in French with his group, Game Time Family, at the Renaissance Hotel in Houston, Texas. Unlike the many hip-hop artists or groups who sang about hardcore "gangsta" topics, Parker wrote lyrics about his life—"an interesting life," as B.U., a member of Game Time Family, told the San Antonio, Texas, *Current* (March 1–7, 2006). "He's been a professional ball player since the age of 14, so he has a life that isn't typical of . . . the ordinary person." Parker's debut album, *Tony Parker* (2007), included a duet with the actor and singer Jamie Foxx and another with the French rapper Don Choa.

In August 2006, on the eve of the 2006 FIBA World Championship, held in cities in Japan, Parker broke his finger during the French national team's exhibition match against Brazil. ("FIBA" is the acronym for "Fédération Internationale de Basketball Amateur," basketball's international governing body.) As a result Parker missed the tournament; in his absence the French squad finished fifth, failing to make the semifinal round. During the Spurs' 2006–07 season, the team defeated the Denver Nuggets, Phoenix Suns, and Utah Jazz to earn a place in the NBA Finals. Parker averaged 18.6 points, 3.2 rebounds, and 5.5 assists per game and was again chosen for the NBA All-Star team. "He's the most mature young guy I've ever been around in my life," Gregg Popovich told Steve Ginsburg for the *Calgary (Alberta, Canada) Herald* (June 15, 2007). Parker averaged 20.8 points per game during the postseason, and in the championship series, in which the Spurs swept the Cleveland Cavaliers, he averaged 24.5 points per game and shot .568 from the field—team highs. Parker was named MVP of the series, which brought the Spurs their third title in five years. Reflecting later on how far he had come since the beginning of his NBA career, he told a reporter for the *Bismarck (North Dakota) Tribune* (June 16, 2007), "There was growing pains for me, but I can't complain because I was in a great organization. But at the same time, you know, Coach Pop was really, really hard on me, always trying to push me and looking for perfection." He added, "I thought I was doing pretty good, being 21, but it was never enough. I could score 14, 15, it was never enough." Parker later thanked his coach for being so hard on him.

In September 2007 in Spain, Parker competed in EuroBasket '07 with the French national team. The team came up short in its bid to compete in the 2008 Beijing Summer Olympics, falling to Slovenia in a qualifying match. Parker scored 31 points in the game, and in the nine-game tournament, he averaged 20.1 points per contest. The following month Parker announced that he would take a two-year sabbatical from the French squad and return for the 2009 EuroBasket tournament. "I'll try to get some rest for my body and spend some time with Eva," he told an Associated Press (October 3, 2007) reporter.

In the 2007–08 NBA season, Parker averaged 18.8 points and 6.0 assists per game. He recorded a career-high average of 22.4 points per game in the play-offs, solidifying his reputation as a clutch player. The Spurs lost to the Los Angeles Lakers in five games at the Western Conference Finals.

In 2003 *People* magazine named Parker one of the world's "50 Most Beautiful People." On July 6, 2007 Parker married Longoria in a civil ceremony in Paris, with the city's mayor, Bertrand Delanoe, officiating. Parker has volunteered for the French branch of the Make-a-Wish Foundation, which grants wishes of children suffering from serious illnesses. He donates 20 tickets to every Spurs home game to local underprivileged youths.

—K.J.P.

Suggested Reading: (Bergen County, New Jersey) *Record* S p10 June 4, 2003; *New York Times* VIII p7 June 8, 2003; *Orange County (California) Register* D p4 April 4, 2000; *Orlando (Florida) Sentinel* D p3 May 8, 2002; (Riverside, California) *Press Enterprise* C p1 May 4, 2004; *San Antonio (Texas) Express-News* C p1 June 29, 2001; *USA Today* C p1 Nov. 28, 2001

Selected Recordings: *Tony Parker*, 2007

Daniel Barry/Getty Images

Paterson, David

May 20, 1954– Governor of New York (Democrat)

Address: State Capitol, Albany, NY 12224

On March 17, 2008 David Paterson was sworn in as the 55th governor of New York State. In addition to being the first African-American to hold that state's highest office, Paterson is the first legally blind person in U.S. history to serve as a governor for more than a few days. Paterson, who had been

lieutenant governor since January 2007, took office one week after the public learned that his predecessor, Governor Eliot Spitzer, had been a customer of a high-priced prostitution service. After Spitzer resigned, Paterson vowed to put the scandal behind him and move forward with the business of running the state. "There is work to be done," he said at his swearing-in ceremony, according to the Associated Press Online (March 18, 2008). "There was an oath to be taken. There's trust that needs to be restored. There are issues that need to be addressed."

Before beginning what turned out to be a 14-month stint as Spitzer's lieutenant governor, Paterson spent two decades as a Democratic state senator, representing a New York City district that includes the Manhattan neighborhood of Harlem. In 2002 he became the first nonwhite state Senate minority leader. Prior to entering politics Paterson, a graduate of Columbia University and the Hofstra University School of Law, worked for the district attorney's office in the New York City borough of Queens. Legally blind since infancy, he has developed what many have called an encyclopedic memory, which enables him to recite speeches and discuss the intricacies of complicated pieces of legislation without notes; he has also acquired ways to "read" people through nonvisual clues. "People are fond of saying of people with disabilities that they are just like everybody else," Paterson told Joel Stashenko for the Associated Press (November 22, 2002). "But that's just something to say to make them feel better. When you have a disability you are not like everyone else. You are uniquely defined by a lack of vision."

The first of the two sons of Basil and Portia (Hairston) Paterson, David Alexander Paterson was born on May 20, 1954 in the New York City borough of Brooklyn. His brother, Daniel, works for the New York State Office of Court Administration. His father is a labor lawyer with a private firm; now 82, he represents the locals of several unions. In the 1960s Basil Paterson served as a New York state senator and in 1978 as a New York City deputy mayor. He was the vice chairman of the Democratic National Committee for six years in the 1970s and, in 1979, became New York's first nonwhite secretary of state. When David Paterson was an infant, an ear infection spread to his optic nerve, leaving him completely blind in his left eye. He has 20/400 vision in his right eye, and while he can see images, he is unable to read for more than a few minutes at a time.

In the 1950s New York City public schools refused to let blind children attend regular classes, and for that reason the Patersons moved to Hempstead, a town on Long Island, New York, where there were no such restrictions. (For a time Paterson's official biographies erroneously stated that he grew up in Harlem.) Surrounded by children with normal vision, Paterson often felt ostracized. Once, he hit a classmate who teased him about his poor sight, earning himself a month of detention. "I went through a lot of periods of depression, but when I was younger, people didn't seek counseling for it," Paterson told Gabe Pressman on the TV program *News Forum* (May 20, 2007). "When I think back on it, I think that's what it was, feelings of a lack of self-esteem." While in elementary school Paterson was "sensitive and mature," Clarice Broderick, his sixth-grade teacher, told Nia-Malika Henderson for *Newsday* (March 12, 2008, on-line), and, his occasional low moods notwithstanding, he often joked with teachers and fellow students. In sixth grade he was the master of ceremonies in his class's production of a play called *Miss Frankenstein*. "He was the star and he knew everyone's lines in the play," Broderick recalled to Henderson. "I told the other students, 'If you forget your lines, David will give you the keyword.'" In 1964, when Basil Paterson made his first foray into politics, David Paterson sometimes helped out at campaign rallies. "He would get up on the sound truck and do all the talking to the crowds, and he was good," the elder Paterson told Juan Gonzalez for the New York *Daily News* (January 24, 2006). "I knew then he had a big future."

At Hempstead High School Paterson was a member of the radio club and the debate team. He graduated in 1971, after only three years. "He got along well with everyone," a fellow student told Henderson. "He was a politician, even at a young age." After high school Paterson attended Columbia University, in New York City, from which he graduated in 1977 with a B.A. degree in history. While in college he worked briefly as a mediator for the Institute for Mediation and Conflict Resolution Inc., which focuses on disputes among residents of the city's Bronx County. For two years beginning in 1976, also when he was an undergraduate, he was a legal assistant with the Municipal Credit Union. In 1981, as a student at the Hofstra University School of Law, in Hempstead, he held the title of assistant grants officer at Bronx Community College; during the next year he directed the Fair Housing Office of New York City's Department of Housing Preservation and Development. In 1983 he earned a J.D. degree. "People mention that he is black and legally blind, but those never have been limiting factors," John Gregory, one of his Hofstra professors, told Henderson. "He saw things writ larger than his personal circumstances."

In his first job after law school, Paterson worked as a criminal-law associate in the Queens district-attorney's office. (While some of his official biographies state that he was an assistant district attorney, others have disputed the accuracy of that title.) During that period Paterson failed the six-hour New York State bar examination. He has blamed that failure on inadequate accommodations for blind or visually impaired test-takers. "I can do some reading on my own, but the bar exam I couldn't, because it was grueling," he told Ben Smith for the *New York Observer* (February 13, 2006). "It was a big problem for me. I didn't realize the time had expired." Paterson's plans to retake the exam never materialized. He has since pushed the state to change the procedures for administration of the bar exam to blind applicants.

Though unable to practice law in New York, Paterson appeared in court as a representative of the Queens prosecutor. He left the district attorney's office in 1985, when he ran for the seat in the New York State Senate representing the 29th Senate District—the same one that his father had held two decades earlier. Paterson won in a special election, held because of the death of the incumbent, and at the age of 31, he became New York's youngest state senator. He earned a reputation for appealing to a broad range of voters. For a time, before redistricting altered his territory (and his district became the 30th), he represented Harlem, whose residents are primarily black and Hispanic; the predominately white Upper West Side; and the area known as Washington Heights, whose mixed population includes a large number of natives of the Dominican Republic. His fellow Democrats in the Senate elected him deputy minority leader in 1985.

In 1993 Paterson had made a bid for the post of New York City's public advocate. Paterson counted on getting more votes from blacks than any of his five competitors in the Democratic primary, held that year in September, but he wound up with only 19 percent of the overall vote; the winner of the primary (and the following general election), Mark Green, a former city consumer-affairs commissioner and a friend of Paterson's, captured 5 percent more than the 40 percent of the overall vote necessary to avoid a runoff. In 1997 Paterson campaigned briefly for the Democratic nomination for Manhattan borough president. He dropped out of the race when it became apparent that C. Virginia Fields, a city councilwoman, had secured the support of most Democratic Party leaders and many donors.

During his early years in the New York State Senate, Paterson gained little notice. He was hampered both by the body's longstanding Republican majority and his status as a young, relatively inexperienced politician. That changed in 2002, when he and two other state senators from Manhattan decided to stage a coup and oust the then–Senate minority leader, Martin Connor. Paterson and his colleagues thought that Connor, who hailed from Brooklyn, was too accepting of the Republican Party's dominance of the legislature. Paterson initially denied rumors that he was interested in getting Connor's job, but in November 2002 he announced that he had enough support to become minority leader, and he assumed that post before year's end. While that position had traditionally been viewed as ineffectual, Paterson set his sights on helping the Democrats take control of the legislature. He achieved success on that front when, in 2004, the party won an additional three seats. "He elevated the office to something it had never been before," C. Virginia Fields told Smith. Despite Paterson's effective leadership, some accused the minority leader of being too obliging in his dealings with opponents, such as Republican leader Joseph Bruno. Some also complained that Paterson, who holds liberal views on most issues, was ambiguous about his stances on such topics as school vouchers and the death penalty.

Earlier, in the mid-1990s, Paterson had met Eliot Spitzer, when the two appeared together on a TV talk show; at that time Spitzer was a partner in a prestigious law firm specializing in antitrust cases. The two debated whether it makes sense for police officers to use high-school yearbook photos in their investigations. "Boy, did we have it out, and yet I thought, 'Boy, this is the most prepared person I think I've ever debated,'" Paterson told Smith. "He really moved me." In January 2006 Spitzer, a Democratic candidate for governor, asked Paterson to become his running mate. In a story for the *Toronto (Ontario, Canada) Star* (March 13, 2008), John Nichols suggested that Spitzer's decision to run with Paterson had been "a political one, designed to strengthen Spitzer's hand as he grabbed for New York's top job after just one high-profile term as state attorney general." Paterson's acceptance of that offer dismayed many Harlem politicians, among them former mayor David N. Dinkins, Congressman Charles B. Rangel, former Manhattan borough president Percy E. Sutton, and Paterson's father, all of whom had already endorsed for lieutenant governor another candidate, Leecia Eve. Nevertheless, Basil Paterson quickly switched allegiance to his son. "He's a remarkable guy . . . ," he told Cara Matthews for Gannett News Services (February 9, 2007). "I've been proud of him all his life." Some political observers questioned why Paterson, who appeared to be in line for the position of Senate majority leader—one of the three most powerful political posts in the state—would entertain the idea of becoming lieutenant governor. Explaining his rationale to Pressman, Paterson said

that he believed that Spitzer could do a lot for New York and that he "wanted to accommodate him."

Spitzer and Paterson were elected in November 2006. Rather than remain in the background, as many previous lieutenant governors had, Paterson took the lead on several key issues. He helped to ensure the passage of a measure that allocated $600 million for stem-cell research during the next 10 years. He also promoted women- and minority-owned businesses and introduced statewide renewable-energy initiatives. "I think my goal is to keep my name from getting added to all those people who never did anything," he said, as quoted by Robert J. McCarthy in the *Buffalo News* (March 6, 2007). According to some sources Paterson sometimes clashed with Spitzer, who was widely described as egotistical and unwilling to share power.

On March 10, 2008, days after federal investigators arrested four men in connection with the Emperor's Club prostitution ring, the *New York Times* reported that Spitzer had been an Emperor's Club client. Spitzer, who was accused of spending many thousands of dollars on high-priced call girls, issued a public apology two days later and announced that, effective March 17, he would step down as governor. Paterson was sworn in that day, becoming the fourth black governor in U.S. history as well as New York's first African-American governor. While he is technically the second legally blind governor in U.S. history, he is the first to serve for any significant length of time. (The blind politician Bob Cowley Riley served as governor of Arkansas for 11 days in 1975, to fill out the term of Dale Bumpers, who had become a U.S. senator.) During his inaugural speech Paterson said he would pick up where Spitzer, who had campaigned as a reformer, left off, citing his desire to create more affordable housing, lower taxes, and boost the economy in the state's northern areas. "I have a vision for New York," he said, as quoted by James T. Madore in the *Chicago Tribune* (March 18, 2008). "It's a New York where achievement is developed only from hard work, where doors are always open and where anyone can achieve." At his swearing-in ceremony, Paterson received a two-minute ovation.

New York State lawmakers from both parties have characterized Paterson as far less combative and more unifying than Spitzer. "There's been tension here for months, and confrontation," Joseph Bruno told Madore. "So, I think there's relief. . . . It's a new day and the sun is shining." "What we are going to do from now on is what we always should have done all along," Paterson said, according to the Associated Press (March 17, 2008). "We're going to work together." By the time he finished his first day on the job, Paterson had signed five bills, among them one that addressed subway safety and another concerning the state's Green Thumb Environmental Program. Generating much more media attention, however, was Paterson's announcement that both he and his wife, the former

Michelle Paige, had engaged in extramarital affairs. Paterson told the *Daily News* that he had had a relationship with another woman from 1999 to 2001, during a period when his marriage "appeared to be going sour," according to the Associated Press (March 18, 2008). He added, "But I went to counseling and we decided we wanted to make it work. Michelle is well aware of what went on."

In April 2008 Paterson worked with state legislators to pass a $121.7 billion budget, avoiding a projected $4.6 billion deficit by cutting spending and raising taxes. That same month he announced that New York had rejected the construction of a natural-gas barge that the company Broadwater Energy had sought to build in Long Island Sound. In doing so he won praise from environmental groups that had opposed the facility. While Paterson has said that he, like Spitzer, supports campaign-finance reforms, some observers have feared that he will not take as tough a stance as his predecessor. On April 29, 2008 Paterson failed to attend events on Reform Day, a forum held in the state capital, Albany, for groups that are committed to pushing for stricter fund-raising laws, among other government reforms. Paterson cited a scheduling conflict as the reason for his absence, and he has insisted that his record proves him to be a reformer.

At a May 2008 press conference, Paterson urged state agencies to amend their regulations and begin recognizing same-sex marriages performed in other jurisdictions. His appeal came roughly three months after a Rochester, New York, appellate court ruled that a Monroe County community college could not deny health benefits to the female spouse of a female employee. (The couple had been married in Canada.) While Paterson's directive could help the state avoid future lawsuits, he has said that he believes gays and lesbians deserve the same rights as heterosexuals. "People who live together for a long time would like to be married—as far as I'm concerned, I think it's beautiful," he said, according to Jeremy W. Peters and Danny Hakim, writing for the *New York Times* (May 30, 2008, online). He added, "It's something that the government should allow for people. It's maybe understood in this generation."

Paterson's first major test as governor came when New York City—the financial capital of the world—assumed center stage in the economic crisis of 2008. With huge losses in tax revenues expected in the wake of Wall Street bankruptcies, near-bankruptcies, and plunging stock prices, Paterson has anticipated correspondingly large deficits in state receipts and has called for sweeping, and potentially unpopular and divisive, budget cuts. In October 2008 he announced that he would run for a full term as governor in 2010.

In his leisure time Paterson enjoys playing basketball and running; in 1999 he finished the New York City marathon. When he and his wife were married, in 1992, Michelle Paterson had a four-year-old daughter, Ashley Dennis, from her first marriage. The couple live in Harlem with Ashley, a college student, and their son, Alex, who attends a public middle school in Manhattan.

—K.J.P.

Suggested Reading: *Buffalo News* A p2 Mar. 12, 2008; *New York Observer* p1+ Feb. 13, 2006; *New York Times* A p25 Mar. 14, 2008; *Newsday* (on-line) Mar. 12, 2008

Gabriel Bouys/AFP/Getty Images

Paul, Ron

Aug. 20, 1935– U.S. representative from Texas (Republican); obstetrician and gynecologist

Address: 203 Cannon House Office Bldg., Washington, DC 20515

"Politicians don't amount to much, but ideas do." That remark, quoted on several dozen Web sites in mid-spring 2008, was made by Ron Paul, a nine-term Republican U.S. congressman from Texas, who in March 2007 announced his bid to be his party's presidential nominee. During the 12 months in which he actively campaigned for that position, Paul—who was well aware that his chances of winning the nomination were minuscule—made use of his newfound prominence to present his highly unorthodox views to audiences nationwide. Thanks in part to the Internet, he received far more attention in 2007–08 than he had in his first run for the nation's highest office, in 1988, when, as the Libertarian candidate, he captured four-10ths of 1 percent of the popular vote, his name appearing on the ballots of 46 states and the District of Columbia. On December 16, 2007 Paul broke the one-day record for on-line campaign fund-raising, collecting $6 million from more than 50,000 donors.

Paul describes himself on his congressional Web site as "the premier advocate for liberty in politics today." Posted on his site are what he has labeled his six "freedom principles": "Rights belong to individuals, not groups. Property should be owned by people, not government. All voluntary associations should be permissible—economic and social. The government's monetary role is to maintain the integrity of the monetary unit, not participate in fraud. [That is, the U.S. should back its currency with gold or silver.] Government exists to protect liberty, not to redistribute wealth or to grant special privileges. The lives and actions of people are their own responsibility, not the government's." Paul maintains, as he explained on his Web site, that every bill introduced by members of Congress "must be examined for its constitutionality; that is, on the basis of whether or not the US Constitution allows the Congress or the Federal Government to engage in the actions described by the proposed legislation. If the Constitution does not allow it, then it must be opposed." His voting record shows that Paul has unfailingly adhered to that maxim. As Christopher Caldwell noted for the *New York Times Magazine* (July 22, 2007), "He has made a habit of objecting to things that no one else objects to."

Before he served his first three full terms in the House of Representatives (1979–85), and during the dozen years before he returned to the House, in 1997, Paul maintained a medical practice as a gynecologist and obstetrician; before he hung up his shingle, he delivered more than 4,000 babies, by his count. While studying economics on his own as an adult, he became a steadfast adherent of the so-called Austrian school of economics, which holds that markets should be free of government interference. In line with that philosophy, Paul advocates the elimination of the U.S. Departments of Commerce, Education, Health and Human Services, Agriculture, Interior, Transportation, Housing and Urban Development, Labor, and Energy; the Food and Drug Administration; the Environmental Protection Agency; and most other federal agencies, all of which, he believes, involve the federal government in activities that should be carried out only with private funds (medical research, for example) or left to the states to oversee. He has proposed abolishing the Federal Bureau of Investigation (FBI) and the Central Intelligence Agency (CIA) as well. Only the Departments of Justice and Defense meet with Paul's approval. He opposes so-called managed-trade agreements and organizations, among them the North American Free Trade Agreement (NAFTA), the General Agreement on Tariffs and Trade (GATT), and the World Trade Organization (WTO), and agencies that intrude in national or international financial affairs (the Federal Reserve Board, the Federal Deposit Insurance Corp., the World Bank, and the International Monetary Fund, to name a few). He has called for a constitutional amendment abolishing the personal income tax, estate tax, and gift tax and another amendment that would deny American citizenship to babies born in the U.S. to noncitizens.

Paul has called for an end to the United States' membership in the United Nations and NATO (the North Atlantic Treaty Organization). While he regards as the government's chief duty the protection of its citizens, their property, and their constitutional rights, he has warned of the dangers and folly of what he regards as the nation's attempt to maintain an "empire" through military might. He opposes the presence on foreign soil of U.S. military bases (currently, there are between 700 and 800) and has introduced legislation calling for the withdrawal of all U.S. troops from South Korea and other foreign countries. He disapproves of the imposition of sanctions against other countries and opposes foreign aid as counterproductive. He voted against military action in Kuwait in 1991, in what is known as the Gulf War, and in Iraq, where the U.S. launched a war in 2003, and he has opposed all legislation allocating additional funds for the latter. Paul was one of only three Republicans who voted against the U.S.A. Patriot Act (in which "U.S.A. Patriot" is an acronym standing for "Uniting and Strengthening America by Providing Appropriate Tools Required to Intercept and Obstruct Terrorism"), which President George W. Bush signed into law in October 2001, in the wake of the September 11, 2001 terrorist acts against the U.S.; Paul also voted against its reauthorization, in 2006. Incensed that he and his House colleagues were called upon to vote on the 500-page U.S.A. Patriot Act in 2001 only an hour after they saw printed copies of the legislation for the first time, Paul introduced a bill that would have amended House rules to ensure that members "have a reasonable amount of time to read legislation that will be voted upon." He has condemned as unconstitutional White House "signing statements"—statements added to bills passed by Congress and signed by the president, in which, as an alternative to vetoing the legislation (which would make it possible for Congress to override the veto), the president offers his own interpretation of what the laws stipulate. (President Bush has signed hundreds of such statements, far more than any previous chief executive.) Such attempts by the Bush administration to weaken the powers of Congress and expand those of the chief executive led Paul to introduce a bill "to restore the Constitution's checks and balances and protections against government abuses as envisioned by the Founding Fathers."

In other matters, in which his positions mirror those of most or many Republicans, Paul has introduced a bill "to provide that human life shall be deemed to exist from conception," and another bill that would "prohibit any Federal official from expending any Federal funds for any population control or population planning program or any family planning activity," as reported on the Library of Congress's Web site www.thomas.loc.gov. He introduced a bill to repeal the Gun-Free School Zones Act and its amendments, and, in accordance with his interpretation of the Second Amendment of the Bill of Rights, he staunchly defends the right of all citizens to own guns. Regarding other issues, Paul's stands set him apart from all or virtually all other Republican members of Congress—and sometimes from all or virtually all Democrats as well. For example, Paul adamantly opposes the federal government's "war on drugs" and believes that the use of marijuana and all other drugs should be legalized. He has never voted "yes" on any legislation that called for using the Social Security Trust Fund surplus for emergency appropriations or any other purpose, and he has voted "no" on all legislation that, with the goal of winning the "war on terror," weakens the Fourth Amendment of the Bill of Rights, which guarantees "the right of the people to be secure in their persons, houses, papers, and effects, against unreasonable searches and seizures." Paul has even voted against issuing congressional medals to Rosa Parks, Pope John Paul II, and Ronald Reagan, since he believes that doing so would constitute an illegal use of tax dollars, and every year he has returned part of the funds allotted for the maintenance of his Washington, D.C., office. "He's just consistent, consistent, consistent," the Wharton County, Texas, Republican Party chairwoman, Debra Medina, told Libby Copeland during an interview for the *Washington Post* (July 9, 2006). "He always talks about the constitution and what the federal government ought to be doing, and he consistently articulates this basic mistrust of big government, [a mistrust] which I think most people have." In a brief video posted on his campaign Web site on March 8, 2008, as quoted by the Associated Press (on-line) the same day, Paul declared, "Though victory in the conventional political sense is not available in the presidential race . . . we must remember [that] elections are short-term efforts. Revolutions are long-term projects," and he urged his supporters to embark on the next phase of what he called "our campaign for liberty." In the latest of his publications, his book *Revolution: A Manifesto* (2008), Paul spelled out his political, social, and economic ideology.

Paul's success at the polls has puzzled some political observers, since none of the bills he has sponsored have passed (most have never reached the floor of the House), and he has consistently voted against farm subsidies, even though his district—which is bigger than Massachusetts—is largely agricultural. Although Paul's district also includes Galveston, which was devastated by a hurricane in 1900, the congressman does not believe that the federal government should give relief money to people in storm-damaged areas, and he voted against a bill that allocated billions of dollars for victims of Hurricane Katrina. "Is bailing out people that chose to live on the coastline a proper function of the federal government?" he asked Libby Copeland. "Why do people in Arizona have to be robbed in order to support the people on the coast?" Despite his distaste for bureaucracy and big government, Paul has earned a reputation for helping constituents "collect Social Security checks, passports, military decorations, immigrant-visa extensions and any emolument to which constituents are entitled by law," as Caldwell wrote. "Ron Paul is a very charismatic person," Tim Delaney, editor of the *Victoria (Texas) Advocate*, a newspaper published in Paul's district, told Caldwell. "He has charm. He does not alter his position ever. His ideals are high. If a little old man calls up from the farm and says, 'I need a wheelchair,' he'll get the damn wheelchair for him." a member of Paul's staff, Jackie Gloor, told Caldwell, "So many times, people say to us, 'We don't like his vote.' But they trust his heart."

The third of the five sons of Howard and Margaret Paul, Ronald Ernest Paul was born on August 20, 1935 in Green Tree, Pennsylvania, a suburb of Pittsburgh. His father, who had only an eighth-grade education, ran a small dairy business. The family lived in a four-room house, in which Paul shared a bedroom with all of his brothers (William, David, Jerrold, and Wayne). As a teenager Paul delivered milk in his community; one of the customers on his route was the retired Hall of Fame baseball player Honus Wagner. At Dormont High School, near Green Tree, Paul was a standout member of the baseball, football, and track teams. In his senior year he was elected student-body president. "He didn't run for it," his wife, the former Carol Wells, a Dormont alumna, told Lisa Anderson for the *Chicago Tribune* (November 13, 2007). "[Other students] wanted him." A knee injury that required surgery around the time of his graduation, in 1953, sidelined Paul from sports temporarily. Raised a Lutheran, he had planned to become a minister, as two of his brothers had, but after he entered Gettysburg College, in Gettysburg, Pennsylvania, Paul decided instead to major in biology. After he earned a B.A. degree, in 1957, he enrolled at the Duke University Medical Center, in Durham, North Carolina; he also got married that year. He received an M.D. degree in 1961 from Duke and then completed his medical internship and residency, in obstetrics and gynecology, at the Henry Ford Hospital, in Detroit, Michigan. He trained further in those specialties from 1965 to 1968 at the University of Pittsburgh.

Meanwhile, as the war in Vietnam escalated, Paul served as a flight surgeon in the U.S. Air Force, from 1963 to 1965, and the Air National Guard, from 1965 to 1968, both within the U.S. and overseas. "I recall doing a lot of physicals on Army warrant officers who wanted to become helicopter pilots and go to Vietnam," he told Caldwell. "They were gung-ho. I've often thought about how many of those people never came back." In 1968 Paul moved with his family to Brazonia County, near Houston in southeastern Texas, where he had been stationed during his final year in the military. He took over the obstetrics and gynecology practice of a retired doctor, and for a while, until a partner joined him, he was the only ob-gyn specialist in the county. By that time Paul had become a follower of the Austrian school of economics, whose leading proponents were Ludwig von Mises (1881–1973); Henry Hazlitt (1894–1993); Friedrich Hayek (1899–1992); and Murray N. Rothbard (1926–95). He also came to believe that the U.S. should back its currency with gold and/or silver reserves—a view he continues to hold. Paul decided to become politically active after President Richard Nixon, in August 1971, announced that wages and prices would be frozen for 90 days and that the United States would no longer exchange gold for currency, as it had been obligated to do throughout its history. Rather, U.S. dollars would be backed by the "faith and credit of the government." "I remember the day very clearly," Paul told S. C. Gwynne for *Texas Monthly* (October 2001). "Nixon closed the gold window. . . . After that day, all money would be political money rather than money of real value. I was astounded."

In 1974, campaigning as an advocate of "freedom, honesty and sound money," according to Caldwell, Paul made his first bid for a seat in the U.S. House of Representatives; he lost to the Democratic incumbent, Robert R. "Bob" Casey. In a special election held in April 1976, after Casey left Congress to join the Federal Maritime Commission, Paul ran successfully against another Democratic candidate, Robert "Bob" Gammage, a Texas state senator, to fill Casey's vacated seat. "I had real difficulty down in Brazoria County . . . ," Gammage told Wade Goodwyn for the National Public Radio program *All Things Considered* (October 7, 2007), "because he'd delivered half the babies in the county." Paul was also helped by radio ads that ran on the morning of the election, in which he accused his opponent of wanting to "turn the rapists and murderers loose," according to Gammage. (That year Paul distanced himself from his fellow Republicans by backing Ronald Reagan, rather than Gerald Ford, for the party's 1976 presidential nomination.) In November 1976, in the regular election, Gammage defeated Paul, by fewer than 300 votes, but two years later, in another contest with Gammage, Paul prevailed. He served three consecutive terms, during which he spoke out against changes in banking rules—adopted in 1980 and 1982—that many believe were responsible for the savings-and-loan collapse of the late 1980s and early 1990s. (More than a thousand savings-and-loan institutions failed. The Federal Savings and Loan Insurance Corp., now defunct, was unable to cover the losses, and the government used billions of taxpayer dollars to make up the difference. The crisis amounted to "the greatest collapse of U.S. financial institutions since the 1930s," according to an *FDIC Banking Review* [December 2000] paper by Timothy Curry and Lynn Shibut.) In 1984 Paul made an unsuccessful try to win a seat in the U.S. Senate, losing in the primary election to Phil

Gramm, a former Democrat who had switched to the GOP.

At the end of the 98th Congress, Paul returned to his ob-gyn practice. In keeping with his libertarian philosophy, he refused to accept Medicare and Medicaid payments for his services; when patients were unable to pay, he provided treatment free of charge. In his spare time he remained active in libertarian politics, and in 1988 he won the Libertarian Party's presidential nomination. Paul campaigned widely, sometimes speaking to gatherings of as few as 10 people. Not surprisingly, he finished a distant third, after the winner, the Republican nominee, Vice President George H. W. Bush, and the Democratic candidate, Governor Michael S. Dukakis of Massachusetts. Paul received 432,000 votes—less than one-half of 1 percent of the total cast—but as a contender he had met many people who later supported his political ambitions. Paul also continued to run the Foundation for Rational Economics and Education (FREE), a nonprofit organization he had founded in 1976, "as a vehicle to increase understanding of economic principles of a free society," according to its Web site. In 1986 he set up the National Endowment for Liberty, as an arm of FREE, "to develop programs that take advantage of the enormous potential of electronic media to pursue the mission of FREE," as the Web site states. He began publishing a newsletter, called the *Ron Paul Political Report* and, later, the *Ron Paul Survival Report*. Also in the 1980s he produced three monographs: *Gold, Peace, and Prosperity: The Birth of a New Currency* (1981) and *Abortion and Liberty* (1983), which he published under the imprint of FREE, and *Case for Gold: A Minority Report of the U.S. Gold Commission* (1982), written with Lewis Lehrman, which was published by the Cato Institute, a libertarian think tank.

In 1995, after Republicans gained control of Congress, Paul met with GOP leaders, in a failed effort to persuade them that he was well positioned to beat the incumbent, Gregory H. "Greg" Laughlin, a conservative Democrat, in the recently redrawn 14th Congressional District, on Texas's Gulf Coast. In June of that year, Laughlin announced that he would run as a Republican. Paul opted to challenge him in the primary, raising money largely from out-of-state libertarians with whom he had forged ties during his years away from Congress. "At first, we kind of blew him off . . . ," the Texas political consultant Royal Masset told Caldwell. "But very quickly, we realized he was getting far more money than anybody." The National Republican Congressional Committee launched a major effort to defeat Paul, enlisting top Republicans—including former president George H. W. Bush, Texas governor George W. Bush, and Congressman Newt Gingrich, the Speaker of the House—to endorse Laughlin; for his part, Paul secured the support of the magazine mogul Steve Forbes (a proponent of a flat tax on all personal and corporate income) and the famed baseball player Nolan Ryan. Paul came in second to Laughlin in the four-way primary contest, but since Laughlin had failed to get a majority of the votes, he and Paul then faced each other in a second primary, which Paul won with 54 percent of the vote. In the general election Paul faced the Democrat Charles "Lefty" Morris, a lawyer who had specialized in personal-injury cases. In that bitterly fought contest, Morris emphasized Paul's most unconventional views; for example, he paid for TV ads showing Paul in 1988 at a conference of the National Organization for the Reform of Marijuana Laws, "pounding on a podium and zealously shouting: 'Let's get rid of the drug dealers by getting rid of all the drug laws,'" as Alex de Marban reported for the *Austin (Texas) Chronicle* (October 31, 1996, on-line). Morris also made public some incendiary portions of Paul's newsletters, including one in which Paul had written, according to Marban, that nearly all black males in the nation's capital were "criminal or semi-criminal" and that, unlike most other 13-year-olds, "black males, age 13, that have been raised on the streets and who have joined criminal gangs are as big, strong, tough, scary, and culpable as any adult [if they have committed crimes] and should be treated as such." Despite such extremist views and his refusal to provide to Morris or the media copies of all his newsletters, Paul won the election with 51 percent of the vote. Paul has held his congressional seat ever since, and in the next three elections, he won by 55, 60, and 68 percent of the votes, respectively. In 2004 he ran unopposed. In 2006 he captured 20 percent more votes than his Democratic challenger, Shane Sklar.

Paul has occasionally found himself aligned with members of the Democratic Party as well as the GOP. In the aftermath of the terrorist attacks of September 11, 2001, he voted to fund the hunt for their assumed mastermind, Osama bin Laden; the following year he was among the six House Republicans and 126 Democrats who voted against giving President Bush authority to invade Iraq. His antiwar stance has won him support from the far left, as has his assertion that the U.S. should not interfere in other countries' internal affairs. "Ultimately, our money, weapons, and interventionist policies never buy us friends for long," Paul wrote in an on-line column, entitled "What Does Regime Change in Iraq Really Mean?," as quoted by Shailagh Murray in the *Wall Street Journal* (March 10, 2003). "And more often we simply arm our future enemies." But Paul has little in common with liberals. "I have a lot of people who correspond with me who come from the left, but I don't go to their events since there's so often more on their plate than just the war," he told Brian Doherty for the Web site *Reason Online* (January 22, 2007). "They have an agenda I don't endorse. I'm interested in reviving that spirit that says conservatives and limited-government constitutionalists can support the antiwar position, can be comfortable without aggressive foreign policy."

On such issues as income taxes and foreign aid, Paul has won praise from the far right. He advocates abolishing Social Security; in his view, despite the trials of the Great Depression, Americans were doing well before 1935, when Congress, spurred by President Franklin D. Roosevelt, established it. "I mean, do you read stories about how many people were laying in the streets and dying and didn't have medical treatment? . . . Prices were low and the country was productive and families took care of themselves and churches built hospitals and there was no starvation," he told Copeland. Speaking about foreign aid, he told Zack Pelta-Heller for the *American Prospect* (June 11, 2007) that Americans "don't need to be forced to pay for foreign welfare at the barrel of a government gun. I don't have the right to take money from you and make you work harder or live less productively, just because I'm sympathetic with the conditions in Darfur." (He was referring to what others have called the genocide of black Africans in Sudan at the hands of that nation's government and its supporters.)

Paul, who opposes abortion, has said that the legality of abortion should be decided by the states, not the federal government. He is against granting amnesty to illegal immigrants and advocates an end to birthright citizenship. Paul has drawn flak from some libertarians for voting in favor of the government's negotiating prices for prescription drugs, an activity prohibited by the Medicare prescription-drug plan, which Congress approved and President George W. Bush signed into law in 2003. "I don't vote for price controls, obviously, but if government has to buy something—even if it shouldn't be buying it!—they have a responsibility to get the best price," he told Doherty. "But most importantly, we shouldn't be in that business [of buying drugs]."

In March 2007 Paul announced that he was running for the 2008 Republican presidential nomination. "Liberty once again must become more important to us than the desire for security and material comfort," he said, according to *World Net Daily* (March 12, 2007, on-line). "Personal safety and economic prosperity can only come as the consequence of liberty. They cannot be provided by an authoritarian government. To expect the government to take care of us from cradle to grave undermines the principles of liberty." Paul told Doherty that the Internet would be a key part of his campaign. "If we don't learn how to use that to its maximum benefit, we won't have a very viable campaign," he said. By July 2007, though polls showed that only a tiny percentage of voters supported his candidacy, Paul was becoming an Internet sensation. He had the most "friends" of any Republican candidate on the social-networking Web site MySpace, and of all the presidential hopefuls, only Barack Obama was attracting more viewers to the video Web site YouTube. Paul's was also one of the most frequently searched-for names on the Internet. In the third quarter of 2007, his campaign raised more than $5 million, putting him ahead of two Republicans, U.S. senator John McCain of Arizona and former governor Mike Huckabee of Arkansas, and two Democratic senators, Joseph Biden of Delaware and Chris Dodd of Connecticut—presidential hopefuls who received more attention than Paul from the national media. "I still don't think it's me as much as the message," Paul told Sarah Liebowitz for the *Concord (New Hampshire) Monitor* (September 30, 2007). "The frustration level is much higher than anybody anticipated. People realize that we are in a period of major change in this country. We are on the verge of a bankruptcy, the dollar is crashing, the foreign policy's in shambles and the people's personal liberties are under attack." On December 16, 2007, the 243d anniversary of the Boston Tea Party, the music promoter Trevor Lyman organized an on-line fund-raiser for Paul; reportedly, more than 50,000 donors contributed a total of $6 million—a record for single-day on-line fundraising.

In March 2008 Paul posted a brief video on his Web site announcing that he was ending his campaign for the presidential nomination. "I don't mind playing a key role in this revolution, but it has to be more than a Ron Paul revolution," he said, according to the Associated Press (March 8, 2008). "Our job now is to plan for the next phase." Paul vowed to continue traveling the country, spreading his message, and raising money for FREE.

Paul's book *The Revolution: A Manifesto* rose immediately to the top of several influential national best-seller lists after its publication, in May 2008. In June he revealed that he intended to use his remaining campaign funds to launch Ron Paul's Campaign for Liberty, an organization dedicated to promoting libertarian ideas and policies. Paul refused to endorse the 2008 Republican nominee for the presidency, U.S. senator John McCain of Arizona, or attend the 2008 Republican National Convention; instead, he staged a "counter-convention" and expressed his approval of several candidates unaffiliated with the two-party system. In September he announced his support for Chuck Baldwin, a member of the Constitution Party. In keeping with his stated beliefs and principles, Paul strongly opposed the so-called government bailout—the federal intervention into the financial system, which came as a response to the economic crisis of 2008—calling it "immoral" and "distastrous." On November 4, 2008, running unopposed, Paul was reelected to his seat in Congress.

Paul's other recent publications include *Mises and Austrian Economics: A Personal View* (2004). A book of his essays, *Ron Paul Speaks* (2008), was compiled and edited by Philip Haddad and Roger Marsh. Paul and his wife live in Lake Jackson, Texas. They have five children—Ronald Paul Jr., Lori Pyeatt, Randall "Rand" Paul, Robert Paul, and Joy Paul-LeBlanc—and many grandchildren.

—K.J.P.

Suggested Reading: *Austin (Texas) Chronicle* (on-line) Oct. 31, 1996; *Chicago Tribune* (on-line) Nov. 13, 2007; *Concord (New Hampshire) Monitor* (on-line) Sep. 30, 2007; *Los Angeles Times* A p12 Nov. 8, 2007; *Fairfield County (Connecticut) Weekly* (on-line) June 21, 2007; *New York Times* (on-line) Oct. 17, 1988; *New York Times Magazine* p26 July 22, 2007; *Politico* (on-line) Oct. 9, 2007; *Washington Post* D p1 July 9, 2006

Selected Books: *Gold, Peace and Prosperity: The Birth of a New Currency*, 1981; *The Case for Gold: A Minority Report of the U.S. Gold Commission*, 1982; *Abortion and Liberty*, 1983; *Freedom Under Seige: The U.S. Constitution After 200 Years*, 1987; *Challenge to Liberty: Coming to Grips with the Abortion Issue*, 1990; *Mises and Austrian Economics: A Personal View*, 2004; *A Foreign Policy of Freedom*, 2007; *The Party System*, 2007; *Ron Paul Speaks*, 2008; *The Revolution: A Manifesto*, 2008

Kevin Winter/Getty Images

Peirce, Kimberly

Sep. 8, 1967– Filmmaker

Address: c/o Creative Artists Agency, 2000 Ave. of the Stars, Los Angeles, CA 90067

Although Kimberly Peirce has co-written only three feature-length screenplays and directed only two full-length films, her ability to tackle controversial subjects has earned her recognition as one of Hollywood's groundbreaking filmmakers.

Peirce's critically acclaimed directorial debut, *Boys Don't Cry* (1999), which was based on the real-life murder of Brandon Teena, a transgendered teen, catapulted her into the Hollywood spotlight. In her second and most recent film, *Stop-Loss* (2008), Peirce shed light on the U.S. military's policy, called stop-loss, of retaining soldiers who have already fulfilled their terms of service.

Peirce was born to teenage parents on September 8, 1967 in Harrisburg, Pennsylvania, where she lived in a trailer park. Her parents separated when she was four years old, and she spent her early childhood being shuttled among relatives in Pennsylvania, New York, and Puerto Rico, before settling in Miami, Florida, where she attended Miami Sunset High School. Peirce developed an interest in photography at an early age. "I actually made Super 8 movies as a kid. Later, I bought my first camera and literally shot everything," she told Ben Barna for *BlackBook* (March 25, 2008, on-line). Peirce, who grew up a tomboy, also became fascinated with notions of masculinity and femininity. "When I was growing up, I always was amazed by women who passed as men—adventurers, sailors, pirates," she recalled to Devin D. O'Leary in an interview for the *Weekly Wire* (February 21, 2000, on-line).

After graduating from high school, in 1985, Peirce enrolled at the University of Chicago, in Illinois. Soon afterward she was forced to leave school, "because my parents wouldn't sign off on my financial aid," as she was quoted as saying in a 2001 interview posted on the *Index* magazine Web site. She then went to the city of Kobe, Japan, where over the next two years she supported herself financially by working as a part-time model, an English teacher, and a photographer. Peirce discovered her passion for moviemaking during a photo-taking tour of Southeast Asia. "Photography didn't feel like enough anymore. I needed narrative movement," she told the interviewer for *Index*. "I wanted to be able to build emotional structures. I wanted something that could match my interests and my enthusiasm." Peirce withdrew the entire $10,000 balance from her bank account and stored it in her sock. She then returned to the U.S. and resumed her undergraduate studies at the University of Chicago. While attending college Peirce spent a significant amount of time in the school's film library, often watching movies by such renowned filmmakers as Federico Fellini, Akira Kurosawa, and Martin Scorsese.

In 1990 Peirce received her bachelor's degree in English and Japanese literature. She subsequently enrolled in the graduate film program at Columbia University, in New York City. While in school she served as an assistant editor on Cheryl Dunye's 16-millimeter short film *Greetings from Africa* (1994). Peirce first garnered critical acclaim with her debut film, *The Last Good Breath* (1994), an experimental 16-millimeter short that she wrote and directed. The movie, which tells the story of two lovers during a world war, was screened at several film festivals and won the second-place prize at the Canada International Film Festival and the Golden Award in the experimental division at the Chicago International Film Festival. During that period she began working on her graduate thesis, which was initially about Pauline Cushman, an African-American spy who posed as a man during the U.S. Civil War. She changed her thesis topic after reading an article in the *Village Voice* about the brutal 1993 murder of Brandon Teena, a biological female who was born Teena Brandon and who identified herself, and dressed, as a man. Peirce was fascinated by Teena's decision to redefine her gender identity. "I felt this total kinship," she told O'Leary. "[I] knew a lot of girls who had passed as boys. [I] was totally in love with the fact that here was this girl, living in a trailer park, [who] didn't have any role models, didn't have much money, and she fully transforms herself into her fantasy of a boy. . . . I wanted to bring her to life."

Peirce immersed herself in learning everything she could about Teena's life. In 1995 she traveled with a group of transsexuals who planned to hold a demonstration vigil in Falls City, Nebraska, where Teena was murdered. While there she visited the farmhouse where Teena's body was found and also attended the trials of Teena's killers: John Lotter, who was sentenced to death for killing Teena and two other people, and Marvin Thomas Nissen, who received a life sentence in exchange for his testimony against Lotter. After returning from her trip, Peirce collaborated with fellow film student Andy Bienen on a screenplay, which she shot and directed in 1995. *Take It Like a Man*, Peirce's 10-minute film, was nominated by the Columbia University faculty for a Princess Grace Award and won an Astrea production grant. Additionally, she served as the editor for the Shawn Atkins animated short *Anastasia and the Queen of Hearts* (1996).

After deciding to turn *Take It Like a Man* into a feature-length movie, Peirce returned to Falls City in July 1996 to conduct more intensive research. She interviewed Brandon Teena's girlfriend Lana Tisdel and met with the coroners and local law-enforcement officials involved in the case. Through her friendship with a court reporter, Peirce gained access to the trial transcripts and exhibit photos; she also obtained Teena's arrest records for petty crimes. Peirce spent more than a year rewriting the screenplay with Bienen, developing it further at the 1997 Sundance Institute Screenwriters' Lab, in Park City, Utah.

Peirce had difficulty getting the project off the ground, not only because of the film's controversial subject matter but also because Peirce, a first-time director, insisted on retaining creative control. The screenplay eventually attracted the attention of the independent film producer Christine Vachon, who provided the movie's initial financing. (IFC Productions, the financing division of the Independent Film Channel, also became an investor in the project.) In addition, Peirce faced the challenge of finding the right person to play the role of Teena. "I needed someone who could not only capture Brandon's spirit, but pass as a guy," she said during an interview for the London *Independent* (March 10, 2000). "I needed an experienced but unknown actor, because otherwise you're always looking at someone playing someone. A lot of young actresses were terrified of being perceived as gay. Then there were girls who wanted to be Brandon but had no idea of what it was to be a boy." After an intensive search, during which Peirce auditioned several "drag kings" (female performance artists who dress as men), transsexuals, and Hollywood starlets, Peirce cast Hilary Swank, a then-obscure actress who had previously appeared on the popular television series *Beverly Hills 90210*. To prepare for the role, Swank cut her shoulder-length hair short; Peirce hired a voice and athletic trainer for Swank and encouraged the actress to get into character by living as a man for several weeks prior to filming.

Boys Don't Cry, as Peirce's film was renamed, was filmed over a 30-day period in and around Dallas, Texas, in late 1998. Peirce landed a distribution deal with executives at Fox Searchlight Pictures, after submitting a powerful 20-minute trailer. At the time there was a public outcry following the 1998 murder of Matthew Shepard, a gay man, in Laramie, Wyoming. "When Brandon was killed, the country wasn't as aware of its own cultural violence as it is now," Peirce told Emma Brockes for the *Irish Times* (May 6, 2000). "Now the corporate financiers are looking at my film and saying, 'Oh my God, you're recognizing a problem that's out there.' But the problem has been out there." Prior to the release of the film, Lana Tisdel filed an invasion-of-privacy lawsuit against the filmmakers and the movie's distributor, alleging the unauthorized use of her name and likeness; she later agreed to an out-of-court settlement. The executives at Fox Searchlight had also settled a claim by the author Aphrodite Jones, whose 1996 nonfiction book about the Brandon Teena murder (*All She Wanted*) had previously been in the process of being developed by Fox Searchlight as a film to star Drew Barrymore.

When *Boys Don't Cry* was released, in October 1999, it received widespread praise from critics. In a review for the *New York Times* (October 1, 1999), Janet Maslin wrote, "*Boys Don't Cry*, a film much tougher and more transfixing than its wan title, understands that this is more than just biography. It reaches out to reveal something about all the lives that Brandon changed forever. At first it would seem that this whole film hangs on the inspired performance of Hilary Swank, a beautiful, lanky actress with *Beverly Hills 90210* to her credit and no residual vanity to come between herself and Brandon. And Ms. Swank, who deserves to be remembered at the end of the year for a devastating portrayal, does account for much of the film's credibility. . . . But this is an ensemble effort, one that draws as much upon Ms. Peirce's insightful over-

view, Jim Denault's streamlined cinematography and the cast's raw emotion to make it work." Paul Tartara wrote for CNN.com (November 23, 1999), "Director-screenwriter Kimberly Peirce's *Boys Don't Cry* is a devastating emotional experience. There's real bravery in this film, the kind that's almost been snuffed in modern films, independent or otherwise."

Boys Don't Cry, which was made on a shoestring budget of $2 million, went on to gross more than $11 million in domestic box-office receipts. For her effort Peirce was honored as best new director by the National Board of Review (NBR) and the Boston Society of Film Critics (BSFC). She and the film's other producers also earned an Independent Spirit Award in the category of best first feature costing more than $500,000 to make. Additionally, Peirce won Las Vegas Film Critics Society awards for best directing and best adapted screenplay. At the 2000 Academy Awards, Swank was honored with a best-actress Oscar, and Chloë Sevigny received an Academy Award nomination for best supporting actress, for her portrayal of Lana Tisdel.

Following the success of *Boys Don't Cry*, Peirce signed a two-year, first-look production deal with New Line Cinema. Soon afterward she began developing the screenplay for a film about the unsolved 1922 murder of William Desmond Taylor, a silent-movie actor and writer. However, film-studio executives shelved the project in 2003 due to budgetary issues. By then the script had already been written, and several well-known actors, including Annette Bening, Ben Kingsley, Evan Rachel Wood, and Hugh Jackman, had been cast. Subsequent to that, Peirce's name was briefly linked to several other film projects, including adaptations of two books: Dave Eggers's *A Heartbreaking Work of Staggering Genius* (2003), which has yet to be made into a film; and Arthur Golden's *Memoirs of a Geisha* (1999), the movie version of which was directed by Rob Marshall in 2005.

Inspired by Hal Ashby's military film comedy/drama *The Last Detail* (1973), Peirce began working on the screenplay for her next film project: a documentary about the Iraq war. In 2003 she traveled across the U.S., armed with a camera, and interviewed several male and female soldiers and their families. "I wanted to make a movie about who the soldiers were that were signing up, why they were signing up, what their experience in combat was, and what their experience coming home was," she told Nathan Rabin in an interview posted on the A.V. Club Web site (March 26, 2008). The project became more personal when Peirce's 18-year-old half-brother, Brett, enlisted and was sent to Iraq. During Brett's first home leave, at Thanksgiving, he returned with several videos that had been filmed by his fellow soldiers. After seeing those videos, Peirce decided to make a full-length feature film rather than a documentary. "I have to admit I would get adrenalized watching [the videos]," she told Katrina Onstad for the *New York Times* (March 23, 2008, on-line). "We've never gotten this close to the soldier experience before. We're literally seeing it, feeling, hearing it, and they're cutting it, so they're seeing their fantasy of themselves. I just knew a movie had to be born from that kind of representation."

Peirce, who often contacted her half-brother through instant messaging, first heard about the controversial stop-loss policy during a conversation with Brett, who told her about a fellow soldier who had been redeployed to Iraq upon completing his tour of duty. She decided to make that practice the focus of the film, after discovering that more than 81,000 soldiers had been involuntarily reenlisted; many of those soldiers deserted their units after fighting their reenlistment unsuccessfully through legal means. Peirce financed her own research and collaborated with Mark Richard on the film's screenplay; the two had met when Peirce expressed interest in adapting Richard's 1990 novel, *The Ice at the Bottom of the World*, for the big screen. By the end of 2005, Peirce had sold the script to Paramount Pictures and MTV Films. Peirce shot the movie in Texas and Morocco. She incorporated in the film video footage from a hand-held camera, with a lot of fast cutting and pulsating music, to give the illusion that those segments were filmed by soldiers.

Released in March 2008, *Stop-Loss* tells the story of a decorated U.S. Army staff sergeant (played by Ryan Phillipe) who is recalled to active duty in Operation Iraqi Freedom and contemplates fleeing the country under a new identity. In a laudatory review for *Rolling Stone* (April 3, 2008, on-line), Peter Travers wrote, "It's been nine years since [Peirce] debuted with *Boys Don't Cry*, but her empathy with society's outsiders is undiminished and fills every frame of *Stop-Loss*. Even when the script slips into sentiment, Peirce sticks with her troubled, questing soldiers, and through this raw and riveting movie, they stick with us." A. O. Scott wrote for the *New York Times* (March 28, 2008), "The commercial failure of last autumn's crop of high-profile Iraq-themed movies—Paul Haggis's *In the Valley of Elah* and Brian De Palma's *Redacted* among them—has hardened into conventional wisdom about the movegoing public's reluctance to engage the war on screen. But those movies did not necessarily deserve their fate, and it would be a shame if *Stop-Loss* were to follow them into oblivion. . . . I say this partly because Ms. Peirce's movie . . . is not only an earnest, issue-driven narrative, but also a feverish entertainment, a passionate, at times overwrought melodrama gaudy with violent actions and emotions. The sober, mournful piety that has characterized a lot of the other fictional features about Iraq—documentaries are another matter—is almost entirely missing from *Stop-Loss*. . . . Not that the movie is unsentimental—far from it—but its messy, chaotic welter of feeling has a tang of authenticity. Instead of high-minded indignation or sorrow, it runs on earthier fuel: sweat, blood, beer, testosterone, loud music and an ideologically indeterminate, freewheeling sense of rage."

Peirce's upcoming film projects include "Sex, Secrets, and Taboo in Suburbia" and an untitled project about New Orleans, Louisiana. Peirce has also directed an episode of the Showtime series *The L Word*, a drama about a group of lesbians. She has been linked romantically with Evren Savci, a graduate student whose fields are gender sociology and Turkish literature. She and Savci live in a beach house in Malibu, California.

—C.C.

Suggested Reading: *Irish Times* p63+ May 6, 2000; *Los Angeles Times* E p1+ Mar. 16, 2008; *New York Times* E p1 Oct. 1, 1999, E p1+ Mar. 28, 2008; *Salon.com* Mar. 9, 2000; University Wire Mar. 27, 2008

Selected Films: *The Last Good Breath*, 1994; *Boys Don't Cry*, 1999; *Stop-Loss*, 2008

Evan Agostini/Getty Images

Peltz, Nelson

June 24, 1942– Business executive; investor

Address: Triarc Group, 280 Park Ave., New York, NY 10017

The 1980s saw the rise of so-called corporate raiders, Wall Street investors who acquired companies with borrowed funds, then paid their creditors and made handsome profits by dismantling the companies and selling their assets. The billionaire investor Nelson Peltz might be called a corporate raider with a difference: rather than breaking up the businesses he acquires, he has earned a reputation for not only keeping them intact but increasing their profitability. His first high-level deal was the 1983 takeover of the wire and cable maker Triangle Industries. In the following decade he and his partner Peter May, forming the company Triarc, successfully entered the fast-food and beverage businesses, selling many of their holdings for a fivefold profit at the start of the new millennium—but only after restoring them to health. In 2005 Peltz, May, and Edward Garden formed the hedge fund Trian, which currently manages over $5 billion in assets, including stakes in such companies as Heinz, Wendy's, and Tiffany & Co. In September 2008 Triarc merged with Wendy's to form one of the nation's largest fast-food chains. Peltz noted to Nancy A. Ruhling for *Lifestyles* (Fall 2005, on-line), "Understanding your customer and understanding what that particular business needs, that's essential. Some need a wider-angle vision, and some need a narrower focus. There's no formula. But they all need a strong ingredient of common sense and getting away from all that clutter; understanding a road map for that business." He added, "You have to say, here's a business. Do I like that business? Do I think that business has a future? Do its products have a future and can they make it in the marketplace, given a Wal-Mart on one side and China on the other? You have to ask questions that you intuitively know the answer to. You can do all your research, but you have to listen to your stomach. It's much more important to feel that you're intuitively on the right track. Then, you do all your work and find out if your investment thesis is appropriate."

Of Jewish lineage, Nelson A. Peltz was born on June 24, 1942, the second of the two children of Maurice Herbert Peltz and the former Claire Wechsler. He grew up in the Cypress Hills section of Brooklyn, New York. His family ran a small business, A. Peltz & Sons, which distributed frozen food and fresh produce to restaurants and other concerns. (The company was founded in 1896 by Nelson Peltz's paternal grandfather, Adolph, who sold presliced apples door-to-door to local residents.) His family later moved to Park Avenue, in the New York City borough of Manhattan. Peltz attended the prestigious Horace Mann preparatory school, located in the affluent Riverdale section of the Bronx, where he was a marginal student.

In 1960 Peltz enrolled in the Wharton School of Business of the University of Pennsylvania to pursue a degree in business administration. The following year he took a leave of absence, returning in 1962 only to drop out after that school year to "be a ski bum," as Ruhling reported. Having landed a job as a teacher at a ski-racing camp in Oregon, Peltz needed money to make the journey, so he drove a truck for his family's business for $200 per week. During that time, as Peltz recalled to Ruhling, "I saw all the opportunities and all the mistakes everybody was making. My father said, 'If you don't like it, why don't you change it?'" Abandoning his original plan, Peltz began acquiring

small food businesses all over the East Coast while his brother, Robert, handled the day-to-day operations of A. Peltz & Sons. By the end of the 1960s, Nelson Peltz had transformed his family's moderately sized business into the largest food-distribution service in the Northeast; he turned the $2.5 million private company into one with annual sales of $50 million. In 1969 he changed the name of A. Peltz & Sons to Flagstaff, the name of a full-service food distributor he had acquired. Peltz served as Flagstaff's president and CEO while his brother acted as chairman of the board. When Flagstaff went public, in 1972, Peltz came into contact with Peter May, his auditor at the accounting firm Peat, Marwick, Mitchell and Co. May, a graduate of the University of Chicago's business school, joined Flagstaff, supplementing Peltz's deal-making skills with operational expertise.

After Flagstaff acquired the Coffee-Mat Corp., a maker of vending machines for beverages and snacks, in 1975, Peltz—by his own admission—became as dedicated to cultivating a playboy lifestyle as he was to working; in the latter part of the 1970s, he was a regular on the Hollywood party circuit and reportedly dated the likes of the actresses Diana Rigg and Victoria Principal. He also became known for throwing wild parties at his summer house in Quogue, Long Island, New York. At the same time, he grew frustrated that his business success was not keeping pace with his social life. A friend of Peltz's recalled to Connie Bruck, the author of *The Predator's Ball*, "Nelson didn't want to be in the food business. He wanted to be a big shot! He wanted to buy Columbia Pictures! He was assiduously cultivating Herbert Siegel [CEO of Chris-Craft Industries], Charlie Bluhdorn [chairman of Gulf + Western], Saul Steinberg [chairman of Reliance Inc.]. He was like the kid who wants to hang out with the varsity football team."

Peltz sold the family food business in 1978 to a group of private investors for approximately $31 million (the Flagstaff Corp. would fall prey to bankruptcy just four years later as a result of soaring interest rates), but he retained control of Coffee-Mat. That company, which had been one of the dominant forces in its industry for many years, almost went bankrupt under Peltz and May. Having seen hard times in business, the two started a consulting practice for struggling firms and began an investment fund that would help them finance future leveraged buyouts, or purchases of companies through loans or bonds. In 1983 Peltz made his first major deal, with the successful takeover of Triangle Industries, a copper-wire and cable manufacturer. (To help finance the deal, he borrowed $10 million and took a second mortgage on his summer house.) By that time he had met the financial wizard Michael Milken, of the now-defunct investment-banking firm Drexel Burnham Lambert, who specialized in providing high-yield bonds to high-level financiers for the purpose of leveraged buyouts of companies. (Popularized by Milken and like-minded "corporate raiders" of the 1980s, high-yield or "junk" bonds were favored by many investors because they normally paid higher yields than better-quality, investment-grade bonds. "Junk" bonds are rated below investment grade because of the low credit quality of their issuers, in contrast to investment-grade bonds, which are issued by low-to-medium-risk lenders such as blue-chip companies. The former pay higher yields in order to attract investors despite the lenders' poor credit ratings. Remembered as the "junk bond king," Milken was later indicted by a federal grand jury and sentenced to 10 years in prison in 1989 for alleged insider trading; he served under two years.)

In the spring of 1985, Milken began planning a takeover of the Chicago, Illinois–based National Can, a company in which the corporate raider Victor Posner had had a controlling stake. After Posner and his fellow raider Carl Icahn (known especially for his hostile takeover of Trans World Airlines that year) deemed the leveraged buyout too risky, Peltz offered to handle the deal. Peltz, describing to Connie Bruck a 1983 meeting with Milken in Beverly Hills, California, recalled, "I said to Mike, I want this deal, I don't want you to finance it for anyone else, I'm not leaving until you agree." After Milken quickly raised $565 million to finance Triangle's takeover of National Can, Peltz and May bought the company for approximately $420 million, in one of the first buyout deals financed entirely by high-yield bonds. The financial analyst Arthur Stupay told Liz Sly for the *Chicago Tribune* (November 25, 1988), "[Peltz and May] were the first ones in America who recognized the values inherent in old-line manufacturing companies. They leveraged themselves to the hilt and it turned into a mega-success."

Instead of selling off parts of National Can and displacing company workers to obtain quick profits, a practice often used by takeover specialists, Peltz and May began to invest money in the company to help finance their next deal. In 1986, after Milken had amassed another $600 million in junk bonds, the partners acquired the packaging company American Can. Stupay said to Sly, "They didn't do what was expected, i.e. carve up National Can. They did the opposite. They put money in, acquired American Can and then went on to buy assets in plastics and [the] glass industry." Peltz and May merged the two companies to form American National Can in 1986. The takeovers of National Can and American Can were made possible by a number of outside factors: in 1986 a decline in interest rates allowed Peltz and May to refinance the National Can debt more cheaply as demand for metal cans increased; and from 1985 to 1987, the company's operating income soared from $131.5 million to $321.9 million, which allowed Triangle to absorb the new debt for the American Can operations without being hurt by the stock-market crash of 1987. By 1988 Peltz and May had turned Triangle Industries into both the largest and the most indebted packaging company in the world, increasing their annual revenues from $264 million to more than $4 billion, with $2.5 billion in debt from bank borrowings and junk bonds. Contrary to rumors circulating on Wall Street at the time that the two would dismantle the properties to finance other business ventures, Peltz and May invested over $300 million in Triangle's metal, glass, and plastic-container businesses in 1986 and 1987, acquiring 26 percent of the metal-container market in the U.S. By taking those measures, they reasoned, they would make their company an ideal candidate for a takeover by a foreign firm.

Indeed, in 1989 Peltz and May sold Triangle for $4.3 billion to the French aluminum producer Pechiney, which paid $1.26 billion to shareholders and agreed to assume the company's $2.5 billion debt, buying back the bonds for 90 percent of their face value. Peltz and May's gains from the deal amounted to $834 million. By that time the stock had risen to $55 a share, giving shareholders a profit worth eight times their investment. Months before the deal it had become known that Peltz and May had increased their holdings in Triangle from 13 percent to 62 percent, leaving company stockholders to wonder at the time of the sale whether the partners had had prior knowledge of the Pechiney buyout. As a result Triangle stockholders sued Peltz and May for alleged insider trading. Though the two denied the allegations, citing the bargain value of Triangle's stock price following the 1987 stock-market crash as the reason they had increased their holdings, they ended up splitting $75 million in settlements with Pechiney. Not long after the deal was made, the junk-bond analyst Bruce Grossman told James Buchan for the London, England, *Financial Times* (November 23, 1988), "If you invest no money and a few years later you make $830 million, you have to have a brain. Their internal rate of return will be a textbook case." Speaking of his success with junk bonds, Peltz later recalled to Ruhling, "It was a brilliant instrument and an instrument that was very necessary. Big companies in those days, like AT&T and GM, could issue long-term debt; smaller guys like me could only borrow from a bank to take over a big company. You needed to get capital on a different basis, and when that capital arrived, it was an eye-opener for me—it was a great facilitator. But once you acquire the business, then you have to make something of it in relatively quick fashion because you have this interest ticking at a pretty high rate."

In the early 1990s Peltz bought the London-based property company Mountleigh, which he hoped to use as a base for future takeovers of major European industries. Plans for selling Mountleigh's buildings were thwarted in 1991, when Peltz and May were censured by the London Stock Exchange for selling half their stake before an earnings announcement that revealed major losses for the company. A year later, following a real-estate market collapse, the company went into receivership and ended up $950 million in debt. Just weeks after the censure, Peltz returned to Florida.

In late 1992 it was announced that Peltz's fellow raider and former leveraged-buyout victim Victor Posner would be forced by a court ruling to sell his controlling stake in the Miami, Florida–based holding company DWG, the parent company of the fast-food restaurant chain Arby's, the soda maker Royal Crown Cola, the textile manufacturer Graniteville, National Propane Gas, and Southeastern Public Service; the ruling came after Posner was accused of plundering company assets for personal expenses. Once it became known on Wall Street that Peltz and May were the company's likely purchasers, DWG's stock almost doubled, to $14.50 per share. In 1993 Peltz and May bought a 29 percent stake in DWG for $72 million and renamed the company Triarc. They explained to reporters at the time, as noted by Phyllis Berman for *Forbes* (May 18, 1998), "We see Triarc as having the ability to be a greater success than National Can." In addition to Triarc, Peltz made a bid in 1994 to buy the Miami Dolphins football franchise from the Robbie family but lost out to the Florida billionaire H. Wayne Huizenga.

Triarc was moderately successful during its first two years of operation. Peltz then began to develop the company into the world's leading beverage conglomerate. In June 1995 Triarc bought Mistic Beverage, a fruit-drink maker that targeted urban youth, for $95 million. Two years later the company purchased the then-struggling beverage company Snapple from Quaker Oats for $300 million. Peltz immediately set about restructuring Snapple's advertising campaign, reviving the enormously popular "Snapple lady" commercials featuring the quirky employee Wendy Kaufman (which Quaker had shelved) and reinstating the offbeat radio personality Howard Stern as a pitchman. Peltz also brought in one of his associates, Michael Weinstein, to help orchestrate changes that included the launching of a new line of fruit juices and exotically flavored teas. Later that year Peltz added the Denver, Colorado–based Cable Car Beverage Corp., maker of Stewart's root beer and Aspen spring water, to his beverage empire. By decade's end he had returned Snapple to profitability. In September 2000 Triarc sold Snapple, along with RC and its other beverage brands, to the London-based Cadbury Schweppes for $1.5 billion, a deal that represented a fivefold return on Triarc's investment—and that Shawn Tully described as "one of the most spectacular deals of the decade." For the year 2000 alone, Peltz's overall compensation exceeded $27 million, with Triarc earning $461.9 million on $87.2 million in revenues, compared to $10.1 million on $770.9 million in 1999. (Throughout his career Peltz has been heavily criticized for being overpaid; he explained to Tully, "I believe in pay for performance. People would be happy to pay a CEO a large amount of comp for doing what I've done with Triarc or Triangle.")

Following Triarc's sale of its beverage companies, Peltz began to focus on expanding his fast-food empire while making bids to acquire struggling companies in other areas. Those included an unsuccessful attempt in 2001 to resurrect the U.S. airline TWA (acquired by American Airlines in April of that year) and a high-profile bid the following year to buy Burger King for $1.9 billion. (Triarc backed out once the fast-food chain set its price at over $2 billion.) In 2004 Triarc acquired an asset-management company, Deerfield Capital, for $86.5 million, receiving 64 percent of the economic interest in the company as well as 90 percent of the company's outstanding voting interests. As part of the deal, Triarc pledged $100 million in capital to develop a new Deerfield multi-strategy hedge fund.

In November 2005 Peltz, May, and Peltz's son-in-law Ed Garden, a former investment banker, launched the hedge fund Trian. In December of that year, Peltz announced that Trian had acquired a 5.4 percent stake in the popular fast-food chain Wendy's; he also used his influence to add three of his associates to Wendy's board of directors in an attempt to turn the company around. Through analyses written on his now-famous "white papers," revealing that Wendy's-owned stores (such as the Canadian doughnut-and-coffee chain Tim Hortons) were generating profit margins of just 9 percent, less than half of the 20 percent posted by Wendy's restaurants, Peltz persuaded board members to spin off 100 percent of Tim Hortons and sell its Baja Fresh Mexican Grill chain in order to achieve greater profit margins with the Wendy's franchise. According to his analyses, the move allowed Wendy's-owned stores to improve their margins while raising Wendy's earnings by $200 million. Peltz also claimed that the stock price should be 40 percent higher, or $75 per share, a change he made upon joining the company's board. "Nelson's white paper was right on target. The activists made the board more aggressive than in the past in pushing management to deal with the issues," Jim Pickett, the chairman of Wendy's, said to Tully.

In early 2006 Trian built up a 4.9 percent stake in CBRL, the owner of the roadside restaurant chain Cracker Barrel. Then, in March of that year, Peltz announced that the company had taken a 5.5 percent stake in Heinz, whose best-known products are baked beans and ketchup. Before he came aboard, Heinz was forced to sell off some of its brands, which included Earth's Best organic baby food and its Weight Watchers products, as a result of falling share prices and a drop in overall net income. In the first quarter after Peltz's arrival, Heinz's stock price recovered, and its net income rose 6 percent, to $205.3 million. In one of the most highly publicized proxy fights of that year, Peltz squared off against Heinz's CEO, William Johnson, over the right to fill board seats in order to restore the company's once-preeminent status among ketchup manufacturers. He pointed out such company missteps as cutting prices and offering large discounts at the end of the quarter to boost sales, when the company could instead have generated greater revenues—according to Peltz—through smart marketing campaigns. In August 2006, with the company's management unable to defend its record, Peltz won two seats on the Heinz board. Later that month Peltz's Trian acquired a 1.2 percent stake, or the equivalent of 2.83 million shares, of the Tribune Co., which owns the *Chicago Tribune*, the *Los Angeles Times*, and other newspapers and television stations.

The year 2007 proved to be one of Peltz's busiest to date. In February he announced that Trian had bought a 5.5 percent stake in Tiffany & Co. for a reported $320 million, with the aim of transforming the company's reputation for exclusiveness into that of an accessible seller of scarves, watches, handbags, and other women's fashion accessories, in the vein of such specialty stores as Hermes and Cartier. (As of mid-October 2008, Trian's stake was 8.4 percent, equivalent to roughly 10.7 million shares.) Peltz noted to Tully, "Women see Tiffany as a place to buy a gift, or where gifts come from in those beautiful blue boxes. But it's not where women go to shop for themselves. And it should be." In March 2007 Trian picked up a 3 percent stake in Cadbury Schweppes for approximately $730 million, with its beverage unit—comprised of Snapple, 7-Up, Dr. Pepper, and other products—accounting for 15 percent of the U.S. soda market. Just a few days later, largely as a result of Peltz's coming on board, Cadbury announced that it would split in two and spin off its U.S. beverage operations. (In May 2008 Cadbury completed the separation; the new company is called the Dr. Pepper Snapple Group.) It was announced in May 2007 that Peltz was stepping down in June as chairman and CEO of Triarc while staying on as a director; he was to receive $50 million upon vacating the post. In July Peltz bought $1.8 billion in shares of Kraft Foods (owner of brands including Nabisco, Oscar Mayer, and Maxwell House), roughly a 3 percent stake of the total equity of the food maker, through Trian. By October 2007 Peltz had raised his stake in Heinz to 6 percent, equivalent to roughly 19 million shares, and increased his stake in Wendy's to 9.8 percent. By late December 2007 Triarc had completed the sale of its investment advisory business, Deerfield Capital, for $145 million. Peltz later lowered his stake in Heinz to 3.1 percent. Thanks to his marketing strategies—many of which he thought up during fast-food outings with his children—Heinz has enjoyed a 16.5 percent increase in sales and a 30.9 percent increase in profits during the past two years.

In April 2008, after more than two years of power struggles and setbacks, Peltz sealed a merger deal with Wendy's worth $2.34 billion; the merger was completed on September 29, 2008. The new company is named Wendy's Arby's Group and trades on the New York Stock Exchange under the symbol WEN. The company, which rivals McDonald's and Burger King among the nation's largest fast-food chains, planned to change its menu to target customers in the 24-to-49-years age demographic rather than those in the 18-to-24 age range, the group it had sought in the past.

His business successes notwithstanding, Peltz said several years ago, according to a writer for the Toronto, Canada, *Globe and Mail* (January 21, 2003), "I'm like old money these days. You see these young guys worth $3 billion to $4 billion, and you think to yourself, 'What have I done wrong?' I feel like the guy who has to say to his kids, 'Go back to work because we can't make ends meet anymore.'"

Peltz "is tanned and well-dressed and quick with sardonic one-liners delivered in a gravelly New York accent," Michael Oneal wrote for the *Chicago Tribune* (August 17, 2006). He owns two of the most expensive homes in the country: his 130-acre, 47,000-square-foot High Winds estate (worth an estimated $16.3 million), the former home of the *Reader's Digest* co-founder DeWitt Wallace, in Bedford, New York, and has 27 rooms, a lake, a waterfall, a professional-quality indoor hockey rink with a Zamboni machine, and albino peacocks; his 44,000-square-foot French Regency–style home, Montsorrel, in Palm Beach, Florida, boasts 17th-century parquet floors from Versailles, two swimming pools, a movie theater, and a 16,000-square-foot mansion for guests. Peltz also has a home in Paris, France, as well as a 727 Boeing airliner at his disposal.

Peltz is involved in a number of philanthropic organizations, including the Prostate Cancer Foundation and the Intrepid Museum Foundation. He is co-chairman of the board of directors of the Simon Wiesenthal Center and chairman of the New York Tolerance Center. "We have to be on watch for intolerance," he told Ruhling. "And I don't just mean antisemitism, I mean intolerance against African-Americans, Hispanics, Asians, and others. The minute you see it, you can't just turn the other cheek. Nobody is born with these feelings in their DNA. This is strictly from their upbringing. Parents have to be aware of what they are teaching their kids." Peltz and his wife, Claudia, a former Ford fashion model, married in 1980 and have eight children; he has two other children from a previous marriage. Speaking to Ruhling about his professional success, he said, "There are a lot of other people—Bill Gates comes to mind—who are a lot more interesting than me. I expected to achieve things, and I don't know that I've achieved anything that spectacular. I don't know if just making money is a great achievement." He added nonetheless, "I'm pleased with the way my life has turned out."

—C.C.

Suggested Reading: *Chicago Tribune* C p1 Nov. 25, 1988; *Columbus (Ohio) Dispatch* C p8 Aug. 1, 2007; *Forbes* p134 May 18, 1998; *Fortune* p76+ Apr. 2, 2007; *Lifestyles* (on-line) Fall 2005; (London) *Financial Times* p33 Nov. 23, 1988, p29 Mar. 9, 2006; (London) *Times* p61 Mar. 14, 2007; *New York Times* C p1+ July 27, 2006;

(Portland, Oregon) *Oregonian* C p13 Oct. 4, 1988; *Time* (on-line) Oct. 21, 1991; Bruck, Connie. *The Predator's Ball: The Junk Bond Raiders and the Man Who Staked Them*, 1988

David Carter, courtesy of Harvard University Press
Irene Pepperberg with Alex

Pepperberg, Irene

Apr. 1, 1949– Animal behaviorist

Address: Dept. of Psychology, Brandeis University, Waltham, MA 02454

"The differences between humans and nonhumans are quantitative, not qualitative," the animal behaviorist Irene Pepperberg said when the Edge Foundation asked her (on-line) its "big question" of 2006: "What's your dangerous idea?" Pepperberg spent 30 years teaching Alex, an African grey parrot whom she bought in an ordinary pet store in Chicago, how to identify objects, colors, and shapes. Alex—whose name was short for "avian learning experiment"—also learned to count to six, express desires, demonstrate an understanding of such concepts as "different," "bigger" and "smaller," "absent" and "present," "none," and "calm down," and sound out combinations of letters such as "SH." Pepperberg believes that Alex, who died in 2007, had the mental capacity of a four- or five-year-old child. While some experts have credited Pepperberg with showing that parrots, contrary to previous belief, may be as intelligent as chimpanzees and dolphins, others have downplayed the significance of her work, insisting that Alex learned through memorization or conditioning. In

addition, some scientists have warned against putting too much stock in the idea that animals are capable of "thinking" and expressing themselves in the same ways as humans. "I never claim that he has language," Pepperberg said of Alex in an interview with David L. Chandler for the *Boston Globe* (May 18, 1998). "You could never have the kind of conversation with him that you would have with another person—a two-way conversation. But he can tell us what he wants, and answer questions posed to him."

Before she entered the field of animal behavior, gaining knowledge on her own, Pepperberg earned a Ph.D. in chemical physics. In addition to dozens of articles for professional journals, she has published two books: *The Alex Studies: Cognitive and Communicative Abilities of Grey Parrots* (2000), and *Alex and Me: How a Scientist and a Parrot Uncovered a Hidden World of Animal Intelligence—and Formed a Deep Bond in the Process* (2008). With Chris Davis, Pepperberg made the video *Alex the Grey in Training Sessions with Professor Irene Pepperberg* (1995). Thanks to Pepperberg's appearances on national TV, Alex became known to millions of people, and when news of his death became public, obituaries about him appeared in periodicals including the *New York Times*, the *Boston Globe*, the London *Independent*, and the *Economist* and on dozens of Web sites and blogs; moreover, the Alex Foundation, which supports Pepperberg's research, received thousands of letters and e-mail messages of condolence.

In an assessment of *The Alex Studies* for the *New York Times Book Review* (January 30, 2000), the ethologist Bernd Heinrich, who has written about the intelligence of ravens based on decades of observations of their behavior, wrote that Pepperberg had proved "that animals have abilities greater than we are led to expect, but these can be revealed only by appropriate research tools. [Pepperberg] succeeds where many others failed, and she convinces us that the details of investigative methods are what matter. Her purpose is not to reveal Alex as a winged Einstein. Instead, she shows that complex mental operations are revealed only by precise methods that match the capabilities investigated. And she demonstrates remarkable parallels between parrots and humans. The core importance of social interaction in both learning and testing is crucial for her results. In that, her studies have relevance far beyond parrots."

Pepperberg was born Irene Maxine Platzblatt on April 1, 1949 in the New York City borough of Brooklyn. The only child of Robert Platzblatt, a biochemist, and the former Yetta Leibowitz, a bookkeeper, she grew up loving animals and reading books about science, such as the biography of the Nobel Prize–winning physicist Marie Curie. When she was four, Pepperberg's father, who was often absent, studying for his master's degree and caring for his ailing mother, gave her a pet budgerigar—commonly called a budgie or parakeet—a type of parrot. Pepperberg continued raising birds throughout her childhood, and when she was in high school, she owned one that she found to be particularly intelligent. In 1969 she graduated from the Massachusetts Institute of Technology (MIT), in Cambridge, Massachusetts, with a B.S. degree in chemistry. Two years later she earned an M.A. degree in chemistry from Harvard University, also in Cambridge, and then began working toward a doctorate in chemical physics, a branch of chemistry that deals with the application of physical principles to the study of chemical systems. She earned her Ph.D. in 1976; her dissertation, written with the surname Pepperberg, was entitled "Molecular Orbital Studies on Boron Hydrides."

Earlier, in 1974, Pepperberg happened to watch three installments of the PBS program *Nova* that dealt with animal communication and became fascinated by that subject. While continuing her research on boron hydrides, she began to study animal behavior and communication. In late 1976 she started a full-time reading regimen in those subjects, focusing on neurobiology, ethology, and psychology. She also read extensively on theories about children's acquisition of language.

In early 1977, at Purdue University, in West Lafayette, Indiana, Pepperberg embarked on research in animal-human communication. (Her then-husband, the physiologist David R. Pepperberg, had taken a job as an assistant professor at the university.) She continued her reading program and, that same year, purchased Alex, a one-year-old African grey parrot, born in captivity, that she found at a Chicago pet store. She chose the bird completely at random. "Otherwise," she told a reporter for *People* magazine (December 13, 1999), "people would say it was specially bred." Using space borrowed from Purdue's Department of Biological Sciences, Pepperberg began conducting experiments on Alex. She was inspired by the work of the British psychologist Nicholas Humphrey and the American primatologist Alison Jolly, who argued that animal intelligence evolved as animals negotiated social hierarchies. In teaching Alex, Pepperberg opted to use the "model-rival" method, developed by the German scientist Dietmar Todt in the 1970s: Pepperberg would teach words and concepts to a laboratory assistant while Alex looked on, an activity called modeling. As he observed the assistant being rewarded for correct answers, the parrot began to compete for Pepperberg's attention. Whenever Alex successfully identified an object, such as a piece of pasta, he was rewarded with that object, not with food he might actually want. Pepperberg did that to avoid the criticism that Alex was merely being conditioned to give correct responses. In September 1979 she became a research associate in biology at Purdue, and in 1982 she joined the school's Department of Psychological Sciences as a lecturer.

In July 1984 Pepperberg became a visiting assistant professor of anthropology at Northwestern University, in Chicago, Illinois. She remained at that school until January 1991. During the 1980s

Alex began to make headlines, and by 1988 he had developed the ability to identify five shapes, seven colors, and the numbers one through six. Pepperberg would show Alex two triangles of different colors, for example, and ask, "What's different?" or "What's the same?," according to Geoffrey Cowley, writing for *Newsweek* (May 23, 1988). Alex would reply, "Color!" or "Shape!" "Basically, we've shown that the parrot is working at the level of the chimpanzee and the dolphin," Pepperberg told William K. Stevens for the *New York Times* News Service, as reported by the Memphis, Tennessee, *Commercial Appeal* (May 31, 1991). In 1991, after 14 years of instruction, Alex could identify an object's name and color about 80 percent of the time. He picked out shapes with 100 percent accuracy, which, Pepperberg concluded, showed that he "understands the questions as well as the abstract concept of category, and that he thinks about the information to come up with an answer," as Stevens wrote. While some scientists had already begun to criticize Pepperberg's findings, warning about the extreme difficulties of determining how nonhuman animals think, James Serpell, then the director of the Companion Animal Research Group at Cambridge University (and currently the director of the Center for the Interaction of Animals and Society at the University of Pennsylvania), praised her efforts. "It is a further indication of how exceptional these birds are in terms of their intellect," he told Stevens.

"Here's a bird that has learned to use English words in relatively meaningful ways," the Rockefeller University zoologist Donald R. Griffin told Clara Germani for the *Christian Science Monitor* (October 27, 1992). "He seems to mean what he says . . . and that is a real revolution, [because] there's a whole 20th-century tradition of minimizing animal thinking or fitting it into rather narrow mental categories like conditioning." (In his 1976 book, *Question of Animal Awareness: Evolutionary Continuity of Mental Experience*, Griffin maintained that the conscious minds of animals resemble those of humans.) By that time Alex had learned more than 90 words, and when Pepperberg would show him a series of adjacent letters, he could "sound out" the word. "Nobody thought that a parrot could really learn to label an object," Pepperberg told Germani. "Everybody knew that parrots could mimic sound, but to make that association between sound and object . . . Only people who had the birds as pets made such claims, there was no scientific evidence." Responding to the charge that Alex was simply memorizing the names of objects, as opposed to learning them, she pointed toward the many bins of objects she used in her experiments and asked, "How could he memorize all of this?" In the early 1990s, according to the *Modesto (California) Bee* (February 16, 1995), Diane Sherman, an occupational therapist from Fresno, California, attended a lecture that Pepperberg gave in Los Angeles. Intrigued by Pepperberg's success with the model-rival technique, she began using the same methods in her work with developmentally disabled children. Sherman's efforts were largely successful, especially among those diagnosed with autism. In January 1991 Pepperberg became an associate professor at the University of Arizona, in Tucson, and in May 1994 she received tenure.

During her 1998 conversation with Chandler, Pepperberg stopped short of saying that Alex had acquired language, but she said that after "working with these birds for 20-some years, there's no question in my mind, on a personal level, that there's consciousness there. But I have not come up with any tests that I believe could show it." She also said that, while parrots are capable of matching the cognitive abilities of a four- or five-year-old child, they exhibit "all the negative, self-centered behavior of a 2- or 3-year-old." She added, "That's why you have so many abandoned parrots." Pepperberg's book *The Alex Studies: Cognitive and Communicative Abilities of Grey Parrots* (2000) described her years of experiments. "Pepperberg's prose is generally clear and straightforward," Edward Kako wrote in a review for *Science* (February 11, 2000). "The book should be accessible to a wide range of audiences, from researchers studying animal behavior to advanced undergraduates in a course that covers relevant material such as animal cognition or the capacities of language-trained animals." *The Alex Studies* appeared on the *Los Angeles Times*'s "Best Nonfiction of 2000" list.

In September 1999 Pepperberg started a two-year stint as a visiting associate professor at MIT. Around the same time, in accordance with her life-long desire to improve the lives of pets, she began designing toys that would stimulate parrots beneficially. Among her collaborators was Benjamin Resner, a children's-software developer, who helped create "InterPet Explorer," a "bird-friendly Web browser that enables parrots to use the Internet to play games, look and squawk at pictures of parrots and other images, listen to music, interact with their owners, and, perhaps, socialize with other parrots in chat rooms," David Abel wrote for the *Boston Globe* (September 26, 2000). In 2002 Pepperberg took an adjunct-professor position at Brandeis University, in Waltham, Massachusetts, and from 2004 to 2005, she was a Bunting fellow at the Radcliffe Institute for Advanced Study, in Cambridge. In May 2005 and February 2006, she published papers in the *Journal of Comparative Psychology* claiming that Alex had acquired the concept of zero.

In September 2007, at the age of 31, Alex died unexpectedly of a heart arrhythmia. "It's devastating to lose an individual you've worked with pretty much every day for 30 years," Pepperberg told John C. Drake for the *Boston Globe* (September 11, 2007). "Someone was working with him eight to 12 hours every day of his life." On the night before he died, Alex told Pepperberg, "You be good. See you tomorrow. I love you," according to *Time* magazine (September 24, 2007). (Other sources reported that

Pepperberg said those words to Alex.) Newspapers around the world ran obituaries of the bird, and Brandeis University issued a statement to the press that read in part, "Alex combined his labels to identify, request, refuse, and categorize more than 100 different items, demonstrating a level and scope of cognitive abilities never expected in an avian species." "Alex has left a significant legacy—not only have he and Dr. Pepperberg and their landmark experiments in modern comparative psychology changed our views of the capabilities of avian minds, but they have forever changed our perception of the term 'bird brains,'" the statement continued. In January 2008 Collins, an imprint of the publishing house HarperCollins, announced plans to release Pepperberg's memoir, tentatively titled *Alex and Me*. The book is due in the fall of 2008.

Pepperberg continues to run the Alex Foundation, which she uses to raise money for her ongoing experiments with two other African grey parrots, Arthur and Griffin. In addition to teaching and renting lab space at Brandeis, she works at Harvard, where she has served as a research associate since 2005. She has written dozens of articles for academic journals and received a number of fellowships and awards, including the Frank A. Beach Comparative Psychology Award, presented by the American Psychological Association, in 2006.

—K.J.P.

Suggested Reading: *Boston Globe* D p1 Sep. 26, 2000; *Concord (New Hampshire) Monitor* Sep. 16, 2007; (Memphis, Tennessee) *Commercial Appeal* B p3 Apr. 19, 2005; *New York Times* A p1 Oct. 9, 1999; *New Yorker* (on-line) May 12, 2008; *USA Today* D p4 May 13, 2008

Selected Books: *The Alex Studies: Cognitive and Communicative Abilities of Grey Parrots*, 2000; *Alex and Me: How a Scientist and a Parrot Uncovered a Hidden World of Animal Intelligence—and Formed a Deep Bond in the Process*, 2008

Perino, Dana

May 9, 1972– White House press secretary

Address: The White House, 1600 Pennsylvania Ave., N.W., Washington, DC 20500

As a young girl Dana Perino learned to herd cattle on her grandparents' Wyoming ranch. Perino, currently the White House press secretary, has said that that skill comes in handy during press briefings, when reporters grill her on such topics as domestic wiretapping and the war in Iraq. "You have to be very alert," Perino told Ronald Kessler for the

Dana Perino

Chip Somodevilla/Getty Images

Web site NewsMax (April 30, 2007), drawing comparisons between tending herds and handling journalists. "You have to be ready to move on a moment's notice. You have to be very flexible, and you have to sort of guide with a gentle hand."

On September 15, 2007, two weeks after President George W. Bush tapped her to replace Tony Snow, who officially stepped down on September 14, Perino became the second woman and second-youngest person ever to hold the office of White House press secretary. (Dee Dee Myers, who served under President Bill Clinton, was both the first female press secretary and the youngest.) Prior to taking over the position, Perino worked as Snow's deputy and periodically filled in at the podium. She was acting press secretary for over a month in March and April 2007, when Snow was forced to undergo treatment for colon cancer. When Snow announced his resignation, Bush said that he had chosen Perino because she is a "smart, capable person who is able to spell out the issues of the day in a way that people . . . can understand," according to *Public Papers of the Presidents* (September 3, 2007). "What I look for in somebody like Dana is somebody who can walk in that Oval Office and give me sound judgment and good advice," Bush added. "And I have found that over the course of the time I've known her, she's capable of doing that. And she's also capable of running the shop that she'll be in charge of."

The older of two girls, Dana Marie Perino was born on May 9, 1972 in Evanston, Wyoming. When she was two the family moved to Parker, a town outside Denver, Colorado. At the age of six, Perino stood on a milk crate, raised an American flag, and declared to her parents, Jan and Leo Perino, "I'm gonna work in the White House," as Chris Barge reported for the *Rocky Mountain News* (March 31, 2007). Perino had become interested in politics and current events by the third grade, when her father started requiring his daughters to read newspaper articles each morning and be prepared to discuss them after school. "I tried to develop the idea that there are always two sides to each story," Leo Perino told Kessler. "We would each argue with our own biases, and then I wanted them to each take the other side just as vehemently." Perino's sister, Angie, recalled to Kessler that she mostly watched and listened while Dana and her father debated with each other.

Perino further honed her speaking skills at Ponderosa High School, in Parker, where she was a member of the school's debate team. She also played the piano and flute. In 1994 she graduated from the University of Southern Colorado (since renamed the University of Colorado-Pueblo) with a bachelor's degree in mass communications. "She's one of those girls who had it all," her college roommate Andrea Aragon told Kessler. Originally wanting to pursue a career in journalism, Perino worked as a reporter for a local radio station while she was in school. "I didn't feel like I was really good at it," she told Kessler. "I liked covering politics, but when I was in the local news market, they also had me covering anything from a house fire to murders. And while those are very important stories to tell, I was not the best one to tell them."

In 1995 Perino earned a master's degree in public-affairs reporting from the University of Illinois at Springfield. As part of the program, she spent six months working as a television reporter for WCIA-TV, covering the Illinois General Assembly. Molly Hall, a bureau chief at the station, told Laura Camper for the Springfield *State Journal-Register* (March 29, 2007) that Perino "really had a fascination for government, really had an intense interest in government." "As a reporter I realized I was conservative politically, and that I was more interested in the policy and issues side of politics," Perino told Peter Roper for the *Pueblo Chieftain* (September 16, 2007), explaining why she eventually chose politics over journalism.

Perino moved to Washington, D.C., in 1995 and made her first foray into politics as a legislative staff aide to the Republican U.S. congressman Scott McInnis of Colorado. Recognizing her talent for dealing with people, McInnis gave Perino the task of sitting outside his office and speaking with unhappy constituents. "Some of their temperatures were very high," McInnis told Howard Kurtz for the *Washington Post* (March 29, 2007). "She could calm them down." Later that year she became the press secretary for U.S. representative Dan Schaefer of Colorado, a position she held for two and a half years, until the lawmaker retired.

After her stint in Schaefer's office, Perino married a businessman, Peter McMahon, and spent a year in his native England before moving to San Diego, California, where she began doing public-relations work for high-tech companies. She took a job with the Gable Group in 1999, then joined the consulting branch of the firm Porter Novelli in January 2001. According to a column by her friend Kevin Brass, published in the *Austin Chronicle* (September 21, 2007), Perino soon quit her job at Porter Novelli, having grown frustrated with "her inability to get any career traction in San Diego. She couldn't even get a job on an interesting City Council race, she complained." Without a job, she moved back to Washington, D.C., where she became a press officer for the Environment and Natural Resources Division of the U.S. Justice Department. She quickly showed her ability to discuss complicated ideas in ways everyone could understand. "She basically was able to take a legal brief, extract the most interesting . . . parts of it and convey it," Susan Whitson, a former deputy director of public affairs at the Justice Department, told Mark Silva for the *Chicago Tribune* (March 30, 2007). Tom Sansonetti, a former assistant attorney general for environmental issues, called Perino "bright and skillful," according to Jon Ward, writing for the *Washington Times* (April 24, 2007). In particular Sansonetti noted her ability to generate media interest in the department's environmental cases, even in the wake of the September 11, 2001 terrorist attacks, when the so-called war on terror dominated headlines.

In 2002 Perino joined the White House press complex and became a spokesperson for the Council on Environmental Quality. She relished the opportunity to work with the Bush administration, as she had long supported the president and his policies. "I have been an advocate for George Bush starting in 1998 when he was still governor of Texas," she told Roper, adding that she believes Bush is the "right leader, at the right time." Brass called Perino a "true believer," adding, "When I talked to her last year, she told me how she had learned to appreciate the president's 'dogged determination' to keep his sights on specific goals and his belief that if you 'say the same thing over and over and over again,' you eventually get your message across." Jim Connaughton, chairman of the Council on Environmental Quality, told Ward that Perino is "more than someone who can just talk well. She brings a lot of intelligence to the issues."

In 2005 then–White House press secretary Scott McClellan offered Perino a job as his deputy. He later promoted Perino to chief deputy, and after he left his post, in April of the following year, his successor, Tony Snow, decided to keep her on his staff. "She understands government as well as anyone I know," Snow, a former Fox News television commentator, told James Gerstenzang for the *Los Angeles Times* (March 31, 2007). "She understands the agencies. She understands the Hill. She understands the press corps." On March 31, 2006 Bush named Perino deputy assistant to the president and deputy press secretary. (Her previous title had been special assistant to the president and deputy press secretary.)

Starting in April 2006 Perino's life became "a whirlwind of meetings with administration officials, travels on Air Force One and press inquiries," Christa Marshall wrote for the *Denver Post* (September 5, 2006). "She wakes at 4:30 a.m. and reads several newspapers while exercising to start a 16-hour day in which she often receives more than 600 e-mails from reporters." In August 2006 Snow went on a late-summer vacation, leaving Perino to take over as the president's chief spokesperson. Marshall noted Perino's calmness during her first press briefing, though the deputy press secretary later admitted to being nervous. "The morning briefing was really tough," Perino told Snow, according to Marshall. "I didn't think I was going to throw up, but I've never worn that much makeup in my life." With Snow out of the office, Perino was able to work more closely with the president, accompanying him to the Gulf Coast to mark the anniversary of Hurricane Katrina. "People should know that he's such a regular guy," Perino told Marshall. "In between policy discussions, he'll ask about my grandparents' ranch and how many cattle they have."

In March 2007 Perino began what was expected to be a three-week stint as acting press secretary, as Snow, who had previously battled cancer, was slated to undergo exploratory surgery. "Dana, you are going to find talents you never knew you had," Snow told Perino, according to Kurtz. "Tony, I hope I can find 15 outfits," she replied. While she had filled in for Snow on occasion in the past, conducting both morning press "gaggles" and televised afternoon briefings, she admitted to not yet being comfortable behind the podium. "If you only gaggle or brief once every five months, it's like doing it for the first time every time," she told Kurtz. "It's really hard."

Others had more confidence in Perino's abilities. Dan Bartlett, a White House counselor, told Kurtz, "She really has become the glue of the press operation. Nobody here has even flinched at the prospect of her stepping into this role during this period. She may be petite, but she brings a lot of punch to the job." Jim Axelrod, a CBS news correspondent, told Kurtz that Perino is "very thorough and very quick about getting back to people. Very often you get the great sound bite from Tony, but the actual follow-up, the in-the-weeds information, that'll come from Dana." Kurtz also praised her ability to "stick to the talking points when necessary," as she did while addressing reports about an aspect of the controversy surrounding Attorney General Alberto Gonzalez's firing of eight U.S. attorneys. Gonzalez "doesn't recall having a recollection about having deliberative discussions about the ongoing process over that two-year period," she said during another meeting with the press, displaying what Kurtz described as her proficiency in the "art of tortured defense."

On the morning of March 27, 2007, Perino was faced with telling reporters that Snow's cancer had returned and spread to his liver. "I was floored," she told Silva. "In all of our conversations about his checkups, I thought it was going to be fine." While she tried to keep her composure, she shed tears while delivering the news. With the length of Snow's absence uncertain, Perino began receiving phone calls of encouragement from fellow government officials. "Put your big-girl panties on," Education Secretary Margaret Spellings told her, according to Kurtz. "In many ways I feel like a student who did not go to class all semester but has to take a final, every day, for the foreseeable future," Perino told Chris Barge.

While Perino's mother told Barge that she had lost sleep worrying about how her daughter would handle reporters' tough questions, the deputy press secretary soon proved she was no pushover. During a briefing in April 2007, when Helen Thomas, a longtime and well-respected member of the White House press corps, asked a number of questions in rapid succession, Perino responded, according to Ward, "Do you want me to answer the question, Helen, or do you want to ask questions? It's really hard to concentrate here. What's your question?" Thomas responded by saying, "You repeat yourself so much that . . ." Perino cut her off by saying, "So do you," before turning to another reporter. Perino told Ward she has "good relationships" with reporters, despite the occasional heated exchange. "I understand that reporters have a job to do, and I understand that they're going to ask really tough questions," she said. "And sometimes, especially when the camera's on, there's a little bit of drama and theatrics. But at the end of the day, I feel like if I can provide the answers that they want in a tone that is reasonable and not aggressive, that is the style I try to bring to the briefing room."

On August 31, 2007 Snow announced that he was stepping down. He told reporters that his decision was based not on his illness but on financial concerns, as he had taken a pay cut when he left the Fox network to work at the White House. Speaking of Snow's departure and her own appointment as his successor, Perino joked to Thomas M. DeFrank for the New York *Daily News* (September 1, 2007), "He leaves very big shoes to fill, and I only wear a size 6." (Snow succumbed to cancer in July 2008.) Perino said that the president had an "ambitious agenda" for his final term, adding, "We are a nation at war, and the press office, the whole team, is going to be here to help support [his] sprint to the finish."

Perino held her first briefing as press secretary on September 18, 2007, when she answered questions regarding Michael B. Mukasey, Bush's nominee to replace Gonzalez as attorney general. In an article for *Time* (October 18, 2007), Massimo Calabresi noted Perino's "easygoing self-confidence," adding that she does not show anxiety, as McClellan did, or come across as being arrogant, the way Ari Fleischer, who served as press secretary during Bush's first term, was thought to have done. "Many of her predecessors came from the antagonistic world of national campaigns, but Perino made her way to the West Wing through a succession of jobs in Congress and the Executive Branch, where life exists beyond the next election and reporters and spokespeople learn to live with—and even respect—the requirements of one another's jobs," Calabresi wrote. Perino admitted to Calabresi that she had taken on her new duties at a difficult time, since the president faced low approval ratings. Speaking with the Fox News host Bill O'Reilly during an installment of *The O'Reilly Factor* (September 26, 2007), Perino said that it was unlikely that Bush would see a "big upswing in the approval polls," adding, "I think that what we are going to do is ask some basic questions. With or without the Congress, we have to offer some solutions. And we have to ask questions: is what we're doing keeping America safe, keeping taxes low, and offering solutions to things that people really care about."

Perino's good looks have helped make her a pop-culture topic of interest. Given her small physical stature—she describes herself as "almost 5-foot-1," according to Silva—White House staff had to lower the pressroom lectern as well as the bas-relief behind it when she took over for Snow. Perino is described as a dog enthusiast, and she reportedly trained her dog, Henry, to bark when asked if former president Bill Clinton should be in prison; growl at the mention of former vice president Al Gore; and—in a trick alluding to Republican claims that the 2004 Democratic presidential nominee "flip-flopped," or showed indecisiveness, on key issues—to retrieve a flip-flop whenever someone says "John Kerry."

—K.J.P.

Suggested Reading: *Chicago Tribune* State and Regional News Mar. 30, 2007; (Denver, Colorado) *Rocky Mountain News* p6 Mar. 31, 2007; *Denver Post* B p2 Sep. 5, 2006; (Fort Lauderdale, Florida) *Sun-Sentinel* A p14 Apr. 1, 2007; NewsMax.com Apr. 30, 2007; *Pueblo (Colorado) Chieftain* Sep. 16, 2007; *Time* (on-line) Oct. 18, 2007; *Washington Post* C p1 Mar. 29, 2007; *Washington Times* A p3 Apr. 24, 2007

Poehler, Amy

Sep. 16, 1971– Comic actress

Address: Saturday Night Live, NBC Studios, 30 Rockefeller Plaza, New York, NY 10112

For seven seasons Amy Poehler has performed a variety of characters on the long-running television show *Saturday Night Live (SNL)*. Her work includes impressions of the real-life figures Hilary Duff, Hillary Rodham Clinton, and Kelly Ripa as well as portrayals of original comic characters, such as the one-legged, hypoglycemic Amber and

Scott Gries/Getty Images

Amy Poehler

the argument-prone Sally Needler. Since 2004 she has been co-host of the *SNL* staple "Weekend Update," first alongside Tina Fey—with whom Poehler formed the first two-woman "Weekend Update" team—and now, since Fey's departure from *SNL*, with Seth Meyers. Poehler has also begun to make her mark on the big screen: in 2004 she turned in a highly lauded performance in *Mean Girls*, written by Fey, and the two co-starred in the 2008 film *Baby Mama*. A common observation about Poehler is one that Fey made in an interview with Donna Freydkin for *USA Today* (March 23, 2007): "Amy is this beautiful girl, but she'd as soon wear goofy teeth and fright wigs."

Amy Poehler was born on September 16, 1971 in Burlington, Massachusetts, to high-school teachers, Bill and Eileen Poehler. Her younger brother, Gary, is now a lawyer. Poehler told Jennifer Wulff and Rebecca Paley for *People* (April 18, 2005) that she was "tomboyish and bossy" as a child rather than being the class cutup. Still, she learned at a young age to banter and tell jokes, since, as she said to the *People* reporters, "my family is pretty witty, so you had to earn your place at the table." Upon graduating from Burlington High School, Poehler enrolled at Boston College, in Massachusetts, where she majored in communications and wanted to become "a teacher, a journalist or an actor," as she recalled for *People*. She joined the Boston College group My Mother's Fleabag, which, according to some sources, is the oldest college improvisational-comedy troupe in the United States. That experience left her "totally intoxicated," she told *People*. "You get one genuine laugh, you just want it again, even if you spend the next 10 years being a waitress." To the chagrin of her parents, she decided to pursue a career as a performer.

After graduating from college, in 1993, Poehler moved to Chicago, Illinois, where she studied improvisation with Second City, the esteemed comedy troupe whose alumni include many onetime *SNL* cast members, among them John Belushi, Bill Murray, Dan Aykroyd, Mike Myers, and Chris Farley. During those years she also honed her skills with Improv Olympics, working under the veteran Del Close, and performed in the troupe Inside Vladimir, alongside the future *SNL* performer and head writer Tina Fey, also a Second City member. The name of that troupe, in which Poehler and Fey were the only two women, "came from a gay porn movie that we saw on the shelf at a mini-mart," Fey told Randy Kennedy for the *New York Times* (October 12, 2004). Poehler said to Phil Rosenthal for the *Chicago Sun-Times* (December 14, 2001), "I always feel like Second City prepared me for writing . . . and Improv-Olympic prepared me for when I do [*SNL*]." In 1996 Poehler became a founding member of the troupe Upright Citizens Brigade, made up mainly of experienced performers. Another founding member, Matt Besser, told Dave Itzkoff for the *New York Times* (March 18, 2007), "We were a group where I think our shortest guy was like 6 foot 1. So it's not just intimidating to perform with us because of our experience, but also because we were literally towering above most people physically." But the diminutive Poehler, he added, "was able to get onstage with us, and that just didn't seem to matter." To help make ends meet in those years, Poehler worked as a waitress, among other jobs.

Shortly after joining that troupe, Poehler moved to New York City, where she performed from time to time on the television show *Late Night with Conan O'Brien*. Around the same time, the cable channel Comedy Central offered the Upright Citizens Brigade their own, eponymous television show, which aired for three seasons beginning in 1998. Poehler and the rest of the troupe, who had moved to New York to film the program, also opened a comedy venue and performance training center. The club remains open; until recently Poehler could be seen there most Sundays perfecting her routines. Also in the late 1990s, Poehler was cast in small roles in a variety of movies, including *Saving Manhattan* (1998), *Deuce Bigalow: Male Gigolo* (1999), and *Wet Hot American Summer* (2001), and television shows, among them *Spin City*.

In September 2001 Poehler debuted as a featured player on *Saturday Night Live*. One of her first notable roles was as Sam, opposite Seth Meyers as Bookie Newton, in the recurring "Li'l Sleuths" sketch, about a pair of young detectives. Meyers had also trained in Chicago; Poehler said to Phil Rosenthal about performing alongside fellow veterans of the Chicago comedy-troupe scene, "This environment, this dorm-room environment, depends a lot on being able to do bits with people. . . . Sometimes I sense a similarity between people from Chicago. . . . It's based on the way we're trained. It's like seeing some dude doing karate and you notice he has the same form as you. You kind of sense they've learned from the same masters." Over the years on *SNL*, Poehler has become known for her impressions of celebrities including Avril Lavigne, Kelly Ripa, Michael Jackson, Sharon Osbourne, Dakota Fanning, and Hilary Duff. She has also created characters, including Sam; Amber, a one-legged woman with gastrointestinal difficulties; and (opposite Meyers) Sally Needler, of the argumentative couple the Needlers.

In 2004 Poehler appeared in two movies, *Envy* and *Mean Girls*, released on the same day. In the former she played the wife of the character portrayed by Jack Black. While that movie—despite an all-star cast that included Ben Stiller, Christopher Walken, and Rachel Weisz—was unsuccessful at the box office, *Mean Girls* was an instant hit and has become a cult classic. Written by Tiny Fey, who also has a role in the movie, *Mean Girls* stars Lindsay Lohan as a 16-year-old in a new high school, where two very different sets of girls try to befriend her. Poehler played Mrs. George, the mother of the girl who leads the Plastics—a trio of pretty, rich, and snobby girls. Though Poehler's role was minor, she stole scenes with her portrayal of an overly permissive mother trying too hard to be cool. The film won Poehler mainstream attention.

Jimmy Fallon left the cast of *SNL* in 2004 to pursue a movie career, creating an opening on *SNL*'s long-running feature "Weekend Update." When Fey—who had come from behind the cameras to co-host the fake-news skit with Fallon—began looking for his successor, she turned to her friend Poehler. Since the inception of *SNL*, "Weekend Update" has been one of its most-watched routines; celebrated cast members of past years, including Chevy Chase, Jane Curtin, and Dennis Miller, first gained significant attention by hosting the segment, which also gave birth to the beloved Gilda Radner characters Emily Litella and Roseanne Roseannadanna. Fey and Poehler became the first female team to serve as hosts for the feature. Because "Weekend Update" is so highly regarded, Poehler was nervous on her first outing, as she told Donna Freydkin: "My knuckles were white. I was so afraid I would swear or blow somebody's joke or that the audience would boo." Her fears notwithstanding, the audience reaction was mainly positive. The Poehler-Fey partnership lasted until Fey left the show, in 2006; Poehler now co-hosts the segment with Seth Meyers.

In 2006 Poehler co-created, executive produced, and provided voice work for the Nickelodeon cable-channel cartoon *The Mighty B!*. The show centers on 10-year-old Bessie Higgenbottom, a "honeybee scout" who sets out to earn more merit badges than any other honeybee in history. Poehler said in a statement quoted by Richard Huff in the New York *Daily News* (December 13, 2006), "Bessie represents the ever-optimistic spaz who believes she can grow up a rock star, actress, politician and brain surgeon all at the same time." Also that year

Poehler had small roles in the movies *Southland Tales* and *Tenacious D in The Pick of Destiny*. In 2007 Poehler lent her voice to another animated character, Snow White, in the movie *Shrek the Third*. In keeping with the *Shrek* series' tradition of parodying fairy-tale characters, Poehler explored hidden facets of her character, as she told Larry Ratliff for the *San Antonio (Texas) Express News* (May 16, 2007): "We always see Snow White as this demure, wonderful lady with activity kind of swirling around her. I thought that like most people I know who have busy homes filled with little people and animals, you have to be a bit of a taskmaster." Also that year Poehler won acclaim for her role in the film *Blades of Glory*. She and her real-life husband, Will Arnett, played a brother-and-sister ice-skating team in competition with the first all-male pairs skating team, played by Will Ferrell and Jon Heder. In addition, Poehler appeared that year in the movies *Mr. Woodcock* and *Wild Girls Gone*.

One of Poehler's most indelible impersonations on *SNL* has been of the U.S. senator and presidential candidate Hillary Rodham Clinton. Writing for *Entertainment Weekly* (March 21, 2008), Clark Collis described Poehler's Clinton as "a wonky bore with a Joker-esque smile." In early 2008, during a televised debate with her Democratic rival, Barack Obama, Clinton referred to a recent skit in which she had been portrayed by Poehler, creating what Poehler described to Collis as a "crazy media frenzy." Days later, Clinton—who had lost a string of primary elections to Obama—won the contests in Texas, Ohio, and Rhode Island, which, as Collis wrote, led "more than one news outlet to credit *SNL* for her comeback."

Fey and Poehler teamed up again in 2008 for the film *Baby Mama*, written and directed by the former *SNL* writer Michael McCullers. Fey played a single, big-city career woman who, at 37, decides to have a baby and is forced to turn to a working-class New Jerseyan—played by Poehler—to carry the child. The film, a box-office success, got a mixed critical reception, but numerous critics found that the acting in *Baby Mama* compensated for the weaknesses of the movie. Joe Neumaier, writing for the New York *Daily News* (April 24, 2008, on-line), found Poehler's performance especially noteworthy: "It's Poehler's physical shenanigans that provide the film's biggest laughs, but in calmer moments she actually straddles a tricky line with finesse. Given the second-act twists, [Poehler's character] can't seem either too stupid, or too normal. In a pleasing contrast to Fey's sharpness, Poehler keeps her performance unpredictable and fuzzy. In this just-add-water comedy, a very funny movie star is born."

Poehler and the comedian Will Arnett, who made a name for himself as the character Gob on the TV show *Arrested Development*, have been married since 2003. Poehler appeared on five episodes of the series as Gob's wife in 2004 and 2005. Poehler and Arnett's first child, a boy named Archie, was born in October 2008.

—F.C.

Suggested Reading: *Chicago Sun-Times* p56 Dec. 14, 2001; *Entertainment Weekly* p22 Mar. 21, 2008; Internet Movie Database Web site; (New York) *Daily News* p103 Dec. 13, 2006, (on-line) Apr. 24, 2008; *San Antonio Express News* G p1 May 16, 2007; *USA Today* E p2 Nov. 26, 2004

Selected Television Shows: *Upright Citizens Brigade*, 1998–2001; *Saturday Night Live*, 2001–; *Arrested Development*, 2004–05; *The Mighty B!*, 2006–

Selected Films: *Saving Manhattan*, 1998; *Deuce Bigalow: Male Gigolo*, 1999; *Wet Hot American Summer*, 2001; *Mean Girls*, 2004; *The Devil and Daniel Webster*, 2004; *Envy*, 2004; *Southland Tales*, 2006; *Tenacious D in The Pick of Destiny*, 2006; *Blades of Glory*, 2007; *Girls Gone Wild*, 2007; *Shrek the Third*, 2007; *Mr. Woodcock*, 2007; *Horton Hears a Who!*, 2008, *Baby Mama*, 2008

Polgar, Susan

Apr. 19, 1969– Chess grandmaster

Address: Susan Polgar Institute for Chess Excellence, Texas Tech University, Box 45080, Lubbock, TX 79409-5080

Susan Polgar has broken major gender barriers in the chess world. In 1986, for example, when she was 17 years old, Polgar became the first woman ever to qualify for the Men's World Championship. The Fédération International des Échecs (FIDE), the game's governing body, refused to let her compete in the championship, and the resulting uproar spurred the organization, which is also known as the World Chess Federation, to change its policy and drop the word "Men's" from the name of the event. In 1991 she became the first woman to earn the title of grandmaster under the same qualifications required of male players. (The FIDE also awards a Women's Grandmaster title, but the qualifications for that are more easily met, and it is thus considered a less prestigious achievement; Polgar reached that milestone at the age of 12.) Polgar frequently jokes that she has never beaten a healthy man, because as soon as she wins a game her male opponent pleads a headache or other ailment to rationalize his loss. Polgar's pioneering efforts have made the chess world a more welcoming place for younger, female players—including her own sister: Judit Polgar, who was named a grandmaster less than a year after Susan, has been the top-ranked female player in the world for several years.

Zsuzsanna Polgár was born on April 19, 1969 in Hungary. (She was nicknamed Zsuzsa in her youth, and many sources still refer to her that way, although she has used the anglicized name Susan Polgar since she moved to the U.S., in the mid-1990s.) Her father, László, was a psychologist, and her mother, Klara, was a foreign-language teacher from Ukraine. In *Psychology Today* (July/August 2005, on-line), Carlin Flora described László and Klara's unusual courtship: "His letters to her weren't filled with reflections on her cherubic beauty or vows of eternal love. Instead, they detailed a pedagogical experiment he was bent on carrying out with his future progeny. After studying the biographies of hundreds of great intellectuals, he had identified a common theme—early and intensive specialization in a particular subject. László thought the public school system could be relied upon to produce mediocre minds. In contrast, he believed he could turn any healthy child into a prodigy. He had already published a book on the subject, *Bring Up Genius!*, and he needed a wife willing to jump on board." Klara was willing, and the couple married in 1967.

When Polgar was nearly four years old, she discovered a chess set in a cabinet and was instantly intrigued by the carved playing pieces. László decided that chess would be a perfect area of focus for his first child and began to teach her the game. (Although some journalists refer to him as an accomplished player, he has repeatedly said that he possesses only average ability.) Within six months Polgar was playing against adult men at the local chess club (almost invariably described by journalists as "smoke-filled") and beating them. A year after she had first picked up a chess piece, she entered her first girl's championship, held in Budapest. So small that she had to sit on a pile of pillows in order to see the board, she emerged from the tournament undefeated, 10–0, despite having been pitted against girls over twice her age.

In 1974 Klara gave birth to Zsofia (sometimes referred to as Sophia), and in 1976 Judit was born. Within a few years the two younger girls, jealous of the attention their elder sister got from László during her daily chess lessons, had also started to play. László and Klara petitioned the Hungarian authorities to allow them to homeschool their daughters, and when given permission they embarked on an ambitious course of math, science, history, literature, and language instruction—coupled with hours of chess each day. Polgar, who is fluent in seven languages, including Esperanto, told Flora, "My dad believed in optimizing early childhood instead of wasting time playing outside or watching TV." The family's apartment was filled with thousands of books on chess, trophies the girls had won, game boards, and a massive file cabinet that contained detailed notes on past games and potential competitors. Occasionally the sisters swam and played table tennis or soccer, and a portion of each day was set aside for relaxing and telling jokes. Polgar told Mark Schwed for the Cox

Paul Truong, courtesy of Susan Polgar

Susan Polgar

News Service (July 31, 2005), "People attacked my father [and] said we didn't play [with toys] enough as children. But children really need and crave food for the mind. They feel good about themselves when they accomplish things."

In August 1982 Polgar won her first world championship, at a tournament for girls under the age of 16, and two years later—despite travel restrictions placed on her by Hungary's Communist government, which made it difficult for her to enter international competition—she was ranked the top female player in the world. After she participated in the 1986 Hungarian National Championship, held in Budapest, she became the first woman to qualify for the Men's World Championship. To be eligible for the potential world championship, a player must have recorded a series of top finishes at predetermined qualifying events and must have achieved an adequate ELO rating from the FIDE. (Although generally capitalized, ELO is not an acronym; it refers to Arpad Elo, the physics professor who devised the ratings method, which calculates the relative skill levels of players in chess and other two-competitor games.)

The players at the Budapest event had been told that the top three finishers would automatically qualify for the World Championship. Polgar paced herself carefully and tied for second with Laszlo Hazai, an international master; grandmaster Ivan Farago placed first. Members of the Hungarian Chess Federation, outraged that a woman had qualified, immediately decided that only the top two finishers would represent Hungary at the world championships, and instead of allowing a tiebreaker, they automatically awarded Hazai the win. The FIDE supported their actions. (Polgar,

who is Jewish, has questioned whether anti-Semitism, as well as sexism, was responsible for the decision.) Later that year Polgar suffered another setback: the FIDE announced that active players who had participated in all-women tournaments would be awarded an extra 100 ELO points, but Polgar was not given the 100 points on the grounds that she had played primarily against men. (László had fought fiercely for her to be allowed to do so, thereby antagonizing the Hungarian Chess Federation and the FIDE.) The move was ostensibly intended to level the playing field between men and women, but Polgar and her supporters believed that the FIDE had acted under pressure from the Soviets, who were used to dominating the game and did not want to see a non-Soviet at the top. With other female players benefiting from the handicap, Polgar was knocked out of the number-one spot in the January 1987 rankings of the world's women players. The FIDE's decision the following year to open the world-championship event to both men and women has been attributed in large part to the outcry over Polgar's exclusion.

In 1988 Polgar, her two sisters, and Ildikó Mádl represented Hungary at the World Chess Olympiad. (The FIDE is a member organization of the International Olympic Committee. The Olympiad is held at two-year intervals, in the autumn of even-numbered years.) The Hungarian team triumphed that year, marking the first time a non-Soviet team had won the gold medal. "It was one of those few things that permanently changes your life," Polgar told Flora. "Until then, we had a lot of doubters and bad-wishers. After that, we became national heroes. . . . We could have a summer house and a car. It was almost like winning the lottery." The sisters returned to the Olympiad in 1990 and repeated their success, silencing those few skeptics who claimed that their first gold-medal win had been a fluke. Some chess aficionados jokingly suggested that the country be renamed "Polgaria."

In early 1991, after qualifying finishes at a series of games in France and Spain, Polgar, who had a stellar ELO rating of more than 2,600, was named a grandmaster. She was the first woman to have been awarded the title under the same standards required of men. (Nona Gaprindashvili had been named a grandmaster by the FIDE in 1978, and Maia Chiburdanidze had been accorded the honor in 1984, but neither of those women had actually met the technical requirements for the title.) At the end of 1991, Judit Polgar also became a grandmaster, becoming—at the age of 15 years and five months—the youngest player in history to do so. (Bobby Fischer, the legendary player who had held the record previously, was one month older when he became a grandmaster, in 1958.)

In 1992 Polgar won the Women's World Blitz and Women's World Rapid Championships. (While a game of conventional chess typically allows each player to complete his or her moves in at least two hours per player, rapid chess limits each player to 25 to 60 minutes, depending on the tournament, and blitz chess to three to five minutes.) In 1994 Polgar married an American computer programmer and moved to New York City. While she had been treated as a luminary in Hungary, in the U.S. her standard of living declined, and she realized she needed to take a job. She found one at a public school in Harlem and discovered that she enjoyed teaching chess. Meanwhile, she continued to play competitively. During the third game of the 1996 World Women's Chess Championship, Polgar, who had the advantage, offered her opponent a draw in order to conserve energy and recuperate for the upcoming matches. In response, the match organizer fined Polgar and her opponent each $25,000 for an intentional early draw. As reported in many sources, her shock and embarrassment were compounded by the presence at the tournament of her husband's parents, whom he had invited without her permission. Despite such pressures she went on to win the championship, thus completing what is known as the triple-crown of chess. (The term refers to the blitz, rapid, and conventionally timed championships.)

Polgar retained the championship until 1999. Then, preparing to defend the title against Xie Jun, a formidable player from China, she asked for a postponement so that she could recuperate from the birth of her first child, a boy. The FIDE agreed to work toward securing a satisfactory date, but after continued disagreement, the organization stripped Polgar of her title and set up a world-championship match between Xie and Alisa Galliamova. (Xie ultimately triumphed.) Polgar later sued the FIDE and was awarded monetary compensation.

Polgar gave birth to a second son in 2000. She retired briefly from competitive chess in order to raise her children and run the Polgar Chess Center, which she had opened with a partner, Paul Truong (a Vietnamese-born chess champion originally named Hoainhan Truong), in 1997 in the New York City borough of Queens. At the center players could take lessons, hear lectures, and play in regular tournaments. Flora wrote, "Susan's feminine touch is apparent at her club, where tea and cakes are served to the mostly male members. 'It's rare to have someone of Susan's stature interacting with amateurs like us. You wouldn't see [famed player Garry] Kasparov sitting here, talking to a normal person,' notes Ruth Arluck, a retired teacher. Truong agrees. 'Susan even insisted on wooden instead of plastic chess pieces. It takes a woman to notice these things.'"

In 2003 Polgar returned to professional chess and was named Grandmaster of the Year by the United States Chess Federation, becoming the first woman ever to receive that honor. Later in the year she became the first woman to win the U.S. Open Blitz Championship. (She won the event in 2005 and 2006 as well.) She became a naturalized U.S. citizen, and in 2004 she helped the American team win a silver medal at that year's Olympiad, which marked the first time the country had been in med-

al contention. (The Chinese team, which included Xie, took home the gold.) Polgar also won two other medals during the tournament: a gold for most points scored and another gold for best overall performance. In 2005 Polgar broke several international chess records, as noted in the *Guinness Book of World Records*. During one 17-hour stretch, she played 1,131 consecutive games against more than 500 opponents—a figure that included 326 simultaneous games. Despite taking no more than a few seconds on each move, she lost only three games. During the event, which took place in a Florida mall, she walked more than nine miles.

Polgar's first marriage dissolved in 2002, and in late 2006, in a quiet, unpublicized ceremony, she married Truong. She has co-written a half-dozen instructional books, including *Alpha Teach Yourself Chess in 24 Hours* (2002), *Chess* (2003), *The ChessCafe Puzzle Book* (2004), *A World Champion's Guide to Chess* (2005), and *Chess Tactics for Champions* (2006). She has also written two memoirs, *Queen of the Kings Game* (1997), published under the name Zsuzsa Polgár (with Jacob Shutzman), and *Breaking Through: How the Polgar Sisters Changed the Game of Chess* (2005), written with Truong. She contributes regularly to *Chess Life* and other magazines and to such Web sites as chesscafe.com.

In 2004 Polgar established a foundation bearing her name; the organization focuses on teaching chess to girls and sponsoring female-only tournaments—the Susan Polgar National Invitational for Girls, the Susan Polgar World Open Chess Championship for Girls, and the Susan Polgar National Open Chess Championship for Girls—to help alleviate some of the pressure they might normally feel in the male-dominated pursuit. Polgar and Truong have also been working on ways to market chess for television. "We want to make chess like tennis or golf," Polgar told Marc Ferris for *Newsday* (November 14, 2003). "There's no reason chess should take a back seat to those sports. It's not a physical activity that can be as attractive for television, like a ballgame, but if it's presented the right way, television will come around."

In 2007 Polgar was elected to the executive board of the U.S. Chess Federation. (In the fall of 2007, controversy erupted in the federation when Samuel H. Sloan, who had lost his seat on the board in the previous election, sued Polgar, Truong, and several others for slander and harassment. Polgar denied the allegations and countersued for libel in August 2008). Also in 2007 Polgar opened the Susan Polgar Institute of Chess Excellence (SPICE) at Texas Tech University and became the coach of the school's highly regarded Knight Raiders chess team. She and Truong have moved to Texas, where they live with Polgar's sons, Tom and Leeam. (The center in Queens remains in operation.) In 2007 she gave the commencement address at Texas Tech.

Regarding Polgar's sisters, Judit Polgar has long topped the list of the world's best female players and often appears on the top-100 list of best players of both genders. She remained in Hungary and is married to a veterinarian. Sophia Polgar, despite being considered the most naturally skilled of the sisters, is raising two sons and currently has little interest in pursuing professional play. She now lives in Israel, has studied art, and is married to an orthopedic surgeon (who is also a grandmaster chess player).

Singly or with Truong, Polgar has won several awards from the organization Chess Journalists of America. Polgar told Roberta T. Vowell for the *Virginian-Pilot* (February 23, 2005), "Chess is, in a way, a small, playful version of life itself. It teaches us to make long-term plans, short-term plans. To think ahead, two, four or 20 moves. . . . That you cannot just live for the moment. It teaches us to be-

come responsible for our actions. It teaches you to look around, to be cautious, to look ahead."

—F.C.

Suggested Reading: Cox News Service July 31, 2005; (New Orleans, Louisiana) *Times-Picayune* A p26 Dec. 22, 1996; *Newsday* A p38 July 25, 1997, A p49 Nov. 14, 2003; *Psychology Today* (on-line) July/Aug. 2005; *Virginian-Pilot* E p1 Feb. 23, 2005

Selected Books: *Queen of the Kings Game,* 1997; *Alpha Teach Yourself Chess in 24 Hours,* 2002; *Chess,* 2003; *The ChessCafe Puzzle Book,* 2004; *A World Champion's Guide to Chess,* 2005; *Breaking Through: How the Polgar Sisters Changed the Game of Chess,* 2005; *Chess Tactics for Champions* 2006

Paul Hawthorne/Getty Images

Power, Samantha

1970– Writer; activist; educator

Address: John F. Kennedy School of Government, Mailbox 14, 79 JFK St., Cambridge, MA 02138

In March 2008 Samantha Power, then an unpaid adviser to the presidential hopeful Barack Obama, was speaking to a journalist when she made an off-the-record comment disparaging Obama's chief rival for the Democratic nomination, Hillary Rodham Clinton. After reports of her comment blanketed the news media, Power was forced to resign

from Obama's campaign staff; perhaps more significantly, the episode threatened to overshadow her noted career as a journalist, activist, educator, and author. At 22 Power began reporting from war zones around the globe for *U.S. News & World Report* and other publications. After earning a law degree and accepting a teaching post at Harvard University's Kennedy School of Government, she channeled her passionate interest in the issue of human rights into her Pulitzer Prize–winning 2002 book, *A Problem from Hell: America and the Age of Genocide.* Her more recent book, *Chasing the Flame: Sergio Vieira de Mello and the Fight to Save the World* (2008), is a biography of the human-rights advocate and longtime United Nations envoy, who was killed in Iraq in 2003.

Samantha J. Power was born in 1970 in Dublin, Ireland. Her mother, Veronica Delaney, a surgeon, wanted to divorce Power's father, a dentist, but was not allowed to do so in the overwhelmingly Catholic country; as a result she left Ireland with her children when Power was nine years old, eventually settling in the United States. Helen Kennedy reported for the New York *Daily News* (March 8, 2008) that Power "lost most of her brogue" while growing up in Atlanta, Georgia, where she developed an enthusiasm for American sports. In high school her skill at playing basketball won her the nickname "Tower of Power."

Power attended Yale University, in New Haven, Connecticut, where she majored in history, played squash on the varsity squad, and aspired to be a sports journalist; she told Kennedy, referring to a famous sportscaster, "All I wanted to be was Bob Costas." Her focus shifted after her freshman year at Yale. She was working as an intern at the Atlanta affiliate of the CBS television network, preparing highlights for a broadcast of a Major League Baseball game, when the live program was interrupted by a news report about Tiananmen Square, in China—where soldiers had opened fire on scores of pro-democracy demonstrators. As quoted by Kennedy, Power recalled, "It was the most shocking thing I had ever seen. I thought, 'Oh, my God. What am I doing with my life?'"

After graduating from Yale, in 1993, Power went to Washington, D.C., to serve as an intern for the Carnegie Endowment for International Peace. That organization's offices were in the same building as those of the publication *U.S. News & World Report.* When she approached a *U.S. News* editor about the possibility of being sent to the war-torn former Yugoslavia as a correspondent, he turned her down but offered to read any stories she sent from the region, where Serbs in Bosnia were carrying out a campaign of "ethnic cleansing" against Muslims. Power accepted that offer and was deeply affected by what she witnessed in Bosnia, as she told Terry Gross for the National Public Radio program *Fresh Air* (June 5, 2003): "There was just something to me surreal and gravely disappointing and disheartening about seeing emaciated men behind barbed wire in concentration camps on the one hand and NATO airplanes flying overhead monitoring the carnage but doing nothing about it on the other. . . . It changed me in that while I had grown up thinking that war was something that had to be avoided at all costs, here was a circumstance where what I wanted—and it wasn't an easy thing to acknowledge that this was what I wanted, but I wanted those NATO planes to do something; that is, I wanted war. And so I think while some people, let's say, on the left in America are really deeply skeptical after Vietnam and so on of the possibility of American power being harnessed for good, I think having gone through that experience and being almost desperate for American power, recognizing that it was American power or nothing, you know, that the Europeans were not themselves going to do anything, makes me perhaps more willing to entertain again the possibility—not the likelihood, but the possibility—that the United States can use its resources for liberal ends." During those years Power wrote articles for *U.S. News* as well as the *Boston Globe*, the *Economist*, and other publications, reporting from trouble spots including East Timor and Rwanda. She next enrolled at Harvard University Law School, in Cambridge, Massachusetts, earning her J.D. degree in 1999. In the previous year she had helped found the Carr Center for Human Rights Policy at Harvard's John F. Kennedy School of Government; she was the center's executive director until 2002. Since 2000 she has been on the faculty of the Kennedy School, where she is currently the Anna Lindh professor of practice of global leadership and public policy.

In 2002 Power published *A Problem from Hell: America and the Age of Genocide.* In that book, which began as a paper she wrote for law school, she analyzed six instances of genocide in the 20th century and the U.S. government's response, or lack thereof, to those tragedies. Peter Ronayne wrote for the journal *Ethics & International Affairs* (2002), "Power reveals the stark record: the United States has rarely missed an opportunity to miss an opportunity to stand against genocide." Beginning with the atrocities committed against Armenians by Turks in 1915, Power discussed the United States government's expressed policy of seeking to maintain neutrality and argued that the policy set the precedent for the nation's responses to subsequent acts of genocide, such as the Holocaust; the Khmer Rouge's murders of millions of Cambodians between 1975 and 1978; the Iraqi leader Saddam Hussein's attempt to eliminate the Kurds during the 1980s; conflict between Serb forces and ethnic Albanians in the Serbian province of Kosovo in the mid-1990s; and the genocide in Rwanda in 1994. Power also told the story of Raphael Lemkin, who lost nearly 50 members of his family during the Holocaust and who in 1943 coined the term "genocide" to give a name to such acts of mass murder, as a way of helping to prevent their occurrence in the future. Power noted that Lemkin's work—which helped bring about the United Nations Convention against Genocide, established in 1948—may have served, ironically, to inhibit responses to mass murder, as observers either resist the drastic action that the word "genocide" seems to call for or debate whether specific cases meet the convention's definition of genocide: "acts committed with the intent to destroy, in whole or in part, a national, ethnical, racial, or religious group, as such." *A Problem from Hell* received critical acclaim and won Power both a National Book Critics Circle Award and the Pulitzer Prize in 2003. While there was some criticism of Power's narrow focus on the role of the United States and what some called her anachronistic view of the United States' power during the early 20th century, critics felt overall that the work was well written, asked pertinent questions, and served as an important treatise on contemporary foreign policy. In a representative review, Laura Secor wrote for the *New York Times* (April 14, 2002): "This vivid and gripping work of American history doubles as a prosecutor's brief: time and again, Power recounts, although the United States had the knowledge and the means to stop genocide abroad, it has not acted. Worse, it has made a resolute commitment to not acting. Washington's record, Power ruefully observes, is not one of failure, but of success."

While Power was promoting her book, a new instance of genocide came to light, in the Darfur region of the Sudan, in Africa. There, members of black farm communities have been systematically slaughtered by the janjaweed, an Arab militia armed largely by the Sudanese government. Power and others have theorized that the atrocities are being committed to open up land for oil exploration and development. Power visited Darfur in 2004 and later discussed the experience with Scott Simon for the program *Weekend Edition* on National Public Radio (August 7, 2004): "It was a kind of tour of hell, I would say. I began in Chad in the camps and heard horrifying tales of decapitation, of children being thrown into fires alive, of rape. There were women who'd actually been branded by the Janjaweeds so they would be marked as having been raped. And then I moved into Sudan, crossed the border into north Darfur, and there I encountered internally displaced people who were too poor or too infirm to make the trek to Chad. They were desperate to get out of Sudan. I encountered bodies lying facedown in a ravine, 14 bodies with 17 bullet casings around them. They were men who had been shot in the back of the head or in the back. I encountered wells that witnesses said had been stuffed with bodies but had subsequently been covered over with sand, so all you could see was the kind of rim of the well and then it was as if they had tried to cover their tracks. It was grim." In 2005 Power edited, with Graham Allison, *Realizing Human Rights: Moving from Inspiration to Impact*, which includes essays by some of the world's leading human-rights activists, among them former president Jimmy Carter.

Also in 2005 Power received a call from the office of Democratic U.S. senator Barack Obama of Illinois, who was then considering a run for the presidency and was seeking advice on foreign policy. According to Paul Gessell, writing for the *Ottawa (Canada) Citizen* (March 6, 2008), Power "had no idea" at the time who Obama was; after hearing from his office, she downloaded footage of his speech at the 2004 Democratic National Convention, during which he referred to continuing poverty and inequality in the U.S. "I had a cry," Power recalled, as quoted by Gessell. "I couldn't believe the speech, couldn't believe the country he was telling me I lived in." Power and Obama met for dinner to discuss points raised in *A Problem from Hell*; the two ended up talking for nearly four hours. "Suddenly," Power recalled to Kennedy, "it was almost midnight and I heard myself saying to him, 'Why don't I just quit my job and work in your office?'" So it was that Power left Harvard for a year to become an adviser for foreign affairs to Obama's presidential campaign; after 2006 she worked with the candidate as an unpaid adviser.

After Power joined the campaign, as Cara Buckley wrote for the *New York Times* (March 16, 2008, on-line), "people who knew her wondered—and worried—whether a person who is so naked about her passions could survive in the political world, where tact and coolness usually trump spontaneity." Those fears were realized in early March 2008, after the campaign had entered the primary season and the race for the Democratic nomination had narrowed to a contest between Obama and Hillary Rodham Clinton. During an interview with the *Scotsman*, Power—expressing her view that Clinton would stop at nothing to win the nomination—called the New York senator a "monster." Power hurriedly explained that her remark was off the record, but the newspaper printed it nonetheless, setting off a political firestorm that ended with Power's resignation from Obama's campaign staff. She later apologized for her remark, which she cal-

led "inexcusable" and "hateful." Obama's victory, on November 4, 2008, in his race for the presidency will probably increase speculation that Power might be welcomed back into his circle of advisers.

Meanwhile, in early 2008, Power had published the book *Chasing the Flame: Sergio Vieira de Mello and the Fight to Save the World*. De Mello was a Brazilian-born U.N. envoy; Power had met him in the 1990s in the Balkans and was immediately struck by his charm, charisma, and passion for human rights. (Vieira de Mello had earlier been described to Power as a cross between Robert F. Kennedy, a U.S. senator and champion of the downtrodden, and the dashing fictional spy James Bond.) After decades of negotiating with governments and rebels alike to protect innocent lives in troubled regions including Rwanda and Cambodia, de Mello was killed by a suicide bomber in Iraq in 2003. Leigh Flayton wrote for *Salon.com* (February 18, 2008), "Power says she sees a strong synergy between Vieira de Mello's principles and Obama's concept of foreign policy—with their emphasis on justice, human rights, security and, perhaps most controversially, direct diplomatic engagement with foreign adversaries." Flayton quoted Power's description of Vieira de Mello: "He is the man for dark times. He had a 35-year head start thinking about how to mend broken people and broken places, these questions that are consuming us now." In a representative review of *Chasing the Flame*, Francis Fukuyama wrote for the *New York Times Book Review* (February 17, 2008), "Power . . . has written a comprehensive biography of Vieira de Mello that explains how his personal evolution paralleled that of the United Nations and how his contradictions and failures were rooted in those of the institution he so loyally served. . . . In the end, the book does not make a persuasive case that the United Nations will ever be able to evolve into an organization that can deploy adequate amounts of hard power or take sides in contentious political disputes. . . . But surely the life and death of Sergio Vieira de Mello is a good place to begin a serious debate about the proper way to manage world order in the future."

Writing for the *Irish Times* (March 4, 2008), Denis Staunton described Power as "tall and willowy, with a translucent complexion and long, flowing, flaxen hair." The diplomat Richard Holbrooke told Cara Buckley about Power, "I've been at parties where people get absolutely giddy when they meet her. She's a real presence—the force and passion. It's mesmerizing." Power, who has nicknamed herself the "genocide chick," was named one of the 100 top scientists and thinkers of 2004 by *Time*; in 2007 she began writing a column for the magazine. In early July 2008 Power married the noted law professor Cass R. Sunstein.

—F.C.

Suggested Reading: *Irish Times* Features p13 July 31, 2007, Features p17 Mar. 4, 2008; (London) *Sunday Times* Features p5 Feb. 24, 2008; New

York *Daily News* p7 Mar. 8, 2008; *New York Times* (on-line) Mar. 16, 2008; *Salon.com* Feb. 18, 2008

Selected Books: *A Problem from Hell: America and the Age of Genocide*, 2002; *Chasing the Flame: Sergio Vieira de Mello and the Fight to Save the World*, 2008

Peter Kramer/Getty Images

Rakim

Jan. 28, 1968– Rapper

Address: c/o Koch Records, 740 Broadway, Seventh Fl., New York, NY 10003

Rakim is one of the most important figures in the history of rap music. In 1985 he formed a partnership with DJ Eric B. to record the songs that would make up the groundbreaking album *Paid in Full* (1987). The album's first single, "Eric B. Is President," was wildly popular among hip-hop aficionados. "Its signature chunky beats, heavy-duty synth bass and flurry of scratches mesmerized listeners," Brolin Winning wrote for *Remix* (May 1, 2004). Though it never received major radio play, the album has sold millions of copies and influenced countless hip-hop artists from the late 1980s to the present day. The duo released three more well-received albums before parting ways in 1992. After the resolution of legal issues that delayed the start of his solo career, Rakim reappeared with *The 18th Letter* in 1997 and, two years later, *The Master*. Following an abortive attempt to record an album on the rapper Dr. Dre's Aftermath label in

2000, Rakim started his own label, G&E Trust, which is slated to release his album *The Seventh Seal* in late 2008.

Rakim Allah was born William Michael Griffin Jr. in the predominantly black town of Wyandanch, Long Island, New York, on January 28, 1968. He grew up with a deep appreciation for jazz, soul music, and rhythm and blues. The famous R&B star Ruth Brown was one of his aunts; his mother, a fan of jazz and opera, enjoyed singing along with records; and his brothers played a variety of musical instruments. Rakim played tenor and baritone saxophone in high school, where he also excelled at football and received good grades. For a time in his teens, he also experimented with drugs and became involved in petty crime and other kinds of trouble. Then, at 16, he joined the sect of Islam called the Nation of Gods and Earths, known popularly as the Five-Percent Nation; at that time he took the name Rakim Allah. Rakim began writing raps while still in high school and caught the attention of Eric Barrier, better known as DJ Eric B., who was then working at the WBLS radio station and seeking an MC with whom he could make music. The two began working together in 1985. ("MC" generally stands for "master of ceremonies"; in the world of hip-hop, it is an acronym for "mic controller".)

In 1986 Rakim and Eric B. released their first single, "Eric B. Is President," a song about Barrier's DJ skills, on Zakia, a small record label based in the New York City neighborhood of Harlem. As DJ, Eric B. composed most of the music and put together the samples and beats while Rakim rapped over them. The single, whose B-side was "My Melody," became an instant underground hit. Various DJs have since remixed the song more than 30 times. Sparsely produced and more heavily reliant on sampling than any other hip-hop song up to that time, the single was like nothing that had come before it. With a rhythmic complexity akin to that of jazz, Rakim delivered a self-reflexive ode to the addictive power of the microphone: "I came in the door / I said it before / I never let the mic magnetize me no more." According to Jess Harvell, writing for *PitchforkMedia.com* (June 2, 2005), "Rakim's innovation was applying a patina of intellectual detachment to rap's most sacred cause: talking . . . about how you're a better rapper than everyone else."

The single attracted the notice of a larger music label, 4th and Broadway Records, which brought out Rakim and Eric B.'s first full-length album, *Paid in Full*, in 1987. Though it did not achieve mainstream success on its initial release, the album later reached platinum status—sales of one million or more units—and is widely regarded as one of the best rap records of all time. "Rakim basically invents modern lyrical technique over the course of *Paid in Full*," Steve Huey wrote for the All Music Guide Web site, "with his complex internal rhymes, literate imagery, velvet-smooth flow, and unpredictable, off-the-beat rhythms."

In the mid-1980s hip-hop music tended to be simple, using rhymes only at the ends of lines to tell easy-to-follow stories. Rakim's lyrics, by contrast, contained metaphors with multiple meanings, assonance, alliteration, internal rhyme schemes, and other devices that had theretofore been used only in literature. Also unprecedented in hip-hop were complex rhythms and seemingly effortless word flow. Rakim has credited his skill in that area to his early exposure to jazz. "I listened to John Coltrane and Thelonious Monk when I was coming up," he told Jim Farber for the New York Daily News (November 18, 1997). "They gave me different timings and rhythms." A decade later he described his songwriting process to Pitchfork-Media.com (October 24, 2007). "When I get a beat," he said, "I can see a million rhythms in the beat. I can see the slowest rhythm in the beat, and I can settle with that and write a song. Or I can look for the most intricate rhythms in the beat, and I can build my style and build my concept on that. That's how I challenge myself, by making sure that when the music comes to me, I'm giving the best of Rakim that I can for that track." Rakim's lyrics are also dense with rhyme and meaning. For example, this short passage from "Eric B. Is President" contains 18 rhyming or otherwise similar-sounding syllables: "I keep the mic at Fahrenheit, freeze MCs, make 'em colder / The listeners system is kicking like solar / As I memorize, advertise like a poet / Keep it goin', when I'm flowin' smooth enough, you know it's rough."

Rakim was also one of the first rappers to express his Islamic beliefs openly in his music. Unlike such soon-to-be-popular rap groups as N.W.A. and Public Enemy, however, he put his love of language before his message, occasionally creating outlandish images in service of a rhyme, as in the track "My Melody": "You scream I'm lazy, you must be crazy / Thought I was a donut, you tried to glaze me." "You don't go to Rakim for political insight, inner turmoil, or sex chat," Jess Harvell wrote. "You go to Rakim for an endless display of pure skill."

Discussing the minimalist production values of Paid in Full, Harvell referred to the record's sound as "hip-hop's garage-rock—a street reaction against the first wave of crossover pop-rap," and Winning described it as "unrelentingly dope: all snappy drum breaks, funky guitar licks, thick bass and rugged cuts." Sampling other songs more heavily than his predecessors had, Barrier in turn created what would become some of the most frequently sampled beats in hip-hop. The second and third singles from the album, "I Ain't No Joke" and "I Know You Got Soul," drew on songs by James Brown and Bobby Byrd. His use of that music set in motion the practice of pillaging old funk records for sounds used in new songs, which continues to this day. It also brought 4th and Broadway label copyright-infringement lawsuits from Brown and Byrd, which were settled out of court but sparked an ongoing debate over the legality and ethics of using sampled sound in hip-hop music.

Rakim and Eric B. signed with Universal Records for their next release, Follow the Leader (1988). The album represented a more refined continuation of the duo's simple beats and sophisticated lyrics. Harvell wrote: "The title track fleshes out Rakim's metaphorical conceit via hellish high-speed-chase music. The beats rattle, the bass seethes, the flutes and strings screech like Blaxploitation crossed with the cheap urgency of an Italian zombie movie. But what's scariest and most exhilarating is how, for all the track's runaway train momentum, it feels inexorable, implacable, utterly in control of itself. Rakim's delivery of the final verse may be the most exciting—at least in terms of breath control—slice of rap the genre has yet delivered."

Rakim and Eric B. were guest artists on the song "Friends" by the R&B musician Jody Watley in 1989, which was the first—and, to date, last—time they made it into the Top 10 on the pop charts. It was also one of the first appearances of a rap artist on a song of another genre. The duo signed a deal with MCA for their next release, Let the Rhythm Hit 'Em (1990), an album that showcased their technical expertise. "As the bass-drum backgrounds wash over him, Rakim sprays out rhymes like a Gatling gun or—in the preferred parlance of rap—like an Uzi," David Hiltbrand wrote for People (August 6, 1990). At the time of the album's release, there was a growing trend toward politics in hip-hop, and though Rakim was far from apolitical, language remained his primary focus. Some critics saw that as a shortcoming. "At a time when West Coast MCs like Ice-T and Ice Cube were mainly interested in getting a political message across," Alex Henderson wrote for the All Music site, "Rakim's goal was showing how much technique he had. . . . There are a few message raps (including 'In the Ghetto'), although Rakim spends most of his time finding tongue-twisting ways to boast and brag about his microphone skills. The overall result is a CD that is enjoyable, yet limited."

The duo's fourth and final release was Don't Sweat the Technique (1992). The record earned good reviews for its flawless production and jazz influences and for the political themes on tracks such as "Casualties of War." Legal and financial disputes caused Rakim and Eric B. to part ways once the album was finished. Rakim told Jim Farber that the trouble had begun when Barrier wanted to record a solo album. "I had to sign [a paper] for him when he wanted to record but when it came time for him to sign for me, he was scared," he said. "We had two albums left on our contract [with MCA]. He thought those albums would be the last and then MCA would just pick me up. I cannot understand that to this day. He's my partner. I would make sure they took care of him. But once he started showing his colors, I just let him get into his own thing."

Rakim began working on a solo album for MCA in 1992. Soon, however, the MCA staff members with whom he worked fell victim to a company purge, then absconded with the unfinished tapes of nine of Rakim's songs and sold them to radio and mix-tape deejays. Almost five years passed before Rakim recorded another album, partly because he was discouraged and partly because of his dislike of the by-then-dominant "gangsta rap" genre. "I didn't want to be labeled as a gangsta because it's majority rules [in music]," he told Farber. "I wanted to go against the grain." He added that at the time of his interview with Farber, late 1997, rap artists seemed "more free to express themselves."

That year, with Universal, Rakim recorded a much-anticipated comeback album, *The 18th Letter*. Debuting at number four on the *Billboard* charts, it was beloved by critics and fans alike. On *The 18th Letter*, Rakim mixed his smooth, laid-back style of rapping with a contemporary technique. "The beats are fresh, the rhymes are solid, the samples are perfect," Ryan Schreiber wrote for *PitchforkMedia.com* (1998). "Rakim is still a master lyricist and he proves it with lines like 'I used to roll up / This is a hold up / Ain't nuthin funny / Stop smiling, be still / Don't nothin move but the money.'" His heavily spiritual follow-up album, *The Master* (1999), was similarly acclaimed, with Angus Batey, writing for the London *Times* (November 27, 1997), hailing Rakim as "his genre's Bob Dylan—a gifted, if often abstract visionary whose followers hang on his every syllable."

Rakim signed to the rapper Dr. Dre's Aftermath Entertainment label in 2000 and began working on an album tentatively titled "Oh, My God." Though he contributed work to songs released by several of his label mates, he shelved his own album in 2003 due to creative differences with Dr. Dre. Later that year Rakim released *Paid in Full: The Platinum Edition*. According to an accompanying press release, the two-disc set included a remastered version of the original album along with "the original mix of 'My Melody' (heretofore unavailable on CD), the enhanced video for 'Paid in Full,'" and "deluxe packaging" featuring "all of the elements of the original album, updated liner notes from essayist Tom Terrell, rare photos and ephemera, plus a special foreword." (In 2004 Rakim and Eric B. sued the Def Jam, Island, and Universal record labels for money owed to them for *Paid in Full*, which was estimated to have sold more than 10 million copies by then.) Rakim signed with Dreamworks to record his next album, but the label dissolved before he could begin work on it.

In 2004, upon his arrival at the Roseland Ballroom, in New York, to play a date with Ghostface (also known as Ghostface Killah) of the Wu Tang Klan, Rakim was arrested on a 2001 warrant associated with a paternity suit. Rakim claimed to have had no prior knowledge of the warrant, arguing that he would not have signed on to play the highly publicized date if he had been a fugitive from justice. The suit—filed by the mother of his then 14-year-old son, a woman with whom he had had a tumultuous relationship and frequent financial disputes—was not the first of its kind. According to

Rakim's attorney, Robert Kaline, the rapper agreed to pay $2,000 in child support "out of an abundance of caution" and was released the next day.

Rakim's live album *The Archive: Live, Lost and Found* (2008) offers, in addition to live recordings, four previously unreleased tracks. Rakim played several dates on the Rock the Bells Tour and the Paid Dues Independent Hip Hop Festival in the summer of 2008, sharing the stage with artists including Mos Def, Ghostface, A Tribe Called Quest, Brother Ali, and the band Rhythm Roots Allstars. The release date of Rakim's newest album, *The Seventh Seal*, was pushed back several times and was most recently set for late 2008.

In his October 24, 2007 interview with *PitchforkMedia.com*, Rakim explained his decision to incorporate a live band in his performances: "The essence of hip-hop is that live band. That's why we had the turntables. When it started, we were scratching live bands. These 60s, 70s funk bands, rock'n'roll—we were taking the records and scratching them. If we would have been in the environment where we had drummers and horn players and guitar players—that's not that common in the ghetto. If we would have had guitar players, bass players, drummers, saxophonists, then you might have seen something different with hip-hop, as far as bands being more incorporated, because that's what it is. I don't want to take the DJ element out of it, but at the same time, I just want to let the crowd know that this is why we sample: that live band. I want them to respect that live band."

As one of hip-hop's pioneers, Rakim sees himself as a custodian of the music's legacy. "At this point in hip-hop, [the history] definitely needs to be expressed a little more and put in front of [fans'] faces so that they won't forget where the essence of hip-hop came from," he told *PitchforkMedia.com* in 2007. "If I'm one of the artists that knows about it then yeah, I'm responsible to keep that alive and keep it in the listeners' faces and give them access to it." In addition to stressing the importance of hip-hop's history, Rakim called upon fans and artists to keep the genre alive. "When they created jazz years ago it was the best thing to happen since fried ice cream," he said in the same interview. "But then you look at it now—it's not so popular as far as [being] universal. . . . The same thing can happen in hip-hop if we take it for granted and don't cherish it."

Rakim currently lives in New York City with his girlfriend and their three children.

—J.E.P.

Suggested Reading: All Music Guide Web site; *Miami (Florida) Times* D p1 Nov. 20, 1997; (New York) *Daily News* p46 Nov. 18, 1997; PitchforkMedia.com Oct. 24, 2007; popmatters.com Nov. 19, 2003; *Remix* p5 May 1, 2004

Selected Recordings: *Paid in Full*, 1987; *Follow the Leader*, 1988; *Let the Rhythm Hit 'Em*, 1990; *Don't Sweat the Technique*, 1992; *The 18th Letter*, 1997; *The Master*, 1999; *The Archive: Live, Lost and Found*, 2008

Courtesy of Le Monde Diplomatique

Ramonet, Ignacio

May 5, 1943– Journalist; activist; educator

Address: Le Monde Diplomatique, 1 Ave. Stephen-Pichon, 75013 Paris, France

"Globalization" refers to the merging of national economies into an international market. The Spanish-born journalist, author, and activist Ignacio Ramonet is best known for his prominent role in the "alter-globalization" movement, a grassroots struggle against what he and his compatriots see as the imposition of unrestrained capitalism and a global political and economic system that disproportionately benefits wealthy countries and classes. Most recently, Ramonet gained attention for his 100 hours of interviews with Fidel Castro, which culminated in the publication of *Fidel Castro: My Life—A Spoken Autobiography*, the most comprehensive volume on the life of the Cuban leader to date. As the editor in chief of the widely respected, Paris, France–based, leftist international-affairs journal *Le Monde Diplomatique* from 1991 to 2008, Ramonet wrote fiery editorials that resulted in the establishment of several important organizations, including ATTAC International, which proposes concrete solutions for what its officials see as the injustices of globalization; the World Social Forum

(the alter-globalization movement's answer to the World Economic Forum), of which Ramonet is one of the main organizers and which has met annually since 2001; and the nongovernmental watchdog group Media Watch Global, which he co-founded in order to counter the corporatization of the media. Through his work at *Le Monde Diplomatique* in the 1990s, Ramonet helped create the slogans "Another world is possible," the motto of the World Social Forum and an answer to the British prime minister Margaret Thatcher's famous statement "There is no alternative" to global free-market capitalism; and "la pensée unique" ("single thought"), one of the terms now commonly used in examining globalization and its perceived inevitability. A professor of media studies and communication theory at Denis Diderot University, in Paris, and an adviser to the United Nations specializing in geopolitics, Ramonet is also a frequent contributor to the Spanish daily *El Pais* and an adviser to the pan–Latin American television network Telesur.

Ignacio Ramonet was born in Redondela, in Galicia, a region of Spain, on May 5, 1943 to Antonio Ramonet, a tailor, and Antonia Miguez. To escape the fascist regime of the country's ruler, Francisco Franco, his family relocated to Tangier, Morocco, in 1946. "I do not belong to the generation whose real battle was fascism-antifascism. That was my parents' generation: my father participated in the Spanish Civil War [on the side that opposed Franco's forces] and my mother was a union militant," he told Rosa Miriam Elizalde for cubanismo.net (October 8, 2006). "The central battle of my generation, during its adolescence and early adulthood, was colonialism/anti-colonialism. Specially the liberation of colonized countries." Ramonet's childhood coincided with Morocco's gaining independence from France, in 1956, and with neighboring Algeria's war for independence from the same country, begun two years earlier; his schoolmates included Algerian refugees whose families had fled oppression in their own country. At a barbershop in Tangier, when he was 12 or 13, Ramonet learned about Cuban revolutionaries' struggle against the military dictatorship in that country. He recalled to Elizalde, "The barber was a man who had been to Cuba many times; he was a Spaniard very fond of the Island. The magazine he set out for his clients was *Bohemia*. With curiosity I began to read *Bohemia* in its salmon-colored pages, the red chronicles relating repressions of the dictatorship. One thing led to another: I discovered the personality of Fidel Castro"—the revolutionary leader who went on to seize power in Cuba in 1959 and hold it for the next five decades. Reading about the oppression of Cuba's people by its own leaders, and about the Cuban revolutionaries' literacy campaigns and agrarian reforms, Ramonet came to believe that "a country isn't sovereign just because it reaches independence but when its people are sovereign and not subjected to any kind of feudality," as he told Omar Gonzalez in an interview for cubanow.net (February 2005).

Ramonet studied at the University of Rabat, in Morocco, and continued his education in France, at the University of Bordeaux III, where he earned an M.A. degree. He went on to teach at several schools in Morocco, including the Collège du Palais Royal à Rabat, where he was on the faculty from 1969 to 1972. Meanwhile, he had launched a network of film societies and embarked upon a career in journalism, both radio and print. He left in 1972 for Paris, where he began teaching at the University of Paris VII and earned a Ph.D. in semiology and in cultural history from the École des Hautes Études en Sciences Sociales; he was a pupil of the eminent philosopher Roland Barthes and the film theorist Christian Metz, among others. At that time he also began contributing film criticism to the French philosopher Jean-Paul Sartre's newly created leftist paper, *Libération*, as well as writing for the influential film journal *Cahiers du Cinéma*. In January 1973, concurrent with his lecturing, he began his long career with *Le Monde Diplomatique*. He started as a contributor to the paper, which had begun in the 1950s as a foreign-affairs supplement to the French daily *Le Monde*. By the time Ramonet began his tenure there, the scholarly and opinionated paper, nicknamed "Le Diplo," had become known as a leftist journal that offered comprehensive foreign-policy and geopolitical analyses. The paper is largely independent of *Le Monde*, as 49 percent of "Le Diplo" is owned by its readers and staff, which "is extremely rare in the press, not only in France but in the world, and . . . guarantees complete independence from all the powers that be, political, media or financial," as Ramonet wrote in its pages (January 1, 2007). Ramonet was elected editorial director and president of the board in 1990 and was reelected to the positions every six years until he resigned, in early 2008. He continues to write for the paper.

In an oft-quoted January 1995 editorial for the paper, Ramonet introduced the idea of "pensée unique," or single thought. "We began to mobilize a group of intellectuals, thinkers, journalists and professors too, around *Le Monde Diplomatique* . . . to try to identify the features of what we today call globalization . . . ," he told Gonzales. "In that stage in which we were trying to identify . . . the adversary's traits, I had proposed that this be called 'single thought.' . . . In truth, single thought is what we call today globalization. This idea that there is only one good way of thinking, one useful way of thinking, one practical way of thinking, one modern way of thinking and that [it] . . . consists in accepting the catalogue of ideas of globalization in economy, in work and in everyday life." Observers trace the development of modern-day globalization to the 1980s, during the conservative governments of Thatcher and U.S. president Ronald Reagan. Its proponents argue that free-market capitalism on an international scale enriches all involved through a trickle-down effect, providing for the democratization of technology and education, which over generations allows communities and nations to develop. Ramonet has characterized globalization as being based on an ideology in which economic considerations trump all others, leading to social Darwinism and ever-increasing discrepancies in wealth between industrialized and Third World nations. "The aim of single thought," Ramonet told Gonzales, "is that people finally accept their own slavery. That's the project: how to make a person voluntarily consent and take part in his own exploitation and in addition, to think he's happy." In a now-famous debate—printed in the journal *Foreign Policy* (September 22, 1999)—between Ramonet and Thomas L. Friedman, a *New York Times* columnist and globalization advocate, Ramonet wrote, "Dazzled by the glimmer of fast profits, the champions of globalization are incapable of taking stock of the future, anticipating the needs of humanity and the environment, planning for the expansion of cities, or slowly reducing inequalities and healing social fractures. . . . The most basic principle [of globalization] is so strong that even a Marxist, caught offguard, would agree: The economic prevails over the political. . . . In this new social order, individuals are divided into 'solvent' or 'nonsolvent'—i.e., apt to integrate into the market or not. The market offers protection to the solvents only. In this new order, where human solidarity is no longer an imperative, the rest are misfits and outcasts."

To Thatcher's famous line "There is no alternative," the alter-globalization movement responded, "Another world is possible." The movement identified globalization as progressing on several fronts: the economic front, in which nations' markets were forced open by more powerful countries as the price of debt relief, and their national resources were forced to be privatized; the ideological/media front, in which globalization was equated with modernization and progress and made to seem inevitable; and, particularly after the September 11, 2001 terrorist attacks on the U.S., the military front, in which the cause of globalization could be advanced by force, as was attempted in Iraq. Ramonet has argued that political sentiments matching those of the alter-globalization movement have been evident in grassroots campaigns throughout Latin America, particularly the Zapatista movement in Mexico led by Subcomandante Marcos and in measures adopted by Venezuelan president Hugo Chavez. "What happened in Latin America at the end of the 1980s? Globally, the military dictatorships that had marked the preceding 20 years in the continent started to disappear and Latin American societies welcomed with relief— the same as the whole world—the disappearance of those terrible regimes . . . ," Ramonet told Gonzales. "But, as soon as those democratic governments started to rule, they accepted globalization's 'solutions' with open arms; they started to privatize massively, to apply the recipes of the International Monetary Fund; and, with time, what we are now seeing took place: deep dissatisfaction in societies which consider that democracy doesn't fulfill its promises. Democracy isn't just the possibility of picking between one party or the other, to take part in civilian liberties; supposedly, it is also the will to create a fairer society, to distribute wealth better, without polarizing and, therefore, allowing greater economic democracy, social democracy, cultural democracy."

Out of those ideas grew three organizations: ATTAC, the World Social Forum, and Media Watch Global. In December 1997, following the collapse of Asian markets, Ramonet wrote in a *Monde Diplomatique* editorial, "Financial globalisation is a law unto itself and it has established a separate supranational state with its own administrative apparatus, its own spheres of influence, its own means of action. That is to say the International Monetary Fund (IMF), the World Bank, the Organization for Economic Cooperation and Development [OECD] and the World Trade Organization (WTO). . . . This artificial world state is a power with no base in society. It is answerable instead to the financial markets and the mammoth business undertakings that are its masters. . . . Absolute freedom of movement for capital undermines democracy and we need to introduce machinery to counter its effects." Warning that "the task of disarming this financial power must be given top priority if the law of the jungle is not to take over completely in the next century," he proposed three solutions— closing down tax havens, increasing taxes on unearned income, and instituting a tax on financial transactions—the last of which, he argued, could be achieved with the adoption of a reform tax, the Tobin tax, named after the Nobel Prize–winning economist James Tobin, who in 1972 advocated it to stabilize markets and generate revenue for the international community. "At 0.1%, the Tobin tax would bring in some $166 billion a year, twice the annual amount needed to abolish the worst poverty by the end of the [20th] century. Many experts have said there would be no particular technical difficulty about introducing this tax. It would spell the end of the . . . dogma subscribed to by all those people who love to tell us that there is no alternative to the present system," Ramonet wrote. He suggested the creation of a global pressure group that would lobby governments to introduce the measure. He wrote, "Why not set up a new worldwide non-governmental organisation, Action for a Tobin Tax to Assist the Citizen (ATTAC)?"

In the summer of 1998, ATTAC, with the acronym standing instead for Association for the Taxation of Financial Transactions for the Aid of Citizens, was formed in France. ATTAC, whose motto is "The world is not for sale," soon became active around the world, addressing many of the concerns of the alter-globalization movement, by calling for democratic control of financial markets; "fair" instead of "free" trade—that is, democratization of global financial organizations including the IMF, World Bank, WTO, and OECD; debt relief rather than austerity measures for poorer countries; defense of public goods and services against privatization; and sustainable development. "At a time when many pundits were writing off the left as dead, ATTAC gave new life and novel forms to traditional left ideals," David Moberg wrote for *In These Times* (May 14, 2001).

One of ATTAC's main projects was the organizing of the World Social Forum. In a *Monde Diplomatique* editorial (January 2006), Ramonet described the World Social Forum (WSF), which was first convened in Porto Alegre, Brazil, in January 2001, as "an international day of reflection" focusing "on rebuilding the internationalism of peoples and an anti-imperialist front." The forum began as a grassroots organizing and strategizing tool against globalization and free trade, operating under the theme "Another World Is Possible"; it aimed to coordinate the efforts of the various alter-globalization forces that were emerging at the time. The WSF was also intended as an alternative to the annual World Economic Forum, which Ramonet described in a 2001 editorial as "the meeting place for the world's new masters, in particular the policy-makers who set the agenda for globalisation." Participants in the WSF have included such well-known thinkers, writers, activists, and statesmen as Arundhati Roy, Naomi Klein, Noam Chomsky, Immanuel Wallerstein, Joseph Stiglitz, Kofi Annan, Gilberto Gil, President Luiz Inácio da Silva of Brazil, and Hugo Chavez. While the WSF has been credited with bringing new ideas to the global conversation, it has also been criticized for being too vague in intent, for lacking follow-through, and, perhaps most significantly in recent years, for allowing well-funded, typically Western-based non-governmental organizations to dominate the agenda, overshadowing grassroots movements. Another problem has been a lack of the sort of media coverage enjoyed by the World Economic Forum.

Ramonet's criticisms of the news media are central to his positions on globalization and the alter-globalization movement. In an editorial entitled "Set the Media Free" (October 2003), he described the news media as being, ideally, "the voice of those who have no voice," a "fourth estate" that is a key element in any healthy democracy. "Over the past 15 years, with the acceleration of globalisation, this fourth estate has been stripped of its potential, and has gradually ceased to function as a counterpower . . . ," he wrote. "Real power is now in the hands of a few global economic groupings and conglomerates that appear to wield more power in world politics than most governments. . . . Globalisation now also means the globalisation of the mass media and the communications-information companies. These big companies are preoccupied with growth, which means that they have to develop relations with the other estates in society, so they no longer claim to act as a fourth estate with a civic objective and a commitment to denouncing human rights abuses." In response to those developments, Ramonet wrote, "we have to create a new estate, a fifth estate, that will let us pit a civic force against this new coalition of rulers."

He added, "Freedom of enterprise cannot be permitted to override people's right to rigorously researched and verified news, nor can it serve as an alibi for the deliberate diffusion of false news and defamation." Ramonet argued that while the choice to cover a story based on one's ability to sell it, particularly to advertisers, or based on one's commercial ties and interests, may be protected by the right to free speech, "these freedoms can only be exercised by media enterprises if they do not infringe other rights that are equally sacred, such as the right of each citizen to have access to uncontaminated news." Ramonet's call for a watchdog group emerged from discussions at the second World Social Forum, in 2002. Media Watch Global, of which he is founder and president, would, as Ramonet wrote in his editorial, "at last give people a peaceful civic weapon against the emerging superpower of the big mass media."

In 2001 Ramonet published a book of his interviews with Subcomandante Marcos, titled *Marcos: La Dignidad Rebelde*. He received far more attention after his 100 hours of interviews with Fidel Castro were published as the book *Fidel Castro: My Life—A Spoken Autobiography* (2008). Ramonet approached Castro with the idea for the project during the 2002 Havana International Book Fair, where Ramonet presented his book *Silent Propaganda*. The two met several times over the next three years; Castro added detailed footnotes and recollections to the resulting manuscript, making for an apparently exhaustive personal account. After the book appeared, Ramonet was relieved of his weekly column at the Spanish paper *La Voz de Galicia*, merely, by his account, for having published interviews with the controversial Cuban leader. In response to criticism that he had lacked the proper skepticism in his interviews with Castro, Ramonet told Elizalde, "Interrogations are for the police. A journalist does not interrogate. A journalist asks questions and the responsibilities for the answers are of the interviewee. I wanted to have a conversation. I have said it often: he never set any condition. . . . Fidel Castro is the most [censored] person in the mass media, they mention him but his words are not heard. That is not right."

Ramonet is the author of a number of other books, among them *Le Chewing-Gum des Yeux, La Golosina Visual, The Tyranny of Communication, The Geopolitics of Chaos, La Post-Television, A World without Direction, Iraq: History of a Disaster,* and *Wars of the 21st Century: New Threats, New Fears*. He teaches media studies and communication theory at Denis Diderot University in Paris and has taught at the Sorbonne and been a visiting scholar at universities in Spain and Latin America. He has received several honorary doctorates and won many prizes for his work, including the Spanish Liber Press Award for best journalist of the year, the Rodolfo Walsh Award in journalism from the University of La Plata in Argentina, and the Spanish Turia Award for contributions to mass media.

Ramonet lives in Paris and is married to Laurence Villaume, a translator. The couple have four children.

—M.M.

Suggested Reading: cubanismo.net Oct. 8, 2006; cubanow.net Feb. 2005

Selected Books: *The Tyranny of Communication*, 1999; *Wars of the 21st Century: New Threats, New Fears*, 2002; *Iraq: History of a Disaster*, 2005; *Fidel Castro: My Life—A Spoken Autobiography*, 2008

Jeff J Mitchell/Getty Images

Rankin, Ian

Apr. 28, 1960– Writer of crime fiction

Address: c/o Enquiries, Orion Publishing Group, Orion House, 5 Upper Saint Martin's Lane, London WC2H 9EA, England

"I always love blurring the edges between what's real and what's fictitious," the Scottish crime writer Ian Rankin said during an interview with Mel Gussow for the *New York Times* (January 3, 2002). "I think fiction gives a structure to the world that we don't always see in our real life." Dubbed "the king of tartan noir" by James Ellroy (himself a best-selling writer of crime fiction), Rankin is among the most popular crime writers in Great Britain, and he has acquired a large readership in the United States as well. The protagonist in 18 of his books is Detective Inspector John Rebus, a member of the police department of Edinburgh, Scotland, the setting for all but one of the Rebus stories. In 2006 Rankin and his antihero accounted for 10 percent of the British market for crime fiction; for a time in 1999, in an unprecedented feat in the United Kingdom, eight of the top 10 books on some best-seller lists were Rankin's. Also categorized as police procedurals, the Rebus novels have been translated into two dozen languages, and adaptations of 10 of them have been broadcast on British television. "Whatever it is that makes a good crime writer, Ian Rankin has it in spades," Arminta Wallace wrote for the *Irish Times* (April 21, 2001).

Reviewers of Rankin's Rebus stories have applauded the author's skill in grappling with topical issues—sectarianism, vigilantism, gang wars among drug peddlers, Internet and corporate crime, smuggling of refugees by prostitution rings, reintroduction into society of pedophiles released from prison, political corruption, anomie among lower-class teenagers—and doing so without being pedantic or moralistic or detracting from the entertainment value of his prose. "The crime novel reinvents itself to take account of what we are scared of in our particular age," Rankin said to Sveinn Bierkir Bjornsson for the *Reykjavik (Iceland) Grapevine* (June 30, 2006). "At the moment we are scared of terrorism, religious intolerance, we are scared of asylum seekers and outsiders who may come and disrupt the fabric of our society as we see it. There is a lot of fear out there and crime fiction lets us explore the things that we are scared of and ask ourselves the question, should we be afraid of them?" Earlier, Rankin told David Lennon for *Europe* (May 2002), "I want to explain Scotland to myself, to fellow Scots, and to the outside world. So far, I'm not sure I've done more than scratch the surface of this bizarre, mixed-up country, but I'll keep trying." Rebus is 40 years old in *Knots and Crosses* (1987), the book in which he makes his debut; in *Exit Music* (2007), the most recent Rebus novel, the detective has reached the mandatory retirement age for Scottish police officers, but he wants to leave the force "no more than the reader wishes him to," as Mark Lawson wrote for the London *Guardian* (September 8, 2007).

"The Rebus novels . . . are looser, hipper, funnier, more down-to-earth than what you'd find in the best contemporary British police procedurals from the likes of Reginald Hill or Ruth Rendell," Charles Taylor wrote for the *New York Times* (February 22, 2004). According to Nicholas Wroe, writing for the London *Guardian* (May 28, 2005), the crime-fiction expert Stephen Knight, a professor at the University of Cardiff, in Wales, has written that traditionally, British crime novels featured "honourable and boring policemen" or detectives like Agatha Christie's Miss Marple, who are "intellectual and mumsie"—that is, motherly. "I think one reason why Rankin has been so successful is that he was the first person to successfully transplant into Britain the mood and the feel of the great American private eye tradition," Knight wrote. "Although Rebus is a policeman, he is a troubled

loner with this mixture of morality and fallibility that seems to provide some deeper insight. Added to this Rankin has provided a very strong sense of place." In 2005 the Crime Writers Association, a British group that Rankin chaired in 1999–2000, awarded him the Diamond Dagger for Lifetime Achievement.

Ian James Rankin was born to James and Isobel Rankin on April 28, 1960 in Cardenden, a coal-mining town in Fife, an administrative area in eastern Scotland. His parents were then in their 40s; each had been widowed previously, and Rankin has one stepsister from his mother's first marriage and another from his father's. James Rankin was a grocery-store clerk and a dock worker; his wife had jobs in school and factory lunchrooms. (Rankin's mother died when he was a college freshman, his father 12 years later.) Neither the Rankins nor anybody they knew owned a car. The family's tiny home in Cardenden was owned by a local housing association, at the same site where several of their relatives lived. "As kids it was great, we were always going in and out, doors were always open to you. I loved it," Rankin told Thomas Quinn for the London *Observer* (September 17, 2006, posted online by the London *Guardian*). During his childhood Rankin and his father enjoyed working together on easy crossword puzzles printed in the local paper. His parents seldom read books, but Rankin made frequent use of Cardenen's public library, and at age seven or so, he started writing for himself—comics at first and then, as he got older, poetry and song lyrics. He won several prizes in poetry contests held by local newspapers. He also kept a diary beginning at age 10 and made daily entries until age 30. Rankin attended the Denend Primary School, in Cardenden; Auchterderran Junior High; and, starting at age 14, Beath High, an academically rigorous school in the nearby town of Cowdenbeath that prepared students for college admission. According to Nicholas Wroe, Rankin's writings at age 15 struck his English teacher, Ron Gillespie, as "evocative and darkly atmospheric." "He was really quite publishable even then," Gillespie said to Wroe.

Rankin was the first person in his family to attend college. In 1978 he entered the University of Edinburgh, where he joined the campus film and poetry clubs. He completed his undergraduate work in 1982, with an M.A. degree in English literature, and for the next three years pursued a doctoral degree in that field at the same university. He never received a Ph.D., however, because instead of completing his dissertation, whose subject was the novels of Muriel Spark, he spent much of his time writing fiction. (He was allowed to use the grant he received from the university to support any endeavor, not only those related to his degree. He wrote "over a thousand pages of my own work and just enough about Muriel Spark for [the school] not to kick me out," he told Wroe.) His first novel, *The Flood*, about a mother and son who are outcasts in their backward, closed-minded coal-mining community, reflects Rankin's interest in using imaginary events and characters to illuminate social issues. Published by a small University of Edinburgh press in 1986 in a print run of a few hundred, the book brought Rankin only £300 (about $440).

Meanwhile, in addition to his literary and academic activities, during the mid-1980s Rankin worked at a series of jobs: grape-picker, swineherd, tax man, alcohol researcher, editor for a hi-fi magazine, college secretary, and singer with a punk band called the Dancing Pigs. During that period, having begun to contemplate a career as a crime writer, he also read books by such veterans of that genre as Ruth Rendell, P. D. James, Reginald Hill, James Ellroy, and Lawrence Block. "The form was flexible," he told Wroe. "I could say everything I wanted to say about the world, and still give readers a pacy, gripping narrative."

In an article for Hachette Book Group USA (March 2007, on-line), Rankin wrote that John Rebus sprang to life in 1985, when the detective was 40 and the writer 24. "It was going to take some time for the pair of us to get to know one another," he continued, "which is why he evolves over the course of the series, not only ageing in real time but also learning from his mistakes, haunted by victims and unresolved cases." Rankin introduced Rebus in his first crime novel, *Knots and Crosses* (1987). (A rebus is a representation of words or syllables in the form of pictures—an eye for "I" or a bee followed by a gun for "begun," for example—or a puzzle that contains such images.) Rebus is the product of a working-class background very similar to Rankin's. Unlike his creator, he left school at 15 and served in the British military; his marriage has ended in divorce, and for long periods he has little face-to-face contact with his only child, a daughter. Although psychologically astute and highly skilled at crime solving, he remains in the lower ranks of the police, by choice and because of his tendency to defy authority. "Rebus knew his place in the food chain: somewhere down among the plankton, the price for years of insubordination and reckless conduct," Rankin wrote in *The Naming of the Dead* (2007). "This seems a fair assessment," Janet Maslin wrote in a review of that book for the *New York Times* (April 2, 2007). "So Rebus tends to be treated dismissively, but sooner or later those who underestimate him wind up sorry. The man is relentless once he shakes off his doldrums and gets into high gear." Rebus smokes heavily and drinks to excess. Except for his job and rock music, he seems to have no interests and no capacity for having fun; his romantic involvements are usually brief. He often broods about difficult social problems. His gruff, world-weary air hides his essential good nature. Nominally a Calvinist, he believes in God and finds solace in places of worship of any denomination. "Stubbornness is Rebus's most deep-seated characteristic," Nicholas Wroe wrote. "All the various ways in which he could improve the quality of his life—which boil down essentially

to his being less impossible—are somehow unthinkable. He stands in everybody else's way, but he stands in his own way too. [He is] difficult, determined, remorseless, honourable, honest, and proud of his lack of charm. . . . The lack of any attempt to be endearing is perhaps Rebus's best feature." Charles Taylor wrote that Rebus is "affable, more sadly resigned than possessed of a hair-trigger temper," and he "carries an air of doughy melancholy balanced by his sarcasm. He has a protective paternal side, particularly with his partner, Detective Sgt. Siobhan Clarke, which doesn't always make their relationship smooth. He also has the sort of smart mouth that sounds great coming from private detectives but always winds up getting a cop in trouble." "I find myself still fascinated by [Rebus], learning from him as well as about him . . . ," Rankin wrote for the Hachette Book Group USA Web site. "Often I'm not sure where I end and he begins, he's become such an integral part of me. When I see the world through his eyes, it becomes both scarier and more exciting."

Partly on the strength of a recommendation from Allan Massie, who, as writer in residence at Edinburgh University, had become acquainted with Rankin, Massie's publisher accepted *Knots and Crosses*, which five other firms had rejected. In *Knots and Crosses* Rebus investigates the abduction of three young girls, with the only clues to their disappearances being knotted strings and crosses made with matches. The book earned Rankin a contract for a sequel but little money. Earlier, in 1986, he had married and moved to London, England. "I had moments of panic all the time," he told Lesley McDowell for the London *Independent* (September 24, 2004). "I still do have moments of panic—you're only as good as your last book. I always panic that it's going to come crashing down around my ears." Unhappy as Londoners and eager to try to live self-sufficiently (by growing their own vegetables, for example), in 1990 he and his wife moved to a dilapidated house with a big yard in rural France, where Rankin devoted himself to writing. His next book, *Hide and Seek*, was published in 1991. It was followed in 1992 by both *Wolfman* (later renamed *Tooth and Nail*) and *A Good Hanging and Other Stories*, a collection of 12 Rebus tales. Sales of his books were modest, and Rankin and his wife had difficulty in making ends meet. In 1992, when his agent suggested that he write a series of mainstream thrillers under a pseudonym, Rankin signed a three-book contract, choosing as his pen name Jack Harvey—Jack being the name of his newborn son and Harvey his wife's surname. The first of the Jack Harvey books, *Witch Hunt*, was published in 1993; the second, *Bleeding Hearts*, in 1994; and the third, *Blood Hunt*, in 1995. "I suppose *Witch Hunt* was an experiment; in fact all the Jack Harvey novels were: they were ways of playing with ideas and structural problems outside the scope of my detective series," Rankin wrote for his Web site. In a review of *Witch Hunt* after it was reissued with Rankin's name as author, Eleanor

Bukowsky wrote for the Mostly Fiction Web site (September 5, 2005), "Although it is a bit long and meanders occasionally, I enjoyed *Witch Hunt.* Rankin explores the intricacies of both police and intelligence work, showing that patience, persistence, and luck are all factors in a successful outcome. Witch is a fascinating uber-assassin, beautiful, changeable, brilliant, and ruthless. Rankin takes pains to humanize her, however, and we learn how she came to be one of the world's most sought-after killers. The ending is a nail-biter, filled with non-stop action and a few surprises to keep the reader off-balance. All in all, its dry humor, varied and well-drawn characters, sharp dialogue, and engrossing depiction of investigative techniques make *Witch Hunt* a winner."

Meanwhile, Rankin had continued to produce his Rebus novels at a brisk pace. *Strip Jack*, published in 1994, is the last of the Rebus books in which Rankin used fictitious settings; the police station, bars, streets, and other sites in its successors are real places. *The Black Book* and *Mortal Causes* were also published in 1994, and *Let It Bleed* in 1995. In 1996 Rankin moved to Edinburgh with his family; he had learned little French and was feeling homesick, and his publisher had suggested that Rankin's Rebus books might be more marketable if the author were living in Scotland.

The turning point in Rankin's career came with *Black and Blue* (1997), the eighth Rebus book, which became an international best-seller—it sold four times as many copies as any of his previous Rebus novels—and won, in Great Britain, the Crime Writers Association Macallan Gold Dagger for fiction. Rankin has attributed the success of *Black and Blue* to a change in his state of mind: while he was writing it, his second son, Kit, was diagnosed with a genetic disorder called Angelman's syndrome, whose symptoms include mental retardation, severely limited or no ability to speak, unprovoked and frequent laughter, seizures, spastic arm movements, and gait problems. The distress and anxiety that that news produced in Rankin and his wife significantly affected his writing. "I do get a lot of [emotional] stuff out in my books," he told Wroe, "and there was a definite shift from *Let It Bleed* . . . to *Black and Blue.* . . . [The latter] was a much bigger, angrier and more questioning book that reflected my personal experience with Kit." In *Black and Blue* Rebus simultaneously investigates three murders that he believes are the work of one killer; meanwhile, he himself becomes subjected to intense media scrutiny regarding an old case involving an apparent miscarriage of justice. Lewis Reed, a reviewer for the London *Sunday Times* (February 1, 1998), called *Black and Blue* "a first-rate and gripping novel" and wrote, "Rankin excels himself here as Rebus comes of age." In an assessment of *Black and Blue* for *Scotland on Sunday* (January 26, 1997), Peter Whitebrook wrote that Rankin's fiction "fizzes with energy." "Essentially, he is a romantic storyteller in the tradition of Robert Louis Stevenson," Whitebrook continued, "yet

at the same time he is a harsh moralist, and the edges of his world are bleak and unforgiving places indeed. . . . His prose is as vivid and terse as the next man's, yet its flexibility and rhythm give it a potential for lyrical expression which is distinctively Rankin's own." In a critique for the *San Francisco Chronicle* (December 14, 1997), Peter Handel labeled the Rebus novels "brilliant" and wrote that the plot of *Black and Blue* "is complex without ever becoming convoluted. . . . The way Rankin orchestrates three seemingly disparate cases—from past and present—into a coherent and plausible whole is the work of a master, as is the bang-up and compelling denouement."

In *The Hanging Garden* (1998), in which Rebus investigates a suspected World War II criminal and a spate of gang violence, the detective suffers a personal blow, when his now-adult daughter, Samantha, is severely injured in a hit-and-run car accident and must spend months in a wheelchair. Rankin has linked that plot element to his learning that his son Kit might never walk. "Just because I was feeling bad, Rebus had to feel bad as well," Rankin told Bjornsson. He also admitted, "I felt really embarrassed about it because I thought that was very petty and small minded of me to do that to my own fictional character." (While Kit, now a teenager, is unable to walk, talk, or feed or dress himself, in a later book Rankin had Samantha make a full recovery.)

The next Rebus novel, *Dead Souls* (1999), was followed by *Set in Darkness* (2000). A London *Sunday Times* Top 10 best-seller, that book finds Rebus searching for the perpetrators of a series of murders connected to the first session of the Scottish Parliament to be held in modern times (in 1999). "I think the books are getting more political as I get older," Rankin told Bjornsson. "A story comes from me getting interested in some big question coming into my head and in order to answer that question or explore that theme, I write a book." Rankin told Lynn Barber for the London *Observer* (November 18, 2007, as posted on-line by the *Guardian*) that the ideas for his plots come to him unbidden, sometimes almost as if they were "channeled" to him. "Even he finds his creative fluency mysterious," Barber wrote. Generally, Rankin has told interviewers, he does not know, until he is well along in the writing of a book, who the culprit will be or the identities of all the characters who will be murdered during the course of the story.

The year 2001 saw the publication of *The Falls*, which, according to Antonia Fraser, writing for the London *Telegraph* (March 19, 2001), shows Rankin "at his brilliant, mordant best, with the dark heart of [Edinburgh] featuring almost as strongly as Rebus himself." Three Rebus novels appeared in 2004: *Resurrection Man*, which won the Edgar Award for best novel and Germany's Deutsche Krimi Prize; *A Question of Blood*; and *Fleshmarket Close* (retitled *Fleshmarket Alley* in the U.S.), named Crime Thriller of the Year at the 2005 British Book Awards ceremony. *The Naming of the*

Dead (2006), which won the same honor, is set at the 2005 meeting of the Group of Eight (G8), which met that year in Edinburgh. In her critique of that novel, Janet Maslin noted that, like most of its predecessors, it contains minor tangential plots, many supporting characters, and much small talk. "These dilatory tactics aren't a drawback; they are among the most likeable features of this top-flight, enduring series," Maslin wrote. "The books use a deceptively casual tone to worm their way into Rebus's thoughts. Although it is de rigueur to know what music a crime-novel star likes to listen to, what a shambles his private life has become, what he eats for breakfast and drinks for dinner, Mr. Rankin gets just as much mileage out of showing how Rebus circles around and around a problem. He meanders very slyly until he's ready to pounce. . . . A book with this many plot elements risks becoming amorphous and overcomplicated. But Mr. Rankin doesn't get lost that way. In his backhanded, reluctant way Rebus winds up uniting all the book's loose ends, and seeing how he accomplishes this is a pleasure. Besides, *The Naming of the Dead* isn't really about its detective plot. It's about Rebus's taking stock, not only of his own past but also of the world around him." *Exit Music*, in which Rebus retires, was published in Great Britain in 2007 and came out in the U.S. in 2008.

Also in 2008 Rankin published *Doors Open*. "Fans of Rankin's successful Inspector Rebus series can stop crying into their whiskies," Melissa McClements wrote in a review for the *Financial Times* (October 13, 2008). "The publication last year of *Exit Music*, the final novel featuring the hard-drinking detective, has not stopped its author writing some excellent new tartan noir." Similarly, John Dugale wrote for the *Sunday Times* (October 5, 2008) that Rankin's latest novel "convincingly shows that he can move with aplomb into another crime form, and tell a story that's typically at once gripping and full of subtle effects, without his depressive detective holding it together."

Rankin assisted in the making of a three-part television documentary series about evil—its nature in various cultures, its causes, and ways of dealing with it—which aired in Great Britain in 2002. In 2004 he and the Scottish singer/songwriter Jackie Leven gave joint performances in which they appeared alternately on stage, with Rankin reading some of his stories and Leven singing his own songs; their two-disk CD, *Jackie Leven Said*, was recorded at one of those concerts. Rankin wrote the text for the guidebook cum memoir *Rebus's Scotland* (2006), which is illustrated with photographs. In 2005 Rankin hosted a 30-minute BBC Four documentary called *Rankin on the Staircase*; inspired by the earlier, eight-part documentary *Death on the Staircase*, it discussed problems inherent in crime writing that blends elements of real-life cases with fiction.

Rankin won a Hawthornden Castle Fellowship in 1988 and a Chandler-Fulbright Award in 1992. He became an Officer of the British Empire in 2002,

and in 2005 *GQ* named him Writer of Year. In 2008 he was named ITV 3 Crime Thriller Author of the Year, for his book *Exit Music*. He lives with his wife, Miranda, and two sons in the upscale Merchiston section of Edinburgh, whose residents also include the writers J. K. Rowling and Alexander McCall Smith. A substantial part of his income pays for daily caregivers for his son Kit, who attends a special school; Rankin and his wife minister to Kit at night and on weekends. The couple donate their services to the organization Special Needs Information Point (Snipinfo.org) and other charitable groups. For a short while on Friday nights, when he is not on promotional tours for his books, Rankin enjoys the company of friends in the Oxford Bar in Edinburgh, John Rebus's favorite watering hole.

—C.S.

Suggested Reading: Hachette Book Group USA Web site Mar. 2007; hackwriters.com 2001; ianrankin.net; *Irish Times* p74 Feb. 14, 1998; (London) *Guardian* (on-line) Sep. 8, 2007, Nov. 18, 2007; (London) *Independent* p24+ Sep. 24, 2004; *New York Times* E p1+ Jan. 3, 2002; powells.com; *Reykjavik (Iceland) Grapevine* (on-line) June 30, 2006

Selected Books: fiction—*The Flood*, 1986; *Knots and Crosses*, 1987; *Hide and Seek*, 1991; *Tooth and Nail*, 1992; *A Good Hanging and Other Stories*, 1992; *Witch Hunt*, 1993; *Bleeding Hearts*, 1994; *Strip Jack*, 1994; *Black Book*, 1994; *Mortal Causes*, 1994; *Blood Hunt*, 1995; *Let It Bleed*, 1995; *Black and Blue*, 1997; *The Hanging Garden*, 1998; *Dead Souls*, 1999; *Set in Darkness*, 2000; *The Falls*, 2001; *Beggars Banquet*, 2002; *Resurrection Man*, 2004; *A Question of Blood*, 2004; *Fleshmarket Close*, 2004; *The Naming of the Dead*, 2006; *Exit Music*, 2007; *Doors Open*, 2008; nonfiction—*Rebus's Scotland*, 2006

Raven-Symone

Dec. 10, 1985– Actress; singer

Address: c/o Hollywood Records, 500 S. Buena Vista St., Burbank, CA 91521

"I think Raven has a very old soul and, in many respects, she is far beyond her years in terms of insight and judgment and the way she views the world," the film producer Debra Martin Chase told Harriette Cole for *Ebony* (March 2007), describing the actress and singer Raven-Symone. "The challenge for her at this point, as it is for all young performers, is to transition her artistry into adulthood and both bring her young fan base along with her and build an older fan base." A show-business vet-

Raven-Symone

Scott Gries/Getty Images

eran who has been in the public eye for most of her 22 years, Raven-Symone first found fame in 1989, when, at the age of three, she joined the cast of the enormously popular NBC sitcom *The Cosby Show*. She portrayed Olivia, the uncommonly smart and sassy step-granddaughter of Heathcliff Huxtable, played by Bill Cosby, until 1992, when the series ended. "She was never quite like the other children [on the show]," Phylicia Rashad, who starred as the Cosby character's wife, Claire Huxtable, told Cole. "It was apparent that she had chosen a direction in life about which she was very definite and would not veer from."

After her work on *The Cosby Show*, Raven-Symone appeared on a number of TV shows, such as *Hangin' with Mr. Cooper*, and acted in several films, most notably *Dr. Dolittle* (1998) and *Dr. Dolittle 2* (2001), both of which starred Eddie Murphy. Despite her steady film and TV work, Raven-Symone did not truly return to the spotlight until 2003, when she became the star of the Disney Channel show *That's So Raven*. For four seasons she played Raven Baxter, a high-school student with the ability to see glimpses of the future. The show was a huge hit, particularly with "tween" girls, aged eight to 12. According to some reports, the series, along with its accompanying merchandise, earned Disney more than $400 million. In addition, Raven-Symone has released four albums, the most recent in April 2008.

Often praised for her work ethic and professionalism, Raven-Symone has eluded the kinds of scandals that have plagued other Hollywood starlets, establishing herself as a role model for young women. "I'm happy that people still care to watch me," she told the Associated Press (March 23,

2008). "It's difficult to grow up and make certain decisions. I'm glad that people still see me as doing the right thing."

The older of two children, Raven-Symone Christina Pearman was born on December 10, 1985 in Atlanta, Georgia. Her father, Christopher, is a musician; her mother, Lydia, is a computer-systems analyst. When she was two she moved with her parents to New York City, where she began modeling and acting in TV commercials. In 1989 she auditioned for the film *Ghost Dad*, which starred Bill Cosby. While she did not get that part—casting executives considered her too young—she soon had another chance to work with Cosby, as the writers for *The Cosby Show* were in the process of developing a new child character. Raven-Symone won the role of Olivia, the stepdaughter of Denise Huxtable (one of Cosby's onscreen daughters), portrayed by Lisa Bonet.

The young actress won high marks for her work on *The Cosby Show*, serving as "a hilarious comedy foil" for Cosby, according to the Queensland, Australia, *Sunday Mail* (July 15, 1990). With the help of her father, Raven-Symone memorized her lines quickly, even though she was not yet old enough to read. "The first day on the set, it was clear that the child WANTED this," Cosby told Cole. "This child was born wanting this, before she could even talk. There's really no need for me to tell her anything. Whatever I could tell her to do, she's done it. Whatever I would warn her to watch out for, she's already watched out for it. She is very smart." Raven-Symone remained part of the cast until 1992, when the show ended its eight-season run. By then she had already become the youngest solo singer to sign a deal with MCA Records, and her first album, *Here's to New Dreams*, was released in 1993.

That same year Raven-Symone played the child who grows up to be Halle Berry's character in the TV miniseries *Queen* and signed on for another sitcom, *Hangin' with Mr. Cooper*. For four seasons, while attending public school in Atlanta, she portrayed Nicole Lee, the daughter of the title character's cousin. In 1994 she earned a role in the film *The Little Rascals*. In 1996, at the age of 10, she worked briefly as a TV reporter, filing positive stories about area youth for Atlanta's NBC affiliate. "You always see a lot of violence and what's going bad in the world," she told Jon Lafayette for *Electronic Media* (April 1, 1996). "I wanted to do something good." In addition to reporting on local affairs, she interviewed such stars as Liza Minnelli and the Atlanta Braves pitcher Tom Glavine. In 1998 she appeared in her first blockbuster film, *Dr. Dolittle*, a comedy starring Eddie Murphy, and three years later she reprised her role as Murphy's daughter, Charisse, in *Dr. Dolittle 2*. Even so, at the age of 15, she was finding it difficult to distance herself in the public mind from Olivia, the character for which she remained best known. "Some people don't believe I am as old as I am now," she told the Detroit *Michigan Chronicle* (July 18, 2001).

"I just have to let them get used to it. They are surprised at how I look now. But this is how 15 year olds look, dress and act. But they're like, 'No, I just saw you on *The Cosby Show* yesterday!' They don't want me to grow up, but it happens."

In 1999 Raven-Symone released her second album, *Undeniable*. The collection featured a version of "With a Child's Heart," a song originally recorded by Michael Jackson, as well as a track called "I Love You," penned by Stevie Wonder, who performed on the album. Calling the album's songs "danceable teen pop," Stephen Thomas Erlewine wrote for the All Music Guide Web site, "While the album is flawed, Symone does prove she can sing." Though she put her acting on hold to focus on music—she even toured with the platinum-selling boy band N' Sync—she found time to appear in *Zenon: Girl of the 21st Century* (1999), a Disney made-for-TV movie.

In 2003 Raven-Symone began work on *That's So Raven*, a Disney show aimed at tween girls. (Around that time she shortened her stage name to Raven, purportedly because her character went by the same name, and she did not want to confuse young fans. She later adopted her full first name once again.) When she auditioned for the show, originally called "Absolutely Psychic," she was slated to play the best friend of the clairvoyant main character. Producers were so impressed by her audition, though, that they reworked the show to center on her.

Since her days on the set of *Hangin' with Mr. Cooper*, Raven-Symone had split her time between Atlanta and Los Angeles, California, and she continued to attend Atlanta's public North Springs High School through her sophomore year. (She received home schooling during her junior and senior years and graduated in 2004.) While her classmates were slow to accept her, expecting her to be conceited, she eventually made friends and enjoyed what she has described as a fairly normal high-school experience. "I didn't get to go to prom, but I made a movie about it," she told Andrew Hampp for the *Columbus (Ohio) Dispatch* (August 16, 2006), referring to *For One Night* (2006), a Lifetime network TV movie in which she starred. The movie tells the true story of a girl who fights against her high school's policy of holding racially segregated proms.

While starring in *That's So Raven*, Raven-Symone appeared in the Disney TV movies *The Cheetah Girls* (2003) and *The Cheetah Girls 2* (2006), playing Galleria, a member of an all-girl teenage band. In 2004 she had a bit part in the feature film *The Princess Diaries 2: Royal Engagement*, singing alongside the actress Julie Andrews, and in 2005 she provided the voice of Monique for Disney's animated TV movie *Kim Possible: So the Drama*. (She had voiced that character on the *Kim Possible* series since 2002.) Meanwhile, *That's So Raven* achieved unprecedented popularity, and by 2006 it had become the most popular basic-cable show among female viewers aged nine to 14. While Disney typically capped its shows at 65 episodes, it extended *That's So Raven* to 100 and sold many items of related merchandise, including a fragrance and cosmetics. "It's corny, good, family-friendly humor," Raven-Symone told Rodney Ho for the *Atlanta Journal-Constitution* (February 6, 2006), describing the show's appeal. Full-figured, at least compared with other, stick-thin Hollywood actresses (such as her onetime roommate, Lindsay Lohan), Raven-Symone won praise for showing young viewers a different standard of beauty. "I'm healthy even though I'm not a size two," she said. "I'm not on the cover of fashion magazines. But I know when I go out, the mothers come up to me and thank me for being a good role model for kids, for girls of all sizes."

Raven-Symone served as a producer during the fourth and final season of *That's So Raven*, and at one point she was even offered a chance to direct an episode. (She turned it down, believing it would be too difficult to act and direct simultaneously.) "A lot of kids start off cute but don't evolve into supreme comediennes," the television director Richard Correll told Denise Abbott for the *Hollywood Reporter* (August 1, 2006). "Raven's just got it—a God-given talent. She's a valuable asset to anyone doing comedy because she lifts everyone's performance. I've been directing sitcoms for 33 years, and I've never come across anyone as strong in terms of both spoken and physical comedy." Raven-Symone spent the summer of 2006 touring in support of her third album, *This Is My Time*, which had been released in 2004. By the time *That's So Raven* ended its run, the show had earned Disney a reported $400 million.

In 2008 Raven-Symone appeared in and produced the film *College Road Trip*, a G-rated comedy starring Martin Lawrence. "When you say 'G' rating, people have such a kiddie connotation put on it," she told Bob Longino for the *Atlanta Journal-Constitution* (March 7, 2008). "But it means general. For everyone. You don't need to cuss or talk about sex or talk about drugs to be entertained." That wholesomeness has apparently carried over into her personal life, and Raven-Symone has thus far avoided the elements of fame that have felled many of her peers.

Raven-Symone won "favorite female TV actress" honors at the 2004 and 2005 Nickelodeon Kids' Choice Awards, and she has also received two NAACP Image Awards. Known for her business acumen, she is said to have followed a five-point plan she drew up at the age of 15. To date, she has accomplished three of her goals, having created a production company, That's So Productions; launched a DVD series; and founded her own Web site, www.Ravensymonepresents.com, which offers tips to young girls. Her remaining two goals are to begin licensing her own merchandise and create her own record label. Raven-Symone has been called a spendthrift, her chief vice involving expensive shoes. She has said that she would like to attend college one day, possibly to study culinary arts. "I like to make it very flavorful and really buttery," she told Kathy Stephenson for the *Salt Lake Tribune* (September 4, 2006), describing the food she cooks. She released her self-titled fourth album in April 2008.

—K.J.P.

Suggested Reading: *Atlanta Journal-Constitution* E p3 Mar. 7, 2008; *Columbus (Ohio) Dispatch* H p1 Aug. 16, 2006; (Durham, North Carolina) *Herald-Sun* C p8 Jan. 15, 2003; *Ebony* p58 Mar. 2007; *Hollywood Reporter* Aug. 1, 2006; *Jet* p60 Sep. 8, 2003; *Toronto Star* M p4 Oct. 14, 2006; *USA Today* D p3 Oct. 26, 1989

Selected Television Shows: *The Cosby Show*, 1989–92; *Hangin' with Mr. Cooper*, 1993–97; *That's So Raven*, 2003–07

Selected Films: *The Little Rascals*, 1994; *Dr. Dolittle*, 1998; *Dr. Dolittle 2*, 2001; *The Princess Diaries 2: Royal Engagement*, 2004; *College Road Trip*, 2008

Selected Recordings: *Here's to New Dreams*, 1993; *Undeniable*, 1999; *This Is My Time*, 2004; *Raven-Symone*, 2008

Courtesy of CFMA Pittsburgh

Ravenstahl, Luke

Feb. 6, 1980– Mayor of Pittsburgh (Democrat)

Address: Office of the Mayor, Rm. 512, City County Bldg., 414 Grant St., Pittsburgh, PA 15219

On September 1, 2006, after the sudden death of Bob O'Connor, the mayor of Pittsburgh, Pennsylvania, Luke Ravenstahl became—at 26—Pittsburgh's 59th mayor and the youngest person in U.S. history to take the top post of a major city. Ravenstahl, who in 2003 had become the youngest person ever elected to Pittsburgh's city council, was already known for bringing ambition and a much-needed youthful perspective to an old steel-driven city that had seen its population and tax base drastically reduced over the last several decades. In late

2005, when the incumbent city-council president, Gene Ricciardi, declined to seek another term, Ravenstahl emerged as a compromise candidate to fill the position after seasoned council members each failed to receive the five votes needed for a majority. Once he assumed office, in January 2006, he began working closely with the newly elected mayor, O'Connor, to reduce Pittsburgh's exorbitant debt and revitalize the city's downtown area. As O'Connor's next-in-line successor, Ravenstahl was sworn in as mayor the night of O'Connor's death. "Ravenstahl is a perfect storm of ambition, political pedigree and luck, and it has taken him far," Morton Coleman, a professor of social work at the University of Pittsburgh, told Ian Urbina for the *New York Times* (September 9, 2006). "But it has also left him with a lot to prove." As mayor, Ravenstahl has worked to fulfill goals put forth by O'Connor, emphasizing a business-oriented approach to alleviating the city's fiscal problems and embracing a "neighborhoods first" theme to facilitate a better rapport between city government and residents. Enormously popular, Ravenstahl won the city's May 2007 Democratic primary with 96 percent of the vote, despite a number of controversies that led observers to blame his youth for some of his poor decisions. On November 6, 2007, in a special mayoral election, Ravenstahl defeated the Republican Mark DeSantis, winning 63 percent of the vote. He explained, according to David M. Brown, writing for the *Pittsburgh Tribune Review* (September 23, 2007), "I don't care if you are 27 or 57, when you walk into the mayor's office, it's an eye-opening experience and one that no textbook or no political background is going to teach you. You are there, and you are learning on the job and that's what I've been able to do over the past year."

The eldest of the three children of Robert and Cindy Ravenstahl, Luke Robert Ravenstahl was born on February 6, 1980 in Pittsburgh and raised in the working-class neighborhood of Summer Hill, on the city's North Side. His father worked his way up the ranks of the city's sewer and water authority before being elected a district judge; his mother worked as a local crossing guard and later became a teacher's aide. Ravenstahl's political ties date back to his grandfather, Robert Ravenstahl Sr., who served as a Democratic ward leader and state representative for the North Side, until he was defeated in 1976 by Tom Murphy. (Murphy went on to become Pittsburgh's mayor, serving from January 1994 until January 2006.) "My family was always involved in public service," Ravenstahl noted to Dan Majors for the *Pittsburgh Post-Gazette* (October 21, 2007), "so it was always something I was involved in and appreciated because of the gratification I know my family received out of public service and helping people." Ravenstahl remembers his father's "getting calls at 10 or 11 o'clock at night when somebody had a question or an issue," as he told Majors. He worked on his father's political campaigns, knocking on doors and handing out literature, beginning when he was 12 or 13.

Ravenstahl attended the prestigious North Catholic High School in the neighborhood of Troy Hill, where he excelled in academics and sports. While there, he took advanced math classes, served as president of the student council, and was quarterback, kicker, and captain of the football team as well as second baseman on the baseball team. His experience on the student council helped reinforce his interest in entering politics. Tim Banner, Ravenstahl's former high-school baseball coach, told Rich Lord for the *Pittsburgh Post-Gazette* (October 8, 2006), "I think baseball taught [Ravenstahl] a lot about keeping on an even keel. If you don't keep your cool, you get in trouble." Banner added, "He had a boyish side to him once in a while, but he was mature. Wherever he was, I didn't have to worry about anything going wrong." In one of the highlights of his athletic career, Ravenstahl hit a game-winning home run during the play-offs. He graduated from North Catholic with honors in 1998.

That year Ravenstahl enrolled at Mercyhurst College, in Erie, Pennsylvania, where he was a kicker for the school football team. A year later he transferred to the University of Pittsburgh, in an unsuccessful attempt to make it as a walk-on player for that school's football team. He eventually settled in at Washington and Jefferson College, in Washington, Pennsylvania, where he set the school record for field goals. John Banaszak, a former defensive lineman for the Pittsburgh Steelers of the National Football League, who coached Ravenstahl at Washington and Jefferson, noted to Lord, "He was a very good kicker. The tougher the kick, or if you were in a situation where time was running out . . . he thrived on that." Banaszak noted to Ian Urbina, "Luke is very mature and doesn't make the same mistake twice." He recalled an instance when Ravenstahl failed to follow instructions for a kickoff during one of his college games: "I chewed him out, and he never disobeyed an instruction the rest of his career. I think he takes that same wisdom with him in politics in that he knows when he is getting good advice and he follows it." During his college years Ravenstahl coached base-

ball at North Catholic and worked summer jobs at the post office, the University of Pittsburgh Medical Center, and the city controller's office. He graduated with honors from Washington and Jefferson in December 2002, earning a B.A. degree in business administration.

Ravenstahl's first job after college was as an account manager for an overnight-shipping firm. During that time he became interested in running for Pittsburgh's city council. "My mom did not like the idea," he recalled to Majors. "Just because of the political world that we live in. Probably, from the mother's point of view, the protective side of things . . . [she] didn't want to see her son, specifically at the age of 23, be exposed to the political world. . . . But that quickly went away when I made my mind up." Over the next several months, Ravenstahl, through the help and support of his family and relatives, mounted a door-to-door, grassroots campaign, emphasizing the city council's need for a fresh voice. The demands of the campaign forced him to skip his college-graduation ceremony, which took place two days before the city's May 2003 Democratic primary—in which he faced the incumbent Barbara Burns for the council's Ward One seat. He easily defeated Burns, and after winning an uncontested general election that November, Ravenstahl became, at 23, the youngest member ever elected to the Pittsburgh city council. For a time after his election, he continued to work for the shipping firm during the day while immersing himself in city-related projects at night, a schedule he has recalled as "overwhelming." City councilman Jim Motznik told Majors, "He spent six months sitting in on budget discussions in my office even before he was sworn in. He didn't give us input, he didn't tell us his opinions. He sat on the couch and he listened and he learned about what the process was all about. It made a huge impression on me."

Ravenstahl assumed his council seat in January 2004. In August of that year, he married Erin Lynn Feith, his longtime girlfriend and high-school sweetheart. Ravenstahl adopted a business-minded approach to his work as a councilman, which included opposition to the state-sponsored Act 47 Recovery Plan, an initiative whose cost-cutting measures included a two-year wage freeze for city employees and a new health-care plan that would require employees to contribute 15 percent toward costs. That December, however, he decided to vote in favor of the plan, after the rest of the council united behind it. In addition to advocating measures aimed at fiscal responsibility, which included a resolution that called for new controls on council spending, Ravenstahl brought a needed youthful perspective to the council, placing a strong emphasis on issues related to Pittsburgh's technological adaptability. He was one of several council members who led the city's entrance into the wireless Internet age, helping to facilitate a plan that allowed laptop users two hours of free Internet access from park benches.

In late 2005 Gene Ricciardi, then president of the nine-member city council, announced that he would resign the presidency by year's end. It was rumored that he was making the move to secure the presidency for his friend, Jim Motznik. Motznik, however, was unable to secure a fifth vote from his colleagues, needed for a majority. When other veteran members each failed to line up the five required votes, including Councilwoman Twanda Carlisle, who also came within a vote of the presidency, Ravenstahl emerged as the council's compromise candidate. On December 6, 2005 he was elected to the presidency by a 5–2 vote; he was unanimously elected to a two-year term in January 2006, after Ricciardi officially relinquished his post.

As council president Ravenstahl worked closely with Bob O'Connor's administration to oppose a nonbinding measure to remove general fiscal oversight by the state, to the displeasure of the politically powerful firefighters' union. (Under the newly amended, state-sponsored Act 47 Recovery Plan, greater controls were put on the firefighters' contract, which included the closing of six fire stations, the freezing of firefighter wages through 2006, and increasing firefighter health-care payments.) He also succeeded in passing legislation for tighter oversight of council members' spending, after an investigation into the discretionary spending habits of Councilwoman Carlisle, who had paid $178,000 to consultants since 2002. Under Ravenstahl's proposal, consultants and temporary employees hired by council members were now required to sign detailed contracts and to show evidence of the work they performed. Council members were also prohibited from transferring money from their staff-salary funds into their allocation accounts for other expenses. Other measures Ravenstahl took as president included the rejection of a city policy that limited staff members' Internet use to 30 minutes per day, and the introduction of legislation to raise money by selling advertising space on city-owned property.

During the summer of 2006, Mayor O'Connor underwent chemotherapy for a rare form of brain cancer. O'Connor, one of Pittsburgh's most beloved mayors in recent years, had developed a reputation as a gregarious figure who would often take strolls through Pittsburgh's residential neighborhoods to talk with citizens about a wide variety of issues. When O'Connor succumbed to his illness, on September 1, 2006, Ravenstahl became the youngest mayor in Pittsburgh's history and the youngest mayor of any major city in the country. On the day after O'Connor's death, Ravenstahl ordered all city flags to be flown at half-mast. He said to Joe Mandak for the Associated Press (September 9, 2006), "Bob O'Connor was a mentor of mine, really a role model for me. To be honest with you, I wouldn't be sitting here as mayor without his help in the council presidency vote last year." Upon being sworn in, Ravenstahl acknowledged that his age would be a source of concern for some. He took im-

mediate action to fulfill goals that had been planned during the O'Connor administration, including the popular "Redd-Up" ("Readying up") campaign, which aimed to clean up and revitalize dilapidated city buildings and houses; nonetheless, Ravenstahl's arrival at City Hall was met with something less than enthusiasm—particularly since he had inherited the bulk of his predecessor's staff. Two weeks into his tenure, he made a high-profile appearance on the *Late Show* with the famed talk-show host David Letterman in an effort to promote the city of Pittsburgh. On the show, referring to his campaign for a seat on the city council, he quipped to Letterman, as noted by Timothy McNulty for the *Pittsburgh Post-Gazette* (September 15, 2006), "There were times, I'll be honest with you, that I got thrown off porches. People would tell me they had sons or daughters [who] were 23 years old and the last thing they'd ever want them to do was become a City Council member." During his visit to New York to film the show, he also met briefly with Mayor Michael Bloomberg to sign a document calling for stricter federal gun controls, which had been signed by dozens of mayors around the country since the spring of 2006.

One of Ravenstahl's first acts as mayor was to tackle "quality-of-life" issues in Pittsburgh by using a "neighborhoods first" approach that focused in turn on each of the city's districts. Through the "Redd-Up" campaign he was able to double the funds raised by the O'Connor administration for the downtown-revitalization project. He told Dan Reynolds for the Pittsburgh *Business Times* (September 18, 2006), "I think our responsibility as a government is not just to clean [residents'] streets and pave their streets and pick up their garbage, but to invest real dollars, real economic development dollars, in those neighborhoods." The recovery plan received a boost when Ravenstahl gained control of the downtown area's property-tax liens at only a fraction of the cost, which helped with a plan to transform condemned property into livable residences. (Over the previous several decades, the shrinking of Pittsburgh's population had resulted in an overabundance of vacant properties and a reduced tax base, leading to blight in certain neighborhoods.) In an effort to facilitate better communication between the city government and residents, Ravenstahl created a 311 telephone line. Initially proposed by O'Connor and inspired by Michael Bloomberg's 311 line in New York, the "Ravenstahl Response Line" handled constituent complaints and queries. Ravenstahl reinstated the city's "beat-cop" program, which helped to deter crime through increased police presence while fostering personal relationships between city residents and members of the police force. Ravenstahl also set out to modernize the city, one of his goals being to make Pittsburgh, generally known as an old steel-mill town rife with pollution, a nationwide leader in the "green" movement. In April 2007, as a result of Ravenstahl's efforts, the publication *Places Rated Almanac*, for the first time since 1985, declared Pittsburgh to be "America's Most Livable City."

As a means of achieving fiscal stability, Ravenstahl created the Blue Ribbon Economic Development team. Early in his mayorship he initiated and hosted a municipal-pension summit at the 108th Annual Convention of the Pennsylvania League of Cities and Municipalities (PLCM), where he addressed pension problems that had plagued city budgets nationwide. As noted by a writer for *US States News* (June 18, 2007), he said, "The pension problem, seen at all levels of government and in local authorities, has become Pennsylvania's version of the national security problem." Ravenstahl submitted balanced-budget proposals that lowered the city's debt and saved another $17 million by reducing the number of Pittsburgh's health-care providers for government employees from three to one. By the end of his first year in office, Ravenstahl's business acumen had resulted in a $42 million budget surplus. Other measures included a pledge to improve relations with legislators in Harrisburg, the state capital, and the signing of a $712,112 contract with officials from the nearby borough of Wilkinsburg, located in Allegheny County, whereby Pittsburgh would provide trash-collection services there. Ravenstahl explained to Jeremy Boren for the *Pittsburgh Tribune Review* (November 17, 2006), "We're going to continue as a city government to look at ways we can cooperate with other municipalities and other entities of government to provide cheaper services and to provide more efficient services to our residents." In May 2007 Ravenstahl ran unopposed in the Democratic primary, winning an astonishing 96 percent of the vote, the largest margin of victory in Pittsburgh's 250-year history.

Despite his many accomplishments, Ravenstahl found himself embroiled in a number of controversies as a city councilman and mayor. The first, referred to by the press as "Heinz-gate," involved his actions at a Pittsburgh Steelers game at Heinz Field on October 31, 2005; then-councilman Ravenstahl was handcuffed for allegedly shoving and shouting profanity at a police officer, who had aggressively handled a crowd of fans waiting to enter the stadium. For several months Ravenstahl dismissed the confrontation to reporters as "much ado about nothing," then owned up to the scuffle in January 2007, admitting that police had handcuffed and detained him. On March 13, 2007 Ravenstahl received widespread criticism for traveling to New York aboard a Boeing 757 private jet owned by the billionaire investor Ron Burkle, co-owner of the Pittsburgh Penguins hockey franchise, on the same day that a development deal was made to secure $290 million toward the building of a casino and new multipurpose arena for the team in the city's impoverished Hill District. The trip prevented Ravenstahl from attending an important meeting with residents of the neighborhood. Early in the day on March 19, Ravenstahl denied having taken the trip, but later that afternoon he admitted to having done

so, saying that he had gone to New York to discuss campaign fund-raising. In June 2007 Ravenstahl sparked the ire of the Pittsburgh city-county Women's Commission after promoting three police officers who had allegedly committed acts of domestic violence. Instead of attending the meetings protesting the appointments, he chose to take part in a charity golf event hosted by the Mario Lemieux Foundation and paid for by the University of Pittsburgh Medical Center (UPMC) and the Pittsburgh Penguins, both of which have business arrangements with the city. After it was disclosed that the participation fees for Ravenstahl and the two UPMC executives accompanying him had totaled around $27,000, he was called in front of Pittsburgh's Ethics Hearing Board, which sought to determine whether he had violated the ethics code. While he was not found guilty of a violation, the panel later recommended that the city impose stricter rules regarding city officials' attendance at charitable events. Later that summer the mayor was criticized for using a sport utility vehicle (SUV), purchased with a federal Homeland Security grant for police purposes, to take his wife to a concert by the country-and-western star Toby Keith. Ravenstahl said to David M. Brown in the fall of 2007, "No matter what decision you make you are always going to have critics. That's just part of being mayor. My skin is a lot thicker today than it was a year ago at this time." Doug Shields, Pittsburgh's current city-council president, noted to Ian Urbina for the *New York Times* (October 8, 2007) about the various controversies, "They were all dumb moves on the mayor's part." He added, "At the same time, I have to admit, none of the mistakes he has made have materially affected the city."

On November 6, 2007 Pittsburgh held a special mayoral election, pitting Ravenstahl against the Republican challenger Mark DeSantis, a businessman and adjunct professor at Carnegie Mellon University; the two had met for seven debates in the months preceding the election. Although DeSantis tried to capitalize on the young mayor's various missteps, winning the backing of the Fraternal Order of Police (FOP) and two major city newspapers, Ravenstahl went on to win easily, garnering more than 63 percent of the vote to DeSantis's 35 percent. (DeSantis, however, won the largest percentage by a Republican in more than 40 years in the city, where Democrats outnumber Republicans five to one.) Ravenstahl will serve out the remaining two years of O'Connor's term, which ends in early 2010. Upon his election victory, Ravenstahl proclaimed to city residents, as noted by Jennifer C. Yates for the Penn Live Web site, "We need to start believing in ourselves once again. We need to start believing in Pittsburgh. Let us recognize Pittsburgh as the great city it is."

In 2008 Ravenstahl focused on his "Green Up Pittsburgh" campaign, expanding the city's beautification efforts by transforming city-owned vacant lots into community green spaces. During the 2008

Stanley Cup play-off run of the Pittsburgh Penguins, he angered the Penguins organization and the athletic-apparel producer Reebok by preventing both from affixing two massive banner advertisements to two downtown buildings. Ravenstahl's chief of staff, Yarone Zober, and city-council members drafted legislation that would have allowed banners on downtown buildings for several weeks, but Ravenstahl halted the plans after alleging that several council members wanted to use the banners for political purposes. In June 2008 Ravenstahl vetoed a campaign-finance-reform measure that would have set a maximum for campaign contributions and given an unfair advantage to independently wealthy candidates. Recently, a state oversight board unanimously approved Ravenstahl's proposed $440 million budget for 2009. Several features in the budget were geared toward paying off the city's $725 million debt.

Ravenstahl and his wife, a beautician, live in a three-bedroom home in Pittsburgh's Summer Hill neighborhood. Both are members of the Roman Catholic Holy Wisdom Parish. Ravenstahl is a passionate sports enthusiast and avid Steelers fan. His favorite movies include the inspirational sports films *Rudy* and *Hoosiers*. Ravenstahl enjoys running in his spare time.

—C.C.

Suggested Reading: *New York Times* A p1+ Sep. 9, 2006, A p13+ Oct. 8, 2007; Pittsburgh Mayor's Office Web site; *Pittsburgh Post-Gazette* A p1+ Oct. 8, 2006, A p1+ Oct. 21, 2007; *Pittsburgh Tribune Review* Sep. 23, 2007

Jim McIsaac/Getty Images

Reyes, José

(RAY-ess, hoh-ZAY)

June 11, 1983– Baseball player

Address: New York Mets, Shea Stadium, 123-01 Roosevelt Ave., Flushing, NY 11368-1699

The shortstop José Reyes is regarded as one of the most exciting young players in baseball and, along with the power-hitting third baseman David Wright, as the cornerstone of the New York Mets franchise. With his unusual blend of speed, base-stealing ability, and power at the plate, he serves as the Mets' leadoff hitter and "igniter—offensively and defensively—especially on offense," as Wright told Tyler Kepner for the *New York Times* (October 19, 2006). "As he goes, we go." Indeed, some view Reyes, who joined the Mets in 2003, as the team in microcosm, in ways positive and negative—a figure representative of the Mets' considerable ability as well as their tendency to squander it on occasion. "That Reyes . . . is the catalyst for the Mets may be an understatement," Billy Witz wrote for the *New York Times* (June 20, 2008, on-line). "He is, actually, the embodiment of the team. The usual descriptions of Reyes—plenty of talent, inconsistent, questionable attention span—are often apt adjectives for the Mets, too." Another writer for the *Times* (July 6, 2008, on-line), Ben Shpigel, observed that Reyes "can be alternately electrifying and petulant, precocious and immature. He turns doubles into triples, then flings his helmet when disagreeing with a managerial move. He throws runners out from his knees, then . . . tosses his glove after making an error. . . . Reyes has been criticized for not reaching base enough, for striking out too much, for celebrating too exuberantly, for not controlling his emotions. No other Met is as regularly dissected or analyzed as . . . he is." No member of the team is more beloved at New York's Shea Stadium, either: Mets fans regularly sing his first name during his at-bats, and his "Learn Spanish with Professor Reyes" segments—in which the Dominican-born Reyes taught Spanish words to fans via a Jumbotron between innings of home games—were popular at the ballpark.

José Bernabé Reyes was born on June 11, 1983 in Villa Gonzalez, in the Dominican Republic, and grew up in nearby Palmar Arriba, a village of about 6,000 residents on the outskirts of Santiago, in the north-central region of the country. His father, José Manuel, worked as a plumber; according to some sources, José Manuel and Reyes's mother, Josefina—known as Rosa—owned a bodega next door to their home during Reyes's childhood. Reyes has a younger sister, whose name has appeared in print and on-line variously as Miosoty, Meosote, and Miosotys. The family lived in a tiny, one-room house with a tin roof, a concrete floor, and an outhouse in the backyard. "We didn't have much, but we always had each other," Reyes told Bob Nightengale for *USA Today* (June 26, 2007, on-line). Reyes first showed an interest in baseball at the age of 10; two or three years later, he became serious about playing the sport. Like many children in the Dominican Republic, he could not afford a baseball glove, instead fashioning one from an empty milk carton. When he was 13 a local scout spotted him playing on a baseball field in his village. "He talked with my father, and he said 'Hey this kid, he has to go to the city [Santiago]—he's got some talent' and my father said okay, let's see what happens," Reyes told Matt Loughlin in an interview posted on the Madison Square Garden (MSG) Web site (August 8, 2003, on-line). Over the next two years, Reyes—by then recognized as the best player in his village—traveled between Palmar Arriba and Santiago to play for a youth league. Taking his father's advice, Reyes, a right-handed hitter by nature, taught himself to hit left-handed in the hope of attracting scouts. A writer for the Web site Jock-Bio.com pointed out that since Reyes's family did not own a TV set, Reyes "never patterned his game after anyone in the big leagues. He was an original in every sense of the word."

At a Major League Baseball (MLB) tryout camp in Santiago in 1999, the 16-year-old Reyes was observed by representatives of four teams, including the Florida Marlins and the Chicago Cubs, but remained unsigned; unimpressed by his hitting and fielding, the scouts also felt that at six feet and 130 pounds, Reyes was simply too scrawny to play professional baseball. But Eddy Toledo, a New York Mets scout who was also present at the tryout, saw potential in Reyes. "There was something special in his face and eyes," Toledo told Lindsay Berra for *ESPN–The Magazine* (October 9, 2006, on-line). "He was so exciting to me." In mid-August, after obtaining approval from Omar Minaya, then the assistant general manager of the Mets and the team's director of international scouting, Toledo offered Reyes a minor-league contract with a $22,000 signing bonus. (Reyes gave half of the money to his parents, who used it to build a new home and renovate—some sources say establish—their bodega.)

At age 17 Reyes headed to the United States to join the Kingsport Mets of the Appalachian League, the New York Mets' rookie-league club, which is based in Tennessee. During Reyes's first professional season (2000–01), his manager, Edgar Alfonzo, designated him the team's starting shortstop, after convincing the Mets' assistant general manager Jim Duquette that Reyes had enough poise to handle playing every day. He appeared in 49 games that season (rookie-league seasons are shorter than those in MLB), finishing with a .250 batting average. In 2001 he was promoted to the

Class-A Capital City Mets of the South Atlantic League. In only his second year of playing professional baseball, he was designated the team's most valuable player, along with first baseman Craig Brazell, after batting .307 with 42 extra-base hits (including 15 triples) and 30 stolen bases. He also performed remarkably well in the field, making only 18 errors. Following his sophomore season in the Mets' minor leagues, he returned to his native country and joined the six-team Dominican Winter League as a reserve player.

Reyes started the 2002 season playing for Port St. Lucie of the Florida State League, the New York Mets' top-level single-A team, before his promotion, in June, to the double-A Binghamton (New York) Mets of the Eastern League. He performed well at both levels, leading the minor leagues with 19 triples (11 in the Florida State League and eight in the Eastern League) while also hitting .288 and recording 26 doubles and 58 stolen bases in 134 games. In addition to being voted to the all-star teams for both leagues, *Baseball America*'s minor-league all-star first team, and the SportsTicker All-Prospect team, Reyes played for the World Team in the Futures All-Star Game, earning most-valuable-player honors as a result of his three-run, game-winning triple. He was also designated the minor-league player of the year by *USA Today* and *Minor League News*; the SportsTicker Teenager of the Year (2002); and the Mets Sterling Organizational Player of the Year.

By 2003 Reyes had bulked up to nearly 200 pounds through an improved diet and exercise regimen. "He might look skinny from afar," Berra wrote, "but his frame is densely packed with muscle." That year he was invited to the Mets' spring-training camp but was soon sidelined by a pulled muscle in his left leg that caused him to miss the first 10 days of exhibition games. He failed to make the major-league club at the time, due to both his injury and his inexperience at the plate. "My offense isn't there—the doubles and triples—because of my leg," he told Peter Abraham for the Westchester County, New York, *Journal News* (March 31, 2003). "I know what I need to do. I have to learn the pitching." After starting the season with the Mets' triple-A affiliate in Norfolk, Virginia, Reyes was called up to the major leagues on June 10, one day shy of his 20th birthday, after the shortstop Rey Sanchez was placed on the disabled list with a thumb injury. In his major-league debut, against the Texas Rangers, Reyes took the leadoff hitter's spot in the third inning and came through with a base hit in his first at-bat, scoring two runs in the game. The same month he hit his first home run—a grand slam—in only his sixth major-league game and drove in five runs in an 8–0 victory against the Anaheim Angels, becoming the second player (after Jack Hamilton) in Mets history whose first major-league home run was a grand slam. Determined to make a good impression off the field as well, Reyes devoted himself to learning English, sometimes asking reporters after interviews how well he had spoken his second language.

Between the end of July and mid-August, Reyes had a 17-game hitting streak—the second-longest in franchise history and the longest by a National League rookie player—during which he had 18 runs scored, five runs batted in (RBIs), six doubles, a triple, a home run, and seven stolen bases. He set a franchise rookie record by recording 39 hits in August and posted the first multiple-home-run game of his major-league career on August 28. Reyes spent the last month of the regular season on the 15-day disabled list, after suffering a severe sprain to his left ankle while sliding into second base during the Mets' 4–1 loss to the Philadelphia Phillies. He finished the season ranked second among rookies in the National League in batting average (.307), fourth in slugging percentage (.434), seventh in hits (84), seventh in on-base percentage (.334), ninth in RBIs (32), 10th in total bases (119), and second in stolen bases (13). He also had a solid defensive season; his 35-game errorless streak was the second-longest by a major-league shortstop in 2003. That year he came in eighth in the National League Rookie of the Year voting. Reyes also had a strong showing in the Dominican Winter League, posting a .302 batting average with 16 runs scored, five doubles, three triples, one home run, and 11 RBIs in 29 regular-season games to help lead the Gigantes del Cibao team into the 2003–04 playoffs. He also hit .422 in 15 play-off games, while driving in nine runs and stealing nine bases.

After a promising rookie campaign, Reyes struggled with injuries during the 2004 season. He was placed on the 15-day disabled list in March with a strained right hamstring, which he re-aggravated several times during his rehabilitation assignments with the single-A Port St. Lucie and the double-A Binghamton teams. When he rejoined the Mets' big-league club, in mid-June, Reyes was designated the team's starting second baseman; Rey Sanchez had been replaced at shortstop by Kazuo Matsui. Reyes made a relatively smooth transition to his new position, hitting .318 with one home run, seven runs batted in, and 11 stolen bases during the month of July, but then suffered a stress fracture in his left fibula in mid-August that resulted in another stint on the 15-day disabled list, which was eventually extended to 60 days. Throughout the 2004 season questions arose concerning Reyes's durability. Returning to the team in late September, he hit in 10 of the last 13 games of the regular season and scored seven runs, five doubles, a triple, two runs batted in, and five stolen bases. In his second major-league season, Reyes, who had missed nearly four months due to injuries, appeared in only 53 games—43 at second base and 10 at shortstop. As the Mets' leadoff hitter, he posted a .255 batting average and a lowly .271 on-base percentage.

The next year was a breakthrough season for Reyes, who returned to shortstop. Under the newly signed manager Willie Randolph, he rebounded from his injuries of 2004, appearing in 161 games—a franchise record previously held by Buddy Harrelson in 1970. He achieved personal-best numbers in several offensive categories, including hits (190), doubles (24), triples (17), home runs (seven), runs batted in (58), and stolen bases (60). Reyes led the major leagues in triples and the National League in stolen bases. His total number of at-bats (696) set a Mets' single-season record; the 60 stolen bases and 17 triples ranked him second on the team's single-season list in both categories. Despite his offensive success, he managed only 27 walks while also committing 18 errors.

In the spring of 2006, the Mets hired the renowned leadoff hitter and former Mets outfielder Rickey Henderson, also the sport's all-time stolen-base leader, as a special instructor for Reyes. The move proved successful, as Reyes increased his on-base percentage by 54 points and collected 53 walks, nearly doubling his total from the previous year. For the second consecutive season, he was the major-league leader in stolen bases (64) and triples (17) and finished the season ranked among the top 10 in the National League in other offensive categories, including hits (194), runs (122), and multi-hit games (56). Reyes told Berra about his approach to stealing bases, "Sometimes I have to wait a couple pitches. Sometimes I say, maybe I'm not going to go. Maybe I'll stay [on base]. But if the pitcher does something wrong, . . . I'm going on his first move. And if I get a jump, forget it." Berra wrote, "If there's one thing [Reyes] learned from Man of Steal Rickey Henderson, . . . it's how to read a pitcher." Reyes received the most votes to be the starting shortstop for the National League in Major League Baseball's All-Star Game, although an injury prevented him from playing; David Eckstein of the St. Louis Cardinals replaced him on the roster. Reyes earned recognition from the Elias Sports Bureau as the first player in the history of baseball to equal or top 122 runs, 194 hits, 19 home runs, and 64 stolen bases in a single season. His offense helped the Mets to capture the National League East division title and qualify for the postseason. In the National League Division Series (NLDS), Reyes played a critical role in each of the Mets' three victories against the Los Angeles Dodgers. He scored the winning run in the first game, drove in the go-ahead run in the second, and hit the game-tying run in the third to help the Mets advance to the 2006 National League Championship Series (NLCS) against the Cardinals. His leadoff home run in the sixth game helped propel the Mets to a 4–2 victory and a seventh and deciding game, in which they lost 3–1 to the Cardinals, who went on to win the World Series against the Detroit Tigers. The nine hits that Reyes collected during the NLCS tied a franchise record. He won the National League Silver Slugger Award for shortstops and finished seventh in the voting for the league's Most Valuable Player award. Another highlight of the 2006 season was the four-year contract extension he signed for more than $23 million, which includes a team option for the year 2011. In November he joined teammate and third baseman David

Wright during Major League Baseball's tour of Japan.

In 2007 the Mets were the early-season favorites to win the National League pennant and advance to the World Series. Reyes continued to work with Henderson, whom the Mets hired as their new first-base coach, and improved on his previous season's totals in walks (from 53 to 77) and stolen bases (from 64 to 78). For the third straight season, he led the National League in the stolen-base category. After putting up a strong offense in the first half of the season, during which he posted a batting average of .307 with four home runs, 35 runs batted in, and 46 stolen bases, Reyes began to develop a reputation for a lack of effort, twice failing to run hard out of the batter's box in July games against the Colorado Rockies and the Houston Astros. Randolph benched him during the four-game series against the Astros when he was thrown out at first base, after failing to run out a ball that was hit down the third-base line and remained in fair territory.

As the season progressed, Reyes continued to struggle offensively. Meanwhile, as late as September 12, 2007, the Mets enjoyed a seven-game lead, with 17 regular-season games remaining. Reyes failed to steal a base over the last 15 games and managed only five hits in 32 at-bats during the final seven games of the season (which all took place at Shea Stadium), against the Washington Nationals, the St. Louis Cardinals, and the Florida Marlins, three teams with records below .500. The Mets, who had been in first place in the National League East for most of the season and seemed headed toward capturing their second straight division title, lost five of the final six games to move into a tie with the Philadelphia Phillies for the National League East division lead, with one regular-season game remaining. The team managed little offense in their 8–1 loss against the last-place Marlins, as Reyes went hitless in five at-bats, eliciting a chorus of boos from the Mets' fans. In their final regular-season game, the Phillies defeated the Washington Nationals, 6–1, to unseat the Mets as NL East division champions and advance to the postseason.

The Mets' defeat capped off a disappointing September, in which the team squandered a seven-game lead, losing 12 of their last 17 games. The team's collapse ranks as the biggest in the history of baseball, as no other major-league team with a lead of seven or more games and 17 games left in the season had failed to finish in first place. Many of the Mets' fans blamed Reyes for the team's failure to win the division title and advance to the play-offs. He also drew criticism for his celebratory antics on the field, which included dancing every time his teammates hit a home run and greeting several of them at the top of the dugout steps with choreographed, signature handshakes. Many opposing teams viewed those exuberant displays as violations of baseball etiquette and signs of disrespect. In a September 2007 game against the Flori-

da Marlins, the catcher Miguel Olivo took exception to a celebratory handshake between Reyes and his then-teammate Lastings Milledge, who had hit two home runs. Olivo incited a bench-clearing brawl, after throwing a punch at Reyes.

After the 2007 season rumors abounded that Reyes would be traded. In November the Mets' general manager, Omar Minaya, publicly announced that he had no intention of trading Reyes, who expressed a desire to remain with the team. During spring training Reyes pledged to tone down his behavior in the dugout. "No more handshakes," he told David Lennon for *Newsday* (February 20, 2008). "People kept saying we got teams fired up when we did those handshakes, so now I want to focus more on baseball." He also eliminated his "Learn Spanish with Professor Reyes" segments. However, sensing that Reyes was unhappy, the Mets center fielder Carlos Beltran encouraged Reyes to be himself. "I tell him 'I want you to be the Reyes that you always have been,'" Beltran told Mark Hale for the *New York Post* (April 17, 2008, on-line). Following a sluggish performance in the first part of the 2008 season, which saw the Mets' manager, Willie Randolph, replaced by Jerry Manuel in June, Reyes rebounded: as of early July he had racked up nine home runs, 22 doubles, 10 triples, and 31 stolen bases. He ended the season with solid offensive statistics, including a .300 batting average, 34 doubles, 18 triples, 49 stolen bases, and 200 hits—the last being a personal best. He also broke the Mets' all-time record for triples (with his 63d in July) and stolen bases (with his 282d in September). Meanwhile, the Mets again squandered a lead in the final stretch of the season—their last at Shea Stadium—and many fans and pundits began calling for one or more of their big-name players to be shown the door.

Despite his promise to focus on the game, Reyes has still shown signs of immaturity. In June 2008, during Manuel's first game as the Mets manager, Reyes experienced tightness in his hamstring after reaching first base and was immediately pulled out of the game. Reyes reacted by throwing his helmet on the ground in disgust. The following month, during a game against the New York Yankees, he threw down his glove and sunglasses after committing a throwing error to first base. His actions drew criticism from Keith Hernandez, a former Mets player and an analyst for the Mets-owned Sports New York (SNY) channel, who called Reyes immature and accused the Mets of babying the shortstop. Reyes confronted Hernandez on the team's charter plane about the remarks; some sources allege that the two nearly came to blows—a claim that Reyes has denied. They have since made peace.

In December 2007 Reyes, an avid video-game player, was named the cover athlete and official spokesperson for the popular video game Major League Baseball 2K8. He has also been named one of the 50 most beautiful people by *People en Español*, the Spanish edition of *People*. He enjoys listening to Latin reggaeton music and has also recorded several reggaeton tracks. During the season Reyes lives in Manhasset, New York, with his girlfriend, Katherine; their two daughters, Katerine and Ashley; and Reyes's parents. He spends the winter months in the Dominican Republican, where he splits his time between his new home in Santiago and his parents' residence in Palmar Arriba.

—B.M.

Suggested Reading: *Baseball Digest* (on-line) Aug. 1, 2007; mets.com; (New York) *Daily News* p90 July 6, 2003; *New York Times* (on-line) Dec. 6, 2007, (on-line) Sep. 30, 2007, (on-line) Sep. 26, 2007; *Sports Illustrated* p54 May 7, 2007

Eliot J. Schechter/Getty Images

Rivers, Doc

Oct. 13, 1961– Basketball coach

Address: Boston Celtics, 226 Causeway St., Fourth Fl., Boston, MA 02114

Glenn "Doc" Rivers, a former player in the National Basketball Association (NBA), has parlayed his talent and knowledge of the game into a successful coaching career. A point guard and floor general known for his strong defensive skills, intelligent command of the backcourt, and charismatic presence, Rivers put up impressive numbers during 13 seasons in the NBA with the Atlanta Hawks (1983–91), Los Angeles Clippers (1991–92), New York Knicks (1992–94), and San Antonio Spurs (1994–96), while playing under such coaching greats as Mike Fratello, Larry Brown, and Pat Riley. Follow-

ing his retirement from active play, in July 1996, he worked as an on-camera basketball analyst for the Turner Sports network and for the Spurs' local television broadcasts before being named, in 1999, as head coach of the Orlando Magic, succeeding the recently retired Hall of Fame coach Chuck Daly. Although the Magic had shared the best record in the Eastern Conference during the lockout-shortened 1998–99 season, the team's general manager, John Gabriel, had traded four of the team's five starters during the following off-season in efforts to rebuild the franchise, which led many sports analysts to write the Magic off before the 1999–2000 season even started. Despite having had no coaching experience at any level, Rivers defied odds and led a team of so-called castoffs to an impressive 41–41 regular-season record, leading a panel of sportswriters in April 2000 to name him the NBA's coach of the year. He led the Magic to the postseason in each of the next three years as coach but was fired in late 2003, after a disastrous 1–10 start to the 2003–04 season. Rivers then worked as a commentator for *The NBA on ABC* for a year before being named head coach of the Boston Celtics, in 2004. In June 2008 Rivers helped the Celtics to crush their perennial rivals, the Los Angeles Lakers, in Game Six of the NBA Finals, and win their league-record 17th NBA championship. In the process, he became the fifth African-American coach in history to take home an NBA title.

Glenn Anton "Doc" Rivers was born on October 13, 1961 in the Maywood area of Chicago, Illinois, into an athletic family. His uncle Jim Brewer played for nine seasons in the NBA with the Cleveland Cavaliers, Phoenix Suns, and Los Angeles Lakers, and his cousin Byron Irvin also played in the NBA. Early on, Rivers learned discipline from his hard-working parents, who also stressed the importance of pride, perseverance, and integrity. His father, Grady, was a Chicago police officer who rose to the rank of lieutenant; his mother, Bettye, was a deeply religious woman who worked on the assembly line at an electronics plant. The family also operated a record store. Rivers's parents' values were demonstrated once when a man tried to steal from the store. "My dad, I thought, was going to kill that guy," Rivers recalled to Tony Massarotti for the *Boston Herald* (December 19, 2007). "And he wasn't mad because he [just] stole. He kept saying to the guy, 'As hard as I work, and you're going to try and steal this from ME?' To me, you had [the contrast of] what was right and what was wrong. It was clear with him. He believed you worked hard. Nothing for free." Despite being exposed in his youth to the rougher elements of his inner-city neighborhood—in part through rides in his father's police cruiser—Rivers escaped trouble, spending his free hours on the basketball court. "I played basketball every single day of my life and I loved it," he recalled to Steve Bulpett for the *Boston Herald* (May 6, 2004). "I never thought about being a pro. I tell kids that all the time. I just played every day." He noted that when he teaches young players at basketball camps, "kids ask me . . . , 'How long did you practice?' I didn't know I was practicing. I didn't call it practice. I'd say, 'Mom, I'm going out to play.' I tell them, 'You guys call it practice. Maybe that's the problem.' We thought it was playing."

Rivers went on to hone his basketball skills under Donald Burnside, who coached him in junior high school. Burnside, an army veteran, ran practices with military-style strictness, even making Rivers and his teammates perform conditioning drills in combat boots. Meanwhile, Rivers played on the same Chicago playgrounds as future NBA stars including Isiah Thomas and Mark Aguirre. Rivers attended Proviso East High School, which had been a scene of race riots in the late 1960s, when Rivers was an elementary-school student. "The [Proviso basketball] team had two white guys and they were criticized for playing with these black guys," Rivers recalled to Bulpett. "And my uncle's sister was dating one of the white guys. It was absolutely crazy. And I'm a second-grader absorbing all this. That had a real impact on me." He added that when Proviso's integrated team won a championship, "the race stuff was gone. I mean, it just disappeared. People shared the same goal for a change instead of looking at perceived differences. It was really a defining moment in my life watching that." An average student in grade school, Rivers had applied himself in preparation for his entrance exam to Proviso and had achieved the second-highest test score of all the applicants. During high school he developed into an all-around basketball player, so quickly that late in his freshman year he made the varsity squad. Rivers got his nickname, "Doc," at a summer basketball camp when the coach, Rick Majerus of the Marquette University team, noticed that he was wearing a T-shirt with the image of the basketball great Julius Erving—also known as "Dr. J." Rivers was named a McDonald's All-American player and became one of the most sought-after recruits in the country.

In 1980 Rivers enrolled at Marquette, a Jesuit college in Milwaukee, Wisconsin. There, he realized that his basketball skills would take him only so far. "Things took a different direction pretty early," he recalled to Steve Bulpett. "I had a professor, Dr. Wolf, my freshman year. I turned in a political science paper, and there was more red on it than blue ink when I got it back. All the information was right. I mean, I did my work. But the spelling and the grammar were horrific, and he decided he was going to deal with it. I remember him saying, 'This will be the best paper you've ever written.' So I rewrote it and it still wasn't right. The next thing you know I'm at his house two times a week for a long time—on that same paper. I was still doing his other work, but he was going to make me write a perfect paper. That's when I saw where I needed to go educationally. Those are the things that change you. I could have said, 'Oh, this guy's [giving me a hard time] because I'm an athlete.' Instead, I said,

'He's right.'" During his time at Marquette, Rivers enjoyed athletic success on the international level. In the 1982 FIBA (International Basketball Federation) World Championship of Basketball, he helped the United States national team to win the silver medal and was named the tournament's most valuable player. Following his junior year at Marquette, he entered the 1983 NBA draft, against the wishes of his parents, who wanted him to complete his education. (Later, in 1985, Rivers earned a degree in pre-law/political science from the university.)

The Atlanta Hawks selected Rivers in the second round of the draft as the 31st overall pick. During his first exhibition game with the team, after losing two front teeth in a collision with his teammate Keith Edmonson, he picked up the teeth, threw them toward the team's bench, and ran downcourt to play defense. "I was trying to make the team," Rivers noted to Bob Hohler for the *Boston Globe* (April 22, 2005). "I wasn't thinking about my teeth." Rivers not only made the team but moved into the starting lineup during his rookie season, after an injury sidelined one of the team's starters. Under the tutelage of the Hawks' newly appointed coach, Mike Fratello, Rivers became a pivotal member of a talented squad that included the future Hall of Fame player Dominique Wilkins. During his eight-year tenure with the Hawks, he set franchise records for single-season assists (823 in 1986–87) and career assists (13,866). He enjoyed stellar seasons in 1986–87, when he averaged a double-double, scoring an average of 12.8 points and providing 10.0 assists per game, and in 1987–88, when he played in the All-Star Game after averaging 14.2 points, 4.6 rebounds, and 9.3 assists per game. In a contest against Seattle on February 4, 1988, he scored a career-high 37 points. The Hawks were title contenders throughout the 1980s, reaching the Eastern Conference semifinals in three straight seasons (1985–86; 1986–87; 1987–88) but falling short each time. Rivers reached the playoffs with the Hawks on two more occasions (1988–89 and 1990–91), but the team failed each time to advance past the first round. In a contest with Boston on May 16, 1988, Rivers set an NBA single-game play-off record for most assists in one half (15).

After averaging a career-high 15.2 points per game during the 1990–91 campaign, Rivers left Atlanta to play for the Los Angeles Clippers. With the addition of Rivers and Head Coach Larry Brown, the team finished the 1991–92 season with a record of 45–37 (the franchise's first winning season in 13 years) and advanced to the play-offs for the first time in 16 years. (They were eliminated in the first round by the Utah Jazz, three games to two.) In the following off-season, Rivers was picked up by the New York Knicks to help add a veteran presence to a talented but inexperienced backcourt that included the fiery shooting guard John Starks. The Knicks, who were led by the renowned head coach Pat Riley and the perennial All-Star center Patrick

Ewing, achieved the best record in the Eastern Conference during the 1992–93 season, due in large part to Rivers's dogged style of play. That season Rivers persevered through a series of injuries that included a separated shoulder, sprained wrist, strained knee, and broken nose. The Knicks advanced through the postseason for a matchup with the Chicago Bulls for the Eastern Conference championship; the Bulls won the series, four games to two. The next season Rivers again hoped to help the Knicks win an NBA championship, but his season ended after only 19 games when he tore the anterior cruciate ligament in his left knee. In that year's play-offs, the Knicks again lost to the Bulls.

The Knicks released Rivers in December 1994. After receiving offers from five other teams, he joined the San Antonio Spurs, a team that included the superstar David Robinson and defensive prodigy Dennis Rodman but, despite faring well during the regular season, consistently fell short in the play-offs. Rivers went on to finish his career with the Spurs as a solid bench performer. Following the end of the 1995–96 season, after playing 13 seasons in the NBA, he announced his retirement. He finished with career averages of 10.9 points, 5.7 assists, and 3.0 rebounds per game.

In July 1996 Rivers went to work as an on-camera NBA analyst for Turner Sports. For a time he also served as an analyst for the Spurs' local television broadcasts. Then, in 1999, he was named head coach of the Orlando Magic, replacing Chuck Daly. With the team's general manager, John Gabriel, having traded most of the Magic's five starters, Rivers faced a daunting task as the new coach. When the team nonetheless ended the season with a 41–41 record, the basketball world took notice, with a panel of sportswriters naming Rivers the NBA's coach of the year. Commenting on his reputation as a "player's coach," the former Magic forward Monty Williams explained to John Denton for *Florida Today* (April 27, 2000), "I think he's that cross between old school and Generation X. He's been around us players to know all the tricks, the attitudes and the spoiled brats of the NBA. But at the same time, he can be hard-core, old school, too."

Rivers led the Magic to the play-offs in each of the following three seasons, but on each occasion the team failed to advance past the first round. "Rivers' .518 career winning percentage might scream mediocrity," Denton wrote in late 2003, "but the job he has done of simply keeping the team afloat has been admirable." Following a dismal 1–10 start to the 2003–04 season, however, the Magic's front office fired Rivers. He returned to the broadcast booth for a year, working as a commentator for *The NBA on ABC*, before becoming the head coach of the Boston Celtics in 2004. He led a veteran Celtics squad that included Paul Pierce, Antoine Walker, and Gary Payton to the first round of the play-offs, only to see them swept in the first round by the Indiana Pacers. The following season he took the team to its first Atlantic Division title

since the 1991–92 season, but the Celtics again failed to deliver in the postseason, duplicating their showing in the previous year by losing to the Pacers in the first round. Following the efforts by the Celtics' general manager, Danny Ainge, to rebuild the team, Rivers entered the 2006–07 season with the difficult task of instructing a much younger and less experienced group of players, which resulted in one of the worst records in franchise history—24–58—putting them second from the bottom in the league. Much criticism came Rivers's way for his alleged lack of commitment to the team; a devoted family man, he has been known to fly across the country regularly to attend his children's various sports events. Ainge quieted fans and the media by giving Rivers another contract extension and by acquiring the much-sought-after free agents Kevin Garnett and Ray Allen from the Minnesota Timberwolves and Seattle Supersonics, respectively.

For the 2007–08 season Rivers developed a coaching strategy that centered on the talents of the team's so-called Big Three (Pierce, Garnett, and Allen) while incorporating a brutally honest style of communicating that helped keep the superstars' egos in check. The Celtics won 29 of their first 32 games. "Doc's very straight up," Garnett told Marc J. Spears for the *Boston Globe* (April 18, 2008). "You know where he's coming from. There's no ifs, ands, or buts about it. He doesn't care who you are, what you've done in this league. For this type of team, if he feels like we are not playing our hardest or he can get more out of us, he says it. He doesn't cater to anyone on this team." The Celtics finished with a league-best 66–16 record—the most franchise victories in a single season since the team won the NBA championship in 1986—and set an NBA record with a 42-game improvement from the previous season, eclipsing the 36-game improvement by the San Antonio Spurs during the 1997–98 season. They carried their momentum into the postseason, defeating the Atlanta Hawks and Cleveland Cavaliers in the first and second rounds, respectively, and then beating the Detroit Pistons in the Eastern Conference Finals, before squaring off against the Los Angeles Lakers in the NBA Finals. Though critics considered Rivers to be overmatched in taking on his Lakers counterpart, the nine-time NBA Finals victor Phil Jackson, the Celtics defeated the Lakers in Game Six, 131–92, to win a record 17th NBA championship. Rivers, who had made the NBA play-offs 10 times as a player without winning a title, became the fifth African-American coach in history to win an NBA crown. "This is a player's game. It always will be, and it really should be," Rivers said to Tom Withers for the Associated Press (June 14, 2008). "[James] Naismith did not invent this game for us to be talking about coaches. It's a players' game and our job is to get the players to play."

Rivers and his wife, Kristen (known as Kris), married in 1986. For the ceremony the wedding party wore pink high-top sneakers. Doc and Kris

Rivers live in Orlando, Florida, with their four children: Jeremiah, Callie, Austin, and Spencer. Jeremiah played basketball for Georgetown University before transferring to play for Indiana University; Callie plays volleyball for the University of Florida. Rivers and his wife, who is white, began dating in college. Early on their relationship prompted racist acts; on one occasion someone slashed the tires of Kris's car and wrote a racial slur on a nearby sidewalk. In 1997 Rivers's house outside San Antonio was burned to the ground in what police judged to be race-related arson. Rivers nonetheless told Tom Enlund for the *Milwaukee Journal Sentinel* (April 28, 2001) that in recent years he and his wife had encountered relatively little hostility because of their different races. "The country as a whole has come a long way," he said. "There are still problems but things have come a long way."

—C.C.

Suggested Reading: Associated Press June 14, 2008, (on-line) Apr. 26, 2000; *Boston Globe* p18 May 30, 2004, A p1 Apr. 22, 2005, D p1 Mar. 12, 2006; *Boston Herald* p108+ May 6, 2004, p76+ Dec. 19, 2007; *Florida Today* Oct. 26, 2003; *International Herald Tribune* p21 June 17, 2008; *Milwaukee Journal Sentinel* Apr. 28, 2001; *New York Times* p2 Nov. 28, 1999; *Orlando (Florida) Sentinel* A p1 Apr. 25, 2001, A p1 Nov. 19, 2003; *Sports Illustrated* p58 Apr. 10, 2000, p30+ June 30, 2008; *Washington Post* E p1 Dec. 18, 2007

Roberts, Robin

Nov. 23, 1960– Television journalist; sportscaster; writer

Address: Good Morning America, *147 Columbus Ave., New York, NY 10023*

After Hurricane Katrina slammed into the U.S. Gulf Coast, in 2005, the ABC-TV newscaster Robin Roberts reported on the disaster at the site of the devastated Mississippi town where she had spent much of her youth. Katrina struck only a few months after Roberts was named co-anchor of the long-running ABC News program *Good Morning America* and three and a half years after she left her dream job, as an anchor for the sports network ESPN. Referring to her repeated visits to her hometown, both as a journalist and as a volunteer in rebuilding efforts, she told Gary Pettus for the Jackson, Mississippi, *Clarion-Ledger* (April 4, 2006), "Personally and professionally, this has been the defining moment for me. I had struggled, I had wondered if I should move from sports to news. When Katrina hit, I looked to the heavens and said, 'Now I get it.'" "Once you've done sports, you can do anything," she told Mike Lacy for the Biloxi, Mississippi, *Sun Herald* (April 25, 2002). "The subject matter has changed, but I have the same journalistic approach whether I'm talking about the Yankees or Osama bin Laden." Currently, Roberts is the only female African-American anchor on morning network television. She began her career in broadcasting during her years as a student at Southeastern Louisiana University, with jobs at local radio stations. For seven years after her college graduation, having resolved to gain experience and hone her skills "in the minors," as she explained to Hal Karp for *Black Enterprise* (April, 1997), she worked for a series of television stations in Mississippi, Tennessee, and Georgia. In 1990, two years after she had rejected a job offer from ESPN because she felt that she was not yet sufficiently pre-

pared, she joined the network as a host and reporter. During the next dozen years, she appeared on programs including *NFL Prime Time, SportsCenter,* and *In the SportsLight* and concurrently, for four years, hosted *Wide World of Sports* on ABC (which, like ESPN, is owned by the Walt Disney Co.). For *Good Morning America,* Roberts has reported from war-torn or otherwise troubled places in the Persian Gulf region and Africa. In March 2007 she hosted a town-hall–style meeting with U.S. senator and Democratic presidential hopeful Hillary Rodham Clinton. Several months later Roberts disclosed on-air that she had been diagnosed with an early stage of breast cancer. She underwent surgery and treatment and included in many of her broadcasts updates about her chemotherapy and her physical and emotional reactions to it. Roberts is the author of the memoir cum inspirational/advice book *From the Heart: Seven Rules to Live By* (2007).

The youngest of four children, Robin Rene Roberts was born to Lawrence Roberts Sr. and Lucy Marion (Tolliver) Roberts on November 23, 1960. Her brother, Lawrence Jr., is a teacher; her sister Sally-Ann is a TV anchor in New Orleans, and her sister Dorothy is a social worker. According to Gary Pettus, her mother (whose given name appears as Lucimarian in some sources) was a member of the Mississippi state board of education; Roberts has credited her mother with teaching her the importance of speaking clearly and grammatically. Her father, a career U.S. Air Force officer, served during World War II with the Tuskegee Airmen, a now-celebrated all-black fighter-pilot squadron. The Robertses lived on a series of air-force bases until Robin was eight, when they settled in the small town of Pass Christian, Mississippi, on the Gulf of Mexico near the Keesler Air Force Base, in Biloxi. "My father taught me that anything is possible . . . ," Roberts told Kimberly C. Roberts for the *Philadelphia Tribune* (June 15, 2007). "In the 1930s he had the nerve to . . . dream about flying when Blacks in this country had very little, if any

Rusty Jarrett/Getty Images for NASCAR

Robin Roberts (center) with her Good Morning America *co-anchor, Diane Sawyer (left), and the race-car driver Jimmie Johnson*

rights. . . . And . . . not only dream it, but make it a reality. . . . We would say, 'I want to do this. I want to do . . . that.' . . . He never looked at us and said, 'You can't do that!' or 'That's impossible!' He was like, 'If that's what you want to do, you have my full support.'" In *From the Heart: Seven Rules to Live By*, Roberts wrote that her parents, who came of age in the 1930s, had experienced racism firsthand but refused to let it hold them back. Her mother, for example, knew that the wives of her husband's fellow air-force officers "didn't want her at their coffee klatches," as Roberts wrote. "She showed up anyway—in a quiet way, asserting her right to be there. My parents never let us use race as an excuse."

Roberts's interest in sports began at an early age. "No matter what sport it was I loved it, loved it, loved it. Loved every aspect of it, seeing how fast I could run, competing against someone else," she told Beth Usewicz for the Women's Sports Foundation Web site. At 10 (12 or 13, according to some sources) she won a Mississippi state bowling competition. She later became proficient at tennis and in the eighth grade, already five feet 10 inches in height, showed unusual skill at basketball. She was the star player on her high-school women's basketball team and drew the attention of college scouts. She won a scholarship from Southeastern Louisiana University, in Hammond, where she played on the Lady Lions basketball team. By that time, as she told Usewicz, she had concluded that her abilities on the court would never reach professional levels. Retaining her desire to be involved with sports, she took the advice of her sister Sally-Ann and decided to make a career as a sportscaster.

She appeared on a campus sports show between classes and basketball practice, and, concurrently, got a job as a disk jockey at a small Hammond radio station that specialized in country-and-western music. She worked at the station every day for an hour or so beginning at 6:00 a.m. and then returned there at noon to write copy. "I scratched a lot of good ole Merle Haggard records before the station let me host a sports show," she told Ylonda Gault Caviness for *Essence* (May 2007). In her junior and senior years, she was named the basketball team's Most Valuable Player. In the latter year her points-per-game average was 15.2, and she was one of only three members of the Lady Lions to average 1,000 or more career points and rebounds. She graduated with a B.A. in communications, cum laude, in 1983.

In the same year Roberts landed a position as a $5.50-per-hour weekend sports anchor at WDAM-TV in Hattiesburg, Mississippi, where her sister had once worked. In taking that job, she had declined an offer to report news for the local ABC affiliate, because she wanted to gain experience in a less high-profile setting. The next year she turned down the chance to serve as a news anchor for WLOX-TV, in Biloxi, Mississippi, in favor of hosting—for a smaller salary—that station's sports segment of the news; she felt, as she told Pettus, that "news" was "a four letter word." In 1986 she became a sports anchor and reporter for WSMV-TV, in Nashville, Tennessee. She told Beth Usewicz that some men expressed skepticism about any woman's ability to cover sports. Among them was a viewer who called the station before her on-air debut. "I told him to let me do a couple of reports and call me back in six months," she said to Usewicz. "In less than half of that time, he called back and said, 'Nah, you are all right.'"

In 1988 Roberts turned down a chance to rise in the sportscasting world, when ESPN asked her to host a show. Although when she was a college student, her ambition had been to work for ESPN by 1990, she felt that she did not have enough experience yet to make the most of the opportunity and gain "staying power," as she put it to Hal Karp. Instead, in 1988 she moved to Atlanta, Georgia, to work at WAGA-TV as a sports reporter, covering major-league games. With her co-host, Mike Roberts (not a relative of hers), she also contributed to Atlanta's highest-rated morning radio show, on WVEE-FM. Her popularity with listeners grew after she beat the National Basketball Association star player Dominique Wilkins in a free-throw shoot-out.

When ESPN again offered her a job, Roberts signed on as an anchorwoman. On January 29, 1990 she became the first African-American female anchor on that network, as the host of the night edition of *SportsCenter*. Within a month she became the first female host of an NFL pregame show, filling in during that broadcast in the absence of the regular host. Soon afterward she received prime-time slots on *Sunday SportsDay* and *NFL Prime-Time*, hosting both for the next five years. In addition, she had her own series, *In the Sportslight*, which premiered in 1995. On that show she conducted interviews and discussed the effects of athletics on the lives of public figures. Also in 1995 Roberts signed a joint $3.9 million contract with ESPN and ABC. She served as a host for ESPN's coverage of the Olympics, for Women's National Basketball Association games from 1997 to 2000, and, in 1999, for *Vintage NBA*, a weekly ESPN program that focused on one sportsman or -woman per episode. Her job also included coverage of professional football and basketball drafts, Ladies Pro Golfing Association competitions, and world tennis events, and she was the first female play-by-play announcer for men's college-basketball games. From 1995 to 2001 she hosted *Wide World of Sports*, which airs on ABC. She also appeared on segments of *Prime Time, Good Morning America,* and *Good Morning America Sunday*.

In April 2002 Roberts was elevated from contributor to news reader on *Good Morning America*, where she had been serving as a fill-in anchor for several months. Her reservations about making the move from ESPN to *Good Morning America* evaporated after she had a conversation with the retired tennis champion Billie Jean King. "She said, 'What, are you an idiot? . . . Go, go. It is a bigger platform for you,'" as Roberts recalled to Usewicz. Concurrently, for three years, she also served as an ABC News correspondent and contributed to Sunday-morning shows on ESPN. In March 2003 she traveled to Kuwait to report on preparations for the impending U.S.-led war in Iraq. "I had no qualms about doing my job and needing to be there [in Ku-

wait] for it," she told Donna Petrozzello for the New York *Daily News* (March 11, 2003). "If you're a journalist, this is the biggest story there is. To see it for yourself and relay that information back to viewers is what the job is meant to be." Other news stories Roberts reported concerned the effectiveness of sky marshals on airplanes; a controversial custody battle involving an adolescent's biological father and the youngster's longtime male caregiver; the effects of the September 11, 2001 terrorist attacks on the New York City suburb of Rockville Center, on Long Island, more than 20 of whose residents died at the World Trade Center that day; debates concerning stem-cell research; and gentrification in the Harlem section of New York City.

In May 2005 Roberts was promoted to third anchor of *Good Morning America*, alongside Diane Sawyer and Charles Gibson. Upon her acceptance of that position, she officially left ESPN, ending her 15-year association with the network. The following August Hurricane Katrina destroyed most of Pass Christian, along with large parts of many other cities in the Gulf Coast states. In the aftermath of the storm, Roberts traveled to Pass Christian with an ABC crew to report on the disaster. Upon her arrival she attempted to find her family before a live broadcast scheduled for 6:00 a.m. that morning. With the help of local police, and with only 15 minutes to spare before she was to face the cameras, she found members of her family alive and unhurt in their home. When she appeared on the air, a question from Gibson about the well-being of her family brought her to tears. "I had just heard of a man who lost his wife in the storm," Roberts recalled for Pettus. "I was grateful my family was safe, but I knew there were countless people waking up that morning not knowing if their family was. That's when everything caught up with me. I believe when people saw me crying, they knew it was bad." Viewer sympathy led ABC to "adopt" Pass Christian, in collaboration with the Salvation Army and the Corporation for National and Community Service. With Roberts reporting, the rebuilding of the town by residents and volunteers was chronicled on *Good Morning America*. In August 2007 Roberts announced on the program that while progress had been made, much restoration work remained.

Earlier, in 2006, Gibson had left *Good Morning America* to host the evening program *ABC World News with Charles Gibson*. With his departure, Roberts and Sawyer became the only all-female team to anchor a morning network show. "For all the talk about competition between women, Diane and Robin clearly like each other and work well together," the former broadcast journalist Carol Jenkins, currently the president of the Women's Media Center, an advocacy group, told Felicia R. Lee for the *New York Times* (November 16, 2006). Victor Neufeld, the senior executive producer of *Paula Zahn Now* on CNN, told Lee that Roberts and Sawyer "are just so relaxed and likeable together," and said, "Robin has this tremendous force of personality as well as being someone you feel you want to hang out with."

In her book, *From the Heart: Seven Rules to Live By*, Roberts described some of what she has learned through her work and in her private life. Kelli Bozeman, in a review of the book for *Mississippi Magazine* (May 1, 2007), wrote, "Roberts' 'rules,' sprinkled throughout *From the Heart*, inspire readers to ready themselves for opportunities, focus on small goals, take chances, be persistent, and keep faith and family close to the heart. But she offers encouragement for breaking the rules as well. 'There is no playbook for your own unique, wonderful life,' she writes. 'Ultimately, you've got to live it for yourself.'" *From the Heart* was published a few months before Roberts learned that she had breast cancer. On July 31, 2007 she revealed that diagnosis on *Good Morning America*. The next month she underwent surgery and then a course of chemotherapy that extended until January 2008. In November 2007, after her hair began to fall out—a common side effect of chemotherapy—she had her head shaved, a process that was filmed and then shown on *Good Morning America*. She began to wear a wig during broadcasts, so as not to distract viewers from the news she was reporting. On a broadcast of *Good Morning America* in April 2008, Roberts removed her wig. "I've taken my cue from people here and from viewers, especially [cancer] survivors . . . who said, 'When it's time to literally flip your wig, you'll know,' " Roberts explained, as quoted by Michael Starr in the *New York Post* (April 22, 2008, on-line). By October 2008 no sign of Roberts's cancer could be detected. That month she earned the 2008 Roswell Park Cancer Institute's Gilda Radner Courage Award. Soon afterward Roberts auctioned off her wig, with the proceeds going to the Bridge Breast Network, an organization that provides services to low-income and uninsured breast-cancer patients.

Among Roberts's many honors are the Daughters of the American Revolution T.V. Award of Merit (1990); the Women at Work Broadcast Journalism Award (1992); the Excellence in Journalism Award, Broadcast Media, from the Center for the Study of Sport in Society, at Northeastern University (1993); and the President's Award from the Women's Sports Foundation (2001). In 2002 she was named Journalist of the Year by *Ebony*.

Speaking of Roberts, Diane Sawyer told Felicia R. Lee, "I think there's nothing more exciting than someone who has a truly good heart and a completely wicked sense of humor." Roberts, who is single, lives on the Upper West Side of Manhattan, in New York City, with her dog, KJ, a Jack Russell terrier. Every morning, she told Scott Ross and Renell Richardson during an interview for the Christian Broadcasting Network (June 19, 2007, on-line), she repeats what she called the "prayer of protection." She also reads selections from *Streams in the Desert*, by L. B. Cowman, a 1920s book of devotionals (passages that aim to enable readers to get closer to God) that once belonged to her maternal grand-

mother. She is a practitioner of the Pilates exercise system.

—W.D.

Suggested Reading: ABC News Web site; *Black Enterprise* p56 Apr. 1997; *Ebony* p118+ Mar. 2006, p192+ May 2007; *Essence* p192 May 2007; (Jackson, Mississippi) *Clarion-Ledger* D p1 Apr. 4, 2006; *Mississippi Magazine* p120+ May 1, 2007; *New York Times* E p3 Nov. 16, 2006; *Philadelphia Tribune* E p6 June 15, 2007; shemadeit.org; *Women's Sports & Fitness* p467 Nov./Dec. 1991; Women's Sports Foundation Web site

Selected Books: *From the Heart: Seven Rules to Live By*, 2007

Tina Mills, courtesy of Tor/Forge Books

Rucker, Rudy

Mar. 22, 1946– Science-fiction writer; mathematician; computer programmer

Address: c/o Susan Protter, 110 W. 40th St., New York, NY 10018

The prolific science-fiction writer Rudy Rucker is credited as one of the founders of cyberpunk, a subgenre that emerged in the 1970s and 1980s and portrays alienated individuals who live in a dystopian future in which advanced science and technology—in the form of globally networked computers, artificial intelligence, and other tools of oppressive governments and omnipresent megacorporations—dominate the world. Rucker published his first cyberpunk novel, *Spacetime Donuts* (1981), years before the term "cyberpunk" was even coined (by Bruce Bethke, who used it as the title of a 1982 short story), and he has since published more than 20 full-length works of science fiction, including the four books in the notable Ware series. He has attracted a loyal readership and inspired a generation of writers who appreciate the real scientific and philosophical theories represented in his books, as well as the attention he devotes to the psyches of his often subversive characters. "Rucker blends the vulgarity of underground comics with some of the hardest ideas in philosophy and physics," Charles Platt wrote for the *Washington Post* (December 25, 1983), shortly after the publication of *Sex Sphere* (1983). "He also writes elegantly and captures the subtlety of human relationships in a realistic context."

In addition to writing fiction, Rucker is a trained mathematician and computer scientist whose academic research has focused on the idea of infinity. He has published a number of textbooks and critically acclaimed nonfiction works on mathematics and computer science. During a brief stint as an employee of the computer-programming company AutoDesk, Rucker designed three programs involving computer animation.

The second of two brothers, Rudolf von Bitter Rucker was born on March 22, 1946 in Louisville, Kentucky. His mother, the German-born Marianne von Bitter Rucker, a descendant of the famous philosopher Georg Hegel, had moved to Philadelphia, Pennsylvania, with her father in 1937; an amateur painter of landscapes, she later took up pottery as well. Rucker's father, Embry Cobb Rucker Sr., was a the owner of a small furniture-manufacturing company and, according to Rucker, "a great storyteller," who at 40 years of age became an Episcopal minister. When Rucker was a boy, his favorite reading materials were comic books by Carl Barks, such as *Donald Duck* and *Uncle Scrooge*. Rucker attended a co-ed boarding school in Germany for eighth grade, then enrolled at an all-male Roman Catholic high school, St. Francis Xavier, back in Louisville. During that time he was interested in works of science fiction and in Beat literature, such as Jack Kerouac's novel *On the Road*, William S. Burroughs's novel *Naked Lunch*, and the poetry of Allen Ginsberg. Rucker was perhaps most influenced by a collection of science-fiction stories by Robert Sheckley, *Untouched by Human Hands*, which he read at age 15 while in the hospital, having ruptured his spleen in an accident involving his backyard swing set. From that point on Rucker knew that he wanted to be a writer of science fiction. Not long afterward he published his first science-fiction story, in the *Chevalier Pegasus*, the literary magazine of a citywide high-school fraternity called the Chevalier Literary Society.

As a teenager, Rucker has said, he had an unusually intense fear of death—to which his accident at 15 and a later mishap with his mother's car probably contributed. Rejecting his father's religion, he dealt with his fear through what he has called his own version of mysticism, a belief in a universal spiritual force alive inside all people. A good student, he won a National Merit Scholarship and applied to Harvard University, writing an admissions essay that argued that life is essentially meaningless. Rucker was admitted to his second choice, Swarthmore College, in Swarthmore, Pennsylvania. His interests leaned toward philosophy and literature; his father persuaded him to study a more practical subject, so he majored in mathematics. While that subject came easily to him, Rucker earned only mediocre grades, as he was given to forgoing his studies in favor of debating with friends, reading books on pop culture, drinking beer, and smoking marijuana. At Swarthmore he met Sylvia Bogsch, whom he married in 1967, after college.

Rucker and his wife entered graduate programs at Rutgers University, in New Brunswick, New Jersey. (Rucker's decision was at least partly fueled by an unwillingness to take part in the Vietnam War.) He earned his M.A. and Ph.D. degrees in mathematics, while she studied French literature. Rucker studied set theory, the branch of mathematical logic pioneered by Georg Cantor, which deals in part with levels of infinity; his dissertation concerned an area of that subject called transfinite set theory. While at Rutgers, Rucker was greatly affected by a meeting with the reclusive Austrian logician Kurt Gödel, whose work influenced contemporary notions of set theory. (The logician was then in residence at the Institute for Advanced Study at Princeton University, in New Jersey.) The meeting rekindled Rucker's interest in mystical philosophy and in the physicist Albert Einstein's work on relativity theory. Their conversation about Gödel's theories concerning time and the notion that individuals are figures in "eternal patterns" also helped ease Rucker's anxiety about death. During their years at Rutgers, Rucker and his wife became the parents of three children: Georgia, Rudy Jr., and Isabel.

After having some difficulty finding a teaching position, Rucker took a job in 1972 at what was then called the State University College at Geneseo, New York, as an assistant professor of mathematics. In one of his courses, Foundations of Geometry, Rucker found the textbook so boring that rather than have his students use it, he distributed the notes he had accumulated over the years while studying the implications of the existence of a fourth dimension. He expanded the notes into the book *Geometry, Relativity and the Fourth Dimension* (1977), which he sold to Dover Books for about $1,000. The small advance helped sustain Rucker's dreams of a career as a writer.

Rucker began writing his first work of fiction the morning after he and Sylvia attended a concert by the rock band the Rolling Stones in 1976. Inspired by what Rucker saw as their radical philosophy of living for the moment, he began what he called a "beatnik science fiction novel," *Spacetime Donuts*.

The book addressed many concepts that have become common science-fiction premises, such as that of people who plug their minds into society's "Big Computer." The acts of the novel's characters—which include using drugs, having casual and/or premarital sex, listening to rock-and-roll music, and other more or less antiestablishment pursuits—were based on Rucker's own experiences as a graduate student; one of the characters is based on Sylvia. Though he was initially unable to publish *Spacetime Donuts* as a book, its first two sections appeared in serialized versions in 1978 and 1979 in a science-fiction magazine called *Unearth*. Then, in 1981, Ace Books published *Spacetime Donuts* as a full-length work of fiction.

After being laid off from his teaching position at Geneseo, Rucker took a visiting professorship at the Mathematics Institute at the University of Heidelberg, in Germany, researching Cantor's continuum hypothesis, which concerns the relative sizes of infinite sets of numbers. After making frustratingly little progress on the problem while at Heidelberg, Rucker wrote *White Light*, a novel about an indifferent mathematics professor who tries to prove Cantor's continuum hypothesis but instead finds himself lying on his floor each afternoon, entering a lucid dreaming state. In that state he imagines himself in a surreal and mathematically oriented world governed by Cantor's infinities. The book, published in 1980 by Ace Books, was the first that Rucker wrote in what he has a called a "transrealist" style.

In his essay "A Transrealist Manifesto," which appeared in the *Bulletin of the Science Fiction Writers of America* in 1983, Rucker encouraged other writers to adopt the transrealist style—that is, to use elements of fantasy to "thicken and intensify" realistic fiction, basing characters on actual people and events on real experiences and writing freely, without knowing in advance how stories would end. According to Rucker, writing in a transrealist style would challenge what he called "consensus reality," or conventional notions of normality. "There are no normal people. . . . Actual people are weird and unpredictable," Rucker wrote, "this is why it is so important to use them as characters instead of the impossibly good and bad paperdolls of mass-culture."

Over the next several years, Rucker published a number of novels in the transrealist style, all of them based to a significant degree on his life and the lives of people he knew. During his second year at Heidelberg, he wrote *Software* (1982), a novel centering on the idea that one's personality can be extracted from one's brain and implanted in hardware units such as robots. *Software* received positive reviews and was awarded the first Philip K. Dick Prize, for the best paperback science-fiction novel of the year. Charles Platt reported that *Software* "dramatized some fairly advanced concepts involving self-replicating artificial intelligence, derived from a paper that Rucker presented to engineers at IBM." He added, "This is science fiction as it should be: authoritative and tightly linked with our real lives and our real future." That novel was followed by three other installments of the Ware series: *Wetware* (1988), which also received a Philip K. Dick Award; *Freeware* (1997); and *Realware* (2000). Though those novels have received mixed assessments over the years, the series as a whole is widely considered one of the most important in science fiction of the past few decades. While at Heidelberg Rucker also began work on a nonfiction book of popular science, called *Infinity and the Mind: the Science and Philosophy of the Infinite*. Published in Germany by Birkhäuser in 1982 and in the United States by Bantam in 1983, the work received positive reviews. A notice in the *New Yorker*, quoted on Amazon.com, read, "Rudy Rucker's *Infinity and the Mind* is a terrific study with real mathematical depth."

Meanwhile, in 1980 Rucker had accepted a job as a teacher of mathematics at Randolph-Macon Woman's College, in Lynchburg, Virginia. Though Rucker was happy to return to the U.S., he and his family were uncomfortable with the southern, religious, conservative world in which they suddenly found themselves, and Rucker clashed with his associates in the school's Mathematics Department. After two years he was fired. Frustrated with the academic world, Rucker briefly joined a punk-rock band called the Dead Pigs. Having recently sold a short-story collection called *The Fifty-Seventh Franz Kafka* (1983) and a novel, *The Sex Sphere* (1983), to Ace Books, he decided to attempt a career as a full-time writer. From 1982 to 1986 Rucker wrote dozens of articles for popular-science magazines and six books, including the nonfiction volume *The Fourth Dimension: A Guided Tour of the Higher Universes* (1984). The book, which contains illustrations and puzzles, was well-received by critics. Along with *Infinity and the Mind*, the book is Rucker's most popular; it has been translated into a dozen languages. He next published *Master of Space and Time* (1984) and *The Secret of Life* (1985). Of the latter, Michael Dirda wrote for the *Washington Post* (June 30, 1985), "This [adolescent] alienation Rucker captures perfectly, along with those sharp moments of dizzying angst that people experience—often late at night or when drunk—when we achingly realize that our lives are slipping by, that yesterday we were in 7th grade and today we are getting married and tomorrow our grandchildren will be playing around our sickbed."

That period, the early to mid-1980s, "marked the birth of cyberpunk science-fiction," Rucker wrote in an autobiographical statement for the San Jose State University Web site, "and I became recognized as a founding father of the movement." In 1983 Rucker was visited by other members of the cyberpunk movement, the writers Bruce Sterling, William Gibson, and Lewis Shiner, who were then in the early stages of their careers and looked to Rucker as a role model. Also in 1983 Rucker met his boyhood hero, Robert Sheckley, when Sheckley dropped by Rucker's house while touring the country in a camper van. Sheckley had read and enjoyed *White Light* as well as a story Rucker had sent to the science-fiction magazine *Omni*, of which Scheckley was an editor. Sheckley's praise helped renew Rucker's pride and belief in his own work.

In 1987 Mariner Books published Rucker's *Mind Tools: The Five Levels of Mathematical Reality*, a nonfiction exploration of mathematical concepts developed in the 20th century, including fractals, information theory, and catastrophe theory. Publishing the book sparked Rucker's interest in teaching math again, and in 1986 he took a position as a professor at San Jose State University (SJSU), in a department that combined mathematics and computer science. Rucker taught courses in the latter subject, although he initially knew very little about it. "Fortunately," he wrote for the SJSU site, "another professor was teaching the same course, and I was able to attend his lectures to help myself figure out what was going on." Learning the subject as he taught, Rucker soon became interested in computer programming, specifically cellular automata, whose applications include computer animation.

At a conference Rucker met John Walker, the founder of the company Autodesk, the maker of the highly successful architectural drawing program Auto-CAD. In 1988 Walker hired him as a programmer, and over the next few years, Rucker worked part-time on three software packages, CA Lab: Rudy Rucker's Cellular Automata; James Gleick's CHAOS: The Software; and BOPPERS: Artificial Life Laboratory. Each of those programs allows users to create computer graphics that "self-generate," or replicate on their own according to laws of cellular reproduction. Though their sales did not match those of Auto-CAD, the programs were well received by the computer programming community. "Rudy Rucker's Cellular Automata Laboratory is not for everyone," Michael J. Miller wrote in a computer-program review for *InfoWorld* (December 11, 1989). "It isn't going to make you more productive or change how you run your business. But Cellular Automata proponents do feel that the technology has applications in such areas as creating realistic animation. In any case, it is fascinating and a lot of fun."

In 1992 Rucker returned to teaching full-time. While in California he socialized and shared ideas with other significant figures in the science-fiction literary community, including the writers Pat Murphy and Mar Laidlaw. He wrote several reviews and short articles for a cyberpunk magazine called *MONDO 2000* and helped put together an anthology of articles, *The MONDO 2000 User's Guide to the New Edge* (1992). Meanwhile, Rucker had also written his first historical science-fiction novel, *The Hollow Earth* (1990), which follows the adventures of a country boy who leaves home, travels down the James River, and meets the writer Edgar Allan Poe, with whom he travels to Antarctica and

into the "hollow earth." Of that work, Jim Hopper wrote for the *San Diego Tribune* (August 31, 1990), "This is a lovely romp, with moods and notions that, as in [the work of Mark] Twain, must be tempered with the cold water of some social hindsight. It's a departure from Rucker's earlier rowdier work, but it shows a lot of finesse." The novel *The Hacker and the Ants* (1994)—the story of a computer programmer who becomes involved with a plot of his evil boss—was based on Rucker's experiences at Autodesk.

In 1999 Rucker published the novel *Saucer Wisdom*, whose narrator supposedly recounts the stories told to him by a friend, Frank Shook; Shook claims to have been abducted by aliens and guided through the events of the coming thousand years. At first, editors at *Wired* magazine had wanted to serialize the story, which they planned to present as if it were factual. After that plan was abandoned, *Saucer Wisdom* was published by Tor Books as a nonfiction science book about the future. The book was well received by critics, but its sales were disappointing, and as a result Rucker's subsequent book advances decreased. Also in 1999 Rucker published *Seek!*, a collection of his essays, followed by *Gnarl!* (2000), a volume of his best short stories, which received mostly positive reviews.

Rucker spent much of his time at SJSU designing software called Pop Framework. The software helps users to write programs for video games—which he finds to be the most interesting area of computer science—for use in Microsoft Windows. He published a textbook, *Software Engineering and Computer Games* (2002), which sheds light on Pop Framework and software engineering in general. "It took me years to organize the material, as programming knowledge has a kind of fractal structure: the details have details with yet more details," Rucker wrote for his Web page on the SJSU site.

Rucker next published *Spaceland* (2002), a novel set in Silicon Valley, and a work of historical fiction, *As Above, So Below: A Novel of Peter Bruegel* (2002), about the life of Rucker's favorite painter, for which Rucker did extensive research in Europe. That work received positive reviews. A *Publishers Weekly* (November 25, 2002) critic wrote, "This is clearly a labor of love and, though sometimes less than graceful, it grapples handily with Bruegel's genius—his ability to wittily and gracefully recreate all human activity, from the sublime to the scatological." The novel met with indifferent sales, which was a significant disappointment for Rucker.

For his 25th book, Rucker wanted to write a work that he could have read to his children when they were young. The result was *Frek and the Elixir* (2004), about a 12-year-old's quest to restore Earth's vanished species in the year 3003. The book earned positive reviews. In the summer of 2004, Rucker decided to retire from teaching and devote his time to writing. (He nonetheless returned to SJSU in the fall of 2005 to teach a course called Computers and Philosophy, on the philosophical implications of computers.)

In 2005 Rucker published *The Lifebox, the Seashell, and the Soul: What Gnarly Computation Taught Me About Ultimate Reality, the Meaning of Life, and How to Be Happy*. In that retrospective look at his life and work, Rucker evoked the concept of the lifebox, a device featured in one of his novels, which reduces a person to a computer-like tool and makes it possible to access his or her personality at will; Rucker used the analogy of the lifebox to suggest that while much about life can be charted through technology, its meaning can be found only when people "[turn] off the machine" and "[open] their hearts." A staff reviewer for *Publishers Weekly*, as quoted on Amazon.com, found the book to be "muddled," writing, "Rucker blissfully spouts his facile pop psychology, but most readers will be lost in the gnarled prose of computer science and bogs of poorly explained mathematical logic." Other recent works of fiction by Rucker include *Mathematicians in Love* (2006), a collection of short stories called *Mad Professor* (2007), and *Postsingular* (2007), a book of interconnected tales. *Mathematicians in Love*, in particular, was met with enthusiastic reviews. In an assessment for the *San Francisco Chronicle* (December 10, 2007), Michael Berry wrote, "[Rucker] keeps the tone light and the action playful, even as his characters grapple with the meaning of tragedy and the ultimate mechanics of the universe. You don't need to be able to solve a differential equation to enjoy *Mathematicians in Love*, a definite high point in Rucker's singular writing career." Critiquing *Postsingular*, Carl Hays wrote for *Booklist* (August 1, 2007), "While Rucker's improbable scenarios sometimes cross the line into pure silliness, his devoted fans and dazzled newcomers to him will revel in his willingness to push technological extrapolation to its soaring limits." According to his home page on San Jose University's Web site, as of mid-October 2008, Rucker was working on a sequel to *Postsingular*. The planned title was "Hylozoic," which refers to hylozoicism (or, more commonly, hylozoism), the belief of some early Greek philosophers that all matter is alive.

In 2007 Rucker founded an on-line science-fiction literary magazine, *Flurb*, on which he has published several stories. He enjoys oil painting and has displayed works at the Live Worms Gallery, in San Francisco, California. He lives with his wife in California.

—M.E.R.

Suggested Reading: 10zenmonkeys.com Mar. 1, 2007; San Jose State University Web Site; *Time* p58 Feb. 8, 1983; *Washington Post* p6 June 30, 1985

Selected Books: *Geometry, Relativity and the Fourth Dimension*, 1977; *White Light*, 1980, 1997; *Spacetime Donuts*, 1981; *Software*, 1982; *Infinity and the Mind*, 1983; *The Fifty-Seventh*

Franz Kafka, 1983; *The Sex Sphere*, 1983; *The Fourth Dimension*, 1984; *Master of Space and Time*, 1984; *The Secret of Life*, 1985; *Mind Tools*, 1987; *Wetware*, 1988; *The Hollow Earth*, 1990; *All the Visions*, 1991; *Transreal!* 1991; *The Hacker and the Ants*, 1994; *Freeware*, 1997; *Seek!*, 1999; *Saucer Wisdom*, 1999; *Gnarl!*, 2000; *Realware*, 2000; *Spaceland*, 2002; *Software Engineering and Computer Games*, 2002; *As Above, So Below: A Novel of Peter Bruegel*, 2002; *Frek and the Elixer*, 2004; *The Lifebox, the Seashell, and the Soul: What Gnarly Computation Taught Me About Ultimate Reality, the Meaning of Life, and How to Be Happy*, 2005; *Mathematicians in Love*, 2006; *Mad Professor*, 2007; *Postsingular*, 2007

Lluis Gene/AFP/Getty Images

Russo, Patricia

June 12, 1953– Former CEO of Alcatel-Lucent Technologies

Address: c/o Schering-Plough Corp. World Headquarters, 2000 Galloping Hill Rd., Kenilworth, NJ 07033-0530

In 2006 Patricia Russo, then the chief executive officer (CEO) of Lucent Technologies, oversaw the complicated merger of Lucent, one of the world's largest telecommunications companies, with the Paris, France–based telecommunications giant Alcatel. In part because of the global economic downturn, the newly formed Alcatel-Lucent has since struggled to meet its profit goals, and Russo was forced to adjust the company's business strategy.

On July 31, 2008 the company reported a net loss of $345.6 million for the second quarter, on revenues that were down 5.2 percent. Apparently as a direct fallout of the sixth straight quarterly loss, Russo resigned from her position as CEO, effective at the end of 2008. She agreed to continue to run the company until a new CEO had been found. (Serge Tchuruk, the chairman of the board, also resigned, as of October 1, 2008.) "Our strategy is taking hold and our results are demonstrating good operational progress. That said, I believe it is the right time for me to step down," Russo said, as quoted in *Submarine Fiber Optic Communications* (August 1, 2008). "The company will benefit from new leadership aligned with a newly composed Board to bring a fresh and independent perspective that will take Alcatel-Lucent to its next level of growth and development in a rapidly changing global market."

Russo, widely known as a brilliant manager and consistently ranked by *Forbes* and *Fortune* as one of the most powerful women in the world, began her career at IBM, as one of only a few women in that firm's marketing and sales departments. Eight years later she joined AT&T, where a decade later she was named vice president and head of national service; in that position she reorganized the company's debt-laden global business-communications system, making it the most profitable division in the company. In 2002, after spending nine months as the president and chief operating officer (COO) of the financially unstable Eastman Kodak Co., Russo took on the job of CEO of AT&T's spin-off company Lucent Technologies, as it was beginning to face major sales losses and plummeting stock prices. In 2004, after several consecutive quarters of reported losses, Lucent's stock sharply increased, a turn of events that was largely credited to the drastic changes that Russo had initiated—including the firing of tens of thousands of employees. Asked by Justin Schack for *Institutional Investor* (International Edition, February 14, 2005) whether she enjoyed weathering the storm with Lucent in the early 2000s, she responded, "I have, as strange as that may sound. I like the opportunity to work with terrific people and sort through complex challenges. And frankly, it feels good when you can see that the decisions you've made in fact have made a difference."

One of seven children, Patricia F. Russo was born on June 12, 1953 into an upper-middle-class family living in Lawrenceville, New Jersey, a suburb of Trenton. Her father was a physician, her mother a homemaker. An energetic child and natural athlete, Russo (her married name) thrived on competition; in games of soccer and other sports with her brothers, she has said, she became adept at "playing along with the guys." At Lawrence High School she was co-captain of the basketball team and captain of the cheerleading squad. Russo attended Georgetown University, in Washington, D.C., where she earned a B.A. degree in political science and history in 1973. That same year she joined the sales and marketing departments at IBM. During her eight years with IBM, Russo was one of very few women responsible for selling mainframe computers for that or any other company. "Early in my career there were some people who didn't believe a woman belonged in sales," she told Olga Kharif for *BusinessWeek* (May 29, 2003, on-line), "but I worked hard on the accounts I was given and made sure I met the customers' needs and focused on producing results for the company. What I found is that results matter—it's hard to argue with them. People who produce results rise to the top."

In 1981 Russo left IBM to work for AT&T, the nation's largest provider of local and long-distance telephone service. At that time the company's dominance of the market had led to a government-mandated breakup. It was divided into seven companies, "Baby Bells," which provided local service, and "Ma Bell," which provided long-distance service. Russo quickly moved up the ranks in the sales and marketing departments. In 1989 she studied advanced management at the Harvard University School of Business, in Cambridge, Massachusetts.

In late 1991 AT&T began a massive reorganization in which its national sales and service divisions were combined. Russo, then AT&T's vice president of national sales, was named vice president of the merged entity, called Global Business Communications Systems. In that role she was assigned the task of restoring the $6 billion unit, which was heavily in debt. Toward that end, Russo extended the company's voice systems—voice mail and voice-messaging technology—to overseas markets. In response to customer complaints regarding the inadequate technical proficiency of AT&T's salespeople, she introduced various training programs. From 1992 to 1996 Russo's actions decreased costs, improved products, increased customer trust, and boosted her unit's revenues by 43 percent, to $5.7 billion, making hers the most profitable division in the company. "It was my first real job where I was in charge, and I had control of all the levers," Russo recalled to Stephanie N. Mehta for *Fortune* (April 15, 2002). "I realized I liked it. I liked the relationship between choosing and planning, and seeing what worked and why."

In January 1996 AT&T announced that it was spinning off its equipment sectors, which included Western Electric and Bell Labs, under the name Lucent Technologies. That move stemmed in part from the reluctance of some of its telecommunications competitors to buy merchandise from a rival. Henry B. Schacht, the recently retired head of Cummins Engine Co., was named Lucent's chief executive officer, Richard McGinn was named president and chief operating officer, and Russo became an executive vice president. Lucent was one of many telecom companies in the late 1990s whose stock prices were propelled upward by the widespread increase in capital spending on wireless and Internet-based networks. Lucent itself began investing in other communications companies and start-ups; it purchased Ascend Communications for $24 billion in 1999. Twice, Lucent declared a reverse stock split (a reduction in the number of its shares, with a concomitant increase in their value). By December 1999 the price of Lucent shares had risen from $27 to a high of $84. Earlier that year, after Carly Fiorina had left Lucent to assume the presidency of Hewlett Packard, Russo had replaced her as executive vice president and chairwoman of Lucent's $24 billion Service Provider Networks Group. That promotion placed Russo in charge of 80,000 employees, whose aggregate responsibility involved the development and sales of products for companies that managed phone and data networks.

A downturn in the value of investments in Internet and wireless-based businesses in the summer of 2000 presented Lucent with major problems. Unlike its competitors Cisco Systems and Nortel, Lucent had failed to invest in optical networking technologies. At the same time demand had dropped for telecommunications products in which Lucent specialized, such as traditional telephone switches. As a result Lucent's sales and earnings decreased. In an effort to stanch further losses, McGinn eliminated Russo's positions and reduced her role in the company. In August 2000 Russo resigned. Three months later Lucent's board ousted McGinn and brought back Schacht (who had left in 1997) in his stead. By that time the value of Lucent's stock had plummeted to less than half of its top price.

Meanwhile, during the months in which Russo was jobless, she read, exercised, painted rooms in her house, and worked as a freelance telecommunications consultant. "There was a time I thought I could be finished, but I found myself champing at the bit," she told Stephanie N. Mehta. "I realized I'm not finished." In January 2001 she reentered the workforce, as chairwoman of Avaya, one of Lucent's spin-off companies. Then, the following April, Russo accepted the positions of president and chief operating officer at Eastman Kodak, which was experiencing significant losses while undergoing a difficult transition from the manufacture and sale of chemical-based photographic film, paper, and other items to products for digital imaging.

About nine months after her arrival at Kodak, Schacht tapped Russo to take his place as president and CEO of Lucent, while he remained chairman. According to Claudia H. Deutsch, writing for the *New York Times* (January 8, 2002), "Most analysts agree that Ms. Russo is running to Lucent Technologies, not away from Kodak," not least because with Kodak's head, Daniel A. Carp, just a few years older than Russo, "her chances of becoming C.E.O. were pretty much zip," as Ulysses Yannas, an analyst with the investment-advice firm Buckman, Buckman & Reid, told Deutsch.

Russo's new job paid an annual salary of $1.2 million and came with a $1.8 million bonus package and $4.7 million in stock options. When Russo officially assumed her duties, on January 7, 2002, she was one of only six female CEOs of Fortune 500 companies. Guided by a business plan Schacht had drawn up, Russo reduced operating expenses by spinning or selling off several businesses. She concentrated on expanding Lucent's so-called mobility business, which develops technology for mobile devices including mobile phones and wireless laptops, and increasing sales of Lucent products to such companies as AT&T, Verizon Wireless, and other Internet service providers. Russo also tried to tailor Lucent's products and services as closely as possible to the needs and desires of customers. "In many ways I am Lucent's chief salesperson," she told *Sales and Marketing Management* (November 1, 2002). "Now more than ever, an experienced, creative, and committed sales team is absolutely critical to our turnaround and success."

Such efforts notwithstanding, by August 23, 2002 the value of Lucent's shares (and those of several other telecommunications companies) had fallen to 90 percent of what they were worth one year earlier. In the quarter that ended on September 30, 2002, Lucent posted a loss of 84 cents per share, or $2.8 billion. By October 2002 the price of Lucent shares had sunk to 58 cents, and Russo announced that 25,000 jobs would be eliminated, reducing Lucent's workforce to 35,000. Commenting three years later on those events, she recalled to a reporter for *Institutional Investor* (February 14, 2005), "So much spending got sucked out of the industry. Thousands of customers disappeared, and those that stayed around dramatically cut back spending. In 2002 revenue was dropping like a rock, and there was nothing we could do about it. So we got very focused on things we could control." In February 2003 Schacht stepped down as Lucent's chairman, and the firm's board of directors appointed Russo to succeed him. *RCR Wireless News* (February 24, 2003) quoted Schacht as saying, "Over the past year, Pat has been dedicated to serving our customers and helped raise customer satisfaction to the highest levels we have seen in years." Russo reiterated Lucent's commitment to end the year in the black. But in July 2003 she reported that revenues for the third fiscal quarter would be about 18 percent below the projected target. A writer for *BusinessWeek* (July 28, 2003) blamed that disappointing result on "a slowdown in the sale of wireless equipment in the U.S., and the unexpected delay of a big contract" on which Lucent had set its sights. Russo predicted that Lucent would not meet its profit targets until 2004. In February 2004 Lucent's board linked a portion of Russo's annual bonus package to Lucent's growth in earnings over the next three years. Observers noted that the change was intended to refocus Russo's priorities on satisfying customers, whose business is required for any growth in earnings to take place, before stockholders, who depend on the growth of the company's stock value, a figure that is not directly linked to its earnings. If Lucent's earnings failed to meet specified targets, Russo would receive only part of her annual bonus.

On September 22, 2004 Russo announced that Lucent had made a turnaround, meeting its profit goals while securing employees' pension funds and health-insurance options. In an interview on CNBC, as quoted by *Total Telecom* (September 22, 2004), Russo explained that the turnaround was largely due to the restructuring of several major aspects of Lucent's business plan. She further noted that she expected future growth in technologies including "next generation convergence networks," technology that allows multiple networks with different communication services to bind together under a single network. She also mentioned plans to capitalize on markets outside the United States, in nations or regions including China, India, Russia, the Caribbean, Latin America, and Eastern Europe.

In the spring of 2006, Russo announced the acquisition of Lucent by its French competitor Alcatel for $13.4 billion. Referred to as a merger, the purchase led to the birth of Alcatel-Lucent, the world's leading telecom-equipment maker. Russo was to become the CEO of the new company, which was valued at $25 billion, and Alcatel's CEO, Serge Tchuruk, was to become its nonexecutive chairman. In a conference call with Leslie Cauley for *USA Today* (April 3, 2006), Russo and Tchuruk said that the consolidation of other telecom companies had inspired their merger. The two executives said that the decrease in costs expected from the consolidation of marketing and administration activities, as well as the projected layoffs of 9,000 workers, might result in savings of as much as $1.7 billion.

Soon, though, Alcatel-Lucent reported having missed its profit goals. In August 2006 the company began a major reorganization of its staff. Its chief operating officer, Frank D'Amelio, and president, Mike Quigley, left the company. By September 2007 Alcatel-Lucent had reported missing its profit marks in three out of four quarters. The same month the company's market value fell to $19.43 billion, down 44 percent in a year. In *Electronic Engineering Times* (September 24, 2007), Balaji Ojo wrote, "Alcatel-Lucent is still plagued by some of the integration and competitive problems identified six months ago by analysts, including persistent customer uncertainty about product road maps, price pressures, poor trading visibility, customer consolidation, poor free cash flow and high debt, which could limit the company's ability to tap the credit market for new financing." In response to media and investor panic, Russo released a statement that read: "Given ongoing dynamics in the rapidly changing telecom industry, the company is taking steps to accelerate the execution of its current restructuring program and to implement additional focused cost reduction plans in markets which require further actions to be taken."

In November 2007 Russo admitted that the Alcatel-Lucent merger had proved to be more disruptive to both customers and employees than she had anticipated. As she told Carol Matlack for *BusinessWeek* (November 29, 2007, on-line), changes in the new company's product line worried customers, and the possibility of job cuts "distracted" workers. Russo also blamed the "aggressive" pricing of Lucent's competitors, Ericsson (ERIC) and Huawei Technologies, which enabled them to secure a greater number of contracts with communications companies, and the failure of Alcatel-Lucent to bring some of its products technologically up to speed. Earlier, on October 31, 2007, Russo had announced that Alcatel-Lucent planned to reduce its workforce by another 4,000 employees by 2009, in an effort to save some $600 million. The news sparked criticism of Russo's leadership. Ojo wrote for the *Electronic Engineering Times* (November 5, 2007), "Here's a reality check: Job cuts won't bring back lost sales or make up for strategic operational mistakes." Nevertheless, Russo predicted a strong finish for the company in the fourth quarter.

In February 2008 Alcatel-Lucent reported fourth-quarter revenues of $7.6 billion—an 18 percent increase over the same period a year before—but with a fourth-quarter loss of $3.8 billion. The loss was largely due to the "revaluation," or the price increase, of the company's wireless data (CDMA) business. Russo was quoted in the *New York Times* (February 9, 2008) as saying that the one-time loss did not reflect consumers' "lack of faith" in the CDMA business in particular, but a broader hesitancy toward the changing market. With a reported net loss of $3.52 billion in Alcatel-Lucent's first year, Russo stated that the recent merger should be considered "a three-year process" and judged for its long-term benefits. She went on to predict that over the next year, the telecommunications market would remain relatively flat or dip slightly lower.

By spring 2008 it was apparent that Alcatel-Lucent had been hurt by the economic turmoil and tight credit market to a greater extent than other telecommunications companies. In April 2008 the company reported that revenues had dropped 0.5 percent ($5.97 billion) from the year earlier, which amounted to a net loss of $280 million. It also reported that its financial condition had been hurt by the weakness of the dollar against the euro. On May 31, 2008 Alcatel-Lucent shareholders voted to let directors of the board remove the CEO by a simple majority rather than a two-thirds vote, a move that seemed to signal members' intent to oust Russo. On June 16 Alcatel-Lucent won a $1 billion contract with China Mobile, China's biggest wireless operator. Nevertheless, on July 29, 2008 the company reported a loss of $1.7 billion, its sixth straight quarterly loss. On the same day Russo resigned from her position as CEO, effective at the end of 2008. Serge Tchuruk, the chairman of the board, also submitted his resignation, effective on

October 1, 2008, and Alcatel-Lucent reported that the firm was changing the composition and reducing the size of its board. In retrospect, a number of observers have noted that Alcatel-Lucent's struggles may have stemmed at least in part from the unanticipated difficulty of merging the contrasting corporate cultures of the two companies, Alcatel and Lucent, difficulties that may have been exacerbated by Russo's decision to hand over leadership to the former management of Lucent, the junior partner, rather than to Alcatel. In September 2008 Alcatel-Lucent announced that Russo would be replaced by Ben Verwaayan, the former CEO of the technology company BT.

While those who know her well have told reporters that Russo has a soft side, the media have emphasized her toughness. Writing for *Fortune* (February 2002), Stephanie N. Mehta noted, "News articles about her have made much of her flawless posture and the precise way she chooses her words. In presentations to analysts and shareholders, she comes across as well prepared and in command, but she shows little of her personality, playing with a poker face that reflects the very serious,

highly visible nature of her job." Russo has sat on the boards of the Xerox Corp., the New Jersey Manufacturers Insurance Co., the Italian American Foundation, and Lucent Technologies Canada Corp. Since 1995 she has maintained an affiliation with the Schering-Plough Corp., serving as the lead director and chairman of the nominating and corporate governance committee and a member of the executive committee. She has received honorary doctoral degrees from Columbia College in South Carolina and the Stevens Institute of Technology. After living in New Jersey for many years, she currently has an office in Paris, France. From her marriage to Frank Russo, in 1983, she has two stepchildren and five stepgrandchildren. In her free time she enjoys playing golf.

—M.E.R.

Suggested Reading: *BusinessWeek* (on-line) May 29, 2003; *Electronic Engineering Times* p17 Sep. 24, 2007; *Fortune* p126 Apr. 15, 2002; *Institutional Investor* (on-line) Feb. 14, 2005; *USA Today* (on-line) Apr. 3, 2006

Sabathia, C. C.

(suh-BATH-ee-uh)

July 21, 1980– Baseball player

Address: Milwaukee Brewers, One Brewers Way, Milwaukee, WI 53214

"Sabathia is the future. He is that rarest commodity in baseball: a left-handed pitcher who throws 95 mph," Sheldon Ocker wrote for the *Akron (Ohio) Beacon Journal* (March 11, 2000). Drafted straight out of high school in 1998 by the Cleveland Indians, C.C. Sabathia played only two years in the minor leagues before becoming one of the dominant, and most intimidating, pitchers in Major League Baseball and a fixture in the Indians' starting rotation. With unusual speed, he diversified his pitching repertoire and mastered his control, while displaying what many have called a maturity far beyond his years. "If it was Sabathia's 95-plus-mph fastball that gained him his chance, it has been his poise that has blown away everyone who has encountered him," Stan McNeal wrote for the *Sporting News* (August 27, 2001). In 2001 he came in second to the Seattle Mariners' Ichiro Suzuki in Rookie of the Year votes. By 2007 he had become one of the youngest pitchers to win 100 career games, and that year he won the American League Cy Young Award for best pitcher. That honor served to quiet those who had maintained that Sabathia pitched too many innings and who believed that, like some other outsized players—Sabathia is six feet, seven inches tall and currently weighs 290

Doug Pensinger/Getty Images

pounds—he would be prone to injury, particularly to his joints. In July 2008 Sabathia was traded to the Milwaukee Brewers, where he continued to shine, leading the team to their first play-off berth in 25 years. Known to fans as the "California Cannon" for the power and speed of his pitches, "California Cool" for his easygoing demeanor, and "Cy Cy" in reference to the Cy Young Award, Sabathia has used his celebrity to share his concern about the shrinking numbers of African-Americans in Major League Baseball and has talked about the need to raise baseball's profile among inner-city youth. "We can all do more," he told a reporter for the Associated Press (March 14, 2007). "Talking about the problem isn't going to solve it. It's time to do something."

The only child of Margie and Carsten Charles Sabathia Sr., Carsten Charles Sabathia Jr. was born on July 21, 1980 in Vallejo, California. His father worked in a warehouse; his mother was a telephone operator. One of his cousins, Demetrius Davis, played tight end for the Los Angeles Raiders football team. "Growing up, I didn't need idols on television," Sabathia told Sheldon Ocker. "I could go to Oakland and watch my cousin. He was my idol." Sabathia is by nature right-handed; he uses that hand for everything but pitching. He began throwing with his left hand while playing T-ball with his father one day when he was five. "I'd just bought two right-handed gloves, but C.C. was throwing like a girl," his father told Paul Hoynes for the *Cleveland (Ohio) Plain Dealer* (February 24, 2002). "I told him to throw left-handed." Sabathia's mother would play catch with him in their garden—but not without a catcher's mask and chest protector. That practice ended on the day when, as a 12-year-old, Sabathia "threw a fastball that about broke my hand, it stung so bad," as his mother recalled to Terry Pluto for the *Akron Beacon Journal* (May 8, 2000). At about that time, Sabathia's parents got divorced. Although he remained close to his father, Sabathia has credited his mother with raising him. "She relates to me. We can just talk to each other about anything," he told Les Carpenter. "My mother, she kept me straight." (To cite one example of their bond, during his rookie season his mother stopped smoking, after promising him that she would quit if he won 10 games.)

At Vallejo Senior High School, Sabathia excelled at both football, in the tight-end position, and baseball. By his own account, he lost only one baseball game in high school: his size and strength, coupled with his control, made his pitches virtually unhittable. He soon gained a reputation as "a hard-throwing and sometimes hot-headed pitcher," as Stan McNeal put it. "I used to get mad when somebody would get a hit off me," Sabathia told McNeal. He recalled to Tom Withers for the Associated Press (March 2, 2001), "All I used to think about was striking guys out and throwing the ball as hard as I could." His senior-year statistics were outstanding: six wins, no losses, a .77 earned-run average, and 82 strikeouts in just over 42 innings. By the time he graduated from high school, Sabathia was considered a major prospect in both baseball and football. As an all-conference tight end, he was offered scholarships to play football at the University of California at Los Angeles (UCLA) and the University of Hawaii. Instead, he joined the Cleveland Indians, who picked him in the first round of the 1998 draft (after 19 other teams had

passed on him) and, thanks to negotiations that his mother handled, offered him a $1.3 million signing bonus. Later, when Tom Withers asked him why he had chosen baseball over football, Sabathia responded, "One-point-three. My mom was making $18,000 a year, so we needed that a lot."

Sabathia started out the 1999 season with the Mahoning Valley Scrappers, a minor-league team whose association with the Indians had begun that year; later in the season he was transferred to the team in Kinston, North Carolina, the advanced Class A affiliate of the Indians. Even though he was fast becoming the organization's number-one prospect, Cleveland officials opted not to rush his entry into major-league play. "He doesn't act like he thinks he's a big deal," Mike Bacsik, one of Sabathia's teammates in Kinston, told Terry Pluto. "You look at him and you know that he's going to be a No. 1 starter in the big leagues. You know that he got the big bonus. You know he's a Top Dog, that he's going to be pushed along. But with him, it doesn't bother you." By the spring of 2000, Sabathia had been promoted to Cleveland's Double-A team in Akron, where he averaged one strikeout per inning. "More than anything, my first few starts were more of an adjustment period," Sabathia told David Lee Morgan Jr. for the *Akron Beacon Journal* (September 2, 1998). "I learned really fast that at this level, you just can't get away with trying to throw the ball right past guys like I did in high school. You have to develop two or three more pitches, and I'm working on that." Sabathia was picked for the 2000 U.S. Olympic baseball team but was called back by the Indians after they learned that he would not be used as a starting pitcher in the Games. In the Futures Game in the major league's All-Star weekend in Atlanta, Georgia, that year, he struck out all three batters he faced.

Instead of moving up to the Indians' Triple-A team in 2001, Sabathia reported for spring training with the Indians. He was the youngest player in the major leagues at that time, and, according to Ocker, "almost from the first day, he was the most talked-about player in camp." Charlie Manuel, who managed the Indians from 2000 to 2002, told Ocker, "C.C. is very coachable. He listens." In his first major-league start, on April 8, 2001, an admittedly nervous Sabathia threw 28 fastballs in a row and pitched five innings. In total during his rookie season, he won 15 of the 19 games that he pitched, thus becoming the first Indians rookie pitcher to win 13 or more games since Dennis Eckersley in 1975. George Vass, writing for *Baseball Digest* (December 1, 2001), described him as "the lone dependable starter in an injury-battered Indians starting staff" and as "the Indians' slump-stopper" and referred to his "undeniable brilliance." Among rookies, his outstanding performance was surpassed that year only by that of Ichiro Suzuki, an outfielder for the Seattle Mariners, who was named Rookie of the Year. Looking back on that season, Sabathia remembered being very conscious of his youthfulness: "It was fun, but I didn't feel like I was part of the team," he said to Sheldon Ocker for the *Akron Beacon Journal* (April 28, 2005). "I think I was the youngest guy by about eight years." In the off-season he signed a contract with the Indians that was worth up to $20 million—at that time the biggest contract ever given to a pitcher with only one year under his belt. With some of his earnings, Sabathia bought his mother a car and a house and persuaded her to quit her telephone-company job, which she had held since age 15.

Sabathia showed up for spring training in 2002 weighing well over 300 pounds. His weight possibly contributed to his disappointing performance during the first half of the season, when he won five games and lost six and had an earned-run average of 5.00 at the end of June. Off the playing field, as Scott Priestle wrote for the *Columbus (Ohio) Dispatch* (June 27, 2003), he behaved "like a kid in a candy store, enjoying the spoils of his newfound fame and fortune." He and his teammate Milton Bradley often went out drinking, and one night Sabathia and a cousin of his were robbed at gunpoint as they left a late-night party in downtown Cleveland; the thieves reportedly stole more than $44,000 in cash and jewelry from the pitcher. Sabathia has referred to that incident as both a turning point and a wake-up call. He finished the season with 149 strikeouts, placing him 10th in the American League in that category. He spent the off-season exercising, dieting, and studying tapes of his performances from the past summer. The pitcher was named to the American League All-Star team in 2003 (he had 13 wins and 141 strikeouts that season) and 2004 (11 wins and 139 strikeouts). Outside baseball, the year 2004 was a difficult one for Sabathia: his father, an uncle, and a close cousin of his died. In the spring of 2005, the Indians signed him to a lucrative contract extension that would keep him in Cleveland through the 2008 season. Over the following two seasons, 2005 and 2006, he put up solid numbers (161 strikeouts and 15 wins in the former year, 172 strikeouts, 44 walks, and a 3.22 ERA in the latter), although minor injuries, including abdominal strain and injuries to a hamstring and a knee, arguably kept him from reaching his full potential.

The next year, 2007, proved to be his best yet. Sabathia, who started in 34 games, led the major leagues in innings pitched (241) and posted career bests in wins (19), earned-run average (3.21), and strikeouts (209), while demonstrating his control and precision by walking only 37 batters. His strikeout-to-walk ratio of 5.65 to one was the second-best for a southpaw in baseball history. At the end of the season, Sabathia won both the Warren Spahn Award for best lefthander in baseball and the American League Cy Young Award, for which he received 19 of a possible 28 first-place votes. Observers noted that, given the poor performance of the Indians' offense, the number of wins Sabathia achieved was remarkable. "Without verbalizing it, he essentially produced a classic 'climb on my back and I'll carry us to the finish line' type of season," Scott Miller wrote for CBS Sports (November 13, 2007, on-line). Cleveland's general manager, Mark Shapiro, told Mike Fitzpatrick for the Associated Press (November 14, 2007), "This year he crossed the final gates of being a true No. 1. C.C. took ownership of what he could control and let go of the things he couldn't control, and that allowed him to really focus pitch to pitch, stay in his delivery and turn into a pitcher instead of just a guy with great potential and a great arm. Maybe the most influential leadership he demonstrated this year was how he handled the stretch of five to seven games where he got almost no run support. He never pointed fingers, never felt sorry for himself, stayed a positive, team-oriented guy and continued to contribute and pull for our team's victories, not worrying about his own individual performance." In the play-offs, however, Sabathia struggled; he lost both games in the American League championship series, and the Indians lost to the eventual World Series champions, the Boston Red Sox. "I can definitely say I was trying to do too much," Sabathia told reporters, according to Miller. "[I'd] try to make the perfect pitch instead of pitching like I did all year, trusting my stuff and letting the ball go."

Toward the end of the 2007 season, the Indians' pitching coach, Carl Willis, told Steve Greenberg for the *Sporting News* (September 13, 2007, on-line) that Sabathia's control is "beyond impressive for a pitcher his size. Guys with long limbs, significant height and wingspans, they have a lot to keep together in their delivery." Modeling himself on the celebrated pitcher Tom Glavine, Sabathia has developed a slider-curveball (sometimes referred to as a "slurve") and an off-speed change-up, which have allowed him to add an element of unpredictability to his repertoire.

On July 7, 2008, after starting the 2008 season with the Indians, Sabathia was traded for four prospects to the Milwaukee Brewers. In what many Clevelanders saw as a classy move, Sabathia placed a big advertisement in the Cleveland *Plain Dealer*, thanking the team, fans, and community for their hospitality in his 10 years there. Moving to the National League, Sabathia remained dominant, posting a 1.65 ERA, 11 wins, and only two losses in seven complete games—three of them shutouts—with the Brewers. His 2008 season totals for both teams were outstanding: 17 wins, 10 losses, a 2.70 ERA, and 251 strikeouts. The Brewers reached the play-offs for the first time since 1982, and although they lost in the first round to the Philadelphia Phillies (who went on to win the World Series), baseball fans from across the U.S. voted him Major League Baseball's Clutch Performer of the Year.

Sabathia has maintained strong ties to his hometown, where residents, teachers, and coaches speak highly of him as a humble and grounded person who has not forgotten his roots. He has contributed both time and money to the local Boys and Girls Club and the North Vallejo Little League. "I want to show [young people]," he told an Associated Press reporter in 2007. "I came from there. These are the fields I played on. There is a way out, and it could be baseball." Sabathia has spoken publicly about the scarcity of African-Americans in Major League Baseball. Only 8.5 percent of the players in 2007 were black—far fewer than when he was a boy. In 2006 he was the only black player on the Indians' starting roster, and the next year he was one of only two African-American starting pitchers in the big leagues (the other was Dontrelle Willis). He believes that Major League Baseball should be promoting the game to inner-city youths who regard basketball as a quicker, more lucrative path to success. "They don't see us playing," he said to a reporter for the Associated Press (March 14, 2007). "When I grew up, I was a pitcher and I liked the Oakland A's. I liked Dave Stewart. I was a big left-handed hitter, so I liked Dave Parker. You had Barry Bonds playing in San Francisco, guys like that. There were a lot of guys to look up to. . . . I don't think people understand that there is a problem. They see players like Jose Reyes and Carlos Delgado and just assume that they're black."

In the off-season Sabathia lives in Fairfield, California, not far from where he grew up, with his wife and high-school sweetheart, Amber, and their two children, Carsten Charles III and Jaeden Arie. He is known for wearing his baseball cap tilted slightly to the right, which he has characterized as "a left-hander's thing."

—M.M.

Suggested Reading: *Akron (Ohio) Beacon Journal* C p1 May 8, 2000, B p1 Feb. 2, 2001, C p1 Mar. 28, 2001; Associated Press Mar. 14, 2007; Cleveland (Ohio) *Plain Dealer* C p1 Feb. 24, 2002; *Seattle Times* Sports Oct. 13, 2001; *Sporting News* (on-line) Sep. 13, 2007

Sandberg, Sheryl

Aug. 28, 1969– Chief operating officer of Facebook

Address: Facebook, 471 Emerson St., Palo Alto, CA 94301-1605

"I want to do things that matter," Sheryl Sandberg told Jessi Hempel for CNNMoney.com (April 11, 2008), less than a month after she joined Facebook Inc. as its first chief operating officer (COO). Inspired by the "facebooks" published each year for incoming students at some colleges, which contain photos of freshmen and information about them, Facebook was founded in 2004 by Mark Zuckerberg, its chief executive officer (CEO), as a social-networking service and Web site. Facebook enables users to set up profiles of themselves, with pictures and background information; post additional photographs, videos, and messages; use applications unique to the site; and join particular social networks, or groups, with selected users, or "friends." The 24-year-old Zuckerberg, who hired the 39-year-old Sandberg, told Carol Hymowitz for the *Wall Street Journal* (April 14, 2008, on-line), "Sheryl and I both believe in building a company that helps people stay connected and makes a positive change in the world." After she graduated with highest honors from Harvard University, in 1991, changing the world for the better—by reducing poverty and improving living standards globally—was the goal of Sandberg's first employer: the World Bank, where she worked with Lawrence H. Summers, one of her former economics professors. She later served as Summers's chief of staff at the U.S. Treasury Department, during Summers's stints there as deputy secretary and then secretary, when Bill Clinton was in the White House. Subsequently, as an executive with Google Inc., she played a major role in the company's phenomenal expansion and influence while also helping to form Google.org and the Google Foundation, which support projects whose ultimate goals are the preservation of Earth's environment and the health of people everywhere. In a description of her that goes far to account for Sandberg's professional achievements and her determination to do good, Summers told Michael J. Ding for the *Harvard Crimson* (March 7, 2008, on-line), "Sheryl is an extraordinarily capable, organized, decisive, and caring person." Sandberg was the youngest person named on *Fortune*'s 2007 list of the 50 most powerful women in business.

Sheryl Kara Sandberg was born on August 28, 1969 to Joel Sandberg, an ophthalmologist, and Adele Sandberg, a teacher of English as a second language. She has one brother, David Sandberg, who is a pediatric neurologist, and one sister, Michelle Sandberg, a pediatrician. At the time of Sheryl Sandberg's birth, her father was a National Institutes of Health researcher in Bethesda, Maryland; when she was two years old, the family moved to North Miami Beach, Florida, where her father joined a private eye-surgery practice. As a youngster she "participated in protest marches, handed out petitions, and worked on letter-writing campaigns to help Soviet Jews," according to Adon Taft, writing for the *Miami Herald* (December 3, 1982, on-line), in an article that centered on her bat mitzvah, a girl's coming-of-age ceremony in Judaism. At that age, 12, she also maintained a correspondence with a penpal, a girl in the Soviet Union. Sandberg attended North Miami Beach High School and then entered Harvard University, in Cambridge, Massachusetts. Impressed by her outstanding work in his class, Lawrence H. Summers, who was then a professor of economics and

Courtesy of eHealthInsurance Services, Inc.

Sheryl Sandberg

political economy, offered to be her adviser for her undergraduate honors thesis, which she wrote on economic factors of domestic violence—in particular, spousal abuse. Summers "made time for me, and he cared about the issue," Sandberg told Liz Willen for bloomberg.com (February 22, 2005). He taught her "to create several models of statistical analysis" to evaluate her research data, as Willen wrote, and he made sure that she was "very rigorous" in her "approach to the data," as Sandberg put it. During her college years Sandberg taught classes in aerobics. "At the end of each class when she had everyone stretch, she'd say, 'Stretch higher, and again higher. See what you can do,'" Adam Freed, a Harvard classmate of hers who worked with Sandberg at Google, told Carol Hymowitz in 2008. "She hasn't changed." When Sandberg graduated from Harvard, in 1991, with an A.B. degree summa cum laude with honors in economics, she won the John H. Williams Prize, awarded to the top student in her major.

After she completed her undergraduate studies, Sandberg joined Summers at the World Bank, where that year (while retaining his Harvard professorship) he had been hired as chief economist and vice president for development economics. Sandberg assisted him in his work as a member of World Bank's loan committee, as a major designer of the strategies for aiding countries in need, and as the director of the bank's research, statistics, and training programs. At one point she traveled to India to help with a World Bank project that aimed to lower or eliminate the incidence of leprosy in that nation. (About 60 percent of leprosy victims worldwide live in India, at least 100,000 new cases are diagnosed there every year, and there are still 1,000 colonies in India in which lepers are isolated from the larger society. Caused by a bacterium, leprosy can be cured with antibiotics.)

In 1993 Sandberg entered the Harvard Business School, where she won a Baker scholarship (awarded to those in the top 5 percent of their class) and a Ford scholarship (for those who receive the highest possible grade in each of their 10 first-year classes). As a graduate student she co-wrote, with V. Kasturi Rangan and Sohel Karim, a paper on marketing strategies for social-change efforts; called "Do Better at Doing Good," it was published in the *Harvard Business Review* (May/June 1996). Sandberg received an M.B.A. degree with highest distinction in 1995. She then spent about a year working for McKinsey & Co., an international management consulting firm. After that she rejoined Summers, who had been named deputy secretary of the U.S. Treasury Department, then headed by Robert E. Rubin, an appointee of President Bill Clinton. As Summers's chief of staff, Sandberg was by his side as he helped to formulate the U.S. government's economic and budget strategies, handled such Treasury Department matters as debt management and tax policies, and worked on international issues. She remained his chief of staff when, in July 1999, Summers succeeded Rubin as treasury secretary. She now assisted Summers as he oversaw the reduction in the federal budget deficit, which resulted in the first budget surplus in the U.S. in 29 years; as he spearheaded efforts to enact the most wide-ranging deregulation of financial institutions in 60 years; and as he worked to reform the International Monetary Fund, secure debt relief for the world's poorest countries, and fight against international money laundering. She also worked with Summers as he expanded the Treasury Department's role in the formulation of U.S. foreign policies, reflecting the increase in globalization and the growing economic interdependence of nations. According to Jessi Hempel, at the Treasury Department Sandberg "gained a reputation for her intellect, organizational abilities and her skills in managing personal relationships." "She was one of the people who kept [the department] together," Lee Sachs, who served as assistant secretary of the treasury for financial markets under Summers, told Hempel. Summers himself told Hempel that Sandberg "never let an event go without a resolution. It made my job easier, and it made me perform better."

When the Clinton administration ended, in January 2001, the now out-of-work Sandberg turned down several job offers from investment banks and instead began investigating possibilities in the technology sector. "I wanted to get into technology, because having viewed the economy from a very macro level that the Treasury Department would view it from, I realized that the growth and the excitement was in technology," she told a writer for *Sales & Marketing Management* (April 2006, on-line). "I really wanted to go to a company that was very mission-based. All my previous jobs were mission-based places." Sandberg found what she was looking for at Google Inc. At that time Google was a relatively small company, with fewer than 300 employees and its offices all in one building. (The company now employs more than 16,000 people and has dozens of offices in Europe, Asia, South America, and Australia as well as the U.S.) When Eric Schmidt, Google's CEO, interviewed her, as she told Jason Goldberg for jobster.blogs.com (February 15, 2006), he gave her what she described as the "best career advice": "The most important thing to get right when selecting a job is how quickly the company is growing," he told her. "Growth creates numerous opportunities for anyone who is contributing to the company's success, whereas when companies stop growing, the careers of everyone, including very talented people, face severe challenges."

After a brief period at Google, Sandberg was named the company's vice president of global online sales and operations, with responsibility for the newly created AdWords program. AdWords made possible the posting of site-specific ads based on each user's geographic location and the key words he or she had chosen for Google searches. The program was a boon for small and midsize businesses; with millions of people using Google daily, they now had greatly increased chances of reaching prospective customers. David Fischer, who was Sandberg's deputy at Google and now holds her position there, told Hempel, "While the rest of us are planning three [financial] quarters ahead, she was thinking about how we jump ahead a number of years." In half a dozen years, Sandberg's staff grew from four to 4,000, according to Carol Hymowitz, and the international on-line sales unit became Google's biggest source of revenue, accounting for more than half of its income.

In 2004 Larry Page and Sergey Brin, Google's founders, resolved to make use of the wealth of intelligence and talent within their company to work toward easing or eradicating two of the world's most serious problems: global warming and poverty; they later added the threat of pandemic disease, drought, or other environmental catastrophes as an area of concern. Page and Brin promised to devote 1 percent of the firm's equity and 1 percent of profits toward that end, along with 20 percent of the work time of self-chosen employees. While maintaining her other responsibilities, Sandberg was placed in charge of Google.org, as the company's philanthropic arm was named (referred to in-house as DotOrg), with the understanding that a search would be launched for a permanent head. In 2005 she helped to set up a foundation to handle the awarding of grants to nonprofit groups and socially progressive corporations. In the difficult process of selecting recipients, Sandberg told Harriet Rubin for the *New York Times* (January 18, 2008), Google.org avoided what she and her colleagues considered mainstream efforts. "If you do things other people could do, you're not adding value," she explained. In February 2006 Google hired Lar-

ry Brilliant, a specialist in preventive medicine, as executive director of Google.org; Sandberg, as a member of the Google Foundation's board, remained active in helping to further Google's charitable goals.

By 2008 Google.org's goals had spawned five initiatives, called RE<C, RechargeIT, Predict and Prevent, Inform and Empower, and SMEs. As described on the Google.org Web site, the aim of RE<C is "to develop electricity from renewable energy sources that is cheaper than electricity produced from coal with a goal of producing one gigawatt of renewable energy capacity—enough to power a city the size of San Francisco—in years, not decades." RechargeIT supports the creation of electrically powered cars and trucks and their widespread use, so that "one day a large portion of the world's vehicles will plug into an electric grid fueled by renewable energy." Predict and Prevent grew out of the fear that "rapid ecological and social changes are increasing the risk of emerging threats, from infectious diseases to drought and other environmental disasters." "This initiative," the Google.org description continued, "will use information and technology to empower communities to predict and prevent emerging threats before they become local, regional, or global crises." Inform and Empower sprang from the belief of Sandberg and her colleagues "that providing meaningful, easily accessible information to citizens and communities, service providers, and policymakers is a key part of creating home-grown solutions to improve the quality of public services"—among them the provision of clean water, sewer systems, and effective schools and medical care. "SMEs" stands for "small and medium-sized enterprises": "SMEs create opportunities for more people to participate in the formal economy"—which includes the services of banks—"and help reduce poverty by creating jobs." As of January 2008, according to its Web site, Google.org had committed more than $75 million in grants and investments to achieve those goals.

In 2007 Sandberg began to consider employment outside Google. Her team there, she told Kara Swisher for All Things Digital (March 10, 2008, online), "was in great shape and I felt like it was time for change for me." Sandberg's friend Roger McNamee, a venture capitalist, and her brother-in-law, Marc Bodnick, a business partner of McNamee's and an investor in Facebook, suggested that she discuss job possibilities with Mark Zuckerberg, Facebook's founder and CEO. Sandberg was already an enthusiastic Facebook user; she had about 600 "friends" at the site and belonged to a dozen groups. Sandberg and Zuckerberg were introduced at a Christmas party, and during the next two months they talked regularly. "It was very philosophical at first and we did not ever talk about a specific job," Sandberg told Swisher. In early March 2008 Zuckerberg announced that he had hired Sandberg to be Facebook's first COO. The attractions of moving to Facebook, Sandberg has said, included its relative newness (the company marked its fourth anniversary in February 2008) and its relative smallness (it currently has 500 employees). "For me that is part of the excitement," she told Brad Stone and Miguel Helft for the *New York Times* (March 5, 2008). "I've loved being part of the process of helping to build Google. The opportunity to help another young company to grow into a global leader is the opportunity of a lifetime."

As of early 2008 Facebook had about 60 million active members (that is, users who had logged in within the past 30 days), among them an increasing number of corporate or business users and political figures, including the presidential candidates Senator Barack Obama of Illinois and Congressman Ron Paul of Texas. Every day, according to the company, 250,000 new users were registering; thus, every week, the membership rolls were growing by about 3 percent. A little more than half of the users were between 18 and 25—an age range considered highly desirable by many sellers of products or services—and, on average, each spent 30 to 45 minutes on the site daily. The number of Facebook pages viewed per month topped 65 billion. A software-development kit enables users to post their own programs; so far, the site offers more than 10,000 such applications, and the total is growing by about 100 each day. The number of groups categorized as regional, work-related, collegiate, or linked to high schools totaled more than 55,000. The vast variety of groups included the more predictable sorts, such as study groups in many subject areas and fans of particular sports, movie genres, and books, as well as more original ones—with such names as West Point Cadets Who Aren't Staunch Republicans, People Who Grew Up with Mountains and Want to Build One in Nebraska, and Students Against Backpacks with Wheels.

When Sandberg began working at Facebook, on March 24, 2008, the company was not earning—and never had earned—as much money as it was spending, according to various sources. As Facebook's COO she took on responsibilities that include increasing ad sales and expanding the business, especially in overseas markets. Her purview also includes public policy and communications and building a business model for Facebook, whose operations have been described as helter-skelter. Facebook has "tremendous potential to connect people, but it needs scale"—that is, growth—"it needs systems and processes to have impact, and I can do that," Sandberg told Hymowitz. According to Kara Swisher, Sandberg "thinks the company needs to focus on scaling operationally, scaling geographically and scaling monetization, and the rest will take care of itself."

Within two weeks of her arrival, according to Carol Hymowitz, Sandberg was "rolling out new management and operations procedures," among them "guidelines for employee performance reviews, processes for identifying and recruiting new employees, and management-training programs."

"It feels like she's been here six months already," Dan Rose, the vice president of business development, told Hymowitz. "She has met every employee, learned what they do, and makes a point of acknowledging people's hard work. The fact that she brings experience makes people feel comfortable."

According to Hymowitz, Sandberg is a "consummate networker." Sandberg described herself to Hymowitz as a "tough-love leader" who seeks to "mentor and demand at the same time, and make it safe to make mistakes." She has sat on the board of directors of eHealthInsurance Services Inc. since 2006. Sandberg's first marriage ended in divorce. In 2004 she married David Goldberg, an entrepreneur-in-residence at Benchmark Capital; previously, he was the vice president and general manager of Yahoo! Music. The couple live in Atherton, California, with their two young children.

—F.C.

Suggested Reading: CNNMoney.com Apr. 11, 2008; Facebook Web site; Google Web site; *New York Times* C p6 Mar. 5, 2008; *Sales and Marketing* Web site Apr. 2006; *Wall Street Journal* (on-line) Mar. 5, 2008, Apr. 14, 2008

Schmidt, Eric

Apr. 27, 1955– CEO and chairman of Google Inc.

Address: Google, 1600 Amphitheatre Pkwy., Mountain View, CA 94043

In August 2001, when the Internet strategist and technology developer Eric Schmidt became the chairman and chief executive officer (CEO) of Google Inc., the three-year-old company was already the number-one search engine on the Web, responding to more than 100 million Internet searches per day by means of its library of 1.3 billion Web pages. Schmidt joined Google's co-founders, Sergey Brin and Larry Page, who had developed the revolutionary technology as graduate students at Stanford University while in their 20s. He brought 20 years of technical experience to Google, four of them as the CEO of Novell, which developed network-operating-system technology in the 1980s. Earlier, Schmidt worked for Sun Microsystems, leading the development of the widely used programming script Java. Sharing executive responsibilities with Page and Brin—and often, according to some observers, playing the role of the sober adult to counter their more free-wheeling management styles—Schmidt has led Google to extraordinary levels of innovation and growth; its share price has risen to over eight times its initial price offering of $85 in 2004. Under Schmidt's management, Google has acquired scores of technology and media companies and developed dozens of new features and applications.

Jung Yeon-Je/AFP/Getty Images

Eric Schmidt

It has also increased its market presence by forging partnerships, licensing both its search technology and its revolutionary target-based advertising technology to companies including Yahoo!, MySpace, the *New York Times*, and MTV. Currently, both of those innovative technologies are nearly ubiquitous on the Web.

By all accounts, Google has secured a spot in the public's consciousness as the best, fastest, most accurate search technology on Earth. It now wields tremendous cultural power by determining, with its algorithms, what information reaches the public fastest in any given Google search. "More than anyone else, Google is defining the new architecture of media and commerce in the digital world," Rob Hof wrote for *BusinessWeek* (April 9, 2007). "The unruly expanse of the Internet and its opportunities cries out for a map, and that's what Google is building out of tens of thousands of server computers around the world that handle quadrillions of bytes of data."

Eric Emerson Schmidt was born on April 27, 1955 in Washington, D.C., and grew up in Blacksburg, Virginia. In interviews he has revealed little about his childhood. His father was a professor of economics at Virginia Tech. As a high-school student, Schmidt excelled at mathematics and science. He attended Princeton University, in New Jersey, where he studied architecture until he concluded that he was "truly terrible" at it, as he told Gary Andrew Poole for the *New York Times* (February 4, 1999). He changed his major to electrical engineering and earned a B.S. degree in that subject in 1976. He earned M.S. and Ph.D. degrees in computer science from the University of California at Berkeley in 1979 and 1982, respectively. While

pursuing his doctorate Schmidt taught part-time at Stanford University, in California. Early in his career he worked as a researcher for companies specializing in information and communications technologies (ICT). His employers included Zilog, Bell Laboratories, and, from 1979 to 1983, Xerox Palo Alto Research Center.

In 1983 Schmidt joined Sun Microsystems as a software manager. He was promoted to vice president and general manager of Sun's software-products division in 1985 and to vice president of the general systems group in 1988. For three years beginning in 1991, he served as president of Sun Technology Enterprises, a division of Sun Microsystems. By the time he returned to the parent company, in 1994, with the title of chief technical officer, Sun had become the nation's leading maker of workstations (high-end microcomputers). Schmidt was the primary strategist in the development of Java technology, a programming language that can run on any computer with a Java virtual machine (software that converts computer codes into computer language and executes them). An advantage of Java technology and Java virtual machines is that they can span multiple computer networks.

In March 1997 Schmidt left Sun to join Novell Inc. as CEO. Based in Provo, Utah, Novell had been a pioneer in the development of network-operating-system technology since the early 1980s. Netware, as Novell's technology is called, allows individuals logged on to the same network to share files and connect to a shared printer. With IPX/SPX protocol, which was specifically designed for the local area networks (LANs) most popular among Internet users, Netware became the dominant networking software in the 1980s and into the Internet boom of the 1990s. Although Novell continued to grow, in part by acquiring networking businesses, it failed to keep pace with other companies, particularly Microsoft, in developing its Internet business. From 1993 to 1999 Novell's market share for network operating systems fell from 44 percent to 19 percent, while during that same period Microsoft increased its market share from 2 to 38 percent. In August 1996, faced with mounting pressure from shareholders, Novell's CEO, Robert Frankenberg, resigned.

Wall Street reacted positively to Novell's choice of Schmidt as Frankenberg's successor: on the day that his appointment was announced, the company's stock price gained 87.5 cents, closing at $9.43 per share. "Novell has to reposition itself as an Internet leader, and Eric brings a lot of credibility to that," Jon Oltsik, a Forrester Research analyst, told Lawrence M. Fisher for the *New York Times* (March 19, 1997). Schmidt promised to create partnerships with software companies, including Sun, and emphasized what he considered Novell's underestimated assets. "Novell has a huge user base, and more people devoted to networking protocols than anyone in the industry," he told Fisher. "They are also moving to the Internet and Java as fast as they can, which was a big selling point for me because I didn't want to go to a place that didn't have the same strategic vision I have."

Two weeks after he was hired, Schmidt publicly disclosed that the company would face a net loss in its second quarter due to poor sales. As Novell's share price dropped, Schmidt announced plans to lay off 1,000 workers—about 18 percent of the workforce—reducing the global payroll to about 4,800. "It's very, very painful for everyone, but it's the right proportion," Schmidt told employees in Dallas, Texas, about the job cuts, as quoted by Steve Lohr in the *New York Times* (July 24, 1997). By July shares of Novell's stock were valued at $6.9375, down from $13 the previous February.

During the summer of 1997, Schmidt directed the integration of Netware with Internet-standard software in a product code called Moab. "It's Netware updated for the 90's," he told Lohr. "And it's something this company should have done two or three years ago." To attract potential employees, Novell spent $130 million renovating its campus; emulating posh technology complexes in Silicon Valley, California, the firm built tennis, volleyball, and basketball courts, a restaurant, a gym, and an espresso bar. In November 1998 Schmidt announced that Novell and Cisco, the leading supplier of networking and network-management equipment, had agreed to make their software and hardware compatible. The collaboration was seen as an effort by Novell to slow Microsoft's dominance of the market. After consecutive quarters showing increasing revenues, on May 2, 2000 Novell surprised investors by announcing significant decreases in revenues in the year's second quarter, to $305 million, down from $316 million the year before, and only marginal profits. Later that month Schmidt announced a plan to package Novell's Web software into bundles to be sold to application-service providers, or ASPs, which would offer rentable e-commerce or Net-collaboration software over the Web. Writing for *BusinessWeek* (May 29, 2000), Jim Kerstetter noted, "If Schmidt can give Novell a new identity, the company could have a brighter future. It has been selling these products for years, but it hasn't been able to establish a reputation as a crucial supplier of Net software." On September 6, 2000 Schmidt eliminated 900 jobs—about 16 percent of Novell's global workforce then—and announced plans to cut quarterly costs further by about $25 million. By November 2000 Novell's stock price had declined significantly, to $6 a share. "We've had a pretty difficult year," Schmidt admitted in a conference call, as quoted by the *New York Times* (November 23, 2000). "We expect sequential growth in 2001, but no year-on-year revenue growth until after 2001."

In March 2001, while remaining with Novell, Schmidt joined the board of directors of Google, whose popularity had skyrocketed since its founding three years earlier by Larry Page and Sergey Brin, during their graduate-student days at Stanford University. The following August Page and Brin asked Schmidt to become Google's CEO. As a Google spokeswoman, Cindy McCaffrey, told Paul Beebe for the *Salt Lake Tribune* (August 7, 2001), Page and Brin had met Schmidt, and been favorably impressed, when contacting him as a reference for a job applicant. Page, Google's founding chief executive, became the firm's president of products, and Brin, the founding president, became president of technology. Google's technology—dubbed "PageRank"—consists of an extremely complex network of algorithms that ranks Web sites on a scale of importance based on the number of links connecting that site with other sites. The result is an objective ranking of Web sites based on relevance. As noted in *BusinessWeek* (September 24, 2001), a survey conducted by the market researcher NPD Group found that 97 percent of Google's users located what they were looking for "every time" or "most of the time," making Google the Internet's most effective search engine.

Schmidt's presence at Google introduced an element of gravity to a company whose corporate culture has from the start been far from conventional. Page, Brin, and Schmidt act as a threesome in which each holds equal weight in making executive decisions. They also strive to involve employees in decision-making—often in large, noisy meetings—encouraging debate and disagreement with the goal of gaining their workers' full commitment to projects. Schmidt recalled to Quentin Hardy for *Forbes* (November 14, 2005) that at a 10-person management meeting he attended early on, he observed the absence of a hierarchical culture in decision-making. "It took me six months to understand how Google works," he told Adi Ignatius for *Time* (February 20, 2006). "The subtleties took a year." The company is known for hiring only highly intelligent people, most of them engineers, and usually with no specific job in mind for them. According to Page and Brin, an unstructured environment nurtures employees' creativity. Toward that end, a ping-pong table serves as the boardroom table, and the company offers free professional in-office massages, on-campus rock concerts, and giant rubber balls as alternative furniture. Employees are encouraged to spend 70 percent of their time on Google's core business, 20 percent on projects that are related to the core business, and 10 percent on projects of their own choosing. Schmidt introduced into that environment a few elements of structure, among them a streamlined accounting system and the scheduling of regular meetings.

In the early 2000s, as Schmidt told Tom Spring for *PC World* (January 30, 2002), Google earned about 50 percent of its profits from sales of its search technology to Yahoo! and other Internet sites. The other half came from paid advertisements that appeared as links alongside related search results. According to Google's Web site, such links benefit both users and advertisers by limiting each ad's exposure to the most receptive audience. In early 2002 Google revamped its ad technology so that companies were charged only when a person clicked on the link, making advertising more cost-effective.

Even as Google's ad technology grew, Schmidt told Robert Weisman for the *Boston Globe* (February 4, 2002) that "search" continued to be Google's main focus. "The mission of the company is [retrieving] all of the world's information," he said. "It's not all the world's information currently available on the Web, it's all of the world's information. So what I do is I sit down every day and I think about, 'What information do I need to get through the day and why isn't it on Google?'"

In the next several years, Google product offerings multiplied, in part thanks to its acquisition of several small start-up tech companies whose engineering teams specialized in product innovations. One such product, Google News, launched in September 2002, offered access to 4,500 news sources. In 2003 Google acquired Pyra Labs, whose engineers created Blogger, Google's provider of Web-logging, or blogging, services. That year Google released its own toolbar, offering a variety of features, including the possibility to use Google to search the Internet without opening a Web browser. On April 1, 2004 Google launched Gmail, a free Web mail service. The following October Google acquired Keyhole Corp., a digital- and satellite-image-mapping company, which provided the technology that would eventually become Google Earth, a search tool that allows users to view three-dimensional images of Earth, including roads and buildings. The year 2005 saw the launches of Google Video, an on-line service that captures closed-caption TV programming and makes it searchable, and Google Maps, an on-line map and navigation provider. Google also began selling its so-called AdSense technology to Blogger users so that they could profit from ads posted on their blogs. Google's creation of so many new products, coupled with rumors about its unconventional work environment, had led to the widely held assumption that the company lacked focus. Schmidt told Adi Ignatius that projecting an image of disorganization a calculated strategy. "We try very hard to look like we're out of control," he explained. "But in fact the company is very measured. And that's part of our secret."

Earlier, in August 2004, Google had made an initial public offering of its stock, with prices starting at $85 per share. In October 2004 Google's first quarterly results as a public company showed revenues of $805.9 million, up 105 percent from the previous year. By November 2005 Google's stocks were selling for about $340 per share. Share prices broke the $700 mark on October 31, 2007. As a result of the subsequent economic downturn, by March 10, 2008 the value of each share was $425, and by October 28, 2008 the figure was about $342 per share.

As Google grew, it began licensing its search and advertisement technologies to such companies as America Online, AOL Europe, Time Warner, Fox Media, Dell, Intuit, eBay, MySpace, and MTV. In October 2006 Google acquired the Internet video-sharing company YouTube.com for a reported $1.65 billion in stock. The next April, in a $3.1 billion deal, Google bought DoubleClick, a company that offers delivery technology and services to advertisers. Such huge purchases notwithstanding, Schmidt told a journalist for *PCMagazine* (May 11, 2007) that Google continued to focus primarily on smaller acquisitions, buying, on average, one startup Internet company per week, as a way of constantly diversifying its portfolio. "No other company has ever grown this much this fast," Quentin Hardy wrote for *Forbes* (October 16, 2006).

In February 2006 Google introduced spreadsheet software, on-line word processing, and a digital payment service, sold for a fraction of the price of Microsoft's Office Suite. At a conference called the Web 2.0 Summit, Schmidt told John Batelle, the founder and chairman of Federated Media Publishing, that Google's applications were fundamentally different from Microsoft's, as quoted by Natali Del Conte in *PC Magazine* (November 9, 2006): "We don't see it as a replacement of Office. The focus we have is not the focus they have. Our focus is on casual sharing and casual collaboration." That year Google also introduced Google Gadgets; similar to Apple Computer's Dashboard widgets, those small applications can be downloaded onto users' desktops.

In November 2007 Schmidt announced an alliance with a number of the leading technology and wireless companies on the development of Android, the first truly open and comprehensive platform for mobile devices. The platform would include an operating system, middleware (which enables programs designed for access to a particular database to access others), user interfaces, and applications. "The best model to get volume is to be open. That's what the Internet has taught us," Schmidt told Todd Spangler for *Multichannel News* (November 12, 2007).

In July 2007 Schmidt announced Google's intention to participate in the upcoming Federal Communications Commission (FCC) auction for $4.6 billion worth of wireless frequencies. Schmidt vowed to pay the asking price for the frequencies if, as came to pass, the FCC agreed to make the spectrum "open access," allowing customers to use the frequencies to run any device or software application. In February 2008 Google bid $4.6 billion; Verizon promptly submitted a bid for $4.74 billion. Although at the end of the auction, Google walked away empty-handed, the company accomplished its goal of adding the "open-access" qualification to the spectrum. Google's interest in the wireless frequencies sparked speculation about the introduction of a possible "Google phone," a challenge to Apple's immensely successful iPhone. After months of rumors, in September 2008 Google and T-Mobile unveiled the T-Mobile G1, which uses both a touch screen and a keyboard and is the first mobile phone to be powered by

Google's Android operating system. The phone went on sale on October 22, 2008 for $179.

Along with abundant praise from computer analysts, advertisers, and Web users, Google has drawn criticism on a number of fronts. In 2004 Google came under fire for failing to secure permission from publishers to scan book pages and store the searchable pages in its database. Though Google tried to quell complaints, the Authors Guild and a group of publishers, including Mc-Graw-Hill, filed lawsuits in 2005. Google temporarily halted the program and released a statement defending it as ultimately beneficial to authors and publishers. The statement also pointed out that only small portions of books could be viewed through the search, and that authors and publishers could choose to exclude their books from the program. On October 28, 2008 Google announced that it had reached a $125 million deal with book publishers to settle the two copyright lawsuits and establish a Book Rights Registry. Under the new registry, users of Google Book Search will be able to build an "on-line bookshelf" and buy licenses to read the full texts of Google's books; libraries, universities, and other organizations will also be able to purchase institutional subscriptions to fully access Google's texts. The registry will ensure that publishers and authors receive compensation from subscription services and ad revenues.

Earlier, in March 2007, Viacom had sued Google for $1 billion, accusing YouTube of willfully infringing on copyrights by allowing users to upload clips of various TV shows. While the lawsuit was still pending, as of late October 2008, Schmidt expressed his belief that the problem would be solved with Google's yet-to-be-released piracy fighter, a tool called Claim Your Content, which would allow owners of content to prove ownership and remove it from the Web.

By April 2007 Google had become the number-one gateway to all Internet sites, used to begin 56 percent of all searches. "In the lives of small-business owners, Google looms as the new Wal-Mart," Justin Martin wrote for *Fortune Small Business* (September 2006). "Many entrepreneurs fear and despise the retailing giant for mistreating vendors and vaporizing small competitors and entire business districts." An Atlanta, Georgia, business owner told Martin that in the months after information about his Internet business disappeared from Google's search results, following Google's adjustments to its logarithms, his revenues fell by 20 percent. "Will the vast commercial landscape of the Net, like so many other tech markets in the past, condense to one dominant force for the foreseeable future? Will we just Google everything?" Rob Hof asked. Schmidt has maintained that Google wants to forge partnerships with media companies, not compete with them, in an effort to improve everyone's business.

In June 2008 Google and Yahoo! agreed to an advertising partnership that would allow Yahoo! to place advertisements sold by Google alongside some of its search results. Some major companies and advertisers—among them Microsoft (Google's rival, which had attempted to purchase Yahoo! for $44.6 billion in February 2008), the Association of National Advertisers, the World Association of Newspapers, and the American Association of World Advertisers—opposed the deal, on the grounds that it would further cement Google's dominance over the search-engine advertising market and push up ad prices. Google and Yahoo! agreed to delay the start of the partnership for 100 days to allow federal regulators to determine whether it violated antitrust laws. Schmidt has said that he anticipated criticism, but that the deal was designed precisely to meet the terms of antitrust laws. As of October 29, 2008 the U.S. Justice Department had not issued a decision about the partnership. Though both companies have said that they would go ahead with the deal by October even if regulators had not completed their investigation, Schmidt recently announced that he would allow regulators more time to arrive at a decision.

In October 2008 Google introduced a new type of e-commerce advertisement that can be used by YouTube viewers to buy digital goods from iTunes or Amazon. The new technology represents an effort by Google to find an advertising model that would make YouTube profitable. In the same month Schmidt announced a 26 percent growth in Google's net income—an increase of $1.35 billion ($4.24 per share). Although the figures showed that, compared with the previous year, Google's growth had slowed considerably, they far exceeded the expectations of investors and seemed to point to Google's ability to withstand the economic downturn.

"A billionaire at 51, Schmidt cuts the typical Silicon Valley figure of somebody's successful, but otherwise average, dad," Adam Lashinsky wrote for *Fortune* (October 2, 2006). "His khakis-and-oxford uniform is standard, as are his wire-frame glasses and Supercuts-inspired hairdo." In August 2006 Schmidt joined the board of directors of Apple Computer Inc. He also serves on the New America Foundation board of directors, and he is a member of the American Academy of Arts and Sciences and the National Academy of Engineering. In 2007 *PC Magazine* placed Schmidt, Page, and Brin at the top of its list of the "Most Important People on the Web." In the half-hour infomercial aired on TV by Democratic U.S. senator Barack Obama of Illinois on October 29, 2008 in his effort to win the presidency, Schmidt spoke in favor of Obama's election.

Schmidt's leisure activities include flying his private plane. He lives in Atherton, California, with his wife, Wendy, and their two children.

—M.E.R.

Suggested Reading: *Business Week* p96 May 29, 2000; *Boston Globe* D p5 Feb. 4, 2002; *Forbes* p108 Oct. 18, 2006; *Fortune* p86 Oct. 2, 2006; *Fortune Small Business* p70 Sep. 2006;

PCWorld.com Jan. 30, 2002; *Time* p36 Feb. 20, 2006, *(*on-line*)* Oct. 2, 2006

Courtesy of Pepper Schwartz

Schwartz, Pepper

May 11, 1945– Sociologist; educator; writer

Address: Dept. of Sociology, University of Washington, 218B Condon Hall, 1100 N.E. Campus Pkwy., Seattle, WA 98195-3340

"I think I know a lot about love," the sociologist Pepper Schwartz told Nicole Brodeur for the *Seattle (Washington) Times* (February 14, 2006). "I have studied it and lived it for thirty years." A professor at the University of Washington, where she has taught since 1972, Schwartz is the author or co-author of 15 books, most of them about love, sex, and other aspects of intimate relationships. *American Couples: Money, Work, Sex* (1983), which she wrote with her colleague Philip Blumstein, established her scholarly reputation, while such books as *The Great Sex Weekend: A 48-Hour Guide to Rekindling Sparks for Bold, Busy, or Bored Lovers* (1997), *201 Questions to Ask Your Kids/201 Questions to Ask Your Parents* (2000), *Everything You Know About Love and Sex Is Wrong* (2001), and *Prime: Adventures and Advice on Sex, Love, and the Sensual Years* (2007) have demonstrated her skills as a popularizer of sociological—and psychological—research. Schwartz has also written or co-written dozens of shorter pieces, among them articles for scholarly journals, seven years' worth of "Sex and Health" columns for the monthly magazine *Glamour*, and eight years' worth of "Talking

about Sex" columns for another monthly, *American Baby*; she has also contributed to publications including the *New York Times, Sexual Health, Psychology Today, Contexts, Ladies' Home Journal, Playboy, Newsweek, Cosmopolitan, Lifetime Magazine,* and *Classmates Magazine,* and for 12 years she was a member of the news staff at KIRO-TV, in Seattle. Schwartz has served as a consultant to the National Academy of Sciences, the American Medical Association, the National Sexuality Resource Center, the dating sites kiss.com and perfectmatch.com, and the health network LLuminari. In addition, she has lectured nationally and internationally and talked on television and radio scores of times on such subjects as communication between parents and children and between men and women; human sexuality; how to maintain personal and family well-being; and women's issues. In 2005 Schwartz received the American Sociological Association's Public Understanding of Sociology Award, which recognizes people who have made "exemplary contributions to the advancement of the public understanding of sociology, sociological research, and scholarship among the general public." Schwartz's work, the award citation read, "demonstrates that sociologists can present research about the most essential aspects of social existence in ways that are understandable and engaging while not betraying underlying methodological and substantive realities. Pepper Schwartz is a model of what sociologists can do to enhance the discipline and help society."

Judith Pepper Schwartz was born in Chicago, Illinois, on May 11, 1945 to Julius J. Schwartz and Gertrude (Puris) Schwartz. As a child she took lessons in horseback riding and developed a passion for that sport that has remained to this day. When she was 11 her mother gave her a booklet about human reproduction, and young Pepper used what she had learned to assure her friend Francie that, contrary to what Francie's mother had told her, masturbation would not lead to eternal damnation. Pleased that she had "saved" Francie, as she recalled to Peter Managhan for the *Chronicle of Higher Education* (September 14, 2007), she started a sex-education group with her mother's help; at meetings that continued for a year, she and a half-dozen of her friends discussed "sex and puberty and our bodies," as she told Managhan.

Schwartz earned a B.A. degree in sociology at Washington University, in St. Louis, Missouri, in 1968; two years later she obtained an M.A. degree there, in the same subject. Schwartz then enrolled at Yale University, in New Haven, Connecticut, with the intention of studying the sociology of law. Yale had accepted its first female undergraduates only three years earlier, and women were still scarce on campus. In that environment Schwartz saw various ways in which gender politics were changing, and she developed an interest in the field of gender studies, which was in its infancy. As a volunteer teaching assistant in a class in sexuality, as she recalled to Claudia Dreifus for the *New*

York Times (April 10, 2007), she was aghast at the sexism, stereotyping, and lopsided morality represented in some of the assigned reading materials. Some of it "made me nuts," as she recalled to Dreifus. "There was all this double-standard stuff about 'bad girls' and 'good girls.' When I scanned the professional literature for alternatives, I couldn't find much. I thought: 'I have to deal with this. This is an area I need to contribute to.'" Dissatisfied as well with the unidimensional treatment of sexuality as a biological phenomenon, Schwartz became fascinated by studies of sexuality within the framework of societal standards. "Many of the earlier sex researchers had been medical doctors," she explained to Dreifus. "For the most part, they looked at sex from a biological standpoint. The other stream was the Kinsey thing"—a reference to the pioneering sexual-behavior surveys conducted in the mid-20th century by Alfred Kinsey, considered to be the "father of sexology"—"which was more an enumeration of sexual acts, but not necessarily meanings—as if all acts were the same as one another. Two researchers I found inspiring were William Simon and John H. Gagnon. They were sociologists. And they believed that to understand sexuality you had to look at how institutions impacted it, that you couldn't separate behavior from a cultural context. People now accept that. But those were new ideas then." At Yale Schwartz earned a second master's degree in 1970 and a Ph.D. in 1974, both in sociology. The title of her doctoral dissertation was "Social Games and Social Roles: Effects of a College Dating System." By the time she completed her doctorate, Schwartz had published two books: *Women at Yale: Liberating a College Campus* (1971), written with another Yale student, the sociologist Janet Lever, and *The Student Guide to Sex on Campus* (1971), written by the the Student Committee on Human Sexuality at Yale, which she co-edited.

In 1972 Schwartz won her first research grant (which she shared with three collaborators, among them the sociologist Philip Blumstein), for a study called "The Communication of Affection." That year she joined the Department of Sociology at the University of Washington (U.W.) at Seattle as an assistant professor. In 1979 U.W. promoted her to associate professor and gave her, in addition, the title of adjunct professor of psychiatry and women's studies; she rose to the rank of full professor in 1988. Earlier, in 1974–75, a U.W. grant supported her research on human sexuality. Her third book, *Sexual Scripts: The Social Construction of Female Sexuality*, written with the sociologist Judith Long Laws, was published in 1977.

That year, with Philip Blumstein, Schwartz won a grant from the National Science Foundation for $236,000 (the equivalent of more than $800,000 in 2008 dollars), to conduct research regarding American couples—specifically, to find out how couples consisting of married heterosexuals, cohabitating heterosexuals, lesbians, or gay males succeeded or failed at maintaining their relationships.

After soliciting volunteers for the study—among them 788 lesbian and 969 gay male couples, populations rarely studied before—Blumstein and Schwartz received back 12,000 completed surveys from 6,000 couples, from which they chose 300 couples for in-depth interviews. About 18 months after the initial survey, those interviewed answered another questionnaire. All the participants lived in New York, Seattle, or San Francisco, California. Among Schwartz and Blumstein's most important findings was that gender played a greater role than sexual orientation in the dynamics of the relationships of married or cohabiting couples. With both heterosexual and homosexual couples, relationships were more likely to end if the male placed greater than usual emphasis on the physical attractiveness of his partner. Infidelity was more detrimental to heterosexual and lesbian relationships than to gay male relationships, in 90 percent of which subjects had had sexual relations with men in addition to their partners. The researchers also found that although 60 percent of wives worked outside the home, virtually all wives did more housework than their spouses. The homosexual relationships tended to be more egalitarian than the heterosexual partnerships. Outward displays of tenderness and affection by men toward their partners correlated more closely with the success of relationships than did frequency of sexual intercourse. In addition, women who were financially independent or could support themselves through jobs were more likely to end their relationships than those who were financially dependent on their mates. "Many unhappy wives stay married because they could not maintain a decent standard of living alone," Schwartz and Blumstein concluded in their book *American Couples: Money, Work, Sex* (1983), in which they described the results of their surveys and interviews.

Carol Tavris, a social psychologist who reviewed *American Couples* for the *New York Times* (October 23, 1983), criticized the study for procedural and theoretical shortcomings: "The sample was biased in the usual ways—respondents were almost entirely white, affluent, moderate-to-liberal, well-educated, professional. This is not a book about immigrant couples, unemployed couples, working-class couples, or minority couples. . . . You will not find here astute, provocative dissection of 'his' and 'her' marriages, as in Jessie Bernard's *The Future of Marriage*; you will not find the eloquence of Studs Terkel's interviewees on the meaning of work. Moreover, the public and professionals alike are past being startled by sheer statistics—Kinsey was the last to get away with that. Without a guiding theory, the authors mistakenly leave out children, who are perhaps the most significant factor in family stress (and pleasure!) and the main reason everyone worries about the high divorce rate." Tavris conceded that "despite these caveats, which are true of all surveys, *American Couples* does offer many findings about modern relationships. Some are truly important."

A *Choice* (April 1984) critic echoed those sentiments, writing that Schwartz and Blumstein's findings "cannot be seen as representative . . . of American couples in general. If we overlook this major shortcoming, we might see the book as offering some interesting and possibly even important material. . . . Despite its limitations, this is a useful book but one which professionals will realize has to be read quite critically." By contrast, Norman Goodman, a sociologist at the State University of New York at Stony Brook, described Schwartz and Blumstein's methodology as "sound," in a review of *American Couples* for the journal *Social Forces* (March 1985), and he pronounced the book to be "interesting, informative, and well-written"; and Francesca M. Cancian, in the *American Journal of Sociology* (November 1984), lauded the book as "impressive," "lively" and "wide-ranging." "Each type of couple gets equal time and equal respect," she wrote. "Part of the effect of this book is that it redefines what constitutes a legitimate American couple."

Schwartz's next book was *Peer Marriage: How Love Between Equals Really Works* (1994). Peer couples, she wrote in an article for *Psychology Today* (September/October 1994), "trade a frustrated, angry relationship with a spouse for one of deep friendship. They may have somewhat tamer sex lives than couples in traditional marriages. They definitely have fewer external sources of validation. And these couples have a closeness that tends to exclude others. But theirs is a collaboration of love and labor that produces profound intimacy and mutual respect. Traditional couples live in separate spheres and have parallel lives. Above all, peer couples live the same life. In doing so, they have found a new way to make love last." Schwartz identified four important characteristics of peer marriages: "The partners do not have more than a 60/40 traditional split of household duties and child raising. The couples do a lot of accounting; the division of duties does not happen naturally on account of our training for traditional male and female roles. These couples ask themselves, 'What wouldn't get done if I didn't do it?' The important thing is they do not get angry. . . . Both partners believe the other has equal influence over important decisions. Both partners feel they have equal control of the family economy and reasonably equal access to discretionary funds. The man does not have automatic veto power. . . . Insofar as we let money determine status in the relationship, it always corrodes equality and friendship. . . . Each person's work is given equal weight in the couple's life plans. Whether or not both partners work, they do not systematically sacrifice one person's work for the other's. The person who earns the least is not the person always given the most housework or child care. These couples consciously consider the role of marriage and their relationship in making their life plans." Schwartz also described most marriages as "near-to-peer" or "near peer," in that both partners felt that although

equality between mates is preferable, theirs was not an equal partnership. "Near-peers say, 'Yeah we believe in equality, and if we could do it, we would,'" she told Mary Jo Kochakian for the *Hartford (Connecticut) Courant* (June 21, 1994), "If you ask them, 'Well then, why don't you do it?' the two things they always say are the things traditional people believe in. The first is that they are investing in his career. . . . They want to maximize income, or don't want to endanger it. [The second is that] they both believe in the female ownership of children."

Soon after the publication of *Peer Marriage*, Schwartz described to Carey Quan Gelernter for the *Seattle Times* (August 21, 1994) how she and her second husband, Arthur M. Skolnik, an architect, maintained their peer marriage, which was then in its 13th year. (Schwartz's first marriage, to John A. Strait, in 1971, ended in divorce.) The couple lived on a large ranch, where they raised horses and llamas, and had a full-time nanny for their preadolescent son and daughter. Schwartz said that she attended all school plays in which her children participated and that she and her husband both attended all parent-teacher conferences, but "for the everyday things, the nanny is there." Schwartz soon found herself publicly taken to task for spending a less-than-average amount of time with her children and for failing to emphasize that the lifestyle she and her family enjoyed depended on their higher-than-average income. She responded to such criticism in a letter to the *Seattle Times* (September 18, 1994), in which she wrote, "I think the people who know me and my husband and family know that we have a tight relationship with our children and that these kids are neither neglected nor unprized. . . . *Peer Marriage* is not about couple selfishness. My husband and I live a lot of our marital life for our kids. But not all of it. First and foremost, people have to function well as a couple so that the marriage is durable and the family doesn't break up. Peer marriage is about ONE way to do this—and I would be the last person in the world to say this is the only way—or the best way for everyone." Schwartz's marriage to Skolnik ended in an amicable divorce in 2001.

In an interview with Jean Blake for the New Orleans, Louisiana, *Times-Picayune* (October 31, 2000), Schwartz discussed unrealistic expectations about love and sex: "Life is tough enough. We don't need to feed ourselves lies (or unwittingly tell them to others). We need to get real, know what relationships really require, and find the solution that is fitted to who we are, rather than a one-size-fits-all approach. Intuitively we know that blanket prescriptions for love and sex can't be right. We are far too quirky and opinionated to feel that there is only one way to conduct our sexual and emotional life." Those statements sum up the premise of Schwartz's next book, *Everything You Know About Love and Sex Is Wrong* (2000). In a conversation with Sandy Naiman for the *Toronto (Ontario) Sun* (April 12, 2001), Schwartz suggested that myths surrounding love and sex have arisen because when one talks to people about those subjects, "you hear things again and again and you begin to believe them because they're moral, you've never thought of the alternative and you assume they should be believed. . . . They may be the accepted wisdom for some people, but it might not be true for you."

Schwartz has written for and acted as a consultant to Web sites including medhelp.org, utango.com, and webmd.com, and she is the "relationship expert" for two subscription-based on-line dating services, kiss.com and perfectmatch.com. For kiss.com Schwartz writes articles and offers advice in a column called "Ask Dr. Pepper." For perfectmatch.com she created a questionnaire designed to match people with apparently compatible personalities. She based the questionnaire on a Myers-Briggs personality test and dubbed it the Duet Total Compatibility System. Her book *Finding Your Perfect Match* (2006), in turn, expands upon the Duet Total Compatibility System.

Schwartz's most recent book is *Prime: Adventures and Advice on Sex, Love, and the Sensual Years* (2007). Judith Newman, writing for *People* (July 16, 2007), lavished praise on the book: "In this relationship manual for those of us old enough to confuse Britney [Spears], Lindsay [Lohan], and Paris [Hilton], Pepper Schwartz . . . doesn't say much we don't already know but she says it with engaging warmth and humor. Her attitude toward relationships for women over 50 will startle some: since we're not looking for the right DNA for children or the right bank account for the house in the Hamptons, we can afford to be more adventurous, because less is at stake. . . . Sometimes sex doesn't have to be a transcendent experience; it can be more like a sandwich: 'You don't love the sandwich; you don't hate the sandwich. You just want to eat the sandwich.' In between dispensing her advice, Schwartz . . . cyber-dates and picks up men on airplanes. She has a rollicking good time, and so do we."

"For someone whose recital of sexual adventures has all of the vigor of Casanova's . . . ," Managhan wrote, "Schwartz is not even vaguely intimidating in person. Her appeal derives not from knock-you-dead looks, but rather from an extraordinary gift for making social contacts. And from her evident vulnerability. She is someone who not only makes the mistakes anyone makes but almost seems willing to make them just so she can relay their lessons to her many readers. Even a famous sexologist, it turns out, can be nervous before a date, hurt by men who say they'll call but never do, and jealous when a flingmate is as cavalier about consorting with others as with oneself." In 2007 U.W.'s Panhellenic Association (the governing body of 16 sororities) named Schwartz the most outstanding teacher in the social sciences and the most engaging lecturer. Her many other honors include the Matrix Award for achievement in education from the organization Women in Communi-

cations, in 1992, and the International Women's Forum Award in Career Achievement in Washington State. In 2008 Schwartz appeared as a guest on television on programs including *Oprah, Dancing with the Stars, The Early Show, The Today Show, Good Morning America,* and *Entertainment Tonight.*

Schwartz lives on her ranch in the foothills of the Cascade Mountains, in Snoqualmie, Washington, where she breeds Rocky Mountain horses. Her daughter, Ryder, and son, Cooper, are now in their 20s.

—T.O.

Suggested Reading: *Chronicle of Higher Education* B p40+ Sep. 14, 2007; *Los Angeles Times* E p3 July 11, 1994; *New York Times* F p6 Apr. 10, 2007; Pepper Schwartz's Web site; *Psychology Today* p48+ July/Aug. 1993; University of Washington Web site; *Washington Post* p8 Oct. 30, 1983; Berger, Bennett M. *Authors of Their Own Lives,* 1990; Schwartz, Pepper. *Prime: Adventures and Advice on Sex, Love, and the Sensual Years,* 2007

Selected Books: *The Student Guide to Sex on Campus* (as co-editor), 1971; *Women at Yale: Liberating a College Campus* (with Janet Lever), 1971; *Sexual Scripts: The Social Construction of Female Sexuality* (with Judith Long Laws), 1977; *American Couples: Money, Work, Sex* (with Philip Blumstein), 1983; *Peer Marriage: How Love Between Equals Really Works,* 1994 (retitled *Love Between Equals: How Peer Marriage Really Works,* 1995); *The Great Sex Weekend* (with Janet Lever), 1997; *What I Learned About Sex: What America's Sex Educators, Counselors, and Therapists Want You to Know* (with Debra Hafner), 1998; *The Love Test* (with Virginia Rutter), 1998; *The Gender of Sexuality* (with Virginia Rutter), 1998; *Everything You Know About Sex and Love Is Wrong,* 2000; *201 Questions to Ask Your Kids/201 Questions to Ask Your Parents,* 2000; *Ten Talks Parents Must Have with Their Children About Sex and Character* (with Dominic Cappello), 2001; *The Lifetime Book of Love and Sex Quizzes,* 2002; *Finding Your Perfect Match,* 2006; *Prime: Adventures and Advice on Sex, Love, and the Sensual Years,* 2007

Kiel Scott, courtesy of Concord Records

Scott, Christian

1983– Jazz trumpeter

Address: c/o Concord Music Group Inc., 23307 Commerce Park Rd., Cleveland, OH 44122

"Pretty consistently I have had people ask me why I'm not playing bebop, or tell me I should be playing bebop," Christian Scott, a 25-year-old, Grammy Award–nominated jazz trumpeter, told R. J. De-Luke for the Albany, New York, *Times Union* (June 22, 2006). He was referring to the style of jazz that was established in the 1940s and is characterized by breakneck melodies and rapid chord changes played by small combos. "But I was born in 1983," he added. "[Bebop] pre-dates my existence by 20, 30, 40 years. . . . It was something that I was practicing and listening to, and in my musical infancy could try to get my foundation together. But it wasn't what was affecting me in my life." Scott, a New Orleans, Louisiana, native, has released two critically acclaimed albums and collaborated with a host of artists of varied genres, including Prince, Randy Jackson, and Jill Scott; he has been compared to prominent jazz trumpet players of the past and present, from Miles Davis to Wynton Marsalis. Scott was mentored by his uncle, the accomplished saxophonist Donald Harrison Jr., who advised him to develop his own style and to limit the influence of other contemporary trumpeters on his playing. Perhaps as a result, Scott learned to play soft, breathy, "round" notes that sometimes sound as close to a human voice as to a brass instrument, and when he was just 16, he made a name for himself when he accompanied his uncle's band on a nationwide tour. The pieces on his two albums to

date, *Rewind That* (2006) and *Anthem* (2007), were deeply influenced by his personal experiences and his views on sociopolitical issues. Suggesting Davis's influence, both of Scott's records—especially *Anthem*—also demonstrate an enthusiasm for infusing jazz with elements from other musical genres, including funk, hip-hop, and indie rock, using heavy guitar riffs, for example, or overlaid rap vocals. Those choices, while eliciting some flak from jazz traditionalists, have also won him popularity and critical praise from those who support such innovation and boundary-pushing. "[Scott] embodies all we have grown to love from past jazz heavyweights while pushing boundaries with today's beboppers," Jake Krolick wrote for the music Web site Jambase.com in the fall of 2007. "When Scott plays his trumpet he blows down jazz barriers but also cultural, economic and emotional obstacles. Scott is one of the most progressive jazz musicians of our time, playing with a unique tone and candor. He is an artist for all the right reasons, who loves his chosen craft as well as embracing indie rock, neo-soul and hip-hop." Scott's first live album, *Live at Newport* (2008), was expected to arrive in stores on November 4, 2008.

Christian Scott was born in 1983 into a New Orleans family chock-full of artists and musicians. His mother, Cara Harrison, had played classical music in high school and college; his father is a visual artist whose work incorporates photography, sculpting, and drawing; and his grandfather Donald Harrison Sr. was both a well-known folk singer and the "big chief" of three Mardi Gras Indian tribes, groups of African-American revelers who for generations have dressed in Native American garb and danced in the Mardi Gras parade in a display of solidarity with the plight of Native Americans. As a young boy Scott's twin brother, Kiel, demonstrated talent as a guitarist, while Scott was more interested in football, baseball, and basketball than in music. (Kiel later became a visual artist and a filmmaker.) But at age 12—a late bloomer by New Orleans standards—Scott decided that he wanted to play trumpet. "I used to get teased all the time because most guys start[ed] playing trumpet or trombone when they were 4 or 5, as soon as they could hold the instrument," Scott told R. J. De-Luke. Although his mother encouraged him to play music, she would have preferred that he play an instrument offering a stronger foundation in chords and harmonics, such as piano, violin, or cello. Soon, though, she became reconciled to his choice of the trumpet and even spent evenings clapping out rhythms for him as he learned. Though not a trained musician, Donald Harrison Sr. also helped Scott by humming classic jazz tunes and asking Scott to play them back to him.

The person who probably influenced Scott's musical development most was Donald Harrison Jr. As Scott began to learn trumpet, Harrison "was stopping by the house between gigs dressed in the most beautiful cream-colored suits the boy had ever seen," as Keith O'Brien wrote for the New Orleans *Times-Picayune* (April 27, 2003). Admiring his uncle's talent and style, Scott asked him for guidance. So Harrison gave his nephew a recording of the jazz trumpeter Clifford Brown playing the song "Donna Lee," by the saxophonist Charlie Parker, who had helped to start bebop and was known for his high-speed, difficult-to-imitate improvisations. Harrison knew that the challenge of learning to play such music would either deter Scott from pursuing jazz or help him develop his own style. "Two weeks later he had learned it," Harrison told Dan Ouellette for *Down Beat* (May 2006). "At that time, I decided to do whatever I could to help him develop." Soon the teacher and student became inseparable, spending whole weekends together; according to Scott's mother, even their mannerisms became almost indistinguishable. "One of the first things that my uncle taught me is how to have musical tact," Scott recalled to Krolick. "All too often young musicians are plagued with the reality of having the skills to play, whereas I was more or less conditioned from the beginning not to worry about whether people thought I could play. It was all about me emoting and being able to come across on an emotional level that made the listener feel what we played."

Scott was a quick learner, impressing his instructors at all levels of his education. During high school he attended the New Orleans Center for Creative Arts (NOCCA), a pre-professional arts-training center that provides, among other educational services, half-day intensive instruction for high-school students in music and other arts. The center's music program boasts such successful alumni as Branford, Wynton, Delfeayo, and Jason Marsalis and Harry Connick Jr. "You're supposed to start there your sophomore or junior year," Scott told Yoshi Kato for the *San Jose (California) Mercury News* (September 13, 2007). "I started in my freshman year, and the curriculum was really easy for me, since I had been hanging out with, and learning from, my uncle." After Scott finished high school, Wynton Marsalis encouraged him to attend the prestigious Juilliard School of Music, in New York City. Instead, not wanting to commit himself to a narrowly focused sound or scene, Scott enrolled at the Berklee School of Music, in Boston, Massachusetts, where he received a full scholarship. "I needed to find out who I was," Scott told Ouellette. "I didn't want to be so defined at my age. I wanted to go into a classroom and see some dude with a mohawk and meet people who were into rock and hip-hop as well as jazz." At Berklee, Scott, along with other first-year students, was required to take a series of placement tests in harmony and ear training. It was common for a student to fail or not finish many of the tests, as most students stopped when they came across parts of the tests they did not understand. Scott was the only student in his class to complete and pass all of the tests, prompting administrators to insist that he be retested; when he passed the second round, some professors gave him tests in individual subjects.

"And after I tested out [of] all of those, they figured I wasn't [messing] around," Scott told Kato.

Meanwhile, in 2000, Scott joined his uncle and the other members of the Donald Harrison Quintet on tour, performing at festivals and concerts across the country, including the New Orleans Jazz and Heritage Festival and the M&T Jazz Fest–Syracuse. Mark Bialczak wrote for the Syracuse, New York, *Post-Standard* (June 24, 2000) that as Scott began playing the tune "Christopher, Jr.," "eyes opened. Jaws dropped. The crowd shrieked. Uncle Don smiled as wide as the stage." Howard Reich, writing for the *Chicago Tribune* (December 14, 2000), described Scott's still-developing style during his show at Chicago's Metropolis Performing Arts Centre: "In the ballad, 'Misty,' he played the first refrain with a gauzy, breathy tone that provided some of his most individualistic music-making of the evening. And the way he dispatched his final 'Misty' solo, taking his time between gestures and ending with a disarmingly simple phrase, pointed to a young musician with poise." Reich also identified some flaws in Scott's performance—"his tendency to rely on familiar scale patterns, relatively simple chord structures and oft-repeated technical stunts"—which, Reich thought, suggested that it may have been too early for Scott to "step into the . . . spotlight." Rick Nowlin, a reporter for the *Pittsburgh Post-Gazette* (June 13, 2001), reviewed a concert at which Scott, who "quite literally just graduated from high school, pretty much stole the show." Those early listeners and reviewers were impressed not only with Scott's technical skills and range but also with the mature style he had developed at such a young age. Some drew parallels between Scott's trumpet playing and the early work of such jazz legends as Miles Davis and Louis Armstrong. They also took note of his ability to produce remarkably soft, "round, fuzzy notes" that did not sound as if they were made by a trumpet. Writing for the Newcastle upon Tyne, England, *Morning Star* (December 27, 2002) about Harrison's album *Kind of New*, on which Scott performed, Chris Searle called the trumpeter's playing "wistfully quiet, note-perfect, almost becalmed . . . [as] if he was mollifying brass, transforming metal into a muted woodwind." Scott produces those sounds, which have also been called "haunting," by means of his circular breathing of warm air through his instrument. To perfect the sound, he took advice from the veteran swing and bop trumpeter Clark Terry and ignored the instructions of textbooks and music teachers. "It took me two years of concentration to come up with that tone . . . ," Scott told Fred Shuster for the *Daily News of Los Angeles* (June 14, 2006). "I like it because it makes the trumpet sound like the human voice." Scott said that his breakthrough came when he decided to focus on capturing a specific sound. "The thing that I tried to emulate was my mother's singing voice," he said.

In 2002 Scott graduated from Berklee with degrees in professional music and film scoring, having completed the five-year program in just two years. The same year Scott released a self-titled, self-produced album and began shopping it to local music stores. After graduating Scott toured regularly with the guitarist Matt Stevens, the tenor saxophonist Walter Smith III, the keyboardist Zaccai Curtis, the bassist Luques Curtis, and the drummer Jamire Williams. In 2003 Scott and his sextet were invited to perform on their own stage at the New Orleans Jazz and Heritage Festival, as the trumpeter had long dreamed of doing. Scott also played more shows with his uncle. Reviewers continued to predict great things for the young man. In 2004, while promoting his self-titled record at a performance at a Virgin music store, Scott was approached by a former distributor for the record label Concord Music Group. Impressed by both the music and the packed crowd, the distributor asked to hear the whole album and urged him to send it to Concord; soon the label offered Scott a record deal. Scott accepted on the condition that he would not be required to play traditional jazz and would be able to incorporate elements from a variety of genres.

Scott was still in Boston when Hurricane Katrina caused flooding that ravaged his hometown in August 2005, an event that affected him deeply as a person and a musician. After the catastrophe Scott's family moved to Houston, Texas, and Scott relocated to New York City, a move he had been contemplating for some time. In March 2006 Concord Records released Scott's major-label debut album, *Rewind That*, which featured Scott's minimalist trumpet lines over Matt Stevens's heavy guitar work. The album consists of 11 tracks, including two covers—Miles Davis's "So What" and "Paradise Found," by Donald Harrison Jr.— and nine original tunes that vary greatly in mood and tempo. Each one was inspired by a personal experience or, according to Scott, a specific conversation. "Rejection" is a somber ballad mourning a painful breakup, while "Suicide" is intended to call attention to trigeminal neuralgia, a rare nerve disease afflicting Scott's mother, which causes pain so intense that it has been dubbed "the suicide disease." The final song on the album, the funk-inflected "Kiel," is dedicated to Scott's twin brother, a visual artist who Scott said is "10 times more talented than I'll ever be," according to Jack W. Hill, writing for the *Arkansas Democrat-Gazette* (September 8, 2006). Scott's uncle is featured on four of the tunes.

Rewind That was met with many rave reviews, with critics praising Scott's ability to draw from Miles Davis's work of the 1970s and 1980s while incorporating elements from a variety of contemporary genres. Scott McLennan wrote for the Massachusetts *Telegram and Gazette* (August 10, 2006) that the album is "full of poise, passion and precision, linking traditional jazz to contemporary grooves." In the Victoria, British Columbia, *Times*

Colonist (May 14, 2006), Joseph Blake identified Scott as "the future of jazz" and as being "wise beyond his years, a thoughtful, less-is-more master of his instrument and a very fine composer of urbane, modern music that is steeped in the blues and jazz tradition of his hometown, but, taking his cues from Miles Davis's electric bands, liberated and fearless enough to establish a new sound with his burnished, muscular playing." Although the vast majority of critics complimented what Ouellette called the trumpeter's "deep, smoky, reson[ant] tone," there were some critics who did not warm to Scott's style. Writing for the Raleigh, North Carolina, *News & Observer* (July 2, 2006), Owen Cordle complained, "Scott's [playing] often seems calculatedly world-weary and bloodless. . . . He's obviously a stronger jazzman than this album indicates. But as it is, there are breathy long tones and a fluffy delivery—the stuff of smooth jazz." By his own account Scott, who greatly values musical freedom, does not mind if some listeners are displeased. He told Fred Shuster, "Everyone wanted me to do a straight-ahead [jazz] album, but that's like meeting a woman and trying to be like her last boyfriend. You've got to be special." In 2006 *Rewind That* received a Grammy nomination for best new jazz album, and Scott was named by *Billboard* magazine as one of its "names to watch." As a result of the exposure from *Rewind That*, such non-jazz artists as Prince and the *American Idol* judge Randy Jackson invited him to collaborate with them; Scott wrote and recorded two songs for Prince's album *Planet Earth* and recorded a track for Jackson's upcoming album, *American Music, Volume 1*. *Ebony* magazine chose Scott as one of its "30 Young Leaders Under 30" in 2007.

Scott and his bandmates toured internationally in 2006 and 2007, performing in jazz clubs and other venues. While on the road, Scott woke up at 6:00 a.m. each day to compose the pieces that would make up his second album, *Anthem*. He told an interviewer for *Down Beat* (June 2007) to expect from that album an even broader array of musical elements than were heard on his first record, including indie rock, classical music, hip-hop, and R&B. Indeed, upon its release, in August 2007, *Anthem* was hailed as an innovative collection that stretched the limits of traditional jazz. Scott told Farai Chideya, host of the National Public Radio program *News and Notes* (September 5, 2007), that he sometimes referred to his music as "razz," a mixture of rock and jazz. Bob Karlovits noted for the *Pittsburgh Tribune-Review* (September 2, 2007), "Christian Scott is heading in the direction Miles Davis would have been, were he still alive. This is not to elevate Scott to the Davis level, but it is to say *Anthem* is an album that looks for a legitimate new direction in music. . . . Scott is a fine trumpet player, but is showing here even more strength as a conceptualist." Scott played cornet and flugelhorn as well as trumpet on the 12 tunes, to add variety to the moods of the album. Most reviewers, however, considered the album as a whole to be significantly darker than his first collection; Charles J. Gans, writing for the Associated Press (August 30, 2007), called the album "edgier and more brooding." As with his first album, Scott drew from both personal experiences and his reactions to sociopolitical issues for each composition's emotional energy. "The thing about *Anthem*," Scott told Kato, "is that it's so tied in to my life and the experiences of the last year and my feelings about what has happened in New Orleans, what hasn't happened in Darfur, what is happening in Iraq. . . . So this music wasn't just about music; it became a musical interpretation of what I was going through." His feelings about the aftermath of Hurricane Katrina inspired several pieces, including "Void" and "Anthem (Antediluvian Adaptation)," the latter of which also features an angry rap from Brother J of the group X-Clan. The title of the ballad "Katrina's Eyes," however, refers not to the hurricane but to Scott's baby daughter. Scott's talent has earned him guest spots as a performer with the singer Jill Scott and the rapper Mos Def. He has said that he would most like to perform with the rock group Radiohead.

Scott has often felt pressure from the critical establishment to conform to the conventional path for jazz musicians. While he seems to have thrived on resisting that pressure, he recognizes a danger for other young musicians in a similar position. Though he agrees that music schools should expose students to the work of past jazz greats, he believes that forcing students to imitate them makes it difficult for them to find their own styles. "The main idea should not be to sound like guys that have already done what they needed to do," Scott told Krolick. "There's another strength, not taught, that makes musicians become individuals."

Scott planned to release his third record, *Live at Newport*, on November 4, 2008. The album features Scott's live performance at the JVC Newport Jazz Festival in Newport, Rhode Island, three songs from his previous two albums, and five new tracks, including "Died In Love," "Isadora," and "The Crawler." The album will be sold with a DVD of Scott's live performances and a behind-the-scenes look at his rehearsals prior to the Newport festival. Scott had small parts in the 2008 films *Leatherheads* and *Rachel Getting Married*.

Scott volunteers regularly for the nonprofit NO/AIDS Task Force in New Orleans. As of the spring of 2006, he shared an apartment in downtown Manhattan with his twin brother, Kiel, a student of filmmaking at New York University.

—M.E.R.

Suggested Reading: *Daily News of Los Angeles* U p6 June 14, 2006; *Down Beat* p29 May 2006; Jambase.com; (New Orleans, Louisiana) *Times-Picayune* Living p1 Apr. 27, 2003; *San Jose Mercury News* Music Sep. 13, 2007

Selected Recordings: *Rewind That*, 2006; *Anthem*, 2007; *Live at Newport*, 2008

Mandel Ngan/AFP/Getty Images

Siegel, Robert

June 26, 1947– Radio journalist; co-host of All Things Considered

Address: National Public Radio, 635 Massachusetts Ave., N.W., Washington, DC 20001

"The thing about Robert Siegel's voice is its familiarity: an easy, neighborly tone that lures the ear without being didactic, that woos the curious without being demanding," Jennifer Barrs wrote for the *Tampa (Florida) Tribune* (January 24, 1995). For more than 20 years, as the host of the award-winning National Public Radio (NPR) evening newsmagazine *All Things Considered*, Siegel has come to occupy a place in the routines of more than 12 million daily listeners, who tune in to upwards of 800 member stations across the country to hear his thorough, conversational explications of events and ideas. In sharp contrast to most commercial radio programs, on which the current trend is to pare down news stories to fit segments lasting mere seconds, *All Things Considered* is known for its intelligent, documentary-style coverage of both headline news and eclectic features, offering a mixture of commentary, reviews, and interviews with experts in various fields, often devoting several minutes to a single story. "[*All Things Considered*] explains events and developments in a manner that assumes that the person listening is intelligent, curious, not an expert, but not a dope, either," Siegel explained to Brian McTavish for the *Kansas City Star* (May 3, 2001). "We're not ambushing people with information. . . . We speak to people, first of all, in a human, rational, normal way. And then we use all the tools of radio—which in commercial radio, alas, are nearly all found in the commercials—to create a real vivid kind of radio journalism." Siegel's interest in broadcast journalism began when, as a freshman at Columbia University, he joined the school's radio station. He worked at several smaller stations before joining the NPR staff, in 1976, as an associate producer. In 1979 he opened NPR's first foreign news bureau, in London, England, and in 1987 he became one of the hosts of *All Things Considered*, for which he continues to cover a wide range of subjects, currently with co-hosts Michele Norris and Melissa Block. While earning several awards for journalistic excellence, Siegel has seen NPR through financial and political crises and played a major part in defining the station's niche on the airwaves. "Public radio occupies a rung in society that is exceptionally important," Siegel told Lynne Weily for United Press International (May 26, 1987). "It is an institution where we build bridges between high culture and mass society. Fitting into that process is something very gratifying."

Robert Charles Siegel was born to Joseph and Edith Ruth (Joffe) Siegel on June 26, 1947 in New York City. He attended Stuyvesant High School before enrolling at Columbia University, in New York. When, during his freshman year, a friend suggested that he become involved in extracurricular activities in order to feel more a part of the school, he joined Columbia's radio station, WKCR-FM. "I got involved in college radio and loved it," Siegel told David Hinckley for the New York *Daily News* (May 3, 2001). "But since everyone said it was a low-rent, dying medium, I assumed I'd have to go into television. Then I found I didn't like television—and radio wasn't dead after all." As an anchor at WKCR Siegel earned the station an award from the Writer's Guild of America East for his coverage of the violent anti–Vietnam War demonstrations at Columbia in 1968. He graduated that same year, and then, from 1968 to 1969, worked as a morning newscaster and telephone talk-show host for WGLI in Babylon, New York, while earning his graduate degree from Columbia University. From 1971 to 1976 he was a reporter, host, and director of news and public affairs for WRVR radio in New York City. He was part of a team that received a Major Armstrong Award for a series called "Rockefeller's Drug Law," which explored New York State's mandatory punishment for drug offenses, including some of the harshest minimum sentences in the country, enacted by Governor Nelson Rockefeller.

In December 1976 Siegel was hired as an associate producer of NPR, where, six months later, he was promoted to public-affairs editor. Founded in 1970, NPR declared its mission to be, among other aims, to "serve the individual," "encourage a sense of active, constructive participation, rather than apathetic helplessness," and "promote personal growth rather than corporate gains." The NPR network, composed of several hundred member stations across the country, is funded mostly through donation drives, along with grants from corporations, foundations, and an allocation from the non-profit Corporation for Public Broadcasting (CPB), established by the federal government. In NPR's early years, before it secured significant corporate sponsorship, the tight budget and small staff made it difficult to put together timely, first-hand reports. Often the station would learn of events from newspapers and broadcast "analysis" stories a day later. In 1979 Siegel opened NPR's first foreign-news bureau, in London, and became the first person to work overseas for NPR at a time when most major news networks had dozens of bureaus around the world. (By the early 2000s, NPR had become known for its coverage of foreign affairs, with 14 foreign bureaus—more than either ABC, CBS, NBC, or the Fox News Channel.) While in London Siegel tried to save money by asking flight attendants or passengers boarding planes to Washington, D.C., to deliver his audiotapes to NPR headquarters.

In 1983, as NPR was undergoing a financial crisis and major changes in personnel, Siegel returned to the United States to become its director of news and information. In February of that year, NPR's president, Frank Mankiewicz, had learned that the company was millions of dollars in debt. NPR was forced to accept a $9.1 million federal loan to avoid bankruptcy; Mankiewicz drastically cut programs and fired nearly a third of NPR's employees over the next several months before resigning under pressure. Siegel told Phil McCombs and Jacqueline Trescott for the *Washington Post* (August 15, 1983) that Mankiewicz "had a record for doing things that in the beginning you couldn't justify," including sending him to London without knowing how NPR would pay for it. In his new position, Siegel oversaw the production of NPR's newsmagazines, *All Things Considered* and *Morning Edition*, in addition to other news programs, and worked to launch the Saturday and Sunday newsmagazine *Weekend Edition*. He was a hands-on director, according to Adam Clayton Powell III, who would eventually succeed Siegel in the position. Powell told Marc Fisher for the *Washington Post* (October 22, 1989) that Siegel "would plunge in every day on how pieces should be edited and so on."

Siegel earned a 1984 Alfred I. DuPont–Columbia University Silver Baton Award for excellence in broadcast journalism for his work on the four-part NPR series "The Most Dangerous Game." Airing in April 1983, the series concerned the history and implications of nuclear programs around the world. Siegel hosted the program's second and third segments, which explored the issue from the perspectives of East and West Germany as well as peace movements in those countries. David Hugh Smith wrote for the *Christian Science Monitor* (April 4, 1983), "The segment on East and West Germany paints an interesting portrait of the German people and how their geographic position affects their perspective about conflict with the Soviet Union."

In 1987 Siegel and the former science reporter Renee Montaigne became the new hosts of NPR's two-hour evening news, commentary, and analysis program, *All Things Considered*, replacing Susan Stamberg and Noah Adams. NPR's first program, *All Things Considered* had always been one of its most popular, noted for its intelligent treatment of complicated issues and for the hosts' conversational, "seen-it-all-before" tone. Siegel expressed his preference for working on air rather than behind the scenes, telling Jeffrey Yorke for the *Washington Post* (March 18, 1987) that the job was "a return to a natural environment after four years in an unnatural one." He later told Yorke (March 27, 1987): "Anybody who has been the news director of NPR would know how easy it would be to relinquish that job. I'm absolutely delighted not to go near those things, not to have those responsibilities. . . . I'm not feeling myself on the bottom of a great avalanche of criticism." Siegel and Montaigne expressed their intention to deepen the show's already in-depth treatment of issues with longer segments. Siegel told Weily, "[*All Things Considered*] gives vent to a breadth of interests. We follow a very, very broad array of stories, meet very interesting people, get to work in radio and actually get paid for this."

When Siegel returned to the airwaves, NPR had stabilized its finances and steadily increased its popularity with listeners. However, the station was receiving increased criticism for what some listeners perceived as a lack of innovation; critics said that NPR was no longer attempting to appeal to new audiences and that there was a sameness to many of its long segments. A Los Angeles, California, station even dropped NPR in 1989, calling the programming "mundane and dull, very traditional, very predictable." Siegel told Fisher that one aspect of the problem might have been the increased competition for entry-level jobs at NPR. "When I came here 13 years ago, I did six months in the newscaster unit, then was made a Washington editor and two years later was sent to London," Siegel said. "[Congressional correspondent] Cokie Roberts was a temp for a year or less and was hired full-time. Now, very bright young people spend maybe three years temping, maybe four or five years in the newscast unit, and only then get to be a reporter. A lot of them leave, and we miss a certain amount of youthful creativity." Discussions continue over how NPR should adapt to a changing audience and culture while maintaining its core listeners and its uniquely in-depth stories.

In March 1992 Siegel interviewed Salman Rushdie, the Indian-British author of *Midnight's Children* (1981) and *The Satanic Verses* (1988) among other novels and short stories. *The Satanic Verses* had been deemed blasphemous by the Ayatollah Khomeini, the spiritual leader of Iran at the time, who issued a fatwa, or religious edict, condemning Rushdie to death. At the time of the interview, Rushdie had been in hiding in Great Britain for three years under the protection of the British se-

cret police. "There is one thing I'd like to say about Salman Rushdie before anything else, and that is that he wrote *Midnight's Children*, a brilliant novel about India that had me in stitches several years ago," Siegel said in his introduction to the segment. "For that book alone, I would want to interview Salman Rushdie and would probably even go to some out-of-the-way hotel and meet some designated intermediary there and then go somewhere else to do it." In the interview Rushdie discussed the difficulties of living in hiding, including the necessity of living and writing apart from most of his possessions; the inconvenience of having to drive three hours in order to take a walk; and his sadness over missing three years of his son's life. Rushdie expressed a hope that the political climate would change for the better and that his situation would thus improve. Even if it did not, Rushdie said, "[T]here will come a point in which I won't live like this anyway." After nine years in hiding, Rushdie emerged on September 25, 1998, after the fatwa was lifted.

In 1994 Siegel edited *The NPR Interviews, 1994*, a print volume containing 100 interviews conducted by the NPR journalists Nina Totenberg, Susan Stamberg, Linda Wertheimer, and Siegel throughout the year. The subjects in the book, published by NPR and Houghton Mifflin in November, include such notable figures as the cartoonist Charles M. Schulz, the photographer Richard Avedon, and the U.S. Supreme Court justice Harry Blackmun. Siegel pored over hundreds of interviews to select those that both read well on the page and reflected the breadth of NPR's subject matter. He told Tim Blangger for the Allentown, Pennsylvania, *Morning Call* (December 31, 1994), "Making a book out of interviews that were conducted for the ear meant deciding just how offensive to the eye we were prepared to be in the interests of authenticity. The decision was to smooth out and sweeten, but not to rewrite." The book was well received, with reviewers noting the timeliness of its publication: in the same month, the newly elected Speaker of the House of Representatives, Newt Gingrich, announced his plans to eliminate funding for CPB due to the "liberal bias" of its programming. In a review of the book, Blangger wrote, "To those looking for evidence of a liberal or conservative NPR bias, this book won't help much. What emerges, however, is a notion that a wide range of subjects represents the sort of material not usually covered by the mainstream media." Siegel edited two subsequent collections of interviews, in 1995 and 1996.

Siegel shared an Alfred I. DuPont–Columbia University Silver Baton Award for 1994/1995 for NPR's extensive daily coverage of the first 100 days of the 104th Congress, following the 1994 elections, which gave Republicans control of both congressional houses for the first time since the 1950s. The daily pieces, which were collectively called "The Changing of the Guard: The Republican Revolution," covered all aspects of the transition, from the struggle to find desks for Republicans' new offices to the details of House Republicans' "Contract with America," a package of legislation that aimed to reduce the size of the federal government by cutting funding to many government programs, such as welfare, the National Endowment for the Arts, and CPB. (Although Republicans succeeded in cutting funding of many programs, CPB funding remained intact.) Throughout those 100 days the hosts of *All Things Considered* obtained analyses and commentary from both sides of the aisle as well as from nonpartisan experts and journalists, offering what was largely seen as balanced coverage. On January 4, 1995, as House Minority Leader Richard Gephardt announced the official transition of majority power from the Democratic to the Republican Party, Siegel commented: "Perhaps a few of those applauding that line were celebrating the peaceful transfer of legislative power, but most seemed to be Republicans celebrating the end of what for them has been 40 years in the wilderness."

Siegel has shrugged off the oft-heard complaint that NPR exhibits a liberal bias. He told Weily, "I think there are biases of journalism which seem particularly liberal. We aggressively question what may be merely accepted elsewhere. If that seems 'liberal,' so be it. But I don't think we're particularly liberal." Moreover, Siegel has pointed out that, in addition to the letters that the station receives complaining about a liberal bias, NPR regularly receives letters complaining about the station's "lack of backbone" in challenging the interests of the world's wealthy and powerful interests. Siegel told Jennifer Barrs, "Often, people just assume you are advancing some kind of agenda. They assume that since journalists are so close to the action, we must be players in it . . . even if you tell them you couldn't care less."

In 1996 Siegel completed a two-part documentary that was broadcast on *All Things Considered* in April, entitled "Murder, Punishment, and Parole in Alabama." Siegel conducted interviews with Alabama prisoners, parole officers, and family members of both prisoners and their victims, to tell the stories of two men who had been sentenced to prison for murder and were up for parole before Alabama's board, which consisted of three political appointees. The documentary revealed many problems with the institution of parole both in Alabama and nationwide. In Alabama, as in many other states, prisons are overcrowded and the state lacks funding to build another facility. Siegel stated, "There's economic pressure on corrections departments to get [inmates] out of prison as soon as possible. But public pressure on prosecutors and judges is to be tough, so they seek and give sentences which, when taken in the aggregate, the state cannot afford. So, the parole board doesn't so much decide who should get parole as which of the many inmates with favorable recommendations in an overpopulated system should not get it." The documentary earned Siegel a Silver Gavel Award from the American Bar Association, in recognition of his exemplary effort to help foster the American public's understanding of the legal system.

Along with the NPR journalist Mara Liasson, Siegel spoke with President Bill Clinton in a pre-scheduled interview on January 21, 1998—the day that the public learned of the president's alleged extramarital affair with the former White House intern Monica Lewinsky. In addition to discussing the federal budget, Clinton's political philosophy, and his efforts to seek peace in the Middle East, Siegel asked Clinton whether there was any truth to the recent allegations. Clinton responded, "I don't know any more about it than I've told you and any more about it really than you do, but I will cooperate. The charges are not true, and I haven't asked anybody to lie." (Shortly afterward Clinton confessed that he and Lewinsky had had an affair.) Years later, Siegel marveled at Clinton's composure during the interview, telling McTavish, "For somebody who was entering obviously the worst period of his public life, I thought he was remarkably unrattled. I didn't think this was somebody who looked distraught to me, by any means."

Despite the significant expansion of its national and international coverage throughout the 1990s and early 2000s, much of the daily behind-the-scenes work at *All Things Considered* has remained the same. Each day starts with planning meetings of hosts and producers, who split up afterward to conduct interviews and pursue stories until airtime, by which point the stories have come together—or have not. Siegel told David Hinckley, "People would be surprised how much of what goes into the show is not ready when we go on the air at 4:00. We may know what we'll be doing at 5:30, but very often it's not finished until right before it goes on." In 2003 NPR received a gift of $230 million upon the death of Joan B. Kroc, the widow of Ray A. Kroc, who built the McDonald's fast-food chain; the enormous donation allowed NPR to create 70 new jobs in its newsroom. Siegel told Jacques Steinberg for the *New York Times* (March 19, 2006) that he does not miss the days when NPR reporters did not have the money to take sources to lunch. "This is a much stronger and more useful organization than it was 30 years ago," Siegel said. "I wouldn't trade that." Siegel noted to Barrs, however, that success and an increased listenership (in 2006 the number of listeners was 25 million, up from 12.5 million a decade earlier) have brought the station new challenges: "[N]ow we've reached this absurd point where, on one hand, we are providing the kinds of programming no else does. And upon succeeding, they want us to go commercial."

Siegel and his *All Things Considered* co-hosts have offered nuanced coverage of the Iraq war. On October 11, 2002 Siegel interviewed Secretary of State Colin Powell about the likelihood that the United States would declare war on Iraq without obtaining a resolution from the United Nations, in the event that Iraq's leader, Saddam Hussein, refused to comply with U.S. demands that it "fully disarm" and allow weapons inspections to take place. "We hope [Hussein] will comply, but I am also sure he will not comply if he doesn't believe that there is a likelihood he will be made to comply," Powell told Siegel. "And that is why it is so important that we not show weakness at this time and the international community comes together. The best way to avoid war is for us to be strong now, both here in the United States and within the United Nations, in order to show that the will of the international community must be obeyed." In March 2003, after the U.N. failed to reach the resolution sought by the Bush administration, the United States declared war on Iraq.

In covering the 2008 presidential primaries, NPR touched on unusual topics, in addition to more traditional news reports and analysis, such as what the candidates' memoirs reveal about their personalities and the ways that the sound of each candidate's name might appeal to voters of different demographics. On July 25, 2007 Siegel interviewed Ron Paul, a Republican U.S. representative from Texas and presidential candidate who espouses libertarian beliefs, about his views on American foreign policy. Siegel served as the moderator for the Democratic presidential debate hosted by NPR that took place in Des Moines, Iowa, on December 4, 2007. Siegel also hosted NPR's extended live coverage of President Bush's final State of the Union Address, on January 29, 2008, and of the "Super Tuesday" elections on February 5, 2008, when the majority of state primary elections were held. Both programs featured interviews with politicians, political scholars, and other analysts. On *All Things Considered* in the summer and fall of 2008, Siegel and his co-host Norris continued to provide in-depth coverage and analysis of major world events: the presidential campaigns of Democrat Barack Obama and Republican John McCain; the 2008 Summer Olympics, held in Beijing, China; Russia's invasion of its neighbor Georgia; the damage wreaked on the southeastern region of the U.S. by Hurricanes Gustav and Ike; and the global economic crisis. On September 1–4, Siegel reported from the Republican National Convention, in St. Paul, Minnesota, where he questioned moderate Republicans about their thoughts on the Republican ticket. Siegel and other reporters at NPR have been credited not only with offering lucid analyses of complicated matters, such as the intricacies of the recent federal takeover of the lending companies Fannie Mae and Freddie Mac, but also with lightening the mood in an increasingly heady and often negative news environment, with tongue-in-cheek stories. For example, on September 10, 2008 Siegel addressed the McCain campaign's labeling as "sexism" a comment made by Obama at a campaign rally: "You know, you can put lipstick on a pig. It's still a pig." Though Obama had meant the metaphor to refer to McCain's promise to bring change to Washington, the McCain campaign accused Obama of referring to vice-presidential candidate Sarah Palin as a pig. (Palin had made a joke about lipstick in one of her speeches.) After broadcasting clips in which politicians, including Vice President Dick Cheney and McCain himself, had used the colloquial metaphor on other occasions, Siegel interviewed Joel Salatin, a farmer and the co-owner of Polyface Farms, while Salatin attempted to apply lipstick to one of his pigs, with comical results. To Siegel's question, "Does the pig look any better with the lipstick on him or her?," Salatin replied, "No. . . . Now, you know, if you put a cummerbund around his loins and some Birkinstocks on his hooves, it might improve him a bit."

During Siegel's tenure on *All Things Considered*, the show has received the Alfred I. DuPont–Columbia University Award, the Overseas Press Club Award, the Major Armstrong Award, the American Women in Radio and Television Award, the Robert F. Kennedy Award, and the *Washington Journalism Review*'s "Best in Business" Award. In 1993 *All Things Considered* became the first public-radio program to be inducted into the Radio Hall of Fame. Siegel lives in Arlington, Virginia, with his wife, Jane Claudia Schwartz, whom he married on June 17, 1973. In his spare time he enjoys reading, playing golf, and watching baseball. He has two grown children, Leah Harriet and Erica Anne. Erica is a candidate for a Ph.D. in Slavic languages and literature at Columbia.

—M.E.R.

Suggested Reading: (Allentown, Pennsylvania) *Morning Call* Entertainment A p52 Oct. 22, 1989; *All Things Considered* (npr.org) Mar. 25, 1992, Apr. 24, 1996, Apr. 26, 1996; *Boston Globe* Living p67 Nov. 17, 1994; *Kansas City Star* FYI E p1 May 3, 2001; *Washington Post Magazine* W p17 Oct. 22, 1989

Selected Books: *NPR Interviews, 1994*; *NPR Interviews, 1995*; *NPR Interviews, 1996*

Simon, David

Sep. 2, 1960– Television writer and producer; journalist

Address: c/o Author Mail, Broadway Books, Doubleday Broadway Group, 1540 Broadway, New York, NY 10036

"There ain't no nostalgia. . . . There's just the street and the game [selling drugs] and what happen here today." Those were the last words uttered by a fictional Baltimore, Maryland, drug dealer known as Cheese (played by the rapper Method Man), prior to his death at the hands of a rival, in the finale of HBO's highly acclaimed crime-drama series *The Wire*. The show, often referred to by crit-

David Simon

Stephen Shugerman/Getty Images

ics during its five-season run (June 2002 to March 2008) as the best show on television, and widely considered to be among the finest TV series ever made, was created by David Simon. A journalist and author, Simon has spent most of his professional life reporting on those involved in or affected by Baltimore's notorious and seemingly unstoppable drug trade, from dealers to police officers to innocent victims. "*The Wire* is dissent," Simon explained to Margaret Talbot for the *New Yorker* (October 22, 2007). "It is perhaps the only storytelling on television that overtly suggests that our political and economic and social constructs are no longer viable, that our leadership has failed us relentlessly, and that no, we are not going to be all right." Simon, a former *Baltimore Sun* reporter who covered the city's police beat from 1983 to 1995, is the author of two much-lauded books: *Homicide: A Year on the Killing Streets* (1991), based on his yearlong experience of following detectives in the Baltimore homicide squad; and *The Corner: A Year in the Life of an Inner-City Neighborhood* (1997, co-authored with Ed Burns), about individuals living near a busy open-air drug market in Baltimore. The first-named book inspired the acclaimed NBC television series *Homicide: Life on the Street* (1993-99), on which Simon served as a writer and producer. *The Corner* was adapted by Simon and the TV writer David Mills into a 2000 HBO miniseries of the same name, which garnered three Emmy Awards. On the strength of those shows' success, Simon was able to realize his ultimate dream: creating a novel for television. *The Wire* transcended the police-drama genre by examining the sociological factors that underlie the modern drug trade. The show explored a different facet of Baltimore each

season, covering, over the course of its run, the drug trade; the port; the city bureaucracy; the school system; and the print news media. Commenting on the worldview expressed by the show, Simon explained to Talbot that *The Wire* is about the devaluing of human beings by "raw, unencumbered capitalism," adding, "Every single moment on the planet, from here on out, human beings are worth less. We are in a post-industrial age. We don't need as many of us as we once did. So, if the first season was about devaluing the cops who knew their beats and the corner boys slinging drugs, then the second was about devaluing the longshoremen and their labor, the third about people who wanted to make changes in the city, and the fourth was about kids who were being prepared, badly, for an economy that no longer really needs them. And the fifth? It's about the people who are supposed to be monitoring all this and sounding the alarm—the journalists. The newsroom I worked in had four hundred and fifty people. Now it's got three hundred. Management says, 'We have to do more with less.' That's the [nonsense] of bean counters who care only about the bottom line. You do *less* with less."

The youngest of the three children of Bernard and Dorothy (Ligeti) Simon, David Judah Simon was born on September 2, 1960 in Washington, D.C. He grew up in a liberal middle-class home in Silver Spring, Maryland, where "books and newspapers were revered and argument was sport," as noted by Janny Scott for the *New York Times* (June 11, 2000). While Simon was raised "in a mostly white world," and "race was rarely discussed" in his home, as Scott reported, belief in equality "was a given" among his family. His father, the national public-relations director for the prominent Jewish service organization B'nai B'rith, had previously written for several newspapers and had friends who were reporters. His mother, a homemaker, had spent several years working for a group called the Negro Student Fund, which provided educational alternatives for students in underperforming public schools. Simon developed an interest in journalism as early as age 12, when his father took him to a local production of the Broadway newsroom comedy *The Front Page*. He went on to attend Bethesda–Chevy Chase High School, in Bethesda, Maryland, where he wrote for the school newspaper.

While at the University of Maryland in College Park, Simon served as editor in chief of the school newspaper, the *Diamondback*. During that time he befriended the future TV writer David Mills, who told Margaret Talbot about Simon's writing and sense of humor, "He had a full-blown writing personality as an undergraduate. He was always getting parking tickets, so he did these rambling, profane, angry pieces about the student ticketers, his nemeses. . . . Though people don't talk much about the humor in *The Wire*, it's there." As a college senior Simon became a stringer for the *Baltimore Sun*, often writing more stories than the paper's full-time staff writers. When he graduated, with a bachelor's degree in journalism, in 1983, the *Sun* immediately took him on as a full-time reporter, assigning him to the frenetic police beat. It was at that point that he began to acquire an understanding of Baltimore's volatile race politics and rampant drug trade. Rebecca Corbett, his first editor at the *Sun* and currently an editor in the Washington bureau of the *New York Times*, explained to Lawrence Lanahan for the *Columbia Journalism Review* (January/February 2008), "[Simon] was writing about the sociology of the city through the prism of the cop beat and the criminal-justice system. And he fairly uniquely looked at the people who we tend to view just as victims or bad guys, and looked at these neighborhoods as real places that we had better understand." In the places where his new job led him, "race was out in the open . . . in a way he had never seen before," as Scott reported. "It was no big deal . . . to walk into a bar in Highlandtown and hear white people talking about black folks, or to meet a black person and be told everything that was wrong with white people, no offense. . . . The biggest crime story was drugs, and intravenous drug use in Baltimore occurred predominantly among African-Americans. To be a decent reporter, [Simon] had to learn to listen to black people."

Simon, who was filing as many as 300 stories a year, gained a great deal of attention in 1987, after writing a much-lauded, five-part series on the notorious Baltimore drug kingpin "Little Melvin" Williams. (After being released from prison, on January 22, 2003, Williams played a recurring role on *The Wire* as a church deacon.) Also in 1987 Simon and other *Baltimore Sun* employees went on strike over benefit cuts. By the time an agreement was reached, Simon had come to feel disillusioned with regard to the newsroom. In 1988, after persuading Edward Tilghman, then Baltimore's police commissioner, to grant him a year's internship with the city's homicide unit, Simon took a 15-month leave of absence from the paper to research and write a book about the detectives' work. He went with detectives to crime scenes and to the houses of victims and suspects, studiously absorbing every facet of the detectives' work, witnessing everything from interrogations of murder suspects to autopsy analyses.

Initially facing skepticism from some of the detectives, Simon eventually won their respect, as he shadowed them over a year in which the city suffered 234 murders. His work culminated in the 1991 book *Homicide: A Year on the Killing Streets*, which garnered widespread praise and received the 1992 Edgar Award for Best Fact Crime Book. Jim Burns wrote in a review for the *Library Journal* (June 1, 1991), "The sociopaths, the crackheads, and their crimes are horrifying, but equal horrors are found in the attitudes of jurors in a case of the shooting and blinding of a policeman and in statistics showing the ultimate legal fates of those apprehended by the unit. Immersing his readers in cases,

procedures, politics, and the detectives' personalities, Simon risks being sabotaged by the sheer scope of his account. Still, for those with strong stomachs and the willingness to work to keep the characters and dramas straight, he has produced a riveting slice of urban life."

After the book's completion, Simon returned to the *Sun*. His stories for the paper displayed his picaresque style, through which he often "turn[ed] obscure murders into full-blown dramatic narratives," as Janny Scott noted. He told Margaret Talbot, "To be a decent city reporter, I had to listen to people who were different from me. I had to not be uncomfortable asking stupid questions or being on the outside. I found I had a knack for walking into situations where I didn't know anything, and just waiting." Meanwhile, *Homicide*, which had become a national best-seller, began to draw interest from Hollywood. It circulated among several directors before catching the eye of the Academy Award–winning writer, director, and producer Barry Levinson, a Baltimore native who had directed films set in that city, including *Diner* (1982) and *Tin Men* (1987). In January 1993 Levinson and the writer-producer Tom Fontana adapted Simon's book for the NBC series *Homicide: Life on the Street*, for which Simon served as both producer and occasional writer; he and his friend David Mills won an award in 1995 from the Writers Guild of America for a Season Two episode they wrote, titled "A Bop Gun," about a tourist killed in front of her family. Commenting on the highly acclaimed—if not widely watched—series, which ran until May 1999, Simon recalled to Mary Alice Blackwell for the *Daily Progressive* (March 23, 2007, on-line), "It was a remarkable drama. It was beautifully acted and well written, but it was designed as entertainment. It did not reflect the book."

Also in 1993 Simon took a second book leave from the *Sun* to begin observing effects of the federal government's declared "war on drugs," from the vantage point of one of the country's most notorious spots for drug sales: the intersection of Fayette and Monroe Streets in Baltimore. Joined by the retired homicide detective and former schoolteacher Ed Burns, Simon spent three years tracking the lives of residents—from the local junkies and drug dealers to activists and families—living within a six-block radius of the intersection. (Ironically, neighborhood activists' demands that police clean up the city resulted in more arrests of users than of dealers.) "My editor on *Homicide*, John Sterling, had the idea," Simon recalled to Neil Drumming for *Entertainment Weekly* (September 22, 2006). "He said, 'Why don't you just go to a corner in the city [and write about it]?' I think he meant just do a neighborhood story." Simon's daily excursions to "the corner"—slang for any scene of frequent drug-related activity—helped him to understand the motivations of those he observed, including drug dealers and addicts. Many of his resulting pieces for the *Sun*, filed after he returned from leave, were written from the point of view of such figures. "I admire journalism where I actually see a nuanced world with complex human beings captured," Simon noted to Lawrence Lanahan. His approach to his subject drew the ire of his editors; in part for that reason, he left the paper in 1995. (He has cited the paper's new management, which took a more bottom-line–oriented approach to publishing, as another reason for his departure.) Immediately after he left the paper, Simon became a full-time writer and producer for *Homicide: Life on the Street.*

In 1997 Simon published *The Corner: A Year in the Life of an Inner-City Neighborhood,* co-written with Burns. The 543-page book centered on the members of one family: Gary McCullough, a self-made businessman turned heroin addict; his ex-wife, Fran Boyd, a mother struggling with her own addiction; and their teenage son, DeAndre McCullough, who at 15 became both a father and a drug dealer. The book was widely praised and was named a Notable Book of the Year by the *New York Times;* Sara Mosle wrote for that newspaper (November 23, 1997), "Despite the obvious virtues of *The Corner*, it remains, finally, a deeply frustrating work. The authors have a fine ear for dialogue, but the book is much too long, mired in detail and filled with policy analysis delivered in a cursing street patois that seems wrongheaded where it's not embarrassing. Still, Simon and Burns display an almost religious regard for individual human lives; it is a respect backed up not by cheap sentiment or easy moralizing but by the dangerous, backbreaking labor of intrepid reporting. They do not always condone their subjects' choices; sympathy is not the same as support. But they prove, as Auden once wrote, 'that the first criterion of success in any human activity, the necessary preliminary, whether to scientific discovery or to artistic vision, is intensity of attention or, less pompously, love.'" In 2000 Simon teamed up again with David Mills to co-write and produce *The Corner* as a six-hour television miniseries for HBO. Directed by Charles S. Dutton, the series was critically acclaimed and received three Emmy Awards, for outstanding directing for miniseries, movie, or special; outstanding writing for a miniseries or a movie; and outstanding miniseries.

In November 2001 Simon and Ed Burns submitted a pilot script to HBO for a gritty police drama called *The Wire*, which was loosely based on their experiences of working for a number of Baltimore institutions, including the newspaper business, the educational system, and the police department. Carolyn Strauss, then the president of HBO Entertainment, was initially hesitant to approve the show, given the cable channel's usual reluctance to air programs similar to those on network television. Nonetheless, Simon was able to convince Strauss that, as she explained to Neil Drumming, "The most challenging and subversive thing that we could do was go right into the networks' backyard." When *The Wire* premiered, in June 2002,

with Simon serving as executive producer and head writer, it was perceived by critics as merely another police procedural, as it focused on the Baltimore police department's investigation—via wiretap—of an extensive drug-dealing network. Over the span of five seasons, however, the show grew to become a sprawling portrait of the many sociological factors that underlie the drug trade. Taking a novelistic approach to storytelling that incorporated contemporary, sometimes unintelligible Baltimore street slang, and featuring nonprofessional actors (many of them former felons) in minor roles to emphasize authenticity, each season of *The Wire* examined a facet of the city of Baltimore: Season One, the drug trade; Season Two, the port and the plight of the working class; Season Three, the city bureaucracy; Season Four, the failings of the educational system; and Season Five, the role of the media. "A wire is something that connects," James Poniewozik wrote in an overview of the series for *Time* (January 14, 2008). "All *The Wire*'s characters face the same forces in a bottom-line, low-margin society, whether they work for a city department, a corporation or a drug cartel. A pusher, a homicide cop, a teacher, a union steward: they're all, in the world of *The Wire*, middlemen getting squeezed for every drop of value by the systems they work for. 'Every day, they matter less as individuals,' says Simon."

Although *The Wire* had a comparatively limited audience of just a few million viewers a week (less than half the number who watched the HBO series *The Sopranos*) and never won any major awards, critics universally praised the show as one of the best ever aired. The program's quality was attributed largely to its writers, who included, in addition to Simon and Burns, some of the most acclaimed crime writers in the country, notably Richard Price, Dennis Lehane, and George Pelecanos. Credit also went to the show's ensemble of actors, among them Dominic West, John Doman, Sonja Sohn, Idris Elba, Wendell Pierce, Andre Royo, and Michael K. Williams, who portrayed characters described by a number of critics as "Dickensian." "When television history is written, little else will rival *The Wire*, a series of such extraordinary depth and ambition that it is, perhaps inevitably, savored only by an appreciative few," Brian Lowry proclaimed for *Variety* (September 7, 2006). In another take on the series, which ended in March 2008, Ken Tucker concluded for *Entertainment Weekly* (March 21, 2008), "In exploring institutions such as local government and the public school system, *The Wire* insisted that no legitimate organization is any less prone to corruption and exploitation than illegal ones. Simon and his writers were making a statement that was a radical, rarely articulated one: Power is essentially evil. From a showbiz point of view, one of *The Wire*'s most enduring triumphs will be that it put more and a greater variety of black faces in major roles than any dramatic series in TV history. . . . Certainly *The Wire* was the best show on the air during its five seasons, and can stand shoulder to shoulder with some of the greatest achievements in series television: *Buffy the Vampire Slayer*, *The Sopranos*, *The Honeymooners*, and *Seinfeld*, among others. And now that it has completed its run, it can be watched forever after in the manner of a work of literature, fulfilling the comparisons from all those reviewers. Just take any one of the fat, season-long DVD collections, each about as thick as your average Balzac novel (the usual *Wire* literary comparison, Charles Dickens, tended to gas on longer than Simon and company did). We can spend a few nights with each 'chapter,' diving into a universe most of us will never experience. For which we can be thankful and grateful on a couple of levels."

In July 2008 Simon and Burns co-wrote and produced a seven-hour miniseries for HBO called *Generation Kill*, based on a 2004 book of the same name by the journalist Evan Wright (who also served as a co-writer). The miniseries, about Wright's experiences as an embedded reporter with the First Reconnaissance Battalion during the invasion of Iraq in 2003, garnered generally favorable reviews. James Poniewozik wrote for *Time* (July 21, 2008) that it "captures the Iraq invasion as searing drama and surreal comedy," adding, "*Kill*'s strength comes from focusing not on why we fight or how, but on who fights for us: volunteers, many from broken homes and troubled 'hoods, who take being lied to as a given and were raised amid low expectations." Nancy Franklin, however, questioned the need for a series that re-traced events already widely reported on, writing for the *New Yorker* (July 21, 2008), "There would certainly be room right now for a drama about the war that emphasized ideas as well as trying to describe the experience, one that went further up the chain of command to the real decision-makers. But *Generation Kill* is lose-lose in that regard: it has too many characters for the writers to be able to do more than create thumbnail sketches, and it seems convinced that verisimilitude and earnest believability—simple accretion of 'slice of life' detail—will add up to drama and watchability. . . . There is very little in *Generation Kill* to distinguish it from other war-is-hell dramas, such as Steven Bochco's 2005 series *Over There*—though civilians never cease to be surprised by the facts of military life."

David Simon has been married to his third wife, Laura Lippman, an award-winning author of detective fiction and a former *Baltimore Sun* reporter, since 2006. They currently live in Baltimore. Simon has a son, Ethan, from his second marriage, to the graphic artist Kayle Tucker. Simon is currently collaborating with the writer and producer Eric Overmyer on a series about musicians living in New Orleans, Louisiana, in the aftermath of Hurricane Katrina, for which HBO has commissioned a pilot episode.

Simon has won numerous honors for his journalistic achievements, including five national and 13 regional awards. In addition to his television

projects, he continues to work as a freelance journalist for publications including the *Washington Post*, the *New Republic*, and *Details* magazine.

—C.C.

Suggested Reading: *Columbia Journalism Review* p22+ Jan./Feb. 2008; *Entertainment Weekly* p54+ Sep. 22, 2006; *New York Times* p1+ June 11, 2000; *New Yorker* p150+ Oct. 22, 2007; *Newsweek* p54+ Jan. 14, 2008; *Seattle Times* Feb. 18, 1999

Selected Books: *Homicide: A Year on the Killing Streets*, 1991; *The Corner: A Year in the Life of an Inner-City Neighborhood* (with Ed Burns), 1997

Selected Television Shows: as writer and producer—*Homicide: Life on the Street*, 1993–99; *The Corner*, 2000; *The Wire*, 2002–08; *Generation Kill*, 2008

Courtesy of William Tung

Simone, Gail

July 29, 1964(?)– Comic-book writer

Address: c/o DC Comics, 1700 Broadway, New York, NY 10019

Gail Simone spent 15 years as a hairstylist in her small Oregon hometown before becoming one of the comic-book industry's most prominent female writers. She first caught the attention of her fellow comic-book readers when she created Women in Refrigerators, a Web site that lists—and protests the roles of—the many female comic-book characters who have functioned chiefly as victims in stories about male heroes. After obtaining her own column on ComicbookResources.com and spending a short time writing comic books based on the popular television show *The Simpsons* for Bongo Comics, Simone wrote several titles for Marvel Comics, including *Deadpool* and the *Marvelous Adventures of Gus Beezer*. In 2003 she joined DC Comics and began her successful four-year run on the *Birds of Prey* series; in 2007 she became the first female regular writer for *Wonder Woman*. Simone has been one of the most outspoken women in the industry with regard to the often-misogynistic treatment of female characters in comic books—a phenomenon that, Simone has said, she felt was changing for the better when she created her Web site, but one that many believe she has helped to improve over the past few years. "I think it's very insulting to have a complete medium where you're cutting out a lot of the audience," she told Dan Phillips for IGN.com (November 13, 2007). "I really feel we have to do a better job, and I think we are doing a better job, even if we have a long way to go. I think that that is really one of the keys to growing an audience. There's no other medium, whether it be TV or movies or anything else, where they cut out whole sections of our population. And we need to recognize that as an industry." Most recently, Simone announced that she is working on a new incarnation of the series *Secret Six*.

The eldest of three children, Gail Simone was born in Florence, Oregon, on July 29 in about 1964. Her family lived on a farm in that small, coastal town. Growing up with little television reception, Simone was a bookworm from a young age. Comic books were among the assortment of literature she read. The first that she picked up were *Archie* and *House of Mystery* comics; she has credited *Justice League of America* with getting her hooked on the world of superheroes. One episode of the 1960s television series *Batman*, in which Batgirl made an appearance, furthered her interest. "Batgirl did it for me," she recalled to Lee Sze Yong for the Singapore *Straits Times* (December 9, 2007). "She had the same red hair [as Simone], and she was punching, kicking and beating bad guys up. . . . Who wouldn't want to be like her?" Simone's avid reading and knowledge of literature allowed her to skip some high-school English courses and instead attend a special class in which the teacher "would assign me reading material like *The Hobbit* and ask me to write a story using that style and my own," she told George Gene Gustines for the *New York Times* (November 27, 2007). She graduated from high school at the age of 16 and went on to attend the University of Oregon, in Eugene. She studied creative writing and theater, crediting the latter with enhancing her facility with fictional characters.

After two years, unable to pay for college any longer, Simone dropped out and began attending a school for cosmetologists. For the next 15 years, she worked as a hairstylist, eventually owning her own salon. Meanwhile, her interest in comics waned. It revived in 1996, when she came across *Kingdom Come*, a four-issue, limited-edition series about a group of aging, iconic superheroes, including Superman and Wonder Woman, who come out of retirement to save the world. "It was really powerful stuff . . . and I was vaguely surprised to learn that there was now a ton of really interesting work being done," Simone said to Dan Koller for the *Dallas Morning News* (May 5, 2006). She began reading comic books again and discussing them with fellow readers in on-line forums.

In 1999, after realizing that most of her favorite superheroines had been subject to tragic and often degrading fates, Simone was inspired to start her Web site, Women in Refrigerators. "There was a character I really liked in a Green Lantern comic, who got murdered off-screen. Kyle [the Green Lantern] comes home and finds her stuffed in the refrigerator. It was actually a well-told story, but a part of me, as a female reader who had seen too many stories like that at the time, I just resented it," she told Stefan Halley for Popsyndicate.com (May 3, 2007). "It made me wonder why this sort of ghoulish, anti-woman violence was such a big trend at the time." With the help of friends, she compiled a list of recurring female comic-book characters who had been "depowered" (or had their superhero abilities taken away); been the victims of rape, torture, or murder; or met other, similarly bleak fates. The list included Batgirl (who became paralyzed), Aquagirl and Elektra (who were both killed), the second Black Canary (who was tortured, made infertile, and depowered), and the original Ms. Marvel, who, as Simone wrote on her site, was "mind-controlled, impregnated by rape, powers and memories stolen, cosmic-powered then depowered, alcoholic—SHEESH!" "Superhero comics are based on wish-fulfillment fantasies," she told Robert Wilonsky for the *Miami New Times* (May 18, 2000). "Bad things happen to male heroes, but they tend to either survive relatively unscathed or die a heroic death. A lot of heroines just get chopped up in the kitchen. There's no wish fulfillment for girls in that." After she finished her list, Simone contacted industry professionals and posted their responses. Women in Refrigerators quickly garnered public attention, and the term "Women in Refrigerators syndrome" has since been added to the comic-book industry vocabulary—used to refer to the death or injury of a female character as a plot device in a story with a male protagonist. The Web site's popularity led to Simone's weekly column on the popular Comic Book Resources Web site. The column, *You'll All Be Sorry!*, often satirized well-known comic books or writers.

The cartoonist, writer, and fellow Comic Book Resources contributor Scott Shaw (whose name has often appeared in published articles with an exclamation point at the end) encouraged Simone to submit work to Bongo Comics, the publishers of the titles based on the popular animated sitcom *The Simpsons*. A fan of the show, Simone followed his advice and began writing for the comic-book series in 2000. During that time she also created and wrote *Killer Princesses*, a miniseries for Oni Press about a sorority of assassins, and wrote an issue of *Noble Causes Extended Family*, a spin-off of the ongoing "superhero soap opera" series *Noble Causes*, for Image Comics. Her work soon led to jobs for Marvel Comics, one of the top American comic-book publishers and the creator of popular superheroes including Spider-Man, Captain America, the Incredible Hulk, Iron Man, the Fantastic Four, and the X-Men. In 2002 Simone started writing for *Deadpool*, a comic featuring the wisecracking mercenary of the same name, working on the series from issue number 65 until its cancellation, due to diminishing sales, four issues later. Marvel wanted to produce a retooled version of the comic, so Simone created *Agent X*, a spin-off about a character much like Deadpool. Simone wrote the new series until issue seven, published in January 2003, when her creative differences with the editor escalated. Later that year she created and wrote the *Marvelous Adventures of Gus Beezer* after the Marvel editor Mike Raicht approached her with the idea of developing a book geared toward children. The three "one-shots" (an industry term for stand-alone stories contained in single issues) featured a young boy with an active imagination as he interacts with famous Marvel heroes including Spider-Man and the Hulk. Wary about the stability of her new career in writing, Simone continued to work as a hairdresser during her initial years in the comic-book industry.

In 2003 Simone moved to Marvel's rival publisher, DC Comics, the home of Superman, Batman, and Wonder Woman. Encouraged by the DC editor Lysa Hawkins, who revealed that she was a fan of the *Killer Princesses* series, Simone submitted a proposal for a new version of the popular DC series *Birds of Prey*. The ongoing series, whose characters are all female, focuses mainly on the superheroines Oracle (formerly Batgirl), Huntress, and Black Canary. Simone won the title and went on to write issues 56 through 108, published in 2007. With her successful and critically praised run on *Birds of Prey*, the writer amassed a solid fan base and cemented her place among the best comic-book writers in the industry. Dan DiDio, DC's former vice president for editorial content and currently its senior vice president and executive editor, praised Simone for her ability to develop memorable female characters. "She has really been able to walk the line by creating strong females that still play out the whole superhero fantasy part as well," he told John Jurgensen for the *Hartford (Connecticut) Courant* (April 16, 2004). Simone wrote several is-

sues of *Action Comics*, a Superman-led series, in 2005 and 2006. She also wrote a 2005 episode of the Cartoon Network animated television series *Justice League Unlimited* as well as issues of the Justice League of America comic *JLA: Classified* in 2006. In addition, that year Simone created and wrote the ongoing *All-New Atom* series, featuring a new version of the longtime DC superhero Atom, and the 12-issue-long *Welcome to Tranquility* series, which centered on a town full of retired superheroes and supervillains.

In April 2007 Simone became the first female ongoing writer for *Wonder Woman* in the series' 66-year history. Simone, who had often told interviewers that her dream job was to work on the series featuring the Amazonian superheroine, was ecstatic upon getting the assignment. Wonder Woman is "just the best kind of person," she told Gustines. "She was a princess who didn't need someone to rescue her. I grew up in an era and a family where women's rights were very important, and the guys didn't tend to stick around too long. She was an amazing role model." Simone's first issue of the series (number 14) was published in November 2007. *Entertainment Weekly* (December 14, 2007) placed *Wonder Woman* on its "Must List," stating, "The comic book's new writer, Gail Simone, dials up the aging series with humor and sass." In his review of Simone's premiere *Wonder Woman* issue, Dan Phillips wrote for IGN.com (November 14, 2007), "Simone's antidote for all that's been ailing this character and title is to—get this—tell a clear, coherent and entertaining story. Simone doesn't undo any of the new status quo or introduce any new developments or themes (at least not yet), she merely steps in and begins telling a story that immediately pulls us in with tight pacing, believable characterization, and most importantly, a feeling of direction—that this tale is actually headed somewhere." He added, "It's finally looking like a good time to be a Wonder Woman fan."

Along with her work on *Wonder Woman*, Simone continues to write the *All-New Atom* series. On April 19, 2008, at the New York Comic Convention, in New York City, Simone announced that she is also working on a new *Secret Six* series, a title—featuring lesser-known villains—that she revived with the 2005 limited-edition *Villains United* series. (The original titles featuring the characters were published in the 1960s and 1980s.) Simone has revealed that the new *Secret Six*, a fan favorite, will feature Catman, Deadshot, Scandal, Ragdoll, and two new characters. She said at the convention, "This is going to be the ballsiest DC book ever, and the greatest thing about it is that it's going to be written by me."

As Simone has gained prominence in the industry, the seeming misogyny that once plagued comic books has diminished greatly. In her 2007 interview with Stefan Halley, she said, "I do believe the industry is waking up. I hate to put it this way, but it's not bitching on websites that will make the most difference. It's success. As more and more women produce comics and commentary and are successful, by critical and/or commercial standards, that's going to smash walls faster than any number of things that have been tried in the past." She added, "And I do believe many of the best commentators on comics right now are women, too many to [list]. It's going to make a difference." When asked about the mark she hopes to leave in the industry, Simone told Halley, "I put a bit of my heart into everything I write. I haven't learned how to hack out a script because an editor needs something on short notice. If I have an artistic legacy, I hope that shines through a little bit." Simone still lives in Florence, with her husband, a travel writer, and their teenage son. Simone has often expressed her interest in working on the Spider-Man, Captain Marvel, and Mary Marvel series.

—M.A.S.

Suggested Reading: IGN Comics (on-line) Nov. 13, 2007; *Miami New Times* Columns May 18, 2000; *New York Times* E p1 Nov. 27, 2007; (Singapore) *Straits Times* (on-line) Dec. 9, 2007

Selected Comic-Book Series: *Killer Princesses*, 2000; *Noble Causes Extended Family*, 2000; *Deadpool*, 2002; *The Marvelous Adventures of Gus Beezer*, 2002; *Birds of Prey*, 2003–07; *Agent X*, 2002–03; *Villains United*, 2005; *Action Comics*, 2005–06; *JLA: Classified*, 2006; *Welcome to Tranquility*, 2006–07; *All New Atom*, 2006– ; *Wonder Woman*, 2007–

Selected Television Shows: *Justice League Unlimited*, 2005

Sinclair, Cameron

Nov. 16(?), 1973– Designer; co-founder and executive director of Architecture for Humanity

Address: Architecture for Humanity, 848 Folsom St., Suite 201, San Francisco, CA 94107

"I really feel that good, innovative and thoughtful design can make a world of difference," the architect Cameron Sinclair, the co-founder and executive director of Architecture for Humanity (AFH), told an interviewer for *DesignBoom* (January 12, 2006, on-line). "Architects can play two roles in society: either create buildings that affect a community for the better or for the worse. Given the choice I think as an industry we strive to improve life whether it be a single family or an entire village. Sadly the design media tends to focus its attention on the dozen or so 'star architects' and in doing so strengthening the general public's view that design is only for the whims of the rich." Sinclair also said, "I am not asking for designers to give up designing for corporate entities, governments or wealthy clients. If anything I want them to continue to do that. But by donating 1% of their time to help those who could benefit from their expertise and wisdom we can make a world of difference." AFH, which Sinclair set up in 1999 with his wife, the journalist Kate Stohr, is a nonprofit organization that offers creative designs for houses and other necessities—chosen primarily through design competitions—to communities facing humanitarian and environmental crises. The impetus for the establishment of AFH was Sinclair and Stohr's growing frustration with traditional architecture's emphasis on both profit and prestige: while many architects strove to win multimillion-dollar projects that benefited only a small number of wealthy individuals, many millions of people around the world continued to lack adequate shelter.

When AFH launched its first design competition, in 1999, the organization consisted only of Sinclair and Stohr, working with a laptop computer in a studio apartment. Thanks to recognition and financial support from like-minded architects, nonprofit organizations, small corporations, and even schoolchildren, by November 2007 AFH was active in 16 countries with 47 regional chapters and a network of more than 5,000 designers. AFH has been instrumental in the provision of housing for refugees from Kosovo, in the former Yugoslavia; mobile HIV/AIDS clinics in South Africa; and reconstruction projects in Southeast Asia following the devastating tsunami of December 2004, and along the United States' Gulf Coast, after Hurricane Katrina, in 2005. The $100,000 TED (Technology Entertainment Design) Award, which Sinclair won in 2006, enabled him to create the Open Architecture Network, an on-line tool, launched in early 2007, that facilitates collaboration among parties involved in humanitarian design and construction projects. *Design Like You Give a Damn: Architectural Responses to Humanitarian Crises* (2006), co-edited by Cameron and Stohr, describes the historical challenges of humanitarian architecture and design and offers dozens of possible solutions to contemporary problems. "If you strip away the theory, ego, and the hype of design, what we all do is provide shelter," Sinclair told a *Fast Company Magazine* (March 20, 2003) interviewer. "Where resources and expertise are scarce, innovative, sustainable and collaborative design can make a difference."

Sinclair has said that the next generation of architects and designers will have to address the growing problem of overpopulation in underdeveloped urban areas. At a lecture he gave in May 2006, Sinclair noted, according to the London *Observer* (May 14, 2006), that one in seven people lived in an overcrowded slum or an "undefined area," such

Peter Foley

Kate Stohr (left) and Cameron Sinclair

as one of the shantytowns that surround some cities, and he cited predictions that in 20 years, that statistic would be one in three. "We need a global architecture revolution," Sinclair has said, as quoted by Michael Kruse in the *St. Petersburg (Florida) Times* (October 1, 2007).

Cameron Sinclair was born in London, England, in 1973 (on November 16, according to unofficial sources). During his childhood he lived at various times in London, upstate New York, and Bath, England, where he attended a boarding school. As a child Sinclair dreamed of pursuing a career in politics or war photography. When he was 10 years old, Desmond Tutu, a South African cleric and activist opponent of apartheid who won the Nobel Peace Prize in 1984, spoke at the church the Sinclairs attended about the troubles of South African communities. Sinclair later recalled Tutu's talk as a significant moment in the development of his social conscience. He was drawn to building design "not because of great cathedrals, but because of bad architecture," as he told Matt Vande Bunte for the *Grand Rapids (Michigan) Press* (November 17, 2007). As a teenager he became interested in the effects of poorly designed public spaces on society and how such designs could be improved.

Sinclair attended the University of Westminster, in London, where he studied architecture and became knowledgeable about social, cultural, and humanitarian aspects of design. After he graduated, in 1995, with honors, Sinclair pursued a master's degree at the Bartlett School of Architecture, also in London. While most of his fellow students and Bartlett professors concentrated on the aesthetic aspects of design and designs with potential for lucrative commissions, Sinclair devoted himself to projects that reflected social consciousness; for his thesis, he wrote about possibilities for sustainable transitional housing for homeless people in New York City, conducting first-hand research there. He recalled to Lucy Siegle for the London *Observer* (May 14, 2006) that one of his Bartlett teachers once told him that he considered designing for the homeless "depressing." "I said I found not designing for the homeless depressing," Sinclair told Siegle. "I was the black sheep of my class," he told Alastair Gordon for the *New York Times* (August 28, 2003).

After he returned to London, Sinclair discovered that his thesis adviser was not pleased with his research. He dropped out of Bartlett in 1997, without completing his degree. That year Sinclair took a job as an assistant architect at Steve Blatz Architects, a large New York City firm. He worked 17 hours a day as a "CAD monkey"—the acronym is for "computer-aided design"—"cutting and pasting buildings together onscreen," as he told Siegle. He contributed to designs of retail stores or sections of stores, including Harvey Nichols, in London; Gum Department Store, in Moscow, Russia; and several stores for the cosmetic companies Clinique and Estée Lauder. Next, for two years beginning in January 1998, Sinclair worked for Christidis Lauster & Radu Architects, in New York, where his projects included an award-winning 30-year rejuvenation plan for Tirgu-Jiu (also spelled Târgu-Jiu), a town in Romania; a redevelopment plan for the Harlem section of New York City; and a health center for UNITE (the Union of Needletrades, Industrial, and Textile Employees). Then, from January 2000 to September 2002, when he was laid off, Sinclair worked as a project architect for Gensler, a huge firm with offices in 30 cities. His Gensler projects included the School at the International Center of Photography, in Manhattan, which opened in 2001, and the transformation of New York City's Fresh Kills landfill into usable public space; he also served on the disaster-recovery team for Lehman Brothers, designing new office space for that investment bank when its headquarters were destroyed during the September 11, 2001 terrorist attacks. Sinclair told Siegle that one day, while designing a display to hold luxury lipstick dispensers for a shopping center in Johannesburg, South Africa, he realized that the majority of Johannesburg citizens would not be able to afford the lipstick. He decided that he wanted to design structures that could be used by the communities that were most in need of help.

Meanwhile, in 1999, an estimated 800,000 Kosovar Albanians returned home to war-ravaged villages and obliterated bridges, roads, and other structures in the aftermath of the violent conflict between Serbian and Yugoslavian security forces and the Kosovo Liberation Army. One evening, while watching television images of returning refugees and their United Nations–provided tents, Sinclair realized that architects and designers could be pivotal in creating inexpensive, durable, well-constructed buildings that would not only provide proper shelter but also empower residents to reconstruct their communities. "Refugee shelter is usually a last-minute, ad hoc affair with little in the way of advance planning," Sinclair told Gordon. On the assumption that he was not the only one interested in the humanitarian applications of design, he used $700 of his savings to launch a competition for designs for temporary housing for the Kosovo refugees with the sponsorship of the London-based relief group War Child—which helped establish communication with refugees and organize a group of experts from relevant nongovernment agencies—and Lauster Radu, an architecture firm that helped establish design criteria for the project. The guidelines required that each structure be strong enough to stand for five years, cost no more than $8,000 to build, accommodate as many as 10 people, and be easy to set up on various terrains. To their surprise, Sinclair and Stohr, who married during that period, received 205 entries from 30 countries. In order to make the winning designs a reality, the couple established and officially registered a new, nonprofit organization, Architecture for Humanity. Sinclair and a panel of four other architects selected 10 winners, five of which later came into being as prototypes. One prototype, designed by an Australian architect, Sean Godsell, resembled a shipping container covered by a canopy. Another, designed by Aziz Valy and her partner Suzan Wines for I-Beam Design, was made of wooden shipping pallets, which are often used to ship supplies to disaster areas. The protypes appeared in an exhibition that toured New York City, London, and Paris in 1999. Disappointingly for Sinclair, none of the designs submitted for the competition were ever built in Kosovo. "We architects enjoy a pat on the back, but unless you build it, it's just an idea," he said to Gordon.

Among the various organizations that were pursuing humanitarian design projects, AFH soon became one of the best-known. Following the September 11, 2001 terrorist attacks on the World Trade Center and the Pentagon, the AFH Web site received a huge surge in hits. Four days after the tragedy, Sinclair received a call from the United Nations high commissioner for refugees, who told him that he was on a list of people available to help with the relief effort anticipated for Afghanistan after the United States began its impending military campaign there. "I told them I hope it's a long list," Sinclair recalled to Gordon, "because I'm a 28-year-old alone in my apartment." He also advised the United Nations about architects and engineers in Pakistan and other nearby areas.

During a trip to South Africa in 1999, Sinclair had witnessed aspects of the toll that the AIDS epidemic had had on that nation. In May 2002, in collaboration with the Van Alen Institute, whose stated mission is to "improve the public realm," AFH announced a competition for designs for a mobile HIV/AIDS clinic to be used in South Africa. By the deadline, November 1, 2002, more than 500 teams from 51 countries had responded. A nine-person jury of architects and medical experts selected four finalists. The first-place design, by Khras Architects of Denmark, was a self-contained clinic made of lightweight local materials, including such self-sustaining features as a satellite dish to capture solar power and a water-collection system, which would give the clinic access to fresh water wherever it went. In 2002–04 the designs were displayed in an exhibition that toured the United States, the United Kingdom, Denmark, and Italy. In the summer of 2004, the four finalists worked in South Africa with the Africa Centre for Health and Population to help realize the designs.

In 2003 Sinclair received the Nice Modernist Award from *Dwell Magazine* for "furthering the development of thoughtful, engaging design." Also in 2003 he launched a lecture tour, dubbed "Design Like You Give a Damn." Over the years Sinclair has spoken about the importance of studying and supporting socially conscious design, giving talks at international conferences including the Fortune Brainstorm Conference, the International Union of Architects World Congress of Architecture, the International Design Conference in Aspen, and the Art Center Design Conference in Pasadena, California. He has donated all of his lecture fees to Architecture for Humanity. After subtracting his travel expenses, Sinclair told Linda Hales for the *Washington Post* (August 6, 2005), his yearly earnings totaled "in the four figures." But as he told a writer for *Interior Design* (2003), accumulating wealth is not his aim. "The work is so fulfilling. . . . And the results of community and humanitarian work will last a lifetime. A possible bonus is that the community remembers you, so you could actually get more projects—paying ones—later."

On December 26, 2004 the second-largest earthquake ever recorded on seismographs erupted in the Indian Ocean. The resulting tsunamis claimed more than 230,000 lives, displaced upwards of a million people, and caused enormous destruction along coastlines of Indonesia, Sri Lanka, India, and Thailand. "This was a key moment, not just for our organization but for the entire movement for socially conscious design," In response, AFH worked with worldchanging.com, a nonprofit on-line magazine, to raise a half-million dollars for projects to aid victims of the tsunamis. Sinclair and Stohr handled several regional projects and coordinated a network of thousands of locally based volunteers. Their largest project, executed in collaboration with five other independent architects, involved rebuilding structures in the Sri Lankan village of Kirinda. In Pottuvil, also in Sri Lanka, AFH worked with the organization Relief International to reconstruct a school; in the process they created a prototype for housing in that area. AFH also helped rebuild structures in the Caddalore and Viluppuram districts of Sri Lanka. By May 2006 AFH had completed five community rebuilding projects in Sri Lanka and three in India.

In 2004 AFH hosted its third global design competition. With the goal of promoting public health and community development as areas of focus for combating the spread of HIV/AIDS in South Africa, AFH asked contestants to design a sports facility and health-education center for women. Out of hundreds of entries, Sinclair and the other judges selected three finalists; a local women's soccer league chose the winning design, by Swee Hong Ng of Pittsburgh, Pennsylvania. That design and others were featured in the March/April 2005 issue of the magazine *International Design*. In 2005, in the wake of the immense destruction caused by Hurricane Katrina along the Gulf Coast of the U.S., Sinclair and AFH teamed up with the East Biloxi Relief Recovery and Revitalization Center and the Gulf Coast Community Design Studio of Mississippi State University to organize several community rebuilding projects. In an unusual approach to the design of affordable, sustainable new homes, the Biloxi Model Home Program paired families who had lost their homes with professional designers. In 2005 four of AFH's HIV/AIDS mobile clinics went into operation in Nigeria. That year, in addition to his continued involvement with tsunami-related projects in Southeast Asia, Sinclair collaborated with the nonprofit organization Kids with Cameras to design and develop a school in Calcutta, India, specializing in leadership skills and the arts.

Sinclair has emphasized that humanitarian architecture and design projects must address the needs, restrictions, and aesthetics of local communities directly. AFH focuses on creating designs in accord with particular nations' budgetary restrictions. Sinclair has defined humanitarian design in far broader terms than simply a response to natural or systematic disasters; as he told an interviewer for the Design Museum Web site, "What a designer does to enrich human life can be defined as humanitarian—if anything our role should be pre-emptive rather than seeking immediate solutions to a crisis." Houses built in geologic fault zones, for example, should be designed so as to withstand earthquakes.

In 2006 TED, a philanthropic community of thinkers and innovators, awarded AFH $100,000. In response, Sinclair created the Open Architecture Network (OAN), an on-line tool that facilitates communication and collaboration among parties involved in all aspects of a design project: designers, architects, engineers, community leaders, nonprofit groups, volunteer organizations, government agencies, technology partners, health-care workers, and educators. According to the OAN web site, "The network has a simple mission: to generate not one idea but the hundreds of thousands of design ideas needed to improve living conditions for all." As of October 2007 the site had attracted more than 3,700 volunteer designers working on about 220 projects. That month the American Institute of Architects honored AFH with an award for "humanitarian efforts in creating opportunities for architects and designers from around the world to help communities in need."

Sinclair's many honors include *Wired* magazine's 2004 Rave Award for Architecture, which he shared with his wife, the World Economic Forum's 2008 Young Global Leader Award, and the Cooper-Hewitt National Design Museum's 2008 Design Patron Award, for demonstrating that "good design can indeed change the world." He has taught courses in architecture at Montana State University and the University of Minnesota, among other schools, and is currently a visiting professor at the University of Southern California. Sinclair and his wife maintain a home in San Francisco, California.

—M.E.R.

Suggested Reading: Architecture for Humanity Web site; *Grand Rapids (Michigan) Press* Business B p1 Nov. 17, 2007; (London) *Observer Magazine* (on-line) May 14, 2006; *New York Times* (on-line) Aug. 28, 2003; *Washington Post* C p1+ Aug. 6, 2005

Selected Books: as co-editor—*Design Like You Give a Damn*, 2006

Thos Robinson/Getty Images for World Science Festival

Sinclair, David A.

*May 6, 1969– Molecular biologist; longevity
researcher; co-founder of Sirtris Pharmaceuticals*

*Address: Dept. of Pathology, Harvard Medical
School, New Rsch. Bldg. Rm. 331, 77 Ave. Louis
Pasteur, Boston, MA 02115*

"Aging is the worst thing that has ever been put
upon humanity," the molecular biologist and longevity researcher David Sinclair told Andrew Rimas for the *Boston Globe* (December 11, 2006).
"When I was three years old, I was horrified by the
idea that my grandparents would die, and then my
parents would die. And then one day I would die."
A Harvard University scientist since 1999 and the
co-founder, in 2004, of Sirtris Pharmaceuticals,
Sinclair has strived to develop drugs that combat
the diseases and disorders that accompany aging,
such as diabetes, cancer, heart disease, Alzheimer's disease, and cataracts. Challenging the
long-held view that the processes of aging are natural and inevitable, Sinclair believes he has discovered a natural chemical compound that may prevent and perhaps even cure age-related diseases,
thereby significantly extending and improving the
life spans of humans. The chemical, called resveratrol, is found in various plants, among them euca-
lyptus, peanuts, and, most abundantly, red grapes.
Based on his studies, which to date have been conducted on yeast cells, roundworms, and rodents,
Sinclair has theorized that resveratrol works by stimulating in cells the natural defense mechanisms
that are normally activated when the cells are faced
with great trauma or stress, prompting them to repair their own DNA; ultimately, such activity

would lead to longer lives for whole organisms.
Sinclair made national headlines in August 2003
when he published in the professional journal *Nature* his finding that resveratrol increased the life
span of yeast cells by up to 70 percent. In 2007
Sirtris Pharmaceuticals began to develop synthetic
compounds whose effects resembled those of resveratrol but were 1,000 times stronger. Formulations of resveratrol and more-potent compounds
have now been tested in human clinical trials. So
far, resveratrol has produced the same sugar-
lowering effect in humans with Type II diabetes as
it has in rodents. Sinclair believes that the drugs
could revolutionize the way humans treat diseases
of aging and extend the lives of humans by five to
10 healthy years. "Cancer, heart disease, diabetes,
cataracts, Alzheimer's. We aim to treat diseases of
aging with a single pill," Sinclair told Rimas. "I
want to see 90-year-olds play squash with their
grandchildren."

The basis of Sinclair's research is a scientific
discovery, made in the 1930s, which showed a link
between caloric restriction and an increased life
span, increased energy, and the delayed onset of
age-related illnesses in rodents. Over the years scientists noted the same connection between caloric
restriction and increased life span in larger animals, such as monkeys, as well as lower life forms,
such as yeast. Many scientists began to theorize
that a diet that contained fewer calories put cells
under such stress that the cells reacted in defense
by repairing DNA damage and becoming more resilient to structural damage. In the mid-1990s, after
Sinclair earned his Ph.D. degree in molecular biology from the University of New South Wales, he
joined a group of researchers, led by Leonard P.
Guarente, based at the Massachusetts Institute of
Technology (MIT), who, along with Cynthia Kenyon, from the University of California, had set out
to discover the specific genes that appeared to be
responsible for the defense reaction. The genes that
Guarente and Sinclair found are called sirtuins. In
his own research lab at Harvard University, Sinclair and his team discovered 18 chemical compounds, called polyphenols, that stimulate sirtuins to produce anti-aging enzymes in yeast cells.
Experiments with those polyphenols showed that
the strongest was resveratrol. Most recent studies
have indicated that resveratrol mimics the physiology of calorie restriction, slows aging, and extends
the lives of rodents.

David A. Sinclair was born on May 6, 1969 and
raised in St. Ives, a suburb of Sydney, Australia.
Both of his parents are biochemists; his father has
worked in the field of information technology
since the 1970s. His only sibling, a younger brother, is a founding partner in a project-management
consulting firm that works with Australia's major
banks. His paternal grandmother, Vera Szigeti, was
only 15 when she gave birth to Sinclair's father
(who anglicized his surname as an adult); she came
to Australia with her teenage son after fleeing Hungary in 1956, during the thwarted grassroots revo-

lution against Hungary's Communist government. In an interview with David Ewing Duncan for *Technology Review* (September/October 2007), Sinclair described his grandmother as "a '60s bohemian who helped raise me and taught me how to think differently and to question dogma." As a boy Sinclair enjoyed setting off explosions with devices that he made from chlorine or gunpowder. "It was rebellious and dangerous. That was the thrill," he told Duncan. At seven, he recalled to Duncan, he thought of 10 ways in which he could change the world, including inventing things "to make money." As a teenager Sinclair liked to wind-surf and race cars. Perhaps more than most young-sters, he was troubled by the inevitable prospect of growing old and dying. "It's a horrible thing to be given consciousness and mortality at the same time," he told Andrew Rimas, referring to what drew him to investigate life-span–enhancing drugs.

Sinclair graduated from St. Ives High School in 1986. He majored in genetics at the University of New South Wales, in Sydney, where he earned a B.S. degree with first-class honors in 1991. He pur-sued a doctorate in molecular biology and genetics at the same school. While he was engaged in his graduate work, which was concerned with gene regulation in yeast, Leonard Guarente, a molecular biologist at MIT, came to the university on a lecture tour, and by chance Sinclair had a chat with him during a communal lunch. During their conversa-tion Sinclair was fascinated to learn that Cynthia Kenyon had discovered that manipulating a gene referred to as *daf2* might significantly lengthen the life spans of roundworms. Guarente was conduct-ing similar experiments on yeast cells. Two of his graduate students had discovered a species of yeast that lived longer than others. Its longevity was due to the activity of a family of genes known by the ac-ronym SIR (silent information regulator), or SIRT in humans. One of the genes is known as SIR2 (SIRT2 in humans).

After he earned his Ph.D., in 1995, Sinclair used the money he gained by selling his car to fly to Massachusetts, where he successfully interviewed for a postdoctoral position in Guarente's lab at Har-vard University. He had greatly impressed his questioners, according to Duncan, by arguing that "scientists studying aging should look for genes that prolong life rather than genes and mechanisms that end it."

In 1997 Sinclair and Guarente discovered that yeast age due to the accumulation of ERCs (an acro-nym for "extrachromosomal rDNA circles"), circu-lar strands of DNA that build up in cells as they age. Not long afterward other scientists in Guar-ente's lab discovered an apparent link between SIR2 and a molecule, called NAD, that is critical in metabolizing food. Because NAD becomes more prevalent in the human body when caloric intake is drastically reduced, the link between SIR2 and NAD suggested that the SIR2 gene accounted for why restricting calories produced anti-aging ef-fects in animals. By adding an extra copy of SIR2, Guarente's team enabled yeast cells to live 30 per-cent longer than average, which appeared to sup-port their overall theory.

In 1999, with Guarente's help, Sinclair joined the faculty of the Department of Pathology at Har-vard Medical School. Sinclair established his own laboratory at Harvard, focusing on the study of sir-tuins, the genes responsible for cells' defense mechanisms. In 2001 Sinclair's investigations of Werner syndrome, a rare genetic disease whose victims age prematurely, led to a significant dis-covery regarding the way that cancerous cells pro-liferate. Scientists had already determined that up to 90 percent of cancerous tumor cells proliferate by replenishing telomeres, protective molecular caps on the ends of chromosomes that are vital in reproduction. Normally, telomeres get smaller when a cell divides, and their disappearance spells the death of the cell. The presence of full-size te-lomeres enables cancer cells to reproduce indefi-nitely. Sinclair's study, described in 2001 in the on-line version of the *Proceedings of the National Academy of Sciences*, suggested that the remaining 10 percent of cancerous cells, which reproduce us-ing a means other than telomeres, may reproduce using a protein called WRN, which is absent in people affected by Werner syndrome. Sinclair's theory is supported by the fact that individuals who suffer from Werner syndrome do not develop most forms of cancer. For years, scientists had been working to create "telomere inhibitors" as a means of halting reproduction of cancerous cells, but Sin-clair's discovery pointed to another possible path-way for scientists to analyze. "It's a warning to all those who think that telomeres inhibitors will be the cure-all," Sinclair told Michael Lasalandra for the *Boston Herald* (March 6, 2001).

In 2003 Sinclair and his research team worked with Konrad Howitz, the director of molecular bi-ology at Biomol, a Pennsylvania-based biochemi-cal company, to screen thousands of molecules, in an effort to discover the proteins that activated cells' anti-aging genes. Biomol discovered 18 mole-cules, called polyphenols, whose presence coin-cided with stimulated sirtuins. Biomol discovered two polyphenols, quercetin and piceatannol, which appeared to strongly stimulate a human sir-tuin. Both proteins were found to be structurally similar to resveratrol, a chemical found in high concentration in the skin of the red grapes used to make wine. Sinclair and Howitz collaborated to test the effect of resveratrol on the life span of yeast. The studies, which were partially funded by the National Institute on Aging, showed that res-veratrol extended the life span of yeast cells by up to 70 percent, and that that extension depended on the SIR2 gene. Sinclair and his research team pub-lished their findings in the on-line version of *Na-ture* in August 2003. Sinclair reasoned that if res-veratrol had a similar effect in humans, it might lead to an entirely new way of looking at medicine. By boosting the body's defenses against disease and cell damage, Sinclair suggested, not only would a person's life span be lengthened, but the quality of health in that individual's last years of life would be improved. "We're talking about the subtle fine tuning of life versus death and these molecules tend to push cells a little bit more toward the survival side of things," Sinclair told Ronald Kotulak for the *Chicago Tribune* (August 25, 2003). "We believe that the survival of a single cell is controlled by the same genes that control the life span of the whole organism. We're really the sum of our parts."

Sinclair's finding was widely covered in the media. *Discover* magazine hailed it as the "discovery of the year," while other publications credited Sinclair with having discovered the "fountain of youth" and heralded red wine as the "elixir of life." Though Sinclair advised that the amount of resveratrol in red wine was not likely to affect a person's life span, many saw the discovery as an explanation for the health benefits long known to be associated with red wine. It also seemed to explain the "French paradox"—the fact that the French, who regularly drink wine and eat a high-fat diet, do not suffer from high levels of cardiovascular disease. Meanwhile, some scientists cautioned against jumping to conclusions regarding the effect of resveratrol on humans, since human cells are much more complicated than yeast cells. "It's great if you're a yeast," Mark Lane, a researcher for the pharmaceuticals company Merck who studies aging in monkeys, told *Newsday* (August 26, 2003). "But it's a big leap from a yeast cell to a human."

Various sources have reported that Sinclair became affiliated with a company that marketed a dietary supplement called Longevinex, each capsule of which was said to contain as much resveratrol as is present in three to four glasses of wine. Sinclair told *Current Biography* that he has never had any connection to the company that sold Longevinex and has never received any money from it.

In the spring of 2004, Christoph Westphal, a venture capitalist who had started several pharmaceutical companies, read about Sinclair's discoveries. That year he and Sinclair founded Sirtris, a pharmaceutical company that aims to develop drugs that target sirtuins, the name given to both genes and enzymes associated with the aging process. Meanwhile, in a July 2004 issue of *Nature*, Sinclair's research team at Harvard published a study showing that resveratrol had a life-extending effect in both fruit flies and roundworms, one that resembled the effect of restricting their caloric intake. The study also showed that unlike the calorie-restricted fruit flies, which exhibited infertility and decreased energy, the fruit flies given resveratrol showed no adverse side effects; indeed, they became more active and produced more fertile eggs per day than previously, and they ate as much as they wanted. "If yeast is a one and humans are a 10, then flies are a nine," Sinclair told Jennifer Lehner for the *Washington Times* (July 16, 2004), comparing the complexity of their respective physiologies.

"We want to move this very quickly." Resveratrol's main drawback, according to Sinclair, was its poor bioavailability—that is, only a tiny portion of a single dose entered an organism's system; thus, in order to be beneficial, it had to be consumed in large quantities. Sinclair and colleagues of his from the University of Connecticut and Brown University hoped to find compounds with properties similar to but far more potent than those of resveratrol.

On November 2, 2006 Sinclair reported in *Nature* the results of a study that demonstrated the anti-aging effects of resveratrol in laboratory mice. That research, conducted with Joseph Baur of Harvard Medical School and Rafael de Cabo of the National Institute on Aging, involved three groups of middle-aged mice. One was fed a standard mouse diet, the second was fed a high-fat, high-calorie diet, and the third was fed a high-fat, high-calorie diet containing resveratrol. While the mice in the second group gained weight, developed fatty livers and heart inflammation, and died young, the mice in the third group gained weight but developed none of the associated health problems. Their physiologies mirrored those of the mice in the first group, and in tests of physical fitness, they outperformed the mice in the other groups. In addition, their risk of death was reduced by 30 percent. "The mice on resveratrol have not just been living longer," Sinclair told James Morgan for the Glasgow, Scotland, *Herald* (November 2, 2006). "They are also living more active, better lives. Their motor skills actually show improvement as they grow older. The health benefits we saw in these mice may mean we can stave off age-related diseases in humans, such as Type 2 diabetes, heart disease and cancer. Only time and research will tell." The results were encouraging for Sinclair, whose aim is not only to lengthen human lives but also to improve them. "[The goal is] to see eventually that an 80-year-old feels like a 50-year-old does today," he told Morgan. Later that month another research team, led by John Auwerx of the Institute of Genetics and Molecular and Cellular Biology in Illkirch, France, reported in the scientific journal *Cell* that their work had corroborated Sinclair's findings: mice treated with resveratrol developed enhanced aerobic capacity, muscles that consumed oxygen more efficiently than those of other mice, and the ability to run twice as far as normal mice without getting tired.

In May 2007 Sirtris made an initial public offering that raised $62 million. (The firm had already acquired more than $103 million in venture funding, some of it from private sources, among them John Henry, the owner of the Boston Red Sox baseball team, and the former Fidelity investment manager Peter Lynch.) In September 2007 Sirtris announced that its researchers had discovered two more genes, SIRT3 and SIRT4, that produce sirtuins; in those cases, the sirtuins are enzymes that help preserve mitochondria, tiny organs (called organelles) within cells that produce energy for the cells and keep them healthy, especially during times of stress or DNA damage. Sinclair noted that SIRT3 and SIRT4 might be additional targets for drugs for treating diseases associated with aging. Also in 2007 Sirtris began clinical trials of SRT501, an enhanced formulation of resveratrol, in patients with diabetes and MELAS syndrome, a rare disorder that leads to fatal deterioration of the brain and muscles. In November of that year, Sirtris announced that it had developed compounds that were 1,000 times more potent than resveratrol and had reversed symptoms of diabetes and reduced sensitivity to insulin in three studies, two involving diabetic mice and the third, diabetic rats. "When you see it work in those three models, you have increased confidence that it will have a universal effect on organisms," Sinclair told Julie Steenhuysen for Reuters (November 29, 2007). Sinclair expressed his hope that the new drugs would be proven effective in treating diabetes as well as most other diseases in the Western world.

More recent studies conducted by Sirtris have shown that in diabetic humans, resveratrol and similar compounds can help lower cholesterol and glucose levels and reduce the risk of a particularly deadly form of prostate cancer. One study conducted by a research team connected with the University of Wisconsin and published in *Public Library of Science* (June 2008) suggested that resveratrol may be effective in mice and people in much lower doses than previously thought necessary, and that a four- or five-ounce glass of wine may contain close to an effective daily dose of resveratrol. Meanwhile, recent studies have cast doubt on whether resveratrol works by activating sirtuins. "The question of how resveratrol is working is an ongoing debate and it will take more studies to get the answer," Sinclair admitted to Nicholas Wade for the *New York Times* (June 4, 2008). Another crucial unresolved issue, for which Sinclair has received significant criticism, is whether caloric restriction actually works the same way in humans as it does in other animals. One of two studies currently being conducted on rhesus monkeys by Richard Weindruch at the University of Wisconsin is beginning to show clear evidence that calorically restricted monkeys were out-living monkeys fed a normal diet, which supports the premise of Sinclair's work. In June 2008 Sirtris was sold to the drug maker GlaxoSmithKline for $720 million. "The upside is so huge that if we are right, the company that dominates the sirtuin space could dominate the pharmaceutical industry and change medicine," Sinclair told Wade. "This will impact humans within a decade," Sinclair predicted to Duncan. "That's why I don't think there is anything more important than this quest. That's why I take chances, and why the controversy is worth it."

Sinclair's honors include the Australian Commonwealth Prize, the Helen Hay Whitney Postdoctoral Award, a special fellowship from the Leukemia Society, a Harvard-Armenise fellowship, an Association for Aging Research fellowship, and the 2004 Genzyme Outstanding Achievement in Biomedical Science Award. He is currently the director of the Paul F. Glenn Laboratories for the Biological Mechanisms of Aging, an associate professor of pathology at Harvard Medical School, and a senior scholar of the Ellison Medical Foundation. Sinclair also co-founded, in 2006, and serves on the board of Genocea Biosciences, a vaccine discovery company whose goal is to prevent infectious diseases, which he co-founded in 2006.

Sinclair lives in West Roxbury, Massachusetts, with his wife, Sandra, who is German; his daughters, Natalie and Madeleine; and his son, Benjamin (who was named for Benjamin Franklin). He used to spend his spare time windsurfing, sailing, and in-line skating; now, he told Rimas, he no longer has time for such activities. "When you're sitting on the potential to treat millions of people's diseases, you can't take time off," he said. "I'm lucky if I have time to shower."

—M.E.R.

Suggested Reading: *Boston Globe* C p2 Dec. 11, 2006; *Boston Herald* p10 Mar. 6, 2001; *Chicago Tribune* p8 Aug. 25, 2003; (Glasgow, Scotland) *Herald* p17 Nov. 2, 2006; *Mass High Tech* p1 Dec. 8, 2003; *New York Times* A p1+ June 4, 2008; *Technology Review* p78+ Sep. 2007; *Washington Times* A p11 July 6, 2004

Sittenfeld, Curtis

Aug. 23, 1975– Writer

Address: Random House Inc., 1745 Broadway, New York, NY 10019

Curtis Sittenfeld's first two novels, *Prep* (2005) and *The Man of My Dreams* (2006), generally fit in the "chick lit" genre, which usually features female characters who are struggling with issues related to love, sex, dieting, careers, and relationships, romantic and otherwise. While those books are not wholly constrained by the genre—especially *Prep*, which also addresses such serious issues as class—Sittenfeld raised the stakes further, and shed the "chick lit" label, with her novel *American Wife* (2008), inspired by the life of First Lady Laura Bush. The book's main character, like her real-life counterpart, is married to a widely unpopular president. There have been some (expected) partisan reactions to the novel, with Democrats saying that the novel is too sympathetic to the Bush family and Republicans countering that Sittenfeld has "smeared" the real president and First Lady. "Detractors from both sides of the aisle might want to veer off message and actually read the book before lobbing grenades . . . ," Connie Schultz wrote for the *Washington Post* (September 7, 2008). "*American Wife* advances the notion that there is more to a president's wife than orchestrated public appear-

Ryan Kurtz, courtesy of Random House
Curtis Sittenfeld

ances. Still a radical notion in Washington, perhaps, but one that women around the country will welcome."

The second of four children (three girls and one boy), Elizabeth Curtis Sittenfeld was born on August 23, 1975 in Cincinnati, Ohio. Her father, Paul, was an investment adviser; her mother, Elizabeth, was an art-history teacher at Seven Hills School, in Cincinnati, which Sittenfeld attended through eighth grade. For high school she enrolled at Groton, an exclusive boarding school near Boston, Massachusetts. Her brother and sisters also attended private schools, but none went to a boarding school; Sittenfeld became interested in Groton after meeting some of the school's recruiters in Cincinnati. She told Samantha Selinger-Morris for the *Sydney (Australia) Morning Herald* (October 1, 2005) that Groton "seemed sort of, like, glamorous and romantic, but also available to adolescents." She added about her time there, "I wouldn't say I was in with the popular kids, but I wasn't a loner either." Sittenfeld's favorite area of study was English; she struggled with some other subjects, including Latin, French, math, and biology. In 1992, during the summer before her senior year at Groton, at the age of 16, Sittenfeld won *Seventeen* magazine's annual fiction contest.

Sittenfeld attended Vassar College, in Poughkeepsie, New York, and then transferred to Stanford University, in California, where she studied creative writing. At Stanford Sittenfeld wrote for the college paper and edited its weekly art magazine. In 1996 she was chosen as one of *Glamour* magazine's "Top 10 College Women." After graduating, in 1997, Sittenfeld pursued journalism, serving as an intern at the *Atlantic Monthly* and then working at the *Charlotte (North Carolina) Observer* and *Fast Company* magazine. "Being a journalist exposes you to so many situations that you would never find yourself in," Sittenfeld told Selinger-Morris. "Like you're in someone's living room and you'd never meet them socially. It's pretty shocking what interviewees tell you about themselves." In 2001 the author received a master's degree from the prestigious Iowa Writers Workshop at the University of Iowa, and in the following year she became the writer-in-residence at St. Albans, an all-boys Christian private school in Washington, D.C. She taught ninth-grade English at the school from 2003 to 2005.

In 2005 Sittenfeld published her first novel, *Prep*, which she had written during her time at St. Albans. *Prep* received rejections from 14 out of 15 publishers; its first printing was only 16,000 copies. Within a month the novel had made it to the *New York Times* best-seller list, where it stayed for nine weeks. *Prep* explores the high-school years of the homely, intelligent Lee Fiora, who is unworldly compared with most of the students at her school. Fiora narrates the story, looking back several years after her college graduation. "The character-driven narrative never lags," Steve Weinberg wrote for the Cleveland, Ohio, *Plain Dealer* (January 23, 2005). "Sittenfeld is superb at rendering dialogue, at physical description, at describing emotions, at floating ideas about human nature, education and the society that invented prep schools." One of the major social phenomena addressed in *Prep* is class. Fiora's father owns a chain of mattress stores, which embarrasses her when she learns about the prestigious and exciting jobs of her classmates' parents. Although the novel received favorable reviews from many top publications—the *New York Times Book Review*, the *New Yorker*, the *Washington Post*, and the *Chicago Tribune*—not everyone found Sittenfeld's debut novel, as Weinberg called it, "irresistible." Writing for the *San Francisco Chronicle* (January 23, 2005), Jesse Berrett declared that the main character's "absolute plainspoken honesty and the elemental nature of so many of Lee's desires make this one of the most tender and accurate portraits of adolescence in recent memory." On the other hand, Berrett wrote, the "endless, unfiltered self-contemplation, a kind of pocket Proustianism, is as exhausting as those all-night conversations where college freshmen compare and contrast world views."

One of the most-written-about aspects of *Prep* had as much to do with Sittenfeld's personal life as with the novel itself. Selinger-Morris, like many reviewers, observed that the heroine's "back story is strikingly similar to the author's. . . . Both are from America's Midwest and attended posh boarding schools in the east. Both are torn about America's class system, yearning for a place on a higher rung and rejecting it outright. Both have an ultra-polite mother and a slightly bawdy father. . . . Like Lee, Sittenfeld was 'enthralled' by a boarding school's promise of privilege, mown athletic fields and co-eds who looked as if they'd stepped out of a toothpaste commercial." Felicia R. Lee wrote for the *New York Times* (January 26, 2005), "While Ms. Sittenfeld merely followed the time-honored advice to 'write what you know,' the question nibbling at her amid the novel's sweet reviews and media attention has been: How much of the first-person book is Curtis and how much is Lee?" In interviews Sittenfeld has stated that no more than 20 percent of her fiction is based on real people and events. The author told Selinger-Morris that she did not set out to examine the more disturbing aspects of her own adolescence when she started writing *Prep*; rather, she said, "boarding school was the only thing I had enough feelings about to fill a book." *Prep* has sold approximately 500,000 copies, and foreign rights have been sold for publication in 25 languages. Paramount has optioned the movie rights to the novel.

In 2006 Sittenfeld published her second novel, *The Man of My Dreams*, which she wrote while also working on *Prep*. "There came this point where it was almost like dating two different people," she told Lev Grossman for *Time* (May 22, 2006). Grossman noted that the books are very different: "Where *Prep* was about love and social class, *Man of My Dreams* is very much a book about love, love, love, but Sittenfeld shows us that there is something fresh to say about the oldest subject in the world." Hannah Gavener, Sittenfeld's protagonist, is—like Lee Fiora—plain; she can also be stubborn and hard to like. Most reviews of the book were mixed, acknowledging Sittenfeld's talent but criticizing her for lacking nuance and creating two-dimensional characters. Whitney Pastorek wrote for *Entertainment Weekly* (May 11, 2006), "Like the boys of *Prep*, the men of *Dreams* exist as archetypes—sensitive, thoughtless, or unattainable; girls (other than Hannah, naturally) tend to be beautiful, confident, and a little bit slutty. The ending is rushed and unsatisfying, despite some obvious, cloying attempts to make it otherwise. As we follow Hannah from her early teens through college and into adulthood, it becomes clear that her personal problems are at least as epic as Lee's and, if anything, less forgivable the older she grows. It's hard to say what compels Sittenfeld to write books about chicks you kinda want to throttle. A writer this articulate could stand to exorcise these ghosts as quickly as possible, and spend her considerable gifts telling stories of people—fully formed, complex, perhaps even welcoming people—who deserve our attention." Responding to such criticism, Sittenfeld told Grossman, "I understand that not everybody likes my characters. . . . I just want to be honest about the way people are." *The Man of My Dreams* has sold about 50,000 copies—10 percent of the sales of *Prep*.

Sittenfeld was perhaps a victim of her own success. Because her debut novel received a lot of praise from readers and reviewers, her sophomore effort—like many writers' second novels—was judged not only on its own merit but also according to how it compared with its predecessor. Another matter complicating the book's reception involved the "chick lit" label that was often placed on Sittenfeld's work, perhaps either prejudicing readers or creating expectations that the novel did not meet. "Sittenfeld's relationship with chick lit has never been quite comfortable—but in a way, chick lit has never been totally comfortable with itself," Grossman wrote. "As a genre it sets itself the task of chronicling the (literarily underserved) lives of contemporary single women—but then, all too often, it suffers a failure of nerve and settles for regurgitating exactly the clichés about boys and shopping and cattiness that it should be rectifying." Sittenfeld herself expressed ambivalence about the genre, telling Grossman, "I almost feel like the premises of plenty of chick-lit books are ones that I would love to read! It's almost like they're not seen as worthy of intelligent treatment."

With her latest novel, *American Wife*, Sittenfeld distanced herself from the "chick lit" label. The novel's main character, who is based on First Lady Laura Bush, has very little in common with the heroines of *Prep* and *The Man of My Dreams*. In the novel, a small-town librarian is courted by a handsome man. The librarian, smart and pretty, is ridden with guilt for having caused the death of a high-school friend in a car accident. (That incident mirrors one in Laura Bush's life.) Her suitor is charming and carefree and clearly adores the librarian. The librarian succumbs to his charms, but with reservations. "In Curtis Sittenfeld's brilliant novel *American Wife*, [the main characters'] names are Alice Lindgren and Charles Blackwell, and they come from Wisconsin," Joe Klein wrote for *Time* (September 15, 2008). "But we also know them, on the evening news, as Laura Welch and George W. Bush from Texas." At its core the book is about the compromises and struggles involved in marriage. Many reviewers noted the subtlety and sensitivity with which Sittenfeld described the relationship and the inner lives of Charles and Alice. "*American Wife* pulls us by our bellies through its imaginary peephole, and allows Sittenfeld and her readers to project a thousand pop-psych analyses and hypotheticals . . . ," Rebecca Traister wrote for *Salon.com* (September 8, 2008). "Wiggling her way under Alice's skin affords us a disconcerting view, of what a flawed, and widely hated, man might look like to a smart woman who loves him." Sittenfeld's nuanced view of her fictional First Lady grew out of her equally thoughtful take on the real one. Speaking to Traister, Sittenfeld elaborated on what she believes to be a "huge question about any first lady and about people in general: How much are we responsible for the behavior of people close to us? . . ." Referring to the 2003 U.S. invasion of Iraq and its aftermath during the Bush presidency, Sittenfeld continued, "People do say that Laura [Bush] has been complicit in the deaths of all these Iraqis. That's an easy thing to say. But let's say you know your husband's a really reckless driver—do you forbid him from driving? Do you steal his keys? Do you divorce him? I think that in life it often seems clearer what other people should do about their problems than what you should do about your problems." Sittenfeld had expressed admiration for Laura Bush in 2004, before she became a published novelist. In an article for *Salon.com* (January 29, 2004) titled "Why I Love Laura Bush," written after she had read a biography of Laura Bush, *The Perfect Wife*, by Ann Gerhart, Sittenfeld wrote that she strongly dislikes President Bush—calling his policies "at best misguided and at worst evil"—but added, "I *love* Laura Bush. In fact, there is no public figure I admire more." Sittenfeld explained that she admired the First Lady's intelligence and unpretentiousness and observed, "Laura Bush's own life resembles a great novel." Deciding that she should write that novel, and wanting to publish it before the end of Bush's presidency, she completed the 558-page work in only 18 months. Sittenfeld revealed to Traister that because she is "obsessed with structure in writing," she "conceived of this book as having four sections, each one built around a major real-life event that happened to Laura Bush. Everything else is made up."

Although *American Wife* is a sensitive portrait of a fictional First Lady, and Sittenfeld has pointed out that only about 15 percent of the story is based on Laura Bush's life, the book aroused controversy as soon as it reached stores (strategically) during the Republican National Convention in September 2008. Even before *American Wife* was officially published, *Radar* magazine put on-line several out-of-context paragraphs from the novel, containing vivid descriptions of sexual acts between the fictional president and First Lady. Other Web sites quickly picked up the material. "I didn't write those scenes to be read by themselves," Sittenfeld told Traister, who pointed out, "It is a testament to the delicacy with which Sittenfeld treats her characters that the W. stand-in, Charlie Blackwell, is so adoring and puppy-doggish a husband—even while remaining so detestable a politician—that the sex actually isn't so hard to stomach." Other controversial passages included those in which Alice gets an abortion, has a bout of diarrhea after drinking too much alcohol, and discovers that her grandmother is a lesbian. Conservative blogs, such as Townhall, made the argument that the book is meant to "smear" the First Lady. Maureen Dowd, an op-ed columnist for the *New York Times* (July 9, 2008), defended Sittenfeld against partisan attacks. (The fact that the well-known Dowd dedicated a column to her work was, Sittenfeld told Traister, "one of the great shocks of my life.") "Ms. Sittenfeld has creatively applied her crayons to all the ambiguous blanks in the coloring book," Dowd wrote. "It isn't an invasion of privacy. Art has always been made out of the stories of kings and queens. . . . Ms. Sittenfeld was not out to sensationalize but to sympathize."

Sittenfeld's book reviews and other short pieces have been published in the *Washington Post*, *Allure*, *Salon.com*, and the *New York Times*, among other periodicals. In March 2008 Sittenfeld married her longtime boyfriend, Matt Carlson, an assistant professor of communications at St. Louis University, in Missouri. The couple live in St. Louis.
—D.K.

Suggested Reading: *Salon* (on-line) Sep. 8, 2008; *San Francisco Chronicle* H p27 June 1, 2006; *Time* p68 May 22, 2006, p59 Sep. 15, 2008

Selected Books: *Prep*, 2005; *The Man of My Dreams*, 2006; *American Wife*, 2008

Frederick M. Brown/Getty Images

Slash

July 23, 1965– Rock musician

Address: c/o RCA Records, 1540 Broadway, New York, NY 10036

With his long ringlets of dark hair and signature top hat, the guitarist Slash, formerly of the popular band Guns N' Roses, is one of the most recognizable figures in the world of rock music. He is also one of rock's archetypes: his rise to the top of the charts during the late 1980s and 1990s was marked by drug addiction, alcoholism, sexual exploits, and infighting among his fellow band members—all of which he has chronicled in his eponymous memoir, published in 2007. (The book's cover declares, "It seems excessive, but that doesn't mean it didn't happen.") While much media attention has been paid to his lifestyle, Slash's talents and musicality are also widely recognized. Jed Gottlieb wrote for the *Boston Herald* (May 18, 2007), "Slash is the sleaziest sleaze-rock guitarist of all time: a Gibson master second only to [Jimmy] Page and [Joe] Perry; a guy who legitimized metal guitar by infusing blues riffs with a genuine punk aesthetic," and Christina Taylor wrote for the Stoke-on-Trent, England, *Sentinel* (June 1, 2007), "Slash has long been established as one of the best guitarists of his generation and continues to set the benchmark for aspiring musicians everywhere." Now a happily married father of two—and reportedly free of his chemical dependencies—Slash is the lead guitarist of the group Velvet Revolver, and he recently appeared as a character in an edition of the blockbuster video game *Guitar Hero*.

The musician was born Saul Hudson on July 23, 1965 in Stoke-on-Trent. (He was given the nickname Slash as a teen, reportedly because he was always dashing around.) His mother, Ola, an African-American costume designer, had met his father, Anthony, a white British painter, during a period in which they were both living in Paris, France. Not long after Slash was born, his mother moved to California to further her career. Her clients included the Pointer Sisters, Ringo Starr, Diana Ross, and John Lennon, among other music luminaries. Slash and his father joined her four years later, and the family settled in the Laurel Canyon section of Los Angeles. In *Slash*, co-written with Anthony Bozza, the musician recalled, "My first memory of Los Angeles is the Doors' 'Light My Fire' blasting from my parents' turntable, every day, all day long." His parents also exposed him, he wrote, "to everything from Beethoven to Led Zeppelin." As demand for his mother's costumes grew, his father found ample work designing album covers for such recording artists as Neil Young and Joni Mitchell. Many musicians lived in Laurel Canyon, known for its artistic, bohemian atmosphere. Slash wrote in his memoir, "The essence of pot and incense usually hung in the air." His parents often took him to concerts, recording studios, and rehearsal spaces, and he developed a love of music at an early age, listening to the radio almost constantly. He was also passionate about drawing. (Mitchell included a series of his animal drawings in an unpublished book of her verse called "The Bestiary.") "He was drawing from the time he could pick up a pencil," his mother told Jeffrey Ressner and Lonn M. Friend for *Rolling Stone* (January 24, 1991, on-line).

Slash's parents separated when he was eight years old, a year after his brother, Albion, was born. Not long after that, his mother began an affair with the famed rocker David Bowie, for whom she had designed costumes. "Bowie came by often, with his wife, Angie, and their son, Zowie, in tow," Slash recalled in his book. "The seventies were unique: it seemed entirely natural for Bowie to bring his wife and son to the home of his lover so that we might all hang out. At the time my mother practiced the same form of transcendental meditation that David did. They chanted before the shrine she maintained in the bedroom." While Slash had some difficulty adjusting to having a new father figure around, he has credited the older musician with teaching him that "being a rock star is the intersection of who you are and who you want to be."

Slash and his brother were shuttled to their maternal grandmother's home, in Hollywood, when Ola was working, and they eventually moved in with her. "I've been shocked at a lot of things I've read where it sounds like I left him on somebody's doorstep in a basket," Ola told Ressner and Friend. "They make it seem as if he never had a family and grew up on the streets like an urchin, but that's not true. It's just part of his image. He's not all leather and tattoos."

During his early teens Slash developed a love for BMX riding and won several competitions in his age division. At around the same time, he began experimenting with drugs and committing petty crimes. If he liked a band, for example, he shoplifted all of their albums from local record stores. He was kicked out of one of the junior high schools he attended for stealing several BMX bikes. "I did wander off at a young age, but it wasn't because of my parents. It was just 'cause I was tripped out and getting into all kinds of stuff," he told Giles Smith for the London *Independent* (July 17, 1995).

Slash and his best friend, Steven Adler—who would later become the drummer of Guns N' Roses—had dreams of starting a rock band, so during the summer before high school, Slash started taking guitar lessons, using an old flamenco guitar that his grandmother had given him. While his instructor, Robert Wolin, taught him the fundamentals, he learned how to improvise and play numbers by his favorite artists and groups—Cheap Trick, AC/DC, Van Halen, Ted Nugent, and Aerosmith—from a bargain-bin book he had picked up called *How to Play Rock Guitar*. He recalled in his memoir, "Finding guitar was like finding myself; it defined me, it gave me purpose. It was a creative outlet that allowed me to understand myself. The turmoil of my adolescence was suddenly secondary; playing guitar gave me focus. I didn't keep a journal; I couldn't seem to vocalize my feelings in a constructive fashion, but the guitar gave me emotional clarity."

When Slash entered Fairfax High School, in 1979, he felt alienated. "I had long hair, and the schools I went to were filled with kids of bankers and real-estate agents," he told Ressner and Friend. "It wasn't like any of them came from the same background I had." He managed, however, to find his own circle of friends, thanks to his guitar playing. He became particularly close to Marc Canter, whose family owned the famous Canter's Deli in Los Angeles, and Matt Cassel, whose father was the veteran character actor Seymour Cassel. (The elder Cassel was responsible for giving Slash his nickname.)

During high school Slash formed his first rock band, Tidus Sloan, which played birthday parties, an occasional Bar Mitzvah, and concerts in the school's auditorium. Slash's time at Fairfax High was cut short when he was expelled for flipping over a teacher's desk. He attended other schools, including Beverly Hills High, before dropping out permanently during his junior year.

Throughout the early 1980s, Slash held a number of odd jobs, including stints at a movie theater, a music store, and Canter's Deli. At the same time he tried to put together a band that could compete with the so-called hair-metal groups, such as Great White and Poison, that were popular at the time. (Hair-metal bands were known as such because of the long, teased, and gelled hairstyles favored by their members; Slash found their music and their posturing vapid.) For the next several years, he played in a variety of bands, including a hard-rock act called Road Crew he founded with Adler and a funk collective known as Black Sheep.

The early history of Guns N' Roses is muddled. Early incarnations of the group were called Rose and Hollywood Rose. In mid-1985 the band—with a new, soon-to-be-iconic name—went on its first club tour, along the West Coast: its members, now considered the classic lineup, included Slash, Adler, Axl Rose, Izzy Stradlin, and Duff McKagen. The band's raw musical style—a hybrid of punk, heavy metal, and classic rock—changed Los Angeles's hair-metal scene seemingly overnight. Slash wrote in his memoir, "There was not a bit of the typical L.A. vibe going on where the goal is to court a record deal. There was no concern for the proper poses or goofy choruses that might spell popular success; which ultimately guaranteed endless hot chicks. That type of calculated rebellion wasn't an option for us; we were too rabid a pack of musically like-minded gutter rats. We were passionate, with a common goal and a very distinct sense of integrity. That was the difference between us and [other bands.]"

In 1986 the group released an independent EP called *Live ?!*@ Like a Suicide*, which featured cover art by Slash. (The recording is often referred to simply as *Live Like a Suicide*.) With a limited release of 10,000 copies, it failed to generate much industry attention. That lack of attention did not last long, however. The band's next effort, for Geffen Records, the full-length *Appetite for Destruction*, released on July 21, 1987, went on to become the biggest-selling debut album of the 1980s and was listed among the top 100 albums of all time by the editors of *Rolling Stone*. Because the band's original album cover, featuring a woman who looked as if she had been sexually violated, was banned from stores, and MTV initially refused to play the graphic video for the debut single, "Welcome to the Jungle," 13 months passed before *Appetite for Destruction* reached the number-one spot on the *Billboard* album charts. To date the album has sold more than 28 million copies worldwide and—with its second cover, which features a styl-

ized cross and skulls representing the band members—reportedly still sells 9,000 copies a week. Besides "Welcome to the Jungle," the album contains the hits "It's So Easy," "Mr. Brownstone," "Paradise City," and "Sweet Child O' Mine." In a review for the All Music Guide Web site, Stephen Thomas Erlewine wrote, "Guns N' Roses' debut, *Appetite for Destruction*, was a turning point for hard rock in the late '80s—it was a dirty, dangerous, and mean record in a time when heavy metal meant nothing but a good time. On the surface, Guns N' Roses may appear to celebrate the same things as their peers—namely, sex, liquor, drugs, and rock & roll—but there is a nasty edge to their songs. . . . [They have] a primal, sleazy sound that adds grit to already grim tales." He concluded, "As good as Rose's lyrics and screeching vocals are, they wouldn't be nearly as effective without the twin-guitar interplay of Slash and Izzy Stradlin who spit out riffs and solos better than any band since the Rolling Stones and that's what makes *Appetite for Destruction* the best metal record of the late '80s." Commenting on the album's 20th anniversary, Slash told a writer for *GQ* (October 2007), "It was blatantly in-your-face about stuff that kids deal with on a daily basis. It was just, like, screaming reality. And it became a badge of honor, like 'This is who I am.' We were like a combustible M-80; we took it all over the edge."

The journey from unknown to star was not easy for Slash. "We started out on the lowest rung of the ladder, as far as club bands are concerned," he told Caroline Ryder for *Swindle* (October 2006). "When we got signed [to Geffen] we were totally [messed] up. We got $7,500 bucks apiece and spent it all on drugs. We had nowhere to live. We were staying in cheap motels. We couldn't find anyone that wanted-ed to produce us and manage us. Then we went on tour opening up for Aerosmith, and everything just sort of worked its way up." While touring—the band worked with such acts as Alice Cooper and Iron Maiden, in addition to Aerosmith—Slash found it easier to cope, but off the road he turned to increasingly dangerous drugs, including heroin. "We'd be on the road and we'd hear we sold a certain number of records," he explained to Ryder. "Then we went back to Hollywood and it's the same [stuff]: living in a cheap apartment and doing drugs all the time, except this time I didn't want to go out because people would recognize me." By his own admission, Slash spent most of the period from 1988 to 1990 abusing heroin and cocaine, and he also developed a problem with alcohol, drinking up to half a gallon of vodka a day, according to some reports. Still, he was able to work; Guns N' Roses released *GN'R Lies* (1988), which consisted of the *Live* EP plus four new tracks, and Slash also did session work for a number of artists, including Iggy Pop, Michael Jackson, Alice Cooper, and Lenny Kravitz (a fellow Fairfax High alumnus).

Guns N' Roses found themselves embroiled in controversies as their popularity increased. *GN'R Lies*, which featured the hit single "Patience" and went on to sell more than 12 million copies worldwide, also contained a song written by Rose called "One in a Million," which attacked—in exceedingly derogatory terms—immigrants, blacks, and homosexuals. As a result, members of the group were collectively referred to as racists; they were barred from participating in a benefit concert for the Gay Men's Health Crisis, in New York City, and were openly criticized onstage by the all-black hard-rock group Living Colour when both bands opened for the Rolling Stones in 1989. Slash, who was never fond of the lyrics in the song, given his ethnic background, explained to Jon Bream for the Minneapolis *Star Tribune* (January 21, 1992), "When I first heard the lyric, I was, like, 'Axl, I know what you're saying, but I don't think people are going to take it right. I know my family isn't going to take it right.'" The Rolling Stones tour was also notable for an incident in which Rose threatened to kick Slash out of the group because of his heroin use. As a peacemaking effort, Slash agreed to address the crowd about the perils of heroin addiction during one of the shows, although he admitted in his memoir that he did so half-heartedly. On January 22, 1990, at the annual American Music Awards, Slash used several expletives during the 20-second, drunken acceptance speech he gave when *Appetite for Destruction* was honored as best rock album of the year. He recalled in his autobiography, "I was overwhelmed by the controversy [that resulted] because to this day the incident still doesn't mean that much to me. I was, however, responsible for the seven-second delay being instituted at all future live award ceremonies; plus Dick Clark wouldn't speak to me for eight years."

The group's next albums, *Use Your Illusion I* and *Use Your Illusion II*, were released simultaneously on September 17, 1991. The albums, which went on to sell some seven million copies each worldwide, marked a major departure from the band's gritty, unpolished hard-rock roots. Incorporating a variety of genres (including blues, country, progressive, and electronica), the *Illusions* albums were deemed both artistically ambitious and brazenly self-indulgent by critics. Slash's guitar playing, however, was universally lauded, with critics impressed by his work on acoustic and flamenco guitars, in addition to his customary Les Paul. After the 28-month *Illusions* promotion tour, during which the band played 192 shows in 27 countries to more than seven million people, Slash officially became an American citizen.

Following the release of Guns N' Roses' next studio album, *The Spaghetti Incident?* (1993), an ill-received covers record, Slash found himself drifting away from the group, disgruntled because Rose had been consistently rejecting material he had written or arranged. When Rose overdubbed Slash's guitar parts for a Guns N' Roses cover of the Rolling Stones song "Sympathy for the Devil," which was featured in the film *Interview with the Vampire* (1994), Slash decided to form a group of his own. Slash's Snakepit, which included Gilby

Clarke and Matt Sorum, released its first album, *It's Five O'clock Somewhere*, in February 1995. Though the album went platinum, it received tepid reviews. J. D. Considine, wrote for *Rolling Stone* (February 23, 1995, on-line), for example, "When he's onstage with Guns N' Roses, it's easy to see Slash as the strong, silent type, happily inscrutable behind his thick mop of curls. Unlike Axl Rose, who seems obsessed with verbalizing his deepest fears, Slash would rather let his fingers do the talking, an approach that has led to some remarkably expressive solos but hasn't told us much about the guitarist's inner life. *It's Five O'clock Somewhere* doesn't alter that image much, either. Even though this is a Slash solo project, the role he plays seems largely the same: He doesn't sing, he doesn't talk, and he generally leaves the lyric writing to others." Slash also worked on other outside projects, including music for Quentin Tarantino's film *Jackie Brown* (1997), while waiting for Rose to complete the material for the next Guns N' Roses album. He explained to Giles Smith, "Axl all of a sudden had this masterplan of how he wanted to approach the next Guns' release. I wanted to go back to doing old style, just heavy Guns N' Roses. But he's still on that long, mountainous trek." In October 1996, in a rambling fax sent to MTV News, Rose officially announced that Slash had left Guns N' Roses and that others in the group were being put on notice; those members departed shortly thereafter, and Slash is said not to have spoken with Rose since the split.

Slash spent the rest of the 1990s and early 2000s as one of the busiest session guitarists in the music business, playing for a wide variety of artists that included Insane Clown Posse, Blackstreet, Chic, Ronnie Wood, and Ray Charles, while contributing to the soundtracks of several films, including *The Kid Stays in the Picture* (2002), about the legendary film producer Robert Evans. In October 2000 Slash released his second Snakepit album, *Ain't Life Grand*, which went platinum. Most critics again made mention of Slash's superb guitar playing but failed to find any promise in the band as a whole. Rob Sheffield wrote for *Rolling Stone* (October 12, 2000), "As the poet [alluding to Axl Rose] once sang, it's hard to hold a candle in the cold November rain—but Slash is still hanging in there, shining the light within his soul as a lucid path back to the days when guitars were guitars, hair was hair. . . . The real problem is that great guitarists need great bands, and the Snakepit dudes are barely functional backup peons who don't even have cool names."

While touring with the hard-rock group AC/DC in 2000, Slash was rushed to the hospital for what he believed was exhaustion. He was instead diagnosed with a heart ailment known as cardiomyopathy and told that he had six weeks to live. He wrote in his memoir, "Fifteen years of overdrinking and drug abuse had swelled [my heart] to one beat short of exploding." Doctors implanted a defibrillator in his chest and advised him to stop drinking and using drugs—advice that he has reportedly since tried to follow.

In April 2002 Slash reunited with former Guns N' Roses bandmates Duff McKagen and Matt Sorum to play a benefit concert for their longtime friend, the drummer Randy Castillo, who had recently died of cancer. Realizing that their chemistry was still good, the three decided to start a new band that initially included Keith Nelson and Josh Todd, from the band Buckcherry. The latter two left after only a few months, and Slash, McKagen, and Sorum embarked on a year-long search for a singer. (They also added a mutual friend, Dave Kushner, on rhythm guitar.) After listening to hundreds of tapes and unsuccessfully auditioning dozens of singers (a project documented by VH1 on a short-lived reality series), they agreed on the former Stone Temple Pilots singer, Scott Weiland. The group settled on the name Velvet Revolver and contributed songs to two film soundtracks, a cover of Pink Floyd's "Money" for *The Italian Job* (2003) and an original song called "Set Me Free" for *The Hulk* (2003). Their first album, *Contraband*, was released in June 2004 and debuted at number one on the *Billboard* album charts. It has sold some four million copies worldwide, and the group won a Grammy Award for best hard-rock performance for the single "Slither."

In March 2006 Rose released a statement to the press claiming that he had once heard Slash make disparaging comments about Weiland, McKagen, and Sorum. While the incident briefly shook the relationship between Slash and his bandmates and put the future of Velvet Revolver in jeopardy, the dispute was eventually resolved, and in July 2007 the group released their sophomore album, *Libertad*. Despite being a commercial disappointment, the album garnered mostly positive reviews. Slash told Jacqui Swift for the London *Sun* (August 3, 2007), "On *Contraband* we barely scratched the surface of what we are capable of. Making *Libertad* we dipped in to see the band's individual and collective talents and we had also blossomed as a band. The relationships between the guys got more personal and we have a real camaraderie going. The sound is more musical and not as aggressive. We played more raw with little over-production. What you're hearing is how we played. It's better and more exciting and so . . . now I have a sense of accomplishment."

In March 2008, after spending the previous month in rehab for undisclosed addictions, Weiland told the audience during a Velvet Revolver show in Glasgow, Scotland, that they were witnessing the band's final tour. Early the next month Slash confirmed reports that Weiland had left the group to rejoin Stone Temple Pilots. Since Weiland's departure, Velvet Revolver has auditioned hundreds of singers, both known and unknown, but has not chosen one. Slash is currently working on a solo album with guest singers and musicians including Izzy Stradlin, Duff McKagen, Lenny Kravitz, Sebastian Bach, Alice Cooper, and Vince Neil.

Slash currently lives in Los Angeles. He and his wife, Perla, have been married since 2000. They have two sons, London (born in 2002) and Cash (born in 2004). His self-titled memoir, written with Anthony Bozza, reached the *New York Times* non-fiction best-seller list soon after its publication. The book focuses largely on his time with Guns N' Roses, attempting to explain the band's breakup and to dispel rumors that the group will one day reunite. It also provides an unflinching look at Slash's addictions and excesses. Ian McCullough wrote for the Sydney, Australia, *Sunday Telegraph* (November 25, 2007), "Considering that at the height of the band's success he was drinking a gallon of vodka a day—and that was before he went out at night—it's remarkable he can remember anything." Alan Light wrote for the *New York Times Book Review* (January 27, 2008, on-line): "Most rock biographies are about getting to the Good Part. There's typically a bit of slogging through the star's unhappy childhood, the revelation of music's true power and a hard-fought rise to the top before the litany of debauchery and depravity begins—the part that fans actually want to read. . . . [*Slash* is] pretty much all Good Part."

In January 2007 Slash was honored with a star on the Rock Walk of Fame, in Los Angeles.

—C.C.

Suggested Reading: *Boston Herald* E p6 May 18, 2007; *Entertainment Weekly* p79 June 4, 2004; (London) *Independent* p4 July 17, 1995; (London) *Sun* Aug. 3, 2007; (Minneapolis) *Star Tribune* E p1 Jan. 21, 1992; *New York Times Book Review* (on-line) Jan. 27, 2008; *Rolling Stone* (on-line) Jan. 24, 1991, June 16, 2004; (Stoke-on-Trent, England) *Sentinel* p6 June 1, 2007; *Swindle* Oct. 2006; (Sydney, Australia) *Sunday Telegraph* p90 Nov. 25, 2007; Slash (with Anthony Bozza). *Slash*, 2007

Selected Recordings: with Guns N' Roses—*Live ?!*@ Like a Suicide*, 1986; *Appetite for Destruction*, 1987; *GN'R Lies*, 1988; *Use Your Illusion I*, 1991; *Use Your Illusion II*, 1991; *The Spaghetti Incident?*, 1993; with Slash's Snakepit—*It's Five O'clock Somewhere*, 1995; *Ain't Life Grand*, 2000; with Velvet Revolver—*Contraband*, 2004; *Libertad*, 2007

Selected Books: *Slash* (with Anthony Bozza), 2007

Snider, Stacey

Apr. 29, 1961– Co-chair and CEO of DreamWorks SKG

Address: DreamWorks SKG, 1000 Flower St., Glendale, CA 91201

Stacey Snider, the co-chairperson of the film production company DreamWorks SKG, "is known in Hollywood as a clear-eyed, organized, tough, resolute, tireless, accessible, script-savvy executive who can handle talent," as Anne Thompson noted for *Variety* (October 7, 2007). Starting her career in the mid-1980s as a mailroom and delivery clerk at a little-known talent agency, Snider went on to join Tri-Star Pictures, rising from director of development to president of production and capturing the zeitgeist with such highly popular films as *Sleepless in Seattle*, *Philadelphia*, *Legends of the Fall*, *Jumanji*, and *Jerry Maguire*. She enjoyed similar success at Universal Pictures, beginning in December 1996 as co-president of production and becoming the company's co-chair less than two years later. When, in November 1999, Snider was named the sole chair and CEO of Universal, she became—at 38—one of only a handful of women ever to run a major film studio. During her tenure there she transformed the once-laggard studio into one of the most profitable in Hollywood; in 2000 alone, Snider and her then-boss, Ron Meyer, Universal Pictures' president and chief operating officer (COO), led the studio as it surpassed the billion-dollar earnings mark for the first time and released a record-breaking string of five number-one films. She greenlighted and oversaw the production of such blockbuster hits as *The Mummy*, *American*

Pie, *Erin Brockovich*, *Meet the Parents*, *How the Grinch Stole Christmas*, *The Fast and the Furious*, and *The Bourne Identity*, along with Oscar-winning films including *Gladiator* and *A Beautiful Mind*. Commenting on her unsentimental approach to the film business, Snider explained to Patrick Goldstein for the *Los Angeles Times* (March 26, 2000), "We're not in the venture capital business. The truth is I don't want to make a lot of risky movies. You want some predictability that can carry you through a few Hail Mary pictures"—that is, films whose box-office returns are largely a matter of luck. "We're excited about working with young filmmakers, but the mandate is: get as many people as possible to see the films."

In December 2000 the *Hollywood Reporter* ranked Snider second on its annual "Women in Entertainment Power 50" list, and in December of the following year, *Entertainment Weekly* named her and Meyer the most powerful duo in Hollywood. "For a skilled corporate executive she still works from her gut," the producer Douglas Wick noted to Josh Young and Gabriel Snyder for *Variety* (September 12–18, 2005). When Universal unsuccessfully attempted to acquire DreamWorks in late 2005, Snider felt dismayed that she would not be able to work with Steven Spielberg, the legendary director who had founded DreamWorks with Jeffrey Katzenberg and David Geffen in 1994; as a result she decided to leave Universal in favor of running the smaller company as chief executive officer and co-chair, with Geffen. Since her arrival, in April 2006, Snider has helped steer DreamWorks to its most successful and profitable period in recent years, with hits including *Transformers* (2007) and the highly praised horror/musical *Sweeney Todd: The Demon Barber of Fleet Street* (2007), among many others. Speaking of Snider's abilities, Spielberg explained to Claudia Eller for the *Los Angeles Times* (February 27, 2006), "Stacey has a unique combination in a film executive in that she recognizes a need to make commercial movies, but also aspires to make art. She recognized that balance is good."

Of Jewish lineage, Stacey Snider was born on April 29, 1961 in Philadelphia, Pennsylvania. Though Snider's parents got divorced early in her childhood (she was raised by her mother), she has recalled being brought up in a loving family. Patrick Goldstein wrote that Snider "credits her parents with grounding her in both culture and business." During her youth Snider became a voracious reader. She received her primary and secondary education at Friends' Central, a Quaker school in Wynnewood, in Lower Merion Township, outside Philadelphia. "The values taught there had a big impact on me. I had classes with wealthy Main Line debutantes and kids from rough Philly neighborhoods, but there were no cliques or bullies. We learned about community and service, which encouraged us to be friends with everyone," she recalled to Patricia R. Olsen for the *New York Times* (January 15, 2006). Snider went on to attend Cornell University, in Ithaca, New York, then transferred during her freshman year to the University of Pennsylvania in order to be closer to her mother, who died by year's end. From that point on she lived on her own, supporting herself throughout college as a hostess, waitress, and busgirl at a Philadelphia restaurant.

While in college Snider took courses in literature as well as history and political science, explaining to Cathy Dunkley for *Variety* (August 27, 2001), "I had more romantic ideas at the beginning. I dreamed of being like a Max Perkins figure [the celebrated editor of F. Scott Fitzgerald and Thomas Wolfe], guiding the career of an important author." She graduated from college in 1982 and moved to the West Coast to attend law school at the University of California at Los Angeles (UCLA). Though Snider has credited law school with teaching her the art of reason, a summer internship at the New York City law firm Kaye, Scholar, Fierman, Hays & Handler left her bored and ended her desire to become a lawyer. She received her J.D. degree from UCLA and passed the bar exam, then decided to pursue a career in the entertainment industry. After trying unsuccessfully to get a job at a film studio, she started working in the mailroom of the Triad Artists talent agency (later purchased by the William Morris Agency). Her job there included delivering packages to clients in various parts of sprawling Los Angeles County. "It was horrible," she recalled to Patrick Goldstein. "They finally limited me to Beverly Hills and Century City because I'd get lost and never come back."

In 1986 Snider was hired as a secretary for the testosterone-fueled production team of Don Simpson and Jerry Bruckheimer, who produced such 1980s pop-culture hits as *Beverly Hills Cop* (1984) and *Top Gun* (1986). Not long afterward she was taken under the wing of the producer Peter Guber and hired as a development executive (a position sometimes called "D-Girl") at the Guber-Peters production company, which Guber had founded with Jon Peters in 1983. Her job entailed reading and evaluating scripts. During that period Snider married and divorced twice. Following Sony's purchase of Guber-Peters, in 1989, the co-founders became co-chairmen of Sony's Columbia Pictures. Guber brought Snider along, giving her the position of executive vice president at Sony's Tri-Star Pictures; in 1992 she became the company's president of production. "She had fire in her belly and a twinkle in her eye," Guber recalled to Goldstein. "She was ambitious and tenacious but she always did her job with style and elegance. She's very self-critical. She's harder on herself than anyone else." As president of production, Snider worked with Tri-Star's chairman, Marc Platt, in overseeing a number of box-office hits, including *Sleepless in Seattle* (1993), *Philadelphia* (1993), *Legends of the Fall* (1994), *Jumanji* (1995), *The Mirror Has Two Faces* (1996), *Jerry Maguire* (1996), and *My Best Friend's Wedding* (1997). During Guber's reign Sony also suffered several high-profile box-office

calamities, forcing the studio to take a $3.2 billion write-off on its losses in 1995. (Kevin Costner's post-apocalyptic science-fiction film *Waterworld*, which cost $175 million and grossed only $88 million at the domestic box office, greatly contributed to the studio's financial woes at the time.)

In December 1996, after marrying and taking maternity leave from Tri-Star earlier in the year, Snider was hired by Casey Silver, the chairman of Universal Pictures, as the studio's co-president of production, along with Platt (who had been forced out of Tri-Star). There, she enjoyed a meteoric series of promotions, becoming sole head of production and then co-chair of the company in less than two years. After co-chair Brian Mulligan left Universal in November 1999 for another position in the studio's parent company, Seagram, Snider became Universal's sole chair. Although Snider's fast rise in Hollywood has largely been credited to her "clarity and decisiveness," as noted by Cathy Dunkley, she has credited Platt with her crash-course schooling in the intricacies of film production. At the time of Snider's arrival as chair at Universal, the studio ranked ninth in domestic box-office grosses, making it among the most unprofitable in the industry. Under the partnership of Snider and Ron Meyer, Universal's president and COO, the company enjoyed one of the quickest turnarounds in the industry's recent history. During Snider's first two years as chair, nine of Universal's films grossed more than $100 million in the U.S. One of the films was Stephen Sommers's *The Mummy* (1999), starring Brendan Frasier and Rachel Weisz, a remake of the 1932 Boris Karloff film about an ancient Egyptian prince who was buried alive. Its 2001 sequel, *The Mummy Returns*, was also very successful financially. Also that year Snider oversaw the launch of the popular *American Pie* series of movies, starring Jason Biggs and Seann William Scott. Other notable films released by Universal during that time included *Jurassic Park III* (2001) and *The Fast and the Furious* (2001). Commenting on the team of Snider and Meyer, Stephen Sommers told a writer for *Entertainment Weekly* (October 26, 2001), "They make a director feel like he's the quarterback and they're two really great coaches."

In 2000 Snider and Meyer helped Universal reach the number-two ranking in box-office grosses among all major studios and led the studio to its first-ever billion-dollar-plus year, largely facilitated by a record-breaking five number-one films in a row. That success, in turn, owed much to the partnerships that Snider had formed with the production companies DreamWorks and Imagine Entertainment. In conjunction with DreamWorks, Universal released the hit comedy *Meet the Parents* (2000) and its sequel *Meet the Fockers* (2004), along with the Oscar-winning films *Gladiator* (2000) and *A Beautiful Mind* (2001), directed by Ridley Scott and Ron Howard, respectively. With Imagine, the production company of Howard and the famous producer Brian Grazer, Universal released the extremely successful hits *How the Grinch Stole Christmas* (2000) and *The Nutty Professor II* (2000). Snider was instrumental in getting Steven Soderbergh's *Erin Brockovich* (2000) made. While several studios had passed on the project after the release of the similar-themed, financially disappointing *A Civil Action* (1998), Snider insisted that Universal push ahead with the project. The film, based on the true story of a single mother's crusade against the West Coast energy giant Pacific Gas and Electric Co., which had contaminated an entire community's water supply, went on to become the biggest sleeper hit of 2000. *Erin Brockovich* garnered five Oscar nominations, with Julia Roberts winning a best-actress Oscar for her portrayal of the title character.

While many studio chiefs take a dictatorial approach to the films they oversee, Snider has mostly refrained from such behavior. (She has, however, been known to add extensive notes to the scripts that she has given directors.) On those occasions when she has deemed it necessary to take a hands-on approach, her input has proved to be invaluable. For example, after viewing a test screening for *Meet the Parents*, Snider recommended to the film's director, Jay Roach, that he add a marriage-proposal scene to satisfy audience expectations of seeing the story's couple (played by Ben Stiller and Teri Polo) solidify their relationship. With that addition, test screenings of the film received more positive feedback. In another instance she decided that a climactic courtroom scene in *Erin Brockovich* should be cut, feeling that the scene was not true to the story; by all accounts, her decision made the film stronger. Snider was also known to reward her team at Universal with bonuses and days off if a film fared well at the box office during its opening weekend.

In 2002, under Snider's leadership, Universal Pictures launched another profitable franchise, with the action thriller *The Bourne Identity*, which starred Matt Damon and was based on the Robert Ludlum novel of the same name. (*The Bourne Supremacy* and *The Bourne Ultimatum* were released in 2004 and 2007, respectively.) Along with its successful films of the late 1990s and early 2000s, Universal had its share of box-office failures, such as *The Adventures of Rocky and Bullwinkle* (2000), *Josie and the Pussycats* (2001), *Captain Corelli's Mandolin* (2001), *The Chronicles of Riddick* (2004), *Thunderbirds* (2004), and the *Bridget Jones* sequel, *Bridget Jones: The Edge of Reason* (2004). As a result, in 2004 the company dropped to sixth in the studio rankings. Snider noted to a writer for *Newsweek* (October 24, 2005), "I've made mistakes in my professional life and I've made mistakes in my personal life. The thing that has always stayed with me is an axiom my dad gave me, which was, adversity breeds character. How you deal with the tough times really defines your character, who you are. But there are definitely times where I feel like 'Alright, enough character . . . I'd like to have some more fun!'"

In May 2004 Universal Pictures (which had become Vivendi Universal in June 2000) merged with the NBC television network to form NBC Universal. In December of the following year, General Electric (GE), owner of NBC Universal, lost its bid to acquire DreamWorks SKG after failing to match the $1.6 billion offer from Viacom, owner of Paramount Pictures. Rumors soon circulated that Snider would leave NBC Universal, as she had become discontented with GE's rigid, bottom-line approach to releasing movies and felt dismayed over the lost opportunity to work further with the acclaimed filmmaker Steven Spielberg, with whom she had developed a number of projects at both Tri-Star and Universal. As quoted by Anne Thompson, at the time that the deal between GE and DreamWorks fell through, Snider quipped to Jeffrey Katzenberg, one of the owners of DreamWorks, "Can you take me in your suitcase?" Katzenberg took the question seriously, and in April 2006 Snider left NBC Universal to take the reins at DreamWorks, in a four-year deal that reportedly paid her between $2.5 and $3 million a year—about half of her salary at NBC Universal. While NBC Universal had her overseeing 16 to 18 films annually, DreamWorks requires her to preside over four to six movies a year. Speaking of her decision to leave Universal, Snider explained to Sharon Waxman for the *New York Times* (February 25, 2006, on-line), "It's about, 'Do you want to be a career executive—another five years at this pace—or do you want to see if there's something that looks different.' It really is, 'Do I wear a dress, or jeans and a sweatshirt?'"

Paramount and DreamWorks have enjoyed one of the most profitable film runs in Hollywood during the two years since Snider's arrival. While DreamWorks has enlisted gifted filmmakers over the years, Snider is seen as providing the strong leadership the company has long lacked. In 2007 she oversaw the production of eight films (up from the six originally projected), which included the Eddie Murphy comedy *Norbit*, the figure-skating spoof *Blades of Glory*, and the recent Michael Bay–helmed summer blockbuster *Transformers*. Executive-produced by Spielberg, *Transformers* was the most profitable film of 2007, grossing $706 million worldwide to date. Snider also helped broker a deal with Warner Bros. to co-finance Tim Burton's *Sweeney Todd: The Demon Barber of Fleet Street*, which received a 2008 Golden Globe Award for best musical or comedy. Snider's 2008 DreamWorks slate included the director Sam Mendes's film version of Richard Yates's 1961 novel, *Revolutionary Road*, starring Leonardo DiCaprio and Kate Winslet; Ben Stiller's war comedy *Tropic Thunder*, starring Robert Downey Jr. and Jack Black; and Spielberg's long-awaited *Indiana Jones 4: The Kingdom of the Crystal Skull*, starring Harrison Ford, Cate Blanchett, and Shia LaBeouf. To Snider's delight, one of her main tasks at DreamWorks is to supply Spielberg with a selection of movies to direct. His next project, a biographical film about Abraham Lincoln, starring Liam Neeson, was scheduled to begin production in early 2009 and to be released by the end of the year. Anne Thompson proclaimed, "Spielberg is still at the apex of the Hollywood pyramid, as he has been for some 30 years. The best that Hollywood has to offer is at his disposal. And that includes Snider." In late 2008 DreamWorks and Universal Pictures reached a seven-year distribution agreement encompassing as many as six releases a year.

Since 1996 Snider has been married to the soundtrack producer Gary Jones. The couple have two daughters, Katie and Natalie, and live in Southern California.

—C.C.

Suggested Reading: *Hollywood Reporter* Mar. 3, 2006; *Los Angeles Times* p18+ Mar. 26, 2000, C p1+ Feb. 27, 2006; *New York Times* C p1+ Jan. 22, 2001, (on-line) Jan. 15, 2006, Feb. 25, 2006; *Time* p52+ July 29, 2002; *Variety* p52+ Sep. 12–18, 2005, p16+ Oct. 1–7, 2007, (on-line) Aug. 27, 2001

Andrew H. Walker/Getty Images for Tishman Speyer

Speyer, Jerry

(SPY-er)

June 23, 1940– Real-estate developer

Address: Tishman Speyer Properties, 45 Rockefeller Plaza, New York, NY 10111

Described by James Traub in the *New York Times Magazine* (December 20, 1998) as "the Anti-

Trump"—a reference to the famously egomaniacal real-estate mega-developer Donald Trump—Jerry Speyer has become one of the most powerful realty figures in New York City, while maintaining a reputation for being generous, publicity-shy, and down-to-earth. Tishman Speyer Properties, the real-estate development company he co-founded with his then–father-in-law, Robert Tishman, in 1978, owns more than 120 office buildings and 11,200 residential units worldwide, including Rockefeller Center and the Chrysler Building, both in New York City; MesseTurm (Fair Tower), a skyscraper in Frankfurt, Germany; and São Paolo, Brazil's Torre Norte (North Tower). Ranked 605th on *Forbes* magazine's 2008 list of the world's billionaires, with a net worth of $2 billion, Speyer is not wholly consumed or defined by his work, as many others at his level of success appear to be: he loves modern art, has been known to wear a Mickey Mouse watch to work, is rumored to be a yo-yo champion, and decorates his desk with toy trucks. As he told Traub, "One thing that sets me apart from the people who are entrepreneurs in this business" is that while "I like to make money . . . that's only part of what makes me happy."

Jerry I. Speyer was born on June 23, 1940 in Milwaukee, Wisconsin, to Ernest and Germaine Speyer. His father, who was Jewish, grew up in Frankfurt and left Germany in 1939, during the height of the Nazi era. Germaine Speyer was Swiss. Jerry Speyer and his younger sister, Vivian, were raised on Riverside Drive in the New York City borough of Manhattan. During his youth Speyer dreamed of becoming a merchant banker, as Traub reported. He attended Columbia University, in New York (where he roomed with the musician Art Garfunkel), earning a B.A. degree in German literature in 1962. Going on to attend Columbia Business School, he received his M.B.A. degree in 1964. While still in school Speyer had married Lynne Tishman, whose father, Robert, was the president of Tishman Realty & Construction. Founded in 1898 by Lynne's grandfather Julius Tishman, the company constructed many prominent New York buildings, including the World Trade Center towers.

Following his graduation and a short stint as the assistant to the vice president of Madison Square Garden, Speyer began working as his father-in-law's assistant in 1966. He climbed the ranks quickly, becoming vice president of the company—and heir apparent—in 1970. Six years later, due to heavy financial losses, the company was forced to liquidate its portfolio. At that time Robert Tishman's brother, Alan, took control of the company. In 1978 Robert Tishman and Speyer transformed the company's finance-and-development unit into Tishman Speyer Properties, with Tishman serving as chairman and Speyer as president and chief executive officer.

Within five years Tishman Speyer had developed 12 projects in New York City; Chicago, Illinois; Houston, Texas; Atlanta, Georgia; and Stamford, Connecticut, with a total worth of $1.2 billion. The company succeeded despite, or because of, risks taken along the way, such as constructing buildings in undeveloped neighborhoods; the foresight Speyer demonstrated in the past has greatly contributed to the success the company enjoys today. For example, in the mid-1980s, after Speyer had begun to feel that the company was building too many structures too quickly, Tishman Speyer began acquiring existing properties. By 1987 the firm owned 25 properties, totaling $4.2 billion. Sensing an imminent drop in the theretofore booming national real-estate market, Speyer soon decided that it was best for the company to develop projects overseas. Its first international project was to be a $150 million complex of apartments and offices in Beijing, China, but plans were dropped after the Tiananmen Square massacre, in 1989, in which Chinese troops killed hundreds of student-led pro-democracy demonstrators. Instead, the company set its sights on Germany, becoming the first U.S. company to develop and build a Class A (or top-quality) office building in the country. Frankfurt's MesseTurm, completed in 1990, was the largest building in Europe at the time. (Its height was surpassed by that of the Commerzbank Tower, in Frankfurt, in 1997.)

Speyer and his wife divorced in 1987, but his business relationship with her father continued. "It was about the most decent divorce I've ever heard of," Robert Tishman told Traub. "There was no reason in the world to destroy what we built up over 20-something years." In 1991 Speyer married Katherine Farley, who had begun working at the company in 1984 in the emerging-markets division. She is currently the senior managing director of emerging markets and global corporate marketing.

Another of Tishman Speyer's international projects, Torre Norte in São Paulo, Brazil, was completed in 1999. It is the country's first commercial building capable of producing energy through a cogeneration plant (which generates both electricity and heat). In 2002 Tishman Speyer was a finalist for the International Real Estate Federation's FIABCI Prix d'Excellence Award. Tishman Speyer completed the new European headquarters for Sony, in Berlin, Germany, in 2000. Designed by the architect Helmut Jahn, the Sony Center consists of eight buildings of various sizes that contain shops, restaurants, museums, movie theaters, office space, and residential apartments. In the center of the buildings is a roofed public space called the Forum. Generally, real-estate developers buy land on which to build or acquire preexisting buildings and set about improving them. Though many developers rely on third parties to design and construct the actual buildings, large developers such as Tishman Speyer have departments specially designated to handle those aspects of the process. For the Sony project Tishman Speyer was selected to reevaluate the existing plans for the buildings, including the design and cost; they reconfigured the buildings and their uses to better suit the Berlin market. For their work on the Sony Center, Tishman Speyer beat out 27 finalists worldwide to win the 2000 International Award for Large Scale Mixed Use from the Urban Land Institute, which recognizes excellence in the full development process of real-estate projects. "I think of real estate as a little bit like cooking or like art," Speyer explained to Traub. "Real estate is dependent on a way of thinking that is very different from the way that, for example, financial engineers look at a project. Financial engineers look at a piece of paper that's 8 1/2 by 11, look at a set of numbers and try to figure out how that relates to demographics or marketplace. But if you're a developer, you have to think about things that move you out of the box— how [a development is] going to affect its place, its landscape or its streetscape."

By far the most notable assets in the Tishman Speyer portfolio are in New York: Rockefeller Center, the Chrysler Building, and the Stuyvesant Town and Peter Cooper Village apartment complexes. In 1995 the Mitsubishi Estate Co., then the owner of Rockefeller Center, decided to sell the 22-acre property after incurring $2 billion in losses and $900 million in debt. After two failed attempts to strike a deal with the company, Speyer was asked to be a partner by Goldman Sachs, a global investment firm that was the principal lender for Mitsubishi, in the firm's purchase of the property. Speyer, who had worked with Goldman's co-chairman Hank Paulson, was chosen along with David Rockefeller, the Italian business mogul Gianni Agnelli, and the Greek shipping tycoon Stavros Niarchos; Speyer and Rockefeller each bought 5 percent of the property, while Agnelli and Niarchos bought 20 percent each. The group bought the mortgage to Rockefeller Center for $306 million and took on $845 million in debt. Speyer, who had often visited Rockefeller Center as a child, was thrilled to own a portion of the landmark. Fourteen of the 19 office buildings that now compose Rockefeller Center were built in the 1930s by John D. Rockefeller Jr. Five of them were added later, in the 1960s and 1970s. Rockefeller Center, a popular tourist attraction, is most famous for its outdoor skating rink, Radio City Music Hall, and the GE Building (or "30 Rock," formerly the RCA Building), home to the television network NBC and the famous Rainbow Room restaurant and nightclub. Speyer told Giles Barrie for the London, England, publication *Property Week* (July 1, 2000, on-line) that Rockefeller Center "was the epicenter of the city when I grew up. It still is. The notion that I would ever have anything to do with those buildings was pretty remote when I was a young man." Speyer was quickly appointed manager of Rockefeller Center and began to make improvements. His plans to add more retail locations to the center attracted owners of major brands, including Banana Republic, Reebok, J. Crew, and Sephora. He opened up the underground shopping area, to let in light from the outside area that contains the skating rink, and replaced the artwork in the buildings with newer pieces. Thanks to Speyer's redesign of the area, Rockefeller Center became profitable again in 1998 and earned $45.3 million in 1999. Only a year later Speyer and the Crown family of Chicago bought the shares owned by Goldman Sachs, Rockefeller, Agnelli, and Niarchos for a total of $1.85 billion and became the owners of Rockefeller Center.

Meanwhile, in 1997, another landmark New York property was up for grabs—the Chrysler Building. That iconic structure, financed by the automobile tycoon Walter Chrysler, was completed in 1930 and was the tallest skyscraper in the world until the Empire State Building was finished, a year later. It is considered by many to be New York's greatest example of Art Deco architecture, a style of design characterized by modern themes (such as the Chrysler Building's automobile theme) and geometric shapes not often associated with buildings. Although a bank owned the building, the land underneath belonged to the Cooper Union for the Advancement of Science and Art, a private college. The winning bid would have to satisfy the school as well as the bank. While other prospective buyers were negotiating with the bank, Speyer contacted Robert Bernhard, a friend and the chairman of Cooper Union. He offered to lease the land from the school for $5.5 million a year, more than the $4.5 million they were asking, and also offered to extend the lease, set to expire in about three decades, to 150 years. With that agreement in place, Speyer approached the bank and won the deal. As he had with Rockefeller Center, he began right away to invest in improvements to the landmark. "We're a for-profit company, with no illusions about what our objectives are," Speyer told Lore Croghan for *Crain's New York Business* (May 15–21, 2000). "But there was a delta point in these transactions, of being able to make money and at the same time restore these properties to their former beauty, dignity and place in the world." In July 2008 the government of Abu Dhabi, the capital city of the United Arab Emirates, bought a 90 percent stake in the Chrysler Building for $800 million. Although Tishman Speyer's share declined to 10 percent, the firm continues to manage and control the property.

Tishman Speyer set a record with its purchase in 2006 of Stuyvesant Town and Peter Cooper Village. Those residential complexes include 110 buildings and more than 11,000 apartments and, at $5.4 billion, became the most expensive property purchase ever made in the United States. (Tishman Speyer's $1.8 billion sale of 666 Fifth Avenue that same year broke the record for the highest price ever paid for a single building in the U.S.) In May 2008 the public learned that Tishman Speyer had denied renewals on the leases of more than 800 tenants of the rent-controlled apartments in the complexes, on the grounds that the residents had primary residences elsewhere, thus violating state and city rent-control laws. Many of those affected

by the denials charged that Tishman Speyer had raised questions about their primary residences in an attempt to drive up the rents on their apartments. Almost half of the cases were later dropped, while a third resulted in tenants' being forced to move.

In recent years Tishman Speyer has incorporated both environmentally friendly and energy-efficient elements in many of its projects. An example is the company's restoration of the Hearst Tower in 2006, which received the first United States Green Building Council's LEED Gold rating, awarded to an occupied office building in New York City. Also, in 2007, Tishman Speyer installed 363 solar panels on the roof of 45 Rockefeller Plaza, making it Manhattan's largest privately owned generating station for solar energy. That same year the famous Rockefeller Center Christmas tree was adorned with LEDs (light emitting diodes), saving "enough electricity each day to power a 2,000-square-foot home for an entire month," as New York City's mayor, Michael Bloomberg, said in a press conference held with Speyer on November 20, 2007.

Speyer's personality and the way he conducts business have earned praise from his colleagues. Kathryn Wylde, the president and chief executive of the Partnership for New York City (a group Speyer chaired in the early 1990s), told Matthew Schuerman for the *New York Observer* (December 18, 2006), "Jerry has deep, deep roots in the financial community. He knows all these people socially. He's a direct, honest man, and these people trust him." The former chairman of Citigroup Inc., Sanford Weill, told Traub, "My feeling is one of complete trust. To feel that you don't have to dot every 'i' and cross every 't' is a great way to deal with people." The influential architect Philip Johnson said to Traub that Speyer "has a lot more esthetic sense than any other developer I know."

Speyer has been collecting contemporary art for more than 40 years. While he often chooses works by relatively unknown artists, some of his favorite artists include such well-known figures as Damien Hirst, Frank Stella, Jeff Koons, and Eric Fischl. "There are two things I really care about when we are developing or redeveloping a building," he told Barrie. "One is the basic architectural plan, the other is the art that goes in the building." Speyer's home (designed by the architects Billie Tsien and Tod Williams), on Manhattan's Upper East Side, is said to have been built around his art collection, which is so expansive that each visitor is given a catalog of the works upon arriving. Barrie reported that Speyer "[prides] himself as a buyer not at auctions, but 'as the paint is drying' on work that he then places in his buildings."

For almost three decades Speyer has been involved with New York community, educational, cultural, and business organizations. He has served as president of the board of trustees of the Dalton School (which his children attended) and as chairman of the board of trustees of Columbia University, the board of directors of the Federal Reserve Bank of New York, and the Real Estate Board of New York. He is currently vice chair of New York Presbyterian Hospital, a member of the Council on Foreign Relations, and an owner of the New York Yankees and is also affiliated with Carnegie Hall and the Economic Club of New York. Perhaps his most notable membership has been with the Museum of Modern Art (MoMA). Invited to join the museum's board in 1982, he became the lead negotiator for the museum's $650 million expansion plan in the 1990s, helping the museum buy the neighboring Dorset Hotel for $50 million, $25 million less than the hotel owners originally asked. Discussing the deal, David Rockefeller, an honorary chairman of MoMA and member of the family who co-founded the museum, told Traub, "I'm not sure that anyone else could have done it." Speyer was promoted from vice chairman to chairman of the board in 2007. Among other charitable contributions, he has given $5 million to MoMA and $10 million to Columbia University. He organized a fund-raiser for the Central Synagogue (of which he is a longtime member) after a fire destroyed most of the building in 1998, and he helped save the Partnership for New York City (a nonprofit group of CEOs, founded by David Rockefeller, that is dedicated to the city's economic growth) by stepping in as chairman in 1992. Speyer's wife, Katherine, serves as vice chair and member of the executive committee of the board for the Lincoln Center for the Performing Arts and as chairman of the Lincoln Center Redevelopment Project.

Most recently, Tishman Speyer acquired a group of buildings in Chicago for $1.72 billion; began construction on an office building in Washington, D.C., that is to be finished in early 2009; announced plans to build a $2 billion township in India; and, in partnership with the family-owned Modell's Sporting Goods, began construction of a large commercial and residential complex in Long Island City, Queens, to be named Gotham Center. The company also teamed up with Morgan Stanley to submit a proposal for the development of Manhattan's West Side Yards. The Metropolitan Transit Authority board, which owns the land, announced on March 26, 2008 that Tishman Speyer, with a bid of a little over $1 billion, had beaten four competitors to win a 99-year lease to the space. Two months later Tishman Speyer abandoned the deal, however, amid concerns about the economy and their failure to attract any financial partners.

Speyer has four children, three (Valerie, Robert, and Holly) with his first wife and one (Laura) with Katherine. His eldest daughter, Valerie, is now the managing director of development for Tishman Speyer and is currently in charge of development for the new Yankee Stadium. His son, Robert, the president, co-CEO, and heir apparent of Tishman Speyer, was in charge of the Stuyvesant Town and Peter Cooper Village purchase. At 68 Speyer, who remains the chairman and co-CEO of the company, has started the process of handing the business over to his son. "Will I still be here at 90? I hope so. Will I be an executive? I sure hope not," he told Jim Packard for the London *Financial Times* (March 13, 2007). "I love what I do, I enjoy it, but I have delegated a lot of responsibility to other people in the company. My son is taking a leading role in the company."

—M.A.S.

Suggested Reading: *New York Times* (on-line) June 2, 2004, p43+ Oct. 10, 1987; *New York Times Magazine* p62+ Dec. 20, 1998; *New York Observer* p11 Dec. 18, 2006; *Property Week* (on-line) July 1, 2000

Courtesy of National Public Radio

Stamberg, Susan

Sep. 7, 1938– Radio journalist

Address: National Public Radio, 635 Massachusetts Ave., N.W., Washington, DC 20001

Susan Stamberg, the first woman ever to anchor a national nightly news program and the self-described "founding mother" of National Public Radio (NPR), did not imagine during her student years that she would have a successful career as a broadcaster. "I grew up on radio," she told Zan Dubin for the *Los Angeles Times* (May 15, 1993). "So to me, saying I wanted to be in radio was like saying I want to be a movie star. I mean, radio was the glamorous medium and it wouldn't have occurred to me that I might ever be able to do it." With her distinctive voice and personality, Stamberg is often credited with the success of the highly popular NPR show *All Things Considered*. She hosted the landmark program for almost 15 years, and when she resigned, an editorial in the *Los Angeles Times* (September 19, 1986) paid tribute to her stature as a newswoman: "[Stamberg] is a thoroughgoing pro, driven by an informed curiosity, well-backgrounded, informal in manner but sharp in her questioning. She is clearly a person who reads, and who thinks, and who wonders and cares about the world around her. Those qualities used to be taken for granted in broadcast news. In an age that has come to be dominated by talking hairdos, they have become all too rare." Stamberg can still be heard on NPR as a special correspondent.

Stamberg was born Susan Levitt to Robert and Anne (Rosenberg) Levitt, Russian-American Jews, on September 7, 1938 in Newark, New Jersey. An only child, she grew up on the Upper West Side of the New York City borough of Manhattan. Her father, who dropped out of school in the sixth grade to help support his family, was a salesman. As a child Stamberg loved listening to the family radio. She told M. J. Van Deventer for the *Oklahoman* (February 17, 2008), "My family didn't get a television until I was a junior in high school. But I always thought radio was the greatest of all media. I think the pictures in your mind's eye from listening are always better than what someone shows you on television. Radio is a wonderful, expansive, embracing medium. As a child, I used to love it when I was ill and I could stay home and listen to all the radio soap operas."

Stamberg attended New York City's High School of Music & Art, now known as the Fiorello H. La-Guardia High School of Music & Art and Performing Arts. (The school is widely known as the setting of the 1980 movie *Fame*.) There, Stamberg studied art. After graduation she enrolled at Barnard College, in New York City, earning a B.A. degree in English literature in 1959. She began graduate studies in English at Brandeis University, in Waltham, Massachusetts, but soon decided that she was tired of academia and dropped out to work as an editorial assistant at *Daedalus*, the official journal of the American Academy of Arts and Sciences. She told Jim Kershner for the Spokane, Washington, *Spokesman Review* (September 21, 1999), "[In the 1950s] your ambition was that you'd have some kind of terrific career and then you'd also be married and have a wonderful family. So I thought I would have some sort of interesting job in publishing . . . newspapers, or books or magazines." On April 14, 1962 she married Louis Collins Stamberg, an employee of the U.S. Department of State whom she had met while at Brandeis. (He had been a Harvard University law student.) The young couple moved to Chevy Chase, a neighborhood in northwest Washington, D.C. (The area borders Chevy Chase, Maryland.)

Stamberg then became an editorial assistant for the *New Republic*, a magazine that covers politics and culture. Then, in 1963, when a friend told her

that WAMU-FM, a local radio station based on the campus of American University, in the nation's capital, was looking for a producer for a weekly public-affairs show, Stamberg applied and was hired. Her on-air debut took place when the weather announcer called in sick and Stamberg filled in for her. When that became a regular occurrence, Stamberg recited weather-related poetry during the broadcast to make her weather reports more interesting.

Stamberg was soon promoted to program director and then station manager. Her duties included recording material both in and out of the studio and transporting and setting up equipment. Later, she began reporting on the air regularly and co-hosted and produced *Kaleidoscope*, a program that featured a variety of segments and interviews.

On January 4, 1970 Stamberg gave birth to a son, Joshua. Sixteen months later she joined the newly formed NPR, a nonprofit organization that produces and distributes news and other programming with no commercials. Hired to edit tapes, Stamberg started reporting news for the network two weeks later. *All Things Considered* debuted on May 3, 1971. The 90-minute weekday-evening show (now expanded to two hours) features a mix of news, reviews, commentary, interviews, and special segments. Stamberg contributed to the program and was chosen to become a host the following year, making her the first woman ever to anchor a national nightly news program. "There were no role models for me," she explained to Robin Updike for the *Seattle Times* (October 8, 1999). "I remember [trying to deepen] my voice when I started because there were objections from station managers that women's voices were not as authoritative." Although she had many critics, she enjoyed the support of Bill Siemering, then the director of programming for NPR, who encouraged her to simply be herself. Stamberg gradually gained confidence, developing one of the most recognized voices on public radio.

Stamberg's voice, with its pronounced New York accent, has been described as possessing "a Big Apple tartness softened by whimsy," according to Paul D. Colford, writing for *Newsday* (May 26, 1993). Donna Perlmutter wrote for the *Los Angeles Times* (April 13, 2001) that Stamberg's tones were "earthy, warm and New Yorkish," while Douglas McCay, in an article for the New Orleans, Louisiana, *Times-Picayune* (June 27, 1993), used the words "warm, cajoling, searching, down-to-earth." Stamberg helped make *All Things Considered* one of the most popular and highly regarded radio programs on the air and prompted the novelist E. L. Doctorow to write in a blurb for one of her books, according to the NPR Web site, that she is "the closest thing to an enlightened humanist on radio."

Stamberg often covered stories about child care and advocated for the show to feature more news concerning women's issues. Having shared her mother-in-law's cranberry-relish recipe on the air at Thanksgiving while at WAMU, she continued to do so after she started working for NPR. The recipe segment became an annual tradition, with the newscaster finding new twists each year—including a musical version performed by the soprano Denise Konicek and a special recitation by the TV personality and businesswoman Martha Stewart. It was later revealed that the recipe, which includes an onion and horseradish among its ingredients, had originally come from the late food critic Craig Claiborne—who claimed during an interview that he was happy that Stamberg had appropriated it.

Stamberg is best known, however, not for such lighthearted segments, but for her interviews. She told Colford, "I'm a natural schmoozer. It is not my lot in life to go sit looking at a computer screen and write all day in this quiet, splendid isolation. I like to get out and scramble with people. That's why I report, that's why I interview." By her own estimation, Stamberg has conducted more than 30,000 interviews during her career with NPR. Her subjects have included such diverse figures as First Lady Laura Bush; the photographer Annie Leibovitz; the civil rights figure Rosa Parks; President Jimmy Carter; the opera star Luciano Pavarotti; the jazz musician Dave Brubeck; and George de Mestral, the inventor of Velcro. She has said that the key to interviewing a subject, besides preparation and research, is to listen carefully to their responses, a skill she feels many of today's interviewers lack. She particularly enjoys interviewing artists, she told Clea Simon for the *Boston Globe* (August 2, 2001), and her least favorite subjects include politicians: "They will never tell me anything they won't tell a thousand other people. There's so much at stake on the smallest slip of the tongue. . . . They're more and more guarded, and I have no interest in that." Anders Gyllenhaal wrote for the *Orlando (Florida) Sentinel*, as reprinted in the *Chicago Tribune* (February 22, 1985), "[Stamberg's] personality pours out over the air in doses that are unusual for newspeople. Willing to giggle openly, ask uncomfortable questions or just let the taped silence coax her subject on, her interviews with heads of state, poets, Nobel Prize winners and the common man and woman are leisurely explorations that often search well beyond the events that brought the focus in the first place."

Thanks in large part to the popularity of *All Things Considered*, NPR, which started with only 63 member stations and 65 employees, has grown substantially. As of October 2008, NPR had upwards of 860 member stations, 750 staff members, and some 26 million listeners every week. "It's become an institution, what began as a wild and wonderful dream on the part of people who'd worked at small public radio stations, mostly at colleges and universities. We built an organization that began as a rickety thing, and now we really are a professional group full of enormous potential," Stamberg told Jennifer Sanderson for the Sioux Falls, South Dakota, *Argus Leader* (July 17, 2002).

In July 1986, after discovering a cancerous lump in her breast, Stamberg had a lumpectomy and underwent radiation treatment. She has since had no recurrence of the cancer. "It gave me a level of compassion that I hadn't had before and a way of understanding pain in other people," she told Helen Forsberg for the *Salt Lake (Utah) Tribune* (April 24, 1994). At the time, she did not discuss her bout with breast cancer publicly. In September 1986 she ended her long run on *All Things Considered*. The following January she returned to NPR to host the new *Weekend Edition Sunday*. The weekly two-hour show featured an array of regular segments, including, at that time, movie reviews by the cartoonist and author Jules Feiffer and recipes from the famed chef Alice Waters. Stamberg's run on *Weekend Edition Sunday* ended two years later, and in 1990 she became a special NPR correspondent, reporting for and occasionally guest-hosting the programs *Morning Edition* and *Weekend Edition Saturday*. Describing that role to Steve Kennedy for *Central PA* magazine (October 2006), she said, "I have been able to follow my own curiosity and report on things, not necessarily news-driven, but areas which absorb and interest me. NPR has been wonderful in permitting that and encouraging that, figuring that if it was interesting to me it will be interesting to our listeners as well. So I'm very lucky for that. I don't have a beat, I don't have any one thing that I do or cover all the time, although I tend to do cultural things."

Stamberg told Steve Hall for the *Buffalo (New York) News* (March 15, 1998) that she believes that NPR is "the most virtuous of all the news organizations." She expressed particular disdain for those outlets that engage in "gotcha journalism," which focuses on embarrassing or scandalous stories involving public figures. Referring to the scandal centering on President Bill Clinton's extramarital affair with Monica Lewinksy, Stamberg told Hall, "The way that story has been covered is so terrifying to me . . . with the continual leaks to the press and everything being rushed on the air so fast. A reporter's job is to dig up facts, poke around, weigh bits of information against each other. In this scandal, generally, we've just been passing information along. That's not reporting."

Stamberg has been awarded seemingly every major prize in the radio industry. She received the Edward R. Murrow Award from the Corporation for Public Broadcasting in 1990 and was inducted into both the Broadcasting and Cable Hall of Fame (1994) and the Radio Hall of Fame (1996). She has been honored with the Radio Club of America's Armstrong Medal, Columbia University's Alfred I. duPont Award (the broadcast equivalent of the Pulitzer Prize), Ohio State University's Golden Anniversary Director's Award, and both the Distinguished Broadcaster Award and the Gracie Tribute Award from American Women in Radio & Television. Stamberg has also received several honorary degrees and has served on the boards of directors of the National Arts Journalism Program at Columbia University's Graduate School of Journalism and the American Institute of Architects, in Washington, D.C. She is currently director emeritus on the board of the PEN/Faulkner Fiction Award Foundation.

Stamberg is the author of *Every Night at Five: Susan Stamberg's All Things Considered Book* (1982) and *Talk: NPR's Susan Stamberg Considers All Things* (1993), which feature interviews and reports from her time on *All Things Considered*. She also co-edited *The Wedding Cake in the Middle of the Road* (1992), a collection of short fiction. (Writers had been asked to pen short stories suitable for reading on the radio; each story had to incorporate the image of a wedding cake abandoned on a roadway.)

Stamberg's husband, who had become a tireless community volunteer after retiring from government service, died in October 2007. Her son, Josh,

an actor, lives in Los Angeles, California, with his wife, the actress Myndy Crist, and their daughter, Vivian. Stamberg, who has no plans to retire as yet, enjoys playing the piano in her spare time. She continues to live in Washington, D.C.

—M.A.S.

Suggested Reading: *Buffalo (New York) News* E p1 Mar. 15, 1998; *Los Angeles Times* F p26 Apr. 13, 2001; *Oklahoman* D p1 Feb. 17, 2008; (Spokane, Washington) *Spokesman Review* D p1 Sep. 21, 1999

Selected Books: *Every Night at Five: Susan Stamberg's All Things Considered Book*, 1982; *Talk: NPR's Susan Stamberg Considers All Things*, 1993

Courtesy of Cass Sunstein

Sunstein, Cass R.

Sep. 21, 1954– Legal scholar; educator; writer

Address: Harvard Law School, 1563 Massachusetts Ave., Cambridge, MA 02138

Cass R. Sunstein is among the best-known legal scholars, theorists, and educators in the U.S. He is "the preeminent legal scholar of our time—the most wide-ranging, the most prolific, the most cited, and the most influential," Elena Kagan, the dean of Harvard Law School, wrote for the school's Web site (February 19, 2008), in announcing that

Sunstein would join the faculty later that year. "His work in any one of the fields he pursues—administrative law and policy, constitutional law and theory, behavioral economics and law, environmental law, to name a non-exhaustive few—would put him in the very front ranks of legal scholars; the combination is singular and breathtaking. He has a gift for framing and discussing issues in ways that invariably gain traction and make progress." Sunstein's areas of expertise include jurisprudence (legal philosophy and theory), regulatory policy, and legal issues connected with affirmative action, censorship, civil rights, the First Amendment, employment and labor practices, animal rights, government welfare programs, federal courts, the U.S. Supreme Court, juries, the separation of powers among branches of the U.S. government, and the American presidency. "His research interests span the legal discipline so widely that his work is relevant to scholars in nearly every field," Paul H. Edelman and Tracey E. George wrote in an article for the *Green Bag: An Entertaining Journal of Law* (Autumn 2007, on-line).

Sunstein has published more than a dozen books and contributed hundreds of articles to newspapers, magazines, and professional journals. He has frequently collaborated with leading thinkers in other fields, such as economics and psychology, and his work reflects his interdisciplinary perspective. A former adviser to Presidents Jimmy Carter and Ronald Reagan, he is often labeled a moderate and credited with interpreting the law in a nonpartisan manner. In the words of a writer for the *Economist* (March 13, 1999), his arguments "are directed at left and right alike." He is an advocate of "judicial minimalism" and believes that courts should avoid broad rulings and proceed slowly in changing laws. In addition to teaching and writing, he has participated in many public discussions and legal processes, regarding, for example, the impeachment of President Bill Clinton, in 1998, which Sunstein actively opposed. He has presented testimony to congressional committees, among them the Senate Judiciary Committee, in connection with Supreme Court nominees. He has also served as a legal adviser to nine nations, among them China, Russia, and South Africa.

Cass Robert Sunstein was born on September 21, 1954 in Salem, Massachusetts, to C. R. Sunstein, a builder, and Marian (Goodrich) Sunstein, a teacher. He and his sister grew up in Newton, a suburb of Boston. After graduating in 1972 from the private Middlesex School, in Concord, Massachusetts, Sunstein enrolled at Harvard University, in Cambridge, Massachusetts, where he was a member of the varsity squash team and sat on the editorial board of the satirical publication the *Harvard Lampoon*. He earned an A.B. degree, magna cum laude, in 1975, then entered Harvard Law School. As a law student he served as the executive editor of the *Harvard Civil Rights–Civil Liberties Law Review* and was on the winning team of an Ames Moot Court Competition, an annual Harvard Law School event. He earned his J.D. degree in 1978, again graduating magna cum laude. The following year Sunstein worked as a law clerk for Judge Benjamin Kaplan of the Supreme Judicial Court of Massachusetts. From 1979 to 1980 he clerked for the U.S. Supreme Court justice Thurgood Marshall, the first African-American to serve on the nation's highest court. (Throughout his tenure, which spanned the years from 1967 to 1991, Marshall was regarded as one of the court's most liberal judges.) From 1980 to 1981, during the final year of the administration of Democratic president Jimmy Carter and the first of Republican president Ronald Reagan, Sunstein was an attorney adviser in the Office of Legal Counsel of the U.S. Justice Department. Among other matters, he focused on issues related to executive privilege.

Sunstein next became an assistant professor of law at the University of Chicago Law School, which, in an article for the *Huffington Post* (March 5, 2008, on-line), he described as "by far the most conservative of the great American law schools." In 1983 he took on an additional assistant professorship, in the university's Department of Political Science, and in 1985 he was made a full professor in both departments. In the mid-1980s he began serving as a visiting professor at Columbia Law School, in New York City, and Harvard. In 1988 he was named Karl N. Llewellyn professor of jurisprudence at the University of Chicago. (In 1993 his title changed to Karl N. Llewellyn distinguished service professor of jurisprudence.) He held that position until 2008, when he announced plans to join the faculty of Harvard Law School and serve as Felix Frankfurter professor of law. Sunstein heads Harvard's new Program on Risk Regulation, which focuses on "low-probability, high-consequence events," such as terrorism and natural disasters. "The nation and the world are facing many unanticipated problems, and policymakers must find ways to protect people from risks without creating

unanticipated side-effects," Sunstein said, according to the Harvard Law School Web site (February 19, 2008). "Our goals are to improve our sense of what the law is now doing—and to see how it might do better." He will continue to teach at the University of Chicago, where, during the winter of the 2008–09 academic year, he will serve as the Harry Kalven visiting professor of law. Over the years Sunstein has taught courses on many legal topics, including constitutional law, legal theory, environmental law and regulation, Social Security and welfare law, and the U.S. Supreme Court.

Sunstein's bibliography includes three legal casebooks: *Administrative Law and Regulatory Policy* (1999), written with Richard B. Stewart, Matthew Spitzer, and Supreme Court justice Stephen G. Breyer; *Constitutional Law* (1986); and *The First Amendment* (1999), the last two of which were written with Geoffrey R. Stone, Louis M. Seidman, Mark V. Tushnet, and Pamela S. Karlan. Sunstein has written or co-written hundreds of articles for newspapers and popular magazines—including *Harper's*, the *New Yorker*, and the *Washington Monthly*—and dozens of professional journals, among them the *Chronicle of Higher Education*, *Social Research*, *Ethics*, the *Harvard Law and Policy Review*, the *Harvard Environmental Law Review*, and the law reviews of many universities. He has also written more than a dozen books spelling out his views on various legal issues. The first, *After the Rights Revolution: Reconceiving the Regulatory State*, was published in 1990. In 1994 his book *Democracy and the Problem of Free Speech*, published the previous year, won the Goldsmith Book Award, an honor bestowed by a division of Harvard's John F. Kennedy School of Government.

In *Legal Reasoning and Political Conflict* (1996), Sunstein argued that judges should make practical decisions on a case-by-case basis, rather than sweeping principle-based determinations. As Joan Biskupic wrote for the *Washington Post* (July 28, 1996), "Sunstein contends that there is greater opportunity for social harmony when judges negotiate their differences, eschew broad abstractions and leave development of national principles to legislators." Sunstein has argued about the Supreme Court's decision in the famous *Roe v. Wade* case, which guaranteed the legal right to abortion, that the Court should have moved incrementally, rather than issuing the absolute and binding judgment that it did. He has claimed that because the ruling polarized public opinion, many other topics, such as gender equality, have become more difficult to debate. "It's absolutely true that if the court goes in the teeth of the public, it can hurt the cause that you're trying to promote," he told J. J. Helland for *Salon.com* (September 12, 2005). In *The Cost of Rights* (1999), written in collaboration with Stephen Holmes, Sunstein argued that it costs the government money to protect so-called negative rights, those that defend individuals against government interference and are often supported by conservatives. That assertion contradicts the popularly held notion that only "positive rights," those that are often backed by liberals and focus on the social and economic rights of citizens, come with a price. "This book is a bracing, head-clearing exercise," the *Economist* (March 13, 1999) reviewer wrote. "Although aimed at American readers, its arguments apply to any liberal democracy. By pointing out the budgetary consequences of rights, the authors also challenge other cherished dichotomies—between fundamental constitutional rights and other lesser legal rights; between rights and responsibilities; and between rights and mere interests."

Sunstein's book *Republic.com* (2001) grew out of his interest in the free-speech issues related to the growth of the Internet. In it, Sunstein warned that the Internet threatens the fundamental requisites of deliberative democracy, because it allows citizens to seek out only information they agree with, eliminating political discourse and promoting what he calls "cyberbalkanization." The book was partially inspired by Sunstein's studies of jury behavior, through which he has found that isolated, like-minded people often spur each other to develop more extreme viewpoints. "Freedom for citizens in a republic 'consists not simply in preference satisfaction but also in the chance to have preferences and beliefs formed under decent conditions . . . after exposure to a sufficient amount of information, and also to an appropriately wide and diverse range of options,'" Carlin Romano wrote for the *Philadelphia Inquirer* (April 12, 2001), summarizing the book's thesis. Romano went on to call Sunstein a "consummate practitioner of his trade, a rat-a-tat-tat issue-spotter who drives home multiple pros and cons of our evolving media marketplace." Sunstein offered similar arguments in *Why Societies Need Dissent* (2003), maintaining that freedom of speech is essential to the health and prosperity of a country.

In 2005 Sunstein published *Radicals in Robes: Why Extreme Right-Wing Courts Are Wrong for America*, the theme of which is the importance of judicial minimalism. In that book Sunstein warned against what he called "fundamentalist" Supreme Court judges—those who believe that the Constitution has a fixed meaning that can be changed only through amendments. "I don't like either form of activism [liberal or conservative]," Sunstein told Tavis Smiley in an interview for Smiley's PBS talk show (September 8, 2005). "I think the court should play a modest role in American government. We have a democracy here, and our basic ground rules should not be set by the Supreme Court." A year earlier Sunstein had published *The Second Bill of Rights: FDR's Unfinished Revolution and Why We Need It More than Ever*, in which he asserted that meaningful citizenship in a democracy should include certain social and economic rights, such as access to sufficient food, adequate housing, proper health care, and a quality education. President Franklin Delano Roosevelt spoke of those rights in his 1944 State of the Union address,

which Sunstein referred to as the "speech of the century." Sunstein stopped short of arguing for amending the Constitution and instead "takes the position, near the end of the book, that we should 'treat the second bill as a set of constitutive commitments, helping define the nation's deepest principles,'" according to Michael DeBow, writing for *Freeman: Ideas on Liberty* (December 2005).

Sunstein's most recent book, *Nudge: Improving Decisions about Health, Wealth, and Happiness* (2008), was co-written with the University of Chicago professor and behavioral economist Richard Thaler. *Nudge* focuses on social policy and calls for a kind of "libertarian paternalism," which, on the surface, sounds like a contradiction in terms. The authors advocate the use of behavioral suggestions aimed at encouraging people to make better choices. One example is the creation of a system whereby drivers are automatically classified as organ donors and must "opt out," or check a box on their driver's licenses, if they do not wish to participate in the program. Such arrangements lead to higher numbers of donors than do those requiring willing participants to "opt in," according to the authors. "Nudging is the new politics," Bryan Appleyard wrote for the London *Sunday Times* (July 6, 2008), praising Sunstein and Thaler for finding middle ground between "top-down, bureaucratic paternalism" and "the cult of the free market," prevailing ideas of government that would place power in the hands of governments and citizens, respectively. Sunstein's other books include *The Partial Constitution* (1993), *Democracy and the Problem of Free Speech* (1995), *Free Markets and Social Justice* (1997), *One Case at a Time: Judicial Minimalism on the Supreme Court* (1999), *Designing Democracy: What Constitutions Do* (2001), *Risk and Reason* (2002), *The Cost-Benefit State* (2002), *Laws of Fear: Beyond the Precautionary Principle* (2005), *Are Judges Political? An Empirical Analysis of the Federal Judiciary* (2005), and *Infotopia: How Many Minds Produce Knowledge* (2006). He has also co-authored, edited, or co-edited several other books.

Sunstein, who serves on the World Wildlife Fund's National Council, was elected to the American Academy of Arts and Sciences in 1992. He is a member of the American Law Institute and has served on several American Bar Association committees. In 2007 he was awarded the prestigious Henry M. Phillips Prize, with which the American Philosophical Association recognizes lifetime achievement in jurisprudence. Sunstein is a strong supporter of and informal legal adviser to the 2008 Democratic presidential candidate, Barack Obama, his friend and former colleague at the University of Chicago. Sunstein is said to have met his current wife, Samantha Power—a Harvard professor who formerly served as Obama's foreign-policy adviser—while working on the candidate's campaign in January 2008. The two were married in July 2008. Sunstein has a college-age daughter, Ellyn Ruddick-Sunstein, from his previous marriage, to Lisa

Ruddick, an English professor at the University of Chicago.

—M.M.

Suggested Reading: *Carnegie Council* (on-line) Sep. 11, 2003; *Economist* p9 Mar. 13, 1999; *Harvard Law School News* (on-line) Feb. 19, 2008; *Huffington Post* (on-line) July 16, 2008; *New York Times* (on-line) Sep. 19, 2004; *Philadelphia Inquirer* Apr. 12, 2001; *Salon.com* Nov. 7, 2007; *Tavis Smiley Show* (on-line) Sep. 8, 2005

Selected Books: *After the Rights Revolution*, 1990; *The Partial Constitution*, 1993; *Democracy and the Problem of Free Speech*, 1995; *Legal Reasoning and Political Conflict*, 1996; *Free Markets and Social Justice*, 1997; *One Case at a Time: Judicial Minimalism on the Supreme Court*, 1999; *The Cost of Rights*, 1999; *Designing Democracy: What Constitutions Do*, 2001; *Republic.com*, 2001; *Risk and Reason*, 2002; *The Cost-Benefit State*, 2002; *Why Societies Need Dissent*, 2003; *The Second Bill of Rights: FDR's Unfinished Revolution and Why We Need It More than Ever*, 2004; *Radicals in Robes: Why Extreme Right-Wing Courts Are Wrong for America*, 2005; *Laws of Fear: Beyond the Precautionary Principle*, 2005; *Are Judges Political? An Empirical Analysis of the Federal Judiciary*, 2005; *Infotopia: How Many Minds Produce Knowledge*, 2006; *Nudge: Improving Decisions about Health, Wealth, and Happiness*, 2008

Courtesy of Johnny Temple

Temple, Johnny

Nov. 3, 1966– Book publisher; musician

Address: Akashic Books, 232 Third St., #B404, Brooklyn, NY 11215

Describing the independent book publisher and musician Johnny Temple, Danny Goldberg, a music producer and record-label executive, told David Daley for the *Hartford (Connecticut) Courant* (May 12, 2002), "He's really got a vision. . . . I've never known of anyone like Johnny, with that renaissance combination of interests and skills." As a bass guitarist, Temple is best known for his work with the indie-rock band Girls Against Boys,

which has toured with such well-known groups as Foo Fighters, Rage Against the Machine, and Fugazi and released songs heard on the soundtracks of movies including *Clerks*, *Series 7: The Contenders*, and *Hedwig and the Angry Inch*. In 1997, after Girls Against Boys signed with a major record label, Temple used money from his advance to found a small, independent publishing company, the Brooklyn, New York–based Akashic Books, dedicated to what the company Web site calls "reverse-gentrification of the literary world"—that is, the distribution of literature ignored by major publishing houses to a readership that extends beyond the educated middle class. The company also aims to provide what it calls "a cure for the common novel." Akashic currently boasts dozens of titles in genres including literary fiction, mystery, crime, nonfiction, African-American interest, and gay and lesbian interest. In addition, Temple has written for several high-profile publications, including the *Nation*.

Johnny Temple was born on November 3, 1966 in Washington, D.C. His father, Ralph J. Temple, a lawyer, served for 13 years as the head of the local chapter of the American Civil Liberties Union (ACLU); his mother was a public defender. Temple grew up in a middle-class, mostly black neighborhood and attended private school until 10th grade, when he transferred of his own volition to a local public high school, Wilson, in the Northwest section of the city. The school "was ten percent white, but that was considered the white public school because it had so many more white kids than [other Washington public schools] . . . ," Temple told Williams Cole and Theodore Hamm for the *Brooklyn Rail-Express* (April 2003). "There was a chasm, you know, academically. In D.C. people will say, 'Oh, Wilson is just as good as any of the private schools.' Well, no it's not, and you really experience the difference in resources between a private school and a public school. It was just really interesting and so much of my life has grown out of that experience—everyone I played music with is from the public school system. I also became really interested in issues of race." While in high school Temple had an internship at an independent reggae record label, RAS Records. After graduating from Wilson, Temple attended Wesleyan University, in Middletown, Connecticut, where he majored in African-American studies. He later earned a master's degree in social work from Columbia University, in New York City. Meanwhile, he had begun playing the bass guitar during his sophomore year of college, and during his junior year he joined a band called Lunchmeat, which included Temple's high-school friends Alexis Fleisig on drums and Scott McCloud on guitar. A few years later the band added the singer Bobby Sullivan, renamed itself Soulside, and was signed to the indie label Dischord. Those developments occurred at about the time Temple received his degree in social work. He told Mary Blume for the *International Herald Tribune* (January 12, 2007), "I loved social work, I loved working with juvenile delinquents, that was my area of focus. . . . I was sort of at a crossroads and I picked rock 'n' roll because I could return to social work, and I still could, but I knew I could never return to rock 'n' roll." Soulside recorded the albums *Trigger* (1988), *Hot Bodi-gram* (1990), and *Soon Come Happy* (1990), breaking up shortly after the last release.

McCloud, Fleisig, and Temple next joined the Fugazi drummer, Brendan Canty, in the studio for a project that culminated in the formation of Girls Against Boys. As McCloud recalled events to Jason Heller for the *Denver (Colorado) Westword* (September 5, 2002), "Girls Against Boys began as basically just an experiment. I think we wanted to give it a little more of a darker edge than Soulside, which was kind of more explosive, you know, more hardcore. We started out with a few studio freakout sessions where we just sort of laid down some weird tracks. It wasn't a real band then. We just kind of fantasized about playing shows. But those sessions did end up becoming that first EP we did, *Nineties Vs. Eighties*." After Canty left the group, Girls Against Boys added another bassist, Eli Janney, who had acted as Soulside's sound technician, and who also added keyboards to the mix. The band—which called itself GVSB for short—released its first album, *Tropic of Scorpio*, in the early 1990s, before signing with the indie label Touch and Go Records. Three full-length albums followed: *Venus Luxure No. 1 Baby* (1994), *Cruise Yourself* (1995), and *House of GVSB* (1996). Girls Against Boys quickly became known for bass-heavy, sexually charged music, with Heidi Sherman remarking for *Rolling Stone* (May 28, 1999), "The band has churned out lo-fi, heavy grooves (they employ two basses) that can transform any club into a carnal pit, dense with sweat and pheromones." Temple told Camille Colatosti for *Witness* (on-line), "Girls Against Boys is both a creative and a social or political project. The music is discordant as far as loud rock music goes. Our musical roots are in the punk rock tradition, but we are not a punk rock band. Still, the passion and aggressiveness of punk informs the band. . . . When the band started in the early 1990s—our first album was in 1991—there was a boys' club mentality in rock music. There are so many more women in rock now than there were 10 years ago, and this is good. But back then we wanted to make a statement about the boys' club. We wanted to say that, even though the band is all men, we aren't part of the boys' club." In 1995, while still with Touch and Go Records, McCloud and Temple began a side project called New Wet Kojak, with Geoff Turner of Gray Matter and Nick Pellecciotto of Edsel. New Wet Kojak has released a self-titled record (1995) as well as *Nasty International* (1997), *Do Things* (2000), and *This Is the Glamorous* (2003).

Following the release of *House of GVSB*, Girls Against Boys left Touch and Go Records for a major label, Geffen Records. Temple resisted the move, explaining to Colatosti, "Now we've signed a contract with Geffen Records. This is not an independent company. It is a major recording corporation. This has helped us get some things that we couldn't get before, like more money so that we can all afford health insurance. But now we have to struggle to stay part of the independent music community. Geffen and other major corporations aren't really part of a music community. They are just trying to make money. Working with them means that we are associated with a business that focuses on the bottom line, and not with an independent label that is interested just in producing good music. The music industry is corrupt, market-driven and it is getting worse. It is disillusioning to work with a company that should be about promoting creativity but isn't." The band's first album with Geffen Records, *Freak*On*Ica* (1998), received mixed reviews. The *Dallas Observer* (May 14, 1998) critic, Keven McAlester, found the album to be overly sanitized, writing, "Girls Against Boys used to be all about sex, and not just in its lyrics (though you'd find plenty there too.) The dueling basses of Eli Janney and Johnny Temple, the slurred come-ons of vocalist Scott McCloud, the preponderance of heavy grooves—all of it once added up to [a] kind of sultry-rock vibe. . . . Its title notwithstanding, *Freak*On*Ica* offers precious little that could be mistaken for sensuality. The deficiency is confusing. . . . Girls Against Boys is capable of writing better songs than these. There's not much of the wit once evidenced in 'Kill the Sexplayer' or 'Cruise Your New Baby Fly Self,' not much of the catchy buzz that once propelled 'Crash 17 (X-Rated Car),' not much of the subdued grind that once carried 'Vera Cruz' and 'Zodiac Love Team.' What's left is . . . well, not much." In stark contrast, Vicki Gilmer wrote for the Minneapolis, Minnesota, *Star Tribune* (August 7, 1998), "Subverting the conventions of lounge and disco music, the Washington, D.C. group's dance-cum-rock music is full of sexual innuendo, punkish vibrancy, and enough electronic manipulation to make it the dirtiest and darkest, but still danceable, soundtrack for the '90s. The band's latest album, *Freak*On*Ica*, recorded at Minneapolis' Seedy Underbelly Studios, is roiled by the twin-bass slaughter of Eli Janney and Johnny Temple, while McCloud's guitar gives the songs enough of a Jurassic stomp to shake the rafters."

After Geffen Records signed Girls Against Boys, the band members received sizable record advances. At first Temple planned to use his share to launch his own record label; after realizing that the business side of music did not appeal to him, he decided to try his hand at publishing. Temple told Sarah Ferguson for the *Village Voice* (June 29, 1999), "Part of what motivated me to . . . invest myself in independent publishing was because my band had made this jump from an independent label to a major one—a system I have absolutely no respect for. That gave me the motivation to create a counterbalance by investing myself in independent art." Akashic Books' first title was a reprint of an underground favorite, *The F**k-Up*, by Arthur Nersesian, in 1997; the book was later picked up by Simon & Schuster. Akashic has since published a wide variety of books, both fiction and nonfiction, many dealing with issues of race, class, or sexuality in urban settings. Temple has attempted not only to publish the work of writers from marginalized groups but to bring literature to a wider audience, telling Mary Blume, "I think that literature should be consumed by more than just the well-educated. Reverse gentrification is the notion that we don't need to just keep trying to sell books to the same people, these people for sure but also more of the population." Temple's venture outside the musical realm allowed him to delve into some of the issues that he had studied in college and graduate school. "I was always struggling with how to satisfy my passion for social justice and social issues," he told Janet Saidi for the *Los Angeles Times* (February 3, 2004), "and I never intended to go into book publishing—it was sort of a whim. I really feel that I've found something that satisfies my interest in politics and race and my various progressive passions." Other Akashic books have included *The Massage* (1999), by Henry Flesh, a novel about a masseuse in New York's gay underworld, and *R&B (Rhythm and Business): The Political Economy of Black Music* (2002), by Norman Kelley.

Mary Blume reported in early 2007 that Akashic "camps with a staff of four in a scruffy room in the former American Can Factory in Brooklyn." Akashic received a major boost in 2002, when Kaylie Jones, the daughter of the famed novelist James Jones, asked Temple to reissue a collection of her late father's short stories, *The Ice Cream Headache and Other Stories* (originally published in 1968) as well as his novel *The Merry Month of May* (1971). Temple was initially hesitant to take on those projects, since, as a small company, Akashic could not offer the same level of distribution as a major publishing house. Unlike bigger, long-established publishing companies, Akashic does not offer large advances but instead relies on a system similar to that of royalties paid by some independent music labels: writers receive half of the profits earned by their books. To save on expenditures, Akashic does not put writers up in expensive hotels or pay their plane fares during book tours; writers often transport themselves by car and stay in inexpensive motels. The appeal of Akashic for many writers is that they have greater agency in the publishing process, including input into their books' cover designs, layout, and marketing campaigns. Every piece of copy related to a book is a collaborative effort between the writer and Akashic. Ron Kovic, the author of the memoir *Born on the Fourth of July*, chose Akashic to reprint that 1976 Vietnam War classic because he was disgusted by the gory cover selected by his previous publisher; with Akashic he was given freer rein to present his book as he wished. Explaining why writers might choose Akashic over major publishing companies, Karin Taylor of the New York Small Press Center told the *Los Angeles Times* (February 3, 2004), "Authors will sometimes choose to go with Johnny Temple because that author knows that Johnny will put his heart, soul and whole effort into that book."

As for Temple's music career, Universal Music Group had purchased Geffen Records in 1999; GVSB subsequently came under pressure to deliver an album that would be accessible to a wider audience. Unwilling to compromise their aesthetic principles, GVSB asked to be released by the company and later signed with an indie label, Jade Tree, which released their first album in four years, *You Can't Fight What You Can't See* (2002). That album was produced by Ted Nicely, who had worked on two of the group's earlier indie albums, *Cruise Yourself* and *House of GVSB*. The new record was in many ways a return to the band's style prior to *Freak*On*Ica*, with a less slick, more insistently powerful sound. "Once we got off Geffen," Temple told Brian Baker for the *Cleveland Scene* (March 7, 2002), "we were free to record the album that we've wanted to record for a couple years. We wanted it to be aggressive, upbeat, raw, with guitars, bass, drums, keyboards, and vocals upfront and urgent." Music aficionados were pleased with the shift away from the *Freak*On*Ica* style; Heller wrote, "With GVSB already somewhat stigmatized by its new major-label association, *Freak*On*Ica* was, for many fans, the final straw. All of the familiar elements of the band's approach were still intact: the black humor, the brooding intensity, the pulverizing beats. And yet, its plastic production and near-pop sensibility steered *Freak*On*Ica* dangerously close to the histrionic shlock dredged up by Nine Inch Nails and Prodigy. . . . *You Can't Fight What You Can't See* . . . is a strong contender for the best yet. Allied with the flourishing independent label Jade Tree, the band is at a point where it has nothing to lose."

Although he now focuses most of his attention on his work for Akashic Books, Temple completed two European tours with Girls Against Boys in 2007. In 2008 he helped organize the third annual Brooklyn Book Festival, which introduced the public to writers and publishers from around the world. Currently, he serves as the chair of the Brooklyn Literary Council.

Temple lives in the Fort Greene section of Brooklyn with his wife and two children. Temple told Amy Freeborn for the *Advertiser* (July 4, 2002), "Being in a band is great but it can't be your only thing. I know for me personally, I'd be pretty miserable if all I did with my life was rock music."

—T.O.

Suggested Reading: *Advertiser* p58 July 4, 2002; *Dallas Observer* (on-line) May 14, 1998; *Denver Westword* (on-line) Sep. 5, 2002; *Hartford*

(Connecticut) Courant p10 May 12, 2002; *International Herald Tribune* (on-line) Jan. 12, 2007; *Los Angeles Times* E p1 Feb. 3, 2004; (Minneapolis, Minnesota) *Star Tribune* E p3 Aug. 7, 1998; *Rolling Stone* (on-line) May 28, 1998; *Village Voice* (on-line) June 29, 1999; *Witness* (on-line) June 2001

Selected Recordings: with Girls Against Boys— *Venus Luxure No. 1 Baby*, 1994; *Cruise Yourself*, 1995; *House of GVSB*, 1996; *Freak*On*Ica*, 1998; *You Can't Fight What You Can't See*, 2002; with Soulside—*Trigger*, 1988; *Hot Bodi-gram*, 1990; *Soon Come Happy*, 1990; with New Wet Kojak— *New Wet Kojak*, 1995; *Nasty International*, 1997; *Do Things*, 2000; *This Is the Glamorous*, 2003

Courtesy of Lhadon Tethong

Tethong, Lhadon

1976(?)– Human-rights activist; executive director of Students for a Free Tibet

Address: Students for a Free Tibet, 602 E. 14th St., Second Fl., New York, NY 10009

Lhadon Tethong is the executive director of Students for a Free Tibet International (SFT), a nonprofit organization with 650 chapters worldwide, which advocates direct, nonviolent action in support of Tibet's independence from China. SFT is one of many activist groups charging China with

human-rights violations and genocidal ambitions in Tibet, a region of Central Asia that it has occupied since 1951; specifically, they accuse Chinese authorities of detaining and harming Tibetan activists, censoring or altering Chinese news reports related to Tibet, and eradicating Buddhist culture in Tibet by relocating non-Buddhist citizens of China to the region. Although Chinese authorities maintain that Tibet has been Chinese territory for centuries, many ethnic Tibetans argue that it is an independent nation—the position taken by the Central Tibetan Administration (CTA), also known as the Tibetan Government in Exile since it relocated to India following a failed 1959 uprising. In seeking to aid Tibetans in their pursuit of independence, groups such as SFT identified the 2008 Summer Olympic Games, held in the Chinese capital of Beijing, as a scene of international interest, and they engaged in large-scale demonstrations there.

Tethong became actively involved in the Tibetan independence movement in 1996, starting a chapter of SFT while attending the University of King's College, in Halifax, Nova Scotia. She drew attention with a speech at the 1998 Tibetan Freedom Concert, in Washington, D.C., and the next year she joined the administrative body of SFT, in New York City, as a program coordinator. There, she became an organizer of many campaigns, nonviolent protests, and other public events. She also became SFT's main voice, frequently quoted in the news media after group demonstrations. Tethong assumed the post of executive director of SFT International in 2004. In August 2007 she visited China to observe the country's preparations for the Olympics and write about them for her blog, BeijingWideOpen.org. Her posts quickly generated international attention—especially after she was detained and forced out of the country by Chinese authorities seeking to censor such information. Tethong also became chair of the Olympics Campaign Working Group of the International Tibet Support Network (ITSN), a global coalition of which SFT is a member. During the 2008 Summer Olympic Games, Tethong again served as the voice of SFT, discussing protests, mounted by her organization, that had resulted in the detentions and/or deportations of members.

Lhadon Tethong was born in about 1976 to Judy and Tsewang Choegyal "T.C." Tethong and raised in Victoria, the capital city of British Columbia, in Canada. Her mother is Canadian; her father was born in Tibet. Tethong grew up hearing about the Tibetan independence movement from her father, who worked in several official posts for the CTA in India. Doug Saunders, writing for the Toronto *Globe and Mail* (March 29, 2008), described Tsewang Tethong as a member of the "inner circle" of Tenzin Gyatso, the current Dalai Lama, or spiritual leader of Tibet. In the 1960s and early 1970s, Tsewang was the Dalai Lama's personal interpreter and assistant representative; he served as a chief coordinator for Tibetan settlements in South India and worked as a Tibetan education deputy. In India he met his future wife; the couple settled in Victoria in 1975. There, Tsewang taught for four years at Lester B. Pearson College and worked for the British Columbia Ministry of Social Services. He was called back to India by the Dalai Lama in 1996, to become his representative in Delhi, and was appointed Tibet's information minister a year later; he served in that post until 2001.

Lhadon Tethong was raised in an environment of activism. Her parents would take the family, which included Tethong's brother and sisters, to the city of Vancouver every March 10 (the anniversary of the 1959 Tibetan uprising) to demonstrate outside the Chinese Embassy. She told Sonya Fatah for the *Toronto Star* (March 19, 2008) that in Canada, raising awareness of the Tibetan cause was challenging. "We used to chant for [the group] Free Tibet and people would come up and ask us what a Tibet was, and what we were giving away for free," she said. Tethong started a chapter of SFT in 1996, while studying history at the University of King's College. A year earlier she had been in India when the Dalai Lama announced the selection of the 11th Panchen Lama, the second-most-revered Tibetan spiritual leader and, according to Tibetan religion, the reincarnation of the enlightened monk Amitabha. Subsequently, the Chinese government took into custody the newly selected Panchen Lama, the then–six-year-old Gedhun Choekyi Nyima, and replaced him with its approved Panchen Lama, prompting outrage from Tibetans and further spurring Tethong into activism. "I remember there being picnics and big celebrations [when the Panchen Lama's selection was announced], and then came the devastating news that the Panchen Lama had been taken away," Tethong told Richard Scheinin for the *San Jose (California) Mercury News* (April 8, 2000). "It's one of the most emotional subjects for Tibetans because it represents that ultimate loss of control that we feel. It brings it all

home . . . the ridiculous lengths that the Chinese will go through to destroy anything Tibetan."

In 1998 Tethong gave a speech about Tibetan independence before a crowd of 66,000 at the third annual Tibetan Freedom Concert, in Washington, D.C., one of a series of festivals held between 1996 and 2001 to raise awareness of—and money for— the Tibetan cause. The festivals were organized by members of the American hip-hop group the Beastie Boys, along with SFT and other groups. After graduating from college, Tethong went to work at the Toronto Stock Exchange, but her interest in Tibetan rights had not faded; in March 1999 she became a program coordinator at SFT's headquarters, in New York City. One of three staff members there, she was responsible for organizing seminars, public-speaking events, and campaigns. She would become one of the organization's most visible public figures, frequently appearing in the media over the next several years as SFT's representative.

In April 1999 Tethong joined a crowd of 600 Tibetans, exiled Chinese, and Taiwanese-Americans at Lafayette Park, in Washington, D.C., to protest China's human-rights violations. That June she spoke at the fourth annual Tibetan Freedom Concert, in Wisconsin. She returned to the U.S. capital in August to protest a World Bank project that would have financed the relocation of 58,000 Chinese farmers into a region known as Qinghai, the birthplace of the Dalai Lama—territory that Tibetans consider part of their homeland. During that protest Tethong addressed the crowd; according to an article in the *Vancouver Sun* (August 31, 1999), she told them, "We are here to help [then–World Bank President] James Wolfensohn, to dispel some myths, a myth that Tibet is a part of China." The World Bank's officials, she said, were "asking for ethnic conflict." The protest was part of an SFT campaign that also involved lobbying, mass e-mailing and faxing, media outreach, and the hanging of a flag over the World Bank building that read, "World Bank Approves China's Genocide in Tibet." In June 2000 World Bank officials announced that they would not fund the Chinese resettlement plan, after determining that the move would have violated the bank's own rules. While it is unclear to what extent such groups as SFT influenced that outcome, the history section on SFT's Web site reads, "In an unprecedented victory, a multi-faceted campaign led by SFT successfully blocks a World Bank project that would have financed the resettlement of 58,000 Chinese colonists into Tibet."

In February 2001 Tethong helped to organize a highly publicized SFT event in Beijing: a protest against a trade meeting between Canadian and Chinese officials. Two Canadian SFT members entered the room where the meeting was in progress and unfurled a banner that read "Free Tibet before Free Trade." On a February 13 Canadian Television News broadcast, Tethong defended the actions of the protestors, telling the news anchor that they "know they did the right thing" and that "this is the kind of action that we have to take to get the issue really on the table." She continued, "We've talked about [planning the protest] for a while. I mean it's very hard not to talk about all sorts of stuff like this when all the talk of trade with China barely has a mention of human rights on the part of the [Canadian] Prime Minister or any of the business leaders."

SFT also took action in 2001 to discourage the International Olympic Committee (IOC) from accepting China's bid to host the 2008 Olympics. Among other actions, SFT members sent to IOC members thousands of postcards depicting a Chinese protestor standing in the path of a government tank, alongside the caption, "Old Beijing, No Olympics," a play on China's slogan "New Beijing, New Olympics." The group also made phone calls, circulated petitions, sent e-mail messages to IOC members, and, when the committee met in Moscow, Russia, to vote on the location for the Games, sent flyers to committee members in their hotel rooms showing a Tibetan monk handcuffed by the Olympic rings logo. Tethong told Linda Robertson for the *Miami Herald* (July 13, 2001), "We figure those against us won't change their minds anyway, but that some voters can be swayed through education." Nonetheless, the IOC announced on July 13, 2001 that the 2008 Games would be held in Beijing. SFT issued a press release that quoted Tethong as saying, "We are outraged that the IOC has chosen to overlook the systematic destruction of Tibetan culture and human rights abuses committed by the Chinese government."

In 2002 Tethong protested with members of SFT and other groups outside the New York City hotel where Hu Jintao, then China's vice president and soon-to-be leader, was staying during a visit with U.S. officials. Jintao has reportedly taken a harsh stance toward Tibetans who protest Chinese rule. Tethong told Stephanie Gaskell for the Associated Press (April 29, 2002), "We want to let him know that he's not welcome here. We want to raise awareness with the American public that the future president of China is responsible for one of the darkest periods in our history." In 2004 SFT and a coalition of Tibetan advocacy groups persuaded the U.S. energy company BP to divest its stake in PetroChina, China's state-owned oil company, which sought to build an oil pipeline in Tibet. During the campaign Tethong met with BP shareholders to discuss China's human-rights issues. That year, after SFT's founder, John Hocevar, left to join the environmental-activist group Greenpeace, SFT's board of directors chose Tethong to succeed him as the organization's executive director.

In February 2006 the Internet company Google Inc. complied with the Chinese government's request to censor information related to Tibet and human rights on a Chinese version of the popular search engine Google.com. SFT protested that development, calling for a Valentine's Day boycott of Google and creating a Web site, NoLuv4Google.com, that encouraged Internet users not to visit the Google site on that day. More than 2,000 people around the world participated in the boycott. According to an Associated Press article available on FoxNews.com (February 15, 2006), officials from Google Inc. defended the censored search engine, calling it a compromise that would give Chinese more access to other information. In November 2006 SFT organized a protest in New Delhi, India, during a visit from Jintao, who by then had become president of China.

SFT staged another headline-making protest in April 2007, when five of its members—four Americans and one Canadian—unfurled banners at a Chinese base camp at Mount Everest, on the Tibet-Nepal border. The action came in response to announcements that the route of the Olympic torch relay would include the top of the mountain, a move seen by SFT and other pro-Tibet activists as an attempt by China to symbolize its claims to Tibet. "The Chinese government hopes to use the 2008 Olympic Games to conceal the brutality of its occupation of Tibet," Tethong, who was in Nepal at the time, told Scott McDonald for the Associated Press State & Local Wire (April 25, 2007). She added, "The International Olympic Committee has no business promoting the Chinese government's political agenda by allowing the torch to be run through Tibet." In August SFT made the news again, successfully circumventing Chinese Internet censorship, when members took live cellphone videos of themselves rappelling down the side of the Great Wall of China with a banner reading "One World, One Dream, Free Tibet 2008." They were able to transmit the videos back to the New York office using the Internet software Skype. The video was subsequently posted on the popular Web site YouTube.com. The Chinese government arrested several of the people involved.

Tethong is perhaps best known for her blog, BeijingWideOpen.org, which she began during a six-day trip to Beijing in August 2007. She had come to China on a tourist visa to observe the country's preparations for the Games; she started the blog to expose "how China is using the Olympics as a tool to cover up their occupation of Tibet and the brutality of their rule," as she put it to Agence France Presse (August 8, 2007). On the blog she posted written observations, video content, and audio clips about China's "propaganda campaign." In one post she called on visitors to the site who planned to attend the Games to stage peaceful protests. In another she posted a letter and video addressing IOC president Jacques Rogge as well as a recording of a phone call she made to the IOC. Her actions netted her an informal meeting with an IOC official, and according to the Agence France Presse article, the blog became "one of the more high-profile actions by a range of rights activists and campaigners who have vowed to ramp-up their activities targeting China as the 2008 Olympic Beijing Games draw closer." Within a few days of her arrival in Beijing, Tethong and a colleague were taken into custody by Chinese authorities, who criticized her actions but did not officially place her under arrest. Within two days she was sent back to Canada. SFT hailed both the arrest of the Great Wall protestors and Tethong's detention as positive developments, owing to the media coverage they generated.

On March 14, 2008 violent protests over Chinese rule, allegedly led by Tibetans, erupted in the Tibetan capital of Lhasa. Chinese and Tibetans were killed; officials on both sides continue to dispute the number of fatalities. Numerous Chinese business establishments were destroyed, apparently the result of arson by Tibetans frustrated over the influx of Chinese into the region. China quelled the riots with swift military action, and Britain, the U.S., and Germany condemned the country for its heavy-handed response. According to Christopher Bodeen, writing for the Associated Press (April 26, 2008), the events in Lhasa "galvanized critics of Beijing's communist regime and threatened to overshadow the Olympics, an object of massive national pride for China." Indeed, after the 2008 Olympic torch relay began, on March 24, the procession was marred in each city by waves of protestors, prompting debate among some world leaders over the merits of a boycott of the Games' opening ceremony.

The relay protests were largely the result of a concentrated effort by the ITSN. At a meeting held by the CTA in 2007, the umbrella group united all the major Tibet organizations in order to focus on demonstrations. In an article for the *Vancouver Sun* (April 19, 2008), Miro Cernetig noted that there are "three women . . . who have been key in making all those Olympic torch protests happen around the world." Cernetig named Kate Woznow, who ran SFT's Olympic protest campaign; Freya Putt, the ITSN Olympics coordinator; and Tethong.

Along with members of the other ITSN groups, Tethong followed the path of the torch relay. Although activists from the Paris-based press-freedom group Reporters Without Borders momentarily disrupted the torch-lighting ceremony in Greece, it was not until the torch reached London that organized protests truly began to affect China's plans for the city-to-city event. In London people from numerous groups attempted to impede the relay and grab the torch or extinguish its flame; according to Jerome Taylor, writing for the Lon*don Independent* (April 7, 2008), the events amounted to "a public relations embarrassment for both the British authorities and for the Chinese, who have desperately tried to bill the 130-day global odyssey as a 'journey of harmony.'" Tethong told Taylor, "Clearly, the journey of harmony is not as harmonious as the Chinese would have liked. Today they lost a huge amount of face and the protests will only get bigger as the torch continues its journey." In Paris the torch had to be extinguished several times due to protests, and on April 7, 2008 three SFT members were arrested for hanging two banners from the Golden Gate Bridge, in San Francis-

co, California, reading "One World One Dream" and "Free Tibet '08." On April 9 the torch passed through San Francisco, where its bearers encountered heavy demonstrations. Tethong gave a speech outside the Chinese Consulate, saying, as quoted by Marcus Wohlsen for the Associated Press (April 19, 2008), "This is about the Chinese government using the torch for political purposes. And we're going to use it right back." At the last moment city authorities had to reroute the torch's path due to security concerns.

In April 2008 Tethong spoke at a press conference held by the software giant Coca-Cola. SFT hoped to persuade the company, one of the main sponsors of the Olympics, to convince China that it should not allow the torch to pass through Tibet, as it was scheduled to do on June 21—as that would lead to further unrest there. According to Joe Guy Collier, writing for t*he Atlanta Journal-Constitution (*April 17, 2008), Tethong said, "Coke will be underwriting bloodshed in Tibet. This is not the time for the torch to go through Tibet." The torch did exactly that, however, amid a heavy security detail. On August 6, two days prior to the opening ceremonies of the Olympic Games, four SFT members hung pro-Tibet banners from light poles outside the site of the ceremonies, the stadium in Beijing known as the Bird's Nest. On the day of the ceremonies, three SFT members were detained after they hung Tibetan flags near the stadium, and the next day five SFT demonstrators were detained in Tiananmen Square after draping themselves in Tibetan flags and lying motionless on the ground in a protest known as a "die in." As quoted on phayul.com (August 9, 2008), Tethong said, "The voices of the Tibetan people will be heard despite the best attempts of the Chinese authorities to silence them."

Protests by SFT and other groups were held throughout the Games. On August 13 SFT members were detained and/or deported after "Free Tibet" banners were raised in Beijing's Chinese Ethnic Culture Park, where a Tibetan cultural exhibit had been set up. SFT claimed that the park was being used as a "tool" to portray peaceful relations between Chinese and Tibetans. "While Tibetan song and dance is on display in Beijing, in Tibet, our culture is under siege and our people are being forcibly kept from speaking out about their repression," Tethong said, as quoted by Bill Schiller in the *Toronto (Ontario, Canada) Star* (August 14, 2008). On August 15 two activists hung a banner near the Beijing headquarters of CCTV, on an outer wall of the building housing China's state-controlled television news service. "While the Chinese government has built a gleaming new building for its official mouthpiece and its public relations strategy has become more sophisticated, the propaganda it uses to maintain its iron-fisted control over Tibet remains the same," Tethong said, as quoted by *Asian Political News* (August 18, 2008). On August 22, two days before the close of the Games, SFT held a press conference declaring the protests a success. On the night of the closing ceremony, China yielded to pressure from the U.S. and Britain to release from detention eight Americans, one Briton, and one German from detention. All 10 had been arrested a week earlier after participating in protests on behalf of SFT and had been sentenced to 10 days of detention. Tethong accused the Chinese government of trying to keep news of the detentions out of the media. According to Jill Drew, writing for the *Washington Post* (August 25, 2008), Tethong said, "After two days of negative publicity over its extra-judicial detention of 10 Tibet supporters, the Chinese government is seeking to suppress a story that would have cast a shadow over the closing ceremony of these Olympic Games, which includes a final propaganda push to legitimize China's rule in Tibet, with Tibetans singing and dancing along with other so-called 'ethnic minorities.'" SFT has continued to protest Chinese rule of Tibet worldwide.

—W.D.

Suggested Reading: (Toronto) *Globe and Mail* (on-line) Mar. 29, 2008; *Toronto Star* AA p3 Aug. 10, 2007, AA p2 Mar. 19, 2008

Ben Russell, courtesy of Grove Atlantic Press

Thomas, Michael

Aug. 21, 1967– Writer; educator

Address: Hunter College, Office 1203, 695 Park Ave., New York, NY 10065

In December 2007, when the *New York Times* published its much-anticipated list of the top 10 books of 2007, the first title listed was *Man Gone Down*, the debut novel by the 39-year-old Michael Thomas—a compelling dissection of the American Dream and racism, celebrated for its poetic language and forceful evocation of life. The novel's content mirrors many of Thomas's own experiences as an African-American man, recounting the main character's attempts to navigate the complicated American racial milieu; to work through the guilt he feels over his biracial children, whom he calls the "wreckage of miscegenation"; and to escape from his perpetual sense of struggle in the often unforgiving city of New York. Among the publications that have championed the novel are the *Washington Post* and *Booklist*, whose review described *Man Gone Down* as "a rhapsodic and piercing post-9/11 lament over aggression, greed, and racism, and a ravishing blues for the soul's unending loneliness."

The youngest of three children, Michael Thomas was born on August 21, 1967 in Boston, Massachusetts, to Thelma and David Milton Thomas. Thelma Thomas, who was originally from Virginia, met her husband, a Boston native, when he was studying philosophy at Boston University. The two began raising their children in Allston, Massachusetts, where Michael attended the Thomas Gardner Elementary School. When busing—the practice of sending children to schools outside their neighborhoods in order to achieve racial integration—began in Boston, in 1974, the Thomases removed Michael from the school and enrolled him in the private Buckingham Browne & Nichols School, in Cambridge, Massachusetts, which he attended through fourth grade. The negotiation between his life at home and life at the private school was difficult: "I had my friends in the neighborhood who didn't understand why we had to go somewhere else to school and then my school friends who didn't understand my life [in my neighborhood]," he told David Mehegan for the *Boston Globe* (March 3, 2007, on-line). "One day I'd be horseback riding and the next it would be breaking windows." Two years later Thelma and David Thomas divorced, and Michael and his siblings stayed with their mother. In 1978 Thelma Thomas and her children moved to Newton, Massachusetts, a more affluent and predominantly white suburb of Boston, where school administrators made Michael take standardized tests repeatedly, apparently not believing that his high scores were legitimate. The school's officials showed skepticism about his knowledge and ability in other ways as well. "In the eighth grade, a guidance counselor wanted to steer me toward vocational and technical [curriculum]," Thomas recalled to Mehegan. "I got put in a remedial reading group. I had read *Hamlet* and mythology in the fifth grade."

During those years Thomas tried to compensate for the absence of his father by reading his father's books. When he was younger, Thomas had listened as his father read classical literature and philosophical texts to him; he considered that ritual to be their special bond. David Thomas expected high achievement from his son. "I was supposed to *be* something," Michael Thomas told Mehegan, "professor, ambassador, president—supposed to go to Harvard. There were good [African-American] models—Charles Hamilton Houston, Thurgood Marshall, [Martin Luther] King, Andrew Young." Referring to a hard-living blues musician, he added, "But I think I had more Leadbelly in me than those folks." Beginning in middle school, Thomas kept journals in which he wrote poems.

After graduating from high school, Thomas attended Connecticut College, in New London, Connecticut, for one semester before dropping out to travel through Europe. He returned to the school after his time abroad but again dropped out. It was at Connecticut College that he met a fellow student, Michaele, a dance major who became his wife in 1993. Together they moved to New York and had three children, who were 11, seven, and six years old in early 2007. At first Thomas tried his hand at music, attempting to become a singer-songwriter. Finding that to be difficult because of his stage fright, he was forced to find odd jobs, including work as a bicycle messenger and carpenter; published sources indicate that he also tried his hand at being a restaurateur and filmmaker. Eventually he began attending Hunter College, in New York, where he earned his bachelor's degree in English literature. He took graduate courses at Brown University, in Providence, Rhode Island, before earning his M.F.A. degree in creative writing at Warren Wilson College, in Swannanoa, North Carolina. After completing his education, he began teaching at his alma mater, Hunter College, where he remains on the faculty.

Although Thomas had been writing poems and short stories for some time, it came as a surprise to him when, in 2002, a friend suggested that one of his stories ought to be expanded into a novel. Thomas, who had never before considered the possibility of writing a novel, set about doing so. After 18 months of writing, he found a literary agent who sent the manuscript to Elisabeth Schmitz, the executive editor at the Grove/Atlantic publishing company. Grove/Atlantic accepted the novel and published it as a paperback rather than as a more expensive hardcover, to make both booksellers and readers more likely to purchase it. Schmitz told Mehegan about *Man Gone Down*, "I read it and fell in love with it. It was the most moving, intelligent, provocative book."

Man Gone Down centers on its 35-year-old, black narrator, a New Yorker who is in a troubled marriage to a white woman and has only four days to come up with $12,000 for his family's rent and his children's tuition—and, in the process, to reestablish his own faith in the American Dream. A floundering writer accustomed to failure, Thomas's protagonist must overcome not only the racial and other societal challenges facing him, but also his personal demons: specifically, his estrangement from his father as a child in 1970s Boston and his being a victim of rape. Thomas's style is unusual, making shifts in chronology and frequent leaps from reality to fantasy. The novelist explained to Mehegan, "The lens through which the narrator sees the world is similar to mine in dealing with memory and the fragmentation of self and consciousness, reconciling or synthesizing the many broken parts."

"It's a tough marketplace for intelligent, literary fiction by a debut writer," Schmitz told Mehegan. Thus, when Kaiama L. Glover published a front-page article in the February 4, 2007 edition of the *New York Times Book Review* in praise of *Man Gone Down*, Schmitz was as surprised as Thomas. Glover extolled Thomas for his negotiation between hopelessness and hope, nihilism and love, egocentrism and vulnerability. Although she acknowledged that the narrator, who refers to himself as Ishmael, "indulges at times in an arrogant self-pity that can undermine sympathy for his plight" and that "*Man Gone Down* might have been shorter," her review was largely glowing. "The scope of Thomas's project is prodigious . . . ," she wrote, "and the end result is an impressive success. He has an exceptional eye for detail, and the poetry of his descriptive digressions—'the heaving surface of the water is what the night sky should be—moving and wild, wavering reflections of buildings on both sides, dark and bright, like thin, shimmering clouds'—provides some respite from the knowledge that the city he loves can truly crush a man's spirit . . . . Thomas seems to have fully embraced the 'write what you know' ethos. And what he knows is how the odds are stacked in America. He knows the unlikelihood of successful black fatherhood. He knows that things are set up to keep the Other poor and the poor in their place. More than anything else, he knows how little but also—fortunately—how much it can take to bring a man down." In December 2007 the *Times* chose *Man Gone Down* as one of the best books of 2007.

Thomas continues to teach at Hunter College. He lives in Brooklyn, New York, with his wife and three children and is currently at work on two new books.

—T.O.

Suggested Reading: *New York Times Book Review* (on-line) Feb. 4, 2007; *Boston Globe* (on-line) Mar. 3, 2007

Selected Books: *Man Gone Down*, 2007

Courtesy of Viking/Penguin

Turin, Luca

Nov. 20, 1953– Biophysicist; scent creator and critic

Address: Flexitral Inc., 4001 Westfax Dr., Chantilly, VA 20151; 11 Herbert St., London NW5 4HA, England

Luca Turin "is not just a fragrance chemist," as Vicki Allan wrote for the Sydney, Australia, *Sunday Herald* (May 21, 2006). "He is one of those unorthodox scientists—originally a biophysicist—who has transcended disciplines and dared to come up with a big theory." That "big theory" proposes that smell is dependent not on the shape of the molecules of the substance emitting an odor, as most scientists believe, but on the speed of vibration of the bonds of that substance's molecules. When Turin introduced his theory, in 1995, specialists in his field immediately labeled him a renegade of olfactory science, and that label has remained: to date, his theory has not been corroborated by any other scientist. At the same time, it has never been disproved, and some of Turin's findings cannot be explained by other theories. Turin is the subject of the biography *The Emperor of Scent: A Story of Perfume, Obsession, and the Last Mystery of the Senses* (2002), by Chandler Burr (who currently critiques fragrance for the *New York Times*). Interested since early childhood in the nature of odors, Turin has taught at University College London, a division of the University of London, in England; acted as a consultant for major perfume producers; and published three books about perfume: *Parfums: Le Guide*, written in French; *The Secret of Scent: Adventures in Per-*

fume and the Science of Smell; and *Perfumes: The Guide*, which is a revised, English version of his first book and was written with his wife, Tania Sanchez. In a review of *The Secret of Scent* for the *New York Times* (December 3, 2006), John Lanchester described Turin as "a brilliantly readable perfume critic" and wrote that he "has an extraordinary gift for writing about smell." Turin is the chief technological officer for Flexitral, a Chantilly, Virginia–based company that uses Turin's odor-prediction technology to develop fragrances far more quickly and less expensively than is possible with traditional methods.

The scent industry accounts for about $14 billion in sales annually. In addition to perfumes (currently, 600 to 1,000 new scents are introduced every year), scents are added to a large array of products, among them soaps and detergents, deodorants and other toiletries, room fresheners, candies, and even new cars. With the costs of many natural scents, such as sandalwood, increasing exponentially in recent years, the quest for artificially created chemical scents has intensified. Thus, potentially, Turin's work could revolutionize the industry.

Luca Turin was born on November 20, 1953 in Beirut, Lebanon, to Adela Mandelli and Duccio Turin, a leading expert in the field known as building or construction economics. Both of his parents, who met in Italy, were Argentinians of Italian descent. Mandelli was a designer for the couturier Lanvin Castillo during the 1950s and 1960s, while Duccio Turin worked as an architect and town planner with the United Nations Refugee Welfare Association; his assignments included designing refugee camps for Palestinians. Soon after Luca Turin's birth, the family settled in Paris, France, where Duccio Turin joined the staff of the Centre Scientifique et Technique du Batiment, which is concerned with the construction of human habitation. In 1957 he resumed working for the United Nations and moved with his family to Geneva, Switzerland, where he and his wife soon divorced.

Luca was extremely unhappy in Geneva, so his mother returned to Paris, where she became the art director for an advertising agency. Meanwhile, at age four, Luca had learned to read, absorbing the reading lessons that his mother was giving to his Spanish nanny. When he was seven his mother rented a beach house on the Côte d'Azur (a famous resort area known in English as the French Riviera). "The moment we arrived in this strange place he set about systematically analyzing the smell of the thyme that grew wild everywhere," his mother recalled to Chandler Burr. Back in Paris, Turin became enamored with science and enjoyed visiting the Palais de la Découverte, a science museum. According to Burr, as a youth "he was famous for boring everyone to death with useless, disconnected facts, like the distance between the earth and the moon in Egyptian cubits."

Turin and his mother later moved to Milan, Italy, where Mandelli had taken a job as the manager of product and image design with Upim, a department store. Later, in 1974, she founded a feminist publishing house for children's books, called Dalla Parte delle Bambine. (It currently operates under the name Du Côte des Filles.)

Earlier, in 1966, Duccio Turin had joined the faculty of the Bartlett School of Architecture at University College London. In 1976 he served as a deputy secretary-general for the United Nations Habitat Conference in Vancouver, Canada. Within days of its conclusion, he was killed in a car crash. The book *Construction and Economic Development: Planning of Human Settlements: Essays in Memory of Duccio Turin*, edited by Otto H. Koenigsberger, was published in 1978.

Luca Turin earned a Ph.D. in physiology and biophysics at University College London in 1982. After his graduation he moved to the south of France, near Nice, to conduct research in marine biology at the Villefranche Marine Station as an employee of the Centre National de Recherche Scientifique. During his free time he often hunted for perfumes in retail shops. At the suggestion of someone he met on one such excursion, he visited Claudine Pillaud, a purveyor of rare perfumes in Menton. Pillaud sold perfumes only to customers whom she liked. At their first meeting Turin impressed her when he correctly identified the principal note in the perfume Bellodgia as carnation. (The ingredients of any perfume are divided into three categories called notes, each of which evaporates at a different rate.) Pillaud sold him a one-ounce tester bottle of Diorama, the first fragrance Christian Dior marketed after World War II, which contained perfume made according to its original formula. Like many other perfumes, in the early 1980s Diorama was being manufactured with cheaper materials; the materials for the original formulations were not only rare but very expensive. "The financial temptation to dilute perfumes is almost irresistible," Turin explained to Burr. Referring to the oil of the agarwood tree, which is used as a base for perfumes, he continued, "I mean, if you can make your oudh go twice as far. . . . Instead of using ten kilos you use five, and given how much this stuff costs per gram, the temptation to futz is just irresistible. It's why Guerlain and Chanel and Jean Patou . . . are so great. Not necessarily expensive perfumes. Just great ones that are never, ever diluted. No tricks, no cheating, no cutting corners. But today all bets are off. When the big fragrance firms take L'Air du Temps and wreck it by having an accountant redraw the formula to take out the expensive ingredients and substitute cheap ones, what they are doing, among other things, is depriving thousands of people throughout the world of the thrill of the memories that are infused with L'Air du Temps, because unless it is the same smell, it won't trigger [a memory]. The pale new reflection may be intellectually, objectively, a reflection . . . but your brain stem isn't electrified. Mem-

ory isn't triggered." Thereafter, during that period, Turin spent a great deal of his money on collector perfumes.

In 1990 an American friend of Turin's told him that the United States Navy was interested in researching and developing sensors to detect odors from enemy submarines in order to trail them, and that the Department of Defense was going to award grants for such studies. Turin applied for a grant, but before he had heard back from the Department of Defense, he was asked to leave the Centre National de Recherche Scientifique, after inadvertently implicating a famed French scientist in a case of fraud. Turin then moved to North Carolina, where he had gotten a position at a branch of the National Institutes of Health (NIH). Soon afterward the funding for the NIH project on which he was working ran out, and he returned to Paris. Unemployed, he began to write perfume reviews, both for his own amusement and as a source of income. The first three fragrances he critiqued were Grace à Rive Gauche, Après l'Ondée, and Vetiver. Of the first he wrote in *Parfums: Le Guide* (as translated into English), "Thanks to Rive Gauche, mortals can at last know the scent of the goddess Diana's bath soap. A true emblem of the 70s, this sumptuous reinterpretation of the innovative metallic note found in the less fortunate Calandre (Paco Rabanne) belongs to the uncrowded category of sculpture-perfumes. Its seamless silvery form, initially hidden by white, powdery notes, soon pierces the clouds and gains height by the hour."

Hermès agreed to publish Turin's collection of reviews, with the title *Parfums: Le Guide*, in 1992. Now out of print (in the French version), it became the best-selling perfume guide in France and caught the attention of the world's seven major perfume producers: International Flavors and Fragrances, Givaudan Roure, Quest International, Firmenich, Haarmann & Reimer, Dragoco, and Takasago. At the invitation of Quest International, Turin visited the company's labs to see how their perfumes were made and voice his opinions on various fragrances.

Still unemployed, Turin moved to Moscow, Russia, after accepting an offer of a visiting professorship from the Moscow State University Institute of Molecular Biology. Soon tiring of that job, he contacted a former professor of his at University College London and secured a teaching job there in 1993. At the same time the U.S. Navy notified Turin that he had won the $60,000 in research funds that he had requested. One day, while perusing a copy of the *Review of Scientific Instruments*, he read about an electron-tunneling spectroscope, a device that measures the vibrations of the molecular bonds of particular substances and thereby indicates the identity of the substances. The mode of operation of the spectroscope led Turin to wonder if, with regard to detecting scents, the nose might work in a similar manner, by somehow distinguishing among molecular vibrations in the act that we call smelling. (An earlier scientist, Malcolm Dyson, suggested in 1938 that the nose operated like a gas chromatograph—an idea that was instantly and universally dismissed.) The accepted theory of the mechanism of the sense of smell centers on the shape of given molecules. Turin questioned the validity of that theory; as he told an interviewer for the London *Daily Mirror* (November 27, 1995), "Smell must be written in molecules, but no one has been able to read that language. It's a bit like an archaeologist trying to decipher hieroglyphics."

Turin acquired the use of a Quest International lab, where he began to test his theory by comparing the scents and vibrations of borane (a compound, not found in nature, composed of hydrogen and boron) and the element sulfur. Turin showed that molecules of borane and sulfur differ in shape but have similar odors and similar vibration speeds; thus, he concluded, vibration must determine the smell. He also found that acetophenone (a chemical, found in several fruits and elsewhere, that is used in the manufacture of fragrances) and deuterated acetophenone (acetophenone to which deuterium, an isotope of hydrogen, has been added) have dissimilar odors and different molecular vibrations yet are the same shape and size. When he submitted a paper describing his hypothesis and experimental results to the prestigious scientific journal *Nature*, the editor rejected it, declaring in a letter, "The major body of the paper is an extremely rambling case-by-case discussion of specific molecules and their shapes. I find this quite unconvincing and virtually irrelevant." In 1996 a far less influential journal, *Chemical Senses*, published Turin's paper.

That year Turin became an outside evaluator for Quest International's fragrances. The company, which was in the process of negotiating a contract to produce Dior fragrances, fired him after he told the French beauty magazine *Votre Beauté* that Dior had unfavorably altered its perfumes by using cheaper ingredients. Quest kept him on briefly, however, to experiment with scent prediction—that is, predicting how a newly created perfume ingredient will smell—and he developed a computer algorithm to analyze the potential scent of a molecule based on its vibrations. Traditionally, in creating new scents, other producers relied on a system of trial and error: technicians had to build molecules, which experts then sniffed, and often, as many as 2,000 molecules were constructed before one or two were deemed satisfactory. That labor-intensive process was extremely costly.

After Turin's association with Quest ended, representatives of another perfume manufacturer, Takasago, met with him once, to talk about developing a machine to create musk-scented molecules, then opted not to deal with him. Burr claimed that the major firms' rejection of Turin stemmed from reasons unrelated to the merits of his approach. "We want to believe that science is dispassionate, objective, and (for those who don't have use for a theological god), omniscient," Burr wrote. "We want to believe that every idea that merits attention is given it. That the good ideas are kept, the bad ones discarded, the industrious rise, the lazy sink, and the hard work and honest data are rewarded. This isn't real. Perhaps unfortunately, perhaps not. Scientists are human. Vested interests beat out new ideas. Egos smother creativity. Personalities clash. Corruption is as common as the survival instinct."

In 2001 a newly launched firm, Flexitral, hired Turin as its chief technological officer. According to its Web site, "The strategy followed by Flexitral since its creation late in 2001 is to identify the fragrance and flavor industry's most pressing needs and answer them by rational odorant design. Flexitral has developed methods to predict the smell of a molecule before it is synthesized. . . . Products were reached after synthetic programs of less than ten molecules." Within the first year, with only $1 million in investments, the company produced two new scents: Acitral and Lioral, which are redolent of lemon and lily-of-the-valley, respectively. Flexitral's products currently include, in addition to Acitral B and Lioral, the jasmine-tinged floral Jasphene, the violet-like Neoctin, the carnation-fragranced Nugenol, the black-currant-like Ribescone, the coumarin-like Coumane, and two rosy-citrus scents, called Tricitrol and Trinalool.

Turin has acknowledged that his theory is more a rebuttal of current theories than an empirically sound explanation of the mechanism of smell. He told Mick O'Hare for *New Scientist* (November 18, 2006), "Every scientist has two jobs—demolition and construction. I've done a good demolition job. . . . Demolition is OK, but what do you construct instead? Empirically the easiest test of vibrational theory would be if different isotopes of the same element smelled different. For example, if you replace hydrogen with heavy hydrogen, the molecular shape is identical but the vibration is different. So do isotopes smell different or not? There's no consensus."

Turin's second book is *The Secret of Scent: Adventures in Perfume and the Science of Smell* (2006). Although most critics acknowledged Turin's ability to write lyrically about perfumes, they often found his scientific explanations of vibration theory and other matters impenetrable. The book "is an admirably sustained feat of evocation," Alex Butterworth wrote for the London *Observer* (May 14, 2006), "and if the cumulative effect is a little heady, there is real poetry here to stimulate our jaded perception." In a review for *Time Out* (May 17, 2006), Leila Dewji wrote, "From the outside, the world of perfume seems glamorous, exotic, and sexy; but once you reduce it to molecular structures, atomic weights, and the Nobel-winning findings of lesser-known Croatian chemists, it all becomes rather laborious and dull. There are pages of incomprehensible diagrams, and it's not always clear which part of the text they're illustrating." The English edition of *Parfums: Le Guide*, which Turin rewrote with his wife, Tania Sanchez, was published in 2008.

Turin has said that fragrance is so important to him that if he had not met a woman who shared his passion for it, he would have stayed unmarried. He and his wife live in London.

—T.O.

Suggested Reading: (London) *Daily Telegraph* p6 June 17, 2006; (London) *Sunday Times* (on-line) Feb. 2, 1997; *New Scientist* p3434 Jan. 3, 1998; *New York Times* p32 Dec. 3, 2006; *Vancouver (Canada) Sun* B p7 Mar. 30, 2004; Burr, Chandler. *The Emperor of Scent*, 2002

Selected Books: *Parfums: Le Guide*, 1992; *The Secret of Scent: Adventures in Perfume and the Science of Smell*, 2006; *Perfumes: The Guide*, 2008

Courtesy of Lydia Villa-Komaroff

Villa-Komaroff, Lydia

(VEE-yuh–KOH-mah-rahf, LID-ee-uh)

Aug. 7, 1947– Molecular biologist; teacher; businesswoman

Address: Cytonome Inc., 27 Drydock Ave., Fifth Fl., Boston, MA 02210

"The two most important things to me are first, that my job be interesting and challenging; and second, by doing my job, I make a difference." By all accounts, Lydia Villa-Komaroff, who expressed this sentiment in an autobiographical sketch she wrote for the Society for the Advancement of Chicanos and Native Americans in Science (SACNAS, 2002,

on-line), has made an indelible difference to humanity as a molecular biologist, educator, college and research-institute administrator, businesswoman—and as a co-founder, in 1973, of SACNAS. The mission of SACNAS, as described on its Web site, is "to encourage Chicano/Latino and Native American students to pursue graduate education and obtain the advanced degrees necessary for science research, leadership, and teaching careers at all levels." Villa-Komaroff, who is of Spanish and Mexican descent, earned a doctoral degree in cell biology from the Massachusetts Institute of Technology (MIT) in 1975, thereby becoming only the third Mexican-American woman in U.S. history to complete a Ph.D. in the sciences.

As a postdoctoral fellow at Harvard University in the late 1970s, Villa-Komaroff contributed to pioneering work by a team headed by the future Nobel laureate Walter Gilbert that demonstrated that bacteria with recombinant DNA can produce insulin, a hormone vital to the production of energy within human cells. Villa-Komaroff went on to conduct research and/or teach at the University of Massachusetts Medical School, Harvard Medical School, Children's Hospital in Boston, and Northwestern University; in the last-named institution, she served as the associate vice president and then vice president of research. She later held that title and that of chief operating officer at the Whitehead Institute for Biomedical Research, an independent research facility affiliated with MIT. She became the chief scientific officer of Cytonome Inc., a developer and manufacturer of medical devices, in 2005; since 2006 she has also served that firm as chief executive officer. "Women can have it all, but not necessarily at the same time," Villa-Komaroff commented to Dyke Hendrickson for *Mass High Tech: The Journal of New England Technology* (March 27, 2006, on-line). "Women's careers aren't always linear. You can accomplish what you want, though not necessarily with the same schedule as men." In 2008 the Museum of Science and Industry in Tampa, Florida, named Villa-Komaroff the National Hispanic Scientist of the Year.

The oldest of six siblings, Villa-Komaroff was born Lydia Villa on August 7, 1947 in Las Vegas, New Mexico (not Nevada), near Santa Fe. According to a family story, while her paternal grandparents were fleeing Mexico during the Mexican Revolution (1911–20), soldiers loyal to the Mexican revolutionary leader Pancho Villa threatened to kill her grandfather. His life was saved by Villa himself: when he learned her grandfather's surname, Villa ordered him to "have lots of sons." Her grandparents' nine sons and three daughters included Villa-Komaroff's father, John Dias Villa. The ancestors of her mother, Drucilla Jaramillo Villa, came to the U.S. from Spain generations ago and settled in the Southwest. Villa-Komaroff's father was a teacher and musician; he played with the Santa Fe Symphony. Her mother was a social worker and teacher. The first in their families to attend college, her parents encouraged their children to get a good education and to follow their dreams. As of the late 1990s, according to the newsletter of the American Society for Cell Biology (ASCB, 1998, on-line), the first of Villa-Komaroff's brothers, Richard, was an investigator for a federal defense agency; her brother Roland (who died in 2003) was a music teacher and jazz musician, and the third, Lorenz, was a fifth-grade teacher; her sister Katherine was a lawyer and the other sister, Dorothea, the vice president of a small bank. "I believe that growing up in a large Mexican-American family taught me the value of collaboration and competition," Villa-Komaroff wrote in her SAC-NAS autobiographical sketch.

When Lydia was five years old, her father brought home a set of the *World Book Encyclopedia*. "He said that everything I wanted to know was in those books," Villa-Komaroff recalled to an interviewer for the book *Journeys of Women in Science and Engineering: No Universal Constants* (1997). "I was very excited by that notion. He bought the books and my mother read to us—that's one of my earliest and warmest childhood memories." Villa-Komaroff's mother and grandmother had a strong interest in nature, particularly in plants, and one of her uncles was a chemist who worked at Sandia Laboratories and then Bell Laboratories. Thanks to their influences, Villa-Komaroff has said, by the age of nine she already knew that she wanted to pursue a career in science.

The summer before her senior year at Santa Fe High School, Villa-Komaroff received a scholarship from the National Science Foundation that enabled her, along with other minority students, to attend the Summer Science Training Program at Texas College, in Tyler, Texas. In 1965, after her high-school graduation, she enrolled at the University of Washington in Seattle. Advised by one professor that chemistry was not a suitable field for women, and fascinated by a course in developmental biology, she changed her major from chemistry to biology during her sophomore year. Her boyfriend at that time, Anthony Komaroff, was a student at the University of Washington Medical School. In 1968, after Komaroff completed his internship in Cambridge, Massachusetts, and began work in Bethesda, Maryland, in the National Office of Regional Medical Programs, Villa-Komaroff transferred to Goucher College, in Towson, Maryland, a women's college (it has since admitted men, too) with "very good chemistry and biology departments," as she told the ASCB interviewer; it was also the sister school of nearby Johns Hopkins University and was affiliated with the National Institutes of Health (NIH) in Bethesda, Maryland. During summers Villa-Komaroff worked in the laboratory of Loretta Leive, an NIH microbiologist; Leive, she told the ASCB interviewer, "browbeat me into applying to MIT for graduate school." Villa-Komaroff graduated cum laude from Goucher with a B.A. degree in biology in 1970. In June of that year, she and Anthony Komaroff married, and that fall Villa-Komaroff enrolled at MIT, in Cam-

bridge—the only graduate school that had accepted her—to pursue a Ph.D. in biology.

Villa-Komaroff and her few female classmates were often subjected to sexist remarks from their male colleagues. "There were some people who didn't think women belonged, but the other women graduate students and I simply avoided them. I must say that I was pretty oblivious to the attitudes of others about my being a woman in science. I guess that was a blessing because I never felt I didn't belong or shouldn't be pursuing something that I loved," she said to the *Journeys of Women in Science and Engineering* interviewer. "I learned early on that it's a very good ploy to act confident even when you're not because then people perceive you as confident, and that makes a big difference." In 1973 Villa-Komaroff co-founded the Society for the Advancement of Chicanos and Native Americans in Science, to encourage Latino and Native American students to pursue careers in science and teaching. "It has always been difficult to maintain a steady level of interest in science in America, and it is especially difficult to get minorities interested in science," she said to Bruce E. Phillips for *Hispanic Engineer* (December 31, 2003).

At MIT, which she has described as "graduate school heaven," Villa-Komaroff decided to specialize in molecular biology rather than developmental biology, after she concluded that the former was "more active," as the ASCB reporter put it. She was mentored there by two professors who shared laboratory space: David Baltimore, who won the Nobel Prize in physiology and medicine in 1975, and Harvey Lodish, now the head of a molecular-biology laboratory at MIT and the Whitehead Institute. Under their supervision Villa-Komaroff began a research project involving polio-virus RNA (ribonucleic acid) and the mechanisms by which the virus produces proteins. Baltimore and Lodish were "demanding, and you [had] to be a self-starter and enjoy competition," she told the ASCB interviewer, but working with them, she said, was "spectacular" and "the most fun part of my life." "Mentors don't always go out of their way for you," she told Dyke Hendrickson; "you often have to approach them. But they generally are experienced and can provide valuable advice and direction." Villa-Komaroff earned her Ph.D. in cell biology in 1975.

Having won a three-year Helen Hay Whitney Postdoctoral Fellowship, Villa-Komaroff next became a research fellow at Harvard University, in Cambridge, Massachusetts. In the laboratory of the biologist Fotis C. Kafatos, she began using recombinant DNA technology, in which a cell's DNA is changed by splicing it and inserting into it strands of DNA from other sources. In 1976 the city of Cambridge, for reasons similar to those voiced by opponents of cloning, banned the use of recombinant DNA, and Villa-Komaroff was forced to continue her research elsewhere; she moved to the Cold Spring Harbor Laboratory, on Long Island, New York, which was headed by James Watson, a co-discoverer of the helical structure of DNA. There, she worked under the microbiologist Tom Maniatis. She returned to Harvard a year later, after the ban on recombinant-DNA studies was lifted, and joined a research team headed by the molecular biologist and future Nobel laureate Walter Gilbert. In 1978 she and her colleagues demonstrated that bacteria modified by recombinant DNA could produce insulin—the first instance in which a human hormone had been created by bacteria.

Also in 1978 Villa-Komaroff left Harvard to join the Department of Molecular Genetics and Microbiology at the University of Massachusetts Medical Center, in Worcester, as an assistant professor; in 1982 she was promoted to associate professor. Two years later a committee composed of members of her department questioned whether to award her tenure (thereby making her employment permanent), because Villa-Komaroff had not published any articles in professional journals since her arrival at the school and thus had not fulfilled one of the requirements for tenure. Villa-Komaroff attributed the absence of papers on her résumé to her heavy teaching schedule, her overcommitment to committee work, and her excessive meticulousness in writing scientific papers. Her fight for tenure ended in her favor, but it strained her relationship with various administrators and professors. For that reason, in 1985 Villa-Komaroff accepted a nontenured position as an associate professor in Harvard Medical School's Department of Neurology. That job came with a lighter teaching load and more time to devote to research. She also worked as a senior research associate at the Children's Hospital in Boston and was appointed the associate director of its mental-retardation research center in 1987. Between 1985 and 1995 Villa-Komaroff coauthored more than 60 scientific papers concerning such topics as growth factors in human brain development and the cell biology of insulin-producing cells. From 1990 to 1993 she also served as the vice president of SACNAS.

Villa-Komaroff and her work were featured in a one-hour documentary called *DNA Detective*, broadcast in 1995 on PBS television stations as part of its Discovering Women series. The film showed Villa-Komaroff investigating a protein that she hypothesized might be responsible for the occurrence of megalencephaly, a rare neurological disorder in which the brain and head of a fetus or infant grow abnormally large. "Things don't always happen the way you want them to" in science, Villa-Komaroff said during the film, in what many sources, quoting a WGBH Educational Foundation press release, described as "a meditation on the value of failure as a tool in science." Also in 1995 she accepted an offer from Northwestern University, in Chicago, Illinois, to join the faculty of the Department of Neurology with the rank of professor. Concurrently, she served as the associate vice president (1995–97) and then vice president (1998–2002) of Northwestern's extensive research programs, which encompassed some 2,000 projects. To prepare for that

administrative job, she took courses at MIT's Sloan School of Management. Her transition from researcher to administrator suited her. "As I got older, I found that I wanted to think about science in a more global way," she explained in 2002 in her SACNAS sketch. "It gave me as much satisfaction to help another scientist find out how to get answers as it did to do my own experiments. Now my job is to help create an environment where other scientists can more easily do their work. I love my job and did not imagine when I was a student that I might one day have a job this satisfying and enjoyable." During her seven years at the school, Villa-Komaroff helped to establish nine new research centers at Northwestern, among them the Institute for Bioengineering and Nanoscience in Advanced Medicine and the Center for Functional Genomics; she was also pivotal in the creation of a clinical-research and training office and a program that provided grants to faculty members and students to travel to research conferences around the world. For much of that time, Villa-Komaroff was apart from her husband, who had remained in Boston. When asked about the separation, she told the ASCB interviewer in 1998, "We were determined to make it work and it has. We get together once every two weeks in either Boston or Chicago. For two workaholics, it may be ideal."

In 2003 Villa-Komaroff left Northwestern to become the vice president of research and chief operating officer at the Whitehead Institute for Biomedical Research. "My job now is to make the place run smoothly so people can do really good science," she told Bruce E. Phillips. Villa-Komaroff also took on lecturing duties at the Sloan School of Management. That year she was named one of the 100 most influential Hispanics in the U.S. by *Hispanic Business* and among the 50 most important Hispanics by *Hispanic Engineer*. She was also elected to the board of directors of Transkaryotic Therapies (TKT), a Cambridge-based biopharmaceutical company specializing in the development of treatments for rare diseases. She played an active role in the sale of the company to Shire Pharmaceuticals Group, a British drug manufacturer, for $1.6 billion in mid-2005. Villa-Komaroff left the Whitehead Institute that year to become the chief scientific officer for Cytonome Inc., in Boston. She was appointed CEO a year later. "We're moving away from research and development and into commercialization, so we need a strong manager," she told Mark Hollmer for the *Boston Business Journal* (January 1, 2007, on-line). The company markets the Gigasort, a device that can sort 144,000 cells per second—seven times faster than other cell-sorters. In one example of how it might be used, the Gigasort can separate useful cells from harmful cells in bone marrow for transplantation into leukemia or lymphoma victims, "to reduce the risk of graft-versus-host disease," in Hollmer's words, which occurs when newly introduced immune-system cells recognize the patient's tissues as "foreign" and attack them.

Villa-Komaroff's career-related activities include service on many committees and groups. Among others, she sat on the advisory board of the National Science Foundation's Biological Sciences Directorate from 1994 to 1999, on the board of directors of the National Center for Genome Resources from 1995 to 2000, and on the American Association for the Advancement of Science from 2000 to 2005. She currently serves on the National Academies of Science and National Academy of Engineering Committee on Women in Science, Engineering and Medicine; the National Research Council Committee on Underrepresented Groups; and the Expansion of the Science and Engineering Workforce Pipeline. She became the chair of the board of trustees of Pine Manor College, a women's school in Brookline, Massachusetts, in 2007.

Villa-Komaroff lives with her husband in Chestnut Hill, Massachusetts. Currently, Anthony Komaroff is a professor of medicine at Harvard Medical School and the editor in chief of Harvard Health Publications. In her leisure time Villa-Komaroff enjoys taking photographs, reading mysteries, and socializing with members of her large extended family, which includes more than 100 first cousins, 17 nieces and nephews, and nine grand-nieces and -nephews.

—M.A.S.

Suggested Reading: American Society for Cell Biology *Newsletter* (on-line) 1998; *Boston Business Journal* (on-line) Dec. 29, 2006; DiversityWorking.com; *Hispanic Engineer* p16 Dec. 31, 2003; SACNAS Web site; *Science* p1902+ Mar. 29, 1996; Women in Technology International Web site; Ambrose, Susan A., and others. *Journeys of Women in Science and Engineering: No Universal Constants*, 1997; *Who's Who in America, 2008*

Roger Hagadone, courtesy of Little, Brown and Co.

von Ziegesar, Cecily

June 27, 1970– Writer

Address: c/o Grand Central Publishing, 237 Park Ave., New York, NY 10017

"I've always been a terrible gossip," Cecily von Ziegesar admitted to Helena de Bertodano for the London *Sunday Telegraph* (March 9, 2003). That statement followed the publication of *You Know You Love Me*, the second novel in von Ziegesar's hit teen series, Gossip Girl, about the escapades of filthy-rich Upper East Side youth. "I love talking about other people and tearing them apart. It's just so addictive. It's supposed to be this big taboo, but it's really like a recreation: everyone does it." Von Ziegesar, a Manhattan native and former student at an elite Upper East Side high school, created the idea for the Gossip Girl series and wrote the first eight books in less than four years, before handing the project off to other writers. (She maintains a significant editing role.) The young-adult novels, narrated by an anonymous blogger who calls herself Gossip Girl, follow the intelligent and beautiful Blair Waldorf and Serena van der Woodsen, students at the fictional Constance Billard School for Girls (widely understood to be based on Nightingale-Bamford, von Ziegesar's alma mater), as they deal with boys, friendships, family, college applications, and pressure to be perfect. While those subjects might seem to be standard fodder for teenage drama, in the case of the Gossip Girl books they are spiced with depictions of unimaginable wealth and extravagance (the text is peppered with such commercial brand names as Prada and Dolce & Gabbana); they also include soap-opera–style plot lines and racy—some would say immoral—content, including casual depictions of teenage sex, heavy drinking, drug use, and bulimia, details that von Ziegesar drew from her own high-school experience. The novels have been wildly popular with teenagers and "tweens" and have infuriated many parents and critics, who argue that the books set negative examples for the 14-through-18-year-olds toward whom they are marketed. Von Ziegesar and others have defended the books on the grounds that they are both realistic and fun to read, not to be taken too seriously or interpreted as examples for the way one should behave. After giving up full-time writing duties for her first series, von Ziegesar created a spin-off series, The It Girl, which follows Jenny Humphrey, a character from the Gossip Girl books. The *Gossip Girl* TV series, based on the books, premiered in the fall of 2007 on the CW network.

Cecily von Ziegesar was born on June 27, 1970 to a wealthy family in the New York City borough of Manhattan. Her father, Franz Albrecht von Ziegesar, worked at Bowne & Co., a financial communications firm, ultimately becoming its chairman and CEO. Her mother is the former Olivia James. Von Ziegesar's parents married three times each, and she has two half-sisters and three half-brothers. Von Ziegesar grew up on Manhattan's Upper West Side and, like her characters, attended a prestigious, private, all-girls high school on the Upper East Side, called Nightingale-Bamford. While she was still in high school, she and her parents moved to Norwalk, Connecticut, where she had to wake up at 6:00 a.m. to commute by train and taxi to New York City to finish out her days at Nightingale-Bamford. At the school she made many of the observations that later served as material for the Gossip Girl series. She told Karen Heller for the *Philadelphia Inquirer* (July 27, 2004) that while she was among the popular students in high school, she was less interested in partying than horseback riding, a sport that took her away from the city on many weekends and gave her a semi-outsider status, even before her move to Connecticut. "But I was friends with all the cool kids," she told Mackenzie Dawson Parks for *Colby Magazine* (Winter 2006, on-line), the alumni publication of Colby College. "I was part of the cool clique—but not completely a part of it, because I kept leaving." Von Ziegesar told de Bertodano about her circle of friends at Nightingale-Bamford, where annual tuition in 2007 was $30,000, "I had some rich and fabulous friends who lived on entire floors of Fifth Avenue apartments. One friend would be flown by Concorde to Paris for fittings with Yves Saint Laurent—but that was a drastic case, an unbelievable indulgence in glamour." While von Ziegesar has contended that many of her depictions of the wealthy Billard teenagers are satirical exaggerations, she also insists that the roots of the material—from pot-smoking in Central Park, to sexual promiscuity, to the bulimic tendencies of her main characters—are drawn directly from life, as is the cavalier tone with which the subjects are discussed. She has said that bulimia among her friends was as common as cigarette smoking, telling Ginia Bellafante for the *New York Times* (August 17, 2003), "I wanted to treat it the way we treated it and not make an issue out of it. That's the way it was for a lot of girls. It was something they dabbled in during high school and got over later."

Von Ziegesar graduated from Nightingale-Bamford in 1988 and attended Colby College, a small liberal-arts school in Waterville, Maine. Upon graduating, in 1992, she spent a year in Budapest, Hungary, working for a local radio station. She returned to the United States to study creative writing at the University of Arizona, where she was

living with her boyfriend until, on a visit to New York, she met an Englishman, Richard Griggs. Within a few months of their meeting, von Ziegesar had moved to north London, England, with Griggs, whom she married shortly afterward. While in London von Ziegesar worked at a publishing company and developed some ideas for stories. In 1998 the couple moved to New York, where von Ziegesar began working for the media company Alloy Entertainment, whose book-packaging division, formerly 17th St. Media, develops ideas and plot lines for fiction series, crafts proposals for publishers, and seeks out writers. That division boasts such hits as the novel *Sisterhood of the Traveling Pants* and the books in the Sweet Valley High series. While an editor at Alloy, von Ziegesar helped develop several book series before writing the proposal for the Gossip Girl novels. When the proposal was accepted by Little, Brown publishers, rather than giving the project to a commissioned writer, she decided to take it on herself. She told Lauren Mechling for the London *Daily Telegraph* (October 17, 2002) that she did not do any research and relied mainly on memory to complete the first book, which took her about four months. "I was just so into it, it came so easily because I felt that I was writing about people that I know," von Ziegesar said. "The girls show more skin these days, but I think, generally, they behave the same way as when I was growing up."

The first installment of the series, *Gossip Girl*, was published in the United States in April 2002 and was quickly dubbed "*Sex and the City* for teenagers," a reference to a popular TV series. The story, narrated by the anonymous blogger Gossip Girl, begins, "Hey people! Ever wondered what the lives of the chosen ones are really like? Well, I'm going to tell you, because I'm one of them. I'm not talking about beautiful models or actors or musical prodigies or mathematical geniuses. I'm talking about the people who are *born to it*—those of us who have everything anyone could possibly wish for and who take it all completely for granted." *Gossip Girl* and the subsequent books in the series—among them *All I Want Is Everything*, *Nobody Does It Better*, and *You're the One That I Want*—were hugely successful, with each installment spending months on the *New York Times* best-seller list for children. Girls and young women flocked to the books, many seeing the tales as an opportunity to escape to an extravagant and largely foreign world, while other readers seemed to genuinely admire the wealthy teens. Von Ziegesar told Mechling after meeting a group of fans who identified with the characters in the books, "Talking to them, I realised it is fiction, but these girls really do exist. They were saying it's like reading about their friends." Indeed, the books seemed to tap into certain realities in the lives of contemporary teenagers that were absent from the pages of other young-adult fiction, which were dominated by artificial plot lines and morals that did not resonate with their readers.

Critical assessments of the books were mixed. Most reviewers agreed that they were entertaining and bound to be popular with teenage girls. Many critics and parents, however, were unhappy that such content was being marketed toward 14-to-18-year-old girls, who might, it was feared, emulate the behavior of the characters. The concerns were exacerbated by reports that the novels' readers were primarily at the younger end of the spectrum, with some as young as nine years old. Von Ziegesar and her supporters have asked that the books be seen not as examples to follow but merely as entertainment for mature young adults, with details based on realities with which they are already familiar. Von Ziegesar told de Bertodano, "My books are really just fun, showing kids behaving and making mistakes in the way real people do. I'm obviously not saying, 'This is how you should act,' but teenagers do these things, so why not show it?" Other critics have similarly pointed out that the readers of the series are more sophisticated than their counterparts from previous generations, having been exposed to adult subject matter through R-rated movies and shows such as *Sex and the City*. Von Ziegesar also noted that her characters' behavior has consequences, telling de Bertodano, "You see the characters embarrassing themselves and throwing up. You see them feeling terrible after a night out. It's all part of a kid's world and it's silly to pretend that it isn't." Moreover, von Ziegesar said to Heather Salerno for the Westchester County, New York, *Journal News* (July 10, 2005) that she had received mostly positive feedback from parents. "They say, 'I'm just thrilled that my daughter is reading,'" von Ziegesar said. "I try not to think about my readers as 14-year-old girls. I don't want to write down to them. I just want them to have something fun to read."

Like the Gossip Girl books, the first novel in Von Ziegesar's spin-off series—The It Girl, published in the fall of 2005—met with both popular success and criticism. The story focuses on Jenny Humphrey, a five-foot-tall, curly-haired, curvaceous Brooklynite, who is portrayed as something of an outsider in the Gossip Girl series. Jenny was expelled from the prestigious Constance Billard school after her reputation was tarnished following affairs with members of the fictional band the Raves; now at Waverly Prep, a prestigious upstate co-ed prep school, she must fight to become the most popular—or the "it"—girl. Cindy Eagen, a senior editor at Little, Brown, explained to *PR Newswire* (September 15, 2004) why she expected the new series to appeal to readers: "Jenny is the perfect character to cross-over into *The It Girl* since *Gossip Girl* fans aspire to be older Serena or Blair, but they relate to Jenny and live vicariously through her stories." A writer for *Publishers Weekly* (October 31, 2005) predicted commercial success for the book but gave it a lukewarm review: "Unfortunately, the zinger-filled Gossip Girl commentary that separated the chapters in the original series is here replaced by rather dull emails sent from students and staff. Still, the author serves up plenty of juicy plotting, and Gossip Girl fans will likely go for this, too." In January 2006 The It Girl appeared at number five on *Publishers Weekly*'s list of best-selling children's series, with Gossip Girl still reigning at number one. Von Ziegesar has so far published seven books in The It Girl series, the most recent of which, *Infamous*, appeared in November 2008. In May 2008 the first book in a new Von Ziegesar series, Gossip Girl: The Carlyles, went on sale. That series follows the dramatic lives of the priveleged Carlyle triplets—Owen, Avery, and Baby—who, after the death of their grandmother, move with their mother from Nantucket Island, in Massachusetts, to the Upper East Side of New York City. Von Ziegesar continues to work for Alloy as an editor and consultant for the series Gossip Girl and The It Girl.

On March 12, 2006 Naomi Wolf, a prominent writer and feminist, published a scathing article in the *New York Times* criticizing not only von Ziegesar's series but the entire current crop of young women's fiction. She condemned the books not only for depicting the characters' sexual promiscuity and drug and alcohol consumption, but for representing a corrupt underlying value system that the characters do not question. "The girls try on adult values and customs as though they were going to wear them forever. The narratives offer the perks of the adult world not as escapist fantasy but in a creepily photorealistic way, just as the book jackets show real girls polished to an unreal gloss," Wolf wrote. In a letter to the editor of the *New York Times* published on March 26, 2006, a high-school sophomore, Eliza Orleans, responded to Wolf and sought to explain the appeal of the books: "True, the books are not intellectual works of genius. The writing style isn't anything to brag about. The story lines are repetitive, revolving around sex, boys, money and, of course, gossip. There are no values whatsoever in the series, and the characters are hardly worthy of admiration. . . . People are drawn to these books because they are deliciously funny. Von Ziegesar is not aiming to change the course of American literature. She is a satirical writer who is poking fun at the absurdity of the consumerist world she has created. After all, isn't a world where teenagers spend nights at the Plaza with rock stars, confused prep school boys make out with bald girls and write awful poetry, lacrosse players steal Viagra and spoiled white girls compete to be the next Audrey Hepburn just a little bit funny? I think so."

Von Ziegesar worked with Josh Schwartz and Stephanie Savage to adapt the Gossip Girl series for TV. *Gossip Girl* premiered in September 2007 on the CW network, with Leighton Meester playing Blair Waldorf, Blake Lively as Serena van der Woodsen, and Kristen Bell as the voice of the blogging narrator. The show, now in its second season, has received mostly good reviews. Like the book series, it has become popular with teenagers while drawing criticism from various conservative, "pro-family" groups for its portrayal of high-school students engaging in what many consider to be immoral activities.

Henry Alford, writing for *Vanity Fair* (May 9, 2006), found that von Ziegesar was "like a dishwasher's rinse cycle of nervous laughter and self-deprecation" who shares few traits with the characters in her novels. The 11th book in the Gossip Girl series, *Don't You Forget About Me*, was published in May 2007; a Gossip Girl prequel, *It Had to Be You*, appeared in October of that year. Those works, like the ninth and 10th Gossip Girl books and the entire The It Girl series, bear von Ziegesar's name as the creator, not the writer. That is because von Ziegesar no longer writes the books herself, though she crafts the plot lines and edits the manuscripts heavily. "I'm a brand now," Von Ziegesar told Alford. She lives in Irvington, New York, with her husband, who is the deputy director of the Public Art Fund, and her young children, Agnes and Oscar. She has a cat named Pony Boy. Asked by Mechling in 2002 if she planned to protect her daughter from the world depicted in her books, von Ziegesar responded, "I would send her to Nightingale-Bamford. I think I got a great educa-tion."

—M.E.R.

Suggested Reading: *American Libraries* p76 Apr. 2007; (London) *Daily Telegraph* p23 Oct. 17, 2002; (London) *Observer* p6 Aug. 25, 2002; (London) *Sunday Telegraph* p2 Mar. 9, 2003 *New York Times* 7 p22 Mar. 12, 2006, E p1 Sep. 12, 2007; *Philadelphia Inquirer* D p1 July 27, 2004

Selected Books: *Gossip Girl*, 2002; *You Know You Love Me*, 2002; *All I Want Is Everything*, 2003; *Because I'm Worth It*, 2003; *I Like It Like That*, 2004; *You're the One That I Want*, 2004; *Nobody Does It Better*, 2005; *Nothing Can Keep Us Together*, 2005; as creator and editor—*The It Girl*, 2005; *Only In Your Dreams*, 2006; *Notorious*, 2006; *Would I Lie to You*, 2006; *Reckless*, 2006; *Unforgettable*, 2007; *Don't You Forget About Me*, 2007; *Lucky*, 2007; *It Had to Be You*, 2007; *Tempted*, 2008; *Infamous*, 2008; *Gossip Girl: The Carlyles*, 2008; *You Just Can't Get Enough*, 2008; *Take a Chance on Me*, 2008

Walters, John P.

Feb. 8, 1952– U.S. drug czar

Address: Office of National Drug Control Policy, 750 17th St. N.W., Washington, D.C. 20503

"There is absolutely no question we are winning," John P. Walters, the director of the White House Office of National Drug Control Policy (ONDCP)—the position popularly known as drug czar—said to Danna Harman for the *Christian Science Monitor* (September 28, 2006). Walters was referring to the United States' national and international efforts to prohibit illegal drug use, trafficking, and smuggling, the campaign often called the "war on drugs." Walters, a longtime combatant in that "war," began his career in government with the National Endowment for the Humanities (NEH) and then the U.S. Department of Education, working for both during the administration of President Ronald Reagan; he next moved to the ONDCP, where he became a senior official under William J. Bennett, then the drug czar for President George H. W. Bush. During the late 1990s Walters served as president of the Philanthropy Roundtable, a national association of more than 600 foundations and individual donors that provides information on all aspects of charitable giving. In 1996 he co-authored the book *Body Count: Moral Poverty . . . and How to Win America's War Against Crime and Drugs*, with Bennett and John J. DiIulio Jr., about the root causes of drug use and crime in the U.S. In May 2001 President George W. Bush nominated

Juan Barreto/AFP/Getty Images

him as director of the ONDCP, with responsibility for coordinating the efforts of all federal drug-control programs.

Walters's policies for reducing drug use and distribution, while credited by many with achieving successes in the war on drugs, have drawn their share of criticism and controversy. Under his get-tough approaches and conservative leadership, drug use among youth has reportedly dropped to its lowest levels since the early 1990s, and the manufacture of hard drugs such as cocaine and heroin have declined steeply. He has helped institute random student drug testing in more than 1,000 schools across the country, spearheaded a national ad campaign informing young people of the destructive powers of drugs, ordered raids on the coca crops in leading cocaine-producing countries, such as Colombia, and worked with the United Nations Commission on Narcotic Drugs in efforts to control chemicals used in the production of synthetic drugs. He has, however, also been widely criticized for his preoccupation with the law-and-order and national-security aspects of drug policy: he has escalated U.S. military involvement in drug-interdiction efforts; left unchanged the 100-to-one disparity between federal sentences for offenses related to crack cocaine and pure powder cocaine, respectively; favored harsh federal prison sentences for marijuana smugglers and repeat drug offenders; emphasized the prosecution of drug users while paying far less attention to drug treatment and education; and opposed federal funding for needle exchanges aimed at reducing the spread of AIDS. In February 2008 he launched the first major federal initiative to combat prescription-drug abuse among teens.

John P. Walters was born on February 8, 1952 in Detroit, Michigan. His father, Vernon, was a U.S. Army lieutenant general who served as the deputy director of the Central Intelligence Agency (CIA) from 1972 to 1976. Walters attended Michigan State University, where he received a B.A. degree in political science, and went on to obtain an M.A. degree from the University of Toronto, in Canada. He taught political science at Michigan State University's James Madison College and then at Boston College, in Massachusetts, before coming to Washington, D.C., in 1982. William Bennett, then head of the National Endowment for the Humanities in the Reagan administration, had personally asked Walters to come work at the organization. "It was supposed to be on a temporary basis," Walters recalled—"with a chuckle"—to a writer for the *National Journal* (June 23, 2001). During his tenure at NEH, Walters served as the acting assistant director and program officer in the Division of Education Programs. In 1985, after Reagan appointed Bennett as the secretary of the Department of Education, Walters followed Bennett there; he began as the assistant to the secretary, heading the Schools Without Drugs prevention program, before being promoted in 1988 to chief of staff and counselor to the secretary. He was also Bennett's representative on the National Drug Policy Board and the Domestic Policy Council's Health Policy Working Group.

In 1988, near the end of the Reagan administration, the Office of National Drug Control Policy was established by the Anti–Drug Abuse Act. The following year, under President George H. W. Bush, Walters began serving as chief of staff for Bennett, who had been chosen to fill the post of ONDCP director—the nation's first official drug czar, a post created in conjunction with Bush's declared war on drugs. A number of factors had sparked that campaign: the drug-related deaths of two high-profile college athletes—the basketball star Len Bias and the football player Don Rogers—within a week in 1986, with the resulting national focus on the dangers of drug use; the use of crack, a cheap and highly addictive form of cocaine, which had reached epidemic proportions in inner cities all over the country by the late 1980s, leading in turn to a major surge in addiction, homelessness, and crime; and the seeming invincibility of international drug kingpins, among them Pablo Escobar of Colombia, who in 1989 had so profited from his cocaine and heroin empire that *Forbes* magazine listed him as the seventh-richest person in the world, even as he reportedly ordered up to 20 murders a day. While serving under Bennett, Walters was instrumental in doubling the federal funding of the war on drugs to $12 billion and helped oversee a major expansion of funding for treatment services. He also worked with a number of governmental agencies to address the national-security aspects of the drug trade, calling for increased military involvement. That would become the main (and most criticized) focus of his drug policy. Walters was the chief architect of the Andean Strategy, a five-year, $2 billion program designed to reduce the amount of illegal drugs entering the United States, which included providing anti-drug intelligence to officials in countries that were principal cocaine sources, such as Colombia, Bolivia, and Peru.

In November 1990 Bennett resigned from the post of drug czar after 19 months in office. (He stated that he had carried out everything he set out to accomplish.) The former Florida governor Bob Martinez was appointed to the position in January 1991. Bush named Walters the deputy director for supply reduction, a position he held at the ONDCP until 1993. During that time he also served as the senior adviser on national-security matters related to drug control. After Martinez stepped down, in January 1993, Walters was briefly the acting drug czar, resigning in protest after President Bill Clinton cut his staff from 146 to 25, as part of a plan to redirect anti-narcotics policy to focus more on prevention and treatment. (By that time Clinton had raised the drug-czar post to Cabinet status.) Walters became a visiting fellow at the Hudson Institute, a conservative think tank, where he continued to write and speak on drug policy. In July 1996 he stirred controversy when he testified before the Senate Judiciary Committee, attacking what he saw as the ineffectiveness of the Clinton administration's efforts to control drug use. As noted by David E. Sanger for the *New York Times* (May 11, 2001), Walters declared that Clinton's policies were "the latest manifestation of the liberals' commitment to a 'therapeutic state' in which government serves as the agent of personal rehabilitation." He urged the committee to establish tougher penalties for drug offenses, including the stiffening of federal laws against marijuana use, and to intensify the battle against drugs at their source, in Latin America; he also called on the committee to oppose federal financing of needle exchanges intended to reduce the spread of AIDS, fearing that such financing would appear to condone illegal drug use. One of his critics, Ethan Nadelmann, the founder and executive director of the Lindesmith Center–Drug Policy Foundation, a New York–based organization that emphasizes drug treatment and rehabilitation over punitive measures, told Sanger, "Anybody can give lip service to drug prevention and addiction, but listen to him and he stands out as a bellicose drug warrior." On the other hand, the Health and Human Services secretary Tommy Thompson, who as governor of Wisconsin had favored treating addiction over building prisons, said to Sanger that Walters was "much more balanced" in his approach to the war on drugs than was often reported.

Also in 1996 Walters co-authored a book, titled *Body Count: Moral Poverty . . . and How to Win America's War Against Crime and Drugs*, with Bennett and the political scientist John DiIulio Jr. The book—about the marriage of crime and drugs in the U.S. and the various societal problems that are their offspring—got mixed responses. Voicing a common criticism, James Lardner wrote for the *New York Times Book Review* (November 3, 1996), "Remember all those 'root causes' that we used to be told about? Things like poverty and unemployment? Forget them. Crime, according to *Body Count*, is caused by 'moral poverty'—'the poverty of being without loving, capable, responsible adults who teach the young right from wrong.' . . . Economics is not a root, not even a twig, in the thinking of Mr. Bennett, Mr. DiIulio and Mr. Walters. Posterity will, I suspect, regard this as the strangest of their omissions. But they will have plenty of company at the bar of judgment. This book's many criticisms of the Clinton Administration notwithstanding, the Democratic Party's abandonment of the jobs issue has been only microscopically less complete than the Republican Party's. In the most important respects, then, *Body Count* can fairly be called not balanced, but, alas, bipartisan." On a more positive note, Gary Rosen wrote in a review for *Commentary* (December 1996), "This is not . . . just a rehash of familiar 'get-tough' policies. Rather, the aim of the authors—who reject such conservative staples as reinstituting chain gangs and stripping prisons of all amenities—is moral accountability. Stern, reliable punishment sends a 'socializing, civilizing message,' they write, while its absence represents yet another instance of adults abdicating their responsibility for guiding the wayward young. . . . Perhaps surprisingly, the authors of *Body Count* are concerned not only about the corrupting influence of drugs in inner-city neighborhoods but about alcohol as well. . . . 'Where broken bottles fill the gutters,' they write, 'social bonds are weakened

and social capital goes down the drain.' If consistency is one test of moral seriousness, Bennett, DiIulio, and Walters pass with flying colors." In 1997 Walters became president of the Philanthropy Roundtable. He held the position until 2001.

In May of that year, President George W. Bush nominated Walters to be the next director of the White House Office of National Drug Control Policy. He was officially sworn in on December 7, 2001, succeeding General Barry McCaffrey as the fifth person to hold the post. As drug czar Walters took on a staff of 150 and a budget of nearly a half-billion dollars. Following his nomination, those opposing his stances had mounted a vigorous campaign against his appointment. Michael Massing, one of his leading critics, described him in an op-ed piece for the *Washington Post* (May 6, 2001) as "a Washington player captivated by the glamour and romance of the drug war," who "seems to be exactly the wrong man for the job." Ethan Nadelmann said to a writer for the *Workplace Substance Abuse Advisor* (May 17, 2001), "John Walters stands for the proposition that drug policy has nothing to do with science or public health. It's all about punishment." However, Calvina L. Fay, executive director of the Drug Free America Foundation in St. Petersburg, Florida, offered praise for Walters, noting to the same writer, "John fully understands what we are up against today in combating substance abuse. He is aware of the well-financed forces that we are besieged with who want to legalize drugs and promote drug use to our children. The mere fact that permissive drug policy groups like the Lindesmith Center are attacking his nomination, demonstrates that he is the right person for this job."

In February 2002 President Bush and Walters unveiled the National Drug Control Strategy, a plan for reducing teen and adult drug use by 10 percent over two years and by 25 percent over five years. One of the strategy's chief focuses was Plan Colombia, a $1.3 billion program dedicated to eradicating the coca crop and cocaine production there. Other focal points of the strategy were to dissuade children and teenagers from trying marijuana and to oppose the use of marijuana for medicinal purposes. "Those who claim marijuana is medicine are lying," Walters explained to Eric Weslander for the Tucson, Arizona, *Citizen* (October 10, 2002). He went on to call medical marijuana "the 21st-century version of snake oil." Marijuana sold today, according to Walters, is much more potent and dangerous than its counterpart of 30 years ago. For that reason, he has favored harsher federal prison sentences for marijuana smugglers. (In July 2007, in a press conference following raids made on marijuana plantations in Mexico, Walters was quoted as calling marijuana growers "violent criminal terrorists.") Elaborating on Walters's strategy, one of his top advisers, David Murray, explained to Ben Wallace-Wells for *Rolling Stone* (December 13, 2007, on-line), "If you're going to have a national office of drug-control policy, you look at the most prevalent drug in the society that's readily available—you don't go after [crystal] meth first thing. You think about it like an epidemiologist, and you go for the vector that's most likely to spread, and that's teen marijuana users." Criticisms of the National Drug Control Strategy include its retaining of the 100-to-one disparity between federal sentences for crack and powder cocaine. (For example, a person found to be in possession of five grams of crack cocaine can receive the same five-year sentence as a person trafficking 500 grams of powder cocaine.) Detractors also noted the strategy's de-emphasizing of treatment programs in favor of the same law-and-order approach taken by the first Bush administration. As noted by Sanger, Walters wrote, "The evidence is that coerced treatment works at least as well as voluntary treatment." (Walters has, however, strongly emphasized religious-based treatment programs and has set in motion the "Access to Recovery" initiative, a grant program funded by the Substance Abuse and Mental Health Services Administration, Center for Substance Abuse Treatment, which provides vouchers to addicts for treatment and recovery-support services.)

While some of his policies have been hotly contested, Walters's accomplishments as drug czar are undeniable. In 2002 he was instrumental in a U.S. Supreme Court ruling that allowed schools to conduct random drug testing among students who wished to participate in school-sponsored extracurricular activities. Commenting on the ruling, Walters explained to Shari Roan for the *Los Angeles Times* (May 21, 2007), "Fifteen years ago, school drug testing was too controversial. People thought the test was going to throw kids out of school or give them a criminal record. The Supreme Court decision was an enormously positive step." He added, "This is an area where doing the right thing for our kids is durable. We can change the face of substance abuse for generations." More than 1,000 schools across the country currently enforce random student drug testing, which has been credited with steering adolescents away from drug experimentation. Also in 2002, Walters—who criticized as too soft the anti-drug ads created by the Partnership for a Drug-Free America during McCaffrey's tenure—spearheaded a new ad campaign, which has apparently been more effective in deterring children and teenagers from drugs. In one ad, titled "Pete's Couch," a teenage narrator says, "I smoked weed and nobody died. I didn't get into a car accident. I didn't OD on heroin the next day. Nothing happened. We sat on Pete's couch for eleven hours." The ad then cuts away to images of other teenagers enjoying themselves while partaking in non-drug-related activities—such as biking and flirting with members of the opposite sex—before returning to the narrator, who, judging those activities to be more fun than smoking marijuana, proclaims, "You have a better shot at dying out in the real world but I'll take my chances out there." Plan Colombia, through its raids on crops, has led to a steep decline in Colombian cultivation of coca and the production of cocaine, as well as the cultivation of opium poppy and the manufacture of heroin. In 2005 alone a record-breaking 170,000 hectares (the equivalent of 419,000 acres) of coca were destroyed, and 225 tons of cocaine hydrochloride and cocaine base were seized, up from 125 tons in 2002.

Under Walters's leadership, youth drug use has also dropped significantly. A study titled *Monitoring the Future Study*, released in December 2006, sponsored by the National Institute on Drug Abuse, and conducted by scientists at the University of Michigan's Institute for Social Resarch, indicated that 840,000 fewer young people (an ONDCP estimate based on a survey of 50,000 teenagers) were using drugs at the time of the report than in 2001, marking a 23 percent reduction. According to the 2007 National Survey on Drug Use and Health, conducted by the Substance Abuse and Mental Health Service Administration's Office of Applied Studies, overall illicit drug use among teens ages 12 to 17 was at a five-year low, at 9.8 percent in 2006, down from 11.6 percent in 2002. Also, over the last five years, teen marijuana use has dropped among many in that age group, as has use of methamphetamine, ecstasy, and LSD. In February 2008 Walters launched the first advertising campaign to combat prescription-drug abuse by teens. The first television ad, shown during Super Bowl XLII, was a direct response to the death of the Oscar-nominated actor Heath Ledger in January 2008—which was a result of an overdose of painkillers, antidepressants, and sleeping pills and was emblematic of the dramatic rise in prescription-drug use nationwide over the last decade. (Since 1990 prescription-drug sales have risen nearly 500 percent.) ONDCP's recent efforts to combat prescription-drug abuse have reportedly been effective to some degree. Commenting on the subject, Walters explained to a writer for *Lab Business Week* (February 10, 2008), "When used as prescribed, prescription painkillers can be tremendously beneficial. But their abuse is becoming a serious public health and addiction problem. We may be unintentionally providing our teens a new way to get high. Most teens who abuse prescription drugs say they get them from home, or from friends and relatives. We need parents to recognize that not all drug threats to their teens come from the street corner. Prescription drugs are in practically every home and parents can have an immediate impact on stopping teen prescription drug abuse." He said to Mary Engel and Daniel Costello for the *Los Angeles Times* (January 26, 2008), "We want people to have access to pain relief that's changed people's lives for the better. We don't want them to fear beneficial medications. But we want to control them, to dispose of them when they're done with them and to talk with their kids."

John P. Walters lives in the Washington, D.C., area. He has founded two nonprofit organizations: the Madison Center, an education think tank, and the New Citizenship Project, an association created to promote greater civic responsibility . He has also served as executive director of the Council on Crime in America, a bipartisan commission on violent crime that runs in conjunction with the New Citizenship Project. Walters and his wife, Mary, have two daughters, Michaela and Rebecca.

—C.C.

Suggested Reading: *Christian Science Monitor* p1+ Sep. 28, 2006; *In These Times* p7 June 11, 2001; *Los Angeles Times* F p1+ May 21, 2007, A p15 Jan. 26, 2008; *National Journal* Social Studies June 2, 2001, White House June 23, 2001; *New York Times* A p20 Apr. 26, 2001, A p20 May 11, 2001; Office of National Drug Control Policy Official Web site; *Rolling Stone* Dec. 13, 2007; *Sheriff* May–June 2004; (Tucson, Arizona) *Citizen* D p1 Oct. 10, 2002; *Weekly Standard* p9 May 21, 2001; *Workplace Substance Abuse Advisor* May 17, 2001

Selected Books: *Body Count: Moral Poverty . . . and How to Win America's War Against Crime and Drugs* (with William J. Bennett and John J. DiIulio Jr.), 1996

Oliver Link, courtesy of Tain Watts

Watts, Jeff "Tain"

Jan. 20, 1960– Jazz drummer

Address: c/o Joel Chriss & Co., 300 Mercer St., New York, NY 10003

Fans of contemporary "straight-ahead" jazz are likely familiar with the work of Jeff "Tain" Watts, one of the most prominent drummers working in the genre today. After gaining attention as part of the trumpeter and composer Wynton Marsalis's quintet in the early 1980s, Watts joined the group led by Marsalis's brother Branford, following the saxophonist to the West Coast in 1992 to become part of Jay Leno's *Tonight Show* band. He later formed groups of his own, releasing five critically acclaimed recordings to date, while contributing to the award-winning albums of the Marsalis brothers, among the more than 100 albums that feature his work. "Watts forges a colossal sound," John Murph wrote for the *Washington Post* (February 5, 2000). "Never one to simply ride the groove, he constantly shifts tempos and breaks up time, sometimes at lightning speed."

Jeff "Tain" Watts was born on January 20, 1960 in Pittsburgh, Pennsylvania. He has said that his family was not particularly musical; his parents did not collect music or even own a record player, and his older brothers bought mainly the music they heard on the radio, such as albums by Stevie Wonder or Aretha Franklin. He took general-music classes as part of his elementary-school curriculum; in the fourth grade, Watts was asked to choose an instrument to play for class, and he picked the trumpet, "because," as he told R. J. DeLuke for the All About Jazz Web site (July 2002, on-line), "it looked fun and cool. You could play some 'legit' music on it, but you could also jam around and have fun with it." Watts's teacher told him that the formation of his teeth would prevent him from playing the trumpet correctly and suggested that he choose another instrument. (Later, after consulting trumpeters who claimed that his teeth were fine for playing the instrument, Watts reached his own conclusion. "What I suspect was, they ran out of trumpets," he told DeLuke. "So I wouldn't cry, they said my teeth were completely wrong.") It was thus that Watts began playing the drums. In the sixth grade he got his own drum set and began to play along with songs on the radio. In those days he was "still pretty much unaware of classic jazz figures," as he told DeLuke, with the exception of big-band musicians such as the drummer Buddy Rich, because "the Big Band thing is easily marketed to schools." When he was 16 or 17, his brother James expanded Watts's musical horizons, giving him jazz-fusion records by artists and groups such as Return to Forever, the Mahavishnu Orchestra, and Herbie Hancock. Thanks to those influences, Watts said for his Web site, "I began a backtracking process that other musicians in my age group share. I'd check out a Chick Corea album, then find out that Chick Corea played with Miles Davis, who played with Charlie Parker, et cetera."

After Watts graduated from high school, he studied classical percussion at nearby Duquesne University, where he focused on the timpani—also known as the kettledrum—and played in operas, musicals, and orchestra concerts. Soon he began to seek other musical settings. "I wanted to be able to perform authentically and accurately on the classical percussion, but also play different styles on the drum set," Watts told R. J. DeLuke. Discovering the work of Harvey Mason, he learned that that jazz drummer had studied at the New England Conservatory and "was capable of all these different things in a studio setting. So I started trying to be versatile. My thirst to explore jazz was pretty much out of that." That "thirst" led Watts to transfer to the Berklee College of Music, in Boston, Massachusetts. There, his fellow students included a number of other future jazz stars, among them the saxophonists Branford Marsalis and Greg Osby and the guitarist Kevin Eubanks.

During 1981, the year that Watts graduated from Berklee, Wynton Marsalis—Branford's younger brother—was organizing a quintet, which would play many of the trumpeter's original compositions as well as classic jazz tunes. (It was among those musicians that Watts received his nickname, "Tain," short for "Chieftain.") The brothers had recruited Kenny Kirkland on piano; despite the availability of more seasoned drummers, Branford knew that Watts was the type of drummer his younger brother was looking for. "I always felt that Tain was the guy," Branford told Ted Panken for Down Beat (November 2002). "I liked how he constructed his [accompanying of] soloists at jam sessions. As opposed to being a complete, thorough historian of the music and playing all the right things at the right time, he played strange things at the right time, imposing his fusion influences on a jazz context. I appreciated that and thought it would be great for Wynton's band." (The Wynton Marsalis Quintet had a number of bassists over the years.) The younger Marsalis spoke with Panken about his impressions of Watts: "My brother liked Tain. There were no auditions. . . . I liked Tain because he was funny, but he has a phenomenal level of talent and intellect. He's a master of form, with perfect pitch and tremendous reflexes. Over the years, he developed a vocabulary that only he plays. All those pieces with time changes and different meters came from playing off of him, because he could do it. It forced me to shape my lines that way, too." Watts told Bob Blumenthal for the Boston Globe (April 23, 1999), "Having to interpret a lot of original music from early on, I was able to develop a less derivative approach. Billy Higgins says that every time you sit behind the drums you learn something, and he's right." Watts stayed with the quintet until 1988, performing on three of Wynton Marsalis's Grammy Award–winning albums of the period: Black Codes (From the Underground) (1985), J Mood (1985), and Marsalis Standard Time—Volume 1 (1986).

In 1988 and 1989 Watts worked variously with the guitarist and singer George Benson, the vocalist Harry Connick Jr., and the pianist McCoy Turner. Then Branford Marsalis invited Watts to join his quartet, which included Kirkland and the bassist Bob Hurst. Watts has played with the quartet on and off ever since and performed on both of the band's Grammy Award–winning albums: I Heard You Twice the First Time (1992) and Contemporary Jazz (2000). (Watts is the only musician to have appeared on every Grammy-winning album by Wynton and Branford Marsalis, respectively.) In 1992, when Branford Marsalis was invited to be the bandleader for the Tonight Show with Jay Leno, he brought his band, including Watts. The gig lasted three years; Watts has said repeatedly that the time he spent in Los Angeles, California, as part of the Tonight Show band was very beneficial, as he had the opportunity to play on the program with a number of musical luminaries, including Lou Rawls, Peter Gabriel, and Elton John. Eventually, though, Watts found his work on the Tonight Show to be both stagnant and all-encompassing. He told Blumenthal about working on the show: "You're even less than a studio musician, because you play in such a narrow scope. It's more purely entertainment, and I felt that the real world of art was going on somewhere else." It was then that Watts began to think more seriously about composing music.

While it is somewhat unusual for a jazz drummer to lead an ensemble (two famous exceptions are Art Blakey and Buddy Rich), Watts decided to try. An early result was the album Megawatts, which was recorded in 1991 but not released until 2003; for that reason Citizen Tain (1999) is considered his first album as leader. The Marsalis brothers (including Delfeayo, a trombonist) and Kirkland performed on the album, as well as the saxophonist Kenny Garrett and bassist Reginald Veal. For the most part critics commended the playing but were less taken with Watts's original compositions. In a representative review, Mark Stryker wrote for the Alberta, Canada, Calgary Herald (October 14, 1999), "The fierce soloing and lively group interaction make up for Watts' rather thin modal compositions. Watts has a curiously bouncy beat for a post-bop drummer, but his time feel and the aggressive looseness with which he drives a band are recognizable, and that's quite an accomplishment in our homogenized era."

In 2002 Watts released his second album as leader, Bar Talk, which featured his band, made up of the saxophonist Ravi Coltrane (son of the sax great John Coltrane), the pianist David Budway, the bassist James Genus, the guitarist Paul Bollenback, and the harmonica player Gregoire Maret; guest musicians on the recording were Branford Marsalis, saxophonist Michael Brecker, guitarist Hiram Bullock, percussionist Robert Thomas Jr., and pianist Joey Calderazzo. Watts spoke with Terry Perkins for the St. Louis (Missouri) Post-Dispatch (December 31, 2003) about the new direction signaled by his sophomore release: "Working on *Bar Talk* really was a transitional effort for me. I was trying to move both my writing and my playing into a more open space, and that's definitely a direction I'm trying to pursue with my current band." Reviewers of *Bar Talk* universally recognized improvement in Watts's compositions, which made up eight of the album's 10 tracks. A representative review, for PR Newswire (May 8, 2002), read, "*Bar Talk* elaborates on *Citizen Tain*'s strengths—and takes them a step further. Where Watts was once a newcomer to jazz composition and band-leading, these days he is a seasoned veteran. *Bar Talk* investigates a wider array of rhythms, and explores more exotic musical terrain through daring arrangements and scorching solos while preserving the clever melodic style and bold rhythmic assurance that made *Citizen Tain* one of 1999's sleeper hits."

Watts's third album, *DeTAINed at the Blue Note*, recorded in February 2004 at the famous New York City jazz club of the title, showcased the work of the alto saxophonist Kenny Garrett, the tenor saxophonist Marcus Strickland, the pianist Dave Kikoski, the bassist Eric Revis, and the guitarist Dave Gilmour. Three years passed before Watts released another studio album, *Folk's Songs*, as leader. His new group, Tain & the Ebonix, includes Strickland, Kikoski, and the bassist Christian McBride. Watts composed seven of the album's 10 tunes. (He was also a guest on his own album, as vocalist "Juan Tainish," who even has his own MySpace page on the Internet.) Bob Karlovits, writing for the *Pittsburgh Tribune Review* (June 10, 2007), found that "Watts has put together a forward-looking band that doesn't take its work lightly. Throughout ['Samo'] and the rest of the album, [the band members] create patterns that drive the songs without ever lapsing into ordinary rhythms. That's not surprising from Watts." James Hale, reviewing *Folk's Songs* for *Down Beat* (September 2007), was impressed by the album, though he found fault with Watts's leadership: "Watts has long since established himself as the exemplar of seamless modern drumming. He has an unparalleled ability to introduce rhythmic nuances and maintain a taut time structure behind soloists. Witness the way he keeps a tough edge on 'Laura Elizabeth' and builds intensity behind pianist David Kikoski. As a bandleader and producer, though, he could benefit from a shade less self-indulgence."

In 2008 Watts performed on *Letter to Herbie*, a survey of various Herbie Hancock compositions; the album, by the Los Angeles–based contemporary jazz pianist and composer John Beasley, reached the top spot on the jazz music charts.

Watts has cited the work of the jazz drummers Elvin Jones, Roy Haynes, Art Blakey, Ed Blackwell, and Max Roach as influences on his own music. He was voted best drummer by *Modern Drummer* magazine in 1988 and 1993. Watts played the role of the drummer Rhythm Jones in Spike Lee's 1990 film, *Mo' Better Blues*. It has been reported that he is dating the trumpeter Laura Kahle, who has per-

formed with him and, since 2005, has aided him as a copyist and arranger.

—F.C.

Suggested Reading: (Alberta, Canada) *Calgary Herald* HL p14 Oct. 14, 1999; All About Jazz Web site July 2002; *Boston Globe* C p17 Apr. 23, 1999; Columbia Records Web site; *Down Beat* p40 Nov. 2002, p70 Sep. 2007; Jeff "Tain" Watts Web site; PR Newswire May 8, 2002; *St. Louis (Missouri) Post Dispatch* p30 Dec. 31, 2003; *Washington Post* C p9 Feb. 5, 2000

Selected Recordings: as bandleader—*Citizen Tain*, 1999; *Bar Talk*, 2002; *Megawatts*, 2003; *DeTAINed at the Blue Note*, 2004; *Folk's Songs*, 2007; with the Wynton Marsalis Quintet—*Black Codes (From the Underground)*, 1985; *J Mood*, 1985; *Marsalis Standard Time—Vol. 1*, 1986; with the Branford Marsalis Quartet—*I Heard You Twice the First Time*, 1992; *Contemporary Jazz*, 2000

Andrea Cipriani Mecchi, courtesy of Simon & Schuster

Weiner, Jennifer

(WYE-ner)

Mar. 28, 1970– Writer

Address: c/o Atria Publicity Dept., Simon & Schuster, 1230 Ave. of the Americas, New York, NY 10020

Jennifer Weiner has helped to popularize "chick lit," a genre of books featuring young, female protagonists struggling to manage their careers, find true love, and reform their eating and spending habits. Weiner has been vocal in defending her work and that of her fellow chick-lit writers against those who use the term disparagingly. She told Ron Hogan for the literary blog Beatrice.com (March 9, 2005), "Writing funny, fast-moving fiction about young women finding their place in the world means your invitation to join the Beautiful Sentence Society will be permanently lost in the mail. The *New York Times* won't review you; the newsweeklies won't write profiles, and don't even get me started on what will happen when you query the *New Yorker*." She elaborated on the theme in a post on her own blog: "The more I think about the increasingly angry divide between ladies who write literature and chicks who write chick lit, the more it seems like a grown-up version of the smart versus pretty games of years ago; like so much jockeying for position in the cafeteria and mocking the girls who are nerdier/sluttier/stupider than you to make yourself feel more secure about your own place in the pecking order." There seems to be little doubt in the minds of Weiner's fans as to her place in the pecking order: some 10 million copies of her books exist in print; each of her titles has landed on the *New York Times* best-seller list; and they have been published in more than 30 countries, including China and Bulgaria.

Jennifer Weiner was born on March 28, 1970 in DeRidder, Louisiana. Two years later she moved to the affluent suburb of Simsbury, Connecticut, with her parents, Lawrence and Fran, and her sister, Molly. The couple later had two more children, Jake and Joe. When Weiner was 16 years old, Lawrence, a psychiatrist, abandoned the family. (Fran, a teacher, later began dating women.) Weiner remembers being unpopular in high school. "It's very funny, there's a bit of revisionist history going on in my home town now," she told Tracy Cochran for *Publishers Weekly* (September 13, 2004). "I spoke at an event there about a year and a half ago and the mother of this boy who had just tormented me and hated me in high school introduced me. He was one of the really popular and good-looking boys. I don't even think I was allowed to make direct eye contact with him. Yet his mother went on and on about what close friends he and I were. . . . The truth was that he would have rather died than speak to me then."

While struggling socially, Weiner was a stellar student, and in 1987 she enrolled at Princeton University, in New Jersey, where she studied writing with such luminaries as Toni Morrison, Joyce Carol Oates, and John McPhee. In 1990 Weiner won Princeton's Academy of American Poets Prize, and the following year she graduated, summa cum laude. Despite her academic and literary achievements, her college years were not completely happy. "I remember every semester in college you go to register for classes and you would get pulled out of line if your parents hadn't paid," she recalled to Cochran. "I remember every goddamned semester

I had to go to the financial aid office and say, 'I don't know where [my father] is and he owes my mom alimony and I don't know what's going on but somebody is going to pay for this.' That somebody wound up being my mother and me. I remember thinking I don't want my life to be like this. I don't want to have to depend on anybody else for my security, financial or otherwise."

After graduating from Princeton, Weiner took a six-week journalism class at the Poynter Institute for Media Studies, in Florida, and accepted a job in central Pennsylvania as an education reporter for the *Centre Daily Times*. She explained on her Web site: "When I was finishing up with college, lo these many years ago, I had an English degree, which meant that I was qualified to do precisely nothing, except compose lovely paragraphs, and speak knowledgeably about French feminist literary theory. . . . I was lucky enough to have John McPhee as a professor, and he was generous enough to give me the best piece of advice ever—go into journalism. 'You'll see a different part of the world. You'll meet all kinds of people. You'll be writing every day, on deadline'—which, of course, turned out to be invaluable when it came time to write fiction."

In addition to her reporting, in 1992 Weiner was assigned by her editors to write a youth-oriented column for the *Centre Daily Times*. The Knight-Ridder news wire began distributing the columns—which covered such topics as safe sex and the challenges facing political candidates seeking the youth vote—to papers all over the country. Meanwhile, Weiner continued writing fiction and was occasionally able to sell short stories to such magazines as *Redbook* and *Seventeen*.

In 1994 Weiner moved to Lexington, Kentucky, to write features for the *Lexington Herald Leader*. In 1995 she moved back to the East Coast to become a general-assignment writer for the *Philadelphia Inquirer*, a major paper that had previously published her columns. Her new editors insisted that she stop writing opinion pieces, and, as she joked on her Web site's timeline, "Realizing that [I'd] pretty much ridden the Gen-X trend into the ground, and after editors and peers gently point out that [I] will not be twentysomething forever, [I] agree." While at the *Philadelphia Inquirer*, Weiner profiled such celebrities as the comedian and actor Adam Sandler and the Mafia wife Victoria Gotti and wrote articles on such diverse topics as the Miss America Pageant, gefilte fish, and drug abuse. Concurrently, in 1998 she became a contributing editor at *Mademoiselle* and made regular appearances as a cultural commentator on a local television show, *Philly After Midnight*.

Weiner was inspired to write her first novel, *Good in Bed* (2001), by events in her own life. "I got dumped," she explained to Bryant Gumbel for CBS News (May 29, 2001). "And my heart was broken. And people with broken hearts are really boring. I mean, you . . . go around sounding like really bad Britney Spears, you know, my heart will never smile again. And there's a gray cloud in my soul. And my friends were getting really sick of listening to me. . . . I was getting really sick of sounding that way, to tell you the truth. And so I said, 'I'm going to write a book about somebody with a broken heart like this and I'm going to make it funny.'" *Good in Bed* tells the story of Cannie Shapiro, a witty young Jewish woman who is humiliated when her ex-boyfriend writes an article for a national magazine about "loving a larger woman" in a weight-obsessed society. Cannie overcomes the embarrassment and ultimately finds romance without compromising herself or losing weight.

Weiner, who has fought her own weight battles for years, submitted sample chapters of *Good in Bed* to more than 20 agents. Most of them immediately refused to represent the young writer; one agreed to try to sell the book only if Weiner rewrote it to make Cannie thinner. Referring to the heroine of a popular 1996 chick-lit book, Weiner told Sara Vilkomerson for the *New York Observer* (July 11, 2005), "I remember thinking, 'Cannie's weight is the plight of the whole book, and if I take it out she's just Bridget Jones at a bat mitzvah.'" Eventually, as Weiner wrote on her Web site, "[I] found what I was looking for—an agent who was in love with what I'd written, who got it on every level, who was going to do her damndest to find my book a happy home. And that, bless her adorable little size-two heart, is exactly what Joanna Pulcini did." Pulcini sold the book in less than a week, for a reported six-figure sum. It quickly landed on the *New York Times* best-seller list and has since been published in more than 15 languages.

While Weiner has often joked that her Princeton professors must be horrified by the popular appeal of her work, she is unabashed by her commercial success. She told Cochran, "If I were to do a Marxist critique, I'd say [there] is a reaction against women gaining power and economic stature in the marketplace. Book sales are flat, chick lit sales are up. And that's scary to a lot of people."

Weiner left the *Philadelphia Inquirer* to promote *Good in Bed* and begin writing her second novel. Like her career, her personal life was undergoing change: in October 2001 she married Adam Bonin, a lawyer, and the pair rented Philadelphia's Mutter Museum, which houses an extensive collection of items concerning medical oddities, for the wedding reception.

In 2002 Weiner's sophomore novel, *In Her Shoes*, was published. It tells the story of two sisters: the professionally successful but frumpy and depressed Rose and the beautiful, dyslexic party girl Maggie. Carole Goldberg wrote for the *Hartford Courant* (November 3, 2002), "This is a Cinderella fable with a wicked stepmother, an ugly stepsister, an unlikely prince, and two heroines who turn out to be each other's fairy godmothers. If you're shopping for a modern fairy tale with plenty of humor and heart, and *In Her Shoes* fits, then wear it." Other reviewers were less favorably impressed. Debra Pickett, for example, wrote for the *Chicago Sun-Times* (November 17, 2002), "The 'hook' that helped propel both of Weiner's books onto the best-seller lists is that her heroines—journalist Cannie Shapiro in *Good in Bed* and lawyer Rose Fuller—are plus-sized women. And the evil women who variously try to steal their men, make them look bad at work and do all sorts of other terrible stuff to them are all thin. The one thing you know about every single female character in Weiner's books is what dress size she wears. And, from that, you can determine virtually everything else about her. Large women are smart and hardworking. They eat right and exercise and always do the right thing. Skinny women are lazy and troubled. . . . They mindlessly step over people, since the world lays out a red carpet for them." Despite the varied critical responses, *In Her Shoes* enjoyed stellar sales, and Weiner, then pregnant with her first child, Lucy Jane, was met by large crowds of fans as she toured to promote the book. In 2005 a big-screen adaptation of *In Her Shoes* was released. The film starred Cameron Diaz as Maggie; Toni Collette (who gained 20 pounds for the role) as Rose; and Shirley MacLaine as Ella, the girls' feisty grandmother. Cameo roles were found for Weiner and her sister, grandmother, and agent. Weiner wrote for the *Philadelphia Inquirer* (September 11, 2005), "There's no easy way to describe what it feels like to sit in the dark and see something you've dreamed up in your head up there on the big screen, larger than life and, in the case of Cameron Diaz, a hundred times better-looking. Surreal doesn't begin to cover it."

Weiner's next book and third *New York Times* best-seller, *Little Earthquakes* (2004), is the story of a group of friends living in Philadelphia and adjusting to pregnancy and new motherhood: Becky, a warmhearted chef with a doting husband and an overbearing mother-in-law; Ayinde, the glamorous wife of a philandering pro basketball star; Kelly, a perky, blond party planner; and Lia, an actress whose baby has died. "After I'd finished *Little Earthquakes*, I found myself missing the characters," Deborah Sussman Susser wrote for the *Washington Post* (September 15, 2004, on-line). "Theirs is a world where young mothers invite strange women in distress into their homes, serve them tea and sympathy and tell them, in essence, 'You go, girlfriend.' It may not be realistic as literary worlds go, but it is reassuring in its warmth and predictability. And judging by the success of chick lit generally and Weiner's books specifically, a lot of us out there are willing—even eager—to suspend our disbelief long enough to enter it." Melinda Bargreen wrote for the *Seattle Times* (September 19, 2004, on-line), "Full of snappy dialogue, *Little Earthquakes* is grown-up chick lit for readers who may be relieved to discover there is life beyond the genre's eternal quest for suitable husbands."

Weiner considered calling her next book—the 2005 tale of a housewife who becomes embroiled in a murder mystery—"Momicide." She decided instead on *Goodnight Nobody*, an allusion to a line in the popular children's book *Goodnight Moon* by Margaret Wise Brown. Kate Klein, the protagonist of *Goodnight Nobody*, is a young mother who finds herself overwhelmed by the demands of her three children. When she discovers one of her neighbors stabbed to death on the floor of her otherwise immaculate kitchen, Kate sees a chance to escape the tedium of suburbia by solving the crime. Some critics found Weiner's venture into the mystery genre disappointing. Missy Schwartz wrote for *Entertainment Weekly* (September 16, 2005, on-line), "Jennifer Weiner has a gift for creating funny, flawed heroines . . . but as a suspense writer, she's still finding her footing. The *Desperate Housewives* gimmick throws *Goodnight Nobody* off focus, robbing us of Weiner's typically razor-sharp originality." Other reviews were more positive. "As with all of Weiner's novels, *Goodnight Nobody* is witty and clever, and Weiner proves that her writing prowess extends beyond chick lit and deeply into the mystery genre," Roberta O'Hara wrote for the Book Reporter Web site. "Although the ending verged on over-the-top, to Weiner's credit it was a huge surprise. The quality of this novel, however, was no surprise. Weiner is gifted and funny, and *Goodnight Nobody* equals her earlier well-received works."

In 2006 Weiner published a short-story collection, *The Guy Not Taken*. Weiner had written the pieces in the volume over the span of several years. Two, "Just Desserts" and "Travels with Nicki," had been written while she was still attending Princeton, while the title story, about a woman who becomes obsessed by her ex-boyfriend's on-line wedding registry, had been originally published in *Glamour* the year before. Many of the stories touched on themes from Weiner's own life, among them divorce, absent fathers, and onerous college tuitions. Carol Memmott wrote for *USA Today* (September 7, 2006), "Jennifer Weiner is resigned to the fact that in some circles she is referred to as the 'Queen of Chick Lit.' But I challenge anyone who says her short-story collection, *The Guy Not Taken*, isn't serious women's fiction. Not that there's anything wrong with chick lit, but the women in these stories are a far cry from the Manolo-obsessed bubbleheads sometimes found in chick lit novels. These women apply healthy doses of self-doubt, loneliness, and misgivings along with their lipgloss and mascara. . . . All the stories in Weiner's collection have that 'Calgon, Take Me Away' quality to which smart women, whose lives are complicated by careers, men, babies, parents, and siblings, can relate."

Weiner's most recent novel, *Certain Girls* (2008), continues the story of Cannie Shapiro from *Good in Bed*. "In her bubbly new novel, *Certain Girls*, Jennifer Weiner achieves the nearly impossible: She makes being a fat, middle-aged woman in America appear not just acceptable but positively delightful," Jennifer Reese wrote for *Entertainment Weekly* (April 4, 2008, on-line). "Cannie was appealing as a lovelorn career girl, but she's even more likable as a sanguine matron with a minivan and a Crock-Pot."

Although most critics were happy to see Cannie return, the respected novelist Jane Smiley wrote in a review for the *Philadelphia Inquirer* (April 6, 2008, on-line), "Just so you know the target audience, Jennifer Weiner's new novel, *Certain Girls*, is about the pinkest book you can imagine. The jacket is pale pink; the endpapers are practically fuchsia. The jacket also sports a fluffy skirt and some very high heels." Smiley continued, "I mention these things because Weiner does not need to be published in pink—her publishers could target a general audience. Weiner is a talented and accomplished novelist, with real stylistic flair, excellent and sometimes laugh-out-loud wit, and good insight into her characters. In her latest novel, she seems boxed in by her chosen genre, and it's a shame, because she's got the intelligence and the ambition to address larger questions than the psychological ups and downs of her nice Jewish characters. For whatever reason, though, she doesn't dare." The review was widely quoted on the Internet and set off renewed debate on the merits of chick lit. Weiner responded during an interview with Jeffrey A. Trachtenberg for the *Wall Street Journal* (April 11, 2008, on-line): "The *Inquirer* has a right to hire whomever they want, and Jane Smiley has a right to her opinions. The only part that surprised me was her taking issue with the pink cover. That's not something I have a lot of control over. Maybe Jane Smiley tells her publisher what cover to give her." Weiner continued, "When an older writer tries to tell a younger writer through a review what kind of career she should be pursuing, it tends to speak to the reviewer's anxieties rather than the book itself. . . . It made me think the book was her jumping off place. But I'll be Jane Smiley's trampoline any day."

While *In Her Shoes* is Weiner's only book thus far to be adapted for the screen, it has been reported that HBO is developing a series based on *Good in Bed*, *Little Earthquakes* is in development at Universal, and DreamWorks has optioned the rights to *The Guy Not Taken*. In early 2008 Weiner signed a two-year, seven-figure deal with ABC to create and produce programs for the company.

Weiner, who had a second daughter, Phoebe Pearl, in 2007, lives with her family in a restored row house in Philadelphia. She told Ellen Futterman for the *St. Louis Post-Dispatch* (November 29, 2006), "If you look at the books I've written, you can sort of chart my life, from being single to getting married to having a baby. But it's not ever all my story because my story is not that interesting. It's more the raw materials of my life and my friends' lives and readers' lives whipped into a meringue of fiction."

—T.O.

Suggested Reading: Beatrice.com Mar. 9, 2005; *Boston Globe* D p6 Oct. 10, 2004; *Chicago Sun-Times* p9 Nov. 17, 2002, p13 Oct. 24, 2004;

Entertainment Weekly (on-line) Sep. 16, 2005, Apr. 4, 2008; *Hartford Courant* G p3 Nov. 3, 2002; *New York Observer* I p11 July 11, 2005; *Philadelphia Inquirer* M p1 Sep. 11, 2005, (on-line) Apr. 6, 2008; *San Francisco Chronicle* D p1 Oct. 30, 2005; *Seattle Times* (on-line) Sep. 19, 2004; *St. Louis Post-Dispatch* E p1 Nov. 29, 2006; *USA Today* D p7 Sep. 29, 2005, D p7 Sep. 7, 2006; *Washington Post* (on-line) Sep. 15, 2004

Selected Books: *Good in Bed*, 2001; *In Her Shoes*, 2002; *Little Earthquakes*, 2004; *Goodnight Nobody*, 2005; *The Guy Not Taken*, 2006; *Certain Girls*, 2008

David Evans, Courtesy of National Geographic

Wells, Spencer

Apr. 6, 1969– Population geneticist; head of the Genographic Project

Address: c/o National Geographic Society, P.O. Box 98199, Washington, DC 20090-8199

"The greatest history book ever written is the one hidden in our DNA," the geneticist Spencer Wells said, as posted on the Web site of the Genographic Project, a five-year initiative to collect 100,000 DNA samples from people around the world. Wells spearheaded the project—which is co-sponsored by the National Geographic Society and IBM, as well as various private donors—in 2005, in an effort to trace mankind's geographic and genetic passage to the present day. The site explains, "The fossil record fixes human origins in Africa, but little is known about the great journey that took *Homo*

sapiens to the far reaches of the Earth. How did we, each of us, end up where we are? Why do we appear in such a wide array of different colors and features? Such questions are even more amazing in light of genetic evidence that we are all related—descended from a common African ancestor who lived only 60,000 years ago. Though eons have passed, the full story remains clearly written in our genes—if only we can read it." The project, while widely lauded by the scientific community, has occasionally met with negative reaction: members of some indigenous groups, for example, have characterized the DNA collection as exploitive. Others are disturbed because population genetics, as Wells's field is known, has challenged certain long-held notions of race—notions he believes are not only socially divisive and harmful, but scientifically incorrect. "People are an interwoven tapestry," Wells told Tania Tan for the Singapore *Straits Times* (July 28, 2007). "There's a little bit of everyone in everyone."

Spencer Wells was born on April 6, 1969 in Georgia and was raised in Lubbock, Texas. His mother was a biologist at Texas Tech University, and his father was a tax attorney. Wells, who aspired as a young child to be a writer or a historian, credits a 1979 PBS series called *Connections* for sparking his interest in science. He spent time in the lab with his mother and realized, "Science was really fun and cool. It's not just about geeky guys in white lab coats, it's about solving puzzles on a daily basis," as he recalled to Jane Gitschier for the Public Library of Science (PLoS) *Genetics Journal* (March 30, 2007, on-line). Wells attended a progressive school that grouped students according to ability rather than age; he typically studied with students older than himself and is often referred to in the media as a prodigy. At age 16 Wells enrolled at the University of Texas, where he majored in biology and worked on an independent study of theoretical population genetics. Elected to the honor society Phi Beta Kappa, Wells finished his undergraduate studies in just three years.

While making plans to attend graduate school at the University of Texas, Wells was invited to study with the famed evolutionary geneticist Richard Lewontin at Harvard University, in Cambridge, Massachusetts. There he earned his Ph.D. degree in population genetics, in 1994, at the age of 25. For his dissertation Wells studied the genome of *Drosophila* (commonly called the fruit fly). He grew increasingly weary of working in a lab, however, and longed to get out in the field and study humans. "At the end of the day I wasn't terribly interested in the population structure of fruit flies," he told Gitschier, "but I had always been interested in human history." (He additionally explained that his grandfather, who died in World War II, had a reputation as a fearless military man: "I think maybe I got some of my love of danger and going to strange places from him.")

Wells went on to conduct postdoctoral research at the Stanford University School of Medicine, in California, where he worked with Luigi Luca Cavalli-Sforza, who is credited with founding the field of human population genetics. While at Stanford Wells became excited about the study of genomic diversity in indigenous populations, as a means of tracking the migration of ancient man.

Questions of human origin and migration had long been explored almost exclusively by cultural anthropologists, who examined relationships among human populations through the disciplines of ethnography, archaeology, and linguistics. That changed greatly in the 1980s, when developments in molecular biology made possible the study of genetic variations at the DNA level. (DNA, or deoxyribonucleic acid, is the genetic material that acts as a blueprint for cells.) While 99.9 percent of DNA is common to all humans, and most of the remaining .1 percent is a mixture of genetic material from a given person's mother and father, there are certain genes that are passed from individual parent to offspring fully intact. Mitochondrial DNA (mtDNA), for example, is passed directly from mother to child, and the Y chromosome is passed unchanged from father to son. When DNA is replicated during cell division, a mutation occasionally occurs; if such a mutation occurs on either the mtDNA or the Y chromosome, that mutation becomes a genetic marker, and it is passed down to all subsequent generations. "If you share a marker with someone, you share an ancestor in the past," Wells explained to a journalist for the *Chicago Tribune* (April 14, 2005). "It's by looking at the pattern of these variances, and connecting people with these markers in networks, that we can trace people around the world."

Geneticists have determined that all modern humans are descended from one woman and one man—dubbed Adam and Eve—who lived in Africa between 60,000 and 200,000 years ago. The notion of our African origins is supported by tests that show "more genetic diversity in a single African village than in the whole world outside Africa," Wells told Greg Callaghan for the *Australian Magazine* (July 30, 2004). Archaeologists have determined that the first wave of humans—probably no more than a couple of thousand—migrated out of Africa to the shores of eastern Asia between 50,000 and 70,000 years ago, when major climate changes affected Africa; all of today's non-Africans share a genetic marker common to that first migrating group. Once in Asia the population split, with some moving into the Middle East and others venturing into India. Scientists have estimated that humans first crossed the Bering Strait into the Americas some 15,000 to 20,000 years ago. "The movement was probably imperceptible," Wells explained to James Shreeve for *National Geographic* (March 1, 2006). "It was less of a journey and probably more like walking a little farther down the beach to get away from the crowd."

Wells's postdoctoral research focused on developing more detailed maps of those ancient migrations by gathering DNA directly from indigenous populations and analyzing it. The Genographic Project Web site explains, "In a shrinking world, mixing populations are scrambling genetic signals. The key to this puzzle is acquiring genetic samples from the world's remaining indigenous and traditional peoples whose ethnic and genetic identities are isolated." Efforts to collect DNA from indigenous populations had been stymied in the past, however, largely for geopolitical and cultural reasons. In the 1990s, for example, Cavalli-Sforza had headed the Human Genome Diversity Project, an effort to collect DNA samples from hundreds of indigenous populations; though the scientific community viewed the enterprise as universally beneficial, many indigenous groups felt exploited. Some raised concerns of intellectual property rights and requested compensation for any medical or commercial use of their DNA. Others found the act of collecting DNA samples antithetical to their cultural or religious beliefs. Still others worried that having concise information about their origins could jeopardize land rights that had been granted on the basis that their ancestors had always occupied a particular area. Because of the controversy, the U.S. government refused to fund the project, which then came to a halt. Wells hoped that in an increasingly globalized world, his own efforts would be better received. (He took particular care to make clear that the DNA samples would not be put to any commercial use.)

In the summer of 1996, Wells traveled to the central Asian nations of Uzbekistan, Kyrgyzstan, and Kazakhstan, areas that had previously been the focus of very little genetic research. He spent five weeks collecting human blood samples from members of 13 indigenous groups, whose ancestors had lived in the same place for centuries. Subjects received analyses of their DNA, and Wells reported that most people were pleased to participate. "People tend to get really excited about that, I find," Wells told Gitschier. "They want to know more. They say 'I'll give you the sample, but make sure you get the information back to me, and tell me what it's all about.'" Wells told Elia Ben-Ari for *BioScience* (February 1999), "[During the 1996 trip] we found evidence of what we think are Middle Eastern genes [moving] eastward along the Silk Road into China," and explained that a certain Y chromosome marker appeared in high frequency in Mongolians, but hardly at all in central Asians, suggesting that although the Mongols had conquered Asia militarily, they "probably didn't leave as strong a genetic impression as they did a cultural and historical one."

Excited by his preliminary data, in 1998 Wells decided to expand his research to include some 25,000 miles of the legendary Silk Road, an intercontinental trade route connecting the imperial court of China, in the East, to the Roman Empire, in the West. Wells and his colleagues dubbed the trip Eurasia '98 and launched a Web site, which they updated from the road with journal entries and photographs. Starting from London, they spent six months driving across Europe through Central Asia, stopping to work with local officials and physicians to collect genetic material—about 50 samples per location. Along the way, the team encountered occasional political difficulties; one notable example took place on the border between Azerbaijan and Iran, during a time when the United States had no formal relations with the latter country. Lacking the credentials to drive across the border, the group split up, with part of the team flying to the Iranian capital, Tehran, and Wells ferrying the car across the Caspian Sea.

At the completion of the trip, Wells was appointed the director of the Population Genetics Research Group, part of the Wellcome Trust Centre for Human Genetics at Oxford University, in England. "Things started to get really exciting scientifically. We had a huge number of samples," Wells told Gitschier. "Every experiment we ran was exciting and new. You're getting these results and they start to make sense. Piecing together migratory patterns." One newly discovered genetic marker that had originated in Mongolia some 800 years ago indicated that 8 percent of the men of central and eastern Asia—and one in 200 men in the world—is a descendant of Genghis Khan, a 13th-century ruler of the Mongolian Empire.

Wells next accepted a position as head researcher at a Massachusetts-based biotechnology company. While there, a producer from the Public Broadcasting Service (PBS) contacted him about making a film explaining his work. The result was *The Journey of Man: A Genetic Odyssey*, a video documentary that followed Wells and a team as they collected DNA samples throughout Africa, Australia, the Middle East, the Himalayas, and the United States. The documentary aired on PBS in the United States in 2001 and internationally on the National Geographic Channel in late 2002. Wells also wrote a companion book of the same title, published in February 2002. In a review for the *New York Times* (March 2, 2003, on-line), Carl Zimmer wrote, "Wells traces our distant history with a mix of clarity and charm that's rare among scientists. He makes the complexities of population genetics wonderfully clear with smart metaphors. And he navigates gracefully from his home waters of genetics into paleontology and climatology and back again."

"At the time I wrote the book, we had sampled maybe 10,000 people around the world, 10,000 out of 6.5 billion," Wells explained on the *Charlie Rose Show* (January 23, 2006). "That's not a great sample size." Thanks in large part to public interest in the book and film, however, the National Geographic Society offered to fund further research, and IBM and the Waitt Family Foundation signed on as well. With backers in place, Wells designed the five-year, $52 million Genographic Project. In addition to creating a vast genetic database for use by scientists, the project, which was officially launched on April 13, 2005, aims to raise awareness about the issues facing indigenous populations and to educate the public about genetics and anthropology. Wells has also invited private individuals to take part by purchasing kits priced at $99.95, which enable them to submit their DNA for testing via a cheek swab. The test results are sent to the purchasers and incorporated into the collective database (if permission is granted). "Your results will reveal your deep ancestry along a single line of direct descent (paternal or maternal) and show the migration paths they followed thousands of years ago. Your results will also place you on a particular branch of the human family tree," Wells wrote for the project Web site. "Your individual results may confirm your expectations of what you believe your deep ancestry to be, or you may be surprised to learn a new story about your genetic background."

A portion of the proceeds from the kits funds the Genographic Legacy Project, which awards grants for the cultural preservation of the participating indigenous groups. Like previous DNA collection efforts, however, the Genographic Project earned significant criticism from various indigenous groups. Debra Harry, the executive director of the Indigenous Council on Biocolonialism (ICBC), told Charlie Furniss for the journal *Geographical* (September 1, 2006), "All over the world we are being killed, we are being displaced. And while this is going on, the Genographic Project is spending millions of dollars on a study that hopes to show the patterns of population migrations. It's hard to see how this is a collaboration. Why don't they bring that money to us and ask us what we really need?" As had been the case with the Human Genome Diversity Project, some tribal leaders expressed concern that the project's findings on human migration would undermine their claims on their native lands and threaten their security. As before, some considered the idea of obtaining genetic material spiritually offensive and disrespectful to their ancestors, and they worried that migratory mapping might contradict beloved traditional stories about their origins. Wells has interpreted such criticisms as politically motivated and paternalistic. "We have encountered little resistance to the project in the field, where we are able to explain the project directly to prospective participants," he told Furniss. "The vast majority of those we have approached—more than 95 percent—have agreed to participate. In parts of North America and Russia, we've even had communities approaching us. Those who have refused have done so because of a fear of needles or something, not because they object to the project."

Wells—dubbed an "explorer-in-residence" for the National Geographic Society—documented many of his genetic discoveries in his second book, *Deep Ancestry: Inside the Genographic Project*, which was published in late 2007. That year Wells was the winner of the Foundation of the Future

Kistler Prize, a $100,000 cash award "given to a scientist or research institution that has, with courage and wisdom, pursued the truth and made original, substantive, and innovative contributions in the study of the connections between the human genome and human society," according to the foundation's Web site.

A press release posted on the Genographic Project's Web site (July 15, 2008) announced that project researchers had discovered a previously unknown mtDNA sequence, containing a deletion—an abnormality in which part of a single chromosome has been lost—that constituted nearly 1 percent of the total mtDNA genome. That variant was unusual, because the deletion exists in a region of the genome that was previously thought to be critical for the replication process. According to the press release, "Comprising nearly 52,000 individual mtDNA genotypes from individuals from approximately 180 countries, the update represents a significant increase over the 21,000 mtDNA genotypes released by the project in 2007." Wells and other project scientists credited the unprecedented size and scope of the project's database, and the correspondingly comprehensive amount of data, for enabling them to make their discovery.

Wells has been featured in several PBS and National Geographic documentaries, including *Explorer: Quest for the Phoenicians* (2004), *The Search for Adam* (2005), and *China's Secret Mummies* (2007). He lives in Washington, D.C., with his wife, the documentary filmmaker Pamela Caragol Wells. He has two daughters, Margot and Sasha, from a previous marriage. In his free time he enjoys skiing, sailing, and taking photographs, among other activities.

To date the Genographic Project has collected more than 30,000 samples from indigenous groups worldwide, and more than 200,000 individuals have submitted their DNA using the kits.

—M.E.R.

Suggested Reading: *Australian Magazine* p1 July 30, 2005; *Bioscience* p98 Feb. 1999; *Charlie Rose Show* Jan. 23, 2006; *Chicago Tribune* C p12 Apr. 14, 2005; *Discover* p32+ Dec. 1, 2004; Genographic Project Web site; *Geographical* p43 Sep. 1, 2006; *National Geographic* p70+ Mar. 1, 2006; *New York Times* A p1 Mar. 7, 2006, (online) Mar. 2, 2003; Public Library of Science *Genetics Journal* (on-line) Mar. 30, 2006; (Singapore) *Straits Times* July 28, 2007

Selected Books: *The Journey of Man: A Genetic Odyssey*, 2002; *Deep Ancestry: Inside the Genographic Project*, 2007

Selected Films: *The Journey of Man: A Genetic Odyssey*, 2001; *Explorer: Quest for the Phoenicians*; 2004; *The Search for Adam*, 2005; *China's Secret Mummies*, 2007

Williams, Juan

Apr. 10, 1954– Print and broadcast journalist; writer

Address: Fox News Channel, 400 N. Capitol St., N.W., Suite 550, Washington, DC 20001

When asked during an interview with Bill Steigerwald for frontpagemagazine.com (September 27, 2006) if he had "turned into a black conservative," the outspoken journalist, author, pundit, and National Public Radio correspondent Juan Williams said, "No. I think I've been pretty consistent. I've always been a guy who has a strong belief in family values, the church, a strong belief in Christ. . . . I've always said education is Number One. These are not things that have just come to me." Since he began his career, as a reporter for the *Washington Post* in the 1970s, Williams has been a vocal critic of post–civil rights era African-American leadership, written extensively on issues regarding religious faith as well as race and politics, and, in print and on numerous television news shows and radio programs, defended controversial conservative figures—actions that might lead one to conclude that he has conservative leanings. But Williams, who has won awards and critical acclaim for his investi-gative journalism, documentaries, books, and radio-show segments, merely believes that many African-American community leaders have not led effectively, and that it is incumbent upon African-Americans to "empower" the black community, as he put it to Steigerwald: "Use your political leverage: vote for both the Democrat[ic] and Republic[can] party. Make them compete for your vote and your attention. Thoroughly empower yourself by educating yourself and preparing yourself for opportunities. That what's imperative for this generation. That's the civil rights movement of the 21st century."

One of three children, Juan Williams was born on April 10, 1954 in Colon, Panama, a seaport city near the Panama Canal. His father, Rogelio, was a Jamaican-born boxing trainer and a follower of Anglican Christianity, a form of the faith with close ties to the Church of England. Williams's sister, Alaina, is 10 years older; when she was about to start high school, "my parents . . . didn't like the way the boys in Panama were looking at that cute, young girl and wanted to make sure that she got an education," Williams told Brian Lamb for *Booknotes* (October 11, 1998, on-line). "And their greatest desire was to get an American education for their children." In 1958, when Williams was four years old, he moved with his mother, sister,

Courtesy of Crown Publishing Group

Juan Williams

and brother to the Bedford-Stuyvesant neighborhood of Brooklyn, New York. His father, who arrived there later, became an accountant, and his mother, Alma, worked as a secretary and seamstress.

Williams has said that growing up as an immigrant in largely black Bedford-Stuyvesant made for an unusual experience. He told a writer for the *Christian Century* (May 31, 2003), "The black experience in this country was new to me as a child. I started exploring the neighborhood, meeting new people—it all had a sense of wonder for me." He has said that one of the most profound observations he made concerned the power of religion in the community; specifically, the church's direct influence on community affairs had an impact on his own perception of faith. "One of the first things I remember noticing was the power and diversity of the church . . . the black church in all this variety seemed omnipresent in my corner of Brooklyn . . . ," he told the *Christian Century*. "People were going to church not only on Sunday but also on Tuesday and Wednesday nights for some auxiliary board meeting, women's meeting or youth group. The black community was defined at the center by the black churches." The Episcopal church to which the Williams family belonged "was extraordinarily supportive of my family, helped my sister and brother in everything from clothes to spending money as they went off to college," Williams told the *Christian Century*. His sister attended Swarthmore College, in Swarthmore, Pennsylvania, and later Harvard University, in Cambridge, Massachusetts; his brother enrolled at New York University Law School.

After attending public school for several years, Williams won a scholarship to Oakwood Friends, a college-preparatory school in Poughkeepsie, New York. He then enrolled at Haverford College, in Haverford, Pennsylvania, where he majored in philosophy and graduated with a bachelor's degree in 1976. That year he also began an internship that would lead to a staff position at the *Washington Post*. He began as a staff writer covering local news; in the early 1980s he made the transition to local and national politics, offering both reportage and commentary, and by the late 1980s he had begun to serve as an editorial columnist.

While he had a successful career at the paper, Williams has suggested that his 23 years there were not always pleasant. In a speech to students at the Reynolds School of Journalism, in Reno, Nevada, as Marti Howill reported for the *Zephyr* (May 2, 2001, on-line), he said, "There was a lot of tension between black and white reporters [in the 1970s]. There was a lot of the tension in society in the newsroom." He himself, he said, was viewed as "a novelty. Here was a black man talking about events at the White House." As a member of the *Washington Post*'s staff, Williams excelled at covering city news, often touching on issues related to the African-American community.

For the *Post* Williams wrote many editorial pieces on such issues as education and black leadership. In an article published on May 17, 1979, for example, he discussed the reputedly poor quality of the predominantly African-American public schools in Washington, D.C., focusing on James Nabrit, a lawyer who had fought segregation in the capital city's public schools 25 years earlier. "In Nabrit's opinion time has produced an unlikely opponent to thwart his victory for a better education for young black Washingtonians," Williams wrote. "That enemy, Nabrit says, is black parents, black children, a mostly black school board and black superintendent now in District schools. They have defeated Nabrit by creating a school system that despite having all of the city's $44 million for education and no evil white racists to point a finger at, drowns Nabrit's victory in a sea of inefficiency and failure. Nabrit, who fought against white officials who relegated black youth to second-class schools, now points to black officials who relegate black youth to second-rate schools 25 years later." Williams has continued to write opinion columns and books citing poor education and leadership within the African-American community as obstacles to blacks' making further strides. During his time at the paper, Williams was also active as an often liberal-leaning pundit in other media, frequently taking part in radio and television shows to discuss political issues.

In 1987 Williams's first book, *Eyes on the Prize: America's Civil Rights Years, 1954–1965*, was published by Viking Press. The book detailed such groundbreaking events as the U.S. Supreme Court decision in *Brown v. Board of Education of Topeka, Kansas*, which sparked the nationwide school-desegregation movement; the 1955 bus boycott in Montgomery, Alabama; the 1963 March on Washington, D.C.; and passage of the Voting Rights Act of 1965. For the book Williams conducted interviews with many leading and lesser-known civil rights activists from the period. The book was written as a companion piece to the Public Broadcasting Service (PBS)–produced documentary series of the same name, which originally aired in 1987.

In 1991 Williams became a controversial figure when he defended the U.S. Supreme Court nominee Clarence Thomas, an African-American with conservative views, who during the confirmation process had been accused by Anita Hill, a former colleague of Thomas's, of sexual harassment. In an op-ed column published on October 10, 1991, Williams wrote that in the previous month, having written about Thomas on several occasions, he had been contacted by staff members of Senate Democrats seeking damaging information of any kind about Thomas. He wrote that the "desperate search for ammunition to shoot down Thomas" was "indiscriminate, mean-spirited mudslinging supported by the so-called champions of fairness: liberal politicians, unions, civil rights groups and women's organizations. . . . Further damaging is the blood-in-the-water response from reputable news operations, notably National Public Radio. They have magnified every question about Thomas into an indictment and sacrificed journalistic balance and integrity for a place in the mob." He declared that Hill had "no credible evidence" against Thomas and had been prompted to speak out by Thomas's political opponents. During the Senate Judiciary Committee hearing on the harassment charges against Thomas, Senator Orrin G. Hatch, a Utah Republican, read aloud from Williams's article.

Only five days after the publication of his scathing piece, Williams found himself in the news, when the Washington Post disclosed in both an editor's note and an article that he was being investigated for alleged sexual improprieties. While the newspaper had been looking into sexual-harassment complaints against him from female staff members prior to publication of the pro-Thomas piece, that inquiry had not been mentioned in the article Williams wrote; as a result, its publication angered still more female employees, who came forward with additional complaints about Williams. The journalist acknowledged his improper conduct and issued an open letter of apology to the staff, quoted by Howard Kurtz in the Washington Post (November 2, 1991): "It pained me to learn during the investigation that I had offended some of you. I have said so repeatedly in the last few weeks, and repeat here: some of my verbal conduct was wrong, I now know that, and I extend my sincerest apology to those whom I offended. I have committed to Post management, and I commit to you—and to myself—to change my ways."

In 1996 Williams began to host the syndicated television news show America's Black Forum, and in the following year he became a regular panelist on the television show Fox News Sunday. He was also featured as a commentator for a variety of other shows on that network, and he currently serves as a news anchor for Fox's weekend daytime live news coverage. Williams was a vocal defender of President Bill Clinton during his impeachment proceedings, in 1998. (Clinton was under investigation for denying his extramarital relationship with a former White House intern, Monica Lewinsky, during grand-jury testimony.) The year 1998 also saw the publication of Williams's book Thurgood Marshall: American Revolutionary, a biography of the first black U.S. Supreme Court justice. Williams had conducted extensive interviews with Marshall over a six-month period in 1989, two years before he retired from the court. (He died in 1993.) Marshall had first gained fame for his role in the civil rights movement, as an attorney for the National Association for the Advancement of Colored People (NAACP) in Brown v. Board of Education and other cases. The book received generally favorable reviews, although it was noted that Williams had focused more on Marshall's early career than on his tenure as a justice. "American Revolutionary is at its weakest in its discussion of Marshall's years on the Court," John O. McGinnis wrote for the National Review (December 7, 1998). "Williams does not have a command of constitutional jurisprudence and frequently turns complex legal issues into political cartoons." Williams has stated that he was unable to obtain certain records held by the NAACP Legal Defense Fund to better document that era of Marshall's life, because Williams's support of Clarence Thomas had not been well received by certain members of the NAACP. Nonetheless, many praised the book; Ruth Conniff, for example, wrote for the Progressive (December 1998) that "in spite of such obstacles, [Williams] has written a terrifically engaging biography. Hours of interviews with Marshall—and with people who knew him—helped Williams put together a wealth of personal anecdotes that illuminate the man and his era. He tells about Marshall's early days in Baltimore, his struggles with Jim Crow [southern segregation laws], and his personal victory over Maryland Law School, when he won the desegregation case against the school that had once kept him out." The book was reissued in 2004, with a new epilogue, to celebrate the 50th anniversary of Brown v. Board of Education.

Williams left the Washington Post in 1999. From 2000 to 2001 he hosted NPR's call-in show Talk of the Nation, bringing the program to cities and towns across the U.S. for monthly radio "town hall" meetings that were conducted in front of live audiences. Those meetings were a part of "The Changing Face of America," a yearlong NPR series focusing on the ways in which Americans were dealing with changes in culture and society in the 21st century; parts of the series aired on the NPR programs *Morning Edition* and *All Things Consid-ered* as well. Williams was also involved in NPR's coverage of the 2000 presidential election, hosting expanded segments of *Talk of the Nation*, which included special Saturday broadcasts. During his time as host, Williams helped the show to achieve an "all time high" in ratings, according to Gretchen Michael, writing for NPR's Web site (August 7, 2001). In 2001 he left the show to become an NPR senior correspondent. He told Michael, "The high caliber guests and the informed people calling ev-eryday made *Talk of the Nation* a joy to host. It has been an honor to sit in that seat and talk with the smartest audience in the radio universe. It was a thrill to be on the air as history was made during the presidential election. Now I look forward to bringing energy and insight to commentary and analysis for NPR [as a senior correspondent]." Wil-liams also covered the 2000 presidential election for Fox News and is currently reporting on the 2008 election campaigns for both NPR and Fox. "It's interesting," Williams told Steigerwald. "On Fox, black people say to me, 'Gee, you're pretty conservative.' White people say, 'Oh, you're the liberal on Fox.' I'm sitting there next to Brit Hume and Bill Kristol, and I'm to the left of them. But in my life even on National Public Radio, people say, 'Yeah, you can be pretty conservative.' So I think it's a lot about where people are coming from and not my political beliefs." Around 2003 Williams became a regular contributor to the NPR program *Day to Day*. In April 2008 Williams signed a new contract with NPR, which allowed him to move from his staff position to that of an on-air news ana-lyst. He thereby gained more freedom to concen-trate on outside work, including a column for the *Wall Street Journal*. He has also continued to con-tribute to *Morning Edition* and *Day to Day*.

In 2003 Williams's book *This Far by Faith: Sto-ries from the African American Religious Experi-ence*, written with Quinton Dixie, was published in conjunction with the airing of a six-part PBS se-ries. In the book Williams explored the connection of powerful African-American churches, as centers of leadership and community organization, to progress made during the civil rights movement. He told the *Christian Century* that his experience with the church while growing up in Brooklyn was the driving force behind the book, saying, "At the heart, *This Far by Faith* is an attempt to understand that childhood immigrant experience of marvel at the church's position in the black community." In 2004 *My Soul Looks Back in Wonder: Voices of the Civil Rights Experience* was published; in it, Wil-liams related the stories of civil rights activists that he had been collecting over the years. The book was part of the Voices of Civil Rights project, a col-laboration between the American Association of Retired Persons (AARP) and the Leadership Con-ference on Civil Rights. "You have this notion of people discovering within themselves that they have the capacity to create social change," Wil-liams said about the book during the July 1, 2004

installment of *Morning Edition*, as quoted on the NPR Web site.

Williams's book detailing his criticisms of the African-American community and culture, *Enough: The Phony Leaders, Dead-End Move-ments, and Culture of Failure That Are Undermin-ing Black America—and What We Can Do About It*, was published in 2006. Inspired by a controver-sial speech that the African-American comedian Bill Cosby gave in 2004 at the NAACP celebration of the 50th anniversary of *Brown v. Board of Edu-cation*, Williams argued that there is a lack of true leadership in the community and a "culture of fail-ure" that dominates many attitudes. He told Steigerwald that the book "is a real call to arms. . . . At the moment we have a 50 percent dropout rate among young black Americans. We have 70 percent of them born out of wedlock. At the same time there are about 25 percent of white children born out of wedlock and 50 percent of Hispanic children. This is a real crisis that is tear-ing apart the foundation of our society—the fami-ly. . . . This is a time when, unfortunately, there are too many black leaders who focus on grievance. The only time you see these guys on TV is when they say somebody has been racist or the police de-partment has done something wrong. All they are doing is complaining and it leads young people to a victim mentality, where they don't think they can succeed in America. They don't think they have a chance. They hear from their leaders that if you're black or Hispanic, you don't have a chance." Some critics agreed with Williams. Glenn Townes wrote for the New York *Amsterdam News* (September 21–27, 2006), "*Enough* is a book that will implore readers to carefully examine the state of Black America and explore how we can improve our own state of affairs and social shortcomings." Others faulted Williams for failing to see the larger pic-ture; Glenn C. Loury, writing for the *Boston Globe* (September 10, 2006), noted, "Any serious consid-eration of why progress for the black poor since 1965 has been so slow and uneven would have to look beyond the 'culture' of black ghetto dwellers, and beyond the public performances of black 'lead-ers,' so as to reckon with larger social, political, and economic developments in American society. Specifically, a serious discussion of reform must consider why the social policy-making process at all levels of government has failed to come to grips with the increasingly dire condition of our nation's most disadvantaged persons. . . . What blacks can do on our own about these problems is not nothing, but it is far less than Williams seems to think."

In an op-ed article published on August 21, 2006 in the *Washington Post*, Williams maintained that popular culture was also detrimental to African-American advancement. "With 50 percent of His-panic children and nearly 70 percent of black chil-dren born to single women today," he wrote, "these young people too often come from fractured fami-lies where there is little time for parenting. Their search for identity and a sense of direction is undermined by a twisted popular culture that focuses on the 'bling-bling' of fast money associated with famous basketball players, rap artists, drug dealers and the idea that women are at their best when flaunting their sexuality and having babies."

In 2007 Williams became involved in a minor controversy when he wrote an article for *Time* (September 28, 2007) defending comments made by the outspoken Fox News talk-show host Bill O'Reilly. In a talk with Williams on a radio show, O'Reilly had said that his visit to Sylvia's, a famous African-American–owned restaurant in the New York City neighborhood of Harlem, "was like going into an Italian restaurant in an all-white suburb in the sense of people were sitting there, and they were ordering and having fun. And there wasn't any kind of craziness at all." Leading political and media figures denounced those comments as racist, feeling that they implied that O'Reilly had expected "craziness" in a black-owned restaurant. O'Reilly and Williams argued that the comments had been taken out of context and claimed to have been having a conversation about preconceived notions concerning race; Williams said that the intention behind O'Reilly's comments was to emphasize that there is a disparity between reality and the portrayals of African-Americans in popular culture. Williams wrote, "O'Reilly says to me that the reality to black life is very different from the lowlife behavior glorified by the rappers. He told me he was at a restaurant in Harlem recently and there was no one shouting profanity, no one threatening people. . . . So imagine how totally astounded I was when I heard O'Reilly was attacked on the basis of that radio conversation as a 'racist.' He was slammed for saying he went to a restaurant in Harlem and had a good time. . . . The attacks on O'Reilly amounted to an effort to take what he said totally out of context in an attempt to brand him a racist by a liberal group that disagrees with much of his politics."

Williams won an Emmy Award for TV documentary writing in 1989 for *From Riot to Recovery* and has received critical praise for documentaries that include *The New Black Power* and *A. Philip Randolph: For Jobs and Freedom*, which aired on PBS in 1990 and 1996, respectively. He hosted *America's Black Forum* for nine years and has appeared on such television shows as *Crossfire, Nightline, Washington Week in Review, Arsenio, Oprah, Capitol Gang Sunday,* and *Sports Century.* Articles by Williams have also appeared *in Newsweek, Fortune,* the *Atlantic Monthly, Ebony,* and other publications. He currently sits on the boards of Haverford College, the Aspen Institute of Communications and Society Program, the Washington Journalism Center, and the New York Civil Rights Coalition. He lives in Washington, D.C., with his wife, Susan Delise, whom he married in 1978. He has three children: Antonio, Raphael, and Regan. Antonio ran unsuccessfully for a seat on the Washington city council in 2006.

—W.D.

Suggested Reading: *Booknotes* (on-line) Oct. 11, 1998; *Christian Century* (on-line) May 31, 2003; *Contemporary Black Biography* vol. 35, 2003; frontpagemagazine.com Sep. 27, 2006; National Public Radio Web site

Selected Books: *Eyes on the Prize: America's Civil Rights Years, 1954-1965,* 1987; *Thurgood Marshall: American Revolutionary,* 1998; *This Far by Faith: Stories from the African American Religious Experience* (with Quinton Dixie), 2003; *My Soul Looks Back in Wonder: Voices of the Civil Rights Experience,* 2004; *Enough: The Phony Leaders, Dead-End Movements, and Culture of Failure That Are Undermining Black America—and What We Can Do About It,* 2006

Selected Radio Shows: as host—*Talk of the Nation,* 2000–01; as correspondent and news analyst—*Morning Edition,* 2001– ; *Day to Day,* 2003–

Selected Television News Shows: as panelist—*Fox News Sunday,* 1997–

Williams, Lauryn

Sep. 11, 1983– Track and field athlete

Address: c/o USA Track & Field, 132 E. Washington St., Suite 800, Indianapolis, IN 46204

"There's something about the big events," the sprinter Lauryn Williams told *Sports Illustrated* (September 3, 2007), days after winning a silver medal at the 2007 World Track and Field Championships, held in Osaka, Japan. "It's do or die, and I did." Over the years Williams has earned a reputation for excelling in big races. In 2004, after becoming a National Collegiate Athletic Association (NCAA) champion in the 100-meter sprint, her signature event, she qualified for the U.S. Olympic team and went on to win a silver medal at that year's Games, held in Athens, Greece. She might have won a second medal, as part of the 4x100-meter relay team, had a botched baton handoff between her and her teammate Marion Jones not resulted in the foursome's being disqualified. After the Olympics Williams was credited with helping to restore credibility to a sport tarnished by drug scandals.

Williams followed her Olympic success with a gold-medal win in the 100-meter sprint at the 2005 World Track and Field Championships. After suffering from a hamstring injury during much of 2006, she won a silver medal at the USA Outdoor Track & Field Championships in July of the following year. While she had been aiming for her first national championship, she viewed her second-

Harry How/Getty Images

Lauryn Williams

place finish as proof that her leg had finally healed. Two months later, in Osaka, she finished so close to Veronica Campbell of Jamaica that five minutes passed before the judges declared a winner. Campbell was ultimately awarded the gold, despite the two runners' having finished with the same official time, 11.01 seconds. In 2008 Williams qualified to compete at the Summer Olympic Games in Beijing, China. She was chosen to anchor the U.S. Women's 400-meter-relay team. During the 400-meter race semifinals, she was again unable to hold on to the baton, dropping it as her teammate Torri Edwards tried to pass it to her. As a result, the U.S. women' team finished last in the event. It was the first time the women's team had missed the Olympic final since 1948.

Lauryn Williams was born on September 11, 1983 in Pittsburgh, Pennsylvania. When she was three years old, her parents—David, a former athlete from the Republic of Trinidad and Tobago, and Donna, a social-studies teacher—divorced. That same year David was diagnosed with leukemia, and his illness left him unemployed and saddled with debt. Williams moved with her mother to Detroit, Michigan, where she lived until she reached sixth grade; she then moved to Rochester, Pennsylvania, where her father had remarried and started a new family. (Three of her seven siblings are from her father's second marriage.) Despite her parents' divorce and father's health problems, Williams told Dejan Kovacevic for the *Pittsburgh Post-Gazette* (August 8, 2004) that she had a "tremendous childhood," adding, "For me, it was like so much of that never happened." Her parents made an effort to stay in touch with each other; throughout her youth Williams lived alternately with her

mother and father, spending her summers visiting the parent she was not living with full-time.

As a young girl Williams tried a number of sports and other physical activities, including karate, ballroom dancing, gymnastics, and basketball, the last of which remained her greatest passion throughout high school. She discovered her knack for running at around the age of 10, when she and her father took a trip to the Carnegie Science Center, in Pittsburgh. An exhibit there allowed visitors to race a moving image of the Olympic sprinter Florence Griffith-Joyner, and Williams set about trying to outpace the image. After what David Williams remembers as six hours, she won. The next day he signed her up for a track meet at a local high school, and she finished first in three events, including the 100-meter sprint. Around the same time Williams began racing neighborhood children in Detroit, and after she defeated every boy and girl on the block, she challenged Ben, the family dog. "I'll never forget that day," her mother told Michelle Kaufman for the *Miami Herald* (August 8, 2004). "She had beaten all her peers, even the boys, so they brought the dog out, and she beat him, too. We took her to a local track club the very next day." (According to some sources, the dog-racing episode took place when Williams was five, not 10.) Racing at the local Police Athletic League track, she earned the nickname "Flash."

By the time Williams was a student at Rochester High School, she had become a standout runner. In 1998, as a freshman, she finished second in two events—the 100- and 200-meter sprints—at the Western Pennsylvania Interscholastic Athletic League (WPIAL) championships. As a sophomore—the same year she attended a prestigious national meet in California—she finished first in both events. She repeated her performance at the statewide Pennsylvania Interscholastic Athletics Association championships, earning two more trophies. As a junior and senior, she successfully defended her local and state 100- and 200-meter titles, and off the track she maintained a 3.55 grade-point average, worked a part-time job, volunteered at a nursing home, and served four consecutive terms as class president. "People sometimes expect that, because of what you do or where you come from or how you look, you can't be smart or involved," Williams, who was the only African-American student in her class, told Kovacevic. "I never liked that. I wanted to do everything."

Throughout high school Williams saw track as little more than a way to stay in shape for basketball season, even though she was a second-string guard who struggled to control the ball. "Lauryn would be the best basketball player ever if she didn't have to use a basketball," her coach, Jen Milne, told Kovacevic. In her senior year Williams began receiving offers for track scholarships. She decided on the University of Miami, where she had taken an instant liking to the women's track coach, Amy Deem. She enrolled there in the fall of 2002, soon after winning two medals—a gold in the 100-

meter sprint and a silver in the 4x100-meter re-lay—at the 2002 World Junior Championships, held in Kingston, Jamaica. Though she fell during the first sprint of her first collegiate practice, she soon began to show improvement. Since she had never learned proper running technique, Williams had to develop a new stride. With Deem's help she fixed her sloppy starts, forward-leaning posture, and wild arm movements, and in 2003 she won two gold medals at the Pan American Games, in Santo Domingo, Dominican Republic. In June 2004, as a junior, she had an undefeated season and won an NCAA championship in the 100-meter sprint.

A month later Williams competed for a spot on the U.S. Olympic team. In the final round of the 100-meter trial, she found herself lined up against two Olympic legends, Marion Jones and Gail Devers, as well as then–world champion Torri Edwards. After stumbling out of the blocks and falling behind the pack, Williams "reached deep down inside . . . and ran my heart out," as she told Kovacevic. She narrowly captured third place, earning a spot on the U.S. team. Williams was also selected for the 4x100-meter relay team. Soon afterward she announced that she would forgo her final year of NCAA eligibility and turn professional. In the weeks leading up to the 2004 Athens Olympics, well-wishers in Detroit, Pittsburgh, and Miami raised roughly $20,000 to send members of Williams's family—including her father, who required regular kidney dialysis treatments—to Greece. (Her father died in October 2008.)

On August 21, 2004, as her family cheered from the stands, Williams came within .03 seconds of an Olympic gold medal, finishing just behind Yuliya Nesterenko of Belarus in the final round of the 100-meter sprint. Nesterenko took the lead in the final 10 meters, and when Williams tried to lean her body over the finish line, she made her move too soon. "There have been people congratulating me," Williams told Kovacevic for the *Pittsburgh Post-Gazette* (November 14, 2004). "They'll go, 'We know you're the real gold medalist because all you did was lean too early.' And I'm, like, that doesn't mean anything. No one gives you a gold medal because you were supposed to do something. To me, that was the hardest part, hearing about what should have happened." Immediately following the race, some expressed doubts about the legitimacy of Nesterenko's win, since she was a virtual unknown who, prior to the Athens Games, had never posted a time better than 11.02 seconds. She finished in less than 11 seconds in each of her four Olympic heats, leading some to speculate that she had used performance-enhancing drugs. She denied those charges, though it was later revealed that she had failed a 2002 drug test.

Days later, competing in her second event of the Athens Games, Williams was involved in a botched baton handoff that cost the 4x100-meter relay team its chance at a medal. Running in the unfamiliar third position—in high school and col-lege, she generally ran the fourth, or anchor, leg—Williams received the baton outside the designated handoff zone, resulting in the team's disqualification. While some charged Jones with running too slowly as she extended the baton, most published accounts blamed Williams for taking off too quickly and failing to wait for her approaching teammate. Williams accepted responsibility, telling Kovacevic (November 14, 2004), "I think it was easy for some people to pin it on her," referring to long-standing allegations that Jones had used banned substances. "She's seen as the bad person, and I'm painted as the brand-new, innocent face in the sport. It couldn't have been my fault because she's the bad, bad girl. I felt really bad because I got to know her as a friend and really respect her. Plus, I really and truly believe that I left early." (In December 2007, two months after she admitted to using performance-enhancing drugs, Jones was stripped of the five medals she won at the 2000 Olympics.) Despite the team's disappointing finish, Williams returned home to a hero's welcome. Residents of Beaver County, Pennsylvania, threw a parade in her honor, and she was a special guest at the first 2004 presidential debate, which was held at the University of Miami. Williams also joined the cycling star Lance Armstrong's "Tour of Hope," which raised money for cancer research, and appeared on TV shows including *Today*. In December 2004 she graduated from college with a degree in finance. She remained in Miami and continued to train with Deem. She spent the summer of 2005 competing on the European professional circuit, and in August she won a gold medal in the 100-meter race at the World Track and Field Championships, in Helsinki, Finland. "Silver feels good, but gold feels great," she told Tim Layden for *Sports Illustrated* (August 15, 2005). She finished the race in 10.93 seconds, .02 seconds slower than what was then her personal best. (Later that month, in Zurich, Switzerland, she posted a time of 10.88 seconds, which remains her fastest time.)

In June 2006 Williams won a silver medal at the 2006 USA Outdoor Track & Field Championships. Two months later she began feeling pain in her left hamstring and withdrew from the European tour; she was unable to compete for much of the following year. In June 2007, one round into the USA Outdoor Track and Field Championships, in Indianapolis, Indiana, she rated her fitness at "about 93 percent," according to Shelly Anderson, writing for the *Pittsburgh Post-Gazette* (June 22, 2007). "I'm on a good track," she added. "I'm not concerned at all." In the final round she ran the 100-meter sprint in 11.16 seconds, good enough for second place. "The final was a disappointment, but I feel like I'm back to normal," she told Anderson for the same newspaper (June 23, 2007). "It's going to be a good summer. I have to count my blessings. I could have been way in the back." Two months later, in Osaka, she ran a neck-and-neck 100-meter race with her Jamaican rival, Veronica Campbell. After five minutes of review, the judges declared

Campbell the winner, though both runners were credited with completing the race in 11.01 seconds. Williams also ran the first leg of the 4x100-meter race, helping the U.S. team win a gold medal. On June 28, 2008 Williams placed third in the final round of the 100-meter Olympic trials, earning a spot on the U.S. team. She broke 11 seconds—something she had not done since 2006—in the quarterfinal, semifinal, and final heats. She was also chosen to compete on the 4x100-meter relay team.

During the 400-meter-race preliminaries at the Games, Williams and Torri Edwards fumbled the baton connection, and the U.S. team came in last. "One of the things we did discuss was knowing the rules and knowing what to do in a situation if everything does go wrong," Williams told Shira Springer for the *Boston Globe* (August 22, 2008). "In '04, I didn't know. Do I stop? Wait? Whatever? We went through the rule book and we knew all the rules and I said, 'In the event that it goes wrong, I'm not walking around the track. I'm never walking around the track again.' Maybe that was foreshadowing or something. I just knew when that stick went down I was not walking to the finish line. I picked it up and I ran. I told my team, 'We are running through the line no matter what.'" Williams finished fourth, with a time of 11.03 seconds, in the women's 100-meter final. The U.S. Olympic men's and women's track and field teams lost in the sprints to the Jamaican team.

Williams, who is listed at five feet three inches tall (some sources say five feet two inches), has been described as being personable. When she is not training or competing, she donates her time to various charitable causes. In 2004 she received the Dapper Dan Sportswoman of the Year Award, and in 2006 she was named the Visa Humanitarian Athlete of the Year. "She is pint-size in her height, but she has a heart that is so overwhelming, it overshadows her petite size," the track legend Jackie Joyner-Kersee told JoAnne Klimovich Harrop for the *Pittsburgh Tribune Review* (November 13, 2005). "She runs against the giants, and she can outrun the giants." Williams is engaged to Talib Humphrey, a former University of Miami fullback. She sometimes visits schools and talks to young people, and as she told Anderson, "I like to tell kids that whatever the case might be—a single-parent family, maybe not a lot of money—they can still do something."

—K.J.P.

Suggested Reading: (Columbia, South Carolina) *State* C p4 Aug. 22, 2004; (London) *Guardian* p22 Aug. 15, 2005; *Miami Herald* C p1 Aug. 8, 2004, Jan. 18, 2007; *Pittsburgh Post-Gazette* D p1 July 15, 2004, A p1 Aug. 26, 2004; *Pittsburgh Tribune Review* Nov. 13, 2005; *Washington Post* D p1 Aug. 9, 2004

Witcover, Jules

July 16, 1927– Writer; political columnist

Address: c/o Johns Hopkins University Press, 2715 N. Charles St., Baltimore, MD 21218-4363

For over five decades the celebrated pundit Jules Witcover worked as a political reporter and columnist for some of the country's most respected newspapers, including the *Los Angeles Times* and the *Washington Post*. Beginning in 1977 he and his fellow columnist Jack Germond co-wrote a popular political column, "Politics Today," for the *Washington Star* (until 1981) and then the *Baltimore Sun*. Appearing five days a week, the column won syndication and appeared in approximately 140 newspapers nationwide for more than 20 years. In addition to reporting, Witcover has published 17 books: five treatises on presidential campaigns (three of them co-authored by Germond), including *85 Days: The Last Campaign of Robert Kennedy* (1969, reprinted in 1988) and *Marathon: The Pursuit of the Presidency, 1972–1976* (1977); 10 books on U.S. politics and history, among them *The Resurrection of Richard Nixon* (1970), *No Way to Pick a President: How Money and Hired Guns Have Debased American Elections* (1999), and *Very Strange Bedfellows: The Short and Unhappy Marriage of Nixon & Agnew* (2007); a political novel, *The Main Chance* (1979); and the memoir *The Making of an Ink-Stained Wretch: Half a Century Pounding the Political Beat* (2005). Since he left the *Sun*, involuntarily, in August 2005—in a cutback representative of many others in newspapers all over the country—Witcover has continued writing for the paper's syndicate, Tribune Media. Timothy Franklin, an editor at the *Baltimore Sun*, declared to Nick Madigan for that newspaper (August 23, 2005) that Witcover is "a Washington institution, and he's extraordinarily knowledgeable about politics and elections." Witcover has been a frequent contributor to other prominent publications, among them *Esquire*, the *Nation*, the *New Republic*, and the *Saturday Review*.

The younger of the two children of Samuel and Sarah "Sadie" (Carpenter) Witcover, Jules Joseph Witcover was born on July 16, 1927 in Union City, New Jersey. His father, who was Jewish "by birth rather than practice," as Witcover wrote in his memoir, ran a one-man auto-body shop; his mother, who was Catholic, was a homemaker. Witcover and his older sister, Marilyn, were raised in their mother's faith. Early on, Witcover displayed an interest in writing. Every Thanksgiving he and one of his cousins would hand out a one-page family newspaper, written in the style of a gossip column. Witcover recalled in his memoir, "We coerced

Jules Witcover

Courtesy of Public Affairs Books

adult relatives into buying ads extolling their businesses and then charged each customer a nickel to read the only copy of the paper, which had to be handed back." He later began writing and distributing a series of neighborhood newspapers. His first, the *Brown Street Rag*, was printed "by using one of those gelatin pads with which operators of neighborhood diners produced their daily menus in purple ink." In 1941 Witcover enrolled at Union Hill High School. Following the Japanese attack on Pearl Harbor on December 7 of that year, which triggered the U.S.'s entry into World War II, he ran his father's auto shop while the elder Witcover worked nights at a nearby defense plant. Although he received good grades throughout high school, he never considered going to college until the class valedictorian, one of his fellow players on the basketball team, persuaded Witcover to apply with him to Columbia University, in New York City. Unaware of Columbia's prestige, he applied and, after performing well on an all-day intelligence test, was accepted at the university.

Witcover attended Columbia for a semester before joining the U.S. Navy. His military career proved to be short-lived: he enlisted on May 8, 1945, known as V-E Day (when Nazi Germany announced its surrender to the Allies), and was called to active duty on August 14, 1945—V-J Day (marking the surrender of Japanese forces). After his official discharge, a year later, Witcover reenrolled at Columbia under the G.I. Bill. He had initially intended to pursue a law degree but decided to follow his dreams of becoming a sportswriter instead. Throughout college he covered sports for the daily *Columbia Spectator*. During that period he also worked part-time at the New York *Daily News*,

sorting through the thousands of entries for the paper's weekly contest, whose participants predicted winners and scores of football games. Commenting on that job, Witcover noted in his memoir, "It was boring and tiring work, but I could console myself by thinking that at least I was working 'in sports.' I was kind of like the guy who had a job in the circus shoveling up manure behind the elephants. Asked why he didn't quit such a disgusting assignment, he replied: 'What? And get out of show business?'" After receiving his A.B. degree from Columbia, in 1949, he started working as a pamphlet writer for a New York insurance company. He then found jobs at two weekly newspapers in Hackensack, New Jersey, first the *Star* and then the *Star-Telegram*, before entering the Columbia Graduate School of Journalism in the fall of 1950.

In 1951 Witcover received his master's degree and got his first job at a daily newspaper, working for the *Providence (Rhode Island) Journal*. He began as a reporter for the paper's city section, then took a position as a copywriter on the night sports desk. Although he yearned to be a sportswriter, his chances of becoming one at the paper seemed remote, so he began pursuing other job opportunities. In 1953 he landed an interim post at the *Newark (New Jersey) Star-Ledger*, a daily owned by the S. I. Newhouse publishing chain. The paper's editor, Philip Hochstein, agreed to take him on for six months before deciding whether to send him to the chain's Washington, D.C., bureau to cover politics. (Witcover had likened the combative nature of politics to that of sports and reasoned that covering it would be just as much fun.) During that trial period, which ended up lasting a year, Witcover learned the ins and outs of tabloid journalism, covering local events. In January 1954 he was promoted to the Washington bureau, where he served as a political correspondent. (In his memoir Witcover compared local coverage to "watching a sideshow at the circus while others were spectators under the big top.") Over the next eight years, Witcover worked the Washington beat for a number of Newhouse papers, including, in New York State, the *Long Island Press*, the *Syracuse Post-Standard*, and the *Syracuse Herald-Journal*, and, in Alabama, the *Huntsville Times*. In that period Alexander "Casey" Jones, then the editor of the *Herald-Journal*, gave Witcover a weekly op-ed column, which allowed him to express his views on national political matters. In 1960 he covered the contest between the U.S. senators Hubert H. Humphrey and John F. Kennedy for the Democratic presidential nomination.

By 1962 Witcover had become a senior correspondent and the chief political writer for the Newhouse National News Service. He was first assigned to the Pentagon to write about daily briefings of Secretary of Defense Robert S. McNamara. In those turbulent times Witcover covered such momentous events as the Cuban Missile Crisis and the assassination of President Kennedy, while reporting on the day-to-day developments of the

Vietnam War. In addition to the Pentagon beat, he covered the struggle for African-American rights and interviewed two of its most important leaders, Martin Luther King Jr. and Malcolm X, both in 1963. In late 1966 Witcover became intimately involved in covering the run-up to the 1968 presidential election. Following President Lyndon B. Johnson's shocking March 1968 announcement of his refusal to seek election to a second full term, Witcover began covering Senator Robert F. Kennedy's bid for the Democratic nomination. Along with several dozen other journalists, photographers, and cameramen, he trailed Kennedy as the candidate made speeches all over the country, and he was among a privileged few who were granted access to some of Kennedy's closed-door conversations. Then, on June 5, 1968, a 24-year-old Palestinian named Sirhan Sirhan shot Kennedy, just moments after the senator had won an important victory in the California primary; Witcover was 30 feet away when he heard the shots. Kennedy was pronounced dead the following day. In his story on the event, Witcover took note of "another hour of mindless tragedy in a nation that cannot or will not keep weapons of death from the hands of madmen who walk its streets."

Recalling the events of the late 1960s as the most memorable of his life, Witcover made them the basis of his entry into book writing. In 1969 he published *85 Days: The Last Campaign of Robert Kennedy,* a chronological account of Kennedy's presidential campaign and a discussion of his legacy. Reviewing the volume for *Book World* (February 2, 1969), W. V. Shannon wrote, "[The author] has produced an admirably balanced, temperate, comprehensive account. He makes clear Kennedy's occasional lapses into demagoguery and expediency as well as his brilliant soaring moments, his moral passion and his private humor."

Later in 1969 Witcover left the Newhouse chain in 1969 to work for the Washington bureau of the *Los Angeles Times.* During his three years with the bureau, he served as a political columnist, reporter, and assistant news editor; his responsibilities also included interviewing job seekers. (Among the many applicants whom Witcover turned away because of their lack of experience in Washington was the then-unknown but soon-to-be-famous Bob Woodward; the two became colleagues at the *Washington Post* several years later.) Witcover spent much of 1969 following Richard Nixon's tumultuous first year in the White House, focusing particularly on the Vietnam War and on the adversarial relationship that Nixon's vice president, Spiro Agnew, had with news reporters and antiwar protesters. In January 1970 Witcover published his second book, *The Resurrection of Richard Nixon,* which covered Nixon's life from his 1962 defeat in the California gubernatorial election to his presidential victory in 1968. The book received generally favorable reviews. A critic wrote for the *New Yorker* (September 5, 1970), "Nothing in this absolutely first-rate account of a remarkable political

comeback is likely to change the reader's estimate of the President. . . . Those who like or admire [him] will find justification for their affection in Mr. Witcover's description of his doggedness and nerve, of his party loyalty and his political astuteness, of his logical mind and simple tastes. Readers who see the President as ambitious, bitter, withdrawn, and, if not unprincipled, lacking an inspiring political vision may well imagine that Mr. Witcover sees him that way, too. The fact is that Mr. Witcover, a thorough, honest reporter who has deftly put together a lot of facts, does not sacrifice complexity to vividness."

Next came two of Witcover's books on Agnew. The first, *White Knight: The Rise of Spiro Agnew* (1972), examines the subject's life from his upbringing in Baltimore, Maryland, and experiences in the military to his struggles as vice president. The book received mixed reviews. Arthur Cooper, in an assessment for *Newsweek* (April 17, 1972), wrote, "Fair and objective this book is, if somewhat windy and crammed with detail. But Agnew probably won't like the book very much. He emerges as a 'sleek,' stern authoritarian whose insensitivity, arrogance and moral absolutism are as boundless as his party loyalty. . . . Yet Witcover is not out to savage Agnew. He credits him with intelligence, the breadth of which has been belied by his public utterances." Walter Jacobson disagreed with Cooper's assertion that the book was a "fair portrait," writing for *Book World* (May 14, 1972), "Agnew-the-Expedient is Witcover's subject, a boorish but clever practitioner of the art of doing what is necessary to get ahead. . . . Witcover is harsh in almost all his judgments; Agnew gets no credit for whatever successes may be in the record." The second book, *A Heartbeat Away: The Investigation and Resignation of Vice President Spiro T. Agnew* (1974), was co-written with the political columnist Richard Cohen and focuses on the money-laundering and tax-evasion scandal that led Agnew to leave office, in 1974.

Meanwhile, following the 1972 presidential election, Witcover had taken a job at the national desk of the *Washington Post.* During his tenure there, from 1973 to 1976, he worked as a political correspondent and reporter, providing in-depth coverage of presidential and vice-presidential politics. That assignment culminated in *Marathon: The Pursuit of the Presidency, 1972–1976* (1977), an exhaustive, 684-page account of the 1976 presidential campaign. Many reviewers commended Witcover's attention to detail and ability to create a coherent narrative from a complex assortment of facts and stories. In a representative review, Wes Daniels wrote for *Library Journal* (July 1977), "This is a highly informative, thoughtful, and entertaining account. . . . Witcover provides both a comprehensive history of the major events of the period and an intelligent analysis of the role of the media in national politics. The fortunes of all contenders for the Republican and Democratic nominations are closely followed, and the race between

[Gerald] Ford and [Jimmy] Carter is covered in detail."

In early 1977 Witcover joined the now-defunct *Washington Star* to start a column with his longtime friend Jack Germond called "Politics Today." Appearing five days a week, the column eventually won syndication in approximately 140 newspapers nationwide; Witcover and Germond would write 6,912 columns together over the next 24 years. (Germond retired in 2001.) After the *Star* folded, in August 1981, after 130 years of publication, both journalists began to write their column for the *Baltimore Sun*. That September Witcover and Germond published the first of the four books they wrote together—*Blue Smoke and Mirrors: How Reagan Won and Why Carter Lost the Election of 1980* (1981). The authors contended that Jimmy Carter had lost his presidential reelection bid because of his failure to free American hostages in Iran before the election. They highlighted turning points in the campaign of Ronald Reagan, including his success in his debate with Carter in Cleveland, Ohio, and examined key primaries and the effects on the election of other world events, including the Soviet invasion of Afghanistan. C. J. Sitomer, writing for the *Christian Science Monitor* (September 14, 1981), called the book "a delightful repast of amusing and often telling anecdotes, as it prances us down the Republican and Democratic primary paths and finally on to the broader general election trail."

In 1985 Witcover and Germond published their second book together, *Wake Us When It's Over: Presidential Politics of 1984*, which focuses chiefly on the Democratic primaries and features analyses of the factors that led to Reagan's reelection. Despite unanimous praise for the authors' reporting skills, the book was criticized for what was seen as its biased viewpoint. Fred Siegel wrote for *Commonweal* (September 6, 1985), "Germond and Witcover are almost exclusively preoccupied with exposing the pseudo-reality of media-based campaigns. . . . [They] are on target in their criticism of media-dominated campaigns; but implicit is the unjustified assumption that had Reagan not been the master of the airwaves, [the Democratic nominee, Walter] Mondale would have been able to win on the issues. Comforting as this notion might be, it is almost certainly wrong." Gary Maloney wrote for the *National Review* (August 9, 1985), "The authors are incapable of accepting the legitimacy of Reagan's mandate for conservatism and the Right's key role in shaping the Emerging Republican Majority; their crabbed view of the American people, and the process by which [the voters] chose Ronald Reagan, remains unredeemed by their fine reporting." Witcover and Germond followed up *Wake Us When It's Over* with *Whose Broad Stripes and Bright Stars?: The Trivial Pursuit of the Presidency, 1988* (1989), a detailed account of the 1988 presidential campaign, and *Mad as Hell: Revolt at the Ballot Box, 1992* (1993), a comprehensive analysis of President Bill Clinton's redefinition of Democratic liberalism and its effects on conservative voters.

Between his collaborations with Germond, Witcover continued to write works of his own, including *Sabotage at Black Tom: Imperial Germany's Secret War in America, 1914-1917* (1989), a thriller-like nonfiction book centered on several acts of terrorism by German saboteurs during World War I, and *Crapshoot: Rolling the Dice on the Vice Presidency: From Adams and Jefferson to Truman and Quayle* (1992), a history of the vice presidency. Witcover next published *The Year the Dream Died: Revisiting 1968 in America* (1997), an account of many of the tumultuous events of 1968, including the assassinations of Martin Luther King Jr. and Robert F. Kennedy, the increasing public anger over America's involvement in the Vietnam War, and the rioting by war protesters and others outside the site of the Democratic National Convention in Chicago. The book received laudatory reviews and was named one of the notable books of 1997 by the *New York Times*. In an assessment for the *New York Times Book Review* (June 22, 1997), Sidney Blumenthal wrote, "Jules Witcover's recreation of the driven politics of 1968, unfolding the drama month by month, is among the most valuable contributions to the recent retrospectives on that centrifugal year."

Next, Witcover expressed his disdain for the methods by which presidential candidates and their running mates have sought office in recent years in *No Way to Pick a President: How Money and Hired Guns Have Debased American Elections* (1999). As noted by Paul Taylor for *Washington Monthly* (October 1, 1999), Witcover set the tone for much of the book by writing in the introduction, "One deplorable fact has become crystal clear: the process by which the nation chooses its leader has been hijacked—by money, ambition, and, yes, the ingenuity of the men and women who practice the art of politics in all its forms." Witcover went on to describe contemporary campaigns as "not an exercise in civic-mindedness but an orgy of no-holds-barred warfare . . . fought out first in a relentless pursuit of campaign money . . . and finally through the new high-tech weapons of mass communication, increasingly under the generalship of mercenaries." Witcover's nostalgia for the presidential campaign strategies of bygone eras was heavily criticized. Fred Barnes observed in a review for the *Weekly Standard* (November 29, 1999), "*No Way to Pick a President* is a sour book—for the simple reason that Witcover . . . now finds more bad than good in presidential campaigns. He's tired of self-selected candidates, amoral political consultants, the deluge of money, cocky but ignorant reporters, the emphasis on television, and the tone and substance of the campaigns themselves. There isn't much about presidential politics he wouldn't uproot, outlaw, or alter." Barnes added that while "you have to agree with a lot of his criticism . . . Witcover's remedies for the ills of presidential politics are drastic, utopian, and elitist." Taylor, by contrast, found much of value in the author's arguments, calling *No Way to Pick A President* a "good, passionate and disheartening book" and adding, "It's vintage Witcover—which means strong reporting, sharp analysis, well-turned anecdotes, revealing interviews and an abiding love of the games, warts and all."

Witcover's most ambitious work to date, the 826-page *Party of the People: A History of the Democrats* (2003), received mixed reviews. Richard Brookhiser wrote for the *New York Times* (November 19, 2003, on-line), "This is a big subject, and [the book] covers it unevenly. At the start Mr. Witcover's survey of the decades before the Civil War is slight and biased, presenting all non-Democrats as mere agents of the rich. . . . At the end Mr. Witcover's account of the Clinton years is remarkably evenhanded. . . . [Witcover] has combed the history books diligently, and he has retrieved many vivid quotations, which stand out from the marsh of his own prose."

In late 2004, while covering the run-up to the presidential election contest between the incumbent, George W. Bush, and Senator John Kerry of Massachusetts, Witcover accepted a "buyout" offer from the *Baltimore Sun*, which ended his tenure as a full-time member of the newspaper's Washington bureau; he reluctantly signed a contract to write his column for the *Sun* once a week (it had been running three times a week since the retirement of Germond). That move, driven by the ever-growing use of the Internet and by other technological breakthroughs in mass communication—and a resulting drop in print circulation—was an example of cutbacks in newspaper staffs all over the country. Then, in August 2005, Witcover's employment at the *Sun* ended altogether, when the paper's management decided not to renew his contract. As he noted in his memoir, Witcover was informed of the decision by letter, which concluded simply, in reference to his 24 years with the paper: "We appreciate your many years of service to *The Sun* and its readers and wish you well in all of your future endeavors." "The coldness of it was what irritated me the most," Witcover told Howard Kurtz for the *Washington Post* (August 23, 2005). Many of his readers believed that his firing was a direct result of his opposition to the Iraq war, which he had expressed prior to the U.S.-led 2003 invasion; Witcover had attacked the Bush administration regularly, particularly over the war, which the Associated Press (August 23, 2005) quoted him as calling "the most wrong-headed foreign policy in my lifetime and the most dangerous."

In November 2005 Witcover published his memoir, *The Making of an Ink-Stained Wretch: Half a Century Pounding the Political Beat*. The book combines the story of Witcover's own life with anecdotes from every presidential election since the early 1960s. In it he reflected on the journalistic trade as a whole, especially the ways in which the roles and styles of reporters have changed over the last half-century. Many reviewers

compared the book to memoirs written by political journalists of the past, with their wealth of "war stories" and accounts of all-night drinking sessions and other classic trappings of the reporter's life. David Yepsen wrote in a review for *Nieman Reports* (Winter 2005), "Witcover pens us a witty book about our trade, grumbles about how things have gone wrong, but then doesn't offer a plan for doing anything about it. . . . Still, after bemoaning some of the things gone wrong with the trade, he concludes charitably: 'All in all, the business of writing about national politics is in as good, if perhaps more sober, hands as it was in my earlier days. Today's crew is probably better educated in various aspects of political science than my gang was, but maybe not quite so well versed in the art of having a helluva good time in the process of writing about it.' Thank you, Jules. And amen."

Witcover's most recent full-length work, *Very Strange Bedfellows: The Short and Unhappy Marriage of Nixon & Agnew*, was published in April 2007. Reviewing the book for the *Washington Times* (June 3, 2007), William F. Gavin pronounced its "fatal flaw" to be that Witcover "has nothing new or interesting to say about Nixon and Agnew or the times they lived in. We've heard all of it before; in fact, we've heard it from Mr. Witcover himself." Gavin nonetheless noted that Witcover "feels deeply about what he writes" and that he "is an old pro [whose] crisp, clear writing style keeps things moving in a fast-paced, organized way." Witcover has also written a work of political fiction, the little-known novel *The Main Chance* (1979), about a multigenerational team of reporters covering the second presidential campaign of a corrupt public figure.

Witcover lives in Washington, D.C., with his second wife, Marion Elizabeth Rodgers, whom he married on June 21, 1997. Rodgers is a specialist in the work of the journalist H. L. Mencken; *Booklist* named her book *Mencken: The American Iconoclast* (2005) one of the best biographies of 2005–06. From Witcover's first marriage, to Marian Laverty, which ended in divorce in 1990 after nearly four decades, he has four children: Paul (the author of two novels, a comic-book series, and a biography of Nora Zeale Hurston), Amy, Julie, and Peter.

—C.C.

Suggested Reading: *Baltimore Sun* C p1 Aug. 23, 2005; *New York Times* p10 Oct. 29, 1989, p19 Jan. 30, 2000; *Washington Monthly* p46 Oct. 1, 1999; *Washington Post* C p1 Aug. 23, 2005; *Washington Times* B p7 June 3, 2007; *Weekly Standard* p30 Nov. 29, 1999; Witcover, Jules. *The Making of an Ink-Stained Wretch: Half a Century Pounding the Political Beat*, 2005

Selected Books: *85 Days: The Last Campaign of Robert Kennedy*, 1969; *The Resurrection of Richard Nixon*, 1970; *White Knight: the Rise of Spiro Agnew*, 1972; *A Heartbeat Away: The Investigation and Resignation of Vice President*

Spiro T. Agnew (with Richard M. Cohen), 1974; *Marathon: The Pursuit of the Presidency, 1972-1976*, 1977; *Blue Smoke and Mirrors: How Reagan Won and Why Carter Lost the Election of 1980* (with Jack W. Germond), 1981; *Wake Us When It's Over: Presidential Politics of 1984* (with Germond), 1985; *Whose Broad Stripes and Bright Stars?: The Trivial Pursuit of the Presidency, 1988* (with Germond), 1989; *Sabotage at Black Tom: Imperial Germany's Secret War in America, 1914-1917*, 1989; *Crapshoot: Rolling the Dice on the Vice Presidency: From Adams and Jefferson to Truman and Quayle*, 1992; *Mad as Hell: Revolt at the Ballot Box, 1992* (with Germond), 1993; *The Year the Dream Died: Revisiting 1968 in America*, 1997; *No Way to Pick a President: How Money and Hired Guns Have Debased American Elections*, 1999; *Party of the People: A History of the Democrats*, 2003; *Very Strange Bedfellows: The Short and Unhappy Marriage of Nixon & Agnew*, 2007; novels—*The Main Chance*, 1979

Michael Lovett, courtesy of G. Schirmer Inc.

Wyner, Yehudi

June 1, 1929– Composer; teacher; pianist

Address: c/o Associated Music Publishers, 445 Bellvale Rd., Chester, NY 10918

"I felt at the time that I had hit the jackpot," the pianist Robert Levin told Richard Dyer for the *Boston Globe* (April 19, 2006), in recalling his first impression of the concerto written for him by his longtime friend Yehudi Wyner. "And now he has, too," Lev-

in added, referring to the news that Wyner, at the age of 74, had won the 2006 Pulitzer Prize for music. The Pulitzer judges recognized Wyner's concerto, subtitled "Chiavi in Mano" ("Keys in Hand" in Italian), as a "distinguished musical composition by an American that had its first performance or recording in the United States" during the year 2005. At its premiere, Wyner's concerto was performed by Levin and the Boston Symphony Orchestra, which had commissioned the work three years earlier. "To me," Levin told Dyer, "what he delivered is a piece of vintage Wyner, rich in emotional communication, eloquence, and vehemence." "Of all my pieces, this one most comprehensively reflects the various sides of me, both the serious and the absurd," Wyner said to the same reporter. Wyner has written more than 70 works for full orchestra, chamber groups, piano, and voice, ranging in length from two minutes (in the cases of such songs as "The Grass Is High" and "Florida Express") to 28 minutes (*Prologue and Narrative* for cello and orchestra). While they are instantly recognizable as 20th/21st-century creations, they reflect, sometimes subtly and other times plainly, Wyner's unusually diverse musical passions and influences, which encompass everything from Christian and Jewish liturgical compositions, Baroque sonatas and contatas, and 19th-century operas to klezmer, pop, jazz, rock, honky-tonk, torch songs, and 12-tone pieces. As the music professor and composer Martin Brody noted in an essay written in 2004 for Associated Music Publishers (which prints and sells scores of Wyner's compositions), "His oeuvre does not neatly divide into periods, genres, or any other categories." Writing for the Raleigh, North Carolina, *News and Observer* (October 19, 2003), David Perkins characterized Wyner's music as "at once deeply thoughtful and full of nervous energy and impatience."

In his essay "Reflections on the Pulitzer Prize" for the Internet magazine *NewMusicBox* (April 27, 2006), Wyner described his compositions as reflections of "emotional and physical states of mind and motion. . . . It is music which seeks to embrace as broad a gamut of experience as I am able to organize in a given musical framework. . . . It is music that does not seek to avoid the influence of all the music I have heard and loved and played and conducted and studied. It permits expression of the raunchy as well as the refined, the trivial as well as the tragic. These statements should not suggest that my music is a collage of references and quotations. Far from it. The references are transformed to reveal something new about the material. . . . I believe that whatever originality my work may have lies in its process of transformation and the significance of unpredictable juxtapositions."

A highly accomplished, Juilliard-trained pianist who has graduate degrees in music, Wyner taught at the college level from 1959 until his retirement from academia, in 2005. In 2008 he began his fifth decade with the Bach Aria Group, as the ensemble's pianist and occasional conductor. In "Reflections on the Pulitzer Prize," he wrote, "My hope is that the prize will stimulate curiosity, and that the curiosity will lead to active engagement with the music for listeners and performers alike. I want my music to be heard and received with an involvement akin to what I feel and imagine as I write it."

Yehudi Wyner was born on June 1, 1929 in Calgary, Alberta, Canada, to Lazar Weiner and Sarah Naomi (Shumiatcher) Weiner. (His parents changed the spelling of their sons' surname to avoid mispronunciation by others.) Wyner grew up with his brother, David, in New York City. His mother was a skilled pianist. His father was a celebrated composer of Jewish liturgical music and Yiddish art songs; an immigrant from the Ukraine, he was also the longtime director of music at the Central Synagogue, a prominent New York City house of worship, and he hosted a weekly radio program called *The Message of Israel*. According to an article about Wyner for the Milken Archive of American Jewish Music (2006, on-line), "Throughout his youth, . . . [his parents'] home was frequented by literati and artists from the Yiddish cultural orbit." Wyner told the music scholar Richard Dyer that he started composing before he turned five. "My father noticed what I was doing at the piano, and he'd write down the little pieces for me," he recalled. Beginning in early childhood, guided by his father, Wyner practiced the piano two or three hours every day—a routine that increased in difficulty as he got older. "It was a very intense and directed professional track," he told Stephen Heyman for the Brandeis University publication *Justice* (as reprinted by University Wire, May 9, 2006, on-line). He told Judith Wershil Hasan for the *New York Times* (August 2, 1981) that the training was "a very painful experience. . . . Later on, I had to struggle to reconcile my natural musical impulses with the vestigial resentment that I was forced to give away the normal pursuits and fellowship of childhood." In one example of his successful efforts at such reconciliation, at a concert held in 1988, six years after his father's death, Wyner performed three preludes for piano composed by Weiner in 1932. In a review of that concert for the *Los Angeles Times* (December 20, 1988), Bruce Burroughs wrote that Wyner played the preludes, which "make real virtuoso demands," with "uncompromising energy, deep respect and the love available only from one to whom this work had been dedicated at the age of 3."

At the private high school he attended, Wyner took no courses in science or math, affording him more time for pianistic pursuits. Concurrently, he studied piano at the Juilliard School of Music, in New York City, which awarded him a diploma in 1946. He told Dyer that he decided to become a composer after leaving Juilliard. "I was pretty sure that the career of a virtuoso pianist was not for me—I didn't want all that traveling and repetition. Also I knew I lacked the kind of commanding memory that a touring virtuoso has to have." After his high-school graduation, Wyner enrolled at Yale University, where he studied under the composers Richard Donovan and Paul Hindemith. As an undergraduate he composed one movement of a concerto for piano and orchestra and had an opportunity to attend a rehearsal of it, under the baton of another student (James Yannatos, now a conductor and composer). "I was so horrified by what it sounded like, by my own ignorance, that I didn't write orchestra work for 25 years!" he told Dyer. Wyner earned three degrees at Yale: an A.B. in 1950; a B.Mus. (bachelor's degree in music) in 1951; and an M.Mus. (master's degree in music) in 1953. The last came one year after he had received an M.A. degree in music from Harvard University, in Cambridge, Massachusetts, where he studied under the composers Randall Thompson and Walter Piston. During that period he spent one summer at the Brandeis Arts Institute in Santa Susana, California, where he met well-regarded Jewish composers, some from Israel, and, according to the Milken Archive article, was "profoundly affected by the founder and director of the institute, Shlomo Bardin, whom he credits with instilling in him . . . a fresh appreciation for Jewish cultural identity."

In 1953 Wyner won a Rome Prize in composition, bestowed by the American Academy in Rome, Italy. Supported by his award money, he spent the next three years at the academy, playing piano and composing music; he also traveled in Italy and elsewhere in Europe. According to Martin Brody, Wyner's experience of other cultures influenced him profoundly, by providing him, in Wyner's words, with a "view of other cultures . . . a connection with the past"; fostering in him "a tolerance and an acceptance of many other ways of life"; and awakening him to "the possibility for integrating, even in an informal way, ideas from all over the world and ideas from all over one's internal landscape, finding things that would be normally regarded as disparate, disorganized or as simply messy; finding that there were ways to have those live together, to be integrated to result in a new synthesis." By the end of his time in Rome, his compositions included a suite, a partita, and a sonata for piano; two chorale preludes for organ; a set of dance variations for wind octet; and choral music set to Psalm 143, which begins "Hear my prayer, O Lord, give ear to my supplications." During the 1950s he and others began to perform some of those works in concerts, in such places as Carnegie Recital Hall, Columbia University, and Town Hall, all in New York City.

In 1957, after his return to the U.S., Wyner began teaching music theory as an instructor at Hebrew Union College, in New York City. He taught at Hofstra College (now University), in Hempstead, New York, in 1959 and at Queens College, a division of the City University of New York, in 1959–60. He served as the music director of the Westchester Reform Temple, a suburban New York synagogue, from 1959 until 1968. In 1960 he won a Guggenheim fellowship and the next year a grant from the

American Institute of Arts and Letters. In 1963 he joined the faculty of Yale; he chaired the composition division of the Department of Music there from 1969 until 1973. Wyner left Yale in 1977 and, the next year, became a professor of music at the State University of New York (SUNY) at Purchase. He taught there until 1989 and served as the dean of music from 1978 to 1982. He told Judith Wershil Hasan in 1981, "I've had the luck of the Irish really. . . . Because of fellowships and major prizes, I have had the privilege of taking years off to cultivate me. In a sense, I'm repaying that privilege now, with service as a teacher, coach and as a dean." In 1989 Wyner made another move, to Brandeis University, in Waltham, Massachusetts, where he remained until he retired from college teaching, in 2005.

Meanwhile, in 1968, Wyner had joined the nine-member Bach Aria Group as keyboardist and sometime conductor, after the ensemble's then-pianist, Paul Ulanowsky, became ill and recommended Wyner as his successor. Founded in 1946 and made up of five instrumentalists and four singers, the group performs Bach contatas, arias from the contatas, and instrumental chamber music. The job gave Wyner the means to devote more time to his own musical interests; as he told Dyer, "The first years of touring . . . brought financial freedom in a way unimaginable for a young composer. My salary from the Bach Aria Group was larger than I earned for an entire year of teaching at Yale." For six summers beginning in 1981, the group held the Bach Aria Festival and Institute at the State University of New York (SUNY) at Stony Brook, on Long Island, offering coaching and lectures as well as concerts. A documentary recorded at the festival in 1983 was broadcast in 1985 on PBS television stations, with the title *In Search of Bach*, to celebrate the 300th anniversary of Bach's birth.

Earlier, in 1967, Wyner's first, 16-year marriage, to the former Nancy Braverman, a mezzo-soprano, had ended in divorce. That same year he married the former Susan M. Davenny, a onetime violinist, who was building a career as a soprano. By his own account, Davenny (who has worked as a conductor in recent years) inspired the composition of a number of his works, among them *Canto Cantabile* (1972), for soprano and concert band; *Memorial Music* (1971–73), for soprano and three flutes; *Intermedio* (1976), for soprano and strings; *Fragments from Antiquity* (1978–81), for soprano and symphony orchestra; five songs set to ancient Chinese and classical romantic poems; and the song cycle *On This Most Voluptuous Night* (1982), for soprano and seven instruments, based on poems by William Carlos Williams.

Others among his compositions from the 1960s, 1970s, and 1980s include the Serenade for seven instruments (1958); *Passover Offering* (1959), for flute, clarinet, cello, and trombone; *Friday Evening Service* (1963; orchestrated, 1992), for cantor, chorus, and organ; *Dances of Atonement* (1976), for violin and piano; *All the Rage* (1980), for flute and

piano; and *O to Be a Dragon* (1989), four songs for women's chorus and piano, set to whimsical poems by Marianne Moore. Wyner also wrote incidental music for two plays: *The Old Glory* (1964), set to a poem by Robert Lowell, which premiered at the American Place Theater, and *The Mirror* (1972–73), set to a fantastical tale by Isaac Bashevis Singer and mounted at the Yale Repertory Theater. *The Mirror* is one of three pieces on an album recorded by Wyner in 2004. Performed by instrumentalists including the flutist Carol Wincenc and the clarinetist Richard Stoltzman, the disk was nominated for two classical-music Grammy Awards, for producer of the year (David Frost) and best small ensemble.

In composing his 28-minute *Prologue and Narrative* for cello and orchestra (1994), Wyner collaborated with the cellist Ralph Kirshbaum, who lives in England. "We would exchange letters, and whenever Ralph came to America for concerts, we would meet and go over passages in detail," Wyner told Richard Dyer (April 11, 1999). "I kept rewriting until both of us were satisfied." The work was introduced to the public in a performance by Kirshbaum and the BBC Philharmonic, which had commissioned it. Another work, *Horntrio* (1997), was written as a sort of appreciation for Brahms's Trio for Horn, Violin, and Piano, one of the rare classical chamber pieces that include the horn. Wyner composed it with the support of the World-Wide Concurrent Premieres and Commissioning Fund, an organization that attempts to generate interest in new music by sponsoring multiple, simultaneous premieres of the works around the around. *Horntrio* debuted at nine locations on December 7, 1997, among them Jordan Hall in Boston, Massachusetts, where it was performed with Wyner on piano, Jean Rife on horn, and James Buswell on violin. "Has any composer since Benjamin Britten played the piano as well as Wyner? How many full-time professional pianists do?" Dyer wrote for the *Boston Globe* (December 9, 1997) after attending the premiere. In the following months 30 additional concerts included the *Horntrio*. Ellen Pfeifer, writing for the *Boston Herald* (December 9, 1997), described the piece as "an intense, mercurial, brilliant affair written in a charged chromatic idiom." Now one of Wyner's most frequently performed pieces, *Horntrio* was among the finalists for the 1998 Pulitzer Prize in music.

In 1999 a program sponsored by the city of Santa Fe, New Mexico, called 20th Century Unlimited, commissioned Wyner to write a vocal piece for the soprano Dominique Labelle. "I've had a lot of experience writing for the voice and making a great effort to get out of the way, but at the same time providing continuity and support," Wyner told Craig Smith for the *Santa Fe New Mexican* (June 4, 1999). "It's a very neat craft; it's very demanding." The commissioned work is the 24-minute song cycle *The Second Madrigal: Voices of Women* for soprano, violin, viola, cello, double bass, and percussion, a set of musical interpretations of poems by or about women collected by Czelaw Milosz in *A Book of Luminous Things*—in particular, from the section of the anthology entitled "Woman's Skin." *The Second Madrigal* was recorded for a 2003 CD that also includes *Horntrio* and Wyner's Quartet for oboe and string trio.

The debut of Wyner's Piano Concerto: "Chiavi in Mano," in early 2005, marked the first concert in over a dozen years at which a Boston composer's work was performed by the city's symphony orchestra with a Boston-based pianist and Mozart specialist (Robert Levin) as the featured soloist. The subtitle refers both to the keys that physically and symbolically give a person use of a house or a car and to the keys of the piano. "As in many of my compositions, simple, familiar musical ideas are the starting point," Wyner explained in a note posted on schirmer.com (December 13, 2004). "A shape, a melodic fragment, a rhythm, a chord, a texture, or a sonority may ignite the appetite for exploration. How such simple insignificant things can be altered, elaborated, extended, and combined becomes the exciting challenge of composition. I also want the finished work to breathe in a natural way, to progress spontaneously, organically, moving toward a transformation of the musical substance in ways unimaginable to me when I began the journey. Transformation is the goal, with

the intention of achieving an altered state of perception and exposure that I am otherwise unable to achieve." Wyner is currently composing a violin concerto for Daniel Stepner, one of the Brandeis University professors who comprise the Lydian String Quartet.

Wyner and his wife live in Medford, Massachusetts. From his first marriage he has two sons, Isaiah and Adam, and a daughter, Cassia. He also has several grandchildren, for whom he wrote a multi-lyric song called "The Button at the Bottom of the Butt." "I'm not sure it's suitable for all children," he told Stephen Heyman.

—M.B.

Suggested Reading: *Boston Globe* N p2 Apr. 11, 1999, C p13 Feb. 18, 2005, F p3 Apr. 19, 2006; Jewish Music WebCenter Nov. 5, 2006; Milken Archive of American Jewish Music; *New York Times* Westchester section p5 Aug. 2, 1981; *Santa Fe New Mexican* P p46 June 4, 1999; Schirmer.com; *Who's Who in America*

Selected Works: *On This Most Voluptuous Night*, 1982; *Prologue and Narrative for Cello and Orchestra*, 1994; *Horntrio*, 1997; *The Second Madrigal: Voices of Women*, 1999; *Chiavo in Mano*, 2005

Yuen Wo Ping

Jan. 1, 1945– Director of martial-arts films; martial-arts and motion-picture stunt choreographer

Address: c/o China Film Group Corp., 31 Xin De Jie, Xi Cheng District, Beijing 100088, China; c/o Casey Silver Productions, 506 Santa Monica Blvd. #322, Santa Monica, CA 90401

Among aficionados of action films made in the Far East, Yuen Wo Ping, as Richard Corliss wrote for *Time* (December 4, 2000), is "revered as the deviser of artful torture for Asia's top actor athletes": Jackie Chan, Jet Li, Michelle Yeoh, and Sammo Hung. A native of mainland China, Yuen was the mastermind behind the extraordinary, gravity-defying acrobatics and balletic fight scenes in two genre-bending, immensely popular films released at the turn of the new millennium: Andy and Larry Wachowski's *The Matrix* (1999) and Ang Lee's *Crouching Tiger, Hidden Dragon* (2000), the latter of which won an Academy Award as best foreign-language film. Steeped in the kung-fu traditions of Hong Kong filmmaking since childhood, Yuen has spent his four-decade professional life on movie sets, both in front of the camera, as an actor, extra, or stuntman, and behind it, as a writer, producer, director, and, most notably, action director—that is, a choreographer of martial-arts sequences. Ac-

cording to the Web site Hong Kong Cinemagic, as of late November 2007, his filmography included 138 titles, including 33 in which he worked in dual or multiple capacities, most frequently as both director and action director. Yuen began his career in cinema in Hong Kong (then a British colony) in 1965, at age 20, with a bit part in *Temple of the Red Lotus* and as a stuntman in *The Lotus Lamp*. He soon landed more substantial roles, in films known to few in the West except fans of kung-fu movies. His first job as action director came in 1971, with the film *Mad Killer*; his first as director came 44 movies later, in 1978, with *Snake in the Eagle's Shadow*, which he choreographed as well. In an interview with David Chute for *LA Weekly* (December 15, 2000), Ang Lee declared that Yuen's distinctive approach to martial-arts and stunt choreography had "revolutionized the kung fu genre," by introducing elements of humor and embracing a "softer," "more fluid" movement style in lieu of what Yuen himself, in an interview with Stuart Husband for the London *Guardian* (December 21, 2000), called the "hard, fast cut-cut-cut of a lot of movies." "I want to bring out the aestheticism of the [martial] art form . . . ," Yuen told Chute. "I want to bring out its beauty by incorporating dance movements, so that the elegance of the gestures can be seen more clearly."

In 2000, with Americans growing more familiar with Yuen's work, Miramax rereleased *Iron Monkey*, one of Yuen's five 2003 films. In a representative review of the film, which Yuen directed and choreographed, Margaret A. McGurk wrote for the *Cincinnati (Ohio) Enquirer* (October 12, 2001) that Yuen's "approach to his kinetic material is gymnastic and ballet-like, not to mention bracingly witty. *Iron Monkey* is chock-full of smart, funny and high-flying martial-arts displays guaranteed to amaze. . . . The simple story encompasses moments of great emotion . . . but mainly serves to frame the astonishing action. Mr. Yuen shows limitless imagination in staging. . . . Those whose taste for Asian action was whetted by *Crouching Tiger* will welcome *Iron Monkey*. So will anybody who just loves a good, old-fashioned adventure." Yuen was the action director for *The Matrix*'s two sequels and for *Kill Bill Volume 1* and *Kill Bill Volume 2*, the latter of which won the American Choreography Award for outstanding achievement in choreographing fights.

The eldest of a dozen children (the number varies in the few English-language sources that mention it),Yuen Wo Ping was born on January 1, 1945 in the city of Guangzhou, in southern China. Many variations of his name have appeared in print, among them Yuen Woo Ping, Wu Ping Yuen, and Yuan Ta Yen. Yuen's father, Yuen Siu Tien (also spelled Yuen Hsiao Tien or Yuen Siu Tin), performed in the Peking (now Beijing) Opera, taught martial arts, and, at times using the given name Simon, appeared in many films, some made by Yuen Wo Ping; as a young actor, Simon Yuen portrayed in several movies the much-celebrated Chinese folk hero Wong Fei Hung (1847–1924), a martial artist, practitioner of traditional medicine, and political and social revolutionary. According to Hong Kong Cinemagic, Yuen Wo Ping has eight brothers, four of whom have, like him, forged careers in the film industry, as scriptwriters, stunt coordinators and choreographers, directors, actors, or producers. One brother, Yuen Cheung Yan, has had parts in many films and choreographed the fight sequnces in *Charlie's Angels* (2000) and other motion pictures. As a child Yuen Wo Ping and his siblings learned from their father the martial art known as *wu xia* (pronounced "woo shah"), a form of acrobatic dancing or "theatrical kung fu," as Yuen called it in his conversation with David Chute. Their father also exposed them to other conventions of Hong Kong action cinema.

In 1965 Yuen Wo Ping entered Hong Kong's emerging film industry, securing jobs as an actor, extra, stunt man, and stunt coordinator. He was cast in minor roles in *The Chinese Boxer* (1970), *Duel of Fists* (1971), and other films emanating from the Shaw Brothers Studio, the largest producer of films in Hong Kong at that time; often, he portrayed "the one who was picked to die first," as he said to Chute. "I was very good at falling down dead." During that period Yuen began to hone his skills in stunt choreography and martial-arts choreography. "I spent lots of time watching my father work," Yuen told Tim Swanson for *Variety* (January 29, 2001/February 4, 2001). "I also paid atten-

tion to the other fight choreographers. I then tried new styles by myself to make the fighting better."

In 1971 Yuen landed his first official credit as a fight choreographer, for the film *Mad Killer*, directed by Ng See Yuen. In the next few years, he served as an extra in a half-dozen films and as fight choreographer for four. Yuen reunited with Ng See Yuen, who had founded the Seasonal Films production company in 1975, and joined Golden Harvest Productions, which had supplanted the Shaw Brothers Studio as the top Hong Kong film producer, to direct his first feature film, *Snake in the Eagle's Shadow* (1978). Starring the then-unknown actor Jackie Chan, *Snake in the Eagle's Shadow* is about a bullied, orphaned school janitor who learns the secrets of "snake-fist" kung fu from an old master (played by Yuen's father) disguised as a beggar while on the run from an "eagle's-claw" kung-fu killer. A big hit in Hong Kong, the film revealed Yuen's talent for mixing clever martial-arts sequences with humor. In Yuen's second feature film, *Drunken Master* (1978), Jackie Chan starred as Wong Fei Hung, portrayed not as the dignified nobleman seen in traditional stories about him but as a rebellious youth who is forced to learn kung fu from a drunkard (Simon Yuen) known for his unmerciful method of instruction. *Drunken Master* transformed the kung-fu genre of filmmaking by "taking some of the grimness out that had been there since Bruce Lee"—a reference to the virtuosic kung-fu film star who died in 1973—and making it "more slapstick, more fun," as Ang Lee told David Chute. In an assessment of *Drunken Master* for the Kung Fu Cinema Web site, Mark Pollard described the movie as "without a doubt . . . the greatest classic kung fu comedy of all time and also the most influential Hong Kong film of the latter half of the 1970s." "The story firmly established stock conventions like the irreverent student-master relationship and the concept of gaining fighting prowess through inebriation that appeared in dozens of subsequent films," Pollard continued. He also wrote that under Yuen's "masterful direction," *Drunken Master* had enabled Jackie Chan "to unleash the full force of his comic and physical genius." With Sammo Hung Kam-Bo (also known as Sammo Hung), Yuen co-directed *The Magnificent Butcher* (1979), a kung-fu movie in which Hung starred.

During the 1980s and early 1990s, Yuen directed and served as martial-arts choreographer for kung-fu action movies featuring such martial-artist luminaries as Donnie Yen Ji-Dan, in *Drunken Tai Chi* (1984); Jet Li, in *The Tai Chi Master* (1993); and Michelle Yeoh, in *Wing Chun* (1994). At around that time Yeon decided to revive *wu xia*, the classic, ballet-like martial art performed in Chinese opera. He choreographed, with Chia Yung Lui, the martial-arts sequences for the director Tsui Hark's *Once Upon a Time in China* (1991) and, working alone, its sequel, *Once Upon a Time in China, Part 2* (1992), about the life of Wong Fei Hung, portrayed by Jet Li. For those films Yuen used the tech-

Woody Wu/AFP/Getty Images

Yuen Wo Ping (right) with the actor Ge You and the actress Zhang Ziyi

nique known as wirework, in which actors are hoisted in the air by means of wire cables, which to some degree also control their movements. As Stuart Husband observed, wirework creates the illusion that a person "can glide, soar, hover, swoop, and [perform] all the other tricks in which birds had previously cornered the market." In an article about the two *Once Upon a Time in China* films for the *Washington Post* (August 15, 2001), Stephen Hunter expressed the opinion that the actors "sail-[ed] through the air on wires more effortlessly than [performers in] any production of *Peter Pan*." Hunter added that what gripped the audience most forcefully was not the wirework but the fights; in sequences designed collaboratively by Jet Li, "an extraordinary gymnast," and the fight choreographers, Li seemed "weirdly able to change direction in midair, or catch himself between pillars in a leg-spread iron cross, or duck a blade by leg-spreading on the ground (ouch!) then skip back to his feet. He frequently takes on gangs of 30 or 40, and he's so fast, elegant and coordinated that he makes you believe in the reality of what you're seeing." Ang Lee told David Chute that in the *Once Upon a Time in China* films, Yuen took "the exhilaration" of the martial-arts sequences "to another level. The style was more operatic than anything he had done before, and his talent for wirework really came to the fore."

Yuen both directed and served as martial-arts director for *Iron Monkey* (1993), a retelling of a Chinese fable about a mysterious masked avenger (the title character, played by Rongguang Yu) reminiscent of the British folk hero Robin Hood. In a review for the *St. Louis (Missouri) Post-Dispatch* (October 12, 2001), Joe Williams described one scene,

in which the film's protagonist, Kei-Ying, manipulates an umbrella, as "a perhaps inadvertent homage to Fred Astaire, while an astounding man-to-man battle atop flaming posts is unlike anything that Western audiences have ever seen." A blockbuster in Hong Kong, *Iron Monkey* attracted little notice in the United States until 2001, when it was rereleased in the States, thanks to efforts on its behalf by the filmmaker Quentin Tarantino, an admirer of Yuen. "Ping is one of my favorite directors," Tarantino told Robert Denerstein for the *Rocky Mountain News* (October 13, 2001). "Iron Monkey is like Zorro, a Chinese Zorro."

Earlier, Yuen got his first taste of Hollywood success, with his martial-arts choreography for *The Matrix* (1999). Conceived by the filmmakers Andy and Larry Wachowski as a futuristic parable that explored conflicting concepts of reality, *The Matrix* blended virtual combat with the fluidity of Asian martial arts. Explaining what had attracted him to the Wachowskis' project, Yuen told Elizabeth Weitzman for *Interview* (April 2001), "When I heard [the Wachowski brothers would] be combining special effects with traditional martial arts, I got very excited. There were movements I had been dreaming about for years that people just couldn't perform. But with the help of advanced technology, I could upgrade the level of action beyond the body's physical limits." To achieve the illusion of seamless, authentic combat, much of which occurred in mid-air, Yuen insisted that the two principal actors, Keanu Reeves and Laurence Fishburne, endure intense kung-fu training. "It was really important for me to have the four months to work with them because none of the actors had an action background," Yuen said to Winnie Chung for Hong Kong's *South China Morning Post* (May 9, 1999). "They didn't know martial arts." To his surprise, the performers, who also had to adjust to logistical complications posed by the wirework (later, the wires were digitally erased), showed aptitude for the new movements. Yuen's choreography for *The Matrix* won praise from both moviegoers and critics. "He does long sequences of fist fights in a way that is balletic and yet it is real fighting. He can get the optimum amount of explosiveness out of action," Ann Hui, a Hong Kong film director, told Rahul Jacob for the *Financial Times* (March 24, 2001). Joan Acocella, in reviewing *The Matrix* for the *New Yorker* (March 26, 2001), described one scene in which Keanu Reeves, "standing on a subway track and happening to notice that a train is bearing down on him, levitates about ten feet into the air, does a backflip, and alights on the subway platform. All of us would like to do this, and such feats leaven the film's violence with a sort of joy." Yuen's choreography in *The Matrix* spawned imitations, such as sequences in the blockbuster animated feature *Shrek* (2001). "I think it is a good thing and it's quite amusing to see a film being copied like that. It is a kind of honour. You have to be good before other people will copy from you," Yuen told Lance Volland for the *Hindu* (June 13, 2003, on-line).

For his choreography for another groundbreaking feature film, Ang Lee's *Crouching Tiger, Hidden Dragon*, Yuen tried "to express the more magical characteristics of the old-fashioned wu xia," as he told Stuart Husband. He integrated magic and sorcery, on one hand, with realistic movements, on the other, to illuminate the characters' humanity. "They fly through the air, but for every leap they make they come back down to earth at some point," he explained to Husband. Effortlessly scaling walls and gliding across treetops, the characters displayed a style of combat, movement, and flight that was largely unknown to Western critics and audiences. Anthony Lane, who reviewed the movie for the *New Yorker* (December 11, 2000), wrote, "The movie is not just the best of its kind; it seems on the verge of creating a new kind," and later added, "You leave the film on air, but you can't decide whether you feel like a 5-year-old coming out of *Peter Pan* or like a Cary Grant fan coming out of *To Catch a Thief*." In a critique for the *Chicago Sun-Times* (December 22, 2000), Roger Ebert described *Crouching Tiger, Hidden Dragon* as "the most exhilarating martial arts movie I have seen. It stirred even the hardened audience at the 8:30 a.m. press screening at [the Cannes Film Festival] last May. There is a sequence near the beginning of the film involving a chase over rooftops, and as the characters run up the sides of walls and leap impossibly from one house to another, the critics applauded, something they rarely do during a film, and I think they were relating to the sheer physical grace of the scene. It is done so lightly, quickly, easily." *Crouching Tiger, Hidden Dragon* set U.S. box-office records for a foreign-language

picture and received many awards. "I did my very best with the choreography but it is beyond my imagination that it would be such a hit," Yuen told Rahul Jacob.

Yuen devised the futuristic stunt sequences for *The Matrix Reloaded* (2003) and *The Matrix Revolutions* (2003) and choreographed the kung-fu artistry in Quentin Tarantino's *Kill Bill: Volume 1* (2003) and *Kill Bill: Volume 2* (2004). In an assessment of the first *Kill Bill*, A. O. Scott described a scene "that cross[ed] the line between jolting and sickening" and then wrote, "Compared with this, the long, intricate climax, during which the Bride takes on 88 yakuza fighters and litters a Tokyo nightclub with their severed limbs and writhing trunks, feels as insouciant and elegant as a show-stopping musical number. Which, in essence, it is, staged with the assistance of the martial-arts maestro Yuen Wo-Ping." In a review of a more recent project of Yuen's, Manohla Dargis wrote for the *New York Times* (May 13, 2005), "The infinitely silly, unconscionably entertaining action film *Unleashed*"—written by Luc Besson and directed by Louis Leterrier—"earns most of its juice from the martial-arts star Jet Li, the eminent martial-arts choreographer Yuen Wo Ping and the fine British actor Bob Hoskins in full terrifying lather."

Yuen's latest film, *The Forbidden Kingdom* (2008), received mostly mixed reviews. "The worst part of martial-arts epic *The Forbidden Kingdom*—in which a kung fu master (Jackie Chan) and a monk (Jet Li) help a time-traveling teen (Michael Angarano) return a magical staff to its owner—isn't the stale story, the fortune-cookie dialogue, or the fizzled pairing of action legends Chan and Li, whose fisticuffs here have all the oomph of a high-speed game of pattycake," Adam Markovitz wrote for *Entertainment Weekly* (April 16, 2008, on-line). "No, it's a moment near the halfway mark when there arrives a gag that involves Chan getting a face full of urine. This kingdom really should be forbidden." Many other critics also expressed disappointment in the failure of Li and Chan to come up with exceptional action scenes. Some were more forgiving. "Once past the clunky prologue, the film is great fun, with a good balance between computer effects and athleticism," David Edelstein wrote for *New York* (April 13, 2008). "The best part is when Chan resurrects his drunken-master fighting style and goes hand-to-hand with the stoic but furious Li." Writing for the *Baltimore Sun* (April 18, 2008), Michael Sragow called Yuen's fight choreography "exhilarating."

—D.J.K.

Suggested Reading:hkcinemagic.com; kungfucinema.com; *LA Weekly* p35+ Dec. 15, 2000; (London) *Financial Times* p11 Mar. 24, 2001; (London) *Guardian* p12 Dec. 21, 2000; lovehkfilm.com; *New Yorker* p100 Mar. 26, 2001; *South China Morning Post* p5 May 9, 1999, p6 May 7, 2003; *Time* p54 Feb. 19, 2001

Selected Films: as director—*Drunken Master*, 1978; *Iron Monkey*, 1993; as stunt choreographer—*The Matrix*, 1999; *Crouching Tiger, Hidden Dragon*, 2000; *The Matrix Reloaded*, 2003; *The Matrix Revolutions*, 2003; *Kill Bill: Volume 1*, 2003; *Kill Bill: Volume 2*, 2004; *The Forbidden Kingdom*, 2008

Zagat, Tim and Nina

Survey and guidebook publishers

Zagat, Tim
(zah-GAT)
June 13, 1940–

Zagat, Nina
Aug. 12, 1942–

Address: Zagat Survey, 4 Columbus Circle, New York, NY 10019

At a dinner party in 1979, Nina and Tim Zagat and their 20 fellow diners had a discussion about reviews of New York City restaurants. They all agreed that the majority were poorly written, often leaving readers baffled about the types and quality of the food served in particular establishments. By the end of the meal, Tim Zagat had developed a questionnaire, with a 30-point scale in four categories: decor, food, service, and cost. The hosts of the dinner and their guests then assessed a total of 75 of their favorite restaurants and rated various features of each on legal-size paper. Each person received a photocopy of the evaluations, free of charge. That egalitarian approach to restaurant recommendations appealed to the Zagats, who had tried it years before, during a two-year stay in Paris, France; as they told Bob Weinstein for *Entrepreneur* (August 1996), "A group of people are more likely to be accurate about a restaurant than one person."

The people at the party then surveyed some of their friends about New York City restaurants; that second set of reviewers then queried others, who did the same in turn. By 1982 the survey, conducted annually by the Zagats for fun, had grown to include 300 restaurants critiqued by approximately 600 people, who came to be known as Zagateers. Also by that time, as Nina Zagat has said on many occasions, their hobby was costing them nearly $12,000 a year and had become very time-consuming, too. She and her husband decided to charge a fee for their survey and have it published professionally. But none of the publishers whom they contacted expressed a willingness to take on their project. Even an uncle of Tim Zagat's who owned a publishing company was wary. "My uncle said his company had printed a guidebook by eminent *New York Times* food critic Craig Clai-

borne," Tim Zagat told Weinstein. "And it never sold more than 30,000 copies a year." The Zagats resolved to publish the book themselves, a decision they regard as perhaps the best—and luckiest—of any they have ever made: once the survey gained in popularity and became a profitable business, they collected all the proceeds, instead of the standard 10 or 15 percent they would have received from a publisher. In 1983 Zagat Survey, as their company is called, sold 7,500 copies of their guide. In 2007, according to Andrew Ross Sorkin in the *New York Times* (January 14, 2008), they sold 5.5 million guides in 100 countries. In addition to *Zagat New York City Restaurants*, Zagat Survey publishes guides that review restaurants in 85 other cities worldwide. Other Zagat guides assess golf courses; nightclubs and other nightlife venues; international hotels, spas, and resorts; New York City theaters; New York City shops; movies ("the 1,000 top films of all time"); and music ("1,000 top albums of all time"). At the turn of the 21st century, Zagat Survey went on-line. As of January 2008 the Web site had 1.5 million registered users. Also that month the Zagat family began seeking a buyer for their company. Within six months, however, they ended their search, having decided to keep the company independent—temporarily, at least. Zagat has a restaurant-and-nightlife software application on the social-networking Web site facebook.com; an arrangement with Google in which the names of Zagat-reviewed restaurants appear on the company's on-line maps; and an agreement with Priceline.com in which Zagat ratings appear on the Priceline home page.

Residents of New York, Tim and Nina Zagat use their guides when they visit other cities, but they never participate in their surveys, because they believe that doing so would result in a conflict of interest and might introduce an element of unfairness into their work. At the same time they have acknowledged that, although they have learned to recognize and weed out responses that seem suspicious, malicious, or dishonest in some other way, such assessments undoubtedly have slipped by them. In the final production stages of each year's New York City restaurant guide, Tim Zagat visits as many as 30 restaurants every night, in order to make sure that the details about each are correct. Annually, he eats at as many as 600. As celebrities in the New York City restaurant scene, the Zagats have received many offers of free meals from eager-to-please chefs, but they have always turned them down.

While the accuracy and legitimacy of the Zagat surveys have been questioned, restaurateurs recognize their importance to many customers. Alan Stillman, the owner of the New York City restaurants Smith & Wollensky and Park Avenue Cafe, told Paul Frumkin for *Nation's Restaurant News* (January 1995), "I know people who own five Zagat guides. They have one at home, one in the car, one in their office. It is the most influential guide. It has

Tim and Nina Zagat

Kazuhiro Nogi/AFP/Getty Images

more impact on sales than the *New York Times* guide to dining." Joe Baum, the owner of the Rainbow Room in New York City, told Frumkin, "I think it's the bible for so many people." "What we have done is empowered hundreds of thousands of people to think that their voice counts, too. It's not just the critic who counts," Tim Zagat told David Leonhardt for the *New York Times* (November 23, 2003). He said to Samantha Miller and Bob Meadows for *People* (September 6, 1999), "We came along at the right time. Wouldn't you rather have 3,000 opinions on whether a place is good than just one?"

Tim Zagat was born Eugene H. Zagat Jr. on June 13, 1940 to Eugene H. Zagat Sr. and the former Cornelia Ernst. He grew up with his sister, Cornelia, in New York City, where he attended the Riverdale Country School, a private prep school in the borough of the Bronx. He then enrolled at Harvard University, in Cambridge, Massachusetts, and received a B.A. degree cum laude in 1961. After his graduation, during the administration of President John F. Kennedy, he worked in Washington, D.C., as a senior staff member of the newly formed Peace Corps; his title was book coordinator, with responsibility for publishing textbooks and organizing, reading, and writing training materials. Nina Zagat was born Nina Irene Safronoff on August 12, 1942 to Samuel Safronoff and his wife, Lily. With her brother, Peter, she grew up in Merrick, Long Island, New York. She attended Vassar College, in Poughkeepsie, New York, and received a B.A. degree cum laude in 1963. The Zagats met while attending law school at Yale University, in New Haven, Connecticut, Nina with the support of the Helen Dwight Reid fellowship for study in international relations

and international law. Tim and Nina were married in 1965.

During that period Tim Zagat worked for NBC News, for which he conducted political surveys connected with the 1964 presidential campaigns of the incumbent, the Democrat Lyndon B. Johnson, and his Republican opponent, Senator Barry Goldwater of Arizona. Immediately after completing their law degrees, in 1966, the Zagats moved to Paris to work in the offices of the law firms they had joined: Hughes, Hubbard & Reed (Tim) and Sterling and Sterling (Nina). During the next two years, Nina Zagat took classes at the renowned Paris culinary school Le Cordon Bleu. The idea of surveying people about which restaurants they preferred, instead of relying on critics for evaluations, came to the Zagats in Paris. Consisting of a single page and titled the *Guide de Guides*, the survey was copied for their friends but never gained wider popularity.

In 1970 the Zagats left Paris to work in the New York City offices of their respective law firms. Six years later Tim joined another firm, Pomerantz, Levy, Haudek & Block. In 1979 the Zagats cofounded Zagat Survey (the name is a registered trademark as well as their company name). For the next few years, their research remained avocational; the couple regarded it simply as a way for them and their friends to gain as much knowledge as possible about the growing number of New York City restaurants. The first professionally published Zagat Survey was printed in 1983. Serving as their own salespeople, the Zagats would drive from one New York bookstore to another in attempts to persuade the owners or managers to carry their guides. Then, in 1986, less than a year after a few cover articles and stories about the survey appeared in newspapers and magazines, sales increased exponentially, to more than 100,000 copies. At the end of 1986, the Zagats hired their first full-time employee. The next year Tim Zagat quit his job—he had been chief litigation counsel for Gulf & Western Industries since 1980—to devote himself to the survey full-time. (Nina Zagat continued working as a lawyer until 1990.)

The success of the New York City restaurant survey led the Zagats, in 1988, to provide similar surveys for restaurants in other cities (among them Washington, D.C.; Los Angeles and San Francisco, California; and Chicago, Illinois) and for hotels, resorts, and spas. Two years later they produced surveys of airlines and car-rental agencies. The year 1992 saw the publication of two nationwide Zagat surveys: *America's 1,000 Top Restaurants* and *America's Best Value Restaurants.*

In the months leading up to the 1992 Democratic National Convention, held that year in New York City, Tim Zagat and other local businesspeople created NY'92—a promotion that enabled the 5,000 delegates and 15,000 members of the press who attended the convention to buy meals at a discount at many of the city's finest restaurants. Zagat persuaded some of the participating restaurants to serve lunches for $19.92—a high price relative to the costs of lunches at most places in the city and elsewhere but substantially less than what those restaurants would normally have charged. NY'92 proved to be a boon to the local economy; its success led to similar promotions in 1993 and 1994. "Tim is an extraordinary asset for New York City and the restaurant community," Joe Baum told Frumkin. "He is willing to put his time and effort on the line to stimulate New York as a major attraction. He fights for what he thinks is right. He's the best kind of leader—he provides solutions for different problems."

In 1999 the Zagats sold one-third of their business for $31 million to a group of investors to raise capital for a new effort: the posting of surveys online. Visitors can vote at the site, and for $19.95 a month, subscribers can access many of the same services offered by the guides, plus regularly updated lists of restaurants and other attractions. Citing one example, the Zagats told Pamela Parseghian for *Nation's Restaurant News* (October 4, 2004), "We can produce—in five minutes or less—the French restaurants on the East Side [of Manhattan] that have fireplaces and are romantic and cost less than $50."

During the summer of 1999, the Zagats hosted a gathering of restaurateurs and other industry professionals to discuss their proposal for a nine-point "diner's bill of rights." No one disputed the inclusion of courteous service, sanitary facilities, and smoke- and cellular-phone– free environments, but some items, among them the rights of diners to bring their own wine to restaurants, complain to managers, and refrain from tipping in some circumstances, sparked controversy. The assumption of such rights, some restaurateurs complained,

would give diners a sense of privilege and perhaps even the expectation of compensation. Drew Nieporent, a New York City restaurant owner, told Frank DiGiacomo for the *New York Observer* (July 19, 1999): "[The Zagat guide] has been an invaluable tool to the restaurant industry. However, what we don't need are people to come into our restaurants looking for problems. The experience should be one of relaxation and civility, not one of what's wrong with this place? Those rights are implicit. They don't need to be written down." By contrast, another restaurateur, who requested anonymity, declared, "There's nothing better than empowering the common people. You'll never get more people on your side than telling a complete idiot that his opinion counts." The restaurateur Danny Meyer told DiGiacomo that he considered the bill of rights "a conversation piece that at its best could foster a better understanding of dining out and could promote dining out."

As of 2007 there were Zagat restaurant guides in print for 85 cities worldwide, and the Zagat surveys were accessible via mobile devices such as Blackberries as well as on-line. Some 120 full-time employees worked in Zagat offices in New York City, and in each city for which a Zagat guide is available, there were two employees, one of which was usually a well-known restaurant critic or reviewer, who copyedited the Zagat reviews and visited surveyed restaurants before publication. The number of Zagateers had increased to about 300,000. Hotels, resorts, and spas in 95 countries are included in Zagat surveys. *Zagat Magazine: Sharing the Experience of Good Living* is available on the Zagat Web site.

In June 2008 the Zagat family ended its six-month search for a buyer. Instead, the company would be allowed to continue its "organic growth," as Tim and Nina Zagat stated in a June 5 press release available on PRNewswire.com. Rejecting some observers' belief that the company's $200 million price tag was too high to attract buyers, the Zagats maintained that the weak economy was a major reason for their failure to sell their company.

Tim Zagat has served on many boards and committees, among them NYC & Co.—nycvisit.com, the city's official tourism site—which he has chaired and worked for as a marketing official. He is the vice president of the national board of directors of the Careers Through the Culinary Arts Program, which is supported by private contributions, and was a director of the NYC Partnership and Chamber of Commerce. Nina Zagat has served on the White House Conference on Travel and Tourism. In 2000 Harvard College named her Entrepreneur of the Year; in 2001 the Star Group named her one of the Leading Women Entrepreneurs of the World, and she was listed among Crain's Top Tech 100, a survey of New York City's most influential people in technology. She has been a member of the corporation of the Culinary Institute of America since 1994. In 2000 both Ernst & Young and Harvard Business School named the Zagats Entrepreneurs of the Year. In 2001 they were inducted into New York University's Entrepreneurship Hall of Fame, and in 2004 *Nation's Restaurant News* named them Innovators of the Year.

When Deborah Solomon interviewed Tim Zagat for the *New York Times* (December 17, 2006), the six-foot two-inch publisher weighed 250 pounds, 50 pounds more than he would have liked. In addition to an apartment overlooking Central Park, in Manhattan, he and his wife own a 160-acre estate two hours north of the city by car. The couple have two sons: Ted, who was the president of Zagat Survey for several years (he left in 2007 to join Univision as a vice president) and John. In 2000 Ted, then 25, completed a survey of nightlife in New York City. Zagat's nightlife surveys currently cover two dozen cities.

—F.C.

Suggested Reading: *Entrepreneur* p120+ Aug. 1996; *Nation's Restaurant News* p223+ Jan. 1995, p136+ Oct. 4, 2004; *New York Times* II p1+ Nov. 23, 2003, C p1+ Jan. 14, 2008; *People* p117+ Sep. 6, 1999; States News Service Feb. 28, 2007; Zagat Web site

Selected Books: *Zagat 2008 America's Top Restaurants*, 2007; *Zagat 2008 Top U.S. Hotels, Resorts & Spas*, 2007; *Zagat 2009 New York City Restaurants*, 2008

Paul J. Richards/AFP/Getty Images

Zoellick, Robert B.

July 25, 1953– President of the World Bank

Address: The World Bank, 1818 H St., N.W., Washington, DC 20433

On July 1, 2007 Robert B. Zoellick began a five-year term as president of the World Bank. A prominent force in both business and the U.S. government, Zoellick has held many positions in the public sphere, beginning with his service from 1985 to 1992 in various capacities in the treasury and state departments. In 1990, as counselor—with the rank of under secretary—to James A. Baker 3d, who was then secretary of state, he played a key role in the peaceful reunification of East and West Germany.

Zoellick was also instrumental in launching the Asia-Pacific Economic Cooperation Forum, effectively opening a huge Asian market to trade with the U.S. He then served as under secretary of state for economic and agricultural affairs in the George H. W. Bush administration, a capacity in which he aggressively pursued U.S. trade interests; he was the principal State Department representative in the negotiation of the North American Free Trade Agreement (NAFTA) and represented the U.S. at the G7 Economic Summits, a yearly policy meeting of the world's economic superpowers. In 1992 Zoellick was appointed White House deputy chief of staff and assistant to the president. Leaving government in 1993, he was appointed executive vice president of Fannie Mae, the largest provider of funds for home purchases in the United States, and also taught at the U.S. Naval Academy. He advised George W. Bush in his successful 2000 presidential run and served as U.S. trade representative from 2001 to 2005, helping to launch the World Trade Organization (WTO) trade round in Doha, Qatar; secure trade-negotiating authority—also known as "fast-track" authority, or FTA—from the U.S. Congress; complete free-trade agreements with 12 countries; and usher China and Taiwan into the WTO. In 2005 he was appointed deputy secretary of state under Condoleezza Rice, leaving that post one year later to work for the private investment bank Goldman Sachs. In 2007 President Bush nominated him as president of the World Bank. In that position he leads an institution charged with the mission of overcoming global poverty.

The second of the two sons of William T. and Gladys Zoellick, Robert Bruce Zoellick was born on July 25, 1953 and grew up in Naperville, Illinois. He graduated from Naperville Central High School in 1971, then attended Swarthmore College, in Swarthmore, Pennsylvania, graduating Phi Beta Kappa in 1975. He went on to study in Cambridge, Massachusetts, obtaining his J.D. degree, magna cum laude, from Harvard Law School in 1981, as well as a master of public policy degree from Harvard University's John F. Kennedy School of Government. Following his graduation from law school, he worked from 1981 to 1982 as a clerk for Judge Patricia Wald of the United States Court of Appeals for the District of Columbia Circuit.

From 1985 to 1992, during the presidential administrations of Ronald Reagan and George H. W. Bush, Zoellick served in a number of positions in the state and treasury departments, including deputy assistant secretary of the treasury for financial institutions policy; counselor to Secretary of State James A. Baker 3d; deputy assistant secretary of state for financial institutions policy; and under secretary of state for economic and agricultural affairs. As counselor under Baker, Zoellick was the U.S. representative in negotiations over the 1990 reunification of East and West Germany. (The two governments, Communist and democratic, respectively, had been separate since 1949, in the early days of the Cold War between the U.S. and the Communist Soviet Union.) Despite misgivings from some NATO (North Atlantic Treaty Organization) allies of the U.S., Zoellick made the case that the existence of Germany as a single, capitalist, Western-style democracy would benefit the region and the world. He has since cited his work with regard to German reunification as one of his proudest achievements. In a 2002 speech at the Reichstag, the seat of Germany's parliament, as quoted by Elizabeth Becker and Edmund L. Andrews for the *New York Times* (February 8, 2003), he said that he felt fortunate "to be among the final cohort of America's cold war diplomats, to have been one of the last of a long line of my countrymen who kept a promise to the German people: a pledge of *Freiheit und Einheit* [freedom and unity]." Zoellick also played an important part in launching the Asia-Pacific Economic Cooperation Forum (APEC) in 1989. Made up of 21 member countries in Asia and the Pacific Rim as well as Australia, North America, and South America, APEC's stated goal is "to further enhance economic growth and prosperity for the region and to strengthen the Asia-Pacific community," according to its Web site.

During those years Zoellick also helped facilitate negotiations for the North American Free Trade Agreement, or NAFTA; Mexican president Carlos Salinas eventually signed the agreement, which went into effect in 1994. In addition to his role in NAFTA, Zoellick pushed for the expansion of free trade around the globe via the World Trade Organization. In 1992 Zoellick was appointed White House deputy chief of staff and assistant to the president, roles in which he advised President Bush on matters relating to trade and foreign policy. He also represented the U.S. in 1991 and 1992 at the G7 Economic Summits, a yearly economic policy meeting among seven economic superpowers: the U.S., the U.K., Canada, Japan, Germany, France, and Italy.

When Zoellick left the government, at the end of the first Bush administration, he received the Distinguished Service Award, the Department of State's highest honor. He was also presented with the Knight Commander's Cross from the German government in recognition of his efforts to unify that country. Turning to the private sector, in 1993 he was appointed executive vice president of the Federal National Mortgage Association, better known as Fannie Mae. Established during the Depression to guarantee funds to mortgage lenders, Fannie Mae was rechartered as a public company by Congress in 1968. Zoellick served in that position until 1997. According to the White House Web site, he "managed the company's affordable housing business; legal, regulatory, government relations activities; and international financial services."

After leaving Fannie Mae, Zoellick found teaching and consulting work. He was a professor of national security at the U.S. Naval Academy, in Annapolis, Maryland, from 1997 to 1998. During those same years, he applied his knowledge of trade and foreign affairs to his work as an international consultant for Goldman Sachs, one of the largest and most profitable investment banks in the country. He was also named a research scholar at the Belfer Center for Science and International Affairs at the John F. Kennedy School of Government. Finally, Zoellick served in that period as a paid consultant on the advisory board of the troubled energy company Enron, holding shares in the company worth between $15,000 and $50,000 but selling them before Enron's 2001 accounting scandal broke—a development that bankrupted the company and wiped out the pensions of 40,000 employees. (Zoellick is one of many members of the second Bush administration to have maintained close ties with Enron.) A Global AIDS Alliance press release of May 29, 2007 pronounced that association to be "significant baggage" for a head of the World Bank.

Also in the 1990s Zoellick became a member of the Project for a New American Century (PNAC), a political think tank dedicated to promoting a neoconservative agenda, including the aggressive pursuit of "American global leadership" and the challenging of "regimes hostile to our interests and values," according to its Web site. In 1998 Zoellick signed a PNAC letter advising President Bill Clinton to take aggressive action to remove Saddam Hussein from power in Iraq. "We believe the U.S. has the authority under existing UN resolutions to take the necessary steps, including military steps, to protect our vital interests in the Gulf," the letter read (January 26, 1998). "In any case, American policy cannot continue to be crippled by a misguided insistence on unanimity in the UN security council." Some commentators view that letter as evidence that the members of the George W. Bush administration, many of whom were among the signatories, had wanted even before Bush took office to invade Iraq—an action taken by the administration in March 2003.

In addition to his work with PNAC, Zoellick served as a board member of the German Marshall Fund and as president of the Center for Strategic and International Studies (CSIS), both international-relations think tanks; as an advisory council member of the World Wildlife Fund, a conservation group; and as a trustee of the Eurasia Foundation, a nonprofit organization dedicated to investing in the developing economies of Eastern Europe and Asia.

Zoellick brought his foreign-policy expertise to the 2000 presidential election campaign, during which he was a member of a group known as "the Vulcans," which advised George W. Bush as part of an effort to show that though he lacked experience in international relations, he had seasoned policy makers working for him. Condoleezza Rice, who had been director for Soviet and East European Affairs of the National Security Council during George H. W. Bush's presidency, led the group. Following Bush's victory in the election, Zoellick resigned from his post at CSIS due to controversy over his political activities. As reported by John Harwood for the *Wall Street Journal* (May 6, 1999), Sam Nunn, the board chairman of CSIS, said in a statement that "the organization preferred its top executive eschew political activities." Zoellick officially reentered government in 2001 as a Bush appointee, along with other "Vulcans": he was named U.S. trade representative, a cabinet-level position in which he advised the president on trade policy.

Zoellick's opinions on trade and foreign policy, while generally consistent with the Republican Party's positions, lack much of the ideological bent of such extreme neoconservatives as Douglas Feith and Donald Rumsfeld. "At first glance, Zoellick could be mistaken for an ideologue, as an evangelist for free trade and a member of the neoconservative vanguard," Tom Barry wrote for the liberal Web site Counterpunch.org (January 14, 2005). "But when his political trajectory is more closely observed, Zoellick is better understood as a can-do member of the Republican foreign policy elite, a diplomat who always keeps his eye on the prize, namely the interests of Corporate America and U.S. global hegemony. Based on his record in the Bush Sr. administration and the current Bush presidency, Zoellick is highly regarded as an astute dealmaker." Zoellick's tendency toward pragmatism and his mistrust of "nation building" sometimes led to disagreements with other members of the Bush administration. Zoellick's own ideology was on display, however, in an essay titled "Campaign 2000: A Republican Foreign Policy," published in *Foreign Affairs* (January/February 2000). In that essay he foreshadowed the Bush administration's use of the word "evil" to describe countries hostile to U.S. interests and touted the superiority of American ideals and principles. "A modern Republican foreign policy recognizes that there is still evil in the world—people who hate America and the ideas for which it stands . . . ," he wrote.

"The United States must remain vigilant and have the strength to defeat its enemies. People driven by enmity or by a need to dominate will not respond to reason or goodwill. They will manipulate civilized rules for uncivilized ends."

As trade representative Zoellick pursued U.S. interests aggressively, attempting to open new markets around the world. When he started in his post, in February 2001, the U.S. and global trade agendas had been stalled for a number of years. No bilateral U.S. trade deals had been completed since the establishment of NAFTA, and the U.S. had a total of three FTA partners (Canada, Mexico, and Israel). The WTO Ministerial Conference in Seattle, Washington, had not launched a new round of global trade negotiations. Zoellick embraced a strategy, which he called "competitive liberalization," of opening markets globally, regionally, and bilaterally; nine months after being sworn in, he helped launch a new global trade round in Doha while successfully steering China and Taiwan's entry into the WTO. In the wake of the September 11, 2001 terrorist attacks on the U.S., Zoellick made a case for trade as part of the Bush administration's so-called war on terror. "The long term war against terrorism has to include trade, openness, and development," he told Becker and Andrews. Zoellick strongly urged Congress to restore fast-track authority, which it did in August 2002. Armed with that authority, he launched a flurry of comprehensive trade deals designed to open markets and support economic reforms in those countries. As U.S. trade representative, he completed 12 FTA deals (with Jordan, Chile, Australia, Singapore, Morocco, Bahrain, and six nations with the Central America–Dominican Free Trade Agreement, or CAFTA-DR: Costa Rica, El Salvador, Nicaragua, Honduras, Guatemala, and the Dominican Republic.) He also launched FTAs that were later completed, with Peru, Panama, and Colombia, and enacted a Basic Trade Agreement with Vietnam. Labor and human-rights groups objected to the CAFTA-DR agreement, mainly because it allowed for free trade with countries that do not meet U.S. labor and environmental standards. Zoellick viewed the agreement in part as a way to support the peaceful growth and stability of fragile Central American democracies that Congress already allowed to export goods duty-free to the U.S. "CAFTA is the opportunity of a lifetime," Zoellick said in a speech to the Heritage Foundation, as quoted by Nikolas Kozloff for Counterpunch.org (November 7, 2006). "If we retreat into isolationism, Daniel Ortega [of Nicaragua], Hugo Chavez, and others like them, leftist autocrats, will advance."

Getting all of the WTO's 140-plus members to reach agreements presented an enormous challenge, given the range of political and economic differences among the nations. Zoellick's frustration was apparent in an op-ed piece he wrote for the London *Financial Times* (September 22, 2003) after WTO talks in Cancún, Mexico, collapsed due to disagreement over issues large and small, particularly those relating to agriculture. "The key division at Cancun was between the can-do and the won't-do," Zoellick wrote. "For over two years, the U.S. has pushed to open markets globally, in our hemisphere, and with sub-regions or individual countries. As WTO members ponder the future, the U.S. will not wait: we will move towards free trade with can-do countries." Zoellick coined the phrase "coalition of the liberalizers" to describe the group of countries that made free-trade agreements (FTAs) with the U.S. in the way he envisioned. He initiated deals with many countries between 2001 and 2005, including many in South America, Central America, and Africa. He frequently invoked the metaphor of a bicycle to justify his constant push for more trade deals, such as in a 2001 speech delivered prior to WTO negotiations at Doha, which stalled largely over U.S. refusals to cut subsidies to its farmers. "The bicycle theory of trade is again in force," he said, as quoted on the Web site of the Office of the United States Trade Representative. "If the trade liberalization process does not move forward, it will, like a bicycle, be pulled down by the political gravity of special interests." Some saw his methods as bold, others as bullying. Andrew Leonard, writing for Salon.com (January 11, 2007), described the bicycle metaphor as fallacious, arguing that "the current standstill is actually a sign of maturity: The developing world is no longer willing to pliantly sign onto deals that screw it over to the advantage of the developed world. . . . Too *much* momentum in one direction is just as likely to inspire a counter-reaction as is no momentum. Protectionist feeling surges when people, or nations, feel they are getting a raw deal, not because no deals are being made at all."

Some critics viewed Zoellick's ostensibly democratic ideals as a smokescreen for pushing exploitative trade practices in the developing world. A September 2000 editorial in the *Economist*, criticizing the WTO, World Bank, and International Monetary Fund, stated: "The decision-making structures of all three institutions continue to ensure that the major industrialised countries, led by the United States, and influenced by their corporations, set the agenda. In the process, the poor are often actively undermined." The editorial listed many indicators that point to worsened poverty since (and, in the author's view, because of) globalization: "According to the UNDP [United Nations Development Program], financial volatility, job and income insecurity, crime, threats to health, food insecurity, loss of cultural diversity, community disintegration and environmental degradation have all increased. The greatest losers from all these trends are the poor."

Another key task for Zoellick in his tenure as trade representative was to balance the demands of large pharmaceutical companies with the need for generic drugs to treat deadly diseases in the developing world. Sebastian Mallaby wrote for the *Washington Post* (August 5, 2002), "Zoellick

quickly saw that the activists were right on this one, and so he socked it to big business. The country-clubbers at the White House gulped a bit. Never mind the naysayers. If Zoellick hadn't gotten out ahead of this issue, AIDS-stricken developing nations would have scuttled the launch of global trade talks in protest at outrageous patent rules." As U.S. trade representative, Zoellick displayed an ability to juggle multiple trade issues by energetically advancing U.S. interests, working collaboratively with his foreign counterparts while promoting the domestic trade agenda. Just months after the high-profile breakdown of talks at Cancún, involving sharp exchanges with Celso Amorim of Brazil, Zoellick embarked on a global shuttle-diplomacy effort to restart the Doha talks, which culminated in a successful WTO meeting in Geneva in August 2004. At the same time that he worked collegially with members of the European Union on the Doha round of negotiations, he filed high-profile dispute cases involving European subsidies for the French-based aircraft company Airbus and what he regarded as unfair European rules regarding biotech food. He also filed the first WTO case against China. As the first U.S. trade representative to visit sub-Saharan Africa, Zoellick placed a special emphasis on the countries of that continent, helping to expand the bipartisan African Growth and Opportunity Act (AGOA) to boost African exports to the U.S. In a summary of his tenure as U.S. trade representative, Bruce Stokes wrote for the *National Journal* (December 4, 2004) that Zoellick had a "commanding presence in the international trade arena throughout President Bush's first term," that his successors' accomplishments would be measured against his own, and that "Zoellick is indisputably one of the most successful members of the first Bush Cabinet." In December 2002 World Trade Organization talks were brought to a standstill when the Bush administration ordered Zoellick to block a proposal that would authorize the sale of generic drugs for diseases other than AIDS, malaria, and tuberculosis. The U.S. was the only country to stand against the proposal. Still, Zoellick issued a promise that the U.S. would not take any country to court over drug-patent laws until the dispute was resolved. The issue remains a source of contention, with most countries urging the U.S. to change its practices out of compassion for the citizens of poor countries affected by disease epidemics.

In 2005 President Bush appointed Zoellick deputy secretary of state under Secretary Condoleezza Rice. The Senate unanimously approved the appointment. In that position he continued to work with China, coining the widely cited phrase "responsible stakeholder" to describe China's potential role in a peaceful system of global relations. He also visited Sudan several times, initiating a project aimed at ending the humanitarian crisis in the African nation's Darfur region. In what appeared to be a major breakthrough, he helped negotiate a peace accord between the government of Sudan and the rebel Sudanese Liberation Army, signed in May 2006. (Following the agreement, rebel groups began to fight among themselves, with the result that many thousands have been killed or made homeless.) After 18 months as deputy secretary, he left his post to work for Goldman Sachs. Though he had been wary from the start of serving as Rice's "alter ego," an aide told Christine Hauser for the *New York Times* (June 19, 2006) that he stayed longer than he had planned in order to work on the peace process in Darfur and greet the visiting Chinese president, Hu Jintao, in April 2006.

Zoellick served as vice chairman, international of the Goldman Sachs Group and as managing director and chairman of Goldman's Board of International Advisors until late May 2007, when President Bush nominated him for the post of president of the World Bank. "Bob Zoellick brings a wealth of experience and energy to this task," Bush (who has reportedly nicknamed him "Z-man") said when announcing his nomination, as quoted in Political Transcript Wire (May 30, 2007). An editorial in the *New York Times* (May 31, 2007), a newspaper that has otherwise been highly critical of the Bush administration, celebrated Zoellick's appointment, calling him "an able diplomat, experienced and interested in the details of development, trade and governance and widely respected in the many countries he has dealt with in his long career as a top State Department official and as America's top trade negotiator." Though some environmental and humanitarian organizations, including the Global AIDS Alliance, expressed displeasure at his nomination, the World Bank's governing board confirmed Zoellick in late June. Zoellick replaced Paul Wolfowitz, who had resigned earlier that year amid a scandal involving favors he had done for Shaha Riza, a subordinate of his at the World Bank, with whom Wolfowitz was romantically involved.

Founded in 1944 as a "facilitator of post-war reconstruction and development," as noted on its Web site, the World Bank is today devoted to "worldwide poverty alleviation." In his first year as president of the World Bank, Zoellick focused the institution's work by laying out six strategic themes: the needs of the poorest countries, those in Africa in particular; fragile and post-conflict states; middle income countries; global and regional public goods; expansion of opportunities for the Arab world; and knowledge and learning. Zoellick received a vote of confidence from big donor countries when they pledged a record $41.7 billion replenishment for the World Bank's fund for the poorest nations. Seeking to address the needs of middle-income countries, Zoellick oversaw the launch of new financial products, a major reduction in loan pricing, and an extension of maturities. He also put the issue of climate change at the center of the World Bank's approach to overcoming poverty. The World Bank launched the Forest Carbon Partnership Facility and the Carbon Partnership Facility as well as the Climate Investment Funds. Anticorruption measures were also integrated into the bank's work, with the launch of the Governance and Anti-Corruption strategy in October 2007. While implementing those measures, Zoellick also quickly mobilized the bank to tackle the global humanitarian crisis caused by rising food prices. In April 2008 he announced the "New Deal for Global Food Policy." He laid out his plan in a speech made to the United Nations System Chief Executives Board for Coordination after a meeting in Bern, Switzerland. "A New Deal must embrace a short, medium and long-term response: support for safety nets such as school feeding, food for work, and conditional cash transfer programs; increased agricultural production; a better understanding of the impact of biofuels and action on the trade front to reduce distorting subsidies, and trade barriers," he said, as quoted on the Web site of the World Bank (April 29, 2008). The bank launched a $1.2 billion rapid-financing facility in May 2008, to address immediate needs, including $200 million in grants targeted at the most vulnerable.

The summer of 2008 saw another international crisis, this one tied closely to the many unregulated activities of mortgage lenders and banks in the U.S. Zoellick warned of the possible negative impact on the developing world of the worsening economy in the U.S. and abroad. "A drop in exports, as well as capital inflow, will trigger a falloff in investments," he said at the International Monetary Fund–World Bank Annual Meeting, as transcribed for the World Bank Web site (October 9, 2008). "Deceleration of growth and deteriorating financial conditions, combined with monetary tightening, will trigger business failures and possibly banking emergencies." Zoellick also said, "We estimate that 44 million additional people will suffer from malnutrition this year as a result of high food prices. And for the children among them, that means lost potential that will never be regained. We cannot let a financial crisis become a human crisis." He called upon the G7 industrialized nations—the U.S., the United Kingdom, Canada, Japan, Germany, France, and Italy—to "help those that are most vulnerable, weaker developing countries slipping toward the edge, and the poorest people with no cushion to sustain in times of trial." The G7 nations, he declared, must take "coherent and reinforcing" actions, such as cutting interest rates worldwide. He also called upon countries other than those in the G7 to help developing nations through the crisis.

Zoellick lives in the Washington, D.C., area with his wife, Sherry.

—J.E.P.

Suggested Reading: BusinessWeek p94+ Mar. 31, 2003; Counterpunch.org Jan 14, 2005; (London) *Guardian* International p15 May 30, 2007; *New Republic* p13+ June 18, 2007; *Nw York Times* (on-line) Health Feb. 8, 2003

Markham Johnson, courtesy of Facebook

Zuckerberg, Mark

May 14, 1984– Founder and CEO of Facebook

*Address: Facebook Inc., 156 University Ave.,
Palo Alto, CA 94301*

If not for his innovative ideas about the myriad possibilities for information sharing over the Internet, Mark Zuckerberg, the 24-year-old CEO of Facebook Inc., might not have passed his art class at Harvard University. As he explained to the technology writer Andy Kessler for Kessler's blog andykessler.com (March 24, 2007), "I was in a lot of trouble, spending my time building Facebook instead of studying." When Zuckerberg found himself unprepared for the class's final exam, which required students to explain the significance of numerous works of art, he turned to the Internet—and his classmates—for help. Before the exam he went to the course Web site, downloaded an image of each art piece, and made a new Web site with a page for each image and a feature through which visitors could make comments. He then e-mailed the site's link to students in the class, and "within an hour or two," his classmates had commented on the images and shared notes with one another, helping Zuckerberg not only to pass the course but to receive an "A." That episode illustrates Zuckerberg's conception of how the Internet, and particularly his site, facebook.com, can be used not only as a social-networking tool but also as a means of information sharing between interconnected groups of people. As he put it to Laura Locke for *Time* (July 17, 2007, on-line), "What we're trying to do is just make it really efficient for people to communicate, get information and share informa-

tion. We always try to emphasize the utility component."

Facebook.com—launched by Zuckerberg and his partners from a Harvard dorm room on February 4, 2004—is a social-networking service and Web site that allows users to set up profiles of themselves, complete with pictures and background information; post additional photographs, videos, and messages; use applications unique to the site; and join unique social networks with selected users, or "friends." Initially geared only toward college students, the Web site had expanded by 2006 to allow anyone with an e-mail address to join. In 2007 Facebook was the number-two social-networking site, behind myspace.com; as of 2008 it was tied with myspace.com for the number-one spot, with 100 million to 110 million active users worldwide, many of them newcomers from the Web site's expanding international market. According to statistics available on its Web site, Facebook is the fourth "most-trafficked" site in the world, with 85 percent of the market share of four-year universities in the U.S. Facebook also has an exclusive advertising deal with Microsoft Corp., annual revenues of about $300 million, a growing staff numbering in the hundreds, and an estimated worth of $15 billion—a valuation set when Microsoft bought a 1.6 percent stake in Facebook for $240 million in October 2007. Zuckerberg is said to be one of America's wealthiest men under 25—his 20 percent stake in Facebook is worth $3 billion—and he has inspired comparisons in the media to the iconic technology entrepreneurs Steve Jobs and Bill Gates, his idols.

The second of four children—and the only son—of a dentist and a psychiatrist, Mark Elliot Zuckerberg was born on May 14, 1984 in Dobbs Ferry, New York. His interest in technology began as early as the sixth grade, when his parents bought him a computer and he began to learn from a book he purchased how to write software programs. He told John Cassidy, writing for the *New Yorker* (May 15, 2006), "I just liked making things. Then I figured out I could make more things if I learned to program." By the end of his ninth-grade year at Ardsley High School, in Ardsley, New York, Zuckerberg had designed a computer version of the popular strategic board game Risk, in which players wage mock battles for land. His game was set in the time of the Roman empire, which he had been studying in school, and featured a virtual version of Julius Caesar so advanced in design that Zuckerberg told Cassidy he had trouble beating it.

Two years later Zuckerberg enrolled at Phillips Exeter Academy, the prestigious boarding prep school in Exeter, New Hampshire, where he would have the first of his many encounters with major software companies. Together with his roommate, Adam D'Angelo (who served as Facebook's chief technical officer until mid-2008), he wrote a downloadable program called Synapse. Known as a "plug-in" because it worked as an addition to an existing program, Synapse selected songs from a user's digital library that were similar to what the user had previously played. The program became very popular, and after the technology Web site Slashdot.com posted a link to it, Zuckerberg was contacted by a number of software companies, including America Online (AOL) and Microsoft. Though the companies expressed interest in purchasing the program, none of them made a formal offer. "What they really wanted was for us to come and work for them," Zuckerberg said to Cassidy. "We didn't want to do that." He told Ellen McGirt for fastcompany.com (May 2007), "It was basically, like, 'You can come work for us, and, oh, we'll also take this thing that you made.'"

In 2002 Zuckerberg and D'Angelo parted ways temporarily, with Zuckerberg heading off to Harvard University, in Cambridge, Massachusetts, and D'Angelo to the California Institute of Technology, in Pasadena, California. While majoring in psychology, Zuckerberg spent his spare time writing new computer programs. In his freshmen year he designed Coursematch, which allowed students to find out who was enrolled in particular classes. In his sophomore year he found himself at odds with Harvard officials after designing a program that many felt was in violation of students' privacy rights. Zuckerberg, frustrated by Harvard's lack of an on-line student directory and by the administration's claims about the difficulty of creating one, decided to prove them wrong. He downloaded pictures of students from Harvard's records and uploaded them onto his new site—facemash.com—for the purpose of having users vote on the physical appeal of each person; votes were used to create a top-10 list. Within a few hours more than 400 people had visited the new site. The site crashed—news sources differ as to whether that happened because of heavy traffic or because Harvard administrators blocked Zuckerberg's Internet access—and complaints about the site from students and faculty brought it to the attention of school officials. After meeting with the Harvard administrative board, Zuckerberg agreed to take the site down and was let off with a warning. For an article in the *Harvard Crimson* (November 6, 2003, on-line), Zuckerberg told S. F. Brickman that the Web site "was basically a mistake. I thought the site was interesting mathematically, theoretically . . . and the idea of it. I didn't mean for it to be released so quickly because I wanted to control people's being offended by it."

Not long afterward Zuckerberg was asked by Divya Narendra and the twin brothers Tyler and Cameron Winklevoss, all Harvard seniors at the time, to work on the coding for a Web site they had conceived. The site, HarvardConnection, was to be the school's version of then-popular social-networking sites such as Friendster.com. Zuckerberg agreed to help finish building the site but did not do so. At around that time, he also began work on his own project, which he intended to model on Harvard's traditional print student directory, known as the "face book." He told Cassidy that his idea was to allow people to put up their own profiles and control the flow of their information: "Obviously, there's no way you can get access to that stuff [personal data] unless people are throwing up profiles, so I wanted to make an application that would allow people to do that, to share as much information as they wanted while having control over what they put up."

In January 2004, during a weeklong break between semesters, Zuckerberg stayed in his dorm and worked late into the night to complete the project. On February 4 he launched the Web site, then known as thefacebook.com ("the" was taken out in 2005), with profiles of himself and his roommates, Chris Hughes (the Facebook co-founder) and Dustin Moskovitz (who served as Facebook's vice president of engineering until the fall of 2008). To expedite the process of signing up members, a link to the site was put on the mailing list for Kirkland House, Zuckerberg's dorm. Soon Kirkland House residents began to join Facebook and inform their friends about it, and after the first day, as Moskovitz told Cassidy, there were "somewhere between twelve hundred and fifteen hundred" profiles. Within the next couple of weeks, requests to open the site up to students at other colleges came pouring in. With the help of Moskovitz, by the end of February facebook.com had expanded to include students from Stanford University, in Palo Alto, California; Columbia University, in New York City; and Yale University, in New Haven, Connecticut. By the end of June, the site had incorporated 40 schools and included 150,000 members. Zuckerberg began to sell ads to generate revenue. (The biggest expense was the $85 monthly payment to rent server space to host the Web site.)

The appeal of Facebook, as Hughes put it to Cassidy, was that it allowed people to represent themselves on-line in more personal ways than on other social-networking sites. "On Facebook, you get to fashion yourself in a new way in a new space," he said. "It's not about changing who you are. It's about emphasizing different aspects of your personality." Indeed, with options allowing users to specify their music, film, literature, and even sexual preferences; establish and join exclusive groups (in most cases, joining a group requires an invitation from the user who set it up); and keep up with friends and acquaintances by visiting their pages, Facebook held immediate appeal for college-age users. Facebook was able to exploit the Internet phenomenon dubbed "Web 2.0" or "Me Media"—names meant to reflect findings such as those of the Pew Internet & American Life Project, according to which, as noted in Cassidy's article, "eighty-seven per cent of Americans between twelve and seventeen years old are online, and more than half of them have created some form of digital content and uploaded it to the Internet: a home page, a blog, a photo album, or a video clip." According to Duncan Watts, a sociologist at Columbia interviewed by Cassidy, voyeurism may play a role in the success of sites such as Facebook. "It's voyeurism and exhibitionism," Watts said. "People like to express themselves, and they are curious about other people."

In the summer of 2004, Zuckerberg, Moskovitz, and another friend from Harvard, Andrew McCollum, moved to Palo Alto, a city in the northern region of California known as Silicon Valley, so named because of the large number of silicon-chip manufacturers, technology businesses, and venture capitalists there. The three partners continued to work on updating the Facebook site, giving access to students at more and more colleges. In Palo Alto Zuckerberg met Sean Parker, one of the founders of Napster, a popular Internet file-sharing service. Parker moved in with Zuckerberg and began to act as an adviser to the young trio, later serving as founding president of Facebook Inc. until 2005. He also introduced Zuckerberg to Peter Thiel, co-founder of PayPal, a highly successful business that manages on-line monetary transactions. After a pitch from Zuckerberg, Thiel, impressed by the promise of Facebook, agreed to invest $500,000 in the project and helped Zuckerberg and his associates to acquire staff. Zuckerberg stated for Forbes.com (September 9, 2006) that Thiel "shared a lot of sense with us. That knowledge helped with the huge transformation we're undergoing and enabled us to hire all these smart engineers. We grew, and we'd never have been able to do any of this if we hadn't come to California."

As a result of those developments, Zuckerberg decided not to return to Harvard for the fall 2004 semester; instead, he continued to explore the possibilities of the Web site. Bill Gates influenced Zuckerberg's decision. Gates, who had dropped out of Harvard in 1975 to set up Microsoft, had spoken in the spring of 2004 to a class Zuckerberg attended. "He really encouraged all of us to take time off school to work on a project," Zuckerberg recalled for the Forbes.com article. "That's a policy at Harvard—you can take as much time off as you want. Gates says to us 'if Microsoft ever falls through I'm going back to Harvard.'"

In September 2004 the Winklevoss brothers and Narendra, the three students who had previously asked Zuckerberg to work on their Web site, HarvardConnection—now called ConnectU—filed a lawsuit seeking damages for what they alleged was theft of their idea; they claimed that Zuckerberg had purposely left his work for them incomplete and stolen their source code. The suit asked the court to shut down Facebook and force the company to reimburse ConnectU for profits resulting from the alleged breach of contract. That lawsuit was dismissed on a technicality (whose details were not covered in the media) but was filed again in 2007. In 2008 the ConnectU founders agreed to receive a cash and stock settlement from Facebook; its details have not been disclosed.

Meanwhile, in November 2004, Facebook passed the one-million-member mark. In early 2005 the operation's headquarters moved from an apartment sublet by the fledgling company to new offices on University Avenue, near the Stanford University campus. A few months later, with about 840 colleges incorporated into the Facebook network, the company received $12.7 million in funding from a venture-capital company, Accel Partners, owned by the Silicon Valley entrepreneur Jim Breyer. Breyer also took a seat on the new company's board, alongside Parker and Thiel. In September 2005 Facebook expanded to include high-school students, and in 2006 the site allowed users from select companies—including Amazon.com, Apple Computer, Electronic Arts, the Gap, Microsoft, PepsiCo., and Teach For America—to register as members. "There's no secret to the companies [we picked]," Melanie Deitch, Facebook's director of marketing, said to Zoe Barton for CNETnews.com (April 28, 2006). "We wanted to get a cross-section of industries, as well as geographies. We wanted to have some diversity to it." She also said that the site had expanded because the main request from users was to allow "out-of-network" people to be allowed to join.

In January 2006 the media conglomerate Viacom Inc. offered to purchase Facebook for $750 million. Zuckerberg asked for $2 billion, a price Viacom rejected. (Earlier, in 2004, Zuckerberg had rejected a deal from Friendster for $10 million.) Yahoo! Inc. came calling next, offering $1 billion for the company. Yahoo! had been struggling to build its own social-networking service and saw Facebook as a means to appeal to a younger, hipper demographic. While Zuckerberg initially agreed to the deal, he later rejected it, when Yahoo! announced slower sales and earnings growth and reduced its offer to $800 million. After he rejected the Yahoo! bid, "critics were accusing him of hubris and foolhardiness," according to Fred Vogelstein, writing for *Wired* (September 6, 2007, on-line). Zuckerberg told McGirt that his decisions were not based solely on monetary amounts. "I'm here to build something for the long term," he said. "Anything else is a distraction."

In September 2006, with Facebook poised to open to all comers, the introduction of new features on the site threw Zuckerberg and his company into a controversy over privacy issues that was reminiscent of his experience with facemash.com a few years earlier. Zuckerberg, who has said that he created Facebook to map people's social relationships in a "social graph," wanted to add features that would allow everyone in a given user's network to view changes to the user's page—for example, new announcements posted by the user or new links to other users. "People already have their friends, acquaintances, and business connections," he explained to Vogelstein. "So rather than building new connections, what we are doing is just mapping them out." The new feature, called News Feed, sent announcements of users' new activities automatically to everyone in their networks.

Announced on September 5, News Feed was met with harsh criticism from users, as it appeared that Facebook "was manipulating and spreading their information without permission," as Vogelstein put it. Amidst a torrent of e-mail messages and other Web-based protests, Zuckerberg issued an apology on September 8 on Facebook's blog, which read: "We really messed this one up. When we launched News Feed and Mini-Feed we were trying to provide you with a stream of information about your social world. Instead, we did a bad job of explaining what the new features were and an even worse job of giving you control of them. I'd like to try to correct those errors now." After the apology and introduction of privacy features allowing users to control the information about them that went into News Feed, the controversy ended. With a more sophisticated information infrastructure in place, Facebook opened to all prospective users. The move was highly successful; according to Vogelstein, "adults, many of whom had yet to sign up on a social network, were drawn to Facebook's relatively staid and conservative structure," and by January 2007 Facebook's membership had grown to nearly 14 million.

The expanded and diversified user base led Facebook to offer more features. While the May 2007 addition of the Facebook Marketplace, essentially a classifieds section, helped to keep users involved with the site, it was Facebook Platform that attracted the most attention. On May 24, 2007 Zuckerberg announced the launch of the platform, which allowed outside venture-capital firms to develop software and integrate it directly into Facebook and let users then pick and choose which applications they wanted—a revolutionary move that gave Facebook an edge over its competitor, Myspace. The appeal of the platform for developers was that popular applications could generate ad revenue. According to Lindsay Blakey and Michael V. Copeland, writing for *Business 2.0 Magazine* (August 23, 2007, re-posted on cnnmoney.com), the applications "have names like FoodFight, Zombies, (fluff)Friends and Fortune Cookie, and they let users indulge in everything from scrawling graffiti and sending virtual cocktails to buying music, brokering loans and joining charitable causes—usually without leaving their Facebook homepages." In one example the writers cited, Jia Shen and Lance Tokuda created an application that organized users' photos into slide shows; the feature became so popular that the two were able to generate more than $200,000 in ad revenue, and eventually they developed 14 other applications with more than 22 million users. There were more than 2,500 new applications on the Facebook site within 10 weeks of the launch and around 6,000 by late 2007. According to Vogelstein, "By turning itself into a platform for new applications, Facebook has launched a whole new branch of the software development industry, just like Bill Gates did with MS-DOS in the 1980s. By allowing developers to charge for their wares or collect the advertising rev-

enue they generate, Zuckerberg set up a system for every programmer to get paid for their efforts."

In the summer of 2007, Andrew Cuomo, the New York state attorney general, began an investigation into whether Facebook's privacy features were sufficient to protect young children from potential predators. Cuomo was concerned that Facebook was misrepresenting itself as a safe social network for minors. In mid-October Cuomo and Facebook announced that they had worked out a "new model to enforce safeguards aimed at protecting its network members, especially children and adolescents, from sexual predators, obscene content and harassment," according to an October 16, 2007 press release on the attorney general's Web site. "Privacy and safety have been a priority since we first built Facebook," Zuckerberg was quoted as saying in the press release. "Our agreement with Attorney General Cuomo will set new industry standards to stop abuse online. We applaud the Attorney General's leadership and are committed to working together to keep Facebook safe."

There has also been controversy over Facebook's introduction in 2007 of a feature allowing anyone, including nonmembers, to search for a user on the Web site or through google.com, a phenomenally popular Internet search engine. In an article for BBC News (September 6, 2007, on-line), the technology writer Om Malik was quoted as saying that the feature "transforms Facebook from being a social network to being a quasi-White Pages of the web." The new search feature spawned caution over what users posted on their profiles, and concerns were raised in the media over employers' ability to view the profiles of potential hires. Facebook officials, however, said that public searches would yield minimal information.

Despite Facebook's almost $300 million in annual revenues (projected by some to rise to $350 million), the company is still struggling to find new ways to increase advertising revenue through the Internet. Robert A. Guth wrote for the Associated Press (October 6, 2008) that much of the Web site's ad money "comes through a display-ad sales agreement with Microsoft Corp., which has a small stake." After Microsoft's October 2007 purchase of $240 million worth of stock in Facebook, the site revealed plans for increasing revenue. In November 2007 Facebook introduced Facebook Ads, a marketing device that enabled businesses to target advertising to specific audiences. The new system made it possible for advertisers to build their own pages and, through a core component called Facebook Beacon, permitted transactions made on advertiser sites by a Facebook user to appear on that user's News Feed. According to a press release on the Facebook Web site, the new system was "a way for businesses to build pages on Facebook to connect with their audiences; an ad system that facilitates the spread of brand messages virally through Facebook Social Ads; and an interface to gather insights into people's activity on Facebook that marketers care about." The move met with criticism; the activist group Moveon.org publicly called Facebook Beacon an invasion of privacy and started an on-line petition against it that read, "Sites like Facebook must respect my privacy. They should not tell my friends what I buy on other sites—or let companies use my name to endorse their products—without my explicit permission." On December 5, 2007 Zuckerberg responded to such complaints, stating on the Facebook blog, "We've made a lot of mistakes building this feature, but we've made even more with how we've handled them. We simply did a bad job with this release, and I apologize for it. While I am disappointed with our mistakes, we appreciate all the feedback we have received from our users." The Facebook team created an option allowing users to turn off Beacon.

In March 2008 Facebook hired as chief operating officer Sheryl Sandberg, previously Google's vice president of global on-line sales and operations. Half a year later Facebook unveiled a new look for its Web site. To avoid an outcry from users who criticized earlier changes to the site, Zuckerberg allowed users the choice of switching back to the old format until September, when the change became permanent. Nevertheless, several petitions opposing the new layout appeared on the Web site after the changes went into effect. In August 2008 BBC News reported that the screenwriter Aaron Sorkin had agreed to make a film about the founders of Facebook. Sorkin, the creator of the television drama *The West Wing*, reportedly opened a Facebook account of his own to gather information for his script.

Despite the seeming stress of being a 24-year-old CEO whose company faces lawsuits, controversy, and media speculation as to whether it will go public, Zuckerberg seems most concerned with developing Facebook to its full potential. When Laura Locke asked him about how he dealt with the pressure of being a "Silicon Valley CEO" running a "hyper-fast paced company," Zuckerberg cited an interview with another one of his idols, Steve Jobs, in which Jobs said that "in order to be doing something like this, you have to really, really like what you're doing, because otherwise it just doesn't make sense." Zuckerberg continued, "The demands and the amount of work that it takes to put something like [Facebook] into place, it's just so much that if you weren't completely into what you were doing and you didn't think it was an important thing, then it would be irrational to spend that much time on it. Part of the reason why this is fun is because we've managed to build a team of really smart people who come from different backgrounds and have different experiences and think in different ways. People constantly try to put us in a bucket: are we trying to sell the company? What are we trying to do? What is the business strategy? People are often more interested in why we're hiring a stock-options administrator. Whereas for me and a lot of people around me, that's not really what we focus on. We're just focused on building things."

Zuckerberg was singled out as the "youngest billionaire bachelor" on the *Forbes* 400 list in 2008. He has been romantically linked to Priscilla Chan, a Facebook technical employee.

—W.D.

Suggested Reading: cnnmoney.com Aug. 23, 2007; forbes.com Sep. 9, 2006; *New Yorker* (on-line) May 15, 2006, Sep.1, 2007; *Time* (on-line) July 17, 2007; *Wired* (on-line) Sep. 6, 2007

Obituaries

Written, unless otherwise noted, by Kieran Dugan

ADAMS, EDITH Apr. 16, 1927–Oct. 15, 2008 Edie Adams was an actress, comedian, and singer who achieved success on Broadway, in television shows and films, in nightclubs, and as the star of a long-running series of Muriel cigar advertisements. She "both embodied and winked at the stereotypes of fetching chanteuse and sexpot blonde," Bruce Weber wrote in the *New York Times* (October 16, 2008) obituary of her. Adams was born Edith Elizabeth (Elizabeth Edith, according to some sources) Enke in Kingston, Pennsylvania. "Adams," which she adopted as an entertainer, was her mother's maiden name. She studied singing at the Juilliard School of Music and took drama classes at Columbia University, in New York City. In 1950 she won the Miss U.S. Television beauty pageant. Her prize, an appearance on-stage with the comedian Milton Berle, led to a guest spot on Berle's weekly TV program, *Texaco Star Theatre*, which in turn landed her a role as a singer on *The Ernie Kovacs Show*, in 1951. Kovacs's hour-long variety show, which moved to New York in 1952, was broadcast nationally. The following year Adams took a break from the show to make her Broadway debut playing Eileen Sherwood in the musical *Wonderful Town*. She and Kovacs married in 1954. Her second Broadway role, as Daisy Mae in *Li'l Abner* in 1956, won her the 1957 Tony Award for best actress in a musical. She played supporting roles in several films, among them *The Apartment* (1960), *Lover Come Back* (1961), *Under the Yum Yum Tree* (1963), *It's a Mad, Mad, Mad, Mad World* (1963), *The Best Man* (1964), and *The Honey Pot* (1967). Earlier, in 1962, Kovacs had been killed in a car crash; unwilling to pay most of his federal taxes, he left hundreds of thousands of dollars in debt to the Internal Revenue Service, which Adams repaid fully several years later by means of her earnings. In 1963 she hosted her own variety show, *Here's Edie*, on ABC. Unusually for that time, she sometimes performed on the show with African-Americans, including Sammy Davis Jr. and Count Basie. *Here's Edie* was nominated for five Emmy Awards, but it was cancelled after one season. During the 1970s and 1980s Adams appeared in many episodes of television series including *The Love Boat, Murder, She Wrote*, and *Designing Women*. For almost two decades she was the face (and body) of Muriel cigars in TV ads; wearing sexy dresses and, in Bruce Weber's words, with "a come-hither moue and a wink," she would whisper, "Pick one up and smoke it sometime" (a variation on the famous Mae West line "Come up and see me sometime") while caressing or dancing with oversize models of cigars. Adams's daughter with Kovac, Mia, died in 1984 at age 22 in a car crash. Her second marriage, to Marty Mills, and third, to the jazz trumpeter Pete Candoli, ended in divorce. Adams died in Los Angeles from pneumonia and cancer. Her son from her marriage to Mills

survived her. See *Current Biography* (1954). — M.A.S.

Obituary *New York Times* A p30 Oct. 16, 2008

ANDERSON, ROBERT O. Apr. 13, 1917–Dec. 2, 2007 Protean businessman; petroleum industry magnate; rancher; philanthropist. Robert O. Anderson established the base of his enormous fortune by building a wildcat stake into one of the U.S.'s largest oil conglomerates, the Atlantic Richfield Oil Corp., which was also known as Arco and since 2000 has been part of BP, the British petroleum giant. Born into an immigrant Swedish banking family in Chicago, Anderson was educated at the University of Chicago's K-12 laboratory school, then participated in its two-year Great Books program before beginning specialized study in economics, in which he received a B.A. degree in 1939. Two years later, exploring for oil in New Mexico, he bought a run-down refinery with a loan from his father. He turned the refinery into a profitable operation and proceeded to parlay it within a decade into Malco Refineries Inc., a company comprising several refineries and a pipeline system. The company became a major independent oil producer when Anderson struck oil at the Empire-Abo field in New Mexico in 1957. Five years later he sold his company to the Atlantic Refining Co. of Philadelphia for shares of Atlantic stock valued at that time at $36,700,000. He was elected to Atlantic's board of directors in 1963 and became chairman of the board and chief executive officer in 1965, when the company was a medium-size East Coast refiner and marketer, ranking 68th on the Fortune 500 list and earning less than 8 percent on its equity. In collaboration with Thornton F. Bradshaw, Atlantic's president, he streamlined the company's cumbersome staff and unwieldy ownership of thousands of service stations, addressed its shortage of crude-oil sources and regional markets, and initiated a modernization program that resulted in a better balance of production, refining, transportation, and marketing operations. In 1966 he negotiated a merger with the Los Angeles–based Richfield Oil Co. to create the Atlantic Richfield Oil Corp., or Arco. Soon Arco was realizing sales of more than a billion dollars and a return on equity of more than 20 percent, and with the acquisition of the Sinclair Oil Co., it became the seventh-largest oil company in the U.S. and the 12th-largest among all U.S. corporations. Trying to contribute to a lessening of the U.S.'s dependence on foreign oil, Anderson was persistent in directing exploratory drilling by Arco in Alaska. After repeated failures, Arco drilling at Prudhoe Bay on Alaska's North Slope in 1967 resulted in the discovery of the largest oil field in North America. Subsequently, in the early and middle 1970s, Anderson led the seven-company effort to develop the Alaskan oil pipeline. He oversaw Arco's investment in other sources of energy, such as tar sands in Canada and oil shale in

Utah, and he pressed for greater U.S. use of nuclear power. During his two decades as chairman and CEO at Arco, Anderson was instrumental, through acquisitions and strategic diversification, in increasing the conglomerate's revenues 20-fold, from $1 billion to more than $20 billion. In 1972 he led Arco's move from New York to new headquarters in Los Angeles, where he oversaw the company's involvement in civic and cultural affairs, including the donation of $3 million toward the cost of a new building at the Los Angeles County Museum of Art. Persuaded by Anderson, the Arco board approved the expenditure of funds to rescue two failing publications, the London *Observer* in 1977 and *Harper's Magazine* in 1980. After leaving Arco, in 1986, Anderson kept a hand in the petroleum industry by serving as chairman and CEO of the Hondo Oil and Gas Co. in Roswell, New Mexico, until 1994. He had numerous holdings in other businesses, from Western apparel to venture capital. His agricultural holdings in Texas and New Mexico included several feedlots and alfalfa farms and approximately 25,000 head of cattle and 11,000 head of sheep on eight ranches. On another ranch he raised Arabian horses. His ranches, farms, and other real estate comprised a total of more than one million acres, making him the biggest individual landholder in the U.S. His other real estate included several residences in New Mexico and Colorado. He chaired the Aspen Institute for Humanistic Studies, in Colorado; cofounded several organizations concerned with environmental issues, including the Worldwatch Institute, in Washington, D.C.; and was one of the elite "free world" movers and shakers making up the international think tank called the Bilderberg Group. A Republican who espoused the ideology of President Ronald Reagan, he was active and financially generous in party affairs, using his clout in the causes of both a smaller federal government and a more comprehensive national energy policy. At one of his philanthropies, the University of New Mexico, the Robert O. Anderson School of Management has been named in his honor. His personal fortune was estimated at $200 million. Anderson died at his home in Roswell, New Mexico, of complications from a fall. He was survived by his wife, Barbara (née Phelps), five daughters, two sons, 20 grandchildren, and five great-grandchildren. See *Current Biography* (1982).

Obituary *New York Times* C p13 Dec. 6, 2007

AOKI, ROCKY Oct. 9, 1938–July 10, 2008 Japanese-born restaurateur. As the founder of the Benihana chain of hibachi-style steakhouses, Rocky Aoki helped to popularize Japanese cuisine internationally, especially in the United States, by making dining a theatrical experience, with chefs throwing knives and flipping food directly onto diners' plates. Born Hiroaki Aoki in Tokyo, Rocky Aoki first visited the United States in 1959 and settled in New York City the following year. After working as a parking-lot attendant and a chauffeur, he rented an ice-cream truck in 1963 and spent a year selling ice cream on the streets of Harlem 13 hours a day. With savings of $10,000 and a $20,000 loan, he opened his first, four-table restaurant (originally called Benihana of To-

kyo) on West 56th Street, near Manhattan's theater district, in 1964. After a slow start, the restaurant quickly paid for itself, and within six months he opened a second restaurant a few blocks from the first. He subsequently opened 10 more restaurants in American cities, including Chicago, and over the following decades, he expanded into Canada, Russia, Thailand, Turkey, Peru, and Japan, creating an empire of some 100 Benihana restaurants. He also launched a chain of sushi restaurants, called Doraku. He resigned as chairman of Benihana National in 1999, after he was accused of insider trading regarding stock he owned in Spectrum Information Technologies. Admitting guilt, he paid a $500,000 fine and served three years' probation. In addition to his business ventures, Aoki was prominently involved in athletics and sportsmanship, as a champion wrestler, record-breaking hot-air balloonist, and world-class race-car and speedboat driver. In addition, with the motto "One Planet, One People," he founded the Manhattan-based Rocky Aoki Foundation, a philanthropic organization that supports medical causes (including research into cancer, juvenile diabetes, and liver diseases), amateur-sports education, environmental protection, and arts programs. He published the book *Saki: Water from Heaven* in 2003. Aoki was married three times and divorced twice and had several extramarital affairs. He died in Manhattan after suffering complications from cancer; the immediate cause of death was pneumonia. His survivors included his third wife, Keiko Ono Aoki, seven children, and several grandchildren. See *Current Biography* (2005).

Obituary *New York Times* C p10 July 12, 2008

ARMSTRONG, ANNE Dec. 27, 1927–July 30, 2008 Politician and diplomat; trailblazing conservative feminist; Republican Party grandee. Anne Armstrong was the first woman to chair the Republican National Committee (1971–73) and the first woman from either major party to deliver a keynote address to a presidential nomination convention (the 1972 Republican National Convention). In another female first, she became a Cabinet-level counselor to President Richard M. Nixon in 1973, a position she retained after Gerald R. Ford succeeded Nixon as president in 1974. In 1976 she was on Ford's vice-presidential "short list" in his unsuccessful election campaign against Jimmy Carter. She was America's first female ambassador to the United Kingdom (1976–77), and she later served as a foreign intelligence adviser to presidents Ronald Reagan and George H. W. Bush. Born Anne Legendre (Katharine Anne, according to Sourcewatch, a project of the Center for Media and Democracy), a native of Louisiana and a graduate of Vassar College, she acquired the name Armstrong—as well as co-ownership of the 50,000-acre Armstrong cattle ranch in Texas—by her marriage to Tobin Armstrong in 1950. She was a registered Democrat until 1952, when she switched her affiliation to the Republican Party. In the Nixon White House in the early 1970s, she created the Office of Women's Programs for the purpose of recruiting more female appointees to high-level government positions. As the Watergate scandal that would force President Nixon to resign from office gathered momentum, she made herself accessible to a hostile press, becoming the administration's "best, brave front to the public," as a *New York Times* reporter observed. In 1980 she co-chaired Ronald Reagan's successful campaign for the presidency. She chaired President Reagan's Foreign Intelligence Advisory Board from 1981 to 1990. President Reagan awarded her the Presidential Medal of Freedom in 1987. After leaving government service Armstrong served as a trustee of the Center for Strategic and International Studies, and she sat on the boards of American Express, Halliburton, Boise Cascade, and General Motors, among other corporations. She was a lobbyist for Baker Botts and for the Parsons Corp., a major recipient, along with Halliburton, of U.S. government civilian contracts connected to the war in Iraq that began in 2003. She was an early financier of Karl Rove's direct mailing company, Karl Rove & Co. U.S. senator Kay Bailey Hutchison was among her protégées. Armstrong died in Houston, Texas, of complications from melanoma. She was predeceased by her husband, Tobin Armstrong. Her survivors included two daughters, three sons, and 13 grandchildren. See *Current Biography* (1976).

Obituary *New York Times* B p6 July 31, 2008

ARNOLD, EDDY May 15, 1918–May 8, 2008 Singer. In his book *Top Country Singles 1944–1993,* Joel Whitburn ranked Eddy Arnold first among the country singles recording artists of his time. A so-called "countrypolitan" crooner with a deep and mellow baritone voice, Arnold delivered folksy sentimental ballads in a polished urbane style, helping to pioneer country's crossover into pop. He had 148 charted country hits, 37 of which made the pop charts as well. During a career of more than half a century, he sold more than 80 million records, and his singles reached the Top 10 echelon in *Billboard*'s charts 92 times and the top spot 28 times. His "I'll Hold You in My Heart (Till I Can Hold You in My Arms)" was number one on the *Billboard* charts for a record 21 weeks in 1947, and the following year his "Bouquet of Roses" was a charted *Billboard* hit for a record 54 weeks. The son of sharecroppers, Arnold billed himself as the Tennessee Ploughboy early in his career. Accompanying himself on the guitar, he sang during the late 1930s on radio stations and in small nightclubs in, successively, Jackson and Memphis, Tennessee, and St. Louis, Missouri. In 1940 he joined Pee Wee King's Golden West Cowboys, and with that western band he sang regularly on radio station WSM in Nashville, Tennessee. After leaving the King band, in 1943, he remained at WSM for five additional years, becoming nationally known as a regular on *Grand Ole Opry,* the NBC radio network's weekly showcase of country-and-western talent, which originated at WSM. At that time he came under the management of Colonel Tom Parker, who later guided the career of Elvis Presley. In 1945, a year after he signed a recording contract with RCA Records (then RCA Victor), his single "Each Minute Feels Like a Million Years" was in the Top Five on the country charts. In 1947 he had his first number-one hit, "It's a Sin." Among his other chart entries in the late 1940s were "Chained to a Memory" and "Just a Little Lovin' Will Go a Long Way." One of his sig-

nature songs, his cover of Tex Owens's "Cattle Call," was the theme song of *Checkerboard Jamboree,* a program he hosted on the Mutual radio network for several years beginning in 1947. On network television, he began making guest appearances in 1948, and he hosted the *Eddy Arnold Show,* a 15-minute CBS variety program, from 1952 to 1956. Playing himself, he co-starred in two musical Western feature films, *Feudin' Rhythm* (1949) and *Hoedown* (1950). He had three singles in the number-one spot on the country charts in 1951: "There's Been a Change in Me," "Kentucky Waltz," and "I Wanna Play House with You." Among his subsequent hits were "Tennessee Stud " and "What's He Doing in My World." Challenged by the rise of rock and roll in the 1950s and 1960s, he modified his country style, adding violins to his musical accompaniment and wearing dapper formal or semi-formal attire in his live appearances in such venues as Las Vegas hotels, the Coconut Grove in Los Angeles and other nightclubs, and Carnegie Hall in Manhattan. In 1965 his "Make the World Go Away" was number one on the country charts and in the Top 10 on the pop charts. In 1966 he was elected to the Country Music Hall of Fame. His six-LP set *Welcome to My World* was released in 1971. He recorded briefly on the MGM label before returning to RCA in 1976 and releasing such hits as "Cowboy" (1976) and "That's What I Get for Loving You" (1980). One of his last television appearances was in the network special *Christmas Time with Eddy Arnold* (1997). Among the last of his 100 albums were *Last of the Love Song Singers* (1993), *Looking Back* (2002), and *After All These Years* (2005). In addition to his career as a singer, Arnold was heavily involved in real-estate development in the Nashville, Tennessee, area. He published an autobiography, *It's a Long Way from Chester County* (1969), and was the subject of two biographies by Don Cusic. He died in a care facility in the Nashville suburb of Cool Springs. His wife, Sally (née Gayhart), predeceased him by two months. He was survived by a son, a daughter, and two grandchildren. See *Current Biography* (1970).

Obituary *New York Times* C p11 May 9, 2008

ARPINO, GERALD Jan. 14, 1923–Oct. 29, 2008 The choreographer Gerald Arpino created modern, daring, and often controversial ballets that helped establish the Joffrey Ballet, which he co-founded, as a world-renowned dance troupe. His work focused on topical issues—nuclear war in *The Clowns* (1968) and AIDS in *Round of Angels* (1983), for example—and incorporated modern elements, as in *Billboards* (1993), a rock ballet set to the music of Prince. Arpino was born in the New York City borough of Richmond (usually called Staten Island) to Italian immigrant parents. He attended Wagner College, on Staten Island, for a year before enlisting in the Coast Guard. Arpino served for three years and, while stationed in Seattle, Washington, met Robert Joffrey. Joffrey was studying ballet and encouraged Arpino to take lessons. Arpino studied several forms of dance in Seattle before returning to New York to attend the School of American Ballet. In the early 1950s he performed in Broadway choruses. In 1956, after Joffrey joined Arpino in New York, the two founded the Joffrey Ballet troupe. Five years later Arpino choreographed his first ballet, *Ropes*. He retired from dancing and soon became the troupe's chief choreographer. During his decades-long career, Arpino created some 40 ballets, many of which are now in the repertoires of ballet companies around the world. Some of his most famous include *Sea Shadow* (1963), *Trinity* (1970), and *Light Rain* (1981). He became artistic director of the company when Joffrey died, in 1988. In 1995, after years of struggling financially, the Joffrey Ballet moved to Chicago, Illinois. Though troubles still plagued the company for a while, the move gave it new life. The Joffrey Ballet was featured in Robert Altman's semi-fictional movie *The Company* (2003), with Malcolm McDowell portraying Arpino (named Alberto Antonelli in the film). Arpino's many honors included the 1974 *Dance Magazine* Award, the Chicago National Association of Dance Masters' 2005 Lifetime Achievement Award, and the Grande Ufficiale dell'Ordine della Stella della Solidarietà Italiana, presented to him by Italian president Carlo Azeglio Ciampi in 2006. Arpino remained the artistic director of the Joffrey Ballet until his retirement, in July 2007. He died in his Chicago home after a long struggle with prostate cancer. He is survived by a cousin and a great-grandnephew. See *Current Biography* (1970). — M.A.S.

Obituary *New York Times* A p30 Oct. 30, 2008

BALL, ROBERT M. Mar. 28, 1914–Jan. 29, 2008 United States government official; Social Security specialist. Robert Myers Ball, whose lifelong involvement in the development and maintenance of the federal old-age- and disability-insurance system began in the late 1930s, was commissioner of Social Security in the U.S. Department of Health, Education, and Welfare (HEW) from 1962 to 1973. After earning an M.A. degree in economics at Wesleyan University, Ball joined the Social Security Administration as a field representative in Newark, New Jersey, in 1939. He rose through the ranks and, after an interruption of three years spent in the private sector, went to Washington, D.C., in 1949 as the assistant director of the administration's Bureau of Old Age and Survivors Insurance. He was promoted to deputy director of that bureau in 1952 and to commissioner of Social Security 10 years later. Ball helped to draft the legislation passed into law as the Medicare Act of 1965, which established a health-insurance program for Americans over the age of 65, and he oversaw the implementation of that program after it went into operation in 1966. After leaving HEW, in 1973, he was a visiting scholar at the Institute of Medicine in the National Academy of Sciences, where he helped to plan Social Security refinements wrought under the administration of President Jimmy Carter. In 1981 U.S. representative Thomas P. O'Neill Jr. appointed him to a bipartisan National Commission on Social Security Reform, assembled under the chairmanship of Alan Greenspan to deal with a looming financial crisis. Pursuant to the recommendations made by the commission in its 1983 report, the Social Security system was buoyed up with a combination of tax increases and benefit reductions. In 1996 Ball served under the chairman-

ship of Edward M. Gramlich on a Social Security advisory council. Gramlich wanted to privatize the system, but Ball succeeded in keeping that issue off the table. Similarly, in 2004 he contributed mightily behind the scenes to the successful opposition to President George W. Bush's proposal to allow younger entrants into the Social Security system to place their Social Security payroll taxes in private accounts. Ball published six books on Social Security, including *Because We're All in This Together* (1989) and the collection of essays *Insuring the Essentials* (2000). At the time of his death, he was writing a memoir. He was survived by his wife, Doris (née McCord), a daughter, three grandchildren, and four great-grandchildren. See *Current Biography* (1968).

Obituary *New York Times* C p10 Feb. 1, 2008

BÉJART, MAURICE Jan. 1, 1927–Nov. 22, 2007 French ballet dancer; choreographer; director. The controversial and influential ballet master Maurice Béjart (originally Maurice Berger), while trained in classical ballet, was an exciting and unabashedly flamboyant and populist innovator, lionized by the mass audiences he attracted—in which young people and other neophytes were heavily represented—and scorned by many conventional critics and veteran balletomanes and even some modern-dance avant-gardists because of what they perceived to be his simplistic iconoclasm, his deliberate attempts to shock, provoke, and be "hip," and his distortions of traditional balletic plots and themes in the service of radical political and social messages. In his version of *Salome*, for example, he assigned the title role to a male dancer; many of his versions of other ballets became antiwar statements, and his costuming often simulated nudity. Béjart began training in ballet as a teenager, partly for therapeutic reasons, because he was not only physically diminutive but frail. After apprenticing with the dance companies of Roland Petit and Mona Inglesby, he became a guest artist with the Royal Swedish Ballet. In Paris in 1953 he founded, in collaboration with Jean Laurent, Les Ballets de l'Étoile, which was later renamed Le Ballet-Théâtre de Paris. In 1959 he began staging operas for the Brussels Opera Company at the Théâtre Royal de la Monnaie in Brussels, Belgium, and he formed his Ballet of the Twentieth Century there in 1960. Over the following years he and his company toured most of Europe, Canada, Japan and other countries in the Far East, and much of Latin America. He and the company made their United States debut in 1971. In the course of his international travels, he converted to Islam. In 1987 he moved the base of his company, along with his Mudra School, to Lausanne, Switzerland, and renamed the company the Béjart Ballet. Among his choreographic works were *Symphonie pour un homme seul* (1955), probably the world's first "musique-concrète" ballet, which made use of taped music and sundry sounds; his highly erotic version of Stravinsky's *Le Sacre du printemps* (1959), widely regarded as his masterpiece, in which 50 dancers writhed en masse, among other novel groupings; his adaptation of Offenbach's *The Tales of Hoffmann* (1962), which included an ostrich character dancing the Charleston; his *The Damnation of Faust* (1963, to music by Berlioz), which featured a striptease; *Ninth Symphony* (1963, to Beethoven's music,), performed with 50 dancers and a full orchestra; *Romeo and Juliet* (1966, to music by Berlioz), in which he accommodated the Shakespearean text to an antiwar and antiauthoritarian message; the religious ballets *Messe pour le temps present* (1967) and *La Nuit obscure* (1968); *Bhakti* (1969, based on a Hindu theme and set to Indian music); the black mass *Notre Faust* (1970, to music by J. S. Bach as well as tango music); *The Firebird* (1970, to Stravinsky's music), a statement on the Vietnam War in favor of the Vietcong; the tour de force *Choreographic Offering* (1971, to music by J. S. Bach); and *Kabuki* (1986). In New York City in 1985, he presented a murder-mystery collage combining campy humor with classical ballet. Béjart wrote several volumes of autobiography and a novel. Jorge Donn, a favorite among his male dancers and his life companion, died of AIDS in 1992. Suffering kidney and cardiac problems, Béjart died at University Hospital in Lausanne, Switzerland. See *Current Biography* (1971).

Obituary *New York Times* Nov. 23, 2007

BENZER, SEYMOUR Oct. 15, 1921–Nov. 30, 2007 Scientist; professor emeritus, California Institute of Technology. A physicist, molecular biologist, and behavioral biologist, Seymour Benzer was a major pioneer in the development of contemporary neuroscience in general and neurogenetics in particular. As a physicist at Purdue University in the mid-1940s, he helped to create the germanium semiconductor, the precursor of the transistor in electronics. As a molecular biologist later in the 1940s, he spent several years conducting postdoctoral research at Caltech under, among others, Max Delbrück, who introduced him to the field of bacteriophage genetics. Back at Purdue in the 1950s, he concentrated on the study of the minute bacterial viruses called phages and in particular on the bacteriophage T4. With his success in mapping rII, a chromosomal region of T4, he, in his own words, bridged "the gap between DNA [as studied by Watson and Crick] and the actual gene structure . . . that corresponds to it." In so doing, he contributed to the eventual realization of the Human Genome Project, the effort to map and sequence the three billion genetic "letters" in the human genome. Benzer changed his focus again in the early 1960s, when he turned his attention to behavioral genetics. In pursuit of that interest, he moved back to Caltech in 1965 to work in close proximity with the psychobiologist Roger W. Sperry. In seeking to trace the neurological connections between genes and the brain and between the brain and behavior, he built on the work done at Caltech several generations before by Thomas Hunt Morgan. Experimenting with fruit flies (drosophilae), he engineered mutations in their genes and noted the effects, especially those connected with behavior. "Once we find the gene in the fly that controls a particular kind of behavior or neurological function, then we look in the human genome to find the corresponding gene in the human," he explained. "Very often these are closely related. The importance is that we can then use the fly as an experimental animal to try to get around the defects—for instance, by applying drugs and screening different kinds of compounds. We do experiments

on the fly which you cannot do on the human to get clues to treatment and understand the mechanism." In the late 1990s Benzer and several colleagues discovered a gene—which they called the "Methuselah"—that enables fruit flies to live about 35 percent longer than those without it. When Benzer was awarded the $50,000 Albany Medical Center Prize in 2006, James J. Barabra, president of the Albany Medical Center, cited him for paving "the way to uncover links between genes and human behavior which have resulted in our improved ability to treat diseases of the brain and central nervous system." Benzer is the subject of Jonathan Weiner's book *Time, Love, Memory: A Great Biologist and His Quest for the Origins of Behavior* (2000). Following the death of his first wife, Dorothy (nee Vlosky), in 1978, Benzer married Carol Miller, who survived him. His other survivors included two daughters from his first marriage, a son from his second, and four grandchildren. Benzer died of a stroke at Huntington Hospital in Pasadena, California. See *Current Biography* (2001).

Obituary *New York Times* D p7 Dec. 8, 2007

BESSMERTNOVA, NATALIA July 19, 1941–Feb.19, 2008 Russian ballerina. Slight but lithe and long-limbed, and soulfully beautiful in visage, Natalia Bessmertnova radiated an intense spiritual quality while epitomizing grace in physical movement. A naturally lyric dancer with flawless technique, she developed into a versatile and powerful dramatic dancer/actress early in her career with Moscow's Bolshoi Ballet, which spanned more than three decades. During most of that time, she worked in close collaboration with the choreographer Yuri Grigorovich, her second husband and the Bolshoi's artistic director from 1964 to 1995. After nine years of preparatory study at the Bolshoi School, where she ranked first in her class, Bessmertnova made her debut dancing with the Bolshoi Ballet in 1961, in a production of *Chopinana* (aka *Les Sylphides*). On that occasion her impact on the audience was, in the words of the ballet historian Gennady Smakov, "potent, especially in the Waltz, where her mysterious delicacy and lingering flights and landings, scarcely touching the boards, evoked . . . the legendary Romantic shades." When she toured the United States and Britain with the Bolshoi Ballet in 1962 and 1963, Bessmertnova appeared only in secondary roles, but critics surmised her greatness. In the *Financial Times* Clement Crisp noted her distinctive "magical quality . . . , a mixture of intensity of feeling and effortless projection of dance ideas" and averred that she was "obviously born to assume the great classical roles and to illuminate and revivify them with her magnificent gifts." Bessmertnova's first leading role was one that would become a signature, the title part in the classic Romantic ballet *Giselle,* which she danced five times between November 1963 and January 1964, when an anonymous journalist reported in *Time* magazine, "Each time she dances she stirs up a storm of acclaim such as the staid old Bolshoi has not seen in years. . . . Bessmertnova seems the very ideal of ballet, the disembodied spirit choreographers dream of, the ethereal figure that explains the whole logic of the dance." In 1965 she danced her first Odette/Odile in *Swan Lake* and was cast as

Masha in Yuri Grigorovich's radical reworking of *The Nutcracker,* and in the following years, she mastered leading female roles in other classics, including Aurora in *The Sleeping Beauty,* Juliet in *Romeo and Juliet,* and Kitri in *Don Quixote,* and in some more recent Soviet classics, including Princess Maria in the 1934 work *The Fountain of Bakhchisarai.* Her first notable credit in a contemporary ballet was her creation in 1964 of Princess Leila in *Leila and Mejnun* (sometimes spelled "Medzhnun"), made for her by the choreographer Kasyan Goleizovsky. In 1965 she was cast as Princess Shirin in Yuri Grigorovich's revival of his 1961 ballet *Legend of Love.* Beginning in 1968—when she married Grigorovich, following her divorce from her first husband—she was the chief inspiration for and creator of leading ballerina roles in his works. Those creations included Phrygia, Spartacus's wife in *Spartacus* (1968), Czarina Anastasia in *Ivan the Terrible* (1975), Valentina in *The Angara* (1976), and Rita in *The Golden Age* (1982), the last role Grigorovich made for her. She was also cast in the female title roles in his reworkings of *Romeo and Juliet* (1979), *Raymonda* (1984), and *Giselle* (1991). When Bessmertnova performed Princess Shirin in *Legend of Love* during the Bolshoi's American tour in 1979, the *New York Times* critic Anna Kisselgoff remarked on the ballerina's "special delicacy—seen in every flutter of a long finger and the skimming quality of her bourrées" as well as "energy below the surface . . . that makes every leap and swift turn thoroughly exciting." Bessmertnova became eligible to retire with a pension in 1989 but continued to perform with the Bolshoi Ballet until 1995, when Yuri Grigorovich was forced to resign as artistic director following a dispute with the company's management, and she resigned in solidarity with him. After leaving the Bolshoi she coached ballerinas in a company directed by her husband in Krasnodar, Russia. She died at a hospital in Moscow. Yuri Grigorovich, who had returned to artistic direction of the Bolshoi Ballet as a member of a triumvirate there in March 2008 at age 81, survived her. Bessmertnova had no children from either of her two marriages. See *Current Biography* (1988).

Obituary *New York Times* C p10 Feb. 20, 2008

BHUTTO, BENAZIR June 21, 1953–Dec. 27, 2007 Pakistani political and governmental leader. Benazir Bhutto was a charismatic, complex, and polarizing figure, an aristocratic populist and brave feminist heroine who was unable to avoid entanglement in the corruption and political intrigue of the culture in which she moved. As prime minister of Pakistan (1988–90, 1993–96), she was the first democratically elected female head of government in an Islamic country in modern times. She chaired the center-left Pakistan People's Party, founded by her father, Zulfikar Ali Bhutto; like him, she became a martyr in her pursuit of that party's avowed "pluralistic liberal" cause. While she was earning a degree in government at Harvard University and pursuing a graduate degree at Oxford University, her father became president (1971–73) and prime minister (1972–77) of Pakistan. In 1977 she returned to her country with the intention of beginning a career in its foreign service. Her father was ousted from power in a military coup

within days of her return, was subsequently incarcerated by a military junta headed by General Zia ul-Haq, and was executed by hanging in 1979. For protesting her father's incarceration, she was repeatedly arrested, and after he was executed, she was placed in detention—alternately in prison and under house arrest—for several years, until 1984, when she was allowed to fly to London for treatment of a serious ear infection. Both of her brothers were political opposition activists, and the younger of the two, Shahnawaz, who was considered a threat to the Zia regime, died under mysterious circumstances—apparently by poisoning—while living in exile on the French Riviera in 1985. Accompanying Shahnawaz's corpse back to Pakistan for burial, Benazir Bhutto was once more placed under house arrest for political agitation. She was released when martial law was relaxed in December 1985. In April 1986 she began holding a series of massive political rallies. In 1987 she agreed to an arranged marriage with the Pakistani businessman Asif Ali Zardari, later explaining that as a Muslim political leader, she would have destroyed her career if she had married for love. (Ultimately, the wheeling and dealing of Zardari—who was nicknamed "Mr. 10 Percent," "for his role as an intermediary in deals involving the Government," according to John F. Burns in the *New York Times* [January 9, 1998]— would prove to be counterproductive in her governments, giving credibility to critics' perception of the widespread existence of kickbacks, embezzlements, money laundering, and nepotism.) General Zia died when the military plane in which he was flying exploded in midair in southern Pakistan in August 1988. Following Zia's death the military regime announced that, for the first time in a decade, free elections would be held. Entering the electoral fray, Benazir Bhutto appealed to the Pakistani masses with her glamorous persona and her campaign promises to remove the remnants of feudalism in Pakistani society, to provide "food, clothing, and shelter for all," and to increase the freedom of women. (Murtaza Bhutto, the elder of her two brothers, a left-wing revolutionary, opposed her candidacy.) When her Pakistan People's Party won a majority of seats in Parliament in November 1988, she was chosen prime minister. In office she generally failed to fulfill her social-welfare and other progressive campaign promises, the reasons being, as she explained, obstruction by conservatives in Parliament and lobbying by vested interests. In August 1990, as allegations of corruption against her government mounted, President Ghulam Ishaq Khan called for new elections. In those elections the Pakistan People's Party lost to the Pakistan Muslim League, headed by Nawaz Sharif, a bitter rival of Bhutto's. In his turn, Sharif was dismissed in the autumn of 1993, and Benazir Bhutto was returned to power in the subsequent elections. During her second term in office, critics' charges of corruption multiplied, and her husband was incarcerated for several years on those charges (without ever facing trial). In November 1996, in elections called for by President Farooq Leghari, Bhutto was defeated by Nawaz Sharif. For eight years beginning in 1999—when the army chief of staff, Pervez Musharraf, ousted Sharif in a military coup and made himself president—Bhutto lived in exile in London and Dubai, in part to escape trial on the charges of corruption. Under American and British auspices, Musharraf in 2007 signed an amnesty agreement for Bhutto, and she made plans to return to Pakistan preparatory to elections in January 2008. Immediately upon her return in October 2007, she narrowly survived a suicide attack that killed 130 of the people lining her motorcade route. In December 2007 assassins succeeded in killing her as she was leaving a rally in Rawalpindi, Pakistan. Bhutto wrote an autobiography, published as *Daughter of the East* in the U.K. in 1988 and as *Daughter of Destiny* in the U.S. in 1989. One week before her assassination, she finished writing *Reconciliation: Islam, Democracy, and the West*, a memoir/history/political manifesto published early in 2008. In that book she identified, by names and cell-phone numbers, the Pakistani intelligence-service operatives who, according to her, would be responsible for her assassination. Bhutto was survived by her husband, a son, and two daughters. Her brother Murtaza was shot to death in a police ambush during her second term as prime minister. See *Current Biography* (1986).

Obituary *New York Times* A p14 Dec. 28, 2007

BISHOP, JOEY Feb. 3, 1919–Oct. 17, 2007 Comedian; actor. The poker-faced and studiously glum standup comic Joey Bishop, a master of the offhand delivery of apparently impromptu quips, rose from nightclub gigs to yeoman work in motion pictures and prominence on television, where he had two network shows of his own. He was perhaps best known as the understated—and last surviving—member of the so-called Rat Pack, the quintet of hip and rowdy entertainers headed by the famed singer Frank Sinatra. Bishop was born Joseph Abraham Gottlieb in the New York City borough of the Bronx and grew up in South Philadelphia. He began his career as a member of a three-man comedy act called the Bishop Brothers, who performed in burlesque, vaudeville, and Jewish summer resorts in the Catskill Mountains. After his two partners were drafted into the U.S. Army, in 1941, he made his debut as a solo entertainer at the El Dumbo nightclub in Cleveland, Ohio. He himself served in the army, from April 1942 until the end of World War II, in 1945, when he resumed his nightclub career. In 1952 Frank Sinatra saw him performing at the Latin Quarter in Manhattan and asked him to open his act at Frank Miller's Riviera, a club in Fort Lee, New Jersey. Bishop thereafter often toured with Sinatra and became a member—along with Peter Lawford, Dean Martin, and Sammy Davis Jr.—of the Rat Pack. In the late 1950s and the 1960s, the five men created a sensation with their largely unscripted performances together as well as their offstage carousing, chiefly at the Sands Hotel in Las Vegas, Nevada; they also made films together. On television, beginning in 1949, Bishop attracted modest attention with a dozen appearances over a period of nine years before becoming a familiar guest, and three-time substitute host, on NBC's daily late-night *Jack Paar Tonight Show* from 1958 to 1962. In the latter year Paar's talk/variety program morphed into the *Tonight Show Starring Johnny Carson*. In competition with Carson's program, Bishop hosted the 90-minute *Joey Bishop Show* on the ABC network from 1967 to 1969. In addition, he starred in a situation comedy, also called the *Joey Bishop Show* (NBC, 1961–64; CBS, 1964–65). During the 1970s and 1980s, he appeared on the Johnny Carson program 10 times, five of them as guest host. He made numerous other appearances on television, as himself on panel and talk/variety shows and in roles in teleplays and episodes in dramatic series. In 1981 he briefly replaced Mickey Rooney in the musical *Sugar Babies* on Broadway. (A non-singer, he instead played the mandolin in that show.) His film career began with minor roles in three 1958 releases: the naval action pictures *The Deep Six* and *Onionhead* and the screen adaptation of Norman Mailer's novel *The Naked and the Dead*. His later screen credits included minor roles in films including *Johnny Cool* (1963) and *Mad Dog Time* (1996) and the role of Eddie's father in *Betsy's Wedding* (1990). With his fellow Rat Packers, he made the films *Ocean's Eleven* (1960), a crime-caper comedy set in Las Vegas, and *Sergeants 3* (1962), a reworking of *Gunga Din* in which the comrades in arms are not Britons in India but U.S. cavalrymen on the western frontier. In the film *The Rat Pack* (1998), Bishop was portrayed by the comedian Bobby Slayton. *Mouse in the Rat Pack*, a biography of him written by Michael Seth Starr, was published in 2002. Bishop was married to the former Sylvia Ruzga from 1941 until her death, in 1999. He died of multiple causes at his home in Newport Beach, California, leaving behind his son, the film and television actor and director Larry Bishop; two grandchildren; and his companion, Nora Garabotti. See *Current Biography* (1962).

Obituary *New York Times* B p6 Oct. 19, 2007

BOURNE, ST. CLAIR Feb. 16, 1943–Dec. 15, 2007 Filmmaker; a trailblazing Harlem-born documentarian known for his inventive and complex yet unintrusive shooting as well as for his compiling and editing techniques. St. Clair Bourne illuminated the African-American experience from an insider's perspective, often focusing on personifications of heroism in the African diaspora and the consequences of instances of cultural and political courage. He was the director and/or producer—and occasionally the writer, or co-writer with Lou Potter—of some 45 films, many of which are empathetic portraits of black men who, in his words, pitted themselves "against the history of the Eurocentric world," who "defined themselves from an Afrocentric point of view," and who "succeeded and overcame opposition" in "trying to find a way." In an interview accompanying a critical essay on Bourne's oeuvre by Clifford Thompson in *Cineaste* (Summer 2001), Bourne told Thompson that his usual approach was "to find out why the person did what they did—they tend to be black achievers—and what price they paid for that." Among Bourne's outstanding works as producer/director are *In Motion: Amiri Baraka* (1993), about that poet, playwright, and "black consciousness" activist, and *John Henrik Clarke: A Great and Mighty Walk* (1996), about that Alabama sharecropper's son, who became an eminent historian, black-studies advocate, and leader of the Pan-Africanist movement. As a director of works produced by others, Bourne realized a crowning achievement with *Paul Robeson: Here I Stand* (1999), a profile of that multitalented athlete, actor, and singer who bravely, if not always prudently, espoused international leftist radicalism in the cause of African-American liberation. Aside from his biographical works, Bourne is probably best known as the director of the theatrical release *Making "Do the Right Thing"* (1989), a "seamless" (as Clifford Thompson put it) behind-the-scenes documentation of Spike Lee's making of his now-classic fictional feature film about racial tension erupting into fatal violence in the Bedford-Stuyvesant section of Brooklyn, New York City. Bourne was the son of a Harlem journalist and a nurse/medical social worker. "I grew up during the civil rights movement and would look at the reality of what was going on and observe that what was being represented on television was incorrect . . . ," he told an interviewer for *Black Camera* in 2006. "They were telling [the story] from a different culture. . . . I felt I could tell the story better." After his expulsion from Georgetown University, following his arrest in a civil rights sit-in, Bourne served in the Peace Corps in Peru for two years. He then earned a dual degree in journalism and political science at Syracuse University and studied filmmaking at Columbia University, where he was again arrested and expelled, for participating in the takeover of the administration building by students demonstrating against the Vietnam War. Soon afterward, in 1968, he was hired by the National Educational Television station in New York City as an associate producer of *Black Journal*, the groundbreaking, then nascent African-American–oriented public-affairs program that became a national, weekly, 30-minute PBS broadcast. In its second year he received the John Rushwurm Citation for "excellence in broadcasting." After he left *Black Journal*, in 1971, he set up his own production company, Chamba Mediaworks, and the Black Film Collective, both in New York. Later he began publishing the newsletter Chamba *Notes*, in hard copy and later also on-line. His first independent narrative documentary was *Let the Church Say Amen!* (1973), in which his camera followed a young Christian seminary graduate in his first steps toward a progressive, denomination-free ministry in ghetto churches. Bourne taught film at Cornell University (1975) and was a guest lecturer (1975–80) at the University of California at Los Angeles. In 1983 he documented, in *The Black and the Green*, a meeting in Belfast, Northern Ireland, of a group of American black activists and Irish Republican Army members. For the PBS TV series *Voices and Visions*, he directed *Langston Hughes: The Dream Keeper* (1988), a "narrative performance" documentary about the life, work, and times of that Harlem Renaissance poet and writer. He later made TV documentaries under other auspices, including several for the *National Geographic Explorer* series, beginning with *The Gullah Connection* (1990). He produced works directed by others, including the Emmy-winning film *Half Past Autumn* (2000), about the life and work of the photojournalist, filmmaker, writer, and musician Gordon Parks. The subjects of other Bourne films include New Orleans brass bands; the Chicago blues scene; expatriate Vietnam War–era black American army deserters living in Stockholm, Sweden; the black cowboy heritage in the American West; and the Black Panthers. He also directed *On the Boulevard*, a made-for-TV love story about an unemployed young musician and a struggling young dancer, and *The Bride Price*, a romantic thriller set in Senegal. In 2001 he directed *Dr. Ben*, a TV documentary about the Egyptologist Josef Ben-Jochannan. He won the Director's View Film Festival's Documentarian Award in 2004 and the Pioneer Award at the Pan African Film and Arts Festival in 2007. In succession, Bourne was married to and divorced from Sylvia Azure Walton and Linda Miller. During most of his later years he lived in Brooklyn, New York City. He died following surgery for a benign brain tumor. See *Current Biography* (2000).

Obituary *New York Times* C p11 Dec. 18, 2007

BOWKER, ALBERT Sep. 8, 1919–Jan. 20, 2008 Educator. Albert Hosmer Bowker gained his reputation as a major figure in American public higher education in a succession of positions, most notably including dean of the graduate school at Stanford University (1959–63), chancellor of the City University of New York (1963–71), and chancellor of the University of California at Berkeley (1971–80). Lettered in mathematical statistics, Bowker was a professor of mathematics and statistics at Stanford before becoming graduate dean. As dean, he demonstrated his administrative skill in coordinating graduate instruction and faculty research in all fields. When he arrived at the City University of New York (CUNY), that public higher-education system comprised four senior colleges and a few community colleges. With his administrative ability and his successful lobbying for increased city and state funding, he built CUNY into the largest urban university in the United States, with 18 campuses offering associate and baccalaureate degrees and a first-rate graduate school offering many doctoral degrees. He also introduced an open-admissions/remedial-education program, which was later terminated. At Berkeley his first priority was to stabilize the campus, a well-known battleground in the student protest and antiwar movements of the time. Once the turbulence was quelled, he concentrated on dealing with reductions in state financing of the university system. A shrewd fundraiser, he was instrumental in increasing financial support from alumni from $3 million in the early 1970s to more than $20 million at the end of his tenure and in establishing the Berkeley Foundation, which raised private capital for several new buildings and projects. He also eliminated many administrative jobs and some departments and programs while overseeing the creation of others, including a women's intercollegiate athletics department and programs in energy and health sciences. Following his tenure at Berkeley, he went to Washington, D.C., as assistant secretary for postsecondary education in the U.S. Department of Education (1980–81). He was dean of the School of Public Affairs at the University of Maryland from 1981 to 1984, when he became executive vice president for central administration at that university. He returned to CUNY as vice president in charge of planning with the university's Research Foundation (1986–93). Following his divorce from his first wife, Elizabeth (née Rempfer), Bowker married Rosedith Sitgreaves. He was predeceased by his wife (as well as his ex-wife) and survived by two daughters, a son, and five grandchildren. He died of pancreatic cancer at a retirement home in Portola Valley, California. See *Current Biography* (1966).

Obituary *New York Times* D p8 Jan. 23, 2008

BRENNAN, EDWARD A. Jan. 16, 1934–Dec. 27, 2007 Retail corporation executive. As chairman and chief executive officer of Sears, Roebuck and Co. from 1986 to 1995, Edward A. Brennan wanted, in his words, "to be remembered as an agent of change that was responsible for the company in an era where the business was evolving." An employee at Sears since 1956 and a high-echelon executive there for more than a decade, Brennan took the helm at a time when the firm was at its peak as the U.S.'s long-time leading retailer, with more than 800 department stores nationwide, a mail-order catalog known as "the consumer's bible," several financial services, including Allstate Insurance and the Discover Card, and annual sales of approximately $25 billion. But the price of its stock was declining, leaving it vulnerable to hostile takeovers, and its competition was fast gaining on it. With the help of Arthur Martinez, his hand-picked successor, Brennan radically restructured and redefined the company and succeeded in bolstering the value of its stock, but several competitors, led by the deep-discount giant Wal-Mart, proceeded to surpass it in sales. By the beginning of the 21st century, Sears, with annual sales of approximately $41 billion, ranked third among American retailers, just behind Kroger and far behind Wal-Mart, which was moving beyond the $200 billion mark. In late 2005 Sears merged with the Kmart chain of stores to form the Sears Holdings Corp., with headquarters in Hoffman Estates, Illinois. (Brennan oversaw Sears's move from the Sears Tower, in Chicago, to that site.) In 2007 the Sears Holdings Corp. ranked sixth among retailers in the U.S., behind Wal-Mart, Home Depot, Costco, Target, and Kroger. Brennan was born in Chicago into what might be called a Sears family: one of his grandfathers worked with its co-founder Richard Sears, and both of his parents, several uncles, and a brother were Sears buyers. He began his career with the company as a sales associate in the Sears store in Madison, Wisconsin, and worked his way up the ranks to become a territorial executive vice president in 1977 and chairman and chief executive officer of the company's whole retail division, the Sears Merchandise Group, in 1981. In 1984 he became chief operating officer of the corporation, constituting not only the Sears Merchandise Group but also the financial-services divisions. He was elected chairman and chief executive officer of Sears and Co. in 1985, and three years later he assumed the presidency as well. After leaving Sears he served on the boards of the McDonald's Corp., the Exelon Corp., and AMR, the parent company of American Airlines. He was executive chairman of the AMR board for a year (2003–04). He also served on the boards of several universities and chaired the board of the Rush University Medical Center in Chicago. The Brennan School of Business at Dominican University in River Forest, Illinois, is named in honor of Brennan and his wife,

Lois, an alumna of the school. He died at his home in the Chicago suburb of Burr Ridge after a brief illness. His survivors included his wife, three sons, three daughters, and 19 grandchildren. See *Current Biography* (1990).

Obituary *New York Times* B p7 Jan. 1, 2008

BUCKLEY, WILLIAM F. JR. Nov. 24, 1925–Feb. 27, 2008 Writer; political pundit; publisher and editor; television host. An urbane and erudite polemicist with a showman's flair, William F. Buckley Jr. founded modern American conservatism, made it the crackpot-free intellectual peer of liberalism in the public forum, and was its most eloquent advocate as it moved out of the fringe with the election of Ronald Reagan to the U.S. presidency in 1980. In the process Buckley came to personify, as Michael Gerson has observed, "the tensions within conservatism," balancing as he did "a wide streak of libertarianism with a vigorous Catholic traditionalism." All the while, in print and public debate, he displayed a mischievous delight in deploying his rapier wit and polysyllabic vocabulary. Buckley began "challenging the New Deal consensus among thinking people" (as Robert Poole put it) in the post–World War II era. In 1955 he founded the fortnightly (originally weekly) journal of opinion *National Review*, modern conservatism's first magazine and long its flagship publication, which has exerted great national influence ever since. In addition to editorials and columns in *National Review*, Buckley wrote a nationally syndicated newspaper column. As the host for 33 years (1966–99) to a Who's Who of political and cultural celebrities on the Emmy-winning public-affairs discussion show *Firing Line*, Buckley was fiercely sharp in debate but unfailingly fair to ideological opponents. The show, broadcast in the New York City metropolitan area until 1971 and then nationally on PBS, was the longest-running program with the same host in TV history. Buckley published 56 books, among them 36 volumes of nonfiction, including such polemical volumes as *Up from Liberalism* (1961), *In Search of Anti-Semitism* (1992), and *Happy Days Were Here Again: Reflections of a Libertarian Journalist* (1993); three accounts of his adventures as a yachtsman; several diaries; and the spiritual and literary autobiographies *Nearer My God* (1997) and *Miles Gone By* (2004), respectively. His 20 books of fiction include 12 popular spy novels in which the protagonist, CIA agent Blackford Oakes, fights for "the survival of the culture of liberty." William Francis Buckley Jr., born into a wealthy Catholic family in Manhattan, was fluent from childhood in Spanish and French as well as English. His early education was under tutors, in boarding schools abroad, and at the Milford (New York) prep school. After service in the U.S. Army, he entered Yale University, where, as captain of the debate team and chairman of the *Yale Daily News*, he began to earn a reputation as a "right-wing firebrand" even beyond the Yale campus. He railed against what he perceived to be the Yale faculty's pervasive practice of imposing a secular liberal ideology on students with the tacit blessing of the administration. After graduating, in 1950, he vented his outrage in *God and Man at Yale* (1951). After a brief stint as a covert agent of the CIA in Mexico City, he was an editor of *American Mercury* magazine (1951–52). In his next book, *McCarthy and His Enemies* (1954), written with his brother-in-law L. Brent Bozell, he defended Senator Joseph McCarthy's anti-Communist crusade, arguing that in alerting Americans to the danger of political subversion, he had performed a patriotic service outweighing the negative aspects of his rough and excessive tactics. At *National Review* Buckley brought converts from the far left (among them Whittaker Chambers and Max Eastman) together with such other established writers as Russell Kirk and Milton Friedman and such younger scholars as Richard Brookhiser to create a new conservative fusion that stressed limited government. He also published the early work of writers including Joan Didion, John Leonard, Gary Wills, Renata Adler, Arlene Croce, and David Brooks. His successful effort to build conservatism into a powerful, intellectually defensible movement was aided by his rejection of the antialtruism of Ayn Rand; the John Birch Society's conspiracy machine; various right-wing forms of knownothingism and anti-Semitsm; and his own early argument in defense of segregation. In 1960 Buckley helped to found the national student activist group Young Americans for Freedom. In 1961 he cofounded the New York Conservative Party. Under Buckley *National Review* was editorially identified with Barry Goldwater's rise to prominence as a Republican presidential contender, in 1964. It was vehemently critical of the Democratic administrations of Presidents Lyndon B. Johnson and Jimmy Carter and expressed unhappiness with aspects of those of the Republican presidents Dwight D. Eisenhower, Richard Nixon, and Gerald R. Ford. Buckley ran for mayor of New York City on the Conservative ticket in 1965, winning 13.4 percent of the vote. In the early 1990s Buckley stepped down as editor in chief of *National Review* to become editor at large. As a libertarian, he for many years advocated the decriminalization of marijuana, and by 1996 he had concluded that the "war on drugs" had proved to be a counterproductive failure. Originally a sanguine supporter of Republican president George W. Bush, Buckley became disappointed (as of 2006) with, in his words, Bush's "absence of effective conservative ideology—with the result that he ended up being very extravagant in domestic spending, extremely tolerant of the excesses of Congress, and, in respect of foreign policy, incapable of bringing together such forces as apparently were necessary to conclude the Iraq challenge." He died at his home in Stamford, Connecticut. He was predeceased by his wife, Patricia (née Taylor), and survived by his son, the author Christopher Buckley, five siblings, and two grandchildren. See *Current Biography* (1982).

Obituary *New York Times* A p1+ Feb. 28, 2008

BUTZ, EARL L. July 3, 1909–Feb.2, 2008 Agricultural economist; U.S. government official; dean emeritus of the School of Agriculture at Purdue University. Earl Butz, a free-market advocate, reached the height of his public career as secretary of agriculture in the cabinets of Republican U.S. presidents Richard Nixon (1971–74) and Gerald R. Ford (1974–76). Butz, a Mormon, grew up on a family farm in Albion,

Indiana. Upon receiving his doctorate in agricultural economics at Purdue University, in 1937, he joined the university faculty as an instructor in agricultural economics; he became a full professor in 1946. At Purdue he headed the Department of Agricultural Economics from 1946 to 1954 and was dean of the School of Agriculture from 1957 to 1967. He was dean of continuing education at Purdue and vice president of the Purdue Research Foundation from 1968 to 1971. On leave from the university from 1954 to 1957, he served under Ezra Taft Benson as assistant secretary of agriculture for marketing and foreign agriculture in the Republican administration of President Dwight D. Eisenhower. In that position he became identified with Benson's conservative policy of cutting back government supports of farm prices. Upon becoming secretary of agriculture, in 1971, he immediately reversed Benson's policies by adding $700 million to the $40 billion already budgeted for 1972 farm subsidies. The general thrust of his regime at the Department of Agriculture, however, was away from New Deal–era federal farm support programs in favor of giving farmers greater freedom in managing their agricultural enterprises, providing them with incentives for greater production, and motivating them to rely on the power of a free market driven by exports. He took a giant step in raising farm incomes and effecting a stronger American farm presence in world export markets when, in 1972, he approved the sale of more than one billion dollars' worth of grain to the Soviet Union. He encouraged greater corn production—and infuriated environmentalists—by telling farmers to "plant from fence row to fence row," and he accelerated the trend away from family farms and toward agribusinesses by telling them to "get big or get out." Butz's breezy style and flair for earthy humor made him popular as an after-dinner speaker but sometimes caused him trouble. For example, he was forced to apologize for a comment about Pope Paul VI he made to American reporters following the 1974 World Food Conference in Rome. The Pope had voiced opposition to "population control" as a way to solve shortages in the international supply of food. In mock Italian, Butz quipped, "He [the Pope] no playa da game, he no maka da rules." More egregiously, in a conversation on a commercial airline flight to California following the Republican National Convention in August 1976, Butz told an obscene joke that was insulting to black men. John W. Dean 3d, who was present, recounted the incident in *Rolling Stone* magazine, identifying the joke teller only as "a Cabinet member." When a subsequent investigative report in *New Times* magazine identified Butz as that member, he was forced to resign as secretary of agriculture, on October 4, 1976. Butz, who lived in West Lafayette, Indiana, continued going regularly to his Purdue University office in the same city until he was well into his 90s. He and his wife, Mary Emma (née Powell), who predeceased him, had two sons, William and Thomas. A week before his death, Butz traveled to Washington, D.C., for a family visit. He died during his sleep there, at his son William's home. See *Current Biography* (1972).

Obituary *New York Times* A p21 Feb. 4, 2008

CAPA, CORNELL Apr. 10, 1918–May 23, 2008 Hungarian-born photojournalist; a self-described "photographer for peace." Cornell Capa, the younger brother of the legendary World War II photographer Robert Capa, had a distinguished career as a socially and politically concerned photographer with *Life* magazine and the agency Magnum Photos as the founder and first director of the International Center of Photography, in Manhattan. He established the center as a repository for the archives of his brother (after Robert was killed in a land-mine explosion in Indochina) and as a public resource for collecting, preserving, and exhibiting the work of other "concerned photographers"—currently, a total of several thousand from around the world. Robert and Cornell Capa—originally surnamed Friedman—were born into an assimilated Jewish family in Budapest. In 1936 Cornell followed Robert to Paris, becoming his printer. The following year the two brothers immigrated to the United States, where Cornell found employment in the darkrooms of the photo agency Pix Inc. and *Life* magazine. His first notable work as a photographer was a photo essay on the 1939 New York World's Fair published in the British magazine *Picture Post*. Naturalized as an American citizen in 1941, he served as an aerial-photo interpreter and public-relations photographer with the U.S. Army Air Forces during World War II. After the war he became a staff photographer with *Life*, and in the mid-1950s he joined Magnum Photos, the agency that had been founded by Henri Cartier-Bresson, David Seymour, and Robert Capa in 1947. His work as a photojournalist over the decades took him from New York to England, the Soviet Union, and Israel (where he covered the Six-Day War in 1967), among other countries. In Latin America he covered the fall of the Péron regime in Argentina and the destruction of the culture of the Amahuaca Indians of Peru. In 1956 *Life* carried his photo essay "A Mission to Forgive," about the families of five Christian missionaries killed by a tribe in Ecuador. His American subjects included the Ford Motor Co., Wall Street entrepreneurs, the treatment of retarded children, and the aging of the population. In politics he covered the election campaigns of Adlai Stevenson, Nelson Rockefeller, John F. Kennedy, and Robert F. Kennedy. He and nine fellow Magnum photographers documented the Kennedy administration's first 100 days in the White House in the book *Let Us Begin* (1961). He also published the books of photographs-and-commentary *Farewell to Eden* (about the Amahuaca Indians, 1964), *The Andean Republics* (1966), *The Concerned Photographer* (1968), *Jerusalem, City of Mankind* (1974), *Capa and Capa: Brothers in Photography* (1990), and *Cornell Capa: Photographs* (1992). In the last he wrote: "I hope . . . I have done some good photo stories with memorable images that make a point and, perhaps, a difference." Capa, who was suffering from Parkinson's disease, died at his home in Manhattan. He was predeceased by his wife, Edith (née Schwartz). See *Current Biography* (2005).

Obituary *New York Times* A p17 May 24, 2008

CARLIN, GEORGE May 12, 1937–June 22, 2008 Comedian. In its 2004 list of the 100 greatest standup comics, the cable-TV network Comedy Central ranked George Carlin second, behind Richard Pryor and ahead of Lenny Bruce. A hip curmudgeon with a misanthropic bent and an ascerbic wit, Carlin thought it was "the duty of the comedian to find out where the line is drawn and cross it deliberately," in his words. Among his favorite targets were religious, political, and social forces inhibiting freedom of speech or obfuscating the meanings of words. He maintained a constant round of engagements in nightclubs, hotels, sites in Las Vegas, Nevada, and other live venues nationwide, appeared in several films, including *Bill and Ted's Excellent Adventure* (1989), and recorded 23 albums, for which he won four Grammy Awards. On TV—where he was nominated for five Emmy Awards—his credits as an actor, writer, and guest performer were myriad; he was the first host of the NBC weekly comedy show *Saturday Night Live* (1975), appeared on NBC's *Tonight Show* 130 times, made 14 HBO specials, and starred as a Manhattan taxicab driver in his own sitcom, *The George Carlin Show* (Fox, January–December 1994). He wrote three books: *Brain Droppings* (1997), *Napalm and Silly Putty* (2001), and *When Will Jesus Bring the Pork Chops?* (2004). Carlin was born in New York City with a love of wordplay and "the gift of gab," as he said, and he grew up streetwise in the Columbia Heights section of Manhattan. "I was always out of step . . . ," he told an Associated Press interviewer early in 2008. "I was always a kind of . . . outlaw rebel." In his early years in nightclubs (at first with Jack Burns as the comedy duo Burns & Carlin) and guest appearances on TV, Carlin was button-down spiffy in his grooming and wardrobe and relatively conservative in his humor. With the emergence of "flower power" in the 1960s, he began to assume a somewhat countercultural style in such characterizations as "Al Sleet, your hippy dippy weatherman," seen on the *Tonight Show*. Deciding to be fully "himself," he grew a beard, let his hair grow long (ultimately wearing it in a ponytail), discarded suit and tie in favor of black T-shirt and jeans, and became outspoken in his routines. His routine "Seven Words You Can Never Say on Television" was included in his third LP, *Class Clown* (1972). When the routine was played on radio station WBAI-FM in New York City, a listener complained to the Federal Communications Commission, which sanctioned the station for broadcasting "indecent" material during hours when children might be listening. The U.S. Supreme Court upheld the FCC's action in 1978. Carlin was the first to point out the oxymoronic potential in such terms as "jumbo shrimp" and "military intelligence." Many of his one-liners were in the form of questions, such as "How come when it's us it's an abortion and when it's a chicken it's an omelet?" and (regarding the Nicaraguan Contras), "If crime fighters fight crime and firefighters fight fire, what do freedom fighters fight?" Carlin was addicted to cocaine for many years, and in his last years he entered rehab for a dependency on Vicodan and alcohol. After a long history of cardiac trouble, Carlin died of heart failure at St. John's Health Center in Santa Monica, California. He was predeceased by his first wife, Brenda (née Hosbrook), and survived by his second wife, Sally Wade, and his daughter, Kelly, from his first marriage. See *Current Biography* (1976).

Obituary *New York Times* C p12 June 24, 2008

CARRUTH, HAYDEN Aug. 3, 1921–Sep. 29, 2008 Hayden Carruth, a critic and editor, was also among the most respected of contemporary American poets. In his more than 30 books of poems, he wrote in a variety of styles about subjects including nature, death, loneliness, and mental illness. "My poems, I think, exist in a state of tension between the love of natural beauty and the fear of natural meaninglessness or absurdity," he once said. In 2003 he wrote, "Regret, acknowledged or not, is the inevitable and in some sense necessary context—the bedrock—of all human thought and activity. Intellectually speaking, it is the ground we stand on." Born and raised in Connecticut, Carruth began writing poetry at a young age with the encouragement of his father, a journalist and newspaper editor. His discovery of jazz at the age of 12 influenced his writing style forever afterward. Carruth earned a bachelor's degree from the University of North Carolina at Chapel Hill in 1943. He then served in Italy with the Army Air Forces during World War II. Upon his return to the U.S., he enrolled at the University of Chicago under the G.I. bill and received a master's degree in English in 1948. Remaining in Chicago, he began writing and criticizing poetry and worked as the editor in chief of *Poetry* magazine (1949–50). He was an associate editor at the University of Chicago Press (1950–51) before moving to New York to take a job as a project manager at Intercultural Publications (1952–53). In 1953, after suffering a nervous breakdown while struggling with alcoholism, he was admitted to Bloomingdale, a private psychiatric hospital in White Plains, New York. He was discharged 18 months later, after undergoing shock therapy. His book-length poem *The Bloomingdale Papers* (1975) was based on his experiences during his treatment, which he claimed had left him worse off than before. Carruth lived for years in his parents' attic, suffering from fear of people and open spaces. He later moved to a cabin in rural Vermont. He earned a living as a freelance editor, book reviewer, and ghostwriter, but poetry remained his passion. Meanwhile, his poems had begun in 1950 to appear in publications including the *Kenyon Review*, the *Virginia Quarterly*, the *Hudson Review*, and *Partisan Review*. Carruth's first book-length collection of poems, *The Crow and the Heart*, was published in 1959. His other collections include *Journey to a Known Place* (1961), *The Norfolk Poems* (1962), *North Winter* (1964), *From Snow and Rock, From Chaos* (1973), and *Brothers, I Loved You All* (1978). From 1977 to 1988 he served as the poetry editor for *Harper's* magazine. He was the poet in residence at Johnson State college, in Vermont, from 1972 to 1974 and an adjunct professor at the University of Vermont from 1975 to 1978. In 1979 Carruth left Vermont to join the English Department faculty at Syracuse University, in Syracuse, New York; he taught there as a professor until 1991. Meanwhile, he continued to write poetry, publishing *The Sleeping Beauty* in 1982 and *Asphalt Georgics* in 1985. His book *Collected Shorter Poems: 1946–91* (1992) won

the National Book Critics' Circle Award in 1992. Another collection, *Scrambled Eggs and Whiskey* (1997), won a National Book Award, a Pulitzer Prize, and a Lannan Literature Award for poetry. His many other honors included the Carl Sandburg Award (1963), the Shelley Award from the Poetry Society of America (1978), and two Guggenheim Foundation fellowships (1965 and 1979). He was named the Vermont poet laureate in 2002. He novel, *Appendix A*, was published in 1963. His first three marriages, to Sara Anderson, Eleanore Ray, and Rose Marie Dorn, ended in divorce. He was preceded in death by a daughter from his first marriage and was survived by his fourth wife, the poet Joe-Anne McLaughlin, whom he married in 1989, and a son from his third marriage. Carruth died in his Munnsville, New York, home after a series of strokes. See *Current Biography* (1992). — M.A.S.

Obituary *New York Times* C p12 Oct. 1, 2008

CHARISSE, CYD Mar. 8, 1922(?)–June 17, 2008 Motion-picture dancer and actress. In MGM Technicolor musicals of the 1940s and 1950s, Cyd Charisse was a strikingly graceful and often sizzling screen presence—"beautiful dynamite," as she was described by Fred Astaire, her dancing partner in *The Band Wagon* (1953), in *Silk Stockings* (1957), and in a brief opening sequence in *Till the Clouds Roll By* (1946). Most prominent among her other partners was Gene Kelly, with whom she danced in *Singin' in the Rain* (1952), *Brigadoon* (1954), and *It's Always Fair Weather* (1957). Cyd Charisse was born Tula Ellice Finklea in Amarillo, Texas. (The name Cyd was a variation of Sid, her nickname from childhood; "Charisse" was the surname of her first husband, the ballet dancer and instructor Nico Charisse.) In Los Angeles, where she was studying ballet in the late 1930s, she joined the Ballet Russe de Monte Carlo. After touring the United States and Europe with the ballet troupe, she returned to Los Angeles and began her Hollywood career with small dancing parts in *Something to Shout About* (1943) and a string of other films that followed. Her first speaking part was that of Deborah in *The Harvey Girls* (1946), and she had star billing for the first time as Mary Chandler in the drama *Tension* (1949). Her subsequent credits included the supporting role of Rosa Senta in the film noir *East Side, West Side* (1949) and the female starring role in one of the three linked love stories set in a rural Mexican village in *Sombrero* (1953). *Silk Stockings* (1957), a musical remake of *Ninotchka* in which she starred as the title character, signaled the end of the musical era in Hollywood. Her next films were *Twilight for the Gods* (1958), in which she starred opposite Rock Hudson as Charlotte King, a passenger on a brigantine in the Pacific who is fleeing a homicide charge, and *Party Girl* (1958), in which she had the title role, the love interest of a Chicago mob lawyer. She had the supporting role of Bianca in Marilyn Monroe's last, unfinished vehicle, *Something's Got to Give* (1962), and the supporting role of Sarita in *The Silencers* (1966), the first of the series of Matt Helm espionage spoofs starring Dean Martin. In musicals, her singing had been dubbed in by others. Following her divorce from Nico Charisse, Cyd Charisse married the singer/actor Tony Martin, with whom she toured the nightclub circuit with a song-and-dance act after her screen career waned. With the assistance of Dick Kleiner, she and Martin wrote the joint autobiography *The Two of Us* (1976). In 1992 she replaced Liliane Montevecchi as the aging and unhappy ballerina in the Broadway musical *Grand Hotel*. Cyd Charisse died at Cedars-Sinai Medical Center in Los Angeles, California, apparently following a heart attack. Her survivors included her husband, Tony Martin, a son from her first marriage, another son from her second marriage, and two grandchildren. See *Current Biography* (1954).

Obituary *New York Times* B p8 June 18, 2008

CHINMOY, SRI Aug. 27, 1931–Oct. 11, 2007 Indian-born mystic and spiritual leader. Independently of each other, the gurus Sri Chinmoy and Swami Prabhupada (the founder of the Hare Krishna movement) were prominent in bringing to the West in the second half of the 20th century the trancelike meditation called bhakti yoga, a technique for finding personal peace and contributing to international harmony through inner surrender to and union with divine power. Believing that "the physical and the spiritual must go together," Sri Chinmoy combined his practice of that ancient "integral" yoga—a discipline transcending religion, including his own Hinduism—with a seemingly preterhuman athleticism and an extraordinary array of prodigious literary, artistic, and musical accomplishments. Regarded by his critics as promotional stunts and gimmicks, his athleticism and other accomplishments helped him to gain thousands of followers. In addition to bhakti yoga, Chinmoy practiced and taught kundalini yoga, a method of achieving what is known as astral projection. Born in east Bengal in what is now Bangladesh, Chinmoy Kumar Ghose entered the Sri Aurobindo Ashram near Pondicherry, in southern India, when he was 12 and remained in that spiritual community for two decades. In 1964 he immigrated permanently to New York City, and three years later he began pursuing his mission full time, establishing meditation centers and lecturing widely in the United States and throughout the world. Beginning in the early 1970s, he directed a meditation group at the United Nations headquarters, in Manhattan, and lectured regularly there. He published, according to his followers, approximately 1,600 books and booklets of prose (including collections of his lectures and meditations) and poetry; composed more than 20,000 pieces of music; played the flute at more than 800 free "peace concerts"; made dozens of musical recordings; produced hundreds of thousands of drawings and paintings; and performed extraordinarily challenging feats in weight-lifting and swimming, among other areas of physical activity. He founded the "world harmony run," a globe-circling marathon relay team, and as a publicly performing strongman, he lifted airplanes and pickup trucks, among other heavy objects, and 8,000 people (individually), ranging from Nelson Mandela and Desmond Tutu to several sumo wrestlers, a score of Nobel laureates, and Hollywood stars. He had approximately 100,000 disciples associated with some 100 of his centers in 60 countries. Mikhail Gorbachev, who headed the Soviet Union before its collapse, was among his admirers, and his followers ranged from the Olympic champion Carl Lewis to the pop or jazz musicians John McLaughlin, Roberta Flack, Carlos Santana, and Clarence Clemmons. Through his service organization called Oneness-Heart-Tears-Smiles, he distributed medical supplies worth millions of dollars to countries in Asia and Africa. Among his numerous books, whose sales have never waned, are such titles as *Yoga and the Spiritual Life* (1970), *Songs of the Soul* (1971), *Kundalini: The Mother Power* (1974), and *The Wisdom of Sri Chinmoy* (2003). Sri Chinmoy, who never married, died of a heart attack at his home in Jamaica Hills in the borough of Queens, New York City, the site of his primary Sri Chinmoy Centre. See *Current Biography* (1976).

Obituary *New York Tmes* C p9 Oct. 13, 2007

CLARKE, ARTHUR C. Dec. 16, 1917–Mar. 19, 2008 British writer. Arthur Charles Clarke was a titan in fantasy and science fiction, a visionary who broke new ground in those genres with more than a score of novels and many short stories offering hypothetical scenarios in space exploration (and its repercussions), future cybernetics and human–robot relations, cosmology (including the role of intellect in the cosmos and its evolutionary implications), and eschatology. While his fertile imagination and fascination with occult symbology often gave his fiction a mystical aspect, Clarke was essentially a rationalist whose visions were extrapolated from his knowledge of physics, mathematics, and astronomy and whose leap of faith was in science/technology as the vehicle for human development beyond terrestrial limits. He believed that "any sufficiently advanced technology is indistinguishable from magic" and that "the only way of discovering the limits of the possible is to venture a little way past them into the impossible." While he was "no metaphysician," as an obituary writer in the *Economist* observed, "he wanted and expected men [and women] to evolve" until they become "like gods." "We shall disappear," he once warned, "if we cannot adapt to an environment that now contains spaceships, computers—and nuclear weapons." Although his reputation among fantasy and science-fiction aficionados rested chiefly on his trove of best-selling books, Clarke was best known to the masses for the motion picture *2001: A Space Odyssey* (1968). That space-adventure film begins with a reference to the birth of primate intelligence and ends with the suggestion of humanity's ultimate emergence as pure intellect. The screenplay for the film, co-written by Clarke and its director, Stanley Kubrick, preceded the novel of the same title (1968), which was written by Kubrick as the filming progressed. In the final scene of the film, a returning astronaut, having been transmogrified through his contact with aliens, orbits Earth as a "Star Child," demonstrating his new powers by destroying the nuclear arsenals of both sides in the Cold War. (The scene was a variation of Clarke's often-iterated view of space exploration as "a moral equivalent of war," providing an outlet for energies otherwise brewing a possible nuclear apocalypse.) The screenplay had been based in part on Clarke's early short story "The Sentinel" (1948), in which astronauts try to pry open a mysterious monolith they have come across on the moon, thereby signaling their presence to the space-traveling aliens who created the artifact. "I can never look now at the Milky Way without wondering from which of those banked clouds of stars the emissaries are coming . . . ," the narrator of the story says. "We have set off the . . . alarm and have nothing to do but wait. I do not think we will have to wait for long." Another important early short story of Clarke's, "Against the Fall of Night" (1948; published as a hardcover novella in 1953), was expanded and revised as *The City and the Stars* (1956). That novel takes place a billion years in the future, in "the desert at the end of time," when a dehydrated Earth has lost most of its population. The young protagonist, Alvin, is one of the few "Uniques," the naturally born and living humans, in Diaspar, a walled technological dystopia run by a central computer, which the humans believe is the only city left on Earth. The other inhabitants are quasi-immortal, their minds quiescently stored in the central computer's memory between periods of computer-generated physical incarnation. All are instinctively insular, fearful of the outside world and of the universe. Alvin escapes and finds one other strange city in the desert world, Lys, a green agrarian oasis whose inhabitants are telepathic and who have their own peculiar pervasive fear, an extreme technophobia. He subsequently travels into deep space and learns of the historical event that explains the origin of Diaspar and Lys: an intergalactic project to create a disembodied intellect that went awry. In another early Clarke novel, *Childhood's End* (1953), alien overlords in the service of the intergalactic "overmind" descend from the heavens in fleets of giant silver starships, an iconic scene copied by others in many motion pictures. The overlords impose a tightly controlled, 200-year "golden age" of unprecedented peace and prosperity on humanity, an age that ends with the destruction of Earth and its inhabitants—save for the children in the final generation, who have been quarantined and spared in preparation for their transition to a higher plane and merger with the cosmic overmind. The themes explored by Clarke in those early works appeared repeatedly in his subsequent fiction, which included the novels *The Nine Billion Names of God* (1967), *Rendezvous with Rama* (1973), *Imperial Earth* (1975), three *Space Odyssey* sequels, and *The Last Theorem* (co-written with Frederick Pohl, 2008). *2010: Odyssey Two* (1982) has a "Lucifer Rising" story line not included in the film version, *2010* (1984). Translated into many languages, his books sold 10s of millions of copies worldwide. As a young man who had served as a radar instructor with the Royal Air Force during World War II, Clarke was a pioneering proponent of the now standard use of geostationary satellites in communications and weather forecasting. His reputation as a scientific expert was established with the nonfiction volumes *Interplanetary Flight* (1950) and *The Exploration of Space* (1951). Among his dozens of later books of nonfiction were *Astounding Days: A Science Fictional Autobiography* (1990) and accounts of his deep-sea scuba diving in the Indian Ocean and exploration of the Great Barrier Reef. He influenced a generation of young people with his television programs *Arthur C. Clarke's Mysterious World* (1980) and *Arthur C. Clarke's World of Strange Powers*

(1985). Following a failed marriage, Clarke settled in the Indian Ocean country of Sri Lanka in 1956; he later acquired Sri Lankan citizenship without losing his British citizenship. Named a KBE (Knight Commander of the Order of the British Empire) in 1998, he did not accept the honor until 2000, after he had successfully defended himself against allegations of pedophilia. He was quoted in the London *Sunday Mirror* (February 1, 1998) as confessing that, unaware of their ages, he had paid boy prostitutes for sex "many, many years ago when I first came here [to Sri Lanka] and the going rate was about two rupees." (He maintained that he could not distinguish adults from teenagers among Sri Lankans males.) Crippled by debilitating postpolio syndrome for many years, Clarke died of respiratory complications in Apollo Hospital in Colombo, Sri Lanka. See *Current Biography* (1966).

Obituary *New York Times* C p12 Mar. 19, 2008

CLEVELAND, HARLAN Jan. 19, 1918–May 30, 2008 Diplomat; educator; author. Harlan Cleveland was an extraordinarily experienced expert on international public affairs. After earning a B.A. in international relations (his only degree) at Princeton University, in 1938, Cleveland was a Rhodes Scholar for a year at Oxford University. His first of many positions with the U.S. government was that of writer with the New Deal's Farm Security Administration. During World War II he was on the U.S. Board of Economic Warfare. After the war he worked in war relief with the Allied Control Commission and the United Nations Relief and Rehabilitation Administration (UNRRA) in Europe. He subsequently directed UNRRA's China program and headed the U.S. Economic Cooperation Administration's aid program to several Southeast Asian countries. After a year (1952–53) as assistant European director of the Mutual Security Agency, a position in which he served as the Washington-based supervisor of the Marshall Plan for European recovery, he was executive editor (1953–55) and publisher (1955–56) of the *Reporter* magazine and dean of the Maxwell Graduate School of Citizenship and Public Affairs at Syracuse University (1956–61). Returning to government service in the 1960s, he was assistant secretary of state for international organization affairs in the administration of President John F. Kennedy and U.S. ambassador to NATO in the administration of President Lyndon B. Johnson. From 1969 to 1974 he was president of the University of Hawaii, and from 1974 to 1980 he directed the Aspen Institute's program in international affairs. From 1980 to 1987 he was the founding dean of the Hubert H. Humphrey Institute of Public Affairs at the University of Minnesota. Later he held, among other positions, the presidency of the World Academy of Art and Science (1991–96). He wrote 11 books, including *The Knowledge Executive: Leadership in an Information Society* (1985), *The Global Common: Policy for the Planet* (1990), and *Birth of a New World: An Open Moment for International Leadership* (1993). Cleveland died at his home in Sterling, Virginia. His survivors included his wife, Lois (nee Burton), a son, a daughter, and a grandchild. See *Current Biography* (1961).

Obituary *New York Times* B p7 June 13, 2008

CROWE, WILLIAM J. Jan. 2, 1925–Oct. 18, 2007 United States Navy admiral. William James Crowe Jr., long an advocate of cooperation between the U.S. Army, Navy, Air Force, and Marine Corps, became the top leader of a unified military command as chairman of the Joint Chiefs of Staff in the Pentagon (1985–89). The independent-minded Crowe won promotion to the highest military ranks partly through the instrumentality of Admiral Elmo Zumwalt, who recognized in him a fellow iconoclast. From 1960 to 1962 Crowe was captain of the diesel attack submarine *U.S.S. Trout*, and he subsequently commanded a submarine division based in San Diego, California. In Vietnam in the early 1970s, he was the senior adviser to the small South Vietnamese naval fleet that plied the waters of the Mekong Delta. From 1974 to 1976 he was assigned to the Pentagon's Internal Security Office as deputy director of naval strategic planning for East Asia and the Pacific. He became commander of a Middle East task force in 1976, commander in chief of NATO forces in southern Europe in 1980, and commander in chief of the Pacific and Indian Ocean unified forces in 1983. As chairman of the Joint Chiefs, he shortened the military chain of command, helped to reduce rivalries among the services, and oversaw American military operations in the Persian Gulf and the Mediterranean, the Reagan administration's partly clandestine support of the anti-Sandinista rebels in Nicaragua, and the U.S. air raid on Libya in 1986, in retaliation for that country's perceived complicity in a terrorist bombing of a discotheque in Berlin, Germany. With deft diplomacy he resolved several international crises, notably the one provoked in 1988 when the captain and crew of the U.S. Navy cruiser *Vincennes* mistook an Iran Air civilian jetliner for a hostile military aircraft and shot it down, killing all 290 passengers. After resigning as chairman of the Joint Chiefs, he studied at the Center for Strategic and International Studies in Washington, D.C., and taught geopolitics at the University of Oklahoma. After serving as U.S. ambassador to the United Kingdom (1994–97), he chaired the executive boards of two related companies founded by Neil Livingstone in Washington, D.C.: Global Options Inc., a security and risk-management company with expertise on such global problems as terrorism and the possible solutions to them, and Executive Action LLC, a firm offering help to companies "under attack by political or business adversaries . . . or being treated unfairly in the media." He also headed the BioPort Corp., manufacturer of anthrax and rabies vaccines. Crowe publicly questioned the build-up to the war in Iraq by the administration of President George H. W. Bush in 1990–91. "A lot of people there don't like us now," he said in December 1990. "Wait until we kill 200,000 or 300,00 Iraqis." In 2004 he joined 26 other former diplomats and military leaders in publicly questioning the ability of the administration of President George W. Bush to handle "the responsibility of global leadership." Crowe died of cardiac arrest at the National Naval Medical Center in Bethesda, Maryland. His survivors included his wife, Shirley, two sons, a daughter, and four grandchildren. See *Current Biography* (1988).

Obituary *New York Times* B p7 Oct. 19, 2007

DARMAN, RICHARD G. May 10, 1943–Jan. 25, 2008 U.S. government official; widely recognized as a brilliant public-policy analyst, strategist, and tactician whose strongest interest was in sound fiscal policy. Richard Gordon "Dick" Darman's career in Washington spanned four Republican administrations and included senior positions in six Cabinet departments during more than two decades beginning in 1970. A protégé of the liberal Republican Elliot L. Richardson and the pragmatic Republican James A. Baker III, he was, as he said, "a registered Republican [for whom] the starting point [was] never party," an attitude that earned him the enmity of party conservatives. In addition, in the course of maneuvering policy measures through bipartisan shoals, he sometimes offended others, Democrats and Republicans, with his alleged "abrasiveness" and his craftiness, a combination that resulted in the coinage of the adjective "Darmanesque" on Capitol Hill. Darman was the scion of a wealthy textile-manufacturing family. After earning an M.B.A. degree at Harvard University, he joined the administration of President Richard M. Nixon; in it, he became special assistant to Elliot L. Richardson in 1970. As the Watergate scandal was building to its climax, Richardson resigned as attorney general in the course of the sudden chain of events in October 1973 known as the Saturday Night Massacre, and Darman did likewise. After working as a private consultant for about two years, Darman returned to government in 1976 as assistant to Under Secretary of Commerce James A. Baker in the administration of President Gerald R. Ford. In that position he participated in international law-of-the sea negotiations that carried over briefly into the Democratic administration of President Jimmy Carter. Darman helped to groom Ronald Reagan for his televised debate with President Carter during Reagan's successful campaign for the presidency in 1980. He subsequently became executive director of Reagan's presidential transition team and principal deputy to chief of staff James A. Baker in the Reagan White House. Positioned by Baker to control the flow of paper in and out of the Oval Office, he quickly evolved into a major White House factotum, helping to prepare President Reagan for major meetings, supervising the drafting of his speeches, and assisting the budget director, David A. Stockman, in the negotiations with congressmen and senators leading to the enactment of the Economic Recovery Tax Act of 1981. By his own account, Stockman's heart was not in that "supply side" accomplishment, which cut taxes while increasing defense spending, and he voiced his qualms to Darman, who told him, famously, "We win it now, we fix it later." Darman subsequently had a hand in persuading President Reagan to relent in his tax-cutting, and he helped to smooth the way to passage of Social Security bailout legislation in 1983. During Reagan's successful campaign for re-election, in 1984, Darman played the role of the Democratic nominee, Walter F. Mondale, in Reagan's practice sessions for his televised debate with Mondale. At the beginning of Reagan's second term, Baker became secretary of the treasury. As Baker's deputy at the Treasury Department, Darman lobbied Capitol Hill for almost two years to win passage of the Tax Reform Act of 1986. That measure, officially sponsored by Democrats, cut individual tax rates but eliminated many tax shelters for the wealthy and increased the tax burden on corporations. Darman left the public sector in April 1987 to become a managing director of the investment banking firm of Shearson, Lehman Brothers, with whom he remained through 1988. During George H. W. Bush's successful campaign for the presidency in 1988—the centerpiece of which was Bush's promise "Read my lips: no new taxes"—Darman played the role of the Democratic nominee, Michael Dukakis, in Bush's practice sessions for his televised debate with Dukakis. As president, Bush named Darman director of the Office of Management and Budget and elevated that office to Cabinet level. Darman's priority as budget director was to get Republicans and Democrats on Capitol Hill to agree on a five-year plan to reduce the federal budget deficit and keep it under control with pay-as-you-go rules. He achieved that goal with a landmark legislative pact that President Bush was persuaded to sign into law in October 1990. In calling for new taxes, the measure broke Bush's vaunted campaign pledge, contributed to the public's cynicism regarding the veracity of its leaders, and was a factor in Bush's loss to the Democratic nominee, Bill Clinton, in the presidential election of 1992. After he again left government employment, Darman was a partner in the Carlyle Group, a private-equity investment firm, and chairman of the AES Corp., a Virginia-based power company. His book, *Who's in Control?: Polar Politics and the Sensible Center*, was published in 1996. Darman, who lived in McLean, Virginia, suffered from acute myelogenous leukemia; he died at Georgetown University Hospital in Washington, D.C. His survivors included his wife, Kathleen, three sons, and a granddaughter. See *Current Biography* (1989).

Obituary *New York Times* A p15 Jan. 26, 2008

DASSIN, JULES Dec. 18, 1911–March 31, 2008 Film director. Jules Dassin was a resilient survivor of the Hollywood political blacklist of the late 1940s and early 1950s. Before his banishment from the American movie studios, Dassin directed several World War II–related melodramas and a string of masterly films noir; subsequently, in exile in Europe, he made such films as the widely imitated caper classic *Rififi*, the more humorous hit movie in the same genre *Topkapi*, and the celebrated comedy *Never on Sunday*, starring his second wife, the Greek actress Melina Mercouri, as a happy prostitute. One of eight children of Jewish immigrants from Russia, Dassin began his career as an actor, at Borscht Belt summer camps and in Manhattan with ARTEF, the Yiddish acronym for a proletarian players' collective founded under the aegis of the Communist daily newspaper *Freiheit*. He was a member of the Communist Party USA for several years, until 1939, when the party's endorsement of the Hitler-Stalin pact disillusioned him. As director of the pro–socialized-medicine play *Medicine Show* on Broadway (1940) and a writer of radio scripts, he came to the attention of Hollywood scouts. Beginning in 1941, he worked in motion pictures for a decade under contract to, successively, the RKO, MGM, Universal-International, and Twentieth Century–Fox studios. His first screen assignment was *The Tell-Tale Heart* (1941), a 20-minute

adaptation of the Poe suspense story. Over the following five years, he directed eight feature films, including *Nazi Agent* (1942), *Reunion in France* (1942), *The Canterville Ghost* (1944), and *A Letter for Evie*. He hit his stride with the gritty naturalistic films *Brute Force* (1947), a violent prison drama starring Burt Lancaster; *The Naked City* (1948), the story of a police manhunt filmed in documentary style on location in New York City; *Thieves' Highway* (1949), a neo-realistic film about racketeering in the trucking industry, filmed on location in California, in which he had a small role; and *Night and the City* (1950), a thriller set in the London underworld. By the time he finished filming *Night and the City* he was persona non grata in the American movie industry, a victim of the blacklist inspired by the Cold War–born so-called Red scare then prevailing in the United States and in particular by the witch-hunting operations of the House Committee on Un-American Activities, commonly known as HUAC. Representing the vanguard of what would soon become known as McCarthyism, the House Un-American Activities Committee began investigating the alleged "Communist faction" in Hollywood in 1947, and by 1950 it was known that Dassin's fellow director Edward Dmytryk was ready to "name names" to the committee, including that of Dassin. With no prospect of further opportunities in Hollywood, Dassin briefly concentrated on directorial work on Broadway and then settled in Europe, living at first in France and Italy and later in Greece. Even across the Atlantic the stigma of the blacklist continued to make him unemployable for several years, until he was offered the opportunity to adapt a crime novel by August le Breton to the screen on a low budget. The result was the French film *Rififi* (1955), a screenplay co-written as well as directed by Dassin about a meticulously planned and successfully executed (up to a point) jewelry-store burglary. Under a pseudonym, Dassin cast himself in the role of one of the four thieves, the weak-willed safecracker César, whose gift of a ring from the heist to his girlfriend enables police to crack the case. *Rififi* brought Dassin the award for best director (shared with Serge Vasiliev) at the Cannes Film Festival in 1955, and the film was a commercial and critical hit in Europe, especially in France, where it broke box-office records. It was a moderate art-cinema success in the United States, where it was at first distributed without Dassin's name attached to it. Dassin's first professional collaboration with Melina Mercouri was his direction of her as a small-town prostitute in *He Who Must Die* (1957), an adaptation of Nikos Kazantzakis's novel about the oppression of Greeks by Turks on the island of Crete in the 1920s. Mercouri starred as a joyously good-hearted trollop in the lighter-veined *Never on Sunday* (1960), a screenplay written by Dassin and produced on a shoestring budget. Dassin co-starred in *Never on Sunday* as a priggish American tourist who tries to reform the Mercouri character. The film was a huge international success, grossing almost $4 million in the United States, where his reputation was enjoying a post–McCarthy era rehabilitation. Mercouri was voted best actress at Cannes, and the film drew five Oscar nominations: one for Mercouri, two (best director and best screenplay) for Dassin, and the others for costumes and theme song.

Dassin subsequently directed Mercouri in starring roles in *Phaedra* (1962) and *Topkapi* (1964). A heist flick lighter-veined than *Rififi*, *Topkapi* was also a great commercial success. In *Topkapi* a gang carries out an ingenious break-in to steal a priceless emerald-encrusted dagger from a glass-enclosed case in the Topkapi Palace Museum in Istanbul, Turkey—with a surprise result. Dassin later directed Mercouri in *Promise of Dawn* (1971) and *A Dream of Passion* (1978). Dassin and Mercouri, who were married in 1966 and who were political activists, were forced to flee Greece when a military junta seized power in 1967, and they lived in Paris until the junta was toppled, in 1974. Dassin's film *The Rehearsal* (1974) was about the student rebellions that led to the junta's ouster. Mercouri served in the Hellenic Parliament beginning in 1974 and as Greek minister of culture from 1981 to 1989. After her death, in 1994, Dassin founded the Melina Mercouri Foundation to continue her work, chiefly her campaign for the return of the so-called Elgin Marbles to Athens. That large collection of sculptures, taken from the Parthenon by Lord Elgin early in the 19th century, is held in the British Museum. In September 2008 a new museum was scheduled to open at the Acropolis in Athens to include plaster casts of the stolen sculptures in anticipation of their return. Dassin directed a total of 22 films, including *The Law* (aka *Where the Hot Wind Blows*, 1959), *Uptight!* (1968), and *Circle of Two* (1980). He died in Hygeia Hospital in Athens, of complications from influenza, according to Agence France-Presse. His daughter, the actress Julie Dassin, from his first marriage, to Beatrice Launer, survived him. His son, the singer Joe Dassin, also from his first marriage, predeceased him. See *Current Biography* (1971).

Obituary *New York Times* A p21 Apr. 1, 2008

DAY, LARAINE Oct. 13, 1920–Nov. 10, 2007 Actress. Laraine Day—named La Raine Johnson at birth—arrived at popularity in the late 1930s and the 1940s as the leading lady in what she described as "B+ movies," especially as the nurse Mary Lamont in the MGM series of five Dr. Kildare movies co-starring Lew Ayres and Lionel Barrymore (1939–41). Her other roles at MGM (where she was under contract from 1938 to 1946) included Croney Cronin, the wisecracking newspaperwoman in *Unholy Partners* (1941), the title part in *The Trial of Mary Dugan* (1941), Gail Farwood in *A Yank on the Burma Road* (1942), Nora Davis, who adopts a British war orphan in *Journey for Margaret* (1942), and Leigh Rand, the tough WAC officer in *Keep Your Powder Dry* (1945). Before signing with MGM, she had starred opposite George O'Brien in three RKO Westerns. She won better roles when she worked for other studios. On loan to United Artists, she impressed critics with her portrayal of Maeve O'Riordan, the sensitive aspiring actress in *My Son, My Son* (1940), and Carol Fisher in Alfred Hitchcock's *Foreign Correspondent* (1940). Again on loan, she returned to RKO to play Dorothy Bryant, the socialite who reforms a playboy/gambler (Cary Grant) in *Mr. Lucky* (1943) and Nancy Monks Blaie Patton, the psychopathic killer in *The Locket* (1946). On loan, this time to Paramount, she was cast as Madeleine in the Gary Cooper vehicle *The Story*

of Dr. Wassell (1944). Under contract with RKO, she starred opposite John Wayne in *Tycoon* (1947). She accrued a total of more than three dozen feature-film credits, among the last of which were the roles of Lydia Price, one of the passengers in the trans-Pacific airline thriller *The High and the Mighty* (1954), Gwen Taylor in *The Toy Tiger* (1956), and the murderously vengeful rejected lover Marian Forbes in *The Third Voice* (1960). Day began her career in regional theater. On television between the early 1950s and the mid-1980s, she was the host of several shows, a guest on many talk/variety programs, and an actress in numerous teleplays and episodes in situation comedies and adventure series. She was married three times and divorced twice, from her first husband, the singer Ray Hendricks, and her second husband, the major-league baseball manager Leo Durocher. As the "First Lady of baseball," she wrote the book *Day with the Giants* (1953). A second book by her, *The America We Love*, was published in 1971. She was predeceased by her third husband, the screenwriter and producer Michael Grilikhes. Among her survivors were several children—at least some of whom were adopted—and many grandchildren and great-grandchildren. She died at the home of her daughter Gigi in Ivins, Utah. See *Current Biography* (1953).

Obituary *New York Times* C p13 Nov. 13, 2007

DE BAKEY, MICHAEL Sep. 7, 1908–July 11, 2008 Physician and surgeon. Michael Ellis De Bakey, the father of modern cardiovascular surgery, was a pioneer in the development of the artificial heart and the creator of scores of devices and procedures now standard in the treatment of strokes and aneurysms as well as heart failure. His first invention, which he came up with as a medical student at Tulane University in 1932, was the roller pump, which became a key component of the heart-lung machine, taking over the function of supplying blood to the brain during surgery. Early on, he also invented an improved blood-transfusion needle, suture scissors, and a colostomy clamp. At the Baylor College of Medicine, in Houston, Texas, during the 1950s, he perfected new, complex procedures for repairing aortic aneurysms and blockages by replacing the diseased segments with grafts of Dacron patches and tubes. (His mother, an immigrant from Lebanon, had taught him to sew when he was a child.) At Baylor in 1963 he created a device facilitating the movement of blood from one heart chamber to another. The following year he became the first surgeon to perform successfully a coronary-bypass operation. His subsequent work at Baylor included the development of a partial artificial heart—the ventricle assist device, or VAD, which he successfully used for the first time in 1966. After Christiaan Bernard of South Africa performed the first human heart transplant, in 1967, De Bakey briefly followed suit, with great wariness. The transplant patients in those days did not survive the operations for long, because their bodies rejected the transplants. After the development of the antirejection drug cyclosporine, De Bakey in 1984 performed his first heart transplant in 14 years. Meanwhile he was experimenting with a whole artificial heart, implanting it in calves. In 1969 his protégé Denton Cooley, without consulting him, took it upon himself to implant the experimental device into a dying human being, unsuccessfully. Cooley's "premature" action shocked De Bakey and sparked one of medicine's best-known and longest feuds, which did not end until almost 40 years later. De-Bakey began teaching surgery at his alma mater, the Tulane University School of Medicine, in 1937. Assigned to the U.S. surgeon general's office during World War II, he helped to develop mobile army surgical units and what became the Veterans Administration's medical-research program, including specialized treatment centers. In 1948 he joined the faculty of the Baylor College of Medicine (then allied to Baylor University, now to the Texas Medical Center), where he became, successively, president and chancellor. In the course of his career, De Bakey operated on more than 60,000 patients—from royalty to Third World peasants—and saved thousands of lives. In Houston and to a lesser degree in his travels around the world, he trained an untold number of surgeons. In his later years he expressed disappointment at not having found the cause of arteriosclerosis. (Doubting that cholesterol was a major factor, he sought a virus or other infectious agent as a cause of the condition.) In addition to more than 1,500 scientific articles, he published several books, including *The Living Heart* (1977) and *The Living Heart Diet* (1984). On December 31, 2005 he successfully underwent a procedure he had developed for repairing a damaged aorta. After the death of his first wife, Diana (née Cooper), in the early 1970s, De Bakey married Katrin Fehlhaber, who survived him. His other survivors included a daughter from his second marriage and two of his four sons from his first marriage. He died at the Methodist Hospital in Houston, Texas. See *Current Biography* (1964).

Obituary *New York Times* p1+ July 13, 2008

DELLO JOIO, NORMAN Jan. 24, 1913–July 24, 2008 Composer; organist; pianist. The descendant of three generations of Italian organists, Norman Dello Joio was a melodically gifted, fine craftsman of a myriad of varied works for orchestra, single instruments, voice, ballet, and opera. Against the atonal tide, he wrote with a neoclassical lyricism, influenced by liturgical music,19th-century opera, jazz, and popular music. Originally named Nicodemo DeGioio, he was born in New York City, the only son of Casimir De-Gioio, an immigrant from Italy, and Antoinette De-Gioio (née Garramone). In early childhood he was introduced to the piano and organ by his father, a prominent organist, pianist, and vocal coach, and he further mastered the organ under the tutelage of his godfather, Pietro Yoon, the organist at St. Patrick's Cathedral. When he was 12 he began spelling his father as organist at Our Lady of Mount Carmel Church in Manhattan, and at 14 he became organist and choir director of St. Mary Star of the Sea Church on City Island, New York City. He also became expert in jazz during his formative years. In the late 1930s and early 1940s, he studied composition under Bernard Wagenaar at the Juilliard School of Music and Paul Hindemith at the Berkshire Music Center and Yale University. He was musical director of the ballet company the Dance Players from 1941 to 1943,

taught at Sarah Lawrence College from 1944 to 1950, and later was dean of the School of Fine and Applied Arts at Boston University. He also worked at the Ford Foundation, helping to set up a program in which young composers were placed in residence in high schools. His early works included *Ballad of Thomas Jefferson* for voice (1943), *Magnificat* for orchestra (1944), *Fantasia on a Gregorian Theme* for violin and piano (1949), and several instrumental sonatas and concertos. He subsequently composed such works as *Song of Affirmation* (1952), a setting of Stephen Vincent Benet's poem "Western Star" for orchestra and voice, the one-act opera *The Ruby* (1955), *To Saint Cecilia* for mixed chorus and brass (1958), and *O Sing Unto the Lord* for male chorus and organ (1959). In 1957 he received the Pulitzer Prize in music for *Meditations on Ecclesiastes* for string orchestra. During the 1950s he devoted several operas to Joan of Arc: *The Triumph of St. Joan*, which he withdrew after a student production at Sarah Lawrence College in 1950; *The Trial at Rouen*, which was televised on the NBC network in 1956; and another titled *The Triumph of St. Joan*, a revision of *The Trial at Rouen*, which premiered at the New York City Opera in 1959. He wrote the score for the NBC documentary *The Louvre,* televised during the 1964–65 season. (He did not win an Emmy Award for that score, as several sources claim.) His ballet credits included the music for Eugene Loring's *Prairie* (1942), Michael Kidd's *On Stage!* (1945), José Limón's *There Is a Time* (1956), and Martha Graham's *Diversion of Angels* (1948), *Seraphic Dialogue* (1951), and *A Time of Snow* (1968). His oeuvre totaled several hundred pieces, including *The Holy Infant's Lullaby* for voice and piano (1962), *Prayers of Cardinal Newman* for mixed chorus and organ (1962), *Scenes from the Louvre* for band (1966), *Homage to Haydn* for orchestra (1969), *The Lamentation of Saul* for voice and various instruments (1970), *Notes from Tom Paine* for chorus a capella (1975), and masses in honor of the Blessed Virgin Mary and the Eucharist. After his formal retirement, in 1979, he continued to compose occasionally. In 1974, following his divorce from his first wife, Grayce Baumgold, in 1971, after three decades of marriage, he married Barbara Bolton, who survived him. His other survivors included, from his first marriage, his sons, Justin and Norman, and his daughter, Victoria; two stepchildren; and three grandchildren. He died in his sleep at his home in East Hampton, New York. See *Current Biography* (1957).

Obituary *New York Times* p24 July 27, 2008

DIDDLEY, BO Dec. 30, 1928–June 2, 2008 Musician. The rhythm-and-blues guitarist/singer/songwriter Bo Diddley was among the black American talents whose seminal contributions to the development of popular music in the second half of the 20th century have been generally underappreciated, although a legion of rock-and-roll musicians have acknowledged his influence in their work. His chief contribution was the "Bo Diddley beat," a syncopated 4/4 or 5/4 pattern, probably originating in West Africa and more directly deriving from the Afro-Cuban clave rhythm and the musical "hambone" game played by African-American children slapping and patting their arms, legs, chests, and heads while chanting rhymes. In its simplest form that beat can be counted out as a two-bar phrase, probably best explained to the lay public with the example of the well-known couplet "Shave and a haircut, two bits." "In his [best] songs," Ben Ratliff wrote in the *New York Times* obituary of Diddley, "[His] booming voice was loaded up with echo and his guitar work came with distortion and a novel bubbling tremolo. The songs were knowing, wisecracking, and full of slang, mother wit, and sexual cockiness." Bo Diddley was born Otha Ellas Bates in McComb, Mississippi. Raised in Chicago, Illinois, by his mother's cousin Gussie McDaniel, he changed his name to Ellas McDaniel in childhood. As a boy, he studied classical violin at a church Sunday school where Gussie McDaniel taught. According to some accounts, he built his first guitar, a square or rectangular instrument, as a vocational-school student in Chicago. (Later, some of his odd-shaped guitars would be custom-built to his specifications by the Gretsch Co.) From the beginning he played the guitar almost as if it were a percussion instrument: "I play drum licks on the guitar," he once said. Dropping out of school, he formed his first band with two friends who played bass and maracas; soon he added a fourth member, a harmonica player. In their early days he and the band gave pass-the-hat performances in Chicago's Maxwell Street open-air market. After they began doing professional gigs in nightclubs on Chicago's South Side, in 1951, the band was expanded to include a pianist. The early band members were all males; later women would be included. Ellas McDaniel adopted the stage name Bo Diddley when he became a recording artist, in the mid-1950s. Whether or not he had already been so nicknamed as a teenager—as some sources claim—the source of the pseudonym is almost without doubt the diddley bow, a makeshift one-stringed instrument of African origin that many black American blues musicians played when they were children. Signing with the Checker label, a subsidiary of Chess Records, in 1955 Diddley released his first single, "Bo Diddley," which was number two on the R&B charts. ("I'm a Man" was on the B-side.) In November 1955 Diddley had his first big break on television, an appearance on Ed Sullivan's popular CBS network show *The Talk of the Town* that he willfully botched. Scheduled by Sullivan to perform a cover of the white singer Tennessee Ernie Ford's hit "Sixteen Tons," he performed "Bo Diddley" instead, infuriating Sullivan and setting the television side of his career back. As a recording artist he reached number 11 on the R&B charts with his second single, "Diddley Daddy," and his other early singles "Pretty Thing," "Crackin' Up," and "I'm Sorry" also sold well. In 1957 the duo Mickey and Sylvia had a pop hit with their recording of his composition "Love Is Strange." In 1959 "Say Man," a single built around good-natured insults exchanged between Bo Diddley and Jerome Green, his sideman on maracas, was number three on the R&B charts, and it became his first and only Top 20 pop hit. His 1962 R&B hit single "You Can't Judge a Book by Its Cover" was written by Willie Dixon. His own original songbook included the numbers "Who Do You Love," "Mona," "Road Runner," "Cops and Robbers," "Uncle John," "The Mule," and "Shave and a Haircut."

Between 1958 and 1963 he recorded 10 albums, including *The Originator*, *Bo Diddley*, *Bo Diddley Is a Gunslinger*, and *Bo Diddley Is a Lover*. In 1963 he toured Great Britain with Little Richard, the Everly Brothers, and the Rolling Stones. In 1964 he released the albums *Bo Diddley's Sixteen All-Time Greatest Hits* and *Two Great Guitars* (with Chuck Berry). In 1967 he recorded a blues album with Muddy Waters and Little Walter and another with Waters and Howlin' Wolf. Among the score of albums he recorded over the following three decades were *Big Bad Bo* (1974), *Ain't It Good to Be Free* (1983), and *Breakin' Through the BS* (1989). *A Man Amongst Men* (1996) was nominated for a Grammy Award. Diddley continued touring until he suffered a stroke in May 2007. He was inducted into the Rock and Roll Hall of Fame in 1987 and the National Academy of Recording Arts and Sciences Hall of Fame in 1998. In the latter year he also received a Grammy Award for lifetime achievement. Among the artists and groups who paid homage to him in their work were Buddy Holly, Johnny Otis, John Lennon, Bruce Springsteen, the Rolling Stones, Donovan, the Monkees, the Who, Elvis Costello, Eric Clapton, U2, the Quicksilver Messenger Service, and George Thorogood. During the last two decades of his life, Bo Diddley lived in Archer, Florida, on 76 acres that included a recording studio. Married four times, he divorced his fourth wife a few years before his death. He died of heart failure in Archer. His survivors included a son, three daughters, a stepson, 15 grandchildren, 15 great-grandchildren, and three great-great-grandchildren. See *Current Biography* (1989).

Obituary *New York Times* A p1+ June 3, 2008

DITH PRAN Sep. 27, 1942–Mar. 30, 2008 Cambodian-born photojournalist; a self-described "one-person crusade . . . for those who did not survive [the Cambodian 'killing fields'] and those who still suffer." Dith Pran was the renowned heroic survivor of the killing fields (a term he coined), created by Pol Pot's ruling party, the Khmer Rouge, during its four-year reign of terror (1975–79) in Cambodia. The Khmer Rouge ("Red Cambodians"), with a rank and file composed of illiterate peasants and young people, were radical agrarian Communist revolutionaries ruthlessly bent on ridding Cambodia (which they renamed Democratic Kampuchea) of all professionals and other educated persons and all vestiges of foreign modernist influence and, beginning in "year zero" (1975), turning it into a classless society by depopulating Phnom Penh, the capital, and other cities and driving the entire population into forced labor in subsistence-farming communes. Under Pol Pot, torture was routine and 1.7 million persons, a fourth of Cambodia's population, died through massacre, execution, exhaustion, illness, or starvation. During the three years preceding Pol Pot's regime (1972–75), Dith Pran had assisted the Pulitzer Prize–winning *New York Times* correspondent Sydney H. Schanberg in covering the civil war in Cambodia. Schanberg's book *The Death and Life of Dith Pran* (1985) was the basis for the Academy Award–winning motion picture *The Killing Fields* (1985), in which Haing S. Ngor played Dith Pran and Sam Waterson played Schanberg. Dith Pran, who was multi-lingual, worked as an interpreter and translator with the U.S. Military Assistance Command in Cambodia from 1962 to 1965, when Norodom Sihanouk, the Cambodian king who was then head of state, broke diplomatic relations with the United States. Dith Pran then found a livelihood in tourism, at a hotel catering to visitors to the Angkor Wat ruins. After Lon Nol seized power in a right-wing coup in March 1970, a civil war broke out between Lon Nol's government forces and the Khmer Rouge. When the war brought tourism to a standstill, Dith Pran turned to working as a guide, interpreter, and translator with foreign war correspondents. After he became the exclusive sidekick of Sydney H. Schanberg, he made photography his better-known metier. As the victory of the Indochinese Communist forces in both Cambodia and adjacent Vietnam neared in the spring of 1975, the United States began swiftly to pull its military and civilian personnel out of both countries and to evacuate a number of indigenous personnel and their families as well. On April 12, 1975 Dith Pran's wife, Ser Moeun, and their four children were evacuated to the United States. (Other members of his family, including three brothers, would die under Pol Pot.) Mistakenly believing that, as Schanberg wrote, when the Khmer Rouge "won their victory they would have what they wanted and would end the terrorism and brutal behavior we had written so often about," Schanberg defied the expressed wishes of his bosses at the New York Times and remained in Phnom Penh with Dith Pran at his side in order to cover the imminent fall of the city to the Khmer Rouge. When that event occurred, on April 17 and 18, 1975, Schanberg and two other American correspondents were among those arrested, in company with Dith Pran, who talked the soldiers who made the arrest out of executing the three journalists, apparently by lying and persuading them that the three were neutral French reporters. Allowed to leave Cambodia, Schanberg spent a year in Burma before returning to New York in May 1976 to become a top editor at the New York Times. Meanwhile Dith Pran remained in Cambodia, enduring hard labor in rural communes, attempted political indoctrination, beatings, and a near-starvation diet for four years, all the while remaining alive by pretending he was an illiterate peasant. After Vietnamese forces invaded Cambodia and a Vietnamese-backed government was announced in Phnom Penh early in 1979, Dith Pran escaped from a commune near Siem Reap. He subsequently trekked more than 50 miles across Cambodia, arriving in October 1979 in a border refugee camp in Thailand. Alerted, Schanberg flew to Thailand to be reunited with the colleague whom he had felt guilty about leaving behind in 1975 to help him move to the United States. In New York Dith Pran became a staff photographer with the New York Times and founded the Dith Pran Holocaust Awareness Project. In 1986 he was naturalized as an American citizen. He was divorced both from his first wife, Ser Moeun Dith (who would be at his bedside when he died) and from his second wife, Kim DePaul. His compilation of memoirs of survivors, Children of Cambodia's Killing Fields (1997), was edited by Kim DePaul. He lived during his final years in Woodbridge, New Jersey, and died of pancreatic cancer at Robert Wood Johnson University Hospital in New Brunswick, New Jersey. His survivors included his companion, Bette Parslow, a daughter, three sons, six grandchildren, and two step-grandchildren. See Current Biography (1996).

Obituary New York Times A p19 Mar. 31, 2008

ELLIOTT, OSBORN Oct. 25, 1924–Sep. 28, 2008 As the editor of Newsweek in the 1960s and 1970s, Osborn "Oz" Elliott revitalized and transformed that newsmagazine from a weaker imitation of Time into a sound competitor. Under his leadership Newsweek became known for advocacy journalism, and by the time he left, in 1976, its circulation had risen from 1.5 million (in 1961) to 2.7 million (that of Time was 3.4 million). Elliott was born and raised in the New York City borough of Manhattan. He attended Harvard College, in Cambridge, Massachusetts, then left to serve in the U.S. Navy aboard the heavy cruiser USS Boston for two years. He earned a bachelor's degree in 1946. Shortly after his college graduation, he became a reporter for the New York Journal of Commerce. Three years later Time—where his first wife, Deirdre M. Spencer, worked in the personnel department—hired him as a contributing editor specializing in business. He was promoted to associate editor in 1952. In 1955 he joined the staff of Newsweek as business editor. He became managing editor in 1959 and then held the title of editor from 1961 to 1969 and 1972 to 1975. (From 1969 to 1976 he held the titles editor in chief, vice chairman, president, chief executive officer, and chairman of the board.) Among the first changes he made were giving reporters bylines—a first for newsmagazines—and ridding the magazine of the backward-running sentences commonly used by Time. (An example from the June 2, 1924 issue of Time: "A ghastly ghoul prowled around a cemetery not far from Paris. Into family chapels went he, robbery of the dead intent upon.") He hired new columnists, including Milton Friedman, Meg Greenfield, Paul Samuelson, and Stewart Alsop, and encouraged more liberal stances. Newsweek began producing in-depth polling on national issues and provided cover stories that examined such topics as the Vietnam War, the civil rights movement, and the women's rights movement. Its first editorial, a 23-page section titled "The Negro in America: What Must Be Done," ran in November 1967 and analyzed the issue of race in the U.S. and suggested ways to integrate African-Americans into all aspects of society. For that section, Newsweek won the Magazine of the Year Award, bestowed by the Columbia University Graduate School of Journalism. In 1969 Elliott became editor in chief and later held the titles of president, chief executive officer and board chairman. When he left the magazine in 1976, New York City mayor Abraham D. Beame asked him to head the city's Office of Economic Opportunity. At the time that Elliott was named deputy mayor for economic development, New York City was struggling with unemployment and near-bankruptcy. He waived his city salary, receiving only a dollar a year, and worked to attract small businesses back into the city. He resigned in 1977 to become dean of the Columbia University Graduate School of Journalism. Though he stepped down in 1986, he remained at the school as the George T. Delacorte professor of magazine journalism until 1994. He authored several books, including *Men at the Top* (1959), which examined the characteristics of America's top executives, and the autobiography *The World of Oz* (1980). He was among the first to be inducted into the American Society of Magazine Editors' Hall of Fame in 1996. Elliott died of cancer in his Manhattan home. His second wife, Inger, three daughters from his first marriage, three stepchildren, two foster sons, 17 grandchildren, and one great-grandchild all survive him. See *Current Biography* (1978).

Obituary *New York Times* A p19 Sep. 29, 2008

FAGLES, ROBERT Sep. 11, 1933–Mar. 26, 2008 Literary scholar; translator; poet; professor emeritus of comparative literature, Princeton University. As a translator who made ancient Greek and Roman classics freshly idiomatic and meaningful while remaining true to the sense and sweep of the original texts, Robert Fagles enjoyed a rare combination of popularity with lay readers and esteem in academe, where his translations became standard texts. Fagles, whose verse translations were usually written in unrhymed six-beat lines, was most admired for his translations of the epic poems of Homer, from the Greek, and Virgil, from the Latin. His books sold more than four million copies worldwide. While teaching English at Yale University, his alma mater, Fagles published his first book, *Complete Poems/Bacchylides* (1961), translated from the Greek. After joining the faculty of Princeton University, he published a translation of the Greek dramatist Aeschylus's trilogy *Oresteia* (1975). In 1972 he published *I Vincent: Poems from the Pictures of Van Gogh,* a volume of his original poems, each of which was an attempt at a linguistic equivalent of the visual impact of a Van Gogh painting. His translations of the Greek dramatist Sophocles' plays *Antigone, Oedipus the King,* and *Oedipus at Colonus* were published together under the title *Three Theban Plays* (1982). His translation of Homer's *Iliad* and *Odyssey* were published in 1990 and 1996, respectively, and his translation of Virgil's *Aeneid* appeared in 2006. Fagles, who became professor emeritus at Princeton University in 2002, died of prostate cancer at his home in Princeton, New Jersey. He was survived by his wife, Lynne (nee Duchovnay), two daughters, and three grandchildren. See *Current Biography* (2006).

Obituary *New York Times* A p15 Mar. 29, 2008

FELKER, CLAY S. Oct. 2, 1925–July 1, 2008 Magazine editor, publisher, and journalist. Clay S. Felker influenced the format and content of modern magazines when he introduced *New York* on the newsstands in the late 1960s. "American journalism would not be what it is today without Clay Felker," the current *New York* editor, Adam Moss, wrote in a July 1, 2008 statement. With a long roster of talented writers, including Tom Wolfe, Jimmy Breslin and Gloria Steinem, Felker's *New York* became one of the first magazines dedicated to the New Journalism of the 1960s, a style of writing in which literary techniques are used to add emotional depth to news stories. Felker was born into a journalistic family in

Webster Groves, Missouri. His father was the managing editor of the *Sporting News* and his mother was the women's editor of the *St. Louis-Dispatch* before she had children. He studied political science at Duke University, in Durham, North Carolina, and spent three years in the navy. After graduation, in 1951, Felker took a job with Time Inc. For six years he wrote sports and political stories for *Life* magazine and helped develop *Sports Illustrated.* He became the features editor of *Esquire* magazine in 1957. Five years later he moved to New York City and worked as a consulting editor for various publishers. His 1963 consulting job for the now-defunct *New York Herald Tribune* led to his hiring as founding editor of the paper's Sunday-supplement magazine, *New York.* After the *Herald Tribune* ceased publication, in 1967, Felker worked to keep that supplement magazine alive, using his severance pay to buy the rights to the name. Along with the graphic designer Milton Glaser, he reimagined the magazine and published the first stand-alone version in 1968. Although initial reception was mixed, the magazine quickly grew in popularity, and other publications soon began imitating its content. "Cities were really down when [Felker] started all this. We had just come out of the fifties, where the cities were slums and people were getting mugged and Chicken Delight wouldn't deliver," Nick Pileggi, who worked as a contributing editor for the magazine in its early years, said during a discussion with other *New York* alumni, as printed in the magazine (July 6, 2008). "All of a sudden, he's writing about all the great stuff about a city: the greatest dry cleaner, the greatest grocery store, where to get the best ice cream. Clay is out there reviewing restaurants. Little ones, cheap ones. None of the newspapers were doing it. And all of that was critically important to the people who wanted to stay in the city." Wolfe, who was the magazine's first staff member, said during the same discussion, "Clay's eye for styles of life and the status groups that created them, his journalist's awareness of such things as hot news, profoundly changed magazine and newspaper publishing in the United States and, for that matter, England. So-called 'city' magazines doing their best to imitate *New York* cropped up all over the country. Newspapers created sections called 'Style,' 'Lifestyle,' . . . all to try to capture some of the *New York* mojo." Among the magazine's most emulated features were its shopping, transportation, and entertainment guides and its profile pieces on prominent figures; also copied was its practice of devoting the first issue of each year to examining the salaries of a variety of New Yorkers, ranging from celebrities to cab drivers. In 1971 Felker helped Steinem and others launch the feminist magazine *Ms.* (In addition to financial backing, he placed a preview of *Ms.* in *New York.*) His magazine acquired the *Village Voice,* a New York weekly newspaper, in 1974. Two years later the Australian press baron Rupert Murdoch made an offer to buy *New York.* Although Felker vehemently refused, the company's principal stockholder, Carter Burden, agreed to the deal. Felker sought in vain to block the decision, and the magazine was sold to Murdoch in 1977. Felker went on to partner with Associated Newspapers to buy *Esquire* magazine, where he served as editor, chief executive and, starting in

1979, publisher. After leaving *Esquire*, in 1981, he became a producer at 20th Century Fox and continued to work as a consultant to other magazines. In 1994 he joined the staff at the University of California's Graduate School of Journalism in Berkeley as a lecturer. Felker's first two marriages, to Leslie Aldridge and then to the actress Pamela Tiffin, ended in divorce. He married the writer Gail Sheehy in 1984. He was diagnosed with throat cancer during his last years and died in his Manhattan home. He is survived by Sheehy, a sister, a daughter, a step-daughter, and three step-grandchildren. See *Current Biography* (1975). — M.A.S.

Obituary *New York Times* A p1+ July 2, 2008

FISCHER, BOBBY Mar. 9, 1943–Jan. 17, 2008 Chess player; international champion (1972–75). Robert James Fischer's reputation as the socially dysfunctional and unpredictable "bad boy of chess" obscured the fact that he was a grandmaster nonpareil, probably unrivaled even by William Steinitz (1836–1900), his Prague-born, naturalized American world-champion predecessor. There was no chess player anywhere more creative than Fischer. Although he was learned in chess history, he tired of what he called the "old chess," with its book-learned and memorized tactics and carefully arranged world championships. He invented Fischer Random, a version of chess in which the grid and the rules were retained but back pieces were lined up haphazardly. Following his victory over the Russian grandmaster Boris Spassky for the world championship in Reykjavik, Iceland, in 1972, his biographer Harold C. Schonberg wrote: "It was Bobby Fischer who had, single-handedly, made the world recognize that chess on its highest level was as competitive as football, as thrilling as a duel to the death, as aesthetically satisfying as a fine work of art, as intellectually demanding as any form of human activity." His reputation for paranoia and bizarre behavior notwithstanding, when he appeared on Dick Cavett's television interview show after his Spassky match, he struck Cavett as funny as well as well-groomed and personable and as having a face that "radiated intelligence," as Cavett recalled in a blog for the *New York Times* (February 8, 2008). A fugitive from U.S. tax authorities, Fischer renounced his U.S. citizenship and became a citizen of Iceland in 2005. Born to a Jewish mother in Chicago and raised in Brooklyn (where he was a high-school dropout), Fischer began playing chess when he was six, was the U.S. junior champion at 13, won the first of his eight U.S. national titles at 14, became the world's youngest grandmaster at 15, and subsequently had a winning streak of 20 games in international competition leading up to his historic confrontation with Spassky in Iceland. That 21-game tournament (July–September 1972)— widely regarded as a proxy battle for the main antagonists of the Cold War, the U.S. and the Soviet Union— brought the insular game of chess to mass popular attention in countries around the world, including the U.S., where the tournament was broadcast in its entirety on public television. (It also made chess competition much more lucrative than before, netting Fischer $250,000 in prize money on that occasion.) Keeping his own counsel while vanquishing an op-ponent fortified with the advice of 35 fellow Russian grandmasters, Fischer was hailed as a "free world" hero—temporarily. His brilliance at chess soon became eclipsed by his strange tendencies toward paranoia and misanthropy. Dropping out of competition, he forfeited his world title by refusing to defend it against Anatoly Karpov in 1975. Aside from an involvement for a number of years until the late 1970s with the Worldwide Church of God, a quirky Pasadena-based millenarian fundamentalist denomination, he also became socially reclusive. He was lured out of his social shell by his love for a young Hungarian woman and out of his professional retirement by the large purse offered by a Yugoslav businessman who sponsored a rematch with Boris Spassky in the Yugoslav republic of Montenegro in 1992. Defeating Spassky in that unofficial event, Fischer won $3.5 million in prize money. The rematch was regarded by the U.S. government as a "commercial project" in violation of an international economic embargo against the government of Slobodan Milosevic. For defying a U.S. Treasury order forbidding his participation in the event, he faced a fine and/or imprisonment. Fleeing into self-imposed exile, he lived at first in Hungary and then in the Philippines. In radio interviews in those countries, he railed against a "stinking" U.S. and its "allies of evil . . . England, Japan, Australia," and he made anti-Semitic statements as well. In July 2004 he was arrested at Narita Airport, in Japan, for attempting to fly to the Philippines on a revoked American passport. After nine months in detention in Japan, he escaped extradition to the United States when Iceland granted him his request for emergency Icelandic citizenship; he settled in Reykjavik. He died of kidney failure in a Reykjavik hospital, leaving behind his companion, the Japanese chess player Miyoko Watai. "He was the pride and sorrow of chess," the British grandmaster and chess journalist Raymond Keene commented. "It's tragic that such a great man descended into madness and anti-Semitism." See *Current Biography* (1994).

Obituary *New York Times* A p1+ Jan. 19, 2008

FOLKMAN, JUDAH Feb. 24, 1933–Jan. 14, 2008 Surgeon and scientist. Moses Judah Folkman was the founding father of anti-angiogenesis—therapy based on inhibiting the generation of new blood vessels— and as such was arguably the most innovative cancer researcher of the second half of the 20th century. Clinical as well as research oncologists seeking a cure for malignant tumors had traditionally concentrated on the abnormal cells themselves and their mitoses. Folkman focused on blocking the concomitantly abnormal blood supply that such cells use to nourish their growth. For many years his approach was widely greeted with skepticism in the scientific and medical professions, but it has led to the development of numerous anti-angiogenic drugs that offer new hope not only to cancer patients but to others with diseases involving abnormal blood-vessel growth, most notably two in ophthalmology: the retinal impairments causing age-related macular degeneration and the loss of vision experienced by some diabetics. In addition, anti-angiogenic drugs may be helpful in reducing the artery plaque that causes heart disease and in treating obesity. At Harvard University Medical School, his alma mater, Folkman was a professor of surgery and cellular biology throughout his career. In addition, he was surgeon-in-chief (1967–81) and subsequently director of the surgical research laboratories and the vascular biology program at Boston's Children's Hospital, the largest and most comprehensive pediatric center in the United States. The son of a Cleveland, Ohio, rabbi, Folkman began aspiring to a career in medicine when, as a child, he accompanied his father in visits to patients at a local hospital. While earning his M.D. degree at Harvard, he helped to develop the atrioventricular implantable pacemaker. His residency in surgery at Massachusetts General Hospital in Boston began in 1957 and was interrupted by service in the U.S. Navy (1960–62). At the National Naval Medical Center in Bethesda, Maryland, he took part in experiments using artificial (silicone) glands for the slow subcutaneous release of drugs, thus contributing to the development, ultimately, of implantable contraceptives. Also at Bethesda, experimenting with blood substitutes in rabbits and mice, he noticed for the first time that "in the absence of blood vessels, there was no tumor growth." Subsequently, when operating on juveniles with cancer at Children's Hospital in Boston, he further noticed, conversely, that in the presence of tumor growth, there was an unusual clustering of blood vessels to sustain and promote the growth. The excessive vascularity, he realized, was triggered by a molecular secretion from the tumor for the purpose of obtaining the nutrition it needed, a matter that would thenceforth demand his attention. In 1971 he published in the *New England Journal of Medicine* what is regarded as the seminal paper in the field of angiogenic research. Widely derided and dismissed, he failed to win government funding, but pharmaceutical and biotechnological companies saw the potential in his research and responded generously. One company, Monsanto, came through in 1974 with $23 million, the largest grant in Harvard Medical School history. Over the following three decades, Folkman and his colleagues at his Harvard laboratory and at Children's Hospital in Boston experimented with a succession of angiogenic inhibitors they discovered, notably endostatin and angiostatin, and others that they synthesized. Their work, abetted by that of others in other laboratories, resulted in more than 30 anti-angiogenic agents, many under license to Entremed Inc., Genentech Inc., and the Celgene Corp. As of early 2008 most of them were awaiting approval by the U.S. Food and Drug Administration. The FDA approved Avastin, in combination with other therapies, for the treatment of metastatic colorectal cancer in 2004, and it subsequently approved the same drug, again in combination, for the treatment of metastatic lung cancer. In 1965 the FDA approved Thalomid in the treatment of multiple myeloma and Lucentis in the treatment of neovascular macular degeneration. Other anti-angiogenic therapies have been authorized in China. Always advising early intervention in cancer therapy, Folkman concentrated in his last years on "biomarkers," body-fluid proteins signaling incipient disease. His work remained little known to the lay public until 1998, when a front-page story in the *New York Times* quoted the

DNA discoverer James Watson as saying that "Judah is going to cure cancer in two years." Folkman commented on that prediction: "I don't think angiogenesis inhibitors will be the cure for cancer. But I do think that they will make cancer more survivable and controllable, especially in conjunction with radiation, chemotherapy, and other treatments." Folkman was the author of *Toward an Understanding of Angiogenesis: Search and Discovery* (1985) and the co-editor, with William D. Figg, of *Angiogenesis: An Integrative Approach from Science to Medicine* (2008). He was the subject of Robert Cooke's book *Dr. Folkman's War: Angiogenesis and the Struggle to Defeat Cancer* (2001). Folkman died, apparently of a heart attack, in Denver, Colorado. His survivors included his wife, Paula (née Prial), two daughters, and a granddaughter. See *Current Biography* (1998).

Obituary *New York Times* p7 Jan. 16, 2008

FOSSETT, STEVE Apr. 22, 1944–Feb. 15, 2008 (date on which he was officially declared dead) Business tycoon and adventure sportsman. In the field of financial services, James Stephen Fossett was known as the founder of Marathon Securities and Lakota Trading Inc., but in the wider world, he was celebrated as a protean risk-taking outdoorsman, a record-breaker in a wide range of activities, most notably sailing and the piloting of every type of aircraft except spaceships. Among his achievements were the first solo crossing of the Pacific Ocean by balloon, the first solo round-the-world flight by balloon, and the first solo nonstop round-the-world flight by nonrefueled fixed-wing airplane. Fossett went missing on September 3, 2007 after taking off alone in a light single-engine Bellanca Citabria Super Decathlon plane from a private airstrip near Smith Valley, Nevada, on what was intended to be a brief pleasure flight. Weeks of intensive search-and-rescue operations by the Civil Air Patrol and others were to no avail, and he was finally declared legally dead by a probate judge in Cook County, Illinois, on February 15, 2008. Fossett, who was born in Tennessee on April 22, 1944, began mountain climbing as a Boy Scout in California, and he did some mountaineering in the Swiss Alps as a vacationing college graduate before earning his master's degree in business administration at Washington University in St. Louis. While making his fortune as a commodities and options broker in Chicago, he increasingly spent his vacation time seeking challenges in adventure sports, swimming the English Channel, running the Boston marathon, auto-racing in the Formula-Atlantic circuit and at Le Mans, and participating in a 100-mile cross-country skiing contest in Canada, a triathlon in Hawaii, and the Iditarod sled-dog race in Alaska. At sea he set more than a score of speed and distance records for vessels under sail, beginning in 1993, when he circumnavigated Ireland in 44 hours and 42 minutes. His accomplishments as skipper of his 125-foot maxi-catamaran *Cheyenne* (originally named *PlayStation*) included record transatlantic and round-the-world marks, both of which were subsequently surpassed by Bruno Peyron in his *Orange II*. Fossett began soaring in high-tech lighter-than-air balloons filled with air or helium in friendly competition with Britain's Richard Branson and Sweden's

Par Lindstrand, the co-pilots of the first balloon to traverse the Atlantic Ocean, in 1987. In emulation, with Tim Cole as his co-pilot, Fossett flew from Canada to Germany by balloon in 1994. The following year, piloting a helium-filled craft, he became the first balloonist to fly solo across the Pacific, traveling 5,438 miles, a distance record in ballooning at that time. His first five attempts to circumnavigate the globe solo by balloon ended prematurely, some with life-threatening mishaps, but in two of those he set world distance records. In another failed round-the-world effort, in 1998, he was the co-pilot with his former competitors, Branson and Lindstrand. (In 1999 Bertrand Piccard and Brian Jones co-piloted the first successful nonstop round-the-world balloon flight.) In his sixth attempt, piloting a helium-filled craft in the summer of 2002, Fossett finally succeeded in becoming the first balloonist to circle the globe solo. The circumnavigation was completed in 13 days and 3 minutes, the absolute round-the-world speed record, but from takeoff to landing, the flight lasted 14 days and 19 hours, allowing Fossett also to claim the records for longest distance flown solo (20,483.25 miles) and longest time solo (355 hours, 50 minutes) in a balloon. As a fixed-wing powered aircraft pilot, Fossett set three transcontinental speed records for non-supersonic jets flying his Cessna Citation X in the United States in 2000 and 2003. In his historic solo flight around the world in the Virgin Atlantic *Global Flyer*, a single-engine jet aircraft, in February-March 2005, his average speed was 342.2 mph, the absolute world record for "speed around the world, nonstop and non-refueled." Again piloting the *Global Flyer* nonstop the following year, he not only went round-the-world eastbound, from Florida to Florida, but then continued on across the Atlantic a second time, to England, setting the absolute world record for "distance without landing" (25,766 miles). He set a new world speed record for airships piloting the Zeppelin NT in 2004. Teamed with Terry Delore, he set 10 official world records while flying gliders. His autobiography, *Chasing the Wind,* was published in 2006. He and his wife, Peggy (nee Viehland), who survived him, had no children. See *Current Biography* (2005).

Obituary *New York Times* B p7 Feb. 16, 2008

FRASER, DOUGLAS A. Dec. 18, 1916–Feb. 23, 2008 As president of the United Automobile Workers union from 1977 to 1983, Douglas A. Fraser helped prevent the Chrysler Corp. from falling into bankruptcy. He also fought for increases in workers'-compensation benefits, unemployment payments, and pensions and for longer vacations and earlier retirement for autoworkers. Fraser was born in Glasgow, Scotland, and came to the United States with his family when he was six years old. The Frasers settled in Detroit, Michigan. Fraser's father worked as an electrician and was a union activist. Fraser dropped out of high school in 1943 to enter the workforce. He was fired from his first two jobs on automobile assembly lines for union organizing. He then found work at a DeSoto plant, owned by Chrysler, and joined the UAW. By the time he was 27, Fraser had been elected president of the local UAW chapter. After a stint in the U.S. Army, he was hired in

1947 as the union's international representative. Walter P. Reuther, the president of the UAW, recruited Fraser as an administrative assistant in 1951. Fraser maintained a close relationship with Reuther and rose to the position of executive board member-at-large in 1962. He was elected vice president of the union in 1970 and president in 1977. A self-described ultraliberal, Fraser was critical of the American automobile industry's reluctance to manufacture smaller, more fuel-efficient vehicles. During his inaugural address, on May 19, 1977, he stated, "The American auto companies have been sitting on their behinds. We do not build a small car that the American public is attracted to, like a Datsun, Toyota, Honda, or Volkswagen." He added that the need to reduce the nation's dependence on foreign oil made it "absolutely indefensible to keep producing gas guzzlers." When Detroit automakers suffered huge financial losses due to rapidly rising fuel prices and the increased popularity of such fuel-efficient Japanese and German cars, Fraser played a role in the drawing up of federal legislation that provided Chrysler with over $1 billion in guaranteed loans, which enabled the company to avoid bankruptcy. After retiring from the UAW presidency, in 1983, Fraser became a professor of labor studies at Wayne State University, in Detroit. He also lectured at other universities, among them Harvard, Columbia, and the University of Michigan. Fraser died at Providence Hospital in Southfield, Michigan. His first wife, née Eva Falk, died in 1970. He was survived by his second wife, Winifred, two daughters, two step-daughters, and several grandchildren. See *Current Biography* (1977).

Obituary *New York Times* B p6 Feb. 25, 2008

GETTY, ESTELLE July 25, 1923–July 22, 2008 Estelle Getty worked in relative obscurity as a stage actress for the better part of four decades before finding in television the comic role for which she became celebrated: that of Sophia Petrillo, the brazen-tongued octogenarian in the NBC hit situation comedy *The Golden Girls* (1985–92). Getty was born Estelle Scher in the borough of Manhattan, New York City, to parents who were Jewish immigrants from Poland. (Her professional name was a variation on Gettleman, her surname after her marriage.) As a teenager she performed a standup comedy routine at a Catskill Mountains resort; she later began acting in settlement-house productions and in Yiddish theater. Over the following years, supporting herself and her family with steady pay from secretarial and other jobs, she acted in community and experimental theaters, regional houses, and summer stock, increasingly in maternal roles as she aged. Her big break came when the playwright/actor Harvey Fierstein wrote for her the character Mrs. Beckoff, the intrusive mother of Arnold Beckoff (played by Fierstein) in *Widows and Children First!*, Fierstein's third play about a flamboyant New York homosexual and female impersonator (Beckoff). With Getty in the cast, *Women and Children First!* opened Off-Off-Broadway in 1979. In 1981 Fierstein conflated his three plays into *Torch Song Trilogy*, which ran briefly Off-Off-Broadway and then Off-Broadway before moving in 1982 to Broadway, where it played for almost three years. Getty was in the original Broadway cast until 1984, when she joined the play's touring company. After the tour reached Los Angeles, she successfully auditioned for the part of Sophia in *The Golden Girls*, adding two decades to her appearance with makeup, a white wig, and such apparel touches as laced-up orthopedic shoes. She was actually 15 months younger than Bea Arthur, who was cast as Dorothy Zbornak, her daughter in the TV show. The premise was that Sophia, who has suffered a stroke (the reason for her uncensored utterances), moves into a household shared by three divorced women (Dorothy and characters played by Betty White and Rue McClanahan), who become the targets of her humorous barbs. The popular show opened in September 1985 and ran on NBC until 1992 and later in syndication. For her role, Getty was nominated for an Emmy Award seven years in a row, winning the award in 1988. She also won a Golden Globe Award, in 1986. She continued to play Sophia in the spin-off sitcom *The Golden Palace* (1992–93) as well as episodes of the shows *Empty Nest*, *Nurses*, and *Ladies Man*. In addition to her stage and television credits, she had a small number of motion-picture roles, including those of the grandmother in *Mask* (1985) and the mother in *Stop! Or My Mother Will Shoot* (1992). With Steve Delsohn, she wrote the autobiography *If I Knew Then What I Know Now . . . So What?* (1988). Getty, who suffered from Lewy body dementia, died at her home on Hollywood Boulevard in Los Angeles. She was predeceased by her husband, Arthur Gettleman, and survived by her sons, Carl and Barry. See *Current Biography* (1990).

Obituary *New York Times* A p19 July 23, 2008

GIROUX, ROBERT Apr. 8, 1914–Sep. 5, 2008 Robert Giroux was a publisher and editor who worked with such renowned literary figures as T. S. Eliot, Jean Stafford, Flannery O'Connor, Jack Kerouac, William Gaddis, and Susan Sontag. He served as partner, editor in chief, and chairman of the publishing house Farrar, Straus & Giroux. During his long, successful career he published the first novels of several authors: Kerouac's *The Town and the City* (1950), Gaddis's *The Recognitions* (1955), Sontag's *The Benefactor* (1963), and Larry Woiwode's *What I'm Going to Do, I Think* (1969). Giroux also published the American edition of George Orwell's *1984* and persuaded William Saroyan to change his film script *The Human Comedy* into a novel (published in 1943). Giroux was born to French-Canadian parents in Jersey City, New Jersey, and attended schools in New York City. He studied journalism at Columbia College until he took courses taught by Raymond Weaver and Mark Van Doren. "Weaver was the first biographer of Herman Melville, and the first person to read the manuscript of [Melville's novel] *Billy Budd*, in 1919," Giroux told Donald Hall for the *New York Times Book Review* in 1980. "This left a mark on me. I thought, 'Imagine discovering a literary masterpiece.'" Giroux decided to become an editor, and he graduated in 1936 with a degree in English and comparative literature. Unable to find a position at a book publishing company, he took a job with CBS. Four years later he got an editing position at Harcourt, Brace & Co. His career was put on hold in

1942, when he joined the U.S. Navy. Giroux served aboard the *U.S.S. Essex*, an aircraft carrier, and reached the rank of lieutenant commander before he was discharged, in 1945. He returned to Harcourt, Brace & Co. and became editor in chief in 1948. At Harcourt, Brace Giroux was encouraged to sign contracts for books he considered worthy that had been rejected by other publishers, among them O'Connor's *Wise Blood* (1952) and Bernard Malamud's *The Natural* (1952). In 1955 he became editor in chief of Farrar, Straus & Co. Many of the writers he had worked with at Harcourt, Brace, including Eliot, O'Connor, and Malamud, followed Giroux to his new firm. In 1964 he was made a partner, and the name of the company was changed to Farrar, Straus & Giroux. He served as vice president from 1955 to 1972 and became chairman of the board in 1973. He was also involved with the National Board of Review of Motion Pictures, a nonprofit organization (not connected to the film industry) that fights movie censorship, acting as president from 1975 to 1982. He wrote several books, among them *The Book Known as Q: A Consideration of Shakespeare's Sonnets* (1982) and *A Deed of Death: The Story Behind the Unsolved Murder of Hollywood Director William Desmond Taylor* (1990). His marriage, to Carmen de Arango in 1952, ended in divorce in 1969. Giroux is survived by three nieces. He died in his sleep in Tinton Falls, New Jersey. See *Current Biography* (1982).

Obituary *New York Times* B p6 Sep. 6, 2008

GOHEEN, ROBERT F. Aug. 15, 1919–Mar. 31, 2008 College administrator; educator; diplomat. As president of Princeton University (1957–72), Robert Francis Goheen oversaw the university's rapid progress in gender, ethnic, and racial diversity and its growth in budget, faculty, campus size, and fields of research. Princeton's relatively peaceful handling of its share of Vietnam War–era student protests was in large measure attributable to his wisdom and flexibility. Appointed by President Jimmy Carter, he was U.S. ambassador to India from 1977 to 1980. Goheen was born in Vengurla, India, where his father was a medical missionary. After service in the U.S. Army, he earned a Ph.D. degree in the classics at Princeton (1948). He was an instructor in classics at Princeton until 1950, when he was named an assistant professor. In 1951 he published the book *The Imagery of Sophocles' Antigone*. For several years beginning in 1953 he directed Princeton's Woodrow Wilson Fellowships program. After leaving Princeton's presidency, in 1972, he served successively as president of the Council on Foundations and president of the Edna McConnell Clark Foundation. Beginning in 1981, following his return from India, he was a senior fellow at Princeton's Woodrow Wilson School of Public and International Affairs and director of the Andrew W. Mellon Fellowships program in the humanities for the Woodrow Wilson National Fellowship Foundation. He died of heart failure in Princeton, New Jersey. His survivors included his wife, Margaret (née Skelly), four daughters, two sons, 18 grandchildren, and six great-grandchildren. See *Current Biography* (1958).

Obituary *New York Times* A p21 Apr. 1, 2008

GOULET, ROBERT Nov. 26, 1933–Oct. 30, 2007 Singer and actor. With his dashing good looks and rich, powerful baritone voice, Robert Gerard Goulet attained star status in Canada before he created, with éclat, the role of Sir Lancelot Du Lac in the hit musical *Camelot* on Broadway (1960–63). *Camelot* seemed doomed to box-office failure until, early in its run, the cast appeared on Ed Sullivan's highly popular weekly CBS television variety program and sang a selection of songs from the show, including Goulet's signature solo, "If Ever I Would Leave You." His *Theatre World* Award–winning portrayal of Lancelot launched a robust and long American career for Goulet as a performer in musical theater, television, motion pictures, and cabaret and as a recording artist. Goulet was born in Lawrence, Massachusetts, and grew up in Edmonton, Alberta, Canada. Before and while studying at the Royal Conservatory of Music in Toronto, he began performing on Canadian television as well as on stage and radio, and he became a national matinee idol as co-host from 1955 to 1959 of *Showtime*, the Canadian Broadcasting Corp.'s leading television variety program at the time. In the years following his success as Lancelot on Broadway, he was a familiar figure on U.S. network television, guest-singing on many variety shows and starring in musical specials and TV adaptations of the musicals *Brigadoon* (1966), *Carousel* (1967), and *Kiss Me Kate* (1968). (The *Brigadoon* production received three Emmy Awards.) As an actor on television, Goulet had supporting and minor roles in many dramatic series; starred as David March, the double agent doing intelligence work for the U.S. in Hitler's Third Reich in the CBS adventure series *The Blue Knight* (1966); co-starred in *Acting Sheriff* (a pilot for an aborted series, 1991); and played himself (sometimes only vocally) in episodes of a number of series, including the animated comic show *The Simpsons* (1993) and the partly animated *TV Funhouse* (2000). In 1996 he recorded a set of award-winning promotional spots for the EPSN network. For many years he toured in starring roles in theatrical revivals. Back on Broadway, he won the Tony Award for best actor for his creation of the character Jacques Bonnard in the musical *The Happy Time* in 1968; played King Arthur in a revival of *Camelot* in 1993; replaced Philip Bosco as George Hay in *Moon Over Buffalo* during the 1995–96 theatrical season; and replaced Daniel Davis as Georges in a revival of *La Cage aux Folles* in 1995. As a cabaret performer he was based in Las Vegas, Nevada, where he performed chiefly at the Sands and Frontier Hotels and where he was one of the city's most honored citizens. He made his theatrical film debut as the voice of one of the characters in the animated feature *Gay Purr-ee* (1962). Later he starred as a misplaced bachelor in the screen comedy *Honeymoon Hotel* (1964); was among the supporting players in the comedies *I'd Rather Be Rich* (1964) and *Naked Gun 2 1/2;* and had minor or cameo roles in several other feature films, including *Beetlejuice* (1988). In a cameo in the picture *Atlantic City* (1980), he parodied himself as a lounge singer. As a recording artist he won a Grammy Award in 1962 for his first two albums, which included the hit single "What Kind of Fool Am I?" His single "My Love Forgive Me" went gold in 1964. Seventeen of his three-score Columbia LPs made the charts between 1962 and 1970. He later recorded on the Harmony, RCA, and MGM labels and his own Rove label, for a career total of approximately 75 albums. After his divorce from Louise Longmore, in 1962, Goulet was married to, in 1963, and divorced from, in 1981, the singer Carol Lawrence. Afflicted with interstitial pulmonary fibrosis, he died at Cedars-Sinai Medical Center in Los Angeles while awaiting a lung transplant. His survivors included his third wife, Vera Novak, a daughter from his first marriage, two sons from his second marriage, and two grandchildren. See *Current Biography* (1962).

Obituary *New York Times* C p11 Oct. 31, 2007

GRAY, SIMON Oct. 21, 1936–Aug. 6, 2008 The writer Simon James Holliday Gray was best known for his plays, which often focused on characters set in the academic or publishing worlds. He was also an accomplished memoirist and, for 20 years, taught English at the University of London. Born in Hampshire, England, three years before the outbreak of World War II, Gray was sent along with his brothers to live with their paternal grandparents in Montreal, Canada, for the duration of the war. After they returned to England, Gray attended Portsmouth Grammar School, in Hampshire, before enrolling in Westminster, a prestigious private school in London. In the early 1950s his family moved to Canada. He earned a B.A. degree in English from Dalhousie University, in Halifax, Nova Scotia, in 1957. He then taught English at a university in Clermont-Ferrand, France, for a year. Gray next enrolled at the Trinity College, a division of the University of Cambridge, in England, and earned an M.A. degree in English with honors in 1961. Having won the Harper-Wood Travelling Studentship, he spent six months in Spain. While there he wrote his first novel, *Colmain*, which was published by Faber in 1963. Gray returned to Cambridge to attend St. John's College and Trinity College as a research student and became a supervisor in English at Trinity. In 1965 he joined the English faculty at the Queen Mary College, a branch of the University of London. In the next few years he published short stories and the novels *Simple People* (1965), *Little Portia* (1967), and *A Comeback for Stark* (1968). When one of his short stories was sold for use on television, Gray wrote the adaptation himself; called *The Caramel Crisis*, it aired on BBC-TV in 1966. After he received a rejection letter for his next television play—about a criminal on the run who agrees to impersonate the mother of a troubled young con artist—he turned the script into *Wise Child*, a drama for the legitimate stage. *Wise Child* debuted in London in 1967, with Alec Guinness in the lead role. It ran successfully there but not on Broadway, where, in 1972, it closed after two days. Gray's television play *Death of a Teddy Bear* (1967), which was based on a 1935 murder case, earned him a Writers' Guild Award. (He later adapted that teleplay for the stage; under the title *Molly*, it was mounted in 1978.) *Butley*, which debuted on the London stage in 1971 and was mounted on Broadway the following year, focused on a single, turbulent day in the life of a university lecturer; it won the London *Evening Standard*'s award for best play of the year. Gray's next play, *Otherwise Engaged*, is about a publisher whose plans to spend the evening listening to a recording of the opera *Parsifal* are dashed by annoying guests. *Otherwise Engaged* opened in London in 1975 and in New York in 1977 and brought Gray awards from the New York Drama Critics Circle and the London *Evening Standard*. His most successful Broadway show, it ran for 309 performances. Gray next wrote *The Rear Column* (1978), *Quartermaine's Terms* (1981), *The Common Pursuit* (1984, televised in 1992), *Melon* (1987), and *Cell Mates* (1995). He continued to teach at Queen Mary College until 1985; he later told Nan Robertson for the *New York Times* (February 28, 1983), "It's extremely depressing not to be making progress with writing a play, and I do really deeply love reading poems and plays and the discipline of doing it for and with students. It's stimulating." His most recent plays included *Just the Late Middle Classes* (1999), *Japes* (2000), *The Old Masters* (2004), and *Little Nell*, the last of which was broadcast on BBC Radio 4 in 2006 and produced for the theater in 2007. Gray wrote three books about the staging of his plays: *An Unnatural Pursuit* (1985), *How's That for Telling Them, Fat Lady?* (1988), and *Fat Chance* (1995). He also wrote the memoirs *The Smoking Diaries* (2004), *The Year of the Jouncer* (2006), and *The Last Cigarette* (2008). Gray died in his North London home, after battling prostate cancer and lung cancer. He is survived by his second wife, Victoria Rothschild. From his first marriage, to Beryl Kevern, he has a son and a daughter, who also survive him. See *Current Biography* (1983). — M.A.S.

Obituary *New York Times* B p6 Aug. 8, 2008

GRIZZARD, GEORGE Apr. 1, 1928–Oct. 2, 2007 Actor. The versatile George Grizzard had scores of acting credits on television and a few in motion pictures, but he regarded theater as his true métier. In his Broadway debut, as Hank Griffin in the crime thriller *The Desperate Hours*, he was cited in *Variety*'s poll of drama critics as the most promising actor of 1955. Subsequently on Broadway he won a *Theatre World* award as Angier Duke in the comedy *The Happiest Millionaire* (1956–57) and was nominated for Tony Awards for his portrayals of Shep Stearns in *The Disenchanted* (1958–59) and Ronnie Johnson in the comedy *Big Fish, Little Fish* (1961). He created the role of Nick, the young biology professor, in the original Broadway production (1962–64) of *Who's Afraid of Virginia Woolf?*, Edward Albee's drama about corrosive marital love/hate, and he won the Tony Award for best actor of 1996 for his depiction of Tobias in a revival of another Albee drama, *A Delicate Balance*, about conflict in a suburban family. In another Albee revival, *Seascape* (2005), he starred as Charlie opposite Frances Sternhagen. Also outstanding among his Broadway credits were his portrayal of the tender/tough Tom in a celebrated revival of *The Glass Menagerie* (1965), his varied performances in the musical revue *Noel Coward's Sweet Potato* (1968), and his multiple comic creations in *You Know I Can't Hear You When the Water's Running* (1967–69) and *California Suite* (1976–77). His other Broadway roles included those of the neurotic Harold Rutland Jr. in the courtroom drama *Face of a Hero* (1960), parts in Lanford Wilson's *The Ging-*

ham Dog (1969) and Donald Freed's *Inquest* (1970), Bernie Dodd in a revival of *The Country Girl* (1972), Lucifer in the comedy *The Creation of the World and Other Business* (1972), King Edward VIII in *Crown Matrimonial* (1973), Tony Cavendish in a revival of *The Royal Family* (1975–76), and Judge Haywood in *Judgment at Nuremberg* (2001). In his last stage performance, Off-Off Broadway in 2006, he created the role of Hank Hadley, the fashion designer turned homosexual activist, in the drawing-room comedy *Regrets Only*. Before his Broadway debut Grizzard was a member of the resident company of the Arena Stage, a theater in the round, in Washington, D.C. He later accrued credits as a classical actor during two seasons with Rosemary Harris's Association of Producing Artists and another two seasons with the Tyrone Guthrie Theatre in Minneapolis, where he offered his interpretations of Chekhov and Shakespeare characters, including Hamlet. He made his motion-picture debut as Lex Porter, a wealthy playboy, in *From the Terrace* (1960). His subsequent screen roles included the villainous Senator Fred Ackerman in *Advise and Consent* (1962), the peace-loving Dr. Norbert Woodley in *Happy Birthday, Wanda June* (1971), the Western oilman Neil Atkinson in *Comes a Horseman* (1978), Leo Gelhorn in *Firepower* (1979), Stanley in *Neil Simon's Seems Like Old Times* (1980), Mr. Thompson in *Bachelor Party* (1984), Fred Leer in *Wonder Boys* (2000), George Blint in *Small Time Crooks* (2000), and John Bradley in *Flags of Our Fathers* (2006). On television he had roles in teleplays on such early anthology showcases as *Goodyear Playhouse*, in some made-for-TV movies, and in episodes in adventure, comedy, and other series, including *Law & Order*. He was nominated for an Emmy Award for his performance as John Adams in the historical miniseries *The Adams Chronicles* (PBS, 1976), and he won an Emmy for his supporting role in the drama *The Oldest Living Graduate* (NBC, 1980). Grizzard died at New York-Presbyterian Hospital/Weill Cornell Medical Center in New York City. He was survived by William Tynan, his companion. See *Current Biography* (1976).

Obituary *New York Times* A p23 Oct. 3, 2007

GUTHMAN, EDWIN O. Aug. 11, 1919–Aug. 31, 2008 Edwin Otto Guthman was a Pulitzer Prize–winning journalist. The son of a grocery sales manager, he was born and raised in Seattle, Washington. He served as editor of his student newspaper at Broadway High School and later wrote for the now-defunct *Seattle Star* while attending the University of Washington. After earning a B.S. degree in journalism, in 1941, Guthman served in the army, where he took part in fighting in North Africa and Italy and was awarded the Purple Heart and Silver Star. He was discharged with the rank of captain in 1945. The following year he rejoined the *Seattle Star* as a general-assignment reporter. He became assistant city editor in 1947 and, later that year, left the *Star* to become a general-assignment and political reporter for the *Seattle Times*. According to an obituary in the *Seattle Weekly* (September 2, 2008, on-line), "Injustice was always on his radar." In 1949 he wrote a series of articles about Melvin Rader, a professor of philosophy at the University of Washington, whom the Washington State legislature's Committee on Un-American Activities, chaired by Representative Albert Canwell of Spokane, had accused of being a Communist. Guthman provided evidence that proved that Rader—who had denied the charge and refused to name others who he knew had joined the Communist Party—had been at a resort in Washington State at the time that a witness claimed Rader had attended a Communist Party training session in New York. Guthman won the 1950 Pulitzer Prize for national reporting for that series, and the Washington State Press Club honored him with its award for distinguished reporting. In 1950–51 he was a Neiman fellow at Harvard University. He continued working for the *Times* until 1961, when, in the administration of President John F. Kennedy, he became the public information director of the U.S. Department of Justice, headed by Attorney General Robert F. Kennedy; he had become acquainted with the latter Kennedy in the 1950s, when he investigated the activities of Dave Beck, the head of the International Brotherhood of Teamsters, who was prosecuted for embezzlement and racketeering and later served jail time for income-tax evasion. In 1962, as a representative of the Justice Department, Guthman watched as angry mobs stoned federal marshals assigned to protect James Meredith, the first African-American to be admitted to the University of Mississippi. In a famous exchange over the phone, when the attorney general asked him, "How's it going down there?," Guthman replied, "Pretty rough. It's getting like the Alamo." Kennedy responded, "Well, you know what happened to those guys, don't you?"—a quip that Guthman later said boosted the his morale and that of others overseeing Meredith's entrance into the university. Guthman later served as Kennedy's spokesman and press secretary during Kennedy's successful run for a seat in the U.S. Senate and for some time afterward. His name appeared on President Richard Nixon's "enemies list," on which he was described as "a highly sophisticated hatchet man against us in '68." In 1965 Guthman became the national-news editor for the *Los Angeles Times*; for 10 years beginning in 1977, he served the *Philadelphia Inquirer* as editorial-page editor. From 1987 to 2007 he taught as a distinguished professor of journalism at the Annenberg School for Communication at the University of Southern California in Los Angeles. He wrote *We Band of Brothers: A Memoir of Robert F. Kennedy* (1971) and co-edited *Robert Kennedy in His Own Words* (1988) and *RFK: Collected Speeches* (1993). He was a founding member of the Los Angeles City Ethics Commission and served as its president during its earliest days (1997–98). In 1993 he was chosen to serve on a three-person independent panel to review the Treasury Department's investigation into the raid of the Branch Davidian compound in Waco, Texas, by federal agents that resulted in the deaths of 82 people. Guthman retired in 2007. He died of amyloidosis in his Los Angeles home. He was predeceased by his wife, JoAnn Cheim, and was survived by three sons, a daughter and five grandchildren. See *Current Biography* (1950). — M.A.S.

Obituary *New York Times* D p8 Sep. 2, 2008

GYGAX, GARY July 27, 1938–March 4, 2008 Game designer; writer. Ernest Gary Gygax was, with Dave Arneson, co-claimant to the title of father of the contemporary interactive role-playing game (RPG). In the early 1970s Gygax, in collaboration with Arneson, developed his signature creation, the sword-and-sorcery RPG *Dungeons & Dragons*, or *D&D*, the most popular and influential entry in hobby-gaming history. *D&D* not only inspired scores of imitative tabletop pen-and-paper games but was a key inspiration in the development of a $1.5 billion electronic-gaming industry. Attracting millions of young gamers, *D&D* helped shape what has been called "the entire geek subculture," which in turn has exerted great influence in the wider world. *D&D* has been described as "interactive storytelling with dice rolls." Moderated by a dungeon master, each of the participants assumes a fictional gothic persona—such as a paladin, wizard, or elf—and embarks on a heroic quest in a Middle Earth virtual world filled with mythical creatures, where the players slay dragons and overcome other obstacles as they proceed in accordance with the rolls of polyhedral dice. "If there is a story to be told," Gygax once explained, "it comes from the interaction of all participants." A high-school dropout, Gygax had been a prodigy at chess and other games from early childhood. He was also steeped in the reading of fantasy and science fiction and interested in the history of the Dark Ages. While he worked as an insurance underwriter in Wisconsin during the 1960s, his favorite hobby was playing miniature war games with his friends. In 1966 he helped to organize the first meeting of the International Federation of Wargamers, which took place in the basement of his home in Lake Geneva, Wisconsin. Two years later he founded the annual hobby-gaming convention Gen Con, and he subsequently formed the Castle and Crusade Society, specializing in medieval-themed variants of war games. With Jeff Perrin, he created one such variant, called *Chainmail*, and published *Chainmail: Rules for Medieval Miniatures* in 1971. At that point Dave Arneson entered the picture, helping Gygax to improve *Chainmail* with scenarios that enhanced "the element of 'role-playing' . . . the feeling of really 'being' a medieval warrior" to an "almost unprecedented" degree, as the games historian Allen Rausch wrote. Together they created *Blackmoor*, which became one of the major settings for *Dungeons & Dragons*. With Don Kaye providing the funding (along with Brian Blume), Kaye and Gygax formed the company TSR Hobbies Inc. (originally called Tactical Studies Rules), which published the first version of *Dungeons & Dragons* in 1974 and *Advanced Dungeons & Dragons*, with far more complex rules, in 1977. A third edition of *D&D* followed. Beginning in 1979 Arneson filed five lawsuits against Gygax and TSR Hobbies Inc.; they were settled out of court in 1981. Independently of TSR Hobbies Inc., Gygax negotiated with the CBS television network the creation of a cartoon series spin-off of *D&D* that ran for three years beginning in 1983. In 1985 Gygax lost control of *D&D* and relinquished his interest in TSR Hobbies Inc., and the company later sued him over the rights to his RPG *Dangerous Journeys*. He returned to writing role-play games in 1999 with *Lejendary Adventures* and six years later to working on

D&D, a fourth edition of which was published in 2008. In addition to his *D&D* players' handbooks, dungeon-masters' guides, and monster manuals, he wrote in his last years five "Gygaxian" books on "how to construct a fantasy world." He also published fantasy novels, most of which were based on RPG scenarios, including the Greyhawk series and, in collaboration with Flint Dille, the Sagard the Barbarian series. He was not directly involved in the production of the motion picture *Dungeons & Dragons* (2001). After his divorce from his first wife, Mary Jo, Gygax in 1987 married Gail Carpenter, who survived him. His other survivors included two sons and three daughters from his first marriage and a son from his second marriage. Diagnosed with an abdominal aortic aneurysm and having suffered two strokes, he died at his home in Lake Geneva, Wisconsin. See *Current Biography* (2007).

Obituary *New York Times* C p11 Mar. 5, 2008

HABASH, GEORGE Aug. 2, 1925–Jan. 26, 2008 Palestinian revolutionary; physician. George Habash was one of the earliest, most radical, and least compromising leaders of the so-called Palestine revolution, the movement calling for armed force in the struggle for "the liberation of Palestine." A pan-Arabist, he viewed that struggle in the context of a wider uprising against Western imperialism and those perceived by him as complicit in it, including Arab regimes as well as Zionists. A Marxist, he held "the Guevara view" of the "revolutionary human being . . . a new breed of man" emerging "among the Arabs as everywhere else." In the early 1950s he co-founded the Arab Nationalist Movement (ANM, sometimes referred to as the Arab Nationalists' Movement), the precursor of the Popular Front for the Liberation of Palestine (PFLP), of which he was the founding secretary general (1967–2000). The PFLP, the second-largest of the factions in the loose affiliation called the Palestine Liberation Organization (PLO), is a secular political/military organization more leftist and hard-line than the larger Al Fatah group co-founded by Yasir Arafat in 1965. Originally, Arafat was a guerrilla chief seeking, in effect, the displacement of Israel from the territory of the historic Palestine, which he viewed as the rightful Palestinian Arab homeland. Over the years Arafat became more conciliatory, seemingly accepting the idea of a two-state solution to the Israeli-Palestinian conflict and signing the Oslo peace accords, which Habash did not accept. A native of Lod (also spelled Lydda) in what is now Israel, Habash was born into a Christian (Greek Orthodox) Arab family that was displaced by the creation of the Israeli state, in 1948. Politically radicalized, he began to discuss with other students "how to return to Palestine" while he was studying medicine at the American University in Beirut, Lebanon. With Hani al Hindi and others, he founded the ANM in 1951 and began recruiting and training guerrillas for attacking targets in Israel. Expelled from Lebanon, he and his ANM associates found a patron in President Gamal Abdel Nasser of Egypt. With the financial backing of Nasser, they set up a medical clinic in Amman, Jordan, that chiefly met the medical needs of the poor, gratis. At the same time it served as a base of operations for creating military/political cells elsewhere, including Saudi Arabia, Kuwait, and Libya (Habash later developed close ties with the Libyan dictator Muammar al-Qaddafi), and for helping to promote Nasser's goal of a pan-Arab superstate that would surround Israel. (The closest Nasser came to that goal was the inclusion of Syria in the United Arab Republic—a k a Egypt—from 1958 to 1961.) Implicated in a plot to overthrow King Hussein of Jordan in 1957, Habash fled to Damascus, Syria, where he set up another medical clinic and remained for six years. Expelled from Syria by the Baathists in 1963, he moved to Lebanon and went underground in Beirut. Trusting in Nasser's plan for a conventional war against Israel, he believed at that time in suspending guerrilla attacks on Israel, a point on which Yasir Arafat disagreed. After Israel defeated the combined forces of Egypt, Jordan, Syria, and Iraq in 1967, in the Six-Day War, Habash and his associates underwent "a full revolution in . . . thought," as he explained: "We decided to adopt the Vietnamese model: a strong political party, complete mobilization of the people, and the principle of not depending on any regime or government." Deploring the "backwardness in the Arab world," he embraced the cause of "the total rebuilding of Arab society." In 1967, after failing to reach an agreement on strategy with Arafat's Al Fatah, he and his associates formed the PFLP, a Marxist-Leninist group dedicated to destroying "the troika of Zionism, imperialism, and Arab reaction." A long series of acts of terrorism by the PFLP (masterminded by Habash's deputy Wadi Haddad rather than Habash, who was more ideologue than tactician) began in 1968 and included passenger-plane hijackings. The most spectacular of the hijackings took place on September 6, 1970, when four planes bound for New York were seized simultaneously. After the passengers disembarked, the planes were blown up, three of them in Jordan, which PFLP guerrillas had been using as a staging ground for commando raids into Israel. Driven out of Jordan by King Hussein's army, Habash and the PFLP moved their base of operations back to Lebanon. After Wadi Haddad's death, in 1978, Habash announced that the PFLP would continue its guerrilla operations but would try to avoid "collateral damage" to civilians and "third-party" groups "not directly aiding Zionism." When Israel invaded Lebanon in 1982, he and the PFLP moved back to Syria, where the regime had changed. Hunted by Israeli military intelligence for decades, Habash narrowly escaped capture on two occasions, in 1973 and 1986. In a debate among Palestinian factions in 1988, he argued that the withdrawal of Israel from Gaza and the West Bank would "solve the problem for the great masses who live there. But we will be misleading ourselves if we believe that this will solve the Palestinian problem." From 1992 on Habash lived in relative quiet in Jordan with his wife, Leila, who had been born there. During the last years of his life, he was hobbled and often bedridden with health problems (including cancer and partial paralysis after brain surgery); at the same time he was marginalized politically by the rise of Palestinian Islamist militant groups, such as Hamas, and by disagreements with elements within his own organization, some more radical than he (several of which became splinter groups) and others more moderate. He resigned as secretary general of the PFLP after the organization came to an agreement with the PLO leadership in 1999 regarding negotiations with Israel. Habash died of a heart attack in Amman, Jordan, days after he had entered Jordan Hospital for surgery. He was survived by his wife and two daughters. See *Current Biography* (1988).

Obituary *New York Times* A p21 Jan. 27, 2008

HARDWICK, ELIZABETH July 27, 1916–Dec. 2, 2007 Author; essayist, short-story writer, and novelist. Kentucky-born Elizabeth Bruce Hardwick was one of the last surviving members of the mid-20th century circle of brilliant, hard-partying Manhattan literati headed by such figures as Edmund Wilson and Philip Rahv and including the likes of Robert Lowell—the celebrated but mentally and emotionally tormented—and tormenting—poet to whom she, genteel and long-suffering, was turbulently married for 23 years (1949–72). Her richest legacy is her trove of informed, thoughtful, often fierce and acerbic literary essays written in a lean, condensed style, including many with illuminating social and cultural criticism, some of it about wronged and tortured women in literature, from Charlotte Brontë and Jane Carlyle to Sylvia Plath. "Although her Proustian-postmodernist novel *Sleepless Nights*, the book-with-buzz of 1979, survives as a revered if neglected classic, her finest work is her criticism and essays," David Gates wrote of Hardwick for *Newsweek* (December 6, 2007). "As [David] Laskin indicates, she was never a confessional writer. You didn't get to know her, only her witty, steely, incisive, and often daring literary voice." Hardwick arrived in New York City in 1939 to pursue graduate studies in literature (never completed) at Columbia University. In 1945 she published her first novel, *The Ghostly Lover*, a partly autobiographical story about a large middle-class Kentucky family with entangled relationships and poor intercommunication told from the perspective of a daughter thwarted in her pursuit of self-realization. In 1955 she published her second novel, *The Simple Truth*, which centered on the trial of a poor, midwestern male college student accused of murdering his rich girlfriend and on the contrasting perspectives of townspeople serving on the jury and two observers from the academic community. Both of those novels drew lukewarm commercial and critical receptions. Hardwick had far greater success with her last and most personal novel, the slim, plotless *Sleepless Nights* (1979), an inventive, nonlineal patchwork of free-associated, episodic memories narrated by her alter ego, an old insomniac woman in a nursing home reflecting on her life. In rave reviews, that book was described as "intelligent," "elegant, wise, tasty," and "subtle and beautiful." In the mid-1940s Hardwick began writing book reviews for Phil Rahv's then highly influential *Partisan Review* and contributing short stories to the *New Yorker* and *Sewanee Review*. (Two of the short stories won O. Henry Memorial Awards and several others were selected for inclusion in other prize-story anthologies.) Hardwick later became a regular contributor to *Harper's* magazine. In 1963, with Jason Epstein, Robert Lowell, and others, she co-founded the *New York Review of Books,* in which her literary es-

says appeared regularly until 2003. Hardwick's essays were collected in *A View of My Own: Essays on Literature and Society* (1962), *Seduction and Betrayal: Women and Literature* (1974), *A New America?* (1978), *Bartleby in Manhattan* (1983), *Sight Readings: American Fiction* (1998), and *American Fictions* (1999). She edited *The Selected Letters of William James* (1980). Her last book was the biography *Herman Melville* (2000). Hardwick taught creative writing at Barnard College from 1964 to 1985 and lived in an apartment on West 67th Street in Manhattan from 1960 until her death. She died in her sleep at Roosevelt Hospital in Manhattan, where she had been admitted for treatment of a minor infection. She was survived by her daughter, Harriet Winslow Lowell. See *Current Biography* (1981).

Obituary *New York Times* A p29 Dec. 5, 2007

HARRISON, GILBERT A. May 8, 1915–Jan. 3, 2008 Magazine publisher and editor; liberal activist. For a score of years beginning in 1953, Gilbert Avery Harrison was owner and editor in chief of the *New Republic* (*TNR*). That distinguished Washington, D.C.–based fortnightly (originally a weekly) was founded in 1914 to "liberalize and leaven American political and social opinion" through topical commentary addressed to a select readership. In its pages the *New Republic* pioneered the transformation of the term "liberal" from its classical laissez-faire denotation to its current usage, including the connotation of a greater openness to government intervention in domestic and world affairs. As the current editor of *TNR*, Franklin Foer, has observed, one of the publication's "historical legacies and obligations" is "to be involved in the ongoing debate over what liberalism means and stands for." In that debate it has on many occasions departed from liberal orthodoxy as defined by that other preeminent American journal of liberal opinion, the *Nation*, the self-described "flagship of the left." Those departures have usually been not on social issues but in centrist or center-left positions on fiscal issues and a hawkish stance in foreign affairs, including the 1991 Persian Gulf war and the war in Iraq. Under Harrison's watch *TNR* was a Cold War hawk but an opponent of the war in Vietnam and a fierce critic of Democratic president Lyndon B. Johnson and Republican president Richard Nixon and their prosecution of that war. In its early years the magazine supported President Theodore Roosevelt's Progressive movement, and for three decades it viewed Soviet Communism positively. In 1932 it backed the Socialist presidential candidate Norman Thomas. Beginning with Franklin D. Roosevelt in 1936, it generally backed Democratic candidates, but in 1968 it refused to support Hubert H. Humphrey, Johnson's hand-picked choice for his successor as president. Instead, it proposed the creation of a peace party with Senator Eugene J. McCarthy as its candidate. (*TNR* again defected from the Democratic fold in the presidential election of 1980, when it endorsed the maverick Republican John B. Anderson, who was running as an Independent, rather than the incumbent president, Jimmy Carter.) Under Harrison, *TNR* was also a strong voice for civil rights. During his last five years as publisher of *TNR*, he also owned the Liveright Publishing

Corp. (1969–74). Harrison served in the U.S. Army Air Forces during World War II and co-founded the American Veterans Committee AVC), a liberal association offering veterans of World War II an alternative to the conservative American Legion and Veterans of Foreign Wars. He served as national vice chairman of the AVC in 1946–47 and as chairman in 1947–48. (The AVC, whose motto was "Citizens First, Veterans Second," is now defunct.) In the course of his travels in pursuit of funding for the AVC, in Chicago in 1950 Harrison met the heiress Anne McCormick Blaine, the great-great-granddaughter of Cyrus McCormick, the inventor of the reaper and founder of the McCormick Harvesting Machine Co., which ultimately merged into the International Harvester Co. He and Anne McCormick Blaine were married in 1951. Two years later they bought the *New Republic*. After the sale of the magazine to Martin H. Peretz, in 1974, Harrison remained on as editor in chief for several months, into 1975, when Peretz moved into that position. Peretz remained editor in chief after selling his shares in *TNR* to others, chiefly the Canadian corporation Can West Media Works International, which became the controlling shareholder in 2007. Gilbert Harrison was the author of two biographies, *A Timeless Affair* (1979), about his wife, and *The Enthusiast* (1983), about Thornton Wilder. Harrison died of congestive heart failure at the Hospice of the Valley in Scottsdale, Arizona. He was predeceased by his wife and survived by three sons, a daughter, and five grandchildren. See *Current Biography* (1949).

Obituary *New York Times* C p14 Jan. 8, 2008

HARTFORD, HUNTINGTON Apr. 18, 1911–May 19, 2008 Heir to the A&P supermarket fortune; aesthete; dilettantish cultural impresario; café society gentleman of leisure. The rich-by-inheritance and prodigal eccentric George Huntington Hartford 2d was the namesake of his paternal grandfather, who founded the Great Atlantic & Pacific Tea Co. with George Gilman in 1859 and gained full control of the giant grocery chain following Gilman's death, in 1901.When his grandfather died, in 1917, Huntington Hartford received in trust 10 percent of the existing shares of A&P stock. Following the deaths of his parents and two uncles, he came into his full inheritance, estimated at $95 million, most of which he would fritter away in myriad short-lived arts and cultural ventures and in the costs of his amorous pursuits, including the more expensive of the divorce settlements that terminated his four marriages. His life and times are recounted by Lisa Rebecca Gubernick in her book *Squandered Fortune* (1990). As a young man Hartford earned a B.S. degree in English at Harvard University; was married to and divorced from his first wife, Mary Lee (née Epling); worked briefly as a reporter for the experimental New York City daily tabloid newspaper *PM* (in which he had invested $100,000); and served in the U.S. Coast Guard during World War II. After the war he settled in Los Angeles, where he founded the Hartford Model Agency in 1947 and began investing in motion-picture productions. In nearby Pacific Palisades in 1949, he created a $600,000 retreat for artists, writers, and composers, and to sustain that colony he founded the Hunting-

ton Hartford Foundation. He produced the films *Hello Out There* (1949) and *Face to Face* (1953), in both of which his second wife, Marjorie Sue (née Steele), starred. He spent $1 million converting an old Los Angeles movie house into the Huntington Hartford Theater, which opened in 1954 with a production of *What Every Woman Knows*, starring Helen Hayes. He also produced several Broadway shows, including *The Master of Thornfield* (1958), his own adaptation of *Jane Eyre*. Between 1961 and 1973 he spent an estimated $8 million publishing the arts and entertainment magazine *Show*. Beginning in 1959 he spent $30 million to buy and develop Hog Island in the Bahamas, which he turned into the jet-set resort Paradise Island (including the Ocean Club, favored by international celebrities); he later sold it for about a third of his investment. Meanwhile he had long been publicly voicing his antipathy to the prevailing hegemony of abstract expressionism in art and amassing a personal collection of representational works, including paintings by Rembrandt, Monet, Turner, and Sargent as well as paintings by Salvador Dali commissioned by him. To house and showcase his collection, he commissioned Edward Durrell Stone to design a 10-story building that would pointedly counter the International modern style in architecture responsible for the starkly rectangular glass-and-steel boxes dominating contemporary metropolitan skylines. The result, costing $7.4 million, was the quirky Huntington Hartford Museum, which opened at 2 Columbus Circle in Manhattan in 1964. While ornamented with porthole-like openings, the white marble structure, with the notable exception of its penthouse overlooking Central Park, had few windows and was variously described as a "queer" architectural "bonbon" and "a die-cut Venetian palazzo on lollipops." Disappointed with the lack of public interest in the museum, Hartford gave the building to Fairleigh Dickinson University in 1969. (It was later acquired by the Gulf & Western conglomerate, which donated it to New York City in 1976. For a quarter of a century thereafter, the building was occupied by New York City's Department of Cultural Affairs; then, in 2003, the city sold it to the Museum of Arts and Design, which made modifications to it before occupying it, in 2008.) Interested in graphology, Hartford founded the Handwriting Institute Inc. and wrote the book *You Are What You Write* (1975). With Herbert Linden, he founded the Oil Shale Corp., a company devoted to researching an alternative way to obtain oil. Now called Tosco, that corporation is currently owned by ConocoPhilips Inc. During his fourth marriage, to Elaine (née Kay), according to his daughter Juliet (from his third marriage, to the former Diane Brown), Hartford descended into a life of dissolute drug abuse. He filed for bankruptcy in 1992 and lived during his final years on a trust fund administered for him. He was living as a recluse in a poor Brooklyn neighborhood when his daughter went to his rescue in 2000; she took him back to the Bahamas with her in 2004. Juliet survived him, as did his son, John, from his second marriage. His daughter Catherine, from his second marriage, predeceased him, as did his son Buzz (from an extramarital one-night stand), who (according to Juliet) committed suicide. Hartford died at the home he shared with Juliet in Lyford Cay, the Bahamas. See *Current Biography* (1959).

Obituary *New York Times* B p8 May 20, 2008

HARTZOG, GEORGE Mar. 17, 1920–June 27, 2008 Government official; lawyer. George Benjamin Hartzog Jr. was director of the U.S. National Park Service from 1964 to 1972. Identified with the expansionist policies of President Lyndon B. Johnson and his secretary of the interior, Stewart L. Udall, Hartzog oversaw the reorganization of the NPS and the doubling of the number of its parks, wildlife refuges, and national monuments. After serving with the U.S. Army during World War II, Hartzog joined the Department of the Interior, the parent department of the NPS, as an attorney. Moving to NPS field assignments, he was assistant superintendent of the Rocky Mountain National Park from 1955 to 1957 and assistant superintendent of the Great Smoky Mountains National Park from 1957 to 1959. As charter superintendent of the Jefferson National Expansion Memorial in St. Louis, Missouri, beginning in 1959, he directed development of that site for more than three years. He served as executive director of Downtown St. Louis Inc., a private urban renewal agency, from July 1962 to February 1963, when he returned to the NPS as associate director in February 1963. Eleven months later, in December 1964, he became director. During his first two years as director, he completed a program called Mission '66, which not only concentrated on the construction of roads and facilities but also added to the NPS system 49 areas, including the Cape Cod National Seashore and the Virgin Islands National Park. He played an important role in drafting and pushing passage of the National Historic Preservation Act of 1966. He devised and in 1966 began implementing Parkscape U.S.A., a six-year program for expanding the NPS to include urban parklands and for making the service generally more relevant to urban society. Hartzog also began accelerating the advancement of women and minorities to positions of authority in the NPS. The first black man to head the U.S. Park Police was Grant Wood, appointed by Hartzog in 1968. Among the others whose careers benefited from the acceleration was Robert Stanton, who would advance over the years from park superintendent and regional director to become the first black director of the NPS (1997–2001). During Hartzog's tenure the NPS acquired 72 new sites covering a total of 2.7 million acres. The greatest of the urban recreation areas acquired were Gateway (New York City) and Golden Gate (San Francisco), both in 1972. After Richard M. Nixon succeeded Lyndon B. Johnson to the presidency, Hartzog had a number of policy disputes with the White House. During the summer of 1972, the superintendent of the Biscayne National Park in Florida revoked a permit allowing a friend of President Nixon's, Charles "Bebe" Rebozo—or a relative of Rebozo's, according to differing accounts—to dock his boat in the park. The incident led Nixon to fire Hartzog, effective December 31, 1972. After leaving government Hartzog practiced law, concentrating on environmental cases. With U.S. senator Alan Bible, he worked on legislation that culminated in the Alaska National Interest Lands Conservation Act of 1980. He published his autobiography, *Battling for the National Parks*, in 1988. Hertzog died at the Virginia Hospital Center in Arlington, of complications of kidney disease and diabetes. He was survived by his wife, Helen (née Carlson), a daughter, two sons, four grandchildren, and a great-granddaughter. See *Current Biography* (1970).

Obituary *New York Times* B p7 July 17, 2008

HAWKINS, A. F. Aug. 31, 1907–Nov. 10, 2007 Democratic politician and government leader. Although he was so fair-skinned that he was often assumed to be a person of predominantly if not strictly European ancestry, Augustus Freeman ("Gus") Hawkins could claim the distinction of being California's first black representative in the U.S. Congress. The Louisiana-born Hawkins received a B.A. degree in economics at the University of California at Los Angeles in 1931. As a member of the California State Assembly (1935–63), he introduced or helped in the passage of such legislation as the Fair Employment Practices Act of 1959. He decided to run for Congress in 1962 because, as he explained, "many of the issues with which I am deeply concerned, such as Medicare and low-cost housing, transcend the national level." He served 14 terms in the U.S. House of Representatives, representing California's 21st Congressional District from 1963 to 1975 and its 29th C.D. from 1975 to 1991. In the House he chaired the Committee on House Administration (during the 97th and 98th Congresses) and the Education and Labor Committee's Subcommittee on Employment Opportunities (during the 98th and 101st Congresses). He also chaired the House/Senate joint committees on printing (during the 96th and 98th Congresses) and on the Library of Congress (during the 97th Congress). In 1971 he became vice chairman of the newly formed Congressional Black Caucus. A civil rights and social-welfare champion, he wrote Title VII of the Civil Rights Act of 1964, the Juvenile Justice and Delinquency Prevention Act of 1974, and the Youth Employment and Demonstration Projects Act of 1977; helped draft the Community Services Act of 1975; and introduced the House version of the Pregnancy Disability Act of 1978. Also in 1978 he was the House floor manager of legislation extending the Comprehensive Employment and Training Act. He was best known as the co-sponsor, with Senator Hubert H. Humphrey, of the Humphrey-Hawkins Full Employment and Balanced Growth Act of 1978. While increasingly opposing President Lyndon B. Johnson's pursuit of the war in Vietnam, he consistently supported Johnson's Great Society programs. Following the 1965 riot in the South Central Los Angeles neighborhood of Watts (the heart of his district), he obtained substantial amounts of federal antipoverty money for his constituents. He later wrote and saw passage of an amendment to the Higher Education Act allocating increased funding for minority colleges and successfully sponsored legislation to continue the School Lunch and Nutrition Program. To approximately the same degree that he supported Johnson's domestic legislation, he opposed that of the administration of President Ronald Reagan during the 1980s. Among his other accomplishments, he succeeded in restoring the honorable discharges of the 170 black soldiers of the U.S. Army's 25th Regiment falsely accused of disorderly conduct in Brownsville, Texas, in 1906. He chose not to seek reelection in 1990. Several years after the death of his first wife, Pegga Adeline (née Smith), Hawkins married Elsie Taylor, who predeceased him. His survivors included two stepdaughters and a stepson. He died in Bethesda, Maryland. Named in his honor is the Augustus F. Hawkins Natural Park, an 8.5-acre green oasis—formerly an industrial wasteland—in the Compton section of Los Angeles County, California. See *Current Biography* (1983).

Obituary *New York Times* B p11 Nov. 14, 2007

HAYES, ISAAC Aug. 20, 1942–Aug. 10, 2008 Singer; songwriter. Isaac Hayes was a major contributor to the version of soul music known as "the Memphis sound," which began to emerge from Stax Records in Memphis, Tennessee, in the late 1960s and early 1970s. In addition to the music he composed and arranged for others at Stax, with his own recordings Hayes was a trendsetter not only in R&B but also in disco and rap music, both of which he anticipated, and he pioneered the creation of the concept album among soul artists. With his breakthrough LP, *Hot Buttered Soul* (1969), Hayes signaled the course of his whole career, breaching industry (and radio-play) custom by recording not three- or four-minute tracks but lengthier offerings, including stretched-out covers of pop and R&B romantic standards embellished by his deep, sensuous voice. He peaked early, with his music for the fast-paced blaxploitation motion picture *Shaft* (1971), which brought him an Academy Award and two Grammys. Unable to read music, Hayes composed at the piano, leaving the notation on paper to others. Born into poverty in Covington, Tennessee, Isaac Lee Hayes Jr. was raised by his maternal grandparents there and in Memphis, Tennessee. While in high school in North Memphis, he sang with various local gospel, rock, and rhythm groups. Teaching himself to play the piano and the saxophone, he subsequently worked musical gigs wherever he could find them in and around Memphis. In 1964 he joined the Memphis-based label Stax Records, also known as Stax/Enterprise. Hired as a sessions musician at Stax, he backed Otis Redding, among other recording artists. He soon became a house composer and arranger as well, in partnership with David Porter. At Stax Records Hayes and Porter composed most of Sam and Dave's hits, including "Soul Man," "When Something Is Wrong with My Baby," and "I Thank You" as well as songs for such artists as Carla Thomas, the Soul Children, and Johnnie Taylor. Together, Hayes and Porter wrote some 200 R&B songs, including "You Don't Know Like I Know" and "Hold On, I'm Coming." Singing and accompanying himself on the organ and backed by a drummer and bass player, Hayes recorded his first album as a solo artist, *Presenting Isaac Hayes*, released by Stax in 1967. That LP drew relatively little attention at first, beginning to gain sales only in the wake of the success of his next album, *Hot Buttered Soul*, two years later. The jacket of *Hot Buttered Soul* showed a flamboyant photograph of Hayes with bald head, dark glasses, bare chest, and a plethora of gold jewelry. The longest

track on the album was Hayes's 18-minute 40-second cover of "By the Time I Get to Phoenix." Several of the cuts became hit singles, including his version of "Walk on By," which crossed over from the R&B to the pop charts, as did his subsequent covers of "Something" and "You've Lost That Loving Feeling." Hayes recorded the soundtrack for *Shaft* in four days with several members of a house band, the Bar-Keys, on a soundstage at Stax. Reflecting the fast action of the movie, the sweeping orchestral arrangement (prefiguring disco) was driven by Charles "Skip" Pitts's relentless wah-wah riffs on the guitar punctuated by a high-hat cymbal, and Hayes's sexy voice was reinforced by breathless backup singers. Released in July 1971 on Stax Records' Enterprise label, the double album *Shaft* became the best-known and best-selling LP in Stax history. It reached the number-one spot on *Billboard*'s 200 chart, where it spent six weeks, and both "Theme from *Shaft*" and the track "Do Your Thing" rose to number one on *Billboard*'s Hot 100 singles chart. At the presentation of the Grammy Awards in March 1972, *Shaft* was honored as the best original score for a motion picture and "Theme from *Shaft*" won the Grammys for best instrumental arrangement and best engineered nonclassical recording. At the Academy Awards ceremony in April 1972, Hayes appeared on stage twice: the first time, wearing a gold chain vest over a bare chest, he performed "Theme from *Shaft*"; later, in a tuxedo, he reappeared to accept the Oscar for best song for "Theme from *Shaft*." Meanwhile, in December 1971, Stax had released the two-record concept album *Black Moses*, the title of which was a label bestowed on Hayes by fans. That album included covers of such songs as "I'll Never Fall in Love Again" and "For the Good Times." In the course of his career, Hayes recorded a score of albums, including *The Isaac Hayes Movement, Live at the Sahara Tahoe, Joy, Chocolate Chip, Juicy Fruit, For the Sake of Love, Don't Let Go, And Once Again,* and *Lifetime Thing*. Several of the LPs were devoted to disco music. In the mid-1970s both Stax Records and Hayes declared bankruptcy, and many of Hayes's assets were liquidated by the U.S. Internal Revenue Service. Hayes subsequently recorded on the ABC, Polydor, Columbia, and Pointblank labels as well as his own label, HBS. In 2002 he was inducted into the Rock 'n' Roll Hall of Fame. In the late 1970s he had a recurring role as the ex-con Gandolph Fitch in the TV series *The Rockford Files*. Hayes had a cameo role in the movie *Shaft* (that of a bartender), and he accrued many acting credits in motion pictures from the early 1980s on. He became best known to a new generation of television viewers as the voice of the character Jerome "Chef" McElroy, a school cook, in the Comedy Central animated series *South Park* from 1997 to 2006; in the latter year the show, which often mocked organized religion, lampooned the Church of Scientology, to which he belonged. (Also in 2006 he suffered a serious stroke.) Hayes did stints as a radio disk jockey, owned two restaurants, published a cookbook, and was engaged in humanitarian work (including the promotion of literacy) through the Isaac Hayes Foundation. He was married four times and had 12 children. His many survivors included his fourth wife, Adowa (whom he met in Ghana), and their son, Kwajdo. He died at home in the Memphis, Tennessee, suburb of Cordova. See *Current Biography* (1972).

Obituary *New York Times* B p6 Aug. 11, 2008

HELMS, JESSE Oct. 18, 1921-July 4, 2008 Jesse A. Helms, a Republican who represented North Carolina in the U.S. Senate, was considered an icon to many political conservatives. During his 31 years in Congress he focused largely on the issues of crime, drug abuse, taxes, and deficit spending. His nickname "Senator No" denoted his practice of blocking nominations and legislation that went against his conservative beliefs. He fought against civil rights and gay rights and introduced a 1973 amendment to the Foreign Assistance Act that blocked funding for international family planning organizations that, in his opinion, promoted abortion. In addition, he sought to reduce or eliminate money for welfare programs and the arts. Helms also enjoyed forcing roll-call votes, which recorded the vote of each senator and often caused Democrats to rethink their stances on controversial cultural issues, such as flag burning and school busing. He was born Jesse Alexander Helms Jr. in Monroe, North Carolina; his first ambition was to become a journalist. He attended college for a brief time before dropping out to work as a reporter for the *News and Observer* in Raleigh, North Carolina. After serving in the Navy during World War II, he became the news and program director at WRAL, a Raleigh radio station, in 1948. Three years later he moved to Washington, D.C., to work in Democratic senator Willis Smith's office as an administrative assistant. Helms also worked for Senator Alton Lennon in 1953 before returning to North Carolina. He became chairman of the North Carolina Bankers Association and, from 1957 to 1961, served on the Raleigh City Council. Starting in 1960 he served as executive vice-president of the Capital Broadcasting Co., a TV and radio company, for 12 years. He provided political commentary on WRAL-TV, the WRAL radio station and the Tobacco Radio Network. In 1972, two years after changing his party registration from Democrat to Republican, he was elected to the U.S. Senate from North Carolina. It was around that time that his political adviser, Tom Ellis, and he established the North Carolina Congressional Club. Later renamed the National Congressional Club, the political action committee was instrumental in raising money and support for conservative candidates. As chairman of the Senate Foreign Relations Committee from 1995 to 2001, Helms pushed for right-wing foreign policy. He adamantly opposed Cuban leader Fidel Castro and his government. In 1996 he, along with Representative Dan Burton, sponsored an act that strengthened the U.S. embargo against Cuba. The Helms- Burton Act was signed into law the following year. Helms consistently won reelection until his retirement, in 2003. He died in Raleigh after years of declining heath. He was survived by his wife, Dorothy, two daughters, a son, seven grandchildren and one great-grandchild. See *Current Biography* (1979).

Obituary *New York Times* A p1+ July 5, 2008

HERRERA CAMPINS, LUIS May 4, 1925–Nov. 9, 2007 President of Venezuela (1979–84); lawyer; journalist; co-founder of the Comite Organizado Para Electiones Independientes (COPEI), also known as the Pardido Social Cristiano, a right-center party inspired in part by Roman Catholic teachings on social justice. Luis Herrera Campíns was a moderately conservative democratic politician whose exceptional probity in government was widely acknowledged even by many members of the Venezuelan left. For his attempt to organize a strike by university students in 1952, he was imprisoned for four months by the dictatorial regime of General Marcos Pérez Jiménez, and he subsequently went into exile in Europe. In exile he and some fellow expatriates published the newspaper *Tiela,* which was clandestinely distributed in Venezuela. When Pérez Jiménez was overthrown, in 1958, Herrera returned to Venezuela and won a seat in the Chamber of Deputies, the lower house of the National Congress. He retained the seat until his election to a five-year term in the presidency, 20 years later. As president he introduced educational reforms and oversaw such major projects as the building of the Caracas subway and the Teresa Carreño arena in Caracas. He assumed the presidency at a time when the economy of oil-rich Venezuela was booming, but oil-export revenues slumped drastically in 1983. In counteraction, he devalued the Venezuelan currency, sparking the beginning of the decline of his political party and paving the way for the rise of Hugo Chávez 15 years later. In an obituary of him on the Internet site *Venezuela News and Views,* Daniel Duquenal, a critic of Herrera and especially of Chávez, blogging (perhaps from Yaracuy) in the Venezuelan provinces, wrote of Herrera: "I never liked him very much. . . . His surprise election gave him an opportunity to effect important changes in Venezuela. But he did not do it and continued on the populist ways of Carlos Andres's preceding term. Thus he had to pay for both terms' mistakes. But he had virtues which today are totally absent from government. If his administration was not exempt [from] corruption, it is an established fact that he did not benefit from it . . . and we are told that some of the privileges reserved for ex-presidents, such as secretary/bodyguard, were removed [in his case]. . . . Herrera Campíns [was] certainly not the best president we had but very likely the most honest." Herrera and his wife, Betty Rafael Urdaneta de Herrera, had five children. He died in Caracas, Venezuela's capital city. See *Current Biography* (1980).

Obituary *New York Times* C p12 Nov. 13, 2007

HESTON, CHARLTON Oct. 4., 1923(?)–Apr. 5, 2008 "If Hollywood had a Mount Rushmore, Heston's face would be on it," the movie-industry publicist Michael Levine once said. Charlton Heston was a colossus of the silver screen, publicly identified with his portrayals of larger-than-life historical figures as well as heroic fictional characters. Those roles, in a total of at least 60 theatrical films, included Moses, Michelangelo, John the Baptist, President Andrew Jackson (twice), Ben-Hur, Marc Antony (twice), rugged American frontiersmen, cowboys, military and naval men, and treasure hunters and other adventurers, among them the time-traveling astronaut George

Taylor, who finds himself marooned in a future planetary society ruled by anthropomorphic apes in the science-fiction fantasy hit *Planet of the Apes* (1968). It is widely accepted that Heston could not have achieved his mythic status without his dedication to his craft as well as such natural endowments as a tall and imposing physique; a handsome, chiseled visage; a deep and sonorous baritone voice; and what his fellow actor Richard Dreyfuss described as "the measured, almost antique rhythm of his speech." The versatile Heston occasionally interpreted less than monumental characters, such as the disgraced ranch foreman Steve Leech in *The Big Country* (1958) and his own favorite role, that of the title character in *Will Penny* (1968), an illiterate and lonely cowhand, whose bleak existence is temporarily warmed by his relationship with a lost mother and son he aids. Heston, a U.S. Army Air Force veteran who studied drama at Northwestern University, began his professional acting career in regional theater, on Broadway (briefly), in live drama on early television, and in principal roles in two independent 16-mm films—*Peer Gynt* and *Julius Caesar*—shot during the 1940s by his college classmate David Bradley. He made his Hollywood debut in the producer Hal Wallis's film noir *Dark City* (1950). That film introduced him to the pioneering producer-director Cecil B. De Mille, who cast him as Ben Braden, the tough circus manager in the star-studded, Academy Award–winning film *The Greatest Show on Earth* (1952). Heston was popularly identified more closely with his second De Mille assignment, his towering portrayal of Moses in the biblical epic *The Ten Commandments* (1956). He became equally if not better known for his role as Judah Ben-Hur, a prince in ancient Roman-occupied Judea who rebels against the Romans, in the director William Wyler's epic *Ben Hur* (1959). *Ben Hur* was a commercial blockbuster and won 11 Academy Awards, including Heston's best-actor prize. Heston was dynamic as Ramon Vargas, a straight-arrow Mexican narcotics detective, in Orson Welles's *Touch of Evil* (1958), a cult film and noir classic. Among his outstanding credits in the 1960s were the title roles in *El Cid* (1961) and *Major Dundee* (1965), John the Baptist in *The Greatest Story Ever Told* (1965), Michelangelo in *The Agony and the Ecstasy* (1965), and the aging professional football quarterback Ron Catlan in *Number One* (1969). In *The Omega Man* (1971), set in a post-apocalyptic future, Heston portrayed Robert Neville, one of the last holdouts against a zombie cult. In another, better-known science-fiction dystopia film, *Soylent Green* (1973), set in a future overpopulated, food-scarce world, he played Robert Thorn, a police detective marked for death by the powers that be when he discovers that dead people are the source of the protein in Soylent, a processed food being rationed to the population. Among his other screen credits in the 1970s were roles in the multigenerational saga *The Hawaiians* (1970), the disaster movies *Airport 1975* (1974) and *Earthquake* (1974), and *Gray Lady Down* (1978). He appeared in at least a dozen films for TV, and he accrued many credits in TV dramas and series. Among those credits was the role of the tycoon Jason Colby in the network prime-time soap opera *Dynasty* (1985) and its spin-off *The Colbys* (1985–87). Heston also often re-turned to acting on stage. He published several books of journals and memoirs, including the autobiography *In the Arena* (1995). As a political activist off screen, he in many ways followed in the footsteps of his friend Ronald Reagan, serving as president of the Screen Actors Guild (1966–71) when he was still a New Deal–style Democrat and later changing his party affiliation to Republican and campaigning for Republican candidates. He became controversial as president of the National Rifle Association (1998–2003), championing Second Amendment rights and inviting gun-control advocates (on two public occasions) to pry his rifle—held above his head—from his "cold dead hands." In the early 2000s, when he was beginning to suffer from symptoms of Alzheimer's disease, he was increasingly vilified and ridiculed by his political enemies, including the independent filmmaker Michael Moore. Flashing an NRA membership card, Moore persuaded Heston to submit to what would be an embarrassing filmed interview included in Moore's documentary film *Bowling for Columbine* (2002). When the old and ailing actor finally perceived that he had been tricked, he responded not in anger but simply by walking away in silence. Heston died at his home in Coldwater Canyon, Los Angeles County, California. He was survived by his wife of 64 years, Lydia (nee Clarke), his son, Fraser (who as a baby played the infant Moses in *The Ten Commandments*), his daughter, Holly Ann, and three grandchildren. See *Current Biography* (1986).

Obituary *New York Times* p1 Apr. 6, 2008, B p7 Apr. 7, 2008

HILLARY, SIR EDMUND July 20, 1919–Jan. 11, 2008 Mountaineer; explorer; philanthropist. On May 29, 1953 two members of a British expedition led by John Hunt became, in tandem, the first mountain climbers to conquer the summit of Mount Everest, the highest peak on Earth, rising 29,035 feet above sea level between Tibet and Nepal. One climber was Tenzing Norgay (sometimes spelled "Norkey"), a professional mountaineer from the Nepalese Sherpa community living in the shadow of Everest's peak; the other was Edmund Percival Hillary, a New Zealander. With their achievement, Hillary and Norgay were trailblazers, inspiring a legion of climbers from around the world to follow in their footsteps. (More than 3,000 succeeded, including Hillary's son, Peter; well over 100 have died in the attempt.) Proud of his feats as a mountaineer and explorer, Hillary was prouder still of his humanitarian and environmental work in behalf of Nepal and the Sherpas, helping the country and the people deal with the social, economic, and environmental changes that came with an invasion that totaled in the hundreds of thousands, including dilettantish trekkers along with serious mountaineers. In the early 1960s he founded the Himalayan Trust, through which he promoted the welfare of Sherpa families and was instrumental in the building of three hospitals, 13 health clinics, more than 30 schools, two airfields, bridges, and other facilities in Nepal. (He raised approximately $250,000 annually for the projects.) Deploring ecological degradation, he persuaded the government of Nepal to pursue a reforestation policy, and he played a major role in bringing about the cleanup of hundreds of tons of accumulated litter left over a period of many years by mountaineers and pressuring the climbers to clean up after themselves henceforth. Born into a family of beekeepers in Auckland, New Zealand, Hillary began co-managing the family's apiary when he was 20, and beekeeping remained his livelihood for almost a score of years. Also when he was 20, he began mountain climbing and immediately knew that he wanted to "spend my life among the mountains and the snow and ice." His first major ascent was of New Zealand's Mount Olivier (7,500 feet), in 1939. He scaled Mount Tapuaenuku ((9,463 feet) in New Zealand's Kaikoura Range in 1944, and Mount Cook, New Zealand's highest peak (12,349 feet), in 1947. Encouraged by his fellow New Zealand mountaineer George Lowe, he subsequently set his sights on the Himalayas in South Asia, the world's highest mountain range. Accompanied by Lowe, he began his Himalayan adventure by taking part in a British reconnaissance expedition on the Tibet-Nepal border headed by Eric Shipton in 1951 and 1952. Members of that expedition succeeded in their ascent of Mukut Parbat (23,760 feet)—an achievement to which Lowe and Hillary made an essential contribution short of the final ridge—but the expedition failed to reach the summit of Cho Oyu (26,906 feet). Most of the members of Shipton's expedition, including Lowe and Hillary, were carried over to form the core of the British Everest expedition headed by John Hunt in 1953. In the years following his ascent of Everest, Hillary led other Himalayan climbs, and he adventured in the Arctic and, especially, the Antarctic. Participating in the Commonwealth Trans-Antarctic Expedition of 1957–58, he led a tractor-motorized New Zealand team in pioneering a new route across the polar plateau. During 1977, traveling by jet boat, he explored India's Ganges River from its mouth almost all of the way to its source. Later in 1977 he suffered a neurological problem that forced him to retire from mountain climbing. He published some dozen books about his life and expeditions, including *High Adventure* (1955) and *Nothing Venture, Nothing Win* (1975). Out of deference to the pride of the Sherpa people, as long as Tenzing Norgay was alive, Hillary publicly adhered to the fiction that the two had set foot on Everest's summit simultaneously. In the memoirs he published just before his death, in 1986, Norgay revealed that Hillary had actually been two or three steps ahead of him in reaching the summit. Hillary confirmed the revelation, and he described the sequence of events in detail in his last book, *The View from the Summit* (1999). Neither he nor Norgay climbed Everest a second time. Hillary's first wife, Louise (née Rose), and his daughter Belinda died in a plane crash in 1975. Fourteen years later he married June Mulgrew (née Anderson), the widow of his close friend Peter Mulgrew. He died of heart failure in Auckland City Hospital, in New Zealand. His wife survived him, along with a son, Peter, and daughter, Sarah, from his first marriage; he also left six grandchildren. See *Current Biography* (1954) and *Current Biography International Yearbook* (2002).

Obituary *New York Times* B p6 Jan. 11, 2008

HILLERMAN, TONY May 27, 1925–Oct. 26, 2008
Novelist. Tony Hillerman was best known for his series of mysteries set in a reservation in the southwestern U.S. That best-selling series followed the Navajo Tribal Police detectives Joe Leaphorn and Jim Chee as they investigate crimes. Praised by book critics as well as members of the Navajo tribe, many of the novels examine the detectives' struggles to maintain their ancient tribal beliefs and customs while working in the contemporary world. Though Hillerman was not Native American, he grew up on a reservation and was fascinated by the Navajo. His aim in writing the series, he said, was to better educate the American public about the lives of Native Americans. "It's always troubled me that the American people are so ignorant of these rich Indian cultures," Hillerman once told an interviewer for *Publishers Weekly*. "I think it's important to show that aspects of ancient Indian ways are still very much alive and are highly germane even to our ways." Anthony Grove Hillerman was born in the small, impoverished town of Sacred Heart, Oklahoma. He grew up on the territorial lands of the Potawatomie tribe in a home that lacked electricity and indoor plumbing and attended schools with Native American children. For a short time beginning in 1942, he took classes at Oklahoma State University in Stillwater. He then enlisted in the army and spent two years fighting in Europe. While on a raid in Germany in 1945, Hillerman stepped on a landmine. His left leg was shattered, and he suffered severe burns and the loss of most of his vision in his left eye. He returned to Oklahoma later that year with a Silver Star, a Bronze Star, and a Purple Heart. He finished college, majoring in journalism, and became a crime reporter for the *Borger (Texas) News-Herald*. He went on to work for newspapers in Lawton, Oklahoma, and Oklahoma City before becoming the Santa Fe, New Mexico, bureau manager for United Press International and executive editor of the *Santa Fe New Mexican*. After 17 years in the newspaper field, Hillerman moved with his family to Albuquerque. He earned his master's degree in English literature from the University of New Mexico in 1966 and became a member of the school's journalism faculty. The mystery that he began writing in his spare time became his first novel, *The Blessing Way*. The book, published by Harper & Row (now HarperCollins) in 1970, was the first of his Navajo Tribal Police series and received critical praise. The other 18 books in the series include *Dance Hall of the Dead* (1973), *People of Darkness* (1980), *The Ghostway* (1984), *Skinwalkers* (1986), *A Thief of Time* (1988), *Talking God* (1989), *Coyote Waits* (1990), *Skeleton Man* (2004), and *The Shape Shifter* (2006). He left his position at the University of New Mexico in the late 1980s to focus full-time on his writing. Along with fiction, Hillerman wrote nonfiction works including *Indian Country: America's Sacred Land* (with Bela Kalman, 1987), *Hillerman Country: A Journey through the Southwest with Tony Hillerman* (with Barney Hillerman, 1991), and *New Mexico, Rio Grande, and Other Essays* (with David Muench, 1992). His memoir, *Seldom Disappointed*, was published in 2001. Among his other honors, *Skinwalkers*—which brought Leaphorn and Chee together—won the Western Writers of America's Golden

Spur Award in 1987, and *Dance Hall of the Dead* won the 1994 Edgar Allan Poe Award for best mystery novel from the Mystery Writers of America. Hillerman was also presented with the Grandmaster Award, the Mystery Writers of America's highest honor, in 1991. By his own account, Hillerman's most treasured honor came from the Navajo Nation, which conferred its status of Special Friend of the Dineh on Hillerman in 1987 for his accurate portrayal of Navajo people and their culture. Hillerman died from pulmonary failure at Presbyterian Hospital in Albuquerque, where he lived. His wife, Marie, and their three daughters and three sons all survived him. See *Current Biography* (1992). — M.A.S.

Obituary *New York Times* B p17 Oct. 28, 2008

HUA GUOFENG Feb. 16, 1921–Aug. 20, 2008 Chinese politician. For several years after the death of Mao Zedong, in 1976, Hua Guofeng (the name has sometimes been spelled Hua Kuofeng) led China; he was ousted in 1980, when Deng Xiaoping succeeded him. Raised poor in China's Shansi Province, he joined the Communist Party as a teenager and enlisted in the Red Army. He served more than 10 years as an officer. Afterward the Communist Party named him a party secretary, first in his home province and then in Hunan Province. He became a supporter of Mao, and in 1958, after Mao became chairman of the Communist Party and head of the government, Hua was promoted to vice governor of Hunan Province and secretary of the Hunan Provincial Committee. Hua's loyalty to Mao was unwavering, even after it became plain that Mao's economic plan, called the Great Leap Forward, had led to the deaths of 10s of millions of Chinese from famine in the 1960s. Within the party Hua was appointed minister of public security in 1975 and later became chairman. In 1976 he was named prime minister, first deputy chairman of the Communist Party, and head of the Central Military Commission. Following Mao's death, in September 1976, Hua assumed leadership of the country as well as the party. During his time as leader, he attempted to boost the economy and revive the school system. He allowed the presentation of films and plays previously censored by the government. Though the Gang of Four, a group of officials that had gained control over the Communist Party during Mao's Great Proletarian Cultural Revolution in 1966, was arrested during Hua's short time in power, some scholars now credit leaders of the military and internal security forces rather than Hua for the decision. He had lost his influence by 1978, relinquished power to Deng in 1980, and stepped down as party chairman in June 1981. He remained a member of the Communist Party's Central Committee until 1997 but was rarely seen in public. Little is known about his family; it is believed that he was survived by a wife and four children. See *Current Biography* (1977). — M.A.S.

Obituary *New York Times* A p21 Aug. 21, 2008

HUMBARD, REX Aug. 13, 1919–Sep. 21, 2007 Radio and television evangelist. Alpha Rex Emmanuel Humbard was a pioneer "electronic evangelist"—as he called himself—famed in particular as the first and for a number of years the most successful of the regularly scheduled televangelists in the U.S. A self-schooled, down-home, Christian preacher in the old-fashioned Bible Belt tradition, the guitar-strumming Humbard earned his divinity credentials not in a seminary but as the scion of a family of itinerant gospel-singing Pentecostal troupers who moved from the revival tent to network radio in the 1940s. He began broadcasting on his own on radio in the late 1940s and on television in 1953, paving the way for such televangelists as Oral Roberts, Jim Bakker, Jimmy Swaggart, Jerry Falwell, and Pat Robertson. (The televised "holiness" crusades of Billy Graham were spectacular but periodic, not fitting a regular broadcast pattern.) Unlike Falwell and Robertson, Humbard had no political agenda; and although touched by scandal, he was, unlike Bakker and Swaggart, not overwhelmingly disgraced by it. His nondenominational Sunday-morning services featured his sermons, delivered in a folksy, storytelling style, and a 40-voice choir, fronted by his wife, Maude Aimee Humbard (née Jones). The televised weekly services were conducted at first in a renovated movie theater in Akron, Ohio, and later in the Cathedral of Tomorrow, a 5,400-seat marble-and-glass megachurch that Humbard built for the purpose, at a cost of $4 million, in Cuyahoga Falls, Ohio. At the peak of his popularity, he reached an estimated audience of eight million through some 600 television stations in the U.S. and Canada and millions more through stations around the world. Among the faithful members of his electronic flock was the pop singer Elvis Presley, at whose funeral he officiated, in 1977. In addition to his Sunday-morning ministry, he conducted in-person Christian crusades, traveling to the sites of the huge revivals with his entourage in his 52-seat jet airplane. For a busy period in the 1960s and early 1970s, he engaged in diversified expansion, acquiring Mackinac College in Michigan, a tall office building in Akron, the Real Form Girdle Co., a plastics company, and an advertising agency, among other enterprises. Overextended, he became financially dependent on loans from the Teamsters Union pension fund through the good graces of Jimmy Hoffa as well as on the sale of unregistered bonds to his flock. He ceased the latter practice when, in 1973, federal and Ohio state securities authorities confronted him with a suit for not revealing to the buyers that he lacked the assets to back the bonds. He survived the financial crisis through the sale of his diversified businesses and other holdings and by raising money with the help of followers who rallied to his support, including such celebrities as the cowboy singer Roy Rogers and his wife, Dale Evans, and the country singers Johnny Cash and June Carter Cash. In the early 1980s Humbard sold the Cathedral of Tomorrow, along with the Akron television station WCOT, to the televangelist Ernest Angley, and he sold the Canton, Ohio, television station WDLI to the Trinity Broadcasting Network. In 1982 he moved his organization to Florida, where he concentrated on producing home videos for direct marketing. Florida also became the base from which he flew to revival sites in Latin America. After living in California for 12 years, he moved back to Florida. Into his last years he taped specials for cable television and made appearances before live audiences. He died in a hospital near his home in Lantana, Florida. His survivors included his wife, Maude Aimee, three sons, a daughter, 10 grandchildren, and 11 great-grandchildren. His son Charles co-founded and serves as president of the Gospel Music Channel on cable television. His son Rex Jr. is president of the Rex Humbard Ministry Inc., and his son Don is the treasurer of the ministry, which continues to sell his many tapes and books, including his two autobiographies, *Miracles in My Life* (1971) and *The Soul-Winning Century: The Humbard Family Legacy* (2006). See *Current Biography* (1972).

Obituary *New York Times* p41 Sep. 23, 2007

HYDE, HENRY J. Apr. 18, 1924–Nov. 29, 2007 Republican U.S. representative from Illinois's Sixth Congressional District (1975–2007); lawyer. Henry John Hyde was an imposing figure in Congress on three counts: his hefty six-foot-four physique, topped in his latter years by a mane of white hair; his fiercely principled and effective championing of causes he believed in and opposition to those he did not; and his reputation for good humor, evenhandedness, and civility in his relations with his ideological opponents. "He's ideologically quite passionate," the liberal Democratic representative Barney Frank once said of him, "but he doesn't allow that passion to make him unfair." Of Irish Catholic descent, Hyde grew up in a Democratic household and voted for Democratic president Harry Truman in 1948. He voted for the Republican president Dwight D. Eisenhower twice before registering as a Republican, in 1958. He served two terms as a representative in the Illinois General Assembly (1967–74), where he was majority leader in the State House of Representatives (1971–72). During that period his reading of Charlie Rice's book *The Vanishing Right to Live* convinced him, as he later said, that abortion is "an evil." Bristling at the common assumption that the conviction was rooted in blind religious faith, he was quoted as saying, "The hell with religion. Let's talk medical facts. The fertilized egg . . . is . . . human life, not a bad tooth to be pulled out. If you leave it alone it will be an old man or old lady some day." As a freshman congressman Hyde was the original sponsor of what is known as the Hyde Amendment, a rider to the annual appropriations bill for Medicaid that prevents the federal government from paying for abortions, except in certain cases. (The ban does not apply to funding by the states, only to the matching federal funds.) Passed into law on October 1, 1976, the amendment has remained in effect in various versions through successive administrations, both Democratic and Republican, ever since. In 1980 the U.S. Supreme Court affirmed the constitutionality of the amendment. In 1993 the amendment was rewritten to expand the exceptions to the ban to include not only "to save the life of the mother" but also cases of rape or incest. Hyde balanced his pro-life stand with support for the federal WIC program (which provides grants to states to address the nutritional needs of women and children); the Family and Medical Leave Act; and legislation aimed at promoting better health care for pregnant women and reducing infant mortality. "He acted on the view that because he opposed abortion, that children would be born in difficult circumstances, and he felt obliged to help

them," Barney Frank observed. Hyde also supported a number of foreign-aid measures, and he was a strong opponent of civil-asset forfeiture laws that allowed federal agencies, district attorneys, and police to confiscate the assets of people suspected of wrongdoing. He supported the Voting Rights Act of 1981 as well as unsuccessful proposals for constitutional amendments requiring a balanced federal budget and outlawing flag burning and same-sex marriage. In 1989 he joined the pro-choice Democrat Barbara Boxer (then a congresswoman) in co-sponsoring legislation penalizing the "baby brokers" who arrange childbirth through surrogate mothers. During congressional hearings on the Iran-Contra scandal in the late 1980s, he was an outspoken defender of the administration of President Ronald Reagan. Under the Republican House Speaker Newt Gingrich in the 1990s, he supported much of the Republicans' so-called Contract with America. He supported the Brady bill and other gun-control legislation. As chairman of the House Judiciary Committee (1995–2001), he led the inquiry that culminated in December 1998 in the House's impeachment of President Bill Clinton on charges of perjury and obstruction of justice arising from the Monica Lewinsky scandal and the Paula Jones lawsuit (although earlier he had stated that he did not believe that "a peccadillo . . . constitutes a high crime and misdemeanor"), and he was the chief House manager in bringing those proceedings to the Senate, which acquitted Clinton in February 1999 (a "jury nullification," in his view). His leadership role in the impeachment proceedings brought him an avalanche of hate mail, death threats, adverse press coverage (including the leak of information regarding an adulterous affair he had had 30 years before), and the need for round-the-clock protection by two Capitol policemen. As chairman of the House International Relations Committee beginning in 2001, he was instrumental in the U.S. government's commitment to a five-year, $5 billion program aimed at combating HIV infection and AIDS around the world. He was instrumental in the passage of the Partial-Birth Abortion Ban Act, signed into law in 2003 and upheld by the U.S. Supreme Court in 2007. He chose not to seek election to a 17th term in Congress in 2006. In retiring, he described himself as "heartbroken" over Republican "instances of corruption" and a "war that seems to have no end" and that "did not create the impression of competence." Hyde died of arrhythmia following heart surgery at Rush University Medical Center in Chicago. He was predeceased by his first wife, Jeanne (nee Simpson), and his eldest son, Henry Jr., and survived by his second wife, Judy (née Wolverton) and two other sons and a daughter from his first marriage. See *Current Biography* (1989).

Obituary *New York Times* B p7 Nov. 30, 2007

JASTROW, ROBERT Sep. 7, 1925–Feb. 8, 2008 Physicist; astronomer; cosmologist; administrator; educator. Robert Jastrow played important roles not only in the U.S.'s exploration of space but also in the academic teaching and mass popularization of Earth science and space studies. After receiving his doctorate in theoretical physics at Columbia University, in 1948, Jastrow conducted postdoctoral research and teaching at several universities, including Yale, before joining the staff of the U.S. Naval Research Laboratory (NRL) in Washington, D.C., in 1954 as a consultant in nuclear physics. At the NRL he soon became involved in the research for Project Vanguard, the first U.S. program for launching an artificial satellite into Earth orbit. After the formation of the National Aeronautics and Space Administration (NASA), in October 1958, he was recruited to head its theoretical division, devoted to basic research in cosmology, astronomy, and planetary sciences. Transferring from NRL, he developed and served as first director of the space-studies group based at the Goddard Space Flight Center in Greenbelt, Maryland, beginning in May 1959. During 1959 he also began a one-year term as chairman of NASA's Lunar Exploration Committee, which established the scientific goals of the Apollo lunar landings. In New York City in 1961, under the auspices of NASA and in association with Columbia University—where he was at that time an adjunct professor of geophysics—he founded the Goddard Institute for Space Studies. With their research in astronomy, atmospheric science, and weather and climate prediction, Jastrow and the scientists under his direction at the Goddard Institute contributed significantly to NASA's Apollo lunar missions and its subsequent Pioneer, Voyager, and Galileo planetary missions. During the lunar missions he was a frequent guest on the CBS and NBC television networks, commenting on those events in terms understandable to lay audiences, and he later hosted scores of CBS programs devoted to the Earth and space sciences. Jastrow directed the Goddard Institute until 1981, when he retired from NASA to become professor of Earth sciences at Dartmouth College, a position he held until 1992. In 1984 he co-founded the George C. Marshall Institute, a Washington, D.C., nonprofit think tank whose purpose is "to conduct assessments of scientific issues affecting public policy." As chairman of that institute, he was an influential figure in public debates on such issues as President Ronald Reagan's Strategic Defense Initiative, popularly known as Star Wars, which he defended. Jastrow was chairman of the board of trustees of the Mount Wilson [Observatory] Institute from 1992 to 2003. He wrote the books *Red Giants and White Dwarfs* (1969), *God and the Astronomers* (1978), *The Enchanted Loom: Mind in the Universe* (1981), and *How to Make Nuclear Weapons Obsolete* (1975), among some dozen books on Earth science, astronomy, the evolution of stars, planets, and life, and space travel and technology. Although he was a professed "agnostic, not a believer," some of his statements were commandeered in the service of the quasi-creationist "intelligent design" movement in cosmology. Jastrow's marriage to Ruth Witenberg in 1967 ended in divorce. He died of complications of pneumonia at his home in Arlington County, Virginia, leaving no immediate survivors. See *Current Biography* (1973).

Obituary *New York Times* D p7 Feb. 12, 2008

JORDAN, HAMILTON Sep. 21, 1944–May 20, 2008
Political strategist and tactician; U.S. president Jimmy Carter's closest adviser. The political wunderkind Hamilton Jordan was the architect of President Carter's ascent from a one-term governorship of Georgia to the White House, where Jordan was Carter's chief of staff. Born in North Carolina, Jordan grew up in Albany, Georgia, his father's hometown. While earning a degree in political science at the University of Georgia at Athens, in 1966, he became a volunteer youth coordinator for peanut farmer and born-again Christian Jimmy Carter, who was then making his first, unsuccessful run for governor of Georgia; he went on to manage Carter's successful gubernatorial campaign four years later. As Governor Carter's executive secretary, he proved to be not only effective at administration but instrumental in pushing progressive legislation through a reluctant General Assembly. In 1972 he drew up a 72-page (80-page, according to some sources) memorandum outlining a game plan for propelling Carter to the post–George McGovern Democratic Party's nomination for the presidency in 1976. The plan was for Carter to write a book explaining his philosophy of government, to begin campaigning early, to meet with foreign leaders on trade missions, to define himself publicly by stages as an "anti-Washington" candidate who carried his own luggage but who could handle national as well as foreign affairs, to win the debt of Democratic candidates across the country by campaigning for them, and to seize momentum in the 1976 primaries by first targeting the early voting states. The plan worked, and, after his victory at the Democratic National Convention in 1976, Carter went on to defeat the Republican presidential incumbent Gerald Ford in the general election, in part by drawing the support of center-right swing voters, including evangelicals and Second Amendment champions. Carter's team, widely named "the Georgia mafia," including Jordan, Bert Lance, and Carter's press secretary, Jody Powell, moved into the White House with him in January 1977. From the beginning Jordan was the president's de facto chief of staff as well as his right-hand point man, and he acquired the formal title of chief of staff in 1979. He played important behind-the-scenes roles in efforts at civil-service reform, in dealing with a Saudi-Egyptian arms package, in repealing a Turkish arms embargo, and in sustaining Carter's nuclear-carrier veto; participated in the Camp David talks resulting in the Egyptian-Israeli Peace Treaty; and was intimately (and frustratingly) involved—during one period abroad at great personal risk—in the effort to resolve the Iranian hostage crisis. His greatest success was in the negotiations leading to congressional approval of the Panama Canal treaties. With his casual lifestyle and penchant for partying, Jordan was less successful socially. Disrespecting Washington's pomp, he was on several occasions accused of breaches of decorum, such as his alleged statement at a state dinner comparing the bosom of the Egyptian ambassador's wife to "the pyramids." After President Carter lost to the Republican Ronald Reagan in the presidential election of 1980, Jordan became a marketing executive with Whittle Communications, invested in the biotechnical divisions of several biomedical companies, and launched a National Football League franchise that became the Jacksonville Jaguars. He published the book *Crisis: The Last Year of the Carter Presidency* in 1982. In 1986 he ran unsuccessfully for the Democratic nomination for

the U.S. Senate in the Georgia primary. From 1987 to 1990 he was chief executive of the Association of Tennis Professionals. Disenchanted with the American two-party system, he, with Ed Rollins, co-managed the unsuccessful presidential bid of the independent candidate H. Ross Perot in 1992. Subsequently he was a member of the founding council of Unity08, Angus King's Internet-based organization for mobilizing voters to nominate a bipartisan presidential ticket in 2008. Jordan was married twice, to Nancy Konigsmark, a teacher, in 1970, and to Dorothy Henry, a pediatric nurse, in 1981. Jordan began a long battle with cancer in 1986, when he was diagnosed with lymphoma. Bouts with melanoma, prostate cancer, and mesothelioma followed. With his wife Dorothy, he founded a summer camp for children with cancer and diabetes near Atlanta, Georgia, and he worked in various anticancer causes. He wrote *No Such Thing as a Bad Day* (2001), a memoir about his struggles with cancer. Jordan died of mesothelioma at home in Atlanta. He was survived by his wife Dorothy, two sons, and a daughter. See *Current Biography* (1977).

Obituary *New York Times* C p12 May 22, 2008

KERR, DEBORAH Sep. 30, 1921–Oct. 16, 2007 Actress. The classy and versatile British actress Deborah Kerr, who is chiefly remembered for her work in motion pictures, excelled in projecting, in the words of her biographer Eric Braun, "moral fortitude concealed by a frail appearance." After she launched her movie career in England, Kerr rose to stardom in American cinema beginning in the late 1940s. During two decades in Hollywood, she was nominated for six Academy Awards, and in retirement, in 1994, she received an Oscar for her lifetime achievement as an "artist of impeccable grace and beauty, a dedicated actress whose motion-picture career always stood for perfection, discipline, and elegance." Her first Academy Award nomination was for her performance as Evelyn Boult, the wife driven to alcoholism in *Edward, My Son* (1949). Cast against type, she drew her second nomination as the nymphomaniacal, adulterous U.S. Army wife Karen Holmes, making what was judged at the time to be torrid love in the surf of a Honolulu beach with the Burt Lancaster character in *From Here to Eternity* (1953). Her third nomination was for her warm and forceful performance as Anna Leonowens, the proper English tutor of the children of the King of Siam in the musical *The King and I* (1956). (She lip-synched her songs, which were dubbed by Marni Nixon.) She received her fourth nomination as Sister Angela, the nun marooned on a Pacific island during World War II with a Marine Corps corporal (Robert Mitchum) in *Heaven Knows, Mr. Allison* (1957), and her fifth as Sibyl Railton-Bell, the spinster with the domineering mother in *Separate Tables* (1958). Her sixth nomination was for her moving performance as Ida Carmody, the long-suffering wife of an Australian sheep drover in *The Sundowners* (1960). Kerr's first screen credit was the role of Jenny Hill in the British film *Major Barbara* (1941). She had roles in eight subsequent screen productions in Britain—including the three characters comprising the female lead in *The Life and Death of Colonel Blimp* (1943) and the role

of the troubled Sister Superior in *Black Narcissus* (1947)—before she immigrated to the United States to star opposite Clark Gable in *The Hucksters* (1947). She went on to accrue a total of four dozen feature-film credits, usually starring roles. They included Portia in *Julius Caesar* (1953), the saintly Sarah Miles in *The End of the Affair* (1955), the Hollywood gossip columnist Sheilah Graham in *Beloved Infidel* (1959), and the profoundly spiritual artist Hannah Jelkes in *The Night of the Iguana* (1964). In *The Innocents* (1961) she was cast as Miss Giddens, the governess who concludes that her two charges are possessed by an evil supernatural entity. In another role as a governess, that of Miss Madrigal in *The Chalk Garden*, her character's wayward past reinforces her determination to prevent the unruly young girl in her charge from taking a similar route. With Cary Grant she starred in the romantic comedies *Dream Wife* (1953) and *The Grass Is Greener* (1960) and the romantic comedy/melodrama *An Affair to Remember* (1957). On Broadway in 1953, in *Tea and Sympathy*, she created the role of Laura Reynolds, the wife of a prep-school housemaster, who offers compassion and, in the end, sexual love to a sensitive schoolboy taunted by his peers and superiors for lacking masculinity, and she reprised that role in the 1956 screen adaptation of the play. Like the play, the film ends with her saying to the schoolboy, famously, "Years from now, when you talk about this—and you will—be kind." After starring with Burt Lancaster in *The Gypsy Moths* (1969) and playing the unsatisfied wife of the Kirk Douglas character in *The Arrangement* (1969), she announced that she was taking a "leave of absence" from film. Returning to Broadway, she created the role of Nancy in *Seascape* in 1975, and she acted in regional theater. On television she played Nurse Primsoll in a TV remake of the film *Witness for the Prosecution* (1982), Sally Wells Grant in the made-for-TV movie *Reunion at Fairborough* (1985), and Emma Harte in the miniseries *A Woman of Substance* (1984) and its sequel, *Hold the Dream* (1986). She returned to cinema in the role of Helen in the feature film *The Assam Garden* (1985). After her divorce from Anthony Bartley, Kerr married the author and screenwriter Peter Viertel, who survived her. Her other survivors included two daughters from her first marriage, a stepdaughter from her second marriage, and three grandchildren. She died in Suffolk, England, of complications from Parkinson's disease. See *Current Biography* (1947).

Obituary *New York Times* B p7 Oct. 19, 2007

KIDD, MICHAEL Aug. 12, 1915–Dec. 23, 2007 Dancer; choreographer; director; actor. With his spirited and exhilarating choreographic inventions—grounded in modern dance as well as ballet and influenced by folk, jazz, pop, and music-hall styles—Michael Kidd entertained stage and screen audiences for half a century and in the process garnered five Tony Awards on Broadway and a special Academy Award in 1997 for "his service in the art of the dance in the art of the screen." The Tony Awards were for his choreography for the original musical comedies *Finian's Rainbow* (1947), *Guys and Dolls* (1951), *Can-Can* (1954), *Li'l Abner* (1957), and *Destry Rides Again* (1960). Among his outstanding Hollywood credits were *The Band Wagon* (1953), *Seven Brides for Seven Brothers* (1954), and the screen adaptations of *Guys and Dolls* (1955) and *Li'l Abner* (1959), films displaying a versatility that ranged from spectacularly acrobatic numbers (most notably the frontier barn-raising hootenanny sequence in *Seven Brides for Seven Brothers*) to more sophisticated and sometimes satirical dances described by critics variously as "blithe," "sleek and steamy," and "sumptuous." Kidd became visible to the moviegoing public as an actor/dancer co-starring with Gene Kelly and Dan Dailey in *It's Always Fair Weather* (1955) and in several less prominent appearances, including that as a choreographer in *Smile* (1975). Born Milton Greenwald in New York City, Kidd made his professional debut dancing on Broadway in the chorus of Max Reinhardt's world premiere production of the spectacular Werfel/Weill Jewish biblical epic *The Eternal Road* in 1937. Subsequently, he toured with Lincoln Kirstein's Ballet Caravan until 1941, when he became a soloist with Eugene Loring's Dance Players. From 1942 through 1946 he was a leading dancer with Antal Dorati's Ballet Theatre (now the American Ballet Theatre). With that troupe he directed and starred in his own original ballet *On Stage!* in 1945. On Broadway, in the wake of his success with *Finian's Rainbow*, he choreographed the original musical comedies *Hold It!* (1948), *Love Life* (1948–49), and *Arms and the Girl* (1950). For *Li'l Abner* and *Destry Rides Again*, he was director as well as choreographer, and he maintained that dual capacity with the original musicals *Wildcat* (1960–61), *Subways Are for Sleeping* (1961–62), *Ben Franklin in Paris* (1964–65), *The Rothschilds* (1970–72), and *Cyrano* (1973). He also co-produced several of the shows, including *Wildcat* and *The Rothschilds*. In his last stint on Broadway, he directed the original musical *The Goodbye Girl* in 1993. His motion-picture choreographic credits began with the British production *Where's Charley?* (1952) and included *Merry Andrew* (1958) and *Hello, Dolly!* (1969). He also contributed choreography to *The Band Wagon* (1953), *Knock on Wood* (1954), and *Star!* (1968), among other films. On rare occasions beginning in the 1970s, he did some choreography and directing and made some appearances on television. After his divorce from his first wife, Mary (née Heater), Kidd married Shelah Hackett. His survivors included Shelah, two daughters from his first marriage, and a daughter and son from his second. He died of cancer at his home in Los Angeles, California. See *Current Biography* (1960).

Obituary *New York Times* C p8 Dec. 25, 2007

KITAJ, R. B. Oct. 29, 1932–Oct. 21, 2007 Robert Brooks Kitaj was an eclectic, chiefly figurative painter, collagist, and graphic artist. (His surname is that of his stepfather, a Viennese refugee; his mother, who was of Russian-Jewish descent, and biological father divorced when he was a toddler.) Without rejecting the painterly brushwork of the abstract expressionists, Kitaj was a superb draftsman and portraitist, best known for the vivid, complex, fragmentally designed semi-pop paintings and drawings in which he pursued historical, literary, autobiographical, and Judaic themes. He rose to prominence in En-

gland, where he lived and worked from 1960 to 1997 with the exception of such periods as the years 1967–70, when he taught at the University of California at Berkeley and at Los Angeles. While eluding strict categorization, in the early 1960s he became loosely identified with the British pop-art movement, which included his friend David Hockney and Eduardo Paolozzi, and subsequently he was part of the School of London, alongside Francis Bacon and Lucian Freud. His canvases and drawings reflected such influences as surrealism, the post-impressionism of Cézanne, Picasso's blue period, the paintings of Matisse and Piet Mondrian, Asian art, and the styles of several filmmakers. They contained allusions to the literary works of Henry James, Franz Kafka, James Joyce, T. S. Eliot, and Ezra Pound, among others, sometimes in what Kitaj called his "history" paintings. Among those works are *The Ohio Gang* (1964), a potpourri of gangsters and other degenerate American figures, *Walter Lippmann* (1966), which has portraits of major-league baseball players and others in addition to that of the title figure, *Hockney, David at Berkeley* (1968), which also has portraits of Kenneth Rexroth and several other Beat and "San Francisco renaissance" poets, *The Autumn of Central Paris (After Walter Benjamin)* (1972–74), a tribute to the German-Jewish intellectual who committed suicide in 1940, and *If Not, Not* (1975–76), a grotesque Bosch-like landscape containing images such as the guardhouse gate at Auschwitz. "A central condition for me has been the murder of the European Jews," Kitaj once said. He subsequently created Degas-like impressionistic pastels and several paintings featuring a Jewish Everyman named Joe Singer. In addition to his two-dimensional works on paper and canvas, he made some fiberglass sculptures. He was stung by the witheringly negative critical response to a retrospective of his work at the Tate Gallery in London in 1994, which various commentators have attributed to the content of the self-written wall labels as well as to the artwork itself. Soon afterward, while visiting his mother on her deathbed in the U.S., he learned that his 47-year-old second wife, the artist Sandra Fisher, had suffered a ruptured brain aneurysm; with Kitaj at her side, Fisher died, a few days later. Kitaj blamed the recent critical attacks for her death, and he retaliated with a series of "agitprop-like tableaux," as David Cohen wrote for the *New York Sun* (October 24, 2007), including the paintings *The Critic Kills* (1996), which was signed "by Ron and Sandra," and *Sandra Three: The Critic Killer Assassinated by his Widower, Even* (1997). In the latter he portrayed the critic as a bug-like creature being exterminated by a firing squad. In 1997 Kitaj left England and returned permanently to the United States, settling in Los Angeles. That move inspired a series of paintings of swimming pools, which he referred to as *My Walden*. A show of 100 of his drawings and paintings at the Marlborough Gallery in New York City in 2000 was titled "How to Reach 67 in Jewish Art." It included *Eclipse of God (After the Uccello Panel Called Breaking Down the Jew's Door)* (1997–2000), *Dreyfus (After Melies)* (1996–2000), and *Circumcision Chair* (1998). He published the books *First Diasporist Manifesto* (1989), with 60 illustrations by him, and *Second Diasporist Manifesto: A*

New Kind of Long Poem in 615 Free Verses (2007). Kitaj's first wife, Elsi (née Roessler), committed suicide in 1969. He died at his home in Los Angeles. His survivors included a son and an adopted daughter from his first marriage, a son from his second marriage, and three grandchildren. See *Current Biography* (1982).

Obituary *New York Times* C p11 Oct. 24, 2007

KNIEVEL, EVEL Oct. 17, 1938–Nov. 30, 2007 Daredevil showman/motorcyclist. Robert Craig "Evel" Knievel, the self-described "last gladiator in the new Rome," wore a signature star-spangled red, white, and blue jumpsuit as he performed death-defying stunts on his sometimes souped-up motorcycles. Most of the stunts were essentially aerobatic feats in which he raced his vehicles up steep ramps to soar over wide chasms or rows of cars or other obstacles. During his relatively brief career (1966–81), Knievel earned millions of dollars and an iconic international reputation. He also broke virtually every bone in his body (except his neck) at least once in a dozen or more mishaps, some of which left him temporarily comatose. Before going solo the Montana-born Knievel barnstormed with his troupe, called Evel Knievel's Motorcycle Daredevils, riding through rings of fire and performing other acts of derring-do. As a solo performer he was by 1967 jumping over as many as 16 automobiles parked side by side between two ramps; later he cleared 19 cars. An early accident occurred on December 31, 1967, when his project was to jump over the row of ornamental fountains in front of the Caesar's Palace casino in Las Vegas, Nevada. On that occasion he successfully completed the 141-foot jump but then lost control of his cycle and crash-landed, sustaining hip, wrist, and ankle fractures, a crushed femur and pelvis, and a concussion. In his most daring stunt, in 1974 he attempted a quarter-mile jump across the Snake River Canyon in Idaho with the help of a parachute and rocket engines strapped to the sides of his Harley-Davidson bike. Because the parachute opened too soon, he failed in that attempt and barely escaped drowning in the Snake River. In 1975 he cleared 13 double-decker buses in Wembley Stadium, in London, England, and 14 Greyhound buses in Kings Island, Ohio. By the time he retired, in March 1981, he had registered a total of some 300 successful jumps, some of which had been televised on *ABC's Wide World of Sports*. George Hamilton portrayed Knievel in the biographical movie *The Evel Knievel Story* (1971); Knievel played himself in the motion picture *Viva Knievel!* (1977); and George Eads was cast in the lead in the made-for-television film *Evel Knievel* (2004). Knievel augmented his income by marketing his image to toy companies and other commercial entities. While he claimed to have earned approximately $40 million, he ended in bankruptcy, for several reasons, including his alleged propensity for gambling, federal and state income-tax prosecutions, and a suit against him won by Sheldon Saltman: angry at unflattering descriptions of him in Saltman's book *Evel Knievel on Tour,* Knievel in 1977 assaulted Saltman with an aluminum baseball bat, shattering the author's left wrist and much of his left arm. At the end of his career, Knievel's body was a patchwork of scar

tissue and surgical metal, including a titanium hip, aluminum plates in his arms, and many pins holding joints and bones together; in some accidents he even broke some of those metal parts. In his last years he was also afflicted with diabetes and idiopathic pulmonary fibrosis, and he suffered two strokes. In addition, he underwent a liver transplant after having been infected with hepatitis C from one of the many blood transfusions he had received. Knievel and his first wife, Linda Jones Bork, separated circa 1990 and subsequently divorced. His marriage to his second wife, Krystal Kennedy, also ended in divorce, but Krystal returned to his side before his death. She was among his survivors, along with four offspring from his first marriage, his sons Kelly and Robbie (who followed him into daredevil motorcycling) and daughters Tracey and Alicia. Knievel died at his home in Clearwater, Florida. See *Current Biography* (1972).

Obituary *New York Times* C p10 Dec. 1, 2007

KORMAN, HARVEY Feb. 15, 1927–May 29, 2008 Comedian. Harvey Herschel Korman described himself, with understatement, as "an actor doing comedy" who could be "funny in a scene or situation." Tall and lean, with a command of precise timing and diction, Korman shone in sketch comedy on television, most famously during a decade as a straight man or second banana on CBS's *The Carol Burnett Show*. For his work on that comedy/variety program, he won four Emmy Awards and one Golden Globe Award. In a parallel, less prolific career in motion pictures, his best-known roles were madcap or humorously corrupt characters in comedies of producer/director/writer/actor Mel Brooks, including the greedy land baron Hedley Lamarr in the Western comedy *Blazing Saddles* (1974), the sadomasochistic psychiatric asylum director Dr. Charles Montague in *High Anxiety* (1977), and Count de Monet (pronounced "Count de Money") in *History of the World: Part I* (1981). After studying at the Goodman School of Drama in Chicago and under Uta Hagen in New York City, Korman spent a dozen years supporting himself at odd jobs while struggling as an actor, chiefly in regional stock. His big break was his performance in the comic skit "Appleby's Office Party" on *The Red Skelton Show* on the CBS television network in December 1961. That led to a regular berth as a featured performer on CBS's *The Danny Kaye Show* (1963–67), on which he played (with a quick learner's ad hoc mastery of accents) roles ranging from a Canadian Mountie to a Nazi prison-camp commandant, a Romany (Gypsy) fiddler, and Dracula's butler. On *The Carol Burnett Show* (1967–77), also on CBS, he rendered broad comic characterizations in 137 episodes. His skits with Burnett included spoofs of old movies, television shows, and TV commercials and the recurring "Ed and Eunice" sketch, in which he and Burnett played a blue-collar couple whose marriage is unsettled by Ed's doltishness and the nagging of Eunice's mother, played by the young comedienne Vickie Lawrence, aged by means of makeup and a gray wig. "Ed and Eunice" was spun off into the NBC situation comedy *Mama's Family* (1983–84; first-run syndication began in 1986). Sketches from *The Carol Burnett Show* were reedited by CBS into the stand-alone program *Carol Burnett and Friends,* which ran in syndication for many years. After leaving *The Carol Burnett Show,* Korman went over to the ABC network, where he made an unsuccessful pilot for his own show in May 1977 and a successful one in January 1978. The situation comedy *The Harvey Korman Show* ran on ABC for only four months, from April to August 1978. Absent from most subsequent incarnations of the Burnett show, Conway returned to the Burnett ensemble in the two-hour CBS special *The Carol Burnett Show: A Reunion* in the fall of 2001. With Tim Conway, another veteran of the Burnett ensemble, Korman toured the United States for several years with their show *Tim Conway and Harvey Korman: Together Again.* Korman's scores of credits on television included guest appearances on many variety shows; the voice of the Great Kazoo on *The Flintstones* (1965–66); roles in such series as *The Lucy Show* (1964–65), *Disneyland* (1965), *The Love Boat* (1976 and 1982–85), and two different *Pink Panther* shows (1982 and 1983); and the role of the comedian Bud Abbott in the made-for-TV movie *Bud and Lou* (1978). After his divorce from Donna Ehlert, Korman married Deborah Fritz, in 1982. He died at the UCLA Medical Center in Los Angeles of complications from the rupture of an abdominal aortic aneurism. His survivors included his second wife, a son and daughter from his first marriage, and two daughters from his second marriage. See *Current Biography* (1979).

Obituary *New York Times* A p19 May 30, 2008

KORNBERG, ARTHUR Mar. 3, 1918–Oct. 26, 2007 Biochemist; Nobel laureate. Arthur Kornberg was honored as a groundbreaking specialist in the biochemistry of genetics. Specifically, he studied the enzymes that catalyze the assembling of the molecules deoxyribonucleic acid (DNA) and ribonucleic acid (RNA). Kornberg and his colleagues discovered how DNA is replicated in a cell, and they were the first scientists to synthesize the process in a test tube. Kornberg decided to devote himself to enzyme research instead of medical practice while he was earning his M.D. degree at the University of Rochester School of Medicine (1937–41). Commissioned an officer in the U.S. Public Health Service in 1942, he was assigned to the National Institutes of Health in Bethesda, Maryland, where he worked in the nutrition section of the physiology division before becoming chief of the enzymes and metabolism section (1947–53). His research at the NIH contributed to the clarification of the processes leading to the formation of the coenzymes flavin adenine dinucleotide (FAD) and diphosphopyridine nucleotide (DPN, now called nicotinamide adenine dinucleotide). As chief of the Department of Microbiology at the Washington University School of Medicine (1953–59), he discovered and isolated an enzyme—which he named DNA polymerase—that catalyzes the formation of polynucleotides from nucleotide triphosphates. For that achievement he shared the 1959 Nobel Prize for physiology or medicine with Severo Ochos, who had discovered the enzyme catalyzing the formation of RNA. In 1959 Kornberg became chief of the Department of Biochemistry at Stanford University, where he continued his research in the biosynthesis of DNA in partnership with Mehran Goulian. Building on work by Robert Sinsheimer, he and Goulian and their colleagues, using as a template a virus that infects the E. coli bacillus, became in 1967 the first scientists to synthesize biologically active DNA in a test tube. After his official retirement, in 1988, Kornberg continued to head a laboratory at Stanford until a few weeks before his death. He wrote the books *For the Love of Enzymes: The Odyssey of a Biochemist* (1989) and *The Golden Helix: Inside Biotech Ventures* (1995). Following the death of his first wife, Sylvy Ruth, in 1986, Kornberg married his second wife, Charlene, who died in 1995. He died of respiratory failure at Stanford Hospital at Stanford University in California. Among his survivors were his third wife, Carolyn Frey Dixon, three sons, and eight grandchildren. His son Roger Kornberg won the 2006 Nobel Prize in chemistry. See *Current Biography* (1968).

Obituary *New York Times* p24 Oct. 28, 2007

LAFONTAINE, DON Aug. 26, 1940–Sep. 1, 2008 Known in the movie industry as "the king of voice-overs" and sometimes as "the voice of God" (or even simply "the V.O.G."), Don LaFontaine wrote and recorded in his resonant baritone the voice-overs for hundreds of thousands of movie trailers, commercials, and promotional ads for television. Occasionally with collaborators, he came up with several phrases that became widely repeated, among them "in a world where . . . ," "one man, one destiny," and "nowhere to run, nowhere to hide." "Don was an absolute treasure to the voice-over industry," Joan Baker, the author of the book Secrets of Voice-Over Success, told Dennis Hevesi for the *New York Times* (September 2, 2008)."He had a unique sound, a voice placed deep in his body." Baker also said that LaFontaine "understood the dynamics of each word and gave each word a musical note that was intuitive, which is why he could perform in so many genres—action, drama, comedy, romance, horror films, science fiction." LaFontaine was born in Duluth, Minnesota; he enlisted in the army soon after his high-school graduation and was assigned to an army band as a recording engineer. After his military discharge he moved to New York City, where he landed a job with the radio producer Floyd Peterson at National Recording Studios in 1962. After LaFontaine made suggestions for the segment of radio advertisement used in the movie *Dr. Strangelove,* Peterson placed him in charge of writing all movie trailers. The two men started a movie-trailer production company in 1963. Two years later, while working on a trailer for *Gunfighters of Casa Grande,* the announcer LaFontaine had hired for the job failed to show up. He recorded the copy himself and, much to his surprise, Columbia Pictures bought the spot the next day. Over the next few years, LaFontaine recorded many voice-overs for radio and started making voice-overs for television and movie-theater trailers as well. In 1976 he started his own production company; his first assignment was for *The Godfather, Part II.* He became head of the trailer department at Paramount Pictures in 1978. In the early 1980s he moved to Los Angeles and resumed working as an independent producer. His voice was heard on promos for such films as *2001: A Space Odyssey* (1968), *The Elephant Man* (1980), *The Terminator* (1984), *Fatal Attraction* (1987), *Home Alone* (1990), *L.A. Confidential* (1997), *There's Something About Mary* (1998), and *Shrek* (2001). He also lent his voice to commercials for Chevrolet, Budweiser, McDonald's, Coca-Cola, Geico, and other companies. In recent years LaFontaine worked out of a home studio, where he often recorded three voice-overs a day. He died in Cedars-Sinai Medical Center in Los Angeles due to complications from a pneumothorax. He was survived by his wife, Nita Whitaker, and three daughters. See *Current Biography* (2004). — M.A.S.

Obituary *New York Times* A p23 Sep. 3, 2008

LAMB, WILLIS JR. July 12, 1913–May 15, 2008 Scientist. The theoretical and experimental physicist Eugene Willis Lamb received the National Medal of Science in 2000 for "his towering contributions to classical and quantum theories of laser radiation and quantum optics and to the proper interpretation of non-relativistic quantum mechanics." Earlier in his career, in 1955, Lamb shared a Nobel Prize in physics for "his discoveries regarding the hyperfine structure of the quantum spectrum" and in particular for his "discovery of the phenomenon called the Lamb shift, which revolutionized the quantum theory of matter," providing crucial experimental support for the emergence of the new theory of quantum electrodynamics (QED). Theoretical laser research by Lamb, reinforcing experimental work by William Bennett, led to his prediction of the existence of what is called the Lamb-Bennett dip, which is used to set laser frequencies precisely. After receiving a B.S. degree in chemistry at the University of California at Berkeley (1934), Lamb earned a Ph.D. degree in theoretical physics there (1938). His research for his dissertation—on the electromagnetic properties of nuclear systems and in particular on the scattering of neutrons by a crystal—was directed by J. Robert Oppenheimer. In that research Lamb partially predicted what became known a score of years later as the Mössbauer effect, also called the Lamb-Dicke-Mössbauer effect. Lamb joined the faculty of Columbia University in 1938 and the staff of the Columbia Radiation Laboratory five years later. From 1943 to 1946 his work at the laboratory was U.S. government-sponsored, defense-related experimentation with microwave frequencies applied to radar. When that work was done, in the summer of 1946, he turned his attention to, and applied his experience with microwaves to, the study of hydrogen, which has the simplest of atoms, with one electron orbiting a central proton in an electromagnetic field. In particular, Lamb concentrated on checking the accuracy of Paul Dirac's predictions regarding the frequencies of radiation enabling the electron to switch from one flight path to another. Dirac's predictions, based on a combination of quantum mechanics and relativity theory, were published in 1928. They included the prediction that two of the orbits could have exactly same energy. Using an apparatus built with the help of R. C. Retherford, a graduate student, Lamb used high-resolution radio resonance techniques to measure the optical radiation in the line of the hydrogen spectrum, announcing his findings in 1947. Hamish Johnston, the editor of *physicsworld.com* (May 20, 2008), succinctly described Lamb's achievement: "Lamb found that the $^2S_1$ electron energy level in hydrogen was slightly higher than the $^2P_1$ energy level. This shift was not predicted by relativistic quantum mechanics, which had been used two decades earlier by Paul Dirac. . . . Instead, the Lamb shift provided crucial evidence for the new theory of QED, which describes the interactions between charged particles in terms of the exchange of photons." In the London *Guardian* (May 24, 2008), Frank Close further explained: "What Lamb had done was to detect the subtle result of quantum physics, not just on the electron and proton, but on the atom's electromagnetic field. It turns out that energy in the electromagnetic field can momentarily convert into matter and antimatter. . . . Lamb was thus the first person to detect that the void is not empty but a seething sea of 'virtual' particles and anti-matter." Hans Bethe was the first physicist to explain, before the end of 1947, that Lamb's finding was the underpinning of contemporary QED, and the Nobel Prize winners Richard Feynman, Julian Swinger, and Sin Itiro Tomonaga elaborated on the same subject a decade later. Polykarp Kusch, the co-recipient of the 1955 Nobel Prize with Lamb, was cited "for his precision [sic] determination of the magnetic moment of the electron." After he left Columbia University, Lamb continued his work in atomic spectroscopy and laser physics at Stanford University (1951–56), and he subsequently held chairs of physics at Oxford University (1956–62) and Yale University (1962–74). In 1974 he became a professor of physics and optical sciences at the University of Arizona, where he remained until his retirement, in 2002. In addition to publishing his collections *Lectures on Masers* (1964), *Lectures on Mössbauer Effect* (1966), and *The Interpretation of Quantum Mechanics* (2001), Lamb co-wrote the book *Laser Physics* (1974). Lamb's first wife, Ursula (née Schaeffer) predeceased him. His subsequent marriage to the physicist Bruria Kaufman ended in divorce. He was survived by his third wife, Elsie (née Wattson), whom he had known for 27 years before their marriage, in January 2008. Lamb died of complications from a gallstone disorder at University Medical Center in Tucson, Arizona. See *Current Biography* (1956).

Obituary New York Times B p7 May 20, 2008

LANTOS, TOM Feb. 1, 1928–Feb. 11, 2008 Democratic U.S. congressman from California (1981–2008). Thomas Peter Lantos, whose constituency included the southwest portion of San Francisco and the northern portion of San Mateo County, was the only Holocaust survivor ever to serve in the U.S. House of Representatives. Lantos brought to his service in the House a dedication to human rights and civil liberties and a perspective on world affairs forged in the crucible of, in his words, "the bloodbath, the cruelty, the death that I saw so many times around me during those few months between March of 1944 and January of 1945," which "made me a very old young man." Early in his congressional tenure, Lantos co-founded and began co-chairing the Human Rights Caucus, a congressional group speaking out for oppressed peoples worldwide, including Christians in Saudi Arabia, the Sudan, and China, Tibetans, Kurds in Iraq, and Buddhist monks and others in Burma. He was also a member of the Congressional Progressive Caucus. While progressive in domestic matters, he was hawkish on Cold War issues, and he often favored U.S. military intervention abroad. He wielded great power as the senior Democratic member of the House Foreign Affairs Committee and even greater power as chairman of that committee beginning in January 2007. He was also a senior member of the Committee on Oversight and Government Reform and the founder of the Congressional Friends of Animals Caucus. A secular Jew, Lantos was born into a family of educators in Budapest, Hungary. After Nazi Germany occupied Hungary in March 1944, the teenage Lantos was interned in a forced-labor camp. He escaped and found refuge in a safe house in Budapest established by Raoul Wallenberg, the Swedish diplomat who used his official status to save thousands of Hungarian Jews. Lantos's father also survived the Holocaust; his mother and other family members did not. After World War II ended, Lantos began his university studies in Budapest. Awarded a Hillel Foundation scholarship in 1947, he immigrated to the U.S. and earned bachelor's and master's degrees in economics at the University of Washington at Seattle. After he was reunited with his childhood girlfriend, Annette Tillemann, also a Holocaust survivor, he married her, in 1950. The couple then moved to the San Francisco Bay Area, where Lantos earned a doctorate in economics at the University of California at Berkeley. For three decades beginning in 1953, he taught economics at San Francisco State University. During that time he provided commentary on international affairs on public television and worked as a consultant to businesspeople and politicians. In 1978–79, on a year's leave of absence from the university, he served as a foreign-policy adviser to Democratic senator Joseph Biden, a presidential hopeful. Running against Democratic incumbent William Royer in California's 11th Congressional District in 1980, Lantos won by 46 to 43 percent; he was sworn in as a member of the House in January 1981. In 13 subsequent elections he was returned to his seat by comfortable margins, as high as 76 percent. (From January 1993 on, following redistricting, he represented California's 12th Congressional District. One of his first acts in Congress was the introduction of a bill, which became law, granting honorary U.S. citizenship to Wallenberg. He strongly supported the 1991 Persian Gulf War, and he was a leader in mustering Democratic participation in the 2002 congressional resolution authorizing the invasion of Iraq, but he later turned against President George W. Bush's Iraq strategy and co-sponsored an unsuccessful resolution opposing the troop buildup in Iraq in 2007. A staunch advocate of Israel, he tried to stop U.S. military aid to Egypt when that country in the early 2000s failed, in his view, to cooperate in blocking the flow of money and arms across the Egyptian border to Hamas in Gaza. Early in 2004 he led the first congressional delegation ever to visit Libya, personally meeting with its leader, Muammar Qaddafi. On his return to the U.S. from that visit, he urged President Bush to lift the existing U.S. sanctions against Libya; the presi-

dent did so later that year. In April 2006 Lantos was among those arrested outside the Sudanese Embassy in Washington, D.C., for protesting against what they called the "genocide" of black African Fur, Masalit, and Zaghawa peoples in Darfur by the government of Sudan and the Arab militias it armed. Lantos infuriated the Bush administration (which was seeking Turkey's cooperation in the Iraq war) when, as Foreign Affairs chairman, he pushed through his committee in October 2007 a bill—never passed—recognizing as genocide the World War I–era Turkish slaughter of Armenians. He also used his chairmanship as a bully pulpit for demanding that Japan apologize for its World War II enslavement of Koreans and others as "comfort women" for its troops. His stands on environmental issues earned him high ratings from conservation groups. Lantos and his wife created a Capitol Hill internship program in which for six years they sponsored 54 Humanity in Action Foundation fellowships. In December 2007 Lantos was diagnosed with esophageal cancer; soon afterward he announced that he would not seek re-election. He died at the National Naval Medical Center in Bethesda, Maryland. His wife, two daughters, 18 grandchildren, and two great-grandchildren survived him. See *Current Biography* (2007).

Obituary *New York Times* D p6 Feb. 12, 2008

LEDERBERG, JOSHUA May 23, 1925–Feb. 2, 2008 Microbiologist; Nobel laureate; professor emeritus, Rockefeller University. A polymathic prodigy, Joshua Lederberg made career-long sustained contributions to the advancement not only of basic microbiology but of medical informatics—the intersection of the information and computer sciences, chemical and biological research, and medicine. As the first demonstrator of proof of bacterial conjugation and the discoverer of bacterial transduction, Lederberg was most renowned as the major pioneer in the development of bacterial genetics, a new science with numerous important medical applications. He was the coiner of the terms "plasmid," a segment of DNA that is separate from chromosomes and capable of replication, and "exobiology," denoting the study of possible life elsewhere in the universe. When he was 16, in 1941, Lederberg matriculated at Columbia College, where as a laboratory assistant to F. J. Ryan, he experimented on the mutation and adaptation of the bread-mold fungus, neurospora. At that time it was generally believed that bacteria had no genes, nuclei, or sex and reproduced by simple cell division. As a graduate student experimenting with two distinct strains of the E. coli bacillus under the supervision of Edward Tatum at Yale University later in the 1940s, Lederberg demonstrated recombination—an exchange of genes producing a third strain—and hence conjugation, "sex life of a sort." Subsequently, at the University of Wisconsin—where he was the founding chairman of the Department of Medical Genetics—Lederberg, assisted by his first wife, Esther Lederberg (née Zimmer), and by the graduate student Norton Zinder, experimented with two strains of the bacterium Salmonella typhimurium that lacked the ability to synthesize the amino acids necessary in sexual recombination. That deficiency ruled out the possibility of an exchange of genetic material by conjugation, yet in those experiments, with the two strains placed in a nutrient broth on either side of a U-tube and separated by a filter, recombinant bacteria appeared and multiplied. Thus did Lederberg, with the help of his associates, prove the phenomenon of transduction, wherein genetic information is carried not by the bacteria themselves but by a bacteriophage, a bacteria-infecting virus. That discovery helped to usher in the age of genetic engineering by manipulation of DNA. Lederberg was elected to the National Academy of Sciences in 1957, and "for his discoveries concerning genetic recombination and the organization of the genetic material of bacteria," he shared the 1958 Nobel Prize for physiology or medicine with Edward Tatum and George Beadle (of the California Institute of Technology). Among the many honors later bestowed on him were the National Medal of Science (1989) and the Presidential Medal of Freedom (2006). In 1959 Lederberg joined the faculty of Stanford University as the founding chairman of the Department of Genetics in the university's School of Medicine. At Stanford he continued to pursue his interests beyond basic microbiological research, establishing a laboratory for the study of life on other planets and advising NASA on ways to carry out its orbital, lunar, and planetary missions without contaminating other celestial bodies with terrestrial microbes or importing alien microbes to Earth. In medical informatics, he contributed to the development of the national SUMEX-AIM biomedical computer network and the DENTRAL program applying artificial intelligence to the solution of problems in chemistry, biology, and medicine. In a weekly column he wrote for the *Washington Post* from 1966 to 1971, "Science and Man," he expounded on his diverse range of ideas and concerns, which included the necessity of controlling nuclear arms, regulating recombinant DNA technology, outlawing germ warfare, and overcoming "blindness to the pace of biological advance and its accessibility to the most perilous genocidal experimentation." He was a science adviser to nine U.S. presidential administrations, beginning with the Eisenhower White House. Lederberg left Stanford to assume the presidency of Rockefeller University in 1978. After retiring as president, in 1990, he continued his research at Rockefeller as a Sackler Foundation scholar and professor emeritus of molecular genetics and informatics. After his first marriage ended in divorce, Lederberg married Marguerite Lederberg (née Hirsch), who survived him. His other survivors included a daughter and a stepson from his second marriage and two grandchildren. He died of pneumonia in New York City. See *Current Biography* (1959).

Obituary *New York Times* B p6 Feb. 5, 2008

LEDGER, HEATH Apr. 4, 1979–Jan. 22, 2008 Actor. The Australian-born Heathcliff Andrew Ledger had barely begun acclimating himself to international superstardom—a status clinched by his understated but powerful portrayal of a guileless, sexually conflicted protagonist in the film *Brokeback Mountain*—when his career was abruptly cut short by his death, at age 28. Untrained in acting, Ledger was naturally blessed not only with matinee-idol good looks but with an intelligence for entering the psyche of a

character and virtually encasing himself in the character's skin as if it were his own. After starring as a teenager in two Australian television series, in 1997 Ledger acquired his first American acting credit, that of Conor, a young Irish prince who unites the Celtic clans to lead them against the invading Romans circa 400 A.D. in the Fox TV network fantasy/adventure series *Roar*, which was filmed in Queensland, Australia. His first motion-picture credits were supporting roles in the Australian productions *Paws* (1997) and *Blackrock* (1997). In the Australian film *Two Hands* (1999), he was cast as Jimmy, a young man pursued by underworld thugs. After making his U.S. film debut, in the lead role of Patrick Verona in the high-school romantic comedy *10 Things I Hate About You* (1999), he rejected further efforts to cast him as a "teen heartthrob" in favor of more brooding roles, in a few as a son trying to define himself in his father's shadow. He had the supporting roles of Gabriel Martin, the idealistic elder son of the Mel Gibson character in the Revolutionary War drama *The Patriot* (2000), and Sonny Grotowski, the severely depressed and finally suicidal prison guard unable to win his father's love in *Monster Ball* (2001) and such starring roles as those of the medieval squire jousting in the disguise of a nobleman in *A Knight's Tale* (2001). His first top-of-the-line big-budget starring vehicle was *The Four Feathers* (2002), a British military drama set in late-19th-century Britain and the Sudan, in which he played the coward-turned-hero Harry Federsham. He starred as the disillusioned priest Alex Fournier intensely pursuing occult knowledge in *The Order* (aka *The Sin Eater*, 2003); the surf-and-skateboard shop owner Skip in *Lords of Dog Town* (2005); and in title roles in *The Brothers Grimm* (2005) and *Casanova* (2005). His most celebrated starring vehicle was *Brokeback Mountain* (2005), in which he played with sensitivity the introverted and laconic Ennis Del Mar, a 1960s Wyoming sheep drover ineptly struggling to process his sexual feelings for another male ranch hand (portrayed by Jake Gyllenhaal). In a press conference in 2005, he explained how he had mastered that role: "I had to go in and discover what was causing [Ennis's] inability to express and to love. . . . [He] was battling himself and his genetic structure . . . his father's and his father's father's opinions, traditions and fears that have been passed down and deeply imbedded in him." The film won many Golden Globe and Academy Awards, and Ledger was nominated for several. He was later cast as Dan in *Candy* (2006) and as Robbie Clark in *I'm Not There* (2007). He directed and was featured in *Black Eyed Dog* (2007), a short film about the British musician Nick Drake, who died of an overdose of an antidepressant drug in 1974 at age 26. (Drake's song "Black Eyed Dog" was inspired by the metaphoric term that the former British prime minister Winston Churchill coined for depression.) In *The Dark Night* (2008), the sequel to *Batman Begins* (2005), Ledger played the comic-book villain the Joker. He was cast as Tom in *The Imaginarium of Dr. Parnassus*, the production of which was suspended when he died. (In the wake of his death, the actors Johnny Depp, Jude Law, and Colin Farrell were being considered in the search for his successor in the role of Tom.) While making *Brokeback Mountain* Ledger became engaged to Michelle Williams, who played his wife in the film. He and Williams had a daughter together, Matilda Rose, born in October 2005. The intimate relationship between Ledger and Williams ended in 2006. Ledger was found dead in the rented apartment in which he had been living in Manhattan. The New York City medical examiner concluded that his death had been caused by "an accidental overdose" of six painkillers and sedatives. See *Current Biography* (2006).

Obituary *New York Times* A p1, B p6 Jan. 23, 2008

LEE, SHERMAN Apr. 19, 1918–July 9, 2008 Museum director. As director of the Cleveland Museum of Art for 25 years (1958–83), Sherman Emery Lee was credited with raising that institution to world-class status. In his obituary in the Cleveland *Plain Dealer*, Steven Litt quoted Philippe de Montebello, the long-time director of New York's Metropolitan Museum of Art, as ranking Lee among "the greatest museum directors America has known," one who will be remembered for "sensational acquisitions that transformed the Cleveland Museum of Art in all fields." Those fields included Asian art, in which Lee was a specialist. While earning his doctorate in art at Western Reserve University (now Case Western Reserve), in Cleveland, Lee worked as an assistant in the Oriental Art Department at the Cleveland Museum of Art (1939–41). He was curator of Far Eastern art at the Detroit Institute of Art from 1941 to 1944, when he enlisted in the U.S. Naval Reserve. When World War II ended, he remained in Japan, serving as the officer in charge of General Douglas MacArthur's Arts and Monuments Division from 1946 to 1948. Back in the United States as a civilian, he was for four years on the staff of the Seattle Art Museum, first as assistant director and then as associate director. Returning to the staff of the Cleveland Museum of Art as curator of Oriental art in 1952, he proceeded to build a collection that one critic called "staggering," including Sung Dynasty scrolls and ceramics, Shang and Chou bronzes, Cham and Kmer sculptures, Japanese folding screens, and a 17th-century Mughal manuscript. Rising through the ranks, Lee became director of the museum in 1958, shortly after it had received $34 million from the estate of Leonard C. Hanna Jr. With that bequest, he bought such masterpieces as Jacques-Louis David's *Cupid and Psyche*, Frederic Edwin Church's *Twilight in the Wilderness*, and Nicolas Poussin's *The Holy Family on the Steps*. During the 1960s he strengthened and expanded the museum's small collection of Spanish paintings, adding an impressive number of works by Goya, Velazquez, and Ribera. The chief criticism launched against Lee was of his wariness regarding the value of much of contemporary Western art, including nonrepresentational abstract expressionism and representational neo-Dada. The Cleveland Museum of Art did not take advantage of opportunities to purchase Pop paintings by Andy Warhol, Jasper Johns, and Roy Lichtenstein, and it did not acquire a Jackson Pollock "action painting" until 1980. After retiring as director of the Cleveland Museum of Art, Lee moved to North Carolina, where he taught at Duke University and the University of North Carolina at Chapel Hill. He wrote more than a dozen books,

including *A History of Far Eastern Art* (1964) and *The Colors of Ink* (1974). In his later years he assisted in curating a number of major exhibitions, including Circa 1942: Art in the Age of Exploration at the National Gallery in Washington, D.C., in 1991 and China: 5,000 Years at the Guggenheim Museum in New York City in 1998. After years of struggling with Parkinson's disease, he died at Carolina Meadows, an assisted-living retirement facility in Chapel Hill. He was predeceased by his wife, Ruth (née Ward), and survived by three daughters, a son, six grandchildren, and two step-grandchildren. See *Current Biography* (1974).

Obituary *New York Times* p11 July 11, 2008

LEVIN, IRA Aug. 27, 1929–Nov. 12, 2007 Novelist and playwright. Ira Levin was "the king of the high-concept thriller," as Peter Guttridge observed in the London *Independent* obituary of him. The New York City–born Levin made unbelievable menace and evil frighteningly believable quotidian reality in elaborately plotted novels combining elements of Gothic horror, the occult, mystery, fantasy, and science fiction. In addition to his seven novels, which sold a total of tens of millions of copies, he wrote 10 plays. He achieved his greatest acclaim with his novel of chilling supernatural suspense *Rosemary's Baby* (1967), in which a young couple, Guy and Rosemary Woodhouse, move into the Bramford, an elegant old Manhattan apartment building, where eccentric neighbors, a coven of devil-worshipers, beguile Guy Woodhouse into conniving in the impregnation of his wife with the seed of Satan. *Rosemary's Baby* sold more than five million copies in the United States alone, was translated into numerous foreign languages, and was made into a highly popular feature film (1968). His next most successful novels, both in print and in their original screen adaptations, were the satire *The Stepford Wives* (1972; film, 1975), in which a group of men in an idyllic Connecticut suburb replace their wives with subservient androids, and *The Boys from Brazil* (1976; film, 1978), about an imagined project by the notorious Nazi physician Josef Mengele, living clandestinely in South America, to clone Adolf Hitler and thus revive the Third Reich. (A revisionist second screen adaptation of *The Stepford Wives* [2004] is generally judged to be far inferior to the first.) Levin won the first of two Edgar Awards with his first novel, *A Kiss Before Dying* (1953), a murder mystery told from three perspectives: that of the cold-bloodedly ambitious college student who murders his wealthy pregnant girlfriend for financial reasons and that of the victim's two sisters, who try to track him down. He ventured into science fiction with *This Perfect Day* (1970), in which the protagonist attempts to escape from a totally computerized future society. In *Sliver* (1991), a woman living in a high-rise, high-tech Manhattan apartment building is justifiably paranoid because she is under intense, constant secret surveillance. His last novel was *Son of Rosemary* (1997), a widely derided sequel to *Rosemary's Baby*. Levin once explained that he was theatrically oriented, "thinking in terms of scenes rather than chapters" and always "really writing for the stage." At the beginning of his career, Levin wrote a television adaptation of Mac Hyman's comic novel *No Time for Sergeants,* about a hillbilly U.S. Air Force draftee. His first play was the stage version of that comedy, which ran on Broadway for 706 performances between 1955 and 1957 and was made into a popular motion picture (1958) starring Andy Griffith. Even more successful was his play *Deathtrap*—a wry, convoluted thriller about an aging playwright who schemes to kill a younger rival and steal his play—which ran on Broadway for 1,793 performances between 1978 and 1982, was nominated for a Tony Award, brought him his second Edgar Award, and was made into a feature film (1982). Far less successful on Broadway were his psychological melodrama *Interlock* (1958), his comedy *Critics Choice* (1960), which was adapted to the big screen three years later, his Freudian melodrama *General Seeger* (1962), his musical *Drat the Cat* (1965, with music by Milton Schafer), and his hard-to-classify *Doctor Cook's Garden* (1968), about a small-town physician who fatally poisons people—a career total of 30—whom he regards as too disabled or too immoral to live. *Doctor Cook's Garden* subsequently became a made-for-TV movie. *Veronica's Room* (1973), in which an elderly couple lure a younger couple into an eerily enchanted room, ran for 76 performances on Broadway. In 2002 Levin was quoted as regretting the plethora of novels and movies with Satanic themes (among them *The Exorcist* and *The Omen*) sparked by *Rosemary's Baby* and contributing to some of the increased strength of religious fundamentalism. "A whole generation . . . has more belief in Satan," he lamented. "I don't believe in Satan." Levin was married to and divorced from Gabrielle Aronsohn (1960–68) and Phyllis Finkel (1979–81). His survivors included three sons from his first marriage and three grandsons. He died in his Manhattan apartment, apparently of a heart attack. See *Current Biography* (1991).

Obituary *New York Times* B p11 Nov. 14, 2007

LUCE, CHARLES F. Aug. 29, 1917–Jan. 26, 2008 Public and private utilities administrator; government official; lawyer. After practicing law in Walla Walla, Washington, for 15 years, Charles F. Luce headed the Bonneville Power Administration (1961–66); served as U.S. undersecretary of the interior (1966–67); and was chairman of the board of the Consolidated Edison Co. of New York Inc., headquartered in Manhattan. The Bonneville Power Administration, an agency of the U.S. Department of Energy based in the Columbia River Valley, operates an extensive electricity-generating and -transmission complex—involving federal dams, a nonfederal nuclear plant, and nonfederal hydroelectric and wind energy facilities—and it markets wholesale electrical power at cost in the Pacific Northwest. Beyond his duties within the Bonneville Power Administration, Luce helped to establish the Pacific Northwest–Pacific Southwest Inter-tie transmission system, and he negotiated the 1964 treaty with Canada for joint development of the Columbia River. As undersecretary of the interior, he successfully pressured midwestern oil companies to rescind a cent-and-a-half rise in the price of gasoline. The Consolidated Edison Co., the biggest private utility in the

United States, was in the years just before Luce arrived there also the most troubled. Accused of charging unusually high rates and of polluting New York City's air, it suffered ill will worsened by an inept public-relations policy. As chairman, Luce moved quickly to ameliorate those problems and to revitalize management and streamline personnel at the company. His control of rates encountered a snag in 1973 and 1974, when the Arab oil embargo caused fuel prices to shoot upward. At that time he tried to keep the cost to customers within limits by sacrificing a dividend expected by shareholders, a tactic strongly protested by the shareholders. In 1977 he and Con Ed drew flak for "negligence" in failing to halt a system-wide blackout that was triggered by two lightning strikes in Westchester County. In 1980 he was a participant in the negotiations in which representatives of Con Ed and other utility companies met with representatives of environmental groups and the federal Environmental Protection Agency and arrived at the model economic/environmental accord known as the Hudson River Peace Treaty. Contributing to the revitalization of the Manhattan neighborhood where Con Ed's offices are located, he was one of the founders of the Union Square Business Improvement District. After the death of his first wife, Helen (née Oden), Luce married Margaret (née Richmond), who survived him. His other survivors included two sons, two daughters, and eight grandchildren. He died of prostate cancer in Torrance, California. See *Current Biography* (1968).

Obituary *New York Times* B p7 Jan. 29, 2008

MAC, BERNIE Oct. 5, 1957–Aug. 9, 2008 The comedian and actor Bernie Mac was best known for his starring role in the hit Fox sitcom *The Bernie Mac Show*, his participation in the Original Kings of Comedy tour, which was partially recorded in a film made by Spike Lee, and his other appearances on the big screen. Mac's humor focused largely on events and people in his life and his ideas about child rearing—particularly, the belief that tough love is the best way to mold youngsters' characters. Mac was born Bernard Jeffrey McCullough in Chicago to a single mother. He knew he wanted to be a comedian from an early age, and his mother encouraged him to pursue his dream. After she died of cancer, when Mac was 16, he moved in with one of his grandmothers in the South Side section of Chicago, where he graduated from Chicago Vocational Career Academy. He worked as a janitor, a furniture mover, and a school-bus driver before landing a job at a General Motors plant in 1977. Still aiming for success as a comedian, he performed at comedy clubs on weekends and entertained passengers on the Chicago subway for tips. After losing his General Motors job, in 1983, Mac was unable to find steady work, and he and his family moved in with relatives. He began performing at bigger clubs, and in 1989, after seeing his act, the comedians Redd Foxx and Slappy White invited him to perform in Las Vegas. The following year Mac won the Miller Lite Comedy Search, a national comedy contest, and was invited to host two shows during the Def Comedy Jam tour. That exposure led to his being cast in minor movie roles, in *Mo' Money*

(1992), *Who's the Man?* (1993), and *House Party 3* (1994). In 1994 he headlined his own comedy tour and appeared in his first dramatic film role, in *Above the Rim.* The next year he starred in his own HBO variety show, *Midnight Mac,* which was cancelled after one season. He continued to appear in films, among them *Friday* (1995), *The Walking Dead* (1995), *Get on the Bus* (1996), and *Don't Be a Menace to South Central While Drinking Your Juice in the Hood* (1996). In 1996 he also debuted on the television sitcom *Moesha* in the recurring role of Uncle Bernie. With Steve Harvey, D.L. Hughley, and Cedric "The Entertainer," he entertained in 1997 in the Original Kings of Comedy tour; with receipts of $59 million, it was the highest-grossing comedy tour in history up until then. Two performances were filmed by Spike Lee for the 2000 film *The Original Kings of Comedy.* Shortly afterward the television writer and producer Larry Wilmore developed a TV series loosely based on Mac's life; with Mac in the title role, *The Bernie Mac Show* ran for five seasons (2001–06) on the Fox television network. The unconventional sitcom, in which Mac played a successful comedian who reluctantly agrees to raise his sister's children while she undergoes treatment for drug addiction, was one of the network's biggest hits. Mac was highly praised for his portrayal of the angry, tough, but kindhearted surrogate father. He was twice nominated for Emmy and Golden Globe Awards and won four NAACP Image Awards and a Television Critics Association Award for his depiction of the character. (The show also won a Peabody Award and an Emmy for outstanding writing for a comedy series.) His work for the silver screen in the 2000s included appearances in *Ocean's Eleven* (2001) and its two sequels; *Charlie's Angels: Full Throttle* (2003); *Bad Santa* (2003); *Mr. 3000* (2004); and *Guess Who* (2005). He wrote the books *I Ain't Scared of You: Bernie Mac on How Life Is* (2001) and the autobiography *Maybe You Never Cry Again* (2003). At the time of his death, Mac had finished several projects that were scheduled for release posthumously, among them *Madagascar: Escape 2 Africa* and *Soul Men.* Mac, who had suffered from an immune-system disorder since 1983, died in Chicago from complications of pneumonia. He was survived by his wife, Rhoda McCullough, and a daughter. See *Current Biography* (2002). — M.A.S.

Obituary *New York Times* A p34 Aug. 10, 2008

MAHESH YOGI, MAHARISHI 1911(?)–Feb. 5, 2008 Hindu spiritual leader. A native of India, Maharishi Mahesh Yogi was the "giggling guru" who introduced to the contemporary world his version of an ancient Vedic consciousness-control technique, which he called Transcendental Meditation, or simply TM. For a price, Mahesh assigned to each of his devotees his or her own special mantra, the inner repetition of which, with eyes closed, ideally induces a state of deep relaxation comparable to what in Western terms might be called self-hypnosis. He viewed TM as a way of "freeing the nervous system of tension" that not only "brings bliss consciousness" to individuals but contributes to peace in the world through its pacific contribution to the collective unconscious. The date of Mahesh's birth is unknown; guesses range from 1911 to 1919. Similarly,

his place in the Indian caste system is in dispute; whatever it was, he rose above his caste in choosing to make himself a maharishi ("great seer"). After studying physics and mathematics at Allahabad University, in northern India, he retreated in the early 1940s into a monastic existence in an ashram in Uttar Kashi, in the Himalayan foothills. There, he was the protégé of the swami Brahmananda Saraswati, known familiarly as Guru Dev, who died circa 1952, bequeathing to Mahesh the mission of keeping alive in Hinduism the technique that Mahesh subsequently trademarked as TM. Following several years of preparation in solitude, Mahesh carried Guru Dev's message throughout India until 1958, when he decided to pursue "the regeneration of the whole world through meditation." After lecturing in Burma, Singapore, and Hawaii, he arrived in California, where he founded the American branch of his Spiritual Regeneration Movement in 1959 with an initial membership of 25 devotees, which quickly multiplied. In Hollywood his movement attracted such actors as Shirley MacLaine, Mia Farrow, Efrem Zimbalist Jr., and Clint Eastwood. Other American celebrities who became devotees included the magician Doug Henning and Mike Love, the lead singer of the pop band the Beach Boys. In 1965 a youth branch of Mahesh's movement, the Student International Meditation Society, was founded at the University of California. The membership of that branch soon swelled into the thousands in the U.S. alone, clinching TM's identification with the counterculture of the time. Financed in large measure by his American followers, Mahesh regularly made world tours, which prominently included the United Kingdom, where he attracted such prominent adherents as the film director David Lynch and the pop musicians Mick Jagger, Marianne Faithfull, Donovan, and, most famously, the Beatles. The Beatles' George Harrison brought Mahesh to the attention of his band mates in 1967. In February 1968 the Fab Four flew to India to place themselves under Mahesh's instruction at his ashram in Rishikesh, but one by one they soon became disillusioned and left, within weeks. Mahesh went on to train a total of some 40,000 teachers of TM, to establish scores of schools and a thousand or more teaching centers, and to attract some five million followers worldwide. Widely regarded as a cultist with a keen business sense, Mahesh at the time of his death had assets estimated at $300 million in the U.S. alone. The American branch of his movement is based in the Maharishi University of Management in Fairfield, Iowa, and Maharishi Vedic Village, north of Fairfield. In Great Britain the base is a meditation community of some 400 members in Skelmersdale, Lancashire, founded in 1980. In the London *Independent* (August 17, 2005), Stephen Khan reported growing discontent in that community over Mahesh's "latest ramblings." Khan cited the explanation for TM's "decline" given by Paul Mason, Mahesh's biographer and himself a faithful meditator: in Mason's view, Mahesh in his last years was realizing that his hopes for the world had "not come true," and that was why he was coming up with "wild ideas" (Khan's paraphrase). Among those ideas was a Sidhi pseudo-levitation technique, dubbed "yogic flying" by Mahesh, in which devotees are instructed to bounce in the air while in the lotus position. Mahesh's first book, *The Science of Being and the Art of Living* (1963), revised repeatedly, has been translated into more than a dozen languages and has sold more than a million copies. Among his other books are *Maharishi Mahesh Yogi on the Bhagavad-Gita* (1984), *Thirty Years Around the World: Dawn of the Age of Enlightenment* (1986), and volumes applying TM to natural law, government, business, and management in general. In 1990 Mahesh took possession of a former Franciscan monastery in Vlodrop, the Netherlands, where he lived the remainder of his years. In his final years he communicated even with his closest associates—including his "minister of science and technology," John Hagelin—only by video or closed-circuit television. He died in his compound at Vlodrop. See *Current Biography* (1972).

Obituary *New York Times* C p10 Feb. 6, 2008

MAILER, NORMAN Jan. 31, 1923–Nov. 10, 2007 Novelist; innovative creative-nonfiction journalist; political and social provocateur. Norman Mailer was a macho and mettlesome writer and public personality whose ego was widely described as being as big as his literary talent and his reputation. A prizefighting aficionado, he liked to think of himself as a claimant to the title of "the Champ" of American letters in his time. He also described himself, in the third person, as having "a fatal taint, a last remaining speck of the one personality he found absolutely insupportable—the nice Jewish boy from Brooklyn." Serving in the U.S. Army during World War II, Mailer never saw combat but nevertheless was able to gather the grist for his first book, *The Naked and the Dead* (1948), a critically acclaimed and best-selling naturalistic war novel filled with raunchy dialogue and antiwar satirical jabs. His next books, *Barbary Shore* (1951) and *The Deer Park* (1955), were political novels reflecting his disillusionment with Communism and his concern with governmental and political trends in the U.S.; *Barbary Shore* was widely panned and sold poorly, while *The Deer Park*, by far the superior of the two, fared little better in its initial reception. In Manhattan's Greenwich Village in the mid-1950s, Mailer co-founded the weekly *Village Voice*. Among his contributions to that newspaper was the essay that became the book *The White Negro* (1957), in which he defined as his heroic ideal the nonconformist "hipster" who sets out on "that uncharted journey into the rebellious imperatives of the self." His first collections of essays, reportage, and other short pieces were *Advertisements for Myself* (1959), *The Presidential Papers* (1963), and *Cannibals and Christians* (1966). Hard-pressed for money, he dashed off *An American Dream* (1965; originally published serially in *Esquire* magazine), a nightmarish novel chronicling two wild sex-, alcohol-, and drug-ridden days in the life of its male chauvinist protagonist, a character that Mailer's feminist foes viewed as a reflection of the author's own demons. His quixotic and unsuccessful 1968 campaign for the Democratic nomination for mayor of New York City—on a secession-from-the-state platform—is detailed in *Running Against the Machine* (1969). For *Life* magazine he wrote a series of articles about NASA's 1969 lunar landing that were includ-

ed in his book *Of a Fire on the Moon* (1970). His reportage on the 1968 Republican and Democratic political conventions for *Esquire* magazine was collected in *Miami and the Siege of Chicago* (1968), and his coverage of the legendary November 1974 Muhammad Ali–George Foreman world heavyweight championship boxing match in Zaire was published as the book *The Fight* (1975). His fifth novel, *Why Are We in Vietnam?* (1967), is about a grizzly-bear hunt in Alaska. His later novels include *Ancient Evenings* (1983), a mythopoeic work set in ancient Egypt, the mystery thriller *Tough Guys Don't Dance* (1984), *Harlot's Ghost* (1991), a basically sympathetic fictionalized history of the CIA, and *The Gospel According to the Son* (1997), a story whose narrator is Jesus Christ. Mailer mixed autobiography with reportage and political commentary in such digressive books as *Armies of the Night* (1968), written in the third-person singular, about his participation in a major anti–Vietnam War demonstration at the Pentagon. That book brought him a Pulitzer Prize, and a National Book Award. He won another Pulitzer Prize, in the fiction category, for *The Executioner's Song* (1979), a work of creative nonfiction in the "new journalism" mode, in which he chronicled the life and death of Gary Gilmore, a convicted murderer executed by the State of Utah in 1976. Lawrence Schiller was Mailer's research collaborator for *The Executioner's Song* as well as for *Oswald's Tale* (1995), a biography of Lee Harvey Oswald, the alleged assassin of President John F. Kennedy. Among Mailer's other biographical subjects were Marilyn Monroe and the young Pablo Picasso. *The Essential Mailer* was published in 1982, the gigantic retrospective anthology *The Time of Our Time* in 1998, and *The Spooky Art: Some Thoughts on Writing* in 2003. Also in 2003 Mailer published *Why Are We at War?*, in which he criticized the administration of President George W. Bush and its war in Iraq. *The Castle in the Forest* (2007) is a novel in the guise of the story of Hitler's childhood and adolescence, told by one of Satan's minions. Mailer also wrote short stories and verse, and with family members and friends, he made several low-budget movies, including *Maidstone* (1970) and *Tough Guys Don't Dance* (1987), based on his 1984 novel. Early in his career Mailer was politically pigeonholed as an anti-Stalinist Marxist; later, his anarchist and libertarian bents came to the fore. In 2004 he told Margo Hammond for the *St. Petersburg Times* that he was "a left conservative," explaining that "the conservative element is that I hate political correctness." Fueling Mailer's notoriety were his attacks on the women's-liberation movement, his feuds with the novelist Gore Vidal and others, his womanizing, his abuse at times of drugs and alcohol, his violent mood swings, his efforts to secure the release from prison of Jack Henry Abbott, who killed a man soon afterward, and his near-fatal stabbing of his second wife, Adele Morales, during an all-night drunken party. He was married six times. His survivors included his sixth wife, Norris Church, and nine children, one of whom was adopted. He died of acute renal failure at Mount Sinai Hospital in New York City. See *Current Biography* (1970).

Obituary *New York Times* p1+ Nov. 11, 2007

MARTIN, DICK Jan. 30, 1922–May 24, 2008 Comedian; director. Dick Martin was the goofy half of the droll comedy team of Rowan and Martin, taking his cues for non sequiturs and other zany quips, including double entendres, from his urbane straight man, Dan Rowan. While established on the nightclub circuit and having had some TV exposure, the team was relatively little known to the wide public until 1967–68, when the NBC network launched *Rowan & Martin's Laugh-In,* an hour-long whirlwind of comic vignettes that soon became the most watched show on American television, topping the Nielsen ratings during the 1968–69 and 1969–70 seasons. It was also a hit on BBC television. Aspiring to a career in Hollywood, Martin had moved from his native Michigan to Los Angeles in 1943, when he was 21 years old. For a time he was on the writing staff of the CBS radio situation comedy *Duffy's Tavern,* and he wrote special material for other shows and several comedians, including Ben Blue, but his default occupation was bartending until 1952, when he formed his partnership with Dan Rowan. Rowan and Martin's first ventures into network television, beginning in 1957, were as guests on a number of shows, including Ed Sullivan's, and during the 1960s they hosted several summer replacement shows. The pilot of the comedy-variety sketch program *Rowan and Martin's Laugh-In* was broadcast by NBC as a special in September 1967, and the show began its regular weekly run in a prime-time Monday-night time slot the following January under the daring creative guidance of executive producer George Schlatter and with such provocative writers as the anarchistic Digby Wolfe, a staff of fast-cutting videotape editors, and a stable of soon-to-be-famous comedians and comediennes, including Goldie Hawn and Lily Tomlin. (The house talent would be mingled with a host of visiting luminaries from show business and politics—from Jack Benny and John Wayne to Richard Nixon—whose importance was downplayed.) The highly innovative and trend-setting program was in Martin's view essentially "cartoon comedy"—rapidly fired single-frame "cartoons." The fast-paced mélange of gags, skits, and blackouts (sometimes partially improvisational) often included sexual innuendoes or irreverent political barbs slyly aimed below the censor's radar. The show's identification with the counterculture of the time was reflected in its use of "psychedelic" colors. During its five-year run (1968–73) *Rowan & Martin's Laugh-In* was nominated for 11 Emmy Awards and won five; Martin shared in four of the nominations and in one of the Emmys. The show influenced NBC in its subsequent creation of *Saturday Night Live,* and its lightning-fast editing together of vignettes, often with no cohesion, inspired the techniques subsequently used in such programs as *Hee Haw* and the cable network MTV in the United States and *Monty Python's Flying Circus* in the United Kingdom. With Rowan, Martin starred in the feature film *The Maltese Bippy* (1969), a comic murder mystery. He later had roles in a score of television series, including the situation comedies *Coach* and *Bob.* Prominent among his numerous directorial credits on television were 11 episodes of *The Bob Newhart Show* (1977–78) and five episodes of *Brothers* (1985–86). Following his divorce from his first wife, Peggy Connolly, Martin married Dolly Read,

whom he divorced in 1975 and remarried in 1978. He died of respiratory complications at a hospital in Santa Monica, California. His survivors included his wife, Dolly, and two sons. See *Current Biography* (1969).

Obituary *New York Times* B p6 May 26, 2008

MCKAY, JIM Sep. 24, 1921–June 7, 2008 Broadcaster. Jim McKay—born James Kenneth McManus—was the first television sportscaster to receive an Emmy Award, in 1968, and he went on to win a total of 13 Emmys over the next 24 years. With consummate professionalism, sensitivity, and understated eloquence, he anchored 12 Olympiads and hosted the ABC network's athletic potpourri *Wide World of Sports,* the most diverse, longest-running, and most successful sports program in television history. He is best remembered for his aplomb at the 1972 Summer Olympic Games, in Munich, Germany, when he was thrust from the role of sportscaster into that of on-the-spot news reporter of a massacre. On the morning of September 5, 1972, "Black September" Palestinian *fedayeen* commandos invaded the living quarters of the Israeli team in Olympic Village, killing two members of the team and taking nine members hostage. For 16 hours beginning on that morning, ABC's cameras were unblinkingly focused on that crisis until it ended in a gunfight at NATO's Fürstenfeldbruck air base near Munich shortly after midnight on September 6. McKay himself was the man on camera without a break for 14 of those hours, finally reporting, sadly, that the nine hostages were "all gone." For his performance on that occasion, he became the first sportscaster ever to win a News Emmy in addition to a Sports Emmy. After earning a B.A. degree in social science and serving in the U.S. Navy, McKay joined the staff of the Baltimore *Evening Sun* newspaper as a reporter in 1946. When the *Evening Sun* began operating WMAR-TV two years later, he became that Baltimore station's charter factotum—producer, director, announcer, writer, and news and sports reporter. In 1950 he was hired by CBS-TV, the CBS network's flagship station in New York City, to host a local early-evening variety show titled *The Real McKay.* To accommodate the title, he agreed to change his surname, and he remained Jim McKay professionally ever thereafter, while keeping his legal name, James McManus, in private life. After *The Real McKay* finished its run, in 1962, McKay performed a variety of chores for CBS-TV and the CBS network, from weather and sports reporting to playing the court reporter on the simulated courtroom-drama series *The Verdict Is Yours* (1957–60). On leave from CBS, he was the moderator of the quiz show *Make the Connection* briefly at NBC in 1955. With CBS he had his first Olympics assignment, covering the 1960 Summer Olympics in Rome. His last assignment at CBS was coverage of the Masters tournament at the Augusta National Golf Club in 1961. Following that event, he moved to the ABC network, at the invitation of Roone Arledge, then ABC Sports' new and innovative executive producer. Arledge recruited him specifically to host *Wide World of Sports,* a weekend anthology series intended by Arledge to cover "a number of sports not normally seen on TV." In that assignment, for a quarter of a century beginning in 1961, McKay traveled the United States and the world covering athletic events in many categories, among them baseball, football, basketball, softball, soccer, cricket, rugby, lacrosse, volleyball, polo, hurling, golf, horse racing and jumping, boxing, wrestling, track and field, auto and motorcycle racing, water and air competitions, tennis and table tennis, ice and roller skating, gymnastics, rodeo, bobsled, dogsled racing, cycling, martial arts, weightlifting, baton twirling, billiards, bridge, chess, climbing, skiing and snowboarding, high-wire walking, skateboarding, Special Olympics, barrel jumping, demolition derbies, and lumberjacking. McKay was the author of two books of memoirs, *My Wide World* (1973) and *The Real McKay* (1998) and the narrator of the HBO autobiographical documentary *Jim McKay: My World in My Words* (2003). In addition to his work on *Wide World of Sports*, he anchored coverage of most major American horse races, including the Kentucky Derby, the Preakness Stakes, and the Belmont Stakes. He raised Thoroughbred horses on his estate in Monckton, Maryland, and he founded the Maryland Million Day races at Pimlico for Maryland-bred horses. McKay died at home in Monckton. His survivors included his wife, Margaret McManus (née Dempsey), a syndicated political and television columnist, his son, Sean McManus, a protégé of Roone Arledge who is president of CBS News and Sports, his daughter, Mary Guba, and three grandchildren. See *Current Biography* (1973).

Obituary *New York Times* p32 June 8, 2008

MELLERS, WILFRID Apr. 26, 1914–May 16, 2008 British musicologist; critic; composer; professor emeritus and founder of the Department of Music, University of York. With contagious joy, Wilfrid Howard Mellers crossed old barriers between purported highbrow and lowbrow genres in music, between the classical European orchestral, chamber, vocal, and choral tradition and jazz, blues, folk, and pop. Giving equal attention to Schubert and the Beatles, Mellers directly influenced generations of British musicians as an enthusiastic teacher, and he exerted a wider influence as a highly readable writer in musicology. Among his score of books are *Music and Society: England and the European Tradition* (1946), *Studies in Contemporary Music* (1947), *Romanticism and the Twentieth Century* (1957), *The Sonata Principle* (1957), volumes three and four of *Man and His Music* (1962), *Music in a New Found Land: Themes and Developments in the History of American Music* (1964), *Caliban Reborn: Renewal in Twentieth Century Music* (1968), *Angels of the Night: Popular Female Singers of Our Time* (1986), *Between Old Worlds and New* (1997), and books on François Couperin, the Beatles, Bob Dylan, Bach, Beethoven, Frederic Mompou, Vaughan Williams, Percy Grainger, Francis Poulenc, and European religious music. Mellers's musicological writings overshadowed his musical compositions, which included chamber music, songs and song cycles, the cantatas *Yeibichai* and *A Ballad for Anyone,* incidental theatrical music, and, most prominently, operatic works, including *The Tragicall History of Christopher Marlowe, The Shepherd's Daughter,* and the masque for puppets *The Trial of the Jewelled Peacock.* Many of his compositions had an edenic, childhood-innocence theme. Elfin in physique and manner, Mellers was captivating in the classroom, exuberantly illustrating his lectures with flourishes at the piano. As a young man studying under F. R. Leavis at Downing College, Cambridge University, in the 1930s, Mellers took a first in English before pursuing a degree in music. During that period he began his long tenure as a contributor to Leavis's literary magazine, *Scrutiny*. His first musical appointment was at Darlington Hall, Cambridge (1938–40). After serving as an extramural lecturer at both Cambridge and the University of Birmingham (1940–46), he returned to Downing College as both supervisor in English and lecturer in music (1946–48). At the University of Birmingham (1948–60) he was a staff tutor in music while earning a doctorate in music and before becoming a senior lecturer. As a visiting professor of music at the University of Pittsburgh in the United States in the early 1960s, he not only lectured on music but conducted a seminar on British theater, poetry, and music of the 17th and 18th centuries. Joining the faculty of the University of York in 1964, he taught in the English Department while founding a Music Department. Departing from the traditional practice in British university music departments, Mellers began by recruiting a faculty, not of musicologists, but of young composers, including David Blake, Peter Ashton, and Bernard Rands, and he gave performance a major place in the curriculum. "Mellers's starting point was that music is not music until it is heard and so there should be no separation between theory and practice," Peter Dickinson wrote for the London *Independent* (May 19, 2008). "With this credo Mellers put contemporary ideas at the center of his new department and, thanks to him, most of these beliefs have penetrated higher education in Britain. . . . Composition was encouraged. . . . Mellers was open to all kinds of musical expression, anticipating the pluralism and multiculturalism of the 21st-century scene. . . . The centre of all this was Mellers himself, whose lecturing technique was uniquely charismatic." In 1981 Mellers retired from teaching and became professor emeritus at York. His many honors included the Order of the British Empire (1982). Mellers was married three times and divorced twice. He had two daughters and a granddaughter by his second wife, Peggy (née Lews), another daughter from another relationship, and five stepchildren by his third wife, Robin Hildyard, who survived him. He died in Scrayingham, North Yorkshire. See *Current Biography* (1962).

Obituary *New York Times* B p7 May 23, 2008

MESKILL, THOMAS J. Jan. 30, 1928–Oct. 29, 2007 Government official; lawyer; federal judge. A generally conservative Republican, Thomas Joseph Meskill was mayor of New Britain, Connecticut (1962–64), a U.S. representative from what was then Connecticut's Sixth Congressional District (1967–71), governor of Connecticut (1971–75), a judge (1975–93), and chief judge (1992–93) on the U.S. Court of Appeals for the Second Circuit. In campaigning for his first term in Congress, Meskill attacked the "boondoggles" of the Lyndon B. Johnson administration's so-called War on Poverty. During his two terms in the House of Representatives, he consistently voted with the House's conservative coalition, receiving a rating of 71 percent from Americans for Constitutional Action in 1968. During his four-year term as governor of Connecticut, he vetoed 229 bills passed by the state legislature (where Democrats were in the majority), including one that would have changed the name of the state's Department of Welfare to the Department of Human Resources. In collaboration with Connecticut's welfare commissioner Henry White, he pursued "tough-love" welfare reform, including "workfare." He was instrumental in transforming the deficit in the state treasury into a surplus and in establishing a lottery as the alternative to a state income tax. During his term as governor, the state Department of Environmental Protection was established, no-fault auto insurance and pension protection were introduced, and off-track betting was legalized. Appalled when Connecticut's 1860 antiabortion law was overturned, in 1972, he compared the ruling to the Supreme Court's *Dred Scott v. Sanford* decision of 1857, which declared that a black slave had no legal rights. Meskill, who suffered from the blood disorder called myelodysplasia, died at Bethesda Memorial Hospital in Boynton Beach, Florida. His survivors included his wife, Mary (Grady) Meskill, three sons, and two daughters. See *Current Biography* (1974).

Obituary *New York Times* D p8 Oct. 30, 2007

METZENBAUM, HOWARD June 4, 1917–Mar. 12, 2008 Democratic U.S. senator from Ohio (1974–75, 1977–95). A self-made millionaire and former labor lawyer and state legislator, Howard Morton Metzenbaum was an unabashed liberal firebrand in the U.S. Senate, a champion of working people and a scourge of big business, including oil companies, the insurance industry, cable-television monopolies, and savings-and-loan associations. The National Rifle Association was another of his targets. An astute master of the rules of order, Metzenbaum made inventive use of such tactics as filibusters and prolonged roll calls to block legislation he opposed—including excessive pork-barreling, tax-loophole bills, and myriad conservative proposals—especially during his early years in the Senate, when the Republicans were in the majority and he was known as "Senator No." Best known nationally as a tenacious and often ferocious questioner in televised hearings of the Senate Judiciary Committee, he also served on committees on the environment, public works, human resources, and intelligence. After the Democrats became the majority in 1986, his clout as a committee member became more positive, and he moved into the chairmanship of important subcommittees, including labor and antitrust panels. As a champion of labor, he successfully sponsored legislation requiring companies to give 60 days' notice of plant closings; he strived to protect or promote the right to strike, workplace safety, and pension plans and fought age discrimination. In consumer protection his concerns ranged from food labeling and baby-formula pricing to control of the cost of energy, including natural gas. As a promoter of gun control, he was the chief Senate sponsor of the so-called Brady Bill, calling for a waiting period for handgun purchases. One of only 10 Jews in the Senate (as of the early 1990s), he quietly but effectively advocated for Israel among his fellow senators when issues in legislative proposals regarding the Middle East and originating in the White House moved him to do so. Metzenbaum earned his fortune through his co-ownership of a Cleveland car-rental business that became one of the largest Avis franchises; a Cleveland airport parking lot that grew into the Airport Parking Co. of America; and the Sun newspaper chain in northeastern Ohio. After personally experiencing anti-Semitism, he led successful fights against ethnic discrimination in a country club and a bank in Cleveland. During the 1940s he served two terms in the Ohio House of Representatives and another two terms in the state Senate. He subsequently managed two successful campaigns for the U.S. Senate by Stephen M. Young. Running for the U.S. Senate himself in 1970, he defeated John Glenn, the veteran Marine combat pilot and famous astronaut, in the Democratic primary but lost to Republican Robert Taft Jr. by a narrow margin in the general election. After the Republican senator William B. Saxbe of Ohio resigned his seat to become the U.S. attorney general late in 1973, John J. Gilligan, the Democratic governor of Ohio, named Metzenbaum to serve the remaining year of Saxbe's Senate term (January 1974–January 1975). Meanwhile, Metzenbaum again faced John Glenn in a rancorous Democratic primary in 1974, during which Metzenbaum asserted that Glenn had "never met a payroll," a statement widely misparaphrased as "never held a job." Insulted, Glenn retorted with what became known as his patriotic "Gold Star Mothers" speech. Glenn, who won the primary and the subsequent general election, did not speak to Metzenbaum—nor Metzenbaum to Glenn—for 10 years, according to reports. (They had a reconciliation of sorts in the mid-1980s.) Defeating Robert Taft Jr. in the 1976 general election, Metzenbaum began his first six-year term as an elected senator in January 1977, and he was reelected in 1982 and 1988. After leaving the Senate, in 1995, he headed the Consumer Federation of America. Metzenbaum died at his home in Aventura, Florida. He was survived by his wife, Shirley (née Turoff), and four daughters. See *Current Biography* (1980).

Obituary *New York Times* A p22 Mar. 14, 2008

MOHAMMED, W. DEEN Oct. 30, 1933–Sep. 9, 2008 W. Deen Mohammed served as the spiritual leader of the American Society of Muslims for almost three decades. A son of the Nation of Islam (NOI) leader Elijah Muhammad, he renounced his father's ideology, which identified white people as devils, and created a more traditional and racially tolerant form of Islam for the black Muslim community. He was born Wallace Deen Muhammad in Detroit, Michigan. His father was a disciple of Wallace D. Fard, the founder of the NOI, who preached that African-Americans are the true children of God and that their true religion is Islam. After Fard disappeared, in 1934, Elijah Muhammad became the leader of the NOI. He proclaimed that Fard had been an incarnation of God and that he himself was the last prophet. His family traveled the country spreading the NOI message and set up headquarters in Chicago. At a young age W. Deen Mohammed began to question his father's beliefs. He was taught Arabic as a child, and his skepticism deepened after he read the Koran. For many years he hid his convictions and instead focused on the love of God that he and his father shared. He became an NOI minister after he completed high school and studied English, history, and social sciences at two local colleges. His refusal to serve in the military led to his imprisonment for three years (1961–64), during which time he studied Sunni Islam. After he regained his freedom, he began to preach about a nonracial, more orthodox version of Islam. His rejection of parts of his father's dogma led Elijah Muhammad several times to expel him from the NOI and then reinstate him. When his father died, in 1975, Mohammed was elected supreme minister of the NOI. Upon becoming an imam the following year, he changed his first name to Warith. (Earlier, he had changed the spelling of his surname.) He renamed the NOI the World Community of al-Islam in the West and, later, the American Muslim Mission. Mohammed welcomed members of other races, emphasized the importance of studying the Koran, and rejected the notion of Fard's divinity. (Louis Farrakhan revived the NOI as a separate organization in 1977.) In 1977 he led what was then the largest pilgrimage of American Muslims to Mecca, Islam's holiest city, in Saudi Arabia. In 1992 he became the first Muslim to deliver the opening prayer in the U.S. Senate, and he led prayers at President Bill Clinton's inaugurations, in 1993 and 1997. He met with world leaders, participating in interfaith dialogues with the Pope in 1996 and 1999. He resigned from his role as leader of the group in 2003, citing his frustration with imams who, according to him, would not seek more religious education and expected members to follow them blindly. Mohammed wrote several books, among them *The Champion We Have in Common: The Dynamic African American Soul*, (2002). He died at his home in Markham, Illinois. It is believed that his fourth wife, eight children, and five stepchildren survive him. See *Current Biography* (2004). — M.A.S.

Obituary *New York Times* B p6 Sep. 10, 2008

MOISEYEV, IGOR Jan. 21, 1906–Nov. 2, 2007 Ukrainian-born Russian ballet dancer; choreographer; director. As the internationally acclaimed founder of the Moiseyev Ballet Company, Igor Alexandrovich Moiseyev introduced to the professional ballet stage a genre of choreographic art based on folk dance. Moiseyev was born in Kiev, the capital of Ukraine, and grew up there, in Paris, and in Moscow, where he graduated from the Bolshoi Theatre's school of ballet in 1924. (Seven years earlier Moscow, the capital of the Russian republic, had also become the capital of the Union of Soviet Socialist Republics, comprising 15 republics, including Ukraine. It remained so until the dissolution of the USSR, in 1991.) As a leading dancer with the Bolshoi Ballet, Moiseyev performed such roles as Phoenix in *The Red Poppy* and Mato in Salammbô. The latter mentioned was choreographed by him, to music by Heinrich Arends, in 1932. *The Footballer* (1930) and *Three Fat Men* (1935)—both to music by Victor Oranasky—

were among the other ballets he choreographed for the Bolshoi. He was maître de ballet of the Bolshoi Ballet from 1936 to 1939, when he left that company, apparently because of the conflict between his proclivity for modernist experimentation and the ruling orthodoxy of Stalinist "social realism." (Two decades later he choreographed—to music by Aram Khachaturian—the ballet *Spartacus,* given its premiere by the Bolshoi Ballet in 1958.) Meanwhile he had found a politically correct outlet for his creativity in his exploration of the folk art and customs, especially the traditional music and dance, of the Soviet Union's numerous ethnic groups. As director of the Moscow Theatre of Folk Art, in 1937 he organized a folk-dance festival, out of which emerged the Moiseyev Ballet Company (originally called the State Academic Dance Ensemble of the Soviet Union). That troupe of dancers, originally 30 in number, tripled in size over the following decades, incorporated in its repertoire the folk dances of countries outside the USSR, and after Stalin's death regularly toured Europe and, beginning in 1958, the United States (where anti-Soviet activists sometimes picketed its performances). Among the works he choreographed for the company were those translated as *Pictures from the Past, Tsam, Regions of the World*, and *Partisans*. The last mentioned, a tribute to Soviet guerrilla fighters in World War II, was the best known. Other works in his company's repertoire included *Bul'ba,* about harvest, *Soccer,* a satire on the sport, and *Two Boys in a Fight*, a novelty wrestling piece. In conjunction with the dance company Moiseyev established a dance academy in Moscow. In addition to his folk-based troupe, he founded and directed for four years (1967–71) the State Ensemble of Classical Ballet. After his marriage to Tamara Zeifert ended in divorce, Moiseyev married Alekseevna Chagadaeva, who survived him. He was also survived by a daughter from his first marriage. He died at a hospital in Moscow. See *Current Biography* (1958).

Obituary *New York Times* B p7 Nov. 3, 2007

MONDAVI, ROBERT June 18, 1913–May 16, 2007 Vintner; chairman emeritus of the Robert Mondavi Corp., which had annual sales of more than nine million cases of wine and annual revues of approximately $468 million at the time the Mondavi family sold the corporation, in 2004. No single person was more responsible for the renaissance of the American wine industry in general and California wine making in particular in the second half of the 20th century than Robert Mondavi, the recognized "patriarch" of the Napa Valley vineyard country. When *Fortune* magazine inducted him into its National Business Hall of Fame, in 1991, its citation read: "Mondavi the innovator was a leader in raising the quality of U.S. wines to world-class standards; Mondavi the promoter was tireless in winning world recognition of those wines." In addition, Mondavi was instrumental in educating Americans in the practice of moderate wine consumption in the home and as an integral part of hospitality and civilized living. After helping his father revive the prestigious but failing Charles Krug Winery, in 1966 Mondavi founded his own Robert Mondavi Winery, with vineyards covering 1,000 acres in Oakville, California. Inspired by his visits to European vineyards and wine cellars, he modeled his improvements in wine making on such vinicultures as those of Bordeaux and the Loire Valley. Using, for example, cold fermentation, small French oak aging casks, and stainless-steel fermenting tanks, he began producing premium wines on a par with the finest that European vintners were offering. Among his greatest successes were his reserve red Cabernet Sauvignon and several white varietals, including his famous "Fumé Blanc" version of Sauvignon Blanc. Robert Gerald Mondavi, better known as Bob Mondavi, was born to Italian immigrant parents in Minnesota, where he was raised until 1923, when the family moved to California. At St. Helena in the Napa Valley, his father, Cesare Mondavi, became part owner of the Sunnyhill Winery, an enterprise that brokered bulk wine, producing it from purchased grapes and selling it to others for bottling. After earning a degree in economics and business administration at Stanford University, Bob joined his father on the production staff at Sunnyhill. In 1943 he and his younger brother Peter—a stricter businessman than Bob, reportedly less inclined to a visionary perspective on wine-making as an art—persuaded their father to buy the Charles Krug Winery, with the understanding that they, the sons, would run that company. So they did, for more than two decades, with Peter in charge of production and Bob handling development, promotion, and marketing. Their differences in philosophy became more acrimonious after the death of their father, in 1959, and the brothers literally came to blows in 1965. At that point Bob left the Charles Krug Winery while retaining a 24 percent share in the company. Within a year he launched Robert Mondavi Winery with the help of others, including two financial partners. His sons, Michael and Timothy (from the first of his two marriages), would soon join him in running his winery. Later his daughter, Marcia (also from his first marriage), would join the management team, in Oakville, California. In 1969 his two partners sold their shares in the Robert Mondavi Winery to the Rainier Companies, controlled at that time by the giant Canadian beer brewer Molson Inc. A long legal dispute with Peter Mondavi ended in 1978 with an out-of-court settlement, which gave Bob the financial wherewithal to buy Rainier/Molson's million shares and obtain the controlling interest in the Robert Mondavi Winery. It also enabled him to acquire a second winery, Woodbridge, in Lodi, California, and thus to include a second label—Woodbridge—under the umbrella of the Robert Mondavi Corp. (Woodbridge is devoted to somewhat less expensive popular/premium wines.) Additional labels would subsequently be included, some of which resulted from joint ventures, including an ultra-premium wine partnership with France's Baron Philippe de Rothschild. In 1990 Bob Mondavi named his sons co-CEOs of the Robert Mondavi Corp. In 1993 the corporation went public, and 11 years later it was sold to Constellation Brands, the international alcoholic beverages conglomerate, for approximately $1 billion. With the help of the writer Paul Chutknow, Bob Mondavi published his autobiography, *Harvest of Joy: My Passion for Excellence*, in 1998. Julia Flynn Siler wrote *The House of Mon-*

davi: The Rise and Fall of an American Wine Dynasy (2007). After his divorce from his first wife, Marjorie (née Declusin), the mother of his three children, Mondavi married Margrit (née Biever). As philanthropists, he and Margrit spent 10s of millions of dollars establishing a wine and food-science institute and a performing-arts center at the University of California at Davis and, with other vintners, Copia: The American Center for Wine, Food, and the Arts in Napa, California. They also co-founded the Oxbow School, a visual-arts center for high-school students, and, with Julia Child, the American Institute for Wine and Food. Mondavi died at his home in Yountville, California. His survivors included his wife, Margrit, his two sons, his daughter, nine grandchildren, and his brother Peter, with whom he had reconciled. See *Current Biography* (1999).

Obituary *New York Times* B p5 May 17, 2008

MOORE, GEORGE E. Feb. 22, 1920–May 19, 2008 Physician and surgeon; medical researcher; educator; administrator. A renowned specialist in oncology, George Eugene Moore began his seminal work in that field as a young intern at the University of Minnesota Hospitals (1946–47), when he made pioneering use of fluorescent and radioactive substances in locating and diagnosing brain tumors. Moore was subsequently the coordinator of cancer studies at the University of Minnesota Medical School until 1953, when he became director of the Roswell Park Cancer Institute, then called the Roswell Park Memorial Institute, in Buffalo, New York. As director, he was instrumental during the following years in building that small and struggling New York State–financed hospital/laboratory complex into a sprawling world-class center of cancer diagnosis, therapy, and research. In 1954 he and his colleagues published the first major study establishing a causal link between the chewing of tobacco and mouth cancer, and he later directed a study of nine brands of filter-tipped cigarettes, the conclusion of which was that advertising claims about the effectiveness of some filters in capturing carcinogens were "almost fraudulent." In the late 1950s and early 1960s, Moore and his colleagues developed the tissue culture RPMI-1640 for growing human tumor cells in test tubes. He oversaw the establishment at Roswell Park of a plant for the mass production of cancer cells *in vitro*; frozen, classified, and stored, that supply of cells became a source drawn upon not only for experiments at the institute itself but for shipment to researchers throughout the world. At Roswell Park Moore also did pioneering experiments with the tumor-suppressing drug TSPA. In addition to his direction of Roswell Park, in 1967 Moore became director of all medical research for the New York State Department of Health, a position to which he soon devoted himself full-time. In 1973 he moved to Denver to join the faculty of the University of Colorado, where he spent the rest of his career. Moore, who lived in Conifer, Colorado, died in Evergreen, Colorado, of bladder cancer. His survivors included his wife, Lorraine (née Hammell), two sons, three daughters, eight grandchildren, and three great-grandchildren. See *Current Biography* (1968).

Obituary *New York Times* B p6 June 14, 2008

MOSEL, TAD May 1, 1922–Aug. 24, 2008 Dramatist. Tad Mosel wrote many television plays during the 1950s. He was best known for *All the Way Home* (1960), the Broadway adaptation of James Agee's autobiographical novel, *A Death in the Family*, which earned Mosel the 1961 Pulitzer Prize for drama. Born George Ault Mosel Jr., he was nicknamed Tad by his father. He discovered theater at the age of 14, when his family moved from Ohio to New York. Mosel studied English at Amherst College, in Massachusetts, and served in the Army Air Forces Weather Service from 1943 to 1946. He went on to attend Yale Drama School and Columbia University. In 1949, in the Broadway comedy *At War with the Army*, he had a nonspeaking role as a lost private trying to find his company. Mosel's first play to be produced was *The Lion Hunters*, which premiered Off-Broadway in 1953. Later that year Fred Coe, then the producer of the NBC show *Television Playhouse*, produced and broadcast Mosel's *The Haven*. Mosel went on to write dozens of other television plays, among them *Other People's Houses* (1953), *Madame Aphrodite* (1953), *My Lost Saints* (1955), and *The Out-of-Towners* (1957). (During that period the major networks often broadcast live performances of plays.) Mosel's adaptation of Robert Sherwood's play *The Petrified Forest* aired on NBC's *Producers' Showcase* in 1955, with Henry Fonda, Lauren Bacall, and Humphrey Bogart in the lead roles. *All the Way Home* opened on Broadway in November 1960 and, along with the Pulitzer, won the 1961 New York Drama Critics Circle Award for the best American play of the Broadway season. Mosel continued to write television plays and wrote the screenplay for the 1967 film *Up the Down Staircase*, adapted from the Bel Kaufman novel. He also wrote the teleplay for a television version of *All the Way Home* (1971) and co-authored, with Gertrude Macy, the biography *Leading Lady: The World and Theater of Katharine Cornell* (1978). Mosel died of cancer in Concord, New Hampshire. He was predeceased by his partner of four decades, Raymond Tatra, and left no immediate relatives. See *Current Biography* (1961). — M.A.S.

Obituary *New York Times* C p11 Aug. 26, 2008

MOTT, STEWART R. Dec. 4, 1937–June 12, 2008 Philanthropist; founder of the Stewart R. Mott Charitable Trust. A self-described "avant-garde philanthropist," Stewart Rawlings Mott was a munificent bankroller of progressive causes, in the areas of human rights, civil liberties, civil rights, feminism, peace, arms reduction, arms control, homosexual rights, sex research, government reform, and population control, including international family planning and reproductive rights. In politics he supported a multitude of candidates, most conspicuously those challenging incumbent presidents, such as the anti–Vietnam War candidates Eugene J. McCarthy, in 1968, and George S. McGovern, in 1972. He was the single largest contributor to McGovern's presidential campaign. An eccentric, he sometimes also funded offbeat pursuits, such as studies of extrasensory perception. The consumer advocate Ralph Nader described Mott as "about the most versatile, imaginative philanthropist of his time. He threw himself into projects and was a pioneer in many fields well before

the large foundations." Mott inherited his fortune from his father, the Michigan entrepreneur Charles Stewart Mott, who was at one time the largest stockholder in the General Motors Corp. After earning a degree in business administration and engaging in graduate work in Greek drama at Columbia University, Stewart R. Mott devoted himself to Planned Parenthood, setting up a birth-control clinic in Flint, Michigan (his birthplace), and serving as an emissary for the national organization, traveling in its behalf across the United States and internationally. He soon became Planned Parenthood's largest single contributor, giving $1.24 million to it and related groups between 1964 and 1968. Offering himself as a consultant to his father's Mott Foundation, a staid organization that concentrated all of its largess on educational and other programs for Flint, he proposed that the foundation would better serve humanity by universalizing three-quarters of its gift-giving and including more progressive causes. After his father rejected his suggestion, he moved to New York City and threw himself into the activities of his own first nonprofit foundation, called Spectemur Agendo ("Let us be known by our deeds," the motto of the Mott family). For Planned Parenthood, his first priority, he worked as a volunteer in the organization's New York office for about a year so that he could learn the mechanics of fund-raising. During that year he raised approximately $3 million. During the late 1960s and early 1970s, he financially supported not only the anti-war Democratic presidential candidates but many peace candidates for lesser offices from both parties. In 1972 he established People Politics, a committee to raise funds to reform the Democratic National Convention to better represent women, blacks, and youths. Some of the $100,000 that he contributed to People Politics, along with funds raised by the committee, were distributed among the National Women's Political Caucus, the National Black Political Caucus, the National Youth Political Caucus, and the Center for Political Reform. Other organizations he supported were the Fund for Peace, SANE (the Committee for a Sane Nuclear Policy), Zero Population Growth, the Center for Corporate Responsibility, the Center for the Study of Democratic Institutions, and Amnesty International. Beginning in the 1980s he concentrated his energy on the the the Stewart R. Mott Charitable Trust, devoted to funding attempts to expose corruption in government and protect constitutional rights. Mott and Kappy Wells, a sculptor, were married in 1979 and divorced in 1999. Mott died at Northern Westchester Hospital in Mount Kisco, New York. His son, Sam, was among his survivors. See *Current Biography* (1975).

Obituary *New York Times* B p6 June 14, 2008

MWANAWASA, LEVY Sep. 3, 1948–Aug. 19, 2008 Zambian politician. Levy Mwanawasa, elected president of Zambia in 2002, died in 2008 while still in office. As president he worked to combat AIDS and government corruption and helped his country's economy grow. He was born in Mufulira in northern Zambia and studied law at the University of Zambia. In 1974 he began practicing at private law firms, and four years later he started his own firm, Mwanawasa and Co., which remained in business until his death. A supporter of the Movement for Multi-Party Democracy, he was appointed solicitor general in 1985, during the administration of President Kenneth Kaunda, and served in that post until 1987. When Frederick Chiluba defeated Kaunda in the 1991 election, Chiluba named Mwanawasa vice president. Only weeks after accepting the position, Mwanawasa suffered multiple injuries in a car crash. The accident left his speech slurred and permanently affected his health. In 1994 he resigned from the vice presidency, complaining of corruption within the administration. Toward the end of Chiluba's second presidential term, he endorsed Mwanawasa as his successor. Mwanawasa narrowly won the 2002 election against 10 opponents, with 29 percent of the votes. He served as minister of defense (2002–03 and 2003 until his death) and as president concurrently. During his presidency he gained admiration from international leaders by fighting corruption and instituting fiscally conservative policies. He attracted foreign investors to Zambia, and a large part of the nation's foreign debt was forgiven. Amid allegations that Chiluba had embezzled money from the Zambian government, Mwanawasa called for his Chiluba's immunity to be lifted, and charges were leveled against him. Before Mwanawasa's reelection, in 2006, he cited the continuing, widespread, grinding poverty in his nation as one of his failures as president. In April 2008, as chairman of the Southern African Development Community, he organized a meeting of the community's 14 nation members (which include Zimbabwe) and condemned Zimbabwe's president, Robert Mugabe, for refusing to accept the results of Zimbabwe's countrywide election, held on March 29, 2008, and for leading his nation into an economic calamity. He died in a hospital in France seven weeks after suffering a stroke. He was survived by his wife, Maureen, and six children. See *Current Biography International Yearbook* (2003). — M.A.S.

Obituary *New York Times* A p21 Aug. 20, 2008

NERINA, NADIA Oct. 21, 1927–Oct. 6, 2008 A principal ballerina with the Royal Ballet (called the Sadler's Wells Ballet until 1956), Nadia Nerina was known for her technical ability—particularly her high, far-reaching jumps—as well as her delicacy, vitality, physical beauty, and charming demeanor, especially in light-hearted roles; she remained one of the company's most popular dancers for a quarter of a century. She was born Nadine Judd in Bloemfontein, South Africa, and began ballet lessons at an early age. In 1945, after a half-dozen years of study with teachers in Durban, South Africa, she traveled to London, England, for further instruction. Two years later she joined the Sadler's Wells Ballet. She soon attracted notice, in the role of the Circus Dancer in Andrée Howard's *Mardi Gras*. She became one of the choreographer Frederick Ashton's favorite dancers after she portrayed the spring fairy in the premiere of Ashton's *Cinderella*, in 1948. She was promoted to principal dancer in 1952 and had leading roles in dances including *The Sleeping Beauty, Coppélia, Giselle, The Firebird, Les Sylphides, Spectre de la Rose, Carnaval, Ondine, Sylvia, Homage to the

Queen, Variations on a Theme by Purcell, Birthday Offering, Don Quixote, Mam'zelle Angot, Ballet Imperial,* and *Petrushka*. After attending the Sadler's Wells company's performance of *The Sleeping Beauty* at the Metropolitan Opera House in New York, John Martin, a dance critic for the *New York Times* (September 23, 1953), wrote, "Miss Nerina is completely adorable. She is pretty as a picture, has great charm and can dance like a million dollars. Her body is beautifully placed, giving her lovely, free arms and an unusually articulated torso. There are simply no problems of movement for her, and never so much as a hint of an ugly one. When Miss Nerina has developed a musical phrase to equal her command of the physical medium, we shall all be fighting to drink Champagne out of her slippers." Nerina danced the role of the main character in Kenneth McMillan's first ballet, *Noctambules* (1956). In 1960 she performed as a guest artist in Russia (then part of the Soviet Union) with both the Kirov Ballet in Leningrad (now Saint Petersburg) and the Bolshoi in Moscow. That year she also debuted in her most famous role, that of Lise in Ashton's celebrated ballet *La Fille Mal Gardée*. In 1963 Nerina performed the title role in *Elektra* (1963), which the choreographer Robert Helpmann had created for her. Her frequent dance partners included Erik Bruhn and David Blair. Many ballet aficionados assumed that Nerina would succeed Margot Fonteyn as the Royal Ballet's star ballerina, but when Rudolf Nureyev defected from Russia and joined the ballet, in 1961, he became Fonteyn's partner and revived her career. Nerina remained a leading dancer with the Royal Ballet until her retirement, in 1969—10 years before Fonteyn's. She moved to Monte Carlo, Monaco, with her husband, Charles Gordon. She is the subject of the book *Ballerina: Portraits and Impressions of Nadia Nerina* (1975), by Clement Crisp. She died at Beaulieu-sur-Mer, near Nice, France. Her only survivor was her husband, whom she married in 1956. See *Current Biography* (1957).— M.A.S.

Obituary *New York Times* B p10 Oct. 11, 2008

NEWMAN, PAUL Jan. 26, 1925–Sep. 26, 2008 Actor; humanitarian. Paul Newman was the 20th-century American cinema's quintessential charismatic anti-hero. In a posthumous tribute for *Time* magazine (on-line), Richard Corliss described Newman as "the iconic movie star of his age," a "most conventionally gorgeous" actor who played against his good looks (including his famously blue eyes) to become a "50-year film eminence by forging a screen personality that was instantly recognizable and virtually unprecedented: the modern American male who radiated equal parts sexuality and menace while taking an easy pleasure in his ability to attract and upset the people he met on screen—and [the] fans . . . who kept coming back to see Paul Newman play cunning variations on 'Paul Newman.'" In addition to acting, Newman competed in amateur and professional auto racing and was engaged in several philanthropies. As a race-car driver, he won a national amateur championship in 1976; after he turned pro, in 1977, he and his team won 107 races and eight series championships. His proudest legacies as a philanthropist are several holiday camps for children with cancer and other life-threatening diseases and New-man's Own, a food company (founded in partnership with A. E. Hotchner in 1982 and run with the help of his daughter Nell, an organic-foods expert) spe-cializing in the likes of oil-and-vinegar dressings, preserves, spaghetti sauce, lemonade, cookies, pop-corn, and other snacks. The profits from Newman's Own—totaling approximately $200 million as of 2008—have gone to various charities. Paul Leonard Newman was born to a Catholic mother and a Jewish father in Cleveland, Ohio. Following World War II service in the U.S. Navy, he began acting at Kenyon College and later studied at the Yale University School of Drama and the Actors Studio in New York City. Beginning in 1952 he was cast in a number of television dramas. On Broadway he made his debut as Alan Seymour in *Picnic* (1953–54), played the psychotic criminal holding a family captive in *The Desperate Hours* (1955), and created the role of Chance Wayne, the ill-starred protagonist of Tennes-see Williams's dark tragedy *Sweet Bird of Youth* (1959–60). After an inauspicious screen debut, as the Greek artisan Basil in the religious costume drama *The Silver Chalice* (1956), Newman broke through as a leading man in film as the protagonist in *Somebody Up There Likes Me* (1956), the life story of the welter-weight prize fighter Rocky Graziano, the success of which landed him a seven-year contract with War-ner Brothers. He began to establish his screen perso-na as a likable scoundrel in the role of the unprinci-pled drifter Ben Quick in *The Long Hot Summer* (1958), the first of the 10 motion pictures in which he shared the screen with Joanne Woodward, his second wife. He followed that performance up with his intense portrayal of the hard-drinking, sexually conflicted Brick Pollitt in the box-office hit *Cat on a Hot Tin Roof* (1958). He was unhappy with the other, mediocre roles offered him by Warner Brothers, and in 1960 he spent $500,000 to extricate himself from his contract. Forthwith he began to explore what he called the "corruptibility level" of human beings in such roles as the unscrupulous pool shark Fast Eddie Felson in *The Hustler* (1961) and a reprise of his por-trayal of Chance Wayne in the somewhat expurgated screen adaptation of *Sweet Birth of Youth* (1962). In the title role in the director Martin Ritt's masterpiece *Hud* (1963), a generational drama set in the contem-porary American West, Newman, playing the self-centered son of a cattle rancher who loses his herd to disease, "was so repellently brilliant as an unre-generate heel that his Oscar nomination [the third of 10] . . . was a foregone conclusion," as Hal Erickson observed in the All Movie Guide (on-line). Newman drew his fourth Academy Award nomination for his performance as Lucas Jackson, an inmate in a Florida prison camp who refuses to the bitter end to conform to the penal system, in *Cool Hand Luke* (1967), a classic in the chain-gang genre that is included in the Library of Congress's National Film Registry. In a change of pace, Newman (as Butch Cassidy) teamed with Robert Redford (as the Sundance Kid) to star in *Butch Cassidy and the Sundance Kid* (1969), a good-natured picaresque comedy/drama based on the es-capades of the legendary Robin Hood–like Western outlaws Robert Parker (Butch Cassidy) and Harry Longbaugh (the Sundance Kid). That film, directed by George Roy Hill, was the highest-grossing West-

ern in motion-picture history. Newman became in-terested in auto racing when he played Frank Capua, the protagonist in the race-track film *Winning* (1969). He and Redford were reunited in Hill's *The Sting* (1973), a Depression-era comedy/drama about two Chicago con men who, in an elaborate ven-geance scam, swindle a huge amount of money from the gambling racketeer responsible for the murder of a friend of theirs. Newman earned his fifth Oscar nomination for his performance as an honest busi-nessman victimized by an irresponsible muckraking journalist in *Absence of Malice* (1981) and his sixth for his portrayal of the alcoholic lawyer in *The Ver-dict.* He won three Academy Awards: in 1986 he was presented with an honorary award "in recognition of his many memorable and compelling screen perfor-mances and for his personal integrity and dedication of this craft"; in 1987 he received the Oscar for best actor for his reprise of the role of Fast Eddie Felton in *The Color of Money* (1986); and in 1994 he was given the Jean Hersholt Humanitarian Award. He ac-crued a total of 55 feature-film credits, including *Ex-odus* (1960), *Harper* (1966), *Slap Shot* (1977), *Fort Apache the Bronx* (1981), and *Mr. and Mrs. Bridge*, which co-starred Woodward (1990). His final Acade-my Award nomination was for his supporting role as John Rooney in *The Road to Perdition* (2002). On television he was nominated for an Emmy Award for his performance as the Stage Manager in a produc-tion of *Our Town* (2003) and won an Emmy for his portrayal of Max Roby in *Empire Falls* (2003). Promi-nent among the several films he directed were *Ra-chel, Rachel* (1968), starring Woodward, and *The Glass Menagerie* (1984), in which Woodward was cast as Amanda Winfield. He and Woodward were married in 1958, following his divorce from his first wife, Jackie Witte. He was survived by Woodward, their three daughters, two daughters from his first marriage, and two grandchildren. His son, Scott, from his first marriage, predeceased him. Although he lent his name prominently to various liberal causes, Newman lived a very private life, far from the glamour of Hollywood. He died—of cancer—at home, in the 18th-century farmhouse near Westport, Connecticut where he and Woodward raised their daughters. See *Current Biography* (1985).

Obituary *New York Times* A p1+ Sep. 28,. 2008

O'NEILL, WILLIAM A. Aug. 11. 1930–Nov. 24, 2007 Democratic governor of Connecticut (1980–91). A low-key and relatively unambitious politician of working-class background, William Atchison O'Neill became governor, as he said, "because of happenstance, luck, and tragedy." After serving six terms in the State House of Representatives, the low-er legislative body of the Connecticut General As-sembly, O'Neill was elected lieutenant governor as the running mate of Ella T. Grasso in her successful bid for election to her second term as governor, in 1978. In December 1981, terminally ill with cancer, Grasso resigned as governor, turning over the office to O'Neill. In serving out the remaining months of Grasso's term, O'Neill described himself as essen-tially a caretaker of her legacy, brokering compro-mises with the state legislature in pursuit of her poli-cies. Elected to a full four-year term as governor in his own right in November 1982, he acted with new self-confidence. When the state's economy began to boom in 1984, he proposed a $4 billion budget with tax increases in only one area, that of transportation. The Democratic-controlled General Assembly passed his legislative package nearly intact, including a program to upgrade Connecticut's roads and bridges to be financed in part by increased gasoline taxes and motor-vehicle fees. The state realized an unexpected $144 million surplus during the fiscal year ending June 30, 1984. The following November Republicans won majorities in both houses of the legislature. Despite that disadvantage, O'Neill worked out impressive compromises with the newly configured state House and Senate. In the first five months of 1985, he signed 200 bills and vetoed only two measures sent to him by the General Assembly. In May 1985 he signed a bipartisan $3.95 billion state budget that included provisions for tax cuts totaling $155 million and a substantial increase in state aid to education. Addressing the opening session of the General Assembly in 1986, he was able to claim that Connecticut had "created the best business climate of all 50 states." He won reelection as governor in November 1986. During his last term as governor, he traveled to Washington, D.C., to support a congressional measure calling for a moratorium on the kind of tax imposed by the state of New York on residents of Connecticut who earn income in New York. He explained in a letter to the *New York Times* in June 1989: "By using a commuter's total income to determine the tax rate on in-state income, New York is really asking for commuters to pay for services they do not use, or use infrequently." He chose not to run for reelection in 1990. O'Neill, who suffered from emphysema, died at his home in East Hampton, Connecticut. He was survived by his wife, the former Nathalie Scott Damon. The couple had no children. See *Current Biography* (1985).

Obituary *New York Times* A p21 Nov. 26, 2007

PALADE, GEORGE E. Nov. 19, 1912–Oct. 7, 2008 Biologist. George Emil Palade was a Nobel Prize–winning pioneer in the field of cell biology. His study of cell structures furthered the understanding of diseases and provided the basis for the biotechnology industry. Palade introduced the use of the electron microscope and helped develop other instruments and techniques to study cell components. Palade was born in Iasi, Romania. He graduated from the University of Bucharest medical school in 1940. He soon decided to focus on basic science and enrolled at the Rockefeller Institute for Medical Research (now Rockefeller University), in New York City. During his time at that school, he began using the recently invented electron microscope to conduct research on cells. He also helped develop cell fractionation, in which components of cells are separated by means of a centrifuge. In the early 1950s Palade discovered the ribosome, the cell's protein manufacturer. Along with his colleagues, he determined the appearance and function of other cell structures, including the mitochondria, the endoplasmic reticulum, and the Golgi complex. He had attained the rank of professor of cell biology when he

left Rockefeller, in 1973, to serve as chairman of Yale University's new Department of Cell Biology. For their contributions to the understanding of cell biology, he shared the 1974 Nobel Prize in Physiology or Medicine with Albert Claude and Christian de Duve. In his Nobel acceptance speech, as quoted by Andrew Pollack in the *New York Times* (October 9, 2008), he said, "Cell biology finally makes possible a century-old dream: that of analysis of diseases at the cellular level, the first step toward their final control." Palade's other honors include the Albert Lasker Basic Research Award (1966), a Gairdner Award (1967), the Horwitz Prize, from Columbia University (1970), and the National Medal of Science (1986). From 1990 to 2001 he served as dean for scientific affairs at the University of California's School of Medicine in San Diego. He retired in 2001. His first wife, Irina Malaxa, died in 1969. Palade is survived by his second wife, Marilyn Gist Farquhar, a daughter, a son, two stepsons, and two grandchildren. See *Current Biography* (1967). — M.A.S.

Obituary *New York Times* B p19 Oct. 10, 2008

PETERSON, OSCAR Aug. 15, 1925–Dec. 23, 2007 Canadian musician; "the Maharaja of the keyboard," as Duke Ellington dubbed him. Long before the emergence of such global pop stars as the singers Céline Dion and Shania Twain, Canada's musical gift to the world was personified in two pianists: Glenn Gould, the eccentric white genius of the classical keyboard, and Oscar Emanuel Peterson, the black titan of the mainstream jazz piano, a legendary crystallizer of jazz genres. An imposing figure even in physique, six feet three inches and hefty, with fingers that flew across the ivories with mercurial speed, Peterson dazzled international audiences for half a century with his powerful swinging style and total command of the instrument. "He had a deep knowledge of jazz history and could play two-fisted stride or complex and intricate bebop," Steve Voce observed in an obituary of Peterson written for the London *Independent*. "His timing and imagination made him one of the great ballad players. He had everything, with only an occasional penchant for rococo decoration to detract from his achievements." A child of immigrants from the West Indies, Peterson grew up in a musical family in Montreal, where he received classical training under the Hungarian-born pianist and composer Paul de Marky, a Liszt aficionado. He initially learned jazz in large measure by listening to big-band swing music on the radio and to recordings, including the pianist Art Tatum's rendition of "Tiger Rag," which marked an epiphany in his early development. The pianist Teddy Wilson and the pianist/singer Nat King Cole and his trio were among later formative influences. Peterson began performing on radio in Canada when he was 14. He later played for five years with the Johnny Holmes Orchestra, then one of Canada's most popular big bands, and in the mid-1940s, he formed a trio specializing in boogie-woogie, his genre of choice before he came under the influence of bop. With that trio he recorded several songs on the RCA Victor label, the first entries in what would become an outstandingly prodigious jazz discography. During a gig at the Alberta Lounge in Montreal in 1949, he was discovered by the American impresario Norman Granz, who became his manager and proceeded to guide his career in a relationship that would last more than three decades, until 1986. At Carnegie Hall, in New York City, in September 1949, Peterson created a sensation when, unannounced, he made his initial surprise appearance with Jazz at the Philharmonic (JATP), Granz's all-star swing-and-bop concert unit. Peterson toured with JATP regularly thereafter, performing in venues across North America and abroad (including several European countries, Japan, Australia, Hong Kong, and the Philippines). With JATP he played alongside Ella Fitzgerald (also managed by Granz) and a changing roster that constituted a virtual Who's Who of the era's preeminent jazz musicians—among others, Louie Bellson, Charlie Parker, Roy Eldridge, Stan Getz, Dizzy Gillespie, Gene Krupa, Illinois Jacquet, and Flip Phillips. Some JATP events were recorded. JATP ended its tours of North America in 1957, but it continued to perform abroad, especially in Europe and Japan, intermittently through the 1960s. Under Granz's management, Peterson performed briefly as a singer, performed and recorded several duets with bassists, and formed a succession of small combos. The best known of those groups was a trio including the guitarist Herb Ellis and the bassist Ray Brown, which often toured with JATP and lasted from 1953 to 1958, when the drummer Ed Thigpen replaced Ellis. Peterson went solo briefly in the late 1960s and early 1970s. During the 1970s he led a trio including the guitarist Joe Pass and the bassist Niels-Henning Ørsted Pedersen. His later collaborations included a duo with the pianist Herbie Hancock, one of his many young protégés, in the 1980s. Peterson made hundreds of recordings, originally released on Granz's Clef, Verve, and Pablo labels, among others. Many have been rereleased in such CD box sets as *Exclusively for My Friends* (1992), *Dimensions* (2003), *Live at the Blue Note* (2004), *Piano Power* (2005), and *Perfect Peterson* (2006), which includes his big 1950s hit "Tenderly." The 10-disk Avid Ideas release *Songbooks Etcetera* (2005) contains 1950s-vintage Peterson-trio coverage of 10 songbooks, including those of Duke Ellington, Cole Porter, George Gershwin, and Richard Rodgers. Peterson composed a number of works, including "Canadiana Suite," "African Suite," "Hymn to Freedom," "When Summer Comes," "Love Ballade," and "She Has Gone," written in memory of Ella Fitzgerald. He taught at York University and was a co-founder of the short-lived Advanced School of Contemporary Music in Toronto. His honors included eight Grammy Awards, many *Down Beat* and *Contemporary Keyboard* poll citations, investiture as a Companion of the Order of Canada, and a Canadian commemorative stamp bearing his image. The CBC TV network broadcast documentaries about him in 2005 and 2006. Peterson did not seem to view race as an especially important factor in jazz, an attitude not universally appreciated in the U.S. Some American critics faulted Peterson for being "glib" and "derivative" in his technical virtuosity and relentlessly "overwhelming" in the force of his playing. His biographer Gene Lees conceded that Peterson was "summational" in his artistry but pointed out that Bach and Mozart were similarly eclectic. Furthermore,

Lees wrote for *Maclean's* (July 1975), Peterson had an identifiable musical vocabulary of his own, and even when he borrowed phrases from others "these alone [could] be electrifying." After suffering a stroke in 1993, Peterson never fully regained the strength of his left hand, with which he had previously played 10ths with ease. With Richard Palmer, he wrote the autobiography *A Jazz Odyssey* (2002). Peterson was married and divorced three times before marrying Kelly Green, who survived him, along with their daughter, Celine. His other survivors included two sons and three daughters from his first marriage and a daughter from his third marriage. He died at his home in the Toronto suburb of Mississauga, Canada. See *Current Biography* (1983).

Obituary *New York Times* C p8 Dec. 25, 2007

POLLACK, SYDNEY July 1, 1934–May 26, 2008 Film director; producer; actor. Sydney Pollack, a bankable professional who thought of himself as a "mainstream" director, made intelligent and often socially relevant movies with mass appeal, including such hits as *They Shoot Horses, Don't They?*, *Absence of Malice*, and the blockbuster *Tootsie*. Originally and occasionally an actor himself, Pollack as a director was adept at working with a host of Hollywood stars, including, among others, Barbra Streisand, Natalie Wood, Meryl Streep, Jane Fonda, Susannah York, Teri Garr, Nicole Kidman, Sally Field, Holly Hunter, Melinda Dillon, Robert Mitchum, Paul Newman, Harrison Ford, Burt Lancaster, Gig Young, Klaus Maria Brandauer, Al Pacino, and Robert Redford, many of whom won or were nominated for Academy Awards for their roles in his films. Redford, his friend from the time they met, when both had their first feature-film roles in *War Hunt* (1962), became the leading man in seven Pollack films, the first—*This Property Is Condemned*—in 1966. Redford played the mountain-man protagonist in Pollack's *Jeremiah Johnson,* a 1972 box-office success. Pollack teamed Redford as an apolitical WASP screenwriter with Barbra Streisand as a Jewish leftist political activist in the days of the Hollywood blacklist in *The Way We Were* (1973), widely ranked among the top screen love stories of all time. In Pollack's espionage thriller *Three Days of the Condor* (1975), Redford was cast as a CIA researcher who is targeted for death after accidentally learning of a renegade agency conspiracy. In *The Electric Horseman* (1979), Pollack cast Redford as a former rodeo rider who retaliates against exploitive businessmen after hiring himself out to advertise a breakfast cereal. The sixth Pollack/Redford collaboration was the panoramically stunning epic *Out of Africa* (1985), based on the Danish author Isak Dinesen's memoir of her 18 years in colonial Kenya (1913–31), running a coffee plantation with her unfaithful and often absent husband and pursuing her enduring but doomed romance with the dashing adventurer Denys Finch-Hatton. *Out of Africa*—which co-starred Redford as Denys and Meryl Streep as Dinesen—was nominated for 11 Academy Awards and won seven, including those for best picture and director. *Havana* (1990) was the last film Pollack and Redford made together. Pollack's first effort as both producer and director—and his first major commercial/critical success—was

They Shoot Horses, Don't They? (1969), a drama about economically desperate Depression-era marathon dancers, which drew 11 Academy Award nominations, including one for Pollack as director and another for Jane Fonda as the lead actress; Gig Young won an Oscar for his supporting role as the cynical and heartless dance emcee. One of Pollack's favorites among his films was the romantic drama *Bobby Deerfield* (1976), starring Al Pacino as a race-car driver reckless of his own life but obsessed with that of his dying beloved (Marthe Keller). Paul Newman was nominated for an Academy Award for his role in *Absence of Malice* (1981), a realistic questioning of journalistic ethics. Most of Pollack's films were romances or dramas or combinations of both. A notable exception was *Tootsie* (1982), a pro-feminist gender-bending comedy in which an unemployed actor, Michael Dorsey (Dustin Hoffman), transforms himself into the female "Dorothy Michaels" in order to get a part in a television soap opera. (In the film Pollack was cast as Dorsey's agent, George Fields.) *Tootsie* drew 10 Academy Award nominations, including those for best picture, best director, best actor, and best screenplay; Jessica Lange won the Oscar for best supporting actress. A protégé of Sanford Meisner at the Neighborhood Playhouse School of the Theater in Manhattan, Pollack assisted Meisner as an instructor at that school while earning his first acting credits on the New York stage in the middle and late 1950s. On television, as an actor he had a dozen roles in dramas and series episodes between 1959 and 1962, and as a director he had 28 credits between 1961 and 1965, including 10 episodes of *Ben Casey* and five dramas on *Bob Hope Presents the Chrysler Theatre*. Kim Stanley, Cliff Robertson, Glenda Farrell, and Shelley Winters won Emmy Awards for roles in television shows that he directed. His first feature film, *The Slender Thread* (1965), about a young volunteer manning a crisis telephone line trying to prevent a female caller from suicide, starred Sidney Poitier and Anne Bancroft; his third, the off-beat Western *The Scalphunters* (1968), starred Burt Lancaster. Among his later box-office successes was the legal drama *The Firm* (1993), starring Tom Cruise, which he also produced. He directed in all a score of feature films, including *Castle Keep* (1969), *The Yakuza* (1969), *Sabrina* (1995), *Random Hearts* (1999)—the last two of which he also produced—and *The Interpreter* (1999). He also took over the directing of *The Swimmer* (1968) after Frank Perry quit that film. His last directorial effort was *Sketches of Frank Gehry* (2005), a documentary about the architect, who was his friend. His late-life credits as an actor included important supporting roles in Robert Altman's *The Player* (1992), Woody Allen's *Husbands and Wives* (1992), Stanley Kubrick's *Eyes Wide Shut* (1999), and Tony Gilroy's *Michael Clayton* (2007). Pollack died of cancer at his home in Pacific Palisades, Los Angeles County, California. He was predeceased by his son, Steven (who was killed in a plane crash), and survived by wife, Claire (née Griswald), his daughters, Rebecca and Rachel, and six grandchildren. See *Current Biography* (1986).

Obituary *New York Times* C p10 May 27, 2008

PYM, FRANCIS Feb. 13, 1922–Mar. 7, 2008 British parliamentarian and statesman. Before he entered the House of Lords, Francis Leslie Pym, also known as Baron Pym, served in the House of Commons for a quarter of a century (1961–87) and was one of the United Kingdom's top Conservative politicians during the 1970s and early 1980s, when he held a succession of leadership roles in Parliament and government under Prime Ministers Edward Heath and Margaret Thatcher. He became best known for his ambivalent relationship with Thatcher, in whose cabinets he served without being a member of her inner circle. He did not share her brand of conservatism, which stressed "individualism" and a strong state role in law and order but a diminished intervention in socioeconomic matters. A self-described centrist, he was lumped by the Thatcherites in the category of "wet Tory" (suggesting weakness), a Conservative Party member who accepts and defends the state "collectivism" that was gradually established in Great Britain under Labour Party leadership in the middle decades of the 20th century. Thatcher, who regarded her roots as "lower" class, once famously said, "The uppers like Pym were always more socialist at heart than the lowers." First elected to the House of Commons from Cambridgeshire in 1961, Pym, a decorated World War II veteran, held that seat until 1983 and then represented Cambridgeshire South East (1983–87) in Parliament. During the 1960s he was successively assistant government whip, opposition whip, and deputy opposition whip in the House of Commons. Under Heath he was chief government whip as well as parliamentary secretary to the treasury department (1970–73) and secretary of state for Northern Ireland (1973–74). When Thatcher assumed the leadership of the Conservative Party, in the mid-1970s (when Labour was in power), he became a member of her shadow cabinet. After she moved into 10 Downing Street, he served in her cabinet as secretary of state for defense (1979–81). He served in brief, concurrent stints as paymaster general, chancellor of the Duchy of Lancaster, leader of the House of Commons, and lord president of the Privy Council (a group of advisers to the queen). He then returned to the Thatcher cabinet in 1982 (at the beginning of the Falklands war, in which Great Britain ended Argentina's attempt to establish its dominion over the Falkland Islands) as secretary of state for foreign and Commonwealth affairs and minister of overseas development. Differences of opinion between Pym and Thatcher came to the fore during the Falklands war, when she objected to his advocacy of "conditional surrender." Repudiating a statement he made during the 1983 election campaign on BBC television ("Landslides don't on the whole produce successful government"), she fired him from her cabinet after her reelection. Retreating to the back benches in the House of Commons, he wrote the book *The Politics of Consent* (1984) and formed a group called the Conservative Centre Forward as vehicles for attacking Thatcherism and promoting his kind of conservatism. In 1987 he was named a life peer and entered the House of Lords as Baron Pym of Sandy. In 1998 he published the memoir *Sentimental Journey*. Pym, who lived in Sandy, Bedfordshire, died at home, according to news reports. He was survived by his wife, Valerie (née Daglish), two sons, and two daughters. See *Current Biography* (1982).

Obituary *New York Times* B p16 Mar. 8, 2008

RAUSCHENBERG, ROBERT Oct. 22, 1925–May 12, 2008 Painter; sculptor; printmaker. The Texas-born Milton "Robert" Rauschenberg was an eclectic and restlessly inventive visual artist, whose style was categorized by many as neo-Dada and proto-Pop. Rauschenberg greatly influenced the art scene on both sides of the Atlantic in the post–World War II decades. Branden Joseph capsuled the salient meaning of Rauschenberg's oeuvre in the title of his book *Random Order: Robert Rauschenberg and the Neo-Avant-Garde* (2003), in which, as the art historian Alexander Alberro wrote, Joseph illuminated neo-Dadaism by showing "how the paradigm of artistic production initiated by the artist in the 1950s and 1960s not only anticipated but also challenged the emergence of a postmodernist subjectivity." Rauschenberg himself said that what he tried to do was "to act in the gap between art and life." In addition to his individually wrought works—the best known of which are the collages and assemblages he called combines, hybrids of paint and three-dimensional objects—Rauschenberg was involved in multimedia and performance-art collaborations, designing sets for Merce Cunningham's dance company (1955–65), for example. In the 1960s he co-founded the organization Experiments in Art and Technology, to promote joint ventures between artists and engineers, and created the scrap-metal sculpture *Oracle* (1962–65), which emitted radio sounds that viewers could change. In 1964 he became the first American to win the Grand Prize at the Venice Biennale. (Two Americans had previously won the painting prize at Venice.) After studying in Paris, at Black Mountain College in North Carolina, and elsewhere, Rauschenberg settled in Manhattan in 1949 and proceeded to become an enfant terrible among the then-dominant "action painters" of the New York School. While respecting the skillful brushwork of those painters, he began moving beyond the limits of their nonrepresentational abstract expressionism and gradually reintroduced in his art the recognizable imagery they had rejected. His early works in New York included such full-scale monoprints as *Female Figure*, produced by shining a sun lamp on a nude model lying on blueprint paper; the large monochromatic works *White Paintings*, *Black Paintings*, and *Red Paintings*; and paintings of black numbers or symbols against white backgrounds. By driving a car over ink and then over a piece of paper, which was then mounted on canvas, his friend the avant-garde composer John Cage participated in the creation of Rauschenberg's *Automobile Tire Print* (1951), a work that revealed the down-to-earth process by which it was made. In a public-relations stunt, Rauschenberg, with the blessing of the abstract-expressionist Willem de Kooning, rubbed out all but vestiges of a drawing by de Kooning to produce *Erased de Kooning Drawing* (1953). In the mid-1950s he began creating such mixed-media works as *Bed* (1955), a quilt sprinkled with red paint, as well as collages of often incongruous combinations of found objects, odds and ends, photographs, and mass-produced images from post-cards, stamps, newspapers, and magazines. There followed fuller three-dimensional works, such as *Curfew* (1958), a semiabstract canvas with a hole containing four Coca-Cola bottles, and *Monogram* (1955–59), consisting of a stuffed Angora goat girdled with an automobile tire and standing on a low platform to which was affixed a collage including a tennis ball, a shirtsleeve, the heel of a shoe, and footprints. One version of *Pelican* (1965) was performance art, in which two skaters wearing huge sail-like wings interacted with a ballet dancer. Later Rauschenberg constructed the not specifically titled collage Rauschenberg Combine. He spent many years working on the gargantuan autobiographical panorama titled *The 1/4 Mile or 2 Furlong Piece*; eventually extending about 1,000 feet with more than 200 adjacent sections, it was exhibited repeatedly as a work-in-progress. Meanwhile, using a transfer-drawing technique, he made prints under the guidance of Tatyana Grossman at her workshop, Universal Limited Art Editions. At the Gemini G.E.L. workshop in Los Angeles, he made lithographs, such as the *Stoned Moon* series (1970). He also made silkscreens, and in his later years he used photographic techniques. In 1983 he received a Grammy Award for the cover he designed for the rock band Talking Heads' album *Speaking in Tongues*. In 1984 he founded the Rauschenberg Overseas Cultural Exchange; for seven years he participated in that program, collaborating with artists and craftsmen worldwide. Late in life he founded Change Inc. to help struggling artists to pay medical bills. Rauschenberg and the artist Susan Weil were married in 1950 and divorced in 1953. After the divorce he had homosexual romantic liaisons with the abstract expressionist Cy Twombly, briefly, and with the painter Jasper Johns, from 1954 to the 1960s. He and Johns shared and traded ideas and are closely linked in art history. In the early 1980s Rauschenberg began a 25-year intimate relationship with the artist Darryl Pottorf. In addition to Greenwich Village in Manhattan, Rauschenberg lived and worked on Captiva Island, off Florida's Gulf Coast. In 2002 he suffered a paralyzing stroke; unable to use his right hand, he trained himself to use the left, signing his work with his thumbprint. He died of heart and respiratory failure on Captiva Island. He was survived by his son, Christopher, an artist, and by Pottorf. See *Current Biography* (1987).

Obituary *New York Times* A p1+ May 14, 2008

ROBBE-GRILLET, ALAIN Aug. 18, 1922–Feb. 18, 2008 French avant-garde writer and filmmaker. Alain Robbe-Grillet was a preeminently influential and controversial artistic innovator, a subversive "anti-novel" novelist and auteur. In France in the decades following World War II, he was the foremost and most radical exponent of the *nouveau roman*, the movement in fiction away from the Balzacian model, with its linear plots, rounded characters, and psychological inner depths, in favor of meticulous and dispassionate perceptions of outer phenomena in the fragmented and time-sequence–flouting way that the mind and imagination operate in various waking and dream states. In the London *Evening Standard* (December 6, 2004), David Sexton described Robbe-

Grillet's novels as "sophisticated linguistic games rather than human dramas," and as such they were fashionable in an era of "'postmodern' occultism," when "Parisian intellectuals such as Roland Barthes and Michel Foucault were involved in the development of Structuralist theory." In an obituary of him in the London *Independent* (February 19, 2008), John Sturrock observed that Robbe-Grillet's career "was built on a sly and amusing paradox: . . . using fiction over and over again to undo the conventions of fiction." Sturrock also noted that Robbe-Grillet's novels grew progressively "more sardonic and extreme, until they were lurid parodies of how the imagination works." In his first published novel, *Les Gommes* (1953; *The Erasers,* 1964), a moderate success among critics, the protagonist, the investigator of what he mistakenly believes to have been a murder, inadvertently becomes the murderer, and his victim may be his own father. Robbe-Grillet's reputation as a major literary figure was launched with his second novel, *Le Voyeur* (1955; *The Voyeur,* 1958), in which the hallucinating male protagonist may or may not have tortured and murdered a young girl. The protagonist of *La Jalousie* (1957; *Jealousy,* 1959) enjoys witnessing, or thinking he is witnessing, his wife's infidelity. That theme was approached more obliquely and opaquely in the work for which Robbe-Grillet became, and remains, best known internationally: the scenario for the elegantly stylized black-and-white motion picture *L'Année dernière à Marienbad* (1961; *Last Year at Marienbad,* 1962), directed by Alain Resnais. New light illuminated the exquisite hermeticism of that enigmatic triangular "love" story—which has beguiled and/or baffled art-cinema critics and aficionados for more than four decades—when Catherine (née Rstakian) Robbe-Grillet, Robbe-Grillet's wife, published *Jeune mariée* (2004), the diary she kept during their first five years of marriage. "The tormented sexual triangles that can be glimpsed in *Marienbad* are here amicably stated," David Sexton noted after reading that book. "Robbe-Grillet was impotent, we soon learn, and preoccupied with sadistic fantasies. . . . For anybody who's ever wondered what on earth *Last Year at Marienbad* was about, here's the human story." Robbe-Grillet made the novelist's creative process itself the theme of his fourth novel, *Dans le labyrinthe* (1959; *In the Labyrinth,* 1960). In the mid-1960s he wrote and directed three black-and-white feature films establishing his reputation as an auteur. The first two films, *L'Immortelle* (The Immortal One, 1963) and *Trans-Europ-Express* (1966), were playful and witty tours de force in inconsistent plot and theme fluctuations. They led logically into the third film, *L'Homme qui ment* (The Man Who Lies, 1968), in which the protagonist, in a castle, invents his own identity, past and present, only to have his words turn against him, resulting in his banishment into the surrounding forest. Robbe-Grillet's subsequent color films—*L'Eden et après* (Eden and After, 1971), *Les Glissments progressifs du plaisir* (Slippery Progressions in Pleasure, 1974), and *Le Jeu avec le feu* (Playing with Fire, 1975)—were generally dismissed by French film critics and historians as "impenetrable" and undermined by "a self-indulgent eroticism." Robbe-Grillet's last films were *La Belle captive* (The Beautiful Captive, 1983) and *Un Bruit qui rend fou* (A Maddening Noise, 1995), which was released in the United States as *The Blue Villa*. Sex slavery and debauchery are rife in Robbe-Grillet's fifth novel, *La Maison de rendez-vous* (1965; same title in English, 1966), set in a Hong Kong brothel, and rape/murders fill his sixth, *Projet pour une révolution à New York* (1970; *Project for a Revolution in New York*, 1972). The first novel he wrote, *Un Régicide*, was not published until 1978. Among his later novels were *Djin* (1981) and *La Réprise* (2001). His last novel, *Un Roman sentimentale,* was published in 2007. He also published an imaginary autobiography in the guise of a fictional trilogy and several novels that were adaptations of screenplays and collages of texts that had appeared elsewhere. In addition, he published a collection of short stories and several collections of essays, including *Pour un nouveau roman* (For a New Novel, 1966), the bible of the *nouveau roman* movement. Robbe-Grillet, who began his career as an agronomist, did extensive international traveling and taught for a time in the United States. He was elected to the Académie Française in 2005 but never took his seat there. He died of heart failure at Caen University Hospital in Caen, France. His wife survived him. See *Current Biography* (1974).

Obituary *New York Times* A p23 Feb. 19, 2008

RUSSERT, TIM May 7, 1950–June 13, 2008 Television journalist. As the NBC network's Washington bureau chief and the moderator of NBC's *Meet the Press*, the most popular of the Sunday morning network-TV public-affairs programs, Tim Russert was for the better part of two decades one of the most visible and arguably the most probing of American journalists. Joe Gandelman, the editor-in-chief of the *Moderate Voice* (on-line), has described Russert as "a journalist's journalist, a centrist's newsman, and someone with a large reservoir of credibility on many fronts" who "got where he was because he was a great interviewer who did his homework, used old-school reporting and interviewing standards, was nimble in adjusting his often-aggressive questions to the answers of his often-spinning guests—and was well connected with excellent sources." Disarmingly genial and ebullient by nature and bearishly avuncular in appearance, Russert interviewed most of the country's political movers and shakers, greeting his guests with his trademark smile before launching into his polite but tenacious interrogations. "Russert's gift," David Remnick observed in the *New Yorker,* "was to employ his bluff, nice-guy, good-son Irish Catholic upstate [New York] persona . . . to offset the avidity with which he would trip up his interlocutors." Another reason for his success, as John Edgerton pointed out in *Broadcasting & Cable* in 2006, was his ability "to cut through Washington jargon and get to the core of the issues and present them in layman's terms." Russert was grounded in, although not beholden to, New York Democratic Party politics. Trained in law, he volunteered to work in Daniel Patrick Moynihan's successful campaign for the U.S. Senate in 1976, and he later ran the senator's district office in Buffalo, New York, and served as his chief of staff in Washington, D.C. He was a full-time adviser to New York governor Mario Cuomo from 1982 to 1984, when he joined the NBC-TV network as a vice president and assistant to Lawrence K. Grossman, president of NBC News. In 1988 Grossman's successor, Michael Gartner, appointed Russert chief of the network's Washington, D.C., bureau. Russert succeeded Garrick Utley as moderator of *Meet the Press* in December 1991. In addition, he appeared as a guest political analyst on other NBC shows, anchored the weekly *Tim Russert Show* on the cable channel MSNBC, moderated a number of political debates, and handled round-the-clock election-night coverage. He won an Emmy Award for his part in NBC's coverage of Ronald Reagan's funeral, in 2004. With William Novak, he wrote the best-selling autobiography *Big Russ and Me* (2004), about his father's influence in his childhood and youth. Some of the 10s of thousands of letters he received in response to that book were collected in *Wisdom of Our Fathers: Lessons and Letters from Daughters and Sons* (2005), also a best-seller. Russert died of cardiac arrest while at work in his Washington office. Among his survivors were his wife, the writer Maureen Orth, a special correspondent for *Vanity Fair* magazine, and his son, Luke. "Russert was defined as much by what he was not as by what he was . . . ," David Remnick wrote. "He was not an ideologue or a cynic. Beyond his family, Russert's passion was politics, and he cared enough about the game to try to keep it, and its players, honest." See *Current Biography* (1997).

Obituary *New York Times* A p1+ June 14, 2008

SAINT LAURENT, YVES Aug. 1, 1936–June 1, 2008 French fashion designer. The Algerian-born Yves Saint Laurent was the successor to Christian Dior as France's leading couturier, reinventing women's wardrobes worldwide during the second half of the 20th century and enjoying unparalleled influence. As Kate Betts observed in *Time* (on-line), he "was widely considered the father of democratized fashion and the designer most often associated with the feminist ideal of empowerment in the 1970s." In 1961, after guiding the House of Dior for a few years after Dior's death, in 1957, Saint Laurent, financed by Pierre Bergé, his lover, set up his own shop, Yves Saint Laurent Couture, in Paris. His designs, especially in the beginning, included diaphanous gowns and tentlike dresses. His chief long-run accomplishment was the adaptation of traditional men's clothing to womenswear, including the pants suit and "le smoking," a version of the tuxedo. He was eclectic in drawing inspiration from such sources as sailors' pea jackets, safari wear, peasant clothing, and Left Bank beatnik street styles. His colors reflected his familiarity with the paintings of Mondrian, Picasso, Braque, Van Gogh, and others as well as Moroccan, Russian, and Chinese sources. In 1966 he took the unusual step of introducing a ready-to-wear line, called Rive Gauche, making his designs available to working-class women and raising the reputation of ready-to-wear in general. He introduced a menswear line in 1974. In addition to apparel, some 100 products were marketed with the YSL label, including scents and such accessories as scarves. In 1993 the Saint Laurent fashion house was sold to Sanofi SA for approximately $600 million; the Gucci Group NV ac-

quired the YSL label six years later. While Saint Laurent designed the haute couture collection in 1999–2000, Tom Ford designed the ready-to-wear line. Saint Laurent retired from designing in 2002. He died from the effects of brain cancer at his home in Paris. Shortly before his death he and Bergé were joined in a "civil act of solidarity." See *Current Biography* (1964).

Obituary *New York Times* A p1+ June 2, 2008

SARDI, VINCENT JR. July 23, 1915–Jan. 4, 2007 New York City restaurateur, small-scale theater-world philanthropist, and "unofficial mayor of Broadway." In 1947 Vincent Sardi Jr. became the owner and manager of Sardi's, the restaurant co-founded a quarter-century earlier on Manhattan's West Side by his father, Vincent Sardi Sr., and mother, Eugenia Sardi. For the next four decades, and then, after a hiatus of about five years, from 1991 until 1997, Vincent Sardi Jr. ran what within a short time of its opening had become a Broadway institution—"the club, mess hall, lounge, post office, saloon and marketplace of the people of the theater," as the publicist Richard Maney described it, in a remark widely quoted in the print and electronic media. Sardi Jr. was born in New York City and educated there, in a Roman Catholic grammar school, a public high school, and then Columbia University. On weekends during his student days, he held mostly menial jobs at his parents' restaurant. After he failed a chemistry course at Columbia, he switched his major from pre-med to business administration, earning a bachelor's degree in 1937. Heeding his father's wishes, he worked for the next two years in food-related departments at the Ritz-Carlton Hotel in Manhattan. In 1939 he took the post of room captain at Sardi's. For four years beginning in 1942, he served in the U.S. Marine Corps, first as the supervisor of a stateside officers' mess, then as the overseer of the construction and operation of a rest camp for members of the 2d Marine Air Wing in Okinawa, Japan, and later as an aide to an American general working in China. In 1947, after his discharge, with the rank of captain, he bought Sardi's from his father and took over its management. In addition to ensuring that the restaurant maintained high standards in its menu, he cultivated supportive relationships with actors and actresses in all stages of their careers. He attended every show that opened on Broadway, revisiting them when they had major cast changes, and he bought four sets of tickets to every show for members of the Sardi's staff, so that they as well as he could greet thespian diners by name and thereby bolster their egos, as he told a *Current Biography* interviewer in 1957. He also extended credit unstintingly to hundreds of actors and actresses down on their luck, some of whom accumulated bills of thousands of dollars over periods as long as 10 years. Moreover, Sardi often sat diners where he thought they could attract the attention of directors or producers, and sat playwrights, directors, and producers where he thought they might be able to work out deals. "The restaurant had a central place in the theater," Gerald Schoenfeld, the president of the Shubert Organization (which in 2008 owned or operated 17 theaters, most of them in Manhattan), told William Grimes for the *New York Times* (January 5, 2007). "You could walk in at lunch and do a day's business, see people you hadn't seen in a long time. You didn't think of going anywhere else." If opening-night reviews of a show were good—"the first 25 copies of *The New York Times* and *The New York Herald Tribune* were rushed over to Sardi's from the printing presses at midnight, with the review pages marked," according to Grimes—celebrations by cast and crew invariably took place at Sardi's. The restaurant's decor famously included (and still includes) hundreds of caricatures of theater personalities. In the 1960s the rising number of crimes on the streets of the theater district and fewer new shows led to a decline in business at Sardi's; at the same time both its physical plant and the qualities of the food and service deteriorated. In 1985 Sardi sold the restaurant; he bought it back in 1991, after its new owners declared bankruptcy. In 1997 he retired and moved to Vermont, leaving the management of the restaurant to his partner, Max Klimavicius. Sardi's résumé includes his appearances as himself in two TV dramas in the 1950s and his co-authorship, with Helen Bryson, of a cookbook, *Curtain Up at Sardi*'s (1957). It also includes two entrepreneurial failures: the East Side Sardi's, which closed its doors in 1968, 10 years after it opened, and a 700-seat dinner theater in Franklin Square, on Long Island, New York, which operated from 1974 through 1976. For several years beginning in the mid-1940s, acting on Sardi's suggestion, the radio station WOR broadcast an hourlong program called *Luncheon at Sardi*'s, in which celebrities were interviewed at their tables. In 2004 the League of American Theatres and Producers (known informally as the Broadway League) recognized Sardi with a Tony Honor for Excellence in Theater. His first two marriages, to Carolyn Euiller and Adelle Ramsey, ended in divorce. Sardi died in a hospital in Berlin, Vermont, of complications of a urinary-tract infection. The next night the lights on Broadway marquees were dimmed for one minute in his memory. Sardi was survived by his third wife, June Keller, whom he married in 1982; two sons; one daughter; nine grandchildren; and several great-grandchildren. Another daughter predeceased him. See *Current Biography* (1957). — M.H.

Obituary *New York Times* B p7 Jan. 5, 2007

SAYRE, FRANCIS JR. Jan. 17, 1915–Oct. 3, 2008 For 27 years the Very Reverend Francis Sayre Jr. served as dean of the Cathedral Church of Saint Peter and Saint Paul, better known as the National Cathedral, in Washington, D.C. He spoke out against McCarthyism, racial segregation, and the Vietnam War. Francis Bowes Sayre Jr. was born in the White House. His mother, Jessie Woodrow Wilson Sayre, was a daughter of President Woodrow Wilson. Sayre Jr. graduated cum laude from Williams College, in Williamstown, Massachusetts, in 1937 with a degree in political science. He received his bachelor of divinity degree in 1940 from the Union Theological Seminary, in New York City. In 1941 he was ordained a deacon of the Episcopal Church and, later that same year, a priest. After serving as a chaplain in the U.S. Navy, he worked in a parish in Cleveland, Ohio, for several years. In 1951, at the age of 36, Sayre became dean of the National Cathedral, an Episcopal house of worship. He was one of the youngest clergymen to ever hold that position. Soon after he became dean, Sayre began to use his pulpit to speak out on social issues. In 1954 he condemned the actions of the Republican U.S. senator Joseph R. McCarthy of Wisconsin during the peak of McCarthy's investigations into Communist influences in the U.S. government and Hollywood; Sayre criticized the American public for allowing McCarthy to capitalize on their fears. Sayre called for an end to school segregation, and when the civil rights movement was gaining momentum in 1957, he encouraged his parishioners to join the cause. He accompanied the Reverend Martin Luther King Jr. during his 1965 voting-rights march from Selma to Montgomery, Alabama. President Eisenhower appointed Sayre chairman of the U.S. Committee for Refugees, a post he held from 1958 to 1961. President Kennedy later named him to the first Equal Opportunity Commission. Sayre oversaw the construction of the National Cathedral's Gloria in Excelsis Tower. He retired from the ministry in 1978. He died at his home on Martha's Vineyard in Massachusetts. His wife, the former Harriet Taft Hart, predeceased him. He was survived by two daughters, two sons, and eight grandchildren. See *Current Biography* (1956). — M.A.S.

Obituary *New York Times* A p27 Oct. 12, 2008

SCHWARTZ, TONY Aug. 19, 1923–June 14, 2008 Media consultant; audio documentarian; advertising designer. No less a figure than Marshall McLuhan regarded Tony Schwartz as a fellow "guru of the electronic age." For all of his achievements in electronic communications, from a great archive of New York City sound recordings to thousands of innovative radio and television spots, Tony Schwartz is commonly identified with one TV commercial: a controversial but highly effective spot that was a factor in the incumbent Democratic president Lyndon B. Johnson's landslide victory over the conservative Republican Barry M. Goldwater in the presidential election of 1964. Designed in collaboration with others at the Doyle Dane Bernbach agency, the commercial began with a little girl counting the petals she is plucking from a daisy. When she reaches the number nine, a sinister male voice replaces hers, counting down the launch of a nuclear missile, ending in an explosion and a mushroom cloud. In a voiceover, President Johnson is heard intoning the words, "These are the stakes! To make a world in which all of God's children can live, or to go into the dark. We must either love each other, or we must die." The ad ended with another voiceover, by the sportscaster Chris Schenkel: "Vote for President Johnson on November 3. The stakes are too high for you to stay home." The name of Goldwater, whose reputation was that of an "extremist" Cold War hawk, was not mentioned, but the implication of the ad was not lost on knowledgeable viewers. Less than one minute long, the spot ran on national television on September 7, 1964 only once before it was pulled following public protests, but it was reshown on news programs and became a landmark in the history of broadcast commercials. A Manhattan native, Schwartz from early manhood (at first using a wire recorder, until the invention of the tape recorder) was recording street sounds of his Hell's Kitchen neighborhood, including ethnic music and singing, children playing games, street vendors hawking their wares, and conversations with taxicab drivers. The first of the many folk singers he recorded (usually in his home studio, because of his agoraphobia) were locals, some of whom at the time were not yet famous, including Pete Seeger and the Weavers, Harry Belafonte, and the street poet Moondog (born Louis Thomas Hardin). He played his recordings on *Around New York*, a weekly radio program that he produced and hosted on the New York City station WNYC from 1945 to 1972. Over the decades he collected his "sound documentaries" on 19 albums on the Folkways and Columbia labels with such titles as *Sounds Outside My House, New York 19, Neuva York, Sounds of My City, A Dog's Life, 123 and a Zing, Zing, Zing*, and *You're Stepping on My Shadow*. (The LPs are now in the catalog of Smithsonian Folkways Recordings.) Beginning in the 1950s Schwartz was approached by a number of advertising agencies to create sounds for their commercials. Among the ads were a familiar promotion for Coca-Cola and spots for a line of Johnson & Johnson baby products. The latter commercials, among others (including one for Bosco chocolate syrup with the sound of a child gulping down chocolate milk) contributed to his reputation as "a great specialist in children's sounds." One of his best-known assignments was a 1963 antismoking ad done for the American Cancer Society that carried the reminder, "Children learn by imitating their parents." The Democratic political campaigns for which he designed ads included the unsuccessful presidential bids of Hubert H. Humphrey, in 1968, and George S. McGovern, in 1972, and Jimmy Carter's successful presidential run in 1976. Also in 1976 he contributed to the successful campaigns of Daniel Patrick Moynihan for election to the U.S. Senate, of Edward M. Kennedy for reelection to the Senate, and of John D. Rockefeller IV for election to the governorship of West Virginia. Crossing party lines, he helped Republican Warren Rudman win a U.S. Senate seat from New Hampshire in 1980. In addition to working for other advertising agencies, Schwartz early in his career founded his own agency, the Weston Co., which became Solow/Weston, and later, for many years, he ran several companies—New Sounds, Environmental Media Consultants, and Planned Reactions—out of his studio in his Manhattan brownstone. Among his projects were sounds designed for several Broadway plays. Because of his agoraphobia, most of his work was done in his home studio, and his lectures at several universities were delivered to the campuses electronically. In 2007 the entire body of his work, including field recordings and commercials, was acquired by the Library of Congress. Eugene DeAnna, the head of recorded sound at the Library of Congress, called it the "aural equivalent of the Family of Man" 1955 photographic collection. Schwartz described his work and the thinking behind it in two books, *The Responsive Chord* (1973) and *Media: The Second God* (1982). Schwartz died at his home in Manhattan of aortic-valve stenosis. His survivors included his wife, Reenah (née Lurie), a daughter, a son, and a grandchild. See *Current Biography* (1985).

Obituary *New York Times* B p6 June 17, 2008

SCOFIELD, PAUL Jan. 21, 1922–Mar. 19, 2008 British actor. Paul Scofield was the quintessential actor's actor, esteemed by his peers perhaps even more highly than he was by critics and audiences. "Of the ten greatest moments in the theater," Richard Burton once said, "eight are Scofield's." In a poll taken in 2004, actors at the Royal Shakespeare Company (RSC), asked to name the greatest stage performance in memory, voted for Scofield's portrayal of King Lear under the direction of Peter Brook (the director with whom Scofield was most closely associated) at Stratford-on-Avon in 1962, during the period when Brook and Scofield were associated with the RSC. (Scofield reprised the Lear role for a film released in 1971.) In the view of John Gielgud, Scofield's best performance was as the fugitive "whiskey priest" in the Brook-directed stage adaptation of Graham Greene's novel *The Power and the Glory* in 1956. Many regarded Scofield's portrayal of Richard II directed by Gielgud in 1952 as the finest Richard of modern times. A tall man with a craggy face and a rich voice, Scofield was able to project intelligence and inner conflict powerfully but understatedly, like a smoldering, controlled volcano. His range was extraordinary, both in the classical repertoire—grounded in large measure in Shakespeare but extending from Marlowe to Gogol, Shaw, Ibsen, Strindberg, and Chekhov, among others—and in contemporary drama, in the British premieres or revivals of works by such playwrights as Jean Anouilh, Charles Dyer, John Osborne, and Terence Rattigan. He attained international stardom with his Tony and Academy Award–winning portrayal of Sir Thomas More in *A Man for All Seasons,* Robert Bolt's character study of the Catholic lord chancellor to King Henry VIII, who chose conscience over king and was executed for refusing to recognize the legitimacy of Henry's leadership of the Church of England. Originally produced in London's West End (1960–61), *A Man for All Seasons* opened at the ANTA Theatre in New York City in November 1961 and ran until July 1963. The motion picture version—one of 16 films Scofield made—was released in 1966. Although his preference always was to act on stage, he also acted for television and won an Emmy Award for his performance as the older and kinder of the female protagonist's two lovers in Alun Owen's television play *Male of the Species* (1969). Scofield made his professional debut in April 1940, on the eve of World War II. During the war, deferred from military service on medical grounds (he had crossed toes), he acted with several repertory companies, often for the entertainment of troops. After the war, recruited by Sir Barry Jackson, he joined the Birmingham Repertory Company, the United Kingdom's leading regional house, where he began his long collaboration with Peter Brook. When Scofield was cast as Tanner in *Man and Superman* in 1945, Brook guided him in learning to infuse the demanding speeches with a "Shavian bristling energy," as Alan Strachan put it for the London *Independent* (March 21, 2008). "The Scofield voice, dark velvet with an arresting rift and stamped by a ringing upper register," Strachan added, "was already unmistakable." When Jackson became artistic director of the festival company at the annual Stratford-on Avon Shakespeare Festival, in 1946, he took Brook and Scofield with him, giving the talents of both wider exposure. As Don Armado in *Love's Labour's Lost* at Stratford in 1946, Scofield, in the words of Strachan, "gave an astonishingly mature tragi-comic portrayal of meditative detachment," and as Mephistopheles in *Doctor Faustus* in 1947, he "breathed the torments of eternity, freezing the blood." During the 1948 Stratford season, Scofield portrayed Hamlet for the first time, demonstrating an ability "to communicate suffering without emotional pitch and toss," as the critic J. C. Trewin observed. He made his debut in London's West End in 1949 as Alexander the Great in *Adventure Story*. For almost two years beginning in January 1950, he played the twins in the West End hit *Ring Around the Moon*, directed by Brook. Among his other credits in greater London (including Hammersmith) in the early 1950s were Pierre in the hit *Venice Preserv'd*, the inner-tormented American protagonist fleeing Nazi-occupied France in *The River Line*, Witwoud in *The Way of the World*, and Paul Gardiner in *A Question of Fact*. Peter Brook directed him as Hamlet in London in 1955 and subsequently on tour. In the West End in 1959, Scofield created the role of the sleazy, hustling show-business agent Johnny Jackson in the Julian Moore/Wolf Mankowitz musical *Expresso Bongo*. His subsequent credits included starring roles in *Timon of Athens* (1966), the comedy *The Government Inspector* (1966), *Amsterdam* (1968), *Uncle Vanya* (1970), *The Captain from Kopenick* (1971), and *Savages* (1973). From the early 1970s on, most of his major performances were at the National Theatre on London's South Bank, where his greatest successes were his searing interpretation of Salieri, Mozart's jealous and resentful rival, in *Amadeus* (1979), and the ebullient title character in *Volpone* (1979). After playing Nat in *I'm Not Rappaport* in New York (1986), he gave an authoritative valedictory performance in the West End as Shotover in Shaw's comedy *Heartbreak House* (1989) before returning to the National Theatre to give a soaring farewell stage performance in the title role of Ibsen's *John Gabriel Borkman* (1996). Scofield was married for 65 years to Joy Parker, an actress who once played Ophelia to his Hamlet. A self-effacing, very private person unspoiled by success, Scofield shunned publicity and the social whirl and lived quietly with his wife in Balcombe, Sussex, 10 miles north of his birthplace, in Hurstpierpoint, Sussex. He accepted the honors of Commander of the British Empire (1956) and Companion of Honour (2001) but turned down knighthood three times. He died of leukemia in a hospital not far from his home, leaving behind his wife, a son, and a daughter. See *Current Biography* (1962).

Obituary *New York Times* B p8 Mar. 21, 2008

SEAMANS, ROBERT C. Oct. 30, 1918–June 28, 2008 Aeronautical engineer. Robert C. Seamans Jr. was largely responsible for organizing and managing NASA's Apollo moon-landing program in the 1960s. After working as the deputy administrator of NASA, he served as secretary of the United States Air Force and, later, became the first administrator of the Energy Research and Development Administration, a forerunner of the Department of Energy. Seamans was born in Salem, Massachusetts. As a boy he was

fascinated with stories of his great-great-great grandfather, Otis Tufts, whose inventions included the steam-powered printing press. Seamans studied engineering at Harvard University and received both his master's degree in aeronautics and his Ph.D. in instrumentology from the Massachusetts Institute of Technology. While doing his doctoral research, Seamans worked with Charles Stark Draper, a pioneer in gyroscope guidance. Together they developed a guided-missile system for the navy that was later used in the Apollo space program. After leaving his teaching post at MIT in 1955, Seamans joined RCA as director of its missile-electronics and -control division in Boston, Massachusetts. He was promoted to chief engineer before leaving to join NASA as associate administrator, in 1960. Five years later he was promoted to deputy administrator. During that period Seamans was instrumental in the decision-making and planning of the Apollo space program. He left NASA in 1968, one year before the Apollo lunar landing, to continue teaching at MIT. Within days of his leaving NASA, President Richard Nixon named him secretary of the U.S. Air Force. He directed the development of new aircraft and missile systems before resigning, in 1973. Seamans then served as president of the National Academy of Engineering for a year before President Gerald Ford appointed him as the first administrator of the new Energy Research and Development Administration, in 1974. He was an advocate for energy conservation and informed Congress of the need for greater production of nuclear power, coal, oil, and natural gas. Seamans returned to MIT in 1977 and became dean of the School of Engineering in 1978, a position he held until his retirement, in 1984. His honors included NASA's Distinguished Service Medal (1965 and 1969) and the U.S. Air Force Academy's Thomas D. White National Defense Award (1980). Seamans died at his home in Beverly Farms, Massachusetts. The cause was a heart attack. He was survived by his wife, Eugenia, three sons, two daughters, 11 grandchildren, and two great-grandchildren. See *Current Biography* (1966). — M.A.S.

Obituary *New York Times* A p21 July 3, 2008

SEITZ, FREDERICK July 4, 1911–Mar. 2, 2008 Physicist; professor emeritus, Rockefeller University; past president, National Academy of Sciences (1962–69). Frederick Seitz was renowned for his early pioneering research in condensed-matter physics, which contributed to the modern quantum theory of the solid state of matter and presaged the development of the electronic transistor, and for his subsequent work as a university administrator. He was also well known for his service as an adviser to industry, the military, and government, and he stirred controversy with some of his positions on public issues, especially his strident leadership in disputing the belief that global warming is occurring at an unnaturally rapid rate. Seitz was a friend of two of the co-inventors of the transistor: William Shockley, whom he met when both were undergraduates in California—Seitz in mathematics at Stanford University, Shockley at Caltech—and John Bardeen, whom he met when pursuing his doctorate in physics at Princeton University. In researching the cohesion of metals at Princeton in 1933, Seitz and his mentor, Eugene Wigner, used for the first time what became known as the Wigner-Seitz unit cell, described in *A Dictionary of Chemistry* (2004) as "a polyhedron in a crystal that is bounded by planes formed by perpendicular bisectors of bonds between lattice sites" and a "concept [that] has been used extensively in the theory of solids." In 1940 Seitz published his influential textbook *The Modern Theory of Solids*. After teaching successively at the University of Rochester and the University of Pennsylvania, in 1942 he joined the faculty of the Carnegie Institute of Technology (now Carnegie Mellon University), in Pittsburgh, as professor of physics and chairman of the Physics Department. While holding those positions for seven years, during World War II he was a member of the National Defense Service Committee, contributing to research on ballistics, armor, radar, and the development of the atomic bomb; after the war he directed a training program in the peaceful uses of atomic energy at the Clinton Laboratories in Oak Ridge, Tennessee. (In his later years he would strongly advocate that the U.S. free itself from dependence on "Muslim" oil by building more nuclear plants.) In 1949 he joined the faculty of the University of Illinois at Urbana as research professor of physics. At Urbana he was instrumental in developing the solid-state research program in the Physics Department, headed the department from 1957 to 1964, and was dean of the graduate school in 1964–65. (The Frederick Seitz Materials Research Laboratory at the university was named in his honor.) After 19 years at the University of Illinois, he served (1968–78) as president of Rockefeller University, the prestigious Manhattan center for research and graduate education in the biomedical sciences. There, he oversaw the introduction of new research programs in the neurosciences, molecular biology, cell biology, and reproductive biology, a joint Ph.D.-M.D. program with Cornell University Medical College, and the establishment of a 1,000-acre Center for Field Research in Ethology and Ecology in Millbrook, New York. In 1978 he began a 10-year relationship (regarded by critics as unseemly) with the R. J. Reynolds tobacco company as a consultant in the disbursement of money for scientific and medical research, including the work of Stanley B. Prusiner, the discoverer of prion, the infective protein causing some brain and neural diseases, including mad-cow disease. Seitz was one of the scientific community's earliest and most vocal Cold War hawks, and as a member of a scientific group advising President Ronald Reagan in the 1980s, he strongly advocated the deployment of the Strategic Defense Initiative, popularly known as Star Wars. In 1984 he co-founded the George C. Marshall Institute for the assessment of scientific issues affecting public policy. In 1995 that institute issued a report dismissing the chances of global warming as "inconsequential." In 1998 Seitz circulated a petition against the Kyoto protocol on global warming that was signed by 15,000 scientists. The petition was accompanied by an eight-page review of research literature that concluded that "predictions of harmful climatic effects due to future increases in greenhouse gases like carbon dioxide are in error and do not conform to current experimental knowledge." Among the many honors bestowed on

Seitz were the National Medal of Science and U.S. Department of Defense and NASA awards. His books include *The Physics of Metals* (1943), *The Science Matrix: The Journey, Travails, Triumphs* (1992), and *On the Frontier: My Life in Science* (1994). Seitz died in the Mary Manning Walsh nursing home in Manhattan. He was predeceased by his wife, Elizabeth (née Marshall) and survived by a son, three grandchildren, and four great-grandchildren. See *Current Biography* (1956).

Obituary *New York Times* B p7 Mar. 6, 2008

SMITH, IAN Apr. 8, 1919–Nov. 20, 2007 The internationally demonized white-supremacist Rhodesian politician and statesman Ian Smith described himself as an "African of British stock." Smith was the prime minister of minority white-ruled Rhodesia (previously Southern Rhodesia, later Zimbabwe Rhodesia, now Zimbabwe) who, in resisting the inexorable wave of black nationalist hegemony in Sub-Saharan Africa, unilaterally declared his country's independence from the British Commonwealth in 1965 and continued to defy international sanctions for 15 years thereafter before agreeing to the election that ushered in the black nationalist government of Robert Mugabe. Writing in the London *Independent* (November 22, 2007), Robert Cornwell described Mugabe as "the revolutionary turned . . . brutal, lunatic totalitarian. . . . Mugabe's tyranny—as with Smith's own feat in stopping history's clock for fifteen years—was just another facet of a continent's tragedy." Smith was born to Scottish immigrants in Southern Rhodesia. As a combat pilot with the Royal Air Force in World War II, he was severely wounded. After the war he returned to Southern Rhodesia to run a farm and enter politics. On the Rhodesia Liberal Party ticket, he won a seat in the Southern Rhodesian legislative assembly in 1948. When the Central African Federation—comprising Southern Rhodesia, Northern Rhodesia (now Zambia), and Nyasaland (now Malawi)—was formed, five years later, he was elected to the federal Parliament as a member of the United Federal Party. In 1961 the Central African Federation broke up and Smith and other white Southern Rhodesians founded the Rhodesian Front Party. He became deputy prime minister and treasury minister of the British crown colony of Southern Rhodesia in 1962 and prime minister in April 1964. In that role he was pressed by British prime minister Harold Wilson to make greater civil and suffrage concessions to Southern Rhodesia's black majority, which constituted 97 percent of the population and was becoming restive. Defiant, Smith on November 11, 1965 unilaterally declared the crown colony, now to be known simply as Rhodesia, independent of the British Commonwealth. The British, with the cooperation of the United States and the United Nations, launched retaliatory embargoes and other sanctions intended to obstruct Rhodesia's importing of oil and its exporting of minerals, tobacco, corn, wheat, and other agricultural products, but the sanctions had little immediate effect in part because of the country's porous border with the sympathetic white-ruled South Africa. More threatened by black nationalist activism, Smith cracked down on black activists, imprisoning thousands and exiling many others, and imposed restrictions on civil rights and freedom of the press. In the early 1970s he waged a bush war against a black nationalist guerrilla army, composed in part of infiltrators from neighboring countries, including Angola. In the mid-1970s Smith began to tire, because of several turns of events. To his great disappointment, the Conservative government of Margaret Thatcher in London was less friendly to him than Harold Wilson had been and was encouraging his opponents. So was the government of the United States, and even South Africa was hedging its support. In addition, in 1975 Portugal's African empire disintegrated, leaving in its wake a newly independent black-ruled Mozambique as a guerrilla sanctuary on Rhodesia's eastern border. Hoping to end the bush war (in which some 30,000 people, mostly blacks, were killed), Smith enlisted the help of several relatively moderate black nationalists, including Bishop Abel Muzorewa, who in June 1979 became interim prime minister of Zimbabwe Rhodesia. In Muzorewa's "government of reconciliation and national unity," Smith was minister without portfolio. Still failing to placate the bush insurgents, and under increased international pressure, Smith in 1980 agreed to a new national election including black political parties. Pursuant to that election, in April 1980 Robert Mugabe, head of the ZANU Party (the Zimbabwe African National Union–Patriotic Front), became prime minister of the independent republic of Zimbabwe, recognized as such by Great Britain. Mugabe, who had been imprisoned by Smith for 10 years, permitted Smith to serve as parliamentary opposition leader for seven years before expelling him from Parliament in 1986. Mugabe declared himself executive president, effective January 1988. Even as Mugabe became more tyrannical he remained lenient toward Smith. While confiscating and redistributing the land of white farmers, for example, he exempted Smith from the confiscation program. Under Mugabe, the country that was once regarded as southern Africa's breadbasket was by late 2007 unable to feed half of its own people, had an inflation rate of 4,000 percent—and rising—and an unemployment rate of 80 percent, and was socially and politically wracked on an unprecedented scale. "It is true," Stephen Glover wrote for the London *Daily Mail* (November 22, 2007), "that Mr. Smith ran a pretty brutal police force, but nothing it did compares in sheer scale with the torture, illegal imprisonment, and intimidation practiced against black Zimbabweans by President Mugabe. . . . Ian Smith helped create a deeply flawed but prosperous country. Robert Mugabe has made it a wasteland." After leaving government Smith published his memoir, *The Great Betrayal*, in 1997. He was predeceased by his wife, Janet (nee Watt), and his son, Eric, and survived by his stepson, Robert, his stepdaughter, Jean, and six grandchildren. After suffering a stroke, he died in a clinic on the outskirts of Cape Town, South Africa. See *Current Biography* (1966).

Obituary *New York Times* A p25 Nov. 21, 2007

SMITH, ROGER B. July 12, 1925–Nov. 29, 2007 Automobile-industry executive. Roger Bonham Smith was chairman of the board and chief executive officer of the General Motors Corp. during the 1980s, a decade when great global and domestic change was beginning to threaten GM's half-century-long status as the world's leading automaker. In accepting change and adapting to it, Smith rightly claimed credit for getting the corporation "ready for the 21st century," with GM sharing its world hegemony neck-and-neck with Japan's Toyota Motor Co. (Both companies reported sales of close to 9.37 million vehicles during 2007.) Lettered in business administration, Smith joined General Motors as an accounting clerk in 1949. He worked his way up to treasurer in 1970, vice president in charge of finance in 1971, and executive vice president in charge of finance, public relations, and government relations in 1974. When he became chairman and CEO, in 1981, General Motors was still by far the world's largest automaker, with a 46 percent share of the U.S. market. (That share had slipped to less than 25 percent by 2008.) Thanks to globalization, imports, especially from Japan, were making inroads on the U.S. market, and Smith correctly anticipated an acceleration of that expansion. In addition, the U.S. government was imposing increasingly tough environmental and safety standards on the industry domestically, and consumers were beginning to demand more efficient, more reasonably priced cars. Addressing those and other challenges, Smith took a number of steps: he oversaw a $40 billion capital spending program that included investments in research and development in automation, robotics, electronics, and other technologies; the building of new assembly plants in Missouri, Indiana, and Michigan; the replacement of conservative and complacent bureaucrats in the General Motors hierarchy with risk-takers; the diversification of GM's operations; the restructuring of its five North American divisions into two umbrella groups; the shifting of virtually all GM car lines from rear-wheel-drive to front-wheel-drive designs to improve efficiency and fuel economy; and the formation of joint strategic ventures with foreign rivals, including Japanese and Korean companies. Among those ventures was New United Motor Manufacturing Inc. (NUMMI), a major collaboration with Toyota, which led to the production of the Chevrolet Nova passenger car at a plant in Fremont, California, in 1985. In that same year Smith's office announced that GM, in an unprecedented cooperative effort with the United Auto Workers, was adding a new GM passenger car unit, the Saturn Corp., that would introduce in the U.S. a radically new, comprehensive auto manufacturing and marketing process, one taking a "clean sheet of paper" approach all the way from technology and labor through sales and service. For the Saturn project, a giant, highly integrated state-of-the-art complex was built at Spring Hill, Tennessee. The first subcompact Saturn rolled off the line at Spring Hill on July 30, 1990, the day before Smith retired as chairman and CEO of GM; within 10 years Saturn had sold 2.2 million vehicles. Smith became known to a wider public—negatively so—through *Roger & Me* (1989), Michael Moore's often humorous documentary film about Moore's efforts to interview Smith about GM's plant closings and layoffs in Flint, Michigan. Smith died in suburban Detroit, Michigan, after a brief illness. He was survived by his wife, Barbara, two sons, two daughters, and six grandchildren. See *Current Biography* (1986).

Obituary *New York Times* C p9 Dec. 1, 2007

SNOW, TONY June 1, 1955–July 12, 2008 Political pundit; radio and television host and news commentator; newspaper columnist; U.S. presidential press secretary. Tony Snow, who generally espoused right-of-center views, brought to political polemics a disarming ease, wit, and affability—"spin with a grin," as Howard Kurtz of the *Washington Post* described his style in handling White House reporters during his 17 months as Republican president George W. Bush's press secretary (2006–07). Earlier, Snow had served as chief speech writer for that president's father, President George H. W. Bush. In the private sector he was highly audible and/or visible as a commentator on National Public Radio and other radio networks and as a guest on numerous public affairs programs on television. From 1996 to 2003 he was the charter host of *Fox News Sunday*, a weekly television interview and roundtable program that Roger Ailes, the president of Fox News, had created specifically as a vehicle for him. From 2003 to 2006 he hosted the *Tony Snow Show*, a daily talk program on Fox News Radio. As the Democratic political strategist Bob Bechel observed, Snow was not "a doctrinaire conservative," but a conservative "with soul." When he was in his early 20s, Robert Anthony Snow began his journalistic career as a writer with the *Greensboro Record* in North Carolina and the Norfolk *Virginian-Pilot* in Virginia and as editorial page editor of the *Newport News Daily Press* in Virginia. He was deputy editor of the *Detroit News* in Michigan from 1984 to 1987, when he became editorial page editor of the *Washington Times*. After four years with the *Times*, he served as chief speech writer for President George H. W. Bush during the elder Bush's last two years in the White House (1991–January 1993). He wrote columns for the *Detroit Free Press* (1993–2000) *and USA Today* (1994–2000), and under contract to Creators Syndicate (1993–2000), he wrote columns published in more than 200 newspapers nationwide. Before hosting his own shows on television and radio, he was for several years the primary substitute host on Rush Limbaugh's call-in radio show, an occasional substitute host on other programs, and a guest on such television shows as *The McLaughlin Group, The MacNeil-Lehrer News Hour, Face the Nation, Crossfire, and Good Morning America*. Diane Rehm, who frequently had him as a panelist on her daily public-affairs roundtable on National Public Radio, was quoted as saying: "Some of these conservatives get really nasty in their political opinions, but Tony is congenial. He says what he has to say but doesn't imply that the rest of the world is worthless." By the time President George W. Bush appointed him his chief press secretary, in April 2006, Snow had already undergone surgery for colon cancer. After the cancer recurred, in March 2007, he underwent surgery again during a leave of absence from the White House. After resigning as presidential press secretary, in September 2007, he worked as a commentator on CNN television and toured as a public speaker. Snow, who lived with his family in Waynewood, Virginia, died in Georgetown Hospital

in Washington, D.C. He was survived by his wife, Jill, and their children, Kendall, Robbie, and Kristi. See *Current Biography* (2006).

Obituary *New York Times* p21 July 13, 2008

SOEHARTO June 8, 1921–Jan. 27, 2008 President of the Republic of Indonesia (1968–98); allegedly one of the most cold-blooded and corrupt dictators of the 20th century. During Indonesia's war for independence from the Netherlands, beginning in 1945, Suharto (spelled "Soeharto" during Dutch colonial times) fought in General Sukarno's army, rising to the rank of regimental commander by August 1949, when the Dutch relinquished control, and lieutenant colonel by December 1950, when an independent republic was declared, with Sukarno as president. During the 1950s and 1960s Suharto continued to rise in the army command, to the rank of major general. Antipathy between pro-Communist Sukarno and anti-Communists in the military high command led in the fall of 1965 to an unsuccessful coup attempt, later officially blamed on Communists, that left six top generals dead. Somehow surviving that failed uprising, Suharto assumed leadership of the army, and he claimed the rank of full general in July 1966; in a six-month campaign of terror, Suharto—who had usurped much of the still-reigning Sukarno's power—purged the country of Communists and suspected Communists, overseeing the killing of as many as half a million people. When Sukarno was forced into retirement, in March 1967, Suharto became acting president. He was inaugurated as president in March 1968, and the Indonesian Parliament reelected him to that position every five years thereafter up to and including 1998. In foreign policy Suharto was aligned with the United States during the Cold War. Domestically, while he oversaw an Indonesian economic expansion exemplary in the developing world, his administration was, according to virtually all reputable sources, egregiously brutal and corrupt, in gross violation of human rights, killing hundreds of thousands of its political opponents, and reportedly responsible for the embezzlement or theft of untold millions if not billions of Euro dollars. As the Asian financial crisis peaked in 1998, Indonesians en masse protested against the Suharto regime, with several hundred of them killed in doing so. Suharto resigned as president in May 1998, two months after his final election to the post. He died in a hospital in Jakarta, Indonesia, of a combination of heart, lung, and kidney failures. He was predeceased by his wife, Siti Hartinah, and survived by his six children, 11 grandchildren, and several greatgrandchildren. See *Current Biography* (1992).

Obituary *New York Times* A p20 Jan. 28, 2008

SOLZHENITSYN, ALEKSANDR Dec. 11, 1918–Aug. 3, 2008 A preeminent figure in 20th-century literature, Aleksandr Solzhenitsyn was a Nobel Prize–winning Russian writer, historian, and dissident who—beginning with his novel *One Day in the Life of Ivan Denisovich* (1962)—brought the Soviet Union's vast system of forced-labor camps, or Gulag Archipelago, as he dubbed it, to the attention of the world. "With his stern visage, lofty brow and full, Old Testament beard, he recalled Tolstoy while suggesting a modern-day Jeremiah, denouncing the evils of the Kremlin and later the mores of the West," Michael T. Kaufman wrote for the *New York Times* (August 4, 2008). His fiction, plays, and poetry drew heavily from his experiences and observations as a Soviet citizen, as a political prisoner for eight years in the late 1940s and early 1950s, as a survivor of cancer, and as an involuntary exile for several years in a town in the Soviet republic of Kazakhstan. The publication of *The Gulag Archipelago* in France in 1973 led to his expulsion from the Soviet Union in 1974; he spent the next 18 years in Cavendish, Vermont, returning to Russia in 1994. Solzhenitsyn was born in Kislovodsk, in the Caucasus, sixth months after his father, a Russian artillery officer during World War I, died in an accident. Aleksandr was raised by his mother in the city of Rostov-on-Don, in southwestern Russia. Although he had wanted since early childhood to be a writer, as a teenager he realized, as he recalled in his Nobel Prize acceptance speech, that his circumstances ruled out the possibility of pursuing a degree in literature at the college level. Instead, he studied physics and math at Rostov State University, graduating in 1941. After German forces attacked Russia, in June 1941, he enlisted in the Russian Army and served as an artillery officer. He was a twice-decorated captain when, in 1945, he was arrested by Soviet agents who accused him of writing remarks critical of the Soviet dictator Joseph Stalin in his private letters to a friend (though he had referred to Stalin "in disguised terms," as he said in his Nobel speech). He was sentenced to eight years in prison and served the full term in several types of facilities, including a special camp for academics, called a *sharashka*, outside Moscow—the setting for his book *The First Circle*. "Probably I would not have survived eight years of the camps if as a mathematician I had not been assigned for three years to a sharashka," he once wrote, as quoted in the *New York Times* (August 4, 2008). In 1953, a month after his release, he was "exiled for life" in Kok Terek, Kazakhstan, in Soviet Central Asia. There, he taught math and physics at a primary school and began writing poems and stories. His struggle with cancer and his successful treatment for the disease, in 1954, inspired him to write *The Cancer Ward*. In 1956 his internal exile was ended, and he moved to Ryazan, where he continued to teach and to write in secret. In 1962, with the approval of Premier Nikita S. Khrushchev, *One Day in the Life of Ivan Denisovich* was included in the Russian literary journal *Novy Mir*. Solzhenitsyn won instant praise, and the novel was soon translated and published around the world. After the change in the Soviet leadership in 1964, the government began to censor Solzhenitsyn's works and treat him with hostility. His manuscripts for *The First Circle* and *The Cancer Ward* were confiscated, and in 1969 he was expelled from the Soviet Writers Union. Fearing that he would be denied reentry into Russia, he did not attend the 1970 Nobel Prize awards ceremony, in Stockholm, Sweden, arranging instead for his acceptance speech to be smuggled there. Since the Soviet government had banned the publication of anything he wrote, other writings of his were similarly smuggled to other countries. *August 1914*, the first of the historical novels in his series (known as "The Red Wheel") about the birth of the Soviet Union, was published in Paris in 1971. In early 1974 the first volume of *The Gulag Archipelago 1918–1956: An Experiment in Literary Investigation* was published in France, in the Russian language; "the greatest and most powerful single indictment of a political regime ever to be leveled in modern times," in the words of the American diplomat George F. Kennan, it contains a history of the prison-camp system and interviews with hundreds of the 60 million people (Solzhenitsyn's estimate) who had passed through it. Within weeks of its publication, Solzhenitsyn was arrested, denounced as a traitor, stripped of his citizenship, and expelled from his native land. In 1976, after a spell in Switzerland, Solzhenitsyn and his family settled in Cavendish, Vermont, where, for the next 18 years, living mostly in isolation, he continued to write. During that period his denunciations of Western culture as spiritually bankrupt and excessively materialistic alienated many of his admirers, as did his criticisms of the "new" Russia after he returned to his native land, in 1994, three years after the dissolution of the Soviet Union. He was awarded Russia's State Prize by President Vladimir Putin in 2007. His books include the novels *November 1916* (1985), *March 1917* (1989), *April 1917* (1991), and the controversial *Two Hundred Years Together* (2003), about the interactions of Jews and Russians and the role of Jews during and after the Russian Revolution as both victims and oppressors. Solzhenitsyn died in Moscow of a stroke or heart attack. He married and divorced his first wife, the chemist Natalia Reshetovskaya, twice. With his second wife, the mathematician Natalia Svetlova, he had three sons. He is survived by Svetlova and his sons, the second of whom, Ignat Solzhenitsyn, is an accomplished conductor and composer. See *Current Biography* (1988). — M.A.S.

Obituary *New York Times* A p1 Aug. 4, 2008

STAFFORD, ROBERT T. Aug. 8, 1913–Dec. 23, 2006 As a Vermont politician whose résumé included two years as governor of the state, 11 years as a U.S. representative, and 17 years as a U.S. senator, Robert T. Stafford dedicated much of his energy for more than 30 years to environmental and educational issues. A Republican, Stafford held many moderate and liberal views and had no reservations about openly disagreeing with members of the GOP. He criticized President Ronald Reagan's efforts to cut low-interest loans for college students and, in 1987, successfully fought to override Reagan's veto of amendments that strengthened the Clean Water Act. In 1988 Congress honored his work on educational loans by renaming the Federal Guaranteed Student Loan Program the Robert T. Stafford Student Loan Program. In 2006 about 14 million college students received so-called Stafford loans. Born in Rutland, Vermont, Stafford received a bachelor's degree in political science from Middlebury College, in Vermont, in 1935 and a law degree from the Boston University School of Law, in Massachusetts, in 1938. In the latter year he joined his father's Rutland law firm as a partner. He served four years in the U.S. Navy during World War II and was elected Rutland County state's attorney in 1946. After another two years of military service, this time in Korea, Stafford was appointed state deputy attorney general in 1953. The following year he was elected attorney general. He held the office of lieutenant governor for two years before successfully running for governor in 1958. In 1960 Stafford was elected to Congress and continued to win reelection until his appointment to the Senate in 1971, following the death of U.S. senator Winston Prouty. He won a special election later that year to serve the five years remaining in Prouty's term, and subsequently won reelection twice. According to an Associated Press obituary, as published in the *New York Times* (December 24, 2006), Stafford rarely made public statements after his retirement. He made an exception in 2000, when, in the words of the Associated Press writer, he "pleaded with the public for civility" during discussions about a Vermont ballot measure that aimed to recognize civil unions of same-sex couples. "I consider that love is one of the great forces in our society and especially in our state of Vermont," Stafford said a few days days before the vote. "It occurs to me that even if a same-sex couple unites in love, what harm does that do anybody or any society? So I felt compelled to come here and say that." Stafford died in Rutland and was survived by his wife, Helen, and their four daughters. See *Current Biography* (1960).

Obituary *New York Times* I p27 Dec. 24, 2006

STEWART, WILLIAM H. May 19, 1921–Apr. 23, 2008 Physician; government official; educator. A career United States Public Health Service officer, William Huffman Stewart became surgeon general of that service in 1965. In the penultimate year of his tenure, 1968, the position of surgeon general was detached from the Public Health Service and placed within what was then the U.S. Department of Health, Education, and Welfare. Carrying forward the anti-cigarette campaign initiated by his immediate predecessor, Luther L. Terry, Stewart commissioned further studies on the link between cigarette smoking and cancer and other diseases, and he successfully helped pressure Congress to pass the Cigarette Labeling and Advertising Act of 1965. That act, effective in January 1966, required a health warning to appear on cigarette packs: "CAUTION: Cigarette Smoking May Be Hazardous to Your Health." Stewart had wanted a stronger warning, but the tobacco-industry lobby persuaded Congress to modify the wording, in addition to forestalling more serious advertising restrictions. In his 1967 surgeon general's report, Stewart declared that smoking is the principal cause of lung cancer and that there was evidence linking smoking to heart disease. (In 1970, after Stewart had resigned as surgeon general, the warning on cigarette packs was strengthened to read, "The Surgeon General Has Determined That Cigarette Smoking Is Dangerous to Your Health." Later, Congress would ban cigarette advertising on radio and television, and surgeons general would warn against not only cigarette smoking but also against secondhand smoke and the use of tobacco in general, including smokeless snuff and chewing tobacco.) As surgeon general, Stewart also crusaded against institutional racism in health care and for fuller health care for the poor. By linking the power of the Civil Rights Act of 1964 to that of the Social Security Act

of 1965, which introduced the Medicare and Medicaid programs, he forced American hospitals still practicing racial discrimination, mostly in the South, to desegregate—or risk loss of U.S. government funds. He was also ahead of his time in his warnings against air and noise pollution and his recommendation that physicians, surgeons, and dentists reduce the bills of their patients by delegating simpler tasks to less-trained but competent assistants. After earning his medical degree under an accelerated World War II program, Stewart served in the U.S. Army Medical Corps as an Army Air Force physician from April 1946 to December 1947. Following his return to civilian life, he completed a residency in pediatrics. Recalled to national service during the Korean War, in 1951, he was soon transferred from the military to the Public Health Service. As a PHS commissioned officer, he directed research in epidemiology until 1953, when he moved to the National Heart Institute in the National Institutes of Health. Subsequently, he was chief of the heart-disease control program at the U.S. Bureau of State Services (1954–56) and assistant director of the National Heart Institute (1956–57). Appointed an assistant to the U.S. surgeon general in 1957, he became chief of the division of public health methods in the Office of the Surgeon General the following year. From 1963 to 1965 he was an assistant on health and medical affairs to the secretary of health, education, and welfare. He was director of the National Heart Institute from August 5 to September 25, 1965. After resigning as surgeon general, in August 1969, he worked at the Medical Center of Louisiana State University in New Orleans, his alma mater, first as chancellor (1969–74), then as professor of pediatrics and head of the Pediatrics Department (1973–77). He also served as secretary of Louisiana's State Department of Health and Human Resources (1974–77). Later, he headed the Department of Preventative Medicine and Public Health at LSU. He died of kidney failure at Ochsner Medical Center in the New Orleans suburb of Metaire, Louisiana. His survivors included his wife, Glendora (née White), two daughters, and five grandchildren. See *Current Biography* (1966).

Obituary *New York Times* A p17 Apr. 29, 2008

STOCKHAUSEN, KARLHEINZ Aug. 22, 1928–Dec. 5, 2007 German composer. Karlheinz Stockhausen, who experimented daringly with musical and nonmusical sounds both natural and synthetic in quest of "a new beauty," was a leading pioneer in the development of electronic music and atonal serial composition. He was arguably the most influential of Germany's post–World War II composers, and he was certainly the most challenging and controversial, hailed as a visionary genius by his admirers, who ranged from his friend Pierre Boulez and Igor Stravinsky to the Beatles, the Grateful Dead, and Miles Davis, and regarded by others as an egomaniacal sensationalist or theatrical buffoon who was derisively dubbed "the mad messiah of modern music." Stockhausen became fascinated with atonal experimentation as a child playing with a small wooden hammer, noting the plinks, plunks, clangs, and other audible results when he hit various objects and surfaces with it. During childhood he also learned to play the piano under the tutelage of a church organist. Orphaned as a teenager, he studied music at a state school at Xanten, Germany. After graduating from the Hochschule für Musik in Cologne, he studied composition under Darius Milhaud and Olivier Messiaen in Paris. Early on he was influenced as a composer by the modular architecture of Gropius and Le Corbusier and by what he called "the Einsteinian concept of the universal formula," and he was always influenced by motion pictures and the paintings of Klee and Mondrian. In beginning his work in electronic music and total serialism in the early 1950s, he adhered to mathematical and psychoacoustical principles, developing concepts of form that dispensed with traditional musical development, repetition, and variation and led to a new system of musical notation. Without totally abandoning conventional notation, over the following years he became progressively more radical in his innovations, less faithful to musical time, more "intuitive" (as he said) and open to improvisation and controlled chance, and more focused on the acoustics of particular concert halls, including large arenas. At times he seemed, in the view of some critics, "to disappear up his own cul-de-sac of experimental noise." While grounded in Catholicism, he drifted deeply into a New Age mysticism fueled by his introduction to East Asian (especially Japanese) thought and music, theosophy, Sufism, the "new revelations" of Jakob Lorber, the works of Jakob Bohme, and Sri Aurobindo's ideas about astral projection, soul evolution, and reincarnation. He took seriously his dreams that he could fly like a bird and that he had come to Earth from a planet in the Sirius star system, and he was sure "that there [was] an angel constantly guiding" him. He first expressed his idea of escaping the bonds of gravity in one of his highly abstract early pieces, *Kreuzspiel* (1951–52). He drew angry protests with the premiere of the vocal work *Gesang der Jünglinge*, the first of his productions in which the sounds converged on the audience from loudspeakers on all sides. Again in *Kontakte* (1959–60), for acoustic piano/percussion and electronic tape, he encircled the audience with loudspeakers with the intention of creating a dizzying auditory effect that he likened to gravitational loss. In *Mikrophonie I* (1964) he fed the taped sounds of a gong hitting household items through electronic filters and potentiometers. In *Stimmung* (1968), based on talismanic chants, he interspersed the harmonics of six voices (entirely in a low B-flat) with allusions to urinating. For live performance by his ensemble in tours that included the United States during the 1960s, he created such works as *Kurzwellen* (1968), in which the instrumentalists interacted with sounds from shortwave radios. He also incorporated shortwave transmissions in another work of that period, *Hymnen,* an electronic collage of national anthems forming a statement of human "oneness" transcending race, religion, and nationality. The major project of his maturity, composed between 1977 and 2002, was the mammoth seven-part operatic cycle *Licht,* a cosmological drama (based on the seven days of the week) in which two positive protagonists, Michael and Eve, are engaged in spiritual warfare with negative forces led by Lucifer. In the 1995 premiere of *Helikopter Streichquartett* (1995), live

musicians hovered above the audience in helicopters. Stockhausen composed 362 individually performed or performable works, among the last of which were those comprising *Klang,* another quasi-operatic cycle, based on the 24 hours of the day. In directing performances by his ensemble (which included several relatives of his), Stockhausen was an authoritarian perfectionist. More often than not he personally controlled the soundboard, using it as an impromptu contributory instrument. Not easily franchisable to other hands, many of his works became known to a wide public during his lifetime, chiefly through radio broadcasts and recordings. (Eight-one CDs are available through Stockhausen Verlag.) In touring with his ensemble, he conducted classes as well as concerts. He was a professor at his alma mater, the Hochschule für Musik in Cologne (1971–77), and a visiting professor at several other schools, including the University of California at Davis (1966–67). In addition, he offered a program of courses at his compound in the village of Kürten, near Bergisch Gladbach, nine miles northeast of Cologne. The compound—dubbed "the Mount Sinai of serialism" by John O'Mahony in the London *Guardian* (September 29, 2001)—includes residences, rehearsal and recording studios, and the headquarters of Stockhausen Verlag and other business offices. In his later years Stockhausen became increasingly reclusive at Kürten, especially after he provoked a storm of outrage in Germany and internationally with his comments on the September 11, 2001 terrorist attacks on the U.S. In a news conference at that time, he was quoted as saying, in translation, that the atrocity, while "a crime . . . of course," was the "biggest work of art there has ever been . . . the greatest work of art that exists cosmologically. . . . Compared to that, we composers are nothing." He later apologized, explaining that what he had said, in effect, or had meant to say, was that the event was "*Lucifer's* greatest work of art." In his personal affairs, from his wardrobe to his conjugal life, Stockhausen was as eccentric as he was in his music. Reportedly a practitioner of polygamy since the mid-1960s, he was married to and divorced from Doris Andreae and Mary Bauermeister before establishing what was reputed to be a common-law ménage à trois with the clarinetist Suzanne Stephens and the flutist Kathinka Pasveer, both of whom survived him. Among the other survivors were six children (including the trumpeter Markus Stockhausen and the saxophonist Simon Stockhausen) from his two legal marriages and several grandchildren. His ex-wife Mary Bauermeister, also a survivor, heads the Stockhausen Foundation. Following a short illness, Stockhausen died of a sudden heart attack at his home in Kürten. See *Current Biography* (1971).

Obituary *New York Times* D p8 Dec. 8, 2007

STUHLINGER, ERNST Dec. 19, 1913–May 25, 2008 German-born physicist; electrical, atomic, and rocket scientist. Ernst Stuhlinger was one of the team of German rocket scientists led by Werner von Braun who were brought to the United States in the wake of World War II and pioneered the development of the U.S. Army's intercontinental-ballistic-missile (ICBM) program and NASA's space program. A close aide of von Braun's, he was the team's chief specialist in guidance and navigation systems for rockets and spacecraft. His most vital contributions to NASA's space program were designs eliminating the need for interplanetary spacecraft to carry and burn unwieldy quantities of chemical fuel on their voyages. Those designs helped to perfect ion propulsion, the process that draws from sunlight the energy to charge electrically a craft's ion engine at relatively low temperatures. Holding a doctorate in physics, Stuhlinger taught at a secondary school in Berlin from 1936 to 1941, when he was conscripted into the Nazi German Army. Fighting on the Eastern front as an infantryman, he survived the battle of Stalingrad. Transferred in 1943 to the German wartime rocket program headed by von Braun, he helped to develop the V2, a rocket bomb with a one-ton warhead and a pre-set guidance system, the first long-range ballistic missile and the most sophisticated weapon used in the European theater in World War II. Beginning in the autumn of 1944, the Germans fired approximately 1,000 V2s, chiefly against London. Traveling at 3,500 mph and arriving out of the stratosphere without warning, they could not be shot down before they hit their targets—with a 50 percent success rate. After World War II, under the aegis of the U.S. Department of State, von Braun and his rocket specialists, including Stuhlinger, immigrated to the United States in what was called Operation Paperclip, beginning in the autumn of 1945. For several years the von Braun team was stationed with the U.S. Army at Fort Bliss, Texas, where it refurbished and launched V2 rockets shipped from Germany, instructed the American military in rocketry, and continued to research potential advances in rocketry. In 1950 the team was transferred to the Redstone Arsenal, in Huntsville, Alabama, where it spent the next six years developing the Army's Redstone rocket, used in the first live nuclear-ballistic-missile tests conducted by the army. It then developed the Jupiter-C, the modified Redstone rocket that launched the West's first earth-orbiting satellite, *Explorer I*, in January 1958. (Stuhlinger created a simple ground-based timing device to initiate the firing of Jupiter-C's second stage and personally pressed the button on the device at precisely the right moment.) The team's work was done under the auspices of the U.S. Army Ballistic Missile Agency (ABMA) and the Army Ordnance Missile Command (AOMC) until July 1960, when President Dwight D. Eisenhower, on site at the Redstone Arsenal, announced the termination of ABMA and AOMC and the creation of a new civilian entity, the National Aeronautics and Space Administration, to be based (originally) in what was to be called the George C. Marshall Space Flight Center at the Redstone Arsenal. Stuhlinger was director of the space-science lab at the Marshall Center from 1960 to 1968, a period during which the von Braun team developed the series of Saturn rockets, climaxing with the Saturn 5, which launched the *Apollo* astronauts who made the first landing on the moon, in 1969. On the eve of that event, in 1968, Stuhlinger was promoted to associate director for science at the Marshall Center. After retiring from that position, in 1975, he became an adjunct professor and senior research scientist at the University of Alabama at Huntsville. While at the Redstone Arsenal, Stuhl-

inger had become a naturalized American citizen, in 1955. He wrote the book *Ion Propulsion for Space Flight* (1964) and co-wrote the biography *Werner von Braun: Crusader for Space* (1993). Stuhlinger died at his home in Huntsville, Alabama, leaving behind his wife, Irmgard (née Lotze), his sons, Tilman and Hans Christoph, and his daughter, Susanne. See *Current Biography* (1957).

Obituary *New York Times* B p5 May 28, 2008

SUMAC, YMA Sep. 13, 1922–Nov. 1, 2008 Peruvian-American singer. A "vocal phenomenon," in the words of Stephen Holden in the *New York Times* (February 26, 1989), whose voice "glided preternaturally across four octaves," as the *Times*'s Douglas Martin put it (November 4, 2008), Yma Sumac enjoyed great success in the United States in the 1950s, with best-selling records and sold-out concerts and nightclub engagements. "In 1950, when *Voice of the Xtabay*, her first album of multi-octave mystical warblings, created a sensation, Miss Sumac was already regarded as something of a camp oddity, albeit one who possessed singular gifts," Holden wrote, after noting that she "always fearlessly straddled the line between the sublime and the ridiculous." While her claim that her range spanned five octaves raised some eyebrows (the average singer's range is two octaves), "few doubted a vocal ability that many experts thought belonged in opera," according to Douglas Martin. In a review for the *New York Herald Tribune* (February 18, 1954) of a concert she gave at Carnegie Hall, in New York City, the composer and critic Virgil Thomson described Sumac as "all at the same time a female baritone, a lyric soprano and a high coloratura." "[She has] a voice of great beauty, and her vocal technique is impeccable," Thomson declared. "She sings very low and warm, very high and bird-like; and her middle range is no less lovely than the extremes of her scale. That scale . . . is no way inhuman or outlandish in sound." In *Playbill.online* (January 3, 2008), Robert Simonson wrote that her career "was suffused with self-manufactured mystery"; partly for that reason, an urban myth arose that her name was really Amy Camus ("Yma" and "Sumac" in reverse) and that she was a native of Brooklyn, New York. At her birth, in Ichocán, a village in the Cajamarca region of the northern Peruvian Andes, Sumac was named Zoila Augusta Emperatriz Chavarri del Castillo. She was the daughter of a full-blooded Indian mother and a father of mixed Spanish and Indian ancestry. Her professional name is a variation on her mother's name; in Quechua, it means "how beautiful!" (In interviews, Sumac maintained that it meant "beautiful flower" or "beautiful girl"; she also said that she had been descended from Incan royalty and consistently lied about her year of birth.) During a festival that Sumac attended as a child, a Peruvian government employee heard her sing, and soon afterward officials at the Department of Education arranged for her to attend a Catholic school for girls in Lima, the nation's capital. There, she attracted the attention of the musician and composer Moisés Vivanco, who directed the Peruvian National Board of Broadcasting. Earlier, Vivanco had formed the Compañia Peruana de Arte, an ensemble of 46 native Peruvian dancers, singers, and instrumentalists, and at his invitation, Sumac began to practice with them. Within months of her radio debut with the group, in 1942, she became its star, performing with them in Argentina and Brazil as well as Peru. Also in 1942 she married Vivanca, who arranged the pieces in her repertoire, most of which were based on Andean folk songs. She made her U.S. debut in 1946 but remained little known in the U.S. until 1950, when Capitol Records released her album *Voice of Xtabay* (a word made up by Capitol marketers, who sought to enhance her exoticism). According to *Current Biography* (December 1955), "With no advertising other than a three-inch item in an obscure journal, the album sold 500,000 copies 'overnight.'" By the end of December 1950, the record had become that year's best-seller, despite competition from recordings by Bing Crosby and other popular singers. Soon afterward Sumac performed at the Hollywood Bowl, in California, before a capacity audience that included movie-industry decision-makers. Thereafter her career blossomed, with an appearance on Broadway, in the short-lived, 1951 musical *Flahooley* (in which the singer Barbara Cook also made her Broadway debut). Sumac also performed on radio and TV; in nightclubs in Las Vegas, Nevada; and elsewhere in New York, at locations including the Roxy Theatre, where in 1951 she shared the stage with the comedian Danny Kaye and Bil Baird's Marionettes. She played an Inca princess in the film *Secret of the Incas* (1954), starring Charlton Heston, and was cast in *Omar Khayyam* (1957), starring Cornel Wilde. From 1961 to 1966, as a member of the Inca Taky Trio, she performed in three dozen cities in Latin America and the Soviet Union and other parts of Europe and Asia. A concert the trio gave in Bucharest, Rumania, was recorded for *Recital*, Sumac's only live album. Her other recordings include *Mambo, Legend of the Sun Valley, Call of the Andes, Queen of Exotica, The Spell of Yma Sumac, Exotic Lure of Yma Sumac, Legend of the Jivaro, The Sun Virgin, Peruvian Queen*, and *Inca Taqui. Yma Rocks!* (1971), produced by Les Baxter, contains westernized arrangements of Incan and other Latin American folk songs. By the time of that album's release, Sumac's popularity had waned. It revived to some extent in the late 1980s and 1990s: the magic act Penn & Teller used her music in two of their shows, in 1987 and 1991, and she was heard on the soundtracks of movies including *Men with Guns* (1997), *The Big Lebowski* (1998), and *Happy, Texas* (1999) and, in the next decade, *Ordinary Decent Criminal* (2000), *Confessions of a Dangerous Mind* (2002), *Death to Smoochy* (2002), *The In-Laws* (2005), and *King of California* (2007). She was a guest on the David Letterman TV show in 1987, and in 1990 she played the role of Heidi in a production of Stephen Sondheim's *Follies* in Long Beach, California. Many crossword aficionados in the United States became familiar with her first name, which was used in many puzzles. In 2006 the Peruvian government honored her with the Orden del Sol, and the National University of San Marcos awarded her the Jorge Basadre Medal. Sumac divorced Vivanco in 1957; they remarried that year and then divorced again in 1965. With Vivanco, Sumac had one son, born in 1949. A naturalized American citizen since 1955, she died in an assisted-living facility in Los Angeles, California. See *Current Biography* (1955). — M.H.

Obituary *New York Times* p32 Nov. 4, 2008

TRUMAN, MARGARET Feb. 17, 1924–Jan. 29, 2008 Daughter of Harry S. Truman, president of the United States from 1945 to 1953; coloratura concert singer; an author best known for her Washington, D.C.–based murder mysteries. Margaret Truman Daniel, as she was known in private life after her marriage, was President Truman's only child. After earning a B.A. degree in history at George Washington University, she made her professional debut as a singer with the Detroit Symphony Orchestra in a concert broadcast on national radio on March 16, 1947. She later made concert tours of the United States with a program of operatic arias, lieder, and light classics. The most publicized moment in her singing career came in December 1950, when the *Washington Post* music critic Paul Hume panned a performance by her at Constitution Hall in Washington, D.C., describing her as "very attractive" but attributing to her "a pleasant voice of little size and fair quality . . . flat a good deal of the time." In the quick retort he mailed to Hume, President Truman famously wrote, "I have just read your lousy review. . . . I never met you, but if I do you'll need a new nose, a lot of beefsteak for black eyes, and perhaps a supporter below!" After she abandoned her singing career, in 1954, Margaret Truman acted in summer stock and for a number of years executed various assignments on television and radio under successive contracts with the NBC and CBS networks. Also in the mid-1950s she hosted a radio program called *Weekday*; a decade later she hosted *International Hour*, a television program of music and dance from around the world, and *Authors in the News*, daily five-minute radio interviews broadcast on more than 100 stations. Her books were all written under the name Margaret Truman. The first was the autobiography *Souvenir* (1956); her second was the coffee-table volume *White House Pets* (1969). Among her later books were the biographies of her father and mother, *Harry S. Truman* (1973) and *Bess W. Truman* (1986), the biographical volumes *Women of Courage* (1976) and *First Ladies* (1996), and *The President's House* (1984), a history of the White House and its occupants. Reviews of her first mystery novel, *Murder in the White House* (1980), a best-seller, included praise for her "sure hand" in creating "a lively Washington scene" on the one hand and, on the other, faint praise for "a certain amount of technical dexterity" in apparent studied emulation of Agatha Christie. Twenty-two subsequent volumes were published in her series, almost all of which are set in venues in and around the District of Columbia, including the Supreme Court, Embassy Row, the Smithsonian Institution, the Kennedy Center, the National Gallery, Union Station, the National Cathedral, and the Library of Congress. The titles range from *Murder on Capitol Hill* (1981) to *Murder on K Street* (2008). In an Associated Press Worldstream obituary, Margaret Stafford wrote that the mystery writer and ghost writer Donald Bain "was rumored to have written Truman's mysteries, but he has denied it." Margaret Truman Daniel, who had lived for four decades on Park Avenue in Manhattan, died at an assisted-living facility in Chicago. The immediate cause of death was an infection. She was predeceased by her husband, the *New York Times* reporter, bureau chief, and managing editor Clifton Daniel, and by her son William W. Daniel (who died in 2000 of injuries suffered when he was struck by a Manhattan taxicab). Her survivors included her sons Clifton T. Daniel, Harrison G. Daniel, and Thomas W. Daniel and five grandchildren. See *Current Biography* (1987).

Obituary *New York Times* B p6 Jan. 30, 2008

WELLER, THOMAS H. June 15, 1915–Aug. 23, 2008 The Nobel Prize–winning virologist Thomas H. Weller helped pave the way for the development of polio vaccines as well as vaccines for other viral diseases. During his research in 1949, he and his colleagues John F. Enders and Frederick C. Robbins discovered that the poliovirus could be grown within human embryonic tissue inside test tubes. Not only did this discredit the theory that the poliovirus could grow only in nervous tissue, but it also eliminated the need for laboratory animals and enabled scientists to monitor the development of the disease closely. Weller, Enders, and Robbins shared the 1954 Nobel Prize in Physiology or Medicine after the creation of the first polio vaccine, by Jonas Salk, in the early 1950s. Weller was also the first scientist to isolate the rubella virus and the varicella zoster viruses, which led to his discovery that the latter were responsible for both chicken pox and shingles. Weller was born in Ann Arbor, Michigan. He received his bachelor's degree from the University of Michigan and earned an M.D. degree in 1940 from the Harvard Medical School, in Boston, Massachusetts, where he had developed an interest in tropical diseases. His clinical training in pediatrics at the Children's Hospital in Boston was interrupted when he joined the Army Medical Corps, in 1942. While in the military he worked on malaria control in the Caribbean. Afterward he became an instructor of tropical public health at Harvard and was named assistant director of the research division of infectious diseases at the Children's Hospital. During that time 10s of thousands of new polio cases were reported each year in the United States. The isolation of the poliovirus by Weller and his colleagues led to the development of both the Salk and the Sabin polio vaccines in the mid-1950s. By the 1970s only a handful of new cases of polio were diagnosed in the U.S., and the disease has since been eradicated from most other parts of the world. Weller was named the Richard Pearson Strong professor of tropical public health at Harvard and the head of the Department of Tropical Public Health (now the Department of Immunology and Infectious Diseases) in 1954. In 1955 he isolated the varicella zoster virus as well as the virus that causes cytomegalic inclusion disease in infants. Seven years later he isolated the virus that causes rubella, or German measles. He revealed in his autobiography, *Growing Pathogens in Tissue Cultures: Fifty Years in Academic Tropical Medicine, Pediatrics and Virology* (2004), that the source of the sample used in isolating the rubella virus was his son, who had contracted German measles in 1960. Weller re-

tired from Harvard in 1985. During the course of his career, he worked with the U.S. Public Health Service, the World Health Organization, the Pan American Health Organization, and the U.S. Agency for International Development. He served as president of the American Society of Tropical Medicine and Hygiene and was honored with the organization's Walter Reed Medal in 1996. Weller died at his home in Needham, Massachusetts. He was survived by his wife, Kathleen, two sons, a daughter, and six grandchildren. See *Current Biography* (1955). — M.A.S.

Obituary *New York Times* D p8 Aug. 27, 2008

WEXLER, JERRY Jan. 10, 1917–Aug. 15, 2008 As a music producer and executive at Atlantic Records, Jerry Wexler cultivated some of the most talented musicians in modern times, among them Ray Charles, Otis Redding, Aretha Franklin, Willie Nelson, Linda Ronstadt, and Bob Dylan. He has also been credited for coining the name of the musical genre known as rhythm and blues. "He played a major role in bringing black music to the masses, and in the evolution of rhythm and blues to soul music," Jim Henke, the vice president and chief curator for the Rock and Roll Hall of Fame, told Bruce Weber for the *New York Times* (August 16, 2008). "Beyond that, he really developed the role of the record producer. Jerry did a lot more than just turn on a tape recorder. He left his stamp on a lot of great music. He had a commercial ear as well as a critical ear." Born Gerald Wexler in New York City, he was raised in a Jewish family in the Manhattan neighborhood of Washington Heights. In his youth he often skipped school to spend time in record stores and Harlem jazz clubs. Hoping to steer him toward a career in writing, his mother enrolled him at the Kansas State College of Agriculture and Applied Science (now Kansas State University), in Manhattan, Kansas. Wexler studied journalism but was more interested in the southern jazz and blues music being performed in Kansas City, Missouri, about 100 miles from the college. He left college for two years to serve in the army during World War II; he was stationed in Texas and Florida during that time. He finished his bachelor's degree in Kansas before moving back to New York City in 1947. There, he found a job as a cub reporter for the music magazine *Billboard*. In 1949, when the magazine's editor decided to change the title of the black popular-music charts, then known as "Race Records," Wexler suggested the name "Rhythm and Blues." His work at *Billboard* soon came to the attention of Ahmet Ertegun and Herb Abramson, the co-founders of Atlantic Records, which was then a small, independent label that worked mainly with black musicians. When Abramson joined the army, in 1953, Ertegun asked Wexler to fill in as co-director of the company. Wexler soon established himself as an ambitious, astute businessman and skilled producer. During his early years with Atlantic, Wexler produced records by artists or groups including Ray Charles, Joe Turner, and the Coasters. "He had an extraordinary insight into talent," Charles said in *Immaculate Funk* (2000), a documentary about Wexler made by Tom Thurman. ("Immaculate funk" was the phrase Wexler used to describe the Atlantic sound.) In the same documentary the singer/songwriter Wilson Pickett said, "How could he understand what was inside of black people like that? But Jerry Wexler did." After Aretha Franklin signed with Atlantic, in 1967, Wexler produced some of her biggest hits, among them "Respect," "Chain of Fools," and "(You Make Me Feel Like) A Natural Woman." Wexler and Ertegun continued to run Atlantic after it was sold to Warner Bros. in 1967. (Abramson had left the firm in 1958.) Wexler continued to work with Willie Nelson and other southern musicians, while Ertegun focused on rock bands—the Rolling Stones, AC/DC, and Led Zepplin. Wexler was vocal about his distaste for rock music, and as the genre continued to rise in popularity in the 1970s, he began to feel alienated at Atlantic. He resigned in 1975 and began working as a freelance producer. During the late 1970s and early 1980s, he worked with Dire Straits, Carlos Santana, and George Michael, and, most notably, produced Bob Dylan's album *Slow Train Coming* (1979). His autobiography, *Rhythm and the Blues* (1993), written with David Ritz, recalled his interactions with legendary musicians and described his tumultuous personal life, which included use of illegal drugs and adulterous affairs. (His first two marriages, to Shirley Kampf and then Renee Pappas, ended in divorce.) Wexler was inducted into the Rock and Roll Hall of Fame in 1987, its second year of operation. He died of congestive heart failure in his home in Sarasota, Florida. He was predeceased by his daughter Anita, from his first marriage. A son and a daughter from that marriage and his third wife, Jean Martin, survived him. See *Current Biography* (2001). — M.A.S.

Obituary *New York Times* A p17 Aug. 16, 2008

WHEELER, JOHN ARCHIBALD July 9, 1911–Apr. 13, 2008 Physicist; cosmologist; professor emeritus, Princeton University. A protégé of Niels Bohr and Albert Einstein, John Archibald Wheeler was himself a titan in theoretical physics and a mentor to such luminaries as Richard Feynman, Kip Thorne, Hugh Everett III, and Jacob Bekenstein. In the 1930s Wheeler introduced the indispensable S-matrix into particle physics and (with Bohr, independently of the similar work of Enrico Fermi) arrived at a general theory of nuclear fission making possible the atomic bomb developed under the aegis of the U.S.'s Manhattan Project during World War II. Over the following decades Wheeler remained in the forefront of visionary physicists seeking to learn the secrets of the universe, from the orderly macrocosmos and what Wheeler called its two "Gates of Time" (the beginning "Big Bang" and the final "Big Crunch") to the microstructures in which a "strange," seemingly "magical" disorder reigns. To that task he brought a fertile and daring imagination and a flair for coining and/or popularizing simple, colorful names for complex phenomena, such as "black hole" in place of "gravitationally completely collapsed star" and "wormhole," denoting a hypothetical tunnel-like shortcut through space-time. One of the major concepts he proposed was the "participatory universe," which included the idea that celestial objects that existed light-years in the past are real today because of our participation as observers of them. Wheeler re-

ceived his Ph.D. degree at Johns Hopkins University in 1933. During the same year he heard Niels Bohr, who was visiting the United States, speak at the Chicago World's Fair. He met Albert Einstein in October 1935, when Einstein took up permanent residence in the United States, and the two later kept in frequent contact in Princeton, New Jersey, where Einstein was a lecturer at the Institute for Advanced Study for almost two decades before his death, in 1955. On a fellowship, Wheeler studied with Bohr in Copenhagen, Denmark, before becoming assistant professor of physics at the University of North Carolina in 1935. He and Bohr subsequently maintained contact, and when Bohr again visited the United States in 1939, the year after Wheeler joined the faculty of Princeton University, they completed their study "The Mechanism of Nuclear Fission." In that paper they proposed their "liquid drop" model of a slow neutron entering the nucleus of a uranium-235 isotope, causing it to split into two smaller drops representing the nuclei of a tellurium-137 atom and a zirconium-97 atom; the consequent emission of neutrons, they showed, resulted in the release of energy that would be realized in practice in the uranium-235 gun-type atomic bomb that destroyed Hiroshima, Japan, on August 6, 1945 and the plutonium-239 implosion-type device that leveled Nagasaki, Japan, three days later. (In nature, plutonium exists only in minute traces; the plutonium in practical use is enriched uranium.) After serving as a consultant on reactor design and procedure at the Manhattan Project's metallurgical laboratory at the University of Chicago, which began producing plutonium in 1942, Wheeler was the chief consultant at the project's Hanford, Washington, site, which began producing plutonium in 1945. Later, after the war, he worked under Edward Teller on Project Matterhorn, which developed the hydrogen-fusion bomb, a thermonuclear device a thousand times more powerful than the atomic-fission bomb. In the early 1950s Wheeler was credited with almost single-handedly reviving interest in Einstein's general theory of relativity. Meanwhile, his rapport with his students always remained his first priority. When his former student Richard Feynman, nanotechnology's "crazy" pioneer, shared a Nobel Prize in 1965 for his "space-time view" of quantum mechanics, Feynman acknowledged that the basic idea had come from Wheeler. After directing the Center for Theoretical Physics at the University of Texas in Austin (1976–86), Wheeler returned to Princeton University as professor emeritus. He co-wrote the 1,280-page textbook *Gravitation* (1973) and wrote, among other books, *Geometrodynamics* (1962), *Frontiers of Time* (1979), *Gravity and Spacetime* (1990), and the autobiographical volumes *At Home in the Universe* (1993) and *Geons, Black Holes, and Quantum Foam: A Life in Physics* (1998). Wheeler died of pneumonia at his home in Hightstown, New Jersey. He was predeceased by his wife, Janette (née Hegner), and survived by two daughters, a son, eight grandchildren, 16 great-grandchildren, six step-grandchildren, and 11 step-great-grandchildren. See *Current Biography* (1970).

Obituary *New York Times* B p7 Apr. 14, 2008

WHITNEY, PHYLLIS A. Sep. 9, 1903–Feb. 8, 2008 Author. Phyllis Ayame Whitney, a prolific writer of best-selling fiction combining romance and gothic suspense, produced 40 adult novels, 14 novels for young people, 19 juvenile mysteries, and approximately 100 short stories over a span of six decades. More than 50 million copies of her books are in print, many in paperback, and the books have been translated into some 30 languages. In addition to the several book awards she received, in 1988 the Mystery Writers of America named her a Grand Master for her lifetime achievement, and in 1990 Malice Domestic Ltd., a fan convention, bestowed an Agatha Award on her, also for lifetime achievement. Whitney, who set her tales in some of the myriad locales where she lived and traveled, was born in Japan, where her father represented an American shipping line. She spent her early childhood there and in China and the Philippines, where her parents operated hotels. Following the deaths of her parents, at age 17 she went to live with an aunt in Chicago, where the plots of her earliest tales were set. Especially in the early years of her career, her protagonists were almost always female. She published her first short story in 1928 and her first book in 1941. That book was *A Place for Ann*, a young-adult novel whose heroine, with friends, organizes a business doing personal-service chores for its customers. *A Star for Ginny* followed in 1942 and *A Window for Julie* in 1943. *The Silver Inkwell* (1945) was written as a guidebook, albeit in fictional guise, for aspiring young writers. The young white heroine of *Willow Hill* (1947) and her high-school classmates deal with the racial integration of a housing project in their neighborhood. ("Most of my writing," Whitney once said, "has been concerned with understanding between people, whether of different races or religions or even the same family.") Her subsequent novels for young people included *Linda's Homecoming* (1950) and *Nobody Likes Trina* (1972), her last book in that genre. Her juvenile books included *Mystery of the Haunted Pool* (1960) and *Mystery of the Hidden Hand* (1963), both of which received the Edgar Award from the Mystery Writers Association of America for the best children's mystery of the year. She published her first adult suspense novel, *Red Is for Murder*, in 1943. The second, the 19th-century romance *The Quicksilver Pool*, did not appear until 1955. In *The Trembling Hills* (1956), one of the great enduring classics among her works, the heroine, Sara Jerome, encounters disturbing supernatural phenomena and lives through the San Francisco earthquake of 1906 in her search for her father and her pursuit of a male love interest already spoken for. Whitney's subsequent adult novels included *Silversword* (1987) and *Feather on the Moon* (1988). In the former, set in Maui, Hawaii, the heroine is denied information (by a malicious aunt) about the fate of her parents; in the latter, a child is kidnapped. Her last adult novel, *Amethyst Dreams* (1997), set on Topsail Island in North Carolina, is about an heiress who goes missing and her best friend's efforts to find her. Several of Whitney's plots involve occult channeling, a subject of great interest to her. In addition to her novels and short stories, she wrote three nonfiction books on the writing of fiction. After her divorce from George A. Garner, Whitney married Lovell F. Jahnke. She was predeceased by Jahnke and survived by a daughter from her first marriage, two grandchildren, and two great-grandchildren. She died of pneumonia in a hospital in Charlottesville, Virginia. See *Current Biography* (1948).

Obituary *New York Times* B p7 Feb. 9, 2008

WICK, CHARLES Z. Oct. 12, 1917–July 20, 2008 Publicist; government official; lawyer. Originally an Independent in politics, Charles Z. Wick became a leading Republican Party fund-raiser because of his friendship with Ronald Reagan. He served as director of the United States Information Agency during President Reagan's two terms in the White House (1981–89). The USIA was essentially a public diplomatic weapon in the Cold War. Launched in 1953 and disbanded in 1999, it employed more than 7,000 people operating in more than 200 posts in 126 countries. From 1978 to 1982 it was known as the International Communications Agency. An arm of the executive branch of the federal government, it was charged with conducting informational and cultural programs promoting the U.S. government's views among populations abroad. Known outside the United States as the U.S. Information Service, it was involved with the International Visitors Program, the Voice of America and other international broadcast services, and the awarding of Fulbright travel grants, among other activities and programs. While earning undergraduate degrees in music and law, Wick supported himself by playing the piano and arranging the music for a dance band that he organized. Born Charles Zwick, he changed his name when, in the early 1940s, he was handling the business and legal affairs of Tommy Dorsey and his orchestra in Los Angeles and New York City. After working for five years (1944–49) in the radio department of the William Morris talent agency in Manhattan, he struck out on his own as an agent for such clients as the musician Benny Goodman, the comedian Pinky Lee, the singer Frances Langford, the actress Sarah Churchill, and the British statesman and author Winston Churchill. Entering the new field of television entertainment in the early 1950s, he founded Charles Wick Associates in New York and Twickenham Studios in London and produced the TV series *Fabian of the Yard*. He also produced the theatrical motion picture *Snow White and the Three Stooges* (1961). He founded the investment firm of Mapleton Associates and co-founded a chain of nursing homes, United Convalescent Hospitals. After Ronald Reagan's victory in the 1980 presidential election, Reagan named Wick co-chairman of the committee that planned and executed the gala inaugural events of January 1981. Wick was nominated to head the U.S. Information Agency in March 1981 and was sworn in the following month. As director of the USIA for eight years, he was credited with winning a greater budget for the agency, expanding its operations, and upgrading the technology of those operations; among his innovations were Radio Martí, the Voice of America's Spanish-language outlet broadcasting American news and opinions to Communist Cuba, and Worldnet, the world's first live international satellite television network. On the negative side, he was criticized for secretly taping his telephone conversations and for installing a security system at his home partly at government expense. (He ultimately reimbursed the government $22,000, its share in the total cost of $32,000.) He denied personal involvement in the Reagan administration's blacklist of 84 public figures—from Jimmy Carter to Ralph Nader—from USIA speaking engagements, agreeing that the list was "un-American." After leaving the USIA, Wick served on the board of Rupert Murdoch's News Corp. and was involved in health-care and real-estate matters. When Ronald Reagan was incapacitated by Alzheimer's disease, Wick and his wife joined Nancy Reagan in her campaign to promote human stem-cell research. He was one of the five honorary pall bearers at Ronald Reagan's funeral, in June 2004. Wick died at his home in Los Angeles, leaving behind his wife, Mary Jane (née Woods), two sons, three daughters, and eight grandchildren. See *Current Biography* (1985).

Obituary *New York Times* B p6 July 24, 2008

WIDMARK, RICHARD Dec. 26, 1914–Mar. 24, 2008 Actor. In the post–World War II years, Richard Widmark joined the likes of Robert Mitchum in bringing to leading and supporting roles in motion pictures "a hardboiled type who [did] not actively court the sympathy of the audience"—as Martin Lewison observed in his mini-biography of Widmark on the Internet Movie Database—and on occasion seemed to have no fear of inviting audience antipathy. With his Academy Award–nominated big-screen debut as Tommy Udo, the giggling psychopathic thug who pushes an old woman in a wheelchair down a stairway to her death in *Kiss of Death* (1947), Widmark established himself overnight as an icon of film noir. In the years that immediately followed, he was often typecast in thrillers as a heavy or semi-heavy, a deeply flawed or troubled character if not an outright villain, but over the course of his career he demonstrated his versatility in a great variety of portrayals, from the U.S. Health Service physician racing against time to track down a criminal carrying the plague in New Orleans in Elia Kazan's *Panic in the Streets* (1950) and the Dauphin in *Saint Joan* (1957) to the American prosecutor in *Judgment at Nuremberg* (1961), the philandering husband in the comedy *The Tunnel of Love* (1968), principal roles in the Westerns *The Alamo* (1960), *Two Rode Together* (1961), and *Cheyenne Autumn* (1964), and the loner police detective sergeant Daniel Madigan, a precursor of Clint Eastwood's Dirty Harry, in *Madigan* (1968). He went on to play Madigan on television, in six 90-minute episodes broadcast on the NBC network during the 1972–73 season. His other television credits included the title roles in the miniseries *Benjamin Franklin* (1974) and *Mr. Horn* (1979) and such TV-movie roles as small-town police chief Joe Steiner in *Blackout* (1985), bayou sheriff Mapes in *A Gathering of Old Men* (1987), and Captain Owen Hayes, an old Texas Ranger who has a long-term adversarial/friendly relationship with an old train- and bank robber (Willie Nelson) in *Once Upon a Train* (1988). Widmark began acting while attending Lake Forest College in Illinois. After earning a degree in drama and political science at Lake Forest, in 1936, and teaching drama there for two years, he went to

New York and acted in radio drama series, beginning with *Aunt Jenny's Real Life Stories* and including *David Harum*, *Stella Dallas*, and *Inner Sanctum*, among other shows. Deferred from military service during World War II on medical grounds (he had a punctured eardrum), he made his Broadway debut as an Army Air Corps lieutenant in the comedy *Kiss and Tell* in 1943. Over the following three years, his Broadway credits included roles in *Get Away Old Man*, *Trio*, *Kiss Them for Me*, and *Daughter*. *Kiss of Death* was his first picture under a seven-year contract with Twentieth Century Fox. Under that contract a score of roles followed, including those of an asthmatic gang leader in *Street with No Name* (1948), a Civil War veteran who becomes an outlaw in *Yellow Sky* (1948), the double-crossing proprietor in *Road House* (1948), the doomed American cabaret hustler in London in *Night and the City* (1950), and the racist convict/patient who taunts a black medical resident (Sidney Poitier) in a prison hospital in *No Way Out* (1950). (Between scenes, he deeply touched Poitier with his repeated apologies.) In changes of pace, he had such sympathetic roles as the good guy warning two parents that their babysitter (Marilyn Monroe) is dangerously disturbed in *Don't Bother to Knock* (1951) and the whaling-ship mate in *Down to the Sea in Ships* (1959). After his contract with Fox expired, he had more control over his choice of pictures, some of which he produced himself. His roles included those of the dedicated court-marshal judge advocate in *Time Limit* (1957), the philandering husband in the comedy *The Tunnel of Love* (1958), the courageous lawyer in *The Trap* (1959), the hawkish destroyer captain in *The Bedford Incident* (1965), a general in the nuclear thriller *Twilight's Last Gleaming* (1977), the malevolent hospital head in *Coma* (1978), and U.S. senator James Stiles in *True Colors* (1991). Widmark was described by those who knew him as a low-keyed, "down-to-earth guy," devoted to his craft but wary of celebrity and shunning publicity, except to further his favorite liberal cause, gun control. He died at his home in Roxbury, Connecticut. He was predeceased by his wife of 55 years, Ora Jean (née Hazelwood), and survived by his second wife, Susan (née Blanshard), a former wife of Henry Fonda; his daughter, Anne Heath Widmark, who was once married to the baseball player Sandy Koufax; his stepdaughter, Amy Fonda Ivers; and his stepson, Marc Weisgal. See *Current Biography* (1963).

Obituary *New York Times* B p6 Mar. 27, 2008

WINSTON, STAN Apr. 7, 1946–June 15, 2008 Make-up and special-effects artist. In a career spanning four decades in motion pictures and television, Stan Winston substantially raised the industry standards for realistic facial prosthetics, animatronics, and robotic design. Winston won Academy Awards for his work on the feature films *Aliens* (1986, for effects, including the 14-foot alien queen), *Terminator 2: Judgment Day* (1991, for makeup and effects, including the slithery futuristic assassin), *Jurassic Park* (1993, for effects, including the rampaging dinosaurs), and *Batman Returns* (1992, for makeup). In addition, he was nominated for Oscars for his work on *Heartbeeps* (1981), *Predator* (1987), *Edward Scissorhands* (1992), *The Lost World* (1997), and *Artificial Intelli-*

gence: *AI* (2001). He worked on a total of more than 40 motion pictures, including *W.C. Fields and Me* (1976), *The Wiz* (1978), *The Thing* (1982), *Monster Squad* (1987), and *The Island of Dr. Moreau* (1996). Shortly before his death he contributed to *Iron Man* (2008), *Indiana Jones and the Kingdom of the Crystal Skull* (2008), and several films in production in 2008, including *Shutter Island* and *Avatar*. He directed four feature films: *Pumpkinhead* (1988), *The Adventures of a Gnome Named Gnom* (1991), *T2 3-D: Battle Across Time* (1996), and *Ghosts* (1997). On television he won Emmy Awards for his makeup work on the productions *Gargoyles* (1972) and *The Autobiography of Miss Jane Whitman* (1974). After apprenticing in the makeup department at Walt Disney Studios for three years (1969–71), Winston established the Stan Winston Studio in 1978. With Scott Ross and director James Cameron, he co-founded Digital Domain, a leader in the production of computer-assisted special effects, in 1993. Winston died of multiple melanoma at his home in Malibu, California. He was survived by his wife, Karen, a son, a daughter, and four grandchildren. See *Current Biography* (2002).

Obituary *New York Times* B p7 June 17, 2008

CLASSIFICATION BY PROFESSION—2008

ACTIVISM
Clooney, George
Hayes, Tyrone B.
Heller, Agnes
Newkirk, Ingrid
Obama, Michelle
Power, Samantha
Ramonet, Ignacio
Sinclair, Cameron
Tethong, Lhadon

AGRICULTURE
Brownback, Sam

ANTHROPOLOGY
McFate, Montgomery

ARCHITECTURE
Nouvel, Jean
Sinclair, Cameron

ART
Ali, Laylah
Arceneaux, Edgar
Carson, David
diCorcia, Philip-Lorca
Estern, Neil
Friedman, Tom
Gibson, Lois
Horsey, David
Jaffee, Al
Newkirk, Kori

ASTRONAUTICS
Bigelow, Robert

ASTRONOMY
Levin, Janna
May, Brian

BUSINESS
Bigelow, Robert
Carson, David
Catz, Safra A.
Corsi, Jerome R.
Deschanel, Caleb
Flay, Bobby
Gopinath, Suhas

Kao, John
Kohl, Herb
Kurzweil, Raymond
Mackey, John
McNerney, James
Medvedev, Dmitry
Mohammed bin Rashid Al Maktoum
Oliver, Garrett
Pandit, Vikram
Peltz, Nelson
Russo, Patricia
Sandberg, Sheryl
Schmidt, Eric
Sinclair, David A.
Snider, Stacey
Speyer, Jerry
Temple, Johnny
Turin, Luca
Villa-Komaroff, Lydia
Zagat, Tim and Nina
Zuckerberg, Mark

COMPUTERS
Kurzweil, Raymond
Rucker, Rudy
Sandberg, Sheryl
Schmidt, Eric
Zuckerberg, Mark

CONSERVATION
Beresford-Kroeger, Diana

DANCE
Ortega, Kenny

ECONOMICS
Zoellick, Robert B.

EDUCATION
Blunt, Roy
Bollinger, Lee C.
Burns, Ed
Capps, Lois
Carson, David
DeCarava, Roy
Feith, Douglas J.
Greider, Carol W.

Harvey, David
Hayes, Tyrone B.
Hellenga, Robert
Heller, Agnes
Hockfield, Susan
Jamail, Joe
Kao, John
Levin, Janna
Melton, Douglas A.
Mitchell, Elvis
Pepperberg, Irene
Polgar, Susan
Power, Samantha
Ramonet, Ignacio
Schwartz, Pepper
Sinclair, David A.
Sittenfeld, Curtis
Sunstein, Cass R.
Thomas, Michael
Turin, Luca
Villa-Komaroff, Lydia
Walters, John P.
Wyner, Yehudi

FASHION
Lhuillier, Monique

FILM
Bridgewater, Dee Dee
Brolin, Josh
Carlos, Wendy
Clooney, George
Deschanel, Caleb
Downey, James
Flight of the Conchords
Ford, Harrison
Garner, Jennifer
Griffin, Kathy
Hee, Dana
Kaufman, Millard
Kitchen, Michael
LaChapelle, David
Lane, Anthony
Maltin, Leonard
Mitchell, Elvis
O'Hara, Kelli
Ortega, Kenny

Page, Ellen
Peirce, Kimberly
Poehler, Amy
Raven-Symone
Snider, Stacey
Weiner, Jennifer
Wells, Spencer
Yuen Wo Ping

FINANCE
Pandit, Vikram

GASTRONOMY
Flay, Bobby
Oliver, Garrett

GOVERNMENT AND
  POLITICS, FOREIGN
Gilani, Yousaf Raza
Golding, Bruce
Johnson, Boris
Medvedev, Dmitry
Mohammed bin Rashid Al
  Maktoum

GOVERNMENT AND
  POLITICS, U.S.
Blunt, Roy
Brownback, Sam
Capps, Lois
Feith, Douglas J.
Giuliani, Rudolph
Jackson Lee, Sheila
Jindal, Bobby
Kao, John
Kelly, Raymond
Kohl, Herb
Kucinich, Dennis J.
McConnell, Mitch
McFate, Montgomery
Mukasey, Michael B.
Obama, Michelle
Paterson, David
Paul, Ron
Perino, Dana
Ravenstahl, Luke
Walters, John P.
Zoellick, Robert B.

JOURNALISM
Brown, Campbell
Bumiller, Elisabeth
Cafferty, Jack
Carroll, E. Jean
Cohen, Roger

Couric, Katie
Faidley, Warren
Horsey, David
Johnson, Boris
Krauthammer, Charles
Lane, Anthony
Maltin, Leonard
Mayer, Jane
Mitchell, Elvis
Norris, Michele
Pareles, Jon
Power, Samantha
Ramonet, Ignacio
Roberts, Robin
Siegel, Robert
Simon, David
Sittenfeld, Curtis
Stamberg, Susan
Weiner, Jennifer
Williams, Juan
Witcover, Jules

LAW
Bollinger, Lee C.
Brownback, Sam
Feith, Douglas J.
Giuliani, Rudolph
Jackson Lee, Sheila
Jamail, Joe
Kelly, Raymond
McFate, Montgomery
Medvedev, Dmitry
Mukasey, Michael B.
Obama, Michelle
Paterson, David
Power, Samantha
Sunstein, Cass R.
Zagat, Tim and Nina
Zoellick, Robert B.

LAW ENFORCEMENT
Burns, Ed
Gibson, Lois
Kelly, Raymond
Walters, John P.

LITERATURE
Beresford-Kroeger, Diana
Corsi, Jerome R.
Couric, Katie
Gessen, Keith
Hellenga, Robert
Johnson, Boris
Kaufman, Millard

Levin, Janna
Meyer, Stephenie
Rankin, Ian
Rucker, Rudy
Simone, Gail
Sittenfeld, Curtis
Thomas, Michael
von Ziegesar, Cecily
Weiner, Jennifer

MATHEMATICS
Rucker, Rudy

MEDICINE
Capps, Lois
Greider, Carol W.
Paul, Ron
Sinclair, David A.

MILITARY
Dunwoody, Ann E.
Kelly, Raymond
Mullen, Mike

MUSIC
Akon
Bridgewater, Dee Dee
Carlos, Wendy
Feist
Flight of the Conchords
Ghostface Killah
Giordani, Marcello
Harvey, PJ
Kurzweil, Raymond
Lockhart, Keith
Malaby, Tony
May, Brian
Mingus, Sue
Monheit, Jane
My Morning Jacket
O'Hara, Kelli
Omarion
Pareles, Jon
Parker, Tony
Rakim
Raven-Symone
Scott, Christian
Slash
Temple, Johnny
Watts, Jeff "Tain"
Wyner, Yehudi

NONFICTION
  Beresford-Kroeger, Diana
  Bollinger, Lee C.
  Brownback, Sam
  Bumiller, Elisabeth
  Carroll, E. Jean
  Cohen, Roger
  Corsi, Jerome R.
  Feith, Douglas J.
  Flay, Bobby
  Gibson, Lois
  Harvey, David
  Hee, Dana
  Heller, Agnes
  Johnson, Boris
  Kao, John
  Kaufman, Millard
  Krauthammer, Charles
  Kurzweil, Raymond
  Levin, Janna
  Maltin, Leonard
  May, Brian
  Mayer, Jane
  Medvedev, Dmitry
  Mingus, Sue
  Newkirk, Ingrid
  Oliver, Garrett
  Pareles, Jon
  Paul, Ron
  Pepperberg, Irene
  Polgar, Susan
  Power, Samantha
  Ramonet, Ignacio
  Rankin, Ian
  Roberts, Robin
  Schwartz, Pepper
  Simon, David
  Slash
  Stamberg, Susan
  Sunstein, Cass R.
  Turin, Luca
  Wells, Spencer
  Williams, Juan
  Witcover, Jules

ORGANIZATIONS
  Couric, Katie
  Jones, Cullen
  Newkirk, Ingrid
  Paul, Ron
  Ramonet, Ignacio
  Sinclair, Cameron

PHILANTHROPY
  Kaká
  Sinclair, Cameron

PHILOSOPHY
  Heller, Agnes

PHOTOGRAPHY
  DeCarava, Roy
  diCorcia, Philip-Lorca
  Faidley, Warren
  LaChapelle, David

PUBLISHING
  Gessen, Keith
  Temple, Johnny
  Zagat, Tim and Nina

RADIO
  Bridgewater, Dee Dee
  Cafferty, Jack
  Golding, Bruce
  Mitchell, Elvis
  Norris, Michele
  Roberts, Robin
  Siegel, Robert
  Stamberg, Susan
  Williams, Juan

SCIENCE
  Beresford-Kroeger, Diana
  Bigelow, Robert
  Greider, Carol W.
  Hayes, Tyrone B.
  Hockfield, Susan
  Kurzweil, Raymond
  Levin, Janna
  Melton, Douglas A.
  Pepperberg, Irene
  Rucker, Rudy
  Schmidt, Eric
  Sinclair, David A.
  Turin, Luca
  Villa-Komaroff, Lydia
  Wells, Spencer

SOCIAL SCIENCES
  Bollinger, Lee C.
  Harvey, David
  Schwartz, Pepper

SPORTS
  Bavetta, Dick
  Bogut, Andrew

Carson, David
Cotto, Miguel
Coughlin, Tom
Ellis, Monta
Fielder, Prince
Francona, Terry
Gagliardi, John
Girardi, Joe
Hatton, Ricky
Hee, Dana
Immelman, Trevor
Johnson, Zach
Jones, Cullen
Kaká
Kuznetsova, Svetlana
Lagat, Bernard
Manning, Eli
Marta
Ovechkin, Alexander
Parker, Tony
Polgar, Susan
Reyes, José
Rivers, Doc
Sabathia, C. C.
Williams, Lauryn

TECHNOLOGY
  Catz, Safra A.
  Russo, Patricia
  Sandberg, Sheryl
  Zuckerberg, Mark

TELEVISION
  Brolin, Josh
  Brown, Campbell
  Burns, Ed
  Cafferty, Jack
  Carroll, E. Jean
  Clooney, George
  Couric, Katie
  Downey, James
  Flay, Bobby
  Flight of the Conchords
  Garner, Jennifer
  Griffin, Kathy
  Hee, Dana
  Johnson, Boris
  Kitchen, Michael
  Maltin, Leonard
  Mitchell, Elvis
  O'Hara, Kelli
  Ortega, Kenny
  Page, Ellen
  Poehler, Amy

Rankin, Ian
Raven-Symone
Roberts, Robin
Simon, David
Watts, Jeff "Tain"

THEATER
Bridgewater, Dee Dee
Brolin, Josh
Flight of the Conchords
Garner, Jennifer
Kitchen, Michael

Letts, Tracy
O'Hara, Kelli
Ortega, Kenny

CUMULATED INDEX 2001–2008

This is the index to the January 2001–November 2008 issues. It also lists obituaries that appear only in yearbooks for the years 2001 to 2008. For the index to the 1940–2005 biographies, see Current Biography Cumulated Index 1940–2005.

3D *see* Massive Attack

Abakanowicz, Magdalena Jan 2001
Abel, Jessica Aug 2007
Abelson, Philip H. obit Yrbk 2004
Abizaid, John Oct 2003
Abraham, Spencer May 2001
Abrams, Jonathan Apr 2006
AC/DC Mar 2005
Acocella, Joan May 2007
Adams, Brock obit Yrbk 2004
Adams, Douglas obit Sep 2001
Adams, Edith obit Yrbk 2008
Adams, William James Jr. *see* Black Eyed Peas
Adams, Yolanda Mar 2002
Aday, Marvin Lee *see* Meat Loaf
Addington, David S. Jan 2007
Adler, Larry obit Oct 2001
Adler, Mortimer J. obit Sep 2001
Aerosmith Jul 2004
Agatston, Arthur Mar 2007
Agnelli, Giovanni obit Jun 2003
Aigner-Clark, Julie Jan 2002
Ailes, Stephen obit Oct 2001
Aitken, Doug Apr 2007
Ajami, Fouad Feb 2007
Akers, Michelle Nov 2004
Akon Jan 2008
Albarn, Damon *see* Blur
Albert, Eddie obit Yrbk 2005
Alexander, Christopher Oct 2003
Ali, Laylah Jul 2008
Alibek, Ken Jun 2002
Alibekov, Kanatjan *see* Alibek, Ken
Alito, Samuel Apr 2006
Alito, Samuel Jr. *see* Alito, Samuel
Aliyev, Heydar obit Jul 2004
Allen, Betsy *see* Cavanna, Betty
Allen, Rick *see* Def Leppard
Allen, Steve obit Jan 2001
Allyson, June obit Yrbk 2006
Alterman, Eric Feb 2007

Altman, Robert obit Yrbk 2007
Alvarez Bravo, Manuel obit Jan 2003
Amado, Jorge obit Oct 2001
Amend, Bill Apr 2003
Ames, Jonathan Oct 2007
Amichai, Yehuda obit Jan 2001
Amies, Hardy obit Aug 2003
Amin, Idi obit Yrbk 2003
Ammons, A. R. obit Jul 2001
Anastasio, Trey *see* Phish
Anderson, Constance obit Apr 2001
Anderson, Don L. Oct 2002
Anderson, Jack obit Yrbk 2006
Anderson, Ray C. May 2005
Anderson, Robert O. obit Yrbk 2008
Anderson, Roy obit Mar 2004
Anderson, Tom *see* Anderson, Tom and DeWolfe, Christopher
Anderson, Tom and DeWolfe, Christopher Jul 2007
Anderson, Wes May 2002
Anderson, William R. obit Yrbk 2007
Anderson, Winston A. Mar 2007
Andre 3000 *see* OutKast
Angeles, Victoria de los obit Aug 2005
Angell, Marcia Nov 2005
Annenberg, Walter H. obit Jan 2003
Anthony, Carmelo Jun 2005
Antonioni, Michelangelo obit Yrbk 2007
Aoki, Rocky Jun 2005 obit Yrbk 2008
apl.de.ap *see* Black Eyed Peas
Appel, Karel obit Yrbk 2006
Appiah, Kwame Anthony Jun 2002
Apple, Fiona Nov 2006
Apple, R. W. Jr. obit Feb 2007
Applebaum, Anne Aug 2004
Arafat, Yasir obit Feb 2005
Arceneaux, Edgar Aug 2008

Archer, Michael D'Angelo *see* D'Angelo
Arledge, Roone obit Apr 2003
Armitage, Kenneth obit May 2002
Armitage, Richard Oct 2003
Armstrong, Anne obit Yrbk 2008
Armstrong, Billie Joe *see* Green Day
Armstrong, J. Sinclair obit Mar 2001
Armstrong, Vic Aug 2003
Arnesen, Liv Jun 2001
Arnold, Eddy obit Yrbk 2008
Arnold, Eve Oct 2005
Arpino, Gerald obit Yrbk 2008
Arrarás, María Celeste Aug 2002
Ash, Mary Kay obit Feb 2002
Ashanti Jan 2003
Ashwell, Rachel Oct 2004
Astor, Brooke obit Yrbk 2007
Atashin, Faegheh *see* Googoosh
Athey, Susan Sep 2007
Atkins, Chet obit Sep 2001
Atkins, Jeffrey *see* Ja Rule
Atkinson, Kate Feb 2007
Auerbach, Arnold obit Yrbk 2007
Augstein, Rudolf obit Jan 2003
Austin, "Stone Cold" Steve Nov 2001
Auth, Tony Feb 2006
Avedon, Richard obit Mar 2005
Azcona Hoyo, José obit Yrbk 2006

Bacher, Robert F. obit Yrbk 2005
Bahcall, John N. obit Yrbk 2007
Bailey, Glenda Oct 2001
Baitz, Jon Robin Aug 2004
Baker, Dusty Apr 2001
Baker, James A. 3d Mar 2007
Bakula, Scott Feb 2002
Balaguer, Joaquín obit Yrbk 2002

Baldwin, Tammy Jun 2005
Ball, Robert M. obit Yrbk 2008
Balthus obit May 2001
Bampton, Rose obit Yrbk 2007
Bancroft, Anne obit Oct 2005 obit Yrbk 2007
Bandaranaike, Sirimavo obit Jan 2001
Banfield, Ashleigh Jul 2002
Banks, Tyra Apr 2007
Bannister, Constance obit Yrbk 2005
Bánzer Suárez, Hugo obit Yrbk 2002
Barber, Patricia Sep 2007
Barber, Ronde see Barber, Tiki and Barber, Ronde
Barber, Tiki see Barber, Tiki and Barber, Ronde
Barber, Tiki and Barber, Ronde Oct 2003
Barbieri, Fedora obit Aug 2003
Barker, Travis see blink-182
Barnard, Christiaan N. obit Nov 2001
Barnes, Brenda May 2006
Barnett, Etta Moten Feb 2002
Barney, Matthew Aug 2003
Barnouw, Erik obit Oct 2001
Barre, Raymond obit Yrbk 2007
Barris, Chuck Mar 2005
Barsamian, David Mar 2007
Bartiromo, Maria Nov 2003
Bartlett, Bruce Jun 2006
Barton, Jacqueline K. Sep 2006
Barzel, Rainer obit Yrbk 2006
Bassler, Bonnie Apr 2003
Bateman, Jason Oct 2005
Bates, Alan obit Yrbk 2004
Baudrillard, Jean obit Yrbk 2007
Bavetta, Dick Mar 2008
Bawer, Bruce Jul 2007
Beach, Edward obit May 2003
Beame, Abraham D. obit Apr 2001
Beane, Billy Jul 2005
Bebey, Francis obit Sep 2001
Beck, Kent Jan 2007
Beckinsale, Kate Aug 2001
Beckman, Arnold O. Jan 2002 obit Yrbk 2004
Bedford, Sybille obit Yrbk 2006
Beehler, Bruce Aug 2006
Beene, Geoffrey obit Mar 2005
Beers, Rand Oct 2004

Behar, Ruth May 2005
Behe, Michael J. Feb 2006
Béjart, Maurice obit Yrbk 2008
Bel Geddes, Barbara obit Yrbk 2005
Belaúnde Terry, Fernando obit Yrbk 2002
Belcher, Angela Jul 2006
Belichick, Bill Sep 2002
Bell, James A. Jul 2006
Bellow, Saul obit Aug 2005
Benchley, Peter obit Jun 2006
Benedict XVI Sep 2005
Bennett, Lerone Jr. Jan 2001
Bennington, Chester see Linkin Park
Bentsen, Lloyd obit Oct 2006
Benyus, Janine M. Mar 2006
Benzer, Seymour May 2001 obit Yrbk 2008
Beresford-Kroeger, Diana Nov 2008
Berg, Patricia Jane obit Yrbk 2007
Berg, Patty see Berg, Patricia Jane
Bergeron, Tom Oct 2007
Bergman, Ingmar obit Sep 2007
Berio, Luciano obit Yrbk 2003
Berle, Milton obit Yrbk 2002
Berlin, Steve see Los Lobos
Berlitz, Charles obit Yrbk 2004
Berman, Lazar obit Yrbk 2005
Bernanke, Ben S. Mar 2006
Bernhard Leopold, consort of Juliana, Queen of the Netherlands obit Mar 2005
Bernstein, Elmer Jun 2003
Berrigan, Philip obit Mar 2003
Berryman, Guy see Coldplay
Berton, Pierre obit Yrbk 2005
Bertozzi, Carolyn R. Jul 2003
Bessmertnova, Natalia obit Yrbk 2008
Bethe, Hans obit Aug 2005
Bethune, Gordon M. Jun 2001
Bettis, Jerome Aug 2006
Bhutto, Benazir obit Apr 2008
Bible, Geoffrey C. Feb 2002
Big Boi see OutKast
Bigelow, Robert Aug 2008
Bilandic, Michael A. obit Apr 2002
Biller, Moe obit Yrbk 2004
Bing, Stanley see Schwartz, Gil
Birendra Bir Bikram Shah Dev, King of Nepal obit Sep 2001

Bishop, Eric see Foxx, Jamie
Bishop, Joey obit Yrbk 2008
Bittman, Mark Feb 2005
Björk Jul 2001
Black Eyed Peas Oct 2006
Black, Jack Feb 2002
Blackburn, Elizabeth H. Jul 2001
Blades, Joan see Blades, Joan and Boyd, Wes
Blades, Joan and Boyd, Wes Aug 2004
Blaine, David Apr 2001
Blake, James Mar 2006
Blakemore, Michael May 2001
Blanco, Kathleen Jun 2004
Blankenship, "Two-Tone" Tommy see My Morning Jacket
Blass, Bill obit Nov 2002
Blind Boys of Alabama Oct 2001
blink-182 Aug 2002
Blitzer, Wolf Feb 2007
Block, Herbert L. obit Jan 2002
Bloomberg, Michael R. Mar 2002
Blount, Winton Malcolm obit Jan 2003
Blum, William May 2007
Blunt, Roy Mar 2008
Blur Nov 2003
Blythe, Stephanie Aug 2004
Bocelli, Andrea Jan 2002
Boehner, John Apr 2006
Bogut, Andrew Jan 2008
Boland, Edward P. obit Feb 2002
Bollinger, Lee C. Feb 2008
Bolten, Joshua Jul 2006
Bolton, John R. Feb 2006
Bond, Julian Jul 2001
Bontecou, Lee Mar 2004
Booker, Cory Feb 2007
Boorstin, Daniel J. obit Yrbk 2004
Borge, Victor obit Mar 2001
Borodina, Olga Feb 2002
Borowitz, Andy Jul 2007
Borst, Lyle B. obit Yrbk 2002
Bosch, Juan obit Feb 2002
Bosselaar, Laure-Anne Sep 2006
Botha, P. W. obit Yrbk 2007
Boudreau, Lou obit Oct 2001
Boulud, Daniel Jan 2005
Bourdain, Anthony Jan 2006
Bourdon, Rob see Linkin Park
Bourne, St. Clair obit Mar 2008
Bowden, Mark Jan 2002

Bowker, Albert obit Yrbk 2008
Boyd, John W. Feb 2001
Boyd, Wes *see* Blades, Joan and Boyd, Wes
Bracken, Eddie obit Feb 2003
Bradley, Ed obit Yrbk 2007
Brady, Tom Aug 2004
Bragg, Rick Apr 2002
Branch, Michelle May 2005
Brando, Marlon obit Yrbk 2004
Bravo, Rose Marie Jun 2004
Brazile, Donna Mar 2006
Breathitt, Edward T. obit Sep 2004
Breen, Edward D. Jul 2004
Brenly, Bob Apr 2002
Brennan, Edward A. obit Yrbk 2008
Brewer, Roy M. obit Yrbk 2006
Bridgewater, Dee Dee Oct 2008
Brier, Bob Sep 2002
Brier, Robert *see* Brier, Bob
Brin, Sergey and Page, Larry Oct 2001
Brinkley, David obit Sep 2003
Brodeur, Martin Nov 2002
Brody, Adrien Jul 2003
Broeg, Bob May 2002
Broemel, Carl *see* My Morning Jacket
Brokaw, Tom Nov 2002
Brolin, Josh Feb 2008
Bronson, Charles obit Mar 2004
Brooks & Dunn Sep 2004
Brooks, David Apr 2004
Brooks, Donald obit Yrbk 2005
Brooks, Geraldine Aug 2006
Brooks, Gwendolyn obit Feb 2001
Brooks, Kix *see* Brooks & Dunn
Brooks, Vincent Jun 2003
Brower, David obit Feb 2001
Brown, Aaron Mar 2003
Brown, Campbell Nov 2008
Brown, Charles L. obit Sep 2004
Brown, Claude obit Apr 2002
Brown, Dan May 2004
Brown, Dee obit Mar 2003
Brown, J. Carter obit Yrbk 2002
Brown, James obit Mar 2007
Brown, Jesse obit Yrbk 2002
Brown, Junior Nov 2004
Brown, Kwame Feb 2002
Brown, Lee P. Sep 2002

Brown, Robert McAfee obit Nov 2001
Brown, Ronald K. May 2002
Brown, Troy Oct 2007
Brownback, Sam Apr 2008
Browning, John obit Jun 2003
Broyhill, Joel T. obit Feb 2007
Brueggemann, Ingar Nov 2001
Brumel, Valery obit Jun 2003
Brunson, Doyle Sep 2007
Bryant, C. Farris obit Yrbk 2002
Brynner, Rock Mar 2005
Bryson, David *see* Counting Crows
Buchanan, Laura *see* King, Florence
Buchholz, Horst obit Aug 2003
Buchwald, Art obit May 2007
Buckingham, Marcus Aug 2006
Buckland, Jon *see* Coldplay
Buckley, Priscilla L. Apr 2002
Buckley, William F. Jr. obit Jun 2008
Budge, Hamer H. obit Yrbk 2003
Bujones, Fernando obit Yrbk 2006
Bumiller, Elisabeth Sep 2008
Bundy, William P. obit Feb 2001
Bunim, Mary-Ellis obit Yrbk 2004 *see* Bunim, Mary-Ellis, and Murray, Jonathan
Bunim, Mary-Ellis, and Murray, Jonathan May 2002
Burford, Anne Gorsuch *see* Gorsuch, Anne
Burgess, Carter L. obit Yrbk 2002
Burnett, Mark May 2001
Burns, Ed May 2008
Burns, Ursula M. Oct 2007
Burroughs, Augusten Apr 2004
Burrows, James Oct 2006
Burrows, Stephen Nov 2003
Burstyn, Mike May 2005
Burtt, Ben May 2003
Bush, George W. Aug 2001
Bush, Laura Jun 2001
Bushnell, Candace Nov 2003
Busiek, Kurt Sep 2005
Butcher, Susan obit Yrbk 2006
Butler, R. Paul *see* Marcy, Geoffrey W., and Butler, R. Paul
Buttons, Red obit Yrbk 2006
Butz, Earl L. obit Yrbk 2008

Caballero, Linda *see* La India
Cactus Jack *see* Foley, Mick
Cafferty, Jack Oct 2008
Calderón, Sila M. Nov 2001
Caldwell, Sarah obit Yrbk 2006
Callaghan, James obit Yrbk 2005
Calle, Sophie May 2001
Camp, John *see* Sandford, John
Campbell, Bebe Moore obit Yrbk 2007
Campbell, Viv *see* Def Leppard
Canada, Geoffrey Feb 2005
Canin, Ethan Aug 2001
Cannon, Howard W. obit Yrbk 2006
Cantwell, Maria Feb 2005
Canty, Brendan *see* Fugazi
Capa, Cornell Jul 2005 obit Yrbk 2008
Capps, Lois Mar 2008
Capriati, Jennifer Nov 2001
Caras, Roger A. obit Jul 2001
Card, Andrew H. Jr. Nov 2003
Carell, Steve Feb 2007
Carell, Steven *see* Carell, Steve
Carey, Ernestine Gilbreth obit Yrbk 2007
Carlin, George obit Oct 2008
Carlos, Walter *see* Carlos, Wendy
Carlos, Wendy Sep 2008
Carlson, Margaret Nov 2003
Carmines, Al obit Yrbk 2005
Carmona, Richard Jan 2003
Carney, Art obit Yrbk 2004
Carone, Nicholas *see* Carone, Nicolas
Carone, Nicolas Jul 2006
Carroll-Abbing, J. Patrick obit Nov 2001
Carroll, Betty Jean *see* Carroll, E. Jean
Carroll, E. Jean Jul 2008
Carroll, Vinnette obit Feb 2003
Carruth, Hayden obit Yrbk 2008
Carson, Anne May 2006
Carson, David Jul 2008
Carson, Johnny obit Jul 2005
Carter, Benny obit Oct 2003
Carter, Jimmy *see* Blind Boys of Alabama
Carter, Majora Oct 2007
Carter, Matthew Oct 2007
Carter, Regina Oct 2003
Carter, Shawn *see* Jay-Z
Carter, Vince Apr 2002

Cartier-Bresson, Henri obit Yrbk 2004
Cary, Frank T. obit May 2006
Casablancas, Julian *see* Strokes
Casey, George W. Jr. Mar 2006
Cash, Johnny obit Jan 2004
Cassini, Oleg obit Yrbk 2006
Castle, Barbara obit Yrbk 2002
Castro, Fidel Jun 2001
Cat Power Oct 2007
Cattrall, Kim Jan 2003
Catz, Safra A. Jan 2008
Cavanagh, Tom Jun 2003
Cavanna, Betty obit Oct 2001
Cave, Nick Jun 2005
Cedric the Entertainer Feb 2004
Cela, Camilo José obit Apr 2002
Celmins, Vija Jan 2005
Chaban-Delmas, Jacques obit Feb 2001
Chafee, Lincoln Jan 2004
Chaikin, Joseph obit Yrbk 2003
Chamberlain, Owen obit Jul 2006
Champion, Will *see* Coldplay
Chandler, Otis obit Yrbk 2006
Chandrasekhar, Sripati obit Sep 2001
Chao, Elaine L. May 2001
Chapman, Duane Mar 2005
Chapman, Steven Curtis Oct 2004
Chappelle, Dave Jun 2004
Charisse, Cyd obit Yrbk 2008
Charles, Eugenia obit Yrbk 2006
Charles, Michael Ray Oct 2005
Charles, Ray obit Yrbk 2004
Chase, Alison Becker Nov 2006
Chase, David Mar 2001
Chauncey, Henry obit Mar 2003
Cheeks, Maurice Feb 2004
Chen, Steve *see* Chen, Steve; Hurley, Chad; and Karim, Jawed
Chen, Steve; Hurley, Chad; and Karim, Jawed Jan 2007
Cheney, Richard B. Jan 2002
Chertoff, Michael Oct 2005
Chesney, Kenny May 2004
Chiang Kai-shek, Mme. *see* Chiang Mei-Ling
Chiang Mei-Ling obit Mar 2004

Chieftains Mar 2004
Child, Julia obit Nov 2004
Chillida, Eduardo obit Yrbk 2002
Chinmoy, Sri obit Yrbk 2008
Chisholm, Shirley obit Apr 2005
Chung, Kyung-Wha Feb 2007
Churchland, Patricia S. May 2003
Claiborne, Liz obit Yrbk 2007
Claremont, Chris Sep 2003
Clark, Kenneth B. obit Sep 2005
Clarke, Arthur C. obit Yrbk 2008
Clarke, Richard May 2006
Clarkson, Kelly Sep 2006
Clarkson, Patricia Aug 2005
Clemens, Roger Aug 2003
Clement, Jemaine *see* Flight of the Conchords
Cleveland, Harlan obit Yrbk 2008
Click and Clack, the Tappet Brothers *see* Magliozzi, Tom and Ray
Clinton, Hillary Rodham Jan 2002
Clooney, George Jul 2008
Clooney, Rosemary obit Nov 2002
Clowes, Daniel Jan 2002
Clyburn, James E. Oct 2001
Coburn, James obit Feb 2003
Coca, Imogene obit Sep 2001
Cochran, Johnnie L. Jr. obit Oct 2005
Cochran, Thad Apr 2002
Coddington, Grace Apr 2005
Coffin, William Sloane obit Yrbk 2006
Cohen, Richard Nov 2007
Cohen, Rob Nov 2002
Cohen, Roger May 2008
Cohen, Sasha Feb 2006
Cohn, Linda Aug 2002
Colbert, Edwin H. obit Feb 2002
Colbert, Gregory Sep 2005
Colbert, Stephen Nov 2006
Coldplay May 2004
Coleman, Cy obit Feb 2005
Coleman, Mary Sue Feb 2007
Coleman, Norman Sep 2004
Coleman, Ronnie Feb 2007
Coleman, Steve Jul 2004
Coles, Dennis *see* Ghostface Killah
Collen, Phil *see* Def Leppard
Collier, Sophia Jul 2002
Collins, Jim Aug 2003

Collins, Patricia Hill Mar 2003
Columbus, Chris Nov 2001
Comden, Betty obit Yrbk 2007
Cometbus, Aaron Mar 2005
Como, Perry obit Jul 2001
Conable, Barber B. obit Sep 2004
Conlee, Jenny *see* Decemberists
Conneff, Kevin *see* Chieftains
Connelly, Jennifer Jun 2002
Conner, Nadine obit Aug 2003
Connor, John T. obit Feb 2001
Conway, Gerry *see* Fairport Convention
Conway, John Horton Sep 2003
Cook, Richard W. Jul 2003
Cooke, Alistair obit Oct 2004
Coontz, Stephanie Jul 2003
Cooper, Anderson Jun 2006
Cooper, Chris Jul 2004
Coppola, Sofia Nov 2003
Corbijn, Anton Jun 2006
Corelli, Franco obit Mar 2004
Corsi, Jerome R. Nov 2008
Corzine, Jon Aug 2006
Cotto, Miguel Feb 2008
Coughlin, Tom Aug 2008
Coulter, Ann Sep 2003
Counsell, Craig Sep 2002
Counting Crows Mar 2003
Couric, Katie Apr 2008
Cowher, Bill Nov 2006
Cox, Archibald obit Yrbk 2004
Cox, Lynne Sep 2004
Coyne, Wayne *see* Flaming Lips
Craig, Daniel Apr 2007
Crain, Jeanne obit Sep 2004
Crandall, Martin *see* Shins
Crane, Eva obit Yrbk 2007
Cranston, Alan obit Mar 2001
Creed May 2002
Creeley, Robert obit Yrbk 2005
Crespin, Regine obit Yrbk 2007
Crick, Francis obit Yrbk 2004
Crittenden, Danielle Jul 2003
Crocker, Ryan Oct 2007
Cromwell, James Aug 2005
Cronyn, Hume obit Yrbk 2003
Croom, Sylvester Jr. Aug 2004
Crosby, John obit Yrbk 2003
Crossfield, A. Scott obit Yrbk 2006
Crowe, William J. obit Yrbk 2008
Cruz, Celia obit Nov 2003

Cruz, Penelope Jul 2001
Cuban, Mark Mar 2001
Culpepper, Daunte Sep 2007
Cummings, Elijah E. Feb 2004
Cunhal, Álvaro obit Yrbk 2005
Currie, Nancy June 2002
Curry, Ann Jun 2004

da Silva, Marta Vieira *see* Marta
Dacre of Glanton, Baron *see* Trevor-Roper, H. R.
Daddy G *see* Massive Attack
Daft, Douglas N. May 2001
Dallek, Robert Sep 2007
Daly, Maureen obit Yrbk 2006
Damasio, Antonio R. Oct 2007
Dan the Automator *see* Nakamura, Dan
Dancer, Stanley obit Yrbk 2005
D'Angelo May 2001
Dangerfield, Rodney obit Feb 2005
Darling, Sharon May 2003
Darman, Richard G. obit Yrbk 2008
Dassin, Jules obit Yrbk 2008
Davidson, Gordon Apr 2005
Davidson, Richard J. Aug 2004
Davis, Benjamin O. Jr. obit Yrbk 2002
Davis, Evelyn Y. Oct 2007
Davis, Glenn obit Yrbk 2005
Davis-Kimball, Jeannine Feb 2006
Davis, Nathanael V. obit Yrbk 2005
Davis, Ossie obit Yrbk 2005
Davis, Shani May 2006
Davis, Wade Jan 2003
Dawdy, Shannon Lee Apr 2006
Day, Laraine obit Yrbk 2008
De Bakey, Michael obit Yrbk 2008
de Branges, Louis Nov 2005
de Hartog, Jan obit Jan 2003
De Jong, Dola obit Sep 2004
de la Rúa, Fernando Apr 2001
de Meuron, Pierre *see* Herzog, Jacques, and de Meuron, Pierre
De Sapio, Carmine obit Yrbk 2004
De Valois, Ninette obit Aug 2001
de Varona, Donna Aug 2003
de Waal, Frans Mar 2006
Deakins, Roger May 2001

Dean, Howard Oct 2002
DeBusschere, Dave obit Yrbk 2003
DeCarava, Roy Aug 2008
DeCarlo, Dan Aug 2001 obit Mar 2002
Decemberists Aug 2007
Deep Throat *see* Felt, W. Mark
Def Leppard Jan 2003
Del Toro, Benicio Sep 2001
Delilah Apr 2005
Dellinger, David obit Yrbk 2004
Dello Joio, Norman obit Yrbk 2008
DeLonge, Tom *see* blink-182
DeLorean, John Z. obit Yrbk 2005
Deloria, Vine Jr. obit Yrbk 2006
Delson, Brad *see* Linkin Park
DeMarcus, Jay *see* Rascal Flatts
DeMille, Nelson Oct 2002
Densen-Gerber, Judianne obit Jul 2003
Derrida, Jacques obit Mar 2005
Desai, Kiran Jan 2007
Deschanel, Caleb Feb 2008
Destiny's Child Aug 2001
Deutsch, Linda Apr 2007
DeWolfe, Christopher *see* Anderson, Tom and DeWolfe, Christopher
Diamond, David obit Yrbk 2005
Diaz, Cameron Apr 2005
Dickerson, Debra Apr 2004
Dickinson, Amy Apr 2004
diCorcia, Philip-Lorca Apr 2008
Diddley, Bo obit Sep 2008
Diebold, John obit Yrbk 2006
Dillon, C. Douglas obit May 2003
Dimon, James Jun 2004
Dionne, E. J. Jr. May 2006
Dirnt, Mike *see* Green Day
Dith Pran obit Yrbk 2008
Djerassi, Carl Oct 2001
Djukanovic, Milo Aug 2001
DMX Aug 2003
Dobbs, Lou Nov 2006
Dodge, Charles Aug 2007
Domini, Amy Nov 2005
Donald, Arnold W. Nov 2005
Donaldson, William Jun 2003
D'Onofrio, Vincent May 2004
Donovan, Billy Feb 2007
Donovan, Carrie obit Feb 2002

Donovan, Landon Jun 2006
Doubilet, David Mar 2003
Doudna, Jennifer Feb 2005
Douglas, Ashanti *see* Ashanti
Douglas, Dave Mar 2006
Douglas, Jerry Aug 2004
Douglas, John E. Jul 2001
Douglas, Mike obit Yrbk 2007
Downey, James Jun 2008
Downey, Jim *see* Downey, James
Drake, James Jul 2005
Drinan, Robert F. obit Yrbk 2007
Drozd, Steven *see* Flaming Lips
Drucker, Eugene *see* Emerson String Quartet
Drucker, Peter F. obit Apr 2006
Duany, Andrés *see* Duany, Andrés and Plater-Zyberk, Elizabeth
Duany, Andrés and Plater-Zyberk, Elizabeth Jan 2006
Dude Love *see* Foley, Mick
Duesberg, Peter H. Jun 2004
Duff, Hilary Feb 2006
Dugan, Alan obit Oct 2004
Duke, Annie Aug 2006
Dungy, Tony Aug 2007
Dunham, Katherine obit Yrbk 2006
Dunlop, John T. obit Sep 2004
Dunn, Jennifer obit Nov 2007
Dunn, Ronnie *see* Brooks & Dunn
Dunne, John Gregory obit Yrbk 2004
Dunst, Kirsten Oct 2001
Dunwoody, Ann E. Nov 2008
Durbin, Richard J. Aug 2006
Duritz, Adam *see* Counting Crows
Dutton, Lawrence *see* Emerson String Quartet
Dwight, Ed Jul 2007
Dworkin, Andrea obit Yrbk 2005

Eagleton, Thomas F. obit Yrbk 2007
Earnhardt, Dale Jr. Jan 2007
Eban, Abba obit Mar 2003
Eberhart, Richard obit Yrbk 2005
Ebsen, Buddy obit Yrbk 2003
Ecevit, Bülent obit Yrbk 2007
Eckert, Robert A. Mar 2003
Eddins, William Feb 2002
Edwards, Bob Sep 2001
Edwards, John R. Oct 2004

Edwards, Ralph obit Yrbk 2006
Egan, Edward M. Jul 2001
Egan, Jennifer Mar 2002
Eggleston, William Feb 2002
Ehlers, Vernon J. Jan 2005
Eiko *see* Eiko and Koma
Eiko and Koma May 2003
Eisner, Will obit May 2005
Elfman, Danny Jan 2007
Elgin, Suzette Haden Aug 2006
Elizabeth, Queen Mother of Great Britain obit Jun 2002
Elling, Kurt Jan 2005
Elliott, Joe *see* Def Leppard
Elliott, Osborn obit Yrbk 2008
Elliott, Sean Apr 2001
Ellis, Albert obit Yrbk 2007
Ellis, Monta Feb 2008
Ellison, Keith Apr 2007
Emanuel, Kerry A. Jan 2007
Emerson String Quartet Jul 2002
Eminem Jan 2001
Engibous, Thomas J. Oct 2003
Ensler, Eve Aug 2002
Epstein, Samuel S. Aug 2001
Epstein, Theo May 2004
Ericsson-Jackson, Aprille J. Mar 2001
Estenssoro, Victor Paz *see* Paz Estenssoro, Victor
Estern, Neil Nov 2008
Etherington, Edwin D. obit Apr 2001
Eugenides, Jeffrey Oct 2003
Eustis, Oskar Oct 2002
Eustis, Paul Jefferson *see* Eustis, Oskar
Evanovich, Janet Apr 2001
Evans, Dale obit Apr 2001
Evans, Donald L. Nov 2001
Eve Jul 2003
Everett, Percival L. Sep 2004
Everett, Rupert Jan 2005
Exon, J. James obit Yrbk 2005
Eyadéma, Etienne Gnassingbé Apr 2002 obit Yrbk 2005
Eyre, Chris May 2003
Eytan, Walter obit Oct 2001

Faber, Sandra Apr 2002
Fadiman, Anne Aug 2005
Fagles, Robert Apr 2006 obit Yrbk 2008
Fahd, King of Saudi Arabia obit Yrbk 2005
Fahd, Prince of Saudi Arabia *see* Fahd, King of Saudi Arabia
Faidley, Warren Feb 2008

Fairclough, Ellen obit Yrbk 2005
Fairport Convention Sep 2005
Falco, Edie Mar 2006
Fallaci, Oriana obit Yrbk 2007
Fallon, Jimmy Jul 2002
Fallon, William J. Jul 2007
Falls, Robert Jan 2004
Falwell, Jerry obit Aug 2007
Fangmeier, Stefen Aug 2004
Farhi, Nicole Nov 2001
Farmer, Paul Feb 2004
Farmer-Paellmann, Deadria Mar 2004
Farrell, Dave *see* Linkin Park
Farrell, Eileen obit Jun 2002
Farrelly, Bobby *see* Farrelly, Peter and Bobby
Farrelly, Peter and Bobby Sep 2001
Fast, Howard obit Jul 2003
Fatal1ty *see* Wendel, Johnathan
Fattah, Chaka Sep 2003
Faulk, Marshall Jan 2003
Faust, Drew Gilpin Jul 2007
Fausto-Sterling, Anne Sep 2005
Fawcett, Joy May 2004
Fay, J. Michael Sep 2001
Fay, Martin *see* Chieftains
Feifel, Herman obit Yrbk 2005
Feist Jun 2008
Feist, Leslie *see* Feist
Feith, Douglas J. Jul 2008
Felker, Clay S. obit Yrbk 2008
Felt, W. Mark Sep 2005
Fenty, Adrian M. Mar 2007
Fenty, Robyn Rihanna *see* Rihanna
Fergie *see* Black Eyed Peas
Ferguson, Maynard obit Yrbk 2006
Ferguson, Stacy *see* Black Eyed Peas
Ferré, Gianfranco obit Yrbk 2007
Ferré, Luis A. obit Mar 2004
Ferrell, Will Feb 2003
Ferrer, Rafael Jul 2001
Ferrera, America Sep 2007
Ferris, Timothy Jan 2001
Fey, Tina Apr 2002
Fiedler, Leslie A. obit Yrbk 2003
Fielder, Prince Jun 2008
Fields, Mark Apr 2005
Finch, Caleb E. Sep 2004
Finch, Jennie Oct 2004
Finckel, David *see* Emerson String Quartet
Firth, Colin Mar 2004

Fischer, Bobby obit Yrbk 2008
Fishman, Jon *see* Phish
Fitzgerald, Geraldine obit Yrbk 2005
Fitzgerald, Patrick J. Jan 2006
Flagg, Fannie Nov 2006
Flaming Lips Oct 2002
Flanagan, Tommy obit Mar 2002
Flay, Bobby May 2008
Fletcher, Arthur obit Yrbk 2005
Flight of the Conchords Mar 2008
Flowers, Vonetta May 2006
Foer, Jonathan Safran Sep 2002
Foley, Mick Sep 2001
Folkman, Judah obit Yrbk 2008
Folon, Jean-Michel obit Yrbk 2006
Foner, Eric Aug 2004
Fong, Hiram L. obit Yrbk 2004
Fong-Torres, Ben Aug 2001
Foote, Shelby obit Yrbk 2005
Ford, Gerald R. obit Feb 2007
Ford, Glenn obit Yrbk 2007
Ford, Harrison Jun 2008
Forrest, Vernon Jul 2002
Forsberg, Peter Nov 2005
Forsee, Gary D. Oct 2005
Forsythe, William Feb 2003
Fortey, Richard Sep 2005
Foss, Joseph Jacob obit Yrbk 2003
Fossett, J. Stephen *see* Fossett, Steve
Fossett, Steve Apr 2005 obit Yrbk 2008
Fountain, Clarence *see* Blind Boys of Alabama
Fowles, John obit Apr 2006
Fox Quesada, Vicente May 2001
Foxx, Jamie May 2005
Fraiture, Nikolai *see* Strokes
Franca, Celia obit Yrbk 2007
Franciosa, Anthony obit Yrbk 2006
Franciosa, Tony *see* Franciosa, Anthony
Francis, Arlene obit Sep 2001
Francisco, Don Feb 2001
Franco, Julio Sep 2006
Francona, Terry Jul 2008
Frank, Reuven obit Yrbk 2006
Frankenheimer, John obit Oct 2002
Franklin, Shirley C. Aug 2002
Franks, Tommy R. Jan 2002

Franzen, Jonathan Sep 2003
Fraser, Brendan Feb 2001
Fraser, Douglas A. obit Yrbk
2008
Fredericks, Henry St. Clair
see Mahal, Taj
Freed, James Ingo obit Yrbk
2006
Freeman, Lucy obit Yrbk
2005
Freeman, Orville L. obit Yrbk
2003
Freston, Tom Aug 2003
Friedan, Betty obit May 2006
Friedlander, Lee May 2006
Friedman, Jane Mar 2001
Friedman, Milton obit Yrbk
2007
Friedman, Tom Oct 2008
Frist, Bill Nov 2002
Froese, Edgar *see* Tangerine
Dream
Froese, Jerome *see* Tangerine
Dream
Frum, David Jun 2004
Fry, Christopher obit Yrbk
2005
Fu, Ping Oct 2006
Fugazi Mar 2002
Fukuyama, Francis Jun 2001
Funk, Chris *see* Decemberists

Gades, Antonio obit Yrbk
2004
Gagliardi, John Jan 2008
Gagne, Eric Jun 2004
Gaines, Donna Jun 2006
Galbraith, James K. Feb 2006
Galbraith, John Kenneth obit
Yrbk 2007
Galinsky, Ellen Oct 2003
Galloway, Joseph L. Sep 2003
Galtieri, Leopoldo obit Yrbk
2003
Gandy, Kim Oct 2001
Garcia, Sergio Mar 2001
Gardner, John W. obit May
2002
Gardner, Rulon Nov 2004
Garfield, Henry *see* Rollins,
Henry
Garner, Jennifer Apr 2008
Garofalo, Janeane Mar 2005
Garrels, Anne Mar 2004
Garrison, Deborah Jan 2001
Gary, Willie E. Apr 2001
Garza, Ed Jun 2002
Garzón, Baltasar Mar 2001
Gaskin, Ina May May 2001
Gates, Melinda Feb 2004
Gates, Robert M. May 2007
Gaubatz, Lynn Feb 2001
Gawande, Atul Mar 2005

Gayle, Helene Jan 2002
Gebel-Williams, Gunther obit
Oct 2001
Geis, Bernard obit Mar 2001
Gelb, Leslie H. Jan 2003
Gennaro, Peter obit Feb 2001
George, Susan Jul 2007
Gerberding, Julie Louise Sep
2004
Gerbner, George obit Yrbk
2006
Germond, Jack W. Jul 2005
Gerson, Michael Feb 2002
Gessen, Keith Sep 2008
Getty, Estelle obit Yrbk 2008
Ghostface Killah Jun 2008
Giamatti, Paul Sep 2005
Giannulli, Mossimo Feb 2003
Gibson, Althea obit Feb 2004
Gibson, Charles Sep 2002
Gibson, Lois Mar 2008
Gibson, Mel Aug 2003
Gierek, Edward obit Oct 2001
Gilani, Yousaf Raza Nov 2008
Gilbreth, Frank B. Jr. obit Jul
2001
Gillingham, Charles *see*
Counting Crows
Gillis, John *see* White Stripes
Gilmore, James S. III Jun 2001
Ginzberg, Eli obit Yrbk 2003
Giordani, Marcello May 2008
Girardi, Joe May 2008
Giroud, Françoise obit Jul
2003
Giroux, Robert obit Yrbk 2008
Giuliani, Rudolph Jan 2008
Giulini, Carlo Maria obit Yrbk
2005
Gladwell, Malcolm Jun 2005
Glass, H. Bentley obit Yrbk
2005
Glavine, Tom Oct 2006
Goff, M. Lee Jun 2001
Goheen, Robert F. obit Yrbk
2008
Gold, Thomas obit Yrbk 2004
Goldberg, Bill Apr 2001
Golden, Thelma Sep 2001
Golding, Bruce Mar 2008
Golding, Orette Bruce *see*
Golding, Bruce
Goldman-Rakic, Patricia Feb
2003
Goldovsky, Boris obit Aug
2001
Goldsman, Akiva Sep 2004
Goldsmith, Jerry May 2001
obit Nov 2004
Goldstine, Herman Heine obit
Yrbk 2004
Golub, Leon obit Yrbk 2004
Gomes, Marcelo May 2007

Gomez, Jaime *see* Black Eyed
Peas
Gondry, Michel May 2007
Gonzales, Alberto R. Apr
2002
Gonzalez, Henry obit Feb
2001
Good, Mary L. Sep 2001
Good, Robert A. obit Yrbk
2003
Goodpaster, Andrew J. obit
Yrbk 2005
Googoosh May 2001
Gopinath, Suhas Jul 2008
Gopnik, Adam Apr 2005
Gopnik, Alison Jan 2007
Gordon, Bruce S. Oct 2005
Gordon, Cyrus H. obit Aug
2001
Gordon, Ed Jul 2005
Gordon, Edmund W. Jun 2003
Gordon, Mike *see* Phish
Gorman, R. C. Jan 2001
Gorsuch, Anne obit Yrbk
2004
Gorton, John Grey obit Yrbk
2002
Gottlieb, Melvin B. obit Mar
2001
Gould, Stephen Jay obit Aug
2002
Goulet, Robert obit Yrbk 2008
Gourdji, Françoise *see*
Giroud, Françoise
Gowdy, Curt obit Yrbk 2006
Gowers, Timothy Jan 2001
Gowers, William Timothy *see*
Gowers, Timothy
Graham, Franklin May 2002
Graham, Katharine obit Oct
2001
Graham, Susan Oct 2005
Graham, Winston obit Yrbk
2003
Grandberry, Omari *see*
Omarion
Granholm, Jennifer M. Oct
2003
Grasso, Richard Oct 2002
Graves, Florence George May
2005
Graves, Morris obit Sep 2001
Gray, L. Patrick obit Yrbk
2005
Gray, Simon obit Yrbk 2008
Gray, Spalding obit Yrbk
2004
Greco, José obit Mar 2001
Green, Adolph obit Mar 2003
Green, Darrell Jan 2001
Green Day Aug 2005
Green, Tom Oct 2003
Greenberg, Jack M. Nov 2001

Greene, Wallace M. obit Aug
2003
Greenstein, Jesse L. obit Yrbk
2003
Greenwood, Colin see
Radiohead
Greenwood, Jonny see
Radiohead
Gregory, Frederick D. Oct
2005
Gregory, Wilton D. Mar 2002
Greider, Carol W. Feb 2008
Griffin Jr., William Michael
see Rakim
Griffin, Kathy Sep 2008
Griffin, Merv obit Yrbk 2007
Griffin, Michael Aug 2005
Griffiths, Martha W. obit Yrbk
2003
Grigg, John obit Apr 2002
Grizzard, George obit Yrbk
2008
Grohl, Dave May 2002
Groopman, Jerome E. Oct
2004
Grossman, Edith Mar 2006
Gruber, Ruth Jun 2001
Gruber, Samuel H. Aug 2004
Grubin, David Aug 2002
Guarente, Leonard P. May
2007
Gudmundsdottir, Björk see
Björk
Guerard, Albert J. obit Mar
2001
Guerrero, Vladimir Jun 2006
Guillen, Ozzie May 2006
Guillermoprieto, Alma Sep
2004
Guinier, Lani Jan 2004
Gunn, Thom obit Yrbk 2004
Gupta, Sanjay Aug 2006
Gursky, Andreas Jul 2001
Guthman, Edwin O. obit Yrbk
2008
Gygax, Gary Mar 2007 obit
Yrbk 2008

Haas, Jonathan Jun 2003
Habash, George obit Yrbk
2008
Hacker see Hackett, Buddy
Hackett, Buddy obit Oct 2003
Hadley, Jerry obit Yrbk 2007
Hadley, Stephen Nov 2006
Hagel, Chuck Aug 2004
Hagen, Uta obit Yrbk 2004
Haggis, Paul Aug 2006
Hahn, Hilary Sep 2002
Hahn, Joseph see Linkin Park
Hailey, Arthur obit Yrbk 2005
Hailsham of St. Marylebone,
Quintin Hogg obit Feb 2002

Hair, Jay D. obit Jan 2003
Halaby, Najeeb E. obit Yrbk
2003
Halasz, Laszlo obit Feb 2002
Halberstam, David obit Jul
2007
Hall, Conrad L. obit May
2003
Hall, Deidre Nov 2002
Hall, Gus obit Jan 2001
Hall, Richard Melville see
Moby
Hall, Steffie see Evanovich,
Janet
Hall, Tex G. May 2005
Hallahan, Patrick see My
Morning Jacket
Hallaren, Mary A. obit Yrbk
2005
Hallström, Lasse Feb 2005
Hamilton, Laird Aug 2005
Hamilton, Tom see
Aerosmith
Hamm, Morgan see Hamm,
Paul and Morgan
Hamm, Paul see Hamm, Paul
and Morgan
Hamm, Paul and Morgan Nov
2004
Hammer, Bonnie Apr 2006
Hammon, Becky Jan 2003
Hammond, Albert Jr. see
Strokes
Hammond, Caleb D. Jr. obit
Yrbk 2006
Hammons, David May 2006
Hampton, Lionel obit Yrbk
2002
Hancock, Graham Feb 2005
Hancock, Trenton Doyle Apr
2006
Hanna, William obit Sep 2001
Hannity, Sean Apr 2005
Hansen, Liane May 2003
Hanson, Mark see Yusuf,
Hamza
Harcourt, Nic Oct 2005
Harden, Marcia Gay Sep 2001
Hardin, Garrett obit Apr 2004
Hardwick, Elizabeth obit Yrbk
2008
Hargis, Billy James obit Yrbk
2005
Hargrove, Marion obit Yrbk
2004
Harjo, Joy Aug 2001
Harper, Ben Jan 2004
Harrer, Heinrich obit Yrbk
2006
Harris, Eva Mar 2004
Harris, Mark obit Yrbk 2007
Harris, Richard obit Yrbk
2003

Harrison, George obit Mar
2002
Harrison, Gilbert A. obit Yrbk
2008
Harrison, Marvin Aug 2001
Harrison, William B. Jr. Mar
2002
Hart, Kitty Carlisle obit Yrbk
2007
Hartford, Huntington obit
Yrbk 2008
Hartke, Vance obit Yrbk 2003
Hartmann, Heidi I. Apr 2003
Hartzog, George obit Yrbk
2008
Harvey, David Aug 2008
Harvey, PJ May 2008
Harvey, Polly Jean see
Harvey, PJ
Hashimoto, Ryutaro obit Yrbk
2006
Haskins, Caryl P. obit Feb
2002
Hass, Robert Feb 2001
Hassenfeld, Alan G. Jul 2003
Hastings, Reed Mar 2006
Hatton, Richard see Hatton,
Ricky
Hatton, Ricky Oct 2008
Hauerwas, Stanley Jun 2003
Haughey, Charles obit Yrbk
2006
Hawkins, A. F. obit Yrbk
2008
Hawkinson, Tim Aug 2005
Hax, Carolyn Nov 2002
Hayden, Melissa obit Yrbk
2006
Hayden, Michael V. Nov 2006
Hayes, Bob obit Jan 2003
Hayes, Edward May 2006
Hayes, Isaac obit Yrbk 2008
Hayes, Tyrone B. May 2008
Haynes, Cornell Jr. see Nelly
Haynes, Todd Jul 2003
Haysbert, Dennis Nov 2006
Headley, Elizabeth see
Cavanna, Betty
Heath, Edward obit Yrbk
2005
Heath, James R. Oct 2003
Hecht, Anthony obit Yrbk
2005
Heckart, Eileen obit Mar 2002
Hee, Dana May 2008
Heilbroner, Robert L. obit
Yrbk 2005
Heilbrun, Carolyn G. obit Feb
2004
Heiskell, Andrew obit Yrbk
2003
Held, Al obit Yrbk 2005
Hellenga, Robert Mar 2008

Heller, Agnes Nov 2008
Helms, Jesse obit Yrbk 2008
Helms, Richard obit Yrbk 2003
Henderson, Donald A. Mar 2002
Henderson, Hazel Nov 2003
Henderson, Joe obit Oct 2001
Henderson, Skitch obit Apr 2006
Hendrickson, Sue Oct 2001
Henriques, Sean Paul see Sean Paul
Henry, Brad Jan 2005
Henry, John W. May 2005
Hepburn, Katharine obit Nov 2003
Herbert, Don obit Yrbk 2007
Herblock see Block, Herbert L.
Hernandez, Dave see Shins
Herndon, J. Marvin Nov 2003
Herrera Campins, Luis obit Yrbk 2008
Herring, Pendleton obit Yrbk 2004
Herring Wonder see Ames, Jonathan
Hersch, Fred Apr 2006
Hertzberg, Arthur obit Yrbk 2006
Herzog, Jacques see Herzog, Jacques, and de Meuron, Pierre
Herzog, Jacques, and de Meuron, Pierre Jun 2002
Heston, Charlton obit Jul 2008
Hewitt, Angela Apr 2007
Hewitt, Lleyton Oct 2002
Hewlett, Sylvia Ann Sep 2002
Heyerdahl, Thor obit Yrbk 2002
Heym, Stefan obit Mar 2002
Heymann, David L. Jul 2004
Hickey, Dave Sep 2007
Hicks, Louise Day obit Jun 2004
Hidalgo, David see Los Lobos
Higgins, Chester Jr. Jun 2002
Higgins, Jack Feb 2007
Hildegarde obit Yrbk 2005
Hill, Andrew Apr 2004 obit Yrbk 2007
Hill, Arthur obit Yrbk 2007
Hill, Dulé Jul 2003
Hill, Faith Mar 2001
Hill, George Roy obit Jun 2003
Hill, Grant Jan 2002
Hill, Herbert obit Yrbk 2004
Hillary, Sir Edmund obit Yrbk 2008

Hillenburg, Stephen Apr 2003
Hiller, Stanley obit Yrbk 2006
Hiller, Wendy obit Yrbk 2003
Hillerman, Tony obit Yrbk 2008
Hines, Gregory obit Yrbk 2003
Hines, Jerome obit Jun 2003
Hinojosa, Maria Feb 2001
Hirschfeld, Al obit Jul 2003
Hobson, Mellody Aug 2005
Hobson Pilot, Ann May 2003
Hockfield, Susan Apr 2008
Hoffman, Philip Seymour May 2001
Hogg, Quintin see Hailsham of St. Marylebone, Quintin Hogg
Holden, Betsy Jul 2003
Holdsclaw, Chamique Feb 2006
Holl, Steven Jul 2004
Holland, Dave Mar 2003
Hollander, Robert B. Sep 2006
Holm, Ian Mar 2002
Hondros, Chris Nov 2004
Hong, Hei-Kyung Nov 2003
Hooker, John Lee obit Sep 2001
Hope, Bob obit Yrbk 2003
Hopkins, Bernard Apr 2002
Hopkins, Nancy May 2002
Hoppus, Mark see blink-182
Horsey, David Sep 2008
Horwich, Frances obit Oct 2001
Hounsfield, Godfrey obit Yrbk 2004
Hounsou, Djimon Aug 2004
Houston, Allan Nov 2003
Houston, James A. obit Yrbk 2005
Howard, Ryan Jul 2007
Howard, Terrence Jun 2007
Howard, Tim Sep 2005
Howe, Harold II obit Yrbk 2003
Howland, Ben Jun 2007
Hoyer, Steny H. Mar 2004
Hoyle, Fred obit Jan 2002
Hrawi, Elias obit Yrbk 2006
Hua Guofeng obit Yrbk 2008
Huckabee, Mike Nov 2005
Hudson, Jennifer May 2007
Hudson, Saul see Slash
Hughes, Barnard obit Yrbk 2006
Hughes, Karen Oct 2001
Hugo, Chad see Neptunes
Hull, Jane Dee Feb 2002
Humbard, Rex obit Yrbk 2008

Hunt Lieberson, Lorraine Jul 2004 obit Yrbk 2006
Hunt, Swanee Mar 2006
Hunter, Charlie Nov 2007
Hunter, Evan obit Yrbk 2005
Hunter, Kermit obit Sep 2001
Hunter, Kim obit Yrbk 2002
Hurley, Chad see Chen, Steve; Hurley, Chad; and Karim, Jawed
Hussein, Saddam obit Apr 2007
Hutton, Betty obit Yrbk 2007
Hyde, Henry J. obit Yrbk 2008

Iakovos, Archbishop obit Yrbk 2005
Ifill, Gwen Sep 2005
Ilitch, Michael Feb 2005
Illich, Ivan obit Yrbk 2003
Immelman, Trevor Oct 2008
Immelt, Jeffrey R. Feb 2004
India.Arie Feb 2002
Inkster, Juli Sep 2002
Irwin, Steve obit Yrbk 2007
Isbin, Sharon Aug 2003
Istomin, Eugene obit Feb 2004
Ive, Jonathan Oct 2006
Ivins, Michael see Flaming Lips
Ivins, Molly obit Yrbk 2007
Iyengar, B. K. S. Jun 2007
Izecson dos Santos Leite, Ricardo see Kaká
Izetbegovic, Alija obit Jun 2004

Ja Rule Jul 2002
Jackman, Hugh Oct 2003
Jackson, Alan Apr 2004
Jackson, Hal Oct 2002
Jackson, Lauren Jun 2003
Jackson Lee, Sheila Nov 2008
Jackson, Maynard H. Jr. obit Yrbk 2003
Jackson, Michael Aug 2005 obit Yrbk 2007
Jackson, Peter Jan 2002
Jackson, Thomas Penfield Jun 2001
Jacobs, Jane obit Yrbk 2006
Jacobs, Paul E. Feb 2007
Jaffee, Al Jul 2008
Jaffee, Allan see Jaffee, Al
Jagger, Janine Apr 2004
Jakes, T.D. Jun 2001
Jamail, Joe Sep 2008
James, Alex see Blur
James, Bill Jun 2004
James, Edgerrin Jan 2002

James, Jim *see* My Morning
  Jacket
James, LeBron Nov 2005
Janeway, Elizabeth obit Yrbk
  2005
Jarecki, Eugene May 2006
Jarring, Gunnar obit Yrbk
  2002
Jarvis, Erich D. May 2003
Jastrow, Robert obit Yrbk
  2008
Jay-Z Aug 2002
Jeffers, Eve Jihan *see* Eve
Jefferts Schori, Katharine Sep
  2006
Jeffery, Vonetta *see* Flowers,
  Vonetta
Jeffords, James Sep 2001
Jenkins, Jerry B. *see* LaHaye,
  Tim and Jenkins, Jerry B.
Jenkins, Roy obit Yrbk 2003
Jennings, Peter obit Sep 2005
Jennings, Waylon obit Apr
  2002
Jensen, Oliver O obit Yrbk
  2005
Jet *see* Urquidez, Benny
Jimenez, Marcos Perez *see*
  Pérez Jiménez, Marcos
Jin, Deborah Apr 2004
Jindal, Bobby Jan 2008
Jindal, Piyush *see* Jindal,
  Bobby
Jobert, Michel obit Yrbk 2002
Johannesen, Grant obit Yrbk
  2005
Johansson, Scarlett Mar 2005
John, Daymond Aug 2007
John Paul II obit Jun 2005
Johnson, Alexander Boris de
  Pfeffel *see* Johnson, Boris
Johnson, Avery Jan 2007
Johnson, Boris Oct 2008
Johnson, Brian *see* AC/DC
Johnson, Claudia Alta obit
  Oct 2007
Johnson, Eddie Bernice Jul
  2001
Johnson, Elizabeth A. Nov
  2002
Johnson, Eric *see* Shins
Johnson, John H. obit Yrbk
  2005
Johnson, Lady Bird *see*
  Johnson, Claudia Alta
Johnson, Philip obit Sep 2005
Johnson, Sheila Crump Jun
  2007
Johnson, Zach Jan 2008
Jones, Bobby Jun 2002
Jones, Chipper May 2001
Jones, Chuck obit May 2002
Jones, Cullen Aug 2008

Jones, Edward P. Mar 2004
Jones, Elaine Jun 2004
Jones, George L. Apr 2007
Jones, Larry Wayne Jr. *see*
  Jones, Chipper
Jones, Norah May 2003
Jones, Sarah Jul 2005
Jones, Scott Jan 2006
Jonze, Spike Apr 2003
Jordan, Hamilton obit Yrbk
  2008
Josefowicz, Leila May 2007
Joyner, Tom Sep 2002
Judd, Jackie Sep 2002
Judd, Jacqueline Dee *see*
  Judd, Jackie
Judson, Olivia Jan 2004
Juliana Queen of the
  Netherlands obit Yrbk 2004
July, Miranda Nov 2007

Kabila, Joseph Sep 2001
Kael, Pauline obit Nov 2001
Kagan, Elena Jun 2007
Kagan, Frederick W. Jul 2007
Kainen, Jacob obit Aug 2001
Kaiser, Philip M. obit Yrbk
  2007
Kaká May 2008
Kamen, Dean Nov 2002
Kane, Joseph Nathan obit Nov
  2002
Kani, John Jun 2001
Kann, Peter R. Mar 2003
Kao, John Oct 2008
Kaptur, Marcy Jan 2003
Kapuściński, Ryszard obit
  Yrbk 2007
Karbo, Karen May 2001
Karim, Jawed *see* Chen,
  Steve; Hurley, Chad; and
  Karim, Jawed
Karle, Isabella Jan 2003
Karon, Jan Mar 2003
Karpinski, Janis Apr 2006
Karsh, Yousuf obit Nov 2002
Karzai, Hamid May 2002
Kase, Toshikazu obit Yrbk
  2004
Kass, Leon R. Aug 2002
Katsav, Moshe Feb 2001
Katz, Jackson Jul 2004
Kaufman, Charlie Jul 2005
Kaufman, Millard Jan 2008
Kavafian, Ani Oct 2006
Kazan, Elia obit Yrbk 2004
Kcho Aug 2001
Keane, Sean *see* Chieftains
Keegan, Robert Jan 2004
Keener, Catherine Oct 2002
Keeshan, Bob obit Yrbk 2004
Keith, Toby Oct 2004
Kelleher, Herb Jan 2001

Keller, Bill Oct 2003
Keller, Marthe Jul 2004
Keller, Thomas Jun 2004
Kelly, Raymond Sep 2008
Kelman, Charles obit Yrbk
  2004
Kempthorne, Dirk Jun 2007
Kennan, George F. obit Yrbk
  2005
Kennedy, Randall Aug 2002
Kennedy, Robert F. Jr. May
  2004
Kent, Jeff May 2003
Kentridge, William Oct 2001
Kenyon, Cynthia Jan 2005
Kepes, György obit Mar 2002
Kerr, Clark obit May 2004
Kerr, Deborah obit Feb 2008
Kerr, Jean obit May 2003
Kerr, Mrs. Walter F *see* Kerr,
  Jean
Kerry, John Sep 2004
Kesey, Ken obit Feb 2002
Ketcham, Hank obit Sep 2001
Keys, Ancel obit Yrbk 2005
Keys, Charlene *see* Tweet
Khalilzad, Zalmay Aug 2006
Kid Rock Oct 2001
Kidd, Chip Jul 2005
Kidd, Jason May 2002
Kidd, Michael obit Yrbk 2008
Kiessling, Laura Aug 2003
Kilbourne, Jean May 2004
Kilpatrick, Kwame M. Apr
  2004
Kim, Jim Yong Nov 2006
King, Alan obit Yrbk 2004
King, Coretta Scott obit Apr
  2006
King, Florence Apr 2006
Kirkpatrick, Jeane obit Yrbk
  2007
Kitaj, R. B. obit Yrbk 2008
Kitchen, Michael Nov 2008
Kittikachorn, Thanom obit
  Yrbk 2004
Klaus, Josef obit Oct 2001
Kleiber, Carlos obit Yrbk 2004
Klein, Naomi Aug 2003
Klein, William Mar 2004
Kleppe, Thomas S. obit Yrbk
  2007
Klinkenborg, Verlyn Jul 2006
Knievel, Evel obit Yrbk 2008
Knievel, Robbie Mar 2005
Knipfel, Jim Mar 2005
Knoll, Andrew H. Apr 2006
Knowles, Beyoncé *see*
  Destiny's Child
Koch, Kenneth obit Yrbk
  2002
Koff, Clea Nov 2004
Koh, Jennifer Sep 2006

Kohl, Herb May 2008
Koizumi, Junichiro Jan 2002
Kolar, Jiri obit Yrbk 2002
Kollek, Teddy obit Yrbk 2007
Koma see Eiko and Koma
Konaré, Alpha Oumar Oct 2001
Koner, Pauline obit Apr 2001
Kopp, Wendy Mar 2003
Korman, Harvey obit Yrbk 2008
Kornberg, Arthur obit Feb 2008
Kos see Moulitsas Zúniga, Markos ("Kos")
Koster, Bo see My Morning Jacket
Kostunica, Vojislav Jan 2001
Kott, Jan obit Mar 2002
Kournikova, Anna Jan 2002
Kovalchuk, Ilya Mar 2007
Kramer, Joey see Aerosmith
Kramer, Stanley obit May 2001
Krause, David W. Feb 2002
Krauthammer, Charles Jan 2008
Krawcheck, Sallie Mar 2006
Kreutzberger, Mario see Francisco, Don
Kripke, Saul Oct 2004
Kristof, Nicholas D. Feb 2006
Krugman, Paul Aug 2001
Krupp, Fred Sep 2007
Kübler-Ross, Elisabeth obit Yrbk 2004
Kucinich, Dennis J. Jul 2008
Kuhn, Bowie obit Yrbk 2007
Kummant, Alexander Jan 2007
Kunitz, Stanley obit Aug 2006
Kurzweil, Raymond Sep 2008
Kushner, Jared Jun 2007
Kushner, Tony Jul 2002
Kusturica, Emir Nov 2005
Kuznetsova, Svetlana Mar 2008
Kyprianou, Spyros obit May 2002

La India May 2002
La Montagne, Margaret see Spellings, Margaret
La Russa, Tony Jul 2003
Labov, William Mar 2006
LaChapelle, David Jun 2008
Lacy, Dan obit Nov 2001
LaDuke, Winona Jan 2003
LaFontaine, Don Sep 2004 obit Yrbk 2008
Lagardère, Jean-Luc obit Aug 2003
Lagat, Bernard Oct 2008

LaHaye, Tim see LaHaye, Tim and Jenkins, Jerry B.
LaHaye, Tim and Jenkins, Jerry B. Jun 2003
Laimbeer, Bill Jan 2006
Laine, Frankie obit Yrbk 2007
Laker, Freddie obit Yrbk 2006
Lally, Joe see Fugazi
Lamb, Willis Jr. obit Yrbk 2008
Lamont, Ann Huntress Feb 2007
Lampert, Edward S. Sep 2005
Landers, Ann obit Nov 2002
Lane, Anthony Nov 2008
Lang, Robert J. Jul 2007
Lange, David obit Yrbk 2005
Langevin, Jim Aug 2005
Lanier, Cathy L. Mar 2007
Lantos, Tom Jul 2007 obit May 2008
Lanzone, Jim May 2007
Lapidus, Morris obit Apr 2001
Lapp, Ralph E. obit Feb 2005
Lara, Brian Feb 2001
Lardner, Ring Jr. obit Feb 2001
Laredo, Ruth obit Yrbk 2005
Lassaw, Ibram obit Yrbk 2004
Lauder, Estée obit Yrbk 2004
Lavigne, Avril Apr 2003
Law, Ty Oct 2002
Lawal, Kase L. Nov 2006
Laws, Hubert Jr. Jul 2007
Lax, Peter D. Oct 2005
Le Clercq, Tanaquil obit Mar 2001
Leakey, Meave Jun 2002
Lederberg, Joshua obit Yrbk 2008
Lederer, Esther Pauline see Landers, Ann
Lederle, John obit Yrbk 2007
Ledger, Heath Jun 2006 obit Yrbk 2008
Lee, Andrea Sep 2003
Lee, Barbara Jun 2004
Lee, Debra L. Jun 2006
Lee, Geddy see Rush
Lee, Jeanette Oct 2002
Lee, Mrs. John G. see Lee, Percy Maxim
Lee, Peggy obit May 2002
Lee, Percy Maxim obit Jan 2003
Lee, Richard C. obit Jun 2003
Lee, Sherman obit Yrbk 2008
LeFrak, Samuel J. obit Yrbk 2003
Legend, John Feb 2007
Lehane, Dennis Oct 2005
Leiter, Al Aug 2002

Lelyveld, Joseph Nov 2005
Lem, Stanislaw obit Yrbk 2006
Lemmon, Jack obit Oct 2001
L'Engle, Madeleine obit Yrbk 2007
Leo, John Sep 2006
Leon, Kenny Nov 2005
Leonard see Hackett, Buddy
Leone, Giovanni obit Feb 2002
Leslie, Chris see Fairport Convention
LeSueur, Larry obit Jun 2003
Lethem, Jonathan Mar 2006
Letterman, David Oct 2002
Letts, Tracy Oct 2008
Levert, Gerald Oct 2003 obit Yrbk 2007
Levin, Carl May 2004
Levin, Ira obit Feb 2008
Levin, Janna Jan 2008
Levine, Mel Nov 2005
LeVox, Gary see Rascal Flatts
Levy, Eugene Jan 2002
Lewis, Ananda Jun 2005
Lewis, David Levering May 2001
Lewis, David S. Jr. obit Yrbk 2004
Lewis, Dorothy Otnow May 2006
Lewis, Flora obit Yrbk 2002
Lewis, John obit Jun 2001
Lewis, Kenneth Apr 2004
Lewis, Marvin Nov 2004
Lewis, Ray Jan 2007
Lewitt, Sol obit Yrbk 2007
Lhuillier, Monique Jun 2008
Li, Jet Jun 2001
Li Lian Jie see Li, Jet
Libeskind, Daniel Jun 2003
Lifeson, Alex see Rush
Lilly, John C. obit Feb 2002
Lilly, Kristine Apr 2004
Lima do Amor, Sisleide see Sissi
Lincoln, Abbey Sep 2002
Lincoln, Blanche Lambert Mar 2002
Lindbergh, Anne Morrow obit Apr 2001
Lindgren, Astrid obit Apr 2002
Lindo, Delroy Mar 2001
Lindsay, John V. obit Mar 2001
Ling, James J. obit Yrbk 2005
Lingle, Linda Jun 2003
Link, O. Winston obit Apr 2001
Linkin Park Mar 2002

Linowitz, Sol M. obit Yrbk 2005
Lipinski, Anne Marie Jul 2004
Lippold, Richard obit Yrbk 2002
Little Steven *see* Van Zandt, Steven
Liu, Lucy Oct 2003
Lloyd, Charles Apr 2002
Locke, Gary Apr 2003
Lockhart, Keith Aug 2008
Logan, Lara Jul 2006
Lohan, Lindsay Nov 2005
Lomax, Alan obit Oct 2002
London, Julie obit Feb 2001
Long, Russell B. obit Yrbk 2003
Long, William Ivey Mar 2004
Lopez, Al obit Yrbk 2006
López Portillo, José obit Yrbk 2004
Lord, Walter obit Yrbk 2002
Los Lobos Oct 2005
Loudon, Dorothy obit Yrbk 2004
Love, John A. obit Apr 2002
Lowell, Mike Sep 2003
Lozano, Conrad *see* Los Lobos
Lucas, George May 2002
Luce, Charles F. obit Yrbk 2008
Luckovich, Mike Jan 2005
Ludacris Jun 2004
Ludlum, Robert obit Jul 2001
Ludwig, Ken May 2004
Luke, Delilah Rene *see* Delilah
Lumet, Sidney Jun 2005
Luns, Joseph M. A. H. obit Yrbk 2002
Lupica, Mike Mar 2001
Lustiger, Jean-Marie obit Yrbk 2007
Lyng, Richard E. obit Jun 2003
Lynne, Shelby Jul 2001

Mac, Bernie Jun 2002 obit Nov 2008
Machado, Alexis Leyva *see* Kcho
MacKaye, Ian *see* Fugazi
MacKenzie, Gisele obit Jul 2004
Mackey, John Nov 2008
MacMitchell, Leslie obit Yrbk 2006
Maddox, Lester obit Yrbk 2003
Madsen, Michael Apr 2004
Magliozzi, Ray *see* Magliozzi, Tom and Ray

Magliozzi, Tom *see* Magliozzi, Tom and Ray
Magliozzi, Tom and Ray Jun 2006
Magloire, Paul E. obit Nov 2001
Maguire, Tobey Sep 2002
Mahal, Taj Nov 2001
Mahesh Yogi, Maharishi obit Yrbk 2008
Mahfouz, Naguib obit Yrbk 2007
Mailer, Norman obit Jan 2008
Maki, Fumihiko Jul 2001
Malaby, Tony Sep 2008
Malina, Joshua Apr 2004
Malley, Matt *see* Counting Crows
Maloney, Carolyn B. Apr 2001
Maloney, Walter E. obit Yrbk 2007
Maltin, Leonard Aug 2008
Manchester, William obit Yrbk 2004
Mankind *see* Foley, Mick
Mankoff, Robert May 2005
Mann, Emily Jun 2002
Manning, Eli Sep 2008
Mansfield, Michael J. *see* Mansfield, Mike
Mansfield, Mike obit Jan 2002
Marceau, Marcel obit Yrbk 2007
Marcinko, Richard Mar 2001
Marcus, Bernie Aug 2007
Marcus, George E. Mar 2006
Marcus, Stanley obit Apr 2002
Marcy, Geoffrey W. *see* Marcy, Geoffrey W., and Butler, R. Paul
Marcy, Geoffrey W., and Butler, R. Paul Nov 2002
Margaret, Princess of Great Britain obit May 2002
Markova, Alicia obit Yrbk 2005
Marks, Leonard H. obit Yrbk 2006
Marlette, Doug Jul 2002 obit Yrbk 2007
Marshall, Burke obit Yrbk 2003
Marshall, Chan *see* Cat Power
Marshall, Charlyn *see* Cat Power
Marshall, Rob Jun 2003
Marta Apr 2008
Martin, A. J. P. *see* Martin, Archer
Martin, Agnes obit Apr 2005

Martin, Archer obit Yrbk 2002
Martin, Chris *see* Coldplay
Martin, Dick obit Yrbk 2008
Martin, George R. R. Jan 2004
Martin, James S. Jr. obit Yrbk 2002
Martin, Jesse L. Jul 2006
Martin, Kenyon Jan 2005
Martin, Kevin J. Aug 2005
Martin, Mark Mar 2001
Martinez, Pedro Jun 2001
Martinez, Rueben Jun 2005
Martinez, Vilma Jul 2004
Martz, Judy Mar 2005
Mary Kay *see* Ash, Mary Kay
Massive Attack Jun 2004
Masters, William H. obit May 2001
Mathers, Marshall *see* Eminem
Mathias, Bob *see* Mathias, Robert Bruce
Mathias, Robert Bruce obit Yrbk 2007
Matisyahu Mar 2007
Matsui, Connie L. Aug 2002
Matsui, Robert T. obit Apr 2005
Matsuzaka, Daisuke Apr 2007
Matta obit Yrbk 2003
Mauch, Gene obit Yrbk 2005
Mauer, Joe Aug 2007
Mauldin, Bill obit Jul 2003
Mauldin, William Henry *see* Mauldin, Bill
May, Brian Oct 2008
Mayer, Jane Oct 2008
Mayne, Thom Oct 2005
Mayr, Ernst obit May 2005
Mays, L. Lowry Aug 2003
Mayweather, Floyd Oct 2004
McBride, Martina Mar 2004
McCain, John S. Mar 2006
McCambridge, Mercedes obit Yrbk 2004
McCann, Renetta May 2005
McCarthy, Eugene J. obit Mar 2006
McCaw, Craig Sep 2001
McCloskey, Robert obit Yrbk 2003
McClurkin, Donnie Apr 2007
McColough, C. Peter obit Yrbk 2007
McConnell, Addison Mitchell *see* McConnell, Mitch
McConnell, John M. *see* McConnell, Mike
McConnell, Mike Apr 2007
McConnell, Mitch Feb 2008
McConnell, Page *see* Phish
McCracken, Craig Feb 2004

McCrary, Tex obit Yrbk 2003
McCurry, Steve Nov 2005
McDonald, Gabrielle Kirk Oct 2001
McDonough, William Jul 2006
McFate, Montgomery Aug 2008
McGhee, George Crews obit Yrbk 2005
McGrady, Tracy Feb 2003
McGrath, Judy Feb 2005
McGraw, Eloise Jarvis obit Mar 2001
McGraw, Phillip Jun 2002
McGraw, Tim Sep 2002
McGreal, Elizabeth see Yates, Elizabeth
McGruder, Aaron Sep 2001
McGuire, Dorothy obit Nov 2001
McIntire, Carl obit Jun 2002
McIntosh, Millicent Carey obit Mar 2001
McKay, Jim obit Yrbk 2008
McKenzie, Bret see Flight of the Conchords
McKeon, Jack Apr 2004
McKinney, Robert obit Yrbk 2001
McLaughlin, John Feb 2004
McLean, Jackie Mar 2001 obit Nov 2006
McLean, John Lenwood see McLean, Jackie
McLurkin, James Sep 2005
McMath, Sid obit Jan 2004
McNabb, Donovan Jan 2004
McNair, Barbara obit Yrbk 2007
McNair, Steve Jan 2005
McNally, Andrew 3d obit Feb 2002
McNeil, John Jun 2007
McNerney, James Mar 2008
McNerney, Walter James Jr. see McNerney, James
McQueen, Alexander Feb 2002
McWhirter, Norris D. obit Yrbk 2004
McWhorter, John H. Feb 2003
Meat Loaf Nov 2006
Mechem, Edwin L. obit Yrbk 2003
Medvedev, Dmitry Jun 2008
Meier, Deborah May 2006
Meiselas, Susan Feb 2005
Mellers, Wilfrid obit Yrbk 2008
Meloy, Colin see Decemberists
Melton, Douglas A. Jun 2008

Mendes, Sam Oct 2002
Menken, Alan Jan 2001
Menotti, Gian Carlo obit Yrbk 2007
Mercer, James see Shins
Merchant, Ismail obit Yrbk 2005
Merchant, Natalie Jan 2003
Meron, Theodor Mar 2005
Merrifield, R. Bruce obit Yrbk 2006
Merrill, Robert obit Feb 2005
Merton, Robert K. obit Yrbk 2003
Meskill, Thomas J. obit Yrbk 2008
Messick, Dale obit Yrbk 2005
Messier, Jean-Marie May 2002
Messing, Debra Aug 2002
Messmer, Pierre obit Yrbk 2007
Meta, Ilir Feb 2002
Metzenbaum, Howard obit Yrbk 2008
Meyer, Cord Jr. obit Aug 2001
Meyer, Danny Jul 2007
Meyer, Edgar Jun 2002
Meyer, Stephenie Oct 2008
Meyers, Nancy Feb 2002
Michel, Sia Sep 2003
Mickelson, Phil Mar 2002
Middelhoff, Thomas Feb 2001
Miller, Ann obit Yrbk 2004
Miller, Arthur obit Jul 2005
Miller, G. William obit Yrbk 2007
Miller, J. Irwin obit Yrbk 2004
Miller, Jason obit Yrbk 2001
Miller, John Aug 2003
Miller, Judith Jan 2006
Miller, Marcus Feb 2006
Miller, Matthew see Matisyahu
Miller, Neal obit Jun 2002
Millionaire, Tony Jul 2005
Millman, Dan Aug 2002
Mills, John obit Yrbk 2005
Milosevic, Slobodan obit Yrbk 2006
Milosz, Czeslaw obit Yrbk 2004
Mingus, Sue Jul 2008
Mink, Patsy T. obit Jan 2003
Minner, Ruth Ann Aug 2001
Mirabal, Robert Aug 2002
Mirvish, Edwin obit Yrbk 2007
Mitchell, Dean Aug 2002
Mitchell, Elvis Jul 2008
Mitchell, Jerry Oct 2007
Mitchell, Pat Aug 2005
Mitha, Tehreema May 2004

Miyazaki, Hayao Apr 2001
Miyazawa, Kiichi obit Yrbk 2007
Moby Apr 2001
Moen, John see Decemberists
Moffo, Anna obit Yrbk 2007
Mohammed bin Rashid Al Maktoum Apr 2008
Mohammed, W. Deen Jan 2004
Mohammed Zahir Shah see Zahir Shah, Mohammed
Moiseiwitsch, Tanya obit Jul 2003
Moiseyev, Igor obit Yrbk 2008
Molina, Alfred Feb 2004
Molloy, Matt see Chieftains
Moloney, Paddy see Chieftains
Mondavi, Robert obit Yrbk 2008
Monheit, Jane Feb 2008
Monk, T. S. Feb 2002
Monseu, Stephanie see Nelson, Keith and Monseu, Stephanie
Monte, Elisa Jun 2007
Montero, Gabriela Jul 2007
Montresor, Beni obit Feb 2002
Moore, Ann Aug 2003
Moore, Dudley obit Yrbk 2002
Moore, Elisabeth Luce obit Yrbk 2002
Moore, George E. obit Yrbk 2008
Moore, Gordon E. Apr 2002
Moore, Paul Jr. obit Yrbk 2003
Moore, Thomas W. obit Yrbk 2007
Moorer, Thomas H. obit Yrbk 2004
Morella, Constance A. Feb 2001
Moretti, Fabrizio see Strokes
Morgan, Tracy Mar 2007
Morial, Marc Jan 2002
Morris, Butch Jul 2005
Morris, Errol Feb 2001
Morris, James T. Mar 2005
Morris, Lawrence see Morris, Butch
Morrison, Philip obit Aug 2005
Mortensen, Viggo Jun 2004
Mos Def Apr 2005
Moseka, Aminata see Lincoln, Abbey
Mosel, Tad obit Yrbk 2008
Moses, Bob see Moses, Robert P.

Moses, Robert P. Apr 2002
Mosley, Sugar Shane Jan 2001
Mosley, Timothy see Timbaland
Moss, Adam Mar 2004
Moss, Frank E. obit Jun 2003
Moss, Randy Jan 2006
Moten, Etta see Barnett, Etta Moten
Motley, Constance Baker obit Feb 2006
Mott, Stewart R. obit Yrbk 2008
Moulitsas Zúniga, Markos ("Kos") Mar 2007
Moynihan, Daniel Patrick obit Yrbk 2003
Muhammad, Warith Deen see Mohammed, W. Deen obit Yrbk 2008
Mukasey, Michael B. Feb 2008
Mulcahy, Anne M. Nov 2002
Mullen, Michael see Mullen, Mike
Mullen, Mike Feb 2008
Murkowski, Frank H. Jul 2003
Murphy, Mark Sep 2004
Murphy, Thomas obit Yrbk 2006
Murray, Bill Sep 2004
Murray, Donald M. Jul 2006
Murray, Elizabeth obit Yrbk 2007
Murray, Jonathan see Bunim, Mary-Ellis, and Murray, Jonathan
Murray, Ty May 2002
Musharraf, Pervaiz see Musharraf, Pervez
Musharraf, Pervez Mar 2001
Musk, Elon Oct 2006
Mwanawasa, Levy obit Yrbk 2008
My Morning Jacket Nov 2008
Mydans, Carl M. obit Yrbk 2004
Mydans, Shelley Smith obit Aug 2002
Myers, Joel N. Apr 2005
Myers, Richard B. Apr 2002

Nabrit, Samuel M. obit Yrbk 2004
Nachtigall, Paul E. Jan 2006
Nagin, C. Ray Jan 2006
Najimy, Kathy Oct 2002
Nakamura, Dan May 2007
Napolitano, Janet Oct 2004
Narayan, R. K. obit Jul 2001
Nash, Steve Mar 2003
Nason, John W. obit Feb 2002
Nasser, Jacques Apr 2001

Nathan, Robert R. obit Nov 2001
Navratilova, Martina Feb 2004
Ne Win obit Yrbk 2003
Neals, Otto Feb 2003
Neeleman, David Sep 2003
Negroponte, John Apr 2003
Nehru, B. K. obit Feb 2002
Nelly Oct 2002
Nelson, Byron obit Yrbk 2007
Nelson, Don May 2007
Nelson, Gaylord obit Yrbk 2005
Nelson, Keith see Nelson, Keith and Monseu, Stephanie
Nelson, Keith and Monseu, Stephanie Jun 2005
Nelson, Marilyn Carlson Oct 2004
Nelson, Stanley May 2005
Neptunes May 2004
Nerina, Nadia obit Yrbk 2008
Neustadt, Richard E. obit Yrbk 2004
Newkirk, Ingrid Apr 2008
Newkirk, Kori Mar 2008
Newman, Arnold obit Yrbk 2006
Newman, J. Wilson obit Yrbk 2003
Newman, Paul obit Yrbk 2008
Newmark, Craig Jun 2005
Newsom, Lee Ann Oct 2004
Newton, Helmut obit Yrbk 2004
Nguyen Van Thieu see Thieu, Nguyen Van
Nicol, Simon see Fairport Convention
Nikolayev, Andrian obit Yrbk 2004
Nilsson, Birgit obit Sep 2006
Nitze, Paul H. obit Mar 2005
Nixon, Agnes Apr 2001
Nofziger, Lyn obit Yrbk 2006
Nooyi, Indra K. Nov 2006
Norman, Christina Nov 2007
Norquist, Grover Oct 2007
Norris, Michele Mar 2008
Norton, Andre obit Yrbk 2005
Norton, Gale A. Jun 2001
Nottage, Lynn Nov 2004
Nouvel, Jean Sep 2008
Novacek, Michael J. Sep 2002
Nowitzki, Dirk Jun 2002
Nozick, Robert obit Apr 2002
Nugent, Ted Apr 2005
Nykvist, Sven obit Yrbk 2007

Obama, Barack Jul 2005
Obama, Michelle Oct 2008

Obote, Milton obit Yrbk 2006
O'Brien, Ed see Radiohead
O'Connor, Carroll obit Sep 2001
O'Connor, Donald obit Apr 2004
O'Day, Anita obit Jan 2007
Ogilvie, Elisabeth obit Yrbk 2007
O'Hair, Madalyn Murray obit Jun 2001
O'Hara, Kelli Oct 2008
Ohno, Apolo Anton Feb 2006
O'Keefe, Sean Jan 2003
Okrent, Daniel Nov 2004
Olin, Lena Jun 2003
Olitski, Jules obit Yrbk 2007
Oliver, Garrett Nov 2008
Ollila, Jorma Aug 2002
Olopade, Olufunmilayo Sep 2006
O'Malley, Sean Patrick Jan 2004
Omarion Feb 2008
O'Neal, Jermaine Jun 2004
O'Neal, Stanley May 2003
O'Neill, Paul H. Jul 2001
O'Neill, William A. obit Yrbk 2008
Oppenheim, Chad Sep 2006
Orbach, Jerry obit Apr 2005
O'Reilly, Bill Oct 2003
Orlean, Susan Jun 2003
Orman, Suze May 2003
Ortega, Kenny Mar 2008
Ortiz, David Aug 2005
Ortner, Sherry B. Nov 2002
Osawa, Sandra Sunrising Jan 2001
Osborne, Barrie M. Feb 2005
Osbourne, Sharon Jan 2001
Osteen, Joel Jan 2006
Oudolf, Piet Apr 2003
Ouma, Kassim Jun 2007
OutKast Apr 2004
Ovechkin, Alexander Jun 2008
Oz, Mehmet C. Apr 2003

Pääbo, Svante Feb 2007
Paar, Jack obit Yrbk 2004
Pace, Peter Jun 2006
Page, Clarence Jan 2003
Page, Ellen May 2008
Page, Larry see Brin, Sergey, and Page, Larry
Paige, Roderick R. Jul 2001
Paik, Nam June obit Yrbk 2006
Palade, George E. obit Yrbk 2008
Palance, Jack obit Feb 2007
Paley, Grace obit Yrbk 2007

Palmeiro, Rafael Aug 2001
Palmer, Violet Nov 2006
Paltrow, Gwyneth Jan 2005
Pandit, Vikram Jun 2008
Panofsky, Wolfgang K. H. obit
    Yrbk 2007
Pareles, Jon Nov 2008
Park, Linda Sue Jun 2002
Park, Rosemary obit Yrbk
    2004
Parker, Mary-Louise Apr 2006
Parker, Robert M. May 2005
Parker, Tony Apr 2008
Parks, Gordon obit Jun 2006
Parks, Rosa obit Jan 2006
Parsons, Richard D. Apr 2003
Pascal, Amy Mar 2002
Patchett, Ann Apr 2003
Paterson, David Jul 2008
Patrick, Danica Oct 2005
Patrick, Deval May 2007
Patterson, Floyd obit Yrbk
    2007
Patty, Sandi Feb 2004
Pau, Peter Feb 2002
Paul, Ron Jun 2008
Paulson, Henry M. Jr. Sep
    2002
Pavarotti, Luciano obit Nov
    2007
Payne, Alexander Feb 2003
Paz Estenssoro, Victor obit
    Sep 2001
Peart, Neil see Rush
Peck, Gregory obit Sep 2003
Peck, M. Scott obit Yrbk 2005
Pegg, Dave see Fairport
    Convention
Peirce, Kimberly Aug 2008
Pekar, Harvey Jan 2004
Pelikan, Jaroslav obit Yrbk
    2006
Pelosi, Nancy Feb 2003
Peltz, Nelson Feb 2008
Pelzer, Dave Mar 2002
Pennington, Ty Feb 2006
Pepperberg, Irene Sep 2008
Perdue, Frank obit Oct 2005
Pérez Jiménez, Marcos obit
    Feb 2002
Pérez, Louie see Los Lobos
Perino, Dana Jan 2008
Perkins, Charles obit Feb
    2001
Perkins, Elizabeth Jan 2007
Perle, Richard Jul 2003
Perry, Joe see Aerosmith
Perry, Tyler Jun 2005
Person, Houston Jun 2003
Perutz, Max obit Apr 2002
Petersen, Wolfgang Jul 2001
Peterson, Martha obit Yrbk
    2006

Peterson, Oscar obit Yrbk
    2008
Petraeus, David H. Apr 2007
Pettibon, Raymond Apr 2005
Pevear, Richard see Pevear,
    Richard and Volokhonsky,
    Larissa
Pevear, Richard and
    Volokhonsky, Larissa Jun
    2006
Peyroux, Madeleine Nov 2005
Phelps, Michael Aug 2004
Phillips, Sam Apr 2001
Phillips, Scott see Creed
Phillips, William obit Yrbk
    2002
Phish Jul 2003
Phoenix see Linkin Park
Piano, Renzo Apr 2001
Picciotto, Guy see Fugazi
Pickering, William H. obit
    Yrbk 2004
Piel, Gerard obit Feb 2005
Pierce, David Hyde Apr 2001
Pierce, John Robinson obit
    Jun 2002
Pierce, Paul Nov 2002
Pierce, Samuel R. Jr. obit Feb
    2001
Pifer, Alan J. obit Yrbk 2006
Pincay, Laffit Sep 2001
Pineda Lindo, Allan see
    Black Eyed Peas
Pingree, Chellie Jan 2005
Pinochet, Augusto obit Yrbk
    2007
Pitt, Harvey Nov 2002
Pitts, Leonard J. Oct 2004
Plater-Zyberk, Elizabeth see
    Duany, Andrés and Plater-
    Zyberk, Elizabeth
Plimpton, George obit Jan
    2004
Plimpton, Martha Apr 2002
Poehler, Amy Aug 2008
Poletti, Charles obit Yrbk
    2002
Polgar, Susan Feb 2008
Polgár, Zsuzsanna see Polgar,
    Susan
Pollack, Sydney obit Sep
    2008
Pollan, Michael Oct 2007
Pollitt, Katha Oct 2002
Pomeroy, Wardell B. obit
    Yrbk 2001
Popeil, Ron Mar 2001
Posen, Zac Jul 2006
Posey, Parker Mar 2003
Poston, Tom obit Yrbk 2007
Potok, Chaim obit Yrbk 2002
Potter, Myrtle S. Aug 2004

Poujade, Pierre obit Yrbk
    2004
Powell, Colin L. Nov 2001
Powell, Kevin Jan 2004
Powell, Michael K. May 2003
Power, Samantha Aug 2008
Prada, Miuccia Feb 2006
Prado, Edgar Sep 2007
Pressel, Morgan Nov 2007
Prigogine, Ilya obit Yrbk 2003
Prince, Charles O. III Jan 2007
Prince-Hughes, Dawn Apr
    2005
Prinze, Freddie Jr. Jan 2003
Profumo, John obit Jun 2006
Prosper, Pierre-Richard Aug
    2005
Proxmire, William obit Mar
    2006
Pryor, Richard obit Apr 2006
Pujols, Albert Sep 2004
Pusey, Nathan M. obit Feb
    2002
Pym, Francis obit Yrbk 2008

Queloz, Didier Feb 2002
Query, Nate see Decemberists
Quine, W. V. obit Mar 2001
Quine, Willard Van Orman
    see Quine, W. V.
Quinn, Aidan Apr 2005
Quinn, Anthony obit Sep
    2001
Quinn, William F. obit Yrbk
    2006

Rabassa, Gregory Jan 2005
Racette, Patricia Feb 2003
Radiohead Jun 2001
Raimi, Sam Jul 2002
Rainier III, Prince of Monaco
    obit Yrbk 2005
Rakic, Patricia Goldman see
    Goldman-Rakic, Patricia
Rakim Aug 2008
Rakoff, David Nov 2007
Rall, Ted May 2002
Ralston, Joseph W. Jan 2001
Ramirez, Manny Jun 2002
Ramirez, Tina Nov 2004
Ramonet, Ignacio Jun 2008
Ramos, Jorge Mar 2004
Rampling, Charlotte Jun 2002
Rampone, Christie Oct 2004
Randall, Lisa May 2006
Randall, Tony obit Yrbk 2004
Randolph, Willie Sep 2005
Rania Feb 2001
Rankin, Ian Jan 2008
Rao, P. V. Narasimha obit
    Yrbk 2005
Rascal Flatts Aug 2003

Ratzinger, Joseph *see* Benedict XVI
Rau, Johannes obit Yrbk 2006
Rauschenberg, Robert obit Aug 2008
Raven *see* Raven-Symone
Raven-Symone Sep 2008
Ravenstahl, Luke Aug 2008
Rawl, Lawrence obit Yrbk 2005
Rawls, Lou obit Oct 2006
Ray, Rachael Aug 2005
Reagan, Ronald obit Sep 2004
Redd, Michael Mar 2005
Redgrave, Vanessa Sep 2003
Redlener, Irwin Nov 2007
Reeve, Christopher obit Jan 2005
Reeves, Dan Oct 2001
Reeves, Dianne Jul 2006
Regan, Donald T. obit Yrbk 2003
Rehnquist, William H. Nov 2003 obit Yrbk 2005
Reich, Walter Aug 2005
Reichs, Kathy Oct 2006
Reid, Antonio *see* Reid, L. A.
Reid, Harry Mar 2003
Reid, L. A. Aug 2001
Reilly, John C. Oct 2004
Reilly, Rick Feb 2005
Reinhardt, Uwe E. Mar 2004
Reinking, Ann Jun 2004
Reitman, Ivan Mar 2001
Rell, M. Jodi Sep 2005
Ressler, Robert K. Feb 2002
Reuss, Henry S. obit Mar 2002
Reuther, Victor obit Yrbk 2004
Revel, Jean Francois obit Yrbk 2006
Reyes, José Aug 2008
Reyes, Silvestre Sep 2007
Reynolds, Glenn Harlan Oct 2007
Reynolds, John W. Jr. obit Mar 2002
Reynoso, Cruz Mar 2002
Rhodes, James A. obit Jul 2001
Rhodes, John J. obit Yrbk 2004
Rhodes, Randi Feb 2005
Rhyne, Charles S. obit Yrbk 2003
Rice, Condoleezza Apr 2001
Richards, Ann obit Yrbk 2007
Richards, Cecile May 2007
Richards, Lloyd obit Yrbk 2007
Richler, Mordecai obit Oct 2001

Richter, Gerhard Jun 2002
Rickey, George W. obit Yrbk 2002
Ricks, Thomas E. Nov 2007
Ridge, Tom Feb 2001
Riefenstahl, Leni obit Yrbk 2004
Riesman, David obit Yrbk 2002
Rihanna Nov 2007
Riley, Terry Apr 2002
Rimm, Sylvia B. Feb 2002
Rimsza, Skip Jul 2002
Rines, Robert H. Jan 2003
Rinfret, Pierre A. obit Yrbk 2006
Riopelle, Jean-Paul obit Yrbk 2002
Ripley, Alexandra obit Yrbk 2004
Ripley, S. Dillon obit Aug 2001
Risen, James Aug 2007
Ritchie, Robert James *see* Kid Rock
Ritter, John obit Yrbk 2004
Rivers, Doc Nov 2008
Rivers, Larry obit Nov 2002
Rizzuto, Phil obit Yrbk 2007
Roach, Max obit Nov 2007
Robards, Jason Jr. obit Mar 2001
Robb, J. D. *see* Roberts, Nora
Robbe-Grillet, Alain obit Yrbk 2008
Robbins, Anthony *see* Robbins, Tony
Robbins, Frederick C. obit Yrbk 2003
Robbins, Tony Jul 2001
Roberts, John G. Feb 2006
Roberts, John G. Jr. *see* Roberts, John G.
Roberts, Nora Sep 2001
Roberts, Robin Feb 2008
Roberts, Tony Oct 2006
Robinson, Arthur H. obit Yrbk 2005
Robinson, Eddie obit Yrbk 2007
Robinson, Janet L. Mar 2003
Robinson, Marilynne Oct 2005
Robinson, Peter Sep 2007
Rochberg, George obit Yrbk 2005
Roche, James M. obit Yrbk 2004
Rockefeller, Laurance S. obit Yrbk 2004
Rockwell, Llewellyn H. Jr. Jun 2007
Roddick, Andy Jan 2004

Roddick, Anita obit Yrbk 2007
Rodino, Peter W. obit Yrbk 2005
Rodriguez, Alex Apr 2003
Rodriguez, Arturo Mar 2001
Rogers, Fred obit Jul 2003
Rogers, William P. obit Mar 2001
Rojas, Rudy Jan 2006
Rollins, Edward J. Mar 2001
Rollins, Henry Sep 2001
Romenesko, Jim Feb 2004
Romer, John Jul 2003
Romero, Anthony Jul 2002
Romney, Mitt Sep 2006
Rooney, Joe Don *see* Rascal Flatts
Rosas, Cesar *see* Los Lobos
Rose, Jalen Mar 2004
Rose, Jim Mar 2003
Rosenfeld, Irene B. Jul 2007
Rosenthal, A. M. obit Sep 2006
Rosenthal, Joe obit Yrbk 2007
Ross, Alex Nov 2007
Ross, Gary May 2004
Ross, Herbert obit Feb 2002
Ross, Robert Oct 2002
Rostow, Eugene V. obit Yrbk 2003
Rostow, Walt W. obit Jul 2003
Rostropovich, Mstislav obit Aug 2007
Rotblat, Joseph obit Feb 2006
Rote, Kyle obit Yrbk 2002
Roth, William V. Jr. obit Yrbk 2004
Rothschild, Baron Guy de obit Yrbk 2007
Rothschild, Miriam obit Yrbk 2005
Rounds, Michael Jun 2006
Rowan, Carl T. obit Jan 2001
Rowland, Kelly *see* Destiny's Child
Rowley, Janet D. Mar 2001
Rowntree, David *see* Blur
Rubenstein, Atoosa Oct 2004
Rubin, Edward M. Jan 2006
Rubin, Rick Sep 2007
Rubin, William S. obit Yrbk 2007
Rucker, Rudy May 2008
Rudd, Phil *see* AC/DC
Rukeyser, Louis obit Nov 2006
Rule, Ja *see* Ja Rule
Rumsfeld, Donald H. Mar 2002
Rus, Daniela Feb 2004
Rusesabagina, Paul May 2005
Rush Feb 2001

Russell, Anna obit Yrbk 2007
Russell, Harold obit Apr 2002
Russell, Kurt Nov 2004
Russert, Tim obit Yrbk 2008
Russo, Patricia May 2008
Rutan, Burt Jun 2005
Ryan, George H. Sep 2001
Ryder, Jonathan *see* Ludlum, Robert
Ryer, Jonathan *see* Ludlum, Robert

Saab, Elie Aug 2004
Sabah, Jaber Al-Ahmad Al-Jaber Al-, Sheik obit Yrbk 2006
Sabathia, C. C. Apr 2008
Safina, Carl Apr 2005
Sagan, Francoise obit Feb 2005
Said, Edward W. obit Feb 2004
Saint Laurent, Yves obit Oct 2008
Salinger, Pierre obit Feb 2005
Sánchez, David Nov 2001
Sandberg, Sheryl Jun 2008
Sanders, Ric *see* Fairport Convention
Sandford, John Mar 2002
Sándor, György obit Yrbk 2006
Sandoval, Jesse *see* Shins
Sanger, Stephen Mar 2004
Santana, Johan Jul 2006
Santos, José Nov 2003
Sapolsky, Robert Jan 2004
Sapp, Warren Sep 2003
Saramago, José Jun 2002
Sardi, Vincent Jr. obit Yrbk 2008
Sarris, Andrew Jan 2007
Savage, Rick *see* Def Leppard
Savimbi, Jonas obit Jun 2002
Sayles Belton, Sharon Jan 2001
Sayre, Francis Jr. obit Yrbk 2008
Scammon, Richard M. obit Sep 2001
Scaturro, Pasquale V. Oct 2005
Scavullo, Francesco obit Yrbk 2004
Scdoris, Rachael Jul 2005
Scelsa, Vin May 2006
Scelsa, Vincent *see* Scelsa, Vin
Schaap, Phil Sep 2001
Schakowsky, Jan Jul 2004
Schell, Maria obit Yrbk 2005
Scheuer, James obit Apr 2006
Schieffer, Bob Aug 2006

Schilling, Curt Oct 2001
Schindler, Alexander M. obit Feb 2001
Schirra, Walter M. obit Yrbk 2007
Schjeldahl, Peter Oct 2005
Schlein, Miriam obit Yrbk 2005
Schlesinger, Arthur M. Jr. obit Aug 2007
Schlesinger, John obit Yrbk 2003
Schmidt, Eric Apr 2008
Schoenberg, Loren Feb 2005
Scholder, Fritz obit Yrbk 2005
Schott, Marge obit Yrbk 2004
Schriever, Bernard obit Yrbk 2005
Schroeder, Frederick R. obit Yrbk 2006
Schroeder, Ted *see* Schroeder, Frederick R.
Schultes, Richard Evans obit Sep 2001
Schultz, Ed Aug 2005
Schwartz, Gil Aug 2007
Schwartz, Pepper Jun 2008
Schwartz, Tony obit Yrbk 2008
Schwarzenegger, Arnold Aug 2004
Schwarzkopf, Elisabeth obit Yrbk 2006
Scofield, Paul obit Yrbk 2008
Scorsese, Martin Jun 2007
Scott, Christian Jan 2008
Scott, George obit Yrbk 2005 *see* Blind Boys of Alabama
Scott, H. Lee Oct 2006
Scott, Jill Jan 2002
Scott, Robert L. Jr. obit Yrbk 2006
Scott, Tony Nov 2004
Scottoline, Lisa Jul 2001
Scully, Vin Oct 2001
Seamans, Robert C. obit Yrbk 2008
Sean Paul Jan 2007
Sears, Martha *see* Sears, William and Martha
Sears, William and Martha Aug 2001
Seau, Junior Sep 2001
Sebelius, Kathleen Nov 2004
Sedaris, Amy Apr 2002
Seitz, Frederick obit Yrbk 2008
Selway, Phil *see* Radiohead
Sembène, Ousmane obit Yrbk 2007
Semel, Terry Jul 2006

Senghor, Léopold Sédar obit Mar 2002
Serrano Súñer, Ramón obit Yrbk 2004
Servan-Schreiber, Jean-Jacques obit Yrbk 2007
Settle, Mary Lee obit Yrbk 2006
Setzer, Philip *see* Emerson String Quartet
Seymour, Lesley Jane Nov 2001
Seymour, Stephanie Oct 2002
Shahade, Jennifer Sep 2005
Shaheen, Jeanne Jan 2001
Shalhoub, Tony Nov 2002
Shapiro, Irving S. obit Nov 2001
Shapiro, Neal May 2003
Shaw, Artie obit Apr 2005
Shawcross, Hartley obit Yrbk 2003
Shearer, Harry Jun 2001
Shearer, Moira obit Yrbk 2006
Sheehan, Cindy May 2007
Sheldon, Sidney obit Yrbk 2007
Shepherd, Michael *see* Ludlum, Robert
Shields, Mark May 2005
Shinoda, Mike *see* Linkin Park
Shins Jun 2007
Shoemaker, Willie obit Apr 2004
Short, Bobby obit Nov 2005
Shriver, Lionel Sep 2005
Shubin, Neil Apr 2007
Shumway, Norman E. obit Yrbk 2006
Shyamalan, M. Night Mar 2003
Siddons, Anne Rivers Jan 2005
Siegel, Robert Jul 2008
Sills, Beverly obit Oct 2007
Silva, Daniel Apr 2007
Silver, Joel Nov 2003
Silverman, Sarah Jul 2006
Simmons, Earl *see* DMX
Simon, Claude obit Yrbk 2005
Simon, David Jun 2008
Simon, Herbert A. obit May 2001
Simon, Paul obit Yrbk 2004
Simone, Gail Nov 2008
Simone, Nina obit Yrbk 2003
Simpson, Lorna Nov 2004
Sin, Jaime obit Yrbk 2005
Sinclair, Cameron Apr 2008
Sinclair, David A. Sep 2008
Sinegal, James D. Aug 2007
Singer, Bryan Apr 2005

Sinopoli, Giuseppe obit Sep 2001
Sisco, Joseph obit Yrbk 2005
Sissi Jun 2001
Sittenfeld, Curtis Nov 2008
Sklansky, David Apr 2007
Slash Mar 2008
Slater, Kelly Jul 2001
Slaughter, Frank obit Yrbk 2006
Slavenska, Mia obit Apr 2003
Smathers, George A. obit Jun 2007
Smiley, Tavis Apr 2003
Smith, Ali Jun 2006
Smith, Amy Jun 2005
Smith, Chesterfield H. obit Yrbk 2003
Smith, Dante Terrell see Mos Def
Smith, Elinor Mar 2001
Smith, Howard K. obit Aug 2002
Smith, Ian obit Feb 2008
Smith, Jeff obit Yrbk 2004
Smith, Kiki Mar 2005
Smith, Lovie Sep 2007
Smith, Maggie Jul 2002
Smith, Orin C. Nov 2003
Smith, Roger B. obit Yrbk 2008
Smith, Steve Sep 2006
Smits, Jimmy May 2006
Smuin, Michael obit Yrbk 2007
Smylie, Robert E. obit Yrbk 2004
Snead, Sam obit Yrbk 2002
Snider, Stacey Apr 2008
Snow, John Aug 2003
Snow, Tony Sep 2006 obit Yrbk 2008
Snyder, Tom obit Yrbk 2007
Soeharto obit Yrbk 2008
Soffer, Olga Jul 2002
Solomon, Phil Oct 2007
Solomon, Susan Jul 2005
Solzhenitsyn, Aleksandr obit Nov 2008
Sontag, Susan obit May 2005
Sothern, Ann obit Aug 2001
Souzay, Gérard obit Yrbk 2004
Spade, Kate Apr 2007
Spahn, Warren obit Yrbk 2004
Spark, Muriel obit Yrbk 2007
Sparks, Nicholas Feb 2001
Spektor, Regina Jul 2007
Spelke, Elizabeth Apr 2006
Spelling, Aaron obit Yrbk 2006
Spellings, Margaret Jun 2005

Spence, Hartzell obit Yrbk 2001
Spencer, John Jan 2001 obit Yrbk 2006
Spencer, Scott Jul 2003
Spergel, David Jan 2005
Speyer, Jerry May 2008
Spillane, Mickey obit Nov 2006
Spiropulu, Maria May 2004
Spitzer, Eliot Mar 2003
Sprewell, Latrell Feb 2001
Squyres, Steven Nov 2006
St. John, Robert obit Yrbk 2003
St. Laurent, Yves see Saint Laurent, Yves
St. Louis, Martin Feb 2007
Stabenow, Debbie Feb 2006
Stackhouse, Jerry Nov 2001
Stafford, Robert T. obit Yrbk 2008
Staley, Dawn Apr 2005
Stamberg, Susan Oct 2008
Stanfield, Robert Lorne obit Yrbk 2004
Stanley, Kim obit Jan 2002
Stanton, Andrew Feb 2004
Stanton, Bill May 2001
Stanton, Frank obit Yrbk 2007
Stapleton, Maureen obit Nov 2006
Stapp, Scott see Creed
Stargell, Willie obit Sep 2001
Starr, Chauncey obit Yrbk 2007
Stassen, Harold E. obit May 2001
Steele, Claude M. Feb 2001
Steele, Michael S. Jul 2004
Steig, William obit Apr 2004
Steiger, Rod obit Yrbk 2002
Stein, Benjamin J. Sep 2001
Stein, Janice Gross Aug 2006
Steingraber, Sandra Sep 2003
Steitz, Joan A. Jun 2007
Stephens, John see Legend, John
Stern, Isaac obit Jan 2002
Stern, Jessica May 2006
Stevens, Ted Oct 2001
Stew Sep 2007
Steward, David L. Nov 2004
Stewart, Alice obit Yrbk 2002
Stewart, James "Bubba" Feb 2005
Stewart, Jon Jul 2004
Stewart, Mark see Stew
Stewart, Thomas obit Yrbk 2007
Stewart, Tony Nov 2006
Stewart, William H. obit Yrbk 2008

Stiefel, Ethan Apr 2004
Stockhausen, Karlheinz obit Yrbk 2008
Stoller, Debbie Aug 2007
Stoltenberg, Gerhard obit Mar 2002
Stolz, Mary obit Yrbk 2007
Stone, W. Clement obit Yrbk 2002
Storch, Gerald L. Jun 2007
Storr, Anthony obit Sep 2001
Stott, John May 2005
Straight, Michael obit Yrbk 2004
Stratton, Dorothy obit Yrbk 2006
Stratton, William G. obit Aug 2001
Straus, Roger W. Jr. obit Yrbk 2004
Streb, Elizabeth Apr 2003
Stringer, Howard Jan 2006
Stroessner, Alfredo obit Yrbk 2007
Strokes Feb 2007
Stroman, Susan Jul 2002
Struzan, Drew Mar 2005
Stuhlinger, Ernst obit Yrbk 2008
Stutz, Geraldine obit Yrbk 2005
Styron, William obit Yrbk 2007
Subandrio obit Apr 2005
Sucksdorff, Arne obit Sep 2001
Sugar, Bert Randolph Nov 2002
Sullivan, Daniel Feb 2003
Sullivan, Leon H. obit Sep 2001
Sumac, Yma obit Yrbk 2008
Summers, Lawrence H. Jul 2002
Summitt, Pat Jun 2005
Sun Wen Apr 2001
Sunstein, Cass R. Oct 2008
Sutherland, Kiefer Mar 2002
Suzuki, Ichiro Jul 2002
Suzuki, Zenko obit Yrbk 2004
Swearingen, John obit Yrbk 2007
Sweeney, Anne Jun 2003
Swinton, Tilda Nov 2001
Syal, Meera Feb 2001

Taboo Nawasha see Black Eyed Peas
Tainish, Juan see Watts, Jeff "Tain"
Taintor, Anne Jun 2005
Tajiri, Satoshi Nov 2001
Talese, Nan Sep 2006

Talley, André Leon Jul 2003
Talmadge, Herman E. obit Jun 2002
Tange, Kenzo obit Yrbk 2005
Tangerine Dream Jan 2005
Tao, Terence Sep 2007
Tarter, Jill Cornell Feb 2001
Tartt, Donna Feb 2003
Tarver, Antonio Jun 2006
Tattersall, Ian Aug 2007
Taufa'ahau, Tupou IV obit Yrbk 2007
Taurasi, Diana Nov 2007
Tauscher, Ellen O. Mar 2001
Taylor, Herman A. Jun 2006
Taylor, Jermain Apr 2006
Taylor, John W. obit Apr 2002
Taylor, Koko Jul 2002
Taylor, Lili Jul 2005
Taylor, Theodore obit Feb 2005
Tebaldi, Renata obit Apr 2005
Tebbel, John obit Mar 2005
Tejada, Miguel Jun 2003
Teller, Edward obit Sep 2004
Temple, Johnny Oct 2008
Tethong, Lhadon Sep 2008
Tetley, Glen obit Yrbk 2007
Thain, John A. May 2004
Thaler, William J. obit Yrbk 2005
Theron, Charlize Nov 2004
Thiam, Aliaune see Akon
Thieu, Nguyen Van obit Jan 2002
Thomas, Dave see Thomas, R. David
Thomas, Michael Feb 2008
Thomas, R. David obit Apr 2002
Thomas, William H. Jan 2006
Thome, Jim Jun 2007
Thompson, Hunter S. obit Yrbk 2005
Thompson, John III Nov 2007
Thompson, John W. Mar 2005
Thompson, Lonnie Jan 2004
Thomson, James A. Nov 2001
Thomson, Kenneth R. obit Yrbk 2006
Thomson, Meldrim Jr. obit Sep 2001
Thurmond, Strom obit Nov 2003
Thyssen-Bornemisza de Kaszan, Baron Hans Heinrich obit Yrbk 2002
Tice, George A. Nov 2003
Tierney, John Aug 2005
Tigerman, Stanley Feb 2001
Tilghman, Shirley M. Jun 2006

Tillerson, Rex Sep 2006
Timbaland Mar 2003
Tisch, Laurence A. obit Yrbk 2004
Titov, Gherman obit Jan 2001
Tobin, James obit May 2002
Toledano, Ralph de obit Yrbk 2007
Toledo, Alejandro Nov 2001
Toles, Thomas G. see Toles, Tom
Toles, Tom Nov 2002
Tolle, Eckhart Feb 2005
Tomlinson, LaDainian Oct 2006
Tre Cool see Green Day
Tremonti, Mark see Creed
Trenet, Charles obit Sep 2001
Trenkler, Freddie obit Yrbk 2001
Trethewey, Natasha Aug 2007
Trevor-Roper, H. R. obit Jul 2003
Tridish, Pete Apr 2004
Trigère, Pauline obit Jul 2002
Tritt, Travis Feb 2004
Trotter, Lloyd Jul 2005
Trout Powell, Eve May 2004
Trout, Robert obit Jan 2001
Trowbridge, Alexander B. obit Yrbk 2006
Troyat, Henri obit Yrbk 2007
Trudeau, Pierre Elliott obit Jan 2001
Truman, David B. obit Yrbk 2004
Truman, Margaret obit Yrbk 2008
Truss, Lynne Jul 2006
Tsui Hark Oct 2001
Tufte, Edward R. Nov 2007
Tull, Tanya Nov 2004
Tureck, Rosalyn obit Yrbk 2003
Turin, Luca Aug 2008
Turner, Mark Nov 2002
Turre, Steve Apr 2001
Tweet Nov 2002
Tyler, Steven see Aerosmith
Tyson, John H. Aug 2001

Underwood, Carrie Mar 2007
Unitas, Johnny obit Yrbk 2002
Uris, Leon obit Yrbk 2003
Urquidez, Benny Nov 2001
Urrea, Luis Alberto Nov 2005
Ustinov, Peter obit Aug 2004

Valdes-Rodriguez, Alisa Jan 2006
Valensi, Nick see Strokes

Valenti, Jack obit Yrbk 2007
Valentine, Bobby Jul 2001
Van Allen, James A. obit Yrbk 2007
Van den Haag, Ernest obit Jul 2002
Van Duyn, Mona obit Nov 2005
Van Exel, Nick Mar 2002
Van Gundy, Jeff May 2001
Van Zandt, Steven Feb 2006
Vance, Cyrus R. obit Apr 2002
Vandiver, S. Ernest obit Yrbk 2005
Vandross, Luther obit Yrbk 2005
Vane, John R. obit Yrbk 2005
Vargas, Elizabeth Apr 2006
Varnay, Astrid obit Yrbk 2007
Varnedoe, Kirk obit Yrbk 2003
Vaughn, Vince Sep 2006
Verdon, Gwen obit Jan 2001
Vick, Michael Nov 2003
Vickrey, Dan see Counting Crows
Vieira, Meredith Apr 2002
Viereck, Peter obit Yrbk 2006
Villa-Komaroff, Lydia Jul 2008
Villaraigosa, Antonio Aug 2007
Vinatieri, Adam Sep 2004
Virilio, Paul Jul 2005
Viscardi, Henry Jr. obit Yrbk 2004
Visser, Lesley Apr 2007
Vitale, Dick Jan 2005
Volokhonsky, Larissa see Pevear, Richard and Volokhonsky, Larissa
von Ziegesar, Cecily Jan 2008
Vonnegut, Kurt obit Aug 2007
Voulkos, Peter obit Aug 2002

Wachowski, Andy see Wachowski, Andy and Larry
Wachowski, Andy and Larry Sep 2003
Wachowski, Larry see Wachowski, Andy and Larry
Wade, Dwyane Apr 2006
Waldheim, Kurt obit Oct 2007
Wales, Jimmy Oct 2006
Walker, Mort Feb 2002
Walker, Olene S. Apr 2005
Wall, Art obit Feb 2002
Wallace, Ben Apr 2004
Wallis, Jim Jul 2005
Walsh, Bill obit Yrbk 2007

Walsh, John Jul 2001
Walters, Barbara Feb 2003
Walters, John P. May 2008
Walters, Vernon A. obit Jul 2002
Walworth, Arthur C. obit Yrbk 2005
Ward, Benjamin obit Yrbk 2002
Ward, Paul L. obit Yrbk 2006
Ward, William E. Nov 2005
Ware, David S. Sep 2003
Warner, Mark R. Oct 2006
Warnke, Paul C. obit Feb 2002
Warren, Rick Oct 2006
Washburn, Bradford obit Yrbk 2007
Washington, Walter E. obit Yrbk 2004
Wasserman, Lew R. obit Yrbk 2002
Wasserstein, Wendy obit Yrbk 2006
Waters, Alice Jan 2004
Watkins, Donald Jan 2003
Watkins, Levi Jr. Mar 2003
Watson, Arthel Lane see Watson, Doc
Watson, Doc Feb 2003
Watson, Emily May 2007
Watts, Jeff "Tain" Apr 2008
Watts, Naomi Mar 2007
Waugh, Auberon obit May 2001
Wayans, Marlon see Wayans, Shawn and Marlon
Wayans, Shawn and Marlon May 2001
Weaver, Dennis obit Yrbk 2006
Weaver, Pat obit Yrbk 2002
Weaver, Sylvester see Weaver, Pat
Webb, Jim Nov 2007
Webb, Karrie Aug 2001
Webber, Chris May 2003
Weber, Dick obit Yrbk 2005
Weinberg, Alvin M. obit Yrbk 2006
Weinberger, Caspar W. obit Jul 2006
Weiner, Jennifer Jul 2008
Weinrig, Gary Lee see Rush
Weinstein, Allen Jun 2006
Weis, Charlie Nov 2007
Weisberg, Jacob Oct 2007
Weiss, Paul obit Yrbk 2002
Weisskopf, Victor F. obit Yrbk 2002
Weitz, John obit Apr 2003
Weizman, Ezer obit Aug 2005

Weizsäcker, Carl F. von obit Yrbk 2007
Wek, Alek Jun 2001
Welch, Stanton Jul 2007
Weller, Thomas H. obit Yrbk 2008
Wells, David May 2004
Wells, Spencer Mar 2008
Wellstone, Paul D. obit Yrbk 2003
Welty, Eudora obit Nov 2001
Wendel, Johnathan Apr 2007
Wendrich, Willeke Jan 2007
Wesley, Valerie Wilson Jun 2002
West, Kanye Aug 2006
Westmoreland, William C. obit Nov 2005
Wexler, Haskell Aug 2007
Wexler, Jerry Jan 2001 obit Yrbk 2008
Weyrich, Paul Feb 2005
Wheeldon, Christopher Mar 2004
Wheeler, John Archibald obit Yrbk 2008
Whipple, Fred L. obit Yrbk 2005
Whitaker, Mark Aug 2003
White, Armond Oct 2006
White, Byron Raymond obit Jul 2002
White, Gilbert F. obit Yrbk 2006
White, Jack see White Stripes
White, John F. obit Yrbk 2005
White, Meg see White Stripes
White, Reggie obit Yrbk 2005
White Stripes Sep 2003
Whitehead, Colson Nov 2001
Whitford, Brad see Aerosmith
Whitford, Bradley Apr 2003
Whitney, Phyllis A. obit Yrbk 2008
Whitson, Peggy Sep 2003
Wick, Charles Z. obit Yrbk 2008
Widmark, Richard obit Yrbk 2008
Wiesenthal, Simon obit Yrbk 2005
Wiggins, James Russell obit Mar 2001
Wilber, Ken Apr 2002
Wilder, Billy obit Yrbk 2002
Wiley, Kehinde Aug 2007
Wilhelm, Hoyt obit Yrbk 2002
Wilkins, Maurice H. F. obit Yrbk 2005
Wilkins, Robert W. obit Yrbk 2003
will.i.am see Black Eyed Peas

Williams, Armstrong May 2004
Williams, Cliff see AC/DC
Williams, Harrison A. Jr. obit Mar 2002
Williams, Juan May 2008
Williams, Lauryn Sep 2008
Williams, Michelle see Destiny's Child
Williams, Pharrell see Neptunes
Williams, Preston Warren II May 2007
Williams, Roy Mar 2007
Williams, Serena see Williams, Venus and Williams, Serena
Williams, Tad Sep 2006
Williams, Ted obit Oct 2002
Williams, Venus see Williams, Venus and Williams, Serena
Williams, Venus and Williams, Serena Feb 2003
Willingham, Tyrone Nov 2002
Willis, Deborah Sep 2004
Willis, Dontrelle Aug 2006
Wilmore, Larry Nov 2007
Wilson, August obit Feb 2006
Wilson, Heather Jul 2006
Wilson, James Q. Aug 2002
Wilson, Kemmons obit Yrbk 2003
Wilson, Luke Feb 2005
Wilson, Marie C. Sep 2004
Wilson, Owen Feb 2003
Wilson, Sloan obit Yrbk 2003
Winchester, Simon Oct 2006
Winsor, Kathleen obit Yrbk 2003
Winston, Stan Jul 2002 obit Nov 2008
Winters, Shelley obit Apr 2006
Wise, Robert obit Apr 2006
Witcover, Jules Apr 2008
Witherspoon, Reese Jan 2004
Woertz, Patricia A. Mar 2007
Woese, Carl R. Jun 2003
Wojciechowska, Maia obit Yrbk 2002
Wolfe, Art Jun 2005
Wolfe, Julia Oct 2003
Wolff, Maritta M. obit Yrbk 2002
Wolfowitz, Paul Feb 2003
Wolfram, Stephen Feb 2005
Wolpoff, Milford Jul 2006
Wong, Andrea Sep 2007
Wong-Staal, Flossie Apr 2001
Wood, Elijah Aug 2002
Wood, Kerry May 2005

Woodcock, Leonard obit Apr 2001
Woods, Donald obit Nov 2001
Woodson, Rod Oct 2004
Woodward, Robert F. obit Yrbk 2001
Wooldridge, Anna Marie *see* Lincoln, Abbey
Wooldridge, Dean E. obit Yrbk 2007
Worth, Irene obit Aug 2002
Wright, Jeffrey May 2002
Wright, Steven May 2003
Wright, Teresa obit Yrbk 2005
Wright, Will Feb 2004
Wright, Winky Jul 2004
Wriston, Walter B. obit Aug 2005
Wrynn, Dylan *see* Tridish, Pete
Wyatt, Jane obit Yrbk 2006
Wylde, Zakk Oct 2004
Wyman, Jane obit Yrbk 2007
Wyman, Thomas obit Yrbk 2003
Wyner, Yehudi Apr 2008

Xenakis, Iannis obit Jul 2001

Yagudin, Alexei Feb 2004
Yard, Molly obit Apr 2006
Yashin, Aleksei *see* Yashin, Alexei
Yashin, Alexei Jan 2003
Yassin, Ahmed obit Yrbk 2004
Yates, Elizabeth obit Nov 2001
Yates, Sidney R. obit Jan 2001
Yeltsin, Boris obit Jun 2007
Yokich, Stephen P. obit Yrbk 2002
Yorke, Thom *see* Radiohead
Young, Angus *see* AC/DC
Young, Kimberly S. Jan 2006
Young, Malcolm *see* AC/DC
Yuen Wo Ping Jan 2008
Yusuf, Hamza Mar 2007

Zagat, Nina *see* Zagat, Tim and Nina
Zagat, Tim *see* Zagat, Tim and Nina
Zagat, Tim and Nina Mar 2008
Zahir Shah, Mohammed obit Yrbk 2007

Zahn, Paula Feb 2002
Zaillian, Steven Oct 2001
Zambello, Francesca May 2003
Zatopek, Emil obit Feb 2001
Zellweger, Renee Feb 2004
Zerhouni, Elias Oct 2003
Zeta-Jones, Catherine Apr 2003
Zhao Ziyang obit Yrbk 2005
Zhu Rongji Jul 2001
Ziegler, Ronald L. obit Jul 2003
Zimmer, Hans Mar 2002
Zindel, Paul obit Yrbk 2007
Zinni, Anthony C. May 2002
Zito, Barry Jul 2004
Zittel, Andrea Aug 2006
Zivojinovich, Alex *see* Rush
Zoellick, Robert B. Jul 2008
Zollar, Jawole Willa Jo Jul 2003
Zorina, Vera obit Yrbk 2003
Zucker, Jeff Jan 2002
Zuckerberg, Mark Jan 2008
Zukerman, Eugenia Jan 2004